Families in America

2015

Families in America

2015

Deirdre A. Gaquin
Mary Meghan Ryan

Lanham, MD

Published in the United States of America
by Bernan Press, a wholly owned subsidiary of
The Rowman & Littlefield Publishing Group, Inc.
4501 Forbes Boulevard, Suite 200
Lanham, Maryland 20706

Bernan Press
800-462-6420
www.rowman.com

ISBN-13: 978-1-59888-767-9
eISBN-13: 978-1-59888-768-6

∞™ The paper used in this publication meets the minimum requirements of
American National Standard for Information Sciences—Permanence of
Paper for Printed Library Materials, ANSI/NISO Z39.48-1992.

Manufactured in the United States of America.

Contents

PREFACE

Most Americans live in families, defined by the Census Bureau as persons related by birth, marriage, or adoption. Family households can include persons who are not family members, and nonfamily households often include persons with close personal relationships. This book includes a selection of data from the American Community Survey that helps us describe American living arrangements, relationships, marriages, births, children, and incomes. Part A includes information on types of households. Part B is about relationships, defining the variety of people who can make up a household. Part C includes details on marital status, marital history, and recent births. Part D summarizes the living arrangements of children and the employment patterns of their parents. Part E includes information about income for the various types of households. Each section includes a large selection of information for the United States, the 50 states, and the District of Columbia. This is followed by a more limited selection of data for 381 metropolitan areas, 980 counties with populations of 50,000 or more, and 795 cities with populations of 50,000 or more.

Although most Americans have always lived in family households, the proportions have changed dramatically over the past half-century. In 1950, nearly 90 percent of households were family households and the proportion remained over 80 percent in 1960 and 1970. The very high birth rates of the baby boom in the 1950s and 1960s were followed by historically low birth rates in the 1970s. The proportion of family households fell to 73.2 percent in 1980 and by 2010 it had dropped to 66.4 percent. As the baby boom population formed new households, the proportion of one-person households increased from 9.3 percent in 1950 to 22.7 percent in 1980. The millennial generation continued this trend and one-person households rose to 26.7 percent in 2010. Family households with children were more than half of families in 1950 through 1980, but dropped to 44.8 percent of families by 2010, as birth rates remained low and hit even lower levels than in the 1970s.

The 2010 census was different from any census in recent memory. All American households answered a simple questionnaire with ten questions. No longer did some people get the "long form" with dozens of detailed questions about employment, education, income, previous residence, housing characteristics, and more. The data gleaned from these important questions have long been used by federal, state, and local governments to evaluate their populations and program needs; by large and small businesses and nonprofit organizations for a variety of planning and location purposes; and by academic researchers to study trends in social and economic conditions. The "long form" has been replaced by the American Community Survey (ACS). Under development for more than a decade, the ACS is an ongoing survey of the American people that is ushering in a new era in social and economic data analysis. The census "long form" provided detailed estimates of social and economic characteristics every ten years. The ACS collects this same information on a rolling basis. It takes 5 years of ACS responses to accumulate a sample almost as large as the census "long form" collected at a single point in time. But data users now have the ability to study these characteristics and trends throughout the decade.

Because the ACS is a sample survey, large numbers of sample cases are needed before reliable estimates can be made for small populations. Each year's sample is large enough to produce estimates for the nation, all the states, most metropolitan areas, and many counties and cities.

The richness of the ACS data can be accessed in varying degrees. Much more subject matter detail is available for large geographic areas partly because reliable estimates for large areas can be produced with smaller samples, and partly because more data must be suppressed for the smaller areas to protect the confidentiality of the respondents. The tables in this book include the ACS 3-year estimates for the period 2011 through 2013. Although 1-year estimates are available for most of the areas in this book, the 3-year estimates were chosen because the book includes very detailed information and the reliability of the estimates is better with the 3-year data.

This book is designed to include a sampling of key information about families, but also to guide users through the process of using the Census Bureau's website to expand on the information included here. The state tables in this book include nearly 500 data items. The metropolitan area, county, and city tables include about 100 data items. The data in the tables are a small selection that show what is available for the counties and cities in the book. Appendix A includes an ACS Table Number for

		Households				
					Family households	
YEAR	Number	Average household size	Percent one-person housholds	Percent in group quarters	Family households as a percent of households	Percent of families with own children under 18 years
	23	24	25	26	27	28
2010	116,716,292	2.6	26.7	2.6	66.4	44.8
2000	105,480,101	2.6	25.8	2.8	68.1	48.2
1990	91,947,410	2.6	24.6	2.7	70.2	47.9
1980	80,389,673	2.8	22.7	2.5	73.2	51.2
1970	63,449,747	3.1	17.6	2.9	80.3	54.9
1960	53,021,061	3.3	13.3	2.8	84.9	56.9
1950	42,857,335	3.4	9.3	3.8	89.4	51.9

Decennial census household data for the United States, 1950–2010

every column enabling users to find the original data on the Census Bureau's website. Much more information is available for analysis of cities and counties or for analysis of specific racial or ethnic groups if those groups have large populations in a particular city or county. Furthermore, the 5-year data include most of the same information for all cities and counties in the nation, no matter how small.

One of the most notable differences between the census "long form" and the ACS is the time frame of the estimates. We are accustomed to the census data that give us specific information every ten years, a snapshot of the country on April 1. The ACS multiyear estimates are different. The data in this book are from the ACS 3-year, 2011–2013 estimates. They are not averages, nor do they represent 2012, the midpoint of the 3-year estimates. They are period estimates with data spread evenly throughout the 3-year survey time period.

Finally, it is always critical to remember that all estimates are subject to sampling error. On the Census Bureau's website, every ACS number is accompanied by its margin of error. In the interests of space and simplicity, this book does not include the margins of error, but all users are encouraged to consult the Census Bureau's website and to understand some basics: small differences are very likely to represent no difference at all; do not draw conclusions from small numbers; use these numbers as a starting point to explore the wealth of information from the ACS.

INTRODUCTION

The American Community Survey (ACS) has ushered in the most substantial change in the decennial census in more than 60 years. It replaced the decennial census long form in 2010, providing more current data throughout the decade by collecting long-form-type information annually rather than only once every 10 years. The ACS provides annual data for states, metropolitan areas, and large cities and counties, and combines 3 years of survey responses (in this book, 2011–2013) to produce data for midsize communities.

The ACS gathers demographic, social, economic, housing and financial information about the nation's people and communities on a continuous basis. The ACS is an ongoing survey conducted by the U.S. Census Bureau in every county, American Indian and Alaska Native Area, and Hawaiian Home Land in the United States. The ACS is also conducted as the Puerto Rico Community Survey in every municipality in Puerto Rico. As the largest survey in the United States, it is the only source of small-area data on a wide range of important social and economic characteristics for all communities in the country. After years of planning, development, and a demonstration period, the ACS began nationwide full implementation in 2005.

Data from the ACS are available on the Census Bureau's website. The ACS main page is www.census.gov/acs/www. More information on methodology can be found at http://www.census.gov/programs-surveys/acs/methodology.html. Additionally, users can also find more guidance here: http://www.census.gov/programs-surveys/acs/guidance.html.

A vast amount of information is collected in the ACS. In this publication, selections of these data have been assembled in various tables by subject and geographic type. The data tables in this book pertain to families and include a selection of characteristics from the ACS in five subject areas:

Living arrangements
Relationships
Marriages and births
Children
Income, poverty, and health insurance

The 3-year estimates from the ACS provide data for areas with populations of 20,000 or more. Because of space limitations and the small population groups in these tables, we have limited the geographic areas to those with populations of 50,000 or more. For each subject area, there is a table with a large selection of data for the United States, the 50 states, and the District of Columbia, followed by a smaller selection of data for 381 metropolitan areas, 980 counties, and 795 cities. Each part begins with a short discussion of some highlights, followed by the detailed tables.

Readers are encouraged to explore the Census Bureau's website to expand on the information contained here and to keep up to date with this constantly changing dataset.

Deirdre A. Gaquin has been a data use consultant to private organizations, government agencies, and universities for more than 30 years. Prior to that, she was Director of Data Access Services at Data Use & Access Laboratories, a pioneer in private sector distribution of federal statistical data. A former President of the Association of Public Data Users, Ms. Gaquin has served on numerous boards, panels, and task forces concerned with federal statistical data and has worked on five decennial censuses. She holds a Master of Urban Planning (MUP) degree from Hunter College. Ms. Gaquin is also an editor of Bernan Press's *County and City Extra; The Who, What, and Where of America; Places, Towns and Townships; The Congressional District Atlas; The Almanac of American Education: Race and Employment in America;* and *State and Metropolitan Area Data Book.*

Mary Meghan Ryan is the senior research editor for Bernan Press. She is also the editor for the *Handbook of U.S. Labor Statistics, State Profiles,* and the associate editor for *Business Statistics of the United States.*

Living Arrangements

PART A. LIVING ARRANGEMENTS

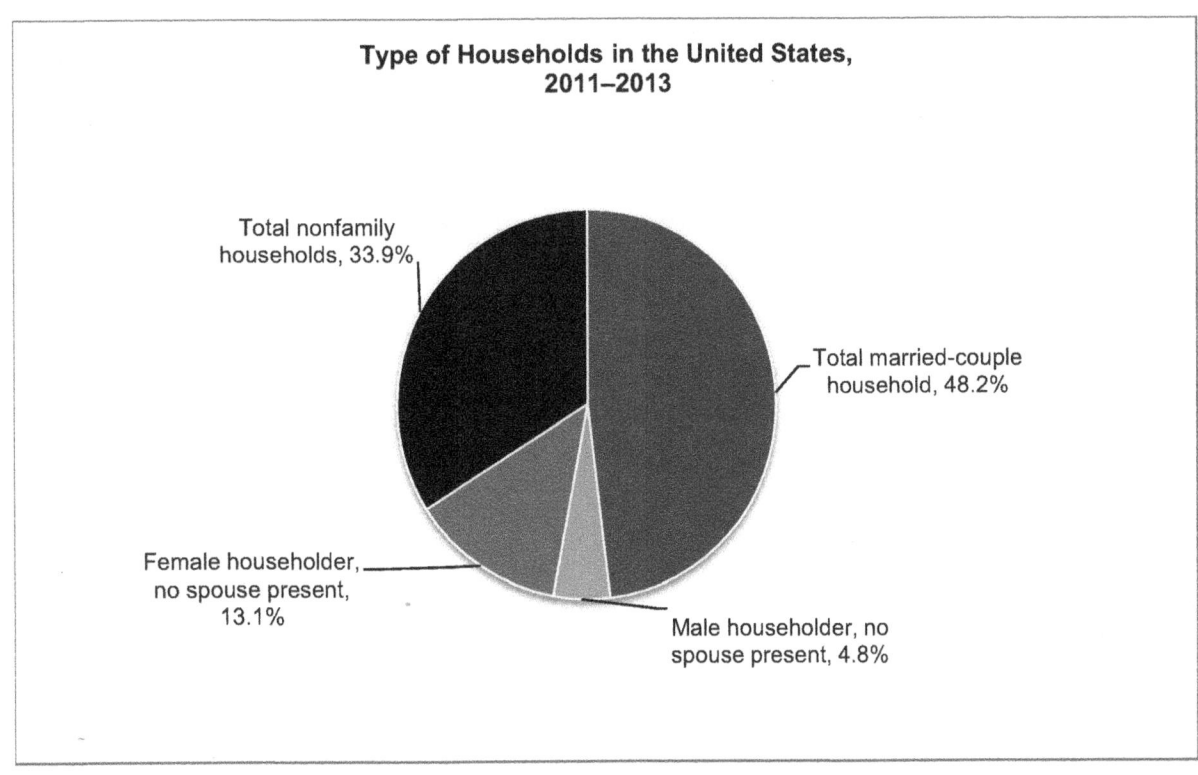

Type of Households in the United States, 2011–2013

Total nonfamily households, 33.9%

Total married-couple household, 48.2%

Female householder, no spouse present, 13.1%

Male householder, no spouse present, 4.8%

Most Americans live in households: groups of people who occupy housing units. Two-thirds of these households are families—people related by birth, marriage, or adoption. Nearly half of the households consist of married couples, with or without other relatives. About 18 percent of households are "other families", unmarried householders living with relatives. Another one-third are nonfamily households, most of them consisting of a householder living alone (27.7 percent of all households). Other nonfamily households can include roommates, boarders, foster children, and unmarried partners. Nearly six percent of households are unmarried partner households. These can be either family or nonfamily households, depending on whether the householder has relatives, making it a family household. About eight percent of the unmarried partners are same-sex partners. Same-sex married couples are included in the count of married-couple families for the first time in the 2013 ACS datasets. Less than one percent of the married-couple family households are same-sex married couples.[1]

Among the states, Utah has the highest proportion of married-couple families—over 60 percent. It also has the lowest proportion of householders living alone, below 20 percent. In the District of Columbia, with an urban population and a recent influx of young single people, 44.7 percent of householders live alone, and only 22.7 percent are married couple family households. There are six metropolitan areas where more than 60 percent of households are married-couple family households. Four are in Utah, one in Florida, and one in Maryland. In three metropolitan areas, the proportion of married-couple families is below 40 percent: New Orleans, LA; Greenville, SC; and Gainesville, FL. In many metropolitan areas, including Washington DC, the level of married-couple families is close to the national average of 48.2 percent of households.

In the United States, 64 percent of householders own their homes. Among householders over 65, fully 78.5 percent are homeowners, while only 33.1 percent of householders under 35 own their homes. In Minnesota, 45.1 percent of householders under 35 are already homeowners, while only 17 percent of these younger householders own their homes in the District

---

[1]See http://www.census.gov/hhes/samesex/ for information on counting same-sex couples.

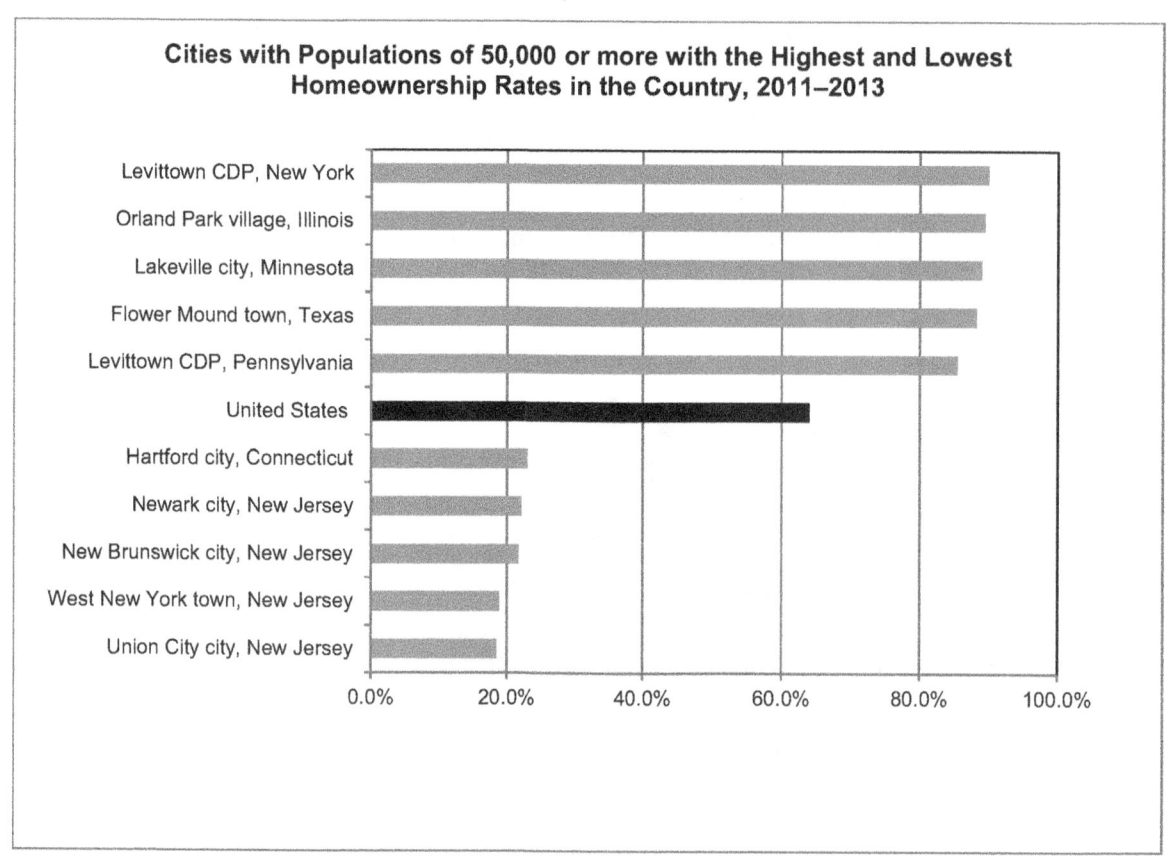

Cities with Populations of 50,000 or more with the Highest and Lowest Homeownership Rates in the Country, 2011–2013

of Columbia. Older householders in all states are more likely to be owners, with nearly half the states having ownership rates over 80 percent among people age 65 and older. South Carolina and West Virginia have the highest rates—over 85 percent—while the District of Columbia and New York are both below 70 percent.

Among cities, the highest homeownership rates are in the outer suburbs. Levittown, NY, outside New York City, has the highest rate—90 percent—followed closely by Orland Park, IL (near Chicago) and Lakeville, MN (near Minneapolis), at 89 percent. Six cities have homeownership rates below 25 percent, five cities in New Jersey plus Hartford, CT. Among these, Union City and West New York, NJ have the lowest rates, both below 20 percent.

Nationally, most householders are between the ages of 35 and 64 (57.9 percent) while 19.3 percent are younger and 22.8 are older. In seven cities—all home to universities or military bases—more than half of the householders are under 35 In four cities, more than 40 percent of householders are 65 or older. Port Charlotte, FL; Georgetown, TX; and Lake Havasu City, AZ are popular retirement destinations, while the fourth of these cities is South Carolina's capital, Columbia.

Table A-1: States—Living Arrangements

State FIPS code	State	Total Households	Family households	Married-couple families		Other families				
			Total family households	Total married-couple families	Married-couple families with children under 18	Total other families	Male householder, no spouse present	Male householder, no spouse present, with children under 18	Female householder, no spouse present	Female householder, no spouse present, with children under 18
	United States...............	115,731,304	76,444,922	55,747,944	24,087,823	20,696,978	5,552,073	3,145,773	15,144,905	9,971,834
1	Alabama.........................	1,837,292	1,236,566	877,131	352,585	359,435	78,039	41,465	281,396	186,204
2	Alaska...........................	250,875	167,553	124,654	58,256	42,899	14,623	9,610	28,276	20,892
4	Arizona.........................	2,381,501	1,560,655	1,124,577	467,578	436,078	128,659	79,316	307,419	210,081
5	Arkansas.......................	1,130,417	755,344	553,817	223,398	201,527	50,444	29,895	151,083	102,886
6	California......................	12,581,722	8,602,735	6,122,335	3,011,597	2,480,400	756,455	421,215	1,723,945	1,088,310
8	Colorado.......................	1,989,371	1,271,180	977,214	438,182	293,966	88,625	55,145	205,341	140,947
9	Connecticut...................	1,348,275	894,728	659,668	283,841	235,060	57,806	29,470	177,254	114,856
10	Delaware.......................	337,245	226,510	162,724	63,678	63,786	16,704	10,510	47,082	30,406
11	District of Columbia.......	268,015	114,484	60,812	23,780	53,672	10,422	5,242	43,250	26,256
12	Florida	7,168,502	4,594,006	3,316,161	1,210,007	1,277,845	328,016	178,049	949,829	599,949
13	Georgia	3,522,934	2,386,724	1,677,631	767,781	709,093	168,761	96,199	540,332	367,525
15	Hawaii..........................	449,296	311,096	231,601	104,244	79,495	24,052	12,393	55,443	31,520
16	Idaho...........................	583,452	404,512	321,679	143,462	82,833	25,891	17,547	56,942	39,779
17	Illinois..........................	4,763,457	3,114,415	2,289,104	1,019,422	825,311	217,971	120,103	607,340	392,735
18	Indiana.........................	2,482,558	1,647,579	1,226,311	514,781	421,268	113,561	69,456	307,707	212,627
19	Iowa.............................	1,227,201	792,745	626,297	252,005	166,448	50,332	32,264	116,116	83,765
20	Kansas..........................	1,109,747	727,902	563,171	246,947	164,731	48,528	30,545	116,203	82,347
21	Kentucky	1,693,399	1,131,310	830,215	339,097	301,095	81,609	47,017	219,486	147,367
22	Louisiana......................	1,715,997	1,127,030	746,288	314,259	380,742	88,115	48,881	292,627	200,491
23	Maine...........................	552,589	345,776	269,688	93,892	76,088	23,613	15,768	52,475	36,186
24	Maryland	2,149,424	1,432,364	1,012,523	451,445	419,841	103,457	57,156	316,384	200,925
25	Massachusetts	2,528,592	1,606,383	1,181,198	515,343	425,185	103,656	50,692	321,529	201,787
26	Michigan	3,815,532	2,489,254	1,824,333	730,812	664,921	173,808	99,204	491,113	317,517
27	Minnesota	2,109,924	1,367,091	1,073,564	453,092	293,527	89,810	55,147	203,717	144,649
28	Mississippi....................	1,086,898	743,178	486,734	203,376	256,444	53,538	29,094	202,906	139,238
29	Missouri........................	2,353,778	1,527,728	1,137,352	460,001	390,376	100,528	60,712	289,848	197,998
30	Montana	405,504	255,929	200,808	74,319	55,121	17,875	11,194	37,246	26,072
31	Nebraska.......................	729,572	472,470	369,775	157,017	102,695	30,903	19,582	71,792	52,130
32	Nevada.........................	995,980	641,060	449,385	199,921	191,675	60,512	35,600	131,163	89,006
33	New Hampshire..............	518,088	346,775	273,749	107,637	73,026	21,673	13,114	51,353	33,884
34	New Jersey.....................	3,181,152	2,203,456	1,615,471	747,084	587,985	156,004	77,084	431,981	260,872
35	New Mexico...................	760,251	494,555	343,336	140,513	151,219	42,386	26,293	108,833	75,674
36	New York.......................	7,214,163	4,594,587	3,162,525	1,399,903	1,432,062	361,667	179,816	1,070,395	653,641
37	North Carolina...............	3,721,358	2,467,843	1,789,108	736,285	678,735	166,110	97,875	512,625	348,274
38	North Dakota.................	291,468	176,378	141,699	56,853	34,679	11,927	7,522	22,752	16,737
39	Ohio.............................	4,551,497	2,920,189	2,132,541	850,725	787,648	202,091	117,763	585,557	396,057
40	Oklahoma......................	1,445,059	959,015	707,880	300,502	251,135	71,460	43,854	179,675	126,113
41	Oregon.........................	1,516,591	959,743	732,053	293,545	227,690	67,964	42,451	159,726	105,689
42	Pennsylvania..................	4,945,140	3,186,145	2,377,594	925,079	808,551	214,497	116,978	594,054	371,655
44	Rhode Island..................	410,347	257,316	180,743	72,196	76,573	19,692	10,597	56,881	36,851
45	South Carolina...............	1,781,957	1,199,885	843,305	331,440	356,580	83,197	45,959	273,383	182,234
46	South Dakota.................	326,086	210,494	163,039	64,529	47,455	15,319	9,866	32,136	24,910
47	Tennessee	2,480,467	1,646,360	1,203,173	490,035	443,187	110,893	62,376	332,294	218,031
48	Texas............................	8,965,352	6,235,820	4,486,257	2,212,772	1,749,563	459,059	263,089	1,290,504	906,665
49	Utah.............................	891,240	667,046	541,105	291,487	125,941	38,112	23,144	87,829	60,043
50	Vermont	256,563	159,883	126,295	45,489	33,588	10,325	6,627	23,263	16,309
51	Virginia.........................	3,026,761	2,033,567	1,527,465	670,367	506,102	130,373	72,111	375,729	242,649
53	Washington	2,634,496	1,694,518	1,300,793	558,150	393,725	119,005	73,235	274,720	182,738
54	West Virginia	739,759	479,062	359,823	127,675	119,239	34,505	19,361	84,734	52,348
55	Wisconsin......................	2,281,781	1,458,497	1,127,742	445,190	330,755	99,617	61,399	231,138	161,507
56	Wyoming.......................	222,679	145,481	115,498	46,249	29,983	9,884	6,788	20,099	14,502

State FIPS code	State	Total Households	Household type						Multi-generational households	
				Nonfamily households						
			Total nonfamily households	Nonfamily households, male householder	Nonfamily households, female householder	Householder living alone	Householder not living alone	Nonfamily households with children under 18	Total multi-generational households	Percent multi-generational households
	United States..............	115,731,304	39,286,382	18,266,678	21,019,704	32,086,699	7,199,683	337,027	4,382,927	3.8
1	Alabama..................	1,837,292	600,726	273,277	327,449	526,111	74,615	3,658	68,469	3.7
2	Alaska....................	250,875	83,322	46,545	36,777	65,166	18,156	790	9,179	3.7
4	Arizona..................	2,381,501	820,846	400,847	419,999	653,590	167,256	7,146	96,245	4.0
5	Arkansas................	1,130,417	375,073	173,868	201,205	318,384	56,689	3,932	36,520	3.2
6	California................	12,581,722	3,978,987	1,887,492	2,091,495	3,064,352	914,635	34,853	711,698	5.7
8	Colorado................	1,989,371	718,191	351,515	366,676	561,418	156,773	5,556	55,515	2.8
9	Connecticut.............	1,348,275	453,547	203,411	250,136	376,810	76,737	2,770	43,638	3.2
10	Delaware	337,245	110,735	48,243	62,492	89,129	21,606	927	14,358	4.3
11	District of Columbia.......	268,015	153,531	69,227	84,304	119,855	33,676	355	8,536	3.2
12	Florida...................	7,168,502	2,574,496	1,182,285	1,392,211	2,104,237	470,259	20,827	274,077	3.8
13	Georgia	3,522,934	1,136,210	524,479	611,731	946,096	190,114	9,122	152,584	4.3
15	Hawaii	449,296	138,200	70,442	67,758	107,962	30,238	1,298	36,203	8.1
16	Idaho....................	583,452	178,940	85,442	93,498	141,636	37,304	1,757	15,346	2.6
17	Illinois....................	4,763,457	1,649,042	759,506	889,536	1,377,539	271,503	13,615	177,328	3.7
18	Indiana..................	2,482,558	834,979	397,568	437,411	693,316	141,663	10,282	77,329	3.1
19	Iowa.....................	1,227,201	434,456	206,171	228,285	355,600	78,856	4,440	22,528	1.8
20	Kansas...................	1,109,747	381,845	179,382	202,463	316,446	65,399	3,734	27,392	2.5
21	Kentucky................	1,693,399	562,089	255,728	306,361	474,673	87,416	5,561	52,898	3.1
22	Louisiana	1,715,997	588,967	281,837	307,130	497,875	91,092	5,268	70,961	4.1
23	Maine....................	552,589	206,813	94,324	112,489	161,476	45,337	1,923	11,102	2.0
24	Maryland	2,149,424	717,060	311,822	405,238	589,214	127,846	5,852	95,420	4.4
25	Massachusetts	2,528,592	922,209	404,910	517,299	729,572	192,637	5,429	84,178	3.3
26	Michigan	3,815,532	1,326,278	620,825	705,453	1,104,765	221,513	12,842	113,475	3.0
27	Minnesota	2,109,924	742,833	349,665	393,168	597,806	145,027	6,671	40,578	1.9
28	Mississippi	1,086,898	343,720	157,576	186,144	299,127	44,593	2,890	52,311	4.8
29	Missouri	2,353,778	826,050	381,763	444,287	682,494	143,556	8,155	68,213	2.9
30	Montana..................	405,504	149,575	74,491	75,084	122,236	27,339	1,164	8,078	2.0
31	Nebraska	729,572	257,102	123,301	133,801	212,146	44,956	2,269	14,613	2.0
32	Nevada	995,980	354,920	187,502	167,418	278,024	76,896	3,926	41,572	4.2
33	New Hampshire	518,088	171,313	81,190	90,123	132,096	39,217	1,867	13,172	2.5
34	New Jersey...............	3,181,152	977,696	426,600	551,096	821,881	155,815	5,954	136,699	4.3
35	New Mexico..............	760,251	265,696	127,271	138,425	219,796	45,900	1,567	31,240	4.1
36	New York................	7,214,163	2,619,576	1,168,250	1,451,326	2,149,703	469,873	15,237	306,055	4.2
37	North Carolina...........	3,721,358	1,253,515	565,935	687,580	1,039,878	213,637	11,193	121,930	3.3
38	North Dakota.............	291,468	115,090	61,040	54,050	91,191	23,899	1,185	4,375	1.5
39	Ohio.....................	4,551,442	1,631,308	750,380	880,928	1,366,241	265,067	16,187	129,733	2.9
40	Oklahoma...............	1,445,059	486,044	230,162	255,882	408,052	77,992	5,097	46,234	3.2
41	Oregon..................	1,516,591	556,848	255,025	301,823	425,939	130,909	5,306	41,577	2.7
42	Pennsylvania.............	4,945,140	1,758,995	791,740	967,255	1,469,925	289,070	14,085	155,058	3.1
44	Rhode Island.............	410,347	153,031	69,596	83,435	123,868	29,163	925	13,305	3.2
45	South Carolina...........	1,781,957	582,072	264,456	317,616	491,496	90,576	4,660	70,676	4.0
46	South Dakota.............	326,086	115,592	58,585	57,007	95,421	20,171	1,120	6,572	2.0
47	Tennessee	2,480,467	834,107	381,303	452,804	705,160	128,947	7,438	87,915	3.5
48	Texas....................	8,965,352	2,729,532	1,321,379	1,408,153	2,246,331	483,201	23,191	442,134	4.9
49	Utah.....................	891,240	224,194	110,169	114,025	175,563	48,631	2,995	36,318	4.1
50	Vermont.................	256,563	96,680	44,151	52,529	72,705	23,975	1,011	4,688	1.8
51	Virginia..................	3,026,761	993,194	453,046	540,148	803,354	189,840	9,207	112,270	3.7
53	Washington..............	2,634,496	939,978	454,621	485,357	731,464	208,514	9,558	75,045	2.8
54	West Virginia	739,759	260,697	120,295	140,402	223,783	36,914	3,020	20,562	2.8
55	Wisconsin................	2,281,781	823,284	388,096	435,188	664,525	158,759	8,498	43,134	1.9
56	Wyoming................	222,679	77,198	39,944	37,254	61,272	15,926	714	3,891	1.7

State FIPS code	State	Unmarried partner households			Subfamilies			Families with children under 18				
								Married-couple families with own children			Other families with own children	
		Total unmarried partner households	Opposite-sex partner households	Same-sex partner households	Total subfamilies	Married-couple subfamilies	Single-parent subfamilies	All married-couple families with own children	Both parents in labor force, percent	One parent in labor force, percent	All other families with own children	Parent is in labor force, percent
	United States...............	6,893,442	6,320,992	572,450	3,807,652	1,152,079	2,655,573	22,468,546	65.9	32.3	11,121,083	83.9
1	Alabama..................	65,739	60,179	5,560	60,762	12,272	48,490	321,333	64.3	33.3	184,693	80.8
2	Alaska....................	20,378	19,460	918	8,080	1,874	6,206	54,988	63.4	34.4	26,440	83.6
4	Arizona...................	167,050	152,275	14,775	88,519	23,895	64,624	431,351	59.3	38.4	244,296	83.8
5	Arkansas.................	52,803	49,485	3,318	34,090	8,904	25,186	205,212	63.7	33.6	110,818	81.0
6	California................	865,734	784,537	81,197	649,429	258,532	390,897	2,788,662	60.8	37.1	1,254,892	82.9
8	Colorado	119,025	107,128	11,897	49,527	14,765	34,762	415,342	65.4	33.1	171,152	86.7
9	Connecticut.............	77,607	71,161	6,446	34,367	10,939	23,428	271,064	71.2	27.8	125,323	86.8
10	Delaware	23,262	21,129	2,133	12,240	2,785	9,455	57,489	71.3	27.0	33,172	88.3
11	District of Columbia.......	19,067	14,567	4,500	6,489	584	5,905	22,252	74.3	23.7	25,451	79.8
12	Florida	441,648	400,130	41,518	218,089	63,596	154,493	1,119,603	66.0	31.9	654,500	85.3
13	Georgia	174,462	155,862	18,600	127,319	28,507	98,812	708,435	64.4	33.8	383,850	83.9
15	Hawaii	29,021	26,083	2,938	35,452	19,223	16,229	90,117	67.9	30.2	31,952	82.6
16	Idaho	32,480	30,946	1,534	14,333	4,676	9,657	135,706	60.9	37.3	50,826	83.6
17	Illinois	271,196	249,442	21,754	156,178	45,215	110,963	961,775	67.4	31.2	434,103	86.9
18	Indiana	151,323	140,758	10,565	65,533	15,629	49,904	479,172	68.2	30.2	244,291	84.5
19	Iowa	77,210	73,542	3,668	19,185	4,658	14,527	241,447	77.8	21.1	105,909	87.1
20	Kansas	58,604	54,961	3,643	25,103	6,285	18,818	234,032	70.4	28.7	99,076	87.1
21	Kentucky	95,804	89,025	6,779	47,282	12,057	35,225	309,483	66.5	30.2	164,338	78.9
22	Louisiana...............	96,602	90,649	5,953	59,786	10,084	49,702	283,919	66.3	31.8	205,609	81.9
23	Maine...................	48,361	44,605	3,756	9,415	3,531	5,884	88,210	71.8	25.8	47,177	80.8
24	Maryland	123,188	112,052	11,136	79,658	21,381	58,277	421,095	72.9	25.9	213,299	88.7
25	Massachusetts	160,495	143,172	17,323	66,819	25,546	41,273	488,913	73.0	25.4	219,278	81.0
26	Michigan	224,600	209,868	14,732	97,792	26,594	71,198	689,117	67.3	30.4	361,679	82.5
27	Minnesota	141,952	130,353	11,599	36,540	10,364	26,176	436,627	77.2	21.8	181,432	87.5
28	Mississippi..............	49,719	46,867	2,852	46,373	6,998	39,375	182,417	66.7	30.9	134,353	81.0
29	Missouri.................	141,737	131,666	10,071	57,413	13,923	43,490	429,874	70.2	27.7	223,052	84.9
30	Montana.................	24,157	23,043	1,114	7,327	2,035	5,292	70,586	68.8	29.4	32,502	86.8
31	Nebraska	41,104	38,745	2,359	13,194	3,055	10,139	150,240	75.1	23.8	64,367	89.7
32	Nevada	72,550	67,430	5,120	35,679	12,528	23,151	186,500	62.8	35.4	106,993	86.8
33	New Hampshire	41,234	38,458	2,776	10,767	3,845	6,922	102,135	72.3	26.1	41,846	84.9
34	New Jersey..............	169,480	155,392	14,088	105,702	40,038	65,664	711,806	67.7	31.2	287,546	85.6
35	New Mexico..............	53,983	49,152	4,831	29,541	6,503	23,038	126,849	60.1	37.3	85,937	82.1
36	New York................	434,407	392,531	41,876	260,806	92,139	168,667	1,318,799	65.1	33.0	698,329	81.7
37	North Carolina..........	195,936	180,176	15,760	103,899	21,871	82,028	684,396	66.2	32.0	379,347	84.2
38	North Dakota...........	19,714	19,126	588	4,103	860	3,243	54,971	75.7	23.4	21,755	87.5
39	Ohio....................	280,067	260,128	19,939	109,738	24,721	85,017	792,021	69.8	28.3	446,387	83.4
40	Oklahoma................	74,268	69,661	4,607	42,432	11,097	31,335	277,345	63.4	34.3	143,775	81.7
41	Oregon..................	111,829	100,787	11,042	36,089	12,582	23,507	276,342	64.5	33.5	130,018	82.0
42	Pennsylvania	293,894	271,709	22,185	127,681	33,871	93,810	869,458	69.8	28.4	418,835	82.0
44	Rhode Island	27,993	25,045	2,948	10,812	3,628	7,184	67,845	74.4	24.4	41,284	83.4
45	South Carolina..........	86,712	81,049	5,663	59,948	10,656	49,292	302,229	66.2	31.4	186,480	83.8
46	South Dakota............	20,396	19,490	906	6,485	1,432	5,053	61,504	79.0	19.6	30,750	87.8
47	Tennessee	127,737	117,862	9,875	74,606	17,932	56,674	448,136	64.5	33.1	234,073	82.2
48	Texas...................	474,534	435,053	39,481	400,616	113,684	286,932	2,038,007	59.9	38.4	975,808	84.3
49	Utah....................	36,758	32,781	3,977	36,345	15,451	20,894	274,904	55.8	43.1	70,622	86.6
50	Vermont	21,762	19,551	2,211	4,024	1,197	2,827	43,136	76.2	22.4	20,805	81.9
51	Virginia.................	157,991	144,882	13,109	95,688	29,596	66,092	627,733	67.4	31.1	264,694	86.1
53	Washington	188,484	171,403	17,081	65,692	23,043	42,649	529,229	62.4	35.9	226,276	82.9
54	West Virginia...........	41,899	39,675	2,224	18,509	5,962	12,547	116,448	60.0	36.3	60,851	74.3
55	Wisconsin...............	151,728	142,748	8,980	38,800	10,612	28,188	426,365	75.3	23.5	201,623	86.2
56	Wyoming.................	15,758	15,213	545	3,396	924	2,472	43,927	68.9	30.0	19,219	86.3

Table A-1: States—Living Arrangements—*Continued*

State FIPS code	State	Total households	Householder is White alone, not Hispanic or Latino, percent	Householder is Black or African American alone, percent	Householder is Hispanic or Latino, percent	Householder is Asian alone, percent	Householder is Some other race alone, percent	Householder is two or more races, percent	Householder is American Indian or Alaska Native alone, percent	Householder is Native Hawaiian or other Pacific Islander alone, percent
	United States	115,731,304	69.8	12.1	12.0	4.2	3.3	1.8	0.7	0.1
1	Alabama	1,837,292	69.6	25.4	2.6	1.0	0.8	1.0	0.5	0.0
2	Alaska	250,875	72.1	3.4	4.9	3.7	1.1	5.0	11.2	0.7
4	Arizona	2,381,501	67.5	4.0	21.8	2.6	4.6	1.8	3.2	0.1
5	Arkansas	1,130,417	77.8	14.9	4.3	1.1	1.4	1.4	0.6	0.1
6	California	12,581,722	50.4	6.5	27.9	12.6	9.4	3.0	0.7	0.3
8	Colorado	1,989,371	76.6	3.7	15.4	2.4	3.4	2.2	0.8	0.1
9	Connecticut	1,348,275	75.2	9.5	11.0	3.3	3.9	1.6	0.2	0.0
10	Delaware	337,245	70.3	19.7	5.7	3.0	1.8	1.4	0.4	0.0
11	District of Columbia	268,015	40.7	46.2	8.0	3.5	2.9	2.2	0.4	0.0
12	Florida	7,168,502	64.9	13.7	18.5	2.1	1.8	1.5	0.3	0.0
13	Georgia	3,522,934	60.0	29.9	6.2	2.8	1.9	1.2	0.3	0.0
15	Hawaii	449,296	31.2	2.2	6.9	39.5	1.1	15.6	0.3	7.6
16	Idaho	583,452	88.2	0.5	7.9	1.1	1.8	1.6	1.1	0.0
17	Illinois	4,763,457	70.1	13.7	10.9	4.2	3.9	1.3	0.2	0.0
18	Indiana	2,482,558	84.3	8.8	4.3	1.4	1.7	1.2	0.2	0.0
19	Iowa	1,227,201	91.6	2.5	3.4	1.5	0.9	0.9	0.3	0.0
20	Kansas	1,109,747	82.9	5.6	7.3	1.9	1.6	1.7	0.8	0.0
21	Kentucky	1,693,399	88.1	7.8	2.1	0.9	0.5	1.1	0.2	0.0
22	Louisiana	1,715,997	63.7	29.9	3.5	1.3	0.8	1.2	0.6	0.0
23	Maine	552,589	96.0	0.7	1.0	0.7	0.1	1.1	0.6	0.0
24	Maryland	2,149,424	58.7	29.1	5.8	5.0	2.2	1.7	0.3	0.0
25	Massachusetts	2,528,592	80.0	6.1	7.9	4.7	3.4	1.8	0.2	0.0
26	Michigan	3,815,532	79.7	13.4	3.1	2.1	0.7	1.4	0.5	0.0
27	Minnesota	2,109,924	87.5	4.5	3.0	3.0	0.9	1.2	0.9	0.0
28	Mississippi	1,086,898	61.7	34.8	1.9	0.7	0.5	0.7	0.3	0.0
29	Missouri	2,353,778	83.5	11.0	2.5	1.4	0.7	1.3	0.4	0.1
30	Montana	405,504	90.9	0.4	2.1	0.6	0.3	1.6	4.7	0.0
31	Nebraska	729,572	86.5	4.3	6.2	1.5	1.5	1.1	0.7	0.1
32	Nevada	995,980	63.1	8.3	19.1	6.4	5.8	2.5	1.0	0.5
33	New Hampshire	518,088	93.9	1.0	2.1	1.9	0.4	1.1	0.2	0.0
34	New Jersey	3,181,152	63.9	13.2	14.6	7.5	4.8	1.6	0.2	0.0
35	New Mexico	760,251	49.2	2.1	40.3	1.1	10.3	2.2	6.4	0.1
36	New York	7,214,163	63.8	14.5	14.5	6.5	6.6	1.8	0.4	0.0
37	North Carolina	3,721,358	69.7	20.8	5.6	1.9	1.8	1.2	1.1	0.0
38	North Dakota	291,468	91.7	1.1	1.6	0.8	0.4	1.0	3.9	0.0
39	Ohio	4,551,497	82.9	12.0	2.3	1.5	0.6	1.3	0.2	0.0
40	Oklahoma	1,445,059	74.2	7.1	6.2	1.4	1.8	5.5	6.1	0.1
41	Oregon	1,516,591	84.3	1.6	7.6	3.2	2.2	2.5	1.1	0.3
42	Pennsylvania	4,945,140	82.7	9.9	4.3	2.3	1.4	1.1	0.2	0.0
44	Rhode Island	410,347	81.1	5.5	9.6	2.4	4.5	1.5	0.5	0.0
45	South Carolina	1,781,957	68.1	26.1	3.5	1.1	1.0	1.0	0.3	0.0
46	South Dakota	326,086	89.3	1.2	2.0	0.7	0.6	1.3	5.7	0.0
47	Tennessee	2,480,467	78.5	15.8	3.1	1.2	1.0	1.2	0.3	0.1
48	Texas	8,965,352	52.8	12.3	29.9	3.7	5.1	1.7	0.5	0.1
49	Utah	891,240	84.5	1.0	10.0	2.0	3.3	1.3	1.0	0.6
50	Vermont	256,563	95.9	0.7	1.1	0.8	0.2	1.2	0.4	0.0
51	Virginia	3,026,761	69.5	18.6	5.8	4.6	1.5	1.8	0.3	0.1
53	Washington	2,634,496	78.4	3.5	7.7	6.4	2.5	2.9	1.2	0.4
54	West Virginia	739,759	94.5	2.8	0.9	0.6	0.1	1.2	0.1	0.0
55	Wisconsin	2,281,781	87.4	5.4	4.0	1.6	1.1	1.0	0.8	0.0
56	Wyoming	222,679	89.1	0.8	6.8	0.7	1.8	1.7	1.6	0.0

Table A-1: States—Living Arrangements—Continued

State FIPS code	State	Total households by household type							
		Total households	Family households, percent	Married-couple family households, percent	Male householder, no spouse, percent	Female householder, no spouse, percent	Nonfamily households, percent	Householder living alone, percent	Nonfamily households, householder not living alone, percent
	United States...............	115,731,304	66.1	48.2	4.8	13.1	33.9	27.7	6.2
1	Alabama........................	1,837,292	67.3	47.7	4.2	15.3	32.7	28.6	4.1
2	Alaska..........................	250,875	66.8	49.7	5.8	11.3	33.2	26.0	7.2
4	Arizona.........................	2,381,501	65.5	47.2	5.4	12.9	34.5	27.4	7.0
5	Arkansas.......................	1,130,417	66.8	49.0	4.5	13.4	33.2	28.2	5.0
6	California......................	12,581,722	68.4	48.7	6.0	13.7	31.6	24.4	7.3
8	Colorado	1,989,371	63.9	49.1	4.5	10.3	36.1	28.2	7.9
9	Connecticut...................	1,348,275	66.4	48.9	4.3	13.1	33.6	27.9	5.7
10	Delaware	337,245	67.2	48.3	5.0	14.0	32.8	26.4	6.4
11	District of Columbia.......	268,015	42.7	22.7	3.9	16.1	57.3	44.7	12.6
12	Florida	7,168,502	64.1	46.3	4.6	13.3	35.9	29.4	6.6
13	Georgia	3,522,934	67.7	47.6	4.8	15.3	32.3	26.9	5.4
15	Hawaii..........................	449,296	69.2	51.5	5.4	12.3	30.8	24.0	6.7
16	Idaho...........................	583,452	69.3	55.1	4.4	9.8	30.7	24.3	6.4
17	Illinois..........................	4,763,457	65.4	48.1	4.6	12.7	34.6	28.9	5.7
18	Indiana.........................	2,482,558	66.4	49.4	4.6	12.4	33.6	27.9	5.7
19	Iowa............................	1,227,201	64.6	51.0	4.1	9.5	35.4	29.0	6.4
20	Kansas..........................	1,109,747	65.6	50.7	4.4	10.5	34.4	28.5	5.9
21	Kentucky	1,693,399	66.8	49.0	4.8	13.0	33.2	28.0	5.2
22	Louisiana	1,715,997	65.7	43.5	5.1	17.1	34.3	29.0	5.3
23	Maine...........................	552,589	62.6	48.8	4.3	9.5	37.4	29.2	8.2
24	Maryland	2,149,424	66.6	47.1	4.8	14.7	33.4	27.4	5.9
25	Massachusetts	2,528,592	63.5	46.7	4.1	12.7	36.5	28.9	7.6
26	Michigan	3,815,532	65.2	47.8	4.6	12.9	34.8	29.0	5.8
27	Minnesota.....................	2,109,924	64.8	50.9	4.3	9.7	35.2	28.3	6.9
28	Mississippi.....................	1,086,898	68.4	44.8	4.9	18.7	31.6	27.5	4.1
29	Missouri........................	2,353,778	64.9	48.3	4.3	12.3	35.1	29.0	6.1
30	Montana........................	405,504	63.1	49.5	4.4	9.2	36.9	30.1	6.7
31	Nebraska	729,572	64.8	50.7	4.2	9.8	35.2	29.1	6.2
32	Nevada.........................	995,980	64.4	45.1	6.1	13.2	35.6	27.9	7.7
33	New Hampshire..............	518,088	66.9	52.8	4.2	9.9	33.1	25.5	7.6
34	New Jersey....................	3,181,152	69.3	50.8	4.9	13.6	30.7	25.8	4.9
35	New Mexico...................	760,251	65.1	45.2	5.6	14.3	34.9	28.9	6.0
36	New York......................	7,214,163	63.7	43.8	5.0	14.8	36.3	29.8	6.5
37	North Carolina...............	3,721,358	66.3	48.1	4.5	13.8	33.7	27.9	5.7
38	North Dakota.................	291,468	60.5	48.6	4.1	7.8	39.5	31.3	8.2
39	Ohio............................	4,551,497	64.2	46.9	4.4	12.9	35.8	30.0	5.8
40	Oklahoma......................	1,445,059	66.4	49.0	4.9	12.4	33.6	28.2	5.4
41	Oregon.........................	1,516,591	63.3	48.3	4.5	10.5	36.7	28.1	8.6
42	Pennsylvania	4,945,140	64.4	48.1	4.3	12.0	35.6	29.7	5.8
44	Rhode Island.................	410,347	62.7	44.0	4.8	13.9	37.3	30.2	7.1
45	South Carolina...............	1,781,957	67.3	47.3	4.7	15.3	32.7	27.6	5.1
46	South Dakota.................	326,086	64.6	50.0	4.7	9.9	35.4	29.3	6.2
47	Tennessee	2,480,467	66.4	48.5	4.5	13.4	33.6	28.4	5.2
48	Texas...........................	8,965,352	69.6	50.0	5.1	14.4	30.4	25.1	5.4
49	Utah............................	891,240	74.8	60.7	4.3	9.9	25.2	19.7	5.5
50	Vermont........................	256,563	62.3	49.2	4.0	9.1	37.7	28.3	9.3
51	Virginia.........................	3,026,761	67.2	50.5	4.3	12.4	32.8	26.5	6.3
53	Washington	2,634,496	64.3	49.4	4.5	10.4	35.7	27.8	7.9
54	West Virginia.................	739,759	64.8	48.6	4.7	11.5	35.2	30.3	5.0
55	Wisconsin	2,281,781	63.9	49.4	4.4	10.1	36.1	29.1	7.0
56	Wyoming.......................	222,679	65.3	51.9	4.4	9.0	34.7	27.5	7.2

Table A-1: States—Living Arrangements—*Continued*

State FIPS code	State	Total White alone, not Hispanic or Latino, households	White alone householders, not Hispanic or Latino, households by household type						
			Family households, percent	Married-couple family households, percent	Male householder, no spouse, percent	Female householder, no spouse, percent	Nonfamily households, percent	Householder living alone, percent	Nonfamily households, householder not living alone, percent
	United States..............	80,761,578	64.3	51.3	3.8	9.2	35.7	29.2	6.5
1	Alabama........................	1,279,191	68.2	54.6	3.8	9.8	31.8	27.8	4.0
2	Alaska...........................	180,800	66.0	53.1	4.6	8.3	34.0	26.4	7.6
4	Arizona.........................	1,608,246	61.8	49.0	3.9	8.9	38.2	30.6	7.5
5	Arkansas.......................	878,946	67.1	52.9	4.1	10.1	32.9	27.8	5.0
6	California......................	6,340,531	60.8	47.8	4.0	9.0	39.2	30.7	8.5
8	Colorado	1,523,285	62.0	50.3	3.7	8.1	38.0	29.8	8.2
9	Connecticut.................	1,013,921	65.0	52.5	3.7	8.8	35.0	29.0	6.0
10	Delaware	237,243	65.6	51.6	4.0	10.0	34.4	27.7	6.7
11	District of Columbia.......	109,043	33.1	29.4	1.2	2.5	66.9	45.7	21.2
12	Florida..........................	4,649,399	60.9	48.6	3.5	8.7	39.1	32.2	6.9
13	Georgia	2,114,807	67.9	55.0	3.7	9.2	32.1	26.5	5.6
15	Hawaii..........................	140,217	62.4	51.9	3.4	7.0	37.6	27.9	9.7
16	Idaho............................	514,313	68.4	55.4	4.0	9.1	31.6	25.3	6.2
17	Illinois..........................	3,339,160	63.7	51.5	3.6	8.6	36.3	30.4	6.0
18	Indiana.........................	2,092,857	66.6	52.1	4.2	10.3	33.4	27.7	5.7
19	Iowa	1,124,131	64.3	52.0	3.8	8.5	35.7	29.5	6.2
20	Kansas..........................	920,463	65.0	52.4	3.8	8.8	35.0	29.2	5.8
21	Kentucky	1,491,596	67.3	51.3	4.6	11.4	32.7	27.7	5.0
22	Louisiana	1,092,854	66.1	51.5	4.5	10.1	33.9	28.2	5.6
23	Maine...........................	530,515	62.6	49.1	4.3	9.2	37.4	29.3	8.1
24	Maryland	1,262,481	66.0	53.5	3.7	8.9	34.0	27.4	6.6
25	Massachusetts	2,021,612	62.2	49.1	3.5	9.6	37.8	30.2	7.7
26	Michigan	3,041,154	65.7	51.9	4.1	9.6	34.3	28.3	6.0
27	Minnesota	1,847,062	64.2	52.6	3.7	7.9	35.8	29.0	6.8
28	Mississippi....................	670,894	69.1	54.4	4.2	10.5	30.9	26.9	4.1
29	Missouri........................	1,965,668	65.5	51.7	4.0	9.8	34.5	28.4	6.1
30	Montana........................	368,754	62.7	50.6	4.0	8.0	37.3	30.5	6.9
31	Nebraska	631,286	63.9	52.2	3.5	8.2	36.1	29.9	6.2
32	Nevada	628,269	60.2	45.8	4.7	9.7	39.8	31.4	8.4
33	New Hampshire	486,290	66.8	53.0	4.0	9.7	33.2	25.7	7.6
34	New Jersey....................	2,031,762	67.1	54.6	3.5	9.0	32.9	27.9	5.0
35	New Mexico..................	374,221	60.7	48.2	3.6	8.9	39.3	32.7	6.6
36	New York.......................	4,599,705	61.2	48.5	3.7	8.9	38.8	31.7	7.1
37	North Carolina..............	2,595,107	66.1	53.5	3.5	9.0	33.9	28.2	5.8
38	North Dakota................	267,373	60.1	49.8	3.6	6.7	39.9	31.8	8.1
39	Ohio.............................	3,773,279	65.0	50.6	4.2	10.2	35.0	29.1	5.9
40	Oklahoma.....................	1,072,905	65.8	51.6	4.2	10.0	34.2	28.9	5.3
41	Oregon.........................	1,278,025	61.9	48.5	3.9	9.5	38.1	29.3	8.8
42	Pennsylvania.................	4,090,201	64.6	51.5	3.9	9.2	35.4	29.5	5.9
44	Rhode Island.................	332,977	61.1	46.4	3.9	10.8	38.9	31.7	7.2
45	South Carolina..............	1,213,071	67.5	54.1	3.9	9.5	32.5	27.1	5.4
46	South Dakota................	291,121	64.0	52.2	4.0	7.8	36.0	29.9	6.1
47	Tennessee	1,947,156	66.9	52.9	4.0	10.0	33.1	27.9	5.2
48	Texas............................	4,730,837	65.7	53.2	3.6	8.8	34.3	28.4	5.9
49	Utah.............................	753,295	74.3	62.0	3.6	8.7	25.7	20.4	5.3
50	Vermont........................	245,957	62.4	49.6	4.0	8.8	37.6	28.4	9.2
51	Virginia.........................	2,103,265	66.3	54.2	3.6	8.6	33.7	27.2	6.5
53	Washington	2,064,881	63.0	50.3	3.9	8.9	37.0	29.0	8.0
54	West Virginia	698,769	65.0	49.4	4.6	11.0	35.0	30.1	4.9
55	Wisconsin.....................	1,994,167	63.4	51.7	3.9	7.9	36.6	29.6	7.0
56	Wyoming......................	198,516	65.1	52.8	4.2	8.1	34.9	27.7	7.1

Table A-1: States—Living Arrangements—*Continued*

State FIPS code	State	Black alone householders, households by household type							
		Total Black alone householder households	Family households, percent	Married-couple family households, percent	Male householder, no spouse, percent	Female householder, no spouse, percent	Nonfamily households, percent	Householder living alone, percent	Nonfamily households, householder not living alone, percent
	United States...............	13,977,892	62.5	27.4	6.1	29.0	37.5	32.8	4.7
1	Alabama.......................	466,927	63.8	28.0	5.0	30.7	36.2	32.6	3.7
2	Alaska.........................	8,484	60.4	35.4	7.1	17.9	39.6	35.0	4.6
4	Arizona.......................	94,759	59.7	29.5	7.2	23.0	40.3	33.5	6.8
5	Arkansas.....................	168,000	61.3	25.8	5.6	29.8	38.7	34.6	4.1
6	California....................	817,218	60.1	27.0	6.8	26.3	39.9	33.7	6.1
8	Colorado	73,354	60.5	32.9	6.2	21.4	39.5	33.1	6.4
9	Connecticut.................	128,428	65.0	27.8	5.3	31.9	35.0	31.5	3.5
10	Delaware	66,457	67.8	33.3	7.2	27.3	32.2	26.9	5.3
11	District of Columbia.......	123,726	50.9	15.3	5.8	29.8	49.1	44.6	4.5
12	Florida	980,767	65.7	30.7	6.3	28.8	34.3	29.3	5.0
13	Georgia	1,053,446	64.3	30.2	5.8	28.2	35.7	31.1	4.6
15	Hawaii	9,826	66.6	52.3	4.9	9.5	33.4	28.1	5.3
16	Idaho	2,643	65.5	43.0	15.6	6.9	34.5	23.8	10.7
17	Illinois	654,458	60.6	23.2	5.8	31.5	39.4	35.1	4.3
18	Indiana	219,262	60.5	24.6	5.9	30.0	39.5	34.9	4.6
19	Iowa	30,802	60.4	25.6	7.4	27.4	39.6	32.6	7.0
20	Kansas........................	62,654	57.7	28.4	5.0	24.3	42.3	35.3	6.9
21	Kentucky	131,418	59.8	25.2	5.3	29.3	40.2	35.2	5.0
22	Louisiana	513,329	64.5	26.4	5.8	32.2	35.5	31.7	3.8
23	Maine.........................	3,685	63.7	37.3	4.7	21.7	36.3	30.4	5.9
24	Maryland	624,433	63.7	31.0	5.6	27.2	36.3	31.7	4.6
25	Massachusetts	155,378	65.7	27.9	7.0	30.8	34.3	28.5	5.8
26	Michigan.....................	510,649	59.6	22.4	6.3	30.9	40.4	36.2	4.2
27	Minnesota	94,944	62.9	25.8	8.2	28.9	37.1	30.4	6.6
28	Mississippi...................	378,312	66.9	27.3	6.0	33.6	33.1	29.3	3.8
29	Missouri......................	258,340	59.5	23.5	5.7	30.3	40.5	35.8	4.7
30	Montana......................	1,426	60.8	31.9	8.8	20.1	39.2	39.2	0.0
31	Nebraska.....................	31,223	58.4	24.7	6.5	27.3	41.6	37.7	3.8
32	Nevada	83,044	59.6	28.0	6.9	24.7	40.4	33.4	7.0
33	New Hampshire	5,393	69.2	38.0	8.7	22.5	30.8	20.6	10.3
34	New Jersey...................	419,710	64.2	28.7	6.7	28.7	35.8	31.7	4.1
35	New Mexico.................	15,967	57.9	30.5	9.0	18.4	42.1	35.5	6.6
36	New York.....................	1,048,430	63.6	25.3	6.8	31.5	36.4	32.2	4.2
37	North Carolina..............	775,675	62.9	28.9	5.6	28.5	37.1	32.1	4.9
38	North Dakota................	3,231	54.0	32.6	9.1	12.4	46.0	34.2	11.7
39	Ohio	546,936	57.4	22.2	5.4	29.7	42.6	38.2	4.5
40	Oklahoma....................	102,536	60.3	27.0	6.7	26.6	39.7	35.0	4.7
41	Oregon	24,420	56.2	25.7	8.8	21.7	43.8	36.9	6.9
42	Pennsylvania	490,615	58.1	22.4	6.0	29.6	41.9	37.4	4.5
44	Rhode Island................	22,557	66.3	27.9	6.6	31.8	33.7	27.5	6.2
45	South Carolina..............	465,851	65.3	29.1	5.8	30.4	34.7	30.8	3.8
46	South Dakota................	3,852	59.5	30.6	12.5	16.4	40.5	31.8	8.7
47	Tennessee	391,766	62.1	26.4	5.7	29.9	37.9	33.6	4.3
48	Texas..........................	1,103,177	63.1	30.3	5.9	26.9	36.9	32.5	4.4
49	Utah...........................	9,014	62.2	36.2	10.0	16.1	37.8	28.4	9.4
50	Vermont......................	1,764	62.0	34.4	13.2	14.5	38.0	22.6	15.5
51	Virginia.......................	561,795	64.8	32.8	5.7	26.3	35.2	30.3	4.9
53	Washington..................	92,442	56.4	29.9	6.8	19.7	43.6	36.3	7.3
54	West Virginia................	20,517	57.2	27.7	6.6	22.9	42.8	38.4	4.4
55	Wisconsin....................	123,176	62.1	19.8	6.7	35.6	37.9	32.4	5.5
56	Wyoming.....................	1,676	65.1	38.7	11.0	15.5	34.9	32.7	2.2

Table A-1: States—Living Arrangements—*Continued*

State FIPS code	State	Hispanic or Latino householders, households by household type							
		Total Hispanic or Latino householder households	Family households, percent	Married-couple family households, percent	Male householder, no spouse, percent	Female householder, no spouse, percent	Nonfamily households, percent	Householder living alone, percent	Nonfamily households, householder not living alone, percent
	United States...............	13,945,351	77.1	47.8	8.9	20.4	22.9	17.1	5.9
1	Alabama........................	47,294	77.7	52.7	9.6	15.4	22.3	14.7	7.5
2	Alaska..........................	12,313	70.0	44.7	7.7	17.6	30.0	24.9	5.1
4	Arizona........................	518,243	76.9	45.9	9.3	21.7	23.1	17.5	5.6
5	Arkansas......................	49,100	79.9	55.5	7.9	16.5	20.1	14.1	6.0
6	California.....................	3,509,217	81.4	51.3	9.7	20.3	18.6	13.1	5.6
8	Colorado	305,517	73.3	47.0	7.8	18.6	26.7	20.2	6.5
9	Connecticut..................	148,742	73.2	37.0	8.2	28.0	26.8	21.0	5.8
10	Delaware	19,350	80.0	50.2	9.3	20.5	20.0	13.1	6.9
11	District of Columbia.......	21,423	51.5	29.0	8.6	13.9	48.5	34.9	13.5
12	Florida	1,325,486	73.1	47.8	7.1	18.1	26.9	20.4	6.5
13	Georgia	217,272	78.8	52.9	10.2	15.6	21.2	14.2	7.0
15	Hawaii.........................	31,215	69.7	47.8	5.9	16.0	30.3	20.2	10.1
16	Idaho..........................	46,147	79.7	55.5	7.8	16.4	20.3	13.3	6.9
17	Illinois.........................	520,363	80.1	52.6	9.8	17.7	19.9	14.9	5.0
18	Indiana........................	105,526	75.7	48.3	9.8	17.6	24.3	18.1	6.2
19	Iowa...........................	41,754	75.3	46.9	9.9	18.5	24.7	16.2	8.4
20	Kansas.........................	81,193	76.8	49.3	10.0	17.5	23.2	17.3	5.9
21	Kentucky......................	34,921	71.4	43.5	11.5	16.4	28.6	18.9	9.7
22	Louisiana	60,184	66.5	41.9	8.8	15.7	33.5	22.9	10.6
23	Maine..........................	5,325	59.8	37.5	5.1	17.2	40.2	25.8	14.5
24	Maryland	125,364	79.3	48.0	13.3	18.0	20.7	13.9	6.8
25	Massachusetts	200,877	71.3	31.5	7.3	32.5	28.7	21.5	7.2
26	Michigan	119,364	73.0	45.7	7.9	19.4	27.0	20.9	6.0
27	Minnesota	64,190	75.2	44.0	11.0	20.2	24.8	17.6	7.2
28	Mississippi....................	20,409	73.4	49.2	9.1	15.1	26.6	18.8	7.8
29	Missouri.......................	58,129	70.9	47.4	7.0	16.5	29.1	21.4	7.7
30	Montana.......................	8,677	66.6	43.2	6.3	17.0	33.4	26.4	7.0
31	Nebraska	45,127	80.2	49.8	12.4	18.0	19.8	14.0	5.8
32	Nevada	190,072	78.0	49.0	10.2	18.8	22.0	16.0	6.0
33	New Hampshire	10,779	72.5	46.2	6.5	19.8	27.5	20.3	7.2
34	New Jersey....................	465,632	76.8	43.1	9.9	23.8	23.2	17.6	5.7
35	New Mexico..................	306,302	70.2	44.1	7.4	18.8	29.8	24.3	5.5
36	New York.....................	1,046,678	71.2	34.9	8.9	27.4	28.8	23.2	5.6
37	North Carolina..............	207,630	78.3	48.9	12.0	17.4	21.7	13.3	8.4
38	North Dakota................	4,659	65.1	40.9	11.5	12.8	34.9	26.3	8.5
39	Ohio...........................	104,668	68.7	38.7	8.6	21.4	31.3	23.0	8.3
40	Oklahoma....................	89,286	77.4	51.5	9.6	16.4	22.6	16.5	6.1
41	Oregon........................	114,797	78.4	51.1	10.0	17.2	21.6	14.5	7.2
42	Pennsylvania	212,672	71.3	35.4	9.2	26.7	28.7	21.9	6.8
44	Rhode Island.................	39,423	74.1	32.9	10.9	30.3	25.9	19.0	6.8
45	South Carolina..............	63,089	76.8	50.3	10.2	16.4	23.2	15.7	7.5
46	South Dakota................	6,484	66.1	36.3	9.5	20.2	33.9	24.2	9.8
47	Tennessee	76,914	75.1	49.1	10.2	15.8	24.9	16.9	8.0
48	Texas..........................	2,680,717	78.6	51.2	7.6	19.8	21.4	16.6	4.8
49	Utah...........................	89,210	81.0	55.7	8.7	16.6	19.0	13.2	5.8
50	Vermont.......................	2,873	57.2	36.0	5.7	15.5	42.8	26.9	16.0
51	Virginia.......................	174,103	77.8	51.9	9.1	16.9	22.2	14.5	7.7
53	Washington	204,092	76.2	48.5	9.1	18.6	23.8	16.6	7.2
54	West Virginia	6,344	65.9	43.7	8.9	13.4	34.1	21.5	12.6
55	Wisconsin	91,120	73.6	43.6	10.5	19.5	26.4	18.5	7.9
56	Wyoming......................	15,085	68.6	46.6	6.5	15.4	31.4	24.8	6.6

State FIPS code	State	Total Asian alone householder households	Family households, percent	Married-couple family households, percent	Male householder, no spouse, percent	Female householder, no spouse, percent	Nonfamily households, percent	Householder living alone, percent	Nonfamily households, householder not living alone, percent
	United States...............	4,839,422	74.2	60.0	4.7	9.5	25.8	19.5	6.3
1	Alabama........................	18,185	68.0	59.1	2.9	6.1	32.0	25.3	6.6
2	Alaska..........................	9,227	74.1	49.3	9.9	14.9	25.9	20.9	5.0
4	Arizona........................	61,944	69.0	55.6	4.9	8.5	31.0	23.4	7.6
5	Arkansas......................	12,275	72.8	59.2	3.3	10.2	27.2	18.7	8.5
6	California.....................	1,589,285	75.0	58.6	5.5	11.0	25.0	18.8	6.1
8	Colorado	46,788	69.5	55.9	3.5	10.2	30.5	23.2	7.3
9	Connecticut..................	44,019	78.5	68.3	3.1	7.0	21.5	16.8	4.7
10	Delaware	10,010	79.0	68.3	3.0	7.7	21.0	14.2	6.8
11	District of Columbia.......	9,476	34.1	26.7	2.2	5.2	65.9	53.4	12.5
12	Florida	148,316	75.3	61.1	4.0	10.2	24.7	18.6	6.1
13	Georgia	99,862	77.6	64.5	4.8	8.4	22.4	17.0	5.4
15	Hawaii.........................	177,532	71.8	53.4	5.4	13.0	28.2	23.8	4.3
16	Idaho...........................	6,280	68.8	60.4	3.2	5.2	31.2	24.0	7.2
17	Illinois	198,015	73.4	62.4	3.6	7.3	26.6	20.0	6.6
18	Indiana	35,855	65.2	55.0	3.5	6.7	34.8	24.8	10.0
19	Iowa............................	17,804	70.2	57.7	4.5	8.1	29.8	19.4	10.4
20	Kansas.........................	21,490	74.0	60.4	3.8	9.7	26.0	18.4	7.6
21	Kentucky	16,064	69.7	55.2	5.5	9.0	30.3	22.3	7.9
22	Louisiana	22,595	69.6	53.8	6.7	9.1	30.4	21.6	8.8
23	Maine..........................	4,049	69.3	53.6	6.0	9.8	30.7	17.8	12.8
24	Maryland	106,963	77.1	65.7	4.0	7.4	22.9	18.6	4.4
25	Massachusetts	118,538	71.5	58.1	4.5	9.0	28.5	19.7	8.7
26	Michigan	78,222	73.7	64.5	3.0	6.3	26.3	19.1	7.1
27	Minnesota	62,743	74.9	56.8	6.3	11.8	25.1	17.9	7.2
28	Mississippi...................	7,908	72.7	63.3	1.7	7.7	27.3	19.9	7.4
29	Missouri.......................	31,949	67.8	58.0	3.1	6.7	32.2	23.4	8.8
30	Montana......................	2,278	53.5	40.9	3.4	9.2	46.5	38.7	7.8
31	Nebraska	10,955	68.0	57.3	3.9	6.8	32.0	22.5	9.4
32	Nevada........................	63,473	72.7	54.2	6.1	12.4	27.3	20.8	6.5
33	New Hampshire	9,663	75.4	67.5	2.1	5.8	24.6	18.5	6.1
34	New Jersey...................	239,580	82.3	71.8	3.6	6.8	17.7	14.2	3.5
35	New Mexico..................	8,658	64.2	49.5	3.5	11.2	35.8	28.1	7.7
36	New York.....................	465,406	72.3	58.0	5.1	9.3	27.7	20.7	6.9
37	North Carolina..............	69,904	75.5	65.2	3.3	6.9	24.5	18.4	6.1
38	North Dakota................	2,410	56.9	44.4	0.7	11.8	43.1	27.8	15.3
39	Ohio............................	67,623	69.1	60.6	2.7	5.8	30.9	23.3	7.6
40	Oklahoma....................	20,046	70.8	56.4	4.7	9.6	29.2	20.0	9.3
41	Oregon	48,633	69.1	55.0	4.4	9.7	30.9	21.8	9.1
42	Pennsylvania	114,230	73.3	61.2	4.5	7.6	26.7	19.8	6.9
44	Rhode Island................	9,737	66.7	47.5	8.0	11.3	33.3	24.4	8.8
45	South Carolina..............	19,769	75.0	61.1	5.0	8.9	25.0	19.0	6.0
46	South Dakota................	2,238	66.4	51.5	9.1	5.8	33.6	20.1	13.5
47	Tennessee	30,144	75.3	62.2	4.3	8.9	24.7	19.3	5.3
48	Texas...........................	327,713	76.7	64.5	4.0	8.2	23.3	17.6	5.6
49	Utah............................	18,211	73.7	60.2	4.7	8.9	26.3	19.3	6.9
50	Vermont.......................	2,175	68.1	58.3	1.9	8.0	31.9	25.4	6.5
51	Virginia........................	139,390	77.8	65.6	4.0	8.2	22.2	16.7	5.5
53	Washington	169,110	69.8	55.9	4.3	9.6	30.2	23.1	7.1
54	West Virginia	4,092	64.6	57.0	0.2	7.4	35.4	25.8	9.6
55	Wisconsin....................	37,022	72.7	56.6	6.0	10.1	27.3	19.8	7.5
56	Wyoming.....................	1,568	49.3	45.9	1.7	1.7	50.7	34.4	16.3

Table A-1: States—Living Arrangements—*Continued*

State FIPS code	State	Householders age 15 to 34, households by household type					
		Total householders age 15 to 34	Married-couple family households, percent	Male householder, no spouse, percent	Female householder, no spouse, percent	Nonfamily householder living alone, percent	Nonfamily households, householder not living alone, percent
	United States...............	22,385,845	37.0	6.8	17.7	22.7	15.7
1	Alabama.....................	347,599	39.1	5.6	22.6	22.2	10.4
2	Alaska.........................	60,460	43.8	7.6	15.0	20.3	13.3
4	Arizona.......................	482,789	35.7	8.6	17.6	22.9	15.2
5	Arkansas.....................	232,983	42.4	6.3	19.1	20.1	12.0
6	California....................	2,437,073	36.7	9.2	16.3	20.0	17.7
8	Colorado.....................	447,640	37.5	6.0	12.4	23.9	20.3
9	Connecticut.................	208,052	34.9	6.6	20.2	22.3	16.1
10	Delaware	57,109	36.3	8.2	19.8	19.8	15.9
11	District of Columbia.......	79,242	16.0	3.2	12.9	40.9	27.0
12	Florida........................	1,135,804	33.6	7.2	19.7	23.9	15.6
13	Georgia	716,435	37.2	6.6	20.2	23.5	12.5
15	Hawaii.........................	83,282	44.4	6.5	12.9	20.5	15.7
16	Idaho..........................	129,095	50.1	5.0	13.7	15.8	15.4
17	Illinois........................	932,492	35.6	6.7	16.5	26.0	15.3
18	Indiana.......................	502,958	39.0	6.3	18.5	22.3	14.0
19	Iowa...........................	266,841	37.9	6.0	14.4	24.1	17.7
20	Kansas........................	252,317	40.2	6.3	15.0	23.1	15.4
21	Kentucky.....................	327,127	41.3	6.4	19.4	20.3	12.7
22	Louisiana	367,466	32.6	6.7	24.7	23.8	12.2
23	Maine.........................	87,543	36.3	6.9	16.4	20.0	20.4
24	Maryland.....................	377,899	35.4	6.8	18.9	23.9	15.0
25	Massachusetts	438,004	31.3	5.3	16.5	23.6	23.3
26	Michigan.....................	671,124	34.8	6.5	19.4	23.0	16.2
27	Minnesota	443,814	38.1	6.2	14.4	23.1	18.2
28	Mississippi...................	203,746	37.6	6.0	27.8	18.8	9.9
29	Missouri......................	488,579	37.9	5.8	18.3	22.9	15.1
30	Montana......................	80,120	37.9	6.7	14.8	22.0	18.6
31	Nebraska.....................	169,629	38.3	6.7	14.6	24.5	15.8
32	Nevada........................	202,711	37.4	8.5	17.9	21.6	14.6
33	New Hampshire	81,666	37.6	6.6	14.9	20.8	20.1
34	New Jersey...................	473,286	39.5	7.8	18.5	20.8	13.4
35	New Mexico..................	149,591	36.8	8.6	21.8	19.5	13.3
36	New York.....................	1,267,044	31.1	6.9	17.7	26.1	18.2
37	North Carolina..............	731,482	37.6	6.2	18.9	22.9	14.4
38	North Dakota................	78,740	35.9	5.6	10.9	26.1	21.5
39	Ohio...........................	853,496	34.9	6.2	20.5	23.7	14.8
40	Oklahoma....................	323,087	41.6	6.8	17.8	21.4	12.5
41	Oregon........................	301,000	37.0	6.2	14.1	20.8	21.9
42	Pennsylvania	834,330	34.7	5.9	17.5	25.2	16.8
44	Rhode Island................	72,077	28.5	7.4	20.1	23.4	20.6
45	South Carolina.............	336,003	36.1	6.6	22.5	21.7	13.2
46	South Dakota................	74,596	37.4	7.8	15.1	24.7	15.0
47	Tennessee....................	486,190	39.2	6.1	19.2	23.0	12.5
48	Texas...........................	2,041,234	39.9	7.0	18.3	22.4	12.4
49	Utah...........................	237,460	58.5	5.2	9.9	13.4	13.1
50	Vermont	43,676	31.8	4.8	15.9	20.3	27.1
51	Virginia.......................	590,258	39.1	5.7	16.5	22.2	16.4
53	Washington..................	549,272	39.3	6.3	13.4	22.5	18.4
54	West Virginia	122,891	39.4	6.4	18.2	23.8	12.2
55	Wisconsin....................	456,995	35.4	6.4	15.7	23.8	18.8
56	Wyoming......................	51,538	41.4	6.6	13.5	21.1	17.3

Table A-1: States—Living Arrangements—*Continued*

State FIPS code	State	Householders age 35 to 64, households by household type					
		Total householders age 35 to 64	Married-couple family households, percent	Male householder, no spouse, percent	Female householder, no spouse, percent	Nonfamily householder living alone, percent	Nonfamily households, householder not living alone, percent
	United States...............	66,971,438	53.7	5.1	13.5	23.2	4.5
1	Alabama......................	1,047,077	52.6	4.6	15.1	24.7	3.0
2	Alaska........................	152,899	53.2	5.8	10.5	24.6	5.8
4	Arizona......................	1,310,711	50.8	5.7	13.9	23.9	5.6
5	Arkansas.....................	621,030	53.0	4.8	13.5	24.8	3.8
6	California....................	7,509,831	54.6	6.0	14.4	19.8	5.2
8	Colorado	1,161,018	54.7	4.7	10.8	24.9	4.8
9	Connecticut.................	817,408	55.4	4.5	13.8	22.1	4.2
10	Delaware	194,503	52.8	5.3	14.9	21.8	5.2
11	District of Columbia.......	139,538	25.6	4.5	18.7	43.6	7.5
12	Florida	3,957,695	50.0	5.2	14.8	24.4	5.6
13	Georgia	2,116,412	52.2	5.0	15.4	23.2	4.1
15	Hawaii.......................	251,430	56.8	5.3	11.6	21.1	5.3
16	Idaho........................	321,081	59.3	5.3	9.8	21.1	4.5
17	Illinois.......................	2,773,859	54.8	4.8	13.1	23.5	3.9
18	Indiana	1,423,791	55.1	4.9	12.2	23.5	4.2
19	Iowa.........................	664,667	58.3	4.6	9.5	23.5	4.0
20	Kansas.......................	609,756	57.4	4.7	10.6	23.7	3.7
21	Kentucky	975,886	54.0	5.2	12.6	24.2	4.0
22	Louisiana	973,733	48.8	5.3	16.5	25.4	3.9
23	Maine........................	324,426	54.0	4.6	9.6	24.7	7.0
24	Maryland	1,310,862	52.2	5.0	15.4	22.9	4.5
25	Massachusetts	1,500,293	53.8	4.5	13.6	23.0	5.0
26	Michigan	2,224,730	53.7	4.9	12.9	24.4	4.2
27	Minnesota	1,204,908	57.5	4.5	9.9	23.6	4.5
28	Mississippi..................	626,529	49.0	5.3	18.6	24.0	3.2
29	Missouri.....................	1,310,449	53.8	4.7	12.3	24.8	4.5
30	Montana.....................	225,986	55.0	4.9	9.2	26.4	4.6
31	Nebraska....................	396,895	58.0	4.3	9.9	24.0	3.8
32	Nevada......................	579,934	48.1	6.5	13.6	25.2	6.5
33	New Hampshire	319,054	58.7	4.3	10.1	21.0	5.9
34	New Jersey..................	1,958,676	56.9	5.1	14.3	19.9	3.8
35	New Mexico.................	427,333	48.5	5.8	14.3	26.3	5.0
36	New York....................	4,272,339	49.8	5.3	16.1	24.1	4.6
37	North Carolina..............	2,153,299	53.0	4.7	14.2	23.8	4.3
38	North Dakota...............	148,496	56.9	4.5	7.8	26.7	4.0
39	Ohio.........................	2,612,241	52.7	4.8	12.6	25.5	4.4
40	Oklahoma...................	784,284	54.2	5.3	12.4	24.1	4.0
41	Oregon	852,502	53.8	4.9	11.1	24.1	6.1
42	Pennsylvania................	2,841,066	54.7	4.8	12.4	23.8	4.3
44	Rhode Island................	240,580	50.3	5.0	14.6	25.2	4.9
45	South Carolina..............	1,015,017	51.7	5.0	15.4	24.0	3.8
46	South Dakota...............	176,353	57.0	4.7	9.8	24.2	4.2
47	Tennessee	1,421,727	53.2	4.8	13.3	24.7	4.0
48	Texas........................	5,230,139	55.5	5.1	14.5	21.2	3.7
49	Utah.........................	488,517	64.6	4.5	10.7	17.0	3.1
50	Vermont	151,001	56.0	4.7	9.2	23.7	6.4
51	Virginia......................	1,785,687	56.1	4.5	12.6	22.4	4.4
53	Washington	1,523,088	54.5	4.8	10.9	23.9	5.8
54	West Virginia	418,095	54.1	5.3	10.8	25.4	4.4
55	Wisconsin	1,300,462	56.3	4.7	10.2	24.0	4.7
56	Wyoming....................	124,145	57.6	4.6	8.8	24.3	4.8

State FIPS code	State	Householders age 65 and older, households by household type					
		Total householders age 65 and older	Married-couple family households, percent	Male householder, no spouse, percent	Female householder, no spouse, percent	Nonfamily householder living alone, percent	Nonfamily households, householder not living alone, percent
	United States...............	26,374,021	43.7	2.3	8.1	43.5	2.5
1	Alabama.........................	442,616	43.1	2.4	10.1	43.0	1.5
2	Alaska...........................	37,516	44.7	3.0	8.4	40.6	3.3
4	Arizona..........................	588,001	48.6	2.1	6.8	39.0	3.6
5	Arkansas........................	276,404	45.4	2.1	8.1	42.5	1.9
6	California.......................	2,634,818	42.8	2.9	9.4	41.3	3.6
8	Colorado	380,713	45.6	1.8	6.3	43.4	2.8
9	Connecticut....................	322,815	41.5	2.3	7.1	46.4	2.7
10	Delaware	85,633	45.8	2.1	7.8	41.4	2.8
11	District of Columbia.......	49,235	25.3	3.2	14.0	53.9	3.7
12	Florida	2,075,003	46.1	2.0	6.8	41.7	3.4
13	Georgia	690,087	44.3	2.4	10.0	41.5	1.9
15	Hawaii	114,584	45.3	4.7	13.6	33.0	3.3
16	Idaho............................	133,276	50.1	1.7	5.9	40.1	2.3
17	Illinois	1,057,106	41.4	2.3	8.5	45.8	2.0
18	Indiana	555,809	44.2	2.1	7.3	44.4	2.0
19	Iowa	295,693	46.5	1.3	4.8	45.7	1.7
20	Kansas	247,674	45.2	1.7	5.7	45.9	1.5
21	Kentucky	390,386	43.1	2.5	8.5	44.2	1.7
22	Louisiana	374,798	40.2	3.2	10.9	43.5	2.1
23	Maine............................	140,620	44.5	1.8	4.9	45.5	3.3
24	Maryland	460,663	42.1	2.6	9.5	43.2	2.5
25	Massachusetts	590,295	40.0	2.3	7.5	47.6	2.6
26	Michigan	919,678	43.2	2.2	8.0	44.4	2.1
27	Minnesota	461,202	46.0	1.6	4.6	45.8	2.1
28	Mississippi.....................	256,623	40.3	3.1	11.7	43.1	1.8
29	Missouri........................	554,750	44.5	2.0	7.1	44.3	2.0
30	Montana........................	99,398	46.5	1.5	4.6	45.2	2.1
31	Nebraska	163,048	45.7	1.5	4.8	46.2	1.8
32	Nevada	213,335	44.3	2.6	7.4	41.3	4.4
33	New Hampshire	117,368	47.6	2.1	5.9	41.0	3.4
34	New Jersey.....................	749,190	41.9	2.6	8.7	44.5	2.3
35	New Mexico....................	183,327	44.1	2.6	8.1	42.6	2.5
36	New York........................	1,674,780	38.3	2.7	9.4	47.0	2.6
37	North Carolina	836,577	44.7	2.2	8.2	43.0	1.9
38	North Dakota.................	64,232	45.0	1.3	3.9	48.2	1.6
39	Ohio	1,085,760	42.3	2.2	7.5	45.9	2.2
40	Oklahoma......................	337,688	44.1	2.3	7.4	44.4	1.9
41	Oregon..........................	363,089	44.8	1.9	6.3	43.6	3.5
42	Pennsylvania	1,269,744	42.0	2.2	7.5	46.0	2.2
44	Rhode Island..................	97,690	40.2	2.3	7.5	47.5	2.5
45	South Carolina	430,937	45.7	2.4	9.6	40.6	1.7
46	South Dakota.................	75,137	46.0	1.7	4.7	45.6	2.1
47	Tennessee	572,550	44.8	2.2	8.7	42.2	2.0
48	Texas............................	1,693,979	45.6	2.7	9.5	40.2	2.0
49	Utah.............................	165,263	52.4	2.2	7.2	36.8	1.4
50	Vermont........................	61,886	44.9	1.8	3.9	45.4	4.0
51	Virginia.........................	650,816	45.4	2.3	8.2	42.0	2.1
53	Washington	562,136	45.4	1.9	6.1	43.3	3.3
54	West Virginia	198,773	42.9	2.3	8.6	44.4	1.8
55	Wisconsin	524,324	44.7	1.7	5.1	46.3	2.2
56	Wyoming.......................	46,996	48.1	1.7	4.8	43.1	2.3

State FIPS code	State	Homeownership rates				Percent of households with one or more persons under 18 years old	Percent of households with one or more persons age 65 or older	Average household size
		Percent of all householders who are owners	Percent of householders age 15 to 34 who are owners	Percent of householders age 35 to 64 who are owners	Percent of householders age 65 and older who are owners			
	United States...............	64.0	33.1	68.7	78.5	32.4	26.0	2.64
1	Alabama......................	69.0	39.0	72.7	83.7	31.8	26.9	2.56
2	Alaska........................	63.0	34.6	69.6	81.7	35.7	17.7	2.80
4	Arizona.......................	62.9	31.7	65.5	82.7	32.1	28.0	2.69
5	Arkansas.....................	66.2	36.3	70.4	82.1	31.9	27.2	2.54
6	California....................	54.2	22.8	57.7	73.2	36.2	25.5	2.96
8	Colorado.....................	64.4	33.5	71.3	79.6	32.2	21.7	2.55
9	Connecticut..................	67.0	33.1	72.1	75.8	32.0	27.3	2.58
10	Delaware	71.4	39.5	75.3	83.8	31.3	28.9	2.64
11	District of Columbia........	41.1	17.0	47.8	61.2	20.8	20.5	2.21
12	Florida........................	65.8	29.9	67.0	83.1	28.0	32.9	2.64
13	Georgia	63.7	33.0	68.6	80.8	35.2	22.7	2.74
15	Hawaii	56.5	19.9	59.8	76.0	33.3	31.5	3.00
16	Idaho	68.7	38.8	74.9	82.9	34.7	25.5	2.69
17	Illinois	66.7	36.5	71.9	79.6	32.5	25.1	2.64
18	Indiana	69.2	40.9	74.3	82.0	32.5	24.9	2.56
19	Iowa	71.8	44.6	78.3	81.5	30.4	26.0	2.43
20	Kansas	66.7	37.1	73.7	79.5	32.8	24.6	2.53
21	Kentucky	67.7	40.0	71.4	81.9	31.8	25.7	2.51
22	Louisiana	66.2	37.3	70.8	82.8	33.2	24.6	2.61
23	Maine..........................	70.8	38.1	76.4	78.3	26.7	28.6	2.34
24	Maryland	66.8	35.8	71.4	78.8	33.3	25.0	2.67
25	Massachusetts	62.0	28.0	68.4	71.1	30.6	26.7	2.53
26	Michigan	71.2	41.0	75.5	82.7	30.4	26.7	2.53
27	Minnesota	71.8	45.4	79.1	78.3	31.3	23.9	2.49
28	Mississippi	68.5	38.1	71.9	84.4	34.5	26.4	2.66
29	Missouri	67.6	39.2	72.7	80.7	30.9	26.0	2.49
30	Montana......................	67.3	34.7	73.4	79.6	27.8	27.2	2.41
31	Nebraska	66.4	38.4	73.4	78.4	31.7	24.2	2.47
32	Nevada	55.2	29.7	57.1	74.2	33.0	25.3	2.73
33	New Hampshire	70.9	37.9	76.4	78.6	30.2	25.8	2.47
34	New Jersey...................	64.9	31.5	68.7	75.9	34.3	27.6	2.73
35	New Mexico..................	68.1	37.3	72.0	84.1	32.1	27.2	2.68
36	New York.....................	53.7	23.5	58.2	65.1	31.2	27.1	2.63
37	North Carolina..............	65.4	33.6	69.9	81.5	32.1	25.2	2.55
38	North Dakota................	65.2	38.5	75.9	73.1	28.2	23.7	2.32
39	Ohio	66.5	36.0	71.1	79.4	30.3	26.4	2.47
40	Oklahoma....................	66.3	37.7	71.3	82.3	32.9	25.8	2.57
41	Oregon	61.1	26.0	66.7	77.0	29.5	27.0	2.51
42	Pennsylvania	69.2	37.6	74.9	77.1	28.9	28.8	2.49
44	Rhode Island.................	60.2	27.6	66.0	70.1	29.4	27.3	2.46
45	South Carolina..............	68.6	37.2	71.9	85.3	31.7	27.3	2.57
46	South Dakota................	67.7	40.7	75.8	75.4	30.8	25.0	2.45
47	Tennessee	66.7	36.0	70.9	82.5	31.4	26.0	2.54
48	Texas..........................	62.4	31.7	68.6	80.4	38.0	22.0	2.84
49	Utah	69.5	44.5	76.4	84.9	42.4	20.9	3.15
50	Vermont	71.2	33.1	78.5	80.0	27.1	27.2	2.34
51	Virginia	66.3	33.6	71.6	81.6	32.9	24.7	2.62
53	Washington	62.4	29.6	68.8	76.9	31.3	24.1	2.56
54	West Virginia................	72.4	41.7	75.4	85.1	27.4	29.8	2.44
55	Wisconsin	67.4	36.9	74.5	76.3	29.7	25.1	2.44
56	Wyoming.....................	69.6	42.1	75.7	83.6	30.7	23.4	2.52

Table A-2: Counties with a Population of 50,000 or More—Living Arrangements

State/County code	Metropolitan area	Total Households	Family households, percent	Married-couple family households, percent	Male householder, no spouse, percent	Female householder, no spouse, percent	Householder living alone, percent	Nonfamily households, householder not living alone, percent	Opposite-sex partner unmarried partner households, percent	Same-sex unmarried partner households, percent	Average household size
00000	**United States**	115,731,304	66.1	48.2	4.8	13.1	27.7	6.2	5.5	0.5	2.6
01000	**Alabama**	1,837,292	67.3	47.7	4.2	15.3	28.6	4.1	3.3	0.3	2.6
01001	Autauga County	20,173	69.1	54.8	2.3	12.0	26.1	4.8	3.0	0.4	2.7
01003	Baldwin County	73,792	69.9	55.3	3.7	10.9	26.0	4.1	3.3	0.2	2.6
01009	Blount County	21,071	74.1	59.1	5.2	9.8	23.7	2.2	2.3	0.5	2.7
01015	Calhoun County	44,756	66.5	46.3	4.6	15.6	28.7	4.8	2.9	0.3	2.6
01031	Coffee County	19,108	67.6	47.9	5.0	14.6	28.7	3.7	3.9	0.2	2.6
01033	Colbert County	22,048	67.5	49.1	4.3	14.0	29.2	3.3	3.0	0.2	2.5
01043	Cullman County	31,720	71.0	54.3	4.7	12.0	25.9	3.1	2.8	0.1	2.5
01045	Dale County	19,359	66.0	46.7	4.6	14.7	29.0	5.0	3.4	0.6	2.5
01049	DeKalb County	24,307	72.3	58.9	4.5	9.0	25.4	2.2	2.2	0.3	2.9
01051	Elmore County	28,342	72.3	55.7	3.1	13.5	25.2	2.5	3.4	0.1	2.7
01055	Etowah County	39,971	69.7	49.0	5.9	14.7	26.9	3.4	3.8	0.2	2.6
01069	Houston County	39,370	67.0	47.4	3.3	16.3	28.9	4.1	3.9	0.2	2.6
01071	Jackson County	20,036	69.3	54.7	4.8	9.8	28.4	2.4	2.9	0.3	2.6
01073	Jefferson County	257,859	63.8	42.3	3.7	17.8	31.8	4.4	3.0	0.4	2.5
01077	Lauderdale County	38,659	65.5	51.0	3.9	10.6	29.7	4.8	2.8	0.6	2.4
01081	Lee County	56,312	62.1	45.2	3.5	13.4	27.5	10.4	3.8	0.3	2.5
01083	Limestone County	32,339	73.3	57.2	3.9	12.2	24.8	1.9	2.3	0.0	2.6
01089	Madison County	134,880	65.2	47.8	4.5	12.9	30.4	4.4	3.7	0.4	2.5
01095	Marshall County	33,795	72.0	53.8	5.0	13.2	25.1	2.9	4.1	0.3	2.8
01097	Mobile County	153,853	67.9	44.4	4.4	19.1	28.2	3.9	3.4	0.5	2.6
01101	Montgomery County	88,380	63.2	37.5	4.9	20.8	31.7	5.0	4.9	0.2	2.5
01103	Morgan County	46,115	68.4	51.3	4.3	12.8	27.9	3.7	3.7	0.7	2.6
01113	Russell County	22,029	63.8	39.8	5.0	19.0	31.6	4.6	3.1	0.4	2.6
01115	St. Clair County	31,840	73.6	58.2	3.6	11.8	22.2	4.2	3.6	0.4	2.6
01117	Shelby County	74,346	71.5	58.3	3.6	9.7	25.4	3.0	2.5	0.2	2.7
01121	Talladega County	31,688	70.0	45.9	5.0	19.1	26.7	3.3	3.6	0.3	2.5
01125	Tuscaloosa County	68,258	66.1	46.7	4.2	15.3	27.8	6.1	2.3	0.1	2.8
01127	Walker County	25,797	70.6	50.9	4.0	15.7	25.8	3.6	2.3	0.5	2.5
02000	**Alaska**	250,875	66.8	49.7	5.8	11.3	26.0	7.2	7.8	0.4	2.8
02020	Anchorage Municipality	104,980	65.8	48.1	5.7	11.9	26.3	7.9	7.5	0.5	2.8
02090	Fairbanks North Star Borough	35,633	62.6	48.9	3.9	9.8	29.1	8.3	7.3	0.3	2.7
02122	Kenai Peninsula Borough	21,418	66.9	52.9	4.6	9.3	27.6	5.6	7.0	0.1	2.6
02170	Matanuska-Susitna Borough	31,368	72.2	57.5	5.5	9.2	21.6	6.2	6.8	0.1	2.9
04000	**Arizona**	2,381,501	65.5	47.2	5.4	12.9	27.4	7.0	6.4	0.6	2.7
04001	Apache County	19,137	68.4	39.9	7.0	21.5	28.2	3.4	6.8	0.1	3.7
04003	Cochise County	48,765	65.6	49.0	4.0	12.6	29.1	5.3	5.1	0.6	2.4
04005	Coconino County	46,614	64.2	45.0	5.9	13.3	23.9	11.8	7.6	0.7	2.7
04007	Gila County	20,721	64.8	47.5	5.8	11.5	31.0	4.3	4.4	0.0	2.5
04013	Maricopa County	1,418,115	65.5	46.8	5.6	13.1	27.2	7.4	6.4	0.7	2.7
04015	Mohave County	80,117	62.8	48.3	3.8	10.6	28.6	8.6	6.7	0.4	2.4
04017	Navajo County	34,237	71.1	46.3	5.6	19.2	25.7	3.2	5.8	0.3	3.1
04019	Pima County	385,524	61.5	43.3	5.4	12.8	30.9	7.5	6.5	0.7	2.5
04021	Pinal County	125,498	72.8	55.0	6.0	11.8	22.3	4.9	6.5	0.7	2.9
04025	Yavapai County	92,332	62.6	49.8	3.3	9.5	31.3	6.1	6.1	0.3	2.3
04027	Yuma County	70,655	77.4	57.4	6.1	13.9	18.7	3.8	6.1	0.1	2.7
05000	**Arkansas**	1,130,417	66.8	49.0	4.5	13.4	28.2	5.0	4.4	0.3	2.5
05007	Benton County	82,689	74.2	61.4	3.3	9.5	20.9	4.9	4.5	0.2	2.8
05031	Craighead County	38,032	67.8	46.8	6.1	14.9	23.9	8.3	5.6	0.6	2.5
05033	Crawford County	23,674	74.6	55.3	5.8	13.5	23.5	1.9	4.0	0.0	2.6
05035	Crittenden County	18,326	69.4	39.1	5.3	25.0	27.3	3.4	5.8	0.1	2.7
05045	Faulkner County	43,076	68.0	52.3	4.8	11.0	23.9	8.1	4.4	0.1	2.6
05051	Garland County	39,748	63.7	46.0	4.5	13.2	29.3	6.9	6.5	0.2	2.4
05069	Jefferson County	28,374	62.5	38.7	5.1	18.7	34.1	3.4	4.2	0.1	2.4
05085	Lonoke County	25,302	73.4	56.7	4.2	12.5	22.1	4.5	4.1	0.4	2.7
05115	Pope County	22,633	67.8	51.8	4.2	11.8	27.8	4.4	3.6	0.2	2.6
05119	Pulaski County	151,923	60.0	40.3	4.0	15.7	34.5	5.5	3.8	0.5	2.5
05125	Saline County	41,774	71.0	55.7	4.8	10.5	24.4	4.6	3.0	0.5	2.7
05131	Sebastian County	49,475	65.4	47.8	5.0	12.6	29.8	4.8	4.2	0.3	2.5
05143	Washington County	80,658	62.7	46.7	4.9	11.2	28.1	9.2	5.7	0.4	2.5
05145	White County	29,337	70.7	55.6	4.0	11.2	25.3	4.0	3.8	0.4	2.6
06000	**California**	12,581,722	68.4	48.7	6.0	13.7	24.4	7.3	6.2	0.6	3.0
06001	Alameda County	550,805	65.1	47.1	5.3	12.7	26.6	8.3	5.7	1.0	2.8
06007	Butte County	84,647	59.7	42.0	5.5	12.1	29.2	11.2	7.4	0.5	2.6
06013	Contra Costa County	380,136	70.6	53.3	5.1	12.3	23.4	6.0	5.3	0.7	2.8
06017	El Dorado County	67,059	70.5	59.7	3.0	7.9	23.6	5.9	4.9	0.3	2.7
06019	Fresno County	291,440	73.0	46.6	8.5	17.9	21.3	5.7	8.1	0.5	3.2
06023	Humboldt County	52,229	56.9	40.3	4.3	12.2	31.5	11.6	10.1	0.8	2.5
06025	Imperial County	47,556	77.2	51.1	6.5	19.5	18.8	4.1	5.4	0.2	3.5
06029	Kern County	256,319	75.3	50.7	8.0	16.7	19.7	5.0	7.8	0.4	3.2
06031	Kings County	41,034	78.0	51.2	7.9	18.9	16.8	5.2	8.6	0.3	3.2

State/ County code	Metropolitan area	Race or Hispanic origin of householder				Age of householder			Percent of households with one or more persons under 18 years old	Percent of households with one or more persons age 65 or older	Percent of all householders who are owners
		Householder is White alone, not Hispanic or Latino, percent	Householder is Black or African American alone, percent	Householder is Hispanic or Latino, percent	Householder is Asian alone, percent	Householders age 15 to 34, percent	Householders age 35 to 64, percent	Householders age 65 and older, percent			
00000	**United States**............	69.8	12.1	12.0	4.2	19.3	57.9	22.8	32.4	26.0	64.0
01000	**Alabama**..................	69.6	25.4	2.6	1.0	18.9	57.0	24.1	31.8	26.9	69.0
01001	Autauga County............	80.3	16.6	0.0	0.0	18.7	59.4	21.9	36.4	25.7	75.4
01003	Baldwin County.............	87.4	7.8	2.5	0.5	14.9	57.1	28.0	28.4	31.2	70.6
01009	Blount County..............	91.2	0.0	5.3	0.0	16.4	57.9	25.7	36.9	28.6	79.3
01015	Calhoun County............	75.0	20.9	2.8	0.0	18.9	56.0	25.1	30.4	29.0	68.6
01031	Coffee County.............	76.0	15.6	5.7	0.0	18.2	57.1	24.7	34.7	27.7	67.6
01033	Colbert County............	80.4	16.9	0.0	0.0	16.3	54.7	29.1	30.0	30.9	71.5
01043	Cullman County............	94.4	0.9	2.9	0.0	18.3	53.8	27.9	30.4	30.1	75.1
01045	Dale County...............	72.5	18.8	4.8	0.0	21.0	55.7	23.4	31.6	25.9	60.7
01049	DeKalb County.............	87.6	1.5	6.9	0.0	13.9	61.2	24.9	31.9	28.4	75.3
01051	Elmore County.............	78.9	16.7	0.0	0.0	18.4	60.3	21.3	34.8	24.9	74.9
01055	Etowah County.............	80.7	15.3	2.2	0.0	15.2	57.9	26.9	32.1	30.9	71.5
01069	Houston County............	71.6	24.0	2.4	0.6	18.9	56.0	25.1	31.4	27.8	64.5
01071	Jackson County............	91.8	3.4	0.0	0.0	13.9	55.4	30.7	28.7	33.1	75.7
01073	Jefferson County..........	53.8	41.2	2.5	1.3	20.8	56.8	22.5	30.7	24.8	63.7
01077	Lauderdale County.........	87.9	9.3	0.0	0.0	19.9	53.0	27.1	28.8	29.9	69.4
01081	Lee County................	70.8	23.6	2.1	2.7	34.1	50.8	15.1	32.0	17.6	60.2
01083	Limestone County..........	82.3	11.6	4.0	0.0	17.4	59.4	23.3	33.2	25.2	75.9
01089	Madison County............	69.0	23.5	3.5	2.1	20.4	59.0	20.6	31.2	23.0	68.0
01095	Marshall County...........	89.2	1.3	7.6	0.0	15.2	57.6	27.3	33.4	30.1	72.9
01097	Mobile County.............	61.5	33.2	2.2	1.7	19.5	57.0	23.5	33.7	26.7	66.2
01101	Montgomery County	42.3	52.8	2.1	1.9	23.6	55.2	21.2	33.1	24.1	60.1
01103	Morgan County.............	81.2	11.5	4.8	0.0	15.4	60.6	24.1	31.2	26.3	71.0
01113	Russell County............	53.3	41.9	0.0	0.0	23.8	54.2	21.9	34.3	25.0	59.4
01115	St. Clair County..........	89.1	8.4	0.0	0.0	17.8	59.2	23.0	36.3	25.6	81.4
01117	Shelby County.............	81.5	11.8	3.9	0.0	18.2	62.2	19.5	35.3	22.3	78.9
01121	Talladega County..........	66.2	31.6	0.0	0.0	15.7	59.0	25.4	33.2	29.1	71.1
01125	Tuscaloosa County.........	67.1	29.4	1.6	1.1	26.0	54.3	19.7	32.2	22.4	63.8
01127	Walker County.............	92.0	5.1	0.0	0.0	14.9	56.5	28.6	31.8	31.2	73.4
02000	**Alaska**...................	72.1	3.4	4.9	3.7	24.1	60.9	15.0	35.7	17.7	63.0
02020	Anchorage Municipality.........	70.3	5.9	6.6	6.0	26.9	59.7	13.5	35.9	16.4	59.1
02090	Fairbanks North Star Borough	79.4	0.0	5.2	1.6	31.9	54.7	13.4	32.1	15.1	58.8
02122	Kenai Peninsula Borough............	86.8	0.0	2.3	0.0	16.9	63.4	19.7	30.1	22.4	72.1
02170	Matanuska-Susitna Borough	87.8	0.9	3.2	0.0	19.5	66.0	14.5	36.4	17.9	75.5
04000	**Arizona**	67.5	4.0	21.8	2.6	20.3	55.0	24.7	32.1	28.0	62.9
04001	Apache County.............	27.6	0.0	5.4	0.0	9.1	62.8	28.1	37.4	31.3	76.3
04003	Cochise County............	66.4	2.8	26.2	0.0	17.2	51.0	31.8	28.7	35.4	67.7
04005	Coconino County...........	64.7	1.2	11.4	1.4	26.4	56.7	16.9	32.1	19.7	59.2
04007	Gila County...............	76.9	0.0	12.5	0.0	11.4	49.3	39.3	24.3	43.1	73.1
04013	Maricopa County...........	68.2	5.1	21.0	3.3	21.7	56.8	21.5	33.6	24.7	60.9
04015	Mohave County.............	86.3	0.6	9.2	0.0	11.8	48.7	39.5	21.6	43.7	67.1
04017	Navajo County.............	54.4	0.0	9.2	0.0	13.3	58.4	28.3	36.2	31.8	70.5
04019	Pima County...............	64.7	3.3	26.4	2.6	21.3	52.4	26.3	28.3	29.7	61.0
04021	Pinal County..............	70.4	3.8	19.9	1.2	17.0	54.5	28.5	35.6	31.9	72.7
04025	Yavapai County............	87.9	0.5	8.5	0.0	11.4	50.4	38.2	20.5	42.1	68.6
04027	Yuma County...............	44.4	1.9	51.2	1.0	21.5	50.3	28.2	41.4	31.8	69.2
05000	**Arkansas**..................	77.8	14.9	4.3	1.1	20.6	54.9	24.5	31.9	27.2	66.2
05007	Benton County	82.6	1.2	10.4	2.9	22.2	56.2	21.5	38.6	23.7	67.0
05031	Craighead County..........	84.0	10.8	2.8	1.0	26.8	54.1	19.1	34.7	22.5	59.4
05033	Crawford County...........	89.1	0.0	5.1	0.0	17.0	59.6	23.5	36.5	25.7	75.3
05035	Crittenden County.........	48.4	47.8	0.0	0.0	20.5	59.6	19.9	37.8	23.7	57.0
05045	Faulkner County...........	84.3	10.3	2.7	0.0	29.4	53.0	17.6	34.5	19.9	63.8
05051	Garland County............	86.6	7.4	2.9	0.0	16.5	52.2	31.3	28.7	35.2	67.6
05069	Jefferson County..........	44.3	52.8	0.0	0.0	19.4	56.0	24.6	31.1	27.5	64.3
05085	Lonoke County.............	89.7	5.1	0.0	0.0	20.8	58.9	20.3	40.6	23.1	70.8
05115	Pope County...............	88.0	3.6	6.0	0.0	20.3	58.3	21.5	31.6	24.5	69.1
05119	Pulaski County............	59.2	33.9	4.2	1.6	22.4	57.4	20.2	26.7	22.6	61.2
05125	Saline County	90.3	4.7	3.1	0.0	18.3	55.3	26.5	32.6	29.7	77.5
05131	Sebastian County..........	77.0	6.2	8.7	4.2	22.0	56.0	22.0	32.9	24.2	60.4
05143	Washington County.........	81.1	2.7	10.3	2.1	33.5	50.1	16.4	33.9	19.0	55.4
05145	White County..............	92.3	3.2	2.6	0.0	21.8	52.8	25.4	34.2	27.8	70.0
06000	**California**	50.4	6.5	27.9	12.6	19.4	59.7	20.9	36.2	25.5	54.2
06001	Alameda County............	41.9	14.1	16.1	24.1	20.2	60.8	19.1	34.2	23.5	52.3
06007	Butte County..............	81.9	1.1	10.8	2.6	22.7	50.4	26.9	26.9	30.0	58.6
06013	Contra Costa County.......	55.8	9.4	17.7	13.8	15.2	62.6	22.1	36.5	26.5	64.7
06017	El Dorado County..........	85.5	0.0	8.2	2.9	10.4	63.1	26.6	29.6	30.5	72.4
06019	Fresno County.............	42.8	5.8	41.4	7.8	22.8	57.2	20.0	43.0	23.9	52.9
06023	Humboldt County...........	84.4	0.0	6.2	1.9	23.0	54.0	23.1	26.5	25.4	54.4
06025	Imperial County...........	19.3	1.5	76.5	1.2	19.8	58.6	21.7	47.2	28.4	55.1
06029	Kern County...............	48.7	6.1	39.7	3.7	23.5	58.3	18.2	45.1	22.1	56.0
06031	Kings County..............	45.6	5.8	43.0	3.7	27.8	54.7	17.5	48.4	20.6	51.1

Table A-2: Counties with a Population of 50,000 or More—Living Arrangements—*Continued*

State/ County code	Metropolitan area	Household type							Opposite-sex partner unmarried partner households, percent	Same-sex unmarried partner households, percent	Average household size
		Total Households	Family households, percent	Married-couple family households, percent	Male householder, no spouse, percent	Female householder, no spouse, percent	Householder living alone, percent	Nonfamily households, householder not living alone, percent			
	California—cont'd										
06033	Lake County	26,848	61.3	40.7	7.4	13.2	29.2	9.5	10.1	0.1	2.4
06037	Los Angeles County	3,233,542	66.8	44.1	6.9	15.8	25.9	7.3	6.3	0.6	3.0
06039	Madera County	42,247	76.1	55.1	5.7	15.3	19.2	4.7	8.1	0.4	3.4
06041	Marin County	102,595	62.4	49.9	2.9	9.6	30.4	7.2	4.9	0.7	2.4
06045	Mendocino County	33,735	59.8	43.7	5.3	10.8	33.1	7.0	7.5	0.4	2.5
06047	Merced County	76,398	76.3	51.0	6.7	18.6	19.0	4.7	7.5	0.2	3.4
06053	Monterey County	125,012	72.5	52.2	6.7	13.5	21.6	6.0	7.5	0.7	3.2
06055	Napa County	48,847	69.1	52.4	5.2	11.4	24.7	6.2	5.1	0.6	2.8
06057	Nevada County	40,859	63.0	50.9	4.2	8.0	29.6	7.3	5.0	0.6	2.4
06059	Orange County	999,563	71.8	54.3	5.5	12.0	21.5	6.7	5.3	0.4	3.0
06061	Placer County	133,988	70.7	56.4	3.8	10.6	23.2	6.1	5.5	0.5	2.7
06065	Riverside County	688,758	73.5	53.6	6.3	13.7	20.6	5.8	6.5	1.0	3.2
06067	Sacramento County	517,066	64.8	43.9	6.1	14.9	27.5	7.6	7.2	0.7	2.8
06069	San Benito County	17,043	78.9	60.1	5.0	13.7	17.5	3.6	6.1	0.1	3.3
06071	San Bernardino County	605,174	75.5	51.4	7.4	16.8	19.9	4.5	6.6	0.4	3.4
06073	San Diego County	1,079,664	66.4	49.1	5.0	12.3	24.9	8.8	5.8	0.7	2.9
06075	San Francisco County	348,751	45.2	33.0	3.6	8.6	38.4	16.4	5.8	2.3	2.3
06077	San Joaquin County	215,707	74.5	51.3	7.1	16.0	20.5	5.1	7.0	0.4	3.2
06079	San Luis Obispo County	102,728	63.4	50.3	3.8	9.2	26.3	10.4	5.9	0.6	2.5
06081	San Mateo County	258,310	67.6	52.6	4.9	10.2	25.3	7.0	5.3	0.6	2.8
06083	Santa Barbara County	141,634	65.4	48.6	5.4	11.4	25.1	9.5	6.2	0.6	2.9
06085	Santa Clara County	614,909	71.4	55.5	5.2	10.7	21.7	6.9	5.3	0.5	2.9
06087	Santa Cruz County	94,218	62.4	47.4	4.8	10.2	26.7	10.9	7.6	0.8	2.7
06089	Shasta County	69,123	65.7	48.4	4.6	12.7	27.6	6.6	6.4	0.4	2.5
06095	Solano County	141,742	71.1	50.1	6.0	15.1	22.7	6.1	6.5	0.6	2.9
06097	Sonoma County	185,259	62.7	46.8	5.1	10.8	28.3	9.0	7.0	1.0	2.6
06099	Stanislaus County	167,863	73.9	50.7	7.0	16.2	20.7	5.4	7.2	0.5	3.1
06101	Sutter County	31,641	74.2	52.9	7.1	14.2	21.2	4.6	7.1	0.6	3.0
06103	Tehama County	23,428	69.4	52.1	4.9	12.3	25.1	5.6	6.9	0.3	2.7
06107	Tulare County	132,911	78.0	52.5	8.6	16.9	17.6	4.4	7.8	0.3	3.4
06109	Tuolumne County	21,846	67.5	52.0	3.9	11.6	28.1	4.4	4.6	0.6	2.3
06111	Ventura County	266,867	73.3	55.5	5.5	12.4	20.7	6.0	5.4	0.5	3.1
06113	Yolo County	70,894	61.8	46.2	4.3	11.3	25.1	13.1	5.6	0.7	2.8
06115	Yuba County	24,745	72.6	50.9	7.4	14.2	20.5	6.9	8.6	0.5	2.9
08000	**Colorado**	1,989,371	63.9	49.1	4.5	10.3	28.2	7.9	5.4	0.6	2.6
08001	Adams County	154,400	70.5	50.6	6.3	13.6	23.2	6.3	6.6	0.6	3.0
08005	Arapahoe County	226,687	65.2	47.7	5.1	12.4	28.7	6.1	5.1	0.5	2.6
08013	Boulder County	121,194	58.9	46.8	4.1	7.9	28.2	12.9	5.8	0.6	2.4
08014	Broomfield County	22,464	66.9	54.8	3.4	8.6	26.5	6.6	4.8	0.7	2.6
08031	Denver County	269,868	47.3	32.9	4.0	10.5	40.6	12.0	6.4	1.4	2.3
08035	Douglas County	105,429	77.2	66.1	3.2	7.9	17.6	5.2	4.5	0.5	2.8
08037	Eagle County	17,648	64.4	53.7	2.9	7.9	25.4	10.1	4.6	0.0	2.9
08041	El Paso County	238,880	68.4	53.2	4.0	11.2	25.5	6.0	4.5	0.4	2.6
08045	Garfield County	20,114	70.8	57.9	3.2	9.7	23.8	5.4	3.9	0.1	2.8
08059	Jefferson County	220,166	64.8	50.2	4.5	10.2	27.7	7.4	5.2	0.6	2.4
08067	La Plata County	21,270	60.6	49.0	3.3	8.2	29.7	9.7	4.8	0.5	2.4
08069	Larimer County	123,203	62.4	50.5	3.8	8.1	25.4	12.2	5.7	0.8	2.5
08077	Mesa County	58,877	67.1	50.6	5.3	11.2	26.1	6.8	4.8	0.2	2.4
08101	Pueblo County	62,136	63.7	44.5	5.7	13.5	30.5	5.8	5.7	0.5	2.5
08123	Weld County	91,683	72.4	56.7	5.4	10.3	21.5	6.2	5.7	0.3	2.8
09000	**Connecticut**	1,348,275	66.4	48.9	4.3	13.1	27.9	5.7	5.3	0.5	2.6
09001	Fairfield County	331,134	69.1	53.1	3.9	12.2	25.6	5.3	4.4	0.4	2.8
09003	Hartford County	346,062	65.1	45.7	4.6	14.9	29.3	5.6	5.1	0.5	2.5
09005	Litchfield County	75,044	66.9	54.2	3.6	9.0	27.4	5.7	4.8	0.4	2.5
09007	Middlesex County	65,563	66.1	53.4	3.9	8.8	28.0	5.9	5.7	0.6	2.4
09009	New Haven County	325,283	64.8	45.5	4.3	15.0	29.6	5.7	5.2	0.5	2.6
09011	New London County	106,911	65.6	48.8	4.9	11.9	28.0	6.4	6.8	0.5	2.5
09013	Tolland County	54,212	67.3	52.8	4.4	10.0	25.6	7.1	7.0	0.5	2.5
09015	Windham County	44,066	67.1	48.5	5.6	13.0	26.9	6.0	7.7	0.3	2.6
10000	**Delaware**	337,245	67.2	48.3	5.0	14.0	26.4	6.4	6.3	0.6	2.6
10001	Kent County	59,341	69.7	49.7	5.0	15.0	24.1	6.2	7.1	0.4	2.7
10003	New Castle County	200,906	66.2	47.0	4.9	14.3	27.3	6.5	6.4	0.5	2.6
10005	Sussex County	76,998	67.7	50.5	5.0	12.2	25.9	6.4	5.3	1.0	2.6
11000	**District of Columbia**	268,015	42.7	22.7	3.9	16.1	44.7	12.6	5.4	1.7	2.2
11001	District of Columbia	268,015	42.7	22.7	3.9	16.1	44.7	12.6	5.4	1.7	2.2
12000	**Florida**	7,168,502	64.1	46.3	4.6	13.3	29.4	6.6	5.6	0.6	2.6
12001	Alachua County	95,996	52.2	37.1	3.9	11.3	33.1	14.7	5.9	0.6	2.5
12005	Bay County	67,664	64.4	47.4	4.6	12.4	28.6	7.1	6.1	0.7	2.5
12009	Brevard County	218,067	63.4	47.1	4.1	12.3	30.5	6.0	5.8	0.3	2.5

State/ County code	Metropolitan area	Race or Hispanic origin of householder				Age of householder			Percent of households with one or more persons under 18 years old	Percent of households with one or more persons age 65 or older	Percent of all householders who are owners
		Householder is White alone, not Hispanic or Latino, percent	Householder is Black or African American alone, percent	Householder is Hispanic or Latino, percent	Householder is Asian alone, percent	Householders age 15 to 34, percent	Householders age 35 to 64, percent	Householders age 65 and older, percent			
	California—cont'd										
06033	Lake County	81.2	2.1	10.9	0.0	15.2	54.8	30.0	27.4	31.8	61.4
06037	Los Angeles County	37.2	10.0	36.5	14.2	19.7	60.8	19.6	35.7	24.7	45.9
06039	Madera County	50.2	2.9	42.5	2.0	18.9	57.3	23.8	41.2	29.0	58.9
06041	Marin County	81.6	1.7	10.1	4.7	9.1	61.7	29.2	30.7	32.5	62.4
06045	Mendocino County	77.6	0.0	14.4	0.0	13.2	58.2	28.6	27.7	32.6	56.7
06047	Merced County	42.0	4.1	46.4	5.6	22.5	58.2	19.3	46.3	24.0	52.2
06053	Monterey County	46.5	2.7	42.2	6.8	21.3	57.5	21.2	41.3	25.5	48.2
06055	Napa County	68.8	1.6	22.3	5.5	14.2	59.2	26.6	32.7	31.0	58.4
06057	Nevada County	90.7	0.0	5.7	0.0	11.2	55.8	33.0	22.6	36.2	72.2
06059	Orange County	55.0	1.8	23.6	17.6	16.8	61.7	21.5	36.7	26.2	57.6
06061	Placer County	81.3	1.0	9.8	5.3	14.7	58.6	26.7	33.2	29.8	69.5
06065	Riverside County	51.7	6.4	34.6	5.2	17.4	59.4	23.3	41.5	28.2	64.7
06067	Sacramento County	56.7	10.2	16.5	12.3	21.7	58.5	19.8	35.1	23.8	55.5
06069	San Benito County	49.2	0.0	45.5	0.0	15.9	64.7	19.4	43.8	24.3	63.1
06071	San Bernardino County	42.6	9.1	39.8	6.4	19.7	62.4	17.9	43.8	22.9	60.7
06073	San Diego County	58.8	5.0	23.9	9.7	22.2	57.4	20.3	33.9	24.4	53.1
06075	San Francisco County	50.9	5.9	11.7	28.3	25.7	54.0	20.3	18.7	24.3	36.0
06077	San Joaquin County	45.6	7.6	31.6	11.9	19.9	60.0	20.1	43.0	24.7	56.9
06079	San Luis Obispo County	78.3	1.5	15.6	2.9	19.9	54.1	26.0	27.1	30.2	56.1
06081	San Mateo County	52.2	2.8	18.5	23.5	15.6	61.6	22.8	32.7	27.6	58.6
06083	Santa Barbara County	60.7	1.7	31.2	4.5	21.6	53.8	24.6	33.2	28.5	51.5
06085	Santa Clara County	44.5	2.8	19.3	31.0	19.2	62.0	18.7	38.8	23.7	56.4
06087	Santa Cruz County	70.8	1.1	22.1	3.7	17.5	59.7	22.8	30.1	25.7	58.1
06089	Shasta County	86.7	0.0	6.2	2.2	15.8	53.9	30.3	27.8	33.6	62.5
06095	Solano County	50.3	14.6	18.1	12.8	18.0	61.1	21.0	36.5	25.4	59.9
06097	Sonoma County	76.9	1.3	16.1	3.5	15.5	59.3	25.2	29.5	28.7	59.3
06099	Stanislaus County	56.6	2.8	33.0	4.7	20.9	58.9	20.2	41.8	24.6	56.6
06101	Sutter County	61.4	1.8	22.2	10.2	20.5	57.4	22.2	39.5	28.0	60.0
06103	Tehama County	80.6	0.0	14.8	0.0	16.6	55.5	27.9	33.4	31.4	67.1
06107	Tulare County	42.8	1.9	50.5	3.3	22.6	58.6	18.8	48.8	23.4	56.3
06109	Tuolumne County	88.0	0.0	6.9	0.0	14.2	51.5	34.3	23.8	38.6	68.8
06111	Ventura County	61.0	1.9	28.5	6.8	15.0	62.0	23.0	38.4	27.5	64.3
06113	Yolo County	58.3	2.7	23.8	11.0	26.8	54.4	18.8	33.7	22.6	51.3
06115	Yuba County	66.2	3.3	19.3	5.4	26.4	55.3	18.3	42.6	22.3	56.2
08000	**Colorado**	76.6	3.7	15.4	2.4	22.5	58.4	19.1	32.2	21.7	64.4
08001	Adams County	63.5	3.0	29.1	2.9	24.2	59.8	16.0	41.3	19.3	64.6
08005	Arapahoe County	70.2	9.6	13.3	4.3	22.3	60.2	17.5	34.6	20.1	61.4
08013	Boulder County	83.8	0.8	9.8	3.9	24.8	57.7	17.5	28.8	19.5	63.0
08014	Broomfield County	82.6	0.0	9.4	5.4	22.9	59.1	18.0	34.7	20.5	66.1
08031	Denver County	64.1	9.4	21.5	3.0	30.7	52.9	16.4	25.0	18.3	49.2
08035	Douglas County	88.4	1.0	5.9	3.4	15.6	69.9	14.5	44.1	16.7	79.6
08037	Eagle County	77.9	0.0	19.5	0.0	21.1	67.7	11.2	34.4	14.2	65.7
08041	El Paso County	76.7	5.7	12.1	2.3	24.6	57.5	17.9	35.3	20.4	63.1
08045	Garfield County	77.3	0.0	21.2	0.0	21.3	63.3	15.3	38.0	18.3	62.2
08059	Jefferson County	84.5	0.8	11.0	2.0	17.9	60.8	21.3	29.4	23.8	70.1
08067	La Plata County	85.1	0.0	9.0	0.0	20.3	60.5	19.2	26.5	22.3	67.0
08069	Larimer County	88.4	0.7	7.6	1.6	25.7	54.3	20.0	28.8	22.4	64.4
08077	Mesa County	87.1	0.0	10.0	0.0	21.0	53.2	25.8	30.0	28.2	70.1
08101	Pueblo County	59.7	0.0	36.9	0.0	18.4	55.9	25.8	31.1	28.6	64.1
08123	Weld County	75.8	0.9	21.0	1.1	24.1	57.9	18.0	38.5	20.6	68.5
09000	**Connecticut**	75.2	9.5	11.0	3.3	15.4	60.6	23.9	32.0	27.3	67.0
09001	Fairfield County	70.7	10.6	13.9	4.3	13.5	62.9	23.6	35.1	27.1	68.2
09003	Hartford County	69.9	12.2	13.0	3.9	16.9	59.2	23.9	31.7	27.1	64.7
09005	Litchfield County	94.1	0.0	2.8	1.1	10.4	63.2	26.4	28.2	29.9	77.0
09007	Middlesex County	89.3	4.3	3.6	0.0	12.8	61.5	25.7	28.4	28.5	75.4
09009	New Haven County	71.2	12.3	12.5	3.0	16.7	59.0	24.3	31.1	27.8	63.0
09011	New London County	83.0	5.0	6.6	3.0	16.9	59.6	23.5	31.2	27.0	66.6
09013	Tolland County	91.2	2.4	3.3	2.4	17.0	61.4	21.6	31.6	25.1	72.6
09015	Windham County	88.3	1.9	8.2	0.0	15.8	62.1	22.0	30.8	25.0	69.3
10000	**Delaware**	70.3	19.7	5.7	3.0	16.9	57.7	25.4	31.3	28.9	71.4
10001	Kent County	69.3	21.4	4.8	0.0	18.8	56.5	24.6	34.1	28.2	70.9
10003	New Castle County	65.7	22.8	6.4	4.1	18.5	60.0	21.5	32.8	24.9	69.1
10005	Sussex County	83.2	10.4	4.7	0.7	11.3	52.6	36.1	25.1	39.8	77.9
11000	**District of Columbia**	40.7	46.2	8.0	3.5	29.6	52.1	18.4	20.8	20.5	41.1
11001	District of Columbia	40.7	46.2	8.0	3.5	29.6	52.1	18.4	20.8	20.5	41.1
12000	**Florida**	64.9	13.7	18.5	2.1	15.8	55.2	28.9	28.0	32.9	65.8
12001	Alachua County	66.9	18.7	8.4	4.6	33.0	48.7	18.3	23.8	20.7	52.9
12005	Bay County	82.3	9.9	4.3	1.4	20.7	54.7	24.7	28.5	27.2	61.0
12009	Brevard County	81.7	9.0	6.8	1.5	12.3	54.6	33.0	24.6	36.8	72.6

Table A-2: Counties with a Population of 50,000 or More—Living Arrangements—*Continued*

State/ County code	Metropolitan area	Total Households	Family households, percent	Married-couple family households, percent	Male householder, no spouse, percent	Female householder, no spouse, percent	Householder living alone, percent	Nonfamily households, householder not living alone, percent	Opposite-sex partner unmarried partner households, percent	Same-sex unmarried partner households, percent	Average household size
	Florida—cont'd										
12011	Broward County	664,304	62.6	42.2	4.6	15.7	30.7	6.7	5.4	1.0	2.7
12015	Charlotte County	69,690	65.4	53.5	4.0	7.9	28.6	5.9	5.2	0.4	2.3
12017	Citrus County	60,419	63.7	51.2	4.2	8.3	30.5	5.8	6.2	0.6	2.3
12019	Clay County	67,362	74.8	56.9	3.9	14.0	19.8	5.4	5.1	0.3	2.9
12021	Collier County	125,417	65.7	52.3	3.9	9.5	29.1	5.2	4.6	0.6	2.6
12023	Columbia County	23,222	63.5	43.8	4.6	15.1	32.9	3.6	5.6	0.1	2.7
12031	Duval County	331,294	62.0	41.9	4.4	15.7	31.5	6.6	5.7	0.5	2.6
12033	Escambia County	111,541	60.5	42.7	4.3	13.6	32.8	6.7	4.7	0.4	2.5
12035	Flagler County	35,363	69.9	58.0	4.0	7.9	24.9	5.2	4.2	0.3	2.8
12053	Hernando County	69,887	68.3	51.7	4.3	12.2	27.4	4.3	4.5	0.5	2.5
12055	Highlands County	39,922	62.4	50.4	2.9	9.1	32.8	4.8	3.3	0.3	2.4
12057	Hillsborough County	475,150	63.6	44.5	5.0	14.1	29.1	7.4	6.0	0.6	2.7
12061	Indian River County	58,531	62.5	48.9	3.5	10.1	32.1	5.4	4.5	0.4	2.4
12069	Lake County	116,703	69.3	56.2	3.7	9.4	25.1	5.6	6.3	0.5	2.6
12071	Lee County	241,201	65.8	51.0	4.5	10.2	28.1	6.1	6.5	0.7	2.6
12073	Leon County	109,939	56.0	38.6	4.3	13.1	29.3	14.7	5.4	0.3	2.4
12081	Manatee County	132,334	64.4	50.9	3.1	10.5	29.0	6.6	5.7	0.7	2.5
12083	Marion County	133,171	65.9	50.1	4.0	11.8	28.1	6.0	5.5	0.3	2.5
12085	Martin County	60,005	63.2	51.2	4.0	8.0	32.1	4.7	4.8	0.2	2.4
12086	Miami-Dade County	832,619	67.9	43.5	6.5	17.9	26.3	5.7	5.6	0.5	3.1
12087	Monroe County	27,676	58.5	46.9	3.8	7.8	31.7	9.8	5.7	1.9	2.6
12089	Nassau County	27,691	73.4	57.5	5.3	10.6	22.8	3.8	5.7	0.2	2.7
12091	Okaloosa County	73,838	66.9	49.8	4.1	13.1	27.5	5.6	5.4	0.3	2.5
12095	Orange County	420,546	63.3	43.2	4.7	15.4	27.8	8.9	6.4	0.8	2.8
12097	Osceola County	89,216	74.5	50.7	5.3	18.5	20.6	4.9	6.5	0.3	3.2
12099	Palm Beach County	524,486	61.9	45.3	4.6	12.0	31.6	6.6	5.7	0.5	2.6
12101	Pasco County	181,681	65.7	51.2	4.3	10.1	28.7	5.6	5.1	0.4	2.6
12103	Pinellas County	399,382	55.1	39.9	3.9	11.4	37.8	7.0	5.7	1.0	2.3
12105	Polk County	218,431	68.8	49.9	4.8	14.1	25.9	5.3	5.6	0.6	2.8
12107	Putnam County	27,484	63.8	46.0	3.6	14.2	30.7	5.4	4.5	0.4	2.6
12109	St. Johns County	76,773	68.6	55.7	3.7	9.1	25.3	6.1	4.5	0.5	2.6
12111	St. Lucie County	106,574	67.3	50.1	4.5	12.7	27.3	5.4	4.9	0.3	2.6
12113	Santa Rosa County	58,224	73.4	58.8	4.0	10.6	20.2	6.4	6.5	0.4	2.6
12115	Sarasota County	172,496	59.9	48.4	3.2	8.3	33.3	6.8	5.2	0.6	2.2
12117	Seminole County	147,153	66.5	49.4	3.6	13.5	27.6	6.0	5.6	0.6	2.9
12119	Sumter County	45,678	68.8	61.7	1.7	5.4	27.4	3.8	2.9	0.3	2.0
12127	Volusia County	195,937	61.1	45.9	4.2	11.0	32.1	6.8	4.9	0.5	2.5
12131	Walton County	23,174	64.8	49.3	5.0	10.4	30.8	4.4	4.9	0.2	2.4
13000	**Georgia**	3,522,934	67.7	47.6	4.8	15.3	26.9	5.4	4.4	0.5	2.7
13013	Barrow County	23,793	76.3	56.1	5.9	14.3	19.4	4.4	6.0	0.4	3.0
13015	Bartow County	34,752	73.2	55.5	4.7	13.0	21.0	5.9	4.3	0.4	2.9
13021	Bibb County	55,832	62.9	37.5	4.4	21.0	32.7	4.4	4.1	0.0	2.7
13031	Bulloch County	25,677	57.5	39.7	3.4	14.5	24.3	18.1	6.2	0.6	2.6
13039	Camden County	18,252	75.8	58.0	5.2	12.6	19.1	5.1	4.9	1.0	2.7
13045	Carroll County	39,787	68.5	48.1	5.5	14.9	25.2	6.3	6.5	0.3	2.7
13047	Catoosa County	23,726	73.5	55.1	6.6	11.8	23.8	2.7	3.4	0.2	2.7
13051	Chatham County	102,953	61.3	41.0	4.2	16.1	31.6	7.0	5.8	0.6	2.6
13057	Cherokee County	76,681	74.1	57.0	4.9	12.2	21.2	4.8	3.8	0.8	2.9
13059	Clarke County	41,856	49.4	32.0	3.7	13.6	34.3	16.3	4.6	0.3	2.6
13063	Clayton County	87,383	65.5	35.3	6.7	23.5	29.3	5.2	5.7	0.4	3.0
13067	Cobb County	264,382	67.1	49.6	4.6	12.8	26.1	6.8	5.0	0.6	2.6
13073	Columbia County	44,510	78.9	62.5	4.6	11.8	18.4	2.6	3.1	0.1	3.0
13077	Coweta County	47,665	74.5	57.9	4.4	12.3	21.5	3.9	3.6	0.4	2.7
13089	DeKalb County	264,038	58.1	36.4	5.0	16.8	34.1	7.8	4.8	1.2	2.6
13095	Dougherty County	35,546	62.9	33.7	5.3	23.8	32.3	4.8	5.8	0.4	2.5
13097	Douglas County	46,306	74.6	49.0	5.9	19.7	20.9	4.5	4.5	0.6	2.9
13103	Effingham County	18,024	77.8	58.9	6.1	12.8	17.1	5.0	4.5	0.3	3.0
13113	Fayette County	37,700	79.8	66.0	3.8	10.0	18.9	1.3	1.8	0.2	2.8
13115	Floyd County	34,168	66.4	48.3	3.9	14.2	28.1	5.5	2.7	0.3	2.7
13117	Forsyth County	57,099	79.7	68.1	2.2	9.4	16.8	3.5	2.0	0.8	3.3
13121	Fulton County	373,461	55.0	36.4	3.6	15.0	37.6	7.4	4.1	0.8	2.5
13127	Glynn County	31,494	68.1	46.0	4.6	17.4	27.5	4.4	4.1	0.3	2.5
13129	Gordon County	19,219	72.0	54.4	4.4	13.2	23.2	4.9	3.1	0.2	2.9
13135	Gwinnett County	268,684	76.3	56.7	5.3	14.2	19.2	4.6	3.8	0.7	3.1
13139	Hall County	60,356	73.2	54.7	5.8	12.6	22.2	4.6	6.2	0.4	3.0
13151	Henry County	69,914	77.2	54.3	5.6	17.3	19.0	3.7	4.3	0.6	3.0
13153	Houston County	52,720	68.7	51.1	3.3	14.3	27.9	3.5	3.7	0.4	2.7
13157	Jackson County	21,316	77.9	60.6	4.7	12.6	17.3	4.8	4.8	0.1	2.8
13179	Liberty County	23,232	73.7	52.9	4.6	16.1	21.2	5.1	4.6	0.2	2.7
13185	Lowndes County	39,711	62.1	41.6	4.0	16.5	27.5	10.4	6.5	0.0	2.8
13215	Muscogee County	71,351	64.2	39.1	4.4	20.7	31.2	4.6	3.8	0.4	2.6
13217	Newton County	33,762	72.1	46.4	6.8	18.9	24.0	3.8	4.4	0.4	3.0
13223	Paulding County	48,165	81.4	63.1	4.4	13.9	15.6	2.9	4.5	0.3	3.0
13245	Richmond County	71,520	60.2	33.9	4.7	21.5	34.5	5.3	4.8	0.5	2.7
13247	Rockdale County	29,053	73.1	49.9	4.8	18.4	23.4	3.6	2.7	0.5	2.9

Table A-2: Counties with a Population of 50,000 or More—Living Arrangements—*Continued*

State/County code	Metropolitan area	Race or Hispanic origin of householder				Age of householder			Percent of households with one or more persons under 18 years old	Percent of households with one or more persons age 65 or older	Percent of all householders who are owners
		Householder is White alone, not Hispanic or Latino, percent	Householder is Black or African American alone, percent	Householder is Hispanic or Latino, percent	Householder is Asian alone, percent	Householders age 15 to 34, percent	Householders age 35 to 64, percent	Householders age 65 and older, percent			
	Florida—cont'd										
12011	Broward County	51.0	22.8	22.2	2.9	15.5	60.8	23.8	31.6	28.1	64.2
12015	Charlotte County	89.3	4.8	4.1	0.9	6.9	43.3	49.8	18.0	53.8	78.6
12017	Citrus County	92.8	2.0	3.3	0.0	7.4	45.8	46.8	18.6	50.5	81.6
12019	Clay County	79.4	9.2	6.7	2.3	14.3	64.1	21.6	36.9	25.4	75.6
12021	Collier County	79.8	4.1	14.8	0.0	9.6	46.6	43.9	21.9	47.5	72.9
12023	Columbia County	80.5	14.1	3.4	0.0	11.9	59.9	28.2	29.3	31.8	70.8
12031	Duval County	60.7	27.6	6.8	3.5	22.8	57.4	19.8	30.0	22.5	60.8
12033	Escambia County	72.2	19.9	3.4	2.1	19.3	54.6	26.1	25.4	29.0	62.2
12035	Flagler County	78.4	11.7	7.0	0.0	8.7	50.6	40.7	21.9	45.3	78.5
12053	Hernando County	86.2	4.4	7.8	0.8	9.9	50.0	40.1	25.2	44.2	77.9
12055	Highlands County	79.4	6.9	11.9	0.0	8.7	41.8	49.5	19.0	53.3	77.0
12057	Hillsborough County	58.1	16.3	21.2	3.2	21.3	58.8	19.9	32.2	23.3	58.6
12061	Indian River County	82.7	7.6	8.2	0.0	11.0	46.2	42.9	21.9	46.9	74.1
12069	Lake County	80.1	7.9	9.2	0.0	12.2	48.1	39.7	26.3	43.2	74.5
12071	Lee County	80.3	6.0	11.7	1.3	12.4	49.7	37.9	24.2	42.0	69.4
12073	Leon County	61.8	29.4	4.9	2.7	34.5	49.0	16.5	26.5	18.9	52.7
12081	Manatee County	81.1	7.1	9.7	1.2	12.1	49.9	38.0	23.4	41.2	70.1
12083	Marion County	78.4	11.1	8.3	1.3	12.0	47.2	40.8	23.0	44.1	74.7
12085	Martin County	87.6	4.2	7.3	0.0	8.5	49.3	42.2	21.2	45.1	74.4
12086	Miami-Dade County	19.1	17.0	63.2	1.6	16.2	60.9	22.9	33.6	29.7	54.5
12087	Monroe County	76.9	4.8	16.5	0.0	12.3	56.7	31.0	19.7	34.3	61.7
12089	Nassau County	89.4	6.5	2.4	0.0	11.1	59.3	29.6	31.4	32.7	76.4
12091	Okaloosa County	80.7	8.1	5.7	3.0	23.5	53.4	23.1	31.2	25.7	64.3
12095	Orange County	51.3	18.7	24.6	4.1	24.4	59.3	16.3	32.0	19.8	55.7
12097	Osceola County	45.5	10.3	41.6	2.5	17.2	62.3	20.5	39.9	25.2	61.6
12099	Palm Beach County	69.8	13.2	14.2	1.9	12.6	52.9	34.6	25.9	38.4	70.1
12101	Pasco County	84.7	4.0	8.9	1.5	12.0	53.7	34.3	26.8	37.9	75.2
12103	Pinellas County	81.9	8.7	5.9	2.2	13.2	54.2	32.6	21.1	35.6	65.1
12105	Polk County	71.7	12.9	13.3	1.3	15.6	53.2	31.3	30.1	35.2	68.8
12107	Putnam County	77.3	14.5	6.6	0.0	13.5	53.5	33.0	25.2	37.0	74.3
12109	St. Johns County	88.6	4.4	3.5	1.9	11.5	61.7	26.9	32.3	30.3	75.6
12111	St. Lucie County	69.2	15.7	12.5	1.2	12.9	53.2	33.9	28.4	37.9	72.2
12113	Santa Rosa County	87.4	4.7	4.1	1.7	17.9	59.5	22.6	34.5	25.6	72.5
12115	Sarasota County	89.4	3.6	5.4	1.0	8.6	46.0	45.4	19.1	49.0	73.6
12117	Seminole County	70.9	10.0	14.1	3.6	16.3	62.8	20.9	30.9	24.8	68.9
12119	Sumter County	93.1	3.3	2.6	0.0	4.1	29.2	66.7	8.4	69.9	89.6
12127	Volusia County	80.7	8.6	8.6	1.2	13.5	52.1	34.4	22.6	37.9	70.3
12131	Walton County	88.9	4.8	4.0	0.0	14.7	57.0	28.2	26.0	30.8	70.0
13000	**Georgia**	60.0	29.9	6.2	2.8	20.3	60.1	19.6	35.2	22.7	63.7
13013	Barrow County	79.3	10.7	6.2	0.0	21.0	61.8	17.2	42.8	21.6	74.9
13015	Bartow County	82.1	10.5	5.2	0.0	18.2	60.7	21.1	36.3	24.0	64.7
13021	Bibb County	45.6	49.0	2.6	1.3	21.3	55.8	22.9	31.8	25.7	53.4
13031	Bulloch County	69.1	26.7	2.4	0.0	36.9	46.0	17.1	30.3	19.6	49.2
13039	Camden County	75.0	17.8	0.0	0.0	25.7	57.4	16.9	41.1	19.8	61.9
13045	Carroll County	77.4	16.1	4.5	0.0	23.2	56.4	20.4	36.3	24.6	64.8
13047	Catoosa County	94.7	0.0	1.3	0.0	17.0	57.4	25.6	36.4	27.9	74.5
13051	Chatham County	56.9	35.2	4.6	2.2	24.6	53.5	22.0	29.6	24.2	55.9
13057	Cherokee County	86.3	5.4	5.8	0.0	15.8	65.5	18.7	40.2	21.3	78.9
13059	Clarke County	59.0	27.4	8.0	3.8	40.8	43.3	15.9	25.3	17.7	42.6
13063	Clayton County	17.0	68.7	9.5	4.1	23.1	64.4	12.5	39.8	16.2	52.4
13067	Cobb County	60.4	26.1	8.6	3.9	22.4	62.0	15.6	35.4	18.3	64.4
13073	Columbia County	76.5	15.2	3.7	3.3	16.0	66.4	17.6	39.8	21.9	77.7
13077	Coweta County	75.8	17.2	4.5	0.0	19.5	61.6	18.8	38.6	22.6	72.9
13089	DeKalb County	36.4	51.3	6.4	4.5	23.1	61.0	14.8	30.4	18.7	68.7
13095	Dougherty County	33.2	63.4	2.0	0.0	23.8	54.0	22.2	32.3	24.6	46.4
13097	Douglas County	51.1	41.0	5.6	0.0	18.0	67.2	14.8	40.7	18.7	68.7
13103	Effingham County	82.9	12.0	0.0	0.0	16.1	66.0	17.8	42.6	21.5	75.6
13113	Fayette County	71.5	18.7	5.0	0.0	7.4	67.5	25.1	36.6	28.3	81.7
13115	Floyd County	77.3	14.1	6.6	0.0	17.8	57.3	24.9	32.4	28.5	62.5
13117	Forsyth County	84.5	2.3	6.4	5.9	10.9	71.7	17.4	47.1	21.6	85.1
13121	Fulton County	46.1	42.5	5.2	5.0	25.5	58.4	16.1	29.6	18.3	52.3
13127	Glynn County	71.0	23.3	4.0	0.0	16.3	56.0	27.7	31.4	30.3	62.6
13129	Gordon County	83.8	4.5	11.0	0.0	18.1	59.4	22.5	34.4	25.8	66.0
13135	Gwinnett County	48.9	25.2	15.0	9.6	19.8	68.1	12.1	44.0	15.9	66.7
13139	Hall County	72.7	7.4	17.5	1.6	18.3	59.6	22.1	38.3	26.1	67.0
13151	Henry County	54.2	37.0	5.1	0.0	15.6	69.0	15.4	43.7	20.0	72.6
13153	Houston County	64.0	28.1	4.9	0.0	22.9	60.2	17.0	37.3	19.9	66.1
13157	Jackson County	86.9	6.8	4.1	0.0	19.5	59.7	20.8	42.4	24.7	77.3
13179	Liberty County	45.0	41.3	10.1	0.0	38.0	49.6	12.4	43.5	13.7	49.6
13185	Lowndes County	57.8	35.7	4.4	0.0	31.3	50.3	18.4	33.5	20.1	50.5
13215	Muscogee County	46.4	45.3	5.4	1.9	23.4	55.5	21.1	35.1	23.2	50.5
13217	Newton County	55.4	39.4	0.0	0.0	14.8	66.3	18.9	40.9	23.2	72.7
13223	Paulding County	78.0	16.0	0.0	0.0	19.1	66.3	14.6	45.8	17.3	79.8
13245	Richmond County	41.9	51.4	3.8	1.7	24.8	54.3	20.9	30.5	23.7	52.7
13247	Rockdale County	45.9	45.9	5.7	0.0	13.3	66.5	20.2	38.4	24.1	69.2

State/County code	Metropolitan area	Household type							Opposite-sex partner unmarried partner households, percent	Same-sex unmarried partner households, percent	Average household size
		Total Households	Family households, percent	Married-couple family households, percent	Male householder, no spouse, percent	Female householder, no spouse, percent	Householder living alone, percent	Nonfamily households, householder not living alone, percent			
	Georgia—cont'd										
13255	Spalding County	22,410	73.7	46.8	4.8	22.1	22.8	3.6	3.8	0.2	2.8
13285	Troup County	24,461	69.3	42.9	5.7	20.8	25.5	5.2	6.6	0.4	2.7
13295	Walker County	25,958	68.7	52.0	4.7	12.1	26.3	5.0	5.2	0.1	2.6
13297	Walton County	29,028	80.0	59.8	5.8	14.3	16.9	3.1	2.7	0.2	2.9
13313	Whitfield County	34,050	74.0	54.3	5.5	14.2	21.7	4.3	3.8	0.4	3.0
15000	**Hawaii**	449,296	69.2	51.5	5.4	12.3	24.0	6.7	5.8	0.7	3.0
15001	Hawaii County	64,825	67.2	47.4	6.8	12.9	25.6	7.3	7.9	0.9	2.9
15003	Honolulu County	308,716	69.9	52.4	5.1	12.4	23.7	6.4	5.0	0.6	3.0
15007	Kauai County	22,653	69.6	54.3	5.6	9.6	22.4	8.0	6.1	1.4	3.0
15009	Maui County	53,050	67.7	50.4	4.8	12.6	25.0	7.3	7.9	0.4	2.9
16000	**Idaho**	583,452	69.3	55.1	4.4	9.8	24.3	6.4	5.3	0.3	2.7
16001	Ada County	153,768	67.9	52.9	5.5	9.5	24.7	7.4	5.1	0.3	2.6
16005	Bannock County	30,239	65.7	50.8	4.3	10.7	27.7	6.5	5.2	0.2	2.7
16019	Bonneville County	36,402	73.0	57.3	4.0	11.7	22.8	4.2	4.0	0.5	2.9
16027	Canyon County	64,534	73.2	56.6	4.1	12.5	22.1	4.6	5.6	0.3	3.0
16055	Kootenai County	55,645	68.7	53.8	4.1	10.7	24.1	7.2	6.9	0.1	2.5
16083	Twin Falls County	28,348	71.3	54.4	5.1	11.8	22.7	6.0	6.2	0.1	2.7
17000	**Illinois**	4,763,457	65.4	48.1	4.6	12.7	28.9	5.7	5.2	0.5	2.6
17001	Adams County	26,569	66.0	52.5	3.3	10.2	29.5	4.4	4.8	0.1	2.5
17007	Boone County	17,605	77.5	62.7	3.4	11.3	18.6	3.9	4.7	0.4	3.1
17019	Champaign County	79,100	53.6	40.0	3.1	10.4	33.2	13.3	5.2	0.6	2.4
17029	Coles County	21,014	56.0	41.1	3.2	11.6	33.0	11.0	8.3	0.1	2.4
17031	Cook County	1,931,524	60.9	40.7	5.0	15.2	32.5	6.6	5.2	0.6	2.7
17037	DeKalb County	37,439	60.6	45.0	4.4	11.2	28.9	10.5	8.3	0.1	2.6
17043	DuPage County	336,540	71.1	57.8	3.8	9.6	24.7	4.2	4.0	0.3	2.7
17063	Grundy County	18,119	72.5	55.6	4.3	12.5	23.6	3.9	4.5	0.5	2.8
17073	Henry County	20,268	68.5	55.1	3.5	9.9	26.3	5.2	6.7	0.4	2.4
17077	Jackson County	23,550	49.0	36.4	3.2	9.5	38.5	12.5	4.7	1.0	2.4
17089	Kane County	170,209	74.4	58.3	5.2	10.9	21.3	4.4	5.3	0.3	3.0
17091	Kankakee County	41,333	67.7	46.9	5.9	15.0	27.1	5.1	6.3	0.5	2.6
17093	Kendall County	38,145	77.5	65.1	3.7	8.6	18.0	4.5	4.3	0.1	3.1
17095	Knox County	21,311	58.4	43.0	4.2	11.3	35.1	6.5	8.2	0.4	2.3
17097	Lake County	242,245	74.0	58.9	4.3	10.8	22.4	3.7	4.2	0.4	2.8
17099	LaSalle County	44,048	65.4	50.0	5.2	10.2	29.2	5.4	7.1	0.1	2.5
17111	McHenry County	108,550	75.3	61.3	4.0	10.0	20.6	4.1	4.8	0.2	2.8
17113	McLean County	64,570	62.0	48.8	3.8	9.4	27.8	10.2	5.3	0.7	2.6
17115	Macon County	45,186	61.6	44.6	4.4	12.6	33.0	5.4	5.9	0.4	2.4
17119	Madison County	106,844	66.4	49.2	5.0	12.2	26.7	6.9	6.7	0.4	2.5
17141	Ogle County	20,770	65.2	54.1	3.4	7.7	28.0	6.8	7.5	0.3	2.5
17143	Peoria County	75,978	61.2	43.6	3.6	14.0	32.9	6.0	5.4	0.6	2.4
17161	Rock Island County	60,724	62.0	45.0	4.4	12.7	33.7	4.3	5.7	0.3	2.4
17163	St. Clair County	102,075	67.0	44.4	4.8	17.8	29.1	3.9	5.3	0.2	2.6
17167	Sangamon County	82,503	62.1	44.2	4.8	13.1	31.5	6.4	5.1	0.4	2.4
17179	Tazewell County	54,416	67.9	54.7	2.9	10.2	27.5	4.6	5.9	0.7	2.5
17183	Vermilion County	31,666	64.6	46.0	4.9	13.7	31.0	4.4	4.4	0.8	2.5
17195	Whiteside County	23,447	66.6	51.5	5.3	9.7	29.4	3.9	6.3	0.3	2.4
17197	Will County	222,313	76.6	60.7	4.7	11.1	19.9	3.5	4.5	0.3	3.0
17199	Williamson County	26,778	67.1	50.8	3.5	12.8	28.7	4.2	4.1	0.6	2.4
17201	Winnebago County	112,759	66.5	47.2	4.7	14.6	28.6	4.9	5.9	0.3	2.6
18000	**Indiana**	2,482,558	66.4	49.4	4.6	12.4	27.9	5.7	5.7	0.4	2.6
18003	Allen County	139,279	64.4	46.5	4.3	13.6	29.7	5.9	5.5	0.4	2.6
18005	Bartholomew County	29,611	68.1	52.0	5.6	10.6	27.1	4.7	4.6	0.5	2.6
18011	Boone County	22,222	73.0	61.1	2.6	9.3	22.3	4.7	4.3	0.2	2.6
18019	Clark County	42,501	66.0	50.1	4.0	11.9	28.1	5.9	5.5	0.5	2.6
18035	Delaware County	46,101	59.8	43.0	3.9	13.0	29.5	10.7	6.2	0.3	2.4
18039	Elkhart County	70,775	72.4	52.6	6.2	13.6	23.4	4.3	6.2	0.3	2.8
18043	Floyd County	28,764	67.7	50.7	3.9	13.1	26.9	5.4	4.8	0.4	2.6
18053	Grant County	27,228	65.1	46.5	3.7	14.9	30.0	4.9	5.9	0.3	2.3
18057	Hamilton County	105,473	73.3	61.6	3.2	8.5	22.3	4.4	4.1	0.4	2.7
18059	Hancock County	25,923	73.4	57.0	5.2	11.2	22.3	4.3	6.5	0.3	2.7
18063	Hendricks County	53,570	75.6	62.0	4.6	9.0	20.6	3.7	5.0	0.2	2.8
18067	Howard County	34,538	64.9	48.7	5.2	11.0	30.4	4.7	5.1	0.2	2.4
18081	Johnson County	52,206	72.4	58.4	3.8	10.1	22.3	5.4	5.7	0.4	2.7
18085	Kosciusko County	28,849	71.0	57.2	5.4	8.4	25.5	3.5	3.8	0.4	2.6
18089	Lake County	181,693	67.4	45.2	5.4	16.8	28.1	4.5	5.4	0.3	2.7
18091	LaPorte County	42,747	65.2	48.2	3.5	13.5	29.1	5.7	6.8	0.4	2.4
18095	Madison County	50,328	64.1	46.6	4.6	12.9	31.2	4.7	5.3	0.6	2.5
18097	Marion County	361,342	58.9	37.2	4.9	16.8	33.9	7.1	6.4	0.8	2.4
18105	Monroe County	53,635	51.4	38.3	3.5	9.6	34.1	14.5	5.3	0.8	2.4
18109	Morgan County	25,788	73.6	60.3	2.3	11.1	20.6	5.8	7.6	0.1	2.7
18127	Porter County	61,781	71.6	55.7	3.6	12.3	23.4	5.0	5.4	0.2	2.6
18141	St. Joseph County	102,659	63.7	46.1	4.3	13.4	29.8	6.5	6.1	0.3	2.5
18157	Tippecanoe County	67,301	57.5	43.8	3.6	10.2	28.8	13.7	6.8	0.4	2.4
18163	Vanderburgh County	73,736	60.5	43.3	4.2	13.0	33.6	5.9	5.5	0.4	2.4

State/ County code	Metropolitan area	Race or Hispanic origin of householder				Age of householder			Percent of households with one or more persons under 18 years old	Percent of households with one or more persons age 65 or older	Percent of all householders who are owners
		Householder is White alone, not Hispanic or Latino, percent	Householder is Black or African American alone, percent	Householder is Hispanic or Latino, percent	Householder is Asian alone, percent	Householders age 15 to 34, percent	Householders age 35 to 64, percent	Householders age 65 and older, percent			
	Georgia—cont'd										
13255	Spalding County	67.2	28.1	0.0	0.0	18.4	57.1	24.4	35.9	29.4	62.6
13285	Troup County	61.4	34.0	1.9	0.0	20.2	58.2	21.6	36.7	25.4	59.5
13295	Walker County	93.6	4.1	0.0	0.0	15.8	58.5	25.7	33.8	28.9	70.7
13297	Walton County	80.0	14.6	2.4	0.0	16.8	62.3	20.8	39.1	25.8	72.7
13313	Whitfield County	70.5	4.2	23.4	0.0	20.4	58.0	21.7	43.2	25.2	64.7
15000	**Hawaii**	31.2	2.2	6.9	39.5	18.5	56.0	25.5	33.3	31.5	56.5
15001	Hawaii County	42.9	0.0	7.7	23.2	13.5	60.2	26.3	30.7	32.2	65.6
15003	Honolulu County	25.8	2.9	6.6	45.8	20.3	53.9	25.8	33.9	31.9	54.2
15007	Kauai County	42.2	0.0	6.7	33.9	13.4	59.7	26.9	31.6	32.9	61.0
15009	Maui County	43.7	0.0	8.3	25.4	16.7	60.9	22.4	33.5	27.9	57.3
16000	**Idaho**	88.2	0.5	7.9	1.1	22.1	55.0	22.8	34.7	25.5	68.7
16001	Ada County	89.9	0.7	5.1	2.1	22.9	58.0	19.1	34.9	21.7	66.7
16005	Bannock County	90.7	0.0	4.9	0.0	27.3	52.7	19.9	34.3	21.9	66.3
16019	Bonneville County	88.5	0.0	8.6	0.0	22.9	55.6	21.5	40.4	23.6	72.1
16027	Canyon County	79.2	0.0	17.5	0.0	23.3	54.8	21.9	40.5	24.8	68.7
16055	Kootenai County	94.0	0.0	2.6	0.0	20.1	55.4	24.5	32.5	27.5	70.7
16083	Twin Falls County	87.1	0.0	9.6	0.0	22.8	52.7	24.5	37.6	27.1	65.2
17000	**Illinois**	70.1	13.7	10.9	4.2	19.6	58.2	22.2	32.5	25.1	66.7
17001	Adams County	95.5	2.8	0.0	0.0	18.6	54.2	27.2	29.0	29.7	70.4
17007	Boone County	82.4	0.0	14.4	0.0	12.4	64.1	23.5	41.1	26.6	83.5
17019	Champaign County	75.1	11.3	3.8	7.9	34.8	47.8	17.4	24.7	19.0	54.9
17029	Coles County	93.6	2.5	1.8	0.0	27.9	48.7	23.4	25.3	25.0	62.1
17031	Cook County	51.9	24.0	17.0	6.0	21.8	57.1	21.0	31.1	24.3	57.1
17037	DeKalb County	85.5	5.4	6.4	2.0	30.5	51.6	17.9	30.8	20.1	59.0
17043	DuPage County	76.1	4.6	9.4	8.7	16.5	62.8	20.7	34.6	23.9	73.8
17063	Grundy County	93.5	0.0	5.2	0.0	19.4	59.2	21.4	37.1	23.5	75.6
17073	Henry County	95.2	0.0	3.5	0.0	15.1	56.6	28.3	27.9	30.4	78.1
17077	Jackson County	78.5	13.3	2.7	2.7	34.1	45.2	20.7	22.9	21.5	51.9
17089	Kane County	69.8	5.2	21.5	2.9	16.8	63.7	19.5	40.4	22.9	74.3
17091	Kankakee County	78.5	13.5	6.4	0.7	18.8	57.6	23.5	35.0	25.8	69.0
17093	Kendall County	79.4	5.9	12.7	0.0	18.7	66.5	14.8	48.1	16.7	84.6
17095	Knox County	90.3	4.9	3.7	0.0	15.6	53.3	31.1	25.8	32.9	67.7
17097	Lake County	72.6	7.0	14.1	5.5	15.4	65.1	19.5	39.8	22.9	74.9
17099	LaSalle County	92.5	0.9	5.5	0.0	16.6	56.6	26.9	28.5	29.1	74.0
17111	McHenry County	88.8	0.0	7.2	2.1	14.0	66.7	19.3	38.2	22.7	81.5
17113	McLean County	84.4	7.0	3.5	4.0	27.9	54.2	17.9	30.6	19.7	66.7
17115	Macon County	82.3	13.8	1.1	0.9	19.1	54.4	26.5	28.6	28.4	68.9
17119	Madison County	88.6	7.8	2.1	0.6	20.0	56.1	23.9	30.6	26.6	71.4
17141	Ogle County	92.1	0.0	5.9	0.0	15.0	59.5	25.5	30.0	28.5	75.7
17143	Peoria County	76.6	16.0	2.8	3.0	23.0	54.3	22.7	29.2	24.9	63.9
17161	Rock Island County	81.9	7.8	7.7	1.3	18.2	54.9	26.9	28.5	29.3	69.3
17163	St. Clair County	66.5	28.8	2.4	0.9	18.3	59.1	22.6	33.5	25.0	67.6
17167	Sangamon County	85.5	10.8	1.3	1.3	20.1	57.1	22.8	29.6	25.3	70.0
17179	Tazewell County	96.5	0.0	1.2	0.0	19.1	55.2	25.7	30.1	27.4	74.7
17183	Vermilion County	85.4	10.8	2.2	0.0	17.2	54.3	28.5	29.8	30.6	71.3
17195	Whiteside County	90.7	0.0	7.3	0.0	15.1	55.3	29.6	29.2	30.9	75.9
17197	Will County	73.4	10.5	11.2	4.1	14.7	66.8	18.4	42.5	21.7	81.9
17199	Williamson County	94.9	2.8	1.0	0.0	18.1	55.0	27.0	30.3	29.3	72.1
17201	Winnebago County	78.2	11.3	7.7	1.8	17.9	58.3	23.7	33.1	26.6	66.5
18000	**Indiana**	84.3	8.8	4.3	1.4	20.3	57.4	22.4	32.5	24.9	69.2
18003	Allen County	80.5	11.7	4.3	2.1	21.9	57.6	20.5	33.2	22.6	69.1
18005	Bartholomew County	89.9	0.0	3.3	4.6	17.3	58.3	24.4	32.9	26.5	71.2
18011	Boone County	94.1	0.0	0.0	0.0	17.1	62.5	20.4	35.6	23.4	77.4
18019	Clark County	88.9	6.6	2.8	0.0	17.8	59.4	22.9	31.4	25.3	72.5
18035	Delaware County	89.3	4.6	1.3	0.8	24.2	50.5	25.3	26.4	27.7	62.6
18039	Elkhart County	83.7	5.0	9.5	0.7	20.0	57.8	22.3	38.9	24.6	72.3
18043	Floyd County	92.5	4.5	1.6	0.0	17.1	60.9	22.0	31.2	24.7	72.3
18053	Grant County	88.0	7.6	2.2	0.0	16.1	55.7	28.2	28.5	30.5	69.5
18057	Hamilton County	88.2	3.9	2.6	4.1	20.4	64.7	15.0	42.6	17.5	79.0
18059	Hancock County	94.6	0.0	0.0	0.0	13.8	64.1	22.0	35.8	24.6	79.2
18063	Hendricks County	91.5	3.8	1.7	0.0	16.9	63.5	19.6	38.8	22.5	82.1
18067	Howard County	88.7	7.4	2.2	0.7	19.2	55.0	25.8	30.5	27.7	69.9
18081	Johnson County	93.5	1.4	2.5	0.0	20.1	58.2	21.7	37.0	24.0	71.6
18085	Kosciusko County	92.6	0.0	5.3	0.0	16.5	58.8	24.7	31.5	26.6	78.8
18089	Lake County	59.3	25.9	13.4	1.0	17.1	59.4	23.5	33.6	26.8	68.8
18091	LaPorte County	87.4	7.7	3.4	0.0	17.6	57.0	25.4	29.1	28.6	71.5
18095	Madison County	90.3	5.8	2.1	0.0	16.5	56.0	27.5	30.0	29.8	68.4
18097	Marion County	63.6	26.2	6.6	1.9	26.8	55.3	17.8	31.5	20.1	54.5
18105	Monroe County	87.5	3.2	2.2	5.1	35.0	47.2	17.9	23.6	19.8	53.3
18109	Morgan County	97.8	0.0	0.0	0.0	16.2	61.1	22.7	34.9	26.2	75.9
18127	Porter County	88.9	3.1	6.1	1.3	17.5	60.9	21.6	34.9	24.6	77.3
18141	St. Joseph County	80.2	12.1	4.7	1.7	20.9	56.6	22.5	30.8	25.1	68.2
18157	Tippecanoe County	82.9	3.9	5.6	6.5	38.0	46.0	16.0	28.5	17.9	53.5
18163	Vanderburgh County	87.0	9.3	1.2	0.0	22.5	54.3	23.2	29.0	25.3	63.7

State/ County code	Metropolitan area	Household type							Opposite-sex partner unmarried partner households, percent	Same-sex unmarried partner households, percent	Average household size
		Total Households	Family households, percent	Married-couple family households, percent	Male householder, no spouse, percent	Female householder, no spouse, percent	Householder living alone, percent	Nonfamily households, householder not living alone, percent			
	Indiana—cont'd										
18167	Vigo County	39,237	61.7	45.7	4.8	11.2	31.3	7.0	6.8	0.8	2.5
18173	Warrick County	22,475	75.2	63.3	2.1	9.8	21.5	3.3	4.0	0.2	2.7
18177	Wayne County	27,966	65.4	47.4	4.2	13.8	28.9	5.7	6.9	0.4	2.4
19000	**Iowa**	1,227,201	64.6	51.0	4.1	9.5	29.0	6.4	6.0	0.3	2.4
19013	Black Hawk County	51,959	58.7	45.7	3.3	9.8	32.2	9.1	6.3	0.4	2.4
19049	Dallas County	26,787	73.2	60.4	3.2	9.6	21.6	5.2	4.5	0.1	2.7
19061	Dubuque County	37,388	64.0	50.9	3.7	9.4	29.7	6.3	4.9	0.2	2.4
19103	Johnson County	55,072	54.9	43.3	3.2	8.3	30.3	14.8	5.9	0.3	2.3
19113	Linn County	85,925	61.9	48.2	3.6	10.0	30.2	7.9	6.4	0.4	2.4
19153	Polk County	174,037	64.8	48.6	4.9	11.3	28.3	6.8	6.6	0.4	2.5
19155	Pottawattamie County	36,339	66.9	48.2	5.2	13.4	27.2	6.0	5.8	0.9	2.5
19163	Scott County	67,063	62.4	47.3	3.7	11.4	31.2	6.4	6.5	0.4	2.5
19169	Story County	35,461	53.2	45.6	2.5	5.1	27.8	19.0	7.2	0.4	2.3
19193	Woodbury County	38,593	65.1	45.9	5.8	13.4	29.4	5.5	7.3	0.3	2.6
20000	**Kansas**	1,109,747	65.6	50.7	4.4	10.5	28.5	5.9	5.0	0.3	2.5
20015	Butler County	24,101	71.7	57.5	5.1	9.1	25.1	3.2	4.4	0.2	2.7
20045	Douglas County	43,325	54.8	41.6	5.1	8.1	29.8	15.3	6.3	0.5	2.4
20091	Johnson County	218,074	67.9	55.0	3.4	9.4	26.4	5.7	4.4	0.4	2.5
20103	Leavenworth County	26,572	71.9	56.5	4.2	11.2	23.3	4.8	4.9	0.2	2.7
20155	Reno County	25,402	65.6	52.1	3.5	10.0	30.0	4.4	4.2	0.4	2.4
20161	Riley County	26,163	54.1	42.6	3.6	7.9	29.8	16.1	5.4	0.3	2.5
20169	Saline County	22,354	64.3	46.6	4.1	13.6	28.6	7.2	7.4	0.2	2.4
20173	Sedgwick County	191,779	64.7	47.2	4.9	12.6	30.1	5.2	4.5	0.4	2.6
20177	Shawnee County	71,073	62.6	46.9	4.3	11.4	30.9	6.5	5.8	0.4	2.5
20209	Wyandotte County	57,653	63.9	38.4	6.6	18.8	29.8	6.3	6.9	0.6	2.7
21000	**Kentucky**	1,693,399	66.8	49.0	4.8	13.0	28.0	5.2	5.3	0.4	2.5
21015	Boone County	43,907	75.0	57.3	5.7	12.0	21.2	3.8	4.2	0.4	2.8
21029	Bullitt County	27,684	74.6	56.2	5.1	13.2	20.6	4.8	7.1	0.7	2.7
21037	Campbell County	35,175	64.3	46.6	4.6	13.0	29.0	6.7	5.7	0.7	2.5
21047	Christian County	25,412	71.5	52.1	3.9	15.5	25.0	3.5	4.8	0.2	2.7
21059	Daviess County	37,787	67.1	51.2	4.7	11.2	28.1	4.9	4.9	0.5	2.5
21067	Fayette County	123,413	57.6	40.8	4.5	12.2	32.8	9.7	5.7	0.6	2.4
21093	Hardin County	39,859	70.8	51.6	4.8	14.4	24.9	4.3	6.7	0.2	2.6
21111	Jefferson County	304,947	61.0	40.9	4.9	15.1	32.5	6.5	5.6	0.6	2.4
21117	Kenton County	61,710	64.4	45.4	5.2	13.8	29.0	6.6	6.9	0.5	2.6
21125	Laurel County	22,916	72.5	53.9	5.3	13.3	23.3	4.2	4.7	0.7	2.6
21145	McCracken County	26,666	62.9	46.1	3.0	13.8	32.5	4.6	4.3	0.5	2.4
21151	Madison County	31,489	64.1	48.3	4.3	11.5	27.6	8.3	5.9	0.4	2.5
21185	Oldham County	19,492	80.8	67.7	4.3	8.8	16.0	3.2	3.1	0.7	2.9
21195	Pike County	25,927	68.0	51.6	4.9	11.6	28.7	3.3	2.9	0.1	2.4
21199	Pulaski County	25,993	68.6	52.3	2.8	13.5	27.6	3.8	4.8	0.2	2.4
21227	Warren County	45,097	63.3	45.4	4.6	13.4	27.9	8.7	5.6	0.2	2.5
22000	**Louisiana**	1,715,997	65.7	43.5	5.1	17.1	29.0	5.3	5.3	0.3	2.6
22001	Acadia Parish	22,837	68.7	47.3	5.0	16.4	26.6	4.7	6.0	0.1	2.7
22005	Ascension Parish	39,206	75.7	56.6	4.5	14.6	20.5	3.8	4.6	0.3	2.8
22015	Bossier Parish	46,409	66.1	46.9	4.4	14.9	30.0	3.8	4.8	0.1	2.6
22017	Caddo Parish	98,380	62.6	36.9	5.3	20.5	33.2	4.1	4.1	0.6	2.6
22019	Calcasieu Parish	74,455	67.7	45.9	5.9	15.9	27.5	4.8	5.2	0.2	2.6
22033	East Baton Rouge Parish	168,221	61.4	38.9	4.9	17.6	30.7	7.8	4.6	0.3	2.6
22045	Iberia Parish	26,553	72.0	46.9	6.5	18.7	23.3	4.7	7.4	0.8	2.7
22051	Jefferson Parish	166,684	62.9	40.7	5.4	16.8	31.7	5.4	6.2	0.4	2.6
22055	Lafayette Parish	87,666	62.3	42.8	5.1	14.5	30.9	6.7	5.6	0.3	2.6
22057	Lafourche Parish	35,009	70.7	51.4	5.1	14.1	23.8	5.5	8.6	0.2	2.7
22063	Livingston Parish	46,833	72.8	53.0	6.7	13.1	22.9	4.3	4.7	0.6	2.8
22071	Orleans Parish	151,790	51.0	26.7	4.7	19.6	40.6	8.4	5.7	0.9	2.4
22073	Ouachita Parish	57,373	65.3	41.9	3.6	19.8	30.4	4.3	3.8	0.3	2.6
22079	Rapides Parish	47,563	65.2	43.8	4.9	16.5	30.7	4.1	4.4	0.4	2.7
22089	St. Charles Parish	18,190	74.0	49.6	4.9	19.4	21.6	4.4	6.1	0.3	2.9
22097	St. Landry Parish	31,235	69.4	44.5	5.7	19.2	26.6	3.9	5.9	0.1	2.6
22099	St. Martin Parish	18,615	70.9	49.0	3.9	18.0	26.0	3.1	4.6	0.4	2.8
22101	St. Mary Parish	20,077	68.0	41.8	6.7	19.5	26.0	6.0	7.2	0.0	2.6
22103	St. Tammany Parish	87,987	73.4	55.3	4.7	13.4	21.7	4.9	4.9	0.3	2.7
22105	Tangipahoa Parish	44,727	68.0	45.2	5.2	17.6	25.6	6.4	6.5	0.0	2.7
22109	Terrebonne Parish	39,604	70.8	48.8	6.9	15.2	23.5	5.6	8.6	0.6	2.8
22113	Vermilion Parish	21,447	71.6	50.7	5.1	15.8	23.9	4.5	6.8	0.3	2.7
22115	Vernon Parish	17,856	74.0	57.0	4.2	12.8	22.8	3.2	3.3	0.0	2.8
23000	**Maine**	552,589	62.6	48.8	4.3	9.5	29.2	8.2	8.1	0.7	2.3
23001	Androscoggin County	44,364	62.1	45.7	4.7	11.6	29.4	8.6	9.0	0.6	2.4
23003	Aroostook County	30,560	63.9	50.9	4.3	8.8	31.0	5.1	6.5	0.5	2.2
23005	Cumberland County	116,882	60.9	47.4	3.8	9.7	30.2	8.9	6.7	1.0	2.4
23009	Hancock County	24,557	59.5	49.1	2.8	7.7	31.6	8.9	8.0	1.0	2.2
23011	Kennebec County	51,331	62.4	48.2	4.1	10.1	29.2	8.3	10.1	0.6	2.3
23017	Oxford County	22,609	64.2	49.9	5.4	9.0	29.3	6.5	7.5	0.5	2.5

State/ County code	Metropolitan area	Race or Hispanic origin of householder				Age of householder			Percent of households with one or more persons under 18 years old	Percent of households with one or more persons age 65 or older	Percent of all householders who are owners
		Householder is White alone, not Hispanic or Latino, percent	Householder is Black or African American alone, percent	Householder is Hispanic or Latino, percent	Householder is Asian alone, percent	Householders age 15 to 34, percent	Householders age 35 to 64, percent	Householders age 65 and older, percent			
	Indiana—cont'd										
18167	Vigo County	90.6	5.0	1.6	0.0	23.0	54.2	22.8	28.8	25.8	62.9
18173	Warrick County	95.0	0.0	0.0	0.0	15.3	61.2	23.5	34.4	25.4	84.5
18177	Wayne County	89.9	4.9	0.0	0.0	18.8	54.7	26.5	31.4	29.2	68.2
19000	**Iowa**	91.6	2.5	3.4	1.5	21.7	54.2	24.1	30.4	26.0	71.8
19013	Black Hawk County	86.4	8.7	2.8	0.0	25.4	50.9	23.6	26.7	25.5	67.7
19049	Dallas County	90.2	0.0	4.1	0.0	24.8	58.0	17.2	38.1	18.5	77.1
19061	Dubuque County	94.5	0.0	1.3	1.1	19.8	56.1	24.1	30.3	26.0	72.1
19103	Johnson County	85.9	4.3	4.2	4.8	38.2	47.1	14.7	27.7	16.0	59.5
19113	Linn County	92.1	3.4	1.7	1.4	23.1	55.4	21.6	31.3	23.5	73.4
19153	Polk County	85.9	5.2	5.1	2.8	25.8	55.9	18.2	35.2	20.4	68.4
19155	Pottawattamie County	92.4	0.0	5.0	0.0	21.4	55.1	23.5	30.0	26.3	69.8
19163	Scott County	86.4	6.9	4.1	1.7	20.9	56.2	22.9	30.9	24.5	67.8
19169	Story County	88.5	1.9	1.9	6.6	41.8	41.5	16.8	23.2	17.7	54.6
19193	Woodbury County	83.6	2.1	10.0	1.8	20.9	56.7	22.3	34.8	24.9	67.8
20000	**Kansas**	82.9	5.6	7.3	1.9	22.7	54.9	22.3	32.8	24.6	66.7
20015	Butler County	94.4	0.0	2.6	0.0	16.5	60.3	23.1	36.4	25.2	74.4
20045	Douglas County	85.7	3.6	3.8	3.3	35.9	47.7	16.4	27.2	18.0	52.7
20091	Johnson County	85.5	4.2	5.2	3.6	22.1	59.1	18.9	36.0	21.0	69.5
20103	Leavenworth County	86.7	6.7	3.1	0.0	16.7	62.1	21.2	37.1	23.3	66.4
20155	Reno County	91.2	2.0	5.2	0.0	18.6	54.6	26.8	29.1	28.7	65.7
20161	Riley County	81.8	6.7	5.4	4.4	50.2	35.8	14.0	28.5	14.6	42.4
20169	Saline County	87.6	3.5	6.1	0.0	23.0	53.1	23.9	31.0	26.6	65.8
20173	Sedgwick County	76.0	9.2	9.3	3.1	23.7	56.3	19.9	33.9	22.5	63.9
20177	Shawnee County	80.6	7.9	7.6	1.0	20.5	55.8	23.7	30.4	26.0	63.7
20209	Wyandotte County	49.9	27.8	18.5	2.0	24.2	56.8	19.0	36.2	22.0	58.8
21000	**Kentucky**	88.1	7.8	2.1	0.9	19.3	57.6	23.1	31.8	25.7	67.7
21015	Boone County	91.0	0.0	0.0	2.1	18.1	63.2	18.7	40.5	21.1	73.7
21029	Bullitt County	96.6	0.0	0.0	0.0	16.5	60.8	22.6	34.3	24.6	82.3
21037	Campbell County	95.0	1.6	1.4	0.0	21.9	56.0	22.1	30.2	24.0	69.2
21047	Christian County	71.0	21.4	5.1	0.0	31.4	49.7	18.8	41.5	22.0	49.7
21059	Daviess County	93.0	4.5	0.0	0.0	19.4	55.5	25.1	31.9	27.6	70.6
21067	Fayette County	76.7	14.6	4.4	3.1	28.9	53.5	17.7	28.7	19.6	54.9
21093	Hardin County	79.6	12.1	3.9	1.8	21.7	59.7	18.6	37.2	21.0	60.8
21111	Jefferson County	73.3	20.2	3.2	1.8	21.0	56.9	22.2	29.7	24.7	62.0
21117	Kenton County	90.9	5.0	2.0	0.0	22.0	58.4	19.6	33.3	21.5	67.0
21125	Laurel County	97.6	0.0	0.0	0.0	18.5	59.7	21.8	33.9	25.2	69.1
21145	McCracken County	86.7	9.9	0.0	0.0	16.5	56.7	26.8	28.0	29.6	67.3
21151	Madison County	92.6	4.3	0.0	0.0	25.8	53.6	20.6	31.1	22.6	59.8
21185	Oldham County	92.2	0.0	0.0	0.0	10.7	70.5	18.8	41.5	21.9	85.2
21195	Pike County	97.8	0.0	0.0	0.0	16.8	58.9	24.3	31.8	27.2	72.9
21199	Pulaski County	96.4	0.0	0.0	0.0	15.6	58.4	26.0	30.3	29.4	69.3
21227	Warren County	84.9	9.6	2.5	1.8	28.4	53.2	18.4	30.5	21.0	58.2
22000	**Louisiana**	63.7	29.9	3.5	1.3	21.4	56.7	21.8	33.2	24.6	66.2
22001	Acadia Parish	80.4	16.9	0.0	0.0	19.3	59.4	21.3	36.4	24.9	70.3
22005	Ascension Parish	74.0	20.9	3.4	0.0	21.5	61.8	16.6	44.5	18.3	80.7
22015	Bossier Parish	73.3	19.2	4.0	0.0	24.5	55.1	20.5	34.7	22.7	67.2
22017	Caddo Parish	51.4	44.7	1.9	0.9	21.3	55.4	23.2	31.0	25.8	61.2
22019	Calcasieu Parish	72.1	22.9	1.9	0.0	21.9	55.9	22.2	35.5	24.9	69.2
22033	East Baton Rouge Parish	51.2	42.1	2.8	2.6	27.2	53.7	19.1	30.4	21.5	60.4
22045	Iberia Parish	64.0	29.6	3.0	0.0	19.4	57.6	23.0	37.0	25.5	71.6
22051	Jefferson Parish	60.4	24.9	10.2	3.1	19.3	57.6	23.1	29.9	26.7	62.3
22055	Lafayette Parish	70.4	23.5	3.4	1.2	25.7	56.7	17.7	34.1	19.4	65.1
22057	Lafourche Parish	81.1	11.9	3.4	0.0	21.0	56.2	22.8	34.0	25.3	76.2
22063	Livingston Parish	91.0	5.2	1.9	0.0	21.1	60.5	18.4	40.2	21.6	80.2
22071	Orleans Parish	35.5	55.8	5.1	2.3	25.2	56.5	18.3	25.8	21.1	46.2
22073	Ouachita Parish	63.1	33.6	1.6	0.0	22.0	55.5	22.5	35.3	24.4	58.8
22079	Rapides Parish	67.1	28.6	2.1	0.0	17.7	57.5	24.8	31.7	28.2	65.2
22089	St. Charles Parish	70.8	22.5	4.7	0.0	14.6	65.5	19.9	40.1	22.0	80.5
22097	St. Landry Parish	58.6	38.3	0.0	0.0	19.8	56.0	24.1	33.8	26.4	69.0
22099	St. Martin Parish	68.9	29.1	0.0	0.0	16.8	61.4	21.8	35.8	24.6	80.4
22101	St. Mary Parish	60.9	29.5	5.1	0.0	18.2	56.8	25.0	35.7	25.8	68.3
22103	St. Tammany Parish	82.9	10.6	3.7	0.0	15.9	61.8	22.3	34.2	26.5	75.9
22105	Tangipahoa Parish	67.9	27.4	2.9	0.0	23.3	56.5	20.2	35.0	24.4	69.0
22109	Terrebonne Parish	73.7	16.4	3.3	0.0	20.5	58.5	21.0	36.2	23.6	73.6
22113	Vermilion Parish	83.7	11.6	0.0	0.0	19.3	58.6	22.1	36.7	24.5	74.8
22115	Vernon Parish	75.5	13.4	6.5	1.5	31.6	50.8	17.5	40.5	20.1	54.2
23000	**Maine**	96.0	0.7	1.0	0.7	15.8	58.7	25.4	26.7	28.6	70.8
23001	Androscoggin County	94.5	0.9	0.0	0.0	18.5	58.4	23.0	30.6	25.3	61.6
23003	Aroostook County	96.9	0.0	0.4	0.0	15.0	55.6	29.4	25.2	32.5	71.1
23005	Cumberland County	94.1	1.8	1.4	1.6	17.1	59.7	23.3	28.0	26.5	67.4
23009	Hancock County	96.8	0.0	0.0	0.0	13.1	59.0	27.9	23.2	31.8	73.8
23011	Kennebec County	96.3	0.0	0.9	0.0	16.4	59.4	24.2	26.3	27.6	70.3
23017	Oxford County	98.3	0.0	0.0	0.0	12.1	61.0	26.9	24.5	30.4	78.2

State/ County code	Metropolitan area	Household type							Opposite- sex partner unmarried partner households, percent	Same-sex unmarried partner households, percent	Average household size
		Total Households	Family households, percent	Married- couple family households, percent	Male householder, no spouse, percent	Female householder, no spouse, percent	Householder living alone, percent	Nonfamily households, householder not living alone, percent			
	Maine—cont'd										
23019	Penobscot County	62,468	61.5	47.9	4.3	9.3	27.7	10.8	8.3	0.6	2.4
23025	Somerset County	21,440	64.5	48.3	4.6	11.5	27.5	8.0	9.9	0.4	2.4
23031	York County	81,490	64.6	51.7	4.3	8.6	27.5	7.9	7.9	0.7	2.4
24000	**Maryland**	2,149,424	66.6	47.1	4.8	14.7	27.4	5.9	5.2	0.5	2.7
24001	Allegany County	28,108	59.6	43.7	4.1	11.8	34.1	6.3	6.3	0.4	2.4
24003	Anne Arundel County	200,839	69.4	52.9	4.8	11.7	24.2	6.4	5.6	0.4	2.7
24005	Baltimore County	312,458	64.6	45.2	4.8	14.5	29.3	6.1	5.2	0.6	2.6
24009	Calvert County	30,749	74.9	58.1	4.2	12.6	21.4	3.7	5.2	0.6	2.9
24013	Carroll County	59,765	74.0	60.9	4.0	9.0	21.7	4.3	4.0	0.5	2.7
24015	Cecil County	36,231	72.6	55.1	4.5	12.9	23.0	4.5	5.2	0.3	2.8
24017	Charles County	51,926	72.3	51.4	4.8	16.1	23.2	4.6	4.6	0.4	2.9
24021	Frederick County	87,397	72.1	56.5	4.5	11.1	22.3	5.7	4.7	0.4	2.7
24025	Harford County	90,912	73.3	56.1	4.6	12.7	22.2	4.4	4.4	0.3	2.7
24027	Howard County	107,263	74.6	59.3	3.7	11.5	20.7	4.7	3.0	0.3	2.8
24031	Montgomery County	361,632	69.0	53.3	4.4	11.3	25.4	5.5	4.4	0.6	2.8
24033	Prince George's County	303,563	65.7	38.1	6.6	20.9	28.4	6.0	5.9	0.5	2.8
24037	St. Mary's County	37,483	74.6	60.8	4.5	9.3	20.9	4.5	4.7	0.3	2.8
24043	Washington County	56,264	66.8	49.0	4.9	13.0	27.0	6.2	6.8	0.7	2.5
24045	Wicomico County	36,388	67.9	46.6	4.4	16.9	25.1	7.1	6.7	0.2	2.7
24047	Worcester County	19,716	65.5	51.8	3.0	10.7	29.1	5.4	5.7	0.4	2.6
24510	Baltimore city	242,243	50.5	23.4	4.7	22.3	40.8	8.7	6.3	0.8	2.5
25000	**Massachusetts**	2,528,592	63.5	46.7	4.1	12.7	28.9	7.6	5.7	0.7	2.5
25001	Barnstable County	93,184	62.3	49.6	3.2	9.5	32.3	5.3	4.3	1.1	2.3
25003	Berkshire County	55,192	59.7	43.7	4.0	11.9	34.6	5.7	6.5	0.5	2.2
25005	Bristol County	210,096	65.4	46.7	4.7	14.1	28.3	6.2	7.1	0.6	2.5
25009	Essex County	285,825	66.7	47.9	4.8	14.0	27.6	5.7	5.8	0.6	2.6
25011	Franklin County	30,085	59.4	44.2	4.9	10.4	30.7	9.9	8.6	0.8	2.3
25013	Hampden County	176,010	65.6	41.9	5.6	18.1	28.4	6.0	7.0	0.5	2.6
25015	Hampshire County	58,766	59.2	45.9	3.7	9.6	30.7	10.1	4.2	1.7	2.3
25017	Middlesex County	583,023	63.8	50.7	3.3	9.8	27.7	8.5	5.1	0.7	2.5
25021	Norfolk County	258,166	65.9	52.6	3.1	10.2	27.8	6.3	4.3	0.6	2.6
25023	Plymouth County	179,345	71.5	54.6	4.2	12.7	23.3	5.2	5.0	0.5	2.7
25025	Suffolk County	289,650	49.1	27.6	4.2	17.3	37.0	13.9	6.0	1.1	2.4
25027	Worcester County	299,474	66.8	49.2	4.7	12.9	26.5	6.6	6.4	0.5	2.6
26000	**Michigan**	3,815,532	65.2	47.8	4.6	12.9	29.0	5.8	5.5	0.4	2.5
26005	Allegan County	41,849	74.0	60.3	3.5	10.2	21.1	4.9	5.3	0.5	2.7
26015	Barry County	22,599	70.2	59.1	3.7	7.4	24.4	5.4	5.0	0.5	2.6
26017	Bay County	43,937	65.1	49.1	4.5	11.5	29.6	5.3	5.9	0.4	2.4
26021	Berrien County	59,108	66.9	49.4	3.9	13.6	29.1	4.0	4.8	0.3	2.6
26025	Calhoun County	52,729	64.7	44.8	4.9	15.1	29.8	5.4	6.7	0.5	2.5
26027	Cass County	19,835	68.2	53.3	5.1	9.8	27.6	4.2	5.7	0.2	2.6
26037	Clinton County	28,716	68.9	56.3	4.1	8.6	24.0	7.0	5.5	0.4	2.6
26045	Eaton County	43,554	64.8	49.9	3.2	11.7	29.9	5.3	5.1	0.5	2.5
26049	Genesee County	164,407	64.7	43.0	5.3	16.3	29.5	5.8	6.8	0.3	2.5
26055	Grand Traverse County	34,069	65.2	51.5	4.0	9.6	28.7	6.1	7.5	0.8	2.5
26065	Ingham County	109,239	55.9	39.0	4.6	12.2	33.1	11.0	6.0	0.5	2.4
26067	Ionia County	21,852	71.7	56.2	5.1	10.4	23.1	5.2	7.7	0.4	2.8
26073	Isabella County	24,572	55.5	40.6	4.2	10.7	26.6	17.8	8.6	0.4	2.6
26075	Jackson County	60,391	66.3	48.2	5.5	12.6	28.2	5.5	6.0	0.3	2.5
26077	Kalamazoo County	99,756	60.1	44.2	4.4	11.6	30.5	9.3	6.6	0.6	2.5
26081	Kent County	230,511	66.4	49.9	4.1	12.4	26.6	6.9	5.9	0.4	2.6
26087	Lapeer County	32,742	74.5	60.1	5.0	9.3	21.3	4.2	5.7	0.0	2.6
26091	Lenawee County	37,994	67.1	52.2	3.9	10.9	27.8	5.1	5.5	0.2	2.5
26093	Livingston County	67,284	74.8	61.6	4.2	9.0	21.2	4.0	4.5	0.4	2.7
26099	Macomb County	332,925	66.6	48.9	4.6	13.0	28.8	4.6	5.2	0.4	2.5
26103	Marquette County	26,554	59.6	48.4	3.6	7.5	31.9	8.5	6.3	0.3	2.4
26111	Midland County	33,543	67.7	55.6	3.5	8.5	26.2	6.1	5.9	0.2	2.5
26115	Monroe County	58,167	70.6	54.1	4.8	11.7	24.8	4.6	5.6	0.4	2.6
26117	Montcalm County	23,164	71.2	55.7	5.1	10.4	24.0	4.8	6.4	0.7	2.6
26121	Muskegon County	64,434	67.2	47.4	4.8	14.9	27.7	5.1	6.8	0.4	2.5
26125	Oakland County	489,684	65.3	50.2	4.1	11.0	29.4	5.3	4.5	0.3	2.5
26139	Ottawa County	94,874	73.8	61.3	3.7	8.7	20.5	5.6	4.5	0.3	2.7
26145	Saginaw County	77,436	64.2	45.2	4.1	14.9	31.2	4.5	5.4	0.3	2.5
26147	St. Clair County	64,196	67.4	51.8	4.7	11.0	26.9	5.7	6.3	0.3	2.5
26149	St. Joseph County	22,653	70.0	53.6	5.1	11.3	25.5	4.4	5.1	0.3	2.7
26155	Shiawassee County	27,486	71.0	54.5	4.9	11.6	24.6	4.4	5.4	0.3	2.5
26157	Tuscola County	20,767	70.6	56.8	4.4	9.4	25.2	4.1	5.7	0.3	2.6

Table A-2: Counties with a Population of 50,000 or More—Living Arrangements—Continued

State/ County code	Metropolitan area	Race or Hispanic origin of householder				Age of householder			Percent of households with one or more persons under 18 years old	Percent of households with one or more persons age 65 or older	Percent of all householders who are owners
		Householder is White alone, not Hispanic or Latino, percent	Householder is Black or African American alone, percent	Householder is Hispanic or Latino, percent	Householder is Asian alone, percent	Householders age 15 to 34, percent	Householders age 35 to 64, percent	Householders age 65 and older, percent			
23019	Penobscot County	95.8	0.0	1.0	0.0	20.0	56.6	23.3	26.8	26.1	65.6
23025	Somerset County	97.6	0.0	0.0	0.0	13.8	61.2	25.0	26.8	30.7	79.0
23031	York County	96.9	0.0	0.9	0.8	14.4	60.0	25.6	27.6	28.4	72.2
24000	**Maryland**	58.7	29.1	5.8	5.0	17.6	61.0	21.4	33.3	25.0	66.8
24001	Allegany County	95.3	3.1	0.0	0.0	17.3	52.7	30.0	24.5	33.0	69.9
24003	Anne Arundel County	76.1	15.1	4.2	2.9	17.4	61.8	20.8	34.5	24.4	73.8
24005	Baltimore County	66.0	25.5	3.1	4.1	17.6	58.1	24.3	30.7	27.7	66.1
24009	Calvert County	82.8	13.1	1.9	0.0	12.2	68.4	19.3	36.8	24.3	80.2
24013	Carroll County	94.0	2.7	1.9	0.0	11.5	64.6	23.9	34.3	27.2	81.1
24015	Cecil County	88.9	6.2	2.8	0.0	16.4	62.6	21.0	35.5	24.1	73.0
24017	Charles County	50.7	41.6	3.1	2.2	15.6	68.1	16.4	37.3	20.7	76.5
24021	Frederick County	81.4	8.6	5.4	3.3	15.4	64.5	20.1	36.3	23.2	74.3
24025	Harford County	81.4	12.0	3.3	2.2	15.1	62.9	22.0	34.7	25.8	79.2
24027	Howard County	61.6	18.8	4.6	13.4	16.3	66.3	17.3	39.4	21.6	73.4
24031	Montgomery County	55.6	16.7	12.7	13.0	16.6	62.4	21.0	35.8	25.0	66.4
24033	Prince George's County	16.9	68.1	10.3	3.4	18.4	64.0	17.6	35.6	21.6	61.8
24037	St. Mary's County	80.0	14.3	2.4	0.0	19.3	62.0	18.6	38.8	21.0	72.8
24043	Washington County	89.1	6.9	2.0	0.0	16.8	58.7	24.5	32.5	27.8	63.8
24045	Wicomico County	70.9	23.1	3.0	0.0	20.4	56.4	23.2	33.8	25.8	64.0
24047	Worcester County	84.4	12.8	0.0	0.0	8.9	54.3	36.8	22.2	40.4	76.3
24510	Baltimore city	32.7	60.1	3.0	2.6	24.8	54.3	20.9	25.6	23.7	47.1
25000	**Massachusetts**	80.0	6.1	7.9	4.7	17.3	59.3	23.3	30.6	26.7	62.0
25001	Barnstable County	94.5	1.6	1.5	0.9	8.5	53.8	37.7	21.4	41.5	78.6
25003	Berkshire County	94.1	1.6	2.0	0.0	12.0	57.9	30.1	24.9	32.6	68.6
25005	Bristol County	87.8	3.3	5.0	1.5	15.3	60.7	23.9	31.2	27.3	62.1
25009	Essex County	80.2	3.4	13.7	2.5	13.9	62.1	24.0	32.8	27.7	62.2
25011	Franklin County	94.7	0.0	1.8	0.0	13.3	62.0	24.7	26.6	28.7	69.0
25013	Hampden County	71.8	7.7	18.3	1.4	16.9	58.6	24.5	32.7	27.5	61.8
25015	Hampshire County	90.2	1.8	4.0	3.2	17.6	58.4	24.0	26.0	27.0	66.4
25017	Middlesex County	80.7	4.2	5.3	8.2	18.9	59.2	21.9	31.0	25.3	62.2
25021	Norfolk County	83.1	5.2	2.8	7.6	14.4	60.9	24.6	32.2	28.2	68.3
25023	Plymouth County	86.8	7.6	2.4	1.0	10.9	64.1	25.0	34.5	28.8	76.6
25025	Suffolk County	54.4	20.4	16.4	8.0	31.6	50.5	17.9	24.7	20.5	35.3
25027	Worcester County	84.3	3.5	7.8	3.3	16.1	62.4	21.5	33.3	25.1	64.8
26000	**Michigan**	79.7	13.4	3.1	2.1	17.6	58.3	24.1	30.4	26.7	71.2
26005	Allegan County	93.0	1.0	4.5	0.0	15.7	61.2	23.0	33.3	25.5	81.1
26015	Barry County	97.0	0.0	0.0	0.0	13.5	60.8	25.7	29.5	28.5	82.4
26017	Bay County	93.5	1.5	3.4	0.0	16.1	57.4	26.5	28.3	28.7	77.5
26021	Berrien County	80.0	14.6	2.8	1.2	15.4	57.7	27.0	29.1	30.6	72.0
26025	Calhoun County	83.0	10.9	3.2	0.0	18.0	56.6	25.4	31.2	27.9	68.7
26027	Cass County	90.1	5.0	2.1	0.0	11.5	60.3	28.2	26.7	31.2	83.8
26037	Clinton County	93.0	1.5	2.9	0.0	17.0	60.0	23.0	30.4	25.4	80.7
26045	Eaton County	87.0	6.9	3.2	0.0	17.0	59.1	23.9	29.5	26.4	70.8
26049	Genesee County	75.0	20.2	2.2	0.7	16.6	58.8	24.6	31.2	26.9	70.2
26055	Grand Traverse County	96.0	0.0	0.0	0.0	16.1	59.3	24.7	27.1	27.8	76.3
26065	Ingham County	76.6	10.7	5.9	4.1	28.6	52.2	19.2	27.7	21.3	57.3
26067	Ionia County	94.9	0.0	2.3	0.0	16.8	60.8	22.5	34.4	24.6	79.1
26073	Isabella County	88.6	1.6	2.6	1.5	34.7	47.1	18.2	27.4	20.2	59.8
26075	Jackson County	90.0	6.4	2.1	0.0	17.0	57.9	25.1	29.9	27.5	70.6
26077	Kalamazoo County	83.2	10.2	2.9	2.1	26.3	52.8	21.0	29.1	23.2	64.5
26081	Kent County	81.2	9.3	6.5	1.6	23.7	56.5	19.8	33.7	21.6	69.0
26087	Lapeer County	95.2	0.0	3.0	0.0	13.4	62.5	24.0	33.2	26.9	82.7
26091	Lenawee County	92.0	0.0	6.2	0.0	15.2	59.2	25.6	29.7	28.3	76.8
26093	Livingston County	96.6	0.0	1.3	0.0	12.3	65.5	22.2	33.8	24.8	84.2
26099	Macomb County	85.0	9.5	1.8	2.3	16.0	59.5	24.5	31.5	27.4	73.9
26103	Marquette County	96.6	0.0	0.5	0.0	20.5	54.6	24.8	23.8	27.2	69.1
26111	Midland County	94.1	0.0	1.6	0.0	17.5	58.1	24.5	30.5	26.2	75.4
26115	Monroe County	94.6	2.1	1.7	0.0	13.7	62.2	24.0	32.1	26.1	78.5
26117	Montcalm County	96.3	0.0	2.2	0.0	16.3	57.9	25.8	31.4	28.6	79.9
26121	Muskegon County	81.8	12.4	3.4	0.0	17.8	58.2	24.0	32.9	26.3	74.8
26125	Oakland County	76.5	14.1	2.7	5.0	16.6	60.7	22.7	30.9	25.5	70.3
26139	Ottawa County	90.0	1.4	5.7	2.2	21.1	57.5	21.4	36.3	23.7	77.3
26145	Saginaw County	75.0	17.4	5.7	0.9	16.5	56.5	27.0	28.9	29.5	72.1
26147	St. Clair County	94.2	2.2	1.9	0.0	14.8	60.1	25.1	29.7	27.3	75.2
26149	St. Joseph County	91.1	2.8	4.3	0.0	17.2	56.3	26.5	32.9	29.4	76.2
26155	Shiawassee County	96.1	0.0	2.0	0.0	16.1	60.1	23.8	31.2	26.8	76.2
26157	Tuscola County	96.1	0.0	1.9	0.0	13.8	58.2	28.0	30.0	30.3	81.5

State/ County code	Metropolitan area	Total Households	Family households, percent	Married-couple family households, percent	Male householder, no spouse, percent	Female householder, no spouse, percent	Householder living alone, percent	Nonfamily households, householder not living alone, percent	Opposite-sex partner unmarried partner households, percent	Same-sex unmarried partner households, percent	Average household size
	Michigan—cont'd										
26159	Van Buren County	28,202	69.5	52.2	5.1	12.2	26.2	4.3	5.3	0.3	2.6
26161	Washtenaw County	136,930	57.3	44.2	3.2	10.0	31.2	11.4	5.3	0.9	2.4
26163	Wayne County	664,432	62.6	37.3	5.6	19.7	32.6	4.8	5.0	0.3	2.7
27000	**Minnesota**	2,109,924	64.8	50.9	4.3	9.7	28.3	6.9	6.2	0.5	2.5
27003	Anoka County	123,536	71.0	55.8	4.6	10.6	23.1	5.9	6.2	0.4	2.7
27013	Blue Earth County	24,394	57.5	47.3	4.4	5.9	29.0	13.5	7.3	0.2	2.5
27019	Carver County	34,062	75.5	64.7	3.5	7.3	20.6	3.9	3.2	0.5	2.7
27025	Chisago County	19,796	72.0	60.6	4.4	7.0	22.1	5.9	8.0	0.2	2.6
27027	Clay County	22,460	65.5	50.6	4.3	10.6	28.1	6.4	6.6	0.7	2.5
27035	Crow Wing County	26,607	67.9	53.6	5.3	9.0	26.0	6.1	6.5	0.3	2.3
27037	Dakota County	155,021	69.6	55.0	4.5	10.1	24.2	6.2	6.8	0.4	2.6
27053	Hennepin County	484,196	57.9	43.3	4.2	10.4	32.9	9.2	5.7	1.1	2.4
27109	Olmsted County	57,515	65.2	52.7	3.4	9.1	28.8	6.0	5.5	0.4	2.5
27111	Otter Tail County	24,082	67.4	56.3	3.7	7.3	28.9	3.7	4.6	0.1	2.3
27123	Ramsey County	205,862	57.9	41.4	4.3	12.3	33.4	8.7	6.7	0.7	2.5
27131	Rice County	22,321	69.5	54.0	3.9	11.6	25.5	4.9	5.8	0.5	2.5
27137	St. Louis County	83,567	58.6	45.0	3.8	9.9	33.5	7.9	6.4	0.5	2.3
27139	Scott County	46,309	76.1	63.8	3.2	9.0	18.6	5.3	5.3	0.3	2.9
27141	Sherburne County	30,134	76.7	62.4	4.4	9.9	17.6	5.7	7.3	0.4	2.9
27145	Stearns County	56,636	64.9	52.8	4.5	7.6	24.7	10.4	7.2	0.1	2.5
27163	Washington County	90,088	73.2	59.3	3.6	10.3	21.8	5.1	5.8	0.4	2.7
27169	Winona County	18,735	59.6	50.6	2.4	6.6	32.2	8.2	4.4	0.3	2.5
27171	Wright County	45,035	77.2	63.0	4.8	9.5	19.0	3.8	6.0	0.3	2.8
28000	**Mississippi**	1,086,898	68.4	44.8	4.9	18.7	27.5	4.1	4.3	0.3	2.7
28033	DeSoto County	58,698	74.5	54.0	5.5	15.1	21.5	4.0	4.7	0.3	2.8
28035	Forrest County	27,793	61.2	38.8	5.3	17.1	29.9	8.9	5.0	0.5	2.6
28047	Harrison County	73,740	65.3	42.9	5.1	17.3	28.6	6.1	5.3	0.5	2.6
28049	Hinds County	88,373	64.7	34.1	6.3	24.4	30.4	4.9	5.0	0.1	2.7
28059	Jackson County	50,317	68.8	47.8	5.3	15.8	25.9	5.2	4.9	0.3	2.8
28067	Jones County	24,600	70.8	49.2	6.2	15.4	24.9	4.4	4.6	0.7	2.7
28071	Lafayette County	15,745	58.4	41.9	5.2	11.3	32.6	9.0	3.0	0.0	2.9
28073	Lamar County	21,763	72.9	53.0	3.6	16.3	21.6	5.5	0.0	0.0	2.6
28075	Lauderdale County	29,823	67.2	41.6	4.0	21.6	29.1	3.7	3.9	0.0	2.6
28081	Lee County	31,877	71.1	49.1	4.5	17.5	24.8	4.0	4.4	0.4	2.6
28087	Lowndes County	23,224	65.4	43.5	3.2	18.6	29.8	4.8	4.3	0.1	2.5
28089	Madison County	36,618	70.6	50.8	4.8	14.9	26.1	3.4	3.0	0.3	2.7
28109	Pearl River County	20,587	70.1	50.1	3.6	16.4	26.2	3.7	4.1	0.1	2.6
28121	Rankin County	53,036	73.4	54.0	4.1	15.3	22.9	3.8	3.0	0.3	2.6
28151	Washington County	17,705	69.7	33.4	5.6	30.8	26.8	3.5	5.5	0.4	2.8
29000	**Missouri**	2,353,778	64.9	48.3	4.3	12.3	29.0	6.1	5.6	0.4	2.5
29019	Boone County	65,822	55.8	42.6	2.9	10.3	30.3	13.9	6.2	0.5	2.4
29021	Buchanan County	32,944	63.8	45.6	5.2	13.0	30.1	6.1	6.1	0.3	2.6
29031	Cape Girardeau County	29,725	64.4	50.5	3.7	10.1	28.3	7.3	5.3	0.4	2.5
29037	Cass County	37,523	73.9	58.6	3.9	11.4	21.4	4.7	4.6	0.3	2.6
29043	Christian County	29,636	76.4	61.6	4.7	10.1	19.7	4.0	5.6	0.1	2.7
29047	Clay County	86,711	67.8	50.4	5.0	12.4	25.9	6.3	6.6	0.5	2.6
29051	Cole County	29,181	65.4	48.9	4.1	12.4	28.8	5.8	5.7	0.7	2.5
29071	Franklin County	39,192	69.7	54.6	5.1	10.0	26.3	4.1	3.4	0.3	2.6
29077	Greene County	116,601	59.6	44.6	4.5	10.5	31.2	9.2	6.0	0.4	2.3
29095	Jackson County	270,803	59.6	39.7	4.4	15.5	33.4	7.0	6.1	0.8	2.5
29097	Jasper County	45,618	65.3	47.6	5.2	12.6	28.7	5.9	6.9	0.5	2.5
29099	Jefferson County	81,398	73.4	56.8	5.0	11.5	21.3	5.4	6.6	0.3	2.7
29101	Johnson County	20,255	64.6	53.1	3.8	7.7	21.8	13.6	7.3	0.3	2.5
29113	Lincoln County	18,848	73.0	56.5	5.5	11.0	22.4	4.5	8.1	0.3	2.8
29145	Newton County	22,208	70.3	57.4	3.9	9.0	24.1	5.6	4.4	0.0	2.6
29165	Platte County	37,163	66.9	52.3	4.6	10.0	27.8	5.3	5.1	0.3	2.5
29169	Pulaski County	15,491	65.7	51.7	3.3	10.7	26.4	8.0	5.2	0.0	2.8
29183	St. Charles County	137,039	73.0	59.5	3.9	9.6	22.7	4.3	5.2	0.3	2.7
29187	St. Francois County	24,548	64.0	47.1	4.6	12.4	30.3	5.7	7.7	0.2	2.3
29189	St. Louis County	401,929	65.1	46.4	4.1	14.6	29.8	5.1	4.7	0.4	2.4
29213	Taney County	20,739	65.5	48.9	4.3	12.3	28.6	6.0	5.4	0.1	2.5
29510	St. Louis city	138,531	46.6	24.5	4.1	18.0	44.1	9.4	6.3	1.0	2.2
30000	**Montana**	405,504	63.1	49.5	4.4	9.2	30.1	6.7	5.7	0.3	2.4
30013	Cascade County	33,326	63.4	48.0	4.9	10.4	31.5	5.1	5.4	0.2	2.4
30029	Flathead County	36,911	65.1	53.9	4.5	6.6	28.9	6.1	5.8	0.2	2.5
30031	Gallatin County	37,070	60.8	50.4	4.5	6.0	26.2	12.9	5.7	0.2	2.4
30049	Lewis and Clark County	26,719	62.7	49.4	4.1	9.2	30.5	6.7	7.2	0.3	2.4
30063	Missoula County	45,834	58.0	43.0	4.6	10.4	30.0	12.0	8.1	0.8	2.4
30111	Yellowstone County	60,423	63.8	47.0	5.1	11.7	29.6	6.6	6.4	0.3	2.5
31000	**Nebraska**	729,572	64.8	50.7	4.2	9.8	29.1	6.2	5.3	0.3	2.5
31055	Douglas County	205,762	61.6	44.3	4.6	12.7	31.7	6.7	5.1	0.5	2.5

State/ County code	Metropolitan area	Race or Hispanic origin of householder				Age of householder			Percent of households with one or more persons under 18 years old	Percent of households with one or more persons age 65 or older	Percent of all householders who are owners
		Householder is White alone, not Hispanic or Latino, percent	Householder is Black or African American alone, percent	Householder is Hispanic or Latino, percent	Householder is Asian alone, percent	Householders age 15 to 34, percent	Householders age 35 to 64, percent	Householders age 65 and older, percent			
	Michigan—cont'd										
26159	Van Buren County	87.8	4.2	5.8	0.0	15.3	59.8	24.8	32.4	28.1	77.4
26161	Washtenaw County	75.2	11.6	3.1	7.6	27.2	54.6	18.2	27.6	20.5	59.5
26163	Wayne County	52.8	39.6	3.9	2.0	16.4	60.2	23.4	31.9	26.3	63.5
27000	**Minnesota**	87.5	4.5	3.0	3.0	21.0	57.1	21.9	31.3	23.9	71.8
27003	Anoka County	89.8	3.5	2.3	2.9	17.7	64.0	18.3	36.3	20.7	80.2
27013	Blue Earth County	93.8	2.0	1.4	0.0	32.3	47.1	20.5	25.5	22.0	66.1
27019	Carver County	93.3	0.0	0.0	0.0	17.2	66.6	16.2	42.0	17.9	80.1
27025	Chisago County	97.5	0.0	0.0	0.0	15.5	62.6	21.9	35.6	24.1	85.2
27027	Clay County	93.8	0.0	2.0	0.0	26.8	52.4	20.7	34.3	22.2	70.0
27035	Crow Wing County	97.7	0.0	0.8	0.0	18.0	53.5	28.5	29.3	31.1	74.8
27037	Dakota County	86.8	4.5	4.4	3.2	20.0	62.1	17.9	35.4	20.2	74.6
27053	Hennepin County	78.5	10.3	4.2	4.8	24.5	56.6	18.9	28.7	20.9	62.7
27109	Olmsted County	88.3	3.3	2.8	4.4	23.1	56.6	20.3	32.1	22.2	73.8
27111	Otter Tail County	96.4	0.0	1.5	0.0	14.6	53.9	31.5	24.7	33.9	79.1
27123	Ramsey County	75.7	9.8	4.9	7.6	25.3	54.4	20.3	28.8	22.4	59.0
27131	Rice County	91.3	0.0	5.0	0.0	19.6	57.0	23.4	34.2	25.8	74.4
27137	St. Louis County	94.7	1.0	0.7	0.6	20.3	54.5	25.1	25.2	27.3	71.4
27139	Scott County	89.3	2.0	2.5	4.9	19.1	66.1	14.8	42.6	17.0	84.6
27141	Sherburne County	95.8	0.0	0.0	0.0	19.7	65.2	15.1	42.3	17.3	81.0
27145	Stearns County	94.2	2.4	1.8	1.1	25.3	53.3	21.5	30.1	23.2	70.8
27163	Washington County	89.8	2.8	2.5	3.9	16.3	63.7	19.9	38.1	22.2	80.2
27169	Winona County	94.9	0.0	0.0	0.0	24.2	51.1	24.7	24.8	26.1	70.5
27171	Wright County	95.0	0.0	0.0	0.0	21.5	60.4	18.1	42.7	19.7	83.4
28000	**Mississippi**	61.7	34.8	1.9	0.7	18.7	57.6	23.6	34.5	26.4	68.5
28033	DeSoto County	72.9	22.1	3.0	0.0	19.6	61.6	18.8	40.5	21.6	74.2
28035	Forrest County	60.3	36.0	2.4	0.0	29.1	49.8	21.1	32.8	23.3	55.3
28047	Harrison County	69.5	22.1	4.2	2.6	23.3	55.5	21.3	34.3	24.1	57.9
28049	Hinds County	31.7	65.8	1.2	0.6	21.5	58.5	20.0	35.6	22.2	58.6
28059	Jackson County	73.3	19.9	3.4	0.0	16.9	60.1	23.0	31.0	25.7	70.6
28067	Jones County	70.8	25.7	0.0	0.0	19.6	55.2	25.2	34.6	27.9	73.3
28071	Lafayette County	76.4	21.3	0.0	0.0	30.0	48.9	21.1	28.6	22.6	58.9
28073	Lamar County	75.0	21.3	0.0	0.0	26.4	55.8	17.8	40.8	21.9	63.0
28075	Lauderdale County	56.6	41.3	0.0	0.0	18.0	57.2	24.8	33.6	27.8	65.1
28081	Lee County	71.0	26.4	0.0	0.0	21.6	55.8	22.6	37.4	25.8	69.7
28087	Lowndes County	55.6	42.3	0.0	0.0	20.0	57.2	22.7	33.3	24.4	60.7
28089	Madison County	60.6	34.8	0.0	0.0	18.8	62.0	19.3	36.9	21.8	71.1
28109	Pearl River County	84.4	11.8	0.0	0.0	14.0	59.4	26.6	32.8	29.3	77.1
28121	Rankin County	78.8	17.6	0.0	0.0	20.3	58.9	20.8	37.6	23.6	74.7
28151	Washington County	30.1	67.4	0.0	0.0	16.2	60.6	23.2	37.4	27.4	55.5
29000	**Missouri**	83.5	11.0	2.5	1.4	20.8	55.7	23.6	30.9	26.0	67.6
29019	Boone County	84.4	7.2	2.2	3.8	35.8	49.3	14.9	27.7	17.3	55.5
29021	Buchanan County	89.6	3.9	4.1	0.0	20.6	55.7	23.8	32.0	25.9	63.3
29031	Cape Girardeau County	90.4	6.9	0.0	0.0	25.5	52.0	22.5	31.1	24.6	64.2
29037	Cass County	92.5	0.0	2.3	0.0	17.0	59.2	23.7	37.7	26.0	76.1
29043	Christian County	95.3	0.0	0.0	0.0	20.3	57.0	22.7	38.4	25.0	72.8
29047	Clay County	87.1	4.7	4.9	1.4	21.6	58.6	19.9	34.6	22.2	69.9
29051	Cole County	88.3	7.5	0.0	1.1	20.1	57.4	22.6	33.8	24.6	66.9
29071	Franklin County	96.9	0.0	0.0	0.0	17.9	58.3	23.8	32.2	26.6	76.3
29077	Greene County	91.9	2.5	1.9	1.3	28.0	49.4	22.5	28.3	25.0	58.4
29095	Jackson County	68.0	23.3	5.6	1.3	23.5	55.6	20.9	29.4	23.1	59.7
29097	Jasper County	90.4	1.6	4.5	0.0	24.9	53.0	22.2	35.4	24.8	64.0
29099	Jefferson County	96.5	0.6	1.3	0.0	18.0	61.9	20.0	36.0	22.8	81.6
29101	Johnson County	89.2	3.9	0.0	0.0	34.0	48.8	17.2	31.2	20.7	60.2
29113	Lincoln County	95.1	1.6	0.0	0.0	20.3	61.2	18.5	39.7	22.5	78.2
29145	Newton County	90.4	0.0	3.0	0.0	18.3	55.0	26.8	32.1	30.0	71.4
29165	Platte County	86.6	6.1	0.0	0.0	21.1	59.2	19.6	33.7	21.5	63.3
29169	Pulaski County	75.6	11.6	7.6	0.0	34.4	51.6	14.0	36.6	16.0	52.2
29183	St. Charles County	91.8	3.8	1.8	0.0	18.5	60.8	20.7	36.6	22.8	80.0
29187	St. Francois County	98.5	0.0	0.0	0.0	20.7	54.3	25.0	31.0	27.2	65.3
29189	St. Louis County	71.6	22.2	1.8	3.0	18.0	57.2	24.8	30.4	27.2	70.4
29213	Taney County	94.5	0.0	2.5	0.0	17.4	53.0	29.6	26.4	34.4	62.7
29510	St. Louis city	48.5	44.4	2.8	2.6	28.3	53.4	18.2	23.6	20.3	44.5
30000	**Montana**	90.9	0.4	2.1	0.6	19.8	55.7	24.5	27.8	27.2	67.3
30013	Cascade County	90.2	0.0	2.6	1.3	22.2	52.7	25.2	30.0	27.7	63.7
30029	Flathead County	95.9	0.0	0.0	0.0	17.4	58.1	24.5	26.7	26.9	71.1
30031	Gallatin County	94.6	0.0	2.5	0.0	31.5	52.0	16.5	27.5	18.5	61.2
30049	Lewis and Clark County	95.0	0.0	1.7	0.0	18.2	59.7	22.1	27.6	25.0	71.4
30063	Missoula County	92.9	0.0	2.0	0.0	29.6	52.1	18.3	26.1	20.5	56.9
30111	Yellowstone County	90.7	0.0	3.3	0.0	21.3	55.5	23.2	31.4	25.6	68.1
31000	**Nebraska**	86.5	4.3	6.2	1.5	23.3	54.4	22.3	31.7	24.2	66.4
31055	Douglas County	77.4	11.3	7.1	2.5	25.9	55.6	18.5	32.7	20.3	61.7

Table A-2: Counties with a Population of 50,000 or More—Living Arrangements—*Continued*

State/ County code	Metropolitan area	Total Households	Family households, percent	Married-couple family households, percent	Male householder, no spouse, percent	Female householder, no spouse, percent	Householder living alone, percent	Nonfamily households, householder not living alone, percent	Opposite-sex partner unmarried partner households, percent	Same-sex unmarried partner households, percent	Average household size
	Nebraska—cont'd										
31079	Hall County	22,290	65.9	49.9	4.5	11.5	27.2	6.9	7.8	0.1	2.7
31109	Lancaster County	115,757	60.6	46.8	4.4	9.4	29.7	9.6	6.6	0.4	2.4
31153	Sarpy County	60,558	73.1	58.2	4.4	10.5	21.9	5.1	5.5	0.3	2.7
32000	**Nevada**	995,980	64.4	45.1	6.1	13.2	27.9	7.7	6.8	0.5	2.7
32003	Clark County	708,369	64.5	43.9	6.5	14.1	27.8	7.7	6.7	0.6	2.8
32007	Elko County	17,527	71.8	58.4	5.8	7.6	21.5	6.7	6.7	0.1	2.9
32019	Lyon County	19,565	69.8	52.7	5.7	11.4	22.8	7.4	10.2	0.3	2.6
32031	Washoe County	162,629	61.8	45.1	5.1	11.6	29.7	8.5	6.9	0.5	2.6
32510	Carson City	21,206	59.3	44.3	2.7	12.3	33.6	7.1	7.0	0.1	2.5
33000	**New Hampshire**	518,088	66.9	52.8	4.2	9.9	25.5	7.6	7.4	0.5	2.5
33001	Belknap County	24,657	68.3	53.4	4.0	10.8	25.1	6.6	8.3	0.2	2.4
33005	Cheshire County	30,601	62.7	48.1	4.9	9.7	27.7	9.5	8.5	0.8	2.4
33009	Grafton County	35,256	62.2	49.0	3.7	9.5	31.1	6.8	5.7	0.4	2.3
33011	Hillsborough County	154,396	67.0	51.6	4.6	10.7	25.3	7.7	7.8	0.5	2.6
33013	Merrimack County	56,496	67.2	53.6	3.9	9.7	25.7	7.1	6.6	0.6	2.5
33015	Rockingham County	117,091	69.7	57.1	3.5	9.0	22.9	7.4	7.0	0.7	2.5
33017	Strafford County	46,617	66.6	50.8	4.6	11.1	23.9	9.5	9.1	0.3	2.5
34000	**New Jersey**	3,181,152	69.3	50.8	4.9	13.6	25.8	4.9	4.9	0.4	2.7
34001	Atlantic County	101,243	67.3	44.9	5.4	17.0	27.5	5.1	5.6	0.5	2.7
34003	Bergen County	335,087	71.6	55.9	4.3	11.4	24.4	3.9	3.4	0.3	2.7
34005	Burlington County	164,194	69.6	53.3	4.6	11.7	25.6	4.8	5.2	0.4	2.7
34007	Camden County	185,772	67.1	45.6	5.0	16.4	27.6	5.3	6.3	0.6	2.7
34009	Cape May County	40,506	64.0	52.0	3.3	8.7	31.2	4.8	4.1	0.8	2.3
34011	Cumberland County	50,047	69.0	43.6	6.1	19.4	24.8	6.2	7.1	0.3	2.9
34013	Essex County	276,690	65.5	39.1	6.3	20.1	29.5	5.0	5.6	0.5	2.8
34015	Gloucester County	103,963	73.0	54.8	5.0	13.2	22.2	4.7	4.9	0.5	2.7
34017	Hudson County	246,114	61.4	37.9	6.3	17.1	29.2	9.4	6.3	0.6	2.6
34019	Hunterdon County	46,512	73.5	62.4	3.1	8.0	21.7	4.8	4.1	0.8	2.6
34021	Mercer County	131,326	67.2	49.5	4.5	13.2	27.4	5.4	4.4	0.4	2.7
34023	Middlesex County	282,106	72.1	55.0	5.0	12.0	23.3	4.6	4.4	0.4	2.8
34025	Monmouth County	233,249	70.2	55.3	4.2	10.7	25.3	4.5	4.5	0.5	2.7
34027	Morris County	180,148	71.8	59.9	3.4	8.6	23.9	4.3	3.8	0.3	2.7
34029	Ocean County	221,050	67.1	53.1	4.3	9.7	29.1	3.9	4.4	0.3	2.6
34031	Passaic County	162,526	73.2	47.5	6.6	19.2	23.2	3.5	5.2	0.3	3.1
34033	Salem County	24,635	67.6	47.7	5.8	14.2	27.2	5.2	6.6	0.2	2.6
34035	Somerset County	114,778	73.6	60.2	3.1	10.2	22.5	4.0	3.6	0.6	2.8
34037	Sussex County	54,103	74.2	60.8	4.0	9.4	21.4	4.4	5.8	0.2	2.7
34039	Union County	185,405	70.7	49.4	5.5	15.8	25.3	4.1	5.3	0.6	2.9
34041	Warren County	41,698	69.8	54.6	4.1	11.1	24.3	5.9	6.2	0.3	2.5
35000	**New Mexico**	760,251	65.1	45.2	5.6	14.3	28.9	6.0	6.5	0.6	2.7
35001	Bernalillo County	262,839	62.0	41.6	6.1	14.3	31.0	6.9	6.7	0.9	2.5
35005	Chaves County	23,423	69.6	47.3	5.8	16.5	26.0	4.4	7.5	0.5	2.7
35009	Curry County	18,241	70.2	50.8	5.1	14.3	25.7	4.0	4.3	0.2	2.7
35013	Doña Ana County	74,145	69.5	47.6	4.8	17.1	23.9	6.6	6.3	0.4	2.8
35015	Eddy County	20,445	67.9	47.7	6.5	13.7	26.4	5.7	7.7	0.1	2.6
35025	Lea County	21,362	74.5	54.2	7.9	12.5	20.8	4.7	6.9	0.8	3.0
35031	McKinley County	17,798	69.1	39.9	5.9	23.3	27.7	3.1	6.3	0.1	4.1
35035	Otero County	23,799	67.3	49.2	4.6	13.5	28.2	4.5	4.7	0.3	2.6
35043	Sandoval County	47,604	70.5	51.9	5.9	12.7	23.5	6.0	6.9	0.8	2.8
35045	San Juan County	39,683	73.0	49.9	6.5	16.6	22.7	4.3	6.4	0.1	3.2
35049	Santa Fe County	60,878	58.1	42.2	4.8	11.1	33.9	8.0	6.8	1.2	2.4
35061	Valencia County	26,477	70.7	52.3	5.6	12.8	24.8	4.5	5.9	0.4	2.8
36000	**New York**	7,214,163	63.7	43.8	5.0	14.8	29.8	6.5	5.4	0.6	2.6
36001	Albany County	122,262	55.9	40.5	3.6	11.8	34.8	9.3	6.9	0.8	2.4
36005	Bronx County	474,703	65.6	27.0	7.5	31.1	30.3	4.1	5.6	0.3	2.9
36007	Broome County	79,275	60.2	44.4	5.0	10.8	32.4	7.5	7.1	0.4	2.4
36009	Cattaraugus County	31,979	62.8	45.9	5.8	11.0	29.9	7.3	7.4	0.4	2.4
36011	Cayuga County	30,755	63.9	46.5	6.4	11.0	29.9	6.2	8.6	0.8	2.5
36013	Chautauqua County	54,416	62.7	46.0	4.0	12.7	30.4	6.9	7.9	0.2	2.3
36015	Chemung County	35,417	62.6	46.1	3.8	12.8	30.3	7.1	6.9	0.2	2.3
36019	Clinton County	32,031	64.1	47.7	5.7	10.7	27.1	8.8	9.5	0.3	2.3
36021	Columbia County	24,960	65.1	48.5	5.0	11.6	27.5	7.4	9.3	1.0	2.4
36027	Dutchess County	106,938	66.5	51.2	3.8	11.5	27.6	5.9	6.0	0.6	2.6
36029	Erie County	380,476	60.5	42.1	4.7	13.7	33.2	6.4	5.7	0.4	2.3
36033	Franklin County	18,802	61.9	45.2	6.4	10.3	30.4	7.6	9.8	0.4	2.4
36035	Fulton County	22,341	65.8	47.8	5.7	12.4	26.6	7.5	8.5	0.6	2.4
36037	Genesee County	24,044	66.9	51.7	4.8	10.5	26.4	6.7	7.2	0.2	2.5
36043	Herkimer County	26,910	65.6	48.1	5.5	12.0	28.6	5.8	8.9	0.4	2.3
36045	Jefferson County	44,651	68.3	51.6	4.7	11.9	25.9	5.8	6.5	0.4	2.5

32 **Families in America**

Table A-2: Counties with a Population of 50,000 or More—Living Arrangements—*Continued*

State/County code	Metropolitan area	Householder is White alone, not Hispanic or Latino, percent	Householder is Black or African American alone, percent	Householder is Hispanic or Latino, percent	Householder is Asian alone, percent	Householders age 15 to 34, percent	Householders age 35 to 64, percent	Householders age 65 and older, percent	Percent of households with one or more persons under 18 years old	Percent of households with one or more persons age 65 or older	Percent of all householders who are owners
	Nebraska—cont'd										
31079	Hall County...............	79.7	0.0	17.4	0.0	23.2	55.6	21.3	36.8	24.4	64.5
31109	Lancaster County.........	88.3	3.1	4.2	3.0	29.6	52.1	18.3	30.4	20.0	59.6
31153	Sarpy County.............	87.4	4.3	5.5	1.5	26.4	57.6	16.0	39.7	17.8	69.3
32000	**Nevada.................**	63.1	8.3	19.1	6.4	20.4	58.2	21.4	33.0	25.3	55.2
32003	Clark County.............	56.9	11.0	21.3	7.8	21.1	58.7	20.2	34.2	24.2	52.7
32007	Elko County.............	75.1	0.0	17.6	0.0	24.4	61.0	14.7	35.1	17.6	69.1
32019	Lyon County.............	84.3	0.0	9.9	0.0	15.3	57.1	27.6	31.8	32.1	70.6
32031	Washoe County..........	75.2	2.2	15.5	4.3	20.7	57.6	21.7	30.8	25.0	56.7
32510	Carson City.............	79.5	0.0	13.9	0.0	16.1	54.1	29.9	25.7	32.8	55.3
33000	**New Hampshire..............**	93.9	1.0	2.1	1.9	15.8	61.6	22.7	30.2	25.8	70.9
33001	Belknap County	97.0	0.0	0.0	0.0	14.8	59.7	25.5	27.1	29.8	73.7
33005	Cheshire County.........	96.8	0.0	0.0	1.2	16.6	57.9	25.5	25.5	28.1	71.5
33009	Grafton County.........	94.2	0.0	0.0	2.3	16.4	57.5	26.1	24.8	28.5	67.0
33011	Hillsborough County......	89.9	2.1	4.0	2.9	17.2	62.7	20.1	32.7	23.1	66.4
33013	Merrimack County........	95.7	0.0	1.1	0.0	13.7	63.8	22.5	30.3	25.8	73.1
33015	Rockingham County........	95.3	0.0	1.7	1.5	14.0	64.6	21.4	32.7	24.8	76.2
33017	Strafford County.........	93.7	0.0	1.9	2.0	21.6	56.9	21.5	30.5	24.2	64.2
34000	**New Jersey ....**	63.9	13.2	14.6	7.5	14.9	61.6	23.6	34.3	27.6	64.9
34001	Atlantic County.........	64.9	15.6	13.5	5.6	15.1	60.2	24.7	33.5	29.4	65.9
34003	Bergen County...........	65.4	5.8	14.2	13.8	12.6	62.4	25.0	33.9	29.7	65.2
34005	Burlington County.......	74.5	14.8	5.0	3.6	13.2	62.2	24.6	33.0	28.2	77.5
34007	Camden County..........	63.9	19.6	11.6	4.4	16.6	60.7	22.7	33.9	26.3	67.5
34009	Cape May County........	91.0	3.4	4.1	0.0	11.6	53.6	34.8	23.5	38.4	75.3
34011	Cumberland County.......	60.7	16.7	21.1	1.3	16.1	59.2	24.7	35.1	28.7	66.7
34013	Essex County............	36.2	41.1	17.4	4.1	17.2	62.1	20.7	36.2	24.5	45.3
34015	Gloucester County.......	83.3	9.6	3.7	2.1	14.1	63.9	22.0	36.4	26.4	80.0
34017	Hudson County...........	36.9	12.3	37.0	13.3	26.4	57.1	16.5	31.8	20.6	31.7
34019	Hunterdon County........	91.0	0.0	4.2	3.1	6.9	69.2	23.8	34.5	27.1	84.4
34021	Mercer County...........	59.7	20.2	11.3	7.9	15.5	61.5	23.0	33.0	26.4	64.8
34023	Middlesex County........	54.9	9.7	15.4	19.2	16.5	62.3	21.2	36.8	25.8	64.9
34025	Monmouth County........	80.3	7.2	7.4	4.4	11.3	64.0	24.7	33.4	28.3	74.9
34027	Morris County...........	79.2	3.0	9.0	8.0	12.0	64.3	23.7	34.8	27.7	75.1
34029	Ocean County............	89.4	2.7	5.7	1.5	11.8	51.7	36.5	28.3	39.9	80.9
34031	Passaic County..........	51.6	13.0	31.4	4.3	14.6	63.2	22.2	38.6	27.2	53.6
34033	Salem County............	80.1	14.1	4.0	0.0	13.9	59.2	26.9	32.8	29.9	71.0
34035	Somerset County.........	66.9	8.5	10.4	13.2	11.2	67.2	21.5	37.5	25.9	77.3
34037	Sussex County...........	92.1	1.5	4.8	1.3	10.3	68.0	21.7	33.5	25.2	84.2
34039	Union County............	48.9	22.1	23.8	4.5	14.9	63.4	21.7	38.1	25.9	58.9
34041	Warren County...........	88.6	3.2	5.2	1.9	13.5	63.8	22.7	32.5	26.6	73.0
35000	**New Mexico..............**	49.2	2.1	40.3	1.1	19.7	56.2	24.1	32.1	27.2	68.1
35001	Bernalillo County	50.2	2.9	40.3	1.9	23.4	55.7	20.9	31.5	23.9	62.3
35005	Chaves County...........	51.3	1.9	45.4	0.0	20.1	54.8	25.1	36.1	29.5	66.0
35009	Curry County............	58.5	7.0	31.2	0.0	29.8	50.3	19.9	36.8	22.3	59.7
35013	Doña Ana County.........	38.3	2.0	57.2	1.0	23.4	53.1	23.5	36.6	26.0	65.1
35015	Eddy County.............	58.8	0.0	37.4	0.0	20.2	55.4	24.5	34.2	26.3	70.3
35025	Lea County..............	50.1	4.5	43.0	0.0	26.1	53.7	20.2	41.5	22.4	69.4
35031	McKinley County	14.6	0.0	14.1	0.0	11.3	62.9	25.8	39.5	28.9	73.1
35035	Otero County............	63.4	3.7	27.1	0.0	21.2	52.4	26.4	29.8	29.9	65.0
35043	Sandoval County.........	56.0	2.6	31.6	0.0	14.6	61.9	23.6	35.4	27.2	81.4
35045	San Juan County.........	52.2	0.0	17.4	0.0	17.8	60.0	22.2	38.2	25.2	75.2
35049	Santa Fe County.........	53.5	0.7	41.5	1.3	13.6	59.4	27.0	24.6	30.3	68.3
35061	Valencia County.........	42.2	0.0	53.1	0.0	16.9	59.4	23.8	36.3	26.9	79.0
36000	**New York ....**	63.8	14.5	14.5	6.5	17.6	59.2	23.2	31.2	27.1	53.7
36001	Albany County...........	79.4	11.0	4.0	4.3	20.4	57.1	22.5	25.1	25.3	58.9
36005	Bronx County............	12.7	34.7	51.7	3.0	18.7	62.1	19.3	39.2	23.4	18.8
36007	Broome County...........	89.9	3.8	2.3	2.9	18.9	54.5	26.6	26.3	29.2	66.4
36009	Cattaraugus County......	94.1	0.8	0.7	0.0	16.8	57.8	25.4	27.7	28.4	70.7
36011	Cayuga County...........	97.0	0.0	0.0	0.0	13.5	59.3	27.2	28.1	30.5	71.9
36013	Chautauqua County.......	92.5	1.5	5.0	0.0	16.8	56.6	26.7	27.8	29.2	69.2
36015	Chemung County..........	92.2	3.8	1.9	0.0	18.7	56.3	25.0	29.0	27.9	68.4
36019	Clinton County..........	96.6	0.0	0.0	0.0	19.7	56.8	23.6	29.3	26.3	68.2
36021	Columbia County.........	92.3	2.3	2.5	0.0	11.3	59.4	29.3	28.5	33.3	73.3
36027	Dutchess County.........	79.6	9.0	7.6	2.9	13.4	62.8	23.8	31.3	27.6	69.1
36029	Erie County.............	80.1	12.9	3.7	1.9	18.1	56.7	25.3	28.1	27.7	64.9
36033	Franklin County.........	91.2	0.0	0.0	0.0	17.0	57.7	25.3	28.9	28.5	73.0
36035	Fulton County...........	96.9	0.0	0.0	0.0	15.4	58.1	26.5	28.9	29.2	70.7
36037	Genesee County..........	93.8	2.0	1.6	0.0	15.7	60.0	24.3	28.9	27.5	72.4
36043	Herkimer County.........	97.9	0.0	0.0	0.0	16.0	56.5	27.6	28.6	30.9	69.5
36045	Jefferson County........	88.4	4.0	4.8	1.1	30.8	50.3	18.9	36.5	21.2	55.3

State/County code	Metropolitan area	Household type							Opposite-sex partner unmarried partner households, percent	Same-sex unmarried partner households, percent	Average household size
		Total Households	Family households, percent	Married-couple family households, percent	Male householder, no spouse, percent	Female householder, no spouse, percent	Householder living alone, percent	Nonfamily households, householder not living alone, percent			
	New York—cont'd										
36047	Kings County	915,398	62.9	37.3	5.8	19.8	29.2	7.9	5.1	0.6	2.8
36051	Livingston County	23,854	65.4	51.1	3.2	11.1	26.9	7.7	7.4	0.1	2.5
36053	Madison County	26,512	66.0	50.5	5.1	10.3	28.7	5.4	7.1	0.2	2.5
36055	Monroe County	297,770	60.9	42.5	4.0	14.3	31.7	7.4	6.2	0.6	2.4
36059	Nassau County	440,640	76.5	60.2	4.4	11.9	20.0	3.5	3.6	0.3	3.0
36061	New York County	734,060	40.6	25.9	3.3	11.3	48.5	11.0	4.4	1.5	2.1
36063	Niagara County	88,548	62.5	44.9	5.1	12.4	32.2	5.3	6.2	0.4	2.4
36065	Oneida County	90,720	61.1	43.4	4.7	13.0	32.7	6.2	7.0	0.7	2.4
36067	Onondaga County	183,894	61.0	43.4	4.2	13.4	32.0	7.0	6.1	0.5	2.4
36069	Ontario County	43,930	66.9	49.7	6.2	11.0	27.0	6.1	7.4	0.5	2.4
36071	Orange County	125,025	71.9	54.5	4.8	12.6	23.4	4.6	5.5	0.5	2.9
36075	Oswego County	44,951	67.5	48.8	5.9	12.8	24.7	7.7	9.6	0.5	2.6
36077	Otsego County	23,669	62.0	47.8	4.6	9.5	28.0	10.1	8.3	0.4	2.4
36079	Putnam County	33,925	77.2	63.9	3.2	10.1	19.9	2.9	3.2	0.4	2.9
36081	Queens County	777,760	66.9	44.2	6.6	16.1	26.8	6.4	4.8	0.4	2.9
36083	Rensselaer County	63,631	62.3	45.8	4.0	12.4	29.5	8.2	8.1	0.5	2.4
36085	Richmond County	164,376	73.2	53.5	5.2	14.5	23.7	3.2	3.2	0.3	2.8
36087	Rockland County	97,959	75.9	60.6	4.3	11.0	20.6	3.5	3.6	0.4	3.2
36089	St. Lawrence County	41,361	63.5	46.7	5.1	11.7	28.9	7.6	8.2	0.2	2.4
36091	Saratoga County	89,235	65.1	52.3	3.9	8.9	27.5	7.4	7.6	0.3	2.4
36093	Schenectady County	57,812	60.5	45.6	3.6	11.3	33.8	5.7	5.6	0.4	2.6
36101	Steuben County	41,494	64.1	47.3	5.2	11.6	29.5	6.4	8.5	0.6	2.3
36103	Suffolk County	496,842	74.9	57.6	4.7	12.7	20.8	4.3	4.3	0.6	3.0
36105	Sullivan County	28,357	62.0	44.9	4.9	12.2	31.3	6.7	8.0	0.8	2.6
36107	Tioga County	19,952	70.6	56.6	3.4	10.7	25.1	4.3	5.4	0.5	2.5
36109	Tompkins County	38,195	53.4	42.8	1.9	8.7	31.4	15.2	7.5	1.4	2.3
36111	Ulster County	69,089	63.4	46.7	5.1	11.6	29.0	7.5	6.7	1.0	2.5
36113	Warren County	27,363	65.0	48.5	3.6	12.8	28.9	6.2	7.8	0.3	2.4
36115	Washington County	24,188	67.6	50.5	4.8	12.2	26.1	6.3	8.7	0.5	2.5
36117	Wayne County	36,334	68.8	53.2	4.9	10.7	25.1	6.2	7.3	0.4	2.5
36119	Westchester County	341,562	69.3	51.1	4.7	13.5	26.9	3.8	4.0	0.4	2.7
37000	**North Carolina**	3,721,358	66.3	48.1	4.5	13.8	27.9	5.7	4.8	0.4	2.6
37001	Alamance County	60,215	67.6	47.5	6.1	14.0	28.3	4.1	4.8	0.4	2.5
37019	Brunswick County	47,735	71.2	55.9	4.9	10.5	24.9	3.9	5.7	0.4	2.3
37021	Buncombe County	100,306	58.8	44.2	3.7	11.0	32.9	8.3	5.7	1.2	2.4
37023	Burke County	33,891	65.9	46.9	5.2	13.8	29.4	4.7	4.5	0.4	2.6
37025	Cabarrus County	64,928	71.7	56.8	3.8	11.1	24.1	4.2	3.7	0.2	2.8
37027	Caldwell County	31,410	64.4	48.3	4.9	11.2	32.7	2.9	3.7	0.1	2.6
37031	Carteret County	28,951	66.5	50.0	4.4	12.1	28.5	5.1	4.7	0.6	2.3
37035	Catawba County	58,222	69.0	52.6	4.9	11.5	25.4	5.6	5.1	0.4	2.6
37037	Chatham County	26,124	70.3	57.4	3.4	9.4	26.3	3.4	2.8	0.7	2.5
37045	Cleveland County	37,398	65.7	47.8	4.9	13.1	30.3	3.9	4.5	0.4	2.6
37047	Columbus County	21,512	64.7	43.5	5.2	16.0	31.2	4.1	5.3	0.3	2.6
37049	Craven County	39,570	70.8	54.9	3.5	12.4	24.6	4.6	4.8	0.3	2.6
37051	Cumberland County	122,870	66.1	43.6	4.1	18.4	28.8	5.1	4.8	0.2	2.6
37057	Davidson County	63,544	68.8	51.8	4.4	12.6	26.5	4.7	5.0	0.3	2.5
37061	Duplin County	22,078	68.0	47.4	6.5	14.1	25.8	6.2	7.4	0.1	2.7
37063	Durham County	112,856	58.4	38.9	4.6	14.9	32.6	9.0	5.7	0.8	2.4
37065	Edgecombe County	20,528	68.5	39.6	4.3	24.6	26.8	4.7	5.5	0.3	2.7
37067	Forsyth County	141,015	63.3	44.6	4.2	14.5	31.2	5.4	4.7	0.5	2.5
37069	Franklin County	23,212	68.6	51.6	4.0	13.1	27.3	4.1	4.2	0.4	2.6
37071	Gaston County	79,682	67.7	47.3	5.2	15.2	27.8	4.5	4.6	0.4	2.6
37077	Granville County	19,936	71.4	50.0	5.3	16.0	25.7	2.9	3.9	0.3	2.7
37081	Guilford County	198,555	63.4	43.0	4.7	15.7	29.7	6.8	4.8	0.5	2.4
37083	Halifax County	21,583	65.9	38.1	5.6	22.2	31.2	2.9	5.1	0.1	2.4
37085	Harnett County	41,481	70.4	52.2	4.4	13.8	24.4	5.2	4.6	0.2	2.9
37087	Haywood County	26,402	66.6	49.1	4.5	13.1	28.2	5.2	6.4	0.3	2.2
37089	Henderson County	45,195	67.5	55.7	3.6	8.2	27.5	5.0	3.6	0.9	2.4
37093	Hoke County	16,622	74.6	51.6	5.4	17.6	22.2	3.2	6.1	0.3	3.0
37097	Iredell County	59,130	73.2	56.1	4.0	13.1	23.0	3.7	4.8	0.1	2.7
37101	Johnston County	60,520	75.2	56.2	5.2	13.8	19.8	5.0	5.4	0.2	2.9
37105	Lee County	21,464	69.5	49.8	5.2	14.5	25.4	5.1	7.3	0.0	2.7
37107	Lenoir County	23,470	65.0	39.6	6.2	19.1	31.0	4.0	5.7	0.2	2.5
37109	Lincoln County	29,924	72.0	57.8	3.9	10.4	23.9	4.0	4.0	0.4	2.6
37119	Mecklenburg County	369,103	62.1	42.8	4.7	14.7	30.3	7.6	5.4	0.5	2.6
37125	Moore County	36,452	67.9	55.8	2.8	9.3	28.5	3.6	3.2	0.3	2.5
37127	Nash County	36,999	66.2	45.8	4.1	16.3	29.2	4.5	5.4	0.2	2.5
37129	New Hanover County	86,545	58.3	42.3	4.8	11.2	31.7	10.0	6.4	0.5	2.3
37133	Onslow County	60,637	72.1	55.2	3.6	13.3	22.3	5.6	4.6	0.3	2.8
37135	Orange County	51,630	60.7	47.3	3.0	10.4	29.4	9.9	4.3	1.2	2.5
37141	Pender County	19,516	71.5	53.9	5.0	12.5	24.1	4.5	3.5	0.3	2.7
37147	Pitt County	66,849	59.6	39.3	3.6	16.7	29.6	10.8	4.8	0.2	2.5
37151	Randolph County	54,059	71.0	53.2	4.7	13.0	25.1	4.0	5.1	0.3	2.6

State/County code	Metropolitan area	Householder is White alone, not Hispanic or Latino, percent	Householder is Black or African American alone, percent	Householder is Hispanic or Latino, percent	Householder is Asian alone, percent	Householders age 15 to 34, percent	Householders age 35 to 64, percent	Householders age 65 and older, percent	Percent of households with one or more persons under 18 years old	Percent of households with one or more persons age 65 or older	Percent of all householders who are owners
	New York—cont'd										
36047	Kings County	40.3	34.1	17.3	8.9	22.3	57.7	20.0	33.5	24.6	29.3
36051	Livingston County	95.5	0.0	1.6	0.0	15.8	58.1	26.1	30.7	28.3	75.8
36053	Madison County	97.4	0.0	0.0	0.0	14.1	60.9	25.0	28.7	28.3	75.2
36055	Monroe County	76.4	13.9	6.2	2.6	19.9	56.5	23.5	29.0	25.7	64.1
36059	Nassau County	71.3	9.8	11.3	6.6	8.9	63.7	27.4	36.5	33.4	79.7
36061	New York County	56.2	13.2	19.0	11.1	26.5	52.2	21.3	18.4	23.3	22.4
36063	Niagara County	89.7	6.5	1.5	0.6	15.3	58.7	25.9	27.1	28.7	70.4
36065	Oneida County	89.7	4.3	2.8	2.1	16.4	56.8	26.8	28.4	29.6	66.1
36067	Onondaga County	83.1	9.9	3.0	2.2	18.5	57.9	23.6	29.4	26.1	65.4
36069	Ontario County	93.7	1.5	3.0	0.0	15.6	59.1	25.3	29.9	28.4	72.2
36071	Orange County	72.9	9.4	14.6	2.1	14.9	64.3	20.8	37.7	24.5	68.5
36075	Oswego County	96.9	0.0	1.4	0.0	15.9	61.3	22.8	31.6	25.3	71.6
36077	Otsego County	96.6	0.0	0.0	0.0	15.9	55.9	28.3	26.1	31.7	73.2
36079	Putnam County	85.6	1.6	10.3	0.0	8.9	68.8	22.4	36.3	26.9	82.8
36081	Queens County	34.7	17.7	24.0	21.2	17.7	60.6	21.7	32.7	27.6	43.3
36083	Rensselaer County	88.5	5.4	3.1	1.6	18.9	59.8	21.3	27.9	24.7	65.6
36085	Richmond County	67.9	10.1	15.1	6.3	13.0	64.3	22.7	36.0	28.3	67.8
36087	Rockland County	69.2	11.3	13.0	5.9	13.6	60.8	25.7	40.0	30.3	69.3
36089	St. Lawrence County	96.7	0.0	0.6	0.8	18.4	57.0	24.6	28.8	27.1	71.3
36091	Saratoga County	95.0	1.2	1.7	1.5	16.1	60.6	23.3	29.4	25.6	72.0
36093	Schenectady County	81.7	9.5	4.2	2.5	15.1	60.0	24.9	28.0	27.5	65.6
36101	Steuben County	95.7	1.6	0.7	0.0	17.1	57.8	25.1	30.0	27.8	70.3
36103	Suffolk County	78.3	6.5	11.8	2.8	10.2	65.0	24.8	36.7	30.0	79.2
36105	Sullivan County	80.6	7.3	10.1	0.0	13.0	61.2	25.8	29.3	29.7	65.7
36107	Tioga County	96.8	0.0	0.0	0.0	14.0	60.3	25.7	28.5	29.2	78.5
36109	Tompkins County	81.0	3.5	3.9	10.0	30.5	50.3	19.2	24.5	22.0	56.1
36111	Ulster County	87.0	3.9	6.6	1.1	13.2	60.9	25.8	27.7	29.6	69.3
36113	Warren County	96.9	0.0	0.0	0.0	13.2	58.8	28.0	26.0	30.7	70.5
36115	Washington County	97.0	0.0	0.0	0.0	13.4	58.7	28.0	30.1	31.1	72.7
36117	Wayne County	93.8	2.6	2.4	0.0	14.0	61.1	24.9	31.5	27.7	80.8
36119	Westchester County	62.5	14.6	17.8	4.6	12.4	62.2	25.4	35.2	29.3	61.3
37000	**North Carolina**	69.7	20.8	5.6	1.9	19.7	57.9	22.5	32.1	25.2	65.4
37001	Alamance County	71.5	18.7	7.7	0.0	18.2	56.8	25.0	31.7	27.8	66.1
37019	Brunswick County	85.7	9.2	2.8	0.0	12.7	52.1	35.2	24.8	39.1	74.3
37021	Buncombe County	88.0	6.3	4.0	0.0	18.7	56.0	25.3	24.7	28.2	62.9
37023	Burke County	88.3	4.8	3.0	1.7	11.4	59.4	29.2	28.9	32.2	71.4
37025	Cabarrus County	75.9	15.5	5.5	0.0	17.3	62.7	20.0	39.1	22.8	71.2
37027	Caldwell County	91.5	4.3	3.3	0.0	12.4	60.2	27.4	26.1	29.8	70.6
37031	Carteret County	88.8	6.3	3.3	0.0	16.8	53.8	29.4	27.5	32.9	70.0
37035	Catawba County	83.7	8.2	5.5	1.7	15.2	59.7	25.2	31.9	28.6	70.1
37037	Chatham County	77.3	12.5	7.8	0.0	11.7	56.1	32.1	26.6	35.5	77.8
37045	Cleveland County	76.9	20.6	1.8	0.0	13.8	58.3	27.9	27.9	31.0	68.0
37047	Columbus County	64.9	28.8	0.0	0.0	13.3	58.2	28.6	29.1	31.9	69.3
37049	Craven County	72.6	19.7	4.9	0.0	24.8	48.7	26.5	32.4	29.8	63.9
37051	Cumberland County	49.8	36.7	8.5	2.1	29.1	54.1	16.8	35.9	19.4	53.2
37057	Davidson County	85.9	8.8	3.9	0.0	15.1	59.7	25.2	31.6	28.4	73.2
37061	Duplin County	58.6	28.2	12.8	0.0	15.5	57.3	27.2	32.5	29.6	67.0
37063	Durham County	49.1	36.6	8.2	4.2	28.1	55.4	16.5	30.0	18.5	53.6
37065	Edgecombe County	41.5	54.3	0.0	0.0	14.9	57.4	27.7	30.3	30.9	62.2
37067	Forsyth County	63.8	26.0	7.5	1.6	20.3	57.8	21.9	31.5	24.6	62.7
37069	Franklin County	66.4	26.0	5.9	0.0	14.8	62.0	23.2	32.9	26.1	74.1
37071	Gaston County	78.5	14.6	4.5	1.0	16.5	60.6	23.0	31.1	26.2	66.8
37077	Granville County	63.9	30.8	0.0	0.0	12.8	65.0	22.2	32.9	25.3	72.5
37081	Guilford County	58.4	32.2	5.0	3.1	22.2	56.8	20.9	32.0	23.4	60.1
37083	Halifax County	43.0	50.7	0.0	0.0	14.4	57.4	28.2	30.4	31.6	61.5
37085	Harnett County	69.6	20.2	7.4	0.0	22.2	58.0	19.8	37.3	21.7	67.0
37087	Haywood County	95.4	0.0	0.0	0.0	14.5	53.5	32.0	27.4	35.1	74.1
37089	Henderson County	89.0	2.7	6.6	0.0	13.6	51.6	34.8	24.3	37.2	73.2
37093	Hoke County	43.8	35.8	9.5	0.0	28.0	57.7	14.3	43.8	15.9	65.8
37097	Iredell County	81.7	11.4	4.4	0.0	15.1	63.0	21.9	34.1	25.0	73.4
37101	Johnston County	74.4	14.8	9.0	0.0	17.2	63.6	19.2	40.1	21.7	71.6
37105	Lee County	66.2	19.4	12.0	0.0	17.4	59.8	22.8	34.4	25.5	66.7
37107	Lenoir County	56.0	37.3	5.1	0.0	14.9	58.5	26.6	30.8	29.7	57.2
37109	Lincoln County	90.0	4.7	4.2	0.0	13.4	62.7	23.9	32.3	27.9	77.0
37119	Mecklenburg County	55.5	30.9	8.3	4.0	25.2	59.7	15.1	33.9	17.4	58.2
37125	Moore County	82.7	11.0	3.5	0.0	13.6	51.6	34.9	25.4	38.4	75.2
37127	Nash County	58.4	36.4	3.7	0.0	15.1	59.2	25.7	31.9	28.7	64.7
37129	New Hanover County	81.1	13.1	3.5	1.0	25.1	52.6	22.3	26.5	24.9	57.1
37133	Onslow County	72.3	16.5	8.6	1.5	41.3	43.6	15.1	42.1	16.8	54.4
37135	Orange County	75.2	11.4	5.2	6.1	25.1	58.0	16.9	30.8	19.2	61.0
37141	Pender County	79.4	14.6	4.2	0.0	12.8	60.6	26.6	28.6	29.2	75.1
37147	Pitt County	59.7	32.8	4.4	1.6	30.7	52.5	16.8	31.3	18.8	53.1
37151	Randolph County	85.3	6.2	6.5	0.0	14.4	61.2	24.4	31.9	27.4	74.1

State/ County code	Metropolitan area	Total Households	Family households, percent	Married-couple family households, percent	Male householder, no spouse, percent	Female householder, no spouse, percent	Householder living alone, percent	Nonfamily households, householder not living alone, percent	Opposite-sex partner unmarried partner households, percent	Same-sex unmarried partner households, percent	Average household size
	North Carolina—cont'd										
37155	Robeson County	45,276	71.2	40.7	6.3	24.3	24.7	4.1	5.9	0.2	2.9
37157	Rockingham County	37,812	67.4	48.0	5.0	14.4	28.1	4.6	5.5	0.1	2.4
37159	Rowan County	51,429	68.5	49.2	4.9	14.4	26.7	4.8	6.3	0.5	2.6
37161	Rutherford County	26,725	71.0	52.1	5.2	13.8	25.8	3.1	4.6	0.3	2.5
37163	Sampson County	22,891	68.2	46.7	6.1	15.5	26.9	4.8	6.1	0.2	2.8
37167	Stanly County	23,454	70.1	51.6	5.1	13.3	27.1	2.9	4.1	0.2	2.5
37171	Surry County	29,814	67.7	50.8	4.6	12.4	29.0	3.3	3.2	0.5	2.4
37179	Union County	68,472	79.5	64.4	4.6	10.5	16.9	3.5	3.3	0.3	3.0
37183	Wake County	355,101	66.4	51.0	3.8	11.6	26.8	6.7	4.5	0.5	2.6
37189	Watauga County	20,213	51.6	42.6	2.0	6.9	28.8	19.6	6.0	0.7	2.3
37191	Wayne County	47,464	67.2	44.2	4.7	18.3	27.3	5.5	5.4	0.2	2.6
37193	Wilkes County	27,543	69.7	53.5	4.2	12.0	26.5	3.8	5.4	0.2	2.5
37195	Wilson County	31,390	66.7	44.0	5.3	17.4	29.3	4.0	4.5	0.4	2.6
38000	**North Dakota**	291,468	60.5	48.6	4.1	7.8	31.3	8.2	6.6	0.2	2.3
38015	Burleigh County	35,384	62.1	49.8	3.2	9.1	30.5	7.4	6.8	0.2	2.3
38017	Cass County	66,844	54.7	42.8	4.6	7.3	33.0	12.2	7.2	0.4	2.3
38035	Grand Forks County	27,870	53.9	43.1	3.7	7.1	34.9	11.2	6.2	0.0	2.3
38101	Ward County	25,386	60.5	48.8	3.8	7.9	31.2	8.3	6.6	0.3	2.5
39000	**Ohio**	4,551,497	64.2	46.9	4.4	12.9	30.0	5.8	5.7	0.4	2.5
39003	Allen County	40,235	65.2	45.4	5.0	14.8	29.1	5.6	7.4	0.4	2.5
39005	Ashland County	20,382	68.8	54.9	4.2	9.6	24.9	6.3	6.5	0.1	2.5
39007	Ashtabula County	39,103	64.7	47.0	5.4	12.3	28.9	6.4	8.9	0.4	2.5
39009	Athens County	22,198	55.8	40.7	5.8	9.3	31.2	13.0	8.0	0.4	2.5
39013	Belmont County	28,229	63.4	50.1	4.6	8.7	32.0	4.6	5.6	0.3	2.3
39017	Butler County	133,836	69.6	52.9	4.6	12.1	24.3	6.1	6.2	0.5	2.7
39023	Clark County	54,405	64.9	46.6	4.5	13.8	29.0	6.1	7.3	0.3	2.5
39025	Clermont County	74,312	71.0	54.9	5.5	10.7	24.1	4.9	4.8	0.3	2.7
39029	Columbiana County	41,708	68.1	51.0	5.2	11.9	26.5	5.4	6.6	0.2	2.5
39035	Cuyahoga County	532,702	57.3	37.3	4.2	15.8	37.2	5.5	5.0	0.6	2.3
39037	Darke County	20,834	66.5	54.0	3.6	8.9	29.7	3.7	4.5	0.2	2.5
39041	Delaware County	65,146	75.6	64.7	3.1	7.8	20.8	3.6	3.7	0.4	2.7
39043	Erie County	32,113	64.4	47.4	4.7	12.4	30.8	4.8	5.1	0.2	2.3
39045	Fairfield County	54,539	72.2	56.6	3.9	11.7	22.6	5.2	6.5	0.5	2.7
39049	Franklin County	471,460	57.7	39.4	4.3	14.1	33.1	9.1	6.7	0.8	2.5
39055	Geauga County	34,563	73.5	62.7	2.1	8.7	22.3	4.2	5.0	0.2	2.7
39057	Greene County	62,776	65.8	52.2	3.1	10.5	28.2	6.0	3.8	0.4	2.5
39061	Hamilton County	326,615	59.0	39.5	4.0	15.5	34.5	6.5	4.8	0.5	2.4
39063	Hancock County	30,566	63.6	49.9	3.9	9.8	31.3	5.0	5.9	0.3	2.4
39077	Huron County	22,324	71.0	54.2	5.6	11.2	23.1	5.9	7.0	0.5	2.6
39081	Jefferson County	27,927	64.7	49.0	4.9	10.9	30.3	5.0	4.6	0.1	2.4
39083	Knox County	22,399	69.7	55.9	4.5	9.3	23.5	6.7	6.0	0.3	2.6
39085	Lake County	93,496	65.1	50.2	4.2	10.7	30.0	5.0	5.4	0.2	2.4
39087	Lawrence County	23,632	68.0	49.3	4.9	13.8	27.5	4.5	5.5	0.8	2.6
39089	Licking County	63,628	70.1	54.8	4.6	10.7	24.8	5.1	6.6	0.5	2.6
39093	Lorain County	116,633	68.2	48.9	5.2	14.0	27.0	4.8	5.2	0.3	2.5
39095	Lucas County	177,296	59.4	38.4	4.8	16.2	33.6	7.0	6.1	0.4	2.4
39099	Mahoning County	97,661	62.4	42.3	4.6	15.5	32.9	4.6	5.7	0.4	2.3
39101	Marion County	24,399	69.0	52.3	4.9	11.7	26.7	4.3	6.9	0.3	2.4
39103	Medina County	65,513	73.0	59.9	4.1	8.9	22.1	4.9	5.4	0.3	2.6
39109	Miami County	40,929	68.9	52.3	5.0	11.6	25.5	5.6	7.2	0.2	2.5
39113	Montgomery County	221,546	60.2	40.3	4.4	15.5	34.4	5.5	5.9	0.6	2.3
39119	Muskingum County	33,959	67.8	47.4	6.1	14.3	26.7	5.5	8.1	0.5	2.5
39129	Pickaway County	19,208	74.1	59.2	4.1	10.8	20.9	5.0	6.5	0.1	2.7
39133	Portage County	60,323	65.7	50.7	3.3	11.8	25.4	8.9	6.8	0.2	2.6
39139	Richland County	48,296	62.6	46.6	3.7	12.3	32.7	4.7	5.3	0.2	2.4
39141	Ross County	28,091	68.7	52.4	4.0	12.3	26.4	4.8	6.1	0.4	2.6
39143	Sandusky County	23,740	67.7	50.7	5.5	11.6	27.9	4.3	6.0	0.1	2.5
39145	Scioto County	29,231	63.0	47.9	4.5	10.6	31.0	6.0	4.6	0.4	2.6
39147	Seneca County	21,393	67.9	52.2	4.8	10.9	27.0	5.1	6.8	0.5	2.5
39151	Stark County	149,912	66.0	48.8	5.2	12.0	29.2	4.9	5.5	0.5	2.4
39153	Summit County	219,214	62.4	45.0	4.0	13.3	31.8	5.8	4.9	0.5	2.4
39155	Trumbull County	86,446	64.3	45.7	5.1	13.5	31.6	4.1	5.3	0.3	2.4
39157	Tuscarawas County	36,274	70.1	54.8	4.5	10.9	25.1	4.8	6.5	0.1	2.5
39159	Union County	18,118	74.1	59.8	4.7	9.5	23.0	2.9	5.3	0.3	2.8
39165	Warren County	77,056	75.6	63.9	4.1	7.6	19.6	4.8	5.1	0.3	2.8
39167	Washington County	25,014	65.4	51.1	3.6	10.7	29.2	5.4	5.3	0.5	2.4
39169	Wayne County	42,804	70.3	57.5	3.9	8.9	25.6	4.1	5.0	0.2	2.6
39173	Wood County	49,481	62.6	49.4	3.6	9.6	28.6	8.8	6.4	0.4	2.5
40000	**Oklahoma**	1,445,059	66.4	49.0	4.9	12.4	28.2	5.4	4.8	0.3	2.6
40017	Canadian County	42,282	74.6	60.2	4.3	10.1	21.8	3.6	4.5	0.4	2.9
40027	Cleveland County	97,575	66.5	50.3	4.9	11.3	25.6	7.8	5.2	0.3	2.6
40031	Comanche County	43,942	64.9	45.7	4.4	14.8	29.3	5.8	5.7	0.3	2.7
40037	Creek County	25,852	71.9	56.2	5.5	10.2	24.8	3.3	3.0	0.2	2.7

Table A-2: Counties with a Population of 50,000 or More—Living Arrangements—*Continued*

State/County code	Metropolitan area	Race or Hispanic origin of householder				Age of householder			Percent of households with one or more persons under 18 years old	Percent of households with one or more persons age 65 or older	Percent of all householders who are owners
		Householder is White alone, not Hispanic or Latino, percent	Householder is Black or African American alone, percent	Householder is Hispanic or Latino, percent	Householder is Asian alone, percent	Householders age 15 to 34, percent	Householders age 35 to 64, percent	Householders age 65 and older, percent			
	North Carolina—cont'd										
37155	Robeson County	32.1	24.4	4.3	0.7	18.7	58.6	22.7	38.1	26.0	63.3
37157	Rockingham County	76.5	17.9	3.4	0.0	13.8	59.5	26.7	29.6	29.4	69.0
37159	Rowan County	78.3	14.3	5.2	0.0	16.0	58.2	25.8	29.9	29.1	67.1
37161	Rutherford County	87.0	9.4	2.7	0.0	13.8	57.4	28.7	32.8	32.5	71.1
37163	Sampson County	60.6	25.3	10.9	0.0	15.3	58.4	26.3	33.1	28.8	72.0
37167	Stanly County	85.8	9.9	0.0	0.0	13.4	59.4	27.2	32.6	29.7	72.2
37171	Surry County	89.4	3.8	6.1	0.0	13.2	57.8	29.0	28.9	31.6	72.1
37179	Union County	79.8	10.7	6.9	0.0	14.8	67.1	18.1	44.3	20.7	79.9
37183	Wake County	66.8	20.6	6.3	5.1	23.1	61.7	15.2	36.7	17.5	64.4
37189	Watauga County	96.5	0.0	0.0	0.0	33.3	45.0	21.7	18.9	23.4	56.1
37191	Wayne County	58.6	32.0	7.4	0.0	21.5	56.6	21.9	34.2	24.8	59.3
37193	Wilkes County	92.1	3.3	0.0	0.0	14.3	55.9	29.8	30.4	32.5	74.4
37195	Wilson County	55.1	36.6	5.7	0.0	14.8	59.6	25.6	30.6	28.5	62.0
38000	**North Dakota**	91.7	1.1	1.6	0.8	27.0	50.9	22.0	28.2	23.7	65.2
38015	Burleigh County	94.2	0.0	0.0	0.0	25.3	52.7	22.0	29.6	23.2	71.3
38017	Cass County	93.0	1.8	1.7	1.6	35.3	49.4	15.4	28.8	16.8	52.9
38035	Grand Forks County	90.7	2.2	2.0	1.9	36.7	45.5	17.8	25.5	19.0	50.6
38101	Ward County	90.7	0.0	2.5	0.0	32.5	46.7	20.7	29.0	21.9	61.1
39000	**Ohio**	82.9	12.0	2.3	1.5	18.8	57.4	23.9	30.3	26.4	66.5
39003	Allen County	84.1	11.3	1.9	0.0	19.2	55.6	25.3	32.6	27.6	67.2
39005	Ashland County	96.9	0.0	0.0	0.0	17.1	56.5	26.4	30.8	28.7	72.2
39007	Ashtabula County	93.6	2.6	2.1	0.0	14.0	59.3	26.7	31.2	29.4	72.0
39009	Athens County	92.5	1.7	0.0	2.9	31.9	48.6	19.5	25.2	21.8	57.0
39013	Belmont County	96.1	2.0	0.0	0.0	16.5	55.6	27.9	24.7	30.8	73.2
39017	Butler County	86.7	6.9	2.9	2.0	19.5	59.4	21.1	34.1	23.6	70.0
39023	Clark County	87.3	9.2	1.7	0.0	17.5	55.3	27.1	30.0	29.5	67.0
39025	Clermont County	95.7	1.2	0.0	0.0	16.5	62.2	21.3	34.7	24.2	73.3
39029	Columbiana County	96.7	1.6	0.0	0.0	15.5	57.5	27.0	30.5	30.1	70.6
39035	Cuyahoga County	63.8	29.0	3.8	2.3	18.1	56.9	25.1	27.3	27.7	59.8
39037	Darke County	97.3	0.0	0.0	0.0	16.4	55.9	27.7	29.8	29.7	73.2
39041	Delaware County	90.3	3.1	1.4	4.1	15.6	66.2	18.1	40.6	20.3	81.3
39043	Erie County	87.1	8.7	2.7	0.0	15.6	56.8	27.5	26.7	30.4	68.7
39045	Fairfield County	90.8	5.1	1.7	1.1	17.5	60.5	22.0	36.5	24.5	71.2
39049	Franklin County	70.7	20.2	3.3	3.6	27.4	56.0	16.6	30.9	18.9	54.0
39055	Geauga County	96.9	0.0	0.0	0.0	10.1	62.9	27.0	30.9	30.8	85.0
39057	Greene County	87.7	6.1	2.0	2.4	21.4	55.1	23.6	29.6	26.1	67.2
39061	Hamilton County	69.0	26.2	1.8	1.8	22.4	55.8	21.8	29.5	23.8	58.8
39063	Hancock County	93.2	1.7	2.9	0.0	19.6	56.5	23.8	28.7	26.4	71.1
39077	Huron County	93.7	0.0	4.0	0.0	16.4	60.0	23.7	35.3	26.7	71.9
39081	Jefferson County	92.5	5.3	0.0	0.0	13.5	55.0	31.4	24.3	33.8	71.5
39083	Knox County	96.8	0.0	0.0	0.0	17.7	56.3	26.0	31.9	28.6	69.5
39085	Lake County	92.3	3.7	2.2	1.2	14.5	59.6	25.9	27.3	29.6	73.6
39087	Lawrence County	96.2	1.8	0.0	0.2	14.7	57.5	27.8	28.6	30.2	74.7
39089	Licking County	94.3	3.0	1.0	0.0	16.9	60.0	23.1	33.4	26.2	72.4
39093	Lorain County	84.0	7.1	6.9	0.0	14.8	60.0	25.2	31.9	27.6	71.3
39095	Lucas County	74.1	19.0	4.3	1.3	21.1	56.7	22.2	29.4	24.4	60.7
39099	Mahoning County	80.5	14.6	3.5	0.0	15.3	55.8	28.9	26.8	31.6	67.8
39101	Marion County	96.2	0.0	0.0	0.0	17.4	55.3	27.4	30.1	29.3	68.0
39103	Medina County	95.6	0.9	1.5	1.0	13.7	62.8	23.5	33.9	26.1	78.7
39109	Miami County	95.6	0.0	0.0	0.0	16.9	56.7	26.4	31.6	28.4	70.4
39113	Montgomery County	74.2	21.0	1.8	1.5	19.6	54.9	25.4	28.8	27.7	60.8
39119	Muskingum County	94.6	3.1	0.0	0.0	18.7	55.9	25.4	31.5	28.3	68.6
39129	Pickaway County	98.1	0.0	0.0	0.0	15.0	61.4	23.5	35.1	27.2	75.6
39133	Portage County	92.5	3.9	1.2	1.3	21.7	56.7	21.6	28.6	24.6	68.0
39139	Richland County	90.8	6.3	0.0	0.0	15.9	55.3	28.9	28.8	31.1	68.8
39141	Ross County	94.3	2.0	0.0	0.0	15.2	60.6	24.2	34.0	27.1	73.2
39143	Sandusky County	89.5	3.0	7.6	0.0	16.8	57.0	26.2	30.8	28.7	74.8
39145	Scioto County	95.7	1.9	0.0	0.0	16.2	56.3	27.5	29.8	30.2	68.9
39147	Seneca County	94.1	0.0	2.9	0.0	17.5	55.8	26.7	30.4	28.5	71.2
39151	Stark County	89.7	6.9	1.2	0.0	16.3	57.4	26.2	29.5	28.8	69.4
39153	Summit County	81.5	13.8	1.2	1.8	18.2	57.6	24.2	29.3	26.8	66.8
39155	Trumbull County	89.5	8.3	0.9	0.0	14.7	56.6	28.8	27.0	31.7	70.4
39157	Tuscarawas County	97.1	1.0	0.0	0.0	16.0	56.6	27.4	30.7	29.4	71.0
39159	Union County	94.7	0.0	0.0	0.0	15.6	65.1	19.3	39.1	21.5	77.9
39165	Warren County	91.8	2.0	1.5	0.0	15.4	64.5	20.1	36.4	22.4	76.5
39167	Washington County	96.4	0.0	0.0	0.0	14.8	56.7	28.5	25.3	30.6	74.9
39169	Wayne County	96.6	1.0	0.9	0.0	17.2	57.5	25.3	31.5	28.0	72.4
39173	Wood County	92.4	2.3	3.2	1.7	23.8	54.6	21.7	29.0	23.1	66.7
40000	**Oklahoma**	74.2	7.1	6.2	1.4	22.4	54.3	23.4	32.9	25.8	66.3
40017	Canadian County	85.3	1.5	5.4	2.1	21.7	58.5	19.8	39.3	22.1	76.9
40027	Cleveland County	80.4	4.3	5.1	2.9	28.3	53.8	17.9	32.9	20.2	66.7
40031	Comanche County	64.4	16.0	9.2	1.9	26.9	52.9	20.2	36.3	21.6	55.6
40037	Creek County	83.4	2.1	2.0	0.0	16.5	56.7	26.8	32.3	29.4	75.3

State/ County code	Metropolitan area	Household type							Opposite-sex partner unmarried partner households, percent	Same-sex unmarried partner households, percent	Average household size
		Total Households	Family households, percent	Married-couple family households, percent	Male householder, no spouse, percent	Female householder, no spouse, percent	Householder living alone, percent	Nonfamily households, householder not living alone, percent			
	Oklahoma—cont'd										
40047	Garfield County	23,298	71.9	54.5	4.6	12.8	24.7	3.4	4.4	0.2	2.6
40051	Grady County	19,593	72.8	56.8	6.1	9.9	23.6	3.6	3.6	0.1	2.7
40101	Muskogee County	26,597	67.8	47.6	5.5	14.7	27.4	4.8	4.2	0.2	2.5
40109	Oklahoma County	286,540	61.6	42.7	5.3	13.6	31.7	6.7	5.0	0.4	2.5
40119	Payne County	29,985	55.1	43.0	3.6	8.5	31.9	13.0	6.2	0.1	2.3
40125	Pottawatomie County	25,983	68.8	52.3	4.5	12.0	27.2	4.0	3.6	0.3	2.6
40131	Rogers County	33,109	75.8	60.2	5.9	9.7	20.7	3.4	3.9	0.3	2.6
40143	Tulsa County	242,168	63.9	45.1	4.7	14.1	30.2	6.0	5.4	0.4	2.5
40145	Wagoner County	27,062	75.0	58.8	5.5	10.7	21.6	3.3	4.0	0.5	2.8
40147	Washington County	20,952	67.2	52.0	3.9	11.3	28.2	4.6	4.9	0.2	2.4
41000	**Oregon**	1,516,591	63.3	48.3	4.5	10.5	28.1	8.6	6.6	0.7	2.5
41003	Benton County	33,298	56.3	45.9	2.5	8.0	29.0	14.7	5.4	0.9	2.4
41005	Clackamas County	147,457	68.7	54.3	4.6	9.8	24.6	6.7	5.1	0.6	2.6
41011	Coos County	25,814	60.3	46.5	4.0	9.8	32.8	6.9	5.7	0.4	2.4
41017	Deschutes County	65,031	65.4	52.0	4.3	9.1	26.2	8.3	6.6	0.5	2.5
41019	Douglas County	43,279	66.9	51.2	4.8	11.0	25.2	7.9	7.5	0.5	2.4
41029	Jackson County	82,737	64.5	48.9	4.5	11.2	28.8	6.7	7.1	0.6	2.5
41033	Josephine County	34,288	64.3	49.7	4.4	10.2	29.7	6.0	6.4	0.6	2.4
41035	Klamath County	27,184	67.2	49.1	7.0	11.1	26.3	6.5	6.2	0.4	2.4
41039	Lane County	144,992	59.0	43.7	4.5	10.8	29.4	11.6	7.2	1.0	2.4
41043	Linn County	44,458	69.0	52.7	4.3	12.0	24.2	6.7	6.2	0.4	2.6
41047	Marion County	113,124	69.3	49.9	5.8	13.5	25.6	5.1	7.3	0.5	2.8
41051	Multnomah County	307,387	54.0	39.0	4.1	10.8	33.3	12.7	8.0	1.4	2.4
41053	Polk County	28,266	67.4	53.9	4.6	8.9	22.8	9.8	6.3	0.5	2.6
41059	Umatilla County	26,640	68.4	50.1	5.9	12.4	26.3	5.4	6.8	0.3	2.7
41067	Washington County	202,958	67.0	52.9	4.1	10.1	25.3	7.7	6.1	0.5	2.7
41071	Yamhill County	33,861	71.8	54.9	5.9	11.0	22.8	5.5	5.7	0.3	2.8
42000	**Pennsylvania**	4,945,140	64.4	48.1	4.3	12.0	29.7	5.8	5.5	0.4	2.5
42001	Adams County	37,829	72.2	58.1	4.2	9.9	23.0	4.8	6.1	0.3	2.6
42003	Allegheny County	525,776	57.8	42.2	3.5	12.0	35.3	6.9	5.1	0.6	2.3
42005	Armstrong County	28,557	67.7	51.7	5.9	10.1	28.4	3.8	5.9	0.3	2.4
42007	Beaver County	70,853	65.1	49.4	4.2	11.5	30.4	4.5	4.7	0.3	2.4
42011	Berks County	153,142	68.2	51.2	5.4	11.6	25.0	6.8	7.2	0.5	2.6
42013	Blair County	50,649	65.2	49.1	4.6	11.4	30.2	4.6	6.5	0.3	2.4
42015	Bradford County	24,152	68.7	53.9	5.4	9.4	25.7	5.6	7.1	0.2	2.6
42017	Bucks County	232,040	71.7	58.1	3.7	9.8	23.9	4.4	3.9	0.6	2.7
42019	Butler County	73,503	67.9	55.8	3.7	8.4	26.5	5.6	4.4	0.3	2.6
42021	Cambria County	57,588	63.8	47.7	4.5	11.6	31.9	4.3	5.0	0.3	2.3
42025	Carbon County	25,959	67.0	51.8	4.3	11.0	27.2	5.8	7.3	0.2	2.5
42027	Centre County	57,447	56.7	46.2	3.9	6.6	27.6	15.7	4.3	0.5	2.4
42029	Chester County	184,958	70.2	58.3	3.4	8.5	23.9	6.0	4.5	0.4	2.7
42033	Clearfield County	31,994	66.7	52.6	4.3	9.8	29.2	4.1	6.2	0.3	2.4
42037	Columbia County	26,023	64.4	50.0	4.4	10.0	26.8	8.8	7.3	0.1	2.4
42039	Crawford County	34,482	66.8	52.5	4.2	10.0	28.0	5.3	6.3	0.5	2.4
42041	Cumberland County	95,166	65.0	52.4	3.9	8.7	29.3	5.7	6.0	0.4	2.4
42043	Dauphin County	108,397	63.6	45.4	4.7	13.5	30.0	6.3	5.9	0.8	2.4
42045	Delaware County	202,972	66.5	47.8	4.5	14.2	28.8	4.7	5.0	0.4	2.7
42049	Erie County	109,733	63.6	46.1	4.1	13.3	30.2	6.2	5.7	0.3	2.4
42051	Fayette County	53,842	64.8	47.4	4.8	12.6	30.9	4.3	6.1	0.1	2.4
42055	Franklin County	58,244	68.4	55.3	4.3	8.8	26.7	4.8	5.8	0.3	2.6
42063	Indiana County	34,162	62.1	49.6	3.8	8.7	29.4	8.5	5.8	0.2	2.4
42069	Lackawanna County	85,513	62.0	45.5	4.6	12.0	32.5	5.4	5.2	0.2	2.4
42071	Lancaster County	193,898	70.3	57.4	3.6	9.3	24.4	5.3	4.7	0.5	2.6
42073	Lawrence County	36,587	65.9	50.1	3.7	12.2	30.0	4.0	4.2	0.1	2.4
42075	Lebanon County	52,068	69.1	53.2	4.5	11.3	26.4	4.5	6.2	0.4	2.5
42077	Lehigh County	133,446	66.6	48.8	4.7	13.1	27.4	6.0	6.6	0.5	2.6
42079	Luzerne County	129,414	63.7	44.9	5.2	13.6	31.7	4.6	5.7	0.3	2.4
42081	Lycoming County	45,584	63.4	48.3	4.2	11.0	29.6	7.0	7.3	0.7	2.4
42085	Mercer County	45,924	66.4	50.3	3.7	12.4	29.7	4.0	5.4	0.1	2.4
42089	Monroe County	58,374	73.9	54.7	6.0	13.2	19.7	6.3	7.1	0.9	2.8
42091	Montgomery County	306,956	67.8	54.9	3.5	9.4	27.0	5.2	4.1	0.5	2.6
42095	Northampton County	112,232	69.4	53.7	4.3	11.4	24.9	5.8	5.8	0.6	2.6
42097	Northumberland County	39,250	64.2	49.1	4.2	10.9	32.0	3.8	6.0	0.2	2.3
42101	Philadelphia County	579,165	52.4	26.8	5.4	20.3	40.0	7.6	5.8	0.6	2.6
42103	Pike County	20,979	71.7	58.1	4.2	9.4	24.2	4.2	5.5	0.4	2.7
42107	Schuylkill County	59,164	65.2	48.6	5.2	11.5	29.4	5.5	7.5	0.2	2.4
42111	Somerset County	29,746	69.7	57.4	4.2	8.1	27.0	3.3	3.8	0.3	2.4
42121	Venango County	22,429	67.1	51.0	4.4	11.7	29.3	3.5	5.7	0.2	2.4
42125	Washington County	83,615	65.8	51.7	3.8	10.2	28.9	5.3	5.8	0.2	2.4
42127	Wayne County	19,527	69.4	55.8	5.0	8.6	26.2	4.4	4.8	0.5	2.5
42129	Westmoreland County	151,279	66.4	51.9	3.9	10.7	29.4	4.1	4.8	0.3	2.3
42133	York County	166,924	69.4	53.4	5.0	11.0	25.3	5.3	6.7	0.5	2.6

State/County code	Metropolitan area	Race or Hispanic origin of householder				Age of householder			Percent of households with one or more persons under 18 years old	Percent of households with one or more persons age 65 or older	Percent of all householders who are owners
		Householder is White alone, not Hispanic or Latino, percent	Householder is Black or African American alone, percent	Householder is Hispanic or Latino, percent	Householder is Asian alone, percent	Householders age 15 to 34, percent	Householders age 35 to 64, percent	Householders age 65 and older, percent			
	Oklahoma—cont'd										
40047	Garfield County	86.2	3.1	5.9	0.0	24.7	51.0	24.3	33.8	27.1	67.2
40051	Grady County	87.0	2.0	3.2	0.0	18.5	55.7	25.8	34.0	27.8	74.6
40101	Muskogee County	65.3	11.8	3.6	0.0	21.0	54.1	24.9	33.3	27.7	66.2
40109	Oklahoma County	66.1	15.0	10.0	2.5	25.7	53.9	20.4	32.5	22.6	58.8
40119	Payne County	84.9	0.0	2.9	3.1	39.4	42.9	17.6	28.0	19.4	50.1
40125	Pottawatomie County	79.4	1.9	3.1	0.0	19.7	54.8	25.5	32.3	28.7	69.8
40131	Rogers County	77.2	0.0	2.9	0.8	17.1	59.9	23.0	36.0	26.2	79.0
40143	Tulsa County	70.8	10.2	7.5	1.8	24.0	55.5	20.5	33.4	22.7	60.1
40145	Wagoner County	79.0	3.4	3.5	0.0	16.6	59.3	24.1	35.9	27.1	81.3
40147	Washington County	80.3	2.7	3.9	0.0	19.4	50.6	30.0	30.9	31.6	72.5
41000	**Oregon**	84.3	1.6	7.6	3.2	19.8	56.2	23.9	29.5	27.0	61.1
41003	Benton County	85.7	0.0	5.4	4.6	29.5	49.5	21.0	24.1	23.7	58.1
41005	Clackamas County	89.1	0.6	4.9	3.0	14.9	61.0	24.1	32.0	27.3	67.8
41011	Coos County	89.6	0.0	3.4	0.0	12.6	52.7	34.6	22.6	38.6	65.6
41017	Deschutes County	91.9	0.0	4.5	1.2	17.1	57.5	25.4	28.0	28.6	63.8
41019	Douglas County	92.2	0.0	3.1	0.0	14.4	52.3	33.3	26.4	38.1	67.6
41029	Jackson County	88.7	0.6	6.9	0.8	17.5	53.1	29.5	27.4	32.5	62.1
41033	Josephine County	91.4	0.0	5.1	0.0	12.7	52.1	35.3	23.2	38.9	65.5
41035	Klamath County	83.8	1.0	8.4	0.0	18.0	53.8	28.3	30.9	31.1	64.1
41039	Lane County	88.6	0.7	5.2	2.0	22.2	52.8	25.0	25.7	28.1	58.3
41043	Linn County	91.8	0.0	4.5	0.9	19.9	52.9	27.2	31.3	30.0	65.0
41047	Marion County	77.8	0.7	15.3	1.8	20.7	55.5	23.8	35.8	26.4	59.1
41051	Multnomah County	78.6	5.1	7.4	5.2	24.7	57.8	17.5	27.0	20.2	53.4
41053	Polk County	86.5	0.0	7.5	1.9	19.7	54.2	26.1	29.7	29.5	63.4
41059	Umatilla County	77.8	0.0	16.6	0.0	19.7	57.5	22.7	36.2	25.9	62.6
41067	Washington County	77.4	1.6	10.2	8.1	22.1	59.3	18.6	35.4	21.4	60.3
41071	Yamhill County	85.9	0.0	9.6	1.6	17.0	56.1	26.9	34.1	29.6	67.4
42000	**Pennsylvania**	82.7	9.9	4.3	2.3	16.9	57.5	25.7	28.9	28.8	69.2
42001	Adams County	94.0	0.9	4.0	0.0	12.4	61.0	26.6	30.6	30.3	77.2
42003	Allegheny County	82.6	12.4	1.2	2.6	19.6	54.5	25.9	25.1	28.5	64.7
42005	Armstrong County	98.5	0.0	0.0	0.0	13.3	56.1	30.5	25.8	33.6	75.3
42007	Beaver County	92.4	5.6	0.9	0.0	13.6	56.3	30.0	25.5	33.1	72.6
42011	Berks County	81.3	4.5	13.0	1.0	16.2	58.8	25.1	32.7	28.0	72.1
42013	Blair County	97.4	1.0	0.6	0.0	15.5	55.7	28.9	28.1	31.7	72.3
42015	Bradford County	97.9	0.0	0.8	0.0	13.2	58.3	28.6	28.2	32.9	74.3
42017	Bucks County	89.0	3.5	3.4	3.2	11.5	63.4	25.1	31.8	28.8	76.9
42019	Butler County	97.1	0.8	0.9	0.8	15.3	59.8	24.9	29.8	27.9	77.2
42021	Cambria County	95.6	2.5	0.8	0.0	13.9	55.3	30.8	24.8	33.6	74.1
42025	Carbon County	95.2	0.0	2.6	0.0	12.7	59.6	27.7	27.9	31.1	75.3
42027	Centre County	90.3	2.2	2.0	4.6	32.0	48.0	19.9	24.1	21.9	60.1
42029	Chester County	85.5	5.4	4.5	3.5	15.4	62.0	22.6	34.2	25.8	74.7
42033	Clearfield County	98.7	0.0	0.0	0.0	13.4	57.4	29.2	27.4	32.0	77.0
42037	Columbia County	95.6	0.0	1.7	0.0	17.6	55.2	27.2	27.0	30.4	69.8
42039	Crawford County	97.7	0.0	0.0	0.0	14.7	57.4	27.9	27.8	31.4	73.8
42041	Cumberland County	92.7	1.8	1.9	2.7	17.7	56.9	25.4	28.6	28.1	70.4
42043	Dauphin County	74.5	16.1	5.7	2.7	19.6	57.5	22.9	30.1	25.4	63.6
42045	Delaware County	74.5	18.8	2.3	3.7	15.2	59.8	25.0	32.2	28.3	69.7
42049	Erie County	90.6	5.9	2.1	0.9	18.9	57.0	24.1	28.5	26.6	66.3
42051	Fayette County	94.9	3.5	0.6	0.0	13.1	58.1	28.8	26.9	32.6	71.5
42055	Franklin County	92.8	3.1	2.8	0.0	16.4	56.3	27.3	31.3	30.4	72.4
42063	Indiana County	96.8	0.0	1.2	0.0	20.6	52.9	26.4	25.2	29.0	71.2
42069	Lackawanna County	92.5	1.7	3.6	1.5	15.2	56.7	28.1	26.5	31.5	66.0
42071	Lancaster County	88.0	3.2	6.8	1.3	18.0	56.5	25.5	31.1	28.5	69.4
42073	Lawrence County	94.6	3.7	0.0	0.0	13.4	56.5	30.2	28.2	32.9	74.2
42075	Lebanon County	89.3	1.7	7.9	0.0	15.9	56.7	27.4	30.5	30.2	71.0
42077	Lehigh County	77.0	5.7	14.3	2.7	16.7	59.3	23.9	31.4	27.3	67.3
42079	Luzerne County	91.6	2.3	5.1	0.7	14.9	56.2	28.9	27.6	32.1	66.8
42081	Lycoming County	94.1	3.3	0.0	0.0	17.5	55.7	26.8	27.3	29.5	70.2
42085	Mercer County	93.1	5.0	0.7	0.0	14.6	54.8	30.6	26.8	33.3	73.5
42089	Monroe County	75.2	11.4	10.3	0.0	12.5	65.5	22.1	34.9	27.3	78.6
42091	Montgomery County	82.2	8.1	3.2	5.5	15.4	59.7	24.9	31.9	28.3	72.6
42095	Northampton County	84.3	4.1	9.0	2.1	14.2	59.2	26.6	31.3	30.3	72.1
42097	Northumberland County	97.9	0.0	1.4	0.0	15.3	55.7	29.0	26.2	32.0	71.3
42101	Philadelphia County	41.1	42.6	10.1	5.4	24.3	54.6	21.0	27.0	24.0	52.4
42103	Pike County	84.7	4.4	9.1	0.0	8.5	62.4	29.1	28.7	34.2	83.4
42107	Schuylkill County	97.1	0.8	1.4	0.0	13.4	57.2	29.4	27.3	32.2	74.1
42111	Somerset County	98.8	0.0	0.0	0.0	12.3	56.6	31.1	26.9	33.8	78.7
42121	Venango County	97.5	0.0	0.0	0.0	12.8	58.9	28.3	28.3	31.3	74.3
42125	Washington County	94.9	2.6	1.0	0.0	13.0	58.6	28.5	27.5	31.8	75.2
42127	Wayne County	97.2	0.0	0.0	0.0	10.2	59.8	30.0	25.3	35.4	79.6
42129	Westmoreland County	96.0	2.0	0.7	0.0	12.9	56.9	30.1	26.0	33.3	76.0
42133	York County	89.7	4.6	4.2	0.9	16.1	59.8	24.2	32.0	27.1	74.0

State/ County code	Metropolitan area	Household type							Opposite-sex partner unmarried partner households, percent	Same-sex unmarried partner households, percent	Average household size
		Total Households	Family households, percent	Married-couple family households, percent	Male householder, no spouse, percent	Female householder, no spouse, percent	Householder living alone, percent	Nonfamily households, householder not living alone, percent			
44000	**Rhode Island**...............	410,347	62.7	44.0	4.8	13.9	30.2	7.1	6.1	0.7	2.5
44003	Kent County.....................	68,743	62.7	47.6	4.7	10.5	31.1	6.2	5.5	0.9	2.4
44005	Newport County................	34,299	61.2	48.0	3.1	10.1	32.4	6.4	4.0	0.5	2.3
44007	Providence County............	238,353	61.7	39.8	5.5	16.4	30.8	7.5	6.8	0.8	2.5
44009	Washington County...........	50,050	66.7	52.4	3.5	10.8	25.8	7.6	5.5	0.4	2.4
45000	**South Carolina**............	1,781,957	67.3	47.3	4.7	15.3	27.6	5.1	4.5	0.3	2.6
45003	Aiken County....................	62,874	67.0	48.1	4.6	14.3	29.0	4.0	3.9	0.5	2.6
45007	Anderson County...............	73,036	70.5	51.5	5.0	14.0	26.0	3.5	3.3	0.1	2.6
45013	Beaufort County................	64,156	68.3	53.7	4.1	10.5	25.9	5.8	4.6	0.4	2.5
45015	Berkeley County................	67,123	72.0	53.2	4.7	14.0	23.1	4.9	4.9	0.4	2.8
45019	Charleston County.............	144,960	58.2	40.0	4.4	13.8	32.2	9.6	4.7	0.4	2.4
45021	Cherokee County...............	20,611	69.7	48.1	5.6	15.9	27.3	3.0	5.8	0.4	2.7
45031	Darlington County..............	26,215	70.6	43.9	6.3	20.5	26.9	2.5	4.1	0.4	2.6
45035	Dorchester County............	51,044	72.4	53.2	4.2	15.0	23.7	3.9	4.5	0.2	2.8
45041	Florence County................	50,903	69.0	44.4	5.3	19.3	27.6	3.5	4.6	0.1	2.7
45043	Georgetown County...........	23,417	69.2	49.5	5.0	14.7	26.5	4.4	4.6	0.2	2.6
45045	Greenville County	175,963	67.7	50.4	4.0	13.3	28.0	4.3	4.2	0.2	2.6
45047	Greenwood County............	26,763	67.8	44.2	5.5	18.1	28.4	3.8	5.3	0.4	2.5
45051	Horry County....................	113,954	64.4	47.9	4.3	12.3	28.9	6.6	6.0	0.3	2.5
45055	Kershaw County................	24,009	70.3	49.4	4.9	16.0	25.8	3.9	4.8	0.1	2.6
45057	Lancaster County..............	28,682	71.3	49.6	3.8	17.8	24.9	3.8	3.4	0.6	2.7
45059	Laurens County.................	24,623	72.6	45.9	7.5	19.1	23.9	3.5	4.4	0.4	2.6
45063	Lexington County..............	104,638	68.8	51.0	4.1	13.7	25.2	6.0	5.3	0.3	2.6
45073	Oconee County.................	30,124	69.4	51.5	5.4	12.4	25.8	4.8	4.6	0.1	2.5
45075	Orangeburg County...........	33,712	64.1	39.2	4.7	20.1	32.7	3.3	3.0	0.2	2.6
45077	Pickens County.................	43,574	65.5	51.1	4.8	9.7	26.8	7.7	4.8	0.2	2.6
45079	Richland County	143,152	61.2	39.9	3.9	17.5	31.5	7.3	4.4	0.5	2.5
45083	Spartanburg County...........	107,394	70.4	48.7	4.6	17.0	25.4	4.3	4.5	0.4	2.6
45085	Sumter County.................	40,068	68.6	44.8	4.9	18.9	27.1	4.2	5.1	0.2	2.6
45091	York County....................	87,303	72.1	54.1	4.1	13.8	23.4	4.5	4.3	0.3	2.6
46000	**South Dakota**	326,086	64.6	50.0	4.7	9.9	29.3	6.2	6.0	0.3	2.5
46099	Minnehaha County.............	68,549	63.8	47.3	5.2	11.3	28.8	7.4	6.1	0.3	2.5
46103	Pennington County.............	40,646	63.6	46.6	5.1	11.9	29.8	6.6	7.2	0.6	2.5
47000	**Tennessee**	2,480,467	66.4	48.5	4.5	13.4	28.4	5.2	4.8	0.4	2.5
47001	Anderson County..............	30,548	63.7	46.2	4.3	13.2	31.5	4.8	5.6	0.3	2.4
47009	Blount County..................	49,016	69.3	56.0	3.0	10.3	26.3	4.4	3.4	0.5	2.5
47011	Bradley County................	37,980	68.6	50.4	5.3	13.0	26.7	4.7	4.8	0.1	2.6
47019	Carter County..................	23,940	66.8	51.7	3.9	11.2	29.9	3.2	4.8	0.2	2.3
47031	Coffee County..................	21,112	68.0	48.5	5.0	14.5	28.2	3.8	7.4	0.1	2.5
47035	Cumberland County...........	23,521	68.8	56.0	4.4	8.5	27.7	3.5	4.6	0.2	2.4
47037	Davidson County	258,580	54.7	36.6	4.1	14.0	36.5	8.8	5.6	0.6	2.4
47043	Dickson County................	18,404	75.3	54.9	5.2	15.2	21.1	3.6	4.7	0.2	2.7
47059	Greene County	28,437	67.9	52.4	3.9	11.6	27.9	4.1	4.9	0.5	2.4
47063	Hamblen County...............	24,138	69.6	49.7	4.7	15.2	25.6	4.7	6.0	0.5	2.6
47065	Hamilton County...............	135,048	65.2	47.3	4.3	13.7	29.5	5.3	4.7	0.6	2.5
47073	Hawkins County	23,044	70.2	54.1	4.5	11.6	26.9	2.9	3.9	0.1	2.4
47089	Jefferson County..............	19,672	71.2	55.5	4.0	11.8	25.5	3.3	5.4	0.3	2.6
47093	Knox County....................	181,195	60.3	46.4	4.1	9.8	32.9	6.8	4.9	0.4	2.4
47107	McMinn County................	20,250	68.6	55.2	4.1	9.3	28.1	3.3	3.8	0.3	2.5
47113	Madison County	35,820	65.9	46.2	3.6	16.1	30.0	4.1	3.6	0.2	2.6
47119	Maury County..................	32,084	67.7	47.8	5.2	14.7	27.4	5.0	5.9	0.4	2.5
47125	Montgomery County...........	64,982	73.7	54.8	4.4	14.6	20.9	5.4	5.4	0.1	2.8
47141	Putnam County.................	29,324	64.5	47.4	5.0	12.0	27.9	7.6	5.4	0.4	2.4
47145	Roane County..................	22,045	67.5	54.3	2.9	10.2	27.7	4.8	4.1	0.2	2.4
47147	Robertson County.............	24,529	73.5	55.9	4.2	13.3	22.5	4.1	5.0	0.7	2.7
47149	Rutherford County.............	97,539	68.9	53.1	4.5	11.3	23.1	8.0	5.1	0.6	2.8
47155	Sevier County	36,794	72.4	55.0	5.0	12.4	23.0	4.6	4.9	0.4	2.5
47157	Shelby County..................	345,099	63.4	37.7	5.1	20.7	31.4	5.2	4.9	0.5	2.7
47163	Sullivan County................	65,836	66.3	50.6	4.3	11.4	28.7	5.0	4.6	0.4	2.3
47165	Sumner County................	61,367	74.9	57.5	5.1	12.3	21.5	3.6	4.1	0.2	2.7
47167	Tipton County..................	21,490	75.6	54.0	4.8	16.8	21.0	3.4	4.7	0.1	2.8
47179	Washington County...........	52,351	63.3	47.6	4.4	11.2	30.9	5.8	4.6	0.4	2.3
47187	Williamson County............	67,254	78.3	68.6	2.4	7.3	19.6	2.1	1.7	0.3	2.9
47189	Wilson County..................	43,349	72.0	56.9	3.5	11.6	24.1	3.9	4.8	0.4	2.7
48000	**Texas**	8,965,352	69.6	50.0	5.1	14.4	25.1	5.4	4.9	0.4	2.8
48001	Anderson County..............	16,637	72.0	52.8	5.3	13.8	25.8	2.2	3.6	0.2	2.7
48005	Angelina County...............	30,485	73.3	50.9	7.0	15.5	22.8	3.9	6.5	0.0	2.8
48021	Bastrop County................	25,223	71.0	56.0	4.3	10.7	23.2	5.8	5.0	0.7	2.9
48027	Bell County.....................	103,001	72.3	52.8	4.2	15.3	24.0	3.7	4.3	0.2	3.1
48029	Bexar County...................	610,174	67.7	45.6	5.4	16.7	26.5	5.8	4.9	0.5	2.8
48037	Bowie County...................	33,457	68.8	46.1	4.8	17.9	26.9	4.3	3.3	0.0	2.6
48039	Brazoria County................	109,826	73.8	56.7	4.5	12.7	22.5	3.7	3.1	0.4	2.9
48041	Brazos County..................	70,418	55.4	39.4	4.2	11.7	28.6	16.0	4.6	0.4	2.6

State/County code	Metropolitan area	Race or Hispanic origin of householder				Age of householder			Percent of households with one or more persons under 18 years old	Percent of households with one or more persons age 65 or older	Percent of all householders who are owners
		Householder is White alone, not Hispanic or Latino, percent	Householder is Black or African American alone, percent	Householder is Hispanic or Latino, percent	Householder is Asian alone, percent	Householders age 15 to 34, percent	Householders age 35 to 64, percent	Householders age 65 and older, percent			
44000	**Rhode Island**............	81.1	5.5	9.6	2.4	17.6	58.6	23.8	29.4	27.3	60.2
44003	Kent County................	93.5	0.0	2.4	1.9	14.6	60.8	24.6	27.9	28.3	70.2
44005	Newport County...........	90.3	3.3	3.0	0.0	13.5	58.7	27.8	25.2	31.1	62.9
44007	Providence County.........	72.4	8.4	14.9	2.9	20.1	57.7	22.2	30.9	25.9	53.4
44009	Washington County........	93.9	0.9	1.7	0.0	14.8	59.7	25.5	27.1	28.3	72.9
45000	**South Carolina**...........	68.1	26.1	3.5	1.1	18.9	57.0	24.2	31.7	27.3	68.6
45003	Aiken County...............	72.4	22.6	3.2	0.8	16.4	57.1	26.6	30.1	29.3	74.0
45007	Anderson County...........	80.2	16.1	2.3	0.6	16.6	57.1	26.3	32.8	29.3	72.8
45013	Beaufort County............	73.9	17.7	6.2	0.0	17.3	47.0	35.7	27.1	38.9	71.2
45015	Berkeley County............	67.9	23.3	4.6	2.2	22.9	58.8	18.3	35.9	22.7	69.3
45019	Charleston County..........	67.8	26.1	3.9	1.2	24.4	53.9	21.7	26.2	24.4	60.7
45021	Cherokee County...........	75.7	21.2	0.0	0.0	17.6	56.5	25.9	33.9	27.5	67.0
45031	Darlington County..........	58.0	39.3	0.0	0.0	15.3	58.0	26.7	32.4	29.4	66.8
45035	Dorchester County..........	68.9	24.1	3.3	1.1	19.1	63.2	17.7	38.9	20.8	69.0
45041	Florence County............	58.2	38.3	1.7	0.0	18.9	56.8	24.4	34.0	27.4	65.9
45043	Georgetown County........	67.8	29.3	0.0	0.0	11.6	51.9	36.4	26.3	39.0	77.5
45045	Greenville County..........	72.8	18.3	6.3	1.8	20.1	57.9	22.0	33.5	25.0	65.6
45047	Greenwood County.........	63.8	29.8	3.1	0.0	19.6	54.5	25.9	31.6	28.6	65.0
45051	Horry County...............	83.0	11.1	3.8	1.0	16.8	54.0	29.2	26.1	32.6	68.4
45055	Kershaw County............	70.6	25.5	2.0	0.0	15.6	59.2	25.2	31.4	28.8	75.6
45057	Lancaster County...........	75.4	21.4	0.0	0.0	15.4	56.8	27.8	32.3	31.4	76.2
45059	Laurens County............	72.3	23.7	0.0	0.0	16.1	58.6	25.4	31.7	28.5	71.5
45063	Lexington County..........	80.1	13.2	4.4	1.2	19.4	60.2	20.4	33.6	24.0	73.7
45073	Oconee County.............	88.6	6.7	3.2	0.0	14.7	53.9	31.4	28.1	34.6	73.8
45075	Orangeburg County.........	37.6	59.1	0.0	0.0	15.4	58.1	26.5	29.5	30.3	68.2
45077	Pickens County.............	89.1	5.7	3.0	1.4	21.3	53.8	24.8	29.0	27.3	69.2
45079	Richland County............	48.1	44.9	3.6	2.1	25.8	56.2	18.0	31.5	20.4	60.5
45083	Spartanburg County........	72.5	21.2	3.9	1.6	18.5	57.9	23.6	34.6	27.2	68.6
45085	Sumter County.............	51.2	43.3	2.6	1.1	21.1	55.8	23.1	34.2	26.2	64.5
45091	York County...............	75.3	18.8	3.4	0.0	19.5	60.4	20.1	37.6	23.2	71.5
46000	**South Dakota**	89.3	1.2	2.0	0.7	22.9	54.1	23.0	30.8	25.0	67.7
46099	Minnehaha County..........	90.2	3.4	2.8	1.0	25.9	55.4	18.8	32.3	20.4	63.6
46103	Pennington County.........	86.5	0.0	3.0	0.6	22.3	55.6	22.1	31.0	24.3	66.1
47000	**Tennessee**	78.5	15.8	3.1	1.2	19.6	57.3	23.1	31.4	26.0	66.7
47001	Anderson County...........	92.1	3.6	2.4	0.0	15.2	56.1	28.7	26.4	30.9	67.7
47009	Blount County..............	93.8	2.4	1.5	0.0	15.2	57.3	27.5	31.4	30.6	72.0
47011	Bradley County.............	90.9	4.1	3.4	0.0	17.8	57.6	24.6	32.3	27.5	65.8
47019	Carter County..............	96.0	1.6	0.0	0.0	16.5	55.5	28.0	28.7	31.8	69.6
47031	Coffee County..............	92.7	2.4	0.0	0.0	18.5	56.0	25.5	30.7	28.6	66.1
47035	Cumberland County	96.9	0.0	0.0	0.0	11.9	48.2	39.9	22.7	44.5	78.4
47037	Davidson County	62.9	26.6	6.6	2.5	27.9	55.2	16.9	26.7	19.3	53.7
47043	Dickson County............	93.5	3.2	0.0	0.0	16.5	59.9	23.6	37.1	26.2	71.9
47059	Greene County.............	95.8	1.5	0.0	0.0	14.0	58.6	27.5	26.9	30.8	72.4
47063	Hamblen County...........	86.5	3.7	7.5	0.0	17.1	54.8	28.1	36.5	30.6	67.4
47065	Hamilton County...........	74.5	19.8	2.8	1.7	19.1	56.9	24.0	30.0	26.7	65.1
47073	Hawkins County	96.5	0.0	0.0	0.0	14.0	59.0	27.0	32.0	30.4	77.1
47089	Jefferson County...........	95.1	0.0	1.8	0.0	15.1	56.1	28.8	28.1	32.5	74.7
47093	Knox County................	85.1	9.8	2.2	1.5	23.7	55.1	21.2	28.2	23.9	63.3
47107	McMinn County............	92.4	4.0	0.0	0.0	16.3	56.0	27.7	29.5	30.8	73.3
47113	Madison County............	61.5	35.0	2.4	0.0	19.1	57.2	23.7	31.3	25.8	65.1
47119	Maury County..............	81.8	12.5	3.7	0.0	19.6	58.6	21.9	30.7	25.1	68.3
47125	Montgomery County	69.3	18.6	7.4	1.8	34.7	51.4	13.8	42.2	16.1	58.9
47141	Putnam County.............	92.0	0.0	3.3	0.0	24.6	51.8	23.6	28.4	26.1	63.0
47145	Roane County..............	92.9	2.7	0.0	0.0	10.4	59.4	30.2	27.2	34.6	75.3
47147	Robertson County..........	86.9	7.8	3.9	0.0	18.1	59.7	22.3	35.0	24.9	75.2
47149	Rutherford County..........	79.1	12.8	4.3	2.3	26.6	57.9	15.4	36.9	17.9	66.8
47155	Sevier County	93.5	0.0	0.0	0.0	16.1	58.7	25.2	31.8	28.8	66.9
47157	Shelby County..............	42.6	50.3	3.8	2.1	21.6	59.9	18.5	33.2	21.5	57.6
47163	Sullivan County............	95.2	2.1	1.1	0.0	14.9	54.0	31.2	28.5	33.5	73.5
47165	Sumner County.............	89.4	6.3	2.2	0.0	17.1	60.6	22.4	38.1	25.8	71.5
47167	Tipton County..............	78.0	18.0	0.0	0.0	15.3	63.8	20.9	40.2	24.0	72.9
47179	Washington County.........	92.5	3.1	1.7	0.0	21.4	53.9	24.7	26.6	27.7	65.8
47187	Williamson County	89.3	4.4	0.0	2.4	12.7	68.4	19.0	41.5	21.3	80.7
47189	Wilson County..............	90.1	5.8	0.0	0.0	15.1	62.7	22.2	35.4	25.1	76.8
48000	**Texas**	52.8	12.3	29.9	3.7	22.8	58.3	18.9	38.0	22.0	62.4
48001	Anderson County...........	75.0	13.3	10.1	0.0	18.1	54.5	27.5	37.0	30.1	70.9
48005	Angelina County...........	70.2	15.2	13.2	0.0	21.4	53.1	25.5	37.1	27.8	65.4
48021	Bastrop County.............	65.9	7.9	24.6	0.0	15.1	63.2	21.7	34.4	25.6	78.3
48027	Bell County.................	55.1	22.5	17.7	2.5	30.2	53.6	16.2	41.9	18.9	55.9
48029	Bexar County...............	36.8	8.1	51.5	2.2	23.9	57.6	18.5	38.1	22.1	58.2
48037	Bowie County..............	71.5	22.5	3.7	0.0	18.7	55.8	25.5	34.8	28.5	65.4
48039	Brazoria County............	59.0	12.4	22.3	5.0	20.3	61.8	17.9	40.8	21.0	73.5
48041	Brazos County..............	64.5	10.5	18.1	5.4	44.3	41.8	13.9	29.8	15.6	45.5

Table A-2: Counties with a Population of 50,000 or More—Living Arrangements—*Continued*

State/ County code	Metropolitan area	Total Households	Family households, percent	Married-couple family households, percent	Male householder, no spouse, percent	Female householder, no spouse, percent	Householder living alone, percent	Nonfamily households, householder not living alone, percent	Opposite-sex partner unmarried partner households, percent	Same-sex unmarried partner households, percent	Average household size
	Texas—cont'd										
48061	Cameron County	119,289	79.3	52.5	5.8	20.9	18.4	2.4	4.2	0.2	3.5
48073	Cherokee County	17,571	73.9	53.5	5.1	15.4	22.4	3.7	2.7	0.4	2.8
48085	Collin County	296,595	73.9	59.8	3.6	10.5	21.1	5.0	4.1	0.5	2.8
48091	Comal County	42,579	74.2	60.4	3.3	10.5	21.6	4.2	3.5	0.7	2.7
48099	Coryell County	20,735	77.4	58.8	3.8	14.8	19.8	2.8	3.4	0.7	3.1
48113	Dallas County	865,833	65.4	43.3	6.0	16.0	28.7	6.0	5.3	0.8	2.8
48121	Denton County	248,495	70.9	55.5	4.3	11.2	22.0	7.1	4.7	0.7	2.8
48135	Ector County	50,488	71.0	47.7	6.7	16.6	23.2	5.8	6.8	0.6	2.8
48139	Ellis County	51,887	79.2	62.2	4.5	12.4	17.2	3.6	4.9	0.2	2.9
48141	El Paso County	258,972	75.1	49.9	5.3	20.0	21.4	3.5	3.5	0.3	3.1
48157	Fort Bend County	196,617	82.7	66.1	4.2	12.4	14.9	2.4	2.9	0.2	3.2
48167	Galveston County	110,891	68.2	51.5	4.0	12.7	26.1	5.6	5.5	0.5	2.7
48181	Grayson County	46,757	67.8	48.9	5.1	13.7	26.9	5.3	5.7	0.6	2.6
48183	Gregg County	45,471	67.2	46.7	4.9	15.7	29.5	3.3	3.8	0.5	2.6
48187	Guadalupe County	47,754	73.7	57.7	3.6	12.4	22.5	3.8	4.1	0.2	2.9
48199	Hardin County	20,958	72.9	57.5	4.2	11.1	23.2	3.9	2.9	0.1	2.6
48201	Harris County	1,452,316	68.2	46.7	6.0	15.6	26.2	5.6	5.3	0.5	2.9
48203	Harrison County	23,810	72.9	54.0	4.6	14.3	24.3	2.9	3.1	0.1	2.8
48209	Hays County	58,385	64.5	49.6	5.2	9.6	23.1	12.4	5.6	0.5	2.8
48213	Henderson County	29,253	68.3	53.1	4.0	11.2	26.5	5.2	3.6	0.2	2.7
48215	Hidalgo County	221,305	81.4	57.4	4.6	19.4	15.9	2.8	2.9	0.3	3.6
48221	Hood County	20,677	69.9	59.7	2.4	7.7	25.6	4.6	3.9	0.7	2.5
48231	Hunt County	30,387	68.4	53.7	4.1	10.5	27.3	4.3	3.8	0.3	2.8
48245	Jefferson County	92,524	63.2	40.3	5.5	17.4	32.7	4.1	3.9	0.3	2.6
48251	Johnson County	52,616	75.2	59.2	6.4	9.6	20.4	4.5	5.8	0.4	2.9
48257	Kaufman County	34,903	78.5	59.3	5.6	13.6	17.9	3.6	5.6	0.5	3.0
48291	Liberty County	24,793	73.6	54.6	5.9	13.0	21.5	4.9	4.7	0.3	2.8
48303	Lubbock County	105,595	62.8	44.4	4.9	13.5	27.8	9.4	5.2	0.4	2.6
48309	McLennan County	85,722	66.6	47.2	4.7	14.7	26.6	6.8	5.3	0.3	2.7
48323	Maverick County	15,932	81.8	56.9	4.0	20.9	17.3	1.0	3.2	0.0	3.4
48329	Midland County	51,528	70.2	52.3	6.0	11.9	24.3	5.5	6.6	0.2	2.8
48339	Montgomery County	166,348	74.4	57.8	4.9	11.7	21.6	4.0	4.8	0.2	2.9
48347	Nacogdoches County	23,437	62.9	43.0	5.2	14.7	31.8	5.3	2.9	0.2	2.6
48355	Nueces County	124,267	68.8	44.7	6.8	17.3	24.6	6.5	6.7	0.3	2.7
48361	Orange County	31,058	71.1	53.0	5.8	12.4	24.9	4.0	5.1	0.2	2.6
48367	Parker County	42,460	75.1	61.0	5.7	8.5	22.0	2.9	3.1	0.0	2.7
48375	Potter County	43,030	64.2	42.0	5.4	16.8	30.4	5.5	6.6	0.3	2.7
48381	Randall County	48,539	68.1	53.2	4.3	10.6	24.7	7.2	4.8	0.3	2.5
48397	Rockwall County	27,460	81.9	67.0	4.2	10.7	15.5	2.6	3.8	0.7	3.0
48401	Rusk County	17,357	68.4	50.0	5.3	13.1	27.8	3.8	4.7	0.2	2.8
48409	San Patricio County	22,401	76.5	52.5	6.7	17.3	19.9	3.6	6.5	0.1	2.9
48423	Smith County	79,115	67.9	49.8	5.1	13.0	26.7	5.4	3.4	0.3	2.7
48427	Starr County	16,062	83.0	53.0	5.3	24.7	15.1	1.9	3.9	0.1	3.8
48439	Tarrant County	663,292	69.0	49.4	5.3	14.4	25.7	5.3	5.5	0.5	2.8
48441	Taylor County	49,155	63.6	47.1	4.4	12.1	29.3	7.1	5.0	0.6	2.6
48451	Tom Green County	42,425	64.6	46.2	4.3	14.1	30.0	5.4	5.6	0.2	2.5
48453	Travis County	417,352	57.1	40.9	4.6	11.6	30.8	12.1	6.6	0.9	2.6
48467	Van Zandt County	18,571	71.0	56.6	3.3	11.1	25.2	3.9	3.7	0.0	2.8
48469	Victoria County	32,192	71.0	49.6	5.1	16.2	24.4	4.6	5.7	0.5	2.7
48471	Walker County	20,450	59.8	42.4	3.3	14.1	31.4	8.8	4.2	0.2	2.3
48479	Webb County	68,033	82.5	53.9	5.9	22.6	14.8	2.7	5.0	0.1	3.8
48485	Wichita County	47,934	65.9	47.0	4.6	14.3	29.8	4.3	6.0	0.3	2.5
48491	Williamson County	157,178	72.8	58.7	4.0	10.2	22.5	4.7	4.3	0.5	2.9
48497	Wise County	20,460	78.0	65.1	3.1	9.9	18.5	3.5	2.6	0.2	2.9
49000	**Utah**	891,240	74.8	60.7	4.3	9.9	19.7	5.5	3.7	0.4	3.2
49003	Box Elder County	16,151	80.5	67.7	4.6	8.3	17.6	1.9	2.4	0.3	3.1
49005	Cache County	35,294	74.3	63.7	2.5	8.0	18.0	7.7	2.5	0.3	3.2
49011	Davis County	96,158	80.9	68.0	3.8	9.1	15.6	3.4	2.2	0.4	3.3
49035	Salt Lake County	346,992	70.3	54.4	5.0	10.9	23.1	6.6	4.8	0.7	3.0
49045	Tooele County	18,245	79.8	64.3	5.2	10.4	16.6	3.6	3.7	0.4	3.3
49049	Utah County	144,795	81.9	70.4	3.3	8.2	12.5	5.5	1.8	0.2	3.6
49053	Washington County	47,346	75.6	62.9	2.8	9.9	19.7	4.7	2.4	0.2	3.0
49057	Weber County	79,490	73.5	56.8	5.1	11.7	21.4	5.1	5.5	0.4	2.9
50000	**Vermont**	256,563	62.3	49.2	4.0	9.1	28.3	9.3	7.6	0.9	2.3
50007	Chittenden County	62,683	59.4	47.5	3.6	8.3	27.0	13.6	7.3	1.1	2.4
50021	Rutland County	25,651	62.0	48.5	4.4	9.2	29.4	8.5	7.6	0.7	2.3
50023	Washington County	24,788	60.7	47.4	3.8	9.6	30.1	9.2	8.4	0.6	2.3
50027	Windsor County	24,785	62.3	50.0	3.6	8.7	29.7	8.0	7.0	0.9	2.2
51000	**Virginia**	3,026,761	67.2	50.5	4.3	12.4	26.5	6.3	4.8	0.4	2.6
51003	Albemarle County	38,250	63.9	53.5	2.3	8.2	29.8	6.2	3.9	0.5	2.5
51013	Arlington County	95,138	46.6	37.1	3.6	5.9	40.4	13.1	4.7	1.1	2.3
51015	Augusta County	28,017	73.9	59.1	5.3	9.6	22.8	3.3	4.7	0.2	2.5

Table A-2: Counties with a Population of 50,000 or More—Living Arrangements—*Continued*

State/County code	Metropolitan area	Race or Hispanic origin of householder				Age of householder			Percent of households with one or more persons under 18 years old	Percent of households with one or more persons age 65 or older	Percent of all householders who are owners
		Householder is White alone, not Hispanic or Latino, percent	Householder is Black or African American alone, percent	Householder is Hispanic or Latino, percent	Householder is Asian alone, percent	Householders age 15 to 34, percent	Householders age 35 to 64, percent	Householders age 65 and older, percent			
	Texas—cont'd										
48061	Cameron County	16.1	0.6	82.2	0.8	18.2	58.4	23.3	48.0	28.0	66.2
48073	Cherokee County	69.8	14.2	13.3	0.0	18.2	54.6	27.2	34.9	30.6	71.2
48085	Collin County	67.4	8.9	11.0	10.6	21.1	65.2	13.7	42.6	16.7	66.2
48091	Comal County	77.0	0.0	19.3	0.0	14.4	59.3	26.3	32.9	30.2	76.2
48099	Coryell County	71.3	12.2	12.5	1.9	27.9	54.6	17.5	44.9	20.1	57.2
48113	Dallas County	41.3	23.9	28.1	5.1	25.8	58.4	15.8	37.4	18.6	51.5
48121	Denton County	69.1	9.3	13.5	5.8	24.9	62.8	12.4	40.7	15.2	64.3
48135	Ector County	46.5	3.5	47.7	0.0	27.1	54.3	18.6	41.3	20.8	65.9
48139	Ellis County	72.2	8.7	17.4	0.0	18.5	62.1	19.3	43.0	22.6	73.1
48141	El Paso County	18.3	3.7	76.0	1.1	22.0	58.2	19.8	44.1	24.0	60.9
48157	Fort Bend County	42.5	20.8	19.5	16.0	16.4	69.6	14.0	47.7	18.6	78.4
48167	Galveston County	64.1	13.5	17.8	3.2	19.0	61.6	19.4	35.4	23.0	67.5
48181	Grayson County	83.2	5.7	7.7	0.8	17.8	56.6	25.6	32.7	29.1	66.2
48183	Gregg County	66.8	19.9	10.9	0.0	23.8	52.5	23.7	34.6	25.9	61.0
48187	Guadalupe County	62.5	6.6	27.8	0.0	17.1	60.0	22.9	38.7	26.5	77.0
48199	Hardin County	88.9	6.0	0.0	0.0	18.3	57.6	24.1	34.0	27.5	78.9
48201	Harris County	40.3	20.3	32.1	6.0	24.6	60.5	14.8	38.9	18.1	55.2
48203	Harrison County	68.4	23.0	7.9	0.0	17.0	58.3	24.7	36.4	28.1	73.6
48209	Hays County	65.5	3.0	28.3	0.0	29.3	55.7	15.0	35.5	18.5	65.2
48213	Henderson County	84.3	6.5	7.6	0.0	15.1	52.2	32.7	28.8	35.7	73.7
48215	Hidalgo County	12.0	0.0	86.2	1.1	21.3	59.1	19.5	52.1	23.9	67.6
48221	Hood County	89.8	0.0	7.4	0.0	15.0	50.0	35.0	27.9	37.4	77.5
48231	Hunt County	80.9	8.4	9.2	0.0	18.6	55.7	25.7	32.2	28.4	69.9
48245	Jefferson County	49.3	33.1	12.9	3.2	21.4	54.9	23.7	32.5	26.3	64.5
48251	Johnson County	81.6	2.4	13.8	0.0	19.0	59.4	21.5	40.5	24.9	73.0
48257	Kaufman County	74.2	11.1	12.3	0.0	19.2	61.8	19.0	44.8	22.8	77.7
48291	Liberty County	76.7	8.6	13.0	0.0	18.7	58.4	22.9	38.2	26.7	76.3
48303	Lubbock County	64.2	6.2	26.2	1.8	31.8	48.7	19.5	32.5	21.8	57.7
48309	McLennan County	64.5	15.4	17.7	1.3	26.1	52.2	21.7	34.0	24.7	59.1
48323	Maverick County	3.7	0.0	95.0	0.0	20.4	58.7	20.9	50.6	26.1	72.2
48329	Midland County	60.8	6.9	30.2	1.3	26.6	55.9	17.5	37.4	20.7	66.1
48339	Montgomery County	77.1	4.3	15.1	2.2	18.1	61.9	20.1	38.3	23.0	71.6
48347	Nacogdoches County	70.1	16.4	10.9	0.0	28.5	49.3	22.2	32.2	24.5	56.9
48355	Nueces County	39.5	4.3	53.9	1.5	22.6	55.9	21.5	35.8	25.0	57.2
48361	Orange County	83.4	9.4	4.7	0.0	18.5	57.7	23.8	32.6	26.2	76.1
48367	Parker County	89.3	0.0	7.5	0.0	13.9	62.8	23.2	34.7	26.3	78.6
48375	Potter County	58.0	8.8	28.5	3.2	26.2	54.0	19.8	36.5	22.2	58.3
48381	Randall County	81.5	2.1	13.4	1.7	24.7	54.3	21.0	33.3	23.3	68.7
48397	Rockwall County	80.3	5.5	11.7	0.0	14.0	67.5	18.5	45.3	20.7	82.6
48401	Rusk County	71.7	17.2	8.9	0.0	14.8	58.4	26.8	32.7	30.2	75.6
48409	San Patricio County	49.4	1.8	47.5	0.0	19.4	56.6	24.0	41.3	27.0	68.4
48423	Smith County	68.9	17.7	11.1	1.0	20.9	54.0	25.1	34.3	27.9	66.0
48427	Starr County	1.8	0.0	98.2	0.0	17.3	61.4	21.3	55.3	27.9	76.1
48439	Tarrant County	58.9	15.6	20.1	3.8	23.5	60.0	16.5	39.0	19.2	60.8
48441	Taylor County	72.3	6.3	18.5	1.6	26.9	50.2	22.9	30.5	25.3	60.1
48451	Tom Green County	64.7	4.3	29.7	0.0	24.9	51.0	24.1	30.9	26.2	61.5
48453	Travis County	59.5	8.2	24.9	5.3	31.5	56.2	12.4	30.9	14.6	51.3
48467	Van Zandt County	88.6	1.9	6.5	0.0	14.3	54.1	31.6	32.4	34.5	79.5
48469	Victoria County	55.7	6.5	35.7	0.0	22.0	55.2	22.8	36.3	26.1	64.9
48471	Walker County	71.1	18.3	8.0	0.0	32.5	44.6	22.9	30.0	25.2	57.4
48479	Webb County	5.1	0.0	93.7	0.0	22.0	62.1	16.0	54.2	21.6	63.2
48485	Wichita County	75.4	9.4	12.3	1.4	25.2	51.3	23.5	33.6	25.9	61.7
48491	Williamson County	70.8	6.0	17.0	4.4	20.4	63.4	16.2	41.3	18.9	68.2
48497	Wise County	84.8	0.0	12.1	0.0	15.9	61.9	22.2	37.7	26.3	80.0
49000	**Utah**	84.5	1.0	10.0	2.0	26.6	54.8	18.5	42.4	20.9	69.5
49003	Box Elder County	91.5	0.0	5.5	0.0	21.9	55.0	23.2	42.0	24.9	78.5
49005	Cache County	89.6	0.0	6.8	1.4	35.0	48.6	16.3	40.2	17.8	65.6
49011	Davis County	88.2	1.2	7.0	2.0	25.3	57.7	17.0	47.6	19.0	77.6
49035	Salt Lake County	79.6	1.5	12.8	3.4	25.8	57.0	17.2	39.4	19.7	66.1
49045	Tooele County	86.2	0.0	9.6	0.0	23.4	61.6	14.9	49.7	17.1	75.3
49049	Utah County	86.9	0.5	9.2	1.3	34.4	50.7	14.9	51.5	17.0	66.5
49053	Washington County	90.5	0.0	6.5	0.0	19.7	47.2	33.1	34.7	36.0	69.8
49057	Weber County	83.0	1.3	12.6	1.2	26.3	53.9	19.8	40.5	22.3	71.0
50000	**Vermont**	95.9	0.7	1.1	0.8	17.0	58.9	24.1	27.1	27.2	71.2
50007	Chittenden County	93.5	1.8	1.4	2.0	24.1	55.9	20.0	27.5	22.1	64.9
50021	Rutland County	97.5	0.0	0.7	0.0	13.9	59.5	26.5	25.7	29.8	69.7
50023	Washington County	95.7	0.0	1.2	0.0	14.6	61.4	24.0	26.9	26.7	72.3
50027	Windsor County	96.6	0.0	0.0	0.0	15.3	57.5	27.3	23.6	30.4	69.7
51000	**Virginia**	69.5	18.6	5.8	4.6	19.5	59.0	21.5	32.9	24.7	66.3
51003	Albemarle County	83.7	8.5	3.3	2.5	19.4	54.9	25.7	29.4	28.2	67.1
51013	Arlington County	70.0	8.5	11.0	8.5	34.8	52.2	13.0	21.1	15.1	44.3
51015	Augusta County	95.5	2.4	0.0	0.0	13.0	57.5	29.6	30.7	32.7	81.2

State/ County code	Metropolitan area	Total Households	Family households, percent	Married-couple family households, percent	Male householder, no spouse, percent	Female householder, no spouse, percent	Householder living alone, percent	Nonfamily households, householder not living alone, percent	Opposite-sex partner unmarried partner households, percent	Same-sex unmarried partner households, percent	Average household size
	Virginia—cont'd										
51019	Bedford County	27,405	72.8	61.0	4.0	7.8	23.3	3.9	3.4	0.6	2.5
51031	Campbell County	21,736	70.7	53.7	4.3	12.6	24.8	4.6	6.1	0.0	2.5
51041	Chesterfield County	113,792	71.1	55.0	4.1	11.9	24.6	4.3	4.8	0.3	2.8
51059	Fairfax County	390,705	71.1	57.6	4.0	9.4	22.7	6.2	3.5	0.5	2.8
51061	Fauquier County	22,920	73.7	62.7	3.4	7.6	20.8	5.5	4.5	0.3	2.9
51067	Franklin County	22,854	72.6	59.5	3.2	9.9	23.5	3.9	4.7	1.1	2.4
51069	Frederick County	29,076	73.4	61.1	3.8	8.5	20.0	6.6	6.7	0.4	2.7
51085	Hanover County	36,707	74.9	60.5	4.0	10.4	20.8	4.3	3.1	0.3	2.7
51087	Henrico County	123,440	63.4	44.7	3.6	15.0	29.7	6.9	5.6	0.5	2.5
51089	Henry County	22,813	67.7	48.6	4.8	14.3	29.7	2.6	4.0	0.0	2.3
51095	James City County	27,291	71.1	57.0	2.7	11.3	24.2	4.7	2.5	0.3	2.5
51107	Loudoun County	109,291	77.5	65.4	3.5	8.6	17.5	5.1	4.3	0.3	3.1
51121	Montgomery County	34,623	55.3	44.2	3.6	7.6	26.2	18.5	6.1	0.5	2.5
51143	Pittsylvania County	25,992	68.4	51.7	4.1	12.7	27.4	4.1	4.5	0.4	2.4
51153	Prince William County	134,783	77.8	60.2	5.7	12.0	17.5	4.7	5.2	0.5	3.2
51161	Roanoke County	38,047	67.2	53.4	4.1	9.7	28.4	4.3	3.9	0.1	2.4
51165	Rockingham County	28,754	72.1	58.5	3.6	10.1	22.6	5.3	4.2	0.9	2.6
51177	Spotsylvania County	42,414	80.0	62.9	4.4	12.7	16.0	4.0	4.7	0.3	3.0
51179	Stafford County	42,736	81.8	66.2	4.1	11.5	15.1	3.1	4.4	0.2	3.1
51191	Washington County	22,589	66.6	52.0	4.8	9.8	29.0	4.4	4.7	0.3	2.4
51199	York County	23,743	78.6	64.8	2.8	11.1	17.8	3.5	2.2	0.2	2.8
51510	Alexandria city	65,294	47.8	36.4	3.8	7.6	42.4	9.9	5.5	1.4	2.2
51550	Chesapeake city	79,431	74.6	54.7	5.0	14.9	21.2	4.2	4.1	0.3	2.8
51650	Hampton city	52,274	62.2	40.0	3.8	18.4	31.5	6.3	4.1	0.4	2.5
51660	Harrisonburg city	15,872	51.3	34.0	6.9	10.4	28.1	20.6	5.1	0.1	2.8
51680	Lynchburg city	28,904	55.6	37.3	3.2	15.1	36.4	8.0	3.5	0.3	2.3
51700	Newport News city	68,120	63.0	38.3	5.9	18.7	30.9	6.1	6.0	0.2	2.5
51710	Norfolk city	86,075	58.2	34.4	5.3	18.5	31.6	10.2	5.7	0.6	2.6
51740	Portsmouth city	36,360	64.4	35.3	6.0	23.1	30.6	5.0	5.0	0.4	2.6
51760	Richmond city	85,303	47.5	23.7	4.9	18.9	40.6	11.9	6.2	1.0	2.3
51770	Roanoke city	41,993	56.1	34.0	4.7	17.4	36.7	7.3	6.1	0.5	2.3
51800	Suffolk city	30,573	73.0	52.4	3.6	16.9	22.7	4.3	4.5	0.5	2.8
51810	Virginia Beach city	164,444	68.6	50.0	3.9	14.7	24.2	7.2	5.6	0.3	2.6
53000	**Washington**	2,634,496	64.3	49.4	4.5	10.4	27.8	7.9	6.5	0.6	2.6
53005	Benton County	66,543	68.7	53.0	4.9	10.8	26.5	4.8	6.4	0.3	2.7
53007	Chelan County	27,196	68.6	54.2	4.2	10.2	25.5	5.9	3.9	0.9	2.7
53009	Clallam County	30,781	60.7	49.4	3.4	7.9	31.0	8.4	6.4	0.5	2.3
53011	Clark County	159,508	69.1	52.5	4.7	11.9	24.0	6.9	6.6	0.6	2.7
53015	Cowlitz County	39,261	66.4	50.3	4.8	11.3	27.0	6.5	8.7	0.3	2.6
53021	Franklin County	24,115	76.6	53.3	7.2	16.1	18.0	5.4	8.5	0.3	3.4
53025	Grant County	30,264	73.3	54.6	5.6	13.0	22.9	3.8	7.5	0.1	3.0
53027	Grays Harbor County	26,915	64.5	46.2	7.8	10.5	29.1	6.3	6.4	0.3	2.6
53029	Island County	32,988	68.8	57.8	2.8	8.3	26.0	5.2	5.0	0.5	2.3
53033	King County	806,762	59.0	46.0	3.9	9.1	31.2	9.7	6.2	1.0	2.4
53035	Kitsap County	98,127	66.6	52.2	4.5	9.9	26.2	7.2	6.7	0.5	2.5
53041	Lewis County	29,461	67.1	50.9	5.8	10.3	27.2	5.8	5.9	0.1	2.5
53045	Mason County	23,395	64.9	51.6	5.1	8.1	27.0	8.1	8.5	0.9	2.5
53053	Pierce County	300,286	66.9	49.6	5.1	12.2	26.3	6.8	6.6	0.5	2.7
53057	Skagit County	45,174	68.6	51.9	4.5	12.3	24.5	6.8	7.0	0.5	2.6
53061	Snohomish County	269,391	67.6	51.9	5.1	10.6	24.9	7.4	6.5	0.6	2.7
53063	Spokane County	187,450	62.6	47.4	4.3	10.8	29.2	8.2	6.6	0.7	2.5
53067	Thurston County	101,098	66.6	50.9	4.7	11.0	26.2	7.2	6.3	0.7	2.5
53071	Walla Walla County	21,413	63.1	49.6	3.7	9.8	31.4	5.5	4.4	0.2	2.5
53073	Whatcom County	78,857	61.8	48.7	2.8	10.3	27.2	11.0	5.7	0.4	2.5
53077	Yakima County	79,266	71.6	51.4	6.2	14.0	22.9	5.5	8.4	0.3	3.1
54000	**West Virginia**	739,759	64.8	48.6	4.7	11.5	30.3	5.0	5.4	0.3	2.4
54003	Berkeley County	40,634	71.1	51.9	6.0	13.2	24.3	4.6	6.7	0.2	2.6
54011	Cabell County	39,626	59.1	41.0	4.6	13.5	33.7	7.2	6.2	0.3	2.4
54033	Harrison County	27,605	65.3	49.5	3.8	12.0	30.8	3.8	4.8	0.4	2.5
54037	Jefferson County	20,053	71.7	55.1	5.5	11.1	21.1	7.2	6.8	0.6	2.7
54039	Kanawha County	82,593	61.3	43.4	4.9	13.0	33.3	5.4	5.7	0.6	2.3
54049	Marion County	22,248	64.4	48.0	4.8	11.7	30.0	5.5	6.0	0.0	2.5
54055	Mercer County	25,946	66.0	49.6	4.4	12.0	29.4	4.6	4.5	0.0	2.4
54061	Monongalia County	36,605	52.4	41.1	3.2	8.1	36.5	11.1	7.2	0.5	2.6
54079	Putnam County	21,582	74.0	58.5	4.2	11.3	21.0	4.9	4.8	0.2	2.6
54081	Raleigh County	31,372	66.1	49.6	4.5	12.0	28.7	5.2	4.5	0.3	2.4
54107	Wood County	35,624	64.1	48.1	4.5	11.5	31.1	4.8	5.8	0.5	2.4
55000	**Wisconsin**	2,281,781	63.9	49.4	4.4	10.1	29.1	7.0	6.3	0.4	2.4
55009	Brown County	99,183	65.2	50.4	4.6	10.2	28.1	6.7	6.9	0.4	2.5
55017	Chippewa County	24,649	67.0	54.7	4.0	8.3	27.0	6.0	6.2	0.7	2.5
55021	Columbia County	22,265	68.8	54.4	4.9	9.5	25.9	5.3	7.0	0.3	2.5
55025	Dane County	208,414	57.6	45.0	3.9	8.8	31.3	11.1	6.3	0.8	2.4
55027	Dodge County	32,702	66.7	54.4	4.7	7.7	28.9	4.3	5.2	0.2	2.6
55035	Eau Claire County	39,900	59.1	47.4	3.8	7.9	30.6	10.3	7.4	0.2	2.4
55039	Fond du Lac County	41,187	66.9	52.7	5.2	9.0	28.0	5.2	7.4	0.5	2.4

State/County code	Metropolitan area	Race or Hispanic origin of householder				Age of householder			Percent of households with one or more persons under 18 years old	Percent of households with one or more persons age 65 or older	Percent of all householders who are owners
		Householder is White alone, not Hispanic or Latino, percent	Householder is Black or African American alone, percent	Householder is Hispanic or Latino, percent	Householder is Asian alone, percent	Householders age 15 to 34, percent	Householders age 35 to 64, percent	Householders age 65 and older, percent			
	Virginia—cont'd										
51019	Bedford County	92.2	5.0	0.0	0.0	11.0	60.4	28.6	28.8	31.8	84.9
51031	Campbell County	84.2	12.6	0.0	0.0	15.8	59.5	24.7	29.3	27.7	75.1
51041	Chesterfield County	69.6	20.4	5.9	2.5	15.2	65.2	19.6	35.7	23.2	76.5
51059	Fairfax County	61.9	9.2	11.5	15.4	18.3	64.5	17.2	37.1	21.3	67.2
51061	Fauquier County	85.8	7.4	4.2	0.0	11.9	63.9	24.2	33.2	27.8	79.8
51067	Franklin County	89.7	6.9	0.0	0.0	13.2	57.8	29.0	30.2	30.9	77.5
51069	Frederick County	89.3	0.0	5.2	0.0	16.6	60.3	23.0	35.4	25.8	78.9
51085	Hanover County	87.4	9.3	1.4	0.0	11.2	64.4	24.5	34.0	27.6	82.0
51087	Henrico County	60.3	28.7	3.9	5.4	20.0	58.8	21.2	33.0	24.5	63.2
51089	Henry County	74.7	20.9	3.1	0.0	14.9	53.8	31.2	26.7	33.9	74.2
51095	James City County	81.3	12.2	3.6	0.0	13.3	52.8	33.9	27.3	37.2	76.8
51107	Loudoun County	67.2	7.7	9.6	13.6	16.9	71.1	11.9	49.5	15.3	76.6
51121	Montgomery County	87.4	3.7	2.3	4.7	35.9	46.8	17.3	25.4	19.3	53.7
51143	Pittsylvania County	79.0	19.2	0.0	0.0	12.5	57.9	29.6	27.6	32.7	78.8
51153	Prince William County	54.5	21.0	15.2	6.8	20.1	67.6	12.3	47.0	16.6	70.2
51161	Roanoke County	90.9	4.5	1.9	0.0	13.2	58.5	28.3	29.6	31.7	76.1
51165	Rockingham County	94.6	1.1	3.3	0.0	13.7	58.4	27.9	30.1	31.3	78.5
51177	Spotsylvania County	76.0	15.1	5.3	2.1	15.7	64.5	19.8	41.3	22.7	76.5
51179	Stafford County	72.5	15.9	7.6	0.0	16.8	68.7	14.4	45.3	18.0	76.6
51191	Washington County	97.3	0.0	0.0	0.0	14.7	56.2	29.1	27.8	32.2	77.9
51199	York County	75.8	13.3	0.0	4.6	17.1	60.9	22.0	38.0	24.9	73.1
51510	Alexandria city	60.4	20.3	11.1	5.6	29.8	56.3	13.9	22.2	15.7	43.0
51550	Chesapeake city	62.5	29.5	4.1	2.6	18.5	63.2	18.3	39.2	22.0	71.0
51650	Hampton city	45.0	48.6	3.3	1.4	22.3	55.6	22.1	30.2	24.7	59.8
51660	Harrisonburg city	74.2	7.2	14.0	0.0	41.5	42.7	15.8	27.9	17.5	34.7
51680	Lynchburg city	64.9	28.7	0.0	0.0	27.2	48.8	24.0	29.4	26.2	51.2
51700	Newport News city	48.9	40.7	5.6	2.3	26.9	53.8	19.2	32.5	22.0	50.8
51710	Norfolk city	48.5	41.1	5.2	2.8	31.1	51.4	17.5	31.8	20.0	43.2
51740	Portsmouth city	44.0	50.7	3.0	0.0	25.0	51.8	23.2	31.3	26.7	54.9
51760	Richmond city	45.0	46.6	4.2	1.9	31.3	49.9	18.8	24.1	21.1	42.8
51770	Roanoke city	68.6	23.7	4.1	1.4	21.2	55.7	23.1	26.4	25.4	54.8
51800	Suffolk city	54.2	40.3	2.6	0.0	15.9	63.7	20.4	37.3	24.2	71.0
51810	Virginia Beach city	69.5	18.2	5.3	5.2	23.4	57.6	19.0	35.3	22.1	63.2
53000	**Washington**	78.4	3.5	7.7	6.4	20.8	57.8	21.3	31.3	24.1	62.4
53005	Benton County	81.2	0.0	12.9	2.1	19.9	57.9	22.2	35.1	24.5	68.4
53007	Chelan County	80.4	0.0	17.5	0.0	16.8	55.2	28.0	29.2	30.3	64.0
53009	Clallam County	89.0	0.0	3.2	0.0	14.0	48.9	37.1	20.7	40.1	69.5
53011	Clark County	86.1	1.6	5.5	3.8	18.0	60.3	21.7	35.0	24.5	64.3
53015	Cowlitz County	90.1	0.0	4.3	0.9	16.8	55.1	28.1	29.3	31.0	66.1
53021	Franklin County	55.4	0.0	40.1	0.0	27.6	58.1	14.3	48.7	17.7	66.7
53025	Grant County	68.0	0.0	27.7	0.0	21.3	53.9	24.8	39.5	26.1	59.7
53027	Grays Harbor County	87.2	0.0	4.9	1.0	14.7	57.9	27.4	27.1	32.4	69.5
53029	Island County	86.8	1.8	4.4	4.0	18.5	51.5	29.9	26.8	33.9	67.7
53033	King County	70.8	5.9	6.5	12.7	23.4	58.7	18.0	29.4	20.5	56.9
53035	Kitsap County	84.0	2.6	4.8	3.9	19.3	57.7	23.0	30.5	26.1	67.2
53041	Lewis County	90.7	0.0	5.2	0.0	15.4	54.4	30.1	28.3	32.2	66.9
53045	Mason County	88.8	0.0	4.3	0.0	13.9	55.6	30.5	24.9	35.2	75.5
53053	Pierce County	75.6	7.2	6.9	5.2	22.1	58.2	19.6	34.4	22.4	61.1
53057	Skagit County	84.3	0.0	10.8	1.3	16.7	56.5	26.8	30.5	31.0	66.4
53061	Snohomish County	79.8	2.5	6.3	7.9	19.4	62.2	18.4	33.8	21.2	65.7
53063	Spokane County	90.2	1.7	3.2	1.8	22.5	55.3	22.2	29.5	24.9	63.3
53067	Thurston County	83.4	2.7	5.3	4.8	19.4	58.5	22.1	30.1	25.2	65.7
53071	Walla Walla County	84.9	0.0	11.8	0.0	17.7	54.8	27.5	27.8	29.9	63.5
53073	Whatcom County	87.2	0.0	4.7	3.2	22.4	54.3	23.3	29.0	25.9	62.9
53077	Yakima County	59.7	0.7	34.2	0.0	20.4	57.8	21.8	41.2	25.6	61.6
54000	**West Virginia**	94.5	2.8	0.9	0.6	16.6	56.5	26.9	27.4	29.8	72.4
54003	Berkeley County	89.4	6.9	2.3	0.0	18.6	61.9	19.5	35.0	23.6	73.3
54011	Cabell County	91.7	5.2	0.0	0.0	22.8	51.5	25.6	25.7	27.9	61.3
54033	Harrison County	95.9	1.3	1.3	0.0	14.9	57.0	28.1	28.7	30.7	74.0
54037	Jefferson County	87.7	6.9	0.0	0.0	17.1	62.0	20.9	34.8	24.2	75.6
54039	Kanawha County	90.1	3.7	0.0	0.9	18.1	55.3	26.6	25.9	29.1	69.4
54049	Marion County	95.4	3.1	0.0	0.0	16.5	54.7	28.9	25.4	31.9	77.5
54055	Mercer County	92.4	5.3	0.0	0.0	16.8	54.0	29.2	29.5	32.3	72.1
54061	Monongalia County	92.0	3.0	1.2	2.9	35.9	47.6	16.4	23.5	18.6	57.5
54079	Putnam County	97.4	0.0	0.0	0.0	14.5	61.6	23.9	35.2	27.0	85.3
54081	Raleigh County	90.0	6.6	0.0	0.0	17.4	54.9	27.7	29.2	29.9	72.3
54107	Wood County	97.4	0.8	0.0	0.0	16.2	55.6	28.1	27.4	31.0	71.6
55000	**Wisconsin**	87.4	5.4	4.0	1.6	20.0	57.0	23.0	29.7	25.1	67.4
55009	Brown County	89.3	1.6	4.3	2.0	21.7	58.2	20.1	32.9	21.6	66.0
55017	Chippewa County	97.8	0.0	0.0	0.0	17.5	57.2	25.3	30.6	27.5	72.4
55021	Columbia County	97.1	0.0	1.3	0.0	15.9	60.2	23.9	29.8	26.4	75.4
55025	Dane County	86.2	4.4	3.9	4.1	29.0	53.6	17.4	27.8	18.8	58.5
55027	Dodge County	95.9	0.0	2.1	0.0	13.7	61.0	25.3	28.2	27.7	73.9
55035	Eau Claire County	95.8	0.0	0.0	2.0	26.5	51.7	21.9	26.1	23.6	62.9
55039	Fond du Lac County	94.5	0.0	3.2	0.0	17.5	57.7	24.8	30.1	26.9	70.6

State/ County code	Metropolitan area	Household type							Opposite-sex partner unmarried partner households, percent	Same-sex unmarried partner households, percent	Average household size
		Total Households	Family households, percent	Married-couple family households, percent	Male householder, no spouse, percent	Female householder, no spouse, percent	Householder living alone, percent	Nonfamily households, householder not living alone, percent			
	Wisconsin—cont'd										
55043	Grant County	19,421	62.0	51.8	3.8	6.4	26.7	11.2	7.8	0.1	2.4
55055	Jefferson County	32,302	67.4	54.6	4.0	8.8	26.2	6.3	6.5	0.1	2.5
55059	Kenosha County	62,333	67.0	48.1	4.8	14.0	26.3	6.6	4.1	0.4	2.6
55063	La Crosse County	45,972	60.4	47.5	3.4	9.5	29.0	10.5	5.7	0.4	2.4
55071	Manitowoc County	33,658	65.2	53.6	3.5	8.1	29.6	5.3	4.8	0.4	2.4
55073	Marathon County	53,167	67.7	54.4	4.8	8.5	26.4	5.9	6.0	0.4	2.5
55079	Milwaukee County	379,860	57.0	35.0	5.1	16.8	35.0	8.0	7.1	0.5	2.5
55087	Outagamie County	69,726	67.6	54.2	4.5	9.0	26.1	6.2	6.9	0.4	2.5
55089	Ozaukee County	34,153	70.9	60.3	2.8	7.8	25.1	4.0	3.9	0.4	2.5
55097	Portage County	27,761	62.7	50.7	4.6	7.4	27.4	9.9	6.5	0.2	2.4
55101	Racine County	74,258	65.7	49.2	4.7	11.8	28.6	5.7	5.7	0.3	2.6
55105	Rock County	63,605	66.6	48.4	5.2	13.0	26.9	6.5	8.1	0.7	2.5
55109	St. Croix County	32,032	72.7	58.6	4.7	9.4	22.4	4.9	5.9	0.4	2.6
55111	Sauk County	25,021	66.0	53.7	3.3	9.0	27.7	6.2	5.4	0.2	2.5
55117	Sheboygan County	46,450	65.5	52.2	4.3	9.0	28.5	6.0	6.7	0.4	2.4
55127	Walworth County	39,668	65.0	50.7	4.9	9.4	26.4	8.6	5.8	0.2	2.5
55131	Washington County	52,156	71.6	58.8	4.4	8.4	24.0	4.4	5.2	0.1	2.5
55133	Waukesha County	153,853	69.8	60.2	3.1	6.6	25.1	5.0	4.2	0.2	2.5
55135	Waupaca County	21,401	67.2	55.4	3.5	8.3	27.3	5.5	7.2	0.4	2.4
55139	Winnebago County	68,043	60.0	47.8	3.7	8.5	32.0	8.0	6.9	0.3	2.4
55141	Wood County	31,740	64.2	51.2	4.1	8.9	30.3	5.5	5.6	0.3	2.3
56000	**Wyoming**	222,679	65.3	51.9	4.4	9.0	27.5	7.2	6.8	0.2	2.5
56021	Laramie County	36,138	66.6	52.8	3.6	10.2	27.1	6.3	5.9	0.2	2.6
56025	Natrona County	31,587	64.8	48.1	6.7	10.0	27.9	7.4	8.0	0.1	2.4

Table A-2: Counties with a Population of 50,000 or More—Living Arrangements—*Continued*

State/ County code	Metropolitan area	Race or Hispanic origin of householder				Age of householder			Percent of households with one or more persons under 18 years old	Percent of households with one or more persons age 65 or older	Percent of all householders who are owners
		Householder is White alone, not Hispanic or Latino, percent	Householder is Black or African American alone, percent	Householder is Hispanic or Latino, percent	Householder is Asian alone, percent	Householders age 15 to 34, percent	Householders age 35 to 64, percent	Householders age 65 and older, percent			
	Wisconsin—cont'd										
55043	Grant County...............	97.4	0.0	1.1	0.0	22.7	51.7	25.6	27.5	27.2	70.4
55055	Jefferson County...........	93.7	0.0	4.5	0.0	17.9	59.2	22.9	32.3	25.4	71.8
55059	Kenosha County	83.2	6.1	8.6	0.0	18.8	61.3	19.9	35.7	22.4	65.9
55063	La Crosse County...........	95.1	0.0	1.1	2.4	24.8	52.8	22.4	27.2	23.9	65.1
55071	Manitowoc County	95.6	0.0	1.7	0.0	15.9	58.6	25.5	27.3	27.8	75.8
55073	Marathon County	94.5	0.0	1.3	0.0	18.8	57.5	23.7	30.5	25.7	72.8
55079	Milwaukee County..........	62.0	24.2	9.6	2.5	25.8	54.6	19.6	30.7	21.7	50.0
55087	Outagamie County	92.4	0.5	2.6	2.0	20.3	59.3	20.3	32.8	22.1	71.3
55089	Ozaukee County.............	95.4	0.0	1.6	0.0	12.2	61.3	26.5	30.8	28.8	77.3
55097	Portage County..............	95.6	0.0	1.5	0.0	23.5	53.8	22.7	26.8	24.3	68.3
55101	Racine County	80.2	9.9	8.1	0.8	16.9	60.2	22.9	31.7	25.6	69.1
55105	Rock County.................	89.1	3.2	4.9	0.8	19.0	58.0	23.0	32.6	25.8	69.1
55109	St. Croix County............	96.6	0.0	0.0	0.0	18.8	62.8	18.4	38.0	20.1	76.8
55111	Sauk County.................	94.5	0.0	3.1	0.0	19.6	55.3	25.2	29.8	27.8	69.8
55117	Sheboygan County	91.8	0.0	3.8	2.9	18.0	57.7	24.3	28.2	26.4	70.8
55127	Walworth County	91.6	0.0	6.4	0.0	18.7	57.8	23.5	30.6	26.3	68.6
55131	Washington County.........	96.5	0.0	0.0	0.0	15.0	61.3	23.7	32.3	25.3	77.4
55133	Waukesha County	93.0	1.2	3.0	2.0	14.1	61.4	24.5	30.4	27.0	76.0
55135	Waupaca County	96.9	0.0	0.0	0.0	15.4	57.8	26.8	29.3	29.2	75.9
55139	Winnebago County	95.0	0.9	2.0	1.5	22.2	55.3	22.5	27.1	23.9	65.6
55141	Wood County................	95.8	0.0	1.6	0.0	16.7	56.5	26.7	26.3	28.4	74.7
56000	**Wyoming ....**	89.1	0.8	6.8	0.7	23.1	55.8	21.1	30.7	23.4	69.6
56021	Laramie County	84.3	2.6	10.8	0.0	22.8	55.9	21.2	31.7	23.5	68.8
56025	Natrona County.............	91.7	0.0	5.3	0.0	25.4	54.7	19.9	32.2	21.5	68.0

Table A-3: Metropolitan Areas—Living Arrangements

CBSA FIPS code	Metropolitan area	Total Households	Family households, percent	Married-couple family households, percent	Male householder, no spouse, percent	Female householder, no spouse, percent	Householder living alone, percent	Nonfamily households, householder not living alone, percent	Opposite-sex partner unmarried partner households, percent	Same-sex unmarried partner households, percent	Average household size
10180	Abilene, TX	60,036	64.1	48.2	3.9	12.0	29.6	6.3	4.7	0.6	2.55
10420	Akron, OH	279,537	63.1	46.2	3.9	13.0	30.4	6.5	5.4	0.4	2.47
10500	Albany, GA	57,949	66.8	40.2	5.7	20.9	29.0	4.2	5.6	0.3	2.61
10540	Albany, OR	44,458	69.0	52.7	4.3	12.0	24.2	6.7	6.2	0.4	2.64
10580	Albany-Schenectady-Troy, NY	345,455	60.6	45.8	3.8	11.0	31.5	7.9	7.2	0.5	2.44
10740	Albuquerque, NM	342,433	63.9	44.0	6.0	13.9	29.5	6.6	6.6	0.8	2.59
10780	Alexandria, LA	54,891	65.5	44.5	4.8	16.2	30.3	4.2	4.7	0.4	2.68
10900	Allentown-Bethlehem-Easton, PA-NJ	313,335	68.1	51.6	4.4	12.0	26.1	5.9	6.3	0.5	2.56
11020	Altoona, PA	50,649	65.2	49.1	4.6	11.4	30.2	4.6	6.5	0.3	2.44
11100	Amarillo, TX	95,116	66.5	48.4	4.7	13.3	27.3	6.2	5.6	0.3	2.60
11180	Ames, IA	35,461	53.2	45.6	2.5	5.1	27.8	19.0	7.2	0.4	2.34
11260	Anchorage, AK	136,348	67.2	50.3	5.7	11.3	25.2	7.5	7.3	0.4	2.80
11460	Ann Arbor, MI	136,930	57.3	44.2	3.2	10.0	31.2	11.4	5.3	0.9	2.44
11500	Anniston-Oxford-Jacksonville, AL	44,756	66.5	46.3	4.6	15.6	28.7	4.8	2.9	0.3	2.56
11540	Appleton, WI	88,039	69.3	56.3	4.6	8.4	24.9	5.9	6.6	0.4	2.56
11700	Asheville, NC	180,105	62.6	48.4	3.8	10.5	30.6	6.8	5.2	1.0	2.35
12020	Athens-Clarke County, GA	68,604	59.1	42.7	3.9	12.4	29.2	11.7	4.4	0.4	2.70
12060	Atlanta-Sandy Springs-Roswell, GA	1,928,087	67.7	47.9	4.8	15.0	26.6	5.7	4.3	0.7	2.78
12100	Atlantic City-Hammonton, NJ	101,243	67.3	44.9	5.4	17.0	27.5	5.1	5.6	0.5	2.65
12220	Auburn-Opelika, AL	56,312	62.1	45.2	3.5	13.4	27.5	10.4	3.8	0.3	2.53
12260	Augusta-Richmond County, GA-SC	207,407	67.8	46.1	4.8	16.9	28.2	4.0	4.1	0.3	2.70
12420	Austin-Round Rock, TX	670,176	62.2	46.6	4.5	11.1	27.8	10.0	5.9	0.8	2.68
12540	Bakersfield, CA	256,319	75.3	50.7	8.0	16.7	19.7	5.0	7.8	0.4	3.22
12580	Baltimore-Columbia-Towson, MD	1,030,802	64.7	45.2	4.6	14.9	28.9	6.4	5.2	0.5	2.60
12620	Bangor, ME	62,468	61.5	47.9	4.3	9.3	27.7	10.8	8.3	0.6	2.35
12700	Barnstable Town, MA	93,184	62.3	49.6	3.2	9.5	32.3	5.3	4.3	1.1	2.28
12940	Baton Rouge, LA	298,592	66.2	44.3	5.4	16.5	27.6	6.1	4.7	0.3	2.65
12980	Battle Creek, MI	52,729	64.7	44.8	4.9	15.1	29.8	5.4	6.7	0.5	2.49
13020	Bay City, MI	43,937	65.1	49.1	4.5	11.5	29.6	5.3	5.9	0.4	2.40
13140	Beaumont-Port Arthur, TX	149,409	66.2	45.6	5.4	15.3	29.7	4.1	4.0	0.3	2.59
13220	Beckley, WV	48,458	66.6	49.1	4.5	13.1	28.3	5.0	4.8	0.3	2.46
13380	Bellingham, WA	78,857	61.8	48.7	2.8	10.3	27.2	11.0	5.7	0.4	2.53
13460	Bend-Redmond, OR	65,031	65.4	52.0	4.3	9.1	26.2	8.3	6.6	0.5	2.48
13740	Billings, MT	65,272	63.8	47.5	4.9	11.3	29.8	6.4	6.2	0.2	2.44
13780	Binghamton, NY	99,227	62.3	46.8	4.7	10.8	30.9	6.8	6.7	0.4	2.40
13820	Birmingham-Hoover, AL	434,226	67.3	48.3	3.7	15.2	28.8	4.0	3.0	0.3	2.56
13900	Bismarck, ND	48,953	63.8	50.8	3.8	9.2	28.8	7.3	7.0	0.2	2.38
13980	Blacksburg-Christiansburg-Radford, VA	68,912	59.3	45.7	4.0	9.7	27.5	13.2	6.0	0.4	2.42
14010	Bloomington, IL	71,559	62.2	48.9	4.0	9.2	28.2	9.7	5.5	0.7	2.53
14020	Bloomington, IN	62,259	54.1	40.6	3.6	9.9	32.7	13.2	5.3	0.8	2.38
14100	Bloomsburg-Berwick, PA	33,303	64.0	50.2	4.1	9.7	28.1	8.0	7.1	0.2	2.43
14260	Boise City, ID	231,308	69.4	53.9	5.1	10.4	24.1	6.5	5.3	0.3	2.71
14460	Boston-Cambridge-Newton, MA-NH	1,759,717	63.4	47.6	3.8	12.1	28.4	8.2	5.4	0.7	2.54
14500	Boulder, CO	121,194	58.9	46.8	4.1	7.9	28.2	12.9	5.8	0.6	2.44
14540	Bowling Green, KY	62,798	65.4	48.9	4.4	12.1	27.5	7.1	5.1	0.2	2.47
14740	Bremerton-Silverdale, WA	98,127	66.6	52.2	4.5	9.9	26.2	7.2	6.7	0.5	2.51
14860	Bridgeport-Stamford-Norwalk, CT	331,134	69.1	53.1	3.9	12.2	25.6	5.3	4.4	0.4	2.76
15180	Brownsville-Harlingen, TX	119,289	79.3	52.5	5.8	20.9	18.4	2.4	4.2	0.2	3.45
15260	Brunswick, GA	43,019	69.5	48.1	5.4	16.0	26.7	3.9	4.2	0.2	2.60
15380	Buffalo-Cheektowaga-Niagara Falls, NY	469,024	60.9	42.6	4.8	13.5	33.0	6.2	5.8	0.4	2.35
15500	Burlington, NC	60,215	67.6	47.5	6.1	14.0	28.3	4.1	4.8	0.4	2.48
15540	Burlington-South Burlington, VT	84,547	61.7	48.9	4.2	8.6	26.2	12.1	7.3	1.0	2.41
15680	California-Lexington Park, MD	37,483	74.6	60.8	4.5	9.3	20.9	4.5	4.7	0.3	2.83
15940	Canton-Massillon, OH	160,825	66.4	49.6	5.1	11.6	28.7	4.9	5.5	0.5	2.45
15980	Cape Coral-Fort Myers, FL	241,201	65.8	51.0	4.5	10.2	28.1	6.1	6.5	0.7	2.64
16020	Cape Girardeau, MO-IL	37,157	64.5	50.0	3.7	10.8	29.0	6.5	4.9	0.4	2.50
16060	Carbondale-Marion, IL	50,328	58.6	44.0	3.4	11.2	33.3	8.1	4.4	0.8	2.40
16180	Carson City, NV	21,206	59.3	44.3	2.7	12.3	33.6	7.1	7.0	0.1	2.47
16220	Casper, WY	31,587	64.8	48.1	6.7	10.0	27.9	7.4	8.0	0.1	2.44
16300	Cedar Rapids, IA	104,084	63.3	49.9	3.7	9.7	29.4	7.3	6.5	0.3	2.45
16540	Chambersburg-Waynesboro, PA	58,244	68.4	55.3	4.3	8.8	26.7	4.8	5.8	0.3	2.56
16580	Champaign-Urbana, IL	91,305	55.5	42.4	3.1	10.0	32.4	12.1	5.3	0.5	2.38
16620	Charleston, WV	95,412	62.6	45.0	4.8	12.8	32.2	5.2	5.7	0.5	2.33
16700	Charleston-North Charleston, SC	263,127	64.4	45.9	4.4	14.1	28.3	7.3	4.7	0.4	2.58
16740	Charlotte-Concord-Gastonia, NC-SC	851,107	67.7	49.2	4.5	13.9	26.7	5.7	4.8	0.4	2.66
16820	Charlottesville, VA	84,100	61.7	49.0	3.1	9.6	30.1	8.2	4.8	0.4	2.48
16860	Chattanooga, TN-GA	208,072	67.4	49.8	4.7	13.0	27.7	4.8	4.5	0.4	2.52

CBSA FIPS code	Metropolitan area	Race or Hispanic origin of householder				Age of householder			Percent of households with one or more persons under 18 years old	Percent of households with one or more persons age 65 or older	Percent of all householders who are owners
		Householder is White alone, not Hispanic or Latino, percent	Householder is Black or African American alone, percent	Householder is Hispanic or Latino, percent	Householder is Asian alone, percent	Householders age 15 to 34, percent	Householders age 35 to 64, percent	Householders age 65 and older, percent			
10180	Abilene, TX	74.7	5.6	17.1	1.3	24.5	50.7	24.8	30.1	27.3	63.8
10420	Akron, OH	83.9	11.6	1.2	1.7	19.0	57.4	23.6	29.2	26.3	67.0
10500	Albany, GA	46.2	50.4	1.8	0.9	20.2	57.6	22.2	33.2	25.4	55.8
10540	Albany, OR	91.8	0.0	4.5	0.9	19.9	52.9	27.2	31.3	30.0	65.0
10580	Albany-Schenectady-Troy, NY	86.1	6.8	3.2	2.6	17.8	59.1	23.1	27.3	25.9	65.3
10740	Albuquerque, NM	50.6	2.7	39.9	1.6	21.4	56.9	21.7	32.3	24.7	66.6
10780	Alexandria, LA	70.0	25.9	1.9	0.0	17.8	57.4	24.8	31.8	27.9	66.8
10900	Allentown-Bethlehem-Easton, PA-NJ	82.7	4.4	10.2	2.2	15.0	59.9	25.0	31.2	28.6	70.4
11020	Altoona, PA	97.4	1.0	0.6	0.0	15.5	55.7	28.9	28.1	31.7	72.3
11100	Amarillo, TX	71.4	5.1	19.9	2.4	25.1	54.1	20.7	34.5	23.1	64.6
11180	Ames, IA	88.5	1.9	1.9	6.6	41.8	41.5	16.8	23.2	17.7	54.6
11260	Anchorage, AK	74.3	4.7	5.8	4.8	25.2	61.1	13.7	36.0	16.8	62.9
11460	Ann Arbor, MI	75.2	11.6	3.1	7.6	27.2	54.6	18.2	27.6	20.5	59.5
11500	Anniston-Oxford-Jacksonville, AL	75.0	20.9	2.8	0.0	18.9	56.0	25.1	30.4	29.0	68.6
11540	Appleton, WI	92.8	0.5	2.6	1.8	19.6	60.0	20.4	33.4	22.1	73.4
11700	Asheville, NC	89.7	4.4	4.2	0.0	16.5	54.5	28.9	25.2	31.7	67.7
12020	Athens-Clarke County, GA	69.9	20.1	5.7	2.9	29.6	51.0	19.4	29.5	21.6	54.8
12060	Atlanta-Sandy Springs-Roswell, GA	55.0	32.4	7.2	4.2	20.6	63.0	16.4	36.6	19.6	63.9
12100	Atlantic City-Hammonton, NJ	64.9	15.6	13.5	5.6	15.1	60.2	24.7	33.5	29.4	65.9
12220	Auburn-Opelika, AL	70.8	23.6	2.1	2.7	34.1	50.8	15.1	32.0	17.6	60.2
12260	Augusta-Richmond County, GA-SC	60.7	33.3	3.3	1.6	18.8	58.7	22.5	32.8	25.6	67.2
12420	Austin-Round Rock, TX	62.9	7.1	23.6	4.5	27.8	58.2	14.0	34.0	16.6	57.7
12540	Bakersfield, CA	48.7	6.1	39.7	3.7	23.5	58.3	18.2	45.1	22.1	56.0
12580	Baltimore-Columbia-Towson, MD	63.0	28.1	3.4	4.1	18.4	59.6	21.9	31.7	25.3	66.2
12620	Bangor, ME	95.8	0.0	1.0	0.0	20.0	56.6	23.3	26.8	26.1	65.6
12700	Barnstable Town, MA	94.5	1.6	1.5	0.9	8.5	53.8	37.7	21.4	41.5	78.6
12940	Baton Rouge, LA	61.5	33.0	2.6	1.7	23.9	56.4	19.7	34.2	22.2	68.3
12980	Battle Creek, MI	83.0	10.9	3.2	0.0	18.0	56.6	25.4	31.2	27.9	68.7
13020	Bay City, MI	93.5	1.5	3.4	0.0	16.1	57.4	26.5	28.3	28.7	77.5
13140	Beaumont-Port Arthur, TX	63.0	23.9	9.5	2.2	20.1	55.8	24.1	32.3	26.7	69.3
13220	Beckley, WV	91.3	5.8	0.7	0.0	16.0	55.7	28.3	28.8	30.7	74.0
13380	Bellingham, WA	87.2	0.0	4.7	3.2	22.4	54.3	23.3	29.0	25.9	62.9
13460	Bend-Redmond, OR	91.9	0.0	4.5	1.2	17.1	57.5	25.4	28.0	28.6	63.8
13740	Billings, MT	91.2	0.0	3.2	0.0	20.6	55.6	23.8	30.7	26.2	68.8
13780	Binghamton, NY	91.3	3.2	2.0	2.4	17.9	55.7	26.4	26.7	29.2	68.9
13820	Birmingham-Hoover, AL	66.8	28.1	2.8	1.1	19.3	58.1	22.7	32.5	25.2	69.6
13900	Bismarck, ND	92.9	0.0	0.0	0.0	24.5	53.6	21.9	29.8	23.5	72.1
13980	Blacksburg-Christiansburg-Radford, VA	90.5	3.9	1.9	2.4	27.1	50.3	22.6	24.4	24.9	60.7
14010	Bloomington, IL	85.6	6.3	3.3	3.6	26.9	54.4	18.7	30.4	20.5	67.7
14020	Bloomington, IN	88.9	2.8	2.0	4.5	32.1	49.1	18.9	24.9	21.0	57.0
14100	Bloomsburg-Berwick, PA	95.8	0.0	1.7	0.0	17.0	55.4	27.6	26.7	30.7	70.7
14260	Boise City, ID	86.7	0.6	8.8	1.6	22.5	57.0	20.6	36.1	23.3	67.5
14460	Boston-Cambridge-Newton, MA-NH	78.6	6.9	7.5	5.8	18.4	59.3	22.3	30.9	25.6	61.1
14500	Boulder, CO	83.8	0.8	9.8	3.9	24.8	57.7	17.5	28.8	19.5	63.0
14540	Bowling Green, KY	88.4	7.1	2.3	1.4	24.8	54.5	20.6	30.8	23.6	63.3
14740	Bremerton-Silverdale, WA	84.0	2.6	4.8	3.9	19.3	57.7	23.0	30.5	26.1	67.2
14860	Bridgeport-Stamford-Norwalk, CT	70.7	10.6	13.9	4.3	13.5	62.9	23.6	35.1	27.1	68.2
15180	Brownsville-Harlingen, TX	16.1	0.6	82.2	0.8	18.2	58.4	23.3	48.0	28.0	66.2
15260	Brunswick, GA	74.9	20.4	3.2	0.0	15.4	56.8	27.8	32.3	30.6	66.9
15380	Buffalo-Cheektowaga-Niagara Falls, NY	81.9	11.7	3.3	1.7	17.6	57.1	25.4	27.9	27.9	65.9
15500	Burlington, NC	71.5	18.7	7.7	0.0	18.2	56.8	25.0	31.7	27.8	66.1
15540	Burlington-South Burlington, VT	94.1	1.4	1.3	1.5	22.1	57.7	20.2	28.6	22.7	67.9
15680	California-Lexington Park, MD	80.0	14.3	2.4	0.0	19.3	62.0	18.6	38.8	21.0	72.8
15940	Canton-Massillon, OH	90.3	6.5	1.2	0.0	16.1	57.6	26.3	29.5	28.9	70.1
15980	Cape Coral-Fort Myers, FL	80.3	6.0	11.7	1.3	12.4	49.7	37.9	24.2	42.0	69.4
16020	Cape Girardeau, MO-IL	89.5	7.9	0.0	0.0	23.2	52.8	23.9	29.9	26.5	67.1
16060	Carbondale-Marion, IL	87.2	7.7	1.8	1.7	25.6	50.4	24.0	26.8	25.7	62.7
16180	Carson City, NV	79.5	0.0	13.9	0.0	16.1	54.1	29.9	25.7	32.8	55.3
16220	Casper, WY	91.7	0.0	5.3	0.0	25.4	54.7	19.9	32.2	21.5	68.0
16300	Cedar Rapids, IA	93.3	2.8	1.4	1.2	21.7	55.9	22.5	31.3	24.4	74.7
16540	Chambersburg-Waynesboro, PA	92.8	3.1	2.8	0.0	16.4	56.3	27.3	31.3	30.4	72.4
16580	Champaign-Urbana, IL	78.1	9.8	3.4	6.9	32.1	49.1	18.8	25.5	20.4	58.3
16620	Charleston, WV	91.3	3.2	0.0	0.8	17.7	56.0	26.3	27.0	29.0	70.6
16700	Charleston-North Charleston, SC	68.0	25.0	4.0	1.4	23.0	56.9	20.1	31.1	23.3	64.5
16740	Charlotte-Concord-Gastonia, NC-SC	68.4	21.8	6.2	2.4	20.2	60.8	19.0	34.9	21.8	66.2
16820	Charlottesville, VA	81.3	12.4	2.9	2.2	21.8	54.4	23.8	27.7	27.0	65.8
16860	Chattanooga, TN-GA	81.4	13.7	2.2	1.3	18.1	57.4	24.5	31.5	27.4	67.9

CBSA FIPS code	Metropolitan area	Total Households	Family households, percent	Married-couple family households, percent	Male householder, no spouse, percent	Female householder, no spouse, percent	Householder living alone, percent	Nonfamily households, householder not living alone, percent	Opposite-sex partner unmarried partner households, percent	Same-sex unmarried partner households, percent	Average household size
					Household type						
16940	Cheyenne, WY	36,138	66.6	52.8	3.6	10.2	27.1	6.3	5.9	0.2	2.56
16980	Chicago-Naperville-										
	Elgin, IL-IN-WI	3,428,165	65.9	47.6	4.7	13.5	28.5	5.6	5.0	0.5	2.73
17020	Chico, CA	84,647	59.7	42.0	5.5	12.1	29.2	11.2	7.4	0.5	2.55
17140	Cincinnati, OH-KY-IN	813,366	65.8	48.3	4.5	13.0	28.4	5.8	5.3	0.4	2.56
17300	Clarksville, TN-KY	96,208	73.0	53.9	4.2	14.9	22.1	4.9	5.3	0.1	2.72
17420	Cleveland, TN	44,851	69.0	51.2	5.2	12.7	26.4	4.6	4.5	0.2	2.55
17460	Cleveland-Elyria, OH	842,907	61.5	43.1	4.3	14.2	33.2	5.2	5.1	0.4	2.40
17660	Coeur d'Alene, ID	55,645	68.7	53.8	4.1	10.7	24.1	7.2	6.9	0.1	2.53
17780	College Station-Bryan, TX	82,557	57.8	41.5	4.2	12.1	28.3	13.9	4.2	0.4	2.66
17820	Colorado Springs, CO	248,206	68.4	53.3	4.0	11.0	25.7	5.9	4.5	0.4	2.63
17860	Columbia, MO	65,822	55.8	42.6	2.9	10.3	30.3	13.9	6.2	0.5	2.42
17900	Columbia, SC	293,972	65.1	45.1	4.1	15.9	28.6	6.3	4.8	0.4	2.55
17980	Columbus, GA-AL	110,280	65.7	42.3	4.5	18.9	29.8	4.5	3.6	0.4	2.66
18020	Columbus, IN	29,611	68.1	52.0	5.6	10.6	27.1	4.7	4.6	0.5	2.62
18140	Columbus, OH	745,038	63.2	46.4	4.2	12.7	29.4	7.4	6.4	0.7	2.55
18580	Corpus Christi, TX	156,303	69.9	46.6	6.6	16.7	24.0	6.0	6.6	0.3	2.74
18700	Corvallis, OR	33,298	56.3	45.9	2.5	8.0	29.0	14.7	5.4	0.9	2.43
18880	Crestview-Fort Walton Beach-										
	Destin, FL	97,012	66.4	49.7	4.3	12.4	28.3	5.3	5.3	0.3	2.47
19060	Cumberland, MD-WV	39,225	57.3	42.5	3.8	11.0	37.8	5.0	5.0	0.4	2.38
19100	Dallas-Fort Worth-Arlington, TX	2,358,062	69.3	50.5	5.2	13.7	25.2	5.5	5.0	0.6	2.80
19140	Dalton, GA	48,263	74.4	54.5	5.9	13.9	21.4	4.2	4.4	0.3	2.92
19180	Danville, IL	31,666	64.6	46.0	4.9	13.7	31.0	4.4	4.4	0.8	2.48
19300	Daphne-Fairhope-Foley, AL	73,792	69.9	55.3	3.7	10.9	26.0	4.1	3.3	0.2	2.55
19340	Davenport-Moline-Rock										
	Island, IA-IL	154,762	63.3	47.9	3.9	11.5	31.4	5.3	6.2	0.3	2.42
19380	Dayton, OH	325,251	62.3	44.1	4.2	14.1	32.1	5.6	5.7	0.5	2.38
19460	Decatur, AL	59,614	68.9	51.2	4.7	13.0	27.6	3.5	3.3	0.5	2.55
19500	Decatur, IL	45,186	61.6	44.6	4.4	12.6	33.0	5.4	5.9	0.4	2.36
19660	Deltona-Daytona Beach-Ormond										
	Beach, FL	231,300	62.4	47.7	4.1	10.5	31.0	6.6	4.8	0.5	2.53
19740	Denver-Aurora-Lakewood, CO	1,020,749	62.5	47.0	4.6	10.9	29.6	7.9	5.6	0.8	2.56
19780	Des Moines-West Des Moines, IA	229,203	66.7	51.1	4.8	10.8	27.0	6.3	6.2	0.3	2.52
19820	Detroit-Warren-Dearborn, MI	1,651,263	65.1	45.5	4.9	14.8	30.0	4.9	4.9	0.4	2.57
20020	Dothan, AL	57,153	67.5	48.1	3.6	15.8	28.6	3.9	4.0	0.1	2.55
20100	Dover, DE	59,341	69.7	49.7	5.0	15.0	24.1	6.2	7.1	0.4	2.74
20220	Dubuque, IA	37,388	64.0	50.9	3.7	9.4	29.7	6.3	4.9	0.2	2.42
20260	Duluth, MN-WI	115,725	59.9	45.6	4.4	9.9	32.7	7.4	6.8	0.5	2.31
20500	Durham-Chapel Hill, NC	206,012	61.1	43.8	4.2	13.1	30.7	8.2	5.0	0.9	2.43
20700	East Stroudsburg, PA	58,374	73.9	54.7	6.0	13.2	19.7	6.3	7.1	0.9	2.84
20740	Eau Claire, WI	64,549	62.1	50.2	3.9	8.1	29.3	8.6	6.9	0.4	2.43
20940	El Centro, CA	47,556	77.2	51.1	6.5	19.5	18.8	4.1	5.4	0.2	3.48
21060	Elizabethtown-Fort Knox, KY	55,483	72.0	52.6	5.5	13.9	23.8	4.2	6.7	0.1	2.65
21140	Elkhart-Goshen, IN	70,775	72.4	52.6	6.2	13.6	23.4	4.3	6.2	0.3	2.77
21300	Elmira, NY	35,417	62.6	46.1	3.8	12.8	30.3	7.1	6.9	0.2	2.33
21340	El Paso, TX	259,952	75.1	49.9	5.3	20.0	21.4	3.5	3.5	0.3	3.13
21500	Erie, PA	109,733	63.6	46.1	4.1	13.3	30.2	6.2	5.7	0.3	2.44
21660	Eugene, OR	144,992	59.0	43.7	4.5	10.8	29.4	11.6	7.2	1.0	2.39
21780	Evansville, IN-KY	125,269	64.9	48.7	4.1	12.2	30.2	4.9	5.0	0.3	2.42
21820	Fairbanks, AK	35,633	62.6	48.9	3.9	9.8	29.1	8.3	7.3	0.3	2.70
22020	Fargo, ND-MN	89,304	57.4	44.7	4.5	8.2	31.8	10.8	7.0	0.5	2.34
22140	Farmington, NM	39,683	73.0	49.9	6.5	16.6	22.7	4.3	6.4	0.1	3.17
22180	Fayetteville, NC	139,492	67.1	44.5	4.2	18.3	28.0	4.9	5.0	0.3	2.60
22220	Fayetteville-Springdale-										
	Rogers, AR-MO	177,790	68.8	54.3	4.1	10.4	24.6	6.6	4.9	0.3	2.66
22380	Flagstaff, AZ	46,614	64.2	45.0	5.9	13.3	23.9	11.8	7.6	0.7	2.71
22420	Flint, MI	164,407	64.7	43.0	5.3	16.3	29.5	5.8	6.8	0.3	2.51
22500	Florence, SC	77,118	69.5	44.2	5.7	19.7	27.3	3.1	4.4	0.2	2.61
22520	Florence-Muscle Shoals, AL	60,707	66.2	50.3	4.0	11.8	29.5	4.3	2.9	0.4	2.39
22540	Fond du Lac, WI	41,187	66.9	52.7	5.2	9.0	28.0	5.2	7.4	0.5	2.39
22660	Fort Collins, CO	123,203	62.4	50.5	3.8	8.1	25.4	12.2	5.7	0.8	2.45
22900	Fort Smith, AR-OK	106,784	68.9	50.8	5.4	12.7	27.2	3.9	4.2	0.2	2.59
23060	Fort Wayne, IN	163,266	65.5	48.1	4.3	13.1	29.0	5.5	5.4	0.4	2.54
23420	Fresno, CA	291,440	73.0	46.6	8.5	17.9	21.3	5.7	8.1	0.5	3.19
23460	Gadsden, AL	39,971	69.7	49.0	5.9	14.7	26.9	3.4	3.8	0.2	2.57
23540	Gainesville, FL	102,097	53.1	37.9	4.0	11.3	32.8	14.0	5.9	0.6	2.47
23580	Gainesville, GA	60,356	73.2	54.7	5.8	12.6	22.2	4.6	6.2	0.4	3.03
23900	Gettysburg, PA	37,829	72.2	58.1	4.2	9.9	23.0	4.8	6.1	0.3	2.57
24020	Glens Falls, NY	51,551	66.2	49.5	4.2	12.5	27.6	6.2	8.2	0.4	2.42
24140	Goldsboro, NC	47,464	67.2	44.2	4.7	18.3	27.3	5.5	5.4	0.2	2.55
24220	Grand Forks, ND-MN	40,497	57.4	45.9	3.5	8.0	33.4	9.3	6.4	0.1	2.30
24260	Grand Island, NE	31,795	67.0	52.5	4.3	10.2	26.6	6.4	7.4	0.1	2.58
24300	Grand Junction, CO	58,877	67.1	50.6	5.3	11.2	26.1	6.8	4.8	0.2	2.44
24340	Grand Rapids-Wyoming, MI	371,148	68.8	53.8	4.1	11.0	24.8	6.4	5.5	0.4	2.65

CBSA FIPS code	Metropolitan area	Race or Hispanic origin of householder				Age of householder			Percent of households with one or more persons under 18 years old	Percent of households with one or more persons age 65 or older	Percent of all householders who are owners
		Householder is White alone, not Hispanic or Latino, percent	Householder is Black or African American alone, percent	Householder is Hispanic or Latino, percent	Householder is Asian alone, percent	Householders age 15 to 34, percent	Householders age 35 to 64, percent	Householders age 65 and older, percent			
16940	Cheyenne, WY..................	84.3	2.6	10.8	0.0	22.8	55.9	21.2	31.7	23.5	68.8
16980	Chicago-Naperville-Elgin, IL-IN-WI...........	61.9	17.1	14.7	5.2	19.5	59.8	20.6	34.0	23.9	64.9
17020	Chico, CA...........................	81.9	1.1	10.8	2.6	22.7	50.4	26.9	26.9	30.0	58.6
17140	Cincinnati, OH-KY-IN............	82.6	12.6	1.9	1.7	19.9	58.8	21.3	32.7	23.6	66.8
17300	Clarksville, TN-KY...............	70.9	18.8	6.3	1.4	32.5	51.2	16.3	41.4	18.9	57.9
17420	Cleveland, TN.....................	91.8	3.5	3.0	0.0	16.8	57.6	25.5	32.0	28.5	67.4
17460	Cleveland-Elyria, OH	73.6	19.9	3.8	1.8	16.5	58.3	25.1	28.6	27.9	65.4
17660	Coeur d'Alene, ID...............	94.0	0.0	2.6	0.0	20.1	55.4	24.5	32.5	27.5	70.7
17780	College Station-Bryan, TX......	65.5	11.2	17.3	4.7	39.8	43.7	16.5	29.9	18.4	50.2
17820	Colorado Springs, CO	77.3	5.5	11.8	2.2	24.1	57.8	18.2	34.9	20.7	63.6
17860	Columbia, MO.....................	84.4	7.2	2.2	3.8	35.8	49.3	14.9	27.7	17.3	55.5
17900	Columbia, SC......................	61.7	31.8	3.7	1.5	21.8	58.0	20.2	32.1	23.1	67.3
17980	Columbus, GA-AL................	52.0	0.0	4.7	1.4	22.3	55.9	21.8	35.0	24.3	55.8
18020	Columbus, IN......................	89.9	152.3	3.3	4.6	17.3	58.3	24.4	32.9	26.5	71.2
18140	Columbus, OH.....................	79.1	13.8	2.5	2.8	23.3	58.2	18.5	32.9	21.0	61.8
18580	Corpus Christi, TX...............	43.1	3.7	50.8	1.4	21.4	55.7	22.9	35.7	26.4	59.8
18700	Corvallis, OR......................	85.7	0.0	5.4	4.6	29.5	49.5	21.0	24.1	23.7	58.1
18880	Crestview-Fort Walton Beach-Destin, FL...........	82.6	7.3	5.3	2.5	21.4	54.2	24.3	29.9	26.9	65.6
19060	Cumberland, MD-WV	95.6	3.2	0.0	0.0	16.0	54.3	29.7	23.3	32.8	64.8
19100	Dallas-Fort Worth-Arlington, TX........	57.2	15.9	20.3	5.0	23.4	60.4	16.2	39.1	19.0	60.3
19140	Dalton, GA.........................	76.2	3.1	19.1	0.0	20.3	58.2	21.5	42.6	25.0	65.6
19180	Danville, IL.........................	85.4	10.8	2.2	0.0	17.2	54.3	28.5	29.8	30.6	71.3
19300	Daphne-Fairhope-Foley, AL..............	87.4	7.8	2.5	0.5	14.9	57.1	28.0	28.4	31.2	70.6
19340	Davenport-Moline-Rock Island, IA-IL.............	86.3	6.2	5.3	1.3	18.8	55.7	25.5	29.4	27.5	70.2
19380	Dayton, OH........................	79.5	15.7	1.7	1.6	19.6	55.2	25.2	29.3	27.5	63.3
19460	Decatur, AL........................	80.4	11.9	3.8	0.0	15.7	60.1	24.2	31.7	26.7	73.2
19500	Decatur, IL.........................	82.3	13.8	1.1	0.9	19.1	54.4	26.5	28.6	28.4	68.9
19660	Deltona-Daytona Beach-Ormond Beach, FL.........	80.3	9.0	8.3	1.3	12.7	51.9	35.4	22.5	39.0	71.6
19740	Denver-Aurora-Lakewood, CO	73.3	5.4	16.3	3.1	22.9	59.5	17.6	32.7	20.0	63.0
19780	Des Moines-West Des Moines, IA......	87.9	4.2	4.5	2.5	24.6	56.6	18.8	35.3	20.9	70.6
19820	Detroit-Warren-Dearborn, MI..........	70.6	22.2	2.9	2.8	16.1	60.5	23.5	31.5	26.3	69.3
20020	Dothan, AL.........................	74.1	22.1	2.1	0.4	17.5	55.9	26.6	30.5	29.1	68.3
20100	Dover, DE...........................	69.3	21.4	4.8	0.0	18.8	56.5	24.6	34.1	28.2	70.9
20220	Dubuque, IA........................	94.5	0.0	1.3	1.1	19.8	56.1	24.1	30.3	26.0	72.1
20260	Duluth, MN-WI.....................	94.6	0.8	0.6	0.6	19.9	55.2	25.0	26.7	27.0	71.6
20500	Durham-Chapel Hill, NC........	60.7	26.4	7.0	4.0	24.2	56.4	19.3	29.6	21.7	59.8
20700	East Stroudsburg, PA............	75.2	11.4	10.3	0.0	12.5	65.5	22.1	34.9	27.3	78.6
20740	Eau Claire, WI.....................	96.6	0.0	0.0	1.4	23.0	53.8	23.2	27.8	25.1	66.6
20940	El Centro, CA......................	19.3	1.5	76.5	1.2	19.8	58.6	21.7	47.2	28.4	55.1
21060	Elizabethtown-Fort Knox, KY	83.0	9.9	3.3	1.4	21.2	59.0	19.8	36.8	22.0	64.4
21140	Elkhart-Goshen, IN..............	83.7	5.0	9.5	0.7	20.0	57.8	22.3	38.9	24.6	69.9
21300	Elmira, NY..........................	92.2	3.8	1.9	0.0	18.7	56.3	25.0	29.0	27.9	68.4
21340	El Paso, TX.........................	18.4	3.7	76.0	1.1	22.0	58.2	19.8	44.1	24.0	61.0
21500	Erie, PA.............................	90.6	5.9	2.1	0.9	18.9	57.0	24.1	28.5	26.6	66.3
21660	Eugene, OR.........................	88.6	0.7	5.2	2.0	22.2	52.8	25.0	25.7	28.1	58.3
21780	Evansville, IN-KY.................	89.7	6.8	1.2	0.0	20.1	56.5	23.4	30.4	25.6	69.5
21820	Fairbanks, AK......................	79.4	0.0	5.2	1.6	31.9	54.7	13.4	32.1	15.1	58.8
22020	Fargo, ND-MN.....................	93.2	1.6	1.7	1.4	33.1	50.1	16.7	30.2	18.2	57.2
22140	Farmington, NM...................	52.2	0.0	17.4	0.0	17.8	60.0	22.2	38.2	25.2	75.2
22180	Fayetteville, NC...................	49.0	36.6	8.6	1.9	29.0	54.5	16.5	36.9	19.0	54.7
22220	Fayetteville-Springdale-Rogers, AR-MO...............	82.4	1.8	10.0	2.3	26.9	53.6	19.5	36.2	21.9	62.3
22380	Flagstaff, AZ.......................	64.7	1.2	11.4	1.4	26.4	56.7	16.9	32.1	19.7	59.2
22420	Flint, MI.............................	75.0	20.2	2.2	0.7	16.6	58.8	24.6	31.2	26.9	70.2
22500	Florence, SC........................	58.2	38.6	1.7	0.0	17.7	57.2	25.2	33.5	28.1	66.2
22520	Florence-Muscle Shoals, AL	85.2	12.1	1.3	0.0	18.6	53.6	27.8	29.2	30.3	70.2
22540	Fond du Lac, WI..................	94.5	0.0	3.2	0.0	17.5	57.7	24.8	30.1	26.9	70.6
22660	Fort Collins, CO	88.4	0.7	7.6	1.6	25.7	54.3	20.0	28.8	22.4	64.4
22900	Fort Smith, AR-OK	78.9	3.7	6.2	2.2	19.4	56.7	23.9	33.8	26.6	67.7
23060	Fort Wayne, IN....................	83.0	10.0	3.9	1.8	21.1	57.7	21.2	33.1	23.2	70.8
23420	Fresno, CA..........................	42.8	5.8	41.4	7.8	22.8	57.2	20.0	43.0	23.9	52.9
23460	Gadsden, AL........................	80.7	15.3	2.2	0.0	15.2	57.9	26.9	32.1	30.9	71.5
23540	Gainesville, FL.....................	68.4	17.7	8.1	4.3	31.7	49.4	18.9	24.1	21.4	54.4
23580	Gainesville, GA	72.7	7.4	17.5	1.6	18.3	59.6	22.1	38.3	26.1	67.0
23900	Gettysburg, PA....................	94.0	0.9	4.0	0.0	12.4	61.0	26.6	30.6	30.3	77.2
24020	Glens Falls, NY....................	97.0	0.6	1.0	0.0	13.3	58.7	28.0	27.9	30.9	71.5
24140	Goldsboro, NC.....................	58.6	32.0	7.4	0.0	21.5	56.6	21.9	34.2	24.8	59.3
24220	Grand Forks, ND-MN............	91.5	1.7	2.8	1.3	31.2	48.3	20.5	26.9	21.9	57.0
24260	Grand Island, NE.................	84.7	0.0	12.7	0.0	21.1	55.4	23.4	34.1	26.2	68.0
24300	Grand Junction, CO	87.1	0.0	10.0	0.0	21.0	53.2	25.8	30.0	28.2	70.1
24340	Grand Rapids-Wyoming, MI.............	85.4	6.2	5.7	1.5	22.0	57.1	21.0	34.0	23.0	72.6

CBSA FIPS code	Metropolitan area	Household type							Opposite-sex partner unmarried partner households, percent	Same-sex unmarried partner households, percent	Average household size
		Total Households	Family households, percent	Married-couple family households, percent	Male householder, no spouse, percent	Female householder, no spouse, percent	Householder living alone, percent	Nonfamily households, householder not living alone, percent			
24420	Grants Pass, OR	34,288	64.3	49.7	4.4	10.2	29.7	6.0	6.4	0.6	2.38
24500	Great Falls, MT	33,326	63.4	48.0	4.9	10.4	31.5	5.1	5.4	0.2	2.38
24540	Greeley, CO	91,683	72.4	56.7	5.4	10.3	21.5	6.2	5.7	0.3	2.80
24580	Green Bay, WI	122,637	65.8	52.1	4.5	9.3	27.6	6.5	6.7	0.4	2.47
24660	Greensboro-High Point, NC	290,426	65.3	45.6	4.8	15.0	28.6	6.0	5.0	0.4	2.47
24780	Greenville, NC	66,849	59.6	39.3	3.6	16.7	29.6	10.8	4.8	0.2	2.49
24860	Greenville-Anderson-Mauldin, SC	317,196	68.4	50.4	4.6	13.4	27.1	4.5	4.1	0.2	2.58
25060	Gulfport-Biloxi-Pascagoula, MS	142,600	67.1	45.3	5.5	16.3	27.3	5.6	5.3	0.4	2.61
25180	Hagerstown-Martinsburg, MD-WV	96,898	68.6	50.2	5.4	13.1	25.9	5.5	6.8	0.5	2.54
25220	Hammond, LA	44,727	68.0	45.2	5.2	17.6	25.6	6.4	6.5	0.0	2.69
25260	Hanford-Corcoran, CA	41,034	78.0	51.2	7.9	18.9	16.8	5.2	8.6	0.3	3.22
25420	Harrisburg-Carlisle, PA	221,682	64.9	49.4	4.4	11.1	29.1	6.0	6.1	0.5	2.41
25500	Harrisonburg, VA	44,626	64.7	49.7	4.8	10.2	24.5	10.7	4.5	0.6	2.68
25540	Hartford-West Hartford-East Hartford, CT	465,837	65.5	47.6	4.5	13.5	28.7	5.8	5.4	0.5	2.50
25620	Hattiesburg, MS	53,856	66.5	45.1	4.5	16.9	26.5	6.9	3.8	0.4	2.64
25860	Hickory-Lenoir-Morganton, NC	137,477	67.3	50.3	5.1	11.9	28.0	4.7	4.5	0.4	2.59
25940	Hilton Head Island-Bluffton-Beaufort, SC	72,993	68.5	52.8	4.4	11.3	25.8	5.7	4.5	0.5	2.57
25980	Hinesville, GA	28,453	74.0	52.2	5.2	16.6	21.1	4.9	4.7	0.4	2.77
26140	Homosassa Springs, FL	60,419	63.7	51.2	4.2	8.3	30.5	5.8	6.2	0.6	2.27
26300	Hot Springs, AR	39,748	63.7	46.0	4.5	13.2	29.3	6.9	6.5	0.2	2.39
26380	Houma-Thibodaux, LA	74,613	70.8	50.0	6.1	14.7	23.7	5.6	8.6	0.4	2.76
26420	Houston-The Woodlands-Sugar Land, TX	2,098,109	70.6	50.5	5.5	14.6	24.4	5.0	4.9	0.4	2.91
26580	Huntington-Ashland, WV-KY-OH	143,092	66.8	49.7	4.9	12.2	28.2	5.0	5.3	0.4	2.49
26620	Huntsville, AL	167,219	66.8	49.6	4.4	12.8	29.3	3.9	3.4	0.3	2.50
26820	Idaho Falls, ID	45,581	74.4	59.1	4.2	11.1	21.5	4.1	3.8	0.4	2.96
26900	Indianapolis-Carmel-Anderson, IN	732,026	65.5	47.7	4.4	13.4	28.6	5.9	5.8	0.6	2.58
26980	Iowa City, IA	64,163	56.5	44.9	3.2	8.4	30.0	13.5	5.8	0.4	2.33
27060	Ithaca, NY	38,195	53.4	42.8	1.9	8.7	31.4	15.2	7.5	1.4	2.34
27100	Jackson, MI	60,391	66.3	48.2	5.5	12.6	28.2	5.5	6.0	0.3	2.50
27140	Jackson, MS	205,918	68.5	43.5	5.3	19.6	27.5	4.0	3.9	0.2	2.69
27180	Jackson, TN	47,525	66.5	47.1	4.2	15.2	29.5	4.0	4.0	0.3	2.63
27260	Jacksonville, FL	511,160	65.5	47.0	4.3	14.2	28.4	6.2	5.4	0.4	2.65
27340	Jacksonville, NC	60,637	72.1	55.2	3.6	13.3	22.3	5.6	4.6	0.3	2.78
27500	Janesville-Beloit, WI	63,605	66.6	48.4	5.2	13.0	26.9	6.5	8.1	0.7	2.47
27620	Jefferson City, MO	56,109	66.5	51.7	3.6	11.2	28.4	5.2	5.6	0.5	2.50
27740	Johnson City, TN	83,609	64.4	49.0	4.5	10.9	30.9	4.7	4.3	0.3	2.31
27780	Johnstown, PA	57,588	63.8	47.7	4.5	11.6	31.9	4.3	5.0	0.3	2.31
27860	Jonesboro, AR	47,325	67.9	47.0	5.9	15.0	24.9	7.1	5.3	0.5	2.54
27900	Joplin, MO	67,826	67.0	50.8	4.7	11.4	27.2	5.8	6.1	0.4	2.54
27980	Kahului-Wailuku-Lahaina, HI	53,102	67.7	50.3	4.8	12.6	25.0	7.4	7.9	0.4	2.93
28020	Kalamazoo-Portage, MI	127,958	62.2	46.0	4.5	11.7	29.6	8.2	6.3	0.6	2.51
28100	Kankakee, IL	41,333	67.7	46.9	5.9	15.0	27.1	5.1	6.3	0.5	2.60
28140	Kansas City, MO-KS	791,116	65.3	48.2	4.4	12.7	28.7	6.0	5.5	0.5	2.54
28420	Kennewick-Richland, WA	90,658	70.8	53.1	5.5	12.2	24.2	4.9	7.0	0.3	2.91
28660	Killeen-Temple, TX	131,248	73.1	54.1	4.3	14.7	23.2	3.7	4.2	0.3	3.02
28700	Kingsport-Bristol-Bristol, TN-VA	128,806	67.2	51.2	4.6	11.4	28.5	4.3	4.5	0.3	2.35
28740	Kingston, NY	69,089	63.4	46.7	5.1	11.6	29.0	7.5	6.7	1.0	2.45
28940	Knoxville, TN	342,017	64.2	49.9	3.9	10.4	30.2	5.6	4.6	0.4	2.42
29020	Kokomo, IN	34,538	64.9	48.7	5.2	11.0	30.4	4.7	5.1	0.2	2.37
29100	La Crosse-Onalaska, WI-MN	53,865	61.9	48.9	3.7	9.4	28.5	9.6	5.8	0.3	2.40
29180	Lafayette, LA	177,118	66.6	45.6	5.2	15.9	27.9	5.5	5.9	0.3	2.63
29200	Lafayette-West Lafayette, IN	78,623	59.0	45.2	3.9	10.0	28.5	12.5	6.8	0.4	2.45
29340	Lake Charles, LA	77,154	67.9	46.5	5.8	15.7	27.4	4.7	5.1	0.2	2.57
29420	Lake Havasu City-Kingman, AZ	80,117	62.8	48.3	3.8	10.6	28.6	8.6	6.7	0.4	2.42
29460	Lakeland-Winter Haven, FL	218,431	68.8	49.9	4.8	14.1	25.9	5.3	5.6	0.6	2.75
29540	Lancaster, PA	193,898	70.3	57.4	3.6	9.3	24.4	5.3	4.7	0.5	2.64
29620	Lansing-East Lansing, MI	181,509	60.1	44.4	4.2	11.5	30.9	9.0	5.7	0.5	2.45
29700	Laredo, TX	68,033	82.5	53.9	5.9	22.6	14.8	2.7	5.0	0.1	3.75
29740	Las Cruces, NM	74,145	69.5	47.6	4.8	17.1	23.9	6.6	6.3	0.4	2.81
29820	Las Vegas-Henderson-Paradise, NV	708,369	64.5	43.9	6.5	14.1	27.8	7.7	6.7	0.6	2.79
29940	Lawrence, KS	43,325	54.8	41.6	5.1	8.1	29.8	15.3	6.3	0.5	2.41
30020	Lawton, OK	46,214	65.2	46.2	4.4	14.5	29.2	5.7	5.8	0.4	2.65
30140	Lebanon, PA	52,068	69.1	53.2	4.5	11.3	26.4	4.5	6.2	0.4	2.53
30300	Lewiston, ID-WA	25,180	65.1	50.8	3.8	10.6	29.0	5.9	6.6	0.2	2.40
30340	Lewiston-Auburn, ME	44,364	62.1	45.7	4.7	11.6	29.4	8.6	9.0	0.6	2.36
30460	Lexington-Fayette, KY	190,748	62.4	45.8	4.4	12.2	29.6	8.0	5.4	0.5	2.45
30620	Lima, OH	40,235	65.2	45.4	5.0	14.8	29.1	5.6	7.4	0.4	2.53
30700	Lincoln, NE	121,906	61.1	47.5	4.4	9.2	29.5	9.4	6.4	0.4	2.43

CBSA FIPS code	Metropolitan area	Householder is White alone, not Hispanic or Latino, percent	Householder is Black or African American alone, percent	Householder is Hispanic or Latino, percent	Householder is Asian alone, percent	Householders age 15 to 34, percent	Householders age 35 to 64, percent	Householders age 65 and older, percent	Percent of households with one or more persons under 18 years old	Percent of households with one or more persons age 65 or older	Percent of all householders who are owners
24420	Grants Pass, OR	91.4	0.0	5.1	0.0	12.7	52.1	35.3	23.2	38.9	65.5
24500	Great Falls, MT	90.2	0.0	2.6	1.3	22.2	52.7	25.2	30.0	27.7	63.7
24540	Greeley, CO	75.8	0.9	21.0	1.1	24.1	57.9	18.0	38.5	20.6	68.5
24580	Green Bay, WI	90.8	1.4	3.7	1.7	20.0	58.6	21.5	31.7	23.2	69.2
24660	Greensboro-High Point, NC	65.7	25.5	5.1	2.3	19.7	58.0	22.3	31.7	24.9	63.9
24780	Greenville, NC	59.7	32.8	4.4	1.6	30.7	52.5	16.8	31.3	18.8	53.1
24860	Greenville-Anderson-Mauldin, SC	76.7	16.5	4.6	1.3	19.1	57.2	23.6	32.6	26.6	68.2
25060	Gulfport-Biloxi-Pascagoula, MS	73.2	19.6	3.8	1.9	20.2	57.5	22.3	33.0	25.3	64.2
25180	Hagerstown-Martinsburg, MD-WV	89.2	6.9	2.1	0.0	17.6	60.1	22.4	33.6	26.1	67.8
25220	Hammond, LA	67.9	27.4	2.9	0.0	23.3	56.5	20.2	35.0	24.4	69.0
25260	Hanford-Corcoran, CA	45.6	5.8	43.0	3.7	27.8	54.7	17.5	48.4	20.6	51.1
25420	Harrisburg-Carlisle, PA	84.2	8.7	3.7	2.5	18.4	57.6	24.0	29.5	26.6	67.8
25500	Harrisonburg, VA	87.3	3.3	7.1	0.0	23.6	52.8	23.6	29.3	26.4	62.9
25540	Hartford-West Hartford-East Hartford, CT	75.1	10.0	10.6	3.4	16.3	59.8	23.9	31.2	27.1	67.1
25620	Hattiesburg, MS	67.8	28.7	2.1	0.0	26.7	52.8	20.5	36.1	23.6	60.8
25860	Hickory-Lenoir-Morganton, NC	87.5	6.0	4.1	1.2	13.6	59.5	26.9	29.5	29.9	71.0
25940	Hilton Head Island-Bluffton-Beaufort, SC	70.4	21.3	6.3	0.0	17.7	48.6	33.7	27.8	36.9	71.4
25980	Hinesville, GA	48.0	38.2	10.6	0.0	35.9	51.9	12.2	43.0	13.8	51.5
26140	Homosassa Springs, FL	92.8	2.0	3.3	0.0	7.4	45.8	46.8	18.6	50.5	81.6
26300	Hot Springs, AR	86.6	7.4	2.9	0.0	16.5	52.2	31.3	28.7	35.2	67.6
26380	Houma-Thibodaux, LA	77.1	14.3	3.3	0.0	20.7	57.4	21.8	35.2	24.4	74.8
26420	Houston-The Woodlands-Sugar Land, TX	46.6	18.1	27.9	6.3	22.7	61.6	15.8	39.6	19.1	60.9
26580	Huntington-Ashland, WV-KY-OH	95.7	2.2	0.6	0.5	17.1	56.4	26.5	29.5	29.5	72.9
26620	Huntsville, AL	71.6	21.2	3.6	1.9	19.8	59.0	21.1	31.5	23.4	69.5
26820	Idaho Falls, ID	88.7	0.0	8.5	0.0	22.7	55.6	21.7	41.4	23.7	74.3
26900	Indianapolis-Carmel-Anderson, IN	78.0	14.4	4.3	1.9	22.3	58.5	19.3	34.4	21.8	65.5
26980	Iowa City, IA	87.1	3.8	4.0	4.2	35.5	48.1	16.4	28.1	17.9	61.4
27060	Ithaca, NY	81.0	3.5	3.9	10.0	30.5	50.3	19.2	24.5	22.0	56.1
27100	Jackson, MI	90.0	6.4	2.1	0.0	17.0	57.9	25.1	29.9	27.5	70.6
27140	Jackson, MS	52.0	44.9	1.5	0.9	20.0	59.0	21.0	36.2	23.4	66.7
27180	Jackson, TN	67.3	29.0	2.5	0.0	19.7	56.3	24.1	31.9	27.0	65.6
27260	Jacksonville, FL	69.4	20.2	6.0	2.9	19.2	59.1	21.7	31.4	24.7	66.1
27340	Jacksonville, NC	72.3	16.5	8.6	1.5	41.3	43.6	15.1	42.1	16.8	54.4
27500	Janesville-Beloit, WI	89.1	3.2	4.9	0.8	19.0	58.0	23.0	32.6	25.8	69.1
27620	Jefferson City, MO	92.1	4.8	1.2	0.7	19.2	57.4	23.4	33.3	25.3	71.8
27740	Johnson City, TN	94.0	2.4	1.6	0.0	19.1	54.4	26.4	27.1	29.6	67.8
27780	Johnstown, PA	95.6	2.5	0.8	0.0	13.9	55.3	30.8	24.8	33.6	74.1
27860	Jonesboro, AR	85.2	10.1	2.5	0.8	24.9	54.3	20.9	34.2	24.1	59.6
27900	Joplin, MO	90.4	1.2	4.0	0.0	22.7	53.6	23.7	34.3	26.5	66.4
27980	Kahului-Wailuku-Lahaina, HI	43.7	0.0	8.3	25.4	16.7	60.9	22.4	33.5	27.9	57.2
28020	Kalamazoo-Portage, MI	84.2	8.9	3.5	1.8	23.9	54.3	21.8	29.8	24.2	67.3
28100	Kankakee, IL	78.5	13.5	6.4	0.7	18.8	57.6	23.5	35.0	25.8	69.0
28140	Kansas City, MO-KS	78.2	12.4	5.7	1.9	21.8	57.7	20.5	33.3	22.8	65.8
28420	Kennewick-Richland, WA	74.3	1.3	20.1	2.0	21.9	58.0	20.1	38.7	22.7	68.0
28660	Killeen-Temple, TX	59.1	19.9	16.6	2.2	29.0	53.9	17.2	41.6	19.9	57.2
28700	Kingsport-Bristol-Bristol, TN-VA	95.7	1.9	1.1	0.3	14.8	55.0	30.2	29.0	32.9	74.3
28740	Kingston, NY	87.0	3.9	6.6	1.1	13.2	60.9	25.8	27.7	29.6	69.3
28940	Knoxville, TN	89.3	6.1	2.1	1.1	19.0	56.1	24.9	28.7	27.8	67.9
29020	Kokomo, IN	88.7	7.4	2.2	0.7	19.2	55.0	25.8	30.5	27.7	69.9
29100	La Crosse-Onalaska, WI-MN	95.5	0.0	1.1	2.1	23.5	53.4	23.1	27.5	24.7	67.3
29180	Lafayette, LA	72.2	22.7	2.6	1.2	22.2	57.9	19.9	35.3	22.2	69.5
29200	Lafayette-West Lafayette, IN	84.8	3.4	5.2	5.6	34.7	47.7	17.6	29.1	19.6	56.8
29340	Lake Charles, LA	73.0	22.2	1.9	0.0	21.5	56.3	22.3	35.6	25.0	69.9
29420	Lake Havasu City-Kingman, AZ	86.3	0.6	9.2	0.0	11.8	48.7	39.5	21.6	43.7	67.1
29460	Lakeland-Winter Haven, FL	71.7	12.9	13.3	1.3	15.6	53.2	31.3	30.1	35.2	68.8
29540	Lancaster, PA	88.0	3.2	6.8	1.3	18.0	56.5	25.5	31.1	28.5	69.4
29620	Lansing-East Lansing, MI	81.7	8.3	4.8	2.9	24.0	55.1	20.9	28.5	23.2	64.2
29700	Laredo, TX	5.1	0.0	93.7	0.0	22.0	62.1	16.0	54.2	21.6	63.2
29740	Las Cruces, NM	38.3	2.0	57.2	1.0	23.4	53.1	23.5	36.6	26.0	65.1
29820	Las Vegas-Henderson-Paradise, NV	56.9	11.0	21.3	7.8	21.1	58.7	20.2	34.2	24.2	52.7
29940	Lawrence, KS	85.7	3.6	3.8	3.3	35.9	47.7	16.4	27.2	18.0	52.7
30020	Lawton, OK	65.1	15.3	9.1	1.8	26.1	53.1	20.7	36.3	22.2	56.6
30140	Lebanon, PA	89.3	1.7	7.9	0.0	15.9	56.7	27.4	30.5	30.2	71.0
30300	Lewiston, ID-WA	93.2	0.0	2.2	0.0	17.2	53.3	29.5	27.0	32.0	68.5
30340	Lewiston-Auburn, ME	94.5	0.9	0.0	0.0	18.5	58.4	23.0	30.6	25.3	61.6
30460	Lexington-Fayette, KY	81.7	11.3	3.6	2.1	24.7	56.4	19.0	30.9	21.3	59.4
30620	Lima, OH	84.1	11.3	1.9	0.0	19.2	55.6	25.3	32.6	27.6	67.2
30700	Lincoln, NE	88.8	3.0	4.0	2.9	29.0	52.2	18.8	30.5	20.5	60.2

CBSA FIPS code	Metropolitan area	Household type							Opposite-sex partner unmarried partner households, percent	Same-sex partner unmarried partner households, percent	Average household size
		Total Households	Family households, percent	Married-couple family households, percent	Male householder, no spouse, percent	Female householder, no spouse, percent	Householder living alone, percent	Nonfamily households, householder not living alone, percent			
30780	Little Rock-North Little Rock-Conway, AR	272,782	64.7	46.8	4.2	13.7	29.7	5.6	3.7	0.5	2.58
30860	Logan, UT-ID	39,485	74.8	64.1	2.9	7.9	18.2	7.0	2.4	0.2	3.15
30980	Longview, TX	76,736	68.5	49.6	4.6	14.3	27.8	3.6	4.3	0.3	2.70
31020	Longview, WA	39,261	66.4	50.3	4.8	11.3	27.0	6.5	8.7	0.3	2.57
31080	Los Angeles-Long Beach-Anaheim, CA	4,233,105	67.9	46.5	6.6	14.9	24.9	7.2	6.0	0.6	3.03
31140	Louisville/Jefferson County, KY-IN	488,439	64.9	46.3	4.8	13.8	29.2	5.9	5.5	0.6	2.51
31180	Lubbock, TX	110,103	63.2	44.7	5.0	13.6	27.7	9.1	5.2	0.4	2.61
31340	Lynchburg, VA	99,221	66.2	50.2	3.9	12.2	28.7	5.1	4.3	0.3	2.45
31420	Macon, GA	83,479	66.6	43.1	4.3	19.3	29.3	4.0	4.5	0.1	2.68
31460	Madera, CA	42,247	76.1	55.1	5.7	15.3	19.2	4.7	8.1	0.4	3.39
31540	Madison, WI	254,930	59.7	47.0	4.0	8.7	30.2	10.1	6.4	0.7	2.37
31700	Manchester-Nashua, NH	154,396	67.0	51.6	4.6	10.7	25.3	7.7	7.8	0.5	2.56
31740	Manhattan, KS	34,309	57.7	46.7	3.2	7.8	29.1	13.2	4.9	0.3	2.56
31860	Mankato-North Mankato, MN	36,910	60.7	49.8	4.2	6.7	28.2	11.1	6.5	0.2	2.46
31900	Mansfield, OH	48,296	62.6	46.6	3.7	12.3	32.7	4.7	5.3	0.2	2.39
32580	McAllen-Edinburg-Mission, TX	221,305	81.4	57.4	4.6	19.4	15.9	2.8	2.9	0.3	3.60
32780	Medford, OR	82,737	64.5	48.9	4.5	11.2	28.8	6.7	7.1	0.6	2.45
32820	Memphis, TN-MS-AR	488,617	66.2	41.2	5.2	19.8	29.1	4.8	4.9	0.4	2.69
32900	Merced, CA	76,398	76.3	51.0	6.7	18.6	19.0	4.7	7.5	0.2	3.35
33100	Miami-Fort Lauderdale-West Palm Beach, FL	2,021,409	64.6	43.5	5.4	15.7	29.1	6.3	5.6	0.7	2.81
33140	Michigan City-La Porte, IN	42,747	65.2	48.2	3.5	13.5	29.1	5.7	6.8	0.4	2.39
33220	Midland, MI	33,543	67.7	55.6	3.5	8.5	26.2	6.1	5.9	0.2	2.46
33260	Midland, TX	52,937	70.3	52.3	6.0	12.0	24.2	5.5	6.7	0.2	2.81
33340	Milwaukee-Waukesha-West Allis, WI	620,022	62.2	44.7	4.4	13.1	31.1	6.8	6.0	0.4	2.48
33460	Minneapolis-St. Paul-Bloomington, MN-WI	1,322,431	64.7	50.1	4.2	10.4	27.9	7.4	6.1	0.7	2.54
33540	Missoula, MT	45,834	58.0	43.0	4.6	10.4	30.0	12.0	8.1	0.8	2.35
33660	Mobile, AL	153,853	67.9	44.4	4.4	19.1	28.2	3.9	3.4	0.5	2.62
33700	Modesto, CA	167,863	73.9	50.7	7.0	16.2	20.7	5.4	7.2	0.5	3.07
33740	Monroe, LA	65,880	65.7	43.2	3.5	19.0	30.1	4.1	3.8	0.3	2.57
33780	Monroe, MI	58,167	70.6	54.1	4.8	11.7	24.8	4.6	5.6	0.4	2.57
33860	Montgomery, AL	140,918	65.9	43.5	4.2	18.2	29.7	4.4	4.3	0.2	2.57
34060	Morgantown, WV	48,954	56.6	45.0	3.9	7.8	34.0	9.4	6.9	0.4	2.56
34100	Morristown, TN	43,810	70.3	52.3	4.4	13.7	25.6	4.1	5.7	0.4	2.57
34580	Mount Vernon-Anacortes, WA	45,174	68.6	51.9	4.5	12.3	24.5	6.8	7.0	0.3	2.57
34620	Muncie, IN	46,101	59.8	43.0	3.9	13.0	29.5	10.7	6.2	0.3	2.38
34740	Muskegon, MI	64,434	67.2	47.4	4.8	14.9	27.7	5.1	6.8	0.4	2.54
34820	Myrtle Beach-Conway-North Myrtle Beach, SC-NC	161,689	66.5	50.3	4.4	11.7	27.7	5.8	5.9	0.3	2.42
34900	Napa, CA	48,847	69.1	52.4	5.2	11.4	24.7	6.2	5.1	0.6	2.75
34940	Naples-Immokalee-Marco Island, FL	125,417	65.7	52.3	3.9	9.5	29.1	5.2	4.6	0.6	2.62
34980	Nashville-Davidson–Murfreesboro–Franklin, TN	650,423	65.4	48.9	4.2	12.4	28.2	6.3	4.9	0.5	2.60
35100	New Bern, NC	48,724	70.4	54.4	3.8	12.3	25.5	4.1	4.4	0.3	2.53
35300	New Haven-Milford, CT	325,283	64.8	45.5	4.3	15.0	29.6	5.7	5.2	0.5	2.56
35380	New Orleans-Metairie, LA	470,694	62.4	39.9	5.0	17.4	31.4	6.2	5.8	0.5	2.56
35620	New York-Newark-Jersey City, NY-NJ-PA	7,067,935	66.1	45.7	5.1	15.3	28.1	5.8	4.6	0.6	2.75
35660	Niles-Benton Harbor, MI	59,108	66.9	49.4	3.9	13.6	29.1	4.0	4.8	0.3	2.55
35840	North Port-Sarasota-Bradenton, FL	304,830	61.9	49.5	3.1	9.3	31.4	6.7	5.4	0.6	2.33
35980	Norwich-New London, CT	106,911	65.6	48.8	4.9	11.9	28.0	6.4	6.8	0.5	2.45
36100	Ocala, FL	133,171	65.9	50.1	4.0	11.8	28.1	6.0	5.5	0.3	2.45
36140	Ocean City, NJ	40,506	64.0	52.0	3.3	8.7	31.2	4.8	4.1	0.8	2.31
36220	Odessa, TX	50,488	71.0	47.7	6.7	16.6	23.2	5.8	6.8	0.6	2.83
36260	Ogden-Clearfield, UT	194,666	78.0	63.5	4.4	10.0	18.1	3.9	3.6	0.4	3.12
36420	Oklahoma City, OK	487,078	65.1	47.6	5.1	12.4	28.7	6.2	4.8	0.4	2.60
36500	Olympia-Tumwater, WA	101,098	66.6	50.9	4.7	11.0	26.2	7.2	6.3	0.7	2.53
36540	Omaha-Council Bluffs, NE-IA	339,603	65.2	48.9	4.5	11.8	28.8	6.0	5.1	0.5	2.56
36740	Orlando-Kissimmee-Sanford, FL	773,618	66.1	47.2	4.4	12.4	26.5	7.4	6.2	0.7	2.82
36780	Oshkosh-Neenah, WI	68,043	60.0	47.8	3.7	8.5	32.0	8.0	6.9	0.3	2.35
36980	Owensboro, KY	44,884	68.1	51.9	4.7	11.4	27.4	4.5	5.0	0.4	2.52
37100	Oxnard-Thousand Oaks-Ventura, CA	266,867	73.3	55.5	5.5	12.4	20.7	6.0	5.4	0.5	3.08
37340	Palm Bay-Melbourne-Titusville, FL	218,067	63.4	47.1	4.1	12.3	30.5	6.0	5.8	0.3	2.48
37460	Panama City, FL	73,411	65.0	47.6	4.9	12.5	28.2	6.8	6.2	0.7	2.49
37620	Parkersburg-Vienna, WV	38,072	64.2	48.1	4.3	11.8	30.7	5.1	6.0	0.5	2.41
37860	Pensacola-Ferry Pass-Brent, FL	169,765	64.9	48.2	4.2	12.6	28.4	6.6	5.3	0.4	2.58
37900	Peoria, IL	152,235	65.2	50.0	3.5	11.6	29.8	5.1	5.4	0.5	2.45

CBSA FIPS code	Metropolitan area	Race or Hispanic origin of householder				Age of householder			Percent of households with one or more persons under 18 years old	Percent of households with one or more persons age 65 or older	Percent of all householders who are owners
		Householder is White alone, not Hispanic or Latino, percent	Householder is Black or African American alone, percent	Householder is Hispanic or Latino, percent	Householder is Asian alone, percent	Householders age 15 to 34, percent	Householders age 35 to 64, percent	Householders age 65 and older, percent			
30780	Little Rock-North Little Rock-Conway, AR	72.2	21.7	3.4	1.3	22.5	56.5	21.0	30.3	23.6	65.6
30860	Logan, UT-ID	90.0	0.0	6.7	1.3	32.9	49.7	17.3	40.5	18.8	67.3
30980	Longview, TX	71.5	17.4	9.1	0.8	20.2	54.6	25.2	33.9	28.0	67.5
31020	Longview, WA	90.1	0.0	4.3	0.9	16.8	55.1	28.1	29.3	31.0	66.1
31080	Los Angeles-Long Beach-Anaheim, CA	41.4	8.1	33.4	15.0	19.0	61.0	20.0	35.9	25.1	48.7
31140	Louisville/Jefferson County, KY-IN	80.6	13.9	2.9	1.3	19.0	58.6	22.3	31.3	25.0	67.4
31180	Lubbock, TX	63.9	6.1	26.8	1.7	31.2	48.9	19.9	32.7	22.2	58.2
31340	Lynchburg, VA	79.2	17.0	1.4	1.1	17.5	55.9	26.6	28.9	29.6	70.9
31420	Macon, GA	54.8	40.9	2.2	1.0	18.8	57.5	23.7	31.8	26.8	61.2
31460	Madera, CA	50.2	2.9	42.5	2.0	18.9	57.3	23.8	41.2	29.0	58.9
31540	Madison, WI	88.3	3.7	3.5	3.4	26.7	54.7	18.6	28.2	20.2	61.5
31700	Manchester-Nashua, NH	89.9	2.1	4.0	2.9	17.2	62.7	20.1	32.7	23.1	66.4
31740	Manhattan, KS	84.7	5.3	5.0	3.4	43.5	40.9	15.6	29.8	16.5	50.5
31860	Mankato-North Mankato, MN	93.5	1.9	2.2	0.0	29.6	49.0	21.5	28.5	22.9	67.8
31900	Mansfield, OH	90.8	6.3	0.0	0.0	15.9	55.3	28.9	28.8	31.1	68.8
32580	McAllen-Edinburg-Mission, TX	12.0	0.0	86.2	1.1	21.3	59.1	19.5	52.1	23.9	67.6
32780	Medford, OR	88.7	0.6	6.9	0.8	17.5	53.1	29.5	27.4	32.5	62.1
32820	Memphis, TN-MS-AR	49.7	44.1	3.4	1.7	20.5	60.2	19.3	34.4	22.4	61.8
32900	Merced, CA	42.0	4.1	46.4	5.6	22.5	58.2	19.3	46.3	24.0	52.2
33100	Miami-Fort Lauderdale-West Palm Beach, FL	42.7	17.9	37.0	2.1	15.0	58.8	26.2	31.0	31.4	61.7
33140	Michigan City-La Porte, IN	87.4	7.7	3.4	0.0	17.6	57.0	25.4	29.1	28.6	71.5
33220	Midland, MI	94.1	0.0	1.6	0.0	17.5	58.1	24.5	30.5	26.2	75.4
33260	Midland, TX	60.8	6.7	30.3	1.2	26.3	55.9	17.7	37.5	20.9	66.3
33340	Milwaukee-Waukesha-West Allis, WI	74.4	15.2	6.8	2.1	21.3	57.2	21.5	30.8	23.7	60.3
33460	Minneapolis-St. Paul-Bloomington, MN-WI	84.0	6.5	3.5	4.2	21.8	59.3	18.9	33.0	21.0	70.0
33540	Missoula, MT	92.9	0.0	2.0	0.0	29.6	52.1	18.3	26.1	20.5	56.9
33660	Mobile, AL	61.5	33.2	2.2	1.7	19.5	57.0	23.5	33.7	26.7	66.2
33700	Modesto, CA	56.6	2.8	33.0	4.7	20.9	58.9	20.2	41.8	24.6	56.6
33740	Monroe, LA	64.2	32.4	1.8	0.0	21.4	55.5	23.2	34.5	25.2	61.4
33780	Monroe, MI	94.6	2.1	1.7	0.0	13.7	62.2	24.0	32.1	26.1	78.5
33860	Montgomery, AL	54.7	40.8	2.0	1.4	21.6	56.9	21.5	33.8	24.7	65.7
34060	Morgantown, WV	93.6	2.3	1.0	2.2	30.4	50.3	19.3	24.8	21.8	62.3
34100	Morristown, TN	90.4	2.9	5.0	0.0	16.2	55.4	28.4	32.8	31.5	70.7
34580	Mount Vernon-Anacortes, WA	84.3	0.0	10.8	1.3	16.7	56.5	26.8	30.5	31.0	66.4
34620	Muncie, IN	89.3	4.6	1.3	0.8	24.2	50.5	25.3	26.4	27.7	62.6
34740	Muskegon, MI	81.8	12.4	3.4	0.0	17.8	58.2	24.0	32.9	26.3	74.8
34820	Myrtle Beach-Conway-North Myrtle Beach, SC-NC	83.8	10.6	3.5	0.9	15.6	53.5	31.0	25.8	34.5	70.1
34900	Napa, CA	68.8	1.6	22.3	5.5	14.2	59.2	26.6	32.7	31.0	58.4
34940	Naples-Immokalee-Marco Island, FL	79.8	4.1	14.8	0.0	9.6	46.6	43.9	21.9	47.5	72.9
34980	Nashville-Davidson—Murfreesboro—Franklin, TN	77.4	15.1	4.4	1.8	22.3	58.8	18.9	32.6	21.5	65.4
35100	New Bern, NC	72.6	20.7	4.3	0.0	22.0	50.0	28.0	31.3	31.4	66.1
35300	New Haven-Milford, CT	71.2	12.3	12.5	3.0	16.7	59.0	24.3	31.1	27.8	63.0
35380	New Orleans-Metairie, LA	56.8	32.9	6.7	2.2	20.4	58.6	21.0	30.5	24.3	61.5
35620	New York-Newark-Jersey City, NY-NJ-PA	54.7	16.7	19.2	8.9	16.7	60.6	22.7	33.3	27.1	51.8
35660	Niles-Benton Harbor, MI	80.0	14.6	2.8	1.2	15.4	57.7	27.0	29.1	30.6	72.0
35840	North Port-Sarasota-Bradenton, FL	85.8	5.1	7.3	1.1	10.1	47.7	42.1	21.0	45.6	72.1
35980	Norwich-New London, CT	83.0	5.0	6.6	3.0	16.9	59.6	23.5	31.2	27.0	66.6
36100	Ocala, FL	78.4	11.1	8.3	1.3	12.0	47.2	40.8	23.0	44.1	74.7
36140	Ocean City, NJ	91.0	3.4	4.1	0.0	11.6	53.6	34.8	23.5	38.4	75.3
36220	Odessa, TX	46.5	3.5	47.7	0.0	27.1	54.3	18.6	41.3	20.8	65.9
36260	Ogden-Clearfield, UT	86.5	1.2	9.1	1.6	25.2	56.1	18.7	44.3	20.9	75.1
36420	Oklahoma City, OK	73.1	10.2	7.8	2.2	24.8	54.7	20.5	33.4	22.8	64.2
36500	Olympia-Tumwater, WA	83.4	2.7	5.3	4.8	19.4	58.5	22.1	30.1	25.2	65.7
36540	Omaha-Council Bluffs, NE-IA	83.0	7.8	5.9	1.8	24.3	56.5	19.2	33.7	21.2	65.7
36740	Orlando-Kissimmee-Sanford, FL	58.7	14.4	22.2	3.4	20.2	58.6	21.2	31.8	24.9	61.7
36780	Oshkosh-Neenah, WI	95.0	0.9	2.0	1.5	22.2	55.3	22.5	27.1	23.9	65.6
36980	Owensboro, KY	93.7	3.9	0.0	0.0	18.9	55.8	25.2	32.1	27.7	72.1
37100	Oxnard-Thousand Oaks-Ventura, CA	61.0	1.9	28.5	6.8	15.0	62.0	23.0	38.4	27.5	64.3
37340	Palm Bay-Melbourne-Titusville, FL	81.7	9.0	6.8	1.5	12.3	54.6	33.0	24.6	36.8	72.6
37460	Panama City, FL	82.7	9.8	4.1	1.3	20.3	54.7	25.0	28.7	27.5	61.9
37620	Parkersburg-Vienna, WV	97.4	0.8	0.0	0.0	16.4	55.1	28.5	27.1	31.1	72.3
37860	Pensacola-Ferry Pass-Brent, FL	77.4	14.7	3.6	2.0	18.8	56.3	24.9	28.5	27.9	65.7
37900	Peoria, IL	86.8	8.2	2.0	1.8	20.4	55.2	24.4	29.9	26.4	70.4

CBSA FIPS code	Metropolitan area	Total Households	Family households, percent	Married-couple family households, percent	Male householder, no spouse, percent	Female householder, no spouse, percent	Householder living alone, percent	Nonfamily households, householder not living alone, percent	Opposite-sex partner unmarried partner households, percent	Same-sex unmarried partner households, percent	Average household size
37980	Philadelphia-Camden-Wilmington, PA-NJ-DE-MD	2,221,792	64.5	45.8	4.5	14.1	29.7	5.8	5.2	0.5	2.63
38060	Phoenix-Mesa-Scottsdale, AZ	1,543,613	66.1	47.5	5.6	13.0	26.8	7.2	6.5	0.7	2.76
38220	Pine Bluff, AR	35,786	64.5	41.7	5.0	17.8	31.9	3.6	4.1	0.3	2.44
38300	Pittsburgh, PA	987,425	61.7	46.6	3.8	11.3	32.4	5.9	5.1	0.4	2.33
38340	Pittsfield, MA	55,192	59.7	43.7	4.0	11.9	34.6	5.7	6.5	0.5	2.23
38540	Pocatello, ID	30,239	65.7	50.8	4.3	10.7	27.7	6.5	5.2	0.2	2.68
38860	Portland-South Portland, ME	213,630	62.4	49.1	4.1	9.3	29.2	8.4	7.3	0.8	2.37
38900	Portland-Vancouver-Hillsboro, OR-WA	874,400	63.4	48.4	4.4	10.6	27.6	9.0	6.7	0.9	2.57
38940	Port St. Lucie, FL	166,579	65.8	50.5	4.3	11.0	29.0	5.2	4.9	0.3	2.56
39140	Prescott, AZ	92,332	62.6	49.8	3.3	9.5	31.3	6.1	6.1	0.3	2.27
39300	Providence-Warwick, RI-MA	620,443	63.6	44.9	4.8	13.9	29.6	6.8	6.4	0.7	2.49
39340	Provo-Orem, UT	147,792	82.0	70.4	3.3	8.3	12.5	5.5	1.8	0.2	3.64
39380	Pueblo, CO	62,136	63.7	44.5	5.7	13.5	30.5	5.8	5.7	0.5	2.51
39460	Punta Gorda, FL	69,690	65.4	53.5	4.0	7.9	28.6	5.9	5.2	0.4	2.28
39540	Racine, WI	74,258	65.7	49.2	4.7	11.8	28.6	5.7	5.7	0.3	2.56
39580	Raleigh, NC	438,833	67.8	51.8	4.0	12.0	25.9	6.4	4.6	0.5	2.65
39660	Rapid City, SD	54,589	65.5	49.5	5.2	10.9	28.1	6.3	7.4	0.5	2.46
39740	Reading, PA	153,142	68.2	51.2	5.4	11.6	25.0	6.8	7.2	0.5	2.61
39820	Redding, CA	69,123	65.7	48.4	4.6	12.7	27.6	6.6	6.4	0.4	2.54
39900	Reno, NV	164,579	61.8	45.1	5.1	11.5	29.7	8.5	6.9	0.5	2.59
40060	Richmond, VA	460,584	65.0	46.1	4.3	14.7	28.6	6.4	5.3	0.5	2.60
40140	Riverside-San Bernardino-Ontario, CA	1,293,932	74.5	52.5	6.8	15.1	20.3	5.2	6.5	0.7	3.29
40220	Roanoke, VA	127,664	65.3	49.0	4.0	12.3	29.3	5.3	4.8	0.5	2.37
40340	Rochester, MN	82,287	66.7	54.3	3.6	8.8	27.7	5.6	5.6	0.3	2.51
40380	Rochester, NY	427,448	62.9	45.1	4.4	13.4	30.0	7.1	6.7	0.6	2.43
40420	Rockford, IL	130,364	68.0	49.3	4.5	14.1	27.2	4.8	5.7	0.3	2.62
40580	Rocky Mount, NC	57,527	67.0	43.6	4.2	19.2	28.4	4.6	5.4	0.3	2.57
40660	Rome, GA	34,168	66.4	48.3	3.9	14.2	28.1	5.5	2.7	0.3	2.69
40900	Sacramento-Roseville–Arden-Arcade, CA	789,007	66.1	47.6	5.2	13.2	26.2	7.7	6.6	0.6	2.73
40980	Saginaw, MI	77,436	64.2	45.2	4.1	14.9	31.2	4.5	5.4	0.3	2.47
41060	St. Cloud, MN	72,125	64.8	52.0	4.7	8.2	25.3	9.9	7.6	0.3	2.51
41100	St. George, UT	47,346	75.6	62.9	2.8	9.9	19.7	4.7	2.4	0.2	3.01
41140	St. Joseph, MO-KS	46,240	65.5	49.4	4.6	11.5	28.9	5.6	5.7	0.4	2.59
41180	St. Louis, MO-IL	1,100,928	65.4	47.4	4.4	13.7	29.1	5.5	5.4	0.4	2.49
41420	Salem, OR	141,390	68.9	50.7	5.6	12.6	25.0	6.0	7.1	0.5	2.72
41500	Salinas, CA	125,012	72.5	52.2	6.7	13.5	21.6	6.0	7.5	0.7	3.24
41540	Salisbury, MD-DE	141,374	66.9	49.0	4.5	13.5	26.5	6.6	5.8	0.7	2.59
41620	Salt Lake City, UT	365,237	70.8	54.9	5.0	10.9	22.8	6.5	4.7	0.7	3.04
41660	San Angelo, TX	43,020	64.8	46.4	4.3	14.0	29.9	5.4	5.6	0.2	2.53
41700	San Antonio-New Braunfels, TX	767,634	69.3	48.4	5.2	15.6	25.4	5.4	4.7	0.5	2.86
41740	San Diego-Carlsbad, CA	1,079,664	66.4	49.1	5.0	12.3	24.9	8.8	5.8	0.7	2.86
41860	San Francisco-Oakland-Hayward, CA	1,640,597	62.4	46.6	4.7	11.2	28.4	9.2	5.5	1.1	2.67
41940	San Jose-Sunnyvale-Santa Clara, CA	631,952	71.6	55.6	5.2	10.7	21.6	6.8	5.4	0.4	2.94
42020	San Luis Obispo-Paso Robles-Arroyo Grande, CA	102,728	63.4	50.3	3.8	9.2	26.3	10.4	5.9	0.6	2.51
42100	Santa Cruz-Watsonville, CA	94,218	62.4	47.4	4.8	10.2	26.7	10.9	7.6	0.8	2.71
42140	Santa Fe, NM	60,878	58.1	42.2	4.8	11.1	33.9	8.0	6.8	1.2	2.35
42200	Santa Maria-Santa Barbara, CA	141,634	65.4	48.6	5.4	11.4	25.1	9.5	6.2	0.6	2.91
42220	Santa Rosa, CA	185,259	62.7	46.8	5.1	10.8	28.3	9.0	7.0	1.0	2.60
42340	Savannah, GA	132,440	65.3	45.2	4.8	15.3	28.4	6.4	5.6	0.5	2.64
42540	Scranton–Wilkes-Barre-Hazleton, PA	225,825	63.2	45.4	5.0	12.8	31.7	5.0	5.6	0.3	2.40
42660	Seattle-Tacoma-Bellevue, WA	1,376,439	62.4	47.9	4.4	10.1	28.9	8.6	6.4	0.8	2.54
42680	Sebastian-Vero Beach, FL	58,531	62.5	48.9	3.5	10.1	32.1	5.4	4.5	0.4	2.37
42700	Sebring, FL	39,922	62.4	50.4	2.9	9.1	32.8	4.8	3.3	0.3	2.41
43100	Sheboygan, WI	46,450	65.5	52.2	4.3	9.0	28.5	6.0	6.7	0.4	2.41
43300	Sherman-Denison, TX	46,757	67.8	48.9	5.1	13.7	26.9	5.3	5.7	0.6	2.55
43340	Shreveport-Bossier City, LA	170,407	64.2	40.7	5.0	18.5	31.8	4.0	4.3	0.4	2.57
43420	Sierra Vista-Douglas, AZ	48,765	65.6	49.0	4.0	12.6	29.1	5.3	5.1	0.6	2.44
43580	Sioux City, IA-NE-SD	64,008	66.9	50.5	5.2	11.1	28.1	5.0	6.4	0.2	2.58
43620	Sioux Falls, SD	91,698	66.0	51.0	4.5	10.6	26.9	7.1	5.8	0.3	2.53
43780	South Bend-Mishawaka, IN-MI	122,494	64.5	47.3	4.4	12.8	29.4	6.1	6.0	0.3	2.50
43900	Spartanburg, SC	118,962	69.8	48.0	4.8	17.0	26.1	4.0	4.6	0.4	2.60
44060	Spokane-Spokane Valley, WA	210,239	63.2	48.2	4.3	10.7	28.9	7.9	6.7	0.7	2.46
44100	Springfield, IL	87,661	62.4	44.9	4.7	12.8	31.3	6.3	5.1	0.4	2.36
44140	Springfield, MA	234,776	64.0	42.9	5.1	16.0	29.0	7.0	6.3	0.8	2.51
44180	Springfield, MO	176,928	65.0	50.2	4.5	10.2	27.5	7.5	5.8	0.3	2.43
44220	Springfield, OH	54,405	64.9	46.6	4.5	13.8	29.0	6.1	7.3	0.3	2.46
44300	State College, PA	57,447	56.7	46.2	3.9	6.6	27.6	15.7	4.3	0.5	2.42
44420	Staunton-Waynesboro, VA	47,155	68.2	51.6	5.2	11.4	27.8	4.0	5.7	0.4	2.41

CBSA FIPS code	Metropolitan area	Race or Hispanic origin of householder				Age of householder			Percent of households with one or more persons under 18 years old	Percent of households with one or more persons age 65 or older	Percent of all householders who are owners
		Householder is White alone, not Hispanic or Latino, percent	Householder is Black or African American alone, percent	Householder is Hispanic or Latino, percent	Householder is Asian alone, percent	Householders age 15 to 34, percent	Householders age 35 to 64, percent	Householders age 65 and older, percent			
37980	Philadelphia-Camden-Wilmington, PA-NJ-DE-MD..............	68.3	20.3	6.2	4.3	17.5	59.5	23.0	31.4	26.4	67.6
38060	Phoenix-Mesa-Scottsdale, AZ	68.4	5.0	20.9	3.1	21.3	56.6	22.1	33.8	25.3	61.9
38220	Pine Bluff, AR..................................	52.1	45.0	0.0	0.0	18.7	56.2	25.1	32.1	27.9	66.3
38300	Pittsburgh, PA.................................	88.6	7.8	1.0	1.6	16.8	56.0	27.3	26.0	30.2	69.5
38340	Pittsfield, MA.................................	94.1	1.6	2.0	0.0	12.0	57.9	30.1	24.9	32.6	68.6
38540	Pocatello, ID...................................	90.7	0.0	4.9	0.0	27.3	52.7	19.9	34.3	21.9	66.3
38860	Portland-South Portland, ME............	95.4	1.2	1.2	1.2	15.9	59.7	24.3	27.7	27.3	69.7
38900	Portland-Vancouver-Hillsboro, OR-WA.....................	82.1	2.6	7.2	5.0	20.6	59.2	20.2	31.6	23.0	60.5
38940	Port St. Lucie, FL	75.8	11.6	10.6	1.0	11.3	51.8	36.9	25.8	40.5	72.9
39140	Prescott, AZ	87.9	0.5	8.5	0.0	11.4	50.4	38.2	20.5	42.1	68.6
39300	Providence-Warwick, RI-MA..............	83.4	4.7	8.0	2.1	16.8	59.3	23.9	30.0	27.3	60.9
39340	Provo-Orem, UT..............................	87.1	0.4	9.1	1.3	34.2	50.7	15.1	51.4	17.2	66.8
39380	Pueblo, CO	59.7	0.0	36.9	0.0	18.4	55.9	25.8	31.1	28.6	64.1
39460	Punta Gorda, FL	89.3	4.8	4.1	0.9	6.9	43.3	49.8	18.0	53.8	78.6
39540	Racine, WI	80.2	9.9	8.1	0.8	16.9	60.2	22.9	31.7	25.6	69.1
39580	Raleigh, NC....................................	67.8	20.1	6.6	4.2	21.8	62.0	16.2	36.9	18.5	65.9
39660	Rapid City, SD	88.3	0.0	2.7	0.5	22.2	55.5	22.3	31.4	24.8	68.0
39740	Reading, PA	81.3	4.5	13.0	1.0	16.2	58.8	25.1	32.7	28.0	72.1
39820	Redding, CA	86.7	0.0	6.2	2.2	15.8	53.9	30.3	27.8	33.6	62.5
39900	Reno, NV	75.5	2.2	15.4	4.2	20.5	57.8	21.8	30.7	25.1	57.1
40060	Richmond, VA.................................	62.9	28.9	3.9	2.6	18.9	59.6	21.5	31.9	24.8	66.1
40140	Riverside-San Bernardino-Ontario, CA....................	47.4	7.6	37.0	5.8	18.5	60.8	20.8	42.6	25.7	62.9
40220	Roanoke, VA...................................	83.9	11.2	2.5	1.1	16.0	57.3	26.7	28.4	29.2	69.8
40340	Rochester, MN	90.9	2.4	2.5	3.1	21.1	56.5	22.4	31.7	24.2	76.1
40380	Rochester, NY	81.9	10.2	5.0	2.0	18.5	57.5	24.1	29.5	26.5	67.7
40420	Rockford, IL	78.7	9.9	8.6	1.7	17.2	59.1	23.7	34.2	26.6	68.8
40580	Rocky Mount, NC............................	52.4	42.7	3.5	0.0	15.0	58.6	26.4	31.3	29.5	63.8
40660	Rome, GA.......................................	77.3	14.1	6.6	0.0	17.8	57.3	24.9	32.4	28.5	62.5
40900	Sacramento—Roseville—Arden-Arcade, CA....................	63.5	7.2	15.4	10.2	20.0	58.5	21.5	34.2	25.3	58.9
40980	Saginaw, MI	75.0	17.4	5.7	0.9	16.5	56.5	27.0	28.9	29.5	72.1
41060	St. Cloud, MN	94.4	2.2	1.6	1.2	25.4	53.5	21.2	31.3	22.9	70.9
41100	St. George, UT................................	90.5	0.0	6.5	0.0	19.7	47.2	33.1	34.7	36.0	69.8
41140	St. Joseph, MO-KS	91.8	3.0	3.1	0.0	19.2	55.8	25.0	31.3	27.1	65.9
41180	St. Louis, MO-IL	77.3	17.8	1.9	1.8	19.5	57.8	22.8	31.4	25.2	70.0
41420	Salem, OR......................................	79.6	0.7	13.8	1.8	20.5	55.2	24.3	34.6	27.0	60.0
41500	Salinas, CA	46.5	2.7	42.2	6.8	21.3	57.5	21.2	41.3	25.5	48.2
41540	Salisbury, MD-DE............................	79.3	15.2	3.6	1.0	13.6	54.1	32.4	27.0	35.7	73.5
41620	Salt Lake City, UT...........................	80.0	1.5	12.6	3.2	25.7	57.2	17.1	40.0	19.5	66.6
41660	San Angelo, TX...............................	64.9	4.3	29.6	0.0	24.9	51.0	24.1	30.9	26.1	61.7
41700	San Antonio-New Braunfels, TX	42.9	7.1	46.8	1.9	22.0	58.1	19.9	37.6	23.5	62.2
41740	San Diego-Carlsbad, CA...................	58.8	5.0	23.9	9.7	22.2	57.4	20.3	33.9	24.4	53.1
41860	San Francisco-Oakland-Hayward, CA.....................	51.1	8.7	15.6	21.3	18.8	60.0	21.3	31.0	25.6	53.3
41940	San Jose-Sunnyvale-Santa Clara, CA.....................	44.6	2.8	20.0	30.2	19.2	62.1	18.8	39.0	23.7	56.6
42020	San Luis Obispo-Paso Robles-Arroyo Grande, CA.............	78.3	1.5	15.6	2.9	19.9	54.1	26.0	27.1	30.2	56.1
42100	Santa Cruz-Watsonville, CA	70.8	1.1	22.1	3.7	17.5	59.7	22.8	30.1	25.7	58.1
42140	Santa Fe, NM	53.5	0.7	41.5	1.3	13.6	59.4	27.0	24.6	30.3	68.3
42200	Santa Maria-Santa Barbara, CA.........	60.7	1.7	31.2	4.5	21.6	53.8	24.6	33.2	28.5	51.5
42220	Santa Rosa, CA...............................	76.9	1.3	16.1	3.5	15.5	59.3	25.2	29.5	28.7	59.3
42340	Savannah, GA.................................	62.2	30.4	4.2	1.9	23.2	55.9	20.9	32.5	23.4	59.5
42540	Scranton—Wilkes-Barre—Hazleton, PA	92.3	2.0	4.3	1.0	15.0	56.5	28.6	27.2	31.8	67.1
42660	Seattle-Tacoma-Bellevue, WA	73.6	5.5	6.5	10.1	22.3	59.3	18.4	31.3	21.0	59.5
42680	Sebastian-Vero Beach, FL	82.7	7.6	8.2	0.0	11.0	46.2	42.9	21.9	46.9	74.1
42700	Sebring, FL.....................................	79.4	6.9	11.9	0.0	8.7	41.8	49.5	19.0	53.3	77.0
43100	Sheboygan, WI	91.8	0.0	3.8	2.9	18.0	57.7	24.3	28.2	26.4	70.8
43300	Sherman-Denison, TX......................	83.2	5.7	7.7	0.8	17.8	56.6	25.6	32.7	29.1	66.2
43340	Shreveport-Bossier City, LA..............	59.0	36.5	2.3	1.0	21.5	55.2	23.4	32.2	25.8	64.5
43420	Sierra Vista-Douglas, AZ	66.4	2.8	26.2	0.0	17.2	51.0	31.8	28.7	35.4	67.7
43580	Sioux City, IA-NE-SD........................	85.1	1.7	9.7	1.4	19.5	57.4	23.1	34.0	25.4	70.3
43620	Sioux Falls, SD	91.8	2.7	2.4	0.9	25.6	55.9	18.5	33.8	20.3	67.3
43780	South Bend-Mishawaka, IN-MI.........	81.8	10.9	4.3	1.4	19.4	57.2	23.4	30.1	26.1	70.7
43900	Spartanburg, SC	71.9	22.2	3.6	1.4	17.9	58.0	24.1	34.2	27.5	69.1
44060	Spokane-Spokane Valley, WA............	90.3	1.6	3.0	1.6	21.3	55.7	23.0	29.4	25.8	64.6
44100	Springfield, IL	86.2	10.2	1.2	1.3	19.7	57.2	23.1	29.7	25.5	70.6
44140	Springfield, MA..............................	76.4	6.3	14.7	1.8	17.1	58.5	24.4	31.0	27.3	63.0
44180	Springfield, MO	93.1	1.8	1.7	0.9	25.3	51.4	23.3	30.9	25.7	63.3
44220	Springfield, OH..............................	87.3	9.2	1.7	0.0	17.5	55.3	27.1	30.0	29.5	67.0
44300	State College, PA............................	90.3	2.2	2.0	4.6	32.0	48.0	19.9	24.1	21.9	60.1
44420	Staunton-Waynesboro, VA...............	91.8	6.0	1.1	0.6	16.2	54.0	29.8	29.4	32.8	71.6

CBSA FIPS code	Metropolitan area	Total Households	Family households, percent	Married-couple family households, percent	Male householder, no spouse, percent	Female householder, no spouse, percent	Householder living alone, percent	Nonfamily households, householder not living alone, percent	Opposite-sex partner unmarried partner households, percent	Same-sex unmarried partner households, percent	Average household size
44700	Stockton-Lodi, CA..............................	215,707	74.5	51.3	7.1	16.0	20.5	5.1	7.0	0.4	3.17
44940	Sumter, SC..	40,068	68.6	44.8	4.9	18.9	27.1	4.2	5.1	0.2	2.63
45060	Syracuse, NY.....................................	255,357	62.7	45.1	4.6	13.0	30.4	6.9	6.8	0.5	2.48
45220	Tallahassee, FL..................................	142,342	58.8	40.0	4.3	14.4	28.9	12.3	5.0	0.3	2.46
45300	Tampa-St. Petersburg-Clearwater, FL .	1,126,100	61.2	44.4	4.4	12.4	32.0	6.8	5.7	0.7	2.49
45460	Terre Haute, IN.................................	63,429	65.0	49.3	4.8	10.9	28.9	6.1	6.1	0.5	2.52
45500	Texarkana, TX-AR..............................	55,516	67.4	45.9	4.5	17.0	28.8	3.8	3.4	0.2	2.57
45540	The Villages, FL................................	45,678	68.8	61.7	1.7	5.4	27.4	3.8	2.9	0.3	2.02
45780	Toledo, OH.......................................	243,127	60.8	42.0	4.5	14.3	32.1	7.1	6.0	0.4	2.43
45820	Topeka, KS..	93,072	64.2	49.4	4.3	10.6	29.9	5.9	5.4	0.3	2.46
45940	Trenton, NJ.......................................	131,326	67.2	49.5	4.5	13.2	27.4	5.4	4.4	0.4	2.66
46060	Tucson, AZ..	385,524	61.5	43.3	5.4	12.8	30.9	7.5	6.5	0.7	2.51
46140	Tulsa, OK..	368,326	66.8	48.9	5.0	12.9	28.1	5.1	5.0	0.4	2.55
46220	Tuscaloosa, AL..................................	81,812	66.1	45.8	4.2	16.1	28.6	5.4	2.3	0.1	2.72
46340	Tyler, TX...	79,115	67.9	49.8	5.1	13.0	26.7	5.4	3.4	0.3	2.65
46520	Urban Honolulu, HI...........................	308,716	69.9	52.4	5.1	12.4	23.7	6.4	5.0	0.6	3.04
46540	Utica-Rome, NY................................	117,630	62.1	44.4	4.9	12.8	31.7	6.1	7.4	0.6	2.41
46660	Valdosta, GA.....................................	51,486	61.9	41.9	4.5	15.5	29.0	9.1	6.0	0.1	2.70
46700	Vallejo-Fairfield, CA..........................	141,742	71.1	50.1	6.0	15.1	22.7	6.1	6.5	0.6	2.89
47020	Victoria, TX.......................................	35,293	70.7	50.1	5.0	15.5	24.8	4.6	5.3	0.4	2.69
47220	Vineland-Bridgeton, NJ	50,047	69.0	43.6	6.1	19.4	24.8	6.2	7.1	0.3	2.89
47260	Virginia Beach-Norfolk-Newport News, VA-NC......................	622,459	67.5	47.1	4.5	15.9	26.2	6.3	4.8	0.4	2.62
47300	Visalia-Porterville, CA........................	132,911	78.0	52.5	8.6	16.9	17.6	4.4	7.8	0.3	3.35
47380	Waco, TX..	91,141	66.3	47.0	4.6	14.7	27.1	6.6	5.2	0.3	2.70
47460	Walla Walla, WA...............................	23,061	63.5	49.8	3.5	10.2	31.0	5.5	4.6	0.3	2.51
47580	Warner Robins, GA............................	66,308	69.3	50.8	3.1	15.4	27.0	3.8	3.4	0.3	2.71
47900	Washington-Arlington-Alexandria, DC-VA-MD-WV	2,106,241	65.7	48.5	4.6	12.7	27.3	6.9	4.8	0.7	2.73
47940	Waterloo-Cedar Falls, IA....................	66,371	61.3	48.9	3.4	9.0	30.9	7.8	5.9	0.4	2.42
48060	Watertown-Fort Drum, NY.................	44,651	68.3	51.6	4.7	11.9	25.9	5.8	6.5	0.4	2.54
48140	Wausau, WI.......................................	53,167	67.7	54.4	4.8	8.5	26.4	5.9	6.0	0.4	2.50
48260	Weirton-Steubenville, WV-OH	50,695	64.5	48.2	4.8	11.4	31.0	4.6	4.7	0.2	2.35
48300	Wenatchee, WA.................................	41,334	71.6	56.4	4.9	10.3	23.1	5.2	5.1	0.7	2.69
48540	Wheeling, WV-OH	60,820	62.3	48.5	4.2	9.6	33.1	4.6	5.5	0.2	2.29
48620	Wichita, KS.......................................	241,484	65.8	49.1	4.9	11.8	29.3	4.9	4.3	0.3	2.59
48660	Wichita Falls, TX...............................	55,471	66.7	49.0	4.5	13.2	29.1	4.2	5.7	0.3	2.46
48700	Williamsport, PA...............................	45,584	63.4	48.3	4.2	11.0	29.6	7.0	7.3	0.7	2.44
48900	Wilmington, NC................................	106,061	60.7	44.5	4.8	11.5	30.3	8.9	5.9	0.4	2.41
49020	Winchester, VA-WV	50,013	62.7	50.1	3.7	8.9	31.1	6.3	5.8	0.4	2.56
49180	Winston-Salem, NC	254,699	65.9	48.4	4.3	13.2	29.3	4.8	4.7	0.4	2.49
49340	Worcester, MA-CT	343,540	66.8	49.1	4.8	12.9	26.6	6.6	6.5	0.5	2.60
49420	Yakima, WA......................................	79,266	71.6	51.4	6.2	14.0	22.9	5.5	8.4	0.3	3.06
49620	York-Hanover, PA..............................	166,924	69.4	53.4	5.0	11.0	25.3	5.3	6.7	0.5	2.57
49660	Youngstown-Warren-Boardman, OH-PA......................	230,031	63.9	45.2	4.6	14.1	31.8	4.3	5.5	0.3	2.34
49700	Yuba City, CA	56,386	73.5	52.1	7.2	14.2	20.9	5.6	7.8	0.5	2.94
49740	Yuma, AZ..	70,655	77.4	57.4	6.1	13.9	18.7	3.8	6.1	0.1	2.74

CBSA FIPS code	Metropolitan area	Race or Hispanic origin of householder				Age of householder			Percent of households with one or more persons under 18 years old	Percent of households with one or more persons age 65 or older	Percent of all householders who are owners
		Householder is White alone, not Hispanic or Latino, percent	Householder is Black or African American alone, percent	Householder is Hispanic or Latino, percent	Householder is Asian alone, percent	Householders age 15 to 34, percent	Householders age 35 to 64, percent	Householders age 65 and older, percent			
44700	Stockton-Lodi, CA	45.6	7.6	31.6	11.9	19.9	60.0	20.1	43.0	24.7	56.9
44940	Sumter, SC	51.2	43.3	2.6	1.1	21.1	55.8	23.1	34.2	26.2	64.5
45060	Syracuse, NY	87.0	7.2	2.5	1.7	17.6	58.8	23.6	29.7	26.2	67.5
45220	Tallahassee, FL	61.0	30.9	4.9	2.1	29.7	51.5	18.7	27.7	21.3	57.5
45300	Tampa-St. Petersburg-Clearwater, FL	72.6	10.8	13.0	2.4	16.2	55.8	28.0	27.0	31.3	64.8
45460	Terre Haute, IN	93.6	3.2	1.2	1.2	20.6	55.4	24.1	29.5	26.9	67.4
45500	Texarkana, TX-AR	71.6	23.1	3.0	0.0	18.3	56.8	24.9	33.7	27.4	66.2
45540	The Villages, FL	93.1	3.3	2.6	0.0	4.1	29.2	66.7	8.4	69.9	89.6
45780	Toledo, OH	79.1	14.4	4.2	1.3	21.3	56.4	22.2	29.5	24.3	63.2
45820	Topeka, KS	83.9	6.1	6.1	0.8	19.0	56.4	24.5	30.8	26.8	67.5
45940	Trenton, NJ	59.7	20.2	11.3	7.9	15.5	61.5	23.0	33.0	26.4	64.8
46060	Tucson, AZ	64.7	3.3	26.4	2.6	21.3	52.4	26.3	28.3	29.7	61.0
46140	Tulsa, OK	73.0	8.1	5.8	1.3	21.4	56.3	22.2	33.5	24.7	66.0
46220	Tuscaloosa, AL	64.8	32.1	1.5	0.9	23.8	55.0	21.2	32.1	23.8	65.7
46340	Tyler, TX	68.9	17.7	11.1	1.0	20.9	54.0	25.1	34.3	27.9	66.0
46520	Urban Honolulu, HI	25.8	2.9	6.6	45.8	20.3	53.9	25.8	33.9	31.9	54.2
46540	Utica-Rome, NY	91.6	3.4	2.3	1.7	16.3	56.7	27.0	28.4	29.9	66.8
46660	Valdosta, GA	59.7	33.5	4.8	1.1	27.9	52.1	20.0	32.5	21.9	54.4
46700	Vallejo-Fairfield, CA	50.3	14.6	18.1	12.8	18.0	61.1	21.0	36.5	25.4	59.9
47020	Victoria, TX	56.8	6.3	35.0	0.0	20.9	55.2	24.0	35.0	27.3	66.7
47220	Vineland-Bridgeton, NJ	60.7	16.7	21.1	1.3	16.1	59.2	24.7	35.1	28.7	66.7
47260	Virginia Beach-Norfolk-Newport News, VA-NC	61.0	30.0	4.3	2.9	22.2	57.1	20.7	33.8	23.8	62.0
47300	Visalia-Porterville, CA	42.8	1.9	50.5	3.3	22.6	58.6	18.8	48.8	23.4	56.3
47380	Waco, TX	64.4	15.9	17.4	1.2	25.0	52.5	22.5	33.7	25.3	60.0
47460	Walla Walla, WA	85.3	0.0	11.5	0.0	16.9	55.0	28.1	27.7	30.4	64.2
47580	Warner Robins, GA	61.8	30.7	5.0	0.0	21.7	60.0	18.3	36.1	21.3	65.9
47900	Washington-Arlington-Alexandria, DC-VA-MD-WV	54.1	25.8	10.2	8.2	20.2	62.3	17.5	34.7	21.1	63.1
47940	Waterloo-Cedar Falls, IA	89.1	6.8	2.3	0.0	23.7	51.3	25.0	27.4	26.7	70.5
48060	Watertown-Fort Drum, NY	88.4	4.0	4.8	1.1	30.8	50.3	18.9	36.5	21.2	55.3
48140	Wausau, WI	94.5	0.0	1.3	0.0	18.8	57.5	23.7	30.5	25.7	72.8
48260	Weirton-Steubenville, WV-OH	94.5	3.6	0.6	0.0	13.2	55.9	30.9	24.8	33.3	72.4
48300	Wenatchee, WA	79.1	0.0	18.3	0.0	17.6	55.0	27.4	31.8	29.5	66.9
48540	Wheeling, WV-OH	96.2	1.9	0.5	0.0	15.6	56.1	28.3	24.6	31.0	72.3
48620	Wichita, KS	79.4	7.4	8.2	2.6	22.3	56.6	21.0	33.8	23.5	65.9
48660	Wichita Falls, TX	77.9	8.2	11.2	1.2	23.5	52.3	24.3	33.1	26.7	64.5
48700	Williamsport, PA	94.1	3.3	0.0	0.0	17.5	55.7	26.8	27.3	29.5	70.2
48900	Wilmington, NC	80.8	13.4	3.6	0.9	22.8	54.1	23.1	26.9	25.7	60.4
49020	Winchester, VA-WV	88.7	4.2	5.1	0.0	16.8	58.7	24.5	28.7	27.0	65.4
49180	Winston-Salem, NC	74.8	17.6	5.7	1.1	17.4	58.6	24.0	31.2	26.7	68.3
49340	Worcester, MA-CT	84.8	3.3	7.8	3.0	16.1	62.4	21.5	33.0	25.1	65.4
49420	Yakima, WA	59.7	0.7	34.2	0.0	20.4	57.8	21.8	41.2	25.6	61.6
49620	York-Hanover, PA	89.7	4.6	4.2	0.9	16.1	59.8	24.2	32.0	27.1	74.0
49660	Youngstown-Warren-Boardman, OH-PA	86.4	10.3	2.0	0.4	14.9	55.9	29.2	26.9	32.0	69.9
49700	Yuba City, CA	63.5	2.5	20.9	8.1	23.1	56.5	20.5	40.9	25.5	58.3
49740	Yuma, AZ	44.4	1.9	51.2	1.0	21.5	50.3	28.2	41.4	31.8	69.2

Table A-4: Cities with a Population of 50,000 or More—Living Arrangements

State/ Place FIPS code	City	Total Households	Family households, percent	Married-couple family households, percent	Male householder, no spouse, percent	Female householder, no spouse, percent	Householder living alone, percent	Nonfamily households, householder not living alone, percent	Opposite-sex partner unmarried partner households, percent	Same-sex unmarried partner households, percent	Average household size
0000000	**United States**	115,731,304	66.1	48.2	4.8	13.1	27.7	6.2	5.5	0.5	2.6
0100000	**Alabama**	1,837,292	67.3	47.7	4.2	15.3	28.6	4.1	3.3	0.3	2.6
0103076	Auburn city	21,528	49.5	36.0	3.4	10.1	31.4	19.1	2.8	0.1	2.5
0107000	Birmingham city	88,251	53.2	25.6	4.2	23.4	40.7	6.0	4.3	0.5	2.3
0120104	Decatur city	22,329	62.2	44.9	4.0	13.3	34.3	3.5	2.5	0.9	2.5
0121184	Dothan city	26,140	65.4	44.7	3.3	17.4	30.1	4.5	3.7	0.2	2.5
0135896	Hoover city	31,941	70.0	56.5	3.0	10.6	26.7	3.3	2.0	0.1	2.6
0137000	Huntsville city	76,624	57.7	38.4	4.7	14.6	37.1	5.2	4.0	0.5	2.3
0150000	Mobile city	75,966	60.3	34.8	4.2	21.4	34.4	5.3	4.2	0.6	2.5
0151000	Montgomery city	79,316	62.0	35.3	5.2	21.6	32.7	5.3	5.2	0.2	2.5
0177256	Tuscaloosa city	31,633	57.9	35.4	4.7	17.8	32.2	9.8	2.7	0.1	2.7
0200000	**Alaska**	250,875	66.8	49.7	5.8	11.3	26.0	7.2	7.8	0.4	2.8
0203000	Anchorage municipality	104,980	65.8	48.1	5.7	11.9	26.3	7.9	7.5	0.5	2.8
0400000	**Arizona**	2,381,501	65.5	47.2	5.4	12.9	27.4	7.0	6.4	0.6	2.7
0404720	Avondale city	22,800	77.4	47.0	7.4	22.9	16.3	6.4	8.3	0.5	3.4
0407940	Buckeye town	15,093	77.4	58.7	5.5	13.2	18.2	4.4	8.1	0.6	3.3
0410670	Casas Adobes CDP	27,586	63.3	47.0	5.1	11.3	30.2	6.5	7.0	0.4	2.5
0411230	Catalina Foothills CDP	23,942	61.3	52.8	2.6	5.9	33.8	4.9	3.4	0.7	2.1
0412000	Chandler city	86,150	70.0	53.3	5.5	11.1	23.0	7.0	6.1	0.4	2.8
0423620	Flagstaff city	23,579	57.8	38.0	7.1	12.7	25.3	17.0	7.5	1.1	2.5
0427400	Gilbert town	70,877	77.9	62.7	4.5	10.7	16.7	5.4	5.3	0.6	3.1
0427820	Glendale city	78,920	67.5	43.7	6.1	17.7	26.0	6.5	8.1	0.7	2.9
0428380	Goodyear city	22,926	79.5	64.1	6.1	9.3	17.5	3.0	4.9	0.3	2.9
0439370	Lake Havasu City city	23,120	64.3	51.2	2.6	10.4	28.0	7.7	6.3	0.7	2.3
0446000	Mesa city	165,911	65.1	45.9	5.9	13.3	27.6	7.3	6.8	0.7	2.7
0454050	Peoria city	58,519	69.7	52.6	5.4	11.8	24.7	5.6	5.9	0.6	2.7
0455000	Phoenix city	519,395	63.2	40.9	6.6	15.6	28.8	8.0	7.5	0.9	2.8
0464210	San Tan Valley CDP	25,396	81.7	64.1	6.0	11.5	14.5	3.9	8.3	0.9	3.5
0465000	Scottsdale city	100,324	57.8	46.1	4.0	7.7	33.6	8.6	4.9	0.4	2.2
0471510	Surprise city	44,079	73.7	58.6	3.9	11.2	22.3	4.0	5.2	0.5	2.8
0473000	Tempe city	63,400	48.2	31.1	5.8	11.3	34.0	17.9	7.5	0.8	2.5
0477000	Tucson city	203,741	55.0	33.5	6.0	15.5	35.6	9.4	7.3	0.8	2.5
0485540	Yuma city	32,624	74.2	54.5	5.9	13.9	21.3	4.5	6.5	0.3	2.7
0500000	**Arkansas**	1,130,417	66.8	49.0	4.5	13.4	28.2	5.0	4.4	0.3	2.5
0515190	Conway city	23,296	59.0	43.4	5.3	10.3	28.7	12.4	6.0	0.2	2.5
0523290	Fayetteville city	32,510	45.5	34.2	3.1	8.2	37.6	16.9	5.6	0.6	2.2
0524550	Fort Smith city	34,617	61.8	42.8	5.1	13.9	32.5	5.7	4.8	0.3	2.5
0535710	Jonesboro city	26,721	64.4	41.5	6.4	16.5	26.1	9.5	5.9	0.7	2.5
0541000	Little Rock city	79,191	56.3	35.7	4.5	16.1	38.1	5.7	3.0	0.5	2.4
0550450	North Little Rock city	24,928	56.6	36.3	2.8	17.4	36.3	7.1	4.1	0.6	2.6
0560410	Rogers city	19,893	70.9	55.2	4.1	11.6	24.9	4.2	5.2	0.3	2.9
0566080	Springdale city	25,021	73.6	49.7	7.6	16.4	22.9	3.5	6.5	0.1	3.0
0600000	**California**	12,581,722	68.4	48.7	6.0	13.7	24.4	7.3	6.2	0.6	3.0
0600562	Alameda city	30,194	61.8	46.0	4.3	11.6	30.0	8.2	4.8	1.7	2.5
0600884	Alhambra city	29,636	67.6	45.7	7.0	14.8	26.1	6.4	3.6	0.6	2.8
0602000	Anaheim city	98,662	75.8	53.4	6.6	15.8	18.1	6.2	6.8	0.2	3.4
0602252	Antioch city	32,688	76.1	51.4	6.0	18.7	18.6	5.3	6.9	0.6	3.2
0602364	Apple Valley town	23,595	77.0	54.2	7.2	15.6	21.2	1.7	5.1	0.1	3.0
0602462	Arcadia city	19,692	75.8	59.2	5.8	10.9	20.5	3.7	2.0	0.1	2.9
0602553	Arden-Arcade CDP	40,059	53.9	36.0	5.2	12.7	38.4	7.8	6.4	0.4	2.3
0603526	Bakersfield city	110,057	74.7	49.9	7.6	17.1	19.5	5.8	7.9	0.4	3.2
0603666	Baldwin Park city	17,169	88.3	56.7	10.2	21.4	9.2	2.5	5.4	0.4	4.4
0604982	Bellflower city	23,265	74.5	45.3	6.9	22.3	21.4	4.1	6.0	0.2	3.3
0606000	Berkeley city	45,931	43.0	32.5	2.3	8.2	36.9	20.2	6.5	1.3	2.3
0608142	Brentwood city	16,311	83.9	66.9	6.7	10.3	12.9	3.2	5.8	0.4	3.3
0608786	Buena Park city	23,413	82.3	58.0	9.0	15.3	12.9	4.9	6.2	0.2	3.5
0608954	Burbank city	40,875	61.3	43.8	5.6	11.9	31.6	7.1	4.2	0.7	2.5
0610046	Camarillo city	22,990	71.2	56.6	4.7	9.9	22.8	6.0	5.5	0.2	2.8
0611194	Carlsbad city	42,938	67.1	54.7	3.2	9.2	26.4	6.5	5.3	0.1	2.5
0611390	Carmichael CDP	25,554	63.3	41.6	6.4	15.4	30.3	6.4	6.2	0.7	2.4
0611530	Carson city	24,975	80.5	53.8	7.5	19.2	16.0	3.5	5.9	0.1	3.7
0611964	Castro Valley CDP	22,028	71.4	54.2	4.2	13.0	22.2	6.4	6.2	0.5	2.7
0612048	Cathedral City city	17,007	66.3	46.3	6.1	14.0	24.4	9.2	5.3	4.4	3.1
0613014	Chico city	34,013	51.3	34.5	4.5	12.3	31.5	17.1	8.7	0.5	2.5
0613210	Chino city	21,280	77.9	58.9	6.4	12.5	18.1	4.0	6.4	0.5	3.4
0613214	Chino Hills city	23,327	80.8	62.8	5.8	12.2	15.8	3.4	6.4	0.5	3.3
0613392	Chula Vista city	77,434	77.1	55.4	5.8	15.8	19.3	3.6	4.6	0.5	3.2
0613588	Citrus Heights city	32,523	62.4	43.7	5.5	13.2	28.2	9.4	7.8	0.7	2.6
0614218	Clovis city	33,631	72.4	51.8	6.1	14.4	22.4	5.2	7.4	0.4	2.9
0614890	Colton city	14,408	77.3	44.0	9.7	23.6	19.3	3.4	7.8	0.6	3.7
0615044	Compton city	23,251	81.0	43.4	9.2	28.4	15.6	3.4	7.0	0.3	4.2
0616000	Concord city	44,995	69.8	50.8	6.4	12.6	23.2	7.0	6.3	0.5	2.7
0616350	Corona city	45,344	79.3	60.2	6.9	12.2	15.6	5.1	6.8	0.4	3.5

State/ Place FIPS code	City	Race or Hispanic origin of householder				Age of householder			Percent of households with one or more persons under 18 years old	Percent of households with one or more persons age 65 or older	Percent of all householders who are owners
		Householder is White alone, not Hispanic or Latino, percent	Householder is Black or African American alone, percent	Householder is Hispanic or Latino, percent	Householder is Asian alone, percent	Householders age 15 to 34, percent	Householders age 35 to 64, percent	Householders age 65 and older, percent			
0000000	**United States**........................	69.8	12.1	12.0	4.2	19.3	57.9	22.8	32.4	26.0	64.0
0100000	**Alabama**.............................	69.6	25.4	2.6	1.0	18.9	57.0	24.1	31.8	26.9	69.0
0103076	Auburn city..........................	74.0	17.6	0.0	5.8	52.4	37.7	9.9	26.6	12.1	44.8
0107000	Birmingham city....................	25.0	70.4	2.5	1.4	23.2	56.0	20.8	25.5	22.6	47.9
0120104	Decatur city.........................	68.9	21.0	7.4	0.0	16.9	58.6	24.6	28.5	26.5	61.4
0121184	Dothan city..........................	65.5	30.0	2.4	0.9	20.9	54.9	24.1	30.5	26.7	59.2
0135896	Hoover city..........................	75.7	14.5	4.1	0.0	22.0	57.0	21.0	34.7	23.7	67.4
0137000	Huntsville city......................	62.6	29.2	4.3	0.0	23.3	54.4	22.4	27.1	24.4	58.8
0150000	Mobile city..........................	48.7	46.8	2.4	1.2	22.8	53.0	24.1	30.3	26.9	56.7
0151000	Montgomery city....................	39.9	54.9	2.2	2.0	24.8	54.3	20.9	33.3	23.8	57.4
0177256	Tuscaloosa city.....................	52.2	43.4	1.9	1.9	30.8	50.4	18.8	27.4	21.8	49.2
0200000	**Alaska**...............................	72.1	3.4	4.9	3.7	24.1	60.9	15.0	35.7	17.7	63.0
0203000	Anchorage municipality...........	70.3	5.9	6.6	6.0	26.9	59.7	13.5	35.9	16.4	59.1
0400000	**Arizona**.............................	67.5	4.0	21.8	2.6	20.3	55.0	24.7	32.1	28.0	62.9
0404720	Avondale city........................	43.5	9.5	41.6	3.3	26.4	63.5	10.2	48.2	15.2	57.6
0407940	Buckeye town........................	64.8	7.0	25.6	0.0	22.7	60.5	16.8	45.4	22.6	65.1
0410670	Casas Adobes CDP..................	81.1	0.0	13.3	0.0	20.6	52.1	27.2	30.4	30.6	68.4
0411230	Catalina Foothills CDP.............	85.9	0.0	7.3	3.7	12.6	51.3	36.1	18.8	39.5	71.0
0412000	Chandler city........................	68.5	5.2	16.9	7.3	22.7	63.1	14.2	38.9	17.1	62.7
0423620	Flagstaff city........................	69.6	1.5	16.0	1.9	39.4	49.0	11.6	31.4	13.1	43.9
0427400	Gilbert town.........................	75.5	3.1	13.3	6.2	21.7	65.7	12.6	46.6	15.0	71.1
0427820	Glendale city........................	59.0	6.8	28.8	3.0	23.2	60.5	16.3	36.7	20.1	56.3
0428380	Goodyear city.......................	66.4	8.0	19.0	4.7	21.8	58.6	19.6	38.5	22.8	68.4
0439370	Lake Havasu City city..............	90.2	0.0	7.4	0.0	11.3	47.7	41.0	19.7	45.6	67.2
0446000	Mesa city............................	73.3	3.7	18.4	1.6	22.4	52.5	25.1	31.7	27.9	59.7
0454050	Peoria city...........................	79.1	3.7	12.2	2.9	16.6	58.6	24.9	34.7	28.3	69.6
0455000	Phoenix city.........................	57.8	7.0	29.4	3.3	24.8	59.7	15.5	36.3	18.4	53.8
0464210	San Tan Valley CDP.................	72.8	4.1	17.8	0.0	28.0	60.1	11.9	54.5	14.7	68.1
0465000	Scottsdale city......................	85.8	1.7	7.4	3.4	18.1	53.2	28.8	21.5	31.6	65.5
0471510	Surprise city.........................	81.0	4.6	11.6	2.0	15.8	51.7	32.5	35.8	36.3	73.2
0473000	Tempe city..........................	68.3	6.2	16.1	5.6	39.1	47.4	13.5	21.8	15.4	43.5
0477000	Tucson city..........................	56.6	4.8	33.0	2.9	27.4	51.9	20.8	28.1	23.6	48.6
0485540	Yuma city............................	44.9	3.1	49.0	0.0	27.2	49.6	23.3	42.8	26.5	59.0
0500000	**Arkansas**...........................	77.8	14.9	4.3	1.1	20.6	54.9	24.5	31.9	27.2	66.2
0515190	Conway city.........................	78.1	15.0	3.2	0.0	37.7	47.7	14.6	31.0	16.4	50.1
0523290	Fayetteville city.....................	84.9	3.9	4.9	0.0	45.8	41.4	12.8	22.9	14.5	40.2
0524550	Fort Smith city......................	69.9	8.6	11.6	5.4	24.8	54.4	20.7	31.7	22.9	51.8
0535710	Jonesboro city......................	78.7	15.0	0.0	1.3	31.1	50.2	18.7	33.9	21.3	53.5
0541000	Little Rock city......................	52.2	39.8	4.8	2.4	23.6	57.0	19.4	29.0	21.5	57.2
0550450	North Little Rock city..............	55.9	37.7	0.0	0.0	25.1	56.2	18.7	27.9	20.9	56.9
0560410	Rogers city..........................	73.7	0.0	20.5	0.0	29.5	53.3	17.2	44.4	18.9	58.1
0566080	Springdale city......................	64.0	3.2	25.2	0.0	31.3	52.8	15.9	48.5	18.2	52.9
0600000	**California**...........................	50.4	6.5	27.9	12.6	19.4	59.7	20.9	36.2	25.5	54.2
0600562	Alameda city........................	52.4	8.5	10.3	25.2	17.5	62.3	20.2	30.0	23.4	47.4
0600884	Alhambra city.......................	13.1	2.0	33.1	50.5	18.7	61.0	20.3	30.0	27.7	39.7
0602000	Anaheim city........................	38.3	3.2	39.7	16.7	21.1	61.2	17.7	43.5	23.1	46.4
0602252	Antioch city.........................	41.1	19.3	25.8	10.0	16.1	67.9	16.0	42.5	21.0	60.3
0602364	Apple Valley town...................	64.2	8.6	22.0	0.0	17.2	53.9	28.9	35.5	33.4	66.8
0602462	Arcadia city.........................	32.4	0.0	9.9	54.7	12.7	63.5	23.8	36.1	32.3	60.9
0602553	Arden-Arcade CDP..................	67.1	9.0	13.9	5.6	22.8	53.8	23.5	26.3	25.9	44.1
0603526	Bakersfield city.....................	45.1	9.4	38.3	5.5	25.8	58.7	15.6	46.5	19.7	55.1
0603666	Baldwin Park city...................	6.7	0.0	73.4	18.6	15.7	68.8	15.4	54.4	25.7	59.3
0604982	Bellflower city.......................	25.9	17.2	45.4	10.0	20.9	64.3	14.8	45.3	20.5	38.4
0606000	Berkeley city........................	62.7	9.7	8.2	15.7	31.3	46.0	22.7	17.3	25.2	42.3
0608142	Brentwood city......................	60.9	4.7	21.9	0.0	13.7	67.2	19.1	48.2	25.9	72.3
0608786	Buena Park city.....................	34.5	4.5	31.0	27.7	14.9	64.5	20.6	42.1	28.7	57.4
0608954	Burbank city........................	61.6	2.5	21.3	10.4	20.0	59.3	20.6	28.9	25.8	41.4
0610046	Camarillo city.......................	69.6	1.7	17.5	9.0	13.9	57.5	28.6	34.6	32.4	70.6
0611194	Carlsbad city........................	80.9	0.0	9.3	0.0	13.1	62.5	24.4	30.5	26.9	60.8
0611390	Carmichael CDP.....................	78.6	5.4	8.8	3.0	16.7	55.4	27.9	28.8	31.3	54.5
0611530	Carson city..........................	12.0	23.3	34.2	22.9	9.2	62.7	28.1	38.9	37.2	76.7
0611964	Castro Valley CDP...................	57.3	7.0	12.2	20.2	14.8	64.3	20.9	33.8	25.5	63.9
0612048	Cathedral City city.................	46.9	3.9	44.9	3.9	14.5	58.4	27.1	41.0	31.0	60.4
0613014	Chico city............................	79.5	2.0	12.6	2.3	35.5	46.1	18.4	27.1	20.8	42.8
0613210	Chino city...........................	34.0	4.6	45.8	12.9	18.5	66.0	15.4	43.3	21.4	70.4
0613214	Chino Hills city.....................	41.0	4.2	41.8	11.8	18.5	66.0	15.4	44.6	17.6	70.4
0613392	Chula Vista city.....................	27.6	5.6	52.0	12.8	19.5	62.2	18.3	44.4	24.0	58.6
0613588	Citrus Heights city..................	77.5	3.6	12.8	3.0	21.2	55.3	23.4	30.5	26.3	53.4
0614218	Clovis city...........................	66.1	2.9	19.9	8.7	20.6	59.9	19.4	41.4	23.0	61.0
0614890	Colton city..........................	18.3	11.9	64.4	5.0	29.6	58.9	11.5	54.2	16.0	53.0
0615044	Compton city........................	1.3	44.1	53.3	0.0	17.1	64.3	18.6	56.1	24.3	53.2
0616000	Concord city........................	59.2	3.9	22.8	10.2	19.5	58.9	21.6	35.7	24.6	60.0
0616350	Corona city..........................	46.7	6.0	34.2	10.8	17.7	68.8	13.5	47.9	19.4	66.3

Table A-4: Cities with a Population of 50,000 or More—Living Arrangements—*Continued*

State/ Place FIPS code	City	Household type							Opposite-sex partner unmarried partner households, percent	Same-sex unmarried partner households, percent	Average household size
		Total Households	Family households, percent	Married-couple family households, percent	Male householder, no spouse, percent	Female householder, no spouse, percent	Householder living alone, percent	Nonfamily households, householder not living alone, percent			
	California—cont'd										
0616532	Costa Mesa city	40,906	58.0	41.9	4.6	11.6	28.4	13.6	8.5	0.4	2.7
0617610	Cupertino city	20,463	78.3	67.8	2.3	8.2	18.2	3.5	1.8	0.2	2.9
0617918	Daly City city	30,866	71.5	51.7	6.8	13.0	20.7	7.8	5.7	0.8	3.3
0618100	Davis city	23,981	49.0	39.4	2.2	7.3	25.1	25.9	6.8	0.7	2.7
0618394	Delano city	10,511	88.6	57.8	10.4	20.4	10.1	1.4	11.8	0.0	4.2
0619192	Diamond Bar city	17,652	82.7	64.0	5.1	13.7	12.7	4.6	3.3	0.2	3.2
0619766	Downey city	32,529	79.1	50.7	9.1	19.3	17.0	3.8	6.6	0.3	3.4
0620802	East Los Angeles CDP	31,230	81.6	45.2	11.0	25.4	14.8	3.7	8.3	0.2	4.2
0621230	Eastvale city	12,618	90.3	74.7	4.2	11.5	7.3	2.4	4.7	0.1	4.4
0621712	El Cajon city	32,751	70.9	44.3	8.3	18.3	23.7	5.4	5.7	0.5	3.0
0622020	Elk Grove city	47,621	80.3	58.5	8.0	13.8	15.5	4.2	5.5	0.4	3.3
0622230	El Monte city	30,355	82.4	51.8	11.5	19.2	14.1	3.5	3.6	0.0	3.8
0622678	Encinitas city	22,931	65.0	55.2	2.3	7.5	24.4	10.7	5.6	0.3	2.6
0622804	Escondido city	44,428	73.2	53.0	7.0	13.2	19.4	7.4	7.5	0.4	3.3
0623182	Fairfield city	34,488	74.7	56.2	6.3	12.2	19.4	5.8	6.4	0.3	3.1
0624477	Florence-Graham CDP	14,311	87.2	44.1	14.9	28.2	9.7	3.1	12.3	0.2	4.5
0624498	Florin CDP	14,994	75.1	41.9	8.5	24.6	20.5	4.5	7.9	0.1	3.4
0624638	Folsom city	25,310	68.2	56.9	4.7	6.6	25.7	6.1	4.8	0.4	2.6
0624680	Fontana city	48,355	84.9	58.7	8.1	18.1	10.9	4.2	8.2	0.5	4.2
0625380	Fountain Valley city	18,672	76.1	58.9	5.3	11.9	18.6	5.3	4.6	0.1	3.0
0626000	Fremont city	71,486	78.7	64.2	4.1	10.4	16.7	4.7	4.3	0.3	3.1
0627000	Fresno city	160,355	69.9	40.8	9.2	19.9	23.1	7.0	8.5	0.6	3.1
0628000	Fullerton city	43,963	71.6	53.4	5.3	12.9	19.7	8.7	5.9	0.3	3.1
0628168	Gardena city	21,173	66.2	42.3	5.7	18.2	29.4	4.3	4.4	0.0	2.8
0629000	Garden Grove city	46,358	79.3	55.0	8.3	16.0	15.1	5.6	5.8	0.4	3.7
0629504	Gilroy city	14,500	81.4	57.0	8.4	15.9	14.8	3.9	7.5	0.2	3.5
0630000	Glendale city	70,310	68.8	50.1	5.5	13.2	26.3	4.9	3.6	0.5	2.7
0630014	Glendora city	16,593	76.7	58.4	5.5	12.8	19.1	4.2	3.8	0.7	3.0
0631596	Hacienda Heights CDP	15,448	81.6	60.4	6.6	14.5	13.7	4.7	5.0	0.6	3.5
0631960	Hanford city	17,368	76.4	51.0	7.8	17.7	19.6	4.0	7.5	0.2	3.1
0632548	Hawthorne city	28,405	67.1	36.9	9.2	21.0	27.1	5.8	6.5	0.3	3.0
0633000	Hayward city	46,111	72.7	49.2	6.9	16.6	20.9	6.3	5.8	0.7	3.2
0633182	Hemet city	30,326	62.3	40.9	6.3	15.1	31.3	6.4	6.2	0.7	2.7
0633434	Hesperia city	26,335	78.8	53.3	10.0	15.5	16.9	4.3	7.6	0.1	3.5
0633588	Highland city	14,642	81.9	55.3	7.1	19.5	14.5	3.7	6.8	0.3	3.7
0636000	Huntington Beach city	74,146	66.7	50.6	5.4	10.7	24.4	8.9	6.0	0.4	2.6
0636056	Huntington Park city	14,717	83.5	45.4	12.6	25.5	12.0	4.5	11.9	0.0	4.0
0636448	Indio city	24,951	77.9	54.0	8.7	15.2	18.3	3.8	9.3	0.3	3.3
0636546	Inglewood city	37,178	66.9	35.4	8.5	23.0	28.8	4.3	7.1	0.3	2.9
0636770	Irvine city	83,228	65.9	52.0	4.0	9.9	24.6	9.4	3.6	0.6	2.7
0637692	Jurupa Valley city	24,650	79.6	56.9	9.5	13.1	15.9	4.6	8.1	0.2	3.9
0639248	Laguna Niguel city	24,139	70.5	59.3	3.4	7.9	24.1	5.4	3.0	0.6	2.7
0639290	La Habra city	18,983	73.2	52.4	7.0	13.9	21.1	5.7	8.4	0.1	3.2
0639486	Lake Elsinore city	14,790	82.9	60.5	7.8	14.6	13.5	3.6	6.7	0.1	3.8
0639496	Lake Forest city	26,690	74.8	60.2	4.5	10.1	20.9	4.3	4.1	0.3	2.9
0639892	Lakewood city	26,383	75.6	52.5	6.8	16.2	20.1	4.3	4.6	1.0	3.1
0640004	La Mesa city	23,575	57.9	40.1	4.4	13.4	33.1	9.0	5.4	1.0	2.4
0640130	Lancaster city	48,092	72.6	48.4	6.3	17.9	22.9	4.4	5.2	0.2	3.1
0641992	Livermore city	29,305	74.7	57.4	6.2	11.2	20.0	5.3	6.1	0.4	2.8
0642202	Lodi city	22,011	68.3	49.3	7.2	11.7	26.4	5.4	6.4	0.5	2.8
0643000	Long Beach city	163,332	60.7	36.8	7.1	16.8	30.6	8.8	7.4	1.4	2.8
0644000	Los Angeles city	1,325,553	59.9	37.7	6.9	15.3	30.3	9.7	7.3	0.7	2.8
0644574	Lynwood city	14,708	87.4	50.6	10.1	26.6	9.7	2.9	10.5	0.4	4.6
0645022	Madera city	16,313	79.4	47.6	7.8	24.0	16.8	3.8	11.3	0.0	3.8
0645484	Manteca city	22,326	74.7	54.0	5.8	14.9	18.6	6.7	8.9	0.4	3.1
0646842	Menifee city	26,826	70.0	55.0	5.8	9.2	24.3	5.8	7.4	0.4	3.0
0646898	Merced city	25,027	70.0	42.1	6.3	21.6	22.9	7.1	6.3	0.3	3.2
0647766	Milpitas city	19,889	79.0	61.1	6.0	11.8	16.2	4.9	3.9	0.3	3.3
0648256	Mission Viejo city	33,571	76.1	64.0	4.7	7.4	19.2	4.6	2.9	0.4	2.8
0648354	Modesto city	68,961	70.0	46.1	6.6	17.3	24.6	5.5	7.7	0.5	2.9
0648816	Montebello city	19,691	72.7	41.8	8.1	22.8	22.8	4.5	5.0	0.7	3.2
0648914	Monterey Park city	18,389	78.3	50.7	7.8	19.8	16.3	5.4	3.1	0.5	3.3
0649270	Moreno Valley city	51,116	83.5	52.5	7.8	23.1	12.4	4.2	8.0	0.8	3.9
0649670	Mountain View city	32,295	57.1	46.0	3.6	7.5	32.9	10.0	6.1	0.5	2.4
0650076	Murrieta city	32,886	75.8	61.9	4.9	9.0	18.6	5.6	5.0	0.0	3.2
0650258	Napa city	28,186	67.1	49.3	5.2	12.5	26.1	6.8	6.6	0.5	2.7
0650398	National City city	15,043	76.6	46.7	7.2	22.8	18.4	5.0	7.0	0.2	3.7
0651182	Newport Beach city	37,920	57.4	46.8	2.5	8.1	32.3	10.3	3.7	0.6	2.3
0652526	Norwalk city	26,907	82.6	52.7	9.8	20.1	13.6	3.8	6.3	0.1	3.9
0652582	Novato city	21,080	65.5	52.8	4.0	8.7	28.4	6.0	5.0	0.5	2.5
0653000	Oakland city	157,168	54.1	32.9	6.0	15.1	35.1	10.8	6.9	1.6	2.5
0653322	Oceanside city	59,590	66.1	49.6	5.3	11.2	25.8	8.0	5.9	0.5	2.9
0653896	Ontario city	46,229	75.0	49.0	7.4	18.6	20.8	4.3	8.3	0.2	3.6
0653980	Orange city	42,852	72.2	52.9	6.3	13.0	19.8	8.0	6.1	0.4	3.1

State/ Place FIPS code	City	Race or Hispanic origin of householder				Age of householder			Percent of households with one or more persons under 18 years old	Percent of households with one or more persons age 65 or older	Percent of all householders who are owners
		Householder is White alone, not Hispanic or Latino, percent	Householder is Black or African American alone, percent	Householder is Hispanic or Latino, percent	Householder is Asian alone, percent	Householders age 15 to 34, percent	Householders age 35 to 64, percent	Householders age 65 and older, percent			
	California—cont'd										
0616532	Costa Mesa city	62.0	1.5	24.4	9.8	27.1	57.4	15.5	29.6	17.7	37.0
0617610	Cupertino city	35.9	0.0	3.6	58.6	10.2	71.6	18.2	48.7	25.0	64.1
0617918	Daly City city	19.6	3.7	21.5	53.1	18.5	58.8	22.7	34.7	30.8	55.8
0618100	Davis city	63.2	1.9	10.3	19.0	37.4	46.0	16.6	27.1	17.9	43.7
0618394	Delano city	5.2	0.0	78.1	13.0	25.0	61.5	13.5	59.5	20.8	51.5
0619192	Diamond Bar city	24.7	4.5	16.5	52.4	12.0	69.2	18.8	39.2	26.2	78.1
0619766	Downey city	23.4	5.4	63.0	7.5	17.7	64.1	18.3	45.9	24.7	49.9
0620802	East Los Angeles CDP	2.0	0.0	95.8	1.6	18.9	62.5	18.6	53.1	25.1	32.8
0621230	Eastvale city	26.8	9.3	33.9	25.9	20.1	73.5	6.5	66.4	15.9	78.9
0621712	El Cajon city	62.3	6.4	22.8	3.5	24.5	55.9	19.5	38.7	23.2	37.9
0622020	Elk Grove city	45.3	11.9	14.7	23.7	16.7	68.9	14.4	48.1	21.5	71.1
0622230	El Monte city	7.3	0.0	61.4	29.9	17.9	62.1	20.0	45.3	29.7	40.3
0622678	Encinitas city	83.3	0.0	9.8	4.6	15.0	62.6	22.4	30.7	26.0	66.4
0622804	Escondido city	55.5	3.1	34.8	5.3	22.2	59.6	18.2	41.8	22.4	48.9
0623182	Fairfield city	44.1	17.0	19.9	13.6	21.8	58.8	19.5	41.2	24.0	55.4
0624477	Florence-Graham CDP	0.0	13.2	85.4	0.0	23.6	63.6	12.9	63.7	20.1	33.3
0624498	Florin CDP	27.1	16.2	24.3	23.2	21.4	59.1	19.4	44.1	26.9	49.6
0624638	Folsom city	74.2	0.0	8.5	13.5	17.1	64.7	18.2	39.6	20.3	67.2
0624680	Fontana city	22.2	11.4	57.4	6.8	20.0	69.2	10.9	56.3	18.4	66.5
0625380	Fountain Valley city	56.7	0.0	11.8	29.5	7.6	60.9	31.5	32.2	38.0	71.1
0626000	Fremont city	31.5	3.9	10.5	49.9	17.2	67.0	15.8	44.8	22.3	62.5
0627000	Fresno city	39.2	9.3	39.3	10.0	26.0	55.6	18.3	42.1	21.7	46.7
0628000	Fullerton city	46.0	3.4	26.0	22.3	24.0	56.6	19.4	35.3	24.3	53.2
0628168	Gardena city	12.1	26.0	27.5	32.7	17.0	59.2	23.9	31.0	30.7	50.6
0629000	Garden Grove city	31.7	1.6	27.7	37.4	14.1	65.2	20.7	43.4	28.3	55.1
0629504	Gilroy city	42.3	0.0	49.0	5.9	18.6	62.0	19.4	48.2	23.2	57.5
0630000	Glendale city	65.9	1.5	14.9	15.6	15.8	59.8	24.4	30.1	31.0	35.9
0630014	Glendora city	64.8	0.0	24.5	7.1	11.1	64.0	24.9	35.1	29.7	69.6
0631596	Hacienda Heights CDP	18.0	0.0	36.4	43.0	10.2	61.5	28.3	33.6	38.5	78.5
0631960	Hanford city	49.3	4.8	39.9	0.0	24.6	56.0	19.5	46.5	22.2	55.3
0632548	Hawthorne city	14.3	32.6	42.0	6.3	27.7	60.2	12.2	41.6	15.9	27.7
0633000	Hayward city	26.5	14.8	31.7	22.1	21.6	60.4	17.9	39.1	24.8	52.5
0633182	Hemet city	62.8	7.1	25.3	2.0	15.5	45.6	38.9	31.8	43.4	57.2
0633434	Hesperia city	51.7	7.1	37.5	0.0	19.9	60.9	19.1	45.5	23.9	60.9
0633588	Highland city	38.6	11.0	40.2	7.8	19.2	64.8	16.0	50.9	19.0	62.9
0636000	Huntington Beach city	72.3	1.0	13.7	10.5	16.1	59.2	24.6	27.7	28.2	58.2
0636056	Huntington Park city	1.8	0.0	96.6	0.0	21.9	66.5	11.6	55.3	18.5	25.1
0636448	Indio city	37.8	2.6	56.0	2.4	19.5	56.2	24.3	43.1	30.5	62.5
0636546	Inglewood city	4.2	56.2	35.9	1.9	19.5	62.4	18.2	39.7	22.7	35.2
0636770	Irvine city	52.8	2.1	8.3	34.5	24.5	60.7	14.9	34.0	18.6	48.4
0637692	Jurupa Valley city	34.4	5.2	56.1	0.0	16.3	65.8	17.9	48.4	23.6	62.6
0639248	Laguna Niguel city	76.1	0.0	11.3	8.0	11.9	66.9	21.1	31.9	24.7	71.6
0639290	La Habra city	39.2	2.5	48.8	8.8	18.9	60.3	20.8	39.9	25.0	53.9
0639486	Lake Elsinore city	47.2	5.4	40.4	0.0	21.8	68.3	9.9	53.8	15.2	63.8
0639496	Lake Forest city	65.4	1.9	16.3	14.4	13.9	68.8	17.3	37.1	21.6	70.0
0639892	Lakewood city	49.5	8.8	24.0	13.6	12.3	68.4	19.3	38.8	25.3	68.9
0640004	La Mesa city	69.2	6.5	15.6	4.2	25.7	51.0	23.2	26.9	26.3	46.1
0640130	Lancaster city	43.6	20.7	30.0	4.2	19.2	63.9	16.9	42.4	20.3	57.4
0641992	Livermore city	74.5	0.0	13.2	8.7	16.8	64.7	18.4	37.2	22.4	69.0
0642202	Lodi city	66.2	0.0	25.1	5.6	20.9	55.9	23.3	37.2	25.6	54.7
0643000	Long Beach city	40.5	14.2	30.6	11.2	22.5	60.6	16.8	34.1	20.2	40.2
0644000	Los Angeles city	38.5	11.3	35.7	12.3	23.5	58.3	18.2	31.8	22.5	36.4
0644574	Lynwood city	0.0	12.9	84.3	0.0	19.9	68.4	11.7	65.3	20.1	46.1
0645022	Madera city	23.5	0.0	68.2	0.0	25.6	57.5	16.9	53.1	21.4	46.8
0645484	Manteca city	57.3	3.7	28.2	7.5	21.5	57.9	20.6	43.3	23.7	58.4
0646842	Menifee city	63.9	6.0	23.2	4.0	17.9	47.5	34.5	35.0	40.8	74.5
0646898	Merced city	42.1	6.2	41.7	8.4	27.6	55.2	17.2	42.8	21.7	42.7
0647766	Milpitas city	19.9	2.8	11.6	63.4	16.4	69.4	14.2	42.0	23.9	64.1
0648256	Mission Viejo city	75.6	1.8	11.8	8.1	8.4	64.7	26.9	34.4	29.9	77.5
0648354	Modesto city	58.4	4.2	27.9	6.1	21.4	57.7	20.8	37.6	24.6	52.3
0648816	Montebello city	14.0	0.0	69.1	15.5	14.0	57.9	28.1	34.7	33.8	46.3
0648914	Monterey Park city	5.6	0.0	29.2	62.6	12.4	59.1	28.5	31.2	39.8	51.1
0649270	Moreno Valley city	24.7	20.9	47.0	5.8	20.0	67.1	12.9	52.3	19.0	60.0
0649670	Mountain View city	53.9	2.0	15.0	26.2	28.2	56.1	15.8	29.3	18.7	41.2
0650076	Murrieta city	62.3	7.7	20.9	6.5	19.7	60.9	19.4	43.1	23.9	66.4
0650258	Napa city	70.1	0.0	25.0	0.0	17.3	58.1	24.6	33.0	27.6	53.0
0650398	National City city	11.8	5.1	61.6	20.1	16.7	62.1	21.2	45.7	28.9	30.2
0651182	Newport Beach city	84.2	0.0	6.2	7.1	16.7	55.4	28.0	22.3	31.2	54.1
0652526	Norwalk city	17.2	5.6	63.0	13.7	17.5	62.6	19.9	47.1	27.4	63.5
0652582	Novato city	76.3	0.0	14.1	0.0	7.7	65.6	26.7	32.9	29.9	66.2
0653000	Oakland city	33.8	29.3	17.1	16.0	22.7	58.1	19.2	28.6	22.4	39.8
0653322	Oceanside city	60.1	5.1	24.9	6.2	21.1	55.8	23.1	32.2	26.5	56.2
0653896	Ontario city	26.7	7.0	59.9	4.8	20.3	64.5	15.2	46.2	19.9	54.8
0653980	Orange city	57.3	1.0	26.7	13.0	17.7	62.3	20.0	36.4	24.9	58.7

State/ Place FIPS code	City	Total Households	Family households, percent	Married-couple family households, percent	Male householder, no spouse, percent	Female householder, no spouse, percent	Householder living alone, percent	Nonfamily households, householder not living alone, percent	Opposite-sex partner unmarried partner households, percent	Same-sex unmarried partner households, percent	Average household size
	California—cont'd										
0654652	Oxnard city	50,877	80.2	54.5	7.4	18.2	14.7	5.1	6.3	0.8	3.9
0655156	Palmdale city	42,163	80.8	51.5	8.2	21.0	14.5	4.7	7.6	0.7	3.7
0655282	Palo Alto city	26,382	64.5	54.7	2.5	7.3	28.9	6.6	3.6	0.4	2.5
0655618	Paramount city	13,575	81.8	50.4	10.2	21.1	15.0	3.2	6.9	0.0	4.0
0656000	Pasadena city	55,153	54.9	40.0	3.9	11.0	34.9	10.2	5.4	0.7	2.4
0656700	Perris city	16,327	87.0	52.7	9.5	24.7	9.7	3.3	7.3	0.7	4.4
0656784	Petaluma city	21,341	65.6	50.6	4.2	10.8	25.9	8.5	6.5	0.9	2.7
0656924	Pico Rivera city	16,794	80.5	51.8	10.7	18.0	16.2	3.2	6.3	0.4	3.8
0657456	Pittsburg city	20,231	74.4	47.0	8.5	18.9	19.3	6.3	6.4	0.4	3.2
0657526	Placentia city	15,718	77.2	58.3	5.8	13.1	16.2	6.6	5.5	0.0	3.3
0657792	Pleasanton city	25,421	78.7	65.2	4.9	8.6	17.5	3.8	3.4	0.5	2.8
0658072	Pomona city	38,699	76.6	49.6	8.7	18.4	17.0	6.4	6.3	0.5	3.8
0658240	Porterville city	16,431	75.3	48.4	8.8	18.2	20.1	4.6	10.3	0.2	3.3
0659444	Rancho Cordova city	23,992	66.9	44.5	5.7	16.7	24.4	8.7	8.3	0.9	2.8
0659451	Rancho Cucamonga city	54,294	74.7	55.3	5.9	13.5	20.8	4.5	4.8	0.5	3.1
0659920	Redding city	34,996	62.8	44.6	4.9	13.3	29.1	8.1	6.3	0.4	2.5
0659962	Redlands city	24,962	66.5	50.8	5.7	10.1	29.6	3.8	4.9	0.1	2.7
0660018	Redondo Beach city	28,267	61.0	47.0	5.7	8.4	30.9	8.1	5.7	0.5	2.4
0660102	Redwood City city	28,520	65.0	49.0	4.6	11.3	27.7	7.3	6.6	0.1	2.7
0660466	Rialto city	25,221	81.7	53.6	7.8	20.3	14.4	3.9	7.2	0.4	4.0
0660620	Richmond city	36,689	65.8	39.9	6.3	19.7	28.5	5.6	7.5	0.5	2.9
0662000	Riverside city	90,709	71.1	49.3	6.0	15.8	21.8	7.1	6.7	0.5	3.3
0662364	Rocklin city	21,307	74.0	55.9	3.4	14.8	20.3	5.7	7.0	0.4	2.7
0662896	Rosemead city	14,547	83.9	56.8	11.2	15.9	12.8	3.4	2.2	0.4	3.7
0662938	Roseville city	45,655	68.7	53.7	3.7	11.4	24.2	7.0	5.9	0.8	2.7
0663218	Rowland Heights CDP	14,753	82.5	58.9	9.3	14.2	12.7	4.8	2.7	0.1	3.5
0664000	Sacramento city	176,504	57.8	36.3	5.8	15.6	33.0	9.2	7.8	1.1	2.7
0664224	Salinas city	40,757	78.0	50.9	9.2	17.8	16.9	5.1	11.1	0.3	3.7
0665000	San Bernardino city	56,996	74.7	40.4	8.9	25.4	20.0	5.4	8.6	0.4	3.6
0665042	San Buenaventura (Ventura) city,	41,616	61.7	43.9	4.8	13.1	29.7	8.6	6.4	0.9	2.6
0665084	San Clemente city	24,368	69.3	56.7	3.7	8.9	25.0	5.7	3.8	0.2	2.6
0666000	San Diego city	476,083	59.3	42.9	4.5	11.9	29.0	11.7	6.0	1.0	2.7
0667000	San Francisco city	348,751	45.2	33.0	3.6	8.6	38.4	16.4	5.8	2.3	2.3
0668000	San Jose city	310,975	73.2	54.4	6.2	12.6	19.7	7.1	6.2	0.5	3.1
0668084	San Leandro city	31,060	66.7	49.0	5.5	12.2	27.6	5.7	4.6	0.6	2.8
0668196	San Marcos city	28,649	68.1	51.1	4.0	13.0	22.8	9.1	6.6	0.5	3.0
0668252	San Mateo city	37,439	62.9	47.3	5.9	9.6	29.6	7.6	5.0	0.4	2.6
0668364	San Rafael city	22,148	62.1	46.3	2.9	12.8	29.2	8.8	5.6	0.8	2.6
0668378	San Ramon city	25,293	76.4	65.9	2.9	7.7	18.0	5.6	3.9	0.5	2.9
0669000	Santa Ana city	73,463	81.2	53.9	9.1	18.2	13.3	5.4	8.4	0.4	4.5
0669070	Santa Barbara city	34,037	55.4	40.5	5.4	9.5	31.7	13.0	8.4	0.6	2.6
0669084	Santa Clara city	42,830	66.1	52.5	4.2	9.4	26.2	7.7	5.0	0.3	2.7
0669088	Santa Clarita city	58,934	75.7	57.0	6.3	12.4	19.1	5.2	5.0	0.3	3.0
0669112	Santa Cruz city	21,154	46.4	34.5	4.7	7.2	32.8	20.8	10.0	1.2	2.5
0669196	Santa Maria city	27,560	75.3	50.6	7.9	16.8	21.1	3.6	6.3	0.2	3.6
0670000	Santa Monica city	46,476	37.3	27.9	2.5	6.8	49.6	13.1	5.6	0.7	1.9
0670098	Santa Rosa city	62,833	62.0	44.2	5.8	12.0	28.9	9.1	8.1	0.8	2.7
0670224	Santee city	19,141	72.9	52.4	4.8	15.7	20.7	6.3	6.3	0.6	2.8
0672016	Simi Valley city	42,134	76.3	59.9	4.7	11.6	18.1	5.6	4.5	0.4	3.0
0673080	South Gate city	23,414	83.7	51.6	10.7	21.4	12.4	3.9	10.6	0.2	4.1
0673262	South San Francisco city	21,003	72.5	55.1	6.4	11.0	22.0	5.5	5.8	0.4	3.1
0673430	South Whittier CDP	15,523	85.2	56.9	8.5	19.8	11.5	3.3	5.6	0.1	3.9
0675000	Stockton city	90,239	73.2	44.6	7.3	21.3	22.2	4.6	7.4	0.5	3.2
0677000	Sunnyvale city	55,066	66.3	54.5	4.6	7.1	25.8	8.0	4.4	0.6	2.6
0678120	Temecula city	31,767	79.9	63.9	4.2	11.7	14.5	5.6	5.6	0.5	3.3
0678582	Thousand Oaks city	45,693	71.7	59.4	4.1	8.1	22.7	5.6	3.9	0.3	2.8
0680000	Torrance city	55,824	69.2	53.0	4.1	12.2	25.8	5.0	3.9	0.6	2.6
0680238	Tracy city	24,129	81.7	63.9	7.8	10.1	13.1	5.2	6.5	0.2	3.5
0680644	Tulare city	18,139	78.1	52.8	8.7	16.6	16.9	5.0	6.4	0.5	3.3
0680812	Turlock city	23,621	72.4	50.6	5.4	16.5	21.2	6.4	5.3	0.2	2.9
0680854	Tustin city	25,021	73.2	50.9	6.8	15.6	20.8	5.9	7.7	0.4	3.1
0681204	Union City city	20,187	81.0	61.6	6.1	13.3	15.6	3.4	5.0	0.3	3.5
0681344	Upland city	26,708	68.2	47.6	4.6	16.0	25.9	5.9	5.4	0.4	2.8
0681554	Vacaville city	31,382	69.4	50.3	5.3	13.8	24.7	5.9	5.7	0.4	2.8
0681666	Vallejo city	40,562	66.8	41.0	6.9	18.9	26.3	6.9	6.9	1.2	2.9
0682590	Victorville city	30,817	79.5	49.3	10.0	20.2	15.4	5.1	5.2	0.8	3.7
0682954	Visalia city	41,647	73.7	49.2	7.7	16.8	21.4	4.9	6.9	0.4	3.0
0682996	Vista city	31,297	68.5	50.3	5.7	12.5	21.2	10.3	7.5	0.5	3.0
0683346	Walnut Creek city	29,377	56.5	46.5	3.7	6.4	36.1	7.3	4.5	0.9	2.2
0683668	Watsonville city	14,110	78.0	52.7	7.1	18.2	19.2	2.8	5.3	0.1	3.7
0684200	West Covina city	30,872	78.9	53.5	6.8	18.6	16.3	4.8	5.8	0.3	3.5
0684550	Westminster city	27,318	77.7	54.9	8.5	14.3	17.8	4.4	4.6	0.6	3.3

Table A-4: Cities with a Population of 50,000 or More—Living Arrangements—*Continued*

State/Place FIPS code	City	Race or Hispanic origin of householder				Age of householder			Percent of households with one or more persons under 18 years old	Percent of households with one or more persons age 65 or older	Percent of all householders who are owners
		Householder is White alone, not Hispanic or Latino, percent	Householder is Black or African American alone, percent	Householder is Hispanic or Latino, percent	Householder is Asian alone, percent	Householders age 15 to 34, percent	Householders age 35 to 64, percent	Householders age 65 and older, percent			
	California—cont'd										
0654652	Oxnard city	25.5	3.8	60.7	8.7	21.0	62.1	16.9	50.4	23.4	54.8
0655156	Palmdale city	32.0	15.3	46.5	4.1	19.3	67.8	12.9	52.6	19.3	60.7
0655282	Palo Alto city	66.7	2.0	5.7	23.1	17.5	55.4	27.1	34.8	30.6	54.8
0655618	Paramount city	8.8	16.5	70.1	3.7	19.0	67.5	13.6	56.4	18.3	39.2
0656000	Pasadena city	46.3	12.0	22.1	17.8	24.8	53.9	21.3	24.6	25.1	43.5
0656700	Perris city	17.6	13.2	65.0	3.5	23.5	66.3	10.2	65.4	14.2	61.6
0656784	Petaluma city	79.1	0.0	14.7	4.1	15.1	61.1	23.8	34.3	26.5	65.9
0656924	Pico Rivera city	8.7	0.0	85.5	3.7	13.2	61.2	25.6	45.0	33.8	68.8
0657456	Pittsburg city	27.4	20.7	32.2	15.2	22.9	60.2	16.9	44.0	22.6	53.2
0657526	Placentia city	53.3	0.0	27.6	15.9	14.5	62.6	22.9	38.5	28.8	64.0
0657792	Pleasanton city	65.7	2.0	7.8	22.3	10.7	68.7	20.6	43.4	24.8	69.6
0658072	Pomona city	19.5	8.9	59.7	10.4	20.2	64.1	15.7	48.0	22.6	52.9
0658240	Porterville city	40.4	0.0	52.1	5.2	24.4	57.2	18.4	50.3	23.5	56.4
0659444	Rancho Cordova city	60.3	11.3	13.5	10.3	21.9	59.1	19.0	34.5	22.5	55.7
0659451	Rancho Cucamonga city	48.4	8.5	30.3	10.8	18.6	66.3	15.1	40.5	20.5	64.2
0659920	Redding city	85.4	0.0	6.2	3.3	20.3	51.0	28.7	29.3	31.3	52.3
0659962	Redlands city	62.7	6.1	22.1	7.0	17.6	57.9	24.4	32.6	26.8	59.4
0660018	Redondo Beach city	70.6	0.0	11.8	11.5	17.2	66.4	16.5	28.0	20.0	52.2
0660102	Redwood City city	55.3	2.7	28.5	11.4	19.6	60.7	19.7	34.0	23.5	50.3
0660466	Rialto city	17.2	18.2	60.7	0.0	18.9	64.2	16.9	52.9	21.6	63.0
0660620	Richmond city	27.1	28.2	27.3	13.9	21.3	59.9	18.9	36.7	23.6	50.9
0662000	Riverside city	42.8	7.3	39.8	6.8	22.4	59.1	18.5	42.0	23.2	55.0
0662364	Rocklin city	73.5	0.0	13.3	7.2	18.7	62.7	18.6	41.8	21.4	64.0
0662896	Rosemead city	8.2	0.0	32.2	57.7	12.2	66.6	21.2	41.7	34.7	46.5
0662938	Roseville city	78.8	0.0	9.9	7.7	19.1	58.2	22.7	35.6	25.5	62.5
0663218	Rowland Heights CDP	14.5	0.0	26.0	57.8	13.2	61.8	25.0	33.6	34.6	68.8
0664000	Sacramento city	44.8	14.6	20.6	15.6	25.4	55.9	18.7	31.9	22.3	47.4
0664224	Salinas city	25.0	1.8	63.9	7.8	25.1	60.8	14.1	51.2	18.5	41.9
0665000	San Bernardino city	25.2	17.6	50.6	4.8	24.1	59.2	16.7	47.5	21.2	47.4
0665042	San Buenaventura (Ventura) city	71.3	1.9	21.8	3.4	15.5	59.8	24.6	30.0	27.9	52.7
0665084	San Clemente city	82.2	0.0	11.9	0.0	13.0	62.3	24.7	34.4	27.1	63.9
0666000	San Diego city	55.5	6.5	21.2	14.1	26.5	55.0	18.4	30.5	22.2	46.9
0667000	San Francisco city	50.9	5.9	11.7	28.3	25.7	54.0	20.3	18.7	24.3	36.0
0668000	San Jose city	38.1	3.5	25.0	31.0	19.1	63.3	17.6	40.6	23.4	56.4
0668084	San Leandro city	35.8	13.9	19.3	27.6	15.6	62.0	22.4	32.1	27.6	55.8
0668196	San Marcos city	63.1	0.0	25.6	7.4	19.3	59.9	20.8	37.5	24.8	59.3
0668252	San Mateo city	56.1	2.5	18.7	19.0	17.0	59.7	23.3	29.0	27.4	51.6
0668364	San Rafael city	72.4	2.4	18.2	4.8	14.3	57.3	28.4	32.1	31.5	52.6
0668378	San Ramon city	51.6	2.8	7.1	35.5	12.4	75.3	12.4	49.2	16.0	68.3
0669000	Santa Ana city	16.4	1.6	68.3	12.7	20.8	64.5	14.7	55.4	22.0	44.6
0669070	Santa Barbara city	66.4	1.7	26.6	3.9	24.8	51.3	24.0	26.8	27.1	39.5
0669084	Santa Clara city	42.6	3.8	13.8	36.9	26.4	58.2	15.4	35.9	18.9	45.7
0669088	Santa Clarita city	62.9	2.8	10.0	26.8	26.4	58.2	15.4	38.7	22.7	45.7
0669112	Santa Cruz city	75.5	2.7	12.9	6.6	27.2	54.2	18.6	23.9	21.0	42.2
0669196	Santa Maria city	35.8	0.0	55.6	5.6	23.1	57.3	19.6	47.1	25.2	49.7
0670000	Santa Monica city	75.7	3.7	9.6	7.9	23.8	54.6	21.6	16.4	23.2	26.4
0670098	Santa Rosa city	71.5	2.2	18.8	4.4	17.3	58.9	23.8	31.7	26.9	52.7
0670224	Santee city	78.7	0.0	12.4	3.6	17.1	64.0	19.0	38.7	21.8	68.8
0672016	Simi Valley city	72.6	1.2	15.3	8.1	13.7	64.5	21.8	38.9	26.0	74.1
0673080	South Gate city	5.3	1.7	92.4	0.0	20.3	65.0	14.6	53.8	22.0	47.5
0673262	South San Francisco city	28.5	2.5	28.6	36.1	17.9	57.8	24.3	35.2	30.7	59.1
0673430	South Whittier CDP	23.8	0.0	66.7	6.0	15.7	66.5	17.7	50.1	25.5	60.7
0675000	Stockton city	30.3	13.1	35.6	18.3	22.7	57.8	19.5	44.8	24.2	49.3
0677000	Sunnyvale city	42.0	2.0	12.5	40.9	26.5	56.3	17.1	36.4	20.7	45.8
0678120	Temecula city	64.9	4.0	19.8	8.4	15.2	69.8	15.0	49.1	19.2	63.8
0678582	Thousand Oaks city	77.1	0.0	11.5	8.7	11.3	61.9	26.8	33.6	30.0	71.8
0680000	Torrance city	48.7	3.4	13.2	31.8	12.2	62.6	25.3	31.0	29.3	55.8
0680238	Tracy city	44.4	8.4	29.2	13.1	18.4	69.9	11.6	50.1	19.5	65.0
0680644	Tulare city	43.0	5.0	48.9	0.0	23.7	58.4	17.9	46.2	21.5	60.4
0680812	Turlock city	62.4	0.0	27.2	5.0	21.3	58.6	20.2	39.1	24.6	52.5
0680854	Tustin city	42.3	0.0	29.2	22.7	23.4	62.2	14.4	41.4	18.7	50.5
0681204	Union City city	20.2	5.3	19.6	48.2	17.9	61.5	20.6	44.8	28.7	63.9
0681344	Upland city	50.7	6.4	32.4	8.2	18.3	61.3	20.4	35.0	24.9	54.9
0681554	Vacaville city	67.5	7.0	16.6	5.5	19.9	59.7	20.4	35.6	23.2	60.6
0681666	Vallejo city	34.4	22.8	18.0	20.8	16.0	63.0	21.0	31.8	26.3	56.9
0682590	Victorville city	34.9	16.5	42.7	5.0	24.9	58.0	17.1	52.8	22.5	59.7
0682954	Visalia city	54.5	2.3	36.7	4.9	23.0	58.3	18.7	44.7	23.7	57.1
0682996	Vista city	56.6	3.8	34.9	3.5	26.5	56.3	17.1	33.2	20.8	47.9
0683346	Walnut Creek city	76.7	0.0	7.4	12.7	14.6	47.0	38.4	23.1	40.3	65.0
0683668	Watsonville city	23.6	0.0	69.8	4.4	18.4	61.3	20.3	50.7	23.8	40.3
0684200	West Covina city	20.9	5.3	46.4	26.4	15.7	61.0	23.2	40.6	31.7	64.5
0684550	Westminster city	35.8	0.0	19.2	42.1	13.1	61.6	25.2	37.4	32.5	54.3

Table A-4: Cities with a Population of 50,000 or More—Living Arrangements—*Continued*

State/ Place FIPS code	City	Total Households	Family households, percent	Married-couple family households, percent	Male householder, no spouse, percent	Female householder, no spouse, percent	Householder living alone, percent	Nonfamily households, householder not living alone, percent	Opposite-sex partner unmarried partner households, percent	Same-sex unmarried partner households, percent	Average household size
	California—cont'd										
0685292	Whittier city	27,218	73.6	50.3	6.9	16.4	21.6	4.8	6.8	0.3	3.1
0686328	Woodland city	19,747	69.4	50.4	4.4	14.6	26.8	3.8	4.2	0.2	2.8
0686832	Yorba Linda city	22,102	81.9	71.0	3.1	7.9	15.6	2.5	2.2	0.3	3.0
0686972	Yuba City city	21,339	73.8	50.4	7.4	16.0	21.0	5.2	7.5	0.7	3.0
0687042	Yucaipa city	17,856	73.1	56.0	4.3	12.8	22.4	4.5	5.2	0.1	2.9
0800000	**Colorado**	1,989,371	63.9	49.1	4.5	10.3	28.2	7.9	5.4	0.6	2.6
0803455	Arvada city	43,581	67.6	51.0	5.2	11.3	26.3	6.1	5.1	0.4	2.5
0804000	Aurora city	122,667	65.0	43.2	6.3	15.6	28.5	6.4	6.6	0.5	2.8
0807850	Boulder city	41,319	42.1	33.8	2.6	5.8	33.1	24.8	6.7	0.7	2.3
0809280	Broomfield city	22,464	66.9	54.8	3.4	8.6	26.5	6.6	4.8	0.7	2.6
0812415	Castle Rock town	17,924	77.2	63.3	3.6	10.3	17.7	5.1	4.8	0.6	2.9
0812815	Centennial city	38,146	74.6	61.3	3.5	9.9	21.1	4.2	3.1	0.5	2.7
0816000	Colorado Springs city	168,914	64.0	48.3	4.1	11.6	29.1	6.9	4.9	0.4	2.5
0820000	Denver city	269,868	47.3	32.9	4.0	10.5	40.6	12.0	6.4	1.4	2.3
0827425	Fort Collins city	57,572	55.0	43.5	3.1	8.4	26.2	18.8	6.2	0.8	2.5
0831660	Grand Junction city	24,208	60.7	44.0	5.5	11.2	30.7	8.5	4.5	0.1	2.3
0832155	Greeley city	33,045	65.8	46.9	6.0	12.9	25.9	8.3	7.4	0.2	2.7
0836410	Highlands Ranch CDP	35,634	78.5	67.0	3.8	7.8	17.3	4.1	4.0	0.5	2.9
0843000	Lakewood city	61,329	57.8	40.9	5.1	11.8	33.5	8.7	5.3	0.6	2.3
0845970	Longmont city	34,011	66.6	49.2	5.8	11.6	26.4	7.0	5.5	0.4	2.6
0846465	Loveland city	29,203	65.1	50.0	6.1	8.9	28.3	6.6	6.4	0.4	2.4
0862000	Pueblo city	42,518	58.6	37.3	6.2	15.1	35.1	6.2	6.3	0.4	2.4
0877290	Thornton city	41,840	73.2	56.0	5.4	11.9	21.5	5.3	6.0	0.4	3.0
0883835	Westminster city	42,004	65.6	48.2	5.8	11.6	26.7	7.8	7.0	0.7	2.6
0900000	**Connecticut**	1,348,275	66.4	48.9	4.3	13.1	27.9	5.7	5.3	0.5	2.6
0908000	Bridgeport city	49,672	63.6	31.5	6.1	26.0	29.4	7.0	7.4	0.7	2.9
0908420	Bristol city	25,063	61.3	44.2	5.5	11.7	31.9	6.8	6.0	0.6	2.4
0918430	Danbury city	29,177	63.4	45.7	6.3	11.4	27.9	8.7	5.4	0.3	2.7
0922700	East Hartford CDP	20,758	62.9	35.2	5.2	22.5	31.1	6.0	6.1	0.4	2.4
0937000	Hartford city	45,038	58.1	19.7	7.0	31.4	35.1	6.8	7.7	0.7	2.6
0946450	Meriden city	23,729	66.3	44.3	4.8	17.3	28.7	5.0	6.3	0.4	2.5
0947515	Milford city	20,828	62.7	49.9	4.0	8.7	31.4	5.9	3.7	0.7	2.5
0950370	New Britain city	27,338	60.6	32.2	6.3	22.2	32.6	6.7	8.2	0.5	2.6
0952000	New Haven city	49,922	54.3	25.9	5.4	23.0	37.4	8.2	6.2	0.9	2.4
0955990	Norwalk city	35,480	59.2	44.0	3.3	11.8	34.5	6.4	4.6	0.5	2.4
0973000	Stamford city	46,190	64.1	47.4	4.3	12.4	29.1	6.8	5.4	0.2	2.7
0974260	Stratford CDP	20,651	65.4	49.8	4.0	11.7	29.5	5.0	5.7	0.6	2.5
0980000	Waterbury city	40,617	63.2	33.7	5.8	23.7	31.0	5.8	7.9	0.3	2.7
0982660	West Hartford CDP	24,894	65.6	51.5	3.2	10.9	28.2	6.3	3.8	0.9	2.5
0982800	West Haven city	20,372	62.6	42.0	2.9	17.7	31.6	5.8	5.6	0.5	2.6
1000000	**Delaware**	337,245	67.2	48.3	5.0	14.0	26.4	6.4	6.3	0.6	2.6
1077580	Wilmington city	28,801	54.5	21.8	6.8	25.8	37.9	7.7	8.0	1.0	2.4
1100000	**District of Columbia**	268,015	42.7	22.7	3.9	16.1	44.7	12.6	5.4	1.7	2.2
1150000	Washington city	268,015	42.7	22.7	3.9	16.1	44.7	12.6	5.4	1.7	2.2
1200000	**Florida**	7,168,502	64.1	46.3	4.6	13.3	29.4	6.6	5.6	0.6	2.6
1200410	Alafaya CDP	26,415	71.0	52.0	4.2	14.7	19.9	9.1	6.8	0.8	2.9
1207300	Boca Raton city	35,965	59.0	46.9	3.8	8.3	33.4	7.6	4.5	0.4	2.4
1207875	Boynton Beach city	28,837	54.0	37.0	4.4	12.6	38.0	7.9	6.3	1.0	2.4
1207950	Bradenton city	20,813	53.4	37.5	3.7	12.2	38.2	8.4	7.2	0.9	2.4
1208150	Brandon CDP	39,342	65.1	45.0	3.4	16.7	26.9	7.9	7.2	0.8	2.7
1210275	Cape Coral city	56,264	72.4	55.4	6.1	10.9	22.0	5.5	7.1	1.2	2.9
1212875	Clearwater city	46,819	54.1	36.3	4.2	13.6	39.3	6.7	5.7	0.9	2.3
1213275	Coconut Creek city	21,845	58.3	43.3	3.7	11.3	34.0	7.7	6.1	0.5	2.5
1214400	Coral Springs city	40,353	77.6	52.0	5.9	19.7	18.3	4.2	6.7	0.4	3.1
1216475	Davie town	32,669	68.9	50.0	4.5	14.3	23.2	7.9	6.1	0.4	2.9
1216525	Daytona Beach city	25,923	45.5	27.5	4.6	13.5	43.2	11.3	4.5	0.1	2.2
1216725	Deerfield Beach city	31,554	53.7	35.1	4.8	13.8	38.3	8.1	4.4	0.6	2.4
1217100	Delray Beach city	26,825	49.3	34.8	4.2	10.4	40.8	9.8	7.1	0.4	2.3
1217200	Deltona city	28,321	72.9	56.0	4.8	12.2	21.7	5.4	6.6	0.6	3.0
1224000	Fort Lauderdale city	72,270	45.9	30.4	4.2	11.3	42.2	11.9	6.6	3.1	2.3
1224125	Fort Myers city	23,333	56.8	35.6	3.8	17.4	36.4	6.8	6.6	0.5	2.6
1224562	Fountainebleau CDP	17,921	69.7	42.0	9.2	18.5	21.7	8.5	8.1	0.9	3.0
1225175	Gainesville city	47,924	40.3	25.3	3.5	11.6	37.7	22.0	6.5	0.3	2.4
1230000	Hialeah city	69,369	74.6	46.1	8.2	20.3	20.6	4.9	7.0	0.2	3.3
1232000	Hollywood city	54,698	59.2	40.1	4.6	14.6	33.0	7.7	6.6	1.2	2.6
1232275	Homestead city	19,455	67.8	43.1	7.3	17.4	24.8	7.4	9.2	0.0	3.2
1235000	Jacksonville city	312,257	62.5	42.0	4.5	16.1	31.2	6.3	5.7	0.5	2.6
1235875	Jupiter town	23,568	62.7	50.7	4.2	7.8	30.1	7.2	5.4	0.4	2.4
1236062	Kendale Lakes CDP	17,974	79.7	51.1	7.6	21.0	16.5	3.7	4.7	0.6	3.3
1236100	Kendall CDP	27,721	63.4	46.6	4.2	12.6	31.6	5.1	3.9	0.3	2.7
1236950	Kissimmee city	20,148	70.6	41.9	4.7	24.1	22.5	6.9	8.0	0.3	3.1

66 Families in America

State/Place FIPS code	City	Race or Hispanic origin of householder				Age of householder			Percent of households with one or more persons under 18 years old	Percent of households with one or more persons age 65 or older	Percent of all householders who are owners
		Householder is White alone, not Hispanic or Latino, percent	Householder is Black or African American alone, percent	Householder is Hispanic or Latino, percent	Householder is Asian alone, percent	Householders age 15 to 34, percent	Householders age 35 to 64, percent	Householders age 65 and older, percent			
	California—cont'd										
0685292	Whittier city	35.1	1.1	58.1	4.8	16.5	61.7	21.8	40.9	26.0	57.4
0686328	Woodland city	52.6	0.0	38.2	0.0	19.5	59.4	21.1	38.9	26.4	54.3
0686832	Yorba Linda city	68.6	0.0	12.0	16.4	7.2	68.6	24.2	36.7	29.9	83.6
0686972	Yuba City city	58.7	2.3	21.1	13.0	22.1	57.0	20.9	39.3	28.0	57.3
0687042	Yucaipa city	73.6	0.0	21.3	0.0	14.0	60.3	25.7	39.3	29.4	72.3
0800000	**Colorado**	76.6	3.7	15.4	2.4	22.5	58.4	19.1	32.2	21.7	64.4
0803455	Arvada city	87.3	0.0	9.4	1.5	16.2	60.3	23.5	31.1	25.9	74.0
0804000	Aurora city	57.0	15.5	20.1	4.2	24.6	59.0	16.4	37.4	19.2	56.3
0807850	Boulder city	85.9	0.0	6.7	4.3	39.5	45.4	15.1	20.4	16.3	48.8
0809280	Broomfield city	82.6	0.0	9.4	5.4	22.9	59.1	18.0	34.7	20.5	66.1
0812415	Castle Rock town	87.9	0.0	8.4	0.0	17.8	68.8	13.4	45.9	14.7	75.7
0812815	Centennial city	86.8	2.4	5.2	3.7	12.8	65.9	21.2	35.4	24.2	81.0
0816000	Colorado Springs city	75.8	5.8	13.2	2.4	25.9	55.7	18.4	32.5	20.6	58.0
0820000	Denver city	64.1	9.4	21.5	3.0	30.7	52.9	16.4	25.0	18.3	49.2
0827425	Fort Collins city	86.2	1.0	8.1	2.3	35.8	49.6	14.6	27.5	16.3	55.1
0831660	Grand Junction city	83.9	0.0	12.7	0.0	25.7	48.9	25.3	28.9	27.5	59.3
0832155	Greeley city	67.2	2.1	27.9	1.2	29.1	51.7	19.3	34.2	21.5	54.8
0836410	Highlands Ranch CDP	87.0	0.0	5.5	5.5	15.3	70.8	14.0	48.2	16.5	79.5
0843000	Lakewood city	77.6	1.1	16.4	2.6	23.3	53.6	23.1	25.8	25.6	57.7
0845970	Longmont city	76.5	0.0	18.4	2.8	21.4	59.4	19.2	34.7	21.6	61.7
0846465	Loveland city	90.0	0.0	6.9	0.0	22.5	53.9	23.6	32.1	26.1	61.7
0862000	Pueblo city	51.5	0.0	45.0	0.0	20.7	53.8	25.5	30.1	28.0	56.3
0877290	Thornton city	69.6	1.5	24.1	4.0	25.4	61.7	12.8	45.2	15.8	69.8
0883835	Westminster city	75.5	1.4	16.4	4.2	23.9	60.0	16.1	34.3	19.8	63.3
0900000	**Connecticut**	75.2	9.5	11.0	3.3	15.4	60.6	23.9	32.0	27.3	67.0
0908000	Bridgeport city	27.7	34.7	34.7	2.9	22.7	59.3	18.0	36.8	21.7	40.6
0908420	Bristol city	85.8	4.0	7.1	0.0	17.4	58.3	24.3	28.6	27.4	66.7
0918430	Danbury city	67.1	6.4	19.8	5.4	18.0	61.4	20.6	29.7	24.2	59.7
0922700	East Hartford CDP	46.3	25.6	22.9	4.3	19.2	59.6	21.2	32.4	25.0	55.1
0937000	Hartford city	16.9	39.3	41.9	2.9	28.3	53.9	17.7	36.0	20.5	23.0
0946450	Meriden city	64.4	9.9	24.2	0.0	18.3	59.5	22.2	29.3	24.9	59.5
0947515	Milford city	87.2	0.0	5.2	3.8	10.1	63.3	26.5	27.9	29.8	77.9
0950370	New Britain city	53.3	9.9	32.6	2.5	24.5	54.9	20.7	32.1	23.9	39.3
0952000	New Haven city	37.5	33.8	22.7	4.8	32.9	48.9	18.2	31.7	20.9	29.7
0955990	Norwalk city	64.3	14.0	18.1	0.0	16.8	61.3	21.9	26.3	25.2	62.0
0973000	Stamford city	59.7	13.7	18.0	7.8	20.8	57.0	22.2	32.8	25.3	55.8
0974260	Stratford CDP	73.1	13.7	10.3	2.6	10.3	59.4	30.3	28.7	33.3	80.0
0980000	Waterbury city	50.5	19.2	27.6	1.5	21.0	58.9	20.1	35.0	23.2	46.2
0982660	West Hartford CDP	81.0	5.5	7.4	4.8	13.9	59.1	27.0	31.7	29.8	72.6
0982800	West Haven city	59.2	22.3	14.5	0.0	18.6	59.6	21.8	32.5	24.6	56.0
1000000	**Delaware**	70.3	19.7	5.7	3.0	16.9	57.7	25.4	31.3	28.9	71.4
1077580	Wilmington city	36.3	52.4	9.1	0.0	25.4	54.0	20.6	31.7	22.8	45.3
1100000	**District of Columbia**	40.7	46.2	8.0	3.5	29.6	52.1	18.4	20.8	20.5	41.1
1150000	Washington city	40.7	46.2	8.0	3.5	29.6	52.1	18.4	20.8	20.5	41.1
1200000	**Florida**	64.9	13.7	18.5	2.1	15.8	55.2	28.9	28.0	32.9	65.8
1200410	Alafaya CDP	53.8	9.1	30.4	0.0	30.7	57.3	11.9	38.6	15.0	63.0
1207300	Boca Raton city	82.3	3.5	10.7	2.2	12.8	54.9	32.3	22.9	35.9	69.0
1207875	Boynton Beach city	64.7	21.2	10.8	0.0	16.1	49.9	34.0	25.1	35.8	64.8
1207950	Bradenton city	74.3	13.4	11.5	0.0	18.0	46.1	35.9	23.2	38.4	52.0
1208150	Brandon CDP	59.0	15.6	19.9	2.4	24.1	59.4	16.5	33.4	19.4	55.1
1210275	Cape Coral city	81.2	2.4	13.9	0.0	12.3	59.1	28.6	32.6	33.7	68.5
1212875	Clearwater city	78.8	8.0	9.6	2.1	16.2	52.7	31.2	23.6	34.0	58.0
1213275	Coconut Creek city	66.2	10.1	17.6	0.0	18.4	52.4	29.2	30.7	32.2	65.9
1214400	Coral Springs city	56.4	16.5	21.2	3.9	14.1	70.3	15.6	44.2	18.8	62.7
1216475	Davie town	60.8	7.6	26.8	4.1	17.2	65.0	17.8	37.4	23.1	72.1
1216525	Daytona Beach city	62.8	28.4	5.5	0.0	25.1	47.8	27.0	17.2	29.1	44.9
1216725	Deerfield Beach city	67.1	18.2	11.4	0.0	15.3	49.1	35.6	24.1	39.9	63.9
1217100	Delray Beach city	73.4	17.6	7.1	1.5	13.0	50.1	36.9	18.4	39.8	64.5
1217200	Deltona city	61.3	9.2	27.9	0.0	14.2	61.0	24.8	32.7	28.9	79.3
1224000	Fort Lauderdale city	61.5	22.3	13.7	1.6	17.9	59.0	23.1	20.4	26.7	52.4
1224125	Fort Myers city	59.7	24.6	13.6	0.0	18.4	52.2	29.4	27.6	32.8	47.7
1224562	Fountainebleau CDP	4.8	0.0	91.9	1.8	21.2	57.7	21.1	30.2	30.2	53.1
1225175	Gainesville city	60.4	21.9	10.4	5.9	45.4	40.8	13.8	17.4	15.1	36.2
1230000	Hialeah city	3.1	2.2	96.0	0.0	11.4	57.7	30.9	35.7	40.1	47.1
1232000	Hollywood city	55.7	14.2	27.0	0.0	15.7	60.8	23.5	28.6	28.1	60.0
1232275	Homestead city	21.5	23.8	55.8	0.0	26.5	59.6	13.9	43.3	17.3	42.0
1235000	Jacksonville city	59.1	29.0	6.9	3.7	22.9	57.5	19.6	30.5	22.3	60.8
1235875	Jupiter town	88.6	0.0	8.0	0.0	11.5	56.1	32.4	25.4	35.0	71.3
1236062	Kendale Lakes CDP	9.6	0.0	87.9	2.3	12.5	63.6	23.9	34.6	33.7	71.6
1236100	Kendall CDP	32.1	4.7	59.4	3.0	12.8	60.7	26.5	27.2	32.4	63.9
1236950	Kissimmee city	29.4	12.6	56.2	3.2	22.7	58.1	19.2	40.4	23.3	43.7

State/ Place FIPS code	City	Total Households	Family households, percent	Married-couple family households, percent	Male householder, no spouse, percent	Female householder, no spouse, percent	Householder living alone, percent	Nonfamily households, householder not living alone, percent	Opposite-sex partner unmarried partner households, percent	Same-sex unmarried partner households, percent	Average household size
	Florida—cont'd										
1238250	Lakeland city	39,030	58.8	39.1	4.6	15.1	33.7	7.5	5.7	0.6	2.5
1239425	Largo city	35,428	50.1	35.2	3.4	11.4	40.7	9.2	7.3	0.7	2.2
1239550	Lauderhill city	23,591	63.0	30.0	5.0	28.0	31.3	5.7	6.2	0.0	2.9
1239925	Lehigh Acres CDP	31,042	75.8	48.4	7.6	19.7	19.2	5.1	9.6	0.3	3.4
1243125	Margate city	21,506	59.4	40.7	3.5	15.2	35.7	4.8	3.8	0.4	2.5
1243975	Melbourne city	32,611	54.2	37.5	3.9	12.8	38.6	7.2	6.0	0.3	2.3
1245000	Miami city	152,200	55.9	31.0	7.0	17.9	36.5	7.6	5.3	0.6	2.7
1245025	Miami Beach city	42,791	43.0	29.2	4.9	8.9	47.4	9.6	5.3	0.6	2.1
1245060	Miami Gardens city	31,327	74.3	36.4	7.9	29.9	22.7	3.0	5.3	0.6	3.5
1245975	Miramar city	38,901	76.8	49.7	4.7	22.5	19.1	4.0	4.4	0.2	3.3
1249450	North Miami city	17,493	64.8	37.5	4.5	22.8	27.7	7.6	7.6	0.2	3.4
1249675	North Port city	22,289	66.8	51.6	5.4	9.8	25.7	7.5	7.4	0.4	2.6
1250750	Ocala city	22,206	58.7	35.5	5.2	18.0	35.1	6.2	6.9	0.3	2.4
1253000	Orlando city	101,436	51.5	29.6	4.4	17.5	37.7	10.7	7.0	1.1	2.4
1254000	Palm Bay city	37,506	68.4	48.0	4.7	15.7	26.4	5.2	5.8	0.2	2.8
1254200	Palm Coast city	27,250	71.0	58.4	4.1	8.5	23.6	5.4	4.3	0.4	2.8
1254350	Palm Harbor CDP	26,084	60.9	49.2	3.2	8.4	32.8	6.3	5.1	1.1	2.3
1255775	Pembroke Pines city	56,685	69.0	50.2	3.7	15.0	27.8	3.3	3.9	0.4	2.8
1255925	Pensacola city	21,797	54.5	35.7	5.3	13.5	37.4	8.1	5.8	0.2	2.4
1256825	Pine Hills CDP	20,051	73.0	38.6	6.8	27.5	21.7	5.4	6.5	0.3	3.4
1257425	Plantation city	32,800	65.6	47.1	4.3	14.1	27.8	6.7	6.1	0.9	2.7
1257900	Poinciana CDP	16,956	80.5	57.7	4.1	18.7	16.5	3.0	4.0	0.7	3.3
1258050	Pompano Beach city	40,395	52.8	32.4	5.5	14.9	38.8	8.4	5.3	0.8	2.5
1258350	Port Charlotte CDP	22,188	62.4	48.0	3.5	10.9	32.5	5.1	4.3	0.8	2.4
1258575	Port Orange city	23,928	61.4	48.3	3.2	9.9	32.0	6.6	4.3	1.0	2.4
1258715	Port St. Lucie city	57,605	74.4	55.8	5.3	13.3	20.5	5.1	5.1	0.3	2.9
1260950	Riverview CDP	24,572	74.0	57.7	5.5	10.9	19.1	6.9	5.9	0.3	3.0
1263000	St. Petersburg city	104,550	53.0	35.1	4.4	13.5	39.3	7.8	6.1	1.4	2.3
1263650	Sanford city	18,011	61.2	36.8	3.7	20.7	32.1	6.7	8.1	0.2	3.0
1264175	Sarasota city	22,814	50.4	35.3	3.6	11.5	38.9	10.7	7.8	0.8	2.2
1268350	Spring Hill CDP	39,055	70.1	52.4	4.7	13.0	25.2	4.7	4.7	0.4	2.6
1269700	Sunrise city	31,683	66.7	44.5	4.5	17.7	28.8	4.6	4.9	0.2	2.8
1270600	Tallahassee city	73,597	47.6	30.1	3.9	13.7	32.7	19.7	5.9	0.4	2.3
1270675	Tamarac city	26,282	58.2	37.3	3.4	17.5	37.2	4.6	5.9	0.4	2.4
1270700	Tamiami CDP	15,419	82.4	59.0	9.2	14.2	13.5	4.1	4.8	0.4	3.5
1271000	Tampa city	140,711	53.8	33.9	4.5	15.5	37.4	8.8	5.7	0.9	2.4
1271569	The Hammocks CDP	15,998	78.7	58.3	3.7	16.7	17.6	3.8	5.7	0.1	3.4
1271625	The Villages CDP	32,073	72.0	69.0	0.5	2.5	24.9	3.1	1.7	0.4	1.8
1272145	Town 'n' Country CDP	29,691	64.8	43.4	5.6	15.8	25.1	10.1	8.7	0.4	2.7
1275812	Wellington village	19,780	78.3	64.4	3.1	10.8	17.6	4.1	4.2	0.1	3.0
1276582	Weston city	20,969	83.3	70.3	3.4	9.7	13.6	3.1	3.2	0.2	3.2
1276600	West Palm Beach city	40,953	51.6	31.1	5.1	15.4	38.4	10.0	7.3	0.6	2.4
1300000	**Georgia**	3,522,934	67.7	47.6	4.8	15.3	26.9	5.4	4.4	0.5	2.7
1301052	Albany city	28,980	60.7	29.5	5.5	25.8	34.1	5.2	6.0	0.3	2.5
1301696	Alpharetta city	22,501	69.8	58.4	2.9	8.5	27.0	3.2	3.0	0.3	2.7
1303440	Athens-Clarke County	41,332	49.2	31.7	3.8	13.7	34.3	16.5	4.7	0.4	2.6
1304000	Atlanta city	181,002	42.8	24.7	3.4	14.8	46.6	10.6	4.1	1.4	2.3
1304204	Augusta-Richmond County	69,773	59.9	33.4	4.7	21.9	34.7	5.3	4.8	0.5	2.7
1310944	Brookhaven city	21,884	47.1	38.0	3.5	5.6	40.1	12.8	7.7	1.1	2.3
1319000	Columbus city	71,351	64.2	39.1	4.4	20.7	31.2	4.6	3.8	0.4	2.6
1342425	Johns Creek city	26,310	81.6	69.8	2.8	9.0	15.8	2.5	2.3	0.1	3.1
1349000	Macon city	32,589	59.6	27.8	4.4	27.4	35.3	5.1	5.1	0.1	2.6
1349756	Marietta city	23,402	55.3	36.0	6.1	13.2	35.6	9.1	6.0	1.0	2.4
1367284	Roswell city	34,348	67.3	53.4	3.4	10.5	28.3	4.4	3.0	0.5	2.7
1368516	Sandy Springs city	42,351	52.4	39.0	3.3	10.1	38.8	8.7	5.8	0.4	2.3
1369000	Savannah city	52,618	55.6	31.3	4.9	19.4	35.4	9.0	6.0	0.7	2.5
1371492	Smyrna city	23,311	54.0	37.9	3.4	12.7	37.2	8.7	7.0	1.0	2.3
1378800	Valdosta city	21,457	52.9	29.1	3.9	20.0	33.1	13.9	7.9	0.1	2.5
1380508	Warner Robins city	26,883	62.4	41.3	3.7	17.4	34.8	2.8	3.5	0.4	2.7
1500000	**Hawaii**	449,296	69.2	51.5	5.4	12.3	24.0	6.7	5.8	0.7	3.0
1571550	Urban Honolulu CDP	127,736	57.4	41.0	4.6	11.8	33.9	8.6	5.2	0.6	2.6
1600000	**Idaho**	583,452	69.3	55.1	4.4	9.8	24.3	6.4	5.3	0.3	2.7
1608830	Boise City city	87,344	59.4	44.3	5.3	9.9	30.6	10.0	5.5	0.5	2.4
1639700	Idaho Falls city	21,016	69.1	50.3	5.1	13.7	26.3	4.6	5.0	0.6	2.7
1652120	Meridian city	27,420	77.9	63.5	5.4	8.9	19.4	2.7	4.9	0.0	2.9
1656260	Nampa city	27,872	72.0	53.1	4.7	14.2	23.2	4.8	6.6	0.2	3.0
1664090	Pocatello city	20,601	61.9	46.2	5.3	10.4	30.5	7.6	5.4	0.3	2.6
1700000	**Illinois**	4,763,457	65.4	48.1	4.6	12.7	28.9	5.7	5.2	0.5	2.6
1702154	Arlington Heights village	30,142	66.9	58.1	2.6	6.2	28.7	4.5	3.2	0.8	2.5
1703012	Aurora city	61,506	73.9	54.7	6.0	13.2	21.0	5.1	5.9	0.2	3.2
1705573	Berwyn city	17,919	71.7	47.2	8.0	16.4	24.3	4.0	8.2	0.7	3.2

State/ Place FIPS code	City	Race or Hispanic origin of householder				Age of householder			Percent of households with one or more persons under 18 years old	Percent of households with one or more persons age 65 or older	Percent of all householders who are owners
		Householder is White alone, not Hispanic or Latino, percent	Householder is Black or African American alone, percent	Householder is Hispanic or Latino, percent	Householder is Asian alone, percent	Householders age 15 to 34, percent	Householders age 35 to 64, percent	Householders age 65 and older, percent			
	Florida—cont'd										
1238250	Lakeland city	69.8	17.9	10.7	0.9	19.1	48.9	31.9	26.3	35.3	54.5
1239425	Largo city	82.4	6.5	7.9	1.8	14.1	50.0	36.0	19.0	37.8	56.6
1239550	Lauderhill city	18.6	36.6	2.8	0.0	12.7	60.9	26.4	34.7	27.3	59.8
1239925	Lehigh Acres CDP	51.6	18.0	27.3	0.0	21.7	58.3	20.0	42.8	24.4	58.9
1243125	Margate city	55.6	21.7	17.0	4.2	12.9	53.6	33.4	27.8	36.7	77.3
1243975	Melbourne city	80.7	8.9	7.2	1.6	17.6	50.5	31.9	22.4	35.4	58.9
1245000	Miami city	15.4	17.7	68.2	1.0	21.4	54.9	23.7	25.9	29.2	31.8
1245025	Miami Beach city	42.1	62.9	242.5	3.6	21.4	54.9	23.7	18.8	24.7	31.8
1245060	Miami Gardens city	3.1	85.9	331.3	5.0	21.4	54.9	23.7	38.1	28.0	31.8
1245975	Miramar city	13.0	47.7	34.7	0.0	18.0	72.8	9.2	47.9	16.3	71.9
1249450	North Miami city	17.5	32.6	15.5	0.0	24.1	64.8	11.1	36.1	24.3	52.1
1249675	North Port city	88.9	5.4	0.0	0.0	12.0	53.2	34.8	31.7	39.5	75.0
1250750	Ocala city	64.0	22.1	10.5	0.0	23.6	47.7	28.7	28.5	30.4	47.9
1253000	Orlando city	49.0	23.1	23.3	3.5	31.5	53.9	14.6	27.3	17.3	37.2
1254000	Palm Bay city	70.6	16.7	11.5	0.0	14.5	59.0	26.5	31.2	31.4	75.1
1254200	Palm Coast city	75.0	13.6	8.2	0.0	9.6	50.6	39.9	24.1	45.0	79.0
1254350	Palm Harbor CDP	92.8	9.2	4.6	0.0	10.0	53.5	36.4	20.6	39.3	72.3
1255775	Pembroke Pines city	35.4	17.6	41.1	5.0	14.3	60.7	25.0	34.3	29.8	72.1
1255925	Pensacola city	68.9	24.5	2.9	0.0	17.2	55.1	27.7	21.6	31.5	59.0
1256825	Pine Hills CDP	15.1	68.2	12.7	2.9	20.2	61.0	18.8	40.6	24.3	54.9
1257425	Plantation city	60.4	17.0	17.5	4.1	16.4	62.2	21.4	30.6	24.6	66.9
1257900	Poinciana CDP	27.2	25.6	44.8	0.0	12.5	61.2	26.3	39.3	33.3	71.7
1258050	Pompano Beach city	63.3	21.7	13.4	0.9	15.3	54.7	30.0	24.2	33.4	53.6
1258350	Port Charlotte CDP	82.0	10.0	5.7	0.0	8.2	48.7	43.1	21.4	45.8	77.2
1258575	Port Orange city	91.9	0.0	3.3	0.0	11.5	52.0	36.5	21.1	40.1	75.4
1258715	Port St. Lucie city	67.9	13.7	15.0	0.0	13.3	59.8	26.8	35.1	31.3	76.5
1260950	Riverview CDP	64.1	17.1	15.2	0.0	20.3	64.9	14.8	41.1	17.7	72.8
1263000	St. Petersburg city	69.4	21.5	5.1	2.3	17.8	57.9	24.3	23.1	27.2	54.7
1263650	Sanford city	54.3	24.7	15.9	3.0	23.0	58.0	19.0	37.1	21.7	54.7
1264175	Sarasota city	72.9	13.4	11.8	0.0	16.2	48.9	34.8	19.6	37.8	53.5
1268350	Spring Hill CDP	82.7	4.6	10.7	0.0	11.6	51.5	36.9	29.8	41.1	75.5
1269700	Sunrise city	42.0	27.2	25.9	0.0	15.7	57.8	26.5	31.8	31.1	69.4
1270600	Tallahassee city	55.9	34.3	5.3	3.3	45.1	40.8	14.1	22.9	16.0	40.3
1270675	Tamarac city	56.1	95.9	14.9	9.1	45.1	40.8	14.1	25.9	43.2	40.3
1270700	Tamiami CDP	0.0	0.0	94.9	0.0	9.7	62.8	27.5	34.8	36.3	76.3
1271000	Tampa city	51.3	24.1	20.1	3.3	24.8	56.5	18.7	27.5	21.4	49.5
1271569	The Hammocks CDP	16.2	9.6	8.5	0.0	11.2	67.3	21.5	38.7	23.4	78.3
1271625	The Villages CDP	98.2	0.0	0.0	0.0	0.0	0.0	0.0	0.0	85.9	0.0
1272145	Town 'n' Country CDP	50.6	7.0	37.3	3.8	20.4	61.0	18.6	29.6	23.8	58.5
1275812	Wellington village	71.7	9.6	13.9	0.0	9.5	69.0	21.5	39.7	25.5	78.8
1276582	Weston city	48.3	0.0	42.9	0.0	8.1	76.7	15.2	49.4	19.0	74.2
1276600	West Palm Beach city	52.4	27.5	17.2	2.5	21.3	53.5	25.2	22.9	29.5	50.8
1300000	**Georgia**	60.0	29.9	6.2	2.8	20.3	60.1	19.6	35.2	22.7	63.7
1301052	Albany city	29.2	67.1	1.9	0.0	26.0	52.8	21.2	32.2	23.6	39.4
1301696	Alpharetta city	71.0	10.0	5.4	12.0	15.8	69.4	14.8	43.3	16.4	64.3
1303440	Athens-Clarke County	58.7	27.5	8.0	3.9	41.2	43.2	15.7	25.3	17.4	42.1
1304000	Atlanta city	43.4	48.6	3.6	3.0	32.0	51.2	16.8	21.0	18.5	44.2
1304204	Augusta-Richmond County	41.3	51.9	3.8	1.8	24.9	54.3	20.8	30.3	23.5	52.3
1310944	Brookhaven city	63.3	13.4	15.9	5.7	32.8	52.9	14.3	21.6	15.5	47.0
1319000	Columbus city	46.4	45.3	5.4	1.9	23.4	55.5	21.1	35.1	23.2	50.5
1342425	Johns Creek city	62.0	11.3	0.0	20.3	9.4	77.0	13.7	50.1	17.5	79.1
1349000	Macon city	31.2	64.9	0.0	0.0	23.6	54.4	22.0	32.0	24.8	41.9
1349756	Marietta city	50.6	33.0	12.8	0.0	29.6	54.2	16.2	28.6	17.3	41.9
1367284	Roswell city	74.2	12.0	9.1	0.0	16.2	65.1	18.7	35.0	21.2	66.6
1368516	Sandy Springs city	61.2	22.2	10.0	4.9	30.1	53.1	16.8	25.0	19.0	45.0
1369000	Savannah city	44.0	49.5	3.8	1.8	27.7	50.1	22.1	27.5	24.6	45.4
1371492	Smyrna city	52.8	33.5	9.0	4.4	30.6	57.1	12.3	27.5	14.1	49.9
1378800	Valdosta city	45.1	48.1	4.2	0.0	39.1	42.4	18.5	29.8	19.3	43.3
1380508	Warner Robins city	54.5	37.3	4.6	0.0	29.1	56.8	14.2	37.3	16.9	56.2
1500000	**Hawaii**	31.2	2.2	6.9	39.5	18.5	56.0	25.5	33.3	31.5	56.5
1571550	Urban Honolulu CDP	23.0	2.2	4.6	54.4	20.4	51.2	28.4	24.9	33.8	41.8
1600000	**Idaho**	88.2	0.5	7.9	1.1	22.1	55.0	22.8	34.7	25.5	68.7
1608830	Boise City city	88.1	1.0	5.2	3.0	24.1	56.9	19.0	29.3	20.8	59.6
1639700	Idaho Falls city	88.7	0.0	8.5	0.0	24.0	52.3	23.7	37.7	25.5	66.0
1652120	Meridian city	91.9	0.0	5.7	0.0	22.2	58.7	19.0	43.4	20.8	73.2
1656260	Nampa city	79.3	0.0	17.3	0.0	24.6	53.6	21.7	41.7	23.9	62.8
1664090	Pocatello city	91.3	0.0	5.3	0.0	32.0	49.8	18.2	32.2	19.5	60.9
1700000	**Illinois**	70.1	13.7	10.9	4.2	19.6	58.2	22.2	32.5	25.1	66.7
1702154	Arlington Heights village	85.6	1.7	4.6	7.5	15.0	57.0	28.1	28.9	30.6	76.0
1703012	Aurora city	51.1	9.5	31.6	6.7	21.6	65.4	13.0	46.1	16.1	68.2
1705573	Berwyn city	43.3	8.9	44.9	0.0	17.2	64.5	18.3	43.1	21.7	59.6

State/ Place FIPS code	City	Total Households	Family households, percent	Married-couple family households, percent	Male householder, no spouse, percent	Female householder, no spouse, percent	Householder living alone, percent	Nonfamily households, householder not living alone, percent	Opposite-sex partner unmarried partner households, percent	Same-sex unmarried partner households, percent	Average household size
	Illinois—cont'd										
1706613	Bloomington city	30,826	59.6	45.3	4.2	10.1	31.4	9.0	6.5	0.8	2.5
1707133	Bolingbrook village	21,757	81.0	63.1	4.8	13.1	15.8	3.2	4.7	0.1	3.4
1712385	Champaign city	32,471	46.7	34.6	2.2	9.9	36.7	16.6	5.1	0.4	2.3
1714000	Chicago city	1,026,014	54.5	32.0	5.4	17.0	36.7	8.8	6.3	0.8	2.6
1714351	Cicero town	21,465	80.7	51.9	9.7	19.1	15.5	3.8	8.7	0.2	3.9
1718823	Decatur city	31,524	57.0	37.2	4.3	15.5	37.3	5.7	6.2	0.5	2.3
1719642	Des Plaines city	22,733	64.1	53.3	1.6	9.1	31.4	4.5	2.7	0.4	2.6
1723074	Elgin city	33,860	70.5	51.2	6.5	12.8	24.0	5.5	6.3	0.4	3.2
1724582	Evanston city	28,929	53.9	40.3	3.5	10.1	37.7	8.4	3.9	1.4	2.3
1735411	Hoffman Estates village	18,281	77.5	63.4	2.5	11.6	18.6	3.9	2.4	0.2	2.9
1738570	Joliet city	46,546	72.7	51.6	6.1	15.0	22.0	5.2	6.8	0.7	3.1
1751089	Mount Prospect village	20,163	70.8	59.4	3.8	7.6	24.5	4.7	3.4	0.3	2.7
1751622	Naperville city	48,758	77.5	66.8	2.7	8.0	18.7	3.8	2.5	0.2	2.9
1753234	Normal town	18,716	53.0	40.7	3.3	9.0	29.5	17.5	3.3	0.9	2.6
1754820	Oak Lawn village	22,037	64.6	48.7	5.0	11.0	31.5	3.9	4.2	0.1	2.6
1754885	Oak Park village	21,616	59.4	46.3	1.9	11.1	35.3	5.3	4.2	0.1	2.4
1756640	Orland Park village	21,556	72.5	61.2	2.3	9.0	23.7	3.8	3.2	0.2	2.7
1757225	Palatine village	25,820	66.2	50.2	5.0	11.0	28.2	5.5	4.7	0.4	2.7
1759000	Peoria city	47,125	57.1	36.7	3.9	16.5	36.7	6.2	5.2	0.8	2.4
1765000	Rockford city	58,444	61.5	38.4	5.0	18.1	32.9	5.6	7.1	0.3	2.5
1768003	Schaumburg village	30,284	60.8	49.0	3.5	8.3	32.8	6.4	4.4	0.8	2.5
1770122	Skokie village	22,821	72.5	55.3	5.2	12.1	24.9	2.6	3.2	0.4	2.8
1772000	Springfield city	50,593	55.8	36.5	4.9	14.4	37.3	6.9	5.6	0.4	2.2
1775484	Tinley Park village	20,836	71.2	57.1	4.3	9.7	23.9	4.9	4.7	0.2	2.7
1779293	Waukegan city	28,899	70.4	44.4	6.3	19.7	24.9	4.7	6.9	0.2	3.0
1781048	Wheaton city	19,066	68.7	58.0	3.7	7.1	26.2	5.1	3.3	0.2	2.7
1800000	**Indiana**	2,482,558	66.4	49.4	4.6	12.4	27.9	5.7	5.7	0.4	2.6
1801468	Anderson city	22,896	56.6	34.8	4.9	17.0	37.8	5.5	6.3	0.5	2.3
1805860	Bloomington city	29,426	36.8	25.5	3.0	8.4	41.2	21.9	5.4	0.9	2.3
1810342	Carmel city	30,700	75.8	66.4	2.1	7.3	19.8	4.4	3.5	0.4	2.7
1820728	Elkhart city	19,906	60.5	33.9	8.7	17.9	32.9	6.6	9.6	0.4	2.6
1822000	Evansville city	50,843	56.6	35.9	4.3	16.3	37.1	6.4	6.0	0.4	2.3
1823278	Fishers town	28,193	75.5	63.8	2.8	8.9	20.5	4.0	3.7	0.4	2.9
1825000	Fort Wayne city	101,455	60.6	40.3	4.8	15.5	33.1	6.3	6.0	0.5	2.5
1827000	Gary city	30,066	61.3	23.9	6.0	31.4	33.9	4.8	6.1	0.3	2.6
1829898	Greenwood city	20,782	63.7	49.0	3.5	11.2	29.2	7.1	6.4	0.2	2.5
1831000	Hammond city	27,836	65.3	39.1	7.2	19.0	29.7	5.0	6.9	0.2	2.8
1836003	Indianapolis city	327,418	58.5	36.8	5.0	16.7	34.1	7.4	6.5	0.8	2.5
1840392	Kokomo city	24,644	58.8	40.0	5.5	13.2	35.6	5.6	6.0	0.3	2.2
1840788	Lafayette city	29,735	57.1	38.4	4.6	14.1	34.2	8.8	8.0	0.8	2.3
1851876	Muncie city	27,719	50.0	31.9	4.1	14.0	34.3	15.7	6.7	0.2	2.2
1854180	Noblesville city	21,716	68.1	55.7	3.4	9.0	27.0	4.9	4.9	0.5	2.6
1871000	South Bend city	39,903	57.0	34.6	4.4	18.0	35.2	7.8	6.5	0.3	2.5
1875428	Terre Haute city	21,276	55.5	36.9	4.6	14.1	36.8	7.6	6.7	1.2	2.4
1900000	**Iowa**	1,227,201	64.6	51.0	4.1	9.5	29.0	6.4	6.0	0.3	2.4
1901855	Ames city	23,425	43.2	37.0	2.1	4.1	31.1	25.7	7.3	0.4	2.3
1912000	Cedar Rapids city	52,195	58.0	42.9	4.0	11.1	33.0	9.0	6.8	0.4	2.4
1916860	Council Bluffs city	24,524	62.2	40.6	5.6	16.0	31.1	6.7	6.9	0.8	2.5
1919000	Davenport city	40,326	57.8	40.1	4.1	13.7	34.5	7.7	7.5	0.6	2.4
1921000	Des Moines city	80,831	60.2	39.5	5.8	14.9	32.3	7.5	7.3	0.5	2.5
1922395	Dubuque city	23,736	55.6	40.7	3.1	11.8	36.1	8.4	6.1	0.3	2.3
1938595	Iowa City city	28,694	44.4	32.7	3.0	8.7	35.3	20.3	4.9	0.2	2.2
1973335	Sioux City city	31,146	63.2	42.3	6.5	14.4	30.8	6.0	7.8	0.2	2.6
1982425	Waterloo city	28,562	56.5	39.6	3.4	13.5	36.4	7.1	6.6	0.6	2.4
1983910	West Des Moines city	24,892	60.5	49.0	2.8	8.8	29.9	9.6	5.6	0.3	2.4
2000000	**Kansas**	1,109,747	65.6	50.7	4.4	10.5	28.5	5.9	5.0	0.3	2.5
2036000	Kansas City city	53,275	63.4	37.3	6.9	19.2	30.1	6.5	7.1	0.6	2.8
2038900	Lawrence city	34,547	50.3	37.0	5.2	8.1	31.9	17.9	6.8	0.6	2.4
2044250	Manhattan city	20,519	47.5	37.0	3.1	7.4	33.1	19.4	5.4	0.4	2.4
2052575	Olathe city	45,809	73.8	60.8	3.9	9.1	20.8	5.4	4.0	0.2	2.8
2053775	Overland Park city	73,829	64.7	51.3	2.5	10.9	30.0	5.3	4.4	0.3	2.4
2064500	Shawnee city	23,656	69.1	56.9	3.7	8.5	24.8	6.1	4.7	0.3	2.7
2071000	Topeka city	52,758	56.7	39.5	4.6	12.6	36.1	7.2	6.3	0.4	2.4
2079000	Wichita city	149,595	61.6	43.4	4.9	13.3	32.5	5.8	4.8	0.3	2.5
2100000	**Kentucky**	1,693,399	66.8	49.0	4.8	13.0	28.0	5.2	5.3	0.4	2.5
2108902	Bowling Green city	23,606	52.6	31.3	5.3	16.0	34.7	12.8	7.0	0.3	2.3
2146027	Lexington-Fayette	123,413	57.6	40.8	4.5	12.2	32.8	9.7	5.7	0.6	2.4
2148006	Louisville/Jefferson county	243,396	60.6	39.1	5.1	16.3	32.8	6.6	5.7	0.6	2.4
2158620	Owensboro city	23,432	60.3	42.6	5.1	12.7	33.9	5.8	5.5	0.6	2.4
2200000	**Louisiana**	1,715,997	65.7	43.5	5.1	17.1	29.0	5.3	5.3	0.3	2.6
2205000	Baton Rouge city	88,508	54.6	29.2	5.4	19.9	34.9	10.6	5.3	0.3	2.5

Table A-4: Cities with a Population of 50,000 or More—Living Arrangements—*Continued*

State/ Place FIPS code	City	Race or Hispanic origin of householder				Age of householder			Percent of households with one or more persons under 18 years old	Percent of households with one or more persons age 65 or older	Percent of all householders who are owners
		Householder is White alone, not Hispanic or Latino, percent	Householder is Black or African American alone, percent	Householder is Hispanic or Latino, percent	Householder is Asian alone, percent	Householders age 15 to 34, percent	Householders age 35 to 64, percent	Householders age 65 and older, percent			
	Illinois—cont'd										
1706613	Bloomington city...............	78.4	10.0	3.9	6.2	25.9	57.2	17.0	30.7	19.0	62.2
1707133	Bolingbrook village	51.8	18.6	19.9	8.9	17.0	70.3	12.7	46.4	17.8	82.5
1712385	Champaign city.................	67.7	14.3	5.6	10.3	41.6	45.1	13.4	21.8	15.2	47.4
1714000	Chicago city.....................	41.3	31.1	20.5	5.7	27.8	54.2	18.0	28.9	21.0	43.9
1714351	Cicero town	14.7	4.5	79.8	0.0	25.7	63.5	10.7	57.3	16.4	50.7
1718823	Decatur city	76.1	19.4	1.2	0.9	21.5	51.5	27.0	27.1	28.8	61.1
1719642	Des Plaines city	77.2	0.0	11.1	10.2	13.8	57.2	29.0	25.9	32.7	79.2
1723074	Elgin city........................	55.3	6.7	32.0	5.3	20.7	62.1	17.2	42.0	21.3	67.2
1724582	Evanston city...................	66.9	16.3	6.5	8.9	24.1	54.4	21.5	27.6	23.8	55.6
1735411	Hoffman Estates village.............	62.5	4.4	10.6	21.2	20.2	64.7	15.1	36.4	21.2	74.4
1738570	Joliet city.......................	60.7	16.9	20.1	0.0	20.8	63.6	15.6	45.0	18.8	71.6
1751089	Mount Prospect village...............	74.4	0.0	10.6	10.0	16.7	58.9	24.5	34.6	26.9	71.4
1751622	Naperville city	75.0	4.3	4.8	14.3	13.9	69.0	17.1	43.3	20.1	76.8
1753234	Normal town	84.7	7.3	4.1	0.0	40.6	43.9	15.5	27.5	16.3	58.5
1754820	Oak Lawn village...............	81.7	6.4	10.1	4.9	16.4	53.4	30.2	27.4	33.0	80.6
1754885	Oak Park village	65.6	6.6	10.3	5.0	16.4	53.4	30.2	32.4	20.3	80.6
1756640	Orland Park village............	87.9	0.0	4.8	0.0	8.4	59.4	32.2	27.4	36.8	89.5
1757225	Palatine village................	74.8	3.2	11.0	10.1	18.8	62.8	18.4	34.9	21.6	66.3
1759000	Peoria city......................	64.9	24.8	3.7	4.4	27.8	51.0	21.2	29.9	23.6	53.9
1765000	Rockford city...................	66.2	19.2	11.2	2.0	21.5	54.8	23.7	33.4	26.1	55.0
1768003	Schaumburg village.............	71.9	4.1	5.0	17.8	24.9	56.3	18.8	29.5	22.0	63.8
1770122	Skokie village	65.4	6.0	6.5	21.3	10.5	61.5	28.1	30.8	34.2	73.5
1772000	Springfield city.................	79.0	16.2	1.5	0.0	21.9	54.7	23.4	26.6	25.6	62.7
1775484	Tinley Park village	86.3	2.9	5.8	0.0	16.8	60.4	22.7	35.3	26.8	85.1
1779293	Waukegan city..................	30.6	22.4	42.6	3.8	26.0	59.6	14.5	45.8	17.6	50.5
1781048	Wheaton city...................	86.7	4.5	3.5	4.7	18.1	59.1	22.8	33.8	24.8	69.3
1800000	**Indiana**	84.3	8.8	4.3	1.4	20.3	57.4	22.4	32.5	24.9	69.2
1801468	Anderson city..................	82.5	11.7	3.2	0.0	20.4	52.3	27.3	28.6	28.9	56.4
1805860	Bloomington city...............	81.0	4.4	3.4	8.4	48.8	35.9	15.3	18.0	16.2	32.9
1810342	Carmel city.....................	86.3	3.1	0.0	7.6	15.5	67.6	16.9	41.0	19.7	77.9
1820728	Elkhart city.....................	69.9	13.1	15.2	0.0	24.5	55.9	19.7	36.8	20.9	50.9
1822000	Evansville city..................	83.6	12.6	1.8	0.0	26.0	51.1	22.9	27.9	25.0	53.9
1823278	Fishers town	84.0	6.1	0.0	4.8	22.3	68.2	9.5	49.0	12.1	85.1
1825000	Fort Wayne city................	75.3	15.5	5.3	2.5	23.4	56.0	20.6	31.9	22.8	62.8
1827000	Gary city........................	11.5	84.0	3.9	0.0	17.5	55.2	27.3	32.9	30.4	52.2
1829898	Greenwood city................	88.8	2.9	0.0	0.0	27.4	51.9	20.7	32.7	22.4	60.7
1831000	Hammond city..................	48.7	22.9	26.5	0.9	21.2	59.7	19.1	38.1	21.6	61.6
1836003	Indianapolis city...............	62.6	27.2	6.7	2.0	27.1	55.3	17.6	31.3	19.9	53.9
1840392	Kokomo city....................	85.4	10.1	2.8	0.9	23.3	51.5	25.2	29.7	26.9	62.4
1840788	Lafayette city...................	83.2	6.4	7.6	1.9	36.8	46.3	16.9	29.3	18.5	48.3
1851876	Muncie city.....................	85.3	6.9	2.0	1.2	33.7	42.8	23.5	22.2	25.4	49.5
1854180	Noblesville city................	90.1	5.1	0.0	0.0	27.4	56.1	16.4	37.8	18.2	71.9
1871000	South Bend city................	63.3	25.3	8.2	1.3	25.1	54.2	20.7	31.1	23.1	60.0
1875428	Terre Haute city...............	87.0	7.7	2.4	0.0	27.4	50.8	21.8	28.6	25.1	54.5
1900000	**Iowa**	91.6	2.5	3.4	1.5	21.7	54.2	24.1	30.4	26.0	71.8
1901855	Ames city.......................	84.0	2.5	2.0	9.9	53.4	33.5	13.1	18.7	13.7	41.5
1912000	Cedar Rapids city..............	90.1	4.6	2.3	1.4	26.6	52.7	20.8	29.3	22.6	68.9
1916860	Council Bluffs city.............	91.2	0.0	6.2	0.0	24.0	53.6	22.4	30.0	24.8	63.9
1919000	Davenport city.................	81.3	10.4	5.3	1.6	25.3	54.0	20.7	30.2	22.5	60.3
1921000	Des Moines city................	77.9	9.4	7.9	3.5	28.1	53.2	18.6	33.5	20.8	62.4
1922395	Dubuque city...................	93.0	0.0	1.3	1.3	21.8	52.9	25.3	26.4	26.9	63.1
1938595	Iowa City city..................	83.4	5.3	4.0	5.9	45.6	39.7	14.7	22.1	15.4	46.8
1973335	Sioux City city.................	80.3	2.7	12.2	2.1	21.9	56.3	21.8	34.6	24.6	64.7
1982425	Waterloo city...................	78.9	15.0	3.7	0.0	25.6	49.7	24.7	27.1	26.6	64.3
1983910	West Des Moines city..........	86.0	3.1	4.6	0.0	34.7	49.6	15.7	33.8	16.8	59.0
2000000	**Kansas**...........................	82.9	5.6	7.3	1.9	22.7	54.9	22.3	32.8	24.6	66.7
2036000	Kansas City city...............	46.9	29.6	19.6	2.0	24.4	56.7	18.9	36.3	22.0	57.8
2038900	Lawrence city...................	83.5	4.2	4.3	4.0	42.1	43.4	14.5	25.0	16.1	46.6
2044250	Manhattan city	80.7	6.7	5.4	5.4	53.7	33.1	13.2	23.9	13.5	39.4
2052575	Olathe city......................	81.9	4.5	8.5	3.7	21.9	64.1	14.0	43.8	15.9	73.6
2053775	Overland Park city.............	83.3	4.8	4.5	5.6	23.8	55.8	20.4	33.0	22.6	63.8
2064500	Shawnee city...................	87.3	4.2	5.3	0.0	21.3	62.4	16.4	39.1	19.0	70.9
2071000	Topeka city.....................	76.2	10.3	8.8	1.2	23.6	53.3	23.1	28.9	25.2	56.0
2079000	Wichita city.....................	71.5	11.2	11.0	3.8	25.0	55.3	19.7	32.6	22.2	59.7
2100000	**Kentucky**.........................	88.1	7.8	2.1	0.9	19.3	57.6	23.1	31.8	25.7	67.7
2108902	Bowling Green city............	78.1	14.7	3.4	2.2	36.3	46.8	16.9	26.7	19.7	37.9
2146027	Lexington-Fayette	76.7	14.6	4.4	3.1	28.9	53.5	17.7	28.7	19.6	54.9
2148006	Louisville/Jefferson	70.9	22.5	3.3	1.7	21.4	57.2	21.4	30.2	24.0	60.5
2158620	Owensboro city................	90.8	6.8	0.0	0.0	20.5	52.7	26.8	30.4	28.7	59.3
2200000	**Louisiana**.........................	63.7	29.9	3.5	1.3	21.4	56.7	21.8	33.2	24.6	66.2
2205000	Baton Rouge city..............	41.4	51.3	2.5	3.1	31.5	48.2	20.2	26.9	22.4	50.4

Table A-4: Cities with a Population of 50,000 or More—Living Arrangements—*Continued*

State/ Place FIPS code	City	Total Households	Family households, percent	Married-couple family households, percent	Male householder, no spouse, percent	Female householder, no spouse, percent	Householder living alone, percent	Nonfamily households, householder not living alone, percent	Opposite-sex partner unmarried partner households, percent	Same-sex unmarried partner households, percent	Average household size
	Louisiana—cont'd										
2208920	Bossier city	25,297	60.2	40.3	3.2	16.7	34.5	5.3	5.3	0.0	2.5
2239475	Kenner city	25,088	64.9	44.8	4.9	15.3	30.6	4.5	4.7	0.1	2.7
2240735	Lafayette city	49,463	56.6	37.3	4.4	14.9	35.2	8.2	4.6	0.6	2.4
2241155	Lake Charles city	29,596	60.0	34.3	5.5	20.3	34.7	5.3	5.2	0.2	2.4
2250115	Metairie CDP	57,794	57.5	40.9	5.3	11.3	35.9	6.6	5.7	0.6	2.4
2255000	New Orleans city	151,790	51.0	26.7	4.7	19.6	40.6	8.4	5.7	0.9	2.4
2270000	Shreveport city	77,774	60.5	32.5	5.1	22.9	35.0	4.4	3.9	0.7	2.5
2300000	**Maine**	552,589	62.6	48.8	4.3	9.5	29.2	8.2	8.1	0.7	2.3
2360545	Portland city	29,992	44.8	31.3	3.4	10.2	39.5	15.6	8.3	1.5	2.1
2400000	**Maryland**	2,149,424	66.6	47.1	4.8	14.7	27.4	5.9	5.2	0.5	2.7
2402825	Aspen Hill CDP	17,336	73.0	49.8	9.1	14.1	21.9	5.1	6.7	0.7	3.0
2404000	Baltimore city	242,243	50.5	23.4	4.7	22.3	40.8	8.7	6.3	0.8	2.5
2407125	Bethesda CDP	25,247	65.3	55.9	2.5	6.9	28.5	6.2	3.2	0.7	2.5
2408775	Bowie city	19,769	71.7	52.6	5.0	14.1	23.8	4.5	2.6	0.6	2.8
2419125	Columbia CDP	40,288	68.4	51.7	4.5	12.3	26.0	5.6	3.9	0.2	2.6
2423975	Dundalk CDP	23,565	63.7	37.7	8.5	17.5	29.5	6.8	7.3	0.8	2.6
2426000	Ellicott City CDP	24,264	80.8	69.2	2.1	9.5	16.3	3.0	2.5	0.2	2.9
2430325	Frederick city	26,277	61.1	40.7	5.2	15.2	30.9	8.0	6.3	0.5	2.5
2431175	Gaithersburg city	22,911	68.6	48.5	5.4	14.7	25.5	5.9	5.4	0.2	2.8
2432025	Germantown CDP	31,504	72.6	52.0	5.1	15.6	24.4	3.0	4.2	0.3	2.9
2432650	Glen Burnie CDP	26,532	62.8	37.6	6.3	18.9	29.8	7.5	6.6	0.3	2.6
2467675	Rockville city	25,063	64.7	52.7	3.7	8.4	28.4	6.9	4.0	0.6	2.5
2472450	Silver Spring CDP	30,459	55.0	38.1	5.6	11.2	35.1	9.9	7.8	1.2	2.5
2478425	Towson CDP	21,105	54.8	41.5	4.2	9.0	36.6	8.7	3.3	0.8	2.4
2481175	Waldorf CDP	25,334	69.0	44.2	4.4	20.3	25.3	5.8	5.2	0.7	2.9
2483775	Wheaton CDP	14,872	72.7	49.2	7.6	15.9	19.6	7.7	7.3	1.2	3.4
2500000	**Massachusetts**	2,528,592	63.5	46.7	4.1	12.7	28.9	7.6	5.7	0.7	2.5
2507000	Boston city	249,728	47.5	26.1	4.1	17.3	37.7	14.8	5.9	1.1	2.4
2509000	Brockton city	32,542	69.4	39.1	7.0	23.3	26.6	4.0	4.5	0.1	2.8
2509210	Brookline CDP	25,891	51.0	41.2	1.8	8.0	36.2	12.8	3.8	1.1	2.2
2511000	Cambridge city	43,642	40.6	29.9	2.2	8.5	40.2	19.1	7.0	1.0	2.1
2513660	Chicopee city	22,732	59.5	39.0	5.9	14.5	33.1	7.5	7.9	0.4	2.4
2523000	Fall River city	38,395	57.1	33.1	4.9	19.1	35.3	7.6	8.5	0.6	2.3
2524960	Framingham CDP	27,182	63.4	46.9	3.6	12.9	30.1	6.4	5.3	0.9	2.4
2529405	Haverhill city	23,816	62.6	41.2	5.7	15.7	29.8	7.7	8.0	0.7	2.5
2534550	Lawrence city	25,857	70.7	29.2	7.5	34.0	23.7	5.6	7.9	0.5	3.0
2537000	Lowell city	39,094	60.9	36.2	5.9	18.8	30.5	8.6	8.5	0.3	2.7
2537490	Lynn city	32,406	66.4	36.3	7.6	22.5	28.3	5.3	7.8	0.5	2.8
2537875	Malden city	22,509	60.5	43.1	3.5	14.0	29.0	10.5	4.1	0.8	2.7
2539835	Medford city	22,111	58.3	45.8	4.3	8.1	27.8	13.9	4.9	1.6	2.5
2545000	New Bedford city	39,300	58.1	33.1	5.5	19.5	34.8	7.1	9.3	0.4	2.4
2545560	Newton city	31,139	69.8	60.6	1.5	7.7	24.7	5.5	3.4	1.1	2.5
2552490	Peabody city	21,593	60.7	46.2	3.4	11.1	34.5	4.8	5.8	0.1	2.4
2555745	Quincy city	39,663	54.1	38.5	4.3	11.3	36.8	9.1	4.8	0.5	2.3
2556585	Revere city	20,471	58.2	37.3	3.8	17.1	33.9	7.9	4.4	1.1	2.6
2562535	Somerville city	32,186	45.4	28.9	4.2	12.3	31.7	22.9	8.0	1.4	2.3
2567000	Springfield city	55,613	64.0	29.6	7.1	27.2	29.7	6.3	7.7	0.5	2.7
2569170	Taunton city	21,655	64.7	44.2	5.3	15.3	29.3	6.0	7.5	0.6	2.6
2572600	Waltham city	24,177	53.0	39.6	4.3	9.0	34.9	12.1	6.7	0.6	2.3
2578972	Weymouth Town city	22,620	59.4	43.8	2.7	13.0	34.1	6.4	5.9	0.7	2.4
2582000	Worcester city	67,973	58.3	33.7	6.2	18.4	32.4	9.3	7.2	0.6	2.5
2600000	**Michigan**	3,815,532	65.2	47.8	4.6	12.9	29.0	5.8	5.5	0.4	2.5
2603000	Ann Arbor city	46,946	42.6	32.8	2.8	6.9	38.3	19.2	4.6	1.4	2.2
2605920	Battle Creek city	20,353	60.7	37.6	4.9	18.3	33.7	5.6	7.5	0.1	2.5
2621000	Dearborn city	31,239	68.0	52.1	5.9	10.1	28.7	3.3	3.0	0.3	3.1
2621020	Dearborn Heights city	20,738	66.9	47.7	5.5	13.7	29.7	3.5	3.0	0.3	2.7
2622000	Detroit city	253,607	57.0	20.9	6.8	29.3	38.2	4.8	5.1	0.3	2.7
2627440	Farmington Hills city	34,166	62.8	50.9	2.9	9.1	33.2	4.0	2.9	0.3	2.3
2629000	Flint city	40,558	55.3	23.2	7.0	25.1	37.8	6.9	8.6	0.4	2.4
2634000	Grand Rapids city	73,080	55.8	35.3	4.5	15.9	33.1	11.1	7.2	0.8	2.5
2642160	Kalamazoo city	27,654	47.6	26.4	4.1	17.1	35.4	17.0	8.7	0.9	2.5
2646000	Lansing city	47,819	53.1	29.6	6.0	17.4	36.7	10.3	6.9	0.6	2.4
2649000	Livonia city	37,215	69.1	56.4	3.1	9.5	26.9	4.1	3.7	0.3	2.5
2659440	Novi city	23,314	63.5	53.8	1.8	7.9	32.1	4.4	5.0	0.4	2.4
2665000	Pontiac city	23,622	58.1	24.0	7.4	26.7	35.1	6.7	8.5	0.2	2.5
2669035	Rochester Hills city	27,770	68.8	58.2	2.9	7.6	26.5	4.8	3.1	0.2	2.6
2670040	Royal Oak city	28,464	45.8	35.6	3.3	6.8	41.7	12.5	5.9	1.2	2.1
2670520	Saginaw city	18,870	59.1	25.3	5.5	28.3	35.8	5.1	6.4	0.3	2.6
2670760	St. Clair Shores city	26,917	57.1	41.7	3.5	11.9	37.5	5.4	5.2	0.4	2.2
2674900	Southfield city	31,403	58.5	33.2	5.3	20.0	37.7	3.9	4.2	0.3	2.3
2676460	Sterling Heights city	49,207	70.7	55.0	6.3	9.5	26.6	2.7	3.4	0.2	2.6
2679000	Taylor city	23,552	66.2	41.0	6.0	19.2	28.2	5.6	6.9	0.4	2.6

State/ Place FIPS code	City	Race or Hispanic origin of householder				Age of householder			Percent of households with one or more persons under 18 years old	Percent of households with one or more persons age 65 or older	Percent of all householders who are owners
		Householder is White alone, not Hispanic or Latino, percent	Householder is Black or African American alone, percent	Householder is Hispanic or Latino, percent	Householder is Asian alone, percent	Householders age 15 to 34, percent	Householders age 35 to 64, percent	Householders age 65 and older, percent			
	Louisiana—cont'd										
2208920	Bossier City city	67.2	23.4	5.2	0.0	28.0	50.2	21.8	34.6	23.4	56.4
2239475	Kenner city	55.9	23.8	15.2	0.0	21.0	54.2	24.8	28.3	28.8	59.8
2240735	Lafayette city	66.0	27.3	3.8	1.7	27.4	53.4	19.2	28.3	21.2	56.7
2241155	Lake Charles city	51.2	42.5	2.3	0.0	24.3	53.6	22.1	31.1	24.6	54.6
2250115	Metairie CDP	74.2	11.0	10.8	2.8	20.7	53.2	26.1	26.0	29.5	60.0
2255000	New Orleans city	35.5	55.8	5.1	2.3	25.2	56.5	18.3	25.8	21.1	46.2
2270000	Shreveport city	44.0	51.7	2.2	1.2	24.0	54.6	21.4	31.3	23.8	55.7
2300000	**Maine**	96.0	0.7	1.0	0.7	15.8	58.7	25.4	26.7	28.6	70.8
2360545	Portland city	89.2	4.8	2.3	2.4	27.1	54.3	18.6	20.5	20.8	43.7
2400000	**Maryland**	58.7	29.1	5.8	5.0	17.6	61.0	21.4	33.3	25.0	66.8
2402825	Aspen Hill CDP	44.6	21.6	21.1	10.2	15.3	60.9	23.8	38.6	27.6	62.0
2404000	Baltimore city	32.7	60.1	3.0	2.6	24.8	54.3	20.9	25.6	23.7	47.1
2407125	Bethesda CDP	80.0	2.8	6.3	9.2	15.0	58.2	26.9	31.3	29.9	67.7
2408775	Bowie city	43.5	48.1	5.0	0.0	9.7	71.7	18.6	36.2	22.4	83.8
2419125	Columbia CDP	55.5	26.2	5.5	11.0	20.3	63.4	16.3	34.0	20.5	65.2
2423975	Dundalk CDP	83.4	10.4	2.5	1.7	18.9	53.5	27.6	30.6	31.9	67.5
2426000	Ellicott City CDP	66.7	9.3	3.8	19.0	10.7	67.2	22.1	43.1	27.0	77.5
2430325	Frederick city	65.8	17.4	10.4	4.4	23.9	58.3	17.8	29.8	20.5	52.4
2431175	Gaithersburg city	46.1	17.2	17.1	17.2	23.8	60.5	15.7	39.7	20.4	57.2
2432025	Germantown CDP	40.7	22.0	17.1	19.2	22.0	69.3	8.7	44.3	13.3	66.3
2432650	Glen Burnie CDP	63.1	25.5	4.0	3.9	23.9	58.0	18.1	32.1	21.7	59.7
2467675	Rockville city	60.1	9.1	9.1	20.0	18.3	58.8	22.9	30.9	26.8	60.1
2472450	Silver Spring CDP	43.6	29.3	18.5	7.2	27.5	59.4	13.1	30.7	15.6	37.9
2478425	Towson CDP	0.0	7.8	2.9	5.4	19.1	54.2	26.7	26.1	28.8	58.9
2481175	Waldorf CDP	34.7	56.3	3.5	3.3	20.0	69.5	10.5	41.4	13.8	66.7
2483775	Wheaton CDP	36.1	19.0	32.8	10.7	21.9	62.5	15.5	43.1	19.5	65.2
2500000	**Massachusetts**	80.0	6.1	7.9	4.7	17.3	59.3	23.3	30.6	26.7	62.0
2507000	Boston city	52.6	22.7	15.1	8.6	33.6	48.9	17.4	23.7	19.9	33.6
2509000	Brockton city	49.3	36.9	7.5	1.5	16.1	62.4	21.5	39.2	26.7	57.0
2509210	Brookline CDP	76.6	2.0	4.3	15.3	29.1	49.1	21.8	24.1	24.7	49.1
2511000	Cambridge city	67.0	10.9	7.5	12.2	37.2	44.9	17.9	16.4	19.3	36.2
2513660	Chicopee city	82.4	2.7	12.9	0.0	19.9	52.8	27.3	27.5	30.0	57.8
2523000	Fall River city	86.5	2.9	5.4	1.6	21.4	54.1	24.5	29.0	27.0	36.1
2524960	Framingham CDP	74.1	6.8	11.0	6.5	21.0	57.6	21.4	30.9	23.9	54.0
2529405	Haverhill city	83.8	2.5	12.5	0.0	16.8	64.0	19.3	33.2	22.8	61.0
2534550	Lawrence city	24.7	8.7	69.4	2.6	24.7	60.6	14.8	42.7	19.8	27.0
2537000	Lowell city	62.4	6.8	15.6	12.9	26.1	56.8	17.1	32.5	21.7	43.0
2537490	Lynn city	54.9	11.1	26.9	5.4	21.5	58.4	20.2	39.6	23.8	46.3
2537875	Malden city	55.8	11.0	9.9	20.7	23.3	60.3	16.4	31.0	20.3	41.1
2539835	Medford city	82.7	7.0	0.0	5.4	25.0	51.9	23.1	23.4	26.4	56.1
2545000	New Bedford city	72.8	6.9	13.9	0.9	21.9	54.4	23.7	29.9	25.7	42.8
2545560	Newton city	82.2	2.7	2.9	11.0	10.7	61.7	27.6	33.7	30.9	69.5
2552490	Peabody city	88.3	0.0	5.2	0.0	11.7	55.6	32.8	25.6	35.9	60.6
2555745	Quincy city	71.5	5.3	3.3	18.3	22.4	54.4	23.1	24.5	26.0	46.7
2556585	Revere city	71.5	5.5	18.0	5.5	15.6	62.6	21.8	28.0	26.1	52.4
2562535	Somerville city	77.7	5.7	7.3	7.7	41.6	41.7	16.6	19.5	18.4	34.9
2567000	Springfield city	42.2	20.4	35.7	1.8	21.6	57.8	20.5	37.2	23.4	47.4
2569170	Taunton city	88.2	5.0	4.5	0.0	16.2	62.2	21.6	29.3	25.7	61.9
2572600	Waltham city	74.3	4.6	9.0	9.9	26.4	53.7	19.9	21.5	23.0	49.5
2578972	Weymouth Town city	88.8	3.5	0.0	4.2	10.7	63.6	25.7	28.5	29.5	67.0
2582000	Worcester city	65.5	10.7	17.4	5.1	24.5	56.7	18.7	31.1	23.0	43.2
2600000	**Michigan**	79.7	13.4	3.1	2.1	17.6	58.3	24.1	30.4	26.7	71.2
2603000	Ann Arbor city	74.8	6.4	3.6	13.2	39.8	42.7	17.6	19.9	19.4	45.2
2605920	Battle Creek city	73.3	17.3	4.6	0.0	22.1	52.9	25.0	34.6	27.0	59.8
2621000	Dearborn city	88.4	4.7	2.6	2.1	17.8	58.1	24.1	39.2	26.8	67.6
2621020	Dearborn Heights city	85.4	7.1	4.0	3.1	17.8	58.1	24.1	32.2	30.3	67.6
2622000	Detroit city	9.9	82.6	5.1	0.9	17.6	59.2	23.1	31.4	26.1	50.5
2627440	Farmington Hills city	68.6	18.9	0.0	9.0	13.8	60.0	26.2	26.4	30.1	62.3
2629000	Flint city	38.8	54.7	3.6	0.0	21.1	58.2	20.7	30.3	23.2	57.0
2634000	Grand Rapids city	68.0	19.0	9.9	1.2	31.0	50.0	19.1	29.5	20.6	54.7
2642160	Kalamazoo city	69.5	20.4	5.6	0.0	37.4	45.4	17.2	26.7	19.0	45.0
2646000	Lansing city	63.3	20.0	9.9	3.2	30.7	52.9	16.4	29.0	18.8	49.4
2649000	Livonia city	91.6	3.7	1.8	2.1	12.4	58.2	29.4	28.3	31.9	83.9
2659440	Novi city	75.4	6.5	1.6	15.4	15.6	62.8	21.7	33.0	23.8	63.9
2665440	Pontiac city	30.7	54.4	11.4	0.0	25.1	56.9	18.0	34.8	21.0	46.8
2669035	Rochester Hills city	82.4	4.2	3.7	8.6	13.8	61.8	24.4	31.4	27.1	75.5
2670040	Royal Oak city	90.0	3.4	2.4	2.7	29.4	52.1	18.5	19.7	20.2	66.2
2670520	Saginaw city	44.5	42.7	10.9	0.0	18.4	62.0	19.7	32.7	22.7	59.0
2670760	St. Clair Shores city	91.0	5.0	1.9	0.9	16.2	54.9	28.9	24.3	30.8	77.7
2674900	Southfield city	24.4	71.1	1.8	0.0	14.9	57.5	27.6	27.0	31.3	47.8
2676460	Sterling Heights city	84.6	6.4	0.0	5.7	15.5	59.0	25.4	31.7	30.1	72.5
2679000	Taylor city	76.2	16.6	4.1	0.0	18.6	58.7	22.7	33.0	26.2	66.5

Table A-4: Cities with a Population of 50,000 or More—Living Arrangements—*Continued*

State/ Place FIPS code	City	Total Households	Family households, percent	Married-couple family households, percent	Male householder, no spouse, percent	Female householder, no spouse, percent	Householder living alone, percent	Nonfamily households, householder not living alone, percent	Opposite-sex partner unmarried partner households, percent	Same-sex unmarried partner households, percent	Average household size
	Michigan—cont'd										
2680700	Troy city	30,542	73.6	62.7	3.1	7.8	23.3	3.1	2.3	0.1	2.7
2684000	Warren city	53,441	63.5	42.4	5.6	15.5	30.7	5.8	7.3	0.6	2.5
2686000	Westland city	33,292	60.1	37.7	4.6	17.8	34.1	5.8	5.0	0.2	2.5
2688940	Wyoming city	27,431	65.5	49.7	5.0	10.8	27.2	7.3	4.6	0.5	2.7
2700000	**Minnesota**	2,109,924	64.8	50.9	4.3	9.7	28.3	6.9	6.2	0.5	2.5
2706382	Blaine city	21,750	73.1	57.5	4.4	11.2	22.3	4.5	4.6	0.2	2.7
2706616	Bloomington city	36,829	58.7	45.3	4.2	9.1	33.9	7.5	5.2	0.7	2.3
2707966	Brooklyn Park city	26,786	71.7	47.9	7.5	16.3	23.6	4.7	7.4	0.8	2.9
2708794	Burnsville city	25,119	60.6	45.6	4.7	10.3	30.9	8.5	7.6	0.3	2.4
2713114	Coon Rapids city	23,641	66.2	49.7	4.4	12.2	26.3	7.5	7.0	0.4	2.6
2717000	Duluth city	34,735	53.3	38.5	3.4	11.4	35.7	11.1	6.6	0.8	2.3
2717288	Eagan city	25,586	68.9	55.2	4.1	9.7	24.8	6.2	5.3	0.6	2.5
2718116	Eden Prairie city	24,396	69.8	57.1	4.8	7.9	25.6	4.6	4.6	0.4	2.5
2735180	Lakeville city	18,773	83.3	70.7	2.6	10.0	12.5	4.2	6.1	0.3	3.1
2740166	Maple Grove city	23,945	75.2	64.7	3.0	7.5	19.9	4.9	2.7	0.3	2.7
2743000	Minneapolis city	165,785	44.7	29.2	3.9	11.5	40.0	15.3	7.1	2.2	2.3
2743252	Minnetonka city	22,287	63.1	51.5	3.2	8.3	31.1	5.9	4.4	0.1	2.3
2751730	Plymouth city	29,552	67.9	56.7	3.2	8.0	26.5	5.6	4.5	0.2	2.4
2754880	Rochester city	43,522	61.5	48.4	3.5	9.6	31.7	6.8	5.7	0.5	2.5
2756896	St. Cloud city	24,619	53.8	38.0	5.0	10.7	29.3	16.9	9.8	0.5	2.5
2758000	St. Paul city	112,289	54.4	34.9	5.2	14.3	35.5	10.1	7.3	0.9	2.5
2771428	Woodbury city	23,527	74.8	62.6	2.2	9.9	19.4	5.9	5.2	0.6	2.7
2800000	**Mississippi**	1,086,898	68.4	44.8	4.9	18.7	27.5	4.1	4.3	0.3	2.7
2829700	Gulfport city	27,407	63.4	37.7	5.7	20.0	30.9	5.7	5.5	0.6	2.5
2836000	Jackson city	62,779	61.5	27.2	6.7	27.6	32.8	5.7	5.6	0.2	2.7
2869280	Southaven city	18,572	70.1	51.7	4.3	14.1	24.6	5.2	5.7	0.7	2.7
2900000	**Missouri**	2,353,778	64.9	48.3	4.3	12.3	29.0	6.1	5.6	0.4	2.5
2906652	Blue Springs city	18,951	74.9	56.3	4.7	13.9	18.7	6.4	7.1	1.0	2.8
2915670	Columbia city	44,069	49.1	36.6	3.2	9.4	33.1	17.7	6.7	0.6	2.4
2924778	Florissant city	21,038	64.4	40.8	4.9	18.7	32.1	3.5	4.7	0.4	2.5
2935000	Independence city	48,778	59.7	41.1	4.4	14.2	34.0	6.2	6.7	0.6	2.4
2937592	Joplin city	21,390	58.7	41.7	5.3	11.7	33.8	7.4	8.3	0.1	2.3
2938000	Kansas City city	191,728	55.7	35.0	4.8	15.8	36.3	8.0	6.0	0.8	2.4
2941348	Lee's Summit city	33,473	74.0	58.9	3.4	11.7	20.9	5.2	5.0	0.7	2.8
2954074	O'Fallon city	29,376	75.2	60.3	3.9	11.0	21.3	3.5	5.2	0.2	2.8
2964082	St. Charles city	26,536	61.4	45.8	2.3	13.2	32.2	6.4	6.9	0.7	2.3
2964550	St. Joseph city	28,245	61.9	42.6	5.3	14.0	31.5	6.6	6.2	0.3	2.6
2965000	St. Louis city	138,531	46.6	24.5	4.1	18.0	44.1	9.4	6.3	1.0	2.2
2965126	St. Peters city	21,113	67.4	55.2	3.8	8.4	27.0	5.5	4.5	0.5	2.6
2970000	Springfield city	71,025	50.6	33.7	5.0	11.9	37.1	12.4	7.3	0.5	2.1
3000000	**Montana**	405,504	63.1	49.5	4.4	9.2	30.1	6.7	5.7	0.3	2.4
3006550	Billings city	43,610	59.9	42.5	4.6	12.8	32.3	7.8	7.0	0.3	2.4
3032800	Great Falls city	24,629	60.5	42.8	5.5	12.1	34.0	5.5	5.5	0.2	2.3
3050200	Missoula city	29,299	49.8	35.4	3.8	10.6	35.1	15.1	9.2	0.6	2.2
3100000	**Nebraska**	729,572	64.8	50.7	4.2	9.8	29.1	6.2	5.3	0.3	2.5
3103950	Bellevue city	19,651	71.8	51.7	5.5	14.6	23.6	4.7	6.1	0.2	2.7
3119595	Grand Island city	18,638	64.3	47.5	4.5	12.2	28.7	7.0	8.3	0.1	2.6
3128000	Lincoln city	105,851	58.7	44.3	4.5	9.9	31.1	10.2	6.8	0.5	2.4
3137000	Omaha city	169,114	59.1	40.5	4.9	13.7	33.9	7.0	5.2	0.6	2.5
3200000	**Nevada**	995,980	64.4	45.1	6.1	13.2	27.9	7.7	6.8	0.5	2.7
3209700	Carson City	21,206	59.3	44.3	2.7	12.3	33.6	7.1	7.0	0.1	2.5
3223770	Enterprise CDP	41,697	67.7	48.5	6.6	12.6	22.1	10.2	8.3	1.0	2.9
3231900	Henderson city	100,943	66.2	48.8	5.7	11.8	26.6	7.2	7.1	0.6	2.6
3240000	Las Vegas city	211,734	64.2	42.5	6.3	15.3	28.7	7.1	6.4	0.5	2.8
3251800	North Las Vegas city	67,487	73.1	49.6	7.1	16.3	20.9	6.0	5.7	0.4	3.3
3254600	Paradise CDP	87,467	55.0	34.0	7.5	13.4	35.9	9.1	7.1	0.9	2.6
3260600	Reno city	89,770	56.2	39.0	5.2	12.0	34.6	9.1	7.0	0.6	2.5
3268400	Sparks city	34,474	63.8	44.1	5.8	13.9	27.4	8.7	7.4	0.4	2.7
3268585	Spring Valley CDP	70,199	58.9	39.4	6.5	13.0	30.6	10.5	7.0	0.6	2.6
3271400	Sunrise Manor CDP	58,498	69.5	43.2	7.9	18.4	23.9	6.6	7.9	0.4	3.2
3300000	**New Hampshire**	518,088	66.9	52.8	4.2	9.9	25.5	7.6	7.4	0.5	2.5
3345140	Manchester city	45,549	56.7	37.3	5.5	13.8	32.7	10.6	9.1	0.6	2.4
3350260	Nashua city	33,885	62.9	46.0	4.5	12.4	28.8	8.3	9.2	1.0	2.5
3400000	**New Jersey**	3,181,152	69.3	50.8	4.9	13.6	25.8	4.9	4.9	0.4	2.7
3403580	Bayonne city	25,649	63.5	39.3	5.2	18.9	30.3	6.2	6.0	0.3	2.5
3410000	Camden city	25,354	64.0	20.0	7.4	36.6	30.5	5.4	10.3	0.2	2.9
3413690	Clifton city	29,055	70.9	51.8	5.7	13.4	26.1	3.0	3.3	0.3	2.9
3419390	East Orange city	25,921	55.0	21.0	6.7	27.3	40.5	4.5	5.7	0.2	2.4
3421000	Elizabeth city	38,987	69.1	36.5	7.9	24.7	24.4	6.6	11.2	0.6	3.2
3432250	Hoboken city	24,670	38.7	29.1	1.7	7.9	38.9	22.4	8.7	0.6	2.0
3436000	Jersey City city	97,364	60.4	37.1	6.0	17.4	30.1	9.5	5.6	1.0	2.6
3451000	Newark city	91,436	63.2	25.7	8.8	28.7	30.3	6.6	8.4	0.3	2.9
3451210	New Brunswick city	13,920	59.6	25.0	9.7	24.9	26.4	14.0	12.0	0.8	3.5

State/Place FIPS code	City	Householder is White alone, not Hispanic or Latino, percent	Householder is Black or African American alone, percent	Householder is Hispanic or Latino, percent	Householder is Asian alone, percent	Householders age 15 to 34, percent	Householders age 35 to 64, percent	Householders age 65 and older, percent	Percent of households with one or more persons under 18 years old	Percent of households with one or more persons age 65 or older	Percent of all householders who are owners
	Michigan—cont'd										
2680700	Troy city	73.4	4.4	1.9	18.4	14.4	61.2	24.4	34.9	28.3	72.9
2684000	Warren city	79.4	13.9	1.1	3.9	17.4	57.1	25.5	29.8	28.3	72.4
2686000	Westland city	74.2	17.4	2.5	3.6	19.3	57.4	23.3	27.5	26.5	59.3
2688940	Wyoming city	76.6	6.5	13.6	0.0	15.0	60.0	25.1	34.5	17.1	72.4
2700000	**Minnesota**	87.5	4.5	3.0	3.0	21.0	57.1	21.9	31.3	23.9	71.8
2706382	Blaine city	87.9	2.7	0.0	5.4	21.4	62.7	15.9	39.5	17.9	84.0
2706616	Bloomington city	83.8	6.8	4.3	3.8	18.2	52.6	29.2	24.5	31.8	68.0
2707966	Brooklyn Park city	57.9	12.3	0.0	4.0	22.5	56.9	20.6	39.1	18.5	61.3
2708794	Burnsville city	81.2	9.6	4.5	0.0	23.4	57.5	19.1	27.8	21.1	63.6
2713114	Coon Rapids city	89.1	5.1	0.0	0.0	20.5	59.3	20.2	33.8	22.7	76.0
2717000	Duluth city	92.4	2.0	0.0	1.2	27.9	49.7	22.4	25.4	23.9	60.5
2717288	Eagan city	83.5	5.4	3.7	5.9	22.9	63.0	14.2	35.0	16.7	70.2
2718116	Eden Prairie city	84.2	4.7	1.9	7.3	19.5	65.5	15.0	36.5	17.2	73.7
2735180	Lakeville city	91.8	0.0	0.0	3.1	15.8	73.1	11.1	48.6	13.5	89.0
2740166	Maple Grove city	89.5	2.0	0.0	5.8	16.9	68.4	14.7	36.3	16.9	84.8
2743000	Minneapolis city	70.1	15.7	6.1	4.4	34.5	52.1	13.5	23.8	15.0	48.4
2743252	Minnetonka city	91.6	3.7	1.4	0.0	16.9	58.1	25.0	26.1	27.0	71.1
2751730	Plymouth city	87.1	3.4	2.5	6.1	18.7	60.9	20.4	31.7	22.7	70.9
2754880	Rochester city	85.5	4.2	3.4	5.5	26.0	53.5	20.5	30.8	22.4	69.7
2756896	St. Cloud city	89.4	6.3	0.0	0.0	36.6	46.6	16.8	25.7	18.5	52.8
2758000	St. Paul city	67.4	14.0	6.6	9.6	30.1	54.4	15.5	30.5	17.7	49.1
2771428	Woodbury city	83.2	5.1	0.0	8.3	20.5	63.0	16.5	41.3	18.3	77.3
2800000	**Mississippi**	61.7	34.8	1.9	0.7	18.7	57.6	23.6	34.5	26.4	68.5
2829700	Gulfport city	57.9	34.6	4.4	0.0	24.4	54.2	21.4	32.4	24.3	52.6
2836000	Jackson city	21.6	76.3	1.2	0.0	23.2	58.1	18.7	35.2	20.6	51.9
2869280	Southaven city	71.5	23.2	0.0	0.0	23.8	58.5	17.7	39.5	19.9	69.0
2900000	**Missouri**	83.5	11.0	2.5	1.4	20.8	55.7	23.6	30.9	26.0	67.6
2906652	Blue Springs city	87.6	6.9	0.0	0.0	20.9	61.9	17.2	38.8	20.1	67.9
2915670	Columbia city	81.5	8.0	2.4	5.5	42.3	44.1	13.5	26.0	15.9	47.6
2924778	Florissant city	68.6	27.8	0.0	0.0	17.0	56.9	26.1	32.5	29.2	71.0
2935000	Independence city	85.6	5.9	5.8	0.9	19.8	53.6	26.6	25.6	29.1	64.7
2937592	Joplin city	89.5	2.9	0.0	0.0	25.5	51.3	23.2	29.8	25.6	56.1
2938000	Kansas City city	60.9	28.0	7.0	2.0	26.9	54.3	18.8	28.5	20.5	55.0
2941348	Lee's Summit city	87.3	8.8	0.0	0.9	18.0	62.0	20.0	39.5	22.1	73.9
2954074	O'Fallon city	90.3	3.7	0.0	0.0	20.7	62.6	16.7	44.7	18.7	79.8
2964082	St. Charles city	88.8	4.8	3.3	0.0	22.8	54.2	23.0	28.7	25.1	65.6
2964550	St. Joseph city	88.2	4.5	4.6	0.0	21.7	54.7	23.6	32.3	25.7	59.6
2965000	St. Louis city	48.5	44.4	2.8	2.6	28.3	53.4	18.2	23.6	20.3	44.5
2965126	St. Peters city	91.5	4.6	0.0	0.0	17.6	61.8	20.6	32.9	22.6	81.0
2970000	Springfield city	90.0	3.3	2.4	1.5	33.9	44.0	22.1	24.4	24.5	45.7
3000000	**Montana**	90.9	0.4	2.1	0.6	19.8	55.7	24.5	27.8	27.2	67.3
3006550	Billings city	89.5	0.0	3.5	0.0	24.1	52.4	23.5	30.4	25.4	62.1
3032800	Great Falls city	89.0	0.0	3.1	0.0	23.6	51.2	25.2	29.5	27.5	61.6
3050200	Missoula city	91.8	0.0	2.6	0.0	35.3	47.4	17.3	22.8	18.8	45.3
3100000	**Nebraska**	86.5	4.3	6.2	1.5	23.3	54.4	22.3	31.7	24.2	66.4
3103950	Bellevue city	82.0	5.5	8.6	0.0	22.5	55.5	22.0	36.7	24.0	66.0
3119595	Grand Island city	76.8	0.0	19.8	0.0	24.6	54.9	20.5	37.1	23.4	61.7
3128000	Lincoln city	87.5	3.4	4.5	3.2	31.2	50.5	18.2	29.5	19.8	57.0
3137000	Omaha city	74.8	12.9	8.1	2.4	26.3	54.4	19.4	30.9	21.2	57.6
3200000	**Nevada**	63.1	8.3	19.1	6.4	20.4	58.2	21.4	33.0	25.3	55.2
3209700	Carson City	79.5	0.0	13.9	0.0	16.1	54.1	29.9	25.7	32.8	55.3
3223770	Enterprise CDP	54.1	8.7	15.5	17.7	28.9	59.7	11.4	38.9	15.7	56.8
3231900	Henderson city	74.5	5.9	10.1	6.9	15.9	59.1	24.9	30.6	29.3	62.0
3240000	Las Vegas city	56.7	12.3	22.3	5.7	19.9	57.8	22.2	34.5	25.7	51.8
3251800	North Las Vegas city	39.3	22.0	29.6	5.5	25.7	60.9	13.4	46.6	18.0	55.5
3254600	Paradise CDP	55.6	9.6	23.4	7.6	22.7	58.7	18.6	29.2	22.1	40.6
3260600	Reno city	73.0	2.5	16.9	5.2	25.2	54.5	20.3	29.9	23.1	46.4
3268400	Sparks city	71.7	2.8	18.4	4.3	18.1	60.2	21.7	34.3	25.0	58.1
3268585	Spring Valley CDP	55.0	10.2	16.3	15.8	24.2	57.6	18.2	28.3	22.7	44.4
3271400	Sunrise Manor CDP	42.1	13.6	38.0	4.4	21.0	61.2	17.9	39.7	22.7	51.2
3300000	**New Hampshire**	93.9	1.0	2.1	1.9	15.8	61.6	22.7	30.2	25.8	70.9
3345140	Manchester city	86.4	3.3	5.6	3.5	24.7	55.6	19.7	27.3	22.7	46.7
3350260	Nashua city	83.1	2.8	7.1	6.0	20.6	59.0	20.5	32.3	23.4	56.1
3400000	**New Jersey**	63.9	13.2	14.6	7.5	14.9	61.6	23.6	34.3	27.6	64.9
3403580	Bayonne city	64.6	8.9	19.0	7.3	18.5	60.4	21.1	33.8	25.7	37.2
3410000	Camden city	5.3	54.2	43.5	0.0	25.4	58.4	16.2	42.3	18.6	38.6
3413690	Clifton city	60.2	4.8	25.9	7.7	14.6	62.0	23.4	32.6	28.3	62.0
3419390	East Orange city	0.0	89.7	5.7	0.0	19.6	60.8	19.6	31.4	23.5	26.4
3421000	Elizabeth city	20.1	20.4	58.5	0.0	24.5	59.0	16.5	42.8	21.7	25.5
3432250	Hoboken city	74.3	0.0	15.7	6.3	45.9	43.2	10.9	17.5	11.4	31.0
3436000	Jersey City city	27.6	24.2	24.3	22.7	28.8	56.5	14.7	31.2	18.7	29.4
3451000	Newark city	12.0	53.6	31.3	1.4	22.8	60.7	16.5	38.5	19.7	24.1
3451210	New Brunswick city	23.9	20.7	48.5	6.0	41.5	46.9	11.6	39.2	13.9	21.7

State/Place FIPS code	City	Total Households	Family households, percent	Married-couple family households, percent	Male householder, no spouse, percent	Female householder, no spouse, percent	Householder living alone, percent	Nonfamily households, householder not living alone, percent	Opposite-sex partner unmarried partner households, percent	Same-sex unmarried partner households, percent	Average household size
	New Jersey—cont'd										
3456550	Passaic city	20,395	72.7	33.1	11.1	28.5	23.5	3.8	8.9	0.2	3.4
3457000	Paterson city	43,383	73.5	33.1	8.5	31.9	23.1	3.4	6.3	0.3	3.3
3458200	Perth Amboy city	16,343	74.6	38.7	13.1	22.8	22.1	3.2	5.6	0.1	3.1
3459190	Plainfield city	14,330	70.7	34.1	9.6	27.1	23.7	5.6	9.8	0.6	3.5
3473110	Toms River CDP	33,420	69.1	51.9	4.8	12.4	26.7	4.2	5.4	0.4	2.6
3474000	Trenton city	28,179	61.9	26.9	8.4	26.7	31.5	6.5	6.4	0.4	2.8
3474630	Union City city	22,367	69.9	32.9	11.0	25.9	23.8	6.3	9.3	0.3	3.0
3476070	Vineland city	20,728	70.5	45.2	6.6	18.6	23.9	5.6	6.9	0.3	2.9
3479610	West New York town	18,394	63.2	36.0	8.5	18.6	27.4	9.4	8.2	0.9	2.8
3500000	**New Mexico**	760,251	65.1	45.2	5.6	14.3	28.9	6.0	6.5	0.6	2.7
3502000	Albuquerque city	222,510	60.4	39.8	6.0	14.5	32.4	7.2	6.7	0.9	2.5
3539380	Las Cruces city	38,254	60.5	39.3	4.4	16.8	30.2	9.4	7.5	0.2	2.6
3563460	Rio Rancho city	32,347	69.3	51.1	6.0	12.2	24.3	6.4	7.6	0.7	2.8
3570500	Santa Fe city	31,604	48.9	33.3	4.7	10.9	41.3	9.8	7.1	1.3	2.2
3600000	**New York**	7,214,163	63.7	43.8	5.0	14.8	29.8	6.5	5.4	0.6	2.6
3601000	Albany city	39,470	42.8	23.9	3.5	15.3	44.1	13.1	7.0	1.0	2.2
3608026	Brentwood CDP	14,243	83.1	50.7	9.4	23.0	12.2	4.7	10.4	0.0	4.2
3611000	Buffalo city	110,374	52.4	24.1	6.3	22.1	39.4	8.2	6.8	0.5	2.3
3615000	Cheektowaga CDP	33,051	59.6	40.6	5.0	14.0	33.6	6.8	6.6	0.1	2.2
3633139	Hempstead village	16,430	67.8	34.0	9.3	24.5	24.6	7.6	8.9	0.2	3.3
3637737	Irondequoit CDP	22,122	60.5	43.8	4.2	12.4	33.7	5.8	4.7	0.6	2.3
3642081	Levittown CDP	16,471	82.7	64.7	6.8	11.2	14.8	2.5	1.6	0.1	3.2
3649121	Mount Vernon city	25,507	62.2	33.1	4.9	24.3	33.0	4.8	5.3	0.2	2.6
3650617	New Rochelle city	28,658	67.8	48.0	7.0	12.9	29.7	2.4	3.7	0.4	2.6
3651000	New York city	3,066,297	59.5	35.6	5.6	18.3	33.1	7.4	4.8	0.7	2.7
3663000	Rochester city	86,413	49.7	20.6	5.0	24.1	40.3	10.0	7.4	0.9	2.3
3665508	Schenectady city	24,507	51.4	31.3	4.1	16.1	40.7	7.8	6.9	0.3	2.6
3673000	Syracuse city	54,520	49.3	23.4	4.9	21.0	40.4	10.3	6.7	0.8	2.4
3674183	Tonawanda CDP	25,636	58.9	43.2	4.1	11.5	35.0	6.1	6.5	0.2	2.3
3676540	Utica city	23,325	55.3	30.9	4.4	20.1	37.2	7.5	7.9	0.8	2.5
3681677	White Plains city	21,471	60.3	42.6	4.4	13.4	34.9	4.8	4.6	0.2	2.6
3684000	Yonkers city	73,092	65.5	39.7	6.0	19.7	31.2	3.3	4.7	0.5	2.7
3700000	**North Carolina**	3,721,358	66.3	48.1	4.5	13.8	27.9	5.7	4.8	0.4	2.6
3702140	Asheville city	36,653	48.4	33.8	2.4	12.2	39.9	11.7	6.6	1.5	2.2
3709060	Burlington city	21,814	61.7	39.1	6.2	16.4	33.6	4.7	4.9	0.4	2.3
3710740	Cary town	53,786	70.7	60.3	3.2	7.2	23.8	5.5	3.7	0.4	2.7
3711800	Chapel Hill town	20,057	53.0	44.0	2.2	6.8	32.8	14.1	4.0	0.7	2.4
3712000	Charlotte city	297,666	60.4	39.7	4.8	15.9	31.5	8.1	5.7	0.5	2.6
3714100	Concord city	28,889	69.0	53.4	3.2	12.4	25.7	5.2	4.8	0.3	2.8
3719000	Durham city	97,515	56.2	35.7	4.7	15.8	34.2	9.7	6.3	0.7	2.4
3722920	Fayetteville city	78,104	64.7	41.5	4.2	19.0	29.6	5.7	4.4	0.3	2.5
3725580	Gastonia city	26,642	69.2	43.8	6.1	19.3	25.3	5.5	5.4	0.4	2.7
3728000	Greensboro city	113,303	57.8	35.9	4.9	17.0	33.9	8.3	5.3	0.6	2.3
3728080	Greenville city	34,944	49.3	29.3	2.2	17.8	33.8	16.9	5.3	0.6	2.4
3731400	High Point city	41,576	64.6	41.1	4.7	18.8	29.3	6.0	5.8	0.3	2.5
3734200	Jacksonville city	20,583	73.9	54.9	4.3	14.8	22.8	3.3	3.3	0.2	2.7
3755000	Raleigh city	165,620	57.0	38.5	4.0	14.5	33.1	9.9	5.3	0.7	2.4
3757500	Rocky Mount city	22,153	64.1	35.7	4.5	24.0	31.9	4.0	4.7	0.5	2.5
3774440	Wilmington city	47,733	50.4	33.6	4.1	12.6	36.3	13.3	7.3	0.6	2.2
3775000	Winston-Salem city	92,302	59.4	37.6	5.3	16.5	34.8	5.8	5.1	0.5	2.4
3800000	**North Dakota**	291,468	60.5	48.6	4.1	7.8	31.3	8.2	6.6	0.2	2.3
3807200	Bismarck city	28,234	56.7	43.3	3.4	10.0	34.8	8.5	7.4	0.3	2.2
3825700	Fargo city	48,440	49.0	36.8	4.3	7.9	36.3	14.8	8.0	0.4	2.2
3832060	Grand Forks city	22,766	48.8	37.7	3.7	7.4	37.9	13.3	6.6	0.1	2.2
3900000	**Ohio**	4,551,497	64.2	46.9	4.4	12.9	30.0	5.8	5.7	0.4	2.5
3901000	Akron city	82,592	54.6	30.0	4.9	19.7	37.6	7.8	6.6	0.6	2.3
3912000	Canton city	29,845	58.4	32.1	6.1	20.2	35.5	6.0	6.9	0.8	2.4
3915000	Cincinnati city	130,360	46.7	23.0	4.3	19.5	44.0	9.4	6.1	0.6	2.2
3916000	Cleveland city	166,093	50.7	21.7	5.6	23.4	42.2	7.1	6.6	0.7	2.3
3918000	Columbus city	327,023	52.8	32.5	4.4	15.8	36.7	10.5	7.3	0.9	2.4
3921000	Dayton city	57,250	50.4	24.4	4.7	21.4	42.3	7.3	7.4	0.8	2.3
3925256	Elyria city	22,819	61.9	37.4	6.7	17.8	30.4	7.7	7.3	0.3	2.3
3933012	Hamilton city	23,789	64.5	39.7	6.9	18.0	29.0	6.4	10.2	0.6	2.6
3940040	Kettering city	24,785	58.5	41.5	4.6	12.4	35.9	5.6	6.6	0.4	2.3
3941664	Lakewood city	24,700	43.9	29.9	3.6	10.4	46.3	9.8	6.3	0.9	2.1
3944856	Lorain city	25,571	64.4	36.8	5.9	21.7	32.4	3.3	5.5	0.4	2.5
3961000	Parma city	32,850	64.5	46.2	5.1	13.3	31.6	3.9	5.1	0.4	2.4
3974118	Springfield city	24,082	57.1	32.9	5.5	18.7	35.4	7.5	8.7	0.4	2.4
3977000	Toledo city	117,008	55.4	31.0	5.2	19.2	36.7	7.9	6.9	0.4	2.4
3988000	Youngstown city	26,296	54.7	23.3	5.4	26.0	39.5	5.8	7.3	0.5	2.3

State/ Place FIPS code	City	Race or Hispanic origin of householder				Age of householder			Percent of households with one or more persons under 18 years old	Percent of households with one or more persons age 65 or older	Percent of all householders who are owners
		Householder is White alone, not Hispanic or Latino, percent	Householder is Black or African American alone, percent	Householder is Hispanic or Latino, percent	Householder is Asian alone, percent	Householders age 15 to 34, percent	Householders age 35 to 64, percent	Householders age 65 and older, percent			
	New Jersey—cont'd										
3456550	Passaic city......................	18.7	15.3	66.4	2.8	22.1	62.0	15.9	49.7	19.6	23.7
3457000	Paterson city.....................	11.2	34.5	53.2	3.1	19.4	62.9	17.8	45.2	24.0	25.5
3458200	Perth Amboy city	16.3	9.3	74.6	0.0	20.1	63.4	16.5	43.5	22.2	33.6
3459190	Plainfield city...................	9.2	54.6	33.7	0.0	20.0	61.3	18.7	44.4	22.5	46.2
3473110	Toms River CDP................	89.1	1.8	4.5	3.9	12.6	60.2	27.1	31.0	30.7	79.8
3474000	Trenton city......................	16.4	57.2	25.7	0.0	22.3	61.5	16.3	38.3	18.6	37.8
3474630	Union City city..................	11.8	5.8	83.7	2.8	22.7	59.6	17.7	40.2	23.2	18.5
3476070	Vineland city.....................	53.7	13.6	32.2	0.0	15.1	60.6	24.3	35.5	28.7	65.5
3479610	West New York town	19.3	3.5	72.4	0.0	23.8	57.7	18.5	33.7	23.0	18.9
3500000	**New Mexico..........................**	49.2	2.1	40.3	1.1	19.7	56.2	24.1	32.1	27.2	68.1
3502000	Albuquerque city	50.7	3.2	39.1	2.1	24.9	54.7	20.4	31.0	23.0	59.4
3539380	Las Cruces city..................	45.5	2.6	48.7	1.4	28.6	48.7	22.8	33.5	24.7	56.4
3563460	Rio Rancho city.................	60.0	3.5	33.1	0.0	18.0	61.2	20.8	38.3	24.1	78.8
3570500	Santa Fe city.....................	56.4	1.0	38.0	2.1	15.9	54.9	29.1	21.8	32.1	59.8
3600000	**New York...........................**	63.8	14.5	14.5	6.5	17.6	59.2	23.2	31.2	27.1	53.7
3601000	Albany city........................	60.0	27.5	6.7	4.9	30.5	49.9	19.7	19.6	22.2	39.5
3608026	Brentwood CDP..................	16.3	18.3	63.5	0.0	16.5	67.1	16.4	54.8	24.1	70.3
3611000	Buffalo city.......................	49.6	36.9	8.9	2.1	26.0	55.6	18.4	28.8	20.5	41.2
3615000	Cheektowaga CDP..............	86.0	9.5	2.2	1.2	16.9	54.4	28.7	24.7	32.0	70.4
3633139	Hempstead village.............	9.8	56.7	31.4	0.0	19.4	60.7	19.9	41.7	24.6	39.6
3637737	Irondequoit CDP................	84.6	8.4	5.6	0.0	14.6	59.3	26.1	26.2	28.6	77.8
3642081	Levittown CDP...................	85.0	0.0	8.2	0.0	8.6	66.0	25.4	39.2	31.7	90.0
3649121	Mount Vernon city.............	21.2	63.0	11.9	1.9	17.5	60.8	21.7	34.2	26.2	38.2
3650617	New Rochelle city..............	55.0	18.0	22.5	3.9	15.2	60.8	24.0	32.5	27.8	50.1
3651000	New York city....................	39.9	23.7	24.6	11.5	21.1	58.2	20.8	30.7	25.0	31.7
3663000	Rochester city	45.8	37.1	14.3	2.1	31.1	53.1	15.8	28.8	17.5	37.8
3665508	Schenectady city...............	63.5	21.0	8.4	3.5	20.7	58.6	20.8	25.8	23.2	46.3
3673000	Syracuse city.....................	58.9	28.3	5.9	4.1	28.7	52.8	18.5	27.6	20.9	38.9
3674183	Tonawanda CDP.................	93.0	2.5	0.0	2.2	18.1	52.7	29.2	23.9	31.3	71.9
3676540	Utica city..........................	71.2	13.5	8.0	5.0	22.5	53.7	23.8	30.9	26.7	47.0
3681677	White Plains city................	56.4	13.6	22.1	6.7	18.7	55.4	25.9	30.5	29.9	52.5
3684000	Yonkers city......................	46.9	19.5	30.0	4.7	17.0	57.5	25.5	33.2	29.4	46.4
3700000	**North Carolina................**	69.7	20.8	5.6	1.9	19.7	57.9	22.5	32.1	25.2	65.4
3702140	Asheville city....................	81.6	12.2	4.3	0.0	24.7	50.4	24.9	22.8	26.9	50.4
3709060	Burlington city..................	59.8	27.4	8.9	0.0	20.8	52.7	26.5	28.5	28.3	55.4
3710740	Cary town.........................	72.5	8.2	5.8	11.9	19.6	65.8	14.6	39.9	17.5	68.2
3711800	Chapel Hill town................	74.6	7.1	4.1	12.7	34.8	48.3	16.8	27.7	18.8	49.9
3712000	Charlotte city....................	50.4	34.9	9.0	4.3	26.7	58.9	14.4	33.5	16.7	54.9
3714100	Concord city......................	73.0	17.4	6.7	0.0	19.1	61.9	19.0	40.4	20.9	66.8
3719000	Durham city......................	44.8	39.7	8.7	4.6	30.8	54.1	15.1	30.1	17.0	48.9
3722920	Fayetteville city.................	44.8	40.9	9.3	2.5	31.6	51.4	17.0	34.0	19.5	48.6
3725580	Gastonia city.....................	61.6	27.6	8.6	0.0	19.5	59.2	21.4	35.9	24.4	53.1
3728000	Greensboro city.................	50.7	40.2	5.1	2.8	27.6	53.5	18.9	30.5	21.0	52.1
3728080	Greenville city...................	56.8	130.2	16.5	8.9	27.6	53.5	18.9	25.6	13.7	52.1
3731400	High Point city	55.8	31.4	6.4	5.3	20.0	59.4	20.6	33.6	23.2	56.0
3734200	Jacksonville city................	60.2	24.2	12.7	0.0	50.6	35.9	13.5	45.0	15.7	37.0
3755000	Raleigh city.......................	59.0	28.4	7.3	4.0	30.2	55.8	14.1	31.5	16.1	52.4
3757500	Rocky Mount city...............	35.3	59.5	3.0	0.0	17.5	55.1	27.4	32.2	30.6	53.8
3774440	Wilmington city.................	75.5	18.2	3.9	1.1	30.4	48.3	21.3	23.0	23.5	44.8
3775000	Winston-Salem city............	52.4	35.2	9.5	1.9	24.1	54.9	21.1	31.1	23.6	55.6
3800000	**North Dakota...................**	91.7	1.1	1.6	0.8	27.0	50.9	22.0	28.2	23.7	65.2
3807200	Bismarck city.....................	94.0	0.0	0.0	0.0	27.2	49.1	23.8	27.1	24.9	66.0
3825700	Fargo city.........................	91.4	2.2	2.1	2.0	39.4	45.3	15.3	25.8	16.5	44.4
3832060	Grand Forks city................	90.0	0.0	2.0	2.2	39.6	43.1	17.3	22.9	18.5	46.5
3900000	**Ohio ....**	82.9	12.0	2.3	1.5	18.8	57.4	23.9	30.3	26.4	66.5
3901000	Akron city.........................	64.7	29.6	1.4	1.7	23.9	54.5	21.6	28.0	23.9	52.5
3912000	Canton city.......................	72.0	22.3	0.0	0.0	21.4	57.4	21.2	31.2	23.4	53.0
3915000	Cincinnati city...................	51.3	43.0	2.2	2.0	31.2	51.2	17.6	25.4	19.3	39.2
3916000	Cleveland city...................	38.3	50.9	7.9	1.7	22.9	56.5	20.6	27.8	23.0	43.0
3918000	Columbus city....................	63.7	26.1	4.0	3.8	32.4	53.1	14.5	29.1	16.5	45.4
3921000	Dayton city.......................	52.1	43.1	2.7	0.7	23.0	55.6	21.4	26.8	24.0	47.7
3925256	Elyria city.........................	79.4	14.4	3.7	0.0	21.5	56.3	22.2	29.1	23.6	59.2
3933012	Hamilton city....................	86.8	8.6	2.7	0.0	21.6	57.3	21.2	32.7	23.9	56.9
3940040	Kettering city....................	92.7	3.4	1.5	1.4	21.3	52.4	26.3	26.8	27.9	60.4
3941664	Lakewood city...................	87.7	6.1	2.6	0.0	30.7	52.5	16.8	21.7	18.9	43.6
3944856	Lorain city.........................	62.6	13.1	21.6	0.0	17.8	56.8	25.5	33.4	27.7	58.3
3961000	Parma city........................	92.7	2.1	2.9	0.0	16.0	55.9	28.2	26.7	30.6	74.5
3974118	Springfield city.................	76.7	19.3	0.0	0.0	22.9	52.6	24.5	30.2	26.7	50.7
3977000	Toledo city........................	65.6	26.5	5.2	1.0	24.2	54.8	21.0	28.4	23.0	53.8
3988000	Youngstown city................	49.8	42.1	6.4	0.0	17.4	56.3	26.3	27.3	29.3	56.5

State/Place FIPS code	City	Total Households	Family households, percent	Married-couple family households, percent	Male householder, no spouse, percent	Female householder, no spouse, percent	Householder living alone, percent	Nonfamily households, householder not living alone, percent	Opposite-sex partner unmarried partner households, percent	Same-sex unmarried partner households, percent	Average household size
4000000	**Oklahoma**	1,445,059	66.4	49.0	4.9	12.4	28.2	5.4	4.8	0.3	2.6
4009050	Broken Arrow city	36,770	76.6	60.7	4.0	11.8	20.3	3.1	4.1	0.4	2.8
4023200	Edmond city	31,566	69.9	57.3	4.6	7.9	23.7	6.4	3.7	0.1	2.6
4041850	Lawton city	34,025	62.3	41.6	4.8	15.9	30.8	6.9	6.6	0.3	2.6
4048350	Midwest City city	23,062	62.5	39.1	6.1	17.3	31.4	6.1	4.8	0.2	2.4
4049200	Moore city	20,954	73.4	52.2	5.8	15.4	21.4	5.2	6.5	0.1	2.7
4052500	Norman city	44,942	56.7	42.3	4.8	9.6	32.2	11.1	5.2	0.6	2.4
4055000	Oklahoma City city	228,435	62.2	43.9	5.2	13.2	31.1	6.6	5.0	0.5	2.6
4075000	Tulsa city	162,775	58.3	37.8	4.9	15.6	34.8	6.9	5.7	0.5	2.4
4100000	**Oregon**	1,516,591	63.3	48.3	4.5	10.5	28.1	8.6	6.6	0.7	2.5
4101000	Albany city	19,370	68.6	47.7	5.3	15.6	25.4	6.0	7.6	0.6	2.6
4101650	Aloha CDP	16,677	74.2	56.9	6.6	10.7	17.7	8.0	7.3	0.3	3.1
4105350	Beaverton city	36,433	59.0	44.4	3.9	10.6	30.7	10.3	6.5	0.3	2.5
4105800	Bend city	32,018	59.7	46.7	4.7	8.3	29.9	10.4	6.5	0.6	2.5
4115800	Corvallis city	21,148	48.0	37.0	2.3	8.6	32.8	19.3	5.8	0.7	2.4
4123850	Eugene city	65,814	50.5	35.9	4.2	10.4	33.0	16.5	7.4	1.4	2.3
4131250	Gresham city	38,931	66.7	43.7	6.0	17.0	26.7	6.7	7.1	0.6	2.8
4134100	Hillsboro city	33,250	68.8	52.4	4.0	12.4	25.4	5.8	5.5	0.2	2.8
4147000	Medford city	29,726	64.7	47.2	5.0	12.5	29.1	6.2	7.8	0.2	2.5
4159000	Portland city	251,027	50.7	37.3	3.8	9.6	35.1	14.2	8.2	1.6	2.3
4164900	Salem city	57,939	64.3	44.7	6.0	13.6	29.7	6.0	6.6	0.5	2.6
4169600	Springfield city	23,734	60.4	41.5	5.0	13.8	29.1	10.5	10.0	0.8	2.5
4200000	**Pennsylvania**	4,945,140	64.4	48.1	4.3	12.0	29.7	5.8	5.5	0.4	2.5
4202000	Allentown city	41,299	63.6	33.7	6.6	23.3	29.4	6.9	10.4	0.8	2.8
4206088	Bethlehem city	29,670	56.4	35.6	5.2	15.5	35.6	8.0	4.6	0.0	2.3
4224000	Erie city	41,187	55.6	33.1	4.3	18.2	36.6	7.8	7.2	0.5	2.3
4241216	Lancaster city	21,416	55.1	29.1	5.6	20.3	35.3	9.6	7.9	0.6	2.6
4242928	Levittown CDP	17,901	74.4	52.0	5.3	17.1	21.7	3.9	5.1	0.6	2.8
4260000	Philadelphia city	579,165	52.4	26.8	5.4	20.3	40.0	7.6	5.8	0.6	2.6
4261000	Pittsburgh city	132,160	46.7	28.6	3.6	14.5	41.3	12.0	6.1	0.9	2.1
4263624	Reading city	30,716	61.7	27.9	8.4	25.4	31.3	7.1	9.1	0.8	2.8
4269000	Scranton city	28,886	56.9	37.4	5.0	14.5	35.8	7.3	6.4	0.1	2.4
4400000	**Rhode Island**	410,347	62.7	44.0	4.8	13.9	30.2	7.1	6.1	0.7	2.5
4419180	Cranston city	29,757	65.0	46.7	5.5	12.8	30.0	5.0	5.2	1.1	2.6
4454640	Pawtucket city	27,855	61.2	35.0	6.6	19.6	33.0	5.8	7.1	0.5	2.5
4459000	Providence city	61,368	56.3	28.6	5.9	21.8	30.8	12.9	7.7	1.1	2.7
4474300	Warwick city	35,283	60.7	45.5	5.1	10.2	32.9	6.4	5.8	1.2	2.3
4500000	**South Carolina**	1,781,957	67.3	47.3	4.7	15.3	27.6	5.1	4.5	0.3	2.6
4513330	Charleston city	52,621	50.3	36.4	2.9	11.0	36.8	12.8	4.9	0.6	2.3
4516000	Columbia city	43,571	51.0	31.1	2.6	17.4	38.5	10.5	4.5	1.1	2.4
4530850	Greenville city	25,667	50.6	32.7	3.8	14.1	41.7	7.8	5.0	0.4	2.2
4548535	Mount Pleasant town	28,423	64.7	52.6	3.7	8.4	27.1	8.2	3.6	0.3	2.5
4550875	North Charleston city, South Carolin	36,567	61.7	35.8	4.8	21.1	30.0	8.3	5.5	0.3	2.6
4561405	Rock Hill city	26,825	62.1	38.1	3.8	20.2	31.7	6.2	5.5	0.3	2.4
4600000	**South Dakota**	326,086	64.6	50.0	4.7	9.9	29.3	6.2	6.0	0.3	2.5
4652980	Rapid City city	27,858	59.7	42.0	5.3	12.4	33.1	7.2	7.5	0.6	2.4
4659020	Sioux Falls city	64,020	62.3	45.4	5.0	11.9	29.6	8.1	5.9	0.4	2.4
4700000	**Tennessee**	2,480,467	66.4	48.5	4.5	13.4	28.4	5.2	4.8	0.4	2.5
4703440	Bartlett city	19,526	80.2	65.0	2.9	12.3	16.5	3.3	2.4	0.3	2.9
4714000	Chattanooga city	69,391	57.2	35.7	4.0	17.5	35.8	7.1	5.2	0.7	2.4
4715160	Clarksville city	50,581	72.2	51.4	4.6	16.2	22.0	5.7	5.2	0.5	2.7
4727740	Franklin city	25,978	66.9	57.0	1.9	7.9	29.8	3.3	1.4	0.3	2.5
4733280	Hendersonville city	20,329	73.0	56.9	4.8	11.3	24.0	3.0	3.4	0.2	2.6
4737640	Jackson city	24,546	60.8	39.6	3.3	18.0	34.5	4.7	3.9	0.2	2.6
4738320	Johnson City city	27,610	55.1	39.8	4.0	11.4	36.7	8.1	5.1	0.7	2.2
4739560	Kingsport city	23,413	61.3	45.0	3.7	12.6	33.9	4.8	3.2	0.6	2.2
4740000	Knoxville city	82,824	47.1	31.5	4.3	11.3	43.3	9.5	5.9	0.5	2.1
4748000	Memphis city	247,638	58.2	28.9	5.4	23.9	35.8	6.0	5.6	0.6	2.6
4751560	Murfreesboro city	43,205	59.6	45.4	3.2	11.0	28.0	12.4	4.9	0.7	2.5
4752006	Nashville-Davidson	249,063	54.2	36.0	4.1	14.1	36.8	8.9	5.6	0.7	2.4
4800000	**Texas**	8,965,352	69.6	50.0	5.1	14.4	25.1	5.4	4.9	0.4	2.8
4801000	Abilene city	42,169	61.7	44.4	4.4	12.9	30.9	7.4	4.9	0.8	2.6
4801924	Allen city	29,396	79.8	65.4	3.0	11.3	16.1	4.1	3.4	0.3	3.1
4803000	Amarillo city	74,851	65.3	45.8	5.0	14.5	28.9	5.9	6.0	0.3	2.6
4804000	Arlington city	133,292	68.1	46.8	5.6	15.7	25.9	6.0	5.2	0.6	2.8
4804462	Atascocita CDP	20,816	81.3	62.4	5.3	13.5	15.2	3.5	3.3	1.0	3.2
4805000	Austin city	342,196	52.3	35.8	4.7	11.8	33.8	13.8	7.1	1.0	2.5
4806128	Baytown city	24,560	71.7	46.3	6.6	18.8	25.5	2.7	5.8	0.4	3.0
4807000	Beaumont city	45,268	60.5	35.1	5.7	19.7	35.1	4.3	3.4	0.4	2.5
4810768	Brownsville city	51,362	79.8	51.3	5.0	23.5	18.9	1.3	3.6	0.3	3.5

Table A-4: Cities with a Population of 50,000 or More—Living Arrangements—*Continued*

State/Place FIPS code	City	Householder is White alone, not Hispanic or Latino, percent	Householder is Black or African American alone, percent	Householder is Hispanic or Latino, percent	Householder is Asian alone, percent	Householders age 15 to 34, percent	Householders age 35 to 64, percent	Householders age 65 and older, percent	Percent of households with one or more persons under 18 years old	Percent of households with one or more persons age 65 or older	Percent of all householders who are owners
		Race or Hispanic origin of householder				Age of householder					
4000000	Oklahoma	74.2	7.1	6.2	1.4	22.4	54.3	23.4	32.9	25.8	66.3
4009050	Broken Arrow city	80.2	4.0	4.6	0.0	19.4	61.3	19.3	38.9	21.6	77.6
4023200	Edmond city	84.5	5.3	2.8	2.7	22.8	58.0	19.2	34.5	21.8	70.8
4041850	Lawton city	58.5	19.9	11.0	2.4	30.5	50.5	19.0	36.3	20.0	48.9
4048350	Midwest City city	67.6	21.0	4.3	0.0	23.6	54.5	21.8	30.7	24.1	57.8
4049200	Moore city	78.7	3.8	6.7	0.0	31.2	53.6	15.2	41.8	16.6	71.0
4052500	Norman city	81.3	4.5	4.2	3.2	33.5	48.7	17.9	26.8	20.0	56.8
4055000	Oklahoma City city	64.0	14.8	11.8	3.1	27.0	54.0	19.0	33.1	21.2	58.4
4075000	Tulsa city	64.6	14.9	9.3	1.9	26.1	53.4	20.6	30.4	22.7	52.5
4100000	Oregon	84.3	1.6	7.6	3.2	19.8	56.2	23.9	29.5	27.0	61.1
4101000	Albany city	88.7	0.0	7.2	0.0	24.6	52.8	22.6	34.1	24.5	60.4
4101650	Aloha CDP	71.3	3.2	15.3	7.2	24.9	61.3	13.8	42.4	16.7	63.9
4105350	Beaverton city	72.8	2.3	11.5	10.8	15.7	54.2	30.1	31.6	20.2	68.5
4105800	Bend city	91.6	0.0	4.9	1.9	20.4	57.2	22.4	29.5	25.6	57.0
4115800	Corvallis city	82.6	0.0	6.7	6.1	38.2	43.2	18.6	21.9	20.5	45.2
4123850	Eugene city	85.5	1.0	6.2	3.4	30.0	48.7	21.4	23.7	23.4	48.1
4131250	Gresham city	77.1	4.0	11.6	2.9	21.0	58.8	20.2	38.1	23.0	52.5
4134100	Hillsboro city	71.2	0.0	14.8	9.6	27.2	57.6	15.2	39.2	17.6	53.8
4147000	Medford city	86.4	0.0	8.7	0.0	22.6	50.3	27.1	31.7	29.5	50.7
4159000	Portland city	78.5	5.4	6.7	5.7	25.7	57.4	16.9	24.8	19.4	52.7
4164900	Salem city	79.0	1.1	12.5	2.8	22.3	55.6	22.2	34.5	24.6	52.4
4169600	Springfield city	86.8	0.0	8.2	0.0	25.1	57.2	17.8	32.4	20.2	52.0
4200000	Pennsylvania	82.7	9.9	4.3	2.3	16.9	57.5	25.7	28.9	28.8	69.2
4202000	Allentown city	51.5	12.1	35.5	0.0	21.7	58.3	20.0	35.8	23.7	47.3
4206088	Bethlehem city	71.3	4.6	0.5	2.2	11.7	57.0	31.4	27.9	27.3	79.3
4224000	Erie city	79.2	14.2	4.4	1.4	25.4	53.6	21.0	27.2	23.5	51.3
4241216	Lancaster city	50.8	14.4	31.7	0.0	30.1	53.6	16.3	32.7	19.1	43.6
4242928	Levittown CDP	92.1	0.0	3.5	0.0	13.2	61.2	25.6	31.3	29.4	85.5
4260000	Philadelphia city	41.1	42.6	10.1	5.4	24.3	54.6	21.0	27.0	24.0	52.4
4261000	Pittsburgh city	68.2	23.7	1.8	4.5	30.9	47.5	21.7	20.6	24.0	47.9
4263624	Reading city	37.0	14.2	49.6	0.0	26.1	55.5	18.4	41.6	20.5	42.2
4269000	Scranton city	85.5	4.4	7.0	2.5	20.1	52.9	26.9	25.6	30.2	50.9
4400000	Rhode Island	81.1	5.5	9.6	2.4	17.6	58.6	23.8	29.4	27.3	60.2
4419180	Cranston city	83.9	3.5	7.6	3.5	14.7	60.6	24.7	29.8	29.4	64.9
4454640	Pawtucket city	62.3	14.0	16.3	0.0	21.4	58.6	20.0	32.1	23.2	44.4
4459000	Providence city	44.8	15.7	33.6	5.3	31.6	53.9	14.5	33.4	18.3	34.8
4474300	Warwick city	92.5	0.0	3.2	2.3	15.3	57.6	27.1	26.2	30.0	71.5
4500000	South Carolina	68.1	26.1	3.5	1.1	18.9	57.0	24.2	31.7	27.3	68.6
4513330	Charleston city	72.5	23.0	2.6	1.2	32.0	48.4	19.6	21.3	22.0	54.0
4516000	Columbia city	52.6	41.1	2.8	2.2	10.9	48.7	40.4	26.2	19.3	74.8
4530850	Greenville city	63.8	30.6	3.2	0.0	28.8	52.2	18.9	25.4	20.4	42.2
4548535	Mount Pleasant town	92.0	3.8	0.0	0.0	18.2	60.9	21.0	32.0	23.9	73.0
4550875	North Charleston city, South Carolin	43.4	44.7	8.0	2.1	29.9	54.5	15.5	34.3	17.1	48.1
4561405	Rock Hill city	56.4	38.0	3.9	0.0	30.7	51.1	18.2	33.8	20.1	51.4
4600000	South Dakota	89.3	1.2	2.0	0.7	22.9	54.1	23.0	30.8	25.0	67.7
4652980	Rapid City city	84.5	0.0	3.3	0.0	24.5	52.0	23.5	30.5	25.4	58.1
4659020	Sioux Falls city	89.2	3.7	3.1	1.2	28.2	53.8	17.9	31.5	19.6	61.1
4700000	Tennessee	78.5	15.8	3.1	1.2	19.6	57.3	23.1	31.4	26.0	66.7
4703440	Bartlett city	79.7	16.6	0.0	0.0	10.0	67.8	22.2	37.8	27.1	82.8
4714000	Chattanooga city	60.1	33.8	3.1	0.0	21.9	54.7	23.4	28.1	25.9	53.4
4715160	Clarksville city	63.8	4.0	10.2	1.8	15.8	51.7	32.5	43.0	14.3	73.2
4727740	Franklin city	85.5	6.3	0.0	3.4	16.3	65.7	18.0	34.5	20.2	68.1
4733280	Hendersonville city	89.3	5.5	0.0	0.0	17.6	61.0	21.4	38.6	25.0	70.4
4737640	Jackson city	52.6	42.8	3.1	0.0	22.6	54.1	23.4	31.1	25.4	56.9
4738320	Johnson City city	88.3	5.7	2.7	0.0	26.6	50.4	23.0	·24.3	26.1	54.9
4739560	Kingsport city	92.5	3.9	0.0	0.0	16.6	51.0	32.4	27.9	34.0	63.9
4740000	Knoxville city	77.7	16.9	2.3	1.2	31.9	47.3	20.8	22.1	22.8	47.9
4748000	Memphis city	33.1	59.8	4.4	1.5	24.9	56.7	18.4	30.7	21.1	49.2
4751560	Murfreesboro city	76.5	15.3	3.4	2.4	34.8	49.7	15.5	30.5	17.4	51.6
4752006	Nashville-Davidson	62.0	27.2	6.7	2.6	28.4	55.0	16.6	26.8	19.0	53.2
4800000	Texas	52.8	12.3	29.9	3.7	22.8	58.3	18.9	38.0	22.0	62.4
4801000	Abilene city	69.4	7.3	20.2	1.9	28.9	48.7	22.3	30.6	24.6	56.0
4801924	Allen city	71.1	7.0	9.0	9.9	17.0	73.4	9.6	51.1	13.4	76.0
4803000	Amarillo city	66.7	6.2	22.8	2.8	26.1	53.2	20.7	35.0	22.8	61.3
4804000	Arlington city	51.9	19.9	21.5	5.5	26.0	58.9	15.1	39.3	17.6	57.2
4804462	Atascocita CDP	57.0	22.0	15.9	4.0	22.9	65.1	12.0	48.7	15.4	78.9
4805000	Austin city	59.1	7.6	25.1	6.0	35.3	53.3	11.4	28.1	13.4	44.4
4806128	Baytown city	45.5	17.7	33.9	0.0	23.4	59.2	17.4	44.7	20.8	59.7
4807000	Beaumont city	38.9	45.7	10.8	3.2	23.3	53.0	23.7	32.0	26.3	59.0
4810768	Brownsville city	7.7	0.0	90.1	0.0	19.4	60.0	20.6	50.8	25.3	61.7

Table A-4: Cities with a Population of 50,000 or More—Living Arrangements—*Continued*

State/ Place FIPS code	City	Total Households	Family households, percent	Married-couple family households, percent	Male householder, no spouse, percent	Female householder, no spouse, percent	Householder living alone, percent	Nonfamily households, householder not living alone, percent	Opposite-sex partner unmarried partner households, percent	Same-sex unmarried partner households, percent	Average household size
	Texas—cont'd										
4810912	Bryan city....................	27,563	58.8	37.5	5.5	15.9	32.3	8.8	5.5	0.4	2.7
4813024	Carrollton city....................	44,313	72.6	54.7	5.3	12.7	22.0	5.4	3.3	0.8	2.8
4813552	Cedar Park city....................	19,007	75.1	61.5	2.7	11.0	20.0	4.9	5.3	0.4	3.0
4815976	College Station city....................	34,015	47.1	35.5	3.5	8.1	28.1	24.8	4.4	0.1	2.6
4816432	Conroe city....................	20,933	68.5	43.9	4.9	19.7	25.8	5.7	7.6	0.0	2.9
4817000	Corpus Christi city....................	112,390	68.5	44.1	6.8	17.5	25.2	6.4	6.5	0.3	2.7
4819000	Dallas city....................	466,448	57.4	35.2	6.3	16.0	34.6	8.1	6.2	1.2	2.6
4819972	Denton city....................	41,890	56.9	39.7	4.9	12.2	27.6	15.5	7.1	0.7	2.6
4820092	DeSoto city....................	19,110	69.9	48.3	3.2	18.4	27.7	2.3	3.0	0.2	2.6
4822660	Edinburg city....................	23,876	74.0	52.2	4.5	17.3	19.6	6.3	4.1	0.4	3.2
4824000	El Paso city....................	219,972	73.2	48.3	5.1	19.8	23.2	3.6	3.3	0.3	3.0
4824768	Euless city....................	20,852	59.3	38.6	7.4	13.3	31.5	9.2	8.0	0.6	2.5
4826232	Flower Mound town....................	21,633	85.2	74.3	2.4	8.4	12.9	2.0	1.8	0.4	3.1
4827000	Fort Worth city....................	266,098	67.4	45.7	5.5	16.2	27.1	5.4	6.4	0.3	2.9
4827684	Frisco city....................	42,844	81.6	67.3	3.9	10.5	15.3	3.0	3.2	0.6	3.0
4829000	Garland city....................	73,915	76.1	52.4	6.0	17.7	20.3	3.6	5.4	0.3	3.1
4829336	Georgetown city....................	21,328	65.5	56.3	2.7	6.6	30.6	3.9	3.0	0.2	2.4
4830464	Grand Prairie city....................	58,172	73.9	51.2	6.3	16.3	21.7	4.4	5.1	0.5	3.1
4832372	Harlingen city....................	20,158	75.4	50.4	6.3	18.8	20.8	3.7	5.8	0.0	3.2
4835000	Houston city....................	788,096	60.8	38.6	5.9	16.3	32.2	7.0	5.6	0.5	2.7
4837000	Irving city....................	83,099	63.2	44.4	6.1	12.7	30.9	5.9	5.0	0.4	2.7
4839148	Killeen city....................	43,715	70.0	47.9	3.4	18.6	25.4	4.6	5.1	0.3	3.1
4841464	Laredo city....................	64,782	82.1	53.9	5.9	22.3	15.1	2.8	7.5	0.7	3.7
4841980	League City city....................	32,597	69.8	58.8	2.7	8.2	23.4	6.8	6.2	0.3	2.7
4842508	Lewisville city....................	38,336	63.6	45.2	5.1	13.2	28.8	7.6	5.3	0.9	2.6
4843888	Longview city....................	30,419	65.8	43.3	5.7	16.8	30.4	3.8	4.1	0.8	2.6
4845000	Lubbock city....................	88,352	60.4	41.1	5.2	14.1	29.5	10.1	5.2	0.4	2.6
4845384	McAllen city....................	41,915	74.4	52.6	5.5	16.2	21.9	3.7	1.8	0.4	3.2
4845744	McKinney city....................	46,836	78.5	62.2	3.8	12.5	16.8	4.7	3.3	0.2	3.0
4846452	Mansfield city....................	19,735	79.4	65.4	4.3	9.7	17.8	2.8	4.8	0.4	3.0
4847892	Mesquite city....................	47,814	75.1	48.1	7.0	19.9	21.5	3.4	5.6	0.1	3.0
4848072	Midland city....................	41,885	69.9	50.3	6.1	13.5	24.3	5.8	7.1	0.2	2.8
4848768	Mission city....................	23,544	82.2	64.3	3.2	14.7	16.2	1.6	1.2	0.1	3.4
4848804	Missouri City city....................	22,733	79.4	60.7	3.9	14.9	18.3	2.3	2.6	0.0	3.0
4850820	New Braunfels city....................	21,656	70.7	52.4	3.0	15.3	24.1	5.2	5.1	0.4	2.8
4852360	North Richland Hills city....................	24,946	70.6	55.0	4.4	11.2	25.5	3.9	3.7	0.5	2.6
4853388	Odessa city....................	38,466	68.8	45.5	6.5	16.8	24.9	6.3	6.9	0.7	2.7
4856000	Pasadena city....................	47,449	72.7	49.0	7.1	16.6	22.8	4.5	6.4	0.1	3.2
4856348	Pearland city....................	33,563	80.4	64.3	3.7	12.4	17.6	2.0	1.8	0.4	2.9
4857176	Pflugerville city....................	18,361	75.0	58.1	3.5	13.4	21.9	3.1	4.6	0.5	2.9
4857200	Pharr city....................	20,380	80.0	53.0	4.4	22.6	16.3	3.7	2.4	0.2	3.6
4858016	Plano city....................	102,489	71.2	57.3	3.9	10.1	23.7	5.0	3.8	0.6	2.6
4858820	Port Arthur city....................	19,584	59.5	34.6	5.5	19.4	35.1	5.4	6.1	0.1	2.7
4861796	Richardson city....................	38,930	68.3	53.0	3.9	11.5	24.6	7.1	4.6	0.7	2.6
4863500	Round Rock city....................	34,930	73.0	57.0	5.0	11.1	22.1	4.9	4.6	0.3	3.1
4863572	Rowlett city....................	18,713	83.8	66.2	4.5	13.0	12.6	3.6	4.6	0.3	3.1
4864472	San Angelo city....................	35,897	62.2	43.0	4.2	15.0	31.6	6.1	6.1	0.3	2.5
4865000	San Antonio city....................	482,686	65.4	42.0	5.5	17.8	28.5	6.2	5.1	0.5	2.8
4865600	San Marcos city....................	18,357	38.0	20.9	4.7	12.4	33.0	29.0	6.8	0.7	2.4
4869596	Spring CDP....................	18,497	75.7	56.7	5.0	13.9	21.2	3.1	4.8	0.5	3.2
4870808	Sugar Land city....................	27,030	82.3	71.0	3.2	8.1	16.3	1.4	0.0	0.0	3.0
4872176	Temple city....................	24,176	67.5	50.4	4.7	12.4	29.3	3.2	3.3	0.2	2.8
4872656	The Woodlands CDP....................	37,421	75.7	66.1	2.8	6.8	21.8	2.5	2.6	0.2	2.8
4874144	Tyler city....................	38,389	60.0	40.1	4.1	15.8	32.7	7.3	4.0	0.3	2.5
4875428	Victoria city....................	23,960	67.5	44.7	5.4	17.3	27.8	4.7	6.3	0.5	2.6
4876000	Waco city....................	46,225	58.5	37.1	5.3	16.2	32.6	8.9	5.4	0.4	2.6
4879000	Wichita Falls city....................	37,377	63.9	43.8	4.3	15.8	31.2	4.9	6.5	0.2	2.4
4900000	**Utah**....................	891,240	74.8	60.7	4.3	9.9	19.7	5.5	3.7	0.4	3.2
4943660	Layton city....................	21,954	79.2	63.2	5.2	10.9	16.4	4.3	2.7	0.4	3.2
4944320	Lehi city....................	12,950	88.5	79.1	2.4	7.1	9.1	2.4	0.0	0.0	4.0
4950150	Millcreek CDP....................	24,471	58.7	45.6	3.5	9.6	31.1	10.2	6.1	0.8	2.5
4955980	Ogden city....................	29,270	65.1	44.2	6.2	14.7	26.3	8.6	7.6	0.5	2.8
4957300	Orem city....................	25,949	78.1	63.3	4.8	10.0	16.0	5.9	1.7	0.4	3.4
4962470	Provo city....................	32,215	71.4	59.0	4.0	8.3	14.0	14.6	2.4	0.2	3.3
4965330	St. George city....................	25,039	71.6	60.5	3.1	8.0	22.3	6.1	3.0	0.1	3.0
4967000	Salt Lake City city....................	74,362	52.5	37.7	4.4	10.3	36.1	11.4	5.6	1.3	2.5
4967440	Sandy city....................	28,748	78.3	64.7	5.5	8.0	17.7	4.0	3.0	0.3	3.1
4970850	South Jordan city....................	15,490	85.7	78.7	2.2	4.9	9.7	4.6	3.2	0.6	3.6
4975360	Taylorsville city....................	19,232	71.7	55.5	3.2	13.0	22.9	5.4	4.8	0.3	3.1
4982950	West Jordan city....................	31,471	77.9	62.2	5.3	10.4	17.8	4.2	4.2	0.5	3.4
4983470	West Valley City city....................	36,434	80.7	55.3	9.5	15.9	15.5	3.8	6.9	0.7	3.6
5000000	**Vermont**....................	256,563	62.3	49.2	4.0	9.1	28.3	9.3	7.6	0.9	2.3

Table A-4: Cities with a Population of 50,000 or More—Living Arrangements—*Continued*

State/ Place FIPS code	City	Race or Hispanic origin of householder				Age of householder			Percent of households with one or more persons under 18 years old	Percent of households with one or more persons age 65 or older	Percent of all householders who are owners
		Householder is White alone, not Hispanic or Latino, percent	Householder is Black or African American alone, percent	Householder is Hispanic or Latino, percent	Householder is Asian alone, percent	Householders age 15 to 34, percent	Householders age 35 to 64, percent	Householders age 65 and older, percent			
	Texas—cont'd										
4810912	Bryan city	51.8	17.2	27.1	2.8	34.8	47.1	18.2	32.8	20.6	47.0
4813024	Carrollton city	53.5	10.7	22.2	11.8	19.7	66.1	14.2	38.3	17.3	61.4
4813552	Cedar Park city	75.8	0.0	13.3	0.0	20.6	66.6	12.9	43.9	14.7	68.5
4815976	College Station city	71.0	6.8	11.9	8.7	58.9	32.2	8.9	24.4	9.7	34.6
4816432	Conroe city	63.2	9.9	25.0	0.0	27.7	52.7	19.6	39.4	22.1	48.0
4817000	Corpus Christi city	39.5	4.7	53.4	1.6	23.5	55.7	20.9	35.6	24.3	55.9
4819000	Dallas city	38.8	26.7	29.8	3.2	30.5	54.0	15.5	32.6	18.0	42.8
4819972	Denton city	68.3	1.4	0.8	3.3	17.1	54.4	28.5	29.5	17.7	62.0
4820092	DeSoto city	19.4	70.1	8.6	0.0	13.9	63.5	22.6	34.5	24.7	64.3
4822660	Edinburg city	11.6	0.0	83.9	3.1	30.9	54.5	14.5	44.0	17.3	54.2
4824000	El Paso city	20.0	4.0	73.9	1.2	22.0	57.1	20.9	41.5	25.0	58.7
4824768	Euless city	62.3	12.6	14.9	8.2	26.4	61.3	12.3	32.3	15.0	41.9
4826232	Flower Mound town	82.4	0.0	6.1	7.0	8.9	82.3	8.8	53.4	12.4	88.3
4827000	Fort Worth city	50.0	20.0	25.4	3.0	26.8	58.0	15.2	40.9	18.0	57.3
4827684	Frisco city	70.2	8.5	3.0	9.2	11.3	65.9	22.8	52.8	13.4	79.2
4829000	Garland city	43.8	13.2	29.5	8.8	20.2	62.1	17.7	43.9	21.0	62.8
4829336	Georgetown city	82.4	2.7	13.4	0.0	14.8	43.5	41.6	24.1	44.5	71.9
4830464	Grand Prairie city	35.4	23.8	33.9	5.1	24.9	64.0	11.1	45.3	14.7	60.9
4832372	Harlingen city	25.3	9.1	5.8	0.0	26.1	59.5	14.3	43.3	28.2	66.2
4835000	Houston city	34.2	25.0	33.5	6.1	27.5	56.3	16.2	33.2	18.9	44.0
4837000	Irving city	38.6	15.4	29.1	15.0	32.2	56.7	11.1	36.7	13.7	37.7
4839148	Killeen city	38.3	35.9	20.1	3.2	37.9	52.9	9.2	45.4	12.1	48.0
4841464	Laredo city	5.2	1.2	4.1	0.0	17.5	66.9	15.6	53.9	21.9	72.1
4841980	League City city	69.7	8.6	14.9	0.0	22.0	64.8	13.2	39.9	15.5	71.5
4842508	Lewisville city	57.8	11.2	21.5	6.5	33.1	55.3	11.6	37.7	13.5	44.0
4843888	Longview city	62.1	23.0	12.5	0.0	24.5	52.3	23.2	35.1	25.3	54.7
4845000	Lubbock city	62.8	7.1	26.5	2.1	34.8	46.3	19.0	31.7	21.1	53.9
4845384	McAllen city	16.3	0.0	79.9	2.7	20.7	60.1	19.2	43.8	23.9	60.5
4845744	McKinney city	70.1	10.5	14.0	4.4	23.1	63.3	13.6	49.9	16.1	67.0
4846452	Mansfield city	68.9	14.5	11.4	0.0	16.2	69.8	14.0	47.3	17.3	77.6
4847892	Mesquite city	46.1	24.2	26.5	3.1	24.5	60.2	15.2	44.6	18.2	58.0
4848072	Midland city	59.0	8.2	30.4	1.3	27.7	54.4	17.9	37.6	21.1	63.4
4848768	Mission city	17.5	13.7	80.0	0.0	17.9	59.6	22.5	49.2	27.1	72.9
4848804	Missouri City city	33.2	40.3	11.7	13.1	9.8	72.0	18.3	39.4	23.2	84.0
4850820	New Braunfels city	69.1	0.0	27.1	0.0	25.1	51.2	23.7	39.3	26.4	65.1
4852356	North Richland Hills city	78.1	4.9	12.4	0.0	23.0	56.6	20.4	33.3	23.2	61.4
4853388	Odessa city	46.7	4.6	45.9	0.0	28.5	53.0	18.4	39.3	20.3	61.1
4856000	Pasadena city	41.9	2.9	52.3	2.1	23.4	60.6	16.1	44.6	19.5	55.0
4856348	Pearland city	51.4	18.7	17.5	0.0	19.3	66.5	14.3	50.0	18.3	79.0
4857176	Pflugerville city	51.3	17.2	24.9	5.1	11.8	75.5	12.7	45.2	15.0	78.2
4857200	Pharr city	0.0	0.0	89.5	0.0	22.9	56.3	20.8	52.5	25.5	58.6
4858016	Plano city	64.3	7.5	10.1	16.0	19.7	64.7	15.6	38.6	18.7	62.2
4858820	Port Arthur city	27.3	42.7	22.6	5.8	23.1	54.0	22.8	34.5	24.5	60.3
4861796	Richardson city	63.6	8.1	12.3	13.8	19.7	60.7	19.5	33.4	22.6	60.1
4863500	Round Rock city	58.3	10.7	23.8	5.0	25.3	65.0	9.7	47.5	12.5	59.9
4863572	Rowlett city	66.4	20.0	44.5	9.4	25.3	65.0	9.7	45.3	19.7	59.9
4864472	San Angelo city	61.6	5.1	32.0	0.0	27.4	47.8	24.8	30.3	26.7	57.6
4865000	San Antonio city	33.7	7.9	55.1	2.2	24.9	56.2	18.9	36.8	22.4	54.4
4865600	San Marcos city	57.8	0.0	35.1	0.0	55.7	32.4	11.9	20.3	13.2	28.8
4869596	Spring CDP	54.3	17.3	23.5	0.0	20.6	67.0	12.4	44.2	16.6	76.9
4870808	Sugar Land city	50.2	7.1	7.7	33.3	12.4	71.1	16.5	40.2	24.0	81.1
4872176	Temple city	63.0	16.0	16.5	0.0	24.1	52.6	23.3	35.6	26.1	57.8
4872656	The Woodlands CDP	79.4	2.6	11.9	4.5	13.8	68.5	17.7	40.9	20.2	72.8
4874144	Tyler city	59.3	23.6	13.8	1.8	26.5	50.1	23.4	31.0	26.3	53.0
4875428	Victoria city	51.0	7.7	39.0	0.0	23.8	53.9	22.3	36.5	25.1	58.8
4876000	Waco city	51.7	22.2	23.2	1.8	33.3	47.2	19.5	32.3	22.3	47.0
4879000	Wichita Falls city	70.5	11.5	14.5	1.8	26.8	50.2	23.0	33.3	25.2	57.3
4900000	**Utah**	84.5	1.0	10.0	2.0	26.6	54.8	18.5	42.4	20.9	69.5
4943660	Layton city	85.0	0.0	8.8	0.0	28.6	56.9	14.6	45.9	16.6	74.3
4944320	Lehi city	91.7	0.0	0.0	0.0	31.0	57.9	11.1	65.0	13.2	80.0
4950150	Millcreek CDP	88.1	0.0	5.3	2.9	23.2	51.9	25.0	28.0	26.5	61.8
4955980	Ogden city	71.3	2.5	22.4	0.0	32.1	49.9	18.0	38.0	20.3	55.4
4957300	Orem city	83.2	0.0	11.9	0.0	34.6	46.9	18.4	44.7	21.2	61.5
4962470	Provo city	78.0	0.0	15.0	2.4	54.2	33.6	12.2	36.2	13.6	40.6
4965330	St. George city	87.6	0.0	8.9	0.0	21.9	45.1	33.0	32.9	35.8	64.7
4967000	Salt Lake City city	74.2	3.0	14.1	4.9	32.9	49.7	17.4	27.6	19.3	48.4
4967440	Sandy city	89.2	0.0	5.2	0.0	16.0	65.2	18.8	40.8	21.4	77.8
4970850	South Jordan city	91.7	0.0	0.0	0.0	20.2	65.4	14.4	48.6	18.3	80.2
4975360	Taylorsville city	76.9	2.0	14.8	0.0	26.2	53.8	20.0	38.9	22.0	69.6
4982950	West Jordan city	79.3	0.0	15.0	2.1	24.6	64.6	10.8	50.9	13.2	74.9
4983470	West Valley City city	60.3	2.7	29.0	4.4	24.7	60.3	14.9	50.3	17.9	67.0
5000000	**Vermont**	95.9	0.7	1.1	0.8	17.0	58.9	24.1	27.1	27.2	71.2

State/ Place FIPS code	City	Total Households	Family households, percent	Married-couple family households, percent	Male householder, no spouse, percent	Female householder, no spouse, percent	Householder living alone, percent	Nonfamily households, householder not living alone, percent	Opposite-sex partner unmarried partner households, percent	Same-sex unmarried partner households, percent	Average household size
5100000	**Virginia**	3,026,761	67.2	50.5	4.3	12.4	26.5	6.3	4.8	0.4	2.6
5101000	Alexandria city	65,294	47.8	36.4	3.8	7.6	42.4	9.9	5.5	1.4	2.2
5103000	Arlington CDP	95,138	46.6	37.1	3.6	5.9	40.4	13.1	5.0	0.5	2.3
5114440	Centreville CDP	24,390	74.2	59.3	4.5	10.4	18.7	7.1	3.5	0.2	3.0
5116000	Chesapeake city	79,431	74.6	54.7	5.0	14.9	21.2	4.2	4.1	0.3	2.8
5121088	Dale City CDP	20,351	82.1	59.6	8.2	14.3	13.8	4.1	5.4	0.1	3.4
5135000	Hampton city	52,274	62.2	40.0	3.8	18.4	31.5	6.3	4.1	0.4	2.5
5135624	Harrisonburg city	15,872	51.3	34.0	6.9	10.4	28.1	20.6	5.1	0.1	2.8
5147672	Lynchburg city	28,904	55.6	37.3	3.2	15.1	36.4	8.0	3.5	0.3	2.3
5156000	Newport News city	68,120	63.0	38.3	5.9	18.7	30.9	6.1	6.0	0.2	2.5
5157000	Norfolk city	86,075	58.2	34.4	5.3	18.5	31.6	10.2	5.7	0.6	2.6
5164000	Portsmouth city	36,360	64.4	35.3	6.0	23.1	30.6	5.0	5.0	0.4	2.6
5166672	Reston CDP	25,598	59.5	48.5	1.7	9.2	31.6	8.9	4.8	0.5	2.4
5167000	Richmond city	85,303	47.5	23.7	4.9	18.9	40.6	11.9	6.2	1.0	2.3
5168000	Roanoke city	41,993	56.1	34.0	4.7	17.4	36.7	7.3	6.1	0.5	2.3
5176432	Suffolk city	30,573	73.0	52.4	3.6	16.9	22.7	4.3	4.5	0.5	2.8
5182000	Virginia Beach city	164,444	68.6	50.0	3.9	14.7	24.2	7.2	5.6	0.3	2.6
5300000	**Washington**	2,634,496	64.3	49.4	4.5	10.4	27.8	7.9	6.5	0.6	2.6
5303180	Auburn city	28,051	64.8	45.8	5.1	13.9	28.1	7.1	7.2	0.3	2.6
5305210	Bellevue city	53,460	64.8	54.2	3.6	7.0	26.5	8.7	4.5	0.3	2.5
5305280	Bellingham city	33,715	48.6	33.9	3.3	11.5	33.8	17.6	4.5	0.3	2.3
5322640	Everett city	41,521	54.2	37.4	4.6	12.1	36.2	9.6	7.4	0.9	2.4
5323515	Federal Way city	33,194	68.1	45.2	6.3	16.6	24.4	7.5	6.5	0.4	2.7
5335275	Kennewick city	27,542	64.5	47.4	4.4	12.7	30.2	5.3	7.2	0.3	2.7
5335415	Kent city	42,213	66.5	47.3	5.1	14.1	27.3	6.2	6.5	0.3	2.9
5335940	Kirkland city	34,592	63.0	50.3	4.5	8.2	30.6	6.4	4.4	0.4	2.4
5338038	Lakewood city	24,204	56.9	40.0	4.5	12.4	36.7	6.3	4.7	0.4	2.4
5343955	Marysville city	21,755	72.6	53.9	6.1	12.6	21.5	5.8	7.5	0.3	2.8
5353545	Pasco city	18,908	76.5	50.9	7.8	17.9	17.7	5.8	8.8	0.3	3.5
5357535	Redmond city	23,651	60.0	51.8	2.4	5.8	30.5	9.5	4.7	0.5	2.4
5357745	Renton city	37,350	58.9	41.4	5.8	11.7	32.0	9.1	8.3	0.3	2.5
5358235	Richland city	20,368	66.1	51.0	4.7	10.4	28.4	5.5	6.1	0.3	2.5
5363000	Seattle city	289,153	44.2	34.2	2.8	7.2	41.3	14.5	7.1	1.8	2.1
5363960	Shoreline city	21,056	61.8	46.8	3.6	11.4	29.9	8.3	5.3	0.6	2.5
5365922	South Hill CDP	18,068	82.1	62.9	5.8	13.4	12.8	5.1	8.0	0.0	3.1
5367000	Spokane city	87,021	55.6	39.2	4.3	12.1	34.4	9.9	7.7	0.9	2.3
5367167	Spokane Valley city	36,909	63.1	46.3	4.8	12.1	30.1	6.8	6.6	0.4	2.4
5370000	Tacoma city	78,223	57.8	39.6	4.9	13.3	33.1	9.0	7.3	1.0	2.5
5374060	Vancouver city	65,418	60.6	42.2	4.3	14.1	30.4	9.1	7.4	0.6	2.5
5380010	Yakima city	32,791	63.1	43.7	5.7	13.6	30.6	6.3	7.5	0.2	2.8
5400000	**West Virginia**	739,759	64.8	48.6	4.7	11.5	30.3	5.0	5.4	0.3	2.4
5414600	Charleston city	22,854	53.3	35.0	4.6	13.7	40.4	6.2	5.4	0.9	2.1
5500000	**Wisconsin**	2,281,781	63.9	49.4	4.4	10.1	29.1	7.0	6.3	0.4	2.4
5502375	Appleton city	28,320	62.8	46.0	5.4	11.3	29.9	7.3	7.9	0.6	2.5
5522300	Eau Claire city	27,077	52.2	39.3	3.6	9.2	34.8	13.0	8.5	0.1	2.3
5531000	Green Bay city	42,623	58.7	40.7	5.3	12.6	32.8	8.5	7.8	0.4	2.4
5537825	Janesville city	26,089	63.6	45.3	4.8	13.5	29.1	7.3	9.4	0.5	2.4
5539225	Kenosha city	37,414	64.5	40.5	5.5	18.4	28.5	7.1	4.7	0.3	2.6
5540775	La Crosse city	20,434	47.6	33.3	4.0	10.3	35.0	17.4	7.2	0.5	2.3
5548000	Madison city	104,028	47.4	34.8	3.7	8.9	37.1	15.5	6.8	1.0	2.2
5553000	Milwaukee city	229,611	55.9	27.5	6.2	22.2	35.3	8.8	8.0	0.5	2.5
5560500	Oshkosh city	25,618	52.2	36.9	3.8	11.4	35.7	12.1	9.0	0.3	2.3
5566000	Racine city	29,727	59.8	37.4	4.9	17.5	33.5	6.8	7.6	0.0	2.6
5584250	Waukesha city	28,349	60.3	46.7	4.0	9.6	31.5	8.2	6.6	0.3	2.4
5585300	West Allis city	27,185	51.6	36.5	4.8	10.3	40.1	8.4	7.7	0.2	2.2
5600000	**Wyoming**	222,679	65.3	51.9	4.4	9.0	27.5	7.2	6.8	0.2	2.5
5613150	Casper city	23,646	62.7	46.3	5.9	10.5	29.1	8.1	8.3	0.1	2.4
5613900	Cheyenne city	24,094	62.1	48.1	3.0	11.0	30.4	7.5	5.8	0.3	2.5

State/ Place FIPS code	City	Householder is White alone, not Hispanic or Latino, percent	Householder is Black or African American alone, percent	Householder is Hispanic or Latino, percent	Householder is Asian alone, percent	Householders age 15 to 34, percent	Householders age 35 to 64, percent	Householders age 65 and older, percent	Percent of households with one or more persons under 18 years old	Percent of households with one or more persons age 65 or older	Percent of all householders who are owners
		Race or Hispanic origin of householder				Age of householder					
5100000	**Virginia**	69.5	18.6	5.8	4.6	19.5	59.0	21.5	32.9	24.7	66.3
5101000	Alexandria city	60.4	20.3	11.1	5.6	29.8	56.3	13.9	22.2	15.7	43.0
5103000	Arlington CDP........................	70.0	8.5	11.0	8.5	24.7	55.5	19.9	21.1	15.1	65.4
5114440	Centreville CDP......................	55.9	8.0	9.8	24.4	21.6	70.8	7.6	44.3	11.8	69.3
5116000	Chesapeake city	62.5	29.5	4.1	2.6	18.5	63.2	18.3	39.2	22.0	71.0
5121088	Dale City CDP	40.3	31.8	19.1	7.0	17.7	70.1	12.2	50.0	18.1	70.3
5135000	Hampton city	45.0	48.6	3.3	1.4	22.3	55.6	22.1	30.2	24.7	59.8
5135624	Harrisonburg city	74.2	7.2	14.0	0.0	41.5	42.7	15.8	27.9	17.5	34.7
5147672	Lynchburg city	64.9	28.7	0.0	0.0	27.2	48.8	24.0	29.4	26.2	51.2
5156000	Newport News city..................	48.9	40.7	5.6	2.3	26.9	53.8	19.2	32.5	22.0	50.8
5157000	Norfolk city	48.5	41.1	5.2	2.8	31.1	51.4	17.5	31.8	20.0	43.2
5164000	Portsmouth city......................	44.0	50.7	3.0	0.0	25.0	51.8	23.2	31.3	26.7	54.9
5166672	Reston CDP............................	71.7	7.6	9.7	8.8	20.5	61.6	17.9	28.9	20.3	59.7
5167000	Richmond city	45.0	46.6	4.2	1.9	31.3	49.9	18.8	24.1	21.1	42.8
5168000	Roanoke city..........................	68.6	23.7	4.1	1.4	21.2	55.7	23.1	26.4	25.4	54.8
5176432	Suffolk city	54.2	40.3	2.6	0.0	15.9	63.7	20.4	37.3	24.2	71.0
5182000	Virginia Beach city..................	69.5	18.2	5.3	5.2	23.4	57.6	19.0	35.3	22.1	63.2
5300000	**Washington**	78.4	3.5	7.7	6.4	20.8	57.8	21.3	31.3	24.1	62.4
5303180	Auburn city	73.6	3.5	8.7	7.6	21.3	59.4	19.3	33.2	22.4	59.7
5305210	Bellevue city	64.1	2.3	3.9	27.1	23.4	56.5	20.1	30.3	23.3	55.2
5305280	Bellingham city.......................	85.6	3.6	6.1	42.9	23.4	56.5	20.1	23.1	23.2	55.2
5322640	Everett city	75.3	3.9	9.4	7.7	25.3	56.9	17.8	28.0	19.8	43.0
5323515	Federal Way city.....................	59.7	10.0	12.1	12.8	21.3	59.2	19.5	34.0	22.8	55.1
5335275	Kennewick city	76.2	0.0	17.2	0.0	23.2	54.7	22.1	36.3	23.6	60.8
5335415	Kent city	58.9	9.7	12.2	13.4	23.7	60.6	15.7	38.5	19.9	51.1
5335940	Kirkland city	79.2	0.0	5.2	11.2	23.2	60.7	16.2	30.9	18.1	63.7
5338038	Lakewood city	60.3	10.6	13.8	8.8	25.5	52.2	22.4	26.1	25.2	46.2
5343955	Marysville city	83.6	0.0	8.2	0.0	23.0	58.1	18.9	38.8	20.5	67.5
5353545	Pasco city..............................	51.6	0.0	43.7	0.0	28.5	58.5	13.1	50.0	16.0	65.2
5357535	Redmond city	61.7	0.0	7.6	24.0	31.3	55.2	13.6	31.6	15.7	50.2
5357745	Renton city	59.1	12.4	8.4	15.7	23.6	60.6	15.8	32.6	18.8	52.2
5358235	Richland city	87.0	0.0	5.9	3.9	20.4	55.2	24.4	31.9	26.0	67.1
5363000	Seattle city	71.6	7.0	5.3	11.7	31.0	52.3	16.7	20.4	18.4	45.8
5363960	Shoreline city	75.1	5.9	5.9	9.7	17.2	57.7	25.0	28.3	28.1	60.9
5365922	South Hill CDP	74.3	6.5	0.0	5.6	22.8	61.5	15.8	48.7	18.8	75.5
5367000	Spokane city	88.3	2.4	3.4	2.4	26.3	51.6	22.0	28.0	24.3	56.3
5367167	Spokane Valley city	91.1	0.0	2.8	0.0	20.9	56.0	23.1	29.3	26.5	60.3
5370000	Tacoma city............................	69.2	10.9	7.0	7.0	24.1	55.9	20.1	29.9	22.8	50.8
5374060	Vancouver city	81.4	2.6	7.4	4.8	21.6	56.0	22.4	31.4	24.9	49.5
5380010	Yakima city	62.8	0.0	31.6	0.0	22.3	54.0	23.8	37.5	26.9	52.3
5400000	**West Virginia**........................	94.5	2.8	0.9	0.6	16.6	56.5	26.9	27.4	29.8	72.4
5414600	Charleston city........................	84.3	7.6	0.0	0.0	20.9	53.2	26.0	23.9	28.4	58.3
5500000	**Wisconsin**.............................	87.4	5.4	4.0	1.6	20.0	57.0	23.0	29.7	25.1	67.4
5502375	Appleton city	90.2	0.0	3.1	3.6	22.3	58.1	19.7	32.8	21.4	68.2
5522300	Eau Claire city	95.5	0.0	0.0	0.0	31.1	49.0	20.0	24.8	21.3	54.2
5531000	Green Bay city........................	83.4	2.5	7.3	2.8	26.1	54.6	19.3	30.5	20.5	57.9
5537825	Janesville city.........................	92.5	0.0	3.5	0.0	22.6	54.4	23.0	32.8	25.0	65.1
5539225	Kenosha city	76.8	9.5	11.7	0.0	22.4	58.6	19.0	37.3	21.0	57.1
5540775	La Crosse city.........................	93.6	0.0	0.0	3.0	34.2	45.3	20.5	21.6	21.7	50.0
5548000	Madison city	81.1	6.0	4.7	6.3	38.7	45.9	15.4	22.4	16.5	48.0
5553000	Milwaukee city	45.6	37.3	12.6	2.4	29.8	54.1	16.1	33.4	18.5	42.2
5560500	Oshkosh city	94.4	0.0	1.9	2.1	27.9	50.0	22.0	25.3	23.3	53.7
5566000	Racine city	62.4	20.7	15.0	0.0	21.8	59.1	19.1	34.7	21.9	54.3
5584250	Waukesha city	84.3	3.3	8.3	2.7	25.4	55.6	19.0	30.1	20.6	58.5
5585300	West Allis city	87.4	3.2	6.4	2.1	26.2	52.1	21.7	24.6	22.9	54.3
5600000	**Wyoming**	89.1	0.8	6.8	0.7	23.1	55.8	21.1	30.7	23.4	69.6
5613150	Casper city.............................	91.0	0.0	5.6	0.0	27.2	52.2	20.5	31.4	21.6	65.5
5613900	Cheyenne city.........................	82.8	3.1	11.1	0.0	25.1	53.9	21.0	30.2	22.9	63.2

Relationships

PART B. RELATIONSHIPS

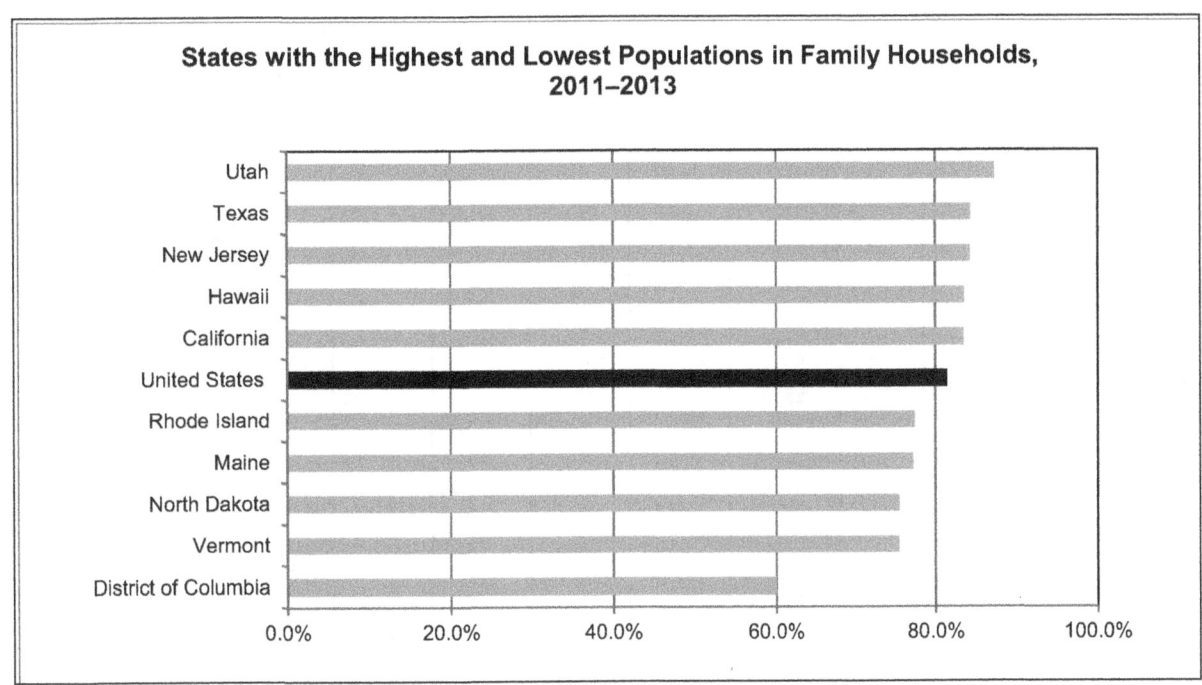

Four out of five Americans live in family households. A family is defined as people who are related by birth, marriage, or adoption. About half of family members—42 percent of the population—are either the householder or spouse of the householder.

In twelve states, more than 45 percent of the people are family householders or their spouses, led by New Hampshire at 47 percent. At the other extreme is the District of Columbia where fewer than 30 percent of residents are family householders or spouses, and only 60 percent of residents live in family households. Thirty-four other cities[1] have fewer than 60 percent of residents in family households, mainly cities with large student or military populations. In Bloomington, IN, barely 40 percent of the people live in family households. In New Brunswick, NJ, 65 percent of residents live in family households but only 21 percent are householders or spouses because of above average proportions of children, other relatives, and nonrelatives who live in family households.

While 81.4 percent of Americans live in family households, there are 100 cities where 90 percent or more live in families. The highest levels are in Eastvale, CA; Lehi, UT; Florence-Graham, CA; and Baldwin Park, CA, all over 95 percent. There are five cities where fewer than half of the residents live in family households, all university towns.

Children of the householder in family households account for 29.9 percent of the population, ranging from 36.7 percent in Utah to 21.9 percent in the District of Columbia. The highest proportion is in Lehi, Utah where 48.6 percent of the residents are children of the householder. Eighteen other cities have levels of 40 percent or more, topped by San Tan Valley, AZ; Perris, CA; Cicero, IL; Florence-Graham, CA; and Pasco, WA, all over 42 percent. In 25 cities, fewer than 20 percent of the residents are children of the householder. Many of these are university towns, but they also include the large cities San Francisco and Seattle.

About one-third of all households are nonfamily households, but they comprise only 16 percent of the population. Many nonfamily householders live alone—about 10 percent of the population. In four cities, more than 20 percent of the people live alone, led by Santa Monica, CA with 25 percent. Large cities with rates above 19 percent include Washington, Atlanta, St. Louis, and Cincinnati.

Only 3.6 percent of Americans are "nonrelatives in nonfamily households"—mostly roommates or unmarried partners. This group accounts for 22.3 percent of the population of Davis, CA, and nearly 20 percent in several other university towns.

---

[1]Only cities with populations of 50,000 or more are included in this book.

Table B-1: States—Relationships

FIPS state code	State	Total population	Population in group quarters	Population in households	Population in family households							
					Total population in family households	Family householders			Spouse in family household	Child in family household		
						Total	Male	Female		Biological child in family household	Adopted child in family household	Stepchild in family household
	United States..............	313,861,723	8,036,874	305,824,849	255,389,986	76,444,922	41,815,505	34,629,417	55,719,115	87,948,196	2,148,298	3,664,067
1	Alabama......................	4,817,624	114,957	4,702,667	3,981,750	1,236,566	664,893	571,673	876,691	1,327,557	35,238	71,782
2	Alaska........................	729,603	26,598	703,005	592,468	167,553	87,545	80,008	124,556	209,237	10,041	11,032
4	Arizona......................	6,548,856	147,514	6,401,342	5,327,635	1,560,655	868,524	692,131	1,123,723	1,825,129	48,118	83,661
5	Arkansas....................	2,949,238	81,252	2,867,986	2,408,672	755,344	407,545	347,799	553,363	777,040	23,490	45,925
6	California...................	38,000,360	812,650	37,187,710	31,715,099	8,602,735	4,775,100	3,827,635	6,118,343	11,395,106	214,600	387,323
8	Colorado....................	5,192,076	117,927	5,074,149	4,115,581	1,271,180	715,785	555,395	976,381	1,367,852	44,706	62,199
9	Connecticut................	3,592,264	119,338	3,472,926	2,909,176	894,728	465,916	428,812	659,326	1,021,251	25,735	32,057
10	Delaware	916,929	25,052	891,877	747,159	226,510	121,278	105,232	162,815	245,408	6,426	10,777
11	District of Columbia........	633,167	40,247	592,920	379,916	114,484	46,976	67,508	60,486	132,031	3,800	2,753
12	Florida.......................	19,319,031	425,915	18,893,116	15,517,553	4,594,006	2,514,306	2,079,700	3,313,543	5,107,204	116,910	239,592
13	Georgia	9,905,993	261,474	9,644,519	8,190,468	2,386,724	1,272,034	1,114,690	1,677,429	2,874,573	77,716	137,566
15	Hawaii.......................	1,390,348	43,359	1,346,989	1,162,058	311,096	173,752	137,344	231,504	365,884	10,825	12,201
16	Idaho........................	1,597,222	29,441	1,567,781	1,331,246	404,512	231,334	173,178	321,695	456,731	13,960	24,202
17	Illinois	12,868,770	299,334	12,569,436	10,516,890	3,114,415	1,740,946	1,373,469	2,287,099	3,764,317	88,418	127,747
18	Indiana......................	6,541,673	188,217	6,353,456	5,305,911	1,647,579	936,462	711,117	1,226,190	1,794,964	53,513	94,925
19	Iowa.........................	3,076,519	100,152	2,976,367	2,427,371	792,745	458,331	334,414	625,999	789,974	23,534	33,893
20	Kansas.......................	2,882,966	79,108	2,803,858	2,324,319	727,902	418,735	309,167	562,706	784,355	25,768	37,456
21	Kentucky....................	4,380,635	126,267	4,254,368	3,563,726	1,131,310	614,999	516,311	829,636	1,158,256	31,432	57,937
22	Louisiana	4,600,933	128,101	4,472,832	3,739,413	1,127,030	553,564	573,466	745,597	1,323,112	26,269	61,974
23	Maine........................	1,328,217	35,581	1,292,636	1,025,574	345,776	185,180	160,596	269,586	300,116	9,789	15,795
24	Maryland....................	5,884,640	141,254	5,743,386	4,823,268	1,432,364	753,906	678,458	1,012,313	1,679,073	38,047	63,319
25	Massachusetts..............	6,648,138	247,261	6,400,877	5,190,544	1,606,383	843,374	763,009	1,180,183	1,806,338	42,409	47,524
26	Michigan....................	9,884,242	226,397	9,657,845	8,000,224	2,489,254	1,385,334	1,103,920	1,823,479	2,745,273	82,643	116,407
27	Minnesota	5,382,376	136,106	5,246,270	4,293,849	1,367,091	779,622	587,469	1,073,612	1,453,682	39,453	51,373
28	Mississippi..................	2,985,181	93,640	2,891,541	2,474,863	743,178	362,404	380,774	486,517	867,811	19,947	43,210
29	Missouri.....................	6,026,255	174,248	5,852,007	4,822,031	1,527,728	847,820	679,908	1,136,229	1,589,516	43,084	86,501
30	Montana.....................	1,006,086	28,801	977,285	786,174	255,929	141,854	114,075	200,677	242,624	8,523	11,325
31	Nebraska....................	1,855,209	51,526	1,803,683	1,483,924	472,470	273,237	199,233	369,509	501,993	15,040	16,957
32	Nevada......................	2,754,148	36,170	2,717,978	2,239,925	641,060	354,441	286,619	448,851	762,200	17,483	40,000
33	New Hampshire	1,321,050	40,719	1,280,331	1,058,358	346,775	192,081	154,694	273,674	330,404	10,444	14,780
34	New Jersey..................	8,867,909	186,582	8,681,327	7,473,789	2,203,456	1,213,896	989,560	1,613,482	2,691,383	55,061	76,838
35	New Mexico.................	2,082,250	42,960	2,039,290	1,706,709	494,555	267,072	227,483	342,838	602,663	16,223	27,868
36	New York....................	19,576,660	584,323	18,992,337	15,643,881	4,594,587	2,356,514	2,238,073	3,160,296	5,634,469	112,647	144,329
37	North Carolina.............	9,749,266	254,224	9,495,042	7,907,401	2,467,843	1,348,818	1,119,025	1,789,690	2,641,695	66,466	121,267
38	North Dakota...............	703,203	26,258	676,945	530,615	176,378	103,274	73,104	141,942	166,905	4,460	7,462
39	Ohio.........................	11,557,868	313,367	11,244,501	9,227,331	2,920,189	1,580,200	1,339,989	2,132,229	3,129,168	77,271	139,984
40	Oklahoma...................	3,817,296	109,851	3,707,445	3,100,922	959,015	527,013	432,002	708,554	1,008,756	32,965	64,537
41	Oregon	3,899,266	87,486	3,811,780	3,054,445	959,743	526,303	433,440	730,979	961,951	30,904	50,721
42	Pennsylvania...............	12,759,859	429,290	12,330,569	10,141,644	3,186,145	1,780,893	1,405,252	2,376,448	3,425,175	82,545	124,275
44	Rhode Island...............	1,050,722	41,009	1,009,713	813,714	257,316	131,699	125,617	180,659	273,214	7,180	9,377
45	South Carolina.............	4,723,923	139,017	4,584,906	3,853,945	1,199,885	633,474	566,411	842,805	1,267,546	34,426	60,592
46	South Dakota...............	834,236	34,008	800,228	656,240	210,494	118,467	92,027	163,124	212,706	6,609	9,248
47	Tennessee	6,449,754	153,968	6,295,786	5,269,562	1,646,360	907,793	738,567	1,203,169	1,713,268	49,239	90,624
48	Texas........................	26,049,971	588,936	25,461,035	21,972,745	6,235,820	3,392,571	2,843,249	4,484,396	7,942,973	164,440	380,938
49	Utah.........................	2,856,839	46,843	2,809,996	2,493,465	667,046	396,187	270,859	541,127	979,844	30,645	37,842
50	Vermont.....................	626,303	25,332	600,971	472,262	159,883	82,268	77,615	126,134	140,852	5,470	5,968
51	Virginia......................	8,184,299	241,971	7,942,328	6,641,604	2,033,567	1,128,996	904,571	1,527,234	2,221,374	49,854	92,356
53	Washington.................	6,896,071	141,037	6,755,034	5,501,379	1,694,518	965,781	728,737	1,299,671	1,811,524	54,952	87,047
54	West Virginia	1,855,392	49,635	1,805,757	1,486,417	479,062	255,880	223,182	359,384	461,361	13,270	23,267
55	Wisconsin...................	5,725,352	148,208	5,577,144	4,527,059	1,458,497	832,317	626,180	1,127,840	1,516,089	41,048	58,039
56	Wyoming....................	575,535	13,963	561,572	459,712	145,481	78,811	66,670	115,402	146,269	5,262	9,295

FIPS state code	State	Population in family households										
		Relative in family household						Nonrelatives in family household				
		Grandchild in family household	Brother or sister in family household	Parent in family household	Parent-in-law in family household	Son-in-law or daughter-in-law in family household	Other relative in family household	Roomer or boarder in family household	Housemate or roommate in family household	Unmarried partner in family household	Foster child in family household	Other nonrelative in family household
	United States............	7,066,977	3,953,805	4,027,262	985,480	1,320,914	5,086,950	629,226	1,195,983	3,047,960	197,249	1,953,582
1	Alabama......................	148,925	56,218	48,009	10,763	18,997	75,517	5,936	13,323	31,699	3,768	20,761
2	Alaska.......................	15,430	9,398	6,573	2,318	2,967	10,579	1,451	3,823	9,382	710	7,418
4	Arizona......................	168,382	95,355	91,400	20,925	30,317	108,947	12,467	29,158	75,675	5,213	48,510
5	Arkansas.....................	78,896	29,070	27,403	6,046	12,155	46,876	4,277	7,751	23,045	2,050	15,941
6	California...................	953,653	708,769	772,914	193,600	246,770	968,927	162,596	245,624	427,331	23,310	293,498
8	Colorado	86,491	52,754	46,805	13,053	18,507	65,923	9,830	23,129	42,052	3,209	31,510
9	Connecticut..................	54,857	39,519	45,245	11,867	11,012	44,858	5,435	12,526	30,606	1,927	18,227
10	Delaware.....................	24,995	10,948	11,217	3,352	2,917	17,288	2,022	3,901	10,556	763	7,264
11	District of Columbia.......	17,816	11,786	5,820	865	979	15,535	1,696	3,253	4,341	50	4,221
12	Florida......................	440,349	290,039	385,321	93,033	100,489	370,994	39,027	93,591	184,009	8,950	140,496
13	Georgia	283,624	144,567	133,764	33,077	39,053	199,545	19,738	39,552	81,211	6,160	56,169
15	Hawaii	62,164	23,866	26,833	7,830	20,865	44,348	8,833	6,609	12,828	567	15,805
16	Idaho........................	25,820	11,772	10,941	2,724	6,402	18,137	2,796	5,969	13,960	1,752	9,873
17	Illinois.....................	274,841	166,330	160,279	36,742	44,166	201,531	15,578	30,520	120,587	7,120	77,200
18	Indiana......................	139,936	53,956	51,963	12,990	20,058	64,976	9,195	20,636	68,504	4,757	41,769
19	Iowa.........................	39,585	17,887	15,035	3,916	6,122	22,370	2,625	7,329	32,353	1,398	12,606
20	Kansas.......................	49,257	22,289	18,880	4,637	7,345	29,679	2,917	9,309	25,994	2,939	12,886
21	Kentucky.....................	112,421	39,668	36,410	8,132	15,190	52,703	3,893	11,432	43,636	5,253	26,417
22	Louisiana....................	155,954	58,127	48,031	9,248	16,419	74,339	4,247	12,579	47,778	1,833	26,876
23	Maine........................	18,153	7,146	9,628	2,632	4,519	8,560	2,077	3,879	18,068	1,023	8,827
24	Maryland	138,886	79,219	79,431	22,050	23,444	107,687	14,863	29,285	55,037	2,339	45,911
25	Massachusetts	101,272	73,294	79,492	22,563	23,930	77,811	10,541	23,751	58,598	4,157	32,298
26	Michigan	191,973	100,937	88,977	19,184	29,682	107,311	12,413	25,248	98,716	6,980	61,747
27	Minnesota	59,560	44,133	30,896	7,971	10,491	43,197	7,648	17,274	59,349	2,584	25,535
28	Mississippi..................	120,180	39,644	27,106	6,129	10,723	53,158	3,533	7,855	26,355	2,324	17,193
29	Missouri.....................	124,965	48,269	46,858	12,424	17,897	61,937	7,082	16,177	60,981	5,409	36,974
30	Montana......................	17,147	7,807	7,309	1,918	3,378	9,191	1,305	4,052	8,546	1,487	4,956
31	Nebraska	24,141	15,123	9,306	1,745	3,497	16,666	1,799	5,576	17,885	2,081	10,136
32	Nevada.......................	55,046	54,191	54,149	13,605	13,047	58,492	7,964	17,274	32,003	1,555	23,005
33	New Hampshire	17,638	8,034	9,534	3,833	4,679	8,686	2,272	3,635	14,991	669	8,310
34	New Jersey...................	154,722	122,909	146,567	39,301	35,047	151,713	18,447	26,490	78,990	4,152	55,231
35	New Mexico...................	63,963	27,884	27,618	4,867	11,224	36,341	2,856	6,793	26,046	1,650	13,320
36	New York.....................	393,800	295,376	314,046	63,763	87,372	396,790	50,035	74,649	185,455	10,855	125,412
37	North Carolina..............	228,199	106,856	97,746	23,747	29,517	141,298	14,472	33,763	88,599	4,890	51,353
38	North Dakota................	8,261	4,681	2,702	737	1,138	3,560	430	1,985	6,751	597	2,626
39	Ohio.........................	234,911	98,586	93,847	21,699	30,191	112,980	10,843	28,960	122,494	6,143	67,836
40	Oklahoma.....................	94,618	39,066	34,783	8,139	16,293	52,462	5,239	13,137	34,726	3,869	24,763
41	Oregon.......................	62,673	37,518	34,886	10,707	16,983	46,671	10,983	24,675	42,289	3,810	28,952
42	Pennsylvania	245,016	117,380	135,700	35,315	35,971	139,227	16,709	25,733	123,214	8,007	64,784
44	Rhode Island.................	17,230	12,474	14,096	2,482	3,510	13,853	1,521	2,496	11,428	775	6,103
45	South Carolina..............	147,551	56,514	53,145	11,447	15,290	76,718	6,694	16,455	41,944	2,536	20,397
46	South Dakota................	14,970	6,156	4,113	809	2,011	8,281	815	2,383	9,510	827	4,184
47	Tennessee...................	171,858	69,690	66,548	16,254	24,075	93,155	7,722	19,371	56,672	4,244	37,313
48	Texas........................	760,933	371,238	365,803	90,491	150,580	505,300	38,506	82,150	237,861	15,500	145,816
49	Utah.........................	61,006	32,552	21,541	7,796	18,657	39,340	8,010	13,914	16,389	1,702	16,054
50	Vermont	7,568	3,420	3,403	957	1,439	3,249	1,348	1,352	6,985	288	3,946
51	Virginia.....................	171,534	96,451	99,394	26,394	30,242	123,871	19,370	34,410	63,945	3,662	47,946
53	Washington...................	103,853	68,572	67,551	19,687	24,098	87,998	20,470	33,460	74,858	6,075	47,045
54	West Virginia................	43,645	17,034	17,558	3,451	8,125	20,235	2,193	4,174	18,253	1,538	13,867
55	Wisconsin....................	70,286	44,012	36,652	7,399	11,637	43,113	5,650	13,184	59,170	3,428	31,015
56	Wyoming......................	8,023	5,321	4,034	866	1,497	5,027	857	2,429	6,305	364	3,280

FIPS state code	State	Total population in nonfamily households	Population in nonfamily households						
			Nonfamily householders						
			Total	Male	Female	Male living alone	Female living alone	Male not living alone	Female not living alone
	United States...............	50,434,863	39,286,382	18,266,678	21,019,704	14,242,580	17,844,119	4,024,098	3,175,585
1	Alabama........................	720,917	600,726	273,277	327,449	231,666	294,445	41,611	33,004
2	Alaska...........................	110,537	83,322	46,545	36,777	35,782	29,384	10,763	7,393
4	Arizona.........................	1,073,707	820,846	400,847	419,999	307,765	345,825	93,082	74,174
5	Arkansas.......................	459,314	375,073	173,868	201,205	141,976	176,408	31,892	24,797
6	California......................	5,472,611	3,978,987	1,887,492	2,091,495	1,376,790	1,687,562	510,702	403,933
8	Colorado	958,568	718,191	351,515	366,676	262,782	298,636	88,733	68,040
9	Connecticut...................	563,750	453,547	203,411	250,136	161,613	215,197	41,798	34,939
10	Delaware.......................	144,718	110,735	48,243	62,492	36,246	52,883	11,997	9,609
11	District of Columbia.......	213,004	153,531	69,227	84,304	51,156	68,699	18,071	15,605
12	Florida	3,375,563	2,574,496	1,182,285	1,392,211	917,697	1,186,540	264,588	205,671
13	Georgia	1,454,051	1,136,210	524,479	611,731	414,717	531,379	109,762	80,352
15	Hawaii	184,931	138,200	70,442	67,758	53,581	54,381	16,861	13,377
16	Idaho............................	236,535	178,940	85,442	93,498	63,966	77,670	21,476	15,828
17	Illinois	2,052,546	1,649,042	759,506	889,536	607,337	770,202	152,169	119,334
18	Indiana	1,047,545	834,979	397,568	437,411	315,826	377,490	81,742	59,921
19	Iowa.............................	548,996	434,456	206,171	228,285	161,325	194,275	44,846	34,010
20	Kansas..........................	479,539	381,845	179,382	202,463	142,509	173,937	36,873	28,526
21	Kentucky	690,642	562,089	255,728	306,361	207,633	267,040	48,095	39,321
22	Louisiana	733,419	588,967	281,837	307,130	229,006	268,869	52,831	38,261
23	Maine...........................	267,062	206,813	94,324	112,489	70,143	91,333	24,181	21,156
24	Maryland	920,118	717,060	311,822	405,238	242,263	346,951	69,559	58,287
25	Massachusetts	1,210,333	922,209	404,910	517,299	303,996	425,576	100,914	91,723
26	Michigan	1,657,621	1,326,278	620,825	705,453	496,657	608,108	124,168	97,345
27	Minnesota	952,421	742,833	349,665	393,168	269,368	328,438	80,297	64,730
28	Mississippi	416,678	343,720	157,576	186,144	131,366	167,761	26,210	18,383
29	Missouri........................	1,029,976	826,050	381,763	444,287	301,792	380,702	79,971	63,585
30	Montana	191,111	149,575	74,491	75,084	59,106	63,130	15,385	11,954
31	Nebraska	319,759	257,102	123,301	133,801	97,387	114,759	25,914	19,042
32	Nevada	478,053	354,920	187,502	167,418	142,576	135,448	44,926	31,970
33	New Hampshire	221,973	171,313	81,190	90,123	59,673	72,423	21,517	17,700
34	New Jersey....................	1,207,538	977,696	426,600	551,096	337,638	484,243	88,962	66,853
35	New Mexico...................	332,581	265,696	127,271	138,425	102,303	117,493	24,968	20,932
36	New York......................	3,348,456	2,619,576	1,168,250	1,451,326	911,281	1,238,422	256,969	212,904
37	North Carolina	1,587,641	1,253,515	565,935	687,580	445,533	594,345	120,402	93,235
38	North Dakota	146,330	115,090	61,040	54,050	46,854	44,337	14,186	9,713
39	Ohio.............................	2,017,170	1,631,308	750,380	880,928	603,154	763,087	147,226	117,841
40	Oklahoma......................	606,523	486,044	230,162	255,882	185,199	222,853	44,963	33,029
41	Oregon.........................	757,335	556,848	255,025	301,823	185,233	240,706	69,792	61,117
42	Pennsylvania	2,188,925	1,758,995	791,740	967,255	633,066	836,859	158,674	130,396
44	Rhode Island	195,999	153,031	69,596	83,435	52,366	71,502	17,230	11,933
45	South Carolina...............	730,961	582,072	264,456	317,616	212,907	278,589	51,549	39,027
46	South Dakota.................	143,988	115,592	58,585	57,007	46,191	49,230	12,394	7,777
47	Tennessee	1,026,224	834,107	381,303	452,804	311,443	393,717	69,860	59,087
48	Texas............................	3,488,290	2,729,532	1,321,379	1,408,153	1,045,836	1,200,495	275,543	207,658
49	Utah.............................	316,531	224,194	110,169	114,025	82,389	93,174	27,780	20,851
50	Vermont........................	128,709	96,680	44,151	52,529	31,211	41,494	12,940	11,035
51	Virginia	1,300,724	993,194	453,046	540,148	347,421	455,933	105,625	84,215
53	Washington	1,253,655	939,978	454,621	485,357	337,251	394,213	117,370	91,144
54	West Virginia	319,340	260,697	120,295	140,402	100,071	123,712	20,224	16,690
55	Wisconsin	1,050,085	823,284	388,096	435,188	300,643	363,882	87,453	71,306
56	Wyoming.......................	101,860	77,198	39,944	37,254	30,890	30,382	9,054	6,872

FIPS state code	State	Population in nonfamily households						Total population	Population in group quarters	Population in households
		Nonrelatives in nonfamily households								
		Total nonrelatives in nonfamily households	Roomer or boarder in nonfamily households	Housemate or roommate in nonfamily households	Unmarried partner in nonfamily households:	Foster child in nonfamily household	Other nonrelatives In nonfamily households			
	United States...............	11,148,481	971,590	4,693,751	3,871,788	38,169	1,573,183	100	2.6	97.4
1	Alabama........................	120,191	11,937	56,206	34,466	716	16,866	100	2.4	97.6
2	Alaska...........................	27,215	2,132	9,998	10,995	80	4,010	100	3.6	96.4
4	Arizona.........................	252,861	20,880	102,344	92,232	990	36,415	100	2.3	97.7
5	Arkansas.......................	84,241	5,880	31,455	30,040	588	16,278	100	2.8	97.2
6	California.......................	1,493,624	166,879	694,095	442,910	4,583	185,157	100	2.1	97.9
8	Colorado.......................	240,377	19,299	115,998	77,812	846	26,422	100	2.3	97.7
9	Connecticut...................	110,203	9,597	39,038	47,196	672	13,700	100	3.3	96.7
10	Delaware	33,983	3,665	12,711	12,675	65	4,867	100	2.7	97.3
11	District of Columbia.......	59,473	5,026	35,122	15,080	18	4,227	100	6.4	93.6
12	Florida..........................	801,067	78,869	331,060	259,694	1,909	129,535	100	2.2	97.8
13	Georgia	317,841	35,964	142,685	93,495	701	44,996	100	2.6	97.4
15	Hawaii..........................	46,731	4,957	19,372	16,109	10	6,283	100	3.1	96.9
16	Idaho...........................	57,595	4,163	24,726	18,478	17	10,211	100	1.8	98.2
17	Illinois..........................	403,504	35,280	156,185	152,526	1,887	57,626	100	2.3	97.7
18	Indiana.........................	212,566	14,977	77,822	82,866	872	36,029	100	2.9	97.1
19	Iowa.............................	114,540	5,687	48,672	44,858	108	15,215	100	3.3	96.7
20	Kansas..........................	97,694	7,161	43,463	33,014	750	13,306	100	2.7	97.3
21	Kentucky	128,553	6,162	46,065	52,719	759	22,848	100	2.9	97.1
22	Louisiana	144,452	9,629	61,941	49,446	691	22,745	100	2.8	97.2
23	Maine...........................	60,249	4,040	17,532	30,327	138	8,212	100	2.7	97.3
24	Maryland	203,058	20,282	82,999	68,494	939	30,344	100	2.4	97.6
25	Massachusetts	288,124	20,528	136,267	102,887	1,351	27,091	100	3.7	96.3
26	Michigan.......................	331,343	20,733	129,699	126,394	1,204	53,313	100	2.3	97.7
27	Minnesota.....................	209,588	12,562	89,575	82,547	497	24,407	100	2.5	97.5
28	Mississippi.....................	72,958	7,915	26,619	23,512	294	14,618	100	3.1	96.9
29	Missouri........................	203,926	12,567	77,229	81,646	526	31,958	100	2.9	97.1
30	Montana........................	41,536	3,081	17,960	15,753	113	4,629	100	2.9	97.1
31	Nebraska	62,657	3,623	25,866	23,474	192	9,502	100	2.8	97.2
32	Nevada.........................	123,133	12,147	50,627	40,883	1,150	18,326	100	1.3	98.7
33	New Hampshire	50,660	2,800	14,348	26,290	66	7,156	100	3.1	96.9
34	New Jersey....................	229,842	22,413	73,727	91,936	524	41,242	100	2.1	97.9
35	New Mexico...................	66,885	6,128	23,552	28,322	146	8,737	100	2.1	97.9
36	New York.......................	728,880	71,327	314,227	250,981	2,415	89,930	100	3.0	97.0
37	North Carolina...............	334,126	31,326	148,566	106,765	1,205	46,264	100	2.6	97.4
38	North Dakota.................	31,240	1,432	13,408	12,789	137	3,474	100	3.7	96.3
39	Ohio.............................	385,862	22,203	143,704	157,740	1,668	60,547	100	2.7	97.3
40	Oklahoma......................	120,479	8,699	49,338	38,633	517	23,292	100	2.9	97.1
41	Oregon	200,487	14,341	92,249	70,495	544	22,858	100	2.2	97.8
42	Pennsylvania	429,930	28,284	163,892	171,678	624	65,452	100	3.4	96.6
44	Rhode Island..................	42,968	3,728	17,000	16,702	46	5,492	100	3.9	96.1
45	South Carolina...............	148,889	13,000	72,012	45,463	953	17,461	100	2.9	97.1
46	South Dakota.................	28,396	1,715	12,110	10,828	105	3,638	100	4.1	95.9
47	Tennessee	192,117	14,135	74,806	71,015	988	31,173	100	2.4	97.6
48	Texas............................	758,758	74,338	325,414	239,263	2,509	117,234	100	2.3	97.7
49	Utah.............................	92,337	10,961	48,973	20,360	639	11,404	100	1.6	98.4
50	Vermont........................	32,029	2,097	11,294	14,899	134	3,605	100	4.0	96.0
51	Virginia.........................	307,530	34,598	138,461	94,240	641	39,590	100	3.0	97.0
53	Washington	313,677	24,215	136,308	114,805	659	37,690	100	2.0	98.0
54	West Virginia	58,643	3,703	18,695	23,929	261	12,055	100	2.7	97.3
55	Wisconsin......................	226,801	11,704	89,475	92,571	692	32,359	100	2.6	97.4
56	Wyoming.......................	24,662	2,821	8,861	9,556	30	3,394	100	2.4	97.6

Table B-1: States—Relationships—*Continued*

FIPS state code	State	Total population in family households	Family householders			Spouse in family household	Child in family household		
			Total	Male	Female		Biological child in family household	Adopted child in family household	Stepchild in family household
	United States..............	81.4	24.4	13.3	11.0	17.8	28.0	0.7	1.2
1	Alabama......................	82.6	25.7	13.8	11.9	18.2	27.6	0.7	1.5
2	Alaska.........................	81.2	23.0	12.0	11.0	17.1	28.7	1.4	1.5
4	Arizona.......................	81.4	23.8	13.3	10.6	17.2	27.9	0.7	1.3
5	Arkansas.....................	81.7	25.6	13.8	11.8	18.8	26.3	0.8	1.6
6	California....................	83.5	22.6	12.6	10.1	16.1	30.0	0.6	1.0
8	Colorado	79.3	24.5	13.8	10.7	18.8	26.3	0.9	1.2
9	Connecticut.................	81.0	24.9	13.0	11.9	18.4	28.4	0.7	0.9
10	Delaware.....................	81.5	24.7	13.2	11.5	17.8	26.8	0.7	1.2
11	District of Columbia........	60.0	18.1	7.4	10.7	9.6	20.9	0.6	0.4
12	Florida	80.3	23.8	13.0	10.8	17.2	26.4	0.6	1.2
13	Georgia	82.7	24.1	12.8	11.3	16.9	29.0	0.8	1.4
15	Hawaii........................	83.6	22.4	12.5	9.9	16.7	26.3	0.8	0.9
16	Idaho.........................	83.3	25.3	14.5	10.8	20.1	28.6	0.9	1.5
17	Illinois........................	81.7	24.2	13.5	10.7	17.8	29.3	0.7	1.0
18	Indiana.......................	81.1	25.2	14.3	10.9	18.7	27.4	0.8	1.5
19	Iowa..........................	78.9	25.8	14.9	10.9	20.3	25.7	0.8	1.1
20	Kansas........................	80.6	25.2	14.5	10.7	19.5	27.2	0.9	1.3
21	Kentucky.....................	81.4	25.8	14.0	11.8	18.9	26.4	0.7	1.3
22	Louisiana	81.3	24.5	12.0	12.5	16.2	28.8	0.6	1.3
23	Maine.........................	77.2	26.0	13.9	12.1	20.3	22.6	0.7	1.2
24	Maryland.....................	82.0	24.3	12.8	11.5	17.2	28.5	0.6	1.1
25	Massachusetts	78.1	24.2	12.7	11.5	17.8	27.2	0.6	0.7
26	Michigan	80.9	25.2	14.0	11.2	18.4	27.8	0.8	1.2
27	Minnesota	79.8	25.4	14.5	10.9	19.9	27.0	0.7	1.0
28	Mississippi...................	82.9	24.9	12.1	12.8	16.3	29.1	0.7	1.4
29	Missouri......................	80.0	25.4	14.1	11.3	18.9	26.4	0.7	1.4
30	Montana	78.1	25.4	14.1	11.3	19.9	24.1	0.8	1.1
31	Nebraska	80.0	25.5	14.7	10.7	19.9	27.1	0.8	0.9
32	Nevada	81.3	23.3	12.9	10.4	16.3	27.7	0.6	1.5
33	New Hampshire	80.1	26.2	14.5	11.7	20.7	25.0	0.8	1.1
34	New Jersey...................	84.3	24.8	13.7	11.2	18.2	30.3	0.6	0.9
35	New Mexico.................	82.0	23.8	12.8	10.9	16.5	28.9	0.8	1.3
36	New York.....................	79.9	23.5	12.0	11.4	16.1	28.8	0.6	0.7
37	North Carolina	81.1	25.3	13.8	11.5	18.4	27.1	0.7	1.2
38	North Dakota...............	75.5	25.1	14.7	10.4	20.2	23.7	0.6	1.1
39	Ohio..........................	79.8	25.3	13.7	11.6	18.4	27.1	0.7	1.2
40	Oklahoma....................	81.2	25.1	13.8	11.3	18.6	26.4	0.9	1.7
41	Oregon.......................	78.3	24.6	13.5	11.1	18.7	24.7	0.8	1.3
42	Pennsylvania	79.5	25.0	14.0	11.0	18.6	26.8	0.6	1.0
44	Rhode Island.................	77.4	24.5	12.5	12.0	17.2	26.0	0.7	0.9
45	South Carolina..............	81.6	25.4	13.4	12.0	17.8	26.8	0.7	1.3
46	South Dakota...............	78.7	25.2	14.2	11.0	19.6	25.5	0.8	1.1
47	Tennessee	81.7	25.5	14.1	11.5	18.7	26.6	0.8	1.4
48	Texas.........................	84.3	23.9	13.0	10.9	17.2	30.5	0.6	1.5
49	Utah..........................	87.3	23.3	13.9	9.5	18.9	34.3	1.1	1.3
50	Vermont......................	75.4	25.5	13.1	12.4	20.1	22.5	0.9	1.0
51	Virginia.......................	81.2	24.8	13.8	11.1	18.7	27.1	0.6	1.1
53	Washington..................	79.8	24.6	14.0	10.6	18.8	26.3	0.8	1.3
54	West Virginia................	80.1	25.8	13.8	12.0	19.4	24.9	0.7	1.3
55	Wisconsin	79.1	25.5	14.5	10.9	19.7	26.5	0.7	1.0
56	Wyoming.....................	79.9	25.3	13.7	11.6	20.1	25.4	0.9	1.6

Table B-1: States—Relationships—*Continued*

FIPS state code	State	Population in family households											
		Relative in family household						Nonrelatives in family household					
		Grandchild in family household	Brother or sister in family household	Parent in family household	Parent-in-law in family household	Son-in-law or daughter-in-law in family household	Other relative in family household	Total nonrelatives in family households	Roomer or boarder in family household	Housemate or roommate in family household	Unmarried partner in family household	Foster child in family household	Other nonrelative in family household
	United States	2.3	1.3	1.3	0.3	0.4	1.6	2.2	0.2	0.4	1.0	0.1	0.6
1	Alabama	3.1	1.2	1.0	0.2	0.4	1.6	1.6	0.1	0.3	0.7	0.1	0.4
2	Alaska	2.1	1.3	0.9	0.3	0.4	1.4	3.1	0.2	0.5	1.3	0.1	1.0
4	Arizona	2.6	1.5	1.4	0.3	0.5	1.7	2.6	0.2	0.4	1.2	0.1	0.7
5	Arkansas	2.7	1.0	0.9	0.2	0.4	1.6	1.8	0.1	0.3	0.8	0.1	0.5
6	California	2.5	1.9	2.0	0.5	0.6	2.5	3.0	0.4	0.6	1.1	0.1	0.8
8	Colorado	1.7	1.0	0.9	0.3	0.4	1.3	2.1	0.2	0.4	0.8	0.1	0.6
9	Connecticut	1.5	1.1	1.3	0.3	0.3	1.2	1.9	0.2	0.3	0.9	0.1	0.5
10	Delaware	2.7	1.2	1.2	0.4	0.3	1.9	2.7	0.2	0.4	1.2	0.1	0.8
11	District of Columbia	2.8	1.9	0.9	0.1	0.2	2.5	2.1	0.3	0.5	0.7	0.0	0.7
12	Florida	2.3	1.5	2.0	0.5	0.5	1.9	2.4	0.2	0.5	1.0	0.0	0.7
13	Georgia	2.9	1.5	1.4	0.3	0.4	2.0	2.0	0.2	0.4	0.8	0.1	0.6
15	Hawaii	4.5	1.7	1.9	0.6	1.5	3.2	3.2	0.6	0.5	0.9	0.0	1.1
16	Idaho	1.6	0.7	0.7	0.2	0.4	1.1	2.2	0.2	0.4	0.9	0.1	0.6
17	Illinois	2.1	1.3	1.2	0.3	0.3	1.6	2.0	0.1	0.2	0.9	0.1	0.6
18	Indiana	2.1	0.8	0.8	0.2	0.3	1.0	2.2	0.1	0.3	1.0	0.1	0.6
19	Iowa	1.3	0.6	0.5	0.1	0.2	0.7	1.8	0.1	0.2	1.1	0.0	0.4
20	Kansas	1.7	0.8	0.7	0.2	0.3	1.0	1.9	0.1	0.3	0.9	0.1	0.4
21	Kentucky	2.6	0.9	0.8	0.2	0.3	1.2	2.1	0.1	0.3	1.0	0.1	0.6
22	Louisiana	3.4	1.3	1.0	0.2	0.4	1.6	2.0	0.1	0.3	1.0	0.0	0.6
23	Maine	1.4	0.5	0.7	0.2	0.3	0.6	2.6	0.2	0.3	1.4	0.1	0.7
24	Maryland	2.4	1.3	1.3	0.4	0.4	1.8	2.5	0.3	0.5	0.9	0.0	0.8
25	Massachusetts	1.5	1.1	1.2	0.3	0.4	1.2	1.9	0.2	0.4	0.9	0.1	0.5
26	Michigan	1.9	1.0	0.9	0.2	0.3	1.1	2.1	0.1	0.3	1.0	0.1	0.6
27	Minnesota	1.1	0.8	0.6	0.1	0.2	0.8	2.1	0.1	0.3	1.1	0.0	0.5
28	Mississippi	4.0	1.3	0.9	0.2	0.4	1.8	1.9	0.1	0.3	0.9	0.1	0.6
29	Missouri	2.1	0.8	0.8	0.2	0.3	1.0	2.1	0.1	0.3	1.0	0.1	0.6
30	Montana	1.7	0.8	0.7	0.2	0.3	0.9	2.0	0.1	0.4	0.8	0.1	0.5
31	Nebraska	1.3	0.8	0.5	0.1	0.2	0.9	2.0	0.1	0.3	1.0	0.1	0.5
32	Nevada	2.0	2.0	2.0	0.5	0.5	2.1	3.0	0.3	0.6	1.2	0.1	0.8
33	New Hampshire	1.3	0.6	0.7	0.3	0.4	0.7	2.3	0.2	0.3	1.1	0.1	0.6
34	New Jersey	1.7	1.4	1.7	0.4	0.4	1.7	2.1	0.2	0.3	0.9	0.0	0.6
35	New Mexico	3.1	1.3	1.3	0.2	0.5	1.7	2.4	0.1	0.3	1.3	0.1	0.6
36	New York	2.0	1.5	1.6	0.3	0.4	2.0	2.3	0.3	0.4	0.9	0.1	0.6
37	North Carolina	2.3	1.1	1.0	0.2	0.3	1.4	2.0	0.1	0.3	0.9	0.1	0.5
38	North Dakota	1.2	0.7	0.4	0.1	0.2	0.5	1.8	0.1	0.3	1.0	0.1	0.4
39	Ohio	2.0	0.9	0.8	0.2	0.3	1.0	2.0	0.1	0.3	1.1	0.1	0.6
40	Oklahoma	2.5	1.0	0.9	0.2	0.4	1.4	2.1	0.1	0.3	0.9	0.1	0.6
41	Oregon	1.6	1.0	0.9	0.3	0.4	1.2	2.8	0.3	0.6	1.1	0.1	0.7
42	Pennsylvania	1.9	0.9	1.1	0.3	0.3	1.1	1.9	0.1	0.2	1.0	0.1	0.5
44	Rhode Island	1.6	1.2	1.3	0.2	0.3	1.3	2.1	0.1	0.2	1.1	0.1	0.6
45	South Carolina	3.1	1.2	1.1	0.2	0.3	1.6	1.9	0.1	0.3	0.9	0.1	0.4
46	South Dakota	1.8	0.7	0.5	0.1	0.2	1.0	2.1	0.1	0.3	1.1	0.1	0.5
47	Tennessee	2.7	1.1	1.0	0.3	0.4	1.4	1.9	0.1	0.3	0.9	0.1	0.6
48	Texas	2.9	1.4	1.4	0.3	0.6	1.9	2.0	0.1	0.3	0.9	0.1	0.6
49	Utah	2.1	1.1	0.8	0.3	0.7	1.4	2.0	0.3	0.5	0.6	0.1	0.6
50	Vermont	1.2	0.5	0.5	0.2	0.2	0.5	2.2	0.2	0.2	1.1	0.0	0.6
51	Virginia	2.1	1.2	1.2	0.3	0.4	1.5	2.1	0.2	0.4	0.8	0.0	0.6
53	Washington	1.5	1.0	1.0	0.3	0.3	1.3	2.6	0.3	0.5	1.1	0.1	0.7
54	West Virginia	2.4	0.9	0.9	0.2	0.4	1.1	2.2	0.1	0.2	1.0	0.1	0.7
55	Wisconsin	1.2	0.8	0.6	0.1	0.2	0.8	2.0	0.1	0.2	1.0	0.1	0.5
56	Wyoming	1.4	0.9	0.7	0.2	0.3	0.9	2.3	0.1	0.4	1.1	0.1	0.6

FIPS state code	State	Total population in nonfamily households	Population in nonfamily households												
			Nonfamily householders							Nonrelatives in nonfamily households					
			Total	Male	Female	Male living alone	Female living alone	Male not living alone	Female not living alone	Total nonrelatives in nonfamily households	Roomer or boarder in nonfamily households	Housemate or roommate in nonfamily households	Unmarried partner in nonfamily households:	Foster child in nonfamily household	Other nonrelatives In nonfamily households
	United States..............	16.1	12.5	5.8	6.7	4.5	5.7	1.3	1.0	3.6	0.3	1.5	1.2	0.0	0.5
1	Alabama.....................	15.0	12.5	5.7	6.8	4.8	6.1	0.9	0.7	2.5	0.2	1.2	0.7	0.0	0.4
2	Alaska........................	15.2	11.4	6.4	5.0	4.9	4.0	1.5	1.0	3.7	0.3	1.4	1.5	0.0	0.5
4	Arizona......................	16.4	12.5	6.1	6.4	4.7	5.3	1.4	1.1	3.9	0.3	1.6	1.4	0.0	0.6
5	Arkansas....................	15.6	12.7	5.9	6.8	4.8	6.0	1.1	0.8	2.9	0.2	1.1	1.0	0.0	0.6
6	California...................	14.4	10.5	5.0	5.5	3.6	4.4	1.3	1.1	3.9	0.4	1.8	1.2	0.0	0.5
8	Colorado....................	18.5	13.8	6.8	7.1	5.1	5.8	1.7	1.3	4.6	0.4	2.2	1.5	0.0	0.5
9	Connecticut...............	15.7	12.6	5.7	7.0	4.5	6.0	1.2	1.0	3.1	0.3	1.1	1.3	0.0	0.4
10	Delaware	15.8	12.1	5.3	6.8	4.0	5.8	1.3	1.0	3.7	0.4	1.4	1.4	0.0	0.5
11	District of Columbia.......	33.6	24.2	10.9	13.3	8.1	10.9	2.9	2.5	9.4	0.8	5.5	2.4	0.0	0.7
12	Florida	17.5	13.3	6.1	7.2	4.8	6.1	1.4	1.1	4.1	0.4	1.7	1.3	0.0	0.7
13	Georgia.....................	14.7	11.5	5.3	6.2	4.2	5.4	1.1	0.8	3.2	0.4	1.4	0.9	0.0	0.5
15	Hawaii	13.3	9.9	5.1	4.9	3.9	3.9	1.2	1.0	3.4	0.4	1.4	1.2	0.0	0.5
16	Idaho........................	14.8	11.2	5.3	5.9	4.0	4.9	1.3	1.0	3.6	0.3	1.5	1.2	0.0	0.6
17	Illinois.......................	15.9	12.8	5.9	6.9	4.7	6.0	1.2	0.9	3.1	0.3	1.2	1.2	0.0	0.4
18	Indiana......................	16.0	12.8	6.1	6.7	4.8	5.8	1.2	0.9	3.2	0.2	1.2	1.3	0.0	0.6
19	Iowa	17.8	14.1	6.7	7.4	5.2	6.3	1.5	1.1	3.7	0.2	1.6	1.5	0.0	0.5
20	Kansas	16.6	13.2	6.2	7.0	4.9	6.0	1.3	1.0	3.4	0.2	1.5	1.1	0.0	0.5
21	Kentucky	15.8	12.8	5.8	7.0	4.7	6.1	1.1	0.9	2.9	0.1	1.1	1.2	0.0	0.5
22	Louisiana	15.9	12.8	6.1	6.7	5.0	5.8	1.1	0.8	3.1	0.2	1.3	1.1	0.0	0.5
23	Maine........................	20.1	15.6	7.1	8.5	5.3	6.9	1.8	1.6	4.5	0.3	1.3	2.3	0.0	0.6
24	Maryland	15.6	12.2	5.3	6.9	4.1	5.9	1.2	1.0	3.5	0.3	1.4	1.2	0.0	0.5
25	Massachusetts	18.2	13.9	6.1	7.8	4.6	6.4	1.5	1.4	4.3	0.3	2.0	1.5	0.0	0.4
26	Michigan	16.8	13.4	6.3	7.1	5.0	6.2	1.3	1.0	3.4	0.2	1.3	1.3	0.0	0.5
27	Minnesota	17.7	13.8	6.5	7.3	5.0	6.1	1.5	1.2	3.9	0.2	1.7	1.5	0.0	0.5
28	Mississippi.................	14.0	11.5	5.3	6.2	4.4	5.6	0.9	0.6	2.4	0.3	0.9	0.8	0.0	0.5
29	Missouri.....................	17.1	13.7	6.3	7.4	5.0	6.3	1.3	1.1	3.4	0.2	1.3	1.4	0.0	0.5
30	Montana.....................	19.0	14.9	7.4	7.5	5.9	6.3	1.5	1.2	4.1	0.3	1.8	1.6	0.0	0.5
31	Nebraska	17.2	13.9	6.6	7.2	5.2	6.2	1.4	1.0	3.4	0.2	1.4	1.3	0.0	0.5
32	Nevada	17.4	12.9	6.8	6.1	5.2	4.9	1.6	1.2	4.5	0.4	1.8	1.5	0.0	0.7
33	New Hampshire	16.8	13.0	6.1	6.8	4.5	5.5	1.6	1.3	3.8	0.2	1.1	2.0	0.0	0.5
34	New Jersey..................	13.6	11.0	4.8	6.2	3.8	5.5	1.0	0.8	2.6	0.3	0.8	1.0	0.0	0.5
35	New Mexico.................	16.0	12.8	6.1	6.6	4.9	5.6	1.2	1.0	3.2	0.3	1.1	1.4	0.0	0.4
36	New York....................	17.1	13.4	6.0	7.4	4.7	6.3	1.3	1.1	3.7	0.4	1.6	1.3	0.0	0.5
37	North Carolina	16.3	12.9	5.8	7.1	4.6	6.1	1.2	1.0	3.4	0.3	1.5	1.1	0.0	0.5
38	North Dakota..............	20.8	16.4	8.7	7.7	6.7	6.3	2.0	1.4	4.4	0.2	1.9	1.8	0.0	0.5
39	Ohio..........................	17.5	14.1	6.5	7.6	5.2	6.6	1.3	1.0	3.3	0.2	1.2	1.4	0.0	0.5
40	Oklahoma...................	15.9	12.7	6.0	6.7	4.9	5.8	1.2	0.9	3.2	0.2	1.3	1.0	0.0	0.6
41	Oregon	19.4	14.3	6.5	7.7	4.8	6.2	1.8	1.6	5.1	0.4	2.4	1.8	0.0	0.6
42	Pennsylvania	17.2	13.8	6.2	7.6	5.0	6.6	1.2	1.0	3.4	0.2	1.3	1.3	0.0	0.5
44	Rhode Island...............	18.7	14.6	6.6	7.9	5.0	6.8	1.6	1.1	4.1	0.4	1.6	1.6	0.0	0.5
45	South Carolina............	15.5	12.3	5.6	6.7	4.5	5.9	1.1	0.8	3.2	0.3	1.5	1.0	0.0	0.4
46	South Dakota..............	17.3	13.9	7.0	6.8	5.5	5.9	1.5	0.9	3.4	0.2	1.5	1.3	0.0	0.4
47	Tennessee	15.9	12.9	5.9	7.0	4.8	6.1	1.1	0.9	3.0	0.2	1.2	1.1	0.0	0.5
48	Texas........................	13.4	10.5	5.1	5.4	4.0	4.6	1.1	0.8	2.9	0.3	1.2	0.9	0.0	0.5
49	Utah.........................	11.1	7.8	3.9	4.0	2.9	3.3	1.0	0.7	3.2	0.4	1.7	0.7	0.0	0.4
50	Vermont	20.6	15.4	7.0	8.4	5.0	6.6	2.1	1.8	5.1	0.3	1.8	2.4	0.0	0.6
51	Virginia	15.9	12.1	5.5	6.6	4.2	5.6	1.3	1.0	3.8	0.4	1.7	1.2	0.0	0.5
53	Washington	18.2	13.6	6.6	7.0	4.9	5.7	1.7	1.3	4.5	0.4	2.0	1.7	0.0	0.5
54	West Virginia	17.2	14.1	6.5	7.6	5.4	6.7	1.1	0.9	3.2	0.2	1.0	1.3	0.0	0.6
55	Wisconsin	18.3	14.4	6.8	7.6	5.3	6.4	1.5	1.2	4.0	0.2	1.6	1.6	0.0	0.6
56	Wyoming....................	17.7	13.4	6.9	6.5	5.4	5.3	1.6	1.2	4.3	0.5	1.5	1.7	0.0	0.6

Table B-1: States—Relationships—*Continued*

FIPS state code	State	Total population in subfamilies	Population in subfamilies									
			In married couple subfamilies				In mother-child subfamily			In father-child subfamily		
			Total in married-couple subfamilies	Husband/wife in a childless subfamily	Husband/wife in a subfamily with children	Child in married-couple subfamily	Total in mother-child subfamilies	Parent in a mother-child subfamily	Child in a mother-child subfamily	Total in father-child subfamilies	Parent in a father-child subfamily	Child in a father-child subfamily
	United States..............	12,054,616	4,153,198	1,902,498	1,317,057	933,643	6,426,173	2,905,997	3,520,176	1,475,245	710,779	764,466
1	Alabama......................	198,713	48,340	20,139	17,028	11,173	125,633	58,557	67,076	24,740	12,658	12,082
2	Alaska........................	26,739	7,857	3,516	2,456	1,885	14,395	6,708	7,687	4,487	2,212	2,275
4	Arizona.......................	298,510	93,132	39,947	29,984	23,201	167,565	72,639	94,926	37,813	17,880	19,933
5	Arkansas.....................	108,132	32,221	13,528	11,637	7,056	59,719	26,895	32,824	16,192	7,439	8,753
6	California....................	2,071,762	909,345	439,404	267,565	202,376	938,726	410,840	527,886	223,691	102,036	121,655
8	Colorado	152,553	53,600	22,004	18,874	12,722	79,263	36,076	43,187	19,690	9,472	10,218
9	Connecticut.................	101,969	37,562	18,337	11,847	7,378	52,623	25,037	27,586	11,784	5,813	5,971
10	Delaware.....................	39,099	10,649	4,503	3,733	2,413	23,366	10,369	12,997	5,084	2,504	2,580
11	District of Columbia.......	20,119	2,197	1,196	551	450	14,595	6,492	8,103	3,327	1,697	1,630
12	Florida	802,641	279,138	147,254	85,249	46,635	426,640	209,488	217,152	96,863	51,434	45,429
13	Georgia	424,792	111,347	50,356	37,384	23,607	261,623	118,769	142,854	51,822	25,240	26,582
15	Hawaii	119,889	71,320	24,178	25,249	21,893	37,066	15,253	21,813	11,503	5,131	6,372
16	Idaho	44,700	17,297	6,508	6,117	4,672	20,459	9,392	11,067	6,944	3,117	3,827
17	Illinois	485,420	157,716	77,599	47,470	32,647	273,696	120,922	152,774	54,008	26,104	27,904
18	Indiana	200,204	56,782	21,076	20,712	14,994	117,095	52,985	64,110	26,327	12,697	13,630
19	Iowa	56,430	15,539	6,202	5,191	4,146	32,872	14,290	18,582	8,019	3,853	4,166
20	Kansas........................	75,571	20,595	8,222	6,908	5,465	43,576	18,596	24,980	11,400	5,048	6,352
21	Kentucky.....................	142,644	43,075	17,176	15,514	10,385	75,352	34,971	40,381	24,217	11,656	12,561
22	Louisiana	197,046	40,133	14,727	15,238	10,168	129,819	58,555	71,264	27,094	13,232	13,862
23	Maine	29,100	12,295	4,752	4,471	3,072	12,987	5,765	7,222	3,818	1,820	1,998
24	Maryland	241,563	73,670	34,027	23,517	16,126	137,675	62,672	75,003	30,218	14,619	15,599
25	Massachusetts	191,812	81,832	40,811	24,233	16,788	89,591	41,356	48,235	20,389	10,053	10,336
26	Michigan	294,414	92,459	39,367	30,486	22,606	164,384	75,823	88,561	37,571	18,550	19,021
27	Minnesota...................	102,759	32,398	15,153	9,925	7,320	54,893	24,611	30,282	15,468	7,133	8,335
28	Mississippi	150,298	27,140	11,518	9,466	6,156	103,607	46,489	57,118	19,551	9,693	9,858
29	Missouri	173,118	49,227	19,745	16,974	12,508	94,836	42,761	52,075	29,055	13,348	15,707
30	Montana.....................	23,681	7,891	3,376	2,623	1,892	12,952	5,930	7,022	2,838	1,414	1,424
31	Nebraska	38,089	10,801	3,491	3,986	3,324	22,151	9,687	12,464	5,137	2,171	2,966
32	Nevada.......................	120,455	49,229	24,662	14,765	9,802	56,952	27,049	29,903	14,274	7,317	6,957
33	New Hampshire.............	30,217	12,342	5,138	4,111	3,093	13,468	6,222	7,246	4,407	2,080	2,327
34	New Jersey...................	315,605	130,220	71,552	34,607	24,061	154,533	70,463	84,070	30,852	14,668	16,184
35	New Mexico.................	102,750	27,824	12,110	9,542	6,172	60,975	28,705	32,270	13,951	6,874	7,077
36	New York	775,498	302,224	152,834	87,550	61,840	390,216	178,452	211,764	83,058	39,242	43,816
37	North Carolina.............	329,018	84,324	35,660	28,777	19,887	198,886	90,969	107,917	45,808	23,150	22,658
38	North Dakota...............	11,566	2,389	1,101	669	619	7,827	2,949	4,878	1,350	618	732
39	Ohio	324,323	85,625	36,298	28,255	21,072	191,218	85,960	105,258	47,480	22,229	25,251
40	Oklahoma...................	134,802	41,840	17,870	14,315	9,655	71,991	32,913	39,078	20,971	9,943	11,028
41	Oregon.......................	108,795	45,376	17,635	15,904	11,837	49,944	23,510	26,434	13,475	6,420	7,055
42	Pennsylvania	384,143	113,742	55,512	33,881	24,349	219,550	98,620	120,930	50,851	25,026	25,825
44	Rhode Island...............	31,284	11,725	5,330	3,731	2,664	16,555	7,616	8,939	3,004	1,263	1,741
45	South Carolina.............	194,810	40,431	17,355	13,743	9,333	129,073	59,271	69,802	25,306	12,627	12,679
46	South Dakota...............	20,986	5,236	2,004	1,732	1,500	11,673	4,888	6,785	4,077	1,802	2,275
47	Tennessee...................	237,995	66,507	26,652	23,370	16,485	137,054	61,577	75,477	34,434	17,226	17,208
48	Texas.........................	1,309,022	432,719	178,870	147,613	106,236	724,630	320,265	404,365	151,673	73,039	78,634
49	Utah	122,671	60,235	20,158	21,986	18,091	51,806	22,525	29,281	10,630	4,938	5,692
50	Vermont	11,228	3,711	1,611	1,168	932	5,905	2,495	3,410	1,612	752	860
51	Virginia......................	292,683	100,777	46,929	32,436	21,412	158,063	72,587	85,476	33,843	16,548	17,295
53	Washington	197,055	78,434	38,815	23,203	16,416	91,440	42,371	49,029	27,221	13,121	14,100
54	West Virginia	61,083	22,707	9,065	8,172	5,470	29,870	14,017	15,853	8,506	4,311	4,195
55	Wisconsin	114,222	35,866	15,630	11,447	8,789	60,786	27,408	33,378	17,570	8,498	9,072
56	Wyoming.....................	12,638	4,157	1,595	1,692	870	6,639	3,237	3,402	1,842	1,063	779

Table B-1: States—Relationships—*Continued*

FIPS state code	State	Total population in subfamilies	In married couple subfamilies				In mother-child subfamily			In father-child subfamily		
			Total in married-couple subfamilies	Husband/wife in a childless subfamily	Husband/wife in a subfamily with children	Child in married-couple subfamily	Total in mother-child subfamilies	Parent in a mother-child subfamily	Child in a mother-child subfamily	Total in father-child subfamilies	Parent in a father-child subfamily	Child in a father-child subfamily
	United States............	3.8	1.3	0.6	0.4	0.3	2.0	0.9	1.1	0.5	0.2	0.2
1	Alabama......................	4.1	1.0	0.4	0.4	0.2	2.6	1.2	1.4	0.5	0.3	0.3
2	Alaska........................	3.7	1.1	0.5	0.3	0.3	2.0	0.9	1.1	0.6	0.3	0.3
4	Arizona......................	4.6	1.4	0.6	0.5	0.4	2.6	1.1	1.4	0.6	0.3	0.3
5	Arkansas.....................	3.7	1.1	0.5	0.4	0.2	2.0	0.9	1.1	0.5	0.3	0.3
6	California...................	5.5	2.4	1.2	0.7	0.5	2.5	1.1	1.4	0.6	0.3	0.3
8	Colorado	2.9	1.0	0.4	0.4	0.2	1.5	0.7	0.8	0.4	0.2	0.2
9	Connecticut.................	2.8	1.0	0.5	0.3	0.2	1.5	0.7	0.8	0.3	0.2	0.2
10	Delaware.....................	4.3	1.2	0.5	0.4	0.3	2.5	1.1	1.4	0.6	0.3	0.3
11	District of Columbia........	3.2	0.3	0.2	0.1	0.1	2.3	1.0	1.3	0.5	0.3	0.3
12	Florida......................	4.2	1.4	0.8	0.4	0.2	2.2	1.1	1.1	0.5	0.3	0.2
13	Georgia	4.3	1.1	0.5	0.4	0.2	2.6	1.2	1.4	0.5	0.3	0.3
15	Hawaii	8.6	5.1	1.7	1.8	1.6	2.7	1.1	1.6	0.8	0.4	0.5
16	Idaho	2.8	1.1	0.4	0.4	0.3	1.3	0.6	0.7	0.4	0.2	0.2
17	Illinois	3.8	1.2	0.6	0.4	0.3	2.1	0.9	1.2	0.4	0.2	0.2
18	Indiana	3.1	0.9	0.3	0.3	0.2	1.8	0.8	1.0	0.4	0.2	0.2
19	Iowa	1.8	0.5	0.2	0.2	0.1	1.1	0.5	0.6	0.3	0.1	0.1
20	Kansas	2.6	0.7	0.3	0.2	0.2	1.5	0.6	0.9	0.4	0.2	0.2
21	Kentucky.....................	3.3	1.0	0.4	0.4	0.2	1.7	0.8	0.9	0.6	0.3	0.3
22	Louisiana....................	4.3	0.9	0.3	0.3	0.2	2.8	1.3	1.5	0.6	0.3	0.3
23	Maine........................	2.2	0.9	0.4	0.3	0.2	1.0	0.4	0.5	0.3	0.1	0.2
24	Maryland	4.1	1.3	0.6	0.4	0.3	2.3	1.1	1.3	0.5	0.2	0.3
25	Massachusetts................	2.9	1.2	0.6	0.4	0.3	1.3	0.6	0.7	0.3	0.2	0.2
26	Michigan	3.0	0.9	0.4	0.3	0.2	1.7	0.8	0.9	0.4	0.2	0.2
27	Minnesota....................	1.9	0.6	0.3	0.2	0.1	1.0	0.5	0.6	0.3	0.1	0.2
28	Mississippi..................	5.0	0.9	0.4	0.3	0.2	3.5	1.6	1.9	0.7	0.3	0.3
29	Missouri.....................	2.9	0.8	0.3	0.3	0.2	1.6	0.7	0.9	0.5	0.2	0.3
30	Montana......................	2.4	0.8	0.3	0.3	0.2	1.3	0.6	0.7	0.3	0.1	0.1
31	Nebraska	2.1	0.6	0.2	0.2	0.2	1.2	0.5	0.7	0.3	0.1	0.2
32	Nevada	4.4	1.8	0.9	0.5	0.4	2.1	1.0	1.1	0.5	0.3	0.3
33	New Hampshire	2.3	0.9	0.4	0.3	0.2	1.0	0.5	0.5	0.3	0.2	0.2
34	New Jersey...................	3.6	1.5	0.8	0.4	0.3	1.7	0.8	0.9	0.3	0.2	0.2
35	New Mexico...................	4.9	1.3	0.6	0.5	0.3	2.9	1.4	1.5	0.7	0.3	0.3
36	New York.....................	4.0	1.5	0.8	0.4	0.3	2.0	0.9	1.1	0.4	0.2	0.2
37	North Carolina..............	3.4	0.9	0.4	0.3	0.2	2.0	0.9	1.1	0.5	0.2	0.2
38	North Dakota................	1.6	0.3	0.2	0.1	0.1	1.1	0.4	0.7	0.2	0.1	0.1
39	Ohio.........................	2.8	0.7	0.3	0.2	0.2	1.7	0.7	0.9	0.4	0.2	0.2
40	Oklahoma.....................	3.5	1.1	0.5	0.4	0.3	1.9	0.9	1.0	0.5	0.3	0.3
41	Oregon.......................	2.8	1.2	0.5	0.4	0.3	1.3	0.6	0.7	0.3	0.2	0.2
42	Pennsylvania	3.0	0.9	0.4	0.3	0.2	1.7	0.8	0.9	0.4	0.2	0.2
44	Rhode Island.................	3.0	1.1	0.5	0.4	0.3	1.6	0.7	0.9	0.3	0.1	0.2
45	South Carolina..............	4.1	0.9	0.4	0.3	0.2	2.7	1.3	1.5	0.5	0.3	0.3
46	South Dakota................	2.5	0.6	0.2	0.2	0.2	1.4	0.6	0.8	0.5	0.2	0.3
47	Tennessee	3.7	1.0	0.4	0.4	0.3	2.1	1.0	1.2	0.5	0.3	0.3
48	Texas........................	5.0	1.7	0.7	0.6	0.4	2.8	1.2	1.6	0.6	0.3	0.3
49	Utah.........................	4.3	2.1	0.7	0.8	0.6	1.8	0.8	1.0	0.4	0.2	0.2
50	Vermont	1.8	0.6	0.3	0.2	0.1	0.9	0.4	0.5	0.3	0.1	0.1
51	Virginia.....................	3.6	1.2	0.6	0.4	0.3	1.9	0.9	1.0	0.4	0.2	0.2
53	Washington	2.9	1.1	0.6	0.3	0.2	1.3	0.6	0.7	0.4	0.2	0.2
54	West Virginia	3.3	1.2	0.5	0.4	0.3	1.6	0.8	0.9	0.5	0.2	0.2
55	Wisconsin....................	2.0	0.6	0.3	0.2	0.2	1.1	0.5	0.6	0.3	0.1	0.2
56	Wyoming......................	2.2	0.7	0.3	0.3	0.2	1.2	0.6	0.6	0.3	0.2	0.1

This page is intentionally left blank

Table B-2: Counties with a Population of 50,000 or More—Relationships

State/ county FIPS code	State/county	Total population	Percent of the population in households	Population in family households, percent					
				Percent in family households	Householder in family household, percent	Spouse in family household, percent	Child in family household (biological, adopted, or stepchild)	Other relative in family household	Nonrelatives in family household
00000	**United States**................................	313,861,723	97.4	81.4	24.4	17.8	29.9	7.2	2.2
01000	**Alabama**..........................	4,817,624	97.6	82.6	25.7	18.2	29.8	7.4	1.6
01001	Autauga County.........................	55,263	99.2	85.6	25.2	20.0	31.1	8.1	1.2
01003	Baldwin County	190,981	98.6	84.2	27.0	21.3	28.3	6.4	1.1
01009	Blount County	57,807	98.9	88.4	27.0	21.6	30.9	7.3	1.6
01015	Calhoun County.........................	117,253	97.8	82.0	25.4	17.7	28.4	8.7	1.7
01031	Coffee County............................	50,906	98.8	84.2	25.4	18.2	31.6	7.1	2.0
01033	Colbert County...........................	54,450	99.2	84.4	27.3	19.9	28.5	7.5	1.2
01043	Cullman County..........................	80,566	98.7	85.6	28.0	21.3	28.2	6.9	1.3
01045	Dale County...............................	50,106	97.7	80.9	25.5	18.0	29.2	7.1	1.1
01049	DeKalb County...........................	71,137	98.8	88.0	24.7	20.1	33.2	8.3	1.8
01051	Elmore County...........................	80,443	93.5	82.7	25.5	19.6	30.3	5.8	1.5
01055	Etowah County	104,188	98.5	84.8	26.7	18.8	29.4	7.9	1.9
01069	Houston County	103,112	99.0	83.7	25.6	18.0	31.6	7.1	1.4
01071	Jackson County	53,078	98.8	85.8	26.1	20.7	31.1	6.8	1.1
01073	Jefferson County.........................	658,601	97.7	80.7	25.0	16.6	30.0	7.7	1.4
01077	Lauderdale County......................	92,693	98.0	80.8	27.3	21.3	26.0	4.7	1.4
01081	Lee County................................	147,537	96.4	74.7	23.7	17.3	26.2	5.7	1.8
01083	Limestone County.......................	87,255	94.9	83.9	27.2	21.2	29.3	5.0	1.3
01089	Madison County..........................	343,112	97.8	81.5	25.6	18.8	29.4	5.9	1.8
01095	Marshall County..........................	94,365	98.9	87.3	25.8	19.3	32.8	7.8	1.6
01097	Mobile County	413,553	97.6	83.5	25.3	16.5	31.3	9.0	1.5
01101	Montgomery County	229,162	96.8	79.8	24.4	14.4	31.1	7.8	2.0
01103	Morgan County...........................	119,953	98.6	84.3	26.3	19.7	30.6	6.2	1.5
01113	Russell County............................	57,438	98.9	81.8	24.5	15.2	30.0	10.6	1.6
01115	St. Clair County..........................	85,261	97.8	85.8	27.5	21.6	27.8	7.1	1.8
01117	Shelby County............................	201,093	98.6	86.3	26.4	21.6	32.0	5.1	1.1
01121	Talladega County........................	81,503	96.2	82.4	27.2	17.9	28.1	7.6	1.7
01125	Tuscaloosa County	198,762	94.8	78.7	22.7	16.0	30.8	7.6	1.6
01127	Walker County............................	66,257	98.6	85.1	27.5	19.8	28.2	7.4	2.3
02000	**Alaska**	729,603	96.4	81.2	23.0	17.1	31.6	6.5	3.1
02020	Anchorage Municipality	298,384	97.3	81.2	23.1	17.0	31.6	6.4	3.1
02090	Fairbanks North Star Borough	99,951	96.1	78.2	22.3	17.4	31.3	4.7	2.5
02122	Kenai Peninsula Borough	56,812	96.8	81.3	25.2	20.0	29.0	4.4	2.6
02170	Matanuska-Susitna Borough	93,641	98.3	85.9	24.2	19.2	33.1	6.5	2.9
04000	**Arizona**	6,548,856	97.7	81.4	23.8	17.2	29.9	7.9	2.6
04001	Apache County...........................	72,378	98.2	88.5	18.1	10.6	41.0	16.2	2.5
04003	Cochise County...........................	131,232	90.8	75.8	24.4	18.2	25.6	5.8	1.8
04005	Coconino County.........................	135,522	93.1	74.4	22.1	15.5	25.8	8.1	2.9
04007	Gila County...............................	53,201	98.3	81.9	25.2	18.2	26.1	10.7	1.7
04013	Maricopa County	3,939,668	98.7	82.2	23.6	16.8	31.1	7.9	2.8
04015	Mohave County..........................	202,857	95.7	76.3	24.8	19.1	23.1	6.8	2.5
04017	Navajo County............................	107,144	97.8	87.2	22.7	14.7	34.2	12.8	2.7
04019	Pima County..............................	992,286	97.5	78.1	23.9	16.8	27.7	7.2	2.5
04021	Pinal County..............................	386,687	94.4	83.0	23.6	17.8	30.7	8.3	2.6
04025	Yavapai County..........................	212,843	98.5	79.0	27.1	21.6	21.4	6.5	2.3
04027	Yuma County.............................	201,595	95.9	86.4	27.1	20.1	31.1	6.1	1.9
05000	**Arkansas**	2,949,238	97.2	81.7	25.6	18.8	28.7	6.8	1.8
05007	Benton County...........................	232,560	98.8	87.0	26.4	21.8	32.0	5.3	1.6
05031	Craighead County.......................	99,927	96.4	79.9	25.8	17.9	27.8	6.5	1.9
05033	Crawford County.........................	61,801	99.0	88.6	28.6	21.2	29.7	6.6	2.5
05035	Crittenden County.......................	50,117	98.5	86.0	25.4	14.4	34.3	9.8	2.1
05045	Faulkner County.........................	118,233	96.0	79.5	24.8	19.0	29.6	4.1	1.9
05051	Garland County..........................	96,900	97.8	79.0	26.1	18.9	24.1	7.6	2.3
05069	Jefferson County.........................	74,611	91.9	75.6	23.8	14.6	27.5	8.1	1.7
05085	Lonoke County...........................	70,051	99.1	87.3	26.5	20.4	31.5	7.1	1.9
05115	Pope County..............................	62,611	94.5	80.3	24.5	18.7	28.8	6.4	1.8
05119	Pulaski County...........................	389,001	98.5	79.3	23.4	15.7	30.4	8.1	1.6
05125	Saline County	112,083	98.7	85.1	26.5	20.7	28.9	7.2	1.9
05131	Sebastian County........................	127,243	98.7	82.0	25.4	18.7	29.9	6.5	1.6
05143	Washington County......................	211,919	96.4	77.4	23.9	17.8	27.8	6.6	1.4
05145	White County.............................	78,404	95.5	82.5	26.5	20.8	27.5	5.1	2.6
06000	**California**	38,000,360	97.9	83.5	22.6	16.1	31.6	10.1	3.0
06001	Alameda County.........................	1,554,725	97.9	80.7	23.1	16.7	28.9	9.5	2.6
06007	Butte County.............................	221,006	97.5	74.1	22.9	16.0	26.2	6.1	3.0
06013	Contra Costa County....................	1,079,460	99.0	85.5	24.9	18.8	31.2	8.2	2.4
06017	El Dorado County........................	181,095	99.0	84.8	26.1	22.1	29.0	5.9	1.7
06019	Fresno County............................	947,942	98.1	86.9	22.4	14.3	36.4	10.3	3.4
06023	Humboldt County........................	134,768	96.8	71.9	22.0	15.7	24.5	6.6	3.1
06025	Imperial County..........................	176,416	93.7	85.5	20.8	13.8	35.1	13.8	1.9
06029	Kern County..............................	856,363	96.4	86.7	22.5	15.2	35.9	9.8	3.3
06031	Kings County.............................	151,445	87.3	78.6	21.1	13.9	33.3	7.4	2.9
06033	Lake County..............................	64,040	98.5	77.7	25.7	17.4	22.8	7.4	4.4
06037	Los Angeles County.....................	9,951,320	98.2	83.6	21.7	14.3	32.1	12.3	3.2

Table B-2: Counties with a Population of 50,000 or More—Relationships—*Continued*

State/county FIPS code	State/county	Population in nonfamily households						Population in subfamilies as a percent of total population					
		Total population in nonfamily households	Nonfamily householders				Nonrelatives in nonfamily households	Total population in subfamilies	In married couple subfamilies			Parent in a parent-child subfamily	Child in a parent-child subfamily
			Total	Male living alone	Female living alone	Householder living with nonrelatives			Total in married-couple subfamilies	Spouse in a married-couple subfamily	Child in married-couple subfamily		
00000	**United States**	16.1	12.5	4.5	5.7	2.3	3.6	3.8	1.3	1.0	0.3	1.2	1.4
01000	**Alabama**	15.0	12.5	4.8	6.1	1.5	2.5	4.1	1.0	0.8	0.2	1.5	1.6
01001	Autauga County	13.5	11.3	4.8	4.7	1.7	2.3	4.2	1.3	1.2	0.2	1.4	1.4
01003	Baldwin County	14.4	11.6	4.3	5.8	1.6	2.8	3.9	1.1	0.8	0.3	1.3	1.6
01009	Blount County	10.5	9.4	4.2	4.4	0.8	1.1	4.6	1.4	1.2	0.2	1.7	1.5
01015	Calhoun County	15.8	12.8	4.7	6.3	1.8	3.0	5.5	1.6	1.3	0.4	1.8	2.0
01031	Coffee County	14.6	12.2	5.3	5.5	1.4	2.4	4.3	0.9	0.7	0.2	1.8	1.7
01033	Colbert County	14.8	13.2	5.3	6.6	1.3	1.7	4.0	1.3	1.0	0.3	1.3	1.4
01043	Cullman County	13.0	11.4	4.7	5.5	1.2	1.6	3.7	1.7	1.4	0.3	1.0	1.0
01045	Dale County	16.8	13.1	5.2	6.0	1.9	3.6	3.7	0.9	0.8	0.1	1.4	1.4
01049	DeKalb County	10.8	9.5	3.9	4.8	0.8	1.4	3.1	1.2	1.0	0.2	0.9	1.0
01051	Elmore County	10.8	9.8	3.5	5.4	0.9	1.1	3.2	0.9	0.8	0.2	1.1	1.2
01055	Etowah County	13.7	11.6	4.3	6.0	1.3	2.1	5.7	2.2	1.6	0.5	1.7	1.8
01069	Houston County	15.3	12.6	4.7	6.3	1.5	2.7	3.7	0.7	0.7	0.1	1.6	1.3
01071	Jackson County	13.0	11.6	4.6	6.1	0.9	1.4	3.1	1.6	1.2	0.3	0.9	0.6
01073	Jefferson County	17.0	14.2	5.4	7.0	1.7	2.8	4.1	0.9	0.7	0.2	1.5	1.7
01077	Lauderdale County	17.2	14.4	4.6	7.8	2.0	2.8	2.0	0.2	0.2	0.0	0.8	0.9
01081	Lee County	21.7	14.5	5.0	5.5	4.0	7.3	0.0	0.0	0.0	0.0	0.0	0.0
01083	Limestone County	10.9	9.9	4.0	5.2	0.7	1.0	3.2	1.0	0.7	0.4	1.0	1.2
01089	Madison County	16.3	13.7	5.6	6.3	1.7	2.6	3.1	0.9	0.7	0.2	1.1	1.1
01095	Marshall County	11.6	10.0	3.7	5.3	1.0	1.5	4.1	1.2	1.1	0.2	1.4	1.4
01097	Mobile County	14.1	12.0	4.6	5.9	1.5	2.1	5.3	1.0	0.7	0.2	2.0	2.4
01101	Montgomery County	17.0	14.2	5.3	7.0	1.9	2.9	4.3	0.5	0.4	0.1	1.7	2.1
01103	Morgan County	14.3	12.1	4.8	5.9	1.4	2.1	3.3	1.0	0.8	0.2	1.0	1.3
01113	Russell County	17.1	13.9	5.6	6.5	1.8	3.2	7.1	1.5	1.2	0.3	2.3	3.3
01115	St. Clair County	12.0	9.9	3.6	4.7	1.6	2.1	4.2	0.9	0.5	0.4	1.7	1.6
01117	Shelby County	12.4	10.5	4.0	5.4	1.1	1.9	2.2	1.0	0.8	0.2	0.7	0.6
01121	Talladega County	13.7	11.7	4.5	5.9	1.3	2.1	4.0	1.3	1.0	0.3	1.3	1.4
01125	Tuscaloosa County	16.1	11.6	4.0	5.6	2.1	4.4	4.2	1.5	1.2	0.3	1.4	1.3
01127	Walker County	13.5	11.5	4.3	5.7	1.4	2.1	4.7	1.4	0.9	0.4	1.5	1.7
02000	**Alaska**	15.2	11.4	4.9	4.0	2.5	3.7	3.7	1.1	0.8	0.3	1.2	1.4
02020	Anchorage Municipality	16.1	12.0	4.7	4.5	2.8	4.1	3.4	1.1	1.0	0.2	1.0	1.2
02090	Fairbanks North Star Borough	17.9	13.3	5.9	4.5	3.0	4.6	2.5	0.7	0.5	0.2	0.9	0.9
02122	Kenai Peninsula Borough	15.5	12.5	5.9	4.5	2.1	3.0	1.5	0.5	0.4	0.1	0.6	0.4
02170	Matanuska-Susitna Borough	12.4	9.3	4.1	3.1	2.1	3.1	3.4	1.4	1.0	0.4	1.0	1.0
04000	**Arizona**	16.4	12.5	4.7	5.3	2.6	3.9	4.6	1.4	1.1	0.4	1.4	1.8
04001	Apache County	9.7	8.3	4.1	3.4	0.9	1.4	10.6	1.8	1.3	0.6	4.1	4.7
04003	Cochise County	15.0	12.8	4.9	6.0	2.0	2.2	3.2	1.1	0.8	0.4	0.9	1.2
04005	Coconino County	18.6	12.3	4.3	4.0	4.1	6.3	6.0	0.7	0.5	0.2	1.9	3.3
04007	Gila County	16.3	13.7	6.0	6.1	1.7	2.6	6.8	2.1	1.7	0.4	2.1	2.5
04013	Maricopa County	16.5	12.4	4.6	5.2	2.6	4.1	4.5	1.6	1.2	0.4	1.3	1.6
04015	Mohave County	19.4	14.7	5.5	5.8	3.4	4.7	3.6	1.0	0.9	0.2	1.1	1.5
04017	Navajo County	10.6	9.2	4.3	3.9	1.0	1.4	9.0	1.9	1.3	0.6	3.1	4.1
04019	Pima County	19.4	14.9	5.5	6.5	2.9	4.5	3.7	1.0	0.7	0.3	1.2	1.6
04021	Pinal County	11.4	8.8	3.4	3.8	1.6	2.6	4.4	1.3	1.1	0.2	1.6	1.5
04025	Yavapai County	19.5	16.2	5.8	7.8	2.6	3.2	4.0	1.3	1.0	0.3	1.1	1.6
04027	Yuma County	9.5	7.9	3.3	3.3	1.3	1.6	4.8	1.6	0.9	0.6	1.0	2.2
05000	**Arkansas**	15.6	12.7	4.8	6.0	1.9	2.9	3.7	1.1	0.9	0.2	1.2	1.4
05007	Benton County	11.8	9.2	3.2	4.2	1.7	2.6	2.9	1.1	0.8	0.3	0.9	0.9
05031	Craighead County	16.5	12.3	3.6	5.5	3.2	4.3	3.0	1.2	0.9	0.4	0.9	0.9
05033	Crawford County	10.4	9.7	4.0	5.0	0.7	0.7	4.6	0.8	0.7	0.1	1.6	2.2
05035	Crittenden County	12.6	11.2	4.7	5.3	1.2	1.4	5.8	1.0	0.7	0.3	1.9	2.8
05045	Faulkner County	16.5	11.7	4.0	4.7	2.9	4.9	2.4	0.9	0.7	0.2	0.8	0.7
05051	Garland County	18.8	14.9	5.2	6.8	2.8	3.9	4.1	1.3	1.1	0.3	1.3	1.4
05069	Jefferson County	16.3	14.3	6.1	6.9	1.3	2.0	5.4	0.6	0.5	0.2	1.9	2.9
05085	Lonoke County	11.8	9.6	3.9	4.1	1.6	2.2	4.2	1.6	1.1	0.5	1.1	1.5
05115	Pope County	14.3	11.6	4.5	5.5	1.6	2.6	3.4	1.5	1.4	0.1	0.9	0.9
05119	Pulaski County	19.2	15.6	5.8	7.7	2.2	3.6	3.4	0.7	0.5	0.2	1.3	1.4
05125	Saline County	13.6	10.8	4.0	5.1	1.7	2.7	3.6	1.1	1.0	0.1	1.3	1.2
05131	Sebastian County	16.7	13.4	5.0	6.6	1.9	3.3	3.9	1.5	1.2	0.4	1.1	1.3
05143	Washington County	19.0	14.2	5.4	5.3	3.5	4.8	3.1	1.3	0.9	0.4	0.6	1.1
05145	White County	13.0	10.9	3.8	5.7	1.5	2.1	2.6	0.7	0.5	0.2	0.9	1.0
06000	**California**	14.4	10.5	3.6	4.4	2.4	3.9	5.5	2.4	1.9	0.5	1.3	1.7
06001	Alameda County	17.2	12.4	4.1	5.3	2.9	4.8	4.7	2.4	2.0	0.4	1.1	1.3
06007	Butte County	23.4	15.4	4.7	6.5	4.3	8.0	2.8	1.3	1.1	0.2	0.8	0.8
06013	Contra Costa County	13.5	10.3	3.4	4.8	2.1	3.2	3.9	1.7	1.4	0.3	1.0	1.2
06017	El Dorado County	14.2	10.9	4.1	4.7	2.2	3.3	3.1	1.5	1.1	0.4	0.8	0.9
06019	Fresno County	11.2	8.3	2.9	3.6	1.8	2.9	5.9	2.2	1.6	0.5	1.6	2.2
06023	Humboldt County	24.9	16.7	6.1	6.1	4.5	8.2	2.8	0.7	0.6	0.1	1.2	0.9
06025	Imperial County	8.2	6.2	2.4	2.7	1.1	2.0	9.4	3.0	2.5	0.5	2.6	3.8
06029	Kern County	9.7	7.4	2.9	3.0	1.5	2.3	5.6	1.9	1.4	0.5	1.7	2.0
06031	Kings County	8.6	6.0	2.1	2.4	1.4	2.7	4.5	1.4	1.0	0.4	1.3	1.8
06033	Lake County	20.7	16.2	6.5	5.7	4.0	4.5	3.2	1.0	0.7	0.3	0.9	1.2
06037	Los Angeles County	14.7	10.8	3.9	4.6	2.4	3.9	6.4	2.8	2.2	0.6	1.6	2.1

Table B-2: Counties with a Population of 50,000 or More—Relationships—*Continued*

State/county FIPS code	State/county	Total population	Percent of the population in households	Population in family households, percent					
				Percent in family households	Householder in family household, percent	Spouse in family household, percent	Child in family household (biological, adopted, or stepchild)	Other relative in family household	Nonrelatives in family household
	California—cont'd								
06039	Madera County.........................	152,255	94.1	85.6	21.1	15.2	33.6	11.5	4.1
06041	Marin County...........................	256,486	96.7	77.7	25.0	20.0	26.4	4.1	2.2
06045	Mendocino County....................	87,333	97.3	77.8	23.1	16.9	26.2	7.7	4.0
06047	Merced County.........................	261,493	97.9	88.5	22.3	14.9	38.7	9.7	3.0
06053	Monterey County......................	425,414	95.2	84.2	21.3	15.4	32.0	11.3	4.3
06055	Napa County............................	139,042	96.5	81.9	24.3	18.3	29.6	6.9	2.8
06057	Nevada County.........................	98,394	98.8	78.6	26.2	21.1	25.6	3.8	1.9
06059	Orange County.........................	3,084,550	98.6	85.8	23.3	17.6	31.6	10.1	3.3
06061	Placer County...........................	361,892	98.9	84.9	26.2	20.9	30.7	5.1	2.0
06065	Riverside County.......................	2,264,491	98.5	87.7	22.4	16.3	34.7	11.2	3.1
06067	Sacramento County...................	1,448,487	98.3	81.6	23.1	15.7	31.1	8.7	3.0
06069	San Benito County.....................	56,867	99.4	91.3	23.6	17.9	34.8	12.1	2.7
06071	San Bernardino County..............	2,076,322	97.8	88.5	22.0	15.0	36.4	11.7	3.4
06073	San Diego County.....................	3,175,313	97.2	80.9	22.6	16.7	30.1	8.9	2.6
06075	San Francisco County................	826,626	97.6	62.5	19.1	13.9	18.2	9.0	2.3
06077	San Joaquin County..................	700,220	97.8	87.4	22.9	15.8	35.4	10.3	3.0
06079	San Luis Obispo County.............	274,106	94.2	73.3	23.7	18.8	24.0	4.7	1.9
06081	San Mateo County.....................	738,114	98.7	83.5	23.7	18.4	29.7	9.1	2.6
06083	Santa Barbara County................	430,616	95.7	78.0	21.5	16.0	28.0	8.5	4.0
06085	Santa Clara County...................	1,836,454	98.2	84.9	23.9	18.6	30.0	9.5	2.9
06087	Santa Cruz County....................	266,908	95.7	75.8	22.0	16.7	27.8	6.0	3.2
06089	Shasta County..........................	178,422	98.4	80.7	25.5	18.7	27.4	5.9	3.1
06095	Solano County..........................	420,628	97.3	84.2	24.0	16.8	31.5	9.0	3.0
06097	Sonoma County........................	491,057	98.1	79.0	23.7	17.6	28.3	6.4	3.0
06099	Stanislaus County.....................	521,597	98.9	87.8	23.8	16.3	35.0	9.5	3.2
06101	Sutter County...........................	94,916	98.9	87.8	24.8	17.6	32.5	10.1	2.9
06103	Tehama County.........................	63,220	98.6	84.5	25.7	19.0	28.4	8.0	3.4
06107	Tulare County...........................	450,964	98.7	90.0	23.0	15.5	37.3	10.5	3.7
06109	Tuolumne County......................	54,209	93.5	77.7	27.2	20.9	20.9	5.9	2.8
06111	Ventura County........................	834,880	98.6	87.0	23.4	17.7	32.5	9.9	3.4
06113	Yolo County.............................	203,504	96.1	73.4	21.5	16.1	27.6	6.4	1.7
06115	Yuba County............................	72,958	98.3	85.9	24.6	17.2	32.4	8.4	3.3
08000	**Colorado**	5,192,076	97.7	79.3	24.5	18.8	28.4	5.5	2.1
08001	Adams County..........................	460,320	99.1	85.9	23.6	17.0	33.0	9.3	3.1
08005	Arapahoe County......................	596,249	99.3	82.7	24.8	18.1	30.9	6.4	2.5
08013	Boulder County........................	305,284	96.7	72.0	23.4	18.5	24.7	3.4	1.9
08014	Broomfield County....................	58,325	99.4	83.9	25.8	21.2	31.3	3.6	2.1
08031	Denver County..........................	634,685	97.6	67.5	20.1	13.9	24.6	7.1	1.8
08035	Douglas County........................	298,924	99.8	89.4	27.2	23.3	34.2	3.1	1.5
08037	Eagle County............................	52,050	99.9	77.6	21.9	18.3	29.0	5.9	2.5
08041	El Paso County..........................	645,787	97.4	82.3	25.3	19.6	30.3	4.8	2.2
08045	Garfield County........................	56,753	98.0	83.8	25.1	20.2	31.9	4.6	1.9
08059	Jefferson County.......................	545,384	98.4	80.0	26.2	20.3	27.3	4.4	1.8
08067	La Plata County........................	52,539	96.4	73.9	24.5	19.7	23.9	3.4	2.3
08069	Larimer County.........................	310,604	97.1	74.9	24.8	20.0	24.7	3.7	1.7
08077	Mesa County............................	147,614	97.4	80.6	26.7	20.2	26.5	4.8	2.4
08101	Pueblo County..........................	160,951	97.0	79.8	24.6	17.2	28.9	6.7	2.4
08123	Weld County............................	263,884	97.4	84.2	25.1	19.7	30.7	6.1	2.5
09000	**Connecticut**	3,592,264	96.7	81.0	24.9	18.4	30.0	5.8	1.9
09001	Fairfield County........................	933,794	98.0	84.0	24.5	18.8	32.0	6.7	2.0
09003	Hartford County.......................	897,426	96.9	80.5	25.1	17.6	30.1	5.9	1.8
09005	Litchfield County......................	187,795	98.2	82.1	26.7	21.7	27.8	4.0	1.8
09007	Middlesex County.....................	165,741	96.2	79.7	26.1	21.1	27.4	3.8	1.3
09009	New Haven County....................	863,217	96.6	80.2	24.4	17.2	30.5	6.3	1.9
09011	New London County..................	274,239	95.3	78.9	25.6	19.0	27.5	4.7	2.0
09013	Tolland County.........................	152,097	89.3	74.3	24.0	18.7	26.5	3.3	1.8
09015	Windham County......................	117,955	95.4	79.7	25.1	18.0	28.6	4.8	3.3
10000	**Delaware**	916,929	97.3	81.5	24.7	17.8	28.6	7.7	2.7
10001	Kent County.............................	167,382	97.0	83.0	24.7	17.6	30.9	7.2	2.7
10003	New Castle County....................	546,059	96.9	80.7	24.4	17.3	29.2	7.5	2.4
10005	Sussex County..........................	203,488	98.5	82.3	25.6	19.2	25.4	8.8	3.4
11000	**District of Columbia**	633,167	93.6	60.0	18.1	9.6	21.9	8.3	2.1
11001	District of Columbia..................	633,167	93.6	60.0	18.1	9.6	21.9	8.3	2.1
12000	**Florida**	19,319,031	97.8	80.3	23.8	17.2	28.3	8.7	2.4
12001	Alachua County........................	251,635	94.0	63.8	19.9	14.2	21.9	6.1	1.7
12005	Bay County..............................	172,251	98.3	80.3	25.3	18.7	27.3	6.4	2.7
12009	Brevard County........................	547,403	98.8	80.5	25.3	18.7	27.1	7.2	2.2
12011	Broward County.......................	1,812,793	99.1	81.4	22.9	15.5	30.9	9.6	2.5
12015	Charlotte County......................	162,283	98.0	78.9	28.1	23.0	19.7	6.1	1.9
12017	Citrus County...........................	139,467	98.4	78.9	27.6	22.2	19.5	6.8	2.8
12019	Clay County.............................	194,268	99.3	87.8	25.9	19.7	33.1	7.2	1.8
12021	Collier County..........................	333,294	98.8	81.6	24.7	19.6	25.2	9.1	3.0
12023	Columbia County......................	67,608	93.2	78.2	21.8	15.1	28.4	10.3	2.5

Table B-2: Counties with a Population of 50,000 or More—Relationships—*Continued*

State/county FIPS code	State/county	Population in nonfamily households						Population in subfamilies as a percent of total population					
		Total population in nonfamily households	Nonfamily householders				Nonrelatives in nonfamily households	Total population in subfamilies	In married couple subfamilies			Parent in a parent-child subfamily	Child in a parent-child subfamily
			Total	Male living alone	Female living alone	Householder living with nonrelatives			Total in married-couple subfamilies	Spouse in a married-couple subfamily	Child in a married-couple subfamily		
	California—cont'd												
06039	Madera County	8.5	6.6	2.8	2.5	1.3	1.9	6.5	2.6	2.0	0.6	1.6	2.3
06041	Marin County	19.1	15.0	4.5	7.7	2.9	4.1	1.8	0.9	0.8	0.1	0.5	0.4
06045	Mendocino County	19.4	15.5	6.1	6.6	2.7	3.9	3.9	1.5	1.0	0.5	1.0	1.4
06047	Merced County	9.4	6.9	2.7	2.8	1.4	2.5	6.0	2.7	2.1	0.6	1.4	1.9
06053	Monterey County	11.0	8.1	2.7	3.7	1.8	2.9	5.9	2.5	2.0	0.5	1.5	2.0
06055	Napa County	14.6	10.9	3.5	5.2	2.2	3.8	3.5	2.1	1.6	0.5	0.6	0.8
06057	Nevada County	20.3	15.4	5.2	7.1	3.0	4.9	2.0	0.9	0.6	0.3	0.6	0.6
06059	Orange County	12.8	9.1	2.9	4.0	2.2	3.7	5.3	2.7	2.0	0.7	1.1	1.5
06061	Placer County	14.0	10.8	3.5	5.1	2.3	3.1	2.8	1.7	1.4	0.3	0.5	0.6
06065	Riverside County	10.8	8.0	2.8	3.5	1.8	2.7	6.9	2.9	2.2	0.7	1.8	2.3
06067	Sacramento County	16.6	12.5	4.1	5.7	2.7	4.1	4.5	1.8	1.4	0.4	1.2	1.5
06069	San Benito County	8.2	6.3	2.4	2.9	1.1	1.8	9.3	4.0	2.4	1.6	2.5	2.8
06071	San Bernardino County	9.3	7.1	2.6	3.2	1.3	2.2	7.1	2.7	2.0	0.7	1.9	2.5
06073	San Diego County	16.3	11.4	3.9	4.5	3.0	4.9	4.5	2.1	1.6	0.5	1.1	1.3
06075	San Francisco County	35.1	23.1	8.2	8.0	6.9	12.0	4.0	2.6	2.2	0.4	0.6	0.8
06077	San Joaquin County	10.3	7.9	2.8	3.5	1.6	2.5	6.2	2.7	2.1	0.7	1.6	1.9
06079	San Luis Obispo County	20.9	13.7	4.1	5.7	3.9	7.2	2.5	1.1	0.9	0.2	0.7	0.7
06081	San Mateo County	15.2	11.3	3.9	5.0	2.5	3.9	4.4	2.5	2.0	0.5	0.9	1.1
06083	Santa Barbara County	17.7	11.4	3.7	4.6	3.1	6.3	4.3	1.9	1.4	0.5	1.1	1.4
06085	Santa Clara County	13.3	9.6	3.4	3.9	2.3	3.7	4.9	2.5	2.1	0.5	1.0	1.4
06087	Santa Cruz County	20.0	13.3	4.1	5.3	3.9	6.7	3.5	1.6	1.2	0.4	0.8	1.1
06089	Shasta County	17.7	13.3	4.4	6.3	2.6	4.4	3.4	1.6	1.2	0.4	0.9	0.9
06095	Solano County	13.0	9.7	3.1	4.5	2.1	3.3	4.6	1.8	1.4	0.4	1.3	1.5
06097	Sonoma County	19.1	14.1	4.2	6.5	3.4	5.0	3.1	1.5	1.1	0.3	0.8	0.9
06099	Stanislaus County	11.2	8.4	3.1	3.6	1.8	2.7	5.3	1.8	1.4	0.4	1.5	2.1
06101	Sutter County	11.1	8.6	3.1	3.9	1.5	2.5	5.9	2.8	2.4	0.4	1.4	1.7
06103	Tehama County	14.1	11.4	4.0	5.3	2.1	2.7	4.7	1.3	0.9	0.4	1.5	1.9
06107	Tulare County	8.7	6.5	2.4	2.8	1.3	2.2	6.5	2.2	1.5	0.7	1.8	2.6
06109	Tuolumne County	15.7	13.1	5.3	6.0	1.8	2.6	2.8	1.6	1.1	0.5	0.6	0.6
06111	Ventura County	11.6	8.5	2.8	3.8	1.9	3.1	5.8	2.7	2.0	0.7	1.4	1.7
06113	Yolo County	22.7	13.3	3.6	5.1	4.6	9.4	3.4	0.9	0.7	0.2	1.0	1.4
06115	Yuba County	12.4	9.3	3.3	3.6	2.3	3.1	5.4	1.9	1.4	0.6	1.6	1.9
08000	**Colorado**	18.5	13.8	5.1	5.8	3.0	4.6	2.9	1.0	0.8	0.2	0.9	1.0
08001	Adams County	13.2	9.9	3.9	3.9	2.1	3.2	5.5	1.9	1.4	0.5	1.6	2.0
08005	Arapahoe County	16.6	13.2	4.8	6.1	2.3	3.3	3.3	1.0	0.9	0.2	1.1	1.1
08013	Boulder County	24.8	16.3	5.3	5.9	5.1	8.5	1.7	0.7	0.6	0.1	0.5	0.5
08014	Broomfield County	15.5	12.7	4.8	5.4	2.6	2.7	2.0	1.0	0.9	0.1	0.4	0.5
08031	Denver County	30.1	22.4	8.2	9.1	5.1	7.7	3.7	1.4	1.0	0.4	1.0	1.3
08035	Douglas County	10.4	8.0	2.6	3.6	1.8	2.4	1.7	0.6	0.4	0.2	0.5	0.6
08037	Eagle County	22.3	12.1	4.7	3.9	3.4	10.2	0.0	0.0	0.0	0.0	0.0	0.0
08041	El Paso County	15.0	11.7	4.3	5.2	2.2	3.4	2.7	0.9	0.7	0.2	0.8	1.0
08045	Garfield County	14.3	10.4	4.7	3.8	1.9	3.9	0.0	0.0	0.0	0.0	0.0	0.0
08059	Jefferson County	18.4	14.2	5.1	6.1	3.0	4.2	2.2	1.0	0.7	0.3	0.6	0.7
08067	La Plata County	22.5	15.9	6.5	5.5	3.9	6.5	1.1	0.3	0.2	0.0	0.4	0.4
08069	Larimer County	22.3	14.9	4.5	5.5	4.9	7.3	2.2	0.8	0.5	0.2	0.6	0.8
08077	Mesa County	16.8	13.1	4.5	5.9	2.7	3.7	2.9	0.9	0.7	0.2	0.9	1.2
08101	Pueblo County	17.2	14.0	5.5	6.3	2.3	3.1	3.4	0.9	0.7	0.2	1.2	1.3
08123	Weld County	13.2	9.6	3.7	3.8	2.1	3.6	3.7	1.1	0.9	0.2	1.2	1.4
09000	**Connecticut**	15.7	12.6	4.5	6.0	2.1	3.1	2.8	1.0	0.8	0.2	0.9	0.9
09001	Fairfield County	14.0	10.9	3.7	5.3	1.9	3.1	3.1	1.3	1.0	0.2	0.9	1.0
09003	Hartford County	16.4	13.4	4.8	6.5	2.2	2.9	2.8	0.9	0.7	0.1	0.9	1.0
09005	Litchfield County	16.2	13.2	4.8	6.1	2.3	2.9	2.7	1.0	0.7	0.3	0.8	0.9
09007	Middlesex County	16.5	13.4	4.7	6.4	2.3	3.1	1.5	0.7	0.6	0.1	0.4	0.4
09009	New Haven County	16.4	13.3	4.7	6.4	2.1	3.1	3.0	1.1	0.9	0.2	1.0	1.0
09011	New London County	16.4	13.4	5.2	5.7	2.5	3.0	2.7	1.2	0.9	0.3	0.6	0.8
09013	Tolland County	15.1	11.7	4.4	4.7	2.5	3.4	1.8	0.9	0.6	0.3	0.4	0.5
09015	Windham County	15.7	12.3	4.3	5.8	2.2	3.4	3.1	0.9	0.7	0.2	1.0	1.1
10000	**Delaware**	15.8	12.1	4.0	5.8	2.4	3.7	4.3	1.2	0.9	0.3	1.4	1.7
10001	Kent County	14.0	10.8	3.5	5.0	2.2	3.2	3.9	1.4	1.1	0.3	1.2	1.4
10003	New Castle County	16.2	12.4	4.2	5.9	2.4	3.8	4.3	1.1	0.8	0.3	1.4	1.8
10005	Sussex County	16.2	12.2	3.7	6.1	2.4	4.0	4.3	1.1	0.9	0.2	1.6	1.7
11000	District of Columbia	33.6	24.2	8.1	10.9	5.3	9.4	3.2	0.3	0.3	0.1	1.3	1.5
11001	District of Columbia	33.6	24.2	8.1	10.9	5.3	9.4	3.2	0.3	0.3	0.1	1.3	1.5
12000	**Florida**	17.5	13.3	4.8	6.1	2.4	4.1	4.2	1.4	1.2	0.2	1.4	1.4
12001	Alachua County	30.1	18.2	5.8	6.8	5.6	11.9	2.9	0.8	0.7	0.2	0.9	1.1
12005	Bay County	18.0	14.0	5.2	6.0	2.8	4.0	3.2	0.8	0.7	0.1	1.2	1.2
12009	Brevard County	18.3	14.6	5.6	6.6	2.4	3.7	4.0	1.5	1.1	0.4	1.4	1.2
12011	Broward County	17.8	13.7	5.1	6.1	2.5	4.1	4.5	1.7	1.4	0.2	1.5	1.4
12015	Charlotte County	19.1	14.8	4.8	7.5	2.6	4.3	3.0	1.0	0.8	0.2	1.2	0.9
12017	Citrus County	19.5	15.7	6.0	7.2	2.5	3.8	3.0	1.5	1.3	0.2	0.7	0.7
12019	Clay County	11.5	8.7	3.3	3.6	1.9	2.8	4.7	2.0	1.5	0.5	1.3	1.5
12021	Collier County	17.1	12.9	4.5	6.5	1.9	4.2	4.1	1.5	1.3	0.2	1.4	1.3
12023	Columbia County	15.0	12.5	5.2	6.1	1.3	2.5	6.2	2.1	1.5	0.6	2.0	2.1

Table B-2: Counties with a Population of 50,000 or More—Relationships—*Continued*

State/county FIPS code	State/county	Total population	Percent of the population in households	Population in family households, percent					
				Percent in family households	Householder in family household, percent	Spouse in family household, percent	Child in family household (biological, adopted, or stepchild)	Other relative in family household	Nonrelatives in family household
	Florida—cont'd								
12031	Duval County............................	879,131	97.9	79.5	23.4	15.8	30.3	8.0	2.1
12033	Escambia County	302,964	93.7	75.1	22.3	15.6	27.4	8.0	1.8
12035	Flagler County	98,578	99.5	84.9	25.1	20.8	26.7	7.9	4.3
12053	Hernando County	173,549	98.9	83.7	27.5	20.9	26.5	6.7	2.2
12055	Highlands County	97,903	98.3	78.9	25.5	20.5	24.0	7.3	1.6
12057	Hillsborough County	1,280,536	98.3	80.1	23.6	16.5	29.6	8.2	2.2
12061	Indian River County	140,509	98.8	79.4	26.0	20.3	25.0	6.7	1.4
12069	Lake County	303,753	98.7	83.5	26.6	21.5	26.6	6.7	2.1
12071	Lee County	645,681	98.5	81.7	24.6	19.1	26.5	8.8	2.8
12073	Leon County	281,268	95.2	67.9	21.9	15.0	24.0	5.1	1.9
12081	Manatee County	334,409	98.6	80.6	25.5	20.1	25.2	7.6	2.2
12083	Marion County	335,036	97.5	80.0	26.2	19.9	24.8	6.9	2.3
12085	Martin County	148,992	97.6	79.4	25.5	20.7	24.8	6.8	1.6
12086	Miami-Dade County	2,592,201	98.3	84.7	21.8	14.0	31.9	14.2	2.9
12087	Monroe County	75,076	97.3	73.8	21.6	17.3	22.2	9.6	3.1
12089	Nassau County	74,868	99.1	86.4	27.1	21.2	27.4	7.7	3.0
12091	Okaloosa County	189,122	97.3	81.3	26.1	19.4	27.8	5.7	2.2
12095	Orange County	1,198,989	97.2	78.8	22.2	15.1	30.7	8.2	2.6
12097	Osceola County	288,077	99.1	88.3	23.1	15.6	35.3	11.3	3.0
12099	Palm Beach County	1,354,932	98.5	79.4	23.9	17.5	27.3	8.1	2.5
12101	Pasco County	470,938	98.5	82.0	25.3	19.8	27.2	7.6	2.1
12103	Pinellas County	922,744	98.1	74.2	23.9	17.2	24.2	6.7	2.2
12105	Polk County	616,447	97.6	83.5	24.4	17.6	29.6	9.2	2.8
12107	Putnam County	73,212	98.0	81.3	24.0	17.3	26.7	10.4	2.9
12109	St. Johns County	202,676	98.7	82.7	26.0	21.1	28.8	5.3	1.4
12111	St. Lucie County........................	283,981	99.0	83.3	25.3	18.8	29.2	7.7	2.5
12113	Santa Rosa County....................	158,486	96.9	84.1	27.0	21.6	29.1	4.2	2.1
12115	Sarasota County........................	386,055	98.6	76.0	26.8	21.6	20.9	4.8	2.0
12117	Seminole County	431,023	99.1	82.9	22.7	16.8	32.9	8.2	2.3
12119	Sumter County	102,372	90.1	73.9	30.7	27.6	10.9	3.9	0.8
12127	Volusia County..........................	497,341	97.8	77.8	24.1	18.1	25.4	7.9	2.4
12131	Walton County	57,715	96.6	79.7	26.0	19.6	24.7	6.3	3.1
13000	**Georgia**	9,905,993	97.4	82.7	24.1	16.9	31.2	8.4	2.0
13013	Barrow County	70,478	99.6	89.4	25.7	18.8	33.9	8.8	2.2
13015	Bartow County	100,659	99.1	86.8	25.3	19.1	30.9	9.1	2.4
13021	Bibb County..............................	155,611	95.6	79.5	22.6	13.5	32.1	9.7	1.6
13031	Bulloch County	72,244	92.3	65.6	20.4	14.2	23.9	5.2	1.9
13039	Camden County	51,089	97.4	85.8	27.1	20.8	32.0	4.6	1.3
13045	Carroll County	111,542	96.4	81.9	24.4	17.2	29.1	8.4	2.7
13047	Catoosa County	65,048	99.2	87.8	26.8	20.0	30.6	7.7	2.8
13051	Chatham County	275,789	95.9	77.3	22.9	15.3	28.9	8.4	1.8
13057	Cherokee County	221,310	99.4	87.5	25.7	19.7	33.1	7.1	1.9
13059	Clarke County............................	120,054	91.5	58.1	17.2	11.2	22.2	6.4	1.1
13063	Clayton County..........................	264,132	98.6	83.9	21.7	11.7	34.7	12.8	3.0
13067	Cobb County.............................	707,248	98.6	82.7	25.1	18.5	30.2	6.9	2.1
13073	Columbia County	131,692	99.6	90.7	26.7	21.1	34.0	7.2	1.7
13077	Coweta County	131,184	99.6	88.5	27.1	21.0	31.9	6.7	1.9
13089	DeKalb County	706,093	97.9	77.5	21.7	13.6	30.1	9.7	2.4
13095	Dougherty County	93,933	95.8	79.1	23.8	12.8	28.5	11.4	2.5
13097	Douglas County	134,505	99.0	88.0	25.7	16.8	32.2	10.5	2.8
13103	Effingham County......................	53,488	99.6	89.6	26.2	19.8	35.0	7.0	1.6
13113	Fayette County	107,680	99.4	91.6	27.9	23.1	33.4	6.2	1.0
13115	Floyd County	95,988	95.9	80.4	23.6	17.1	29.1	8.5	2.0
13117	Forsyth County	188,590	99.7	91.2	24.1	20.6	37.5	7.3	1.7
13121	Fulton County............................	970,400	96.6	74.1	21.2	14.0	29.5	7.8	1.6
13127	Glynn County............................	80,882	98.4	83.5	26.5	17.9	28.4	8.1	2.6
13129	Gordon County..........................	55,634	98.8	86.0	24.9	18.7	32.5	7.4	2.4
13135	Gwinnett County	841,658	99.4	89.3	24.4	18.1	36.2	8.5	2.2
13139	Hall County...............................	185,229	98.7	87.4	23.8	17.8	33.6	8.9	3.2
13151	Henry County	208,966	99.6	90.4	25.8	18.3	34.4	9.1	2.8
13153	Houston County	145,957	99.0	85.7	24.8	18.5	33.3	7.8	1.3
13157	Jackson County..........................	60,692	98.7	88.4	27.4	21.3	30.6	7.9	1.2
13179	Liberty County...........................	64,919	97.2	85.4	26.4	19.0	33.6	5.4	1.1
13185	Lowndes County........................	113,129	96.6	75.8	21.8	14.5	31.4	6.6	1.4
13215	Muscogee County......................	198,498	94.3	78.4	23.1	14.0	31.9	7.4	1.9
13217	Newton County	101,497	98.5	87.2	24.0	15.5	32.1	13.0	2.7
13223	Paulding County	145,229	99.5	91.9	27.0	20.9	34.2	7.5	2.4
13245	Richmond County	201,960	95.8	78.6	21.3	12.0	32.7	10.4	2.2
13247	Rockdale County	86,070	99.1	88.0	24.7	16.8	33.1	10.9	2.4
13255	Spalding County	63,947	98.0	87.5	25.8	16.4	30.7	12.9	1.6
13285	Troup County	68,433	97.7	84.0	24.8	15.2	31.7	9.4	3.0
13295	Walker County...........................	68,299	98.1	83.5	26.1	19.7	27.0	8.4	2.2
13297	Walton County	84,851	99.2	90.8	27.4	20.5	32.3	8.8	1.8
13313	Whitfield County	103,003	98.9	88.0	24.5	17.9	34.5	8.8	2.2

Table B-2: Counties with a Population of 50,000 or More—Relationships—*Continued*

State/county FIPS code	State/county	Population in nonfamily households						Population in subfamilies as a percent of total population					
		Total population in nonfamily households	Nonfamily householders				Nonrelatives in nonfamily households	Total population in subfamilies	In married couple subfamilies			Parent in a parent-child subfamily	Child in a parent-child subfamily
			Total	Male living alone	Female living alone	Householder living with nonrelatives			Total in married-couple subfamilies	Spouse in a married-couple subfamily	Child in married-couple subfamily		
	Florida—cont'd												
12031	Duval County	18.4	14.3	5.2	6.6	2.5	4.0	4.2	1.1	0.9	0.2	1.5	1.6
12033	Escambia County	18.6	14.5	5.3	6.7	2.5	4.1	4.3	1.5	1.1	0.4	1.3	1.6
12035	Flagler County	14.6	10.8	3.0	5.9	1.9	3.8	4.0	1.3	1.2	0.1	1.4	1.4
12053	Hernando County	15.2	12.8	4.7	6.3	1.7	2.4	3.6	1.2	0.9	0.3	1.1	1.2
12055	Highlands County	19.5	15.3	5.5	7.9	2.0	4.2	4.1	1.2	1.0	0.3	1.1	1.7
12057	Hillsborough County	18.2	13.5	4.8	5.9	2.7	4.7	3.9	1.3	1.0	0.2	1.2	1.4
12061	Indian River County	19.4	15.6	5.2	8.2	2.2	3.8	3.1	1.4	1.2	0.3	1.0	0.7
12069	Lake County	15.2	11.8	3.7	5.9	2.1	3.4	3.9	1.2	0.9	0.3	1.3	1.3
12071	Lee County	16.8	12.8	4.3	6.2	2.3	4.0	3.7	1.7	1.6	0.1	1.1	0.8
12073	Leon County	27.2	17.2	4.8	6.6	5.7	10.0	2.1	0.4	0.3	0.0	0.7	1.0
12081	Manatee County	18.0	14.1	4.7	6.8	2.6	3.9	3.3	0.9	0.7	0.1	1.3	1.2
12083	Marion County	17.5	13.6	4.5	6.6	2.4	3.9	3.4	1.1	0.9	0.2	1.1	1.2
12085	Martin County	18.2	14.8	5.5	7.5	1.9	3.4	2.4	0.6	0.5	0.1	1.0	0.8
12086	Miami-Dade County	13.5	10.3	3.9	4.6	1.8	3.2	6.2	2.5	2.1	0.4	1.8	1.8
12087	Monroe County	23.5	15.3	6.5	5.2	3.6	8.2	2.8	1.2	1.1	0.2	1.0	0.6
12089	Nassau County	12.7	9.8	3.7	4.7	1.4	2.9	4.3	1.5	1.1	0.3	1.4	1.4
12091	Okaloosa County	16.0	12.9	5.8	5.0	2.2	3.0	2.9	1.0	0.8	0.2	0.9	1.1
12095	Orange County	18.4	12.9	4.7	5.0	3.1	5.6	4.0	1.4	1.1	0.2	1.3	1.3
12097	Osceola County	10.7	7.9	3.1	3.3	1.5	2.8	6.2	2.3	2.0	0.3	2.1	1.8
12099	Palm Beach County	19.2	14.8	4.7	7.5	2.5	4.4	3.5	1.2	1.0	0.2	1.2	1.2
12101	Pasco County	16.5	13.2	4.7	6.4	2.2	3.3	3.8	1.3	1.1	0.2	1.3	1.2
12103	Pinellas County	23.9	19.4	7.0	9.4	3.0	4.5	3.2	1.0	0.8	0.2	1.1	1.1
12105	Polk County	14.0	11.1	3.8	5.3	1.9	3.0	5.0	1.6	1.3	0.3	1.6	1.8
12107	Putnam County	16.7	13.6	5.3	6.3	2.0	3.1	6.1	0.9	0.7	0.1	2.2	3.1
12109	St. Johns County	16.0	11.9	3.7	5.9	2.3	4.1	2.5	0.7	0.6	0.1	0.9	0.9
12111	St. Lucie County	15.6	12.3	4.3	5.9	2.0	3.4	3.9	1.3	1.1	0.2	1.4	1.1
12113	Santa Rosa County	12.8	9.8	3.5	3.9	2.4	3.0	3.1	0.8	0.6	0.2	1.0	1.3
12115	Sarasota County	22.6	17.9	5.6	9.3	3.0	4.7	2.2	0.5	0.4	0.1	0.9	0.9
12117	Seminole County	16.2	11.4	4.2	5.2	2.0	4.7	4.1	1.5	1.3	0.2	1.5	1.2
12119	Sumter County	16.2	13.9	4.3	7.9	1.7	2.3	0.0	0.0	0.0	0.0	0.0	0.0
12127	Volusia County	20.0	15.3	5.4	7.3	2.7	4.6	3.7	1.2	0.9	0.2	1.3	1.3
12131	Walton County	16.9	14.1	5.8	6.6	1.8	2.7	3.7	1.7	1.3	0.5	1.0	0.9
13000	**Georgia**	14.7	11.5	4.2	5.4	1.9	3.2	4.3	1.1	0.9	0.2	1.5	1.7
13013	Barrow County	10.3	8.0	2.7	3.9	1.5	2.2	6.2	2.4	1.9	0.6	1.8	1.9
13015	Bartow County	12.3	9.3	3.0	4.2	2.0	3.0	5.1	1.4	1.0	0.4	1.4	2.3
13021	Bibb County	16.0	13.3	4.8	6.9	1.6	2.7	5.0	0.5	0.4	0.1	2.1	2.4
13031	Bulloch County	26.6	15.1	4.2	4.4	6.5	11.5	0.0	0.0	0.0	0.0	0.0	0.0
13039	Camden County	11.6	8.7	3.6	3.2	1.8	3.0	0.0	0.0	0.0	0.0	0.0	0.0
13045	Carroll County	14.5	11.2	4.4	4.6	2.3	3.3	5.3	1.4	0.9	0.5	1.4	2.5
13047	Catoosa County	11.3	9.7	3.5	5.1	1.0	1.6	0.0	0.0	0.0	0.0	0.0	0.0
13051	Chatham County	18.7	14.4	5.3	6.5	2.6	4.2	4.1	0.8	0.6	0.1	1.6	1.7
13057	Cherokee County	11.9	9.0	3.2	4.1	1.6	2.9	3.6	1.8	1.3	0.5	0.8	1.0
13059	Clarke County	33.5	17.7	4.5	7.4	5.7	15.8	2.7	1.0	0.8	0.2	0.9	0.8
13063	Clayton County	14.8	11.4	4.4	5.3	1.7	3.4	6.1	1.1	0.9	0.2	2.2	2.8
13067	Cobb County	15.9	12.3	4.0	5.7	2.6	3.6	3.6	1.1	1.0	0.2	1.1	1.4
13073	Columbia County	8.9	7.1	2.8	3.5	0.9	1.8	3.7	1.0	0.7	0.3	1.5	1.1
13077	Coweta County	11.1	9.3	3.4	4.4	1.4	1.8	4.5	1.7	1.3	0.5	1.2	1.5
13089	DeKalb County	20.4	15.7	5.4	7.4	2.9	4.7	4.7	0.9	0.8	0.1	1.7	2.1
13095	Dougherty County	16.8	14.0	4.9	7.3	1.8	2.7	4.4	0.5	0.4	0.1	1.7	2.2
13097	Douglas County	11.0	8.7	3.3	3.9	1.5	2.3	5.6	1.2	0.9	0.3	1.8	2.7
13103	Effingham County	10.0	7.5	2.7	3.1	1.7	2.5	2.9	0.5	0.4	0.1	1.2	1.2
13113	Fayette County	7.8	7.1	2.5	4.1	0.5	0.7	3.9	0.9	0.7	0.2	1.3	1.7
13115	Floyd County	15.5	12.0	4.1	5.9	2.0	3.5	5.1	1.9	1.5	0.4	1.4	1.8
13117	Forsyth County	8.4	6.1	2.2	2.9	1.1	2.3	3.8	1.7	1.6	0.1	1.2	0.9
13121	Fulton County	22.5	17.3	6.6	7.8	2.9	5.2	3.2	0.6	0.6	0.1	1.3	1.3
13127	Glynn County	14.8	12.4	4.9	5.8	1.7	2.4	5.8	1.0	0.7	0.3	2.1	2.7
13129	Gordon County	12.9	9.7	3.4	4.6	1.7	3.2	3.6	2.4	2.0	0.4	0.6	0.6
13135	Gwinnett County	10.1	7.6	2.7	3.4	1.5	2.5	4.0	1.6	1.3	0.3	1.1	1.2
13139	Hall County	11.4	8.7	3.2	4.1	1.5	2.6	4.8	2.1	1.4	0.7	1.4	1.3
13151	Henry County	9.2	7.6	2.6	3.7	1.2	1.6	5.8	1.5	1.2	0.3	1.9	2.4
13153	Houston County	13.3	11.3	4.5	5.5	1.3	2.0	4.0	0.8	0.7	0.1	1.6	1.6
13157	Jackson County	10.3	7.8	2.8	3.3	1.7	2.5	4.1	1.2	1.1	0.2	1.1	1.8
13179	Liberty County	11.7	9.4	4.0	3.6	1.8	2.3	0.0	0.0	0.0	0.0	0.0	0.0
13185	Lowndes County	20.8	13.3	4.8	4.9	3.7	7.5	4.1	1.3	0.9	0.4	1.4	1.4
13215	Muscogee County	15.9	12.9	4.9	6.4	1.6	3.0	4.1	0.5	0.4	0.1	1.8	1.8
13217	Newton County	11.2	9.3	3.7	4.3	1.3	2.0	7.6	1.0	0.9	0.1	2.8	3.8
13223	Paulding County	7.6	6.2	2.0	3.2	1.0	1.5	3.7	1.8	1.0	0.8	0.9	1.1
13245	Richmond County	17.2	14.1	5.5	6.7	1.9	3.1	4.7	0.3	0.2	0.1	2.1	2.3
13247	Rockdale County	11.1	9.1	3.6	4.3	1.2	2.0	5.7	2.0	1.2	0.8	1.8	1.9
13255	Spalding County	10.6	9.2	3.6	4.4	1.2	1.3	5.7	0.7	0.6	0.1	2.2	2.9
13285	Troup County	13.7	11.0	4.3	4.8	1.9	2.7	4.8	1.3	0.9	0.4	1.7	1.8
13295	Walker County	14.6	11.9	4.4	5.6	1.9	2.7	5.2	1.8	1.4	0.4	1.5	2.0
13297	Walton County	8.4	6.9	2.4	3.3	1.1	1.5	4.9	2.1	1.8	0.3	1.3	1.5
13313	Whitfield County	11.0	8.6	3.5	3.7	1.4	2.4	5.3	1.5	1.2	0.3	2.0	1.8

State/county FIPS code	State/county	Total population	Percent of the population in households	Population in family households, percent					
				Percent in family households	Householder in family household, percent	Spouse in family household, percent	Child in family household (biological, adopted, or stepchild)	Other relative in family household	Nonrelatives in family household
15000	**Hawaii**...............................	1,390,348	96.9	83.6	22.4	16.7	28.0	13.4	3.2
15001	Hawaii County.............................	188,761	98.4	83.2	23.1	16.3	27.8	12.0	4.0
15003	Honolulu County...........................	974,683	96.2	83.6	22.1	16.6	28.1	13.8	2.9
15007	Kauai County..............................	68,546	98.8	84.6	23.0	17.9	28.0	12.6	3.2
15009	Maui County...............................	158,269	98.3	83.6	22.7	16.9	27.3	12.7	4.0
16000	**Idaho**.................................	1,597,222	98.2	83.3	25.3	20.1	31.0	4.7	2.2
16001	Ada County................................	408,785	98.1	82.0	25.5	19.9	29.9	4.5	2.1
16005	Bannock County............................	83,487	97.1	80.6	23.8	18.4	32.5	4.2	1.7
16019	Bonneville County.........................	106,737	98.7	87.6	24.9	19.5	36.8	4.2	2.0
16027	Canyon County.............................	194,687	98.4	87.3	24.3	18.7	34.9	6.4	3.0
16055	Kootenai County...........................	142,541	98.9	82.5	26.8	21.0	27.1	5.0	2.5
16083	Twin Falls County.........................	78,846	98.5	84.2	25.6	19.6	31.3	5.4	2.3
17000	**Illinois**..............................	12,868,770	97.7	81.7	24.2	17.8	30.9	6.9	2.0
17001	Adams County..............................	67,185	97.9	81.8	26.1	20.8	29.2	3.7	2.0
17007	Boone County..............................	54,013	99.4	90.4	25.3	20.2	33.3	9.5	2.1
17019	Champaign County..........................	203,586	92.0	63.9	20.8	15.6	22.8	3.3	1.3
17029	Coles County..............................	53,705	91.9	67.6	21.9	16.1	23.6	4.0	1.9
17031	Cook County...............................	5,227,094	98.3	80.2	22.5	15.0	31.1	9.6	2.0
17037	DeKalb County.............................	104,614	94.1	73.4	21.7	16.1	29.4	4.2	2.1
17043	DuPage County.............................	927,775	98.7	86.1	25.8	20.9	33.0	5.0	1.4
17063	Grundy County.............................	50,168	99.5	87.8	26.2	20.1	34.6	4.6	2.4
17073	Henry County..............................	50,110	98.5	82.9	27.7	22.0	28.3	2.5	2.4
17077	Jackson County............................	60,078	92.8	62.2	19.2	14.2	22.2	5.2	1.4
17089	Kane County...............................	521,561	98.9	88.2	24.3	19.0	34.7	8.0	2.2
17091	Kankakee County...........................	112,795	95.3	80.7	24.8	17.2	30.8	5.4	2.5
17093	Kendall County............................	118,045	99.8	90.3	25.0	21.0	37.7	5.4	1.1
17095	Knox County...............................	52,331	91.8	71.8	23.8	17.5	24.4	3.0	3.0
17097	Lake County...............................	701,763	97.5	86.8	25.5	20.3	33.6	5.6	1.7
17099	LaSalle County............................	112,871	97.4	80.9	25.5	19.5	29.0	4.4	2.5
17111	McHenry County............................	307,684	99.5	88.9	26.6	21.6	34.0	4.9	1.8
17113	McLean County.............................	172,548	95.3	73.7	23.2	18.2	27.1	3.7	1.5
17115	Macon County..............................	109,942	96.8	77.6	25.3	18.2	27.3	4.8	2.1
17119	Madison County............................	267,870	98.0	80.8	26.5	19.7	27.6	4.8	2.2
17141	Ogle County...............................	52,796	98.9	82.0	25.6	21.3	30.1	2.8	2.2
17143	Peoria County.............................	187,463	97.3	78.1	24.8	17.7	29.0	4.8	1.9
17161	Rock Island County........................	147,397	97.0	79.1	25.5	18.5	28.0	4.9	2.2
17163	St. Clair County..........................	268,596	98.6	83.7	25.5	16.8	32.9	6.4	2.1
17167	Sangamon County...........................	199,109	97.8	78.5	25.7	18.3	27.9	4.2	2.3
17179	Tazewell County...........................	136,078	98.3	83.2	27.1	21.8	28.4	3.4	2.4
17183	Vermilion County..........................	80,809	97.2	80.7	25.3	17.9	29.5	5.7	2.4
17195	Whiteside County..........................	57,870	98.2	82.6	27.0	20.7	28.2	4.0	2.6
17197	Will County...............................	681,537	98.8	89.7	25.0	19.8	36.9	6.3	1.7
17199	Williamson County.........................	66,791	97.3	81.5	26.9	20.3	27.8	5.0	1.5
17201	Winnebago County..........................	292,054	98.6	83.3	25.7	18.2	30.7	6.0	2.7
18000	**Indiana**...............................	6,541,673	97.1	81.1	25.2	18.7	29.7	5.3	2.2
18003	Allen County..............................	360,698	98.5	81.4	24.9	18.0	31.8	4.7	2.0
18005	Bartholomew County........................	78,740	98.7	84.1	25.6	19.6	29.1	6.5	3.2
18011	Boone County..............................	59,100	99.0	86.7	27.4	22.9	31.7	3.5	1.2
18019	Clark County..............................	112,156	98.5	82.3	25.0	19.0	30.1	6.6	1.6
18035	Delaware County...........................	117,570	93.2	70.1	23.4	16.9	23.9	4.0	1.8
18039	Elkhart County............................	199,449	98.2	86.2	25.7	18.6	32.9	6.0	3.1
18043	Floyd County..............................	75,548	98.4	83.3	25.8	19.2	31.1	5.6	1.6
18053	Grant County..............................	69,387	91.8	74.9	25.5	18.3	25.2	3.7	2.2
18057	Hamilton County...........................	289,719	99.5	87.8	26.7	22.4	34.1	3.4	1.2
18059	Hancock County............................	70,981	99.1	87.4	26.8	20.9	33.1	4.7	1.9
18063	Hendricks County..........................	151,098	98.0	87.8	26.8	22.0	33.4	3.9	1.7
18067	Howard County.............................	82,834	98.6	81.7	27.1	20.4	27.7	4.1	2.6
18081	Johnson County............................	143,448	98.4	85.7	26.3	21.3	30.3	5.8	2.0
18085	Kosciusko County..........................	77,674	97.9	85.2	26.4	21.2	30.8	4.8	2.0
18089	Lake County...............................	493,136	98.8	84.4	24.8	16.6	34.0	7.1	1.9
18091	LaPorte County............................	111,228	91.8	75.9	25.0	18.5	25.8	4.5	2.0
18095	Madison County............................	130,630	94.7	78.0	24.7	18.0	27.3	5.6	2.4
18097	Marion County.............................	919,356	98.2	77.7	23.2	14.6	30.0	7.0	3.0
18105	Monroe County.............................	141,149	90.1	59.4	19.5	14.5	20.4	3.2	1.8
18109	Morgan County.............................	69,463	98.9	86.5	27.3	22.3	29.3	5.7	1.8
18127	Porter County.............................	165,919	97.8	84.5	26.7	20.7	30.3	4.9	2.0
18141	St. Joseph County.........................	266,624	95.7	78.2	24.5	17.8	29.1	4.7	2.1
18157	Tippecanoe County.........................	177,741	92.3	67.1	21.8	16.5	23.8	3.2	1.8
18163	Vanderburgh County........................	180,798	95.9	76.4	24.7	17.6	26.9	5.0	2.2
18167	Vigo County...............................	108,373	91.1	73.1	22.3	16.5	26.6	4.8	2.8
18173	Warrick County............................	60,585	98.7	87.7	27.9	23.4	29.8	4.8	1.8
18177	Wayne County..............................	68,308	96.0	78.8	26.8	19.3	25.4	4.9	2.4
19000	**Iowa**..................................	3,076,519	96.7	78.9	25.8	20.3	27.5	3.4	1.8

Table B-2: Counties with a Population of 50,000 or More—Relationships—*Continued*

State/county FIPS code	State/county	Population in nonfamily households						Population in subfamilies as a percent of total population					
		Total population in nonfamily households	Nonfamily householders				Nonrelatives in nonfamily households	Total population in subfamilies	In married couple subfamilies			Parent in a parent-child subfamily	Child in a parent-child subfamily
			Total	Male living alone	Female living alone	Householder living with nonrelatives			Total in married-couple subfamilies	Spouse in a married-couple subfamily	Child in married-couple subfamily		
15000	**Hawaii**..............	13.3	9.9	3.9	3.9	2.2	3.4	8.6	5.1	3.6	1.6	1.5	2.0
15001	Hawaii County..............	15.2	11.3	4.4	4.4	2.5	4.0	7.4	4.3	2.9	1.4	1.4	1.7
15003	Honolulu County..............	12.6	9.5	3.7	3.8	2.0	3.1	8.9	5.4	3.7	1.6	1.4	2.1
15007	Kauai County..............	14.2	10.1	3.5	3.9	2.7	4.1	8.2	3.8	2.8	1.0	1.9	2.6
15009	Maui County..............	14.7	10.8	4.4	4.0	2.5	3.8	8.7	5.3	3.6	1.7	1.6	1.9
16000	**Idaho**..............	14.8	11.2	4.0	4.9	2.3	3.6	2.8	1.1	0.8	0.3	0.8	0.9
16001	Ada County..............	16.2	12.1	3.8	5.5	2.8	4.1	2.3	0.8	0.7	0.2	0.6	0.8
16005	Bannock County..............	16.5	12.4	4.7	5.4	2.4	4.0	2.3	1.1	0.8	0.3	0.5	0.7
16019	Bonneville County..............	11.1	9.2	3.7	4.1	1.4	1.9	2.5	1.2	0.8	0.5	0.7	0.6
16027	Canyon County..............	11.1	8.9	3.1	4.2	1.5	2.3	4.7	2.0	1.4	0.6	1.3	1.4
16055	Kootenai County..............	16.4	12.2	4.1	5.3	2.8	4.2	3.0	0.9	0.6	0.2	0.9	1.2
16083	Twin Falls County..............	14.3	10.3	3.4	4.7	2.2	3.9	3.5	1.3	1.0	0.3	1.0	1.2
17000	**Illinois**..............	15.9	12.8	4.7	6.0	2.1	3.1	3.8	1.2	1.0	0.3	1.1	1.4
17001	Adams County..............	16.1	13.4	4.9	6.7	1.7	2.7	2.2	0.3	0.2	0.1	1.0	1.0
17007	Boone County..............	9.0	7.3	3.1	3.0	1.3	1.7	7.8	2.4	1.6	0.7	2.6	2.8
17019	Champaign County..............	28.1	18.0	6.2	6.6	5.1	10.1	1.7	0.6	0.3	0.2	0.6	0.6
17029	Coles County..............	24.3	17.2	5.8	7.1	4.3	7.1	0.0	0.0	0.0	0.0	0.0	0.0
17031	Cook County..............	18.1	14.5	5.2	6.8	2.4	3.7	5.0	1.6	1.3	0.3	1.5	1.9
17037	DeKalb County..............	20.7	14.1	4.9	5.4	3.8	6.6	2.4	0.4	0.3	0.0	1.0	1.1
17043	DuPage County..............	12.6	10.5	3.7	5.2	1.5	2.1	2.9	1.4	1.1	0.2	0.7	0.8
17063	Grundy County..............	11.6	9.9	4.2	4.3	1.4	1.7	2.3	0.7	0.4	0.3	0.7	0.9
17073	Henry County..............	15.6	12.7	5.2	5.5	2.1	2.9	1.6	0.3	0.2	0.1	0.6	0.7
17077	Jackson County..............	30.6	20.0	7.5	7.5	4.9	10.6	2.3	0.3	0.3	0.0	1.0	0.9
17089	Kane County..............	10.7	8.4	3.0	3.9	1.4	2.3	4.5	1.8	1.3	0.4	1.2	1.5
17091	Kankakee County..............	14.6	11.8	4.1	5.9	1.9	2.7	3.5	0.6	0.4	0.1	1.4	1.6
17093	Kendall County..............	9.5	7.3	3.0	2.9	1.5	2.2	4.2	1.7	1.5	0.2	1.2	1.3
17095	Knox County..............	20.0	16.9	6.3	8.0	2.6	3.1	1.9	0.5	0.3	0.1	0.7	0.8
17097	Lake County..............	10.7	9.0	3.5	4.3	1.3	1.7	3.1	1.3	0.9	0.3	0.8	1.1
17099	LaSalle County..............	16.5	13.5	5.1	6.2	2.1	3.0	2.8	1.1	0.7	0.5	0.7	0.9
17111	McHenry County..............	10.5	8.7	3.4	3.9	1.4	1.9	3.2	1.4	1.2	0.3	0.7	1.0
17113	McLean County..............	21.6	14.2	4.7	5.7	3.8	7.4	2.1	0.6	0.4	0.2	0.7	0.8
17115	Macon County..............	19.2	15.8	5.9	7.7	2.2	3.5	3.9	0.9	0.8	0.2	1.3	1.7
17119	Madison County..............	17.2	13.4	4.7	6.0	2.7	3.8	2.9	1.0	0.8	0.2	0.8	1.1
17141	Ogle County..............	16.9	13.7	5.1	5.9	2.7	3.2	1.5	0.2	0.2	0.0	0.6	0.7
17143	Peoria County..............	19.2	15.7	6.3	7.0	2.4	3.4	2.5	0.7	0.5	0.2	0.9	0.9
17161	Rock Island County..............	17.9	15.7	6.2	7.7	1.8	2.2	3.0	0.9	0.7	0.2	1.0	1.2
17163	St. Clair County..............	14.9	12.5	4.8	6.2	1.5	2.3	3.6	0.5	0.4	0.1	1.4	1.6
17167	Sangamon County..............	19.3	15.7	5.5	7.6	2.6	3.6	1.7	0.4	0.3	0.1	0.6	0.7
17179	Tazewell County..............	15.0	12.9	5.1	5.9	1.9	2.2	2.1	0.6	0.4	0.2	0.7	0.8
17183	Vermilion County..............	16.4	13.9	5.9	6.2	1.7	2.6	3.2	0.6	0.5	0.2	1.2	1.4
17195	Whiteside County..............	15.6	13.5	5.2	6.8	1.6	2.1	2.2	0.5	0.4	0.1	0.8	0.9
17197	Will County..............	9.2	7.6	2.9	3.5	1.2	1.6	3.6	1.4	1.1	0.3	1.0	1.2
17199	Williamson County..............	15.7	13.2	4.7	6.8	1.7	2.5	2.3	0.8	0.6	0.1	0.9	0.7
17201	Winnebago County..............	15.3	12.9	5.2	5.9	1.9	2.4	3.5	1.0	0.8	0.2	1.1	1.4
18000	**Indiana**..............	16.0	12.8	4.8	5.8	2.2	3.2	3.1	0.9	0.6	0.2	1.0	1.2
18003	Allen County..............	17.1	13.7	5.4	6.0	2.3	3.3	2.6	0.7	0.5	0.2	0.8	1.0
18005	Bartholomew County..............	14.6	12.0	4.2	6.1	1.8	2.6	3.4	1.9	1.4	0.5	0.8	0.7
18011	Boone County..............	12.3	10.2	3.7	4.7	1.8	2.2	1.9	0.8	0.5	0.2	0.5	0.7
18019	Clark County..............	16.2	12.9	4.7	6.0	2.2	3.3	4.5	1.0	0.8	0.3	1.7	1.7
18035	Delaware County..............	23.1	15.8	4.9	6.6	4.2	7.4	2.6	0.8	0.5	0.2	0.8	1.0
18039	Elkhart County..............	12.0	9.8	3.6	4.7	1.5	2.2	3.8	1.5	0.9	0.6	1.0	1.3
18043	Floyd County..............	15.1	12.3	4.4	5.9	2.1	2.8	2.7	0.7	0.6	0.1	1.0	1.1
18053	Grant County..............	16.8	13.7	4.9	6.8	1.9	3.1	0.0	0.0	0.0	0.0	0.0	0.0
18057	Hamilton County..............	11.6	9.7	3.7	4.4	1.6	1.9	1.7	0.6	0.5	0.1	0.5	0.6
18059	Hancock County..............	11.7	9.7	3.7	4.4	1.6	1.9	0.0	0.0	0.0	0.0	0.0	0.0
18063	Hendricks County..............	10.2	8.6	2.5	4.8	1.3	1.5	2.5	1.3	1.0	0.3	0.5	0.7
18067	Howard County..............	16.9	14.6	5.7	7.0	2.0	2.2	1.7	0.2	0.2	0.1	0.6	0.8
18081	Johnson County..............	12.7	10.1	3.5	4.6	2.0	2.6	3.7	1.0	0.6	0.4	1.1	1.6
18085	Kosciusko County..............	12.7	10.8	4.1	5.4	1.3	2.0	2.9	0.5	0.4	0.2	1.0	1.4
18089	Lake County..............	14.4	12.0	4.7	5.7	1.7	2.4	4.1	0.9	0.7	0.2	1.4	1.7
18091	LaPorte County..............	15.9	13.4	5.3	5.9	2.2	2.5	3.0	0.8	0.5	0.3	0.7	1.5
18095	Madison County..............	16.7	13.8	5.4	6.6	1.8	2.9	3.1	0.8	0.6	0.2	1.2	1.2
18097	Marion County..............	20.4	16.1	6.2	7.1	2.8	4.3	3.5	0.5	0.4	0.1	1.4	1.6
18105	Monroe County..............	30.6	18.5	6.2	6.7	5.5	12.1	1.5	0.6	0.5	0.1	0.5	0.4
18109	Morgan County..............	12.5	9.8	3.6	4.0	2.2	2.7	4.4	1.6	1.0	0.6	1.1	1.7
18127	Porter County..............	13.3	10.6	4.3	4.5	1.9	2.7	3.1	1.0	0.7	0.3	1.0	1.1
18141	St. Joseph County..............	17.5	14.0	5.1	6.4	2.5	3.5	2.6	0.6	0.5	0.1	0.9	1.1
18157	Tippecanoe County..............	25.2	16.1	5.3	5.6	5.2	9.1	1.9	0.9	0.7	0.2	0.5	0.6
18163	Vanderburgh County..............	19.5	16.1	6.0	7.7	2.4	3.4	2.6	0.9	0.7	0.2	0.8	0.9
18167	Vigo County..............	18.0	13.9	4.8	6.5	2.5	4.2	2.8	0.9	0.7	0.2	1.0	0.9
18173	Warrick County..............	11.0	9.2	3.8	4.2	1.2	1.8	0.0	0.0	0.0	0.0	0.0	0.0
18177	Wayne County..............	17.2	14.2	5.6	6.3	2.3	3.0	2.4	0.6	0.5	0.1	0.8	1.1
19000	**Iowa**..............	17.8	14.1	5.2	6.3	2.6	3.7	1.8	0.5	0.4	0.1	0.6	0.7

State/county FIPS code	State/county	Total population	Percent of the population in households	Population in family households, percent					
				Percent in family households	Householder in family household, percent	Spouse in family household, percent	Child in family household (biological, adopted, or stepchild)	Other relative in family household	Nonrelatives in family household
	Iowa—cont'd								
19013	Black Hawk County	131,862	95.4	72.8	23.1	18.0	25.9	4.1	1.6
19049	Dallas County	72,157	99.1	85.6	27.2	22.3	32.5	2.0	1.6
19061	Dubuque County	95,073	95.3	77.0	25.2	20.0	28.1	2.5	1.3
19103	Johnson County	136,353	94.0	66.2	22.2	17.4	23.1	2.1	1.5
19113	Linn County	215,096	97.7	78.0	24.7	19.4	27.9	4.3	1.7
19153	Polk County	444,498	97.9	80.6	25.4	19.0	29.3	4.9	2.0
19155	Pottawattamie County	93,006	97.6	81.3	26.1	18.8	28.5	5.5	2.4
19163	Scott County	168,685	98.1	79.5	24.8	18.9	30.4	3.7	1.7
19169	Story County	91,623	90.8	60.0	20.6	17.7	19.5	1.4	0.9
19193	Woodbury County	102,284	97.2	80.8	24.6	17.3	30.7	5.3	2.9
20000	**Kansas**	2,882,966	97.3	80.6	25.2	19.5	29.4	4.6	1.9
20015	Butler County	65,798	96.9	84.9	26.3	21.1	31.1	4.4	2.1
20045	Douglas County	113,246	92.1	64.4	21.0	15.8	21.9	3.9	1.9
20091	Johnson County	559,881	99.1	83.6	26.4	21.4	30.9	3.3	1.5
20103	Leavenworth County	77,668	92.1	80.5	24.6	19.3	31.0	4.0	1.5
20155	Reno County	64,278	95.7	79.7	25.9	20.6	28.5	3.0	1.7
20161	Riley County	74,893	87.8	59.3	18.9	15.1	21.1	2.4	1.8
20169	Saline County	55,751	97.3	79.5	25.8	18.6	28.2	4.8	2.2
20173	Sedgwick County	503,189	98.7	82.3	24.7	17.9	32.2	5.8	1.7
20177	Shawnee County	178,942	97.5	79.0	24.9	18.6	28.6	5.0	1.9
20209	Wyandotte County	159,183	99.2	82.2	23.1	13.9	33.2	9.0	2.9
21000	**Kentucky**	4,380,635	97.1	81.4	25.8	18.9	28.5	6.0	2.1
21015	Boone County	123,103	99.2	88.3	26.8	20.3	34.8	4.9	1.5
21029	Bullitt County	76,004	99.6	88.2	27.2	20.5	31.5	6.0	3.1
21037	Campbell County	90,939	96.9	79.3	24.9	18.0	28.9	5.6	2.1
21047	Christian County	74,411	92.2	80.8	24.4	17.9	31.9	4.9	1.5
21059	Daviess County	97,723	97.4	82.0	25.9	19.7	28.7	5.9	1.7
21067	Fayette County	304,998	95.8	71.7	23.3	16.5	24.9	5.1	1.9
21093	Hardin County	107,602	96.6	83.7	26.2	19.1	30.6	5.3	2.4
21111	Jefferson County	751,312	98.0	78.3	24.7	16.6	28.7	6.2	2.0
21117	Kenton County	161,685	98.7	81.5	24.6	17.3	31.6	5.5	2.5
21125	Laurel County	59,456	98.7	86.1	27.9	20.7	28.3	7.1	2.0
21145	McCracken County	65,611	98.1	80.3	25.6	18.7	27.7	6.6	1.8
21151	Madison County	84,817	93.5	74.5	23.8	17.9	24.8	5.7	2.3
21185	Oldham County	61,507	92.9	85.7	25.6	21.5	33.5	3.7	1.3
21195	Pike County	64,042	98.3	83.4	27.5	20.9	27.0	6.7	1.3
21199	Pulaski County	63,648	98.4	83.5	28.0	21.4	27.1	5.1	1.9
21227	Warren County	116,890	94.7	75.5	24.4	17.3	26.8	4.7	2.3
22000	**Louisiana**	4,600,933	97.2	81.3	24.5	16.2	30.7	7.9	2.0
22001	Acadia Parish	61,975	98.3	84.3	25.3	17.6	30.9	7.2	3.3
22005	Ascension Parish	112,187	99.3	88.6	26.4	19.7	34.4	5.9	2.2
22015	Bossier Parish	122,319	98.0	83.1	25.1	17.8	29.6	8.4	2.2
22017	Caddo Parish	256,294	97.9	81.3	24.0	14.1	31.4	9.4	2.3
22019	Calcasieu Parish	194,437	98.1	82.9	25.9	17.6	31.0	6.7	1.7
22033	East Baton Rouge Parish	443,675	97.8	77.6	23.3	14.8	29.4	8.3	1.9
22045	Iberia Parish	73,705	98.8	86.4	26.0	16.8	33.4	7.1	3.2
22051	Jefferson Parish	434,246	99.2	81.7	24.1	15.6	30.3	9.3	2.3
22055	Lafayette Parish	227,326	97.7	79.0	24.0	16.5	30.1	6.3	2.0
22057	Lafourche Parish	97,008	97.9	84.0	25.5	18.5	30.5	7.2	2.4
22063	Livingston Parish	132,025	99.2	87.1	25.8	18.7	32.3	7.5	2.8
22071	Orleans Parish	369,765	96.5	70.7	20.9	10.9	28.1	8.7	2.0
22073	Ouachita Parish	155,394	94.6	79.2	24.1	15.5	31.1	6.9	1.6
22079	Rapides Parish	132,432	96.8	81.7	23.4	15.7	33.6	7.5	1.5
22089	St. Charles Parish	52,520	98.9	88.1	25.6	17.2	35.1	8.6	1.5
22097	St. Landry Parish	83,447	98.5	85.0	26.0	16.7	34.6	6.0	1.7
22099	St. Martin Parish	52,834	99.4	87.1	25.0	17.4	35.4	8.0	1.4
22101	St. Mary Parish	53,754	98.3	83.5	25.4	15.7	31.3	8.7	2.5
22103	St. Tammany Parish	239,452	99.0	86.7	27.0	20.3	31.6	6.4	1.4
22105	Tangipahoa Parish	123,918	97.1	81.7	24.5	16.2	30.2	8.3	2.4
22109	Terrebonne Parish	112,031	98.8	85.9	25.0	17.3	32.8	7.5	3.2
22113	Vermilion Parish	58,730	99.1	86.1	26.1	18.4	31.3	7.2	3.2
22115	Vernon Parish	52,968	95.8	85.1	24.9	19.2	32.8	6.9	1.3
23000	**Maine**	1,328,217	97.3	77.2	26.0	20.3	24.5	3.8	2.6
23001	Androscoggin County	107,556	97.2	77.4	25.6	18.9	26.4	3.5	3.0
23003	Aroostook County	70,728	97.0	78.7	27.6	21.9	23.4	3.6	2.1
23005	Cumberland County	283,955	97.0	75.9	25.1	19.6	25.4	3.8	2.1
23009	Hancock County	54,647	97.0	73.9	26.7	22.0	21.0	2.5	1.6
23011	Kennebec County	121,548	97.1	77.3	26.4	20.3	23.9	3.6	3.2
23017	Oxford County	57,527	98.7	80.1	25.2	19.5	27.3	5.4	2.8
23019	Penobscot County	153,550	95.4	73.4	25.0	19.5	22.6	3.8	2.5
23025	Somerset County	51,796	98.7	79.8	26.7	19.8	25.3	4.8	3.2
23031	York County	198,904	98.6	80.1	26.5	21.2	26.0	3.8	2.5
24000	**Maryland**	5,884,640	97.6	82.0	24.3	17.2	30.3	7.7	2.5
24001	Allegany County	73,962	89.5	70.7	22.7	16.7	24.4	4.5	2.5

Table B-2: Counties with a Population of 50,000 or More—Relationships—*Continued*

State/county FIPS code	State/county	Population in nonfamily households						Population in subfamilies as a percent of total population					
		Total population in nonfamily households	Nonfamily householders				Nonrelatives in nonfamily households	Total population in subfamilies	In married couple subfamilies			Parent in a parent-child subfamily	Child in a parent-child subfamily
			Total	Male living alone	Female living alone	Householder living with nonrelatives			Total in married-couple subfamilies	Spouse in a married-couple subfamily	Child in married-couple subfamily		
	Iowa—cont'd												
19013	Black Hawk County	22.6	16.3	5.8	6.9	3.6	6.4	2.1	0.5	0.3	0.1	0.7	0.9
19049	Dallas County	13.5	10.0	3.2	4.9	1.9	3.6	1.3	0.9	0.5	0.4	0.2	0.2
19061	Dubuque County	18.3	14.2	5.4	6.3	2.5	4.2	1.3	0.2	0.2	0.0	0.4	0.7
19103	Johnson County	27.8	18.2	5.6	6.7	6.0	9.6	0.0	0.0	0.0	0.0	0.0	0.0
19113	Linn County	19.7	15.2	5.8	6.3	3.2	4.5	2.3	0.5	0.4	0.1	0.9	0.9
19153	Polk County	17.3	13.8	4.9	6.2	2.7	3.5	2.5	0.8	0.6	0.2	0.8	0.9
19155	Pottawattamie County	16.3	12.9	4.5	6.1	2.3	3.3	2.8	0.9	0.8	0.2	0.8	1.0
19163	Scott County	18.6	14.9	5.7	6.7	2.5	3.7	2.1	0.4	0.3	0.1	0.8	0.9
19169	Story County	30.7	18.1	5.3	5.5	7.3	12.6	0.5	0.2	0.1	0.1	0.2	0.2
19193	Woodbury County	16.4	13.2	5.0	6.1	2.1	3.2	2.9	0.9	0.5	0.4	1.0	1.0
20000	**Kansas**	16.6	13.2	4.9	6.0	2.3	3.4	2.6	0.7	0.5	0.2	0.8	1.1
20015	Butler County	12.0	10.4	3.9	5.3	1.2	1.6	2.5	0.6	0.4	0.3	0.9	0.9
20045	Douglas County	27.7	17.3	4.7	6.7	5.9	10.4	1.7	0.2	0.2	0.0	0.6	0.8
20091	Johnson County	15.5	12.5	4.2	6.1	2.2	3.0	1.8	0.7	0.6	0.1	0.5	0.6
20103	Leavenworth County	11.6	9.6	3.5	4.4	1.6	2.0	2.5	1.0	0.8	0.2	0.6	0.9
20155	Reno County	16.0	13.6	5.2	6.7	1.8	2.4	0.0	0.0	0.0	0.0	0.0	0.0
20161	Riley County	28.5	16.0	5.2	5.2	5.6	12.5	0.0	0.0	0.0	0.0	0.0	0.0
20169	Saline County	17.8	14.3	5.2	6.2	2.9	3.5	2.3	0.3	0.2	0.0	0.8	1.2
20173	Sedgwick County	16.3	13.5	5.6	5.8	2.0	2.9	3.4	0.8	0.6	0.2	1.2	1.5
20177	Shawnee County	18.4	14.9	5.4	6.9	2.6	3.6	3.0	0.9	0.6	0.3	0.9	1.2
20209	Wyandotte County	16.9	13.1	5.0	5.8	2.3	3.9	4.8	1.0	0.8	0.3	1.6	2.1
21000	**Kentucky**	15.8	12.8	4.7	6.1	2.0	2.9	3.3	1.0	0.7	0.2	1.1	1.2
21015	Boone County	10.9	8.9	3.5	4.0	1.3	2.0	2.7	1.1	1.0	0.2	0.7	0.8
21029	Bullitt County	11.3	9.3	3.7	3.8	1.7	2.1	3.1	0.4	0.3	0.1	1.3	1.4
21037	Campbell County	17.6	13.8	4.6	6.7	2.6	3.7	2.7	0.9	0.7	0.1	0.7	1.1
21047	Christian County	11.4	9.7	4.1	4.4	1.2	1.6	3.2	1.4	0.9	0.5	0.9	0.9
21059	Daviess County	15.5	12.7	4.4	6.4	1.9	2.7	3.4	0.9	0.8	0.1	1.2	1.3
21067	Fayette County	24.1	17.2	5.9	7.4	3.9	6.9	2.1	0.7	0.5	0.2	0.7	0.8
21093	Hardin County	12.9	10.8	4.1	5.1	1.6	2.1	3.5	1.2	0.9	0.3	1.1	1.2
21111	Jefferson County	19.7	15.8	5.7	7.5	2.6	3.8	3.2	0.6	0.5	0.2	1.2	1.3
21117	Kenton County	17.1	13.6	5.1	6.0	2.5	3.5	2.7	0.7	0.5	0.2	1.0	1.1
21125	Laurel County	12.6	10.6	4.0	5.0	1.6	2.0	4.9	1.4	1.0	0.3	1.5	2.0
21145	McCracken County	17.8	15.1	5.5	7.7	1.9	2.7	3.7	0.7	0.5	0.3	1.6	1.4
21151	Madison County	19.0	13.3	4.3	6.0	3.1	5.7	2.6	0.5	0.4	0.1	0.9	1.2
21185	Oldham County	7.2	6.1	2.1	2.9	1.0	1.1	2.3	1.0	0.8	0.2	0.7	0.6
21195	Pike County	14.8	12.9	4.7	7.0	1.3	1.9	4.7	1.2	0.9	0.3	1.7	1.8
21199	Pulaski County	14.9	12.8	4.8	6.5	1.6	2.1	2.7	0.4	0.3	0.1	1.1	1.2
21227	Warren County	19.1	14.2	4.8	6.0	3.4	5.0	2.0	0.4	0.3	0.1	0.7	1.0
22000	**Louisiana**	15.9	12.8	5.0	5.8	2.0	3.1	4.3	0.9	0.7	0.2	1.6	1.9
22001	Acadia Parish	13.9	11.5	4.5	5.3	1.7	2.4	4.9	0.6	0.5	0.1	1.9	2.4
22005	Ascension Parish	10.7	8.5	3.7	3.5	1.3	2.2	3.9	1.2	0.9	0.3	1.2	1.4
22015	Bossier Parish	14.9	12.8	5.5	5.9	1.5	2.1	5.3	1.5	1.0	0.5	1.8	2.0
22017	Caddo Parish	16.7	14.3	5.7	7.1	1.6	2.3	4.9	0.7	0.5	0.2	2.0	2.2
22019	Calcasieu Parish	15.2	12.4	4.6	5.9	1.8	2.8	4.3	1.0	0.6	0.3	1.5	1.8
22033	East Baton Rouge Parish	20.1	14.6	5.2	6.5	3.0	5.5	4.3	0.5	0.4	0.2	1.6	2.1
22045	Iberia Parish	12.3	10.1	4.2	4.2	1.7	2.3	5.2	0.9	0.7	0.2	1.8	2.6
22051	Jefferson Parish	17.5	14.3	5.4	6.7	2.1	3.2	4.7	1.2	0.9	0.3	1.7	1.9
22055	Lafayette Parish	18.8	14.5	5.6	6.3	2.6	4.3	3.2	0.7	0.5	0.2	1.2	1.2
22057	Lafourche Parish	13.9	10.6	4.0	4.5	2.0	3.3	4.5	0.9	0.7	0.2	1.6	2.0
22063	Livingston Parish	12.2	9.6	4.2	4.0	1.5	2.5	3.9	1.1	0.9	0.2	1.4	1.4
22071	Orleans Parish	25.8	20.1	7.9	8.7	3.5	5.7	3.8	0.6	0.4	0.1	1.5	1.7
22073	Ouachita Parish	15.3	12.8	4.3	7.0	1.6	2.5	4.3	0.6	0.4	0.2	1.7	2.0
22079	Rapides Parish	15.1	12.5	4.9	6.2	1.5	2.6	3.7	0.6	0.4	0.2	1.5	1.6
22089	St. Charles Parish	10.8	9.0	3.8	3.7	1.5	1.8	4.7	1.5	1.4	0.1	1.5	1.6
22097	St. Landry Parish	13.5	11.4	4.7	5.2	1.5	2.0	3.4	0.4	0.4	0.1	1.4	1.5
22099	St. Martin Parish	12.3	10.3	5.1	4.0	1.1	2.1	0.0	0.0	0.0	0.0	0.0	0.0
22101	St. Mary Parish	14.8	12.0	4.5	5.2	2.2	2.8	5.6	1.0	0.7	0.3	2.2	2.4
22103	St. Tammany Parish	12.3	9.8	3.5	4.5	1.8	2.5	3.2	1.0	0.8	0.2	1.0	1.1
22105	Tangipahoa Parish	15.4	11.6	4.4	4.8	2.3	3.8	4.5	1.4	0.9	0.5	1.5	1.7
22109	Terrebonne Parish	13.0	10.3	4.4	3.9	2.0	2.7	4.7	1.0	0.7	0.3	1.6	2.1
22113	Vermilion Parish	13.0	10.4	4.0	4.7	1.6	2.6	3.6	1.1	0.7	0.3	1.2	1.3
22115	Vernon Parish	10.7	8.8	4.0	3.7	1.1	1.9	3.8	1.9	1.7	0.1	1.0	1.0
23000	**Maine**	20.1	15.6	5.3	6.9	3.4	4.5	2.2	0.9	0.7	0.2	0.6	0.7
23001	Androscoggin County	19.8	15.6	5.2	6.9	3.5	4.1	2.5	0.7	0.5	0.2	0.7	1.1
23003	Aroostook County	18.3	15.6	6.0	7.4	2.2	2.7	1.6	0.5	0.4	0.2	0.4	0.6
23005	Cumberland County	21.1	16.1	5.0	7.4	3.6	5.1	2.2	1.1	0.9	0.2	0.5	0.6
23009	Hancock County	23.1	18.2	6.0	8.2	4.0	4.9	1.5	0.6	0.4	0.2	0.4	0.5
23011	Kennebec County	19.8	15.9	5.6	6.7	3.5	4.0	1.8	0.8	0.6	0.2	0.4	0.6
23017	Oxford County	18.5	14.1	5.3	6.3	2.5	4.5	3.4	1.2	0.9	0.3	1.2	1.0
23019	Penobscot County	22.0	15.7	5.0	6.2	4.4	6.4	1.9	0.7	0.6	0.2	0.6	0.6
23025	Somerset County	18.9	14.7	6.1	5.2	3.3	4.2	2.0	0.9	0.7	0.2	0.5	0.5
23031	York County	18.5	14.5	4.6	6.7	3.2	4.0	2.5	1.3	0.9	0.4	0.5	0.7
24000	**Maryland**	15.6	12.2	4.1	5.9	2.2	3.5	4.1	1.3	1.0	0.3	1.3	1.5
24001	Allegany County	18.8	15.3	5.5	7.4	2.4	3.4	3.0	0.7	0.6	0.1	1.0	1.2

Table B-2: Counties with a Population of 50,000 or More—Relationships—*Continued*

State/county FIPS code	State/county	Total population	Percent of the population in households	Population in family households, percent					
				Percent in family households	Householder in family household, percent	Spouse in family household, percent	Child in family household (biological, adopted, or stepchild)	Other relative in family household	Nonrelatives in family household
	Maryland—cont'd								
24003	Anne Arundel County	550,181	97.3	82.8	25.3	19.3	29.7	6.3	2.2
24005	Baltimore County	817,791	97.4	80.3	24.7	17.3	29.2	7.0	2.2
24009	Calvert County	89,825	99.3	89.0	25.6	19.9	33.8	6.8	3.0
24013	Carroll County	167,348	97.9	86.2	26.4	21.8	31.6	4.6	1.7
24015	Cecil County	101,733	98.6	86.3	25.8	19.6	32.1	6.1	2.6
24017	Charles County	150,956	98.9	86.8	24.9	17.7	34.3	7.6	2.3
24021	Frederick County	239,407	98.2	85.4	26.3	20.6	31.4	5.2	1.9
24025	Harford County	248,145	99.1	87.3	26.9	20.5	31.9	6.2	1.7
24027	Howard County	299,188	99.3	87.7	26.7	21.3	32.3	6.1	1.4
24031	Montgomery County	1,004,242	99.1	84.8	24.9	19.2	30.9	7.2	2.6
24033	Prince George's County	881,876	97.8	82.0	22.6	13.1	31.5	11.3	3.5
24037	St. Mary's County	108,794	97.5	86.5	25.7	20.9	31.5	6.5	1.9
24043	Washington County	149,159	94.0	78.7	25.2	18.5	27.1	5.4	2.6
24045	Wicomico County	100,481	95.9	79.5	24.6	16.8	29.2	5.7	3.3
24047	Worcester County	51,537	98.7	80.9	25.0	19.7	28.6	5.5	2.1
24510	Baltimore city	621,836	96.0	70.8	19.7	9.1	28.1	10.9	3.0
25000	**Massachusetts**	6,648,138	96.3	78.1	24.2	17.8	28.5	5.7	1.9
25001	Barnstable County	215,112	98.6	79.0	27.0	21.4	24.6	4.1	1.9
25003	Berkshire County	130,069	94.8	74.7	25.3	18.6	24.9	3.8	2.1
25005	Bristol County	550,965	96.9	80.6	25.0	17.8	29.8	5.7	2.3
25009	Essex County	756,508	97.6	82.2	25.2	18.1	30.2	6.5	2.3
25011	Franklin County	71,450	97.9	75.1	25.0	18.6	24.7	4.2	2.6
25013	Hampden County	466,313	97.0	80.8	24.7	15.8	30.9	6.7	2.7
25015	Hampshire County	159,744	86.0	64.3	21.8	16.8	20.6	3.4	1.6
25017	Middlesex County	1,537,150	96.1	77.7	24.2	19.2	27.8	5.0	1.5
25021	Norfolk County	682,501	97.2	81.2	24.9	19.9	30.3	4.9	1.1
25023	Plymouth County	499,449	97.6	85.0	25.7	19.6	31.8	6.2	1.8
25025	Suffolk County	745,716	93.7	64.1	19.1	10.7	24.0	7.9	2.3
25027	Worcester County	805,989	96.7	80.9	24.8	18.3	30.3	5.3	2.2
26000	**Michigan**	9,884,242	97.7	80.9	25.2	18.4	29.8	5.4	2.1
26005	Allegan County	111,987	99.0	86.6	27.7	22.5	30.5	3.8	2.1
26015	Barry County	59,018	98.8	84.9	26.9	22.6	29.5	4.3	1.6
26017	Bay County	106,984	98.6	81.3	26.7	20.2	28.4	4.1	2.0
26021	Berrien County	155,871	96.8	82.0	25.4	18.7	30.3	5.5	2.0
26025	Calhoun County	135,120	97.2	80.5	25.3	17.5	29.3	5.7	2.7
26027	Cass County	52,167	99.2	84.6	25.9	20.3	30.5	5.8	2.0
26037	Clinton County	76,263	99.0	82.6	26.0	21.3	29.6	4.2	1.5
26045	Eaton County	108,107	98.5	81.4	26.1	20.1	29.5	3.9	1.9
26049	Genesee County	418,306	98.7	81.8	25.4	16.9	31.3	5.9	2.3
26055	Grand Traverse County	89,048	95.7	79.1	24.9	19.8	27.1	4.7	2.6
26065	Ingham County	281,972	93.4	68.7	21.6	15.1	25.3	4.4	2.2
26067	Ionia County	63,944	93.9	82.1	24.5	19.3	30.3	5.6	2.4
26073	Isabella County	70,554	90.9	60.9	19.3	14.1	22.3	3.0	2.1
26075	Jackson County	160,122	94.2	78.8	25.0	18.2	28.2	5.2	2.2
26077	Kalamazoo County	254,678	96.7	74.7	23.6	17.3	27.4	4.1	2.3
26081	Kent County	614,495	98.3	81.7	24.9	18.7	31.1	4.6	2.4
26087	Lapeer County	88,226	97.9	86.4	27.6	22.4	30.0	4.7	1.8
26091	Lenawee County	99,211	94.6	79.2	25.7	20.0	27.4	4.1	2.0
26093	Livingston County	183,309	99.3	88.3	27.4	22.7	32.5	4.0	1.7
26099	Macomb County	848,455	99.0	83.6	26.1	19.2	30.7	5.9	1.7
26103	Marquette County	67,643	93.2	71.4	23.4	19.0	24.5	2.9	1.6
26111	Midland County	83,971	98.4	82.5	27.0	22.3	28.0	3.2	2.0
26115	Monroe County	150,944	99.2	85.2	27.2	20.8	30.8	4.3	2.0
26117	Montcalm County	63,137	95.7	82.5	26.1	20.3	28.7	4.1	3.2
26121	Muskegon County	170,362	96.1	81.0	25.4	17.9	29.7	5.3	2.7
26125	Oakland County	1,221,103	99.1	82.3	26.2	20.1	29.8	4.7	1.5
26139	Ottawa County	269,384	96.6	84.3	26.0	21.7	31.0	3.7	2.0
26145	Saginaw County	197,832	96.8	80.0	25.1	17.6	29.7	5.3	2.2
26147	St. Clair County	160,878	99.0	83.0	26.9	20.6	28.7	4.6	2.2
26149	St. Joseph County	60,958	98.8	85.0	26.0	19.9	30.9	5.7	2.5
26155	Shiawassee County	69,400	98.9	85.1	28.1	21.5	29.0	3.9	2.5
26157	Tuscola County	54,760	97.6	84.6	26.8	21.6	28.7	5.0	2.6
26159	Van Buren County	75,582	98.3	84.7	25.9	19.5	30.5	5.7	3.0
26161	Washtenaw County	351,345	94.9	70.3	22.3	17.2	25.7	3.6	1.6
26163	Wayne County	1,789,819	98.8	82.2	23.2	13.8	33.9	9.0	2.3
27000	**Minnesota**	5,382,376	97.5	79.8	25.4	19.9	28.7	3.6	2.1
27003	Anoka County	336,345	99.1	85.4	26.1	20.5	32.1	4.7	2.1
27013	Blue Earth County	64,962	93.4	67.3	21.6	17.8	23.5	2.2	2.1
27019	Carver County	94,088	99.1	88.5	27.3	23.4	34.7	2.0	1.0
27025	Chisago County	53,665	96.6	83.8	26.5	22.4	29.9	2.4	2.5
27027	Clay County	60,236	93.3	76.4	24.4	18.6	27.9	2.8	2.8
27035	Crow Wing County	62,934	98.7	81.9	28.7	22.6	26.2	2.4	2.0
27037	Dakota County	405,158	99.3	84.6	26.6	21.1	31.6	3.3	1.9
27053	Hennepin County	1,184,060	97.9	75.1	23.7	17.7	27.1	4.6	2.0

State/county FIPS code	State/county	Population in nonfamily households						Population in subfamilies as a percent of total population					
		Total population in nonfamily households	Nonfamily householders				Nonrelatives in nonfamily households	Total population in subfamilies	In married couple subfamilies			Parent in a parent-child subfamily	Child in a parent-child subfamily
			Total	Male living alone	Female living alone	Householder living with nonrelatives			Total in married-couple subfamilies	Spouse in a married-couple subfamily	Child in a married-couple subfamily		
	Maryland—cont'd												
24003	Anne Arundel County	14.5	11.2	3.8	5.0	2.3	3.3	3.5	1.2	0.9	0.3	1.0	1.3
24005	Baltimore County	17.1	13.5	4.3	6.9	2.3	3.6	3.7	1.0	0.8	0.2	1.3	1.4
24009	Calvert County	10.3	8.6	3.5	3.9	1.3	1.7	4.4	2.3	1.7	0.6	1.1	1.1
24013	Carroll County	11.7	9.3	3.1	4.7	1.5	2.4	3.1	1.0	0.8	0.2	0.9	1.2
24015	Cecil County	12.3	9.8	3.8	4.4	1.6	2.5	4.6	1.8	1.4	0.4	1.3	1.4
24017	Charles County	12.1	9.5	3.2	4.8	1.6	2.6	4.8	1.4	1.1	0.3	1.5	1.9
24021	Frederick County	12.9	10.2	3.3	4.8	2.1	2.7	3.1	1.1	0.9	0.2	0.7	1.2
24025	Harford County	11.8	9.8	3.5	4.7	1.6	2.1	3.7	1.5	1.1	0.5	0.9	1.2
24027	Howard County	11.6	9.1	3.3	4.1	1.7	2.5	3.7	1.7	1.4	0.3	0.9	1.1
24031	Montgomery County	14.3	11.2	3.4	5.7	2.0	3.1	3.2	1.4	1.2	0.2	0.8	0.9
24033	Prince George's County	15.8	11.8	4.1	5.7	2.1	3.9	6.1	1.7	1.3	0.4	2.1	2.3
24037	St. Mary's County	11.0	8.8	3.7	3.5	1.6	2.2	3.3	1.0	0.8	0.3	1.2	1.0
24043	Washington County	15.3	12.5	4.6	5.6	2.3	2.8	3.4	1.1	0.9	0.2	0.9	1.4
24045	Wicomico County	16.4	11.6	3.8	5.3	2.6	4.8	2.8	0.7	0.6	0.1	1.1	0.9
24047	Worcester County	17.7	13.2	4.1	7.0	2.1	4.5	3.6	0.8	0.7	0.1	1.7	1.1
24510	Baltimore city	25.2	19.3	6.6	9.3	3.4	5.9	5.8	0.8	0.6	0.2	2.3	2.8
25000	**Massachusetts**	18.2	13.9	4.6	6.4	2.9	4.3	2.9	1.2	1.0	0.3	0.8	0.9
25001	Barnstable County	19.5	16.3	5.4	8.6	2.3	3.2	2.4	1.1	0.9	0.2	0.6	0.7
25003	Berkshire County	20.1	17.1	5.8	8.8	2.4	3.0	1.9	0.4	0.4	0.0	0.7	0.7
25005	Bristol County	16.3	13.2	4.7	6.1	2.4	3.1	3.2	1.5	1.1	0.4	0.8	0.9
25009	Essex County	15.4	12.6	4.1	6.3	2.2	2.8	3.3	1.4	1.1	0.3	0.8	1.1
25011	Franklin County	22.8	17.1	5.4	7.6	4.2	5.7	2.3	1.0	0.7	0.3	0.6	0.7
25013	Hampden County	16.2	13.0	4.6	6.1	2.3	3.2	3.7	1.0	0.9	0.2	1.3	1.4
25015	Hampshire County	21.7	15.0	4.9	6.4	3.7	6.7	1.8	0.5	0.4	0.1	0.6	0.7
25017	Middlesex County	18.4	13.7	4.5	6.0	3.2	4.7	2.5	1.4	1.1	0.3	0.5	0.6
25021	Norfolk County	16.1	12.9	4.0	6.5	2.4	3.2	2.4	1.3	1.1	0.2	0.5	0.6
25023	Plymouth County	12.6	10.2	3.3	5.1	1.9	2.4	3.7	1.4	1.1	0.3	1.1	1.3
25025	Suffolk County	29.6	19.8	6.2	8.2	5.4	9.9	3.3	1.0	0.8	0.2	1.1	1.1
25027	Worcester County	15.9	12.3	4.3	5.5	2.5	3.5	2.7	1.1	0.9	0.2	0.8	0.8
26000	**Michigan**	16.8	13.4	5.0	6.2	2.2	3.4	3.0	0.9	0.7	0.2	1.0	1.1
26005	Allegan County	12.4	9.7	4.0	3.9	1.8	2.7	2.1	0.4	0.3	0.1	0.7	1.0
26015	Barry County	13.9	11.4	4.8	4.5	2.1	2.5	2.5	1.3	1.1	0.2	0.6	0.6
26017	Bay County	17.3	14.3	5.6	6.6	2.2	2.9	2.1	0.6	0.5	0.1	0.6	0.9
26021	Berrien County	14.8	12.6	4.8	6.2	1.5	2.3	2.7	0.6	0.5	0.1	1.0	1.1
26025	Calhoun County	16.6	13.8	5.2	6.4	2.1	2.9	3.8	1.2	0.9	0.3	1.2	1.4
26027	Cass County	14.7	12.1	5.0	5.5	1.6	2.6	3.7	1.5	1.2	0.3	1.2	1.0
26037	Clinton County	16.5	11.7	4.4	4.7	2.6	4.8	2.1	1.1	0.8	0.3	0.5	0.6
26045	Eaton County	17.1	14.2	5.1	6.9	2.1	2.9	2.2	0.9	0.7	0.2	0.7	0.6
26049	Genesee County	16.9	13.9	5.2	6.4	2.3	3.0	3.4	0.7	0.6	0.2	1.2	1.5
26055	Grand Traverse County	16.6	13.3	4.7	6.3	2.3	3.3	3.0	0.8	0.7	0.1	1.2	1.0
26065	Ingham County	24.8	17.1	5.6	7.2	4.3	7.7	2.4	0.7	0.5	0.2	0.7	0.9
26067	Ionia County	11.8	9.7	3.9	4.0	1.8	2.1	3.6	1.7	1.1	0.6	1.0	0.9
26073	Isabella County	30.0	15.5	4.1	5.2	6.2	14.5	1.8	0.5	0.5	0.0	0.7	0.6
26075	Jackson County	15.4	12.7	4.7	5.9	2.1	2.7	2.6	0.4	0.3	0.1	1.0	1.1
26077	Kalamazoo County	22.1	15.6	5.4	6.6	3.7	6.5	2.2	0.5	0.4	0.1	0.8	0.9
26081	Kent County	16.6	12.6	4.3	5.7	2.6	4.0	2.4	0.7	0.5	0.2	0.8	0.9
26087	Lapeer County	11.5	9.5	3.8	4.1	1.6	2.0	3.6	1.5	1.0	0.5	1.0	1.1
26091	Lenawee County	15.3	12.6	5.1	5.6	2.0	2.7	2.9	0.8	0.5	0.3	0.8	1.3
26093	Livingston County	11.0	9.3	3.8	4.0	1.5	1.8	2.1	1.0	0.7	0.3	0.6	0.6
26099	Macomb County	15.4	13.1	4.9	6.4	1.8	2.3	3.3	1.3	1.0	0.3	0.9	1.0
26103	Marquette County	21.8	15.9	5.9	6.6	3.3	5.9	0.0	0.0	0.0	0.0	0.0	0.0
26111	Midland County	15.9	12.9	4.6	5.8	2.4	3.0	1.8	0.5	0.4	0.1	0.5	0.8
26115	Monroe County	14.0	11.3	4.5	5.0	1.8	2.7	3.4	0.7	0.5	0.2	1.2	1.5
26117	Montcalm County	13.3	10.6	4.0	4.8	1.8	2.7	2.3	1.3	1.0	0.2	0.4	0.6
26121	Muskegon County	15.0	12.4	4.7	5.8	1.9	2.6	3.1	0.9	0.6	0.3	1.0	1.2
26125	Oakland County	16.7	13.9	5.1	6.7	2.1	2.8	2.4	1.0	0.8	0.2	0.6	0.7
26139	Ottawa County	12.4	9.2	3.1	4.1	2.0	3.1	2.4	0.8	0.5	0.2	0.7	0.9
26145	Saginaw County	16.8	14.0	5.4	6.8	1.8	2.8	3.0	0.8	0.6	0.2	1.1	1.2
26147	St. Clair County	16.0	13.0	4.9	5.8	2.3	3.0	2.9	1.5	1.1	0.4	0.7	0.8
26149	St. Joseph County	13.8	11.1	4.2	5.3	1.6	2.7	3.6	1.3	0.8	0.4	1.1	1.2
26155	Shiawassee County	13.9	11.5	4.3	5.4	1.7	2.4	2.1	0.6	0.5	0.2	0.6	0.9
26157	Tuscola County	13.0	11.1	4.6	5.0	1.6	1.8	3.9	1.4	1.0	0.3	1.3	1.3
26159	Van Buren County	13.5	11.4	4.4	5.4	1.6	2.2	3.5	0.8	0.6	0.2	1.1	1.6
26161	Washtenaw County	24.6	16.6	5.4	6.8	4.5	8.0	1.8	0.8	0.6	0.2	0.5	0.5
26163	Wayne County	16.6	13.9	5.5	6.6	1.8	2.7	4.6	1.1	0.8	0.2	1.7	1.8
27000	**Minnesota**	17.7	13.8	5.0	6.1	2.7	3.9	1.9	0.6	0.5	0.1	0.6	0.7
27003	Anoka County	13.7	10.7	3.9	4.6	2.2	3.0	3.2	1.0	0.8	0.2	1.0	1.2
27013	Blue Earth County	26.1	16.0	5.0	5.9	5.1	10.2	0.7	0.0	0.0	0.0	0.3	0.3
27019	Carver County	10.5	8.9	3.2	4.3	1.4	1.6	1.5	0.5	0.4	0.1	0.5	0.6
27025	Chisago County	12.8	10.3	3.9	4.2	2.2	2.5	1.7	0.8	0.6	0.2	0.4	0.5
27027	Clay County	16.9	12.9	5.0	5.5	2.4	4.0	0.0	0.0	0.0	0.0	0.0	0.0
27035	Crow Wing County	16.8	13.6	4.9	6.1	2.6	3.2	1.5	0.5	0.4	0.2	0.4	0.5
27037	Dakota County	14.7	11.6	3.9	5.4	2.4	3.1	1.8	0.6	0.5	0.1	0.5	0.6
27053	Hennepin County	22.8	17.2	5.9	7.5	3.8	5.6	1.9	0.6	0.5	0.1	0.6	0.8

State/ county FIPS code	State/county	Total population	Percent of the population in households	Population in family households, percent					
				Percent in family households	Householder in family household, percent	Spouse in family household, percent	Child in family household (biological, adopted, or stepchild)	Other relative in family household	Nonrelatives in family household
	Minnesota—cont'd								
27109	Olmsted County	147,436	98.0	81.1	25.4	20.5	29.9	3.2	2.1
27111	Otter Tail County	57,417	97.8	82.1	28.3	23.6	26.0	2.4	1.8
27123	Ramsey County	520,903	96.9	75.3	22.9	16.4	28.7	5.2	2.2
27131	Rice County	64,928	86.0	73.6	23.9	18.6	26.0	2.6	2.5
27137	St. Louis County	200,420	95.2	72.4	24.4	18.8	24.0	3.0	2.1
27139	Scott County	134,952	99.0	88.2	26.1	21.9	35.1	3.4	1.8
27141	Sherburne County	89,644	97.8	87.2	25.8	21.1	33.6	4.4	2.3
27145	Stearns County	151,622	94.4	75.1	24.2	19.7	27.3	2.4	1.4
27163	Washington County	243,992	98.6	86.2	27.0	21.9	32.3	2.9	2.0
27169	Winona County	51,277	91.2	69.5	21.8	18.5	25.5	2.5	1.3
27171	Wright County	127,422	99.1	89.3	27.3	22.2	34.9	2.4	2.5
28000	**Mississippi**	2,985,181	96.9	82.9	24.9	16.3	31.2	8.6	1.9
28033	DeSoto County	166,132	99.5	88.2	26.3	19.0	33.6	7.0	2.3
28035	Forrest County	76,670	94.9	74.5	22.2	14.0	28.3	8.3	1.7
28047	Harrison County	193,684	97.4	80.6	24.9	16.3	28.4	8.5	2.4
28049	Hinds County	247,117	96.9	81.2	23.1	12.2	33.4	10.5	2.0
28059	Jackson County	140,231	99.1	85.4	24.7	17.2	31.9	9.7	2.0
28067	Jones County	68,514	97.5	84.7	25.4	17.6	30.6	8.6	2.5
28071	Lafayette County	50,093	90.0	66.1	18.4	13.2	25.6	7.4	1.6
28073	Lamar County	57,860	99.3	84.8	27.4	20.1	31.5	4.8	1.0
28075	Lauderdale County	80,361	95.2	80.7	25.0	15.6	30.1	7.8	2.2
28081	Lee County	84,800	98.8	86.0	26.7	18.5	32.0	7.1	1.7
28087	Lowndes County	59,749	97.4	81.0	25.4	16.9	29.7	7.5	1.5
28089	Madison County	98,696	98.2	85.6	26.2	19.0	32.1	7.0	1.4
28109	Pearl River County	55,319	97.7	84.7	26.1	18.4	30.3	8.6	1.4
28121	Rankin County	145,200	95.8	84.3	26.8	19.8	30.4	5.8	1.6
28151	Washington County	50,077	98.9	86.3	24.7	11.9	35.2	12.6	2.1
29000	**Missouri**	6,026,255	97.1	80.0	25.4	18.9	28.5	5.2	2.1
29019	Boone County	168,383	94.5	67.7	21.8	16.7	24.2	3.4	1.6
29021	Buchanan County	89,603	95.8	78.7	23.5	16.7	28.0	8.4	2.0
29031	Cape Girardeau County	76,941	95.3	76.9	24.9	19.6	26.7	4.1	1.6
29037	Cass County	100,281	98.9	87.0	27.7	21.9	30.9	4.9	1.6
29043	Christian County	79,805	99.2	88.4	28.4	22.9	31.3	3.6	2.3
29047	Clay County	227,741	98.8	83.1	25.8	19.2	30.7	5.0	2.4
29051	Cole County	76,535	93.8	77.4	24.9	18.5	26.7	5.1	2.2
29071	Franklin County	101,629	99.2	85.3	26.9	21.0	29.9	5.7	1.9
29077	Greene County	280,591	96.1	73.8	24.8	18.5	24.4	4.3	1.8
29095	Jackson County	677,502	98.3	78.1	23.8	15.9	29.7	6.3	2.4
29097	Jasper County	116,594	98.0	81.7	25.6	18.6	27.7	6.5	3.3
29099	Jefferson County	220,443	99.1	86.8	27.1	21.0	31.7	4.6	2.4
29101	Johnson County	54,177	92.3	72.9	24.2	19.8	24.4	2.6	1.9
29113	Lincoln County	53,435	98.7	87.1	25.8	19.9	32.2	6.4	2.8
29145	Newton County	58,897	98.3	84.5	26.5	21.7	29.5	5.2	1.6
29165	Platte County	92,089	99.0	82.8	27.0	21.0	28.6	4.9	1.3
29169	Pulaski County	53,489	82.0	67.9	19.0	15.1	28.7	3.4	1.8
29183	St. Charles County	368,984	98.3	86.2	27.1	22.1	31.9	3.5	1.6
29187	St. Francois County	65,881	87.2	70.5	23.9	17.5	23.5	3.1	2.5
29189	St. Louis County	1,000,363	98.1	81.5	26.2	18.6	30.2	4.8	1.8
29213	Taney County	53,114	96.7	78.7	25.6	18.8	25.8	5.8	2.8
29510	St. Louis city	318,892	96.4	67.4	20.2	10.6	26.4	7.9	2.3
30000	**Montana**	1,006,086	97.1	78.1	25.4	19.9	26.1	4.6	2.0
30013	Cascade County	81,975	96.8	78.8	25.8	19.5	26.7	4.5	2.3
30029	Flathead County	91,960	98.7	81.1	26.1	21.6	27.7	4.2	1.5
30031	Gallatin County	92,907	95.9	71.8	24.3	20.1	23.0	2.6	1.8
30049	Lewis and Clark County	64,819	97.4	78.0	25.9	20.2	26.2	3.8	2.0
30063	Missoula County	111,024	97.0	71.8	23.9	17.9	24.0	3.6	2.4
30111	Yellowstone County	151,974	97.5	79.2	25.4	18.7	27.4	5.3	2.6
31000	**Nebraska**	1,855,209	97.2	80.0	25.5	19.9	28.8	3.8	2.0
31055	Douglas County	531,000	97.7	79.2	23.9	17.1	30.9	5.1	2.2
31079	Hall County	60,140	98.5	81.8	24.4	18.3	30.5	4.2	4.3
31109	Lancaster County	293,380	95.5	74.3	23.9	18.4	26.5	3.2	2.2
31153	Sarpy County	165,919	99.2	87.1	26.7	21.3	33.3	4.1	1.7
32000	**Nevada**	2,754,148	98.7	81.3	23.3	16.3	29.8	9.0	3.0
32003	Clark County	1,997,371	98.9	81.9	22.9	15.5	30.6	9.8	3.1
32007	Elko County	50,904	98.3	85.7	24.7	19.9	31.7	7.6	1.9
32019	Lyon County	51,450	99.4	84.6	26.5	20.1	26.5	8.1	3.3
32031	Washoe County	429,241	98.4	78.5	23.4	17.1	28.3	7.1	2.6
32510	Carson City	54,481	96.1	76.2	23.1	17.2	26.8	6.5	2.6
33000	**New Hampshire**	1,321,050	96.9	80.1	26.2	20.7	26.9	4.0	2.3
33001	Belknap County	60,268	98.5	82.1	27.9	22.0	25.6	4.1	2.5
33005	Cheshire County	76,723	93.7	73.5	25.0	19.3	23.4	3.0	2.7
33009	Grafton County	89,268	92.2	73.3	24.6	19.3	23.7	3.6	2.1
33011	Hillsborough County	402,979	97.9	81.6	25.7	19.7	29.1	4.8	2.3

Table B-2: Counties with a Population of 50,000 or More—Relationships—*Continued*

State/ county FIPS code	State/county	Population in nonfamily households						Population in subfamilies as a percent of total population					
		Total population in nonfamily households	Nonfamily householders				Nonrelatives in nonfamily households	Total population in subfamilies	In married couple subfamilies			Parent in a parent-child subfamily	Child in a parent-child subfamily
			Total	Male living alone	Female living alone	Householder living with nonrelatives			Total in married-couple subfamilies	Spouse in a married-couple subfamily	Child in a married-couple subfamily		
	Minnesota—cont'd												
27109	Olmsted County	16.9	13.6	4.5	6.7	2.3	3.3	1.8	0.6	0.5	0.1	0.6	0.6
27111	Otter Tail County	15.7	13.7	5.3	6.8	1.6	2.0	1.3	0.5	0.4	0.1	0.3	0.5
27123	Ramsey County	21.6	16.6	5.7	7.5	3.4	5.0	2.5	0.9	0.7	0.2	0.7	0.9
27131	Rice County	12.4	10.5	4.6	4.2	1.7	1.9	1.3	0.3	0.2	0.1	0.4	0.6
27137	St. Louis County	22.8	17.2	6.9	7.1	3.3	5.6	1.4	0.4	0.3	0.0	0.5	0.6
27139	Scott County	10.7	8.2	3.1	3.3	1.8	2.5	1.9	1.0	0.8	0.2	0.4	0.4
27141	Sherburne County	10.6	7.8	3.1	2.9	1.9	2.7	2.7	1.4	1.2	0.2	0.7	0.6
27145	Stearns County	19.3	13.1	4.4	4.9	3.9	6.2	1.0	0.4	0.3	0.1	0.3	0.4
27163	Washington County	12.4	9.9	3.4	4.6	1.9	2.4	2.0	0.6	0.5	0.1	0.7	0.7
27169	Winona County	21.7	14.8	5.5	6.2	3.0	6.9	1.6	0.2	0.2	0.1	0.9	0.5
27171	Wright County	9.8	8.1	3.3	3.5	1.3	1.8	1.6	0.4	0.3	0.1	0.5	0.6
28000	**Mississippi**	14.0	11.5	4.4	5.6	1.5	2.4	5.0	0.9	0.7	0.2	1.9	2.2
28033	DeSoto County	11.3	9.0	3.3	4.3	1.4	2.3	4.3	1.2	1.0	0.2	1.4	1.6
28035	Forrest County	20.4	14.1	4.7	6.2	3.2	6.3	4.5	1.4	1.0	0.3	1.5	1.7
28047	Harrison County	16.8	13.2	5.4	5.5	2.3	3.6	4.3	1.4	1.1	0.2	1.4	1.6
28049	Hinds County	15.7	12.6	4.6	6.2	1.8	3.1	6.3	0.6	0.5	0.2	2.6	3.1
28059	Jackson County	13.8	11.2	4.4	4.9	1.9	2.6	5.1	1.3	1.1	0.2	1.7	2.1
28067	Jones County	12.7	10.5	3.6	5.3	1.6	2.3	4.5	0.7	0.6	0.1	1.8	2.0
28071	Lafayette County	23.8	13.1	4.6	5.7	2.8	10.7	0.0	0.0	0.0	0.0	0.0	0.0
28073	Lamar County	14.5	10.2	3.6	4.5	2.1	4.3	0.0	0.0	0.0	0.0	0.0	0.0
28075	Lauderdale County	14.4	12.2	4.8	5.9	1.4	2.3	5.1	1.7	1.3	0.4	1.7	1.7
28081	Lee County	12.8	10.8	3.8	5.5	1.5	1.9	3.8	0.6	0.5	0.0	1.5	1.7
28087	Lowndes County	16.5	13.5	5.6	6.0	1.9	3.0	0.0	0.0	0.0	0.0	0.0	0.0
28089	Madison County	12.6	10.9	4.4	5.3	1.2	1.7	3.8	0.6	0.4	0.2	1.6	1.7
28109	Pearl River County	13.0	11.1	3.7	6.1	1.4	1.9	6.8	2.6	1.6	1.0	1.9	2.4
28121	Rankin County	11.4	9.7	3.6	4.8	1.4	1.7	3.5	1.3	1.0	0.3	1.0	1.2
28151	Washington County	12.5	10.7	4.1	5.3	1.2	1.8	7.6	1.1	1.1	0.1	2.9	3.6
29000	**Missouri**	17.1	13.7	5.0	6.3	2.4	3.4	2.9	0.8	0.6	0.2	0.9	1.1
29019	Boone County	26.8	17.3	5.1	6.7	5.4	9.5	1.7	0.2	0.2	0.0	0.6	0.8
29021	Buchanan County	17.1	13.3	4.7	6.3	2.2	3.8	4.4	1.0	0.8	0.2	1.6	1.8
29031	Cape Girardeau County	18.4	13.8	5.0	6.0	2.8	4.7	2.8	0.8	0.6	0.2	1.0	1.0
29037	Cass County	12.0	9.8	3.3	4.7	1.8	2.2	3.5	0.8	0.5	0.3	1.2	1.5
29043	Christian County	10.8	8.8	3.0	4.3	1.5	2.0	2.5	0.4	0.2	0.1	1.0	1.2
29047	Clay County	15.7	12.2	4.3	5.5	2.4	3.5	2.9	0.7	0.6	0.1	0.9	1.3
29051	Cole County	16.4	13.2	4.8	6.2	2.2	3.2	3.5	1.2	0.7	0.5	1.0	1.2
29071	Franklin County	13.9	11.7	4.9	5.2	1.6	2.2	3.1	1.2	0.8	0.4	0.9	0.9
29077	Greene County	22.3	16.8	5.5	7.5	3.8	5.5	2.1	0.8	0.6	0.2	0.6	0.7
29095	Jackson County	20.2	16.1	6.0	7.3	2.8	4.1	3.0	0.6	0.5	0.1	1.0	1.3
29097	Jasper County	16.2	13.6	5.1	6.1	2.3	2.7	3.9	1.6	1.2	0.4	0.9	1.4
29099	Jefferson County	12.3	9.8	4.0	3.8	2.0	2.5	3.0	0.7	0.5	0.2	1.2	1.2
29101	Johnson County	19.4	13.2	4.4	3.8	5.1	6.2	1.2	0.3	0.3	0.0	0.3	0.5
29113	Lincoln County	11.6	9.5	4.5	3.4	1.6	2.1	3.9	2.3	1.8	0.5	0.7	0.9
29145	Newton County	13.8	11.2	4.6	4.5	2.1	2.6	2.9	1.3	0.8	0.5	0.7	0.9
29165	Platte County	16.2	13.4	5.0	6.3	2.1	2.8	2.8	1.1	0.8	0.3	0.7	1.0
29169	Pulaski County	14.1	9.9	4.5	3.1	2.3	4.2	0.0	0.0	0.0	0.0	0.0	0.0
29183	St. Charles County	12.0	10.0	3.6	4.8	1.6	2.0	2.2	0.7	0.5	0.2	0.7	0.8
29187	St. Francois County	16.7	13.4	5.2	6.1	2.1	3.3	2.0	0.1	0.1	0.0	0.7	1.2
29189	St. Louis County	16.6	14.0	4.8	7.2	2.0	2.6	2.8	0.8	0.6	0.2	0.9	1.1
29213	Taney County	18.0	13.5	4.5	6.7	2.3	4.5	0.0	0.0	0.0	0.0	0.0	0.0
29510	St. Louis city	29.0	23.2	9.0	10.1	4.1	5.8	3.4	0.5	0.4	0.1	1.3	1.6
30000	**Montana**	19.0	14.9	5.9	6.3	2.7	4.1	2.4	0.8	0.6	0.2	0.7	0.8
30013	Cascade County	18.0	14.9	6.1	6.7	2.1	3.1	2.3	1.1	0.8	0.3	0.6	0.6
30029	Flathead County	17.7	14.0	5.2	6.4	2.4	3.6	1.8	0.7	0.6	0.1	0.6	0.5
30031	Gallatin County	24.1	15.6	5.3	5.1	5.2	8.5	0.0	0.0	0.0	0.0	0.0	0.0
30049	Lewis and Clark County	19.4	15.4	5.8	6.8	2.8	4.1	2.0	0.9	0.7	0.2	0.5	0.6
30063	Missoula County	25.2	17.4	6.1	6.3	5.0	7.9	1.6	0.5	0.3	0.1	0.5	0.6
30111	Yellowstone County	18.3	14.4	5.3	6.5	2.6	3.9	2.7	0.9	0.7	0.2	0.9	0.9
31000	**Nebraska**	17.2	13.9	5.2	6.2	2.4	3.4	2.1	0.6	0.4	0.2	0.6	0.8
31055	Douglas County	18.6	14.9	5.6	6.7	2.6	3.7	2.6	0.7	0.5	0.2	0.8	1.0
31079	Hall County	16.8	12.7	4.4	5.7	2.6	4.1	1.8	1.0	0.7	0.3	0.3	0.4
31109	Lancaster County	21.2	15.5	5.3	6.4	3.8	5.6	1.6	0.4	0.3	0.1	0.5	0.7
31153	Sarpy County	12.1	9.8	3.7	4.2	1.8	2.3	2.5	0.8	0.5	0.3	0.8	0.9
32000	**Nevada**	17.4	12.9	5.2	4.9	2.8	4.5	4.4	1.8	1.4	0.4	1.2	1.3
32003	Clark County	17.0	12.6	5.0	4.8	2.7	4.4	4.7	1.9	1.6	0.4	1.3	1.4
32007	Elko County	12.6	9.7	4.1	3.4	2.3	2.9	4.9	3.3	2.0	1.3	0.8	0.8
32019	Lyon County	14.8	11.5	4.2	4.5	2.8	3.3	0.0	0.0	0.0	0.0	0.0	0.0
32031	Washoe County	19.9	14.5	5.8	5.5	3.2	5.4	3.6	1.5	1.2	0.3	1.0	1.1
32510	Carson City	19.9	15.8	6.2	6.9	2.8	4.1	3.9	0.8	0.7	0.0	1.3	1.8
33000	**New Hampshire**	16.8	13.0	4.5	5.5	3.0	3.8	2.3	0.9	0.7	0.2	0.6	0.7
33001	Belknap County	16.3	13.0	5.0	5.3	2.7	3.4	1.1	0.0	0.0	0.0	0.6	0.5
33005	Cheshire County	20.3	14.9	4.6	6.5	3.8	5.4	1.7	0.7	0.5	0.1	0.5	0.5
33009	Grafton County	18.9	14.9	5.3	7.0	2.7	4.0	1.8	0.7	0.6	0.1	0.5	0.9
33011	Hillsborough County	16.4	12.7	4.6	5.1	3.0	3.7	2.8	1.2	0.9	0.3	0.8	0.9

Part B — Relationships 111

State/ county FIPS code	State/county	Total population	Percent of the population in households	Population in family households, percent					
				Percent in family households	Householder in family household, percent	Spouse in family household, percent	Child in family household (biological, adopted, or stepchild)	Other relative in family household	Nonrelatives in family household
	New Hampshire—cont'd								
33013	Merrimack County	146,807	95.6	79.5	25.9	20.6	26.4	3.9	2.8
33015	Rockingham County	297,728	99.2	83.6	27.4	22.5	28.3	3.6	1.8
33017	Strafford County	124,319	93.4	76.0	25.0	19.0	26.1	3.5	2.4
34000	**New Jersey**	8,867,909	97.9	84.3	24.8	18.2	31.8	7.3	2.1
34001	Atlantic County	275,339	97.5	82.7	24.8	16.4	29.7	9.0	2.8
34003	Bergen County	919,049	98.8	86.5	26.1	20.4	31.7	6.9	1.4
34005	Burlington County	451,071	97.3	83.9	25.3	19.4	31.5	6.0	1.6
34007	Camden County	513,404	98.6	84.1	24.3	16.5	33.4	7.7	2.2
34009	Cape May County	96,305	97.2	79.2	26.9	21.9	24.3	4.6	1.6
34011	Cumberland County	157,658	91.9	79.1	21.9	13.8	31.0	8.8	3.6
34013	Essex County	787,615	97.3	82.3	23.0	13.7	33.6	9.2	2.7
34015	Gloucester County	289,837	98.3	86.2	26.2	19.6	32.6	5.9	1.8
34017	Hudson County	652,921	98.9	78.7	23.1	14.3	28.2	10.4	2.6
34019	Hunterdon County	126,505	96.2	84.5	27.0	22.9	29.6	3.5	1.4
34021	Mercer County	369,019	94.8	80.1	23.9	17.6	29.9	6.7	1.9
34023	Middlesex County	822,933	96.9	84.8	24.7	18.9	31.4	8.0	1.9
34025	Monmouth County	629,754	98.9	85.7	26.0	20.4	32.3	5.4	1.6
34027	Morris County	497,591	98.1	85.8	26.0	21.7	31.8	4.7	1.5
34029	Ocean County	581,223	98.7	84.3	25.5	20.2	31.5	5.0	2.1
34031	Passaic County	504,475	98.1	87.5	23.6	15.2	35.7	10.7	2.3
34033	Salem County	65,651	97.7	82.6	25.4	17.9	30.2	7.1	2.1
34035	Somerset County	328,432	98.7	87.5	25.7	21.0	32.9	6.1	1.6
34037	Sussex County	147,114	98.6	87.2	27.3	22.4	31.7	4.2	1.7
34039	Union County	544,223	98.7	86.4	24.1	16.8	33.5	8.9	3.0
34041	Warren County	107,790	98.0	83.8	27.0	21.3	29.6	4.3	1.6
35000	**New Mexico**	2,082,250	97.9	82.0	23.8	16.5	31.1	8.3	2.4
35001	Bernalillo County	672,027	98.4	79.8	24.3	16.3	29.5	7.3	2.5
35005	Chaves County	65,749	96.7	83.9	24.8	16.8	33.4	6.3	2.6
35009	Curry County	50,328	97.9	84.4	25.5	18.4	32.3	5.9	2.3
35013	Do±a Ana County	213,395	97.7	83.2	24.2	16.5	33.1	7.4	2.1
35015	Eddy County	54,646	98.6	83.9	25.4	17.8	31.4	6.9	2.4
35025	Lea County	66,424	97.2	86.8	24.0	17.5	33.6	9.4	2.3
35031	McKinley County	73,175	99.0	90.0	16.8	9.8	42.5	18.3	2.7
35035	Otero County	65,678	95.6	81.8	24.4	17.8	30.4	7.4	1.9
35043	Sandoval County	135,387	99.5	86.4	24.8	18.3	32.5	8.1	2.7
35045	San Juan County	127,620	98.7	88.4	22.7	15.5	34.7	13.1	2.3
35049	Santa Fe County	146,429	97.8	75.8	24.2	17.6	25.2	6.6	2.2
35061	Valencia County	76,583	97.9	85.4	24.4	18.0	32.8	7.5	2.7
36000	**New York**	19,576,660	97.0	79.9	23.5	16.1	30.1	7.9	2.3
36001	Albany County	305,890	94.4	71.2	22.3	16.2	26.1	4.7	1.9
36005	Bronx County	1,407,535	97.0	83.0	22.1	9.1	36.2	12.6	3.0
36007	Broome County	198,379	94.7	74.1	24.0	17.7	26.1	3.9	2.3
36009	Cattaraugus County	79,321	96.6	77.7	25.3	18.5	28.0	3.4	2.5
36011	Cayuga County	79,610	95.3	78.4	24.7	17.8	27.8	5.3	2.8
36013	Chautauqua County	133,584	95.1	76.3	25.5	18.7	26.0	3.9	2.2
36015	Chemung County	88,864	93.0	74.6	25.0	18.2	26.0	4.1	1.4
36019	Clinton County	81,666	90.4	72.2	25.1	18.6	23.0	2.9	2.5
36021	Columbia County	62,445	96.0	77.9	26.0	19.4	25.2	4.8	2.6
36027	Dutchess County	297,435	93.8	78.6	23.9	18.5	29.5	4.9	1.8
36029	Erie County	919,332	96.9	76.9	25.0	17.4	28.8	4.0	1.7
36033	Franklin County	51,699	87.9	70.6	22.5	16.5	25.3	3.6	2.6
36035	Fulton County	54,941	97.6	79.6	26.8	19.4	25.6	4.9	2.9
36037	Genesee County	59,796	98.5	81.6	26.9	20.8	28.1	3.8	1.9
36043	Herkimer County	64,442	97.9	80.8	27.4	20.0	26.5	3.9	3.0
36045	Jefferson County	119,580	94.8	80.1	25.5	19.2	29.3	3.8	2.3
36047	Kings County	2,567,201	98.5	80.9	22.4	13.3	32.0	11.0	2.2
36051	Livingston County	64,875	90.5	72.6	24.0	18.7	24.6	3.1	2.1
36053	Madison County	72,543	92.7	77.1	24.1	18.4	28.1	4.4	2.1
36055	Monroe County	748,221	96.4	76.8	24.2	16.9	28.7	4.8	2.1
36059	Nassau County	1,348,563	98.4	89.0	25.0	19.7	33.9	8.4	2.0
36061	New York County	1,618,266	96.3	60.0	18.4	11.7	21.0	7.3	1.6
36063	Niagara County	214,928	98.1	79.7	25.7	18.5	28.9	4.1	2.5
36065	Oneida County	233,856	94.3	76.0	23.7	16.9	29.1	4.2	2.0
36067	Onondaga County	467,650	95.9	76.5	24.0	17.1	28.7	4.7	2.1
36069	Ontario County	108,760	96.4	79.5	27.0	20.0	25.9	4.0	2.6
36071	Orange County	374,662	96.8	85.4	24.0	18.2	35.3	5.7	2.2
36075	Oswego County	121,594	96.2	80.1	25.0	18.0	29.3	4.7	3.0
36077	Otsego County	61,879	91.3	71.1	23.7	18.3	23.8	3.5	1.7
36079	Putnam County	99,731	97.6	88.4	26.3	21.8	32.7	5.9	1.7
36081	Queens County	2,276,634	98.8	83.9	22.8	15.1	30.0	12.8	3.1
36083	Rensselaer County	159,767	96.3	77.1	24.8	18.3	27.8	4.2	2.0
36085	Richmond County	471,486	98.4	87.5	25.5	18.6	34.2	7.7	1.4
36087	Rockland County	318,064	97.8	88.6	23.4	18.7	37.5	6.8	2.3
36089	St. Lawrence County	112,180	89.8	72.5	23.4	17.1	25.2	4.2	2.5

Table B-2: Counties with a Population of 50,000 or More—Relationships—*Continued*

State/county FIPS code	State/county	Population in nonfamily households						Population in subfamilies as a percent of total population					
		Total population in nonfamily households	Nonfamily householders				Nonrelatives in nonfamily households	Total population in subfamilies	In married couple subfamilies			Parent in a parent-child subfamily	Child in a parent-child subfamily
			Total	Male living alone	Female living alone	Householder living with nonrelatives			Total in married-couple subfamilies	Spouse in a married-couple subfamily	Child in married-couple subfamily		
	New Hampshire—cont'd												
33013	Merrimack County	16.1	12.6	4.4	5.5	2.7	3.5	2.5	0.7	0.5	0.2	0.9	1.0
33015	Rockingham County	15.6	11.9	4.0	5.0	2.9	3.6	2.3	1.1	0.8	0.3	0.5	0.6
33017	Strafford County	17.4	12.5	3.7	5.3	3.6	4.9	2.0	1.1	0.9	0.2	0.4	0.5
34000	**New Jersey**	13.6	11.0	3.8	5.5	1.8	2.6	3.6	1.5	1.2	0.3	1.0	1.1
34001	Atlantic County	14.7	12.0	4.5	5.7	1.9	2.7	5.1	1.7	1.3	0.3	1.5	2.0
34003	Bergen County	12.3	10.3	3.5	5.4	1.4	1.9	3.1	1.8	1.5	0.3	0.6	0.7
34005	Burlington County	13.5	11.1	3.7	5.6	1.7	2.4	3.4	1.1	0.8	0.3	1.1	1.3
34007	Camden County	14.5	11.9	4.0	6.1	1.9	2.6	4.1	1.2	1.0	0.3	1.4	1.5
34009	Cape May County	18.0	15.1	5.2	7.9	2.0	2.8	2.9	1.3	0.9	0.4	0.7	0.9
34011	Cumberland County	12.8	9.8	3.2	4.7	2.0	3.0	5.5	1.0	0.7	0.2	2.1	2.5
34013	Essex County	15.0	12.1	4.4	5.9	1.8	2.9	3.9	1.1	0.9	0.2	1.3	1.5
34015	Gloucester County	12.1	9.7	3.4	4.6	1.7	2.5	3.3	1.0	0.8	0.2	1.1	1.2
34017	Hudson County	20.2	14.6	5.3	5.7	3.5	5.6	4.4	1.8	1.5	0.3	1.2	1.4
34019	Hunterdon County	11.8	9.7	3.3	4.7	1.8	2.0	2.1	1.4	0.8	0.5	0.3	0.4
34021	Mercer County	14.7	11.7	4.0	5.7	1.9	3.1	2.9	1.1	0.9	0.2	0.9	1.0
34023	Middlesex County	12.1	9.6	3.2	4.8	1.6	2.5	4.1	2.3	2.0	0.3	0.8	1.0
34025	Monmouth County	13.2	11.1	3.7	5.7	1.7	2.2	2.7	1.3	1.0	0.3	0.6	0.7
34027	Morris County	12.4	10.2	3.6	5.0	1.5	2.1	2.0	1.3	1.1	0.3	0.3	0.4
34029	Ocean County	14.4	12.5	3.9	7.1	1.5	1.9	2.9	1.1	0.8	0.3	0.7	1.0
34031	Passaic County	10.6	8.6	3.2	4.3	1.1	1.9	5.3	2.0	1.6	0.4	1.5	1.8
34033	Salem County	15.1	12.1	4.5	5.7	1.9	2.9	4.6	1.2	1.0	0.2	1.8	1.6
34035	Somerset County	11.2	9.2	2.9	4.9	1.4	2.0	2.7	1.6	1.3	0.3	0.6	0.6
34037	Sussex County	11.3	9.5	3.9	4.0	1.6	1.9	2.3	1.1	0.9	0.2	0.5	0.7
34039	Union County	12.3	10.0	3.4	5.2	1.4	2.3	3.8	1.3	1.2	0.1	1.2	1.3
34041	Warren County	14.2	11.7	3.7	5.7	2.3	2.5	2.0	0.8	0.6	0.2	0.4	0.7
35000	**New Mexico**	16.0	12.8	4.9	5.6	2.2	3.2	4.9	1.3	1.0	0.3	1.7	1.9
35001	Bernalillo County	18.6	14.9	5.5	6.6	2.7	3.8	3.9	1.2	1.0	0.2	1.3	1.4
35005	Chaves County	12.9	10.8	3.9	5.3	1.6	2.1	3.6	1.0	0.7	0.3	1.3	1.3
35009	Curry County	13.5	10.8	4.4	4.9	1.5	2.8	0.0	0.0	0.0	0.0	0.0	0.0
35013	Do±a Ana County	14.5	10.6	3.6	4.7	2.3	3.9	5.4	1.3	1.0	0.3	1.8	2.4
35015	Eddy County	14.7	12.0	5.0	4.9	2.1	2.7	4.1	1.0	0.9	0.2	1.5	1.7
35025	Lea County	10.4	8.2	3.5	3.1	1.5	2.2	6.2	2.1	1.6	0.5	1.8	2.3
35031	McKinley County	8.9	7.5	3.4	3.4	0.8	1.4	12.8	2.4	1.7	0.7	5.2	5.2
35035	Otero County	13.9	11.8	5.6	4.6	1.6	2.0	5.7	0.6	0.5	0.1	2.3	2.9
35043	Sandoval County	13.1	10.4	3.8	4.4	2.1	2.7	5.4	1.8	1.3	0.5	1.6	2.0
35045	San Juan County	10.3	8.4	3.6	3.5	1.3	1.9	7.9	1.9	1.2	0.7	2.7	3.3
35049	Santa Fe County	22.0	17.4	5.8	8.3	3.3	4.6	3.3	1.1	0.9	0.2	1.1	1.1
35061	Valencia County	12.4	10.1	3.9	4.6	1.6	2.3	4.8	1.4	1.2	0.2	1.8	1.6
36000	**New York**	17.1	13.4	4.7	6.3	2.4	3.7	4.0	1.5	1.2	0.3	1.1	1.3
36001	Albany County	23.1	17.6	6.2	7.7	3.7	5.5	2.4	0.6	0.5	0.1	0.8	0.9
36005	Bronx County	14.0	11.6	4.3	5.9	1.4	2.3	6.0	1.4	1.1	0.3	2.2	2.4
36007	Broome County	20.7	15.9	5.5	7.4	3.0	4.7	1.9	0.9	0.6	0.3	0.5	0.5
36009	Cattaraugus County	18.9	15.0	6.0	6.0	2.9	3.9	2.0	0.7	0.5	0.2	0.6	0.7
36011	Cayuga County	17.0	14.0	5.3	6.3	2.4	3.0	3.0	0.6	0.5	0.2	1.2	1.2
36013	Chautauqua County	18.7	15.2	5.7	6.6	2.8	3.5	2.4	0.7	0.4	0.2	0.8	1.0
36015	Chemung County	18.4	14.9	5.3	6.7	2.8	3.5	2.6	1.2	0.7	0.4	0.6	0.8
36019	Clinton County	18.2	14.1	4.6	6.0	3.5	4.1	1.6	0.4	0.3	0.1	0.4	0.7
36021	Columbia County	18.1	13.9	5.0	6.0	3.0	4.1	2.5	0.9	0.8	0.1	0.8	0.8
36027	Dutchess County	15.2	12.0	4.3	5.6	2.1	3.2	2.5	1.0	0.8	0.2	0.7	0.8
36029	Erie County	20.0	16.4	5.7	8.0	2.6	3.6	1.9	0.6	0.5	0.1	0.6	0.7
36033	Franklin County	17.3	13.9	4.8	6.3	2.8	3.5	2.1	0.4	0.3	0.1	0.9	0.9
36035	Fulton County	18.1	13.9	5.1	5.7	3.1	4.2	2.8	1.3	1.0	0.3	0.6	0.9
36037	Genesee County	16.9	13.3	5.4	5.2	2.7	3.6	2.0	0.6	0.5	0.2	0.6	0.8
36043	Herkimer County	17.1	14.4	5.6	6.4	2.4	2.7	2.5	1.2	0.8	0.4	0.5	0.8
36045	Jefferson County	14.6	11.9	4.5	5.2	2.2	2.8	2.3	0.6	0.4	0.2	0.7	0.9
36047	Kings County	17.6	13.2	4.2	6.2	2.8	4.4	5.4	1.9	1.5	0.4	1.5	2.0
36051	Livingston County	17.9	12.7	4.2	5.6	2.8	5.2	1.4	0.6	0.4	0.2	0.3	0.4
36053	Madison County	15.6	12.4	5.1	5.4	2.0	3.2	2.3	1.1	0.8	0.3	0.7	0.9
36055	Monroe County	19.6	15.6	5.5	7.1	3.0	4.1	2.6	0.9	0.7	0.2	0.8	0.9
36059	Nassau County	9.5	7.7	2.4	4.2	1.2	1.8	4.3	2.3	1.8	0.5	0.9	1.1
36061	New York County	36.3	27.0	9.2	12.7	5.0	9.3	3.1	0.9	0.8	0.1	1.1	1.1
36063	Niagara County	18.3	15.5	5.9	7.3	2.2	2.9	2.5	0.6	0.5	0.1	0.9	1.0
36065	Oneida County	18.4	15.1	5.9	6.8	2.4	3.3	2.4	1.0	0.7	0.3	0.6	0.7
36067	Onondaga County	19.4	15.3	5.6	7.0	2.7	4.1	2.5	0.8	0.6	0.2	0.8	0.9
36069	Ontario County	16.9	13.4	4.7	6.3	2.5	3.6	1.8	0.5	0.4	0.1	0.6	0.7
36071	Orange County	11.3	9.4	3.5	4.3	1.5	2.0	3.0	1.1	0.8	0.3	0.9	1.1
36075	Oswego County	16.1	12.0	4.4	4.7	2.9	4.1	2.8	0.9	0.6	0.3	1.0	0.9
36077	Otsego County	20.2	14.5	4.7	5.9	3.8	5.6	2.4	1.0	0.8	0.2	0.6	0.8
36079	Putnam County	9.2	7.7	3.0	3.8	1.0	1.5	4.3	2.8	2.0	0.8	0.6	0.9
36081	Queens County	14.9	11.3	3.9	5.3	2.2	3.6	6.1	2.9	2.4	0.5	1.4	1.8
36083	Rensselaer County	19.2	15.0	5.5	6.2	3.3	4.1	1.8	0.5	0.4	0.1	0.6	0.7
36085	Richmond County	10.9	9.4	3.3	4.9	1.1	1.5	4.2	1.9	1.4	0.5	0.9	1.4
36087	Rockland County	9.2	7.4	2.5	3.8	1.1	1.8	3.3	1.4	1.1	0.3	0.9	1.0
36089	St. Lawrence County	17.3	13.5	4.8	5.8	2.8	3.9	2.6	0.9	0.6	0.2	0.8	0.9

Table B-2: Counties with a Population of 50,000 or More—Relationships—*Continued*

State/county FIPS code	State/county	Total population	Percent of the population in households	Population in family households, percent					
				Percent in family households	Householder in family household, percent	Spouse in family household, percent	Child in family household (biological, adopted, or stepchild)	Other relative in family household	Nonrelatives in family household
	New York—cont'd								
36091	Saratoga County	222,411	98.1	80.5	26.1	21.0	27.8	3.7	1.9
36093	Schenectady County	155,046	97.2	78.9	22.6	17.0	32.3	5.4	1.6
36101	Steuben County	98,955	98.2	80.1	26.9	19.8	27.1	3.6	2.8
36103	Suffolk County	1,499,091	97.9	87.5	24.8	19.1	32.9	8.4	2.3
36105	Sullivan County	76,861	94.5	77.4	22.9	16.7	29.8	5.4	2.6
36107	Tioga County	50,556	98.9	85.4	27.9	22.4	28.3	4.3	2.5
36109	Tompkins County	102,726	86.9	60.2	19.9	15.8	19.3	2.4	2.8
36111	Ulster County	181,806	93.2	75.4	24.1	17.7	26.2	5.2	2.2
36113	Warren County	65,516	98.7	80.8	27.1	20.3	26.1	4.8	2.5
36115	Washington County	63,262	94.9	79.7	25.8	19.3	26.1	4.9	3.5
36117	Wayne County	92,913	98.0	83.0	26.9	20.8	28.6	4.9	1.8
36119	Westchester County	962,233	97.1	84.2	24.6	18.1	32.0	7.1	2.3
37000	**North Carolina**	9,749,266	97.4	81.1	25.3	18.4	29.0	6.4	2.0
37001	Alamance County	153,623	97.1	82.3	26.5	18.5	28.6	6.5	2.1
37019	Brunswick County	112,588	99.2	84.7	30.2	23.7	22.8	5.5	2.5
37021	Buncombe County	244,612	97.0	74.7	24.1	18.2	25.5	5.0	1.9
37023	Burke County	90,340	96.7	80.8	24.7	17.6	28.3	7.7	2.5
37025	Cabarrus County	184,170	99.2	86.5	25.3	20.0	33.0	6.3	1.9
37027	Caldwell County	82,078	98.7	83.3	24.7	18.4	29.3	8.5	2.5
37031	Carteret County	67,858	98.4	80.9	28.4	21.3	24.2	5.1	2.0
37035	Catawba County	154,416	98.4	83.8	26.0	19.8	30.0	5.9	2.1
37037	Chatham County	65,991	98.7	84.9	27.8	22.8	26.8	5.2	2.2
37045	Cleveland County	97,367	98.2	82.9	25.3	18.4	28.9	8.3	2.0
37047	Columbus County	57,558	95.2	80.2	24.2	16.2	29.1	9.3	1.4
37049	Craven County	104,791	96.1	82.8	26.7	20.6	27.6	5.8	2.1
37051	Cumberland County	324,222	96.8	81.3	25.0	16.5	31.1	6.7	2.0
37057	Davidson County	163,190	98.8	83.9	26.8	20.2	28.7	6.2	2.0
37061	Duplin County	59,900	98.7	82.5	25.1	17.6	30.4	6.7	2.8
37063	Durham County	282,112	95.2	73.2	23.3	15.6	25.9	6.1	2.2
37065	Edgecombe County	55,797	97.6	83.7	25.2	14.6	32.2	9.5	2.2
37067	Forsyth County	357,815	97.2	79.7	25.0	17.6	29.3	5.9	2.0
37069	Franklin County	61,672	97.2	83.5	25.8	19.5	29.6	6.4	2.1
37071	Gaston County	208,105	98.6	84.0	25.9	18.1	30.1	7.8	2.0
37077	Granville County	57,957	93.3	81.8	24.5	17.1	29.6	8.4	2.2
37081	Guilford County	500,931	96.9	78.6	25.1	17.0	28.6	6.0	1.8
37083	Halifax County	53,903	97.2	82.2	26.4	15.4	28.1	9.9	2.4
37085	Harnett County	122,124	97.2	84.3	23.9	17.8	34.2	6.1	2.3
37087	Haywood County	58,883	98.9	81.1	29.9	22.2	22.5	4.9	1.6
37089	Henderson County	108,386	98.7	82.5	28.2	23.3	24.4	5.0	1.6
37093	Hoke County	50,441	97.7	87.5	24.6	17.0	34.2	9.3	2.5
37097	Iredell County	162,762	99.2	87.3	26.6	20.4	31.7	6.3	2.2
37101	Johnston County	175,172	98.9	87.4	26.0	19.5	34.2	5.7	2.1
37105	Lee County	59,471	98.1	84.2	25.1	18.2	31.8	6.8	2.3
37107	Lenoir County	59,175	98.1	81.8	25.8	15.8	29.4	8.4	2.4
37109	Lincoln County	79,278	99.1	86.4	27.2	21.8	27.9	8.2	1.3
37119	Mecklenburg County	967,906	98.4	79.1	23.7	16.3	29.9	7.0	2.1
37125	Moore County	90,439	98.8	83.6	27.4	22.6	27.1	5.5	1.1
37127	Nash County	95,497	97.6	81.7	25.7	17.7	29.8	6.8	1.8
37129	New Hanover County	209,492	96.8	73.4	24.1	17.5	24.4	5.1	2.4
37133	Onslow County	182,352	92.4	79.9	24.0	18.3	31.5	4.1	2.0
37135	Orange County	137,927	92.6	70.4	22.7	17.7	24.8	3.6	1.6
37141	Pender County	54,337	97.3	84.3	25.7	19.4	29.9	7.0	2.3
37147	Pitt County	172,672	96.5	72.9	23.1	15.2	27.3	6.1	1.2
37151	Randolph County	142,386	99.0	86.0	26.9	20.2	29.8	6.9	2.2
37155	Robeson County	135,080	97.3	85.2	23.9	13.5	33.1	11.7	3.0
37157	Rockingham County	92,573	98.6	82.4	27.5	19.6	26.9	6.6	1.8
37159	Rowan County	138,140	96.9	82.6	25.5	18.4	29.4	6.8	2.5
37161	Rutherford County	67,224	98.2	84.9	28.2	20.6	26.0	7.5	2.6
37163	Sampson County	63,924	98.5	84.3	24.4	16.8	30.7	10.5	1.9
37167	Stanly County	60,530	96.6	83.1	27.1	19.9	28.2	5.8	1.9
37171	Surry County	73,402	98.7	83.7	27.5	20.7	28.6	5.4	1.6
37179	Union County	208,808	99.0	90.4	26.1	21.1	35.1	6.7	1.4
37183	Wake County	951,834	97.6	81.1	24.8	19.1	30.5	5.1	1.7
37189	Watauga County	52,026	90.2	57.9	20.0	16.4	16.5	3.6	1.4
37191	Wayne County	124,262	97.6	81.7	25.7	16.8	29.5	6.9	2.7
37193	Wilkes County	69,144	98.5	84.5	27.8	21.2	27.1	6.1	2.4
37195	Wilson County	81,624	98.1	83.0	25.7	17.0	30.8	7.2	2.3
38000	**North Dakota**	703,203	96.3	75.5	25.1	20.2	25.4	3.0	1.8
38015	Burleigh County	85,907	96.5	76.6	25.6	20.4	26.4	2.6	1.6
38017	Cass County	157,420	96.9	70.7	23.2	18.2	24.7	3.1	1.5
38035	Grand Forks County	67,773	92.8	67.1	22.2	17.6	22.8	2.5	1.9
38101	Ward County	65,911	95.9	75.8	23.3	19.0	27.7	3.9	1.8
39000	**Ohio**	11,557,868	97.3	79.8	25.3	18.4	29.0	5.1	2.0
39003	Allen County	105,528	96.3	80.0	24.9	17.3	29.3	5.8	2.7

114 Families in America

State/county FIPS code	State/county	Population in nonfamily households						Population in subfamilies as a percent of total population					
		Total population in nonfamily households	Nonfamily householders				Nonrelatives in nonfamily households	Total population in subfamilies	In married couple subfamilies			Parent in a parent-child subfamily	Child in a parent-child subfamily
			Total	Male living alone	Female living alone	Householder living with nonrelatives			Total in married-couple subfamilies	Spouse in a married-couple subfamily	Child in married-couple subfamily		
	New York—cont'd												
36091	Saratoga County	17.6	14.0	4.8	6.3	3.0	3.6	1.8	0.8	0.5	0.4	0.5	0.5
36093	Schenectady County	18.2	14.7	5.6	7.0	2.1	3.5	3.4	1.2	1.1	0.2	1.1	1.0
36101	Steuben County	18.1	15.1	5.9	6.5	2.7	3.0	2.1	0.8	0.5	0.3	0.5	0.8
36103	Suffolk County	10.4	8.3	2.8	4.0	1.4	2.1	4.8	2.1	1.6	0.5	1.1	1.5
36105	Sullivan County	17.1	14.0	5.5	6.0	2.5	3.1	3.3	1.0	0.8	0.2	1.1	1.3
36107	Tioga County	13.5	11.6	4.2	5.7	1.7	1.9	2.7	1.7	1.0	0.6	0.5	0.6
36109	Tompkins County	26.7	17.3	5.1	6.6	5.6	9.4	1.5	0.6	0.5	0.1	0.4	0.5
36111	Ulster County	17.8	13.9	4.8	6.3	2.9	3.9	2.3	0.9	0.7	0.2	0.7	0.7
36113	Warren County	17.9	14.6	5.0	7.0	2.6	3.3	0.0	0.0	0.0	0.0	0.0	0.0
36115	Washington County	15.2	12.4	4.1	5.8	2.4	2.8	2.7	0.9	0.7	0.3	0.8	0.9
36117	Wayne County	15.0	12.2	4.6	5.2	2.4	2.8	3.1	0.8	0.4	0.3	0.9	1.4
36119	Westchester County	13.0	10.9	3.7	5.9	1.3	2.1	3.3	1.8	1.4	0.4	0.7	0.8
37000	**North Carolina**	16.3	12.9	4.6	6.1	2.2	3.4	3.4	0.9	0.7	0.2	1.2	1.3
37001	Alamance County	14.9	12.7	4.2	6.9	1.6	2.2	3.2	0.7	0.6	0.1	1.2	1.3
37019	Brunswick County	14.5	12.2	4.0	6.5	1.7	2.3	2.6	0.6	0.5	0.1	1.0	1.0
37021	Buncombe County	22.4	16.9	5.4	8.1	3.4	5.5	2.7	0.9	0.7	0.2	0.9	1.0
37023	Burke County	15.8	12.8	4.7	6.4	1.8	3.0	4.5	1.7	1.4	0.3	1.6	1.3
37025	Cabarrus County	12.7	10.0	3.4	5.1	1.5	2.7	4.1	1.2	0.9	0.4	1.4	1.4
37027	Caldwell County	15.4	13.6	5.9	6.6	1.1	1.8	3.8	1.8	1.7	0.1	1.0	1.0
37031	Carteret County	17.4	14.3	5.5	6.7	2.2	3.1	2.6	1.1	0.9	0.2	0.8	0.7
37035	Catawba County	14.6	11.7	4.1	5.4	2.1	2.9	3.1	0.9	0.7	0.2	1.0	1.2
37037	Chatham County	13.8	11.8	3.9	6.5	1.4	2.0	0.0	0.0	0.0	0.0	0.0	0.0
37045	Cleveland County	15.3	13.2	5.1	6.6	1.5	2.2	4.5	1.2	1.0	0.2	1.5	1.8
37047	Columbus County	15.1	13.2	5.0	6.6	1.5	1.9	5.2	2.2	1.6	0.5	1.3	1.7
37049	Craven County	13.3	11.0	3.7	5.5	1.7	2.2	3.8	0.6	0.4	0.1	1.5	1.8
37051	Cumberland County	15.6	12.9	5.2	5.7	1.9	2.7	3.8	1.0	0.6	0.4	1.2	1.6
37057	Davidson County	15.0	12.2	4.4	6.0	1.8	2.8	3.5	1.6	1.2	0.4	0.8	1.0
37061	Duplin County	16.2	11.8	4.1	5.4	2.3	4.4	3.3	0.4	0.4	0.1	1.6	1.4
37063	Durham County	22.0	16.7	5.5	7.5	3.6	5.4	2.9	0.2	0.2	0.1	1.2	1.5
37065	Edgecombe County	13.9	11.6	4.3	5.5	1.7	2.3	4.8	0.8	0.7	0.2	1.9	2.0
37067	Forsyth County	17.5	14.4	5.2	7.1	2.1	3.1	2.8	0.6	0.4	0.2	1.0	1.2
37069	Franklin County	13.7	11.8	4.9	5.4	1.5	1.9	0.0	0.0	0.0	0.0	0.0	0.0
37071	Gaston County	14.6	12.4	4.7	5.9	1.7	2.3	3.8	1.1	0.8	0.3	1.2	1.5
37077	Granville County	11.5	9.9	4.3	4.5	1.0	1.7	4.9	0.9	0.9	0.0	2.1	1.9
37081	Guilford County	18.3	14.5	4.8	7.0	2.7	3.8	2.9	0.7	0.6	0.1	1.0	1.3
37083	Halifax County	15.0	13.6	5.1	7.4	1.2	1.4	5.4	0.4	0.3	0.1	1.9	3.2
37085	Harnett County	12.9	10.1	4.1	4.2	1.8	2.8	3.3	0.7	0.6	0.1	1.3	1.3
37087	Haywood County	17.8	15.0	5.5	7.1	2.3	2.9	2.6	0.5	0.5	0.0	0.9	1.2
37089	Henderson County	16.2	13.5	4.7	6.8	2.1	2.6	3.6	0.8	0.6	0.2	1.4	1.3
37093	Hoke County	10.1	8.4	3.3	4.0	1.0	1.8	5.6	0.9	0.6	0.2	2.2	2.5
37097	Iredell County	12.0	9.7	3.7	4.7	1.3	2.2	3.3	1.0	0.8	0.2	1.1	1.2
37101	Johnston County	11.6	8.6	2.7	4.1	1.7	3.0	3.2	1.1	0.9	0.2	1.1	1.1
37105	Lee County	13.9	11.0	3.8	5.3	1.9	2.9	4.5	1.2	0.9	0.3	1.4	1.9
37107	Lenoir County	16.3	13.9	4.7	7.6	1.6	2.4	0.0	0.0	0.0	0.0	0.0	0.0
37109	Lincoln County	12.7	10.6	3.8	5.2	1.5	2.1	4.4	1.0	0.8	0.2	1.4	2.0
37119	Mecklenburg County	19.3	14.5	5.0	6.5	2.9	4.9	3.5	0.9	0.7	0.2	1.2	1.4
37125	Moore County	15.2	12.9	4.5	7.0	1.4	2.2	3.0	0.7	0.5	0.2	1.0	1.3
37127	Nash County	15.9	13.1	4.6	6.8	1.8	2.8	4.4	0.5	0.3	0.2	1.8	2.1
37129	New Hanover County	23.4	17.2	5.3	7.8	4.1	6.2	2.4	0.9	0.6	0.3	0.7	0.8
37133	Onslow County	12.5	9.3	3.6	3.8	1.9	3.3	2.2	0.7	0.5	0.2	0.8	0.5
37135	Orange County	22.2	14.7	5.2	5.8	3.7	7.5	1.8	0.6	0.4	0.2	0.7	0.5
37141	Pender County	13.0	10.3	4.6	4.0	1.6	2.8	4.4	1.4	1.4	0.1	1.4	1.6
37147	Pitt County	23.6	15.6	4.8	6.7	4.2	8.0	3.3	0.5	0.4	0.1	1.3	1.5
37151	Randolph County	13.0	11.0	4.3	5.2	1.5	2.0	3.8	1.1	0.9	0.2	1.2	1.6
37155	Robeson County	12.1	9.6	3.6	4.7	1.4	2.5	6.8	0.9	0.7	0.1	2.7	3.2
37157	Rockingham County	16.2	13.3	4.5	7.0	1.9	2.8	3.2	0.6	0.5	0.1	1.3	1.3
37159	Rowan County	14.3	11.7	4.2	5.7	1.8	2.6	3.1	0.9	0.8	0.1	1.0	1.2
37161	Rutherford County	13.3	11.5	4.3	5.9	1.2	1.8	3.9	0.3	0.2	0.1	1.8	1.7
37163	Sampson County	14.1	11.4	3.8	5.8	1.7	2.8	6.9	2.3	1.3	0.9	2.0	2.7
37167	Stanly County	13.5	11.6	5.3	5.2	1.1	1.8	4.3	0.6	0.4	0.1	1.8	1.9
37171	Surry County	15.0	13.1	4.8	7.0	1.3	1.9	3.0	1.4	0.9	0.5	0.8	0.9
37179	Union County	8.6	6.7	2.4	3.2	1.2	1.9	3.7	1.3	1.1	0.2	1.0	1.4
37183	Wake County	16.5	12.5	4.3	5.7	2.5	4.0	2.2	0.7	0.5	0.1	0.7	0.8
37189	Watauga County	32.3	18.8	5.6	5.6	7.6	13.4	1.7	0.9	0.4	0.5	0.4	0.4
37191	Wayne County	15.9	12.5	4.9	5.6	2.1	3.4	3.0	0.3	0.2	0.0	1.1	1.6
37193	Wilkes County	14.1	12.1	4.8	5.8	1.5	2.0	3.1	0.7	0.6	0.1	1.2	1.2
37195	Wilson County	15.0	12.8	4.6	6.7	1.5	2.2	3.4	1.1	0.8	0.3	1.1	1.2
38000	**North Dakota**	20.8	16.4	6.7	6.3	3.4	4.4	1.6	0.3	0.3	0.1	0.5	0.8
38015	Burleigh County	19.8	15.6	5.7	6.8	3.0	4.2	1.8	0.5	0.4	0.1	0.6	0.7
38017	Cass County	26.1	19.2	7.1	7.0	5.2	6.9	1.6	0.3	0.2	0.1	0.5	0.7
38035	Grand Forks County	25.7	19.0	7.5	6.9	4.6	6.8	0.0	0.0	0.0	0.0	0.0	0.0
38101	Ward County	20.2	15.2	7.0	5.0	3.2	4.9	0.0	0.0	0.0	0.0	0.0	0.0
39000	**Ohio**	17.5	14.1	5.2	6.6	2.3	3.3	2.8	0.7	0.6	0.2	0.9	1.1
39003	Allen County	16.3	13.3	4.9	6.2	2.1	3.0	3.1	0.5	0.4	0.1	1.2	1.4

Table B-2: Counties with a Population of 50,000 or More—Relationships—*Continued*

State/county FIPS code	State/county	Total population	Percent of the population in households	Population in family households, percent					
				Percent in family households	Householder in family household, percent	Spouse in family household, percent	Child in family household (biological, adopted, or stepchild)	Other relative in family household	Nonrelatives in family household
	Ohio—cont'd								
39005	Ashland County	53,179	96.0	80.5	26.4	21.2	27.5	4.0	1.5
39007	Ashtabula County	100,391	96.6	79.3	25.2	18.3	27.7	5.4	2.8
39009	Athens County	64,746	85.2	59.2	19.1	14.1	19.2	4.7	2.2
39013	Belmont County	69,740	94.2	77.1	25.7	20.3	25.3	4.0	1.8
39017	Butler County	370,842	96.9	82.5	25.1	19.1	30.6	5.6	2.1
39023	Clark County	137,031	97.7	80.4	25.8	18.5	28.1	5.7	2.4
39025	Clermont County	199,290	99.1	85.6	26.5	20.4	31.4	4.9	2.4
39029	Columbiana County	106,535	96.5	81.3	26.7	20.1	27.0	5.3	2.3
39035	Cuyahoga County	1,266,434	97.7	76.7	24.1	15.6	29.4	5.9	1.7
39037	Darke County	52,514	98.8	83.7	26.4	21.5	30.9	3.7	1.2
39041	Delaware County	181,601	98.4	88.3	27.1	23.2	33.3	3.2	1.4
39043	Erie County	76,357	98.2	80.6	27.1	20.0	26.6	5.1	1.9
39045	Fairfield County	147,901	98.2	85.5	26.6	20.9	31.5	4.2	2.2
39049	Franklin County	1,195,915	97.8	75.4	22.8	15.5	28.8	6.0	2.3
39055	Geauga County	93,729	99.1	87.5	27.1	23.1	32.5	3.3	1.3
39057	Greene County	163,425	94.2	77.5	25.3	20.1	26.7	3.8	1.6
39061	Hamilton County	802,659	97.7	76.8	24.0	16.1	29.3	5.7	1.7
39063	Hancock County	75,519	97.5	79.5	25.8	20.1	26.6	3.3	3.8
39077	Huron County	59,110	98.8	84.3	26.8	20.4	30.6	4.6	2.0
39081	Jefferson County	68,400	96.4	79.5	26.4	19.9	25.9	5.1	2.1
39083	Knox County	60,967	94.1	79.8	25.6	20.6	27.9	4.0	1.6
39085	Lake County	229,760	98.7	81.9	26.5	20.5	29.0	4.3	1.7
39087	Lawrence County	62,144	98.9	84.5	25.9	18.7	28.7	8.9	2.3
39089	Licking County	167,777	97.8	84.0	26.6	20.8	29.6	4.4	2.5
39093	Lorain County	302,084	96.6	81.8	26.3	18.9	29.1	5.4	2.1
39095	Lucas County	437,788	97.7	77.0	24.0	15.5	29.5	5.7	2.2
39099	Mahoning County	235,449	96.6	78.4	25.9	17.6	28.2	5.0	1.8
39101	Marion County	66,221	89.7	76.2	25.4	19.2	23.9	4.7	3.0
39103	Medina County	174,016	99.2	86.7	27.5	22.6	31.3	3.9	1.4
39109	Miami County	103,114	99.1	83.9	27.3	20.8	29.5	4.2	2.0
39113	Montgomery County	536,342	96.6	76.9	24.8	16.6	27.9	5.3	2.3
39119	Muskingum County	85,795	97.6	81.9	26.9	18.6	27.4	5.4	3.6
39129	Pickaway County	56,220	92.6	81.0	25.3	20.2	26.6	6.6	2.4
39133	Portage County	163,945	95.9	77.2	24.2	18.7	27.8	4.6	1.9
39139	Richland County	122,485	94.4	76.9	24.7	18.4	26.1	5.2	2.4
39141	Ross County	77,677	92.2	78.2	24.9	19.0	26.9	5.1	2.4
39143	Sandusky County	60,382	97.9	82.9	26.6	19.9	29.2	4.9	2.3
39145	Scioto County	78,661	95.3	77.8	23.4	17.8	26.1	7.6	2.8
39147	Seneca County	56,121	94.2	79.0	25.9	19.9	27.9	2.9	2.5
39151	Stark County	375,015	97.6	81.5	26.4	19.5	29.0	4.6	2.0
39153	Summit County	541,408	98.2	79.4	25.3	18.2	28.6	5.6	1.8
39155	Trumbull County	207,583	98.0	81.2	26.8	19.0	28.2	5.4	1.7
39157	Tuscarawas County	92,504	98.7	84.7	27.5	21.4	29.5	4.4	2.0
39159	Union County	53,063	93.9	83.7	25.3	20.3	32.0	3.8	2.4
39165	Warren County	217,295	97.5	86.5	26.8	22.7	32.5	3.3	1.2
39167	Washington County	61,449	97.2	80.1	26.6	20.8	25.9	4.9	1.9
39169	Wayne County	114,889	96.5	83.6	26.2	21.4	30.0	4.1	2.0
39173	Wood County	128,433	94.7	74.2	24.1	19.0	26.3	2.9	1.9
40000	**Oklahoma**	3,817,296	97.1	81.2	25.1	18.6	29.0	6.4	2.1
40017	Canadian County	122,738	98.3	87.7	25.7	20.8	34.1	5.7	1.5
40027	Cleveland County	265,505	95.8	78.5	24.5	18.5	27.5	6.0	2.0
40031	Comanche County	125,849	92.6	76.7	22.7	15.9	28.6	6.8	2.6
40037	Creek County	70,521	98.7	86.6	26.4	20.6	30.0	7.8	1.8
40047	Garfield County	61,353	97.1	84.5	27.3	20.7	28.5	6.0	2.0
40051	Grady County	53,187	98.7	86.9	26.8	21.1	30.3	6.2	2.5
40101	Muskogee County	70,503	94.8	80.0	25.6	17.9	27.9	6.8	1.9
40109	Oklahoma County	742,641	98.0	79.0	23.8	16.5	29.6	7.1	2.1
40119	Payne County	78,403	89.5	64.7	21.1	16.6	21.7	3.2	2.1
40125	Pottawatomie County	70,693	94.8	80.9	25.3	19.2	28.5	5.8	2.2
40131	Rogers County	88,351	98.7	88.0	28.4	22.6	30.0	5.2	1.8
40143	Tulsa County	615,059	98.6	81.0	25.1	17.8	30.1	5.7	2.3
40145	Wagoner County	74,949	99.6	88.7	27.1	21.2	31.9	6.6	1.8
40147	Washington County	51,602	98.5	82.3	27.3	21.1	27.9	4.1	2.0
41000	**Oregon**	3,899,266	97.8	78.3	24.6	18.7	26.8	5.4	2.8
41003	Benton County	86,346	93.8	66.4	21.7	17.6	20.6	4.4	2.1
41005	Clackamas County	383,890	99.3	83.5	26.4	20.8	29.2	5.0	2.1
41011	Coos County	62,559	98.3	77.5	24.9	19.2	22.6	7.7	3.2
41017	Deschutes County	162,547	99.2	80.1	26.2	20.9	26.4	4.4	2.3
41019	Douglas County	107,133	98.4	81.0	27.0	20.7	24.4	5.8	3.0
41029	Jackson County	206,619	98.1	80.1	25.8	19.3	25.9	5.4	3.7
41033	Josephine County	82,920	98.5	80.5	26.6	20.4	24.6	5.6	3.4
41035	Klamath County	66,099	98.5	81.7	27.7	20.3	26.1	5.4	2.4
41039	Lane County	354,738	97.7	73.2	24.1	17.9	23.6	4.2	3.3
41043	Linn County	118,450	98.9	83.4	25.9	19.8	27.8	6.7	3.2

State/county FIPS code	State/county	Population in nonfamily households						Population in subfamilies as a percent of total population					
		Total population in nonfamily households	Nonfamily householders				Nonrelatives in nonfamily households	Total population in subfamilies	In married couple subfamilies			Parent in a parent-child subfamily	Child in a parent-child subfamily
			Total	Male living alone	Female living alone	Householder living with nonrelatives			Total in married-couple subfamilies	Spouse in a married-couple subfamily	Child in married-couple subfamily		
	Ohio—cont'd												
39005	Ashland County	15.5	12.0	4.6	4.9	2.4	3.5	2.4	0.9	0.7	0.3	0.6	0.8
39007	Ashtabula County	17.2	13.8	5.0	6.2	2.5	3.5	3.3	0.7	0.4	0.2	1.2	1.4
39009	Athens County	25.9	15.2	5.4	5.3	4.4	10.8	2.2	0.4	0.3	0.1	0.8	1.0
39013	Belmont County	17.1	14.8	5.8	7.2	1.9	2.3	2.0	0.7	0.5	0.1	0.6	0.7
39017	Butler County	14.5	11.0	3.8	4.9	2.2	3.5	2.8	0.9	0.7	0.2	0.9	1.0
39023	Clark County	17.4	13.9	5.1	6.4	2.4	3.4	3.3	1.3	1.0	0.3	0.8	1.2
39025	Clermont County	13.5	10.8	4.1	4.8	1.8	2.7	2.8	0.9	0.6	0.3	0.9	1.0
39029	Columbiana County	15.2	12.5	4.9	5.5	2.1	2.7	3.6	0.8	0.6	0.2	1.1	1.6
39035	Cuyahoga County	21.0	18.0	6.7	9.0	2.3	3.0	2.9	0.6	0.5	0.1	1.0	1.2
39037	Darke County	15.1	13.3	5.5	6.3	1.5	1.8	2.0	0.6	0.4	0.2	0.6	0.7
39041	Delaware County	10.2	8.8	3.2	4.3	1.3	1.4	2.0	0.7	0.7	0.1	0.6	0.7
39043	Erie County	17.6	15.0	6.3	6.7	2.0	2.6	2.5	0.7	0.5	0.2	0.8	1.0
39045	Fairfield County	12.6	10.2	3.5	4.8	1.9	2.4	2.8	0.8	0.6	0.1	0.9	1.1
39049	Franklin County	22.5	16.7	5.9	7.1	3.6	5.8	3.0	0.8	0.6	0.1	1.0	1.2
39055	Geauga County	11.6	9.8	3.6	4.7	1.5	1.8	2.1	1.2	0.7	0.5	0.3	0.5
39057	Greene County	16.6	13.1	5.1	5.8	2.3	3.5	2.3	0.7	0.6	0.1	0.7	0.9
39061	Hamilton County	20.9	16.7	6.1	7.9	2.6	4.3	3.2	0.7	0.5	0.2	1.2	1.4
39063	Hancock County	18.0	14.7	5.8	6.9	2.0	3.3	0.0	0.0	0.0	0.0	0.0	0.0
39077	Huron County	14.4	10.9	3.9	4.8	2.2	3.5	2.8	0.4	0.2	0.2	1.0	1.4
39081	Jefferson County	17.0	14.4	5.0	7.4	2.0	2.6	2.7	0.8	0.6	0.1	0.9	1.1
39083	Knox County	14.4	11.1	3.6	5.0	2.5	3.2	2.1	0.6	0.4	0.2	0.7	0.8
39085	Lake County	16.7	14.2	5.5	6.7	2.0	2.5	2.1	0.9	0.7	0.3	0.6	0.6
39087	Lawrence County	14.4	12.2	4.2	6.3	1.7	2.2	5.3	1.9	1.4	0.5	1.6	1.9
39089	Licking County	13.8	11.3	4.2	5.2	1.9	2.5	2.4	0.4	0.3	0.1	0.9	1.1
39093	Lorain County	14.9	12.3	4.3	6.1	1.9	2.6	3.2	0.8	0.6	0.2	1.1	1.3
39095	Lucas County	20.7	16.5	6.2	7.5	2.8	4.2	2.9	0.4	0.3	0.1	1.1	1.4
39099	Mahoning County	18.2	15.6	5.8	7.8	1.9	2.6	2.6	0.5	0.4	0.1	0.9	1.1
39101	Marion County	13.5	11.4	4.2	5.6	1.6	2.0	3.4	1.1	0.7	0.4	0.8	1.4
39103	Medina County	12.6	10.2	3.6	4.7	1.9	2.4	2.8	1.2	0.7	0.5	0.7	0.9
39109	Miami County	15.1	12.4	4.6	5.5	2.2	2.8	2.5	1.1	0.8	0.3	0.7	0.7
39113	Montgomery County	19.7	16.5	6.2	8.1	2.3	3.2	2.6	0.6	0.4	0.1	0.9	1.1
39119	Muskingum County	15.7	12.7	4.4	6.2	2.2	3.0	2.4	0.8	0.6	0.2	0.7	0.9
39129	Pickaway County	11.5	8.9	3.4	3.8	1.7	2.7	4.9	1.3	0.8	0.5	1.4	2.3
39133	Portage County	18.7	12.6	4.5	4.9	3.3	6.1	2.8	1.1	0.9	0.3	0.9	0.8
39139	Richland County	17.5	14.7	5.6	7.3	1.8	2.7	2.8	0.8	0.6	0.2	0.9	1.1
39141	Ross County	13.9	11.3	4.8	4.8	1.7	2.6	4.1	0.9	0.7	0.2	1.4	1.8
39143	Sandusky County	15.0	12.7	4.8	6.2	1.7	2.3	3.4	0.9	0.5	0.4	1.2	1.3
39145	Scioto County	17.5	13.7	4.9	6.6	2.2	3.8	5.1	1.4	1.0	0.4	1.8	1.9
39147	Seneca County	15.2	12.3	4.4	5.9	1.9	3.0	2.4	0.7	0.6	0.1	0.8	1.0
39151	Stark County	16.1	13.6	5.0	6.7	1.9	2.5	2.5	0.5	0.4	0.1	0.9	1.1
39153	Summit County	18.8	15.2	5.8	7.1	2.4	3.6	2.8	0.7	0.5	0.2	1.0	1.1
39155	Trumbull County	16.8	14.9	5.7	7.4	1.7	1.9	3.0	0.8	0.6	0.2	0.9	1.2
39157	Tuscarawas County	14.0	11.7	3.7	6.2	1.9	2.2	1.8	0.4	0.3	0.0	0.7	0.8
39159	Union County	10.2	8.9	3.7	4.1	1.0	1.3	0.0	0.0	0.0	0.0	0.0	0.0
39165	Warren County	11.0	8.7	3.0	4.0	1.7	2.3	1.7	0.6	0.5	0.1	0.5	0.6
39167	Washington County	17.1	14.1	5.6	6.3	2.2	3.0	3.4	0.9	0.8	0.2	1.1	1.4
39169	Wayne County	12.9	11.1	4.3	5.2	1.5	1.8	2.6	0.8	0.5	0.3	0.8	1.0
39173	Wood County	20.5	14.4	5.0	6.0	3.4	6.1	1.6	0.4	0.2	0.2	0.7	0.6
40000	**Oklahoma**	15.9	12.7	4.9	5.8	2.0	3.2	3.5	1.1	0.8	0.3	1.1	1.3
40017	Canadian County	10.6	8.8	3.5	4.0	1.2	1.8	2.5	0.7	0.6	0.1	1.0	0.9
40027	Cleveland County	17.3	12.3	4.2	5.2	2.9	5.0	3.2	1.4	1.1	0.3	0.8	1.0
40031	Comanche County	15.9	12.3	5.2	5.0	2.0	3.7	4.3	1.1	0.8	0.3	1.5	1.7
40037	Creek County	12.1	10.3	4.3	4.7	1.2	1.8	4.5	1.9	1.4	0.5	1.3	1.4
40047	Garfield County	12.6	10.7	4.2	5.2	1.3	1.9	2.4	0.5	0.4	0.1	0.8	1.1
40051	Grady County	11.7	10.0	3.8	4.9	1.3	1.7	3.4	1.0	0.8	0.3	1.2	1.1
40101	Muskogee County	14.8	12.1	4.9	5.4	1.8	2.6	3.8	1.0	0.8	0.2	1.3	1.6
40109	Oklahoma County	19.0	14.8	5.5	6.8	2.6	4.2	3.9	1.1	0.8	0.2	1.3	1.5
40119	Payne County	24.8	17.2	5.8	6.4	5.0	7.6	1.9	0.5	0.5	0.0	0.6	0.8
40125	Pottawatomie County	13.9	11.5	4.4	5.6	1.5	2.5	3.5	1.4	0.9	0.5	0.9	1.3
40131	Rogers County	10.6	9.1	3.2	4.5	1.3	1.6	3.1	1.0	0.8	0.3	0.9	1.2
40143	Tulsa County	17.6	14.2	5.3	6.6	2.4	3.4	2.9	0.9	0.7	0.2	0.9	1.1
40145	Wagoner County	10.9	9.0	3.8	4.0	1.2	1.9	3.9	1.4	1.0	0.4	1.2	1.4
40147	Washington County	16.1	13.3	3.9	7.5	1.9	2.8	1.7	0.6	0.5	0.2	0.5	0.5
41000	**Oregon**	19.4	14.3	4.8	6.2	3.4	5.1	2.8	1.2	0.9	0.3	0.8	0.9
41003	Benton County	27.4	16.8	4.9	6.3	5.7	10.6	1.7	0.9	0.6	0.2	0.4	0.4
41005	Clackamas County	15.8	12.0	3.8	5.7	2.6	3.7	2.9	1.5	1.0	0.5	0.6	0.8
41011	Coos County	20.8	16.4	6.2	7.3	2.9	4.4	4.4	1.5	1.4	0.1	1.4	1.5
41017	Deschutes County	19.1	13.8	4.4	6.1	3.3	5.3	2.0	1.0	0.8	0.2	0.5	0.5
41019	Douglas County	17.4	13.4	5.1	5.0	3.2	4.1	3.1	1.8	1.2	0.6	0.6	0.7
41029	Jackson County	18.0	14.2	4.9	6.6	2.7	3.8	2.9	1.1	0.8	0.3	0.9	0.9
41033	Josephine County	18.0	14.8	5.0	7.3	2.5	3.2	3.1	1.6	0.9	0.7	0.6	1.0
41035	Klamath County	16.7	13.5	5.5	5.3	2.7	3.3	3.2	1.0	0.8	0.2	1.0	1.1
41039	Lane County	24.5	16.7	5.2	6.8	4.7	7.8	2.3	0.7	0.5	0.2	0.8	0.9
41043	Linn County	15.6	11.6	4.1	5.0	2.5	3.9	4.0	2.1	1.5	0.7	0.9	0.9

State/ county FIPS code	State/county	Total population	Percent of the population in households	Population in family households, percent					
				Percent in family households	Householder in family household, percent	Spouse in family household, percent	Child in family household (biological, adopted, or stepchild)	Other relative in family household	Nonrelatives in family household
	Oregon—cont'd								
41047	Marion County	320,956	96.8	82.9	24.4	17.5	31.2	6.3	3.4
41051	Multnomah County	757,738	97.5	70.8	21.9	15.8	24.4	5.6	3.0
41053	Polk County	76,378	97.4	80.5	25.0	19.8	29.9	3.6	2.2
41059	Umatilla County	76,761	94.3	80.7	23.7	17.4	30.2	6.3	3.1
41067	Washington County	547,336	98.7	82.2	24.9	19.6	30.3	5.1	2.4
41071	Yamhill County	100,354	94.6	81.8	24.2	18.5	28.1	6.9	4.1
42000	**Pennsylvania**	12,759,859	96.6	79.5	25.0	18.6	28.5	5.6	1.9
42001	Adams County	101,589	95.9	83.0	26.9	21.7	27.4	4.8	2.2
42003	Allegheny County	1,229,582	97.2	74.9	24.7	18.0	26.5	4.2	1.4
42005	Armstrong County	68,373	98.9	83.5	28.3	21.7	26.8	4.3	2.5
42007	Beaver County	170,263	98.3	81.5	27.1	20.5	27.2	5.2	1.4
42011	Berks County	412,916	96.8	81.5	25.3	19.0	29.7	5.3	2.3
42013	Blair County	126,839	97.4	80.8	26.0	19.6	27.5	5.1	2.5
42015	Bradford County	62,704	98.8	83.5	26.4	20.7	28.1	5.4	2.8
42017	Bucks County	626,612	98.5	85.9	26.5	21.5	31.1	5.3	1.3
42019	Butler County	185,098	97.0	81.1	27.0	22.2	27.3	3.5	1.1
42021	Cambria County	141,536	94.0	76.8	25.9	19.4	26.2	3.8	1.5
42025	Carbon County	64,983	98.6	82.6	26.8	20.6	27.5	4.7	3.0
42027	Centre County	155,032	89.6	61.8	21.0	17.2	19.4	2.7	1.5
42029	Chester County	506,406	97.0	82.8	25.6	21.3	30.5	4.1	1.3
42033	Clearfield County	81,392	93.5	78.5	26.2	20.6	25.5	4.0	2.1
42037	Columbia County	66,855	94.5	74.1	25.1	19.4	23.7	4.1	1.8
42039	Crawford County	87,719	95.9	80.3	26.2	20.6	27.8	3.5	2.2
42041	Cumberland County	239,118	94.4	77.3	25.9	20.9	25.3	3.3	1.9
42043	Dauphin County	269,939	97.4	79.6	25.6	18.3	28.0	5.6	2.2
42045	Delaware County	560,577	96.1	81.6	24.1	17.3	31.4	7.1	1.7
42049	Erie County	280,679	95.5	77.8	24.9	17.9	28.3	4.7	2.0
42051	Fayette County	135,598	96.6	80.2	25.7	18.8	27.5	5.8	2.4
42055	Franklin County	151,467	98.5	83.6	26.3	21.2	29.1	4.7	2.2
42063	Indiana County	88,128	93.3	73.0	24.1	19.3	24.4	3.7	1.5
42069	Lackawanna County	214,281	96.1	77.8	24.8	18.1	27.9	5.5	1.5
42071	Lancaster County	526,549	97.3	83.7	25.9	21.1	30.5	4.5	1.7
42073	Lawrence County	89,827	97.3	81.3	26.9	20.4	27.4	5.2	1.4
42075	Lebanon County	135,119	97.6	83.2	26.6	20.4	29.0	4.7	2.5
42077	Lehigh County	354,364	97.4	82.0	25.1	18.4	30.2	6.3	2.2
42079	Luzerne County	320,894	96.2	79.1	25.7	18.1	27.4	6.0	2.0
42081	Lycoming County	116,921	95.3	77.3	24.7	18.8	26.5	5.1	2.1
42085	Mercer County	115,650	93.8	78.7	26.4	20.0	26.6	3.7	2.1
42089	Monroe County	168,469	98.4	85.9	25.6	19.0	31.8	6.9	2.7
42091	Montgomery County	808,846	97.4	82.6	25.7	20.8	30.0	4.7	1.3
42095	Northampton County	299,174	96.4	81.9	26.0	20.1	28.8	5.0	2.0
42097	Northumberland County	94,366	94.6	77.9	26.7	20.5	24.8	3.8	2.1
42101	Philadelphia County	1,546,770	96.7	73.3	19.6	10.0	30.3	11.2	2.3
42103	Pike County	56,964	99.2	86.5	26.4	21.5	30.3	5.6	2.7
42107	Schuylkill County	147,303	95.3	78.6	26.2	19.5	26.4	4.4	2.1
42111	Somerset County	76,995	93.7	80.2	26.9	22.2	26.1	3.7	1.2
42121	Venango County	54,304	97.7	82.2	27.7	21.1	25.8	4.8	2.8
42125	Washington County	208,253	97.5	80.8	26.4	20.8	27.6	4.2	1.9
42127	Wayne County	51,852	92.6	79.0	26.2	21.1	25.8	4.7	1.4
42129	Westmoreland County	363,379	97.6	81.4	27.7	21.6	26.6	4.0	1.7
42133	York County	437,720	98.0	83.5	26.5	20.3	29.2	5.0	2.4
44000	**Rhode Island**	1,050,722	96.1	77.4	24.5	17.2	27.6	6.1	2.1
44003	Kent County	165,121	99.0	80.2	26.1	19.8	27.4	5.1	1.8
44005	Newport County	82,310	96.2	76.1	25.5	20.0	24.5	4.5	1.7
44007	Providence County	628,033	95.8	76.8	23.4	15.1	28.5	7.3	2.5
44009	Washington County	126,187	94.8	77.3	26.4	20.8	25.9	3.1	1.1
45000	**South Carolina**	4,723,923	97.1	81.6	25.4	17.8	28.8	7.6	1.9
45003	Aiken County	163,151	98.1	83.3	25.8	18.6	29.8	7.6	1.4
45007	Anderson County	189,510	98.8	85.2	27.2	19.8	29.0	7.5	1.6
45013	Beaufort County	168,024	96.7	80.2	26.1	20.4	26.0	6.1	1.7
45015	Berkeley County	189,319	98.1	85.7	25.5	18.8	31.6	7.6	2.1
45019	Charleston County	365,198	96.6	73.4	23.1	15.8	26.0	6.9	1.7
45021	Cherokee County	55,756	98.5	85.5	25.7	17.9	30.2	9.1	2.6
45031	Darlington County	68,129	98.2	85.5	27.2	16.9	29.2	10.6	1.5
45035	Dorchester County	142,599	98.7	86.7	25.9	19.0	32.8	7.1	1.9
45041	Florence County	137,921	97.6	84.1	25.5	16.4	30.2	10.2	1.8
45043	Georgetown County	60,286	99.0	84.5	26.9	19.2	27.2	9.6	1.6
45045	Greenville County	466,628	97.5	82.8	25.5	19.0	30.3	6.4	1.6
45047	Greenwood County	69,772	96.4	81.5	26.0	17.2	29.4	6.5	2.4
45051	Horry County	282,409	99.1	80.1	26.0	19.3	24.7	7.2	2.8
45055	Kershaw County	62,253	99.3	86.1	27.1	19.0	29.5	8.6	1.9
45057	Lancaster County	79,130	97.5	84.6	25.8	17.9	30.4	8.4	1.9
45059	Laurens County	66,285	96.2	84.6	27.0	17.0	28.8	9.8	1.9
45063	Lexington County	270,190	98.9	83.6	26.6	19.7	29.1	6.3	1.9

Table B-2: Counties with a Population of 50,000 or More—Relationships—*Continued*

| State/ county FIPS code | State/county | Population in nonfamily households | | | | | | Population in subfamilies as a percent of total population | | | | | |
| | | Total population in nonfamily households | Nonfamily householders | | | | Nonrelatives in nonfamily households | Total population in subfamilies | In married couple subfamilies | | | Parent in a parent-child subfamily | Child in a parent-child subfamily |
			Total	Male living alone	Female living alone	Householder living with nonrelatives			Total in married-couple subfamilies	Spouse in a married-couple subfamily	Child in married-couple subfamily		
	Oregon—cont'd												
41047	Marion County	13.9	10.8	3.5	5.5	1.8	3.0	3.1	1.2	0.9	0.3	0.9	1.0
41051	Multnomah County	26.7	18.7	6.2	7.3	5.2	8.1	2.7	1.1	0.9	0.2	0.8	0.8
41053	Polk County	16.9	12.1	3.3	5.1	3.6	4.8	1.9	0.9	0.7	0.2	0.5	0.5
41059	Umatilla County	13.7	11.0	4.3	4.8	1.9	2.7	2.8	0.7	0.4	0.3	0.9	1.2
41067	Washington County	16.5	12.2	4.0	5.4	2.8	4.3	2.3	1.1	0.8	0.2	0.6	0.6
41071	Yamhill County	12.8	9.5	3.1	4.5	1.8	3.2	4.1	2.1	1.4	0.7	1.0	1.1
42000	**Pennsylvania**	17.2	13.8	5.0	6.6	2.3	3.4	3.0	0.9	0.7	0.2	1.0	1.2
42001	Adams County	12.8	10.3	4.0	4.6	1.8	2.5	2.8	1.2	1.0	0.2	0.7	0.9
42003	Allegheny County	22.3	18.1	6.4	8.7	3.0	4.2	2.1	0.6	0.5	0.1	0.7	0.8
42005	Armstrong County	15.4	13.5	5.1	6.7	1.6	1.9	2.0	0.6	0.5	0.1	0.6	0.7
42007	Beaver County	16.9	14.5	5.0	7.6	1.9	2.3	3.0	0.7	0.6	0.1	1.0	1.2
42011	Berks County	15.3	11.8	4.0	5.3	2.5	3.5	3.3	1.2	0.9	0.3	1.0	1.1
42013	Blair County	16.7	13.9	5.2	6.9	1.8	2.8	2.4	0.7	0.5	0.2	0.8	0.8
42015	Bradford County	15.3	12.1	4.4	5.5	2.2	3.3	3.3	1.0	0.7	0.3	1.1	1.2
42017	Bucks County	12.6	10.5	3.8	5.1	1.6	2.1	3.1	1.2	0.9	0.3	0.8	1.1
42019	Butler County	16.0	12.7	5.1	5.4	2.2	3.2	1.8	0.6	0.5	0.1	0.5	0.6
42021	Cambria County	17.2	14.7	5.5	7.5	1.8	2.4	1.9	0.6	0.5	0.1	0.6	0.7
42025	Carbon County	16.1	13.2	5.0	5.9	2.3	2.9	3.1	1.1	1.1	0.0	1.0	1.0
42027	Centre County	27.8	16.0	4.9	5.4	5.8	11.7	0.9	0.3	0.3	0.0	0.3	0.3
42029	Chester County	14.2	10.9	3.6	5.1	2.2	3.3	2.4	0.9	0.8	0.2	0.6	0.8
42033	Clearfield County	15.0	13.1	5.2	6.3	1.6	1.9	1.9	0.5	0.4	0.1	0.6	0.8
42037	Columbia County	20.4	13.9	4.2	6.3	3.4	6.6	2.1	0.9	0.7	0.2	0.6	0.6
42039	Crawford County	15.6	13.1	5.0	6.0	2.1	2.5	2.0	0.8	0.7	0.1	0.5	0.7
42041	Cumberland County	17.1	13.9	5.0	6.6	2.3	3.2	2.2	0.8	0.6	0.2	0.6	0.8
42043	Dauphin County	17.7	14.6	5.0	7.1	2.5	3.1	3.2	0.7	0.5	0.1	1.0	1.5
42045	Delaware County	14.4	12.1	4.1	6.3	1.7	2.3	3.6	1.0	0.8	0.2	1.2	1.4
42049	Erie County	17.7	14.2	5.4	6.5	2.4	3.5	2.9	0.8	0.6	0.2	0.9	1.2
42051	Fayette County	16.3	14.0	5.5	6.8	1.7	2.4	2.9	0.9	0.7	0.2	1.0	1.0
42055	Franklin County	14.9	12.1	4.1	6.2	1.9	2.8	2.3	0.7	0.5	0.1	0.8	0.9
42063	Indiana County	20.3	14.7	5.5	5.9	3.3	5.6	2.2	0.5	0.4	0.1	0.8	1.0
42069	Lackawanna County	18.3	15.1	5.3	7.7	2.2	3.2	2.8	1.1	0.9	0.3	0.7	0.9
42071	Lancaster County	13.6	10.9	3.8	5.2	2.0	2.6	2.7	1.0	0.7	0.3	0.7	1.0
42073	Lawrence County	16.0	13.9	5.1	7.1	1.6	2.2	3.1	0.5	0.4	0.1	1.2	1.4
42075	Lebanon County	14.4	11.9	4.2	6.0	1.7	2.5	2.0	0.3	0.3	0.1	0.7	1.0
42077	Lehigh County	15.4	12.6	4.6	5.7	2.2	2.8	3.6	0.9	0.8	0.1	1.1	1.6
42079	Luzerne County	17.1	14.6	5.6	7.2	1.9	2.5	3.1	1.1	0.8	0.3	1.0	1.0
42081	Lycoming County	18.0	14.3	5.1	6.4	2.7	3.7	2.9	1.1	0.7	0.4	0.7	1.0
42085	Mercer County	15.2	13.4	5.2	6.6	1.6	1.8	2.1	0.8	0.6	0.2	0.6	0.7
42089	Monroe County	12.5	9.0	3.2	3.6	2.2	3.4	4.2	1.7	1.5	0.3	1.2	1.2
42091	Montgomery County	14.8	12.2	4.2	6.0	2.0	2.6	2.4	1.0	0.8	0.2	0.7	0.8
42095	Northampton County	14.5	11.5	3.8	5.5	2.2	3.0	2.9	0.9	0.7	0.3	1.0	1.0
42097	Northumberland County	16.7	14.9	6.4	6.9	1.6	1.8	2.0	0.9	0.6	0.3	0.5	0.6
42101	Philadelphia County	23.4	17.8	6.5	8.5	2.8	5.5	5.9	1.1	0.8	0.2	2.2	2.6
42103	Pike County	12.6	10.4	3.7	5.2	1.5	2.2	0.0	0.0	0.0	0.0	0.0	0.0
42107	Schuylkill County	16.7	14.0	5.4	6.4	2.2	2.8	2.9	0.8	0.6	0.2	0.9	1.1
42111	Somerset County	13.5	11.7	4.6	5.8	1.3	1.8	2.0	0.7	0.5	0.2	0.6	0.7
42121	Venango County	15.5	13.6	5.3	6.8	1.5	1.9	2.7	1.0	0.7	0.3	0.9	0.9
42125	Washington County	16.7	13.7	4.9	6.8	2.1	3.0	2.0	0.7	0.6	0.2	0.6	0.6
42127	Wayne County	13.5	11.5	4.9	4.9	1.6	2.0	1.6	0.4	0.4	0.0	0.6	0.6
42129	Westmoreland County	16.1	14.0	5.1	7.1	1.7	2.1	2.0	0.7	0.5	0.2	0.6	0.7
42133	York County	14.5	11.7	4.4	5.3	2.0	2.8	2.9	0.9	0.8	0.2	0.9	1.1
44000	**Rhode Island**	18.7	14.6	5.0	6.8	2.8	4.1	3.0	1.1	0.9	0.3	0.8	1.0
44003	Kent County	18.8	15.5	5.5	7.5	2.6	3.3	2.9	1.4	1.0	0.4	0.7	0.9
44005	Newport County	20.0	16.2	5.5	8.0	2.7	3.9	2.4	0.8	0.5	0.3	0.7	0.8
44007	Providence County	18.9	14.5	5.0	6.7	2.9	4.4	3.4	1.1	0.9	0.2	1.0	1.2
44009	Washington County	17.5	13.2	4.3	5.9	3.0	4.3	1.9	1.2	0.9	0.2	0.3	0.5
45000	**South Carolina**	15.5	12.3	4.5	5.9	1.9	3.2	4.1	0.9	0.7	0.2	1.5	1.7
45003	Aiken County	14.8	12.7	4.8	6.4	1.5	2.1	4.1	1.3	0.9	0.4	1.5	1.3
45007	Anderson County	13.5	11.4	4.5	5.5	1.3	2.2	4.1	0.8	0.7	0.2	1.5	1.8
45013	Beaufort County	16.5	12.1	3.6	6.3	2.2	4.4	3.2	1.0	0.8	0.2	1.3	0.9
45015	Berkeley County	12.5	9.9	3.6	4.6	1.7	2.5	4.5	0.7	0.6	0.1	1.8	1.9
45019	Charleston County	23.2	16.6	5.4	7.4	3.8	6.6	2.6	0.3	0.2	0.1	1.0	1.3
45021	Cherokee County	12.9	11.2	5.1	5.0	1.1	1.7	5.1	1.9	1.5	0.5	1.7	1.4
45031	Darlington County	12.7	11.3	4.6	5.7	1.0	1.4	7.3	1.6	1.3	0.3	2.1	3.6
45035	Dorchester County	12.0	9.9	3.8	4.7	1.4	2.2	4.6	0.8	0.6	0.2	1.6	2.2
45041	Florence County	13.6	11.4	4.3	5.9	1.3	2.1	6.6	1.4	1.2	0.2	2.4	2.8
45043	Georgetown County	14.6	12.0	3.7	6.5	1.7	2.6	6.2	1.4	1.1	0.3	2.1	2.7
45045	Greenville County	14.7	12.2	4.5	6.0	1.6	2.5	3.4	0.8	0.7	0.1	1.2	1.4
45047	Greenwood County	14.9	12.4	4.6	6.3	1.5	2.5	3.5	1.3	0.9	0.4	1.1	1.1
45051	Horry County	19.1	14.3	5.0	6.7	2.7	4.7	3.9	0.8	0.6	0.2	1.6	1.6
45055	Kershaw County	13.3	11.5	4.5	5.5	1.5	1.8	3.8	0.6	0.4	0.2	1.5	1.8
45057	Lancaster County	12.9	10.4	4.5	4.6	1.4	2.5	3.0	0.5	0.5	0.1	1.4	1.1
45059	Laurens County	11.7	10.2	3.7	5.1	1.3	1.5	6.0	1.2	1.0	0.3	2.2	2.5
45063	Lexington County	15.3	12.1	4.6	5.2	2.3	3.2	3.2	1.1	0.8	0.2	1.0	1.2

Table B-2: Counties with a Population of 50,000 or More—Relationships—*Continued*

State/county FIPS code	State/county	Total population	Percent of the population in households	Population in family households, percent					
				Percent in family households	Householder in family household, percent	Spouse in family household, percent	Child in family household (biological, adopted, or stepchild)	Other relative in family household	Nonrelatives in family household
	South Carolina—cont'd								
45073	Oconee County	74,634	99.1	83.0	28.0	20.9	26.4	5.0	2.7
45075	Orangeburg County	91,368	96.7	81.4	23.6	14.6	29.3	12.6	1.4
45077	Pickens County	119,674	93.5	75.4	23.9	18.6	25.3	5.5	2.2
45079	Richland County	394,174	92.0	72.9	22.2	14.5	28.3	6.3	1.6
45083	Spartanburg County	288,628	97.4	83.8	26.2	18.1	30.2	7.3	2.0
45085	Sumter County	107,884	97.7	83.9	25.5	16.7	30.3	9.0	2.3
45091	York County	234,716	98.3	85.6	26.8	20.2	30.8	6.4	1.5
46000	**South Dakota**	834,236	95.9	78.7	25.2	19.6	27.4	4.4	2.1
46099	Minnehaha County	175,693	97.1	78.8	24.9	18.5	29.4	4.0	2.1
46103	Pennington County	104,195	96.9	78.8	24.8	18.1	27.8	5.2	2.9
47000	**Tennessee**	6,449,754	97.6	81.7	25.5	18.7	28.7	6.8	1.9
47001	Anderson County	75,379	98.4	81.2	25.8	18.9	28.5	6.0	2.0
47009	Blount County	124,257	98.4	83.5	27.3	22.1	27.3	5.5	1.2
47011	Bradley County	100,951	97.1	82.5	25.8	18.9	27.9	7.2	2.7
47019	Carter County	57,390	97.1	81.5	27.9	21.7	25.2	4.7	2.0
47031	Coffee County	53,151	98.7	84.0	27.0	19.5	27.2	7.5	2.9
47035	Cumberland County	57,023	98.7	83.6	28.4	23.0	23.1	6.6	2.6
47037	Davidson County	647,670	96.4	72.5	21.8	14.6	26.7	7.3	2.1
47043	Dickson County	50,180	98.8	88.2	27.6	20.1	32.8	6.0	1.7
47059	Greene County	68,612	97.4	81.9	28.2	21.6	24.3	6.0	1.8
47063	Hamblen County	62,888	98.8	84.6	26.7	19.2	27.7	8.6	2.4
47065	Hamilton County	345,000	97.1	80.3	25.5	18.5	27.6	6.9	1.7
47073	Hawkins County	56,689	99.1	85.6	28.5	22.0	26.5	6.7	2.0
47089	Jefferson County	52,016	97.0	83.5	26.9	20.9	27.2	5.7	2.8
47093	Knox County	440,800	97.3	76.9	24.8	19.1	25.9	5.3	1.7
47107	McMinn County	52,378	98.0	84.2	26.5	21.4	27.9	6.5	1.8
47113	Madison County	98,423	95.9	81.0	24.0	16.8	31.3	7.6	1.4
47119	Maury County	82,412	98.5	83.6	26.3	18.5	30.2	6.3	2.2
47125	Montgomery County	182,002	98.1	85.8	26.3	19.6	32.4	5.2	2.3
47141	Putnam County	73,128	95.7	78.3	25.9	19.2	25.1	6.1	2.0
47145	Roane County	53,443	98.7	82.9	27.8	22.4	25.7	5.9	1.1
47147	Robertson County	66,962	98.8	87.0	26.9	20.6	29.8	7.7	2.0
47149	Rutherford County	274,720	98.1	82.4	24.5	18.9	31.5	5.6	1.9
47155	Sevier County	92,421	98.9	85.3	28.8	21.9	25.6	6.6	2.4
47157	Shelby County	937,748	98.2	81.7	23.3	13.9	33.2	9.2	2.1
47163	Sullivan County	156,729	98.2	81.5	27.8	21.2	25.2	5.8	1.6
47165	Sumner County	166,167	99.2	88.0	27.7	21.2	30.6	6.3	2.2
47167	Tipton County	61,501	98.8	88.7	26.4	18.9	31.7	9.6	2.1
47179	Washington County	124,818	96.1	77.5	26.5	19.9	25.0	4.4	1.7
47187	Williamson County	193,418	99.7	90.9	27.2	23.8	35.2	3.5	1.3
47189	Wilson County	119,254	98.8	86.0	26.2	20.6	29.8	7.5	2.0
48000	**Texas**	26,049,971	97.7	84.3	23.9	17.2	32.6	8.6	2.0
48001	Anderson County	58,141	77.6	68.7	20.6	14.9	24.8	5.2	3.1
48005	Angelina County	87,416	96.5	85.6	25.6	17.6	31.2	8.7	2.5
48021	Bastrop County	75,240	97.1	84.1	23.8	18.7	31.6	8.4	1.7
48027	Bell County	322,242	97.4	86.1	23.1	16.9	34.8	8.5	2.7
48029	Bexar County	1,785,855	98.1	83.9	23.1	15.5	33.4	9.6	2.1
48037	Bowie County	93,124	94.3	80.8	24.7	16.7	28.7	8.4	2.4
48039	Brazoria County	324,596	96.8	86.1	25.0	19.2	33.4	7.3	1.2
48041	Brazos County	200,367	92.8	64.9	19.5	13.8	24.2	5.6	1.8
48061	Cameron County	415,191	99.1	92.1	22.8	15.1	39.8	12.6	1.9
48073	Cherokee County	51,000	94.7	84.3	25.5	18.4	31.6	7.4	1.4
48085	Collin County	834,110	99.5	87.8	26.3	21.2	33.1	5.8	1.5
48091	Comal County	114,879	99.0	87.3	27.5	22.4	28.5	6.7	2.2
48099	Coryell County	76,522	82.8	75.1	21.0	15.9	30.6	6.0	1.7
48113	Dallas County	2,447,575	98.8	83.4	23.1	15.3	32.8	9.9	2.2
48121	Denton County	707,550	98.3	84.1	24.9	19.5	32.0	6.2	1.6
48135	Ector County	144,559	98.8	85.8	24.8	16.6	33.8	7.7	2.9
48139	Ellis County	154,083	98.9	90.4	26.7	20.9	33.0	7.8	2.1
48141	El Paso County	824,916	98.3	88.7	23.6	15.6	37.3	10.6	1.7
48157	Fort Bend County	628,443	99.1	92.6	25.9	20.7	36.4	8.3	1.3
48167	Galveston County	301,092	98.4	83.6	25.1	19.0	30.9	6.8	1.8
48181	Grayson County	121,768	98.1	82.4	26.0	18.9	28.5	6.7	2.2
48183	Gregg County	122,712	96.6	82.8	24.9	17.3	29.8	8.4	2.4
48187	Guadalupe County	139,668	98.7	87.8	25.2	19.8	33.4	7.7	1.7
48199	Hardin County	55,223	99.2	87.3	27.7	21.8	28.8	7.6	1.5
48201	Harris County	4,255,830	99.1	85.3	23.3	15.9	34.2	9.7	2.2
48203	Harrison County	67,137	98.0	86.5	25.9	19.0	30.7	9.9	1.1
48209	Hays County	169,603	96.1	76.2	22.2	17.1	28.7	6.4	1.8
48213	Henderson County	78,765	98.5	83.4	25.4	19.7	28.8	8.0	1.6
48215	Hidalgo County	805,497	98.9	92.6	22.4	15.8	40.8	12.5	1.3
48221	Hood County	52,194	98.7	83.8	27.7	23.6	25.4	5.3	1.9
48231	Hunt County	86,906	97.0	83.6	23.9	18.7	30.1	8.8	2.0

Table B-2: Counties with a Population of 50,000 or More—Relationships—*Continued*

| State/county FIPS code | State/county | Population in nonfamily households | | | | | | Population in subfamilies as a percent of total population | | | | | |
| | | Total population in nonfamily households | Nonfamily householders | | | | Nonrelatives in nonfamily households | Total population in subfamilies | In married couple subfamilies | | | Parent in a parent-child subfamily | Child in a parent-child subfamily |
			Total	Male living alone	Female living alone	Householder living with nonrelatives			Total in married-couple subfamilies	Spouse in a married-couple subfamily	Child in married-couple subfamily		
	South Carolina—cont'd												
45073	Oconee County	16.1	12.4	4.4	6.0	1.9	3.7	1.7	0.4	0.3	0.1	0.6	0.6
45075	Orangeburg County	15.3	13.3	5.5	6.6	1.2	2.1	7.8	0.8	0.5	0.3	3.0	3.9
45077	Pickens County	18.2	12.5	4.5	5.3	2.8	5.6	2.9	1.0	0.8	0.2	0.7	1.2
45079	Richland County	19.1	14.1	4.8	6.6	2.6	5.0	3.3	0.5	0.4	0.1	1.3	1.5
45083	Spartanburg County	13.6	11.0	4.1	5.3	1.6	2.6	3.9	1.0	0.7	0.3	1.4	1.5
45085	Sumter County	13.8	11.6	4.4	5.7	1.6	2.2	4.7	0.3	0.2	0.1	1.8	2.6
45091	York County	12.7	10.4	4.0	4.7	1.7	2.3	3.2	0.8	0.6	0.2	1.2	1.2
46000	**South Dakota**	17.3	13.9	5.5	5.9	2.4	3.4	2.5	0.6	0.4	0.2	0.8	1.1
46099	Minnehaha County	18.3	14.1	5.1	6.1	2.9	4.2	2.0	0.8	0.6	0.3	0.6	0.6
46103	Pennington County	18.0	14.2	5.2	6.5	2.6	3.8	2.9	0.4	0.3	0.1	1.1	1.4
47000	**Tennessee**	15.9	12.9	4.8	6.1	2.0	3.0	3.7	1.0	0.8	0.3	1.2	1.4
47001	Anderson County	17.3	14.7	5.4	7.3	2.0	2.5	3.3	0.8	0.5	0.2	1.1	1.4
47009	Blount County	14.9	12.1	4.3	6.1	1.7	2.8	2.5	1.0	0.8	0.2	0.7	0.8
47011	Bradley County	14.6	11.8	4.5	5.5	1.8	2.8	4.4	2.0	1.4	0.6	1.2	1.2
47019	Carter County	15.6	13.8	5.0	7.5	1.3	1.8	3.3	0.5	0.5	0.0	1.4	1.4
47031	Coffee County	14.7	12.7	5.8	5.4	1.5	2.0	4.1	2.0	1.3	0.6	0.9	1.3
47035	Cumberland County	15.1	12.8	4.9	6.6	1.4	2.3	3.5	1.0	0.8	0.2	1.2	1.3
47037	Davidson County	23.9	18.1	6.5	8.1	3.5	5.8	3.4	0.8	0.7	0.1	1.2	1.4
47043	Dickson County	10.7	9.1	3.2	4.6	1.3	1.6	3.7	1.0	0.8	0.3	1.2	1.4
47059	Greene County	15.5	13.3	5.6	6.0	1.7	2.2	3.4	1.0	0.8	0.2	1.0	1.4
47063	Hamblen County	14.2	11.7	4.4	5.4	1.8	2.6	4.4	2.1	1.7	0.4	1.0	1.3
47065	Hamilton County	16.8	13.6	4.8	6.7	2.1	3.2	3.2	1.0	0.8	0.2	1.1	1.1
47073	Hawkins County	13.5	12.1	5.7	5.3	1.2	1.4	3.4	0.9	0.7	0.1	1.3	1.3
47089	Jefferson County	13.5	10.9	4.2	5.5	1.2	2.6	3.7	0.6	0.6	0.1	1.6	1.4
47093	Knox County	20.4	16.3	6.0	7.5	2.8	4.1	2.5	0.7	0.6	0.2	0.8	1.0
47107	McMinn County	13.8	12.1	5.1	5.7	1.3	1.7	3.2	0.2	0.2	0.0	1.7	1.3
47113	Madison County	14.9	12.4	4.6	6.3	1.5	2.5	3.1	0.8	0.6	0.2	1.1	1.2
47119	Maury County	14.9	12.6	4.5	6.2	1.9	2.4	3.4	1.0	0.7	0.3	1.1	1.2
47125	Montgomery County	12.3	9.4	3.6	3.9	1.9	2.9	2.4	0.8	0.6	0.3	0.8	0.8
47141	Putnam County	17.4	14.2	5.1	6.1	3.0	3.2	3.9	2.1	1.0	1.0	0.8	1.0
47145	Roane County	15.8	13.4	5.2	6.2	2.0	2.4	4.3	0.9	0.7	0.2	1.6	1.8
47147	Robertson County	11.8	9.7	3.4	4.8	1.5	2.0	5.4	1.5	1.1	0.4	1.3	2.6
47149	Rutherford County	15.6	11.0	3.7	4.5	2.8	4.6	3.2	0.9	0.8	0.2	1.0	1.3
47155	Sevier County	13.6	11.0	4.1	5.1	1.8	2.6	3.8	0.5	0.4	0.1	1.6	1.8
47157	Shelby County	16.5	13.5	5.2	6.4	1.9	3.0	4.7	0.7	0.5	0.2	1.8	2.2
47163	Sullivan County	16.7	14.2	4.7	7.3	2.1	2.5	3.8	1.4	1.0	0.4	1.0	1.4
47165	Sumner County	11.2	9.3	3.0	4.9	1.3	2.0	4.2	1.7	1.3	0.4	1.2	1.2
47167	Tipton County	10.1	8.5	3.6	3.7	1.2	1.6	6.7	1.6	1.2	0.4	2.2	2.9
47179	Washington County	18.6	15.4	6.0	7.0	2.4	3.2	2.4	0.9	0.6	0.2	0.7	0.8
47187	Williamson County	8.7	7.5	2.1	4.7	0.7	1.2	1.9	0.7	0.6	0.1	0.6	0.5
47189	Wilson County	12.7	10.2	3.8	5.0	1.4	2.6	4.3	2.1	1.6	0.5	1.1	1.1
48000	**Texas**	13.4	10.5	4.0	4.6	1.9	2.9	5.0	1.7	1.3	0.4	1.5	1.9
48001	Anderson County	8.9	8.0	3.1	4.3	0.6	0.9	3.1	0.8	0.7	0.1	1.4	0.9
48005	Angelina County	10.9	9.3	3.2	4.8	1.3	1.6	5.2	1.7	1.2	0.5	1.6	2.0
48021	Bastrop County	12.9	9.7	3.4	4.4	1.9	3.2	4.4	1.5	1.3	0.2	1.3	1.6
48027	Bell County	11.3	8.8	3.6	4.1	1.2	2.5	3.9	1.4	1.2	0.2	1.4	1.1
48029	Bexar County	14.2	11.0	4.3	4.8	2.0	3.2	6.0	2.1	1.5	0.5	1.8	2.2
48037	Bowie County	13.5	11.2	4.3	5.3	1.6	2.3	5.1	0.7	0.6	0.1	2.1	2.3
48039	Brazoria County	10.8	8.9	3.8	3.8	1.2	1.9	4.4	1.6	1.1	0.5	1.4	1.5
48041	Brazos County	27.9	15.7	5.0	5.0	5.6	12.2	2.6	0.6	0.4	0.2	0.9	1.1
48061	Cameron County	7.0	6.0	2.2	3.1	0.7	1.0	9.2	3.2	2.3	0.9	2.4	3.5
48073	Cherokee County	10.4	9.0	3.6	4.1	1.3	1.5	3.4	0.6	0.5	0.0	1.1	1.6
48085	Collin County	11.7	9.3	3.4	4.1	1.8	2.5	3.2	1.4	1.0	0.3	0.9	0.9
48091	Comal County	11.7	9.6	3.6	4.5	1.5	2.2	4.0	2.1	1.7	0.4	0.8	1.1
48099	Coryell County	7.7	6.1	2.5	2.9	0.8	1.6	2.1	0.7	0.6	0.1	0.8	0.5
48113	Dallas County	15.4	12.3	4.7	5.5	2.1	3.1	5.2	1.7	1.3	0.4	1.6	1.9
48121	Denton County	14.2	10.2	3.5	4.2	2.5	4.0	3.2	1.2	0.9	0.2	1.0	1.0
48135	Ector County	13.0	10.1	3.9	4.2	2.0	2.9	5.6	1.7	1.2	0.5	1.6	2.4
48139	Ellis County	8.5	7.0	2.5	3.3	1.2	1.5	4.8	1.1	0.9	0.3	1.4	2.3
48141	El Paso County	9.5	7.8	3.2	3.5	1.1	1.7	6.9	2.1	1.5	0.5	2.0	2.8
48157	Fort Bend County	6.5	5.4	2.0	2.7	0.8	1.1	4.6	1.6	1.4	0.2	1.3	1.7
48167	Galveston County	14.8	11.7	4.6	5.1	2.1	3.1	3.8	1.0	0.8	0.2	1.4	1.5
48181	Grayson County	15.6	12.4	4.3	6.1	2.1	3.3	3.9	1.5	1.1	0.4	1.2	1.2
48183	Gregg County	13.9	12.1	4.8	6.1	1.2	1.7	4.6	1.1	0.8	0.3	1.6	1.9
48187	Guadalupe County	10.9	9.0	3.4	4.3	1.3	1.9	5.9	1.6	1.2	0.4	1.8	2.5
48199	Hardin County	11.9	10.3	4.6	4.3	1.5	1.6	5.1	1.2	0.7	0.5	1.4	2.5
48201	Harris County	13.8	10.8	4.4	4.5	1.9	2.9	5.1	1.6	1.3	0.3	1.4	1.9
48203	Harrison County	11.5	9.6	3.8	4.8	1.0	1.9	4.8	0.7	0.5	0.2	2.0	2.0
48209	Hays County	19.9	12.2	3.8	4.1	4.3	7.7	3.4	1.2	1.0	0.2	0.9	1.2
48213	Henderson County	15.0	11.8	4.4	5.5	1.9	3.3	4.7	2.0	1.4	0.5	1.4	1.3
48215	Hidalgo County	6.3	5.1	1.9	2.4	0.8	1.2	9.6	4.1	2.6	1.5	2.1	3.3
48221	Hood County	14.9	11.9	4.6	5.5	1.8	2.9	2.1	0.5	0.5	0.1	0.8	0.8
48231	Hunt County	13.4	11.1	4.2	5.3	1.5	2.4	5.9	1.4	1.0	0.4	2.1	2.3

Table B-2: Counties with a Population of 50,000 or More—Relationships—*Continued*

State/county FIPS code	State/county	Total population	Percent of the population in households	Population in family households, percent					
				Percent in family households	Householder in family household, percent	Spouse in family household, percent	Child in family household (biological, adopted, or stepchild)	Other relative in family household	Nonrelatives in family household
	Texas—cont'd								
48245	Jefferson County	252,321	93.7	77.7	23.2	14.8	29.9	8.1	1.8
48251	Johnson County	153,346	98.1	87.4	25.8	20.3	30.0	9.1	2.2
48257	Kaufman County	106,842	98.7	90.0	25.7	19.3	32.2	9.9	3.0
48291	Liberty County	76,398	92.0	81.3	23.9	17.7	27.9	9.5	2.2
48303	Lubbock County	286,228	95.9	76.2	23.2	16.4	28.5	6.4	1.8
48309	McLennan County	239,642	96.2	79.8	23.8	16.9	30.3	6.7	2.1
48323	Maverick County	55,496	98.4	92.8	23.5	16.3	40.2	11.5	1.4
48329	Midland County	146,085	98.8	85.5	24.8	18.4	31.6	8.7	2.0
48339	Montgomery County	485,225	99.4	88.2	25.5	19.8	33.5	7.2	2.1
48347	Nacogdoches County	65,586	91.7	75.2	22.5	15.4	28.5	7.1	1.8
48355	Nueces County	347,585	97.9	83.5	24.6	16.0	31.0	9.6	2.3
48361	Orange County	82,762	99.1	86.3	26.7	19.9	30.1	7.4	2.2
48367	Parker County	119,771	97.3	86.8	26.6	21.6	30.7	6.1	1.8
48375	Potter County	122,044	94.7	79.4	22.6	14.9	31.9	7.6	2.4
48381	Randall County	125,013	98.3	81.7	26.4	20.7	28.2	4.9	1.5
48397	Rockwall County	83,152	99.1	92.0	27.1	22.1	34.8	5.8	2.2
48401	Rusk County	53,780	91.5	79.1	22.1	16.1	29.4	9.0	2.5
48409	San Patricio County	65,251	98.8	89.3	26.3	18.0	34.2	8.3	2.5
48423	Smith County	214,529	97.8	82.5	25.1	18.4	29.4	8.1	1.5
48427	Starr County	61,737	99.0	93.9	21.6	13.8	43.1	14.0	1.5
48439	Tarrant County	1,880,361	98.8	85.1	24.3	17.4	33.2	8.0	2.2
48441	Taylor County	133,616	95.6	77.8	23.4	17.3	28.2	6.7	2.2
48451	Tom Green County	113,427	94.4	78.1	24.1	17.2	27.4	7.3	2.1
48453	Travis County	1,093,138	97.9	73.9	21.8	15.6	27.2	7.0	2.4
48467	Van Zandt County	52,518	98.6	85.6	25.1	20.0	30.5	8.4	1.5
48469	Victoria County	88,949	98.5	85.8	25.7	18.0	30.9	8.5	2.8
48471	Walker County	68,528	68.2	51.9	17.8	12.5	17.5	3.4	0.7
48479	Webb County	258,973	98.6	92.7	21.7	14.1	41.3	13.5	2.1
48485	Wichita County	131,403	89.5	75.2	24.1	17.2	26.7	5.2	2.0
48491	Williamson County	456,571	99.1	87.1	25.1	20.2	34.0	6.1	1.8
48497	Wise County	60,412	98.4	89.0	26.4	22.0	29.9	8.7	1.9
49000	**Utah**	2,856,839	98.4	87.3	23.3	18.9	36.7	6.3	2.0
49003	Box Elder County	50,425	99.2	91.8	25.8	21.6	38.9	4.5	1.0
49005	Cache County	115,779	96.5	83.5	22.6	19.4	36.5	3.6	1.2
49011	Davis County	316,562	99.5	92.2	24.6	20.7	40.3	5.1	1.6
49035	Salt Lake County	1,063,941	98.8	85.4	22.9	17.7	34.5	7.7	2.5
49045	Tooele County	59,961	99.3	91.4	24.3	19.6	39.6	6.4	1.4
49049	Utah County	540,635	97.5	88.9	21.9	18.9	41.0	5.5	1.6
49053	Washington County	144,664	98.6	86.9	24.7	20.6	33.7	6.3	1.6
49057	Weber County	236,368	98.6	86.9	24.7	19.1	35.0	5.9	2.2
50000	**Vermont**	626,303	96.0	75.4	25.5	20.1	24.3	3.2	2.2
50007	Chittenden County	158,543	93.9	70.0	23.5	18.7	23.6	2.8	1.4
50021	Rutland County	60,943	96.1	75.5	26.1	20.5	22.6	3.7	2.6
50023	Washington County	59,408	96.3	75.0	25.3	19.7	24.9	2.9	2.2
50027	Windsor County	56,259	98.1	77.4	27.4	22.1	23.2	2.8	2.0
51000	**Virginia**	8,184,299	97.0	81.2	24.8	18.7	28.9	6.7	2.1
51003	Albemarle County	101,974	92.2	75.0	24.0	20.1	24.5	4.6	1.8
51013	Arlington County	220,785	98.6	64.3	20.1	15.9	20.2	6.2	1.8
51015	Augusta County	73,768	94.7	83.3	28.1	22.5	26.5	4.5	1.7
51019	Bedford County	69,584	99.5	86.8	28.7	24.0	27.9	4.7	1.5
51031	Campbell County	55,161	99.1	85.4	27.8	21.1	27.3	6.9	2.3
51041	Chesterfield County	323,984	98.7	86.1	25.0	19.3	33.2	6.5	2.2
51059	Fairfax County	1,117,918	99.2	85.7	24.8	20.1	31.1	7.4	2.2
51061	Fauquier County	66,596	99.4	87.7	25.4	21.5	31.9	7.4	1.6
51067	Franklin County	56,344	97.2	84.4	29.5	24.2	24.4	4.5	1.9
51069	Frederick County	80,417	98.6	85.5	26.5	22.1	30.1	4.8	2.0
51085	Hanover County	100,693	98.0	86.8	27.3	22.1	31.0	5.2	1.2
51087	Henrico County	314,780	99.3	80.8	24.9	17.6	30.4	6.2	1.7
51089	Henry County	52,917	98.8	83.6	29.2	21.1	25.8	6.0	1.5
51095	James City County	69,149	98.6	84.0	28.0	22.4	26.9	5.1	1.5
51107	Loudoun County	337,766	99.6	89.7	25.1	21.2	35.2	6.0	2.2
51121	Montgomery County	95,409	90.5	60.4	20.1	16.0	18.5	4.3	1.5
51143	Pittsylvania County	62,791	98.6	83.5	28.3	21.3	25.4	6.9	1.5
51153	Prince William County	429,316	99.1	90.0	24.4	18.9	35.6	8.2	2.8
51161	Roanoke County	93,140	97.8	82.4	27.5	21.8	26.1	5.8	1.2
51165	Rockingham County	77,407	97.9	85.1	26.8	21.7	29.5	5.7	1.4
51177	Spotsylvania County	125,888	99.7	90.8	26.9	21.2	34.3	6.2	2.1
51179	Stafford County	134,396	97.2	90.1	26.0	21.1	35.0	6.1	2.0
51191	Washington County	54,811	97.2	81.0	27.4	21.4	25.1	5.8	1.3
51199	York County	66,142	98.7	89.4	28.2	23.3	31.7	5.3	0.8
51510	Alexandria city	146,690	99.1	68.3	21.3	16.3	21.5	7.1	2.2
51550	Chesapeake city	228,092	97.3	86.5	26.0	19.1	31.8	7.7	1.9
51650	Hampton city	136,507	96.8	78.1	23.8	15.4	28.8	7.7	2.4
51660	Harrisonburg city	50,759	86.0	52.1	16.0	10.7	19.5	4.3	1.7

Table B-2: Counties with a Population of 50,000 or More—Relationships—*Continued*

State/county FIPS code	State/county	Population in nonfamily households						Population in subfamilies as a percent of total population					
		Total population in nonfamily households	Nonfamily householders				Nonrelatives in nonfamily households	Total population in subfamilies	In married couple subfamilies			Parent in a parent-child subfamily	Child in a parent-child subfamily
			Total	Male living alone	Female living alone	Householder living with nonrelatives			Total in married-couple subfamilies	Spouse in a married-couple subfamily	Child in married-couple subfamily		
	Texas—cont'd												
48245	Jefferson County	15.9	13.5	5.6	6.4	1.5	2.4	4.3	1.5	1.2	0.3	1.4	1.5
48251	Johnson County	10.7	8.5	3.1	3.9	1.5	2.2	5.7	1.9	1.3	0.6	1.6	2.2
48257	Kaufman County	8.7	7.0	2.6	3.3	1.2	1.7	6.4	1.9	1.5	0.4	2.1	2.5
48291	Liberty County	10.7	8.6	3.6	3.4	1.6	2.1	6.9	1.6	0.9	0.7	1.8	3.4
48303	Lubbock County	19.6	13.7	4.5	5.8	3.5	5.9	4.1	0.8	0.6	0.2	1.5	1.8
48309	McLennan County	16.4	11.9	4.3	5.2	2.4	4.5	4.4	1.1	0.8	0.3	1.5	1.8
48323	Maverick County	5.6	5.2	2.0	2.9	0.3	0.4	9.1	3.4	2.4	1.0	2.3	3.3
48329	Midland County	13.2	10.5	4.1	4.5	1.9	2.7	5.3	1.6	1.2	0.4	1.6	2.2
48339	Montgomery County	11.2	8.8	3.0	4.4	1.4	2.4	3.9	1.5	1.3	0.2	1.1	1.2
48347	Nacogdoches County	16.5	13.3	4.7	6.7	1.9	3.2	3.9	0.9	0.8	0.2	1.3	1.7
48355	Nueces County	14.4	11.1	4.3	4.5	2.3	3.2	6.1	1.5	1.2	0.4	2.0	2.6
48361	Orange County	12.8	10.8	4.6	4.7	1.5	2.0	5.1	1.5	1.1	0.4	1.5	2.1
48367	Parker County	10.4	8.8	3.5	4.3	1.0	1.6	3.2	0.7	0.5	0.2	1.3	1.2
48375	Potter County	15.3	12.6	5.1	5.6	1.9	2.6	4.4	1.3	1.1	0.2	1.4	1.8
48381	Randall County	16.6	12.4	4.1	5.5	2.8	4.2	2.5	0.4	0.3	0.1	0.9	1.2
48397	Rockwall County	7.1	6.0	1.9	3.2	0.9	1.2	3.7	0.8	0.7	0.0	1.4	1.5
48401	Rusk County	12.5	10.2	4.7	4.3	1.2	2.3	5.9	2.1	1.5	0.7	1.8	2.0
48409	San Patricio County	9.6	8.1	3.1	3.7	1.2	1.5	4.0	0.7	0.5	0.2	1.5	1.7
48423	Smith County	15.3	11.8	4.0	5.8	2.0	3.4	4.1	1.5	1.0	0.5	1.2	1.4
48427	Starr County	5.1	4.4	1.4	2.5	0.5	0.7	12.2	5.6	4.2	1.5	3.1	3.5
48439	Tarrant County	13.7	10.9	4.2	4.9	1.9	2.8	4.6	1.6	1.3	0.4	1.3	1.6
48441	Taylor County	17.8	13.4	5.0	5.8	2.6	4.4	3.8	0.8	0.7	0.1	1.3	1.7
48451	Tom Green County	16.3	13.3	5.2	6.0	2.0	3.1	4.2	0.9	0.5	0.3	1.6	1.8
48453	Travis County	24.0	16.4	5.7	6.0	4.6	7.6	3.3	1.1	0.9	0.3	1.0	1.2
48467	Van Zandt County	13.0	10.3	4.5	4.4	1.4	2.8	4.3	1.4	1.2	0.2	1.5	1.4
48469	Victoria County	12.7	10.5	4.6	4.2	1.7	2.2	5.4	1.0	0.7	0.3	1.9	2.6
48471	Walker County	16.3	12.0	4.3	5.1	2.6	4.3	0.0	0.0	0.0	0.0	0.0	0.0
48479	Webb County	5.9	4.6	1.9	2.0	0.7	1.3	9.3	3.0	2.0	1.1	2.5	3.8
48485	Wichita County	14.3	12.4	4.7	6.2	1.6	1.9	2.4	0.5	0.4	0.1	0.8	1.1
48491	Williamson County	12.0	9.4	3.3	4.5	1.6	2.6	3.9	1.9	1.4	0.5	1.0	1.0
48497	Wise County	9.5	7.4	3.1	3.1	1.2	2.0	6.0	1.7	1.3	0.3	2.1	2.2
49000	**Utah**	11.1	7.8	2.9	3.3	1.7	3.2	4.3	2.1	1.5	0.6	1.0	1.2
49003	Box Elder County	7.4	6.3	2.4	3.2	0.6	1.1	3.3	1.2	0.8	0.4	0.8	1.4
49005	Cache County	13.0	7.8	2.5	3.0	2.3	5.2	2.0	0.9	0.5	0.4	0.5	0.6
49011	Davis County	7.3	5.8	2.2	2.5	1.0	1.6	4.2	1.9	1.4	0.5	1.0	1.2
49035	Salt Lake County	13.4	9.7	3.6	3.9	2.2	3.7	5.1	2.5	1.7	0.7	1.2	1.4
49045	Tooele County	7.9	6.1	2.4	2.6	1.1	1.7	4.0	1.3	0.7	0.6	1.2	1.5
49049	Utah County	8.6	4.8	1.4	1.9	1.5	3.8	4.1	2.5	1.6	0.8	0.7	0.9
49053	Washington County	11.6	8.0	2.5	3.9	1.5	3.6	3.7	2.0	1.4	0.6	0.8	1.0
49057	Weber County	11.7	8.9	3.5	3.7	1.7	2.8	4.0	1.5	1.1	0.4	1.0	1.6
50000	**Vermont**	20.6	15.4	5.0	6.6	3.8	5.1	1.8	0.6	0.4	0.1	0.5	0.7
50007	Chittenden County	23.9	16.1	4.6	6.0	5.4	7.8	1.6	0.6	0.4	0.1	0.4	0.6
50021	Rutland County	20.7	16.0	4.8	7.6	3.6	4.7	2.3	0.9	0.7	0.2	0.6	0.9
50023	Washington County	21.3	16.4	5.5	7.1	3.8	4.9	1.6	0.4	0.3	0.2	0.5	0.6
50027	Windsor County	20.6	16.6	5.6	7.5	3.5	4.0	1.8	0.3	0.3	0.1	0.6	0.8
51000	**Virginia**	15.9	12.1	4.2	5.6	2.3	3.8	3.6	1.2	1.0	0.3	1.1	1.3
51003	Albemarle County	17.2	13.5	4.2	7.0	2.3	3.7	2.8	0.8	0.6	0.2	0.9	1.1
51013	Arlington County	34.3	23.0	8.2	9.2	5.6	11.3	2.3	1.2	1.0	0.2	0.6	0.5
51015	Augusta County	11.5	9.9	4.0	4.7	1.3	1.5	3.3	1.2	0.8	0.4	1.0	1.1
51019	Bedford County	12.7	10.7	4.2	5.0	1.5	2.0	2.9	1.8	1.4	0.4	0.6	0.5
51031	Campbell County	13.7	11.6	4.2	5.6	1.8	2.1	3.8	1.4	0.9	0.4	1.3	1.2
51041	Chesterfield County	12.6	10.2	3.4	5.2	1.5	2.4	3.4	0.9	0.8	0.2	1.2	1.2
51059	Fairfax County	13.5	10.1	3.4	4.5	2.2	3.4	3.7	2.0	1.7	0.3	0.8	0.9
51061	Fauquier County	11.7	9.1	3.4	3.8	1.9	2.6	5.1	1.9	1.4	0.5	1.5	1.7
51067	Franklin County	12.8	11.1	4.7	4.8	1.6	1.7	3.4	0.7	0.5	0.2	1.3	1.4
51069	Frederick County	13.1	9.6	3.1	4.1	2.4	3.4	3.4	1.5	1.2	0.3	1.0	0.9
51085	Hanover County	11.1	9.1	3.3	4.3	1.6	2.0	2.9	1.1	0.8	0.3	0.8	1.0
51087	Henrico County	18.5	14.4	4.5	7.1	2.7	4.2	3.0	0.6	0.5	0.1	1.1	1.3
51089	Henry County	15.2	13.9	5.7	7.1	1.1	1.3	2.8	0.8	0.6	0.1	0.8	1.2
51095	James City County	14.6	11.4	3.6	6.0	1.8	3.2	3.3	1.2	1.0	0.3	0.9	1.2
51107	Loudoun County	9.9	7.3	2.6	3.0	1.6	2.6	3.2	1.7	1.3	0.4	0.7	0.8
51121	Montgomery County	30.1	16.2	4.4	5.1	6.7	13.9	1.7	1.2	0.9	0.3	0.3	0.3
51143	Pittsylvania County	15.1	13.1	5.0	6.4	1.7	2.0	3.9	0.5	0.5	0.0	1.2	2.2
51153	Prince William County	9.1	7.0	2.6	2.9	1.5	2.2	4.6	1.7	1.4	0.3	1.3	1.6
51161	Roanoke County	15.3	13.4	3.9	7.7	1.8	2.0	3.9	1.7	1.0	0.7	0.9	1.3
51165	Rockingham County	12.9	10.3	3.1	5.3	2.0	2.5	3.1	0.6	0.5	0.1	1.1	1.5
51177	Spotsylvania County	8.9	6.7	2.1	3.3	1.4	2.2	4.5	0.9	0.7	0.2	1.7	1.8
51179	Stafford County	7.1	5.8	2.0	2.7	1.0	1.3	3.2	1.2	1.0	0.3	0.8	1.1
51191	Washington County	16.1	13.8	5.0	7.0	1.8	2.4	2.4	0.9	0.8	0.1	0.7	0.7
51199	York County	9.4	7.7	2.5	3.9	1.3	1.7	2.6	0.9	0.8	0.1	0.9	0.8
51510	Alexandria city	30.8	23.2	7.9	10.9	4.4	7.6	2.3	0.9	0.7	0.1	0.7	0.7
51550	Chesapeake city	10.8	8.8	3.0	4.4	1.5	2.0	5.4	1.8	1.3	0.5	1.6	2.0
51650	Hampton city	18.7	14.5	5.5	6.6	2.4	4.2	4.5	1.1	0.8	0.2	1.6	1.8
51660	Harrisonburg city	33.8	15.2	3.5	5.3	6.5	18.6	0.0	0.0	0.0	0.0	0.0	0.0

Table B-2: Counties with a Population of 50,000 or More—Relationships—*Continued*

State/county FIPS code	State/county	Total population	Percent of the population in households	Population in family households, percent					
				Percent in family households	Householder in family household, percent	Spouse in family household, percent	Child in family household (biological, adopted, or stepchild)	Other relative in family household	Nonrelatives in family household
	Virginia—cont'd								
51680	Lynchburg city........................	77,157	86.6	64.4	20.8	13.9	24.0	4.1	1.7
51700	Newport News city..................	181,043	95.3	77.4	23.7	14.4	29.6	6.5	3.2
51710	Norfolk city..........................	245,262	89.8	69.0	20.4	12.1	26.0	7.9	2.5
51740	Portsmouth city.....................	96,209	97.2	81.0	24.3	13.3	30.6	10.5	2.3
51760	Richmond city.......................	210,453	95.0	64.3	19.3	9.6	24.0	8.8	2.7
51770	Roanoke city........................	97,654	97.8	75.0	24.1	14.7	26.7	6.6	2.8
51800	Suffolk city..........................	85,228	98.9	87.3	26.2	18.9	33.0	7.5	1.8
51810	Virginia Beach city.................	445,561	97.6	82.2	25.3	18.4	30.2	6.3	1.9
53000	**Washington**......................	6,896,071	98.0	79.8	24.6	18.8	28.3	5.4	2.6
53005	Benton County......................	182,460	99.0	85.0	25.1	19.3	32.7	5.5	2.4
53007	Chelan County.......................	73,609	98.4	83.6	25.4	19.9	30.4	6.1	1.8
53009	Clallam County......................	72,014	98.4	76.0	25.9	21.1	22.4	4.4	2.3
53011	Clark County.........................	438,194	99.1	84.3	25.1	19.1	31.7	5.6	2.8
53015	Cowlitz County......................	102,009	98.9	82.7	25.6	19.3	27.7	6.1	3.9
53021	Franklin County.....................	85,186	97.3	88.4	21.7	15.1	40.7	7.9	3.0
53025	Grant County........................	91,363	98.8	88.0	24.3	18.0	36.0	6.6	3.2
53027	Grays Harbor County...............	71,720	95.6	78.7	24.2	17.4	26.4	7.6	3.0
53029	Island County........................	79,027	97.5	81.8	28.7	24.2	24.1	2.9	1.9
53033	King County..........................	2,007,779	98.2	75.8	23.7	18.4	26.0	5.3	2.4
53035	Kitsap County.......................	254,326	96.8	80.2	25.7	20.1	27.6	4.2	2.6
53041	Lewis County........................	75,431	98.5	82.3	26.2	19.9	27.1	6.0	3.1
53045	Mason County.......................	60,717	97.8	79.7	25.0	20.0	26.1	5.6	3.1
53053	Pierce County.......................	811,730	98.0	81.9	24.7	18.3	30.5	5.5	2.8
53057	Skagit County.......................	118,225	98.4	82.6	26.2	19.8	27.5	5.5	3.6
53061	Snohomish County..................	733,797	98.6	82.6	24.8	19.1	29.9	5.9	2.9
53063	Spokane County.....................	476,295	96.6	77.2	24.6	18.7	27.1	4.3	2.5
53067	Thurston County....................	259,144	98.6	81.5	26.0	19.9	28.4	4.9	2.4
53071	Walla Walla County.................	59,481	90.8	74.2	22.7	17.7	27.4	4.3	2.0
53073	Whatcom County....................	204,880	97.4	74.9	23.8	18.7	25.7	4.6	2.2
53077	Yakima County......................	246,498	98.5	86.6	23.0	16.5	35.2	8.8	3.1
54000	**West Virginia**....................	1,855,392	97.3	80.1	25.8	19.4	26.8	5.9	2.2
54003	Berkeley County.....................	107,192	99.0	85.2	27.0	19.7	29.9	5.0	3.7
54011	Cabell County.......................	96,878	95.9	74.3	24.2	16.8	26.0	5.5	1.9
54033	Harrison County.....................	69,151	98.7	82.7	26.1	19.6	27.3	6.5	3.2
54037	Jefferson County....................	54,653	97.5	83.3	26.3	20.1	27.5	7.3	2.1
54039	Kanawha County....................	191,789	98.3	78.8	26.4	18.7	26.3	5.3	2.1
54049	Marion County......................	56,793	98.0	81.0	25.2	18.7	28.3	6.8	1.9
54055	Mercer County......................	62,271	98.0	81.0	27.5	20.7	25.3	5.8	1.7
54061	Monongalia County.................	100,491	93.0	65.4	19.1	14.9	24.9	5.0	1.5
54079	Putnam County......................	56,441	99.5	86.5	28.3	22.2	29.5	4.6	1.9
54081	Raleigh County......................	79,090	95.1	78.8	26.2	19.7	25.4	5.3	2.2
54107	Wood County........................	86,690	99.0	81.0	26.3	19.8	26.9	5.2	2.7
55000	**Wisconsin**........................	5,725,352	97.4	79.1	25.5	19.7	28.2	3.7	2.0
55009	Brown County.......................	252,672	97.1	79.9	25.6	19.8	29.3	3.3	1.9
55017	Chippewa County...................	62,953	96.0	79.9	26.2	21.4	27.2	2.9	2.2
55021	Columbia County....................	56,626	97.4	82.6	27.1	21.4	29.0	2.7	2.5
55025	Dane County.........................	503,273	97.2	72.4	23.9	18.6	25.4	2.9	1.7
55027	Dodge County.......................	88,552	94.4	79.5	24.6	20.1	28.4	4.2	2.1
55035	Eau Claire County...................	100,600	95.7	72.8	23.4	18.8	26.5	2.3	1.7
55039	Fond du Lac County.................	101,771	96.7	80.7	27.1	21.4	26.8	2.8	2.7
55043	Grant County........................	51,101	92.3	71.0	23.6	19.6	23.6	2.2	2.0
55055	Jefferson County....................	84,255	95.7	79.9	25.8	21.0	27.7	3.4	2.0
55059	Kenosha County.....................	167,416	97.3	81.4	25.0	17.9	30.3	5.6	2.6
55063	La Crosse County...................	116,074	95.5	72.9	23.9	18.9	25.5	2.7	1.9
55071	Manitowoc County..................	80,867	98.6	81.3	27.1	22.4	28.0	2.5	1.2
55073	Marathon County...................	134,875	98.6	83.0	26.7	21.5	29.9	2.7	2.2
55079	Milwaukee County..................	953,901	97.7	75.8	22.7	13.9	30.4	6.4	2.3
55087	Outagamie County..................	179,023	98.2	82.6	26.3	21.1	30.4	2.9	1.9
55089	Ozaukee County....................	86,928	99.0	85.3	27.8	23.6	30.3	2.6	0.9
55097	Portage County.....................	70,277	95.1	73.9	24.8	20.0	24.7	2.3	2.1
55101	Racine County.......................	194,897	97.4	81.1	25.0	18.8	30.6	4.9	1.7
55105	Rock County.........................	160,359	98.0	81.5	26.4	19.1	27.9	4.7	3.4
55109	St. Croix County....................	85,371	99.0	86.4	27.3	21.9	32.2	3.3	1.7
55111	Sauk County.........................	62,727	98.5	81.6	26.3	21.3	28.4	3.4	2.1
55117	Sheboygan County..................	115,067	97.2	80.2	26.4	21.0	27.8	3.2	1.8
55127	Walworth County...................	102,952	97.3	78.9	25.0	19.5	28.0	4.5	1.8
55131	Washington County.................	132,482	99.1	85.7	28.2	23.2	30.3	2.6	1.4
55133	Waukesha County..................	392,338	98.7	84.2	27.4	23.6	29.8	2.3	1.1
55135	Waupaca County....................	52,233	97.0	80.5	27.5	22.6	25.6	2.7	2.2
55139	Winnebago County.................	168,618	94.9	74.0	24.2	19.3	25.5	3.1	1.9
55141	Wood County........................	74,313	98.7	80.6	27.4	21.8	27.2	2.4	1.7
56000	**Wyoming**.........................	575,535	97.6	79.9	25.3	20.1	27.9	4.3	2.3
56021	Laramie County.....................	94,294	98.2	81.2	25.5	20.2	28.7	4.2	2.5
56025	Natrona County.....................	78,671	98.0	79.7	26.0	19.2	26.9	5.2	2.4

Table B-2: Counties with a Population of 50,000 or More—Relationships—*Continued*

State/county FIPS code	State/county	Population in nonfamily households						Population in subfamilies as a percent of total population					
		Total population in nonfamily households	Nonfamily householders				Nonrelatives in nonfamily households	Total population in subfamilies	In married couple subfamilies			Parent in a parent-child subfamily	Child in a parent-child subfamily
			Total	Male living alone	Female living alone	Householder living with nonrelatives			Total in married-couple subfamilies	Spouse in a married-couple subfamily	Child in married-couple subfamily		
	Virginia—cont'd												
51680	Lynchburg city	22.2	16.6	6.4	7.2	3.0	5.5	2.3	0.2	0.2	0.0	0.9	1.2
51700	Newport News city	17.8	13.9	5.1	6.6	2.3	3.9	3.9	0.7	0.6	0.2	1.4	1.7
51710	Norfolk city	20.8	14.7	5.2	5.9	3.6	6.1	4.3	0.9	0.8	0.2	1.6	1.8
51740	Portsmouth city	16.2	13.5	5.2	6.4	1.9	2.7	5.6	0.9	0.8	0.1	2.1	2.5
51760	Richmond city	30.7	21.3	7.2	9.2	4.8	9.4	3.1	0.5	0.4	0.1	1.4	1.2
51770	Roanoke city	22.8	18.9	7.1	8.7	3.1	3.9	3.5	0.9	0.5	0.4	1.2	1.5
51800	Suffolk city	11.6	9.7	3.8	4.3	1.5	1.9	4.1	0.6	0.5	0.1	1.7	1.8
51810	Virginia Beach city	15.4	11.6	3.9	5.0	2.6	3.8	3.6	1.3	1.0	0.3	1.1	1.3
53000	**Washington**	18.2	13.6	4.9	5.7	3.0	4.5	2.9	1.1	0.9	0.2	0.8	0.9
53005	Benton County	14.0	11.4	4.6	5.0	1.7	2.6	3.6	1.5	1.0	0.4	1.0	1.2
53007	Chelan County	14.8	11.6	3.9	5.6	2.2	3.2	3.5	1.6	1.4	0.3	1.0	0.8
53009	Clallam County	22.4	16.8	5.8	7.4	3.6	5.6	2.0	0.3	0.2	0.1	0.9	0.7
53011	Clark County	14.8	11.3	3.9	4.9	2.5	3.5	3.3	1.3	1.0	0.3	1.0	1.0
53015	Cowlitz County	16.2	12.9	4.2	6.2	2.5	3.3	3.8	0.9	0.8	0.1	1.2	1.6
53021	Franklin County	8.9	6.6	2.9	2.2	1.5	2.3	4.7	2.2	1.9	0.3	1.1	1.3
53025	Grant County	10.8	8.8	3.4	4.1	1.3	2.0	3.8	1.6	1.2	0.4	1.1	1.2
53027	Grays Harbor County	16.9	13.3	4.8	6.1	2.4	3.6	3.3	1.2	1.1	0.1	1.0	1.1
53029	Island County	15.7	13.0	4.7	6.2	2.2	2.7	1.4	0.9	0.8	0.1	0.2	0.3
53033	King County	22.4	16.5	6.0	6.6	3.9	5.9	2.5	1.2	1.0	0.2	0.6	0.7
53035	Kitsap County	16.7	12.9	4.5	5.6	2.8	3.8	2.2	1.0	0.8	0.2	0.6	0.7
53041	Lewis County	16.2	12.9	4.8	5.8	2.3	3.3	3.6	1.3	0.9	0.5	1.0	1.3
53045	Mason County	18.1	13.5	5.4	5.0	3.1	4.6	3.1	1.0	0.8	0.2	1.1	1.0
53053	Pierce County	16.0	12.2	4.5	5.2	2.5	3.8	3.2	1.3	0.9	0.3	0.9	1.0
53057	Skagit County	15.8	12.0	4.1	5.3	2.6	3.8	2.9	0.9	0.7	0.2	1.0	1.0
53061	Snohomish County	16.0	11.9	4.3	4.9	2.7	4.1	2.6	1.1	1.0	0.2	0.7	0.8
53063	Spokane County	19.5	14.7	5.1	6.4	3.2	4.8	2.3	0.7	0.6	0.1	0.7	0.9
53067	Thurston County	17.1	13.0	4.3	5.9	2.8	4.0	2.1	0.7	0.5	0.2	0.7	0.7
53071	Walla Walla County	16.6	13.3	4.7	6.6	2.0	3.3	0.0	0.0	0.0	0.0	0.0	0.0
53073	Whatcom County	22.4	14.7	5.0	5.5	4.2	7.7	2.4	0.9	0.8	0.1	0.8	0.7
53077	Yakima County	11.9	9.1	3.3	4.1	1.8	2.8	6.1	1.6	1.2	0.4	2.0	2.5
54000	**West Virginia**	17.2	14.1	5.4	6.7	2.0	3.2	3.3	1.2	0.9	0.3	1.0	1.1
54003	Berkeley County	13.8	10.9	4.5	4.7	1.8	2.8	2.8	0.9	0.6	0.3	1.0	0.9
54011	Cabell County	21.6	16.7	6.1	7.7	2.9	4.9	2.1	0.9	0.7	0.2	0.7	0.6
54033	Harrison County	16.0	13.8	5.7	6.6	1.5	2.2	4.9	3.0	2.2	0.9	0.8	1.0
54037	Jefferson County	14.1	10.4	3.5	4.2	2.6	3.8	4.7	1.9	1.6	0.3	1.1	1.7
54039	Kanawha County	19.6	16.7	6.2	8.2	2.3	2.9	2.7	1.0	0.8	0.2	0.8	0.9
54049	Marion County	17.0	13.9	5.1	6.7	2.2	3.0	4.3	1.9	1.6	0.3	1.1	1.3
54055	Mercer County	17.0	14.1	4.6	7.6	1.9	2.8	2.8	0.6	0.5	0.1	1.0	1.3
54061	Monongalia County	27.6	17.3	6.5	6.8	4.0	10.2	1.8	0.5	0.5	0.0	0.8	0.4
54079	Putnam County	13.0	9.9	2.8	5.2	1.9	3.1	0.0	0.0	0.0	0.0	0.0	0.0
54081	Raleigh County	16.3	13.5	5.0	6.4	2.1	2.8	3.1	0.7	0.6	0.1	1.0	1.3
54107	Wood County	18.0	14.8	5.3	7.5	2.0	3.2	3.0	0.8	0.6	0.2	1.1	1.2
55000	**Wisconsin**	18.3	14.4	5.3	6.4	2.8	4.0	2.0	0.6	0.5	0.2	0.6	0.7
55009	Brown County	17.3	13.7	5.1	6.0	2.6	3.6	1.9	0.5	0.3	0.2	0.7	0.7
55017	Chippewa County	16.1	12.9	5.1	5.5	2.3	3.1	1.8	0.8	0.5	0.3	0.5	0.5
55021	Columbia County	14.8	12.3	4.8	5.4	2.1	2.6	1.2	0.4	0.3	0.1	0.4	0.4
55025	Dane County	24.8	17.5	5.7	7.2	4.6	7.3	1.2	0.4	0.3	0.1	0.4	0.5
55027	Dodge County	14.9	12.3	5.3	5.4	1.6	2.6	2.7	0.9	0.7	0.2	0.9	0.9
55035	Eau Claire County	22.9	16.2	5.1	7.0	4.1	6.7	1.0	0.4	0.3	0.1	0.4	0.3
55039	Fond du Lac County	15.9	13.4	5.2	6.1	2.1	2.5	1.6	0.6	0.4	0.1	0.4	0.6
55043	Grant County	21.3	14.4	4.6	5.5	4.3	6.9	1.0	0.3	0.2	0.1	0.3	0.4
55055	Jefferson County	15.8	12.5	4.7	5.4	2.4	3.3	1.9	0.4	0.3	0.1	0.6	0.9
55059	Kenosha County	16.0	12.3	4.7	5.1	2.5	3.7	3.3	1.0	0.7	0.3	1.0	1.3
55063	La Crosse County	22.6	15.7	5.0	6.5	4.2	6.9	1.1	0.2	0.1	0.1	0.4	0.5
55071	Manitowoc County	17.3	14.5	6.3	6.0	2.2	2.8	1.2	0.3	0.3	0.0	0.4	0.4
55073	Marathon County	15.6	12.7	4.6	5.8	2.3	2.9	1.4	0.6	0.5	0.1	0.4	0.4
55079	Milwaukee County	21.8	17.1	6.1	7.8	3.2	4.7	3.1	0.7	0.6	0.1	1.1	1.3
55087	Outagamie County	15.6	12.6	4.9	5.3	2.4	3.0	1.7	0.7	0.5	0.2	0.4	0.6
55089	Ozaukee County	13.7	11.4	3.7	6.2	1.6	2.3	1.2	0.7	0.5	0.2	0.2	0.3
55097	Portage County	21.2	14.7	4.7	6.1	3.9	6.5	1.2	0.5	0.4	0.1	0.4	0.4
55101	Racine County	16.4	13.1	4.8	6.2	2.2	3.3	2.9	1.0	0.8	0.1	0.9	1.0
55105	Rock County	16.5	13.3	4.5	6.2	2.6	3.2	3.3	1.2	0.9	0.4	0.9	1.2
55109	St. Croix County	12.6	10.2	3.8	4.6	1.8	2.4	2.6	0.7	0.5	0.2	1.0	0.9
55111	Sauk County	17.0	13.5	4.9	6.2	2.5	3.4	1.6	0.4	0.3	0.1	0.6	0.6
55117	Sheboygan County	17.0	13.9	5.4	6.1	2.4	3.0	1.4	0.5	0.4	0.1	0.4	0.5
55127	Walworth County	18.4	13.5	4.4	5.8	3.3	4.9	3.4	1.5	0.9	0.6	0.8	1.1
55131	Washington County	13.4	11.2	3.8	5.6	1.7	2.2	1.6	0.8	0.6	0.3	0.4	0.4
55133	Waukesha County	14.5	11.8	3.9	5.9	2.0	2.7	1.3	0.7	0.5	0.2	0.3	0.3
55135	Waupaca County	16.5	13.4	5.3	5.9	2.3	3.1	1.5	0.4	0.3	0.1	0.5	0.6
55139	Winnebago County	20.9	16.2	5.8	7.1	3.2	4.7	1.5	0.5	0.3	0.1	0.5	0.6
55141	Wood County	18.1	15.3	5.4	7.5	2.4	2.8	1.4	0.4	0.3	0.1	0.4	0.5
56000	**Wyoming**	17.7	13.4	5.4	5.3	2.8	4.3	2.2	0.7	0.6	0.2	0.7	0.7
56021	Laramie County	17.1	12.8	5.1	5.3	2.4	4.3	2.2	0.5	0.4	0.1	0.9	0.8
56025	Natrona County	18.3	14.1	6.0	5.2	3.0	4.2	1.9	0.9	0.7	0.1	0.5	0.6

FIPS CBSA code	State	Total population	Percent of the population in households	Population in family households, percent					
				Percent in family households	Householder in family household, percent	Spouse in family household, percent	Child in family household (biological, adopted, or stepchild)	Other relative in family household	Nonrelatives in family household
10180	Abilene, TX...............	167,165	91.7	75.1	23.0	17.3	26.8	6.1	1.9
10420	Akron, OH...............	705,353	97.7	78.9	25.0	18.3	28.4	5.4	1.8
10500	Albany, GA...............	156,956	96.3	81.8	24.6	14.8	29.8	10.3	2.2
10540	Albany, OR...............	118,450	98.9	83.4	25.9	19.8	27.8	6.7	3.2
10580	Albany-Schenectady-Troy, NY......	875,306	96.2	76.3	23.9	18.1	27.9	4.5	1.9
10740	Albuquerque, NM...............	900,044	98.5	81.3	24.3	16.7	30.2	7.4	2.6
10780	Alexandria, LA...............	154,490	95.1	80.4	23.3	15.8	32.5	7.2	1.6
10900	Allentown-Bethlehem-Easton, PA-NJ......	826,311	97.2	82.3	25.8	19.6	29.4	5.4	2.1
11020	Altoona, PA...............	126,839	97.4	80.8	26.0	19.6	27.5	5.1	2.5
11100	Amarillo, TX...............	256,766	96.5	80.7	24.6	18.0	30.0	6.1	1.9
11180	Ames, IA...............	91,623	90.8	60.0	20.6	17.7	19.5	1.4	0.9
11260	Anchorage, AK...............	392,025	97.5	82.3	23.4	17.5	31.9	6.4	3.1
11460	Ann Arbor, MI...............	351,345	94.9	70.3	22.3	17.2	25.7	3.6	1.6
11500	Anniston-Oxford-Jacksonville, AL......	117,253	97.8	82.0	25.4	17.7	28.4	8.7	1.7
11540	Appleton, WI...............	228,676	98.5	83.9	26.7	21.7	31.0	2.9	1.7
11700	Asheville, NC...............	432,791	97.6	77.8	26.1	20.2	24.8	4.9	1.8
12020	Athens-Clarke County, GA...............	196,309	94.5	69.5	20.6	14.9	26.2	6.3	1.4
12060	Atlanta-Sandy Springs-Roswell, GA......	5,450,291	98.4	83.7	23.9	16.9	32.1	8.6	2.1
12100	Atlantic City-Hammonton, NJ......	275,339	97.5	82.7	24.8	16.4	29.7	9.0	2.8
12220	Auburn-Opelika, AL...............	147,537	96.4	74.7	23.7	17.3	26.2	5.7	1.8
12260	Augusta-Richmond County, GA-SC......	575,818	97.3	83.5	24.4	16.6	31.9	8.7	1.8
12420	Austin-Round Rock, TX...............	1,833,344	97.8	77.9	22.7	17.0	29.2	6.8	2.1
12540	Bakersfield, CA...............	856,363	96.4	86.7	22.5	15.2	35.9	9.8	3.3
12580	Baltimore-Columbia-Towson, MD......	2,752,965	97.5	80.6	24.2	16.9	29.8	7.4	2.2
12620	Bangor, ME...............	153,550	95.4	73.4	25.0	19.5	22.6	3.8	2.5
12700	Barnstable Town, MA...............	215,112	98.6	79.0	27.0	21.4	24.6	4.1	1.9
12940	Baton Rouge, LA...............	814,572	97.2	80.9	24.3	16.2	30.5	7.7	2.1
12980	Battle Creek, MI...............	135,120	97.2	80.5	25.3	17.5	29.3	5.7	2.7
13020	Bay City, MI...............	106,984	98.6	81.3	26.7	20.2	28.4	4.1	2.0
13140	Beaumont-Port Arthur, TX...............	404,580	95.6	80.9	24.5	16.8	29.6	8.2	1.8
13220	Beckley, WV...............	124,898	95.3	79.6	25.9	19.1	26.2	6.2	2.3
13380	Bellingham, WA...............	204,980	97.4	74.9	23.8	18.7	25.7	4.6	2.2
13460	Bend-Redmond, OR...............	162,547	99.2	80.1	26.2	20.9	26.4	4.4	2.3
13740	Billings, MT...............	163,042	97.6	79.3	25.5	19.0	27.2	5.0	2.5
13780	Binghamton, NY...............	248,935	95.6	76.4	24.8	18.7	26.5	4.0	2.4
13820	Birmingham-Hoover, AL...............	1,135,513	97.9	83.0	25.7	18.5	30.2	7.2	1.5
13900	Bismarck, ND...............	120,346	96.9	78.2	26.0	20.6	26.6	3.2	1.8
13980	Blacksburg-Christiansburg-Radford, VA......	179,439	92.8	67.6	22.8	17.6	20.7	4.8	1.8
14010	Bloomington, IL...............	189,028	95.6	74.4	23.5	18.5	27.1	3.6	1.6
14020	Bloomington, IN...............	162,519	91.3	62.9	20.7	15.5	21.2	3.6	1.7
14100	Bloomsburg-Berwick, PA...............	85,322	94.9	74.7	25.0	19.5	24.4	4.2	1.7
14260	Boise City, ID...............	638,510	98.3	83.7	25.1	19.5	31.5	5.1	2.5
14460	Boston-Cambridge-Newton, MA-NH......	4,643,371	96.4	77.9	24.0	18.0	28.4	5.7	1.8
14500	Boulder, CO...............	305,284	96.7	72.0	23.4	18.5	24.7	3.4	1.9
14540	Bowling Green, KY...............	162,070	95.6	78.2	25.3	18.8	27.4	4.7	2.0
14740	Bremerton-Silverdale, WA...............	254,326	96.8	80.2	25.7	20.1	27.6	4.2	2.6
14860	Bridgeport-Stamford-Norwalk, CT......	933,794	98.0	84.0	24.5	18.8	32.0	6.7	2.0
15180	Brownsville-Harlingen, TX...............	415,191	99.1	92.1	22.8	15.1	39.8	12.6	1.9
15260	Brunswick, GA...............	113,411	98.7	84.9	26.3	18.2	28.9	9.0	2.4
15380	Buffalo-Cheektowaga-Niagara Falls, NY......	1,134,260	97.1	77.4	25.2	17.6	28.8	4.0	1.8
15500	Burlington, NC...............	153,623	97.1	82.3	26.5	18.5	28.6	6.5	2.1
15540	Burlington-South Burlington, VT......	213,754	95.2	73.3	24.4	19.3	24.9	3.2	1.5
15680	California-Lexington Park, MD......	108,794	97.5	86.5	25.7	20.9	31.5	6.5	1.9
15940	Canton-Massillon, OH...............	403,589	97.6	81.7	26.5	19.8	28.9	4.6	2.0
15980	Cape Coral-Fort Myers, FL...............	645,681	98.5	81.7	24.6	19.1	26.5	8.8	2.8
16020	Cape Girardeau, MO-IL...............	96,940	95.6	77.9	24.7	19.2	27.5	4.7	1.7
16060	Carbondale-Marion, IL...............	126,869	95.1	72.4	23.3	17.4	25.1	5.1	1.5
16180	Carson City, NV...............	54,481	96.1	76.2	23.1	17.2	26.8	6.5	2.6
16220	Casper, WY...............	78,671	98.0	79.7	26.0	19.2	26.9	5.2	2.4
16300	Cedar Rapids, IA...............	261,634	97.4	78.8	25.2	19.9	27.9	4.0	1.8
16540	Chambersburg-Waynesboro, PA...............	151,467	98.5	83.6	26.3	21.2	29.1	4.7	2.2
16580	Champaign-Urbana, IL...............	234,055	92.9	66.4	21.7	16.6	23.6	3.2	1.4
16620	Charleston, WV...............	225,490	98.5	79.8	26.5	19.0	26.6	5.6	2.1
16700	Charleston-North Charleston, SC......	697,116	97.5	79.5	24.3	17.3	28.9	7.2	1.8
16740	Charlotte-Concord-Gastonia, NC-SC......	2,295,703	98.5	83.1	25.1	18.3	30.8	7.0	2.0
16820	Charlottesville, VA...............	222,601	93.6	73.0	23.3	18.4	24.1	5.4	1.8
16860	Chattanooga, TN-GA...............	537,584	97.5	82.1	26.1	19.3	27.5	7.3	1.9
16940	Cheyenne, WY...............	94,294	98.2	81.2	25.5	20.2	28.7	4.2	2.5
16980	Chicago-Naperville-Elgin, IL-IN-WI......	9,514,212	98.4	83.1	23.8	17.2	32.4	7.9	1.9
17020	Chico, CA...............	221,006	97.5	74.1	22.9	16.0	26.2	6.1	3.0
17140	Cincinnati, OH-KY-IN...............	2,129,899	97.9	81.4	25.1	18.5	30.6	5.3	1.9
17300	Clarksville, TN-KY...............	270,705	96.5	84.4	25.9	19.2	31.8	5.3	2.2
17420	Cleveland, TN...............	117,637	97.3	82.9	26.3	19.5	27.1	7.3	2.6
17460	Cleveland-Elyria, OH...............	2,066,023	97.8	79.4	25.1	17.6	29.6	5.4	1.7
17660	Coeur d'Alene, ID...............	142,541	98.9	82.5	26.8	21.0	27.1	5.0	2.5

| FIPS CBSA code | State | Population in nonfamily households | | | | | | Population in subfamilies as a percent of total population | | | | | |
| | | Total population in nonfamily households | Nonfamily householders | | | | Nonrelatives in nonfamily households | Total population in subfamilies | In married couple subfamilies | | | Parent in a parent-child subfamily | Child in a parent-child subfamily |
			Total	Male living alone	Female living alone	Householder living with nonrelatives			Total in married-couple subfamilies	Spouse in a married-couple subfamily	Child in married-couple subfamily		
10180	Abilene, TX	16.6	12.9	4.9	5.7	2.3	3.7	3.4	0.7	0.5	0.1	1.1	1.6
10420	Akron, OH	18.8	14.6	5.5	6.5	2.6	4.2	2.8	0.8	0.6	0.2	1.0	1.0
10500	Albany, GA	14.5	12.3	4.4	6.3	1.5	2.2	4.4	0.7	0.5	0.1	1.7	2.1
10540	Albany, OR	15.6	11.6	4.1	5.0	2.5	3.9	4.0	2.1	1.5	0.7	0.9	0.9
10580	Albany-Schenectady-Troy, NY	19.9	15.6	5.6	6.9	3.1	4.3	2.4	0.8	0.6	0.2	0.8	0.8
10740	Albuquerque, NM	17.2	13.7	5.1	6.1	2.5	3.4	4.2	1.3	1.1	0.2	1.4	1.5
10780	Alexandria, LA	14.7	12.2	4.9	5.9	1.5	2.5	3.7	0.7	0.5	0.2	1.4	1.5
10900	Allentown-Bethlehem-Easton, PA-NJ	15.0	12.1	4.2	5.7	2.2	2.9	3.1	0.9	0.8	0.2	1.0	1.2
11020	Altoona, PA	16.7	13.9	5.2	6.9	1.8	2.8	2.4	0.7	0.5	0.2	0.8	0.8
11100	Amarillo, TX	15.8	12.4	4.6	5.5	2.3	3.3	3.4	0.8	0.7	0.1	1.1	1.5
11180	Ames, IA	30.7	18.1	5.3	5.5	7.3	12.6	0.5	0.2	0.1	0.1	0.2	0.2
11260	Anchorage, AK	15.2	11.4	4.6	4.2	2.6	3.8	3.4	1.2	1.0	0.2	1.0	1.2
11460	Ann Arbor, MI	24.6	16.6	5.4	6.8	4.5	8.0	1.8	0.8	0.6	0.2	0.5	0.5
11500	Anniston-Oxford-Jacksonville, AL	15.8	12.8	4.7	6.3	1.8	3.0	5.5	1.6	1.3	0.4	1.8	2.0
11540	Appleton, WI	14.6	11.8	4.6	5.0	2.3	2.7	1.6	0.7	0.5	0.2	0.4	0.5
11700	Asheville, NC	19.8	15.6	5.2	7.5	2.8	4.3	2.9	0.8	0.6	0.2	1.0	1.1
12020	Athens-Clarke County, GA	25.1	14.3	4.0	6.2	4.1	10.8	3.1	1.1	0.9	0.2	1.0	1.0
12060	Atlanta-Sandy Springs-Roswell, GA	14.7	11.4	4.1	5.3	2.0	3.3	4.3	1.3	1.0	0.2	1.4	1.7
12100	Atlantic City-Hammonton, NJ	14.7	12.0	4.5	5.7	1.9	2.7	5.1	1.7	1.3	0.3	1.5	2.0
12220	Auburn-Opelika, AL	21.7	14.5	5.0	5.5	4.0	7.3	0.0	0.0	0.0	0.0	0.0	0.0
12260	Augusta-Richmond County, GA-SC	13.8	11.6	4.5	5.6	1.4	2.2	4.3	0.8	0.6	0.2	1.7	1.8
12420	Austin-Round Rock, TX	19.9	13.8	4.8	5.4	3.7	6.1	3.6	1.4	1.1	0.3	1.0	1.2
12540	Bakersfield, CA	9.7	7.4	2.9	3.0	1.5	2.3	5.6	1.9	1.4	0.5	1.7	2.0
12580	Baltimore-Columbia-Towson, MD	16.9	13.2	4.5	6.4	2.4	3.7	4.1	1.1	0.8	0.3	1.4	1.6
12620	Bangor, ME	22.0	15.7	5.0	6.2	4.4	6.4	1.9	0.7	0.6	0.2	0.6	0.6
12700	Barnstable Town, MA	19.5	16.3	5.4	8.6	2.3	3.2	2.4	1.1	0.9	0.2	0.6	0.7
12940	Baton Rouge, LA	16.3	12.4	4.7	5.5	2.2	4.0	4.3	0.7	0.5	0.2	1.6	2.0
12980	Battle Creek, MI	16.6	13.8	5.2	6.4	2.1	2.9	3.8	1.2	0.9	0.3	1.2	1.4
13020	Bay City, MI	17.3	14.3	5.6	6.6	2.2	2.9	2.1	0.6	0.5	0.1	0.6	0.9
13140	Beaumont-Port Arthur, TX	14.7	12.5	5.2	5.7	1.5	2.3	4.9	1.4	1.1	0.3	1.5	2.0
13220	Beckley, WV	15.7	12.9	5.0	6.0	2.0	2.8	3.5	1.2	0.9	0.3	1.1	1.2
13380	Bellingham, WA	22.4	14.7	5.0	5.5	4.2	7.7	2.4	0.9	0.8	0.1	0.8	0.7
13460	Bend-Redmond, OR	19.1	13.8	4.4	6.1	3.3	5.3	2.0	1.0	0.8	0.2	0.5	0.5
13740	Billings, MT	18.3	14.5	5.3	6.6	2.6	3.8	2.6	0.9	0.6	0.2	0.9	0.9
13780	Binghamton, NY	19.2	15.0	5.2	7.1	2.7	4.2	2.1	1.0	0.7	0.3	0.5	0.5
13820	Birmingham-Hoover, AL	14.9	12.5	4.9	6.2	1.5	2.4	3.9	1.0	0.7	0.2	1.4	1.5
13900	Bismarck, ND	18.7	14.7	5.4	6.3	3.0	4.0	2.0	0.5	0.4	0.1	0.6	0.9
13980	Blacksburg-Christiansburg-Radford, VA	25.2	15.6	4.8	5.8	5.1	9.6	2.2	0.9	0.6	0.3	0.6	0.7
14010	Bloomington, IL	21.2	14.3	4.9	5.8	3.7	6.9	2.0	0.5	0.4	0.2	0.7	0.8
14020	Bloomington, IN	28.4	17.6	6.2	6.4	5.1	10.8	1.8	0.7	0.6	0.2	0.6	0.5
14100	Bloomsburg-Berwick, PA	20.1	14.1	4.3	6.6	3.1	6.1	2.3	1.1	0.8	0.2	0.6	0.6
14260	Boise City, ID	14.6	11.1	3.7	5.1	2.4	3.5	3.1	1.2	0.9	0.3	0.9	1.0
14460	Boston-Cambridge-Newton, MA-NH	18.5	13.9	4.4	6.3	3.1	4.7	2.8	1.3	1.0	0.3	0.7	0.8
14500	Boulder, CO	24.8	16.3	5.3	5.9	5.1	8.5	1.7	0.7	0.6	0.1	0.5	0.5
14540	Bowling Green, KY	17.5	13.4	4.8	5.9	2.8	4.0	1.9	0.5	0.4	0.1	0.6	0.8
14740	Bremerton-Silverdale, WA	16.7	12.9	4.5	5.6	2.8	3.8	2.2	1.0	0.8	0.2	0.6	0.7
14860	Bridgeport-Stamford-Norwalk, CT	14.0	10.9	3.7	5.3	1.9	3.1	3.1	1.3	1.0	0.2	0.9	1.0
15180	Brownsville-Harlingen, TX	7.0	6.0	2.2	3.1	0.7	1.0	9.2	3.2	2.3	0.9	2.4	3.5
15260	Brunswick, GA	13.8	11.6	4.6	5.5	1.5	2.2	6.1	1.0	0.8	0.2	2.4	2.4
15380	Buffalo-Cheektowaga-Niagara Falls, NY	19.7	16.2	5.8	7.9	2.6	3.5	2.0	0.6	0.5	0.1	0.7	0.7
15500	Burlington, NC	14.9	12.7	4.2	6.9	1.6	2.2	3.2	0.7	0.6	0.1	1.2	1.3
15540	Burlington-South Burlington, VT	21.9	15.1	4.4	6.0	4.8	6.7	1.9	0.6	0.4	0.2	0.5	0.8
15680	California-Lexington Park, MD	11.0	8.8	3.7	3.5	1.6	2.2	3.3	1.0	0.8	0.3	1.2	1.0
15940	Canton-Massillon, OH	15.9	13.4	4.9	6.5	2.0	2.5	2.5	0.5	0.4	0.1	0.9	1.1
15980	Cape Coral-Fort Myers, FL	16.8	12.8	4.3	6.2	2.3	4.0	3.7	1.7	1.6	0.1	1.1	0.8
16020	Cape Girardeau, MO-IL	17.8	13.6	5.2	5.9	2.5	4.2	2.7	0.8	0.6	0.2	0.9	0.9
16060	Carbondale-Marion, IL	22.8	16.4	6.1	7.1	3.2	6.4	2.3	0.6	0.5	0.1	0.9	0.8
16180	Carson City, NV	19.9	15.8	6.2	6.9	2.8	4.1	3.9	0.8	0.7	0.0	1.3	1.8
16220	Casper, WY	18.3	14.1	6.0	5.2	3.0	4.2	1.9	0.9	0.7	0.1	0.5	0.6
16300	Cedar Rapids, IA	18.6	14.6	5.7	6.0	2.9	4.0	2.1	0.5	0.4	0.1	0.8	0.8
16540	Chambersburg-Waynesboro, PA	14.9	12.1	4.1	6.2	1.9	2.8	2.3	0.7	0.5	0.1	0.8	0.9
16580	Champaign-Urbana, IL	26.4	17.3	6.0	6.6	4.7	9.1	1.7	0.5	0.3	0.2	0.6	0.6
16620	Charleston, WV	18.6	15.8	5.9	7.7	2.2	2.8	3.0	1.0	0.8	0.2	0.9	1.1
16700	Charleston-North Charleston, SC	18.0	13.4	4.6	6.1	2.8	4.6	3.5	0.5	0.4	0.1	1.3	1.7
16740	Charlotte-Concord-Gastonia, NC-SC	15.4	12.0	4.3	5.6	2.1	3.4	3.6	1.0	0.8	0.2	1.2	1.4
16820	Charlottesville, VA	20.5	14.5	4.7	6.7	3.1	6.0	3.4	1.0	0.8	0.2	1.0	1.3
16860	Chattanooga, TN-GA	15.4	12.6	4.6	6.2	1.9	2.8	3.7	1.1	0.8	0.2	1.2	1.4
16940	Cheyenne, WY	17.1	12.8	5.1	5.3	2.4	4.3	2.2	0.5	0.4	0.1	0.9	0.8
16980	Chicago-Naperville-Elgin, IL-IN-WI	15.3	12.3	4.5	5.7	2.0	3.0	4.3	1.4	1.2	0.3	1.3	1.6
17020	Chico, CA	23.4	15.4	4.7	6.5	4.3	8.0	2.8	1.3	1.1	0.2	0.8	0.8
17140	Cincinnati, OH-KY-IN	16.5	13.1	4.8	6.1	2.2	3.4	3.0	0.9	0.7	0.2	1.0	1.1
17300	Clarksville, TN-KY	12.1	9.6	3.7	4.1	1.7	2.5	2.7	1.0	0.6	0.3	0.8	0.9
17420	Cleveland, TN	14.5	11.8	4.7	5.4	1.7	2.6	4.4	1.8	1.3	0.5	1.2	1.3
17460	Cleveland-Elyria, OH	18.5	15.7	5.8	7.7	2.1	2.8	2.8	0.8	0.6	0.2	0.9	1.1
17660	Coeur d'Alene, ID	16.4	12.2	4.1	5.3	2.8	4.2	3.0	0.9	0.6	0.2	0.9	1.2

FIPS CBSA code	State	Total population	Percent of the population in households	Population in family households, percent					
				Percent in family households	Householder in family household, percent	Spouse in family household, percent	Child in family household (biological, adopted, or stepchild)	Other relative in family household	Nonrelatives in family household
17780	College Station-Bryan, TX	234,165	93.7	68.2	20.4	14.6	25.2	6.2	1.8
17820	Colorado Springs, CO	669,116	97.4	82.4	25.4	19.8	30.2	4.8	2.2
17860	Columbia, MO	168,383	94.5	67.7	21.8	16.7	24.2	3.4	1.6
17900	Columbia, SC	784,970	95.4	78.4	24.4	16.8	28.7	6.8	1.7
17980	Columbus, GA-AL	308,712	94.9	79.8	23.5	15.1	31.7	7.9	1.7
18020	Columbus, IN	78,740	98.7	84.1	25.6	19.6	29.1	6.5	3.2
18140	Columbus, OH	1,945,807	97.5	79.1	24.2	17.7	29.4	5.4	2.3
18580	Corpus Christi, TX	436,731	98.0	84.3	25.0	16.7	31.0	9.3	2.3
18700	Corvallis, OR	86,346	93.8	66.4	21.7	17.6	20.6	4.4	2.1
18880	Crestview-Fort Walton Beach-Destin, FL	246,837	97.1	80.9	26.1	19.5	27.1	5.9	2.4
19060	Cumberland, MD-WV	101,878	91.6	72.4	22.0	16.4	26.6	5.3	2.1
19100	Dallas-Fort Worth-Arlington, TX	6,694,889	98.8	85.1	24.4	17.8	32.7	8.2	2.0
19140	Dalton, GA	142,365	99.0	88.1	25.2	18.4	33.7	8.3	2.5
19180	Danville, IL	80,809	97.2	80.7	25.3	17.9	29.5	5.7	2.4
19300	Daphne-Fairhope-Foley, AL	190,981	98.6	84.2	27.0	21.3	28.3	6.4	1.1
19340	Davenport-Moline-Rock Island, IA-IL	382,446	97.8	80.0	25.6	19.4	29.0	4.0	2.0
19380	Dayton, OH	802,881	96.4	78.0	25.3	17.9	27.9	4.9	2.1
19460	Decatur, AL	153,759	98.7	84.6	26.7	19.9	30.3	6.3	1.3
19500	Decatur, IL	109,942	96.8	77.6	25.3	18.2	27.3	4.8	2.1
19660	Deltona-Daytona Beach-Ormond Beach, FL	595,919	98.1	79.0	24.2	18.5	25.6	7.9	2.7
19740	Denver-Aurora-Lakewood, CO	2,648,027	98.7	79.8	24.1	18.1	29.3	6.2	2.1
19780	Des Moines-West Des Moines, IA	590,003	97.9	81.7	25.9	19.8	29.7	4.3	1.9
19820	Detroit-Warren-Dearborn, MI	4,291,790	98.9	82.9	25.1	17.5	31.7	6.7	1.9
20020	Dothan, AL	147,284	99.0	83.9	26.2	18.7	30.5	6.9	1.7
20100	Dover, DE	167,382	97.0	83.0	24.7	17.6	30.9	7.2	2.7
20220	Dubuque, IA	95,073	95.3	77.0	25.2	20.0	28.1	2.5	1.3
20260	Duluth, MN-WI	279,787	95.4	73.8	24.8	18.9	24.7	3.1	2.3
20500	Durham-Chapel Hill, NC	525,375	95.2	74.6	24.0	17.2	25.9	5.5	2.1
20700	East Stroudsburg, PA	168,469	98.4	85.9	25.6	19.0	31.8	6.9	2.7
20740	Eau Claire, WI	163,553	95.8	75.5	24.5	19.8	26.8	2.6	1.9
20940	El Centro, CA	176,416	93.7	85.5	20.8	13.8	35.1	13.8	1.9
21060	Elizabethtown-Fort Knox, KY	151,070	97.3	84.8	26.4	19.3	31.0	5.6	2.5
21140	Elkhart-Goshen, IN	199,449	98.2	86.2	25.7	18.6	32.9	6.0	3.1
21300	Elmira, NY	88,864	93.0	74.6	25.0	18.2	26.0	4.1	1.4
21340	El Paso, TX	828,372	98.2	88.7	23.6	15.6	37.3	10.6	1.7
21500	Erie, PA	280,679	95.5	77.8	24.9	17.9	28.3	4.7	2.0
21660	Eugene, OR	354,738	97.7	73.2	24.1	17.9	23.6	4.2	3.3
21780	Evansville, IN-KY	313,368	96.9	80.2	26.0	19.5	27.7	5.0	2.0
21820	Fairbanks, AK	99,951	96.1	78.2	22.3	17.4	31.3	4.7	2.5
22020	Fargo, ND-MN	217,656	95.9	72.3	23.6	18.3	25.6	3.0	1.9
22140	Farmington, NM	127,620	98.7	88.4	22.7	15.5	34.7	13.1	2.3
22180	Fayetteville, NC	374,663	97.0	82.1	25.0	16.6	31.5	7.1	2.0
22220	Fayetteville-Springdale-Rogers, AR-MO	482,916	97.8	82.9	25.3	20.0	30.0	5.9	1.7
22380	Flagstaff, AZ	135,522	93.1	74.4	22.1	15.5	25.8	8.1	2.9
22420	Flint, MI	418,306	98.7	81.8	25.4	16.9	31.3	5.9	2.3
22500	Florence, SC	206,050	97.8	84.5	26.0	16.5	29.9	10.4	1.7
22520	Florence-Muscle Shoals, AL	147,143	98.4	82.1	27.3	20.8	27.0	5.8	1.3
22540	Fond du Lac, WI	101,771	96.7	80.7	27.1	21.4	26.8	2.8	2.7
22660	Fort Collins, CO	310,604	97.1	74.9	24.8	20.0	24.7	3.7	1.7
22900	Fort Smith, AR-OK	280,517	98.5	84.3	26.2	19.3	29.7	6.9	2.0
23060	Fort Wayne, IN	421,753	98.5	82.0	25.3	18.6	31.5	4.5	2.0
23420	Fresno, CA	947,942	98.1	86.9	22.4	14.3	36.4	10.3	3.4
23460	Gadsden, AL	104,188	98.5	84.8	26.7	18.8	29.4	7.9	1.9
23540	Gainesville, FL	268,559	93.9	64.8	20.2	14.5	22.2	6.1	1.8
23580	Gainesville, GA	185,229	98.7	87.4	23.8	17.8	33.6	8.9	3.2
23900	Gettysburg, PA	101,589	95.9	83.0	26.9	21.7	27.4	4.8	2.2
24020	Glens Falls, NY	128,778	96.8	80.2	26.5	19.8	26.1	4.8	3.0
24140	Goldsboro, NC	124,262	97.6	81.7	25.7	16.8	29.5	6.9	2.7
24220	Grand Forks, ND-MN	99,284	93.7	71.0	23.4	18.6	24.5	2.5	1.9
24260	Grand Island, NE	83,431	98.5	82.2	25.5	19.9	29.5	3.7	3.6
24300	Grand Junction, CO	147,614	97.4	80.6	26.7	20.2	26.5	4.8	2.4
24340	Grand Rapids-Wyoming, MI	1,006,034	97.7	82.6	25.4	19.8	30.8	4.3	2.3
24420	Grants Pass, OR	82,920	98.5	80.5	26.6	20.4	24.6	5.6	3.4
24500	Great Falls, MT	81,975	96.8	78.8	25.8	19.5	26.7	4.5	2.3
24540	Greeley, CO	263,884	97.4	84.2	25.1	19.7	30.7	6.1	2.5
24580	Green Bay, WI	310,707	97.5	80.5	26.0	20.6	29.0	3.2	1.8
24660	Greensboro-High Point, NC	735,890	97.5	80.5	25.8	18.0	28.6	6.3	1.9
24780	Greenville, NC	172,672	96.5	72.9	23.1	15.2	27.3	6.1	1.2
24860	Greenville-Anderson-Mauldin, SC	842,097	97.1	82.4	25.8	19.0	29.2	6.8	1.7
25060	Gulfport-Biloxi-Pascagoula, MS	379,080	98.2	82.8	25.2	17.0	29.6	8.7	2.2
25180	Hagerstown-Martinsburg, MD-WV	256,351	96.1	81.4	25.9	19.0	28.3	5.2	3.0
25220	Hammond, LA	123,918	97.1	81.7	24.5	16.2	30.2	8.3	2.4
25260	Hanford-Corcoran, CA	151,445	87.3	78.6	21.1	13.9	33.3	7.4	2.9
25420	Harrisburg-Carlisle, PA	554,772	96.2	78.9	25.9	19.8	26.8	4.4	2.0
25500	Harrisonburg, VA	128,166	93.2	72.0	22.5	17.4	25.5	5.1	1.5

Table B-3: Metropolitan Areas—Relationships—*Continued*

FIPS CBSA code	State	Total population in nonfamily households	Nonfamily householders				Nonrelatives in nonfamily households	Total population in subfamilies	In married couple subfamilies			Parent in a parent-child subfamily	Child in a parent-child subfamily
			Total	Male living alone	Female living alone	Householder living with nonrelatives			Total in married-couple subfamilies	Spouse in a married-couple subfamily	Child in a married-couple subfamily		
17780	College Station-Bryan, TX	25.4	14.9	4.9	5.0	4.9	10.5	2.9	0.7	0.5	0.2	1.0	1.2
17820	Colorado Springs, CO	15.1	11.7	4.3	5.2	2.2	3.3	2.7	0.9	0.7	0.2	0.8	1.0
17860	Columbia, MO	26.8	17.3	5.1	6.7	5.4	9.5	1.7	0.2	0.2	0.0	0.6	0.8
17900	Columbia, SC	17.0	13.1	4.7	6.0	2.3	3.9	3.6	0.8	0.6	0.2	1.4	1.5
17980	Columbus, GA-AL	15.2	12.3	4.7	6.0	1.6	2.9	4.6	0.9	0.7	0.2	1.8	2.0
18020	Columbus, IN	14.6	12.0	4.2	6.1	1.8	2.6	3.4	1.9	1.4	0.5	0.8	0.7
18140	Columbus, OH	18.4	14.1	5.1	6.2	2.8	4.3	2.9	0.8	0.6	0.2	1.0	1.1
18580	Corpus Christi, TX	13.7	10.8	4.2	4.4	2.2	3.0	5.6	1.4	1.0	0.3	1.9	2.4
18700	Corvallis, OR	27.4	16.8	4.9	6.3	5.7	10.6	1.7	0.9	0.6	0.2	0.4	0.4
18880	Crestview-Fort Walton Beach-Destin, FL	16.2	13.2	5.8	5.3	2.1	3.0	3.1	1.1	0.9	0.2	0.9	1.0
19060	Cumberland, MD-WV	19.2	16.5	6.6	7.9	1.9	2.7	3.7	0.7	0.6	0.1	1.6	1.3
19100	Dallas-Fort Worth-Arlington, TX	13.7	10.8	4.0	4.8	1.9	2.9	4.5	1.5	1.2	0.4	1.4	1.6
19140	Dalton, GA	11.0	8.7	3.5	3.7	1.4	2.3	5.0	1.6	1.3	0.3	1.7	1.7
19180	Danville, IL	16.4	13.9	5.9	6.2	1.7	2.6	3.2	0.6	0.5	0.2	1.2	1.4
19300	Daphne-Fairhope-Foley, AL	14.4	11.6	4.3	5.8	1.6	2.8	3.9	1.1	0.8	0.3	1.3	1.6
19340	Davenport-Moline-Rock Island, IA-IL	17.7	14.8	5.8	6.9	2.1	2.9	2.4	0.6	0.5	0.1	0.8	1.0
19380	Dayton, OH	18.5	15.3	5.7	7.3	2.3	3.2	2.5	0.6	0.5	0.1	0.9	1.0
19460	Decatur, AL	14.1	12.0	4.9	5.8	1.3	2.1	3.6	1.0	0.8	0.2	1.2	1.3
19500	Decatur, IL	19.2	15.8	5.9	7.7	2.2	3.5	3.9	0.9	0.8	0.2	1.3	1.7
19660	Deltona-Daytona Beach-Ormond Beach, FL	19.1	14.6	5.0	7.1	2.6	4.5	3.8	1.2	1.0	0.2	1.3	1.3
19740	Denver-Aurora-Lakewood, CO	18.9	14.5	5.3	6.1	3.0	4.4	3.3	1.2	0.9	0.3	1.0	1.1
19780	Des Moines-West Des Moines, IA	16.3	12.9	4.6	5.9	2.5	3.3	2.2	0.8	0.5	0.2	0.7	0.8
19820	Detroit-Warren-Dearborn, MI	16.0	13.4	5.1	6.4	1.9	2.6	3.5	1.1	0.9	0.2	1.1	1.3
20020	Dothan, AL	15.1	12.6	4.8	6.2	1.5	2.5	3.5	0.8	0.6	0.1	1.4	1.3
20100	Dover, DE	14.0	10.8	3.5	5.0	2.2	3.2	3.9	1.4	1.1	0.3	1.2	1.4
20220	Dubuque, IA	18.3	14.2	5.4	6.3	2.5	4.2	1.3	0.2	0.2	0.0	0.4	0.7
20260	Duluth, MN-WI	21.6	16.6	6.5	7.0	3.1	5.0	1.6	0.5	0.4	0.1	0.5	0.6
20500	Durham-Chapel Hill, NC	20.6	15.3	5.2	6.8	3.2	5.3	2.6	0.4	0.3	0.1	1.0	1.2
20700	East Stroudsburg, PA	12.5	9.0	3.2	3.6	2.2	3.4	4.2	1.7	1.5	0.3	1.2	1.2
20740	Eau Claire, WI	20.3	15.0	5.1	6.4	3.4	5.3	1.4	0.5	0.4	0.2	0.4	0.4
20940	El Centro, CA	8.2	6.2	2.4	2.7	1.1	2.0	9.4	3.0	2.5	0.5	2.6	3.8
21060	Elizabethtown-Fort Knox, KY	12.5	10.3	3.9	4.8	1.5	2.2	3.6	1.1	0.8	0.3	1.2	1.2
21140	Elkhart-Goshen, IN	12.0	9.8	3.6	4.7	1.5	2.2	3.8	1.5	0.9	0.6	1.0	1.3
21300	Elmira, NY	18.4	14.9	5.3	6.7	2.8	3.5	2.6	1.2	0.7	0.4	0.6	0.8
21340	El Paso, TX	9.5	7.8	3.2	3.5	1.1	1.7	7.0	2.1	1.5	0.5	2.0	2.9
21500	Erie, PA	17.7	14.2	5.4	6.5	2.4	3.5	2.9	0.8	0.6	0.2	0.9	1.2
21660	Eugene, OR	24.5	16.7	5.2	6.8	4.7	7.8	2.3	0.7	0.5	0.2	0.8	0.9
21780	Evansville, IN-KY	16.7	14.0	5.4	6.7	1.9	2.7	2.8	0.9	0.6	0.2	0.9	0.9
21820	Fairbanks, AK	17.9	13.3	5.9	4.5	3.0	4.6	2.5	0.7	0.5	0.2	0.9	0.9
22020	Fargo, ND-MN	23.6	17.5	6.5	6.6	4.4	6.1	1.5	0.3	0.2	0.1	0.6	0.7
22140	Farmington, NM	10.3	8.4	3.6	3.5	1.3	1.9	7.9	1.9	1.2	0.7	2.7	3.3
22180	Fayetteville, NC	14.8	12.3	4.9	5.5	1.8	2.6	4.1	1.0	0.6	0.4	1.3	1.7
22220	Fayetteville-Springdale-Rogers, AR-MO	14.9	11.5	4.3	4.7	2.4	3.4	3.1	1.2	0.9	0.4	0.8	1.1
22380	Flagstaff, AZ	18.6	12.3	4.3	4.0	4.1	6.3	6.0	0.7	0.5	0.2	1.9	3.3
22420	Flint, MI	16.9	13.9	5.2	6.4	2.3	3.0	3.4	0.7	0.6	0.2	1.2	1.5
22500	Florence, SC	13.3	11.4	4.4	5.9	1.2	1.9	6.9	1.5	1.2	0.2	2.3	3.1
22520	Florence-Muscle Shoals, AL	16.3	13.9	4.8	7.3	1.8	2.4	2.8	0.6	0.5	0.1	1.0	1.1
22540	Fond du Lac, WI	15.9	13.4	5.2	6.1	2.1	2.5	1.6	0.6	0.4	0.1	0.4	0.6
22660	Fort Collins, CO	22.3	14.9	4.5	5.5	4.9	7.3	2.2	0.8	0.5	0.2	0.6	0.8
22900	Fort Smith, AR-OK	14.3	11.8	4.6	5.8	1.5	2.4	3.9	1.4	1.1	0.3	1.2	1.4
23060	Fort Wayne, IN	16.5	13.4	5.3	6.0	2.1	3.1	2.6	0.7	0.5	0.2	0.8	1.0
23420	Fresno, CA	11.2	8.3	2.9	3.6	1.8	2.9	5.9	2.2	1.6	0.5	1.6	2.2
23460	Gadsden, AL	13.7	11.6	4.3	6.0	1.3	2.1	5.7	2.2	1.6	0.5	1.7	1.8
23540	Gainesville, FL	29.1	17.8	5.8	6.7	5.3	11.3	2.8	0.8	0.7	0.2	1.0	1.0
23580	Gainesville, GA	11.4	8.7	3.2	4.1	1.5	2.6	4.8	2.1	1.4	0.7	1.4	1.3
23900	Gettysburg, PA	12.8	10.3	4.0	4.6	1.8	2.5	2.8	1.2	1.0	0.2	0.7	0.9
24020	Glens Falls, NY	16.6	13.5	4.6	6.4	2.5	3.1	2.6	0.7	0.5	0.2	0.9	1.0
24140	Goldsboro, NC	15.9	12.5	4.9	5.6	2.1	3.4	3.0	0.3	0.2	0.0	1.1	1.6
24220	Grand Forks, ND-MN	22.8	17.4	7.0	6.6	3.8	5.4	1.7	0.4	0.3	0.1	0.5	0.8
24260	Grand Island, NE	16.2	12.6	4.5	5.6	2.4	3.7	1.7	0.9	0.6	0.3	0.3	0.4
24300	Grand Junction, CO	16.8	13.1	4.5	5.9	2.7	3.7	2.9	0.9	0.7	0.2	0.9	1.2
24340	Grand Rapids-Wyoming, MI	15.1	11.5	4.0	5.1	2.4	3.6	2.4	0.8	0.6	0.2	0.7	0.9
24420	Grants Pass, OR	18.0	14.8	5.0	7.3	2.5	3.2	3.1	1.6	0.9	0.7	0.6	1.0
24500	Great Falls, MT	18.0	14.9	6.1	6.7	2.1	3.1	2.3	1.1	0.8	0.3	0.6	0.6
24540	Greeley, CO	13.2	9.6	3.7	3.8	2.1	3.6	3.7	1.1	0.9	0.2	1.2	1.4
24580	Green Bay, WI	17.0	13.5	5.1	5.8	2.6	3.5	1.8	0.5	0.4	0.2	0.6	0.7
24660	Greensboro-High Point, NC	17.0	13.7	4.6	6.7	2.4	3.3	3.1	0.8	0.6	0.1	1.0	1.3
24780	Greenville, NC	23.6	15.6	4.8	6.7	4.2	8.0	3.3	0.5	0.4	0.1	1.3	1.5
24860	Greenville-Anderson-Mauldin, SC	14.7	11.9	4.5	5.7	1.7	2.8	3.7	0.9	0.7	0.2	1.3	1.5
25060	Gulfport-Biloxi-Pascagoula, MS	15.4	12.4	5.0	5.3	2.1	3.0	4.6	1.2	1.0	0.2	1.5	1.8
25180	Hagerstown-Martinsburg, MD-WV	14.7	11.9	4.6	5.2	2.1	2.8	3.1	1.0	0.8	0.2	0.9	1.2
25220	Hammond, LA	15.4	11.6	4.4	4.8	2.3	3.8	4.5	1.4	0.9	0.5	1.5	1.7
25260	Hanford-Corcoran, CA	8.6	6.0	2.1	2.4	1.4	2.7	4.5	1.4	1.0	0.4	1.3	1.8
25420	Harrisburg-Carlisle, PA	17.3	14.0	5.0	6.6	2.4	3.2	2.7	0.8	0.6	0.2	0.8	1.2
25500	Harrisonburg, VA	21.2	12.3	3.3	5.3	3.7	8.9	2.4	0.5	0.4	0.1	0.8	1.1

FIPS CBSA code	State	Total population	Percent of the population in households	Population in family households, percent					
				Percent in family households	Householder in family household, percent	Spouse in family household, percent	Child in family household (biological, adopted, or stepchild)	Other relative in family household	Nonrelatives in family household
25540	Hartford-West Hartford-East Hartford, CT	1,215,264	95.9	79.6	25.1	18.2	29.3	5.3	1.7
25620	Hattiesburg, MS................	146,684	97.0	79.6	24.4	16.6	29.9	7.2	1.5
25860	Hickory-Lenoir-Morganton, NC	363,844	97.9	82.9	25.4	19.0	29.2	7.0	2.2
25940	Hilton Head Island-Bluffton-Beaufort, SC	193,980	96.8	80.6	25.8	19.7	26.5	6.8	1.8
25980	Hinesville, GA................	80,915	97.4	86.0	26.0	18.3	34.0	6.4	1.3
26140	Homosassa Springs, FL................	139,467	98.4	78.9	27.6	22.2	19.5	6.8	2.8
26300	Hot Springs, AR................	96,900	97.8	79.0	26.1	18.9	24.1	7.6	2.3
26380	Houma-Thibodaux, LA................	209,039	98.4	85.0	25.3	17.8	31.7	7.3	2.8
26420	Houston-The Woodlands-Sugar Land, TX	6,180,966	98.8	86.1	23.9	17.1	34.0	9.0	2.0
26580	Huntington-Ashland, WV-KY-OH................	364,624	97.9	81.8	26.2	19.5	27.5	6.6	2.0
26620	Huntsville, AL................	430,367	97.2	82.0	25.9	19.3	29.4	5.7	1.7
26820	Idaho Falls, ID................	136,326	98.9	88.4	24.9	19.8	37.9	4.0	1.9
26900	Indianapolis-Carmel-Anderson, IN................	1,931,065	98.0	81.7	24.8	18.1	30.7	5.7	2.4
26980	Iowa City, IA................	158,281	94.6	68.4	22.9	18.1	23.5	2.3	1.6
27060	Ithaca, NY................	102,726	86.9	60.2	19.9	15.8	19.3	2.4	2.8
27100	Jackson, MI................	160,122	94.2	78.8	25.0	18.2	28.2	5.2	2.2
27140	Jackson, MS................	575,554	96.3	82.9	24.5	15.6	32.3	8.7	1.8
27180	Jackson, TN................	130,242	95.8	81.1	24.3	17.1	30.9	7.3	1.6
27260	Jacksonville, FL................	1,377,993	98.1	81.5	24.3	17.4	30.3	7.5	2.0
27340	Jacksonville, NC................	182,352	92.4	79.9	24.0	18.3	31.5	4.1	2.0
27500	Janesville-Beloit, WI................	160,359	98.0	81.5	26.4	19.1	27.9	4.7	3.4
27620	Jefferson City, MO................	150,394	93.2	78.0	24.8	19.2	27.2	4.6	2.1
27740	Johnson City, TN................	200,412	96.5	79.0	26.9	20.4	25.5	4.5	1.7
27780	Johnstown, PA................	141,536	94.0	76.8	25.9	19.4	26.2	3.8	1.5
27860	Jonesboro, AR................	124,208	96.8	80.8	25.9	18.0	27.7	7.1	2.1
27900	Joplin, MO................	175,491	98.1	82.7	25.9	19.6	28.3	6.1	2.8
27980	Kahului-Wailuku-Lahaina, HI................	158,358	98.3	83.6	22.7	16.9	27.3	12.7	4.0
28020	Kalamazoo-Portage, MI................	330,260	97.1	77.0	24.1	17.8	28.1	4.5	2.5
28100	Kankakee, IL................	112,795	95.3	80.7	24.8	17.2	30.8	5.4	2.5
28140	Kansas City, MO-KS................	2,039,318	98.5	81.7	25.3	18.7	30.4	5.2	2.1
28420	Kennewick-Richland, WA................	267,646	98.5	86.1	24.0	18.0	35.2	6.2	2.6
28660	Killeen-Temple, TX................	418,864	94.8	84.1	22.9	17.0	33.8	8.0	2.5
28700	Kingsport-Bristol-Bristol, TN-VA................	308,921	98.1	82.2	28.0	21.3	25.5	5.8	1.6
28740	Kingston, NY................	181,806	93.2	75.4	24.1	17.7	26.2	5.2	2.2
28940	Knoxville, TN................	847,916	97.6	79.9	25.9	20.2	26.5	5.7	1.6
29020	Kokomo, IN................	82,834	98.6	81.7	27.1	20.4	27.7	4.1	2.6
29100	La Crosse-Onalaska, WI-MN................	134,915	96.0	74.5	24.7	19.6	25.6	2.7	1.9
29180	Lafayette, LA................	474,570	98.3	82.6	24.9	17.0	31.5	6.9	2.4
29200	Lafayette-West Lafayette, IN................	206,667	93.3	69.4	22.5	17.2	24.4	3.5	1.9
29340	Lake Charles, LA................	201,613	98.2	83.1	26.0	17.8	30.9	6.8	1.7
29420	Lake Havasu City-Kingman, AZ................	202,857	95.7	76.3	24.8	19.1	23.1	6.8	2.5
29460	Lakeland-Winter Haven, FL................	616,447	97.6	83.5	24.4	17.6	29.6	9.2	2.8
29540	Lancaster, PA................	526,549	97.3	83.7	25.9	21.1	30.5	4.5	1.7
29620	Lansing-East Lansing, MI................	466,342	95.5	73.9	23.4	17.3	26.9	4.2	2.0
29700	Laredo, TX................	258,973	98.6	92.7	21.7	14.1	41.3	13.5	2.1
29740	Las Cruces, NM................	213,395	97.7	83.2	24.2	16.5	33.1	7.4	2.1
29820	Las Vegas-Henderson-Paradise, NV................	1,997,371	98.9	81.9	22.9	15.5	30.6	9.8	3.1
29940	Lawrence, KS................	113,246	92.1	64.4	21.0	15.8	21.9	3.9	1.9
30020	Lawton, OK................	132,007	92.9	77.1	22.8	16.1	28.4	7.0	2.7
30140	Lebanon, PA................	135,119	97.6	83.2	26.6	20.4	29.0	4.7	2.5
30300	Lewiston, ID-WA................	61,607	97.9	80.5	26.6	20.8	25.9	5.1	2.1
30340	Lewiston-Auburn, ME................	107,556	97.2	77.4	25.6	18.9	26.4	3.5	3.0
30460	Lexington-Fayette, KY................	484,246	96.5	76.4	24.6	18.0	26.7	5.1	2.0
30620	Lima, OH................	105,528	96.3	80.0	24.9	17.3	29.3	5.8	2.7
30700	Lincoln, NE................	310,311	95.3	74.5	24.0	18.6	26.6	3.1	2.2
30780	Little Rock-North Little Rock-Conway, AR	717,700	98.2	81.3	24.6	17.8	30.2	7.1	1.7
30860	Logan, UT-ID................	128,602	96.8	84.4	23.0	19.7	37.0	3.5	1.2
30980	Longview, TX................	216,399	95.7	82.6	24.3	17.6	29.7	8.5	2.6
31020	Longview, WA................	102,009	98.9	82.7	25.6	19.3	27.7	6.1	3.9
31080	Los Angeles-Long Beach-Anaheim, CA................	13,035,870	98.3	84.1	22.1	15.1	32.0	11.7	3.2
31140	Louisville/Jefferson County, KY-IN................	1,252,860	98.0	81.0	25.3	18.0	29.6	6.1	2.0
31180	Lubbock, TX................	299,428	96.0	76.8	23.3	16.4	28.7	6.6	1.9
31340	Lynchburg, VA................	255,129	95.1	78.9	25.8	19.5	26.4	5.4	1.8
31420	Macon, GA................	232,218	96.2	81.9	24.0	15.6	31.4	9.1	1.9
31460	Madera, CA................	152,255	94.1	85.6	21.1	15.2	33.6	11.5	4.1
31540	Madison, WI................	620,655	97.4	74.4	24.5	19.3	26.0	2.9	1.8
31700	Manchester-Nashua, NH................	402,979	97.9	81.6	25.7	19.7	29.1	4.8	2.3
31740	Manhattan, KS................	97,261	90.3	65.1	20.4	16.6	24.1	2.5	1.6
31860	Mankato-North Mankato, MN................	97,949	92.6	69.7	22.9	18.8	23.8	2.1	2.0
31900	Mansfield, OH................	122,485	94.4	76.9	24.7	18.4	26.1	5.2	2.4
32580	McAllen-Edinburg-Mission, TX................	805,497	98.9	92.6	22.4	15.8	40.8	12.5	1.3
32780	Medford, OR................	206,619	98.1	80.1	25.8	19.3	25.9	5.4	3.7
32820	Memphis, TN-MS-AR................	1,338,445	98.2	83.2	24.2	15.0	32.9	8.9	2.1
32900	Merced, CA................	261,493	97.9	88.5	22.3	14.9	38.7	9.7	3.0

| FIPS CBSA code | State | Population in nonfamily households | | | | | | Population in subfamilies as a percent of total population | | | | | |
| | | Total population in nonfamily households | Nonfamily householders | | | | Nonrelatives in nonfamily households | Total population in subfamilies | In married couple subfamilies | | | Parent in a parent-child subfamily | Child in a parent-child subfamily |
			Total	Male living alone	Female living alone	Householder living with nonrelatives			Total in married-couple subfamilies	Spouse in a married-couple subfamily	Child in married-couple subfamily		
25540	Hartford-West Hartford-East Hartford, CT	16.2	13.2	4.7	6.3	2.2	3.0	2.5	0.8	0.7	0.1	0.8	0.9
25620	Hattiesburg, MS................................	17.4	12.3	4.3	5.4	2.5	5.1	4.3	1.2	0.9	0.3	1.4	1.7
25860	Hickory-Lenoir-Morganton, NC	15.0	12.4	4.7	5.9	1.8	2.6	3.8	1.4	1.2	0.2	1.2	1.2
25940	Hilton Head Island-Bluffton-Beaufort, SC	16.2	11.9	3.7	6.0	2.2	4.3	3.4	0.9	0.7	0.2	1.4	1.0
25980	Hinesville, GA................................	11.5	9.1	3.8	3.7	1.7	2.3	0.0	0.0	0.0	0.0	0.0	0.0
26140	Homosassa Springs, FL........................	19.5	15.7	6.0	7.2	2.5	3.8	3.0	1.5	1.3	0.2	0.7	0.7
26300	Hot Springs, AR..............................	18.8	14.9	5.2	6.8	2.8	3.9	4.1	1.3	1.1	0.3	1.3	1.4
26380	Houma-Thibodaux, LA..........................	13.4	10.4	4.2	4.2	2.0	3.0	4.6	0.9	0.7	0.3	1.6	2.0
26420	Houston-The Woodlands-Sugar Land, TX....	12.6	10.0	4.0	4.3	1.7	2.7	4.9	1.6	1.2	0.3	1.5	1.8
26580	Huntington-Ashland, WV-KY-OH................	16.1	13.0	4.7	6.4	2.0	3.0	3.4	1.1	0.8	0.2	1.2	1.2
26620	Huntsville, AL...............................	15.2	12.9	5.3	6.1	1.5	2.3	3.1	0.9	0.7	0.2	1.1	1.1
26820	Idaho Falls, ID..............................	10.4	8.6	3.4	3.8	1.4	1.9	2.4	1.1	0.7	0.4	1.0	0.6
26900	Indianapolis-Carmel-Anderson, IN.............	16.3	13.1	5.0	5.9	2.2	3.2	3.1	0.7	0.5	0.2	1.1	1.3
26980	Iowa City, IA................................	26.2	17.6	5.6	6.6	5.5	8.6	1.0	0.3	0.2	0.1	0.3	0.4
27060	Ithaca, NY...................................	26.7	17.3	5.1	6.6	5.6	9.4	1.5	0.6	0.5	0.1	0.4	0.5
27100	Jackson, MI..................................	15.4	12.7	4.7	5.9	2.1	2.7	2.6	0.4	0.3	0.1	1.0	1.1
27140	Jackson, MS..................................	13.5	11.3	4.3	5.6	1.4	2.2	5.3	0.8	0.6	0.2	2.1	2.4
27180	Jackson, TN..................................	14.7	12.2	4.5	6.2	1.5	2.5	3.1	0.9	0.7	0.2	1.0	1.2
27260	Jacksonville, FL.............................	16.6	12.8	4.6	5.9	2.3	3.8	4.1	1.2	1.0	0.2	1.4	1.5
27340	Jacksonville, NC.............................	12.5	9.3	3.6	3.8	1.9	3.3	2.2	0.7	0.5	0.2	0.8	0.6
27500	Janesville-Beloit, WI........................	16.5	13.3	4.5	6.2	2.6	3.2	3.3	1.2	0.9	0.4	0.9	1.2
27620	Jefferson City, MO...........................	15.2	12.5	4.6	6.0	1.9	2.7	2.9	0.9	0.6	0.3	0.9	1.0
27740	Johnson City, TN.............................	17.5	14.9	5.7	7.2	2.0	2.6	2.4	0.7	0.6	0.2	0.8	0.9
27780	Johnstown, PA................................	17.2	14.7	5.5	7.5	1.8	2.4	1.9	0.6	0.5	0.1	0.6	0.7
27860	Jonesboro, AR................................	16.0	12.2	3.9	5.6	2.7	3.8	3.4	1.4	1.0	0.4	0.9	1.1
27900	Joplin, MO...................................	15.4	12.8	4.9	5.6	2.2	2.6	3.6	1.5	1.1	0.4	0.9	1.2
27980	Kahului-Wailuku-Lahaina, HI..................	14.7	10.8	4.4	4.0	2.5	3.8	8.7	5.3	3.6	1.7	1.6	1.9
28020	Kalamazoo-Portage, MI........................	20.1	14.6	5.1	6.3	3.2	5.5	2.5	0.6	0.4	0.2	0.9	1.0
28100	Kankakee, IL.................................	14.6	11.8	4.1	5.9	1.9	2.7	3.5	0.6	0.4	0.1	1.4	1.6
28140	Kansas City, MO-KS...........................	16.8	13.5	4.9	6.2	2.3	3.3	2.8	0.8	0.6	0.2	0.9	1.2
28420	Kennewick-Richland, WA.......................	12.4	9.9	4.1	4.1	1.7	2.5	4.0	1.7	1.3	0.4	1.0	1.2
28660	Killeen-Temple, TX...........................	10.7	8.4	3.4	3.9	1.1	2.3	3.6	1.3	1.1	0.2	1.3	1.0
28700	Kingsport-Bristol-Bristol, TN-VA.............	15.9	13.7	4.9	7.0	1.8	2.2	3.4	1.2	1.0	0.3	0.9	1.2
28740	Kingston, NY.................................	17.8	13.9	4.8	6.3	2.9	3.9	2.3	0.9	0.7	0.2	0.7	0.7
28940	Knoxville, TN................................	17.7	14.4	5.4	6.8	2.3	3.2	3.0	0.8	0.6	0.2	1.0	1.2
29020	Kokomo, IN...................................	16.9	14.6	5.7	7.0	2.0	2.2	1.7	0.2	0.2	0.1	0.6	0.8
29100	La Crosse-Onalaska, WI-MN....................	21.5	15.2	4.9	6.5	3.8	6.3	1.1	0.2	0.1	0.1	0.4	0.5
29180	Lafayette, LA................................	15.7	12.4	5.0	5.4	2.1	3.3	4.0	0.8	0.6	0.2	1.5	1.7
29200	Lafayette-West Lafayette, IN.................	23.9	15.6	5.3	5.6	4.7	8.3	2.1	0.9	0.7	0.2	0.5	0.7
29340	Lake Charles, LA.............................	15.1	12.3	4.6	5.9	1.8	2.8	4.3	1.0	0.6	0.4	1.5	1.8
29420	Lake Havasu City-Kingman, AZ.................	19.4	14.7	5.5	5.8	3.4	4.7	3.6	1.0	0.9	0.2	1.1	1.5
29460	Lakeland-Winter Haven, FL....................	14.0	11.1	3.8	5.3	1.9	3.0	5.0	1.6	1.3	0.3	1.6	1.8
29540	Lancaster, PA................................	13.6	10.9	3.8	5.2	2.0	2.6	2.7	1.0	0.7	0.3	0.7	1.0
29620	Lansing-East Lansing, MI.....................	21.6	15.5	5.3	6.7	3.5	6.1	2.3	0.8	0.6	0.2	0.7	0.8
29700	Laredo, TX...................................	5.9	4.6	1.9	2.0	0.7	1.3	9.3	3.0	2.0	1.1	2.5	3.8
29740	Las Cruces, NM...............................	14.5	10.6	3.6	4.7	2.3	3.9	5.4	1.3	1.0	0.3	1.8	2.4
29820	Las Vegas-Henderson-Paradise, NV.............	17.0	12.6	5.0	4.8	2.7	4.4	4.7	1.9	1.6	0.4	1.3	1.4
29940	Lawrence, KS.................................	27.7	17.3	4.7	6.7	5.9	10.4	1.7	0.2	0.2	0.0	0.6	0.8
30020	Lawton, OK...................................	15.8	12.2	5.1	5.1	2.0	3.6	4.5	1.3	0.9	0.4	1.5	1.7
30140	Lebanon, PA..................................	14.4	11.9	4.2	6.0	1.7	2.5	2.0	0.3	0.3	0.1	0.7	1.0
30300	Lewiston, ID-WA..............................	17.5	14.2	5.1	6.7	2.4	3.2	3.1	1.2	0.9	0.3	0.9	1.0
30340	Lewiston-Auburn, ME..........................	19.8	15.6	5.2	6.9	3.5	4.1	2.5	0.7	0.5	0.2	0.7	1.1
30460	Lexington-Fayette, KY........................	20.2	14.8	5.0	6.7	3.2	5.3	2.3	0.6	0.5	0.1	0.8	0.9
30620	Lima, OH.....................................	16.3	13.3	4.9	6.2	2.1	3.0	3.1	0.5	0.4	0.1	1.2	1.4
30700	Lincoln, NE..................................	20.7	15.3	5.3	6.3	3.7	5.5	1.6	0.4	0.3	0.1	0.5	0.6
30780	Little Rock-North Little Rock-Conway, AR	16.9	13.4	5.0	6.3	2.1	3.5	3.4	0.9	0.7	0.2	1.2	1.3
30860	Logan, UT-ID.................................	12.4	7.7	2.5	3.1	2.1	4.7	2.1	1.0	0.6	0.4	0.5	0.6
30980	Longview, TX.................................	13.1	11.2	4.5	5.4	1.3	2.0	4.8	1.4	1.0	0.4	1.6	1.9
31020	Longview, WA.................................	16.2	12.9	4.2	6.2	2.5	3.3	3.8	0.9	0.8	0.1	1.2	1.6
31080	Los Angeles-Long Beach-Anaheim, CA...........	14.2	10.4	3.6	4.4	2.3	3.8	6.2	2.7	2.1	0.6	1.5	1.9
31140	Louisville/Jefferson County, KY-IN...........	16.9	13.7	4.9	6.4	2.3	3.3	3.3	0.8	0.6	0.2	1.2	1.3
31180	Lubbock, TX..................................	19.2	13.5	4.4	5.7	3.3	5.7	4.2	0.8	0.6	0.2	1.6	1.9
31340	Lynchburg, VA................................	16.2	13.1	5.0	6.1	2.0	3.1	3.1	1.1	0.8	0.3	1.0	1.0
31420	Macon, GA....................................	14.2	12.0	4.5	6.1	1.4	2.3	4.6	0.5	0.3	0.1	1.9	2.3
31460	Madera, CA...................................	8.5	6.6	2.8	2.5	1.3	1.9	6.5	2.6	2.0	0.6	1.6	2.3
31540	Madison, WI..................................	23.0	16.6	5.5	6.9	4.2	6.4	1.2	0.4	0.3	0.1	0.4	0.5
31700	Manchester-Nashua, NH........................	16.4	12.7	4.6	5.1	3.0	3.7	2.8	1.2	0.9	0.3	0.8	0.9
31740	Manhattan, KS................................	25.2	14.9	5.1	5.2	4.6	10.2	0.0	0.0	0.0	0.0	0.0	0.0
31860	Mankato-North Mankato, MN....................	23.0	14.8	4.7	5.9	4.2	8.2	1.0	0.1	0.1	0.0	0.4	0.5
31900	Mansfield, OH................................	17.5	14.7	5.6	7.3	1.8	2.7	2.8	0.8	0.6	0.2	1.1	1.1
32580	McAllen-Edinburg-Mission, TX.................	6.3	5.1	1.9	2.4	0.8	1.2	9.6	4.1	2.6	1.5	2.1	3.3
32780	Medford, OR..................................	18.0	14.2	4.9	6.6	2.7	3.8	2.9	1.1	0.8	0.3	0.9	0.9
32820	Memphis, TN-MS-AR............................	15.1	12.4	4.8	5.9	1.7	2.7	4.8	0.8	0.6	0.2	1.7	2.2
32900	Merced, CA...................................	9.4	6.9	2.7	2.8	1.4	2.5	6.0	2.7	2.1	0.6	1.4	1.9

FIPS CBSA code	State	Total population	Percent of the population in households	Population in family households, percent					
				Percent in family households	Householder in family household, percent	Spouse in family household, percent	Child in family household (biological, adopted, or stepchild)	Other relative in family household	Nonrelatives in family household
33100	Miami-Fort Lauderdale-West Palm Beach, FL	5,759,926	98.6	82.4	22.7	15.3	30.5	11.3	2.7
33140	Michigan City-La Porte, IN............	111,228	91.8	75.9	25.0	18.5	25.8	4.5	2.0
33220	Midland, MI............................	83,971	98.4	82.5	27.0	22.3	28.0	3.2	2.0
33260	Midland, TX............................	150,484	98.8	85.6	24.7	18.3	31.9	8.6	2.0
33340	Milwaukee-Waukesha-West Allis, WI	1,565,649	98.1	79.3	24.6	17.7	30.2	4.9	1.9
33460	Minneapolis-St. Paul-Bloomington, MN-WI ..	3,423,425	98.2	80.5	25.0	19.4	29.9	4.1	2.1
33540	Missoula, MT............................	111,024	97.0	71.8	23.9	17.9	24.0	3.6	2.4
33660	Mobile, AL..............................	413,553	97.6	83.5	25.3	16.5	31.3	9.0	1.5
33700	Modesto, CA............................	521,597	98.9	87.8	23.8	16.3	35.0	9.5	3.2
33740	Monroe, LA.............................	177,895	95.0	79.9	24.3	16.0	31.1	6.9	1.6
33780	Monroe, MI.............................	150,944	99.2	85.2	27.2	20.8	30.8	4.3	2.0
33860	Montgomery, AL.........................	375,756	96.5	81.4	24.7	16.3	31.1	7.6	1.8
34060	Morgantown, WV.........................	134,305	93.2	69.0	20.6	16.3	25.2	5.1	1.8
34100	Morristown, TN.........................	114,904	98.0	84.1	26.8	20.0	27.5	7.3	2.5
34580	Mount Vernon-Anacortes, WA.............	118,225	98.4	82.6	26.2	19.8	27.5	5.5	3.6
34620	Muncie, IN.............................	117,570	93.2	70.1	23.4	16.9	23.9	4.0	1.8
34740	Muskegon, MI...........................	170,362	96.1	81.0	25.4	17.9	29.7	5.3	2.7
34820	Myrtle Beach-Conway-North Myrtle Beach, SC-NC	394,997	99.2	81.4	27.2	20.6	24.2	6.7	2.7
34900	Napa, CA...............................	139,042	96.5	81.9	24.3	18.3	29.6	6.9	2.8
34940	Naples-Immokalee-Marco Island, FL	333,294	98.8	81.6	24.7	19.6	25.2	9.1	3.0
34980	Nashville-Davidson–Murfreesboro–Franklin, TN	1,727,612	97.8	81.0	24.6	18.4	29.5	6.5	2.0
35100	New Bern, NC...........................	128,151	96.2	82.9	26.8	20.6	27.2	6.3	2.0
35300	New Haven-Milford, CT..................	863,217	96.6	80.2	24.4	17.2	30.5	6.3	1.9
35380	New Orleans-Metairie, LA...............	1,227,529	98.3	80.2	23.9	15.3	30.6	8.5	1.9
35620	New York-Newark-Jersey City, NY-NJ-PA......	19,839,700	97.9	82.5	23.6	16.3	31.6	8.9	2.2
35660	Niles-Benton Harbor, MI................	155,871	96.8	82.0	25.4	18.7	30.3	5.5	2.0
35840	North Port-Sarasota-Bradenton, FL	720,464	98.6	78.1	26.2	20.9	22.9	6.1	2.1
35980	Norwich-New London, CT................	274,239	95.3	78.9	25.6	19.0	27.5	4.7	2.0
36100	Ocala, FL..............................	335,036	97.5	80.0	26.2	19.9	24.8	6.9	2.3
36140	Ocean City, NJ.........................	96,305	97.2	79.2	26.9	21.9	24.3	4.6	1.6
36220	Odessa, TX.............................	144,559	98.8	85.8	24.8	16.6	33.8	7.7	2.9
36260	Ogden-Clearfield, UT...................	613,230	99.2	90.2	24.8	20.2	38.2	5.3	1.8
36420	Oklahoma City, OK......................	1,297,831	97.6	80.7	24.4	17.9	29.8	6.6	2.0
36500	Olympia-Tumwater, WA..................	259,144	98.6	81.5	26.0	19.9	28.4	4.9	2.4
36540	Omaha-Council Bluffs, NE-IA	885,819	98.0	81.5	25.0	18.8	30.9	4.8	2.1
36740	Orlando-Kissimmee-Sanford, FL	2,221,842	98.0	81.5	23.0	16.4	31.2	8.4	2.5
36780	Oshkosh-Neenah, WI	168,618	94.9	74.0	24.2	19.3	25.5	3.1	1.9
36980	Owensboro, KY.........................	115,877	97.7	82.8	26.4	20.0	28.9	5.8	1.8
37100	Oxnard-Thousand Oaks-Ventura, CA.......	834,880	98.6	87.0	23.4	17.7	32.5	9.9	3.4
37340	Palm Bay-Melbourne-Titusville, FL	547,403	98.8	80.5	25.3	18.7	27.1	7.2	2.2
37460	Panama City, FL........................	187,992	97.3	79.8	25.4	18.6	26.6	6.4	2.7
37620	Parkersburg-Vienna, WV.................	92,464	99.0	80.9	26.4	19.9	26.9	5.0	2.6
37860	Pensacola-Ferry Pass-Brent, FL	461,450	94.8	78.2	23.9	17.7	28.0	6.7	1.9
37900	Peoria, IL.............................	381,059	97.7	81.0	26.0	20.0	29.0	3.9	2.1
37980	Philadelphia-Camden-Wilmington, PA-NJ-DE-MD	6,016,966	97.3	80.8	23.8	16.9	30.9	7.3	1.9
38060	Phoenix-Mesa-Scottsdale, AZ............	4,326,355	98.4	82.3	23.6	16.9	31.1	8.0	2.7
38220	Pine Bluff, AR.........................	97,302	89.6	74.7	23.7	15.3	26.7	7.4	1.5
38300	Pittsburgh, PA.........................	2,360,546	97.3	77.9	25.8	19.5	26.8	4.3	1.5
38340	Pittsfield, MA.........................	130,069	94.8	74.7	25.3	18.6	24.9	3.8	2.1
38540	Pocatello, ID..........................	83,487	97.1	80.6	23.8	18.4	32.5	4.2	1.7
38860	Portland-South Portland, ME............	517,920	97.8	77.7	25.8	20.3	25.6	3.8	2.3
38900	Portland-Vancouver-Hillsboro, OR-WA........	2,288,014	98.3	79.1	24.2	18.5	28.3	5.4	2.7
38940	Port St. Lucie, FL	432,973	98.5	82.0	25.3	19.4	27.7	7.4	2.2
39140	Prescott, AZ...........................	212,843	98.5	79.0	27.1	21.6	21.4	6.5	2.3
39300	Providence-Warwick, RI-MA..............	1,601,687	96.4	78.5	24.6	17.4	28.3	5.9	2.2
39340	Provo-Orem, UT........................	550,979	97.5	89.0	22.0	18.9	41.0	5.5	1.6
39380	Pueblo, CO.............................	160,951	97.0	79.8	24.6	17.2	28.9	6.7	2.4
39460	Punta Gorda, FL........................	162,283	98.0	78.9	28.1	23.0	19.7	6.1	1.9
39540	Racine, WI.............................	194,897	97.4	81.1	25.0	18.8	30.6	4.9	1.7
39580	Raleigh, NC............................	1,188,678	97.8	82.1	25.0	19.1	31.0	5.2	1.8
39660	Rapid City, SD.........................	138,852	96.8	79.8	25.8	19.5	27.2	4.4	2.9
39740	Reading, PA............................	412,916	96.8	81.5	25.3	19.0	29.7	5.3	2.3
39820	Redding, CA............................	178,422	98.4	80.7	25.5	18.7	27.4	5.9	3.1
39900	Reno, NV...............................	433,609	98.4	78.5	23.5	17.2	28.2	7.1	2.6
40060	Richmond, VA...........................	1,232,639	97.0	79.9	24.3	17.2	29.5	6.8	2.0
40140	Riverside-San Bernardino-Ontario, CA........	4,340,813	98.2	88.1	22.2	15.7	35.5	11.5	3.3
40220	Roanoke, VA............................	310,128	97.4	80.5	26.9	20.2	26.1	5.5	1.8
40340	Rochester, MN..........................	209,997	98.2	82.2	26.1	21.3	29.9	2.9	1.9
40380	Rochester, NY..........................	1,082,536	96.0	77.5	24.8	17.8	28.1	4.6	2.1
40420	Rockford, IL...........................	346,067	98.7	84.4	25.6	18.6	31.1	6.5	2.6
40580	Rocky Mount, NC.......................	151,294	97.6	82.5	25.5	16.6	30.7	7.8	1.9
40660	Rome, GA...............................	95,988	95.9	80.4	23.6	17.1	29.1	8.5	2.0

| | | | Population in nonfamily households | | | | | Population in subfamilies as a percent of total population | | | | | |
| | | | | Nonfamily householders | | | | | In married couple subfamilies | | | | |
FIPS CBSA code	State	Total population in nonfamily households	Total	Male living alone	Female living alone	Householder living with nonrelatives	Nonrelatives in nonfamily households	Total population in subfamilies	Total in married-couple subfamilies	Spouse in a married-couple subfamily	Child in a married-couple subfamily	Parent in a parent-child subfamily	Child in a parent-child subfamily
33100	Miami-Fort Lauderdale-West Palm Beach, FL	16.2	12.4	4.5	5.7	2.2	3.8	5.0	1.9	1.6	0.3	1.6	1.5
33140	Michigan City-La Porte, IN	15.9	13.4	5.3	5.9	2.2	2.5	3.0	0.8	0.5	0.3	0.7	1.5
33220	Midland, MI	15.9	12.9	4.6	5.8	2.4	3.0	1.8	0.5	0.4	0.1	0.5	0.8
33260	Midland, TX	13.1	10.4	4.0	4.5	1.9	2.7	5.2	1.5	1.1	0.4	1.5	2.2
33340	Milwaukee-Waukesha-West Allis, WI	18.8	15.0	5.2	7.1	2.7	3.8	2.4	0.7	0.6	0.2	0.8	0.9
33460	Minneapolis-St. Paul-Bloomington, MN-WI	17.7	13.6	4.8	6.0	2.8	4.1	2.1	0.7	0.6	0.2	0.6	0.8
33540	Missoula, MT	25.2	17.4	6.1	6.3	5.0	7.9	1.6	0.5	0.3	0.1	0.5	0.6
33660	Mobile, AL	14.1	12.0	4.6	5.9	1.5	2.1	5.3	1.0	0.7	0.2	2.0	2.4
33700	Modesto, CA	11.2	8.4	3.1	3.6	1.8	2.7	5.3	1.8	1.4	0.4	1.5	2.1
33740	Monroe, LA	15.1	12.7	4.4	6.8	1.5	2.4	4.1	0.6	0.4	0.2	1.6	1.9
33780	Monroe, MI	14.0	11.3	4.5	5.0	1.8	2.7	3.4	0.7	0.5	0.2	1.2	1.5
33860	Montgomery, AL	15.1	12.8	4.8	6.3	1.6	2.3	4.1	0.7	0.6	0.1	1.6	1.9
34060	Morgantown, WV	24.1	15.8	5.8	6.5	3.4	8.3	2.1	0.8	0.7	0.1	0.8	0.5
34100	Morristown, TN	13.9	11.3	4.3	5.4	1.6	2.6	4.1	1.4	1.2	0.3	1.3	1.4
34580	Mount Vernon-Anacortes, WA	15.8	12.0	4.1	5.3	2.6	3.8	2.9	0.9	0.7	0.2	1.0	1.0
34620	Muncie, IN	23.1	15.8	4.9	6.6	4.2	7.4	2.6	0.8	0.5	0.2	0.8	1.0
34740	Muskegon, MI	15.0	12.4	4.7	5.8	1.9	2.6	3.1	0.9	0.6	0.3	1.0	1.2
34820	Myrtle Beach-Conway-North Myrtle Beach, SC-NC	17.8	13.7	4.7	6.6	2.4	4.0	3.5	0.7	0.6	0.1	1.4	1.4
34900	Napa, CA	14.6	10.9	3.5	5.2	2.2	3.8	3.5	2.1	1.6	0.5	0.6	0.8
34940	Naples-Immokalee-Marco Island, FL	17.1	12.9	4.5	6.5	1.9	4.2	4.1	1.5	1.3	0.2	1.4	1.3
34980	Nashville-Davidson–Murfreesboro–Franklin, TN	16.8	13.0	4.6	6.0	2.4	3.8	3.5	1.1	0.8	0.3	1.1	1.3
35100	New Bern, NC	13.3	11.3	3.9	5.8	1.6	2.1	3.9	0.9	0.6	0.2	1.4	1.6
35300	New Haven-Milford, CT	16.4	13.3	4.7	6.4	2.1	3.1	3.0	1.1	0.9	0.2	1.0	1.0
35380	New Orleans-Metairie, LA	18.1	14.4	5.6	6.5	2.4	3.6	4.1	1.0	0.8	0.2	1.5	1.7
35620	New York-Newark-Jersey City, NY-NJ-PA	15.4	12.1	4.1	5.9	2.0	3.3	4.3	1.8	1.5	0.3	1.2	1.4
35660	Niles-Benton Harbor, MI	14.8	12.6	4.8	6.2	1.5	2.3	2.7	0.6	0.5	0.1	1.0	1.1
35840	North Port-Sarasota-Bradenton, FL	20.4	16.1	5.2	8.1	2.8	4.3	2.7	0.6	0.6	0.1	1.1	1.0
35980	Norwich-New London, CT	16.4	13.4	5.2	5.7	2.5	3.0	2.7	1.2	0.9	0.3	0.6	0.8
36100	Ocala, FL	17.5	13.6	4.5	6.6	2.4	3.9	3.4	1.1	0.9	0.2	1.1	1.2
36140	Ocean City, NJ	18.0	15.1	5.2	7.9	2.0	2.8	2.9	1.3	0.9	0.4	0.7	0.9
36220	Odessa, TX	13.0	10.1	3.9	4.2	2.0	2.9	5.6	1.7	1.2	0.5	1.6	2.4
36260	Ogden-Clearfield, UT	9.0	7.0	2.7	3.0	1.3	2.0	4.1	1.7	1.3	0.5	1.0	1.3
36420	Oklahoma City, OK	16.9	13.1	4.9	5.9	2.3	3.8	3.6	1.1	0.9	0.2	1.2	1.3
36500	Olympia-Tumwater, WA	17.1	13.0	4.3	5.9	2.8	4.0	2.1	0.7	0.5	0.2	0.7	0.7
36540	Omaha-Council Bluffs, NE-IA	16.5	13.3	5.0	6.0	2.3	3.2	2.6	0.8	0.5	0.2	0.8	1.0
36740	Orlando-Kissimmee-Sanford, FL	16.6	11.8	4.3	5.0	2.6	4.8	4.3	1.5	1.2	0.2	1.4	1.4
36780	Oshkosh-Neenah, WI	20.9	16.2	5.8	7.1	3.2	4.7	1.5	0.5	0.3	0.1	0.5	0.6
36980	Owensboro, KY	14.8	12.4	4.5	6.1	1.7	2.5	3.4	1.0	0.8	0.2	1.2	1.2
37100	Oxnard-Thousand Oaks-Ventura, CA	11.6	8.5	2.8	3.8	1.9	3.1	5.8	2.7	2.0	0.7	1.4	1.7
37340	Palm Bay-Melbourne-Titusville, FL	18.3	14.6	5.6	6.6	2.4	3.7	4.0	1.5	1.1	0.4	1.4	1.2
37460	Panama City, FL	17.5	13.7	5.2	5.8	2.7	3.8	3.2	0.8	0.7	0.1	1.2	1.2
37620	Parkersburg-Vienna, WV	18.1	14.7	5.3	7.3	2.1	3.4	2.9	0.7	0.6	0.2	1.0	1.1
37860	Pensacola-Ferry Pass-Brent, FL	16.6	12.9	4.7	5.8	2.4	3.7	3.9	1.2	0.9	0.3	1.2	1.5
37900	Peoria, IL	16.6	13.9	5.6	6.3	2.0	2.7	2.3	0.7	0.5	0.2	0.8	0.8
37980	Philadelphia-Camden-Wilmington, PA-NJ-DE-MD	16.5	13.1	4.6	6.4	2.1	3.4	4.0	1.1	0.8	0.2	1.3	1.6
38060	Phoenix-Mesa-Scottsdale, AZ	16.1	12.1	4.5	5.1	2.6	4.0	4.5	1.5	1.2	0.4	1.4	1.6
38220	Pine Bluff, AR	14.9	13.1	5.5	6.2	1.3	1.9	4.5	0.5	0.4	0.1	1.6	2.4
38300	Pittsburgh, PA	19.4	16.0	5.8	7.8	2.4	3.4	2.2	0.6	0.5	0.1	0.7	0.8
38340	Pittsfield, MA	20.1	17.1	5.8	8.8	2.4	3.0	1.9	0.4	0.4	0.0	0.7	0.7
38540	Pocatello, ID	16.5	12.4	4.7	5.4	2.4	4.0	2.3	1.1	0.8	0.3	0.5	0.7
38860	Portland-South Portland, ME	20.1	15.5	4.9	7.1	3.5	4.6	2.3	1.2	0.9	0.3	0.6	0.6
38900	Portland-Vancouver-Hillsboro, OR-WA	19.2	14.0	4.6	5.9	3.4	5.2	2.9	1.3	0.9	0.3	0.8	0.8
38940	Port St. Lucie, FL	16.5	13.1	4.7	6.5	2.0	3.4	3.4	1.1	0.9	0.2	1.3	1.0
39140	Prescott, AZ	19.5	16.2	5.8	7.8	2.6	3.2	4.0	1.3	1.0	0.3	1.1	1.6
39300	Providence-Warwick, RI-MA	17.8	14.1	4.9	6.6	2.6	3.7	3.0	1.3	0.9	0.3	0.8	1.0
39340	Provo-Orem, UT	8.6	4.8	1.4	1.9	1.5	3.7	4.1	2.4	1.6	0.8	0.7	0.9
39380	Pueblo, CO	17.2	14.0	5.5	6.3	2.3	3.1	3.4	0.9	0.7	0.2	1.2	1.3
39460	Punta Gorda, FL	19.1	14.8	4.8	7.5	2.6	4.3	3.0	1.0	0.8	0.2	1.2	0.9
39540	Racine, WI	16.4	13.1	4.8	6.2	2.2	3.3	2.9	1.0	0.8	0.1	0.9	1.0
39580	Raleigh, NC	15.6	11.9	4.1	5.5	2.4	3.7	2.4	0.7	0.6	0.1	0.8	0.9
39660	Rapid City, SD	17.0	13.5	5.0	6.0	2.5	3.5	2.3	0.3	0.3	0.0	0.9	1.1
39740	Reading, PA	15.3	11.8	4.0	5.3	2.5	3.5	3.3	1.2	0.9	0.3	1.0	1.1
39820	Redding, CA	17.7	13.3	4.4	6.3	2.6	4.4	3.4	1.6	1.2	0.4	0.9	0.9
39900	Reno, NV	19.9	14.5	5.8	5.5	3.2	5.4	3.6	1.5	1.2	0.3	1.0	1.1
40060	Richmond, VA	17.1	13.1	4.4	6.3	2.4	4.0	3.3	0.8	0.6	0.2	1.2	1.3
40140	Riverside-San Bernardino-Ontario, CA	10.1	7.6	2.7	3.3	1.6	2.5	7.0	2.8	2.1	0.7	1.8	2.4
40220	Roanoke, VA	16.9	14.3	5.1	7.0	2.2	2.6	3.4	1.1	0.7	0.5	1.0	1.3
40340	Rochester, MN	16.0	13.0	4.5	6.3	2.2	3.0	1.7	0.5	0.4	0.1	0.5	0.6
40380	Rochester, NY	18.5	14.6	5.2	6.6	2.8	3.9	2.5	0.8	0.6	0.2	0.7	0.9
40420	Rockford, IL	14.3	12.1	4.8	5.4	1.8	2.3	4.2	1.2	0.9	0.3	1.3	1.6
40580	Rocky Mount, NC	15.2	12.5	4.5	6.3	1.7	2.6	4.5	0.6	0.4	0.2	1.8	2.1
40660	Rome, GA	15.5	12.0	4.1	5.9	2.0	3.5	5.1	1.9	1.5	0.4	1.4	1.8

FIPS CBSA code	State	Total population	Percent of the population in households	Population in family households, percent					
				Percent in family households	Householder in family household, percent	Spouse in family household, percent	Child in family household (biological, adopted, or stepchild)	Other relative in family household	Nonrelatives in family household
40900	Sacramento–Roseville–Arden-Arcade, CA....	2,194,978	98.2	81.7	23.7	17.1	30.5	7.7	2.6
40980	Saginaw, MI..	197,832	96.8	80.0	25.1	17.6	29.7	5.3	2.2
41060	St. Cloud, MN..	190,590	95.1	76.0	24.5	19.7	27.6	2.5	1.7
41100	St. George, UT..	144,664	98.6	86.9	24.7	20.6	33.7	6.3	1.6
41140	St. Joseph, MO-KS..	127,773	93.7	78.0	23.7	17.8	27.4	7.0	2.0
41180	St. Louis, MO-IL..	2,797,021	98.0	81.5	25.8	18.6	30.0	5.2	2.0
41420	Salem, OR..	397,334	96.9	82.4	24.5	18.0	31.0	5.8	3.2
41500	Salinas, CA..	425,414	95.2	84.2	21.3	15.4	32.0	11.3	4.3
41540	Salisbury, MD-DE..	381,780	96.0	79.5	24.8	18.1	26.3	7.3	3.1
41620	Salt Lake City, UT..	1,123,902	98.8	85.7	23.0	17.8	34.7	7.7	2.5
41660	San Angelo, TX..	115,239	94.5	78.3	24.2	17.3	27.5	7.3	2.1
41700	San Antonio-New Braunfels, TX..	2,234,884	98.1	84.7	23.8	16.6	32.9	9.3	2.1
41740	San Diego-Carlsbad, CA..	3,175,313	97.2	80.9	22.6	16.7	30.1	8.9	2.6
41860	San Francisco-Oakland-Hayward, CA..	4,455,411	98.2	78.8	23.0	17.1	27.5	8.7	2.5
41940	San Jose-Sunnyvale-Santa Clara, CA..	1,893,321	98.3	85.1	23.9	18.5	30.2	9.6	2.9
42020	San Luis Obispo-Paso Robles-Arroyo Grande, CA..	274,106	94.2	73.3	23.7	18.8	24.0	4.7	1.9
42100	Santa Cruz-Watsonville, CA..	266,908	95.7	75.8	22.0	16.7	27.8	6.0	3.2
42140	Santa Fe, NM..	146,429	97.8	75.8	24.2	17.6	25.2	6.6	2.2
42200	Santa Maria-Santa Barbara, CA..	430,616	95.7	78.0	21.5	16.0	28.0	8.5	4.0
42220	Santa Rosa, CA..	491,057	98.1	79.0	23.7	17.6	28.3	6.4	3.0
42340	Savannah, GA..	361,495	96.8	80.4	23.9	16.6	30.3	7.9	1.8
42540	Scranton–Wilkes-Barre–Hazleton, PA..	563,295	96.2	78.7	25.3	18.2	27.6	5.8	1.8
42660	Seattle-Tacoma-Bellevue, WA..	3,553,306	98.2	78.6	24.2	18.6	27.8	5.4	2.6
42680	Sebastian-Vero Beach, FL..	140,509	98.8	79.4	26.0	20.3	25.0	6.7	1.4
42700	Sebring, FL..	97,903	98.3	78.9	25.5	20.5	24.0	7.3	1.6
43100	Sheboygan, WI..	115,067	97.2	80.2	26.4	21.0	27.8	3.2	1.8
43300	Sherman-Denison, TX..	121,768	98.1	82.4	26.0	18.9	28.5	6.7	2.2
43340	Shreveport-Bossier City, LA..	446,536	98.0	82.1	24.5	15.5	30.9	9.0	2.2
43420	Sierra Vista-Douglas, AZ..	131,232	90.8	75.8	24.4	18.2	25.6	5.8	1.8
43580	Sioux City, IA-NE-SD..	168,778	97.8	82.4	25.4	19.2	30.9	4.7	2.3
43620	Sioux Falls, SD..	237,980	97.5	80.4	25.4	19.6	29.9	3.5	1.9
43780	South Bend-Mishawaka, IN-MI..	318,791	96.2	79.2	24.8	18.2	29.3	4.9	2.1
43900	Spartanburg, SC..	316,949	97.5	83.7	26.2	18.0	30.0	7.5	2.0
44060	Spokane-Spokane Valley, WA..	532,727	96.9	77.8	24.9	19.0	27.0	4.4	2.5
44100	Springfield, IL..	211,784	97.8	78.7	25.8	18.6	27.9	4.2	2.2
44140	Springfield, MA..	626,057	94.2	76.6	24.0	16.0	28.2	5.9	2.5
44180	Springfield, MO..	444,527	96.8	78.6	25.9	20.0	26.6	4.4	1.9
44220	Springfield, OH..	137,031	97.7	80.4	25.8	18.5	28.1	5.7	2.4
44300	State College, PA..	155,032	89.6	61.8	21.0	17.2	19.4	2.7	1.5
44420	Staunton-Waynesboro, VA..	119,033	95.5	81.0	27.0	20.5	26.3	4.8	2.4
44700	Stockton-Lodi, CA..	700,220	97.8	87.4	22.9	15.8	35.4	10.3	3.0
44940	Sumter, SC..	107,884	97.7	83.9	25.5	16.7	30.3	9.0	2.3
45060	Syracuse, NY..	661,787	95.6	77.2	24.2	17.4	28.8	4.6	2.3
45220	Tallahassee, FL..	373,245	93.9	70.1	22.4	15.2	25.2	5.6	1.7
45300	Tampa-St. Petersburg-Clearwater, FL..	2,847,767	98.3	78.7	24.2	17.5	27.3	7.5	2.2
45460	Terre Haute, IN..	172,447	92.8	76.5	23.9	18.1	26.8	5.0	2.7
45500	Texarkana, TX-AR..	149,579	95.5	81.4	25.0	17.1	29.3	7.9	2.0
45540	The Villages, FL..	102,372	90.1	73.9	30.7	27.6	10.9	3.9	0.8
45780	Toledo, OH..	608,753	97.1	77.1	24.3	16.8	29.0	5.0	2.1
45820	Topeka, KS..	234,556	97.8	80.4	25.5	19.6	28.5	4.9	1.9
45940	Trenton, NJ..	369,019	94.8	80.1	23.9	17.6	29.9	6.7	1.9
46060	Tucson, AZ..	992,286	97.5	78.1	23.9	16.8	27.7	7.2	2.5
46140	Tulsa, OK..	953,120	98.5	82.8	25.8	18.9	29.9	6.0	2.2
46220	Tuscaloosa, AL..	233,522	95.3	79.5	23.1	16.1	30.6	8.1	1.6
46340	Tyler, TX..	214,529	97.8	82.5	25.1	18.4	29.4	8.1	1.5
46520	Urban Honolulu, HI..	974,683	96.2	83.6	22.1	16.6	28.1	13.8	2.9
46540	Utica-Rome, NY..	298,298	95.1	77.0	24.5	17.6	28.6	4.1	2.2
46660	Valdosta, GA..	143,281	97.1	77.0	22.2	15.0	30.4	7.8	1.6
46700	Vallejo-Fairfield, CA..	420,628	97.3	84.2	24.0	16.8	31.5	9.0	3.0
47020	Victoria, TX..	96,291	98.6	85.6	25.9	18.4	30.2	8.4	2.7
47220	Vineland-Bridgeton, NJ..	157,658	91.9	79.1	21.9	13.8	31.0	8.8	3.6
47260	Virginia Beach-Norfolk-Newport News, VA-NC..	1,697,545	96.2	80.7	24.8	17.3	29.4	7.1	2.1
47300	Visalia-Porterville, CA..	450,964	98.7	90.0	23.0	15.5	37.3	10.5	3.7
47380	Waco, TX..	257,293	95.7	79.4	23.5	16.7	30.3	6.9	2.1
47460	Walla Walla, WA..	63,502	91.2	74.6	23.0	18.0	27.1	4.2	2.2
47580	Warner Robins, GA..	185,028	97.0	83.9	24.8	18.2	31.8	7.6	1.5
47900	Washington-Arlington-Alexandria, DC-VA-MD-WV..	5,861,318	98.2	81.7	23.6	17.4	30.3	7.9	2.5
47940	Waterloo-Cedar Falls, IA..	168,747	95.3	74.7	24.1	19.3	26.2	3.5	1.5
48060	Watertown-Fort Drum, NY..	119,580	94.8	80.1	25.5	19.2	29.3	3.8	2.3
48140	Wausau, WI..	134,875	98.6	83.0	26.7	21.5	29.9	2.7	2.2
48260	Weirton-Steubenville, WV-OH..	122,629	97.0	79.9	26.6	19.9	25.8	5.4	2.2
48300	Wenatchee, WA..	112,796	98.7	85.6	26.3	20.6	30.9	5.5	2.3

FIPS CBSA code	State	Population in nonfamily households						Population in subfamilies as a percent of total population					
		Total population in nonfamily households	Nonfamily householders				Nonrelatives in nonfamily households	Total population in subfamilies	In married couple subfamilies			Parent in a parent-child subfamily	Child in a parent-child subfamily
			Total	Male living alone	Female living alone	Householder living with nonrelatives			Total in married-couple subfamilies	Spouse in a married-couple subfamily	Child in married-couple subfamily		
40900	Sacramento–Roseville–Arden-Arcade, CA.....	16.6	12.2	4.0	5.5	2.8	4.4	4.0	1.7	1.3	0.4	1.0	1.3
40980	Saginaw, MI...............................	16.8	14.0	5.4	6.8	1.8	2.8	3.0	0.8	0.6	0.2	1.1	1.2
41060	St. Cloud, MN............................	19.1	13.3	4.6	5.0	3.8	5.7	1.3	0.4	0.3	0.1	0.3	0.5
41100	St. George, UT...........................	11.6	8.0	2.5	3.9	1.5	3.6	3.7	2.0	1.4	0.6	0.8	1.0
41140	St. Joseph, MO-KS........................	15.7	12.5	4.5	6.0	2.0	3.3	4.0	1.1	0.9	0.2	1.4	1.5
41180	St. Louis, MO-IL.........................	16.5	13.6	5.0	6.4	2.2	2.9	2.9	0.8	0.6	0.2	1.0	1.2
41420	Salem, OR................................	14.4	11.1	3.5	5.4	2.2	3.4	2.9	1.2	0.9	0.3	0.8	0.9
41500	Salinas, CA..............................	11.0	8.1	2.7	3.7	1.8	2.9	5.9	2.5	2.0	0.5	1.5	2.0
41540	Salisbury, MD-DE.........................	16.4	12.3	3.8	6.0	2.4	4.2	3.8	0.9	0.8	0.1	1.5	1.5
41620	Salt Lake City, UT.......................	13.1	9.5	3.6	3.8	2.1	3.6	5.0	2.4	1.7	0.7	1.2	1.4
41660	San Angelo, TX...........................	16.2	13.2	5.2	6.0	2.0	3.1	4.2	0.8	0.5	0.3	1.6	1.8
41700	San Antonio-New Braunfels, TX............	13.5	10.6	4.1	4.6	1.8	2.9	5.9	2.1	1.5	0.5	1.7	2.1
41740	San Diego-Carlsbad, CA...................	16.3	11.4	3.9	4.5	3.0	4.9	4.5	2.1	1.6	0.5	1.1	1.3
41860	San Francisco-Oakland-Hayward, CA	19.4	13.9	4.7	5.8	3.4	5.5	4.2	2.2	1.8	0.4	0.9	1.1
41940	San Jose-Sunnyvale-Santa Clara, CA	13.2	9.5	3.4	3.8	2.3	3.7	5.1	2.6	2.1	0.5	1.1	1.4
42020	San Luis Obispo-Paso Robles-Arroyo Grande, CA.............................	20.9	13.7	4.1	5.7	3.9	7.2	2.5	1.1	0.9	0.2	0.7	0.7
42100	Santa Cruz-Watsonville, CA...............	20.0	13.3	4.1	5.3	3.9	6.7	3.5	1.6	1.2	0.4	0.8	1.1
42140	Santa Fe, NM.............................	22.0	17.4	5.8	8.3	3.3	4.6	3.3	1.1	0.9	0.2	1.1	1.1
42200	Santa Maria-Santa Barbara, CA............	17.7	11.4	3.7	4.6	3.1	6.3	4.3	1.9	1.4	0.5	1.1	1.4
42220	Santa Rosa, CA...........................	19.1	14.1	4.2	6.5	3.4	5.0	3.1	1.5	1.1	0.3	0.8	0.9
42340	Savannah, GA.............................	16.4	12.7	4.6	5.8	2.3	3.7	3.9	0.7	0.6	0.1	1.5	1.7
42540	Scranton–Wilkes-Barre–Hazleton, PA.......	17.5	14.7	5.4	7.3	2.0	2.8	3.0	1.1	0.9	0.3	0.9	1.0
42660	Seattle-Tacoma-Bellevue, WA..............	19.6	14.6	5.3	5.9	3.3	5.1	2.7	1.2	1.0	0.2	0.7	0.8
42680	Sebastian-Vero Beach, FL.................	19.4	15.6	5.2	8.2	2.2	3.8	3.1	1.4	1.2	0.3	1.0	0.7
42700	Sebring, FL..............................	19.5	15.3	5.5	7.9	2.0	4.2	4.1	1.2	1.0	0.3	1.1	1.7
43100	Sheboygan, WI............................	17.0	13.9	5.4	6.1	2.4	3.0	1.4	0.5	0.4	0.1	0.4	0.5
43300	Sherman-Denison, TX......................	15.6	12.4	4.3	6.1	2.1	3.3	3.9	1.5	1.1	0.4	1.2	1.2
43340	Shreveport-Bossier City, LA..............	15.9	13.7	5.6	6.5	1.5	2.2	4.9	1.0	0.7	0.3	1.9	2.0
43420	Sierra Vista-Douglas, AZ.................	15.0	12.8	4.9	6.0	2.0	2.2	3.2	1.1	0.8	0.4	0.9	1.2
43580	Sioux City, IA-NE-SD.....................	15.3	12.6	4.7	5.9	1.9	2.8	2.6	0.9	0.6	0.3	0.8	0.9
43620	Sioux Falls, SD..........................	17.1	13.1	4.9	5.4	2.7	4.0	1.8	0.7	0.5	0.2	0.5	0.5
43780	South Bend-Mishawaka, IN-MI..............	17.0	13.7	5.1	6.2	2.3	3.4	2.8	0.7	0.6	0.1	1.0	1.1
43900	Spartanburg, SC..........................	13.8	11.3	4.2	5.6	1.5	2.5	3.9	1.1	0.8	0.3	1.4	1.5
44060	Spokane-Spokane Valley, WA...............	19.1	14.5	5.1	6.2	3.1	4.6	2.4	0.8	0.6	0.2	0.7	0.8
44100	Springfield, IL..........................	19.1	15.4	5.4	7.5	2.6	3.6	1.7	0.4	0.3	0.1	0.6	0.7
44140	Springfield, MA..........................	17.6	13.5	4.7	6.2	2.6	4.1	3.2	0.9	0.7	0.2	1.1	1.2
44180	Springfield, MO..........................	18.2	13.9	4.7	6.3	3.0	4.2	2.4	0.8	0.6	0.2	0.7	0.9
44220	Springfield, OH..........................	17.4	13.9	5.1	6.4	2.4	3.4	3.3	1.3	1.0	0.3	0.8	1.2
44300	State College, PA........................	27.8	16.0	4.9	5.4	5.8	11.7	0.9	0.3	0.3	0.0	0.3	0.3
44420	Staunton-Waynesboro, VA..................	14.5	12.6	4.6	6.4	1.6	2.0	2.8	1.0	0.7	0.3	0.9	1.0
44700	Stockton-Lodi, CA........................	10.3	7.9	2.8	3.5	1.6	2.5	6.2	2.7	2.1	0.7	1.6	1.9
44940	Sumter, SC...............................	13.8	11.6	4.4	5.7	1.6	2.2	4.7	0.3	0.2	0.1	1.8	2.6
45060	Syracuse, NY.............................	18.4	14.4	5.3	6.4	2.7	4.0	2.5	0.9	0.6	0.2	0.8	0.9
45220	Tallahassee, FL..........................	23.8	15.7	4.8	6.2	4.7	8.1	2.8	0.6	0.5	0.1	0.9	1.3
45300	Tampa-St. Petersburg-Clearwater, FL..........	19.6	15.3	5.5	7.2	2.7	4.2	3.6	1.2	1.0	0.2	1.2	1.3
45460	Terre Haute, IN..........................	16.3	12.9	4.6	6.0	2.2	3.5	3.0	1.3	0.9	0.4	0.8	0.8
45500	Texarkana, TX-AR.........................	14.1	12.1	4.8	5.9	1.4	2.0	5.1	0.9	0.9	0.1	2.0	2.2
45540	The Villages, FL.........................	16.2	13.9	4.3	7.9	1.7	2.3	0.0	0.0	0.0	0.0	0.0	0.0
45780	Toledo, OH...............................	20.1	15.6	5.8	7.0	2.8	4.4	2.6	0.4	0.3	0.1	1.0	1.2
45820	Topeka, KS...............................	17.4	14.2	5.3	6.5	2.4	3.2	3.0	0.9	0.6	0.3	0.9	1.2
45940	Trenton, NJ..............................	14.7	11.7	4.0	5.7	1.9	3.1	2.9	1.1	0.9	0.2	0.9	1.0
46060	Tucson, AZ...............................	19.4	14.9	5.5	6.5	2.9	4.5	3.7	1.0	0.7	0.3	1.2	1.6
46140	Tulsa, OK................................	15.7	12.8	4.9	6.0	2.0	2.9	3.3	1.1	0.8	0.2	1.0	1.2
46220	Tuscaloosa, AL...........................	15.8	11.9	4.2	5.8	1.9	3.9	4.3	1.3	1.1	0.3	1.5	1.4
46340	Tyler, TX................................	15.3	11.8	4.0	5.8	2.0	3.4	4.1	1.5	1.0	0.5	1.2	1.4
46520	Urban Honolulu, HI.......................	12.6	9.5	3.7	3.8	2.0	3.1	8.9	5.4	3.7	1.6	1.4	2.1
46540	Utica-Rome, NY...........................	18.1	14.9	5.8	6.7	2.4	3.2	2.4	1.0	0.7	0.3	0.6	0.7
46660	Valdosta, GA.............................	20.1	13.7	5.1	5.4	3.3	6.4	4.9	1.3	1.0	0.3	1.6	1.9
46700	Vallejo-Fairfield, CA....................	13.0	9.7	3.1	4.5	2.1	3.3	4.6	1.8	1.4	0.4	1.3	1.5
47020	Victoria, TX.............................	13.0	10.8	4.7	4.3	1.7	2.2	5.2	0.9	0.7	0.2	1.8	2.5
47220	Vineland-Bridgeton, NJ...................	12.8	9.8	3.2	4.7	2.0	3.0	5.5	1.0	0.7	0.2	2.1	2.5
47260	Virginia Beach-Norfolk-Newport News, VA-NC	15.5	11.9	4.2	5.4	2.3	3.6	4.1	1.1	0.9	0.2	1.4	1.6
47300	Visalia-Porterville, CA..................	8.7	6.5	2.4	2.8	1.3	2.2	6.5	2.2	1.5	0.7	1.8	2.6
47380	Waco, TX.................................	16.2	11.9	4.3	5.3	2.3	4.3	4.6	1.2	0.9	0.3	1.6	1.8
47460	Walla Walla, WA..........................	16.6	13.3	4.7	6.6	2.0	3.3	0.0	0.0	0.0	0.0	0.0	0.0
47580	Warner Robins, GA........................	13.1	11.0	4.4	5.2	1.3	2.1	3.8	0.7	0.7	0.1	1.4	1.6
47900	Washington-Arlington-Alexandria, DC-VA-MD-WV.......................	16.5	12.3	4.2	5.7	2.5	4.2	3.9	1.5	1.2	0.3	1.1	1.3
47940	Waterloo-Cedar Falls, IA.................	20.7	15.2	5.5	6.6	3.1	5.4	1.8	0.5	0.3	0.1	0.6	0.7
48060	Watertown-Fort Drum, NY..................	14.6	11.9	4.5	5.2	2.2	2.8	2.3	0.6	0.4	0.2	0.7	0.9
48140	Wausau, WI...............................	15.6	12.7	4.6	5.8	2.3	2.9	1.4	0.6	0.5	0.1	0.4	0.4
48260	Weirton-Steubenville, WV-OH..............	17.1	14.7	5.2	7.6	1.9	2.4	3.2	1.4	1.1	0.3	0.8	1.0
48300	Wenatchee, WA............................	13.1	10.4	3.4	5.1	1.9	2.7	3.3	1.4	1.1	0.3	0.9	0.9

Table B-3: Metropolitan Areas—Relationships—*Continued*

FIPS CBSA code	State	Total population	Percent of the population in households	Population in family households, percent					
				Percent in family households	Householder in family household, percent	Spouse in family household, percent	Child in family household (biological, adopted, or stepchild)	Other relative in family household	Nonrelatives in family household
48540	Wheeling, WV-OH	146,397	95.3	77.0	25.9	20.1	25.0	4.0	2.0
48620	Wichita, KS	635,312	98.3	82.6	25.0	18.7	31.7	5.4	1.8
48660	Wichita Falls, TX	150,692	90.7	76.6	24.6	18.1	26.8	5.2	2.0
48700	Williamsport, PA	116,921	95.3	77.3	24.7	18.8	26.5	5.1	2.1
48900	Wilmington, NC	263,829	96.9	75.7	24.4	17.9	25.5	5.5	2.4
49020	Winchester, VA-WV	130,957	97.9	80.1	23.9	19.0	29.3	6.0	1.9
49180	Winston-Salem, NC	647,433	98.0	81.8	25.9	19.0	28.8	5.9	2.1
49340	Worcester, MA-CT	923,944	96.5	80.7	24.9	18.2	30.1	5.2	2.3
49420	Yakima, WA	246,498	98.5	86.6	23.0	16.5	35.2	8.8	3.1
49620	York-Hanover, PA	437,720	98.0	83.5	26.5	20.3	29.2	5.0	2.4
49660	Youngstown-Warren-Boardman, OH-PA......	558,682	96.5	79.5	26.3	18.6	27.9	4.9	1.8
49700	Yuba City, CA	167,874	98.7	87.0	24.7	17.4	32.5	9.4	3.1
49740	Yuma, AZ...	201,595	95.9	86.4	27.1	20.1	31.1	6.1	1.9

FIPS CBSA code	State	Population in nonfamily households						Population in subfamilies as a percent of total population					
		Total population in nonfamily households	Nonfamily householders				Nonrelatives in nonfamily households	Total population in subfamilies	In married couple subfamilies			Parent in a parent-child subfamily	Child in a parent-child subfamily
			Total	Male living alone	Female living alone	Householder living with nonrelatives			Total in married-couple subfamilies	Spouse in a married-couple subfamily	Child in married-couple subfamily		
48540	Wheeling, WV-OH	18.3	15.7	6.0	7.7	1.9	2.6	2.1	0.8	0.6	0.2	0.6	0.8
48620	Wichita, KS	15.7	13.0	5.3	5.8	1.8	2.7	3.2	0.7	0.5	0.2	1.1	1.4
48660	Wichita Falls, TX	14.1	12.3	4.6	6.1	1.5	1.9	2.5	0.5	0.4	0.1	0.9	1.1
48700	Williamsport, PA	18.0	14.3	5.1	6.4	2.7	3.7	2.9	1.1	0.7	0.4	0.7	1.0
48900	Wilmington, NC	21.3	15.8	5.2	7.0	3.6	5.5	2.9	1.0	0.8	0.3	0.9	0.9
49020	Winchester, VA-WV	17.9	14.3	5.7	6.1	2.4	3.6	3.3	1.9	1.5	0.4	0.7	0.7
49180	Winston-Salem, NC	16.2	13.4	4.9	6.7	1.9	2.8	3.2	0.9	0.7	0.2	1.0	1.2
49340	Worcester, MA-CT	15.8	12.3	4.3	5.6	2.4	3.5	2.7	1.1	0.9	0.2	0.8	0.8
49420	Yakima, WA	11.9	9.1	3.3	4.1	1.8	2.8	6.1	1.6	1.2	0.4	2.0	2.5
49620	York-Hanover, PA	14.5	11.7	4.4	5.3	2.0	2.8	2.9	0.9	0.8	0.2	0.9	1.1
49660	Youngstown-Warren-Boardman, OH-PA	17.0	14.9	5.7	7.4	1.8	2.2	2.6	0.7	0.5	0.2	0.9	1.1
49700	Yuba City, CA	11.7	8.9	3.2	3.8	1.9	2.8	5.7	2.4	1.9	0.5	1.5	1.8
49740	Yuma, AZ	9.5	7.9	3.3	3.3	1.3	1.6	4.8	1.6	0.9	0.6	1.0	2.2

Table B-4: Cities with a Population of 50,000 or More—Relationships

State/ place FIPS code	State/place	Total population	Percent of the population in households	Population in family households, percent					
				Percent in family households	Householder in family household, percent	Spouse in family household, percent	Child in family household (biological, adopted, or stepchild)	Other relative in family household	Nonrelatives in family household
0000000	**United States**.............................	313,861,723	97.4	81.4	24.4	17.8	29.9	7.2	2.2
0100000	**Alabama**.............................	4,817,624	97.6	82.6	25.7	18.2	29.8	7.4	1.6
0103076	Auburn city.............................	56,849	92.6	59.0	18.7	13.7	20.7	4.4	1.4
0107000	Birmingham city.............................	211,612	96.0	72.2	22.2	10.6	28.6	9.0	1.8
0120104	Decatur city.............................	55,801	98.3	80.6	24.9	17.9	30.5	5.9	1.5
0121184	Dothan city.............................	67,370	98.6	82.1	25.4	17.3	31.0	7.2	1.1
0135896	Hoover city.............................	83,154	99.5	86.1	26.9	21.6	31.7	4.7	1.2
0137000	Huntsville city.............................	183,702	96.5	75.5	24.1	16.0	27.2	6.4	1.8
0150000	Mobile city.............................	194,878	95.6	77.3	23.5	13.6	30.2	8.6	1.5
0151000	Montgomery city.............................	204,478	97.0	79.3	24.1	13.6	31.4	8.0	2.1
0177256	Tuscaloosa city.............................	93,757	89.8	68.2	19.5	12.0	27.7	7.3	1.6
0200000	**Alaska**.............................	729,603	96.4	81.2	23.0	17.1	31.6	6.5	3.1
0203000	Anchorage municipality.............................	298,384	97.3	81.2	23.1	17.0	31.6	6.4	3.1
0400000	**Arizona**.............................	6,548,856	97.7	81.4	23.8	17.2	29.9	7.9	2.6
0404720	Avondale city.............................	78,039	99.8	90.1	22.6	13.7	36.0	14.5	3.4
0407940	Buckeye town.............................	54,582	89.7	82.0	21.4	16.2	32.8	9.3	2.3
0410670	Casas Adobes CDP.............................	69,663	98.6	80.5	25.1	18.7	28.7	5.4	2.6
0411230	Catalina Foothills CDP.............................	51,420	99.6	78.9	28.6	24.6	21.5	3.3	1.0
0412000	Chandler city.............................	244,864	99.7	85.5	24.6	18.8	33.2	6.6	2.4
0423620	Flagstaff city.............................	67,418	87.6	62.6	20.2	13.3	21.9	4.6	2.6
0427400	Gilbert town.............................	221,741	99.8	90.2	24.9	20.0	38.0	5.3	2.0
0427820	Glendale city.............................	231,760	98.4	84.0	23.0	14.8	33.5	9.4	3.3
0428380	Goodyear city.............................	69,902	94.4	86.1	26.1	21.1	31.7	4.9	2.3
0439370	Lake Havasu City city.............................	52,834	99.6	79.6	28.1	22.5	20.5	6.3	2.2
0446000	Mesa city.............................	451,306	99.2	82.3	23.9	16.9	31.0	7.3	3.2
0454050	Peoria city.............................	159,667	99.2	85.2	25.5	19.3	31.6	6.6	2.3
0455000	Phoenix city.............................	1,488,669	98.9	81.7	22.0	14.3	32.6	9.4	3.4
0464210	San Tan Valley CDP.............................	89,440	100.0	93.0	23.2	18.0	43.2	5.9	2.7
0465000	Scottsdale city.............................	223,410	99.3	74.5	26.0	20.7	22.7	3.9	1.2
0471510	Surprise city.............................	121,343	99.7	88.3	26.8	21.2	31.4	6.9	2.0
0473000	Tempe city.............................	166,114	94.0	61.5	18.4	11.8	22.1	6.2	3.1
0477000	Tucson city.............................	524,904	95.8	72.4	21.3	13.0	27.7	7.6	2.7
0485540	Yuma city.............................	92,902	94.4	83.5	26.1	18.9	30.8	5.5	2.3
0500000	**Arkansas**.............................	2,949,238	97.2	81.7	25.6	18.8	28.7	6.8	1.8
0515190	Conway city.............................	62,879	92.5	69.7	21.8	16.2	27.7	2.3	1.7
0523290	Fayetteville city.............................	77,201	91.2	58.5	19.2	14.4	19.5	4.7	0.8
0524550	Fort Smith city.............................	87,476	98.5	79.2	24.4	16.8	29.7	6.5	1.7
0535710	Jonesboro city.............................	70,378	95.2	76.9	24.5	16.0	27.7	6.7	2.0
0541000	Little Rock city.............................	196,435	98.2	76.7	22.7	14.5	29.3	8.9	1.4
0550450	North Little Rock city.............................	64,749	99.0	77.2	21.8	13.6	31.4	8.0	2.3
0560410	Rogers city.............................	58,968	99.1	86.9	23.9	18.7	34.8	6.8	2.8
0566080	Springdale city.............................	75,825	98.8	88.5	24.3	16.5	35.9	9.7	2.0
0600000	**California**.............................	38,000,360	97.9	83.5	22.6	16.1	31.6	10.1	3.0
0600562	Alameda city.............................	75,587	98.5	78.4	24.7	18.5	26.5	6.6	2.0
0600884	Alhambra city.............................	84,177	99.2	83.4	23.8	16.0	27.3	14.1	2.3
0602000	Anaheim city.............................	342,913	98.6	88.4	21.8	15.3	34.3	13.5	3.4
0602252	Antioch city.............................	105,422	99.3	89.3	23.6	16.0	35.4	10.8	3.4
0602364	Apple Valley town.............................	70,510	99.3	90.4	25.8	18.2	32.9	9.7	3.8
0602462	Arcadia city.............................	57,121	99.5	89.1	26.1	20.4	29.4	12.3	0.9
0602553	Arden-Arcade CDP.............................	91,456	98.6	73.2	23.6	15.9	26.1	5.2	2.5
0603526	Bakersfield city.............................	358,184	98.9	88.2	22.9	15.4	36.9	9.7	3.2
0603666	Baldwin Park city.............................	76,279	99.4	95.3	19.9	12.7	37.9	21.5	3.3
0604982	Bellflower city.............................	77,320	99.1	88.7	22.4	13.6	37.9	11.7	3.0
0606000	Berkeley city.............................	115,349	89.9	51.6	17.1	13.0	16.0	3.8	1.7
0608142	Brentwood city.............................	53,776	99.7	93.4	25.4	20.3	35.4	8.5	3.7
0608786	Buena Park city.............................	82,196	99.0	90.9	23.4	16.3	35.0	12.8	3.4
0608954	Burbank city.............................	104,302	99.5	80.3	24.0	17.2	28.6	8.7	1.8
0610046	Camarillo city.............................	65,853	99.2	85.4	24.8	19.8	31.2	6.4	3.1
0611194	Carlsbad city.............................	109,270	99.5	82.9	26.4	21.5	29.5	4.0	1.5
0611390	Carmichael CDP.............................	62,812	98.1	79.7	25.8	16.9	28.0	6.0	3.1
0611530	Carson city.............................	92,277	99.1	92.3	21.8	14.6	34.6	17.1	4.2
0611964	Castro Valley CDP.............................	61,062	98.0	84.6	25.8	19.5	29.3	7.7	2.4
0612048	Cathedral City city.............................	52,532	99.2	84.2	21.5	14.9	34.2	11.3	2.3
0613014	Chico city.............................	87,372	96.2	64.6	20.0	13.4	23.9	4.6	2.7
0613210	Chino city.............................	80,191	89.3	82.1	20.7	15.6	33.5	9.5	2.8
0613214	Chino Hills city.............................	76,173	99.8	92.3	24.7	19.3	38.4	8.2	1.6
0613392	Chula Vista city.............................	252,591	99.3	90.8	23.6	16.9	36.4	11.1	2.8
0613588	Citrus Heights city.............................	84,614	99.3	79.5	24.0	16.7	28.2	7.3	3.4
0614218	Clovis city.............................	98,563	99.5	87.6	24.7	17.8	36.2	6.2	2.7
0614890	Colton city.............................	53,022	99.2	91.5	21.0	12.0	40.9	13.9	3.8
0615044	Compton city.............................	97,495	99.3	92.6	19.3	10.3	40.3	18.4	4.3
0616000	Concord city.............................	124,746	99.0	84.0	25.2	18.3	30.3	7.1	3.2
0616350	Corona city.............................	157,368	99.6	91.5	22.9	17.3	38.5	10.0	2.8

Table B-4: Cities with a Population of 50,000 or More—Relationships—*Continued*

State/place FIPS code	State/place	Population in nonfamily households						Population in subfamilies as a percent of total population					
		Total population in nonfamily households	Nonfamily householders				Nonrelatives in nonfamily households	Total population in subfamilies	In married couple subfamilies			Parent in a parent-child subfamily	Child in a parent-child subfamily
			Total	Male living alone	Female living alone	Householder living with nonrelatives			Total in married-couple subfamilies	Spouse in a married-couple subfamily	Child in a married-couple subfamily		
0000000	**United States**........................	16.1	12.5	4.5	5.7	2.3	3.6	3.8	1.3	1.0	0.3	1.2	1.4
0100000	**Alabama**............................	15.0	12.5	4.8	6.1	1.5	2.5	4.1	1.0	0.8	0.2	1.5	1.6
0103076	Auburn city..........................	33.6	19.1	5.3	6.6	7.2	14.5	0.0	0.0	0.0	0.0	0.0	0.0
0107000	Birmingham city.....................	23.8	19.5	7.9	9.1	2.5	4.3	4.7	0.4	0.4	0.1	2.0	2.3
0120104	Decatur city.........................	17.7	15.1	5.8	7.9	1.4	2.5	2.9	0.5	0.5	0.1	1.1	1.2
0121184	Dothan city..........................	16.5	13.4	4.6	7.1	1.7	3.1	3.1	0.6	0.6	0.1	1.3	1.1
0135896	Hoover city..........................	13.4	11.5	4.3	6.0	1.3	1.9	0.0	0.0	0.0	0.0	0.0	0.0
0137000	Huntsville city.......................	21.0	17.6	7.2	8.3	2.2	3.3	3.3	1.1	0.8	0.3	1.1	1.1
0150000	Mobile city..........................	18.4	15.5	5.7	7.7	2.1	2.9	4.5	0.6	0.5	0.1	1.8	2.1
0151000	Montgomery city.....................	17.8	14.7	5.4	7.3	2.1	3.0	4.3	0.5	0.3	0.1	1.8	2.1
0177256	Tuscaloosa city......................	21.6	14.2	4.3	6.6	3.3	7.4	3.4	1.2	1.1	0.1	1.3	1.0
0200000	**Alaska**.............................	15.2	11.4	4.9	4.0	2.5	3.7	3.7	1.1	0.8	0.3	1.2	1.4
0203000	Anchorage municipality..............	16.1	12.0	4.7	4.5	2.8	4.1	3.4	1.1	1.0	0.2	1.0	1.2
0400000	**Arizona**............................	16.4	12.5	4.7	5.3	2.6	3.9	4.6	1.4	1.1	0.4	1.4	1.8
0404720	Avondale city........................	9.7	6.6	2.8	2.0	1.9	3.1	9.9	1.8	1.6	0.1	3.2	4.9
0407940	Buckeye town........................	7.7	6.2	2.3	2.7	1.2	1.5	4.4	2.8	1.7	1.0	0.9	0.7
0410670	Casas Adobes CDP...................	18.0	14.5	4.5	7.5	2.6	3.5	2.7	1.1	0.7	0.5	0.7	0.9
0411230	Catalina Foothills CDP...............	20.7	18.0	6.7	9.1	2.3	2.7	0.0	0.0	0.0	0.0	0.0	0.0
0412000	Chandler city........................	14.2	10.6	4.1	4.0	2.5	3.6	3.7	1.1	0.9	0.2	1.1	1.5
0423620	Flagstaff city........................	25.0	14.8	4.4	4.4	5.9	10.2	2.2	0.3	0.2	0.1	0.8	1.2
0427400	Gilbert town.........................	9.7	7.1	2.4	3.0	1.7	2.6	3.1	2.0	1.3	0.7	0.5	0.6
0427820	Glendale city........................	14.4	11.1	4.3	4.5	2.2	3.3	6.1	1.9	1.5	0.4	1.9	2.3
0428380	Goodyear city.......................	8.3	6.7	3.0	2.7	1.0	1.6	0.0	0.0	0.0	0.0	0.0	0.0
0439370	Lake Havasu City city...............	19.9	15.6	6.3	6.0	3.4	4.3	4.2	1.2	1.1	0.1	1.3	1.7
0446000	Mesa city............................	17.0	12.8	4.7	5.5	2.7	4.2	3.9	1.3	1.0	0.3	1.2	1.4
0454050	Peoria city...........................	13.9	11.1	3.6	5.5	2.1	2.8	4.1	1.9	1.3	0.6	1.1	1.1
0455000	Phoenix city.........................	17.2	12.9	5.0	5.0	2.8	4.3	5.5	1.7	1.3	0.4	1.8	2.1
0464210	San Tan Valley CDP..................	7.0	5.2	1.8	2.3	1.1	1.8	0.0	0.0	0.0	0.0	0.0	0.0
0465000	Scottsdale city.......................	24.8	18.9	6.5	8.6	3.9	5.8	1.7	0.7	0.6	0.1	0.5	0.5
0471510	Surprise city.........................	11.4	9.6	3.6	4.5	1.5	1.8	4.4	1.6	1.2	0.4	1.1	1.7
0473000	Tempe city..........................	32.5	19.8	7.2	5.8	6.8	12.7	2.5	1.2	1.0	0.2	0.6	0.7
0477000	Tucson city..........................	23.4	17.5	6.6	7.2	3.6	5.9	3.7	0.8	0.6	0.2	1.3	1.6
0485540	Yuma city...........................	11.0	9.1	3.6	3.8	1.6	1.9	3.6	1.1	0.7	0.4	0.8	1.7
0500000	**Arkansas**...........................	15.6	12.7	4.8	6.0	1.9	2.9	3.7	1.1	0.9	0.2	1.2	1.4
0515190	Conway city.........................	22.8	15.2	4.8	5.8	4.6	7.6	0.0	0.0	0.0	0.0	0.0	0.0
0523290	Fayetteville city......................	32.7	22.9	8.2	7.6	7.1	9.8	1.3	0.2	0.1	0.1	0.4	0.7
0524550	Fort Smith city.......................	19.3	15.1	5.6	7.2	2.3	4.2	4.2	2.1	1.5	0.5	1.0	1.1
0535710	Jonesboro city.......................	18.3	13.5	3.6	6.3	3.6	4.8	3.7	1.6	1.1	0.5	1.0	1.1
0541000	Little Rock city.......................	21.5	17.6	6.4	8.9	2.3	3.9	3.1	0.4	0.4	0.1	1.3	1.4
0550450	North Little Rock city................	21.8	16.7	6.6	7.4	2.7	5.1	3.9	0.3	0.3	0.0	1.5	2.0
0560410	Rogers city...........................	12.2	9.8	3.3	5.1	1.4	2.4	3.1	1.2	0.9	0.3	0.9	1.1
0566080	Springdale city.......................	10.3	8.7	3.6	3.9	1.2	1.6	5.7	2.4	1.7	0.8	1.2	2.0
0600000	**California**..........................	14.4	10.5	3.6	4.4	2.4	3.9	5.5	2.4	1.9	0.5	1.3	1.7
0600562	Alameda city........................	20.1	15.2	4.9	7.1	3.3	4.9	3.1	1.7	1.5	0.2	0.6	0.9
0600884	Alhambra city........................	15.7	11.4	4.0	5.2	2.2	4.3	6.2	3.6	3.0	0.6	1.2	1.4
0602000	Anaheim city........................	10.2	7.0	2.2	3.0	1.8	3.2	7.7	3.7	2.8	0.8	1.7	2.3
0602252	Antioch city.........................	10.0	7.4	2.2	3.6	1.6	2.6	4.6	2.2	1.7	0.5	1.2	1.2
0602364	Apple Valley town....................	8.8	7.7	3.0	4.1	0.6	1.2	6.3	3.3	2.5	0.8	1.4	1.6
0602462	Arcadia city..........................	10.4	8.3	2.4	4.7	1.3	2.1	4.8	3.7	3.2	0.5	0.5	0.6
0602553	Arden-Arcade CDP..................	25.5	20.2	7.0	9.8	3.4	5.3	1.9	0.5	0.3	0.2	0.7	0.7
0603526	Bakersfield city......................	10.8	7.8	2.8	3.2	1.8	3.0	5.1	1.8	1.4	0.5	1.5	1.8
0603666	Baldwin Park city....................	4.1	2.6	1.0	1.1	0.6	1.4	12.2	5.8	4.5	1.3	3.0	3.5
0604982	Bellflower city........................	10.4	7.7	3.0	3.4	1.2	2.7	6.2	2.2	1.8	0.4	1.9	2.1
0606000	Berkeley city.........................	38.3	22.7	6.7	8.0	8.0	15.6	1.5	0.7	0.6	0.1	0.4	0.4
0608142	Brentwood city......................	6.4	4.9	1.3	2.6	1.0	1.5	2.9	1.7	1.3	0.4	0.6	0.6
0608786	Buena Park city......................	8.1	5.0	1.5	2.1	1.4	3.1	6.0	3.2	2.6	0.6	1.3	1.5
0608954	Burbank city.........................	19.2	15.2	5.6	6.8	2.8	4.0	3.7	2.4	2.0	0.4	0.6	0.7
0610046	Camarillo city........................	13.8	10.1	3.1	4.8	2.1	3.7	3.8	2.0	1.5	0.5	0.9	0.9
0611194	Carlsbad city.........................	16.6	12.9	4.4	5.9	2.5	3.7	1.2	0.7	0.5	0.2	0.3	0.3
0611390	Carmichael CDP......................	18.4	14.9	4.9	7.4	2.6	3.5	0.0	0.0	0.0	0.0	0.0	0.0
0611530	Carson city..........................	6.8	5.3	1.8	2.5	0.9	1.5	9.2	4.8	3.5	1.3	2.0	2.4
0611964	Castro Valley CDP....................	13.4	10.3	3.3	4.7	2.3	3.0	3.3	1.6	1.4	0.2	0.8	0.9
0612048	Cathedral City city..................	15.0	10.9	4.2	3.7	3.0	4.1	5.2	1.6	1.3	0.3	1.6	2.1
0613014	Chico city...........................	31.6	19.0	5.3	7.0	6.7	12.6	0.0	0.0	0.0	0.0	0.0	0.0
0613210	Chino city...........................	7.2	5.9	2.0	2.8	1.1	1.3	6.2	2.7	2.2	0.4	1.6	2.0
0613214	Chino Hills city......................	7.5	5.9	2.1	2.7	1.0	1.7	6.6	2.8	2.3	0.5	1.7	2.1
0613392	Chula Vista city......................	8.5	7.0	2.5	3.4	1.1	1.5	6.3	3.1	2.5	0.5	1.5	1.7
0613588	Citrus Heights city...................	19.7	14.5	3.8	7.0	3.6	5.3	4.3	1.7	1.4	0.4	1.2	1.4
0614218	Clovis city...........................	11.9	9.4	3.5	4.1	1.8	2.5	2.5	1.0	0.9	0.2	0.6	0.8
0614890	Colton city...........................	7.6	6.2	2.6	2.7	0.9	1.5	10.2	3.6	2.7	0.9	2.7	3.9
0615044	Compton city........................	6.7	4.5	1.4	2.3	0.8	2.2	11.3	3.3	2.4	0.9	3.3	4.7
0616000	Concord city.........................	14.9	10.9	4.0	4.4	2.5	4.0	3.7	1.9	1.4	0.5	0.9	0.9
0616350	Corona city..........................	8.1	6.0	1.9	2.6	1.5	2.1	5.7	2.7	2.2	0.5	1.4	1.6

Table B-4: Cities with a Population of 50,000 or More—Relationships—*Continued*

State/place FIPS code	State/place	Total population	Percent of the population in households	Population in family households, percent					
				Percent in family households	Householder in family household, percent	Spouse in family household, percent	Child in family household (biological, adopted, or stepchild)	Other relative in family household	Nonrelatives in family household
	California—cont'd								
0616532	Costa Mesa city	111,623	98.3	75.3	21.3	15.4	28.0	6.7	3.9
0617610	Cupertino city	59,701	99.3	90.0	26.8	23.3	34.3	5.0	0.5
0617918	Daly City city	103,685	99.3	85.7	21.3	15.6	29.5	16.2	3.2
0618100	Davis city	65,890	96.7	55.9	17.8	14.6	20.7	1.9	0.9
0618394	Delano city	52,817	84.1	81.5	17.6	11.5	37.5	11.1	3.8
0619192	Diamond Bar city	56,171	99.7	91.8	26.0	20.1	33.8	10.3	1.7
0619766	Downey city	112,814	99.3	91.7	22.8	14.5	38.4	12.8	3.2
0620802	East Los Angeles CDP	130,546	99.8	93.4	19.5	10.7	39.3	18.8	5.1
0621230	Eastvale city	54,942	100.0	97.0	20.7	17.0	39.8	16.3	3.1
0621712	El Cajon city	101,467	97.1	85.0	22.9	14.2	35.3	8.8	3.7
0622020	Elk Grove city	158,378	99.4	91.3	24.1	17.6	36.8	10.3	2.5
0622230	El Monte city	114,986	99.0	92.8	21.8	13.5	35.0	19.3	3.1
0622678	Encinitas city	60,915	99.5	80.4	24.5	20.8	27.5	5.2	2.5
0622804	Escondido city	147,487	98.5	86.9	22.1	16.0	32.8	11.5	4.5
0623182	Fairfield city	107,653	98.0	86.8	23.9	18.0	32.7	9.4	2.7
0624477	Florence-Graham CDP	63,750	99.9	95.6	19.6	9.8	42.4	18.8	5.1
0624498	Florin CDP	50,821	99.1	89.2	22.1	12.4	36.0	14.2	4.4
0624638	Folsom city	73,009	91.1	77.3	23.6	19.7	30.1	2.5	1.3
0624680	Fontana city	201,293	99.7	94.1	20.4	14.1	40.9	15.6	3.0
0625380	Fountain Valley city	56,351	99.1	88.2	25.2	19.4	30.5	10.9	2.3
0626000	Fremont city	221,275	99.2	89.9	25.4	20.6	32.1	9.8	2.0
0627000	Fresno city	505,649	98.2	85.1	22.2	12.9	36.1	10.3	3.6
0628000	Fullerton city	138,010	97.5	83.3	22.8	17.0	31.1	9.0	3.4
0628168	Gardena city	59,568	98.7	84.5	23.5	15.0	32.3	11.2	2.5
0629000	Garden Grove city	174,167	98.8	90.0	21.1	14.6	33.4	17.0	4.0
0629504	Gilroy city	50,636	98.8	90.9	23.3	16.2	35.5	11.8	4.1
0630000	Glendale city	194,450	99.2	85.3	24.9	18.2	30.7	9.9	1.5
0630014	Glendora city	50,762	98.1	88.2	25.1	19.2	34.2	7.9	1.8
0631596	Hacienda Heights CDP	53,990	99.7	92.3	23.4	17.2	32.3	16.9	2.6
0631960	Hanford city	54,461	98.7	89.3	24.4	16.7	37.5	7.3	3.4
0632548	Hawthorne city	85,597	99.3	85.8	22.3	12.2	36.6	11.1	3.5
0633000	Hayward city	149,286	98.1	86.6	22.5	15.1	31.3	14.0	3.8
0633182	Hemet city	81,124	99.1	81.7	23.3	15.4	30.2	9.7	3.1
0633434	Hesperia city	91,783	100.0	91.1	22.6	15.3	36.7	11.8	3.8
0633588	Highland city	54,020	99.7	93.1	22.2	15.0	38.2	14.3	3.3
0636000	Huntington Beach city	195,094	99.5	81.9	25.3	19.3	28.3	6.6	2.4
0636056	Huntington Park city	58,654	99.7	93.6	21.0	11.3	40.3	16.2	4.9
0636448	Indio city	82,355	98.9	90.5	23.6	16.4	34.3	12.1	4.2
0636546	Inglewood city	111,121	98.3	85.1	22.4	11.7	35.3	12.4	3.4
0636770	Irvine city	228,813	96.8	77.7	24.0	18.9	28.3	5.1	1.3
0637692	Jurupa Valley city	97,212	99.1	92.2	20.2	14.3	37.0	16.7	4.0
0639248	Laguna Niguel city	64,247	99.5	85.8	26.5	22.4	30.4	4.7	1.8
0639290	La Habra city	61,339	99.3	88.5	22.7	16.1	34.5	11.3	3.9
0639486	Lake Elsinore city	55,983	99.7	93.2	21.9	16.0	36.9	14.7	3.7
0639496	Lake Forest city	78,840	99.2	88.6	25.3	20.5	31.9	8.4	2.5
0639892	Lakewood city	80,794	99.8	89.7	24.7	17.2	33.6	11.0	3.2
0640004	La Mesa city	58,178	98.7	76.7	23.5	16.4	27.8	6.9	2.2
0640130	Lancaster city	158,783	95.0	84.6	22.0	14.6	35.0	10.4	2.6
0641992	Livermore city	83,665	99.5	87.7	26.2	20.0	31.8	7.0	2.8
0642202	Lodi city	63,105	98.9	85.5	23.8	17.2	34.6	7.2	2.7
0643000	Long Beach city	467,580	98.2	80.0	21.2	12.9	32.0	10.7	3.2
0644000	Los Angeles city	3,852,816	97.8	78.5	20.6	13.0	29.7	11.8	3.5
0644574	Lynwood city	70,657	96.1	92.3	18.2	10.4	41.2	17.8	4.6
0645022	Madera city	62,581	99.3	92.2	20.7	12.3	39.4	14.2	5.5
0645484	Manteca city	70,732	99.2	88.0	23.6	16.9	35.7	8.6	3.1
0646842	Menifee city	81,535	99.8	86.9	23.0	18.1	32.0	9.9	4.0
0646898	Merced city	80,459	98.6	84.6	21.8	13.2	37.0	10.3	2.4
0647766	Milpitas city	68,568	96.9	87.4	22.9	17.7	29.5	13.6	3.6
0648256	Mission Viejo city	95,136	98.5	87.6	26.9	22.5	30.7	6.3	1.3
0648354	Modesto city	203,544	98.5	85.5	23.7	15.7	33.4	9.3	3.5
0648816	Montebello city	63,234	99.2	87.9	22.6	12.8	32.9	16.6	3.0
0648914	Monterey Park city	60,870	99.5	89.2	23.7	15.2	30.1	17.4	2.8
0649270	Moreno Valley city	198,896	99.6	93.6	21.4	13.5	38.5	16.0	4.2
0649670	Mountain View city	76,478	99.6	75.5	24.1	19.3	25.0	5.1	2.0
0650076	Murrieta city	106,359	99.5	89.3	23.4	19.2	34.7	9.5	2.4
0650258	Napa city	78,352	98.4	82.6	24.1	17.8	31.0	6.7	3.1
0650398	National City city	59,467	92.2	84.3	19.4	11.7	34.2	15.6	3.4
0651182	Newport Beach city	86,697	99.7	74.0	25.1	20.5	24.1	3.6	0.7
0652526	Norwalk city	106,310	98.4	92.6	20.9	13.3	36.8	17.8	3.8
0652582	Novato city	53,368	98.7	81.7	25.9	20.7	28.8	4.5	1.9
0653000	Oakland city	401,278	98.2	73.4	21.2	12.9	26.5	9.7	3.1
0653322	Oceanside city	171,210	99.5	82.6	23.0	17.3	29.4	9.8	3.1
0653896	Ontario city	166,804	99.6	90.8	20.8	13.6	37.2	14.4	4.8
0653980	Orange city	139,199	95.1	81.7	22.2	16.3	29.6	10.4	3.2

Table B-4: Cities with a Population of 50,000 or More—Relationships—*Continued*

State/ place FIPS code	State/place	Population in nonfamily households						Population in subfamilies as a percent of total population					
		Total population in nonfamily households	Nonfamily householders				Nonrelatives in nonfamily households	Total population in subfamilies	In married couple subfamilies			Parent in a parent-child subfamily	Child in a parent-child subfamily
			Total	Male living alone	Female living alone	Householder living with nonrelatives			Total in married-couple subfamilies	Spouse in a married-couple subfamily	Child in married-couple subfamily		
	California—cont'd												
0616532	Costa Mesa city	23.0	15.4	5.0	5.4	5.0	7.6	3.5	1.7	1.2	0.5	0.8	1.0
0617610	Cupertino city	9.3	7.5	2.4	3.8	1.2	1.9	0.0	0.0	0.0	0.0	0.0	0.0
0617918	Daly City city	13.5	8.5	3.1	3.1	2.3	5.0	8.4	4.9	4.3	0.6	1.6	1.8
0618100	Davis city	40.8	18.6	3.4	5.8	9.4	22.3	0.0	0.0	0.0	0.0	0.0	0.0
0618394	Delano city	2.6	2.3	0.7	1.3	0.3	0.3	8.0	4.0	3.0	0.9	1.7	2.4
0619192	Diamond Bar city	7.8	5.4	1.4	2.6	1.4	2.4	4.7	2.2	2.0	0.2	0.8	1.6
0619766	Downey city	7.6	6.0	2.4	2.5	1.1	1.6	7.2	2.9	2.3	0.6	2.0	2.3
0620802	East Los Angeles CDP	6.5	4.4	1.6	1.9	0.9	2.1	11.3	4.1	2.6	1.5	3.0	4.3
0621230	Eastvale city	3.0	2.2	0.9	0.8	0.5	0.8	8.5	5.4	4.4	1.0	1.3	1.9
0621712	El Cajon city	12.2	9.4	3.3	4.4	1.7	2.8	3.5	1.9	1.5	0.3	0.8	0.8
0622020	Elk Grove city	8.1	5.9	1.7	3.0	1.3	2.2	5.8	3.0	2.6	0.4	1.2	1.5
0622230	El Monte city	6.2	4.6	1.7	2.0	0.9	1.5	10.2	5.9	5.0	1.0	1.8	2.4
0622678	Encinitas city	19.0	13.2	4.1	5.0	4.0	5.9	2.7	2.0	1.4	0.6	0.3	0.4
0622804	Escondido city	11.6	8.1	2.3	3.5	2.2	3.6	6.3	2.4	1.7	0.7	1.8	2.2
0623182	Fairfield city	11.2	8.1	2.2	4.0	1.9	3.1	4.8	1.6	1.3	0.3	1.5	1.7
0624477	Florence-Graham CDP	4.3	2.9	0.8	1.4	0.7	1.4	10.9	4.7	3.5	1.3	2.6	3.6
0624498	Florin CDP	9.9	7.4	2.7	3.3	1.3	2.6	7.5	2.8	2.0	0.8	1.9	2.7
0624638	Folsom city	13.9	11.0	3.4	5.5	2.1	2.9	0.0	0.0	0.0	0.0	0.0	0.0
0624680	Fontana city	5.6	3.6	1.1	1.6	1.0	2.0	10.3	5.2	3.7	1.5	2.2	2.9
0625380	Fountain Valley city	10.9	7.9	2.5	3.6	1.8	3.0	4.6	2.4	1.8	0.6	1.1	1.2
0626000	Fremont city	9.3	6.9	2.5	2.9	1.5	2.4	5.2	3.3	2.9	0.5	0.9	1.0
0627000	Fresno city	13.1	9.6	3.3	4.1	2.2	3.5	5.6	1.9	1.5	0.4	1.6	2.1
0628000	Fullerton city	14.2	9.0	3.0	3.3	2.8	5.2	4.5	2.3	1.8	0.5	1.0	1.2
0628168	Gardena city	14.2	12.0	5.1	5.4	1.5	2.2	4.8	2.4	2.0	0.3	1.1	1.4
0629000	Garden Grove city	8.8	5.5	1.5	2.5	1.5	3.2	8.7	4.8	3.5	1.3	1.6	2.3
0629504	Gilroy city	7.8	5.3	1.9	2.3	1.1	2.5	6.7	2.1	1.4	0.6	2.0	2.7
0630000	Glendale city	14.0	11.3	3.7	5.8	1.8	2.7	4.7	3.5	3.0	0.5	0.6	0.6
0630014	Glendora city	9.9	7.6	2.5	3.8	1.4	2.3	4.3	2.2	1.7	0.4	1.0	1.1
0631596	Hacienda Heights CDP	7.3	5.3	1.3	2.7	1.3	2.1	11.1	6.3	4.9	1.4	2.0	2.8
0631960	Hanford city	9.4	7.5	2.7	3.5	1.3	1.9	4.8	1.6	1.2	0.4	1.4	1.9
0632548	Hawthorne city	13.6	10.9	4.5	4.5	1.9	2.7	5.4	2.1	1.6	0.4	1.5	1.8
0633000	Hayward city	11.5	8.4	2.5	3.9	2.0	3.1	7.3	4.1	3.4	0.7	1.5	1.7
0633182	Hemet city	17.4	14.1	4.5	7.2	2.4	3.3	5.2	2.2	1.3	0.9	1.3	1.7
0633434	Hesperia city	8.9	6.1	2.1	2.8	1.2	2.8	7.3	2.5	1.7	0.7	2.1	2.8
0633588	Highland city	6.6	4.9	1.7	2.2	1.0	1.7	10.6	2.7	1.7	1.0	3.5	4.4
0636000	Huntington Beach city	17.6	12.7	4.4	4.9	3.4	4.9	3.6	1.8	1.3	0.5	0.9	1.0
0636056	Huntington Park city	6.1	4.1	1.4	1.6	1.1	2.0	9.7	3.1	2.1	1.0	2.8	3.8
0636448	Indio city	8.4	6.7	2.1	3.4	1.2	1.7	7.2	2.1	1.8	0.4	2.1	3.0
0636546	Inglewood city	13.2	11.1	4.0	5.6	1.4	2.1	6.6	2.0	1.6	0.4	2.1	2.4
0636770	Irvine city	19.1	12.4	4.3	4.6	3.4	6.7	1.6	1.4	1.2	0.2	0.1	0.2
0637692	Jurupa Valley city	6.9	5.2	1.7	2.3	1.2	1.7	12.4	6.1	4.4	1.7	2.7	3.5
0639248	Laguna Niguel city	13.7	11.1	3.0	6.0	2.0	2.7	0.0	0.0	0.0	0.0	0.0	0.0
0639290	La Habra city	10.8	8.3	2.7	3.9	1.8	2.5	5.9	1.4	1.1	0.3	2.0	2.6
0639486	Lake Elsinore city	6.5	4.5	1.9	1.7	0.9	2.0	10.3	3.5	2.9	0.6	2.8	4.0
0639496	Lake Forest city	10.7	8.5	3.0	4.1	1.5	2.1	4.1	2.4	1.8	0.6	0.8	0.9
0639892	Lakewood city	10.2	8.0	2.9	3.7	1.4	2.2	5.7	2.4	1.8	0.6	1.4	1.9
0640004	La Mesa city	22.0	17.1	5.4	8.0	3.7	5.0	2.1	1.2	1.0	0.2	0.5	0.4
0640130	Lancaster city	10.4	8.3	3.1	3.8	1.3	2.1	6.5	2.3	1.7	0.6	1.6	2.5
0641992	Livermore city	11.8	8.8	3.3	3.7	1.9	3.0	4.0	1.8	1.5	0.3	1.0	1.1
0642202	Lodi city	13.5	11.1	3.7	5.5	1.9	2.4	4.1	1.8	1.3	0.5	1.0	1.3
0643000	Long Beach city	18.2	13.7	5.1	5.6	3.1	4.5	5.4	1.8	1.4	0.4	1.6	2.0
0644000	Los Angeles city	19.3	13.8	5.0	5.4	3.3	5.5	5.8	2.3	1.8	0.5	1.5	1.9
0644574	Lynwood city	3.8	2.6	0.9	1.1	0.6	1.2	11.9	3.5	2.8	0.7	3.6	4.8
0645022	Madera city	7.2	5.4	2.5	1.9	1.0	1.8	6.8	1.9	1.4	0.5	2.1	2.8
0645484	Manteca city	11.2	8.0	2.4	3.5	2.1	3.2	6.6	2.9	2.0	0.9	1.7	1.9
0646842	Menifee city	12.9	9.9	3.2	4.8	1.9	3.0	6.4	3.8	3.1	0.6	1.4	1.2
0646898	Merced city	14.0	9.3	3.2	4.0	2.2	4.6	6.6	2.7	2.0	0.7	1.7	2.2
0647766	Milpitas city	9.5	6.1	2.1	2.6	1.4	3.4	7.4	4.6	3.8	0.9	1.2	1.5
0648256	Mission Viejo city	10.9	8.4	2.6	4.2	1.6	2.5	4.3	2.5	1.8	0.7	0.7	1.1
0648354	Modesto city	13.0	10.2	4.0	4.4	1.9	2.8	5.4	1.6	1.2	0.4	1.6	2.2
0648816	Montebello city	11.3	8.5	2.8	4.3	1.4	2.8	8.9	3.2	2.3	0.9	2.5	3.2
0648914	Monterey Park city	10.4	6.5	2.4	2.5	1.6	3.8	9.0	5.9	5.0	0.9	1.3	1.8
0649270	Moreno Valley city	6.0	4.3	1.7	1.5	1.1	1.7	10.9	4.5	3.3	1.2	2.7	3.7
0649670	Mountain View city	24.1	18.1	7.1	6.8	4.2	5.9	1.9	1.0	1.0	0.1	0.4	0.4
0650076	Murrieta city	10.2	7.5	1.9	3.9	1.7	2.7	4.9	2.5	2.2	0.4	1.1	1.2
0650258	Napa city	15.8	11.8	3.6	5.8	2.4	4.0	3.0	1.8	1.3	0.6	0.5	0.6
0650398	National City city	7.9	5.9	2.1	2.5	1.3	2.0	9.2	4.3	3.1	1.2	2.1	2.8
0651182	Newport Beach city	25.7	18.6	6.2	7.9	4.5	7.0	0.0	0.0	0.0	0.0	0.0	0.0
0652526	Norwalk city	5.8	4.4	1.4	2.1	1.0	1.4	9.4	4.2	3.0	1.2	2.3	3.0
0652582	Novato city	17.0	13.6	4.6	6.6	2.4	3.4	0.0	0.0	0.0	0.0	0.0	0.0
0653000	Oakland city	24.8	18.0	5.9	7.8	4.2	6.8	4.5	1.6	1.3	0.3	1.3	1.6
0653322	Oceanside city	16.9	11.8	4.1	4.9	2.8	5.1	6.0	2.3	1.7	0.6	1.6	2.1
0653896	Ontario city	8.8	6.9	2.6	3.2	1.2	1.8	8.8	2.8	2.3	0.5	2.7	3.3
0653980	Orange city	13.4	8.6	2.8	3.3	2.5	4.8	5.6	2.9	2.3	0.6	1.3	1.4

State/ place FIPS code	State/place	Total population	Percent of the population in households	Population in family households, percent					
				Percent in family households	Householder in family household, percent	Spouse in family household, percent	Child in family household (biological, adopted, or stepchild)	Other relative in family household	Nonrelatives in family household
	California—cont'd								
0654652	Oxnard city	201,380	99.3	91.8	20.3	13.7	35.4	17.2	5.2
0655156	Palmdale city	155,567	99.9	92.3	21.9	14.0	40.0	12.4	4.0
0655282	Palo Alto city	66,029	99.2	80.9	25.8	22.0	28.9	3.6	0.6
0655618	Paramount city	54,714	99.4	93.5	20.3	12.4	40.5	16.7	3.6
0656000	Pasadena city	138,658	97.2	72.9	21.8	15.9	24.4	8.9	1.9
0656700	Perris city	71,279	99.6	94.9	19.9	12.0	42.9	15.8	4.2
0656784	Petaluma city	58,835	98.9	82.0	23.8	18.2	31.7	5.9	2.4
0656924	Pico Rivera city	63,541	99.2	92.8	21.3	13.6	34.9	19.2	3.8
0657456	Pittsburg city	65,616	99.5	88.6	22.9	14.6	35.2	12.4	3.5
0657526	Placentia city	51,885	99.0	88.9	23.4	17.6	33.4	10.7	3.8
0657792	Pleasanton city	72,488	99.5	90.2	27.6	22.9	33.6	4.8	1.3
0658072	Pomona city	150,646	96.6	87.3	19.7	12.7	36.9	14.5	3.5
0658240	Porterville city	54,947	97.6	87.6	22.5	14.5	39.7	7.2	3.7
0659444	Rancho Cordova city	66,931	99.3	83.0	24.0	16.0	31.1	8.1	3.8
0659451	Rancho Cucamonga city	169,898	98.2	87.8	23.9	17.6	35.9	8.4	2.0
0659920	Redding city	90,713	97.6	76.9	24.2	17.1	27.3	5.3	3.0
0659962	Redlands city	69,715	96.2	82.0	23.8	18.2	31.0	6.4	2.6
0660018	Redondo Beach city	67,455	99.8	78.7	25.6	19.8	25.6	5.9	1.8
0660102	Redwood City city	79,316	98.0	81.3	23.4	17.7	30.7	6.9	2.7
0660466	Rialto city	101,434	99.3	92.9	20.3	13.3	39.2	15.9	4.2
0660620	Richmond city	106,465	98.6	83.3	22.7	13.7	30.9	12.6	3.5
0662000	Riverside city	313,050	96.5	84.1	20.6	14.3	34.8	11.3	3.1
0662364	Rocklin city	58,980	98.9	86.6	26.7	20.0	33.9	3.8	2.1
0662896	Rosemead city	54,332	99.1	92.7	22.5	15.0	30.3	21.4	3.6
0662938	Roseville city	124,617	99.2	84.5	25.2	19.6	32.6	5.2	1.9
0663218	Rowland Heights CDP	51,604	99.6	90.5	23.6	16.8	29.8	16.9	3.3
0664000	Sacramento city	475,536	98.3	77.5	21.4	13.4	29.6	10.0	3.1
0664224	Salinas city	154,135	98.5	89.9	20.6	13.4	36.9	13.6	5.4
0665000	San Bernardino city	212,886	95.8	86.7	20.0	10.8	37.9	13.7	4.2
0665042	San Buenaventura (Ventura) city, Cal	108,320	98.4	79.0	23.7	16.9	28.9	6.9	2.5
0665084	San Clemente city	64,696	99.5	85.2	26.1	21.4	31.1	4.5	2.1
0666000	San Diego city	1,337,522	97.1	75.6	21.1	15.3	28.2	8.8	2.3
0667000	San Francisco city	826,626	97.6	62.5	19.1	13.9	18.2	9.0	2.3
0668000	San Jose city	983,775	98.5	86.4	23.1	17.2	31.0	11.4	3.7
0668084	San Leandro city	86,929	99.3	84.5	23.8	17.6	29.4	11.9	1.7
0668196	San Marcos city	87,119	98.9	84.2	22.4	16.8	31.8	10.3	2.9
0668252	San Mateo city	99,768	98.5	79.6	23.6	17.6	27.3	8.5	2.5
0668364	San Rafael city	58,525	96.6	77.3	23.5	17.4	26.7	6.5	3.2
0668378	San Ramon city	73,764	99.8	89.4	26.2	22.5	35.6	4.7	0.5
0669000	Santa Ana city	331,328	98.6	92.1	18.0	11.9	35.4	19.0	7.7
0669070	Santa Barbara city	89,541	98.1	73.2	21.0	15.4	23.9	7.2	5.7
0669084	Santa Clara city	119,075	97.0	80.1	23.8	18.9	27.3	7.7	2.4
0669088	Santa Clarita city	178,600	99.0	88.3	25.0	18.9	34.6	7.2	2.6
0669112	Santa Cruz city	62,082	85.9	52.0	15.8	11.8	18.5	3.5	2.4
0669196	Santa Maria city	101,229	99.0	90.0	20.5	13.8	35.5	14.6	5.7
0670000	Santa Monica city	91,579	98.1	56.2	18.9	14.2	18.7	3.1	1.3
0670098	Santa Rosa city	170,493	98.2	79.5	22.8	16.2	30.2	6.9	3.4
0670224	Santee city	55,347	97.9	85.3	25.2	18.1	33.9	5.7	2.4
0672016	Simi Valley city	125,577	99.4	88.7	25.6	20.0	32.4	8.2	2.4
0673080	South Gate city	95,326	99.9	94.5	20.6	12.5	39.9	17.0	4.5
0673262	South San Francisco city	65,434	98.9	87.6	23.3	17.5	31.4	12.4	3.0
0673430	South Whittier CDP	61,160	99.5	94.2	21.6	14.4	39.1	15.4	3.7
0675000	Stockton city	296,853	97.8	87.5	22.3	13.5	36.4	12.0	3.4
0677000	Sunnyvale city	145,871	99.4	82.2	25.0	20.5	27.2	7.5	2.0
0678120	Temecula city	104,754	99.9	91.1	24.2	19.5	38.3	6.8	2.2
0678582	Thousand Oaks city	128,136	98.4	85.3	25.6	21.3	30.8	5.6	2.1
0680000	Torrance city	146,879	99.1	85.0	26.3	20.1	31.0	6.1	1.5
0680238	Tracy city	84,327	99.7	91.6	23.4	18.6	37.1	9.8	2.8
0680644	Tulare city	60,631	99.5	90.5	23.4	16.0	37.2	10.5	3.5
0680812	Turlock city	69,740	99.0	86.2	24.5	17.1	35.5	7.0	2.1
0680854	Tustin city	77,464	99.1	87.6	23.6	16.5	32.3	11.5	3.6
0681204	Union City city	71,602	99.0	91.9	22.8	17.3	33.1	16.2	2.5
0681344	Upland city	75,017	99.0	84.7	24.3	16.9	33.4	7.8	2.2
0681554	Vacaville city	93,796	92.2	78.4	23.2	16.7	30.1	6.2	2.1
0681666	Vallejo city	117,844	98.7	83.7	23.0	14.2	30.5	12.0	4.0
0682590	Victorville city	119,725	96.0	88.4	20.5	12.7	38.5	13.3	3.5
0682954	Visalia city	126,760	98.8	87.5	24.2	16.3	34.2	9.4	3.5
0682996	Vista city	96,008	98.1	82.4	22.3	16.4	28.6	11.4	3.7
0683346	Walnut Creek city	65,770	98.4	74.7	25.3	20.8	22.9	4.4	1.4
0683668	Watsonville city	51,968	99.2	92.1	21.2	13.9	40.8	11.7	4.6
0684200	West Covina city	107,343	99.3	91.0	22.7	15.4	34.8	15.5	2.6
0684550	Westminster city	91,344	99.4	90.3	23.3	16.4	32.0	14.4	4.3
0685292	Whittier city	86,222	98.0	87.1	23.2	15.8	35.5	9.1	3.4
0686328	Woodland city	56,181	98.0	85.3	24.4	17.8	32.2	8.9	1.9
0686832	Yorba Linda city	66,386	99.6	92.4	27.3	23.6	35.4	5.2	1.0

State/ place FIPS code	State/place	Population in nonfamily households						Population in subfamilies as a percent of total population					
		Total population in nonfamily households	Nonfamily householders				Nonrelatives in nonfamily households	Total population in subfamilies	In married couple subfamilies			Parent in a parent-child subfamily	Child in a parent-child subfamily
			Total	Male living alone	Female living alone	Householder living with nonrelatives			Total in married-couple subfamilies	Spouse in a married-couple subfamily	Child in a married-couple subfamily		
	California—cont'd												
0654652	Oxnard city	7.5	5.0	1.7	2.0	1.3	2.5	10.3	4.5	3.3	1.2	2.5	3.3
0655156	Palmdale city	7.6	5.2	2.1	1.9	1.3	2.4	7.9	2.2	1.6	0.6	2.4	3.2
0655282	Palo Alto city	18.3	14.2	4.8	6.8	2.7	4.1	1.4	1.0	0.8	0.1	0.2	0.2
0655618	Paramount city	6.0	4.5	1.6	2.1	0.8	1.4	9.4	3.8	2.6	1.3	2.5	3.1
0656000	Pasadena city	24.2	17.9	6.3	7.6	4.1	6.3	4.2	1.7	1.3	0.4	1.1	1.4
0656700	Perris city	4.7	3.0	1.2	1.1	0.8	1.7	10.0	3.9	2.5	1.4	2.7	3.4
0656784	Petaluma city	16.9	12.5	3.1	6.3	3.1	4.4	3.7	1.7	1.5	0.2	0.9	1.0
0656924	Pico Rivera city	6.5	5.1	1.8	2.4	0.9	1.3	11.7	5.8	4.2	1.6	2.7	3.2
0657456	Pittsburg city	10.9	7.9	2.4	3.5	1.9	3.0	5.8	1.8	1.5	0.4	1.7	2.2
0657526	Placentia city	10.1	6.9	2.0	2.9	2.0	3.2	6.1	3.9	3.0	0.9	1.1	1.1
0657792	Pleasanton city	9.3	7.5	2.6	3.5	1.3	1.9	1.4	0.7	0.5	0.1	0.3	0.3
0658072	Pomona city	9.3	6.0	2.0	2.3	1.6	3.2	8.7	3.4	2.6	0.9	2.3	3.0
0658240	Porterville city	10.0	7.4	2.8	3.2	1.4	2.6	5.1	2.0	1.3	0.7	1.3	1.8
0659444	Rancho Cordova city	16.3	11.9	4.2	4.6	3.1	4.5	3.8	1.4	1.1	0.3	1.1	1.3
0659451	Rancho Cucamonga city	10.4	8.1	3.4	3.3	1.5	2.3	4.3	2.3	2.0	0.3	1.0	1.0
0659920	Redding city	20.7	14.3	4.3	6.9	3.1	6.3	2.8	1.2	1.1	0.1	0.8	0.8
0659962	Redlands city	14.1	12.0	3.9	6.7	1.4	2.1	3.6	1.8	1.2	0.5	0.7	1.1
0660018	Redondo Beach city	21.1	16.3	6.5	6.4	3.4	4.7	2.1	1.4	1.2	0.2	0.3	0.4
0660102	Redwood City city	16.7	12.6	4.7	5.3	2.6	4.1	3.5	1.8	1.5	0.3	0.7	1.0
0660466	Rialto city	6.5	4.5	1.6	2.0	1.0	1.9	11.2	4.5	2.9	1.6	2.8	4.0
0660620	Richmond city	15.3	11.8	4.2	5.6	1.9	3.5	6.0	1.8	1.4	0.4	2.0	2.2
0662000	Riverside city	12.4	8.4	3.0	3.3	2.1	4.0	7.6	3.2	2.3	0.9	1.9	2.5
0662364	Rocklin city	12.2	9.4	3.5	3.8	2.0	2.9	0.0	0.0	0.0	0.0	0.0	0.0
0662896	Rosemead city	6.4	4.3	1.4	2.0	0.9	2.1	10.8	7.3	6.2	1.1	1.6	1.8
0662938	Roseville city	14.7	11.5	3.5	5.4	2.6	3.3	2.8	2.0	1.7	0.3	0.4	0.4
0663218	Rowland Heights CDP	9.2	5.0	1.4	2.2	1.4	4.1	8.9	5.5	4.7	0.8	1.7	1.8
0664000	Sacramento city	20.7	15.7	5.3	6.9	3.4	5.0	5.2	2.2	1.7	0.5	1.3	1.6
0664224	Salinas city	8.6	5.8	1.9	2.5	1.4	2.8	7.2	3.1	2.5	0.6	1.7	2.3
0665000	San Bernardino city	9.1	6.8	2.4	3.0	1.4	2.3	7.6	1.9	1.4	0.5	2.4	3.3
0665042	San Buenaventura (Ventura) city, Cal	19.4	14.7	5.0	6.4	3.3	4.7	3.9	1.6	1.4	0.3	1.0	1.3
0665084	San Clemente city	14.3	11.6	3.8	5.6	2.1	2.8	0.0	0.0	0.0	0.0	0.0	0.0
0666000	San Diego city	21.5	14.5	5.1	5.2	4.2	7.0	4.3	2.0	1.6	0.5	1.0	1.3
0667000	San Francisco city	35.1	23.1	8.2	8.0	6.9	12.0	4.0	2.6	2.2	0.4	0.6	0.8
0668000	San Jose city	12.1	8.5	2.9	3.3	2.2	3.7	6.0	3.0	2.4	0.6	1.3	1.7
0668084	San Leandro city	14.9	11.9	4.4	5.5	2.0	3.0	6.1	3.2	2.9	0.4	1.3	1.5
0668196	San Marcos city	14.7	10.5	2.8	4.7	3.0	4.2	5.2	2.6	2.1	0.5	1.2	1.3
0668252	San Mateo city	18.9	13.9	4.9	6.2	2.8	5.0	3.4	1.9	1.6	0.3	0.7	0.7
0668364	San Rafael city	19.4	14.4	4.0	7.1	3.3	5.0	0.0	0.0	0.0	0.0	0.0	0.0
0668378	San Ramon city	10.4	8.1	2.4	3.7	1.9	2.3	1.9	1.4	1.3	0.1	0.3	0.3
0669000	Santa Ana city	6.5	4.2	1.3	1.6	1.2	2.4	11.4	5.1	3.7	1.5	2.5	3.7
0669070	Santa Barbara city	24.9	17.0	5.3	6.8	4.9	7.9	4.0	1.7	1.2	0.5	1.1	1.2
0669084	Santa Clara city	16.9	12.2	5.3	4.1	2.8	4.7	3.9	1.9	1.7	0.3	0.9	1.0
0669088	Santa Clarita city	10.7	8.0	2.7	3.6	1.7	2.7	2.6	1.3	1.1	0.2	0.6	0.7
0669112	Santa Cruz city	33.9	18.3	5.0	6.2	7.1	15.6	0.0	0.0	0.0	0.0	0.0	0.0
0669196	Santa Maria city	8.9	6.7	2.6	3.1	1.0	2.2	7.2	3.4	2.5	0.9	1.6	2.2
0670000	Santa Monica city	41.9	31.8	11.3	13.9	6.6	10.1	0.0	0.0	0.0	0.0	0.0	0.0
0670098	Santa Rosa city	18.7	14.0	4.1	6.5	3.4	4.7	3.9	1.7	1.3	0.4	1.0	1.2
0670224	Santee city	12.5	9.4	2.9	4.3	2.2	3.2	2.1	0.6	0.4	0.2	0.7	0.8
0672016	Simi Valley city	10.7	8.0	2.3	3.8	1.9	2.7	4.4	2.2	1.8	0.5	1.0	1.1
0673080	South Gate city	5.4	4.0	1.2	1.8	1.0	1.4	10.5	4.1	2.9	1.2	2.8	3.6
0673262	South San Francisco city	11.4	8.8	3.1	4.0	1.8	2.5	6.8	3.9	3.0	0.8	1.3	1.7
0673430	South Whittier CDP	5.3	3.7	1.0	1.9	0.8	1.6	8.3	4.9	3.7	1.2	1.7	1.8
0675000	Stockton city	10.3	8.1	3.0	3.7	1.4	2.2	7.0	2.8	2.1	0.7	1.9	2.4
0677000	Sunnyvale city	17.2	12.7	4.9	4.9	3.0	4.5	3.6	1.7	1.4	0.3	0.8	1.1
0678120	Temecula city	8.8	6.1	1.9	2.5	1.7	2.7	4.3	1.6	1.3	0.3	1.1	1.6
0678582	Thousand Oaks city	13.0	10.1	3.1	5.1	2.0	2.9	3.2	1.7	1.1	0.6	0.7	0.9
0680000	Torrance city	14.2	11.7	4.2	5.6	1.9	2.4	2.4	1.3	1.0	0.3	0.5	0.5
0680238	Tracy city	8.1	5.2	1.9	1.8	1.5	2.9	5.4	2.4	1.9	0.5	1.3	1.7
0680644	Tulare city	9.0	6.6	2.2	2.9	1.5	2.4	6.1	2.0	1.4	0.6	1.6	2.5
0680812	Turlock city	12.8	9.4	3.1	4.1	2.2	3.5	3.7	0.9	0.7	0.2	1.1	1.8
0680854	Tustin city	11.5	8.7	2.6	4.2	1.9	2.9	5.6	2.9	2.2	0.7	1.3	1.4
0681204	Union City city	7.1	5.4	1.9	2.5	1.0	1.7	9.1	7.0	5.5	1.5	1.0	1.1
0681344	Upland city	14.3	11.3	3.8	5.4	2.1	3.0	4.6	1.6	1.3	0.4	1.4	1.6
0681554	Vacaville city	13.8	10.2	3.7	4.6	2.0	3.6	3.4	1.4	0.9	0.5	0.9	1.1
0681666	Vallejo city	15.1	11.4	3.8	5.3	2.4	3.6	5.8	2.6	2.1	0.5	1.4	1.8
0682590	Victorville city	7.6	5.3	1.9	2.1	1.3	2.3	8.6	2.5	1.8	0.7	2.4	3.7
0682954	Visalia city	11.3	8.6	3.1	3.9	1.6	2.7	5.3	1.8	1.3	0.5	1.5	2.0
0682996	Vista city	15.7	10.3	3.6	3.3	3.4	5.4	4.7	2.2	1.6	0.6	1.1	1.4
0683346	Walnut Creek city	23.7	19.4	5.2	10.9	3.3	4.3	0.0	0.0	0.0	0.0	0.0	0.0
0683668	Watsonville city	7.1	6.0	2.0	3.3	0.8	1.1	6.2	2.7	1.9	0.8	1.4	2.1
0684200	West Covina city	8.3	6.1	1.9	2.8	1.4	2.2	7.7	3.7	2.9	0.7	1.9	2.2
0684550	Westminster city	9.1	6.7	2.2	3.2	1.3	2.4	7.1	4.0	3.4	0.6	1.3	1.7
0685292	Whittier city	10.9	8.3	2.8	4.0	1.5	2.5	5.3	2.2	1.7	0.5	1.6	1.5
0686328	Woodland city	12.7	10.8	4.0	5.5	1.3	1.9	4.7	1.4	1.2	0.2	1.4	1.9
0686832	Yorba Linda city	7.2	6.0	2.0	3.2	0.8	1.2	2.7	1.6	1.2	0.3	0.6	0.6

Table B-4: Cities with a Population of 50,000 or More—Relationships—*Continued*

State/ place FIPS code	State/place	Total population	Percent of the population in households	Population in family households, percent					
				Percent in family households	Householder in family household, percent	Spouse in family household, percent	Child in family household (biological, adopted, or stepchild)	Other relative in family household	Nonrelatives in family household
	California—cont'd								
0686972	Yuba City city	65,052	98.9	87.4	24.2	16.5	31.7	11.8	3.2
0687042	Yucaipa city	52,309	98.8	87.4	25.0	19.1	34.0	6.3	3.1
0800000	**Colorado**	5,192,076	97.7	79.3	24.5	18.8	28.4	5.5	2.1
0803455	Arvada city	109,590	99.5	82.8	26.9	20.2	28.6	5.0	2.1
0804000	Aurora city	339,256	99.3	83.4	23.5	15.5	32.5	8.6	3.3
0807850	Boulder city	101,871	91.7	50.0	17.1	13.6	16.2	1.7	1.4
0809280	Broomfield city	58,325	99.4	83.9	25.8	21.2	31.3	3.6	2.1
0812415	Castle Rock town	51,503	99.1	88.7	26.9	21.8	34.9	3.5	1.6
0812815	Centennial city	104,116	99.2	87.4	27.3	22.4	31.5	4.4	1.8
0816000	Colorado Springs city	433,619	98.5	80.3	24.9	18.8	29.4	4.9	2.3
0820000	Denver city	634,685	97.6	67.5	20.1	13.9	24.6	7.1	1.8
0827425	Fort Collins city	148,975	95.0	65.8	21.2	16.8	22.5	3.4	1.8
0831660	Grand Junction city	59,778	94.9	73.7	24.6	18.1	23.7	5.1	2.2
0832155	Greeley city	95,338	94.2	77.0	22.8	16.4	28.0	6.2	3.6
0836410	Highlands Ranch CDP	104,369	100.0	90.9	26.8	22.9	36.4	3.2	1.7
0843000	Lakewood city	145,619	97.3	74.1	24.4	17.1	24.9	5.7	2.0
0845970	Longmont city	88,710	99.3	82.9	25.5	19.0	30.8	5.6	2.1
0846465	Loveland city	70,243	99.3	81.3	27.0	21.0	27.9	3.8	1.7
0862000	Pueblo city	107,931	95.7	75.8	23.1	14.7	28.5	7.0	2.5
0877290	Thornton city	124,487	99.6	88.2	24.6	18.8	34.6	7.5	2.7
0883835	Westminster city	109,301	99.6	82.5	25.2	18.6	28.9	6.9	2.9
0900000	**Connecticut**	3,592,264	96.7	81.0	24.9	18.4	30.0	5.8	1.9
0908000	Bridgeport city	146,630	97.0	80.3	21.5	10.4	33.1	12.3	2.9
0908420	Bristol city	60,571	98.7	79.1	25.4	18.5	28.0	5.1	2.1
0918430	Danbury city	82,828	95.6	76.9	22.3	16.0	26.3	9.5	2.7
0922700	East Hartford CDP	51,253	98.8	80.6	25.5	14.3	30.2	8.8	1.9
0937000	Hartford city	125,188	93.5	74.6	20.9	7.2	33.2	10.1	3.2
0946450	Meriden city	60,588	98.3	82.4	26.0	17.1	28.7	7.6	3.0
0947515	Milford city	51,629	99.1	81.1	25.3	20.2	29.6	5.0	1.0
0950370	New Britain city	73,079	95.8	77.0	22.7	12.2	30.5	8.2	3.4
0952000	New Haven city	130,794	92.4	70.1	20.7	9.9	28.5	8.5	2.5
0955990	Norwalk city	87,181	99.1	78.5	24.1	17.9	26.8	7.6	2.2
0973000	Stamford city	125,134	99.0	81.6	23.7	17.5	29.5	7.9	3.1
0974260	Stratford CDP	51,992	99.3	83.2	26.0	19.9	28.7	6.7	2.0
0980000	Waterbury city	109,871	98.2	81.8	23.4	12.4	34.4	8.5	3.1
0982660	West Hartford CDP	63,366	96.8	80.0	25.8	20.2	29.0	3.6	1.5
0982800	West Haven city	55,247	94.6	77.1	23.1	15.5	29.7	6.6	2.2
1000000	**Delaware**	916,929	97.3	81.5	24.7	17.8	28.6	7.7	2.7
1077580	Wilmington city	71,255	96.3	73.6	22.0	8.8	28.0	11.3	3.5
1100000	**District of Columbia**	633,167	93.6	60.0	18.1	9.6	21.9	8.3	2.1
1150000	Washington city	633,167	93.6	60.0	18.1	9.6	21.9	8.3	2.1
1200000	**Florida**	19,319,031	97.8	80.3	23.8	17.2	28.3	8.7	2.4
1200410	Alafaya CDP	77,230	99.8	84.7	24.3	17.8	33.6	6.1	3.0
1207300	Boca Raton city	87,902	96.2	73.2	24.1	19.2	23.7	5.1	1.0
1207875	Boynton Beach city	70,040	98.7	74.8	22.3	15.3	25.5	9.4	2.3
1207950	Bradenton city	50,744	97.1	72.5	21.9	15.3	25.5	8.4	1.3
1208150	Brandon CDP	108,157	97.2	79.8	23.7	16.4	30.9	6.8	1.9
1210275	Cape Coral city	161,692	99.7	86.9	25.2	19.2	31.8	8.5	2.2
1212875	Clearwater city	108,966	97.5	72.5	23.2	15.6	24.8	6.6	2.4
1213275	Coconut Creek city	55,287	99.5	78.1	23.0	17.0	28.5	7.3	2.3
1214400	Coral Springs city	125,170	99.8	90.5	25.0	16.7	37.8	8.6	2.3
1216475	Davie town	95,340	98.8	83.3	23.6	17.2	33.2	7.4	2.0
1216525	Daytona Beach city	61,755	93.9	61.2	19.1	11.7	21.2	7.3	2.0
1216725	Deerfield Beach city	77,267	98.7	73.8	21.9	14.3	25.2	10.7	1.6
1217100	Delray Beach city	62,645	98.5	70.3	21.1	14.9	21.6	10.4	2.3
1217200	Deltona city	85,694	99.8	87.9	24.1	18.4	32.8	10.3	2.3
1224000	Fort Lauderdale city	170,600	98.4	67.4	19.5	12.9	23.8	8.8	2.4
1224125	Fort Myers city	65,911	93.0	72.6	20.1	12.6	25.8	11.5	2.6
1224562	Fountainebleau CDP	53,397	99.9	84.6	23.4	14.1	27.2	16.5	3.3
1225175	Gainesville city	126,653	89.0	47.4	15.2	9.5	16.3	5.0	1.4
1230000	Hialeah city	231,962	99.2	88.8	22.3	13.7	30.7	18.1	4.0
1232000	Hollywood city	145,092	99.2	79.3	22.3	15.2	28.7	10.0	3.2
1232275	Homestead city	63,250	99.4	84.9	20.8	13.4	36.0	11.7	3.0
1235000	Jacksonville city	836,087	97.8	80.0	23.4	15.6	30.7	8.1	2.2
1235875	Jupiter town	57,226	99.4	78.8	25.8	20.9	25.1	5.3	1.7
1236062	Kendale Lakes CDP	59,449	99.6	91.3	24.1	15.4	31.7	16.9	3.2
1236100	Kendall CDP	73,844	99.5	83.2	23.8	17.4	30.5	9.8	1.6
1236950	Kissimmee city	63,317	99.3	85.8	22.5	13.4	34.5	12.2	3.3
1238250	Lakeland city	99,843	95.6	74.9	23.0	15.3	26.1	8.4	2.2
1239425	Largo city	78,007	97.7	69.5	22.7	15.9	22.3	6.1	2.4
1239550	Lauderhill city	69,079	99.1	83.2	21.5	10.3	35.9	11.7	3.8
1239925	Lehigh Acres CDP	107,049	99.8	90.1	22.0	14.0	37.8	12.2	4.1

Table B-4: Cities with a Population of 50,000 or More—Relationships—*Continued*

State/place FIPS code	State/place	Population in nonfamily households						Population in subfamilies as a percent of total population					
		Total population in nonfamily households	Nonfamily householders				Nonrelatives in nonfamily households	Total population in subfamilies	In married couple subfamilies			Parent in a parent-child subfamily	Child in a parent-child subfamily
			Total	Male living alone	Female living alone	Householder living with nonrelatives			Total in married-couple subfamilies	Spouse in a married-couple subfamily	Child in married-couple subfamily		
	California—cont'd												
0686972	Yuba City city.........................	11.5	8.6	3.1	3.8	1.7	2.9	6.6	3.2	2.8	0.5	1.6	1.8
0687042	Yucaipa city...........................	11.4	9.2	3.4	4.3	1.5	2.2	5.1	1.8	1.3	0.5	1.5	1.7
0800000	**Colorado**	18.5	13.8	5.1	5.8	3.0	4.6	2.9	1.0	0.8	0.2	0.9	1.0
0803455	Arvada city............................	16.7	12.9	4.8	5.7	2.4	3.8	2.7	0.8	0.5	0.2	0.9	1.0
0804000	Aurora city............................	16.0	12.6	4.6	5.7	2.3	3.3	5.0	1.7	1.3	0.3	1.6	1.7
0807850	Boulder city...........................	41.7	23.5	6.3	7.2	10.1	18.2	0.0	0.0	0.0	0.0	0.0	0.0
0809280	Broomfield city.......................	15.5	12.7	4.8	5.4	2.6	2.7	2.0	1.0	0.9	0.1	0.4	0.5
0812415	Castle Rock town.....................	10.4	7.9	2.3	3.9	1.8	2.4	0.0	0.0	0.0	0.0	0.0	0.0
0812815	Centennial city........................	11.7	9.3	2.8	4.9	1.6	2.4	2.3	0.8	0.7	0.1	0.7	0.8
0816000	Colorado Springs city...............	18.2	14.0	5.2	6.2	2.7	4.2	2.7	0.9	0.7	0.2	0.8	1.0
0820000	Denver city............................	30.1	22.4	8.2	9.1	5.1	7.7	3.7	1.4	1.0	0.4	1.0	1.3
0827425	Fort Collins city......................	29.2	17.4	4.3	5.8	7.3	11.8	1.9	0.7	0.5	0.2	0.5	0.7
0831660	Grand Junction city..................	21.2	15.9	5.5	6.9	3.5	5.3	2.5	1.1	0.7	0.4	0.6	0.8
0832155	Greeley city...........................	17.2	11.9	3.8	5.1	2.9	5.3	3.4	1.2	0.9	0.3	0.8	1.3
0836410	Highlands Ranch CDP................	9.0	7.3	2.4	3.6	1.4	1.7	1.3	0.5	0.3	0.1	0.4	0.4
0843000	Lakewood city........................	23.2	17.8	6.4	7.7	3.7	5.4	2.3	0.9	0.7	0.2	0.7	0.8
0845970	Longmont city........................	16.4	12.8	5.0	5.1	2.7	3.6	3.3	1.1	0.9	0.2	1.1	1.1
0846465	Loveland city.........................	17.9	14.5	4.5	7.3	2.7	3.4	2.5	0.9	0.7	0.3	0.7	0.9
0862000	Pueblo city............................	19.8	16.3	6.1	7.7	2.5	3.5	3.2	0.8	0.7	0.1	1.2	1.2
0877290	Thornton city.........................	11.4	9.0	3.4	3.8	1.8	2.4	4.1	1.6	1.2	0.5	1.1	1.3
0883835	Westminster city......................	17.1	13.2	4.5	5.8	3.0	3.9	3.5	2.1	1.6	0.5	0.7	0.7
0900000	**Connecticut**.........................	15.7	12.6	4.5	6.0	2.1	3.1	2.8	1.0	0.8	0.2	0.9	0.9
0908000	Bridgeport city........................	16.7	12.3	4.6	5.4	2.4	4.3	5.5	1.2	0.9	0.2	1.9	2.4
0908420	Bristol city.............................	19.6	16.0	5.3	7.9	2.8	3.6	2.7	1.2	1.0	0.2	0.7	0.8
0918430	Danbury city..........................	18.8	12.9	4.2	5.6	3.1	5.9	4.2	1.3	0.9	0.3	1.4	1.5
0922700	East Hartford CDP....................	18.3	15.0	6.9	5.7	2.4	3.2	0.0	0.0	0.0	0.0	0.0	0.0
0937000	Hartford city..........................	18.9	15.1	6.1	6.5	2.4	3.8	5.4	0.8	0.6	0.2	2.1	2.4
0946450	Meriden city..........................	15.9	13.2	5.6	5.6	2.0	2.7	4.1	0.9	0.6	0.3	1.5	1.7
0947515	Milford city...........................	18.0	15.1	4.5	8.2	2.4	3.0	2.6	1.0	0.6	0.4	0.8	0.7
0950370	New Britain city......................	18.9	14.7	5.3	6.9	2.5	4.1	3.9	1.2	1.1	0.0	1.3	1.5
0952000	New Haven city.......................	22.3	17.4	6.7	7.6	3.1	4.9	3.5	0.6	0.4	0.2	1.4	1.4
0955990	Norwalk city..........................	20.6	16.6	6.3	7.7	2.6	4.0	3.5	1.4	1.1	0.3	1.0	1.1
0973000	Stamford city.........................	17.4	13.3	4.0	6.8	2.5	4.1	3.0	1.2	1.1	0.1	0.9	0.9
0974260	Stratford CDP.........................	16.1	13.7	4.7	7.1	2.0	2.4	4.1	2.8	2.1	0.7	0.6	0.7
0980000	Waterbury city........................	16.5	13.6	5.3	6.1	2.1	2.9	3.7	1.2	1.0	0.2	1.2	1.3
0982660	West Hartford CDP...................	16.8	13.5	3.6	7.5	2.5	3.3	1.6	0.4	0.4	0.0	0.6	0.6
0982800	West Haven city......................	17.4	13.8	5.5	6.1	2.2	3.6	0.0	0.0	0.0	0.0	0.0	0.0
1000000	**Delaware**	15.8	12.1	4.0	5.8	2.4	3.7	4.3	1.2	0.9	0.3	1.4	1.7
1077580	Wilmington city......................	22.8	18.4	6.3	9.0	3.1	4.4	6.1	0.8	0.7	0.1	2.3	2.9
1100000	**District of Columbia**..............	33.6	24.2	8.1	10.9	5.3	9.4	3.2	0.3	0.3	0.1	1.3	1.5
1150000	Washington city......................	33.6	24.2	8.1	10.9	5.3	9.4	3.2	0.3	0.3	0.1	1.3	1.5
1200000	**Florida**..............................	17.5	13.3	4.8	6.1	2.4	4.1	4.2	1.4	1.2	0.2	1.4	1.4
1200410	Alafaya CDP...........................	15.1	9.9	3.7	3.1	3.1	5.2	0.0	0.0	0.0	0.0	0.0	0.0
1207300	Boca Raton city.......................	22.9	16.8	6.0	7.6	3.1	6.2	0.0	0.0	0.0	0.0	0.0	0.0
1207875	Boynton Beach city...................	23.9	18.9	6.4	9.3	3.3	5.0	4.3	2.0	1.6	0.4	1.3	1.1
1207950	Bradenton city........................	24.6	19.1	6.3	9.4	3.4	5.5	3.4	0.8	0.7	0.2	1.5	1.1
1208150	Brandon CDP..........................	17.4	12.7	3.9	5.9	2.9	4.7	3.6	1.1	0.9	0.2	1.3	1.2
1210275	Cape Coral city.......................	12.8	9.6	3.4	4.2	1.9	3.2	4.5	2.3	2.1	0.2	1.4	0.8
1212875	Clearwater city.......................	24.9	19.7	7.1	9.8	2.9	5.2	3.5	0.8	0.7	0.0	1.5	1.2
1213275	Coconut Creek city...................	21.4	16.5	5.4	8.1	3.0	4.9	0.0	0.0	0.0	0.0	0.0	0.0
1214400	Coral Springs city....................	9.3	7.2	2.8	3.1	1.3	2.1	4.7	2.2	1.8	0.4	1.4	1.2
1216475	Davie town............................	15.5	10.7	4.0	4.0	2.7	4.9	3.6	1.8	1.6	0.2	1.0	0.8
1216525	Daytona Beach city..................	32.7	22.9	8.7	9.4	4.8	9.8	0.0	0.0	0.0	0.0	0.0	0.0
1216725	Deerfield Beach city..................	24.9	18.9	6.1	9.5	3.3	6.0	4.8	1.9	1.7	0.2	1.4	1.4
1217100	Delray Beach city.....................	28.2	21.7	7.5	10.0	4.2	6.5	5.1	0.9	0.8	0.1	2.0	2.2
1217200	Deltona city...........................	11.9	8.9	3.1	4.0	1.8	2.9	6.3	1.5	1.0	0.5	2.2	2.6
1224000	Fort Lauderdale city..................	31.0	22.9	9.8	8.1	5.0	8.1	4.3	0.8	0.7	0.1	1.7	1.9
1224125	Fort Myers city........................	20.4	15.3	5.8	7.1	2.4	5.1	5.8	2.4	2.2	0.2	1.8	1.6
1224562	Fountainebleau CDP..................	15.3	10.2	2.1	5.2	2.9	5.2	5.6	3.7	3.3	0.4	1.1	0.8
1225175	Gainesville city.......................	41.6	22.6	6.9	7.3	8.3	19.0	1.9	0.5	0.5	0.0	0.7	0.7
1230000	Hialeah city...........................	10.4	7.6	2.5	3.6	1.5	2.8	8.1	4.1	3.3	0.7	2.0	2.0
1232000	Hollywood city.......................	19.9	15.4	5.9	6.5	2.9	4.5	5.1	2.6	2.4	0.2	1.2	1.2
1232275	Homestead city.......................	14.5	9.9	3.5	4.1	2.3	4.6	0.0	0.0	0.0	0.0	0.0	0.0
1235000	Jacksonville city......................	17.8	14.0	5.2	6.5	2.3	3.8	4.4	1.1	0.9	0.2	1.5	1.7
1235875	Jupiter town...........................	20.7	15.4	5.0	7.4	2.9	5.3	0.0	0.0	0.0	0.0	0.0	0.0
1236062	Kendale Lakes CDP...................	8.4	6.1	1.8	3.2	1.1	2.3	6.0	3.1	2.8	0.3	1.5	1.3
1236100	Kendall CDP...........................	16.4	13.8	4.8	7.1	1.9	2.6	3.8	2.1	1.6	0.5	0.9	0.8
1236950	Kissimmee city........................	13.4	9.4	4.1	3.1	2.2	4.1	6.2	1.7	1.7	0.1	2.3	2.2
1238250	Lakeland city.........................	20.7	16.1	5.2	8.0	2.9	4.6	4.5	0.7	0.6	0.0	1.9	2.0
1239425	Largo city.............................	28.2	22.7	7.9	10.6	4.2	5.5	0.0	0.0	0.0	0.0	0.0	0.0
1239550	Lauderhill city........................	15.9	12.6	4.2	6.5	1.9	3.2	5.1	1.0	0.7	0.2	2.0	2.0
1239925	Lehigh Acres CDP.....................	9.8	7.0	2.6	3.0	1.5	2.8	4.9	1.8	1.7	0.1	1.9	1.3

State/ place FIPS code	State/place	Total population	Percent of the population in households	Population in family households, percent					
				Percent in family households	Householder in family household, percent	Spouse in family household, percent	Child in family household (biological, adopted, or stepchild)	Other relative in family household	Nonrelatives in family household
	Florida—cont'd								
1243125	Margate city...............	54,881	99.7	79.4	23.3	16.0	28.7	9.0	2.3
1243975	Melbourne city............	77,033	97.2	73.6	23.0	15.8	25.4	7.3	2.1
1245000	Miami city.................	414,144	97.7	76.5	20.5	11.3	27.5	14.1	3.1
1245025	Miami Beach city.........	90,574	98.9	64.9	20.3	13.7	20.8	7.9	2.0
1245060	Miami Gardens city.......	110,703	98.8	90.1	21.0	10.3	37.3	18.5	3.0
1245975	Miramar city..............	128,016	99.9	91.0	23.4	14.9	36.1	14.1	2.5
1249450	North Miami city.........	60,673	97.2	83.4	18.7	10.9	35.1	15.4	3.3
1249675	North Port city...........	58,427	99.8	82.4	25.5	19.7	29.0	5.4	2.7
1250750	Ocala city.................	57,104	94.4	74.5	22.8	13.7	28.9	6.5	2.6
1253000	Orlando city..............	249,774	98.0	70.8	20.9	12.0	27.8	7.4	2.5
1254000	Palm Bay city.............	104,180	99.4	85.0	24.6	17.2	29.9	10.4	2.9
1254200	Palm Coast city..........	77,618	99.8	85.7	24.9	20.4	28.2	7.6	4.6
1254350	Palm Harbor CDP.........	59,290	99.0	77.8	26.8	21.6	23.3	5.2	0.9
1255775	Pembroke Pines city......	159,754	99.5	86.3	24.5	17.6	32.4	9.5	2.3
1255925	Pensacola city............	52,367	98.8	75.0	22.7	14.8	28.6	7.7	1.2
1256825	Pine Hills CDP............	67,604	99.8	87.7	21.6	11.2	36.9	13.3	4.6
1257425	Plantation city...........	88,355	99.5	83.2	24.3	17.6	29.9	8.3	3.1
1257900	Poinciana CDP............	55,444	100.0	92.2	24.6	17.4	35.1	12.9	2.2
1258050	Pompano Beach city......	103,040	96.3	71.6	20.7	12.8	26.2	9.2	2.6
1258350	Port Charlotte CDP.......	54,081	99.1	80.2	25.6	19.9	24.0	8.3	2.5
1258575	Port Orange city.........	56,821	99.7	78.8	25.9	20.3	25.3	5.8	1.5
1258715	Port St. Lucie city........	169,051	99.6	88.1	25.3	19.0	33.2	8.4	2.1
1260950	Riverview CDP............	73,092	99.7	87.3	24.9	19.3	34.1	7.3	1.8
1263000	St. Petersburg city.......	247,742	97.6	73.0	22.4	14.7	26.1	7.4	2.4
1263650	Sanford city..............	54,869	97.3	80.4	20.1	12.1	34.6	11.1	2.5
1264175	Sarasota city.............	52,888	93.9	66.0	21.7	15.6	20.2	5.7	2.8
1268350	Spring Hill CDP...........	102,706	98.8	84.9	26.7	20.0	29.2	7.3	1.8
1269700	Sunrise city..............	88,427	99.3	84.6	23.9	16.0	31.2	11.2	2.3
1270600	Tallahassee city..........	185,675	92.9	58.1	18.9	11.9	20.8	4.4	2.1
1270675	Tamarac city.............	62,479	99.6	78.9	24.5	15.7	27.5	9.1	2.1
1270700	Tamiami CDP.............	54,267	99.4	91.8	23.4	16.7	32.0	17.0	2.7
1271000	Tampa city...............	349,429	96.6	72.0	21.7	13.6	27.3	7.3	2.2
1271569	The Hammocks CDP......	54,329	99.6	91.0	23.2	17.2	35.6	12.8	2.3
1272145	Town 'n' Country CDP....	80,136	99.7	79.7	24.0	16.0	27.5	9.9	2.3
1275812	Wellington village........	58,835	100.0	90.5	26.3	21.7	35.3	5.3	1.9
1276582	Weston city..............	67,600	100.0	93.2	25.9	21.9	39.5	4.8	1.2
1276600	West Palm Beach city....	101,715	97.2	68.7	20.8	12.5	25.1	8.1	2.3
1300000	**Georgia**...............	9,905,993	97.4	82.7	24.1	16.9	31.2	8.4	2.0
1301052	Albany city...............	77,006	95.0	77.3	22.9	11.2	28.9	11.9	2.4
1301696	Alpharetta city...........	61,234	99.9	86.7	25.6	21.2	35.4	3.9	0.5
1303440	Athens-Clarke County.....	118,711	91.5	57.8	17.1	11.1	22.1	6.4	1.1
1304000	Atlanta city..............	441,064	92.9	61.2	17.6	10.1	23.0	8.9	1.6
1304204	Augusta-Richmond County..	196,381	95.7	78.3	21.3	11.8	32.6	10.4	2.2
1310944	Brookhaven city..........	50,114	98.2	67.1	20.6	16.5	22.5	5.2	2.3
1319000	Columbus city............	198,498	94.3	78.4	23.1	14.0	31.9	7.4	1.9
1342425	Johns Creek city..........	81,494	100.0	93.0	26.4	22.3	37.7	6.1	0.5
1349000	Macon city...............	91,043	94.3	77.0	21.3	9.9	33.2	10.8	1.7
1349756	Marietta city.............	58,356	95.2	71.9	22.2	14.5	24.8	7.4	3.0
1367284	Roswell city..............	92,963	99.5	84.2	24.9	19.8	31.4	5.7	2.4
1368516	Sandy Springs city.......	98,702	99.6	73.1	22.5	16.8	26.6	5.5	1.7
1369000	Savannah city............	141,786	94.2	72.1	20.6	11.7	28.4	9.9	1.5
1371492	Smyrna city..............	52,699	99.6	74.6	23.9	16.8	26.2	5.4	2.3
1378800	Valdosta city.............	56,757	96.0	67.4	20.0	10.9	28.7	6.2	1.7
1380508	Warner Robins city.......	71,683	99.6	83.8	23.4	15.3	34.7	8.5	1.8
1500000	**Hawaii**................	1,390,348	96.9	83.6	22.4	16.7	28.0	13.4	3.2
1571550	Urban Honolulu CDP......	344,907	96.0	75.5	21.3	15.1	23.3	13.4	2.4
1600000	**Idaho**.................	1,597,222	98.2	83.3	25.3	20.1	31.0	4.7	2.2
1608830	Boise City city...........	211,880	98.5	75.5	24.5	18.3	26.2	4.5	2.0
1639700	Idaho Falls city..........	57,992	97.9	84.4	25.1	18.2	34.0	4.6	2.6
1652120	Meridian city.............	80,643	99.6	90.7	26.5	21.5	36.0	4.2	2.5
1656260	Nampa city...............	84,361	97.9	86.3	23.8	17.7	36.5	5.3	3.1
1664090	Pocatello city............	54,542	97.2	77.7	23.4	17.4	31.0	3.9	1.9
1700000	**Illinois**...............	12,868,770	97.7	81.7	24.2	17.8	30.9	6.9	2.0
1702154	Arlington Heights village..	75,595	98.7	83.3	26.7	23.1	29.7	3.1	0.8
1703012	Aurora city...............	198,312	99.2	88.2	22.9	17.0	36.4	9.1	2.8
1705573	Berwyn city..............	56,747	99.8	88.9	22.6	14.8	36.6	12.0	2.9
1706613	Bloomington city.........	77,901	97.2	75.9	23.6	18.0	28.6	4.1	1.7
1707133	Bolingbrook village.......	73,809	99.6	92.5	23.9	18.6	37.6	10.2	2.2
1712385	Champaign city...........	82,641	90.1	56.3	18.3	13.6	19.9	3.5	0.9
1714000	Chicago city..............	2,711,992	98.0	75.6	20.6	12.1	29.3	11.3	2.3
1714351	Cicero town..............	84,058	99.5	92.9	20.6	13.1	42.6	13.5	3.1
1718823	Decatur city..............	75,297	95.6	73.6	23.9	15.3	26.2	5.6	2.6
1719642	Des Plaines city..........	58,937	98.6	82.6	24.7	20.5	29.5	6.0	1.9

Table B-4: Cities with a Population of 50,000 or More—Relationships—*Continued*

State/place FIPS code	State/place	Population in nonfamily households						Population in subfamilies as a percent of total population					
		Total population in nonfamily households	Nonfamily householders				Nonrelatives in nonfamily households	Total population in subfamilies	In married couple subfamilies			Parent in a parent-child subfamily	Child in a parent-child subfamily
			Total	Male living alone	Female living alone	Householder living with nonrelatives			Total in married-couple subfamilies	Spouse in a married-couple subfamily	Child in married-couple subfamily		
	Florida—cont'd												
1243125	Margate city	20.3	15.9	5.3	8.7	1.9	4.4	4.2	0.9	0.8	0.1	1.8	1.5
1243975	Melbourne city	23.6	19.4	6.9	9.5	3.0	4.2	3.0	1.2	0.9	0.2	1.1	0.7
1245000	Miami city	21.2	16.2	6.9	6.5	2.8	5.0	5.4	1.5	1.2	0.3	1.9	1.9
1245025	Miami Beach city	34.0	26.9	12.6	9.7	4.5	7.1	24.5	7.0	5.6	1.4	8.6	8.9
1245060	Miami Gardens city	8.7	7.3	2.6	3.9	0.9	1.4	20.0	5.7	4.6	1.1	7.1	7.3
1245975	Miramar city	8.9	7.0	3.0	2.8	1.2	1.8	6.1	2.4	1.9	0.4	2.0	1.7
1249450	North Miami city	13.8	10.2	3.8	4.2	2.2	3.7	5.5	1.6	0.8	0.8	2.0	1.9
1249675	North Port city	17.4	12.7	4.9	5.0	2.9	4.8	0.0	0.0	0.0	0.0	0.0	0.0
1250750	Ocala city	19.8	16.1	5.0	8.6	2.4	3.8	0.0	0.0	0.0	0.0	0.0	0.0
1253000	Orlando city	27.2	19.7	7.2	8.1	4.3	7.5	3.5	0.8	0.6	0.1	1.4	1.3
1254000	Palm Bay city	14.4	11.4	4.2	5.3	1.9	3.0	6.9	2.9	2.0	0.9	2.1	1.9
1254200	Palm Coast city	14.1	10.2	2.5	5.8	1.9	3.9	3.0	1.2	1.1	0.1	1.1	0.7
1254350	Palm Harbor CDP	21.2	17.2	5.2	9.2	2.8	4.0	0.0	0.0	0.0	0.0	0.0	0.0
1255775	Pembroke Pines city	13.2	11.0	3.6	6.2	1.2	2.2	4.1	2.3	2.1	0.1	0.9	0.9
1255925	Pensacola city	23.9	19.0	6.6	9.0	3.4	4.9	4.1	2.2	1.8	0.5	0.8	1.1
1256825	Pine Hills CDP	12.1	8.0	2.5	3.9	1.6	4.1	5.8	1.5	1.2	0.3	2.3	2.0
1257425	Plantation city	16.4	12.8	4.3	6.0	2.5	3.6	3.5	1.4	1.2	0.1	1.2	1.0
1257900	Poinciana CDP	7.7	6.0	2.2	2.9	0.9	1.8	0.0	0.0	0.0	0.0	0.0	0.0
1258050	Pompano Beach city	24.8	18.5	7.2	8.0	3.3	6.3	4.0	1.1	1.0	0.1	1.6	1.3
1258350	Port Charlotte CDP	18.9	15.4	4.6	8.7	2.1	3.5	4.8	1.8	1.4	0.3	1.7	1.3
1258575	Port Orange city	20.9	16.2	5.2	8.3	2.8	4.6	0.0	0.0	0.0	0.0	0.0	0.0
1258715	Port St. Lucie city	11.5	8.7	3.1	3.9	1.7	2.7	4.2	1.2	1.0	0.2	1.6	1.4
1260950	Riverview CDP	12.4	8.7	2.6	3.8	2.3	3.7	2.5	0.4	0.4	0.1	1.0	1.1
1263000	St. Petersburg city	24.5	19.9	7.6	9.0	3.3	4.7	3.6	0.6	0.5	0.1	1.5	1.5
1263650	Sanford city	16.9	12.7	4.9	5.6	2.2	4.2	6.7	1.9	1.6	0.3	2.7	2.1
1264175	Sarasota city	27.8	21.4	6.5	10.3	4.6	6.4	0.0	0.0	0.0	0.0	0.0	0.0
1268350	Spring Hill CDP	13.9	11.4	4.3	5.3	1.8	2.5	3.6	1.1	0.8	0.3	1.2	1.3
1269700	Sunrise city	14.7	11.9	3.6	6.7	1.6	2.8	5.0	1.9	1.7	0.1	1.7	1.4
1270600	Tallahassee city	34.8	20.8	5.5	7.5	7.8	14.1	1.4	0.2	0.2	0.0	0.5	0.8
1270675	Tamarac city	20.7	17.6	5.9	9.7	1.9	3.1	4.3	0.6	0.6	0.0	1.5	2.3
1270700	Tamiami CDP	7.5	5.0	1.8	2.0	1.2	2.5	8.6	5.4	4.6	0.8	1.8	1.4
1271000	Tampa city	24.6	18.6	7.2	7.8	3.6	5.9	2.8	0.6	0.5	0.1	1.1	1.1
1271569	The Hammocks CDP	8.5	6.3	2.5	2.7	1.1	2.3	5.6	3.2	2.5	0.6	1.4	1.1
1272145	Town 'n' Country CDP	20.0	13.1	4.3	5.0	3.8	6.9	4.4	1.3	1.3	0.0	1.4	1.7
1275812	Wellington village	9.5	7.3	1.6	4.3	1.4	2.2	0.0	0.0	0.0	0.0	0.0	0.0
1276582	Weston city	6.8	5.2	1.6	2.6	1.0	1.6	0.0	0.0	0.0	0.0	0.0	0.0
1276600	West Palm Beach city	28.5	19.5	6.8	8.6	4.0	9.0	3.8	0.6	0.6	0.0	1.6	1.6
1300000	**Georgia**	14.7	11.5	4.2	5.4	1.9	3.2	4.3	1.1	0.9	0.2	1.5	1.7
1301052	Albany city	17.7	14.8	5.2	7.6	2.0	3.0	4.4	0.5	0.4	0.1	1.6	2.3
1301696	Alpharetta city	13.2	11.1	3.9	6.0	1.2	2.1	0.0	0.0	0.0	0.0	0.0	0.0
1303440	Athens-Clarke County	33.7	17.7	4.5	7.4	5.8	16.0	2.7	1.0	0.8	0.2	0.9	0.8
1304000	Atlanta city	31.7	23.5	9.4	9.8	4.3	8.2	3.5	0.5	0.3	0.1	1.5	1.6
1304204	Augusta-Richmond County	17.4	14.2	5.6	6.7	1.9	3.2	4.5	0.3	0.2	0.1	2.0	2.2
1310944	Brookhaven city	31.1	23.1	7.6	10.0	5.6	8.0	0.0	0.0	0.0	0.0	0.0	0.0
1319000	Columbus city	15.9	12.9	4.9	6.4	1.6	3.0	4.1	0.5	0.4	0.1	1.8	1.8
1342425	Johns Creek city	7.0	5.9	2.1	3.1	0.8	1.1	0.0	0.0	0.0	0.0	0.0	0.0
1349000	Macon city	17.3	14.5	5.0	7.6	1.8	2.8	5.3	0.3	0.3	0.0	2.3	2.7
1349756	Marietta city	23.3	17.9	6.0	8.2	3.7	5.4	0.0	0.0	0.0	0.0	0.0	0.0
1367284	Roswell city	15.3	12.1	4.2	6.3	1.6	3.2	1.2	0.8	0.7	0.1	0.3	0.2
1368516	Sandy Springs city	26.6	20.4	6.8	9.9	3.7	6.1	0.0	0.0	0.0	0.0	0.0	0.0
1369000	Savannah city	22.1	16.5	5.9	7.2	3.3	5.6	4.7	0.8	0.6	0.1	1.8	2.0
1371492	Smyrna city	25.0	20.3	6.5	9.9	3.9	4.7	0.0	0.0	0.0	0.0	0.0	0.0
1378800	Valdosta city	28.6	17.8	6.1	6.4	5.3	10.8	0.0	0.0	0.0	0.0	0.0	0.0
1380508	Warner Robins city	15.8	14.1	6.3	6.8	1.1	1.7	4.6	1.0	0.8	0.2	1.7	1.8
1500000	**Hawaii**	13.3	9.9	3.9	3.9	2.2	3.4	8.6	5.1	3.6	1.6	1.5	2.0
1571550	Urban Honolulu CDP	20.6	15.8	6.3	6.3	3.2	4.8	7.6	5.0	3.5	1.5	1.1	1.6
1600000	**Idaho**	14.8	11.2	4.0	4.9	2.3	3.6	2.8	1.1	0.8	0.3	0.8	0.9
1608830	Boise City city	23.0	16.7	5.4	7.2	4.1	6.3	2.3	0.8	0.6	0.2	0.7	0.8
1639700	Idaho Falls city	13.5	11.2	4.4	5.1	1.7	2.3	2.2	1.0	0.6	0.3	0.6	0.6
1652120	Meridian city	8.9	7.5	1.8	4.8	0.9	1.3	0.0	0.0	0.0	0.0	0.0	0.0
1656260	Nampa city	11.6	9.3	3.1	4.6	1.6	2.3	3.8	1.6	1.1	0.5	1.0	1.2
1664090	Pocatello city	19.6	14.4	5.1	6.4	2.9	5.2	2.2	1.1	0.7	0.4	0.5	0.6
1700000	**Illinois**	15.9	12.8	4.7	6.0	2.1	3.1	3.8	1.2	1.0	0.3	1.1	1.4
1702154	Arlington Heights village	15.4	13.2	4.3	7.1	1.8	2.2	0.0	0.0	0.0	0.0	0.0	0.0
1703012	Aurora city	11.0	8.1	3.2	3.4	1.6	2.9	5.6	2.1	1.7	0.4	1.5	2.0
1705573	Berwyn city	10.9	8.9	4.2	3.5	1.3	2.0	8.5	2.3	1.9	0.4	2.9	3.3
1706613	Bloomington city	21.3	16.0	5.6	6.8	3.5	5.3	1.8	0.1	0.0	0.0	0.8	0.9
1707133	Bolingbrook village	7.1	5.6	2.3	2.3	0.9	1.5	6.1	3.1	2.2	0.9	1.4	1.6
1712385	Champaign city	33.8	21.0	7.6	6.9	6.5	12.8	0.0	0.0	0.0	0.0	0.0	0.0
1714000	Chicago city	22.4	17.2	6.4	7.5	3.3	5.1	5.7	1.5	1.2	0.3	1.8	2.3
1714351	Cicero town	6.6	4.9	2.5	1.5	1.0	1.7	7.6	3.6	2.7	0.9	1.8	2.2
1718823	Decatur city	22.0	18.0	7.0	8.6	2.4	4.0	4.5	1.0	0.8	0.2	1.5	2.0
1719642	Des Plaines city	16.1	13.9	5.3	6.8	1.7	2.2	2.5	0.9	0.7	0.2	0.7	0.8

Table B-4: Cities with a Population of 50,000 or More—Relationships—*Continued*

State/ place FIPS code	State/place	Total population	Percent of the population in households	Population in family households, percent					
				Percent in family households	Householder in family household, percent	Spouse in family household, percent	Child in family household (biological, adopted, or stepchild)	Other relative in family household	Nonrelatives in family household
	Illinois—cont'd								
1723074	Elgin city..................	110,603	98.3	86.6	21.6	15.6	36.3	10.8	2.4
1724582	Evanston city..................	75,310	90.6	67.6	20.7	15.6	24.7	5.4	1.3
1735411	Hoffman Estates village..................	52,342	99.6	89.9	27.1	22.0	32.5	7.3	1.0
1738570	Joliet city..................	147,738	98.3	87.4	22.9	16.2	37.6	7.8	2.8
1751089	Mount Prospect village..................	54,596	99.7	86.5	26.2	22.0	32.1	5.5	0.8
1751622	Naperville city..................	143,940	98.3	89.0	26.2	22.7	35.8	3.3	0.9
1753234	Normal town..................	54,487	89.4	58.8	18.2	13.8	22.5	3.3	1.0
1754820	Oak Lawn village..................	56,975	99.0	83.1	25.0	18.8	31.4	6.3	1.6
1754885	Oak Park village..................	51,976	99.0	79.4	24.7	19.4	30.2	3.5	1.5
1756640	Orland Park village..................	57,538	99.2	87.1	27.2	22.9	31.2	5.0	0.9
1757225	Palatine village..................	69,096	99.7	84.3	24.8	18.8	31.8	6.2	2.8
1759000	Peoria city..................	115,814	96.6	75.3	23.2	15.0	29.6	5.5	2.0
1765000	Rockford city..................	151,272	97.5	79.9	23.8	14.9	32.0	6.5	2.8
1768003	Schaumburg village..................	74,541	99.4	79.8	24.7	20.0	27.9	6.1	1.0
1770122	Skokie village..................	65,079	98.8	87.8	25.4	19.4	30.5	11.6	0.9
1772000	Springfield city..................	117,008	96.7	73.5	24.1	15.7	26.4	4.7	2.6
1775484	Tinley Park village..................	56,867	99.9	87.3	26.1	21.0	33.3	6.1	0.9
1779293	Waukegan city..................	88,963	97.7	86.2	22.9	14.4	35.4	10.8	2.7
1781048	Wheaton city..................	53,442	94.6	80.7	24.5	20.6	30.4	4.2	1.0
1800000	**Indiana**..................	6,541,673	97.1	81.1	25.2	18.7	29.7	5.3	2.2
1801468	Anderson city..................	55,638	95.2	73.5	23.3	14.2	26.7	6.7	2.7
1805860	Bloomington city..................	80,385	82.9	40.8	13.5	9.4	13.6	2.6	1.6
1810342	Carmel city..................	83,797	99.5	88.9	27.8	24.1	33.6	2.7	0.7
1820728	Elkhart city..................	51,640	98.6	79.7	23.3	12.7	32.4	6.5	4.8
1822000	Evansville city..................	120,250	96.1	74.0	23.9	15.3	26.4	6.1	2.3
1823278	Fishers town..................	82,238	100.0	90.0	25.9	21.8	37.2	3.4	1.6
1825000	Fort Wayne city..................	254,606	98.1	78.7	24.1	16.1	31.0	5.1	2.3
1827000	Gary city..................	78,991	99.0	81.7	23.3	9.1	36.3	10.4	2.5
1829898	Greenwood city..................	52,783	99.1	81.6	25.1	19.1	29.0	6.3	2.1
1831000	Hammond city..................	79,562	98.8	84.2	22.8	13.8	36.0	9.5	2.2
1836003	Indianapolis city..................	833,900	98.1	77.3	23.0	14.4	29.8	7.1	3.0
1840392	Kokomo city..................	56,195	98.2	77.4	25.8	17.7	27.0	4.2	2.7
1840788	Lafayette city..................	70,156	98.1	74.5	24.2	16.2	27.2	4.5	2.5
1851876	Muncie city..................	69,868	89.0	58.1	19.8	12.8	19.9	4.1	1.5
1854180	Noblesville city..................	57,260	98.7	84.4	25.8	21.4	32.6	2.9	1.6
1871000	South Bend city..................	100,157	97.6	75.8	22.7	13.8	30.8	6.2	2.3
1875428	Terre Haute city..................	60,763	85.3	65.3	19.4	12.9	24.3	5.3	3.4
1900000	**Iowa**..................	3,076,519	96.7	78.9	25.8	20.3	27.5	3.4	1.8
1901855	Ames city..................	61,035	86.8	47.3	16.6	14.1	14.6	1.3	0.7
1912000	Cedar Rapids city..................	128,122	97.3	74.9	23.6	17.5	27.1	4.7	1.9
1916860	Council Bluffs city..................	62,152	96.6	77.8	24.5	16.1	28.2	5.9	3.1
1919000	Davenport city..................	101,321	97.1	75.7	23.0	16.0	29.7	4.7	2.3
1921000	Des Moines city..................	206,571	97.2	77.7	23.6	15.4	29.1	7.0	2.6
1922395	Dubuque city..................	58,032	92.8	68.8	22.7	16.6	24.7	3.1	1.6
1938595	Iowa City city..................	70,304	90.3	53.3	18.1	13.4	18.0	2.5	1.2
1973335	Sioux City city..................	82,658	96.6	79.3	23.8	15.9	30.2	6.0	3.3
1982425	Waterloo city..................	68,341	98.4	75.4	23.6	16.5	27.6	5.5	2.2
1983910	West Des Moines city..................	59,644	99.4	77.6	25.3	20.3	27.6	3.7	0.7
2000000	**Kansas**..................	2,882,966	97.3	80.6	25.2	19.5	29.4	4.6	1.9
2036000	Kansas City city..................	147,348	99.3	82.0	22.9	13.5	33.2	9.4	3.0
2038900	Lawrence city..................	89,825	90.9	59.4	19.3	14.1	20.0	3.9	2.0
2044250	Manhattan city..................	55,483	89.0	53.5	17.6	13.9	17.6	2.3	2.1
2052575	Olathe city..................	130,057	98.8	86.8	26.0	21.3	34.0	4.1	1.3
2053775	Overland Park city..................	178,731	99.2	81.8	26.7	21.1	29.4	3.1	1.4
2064500	Shawnee city..................	63,636	99.3	84.7	25.7	21.1	33.1	3.0	1.9
2071000	Topeka city..................	127,911	96.8	74.7	23.4	16.4	27.4	5.5	2.0
2079000	Wichita city..................	385,154	98.4	80.2	23.9	16.9	31.6	6.1	1.7
2100000	**Kentucky**..................	4,380,635	97.1	81.4	25.8	18.9	28.5	6.0	2.1
2108902	Bowling Green city..................	60,515	89.8	64.2	20.5	12.1	24.3	4.6	2.8
2146027	Lexington-Fayette..................	304,998	95.8	71.7	23.3	16.5	24.9	5.1	1.9
2148006	Louisville/Jefferson County..................	605,429	97.8	78.0	24.3	15.7	29.1	6.7	2.1
2158620	Owensboro city..................	58,082	96.7	77.2	24.3	17.3	27.7	5.9	2.0
2200000	**Louisiana**..................	4,600,933	97.2	81.3	24.5	16.2	30.7	7.9	2.0
2205000	Baton Rouge city..................	229,491	96.3	71.1	21.0	11.2	27.4	9.4	2.1
2208920	Bossier City city..................	65,107	97.0	78.9	23.4	15.7	28.8	9.1	1.9
2239475	Kenner city..................	66,891	99.3	83.2	24.3	16.6	29.8	10.6	1.7
2240735	Lafayette city..................	122,997	96.5	73.1	22.8	15.0	27.3	6.6	1.5
2241155	Lake Charles city..................	73,437	95.7	76.4	24.2	13.9	29.3	7.4	1.6
2250115	Metairie CDP..................	139,626	99.7	77.7	23.8	16.8	27.5	7.5	2.2
2255000	New Orleans city..................	369,765	96.5	70.7	20.9	10.9	28.1	8.7	2.0
2270000	Shreveport city..................	201,397	97.7	80.0	23.4	12.5	32.2	9.7	2.3
2300000	**Maine**..................	1,328,217	97.3	77.2	26.0	20.3	24.5	3.8	2.6
2360545	Portland city..................	66,230	97.0	61.5	20.3	14.3	20.7	4.0	2.2

Table B-4: Cities with a Population of 50,000 or More—Relationships—*Continued*

State/ place FIPS code	State/place	Population in nonfamily households						Population in subfamilies as a percent of total population					
		Total population in nonfamily households	Nonfamily householders				Nonrelatives in nonfamily households	Total population in subfamilies	In married couple subfamilies			Parent in a parent-child subfamily	Child in a parent-child subfamily
			Total	Male living alone	Female living alone	Householder living with nonrelatives			Total in married-couple subfamilies	Spouse in a married-couple subfamily	Child in married-couple subfamily		
	Illinois—cont'd												
1723074	Elgin city	11.7	9.0	2.9	4.4	1.7	2.6	6.4	2.5	2.0	0.5	1.7	2.2
1724582	Evanston city	22.9	17.7	6.0	8.5	3.2	5.2	2.6	0.8	0.7	0.1	0.7	1.1
1735411	Hoffman Estates village	9.7	7.8	3.4	3.1	1.4	1.9	3.5	2.1	1.8	0.3	0.7	0.8
1738570	Joliet city	10.9	8.6	3.1	3.8	1.7	2.3	4.6	2.0	1.7	0.4	1.2	1.4
1751089	Mount Prospect village	13.2	10.8	3.5	5.5	1.7	2.4	2.9	1.5	1.3	0.2	0.7	0.7
1751622	Naperville city	9.4	7.6	2.4	3.9	1.3	1.7	1.6	1.0	0.9	0.1	0.3	0.3
1753234	Normal town	30.6	16.2	4.7	5.4	6.0	14.5	2.2	1.0	0.6	0.4	0.6	0.6
1754820	Oak Lawn village	15.9	13.7	4.3	7.9	1.5	2.2	3.8	1.3	1.1	0.3	1.0	1.5
1754885	Oak Park village	19.6	16.9	5.7	8.9	2.2	2.7	4.2	1.5	1.2	0.3	1.1	1.6
1756640	Orland Park village	12.1	10.3	2.4	6.5	1.4	1.8	0.0	0.0	0.0	0.0	0.0	0.0
1757225	Palatine village	15.4	12.6	4.8	5.7	2.1	2.7	3.9	1.3	0.9	0.4	1.1	1.5
1759000	Peoria city	21.3	17.5	7.0	8.0	2.5	3.8	2.4	0.8	0.5	0.3	0.7	0.9
1765000	Rockford city	17.6	14.9	5.7	7.0	2.2	2.7	3.7	0.8	0.6	0.2	1.3	1.7
1768003	Schaumburg village	19.6	15.9	4.9	8.4	2.6	3.7	0.0	0.0	0.0	0.0	0.0	0.0
1770122	Skokie village	11.0	9.6	3.2	5.5	0.9	1.4	0.0	0.0	0.0	0.0	0.0	0.0
1772000	Springfield city	23.2	19.1	6.7	9.4	3.0	4.1	1.7	0.5	0.4	0.1	0.6	0.6
1775484	Tinley Park village	12.6	10.6	3.2	5.6	1.8	2.0	0.0	0.0	0.0	0.0	0.0	0.0
1779293	Waukegan city	11.5	9.6	4.4	3.6	1.5	1.9	6.0	1.4	1.1	0.3	2.1	2.6
1781048	Wheaton city	13.9	11.2	3.3	6.1	1.8	2.7	2.3	1.7	1.3	0.5	0.3	0.3
1800000	**Indiana**	16.0	12.8	4.8	5.8	2.2	3.2	3.1	0.9	0.6	0.2	1.0	1.2
1801468	Anderson city	21.7	17.8	6.9	8.7	2.3	3.9	3.2	0.6	0.5	0.2	1.3	1.3
1805860	Bloomington city	42.2	23.1	7.2	7.9	8.0	19.0	0.0	0.0	0.0	0.0	0.0	0.0
1810342	Carmel city	10.6	8.9	3.0	4.2	1.6	1.7	0.0	0.0	0.0	0.0	0.0	0.0
1820728	Elkhart city	18.9	15.2	5.5	7.2	2.5	3.6	4.0	1.2	0.9	0.4	1.2	1.5
1822000	Evansville city	22.1	18.4	6.8	8.9	2.7	3.7	3.1	0.9	0.6	0.2	1.1	1.2
1823278	Fishers town	10.0	8.4	3.6	3.4	1.4	1.6	0.0	0.0	0.0	0.0	0.0	0.0
1825000	Fort Wayne city	19.4	15.7	6.2	7.0	2.5	3.7	2.9	0.9	0.6	0.2	0.9	1.1
1827000	Gary city	17.3	14.7	5.4	7.5	1.8	2.6	5.1	0.4	0.4	0.0	2.1	2.6
1829898	Greenwood city	17.6	14.3	4.9	6.6	2.8	3.3	3.6	2.0	1.2	0.7	0.8	0.8
1831000	Hammond city	14.5	12.1	5.3	5.0	1.8	2.4	5.9	1.3	1.0	0.4	2.2	2.4
1836003	Indianapolis city	20.8	16.3	6.2	7.1	2.9	4.5	3.4	0.5	0.4	0.1	1.4	1.6
1840392	Kokomo city	20.7	18.1	7.2	8.4	2.4	2.7	1.4	0.2	0.2	0.1	0.6	0.6
1840788	Lafayette city	23.6	18.2	6.9	7.6	3.7	5.4	0.0	0.0	0.0	0.0	0.0	0.0
1851876	Muncie city	30.9	19.8	5.8	7.8	6.2	11.0	2.0	0.5	0.3	0.1	0.7	0.8
1854180	Noblesville city	14.2	12.1	4.4	5.9	1.9	2.2	0.0	0.0	0.0	0.0	0.0	0.0
1871000	South Bend city	21.8	17.1	6.1	8.0	3.1	4.6	3.3	0.5	0.4	0.1	1.3	1.5
1875428	Terre Haute city	20.0	15.6	5.4	7.5	2.7	4.5	3.0	0.7	0.5	0.1	1.2	1.2
1900000	**Iowa**	17.8	14.1	5.2	6.3	2.6	3.7	1.8	0.5	0.4	0.1	0.6	0.7
1901855	Ames city	39.5	21.8	6.2	5.8	9.9	17.7	0.0	0.0	0.0	0.0	0.0	0.0
1912000	Cedar Rapids city	22.4	17.1	6.2	7.3	3.7	5.3	2.5	0.7	0.6	0.2	0.9	0.9
1916860	Council Bluffs city	18.9	14.9	5.0	7.2	2.6	4.0	3.1	1.1	0.9	0.2	0.9	1.2
1919000	Davenport city	21.4	16.8	6.8	6.9	3.1	4.6	2.6	0.5	0.3	0.1	1.0	1.1
1921000	Des Moines city	19.5	15.6	5.8	6.8	2.9	4.0	3.6	1.0	0.7	0.4	1.1	1.4
1922395	Dubuque city	24.0	18.2	6.6	8.2	3.4	5.8	1.6	0.1	0.1	0.0	0.6	0.9
1938595	Iowa City city	37.0	22.7	6.7	7.7	8.3	14.4	0.0	0.0	0.0	0.0	0.0	0.0
1973335	Sioux City city	17.3	13.9	5.3	6.3	2.2	3.4	3.2	1.1	0.6	0.5	1.1	1.1
1982425	Waterloo city	23.0	18.2	6.7	8.5	3.0	4.9	2.5	0.4	0.3	0.1	0.9	1.2
1983910	West Des Moines city	21.8	16.5	5.9	6.5	4.0	5.3	1.7	0.8	0.6	0.2	0.4	0.5
2000000	**Kansas**	16.6	13.2	4.9	6.0	2.3	3.4	2.6	0.7	0.5	0.2	0.8	1.1
2036000	Kansas City city	17.3	13.2	5.1	5.8	2.4	4.0	4.8	1.0	0.7	0.2	1.7	2.2
2038900	Lawrence city	31.6	19.1	4.8	7.4	6.9	12.4	1.5	0.2	0.2	0.0	0.6	0.7
2044250	Manhattan city	35.6	19.4	6.0	6.2	7.2	16.1	0.0	0.0	0.0	0.0	0.0	0.0
2052575	Olathe city	12.0	9.2	2.9	4.4	1.9	2.8	2.3	1.0	0.7	0.3	0.6	0.8
2053775	Overland Park city	17.4	14.6	4.8	7.6	2.2	2.9	1.9	0.8	0.7	0.1	0.5	0.6
2064500	Shawnee city	14.6	11.5	4.1	5.1	2.3	3.1	0.0	0.0	0.0	0.0	0.0	0.0
2071000	Topeka city	22.1	17.9	6.4	8.5	3.0	4.2	3.1	1.0	0.7	0.3	0.9	1.3
2079000	Wichita city	18.2	14.9	6.3	6.4	2.3	3.3	3.5	0.8	0.7	0.2	1.1	1.5
2100000	**Kentucky**	15.8	12.8	4.7	6.1	2.0	2.9	3.3	1.0	0.7	0.2	1.1	1.2
2108902	Bowling Green city	25.6	18.5	6.2	7.3	5.0	7.1	1.3	0.1	0.1	0.0	0.5	0.7
2146027	Lexington-Fayette	24.1	17.2	5.9	7.4	3.9	6.9	2.1	0.7	0.5	0.2	0.7	0.8
2148006	Louisville/Jefferson County	19.8	15.9	5.8	7.4	2.7	4.0	3.5	0.7	0.6	0.2	1.3	1.5
2158620	Owensboro city	19.5	16.0	5.1	8.5	2.3	3.5	3.2	0.7	0.5	0.2	1.2	1.3
2200000	**Louisiana**	15.9	12.8	5.0	5.8	2.0	3.1	4.3	0.9	0.7	0.2	1.6	1.9
2205000	Baton Rouge city	25.2	17.5	6.0	7.5	4.1	7.7	4.4	0.4	0.3	0.2	1.7	2.3
2208920	Bossier City city	18.2	15.5	6.2	7.2	2.1	2.7	4.9	1.9	1.1	0.8	1.5	1.5
2239475	Kenner city	16.2	13.2	5.0	6.5	1.7	3.0	5.2	1.1	1.0	0.2	1.9	2.2
2240735	Lafayette city	23.4	17.5	6.2	8.0	3.3	5.9	2.8	0.4	0.3	0.1	1.2	1.2
2241155	Lake Charles city	19.4	16.1	6.4	7.6	2.1	3.3	4.3	0.3	0.2	0.1	1.9	2.2
2250115	Metairie CDP	22.0	17.6	6.6	8.2	2.8	4.4	2.9	0.9	0.8	0.2	1.0	1.0
2255000	New Orleans city	25.8	20.1	7.9	8.7	3.5	5.7	3.8	0.6	0.4	0.1	1.5	1.7
2270000	Shreveport city	17.7	15.2	5.9	7.6	1.7	2.4	4.9	0.5	0.4	0.2	2.0	2.3
2300000	**Maine**	20.1	15.6	5.3	6.9	3.4	4.5	2.2	0.9	0.7	0.2	0.6	0.7
2360545	Portland city	35.5	25.0	8.1	9.8	7.1	10.5	2.2	0.9	0.6	0.3	0.6	0.7

State/place FIPS code	State/place	Total population	Percent of the population in households	Population in family households, percent					
				Percent in family households	Householder in family household, percent	Spouse in family household, percent	Child in family household (biological, adopted, or stepchild)	Other relative in family household	Nonrelatives in family household
2400000	**Maryland**	5,884,640	97.6	82.0	24.3	17.2	30.3	7.7	2.5
2402825	Aspen Hill CDP............................	53,130	99.2	87.1	23.8	16.4	30.1	11.5	5.3
2404000	Baltimore city............................	621,836	96.0	70.8	19.7	9.1	28.1	10.9	3.0
2407125	Bethesda CDP............................	63,374	98.8	81.6	26.0	22.4	29.2	3.0	1.0
2408775	Bowie city............................	56,160	99.4	86.6	25.3	18.5	34.5	6.7	1.7
2419125	Columbia CDP............................	103,683	99.5	84.5	26.6	20.3	30.4	5.5	1.8
2423975	Dundalk CDP............................	61,374	99.5	81.7	24.5	14.4	29.9	9.7	3.1
2426000	Ellicott City CDP............................	69,647	99.6	91.4	28.1	24.1	33.9	4.3	1.0
2430325	Frederick city............................	66,427	97.6	78.1	24.2	15.8	28.5	6.8	2.9
2431175	Gaithersburg city............................	63,360	99.4	85.1	24.8	17.5	32.4	7.5	2.8
2432025	Germantown CDP............................	90,676	99.9	88.9	25.2	18.1	35.1	8.4	2.2
2432650	Glen Burnie CDP............................	68,693	98.8	80.7	24.3	14.6	29.6	9.7	2.5
2467675	Rockville city............................	63,106	98.6	80.0	25.7	20.8	26.7	5.2	1.5
2472450	Silver Spring CDP............................	76,716	99.6	75.8	21.8	15.1	26.8	7.9	4.2
2478425	Towson CDP............................	58,186	85.6	62.9	19.9	15.0	23.1	3.8	1.1
2481175	Waldorf CDP............................	72,720	99.6	85.3	24.0	15.4	35.8	7.5	2.7
2483775	Wheaton CDP............................	50,727	99.5	86.3	21.3	14.3	30.9	14.8	5.0
2500000	**Massachusetts**...........................	6,648,138	96.3	78.1	24.2	17.8	28.5	5.7	1.9
2507000	Boston city............................	637,625	92.8	61.6	18.6	10.3	23.2	7.5	2.0
2509000	Brockton city............................	93,971	98.3	85.6	24.0	13.4	34.9	11.0	2.2
2509210	Brookline CDP............................	58,918	96.9	65.9	22.4	18.0	22.0	2.6	1.0
2511000	Cambridge city............................	106,355	83.9	47.0	16.7	12.3	14.0	3.1	0.9
2513660	Chicopee city............................	55,615	97.7	77.4	24.3	15.8	27.4	6.6	3.2
2523000	Fall River city............................	88,714	98.3	75.8	24.7	14.4	29.1	5.3	2.2
2524960	Framingham CDP............................	69,931	95.0	77.5	24.7	18.3	26.6	6.2	1.7
2529405	Haverhill city............................	61,732	98.1	80.0	24.1	16.0	29.9	6.9	3.1
2534550	Lawrence city............................	77,267	98.8	86.1	23.7	9.7	36.8	12.6	3.4
2537000	Lowell city............................	108,210	95.7	77.1	22.0	13.0	30.6	8.1	3.3
2537490	Lynn city............................	91,171	99.2	84.6	23.6	12.8	33.0	10.2	5.0
2537875	Malden city............................	60,213	99.4	77.9	22.6	16.1	27.2	10.1	1.9
2539835	Medford city............................	56,887	96.0	70.3	22.7	17.8	22.6	6.0	1.3
2545000	New Bedford city............................	94,899	97.9	76.4	24.1	13.8	28.4	5.9	4.2
2545560	Newton city............................	87,018	90.5	77.1	25.0	21.7	27.3	1.8	1.2
2552490	Peabody city............................	51,790	98.9	80.1	25.3	19.3	27.1	6.8	1.6
2555745	Quincy city............................	93,025	98.7	73.9	23.1	16.1	25.6	7.6	1.5
2556585	Revere city............................	53,235	99.5	78.8	22.4	14.0	29.5	9.5	3.5
2562535	Somerville city............................	77,739	96.3	58.0	18.8	11.9	18.6	6.2	2.6
2567000	Springfield city............................	153,593	96.5	80.0	23.2	10.8	33.5	9.3	3.3
2569170	Taunton city............................	55,975	98.7	82.4	25.0	16.8	29.9	7.6	3.0
2572600	Waltham city............................	61,803	88.3	63.4	20.7	15.4	19.9	5.8	1.6
2578972	Weymouth Town city............................	54,835	99.1	78.9	24.5	18.2	29.4	5.2	1.6
2582000	Worcester city............................	182,386	93.9	72.9	21.7	12.7	28.4	7.2	3.0
2600000	**Michigan**...........................	9,884,242	97.7	80.9	25.2	18.4	29.8	5.4	2.1
2603000	Ann Arbor city............................	116,173	90.5	51.5	17.2	13.2	17.8	2.0	1.3
2605920	Battle Creek city............................	51,938	97.6	79.2	23.8	14.9	31.8	5.5	3.2
2621000	Dearborn city............................	96,609	99.7	87.8	22.0	16.8	39.4	8.5	1.0
2621020	Dearborn Heights city............................	56,979	98.9	85.0	24.3	17.4	35.0	6.7	1.6
2622000	Detroit city............................	696,922	98.2	79.6	20.7	7.6	35.3	13.1	2.9
2627440	Farmington Hills city............................	80,760	98.7	80.8	26.6	21.5	27.2	4.8	0.8
2629000	Flint city............................	100,513	97.3	75.4	22.3	9.5	32.1	8.6	2.9
2634000	Grand Rapids city............................	190,558	96.2	71.9	21.4	13.6	28.7	5.3	3.0
2642160	Kalamazoo city............................	75,122	90.3	58.5	17.5	9.7	23.7	4.6	3.0
2646000	Lansing city............................	113,629	99.2	72.4	22.3	12.6	27.9	6.8	2.8
2649000	Livonia city............................	95,758	98.5	84.3	26.8	21.9	30.3	3.9	1.3
2659440	Novi city............................	56,939	99.4	82.4	26.0	22.2	30.5	2.5	1.3
2665440	Pontiac city............................	59,706	96.9	76.9	23.0	9.4	32.2	9.4	2.9
2669035	Rochester Hills city............................	72,278	98.6	84.1	26.4	22.3	30.9	3.5	1.0
2670040	Royal Oak city............................	58,543	99.5	64.8	22.2	17.2	20.7	3.5	1.1
2670520	Saginaw city............................	50,701	97.5	79.2	22.0	9.5	34.4	10.0	3.3
2670760	St. Clair Shores city............................	59,847	99.5	77.2	25.7	18.7	26.4	4.9	1.5
2674900	Southfield city............................	72,570	98.1	77.8	25.3	14.5	28.0	8.1	1.9
2676460	Sterling Heights city............................	130,523	99.3	87.1	26.7	20.6	30.4	8.1	1.3
2679000	Taylor city............................	62,232	98.8	83.1	25.1	15.5	31.7	8.4	2.4
2680700	Troy city............................	82,168	99.6	88.2	27.4	23.4	30.8	5.8	1.0
2684000	Warren city............................	134,349	99.1	81.8	25.3	16.8	30.7	6.9	2.1
2686000	Westland city............................	83,090	98.9	79.6	24.1	15.1	30.7	7.1	2.7
2688940	Wyoming city............................	73,386	99.4	82.5	24.5	18.4	29.8	6.6	3.1
2700000	**Minnesota**...........................	5,382,376	97.5	79.8	25.4	19.9	28.7	3.6	2.1
2706382	Blaine city............................	59,340	99.7	87.5	26.8	21.0	34.4	3.9	1.5
2706616	Bloomington city............................	85,407	98.8	76.4	25.3	19.6	25.0	4.5	2.0
2707966	Brooklyn Park city............................	77,676	99.7	87.7	24.7	16.5	33.8	9.3	3.4
2708794	Burnsville city............................	61,052	99.3	78.1	24.9	18.8	28.4	3.8	2.1
2713114	Coon Rapids city............................	61,843	99.4	82.0	25.3	18.9	31.0	4.8	2.0
2717000	Duluth city............................	86,191	92.3	64.5	21.5	15.6	23.1	2.3	2.0

State/place FIPS code	State/place	Total population in nonfamily households	Nonfamily householders Total	Male living alone	Female living alone	Householder living with nonrelatives	Nonrelatives in nonfamily households	Total population in subfamilies	Total in married-couple subfamilies	Spouse in a married-couple subfamily	Child in married-couple subfamily	Parent in a parent-child subfamily	Child in a parent-child subfamily
2400000	**Maryland**	15.6	12.2	4.1	5.9	2.2	3.5	4.1	1.3	1.0	0.3	1.3	1.5
2402825	Aspen Hill CDP	12.0	8.8	2.2	4.9	1.7	3.2	6.0	1.7	1.4	0.2	1.9	2.4
2404000	Baltimore city	25.2	19.3	6.6	9.3	3.4	5.9	5.8	0.8	0.6	0.2	2.3	2.8
2407125	Bethesda CDP	17.2	13.8	4.1	7.2	2.5	3.4	0.0	0.0	0.0	0.0	0.0	0.0
2408775	Bowie city	12.8	10.0	3.0	5.3	1.6	2.8	3.0	1.4	1.1	0.3	0.7	0.8
2419125	Columbia CDP	14.9	12.3	4.5	5.6	2.2	2.7	0.0	0.0	0.0	0.0	0.0	0.0
2423975	Dundalk CDP	17.8	13.9	5.1	6.2	2.6	3.9	3.9	1.3	1.0	0.4	1.3	1.3
2426000	Ellicott City CDP	8.2	6.7	2.3	3.3	1.0	1.5	2.1	1.3	1.0	0.3	0.3	0.5
2430325	Frederick city	19.4	15.4	4.7	7.5	3.2	4.1	3.7	1.0	0.9	0.1	0.8	1.9
2431175	Gaithersburg city	14.3	11.3	3.7	5.5	2.1	2.9	0.0	0.0	0.0	0.0	0.0	0.0
2432025	Germantown CDP	11.0	9.5	3.3	5.1	1.0	1.5	3.5	2.2	1.9	0.4	0.6	0.7
2432650	Glen Burnie CDP	18.1	14.4	5.3	6.1	2.9	3.7	6.0	1.9	1.4	0.5	1.8	2.4
2467675	Rockville city	18.7	14.0	5.2	6.1	2.8	4.7	2.4	0.7	0.7	0.0	0.9	0.8
2472450	Silver Spring CDP	23.8	17.9	6.2	7.8	3.9	5.9	2.3	0.9	0.7	0.1	0.6	0.8
2478425	Towson CDP	22.7	16.4	4.6	8.6	3.1	6.3	0.0	0.0	0.0	0.0	0.0	0.0
2481175	Waldorf CDP	14.3	10.8	2.9	5.9	2.0	3.5	5.0	0.6	0.4	0.1	2.0	2.5
2483775	Wheaton CDP	13.2	8.0	2.5	3.2	2.3	5.2	7.7	2.7	2.1	0.6	2.2	2.8
2500000	**Massachusetts**	18.2	13.9	4.6	6.4	2.9	4.3	2.9	1.2	1.0	0.3	0.8	0.9
2507000	Boston city	31.2	20.6	6.3	8.5	5.8	10.7	3.0	0.9	0.8	0.1	1.1	1.1
2509000	Brockton city	12.7	10.6	4.1	5.1	1.4	2.1	5.8	1.6	1.4	0.3	2.0	2.2
2509210	Brookline CDP	31.1	21.5	4.3	11.6	5.6	9.5	0.0	0.0	0.0	0.0	0.0	0.0
2511000	Cambridge city	36.9	24.4	7.6	8.9	7.8	12.6	0.9	0.5	0.4	0.1	0.2	0.2
2513660	Chicopee city	20.4	16.6	6.0	7.5	3.0	3.8	5.4	1.5	1.2	0.3	1.9	2.0
2523000	Fall River city	22.6	18.6	6.7	8.5	3.3	4.0	2.6	1.3	1.1	0.2	0.7	0.7
2524960	Framingham CDP	17.5	14.2	5.1	6.6	2.5	3.3	2.4	1.8	1.4	0.4	0.3	0.4
2529405	Haverhill city	18.1	14.4	4.7	6.8	3.0	3.6	3.5	1.1	0.9	0.2	0.9	1.5
2534550	Lawrence city	12.7	9.8	3.6	4.3	1.9	2.9	5.6	1.5	1.4	0.1	1.9	2.3
2537000	Lowell city	18.7	14.1	6.3	4.8	3.1	4.5	3.7	1.6	1.3	0.3	0.9	1.2
2537490	Lynn city	14.6	11.9	4.5	5.5	1.9	2.6	5.4	1.9	1.5	0.4	1.5	2.0
2537875	Malden city	21.5	14.8	5.2	5.6	3.9	6.7	4.6	2.9	2.5	0.4	0.6	1.1
2539835	Medford city	25.6	16.2	4.1	6.7	5.4	9.4	0.0	0.0	0.0	0.0	0.0	0.0
2545000	New Bedford city	21.5	17.4	6.6	7.8	2.9	4.1	2.4	0.9	0.7	0.2	0.7	0.8
2545560	Newton city	13.4	10.8	3.2	5.7	2.0	2.6	0.0	0.0	0.0	0.0	0.0	0.0
2552490	Peabody city	18.8	16.4	5.1	9.3	2.0	2.5	0.0	0.0	0.0	0.0	0.0	0.0
2555745	Quincy city	24.9	19.6	6.5	9.2	3.9	5.3	3.7	2.2	1.8	0.4	0.7	0.8
2556585	Revere city	20.6	16.1	6.3	6.8	3.0	4.5	5.2	1.8	1.3	0.6	1.7	1.7
2562535	Somerville city	38.3	22.6	6.0	7.1	9.5	15.6	3.3	1.7	1.2	0.4	0.8	0.9
2567000	Springfield city	16.5	13.0	4.9	5.8	2.3	3.4	4.6	0.8	0.7	0.1	1.7	2.0
2569170	Taunton city	16.3	13.7	4.8	6.6	2.3	2.6	4.4	1.0	0.9	0.1	1.5	1.8
2572600	Waltham city	24.9	18.4	5.4	8.2	4.7	6.5	1.8	1.2	0.8	0.3	0.3	0.3
2578972	Weymouth Town city	20.2	16.7	5.7	8.4	2.6	3.5	0.0	0.0	0.0	0.0	0.0	0.0
2582000	Worcester city	21.0	15.5	5.1	6.9	3.5	5.4	2.9	1.2	1.1	0.2	0.8	0.8
2600000	**Michigan**	16.8	13.4	5.0	6.2	2.2	3.4	3.0	0.9	0.7	0.2	1.0	1.1
2603000	Ann Arbor city	39.0	23.2	6.7	8.8	7.7	15.8	0.9	0.4	0.3	0.1	0.2	0.3
2605920	Battle Creek city	18.5	15.4	5.3	7.9	2.2	3.1	3.8	1.2	0.8	0.3	1.3	1.3
2621000	Dearborn city	12.0	10.3	4.3	5.0	1.1	1.6	5.1	2.6	2.1	0.6	1.2	1.3
2621020	Dearborn Heights city	13.9	12.1	4.9	5.9	1.3	1.8	8.7	4.4	3.5	1.0	2.1	2.1
2622000	Detroit city	18.6	15.7	6.7	7.2	1.8	3.0	6.6	0.9	0.7	0.2	2.7	3.0
2627440	Farmington Hills city	17.9	15.7	6.1	7.9	1.7	2.2	2.1	1.0	0.8	0.2	0.5	0.6
2629000	Flint city	22.0	18.0	7.8	7.5	2.8	3.9	4.4	0.6	0.4	0.2	1.8	2.1
2634000	Grand Rapids city	24.3	17.0	5.6	7.1	4.3	7.3	2.9	0.4	0.3	0.0	1.1	1.4
2642160	Kalamazoo city	31.8	19.3	5.7	7.3	6.3	12.5	2.6	0.4	0.3	0.1	1.1	1.1
2646000	Lansing city	26.7	19.7	6.8	8.6	4.3	7.0	3.8	1.0	0.8	0.2	1.3	1.5
2649000	Livonia city	14.3	12.0	4.4	6.0	1.6	2.3	2.1	0.9	0.7	0.2	0.7	0.6
2659440	Novi city	16.9	14.9	5.7	7.4	1.8	2.0	0.0	0.0	0.0	0.0	0.0	0.0
2665440	Pontiac city	20.0	16.6	6.4	7.6	2.7	3.5	4.9	1.5	0.9	0.6	1.6	1.8
2669035	Rochester Hills city	14.5	12.0	4.2	6.0	1.8	2.5	2.2	1.4	1.3	0.1	0.3	0.4
2670040	Royal Oak city	34.7	26.4	8.9	11.4	6.1	8.3	0.0	0.0	0.0	0.0	0.0	0.0
2670520	Saginaw city	18.3	15.2	6.7	6.6	1.9	3.0	5.7	1.0	0.6	0.4	2.3	2.4
2670760	St. Clair Shores city	22.3	19.3	6.8	10.0	2.4	3.0	1.4	0.7	0.6	0.1	0.3	0.3
2674900	Southfield city	20.3	18.0	5.8	10.5	1.7	2.3	2.9	0.6	0.5	0.1	1.1	1.2
2676460	Sterling Heights city	12.2	11.0	4.4	5.6	1.0	1.1	4.2	2.4	2.1	0.3	0.8	1.0
2679000	Taylor city	15.7	12.8	4.8	5.8	2.1	2.9	4.5	1.0	0.9	0.2	1.7	1.7
2680700	Troy city	11.4	9.8	3.4	5.2	1.2	1.6	2.5	1.9	1.7	0.3	0.3	0.3
2684000	Warren city	17.3	14.5	5.7	6.5	2.3	2.8	3.6	1.2	0.9	0.3	1.2	1.2
2686000	Westland city	19.3	16.0	5.6	8.1	2.3	3.4	3.3	1.3	1.0	0.3	1.0	1.0
2688940	Wyoming city	16.9	12.9	4.9	5.2	2.7	4.0	4.0	1.9	1.2	0.7	1.0	1.2
2700000	**Minnesota**	17.7	13.8	5.0	6.1	2.7	3.9	1.9	0.6	0.5	0.1	0.6	0.7
2706382	Blaine city	12.2	9.8	3.2	5.0	1.7	2.4	2.5	1.3	1.0	0.3	0.6	0.6
2706616	Bloomington city	22.5	17.8	5.9	8.7	3.2	4.6	1.9	1.0	0.8	0.2	0.4	0.4
2707966	Brooklyn Park city	12.0	9.8	3.6	4.6	1.6	2.2	1.9	0.4	0.3	0.1	0.6	0.9
2708794	Burnsville city	21.2	16.2	5.5	7.2	3.5	5.0	2.8	1.0	0.7	0.3	0.9	0.9
2713114	Coon Rapids city	17.4	12.9	4.6	5.4	2.9	4.4	3.7	1.0	0.7	0.2	1.3	1.4
2717000	Duluth city	27.8	18.8	6.5	7.9	4.5	9.0	0.8	0.2	0.2	0.0	0.3	0.3

Table B-4: Cities with a Population of 50,000 or More—Relationships—*Continued*

State/ place FIPS code	State/place	Total population	Percent of the population in households	Population in family households, percent					
				Percent in family households	Householder in family household, percent	Spouse in family household, percent	Child in family household (biological, adopted, or stepchild)	Other relative in family household	Nonrelatives in family household
	Minnesota—cont'd								
2717288	Eagan city	64,956	99.7	83.9	27.2	21.8	30.5	2.8	1.7
2718116	Eden Prairie city	62,164	99.7	85.7	27.4	22.3	31.3	3.6	1.1
2735180	Lakeville city	57,487	99.9	92.9	27.2	23.1	37.6	3.7	1.4
2740166	Maple Grove city	64,337	99.9	88.3	28.0	24.1	32.6	2.8	0.8
2743000	Minneapolis city	393,661	95.4	61.9	18.8	12.3	22.7	5.6	2.5
2743252	Minnetonka city	51,028	99.2	80.0	27.5	22.5	26.3	2.4	1.2
2751730	Plymouth city	72,864	98.7	82.6	27.5	22.9	28.3	3.0	0.9
2754880	Rochester city	109,324	97.4	78.3	24.5	19.2	29.1	3.4	2.2
2756896	St. Cloud city	65,789	91.9	64.2	20.1	14.4	23.4	4.1	2.2
2758000	St. Paul city	291,527	96.9	73.6	21.0	13.4	30.2	6.5	2.5
2771428	Woodbury city	64,536	99.5	87.3	27.3	22.7	33.7	2.4	1.2
2800000	**Mississippi**	2,985,181	96.9	82.9	24.9	16.3	31.2	8.6	1.9
2829700	Gulfport city	69,960	97.6	79.7	24.8	14.6	28.4	9.2	2.6
2836000	Jackson city	174,371	96.5	79.1	22.2	9.8	34.2	10.8	2.2
2869280	Southaven city	50,351	99.5	85.4	25.9	18.9	32.7	5.5	2.5
2900000	**Missouri**	6,026,255	97.1	80.0	25.4	18.9	28.5	5.2	2.1
2906652	Blue Springs city	53,049	99.6	87.2	26.8	20.2	33.6	4.3	2.4
2915670	Columbia city	113,216	92.1	59.7	19.1	14.3	22.0	2.8	1.5
2924778	Florissant city	52,385	98.5	82.4	25.9	16.5	32.6	5.2	2.2
2935000	Independence city	117,098	98.9	78.7	24.9	17.1	27.6	6.3	2.9
2937592	Joplin city	51,188	96.6	75.6	24.5	17.7	25.1	5.7	2.7
2938000	Kansas City city	464,448	98.1	74.8	23.0	14.4	28.5	6.5	2.3
2941348	Lee's Summit city	92,873	99.2	87.6	26.7	21.2	34.0	4.2	1.6
2954074	O'Fallon city	81,901	99.6	89.2	27.0	21.6	35.8	2.9	2.0
2964082	St. Charles city	66,704	91.7	73.2	24.4	18.2	25.4	3.5	1.7
2964550	St. Joseph city	77,140	95.1	76.9	22.7	15.6	27.6	9.1	2.0
2965000	St. Louis city	318,892	96.4	67.4	20.2	10.6	26.4	7.9	2.3
2965126	St. Peters city	54,096	99.6	84.1	26.3	21.7	30.6	4.1	1.3
2970000	Springfield city	162,229	93.6	64.2	22.1	14.8	21.0	4.3	2.0
3000000	**Montana**	1,006,086	97.1	78.1	25.4	19.9	26.1	4.6	2.0
3006550	Billings city	107,208	96.8	76.0	24.4	17.3	26.6	5.0	2.8
3032800	Great Falls city	59,091	97.5	77.6	25.2	18.0	26.5	5.2	2.7
3050200	Missoula city	68,425	95.5	63.4	21.3	15.4	21.6	2.8	2.4
3100000	**Nebraska**	1,855,209	97.2	80.0	25.5	19.9	28.8	3.8	2.0
3103950	Bellevue city	52,712	99.8	86.8	26.8	19.3	33.3	5.2	2.3
3119595	Grand Island city	50,002	98.3	81.2	24.0	17.6	30.4	4.3	4.9
3128000	Lincoln city	265,470	95.1	72.6	23.4	17.6	26.0	3.3	2.3
3137000	Omaha city	428,781	97.5	77.4	23.3	15.9	30.0	5.6	2.5
3200000	**Nevada**	2,754,148	98.7	81.3	23.3	16.3	29.8	9.0	3.0
3209700	Carson City	54,481	96.1	76.2	23.1	17.2	26.8	6.5	2.6
3223770	Enterprise CDP	120,695	99.9	83.5	23.4	16.8	29.4	11.4	2.4
3231900	Henderson city	265,376	99.4	82.4	25.2	18.6	28.8	7.1	2.6
3240000	Las Vegas city	595,906	98.6	81.8	22.8	15.1	30.9	9.7	3.3
3251800	North Las Vegas city	222,967	99.0	87.5	22.1	15.0	36.3	10.9	3.2
3254600	Paradise CDP	224,728	99.3	76.0	21.4	13.1	28.1	9.5	3.9
3260600	Reno city	230,785	97.3	74.2	21.9	15.1	27.9	6.6	2.6
3268400	Sparks city	92,145	99.6	80.5	23.9	16.7	29.0	8.8	2.2
3268585	Spring Valley CDP	185,027	99.9	78.0	22.4	14.9	27.4	10.4	3.0
3271400	Sunrise Manor CDP	184,599	99.9	87.0	22.0	13.7	35.0	12.0	4.2
3300000	**New Hampshire**	1,321,050	96.9	80.1	26.2	20.7	26.9	4.0	2.3
3345140	Manchester city	110,168	97.5	74.2	23.5	15.4	26.4	6.0	2.9
3350260	Nashua city	86,851	97.9	79.3	24.5	18.0	28.0	5.7	3.1
3400000	**New Jersey**	8,867,909	97.9	84.3	24.8	18.2	31.8	7.3	2.1
3403580	Bayonne city	64,465	99.5	81.0	25.3	15.7	30.1	7.8	2.1
3410000	Camden city	77,311	96.5	81.7	21.0	6.5	38.9	11.8	3.5
3413690	Clifton city	85,027	98.9	87.5	24.2	17.5	35.1	8.9	1.8
3419390	East Orange city	64,398	98.3	77.7	22.1	8.5	30.9	13.1	3.1
3421000	Elizabeth city	126,778	98.2	85.4	21.2	11.2	35.3	12.1	5.5
3432250	Hoboken city	51,901	97.1	50.9	18.4	13.9	15.2	2.6	0.8
3436000	Jersey City city	254,872	98.9	78.2	23.1	14.1	28.2	10.6	2.2
3451000	Newark city	277,849	95.0	78.9	20.8	8.4	34.0	11.7	4.0
3451210	New Brunswick city	55,646	86.5	65.7	14.9	6.2	24.5	11.7	8.4
3456550	Passaic city	70,531	99.4	89.5	21.0	9.8	41.3	12.8	4.6
3457000	Paterson city	145,800	98.4	88.7	21.9	9.7	37.9	16.6	2.7
3458200	Perth Amboy city	51,757	98.8	89.3	23.6	12.1	35.4	14.4	3.8
3459190	Plainfield city	50,304	98.4	85.4	20.1	9.5	30.1	17.2	8.4
3473110	Toms River CDP	89,495	98.3	84.8	25.8	19.5	31.8	5.5	2.2
3474000	Trenton city	84,359	93.3	76.6	20.7	8.8	32.6	11.0	3.6
3474630	Union City city	67,855	99.2	86.1	23.0	10.8	31.7	15.6	5.0
3476070	Vineland city	60,994	97.1	84.0	23.9	15.1	34.5	7.9	2.5
3479610	West New York town	51,411	100.0	81.8	22.6	12.8	29.6	12.2	4.6

Table B-4: Cities with a Population of 50,000 or More—Relationships—*Continued*

State/ place FIPS code	State/place	Population in nonfamily households						Population in subfamilies as a percent of total population					
		Total population in nonfamily households	Nonfamily householders				Nonrelatives in nonfamily households	Total population in subfamilies	In married couple subfamilies			Parent in a parent-child subfamily	Child in a parent-child subfamily
			Total	Male living alone	Female living alone	Householder living with nonrelatives			Total in married-couple subfamilies	Spouse in a married-couple subfamily	Child in a married-couple subfamily		
	Minnesota—cont'd												
2717288	Eagan city	15.8	12.2	4.5	5.3	2.5	3.5	0.0	0.0	0.0	0.0	0.0	0.0
2718116	Eden Prairie city	14.0	11.9	4.0	6.0	1.8	2.1	0.0	0.0	0.0	0.0	0.0	0.0
2735180	Lakeville city	7.0	5.5	2.3	1.8	1.4	1.5	0.0	0.0	0.0	0.0	0.0	0.0
2740166	Maple Grove city	11.6	9.2	3.1	4.3	1.8	2.3	0.0	0.0	0.0	0.0	0.0	0.0
2743000	Minneapolis city	33.5	23.3	8.1	8.7	6.4	10.2	2.3	0.5	0.4	0.2	0.8	1.0
2743252	Minnetonka city	19.2	16.1	5.1	8.4	2.6	3.0	0.0	0.0	0.0	0.0	0.0	0.0
2751730	Plymouth city	16.1	13.0	4.0	6.8	2.3	3.0	1.1	0.2	0.2	0.0	0.4	0.5
2754880	Rochester city	19.1	15.3	4.9	7.7	2.7	3.8	1.9	0.7	0.5	0.2	0.6	0.7
2756896	St. Cloud city	27.7	17.3	5.2	5.8	6.3	10.4	0.0	0.0	0.0	0.0	0.0	0.0
2758000	St. Paul city	23.3	17.6	6.3	7.3	3.9	5.8	3.1	1.1	0.8	0.3	0.9	1.1
2771428	Woodbury city	12.2	9.2	2.6	4.5	2.1	3.0	0.0	0.0	0.0	0.0	0.0	0.0
2800000	**Mississippi**	14.0	11.5	4.4	5.6	1.5	2.4	5.0	0.9	0.7	0.2	1.9	2.2
2829700	Gulfport city	17.9	14.3	5.9	6.2	2.2	3.6	4.1	1.2	0.8	0.4	1.2	1.7
2836000	Jackson city	17.4	13.8	5.1	6.7	2.0	3.6	6.3	0.4	0.4	0.1	2.6	3.3
2869280	Southaven city	14.1	11.0	3.4	5.7	1.9	3.1	3.5	1.1	0.7	0.3	1.0	1.4
2900000	**Missouri**	17.1	13.7	5.0	6.3	2.4	3.4	2.9	0.8	0.6	0.2	0.9	1.1
2906652	Blue Springs city	12.3	9.0	3.0	3.7	2.3	3.4	1.5	0.4	0.3	0.1	0.5	0.6
2915670	Columbia city	32.4	19.8	5.7	7.2	6.9	12.6	1.2	0.1	0.1	0.0	0.5	0.6
2924778	Florissant city	16.0	14.3	5.0	7.9	1.4	1.7	3.8	1.2	1.0	0.3	1.2	1.4
2935000	Independence city	20.2	16.8	6.4	7.8	2.6	3.4	2.8	0.9	0.7	0.2	0.8	1.1
2937592	Joplin city	21.0	17.2	5.9	8.2	3.1	3.7	3.3	1.4	1.1	0.3	0.8	1.1
2938000	Kansas City city	23.4	18.3	6.8	8.2	3.3	5.0	3.1	0.5	0.4	0.1	1.1	1.5
2941348	Lee's Summit city	11.6	9.4	2.9	4.6	1.9	2.3	2.5	0.8	0.5	0.3	0.8	0.9
2954074	O'Fallon city	10.4	8.9	3.2	4.4	1.3	1.5	2.2	0.6	0.4	0.2	0.8	0.9
2964082	St. Charles city	18.5	15.4	6.0	6.8	2.5	3.1	1.9	0.4	0.3	0.1	0.7	0.9
2964550	St. Joseph city	18.2	13.9	4.8	6.7	2.4	4.2	5.0	1.1	0.9	0.2	1.8	2.0
2965000	St. Louis city	29.0	23.2	9.0	10.1	4.1	5.8	3.4	0.5	0.4	0.1	1.3	1.6
2965126	St. Peters city	15.5	12.7	3.4	7.2	2.2	2.8	2.6	0.9	0.6	0.4	0.8	0.9
2970000	Springfield city	29.4	21.6	6.9	9.3	5.4	7.7	1.9	0.6	0.5	0.1	0.6	0.6
3000000	**Montana**	19.0	14.9	5.9	6.3	2.7	4.1	2.4	0.8	0.6	0.2	0.7	0.8
3006550	Billings city	20.9	16.3	5.7	7.4	3.2	4.6	2.8	0.8	0.6	0.2	1.0	1.0
3032800	Great Falls city	19.9	16.5	6.4	7.8	2.3	3.4	2.8	1.3	1.0	0.3	0.7	0.7
3050200	Missoula city	32.1	21.5	7.3	7.8	6.5	10.6	0.0	0.0	0.0	0.0	0.0	0.0
3100000	**Nebraska**	17.2	13.9	5.2	6.2	2.4	3.4	2.1	0.6	0.4	0.2	0.6	0.8
3103950	Bellevue city	13.0	10.5	3.9	4.9	1.7	2.5	3.2	1.1	0.7	0.3	0.9	1.2
3119595	Grand Island city	17.1	13.3	4.7	6.0	2.6	3.8	2.0	1.1	0.8	0.3	0.4	0.5
3128000	Lincoln city	22.5	16.5	5.5	6.9	4.1	6.0	1.6	0.4	0.4	0.1	0.5	0.6
3137000	Omaha city	20.1	16.1	6.1	7.2	2.8	4.0	2.9	0.8	0.6	0.3	0.9	1.1
3200000	**Nevada**	17.4	12.9	5.2	4.9	2.8	4.5	4.4	1.8	1.4	0.4	1.2	1.3
3209700	Carson City	19.9	15.8	6.2	6.9	2.8	4.1	3.9	0.8	0.7	0.0	1.3	1.8
3223770	Enterprise CDP	16.5	11.2	4.2	3.5	3.5	5.3	4.1	2.1	1.9	0.2	1.0	1.0
3231900	Henderson city	17.0	12.8	4.3	5.8	2.7	4.2	3.8	1.5	1.3	0.2	1.2	1.1
3240000	Las Vegas city	16.9	12.7	5.2	5.0	2.5	4.1	4.7	1.7	1.4	0.3	1.5	1.5
3251800	North Las Vegas city	11.5	8.1	3.3	3.1	1.8	3.3	5.7	2.5	1.9	0.6	1.4	1.7
3254600	Paradise CDP	23.3	17.5	8.0	5.9	3.5	5.8	4.1	1.8	1.5	0.3	1.0	1.2
3260600	Reno city	23.1	17.0	7.0	6.5	3.6	6.1	3.1	1.1	0.9	0.2	1.0	0.9
3268400	Sparks city	19.1	13.5	4.5	5.7	3.3	5.6	5.0	2.9	2.0	0.9	1.0	1.1
3268585	Spring Valley CDP	21.9	15.6	5.7	5.9	4.0	6.3	4.3	2.1	1.7	0.4	1.1	1.1
3271400	Sunrise Manor CDP	13.0	9.7	4.0	3.6	2.1	3.3	6.5	2.6	2.0	0.6	1.7	2.2
3300000	**New Hampshire**	16.8	13.0	4.5	5.5	3.0	3.8	2.3	0.9	0.7	0.2	0.6	0.7
3345140	Manchester city	23.3	17.9	6.8	6.7	4.4	5.5	2.1	0.7	0.5	0.1	0.7	0.8
3350260	Nashua city	18.6	14.5	5.1	6.1	3.2	4.1	3.9	1.6	1.2	0.4	1.0	1.4
3400000	**New Jersey**	13.6	11.0	3.8	5.5	1.8	2.6	3.6	1.5	1.2	0.3	1.0	1.1
3403580	Bayonne city	18.6	14.5	6.4	5.6	2.5	4.0	3.5	1.6	1.4	0.2	0.8	1.0
3410000	Camden city	14.8	11.8	4.2	5.8	1.8	3.0	5.7	0.4	0.4	0.0	2.4	2.9
3413690	Clifton city	11.4	9.9	4.1	4.9	1.0	1.5	4.4	2.2	2.0	0.3	1.1	1.1
3419390	East Orange city	20.6	18.1	6.4	9.9	1.8	2.5	6.1	0.5	0.4	0.1	2.6	3.0
3421000	Elizabeth city	12.9	9.5	3.8	3.7	2.0	3.4	5.5	1.9	1.7	0.3	1.7	1.9
3432250	Hoboken city	46.2	29.1	7.7	10.7	10.7	17.1	0.0	0.0	0.0	0.0	0.0	0.0
3436000	Jersey City city	20.8	15.1	5.8	5.6	3.6	5.7	4.3	1.8	1.5	0.2	1.2	1.4
3451000	Newark city	16.1	12.1	4.5	5.5	2.2	4.0	4.8	0.8	0.7	0.1	1.9	2.1
3451210	New Brunswick city	20.8	10.1	3.0	3.6	3.5	10.7	4.9	0.5	0.5	0.0	1.8	2.6
3456550	Passaic city	9.9	7.9	3.3	3.5	1.1	2.0	6.0	1.2	1.0	0.2	2.3	2.5
3457000	Paterson city	9.7	7.9	2.9	4.0	1.0	1.8	7.9	2.6	2.1	0.5	2.5	2.8
3458200	Perth Amboy city	9.5	8.0	2.6	4.4	1.0	1.5	6.7	2.1	1.8	0.3	2.0	2.6
3459190	Plainfield city	13.0	8.3	2.9	3.8	1.6	4.7	7.4	1.4	1.1	0.4	2.6	3.3
3473110	Toms River CDP	13.5	11.6	4.3	5.7	1.6	1.9	3.2	1.7	1.2	0.4	0.7	0.8
3474000	Trenton city	16.7	12.7	5.3	5.2	2.2	3.9	5.2	0.7	0.7	0.0	2.1	2.4
3474630	Union City city	13.1	9.9	3.7	4.1	2.1	3.2	5.8	1.6	1.3	0.3	1.8	2.4
3476070	Vineland city	13.0	10.0	2.8	5.4	1.9	3.0	5.3	0.6	0.4	0.2	2.3	2.3
3479610	West New York town	18.1	13.2	4.8	5.0	3.4	5.0	5.0	1.8	1.3	0.6	1.6	1.7

State/place FIPS code	State/place	Total population	Percent of the population in households	Population in family households, percent					
				Percent in family households	Householder in family household, percent	Spouse in family household, percent	Child in family household (biological, adopted, or stepchild)	Other relative in family household	Nonrelatives in family household
3500000	**New Mexico**....................	2,082,250	97.9	82.0	23.8	16.5	31.1	8.3	2.4
3502000	Albuquerque city...............	554,305	98.9	78.9	24.2	15.9	29.5	6.7	2.5
3539380	Las Cruces city..................	100,818	98.0	76.7	23.0	14.9	31.2	5.2	2.5
3563460	Rio Rancho city.................	90,806	99.7	85.8	24.7	18.3	34.2	5.4	3.1
3570500	Santa Fe city....................	69,374	98.0	68.3	22.3	15.2	22.7	6.0	2.0
3600000	**New York**........................	19,576,660	97.0	79.9	23.5	16.1	30.1	7.9	2.3
3601000	Albany city.......................	98,261	89.4	57.4	17.2	9.6	22.1	6.7	1.7
3608026	Brentwood CDP.................	60,374	97.9	91.9	19.6	11.9	33.1	19.2	8.1
3611000	Buffalo city......................	259,574	96.5	71.0	22.3	10.2	30.0	6.2	2.3
3615000	Cheektowaga CDP.............	75,494	98.1	76.7	26.1	17.6	27.6	3.7	1.7
3633139	Hempstead village............	54,763	98.3	82.1	20.3	10.2	29.8	16.2	5.5
3637737	Irondequoit CDP...............	51,531	99.0	79.1	26.0	18.8	27.7	5.1	1.4
3642081	Levittown CDP..................	52,147	99.8	93.3	26.1	20.4	36.1	9.1	1.5
3649121	Mount Vernon city............	67,899	98.9	82.4	23.4	12.4	32.4	12.0	2.3
3650617	New Rochelle city..............	78,476	95.9	82.9	24.8	17.3	31.5	7.3	1.9
3651000	New York city...................	8,341,122	97.9	78.4	21.9	13.1	30.1	10.8	2.4
3663000	Rochester city	210,481	95.4	69.0	20.4	8.4	29.3	7.7	3.2
3665508	Schenectady city...............	65,993	94.9	71.5	19.1	12.1	32.4	5.5	2.4
3673000	Syracuse city....................	144,443	89.9	64.1	18.6	8.7	27.1	7.1	2.6
3674183	Tonawanda CDP................	58,181	99.1	77.6	25.9	19.1	28.1	3.2	1.3
3676540	Utica city.........................	61,915	95.1	74.2	20.8	11.9	32.9	6.6	2.0
3681677	White Plains city...............	57,480	97.2	79.2	22.5	15.8	28.0	10.5	2.3
3684000	Yonkers city.....................	198,615	98.5	84.1	24.1	14.6	32.3	10.2	2.8
3700000	**North Carolina**................	9,749,266	97.4	81.1	25.3	18.4	29.0	6.4	2.0
3702140	Asheville city....................	86,009	95.5	65.1	20.6	14.3	24.1	4.1	1.9
3709060	Burlington city..................	51,890	98.2	79.6	25.9	16.1	29.2	6.3	2.0
3710740	Cary town........................	146,161	99.8	85.9	26.0	22.3	31.9	4.1	1.6
3711800	Chapel Hill town...............	58,174	83.5	55.4	18.3	15.2	18.8	2.0	1.2
3712000	Charlotte city...................	774,433	98.3	77.9	23.2	15.3	29.8	7.3	2.2
3714100	Concord city.....................	82,067	98.7	84.6	24.3	18.9	33.4	5.7	2.3
3719000	Durham city......................	239,666	95.8	72.0	22.9	14.6	25.9	6.2	2.4
3722920	Fayetteville city................	202,576	95.5	78.9	24.9	16.0	29.7	6.4	1.8
3725580	Gastonia city....................	72,645	97.9	83.8	25.4	15.9	32.9	7.2	2.4
3728000	Greensboro city................	276,311	95.8	73.8	23.7	14.7	27.3	6.2	1.9
3728080	Greenville city..................	87,771	93.7	59.9	19.6	11.3	22.8	5.1	1.1
3731400	High Point city..................	107,659	96.9	79.8	25.0	16.0	30.4	6.2	2.2
3734200	Jacksonville city................	68,987	81.8	72.2	22.1	16.0	29.4	3.3	1.5
3755000	Raleigh city......................	423,198	95.0	71.9	22.3	15.0	27.2	5.3	2.0
3757500	Rocky Mount city..............	57,267	97.2	80.1	24.8	13.7	30.7	8.3	2.5
3774440	Wilmington city................	110,079	95.5	65.2	21.8	14.5	21.8	4.7	2.3
3775000	Winston-Salem city...........	234,231	95.9	76.5	23.4	14.8	29.4	6.6	2.2
3800000	**North Dakota**..................	703,203	96.3	75.5	25.1	20.2	25.4	3.0	1.8
3807200	Bismarck city....................	64,878	97.0	73.0	24.7	18.9	24.7	3.0	1.8
3825700	Fargo city........................	110,474	95.6	64.4	21.5	16.1	21.9	3.4	1.5
3832060	Grand Forks city...............	53,725	92.2	62.2	20.7	15.9	21.0	2.6	1.9
3900000	**Ohio**..............................	11,557,868	97.3	79.8	25.3	18.4	29.0	5.1	2.0
3901000	Akron city........................	198,559	97.3	72.8	22.7	12.5	27.6	7.2	2.8
3912000	Canton city......................	72,782	96.3	75.6	24.0	13.2	29.5	6.5	2.4
3915000	Cincinnati city..................	296,805	95.6	65.3	20.5	10.0	26.7	6.1	1.9
3916000	Cleveland city...................	391,317	96.6	71.6	21.5	9.2	29.9	8.4	2.6
3918000	Columbus city...................	810,387	97.4	71.4	21.3	13.1	27.7	6.7	2.6
3921000	Dayton city......................	143,429	90.5	66.2	20.1	9.7	26.1	7.2	3.0
3925256	Elyria city........................	54,114	98.5	78.1	26.1	15.8	27.8	6.0	2.5
3933012	Hamilton city...................	62,296	97.4	80.6	24.6	15.3	29.7	7.4	3.6
3940040	Kettering city...................	56,314	99.1	77.3	25.8	18.3	27.2	3.7	2.3
3941664	Lakewood city...................	51,385	99.4	66.5	21.1	14.4	25.9	3.6	1.5
3944856	Lorain city.......................	63,800	98.9	83.1	25.8	15.0	31.4	7.2	3.6
3961000	Parma city.......................	80,699	98.6	82.1	26.3	18.8	30.4	5.0	1.7
3974118	Springfield city.................	59,930	95.3	73.6	23.0	13.3	28.3	6.1	2.9
3977000	Toledo city.......................	283,726	97.3	73.8	22.8	12.8	29.0	6.7	2.5
3988000	Youngstown city...............	65,724	91.2	70.1	21.9	9.2	28.2	8.4	2.4
4000000	**Oklahoma**......................	3,817,296	97.1	81.2	25.1	18.6	29.0	6.4	2.1
4009050	Broken Arrow city.............	101,915	99.5	89.2	27.6	21.9	33.4	4.4	1.9
4023200	Edmond city.....................	85,000	98.0	82.6	25.9	21.4	30.1	4.2	0.9
4041850	Lawton city......................	97,965	91.2	73.7	21.6	14.1	28.3	6.8	2.8
4048350	Midwest City city..............	56,073	99.5	80.2	25.7	16.2	28.9	6.8	2.6
4049200	Moore city.......................	57,668	99.3	86.8	26.7	19.2	31.4	6.8	2.7
4052500	Norman city.....................	115,886	93.6	68.6	22.0	16.6	23.0	4.9	2.2
4055000	Oklahoma City city............	600,044	98.0	79.6	23.7	16.7	30.1	7.3	1.9
4075000	Tulsa city.........................	395,209	98.2	76.9	24.0	15.6	28.7	6.1	2.5
4100000	**Oregon**..........................	3,899,266	97.8	78.3	24.6	18.7	26.8	5.4	2.8
4101000	Albany city.......................	51,449	98.5	82.8	25.8	17.9	29.7	5.4	4.0
4101650	Aloha CDP.......................	51,674	99.0	86.6	23.9	18.4	33.6	7.9	2.8

Table B-4: Cities with a Population of 50,000 or More—Relationships—*Continued*

State/place FIPS code	State/place	Population in nonfamily households						Population in subfamilies as a percent of total population					
		Total population in nonfamily households	Nonfamily householders				Nonrelatives in nonfamily households	Total population in subfamilies	In married couple subfamilies			Parent in a parent-child subfamily	Child in a parent-child subfamily
			Total	Male living alone	Female living alone	Householder living with nonrelatives			Total in married-couple subfamilies	Spouse in a married-couple subfamily	Child in married-couple subfamily		
3500000	**New Mexico**	16.0	12.8	4.9	5.6	2.2	3.2	4.9	1.3	1.0	0.3	1.7	1.9
3502000	Albuquerque city	20.0	15.9	5.8	7.2	2.9	4.1	3.5	1.1	0.9	0.2	1.2	1.3
3539380	Las Cruces city	21.2	15.0	4.9	6.5	3.5	6.2	3.0	0.7	0.5	0.2	1.0	1.3
3563460	Rio Rancho city	14.0	10.9	3.8	4.9	2.3	3.0	3.4	1.5	1.1	0.4	1.0	0.8
3570500	Santa Fe city	29.6	23.3	7.3	11.5	4.5	6.4	2.7	1.1	0.9	0.2	0.8	0.8
3600000	**New York**	17.1	13.4	4.7	6.3	2.4	3.7	4.0	1.5	1.2	0.3	1.1	1.3
3601000	Albany city	32.0	23.0	8.1	9.6	5.3	9.0	3.3	0.4	0.4	0.0	1.2	1.7
3608026	Brentwood CDP	6.0	4.0	1.5	1.4	1.1	2.0	11.2	3.6	2.5	1.1	3.3	4.4
3611000	Buffalo city	25.4	20.2	7.8	9.0	3.5	5.2	2.6	0.7	0.6	0.1	1.0	1.0
3615000	Cheektowaga CDP	21.5	17.7	5.8	8.9	3.0	3.8	0.0	0.0	0.0	0.0	0.0	0.0
3633139	Hempstead village	16.2	9.7	3.2	4.1	2.3	6.5	8.2	2.6	1.9	0.7	2.5	3.1
3637737	Irondequoit CDP	20.0	17.0	5.5	9.0	2.5	3.0	2.9	0.7	0.6	0.1	0.9	1.2
3642081	Levittown CDP	6.5	5.5	2.2	2.4	0.8	1.1	5.0	3.8	2.9	0.9	0.6	0.7
3649121	Mount Vernon city	16.5	14.2	5.0	7.3	1.8	2.3	5.9	1.4	1.0	0.3	2.2	2.4
3650617	New Rochelle city	13.0	11.7	4.1	6.8	0.9	1.3	3.1	1.2	1.0	0.2	0.9	0.9
3651000	New York city	19.5	14.9	5.1	7.1	2.7	4.6	5.2	1.9	1.6	0.3	1.5	1.8
3663000	Rochester city	26.4	20.7	8.7	7.9	4.1	5.7	3.6	0.8	0.6	0.2	1.2	1.6
3665508	Schenectady city	23.4	18.0	7.2	8.0	2.9	5.4	3.4	0.9	0.8	0.1	1.2	1.3
3673000	Syracuse city	25.7	19.1	7.4	7.8	3.9	6.6	3.4	0.6	0.5	0.1	1.2	1.6
3674183	Tonawanda CDP	21.5	18.1	6.1	9.3	2.7	3.4	0.0	0.0	0.0	0.0	0.0	0.0
3676540	Utica city	20.9	16.8	6.7	7.3	2.8	4.1	3.3	1.3	1.0	0.3	0.9	1.1
3681677	White Plains city	18.0	14.8	4.9	8.2	1.8	3.2	5.4	3.2	2.4	0.8	1.2	1.1
3684000	Yonkers city	14.4	12.7	4.7	6.8	1.2	1.7	4.3	2.1	1.7	0.4	1.0	1.2
3700000	**North Carolina**	16.3	12.9	4.6	6.1	2.2	3.4	3.4	0.9	0.7	0.2	1.2	1.3
3702140	Asheville city	30.4	22.0	6.5	10.5	5.0	8.4	1.7	0.5	0.5	0.0	0.6	0.6
3709060	Burlington city	18.6	16.1	4.6	9.6	2.0	2.5	0.0	0.0	0.0	0.0	0.0	0.0
3710740	Cary town	13.9	10.8	3.7	5.0	2.0	3.1	1.8	1.0	0.9	0.1	0.4	0.5
3711800	Chapel Hill town	28.0	16.2	5.1	6.2	4.9	11.8	0.0	0.0	0.0	0.0	0.0	0.0
3712000	Charlotte city	20.5	15.2	5.3	6.8	3.1	5.3	3.6	0.8	0.6	0.2	1.3	1.5
3714100	Concord city	14.1	10.9	3.4	5.7	1.8	3.2	0.0	0.0	0.0	0.0	0.0	0.0
3719000	Durham city	23.8	17.8	5.9	8.0	3.9	5.9	2.8	0.2	0.2	0.0	1.1	1.4
3722920	Fayetteville city	16.6	13.6	5.3	6.1	2.2	3.0	3.1	0.6	0.3	0.3	1.1	1.5
3725580	Gastonia city	14.1	11.3	4.0	5.3	2.0	2.8	3.5	0.7	0.5	0.2	1.3	1.5
3728000	Greensboro city	22.0	17.3	5.6	8.3	3.4	4.7	2.7	0.6	0.5	0.1	0.9	1.2
3728080	Greenville city	33.9	20.2	5.2	8.3	6.7	13.7	8.4	1.7	1.6	0.2	3.0	3.7
3731400	High Point city	17.1	13.7	4.2	7.1	2.3	3.4	3.1	0.7	0.5	0.1	1.0	1.4
3734200	Jacksonville city	9.5	7.8	3.1	3.7	1.0	1.8	0.0	0.0	0.0	0.0	0.0	0.0
3755000	Raleigh city	23.1	16.8	5.5	7.5	3.9	6.3	1.7	0.2	0.2	0.0	0.7	0.8
3757500	Rocky Mount city	17.1	13.9	4.8	7.5	1.5	3.2	0.0	0.0	0.0	0.0	0.0	0.0
3774440	Wilmington city	30.3	21.5	6.1	9.6	5.8	8.7	2.4	0.7	0.6	0.1	0.8	0.8
3775000	Winston-Salem city	19.4	16.0	5.6	8.1	2.3	3.4	2.9	0.5	0.4	0.1	1.1	1.4
3800000	**North Dakota**	20.8	16.4	6.7	6.3	3.4	4.4	1.6	0.3	0.3	0.1	0.5	0.8
3807200	Bismarck city	24.0	18.8	6.4	8.7	3.7	5.2	0.0	0.0	0.0	0.0	0.0	0.0
3825700	Fargo city	31.2	22.4	7.8	8.1	6.5	8.8	0.0	0.0	0.0	0.0	0.0	0.0
3832060	Grand Forks city	30.0	21.7	8.3	7.8	5.6	8.3	0.0	0.0	0.0	0.0	0.0	0.0
3900000	**Ohio**	17.5	14.1	5.2	6.6	2.3	3.3	2.8	0.7	0.6	0.2	0.9	1.1
3901000	Akron city	24.5	18.9	7.7	8.0	3.2	5.6	3.2	0.7	0.5	0.2	1.2	1.4
3912000	Canton city	20.7	17.0	6.4	8.1	2.5	3.7	3.1	0.3	0.3	0.0	1.0	1.8
3915000	Cincinnati city	30.4	23.4	9.2	10.1	4.1	6.9	3.0	0.3	0.2	0.1	1.2	1.5
3916000	Cleveland city	25.1	20.9	8.7	9.2	3.0	4.2	4.1	0.4	0.3	0.1	1.6	2.0
3918000	Columbus city	26.0	19.1	6.9	7.9	4.3	7.0	3.2	0.9	0.7	0.1	1.1	1.3
3921000	Dayton city	24.4	19.8	8.0	8.9	2.9	4.6	2.9	0.5	0.3	0.2	1.0	1.4
3925256	Elyria city	20.4	16.1	4.7	8.1	3.3	4.3	0.0	0.0	0.0	0.0	0.0	0.0
3933012	Hamilton city	16.8	13.5	4.4	6.7	2.5	3.2	2.8	0.9	0.6	0.2	0.9	1.0
3940040	Kettering city	21.8	18.3	6.7	9.1	2.5	3.6	2.1	0.5	0.4	0.1	0.7	0.8
3941664	Lakewood city	32.9	27.0	9.6	12.6	4.7	5.9	0.0	0.0	0.0	0.0	0.0	0.0
3944856	Lorain city	15.8	14.3	5.4	7.5	1.3	1.5	3.9	0.9	0.6	0.3	1.4	1.6
3961000	Parma city	16.6	14.4	5.6	7.3	1.6	2.1	2.7	1.2	1.0	0.2	0.7	0.8
3974118	Springfield city	21.7	17.2	6.6	7.7	3.0	4.5	2.9	0.9	0.7	0.1	0.8	1.2
3977000	Toledo city	23.5	18.4	7.0	8.1	3.3	5.1	3.3	0.4	0.3	0.1	1.3	1.6
3988000	Youngstown city	21.1	18.1	7.2	8.6	2.3	3.0	4.2	0.4	0.3	0.1	1.5	2.3
4000000	**Oklahoma**	15.9	12.7	4.9	5.8	2.0	3.2	3.5	1.1	0.8	0.3	1.1	1.3
4009050	Broken Arrow city	10.3	8.5	3.2	4.1	1.1	1.9	2.6	0.8	0.7	0.1	0.9	1.0
4023200	Edmond city	15.4	11.2	3.6	5.2	2.4	4.2	1.2	0.6	0.5	0.0	0.4	0.3
4041850	Lawton city	17.5	13.1	5.4	5.3	2.4	4.4	4.1	1.2	0.8	0.4	1.3	1.6
4048350	Midwest City city	19.2	15.4	5.5	7.4	2.5	3.8	3.6	1.2	0.7	0.5	1.2	1.1
4049200	Moore city	12.6	9.7	3.7	4.1	1.9	2.9	3.6	1.1	0.8	0.3	1.2	1.3
4052500	Norman city	24.9	16.8	5.5	6.9	4.3	8.1	2.0	0.9	0.7	0.2	0.5	0.6
4055000	Oklahoma City city	18.4	14.4	5.4	6.4	2.5	4.0	4.0	1.2	1.0	0.2	1.3	1.5
4075000	Tulsa city	21.3	17.2	6.5	7.9	2.8	4.1	2.9	0.8	0.7	0.1	1.0	1.2
4100000	**Oregon**	19.4	14.3	4.8	6.2	3.4	5.1	2.8	1.2	0.9	0.3	0.8	0.9
4101000	Albany city	15.7	11.8	4.7	4.9	2.3	3.9	2.4	0.6	0.4	0.2	0.9	0.8
4101650	Aloha CDP	12.5	8.3	2.3	3.4	2.6	4.2	4.7	1.7	1.6	0.1	1.5	1.5

Table B-4: Cities with a Population of 50,000 or More—Relationships—*Continued*

State/ place FIPS code	State/place	Total population	Percent of the population in households	Population in family households, percent					
				Percent in family households	Householder in family household, percent	Spouse in family household, percent	Child in family household (biological, adopted, or stepchild)	Other relative in family household	Nonrelatives in family household
	Oregon—cont'd								
4105350	Beaverton city	92,560	99.1	76.6	23.2	17.6	27.8	5.3	2.7
4105800	Bend city	79,278	99.2	75.7	24.1	18.9	27.1	3.9	1.6
4115800	Corvallis city	54,963	90.5	56.3	18.5	14.3	17.9	3.8	1.8
4123850	Eugene city	158,169	95.7	62.8	21.0	15.0	21.2	2.7	2.9
4131250	Gresham city	108,610	98.5	82.9	23.9	15.5	31.5	8.6	3.4
4134100	Hillsboro city	95,574	98.5	84.6	23.9	18.2	31.5	8.0	3.0
4147000	Medford city	76,666	97.8	80.6	25.1	18.0	27.4	5.6	4.5
4159000	Portland city	603,047	97.2	67.5	21.1	15.5	22.8	5.1	2.9
4164900	Salem city	158,709	94.7	78.2	23.5	16.3	30.5	4.8	3.2
4169600	Springfield city	59,961	99.2	78.0	23.9	16.4	27.6	5.9	4.2
4200000	**Pennsylvania**	12,759,859	96.6	79.5	25.0	18.6	28.5	5.6	1.9
4202000	Allentown city	118,678	95.6	80.0	22.1	11.7	32.7	9.4	4.0
4206088	Bethlehem city	75,041	92.0	69.6	22.3	14.0	26.3	5.1	1.8
4224000	Erie city	101,083	95.1	72.3	22.7	13.2	27.7	6.2	2.5
4241216	Lancaster city	59,354	92.8	71.7	19.9	10.5	29.6	8.2	3.5
4242928	Levittown CDP	50,533	99.6	88.8	26.4	18.3	32.8	8.2	3.0
4260000	Philadelphia city	1,546,770	96.7	73.3	19.6	10.0	30.3	11.2	2.3
4261000	Pittsburgh city	305,999	92.2	60.7	20.2	12.4	21.5	4.8	1.8
4263624	Reading city	87,987	96.8	79.9	21.5	9.6	35.3	9.4	4.0
4269000	Scranton city	75,943	92.7	71.3	21.6	14.1	27.5	6.0	2.1
4400000	**Rhode Island**	1,050,722	96.1	77.4	24.5	17.2	27.6	6.1	2.1
4419180	Cranston city	80,532	94.2	78.6	24.0	17.3	28.8	6.2	2.3
4454640	Pawtucket city	71,144	99.3	81.0	24.0	13.7	30.2	9.0	4.2
4459000	Providence city	178,139	92.1	68.9	19.4	9.8	28.4	8.8	2.5
4474300	Warwick city	82,032	99.1	78.9	26.1	19.5	26.5	4.9	1.8
4500000	**South Carolina**	4,723,923	97.1	81.6	25.4	17.8	28.8	7.6	1.9
4513330	Charleston city	125,655	95.4	65.0	21.1	15.2	22.1	5.3	1.2
4516000	Columbia city	131,949	77.6	54.6	16.9	10.3	21.4	4.6	1.4
4530850	Greenville city	60,697	92.8	66.8	21.4	13.9	24.5	5.8	1.2
4548535	Mount Pleasant town	72,089	99.3	79.8	25.5	20.7	29.1	3.4	1.1
4550875	North Charleston city	101,969	94.2	75.7	22.1	12.8	30.8	7.7	2.3
4561405	Rock Hill city	68,284	95.5	76.8	24.4	15.1	28.3	7.0	2.0
4600000	**South Dakota**	834,236	95.9	78.7	25.2	19.6	27.4	4.4	2.1
4652980	Rapid City city	69,815	95.6	74.9	23.8	16.6	26.3	5.0	3.1
4659020	Sioux Falls city	160,548	97.0	77.1	24.8	18.1	28.3	3.8	2.0
4700000	**Tennessee**	6,449,754	97.6	81.7	25.5	18.7	28.7	6.8	1.9
4703440	Bartlett city	57,930	98.7	90.1	27.0	22.1	34.2	5.9	0.8
4714000	Chattanooga city	172,110	95.6	73.8	23.0	14.4	26.8	7.7	1.9
4715160	Clarksville city	140,628	97.8	84.7	26.0	18.6	32.3	5.3	2.6
4727740	Franklin city	66,542	99.2	84.3	26.1	22.0	32.0	3.1	1.0
4733280	Hendersonville city	53,166	99.7	88.0	27.9	21.7	31.5	5.3	1.6
4737640	Jackson city	67,238	94.2	76.8	22.2	14.4	31.2	7.7	1.3
4738320	Johnson City city	64,466	93.9	70.1	23.6	17.1	22.9	4.6	1.9
4739560	Kingsport city	52,990	98.1	78.2	27.1	19.8	24.5	5.3	1.6
4740000	Knoxville city	182,034	94.8	64.1	21.4	14.4	20.6	5.9	1.8
4748000	Memphis city	653,020	97.7	78.2	22.1	11.0	32.4	10.3	2.5
4751560	Murfreesboro city	114,233	95.9	72.8	22.6	17.4	28.1	3.5	1.2
4752006	Nashville-Davidson	623,895	96.3	72.1	21.7	14.3	26.6	7.4	2.1
4800000	**Texas**	26,049,971	97.7	84.3	23.9	17.2	32.6	8.6	2.0
4801000	Abilene city	121,508	89.3	71.6	21.4	15.4	26.0	6.6	2.2
4801924	Allen city	89,801	99.8	91.4	26.1	21.5	36.7	5.6	1.4
4803000	Amarillo city	195,277	99.0	82.6	25.0	17.6	31.4	6.4	2.2
4804000	Arlington city	375,555	99.1	84.5	24.2	16.5	33.4	8.0	2.4
4804462	Atascocita CDP	68,146	96.5	89.5	24.8	19.3	36.5	7.1	1.8
4805000	Austin city	862,876	97.7	69.6	20.8	14.2	25.4	6.8	2.5
4806128	Baytown city	73,725	99.2	88.3	23.9	15.8	36.2	10.2	2.3
4807000	Beaumont city	117,494	96.3	78.6	23.3	13.4	30.9	9.2	1.8
4810768	Brownsville city	180,302	99.1	92.6	22.7	14.6	41.0	12.5	1.9
4810912	Bryan city	77,932	95.3	73.6	20.8	13.5	28.7	8.2	2.5
4813024	Carrollton city	124,940	99.6	87.2	25.8	19.4	33.1	7.6	1.3
4813552	Cedar Park city	57,582	99.7	89.4	24.8	20.3	36.7	6.4	1.2
4815976	College Station city	97,885	89.1	52.0	16.4	12.2	18.5	3.3	1.6
4816432	Conroe city	61,463	97.1	82.8	23.3	15.1	32.6	8.7	3.2
4817000	Corpus Christi city	312,153	97.7	83.1	24.7	15.9	30.9	9.3	2.3
4819000	Dallas city	1,239,268	98.5	78.1	21.6	13.2	30.7	10.3	2.4
4819972	Denton city	120,858	91.5	65.9	19.7	13.8	22.8	7.7	1.9
4820092	DeSoto city	50,903	99.1	86.8	26.3	18.1	34.3	7.2	1.1
4822660	Edinburg city	78,932	97.8	86.7	22.4	15.7	38.6	8.4	1.5
4824000	El Paso city	671,058	98.8	88.1	24.0	15.8	36.4	10.2	1.6
4824768	Euless city	52,725	99.7	78.8	23.4	15.3	29.5	8.3	2.3
4826232	Flower Mound town	67,545	99.8	94.1	27.3	23.8	38.3	3.6	1.2
4827000	Fort Worth city	777,512	98.2	84.4	23.1	15.6	33.7	9.5	2.4
4827684	Frisco city	129,551	99.8	92.2	27.0	22.1	37.7	4.1	1.2

Table B-4: Cities with a Population of 50,000 or More—Relationships—*Continued*

State/place FIPS code	State/place	Population in nonfamily households						Population in subfamilies as a percent of total population					
		Total population in nonfamily households	Nonfamily householders				Nonrelatives in nonfamily households	Total population in subfamilies	In married couple subfamilies			Parent in a parent-child subfamily	Child in a parent-child subfamily
			Total	Male living alone	Female living alone	Householder living with nonrelatives			Total in married-couple subfamilies	Spouse in a married-couple subfamily	Child in married-couple subfamily		
	Oregon—cont'd												
4105350	Beaverton city	22.5	16.2	5.5	6.6	4.1	6.3	2.1	1.1	1.0	0.1	0.6	0.5
4105800	Bend city	23.6	16.3	4.7	7.3	4.2	7.3	0.0	0.0	0.0	0.0	0.0	0.0
4115800	Corvallis city	34.2	20.0	5.4	7.2	7.4	14.2	0.0	0.0	0.0	0.0	0.0	0.0
4123850	Eugene city	32.9	20.6	5.9	7.9	6.9	12.3	0.9	0.2	0.2	0.0	0.4	0.3
4131250	Gresham city	15.6	12.0	4.3	5.3	2.4	3.6	4.6	1.2	1.0	0.2	1.6	1.8
4134100	Hillsboro city	13.9	10.9	3.7	5.1	2.0	3.0	4.1	1.5	1.0	0.5	1.4	1.3
4147000	Medford city	17.2	13.7	4.9	6.4	2.4	3.5	3.1	0.9	0.7	0.2	1.1	1.1
4159000	Portland city	29.8	20.5	6.7	7.9	5.9	9.3	2.3	1.1	0.9	0.2	0.6	0.6
4164900	Salem city	16.5	13.0	4.1	6.7	2.2	3.5	2.2	0.6	0.5	0.1	0.8	0.8
4169600	Springfield city	21.2	15.7	5.2	6.3	4.2	5.5	4.3	0.8	0.4	0.3	1.6	1.9
4200000	**Pennsylvania**	17.2	13.8	5.0	6.6	2.3	3.4	3.0	0.9	0.7	0.2	1.0	1.2
4202000	Allentown city	15.6	12.7	4.9	5.4	2.4	3.0	5.7	1.0	1.0	0.1	1.9	2.8
4206088	Bethlehem city	22.4	17.2	5.8	8.2	3.2	5.2	2.5	0.4	0.4	0.1	1.1	1.0
4224000	Erie city	22.8	18.1	7.1	7.9	3.2	4.7	3.3	0.7	0.5	0.2	1.2	1.5
4241216	Lancaster city	21.1	16.2	5.8	6.9	3.5	4.8	5.2	1.2	0.8	0.4	1.5	2.5
4242928	Levittown CDP	10.8	9.1	3.2	4.5	1.4	1.8	5.2	1.5	0.9	0.6	1.7	2.1
4260000	Philadelphia city	23.4	17.8	6.5	8.5	2.8	5.5	5.9	1.1	0.8	0.2	2.2	2.6
4261000	Pittsburgh city	31.5	23.0	7.9	10.0	5.2	8.5	2.5	0.5	0.4	0.1	0.9	1.1
4263624	Reading city	16.9	13.4	5.0	5.9	2.5	3.5	5.6	1.3	1.0	0.3	1.9	2.4
4269000	Scranton city	21.4	16.4	6.1	7.5	2.8	5.0	3.1	1.1	0.8	0.3	0.8	1.2
4400000	**Rhode Island**	18.7	14.6	5.0	6.8	2.8	4.1	3.0	1.1	0.9	0.3	0.8	1.0
4419180	Cranston city	15.6	12.9	4.5	6.6	1.8	2.7	2.5	0.8	0.6	0.2	0.7	1.1
4454640	Pawtucket city	18.3	15.2	6.0	7.0	2.3	3.1	4.9	1.7	1.4	0.3	1.5	1.7
4459000	Providence city	23.1	15.1	5.3	5.4	4.4	8.1	3.6	1.0	0.8	0.3	1.1	1.4
4474300	Warwick city	20.1	16.9	5.5	8.6	2.8	3.2	2.7	1.3	1.0	0.3	0.7	0.7
4500000	**South Carolina**	15.5	12.3	4.5	5.9	1.9	3.2	4.1	0.9	0.7	0.2	1.5	1.7
4513330	Charleston city	30.5	20.8	6.3	9.1	5.4	9.7	2.1	0.4	0.3	0.1	0.7	1.0
4516000	Columbia city	23.0	16.2	5.8	6.9	3.5	6.8	2.0	0.2	0.2	0.0	0.8	1.0
4530850	Greenville city	26.0	20.9	7.5	10.1	3.3	5.1	2.0	0.1	0.1	0.0	0.9	1.0
4548535	Mount Pleasant town	19.5	13.9	3.5	7.2	3.2	5.6	0.0	0.0	0.0	0.0	0.0	0.0
4550875	North Charleston city	18.5	13.7	4.9	5.8	3.0	4.8	3.6	0.2	0.1	0.1	1.4	2.0
4561405	Rock Hill city	18.7	14.9	5.5	7.0	2.4	3.8	2.9	0.6	0.5	0.1	1.1	1.2
4600000	**South Dakota**	17.3	13.9	5.5	5.9	2.4	3.4	2.5	0.6	0.4	0.2	0.8	1.1
4652980	Rapid City city	20.7	16.1	5.6	7.6	2.9	4.6	0.0	0.0	0.0	0.0	0.0	0.0
4659020	Sioux Falls city	19.9	15.0	5.2	6.6	3.2	4.9	1.6	0.4	0.4	0.0	0.6	0.6
4700000	**Tennessee**	15.9	12.9	4.8	6.1	2.0	3.0	3.7	1.0	0.8	0.3	1.2	1.4
4703440	Bartlett city	8.6	6.7	2.5	3.0	1.1	1.9	3.7	1.2	0.8	0.4	1.3	1.2
4714000	Chattanooga city	21.8	17.3	6.2	8.2	2.8	4.5	3.1	0.7	0.6	0.1	1.2	1.2
4715160	Clarksville city	13.1	10.0	3.8	4.1	2.1	3.1	3.8	1.3	1.0	0.3	0.9	1.5
4727740	Franklin city	15.0	12.9	3.5	8.2	1.3	2.0	0.0	0.0	0.0	0.0	0.0	0.0
4733280	Hendersonville city	11.7	10.3	3.4	5.8	1.1	1.4	3.0	0.8	0.6	0.2	1.1	1.1
4737640	Jackson city	17.4	14.3	5.0	7.6	1.7	3.1	0.0	0.0	0.0	0.0	0.0	0.0
4738320	Johnson City city	23.8	19.2	7.3	8.5	3.5	4.6	2.0	1.1	0.8	0.3	0.5	0.5
4739560	Kingsport city	19.9	17.1	5.4	9.6	2.1	2.8	4.4	1.3	1.0	0.3	1.2	2.0
4740000	Knoxville city	30.6	24.1	9.1	10.6	4.3	6.6	2.4	0.6	0.5	0.1	0.8	1.0
4748000	Memphis city	19.5	15.9	6.2	7.4	2.3	3.6	5.0	0.5	0.4	0.1	2.0	2.5
4751560	Murfreesboro city	23.0	15.3	4.6	6.0	4.7	7.8	0.0	0.0	0.0	0.0	0.0	0.0
4752006	Nashville-Davidson	24.2	18.3	6.6	8.1	3.6	5.9	3.4	0.8	0.7	0.1	1.2	1.4
4800000	**Texas**	13.4	10.5	4.0	4.6	1.9	2.9	5.0	1.7	1.3	0.4	1.5	1.9
4801000	Abilene city	17.7	13.3	5.0	5.8	2.6	4.4	3.7	0.7	0.5	0.1	1.3	1.8
4801924	Allen city	8.4	6.6	2.1	3.2	1.3	1.8	0.0	0.0	0.0	0.0	0.0	0.0
4803000	Amarillo city	16.4	13.3	4.9	6.2	2.2	3.1	3.7	0.9	0.8	0.2	1.2	1.6
4804000	Arlington city	14.6	11.3	4.4	4.8	2.1	3.3	4.7	1.7	1.2	0.5	1.5	1.5
4804462	Atascocita CDP	7.1	5.7	2.6	2.0	1.1	1.3	5.1	1.0	0.9	0.1	2.1	2.1
4805000	Austin city	28.1	18.9	6.6	6.8	5.5	9.2	3.1	1.1	0.8	0.3	0.9	1.1
4806128	Baytown city	10.9	9.4	4.2	4.3	0.9	1.5	7.0	1.6	1.3	0.4	2.6	2.8
4807000	Beaumont city	17.7	15.2	6.0	7.5	1.7	2.5	4.0	1.4	1.1	0.3	1.3	1.3
4810768	Brownsville city	6.5	5.8	2.2	3.2	0.4	0.8	7.8	3.1	2.3	0.8	2.0	2.7
4810912	Bryan city	21.6	14.6	5.7	5.8	3.1	7.1	4.2	0.6	0.5	0.1	1.6	2.0
4813024	Carrollton city	12.4	9.7	3.3	4.5	1.9	2.7	4.1	1.5	1.3	0.2	1.3	1.4
4813552	Cedar Park city	10.3	8.2	2.4	4.2	1.6	2.1	6.2	4.3	2.7	1.6	1.1	0.9
4815976	College Station city	37.1	18.4	4.9	4.9	8.6	18.7	0.0	0.0	0.0	0.0	0.0	0.0
4816432	Conroe city	14.3	10.7	2.9	5.9	1.9	3.5	4.0	0.8	0.5	0.3	1.6	1.6
4817000	Corpus Christi city	14.6	11.4	4.5	4.6	2.3	3.2	5.8	1.4	1.1	0.4	1.9	2.5
4819000	Dallas city	20.4	16.0	6.3	6.7	3.0	4.4	5.1	1.6	1.3	0.3	1.6	1.9
4819972	Denton city	25.6	14.9	4.3	5.3	5.4	10.6	0.9	0.4	0.3	0.1	0.3	0.2
4820092	DeSoto city	12.3	11.3	3.2	7.2	0.9	1.0	0.0	0.0	0.0	0.0	0.0	0.0
4822660	Edinburg city	11.2	7.8	3.0	2.9	1.9	3.3	5.6	3.6	2.2	1.4	0.9	1.1
4824000	El Paso city	10.7	8.8	3.6	4.1	1.2	1.9	6.1	1.9	1.4	0.5	1.8	2.4
4824768	Euless city	20.8	16.1	6.3	6.2	3.6	4.7	0.0	0.0	0.0	0.0	0.0	0.0
4826232	Flower Mound town	5.6	4.8	1.6	2.6	0.6	0.9	0.0	0.0	0.0	0.0	0.0	0.0
4827000	Fort Worth city	13.9	11.1	4.2	5.1	1.9	2.7	5.6	1.9	1.4	0.5	1.7	2.1
4827684	Frisco city	7.6	6.1	2.4	2.7	1.0	1.5	1.6	0.5	0.5	0.0	0.6	0.5

State/place FIPS code	State/place	Total population	Percent of the population in households	Population in family households, percent					
				Percent in family households	Householder in family household, percent	Spouse in family household, percent	Child in family household (biological, adopted, or stepchild)	Other relative in family household	Nonrelatives in family household
	Texas—cont'd								
4829000	Garland city	232,843	99.7	90.3	24.2	16.8	36.2	10.7	2.3
4829336	Georgetown city	52,560	96.6	79.7	26.6	23.1	22.8	6.2	1.0
4830464	Grand Prairie city	181,209	99.9	89.4	23.7	16.4	35.8	11.0	2.4
4832372	Harlingen city	65,653	98.4	89.3	23.2	15.5	38.5	10.1	2.0
4835000	Houston city	2,162,268	98.5	80.2	22.2	14.1	31.6	10.2	2.2
4837000	Irving city	224,676	99.6	82.6	23.4	16.4	31.0	9.3	2.5
4839148	Killeen city	134,483	99.8	87.0	22.7	15.7	36.9	8.7	2.9
4841464	Laredo city	244,586	98.5	92.4	21.7	14.2	41.0	13.5	2.1
4841980	League City city	88,817	99.5	84.6	25.6	21.6	33.3	3.2	0.9
4842508	Lewisville city	99,440	99.5	81.6	24.5	17.3	31.4	6.4	2.1
4843888	Longview city	81,647	96.0	81.2	24.5	16.3	29.8	8.5	2.1
4845000	Lubbock city	236,488	95.4	74.0	22.6	15.3	27.6	6.5	2.0
4845384	McAllen city	135,132	99.2	89.1	23.1	16.4	35.8	12.1	1.8
4845744	McKinney city	143,089	98.5	89.4	25.7	20.4	34.9	6.7	1.7
4846452	Mansfield city	59,186	99.3	91.2	26.5	21.7	37.6	3.8	1.6
4847892	Mesquite city	142,744	99.5	89.5	25.1	16.1	35.6	10.4	2.3
4848072	Midland city	119,171	98.6	85.2	24.6	17.6	31.5	9.3	2.3
4848768	Mission city	80,306	99.8	93.9	24.1	18.8	40.0	10.7	0.4
4848804	Missouri City city	68,310	99.6	91.2	26.4	20.2	35.3	8.4	1.0
4850820	New Braunfels city	61,166	98.4	85.4	25.0	18.4	32.9	7.1	2.0
4852356	North Richland Hills city	65,683	99.6	86.4	26.8	20.9	31.3	5.8	1.6
4853388	Odessa city	107,279	98.4	84.0	24.7	16.3	33.2	7.0	2.8
4856000	Pasadena city	152,030	99.4	88.6	22.7	15.2	37.3	10.7	2.7
4856348	Pearland city	98,123	99.6	92.0	27.5	21.8	35.6	6.2	0.8
4857176	Pflugerville city	52,704	99.6	89.6	26.1	20.1	35.6	6.5	1.2
4857200	Pharr city	72,939	100.0	93.0	22.4	14.6	40.7	14.2	1.2
4858016	Plano city	271,135	99.7	86.0	26.9	21.5	31.0	5.4	1.2
4858820	Port Arthur city	54,233	98.7	80.6	21.5	12.7	34.3	9.6	2.5
4861796	Richardson city	103,204	99.1	82.6	25.8	19.9	29.6	5.9	1.4
4863500	Round Rock city	107,178	99.5	88.1	23.8	18.4	37.0	6.5	2.4
4863572	Rowlett city	58,818	99.4	93.0	26.6	21.3	35.7	7.7	1.6
4864472	San Angelo city	96,093	93.6	76.0	23.3	15.9	27.3	7.4	2.1
4865000	San Antonio city	1,383,716	98.3	82.7	22.8	14.6	33.2	9.9	2.2
4865600	San Marcos city	50,610	88.5	46.1	13.8	7.9	15.9	7.0	1.5
4869596	Spring CDP	58,321	100.0	90.7	24.0	18.0	36.9	9.0	2.7
4870808	Sugar Land city	82,204	98.5	92.0	27.1	23.5	31.8	9.3	0.3
4872176	Temple city	69,024	97.7	84.1	23.6	17.7	32.4	8.3	2.0
4872656	The Woodlands CDP	105,177	99.6	89.6	26.9	23.5	35.6	3.1	0.5
4874144	Tyler city	99,404	96.0	75.6	23.2	15.4	27.4	8.0	1.6
4875428	Victoria city	64,246	98.3	83.7	25.2	16.8	30.6	7.8	3.3
4876000	Waco city	127,808	93.7	72.4	21.2	13.4	29.0	6.5	2.3
4879000	Wichita Falls city	104,440	86.9	71.8	22.9	15.8	26.0	5.0	2.2
4900000	**Utah**	2,856,839	98.4	87.3	23.3	18.9	36.7	6.3	2.0
4943660	Layton city	69,202	99.9	91.4	25.1	20.1	37.7	6.4	2.1
4944320	Lehi city	51,906	99.8	95.9	22.1	19.7	48.6	4.5	1.0
4950150	Millcreek CDP	62,441	98.6	75.7	23.0	18.0	26.9	5.8	1.9
4955980	Ogden city	83,830	96.6	79.7	22.7	15.6	31.6	6.5	3.2
4957300	Orem city	90,642	97.9	87.6	22.4	18.2	37.2	7.9	2.0
4962470	Provo city	115,427	92.0	72.0	19.9	16.5	27.6	5.7	2.4
4965330	St. George city	75,361	98.6	83.6	23.8	20.3	31.9	5.9	1.7
4967000	Salt Lake City city	189,601	97.2	70.9	20.6	14.7	26.3	7.1	2.2
4967440	Sandy city	89,457	99.5	89.9	25.2	20.8	36.9	5.4	1.7
4970850	South Jordan city	56,225	100.0	93.6	23.6	21.6	39.3	6.9	2.2
4975360	Taylorsville city	60,146	99.8	87.8	22.9	18.0	34.4	9.7	2.8
4982950	West Jordan city	108,311	99.5	91.3	22.6	18.0	39.6	9.1	2.0
4983470	West Valley City city	132,285	99.8	92.8	22.2	15.3	37.3	13.3	4.6
5000000	**Vermont**	626,303	96.0	75.4	25.5	20.1	24.3	3.2	2.2
5100000	**Virginia**	8,184,299	97.0	81.2	24.8	18.7	28.9	6.7	2.1
5101000	Alexandria city	146,690	99.1	68.3	21.3	16.3	21.5	7.1	2.2
5103000	Arlington CDP	220,785	98.6	64.3	20.1	15.9	20.2	6.2	1.8
5114440	Centreville CDP	72,688	100.0	88.0	24.9	19.8	34.3	7.6	1.3
5116000	Chesapeake city	228,092	97.3	86.5	26.0	19.1	31.8	7.7	1.9
5121088	Dale City CDP	68,876	100.0	92.6	24.2	17.3	37.9	10.4	2.7
5135000	Hampton city	136,507	96.8	78.1	23.8	15.4	28.8	7.7	2.4
5135624	Harrisonburg city	50,759	86.0	52.1	16.0	10.7	19.5	4.3	1.7
5147672	Lynchburg city	77,157	86.6	64.4	20.8	13.9	24.0	4.1	1.7
5156000	Newport News city	181,043	95.3	77.4	23.7	14.4	29.6	6.5	3.2
5157000	Norfolk city	245,262	89.8	69.0	20.4	12.1	26.0	7.9	2.5
5164000	Portsmouth city	96,209	97.2	81.0	24.3	13.3	30.6	10.5	2.3
5166672	Reston CDP	61,929	99.6	77.8	24.6	20.1	26.6	4.6	1.9
5167000	Richmond city	210,453	95.0	64.3	19.3	9.6	24.0	8.8	2.7
5168000	Roanoke city	97,654	97.8	75.0	24.1	14.7	26.7	6.6	2.8
5176432	Suffolk city	85,228	98.9	87.3	26.2	18.9	33.0	7.5	1.8

Table B-4: Cities with a Population of 50,000 or More—Relationships—*Continued*

State/ place FIPS code	State/place	Population in nonfamily households						Population in subfamilies as a percent of total population					
		Total population in nonfamily households	Nonfamily householders				Nonrelatives in nonfamily households	Total population in subfamilies	In married couple subfamilies			Parent in a parent-child subfamily	Child in a parent-child subfamily
			Total	Male living alone	Female living alone	Householder living with nonrelatives			Total in married-couple subfamilies	Spouse in a married-couple subfamily	Child in married-couple subfamily		
	Texas—cont'd												
4829000	Garland city	9.4	7.6	2.7	3.7	1.1	1.9	6.1	1.9	1.5	0.4	1.9	2.3
4829336	Georgetown city	17.0	14.0	5.1	7.3	1.6	3.0	2.7	1.3	1.0	0.3	0.7	0.7
4830464	Grand Prairie city	10.5	8.4	3.6	3.4	1.4	2.1	6.3	2.4	1.8	0.6	1.7	2.2
4832372	Harlingen city	9.1	7.5	2.7	3.7	1.1	1.6	6.7	2.3	1.7	0.7	1.7	2.6
4835000	Houston city	18.3	14.3	5.8	5.9	2.6	4.0	5.0	1.5	1.1	0.3	1.6	2.0
4837000	Irving city	16.9	13.6	5.7	5.8	2.2	3.3	4.2	1.7	1.3	0.4	1.1	1.3
4839148	Killeen city	12.9	9.8	4.5	3.7	1.5	3.1	4.2	1.0	0.9	0.1	1.8	1.5
4841464	Laredo city	6.1	4.7	2.0	2.0	0.8	1.4	0.6	0.2	0.1	0.0	0.2	0.2
4841980	League City city	14.8	11.1	3.3	5.3	2.5	3.7	1.2	0.2	0.1	0.0	0.6	0.5
4842508	Lewisville city	17.9	14.0	4.9	6.2	2.9	3.8	2.9	0.7	0.6	0.1	1.0	1.2
4843888	Longview city	14.8	12.8	5.3	6.1	1.4	2.1	4.4	1.0	0.8	0.3	1.5	1.9
4845000	Lubbock city	21.4	14.8	4.7	6.3	3.8	6.6	4.1	0.7	0.5	0.2	1.4	1.9
4845384	McAllen city	10.1	7.9	3.1	3.7	1.2	2.1	7.4	2.9	2.0	0.9	1.8	2.8
4845744	McKinney city	9.1	7.0	2.3	3.2	1.5	2.1	4.2	1.7	1.1	0.5	1.2	1.3
4846452	Mansfield city	8.1	6.9	3.2	2.7	0.9	1.2	0.0	0.0	0.0	0.0	0.0	0.0
4847892	Mesquite city	10.0	8.4	3.0	4.2	1.2	1.7	6.6	2.2	1.4	0.7	2.0	2.4
4848072	Midland city	13.3	10.6	3.8	4.7	2.0	2.8	5.5	1.8	1.3	0.5	1.5	2.2
4848768	Mission city	5.9	5.2	1.9	2.9	0.5	0.6	8.1	5.4	2.6	2.8	1.2	1.5
4848804	Missouri City city	8.4	6.8	1.9	4.2	0.8	1.5	5.7	1.1	0.9	0.3	2.0	2.6
4850820	New Braunfels city	12.9	10.4	3.3	5.3	1.8	2.6	4.9	2.4	2.0	0.4	1.1	1.5
4852356	North Richland Hills city	13.1	11.2	4.0	5.6	1.5	2.0	2.1	0.6	0.4	0.1	0.8	0.8
4853388	Odessa city	14.4	11.2	4.1	4.8	2.3	3.2	4.9	1.3	1.0	0.4	1.4	2.2
4856000	Pasadena city	10.8	8.5	3.6	3.5	1.4	2.3	6.3	2.0	1.4	0.6	2.0	2.3
4856348	Pearland city	7.5	6.7	2.5	3.5	0.7	0.9	3.3	0.8	0.7	0.1	1.3	1.2
4857176	Pflugerville city	10.0	8.7	3.6	4.0	1.1	1.3	0.0	0.0	0.0	0.0	0.0	0.0
4857200	Pharr city	7.0	5.6	1.7	2.8	1.0	1.4	9.8	2.4	1.6	0.8	2.8	4.6
4858016	Plano city	13.7	10.9	3.8	5.2	1.9	2.8	3.0	1.2	1.0	0.2	0.8	1.0
4858820	Port Arthur city	18.1	14.6	6.3	6.4	2.0	3.4	6.1	2.0	1.5	0.6	1.9	2.2
4861796	Richardson city	16.5	11.9	4.3	5.0	2.7	4.6	3.0	1.9	1.4	0.4	0.5	0.6
4863500	Round Rock city	11.4	8.8	2.9	4.3	1.6	2.6	3.5	1.7	1.6	0.2	0.8	1.0
4863572	Rowlett city	6.5	5.2	1.8	2.2	1.2	1.3	6.3	3.2	2.9	0.3	1.4	1.7
4864472	San Angelo city	17.6	14.1	5.2	6.6	2.3	3.5	4.0	0.7	0.5	0.2	1.5	1.8
4865000	San Antonio city	15.6	12.1	4.7	5.2	2.2	3.5	6.2	2.0	1.5	0.5	1.9	2.3
4865600	San Marcos city	42.4	22.5	6.2	5.8	10.5	19.9	0.0	0.0	0.0	0.0	0.0	0.0
4869596	Spring CDP	9.3	7.7	3.7	3.0	1.0	1.6	0.0	0.0	0.0	0.0	0.0	0.0
4870808	Sugar Land city	6.5	5.8	2.0	3.4	0.5	0.7	4.8	2.5	2.2	0.4	1.1	1.2
4872176	Temple city	13.6	11.4	4.0	6.3	1.1	2.3	3.9	1.6	1.5	0.1	1.4	1.0
4872656	The Woodlands CDP	10.0	8.6	2.8	5.0	0.9	1.3	0.0	0.0	0.0	0.0	0.0	0.0
4874144	Tyler city	20.4	15.5	4.9	7.8	2.8	5.0	3.8	1.5	1.0	0.5	1.0	1.4
4875428	Victoria city	14.5	12.1	5.5	4.8	1.8	2.4	4.9	0.2	0.1	0.1	2.0	2.8
4876000	Waco city	21.3	15.0	5.4	6.4	3.2	6.3	3.8	0.5	0.4	0.1	1.6	1.8
4879000	Wichita Falls city	15.0	12.9	4.8	6.4	1.7	2.1	2.3	0.4	0.3	0.0	0.8	1.1
4900000	**Utah**	11.1	7.8	2.9	3.3	1.7	3.2	4.3	2.1	1.5	0.6	1.0	1.2
4943660	Layton city	8.5	6.6	2.6	2.6	1.4	1.9	5.5	1.8	1.4	0.4	1.7	2.0
4944320	Lehi city	3.9	2.9	1.2	1.0	0.6	1.0	4.3	3.0	2.2	0.7	0.6	0.7
4950150	Millcreek CDP	23.0	16.2	5.3	6.9	4.0	6.8	3.1	1.3	1.0	0.3	0.9	0.9
4955980	Ogden city	17.0	12.2	4.6	4.5	3.0	4.8	4.2	1.6	1.1	0.5	1.0	1.5
4957300	Orem city	10.3	6.3	1.8	2.8	1.7	4.0	5.4	3.1	1.8	1.3	1.0	1.3
4962470	Provo city	20.0	8.0	1.7	2.2	4.1	12.0	3.8	2.3	1.5	0.8	0.8	0.8
4965330	St. George city	15.0	9.4	2.3	5.1	2.0	5.5	3.8	1.7	1.1	0.6	0.9	1.3
4967000	Salt Lake City city	26.3	18.6	7.3	6.9	4.5	7.7	3.8	1.6	1.1	0.5	1.1	1.1
4967440	Sandy city	9.6	7.0	2.7	3.0	1.3	2.6	4.0	2.3	1.8	0.6	0.8	0.9
4970850	South Jordan city	6.4	3.9	1.5	1.2	1.3	2.5	5.5	3.8	2.6	1.2	0.7	1.0
4975360	Taylorsville city	12.0	9.0	3.4	3.9	1.7	3.0	5.9	2.7	1.8	0.9	1.6	1.6
4982950	West Jordan city	8.1	6.4	2.6	2.5	1.2	1.7	6.8	2.9	2.1	0.8	1.8	2.1
4983470	West Valley City city	7.0	5.3	2.2	2.1	1.1	1.7	8.5	3.9	2.7	1.2	1.8	2.8
5000000	**Vermont**	20.6	15.4	5.0	6.6	3.8	5.1	1.8	0.6	0.4	0.1	0.5	0.7
5100000	**Virginia**	15.9	12.1	4.2	5.6	2.3	3.8	3.6	1.2	1.0	0.3	1.1	1.3
5101000	Alexandria city	30.8	23.2	7.9	10.9	4.4	7.6	2.3	0.9	0.7	0.1	0.7	0.7
5103000	Arlington CDP	34.3	23.0	8.2	9.2	5.6	11.3	2.3	1.2	1.0	0.2	0.6	0.5
5114440	Centreville CDP	12.0	8.7	2.4	3.9	2.4	3.4	0.0	0.0	0.0	0.0	0.0	0.0
5116000	Chesapeake city	10.8	8.8	3.0	4.4	1.5	2.0	5.4	1.8	1.3	0.5	1.6	2.0
5121088	Dale City CDP	7.4	5.3	1.6	2.5	1.2	2.1	6.6	2.2	1.9	0.3	2.0	2.5
5135000	Hampton city	18.7	14.5	5.5	6.6	2.4	4.2	4.5	1.1	0.8	0.2	1.6	1.8
5135624	Harrisonburg city	33.8	15.2	3.5	5.3	6.5	18.6	0.0	0.0	0.0	0.0	0.0	0.0
5147672	Lynchburg city	22.2	16.6	6.4	7.2	3.0	5.5	2.3	0.2	0.2	0.0	0.9	1.2
5156000	Newport News city	17.8	13.9	5.1	6.6	2.3	3.9	3.9	0.7	0.6	0.2	1.4	1.7
5157000	Norfolk city	20.8	14.7	5.2	5.9	3.6	6.1	4.3	0.9	0.8	0.2	1.6	1.8
5164000	Portsmouth city	16.2	13.5	5.2	6.4	1.9	2.7	5.6	0.9	0.8	0.1	2.1	2.5
5166672	Reston CDP	21.8	16.8	5.4	7.6	3.7	5.1	2.4	0.9	0.7	0.2	0.7	0.8
5167000	Richmond city	30.7	21.3	7.2	9.2	4.8	9.4	3.1	0.5	0.4	0.1	1.4	1.2
5168000	Roanoke city	22.8	18.9	7.1	8.7	3.1	3.9	3.5	0.9	0.5	0.4	1.2	1.5
5176432	Suffolk city	11.6	9.7	3.8	4.3	1.5	1.9	4.1	0.6	0.5	0.1	1.7	1.8

State/ place FIPS code	State/place	Total population	Percent of the population in households	Population in family households, percent					
				Percent in family households	Householder in family household, percent	Spouse in family household, percent	Child in family household (biological, adopted, or stepchild)	Other relative in family household	Nonrelatives in family household
	Virginia—cont'd								
5182000	Virginia Beach city..................................	445,561	97.6	82.2	25.3	18.4	30.2	6.3	1.9
5300000	**Washington**	6,896,071	98.0	79.8	24.6	18.8	28.3	5.4	2.6
5303180	Auburn city...	72,754	99.2	81.8	25.0	17.6	29.4	6.2	3.6
5305210	Bellevue city...	132,131	99.0	79.5	26.2	21.8	25.4	4.4	1.7
5305280	Bellingham city..	82,128	94.1	59.0	19.9	14.0	20.2	3.3	1.5
5322640	Everett city...	104,532	96.4	72.5	21.5	15.0	26.7	6.3	3.0
5323515	Federal Way city......................................	91,788	99.1	83.5	24.6	16.4	30.5	8.4	3.7
5335275	Kennewick city..	76,115	98.0	82.4	23.3	17.3	32.8	6.0	3.0
5335415	Kent city...	122,748	98.4	83.7	22.9	16.2	32.2	9.7	2.7
5335940	Kirkland city..	83,333	99.1	80.0	26.2	20.9	26.8	3.8	2.3
5338038	Lakewood city...	58,885	98.1	76.6	23.4	16.5	27.7	6.6	2.4
5343955	Marysville city...	62,311	99.3	86.5	25.4	18.8	32.6	5.9	3.8
5353545	Pasco city...	66,289	99.3	90.0	21.8	14.6	42.2	7.8	3.5
5357535	Redmond city..	56,526	99.4	76.2	25.1	21.4	26.0	3.1	0.6
5357745	Renton city...	95,600	99.2	77.9	23.0	16.2	27.8	6.7	4.2
5358235	Richland city...	51,430	99.4	82.4	26.2	20.1	30.6	3.4	2.1
5363000	Seattle city...	636,270	96.3	60.8	20.1	15.6	18.9	4.1	2.2
5363960	Shoreline city..	54,312	96.6	75.9	24.0	18.2	25.3	6.6	1.9
5365922	South Hill CDP...	55,286	99.9	91.8	26.8	20.6	37.3	4.5	2.6
5367000	Spokane city...	209,876	96.6	72.1	23.1	16.2	25.7	4.5	2.6
5367167	Spokane Valley city..................................	90,817	99.1	80.1	25.7	18.9	28.0	4.7	2.9
5370000	Tacoma city..	201,893	97.3	75.6	22.4	15.4	28.1	6.4	3.2
5374060	Vancouver city...	165,613	98.5	77.9	23.9	16.6	28.7	6.1	2.6
5380010	Yakima city...	92,995	97.2	80.7	22.2	15.3	32.0	8.1	3.0
5400000	**West Virginia**..	1,855,392	97.3	80.1	25.8	19.4	26.8	5.9	2.2
5414600	Charleston city..	50,984	95.7	71.6	23.9	15.7	25.7	4.6	1.7
5500000	**Wisconsin**...	5,725,352	97.4	79.1	25.5	19.7	28.2	3.7	2.0
5502375	Appleton city..	72,693	96.5	78.5	24.4	18.0	30.4	3.5	2.0
5522300	Eau Claire city...	66,824	93.9	65.5	21.1	15.9	24.2	2.3	2.0
5531000	Green Bay city...	104,623	96.8	74.9	23.9	16.6	27.8	4.3	2.3
5537825	Janesville city..	63,614	99.0	79.9	26.1	18.4	26.9	4.3	4.3
5539225	Kenosha city...	99,844	96.8	79.7	24.2	15.1	31.8	5.6	3.0
5540775	La Crosse city..	51,448	90.9	57.4	18.9	13.3	19.8	2.8	2.6
5548000	Madison city...	240,301	95.1	60.8	20.5	15.1	20.7	2.7	1.8
5553000	Milwaukee city..	598,325	97.3	75.1	21.5	10.5	32.2	8.0	3.0
5560500	Oshkosh city...	66,526	88.5	62.9	20.1	14.3	22.5	3.5	2.4
5566000	Racine city..	78,287	98.2	78.7	22.7	14.2	33.1	6.4	2.2
5584250	Waukesha city...	70,865	95.9	74.7	24.1	18.5	28.1	2.4	1.5
5585300	West Allis city..	60,619	98.5	72.1	23.1	16.4	25.9	4.6	2.1
5600000	**Wyoming**	575,535	97.6	79.9	25.3	20.1	27.9	4.3	2.3
5613150	Casper city..	57,913	98.2	78.4	25.6	18.8	26.9	4.5	2.6
5613900	Cheyenne city...	61,417	98.7	78.7	24.4	19.0	28.8	3.8	2.8

Table B-4: Cities with a Population of 50,000 or More—Relationships—*Continued*

State/ place FIPS code	State/place	Population in nonfamily households						Population in subfamilies as a percent of total population					
		Total population in nonfamily households	Nonfamily householders				Nonrelatives in nonfamily households	Total population in subfamilies	In married couple subfamilies			Parent in a parent-child subfamily	Child in a parent-child subfamily
			Total	Male living alone	Female living alone	Householder living with nonrelatives			Total in married-couple subfamilies	Spouse in a married-couple subfamily	Child in married-couple subfamily		
	Virginia—cont'd												
5182000	Virginia Beach city......................	15.4	11.6	3.9	5.0	2.6	3.8	3.6	1.3	1.0	0.3	1.1	1.3
5300000	**Washington**............................	18.2	13.6	4.9	5.7	3.0	4.5	2.9	1.1	0.9	0.2	0.8	0.9
5303180	Auburn city..............................	17.4	13.6	5.6	5.2	2.7	3.8	3.0	0.9	0.9	0.0	1.0	1.1
5305210	Bellevue city............................	19.4	14.3	5.3	5.5	3.5	5.2	1.8	1.2	1.1	0.1	0.3	0.3
5305280	Bellingham city.........................	35.2	21.1	6.7	7.2	7.2	14.1	2.9	1.9	1.8	0.1	0.5	0.5
5322640	Everett city..............................	23.9	18.2	7.6	6.8	3.8	5.7	2.5	1.0	0.8	0.2	0.8	0.8
5323515	Federal Way city........................	15.6	11.5	4.0	4.8	2.7	4.1	4.4	1.8	1.5	0.3	1.1	1.4
5335275	Kennewick city..........................	15.6	12.8	5.0	5.9	1.9	2.7	3.7	1.8	1.2	0.6	0.9	1.0
5335415	Kent city.................................	14.7	11.5	4.7	4.7	2.1	3.2	5.5	3.0	2.2	0.8	1.2	1.3
5335940	Kirkland city.............................	19.1	15.4	5.2	7.5	2.6	3.8	2.0	1.2	1.0	0.2	0.4	0.4
5338038	Lakewood city...........................	21.5	17.7	7.6	7.5	2.6	3.8	0.0	0.0	0.0	0.0	0.0	0.0
5343955	Marysville city..........................	12.8	9.6	3.4	4.1	2.0	3.3	2.4	0.8	0.5	0.3	0.6	1.0
5353545	Pasco city...............................	9.3	6.7	2.7	2.4	1.6	2.6	4.4	2.0	1.7	0.3	1.0	1.4
5357535	Redmond city...........................	23.2	16.8	6.7	6.1	4.0	6.4	0.0	0.0	0.0	0.0	0.0	0.0
5357745	Renton city..............................	21.4	16.1	6.4	6.1	3.6	5.3	3.5	2.3	1.6	0.7	0.6	0.5
5358235	Richland city............................	17.1	13.4	5.8	5.5	2.2	3.6	0.0	0.0	0.0	0.0	0.0	0.0
5363000	Seattle city..............................	35.5	25.4	8.9	9.9	6.6	10.1	1.5	0.7	0.6	0.1	0.4	0.5
5363960	Shoreline city...........................	20.7	14.8	4.9	6.6	3.2	5.8	4.1	2.7	2.1	0.6	0.6	0.8
5365922	South Hill CDP..........................	8.1	5.9	2.0	2.2	1.7	2.2	2.5	1.1	1.1	0.1	0.6	0.8
5367000	Spokane city............................	24.5	18.4	6.2	8.1	4.1	6.1	2.2	0.6	0.5	0.1	0.8	0.9
5367167	Spokane Valley city.....................	19.0	15.0	5.7	6.5	2.8	4.0	3.1	1.2	0.9	0.3	0.9	1.0
5370000	Tacoma city.............................	21.7	16.3	5.4	7.4	3.5	5.4	3.2	1.1	0.9	0.2	1.0	1.1
5374060	Vancouver city..........................	20.6	15.6	5.4	6.6	3.6	5.0	3.6	1.3	1.0	0.2	1.1	1.2
5380010	Yakima city..............................	16.6	13.0	4.5	6.3	2.2	3.5	6.0	1.1	0.8	0.3	2.2	2.7
5400000	**West Virginia**.........................	17.2	14.1	5.4	6.7	2.0	3.2	3.3	1.2	0.9	0.3	1.0	1.1
5414600	Charleston city..........................	24.2	20.9	8.3	9.8	2.8	3.3	2.5	1.0	0.7	0.3	0.7	0.8
5500000	**Wisconsin**.............................	18.3	14.4	5.3	6.4	2.8	4.0	2.0	0.6	0.5	0.2	0.6	0.7
5502375	Appleton city...........................	18.0	14.5	5.5	6.2	2.9	3.5	2.1	1.1	0.8	0.4	0.4	0.6
5522300	Eau Claire city..........................	28.3	19.4	5.7	8.4	5.3	9.0	1.1	0.3	0.2	0.1	0.4	0.4
5531000	Green Bay city..........................	21.9	16.8	6.6	6.7	3.5	5.0	2.6	0.8	0.5	0.3	0.9	0.9
5537825	Janesville city...........................	19.1	14.9	4.6	7.3	3.0	4.2	3.8	1.0	0.8	0.2	1.2	1.6
5539225	Kenosha city............................	17.1	13.3	5.0	5.6	2.7	3.8	3.0	0.8	0.6	0.2	1.0	1.3
5540775	La Crosse city...........................	33.4	20.8	5.8	8.1	6.9	12.6	0.0	0.0	0.0	0.0	0.0	0.0
5548000	Madison city............................	34.4	22.8	7.3	8.7	6.7	11.6	0.6	0.1	0.1	0.0	0.2	0.3
5553000	Milwaukee city..........................	22.1	16.9	6.2	7.4	3.4	5.2	3.8	0.6	0.5	0.1	1.5	1.8
5560500	Oshkosh city............................	25.7	18.4	6.4	7.4	4.7	7.2	0.0	0.0	0.0	0.0	0.0	0.0
5566000	Racine city..............................	19.6	15.3	5.8	6.9	2.6	4.3	3.4	0.9	0.8	0.1	1.1	1.4
5584250	Waukesha city..........................	21.2	15.9	5.5	7.1	3.3	5.3	0.0	0.0	0.0	0.0	0.0	0.0
5585300	West Allis city...........................	26.4	21.7	8.0	10.0	3.7	4.7	2.6	1.1	0.9	0.2	0.7	0.8
5600000	**Wyoming**..............................	17.7	13.4	5.4	5.3	2.8	4.3	2.2	0.7	0.6	0.2	0.7	0.7
5613150	Casper city..............................	19.8	15.2	6.2	5.7	3.3	4.6	0.0	0.0	0.0	0.0	0.0	0.0
5613900	Cheyenne city...........................	20.0	14.9	5.5	6.4	2.9	5.2	0.0	0.0	0.0	0.0	0.0	0.0

Marriages and Births

PART C. MARRIAGES AND BIRTHS

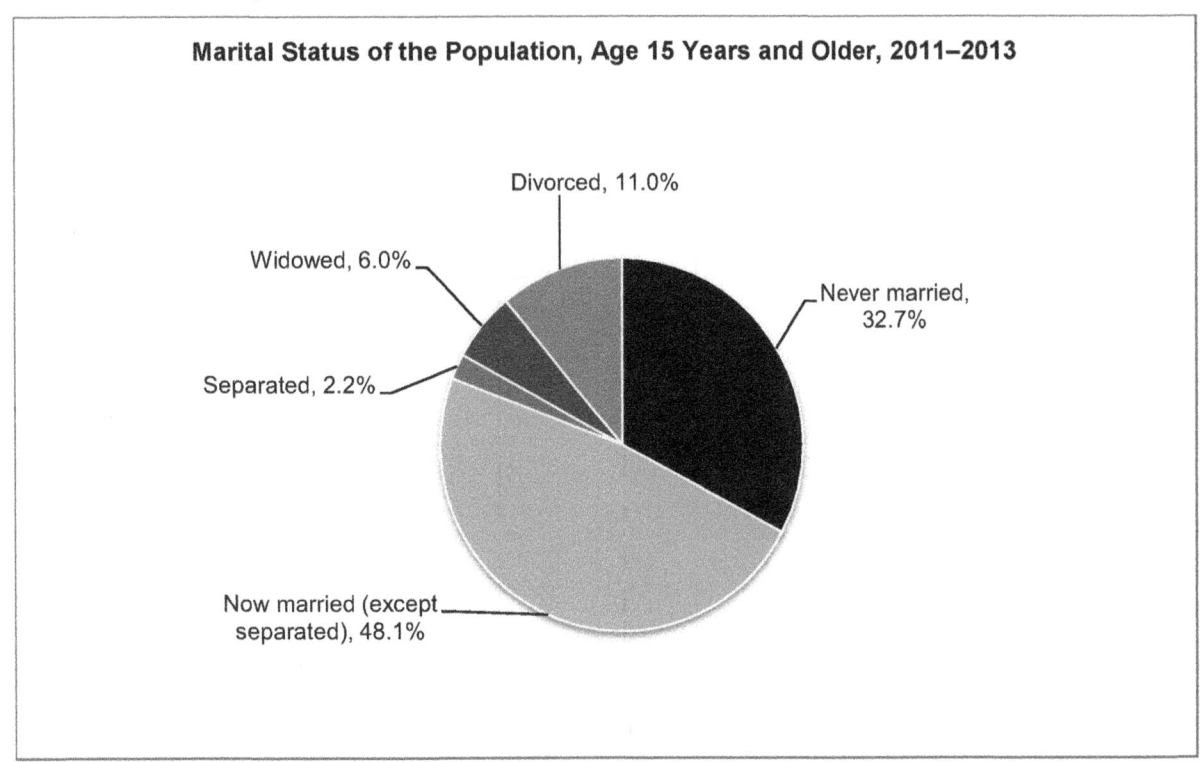

Marital Status of the Population, Age 15 Years and Older, 2011–2013

Divorced, 11.0%

Widowed, 6.0%

Never married, 32.7%

Separated, 2.2%

Now married (except separated), 48.1%

Just under half of the population aged 15 and older are married—49.9 percent of men and 46.4 percent of women. Thirty-six percent of men have never married, compared with 29.6 percent of women, while higher proportions of women are widowed or divorced. Among women, 9.2 percent are widowed and 12.3 percent are divorced, while 2.6 percent of men are widowed and 9.7 percent are divorced.

In 21 states, more than half of adults are currently married, topped by Utah and Idaho with over 55 percent. In the District of Columbia, with its large proportion of nonfamily households, only 26 percent of adult residents are married. Among the states, four have proportions of currently married people below 45 percent: Louisiana, New York, Mississippi, and Rhode Island. Maine and Nevada have the highest proportions of divorced people, both 14.1 percent. The lowest proportions were in New York and New Jersey, both under 9 percent. Nationally, 32.7 percent of adults have never married, ranging from 57.5 percent in the District of Columbia to 26 percent in Idaho.

Three out of four ever-married people have been married once, and 5.1 percent have been married three or more times. In Arkansas, 10.4 percent have been married three or more times, followed by Oklahoma with 9.8 percent. Idaho, Tennessee, Nevada, Wyoming, and Alabama also had high rates of people

who had been married three of more times, all over 8 percent. The lowest rates were in New Jersey, the District of Columbia, New York, and Massachusetts, all at 2 percent or lower.

In the United States, 5.3 percent of women gave birth during the year before their interview. In Utah, 7.4 percent of women had births and the proportion was over 6 percent in 9 states. Less than 4 percent of women in Vermont gave birth, and 11 other states had levels below 5 percent. 64.1 percent of these new mothers were married, and an additional 10.1 percent were unmarried partners. The percent of new mothers who were married ranged from 83.8 percent in Utah to 50.9 percent in Louisiana. The percent who were unmarried partners ranged from 17.3 percent in South Dakota to 5.3 percent in Utah.

Most new mothers are between the ages of 20 and 34—73.8 percent of women who gave birth—with 5.5 percent of births to teenage women and 20.7 percent to women 35 and over. In New Mexico, Mississippi, and Texas, 8 percent or more of births were to teenage mothers, while less than 3 percent of new mothers in New Jersey and Massachusetts were teenagers. In the District of Columbia, 30.7 percent of births were to women aged 35 or older, followed closely by Massachusetts at 29.6 percent. Arkansas had the lowest proportion of older mothers—at 11.6 percent—while Wyoming, Oklahoma, and Mississippi had levels below 13 percent.

Table C-1: States—Marriages and Births

State FIPS code	State	Marital status						Marital status, percent				
		Total population 15 years and older	Never married	Now married (except separated)	Separated	Widowed	Divorced	Never married	Now married (except separated)	Separated	Widowed	Divorced
	United States............	252,732,021	82,721,646	121,534,747	5,570,499	15,040,963	27,864,166	32.7	48.1	2.2	6.0	11.0
1	Alabama......................	3,891,144	1,147,168	1,876,518	99,490	278,399	489,569	29.5	48.2	2.6	7.2	12.6
2	Alaska........................	571,984	193,808	276,636	10,960	21,794	68,786	33.9	48.4	1.9	3.8	12.0
4	Arizona.......................	5,201,287	1,693,062	2,467,308	101,747	288,448	650,722	32.6	47.4	2.0	5.5	12.5
5	Arkansas.....................	2,355,484	636,452	1,189,168	55,505	161,813	312,546	27.0	50.5	2.4	6.9	13.3
6	California....................	30,396,377	11,098,801	14,077,875	716,891	1,548,251	2,954,559	36.5	46.3	2.4	5.1	9.7
8	Colorado.....................	4,156,448	1,291,498	2,105,359	68,674	188,286	502,631	31.1	50.7	1.7	4.5	12.1
9	Connecticut..................	2,944,753	992,153	1,416,498	42,997	179,158	313,947	33.7	48.1	1.5	6.1	10.7
10	Delaware.....................	746,911	248,655	351,847	14,343	46,047	86,019	33.3	47.1	1.9	6.2	11.5
11	District of Columbia.......	541,211	311,412	140,452	12,367	25,274	51,706	57.5	26.0	2.3	4.7	9.6
12	Florida	16,009,758	4,987,436	7,376,641	408,693	1,141,946	2,095,042	31.2	46.1	2.6	7.1	13.1
13	Georgia	7,829,101	2,619,745	3,671,122	200,613	438,321	899,300	33.5	46.9	2.6	5.6	11.5
15	Hawaii........................	1,133,822	375,737	567,323	15,920	68,947	105,895	33.1	50.0	1.4	6.1	9.3
16	Idaho.........................	1,238,968	321,608	683,437	15,587	64,317	154,019	26.0	55.2	1.3	5.2	12.4
17	Illinois.......................	10,343,979	3,584,205	4,939,645	183,486	615,741	1,020,902	34.7	47.8	1.8	6.0	9.9
18	Indiana	5,222,309	1,575,578	2,593,812	77,899	315,476	659,544	30.2	49.7	1.5	6.0	12.6
19	Iowa..........................	2,474,777	710,019	1,304,972	32,413	155,715	271,658	28.7	52.7	1.3	6.3	11.0
20	Kansas........................	2,276,556	649,296	1,192,217	33,712	134,443	266,888	28.5	52.4	1.5	5.9	11.7
21	Kentucky	3,531,594	983,374	1,765,941	80,422	235,854	466,003	27.8	50.0	2.3	6.7	13.2
22	Louisiana.....................	3,668,677	1,264,384	1,611,587	103,333	245,733	443,640	34.5	43.9	2.8	6.7	12.1
23	Maine	1,112,439	307,624	565,181	12,156	70,172	157,306	27.7	50.8	1.1	6.3	14.1
24	Maryland	4,770,688	1,675,713	2,219,699	121,088	273,473	480,715	35.1	46.5	2.5	5.7	10.1
25	Massachusetts	5,500,845	1,979,379	2,560,736	106,312	322,978	531,440	36.0	46.6	1.9	5.9	9.7
26	Michigan	8,028,676	2,611,970	3,862,135	120,111	499,432	935,028	32.5	48.1	1.5	6.2	11.6
27	Minnesota	4,318,219	1,360,025	2,251,029	50,105	223,666	433,214	31.5	52.1	1.2	5.2	10.0
28	Mississippi	2,365,073	786,571	1,056,929	75,004	165,934	280,635	33.3	44.7	3.2	7.0	11.9
29	Missouri......................	4,859,594	1,447,492	2,412,995	92,967	312,512	593,628	29.8	49.7	1.9	6.4	12.2
30	Montana	820,867	230,639	424,984	10,632	50,562	104,050	28.1	51.8	1.3	6.2	12.7
31	Nebraska	1,466,890	431,101	777,273	19,255	84,887	154,374	29.4	53.0	1.3	5.8	10.5
32	Nevada	2,204,875	710,387	1,012,385	55,438	115,411	311,254	32.2	45.9	2.5	5.2	14.1
33	New Hampshire	1,097,738	317,860	575,509	14,114	59,204	131,051	29.0	52.4	1.3	5.4	11.9
34	New Jersey...................	7,192,367	2,445,174	3,529,497	144,771	454,408	618,517	34.0	49.1	2.0	6.3	8.6
35	New Mexico..................	1,655,442	556,170	755,730	31,539	97,083	214,920	33.6	45.7	1.9	5.9	13.0
36	New York.....................	16,065,870	6,102,939	7,128,040	440,476	990,880	1,403,535	38.0	44.4	2.7	6.2	8.7
37	North Carolina	7,842,120	2,429,374	3,835,191	247,106	487,061	843,388	31.0	48.9	3.2	6.2	10.8
38	North Dakota................	571,203	180,502	297,093	5,035	34,073	54,500	31.6	52.0	0.9	6.0	9.5
39	Ohio..........................	9,357,346	2,933,048	4,500,796	172,933	609,058	1,141,511	31.3	48.1	1.8	6.5	12.2
40	Oklahoma....................	3,027,585	827,652	1,533,009	65,503	197,636	403,785	27.3	50.6	2.2	6.5	13.3
41	Oregon.......................	3,186,598	957,055	1,576,718	59,636	174,537	418,652	30.0	49.5	1.9	5.5	13.1
42	Pennsylvania	10,514,479	3,499,853	5,043,094	230,570	744,604	996,358	33.3	48.0	2.2	7.1	9.5
44	Rhode Island................	873,678	311,664	390,475	16,903	56,348	98,288	35.7	44.7	1.9	6.4	11.2
45	South Carolina..............	3,824,255	1,214,794	1,807,969	131,892	263,726	405,874	31.8	47.3	3.4	6.9	10.6
46	South Dakota................	662,338	199,573	343,356	7,885	39,706	71,818	30.1	51.8	1.2	6.0	10.8
47	Tennessee	5,211,459	1,507,783	2,572,766	120,019	339,864	671,027	28.9	49.4	2.3	6.5	12.9
48	Texas.........................	20,196,175	6,410,488	9,968,532	551,932	1,051,139	2,214,084	31.7	49.4	2.7	5.2	11.0
49	Utah..........................	2,102,136	617,315	1,173,084	34,298	78,848	198,591	29.4	55.8	1.6	3.8	9.4
50	Vermont......................	525,206	163,639	262,737	6,874	28,485	63,471	31.2	50.0	1.3	5.4	12.1
51	Virginia	6,634,998	2,106,018	3,314,099	170,059	370,632	674,190	31.7	49.9	2.6	5.6	10.2
53	Washington	5,573,172	1,710,607	2,804,314	94,587	275,753	687,911	30.7	50.3	1.7	4.9	12.3
54	West Virginia	1,538,216	421,822	768,932	25,816	120,840	200,806	27.4	50.0	1.7	7.9	13.1
55	Wisconsin....................	4,636,493	1,457,652	2,358,290	52,914	269,609	498,028	31.4	50.9	1.1	5.8	10.7
56	Wyoming.....................	459,841	125,192	243,812	7,517	24,479	58,841	27.2	53.0	1.6	5.3	12.8

Table C-1: States—Marriages and Births—*Continued*

State FIPS code	State	Male, marital status						Male, marital status, percent				
		Male population 15 years and older	Never married	Now married (except separated)	Separated	Widowed	Divorced	Never married	Now married (except separated)	Separated	Widowed	Divorced
	United States.............	123,212,971	44,340,348	61,460,280	2,286,374	3,161,454	11,964,515	36.0	49.9	1.9	2.6	9.7
1	Alabama......................	1,862,214	604,903	947,538	38,119	56,538	215,116	32.5	50.9	2.0	3.0	11.6
2	Alaska........................	299,425	114,331	140,963	4,913	5,601	33,617	38.2	47.1	1.6	1.9	11.2
4	Arizona.......................	2,569,288	929,456	1,251,029	43,737	66,376	278,690	36.2	48.7	1.7	2.6	10.8
5	Arkansas.....................	1,143,822	347,177	601,314	23,358	31,974	139,999	30.4	52.6	2.0	2.8	12.2
6	California....................	15,012,016	6,036,593	7,142,710	288,390	319,313	1,225,010	40.2	47.6	1.9	2.1	8.2
8	Colorado.....................	2,075,336	722,536	1,065,227	29,217	43,686	214,670	34.8	51.3	1.4	2.1	10.3
9	Connecticut..................	1,419,698	524,731	712,640	16,769	38,239	127,319	37.0	50.2	1.2	2.7	9.0
10	Delaware.....................	357,481	128,314	176,873	6,317	10,832	35,145	35.9	49.5	1.8	3.0	9.8
11	District of Columbia.......	253,125	148,274	71,916	5,631	5,226	22,078	58.6	28.4	2.2	2.1	8.7
12	Florida	7,757,981	2,708,566	3,736,509	168,683	246,547	897,676	34.9	48.2	2.2	3.2	11.6
13	Georgia	3,780,350	1,377,627	1,859,074	82,453	89,051	372,145	36.4	49.2	2.2	2.4	9.8
15	Hawaii	568,002	212,998	286,338	7,444	13,439	47,783	37.5	50.4	1.3	2.4	8.4
16	Idaho	616,275	180,256	345,434	6,082	14,299	70,204	29.2	56.1	1.0	2.3	11.4
17	Illinois.......................	5,027,821	1,896,476	2,498,531	75,016	123,716	434,082	37.7	49.7	1.5	2.5	8.6
18	Indiana.......................	2,546,882	846,382	1,308,415	32,074	67,466	292,545	33.2	51.4	1.3	2.6	11.5
19	Iowa..........................	1,216,354	389,640	656,573	13,402	31,214	125,525	32.0	54.0	1.1	2.6	10.3
20	Kansas........................	1,123,515	358,306	602,755	14,508	29,703	118,243	31.9	53.6	1.3	2.6	10.5
21	Kentucky.....................	1,719,880	539,896	888,747	34,101	50,147	206,989	31.4	51.7	2.0	2.9	12.0
22	Louisiana.....................	1,775,133	667,030	820,785	41,047	52,994	193,277	37.6	46.2	2.3	3.0	10.9
23	Maine.........................	539,761	165,444	283,125	4,815	15,925	70,452	30.7	52.5	0.9	3.0	13.1
24	Maryland	2,282,623	854,863	1,124,744	51,228	55,909	195,879	37.5	49.3	2.2	2.4	8.6
25	Massachusetts	2,634,936	1,019,503	1,291,626	43,491	67,924	212,392	38.7	49.0	1.7	2.6	8.1
26	Michigan	3,901,469	1,395,125	1,934,894	49,023	105,726	416,701	35.8	49.6	1.3	2.7	10.7
27	Minnesota	2,129,781	741,465	1,128,332	20,709	46,684	192,591	34.8	53.0	1.0	2.2	9.0
28	Mississippi...................	1,134,219	409,009	539,254	30,380	33,228	122,348	36.1	47.5	2.7	2.9	10.8
29	Missouri......................	2,357,488	772,594	1,213,443	40,177	66,486	264,788	32.8	51.5	1.7	2.8	11.2
30	Montana......................	410,108	130,927	214,682	4,749	11,459	48,291	31.9	52.3	1.2	2.8	11.8
31	Nebraska.....................	722,428	235,623	391,823	8,597	17,936	68,449	32.6	54.2	1.2	2.5	9.5
32	Nevada.......................	1,106,651	396,730	513,622	22,997	27,271	146,031	35.8	46.4	2.1	2.5	13.2
33	New Hampshire	537,698	171,125	290,899	5,708	12,622	57,344	31.8	54.1	1.1	2.3	10.7
34	New Jersey...................	3,469,363	1,288,256	1,790,877	57,045	91,176	242,009	37.1	51.6	1.6	2.6	7.0
35	New Mexico..................	813,817	299,119	386,360	11,441	22,861	94,036	36.8	47.5	1.4	2.8	11.6
36	New York.....................	7,698,201	3,153,247	3,610,440	168,500	201,857	564,157	41.0	46.9	2.2	2.6	7.3
37	North Carolina..............	3,776,005	1,286,263	1,935,486	104,944	96,370	352,942	34.1	51.3	2.8	2.6	9.3
38	North Dakota................	290,486	104,470	150,516	2,344	6,638	26,518	36.0	51.8	0.8	2.3	9.1
39	Ohio..........................	4,524,839	1,554,358	2,264,349	73,349	133,004	499,779	34.4	50.0	1.6	2.9	11.0
40	Oklahoma....................	1,486,092	458,398	772,937	27,370	43,566	183,821	30.8	52.0	1.8	2.9	12.4
41	Oregon.......................	1,564,755	522,822	795,978	25,096	38,658	182,201	33.4	50.9	1.6	2.5	11.6
42	Pennsylvania	5,082,914	1,848,138	2,547,143	99,380	158,125	430,128	36.4	50.1	2.0	3.1	8.5
44	Rhode Island................	417,748	162,824	197,836	6,484	10,595	40,009	39.0	47.4	1.6	2.5	9.6
45	South Carolina..............	1,839,923	638,359	913,013	55,538	55,667	177,346	34.7	49.6	3.0	3.0	9.6
46	South Dakota................	330,968	111,201	173,129	3,347	8,120	35,171	33.6	52.3	1.0	2.5	10.6
47	Tennessee....................	2,511,894	801,417	1,294,128	49,233	69,076	298,040	31.9	51.5	2.0	2.7	11.9
48	Texas.........................	9,951,393	3,481,018	5,079,505	220,535	222,103	948,232	35.0	51.0	2.2	2.2	9.5
49	Utah..........................	1,048,510	339,946	588,766	14,115	17,184	88,499	32.4	56.2	1.3	1.6	8.4
50	Vermont......................	256,552	88,203	130,870	3,092	5,785	28,602	34.4	51.0	1.2	2.3	11.1
51	Virginia......................	3,230,845	1,128,878	1,673,480	70,902	75,168	282,417	34.9	51.8	2.2	2.3	8.7
53	Washington..................	2,764,295	949,842	1,417,060	41,990	59,835	295,568	34.4	51.3	1.5	2.2	10.7
54	West Virginia................	752,757	235,162	387,274	11,176	25,332	93,813	31.2	51.4	1.5	3.4	12.5
55	Wisconsin....................	2,285,832	790,226	1,187,704	23,281	57,106	227,515	34.6	52.0	1.0	2.5	10.0
56	Wyoming.....................	234,022	72,301	123,614	4,077	5,697	28,333	30.9	52.8	1.7	2.4	12.1

Table C-1: States—Marriages and Births—*Continued*

State FIPS code	State	Female, marital status						Female, marital status, percent				
		Female population 15 years and older	Never married	Now married (except separated	Separated	Widowed	Divorced	Never married	Now married (except separated	Separated	Widowed	Divorced
	United States...............	129,519,050	38,381,298	60,074,467	3,284,125	11,879,509	15,899,651	29.6	46.4	2.5	9.2	12.3
1	Alabama......................	2,028,930	542,265	928,980	61,371	221,861	274,453	26.7	45.8	3.0	10.9	13.5
2	Alaska........................	272,559	79,477	135,673	6,047	16,193	35,169	29.2	49.8	2.2	5.9	12.9
4	Arizona.......................	2,631,999	763,606	1,216,279	58,010	222,072	372,032	29.0	46.2	2.2	8.4	14.1
5	Arkansas.....................	1,211,662	289,275	587,854	32,147	129,839	172,547	23.9	48.5	2.7	10.7	14.2
6	California....................	15,384,361	5,062,208	6,935,165	428,501	1,228,938	1,729,549	32.9	45.1	2.8	8.0	11.2
8	Colorado.....................	2,081,112	568,962	1,040,132	39,457	144,600	287,961	27.3	50.0	1.9	6.9	13.8
9	Connecticut..................	1,525,055	467,422	703,858	26,228	140,919	186,628	30.6	46.2	1.7	9.2	12.2
10	Delaware	389,430	120,341	174,974	8,026	35,215	50,874	30.9	44.9	2.1	9.0	13.1
11	District of Columbia........	288,086	163,138	68,536	6,736	20,048	29,628	56.6	23.8	2.3	7.0	10.3
12	Florida	8,251,777	2,278,870	3,640,132	240,010	895,399	1,197,366	27.6	44.1	2.9	10.9	14.5
13	Georgia	4,048,751	1,242,118	1,812,048	118,160	349,270	527,155	30.7	44.8	2.9	8.6	13.0
15	Hawaii	565,820	162,739	280,985	8,476	55,508	58,112	28.8	49.7	1.5	9.8	10.3
16	Idaho	622,693	141,352	338,003	9,505	50,018	83,815	22.7	54.3	1.5	8.0	13.5
17	Illinois	5,316,158	1,687,729	2,441,114	108,470	492,025	586,820	31.7	45.9	2.0	9.3	11.0
18	Indiana	2,675,427	729,196	1,285,397	45,825	248,010	366,999	27.3	48.0	1.7	9.3	13.7
19	Iowa	1,258,423	320,379	648,399	19,011	124,501	146,133	25.5	51.5	1.5	9.9	11.6
20	Kansas	1,153,041	290,990	589,462	19,204	104,740	148,645	25.2	51.1	1.7	9.1	12.9
21	Kentucky	1,811,714	443,478	877,194	46,321	185,707	259,014	24.5	48.4	2.6	10.3	14.3
22	Louisiana	1,893,544	597,354	790,802	62,286	192,739	250,363	31.5	41.8	3.3	10.2	13.2
23	Maine	572,678	142,180	282,056	7,341	54,247	86,854	24.8	49.3	1.3	9.5	15.2
24	Maryland	2,488,065	820,850	1,094,955	69,860	217,564	284,836	33.0	44.0	2.8	8.7	11.4
25	Massachusetts	2,865,909	959,876	1,269,110	62,821	255,054	319,048	33.5	44.3	2.2	8.9	11.1
26	Michigan	4,127,207	1,216,845	1,927,241	71,088	393,706	518,327	29.5	46.7	1.7	9.5	12.6
27	Minnesota	2,188,438	618,740	1,122,697	29,396	176,982	240,623	28.3	51.3	1.3	8.1	11.0
28	Mississippi...................	1,230,854	377,562	517,675	44,624	132,706	158,287	30.7	42.1	3.6	10.8	12.9
29	Missouri	2,502,106	674,898	1,199,552	52,790	246,026	328,840	27.0	47.9	2.1	9.8	13.1
30	Montana......................	410,759	99,712	210,302	5,883	39,103	55,759	24.3	51.2	1.4	9.5	13.6
31	Nebraska	744,462	195,478	385,450	10,658	66,951	85,925	26.3	51.8	1.4	9.0	11.5
32	Nevada	1,098,224	313,657	498,763	32,441	88,140	165,223	28.6	45.4	3.0	8.0	15.0
33	New Hampshire	560,040	146,735	284,610	8,406	46,582	73,707	26.2	50.8	1.5	8.3	13.2
34	New Jersey....................	3,723,004	1,156,918	1,738,620	87,726	363,232	376,508	31.1	46.7	2.4	9.8	10.1
35	New Mexico	841,625	257,051	369,370	20,098	74,222	120,884	30.5	43.9	2.4	8.8	14.4
36	New York	8,367,669	2,949,692	3,517,600	271,976	789,023	839,378	35.3	42.0	3.3	9.4	10.0
37	North Carolina...............	4,066,115	1,143,111	1,899,705	142,162	390,691	490,446	28.1	46.7	3.5	9.6	12.1
38	North Dakota.................	280,717	76,032	146,577	2,691	27,435	27,982	27.1	52.2	1.0	9.8	10.0
39	Ohio..........................	4,832,507	1,378,690	2,236,447	99,584	476,054	641,732	28.5	46.3	2.1	9.9	13.3
40	Oklahoma....................	1,541,493	369,254	760,072	38,133	154,070	219,964	24.0	49.3	2.5	10.0	14.3
41	Oregon	1,621,843	434,233	780,740	34,540	135,879	236,451	26.8	48.1	2.1	8.4	14.6
42	Pennsylvania.................	5,431,565	1,651,715	2,495,951	131,190	586,479	566,230	30.4	46.0	2.4	10.8	10.4
44	Rhode Island.................	455,930	148,840	192,639	10,419	45,753	58,279	32.6	42.3	2.3	10.0	12.8
45	South Carolina...............	1,984,332	576,435	894,956	76,354	208,059	228,528	29.0	45.1	3.8	10.5	11.5
46	South Dakota.................	331,370	88,372	170,227	4,538	31,586	36,647	26.7	51.4	1.4	9.5	11.1
47	Tennessee	2,699,565	706,366	1,278,638	70,786	270,788	372,987	26.2	47.4	2.6	10.0	13.8
48	Texas.........................	10,244,782	2,929,470	4,889,027	331,397	829,036	1,265,852	28.6	47.7	3.2	8.1	12.4
49	Utah	1,053,626	277,369	584,318	20,183	61,664	110,092	26.3	55.5	1.9	5.9	10.4
50	Vermont	268,654	75,436	131,867	3,782	22,700	34,869	28.1	49.1	1.4	8.4	13.0
51	Virginia	3,404,153	977,140	1,640,619	99,157	295,464	391,773	28.7	48.2	2.9	8.7	11.5
53	Washington	2,808,877	760,765	1,387,254	52,597	215,918	392,343	27.1	49.4	1.9	7.7	14.0
54	West Virginia	785,459	186,660	381,658	14,640	95,508	106,993	23.8	48.6	1.9	12.2	13.6
55	Wisconsin	2,350,661	667,426	1,170,586	29,633	212,503	270,513	28.4	49.8	1.3	9.0	11.5
56	Wyoming	225,819	52,891	120,198	3,440	18,782	30,508	23.4	53.2	1.5	8.3	13.5

Table C-1: States—Marriages and Births—*Continued*

State FIPS code	State	Median age at first marriage		Number of times married, men				Number of times married, men, as a percent of ever-married men		
		Male	Female	Ever-married men	Married once	Married two times	Married three or more times	Married once	Married two times	Married three or more times
	United States..............	29.1	27.1	78,872,623	59,352,926	15,341,416	4,178,281	75.3	19.5	5.3
1	Alabama........................	27.6	26.0	1,257,311	854,979	291,657	110,675	68.0	23.2	8.8
2	Alaska..........................	27.8	25.5	185,094	134,310	39,059	11,725	72.6	21.1	6.3
4	Arizona........................	28.9	26.9	1,639,832	1,183,291	346,545	109,996	72.2	21.1	6.7
5	Arkansas......................	26.6	25.1	796,645	522,409	190,673	83,563	65.6	23.9	10.5
6	California.....................	30.0	27.8	8,975,423	7,143,759	1,483,755	347,909	79.6	16.5	3.9
8	Colorado.......................	28.6	26.5	1,352,800	1,000,572	281,934	70,294	74.0	20.8	5.2
9	Connecticut...................	30.5	28.9	894,967	718,253	152,427	24,287	80.3	17.0	2.7
10	Delaware......................	29.9	28.2	229,167	170,694	47,983	10,490	74.5	20.9	4.6
11	District of Columbia.......	30.3	30.3	104,851	85,334	16,781	2,736	81.4	16.0	2.6
12	Florida.........................	30.0	27.9	5,049,415	3,526,151	1,162,221	361,043	69.8	23.0	7.2
13	Georgia........................	28.8	27.0	2,402,723	1,729,105	513,523	160,095	72.0	21.4	6.7
15	Hawaii.........................	28.3	26.4	355,004	281,920	60,670	12,414	79.4	17.1	3.5
16	Idaho...........................	26.2	24.7	436,019	302,959	97,605	35,455	69.5	22.4	8.1
17	Illinois.........................	29.7	27.9	3,131,345	2,469,938	536,443	124,964	78.9	17.1	4.0
18	Indiana	28.0	26.3	1,700,500	1,210,249	366,511	123,740	71.2	21.6	7.3
19	Iowa............................	27.8	26.0	826,714	636,988	149,821	39,905	77.1	18.1	4.8
20	Kansas.........................	27.2	25.8	765,209	563,186	153,059	48,964	73.6	20.0	6.4
21	Kentucky	27.3	25.7	1,179,984	818,739	267,621	93,624	69.4	22.7	7.9
22	Louisiana......................	28.8	27.1	1,108,103	799,759	237,199	71,145	72.2	21.4	6.4
23	Maine..........................	29.1	26.9	374,317	268,576	83,422	22,319	71.8	22.3	6.0
24	Maryland......................	29.9	28.2	1,427,760	1,102,369	275,077	50,314	77.2	19.3	3.5
25	Massachusetts	30.6	29.2	1,615,433	1,332,971	245,592	36,870	82.5	15.2	2.3
26	Michigan	29.4	27.3	2,506,344	1,885,336	499,528	121,480	75.2	19.9	4.8
27	Minnesota.....................	29.0	26.8	1,388,316	1,130,245	217,835	40,236	81.4	15.7	2.9
28	Mississippi....................	28.1	26.4	725,210	503,160	165,230	56,820	69.4	22.8	7.8
29	Missouri.......................	28.2	26.5	1,584,894	1,118,255	350,170	116,469	70.6	22.1	7.3
30	Montana.......................	28.4	26.0	279,181	198,717	62,089	18,375	71.2	22.2	6.6
31	Nebraska......................	27.4	26.0	486,805	382,124	84,935	19,746	78.5	17.4	4.1
32	Nevada.........................	28.6	26.4	709,921	490,407	161,131	58,383	69.1	22.7	8.2
33	New Hampshire	29.6	27.1	366,573	275,955	73,994	16,624	75.3	20.2	4.5
34	New Jersey....................	30.4	28.6	2,181,107	1,807,033	328,246	45,828	82.8	15.0	2.1
35	New Mexico...................	28.0	26.5	514,698	377,981	104,335	32,382	73.4	20.3	6.3
36	New York......................	30.7	29.2	4,544,954	3,748,759	685,510	110,685	82.5	15.1	2.4
37	North Carolina...............	28.3	26.6	2,489,742	1,818,976	529,796	140,970	73.1	21.3	5.7
38	North Dakota.................	27.6	26.0	186,016	152,092	28,460	5,464	81.8	15.3	2.9
39	Ohio............................	29.0	27.0	2,970,481	2,188,661	613,729	168,091	73.7	20.7	5.7
40	Oklahoma.....................	26.8	25.2	1,027,694	686,624	241,696	99,374	66.8	23.5	9.7
41	Oregon.........................	29.0	27.1	1,041,933	729,762	233,249	78,922	70.0	22.4	7.6
42	Pennsylvania	29.9	28.1	3,234,776	2,566,907	562,854	105,015	79.4	17.4	3.2
44	Rhode Island.................	30.8	29.3	254,924	201,483	46,730	6,711	79.0	18.3	2.6
45	South Carolina...............	28.8	27.3	1,201,564	864,914	262,770	73,880	72.0	21.9	6.1
46	South Dakota.................	27.7	25.7	219,767	173,066	37,089	9,612	78.7	16.9	4.4
47	Tennessee	27.7	26.1	1,710,477	1,168,507	398,641	143,329	68.3	23.3	8.4
48	Texas...........................	27.9	26.1	6,470,375	4,780,073	1,283,115	407,187	73.9	19.8	6.3
49	Utah............................	25.9	23.8	708,564	550,319	120,872	37,373	77.7	17.1	5.3
50	Vermont.......................	30.7	28.4	168,349	126,676	35,438	6,235	75.2	21.1	3.7
51	Virginia........................	29.0	27.0	2,101,967	1,580,023	422,618	99,326	75.2	20.1	4.7
53	Washington	28.4	26.4	1,814,453	1,329,782	374,019	110,652	73.3	20.6	6.1
54	West Virginia.................	27.7	26.0	517,595	365,023	116,430	36,142	70.5	22.5	7.0
55	Wisconsin.....................	28.9	26.9	1,495,606	1,182,899	264,109	48,598	79.1	17.7	3.2
56	Wyoming.......................	26.8	25.3	161,721	112,656	37,220	11,845	69.7	23.0	7.3

Table C-1: States—Marriages and Births—*Continued*

State FIPS code	State	Number of times married, women				Number of times married, women, as a percent of ever-married women			Median duration of current marriage (years) (for now married or separated)
		Ever-married women	Married once	Married two times	Married three or more times	Married once	Married two times	Married three or more times	
	United States...............	91,137,752	68,863,682	17,599,413	4,674,657	75.6	19.3	5.1	19.3
1	Alabama.........................	1,486,665	1,024,574	340,743	121,348	68.9	22.9	8.2	19.6
2	Alaska...........................	193,082	138,106	42,574	12,402	71.5	22.0	6.4	16.1
4	Arizona..........................	1,868,393	1,337,026	404,890	126,477	71.6	21.7	6.8	19.0
5	Arkansas........................	922,387	603,645	222,990	95,752	65.4	24.2	10.4	18.7
6	California.......................	10,322,153	8,225,560	1,713,555	383,038	79.7	16.6	3.7	18.2
8	Colorado	1,512,150	1,106,548	319,376	86,226	73.2	21.1	5.7	17.6
9	Connecticut....................	1,057,633	860,328	170,540	26,765	81.3	16.1	2.5	20.7
10	Delaware	269,089	201,752	55,730	11,607	75.0	20.7	4.3	20.8
11	District of Columbia.......	124,948	105,442	17,239	2,267	84.4	13.8	1.8	12.2
12	Florida	5,972,907	4,230,948	1,349,158	392,801	70.8	22.6	6.6	20.2
13	Georgia	2,806,633	2,026,373	599,080	181,180	72.2	21.3	6.5	17.5
15	Hawaii...........................	403,081	327,271	63,944	11,866	81.2	15.9	2.9	18.2
16	Idaho............................	481,341	329,630	109,746	41,965	68.5	22.8	8.7	18.4
17	Illinois	3,628,429	2,874,533	617,755	136,141	79.2	17.0	3.8	20.0
18	Indiana..........................	1,946,231	1,382,307	422,548	141,376	71.0	21.7	7.3	19.7
19	Iowa.............................	938,044	715,783	177,369	44,892	76.3	18.9	4.8	21.7
20	Kansas...........................	862,051	626,255	177,602	58,194	72.6	20.6	6.8	19.6
21	Kentucky	1,368,236	950,655	310,002	107,579	69.5	22.7	7.9	19.5
22	Louisiana	1,296,190	950,715	267,973	77,502	73.3	20.7	6.0	19.0
23	Maine............................	430,498	309,942	96,245	24,311	72.0	22.4	5.6	22.1
24	Maryland	1,667,215	1,309,633	303,229	54,353	78.6	18.2	3.3	18.7
25	Massachusetts	1,906,033	1,591,179	277,188	37,666	83.5	14.5	2.0	20.4
26	Michigan	2,910,362	2,200,895	568,524	140,943	75.6	19.5	4.8	21.1
27	Minnesota	1,569,698	1,272,877	252,224	44,597	81.1	16.1	2.8	20.9
28	Mississippi.....................	853,292	600,551	189,381	63,360	70.4	22.2	7.4	19.2
29	Missouri.........................	1,827,208	1,289,873	401,433	135,902	70.6	22.0	7.4	20.0
30	Montana........................	311,047	220,299	68,793	21,955	70.8	22.1	7.1	21.2
31	Nebraska	548,984	426,732	98,655	23,597	77.7	18.0	4.3	21.0
32	Nevada..........................	784,567	537,726	181,525	65,316	68.5	23.1	8.3	16.4
33	New Hampshire	413,305	313,897	82,003	17,405	75.9	19.8	4.2	21.1
34	New Jersey.....................	2,566,086	2,159,016	362,802	44,268	84.1	14.1	1.7	20.1
35	New Mexico....................	584,574	426,544	122,066	35,964	73.0	20.9	6.2	19.8
36	New York.......................	5,417,977	4,528,062	787,727	102,188	83.6	14.5	1.9	20.0
37	North Carolina...............	2,923,004	2,130,542	629,568	162,894	72.9	21.5	5.6	18.9
38	North Dakota.................	204,685	163,748	34,259	6,678	80.0	16.7	3.3	21.3
39	Ohio.............................	3,453,817	2,558,722	701,356	193,739	74.1	20.3	5.6	20.9
40	Oklahoma......................	1,172,239	777,132	279,897	115,210	66.3	23.9	9.8	18.2
41	Oregon..........................	1,187,610	824,929	268,839	93,842	69.5	22.6	7.9	19.1
42	Pennsylvania	3,779,850	3,027,262	640,091	112,497	80.1	16.9	3.0	22.1
44	Rhode Island..................	307,090	248,413	51,506	7,171	80.9	16.8	2.3	20.8
45	South Carolina...............	1,407,897	1,026,288	300,701	80,908	72.9	21.4	5.7	19.9
46	South Dakota.................	242,998	189,056	43,204	10,738	77.8	17.8	4.4	22.4
47	Tennessee	1,993,199	1,360,517	462,782	169,900	68.3	23.2	8.5	19.0
48	Texas............................	7,315,312	5,404,178	1,463,244	447,890	73.9	20.0	6.1	17.2
49	Utah.............................	776,257	594,809	137,217	44,231	76.6	17.7	5.7	16.5
50	Vermont	193,218	147,119	38,596	7,503	76.1	20.0	3.9	22.3
51	Virginia	2,427,013	1,844,591	473,804	108,618	76.0	19.5	4.5	18.6
53	Washington	2,048,112	1,486,797	432,117	129,198	72.6	21.1	6.3	18.3
54	West Virginia	598,799	421,822	135,607	41,370	70.4	22.6	6.9	21.9
55	Wisconsin	1,683,235	1,333,292	293,174	56,769	79.2	17.4	3.4	21.5
56	Wyoming.......................	172,928	119,788	38,842	14,298	69.3	22.5	8.3	19.1

Table C-1: States—Marriages and Births—*Continued*

State FIPS code	State	Married, divorced, or widowed during the last year							
		Men				Women			
		Ever married men	Married last year	Divorced last year	Widowed last year	Ever married women	Married last year	Divorced last year	Widowed last year
	United States...............	78,872,623	2,191,668	1,116,102	437,388	91,137,752	2,131,250	1,234,559	990,003
1	Alabama......................	1,257,311	36,441	21,954	8,567	1,486,665	36,409	24,588	21,016
2	Alaska........................	185,094	7,110	2,873	689	193,082	6,673	3,111	1,198
4	Arizona.......................	1,639,832	46,564	22,720	8,317	1,868,393	45,192	27,068	17,772
5	Arkansas.....................	796,645	26,399	14,769	4,468	922,387	25,013	16,198	10,702
6	California....................	8,975,423	255,463	112,183	41,074	10,322,153	243,756	124,062	103,450
8	Colorado	1,352,800	45,813	23,706	6,407	1,512,150	43,696	23,473	13,089
9	Connecticut.................	894,967	20,886	11,720	4,639	1,057,633	20,623	12,865	11,087
10	Delaware	229,167	6,135	2,673	1,305	269,089	6,321	3,334	2,802
11	District of Columbia.......	104,851	5,877	2,511	492	124,948	4,880	2,009	1,220
12	Florida.......................	5,049,415	120,178	71,988	31,589	5,972,907	117,335	83,658	72,549
13	Georgia	2,402,723	74,793	38,489	13,748	2,806,633	71,332	43,182	29,605
15	Hawaii	355,004	11,966	4,420	1,775	403,081	11,478	4,189	4,975
16	Idaho.........................	436,019	12,756	6,964	1,705	481,341	12,851	7,482	4,070
17	Illinois.......................	3,131,345	78,998	39,503	17,120	3,628,429	76,722	42,494	38,386
18	Indiana.......................	1,700,500	50,017	28,055	10,447	1,946,231	48,992	28,827	21,374
19	Iowa..........................	826,714	21,102	12,173	4,876	938,044	21,202	11,575	10,756
20	Kansas	765,209	23,880	11,842	4,713	862,051	22,315	14,084	9,845
21	Kentucky	1,179,984	32,849	21,423	8,011	1,368,236	32,616	22,379	15,815
22	Louisiana	1,108,103	30,843	15,782	7,242	1,296,190	29,385	20,303	16,953
23	Maine........................	374,317	8,845	6,544	2,559	430,498	9,633	5,717	4,244
24	Maryland	1,427,760	39,525	21,302	6,815	1,667,215	38,562	23,168	17,288
25	Massachusetts	1,615,433	40,383	17,461	7,670	1,906,033	40,373	21,632	20,456
26	Michigan	2,506,344	62,023	36,862	15,344	2,910,362	62,131	39,442	34,405
27	Minnesota	1,388,316	36,510	15,034	6,663	1,569,698	36,315	17,044	14,327
28	Mississippi	725,210	21,939	12,119	5,041	853,292	20,805	13,939	11,194
29	Missouri......................	1,584,894	43,760	23,453	10,166	1,827,208	43,601	26,582	21,273
30	Montana	279,181	7,588	4,147	1,353	311,047	7,465	4,951	3,267
31	Nebraska	486,805	13,871	7,223	2,732	548,984	13,429	7,126	5,608
32	Nevada	709,921	20,732	13,370	3,537	784,567	20,493	13,043	8,181
33	New Hampshire	366,573	8,467	4,584	1,502	413,305	8,518	6,363	3,350
34	New Jersey..................	2,181,107	50,472	22,777	12,640	2,566,086	48,030	25,766	27,419
35	New Mexico.................	514,698	15,802	7,796	3,010	584,574	14,400	9,025	6,494
36	New York....................	4,544,954	117,947	51,097	24,477	5,417,977	114,709	62,119	60,781
37	North Carolina.............	2,489,742	72,517	35,864	13,823	2,923,004	70,138	38,942	31,787
38	North Dakota...............	186,016	6,649	2,158	779	204,685	6,052	2,297	2,237
39	Ohio..........................	2,970,481	74,118	41,157	19,442	3,453,817	75,077	46,729	40,427
40	Oklahoma...................	1,027,694	33,876	19,634	6,164	1,172,239	33,030	19,734	12,827
41	Oregon.......................	1,041,933	26,444	14,846	5,542	1,187,610	26,339	18,458	13,226
42	Pennsylvania	3,234,776	77,067	38,789	22,275	3,779,850	74,284	39,417	47,753
44	Rhode Island...............	254,924	5,696	3,522	1,405	307,090	5,373	3,585	3,947
45	South Carolina.............	1,201,564	34,168	16,167	8,058	1,407,897	32,807	18,419	17,410
46	South Dakota...............	219,767	6,746	3,208	1,087	242,998	6,383	3,095	2,386
47	Tennessee	1,710,477	49,663	29,403	10,889	1,993,199	50,075	30,950	24,394
48	Texas.........................	6,470,375	205,901	99,911	31,798	7,315,312	199,469	113,915	71,735
49	Utah	708,564	28,141	11,437	3,034	776,257	27,783	12,289	5,259
50	Vermont......................	168,349	3,866	2,221	783	193,218	3,771	2,139	1,581
51	Virginia.......................	2,101,967	61,570	29,817	10,593	2,427,013	57,994	30,710	25,474
53	Washington	1,814,453	54,808	27,973	8,572	2,048,112	52,813	31,955	17,409
54	West Virginia	517,595	13,767	8,117	3,891	598,799	13,623	9,574	7,682
55	Wisconsin	1,495,606	35,498	19,515	7,328	1,683,235	35,715	18,825	18,036
56	Wyoming.....................	161,721	5,239	2,846	1,232	172,928	5,269	2,728	1,482

Table C-1: States—Marriages and Births—*Continued*

State FIPS code	State	Married, divorced or widowed during the last year, percent						Total women age 15 to 50 years
		Men, as a percent of ever-married men			Women, as a percent of ever-married women			
		Married last year	Divorced last year	Widowed last year	Married last year	Divorced last year	Widowed last year	
	United States...............	2.8	1.4	0.6	2.3	1.4	1.1	76,155,872
1	Alabama..........................	2.9	1.7	0.7	2.4	1.7	1.4	1,165,746
2	Alaska............................	3.8	1.6	0.4	3.5	1.6	0.6	176,655
4	Arizona...........................	2.8	1.4	0.5	2.4	1.4	1.0	1,536,237
5	Arkansas.........................	3.3	1.9	0.6	2.7	1.8	1.2	692,569
6	California........................	2.8	1.2	0.5	2.4	1.2	1.0	9,553,926
8	Colorado.........................	3.4	1.8	0.5	2.9	1.6	0.9	1,267,458
9	Connecticut.....................	2.3	1.3	0.5	1.9	1.2	1.0	864,070
10	Delaware	2.7	1.2	0.6	2.3	1.2	1.0	221,083
11	District of Columbia........	5.6	2.4	0.5	3.9	1.6	1.0	193,803
12	Florida	2.4	1.4	0.6	2.0	1.4	1.2	4,449,952
13	Georgia	3.1	1.6	0.6	2.5	1.5	1.1	2,525,451
15	Hawaii	3.4	1.2	0.5	2.8	1.0	1.2	319,934
16	Idaho.............................	2.9	1.6	0.4	2.7	1.6	0.8	369,379
17	Illinois............................	2.5	1.3	0.5	2.1	1.2	1.1	3,162,329
18	Indiana...........................	2.9	1.6	0.6	2.5	1.5	1.1	1,558,798
19	Iowa	2.6	1.5	0.6	2.3	1.2	1.1	705,099
20	Kansas	3.1	1.5	0.6	2.6	1.6	1.1	669,908
21	Kentucky	2.8	1.8	0.7	2.4	1.6	1.2	1,041,060
22	Louisiana	2.8	1.4	0.7	2.3	1.6	1.3	1,126,108
23	Maine.............................	2.4	1.7	0.7	2.2	1.3	1.0	298,992
24	Maryland	2.8	1.5	0.5	2.3	1.4	1.0	1,476,529
25	Massachusetts	2.5	1.1	0.5	2.1	1.1	1.1	1,666,805
26	Michigan	2.5	1.5	0.6	2.1	1.4	1.2	2,327,914
27	Minnesota	2.6	1.1	0.5	2.3	1.1	0.9	1,277,310
28	Mississippi	3.0	1.7	0.7	2.4	1.6	1.3	724,800
29	Missouri	2.8	1.5	0.6	2.4	1.5	1.2	1,426,918
30	Montana.........................	2.7	1.5	0.5	2.4	1.6	1.1	223,088
31	Nebraska	2.8	1.5	0.6	2.4	1.3	1.0	432,821
32	Nevada	2.9	1.9	0.5	2.6	1.7	1.0	667,295
33	New Hampshire	2.3	1.3	0.4	2.1	1.5	0.8	311,299
34	New Jersey......................	2.3	1.0	0.6	1.9	1.0	1.1	2,149,755
35	New Mexico....................	3.1	1.5	0.6	2.5	1.5	1.1	483,237
36	New York........................	2.6	1.1	0.5	2.1	1.1	1.1	4,921,807
37	North Carolina................	2.9	1.4	0.6	2.4	1.3	1.1	2,387,385
38	North Dakota..................	3.6	1.2	0.4	3.0	1.1	1.1	161,588
39	Ohio	2.5	1.4	0.7	2.2	1.4	1.2	2,710,248
40	Oklahoma.......................	3.3	1.9	0.6	2.8	1.7	1.1	898,579
41	Oregon	2.5	1.4	0.5	2.2	1.6	1.1	919,777
42	Pennsylvania...................	2.4	1.2	0.7	2.0	1.0	1.3	2,981,873
44	Rhode Island...................	2.2	1.4	0.6	1.7	1.2	1.3	258,792
45	South Carolina................	2.8	1.3	0.7	2.3	1.3	1.2	1,134,527
46	South Dakota..................	3.1	1.5	0.5	2.6	1.3	1.0	187,109
47	Tennessee	2.9	1.7	0.6	2.5	1.6	1.2	1,562,075
48	Texas.............................	3.2	1.5	0.5	2.7	1.6	1.0	6,524,003
49	Utah	4.0	1.6	0.4	3.6	1.6	0.7	712,683
50	Vermont.........................	2.3	1.3	0.5	2.0	1.1	0.8	144,883
51	Virginia...........................	2.9	1.4	0.5	2.4	1.3	1.0	2,039,556
53	Washington	3.0	1.5	0.5	2.6	1.6	0.9	1,659,615
54	West Virginia..................	2.7	1.6	0.8	2.3	1.6	1.3	417,010
55	Wisconsin	2.4	1.3	0.5	2.1	1.1	1.1	1,337,285
56	Wyoming........................	3.2	1.8	0.8	3.0	1.6	0.9	130,749

Table C-1: States—Marriages and Births—*Continued*

			Women who have given birth in the past 12 months								
			Women who had a birth in the past 12 months:								
State FIPS code	State	Total women who had a birth in the past year	Now married (including separated and spouse absent):				Unmarried (never married, widowed, and divorced)				Partner in an unmarried partner household
			Total now married	Age 15-19 now married	Age 20-34 now married	Age 35-50 now married	Total unmarried	Age 15-19 unmarried	Age 20-34 unmarried	Age 35-50 unmarried	
	United States..............	4,059,693	2,602,787	30,841	1,894,323	677,623	1,456,906	191,013	1,101,457	164,436	410,667
1	Alabama......................	63,947	37,678	508	30,149	7,021	26,269	4,010	20,077	2,182	3,983
2	Alaska........................	11,008	6,861	51	4,700	2,110	4,147	357	3,392	398	1,613
4	Arizona......................	86,043	52,238	695	37,875	13,668	33,805	4,364	25,006	4,435	10,371
5	Arkansas....................	37,538	23,511	620	19,500	3,391	14,027	1,979	11,098	950	3,569
6	California...................	500,839	331,268	4,542	225,604	101,122	169,571	20,663	126,892	22,016	51,480
8	Colorado....................	70,157	50,999	782	37,839	12,378	19,158	2,324	14,199	2,635	5,987
9	Connecticut................	38,505	25,230	93	16,887	8,250	13,275	1,306	10,033	1,936	3,294
10	Delaware....................	11,713	7,334	37	4,968	2,329	4,379	433	3,393	553	1,279
11	District of Columbia........	8,195	4,262	0	2,325	1,937	3,933	265	3,087	581	579
12	Florida	214,789	126,065	1,025	87,441	37,599	88,724	10,296	66,114	12,314	23,081
13	Georgia	140,175	84,968	1,190	60,755	23,023	55,207	7,233	40,830	7,144	12,408
15	Hawaii	20,518	13,963	67	10,158	3,738	6,555	908	4,906	741	2,151
16	Idaho........................	25,029	18,478	190	15,268	3,020	6,551	1,025	5,171	355	2,238
17	Illinois......................	159,163	100,611	546	71,810	28,255	58,552	8,262	44,024	6,266	15,908
18	Indiana......................	86,697	52,772	543	41,191	11,038	33,925	5,478	26,420	2,027	9,756
19	Iowa.........................	38,420	26,179	164	21,024	4,991	12,241	1,227	9,885	1,129	4,658
20	Kansas.......................	43,388	30,029	472	23,381	6,176	13,359	1,957	9,709	1,693	4,147
21	Kentucky....................	55,799	35,934	824	28,441	6,669	19,865	3,016	15,020	1,829	5,609
22	Louisiana...................	61,694	31,374	693	25,106	5,575	30,320	3,088	24,366	2,866	6,700
23	Maine.......................	14,126	9,052	57	7,093	1,902	5,074	487	3,959	628	2,399
24	Maryland....................	77,734	49,140	212	33,193	15,735	28,594	3,717	21,573	3,304	7,395
25	Massachusetts	76,317	52,718	185	33,363	19,170	23,599	2,030	18,170	3,399	7,125
26	Michigan	120,332	72,982	699	54,629	17,654	47,350	6,103	36,665	4,582	15,315
27	Minnesota..................	73,145	51,785	269	39,110	12,406	21,360	3,132	16,594	1,634	8,606
28	Mississippi.................	38,562	19,982	230	16,185	3,567	18,580	2,901	14,346	1,333	2,789
29	Missouri.....................	79,174	48,907	480	37,342	11,085	30,267	4,795	23,230	2,242	8,787
30	Montana....................	12,133	8,226	95	6,434	1,697	3,907	439	3,083	385	1,530
31	Nebraska....................	26,523	19,047	141	15,117	3,789	7,476	897	5,862	717	3,039
32	Nevada......................	35,819	23,415	237	16,713	6,465	12,404	1,671	9,035	1,698	5,224
33	New Hampshire	14,198	10,120	163	7,036	2,921	4,078	310	3,094	674	1,635
34	New Jersey..................	106,149	73,612	279	48,907	24,426	32,537	2,732	24,661	5,144	9,075
35	New Mexico.................	28,624	15,170	277	11,714	3,179	13,454	2,097	9,820	1,537	3,915
36	New York....................	238,783	156,433	974	100,678	54,781	82,350	7,975	62,735	11,640	21,986
37	North Carolina..............	129,666	81,651	1,351	59,784	20,516	48,015	6,246	36,507	5,262	12,147
38	North Dakota...............	10,634	7,264	123	5,995	1,146	3,370	409	2,655	306	1,489
39	Ohio.........................	143,799	85,525	830	65,709	18,986	58,274	6,948	45,503	5,823	16,739
40	Oklahoma...................	53,499	34,122	857	27,866	5,399	19,377	2,867	15,142	1,368	6,289
41	Oregon......................	46,190	31,454	137	23,457	7,860	14,736	1,613	11,071	2,052	5,474
42	Pennsylvania...............	145,804	88,606	490	63,664	24,452	57,198	7,687	43,998	5,513	16,381
44	Rhode Island...............	11,802	6,606	7	4,799	1,800	5,196	721	3,938	537	1,671
45	South Carolina.............	62,075	33,874	363	25,493	8,018	28,201	3,643	22,027	2,531	5,334
46	South Dakota...............	12,910	7,997	150	6,581	1,266	4,913	633	3,770	510	2,233
47	Tennessee..................	85,067	51,168	662	39,136	11,370	33,899	5,013	25,673	3,213	8,390
48	Texas........................	394,149	256,120	6,238	190,336	59,546	138,029	25,322	97,411	15,296	32,239
49	Utah.........................	52,519	43,987	393	36,684	6,910	8,532	1,300	6,429	803	2,809
50	Vermont.....................	5,685	3,803	3	2,672	1,128	1,882	264	1,495	123	815
51	Virginia......................	107,321	73,626	730	53,153	19,743	33,695	4,361	25,975	3,359	8,659
53	Washington	89,711	64,304	542	47,733	16,029	25,407	3,270	18,680	3,457	10,630
54	West Virginia...............	18,573	11,323	200	9,241	1,882	7,250	840	5,755	655	1,825
55	Wisconsin...................	67,811	45,764	384	35,671	9,709	22,047	2,194	17,286	2,567	8,944
56	Wyoming....................	7,242	5,250	41	4,413	796	1,992	205	1,693	94	968

Table C-1: States—Marriages and Births—*Continued*

State FIPS code	State	Total women who had a birth in the past year	Women who have given birth in the past 12 months								
			Women who had a birth in the past 12 months as a percent of all women age 15 to 50								
			Now married (including separated and spouse absent):				Unmarried (never married, widowed, and divorced)				
			Total now married	Age 15-19 now married	Age 20-34 now married	Age 35-50 now married	Total unmarried	Age 15-19 unmarried	Age 20-34 unmarried	Age 35-50 unmarried	Partner in an unmarried partner household
	United States............	5.3	3.4	0.0	2.5	0.9	1.9	0.3	1.4	0.2	0.5
1	Alabama....................	5.5	3.2	0.0	2.6	0.6	2.3	0.3	1.7	0.2	0.3
2	Alaska......................	6.2	3.9	0.0	2.7	1.2	2.3	0.2	1.9	0.2	0.9
4	Arizona....................	5.6	3.4	0.0	2.5	0.9	2.2	0.3	1.6	0.3	0.7
5	Arkansas..................	5.4	3.4	0.1	2.8	0.5	2.0	0.3	1.6	0.1	0.5
6	California.................	5.2	3.5	0.0	2.4	1.1	1.8	0.2	1.3	0.2	0.5
8	Colorado	5.5	4.0	0.1	3.0	1.0	1.5	0.2	1.1	0.2	0.5
9	Connecticut..............	4.5	2.9	0.0	2.0	1.0	1.5	0.2	1.2	0.2	0.4
10	Delaware	5.3	3.3	0.0	2.2	1.1	2.0	0.2	1.5	0.3	0.6
11	District of Columbia........	4.2	2.2	0.0	1.2	1.0	2.0	0.1	1.6	0.3	0.3
12	Florida....................	4.8	2.8	0.0	2.0	0.8	2.0	0.2	1.5	0.3	0.5
13	Georgia....................	5.6	3.4	0.0	2.4	0.9	2.2	0.3	1.6	0.3	0.5
15	Hawaii......................	6.4	4.4	0.0	3.2	1.2	2.0	0.3	1.5	0.2	0.7
16	Idaho......................	6.8	5.0	0.1	4.1	0.8	1.8	0.3	1.4	0.1	0.6
17	Illinois...................	5.0	3.2	0.0	2.3	0.9	1.9	0.3	1.4	0.2	0.5
18	Indiana....................	5.6	3.4	0.0	2.6	0.7	2.2	0.4	1.7	0.1	0.6
19	Iowa.......................	5.4	3.7	0.0	3.0	0.7	1.7	0.2	1.4	0.2	0.7
20	Kansas.....................	6.5	4.5	0.1	3.5	0.9	2.0	0.3	1.4	0.3	0.6
21	Kentucky...................	5.4	3.5	0.1	2.7	0.6	1.9	0.3	1.4	0.2	0.5
22	Louisiana	5.5	2.8	0.1	2.2	0.5	2.7	0.3	2.2	0.3	0.6
23	Maine......................	4.7	3.0	0.0	2.4	0.6	1.7	0.2	1.3	0.2	0.8
24	Maryland	5.3	3.3	0.0	2.2	1.1	1.9	0.3	1.5	0.2	0.5
25	Massachusetts	4.6	3.2	0.0	2.0	1.2	1.4	0.1	1.1	0.2	0.4
26	Michigan	5.2	3.1	0.0	2.3	0.8	2.0	0.3	1.6	0.2	0.7
27	Minnesota	5.7	4.1	0.0	3.1	1.0	1.7	0.2	1.3	0.1	0.7
28	Mississippi................	5.3	2.8	0.0	2.2	0.5	2.6	0.4	2.0	0.2	0.4
29	Missouri...................	5.5	3.4	0.0	2.6	0.8	2.1	0.3	1.6	0.2	0.6
30	Montana....................	5.4	3.7	0.0	2.9	0.8	1.8	0.2	1.4	0.2	0.7
31	Nebraska...................	6.1	4.4	0.0	3.5	0.9	1.7	0.2	1.4	0.2	0.7
32	Nevada.....................	5.4	3.5	0.0	2.5	1.0	1.9	0.3	1.4	0.3	0.8
33	New Hampshire	4.6	3.3	0.1	2.3	0.9	1.3	0.1	1.0	0.2	0.5
34	New Jersey.................	4.9	3.4	0.0	2.3	1.1	1.5	0.1	1.1	0.2	0.4
35	New Mexico.................	5.9	3.1	0.1	2.4	0.7	2.8	0.4	2.0	0.3	0.8
36	New York...................	4.9	3.2	0.0	2.0	1.1	1.7	0.2	1.3	0.2	0.4
37	North Carolina............	5.4	3.4	0.1	2.5	0.9	2.0	0.3	1.5	0.2	0.5
38	North Dakota..............	6.6	4.5	0.1	3.7	0.7	2.1	0.3	1.6	0.2	0.9
39	Ohio.......................	5.3	3.2	0.0	2.4	0.7	2.2	0.3	1.7	0.2	0.6
40	Oklahoma...................	6.0	3.8	0.1	3.1	0.6	2.2	0.3	1.7	0.2	0.7
41	Oregon.....................	5.0	3.4	0.0	2.6	0.9	1.6	0.2	1.2	0.2	0.6
42	Pennsylvania..............	4.9	3.0	0.0	2.1	0.8	1.9	0.3	1.5	0.2	0.5
44	Rhode Island..............	4.6	2.6	0.0	1.9	0.7	2.0	0.3	1.5	0.2	0.6
45	South Carolina............	5.5	3.0	0.0	2.2	0.7	2.5	0.3	1.9	0.2	0.5
46	South Dakota..............	6.9	4.3	0.1	3.5	0.7	2.6	0.3	2.0	0.3	1.2
47	Tennessee	5.4	3.3	0.0	2.5	0.7	2.2	0.3	1.6	0.2	0.5
48	Texas......................	6.0	3.9	0.1	2.9	0.9	2.1	0.4	1.5	0.2	0.5
49	Utah.......................	7.4	6.2	0.1	5.1	1.0	1.2	0.2	0.9	0.1	0.4
50	Vermont....................	3.9	2.6	0.0	1.8	0.8	1.3	0.2	1.0	0.1	0.6
51	Virginia...................	5.3	3.6	0.0	2.6	1.0	1.7	0.2	1.3	0.2	0.4
53	Washington................	5.4	3.9	0.0	2.9	1.0	1.5	0.2	1.1	0.2	0.6
54	West Virginia	4.5	2.7	0.0	2.2	0.5	1.7	0.2	1.4	0.2	0.4
55	Wisconsin	5.1	3.4	0.0	2.7	0.7	1.6	0.2	1.3	0.2	0.7
56	Wyoming....................	5.5	4.0	0.0	3.4	0.6	1.5	0.2	1.3	0.1	0.7

Table C-1: States—Marriages and Births—*Continued*

State FIPS code	State	Marital status of women who had a birth in the past year				Women who had a birth in the last year as a percent of all women in their age group			
		All women who had a birth in the past year	Married women who had a birth in the past year as a percent of all women who had a birth	All unmarried women who had a birth in the past year as a percent of all women who had a birth	Partners in unmarried partner households who had a birth in the past year as a percent of all women who had a birth	All women age 15 to 50	Age 15 to 19	Age 20 to 34	Age 35 to 50
	United States...............	4,059,693	64.1	35.9	10.1	5.3	2.1	9.4	2.5
1	Alabama........................	63,947	58.9	41.1	6.2	5.5	2.8	10.3	1.8
2	Alaska..........................	11,008	62.3	37.7	14.7	6.2	1.7	10.3	3.4
4	Arizona........................	86,043	60.7	39.3	12.1	5.6	2.3	9.6	2.7
5	Arkansas......................	37,538	62.6	37.4	9.5	5.4	2.7	10.5	1.4
6	California......................	500,839	66.1	33.9	10.3	5.2	1.9	8.7	3.0
8	Colorado......................	70,157	72.7	27.3	8.5	5.5	1.9	9.6	2.7
9	Connecticut..................	38,505	65.5	34.5	8.6	4.5	1.1	8.2	2.5
10	Delaware......................	11,713	62.6	37.4	10.9	5.3	1.6	9.1	2.9
11	District of Columbia.......	8,195	52.0	48.0	7.1	4.2	1.3	5.1	3.8
12	Florida.........................	214,789	58.7	41.3	10.7	4.8	2.0	8.4	2.4
13	Georgia........................	140,175	60.6	39.4	8.9	5.6	2.4	9.8	2.6
15	Hawaii.........................	20,518	68.1	31.9	10.5	6.4	2.4	10.8	3.2
16	Idaho..........................	25,029	73.8	26.2	8.9	6.8	2.2	12.9	2.2
17	Illinois.........................	159,163	63.2	36.8	10.0	5.0	2.0	8.7	2.5
18	Indiana........................	86,697	60.9	39.1	11.3	5.6	2.7	10.4	1.9
19	Iowa...........................	38,420	68.1	31.9	12.1	5.4	1.3	10.4	2.0
20	Kansas.........................	43,388	69.2	30.8	9.6	6.5	2.4	11.5	2.8
21	Kentucky......................	55,799	64.4	35.6	10.1	5.4	2.7	10.1	1.8
22	Louisiana......................	61,694	50.9	49.1	10.9	5.5	2.5	9.9	1.8
23	Maine..........................	14,126	64.1	35.9	17.0	4.7	1.3	9.7	1.8
24	Maryland......................	77,734	63.2	36.8	9.5	5.3	2.0	9.1	2.8
25	Massachusetts	76,317	69.1	30.9	9.3	4.6	1.0	7.5	3.0
26	Michigan......................	120,332	60.7	39.3	12.7	5.2	2.0	9.7	2.1
27	Minnesota....................	73,145	70.8	29.2	11.8	5.7	1.9	10.4	2.5
28	Mississippi....................	38,562	51.8	48.2	7.2	5.3	2.9	10.1	1.6
29	Missouri.......................	79,174	61.8	38.2	11.1	5.5	2.7	10.0	2.1
30	Montana.......................	12,133	67.8	32.2	12.6	5.4	1.7	10.0	2.2
31	Nebraska......................	26,523	71.8	28.2	11.5	6.1	1.6	11.2	2.5
32	Nevada........................	35,819	65.4	34.6	14.6	5.4	2.2	9.1	2.7
33	New Hampshire.............	14,198	71.3	28.7	11.5	4.6	1.0	8.8	2.4
34	New Jersey...................	106,149	69.3	30.7	8.5	4.9	1.1	8.8	2.9
35	New Mexico..................	28,624	53.0	47.0	13.7	5.9	3.3	10.5	2.3
36	New York.....................	238,783	65.5	34.5	9.2	4.9	1.4	7.8	3.0
37	North Carolina..............	129,666	63.0	37.0	9.4	5.4	2.4	9.9	2.4
38	North Dakota................	10,634	68.3	31.7	14.0	6.6	2.3	11.4	2.3
39	Ohio...........................	143,799	59.5	40.5	11.6	5.3	2.0	10.0	2.0
40	Oklahoma.....................	53,499	63.8	36.2	11.8	6.0	3.0	10.9	1.8
41	Oregon........................	46,190	68.1	31.9	11.9	5.0	1.5	8.8	2.4
42	Pennsylvania.................	145,804	60.8	39.2	11.2	4.9	1.9	8.8	2.2
44	Rhode Island.................	11,802	56.0	44.0	14.2	4.6	1.9	8.2	2.1
45	South Carolina..............	62,075	54.6	45.4	8.6	5.5	2.6	10.0	2.1
46	South Dakota................	12,910	61.9	38.1	17.3	6.9	2.7	12.8	2.3
47	Tennessee....................	85,067	60.2	39.8	9.9	5.4	2.8	10.0	2.1
48	Texas..........................	394,149	65.0	35.0	8.2	6.0	3.4	10.3	2.6
49	Utah...........................	52,519	83.8	16.2	5.3	7.4	1.6	12.9	2.9
50	Vermont.......................	5,685	66.9	33.1	14.3	3.9	1.2	7.3	1.9
51	Virginia........................	107,321	68.6	31.4	8.1	5.3	1.9	9.3	2.5
53	Washington	89,711	71.7	28.3	11.8	5.4	1.7	9.4	2.7
54	West Virginia	18,573	61.0	39.0	9.8	4.5	1.9	8.9	1.3
55	Wisconsin.....................	67,811	67.5	32.5	13.2	5.1	1.4	9.6	2.1
56	Wyoming......................	7,242	72.5	27.5	13.4	5.5	1.4	10.4	1.6

Table C-2: Counties with a Population of 50,000 or More—Marriages and Births

State/county FIPS code	State/County	Total population 15 years and older	Marital status, percent			Male population 15 years and older	Male, marital status, percent			Female population 15 years and older	Female, marital status, percent		
			Never married	Now married (except separated)	Separated, widowed, or divorced		Never married	Now married (except separated)	Separated, widowed, or divorced		Never married	Now married (except separated)	Separated, widowed, or divorced
00000	United States............................	252,732,021	32.7	48.1	19.2	123,212,971	36.0	49.9	14.1	129,519,050	29.6	46.4	24.0
01000	Alabama..................................	3,891,144	29.5	48.2	22.3	1,862,214	32.5	50.9	16.6	2,028,930	26.7	45.8	27.5
01001	Autauga County	43,576	24.5	53.2	22.3	20,966	27.2	55.7	17.2	22,610	22.0	51.0	27.0
01003	Baldwin County	155,044	23.3	55.5	21.2	75,202	26.6	57.3	16.1	79,842	20.2	53.7	26.1
01009	Blount County	46,362	20.5	58.2	21.3	22,691	24.6	59.2	16.2	23,671	16.5	57.3	26.2
01015	Calhoun County	95,402	27.9	46.8	25.3	45,186	31.1	49.0	20.0	50,216	25.0	44.9	30.1
01031	Coffee County	40,784	26.2	49.5	24.3	19,915	28.8	52.3	18.9	20,869	23.7	46.8	29.5
01033	Colbert County	44,801	25.0	51.1	23.9	21,214	27.2	55.3	17.5	23,587	23.1	47.4	29.6
01043	Cullman County	65,294	19.3	58.9	21.8	32,085	21.8	61.2	17.0	33,209	16.8	56.7	26.5
01045	Dale County..............................	40,086	26.1	49.1	24.9	19,579	30.3	51.2	18.6	20,507	22.1	47.1	30.8
01049	DeKalb County	56,873	23.9	55.0	21.1	27,121	26.5	57.4	16.1	29,752	21.6	52.7	25.6
01051	Elmore County	64,874	26.5	51.7	21.8	31,270	30.9	52.3	16.7	33,604	22.4	51.1	26.5
01055	Etowah County	85,085	26.0	49.7	24.3	40,492	29.7	51.2	19.2	44,593	22.6	48.4	29.0
01069	Houston County	82,329	27.6	48.1	24.4	38,673	31.3	51.5	17.2	43,656	24.3	45.0	30.7
01071	Jackson County	43,642	21.6	53.9	24.5	21,352	24.6	55.8	19.6	22,290	18.7	52.2	29.1
01073	Jefferson County	530,342	33.0	44.3	22.7	246,404	35.6	47.8	16.6	283,938	30.8	41.2	28.0
01077	Lauderdale County	76,817	25.9	53.1	21.0	36,153	28.0	57.1	14.9	40,664	24.0	49.5	26.4
01081	Lee County	120,747	39.7	44.3	16.1	59,314	43.5	45.5	11.0	61,433	35.9	43.1	21.0
01083	Limestone County	70,144	24.5	55.9	19.6	35,152	28.9	56.7	14.4	34,992	20.2	55.0	24.8
01089	Madison County	278,232	31.0	49.1	19.9	134,899	34.1	51.0	14.9	143,333	28.0	47.4	24.6
01095	Marshall County	74,864	24.8	51.9	23.3	36,558	28.9	53.5	17.6	38,306	20.8	50.4	28.8
01097	Mobile County	329,814	32.4	44.8	22.9	155,738	35.3	47.7	16.9	174,076	29.7	42.1	28.2
01101	Montgomery County	182,289	38.9	38.8	22.4	84,844	41.0	42.5	16.4	97,445	37.0	35.5	27.5
01103	Morgan County	96,608	24.5	52.2	23.4	46,854	28.0	54.3	17.6	49,754	21.1	50.1	28.8
01113	Russell County	45,289	31.6	44.1	24.3	21,704	33.6	48.5	17.9	23,585	29.7	40.1	30.2
01115	St. Clair County	68,662	20.7	56.3	23.0	33,871	23.6	58.0	18.4	34,791	17.9	54.7	27.4
01117	Shelby County	159,438	24.9	57.0	18.1	76,911	26.3	60.2	13.5	82,527	23.7	54.0	22.4
01121	Talladega County	66,248	27.8	47.5	24.7	32,070	31.1	49.8	19.1	34,178	24.7	45.3	30.0
01125	Tuscaloosa County	163,563	40.3	42.2	17.5	78,088	42.8	44.6	12.5	85,475	37.9	39.9	22.1
01127	Walker County	54,162	23.2	51.0	25.8	26,058	27.4	53.4	19.2	28,104	19.3	48.7	32.0
02000	Alaska	571,984	33.9	48.4	17.8	299,425	38.2	47.1	14.7	272,559	29.2	49.8	21.1
02020	Anchorage Municipality	235,095	35.3	47.4	17.3	119,334	39.8	46.4	13.8	115,761	30.5	48.5	20.9
02090	Fairbanks North Star Borough	78,574	34.9	47.9	17.2	42,045	40.1	46.0	13.9	36,529	29.0	50.0	21.0
02122	Kenai Peninsula Borough	46,027	27.4	52.6	19.9	24,319	31.4	51.6	17.0	21,708	23.0	53.8	23.2
02170	Matanuska-Susitna Borough	71,925	27.3	54.1	18.6	37,201	31.8	51.7	16.5	34,724	22.4	56.6	20.9
04000	Arizona	5,201,287	32.6	47.4	20.0	2,569,288	36.2	48.7	15.1	2,631,999	29.0	46.2	24.8
04001	Apache County..........................	54,293	46.9	34.7	18.4	26,965	49.3	35.8	14.9	27,328	44.4	33.6	21.9
04003	Cochise County	106,607	28.2	49.3	22.4	54,582	34.5	47.7	17.8	52,025	21.6	51.0	27.3
04005	Coconino County.......................	110,185	43.6	42.0	14.4	54,106	45.5	42.9	11.6	56,079	41.7	41.2	17.1
04007	Gila County	44,055	23.3	50.1	26.6	21,662	26.1	51.8	22.1	22,393	20.5	48.5	31.0
04013	Maricopa County.......................	3,097,230	33.7	47.1	19.1	1,518,930	37.3	48.6	14.1	1,578,300	30.3	45.8	24.0
04015	Mohave County.........................	170,100	24.0	48.8	27.2	85,570	27.9	48.8	23.3	84,530	20.0	48.8	31.2
04017	Navajo County	81,770	36.0	44.5	19.4	40,782	39.3	46.5	14.2	40,988	32.8	42.6	24.6
04019	Pima County	808,251	33.7	44.7	21.6	394,525	37.4	46.2	16.4	413,726	30.1	43.4	26.6
04021	Pinal County	302,734	29.0	50.8	20.2	159,594	32.8	51.5	15.7	143,140	24.7	50.0	25.3
04025	Yavapai County	181,345	21.1	54.1	24.8	87,886	25.3	55.9	18.7	93,459	17.0	52.4	30.6
04027	Yuma County	156,471	27.2	56.1	16.6	80,137	31.1	55.8	13.1	76,334	23.2	56.5	20.3
05000	Arkansas	2,355,484	27.0	50.5	22.5	1,143,822	30.4	52.6	17.1	1,211,662	23.9	48.5	27.6
05007	Benton County	178,320	23.2	60.3	16.5	87,393	27.2	61.5	11.3	90,927	19.3	59.2	21.6
05031	Craighead County......................	79,110	29.8	49.2	21.0	37,930	33.4	51.5	15.1	41,180	26.5	47.2	26.3
05033	Crawford County	48,870	21.4	56.8	21.7	23,791	25.0	58.8	16.2	25,079	18.1	55.0	27.0
05035	Crittenden County	38,427	35.6	41.1	23.4	17,910	36.9	45.2	17.9	20,517	34.4	37.5	28.1
05045	Faulkner County	94,120	32.2	50.4	17.4	45,571	34.8	51.6	13.6	48,549	29.7	49.2	21.0
05051	Garland County	80,388	22.7	49.6	27.7	38,327	26.3	52.0	21.6	42,061	19.4	47.3	33.3
05069	Jefferson County	60,255	36.3	40.0	23.7	29,192	40.3	41.5	18.1	31,063	32.5	38.6	28.9
05085	Lonoke County	54,280	22.2	56.8	20.9	26,375	24.9	59.5	15.6	27,905	19.7	54.3	26.0
05115	Pope County	50,372	28.5	51.2	20.3	24,655	32.4	53.7	13.9	25,717	24.8	48.9	26.4
05119	Pulaski County	310,480	34.8	42.7	22.5	146,989	38.2	45.3	16.5	163,491	31.7	40.5	27.9
05125	Saline County	89,723	21.8	55.8	22.4	43,731	24.4	58.3	17.3	45,992	19.3	53.5	27.2
05131	Sebastian County	100,646	25.8	50.3	23.9	48,870	30.1	51.9	18.0	51,776	21.8	48.7	29.5
05143	Washington County....................	166,112	33.4	48.9	17.7	82,468	36.2	50.0	13.8	83,644	30.7	47.9	21.5
05145	White County	62,857	25.6	55.1	19.2	30,585	26.8	58.9	14.4	32,272	24.6	51.5	23.9
06000	California	30,396,377	36.5	46.3	17.2	15,012,016	40.2	47.6	12.2	15,384,361	32.9	45.1	22.0
06001	Alameda County........................	1,268,852	36.6	47.2	16.3	616,212	39.5	49.0	11.5	652,640	33.8	45.5	20.8
06007	Butte County	183,730	35.6	42.0	22.3	90,333	40.5	43.1	16.5	93,397	30.9	41.0	28.0
06013	Contra Costa County..................	865,498	30.9	51.4	17.7	417,902	34.0	53.6	12.5	447,596	28.1	49.4	22.6
06017	El Dorado County	149,569	24.8	56.9	18.3	74,671	28.3	57.5	14.3	74,898	21.3	56.4	22.3
06019	Fresno County	715,918	37.8	44.1	18.1	354,962	41.5	45.1	13.4	360,956	34.2	43.1	22.7
06023	Humboldt County	112,904	38.5	40.4	21.0	56,309	42.4	41.0	16.6	56,595	34.7	39.9	25.4
06025	Imperial County	134,231	36.6	45.2	18.1	69,144	41.1	45.1	13.8	65,087	31.9	45.4	22.7
06029	Kern County	643,446	35.8	46.4	17.8	332,082	39.8	46.4	13.7	311,364	31.6	46.4	22.0
06031	Kings County	116,037	36.2	44.5	19.3	66,823	41.6	41.6	16.8	49,214	28.8	48.5	22.6

Table C-2: Counties with a Population of 50,000 or More—Marriages and Births—*Continued*

State/ county FIPS code	State/County	Total women age 15 to 50 years	Percent of all women who had a birth in the past year	Percent of women who had a birth who were married (including separated and spouse absent):	Percent of women who had a birth who were partners in an unmarried partner household	Age of women who had a birth in the last year as a percent of all women who had a birth			Women who had a birth in the last year as a percent of all women in their age group		
						Age 15 to 19	Age 20 to 34	Age 35 to 50	Age 15 to 19	Age 20 to 34	Age 35 to 50
00000	**United States**....................	76,155,872	5.3	64.1	10.1	5.5	73.8	20.7	2.1	9.4	2.5
01000	**Alabama**...............	1,165,746	5.5	58.9	6.2	7.1	78.5	14.4	2.8	10.3	1.8
01001	Autauga County	13,622	3.8	60.5	9.4	6.3	85.0	8.8	1.7	8.6	0.7
01003	Baldwin County	42,338	5.8	67.0	3.8	5.8	68.9	25.3	2.6	10.5	3.0
01009	Blount County	12,972	7.5	69.2	4.3	6.2	91.1	2.8	3.2	18.3	0.4
01015	Calhoun County	28,048	3.9	60.6	3.0	17.6	63.7	18.8	5.0	5.8	1.7
01031	Coffee County	12,102	5.5	28.5	13.0	2.6	91.2	6.2	1.1	12.7	0.7
01033	Colbert County	12,513	2.9	73.6	0.0	8.4	91.6	0.0	1.7	7.0	0.0
01043	Cullman County	18,140	5.1	69.1	9.5	5.9	69.9	24.2	2.4	9.0	2.5
01045	Dale County	11,713	5.9	58.0	5.6	17.6	74.2	8.2	7.7	10.1	1.1
01049	DeKalb County	17,369	4.3	84.3	2.3	6.0	74.3	19.7	1.3	9.1	1.9
01051	Elmore County	20,534	4.7	78.4	6.6	3.6	81.8	14.6	1.3	9.7	1.5
01055	Etowah County	24,331	4.3	60.1	10.1	10.0	78.1	11.9	3.2	8.6	1.1
01069	Houston County	24,620	5.6	56.5	6.0	5.2	80.0	14.7	2.3	10.9	1.8
01071	Jackson County	11,757	2.8	58.3	0.6	7.7	69.1	23.1	1.6	5.0	1.3
01073	Jefferson County	164,359	6.1	55.2	5.1	7.4	76.7	15.9	3.5	10.5	2.2
01077	Lauderdale County	22,116	4.9	68.9	4.6	0.0	90.8	9.2	0.0	10.7	1.0
01081	Lee County	42,140	4.4	70.7	10.3	11.5	81.0	7.5	3.3	7.1	1.0
01083	Limestone County	20,427	5.5	69.2	12.5	8.1	83.0	8.9	3.2	11.7	1.0
01089	Madison County	86,036	4.8	67.2	11.5	6.0	84.0	10.1	2.1	9.8	1.1
01095	Marshall County	21,384	6.3	52.2	5.1	12.9	72.3	14.8	6.1	11.4	2.0
01097	Mobile County	101,514	5.0	52.1	9.0	6.8	78.0	15.1	2.5	9.1	1.8
01101	Montgomery County	58,964	5.9	37.2	15.1	10.4	78.9	10.7	4.3	10.4	1.5
01103	Morgan County	28,029	4.9	76.0	3.8	11.3	67.6	21.2	3.8	8.8	2.2
01113	Russell County	14,042	7.2	41.6	1.0	14.3	75.9	9.8	8.1	11.7	1.7
01115	St. Clair County	20,104	5.5	81.5	3.9	7.2	79.7	13.1	3.1	11.0	1.5
01117	Shelby County	50,281	4.1	84.1	4.6	0.5	80.0	19.5	0.2	8.5	1.7
01121	Talladega County	18,915	4.7	51.6	3.0	5.9	92.3	1.8	2.1	10.8	0.2
01125	Tuscaloosa County	56,040	5.4	69.6	1.0	2.4	83.8	13.8	0.8	9.2	2.2
01127	Walker County	14,870	5.9	45.3	2.3	8.9	85.4	5.8	3.9	13.2	0.7
02000	**Alaska**..................	176,655	6.2	62.3	14.7	3.7	73.5	22.8	1.7	10.3	3.4
02020	Anchorage Municipality	77,456	5.5	64.8	13.2	3.1	74.7	22.2	1.3	8.9	2.9
02090	Fairbanks North Star Borough	25,087	6.6	76.8	12.3	2.2	64.2	33.5	1.2	8.6	5.7
02122	Kenai Peninsula Borough	11,872	7.0	62.1	15.0	0.0	77.3	22.7	0.0	13.5	3.5
02170	Matanuska-Susitna Borough	22,050	4.9	69.6	10.6	1.9	76.0	22.2	0.6	9.4	2.4
04000	**Arizona**................	1,536,237	5.6	60.7	12.1	5.9	73.1	21.0	2.3	9.6	2.7
04001	Apache County	16,607	5.9	42.3	6.8	6.9	73.0	20.1	2.1	11.0	2.8
04003	Cochise County	27,301	4.4	63.0	17.6	17.7	74.7	7.7	4.7	8.0	0.8
04005	Coconino County	36,927	5.2	43.8	12.2	8.7	64.6	26.7	2.1	7.3	4.3
04007	Gila County	9,622	6.7	31.8	30.6	7.3	84.6	8.1	3.1	15.0	1.2
04013	Maricopa County	970,297	5.7	62.3	10.9	5.4	71.5	23.1	2.3	9.6	3.0
04015	Mohave County	36,464	4.4	67.4	15.4	3.4	74.4	22.2	1.0	8.6	2.1
04017	Navajo County	22,751	8.1	35.8	7.1	7.2	76.4	16.4	3.4	15.6	3.1
04019	Pima County	230,793	5.2	57.8	15.8	5.1	78.1	16.8	1.8	9.2	2.1
04021	Pinal County	79,409	5.2	61.7	15.2	5.2	70.8	24.1	1.9	8.8	2.8
04025	Yavapai County	37,210	5.2	62.2	9.1	18.6	71.8	9.6	6.8	9.9	1.0
04027	Yuma County	44,952	6.2	67.9	17.0	6.5	77.8	15.8	2.4	11.3	2.4
05000	**Arkansas**	692,569	5.4	62.6	9.5	6.9	81.5	11.6	2.7	10.5	1.4
05007	Benton County	56,354	5.0	77.7	5.6	4.3	78.4	17.3	1.7	9.4	1.9
05031	Craighead County	25,773	5.9	71.4	8.4	1.5	94.2	4.2	0.6	11.9	0.6
05033	Crawford County	14,249	6.8	49.6	7.8	3.1	92.4	4.5	1.5	15.6	0.7
05035	Crittenden County	12,788	6.0	33.8	11.1	18.5	66.1	15.4	8.0	9.5	2.1
05045	Faulkner County	32,274	5.4	68.8	4.0	2.0	90.5	7.6	0.7	10.1	1.1
05051	Garland County	20,450	4.7	63.2	6.8	4.4	88.0	7.6	1.4	10.6	0.8
05069	Jefferson County	17,526	3.6	38.9	11.1	4.6	78.5	17.0	1.1	6.7	1.5
05085	Lonoke County	17,310	7.7	77.0	3.7	5.8	83.8	10.4	3.2	16.0	1.7
05115	Pope County	15,470	5.6	81.8	2.5	20.9	72.5	6.6	7.4	9.2	0.9
05119	Pulaski County	96,724	4.5	64.3	7.2	2.7	83.8	13.5	1.0	8.5	1.4
05125	Saline County	25,906	4.3	64.2	2.9	5.4	89.3	5.3	1.9	9.2	0.5
05131	Sebastian County	29,898	5.4	66.7	9.8	8.9	77.8	13.3	3.6	9.6	1.7
05143	Washington County	55,965	4.9	71.8	9.1	6.3	77.8	15.9	2.0	7.9	2.1
05145	White County	19,095	5.7	72.0	5.5	1.7	81.6	16.7	0.6	10.4	2.4
06000	**California**	9,553,926	5.2	66.1	10.3	5.0	70.4	24.6	1.9	8.7	3.0
06001	Alameda County	407,715	5.0	76.8	7.6	1.7	68.4	29.8	0.8	8.1	3.3
06007	Butte County	52,654	5.6	66.2	11.4	7.4	70.3	22.2	2.7	8.3	3.4
06013	Contra Costa County	261,288	5.4	69.9	8.9	2.8	67.5	29.7	1.1	9.7	3.3
06017	El Dorado County	37,949	4.9	78.9	4.1	0.0	61.5	38.5	0.0	8.9	3.7
06019	Fresno County	234,380	6.1	63.9	10.9	4.4	78.8	16.8	1.7	10.6	2.6
06023	Humboldt County	32,580	5.2	66.1	13.0	1.2	74.7	24.1	0.4	8.1	3.3
06025	Imperial County	41,289	7.2	49.9	10.0	7.5	75.9	16.5	3.3	13.0	2.9
06029	Kern County	204,900	6.8	56.5	14.3	10.4	76.0	13.6	4.4	11.8	2.3
06031	Kings County	33,011	7.9	52.5	11.9	10.9	74.9	14.2	5.4	13.1	2.9

State/county FIPS code	State/County	Total population 15 years and older	Marital status, percent			Male population 15 years and older	Male, marital status, percent			Female population 15 years and older	Female, marital status, percent		
			Never married	Now married (except separated)	Separated, widowed, or divorced		Never married	Now married (except separated)	Separated, widowed, or divorced		Never married	Now married (except separated)	Separated, widowed, or divorced
	California—cont'd												
06033	Lake County	53,335	28.4	46.1	25.5	26,685	33.1	46.7	20.1	26,650	23.6	45.4	30.9
06037	Los Angeles County	8,027,896	41.6	42.2	16.2	3,924,796	45.0	43.8	11.2	4,103,100	38.3	40.6	21.1
06039	Madera County	116,469	37.1	46.3	16.6	55,814	39.8	48.7	11.5	60,655	34.6	44.1	21.4
06041	Marin County	212,352	27.9	51.7	20.4	103,609	31.5	54.0	14.5	108,743	24.4	49.5	26.1
06045	Mendocino County	71,632	29.4	45.8	24.8	35,648	34.6	46.0	19.4	35,984	24.2	45.6	30.2
06047	Merced County	195,260	37.6	45.5	17.0	98,111	41.7	46.0	12.2	97,149	33.3	44.9	21.7
06053	Monterey County	330,266	37.6	47.4	15.0	169,924	42.0	46.4	11.6	160,342	33.0	48.5	18.6
06055	Napa County	113,529	30.3	50.2	19.5	56,258	33.5	53.1	13.4	57,271	27.1	47.4	25.5
06057	Nevada County	84,067	24.6	52.8	22.7	41,275	28.7	54.3	17.0	42,792	20.6	51.3	28.1
06059	Orange County	2,485,754	34.0	49.9	16.1	1,219,431	37.7	51.4	10.9	1,266,323	30.3	48.5	21.2
06061	Placer County	291,995	25.8	55.7	18.6	141,143	29.6	57.7	12.7	150,852	22.2	53.8	24.0
06065	Riverside County	1,757,766	33.6	48.3	18.0	869,722	37.2	49.5	13.2	888,044	30.1	47.2	22.7
06067	Sacramento County	1,149,146	35.0	44.5	20.5	556,081	38.8	46.4	14.8	593,065	31.4	42.7	25.9
06069	San Benito County	43,870	29.4	52.7	17.9	21,862	33.6	52.9	13.5	22,008	25.2	52.4	22.4
06071	San Bernardino County	1,596,565	36.7	45.4	17.9	787,552	39.8	46.8	13.3	809,013	33.6	44.1	22.3
06073	San Diego County	2,572,530	35.9	47.0	17.1	1,287,094	40.3	47.9	11.8	1,285,436	31.4	46.1	22.5
06075	San Francisco County	732,604	46.5	38.1	15.3	372,667	51.1	38.3	10.7	359,937	41.8	38.0	20.1
06077	San Joaquin County	535,071	34.4	47.6	18.0	263,808	37.9	48.8	13.4	271,263	31.0	46.4	22.6
06079	San Luis Obispo County	232,320	34.1	48.2	17.7	118,559	38.5	48.5	13.0	113,761	29.7	47.8	22.5
06081	San Mateo County	602,473	32.1	51.3	16.6	294,131	35.9	52.8	11.3	308,342	28.5	49.9	21.7
06083	Santa Barbara County	349,349	38.9	44.9	16.2	174,797	42.6	45.6	11.8	174,552	35.1	44.2	20.7
06085	Santa Clara County	1,470,766	32.7	53.1	14.1	735,618	36.5	53.9	9.6	735,148	29.0	52.4	18.7
06087	Santa Cruz County	221,276	38.9	44.5	16.6	109,309	42.5	45.7	11.8	111,967	35.4	43.2	21.4
06089	Shasta County	146,570	27.0	49.6	23.3	71,333	31.3	51.0	17.7	75,237	23.0	48.3	28.6
06095	Solano County	338,805	33.7	46.8	19.4	168,029	37.4	48.1	14.5	170,776	30.1	45.6	24.3
06097	Sonoma County	405,248	32.2	46.6	21.2	197,656	36.2	48.5	15.2	207,592	28.5	44.7	26.9
06099	Stanislaus County	401,606	34.0	47.8	18.1	196,710	38.2	48.9	12.9	204,896	30.1	46.8	23.2
06101	Sutter County	73,792	29.4	52.5	18.2	36,483	33.5	53.4	13.1	37,309	25.3	51.5	23.1
06103	Tehama County	50,562	26.2	51.3	22.5	24,964	29.7	52.2	18.1	25,598	22.7	50.5	26.8
06107	Tulare County	330,027	35.2	48.3	16.6	164,388	38.8	49.7	11.5	165,639	31.6	46.9	21.5
06109	Tuolumne County	46,822	24.8	52.4	22.9	24,688	29.5	50.4	20.1	22,134	19.5	54.5	26.0
06111	Ventura County	664,319	32.2	50.4	17.4	327,635	36.0	51.6	12.4	336,684	28.5	49.3	22.2
06113	Yolo County	166,411	41.9	42.7	15.4	80,168	43.8	45.7	10.6	86,243	40.1	39.9	20.0
06115	Yuba County	55,388	28.9	50.2	20.9	27,774	31.7	50.8	17.5	27,614	26.0	49.6	24.3
08000	**Colorado**	4,156,448	31.1	50.7	18.3	2,075,336	34.8	51.3	13.9	2,081,112	27.3	50.0	22.7
08001	Adams County	349,592	31.0	50.4	18.6	174,914	34.5	50.9	14.6	174,678	27.5	49.9	22.6
08005	Arapahoe County	472,278	31.0	49.8	19.2	229,366	34.2	51.7	14.1	242,912	28.0	47.9	24.1
08013	Boulder County	252,792	37.2	47.7	15.2	126,358	40.4	48.6	11.0	126,434	34.0	46.7	19.3
08014	Broomfield County	45,498	27.6	56.5	15.9	22,352	30.3	58.7	11.0	23,146	25.0	54.3	20.7
08031	Denver County	517,861	41.8	38.5	19.7	258,098	45.0	39.5	15.4	259,763	38.5	37.4	24.0
08035	Douglas County	225,332	21.8	64.2	14.1	110,499	23.7	66.6	9.6	114,833	19.8	61.8	18.4
08037	Eagle County	41,678	36.5	50.4	13.1	22,428	41.5	47.6	10.9	19,250	30.7	53.6	15.7
08041	El Paso County	507,864	28.4	53.7	17.9	253,410	32.7	54.2	13.1	254,454	24.2	53.2	22.6
08045	Garfield County	43,912	26.8	56.1	17.1	22,526	30.5	54.5	15.1	21,386	22.9	57.8	19.3
08059	Jefferson County	448,848	28.3	52.2	19.5	221,607	32.5	53.0	14.5	227,241	24.2	51.5	24.3
08067	La Plata County	43,976	32.0	49.7	18.4	22,153	36.5	49.6	13.8	21,823	27.3	49.7	22.9
08069	Larimer County	256,728	33.6	50.9	15.6	127,026	36.8	51.9	11.4	129,702	30.4	49.9	19.7
08077	Mesa County	119,314	26.9	52.7	20.3	58,819	32.3	53.5	14.2	60,495	21.7	52.0	26.2
08101	Pueblo County	129,266	30.4	46.4	23.1	63,040	33.7	47.6	18.8	66,226	27.3	45.4	27.3
08123	Weld County	202,984	28.4	54.8	16.8	101,340	31.0	54.9	14.1	101,644	25.8	54.6	19.6
09000	**Connecticut**	2,944,753	33.7	48.1	18.2	1,419,698	37.0	50.2	12.8	1,525,055	30.6	46.2	23.2
09001	Fairfield County	749,174	32.5	50.9	16.6	360,364	35.2	53.5	11.3	388,810	30.0	48.5	21.5
09003	Hartford County	735,003	34.7	46.2	19.1	351,942	38.3	48.5	13.3	383,061	31.4	44.2	24.4
09005	Litchfield County	157,147	26.6	54.3	19.1	76,406	30.4	56.1	13.5	80,741	23.0	52.5	24.5
09007	Middlesex County	138,613	29.6	52.6	17.8	66,900	32.0	55.2	12.8	71,713	27.4	50.1	22.4
09009	New Haven County	711,413	36.4	44.9	18.8	338,939	39.8	47.2	13.0	372,474	33.2	42.7	24.0
09011	New London County	227,573	31.3	49.5	19.1	113,179	35.3	49.9	14.8	114,394	27.4	49.2	23.4
09013	Tolland County	128,388	37.5	46.4	16.0	64,127	40.3	46.7	13.0	64,261	34.8	46.2	19.1
09015	Windham County	97,442	33.6	46.7	19.7	47,841	37.6	47.8	14.6	49,601	29.7	45.7	24.6
10000	**Delaware**	746,911	33.3	47.1	19.6	357,481	35.9	49.5	14.6	389,430	30.9	44.9	24.2
10001	Kent County	133,550	31.6	48.1	20.4	63,445	33.2	50.7	16.1	70,105	30.1	45.7	24.2
10003	New Castle County	443,910	36.1	45.9	18.0	212,378	38.7	48.3	12.9	231,532	33.8	43.6	22.6
10005	Sussex County	169,451	27.2	49.6	23.2	81,658	30.6	51.5	17.9	87,793	24.0	47.8	28.2
11000	**District of Columbia**	541,211	57.5	26.0	16.5	253,125	58.6	28.4	13.0	288,086	56.6	23.8	19.6
11001	District of Columbia	541,211	57.5	26.0	16.5	253,125	58.6	28.4	13.0	288,086	56.6	23.8	19.6
12000	**Florida**	16,009,758	31.2	46.1	22.8	7,757,981	34.9	48.2	16.9	8,251,777	27.6	44.1	28.3
12001	Alachua County	213,788	47.0	36.6	16.4	102,390	49.2	38.1	12.7	111,398	44.9	35.2	19.9
12005	Bay County	140,899	26.7	49.2	24.1	69,555	30.8	49.6	19.6	71,344	22.6	48.9	28.5
12009	Brevard County	462,383	26.6	48.0	25.4	223,882	30.8	50.0	19.3	238,501	22.7	46.2	31.1
12011	Broward County	1,486,490	33.9	42.9	23.3	714,290	37.8	45.4	16.8	772,200	30.2	40.5	29.3
12015	Charlotte County	144,449	18.8	55.3	25.9	69,446	21.8	58.9	19.3	75,003	16.0	52.0	32.0

Table C-2: Counties with a Population of 50,000 or More—Marriages and Births—*Continued*

State/county FIPS code	State/County	Total women age 15 to 50 years	Percent of all women who had a birth in the past year	Percent of women who had a birth who were married (including separated and spouse absent):	Percent of women who had a birth who were partners in an unmarried partner household	Age of women who had a birth in the last year as a percent of all women who had a birth			Women who had a birth in the last year as a percent of all women in their age group		
						Age 15 to 19	Age 20 to 34	Age 35 to 50	Age 15 to 19	Age 20 to 34	Age 35 to 50
	California—cont'd										
06033	Lake County	12,608	8.4	38.1	27.8	16.2	81.8	2.0	9.8	17.7	0.4
06037	Los Angeles County	2,614,445	4.8	60.4	11.1	5.2	67.4	27.4	1.9	7.5	3.0
06039	Madera County	38,238	6.7	52.4	11.5	12.3	67.9	19.9	5.9	10.6	3.1
06041	Marin County	53,189	5.5	82.0	5.2	1.8	61.1	37.1	0.8	11.3	3.6
06045	Mendocino County	17,998	5.4	60.8	12.6	6.4	69.5	24.1	2.5	9.4	2.9
06047	Merced County	64,288	6.4	65.0	13.4	10.1	71.9	18.0	3.7	10.6	2.9
06053	Monterey County	100,599	6.3	66.8	13.3	6.9	66.6	26.5	2.9	9.4	4.1
06055	Napa County	31,853	5.1	72.1	7.7	2.7	65.8	31.4	1.0	8.7	3.5
06057	Nevada County	18,649	3.4	79.7	6.4	0.0	71.3	28.7	0.0	6.9	1.9
06059	Orange County	785,299	4.8	73.2	8.5	3.5	67.8	28.8	1.2	8.0	3.0
06061	Placer County	82,193	4.5	76.3	7.8	1.5	72.1	26.3	0.5	9.0	2.4
06065	Riverside County	558,064	5.8	60.3	13.0	7.9	72.1	20.0	2.9	10.2	2.7
06067	Sacramento County	365,354	5.3	61.5	14.3	4.4	78.4	17.2	1.8	9.4	2.1
06069	San Benito County	14,024	6.0	73.0	4.2	7.1	71.3	21.6	2.7	11.2	2.8
06071	San Bernardino County	534,890	6.0	60.0	10.6	5.7	75.5	18.8	2.2	10.6	2.7
06073	San Diego County	805,703	5.1	77.0	6.4	4.4	72.7	22.9	1.8	8.3	2.8
06075	San Francisco County	226,683	3.7	79.6	4.3	0.1	51.3	48.5	0.1	3.7	4.3
06077	San Joaquin County	171,385	6.4	61.6	10.0	6.7	76.0	17.4	2.7	11.6	2.6
06079	San Luis Obispo County	61,624	4.6	71.0	10.5	4.2	70.0	25.8	1.1	7.3	3.1
06081	San Mateo County	177,377	5.0	79.2	7.8	1.7	60.4	38.0	0.7	7.6	3.8
06083	Santa Barbara County	107,256	5.1	71.7	8.2	7.5	69.5	23.1	2.2	7.6	3.1
06085	Santa Clara County	464,029	5.7	78.1	6.2	2.9	66.0	31.1	1.4	9.3	3.7
06087	Santa Cruz County	67,391	4.5	65.5	10.0	2.9	70.9	26.2	0.8	7.4	2.9
06089	Shasta County	38,644	3.7	70.1	17.3	5.2	78.4	16.4	1.4	7.1	1.4
06095	Solano County	101,096	5.2	60.7	14.7	5.1	74.9	20.0	1.9	9.2	2.3
06097	Sonoma County	112,766	5.1	63.3	13.5	2.3	69.2	28.5	0.8	8.6	3.2
06099	Stanislaus County	128,351	6.0	62.2	15.1	7.2	79.2	13.6	2.8	11.2	1.9
06101	Sutter County	22,438	6.2	63.8	7.0	9.3	75.1	15.6	4.0	10.9	2.2
06103	Tehama County	13,693	5.0	53.0	21.8	14.9	85.1	0.0	4.8	10.6	0.0
06107	Tulare County	109,902	7.2	57.4	18.1	7.4	80.0	12.6	3.2	13.2	2.3
06109	Tuolumne County	9,399	4.7	49.0	43.5	7.5	78.1	14.4	2.3	8.8	1.6
06111	Ventura County	201,691	5.1	70.3	5.7	5.2	71.1	23.7	1.8	9.1	2.7
06113	Yolo County	57,978	4.2	63.9	7.2	5.5	62.3	32.1	1.3	5.5	4.0
06115	Yuba County	17,278	8.0	64.3	13.4	8.5	81.1	10.4	5.0	13.8	2.1
08000	**Colorado**	1,267,458	5.5	72.7	8.5	4.4	74.2	21.4	1.9	9.6	2.7
08001	Adams County	116,539	6.7	70.4	9.7	6.4	76.4	17.2	3.5	11.6	2.7
08005	Arapahoe County	149,877	5.8	72.9	10.0	2.2	75.5	22.3	1.0	10.6	2.8
08013	Boulder County	78,926	4.6	79.3	7.9	4.3	57.3	38.3	1.3	6.1	4.3
08014	Broomfield County	14,768	6.2	70.3	0.0	2.5	76.7	20.8	1.5	11.0	2.8
08031	Denver County	173,606	5.3	68.2	5.4	4.1	68.8	27.2	2.4	7.1	3.7
08035	Douglas County	74,518	4.9	87.7	5.2	3.6	72.6	23.8	1.3	11.7	2.1
08037	Eagle County	13,275	4.6	88.0	0.0	9.3	69.2	21.6	3.4	8.1	2.1
08041	El Paso County	158,968	6.0	79.5	5.4	4.2	79.5	16.3	1.9	10.9	2.3
08045	Garfield County	13,700	3.9	85.3	6.3	0.0	77.1	22.9	0.0	7.9	1.9
08059	Jefferson County	126,112	4.3	73.5	8.0	2.3	67.2	30.5	0.8	7.3	2.7
08067	La Plata County	12,710	4.1	77.2	16.3	0.0	61.5	38.5	0.0	6.3	3.6
08069	Larimer County	78,189	5.1	75.5	10.3	4.0	75.4	20.5	1.4	8.1	2.7
08077	Mesa County	33,239	7.1	63.0	17.2	8.9	89.4	1.7	4.1	14.5	0.3
08101	Pueblo County	36,427	5.6	61.2	9.0	10.1	76.7	13.2	3.8	10.2	1.7
08123	Weld County	64,889	7.3	60.3	9.3	1.8	82.1	16.1	0.9	13.9	2.7
09000	**Connecticut**	864,070	4.5	65.5	8.6	3.6	69.9	26.5	1.1	8.2	2.5
09001	Fairfield County	224,540	4.5	76.2	6.2	3.7	59.8	36.5	1.2	7.7	3.3
09003	Hartford County	215,026	5.4	59.3	8.7	4.5	70.3	25.2	1.8	9.6	2.9
09005	Litchfield County	40,568	3.3	75.5	2.3	0.0	78.5	21.5	0.0	7.8	1.3
09007	Middlesex County	38,339	3.5	86.6	1.9	0.0	75.2	24.8	0.0	7.6	1.7
09009	New Haven County	213,493	4.3	57.9	8.7	4.1	73.0	22.9	1.2	7.9	2.2
09011	New London County	63,970	4.4	65.3	18.8	3.0	78.1	18.9	0.9	8.9	1.7
09013	Tolland County	39,207	2.2	78.6	2.9	0.0	85.2	14.8	0.0	4.8	0.8
09015	Windham County	28,927	4.0	49.5	21.7	2.3	84.2	13.5	0.6	8.9	1.1
10000	**Delaware**	221,083	5.3	62.6	10.9	4.0	71.4	24.6	1.6	9.1	2.9
10001	Kent County	41,134	6.4	60.7	7.5	4.8	67.2	28.0	2.1	10.1	4.1
10003	New Castle County	139,376	5.1	64.9	12.6	2.9	71.1	26.0	1.1	8.6	3.0
10005	Sussex County	40,573	5.0	56.9	9.3	6.9	77.7	15.4	2.7	9.9	1.6
11000	**District of Columbia**	193,803	4.2	52.0	7.1	3.2	66.0	30.7	1.3	5.1	3.8
11001	District of Columbia	193,803	4.2	52.0	7.1	3.2	66.0	30.7	1.3	5.1	3.8
12000	**Florida**	4,449,952	4.8	58.7	10.7	5.3	71.5	23.2	2.0	8.4	2.4
12001	Alachua County	73,515	3.0	67.4	9.6	3.2	84.0	12.8	0.6	4.5	1.3
12005	Bay County	39,662	6.5	59.2	8.3	5.6	82.3	12.1	3.3	12.4	1.7
12009	Brevard County	113,631	4.4	67.0	8.9	6.1	73.2	20.7	2.0	8.5	1.9
12011	Broward County	448,739	4.7	60.0	11.3	4.8	68.6	26.7	1.8	8.2	2.6
12015	Charlotte County	24,729	4.4	54.5	4.7	6.6	78.9	14.5	2.0	10.2	1.2

Table C-2: Counties with a Population of 50,000 or More—Marriages and Births—*Continued*

State/county FIPS code	State/County	Total population 15 years and older	Marital status, percent			Male population 15 years and older	Male, marital status, percent			Female population 15 years and older	Female, marital status, percent		
			Never married	Now married (except separated)	Separated, widowed, or divorced		Never married	Now married (except separated)	Separated, widowed, or divorced		Never married	Now married (except separated)	Separated, widowed, or divorced
	Florida—cont'd												
12017	Citrus County	122,172	18.6	54.7	26.7	58,711	22.0	57.0	21.0	63,461	15.5	52.5	32.0
12019	Clay County	155,096	26.3	53.5	20.3	75,128	28.9	56.1	15.0	79,968	23.8	51.0	25.2
12021	Collier County	281,278	24.7	52.5	22.8	137,551	28.8	55.8	15.4	143,727	20.7	49.5	29.8
12023	Columbia County	55,162	31.5	44.4	24.2	28,417	36.8	44.8	18.5	26,745	25.9	43.9	30.2
12031	Duval County	708,451	34.4	43.0	22.7	339,145	37.8	45.2	17.0	369,306	31.2	40.9	27.9
12033	Escambia County	249,428	34.4	41.9	23.7	122,949	38.6	43.0	18.4	126,479	30.3	40.9	28.8
12035	Flagler County	83,130	23.3	54.3	22.4	39,354	25.1	57.9	17.1	43,776	21.8	51.0	27.2
12053	Hernando County	146,571	22.0	53.3	24.7	69,387	24.9	55.8	19.3	77,184	19.3	51.0	29.7
12055	Highlands County	83,327	21.6	52.2	26.2	40,408	24.9	53.0	22.1	42,919	18.4	51.4	30.1
12057	Hillsborough County	1,032,503	34.2	45.1	20.7	498,101	37.2	47.5	15.2	534,402	31.5	42.7	25.8
12061	Indian River County	119,783	22.4	52.2	25.4	57,063	27.7	54.7	17.7	62,720	17.6	49.9	32.4
12069	Lake County	252,657	23.9	55.0	21.1	120,778	27.4	56.5	16.0	131,879	20.6	53.7	25.7
12071	Lee County	543,015	26.0	50.3	23.7	264,117	29.5	52.0	18.5	278,898	22.6	48.7	28.6
12073	Leon County	236,194	46.1	38.4	15.5	111,037	48.1	40.6	11.4	125,157	44.5	36.4	19.1
12081	Manatee County	278,799	24.9	52.4	22.7	133,368	28.7	55.0	16.3	145,431	21.4	50.0	28.6
12083	Marion County	282,988	23.9	51.0	25.0	134,273	26.7	54.0	19.4	148,715	21.5	48.4	30.2
12085	Martin County	128,244	24.6	50.9	24.5	63,298	29.4	51.7	18.9	64,946	19.8	50.2	30.0
12086	Miami-Dade County	2,139,399	36.7	41.1	22.2	1,027,808	40.4	43.9	15.7	1,111,591	33.2	38.6	28.2
12087	Monroe County	65,777	30.9	45.5	23.6	34,969	36.1	44.6	19.3	30,808	24.9	46.6	28.5
12089	Nassau County	62,146	22.8	55.1	22.1	30,237	26.4	56.7	16.9	31,909	19.5	53.6	27.0
12091	Okaloosa County	153,823	27.5	51.6	20.9	77,738	33.1	51.1	15.8	76,085	21.8	52.2	26.0
12095	Orange County	969,229	39.0	42.0	18.9	473,108	42.9	43.6	13.6	496,121	35.4	40.6	24.0
12097	Osceola County	227,951	32.9	45.2	21.9	110,807	36.5	47.7	15.8	117,144	29.6	42.8	27.6
12099	Palm Beach County	1,132,782	30.6	46.5	22.9	542,846	34.4	49.3	16.4	589,936	27.1	43.9	29.0
12101	Pasco County	390,324	24.7	51.3	24.0	187,541	28.0	53.8	18.2	202,783	21.6	49.1	29.3
12103	Pinellas County	791,658	29.0	43.9	27.1	375,891	33.0	46.4	20.6	415,767	25.4	41.6	33.1
12105	Polk County	498,335	29.6	48.0	22.4	241,644	33.4	50.2	16.4	256,691	26.1	45.9	28.0
12107	Putnam County	59,772	26.7	46.5	26.8	29,150	28.7	48.0	23.3	30,622	24.8	45.0	30.1
12109	St. Johns County	165,914	25.5	54.0	20.6	79,746	28.5	56.3	15.2	86,168	22.6	51.8	25.6
12111	St. Lucie County	233,726	26.5	50.0	23.6	112,711	29.7	52.1	18.2	121,015	23.4	48.0	28.6
12113	Santa Rosa County	128,235	24.5	55.9	19.6	65,253	28.5	56.6	14.9	62,982	20.3	55.2	24.5
12115	Sarasota County	337,885	22.2	52.4	25.4	159,730	25.3	55.5	19.2	178,155	19.3	49.7	31.0
12117	Seminole County	354,386	33.2	45.6	21.2	169,696	37.3	47.9	14.9	184,690	29.5	43.4	27.1
12119	Sumter County	95,580	14.3	63.2	22.5	48,966	19.3	63.1	17.6	46,614	9.1	63.3	27.6
12127	Volusia County	422,521	28.0	46.4	25.6	204,170	31.9	48.5	19.6	218,351	24.3	44.4	31.3
12131	Walton County	47,851	24.0	51.6	24.4	24,353	28.5	51.2	20.3	23,498	19.3	52.0	28.7
13000	**Georgia**	7,829,101	33.5	46.9	19.6	3,780,350	36.4	49.2	14.4	4,048,751	30.7	44.8	24.6
13013	Barrow County	54,022	27.2	53.8	19.0	26,513	31.8	55.3	12.9	27,509	22.8	52.3	24.9
13015	Bartow County	78,770	26.2	53.2	20.6	38,470	29.6	56.0	14.3	40,300	22.8	50.6	26.6
13021	Bibb County	122,418	39.5	37.8	22.6	56,691	42.2	41.3	16.5	65,727	37.2	34.9	28.0
13031	Bulloch County	59,973	48.4	36.6	15.0	29,563	51.5	37.7	10.9	30,410	45.5	35.5	19.0
13039	Camden County	40,055	27.9	56.0	16.1	20,464	32.2	55.8	12.0	19,591	23.5	56.2	20.3
13045	Carroll County	88,434	31.8	46.7	21.5	42,207	34.6	48.4	17.1	46,227	29.3	45.1	25.5
13047	Catoosa County	52,170	22.8	55.5	21.6	24,817	25.7	56.9	17.4	27,353	20.2	54.3	25.5
13051	Chatham County	223,475	37.6	40.8	21.6	106,578	41.1	43.5	15.4	116,897	34.5	38.3	27.3
13057	Cherokee County	171,471	25.2	55.6	19.2	83,680	28.3	57.7	14.1	87,791	22.2	53.6	24.1
13059	Clarke County	101,952	56.5	29.9	13.6	47,950	57.9	33.0	9.0	54,002	55.3	27.0	17.7
13063	Clayton County	200,751	43.0	35.2	21.8	93,440	44.3	38.4	17.3	107,311	41.9	32.5	25.6
13067	Cobb County	559,445	32.5	50.8	16.7	268,137	34.9	53.0	12.1	291,308	30.3	48.8	20.9
13073	Columbia County	102,830	25.7	58.5	15.7	49,387	27.8	61.5	10.7	53,443	23.8	55.8	20.4
13077	Coweta County	102,546	25.4	58.0	16.6	49,599	27.7	60.1	12.2	52,947	23.3	55.9	20.8
13089	DeKalb County	563,786	41.7	38.3	20.0	264,739	44.2	41.5	14.2	299,047	39.4	35.5	25.1
13095	Dougherty County	73,850	41.8	34.8	23.3	33,436	43.4	39.8	16.8	40,414	40.5	30.7	28.7
13097	Douglas County	103,917	32.1	47.6	20.3	48,859	34.1	51.2	14.7	55,058	30.4	44.4	25.2
13103	Effingham County	41,451	25.5	54.0	20.6	20,277	28.6	56.7	14.8	21,174	22.5	51.4	26.1
13113	Fayette County	87,041	24.7	60.1	15.2	41,536	27.7	63.4	8.9	45,505	22.0	57.1	20.9
13115	Floyd County	76,891	28.4	48.0	23.6	36,477	31.2	51.6	17.2	40,414	26.0	44.6	29.4
13117	Forsyth County	141,426	24.4	59.7	16.0	69,452	27.3	61.7	11.0	71,974	21.5	57.7	20.8
13121	Fulton County	779,067	43.3	38.4	18.2	375,767	46.9	40.4	12.7	403,300	40.0	36.6	23.4
13127	Glynn County	65,111	28.9	48.1	23.0	30,406	32.8	50.2	17.0	34,705	25.6	46.2	28.2
13129	Gordon County	43,381	24.4	53.3	22.4	21,151	26.7	56.3	16.9	22,230	22.1	50.3	27.5
13135	Gwinnett County	643,164	32.2	52.7	15.0	312,552	35.0	55.2	9.8	330,612	29.7	50.3	20.0
13139	Hall County	142,844	28.7	50.7	20.5	70,923	31.9	52.2	16.0	71,921	25.7	49.3	25.0
13151	Henry County	161,554	30.0	50.6	19.4	75,853	32.0	55.3	12.8	85,701	28.2	46.4	25.3
13153	Houston County	113,871	29.0	51.3	19.6	54,891	31.4	54.4	14.1	58,980	26.8	48.5	24.7
13157	Jackson County	47,414	21.8	58.7	19.4	23,172	24.6	60.8	14.6	24,242	19.2	56.7	24.1
13179	Liberty County	48,286	27.9	55.5	16.6	24,015	31.9	54.6	13.4	24,271	24.0	56.3	19.8
13185	Lowndes County	89,505	40.3	40.0	19.8	43,552	44.2	40.9	14.9	45,953	36.6	39.1	24.3
13215	Muscogee County	157,052	37.5	39.0	23.5	75,785	42.9	40.2	16.9	81,267	32.4	38.0	29.6
13217	Newton County	78,237	34.0	43.5	22.5	36,377	36.7	47.5	15.8	41,860	31.7	40.1	28.3
13223	Paulding County	110,457	24.3	59.4	16.2	53,289	26.8	61.4	11.8	57,168	22.0	57.6	20.4
13245	Richmond County	160,645	41.2	34.7	24.1	77,100	44.2	37.2	18.7	83,545	38.5	32.4	29.1
13247	Rockdale County	67,728	31.9	48.2	20.0	31,591	34.2	53.0	12.8	36,137	29.8	43.9	26.3
13255	Spalding County	50,486	31.2	45.9	22.8	24,080	35.3	48.0	16.8	26,406	27.6	44.1	28.4

Table C-2: Counties with a Population of 50,000 or More—Marriages and Births—*Continued*

State/ county FIPS code	State/County	Total women age 15 to 50 years	Percent of all women who had a birth in the past year	Percent of women who had a birth who were married (including separated and spouse absent):	Percent of women who had a birth who were partners in an unmarried partner household	Age of women who had a birth in the last year as a percent of all women who had a birth			Women who had a birth in the last year as a percent of all women in their age group		
						Age 15 to 19	Age 20 to 34	Age 35 to 50	Age 15 to 19	Age 20 to 34	Age 35 to 50
	Florida—cont'd										
12017	Citrus County	22,401	3.5	55.2	20.1	10.1	74.7	15.2	2.3	8.0	1.0
12019	Clay County	48,059	3.5	43.2	20.5	14.6	65.3	20.1	3.5	6.3	1.4
12021	Collier County	61,910	4.8	55.2	11.1	9.3	67.0	23.7	3.4	8.5	2.3
12023	Columbia County	14,124	3.3	41.0	13.1	0.6	95.1	4.2	0.2	7.8	0.3
12031	Duval County	225,800	5.4	59.6	8.4	3.4	77.2	19.4	1.5	9.2	2.4
12033	Escambia County	71,065	5.0	64.6	8.4	6.8	71.4	21.8	2.3	7.8	2.7
12035	Flagler County	18,704	4.6	84.4	0.0	1.2	83.9	15.0	0.4	10.4	1.4
12053	Hernando County	33,728	4.8	37.7	25.1	0.0	80.4	19.6	0.0	10.9	1.9
12055	Highlands County	16,081	5.1	55.9	10.5	0.0	85.7	14.3	0.0	11.4	1.6
12057	Hillsborough County	330,686	4.7	64.2	8.4	4.8	72.0	23.2	1.8	7.8	2.5
12061	Indian River County	25,881	5.5	62.4	17.6	3.6	69.7	26.7	1.5	10.3	2.9
12069	Lake County	60,324	5.1	57.8	21.5	10.2	70.7	19.0	3.8	9.7	2.0
12071	Lee County	127,828	4.7	57.8	12.7	7.3	70.4	22.4	2.5	8.3	2.2
12073	Leon County	85,016	3.6	65.3	8.2	5.8	74.0	20.2	1.3	5.0	2.4
12081	Manatee County	66,376	4.7	61.2	12.3	4.8	72.5	22.7	1.7	8.8	2.2
12083	Marion County	65,720	5.8	47.4	14.0	6.3	77.2	16.5	2.8	11.4	2.0
12085	Martin County	26,199	4.9	44.9	9.9	1.2	66.9	31.9	0.4	9.0	3.1
12086	Miami-Dade County	661,515	4.4	59.9	8.4	5.0	65.3	29.8	1.8	7.0	2.8
12087	Monroe County	15,403	6.0	57.2	13.6	1.9	63.4	34.7	1.4	9.6	4.0
12089	Nassau County	16,250	5.9	68.1	11.1	0.0	76.0	24.0	0.0	13.0	2.8
12091	Okaloosa County	43,314	5.7	70.3	15.0	3.0	79.4	17.5	1.5	10.1	2.3
12095	Orange County	328,337	5.1	53.0	12.9	5.5	68.0	26.5	2.2	7.6	3.2
12097	Osceola County	74,284	6.5	55.2	12.9	8.0	76.2	15.8	3.8	12.4	2.2
12099	Palm Beach County	293,542	5.3	56.9	9.8	5.2	71.4	23.4	2.1	9.9	2.6
12101	Pasco County	100,398	4.8	59.4	13.1	3.4	68.7	28.0	1.2	8.9	2.7
12103	Pinellas County	196,752	4.7	51.3	11.9	4.3	77.8	17.8	1.8	9.4	1.7
12105	Polk County	137,163	5.7	53.3	13.9	6.7	75.8	17.4	2.8	10.4	2.2
12107	Putnam County	14,733	4.4	44.2	20.7	5.0	84.4	10.6	1.4	9.4	1.0
12109	St. Johns County	46,292	2.6	90.8	2.1	0.0	69.0	31.0	0.0	5.3	1.5
12111	St. Lucie County	60,588	5.3	59.9	6.2	1.5	80.9	17.6	0.6	10.8	1.9
12113	Santa Rosa County	36,346	5.9	78.0	9.3	4.1	73.9	22.0	1.8	11.6	2.6
12115	Sarasota County	66,896	4.4	64.1	5.3	12.3	60.2	27.5	4.2	7.4	2.4
12117	Seminole County	110,098	4.9	58.7	9.7	3.8	70.5	25.8	1.4	8.5	2.7
12119	Sumter County	8,825	3.9	73.1	2.3	7.3	80.4	12.3	2.0	8.8	0.9
12127	Volusia County	103,532	4.2	52.9	11.8	4.5	70.1	25.4	1.5	7.4	2.3
12131	Walton County	11,979	6.8	70.2	10.1	3.9	83.0	13.0	2.2	14.6	1.8
13000	**Georgia**	2,525,451	5.6	60.6	8.9	6.0	72.5	21.5	2.4	9.8	2.6
13013	Barrow County	17,252	5.5	85.9	4.9	18.1	55.3	26.6	9.0	6.9	3.2
13015	Bartow County	0	0.0	0.0	0.0	0.0	0.0	0.0	0.0	0.0	0.0
13021	Bibb County	38,834	5.2	43.4	3.4	11.6	74.6	13.8	3.8	8.9	1.7
13031	Bulloch County	21,621	4.3	67.4	10.7	2.8	83.9	13.3	0.6	7.2	2.0
13039	Camden County	12,663	6.1	39.7	12.1	0.0	94.1	5.9	0.0	12.6	0.8
13045	Carroll County	29,568	7.7	61.7	6.1	8.9	70.4	20.7	3.9	12.5	4.0
13047	Catoosa County	15,429	6.8	49.4	12.7	0.0	86.9	13.1	0.0	15.4	1.8
13051	Chatham County	71,656	5.4	45.6	13.0	5.8	80.9	13.3	2.3	8.9	1.9
13057	Cherokee County	0	0.0	0.0	0.0	0.0	0.0	0.0	0.0	0.0	0.0
13059	Clarke County	39,914	3.7	53.3	7.9	14.2	63.4	22.4	2.4	4.3	3.5
13063	Clayton County	73,988	5.7	46.1	14.9	10.2	68.1	21.8	4.5	9.1	2.8
13067	Cobb County	189,142	4.6	67.6	13.1	4.5	64.3	31.2	1.7	7.5	3.0
13073	Columbia County	33,530	5.2	82.4	2.6	0.3	74.5	25.2	0.1	10.0	2.7
13077	Coweta County	33,330	6.8	73.6	7.5	5.0	73.9	21.1	2.5	13.7	2.9
13089	DeKalb County	195,064	5.9	58.6	8.0	3.5	74.0	22.4	1.9	9.8	3.0
13095	Dougherty County	24,544	7.6	29.4	17.6	1.2	83.7	15.1	0.6	13.7	2.9
13097	Douglas County	36,078	6.5	63.1	17.6	2.3	65.1	32.7	1.0	12.2	4.2
13103	Effingham County	13,275	4.5	89.0	2.0	0.0	81.5	18.5	0.0	9.8	1.7
13113	Fayette County	24,897	3.6	61.8	10.8	0.0	76.3	23.7	0.0	10.2	1.6
13115	Floyd County	0	0.0	0.0	0.0	0.0	0.0	0.0	0.0	0.0	0.0
13117	Forsyth County	46,678	5.0	85.6	1.2	0.0	71.4	28.6	0.0	12.0	2.5
13121	Fulton County	267,135	4.4	59.1	6.9	5.1	70.7	24.2	1.8	7.1	2.5
13127	Glynn County	18,837	3.8	40.9	13.4	14.9	71.2	13.8	4.5	6.6	1.2
13129	Gordon County	13,502	6.5	70.0	1.0	18.0	58.1	23.9	8.6	9.6	3.3
13135	Gwinnett County	225,260	4.7	72.7	10.8	5.2	65.8	29.0	1.8	8.3	2.7
13139	Hall County	43,871	6.6	65.3	13.1	5.7	75.9	18.4	2.6	12.5	2.7
13151	Henry County	56,766	4.4	77.0	6.3	1.6	67.9	30.5	0.5	9.0	2.7
13153	Houston County	37,304	4.9	68.8	8.3	1.4	90.5	8.1	0.5	10.4	0.9
13157	Jackson County	14,786	5.4	85.9	0.4	2.6	80.9	16.5	1.1	11.7	1.8
13179	Liberty County	17,285	8.8	62.6	12.9	10.5	85.3	4.1	8.7	13.9	1.0
13185	Lowndes County	31,160	5.1	52.2	8.1	6.3	79.6	14.2	1.9	8.3	2.1
13215	Muscogee County	50,371	6.8	54.5	9.8	8.8	79.9	11.3	4.5	11.8	1.9
13217	Newton County	26,818	7.1	40.8	5.2	7.6	75.2	17.2	3.5	14.7	2.5
13223	Paulding County	39,146	4.4	80.0	2.7	0.0	86.9	13.1	0.0	10.6	1.1
13245	Richmond County	51,295	5.8	37.1	1.5	9.5	82.2	8.3	4.6	9.8	1.2
13247	Rockdale County	21,821	5.4	62.7	4.1	2.5	85.4	12.1	0.9	12.6	1.3
13255	Spalding County	14,893	4.3	53.9	0.0	0.0	76.4	23.6	0.0	7.4	2.4

Table C-2: Counties with a Population of 50,000 or More—Marriages and Births—*Continued*

State/county FIPS code	State/County	Total population 15 years and older	Marital status, percent			Male population 15 years and older	Male, marital status, percent			Female population 15 years and older	Female, marital status, percent		
			Never married	Now married (except separated)	Separated, widowed, or divorced		Never married	Now married (except separated)	Separated, widowed, or divorced		Never married	Now married (except separated)	Separated, widowed, or divorced
	Georgia—cont'd												
13285	Troup County	53,823	32.2	42.6	25.2	25,694	36.1	45.0	18.8	28,129	28.7	40.3	31.0
13295	Walker County	55,438	23.6	52.2	24.2	27,026	28.4	54.4	17.2	28,412	19.1	50.2	30.8
13297	Walton County	66,808	25.6	56.8	17.6	31,928	28.3	59.3	12.5	34,880	23.2	54.5	22.3
13313	Whitfield County	79,329	26.4	51.2	22.4	39,287	29.8	52.9	17.3	40,042	23.1	49.5	27.5
15000	**Hawaii**	1,133,822	33.1	50.0	16.8	568,002	37.5	50.4	12.1	565,820	28.8	49.7	21.6
15001	Hawaii County	153,933	33.0	47.7	19.4	76,595	37.0	48.3	14.8	77,338	29.0	47.1	23.9
15003	Honolulu County	795,585	33.8	50.2	16.1	399,577	38.3	50.4	11.3	396,008	29.2	49.9	20.9
15007	Kauai County	55,875	29.7	52.8	17.5	27,644	33.6	53.2	13.2	28,231	25.9	52.4	21.8
15009	Maui County	128,340	31.0	50.8	18.2	64,145	35.0	51.6	13.3	64,195	27.0	49.9	23.1
16000	**Idaho**	1,238,968	26.0	55.2	18.9	616,275	29.2	56.1	14.7	622,693	22.7	54.3	23.0
16001	Ada County	320,439	28.3	53.8	18.0	159,418	31.7	55.4	13.0	161,021	24.9	52.2	22.9
16005	Bannock County	64,315	28.8	51.4	19.8	31,753	32.1	51.5	16.4	32,562	25.5	51.4	23.1
16019	Bonneville County	78,280	24.5	56.1	19.4	38,474	27.9	56.7	15.4	39,806	21.2	55.5	23.3
16027	Canyon County	144,517	26.2	54.6	19.2	70,593	29.2	57.0	13.9	73,924	23.4	52.4	24.3
16055	Kootenai County	114,226	23.9	55.4	20.6	55,807	27.3	57.1	15.6	58,419	20.8	53.8	25.4
16083	Twin Falls County	60,437	24.7	54.8	20.5	29,483	28.2	56.8	15.0	30,954	21.4	52.9	25.7
17000	**Illinois**	10,343,979	34.7	47.8	17.6	5,027,821	37.7	49.7	12.6	5,316,158	31.7	45.9	22.3
17001	Adams County	54,520	27.3	52.7	19.9	26,222	29.7	55.8	14.5	28,298	25.1	49.9	25.0
17007	Boone County	41,924	26.9	56.3	16.8	20,756	28.8	57.7	13.4	21,168	25.1	54.8	20.1
17019	Champaign County	170,926	46.3	39.4	14.3	85,168	49.4	40.2	10.4	85,758	43.2	38.6	18.2
17029	Coles County	45,843	41.2	39.3	19.5	21,818	43.6	42.3	14.1	24,025	39.1	36.5	24.4
17031	Cook County	4,224,010	41.2	41.7	17.1	2,024,134	44.0	44.3	11.6	2,199,876	38.5	39.3	22.1
17037	DeKalb County	85,500	43.6	41.0	15.4	41,957	45.1	42.4	12.5	43,543	42.1	39.7	18.2
17043	DuPage County	745,439	29.7	55.5	14.8	362,209	32.5	57.6	9.9	383,230	27.0	53.5	19.4
17063	Grundy County	38,858	29.3	53.3	17.4	19,059	33.5	53.5	13.0	19,799	25.3	53.2	21.5
17073	Henry County	40,646	23.7	56.1	20.3	19,923	26.5	56.6	16.9	20,723	21.0	55.6	23.5
17077	Jackson County	51,124	48.2	35.6	16.1	25,744	53.3	36.2	10.5	25,380	43.1	35.1	21.8
17089	Kane County	400,385	30.5	54.0	15.6	198,027	33.7	54.8	11.5	202,358	27.3	53.2	19.5
17091	Kankakee County	89,841	34.0	45.7	20.3	43,546	38.0	47.7	14.2	46,295	30.2	43.7	26.1
17093	Kendall County	87,501	27.4	59.3	13.3	42,915	29.9	59.5	10.6	44,586	24.9	59.2	15.9
17095	Knox County	43,549	31.5	44.1	24.4	21,809	36.2	45.0	18.8	21,740	26.8	43.3	30.0
17097	Lake County	551,268	29.7	55.3	15.1	273,117	33.2	56.1	10.7	278,151	26.2	54.4	19.4
17099	LaSalle County	92,137	28.8	50.6	20.6	46,108	33.3	51.6	15.2	46,029	24.4	49.7	26.0
17111	McHenry County	242,738	26.9	57.7	15.4	120,107	29.7	59.0	11.3	122,631	24.2	56.5	19.3
17113	McLean County	140,279	38.2	47.1	14.7	67,587	40.5	49.0	10.5	72,692	36.1	45.4	18.6
17115	Macon County	89,332	29.5	47.9	22.6	42,218	32.6	50.6	16.9	47,114	26.7	45.6	27.8
17119	Madison County	218,213	29.1	50.5	20.5	105,149	32.5	52.2	15.3	113,064	25.9	48.9	25.2
17141	Ogle County	42,629	25.9	54.5	19.6	21,075	29.6	55.3	15.1	21,554	22.2	53.7	24.1
17143	Peoria County	150,059	35.6	46.3	18.0	71,776	38.3	48.1	13.7	78,283	33.3	44.7	22.0
17161	Rock Island County	119,797	29.1	48.5	22.4	58,343	32.9	51.0	16.1	61,454	25.6	46.2	28.3
17163	St. Clair County	213,856	34.4	44.7	20.9	101,746	36.2	48.2	15.7	112,110	32.9	41.5	25.6
17167	Sangamon County	160,572	30.8	47.4	21.8	75,889	33.3	50.1	16.6	84,683	28.5	45.0	26.5
17179	Tazewell County	109,795	24.2	55.9	19.9	53,866	28.2	57.0	14.8	55,929	20.3	54.9	24.8
17183	Vermilion County	64,579	28.6	47.5	24.0	31,761	32.8	47.7	19.5	32,818	24.5	47.2	28.3
17195	Whiteside County	46,975	25.0	53.4	21.6	22,925	28.4	55.5	16.1	24,050	21.7	51.4	26.9
17197	Will County	526,508	30.5	54.8	14.7	259,133	33.2	56.4	10.5	267,375	27.9	53.2	18.9
17199	Williamson County	54,598	24.2	53.0	22.8	26,789	27.7	55.6	16.7	27,809	20.8	50.5	28.7
17201	Winnebago County	233,228	31.1	48.1	20.8	112,707	34.2	49.9	15.9	120,521	28.1	46.4	25.5
18000	**Indiana**	5,222,309	30.2	49.7	20.2	2,546,882	33.2	51.4	15.4	2,675,427	27.3	48.0	24.7
18003	Allen County	280,799	31.1	48.9	20.0	135,542	33.8	51.0	15.1	145,257	28.5	46.9	24.6
18005	Bartholomew County	62,536	25.7	53.0	21.3	30,846	29.8	55.0	15.1	31,690	21.6	51.0	27.4
18011	Boone County	45,946	21.5	60.8	17.8	22,619	23.3	63.7	13.0	23,327	19.7	57.9	22.4
18019	Clark County	90,321	27.4	49.6	23.1	43,539	29.9	52.5	17.6	46,782	25.0	46.9	28.2
18035	Delaware County	98,978	38.2	42.4	19.3	46,965	41.6	44.5	13.9	52,013	35.2	40.6	24.2
18039	Elkhart County	152,256	28.7	52.3	19.0	74,514	30.9	54.9	14.2	77,742	26.7	49.8	23.5
18043	Floyd County	60,937	27.9	49.7	22.3	29,264	30.6	53.0	16.4	31,673	25.5	46.7	27.8
18053	Grant County	57,302	31.1	46.2	22.7	27,167	32.9	50.0	17.2	30,135	29.5	42.8	27.7
18057	Hamilton County	218,818	23.9	61.9	14.2	105,321	25.5	64.3	10.2	113,497	22.4	59.7	17.9
18059	Hancock County	56,551	25.7	54.4	19.8	27,755	29.4	55.7	14.8	28,796	22.2	53.2	24.7
18063	Hendricks County	117,865	23.5	59.4	17.0	58,415	26.4	61.6	12.0	59,450	20.8	57.3	21.9
18067	Howard County	67,111	24.8	52.6	22.6	31,808	26.2	54.5	19.3	35,303	23.5	50.9	25.5
18081	Johnson County	112,782	24.3	57.4	18.4	54,636	27.3	58.9	13.9	58,146	21.5	55.9	22.6
18085	Kosciusko County	61,799	25.3	56.3	18.4	30,700	28.0	57.8	14.2	31,099	22.7	54.8	22.5
18089	Lake County	391,202	34.5	45.0	20.5	186,251	37.5	47.5	15.0	204,951	31.9	42.7	25.5
18091	LaPorte County	90,895	30.2	48.2	21.6	47,284	35.4	46.6	17.9	43,611	24.6	49.9	25.5
18095	Madison County	106,359	28.5	47.0	24.5	52,783	33.6	46.9	19.5	53,576	23.4	47.2	29.4
18097	Marion County	724,776	38.4	40.1	21.6	344,127	41.0	42.5	16.4	380,649	36.0	37.9	26.2
18105	Monroe County	121,961	49.2	35.6	15.2	60,196	52.6	36.1	11.3	61,765	45.9	35.1	18.9
18109	Morgan County	55,433	22.5	58.3	19.2	27,153	24.9	59.9	15.1	28,280	20.1	56.7	23.1
18127	Porter County	134,319	28.2	53.7	18.1	65,507	31.7	55.6	12.7	68,812	24.8	52.0	23.2
18141	St. Joseph County	213,022	34.0	46.7	19.3	101,852	36.7	48.8	14.5	111,170	31.6	44.7	23.7
18157	Tippecanoe County	146,763	42.9	42.4	14.7	74,950	47.2	41.7	11.0	71,813	38.4	43.0	18.5
18163	Vanderburgh County	147,363	31.6	46.0	22.4	70,313	34.9	48.3	16.9	77,050	28.6	43.9	27.5

State/county FIPS code	State/County	Total women age 15 to 50 years	Percent of all women who had a birth in the past year	Percent of women who had a birth who were married (including separated and spouse absent):	Percent of women who had a birth who were partners in an unmarried partner household	Age of women who had a birth in the last year as a percent of all women who had a birth			Women who had a birth in the last year as a percent of all women in their age group		
						Age 15 to 19	Age 20 to 34	Age 35 to 50	Age 15 to 19	Age 20 to 34	Age 35 to 50
	Georgia—cont'd										
13285	Troup County	16,714	6.0	33.9	17.8	10.1	80.9	9.0	4.6	11.4	1.2
13295	Walker County	15,390	7.7	60.4	18.5	9.0	82.2	8.8	5.1	16.4	1.4
13297	Walton County	21,287	4.8	52.6	12.0	11.6	80.1	8.3	3.7	10.5	0.8
13313	Whitfield County	24,574	5.5	64.9	13.3	9.1	77.8	13.1	3.5	10.7	1.6
15000	**Hawaii**	319,934	6.4	68.1	10.5	4.8	73.4	21.8	2.4	10.8	3.2
15001	Hawaii County	40,754	5.9	55.0	18.3	5.3	79.6	15.0	2.2	11.3	2.0
15003	Honolulu County	228,294	6.5	72.2	8.0	4.5	71.6	23.9	2.5	10.4	3.6
15007	Kauai County	14,691	5.7	77.9	1.9	3.2	80.3	16.5	1.4	11.5	2.0
15009	Maui County	36,178	6.5	51.5	21.0	6.0	76.2	17.8	3.1	12.5	2.4
16000	**Idaho**	369,379	6.8	73.8	8.9	4.9	81.7	13.5	2.2	12.9	2.2
16001	Ada County	99,368	5.3	75.8	7.8	3.0	84.8	12.2	1.2	10.4	1.5
16005	Bannock County	20,146	5.5	77.0	6.8	2.6	86.0	11.4	1.0	9.9	1.7
16019	Bonneville County	24,639	8.9	75.2	8.8	3.0	79.1	17.9	1.7	16.1	3.9
16027	Canyon County	46,854	7.7	71.1	6.7	8.5	83.2	8.3	4.2	15.4	1.5
16055	Kootenai County	32,195	8.6	71.4	8.7	6.7	68.1	25.2	4.2	14.2	4.8
16083	Twin Falls County	17,951	7.5	48.9	24.2	9.9	84.6	5.6	5.2	14.1	1.0
17000	**Illinois**	3,162,329	5.0	63.2	10.0	5.5	72.8	21.7	2.0	8.7	2.5
17001	Adams County	14,824	6.2	43.9	15.9	12.7	65.4	22.0	5.6	9.7	3.1
17007	Boone County	12,639	7.2	76.8	6.1	19.7	65.3	15.0	8.4	13.9	2.2
17019	Champaign County	58,136	3.1	71.6	7.5	6.9	78.8	14.3	1.2	4.6	1.4
17029	Coles County	15,052	3.3	55.6	17.0	5.4	83.6	11.0	1.0	5.4	1.2
17031	Cook County	1,354,385	5.1	61.2	8.2	5.0	69.9	25.1	2.0	7.8	3.0
17037	DeKalb County	29,949	5.3	60.6	13.2	0.0	83.2	16.8	0.0	8.9	2.7
17043	DuPage County	224,121	4.7	79.7	7.1	5.5	67.8	26.6	1.8	8.3	2.6
17063	Grundy County	11,975	4.2	74.2	8.8	4.2	84.6	11.2	1.3	8.7	1.0
17073	Henry County	10,604	6.3	53.5	17.3	13.0	66.8	20.2	5.4	11.1	2.7
17077	Jackson County	16,504	3.3	78.6	12.7	0.9	75.3	23.8	0.2	4.9	2.8
17089	Kane County	127,016	5.5	66.5	10.5	3.4	71.7	24.8	1.3	10.4	2.8
17091	Kankakee County	26,904	4.7	52.7	12.6	9.7	76.5	13.8	3.1	8.6	1.5
17093	Kendall County	31,021	4.7	86.0	0.3	0.0	89.6	10.4	0.0	11.6	1.0
17095	Knox County	10,736	5.9	61.5	15.5	2.8	85.6	11.5	1.1	11.9	1.6
17097	Lake County	167,573	4.8	71.2	7.6	3.5	71.2	25.3	1.1	9.9	2.5
17099	LaSalle County	24,158	5.0	56.9	17.1	4.2	72.4	23.4	1.4	9.1	2.5
17111	McHenry County	74,403	4.3	70.1	7.9	6.4	66.2	27.3	1.8	8.7	2.3
17113	McLean County	48,175	4.0	55.6	11.4	8.4	81.3	10.4	2.2	6.6	1.1
17115	Macon County	25,347	5.4	42.6	15.0	11.4	80.2	8.4	4.4	10.5	1.0
17119	Madison County	64,235	5.6	67.9	11.8	2.2	81.8	16.0	1.0	10.7	2.0
17141	Ogle County	11,714	5.8	68.8	9.0	1.2	92.6	6.2	0.5	14.8	0.7
17143	Peoria County	44,912	5.7	43.0	13.2	5.2	77.9	17.0	2.1	10.0	2.3
17161	Rock Island County	32,604	6.4	59.3	14.2	1.9	88.5	9.6	0.9	13.1	1.4
17163	St. Clair County	66,033	4.4	61.8	14.3	2.1	74.5	23.4	0.7	8.0	2.3
17167	Sangamon County	47,019	4.6	61.7	9.9	2.8	81.4	15.8	1.0	9.0	1.6
17179	Tazewell County	30,326	5.4	75.0	10.6	2.3	83.5	14.2	1.0	11.3	1.6
17183	Vermilion County	17,390	5.5	54.0	22.4	6.9	88.8	4.3	2.5	12.3	0.5
17195	Whiteside County	12,065	7.1	46.1	15.9	15.4	70.4	14.2	7.3	13.5	2.1
17197	Will County	170,740	5.3	70.4	6.0	8.4	67.0	24.7	2.9	10.1	2.6
17199	Williamson County	14,975	5.2	48.2	16.8	4.0	85.6	10.4	1.7	10.7	1.2
17201	Winnebago County	67,974	5.2	51.2	13.2	7.1	75.6	17.3	2.7	9.7	2.0
18000	**Indiana**	1,558,798	5.6	60.9	11.3	6.9	78.0	15.1	2.7	10.4	1.9
18003	Allen County	87,133	6.2	55.0	8.6	7.8	76.5	15.7	3.4	11.3	2.2
18005	Bartholomew County	17,937	5.7	61.6	13.6	0.0	83.2	16.8	0.0	12.2	2.0
18011	Boone County	13,727	6.1	86.3	1.5	4.2	71.2	24.6	1.7	13.0	2.9
18019	Clark County	26,868	5.7	59.7	7.1	11.7	73.7	14.6	5.4	10.1	1.8
18035	Delaware County	31,498	4.4	66.7	13.8	7.7	77.1	15.2	1.8	7.1	2.0
18039	Elkhart County	45,931	7.9	60.8	12.8	10.8	77.4	11.8	5.8	14.9	2.1
18043	Floyd County	17,748	4.6	63.2	7.9	2.3	89.2	8.5	0.8	10.4	0.9
18053	Grant County	16,675	3.7	26.8	14.6	13.0	78.2	8.8	2.7	6.9	0.8
18057	Hamilton County	73,429	6.0	85.3	5.9	8.0	54.8	37.2	3.4	9.5	4.3
18059	Hancock County	16,506	3.9	88.4	10.5	0.0	81.0	19.0	0.0	9.2	1.4
18063	Hendricks County	36,054	4.7	79.5	4.9	6.4	74.9	18.6	2.2	9.9	1.8
18067	Howard County	18,298	6.8	63.2	6.7	11.1	74.6	14.3	5.3	13.0	2.1
18081	Johnson County	34,407	4.6	73.0	10.9	4.1	71.5	24.4	1.4	8.3	2.4
18085	Kosciusko County	17,673	4.4	68.9	11.0	7.5	84.8	7.7	2.2	9.4	0.8
18089	Lake County	116,793	5.4	47.0	12.5	6.5	80.1	13.4	2.4	10.6	1.6
18091	LaPorte County	23,475	4.9	55.9	17.1	5.8	76.0	18.3	2.1	9.4	1.9
18095	Madison County	29,261	5.3	55.0	12.4	8.1	77.8	14.0	3.1	10.3	1.6
18097	Marion County	240,234	6.1	53.8	12.2	6.5	78.4	15.1	3.4	10.2	2.3
18105	Monroe County	42,924	4.2	69.2	3.2	2.1	78.3	19.6	0.5	5.9	3.1
18109	Morgan County	16,029	4.8	68.1	6.1	0.0	100.0	0.0	0.0	13.1	0.0
18127	Porter County	39,769	5.7	64.6	8.2	4.6	85.7	9.8	1.9	12.2	1.2
18141	St. Joseph County	65,259	5.3	55.8	11.1	7.9	76.8	15.3	2.7	9.6	2.0
18157	Tippecanoe County	49,077	5.1	68.6	18.1	2.4	86.0	11.6	0.8	8.2	2.0
18163	Vanderburgh County	43,819	4.7	56.8	16.1	6.6	82.5	11.0	2.2	8.5	1.3

State/county FIPS code	State/County	Total population 15 years and older	Marital status, percent — Never married	Marital status, percent — Now married (except separated)	Marital status, percent — Separated, widowed, or divorced	Male population 15 years and older	Male, marital status, percent — Never married	Male, marital status, percent — Now married (except separated)	Male, marital status, percent — Separated, widowed, or divorced	Female population 15 years and older	Female, marital status, percent — Never married	Female, marital status, percent — Now married (except separated)	Female, marital status, percent — Separated, widowed, or divorced
	Indiana—cont'd												
18167	Vigo County	89,402	35.3	42.7	22.1	45,254	39.1	43.1	17.8	44,148	31.3	42.2	26.5
18173	Warrick County	48,028	20.4	61.7	17.9	23,368	23.7	63.0	13.2	24,660	17.2	60.5	22.3
18177	Wayne County	55,723	26.1	49.6	24.3	26,762	29.3	50.7	20.0	28,961	23.2	48.5	28.3
19000	**Iowa**	2,474,777	28.7	52.7	18.6	1,216,354	32.0	54.0	14.0	1,258,423	25.5	51.5	23.0
19013	Black Hawk County	108,127	36.6	45.8	17.6	52,274	39.8	47.2	13.0	55,853	33.6	44.6	21.9
19049	Dallas County	54,361	23.2	61.0	15.8	26,511	23.6	63.0	13.4	27,850	22.8	59.1	18.1
19061	Dubuque County	76,690	31.6	51.7	16.8	37,486	33.9	53.5	12.6	39,204	29.3	49.9	20.8
19103	Johnson County	113,189	44.0	44.2	11.8	56,218	46.7	44.7	8.5	56,971	41.2	43.7	15.1
19113	Linn County	171,829	30.2	50.3	19.5	84,045	32.5	51.5	16.0	87,784	27.9	49.2	22.9
19153	Polk County	349,180	30.4	51.2	18.4	169,713	32.9	53.1	14.0	179,467	28.0	49.4	22.5
19155	Pottawattamie County	74,667	29.1	49.7	21.2	36,312	33.8	51.1	15.1	38,355	24.7	48.3	27.0
19163	Scott County	134,515	30.7	49.2	20.2	65,314	33.8	50.4	15.8	69,201	27.7	47.9	24.3
19169	Story County	78,093	47.1	42.5	10.4	40,310	51.7	41.6	6.7	37,783	42.2	43.5	14.3
19193	Woodbury County	79,689	31.0	47.5	21.5	38,862	34.9	48.0	17.1	40,827	27.3	47.0	25.7
20000	**Kansas**	2,276,556	28.5	52.4	19.1	1,123,515	31.9	53.6	14.5	1,153,041	25.2	51.1	23.6
20015	Butler County	51,577	24.2	56.2	19.7	25,733	27.9	56.6	15.6	25,844	20.5	55.7	23.8
20045	Douglas County	95,061	46.7	39.8	13.5	47,071	49.3	41.2	9.5	47,990	44.2	38.4	17.4
20091	Johnson County	438,967	26.6	56.8	16.6	211,763	28.3	60.0	11.7	227,204	25.0	53.9	21.1
20103	Leavenworth County	61,648	27.0	53.0	20.0	33,287	31.7	50.7	17.6	28,361	21.4	55.6	22.9
20155	Reno County	51,721	24.2	54.0	21.8	25,728	27.5	55.0	17.5	25,993	20.9	53.0	26.1
20161	Riley County	62,939	50.7	38.7	10.6	33,561	55.1	37.1	7.7	29,378	45.7	40.4	13.9
20169	Saline County	44,321	28.3	48.6	23.1	21,694	32.0	50.1	17.9	22,627	24.7	47.1	28.2
20173	Sedgwick County	389,960	30.1	49.7	20.2	191,240	33.4	51.4	15.3	198,720	26.9	48.1	25.0
20177	Shawnee County	142,174	28.5	49.7	21.8	67,974	32.4	51.1	16.5	74,200	24.9	48.5	26.6
20209	Wyandotte County	120,754	36.0	41.1	22.9	59,030	39.3	42.3	18.4	61,724	32.8	40.0	27.2
21000	**Kentucky**	3,531,594	27.8	50.0	22.2	1,719,880	31.4	51.7	16.9	1,811,714	24.5	48.4	27.1
21015	Boone County	93,964	24.9	57.0	18.1	46,162	27.7	59.4	12.9	47,802	22.2	54.7	23.1
21029	Bullitt County	60,923	24.3	53.2	22.5	29,813	26.9	54.8	18.3	31,110	21.9	51.7	26.4
21037	Campbell County	73,918	32.7	47.3	20.0	35,842	36.4	48.7	14.8	38,076	29.2	46.0	24.9
21047	Christian County	55,903	29.9	52.0	18.2	29,142	37.8	49.3	12.9	26,761	21.2	54.9	23.9
21059	Daviess County	77,884	25.5	52.4	22.1	37,326	28.8	55.1	16.1	40,558	22.4	49.9	27.6
21067	Fayette County	250,142	38.1	43.2	18.8	121,843	41.3	44.6	14.1	128,299	35.0	41.8	23.2
21093	Hardin County	84,462	26.0	53.1	20.9	41,714	29.9	54.3	15.8	42,748	22.2	51.9	25.9
21111	Jefferson County	607,311	33.9	43.7	22.4	289,120	37.5	46.1	16.5	318,191	30.6	41.6	27.7
21117	Kenton County	128,048	32.2	46.2	21.6	62,630	35.6	47.1	17.3	65,418	28.9	45.4	25.7
21125	Laurel County	47,589	20.9	54.5	24.5	23,044	25.3	56.2	18.5	24,545	16.8	53.0	30.2
21145	McCracken County	53,707	25.5	48.4	26.2	25,395	28.6	52.4	19.0	28,312	22.6	44.8	32.6
21151	Madison County	69,775	33.9	45.8	20.4	33,716	37.0	47.0	16.0	36,059	30.9	44.6	24.5
21185	Oldham County	48,232	25.6	58.3	16.1	25,627	29.0	56.2	14.8	22,605	21.9	60.6	17.6
21195	Pike County	52,659	19.6	53.5	26.9	25,542	23.6	55.6	20.8	27,117	15.8	51.6	32.6
21199	Pulaski County	51,673	20.7	54.5	24.9	24,986	24.2	57.2	18.6	26,687	17.3	51.9	30.7
21227	Warren County	94,845	35.3	45.6	19.2	45,666	37.8	47.8	14.5	49,179	33.0	43.5	23.5
22000	**Louisiana**	3,668,677	34.5	43.9	21.6	1,775,133	37.6	46.2	16.2	1,893,544	31.5	41.8	26.7
22001	Acadia Parish	48,152	30.9	48.2	20.9	23,100	34.7	51.6	13.7	25,052	27.5	45.0	27.5
22005	Ascension Parish	85,355	27.6	54.8	17.6	41,584	29.3	57.6	13.1	43,771	26.1	52.1	21.8
22015	Bossier Parish	96,159	28.8	49.2	22.0	46,934	31.4	51.7	16.9	49,225	26.2	46.9	26.9
22017	Caddo Parish	203,685	37.0	39.2	23.8	95,348	39.8	42.7	17.5	108,337	34.5	36.2	29.3
22019	Calcasieu Parish	154,044	30.5	46.9	22.6	74,202	33.3	49.3	17.4	79,842	27.9	44.6	27.5
22033	East Baton Rouge Parish	358,418	41.1	39.0	19.9	169,680	44.1	41.2	14.7	188,738	38.4	37.0	24.6
22045	Iberia Parish	57,277	32.3	46.6	21.2	27,615	36.3	48.0	15.7	29,662	28.5	45.2	26.3
22051	Jefferson Parish	353,789	35.2	42.3	22.4	170,293	38.3	45.6	16.1	183,496	32.4	39.3	28.3
22055	Lafayette Parish	181,417	36.1	44.1	19.8	87,709	38.1	46.9	15.0	93,708	34.2	41.5	24.3
22057	Lafourche Parish	77,783	30.9	48.1	21.0	37,859	34.9	49.2	15.8	39,924	27.1	47.1	25.8
22063	Livingston Parish	102,633	26.2	51.6	22.3	50,069	28.6	54.5	16.9	52,564	23.9	48.7	27.4
22071	Orleans Parish	304,686	48.8	30.1	21.1	144,452	51.6	32.5	15.9	160,234	46.3	27.9	25.8
22073	Ouachita Parish	121,831	36.0	42.3	21.7	57,329	40.1	44.9	14.9	64,502	32.4	39.9	27.7
22079	Rapides Parish	104,334	32.3	42.7	25.0	49,585	37.2	44.0	18.8	54,749	27.9	41.5	30.6
22089	St. Charles Parish	41,367	31.3	48.3	20.4	20,282	33.1	50.9	16.0	21,085	29.6	45.8	24.6
22097	St. Landry Parish	64,556	33.2	45.1	21.6	30,255	35.6	47.0	17.4	34,301	31.2	43.5	25.3
22099	St. Martin Parish	41,470	31.5	47.6	20.8	20,106	33.9	50.0	16.1	21,364	29.3	45.4	25.3
22101	St. Mary Parish	42,590	32.9	43.2	23.9	20,989	36.1	46.8	17.1	21,601	29.9	39.7	30.5
22103	St. Tammany Parish	190,056	25.9	54.4	19.7	91,326	28.8	56.7	14.5	98,730	23.3	52.2	24.5
22105	Tangipahoa Parish	98,050	34.3	44.2	21.6	46,630	37.7	46.6	15.8	51,420	31.2	42.0	26.8
22109	Terrebonne Parish	87,639	32.0	47.0	21.0	42,944	34.9	48.3	16.8	44,695	29.2	45.8	25.0
22113	Vermilion Parish	45,320	26.1	50.8	23.1	21,611	27.7	53.0	19.4	23,709	24.6	48.9	26.5
22115	Vernon Parish	40,386	25.7	56.0	18.3	21,064	31.2	56.6	12.2	19,322	19.7	55.3	25.0
23000	**Maine**	1,112,439	27.7	50.8	21.5	539,761	30.7	52.5	16.9	572,678	24.8	49.3	25.9
23001	Androscoggin County	87,615	29.6	48.4	22.0	42,503	32.7	49.8	17.5	45,112	26.6	47.1	26.3
23003	Aroostook County	59,793	24.5	54.0	21.5	29,151	27.6	55.8	16.5	30,642	21.5	52.3	26.2
23005	Cumberland County	237,360	30.7	49.5	19.7	114,141	33.7	51.9	14.4	123,219	28.0	47.3	24.7
23009	Hancock County	46,698	24.7	53.5	21.8	22,693	27.1	55.7	17.2	24,005	22.3	51.4	26.2
23011	Kennebec County	101,568	26.5	50.4	23.1	49,193	29.4	51.7	18.8	52,375	23.8	49.1	27.1
23017	Oxford County	48,106	27.4	49.9	22.7	23,726	30.7	51.6	17.8	24,380	24.2	48.3	27.5

Table C-2: Counties with a Population of 50,000 or More—Marriages and Births—*Continued*

State/county FIPS code	State/County	Total women age 15 to 50 years	Percent of all women who had a birth in the past year	Percent of women who had a birth who were married (including separated and spouse absent):	Percent of women who had a birth who were partners in an unmarried partner household	Age of women who had a birth in the last year as a percent of all women who had a birth			Women who had a birth in the last year as a percent of all women in their age group		
						Age 15 to 19	Age 20 to 34	Age 35 to 50	Age 15 to 19	Age 20 to 34	Age 35 to 50
	Indiana—cont'd										
18167	Vigo County	25,778	5.3	57.2	4.5	8.3	79.2	12.4	2.8	9.1	1.7
18173	Warrick County	13,544	5.5	66.9	12.9	0.0	80.5	19.5	0.0	12.1	2.2
18177	Wayne County	15,185	6.7	46.4	18.2	9.8	83.6	6.6	4.4	14.3	1.0
19000	**Iowa**	705,099	5.4	68.1	12.1	3.6	80.5	15.9	1.3	10.4	2.0
19013	Black Hawk County	33,331	5.4	58.7	9.6	3.8	90.7	5.6	1.3	9.9	0.9
19049	Dallas County	18,154	5.6	85.0	10.6	1.1	81.2	17.8	0.5	11.0	2.1
19061	Dubuque County	21,801	6.1	70.1	18.2	1.6	82.0	16.4	0.6	12.2	2.3
19103	Johnson County	39,636	4.4	71.9	11.7	0.0	76.5	23.5	0.0	6.3	3.4
19113	Linn County	51,639	5.7	70.9	6.2	4.6	78.0	17.4	1.9	10.4	2.3
19153	Polk County	112,387	6.4	71.7	6.7	3.9	79.5	16.6	2.0	11.3	2.5
19155	Pottawattamie County	21,395	5.2	54.4	10.2	0.0	86.6	13.4	0.0	11.0	1.5
19163	Scott County	40,346	4.1	72.5	11.0	5.5	74.1	20.5	1.7	7.3	1.9
19169	Story County	26,203	2.9	87.8	8.9	0.4	86.3	13.4	0.1	4.5	1.6
19193	Woodbury County	24,030	6.1	52.4	15.5	6.0	86.3	7.6	2.5	12.0	1.1
20000	**Kansas**	669,908	6.5	69.2	9.6	5.6	76.3	18.1	2.4	11.5	2.8
20015	Butler County	14,814	6.9	66.7	6.3	16.3	65.4	18.3	6.4	12.3	2.7
20045	Douglas County	33,320	4.5	70.1	9.7	4.3	74.0	21.7	1.2	6.1	3.3
20091	Johnson County	137,315	5.9	82.7	5.2	1.8	77.8	20.4	0.8	11.4	2.6
20103	Leavenworth County	16,563	5.9	70.9	11.9	2.9	77.2	19.8	1.2	12.1	2.5
20155	Reno County	13,465	6.2	71.1	9.5	0.0	87.2	12.8	0.0	12.9	1.8
20161	Riley County	22,385	5.5	86.0	1.3	2.8	93.6	3.6	0.8	8.4	1.0
20169	Saline County	12,526	6.6	62.8	2.5	0.0	74.2	25.8	0.0	11.6	3.9
20173	Sedgwick County	119,586	6.2	66.9	6.9	4.6	82.4	13.0	2.1	11.6	2.0
20177	Shawnee County	40,587	6.2	63.2	13.6	6.4	82.4	11.2	2.9	11.8	1.6
20209	Wyandotte County	38,181	5.7	51.4	10.5	5.4	77.3	17.3	2.3	9.6	2.4
21000	**Kentucky**	1,041,060	5.4	64.4	10.1	6.9	77.9	15.2	2.7	10.1	1.8
21015	Boone County	30,152	6.2	70.1	6.1	1.5	85.5	13.0	0.8	14.0	1.6
21029	Bullitt County	18,598	4.7	57.1	7.4	5.0	62.9	32.2	1.7	8.1	3.1
21037	Campbell County	22,161	5.1	67.6	8.0	0.0	92.2	7.8	0.0	10.4	0.9
21047	Christian County	17,304	8.4	63.3	13.7	10.3	70.7	19.0	7.5	11.7	4.3
21059	Daviess County	22,455	5.4	60.6	14.2	13.8	82.7	3.4	5.8	10.8	0.4
21067	Fayette County	82,464	5.2	72.1	12.6	4.7	80.8	14.5	2.0	8.5	2.0
21093	Hardin County	25,595	6.4	70.0	8.6	2.3	81.9	15.8	1.1	12.8	2.3
21111	Jefferson County	182,765	5.2	59.8	7.9	5.9	72.7	21.4	2.5	8.7	2.5
21117	Kenton County	39,726	6.6	56.6	10.5	9.1	79.7	11.2	5.0	12.1	1.7
21125	Laurel County	14,174	6.7	59.1	7.5	8.4	82.7	8.9	4.6	13.6	1.3
21145	McCracken County	14,826	4.3	72.2	0.0	3.4	88.3	8.3	1.2	9.4	0.8
21151	Madison County	23,009	5.0	75.7	6.3	10.4	77.8	11.9	3.2	8.4	1.6
21185	Oldham County	13,531	3.6	88.8	0.0	2.6	71.5	25.9	0.6	9.5	1.7
21195	Pike County	14,971	4.6	76.1	0.0	13.0	65.5	21.4	4.8	7.8	2.0
21199	Pulaski County	13,948	6.7	53.2	14.5	2.5	88.2	9.4	1.3	15.2	1.3
21227	Warren County	32,007	3.7	52.1	9.5	12.6	70.9	16.5	2.5	6.1	1.6
22000	**Louisiana**	1,126,108	5.5	50.9	10.9	6.1	80.2	13.7	2.5	9.9	1.8
22001	Acadia Parish	14,833	5.4	49.8	12.8	5.9	78.6	15.6	2.2	10.0	1.9
22005	Ascension Parish	28,634	7.2	61.0	10.4	2.8	90.1	7.0	1.5	16.6	1.1
22015	Bossier Parish	30,262	6.7	64.3	6.9	7.7	75.0	17.3	4.1	11.2	2.7
22017	Caddo Parish	62,465	5.7	39.2	7.8	4.6	80.0	15.4	2.0	10.0	2.1
22019	Calcasieu Parish	46,690	6.0	44.5	12.9	9.7	78.1	12.2	4.2	10.6	1.8
22033	East Baton Rouge Parish	118,655	4.5	54.9	5.5	8.1	81.5	10.4	2.6	7.5	1.3
22045	Iberia Parish	17,515	7.0	42.5	31.6	3.1	90.7	6.3	1.6	14.9	1.0
22051	Jefferson Parish	104,230	5.3	47.4	16.9	6.1	80.0	13.9	2.8	9.6	1.7
22055	Lafayette Parish	59,402	5.8	61.3	8.0	2.5	81.2	16.2	1.2	10.0	2.4
22057	Lafourche Parish	23,783	4.6	56.3	20.0	5.4	88.7	5.9	1.8	9.4	0.6
22063	Livingston Parish	33,167	5.7	51.3	15.6	4.4	78.0	17.6	1.8	11.0	2.2
22071	Orleans Parish	99,700	5.2	39.4	11.7	2.0	74.6	23.4	0.9	7.6	3.2
22073	Ouachita Parish	39,195	5.4	36.0	6.3	9.7	81.9	8.4	3.7	9.9	1.1
22079	Rapides Parish	31,551	4.2	59.7	6.1	7.3	82.5	10.3	2.2	8.4	1.0
22089	St. Charles Parish	12,777	6.4	45.9	8.7	15.1	56.0	28.9	7.1	9.5	3.8
22097	St. Landry Parish	19,549	8.3	47.6	9.1	3.6	84.7	11.7	2.1	16.9	2.2
22099	St. Martin Parish	12,532	7.5	56.6	15.0	0.7	91.7	7.6	0.5	15.7	1.3
22101	St. Mary Parish	12,658	7.4	45.0	8.6	8.0	84.2	7.8	4.3	15.1	1.3
22103	St. Tammany Parish	56,208	5.3	63.5	4.7	2.8	81.7	15.5	1.1	11.9	1.7
22105	Tangipahoa Parish	31,157	3.4	67.6	4.0	2.9	76.3	20.7	0.7	5.5	1.8
22109	Terrebonne Parish	27,324	5.6	55.7	20.7	6.6	80.8	12.5	3.0	10.2	1.6
22113	Vermilion Parish	13,871	6.9	53.1	15.0	13.2	84.7	2.1	6.9	13.9	0.3
22115	Vernon Parish	12,848	7.0	77.5	3.9	12.7	80.3	7.0	7.4	11.4	1.3
23000	**Maine**	298,992	4.7	64.1	17.0	3.9	78.2	17.9	1.3	9.7	1.8
23001	Androscoggin County	25,401	5.7	59.1	25.2	1.3	90.7	8.0	0.6	12.4	1.0
23003	Aroostook County	14,814	4.3	64.9	20.1	2.8	83.2	14.0	0.8	10.2	1.2
23005	Cumberland County	68,038	4.5	69.4	9.5	3.1	76.3	20.6	1.0	9.0	1.9
23009	Hancock County	11,509	3.8	55.7	23.2	3.0	86.9	10.1	0.9	9.3	0.7
23011	Kennebec County	27,387	4.5	60.6	18.2	2.3	77.7	20.0	0.7	9.1	1.9
23017	Oxford County	12,066	5.2	58.8	7.8	7.3	82.4	10.3	2.8	11.7	1.1

Table C-2: Counties with a Population of 50,000 or More—Marriages and Births—*Continued*

State/county FIPS code	State/County	Total population 15 years and older	Marital status, percent — Never married	Marital status, percent — Now married (except separated)	Marital status, percent — Separated, widowed, or divorced	Male population 15 years and older	Male, marital status, percent — Never married	Male, marital status, percent — Now married (except separated)	Male, marital status, percent — Separated, or divorced	Female population 15 years and older	Female, marital status, percent — Never married	Female, marital status, percent — Now married (except separated)	Female, marital status, percent — Separated, widowed, or divorced
	Maine—cont'd												
23019	Penobscot County......................	129,678	30.7	48.2	21.2	63,501	34.3	48.9	16.9	66,177	27.3	47.5	25.2
23025	Somerset County	43,207	25.1	50.2	24.7	21,261	28.5	51.0	20.5	21,946	21.8	49.4	28.7
23031	York County...............................	165,711	26.6	53.3	20.2	79,730	29.0	55.2	15.8	85,981	24.3	51.5	24.2
24000	**Maryland ....**	4,770,688	35.1	46.5	18.3	2,282,623	37.5	49.3	13.3	2,488,065	33.0	44.0	23.0
24001	Allegany County	63,165	35.3	42.1	22.6	32,872	40.9	41.5	17.6	30,293	29.2	42.7	28.1
24003	Anne Arundel County.................	444,788	30.2	51.2	18.6	218,395	33.3	52.8	13.9	226,393	27.2	49.7	23.0
24005	Baltimore County.......................	670,962	34.4	45.7	19.9	312,343	36.3	49.4	14.3	358,619	32.8	42.5	24.7
24009	Calvert County...........................	72,242	29.9	52.9	17.2	35,235	33.1	54.0	12.9	37,007	26.8	51.9	21.3
24013	Carroll County............................	136,043	27.0	56.0	17.0	66,535	29.8	58.3	11.9	69,508	24.4	53.7	21.9
24015	Cecil County...............................	81,578	28.2	52.7	19.1	40,180	31.5	54.3	14.2	41,398	25.1	51.1	23.8
24017	Charles County...........................	120,020	33.9	49.0	17.2	56,967	36.0	52.1	11.9	63,053	31.9	46.1	22.0
24021	Frederick County........................	191,419	28.4	54.6	17.0	93,462	30.6	56.7	12.8	97,957	26.4	52.6	21.0
24025	Harford County..........................	200,278	28.1	54.7	17.3	96,842	30.7	57.2	12.1	103,436	25.6	52.3	22.1
24027	Howard County..........................	238,192	28.3	57.6	14.1	115,506	30.6	59.5	9.9	122,686	26.1	55.8	18.1
24031	Montgomery County	806,692	31.8	53.1	15.1	383,123	34.1	56.3	9.5	423,569	29.6	50.2	20.1
24033	Prince George's County..............	712,822	43.3	37.7	19.1	337,755	45.4	40.6	14.0	375,067	41.4	35.0	23.6
24037	St. Mary's County.......................	85,721	28.3	56.5	15.2	42,528	30.3	58.4	11.4	43,193	26.3	54.7	19.0
24043	Washington County....................	121,566	29.5	48.8	21.7	62,134	34.0	49.0	17.0	59,432	24.7	48.6	26.7
24045	Wicomico County.......................	81,867	36.0	44.4	19.6	38,516	38.9	47.6	13.5	43,351	33.4	41.7	24.9
24047	Worcester County.......................	43,877	28.2	48.8	23.0	21,255	33.3	51.4	15.3	22,622	23.4	46.5	30.2
24510	Baltimore city............................	510,014	52.1	26.0	21.9	236,383	53.6	29.1	17.3	273,631	50.8	23.4	25.9
25000	**Massachusetts........................**	5,500,845	36.0	46.6	17.5	2,634,936	38.7	49.0	12.3	2,865,909	33.5	44.3	22.2
25001	Barnstable County	186,612	26.2	52.8	21.1	87,879	30.1	56.1	13.8	98,733	22.7	49.8	27.5
25003	Berkshire County	110,898	31.9	45.7	22.4	52,819	35.0	48.1	16.9	58,079	29.1	43.5	27.3
25005	Bristol County............................	453,754	33.6	46.6	19.8	217,412	36.9	49.3	13.8	236,342	30.6	44.1	25.3
25009	Essex County..............................	617,521	33.1	48.4	18.5	292,843	36.3	51.2	12.5	324,678	30.3	45.9	23.8
25011	Franklin County	60,584	31.0	46.7	22.3	29,367	34.3	48.7	17.0	31,217	27.9	44.9	27.3
25013	Hampden County	378,959	37.0	42.6	20.5	180,019	39.9	45.8	14.3	198,940	34.3	39.7	26.0
25015	Hampshire County	139,215	42.8	40.7	16.5	64,245	44.2	43.5	12.2	74,970	41.5	38.3	20.2
25017	Middlesex County	1,272,173	34.9	50.2	14.8	614,251	37.6	52.2	10.2	657,922	32.4	48.4	19.2
25021	Norfolk County..........................	559,008	32.1	52.1	15.8	264,229	33.7	55.6	10.7	294,779	30.6	49.0	20.4
25023	Plymouth County........................	404,840	30.5	51.4	18.1	194,284	33.7	53.8	12.4	210,556	27.6	49.2	23.3
25025	Suffolk County...........................	636,864	54.3	29.8	15.9	304,705	55.8	32.3	11.9	332,159	52.9	27.5	19.6
25027	Worcester County.......................	657,756	33.3	48.0	18.7	321,373	36.5	49.6	13.9	336,383	30.2	46.5	23.2
26000	**Michigan ....**	8,028,676	32.5	48.1	19.4	3,901,469	35.8	49.6	14.6	4,127,207	29.5	46.7	23.8
26005	Allegan County	88,649	24.0	58.4	17.6	43,821	27.3	59.5	13.2	44,828	20.7	57.4	21.9
26015	Barry County..............................	47,797	23.3	58.3	18.4	23,909	26.7	57.8	15.5	23,888	19.8	58.8	21.3
26017	Bay County................................	88,195	29.1	50.6	20.4	42,791	33.9	51.7	14.4	45,404	24.5	49.5	26.0
26021	Berrien County...........................	126,545	29.9	49.4	20.7	61,026	32.7	52.0	15.3	65,519	27.3	47.0	25.7
26025	Calhoun County..........................	108,982	29.4	46.7	23.9	52,462	33.5	47.5	19.0	56,520	25.6	45.9	28.5
26027	Cass County	42,701	25.2	53.2	21.6	21,162	27.5	53.6	18.9	21,539	22.8	52.8	24.4
26037	Clinton County...........................	61,636	28.6	54.5	16.9	30,229	31.4	54.5	14.1	31,407	26.0	54.4	19.6
26045	Eaton County.............................	88,510	28.1	51.6	20.3	42,942	30.9	54.2	14.9	45,568	25.4	49.2	25.4
26049	Genesee County.........................	335,571	33.2	44.3	22.5	159,164	35.9	46.7	17.4	176,407	30.8	42.2	27.0
26055	Grand Traverse County...............	73,672	28.8	51.4	19.9	36,098	33.2	51.8	15.0	37,574	24.5	51.0	24.5
26065	Ingham County	234,111	44.0	39.1	16.9	112,262	46.7	40.4	12.9	121,849	41.5	38.0	20.5
26067	Ionia County..............................	51,437	30.1	51.0	18.8	27,659	35.5	48.3	16.2	23,778	23.9	54.2	21.9
26073	Isabella County..........................	60,302	50.4	34.9	14.7	29,009	51.9	36.4	11.8	31,293	49.1	33.5	17.4
26075	Jackson County...........................	130,470	30.6	47.2	22.2	66,604	34.6	46.5	19.0	63,866	26.5	48.0	25.5
26077	Kalamazoo County	207,387	37.4	44.4	18.1	100,403	40.5	46.2	13.3	106,984	34.6	42.8	22.7
26081	Kent County	483,226	33.6	49.8	16.5	234,362	36.7	51.1	12.2	248,864	30.8	48.6	20.6
26087	Lapeer County	72,074	25.3	57.5	17.1	36,120	28.8	57.5	13.7	35,954	21.7	57.6	20.6
26091	Lenawee County.........................	81,214	29.2	51.1	19.6	40,849	33.5	51.4	15.2	40,365	25.0	50.9	24.1
26093	Livingston County.......................	147,934	25.0	58.2	16.8	73,337	28.6	58.3	13.1	74,597	21.6	58.1	20.4
26099	Macomb County.........................	693,903	31.0	49.7	19.3	333,208	34.7	51.8	13.5	360,695	27.6	47.6	24.8
26103	Marquette County	57,579	36.0	46.9	17.1	28,859	38.9	46.9	14.2	28,720	33.1	46.9	20.0
26111	Midland County..........................	68,448	25.4	56.8	17.7	33,488	28.7	57.7	13.6	34,960	22.3	56.0	21.7
26115	Monroe County	122,532	26.8	53.4	19.8	59,900	30.7	54.5	14.8	62,632	23.0	52.3	24.7
26117	Montcalm County.......................	51,123	26.5	53.5	20.0	26,376	29.9	53.8	16.3	24,747	22.9	53.1	24.0
26121	Muskegon County	136,365	31.4	46.9	21.6	66,632	34.6	48.3	17.2	69,733	28.4	45.7	25.9
26125	Oakland County..........................	995,254	30.0	52.1	17.9	477,069	32.9	54.3	12.9	518,185	27.4	50.0	22.5
26139	Ottawa County...........................	212,961	29.8	56.6	13.6	103,478	31.8	58.5	9.7	109,483	27.9	54.8	17.3
26145	Saginaw County.........................	161,364	32.9	45.7	21.3	77,088	36.5	47.8	15.7	84,276	29.7	43.8	26.5
26147	St. Clair County..........................	131,284	26.1	53.2	20.6	64,566	29.2	54.4	16.4	66,718	23.2	52.1	24.7
26149	St. Joseph County.......................	48,104	25.2	53.3	21.5	23,621	28.7	54.8	16.5	24,483	21.9	51.8	26.3
26155	Shiawassee County.....................	56,644	26.7	54.5	18.8	27,685	30.6	55.9	13.5	28,959	22.9	53.2	23.8
26157	Tuscola County	45,144	25.9	55.2	18.9	22,474	28.7	56.8	14.5	22,670	23.2	53.6	23.3
26159	Van Buren County.......................	60,349	26.9	51.1	22.0	29,721	31.4	51.4	17.2	30,628	22.5	50.9	26.6
26161	Washtenaw County.....................	292,935	41.8	43.8	14.4	143,391	45.0	44.9	10.1	149,544	38.7	42.8	18.5
26163	Wayne County............................	1,429,854	40.8	38.1	21.1	677,237	43.9	40.4	15.7	752,617	38.0	36.1	25.9
27000	**Minnesota................................**	4,318,219	31.5	52.1	16.4	2,129,781	34.8	53.0	12.2	2,188,438	28.3	51.3	20.4
27003	Anoka County	266,973	29.6	54.0	16.3	132,808	32.7	54.7	12.6	134,165	26.6	53.3	20.1

State/county FIPS code	State/County	Total women age 15 to 50 years	Percent of all women who had a birth in the past year	Percent of women who had a birth who were married (including separated and spouse absent):	Percent of women who had a birth who were partners in an unmarried partner household	Age of women who had a birth in the last year as a percent of all women who had a birth			Women who had a birth in the last year as a percent of all women in their age group		
						Age 15 to 19	Age 20 to 34	Age 35 to 50	Age 15 to 19	Age 20 to 34	Age 35 to 50
	Maine—cont'd										
23019	Penobscot County	37,117	4.5	58.6	16.6	1.4	89.7	8.9	0.5	9.7	0.9
23025	Somerset County	11,047	3.9	50.6	20.1	4.7	90.6	4.7	1.3	9.8	0.4
23031	York County	44,757	5.0	70.6	17.8	6.1	63.8	30.0	2.2	8.7	3.0
24000	**Maryland**	1,476,529	5.3	63.2	9.5	5.1	70.5	24.5	2.0	9.1	2.8
24001	Allegany County	15,607	4.6	60.5	26.3	4.2	73.8	21.9	1.1	8.2	2.4
24003	Anne Arundel County	134,170	5.6	73.0	8.3	5.0	72.8	22.2	2.3	10.0	2.6
24005	Baltimore County	204,331	4.9	68.4	10.5	4.8	68.2	27.0	1.8	8.0	3.0
24009	Calvert County	21,892	3.5	77.5	8.8	1.2	75.7	23.2	0.2	8.2	1.6
24013	Carroll County	38,915	4.5	57.9	10.9	3.7	71.9	24.4	1.0	9.8	2.2
24015	Cecil County	24,490	4.2	74.2	11.9	7.5	78.7	13.7	2.5	9.0	1.2
24017	Charles County	40,559	4.5	51.3	12.3	5.7	65.2	29.1	1.8	8.3	2.6
24021	Frederick County	59,276	4.4	77.6	6.5	2.6	76.5	20.9	0.8	9.1	1.8
24025	Harford County	59,170	6.0	72.8	7.4	3.2	69.8	27.0	1.4	11.2	3.3
24027	Howard County	75,290	5.2	84.8	1.7	2.1	68.3	29.7	0.8	10.0	3.1
24031	Montgomery County	249,195	5.5	76.2	7.9	2.6	64.2	33.2	1.2	9.1	3.7
24033	Prince George's County	236,974	5.2	50.3	14.4	5.3	73.4	21.3	2.1	9.0	2.5
24037	St. Mary's County	27,590	6.0	61.4	6.4	1.4	79.9	18.7	0.6	12.3	2.4
24043	Washington County	32,972	5.5	57.6	8.3	2.2	81.7	16.1	0.9	11.5	1.8
24045	Wicomico County	25,859	5.6	65.5	5.4	15.4	74.1	10.6	5.0	9.4	1.6
24047	Worcester County	9,899	4.8	56.6	14.3	0.0	57.5	42.5	0.0	7.4	4.0
24510	Baltimore city	170,330	5.9	37.8	8.2	10.3	69.4	20.3	5.2	8.1	3.2
25000	**Massachusetts**	1,666,805	4.6	69.1	9.3	2.9	67.5	29.6	1.0	7.5	3.0
25001	Barnstable County	39,792	2.8	66.1	14.7	0.0	77.7	22.3	0.0	6.0	1.2
25003	Berkshire County	28,608	4.7	52.9	22.1	7.3	60.9	31.9	2.1	7.6	3.3
25005	Bristol County	134,969	4.7	56.4	14.1	2.0	78.0	20.1	0.7	9.5	2.0
25009	Essex County	181,736	4.9	63.8	11.1	3.0	69.8	27.2	1.0	9.0	2.8
25011	Franklin County	15,690	3.3	60.3	19.7	9.9	76.4	13.7	2.4	6.8	0.9
25013	Hampden County	113,366	4.5	49.4	11.5	7.3	76.1	16.7	2.1	8.3	1.7
25015	Hampshire County	46,585	2.5	81.3	8.5	0.0	64.8	35.2	0.0	3.6	2.7
25017	Middlesex County	392,424	4.9	83.0	5.4	2.2	60.6	37.2	0.9	7.0	4.0
25021	Norfolk County	166,486	4.8	87.7	4.2	0.2	62.0	37.8	0.1	7.8	3.8
25023	Plymouth County	115,390	4.6	64.9	8.9	3.9	63.6	32.6	1.2	8.5	2.9
25025	Suffolk County	229,489	4.2	57.0	7.1	3.9	69.7	26.5	1.3	5.2	3.4
25027	Worcester County	196,652	4.9	66.7	13.5	3.0	72.4	24.7	1.0	9.4	2.5
26000	**Michigan**	2,327,914	5.2	60.7	12.7	5.7	75.9	18.5	2.0	9.7	2.1
26005	Allegan County	24,983	5.9	70.7	10.0	8.8	79.6	11.6	3.4	12.6	1.4
26015	Barry County	12,603	6.3	65.7	12.1	0.8	80.4	18.8	0.3	14.1	2.4
26017	Bay County	23,199	5.4	43.9	17.9	3.3	90.1	6.7	1.3	12.1	0.8
26021	Berrien County	34,589	4.5	58.0	10.8	2.5	82.4	15.1	0.7	9.6	1.4
26025	Calhoun County	31,098	4.7	58.9	16.7	4.6	75.7	19.7	1.5	8.8	2.0
26027	Cass County	10,807	4.1	69.5	10.9	10.9	85.2	3.9	2.7	10.2	0.3
26037	Clinton County	18,197	4.4	58.7	12.8	1.7	80.7	17.6	0.5	9.2	1.6
26045	Eaton County	25,041	5.2	65.7	7.2	3.5	75.1	21.4	1.3	10.0	2.4
26049	Genesee County	99,072	4.4	44.7	17.2	9.5	76.7	13.8	3.0	8.6	1.3
26055	Grand Traverse County	19,685	5.9	66.2	16.7	0.0	70.5	29.5	0.0	10.4	3.7
26065	Ingham County	79,054	4.9	63.1	10.4	7.6	72.0	20.4	2.1	7.2	3.1
26067	Ionia County	13,820	5.7	70.1	14.4	4.3	74.7	21.1	1.6	11.2	2.6
26073	Isabella County	21,973	3.9	55.1	16.3	4.3	80.5	15.2	0.8	5.8	2.4
26075	Jackson County	35,164	5.0	48.5	13.3	5.2	84.4	10.4	1.7	11.1	1.1
26077	Kalamazoo County	66,046	4.8	61.2	18.1	3.7	80.8	15.4	1.2	8.1	2.0
26081	Kent County	153,398	6.0	71.9	8.9	4.3	76.7	19.0	1.9	10.3	2.7
26087	Lapeer County	19,467	6.0	51.8	17.5	6.3	73.8	19.9	2.3	13.1	2.4
26091	Lenawee County	21,702	4.2	54.9	19.7	8.6	78.3	13.1	2.4	8.8	1.2
26093	Livingston County	41,917	4.4	81.2	9.4	3.1	79.8	17.2	0.9	11.0	1.4
26099	Macomb County	201,554	4.8	60.8	14.7	1.5	84.1	14.4	0.6	10.3	1.4
26103	Marquette County	16,233	3.1	76.3	12.4	8.0	72.3	19.7	1.5	4.7	1.6
26111	Midland County	19,235	6.0	82.1	10.6	3.0	83.4	13.6	1.3	13.2	1.7
26115	Monroe County	34,315	6.9	74.9	11.5	4.3	78.7	17.0	2.0	14.8	2.4
26117	Montcalm County	13,659	6.6	51.8	21.9	12.6	60.9	26.5	5.9	10.2	3.8
26121	Muskegon County	38,887	5.3	49.9	21.5	5.9	79.8	14.4	2.0	10.5	1.7
26125	Oakland County	291,576	5.4	69.6	8.7	4.6	68.6	26.8	1.8	9.9	2.9
26139	Ottawa County	67,810	5.8	63.9	15.8	6.7	86.3	6.9	2.2	12.2	1.0
26145	Saginaw County	45,366	4.3	49.6	9.6	11.9	74.1	14.1	3.3	7.9	1.4
26147	St. Clair County	35,908	4.7	60.3	21.5	9.1	75.2	15.7	2.9	10.0	1.5
26149	St. Joseph County	13,146	6.6	59.3	15.6	3.9	77.8	18.3	1.6	12.7	2.7
26155	Shiawassee County	15,622	5.1	71.4	17.5	4.1	85.0	10.9	1.4	11.6	1.2
26157	Tuscola County	11,792	4.9	70.8	10.9	12.3	70.1	17.6	4.1	9.3	1.8
26159	Van Buren County	16,365	4.3	69.6	8.9	0.7	85.2	14.1	0.2	9.6	1.3
26161	Washtenaw County	96,980	3.8	69.6	7.5	3.1	69.8	27.1	0.8	5.5	2.8
26163	Wayne County	437,777	5.6	48.1	11.5	8.4	72.0	19.6	3.3	10.0	2.5
27000	**Minnesota**	1,277,310	5.7	70.8	11.8	4.6	76.2	19.2	1.9	10.4	2.5
27003	Anoka County	82,265	6.1	72.5	10.9	3.5	77.1	19.4	1.6	12.3	2.4

State/ county FIPS code	State/County	Total population 15 years and older	Marital status, percent			Male population 15 years and older	Male, marital status, percent			Female population 15 years and older	Female, marital status, percent		
			Never married	Now married (except separated)	Separated, widowed, or divorced		Never married	Now married (except separated)	Separated, widowed, or divorced		Never married	Now married (except separated)	Separated, widowed, or divorced
	Minnesota—cont'd												
27013	Blue Earth County	54,173	43.9	44.0	12.1	27,022	47.8	43.7	8.5	27,151	40.1	44.3	15.6
27019	Carver County	71,688	24.4	63.1	12.4	35,336	27.4	64.1	8.5	36,352	21.6	62.2	16.3
27025	Chisago County	43,109	26.6	58.1	15.3	22,247	31.5	56.0	12.5	20,862	21.4	60.3	18.2
27027	Clay County	48,627	36.3	47.9	15.7	23,738	38.4	50.1	11.5	24,889	34.3	45.9	19.8
27035	Crow Wing County	51,205	24.3	57.8	17.9	25,352	27.0	58.7	14.4	25,853	21.7	57.0	21.3
27037	Dakota County	319,764	29.3	55.3	15.4	155,637	31.7	57.1	11.2	164,127	27.1	53.6	19.3
27053	Hennepin County	960,526	37.2	46.6	16.2	468,918	40.3	47.6	12.1	491,608	34.3	45.5	20.2
27109	Olmsted County	116,276	30.1	54.5	15.4	56,279	33.0	56.5	10.5	59,997	27.3	52.6	20.1
27111	Otter Tail County	47,384	23.2	59.6	17.2	23,612	27.3	60.9	11.7	23,772	19.0	58.4	22.6
27123	Ramsey County	419,225	39.0	43.8	17.2	201,040	42.1	45.4	12.5	218,185	36.2	42.3	21.5
27131	Rice County	52,838	35.3	48.6	16.2	27,015	38.8	47.9	13.4	25,823	31.6	49.3	19.1
27137	St. Louis County	168,246	33.0	47.1	19.9	84,103	37.2	47.4	15.4	84,143	28.9	46.9	24.3
27139	Scott County	101,503	25.9	61.0	13.1	50,267	28.5	61.6	9.8	51,236	23.4	60.4	16.2
27141	Sherburne County	68,815	27.5	57.7	14.7	35,133	31.0	57.1	11.9	33,682	23.9	58.4	17.7
27145	Stearns County	122,631	36.5	50.4	13.1	61,639	39.9	50.0	10.2	60,992	33.0	50.9	16.1
27163	Washington County	192,496	27.7	57.4	14.8	94,504	31.0	58.3	10.6	97,992	24.6	56.5	18.9
27169	Winona County	43,464	41.7	45.1	13.1	21,259	45.7	44.3	10.0	22,205	37.9	45.9	16.1
27171	Wright County	95,852	24.7	61.7	13.6	47,864	27.8	62.8	9.4	47,988	21.6	60.5	17.8
28000	**Mississippi**	2,365,073	33.3	44.7	22.1	1,134,219	36.1	47.5	16.4	1,230,854	30.7	42.1	27.3
28033	DeSoto County	128,532	27.0	52.7	20.2	61,385	30.0	55.5	14.5	67,147	24.3	50.2	25.5
28035	Forrest County	61,375	39.9	39.1	21.1	28,756	41.7	41.8	16.5	32,619	38.2	36.7	25.1
28047	Harrison County	153,608	31.2	46.0	22.8	75,827	35.5	47.7	16.8	77,781	27.0	44.4	28.5
28049	Hinds County	194,350	43.3	34.7	22.0	89,390	45.0	38.7	16.3	104,960	41.9	31.3	26.8
28059	Jackson County	111,371	29.4	48.4	22.2	54,348	31.9	49.8	18.3	57,023	27.0	47.0	26.0
28067	Jones County	53,852	29.5	48.4	22.1	25,731	31.3	52.6	16.1	28,121	27.9	44.6	27.5
28071	Lafayette County	42,565	49.1	34.4	16.4	20,800	50.9	36.7	12.5	21,765	47.4	32.3	20.2
28073	Lamar County	45,356	28.9	53.0	18.0	21,588	31.2	55.4	13.4	23,768	26.9	50.9	22.2
28075	Lauderdale County	63,966	33.7	43.1	23.1	30,621	36.5	45.0	18.5	33,345	31.2	41.5	27.3
28081	Lee County	66,110	27.8	50.0	22.1	30,913	30.8	54.1	15.1	35,197	25.3	46.4	28.3
28087	Lowndes County	47,525	32.6	44.8	22.6	22,252	34.3	49.3	16.4	25,273	31.0	40.9	28.1
28089	Madison County	77,353	31.9	51.8	16.3	36,287	33.4	55.6	10.9	41,066	30.6	48.4	20.9
28109	Pearl River County	44,224	25.4	50.9	23.7	21,548	28.3	56.4	15.3	22,676	22.6	45.7	31.7
28121	Rankin County	115,111	26.0	53.5	20.6	54,478	29.0	56.5	14.5	60,633	23.2	50.8	26.0
28151	Washington County	38,822	40.9	34.3	24.7	17,625	42.5	38.6	18.9	21,197	39.6	30.8	29.6
29000	**Missouri**	4,859,594	29.8	49.7	20.6	2,357,488	32.8	51.5	15.8	2,502,106	27.0	47.9	25.1
29019	Boone County	138,707	43.3	42.0	14.7	66,065	44.9	44.6	10.5	72,642	41.9	39.7	18.4
29021	Buchanan County	72,225	31.9	45.3	22.8	36,042	35.9	46.8	17.3	36,183	27.9	43.8	28.3
29031	Cape Girardeau County	62,758	31.3	50.1	18.6	29,921	34.9	52.4	12.7	32,837	28.0	48.0	24.0
29037	Cass County	78,862	21.9	57.8	20.3	37,995	24.2	59.9	15.9	40,867	19.8	55.8	24.3
29043	Christian County	61,918	20.9	61.1	18.0	29,955	23.6	63.0	13.4	31,963	18.4	59.4	22.2
29047	Clay County	179,471	27.3	51.5	21.2	86,913	30.5	53.2	16.3	92,558	24.2	49.9	25.9
29051	Cole County	61,752	30.3	49.3	20.4	31,083	34.5	49.7	15.7	30,669	25.9	49.0	25.1
29071	Franklin County	81,323	23.8	55.9	20.2	39,916	27.6	56.3	16.1	41,407	20.2	55.5	24.2
29077	Greene County	230,756	31.0	47.5	21.5	111,101	33.9	49.6	16.6	119,655	28.3	45.6	26.1
29095	Jackson County	539,598	35.1	43.0	21.9	257,595	37.5	45.7	16.9	282,003	32.9	40.6	26.5
29097	Jasper County	91,415	26.5	51.0	22.4	44,262	29.8	53.4	16.7	47,153	23.5	48.8	27.8
29099	Jefferson County	175,607	25.3	55.0	19.6	86,267	28.7	55.7	15.6	89,340	22.1	54.4	23.5
29101	Johnson County	44,025	34.9	50.5	14.6	22,462	38.8	48.5	12.6	21,563	30.8	52.6	16.6
29113	Lincoln County	41,488	24.3	54.8	20.9	20,506	26.9	54.4	18.7	20,982	21.9	55.2	22.9
29145	Newton County	46,824	22.0	57.5	20.5	22,863	25.7	58.0	16.4	23,961	18.6	57.0	24.4
29165	Platte County	73,875	26.0	55.4	18.6	36,064	28.9	57.6	13.6	37,811	23.3	53.3	23.3
29169	Pulaski County	42,763	39.5	46.0	14.5	24,695	47.0	41.4	11.6	18,068	29.2	52.3	18.5
29183	St. Charles County	292,447	26.2	57.8	15.9	142,191	28.6	59.7	11.7	150,256	23.9	56.1	19.9
29187	St. Francois County	54,236	28.0	46.1	25.8	29,625	35.2	42.8	22.1	24,611	19.4	50.2	30.4
29189	St. Louis County	814,138	32.2	48.5	19.3	378,864	34.4	52.3	13.2	435,274	30.3	45.1	24.6
29213	Taney County	43,624	26.7	49.5	23.8	20,896	31.6	50.9	17.4	22,728	22.2	48.2	29.6
29510	St. Louis city	263,545	50.0	28.5	21.5	125,635	52.7	30.4	16.9	137,910	47.5	26.9	25.7
30000	**Montana**	820,867	28.1	51.8	20.1	410,108	31.9	52.3	15.7	410,759	24.3	51.2	24.5
30013	Cascade County	66,347	26.9	52.0	21.2	32,911	30.8	53.3	15.9	33,436	23.0	50.6	26.4
30029	Flathead County	74,714	22.9	55.6	21.5	37,111	26.1	57.2	16.7	37,603	19.8	54.0	26.2
30031	Gallatin County	76,631	37.3	50.0	12.8	39,717	42.6	48.6	8.8	36,914	31.5	51.4	17.0
30049	Lewis and Clark County	52,886	26.8	52.1	21.1	25,933	31.9	52.6	15.5	26,953	21.9	51.6	26.4
30063	Missoula County	92,781	36.9	44.8	18.3	46,245	39.5	44.5	15.9	46,536	34.2	45.0	20.7
30111	Yellowstone County	122,078	28.3	49.4	22.3	59,002	31.8	51.1	17.1	63,076	25.0	47.7	27.3
31000	**Nebraska**	1,466,890	29.4	53.0	17.6	722,428	32.6	54.2	13.1	744,462	26.3	51.8	22.0
31055	Douglas County	414,613	34.9	46.9	18.2	201,843	38.0	48.8	13.2	212,770	31.9	45.2	22.9
31079	Hall County	46,439	27.4	52.3	20.3	23,136	30.5	53.5	16.0	23,303	24.3	51.2	24.5
31109	Lancaster County	235,584	35.9	47.9	16.2	117,486	39.4	48.4	12.2	118,098	32.5	47.4	20.1
31153	Sarpy County	125,917	27.0	58.5	14.6	62,272	29.5	59.8	10.7	63,645	24.5	57.2	18.3
32000	**Nevada**	2,204,875	32.2	45.9	21.9	1,106,651	35.8	46.4	17.7	1,098,224	28.6	45.4	26.0
32003	Clark County	1,590,689	33.6	44.7	21.7	795,724	37.0	45.5	17.5	794,965	30.1	43.9	26.0
32007	Elko County	38,906	26.5	57.2	16.3	20,250	30.4	56.1	13.6	18,656	22.3	58.4	19.3
32019	Lyon County	41,589	23.7	51.9	24.4	20,644	27.1	51.6	21.3	20,945	20.3	52.1	27.5

Table C-2: Counties with a Population of 50,000 or More—Marriages and Births—*Continued*

State/ county FIPS code	State/County	Total women age 15 to 50 years	Percent of all women who had a birth in the past year	Percent of women who had a birth who were married (including separated and spouse absent):	Percent of women who had a birth who were partners in an unmarried partner household	Age of women who had a birth in the last year as a percent of all women who had a birth			Women who had a birth in the last year as a percent of all women in their age group		
						Age 15 to 19	Age 20 to 34	Age 35 to 50	Age 15 to 19	Age 20 to 34	Age 35 to 50
	Minnesota—cont'd										
27013	Blue Earth County	17,613	4.1	51.5	28.6	9.6	79.9	10.5	2.2	6.2	1.5
27019	Carver County	23,263	5.3	87.4	1.8	5.6	60.6	33.9	2.0	9.9	3.4
27025	Chisago County	12,254	5.2	71.2	18.0	1.1	86.6	12.3	0.4	13.6	1.2
27027	Clay County	16,062	6.1	67.1	11.3	1.6	74.4	24.0	0.5	9.2	4.5
27035	Crow Wing County	12,916	5.3	69.1	18.6	0.9	92.8	6.3	0.3	11.9	0.7
27037	Dakota County	99,749	5.5	71.8	10.2	4.3	73.6	22.1	1.8	10.4	2.5
27053	Hennepin County	300,959	6.0	70.2	8.6	5.4	71.7	22.9	2.7	9.2	3.3
27109	Olmsted County	35,059	6.2	81.4	15.9	0.0	70.1	29.9	0.0	9.8	4.3
27111	Otter Tail County	10,838	6.7	62.3	30.0	4.0	81.6	14.4	1.7	14.6	2.0
27123	Ramsey County	132,473	6.1	64.9	11.0	5.6	75.2	19.2	2.5	9.4	3.0
27131	Rice County	15,393	3.9	72.9	10.2	3.6	69.9	26.4	0.7	6.6	2.7
27137	St. Louis County	44,902	4.2	68.0	11.6	4.5	84.1	11.4	1.2	8.0	1.2
27139	Scott County	34,188	5.8	89.6	1.7	0.3	81.3	18.5	0.1	13.3	2.1
27141	Sherburne County	22,032	5.9	80.8	1.8	4.5	75.3	20.1	1.8	12.3	2.4
27145	Stearns County	37,916	4.5	72.6	20.8	2.4	81.9	15.7	0.6	8.2	1.9
27163	Washington County	58,315	4.5	79.9	8.1	2.5	70.3	27.2	0.8	8.9	2.4
27169	Winona County	13,542	4.4	77.3	6.3	5.6	82.5	11.9	1.2	7.3	1.7
27171	Wright County	31,121	6.5	84.0	4.9	0.2	87.9	11.9	0.1	15.0	1.6
28000	**Mississippi**	724,800	5.3	51.8	7.2	8.1	79.2	12.7	2.9	10.1	1.6
28033	DeSoto County	42,549	5.0	67.5	12.4	2.1	78.4	19.4	0.8	10.3	2.0
28035	Forrest County	21,209	4.5	42.8	9.1	3.8	81.9	14.3	1.1	7.2	1.9
28047	Harrison County	47,107	4.8	56.2	14.0	5.8	82.8	11.5	2.2	8.9	1.3
28049	Hinds County	65,499	5.4	33.9	4.2	14.2	79.9	5.9	5.0	9.5	0.8
28059	Jackson County	33,730	5.1	56.4	2.9	13.5	70.6	15.9	5.1	8.9	1.8
28067	Jones County	15,810	9.0	50.2	12.1	12.5	77.3	10.2	6.6	16.7	2.2
28071	Lafayette County	15,207	4.0	54.2	0.0	0.0	90.2	9.8	0.0	7.7	1.4
28073	Lamar County	15,462	4.7	79.4	0.8	0.0	87.5	12.5	0.0	8.9	1.4
28075	Lauderdale County	18,997	6.3	57.0	4.0	14.4	79.9	5.7	6.3	11.9	0.8
28081	Lee County	20,924	5.3	58.9	11.3	5.3	74.6	20.1	2.1	9.4	2.3
28087	Lowndes County	14,888	6.9	52.7	1.9	10.5	79.0	10.4	5.1	12.5	1.7
28089	Madison County	25,129	5.7	57.0	0.4	8.4	80.7	10.9	3.5	11.5	1.4
28109	Pearl River County	12,561	5.0	92.0	7.1	0.0	86.5	13.5	0.0	11.7	1.4
28121	Rankin County	37,019	5.2	69.2	2.5	2.3	86.9	10.8	1.0	10.8	1.2
28151	Washington County	12,336	5.1	9.7	7.1	23.9	71.2	4.9	7.7	9.1	0.6
29000	**Missouri**	1,426,918	5.5	61.8	11.1	6.7	76.5	16.8	2.7	10.0	2.1
29019	Boone County	50,400	4.8	73.3	5.7	9.3	74.7	16.0	3.0	6.8	2.4
29021	Buchanan County	20,650	5.6	48.3	11.2	12.8	72.3	15.0	5.1	8.9	2.0
29031	Cape Girardeau County	19,356	5.8	49.3	2.9	3.7	85.7	10.6	1.4	10.4	1.6
29037	Cass County	23,133	4.9	68.3	7.7	8.8	81.4	9.7	2.9	10.8	1.0
29043	Christian County	19,057	4.8	68.0	5.2	8.9	67.4	23.7	3.2	8.1	2.5
29047	Clay County	56,722	5.5	67.6	14.0	8.2	65.9	25.9	3.5	8.9	3.1
29051	Cole County	17,877	6.9	49.0	11.3	2.3	85.7	12.0	1.1	14.2	1.9
29071	Franklin County	23,035	5.7	56.3	16.8	7.7	72.9	19.4	3.3	10.6	2.4
29077	Greene County	70,642	5.3	65.3	12.7	6.5	75.5	18.1	2.6	8.1	2.6
29095	Jackson County	166,622	5.7	52.7	12.0	6.6	78.4	15.0	3.0	9.9	2.0
29097	Jasper County	27,960	6.3	61.8	8.2	2.4	77.8	19.8	1.1	10.9	3.0
29099	Jefferson County	52,554	6.2	54.5	22.8	6.3	76.6	17.2	3.0	12.0	2.2
29101	Johnson County	14,683	6.1	68.0	8.8	2.4	84.0	13.7	0.9	9.7	2.6
29113	Lincoln County	12,739	5.1	73.7	15.5	2.3	87.6	10.0	0.8	11.1	1.1
29145	Newton County	13,075	6.3	71.3	0.0	3.4	83.4	13.2	1.4	13.5	1.8
29165	Platte County	22,453	5.4	75.9	6.4	3.7	64.7	31.6	1.4	9.5	3.5
29169	Pulaski County	12,685	5.7	96.4	1.6	2.9	89.8	7.3	0.8	11.0	1.3
29183	St. Charles County	90,063	4.9	74.6	9.5	2.0	75.0	23.0	0.7	9.2	2.4
29187	St. Francois County	13,329	5.7	56.5	19.7	23.5	73.7	2.8	10.0	9.9	0.4
29189	St. Louis County	237,321	5.3	66.7	9.3	4.5	67.8	27.6	1.7	8.9	3.2
29213	Taney County	12,232	5.7	60.4	11.6	23.7	65.9	10.4	9.3	9.1	1.4
29510	St. Louis city	87,421	5.4	43.4	6.5	9.6	75.1	15.4	4.6	7.8	2.2
30000	**Montana**	223,088	5.4	67.8	12.6	4.4	78.4	17.2	1.7	10.0	2.2
30013	Cascade County	18,379	5.6	65.1	8.2	4.7	89.2	6.1	1.9	11.0	0.8
30029	Flathead County	19,958	6.2	77.0	5.3	0.8	95.6	3.6	0.3	15.0	0.5
30031	Gallatin County	24,230	4.0	84.5	9.0	4.6	67.9	27.5	1.4	5.5	3.0
30049	Lewis and Clark County	14,480	4.7	75.4	11.1	0.0	81.8	18.2	0.0	9.5	1.8
30063	Missoula County	28,991	4.2	67.3	21.1	3.7	79.1	17.3	1.2	6.4	2.0
30111	Yellowstone County	35,465	4.8	61.5	19.0	4.7	76.1	19.2	1.7	8.4	2.1
31000	**Nebraska**	432,821	6.1	71.8	11.5	3.9	79.1	17.0	1.6	11.2	2.5
31055	Douglas County	133,394	5.5	71.2	8.4	3.3	78.1	18.5	1.4	9.3	2.5
31079	Hall County	13,513	7.4	41.4	22.0	11.8	79.2	9.1	5.6	14.4	1.5
31109	Lancaster County	74,313	6.2	69.1	13.8	3.8	78.0	18.1	1.6	9.9	3.1
31153	Sarpy County	41,968	7.0	79.1	11.1	1.5	81.0	17.6	0.8	13.6	2.7
32000	**Nevada**	667,295	5.4	65.4	14.6	5.3	71.9	22.8	2.2	9.1	2.7
32003	Clark County	497,333	5.3	65.8	14.1	5.5	69.7	24.8	2.3	8.6	2.9
32007	Elko County	12,059	7.6	61.3	17.7	0.8	90.7	8.6	0.4	16.2	1.5
32019	Lyon County	10,802	5.2	55.2	25.4	14.3	65.6	20.1	4.7	9.6	2.1

Table C-2: Counties with a Population of 50,000 or More—Marriages and Births—*Continued*

State/county FIPS code	State/County	Total population 15 years and older	Marital status, percent			Male population 15 years and older	Male, marital status, percent			Female population 15 years and older	Female, marital status, percent		
			Never married	Now married (except separated)	Separated, widowed, or divorced		Never married	Now married (except separated)	Separated, widowed, or divorced		Never married	Now married (except separated)	Separated, widowed, or divorced
	Nevada—cont'd												
32031	Washoe County	347,325	31.8	46.6	21.6	174,160	36.1	46.5	17.4	173,165	27.5	46.7	25.8
32510	Carson City	44,972	28.2	46.0	25.8	22,931	34.4	45.7	19.8	22,041	21.7	46.2	32.1
33000	**New Hampshire**	1,097,738	29.0	52.4	18.6	537,698	31.8	54.1	14.1	560,040	26.2	50.8	23.0
33001	Belknap County	50,453	24.6	54.4	21.0	24,420	27.4	54.9	17.6	26,033	22.0	53.9	24.1
33005	Cheshire County	64,915	32.5	47.7	19.8	31,316	34.4	49.2	16.4	33,599	30.7	46.3	23.0
33009	Grafton County	76,371	34.0	48.1	18.0	37,453	35.5	50.1	14.3	38,918	32.5	46.1	21.4
33011	Hillsborough County	329,089	30.5	51.3	18.3	162,002	34.0	52.3	13.7	167,087	27.0	50.2	22.7
33013	Merrimack County	122,159	28.9	51.6	19.5	59,643	31.2	53.4	15.4	62,516	26.7	49.9	23.4
33015	Rockingham County	246,279	25.8	57.0	17.2	121,022	28.7	59.2	12.0	125,257	22.9	54.9	22.2
33017	Strafford County	103,779	34.4	47.7	17.9	49,853	37.4	50.2	12.4	53,926	31.6	45.5	22.9
34000	**New Jersey**	7,192,367	34.0	49.1	16.9	3,469,363	37.1	51.6	11.2	3,723,004	31.1	46.7	22.2
34001	Atlantic County	224,182	34.9	45.4	19.7	107,248	37.9	48.3	13.8	116,934	32.2	42.7	25.1
34003	Bergen County	753,690	30.0	54.0	16.0	360,004	33.2	56.9	9.9	393,686	27.1	51.4	21.5
34005	Burlington County	368,369	31.2	50.5	18.3	179,929	35.4	52.3	12.3	188,440	27.2	48.8	24.0
34007	Camden County	412,621	37.2	44.5	18.3	196,592	40.1	48.1	11.8	216,029	34.7	41.1	24.2
34009	Cape May County	82,034	27.1	54.4	18.5	39,750	31.5	56.6	12.0	42,284	23.1	52.3	24.6
34011	Cumberland County	126,111	40.8	38.8	20.3	65,053	44.7	39.2	16.1	61,058	36.7	38.5	24.8
34013	Essex County	627,076	42.7	39.3	18.0	296,637	45.1	42.5	12.4	330,439	40.5	36.5	23.0
34015	Gloucester County	233,856	31.7	51.2	17.1	112,154	34.6	54.0	11.4	121,702	29.0	48.6	22.3
34017	Hudson County	540,200	42.0	40.9	17.1	266,674	45.6	42.5	11.9	273,526	38.5	39.3	22.2
34019	Hunterdon County	104,467	27.7	58.0	14.2	51,963	31.0	59.0	10.0	52,504	24.5	57.0	18.4
34021	Mercer County	301,670	36.6	47.2	16.1	146,304	40.4	48.6	10.9	155,366	33.1	45.9	21.0
34023	Middlesex County	670,360	33.8	51.5	14.7	326,822	37.6	53.4	9.0	343,538	30.3	49.6	20.2
34025	Monmouth County	513,088	30.4	53.2	16.4	246,976	33.4	56.0	10.6	266,112	27.7	50.5	21.7
34027	Morris County	404,739	28.4	57.0	14.6	196,227	31.3	59.3	9.4	208,512	25.8	54.8	19.4
34029	Ocean County	466,722	26.4	53.2	20.4	220,305	29.8	56.6	13.5	246,417	23.4	50.1	26.6
34031	Passaic County	401,575	39.9	43.9	16.1	192,693	42.4	46.9	10.7	208,882	37.6	41.2	21.2
34033	Salem County	53,439	31.7	46.8	21.5	25,519	34.7	49.5	15.8	27,920	29.0	44.4	26.6
34035	Somerset County	264,209	28.7	56.3	15.0	127,393	31.3	59.5	9.1	136,816	26.2	53.4	20.4
34037	Sussex County	120,703	27.3	56.9	15.8	59,657	31.1	56.9	12.0	61,046	23.5	56.9	19.5
34039	Union County	435,122	36.6	46.6	16.7	209,037	38.7	49.8	11.5	226,085	34.7	43.7	21.6
34041	Warren County	88,134	27.0	54.7	18.3	42,426	29.8	57.5	12.7	45,708	24.3	52.1	23.6
35000	**New Mexico**	1,655,442	33.6	45.7	20.8	813,817	36.8	47.5	15.8	841,625	30.5	43.9	25.6
35001	Bernalillo County	539,892	35.1	44.0	20.9	262,443	38.4	46.0	15.6	277,449	31.9	42.2	25.9
35005	Chaves County	50,868	30.6	47.9	21.5	24,959	34.4	50.7	14.9	25,909	27.0	45.2	27.8
35009	Curry County	38,530	29.1	52.0	18.8	19,850	33.7	53.2	13.1	18,680	24.3	50.7	25.0
35013	Do±a Ana County	166,751	35.4	45.8	18.8	81,186	39.3	47.6	13.2	85,565	31.8	44.1	24.1
35015	Eddy County	42,863	29.3	49.2	21.5	21,656	32.7	51.0	16.4	21,207	25.9	47.4	26.7
35025	Lea County	49,698	29.3	54.0	16.8	25,622	33.0	53.6	13.3	24,076	25.3	54.3	20.4
35031	McKinley County	54,579	51.5	33.2	15.3	25,860	54.8	35.5	9.7	28,719	48.4	31.2	20.3
35035	Otero County	51,828	28.2	49.5	22.3	26,412	33.1	50.0	16.9	25,416	23.1	49.0	28.0
35043	Sandoval County	106,914	31.3	50.0	18.7	51,817	33.2	51.4	15.4	55,097	29.5	48.7	21.8
35045	San Juan County	97,470	36.1	46.1	17.8	48,145	39.2	47.8	13.0	49,325	33.1	44.4	22.5
35049	Santa Fe County	121,789	30.4	46.8	22.7	59,042	33.3	49.9	16.8	62,747	27.7	44.0	28.3
35061	Valencia County	60,569	29.9	49.0	21.2	30,379	31.8	50.7	17.5	30,190	27.9	47.2	24.9
36000	**New York**	16,065,870	38.0	44.4	17.6	7,698,201	41.0	46.9	12.1	8,367,669	35.3	42.0	22.7
36001	Albany County	258,095	41.8	41.2	17.0	123,506	44.6	43.6	11.8	134,589	39.2	38.9	21.8
36005	Bronx County	1,103,175	48.9	30.3	20.8	507,347	51.8	34.1	14.2	595,828	46.5	27.1	26.4
36007	Broome County	166,287	35.4	44.8	19.7	80,691	39.0	46.0	15.0	85,596	32.0	43.7	24.2
36009	Cattaraugus County	64,381	29.0	48.1	22.9	31,557	31.9	49.7	18.4	32,824	26.3	46.5	27.2
36011	Cayuga County	66,169	31.3	46.3	22.4	33,861	35.8	46.8	17.4	32,308	26.6	45.8	27.6
36013	Chautauqua County	110,474	30.7	48.0	21.3	54,262	34.8	49.6	15.5	56,212	26.7	46.4	26.9
36015	Chemung County	72,582	30.7	48.7	20.6	35,934	35.2	50.1	14.7	36,648	26.3	47.4	26.3
36019	Clinton County	69,349	34.5	47.8	17.8	35,697	38.4	47.8	13.9	33,652	30.3	47.7	22.0
36021	Columbia County	52,880	28.9	49.3	21.8	26,482	32.4	50.8	16.8	26,398	25.4	47.8	26.8
36027	Dutchess County	247,613	34.8	47.9	17.3	122,565	38.0	49.5	12.5	125,048	31.6	46.4	22.0
36029	Erie County	762,241	36.2	44.4	19.4	364,153	39.6	46.5	13.9	398,088	33.0	42.6	24.4
36033	Franklin County	43,375	36.1	42.6	21.2	24,312	43.4	40.3	16.3	19,063	26.8	45.6	27.6
36035	Fulton County	45,449	27.5	50.9	21.6	22,414	32.5	51.5	16.0	23,035	22.7	50.3	27.1
36037	Genesee County	49,477	27.5	52.5	19.9	24,595	32.4	52.8	14.8	24,882	22.8	52.2	25.0
36043	Herkimer County	53,253	28.1	50.9	20.9	26,114	31.3	53.4	15.3	27,139	25.1	48.5	26.4
36045	Jefferson County	93,603	28.8	53.2	18.0	48,702	34.7	51.2	14.1	44,901	22.4	55.4	22.2
36047	Kings County	2,060,772	43.9	39.7	16.4	957,029	45.9	43.5	10.5	1,103,743	42.1	36.3	21.5
36051	Livingston County	54,751	34.9	47.4	17.7	27,251	35.7	49.7	14.6	27,500	34.2	45.0	20.8
36053	Madison County	60,308	34.3	46.9	18.9	29,418	37.5	48.1	14.3	30,890	31.1	45.7	23.2
36055	Monroe County	614,103	37.4	44.1	18.5	292,869	40.2	46.4	13.3	321,234	34.8	41.9	23.2
36059	Nassau County	1,102,887	31.7	53.0	15.2	527,612	35.1	55.8	9.1	575,275	28.7	50.5	20.8
36061	New York County	1,416,236	51.1	32.2	16.7	660,733	53.4	34.9	11.7	755,503	49.2	29.7	21.1
36063	Niagara County	178,506	32.2	47.0	20.8	85,981	35.7	48.8	15.5	92,525	29.0	45.2	25.7
36065	Oneida County	192,687	34.1	43.7	22.2	95,521	38.2	44.8	17.0	97,166	29.9	42.7	27.3
36067	Onondaga County	382,341	36.4	44.5	19.1	182,173	38.8	46.8	14.3	200,168	34.1	42.4	23.5
36069	Ontario County	89,734	29.1	51.2	19.7	43,416	31.6	52.9	15.5	46,318	26.6	49.6	23.7
36071	Orange County	292,912	33.2	50.3	16.5	145,494	37.4	51.3	11.3	147,418	29.1	49.3	21.5

State/county FIPS code	State/County	Total women age 15 to 50 years	Percent of all women who had a birth in the past year	Percent of women who had a birth who were married (including separated and spouse absent):	Percent of women who had a birth who were partners in an unmarried partner household	Age of women who had a birth in the last year as a percent of all women who had a birth			Women who had a birth in the last year as a percent of all women in their age group		
						Age 15 to 19	Age 20 to 34	Age 35 to 50	Age 15 to 19	Age 20 to 34	Age 35 to 50
	Nevada—cont'd										
32031	Washoe County	102,491	5.5	71.2	12.2	4.6	75.7	19.7	1.9	9.6	2.5
32510	Carson City	11,410	4.2	75.8	2.5	8.3	82.7	9.0	2.2	8.9	0.8
33000	**New Hampshire**	311,299	4.6	71.3	11.5	3.3	71.3	25.3	1.0	8.8	2.4
33001	Belknap County	12,746	3.2	50.2	16.7	2.9	42.2	54.9	0.6	3.9	3.5
33005	Cheshire County	18,584	4.7	71.7	18.5	0.0	76.5	23.5	0.0	9.7	2.6
33009	Grafton County	21,412	5.8	67.9	6.5	0.6	57.5	41.8	0.2	8.0	5.8
33011	Hillsborough County	97,795	4.8	74.4	11.5	4.5	74.4	21.1	1.6	9.6	2.1
33013	Merrimack County	34,082	3.8	68.6	8.3	8.6	71.1	20.3	2.2	7.4	1.6
33015	Rockingham County	68,958	4.4	77.0	5.8	0.2	73.5	26.3	0.1	9.8	2.2
33017	Strafford County	32,947	4.1	67.2	14.6	4.6	74.0	21.5	1.1	7.0	2.3
34000	**New Jersey**	2,149,755	4.9	69.3	8.5	2.8	69.3	27.9	1.1	8.8	2.9
34001	Atlantic County	65,716	4.4	58.8	15.2	3.4	75.3	21.3	1.1	8.6	2.0
34003	Bergen County	218,087	3.9	83.5	5.0	2.5	59.7	37.8	0.7	6.6	2.9
34005	Burlington County	104,910	4.7	76.7	5.1	1.3	73.0	25.7	0.4	9.3	2.4
34007	Camden County	126,162	6.1	60.3	9.7	4.5	71.1	24.4	2.1	10.6	3.2
34009	Cape May County	18,730	5.4	75.8	2.2	5.9	80.5	13.6	2.4	11.3	1.5
34011	Cumberland County	35,544	5.9	52.5	8.3	4.4	83.7	11.9	1.9	11.8	1.6
34013	Essex County	202,025	5.2	52.0	9.8	2.6	68.3	29.1	1.0	8.7	3.2
34015	Gloucester County	70,905	4.5	74.0	6.2	4.9	68.6	26.5	1.6	8.2	2.5
34017	Hudson County	182,244	5.4	71.3	10.0	2.8	70.7	26.5	1.6	7.7	3.4
34019	Hunterdon County	27,668	4.5	87.8	4.4	0.0	47.9	52.1	0.0	8.0	4.1
34021	Mercer County	92,157	4.4	67.7	5.9	4.3	67.6	28.0	1.3	7.6	2.7
34023	Middlesex County	208,240	5.0	76.7	7.7	2.2	69.3	28.5	0.8	8.5	3.1
34025	Monmouth County	146,329	4.7	64.2	13.7	4.8	66.7	28.4	1.5	9.2	2.6
34027	Morris County	117,136	3.8	88.7	6.5	0.8	64.6	34.6	0.2	7.5	2.5
34029	Ocean County	119,256	5.6	79.0	5.9	0.5	75.0	24.5	0.2	10.7	2.9
34031	Passaic County	127,107	5.0	62.2	6.3	3.2	75.6	21.2	1.2	9.3	2.4
34033	Salem County	15,047	6.4	36.1	25.7	3.2	86.2	10.6	1.4	14.3	1.5
34035	Somerset County	78,848	4.9	82.2	6.8	3.2	57.8	39.0	1.1	8.6	3.5
34037	Sussex County	33,825	4.4	84.7	8.2	0.0	75.5	24.5	0.0	10.5	2.0
34039	Union County	134,597	5.8	59.2	12.4	2.0	71.7	26.3	0.9	10.8	3.2
34041	Warren County	25,222	5.2	66.3	7.1	8.9	57.8	33.3	3.2	8.9	3.3
35000	**New Mexico**	483,237	5.9	53.0	13.7	8.3	75.2	16.5	3.3	10.5	2.3
35001	Bernalillo County	164,333	5.6	59.6	13.9	4.2	76.8	18.9	1.8	9.6	2.5
35005	Chaves County	14,695	8.5	52.0	29.4	10.5	78.3	11.1	5.3	15.7	2.3
35009	Curry County	11,897	8.8	53.3	12.0	13.3	78.3	8.4	8.8	14.2	1.9
35013	Do±a Ana County	53,570	6.3	46.3	9.6	9.4	74.1	16.5	3.5	10.4	2.7
35015	Eddy County	11,852	7.8	35.2	25.5	10.7	70.7	18.6	5.4	13.0	3.5
35025	Lea County	15,081	7.7	47.9	9.8	25.9	60.6	13.5	12.8	10.7	2.6
35031	McKinley County	18,499	6.0	25.4	8.5	2.3	82.7	15.0	0.8	12.0	2.2
35035	Otero County	14,528	8.8	37.9	9.3	13.5	80.7	5.8	8.8	15.8	1.2
35043	Sandoval County	31,033	5.9	68.7	8.1	1.4	70.9	27.7	0.6	10.9	3.5
35045	San Juan County	29,972	5.1	56.8	12.3	5.9	79.9	14.1	2.1	9.4	1.7
35049	Santa Fe County	31,238	4.1	62.9	7.0	15.1	73.5	11.4	4.7	7.8	0.9
35061	Valencia County	17,292	6.5	54.7	12.3	11.7	73.8	14.5	4.7	12.5	2.1
36000	**New York**	4,921,807	4.9	65.5	9.2	3.7	68.4	27.8	1.4	7.8	3.0
36001	Albany County	78,737	3.5	64.1	13.6	2.3	66.6	31.1	0.5	5.2	2.7
36005	Bronx County	382,845	5.7	43.8	9.6	5.7	71.6	22.7	2.4	9.2	3.1
36007	Broome County	46,412	4.0	62.7	20.8	5.1	70.3	24.6	1.2	6.6	2.4
36009	Cattaraugus County	17,791	4.5	56.9	18.7	2.3	87.2	10.5	0.6	10.2	1.0
36011	Cayuga County	17,070	5.3	48.8	19.0	0.0	74.5	25.5	0.0	10.0	2.9
36013	Chautauqua County	29,742	5.3	56.6	19.3	9.7	74.6	15.7	3.1	9.9	1.9
36015	Chemung County	19,532	5.0	62.0	18.1	10.5	73.3	16.1	3.6	9.1	1.8
36019	Clinton County	19,585	3.6	61.6	11.5	0.0	80.7	19.3	0.0	7.0	1.6
36021	Columbia County	12,901	3.8	70.5	18.3	4.7	74.9	20.4	1.3	8.4	1.5
36027	Dutchess County	71,370	3.7	67.5	10.0	3.3	65.8	30.8	0.8	6.6	2.5
36029	Erie County	217,587	4.8	61.5	12.9	2.9	75.2	21.9	1.0	8.6	2.4
36033	Franklin County	10,438	6.4	41.6	17.7	3.7	81.7	14.5	1.7	13.0	2.0
36035	Fulton County	11,994	4.3	43.4	17.3	10.2	75.1	14.6	3.1	8.5	1.3
36037	Genesee County	13,088	4.8	65.8	8.3	3.4	88.5	8.2	1.2	10.7	0.8
36043	Herkimer County	14,124	6.5	45.7	33.0	4.5	74.2	21.3	1.9	12.4	3.0
36045	Jefferson County	28,116	8.0	76.5	11.1	5.8	82.0	12.2	3.9	13.3	2.5
36047	Kings County	702,970	5.3	64.9	6.5	4.0	68.2	27.8	2.0	7.7	3.6
36051	Livingston County	15,722	3.9	57.4	25.2	1.3	83.9	14.8	0.3	8.3	1.4
36053	Madison County	17,532	3.8	67.5	16.9	2.2	76.1	21.7	0.4	7.8	1.9
36055	Monroe County	184,671	5.1	54.1	9.6	4.2	74.8	21.0	1.5	9.0	2.5
36059	Nassau County	314,027	4.4	80.1	3.1	1.3	64.9	33.8	0.4	7.9	3.0
36061	New York County	481,626	3.4	73.2	5.6	2.6	58.7	38.8	1.1	3.7	3.5
36063	Niagara County	48,940	5.8	48.6	18.2	7.1	72.4	20.5	2.9	10.3	2.6
36065	Oneida County	52,333	5.4	58.0	18.9	6.6	72.7	20.8	2.3	9.9	2.5
36067	Onondaga County	114,853	5.0	55.9	13.2	4.9	78.9	16.3	1.6	9.5	1.9
36069	Ontario County	24,531	5.5	70.1	12.2	2.7	66.0	31.3	1.0	9.8	3.6
36071	Orange County	89,325	5.4	69.3	11.2	6.4	64.1	29.5	2.2	9.6	3.3

State/county FIPS code	State/County	Total population 15 years and older	Marital status, percent			Male population 15 years and older	Male, marital status, percent			Female population 15 years and older	Female, marital status, percent		
			Never married	Now married (except separated)	Separated, widowed, or divorced		Never married	Now married (except separated)	Separated, widowed, or divorced		Never married	Now married (except separated)	Separated, widowed, or divorced
	New York—cont'd												
36075	Oswego County	99,832	32.8	46.8	20.4	49,561	36.9	46.5	16.6	50,271	28.7	47.2	24.1
36077	Otsego County	53,151	36.0	45.5	18.4	25,589	38.9	46.4	14.7	27,562	33.4	44.7	21.9
36079	Putnam County	81,823	28.1	57.7	14.1	40,630	32.2	58.1	9.8	41,193	24.2	57.4	18.4
36081	Queens County	1,886,898	38.4	44.9	16.8	905,439	41.9	47.4	10.7	981,459	35.0	42.6	22.4
36083	Rensselaer County	132,947	36.5	46.0	17.5	65,145	40.5	46.9	12.5	67,802	32.7	45.0	22.2
36085	Richmond County	383,484	34.0	50.3	15.7	183,235	37.4	53.4	9.2	200,249	30.9	47.5	21.6
36087	Rockland County	244,763	32.7	52.9	14.5	118,334	35.4	54.8	9.7	126,429	30.1	51.0	18.9
36089	St. Lawrence County	92,886	36.4	44.6	19.0	47,048	40.5	45.0	14.6	45,838	32.2	44.2	23.6
36091	Saratoga County	182,635	27.8	53.9	18.3	89,229	30.7	55.3	14.0	93,406	25.0	52.5	22.5
36093	Schenectady County	126,690	34.9	45.6	19.5	60,746	38.3	47.8	13.9	65,944	31.8	43.6	24.6
36101	Steuben County	80,563	25.9	51.6	22.5	39,710	28.5	52.4	19.0	40,853	23.4	50.8	25.8
36103	Suffolk County	1,219,326	32.0	51.7	16.2	594,454	35.7	53.8	10.5	624,872	28.5	49.8	21.7
36105	Sullivan County	63,139	33.2	45.3	21.5	32,099	37.1	45.3	17.6	31,040	29.1	45.3	25.6
36107	Tioga County	41,347	24.8	57.3	17.9	20,272	28.7	59.7	11.7	21,075	21.1	55.0	23.9
36109	Tompkins County	89,613	48.3	38.9	12.8	43,819	52.3	39.8	7.9	45,794	44.4	38.0	17.6
36111	Ulster County	153,644	33.8	46.9	19.3	76,116	37.0	48.3	14.7	77,528	30.6	45.5	23.9
36113	Warren County	55,143	27.7	49.9	22.4	26,670	30.6	53.5	15.9	28,473	25.0	46.5	28.5
36115	Washington County	52,929	29.4	48.7	21.8	27,319	34.3	49.2	16.5	25,610	24.3	48.2	27.5
36117	Wayne County	75,615	26.1	54.3	19.5	37,301	28.5	55.8	15.7	38,314	23.8	52.8	23.3
36119	Westchester County	778,189	33.8	49.8	16.3	369,853	36.1	53.4	10.6	408,336	31.8	46.6	21.6
37000	**North Carolina**	7,842,120	31.0	48.9	20.1	3,776,005	34.1	51.3	14.7	4,066,115	28.1	46.7	25.2
37001	Alamance County	124,385	29.8	48.9	21.3	58,265	31.5	53.5	15.0	66,120	28.4	44.9	26.7
37019	Brunswick County	95,315	19.2	57.9	22.9	45,763	22.0	60.0	18.1	49,552	16.7	55.9	27.4
37021	Buncombe County	203,995	30.6	46.3	23.1	97,169	34.5	49.2	16.3	106,826	27.0	43.7	29.4
37023	Burke County	75,007	29.6	46.8	23.6	37,267	34.9	47.8	17.3	37,740	24.5	45.7	29.8
37025	Cabarrus County	143,056	26.9	54.7	18.4	68,638	29.6	58.0	12.4	74,418	24.4	51.7	23.9
37027	Caldwell County	67,789	23.7	49.2	27.1	33,199	28.8	50.2	21.0	34,590	18.8	48.3	32.9
37031	Carteret County	57,385	23.1	53.5	23.5	27,881	26.9	54.4	18.7	29,504	19.4	52.6	28.0
37035	Catawba County	124,822	27.0	51.6	21.4	60,402	29.7	53.6	16.7	64,420	24.4	49.8	25.9
37037	Chatham County	54,251	22.7	58.1	19.1	26,060	25.3	60.8	13.9	28,191	20.4	55.6	24.0
37045	Cleveland County	79,245	29.4	48.8	21.9	37,551	32.3	51.4	16.3	41,694	26.7	46.4	26.9
37047	Columbus County	46,921	29.3	45.5	25.1	23,055	35.3	45.4	19.3	23,866	23.6	45.6	30.7
37049	Craven County	84,180	26.0	55.1	18.9	42,419	29.8	56.8	13.5	41,761	22.2	53.3	24.5
37051	Cumberland County	251,638	31.7	47.2	21.1	120,902	35.5	49.4	15.1	130,736	28.2	45.2	26.6
37057	Davidson County	132,099	24.5	53.2	22.3	63,902	28.4	55.7	16.0	68,197	20.9	50.9	28.2
37061	Duplin County	47,325	32.0	47.3	20.7	23,148	34.7	48.5	16.8	24,177	29.4	46.2	24.5
37063	Durham County	228,523	39.5	42.5	17.9	108,244	41.6	44.9	13.5	120,279	37.7	40.4	21.9
37065	Edgecombe County	44,860	36.3	39.4	24.3	20,366	37.7	43.1	19.2	24,494	35.1	36.4	28.5
37067	Forsyth County	286,010	34.2	46.5	19.3	133,417	36.0	49.9	14.1	152,593	32.6	43.5	23.9
37069	Franklin County	49,553	28.0	51.1	20.9	24,249	30.8	51.7	17.5	25,304	25.3	50.6	24.2
37071	Gaston County	167,592	27.9	48.7	23.4	80,032	31.2	51.3	17.5	87,560	24.9	46.3	28.8
37077	Granville County	47,429	31.7	46.3	22.0	24,351	34.8	46.3	18.9	23,078	28.4	46.2	25.3
37081	Guilford County	405,161	35.7	45.2	19.1	189,458	37.9	48.9	13.2	215,703	33.8	41.9	24.3
37083	Halifax County	44,061	34.5	39.4	26.1	20,755	38.8	42.7	18.5	23,306	30.6	36.5	32.9
37085	Harnett County	93,488	29.8	50.1	20.2	45,511	33.2	50.6	16.2	47,977	26.5	49.6	23.9
37087	Haywood County	50,063	21.9	54.2	23.9	24,071	25.3	58.0	16.8	25,992	18.7	50.7	30.6
37089	Henderson County	89,911	20.2	59.1	20.7	42,988	23.6	62.4	14.0	46,923	17.1	56.1	26.7
37093	Hoke County	37,550	31.0	50.3	18.6	18,105	34.7	51.0	14.3	19,445	27.6	49.7	22.7
37097	Iredell County	129,981	27.6	54.0	18.4	63,421	30.7	56.3	13.1	66,560	24.7	51.8	23.5
37101	Johnston County	135,377	25.9	53.4	20.6	65,687	29.6	55.6	14.8	69,690	22.5	51.3	26.2
37105	Lee County	46,611	31.2	49.5	19.4	22,660	36.3	49.7	14.0	23,951	26.3	49.2	24.5
37107	Lenoir County	47,873	31.3	41.9	26.8	22,412	34.7	44.4	20.8	25,461	28.3	39.7	32.0
37109	Lincoln County	64,256	23.0	57.3	19.7	31,539	26.3	61.1	12.6	32,717	19.8	53.6	26.6
37119	Mecklenburg County	762,948	37.6	44.8	17.5	362,892	39.5	48.2	12.3	400,056	35.9	41.8	22.3
37125	Moore County	74,068	20.4	57.4	22.2	35,225	24.3	59.6	16.1	38,843	16.9	55.4	27.7
37127	Nash County	77,317	31.7	46.1	22.3	36,825	34.2	48.6	17.2	40,492	29.4	43.8	26.8
37129	New Hanover County	175,067	35.2	45.3	19.5	83,829	37.7	47.3	15.0	91,238	33.0	43.4	23.6
37133	Onslow County	141,182	29.9	53.3	16.8	77,599	37.7	49.8	12.5	63,583	20.5	57.6	22.0
37135	Orange County	114,631	41.2	45.0	13.8	53,920	42.1	48.1	9.8	60,711	40.3	42.3	17.4
37141	Pender County	44,395	26.2	53.5	20.3	22,086	28.5	54.0	17.5	22,309	23.9	53.1	23.0
37147	Pitt County	140,538	43.3	39.5	17.2	64,834	45.0	43.0	11.9	75,704	41.9	36.5	21.6
37151	Randolph County	114,115	24.0	53.6	22.4	55,630	27.3	55.6	17.2	58,485	20.9	51.7	27.4
37155	Robeson County	105,240	38.4	38.7	22.9	50,253	41.8	40.9	17.3	54,987	35.3	36.6	28.1
37157	Rockingham County	76,464	25.4	49.7	25.0	36,395	27.6	53.6	18.8	40,069	23.3	46.1	30.6
37159	Rowan County	111,688	27.9	49.0	23.1	54,564	32.7	50.5	16.8	57,124	23.3	47.6	29.1
37161	Rutherford County	55,232	23.2	52.3	24.5	26,589	26.6	56.0	17.4	28,643	20.1	48.9	31.0
37163	Sampson County	50,616	30.7	46.1	23.1	24,649	34.2	50.4	15.4	25,967	27.4	42.1	30.5
37167	Stanly County	49,499	26.8	51.0	22.2	24,615	30.7	52.1	17.3	24,884	23.0	49.9	27.1
37171	Surry County	59,816	23.3	54.1	22.6	28,932	28.3	55.3	16.4	30,884	18.6	52.9	28.5
37179	Union County	158,094	25.7	59.8	14.5	77,000	28.0	61.3	10.7	81,094	23.5	58.4	18.0
37183	Wake County	747,615	32.9	51.5	15.6	359,946	36.0	53.6	10.4	387,669	30.1	49.5	20.4
37189	Watauga County	46,284	48.0	39.0	13.0	22,901	50.6	39.9	9.5	23,383	45.5	38.1	16.3
37191	Wayne County	98,843	31.7	45.0	23.3	47,872	35.9	47.5	16.6	50,971	27.8	42.6	29.6
37193	Wilkes County	56,931	24.0	54.4	21.6	27,629	27.4	55.2	17.4	29,302	20.8	53.7	25.5
37195	Wilson County	65,232	31.2	45.7	23.0	30,459	34.6	48.5	16.8	34,773	28.3	43.3	28.5

Table C-2: Counties with a Population of 50,000 or More—Marriages and Births—*Continued*

State/county FIPS code	State/County	Total women age 15 to 50 years	Percent of all women who had a birth in the past year	Percent of women who had a birth who were married (including separated and spouse absent):	Percent of women who had a birth who were partners in an unmarried partner household	Age of women who had a birth in the last year as a percent of all women who had a birth			Women who had a birth in the last year as a percent of all women in their age group		
						Age 15 to 19	Age 20 to 34	Age 35 to 50	Age 15 to 19	Age 20 to 34	Age 35 to 50
	New York—cont'd										
36075	Oswego County	29,583	4.5	45.9	23.1	8.7	64.3	27.0	2.2	7.5	2.7
36077	Otsego County	15,180	4.1	69.5	17.9	2.4	76.7	20.9	0.5	7.4	2.4
36079	Putnam County	23,153	2.8	81.7	3.4	0.0	45.0	55.0	0.0	4.2	2.8
36081	Queens County	595,089	5.1	71.1	5.8	2.7	67.7	29.5	1.3	7.8	3.4
36083	Rensselaer County	38,432	3.7	57.5	14.2	9.3	79.6	11.1	2.5	7.2	0.9
36085	Richmond County	116,217	4.6	73.8	8.2	3.8	68.1	28.1	1.3	7.8	2.7
36087	Rockland County	72,054	7.1	81.8	6.4	3.2	66.7	30.1	1.4	12.3	4.6
36089	St. Lawrence County	26,356	5.2	54.7	16.6	7.4	76.4	16.2	2.1	9.6	2.1
36091	Saratoga County	52,107	4.5	74.9	11.1	3.1	67.9	29.0	1.0	8.2	2.6
36093	Schenectady County	36,787	4.9	72.8	4.7	0.2	83.4	16.4	0.1	10.2	1.8
36101	Steuben County	21,691	6.5	55.8	29.8	5.0	79.8	15.2	2.2	13.6	2.1
36103	Suffolk County	357,497	4.6	75.1	7.7	2.1	60.1	37.9	0.7	7.7	3.5
36105	Sullivan County	16,728	5.7	54.8	20.5	8.5	70.1	21.4	3.2	10.6	2.6
36107	Tioga County	10,968	5.9	66.2	12.2	0.0	82.3	17.7	0.0	13.7	2.1
36109	Tompkins County	30,408	4.3	73.8	13.9	2.8	80.6	16.7	0.5	7.1	2.5
36111	Ulster County	41,755	4.5	62.2	18.2	2.5	69.3	28.1	0.8	8.1	2.7
36113	Warren County	14,548	3.2	43.5	23.9	12.6	87.4	0.0	2.9	7.6	0.0
36115	Washington County	13,386	4.6	64.2	6.1	1.8	80.0	18.2	0.6	9.8	1.7
36117	Wayne County	20,534	4.8	71.8	10.4	3.6	81.4	15.0	1.2	10.8	1.5
36119	Westchester County	228,815	5.4	73.7	6.6	3.9	56.4	39.7	1.4	8.5	4.3
37000	**North Carolina**	2,387,385	5.4	63.0	9.4	5.9	74.3	19.9	2.4	9.9	2.4
37001	Alamance County	37,849	4.4	53.0	3.8	2.4	74.4	23.2	0.7	8.4	2.2
37019	Brunswick County	21,233	6.1	63.3	27.0	5.4	86.0	8.5	2.9	13.8	1.0
37021	Buncombe County	57,175	4.0	59.0	12.1	7.2	71.0	21.9	2.6	6.6	1.9
37023	Burke County	19,780	3.8	71.2	8.3	14.5	64.4	21.2	3.9	6.9	1.6
37025	Cabarrus County	46,153	6.1	69.1	4.8	10.4	69.6	20.0	4.9	11.7	2.4
37027	Caldwell County	18,541	5.4	53.4	9.8	16.0	64.2	19.8	6.8	9.8	2.1
37031	Carteret County	14,244	4.3	62.3	4.1	9.6	82.5	8.0	3.2	9.0	0.7
37035	Catawba County	35,961	4.1	82.1	8.9	0.0	73.4	26.6	0.0	8.2	2.2
37037	Chatham County	13,354	7.0	74.7	5.2	1.1	50.9	48.1	0.7	10.5	6.0
37045	Cleveland County	22,608	3.8	67.8	4.7	8.6	72.4	19.0	2.2	7.2	1.5
37047	Columbus County	12,368	6.3	40.6	14.1	17.1	75.6	7.4	6.9	12.3	1.0
37049	Craven County	22,670	7.1	81.5	8.6	1.4	88.5	10.1	0.8	13.1	1.8
37051	Cumberland County	86,023	6.1	71.9	8.4	7.1	80.6	12.3	3.4	10.2	1.9
37057	Davidson County	37,974	5.0	58.5	1.7	13.9	62.2	23.9	5.3	8.7	2.4
37061	Duplin County	13,251	6.7	52.1	8.7	7.7	85.1	7.2	3.9	13.7	1.1
37063	Durham County	0	0.0	0.0	0.0	0.0	0.0	0.0	0.0	0.0	0.0
37065	Edgecombe County	13,340	3.6	33.4	20.5	17.1	69.1	13.8	4.5	6.3	1.1
37067	Forsyth County	89,660	4.6	62.8	12.1	7.2	77.1	15.7	2.3	8.5	1.6
37069	Franklin County	14,163	3.2	73.5	3.6	0.0	84.9	15.1	0.0	7.2	1.0
37071	Gaston County	50,047	5.2	57.4	12.6	7.0	82.4	10.6	2.8	11.2	1.1
37077	Granville County	13,030	8.2	50.5	13.1	3.7	61.1	35.2	2.5	13.9	5.5
37081	Guilford County	131,501	5.6	63.2	12.1	3.0	74.4	22.5	1.2	9.8	2.9
37083	Halifax County	11,892	6.7	34.7	16.8	6.9	83.4	9.7	3.1	14.7	1.4
37085	Harnett County	31,030	5.0	75.2	10.4	3.4	77.1	19.5	1.2	8.9	2.3
37087	Haywood County	12,342	4.6	76.1	4.8	12.7	73.9	13.4	4.6	9.6	1.2
37089	Henderson County	20,925	6.3	87.3	1.2	7.7	64.4	27.9	4.1	10.4	3.5
37093	Hoke County	13,504	5.9	64.9	1.0	13.6	69.7	16.7	5.9	9.2	2.4
37097	Iredell County	38,691	3.9	73.8	8.9	4.1	77.7	18.3	1.2	8.6	1.4
37101	Johnston County	42,696	5.4	58.3	7.9	6.5	83.7	9.8	2.5	12.6	1.0
37105	Lee County	13,577	5.8	57.2	21.1	4.3	91.2	4.5	1.8	13.1	0.6
37107	Lenoir County	13,096	6.9	35.0	27.8	2.9	93.7	3.5	1.2	16.9	0.5
37109	Lincoln County	18,091	5.5	57.1	5.5	2.5	75.6	21.9	1.1	11.9	2.3
37119	Mecklenburg County	267,040	5.4	63.2	7.2	4.4	69.2	26.4	2.1	8.6	3.2
37125	Moore County	18,473	3.8	67.9	4.5	11.2	66.8	22.0	3.1	7.1	1.6
37127	Nash County	21,998	6.6	42.1	9.0	19.4	72.9	7.7	8.4	13.1	1.0
37129	New Hanover County	53,551	5.0	66.0	15.6	6.6	71.0	22.4	2.3	7.7	2.7
37133	Onslow County	44,815	9.6	81.4	12.3	8.0	88.2	3.8	7.4	14.7	1.1
37135	Orange County	40,148	5.4	62.2	13.4	4.4	64.4	31.2	1.3	7.7	4.6
37141	Pender County	12,295	3.7	45.7	0.0	22.3	46.1	31.6	5.3	5.0	2.3
37147	Pitt County	50,933	4.1	45.9	10.7	1.7	85.6	12.7	0.4	7.2	1.5
37151	Randolph County	32,652	4.8	57.4	5.1	1.3	75.9	22.9	0.5	9.8	2.2
37155	Robeson County	33,404	6.5	40.0	7.6	14.3	76.1	9.6	6.1	11.9	1.4
37157	Rockingham County	20,910	5.0	55.2	25.8	1.0	81.5	17.6	0.4	11.5	1.7
37159	Rowan County	31,567	4.2	56.5	13.7	7.2	80.6	12.2	2.2	8.4	1.1
37161	Rutherford County	14,486	6.3	52.0	10.9	10.0	75.4	14.6	4.7	12.6	1.8
37163	Sampson County	14,463	4.8	59.6	4.4	0.7	83.0	16.3	0.2	10.3	1.6
37167	Stanly County	13,331	3.3	32.3	4.6	13.8	83.7	2.5	2.8	7.4	0.2
37171	Surry County	16,061	5.0	61.0	8.1	9.5	76.1	14.4	3.7	11.0	1.4
37179	Union County	51,541	7.4	79.9	2.5	5.7	63.3	31.0	2.6	14.9	4.3
37183	Wake County	258,156	5.0	73.2	9.3	2.2	73.5	24.3	0.9	9.2	2.6
37189	Watauga County	15,273	3.0	55.8	31.7	4.1	73.5	22.4	0.6	4.3	2.6
37191	Wayne County	29,047	5.6	60.8	5.8	2.3	87.2	10.5	1.0	11.5	1.3
37193	Wilkes County	15,039	4.1	32.7	29.6	0.3	96.9	2.8	0.1	10.8	0.2
37195	Wilson County	18,949	6.3	52.2	1.4	6.9	78.3	14.8	3.0	12.5	2.0

State/ county FIPS code	State/County	Total population 15 years and older	Marital status, percent			Male population 15 years and older	Male, marital status, percent			Female population 15 years and older	Female, marital status, percent		
			Never married	Now married (except separated)	Separated, widowed, or divorced		Never married	Now married (except separated)	Separated, widowed, or divorced		Never married	Now married (except separated)	Separated, widowed, or divorced
38000	**North Dakota**............................	571,203	31.6	52.0	16.4	290,486	36.0	51.8	12.2	280,717	27.1	52.2	20.7
38015	Burleigh County............................	69,501	30.7	52.7	16.6	33,979	33.7	54.4	11.9	35,522	27.8	51.0	21.1
38017	Cass County................................	128,233	38.5	47.0	14.5	64,757	41.9	47.1	11.0	63,476	35.1	46.8	18.0
38035	Grand Forks County........................	56,354	41.5	44.3	14.2	29,161	45.9	43.6	10.5	27,193	36.7	45.1	18.2
38101	Ward County................................	52,735	33.3	50.6	16.1	27,702	39.6	48.3	12.1	25,033	26.2	53.2	20.6
39000	**Ohio**..	9,357,346	31.3	48.1	20.6	4,524,839	34.4	50.0	15.6	4,832,507	28.5	46.3	25.2
39003	Allen County................................	84,841	32.8	45.4	21.7	42,615	37.3	46.5	16.2	42,226	28.3	44.4	27.3
39005	Ashland County............................	43,085	27.2	53.9	18.8	20,841	30.3	55.3	14.4	22,244	24.3	52.7	23.0
39007	Ashtabula County..........................	81,667	27.1	47.7	25.2	40,754	30.6	49.5	19.9	40,913	23.5	46.0	30.5
39009	Athens County..............................	56,456	50.2	34.3	15.4	28,157	53.1	34.4	12.6	28,299	47.4	34.3	18.2
39013	Belmont County............................	58,928	26.5	50.6	22.9	29,944	31.5	50.6	17.9	28,984	21.3	50.5	28.1
39017	Butler County	294,972	30.5	50.5	18.9	142,772	33.3	52.3	14.4	152,200	27.9	48.9	23.2
39023	Clark County................................	110,855	27.9	48.9	23.2	53,047	32.0	50.9	17.1	57,808	24.2	47.0	28.8
39025	Clermont County..........................	158,165	26.2	54.4	19.4	77,218	28.9	55.7	15.4	80,947	23.7	53.2	23.1
39029	Columbiana County........................	88,007	25.0	51.7	23.3	43,999	28.3	52.5	19.2	44,008	21.6	51.0	27.4
39035	Cuyahoga County..........................	1,038,802	37.6	40.6	21.8	486,487	40.5	43.6	15.9	552,315	35.0	38.0	27.1
39037	Darke County	41,917	24.2	55.3	20.4	20,399	27.5	56.6	15.8	21,518	21.1	54.1	24.8
39041	Delaware County..........................	138,514	23.1	63.2	13.7	67,583	24.5	64.8	10.8	70,931	21.8	61.7	16.5
39043	Erie County..................................	63,030	27.1	50.9	22.0	30,551	30.1	52.8	17.1	32,479	24.3	49.1	26.6
39045	Fairfield County............................	117,657	26.6	54.7	18.7	58,106	29.2	56.1	14.7	59,551	24.1	53.2	22.7
39049	Franklin County............................	955,748	38.7	42.1	19.2	459,853	41.6	44.1	14.3	495,895	36.0	40.3	23.7
39055	Geauga County............................	75,139	25.4	59.8	14.8	36,437	27.3	62.2	10.5	38,702	23.6	57.5	18.9
39057	Greene County............................	135,040	32.4	50.8	16.8	65,256	34.5	53.5	12.0	69,784	30.4	48.3	21.3
39061	Hamilton County..........................	646,531	37.7	42.4	19.9	306,839	40.3	45.2	14.5	339,692	35.3	39.9	24.7
39063	Hancock County............................	61,124	27.6	52.1	20.3	29,575	30.9	53.6	15.6	31,549	24.5	50.6	24.8
39077	Huron County..............................	46,877	26.1	53.3	20.6	22,935	29.5	54.9	15.6	23,942	22.9	51.7	25.4
39081	Jefferson County..........................	57,505	28.5	49.6	21.9	27,443	31.4	52.2	16.3	30,062	25.9	47.2	26.9
39083	Knox County................................	49,246	27.2	53.5	19.3	23,751	28.8	55.8	15.5	25,495	25.7	51.4	22.9
39085	Lake County................................	189,555	27.9	51.8	20.3	91,579	31.5	53.5	14.9	97,976	24.5	50.2	25.2
39087	Lawrence County..........................	50,474	25.6	49.7	24.7	24,340	29.6	51.9	18.5	26,134	21.8	47.7	30.5
39089	Licking County..............................	134,466	26.1	53.6	20.3	64,978	29.2	54.2	16.5	69,488	23.2	53.0	23.8
39093	Lorain County..............................	244,684	30.4	49.4	20.2	119,210	34.0	51.0	15.0	125,474	27.0	47.8	25.2
39095	Lucas County................................	352,803	36.8	40.9	22.3	168,852	40.4	42.6	17.0	183,951	33.6	39.2	27.2
39099	Mahoning County..........................	195,612	31.6	44.9	23.5	93,827	35.5	47.7	16.8	101,785	28.1	42.4	29.6
39101	Marion County..............................	54,622	27.0	49.9	23.1	29,675	33.4	47.2	19.4	24,947	19.4	53.1	27.5
39103	Medina County............................	139,409	24.3	58.4	17.3	68,194	26.8	59.4	13.8	71,215	22.0	57.4	20.5
39109	Miami County	83,035	24.6	54.1	21.3	40,374	27.9	55.5	16.6	42,661	21.5	52.7	25.7
39113	Montgomery County......................	436,070	32.8	43.4	23.8	206,830	35.9	46.3	17.9	229,240	30.0	40.8	29.2
39119	Muskingum County........................	69,315	28.2	48.5	23.2	33,192	31.9	50.7	17.3	36,123	24.8	46.5	28.6
39129	Pickaway County..........................	45,767	27.0	53.1	19.9	24,286	31.5	51.9	16.6	21,481	21.9	54.4	23.6
39133	Portage County............................	138,022	36.8	46.3	16.9	66,525	38.3	48.1	13.6	71,497	35.4	44.6	19.9
39139	Richland County............................	100,442	28.7	47.1	24.2	50,607	33.8	47.3	18.9	49,835	23.6	46.8	29.6
39141	Ross County................................	63,624	27.4	49.7	22.9	33,567	31.6	47.2	21.2	30,057	22.7	52.4	24.8
39143	Sandusky County..........................	48,581	26.5	51.2	22.3	23,623	30.1	54.1	15.7	24,958	23.0	48.5	28.5
39145	Scioto County..............................	64,222	29.0	47.3	23.7	31,478	34.2	47.9	17.9	32,744	24.0	46.7	29.3
39147	Seneca County..............................	45,489	29.4	50.7	19.8	22,408	32.8	52.1	15.1	23,081	26.1	49.4	24.5
39151	Stark County................................	306,576	28.8	49.7	21.6	146,643	31.6	52.0	16.5	159,933	26.2	47.6	26.2
39153	Summit County............................	443,655	32.6	46.9	20.5	212,221	35.5	49.4	15.0	231,434	29.9	44.7	25.5
39155	Trumbull County..........................	171,415	28.7	48.7	22.6	82,474	31.5	51.6	16.9	88,941	26.2	46.0	27.8
39157	Tuscarawas County........................	74,741	23.3	54.8	21.9	36,274	26.6	57.1	16.3	38,467	20.3	52.6	27.1
39159	Union County..............................	41,499	25.5	55.2	19.3	19,477	25.8	59.8	14.4	22,022	25.2	51.1	23.7
39165	Warren County............................	169,382	23.2	60.8	16.0	84,640	27.3	60.5	12.2	84,742	19.1	61.1	19.8
39167	Washington County........................	51,322	24.8	52.9	22.4	24,882	28.8	53.5	17.7	26,440	21.0	52.3	26.7
39169	Wayne County..............................	91,070	26.9	55.8	17.3	44,557	29.9	57.4	12.7	46,513	23.9	54.3	21.8
39173	Wood County..............................	106,488	35.8	47.8	16.4	51,730	38.0	49.9	12.1	54,758	33.7	45.9	20.4
40000	**Oklahoma**	3,027,585	27.3	50.6	22.0	1,486,092	30.8	52.0	17.1	1,541,493	24.0	49.3	26.7
40017	Canadian County..........................	95,424	23.5	56.4	20.1	47,137	26.8	56.9	16.3	48,287	20.3	55.8	23.9
40027	Cleveland County..........................	214,843	32.5	49.5	18.0	106,549	36.1	50.1	13.8	108,294	28.9	48.9	22.2
40031	Comanche County........................	99,469	30.7	46.1	23.2	51,743	36.5	46.3	17.2	47,726	24.5	45.8	29.8
40037	Creek County..............................	56,367	22.7	55.3	22.0	27,611	25.4	56.3	18.3	28,756	20.0	54.4	25.5
40047	Garfield County............................	48,057	21.8	55.6	22.6	23,740	26.7	56.4	16.9	24,317	17.0	54.9	28.1
40051	Grady County..............................	42,345	21.8	56.8	21.3	20,674	24.9	59.2	15.9	21,671	18.9	54.6	26.5
40101	Muskogee County........................	55,950	25.6	49.7	24.7	27,009	29.7	50.9	19.5	28,941	21.8	48.5	29.7
40109	Oklahoma County..........................	581,401	31.7	46.4	21.9	281,038	34.9	48.1	17.0	300,363	28.7	44.7	26.6
40119	Payne County..............................	65,442	43.4	42.0	14.6	33,422	46.7	41.9	11.4	32,020	40.0	42.1	17.9
40125	Pottawatomie County......................	56,243	24.7	52.3	23.0	26,359	26.9	55.6	17.5	29,884	22.8	49.4	27.8
40131	Rogers County..............................	70,306	21.5	60.0	18.5	34,623	24.5	61.1	14.4	35,683	18.6	58.9	22.4
40143	Tulsa County................................	482,898	29.6	48.4	22.0	232,076	32.7	50.8	16.5	250,822	26.7	46.2	27.1
40145	Wagoner County..........................	58,908	23.0	57.0	20.0	28,949	26.2	57.4	16.5	29,959	20.0	56.7	23.4
40147	Washington County........................	41,423	22.2	55.1	22.7	19,466	25.6	58.8	15.6	21,957	19.1	51.8	29.1
41000	**Oregon**....................................	3,186,598	30.0	49.5	20.5	1,564,755	33.4	50.9	15.7	1,621,843	26.8	48.1	25.1
41003	Benton County	74,251	41.8	43.5	14.7	37,374	45.1	43.8	11.1	36,877	38.5	43.1	18.4
41005	Clackamas County........................	313,163	25.7	54.8	19.5	153,113	28.9	56.5	14.6	160,050	22.6	53.1	24.2

Table C-2: Counties with a Population of 50,000 or More—Marriages and Births—Continued

State/ county FIPS code	State/County	Total women age 15 to 50 years	Percent of all women who had a birth in the past year	Percent of women who had a birth who were married (including separated and spouse absent):	Percent of women who had a birth who were partners in an unmarried partner household	Age of women who had a birth in the last year as a percent of all women who had a birth			Women who had a birth in the last year as a percent of all women in their age group		
						Age 15 to 19	Age 20 to 34	Age 35 to 50	Age 15 to 19	Age 20 to 34	Age 35 to 50
38000	**North Dakota**	161,588	6.6	68.3	14.0	5.0	81.3	13.7	2.3	11.4	2.3
38015	Burleigh County	20,399	5.8	62.8	14.8	0.0	85.0	15.0	0.0	10.4	2.2
38017	Cass County	42,236	6.2	75.9	5.5	3.1	80.0	16.9	1.5	9.6	3.0
38035	Grand Forks County	17,810	5.6	62.7	23.5	9.8	83.5	6.7	3.4	8.6	1.2
38101	Ward County	15,221	7.2	76.3	14.7	6.6	79.5	14.0	3.9	10.7	2.9
39000	**Ohio**	2,710,248	5.3	59.5	11.6	5.4	77.3	17.3	2.0	10.0	2.0
39003	Allen County	23,036	6.4	44.0	14.6	12.7	76.9	10.4	5.6	12.0	1.5
39005	Ashland County	12,153	6.1	79.6	1.8	7.6	75.5	16.9	2.8	11.5	2.4
39007	Ashtabula County	21,404	6.6	47.9	26.4	8.1	76.4	15.4	3.6	13.6	2.1
39009	Athens County	19,667	2.1	47.4	22.2	6.0	84.0	10.0	0.6	3.5	0.8
39013	Belmont County	13,944	2.9	60.0	17.0	9.8	61.5	28.8	2.2	4.5	1.7
39017	Butler County	91,508	5.7	59.4	11.3	6.3	77.1	16.6	2.3	10.7	2.2
39023	Clark County	30,619	4.5	42.9	17.1	5.3	85.4	9.3	1.6	9.7	0.9
39025	Clermont County	46,450	5.3	78.2	6.9	4.4	75.2	20.5	1.7	10.6	2.2
39029	Columbiana County	22,468	7.8	54.8	13.9	6.2	75.8	17.9	3.5	15.5	2.9
39035	Cuyahoga County	299,946	4.8	51.5	11.4	6.5	73.4	20.2	2.3	8.6	2.2
39037	Darke County	10,978	6.2	72.2	6.0	3.5	83.6	12.9	1.5	13.5	1.7
39041	Delaware County	44,417	5.2	84.1	5.4	0.0	65.8	34.2	0.0	10.8	3.3
39043	Erie County	16,447	5.2	54.4	17.5	3.1	88.2	8.6	1.2	11.6	1.0
39045	Fairfield County	34,721	5.2	73.3	12.3	5.4	79.1	15.5	2.0	11.8	1.6
39049	Franklin County	0	0.0	0.0	0.0	0.0	0.0	0.0	0.0	0.0	0.0
39055	Geauga County	19,542	5.3	84.8	12.1	3.5	70.1	26.4	1.0	11.9	2.8
39057	Greene County	40,441	4.9	72.9	10.8	3.3	76.2	20.5	1.0	8.7	2.5
39061	Hamilton County	195,972	5.6	54.9	7.5	4.6	80.7	14.7	1.9	10.1	1.9
39063	Hancock County	17,766	5.0	60.3	24.3	10.4	69.2	20.4	3.6	8.0	2.4
39077	Huron County	13,407	4.2	64.0	16.6	0.0	94.9	5.1	0.0	10.5	0.5
39081	Jefferson County	14,893	4.8	57.9	16.5	10.5	72.6	16.9	3.2	8.7	1.8
39083	Knox County	14,166	5.1	83.9	14.0	1.8	85.5	12.7	0.5	10.3	1.6
39085	Lake County	50,514	4.0	62.1	14.3	1.7	79.3	19.0	0.5	8.6	1.6
39087	Lawrence County	14,011	5.2	79.3	5.8	4.0	94.9	1.1	1.6	12.6	0.1
39089	Licking County	39,106	5.7	72.8	4.4	3.1	71.4	25.5	1.2	10.5	3.1
39093	Lorain County	67,686	4.7	48.0	14.8	7.8	76.8	15.4	2.4	9.6	1.5
39095	Lucas County	105,978	5.0	52.3	12.5	4.1	82.0	13.9	1.5	9.5	1.6
39099	Mahoning County	50,386	4.5	47.0	10.0	8.3	73.3	18.4	2.5	8.4	1.8
39101	Marion County	13,072	6.2	41.8	28.0	17.6	71.3	11.0	8.1	11.0	1.5
39103	Medina County	40,038	5.0	76.9	10.8	3.6	72.2	24.2	1.3	10.9	2.3
39109	Miami County	22,714	3.8	79.7	7.9	0.1	74.9	25.0	0.0	7.7	2.0
39113	Montgomery County	125,978	5.2	48.9	14.0	5.9	81.8	12.3	2.2	10.0	1.5
39119	Muskingum County	19,757	4.6	53.4	25.4	5.6	88.1	6.3	1.7	10.4	0.6
39129	Pickaway County	12,353	5.4	91.4	6.2	5.6	80.5	13.8	2.0	12.3	1.5
39133	Portage County	43,724	4.2	54.3	15.8	6.2	74.8	18.9	1.4	7.1	2.2
39139	Richland County	25,617	5.7	55.9	14.6	10.9	80.8	8.3	4.5	11.7	1.0
39141	Ross County	16,210	5.2	62.7	5.6	11.4	74.9	13.7	4.1	10.1	1.5
39143	Sandusky County	13,054	5.7	60.5	10.0	4.3	85.3	10.4	1.7	12.2	1.3
39145	Scioto County	17,831	5.6	38.0	2.9	6.7	75.1	18.2	2.5	10.5	2.3
39147	Seneca County	12,595	4.0	72.4	21.5	3.0	87.5	9.5	0.7	8.6	0.9
39151	Stark County	84,357	5.6	54.3	12.8	2.9	86.1	11.0	1.1	12.0	1.3
39153	Summit County	126,811	5.1	56.3	10.0	5.5	78.6	15.9	2.0	9.9	1.8
39155	Trumbull County	44,339	3.8	51.0	12.6	11.8	68.8	19.4	3.1	6.8	1.5
39157	Tuscarawas County	20,129	3.9	71.0	8.2	2.2	80.1	17.7	0.6	7.9	1.5
39159	Union County	14,294	4.4	74.3	2.7	7.7	70.3	22.0	2.7	7.9	2.0
39165	Warren County	50,965	4.6	73.7	16.4	3.4	80.2	16.4	1.1	10.9	1.4
39167	Washington County	13,384	4.9	73.5	6.7	5.3	92.7	2.0	1.8	11.8	0.2
39169	Wayne County	25,627	6.3	72.5	13.3	3.0	76.2	20.8	1.1	12.2	3.0
39173	Wood County	33,566	4.2	74.6	4.3	5.3	67.9	26.8	1.2	6.5	3.1
40000	**Oklahoma**	898,579	6.0	63.8	11.8	7.0	80.4	12.6	3.0	10.9	1.8
40017	Canadian County	29,684	6.3	70.0	15.0	1.9	82.5	15.6	0.9	12.9	2.2
40027	Cleveland County	69,545	4.9	82.7	2.3	4.0	80.9	15.2	1.4	8.2	2.0
40031	Comanche County	30,712	6.6	61.5	8.7	6.4	86.3	7.2	3.2	11.9	1.2
40037	Creek County	15,438	5.2	65.8	4.0	8.6	80.7	10.7	3.1	10.6	1.2
40047	Garfield County	13,213	5.8	65.7	17.2	7.5	88.3	4.2	3.5	10.9	0.6
40051	Grady County	12,446	4.7	76.6	7.2	4.4	77.1	18.4	1.4	9.2	1.9
40101	Muskogee County	16,070	6.9	49.0	10.2	13.7	79.8	6.6	6.5	13.0	1.1
40109	Oklahoma County	183,124	6.6	63.3	11.2	7.0	80.1	12.9	3.8	11.3	2.1
40119	Payne County	22,213	5.7	48.7	41.2	10.9	76.2	12.9	3.4	7.8	2.7
40125	Pottawatomie County	17,262	6.3	61.1	9.9	6.8	83.9	9.3	2.9	12.3	1.4
40131	Rogers County	20,812	5.4	61.6	13.4	8.2	72.6	19.2	2.9	10.4	2.2
40143	Tulsa County	151,048	5.9	63.5	12.2	6.4	79.6	14.0	2.9	10.6	1.9
40145	Wagoner County	17,339	4.8	70.6	11.0	2.6	74.1	23.3	0.9	9.1	2.4
40147	Washington County	11,142	6.5	68.6	19.9	1.4	89.5	9.1	0.6	14.0	1.4
41000	**Oregon**	919,777	5.0	68.1	11.9	3.8	74.8	21.5	1.5	8.8	2.4
41003	Benton County	22,846	3.4	69.7	5.1	4.4	78.3	17.3	0.8	5.2	1.8
41005	Clackamas County	87,007	4.5	80.2	5.8	1.8	75.6	22.6	0.6	9.2	2.1

State/county FIPS code	State/County	Total population 15 years and older	Marital status, percent			Male population 15 years and older	Male, marital status, percent			Female population 15 years and older	Female, marital status, percent		
			Never married	Now married (except separated)	Separated, widowed, or divorced		Never married	Now married (except separated)	Separated, widowed, or divorced		Never married	Now married (except separated)	Separated, widowed, or divorced
	Oregon—cont'd												
41011	Coos County	53,069	23.1	49.3	27.7	26,062	26.5	51.0	22.5	27,007	19.8	47.5	32.7
41017	Deschutes County	132,615	24.6	54.1	21.3	64,987	27.6	55.4	17.0	67,628	21.7	53.0	25.4
41019	Douglas County	89,921	21.7	52.8	25.5	44,063	24.6	54.1	21.3	45,858	19.0	51.5	29.5
41029	Jackson County	170,026	26.4	50.6	23.0	82,343	29.2	53.6	17.2	87,683	23.9	47.7	28.4
41033	Josephine County	69,540	23.2	51.8	25.0	33,584	27.3	53.7	19.0	35,956	19.3	50.1	30.6
41035	Klamath County	54,308	24.3	52.7	23.0	26,876	27.2	52.9	19.9	27,432	21.5	52.5	26.0
41039	Lane County	298,345	33.3	45.1	21.5	145,224	37.4	46.4	16.1	153,121	29.4	43.9	26.6
41043	Linn County	95,096	25.7	53.7	20.6	46,670	28.5	55.7	15.7	48,426	23.0	51.7	25.3
41047	Marion County	251,822	30.2	49.6	20.2	124,334	33.5	50.9	15.6	127,488	27.1	48.4	24.6
41051	Multnomah County	628,554	38.9	41.8	19.3	308,569	42.1	43.1	14.8	319,985	35.8	40.6	23.6
41053	Polk County	61,461	30.2	51.6	18.2	29,212	32.1	54.3	13.6	32,249	28.5	49.2	22.3
41059	Umatilla County	59,909	29.6	49.6	20.8	31,461	34.5	48.0	17.5	28,448	24.3	51.3	24.5
41067	Washington County	433,016	29.5	52.7	17.9	210,892	32.8	54.3	12.8	222,124	26.3	51.1	22.7
41071	Yamhill County	80,485	28.6	52.2	19.2	40,000	32.0	53.7	14.4	40,485	25.3	50.8	24.0
42000	**Pennsylvania**	10,514,479	33.3	48.0	18.8	5,082,914	36.4	50.1	13.5	5,431,565	30.4	46.0	23.6
42001	Adams County	83,971	27.2	55.4	17.3	41,141	29.7	57.2	13.1	42,830	24.9	53.8	21.4
42003	Allegheny County	1,034,657	35.7	44.9	19.3	491,141	39.2	47.5	13.3	543,516	32.7	42.6	24.7
42005	Armstrong County	57,404	24.1	53.6	22.2	28,353	28.2	55.1	16.7	29,051	20.2	52.2	27.6
42007	Beaver County	142,495	27.1	51.2	21.7	68,017	29.6	54.2	16.1	74,478	24.7	48.4	26.9
42011	Berks County	334,186	31.2	49.6	19.2	162,594	33.9	51.7	14.4	171,592	28.6	47.5	23.8
42013	Blair County	104,948	28.0	50.0	22.0	50,375	31.3	52.3	16.4	54,573	25.0	47.9	27.1
42015	Bradford County	51,216	25.5	53.5	21.0	25,179	29.0	54.9	16.1	26,037	22.1	52.2	25.7
42017	Bucks County	514,910	28.1	55.1	16.8	249,984	31.6	57.0	11.4	264,926	24.8	53.4	21.8
42019	Butler County	153,083	27.1	55.5	17.4	75,146	30.1	56.6	13.3	77,937	24.2	54.5	21.3
42021	Cambria County	119,041	30.3	48.3	21.5	58,677	34.5	49.9	15.5	60,364	26.1	46.6	27.2
42025	Carbon County	54,231	26.4	52.5	21.1	26,721	29.8	54.8	15.4	27,510	23.2	50.2	26.6
42027	Centre County	135,180	46.6	41.1	12.4	70,397	50.2	40.5	9.3	64,783	42.6	41.8	15.6
42029	Chester County	406,458	29.1	55.8	15.2	197,792	31.5	57.9	10.7	208,666	26.8	53.7	19.5
42033	Clearfield County	68,654	26.9	52.3	20.9	35,673	31.7	51.7	16.7	32,981	21.7	52.9	25.4
42037	Columbia County	56,944	33.3	48.1	18.6	26,956	35.8	50.6	13.7	29,988	31.1	45.8	23.1
42039	Crawford County	72,066	26.8	52.4	20.8	34,633	29.4	54.8	15.8	37,433	24.4	50.1	25.5
42041	Cumberland County	198,859	29.7	52.4	17.9	97,070	32.8	53.9	13.2	101,789	26.7	50.9	22.4
42043	Dauphin County	219,649	33.5	48.0	18.4	105,099	36.6	50.3	13.1	114,550	30.7	46.0	23.3
42045	Delaware County	456,189	36.2	45.9	17.9	215,790	38.7	49.1	12.2	240,399	33.9	42.9	23.1
42049	Erie County	229,567	34.7	46.6	18.8	111,875	37.6	48.7	13.7	117,692	31.9	44.5	23.6
42051	Fayette County	113,800	29.5	48.0	22.4	55,713	34.5	48.7	16.8	58,087	24.8	47.4	27.8
42055	Franklin County	122,040	25.5	54.8	19.7	59,150	27.7	58.2	14.1	62,890	23.4	51.6	25.0
42063	Indiana County	74,716	35.2	47.6	17.1	37,122	38.2	48.5	13.3	37,594	32.3	46.8	20.9
42069	Lackawanna County	178,870	33.1	46.3	20.5	85,382	35.3	49.6	15.1	93,488	31.2	43.3	25.5
42071	Lancaster County	419,972	29.0	55.3	15.7	202,765	31.6	57.5	11.0	217,207	26.6	53.3	20.1
42073	Lawrence County	74,743	27.8	50.8	21.4	35,710	31.7	53.4	14.9	39,033	24.2	48.5	27.3
42075	Lebanon County	109,387	27.5	52.1	20.5	52,807	30.6	54.8	14.6	56,580	24.5	49.5	26.0
42077	Lehigh County	287,128	32.7	48.4	19.0	137,949	35.5	50.6	13.9	149,179	30.1	46.3	23.6
42079	Luzerne County	269,100	33.0	46.1	20.9	131,311	37.3	48.1	14.6	137,789	28.8	44.2	27.0
42081	Lycoming County	97,034	30.3	48.3	21.4	47,348	34.3	49.5	16.1	49,686	26.4	47.1	26.5
42085	Mercer County	96,457	28.5	50.0	21.5	47,273	32.5	51.1	16.4	49,184	24.6	48.9	26.5
42089	Monroe County	138,895	33.1	49.8	17.1	68,081	36.4	51.6	12.0	70,814	29.8	48.1	22.1
42091	Montgomery County	660,227	30.0	53.9	16.1	316,788	32.8	56.5	10.7	343,439	27.4	51.4	21.2
42095	Northampton County	247,615	30.3	51.5	18.1	119,984	34.3	53.5	12.2	127,631	26.6	49.7	23.7
42097	Northumberland County	79,085	27.9	51.6	20.5	39,901	33.7	51.2	15.1	39,184	22.0	52.0	26.0
42101	Philadelphia County	1,257,813	52.2	28.7	19.1	583,308	54.8	31.6	13.7	674,505	50.1	26.2	23.7
42103	Pike County	47,589	27.0	54.9	18.2	23,568	30.5	55.4	14.1	24,021	23.5	54.3	22.2
42107	Schuylkill County	123,536	29.3	48.9	21.8	62,736	34.7	48.6	16.7	60,800	23.7	49.1	27.1
42111	Somerset County	65,330	25.2	55.0	19.8	33,967	30.8	53.5	15.8	31,363	19.2	56.6	24.2
42121	Venango County	45,169	25.7	53.0	21.3	22,020	29.1	55.4	15.4	23,149	22.4	50.6	26.9
42125	Washington County	174,126	27.5	51.8	20.7	84,130	30.2	54.6	15.2	89,996	25.0	49.1	25.8
42127	Wayne County	44,363	26.2	52.9	20.8	23,574	31.2	50.9	17.9	20,789	20.6	55.2	24.2
42129	Westmoreland County	306,784	26.4	53.0	20.5	148,383	29.9	55.5	14.6	158,401	23.2	50.7	26.1
42133	York County	355,540	28.1	52.6	19.3	173,776	30.9	54.3	14.8	181,764	25.5	51.0	23.6
44000	**Rhode Island**	873,678	35.7	44.7	19.6	417,748	39.0	47.4	13.7	455,930	32.6	42.3	25.1
44003	Kent County	138,507	29.2	49.7	21.2	65,885	32.6	52.6	14.8	72,622	26.0	47.1	26.9
44005	Newport County	69,539	30.2	50.5	19.3	33,639	32.8	53.5	13.7	35,900	27.8	47.6	24.6
44007	Providence County	517,263	39.6	40.5	19.9	247,195	43.0	43.1	13.8	270,068	36.4	38.2	25.4
44009	Washington County	107,254	31.2	51.5	17.3	51,526	33.8	54.0	12.2	55,728	28.8	49.1	22.1
45000	**South Carolina**	3,824,255	31.8	47.3	21.0	1,839,923	34.7	49.6	15.7	1,984,332	29.0	45.1	25.8
45003	Aiken County	132,613	28.9	49.3	21.9	63,128	31.5	52.7	15.8	69,485	26.5	46.2	27.4
45007	Anderson County	152,535	26.1	51.8	22.1	72,747	28.2	54.6	17.2	79,788	24.1	49.3	26.6
45013	Beaufort County	138,760	26.0	53.3	20.7	68,090	30.1	55.1	14.8	70,670	22.0	51.6	26.4
45015	Berkeley County	149,895	30.0	50.8	19.2	74,386	33.5	52.1	14.3	75,509	26.5	49.5	24.0
45019	Charleston County	301,473	37.8	41.2	21.0	144,696	40.8	43.1	16.1	156,777	35.0	39.5	25.5
45021	Cherokee County	44,571	30.1	49.0	20.9	21,282	33.2	50.2	16.6	23,289	27.2	47.9	24.8
45031	Darlington County	54,924	33.1	45.3	21.6	25,560	34.8	49.6	15.7	29,364	31.6	41.6	26.8
45035	Dorchester County	111,417	27.7	52.2	20.1	53,965	31.1	54.1	14.8	57,452	24.6	50.4	25.0

State/ county FIPS code	State/County	Total women age 15 to 50 years	Percent of all women who had a birth in the past year	Percent of women who had a birth who were married (including separated and spouse absent):	Percent of women who had a birth who were partners in an unmarried partner household	Age of women who had a birth in the last year as a percent of all women who had a birth			Women who had a birth in the last year as a percent of all women in their age group		
						Age 15 to 19	Age 20 to 34	Age 35 to 50	Age 15 to 19	Age 20 to 34	Age 35 to 50
	Oregon—cont'd										
41011	Coos County	11,839	6.3	64.2	1.9	5.2	91.5	3.3	2.4	14.1	0.5
41017	Deschutes County	36,225	4.6	69.3	4.5	3.5	64.1	32.4	1.3	7.5	3.1
41019	Douglas County	21,090	5.3	61.6	13.6	10.4	68.1	21.5	4.0	9.0	2.4
41029	Jackson County	44,231	4.2	53.0	27.4	4.6	82.9	12.5	1.4	8.2	1.2
41033	Josephine County	15,907	5.9	78.2	19.9	0.0	89.1	10.9	0.0	13.5	1.4
41035	Klamath County	14,135	7.9	45.2	23.4	0.0	81.2	18.8	0.0	15.9	3.3
41039	Lane County	84,737	4.4	62.9	11.4	0.6	82.6	16.8	0.2	7.9	1.9
41043	Linn County	26,388	4.3	76.8	2.8	0.6	77.1	22.3	0.2	7.9	2.2
41047	Marion County	74,514	6.0	55.3	19.0	13.1	65.2	21.7	5.2	9.0	3.1
41051	Multnomah County	204,402	4.6	72.5	8.5	2.5	69.0	28.5	1.2	6.6	3.1
41053	Polk County	18,770	4.8	71.1	13.7	8.7	83.2	8.1	2.1	10.0	0.9
41059	Umatilla County	16,510	6.7	72.8	11.8	8.1	75.9	16.0	3.4	12.5	2.5
41067	Washington County	139,983	5.7	71.4	11.5	1.1	72.8	26.1	0.5	9.9	3.2
41071	Yamhill County	23,444	4.4	90.2	0.5	4.0	80.1	16.0	1.1	8.8	1.6
42000	**Pennsylvania**	2,981,873	4.9	60.8	11.2	5.6	73.8	20.6	1.9	8.8	2.2
42001	Adams County	22,854	4.5	71.4	6.5	10.1	72.3	17.6	2.8	8.8	1.7
42003	Allegheny County	289,577	4.8	64.1	11.2	3.8	73.8	22.3	1.4	8.0	2.5
42005	Armstrong County	14,109	3.7	52.4	26.1	9.1	80.3	10.6	2.5	8.2	0.8
42007	Beaver County	36,343	4.6	62.8	6.8	10.3	75.9	13.8	3.4	9.0	1.3
42011	Berks County	97,776	5.4	59.2	11.6	4.7	79.1	16.1	1.7	11.1	1.9
42013	Blair County	28,059	4.3	62.3	16.7	6.4	71.5	22.1	2.1	7.7	2.1
42015	Bradford County	12,989	5.1	50.2	20.3	5.6	74.5	19.8	1.9	10.3	2.1
42017	Bucks County	142,668	4.6	77.1	6.2	1.4	68.3	30.4	0.4	8.9	2.8
42019	Butler County	42,101	4.4	74.7	9.1	7.2	63.6	29.3	2.1	7.9	2.6
42021	Cambria County	29,294	4.8	56.1	20.3	7.7	77.1	15.1	2.5	9.5	1.6
42025	Carbon County	13,703	3.1	38.3	20.9	0.0	86.3	13.7	0.0	7.2	0.9
42027	Centre County	43,139	3.7	64.9	18.7	3.8	76.3	19.9	0.7	5.4	2.5
42029	Chester County	119,118	4.9	76.5	9.0	3.1	71.0	25.8	1.0	9.6	2.6
42033	Clearfield County	16,642	4.8	56.3	12.9	7.8	72.8	19.4	2.8	9.7	1.9
42037	Columbia County	17,116	3.6	61.0	28.5	5.4	86.7	8.0	1.0	7.3	0.7
42039	Crawford County	19,902	6.0	76.3	13.1	3.2	80.3	16.5	1.2	12.7	2.2
42041	Cumberland County	55,903	4.7	69.9	11.3	3.0	83.8	13.2	0.9	9.8	1.4
42043	Dauphin County	63,867	5.6	52.4	15.5	8.1	71.5	20.4	3.6	9.4	2.5
42045	Delaware County	135,586	5.2	59.5	7.9	3.6	69.0	27.4	1.2	8.9	3.2
42049	Erie County	65,841	4.1	47.0	10.4	2.9	75.7	21.4	0.8	7.3	2.1
42051	Fayette County	29,158	4.5	52.4	16.4	8.3	79.6	12.1	2.9	9.5	1.1
42055	Franklin County	34,015	4.9	78.2	9.6	0.0	63.7	36.3	0.0	8.1	3.8
42063	Indiana County	21,056	4.2	73.1	10.3	7.5	69.3	23.2	1.6	6.7	2.6
42069	Lackawanna County	49,243	4.1	64.2	14.1	7.7	69.1	23.2	2.2	6.9	2.1
42071	Lancaster County	121,369	6.5	70.4	8.3	5.1	79.1	15.8	2.2	12.5	2.3
42073	Lawrence County	19,119	4.0	63.5	8.6	8.7	73.1	18.2	2.4	7.9	1.5
42075	Lebanon County	29,825	5.9	63.7	12.7	4.4	88.5	7.1	1.8	13.2	0.9
42077	Lehigh County	84,335	5.1	55.4	13.1	6.2	76.6	17.2	2.2	9.8	1.9
42079	Luzerne County	71,051	4.9	45.4	16.4	5.4	82.3	12.2	1.9	10.1	1.3
42081	Lycoming County	26,386	5.4	55.0	19.1	2.0	78.7	19.3	0.8	10.1	2.3
42085	Mercer County	24,554	5.2	57.0	13.8	4.1	80.3	15.5	1.4	10.8	1.7
42089	Monroe County	40,397	3.5	60.7	7.9	0.0	77.1	22.9	0.0	7.9	1.7
42091	Montgomery County	188,887	4.4	84.8	5.0	1.3	65.4	33.4	0.4	7.6	3.0
42095	Northampton County	68,974	4.6	65.9	14.2	2.1	72.7	25.1	0.6	8.8	2.4
42097	Northumberland County	19,235	5.2	58.0	24.9	4.4	86.3	9.3	1.9	11.5	1.0
42101	Philadelphia County	423,500	5.3	38.1	9.8	12.2	68.8	18.9	5.2	7.3	2.7
42103	Pike County	12,117	6.2	72.4	6.0	0.0	88.4	11.6	0.0	18.2	1.4
42107	Schuylkill County	30,325	4.7	59.7	20.4	3.1	70.5	26.4	1.1	9.0	2.5
42111	Somerset County	15,020	5.6	70.9	18.7	4.0	84.3	11.8	1.7	12.8	1.3
42121	Venango County	11,134	4.8	52.7	30.6	7.2	80.9	11.9	2.5	10.1	1.2
42125	Washington County	45,305	5.0	67.5	7.6	2.8	80.2	17.0	1.0	10.8	1.8
42127	Wayne County	9,634	3.3	68.5	11.2	2.2	73.5	24.3	0.5	7.3	1.6
42129	Westmoreland County	76,135	3.6	68.8	9.7	2.0	80.5	17.5	0.5	7.9	1.2
42133	York County	102,200	4.7	57.4	14.3	7.4	79.5	13.1	2.6	9.9	1.3
44000	**Rhode Island**	258,792	4.6	56.0	14.2	6.2	74.0	19.8	1.9	8.2	2.1
44003	Kent County	37,534	4.4	62.6	11.3	7.9	82.6	9.5	2.8	9.5	0.9
44005	Newport County	18,426	3.9	74.3	10.5	3.9	72.6	23.5	1.0	7.5	1.9
44007	Providence County	161,485	4.9	50.0	16.2	6.8	75.3	17.9	2.4	8.5	2.1
44009	Washington County	30,189	3.3	73.9	9.0	0.0	68.5	31.5	0.0	6.3	2.3
45000	**South Carolina**	1,134,527	5.5	54.6	8.6	6.5	76.6	17.0	2.6	10.0	2.1
45003	Aiken County	37,510	4.5	69.2	0.9	10.6	75.3	14.1	3.4	8.2	1.4
45007	Anderson County	43,732	5.9	61.9	6.7	4.5	75.1	20.4	1.9	11.5	2.6
45013	Beaufort County	34,128	6.9	80.5	5.3	1.6	85.6	12.8	0.9	13.4	2.1
45015	Berkeley County	46,941	5.5	60.5	7.4	9.6	78.1	12.4	4.2	10.0	1.5
45019	Charleston County	92,946	4.6	54.7	4.0	7.3	77.1	15.6	2.9	7.1	1.8
45021	Cherokee County	13,549	9.3	35.3	13.3	16.4	74.9	8.7	11.1	17.4	1.7
45031	Darlington County	16,046	6.5	39.5	27.4	12.6	69.5	17.9	5.8	11.9	2.4
45035	Dorchester County	36,188	5.1	70.3	8.3	1.4	77.9	20.7	0.5	9.9	2.2

State/ county FIPS code	State/County	Total population 15 years and older	Marital status, percent			Male population 15 years and older	Male, marital status, percent			Female population 15 years and older	Female, marital status, percent		
			Never married	Now married (except separated)	Separated, widowed, or divorced		Never married	Now married (except separated)	Separated, widowed, or divorced		Never married	Now married (except separated)	Separated, widowed, or divorced
	South Carolina—cont'd												
45041	Florence County.........................	109,747	33.3	45.3	21.5	50,390	35.4	49.8	14.8	59,357	31.5	41.4	27.1
45043	Georgetown County..................	50,149	28.9	49.2	21.9	23,533	31.0	53.3	15.7	26,616	27.1	45.5	27.4
45045	Greenville County	373,623	30.4	50.4	19.2	179,408	32.4	53.6	14.0	194,215	28.4	47.5	24.1
45047	Greenwood County..................	56,255	32.7	45.1	22.2	25,804	31.9	49.7	18.4	30,451	33.3	41.3	25.5
45051	Horry County.............................	235,760	28.6	49.5	21.9	114,008	32.1	51.4	16.4	121,752	25.2	47.7	27.1
45055	Kershaw County........................	49,783	27.8	49.6	22.6	23,581	31.7	53.3	15.0	26,202	24.3	46.2	29.5
45057	Lancaster County......................	64,160	28.8	47.2	24.0	31,320	32.2	49.0	18.8	32,840	25.5	45.6	28.9
45059	Laurens County.........................	53,638	31.8	46.0	22.3	25,608	33.5	48.4	18.2	28,030	30.2	43.8	26.1
45063	Lexington County......................	216,434	27.5	52.0	20.5	104,366	31.1	53.6	15.3	112,068	24.1	50.6	25.3
45073	Oconee County..........................	61,839	24.5	53.0	22.5	30,131	28.2	54.7	17.1	31,708	20.9	51.4	27.7
45075	Orangeburg County..................	74,095	38.2	38.5	23.2	34,036	39.4	43.1	17.6	40,059	37.3	34.7	28.1
45077	Pickens County..........................	99,913	35.5	47.3	17.3	49,418	38.9	48.4	12.7	50,495	32.1	46.2	21.7
45079	Richland County	321,331	42.4	38.9	18.7	154,967	46.0	40.7	13.3	166,364	39.0	37.2	23.8
45083	Spartanburg County..................	231,290	29.9	48.7	21.4	110,789	32.8	51.1	16.1	120,501	27.3	46.5	26.2
45085	Sumter County...........................	85,243	33.0	44.8	22.2	40,740	35.9	47.8	16.3	44,503	30.4	42.1	27.5
45091	York County...............................	185,746	27.9	54.0	18.1	88,182	29.7	56.6	13.7	97,564	26.2	51.7	22.0
46000	**South Dakota ....**	662,338	30.1	51.8	18.0	330,968	33.6	52.3	14.1	331,370	26.7	51.4	22.0
46099	Minnehaha County.....................	138,723	32.7	49.6	17.8	68,914	35.8	50.0	14.2	69,809	29.6	49.1	21.3
46103	Pennington County....................	82,739	29.6	48.7	21.7	40,958	33.1	49.4	17.4	41,781	26.2	48.0	25.8
47000	**Tennessee ....**	5,211,459	28.9	49.4	21.7	2,511,894	31.9	51.5	16.6	2,699,565	26.2	47.4	26.5
47001	Anderson County.......................	62,149	26.8	48.1	25.1	29,837	30.9	49.9	19.2	32,312	23.0	46.3	30.7
47009	Blount County............................	102,282	22.1	56.4	21.5	49,012	25.9	59.0	15.1	53,270	18.7	53.9	27.4
47011	Bradley County	81,893	26.0	50.5	23.5	39,371	29.1	51.4	19.5	42,522	23.2	49.6	27.1
47019	Carter County............................	48,225	22.2	54.3	23.5	23,197	24.6	56.7	18.7	25,028	20.0	52.0	28.0
47031	Coffee County............................	42,711	23.9	51.8	24.4	20,272	27.3	52.3	20.4	22,439	20.8	51.3	27.9
47035	Cumberland County...................	48,360	17.1	58.1	24.9	23,229	20.7	58.8	20.5	25,131	13.7	57.4	28.9
47037	Davidson County........................	527,171	39.8	39.6	20.6	252,078	42.0	42.6	15.4	275,093	37.8	36.9	25.3
47043	Dickson County..........................	40,068	23.8	52.9	23.4	19,405	27.3	56.4	16.2	20,663	20.4	49.5	30.1
47059	Greene County...........................	57,048	22.5	54.9	22.6	27,568	25.6	57.8	16.6	29,480	19.5	52.2	28.3
47063	Hamblen County........................	50,542	22.6	51.4	26.0	24,216	26.8	55.2	18.0	26,326	18.8	47.9	33.3
47065	Hamilton County	283,606	30.5	48.0	21.4	134,766	33.9	50.8	15.3	148,840	27.5	45.6	27.0
47073	Hawkins County.........................	46,681	20.7	55.3	24.1	22,530	24.0	55.8	20.2	24,151	17.5	54.8	27.7
47089	Jefferson County........................	42,956	25.0	53.7	21.3	20,970	28.2	56.3	15.5	21,986	22.0	51.2	26.7
47093	Knox County..............................	361,370	31.0	49.5	19.4	173,612	34.3	51.2	14.6	187,758	28.1	48.0	24.0
47107	McMinn County	42,810	23.2	53.6	23.3	20,491	27.4	54.8	17.8	22,319	19.3	52.5	28.2
47113	Madison County.........................	79,173	32.5	44.6	22.9	36,911	33.9	48.6	17.5	42,262	31.2	41.1	27.6
47119	Maury County............................	65,823	27.0	48.7	24.3	31,311	29.1	51.4	19.5	34,512	25.2	46.2	28.7
47125	Montgomery County..................	139,074	26.2	55.2	18.6	68,372	29.9	55.8	14.4	70,702	22.7	54.5	22.7
47141	Putnam County..........................	60,164	30.0	49.6	20.4	29,071	35.2	51.0	13.8	31,093	25.1	48.3	26.6
47145	Roane County	44,739	20.7	55.9	23.4	21,700	24.1	58.7	17.2	23,039	17.6	53.2	29.2
47147	Robertson County......................	52,684	22.7	56.3	21.0	25,733	24.7	59.7	15.6	26,951	20.8	53.0	26.2
47149	Rutherford County.....................	215,916	31.3	50.7	18.1	105,851	34.9	51.1	14.0	110,065	27.8	50.2	22.0
47155	Sevier County.............................	76,027	22.7	55.6	21.7	36,697	26.1	58.2	15.7	39,330	19.5	53.2	27.3
47157	Shelby County............................	737,262	40.2	38.4	21.4	346,008	42.7	41.2	16.1	391,254	38.1	35.9	26.0
47163	Sullivan County..........................	130,785	21.0	53.9	25.0	62,491	24.3	56.7	18.9	68,294	18.0	51.4	30.7
47165	Sumner County..........................	132,624	23.3	56.3	20.4	63,915	26.5	59.4	14.1	68,709	20.3	53.4	26.2
47167	Tipton County............................	48,265	27.7	52.0	20.3	23,503	29.9	54.0	16.1	24,762	25.6	50.1	24.3
47179	Washington County....................	104,189	27.8	50.8	21.4	50,266	31.1	52.4	16.5	53,923	24.8	49.4	25.8
47187	Williamson County	147,792	21.4	65.5	13.1	71,117	23.7	67.8	8.5	76,675	19.2	63.3	17.4
47189	Wilson County............................	95,152	23.8	55.9	20.3	46,248	26.3	59.0	14.7	48,904	21.4	53.0	25.6
48000	**Texas ....**	20,196,175	31.7	49.4	18.9	9,951,393	35.0	51.0	14.0	10,244,782	28.6	47.7	23.7
48001	Anderson County.......................	48,701	29.8	43.8	26.4	30,736	36.3	40.7	23.0	17,965	18.7	49.2	32.1
48005	Angelina County........................	68,142	26.8	50.0	23.2	33,135	30.2	51.1	18.6	35,007	23.5	49.0	27.5
48021	Bastrop County..........................	59,064	26.4	52.7	20.9	30,098	30.0	52.9	17.1	28,966	22.7	52.4	24.9
48027	Bell County................................	244,727	29.7	51.4	19.0	120,983	34.7	51.4	13.9	123,744	24.7	51.3	23.9
48029	Bexar County.............................	1,388,469	34.6	45.3	20.1	675,847	37.9	47.6	14.5	712,622	31.4	43.2	25.4
48037	Bowie County.............................	74,648	29.4	45.8	24.8	37,392	34.6	45.4	20.0	37,256	24.2	46.1	29.6
48039	Brazoria County.........................	250,409	26.8	54.4	18.8	126,911	30.0	55.1	14.9	123,498	23.5	53.8	22.7
48041	Brazos County	165,210	50.1	36.8	13.1	83,686	53.7	36.9	9.4	81,524	46.4	36.8	16.8
48061	Cameron County........................	303,059	32.5	49.0	18.5	143,095	34.9	52.6	12.5	159,964	30.3	45.8	23.9
48073	Cherokee County.......................	40,136	28.0	51.3	20.7	20,480	32.4	52.3	15.3	19,656	23.5	50.1	26.3
48085	Collin County.............................	639,900	26.2	59.0	14.8	311,055	28.9	61.0	10.1	328,845	23.7	57.1	19.2
48091	Comal County............................	93,365	23.8	59.0	17.2	45,383	25.7	60.6	13.6	47,982	22.0	57.5	20.5
48099	Coryell County...........................	59,070	30.2	49.0	20.9	28,836	36.6	48.8	14.6	30,234	24.0	49.1	26.9
48113	Dallas County............................	1,885,175	36.3	45.2	18.6	923,485	39.4	47.3	13.3	961,690	33.2	43.1	23.6
48121	Denton County..........................	548,308	30.7	53.6	15.7	266,866	32.8	55.9	11.3	281,442	28.8	51.4	19.8
48135	Ector County.............................	108,613	30.1	48.6	21.3	53,866	33.7	49.9	16.3	54,747	26.5	47.3	26.1
48139	Ellis County...............................	118,791	25.2	57.4	17.4	57,768	27.7	60.0	12.4	61,023	22.9	54.9	22.1
48141	El Paso County...........................	624,662	32.5	47.4	20.2	301,665	35.6	50.0	14.4	322,997	29.6	44.9	25.6
48157	Fort Bend County.......................	479,389	27.6	59.2	13.2	232,611	29.6	61.6	8.8	246,778	25.7	56.9	17.4
48167	Galveston County......................	238,762	28.3	51.3	20.4	117,069	32.0	52.8	15.2	121,693	24.7	49.9	25.4
48181	Grayson County.........................	97,708	25.4	50.9	23.7	46,818	27.8	52.9	19.2	50,890	23.1	49.1	27.8
48183	Gregg County............................	96,085	28.7	48.3	23.0	46,482	33.3	49.8	16.8	49,603	24.4	46.8	28.8

Table C-2: Counties with a Population of 50,000 or More—Marriages and Births—*Continued*

State/county FIPS code	State/County	Total women age 15 to 50 years	Percent of all women who had a birth in the past year	Percent of women who had a birth who were married (including separated and spouse absent):	Percent of women who had a birth who were partners in an unmarried partner household	Age of women who had a birth in the last year as a percent of all women who had a birth			Women who had a birth in the last year as a percent of all women in their age group		
						Age 15 to 19	Age 20 to 34	Age 35 to 50	Age 15 to 19	Age 20 to 34	Age 35 to 50
	South Carolina—cont'd										
45041	Florence County	34,334	6.0	52.5	12.2	4.7	73.3	22.0	2.1	10.5	3.0
45043	Georgetown County	12,035	6.4	29.2	7.8	8.5	77.7	13.8	4.3	12.7	1.8
45045	Greenville County	115,094	5.3	60.5	8.4	6.9	68.3	24.9	2.8	8.7	2.9
45047	Greenwood County	17,403	5.6	29.5	9.6	0.6	75.2	24.2	0.2	10.1	3.2
45051	Horry County	63,999	5.2	46.4	9.0	8.9	80.3	10.8	3.9	10.0	1.2
45055	Kershaw County	13,890	6.1	69.5	2.6	0.0	83.5	16.5	0.0	13.1	2.1
45057	Lancaster County	17,326	4.9	63.8	6.3	3.0	74.9	22.1	1.2	9.7	2.2
45059	Laurens County	15,684	3.9	50.2	11.2	6.0	84.9	9.1	1.7	8.4	0.8
45063	Lexington County	65,700	5.1	69.6	11.6	4.8	80.0	15.2	1.9	10.1	1.6
45073	Oconee County	15,726	5.5	69.6	3.1	3.7	81.2	15.2	1.5	11.4	1.8
45075	Orangeburg County	22,602	7.0	18.4	7.5	10.9	77.9	11.3	5.0	12.7	1.9
45077	Pickens County	30,641	3.5	69.9	16.7	3.7	83.8	12.5	0.7	6.6	1.2
45079	Richland County	108,451	4.8	45.3	7.6	6.0	73.0	21.1	1.9	7.5	2.6
45083	Spartanburg County	69,450	6.3	59.4	8.7	9.0	73.3	17.8	3.9	11.5	2.5
45085	Sumter County	25,753	6.1	40.9	18.6	2.5	88.0	9.5	1.1	12.1	1.4
45091	York County	59,518	5.7	74.5	5.3	3.2	72.7	24.1	1.3	10.8	2.9
46000	**South Dakota**	187,109	6.9	61.9	17.3	6.1	80.2	13.8	2.7	12.8	2.3
46099	Minnehaha County	42,708	7.1	63.6	17.0	0.0	85.8	14.2	0.0	13.3	2.5
46103	Pennington County	23,582	6.0	49.4	19.9	18.8	76.2	5.0	8.5	10.5	0.7
47000	**Tennessee**	1,562,075	5.4	60.2	9.9	6.7	76.2	17.1	2.8	10.0	2.1
47001	Anderson County	16,685	4.1	57.8	18.5	8.6	73.9	17.5	2.7	8.1	1.5
47009	Blount County	28,112	4.6	80.3	5.3	4.4	87.9	7.7	1.4	10.8	0.7
47011	Bradley County	24,364	8.7	55.9	11.2	8.8	75.5	15.7	5.4	16.0	3.0
47019	Carter County	13,265	4.3	70.1	11.4	8.3	84.3	7.4	3.0	8.9	0.7
47031	Coffee County	12,565	3.6	61.7	29.8	8.5	84.7	6.8	2.1	7.7	0.5
47035	Cumberland County	10,721	4.8	62.4	14.1	4.3	95.7	0.0	1.4	12.3	0.0
47037	Davidson County	177,578	5.0	61.3	11.4	3.7	73.9	22.4	1.8	7.4	2.9
47043	Dickson County	11,970	3.9	88.1	5.2	3.9	86.6	9.5	1.2	8.5	0.8
47059	Greene County	15,238	3.2	64.1	8.4	17.8	79.0	3.3	4.3	6.8	0.2
47063	Hamblen County	13,996	4.4	76.6	12.1	7.7	80.8	11.5	2.8	9.3	1.0
47065	Hamilton County	83,315	5.5	53.0	10.1	8.3	70.3	21.4	3.5	9.1	2.7
47073	Hawkins County	12,584	4.5	58.5	8.0	3.0	85.6	11.4	1.0	10.5	1.0
47089	Jefferson County	11,810	4.2	37.7	5.2	24.8	66.9	8.3	7.4	7.2	0.7
47093	Knox County	112,304	5.3	64.2	16.3	6.8	79.1	14.1	2.8	9.4	1.7
47107	McMinn County	11,742	4.8	77.7	6.1	17.5	77.1	5.4	6.0	9.4	0.5
47113	Madison County	24,606	4.8	51.8	14.1	7.3	80.4	12.3	2.3	8.8	1.4
47119	Maury County	19,424	5.4	62.8	0.0	9.4	73.7	16.9	4.3	9.3	2.0
47125	Montgomery County	49,555	7.0	77.0	5.9	5.4	78.3	16.3	3.2	11.2	3.0
47141	Putnam County	18,443	2.7	51.8	14.0	7.3	72.3	20.4	1.3	4.3	1.4
47145	Roane County	11,143	3.8	39.3	5.4	0.0	90.6	9.4	0.0	9.4	0.7
47147	Robertson County	16,101	6.3	73.7	10.0	9.8	62.5	27.6	5.0	10.3	3.6
47149	Rutherford County	74,785	5.3	67.2	8.5	6.8	77.6	15.6	2.7	9.1	2.0
47155	Sevier County	21,177	6.9	38.4	11.6	18.2	81.8	0.0	10.0	14.8	0.0
47157	Shelby County	242,241	7.2	44.0	9.7	6.0	70.2	23.7	3.1	11.8	4.0
47163	Sullivan County	34,384	5.0	59.2	7.7	6.5	85.2	8.3	2.6	11.6	0.8
47165	Sumner County	39,735	4.7	78.6	4.9	1.1	89.7	9.3	0.4	11.2	0.9
47167	Tipton County	15,034	7.3	62.9	11.2	1.3	77.2	21.5	0.6	14.6	3.4
47179	Washington County	30,823	3.5	61.9	11.0	2.8	85.0	12.2	0.7	6.9	1.0
47187	Williamson County	46,586	4.7	86.9	3.3	0.0	63.4	36.6	0.0	10.3	3.1
47189	Wilson County	28,496	4.9	72.9	11.1	6.5	86.6	7.0	2.5	11.9	0.7
48000	**Texas**	6,524,003	6.0	65.0	8.2	8.0	73.0	19.0	3.4	10.3	2.6
48001	Anderson County	9,609	8.4	68.9	7.2	11.5	61.0	27.5	7.4	12.1	5.1
48005	Angelina County	20,425	5.9	63.1	14.8	9.6	84.5	5.9	4.2	11.8	0.8
48021	Bastrop County	16,301	5.4	82.6	3.2	0.0	78.7	21.3	0.0	11.5	2.4
48027	Bell County	84,433	4.9	81.1	4.0	4.1	84.0	11.9	1.6	8.4	1.5
48029	Bexar County	458,882	6.1	63.7	8.7	7.5	73.5	19.0	3.3	10.2	2.8
48037	Bowie County	20,727	7.7	62.7	14.3	17.8	61.3	20.9	9.1	11.7	3.6
48039	Brazoria County	78,875	7.5	68.7	1.6	7.2	68.6	24.3	4.0	13.0	3.9
48041	Brazos County	61,540	4.8	70.3	6.0	6.1	74.2	19.6	1.9	6.1	3.6
48061	Cameron County	102,159	6.5	56.1	6.9	13.6	71.8	14.6	5.1	11.5	2.2
48073	Cherokee County	10,728	4.8	59.2	1.4	0.0	90.1	9.9	0.0	10.3	1.1
48085	Collin County	220,542	5.9	75.8	7.5	1.7	70.8	27.6	0.8	11.7	3.2
48091	Comal County	25,311	5.8	51.6	14.9	7.1	84.9	8.1	2.8	14.0	0.9
48099	Coryell County	21,823	6.0	71.9	3.1	4.0	83.0	13.0	2.4	10.3	1.9
48113	Dallas County	0	0.0	0.0	0.0	0.0	0.0	0.0	0.0	0.0	0.0
48121	Denton County	195,974	4.5	66.6	8.3	3.9	74.0	22.1	1.4	8.2	2.2
48135	Ector County	35,221	11.8	59.0	15.3	4.4	87.9	7.6	3.6	21.9	2.4
48139	Ellis County	37,626	5.7	64.3	8.6	5.1	83.3	11.5	1.9	12.2	1.5
48141	El Paso County	207,729	6.0	64.1	5.9	9.3	72.6	18.2	3.6	10.2	2.7
48157	Fort Bend County	160,586	5.7	79.2	2.5	6.0	71.9	22.1	2.3	11.3	2.5
48167	Galveston County	72,397	5.9	62.7	11.3	10.7	72.5	16.7	4.6	10.6	2.1
48181	Grayson County	27,825	5.2	52.5	2.4	17.0	69.3	13.6	5.8	9.0	1.6
48183	Gregg County	29,025	6.0	59.4	19.6	8.3	82.9	8.9	3.6	11.3	1.2

State/ county FIPS code	State/County	Total population 15 years and older	Marital status, percent			Male population 15 years and older	Male, marital status, percent			Female population 15 years and older	Female, marital status, percent		
			Never married	Now married (except separated)	Separated, widowed, or divorced		Never married	Now married (except separated)	Separated, widowed, or divorced		Never married	Now married (except separated)	Separated, widowed, or divorced
	Texas—cont'd												
48187	Guadalupe County.....................	108,949	26.9	54.3	18.9	52,784	29.7	56.8	13.5	56,165	24.2	51.9	23.9
48199	Hardin County.........................	43,685	20.8	58.7	20.5	21,323	22.7	60.7	16.6	22,362	18.9	56.8	24.2
48201	Harris County..........................	3,267,485	35.4	46.9	17.7	1,616,492	38.6	48.5	12.9	1,650,993	32.3	45.3	22.4
48203	Harrison County.......................	52,923	28.1	50.7	21.2	25,626	30.8	53.1	16.1	27,297	25.4	48.5	26.1
48209	Hays County............................	135,370	38.9	45.9	15.2	67,179	42.1	45.9	11.9	68,191	35.6	45.9	18.5
48213	Henderson County.....................	64,276	21.9	52.4	25.7	30,878	24.5	53.8	21.7	33,398	19.5	51.1	29.3
48215	Hidalgo County........................	573,696	31.5	52.4	16.1	275,675	33.9	55.4	10.7	298,021	29.3	49.7	21.0
48221	Hood County...........................	42,941	16.3	60.4	23.3	21,013	18.7	62.4	18.9	21,928	14.0	58.6	27.4
48231	Hunt County............................	69,430	25.9	50.5	23.6	33,992	29.4	52.6	18.1	35,438	22.6	48.6	28.9
48245	Jefferson County......................	202,411	33.3	42.9	23.8	103,623	36.8	44.4	18.8	98,788	29.7	41.3	29.1
48251	Johnson County........................	119,408	23.6	56.9	19.5	59,134	27.2	57.8	15.0	60,274	20.0	56.1	23.9
48257	Kaufman County.......................	81,881	25.2	55.1	19.7	39,752	27.1	57.8	15.1	42,129	23.3	52.6	24.1
48291	Liberty County.........................	60,486	28.1	50.1	21.8	29,419	30.4	52.8	16.8	31,067	25.9	47.6	26.5
48303	Lubbock County.......................	227,440	37.4	43.9	18.7	111,588	40.9	45.4	13.7	115,852	34.1	42.5	23.4
48309	McLennan County	189,515	33.7	46.2	20.1	90,977	36.3	48.9	14.8	98,538	31.3	43.7	24.9
48323	Maverick County.......................	40,465	31.0	51.9	17.1	19,721	34.3	55.1	10.6	20,744	27.8	48.8	23.4
48329	Midland County........................	112,078	29.5	53.1	17.4	54,910	33.4	53.5	13.1	57,168	25.8	52.6	21.6
48339	Montgomery County	375,607	25.8	55.7	18.5	184,158	28.5	58.0	13.5	191,449	23.2	53.4	23.4
48347	Nacogdoches County..................	52,633	39.6	42.5	18.0	24,787	41.2	48.2	10.6	27,846	38.2	37.3	24.5
48355	Nueces County.........................	273,581	32.8	45.7	21.6	133,181	36.2	47.8	16.0	140,400	29.5	43.6	26.9
48361	Orange County.........................	65,979	24.2	53.6	22.1	32,234	27.8	53.9	18.4	33,745	20.9	53.4	25.7
48367	Parker County..........................	95,812	22.4	56.8	20.8	48,116	26.1	57.6	16.4	47,696	18.8	56.0	25.3
48375	Potter County..........................	93,313	32.0	43.3	24.7	47,790	35.4	43.9	20.7	45,523	28.4	42.6	29.0
48381	Randall County.........................	99,142	27.3	54.7	18.0	47,727	30.2	56.9	12.8	51,415	24.5	52.6	22.9
48397	Rockwall County.......................	63,488	22.6	60.7	16.7	31,013	25.4	63.7	10.9	32,475	19.9	57.9	22.2
48401	Rusk County............................	43,393	28.1	46.0	25.9	23,169	30.5	48.3	21.2	20,224	25.4	43.3	31.3
48409	San Patricio County...................	50,578	29.1	49.6	21.3	25,033	33.1	52.1	14.8	25,545	25.1	47.2	27.8
48423	Smith County...........................	169,149	27.2	50.8	22.0	80,430	29.3	54.2	16.5	88,719	25.3	47.8	26.9
48427	Starr County............................	44,503	32.0	47.9	20.0	21,293	36.1	49.9	14.0	23,210	28.3	46.1	25.6
48439	Tarrant County.........................	1,445,534	31.3	49.4	19.3	700,452	34.0	51.8	14.3	745,082	28.7	47.2	24.1
48441	Taylor County..........................	106,036	32.4	47.6	20.1	51,218	35.4	49.8	14.8	54,818	29.5	45.4	25.0
48451	Tom Green County.....................	90,936	31.1	46.5	22.4	44,362	34.3	48.0	17.7	46,574	28.0	45.2	26.8
48453	Travis County...........................	873,966	40.0	43.4	16.6	439,269	43.6	44.2	12.2	434,697	36.3	42.6	21.1
48467	Van Zandt County......................	42,410	22.3	53.4	24.2	20,801	26.9	54.3	18.8	21,609	17.9	52.6	29.5
48469	Victoria County........................	69,473	28.1	48.9	23.0	33,597	32.6	50.1	17.3	35,876	23.9	47.8	28.3
48471	Walker County.........................	59,599	40.4	38.3	21.3	36,101	42.8	35.9	21.3	23,498	36.7	42.0	21.3
48479	Webb County...........................	183,744	36.0	47.3	16.7	88,085	38.2	50.9	10.9	95,659	34.0	44.0	22.0
48485	Wichita County.........................	106,091	32.3	46.2	21.5	54,771	37.8	45.4	16.8	51,320	26.5	47.0	26.6
48491	Williamson County	349,237	26.4	57.2	16.4	169,717	29.0	59.8	11.2	179,520	23.9	54.7	21.4
48497	Wise County............................	47,890	21.3	59.1	19.7	24,053	26.2	59.6	14.2	23,837	16.3	58.5	25.2
49000	**Utah**	2,102,136	29.4	55.8	14.8	1,048,510	32.4	56.2	11.4	1,053,626	26.3	55.5	18.2
49003	Box Elder County	36,342	22.7	63.3	14.0	18,240	26.5	63.3	10.3	18,102	18.9	63.3	17.8
49005	Cache County...........................	84,831	33.7	56.1	10.2	41,910	35.9	57.3	6.8	42,921	31.6	54.8	13.6
49011	Davis County	225,465	25.1	61.6	13.3	112,037	28.2	61.9	9.8	113,428	21.9	61.3	16.7
49035	Salt Lake County.......................	804,548	31.3	52.0	16.7	402,162	34.5	52.2	13.3	402,386	28.2	51.8	20.0
49045	Tooele County..........................	42,052	25.5	59.3	15.2	20,832	26.8	61.2	11.9	21,220	24.3	57.4	18.3
49049	Utah County............................	377,685	32.0	58.1	9.9	187,923	34.2	58.9	7.0	189,762	29.8	57.4	12.7
49053	Washington County....................	108,947	23.6	59.1	17.4	53,257	26.2	60.7	13.0	55,690	21.0	57.5	21.5
49057	Weber County..........................	177,126	27.2	54.4	18.3	88,194	30.9	54.8	14.4	88,932	23.6	54.1	22.3
50000	**Vermont**...............................	525,206	31.2	50.0	18.8	256,552	34.4	51.0	14.6	268,654	28.1	49.1	22.8
50007	Chittenden County.....................	133,661	39.0	46.3	14.7	64,567	41.3	47.5	11.2	69,094	36.9	45.3	17.8
50021	Rutland County.........................	51,794	29.5	50.3	20.2	25,200	33.7	50.9	15.4	26,594	25.6	49.7	24.8
50023	Washington County....................	49,735	29.1	49.0	21.9	24,396	32.4	50.3	17.2	25,339	25.9	47.7	26.4
50027	Windsor County........................	47,473	25.2	54.4	20.4	23,091	28.0	55.1	17.0	24,382	22.7	53.7	23.7
51000	**Virginia**	6,634,998	31.7	49.9	18.3	3,230,845	34.9	51.8	13.3	3,404,153	28.7	48.2	23.1
51003	Albemarle County......................	83,997	32.9	51.8	15.3	39,509	35.7	54.6	9.8	44,488	30.5	49.4	20.2
51013	Arlington County.......................	189,378	45.9	41.7	12.4	94,634	47.9	43.2	8.9	94,744	44.0	40.2	15.9
51015	Augusta County........................	61,536	23.5	56.6	19.9	31,114	28.6	54.9	16.5	30,422	18.3	58.4	23.3
51019	Bedford County........................	57,544	21.2	61.1	17.7	28,427	24.4	62.9	12.7	29,117	18.1	59.3	22.5
51031	Campbell County.......................	45,744	24.7	54.2	21.1	21,827	25.7	58.2	16.1	23,917	23.8	50.5	25.7
51041	Chesterfield County....................	257,810	30.2	51.6	18.2	121,843	32.6	54.5	13.0	135,967	28.1	49.1	22.8
51059	Fairfax County..........................	893,062	30.4	56.0	13.6	438,415	33.2	57.6	9.2	454,647	27.8	54.4	17.8
51061	Fauquier County........................	53,376	25.1	57.2	17.7	25,910	28.1	59.0	12.9	27,466	22.2	55.5	22.3
51067	Franklin County........................	47,052	22.5	59.3	18.2	23,125	25.7	61.1	13.3	23,927	19.4	57.6	23.0
51069	Frederick County.......................	64,395	23.8	58.3	17.9	31,658	26.2	58.9	14.9	32,737	21.5	57.8	20.7
51085	Hanover County........................	81,586	24.4	57.5	18.1	39,295	27.6	59.5	13.0	42,291	21.5	55.7	22.9
51087	Henrico County.........................	252,848	32.4	46.9	20.8	116,660	34.7	51.3	14.0	136,188	30.3	43.1	26.6
51089	Henry County	44,107	23.2	52.3	24.5	20,931	26.7	54.4	19.0	23,176	20.0	50.4	29.6
51095	James City County.....................	57,213	22.7	58.9	18.4	27,522	25.7	62.3	12.0	29,691	19.9	55.7	24.4
51107	Loudoun County.......................	251,263	25.8	61.7	12.5	123,310	27.7	63.3	9.0	127,953	23.9	60.2	15.9
51121	Montgomery County...................	82,892	47.6	39.4	13.0	42,893	52.2	38.2	9.5	39,999	42.7	40.6	16.7
51143	Pittsylvania County....................	52,434	24.5	53.1	22.4	25,575	28.4	55.3	16.3	26,859	20.8	51.0	28.2
51153	Prince William County.................	326,257	30.2	54.8	14.9	161,063	33.7	55.8	10.4	165,194	26.9	53.8	19.3

State/ county FIPS code	State/County	Total women age 15 to 50 years	Percent of all women who had a birth in the past year	Percent of women who had a birth who were married (including separated and spouse absent):	Percent of women who had a birth who were partners in an unmarried partner household	Age of women who had a birth in the last year as a percent of all women who had a birth			Women who had a birth in the last year as a percent of all women in their age group		
						Age 15 to 19	Age 20 to 34	Age 35 to 50	Age 15 to 19	Age 20 to 34	Age 35 to 50
	Texas—cont'd										
48187	Guadalupe County...............	34,752	6.2	65.9	11.4	10.6	65.5	23.9	4.2	11.2	3.1
48199	Hardin County....................	12,760	6.1	57.2	0.0	27.2	69.0	3.9	11.8	10.7	0.5
48201	Harris County.....................	1,108,699	6.1	64.4	8.4	7.9	72.3	19.8	3.7	10.0	2.8
48203	Harrison County..................	15,653	6.9	48.0	8.0	0.0	90.1	9.9	0.0	14.2	1.6
48209	Hays County......................	46,556	3.5	60.3	8.0	10.8	69.4	19.8	2.5	5.1	1.9
48213	Henderson County...............	16,981	5.6	67.0	9.6	3.4	78.4	18.2	1.3	11.6	2.1
48215	Hidalgo County..................	203,986	7.4	72.8	4.0	10.5	74.9	14.6	4.6	13.0	2.6
48221	Hood County......................	9,989	6.3	83.2	2.2	9.6	81.6	8.8	4.9	12.5	1.2
48231	Hunt County......................	20,239	4.3	63.3	6.8	9.1	81.2	9.8	2.7	8.7	0.9
48245	Jefferson County.................	57,834	5.7	52.8	9.9	13.5	74.4	12.1	5.3	9.6	1.6
48251	Johnson County..................	36,158	5.5	77.2	12.0	6.1	81.0	12.9	2.3	11.4	1.5
48257	Kaufman County.................	26,241	5.6	59.7	7.0	11.6	73.6	14.8	4.6	10.7	1.8
48291	Liberty County...................	19,446	6.3	55.5	1.6	13.7	74.0	12.2	6.8	10.8	1.7
48303	Lubbock County.................	75,553	4.9	65.3	6.2	9.1	75.5	15.4	3.0	7.4	2.2
48309	McLennan County...............	60,677	5.1	61.3	9.8	9.8	74.6	15.6	3.0	8.2	2.1
48323	Maverick County................	13,281	7.6	62.1	4.0	10.6	69.1	20.3	4.2	13.4	3.7
48329	Midland County..................	35,992	6.3	77.8	4.7	8.2	83.4	8.4	3.7	11.3	1.3
48339	Montgomery County............	117,249	5.3	73.8	8.4	5.0	73.1	21.9	1.9	10.1	2.4
48347	Nacogdoches County...........	18,128	4.6	48.1	16.0	15.2	75.9	8.9	3.3	7.4	1.3
48355	Nueces County...................	84,679	5.4	49.8	10.0	7.5	83.9	8.5	2.9	10.3	1.1
48361	Orange County...................	19,360	4.5	46.7	14.6	9.1	75.2	15.7	2.7	8.7	1.5
48367	Parker County....................	27,810	5.3	69.8	1.5	17.8	70.3	12.0	6.1	10.9	1.3
48375	Potter County....................	28,419	6.6	58.6	12.1	13.0	72.0	15.0	6.0	10.3	2.5
48381	Randall County..................	31,034	6.2	63.7	13.0	3.1	80.9	16.0	1.4	11.4	2.4
48397	Rockwall County................	20,353	6.6	61.9	3.5	9.3	86.1	4.6	4.3	16.5	0.6
48401	Rusk County.....................	11,209	7.4	45.8	2.9	24.0	61.7	14.3	11.5	11.6	2.3
48409	San Patricio County............	15,109	9.1	44.1	16.7	8.1	75.4	16.4	4.7	16.9	3.4
48423	Smith County....................	51,559	6.2	61.4	5.8	9.3	77.3	13.4	4.1	10.8	2.0
48427	Starr County.....................	15,448	6.1	51.0	13.3	3.1	84.1	12.8	1.0	12.7	1.9
48439	Tarrant County..................	488,306	5.9	60.7	12.0	7.4	75.5	17.1	3.3	10.5	2.3
48441	Taylor County...................	33,732	6.0	60.5	14.3	10.1	87.8	2.2	4.0	10.8	0.4
48451	Tom Green County..............	27,494	4.6	77.1	7.7	10.0	86.4	3.6	3.1	8.2	0.4
48453	Travis County....................	303,423	5.3	70.1	8.6	4.4	70.1	25.4	2.1	7.6	3.3
48467	Van Zandt County..............	10,943	5.4	78.9	8.3	5.6	79.8	14.6	2.0	12.2	1.6
48469	Victoria County.................	20,495	4.6	46.7	21.1	9.0	85.2	5.8	3.0	9.1	0.6
48471	Walker County..................	15,475	5.6	42.0	10.1	38.4	48.6	13.0	8.2	6.4	2.3
48479	Webb County....................	67,047	6.8	62.1	7.3	11.5	75.2	13.3	4.5	12.4	2.2
48485	Wichita County..................	30,028	5.3	64.6	19.5	13.3	72.5	14.1	5.0	8.1	1.9
48491	Williamson County..............	0	0.0	0.0	0.0	0.0	0.0	0.0	0.0	0.0	0.0
48497	Wise County.....................	13,812	6.2	90.7	2.9	1.7	94.9	3.4	0.7	16.4	0.4
49000	**Utah**	712,683	7.4	83.8	5.3	3.2	82.1	14.7	1.6	12.9	2.9
49003	Box Elder County...............	11,227	7.6	85.7	3.5	7.3	74.7	18.1	3.5	13.6	3.2
49005	Cache County...................	31,312	7.4	88.2	7.6	3.6	79.5	16.9	1.5	11.1	4.4
49011	Davis County....................	77,232	7.0	91.2	0.0	2.6	85.6	11.8	1.2	13.6	2.0
49035	Salt Lake County................	271,851	7.0	78.8	6.5	4.0	77.3	18.7	2.1	11.4	3.3
49045	Tooele County...................	14,711	6.1	66.6	10.9	0.0	87.0	13.0	0.0	13.8	1.8
49049	Utah County.....................	143,345	8.5	92.1	3.4	1.1	86.9	11.9	0.5	14.3	3.2
49053	Washington County............	30,394	7.1	84.6	4.1	7.8	77.5	14.7	3.2	12.3	2.8
49057	Weber County...................	57,774	7.3	78.1	9.0	3.6	84.8	11.6	1.9	13.2	2.2
50000	**Vermont**	144,883	3.9	66.9	14.3	4.7	73.3	22.0	1.2	7.3	1.9
50007	Chittenden County..............	42,729	4.0	81.3	7.0	0.1	65.5	34.4	0.0	5.9	3.6
50021	Rutland County..................	13,242	3.6	56.7	25.4	5.5	85.0	9.5	1.3	8.0	0.7
50023	Washington County............	13,231	3.2	68.6	12.0	3.3	70.3	26.4	0.8	6.2	1.7
50027	Windsor County.................	11,646	4.7	53.0	16.2	16.2	72.7	11.1	5.8	9.1	1.1
51000	**Virginia**	2,039,556	5.3	68.6	8.1	4.7	73.7	21.5	1.9	9.3	2.5
51003	Albemarle County..............	25,340	4.9	75.5	6.7	3.0	76.3	20.7	0.7	9.5	2.4
51013	Arlington County................	67,617	5.1	79.4	1.5	5.8	53.9	40.2	5.4	4.8	5.5
51015	Augusta County.................	15,561	5.7	68.2	14.5	0.0	84.5	15.5	0.0	14.1	1.7
51019	Bedford County.................	14,539	4.8	75.4	5.3	0.0	87.8	12.2	0.0	13.2	1.1
51031	Campbell County...............	12,858	3.8	75.1	14.4	5.2	80.8	14.0	1.2	8.3	1.1
51041	Chesterfield County............	81,932	4.4	73.2	10.8	3.5	81.3	15.2	1.1	9.6	1.4
51059	Fairfax County...................	282,831	5.5	83.1	3.1	2.1	63.7	34.2	0.9	8.9	3.9
51061	Fauquier County................	15,385	5.8	53.2	8.7	6.9	83.1	10.0	2.6	14.9	1.1
51067	Franklin County.................	11,839	6.8	69.7	10.4	9.4	66.8	23.8	4.3	12.3	3.3
51069	Frederick County...............	19,031	6.1	74.8	9.5	8.0	70.9	21.1	3.6	11.9	2.5
51085	Hanover County................	23,732	4.3	86.7	4.7	0.0	72.6	27.4	0.0	10.3	2.2
51087	Henrico County.................	80,785	5.4	66.1	7.4	3.9	74.3	21.9	1.7	9.7	2.5
51089	Henry County....................	11,291	6.0	70.3	6.1	5.0	88.7	6.3	2.3	15.1	0.7
51095	James City County.............	14,191	5.4	90.5	6.5	3.0	69.6	27.5	1.3	9.5	3.1
51107	Loudoun County................	90,070	5.7	86.4	3.8	1.1	70.3	28.7	0.5	11.9	3.0
51121	Montgomery County...........	27,833	3.4	87.6	12.2	0.0	85.9	14.1	0.0	5.6	1.7
51143	Pittsylvania County............	13,160	3.4	56.1	16.3	9.0	82.4	8.6	2.2	7.8	0.6
51153	Prince William County.........	113,531	6.7	74.1	6.0	2.4	70.9	26.7	1.3	11.9	3.7

Table C-2: Counties with a Population of 50,000 or More—Marriages and Births—*Continued*

State/ county FIPS code	State/County	Total population 15 years and older	Marital status, percent			Male population 15 years and older	Male, marital status, percent			Female population 15 years and older	Female, marital status, percent		
			Never married	Now married (except separated)	Separated, widowed, or divorced		Never married	Now married (except separated)	Separated, widowed, or divorced		Never married	Now married (except separated)	Separated, widowed, or divorced
	Virginia—cont'd												
51161	Roanoke County	77,156	22.1	56.0	21.9	36,343	24.3	61.3	14.4	40,813	20.2	51.3	28.5
51165	Rockingham County	62,710	25.4	56.1	18.4	30,402	28.6	57.9	13.5	32,308	22.4	54.5	23.1
51177	Spotsylvania County	98,556	26.9	57.4	15.7	47,575	28.9	60.1	11.0	50,981	25.0	54.9	20.0
51179	Stafford County	104,521	28.6	57.8	13.6	52,456	31.9	58.5	9.6	52,065	25.3	57.1	17.6
51191	Washington County	46,027	23.1	53.9	23.0	22,475	26.1	56.4	17.5	23,552	20.3	51.5	28.2
51199	York County	52,986	24.6	61.7	13.8	25,968	27.4	63.6	9.0	27,018	21.8	59.8	18.4
51510	Alexandria city	124,035	40.2	44.0	15.8	59,747	41.9	46.3	11.7	64,288	38.5	41.8	19.7
51550	Chesapeake city	181,560	29.2	52.4	18.5	87,594	32.2	54.2	13.6	93,966	26.4	50.7	22.9
51650	Hampton city	111,395	36.9	40.8	22.2	52,739	40.0	43.4	16.6	58,656	34.2	38.5	27.3
51660	Harrisonburg city	43,933	60.2	26.9	12.9	20,450	60.0	29.4	10.6	23,483	60.4	24.8	14.8
51680	Lynchburg city	64,373	45.7	36.2	18.1	29,783	49.5	39.1	11.4	34,590	42.5	33.6	23.9
51700	Newport News city	144,476	37.0	40.7	22.3	69,006	40.9	43.0	16.1	75,470	33.4	38.6	28.0
51710	Norfolk city	201,984	46.0	33.8	20.2	105,558	51.3	33.7	15.0	96,426	40.3	33.9	25.8
51740	Portsmouth city	76,896	38.1	36.4	25.5	36,580	42.9	39.1	18.0	40,316	33.7	34.0	32.3
51760	Richmond city	176,537	52.0	25.7	22.3	83,098	55.5	27.9	16.6	93,439	48.9	23.7	27.4
51770	Roanoke city	79,227	34.7	39.5	25.8	37,193	38.5	42.7	18.8	42,034	31.3	36.7	31.9
51800	Suffolk city	67,076	28.5	50.8	20.6	31,856	29.8	53.5	16.7	35,220	27.4	48.4	24.2
51810	Virginia Beach city	358,884	31.6	49.5	18.8	174,285	35.9	51.3	12.7	184,599	27.5	47.9	24.6
53000	**Washington**	5,573,172	30.7	50.3	19.0	2,764,295	34.4	51.3	14.4	2,808,877	27.1	49.4	23.5
53005	Benton County	141,529	27.9	52.9	19.2	70,598	31.6	53.8	14.6	70,931	24.3	52.1	23.7
53007	Chelan County	58,833	27.3	54.3	18.5	29,043	31.8	54.7	13.5	29,790	22.8	53.9	23.3
53009	Clallam County	61,621	24.8	51.9	23.3	30,253	26.7	54.1	19.1	31,368	23.0	49.7	27.4
53011	Clark County	344,538	28.0	52.1	19.9	168,485	31.1	53.4	15.5	176,053	25.0	50.9	24.2
53015	Cowlitz County	82,049	26.1	51.1	22.8	40,382	29.7	53.5	16.7	41,667	22.5	48.8	28.7
53021	Franklin County	60,314	33.8	49.6	16.7	31,722	37.0	49.5	13.5	28,592	30.2	49.6	20.2
53025	Grant County	67,924	29.4	52.6	18.0	34,449	32.8	53.3	13.9	33,475	26.0	51.8	22.3
53027	Grays Harbor County	59,234	28.0	47.6	24.4	30,414	33.5	47.1	19.3	28,820	22.2	48.0	29.8
53029	Island County	66,029	20.9	61.0	18.1	32,673	24.8	61.3	13.9	33,356	17.0	60.7	22.3
53033	King County	1,651,191	34.4	48.8	16.8	819,695	38.0	49.7	12.3	831,496	30.8	47.9	21.2
53035	Kitsap County	209,342	27.9	52.5	19.6	106,445	33.1	52.7	14.2	102,897	22.5	52.3	25.2
53041	Lewis County	61,706	24.9	52.1	23.1	30,695	29.5	52.5	18.0	31,011	20.2	51.6	28.1
53045	Mason County	50,839	24.1	51.3	24.7	26,200	30.2	50.3	19.5	24,639	17.5	52.3	30.2
53053	Pierce County	646,729	30.2	49.7	20.1	318,149	33.7	50.5	15.7	328,580	26.8	48.9	24.3
53057	Skagit County	95,740	25.6	53.0	21.3	47,266	29.1	55.5	15.4	48,474	22.3	50.6	27.1
53061	Snohomish County	590,091	29.4	51.4	19.2	294,237	33.6	52.4	13.9	295,854	25.3	50.4	24.3
53063	Spokane County	386,192	30.7	48.6	20.6	189,467	34.1	49.7	16.3	196,725	27.6	47.6	24.8
53067	Thurston County	211,206	27.8	52.1	20.1	101,571	30.7	53.5	15.8	109,635	25.2	50.8	24.0
53071	Walla Walla County	48,742	33.2	46.7	20.0	24,947	37.9	47.3	14.7	23,795	28.3	46.1	25.5
53073	Whatcom County	170,226	34.1	48.1	17.8	83,737	37.5	50.0	12.5	86,489	30.8	46.3	23.0
53077	Yakima County	183,851	32.2	49.0	18.8	91,548	36.0	50.1	14.0	92,303	28.4	48.0	23.6
54000	**West Virginia**	1,538,216	27.4	50.0	22.6	752,757	31.2	51.4	17.3	785,459	23.8	48.6	27.6
54003	Berkeley County	85,251	26.4	52.7	20.8	41,610	28.7	54.0	17.3	43,641	24.2	51.5	24.3
54011	Cabell County	80,704	31.1	43.2	25.7	38,774	35.4	44.4	20.2	41,930	27.2	42.0	30.8
54033	Harrison County	56,825	24.0	53.0	23.0	27,257	26.9	56.0	17.1	29,568	21.3	50.3	28.5
54037	Jefferson County	43,988	28.1	54.5	17.4	21,536	29.8	56.5	13.7	22,452	26.5	52.5	20.9
54039	Kanawha County	159,090	26.8	47.6	25.6	75,665	30.9	50.4	18.7	83,425	23.1	45.1	31.8
54049	Marion County	47,324	29.2	49.4	21.4	22,886	32.9	53.3	13.8	24,438	25.7	45.7	28.6
54055	Mercer County	51,628	24.4	52.2	23.4	24,406	28.6	55.5	15.9	27,222	20.7	49.2	30.1
54061	Monongalia County	86,958	49.2	36.5	14.2	44,864	53.3	36.4	10.3	42,094	44.9	36.7	18.3
54079	Putnam County	45,402	21.5	57.5	21.1	22,123	24.0	60.8	15.2	23,279	19.0	54.3	26.7
54081	Raleigh County	65,236	25.6	51.4	22.9	32,637	30.8	50.6	18.6	32,599	20.5	52.3	27.2
54107	Wood County	71,412	25.6	51.1	23.3	34,025	29.6	53.4	17.1	37,387	21.9	49.0	29.1
55000	**Wisconsin**	4,636,493	31.4	50.9	17.7	2,285,832	34.6	52.0	13.5	2,350,661	28.4	49.8	21.8
55009	Brown County	200,749	31.9	51.9	16.3	98,799	34.5	52.8	12.7	101,950	29.3	51.0	19.7
55017	Chippewa County	50,871	25.3	54.7	20.0	26,570	30.6	52.7	16.7	24,301	19.4	56.9	23.7
55021	Columbia County	45,985	25.7	54.3	20.1	23,397	29.0	54.4	16.6	22,588	22.3	54.0	23.7
55025	Dane County	412,681	37.7	47.4	14.8	202,792	40.0	48.9	11.0	209,889	35.5	46.0	18.5
55027	Dodge County	73,142	29.2	51.3	19.4	38,469	34.1	49.5	16.3	34,673	23.8	53.3	22.9
55035	Eau Claire County	83,410	37.0	46.6	16.4	40,321	39.6	48.2	12.3	43,089	34.6	45.2	20.2
55039	Fond du Lac County	83,219	27.8	54.1	18.1	40,651	31.1	55.1	13.8	42,568	24.6	53.1	22.3
55043	Grant County	42,341	35.1	49.4	15.5	22,029	41.4	47.4	11.2	20,312	28.2	51.6	20.2
55055	Jefferson County	68,304	29.2	53.7	17.1	33,792	32.5	54.9	12.6	34,512	26.0	52.5	21.5
55059	Kenosha County	133,176	32.2	48.5	19.3	65,305	36.1	50.0	13.9	67,871	28.4	47.1	24.5
55063	La Crosse County	96,081	36.8	47.1	16.0	46,456	38.6	49.1	12.3	49,625	35.2	45.4	19.5
55071	Manitowoc County	66,648	25.9	55.5	18.7	32,868	29.3	56.6	14.1	33,780	22.5	54.3	23.2
55073	Marathon County	108,446	26.7	55.6	17.8	54,067	30.1	56.3	13.6	54,379	23.3	54.8	21.9
55079	Milwaukee County	756,099	43.5	38.0	18.4	360,193	45.9	40.2	13.9	395,906	41.4	36.1	22.5
55087	Outagamie County	142,661	28.4	55.2	16.4	70,591	32.4	55.6	12.0	72,070	24.5	54.9	20.6
55089	Ozaukee County	71,034	24.2	59.8	15.9	34,524	27.2	63.2	9.5	36,510	21.4	56.6	22.0
55097	Portage County	58,623	35.4	49.6	15.1	29,087	38.7	50.0	11.3	29,536	32.1	49.2	18.7
55101	Racine County	155,723	31.8	49.4	18.8	76,472	34.8	51.0	14.2	79,251	28.9	47.8	23.3
55105	Rock County	128,243	28.8	50.9	20.3	62,357	31.9	52.8	15.3	65,886	25.8	49.1	25.1
55109	St. Croix County	66,326	26.1	58.3	15.6	32,927	28.7	59.4	11.8	33,399	23.5	57.2	19.3
55111	Sauk County	50,541	26.1	55.4	18.5	25,070	31.0	56.0	13.0	25,471	21.3	54.8	23.9

State/ county FIPS code	State/County	Total women age 15 to 50 years	Percent of all women who had a birth in the past year	Percent of women who had a birth who were married (including separated and spouse absent):	Percent of women who had a birth who were partners in an unmarried partner household	Age of women who had a birth in the last year as a percent of all women who had a birth			Women who had a birth in the last year as a percent of all women in their age group		
						Age 15 to 19	Age 20 to 34	Age 35 to 50	Age 15 to 19	Age 20 to 34	Age 35 to 50
	Virginia—cont'd										
51161	Roanoke County	20,760	4.9	78.3	4.5	3.5	69.0	27.5	1.2	9.6	2.7
51165	Rockingham County	17,636	5.1	69.4	2.3	13.9	69.8	16.3	4.5	9.6	1.8
51177	Spotsylvania County..................	31,949	6.7	56.6	2.9	7.6	71.0	21.4	3.5	12.9	2.9
51179	Stafford County	35,056	4.7	88.3	2.7	1.5	78.4	20.1	0.4	10.7	1.9
51191	Washington County...................	12,008	6.2	54.0	17.5	23.4	63.8	12.8	10.7	11.2	1.6
51199	York County............................	15,739	5.6	81.5	3.6	2.1	73.0	24.8	0.7	12.0	2.8
51510	Alexandria city	44,183	5.5	84.1	8.1	2.8	72.9	24.3	3.0	7.8	3.0
51550	Chesapeake city	57,339	5.0	64.7	6.8	3.1	78.6	18.3	1.1	10.1	2.0
51650	Hampton city	35,267	4.3	38.0	7.4	17.9	66.7	15.4	5.4	6.2	1.6
51660	Harrisonburg city	18,698	2.4	57.3	2.7	29.3	60.0	10.7	2.5	2.8	1.3
51680	Lynchburg city.........................	22,190	5.7	80.2	4.7	0.0	92.4	7.6	0.0	10.4	1.5
51700	Newport News city	48,141	6.0	51.5	9.7	8.6	73.1	18.3	3.9	9.0	2.9
51710	Norfolk city	63,621	6.3	58.9	4.1	5.4	81.7	12.9	2.7	9.6	2.4
51740	Portsmouth city........................	23,851	6.0	52.9	19.5	3.6	78.9	17.6	1.9	9.6	2.6
51760	Richmond city..........................	60,164	4.6	47.8	11.9	2.8	80.5	16.8	1.0	6.7	2.3
51770	Roanoke city	23,912	6.8	54.9	9.6	12.6	66.6	20.8	8.4	9.9	3.2
51800	Suffolk city.............................	21,237	5.6	61.0	5.2	4.6	79.0	16.4	2.1	11.6	1.9
51810	Virginia Beach city....................	115,588	5.4	72.3	7.7	2.8	80.9	16.3	1.3	9.7	2.1
53000	**Washington**	1,659,615	5.4	71.7	11.8	4.2	74.0	21.7	1.7	9.4	2.7
53005	Benton County	42,174	5.2	74.1	10.4	2.9	86.3	10.8	1.0	10.7	1.3
53007	Chelan County	16,045	4.6	62.3	14.8	20.2	66.4	13.4	5.9	7.5	1.4
53009	Clallam County	12,767	5.8	66.1	7.0	0.0	81.2	18.8	0.0	11.7	2.4
53011	Clark County	104,634	6.0	70.6	13.2	4.9	79.9	15.2	2.1	12.1	1.9
53015	Cowlitz County	21,980	6.9	39.9	27.1	20.2	69.6	10.2	9.4	12.4	1.5
53021	Franklin County	20,080	7.7	72.0	18.0	0.0	78.2	21.8	0.0	13.2	4.3
53025	Grant County...........................	20,557	5.6	64.6	16.2	13.1	59.8	27.1	4.3	8.1	3.7
53027	Grays Harbor County	14,198	5.4	67.5	18.1	18.4	65.8	15.8	6.6	9.0	1.9
53029	Island County..........................	15,837	5.9	84.0	13.8	0.0	83.5	16.5	0.0	11.5	2.2
53033	King County	518,477	5.3	76.0	9.4	2.5	69.2	28.3	1.2	8.4	3.3
53035	Kitsap County	56,459	6.0	82.7	7.4	0.0	82.4	17.6	0.0	11.8	2.4
53041	Lewis County...........................	15,798	4.3	72.3	15.4	6.2	66.2	27.6	1.8	7.2	2.6
53045	Mason County	11,617	5.8	51.1	12.0	3.1	53.7	43.2	1.3	7.8	5.3
53053	Pierce County	201,320	5.6	70.9	12.8	5.0	77.1	17.9	2.2	10.0	2.3
53057	Skagit County..........................	25,431	5.9	55.4	32.3	3.8	79.0	17.2	1.5	11.4	2.3
53061	Snohomish County	179,440	4.7	76.2	9.7	1.8	74.0	24.2	0.7	8.7	2.4
53063	Spokane County	114,636	4.9	71.2	10.7	3.4	82.8	13.8	1.2	9.0	1.6
53067	Thurston County	63,057	5.5	73.5	13.3	4.8	69.8	25.3	1.9	9.2	3.2
53071	Walla Walla County	13,222	3.7	62.0	17.4	2.2	86.7	11.0	0.4	7.9	1.0
53073	Whatcom County	51,263	4.6	72.9	5.6	2.3	72.9	24.7	0.7	7.2	3.0
53077	Yakima County	56,601	6.9	57.2	12.3	13.6	70.4	16.0	5.7	11.3	2.7
54000	**West Virginia**.......................	417,010	4.5	61.0	9.8	5.6	80.7	13.7	1.9	8.9	1.3
54003	Berkeley County.......................	26,405	5.3	71.3	11.7	0.0	86.4	13.6	0.0	11.7	1.5
54011	Cabell County..........................	23,300	4.8	70.6	8.3	8.3	71.2	20.6	2.8	7.4	2.6
54033	Harrison County.......................	15,342	6.2	88.1	2.9	2.5	87.2	10.3	1.2	13.7	1.3
54037	Jefferson County......................	13,509	4.0	70.7	11.6	0.0	76.8	23.2	0.0	8.1	1.9
54039	Kanawha County......................	42,456	3.8	52.4	14.3	6.4	86.0	7.6	2.0	7.9	0.6
54049	Marion County.........................	12,940	3.1	71.5	8.8	3.4	87.7	8.8	0.7	6.5	0.6
54055	Mercer County.........................	13,835	4.7	55.9	16.6	2.1	89.2	8.7	0.7	10.5	0.9
54061	Monongalia County...................	28,437	4.4	43.5	7.8	1.9	76.3	21.8	0.6	6.0	3.4
54079	Putnam County........................	12,874	7.0	65.7	3.9	11.9	73.1	15.0	6.7	14.3	2.0
54081	Raleigh County	16,719	3.4	77.4	5.3	0.0	79.1	20.9	0.0	6.4	1.5
54107	Wood County	19,550	5.3	45.8	20.8	17.2	71.9	10.9	7.3	9.7	1.2
55000	**Wisconsin**............................	1,337,285	5.1	67.5	13.2	3.8	78.1	18.1	1.4	9.6	2.1
55009	Brown County..........................	61,183	6.0	59.1	17.4	6.6	77.0	16.4	2.8	11.0	2.2
55017	Chippewa County.....................	12,915	5.8	76.4	19.3	7.0	88.0	5.1	3.1	12.8	0.6
55021	Columbia County......................	12,029	5.1	71.1	18.6	1.3	74.3	24.4	0.5	10.5	2.5
55025	Dane County	133,358	4.5	75.7	7.1	2.6	77.0	20.3	0.9	7.2	2.3
55027	Dodge County	18,154	4.9	55.3	7.7	2.3	79.9	17.8	0.8	10.8	1.7
55035	Eau Claire County.....................	26,838	4.3	65.3	12.1	2.9	77.7	19.4	0.8	6.6	2.5
55039	Fond du Lac County...................	23,293	5.1	68.2	20.4	1.3	78.9	19.9	0.5	10.0	2.2
55043	Grant County...........................	11,043	5.5	67.3	23.5	5.3	76.0	18.7	1.6	9.6	2.7
55055	Jefferson County......................	20,145	5.0	80.8	8.2	0.0	88.8	11.2	0.0	11.6	1.2
55059	Kenosha County.......................	40,955	4.3	65.6	7.3	6.4	70.2	23.5	1.8	7.7	2.2
55063	La Crosse County......................	29,712	4.4	73.1	17.8	2.3	72.5	25.2	0.6	6.9	3.1
55071	Manitowoc County....................	17,149	4.9	81.4	5.5	9.3	68.1	22.6	2.9	9.1	2.3
55073	Marathon County......................	30,343	5.5	75.7	19.6	1.5	75.1	23.4	0.6	10.8	2.7
55079	Milwaukee County.....................	246,643	5.2	52.1	14.4	4.9	75.5	19.6	1.9	8.3	2.5
55087	Outagamie County....................	42,860	5.2	77.9	16.0	0.8	82.3	16.9	0.3	10.6	1.9
55089	Ozaukee County.......................	18,665	4.6	87.4	5.7	0.0	71.9	28.1	0.0	10.2	2.5
55097	Portage County........................	17,800	3.7	73.4	20.7	1.1	75.5	23.4	0.2	6.1	2.3
55101	Racine County	44,682	4.7	56.8	16.7	5.5	80.4	14.1	1.9	9.9	1.4
55105	Rock County............................	37,978	6.4	64.6	11.0	4.5	75.3	20.1	2.1	12.2	2.8
55109	St. Croix County	20,413	6.9	81.8	10.1	4.3	85.9	9.8	2.3	16.4	1.3
55111	Sauk County	13,440	5.2	69.6	8.8	3.3	86.2	10.5	1.3	11.4	1.1

Table C-2: Counties with a Population of 50,000 or More—Marriages and Births—*Continued*

State/ county FIPS code	State/County	Total population 15 years and older	Marital status, percent			Male population 15 years and older	Male, marital status, percent			Female population 15 years and older	Female, marital status, percent		
			Never married	Now married (except separated	Separated, widowed, or divorced		Never married	Now married (except separated	Separated, widowed, or divorced		Never married	Now married (except separated	Separated, widowed, or divorced
	Wisconsin—cont'd												
55117	Sheboygan County	93,201	27.5	54.4	18.1	46,511	30.9	54.7	14.3	46,690	24.0	54.1	21.8
55127	Walworth County	83,791	30.9	50.9	18.2	41,503	34.3	52.2	13.4	42,288	27.6	49.5	22.9
55131	Washington County	106,640	24.1	59.7	16.2	52,608	27.5	60.7	11.8	54,032	20.8	58.8	20.4
55133	Waukesha County	319,137	24.9	59.9	15.2	155,493	28.0	61.6	10.3	163,644	22.0	58.3	19.8
55135	Waupaca County	42,969	22.7	57.1	20.2	21,589	26.0	57.9	16.1	21,380	19.4	56.2	24.4
55139	Winnebago County	138,705	33.0	48.8	18.2	69,417	36.9	49.0	14.2	69,288	29.2	48.6	22.2
55141	Wood County	60,744	24.6	55.0	20.4	29,840	28.3	56.7	15.1	30,904	21.0	53.4	25.6
56000	**Wyoming**	459,841	27.2	53.0	19.8	234,022	30.9	52.8	16.3	225,819	23.4	53.2	23.4
56021	Laramie County	75,309	25.7	53.7	20.6	37,708	29.5	54.4	16.1	37,601	21.8	53.0	25.2
56025	Natrona County	62,878	27.5	51.8	20.7	31,548	30.7	50.9	18.4	31,330	24.2	52.6	23.1

Table C-2: Counties with a Population of 50,000 or More—Marriages and Births—*Continued*

State/county FIPS code	State/County	Total women age 15 to 50 years	Percent of all women who had a birth in the past year	Percent of women who had a birth who were married (including separated and spouse absent):	Percent of women who had a birth who were partners in an unmarried partner household	Age of women who had a birth in the last year as a percent of all women who had a birth			Women who had a birth in the last year as a percent of all women in their age group		
						Age 15 to 19	Age 20 to 34	Age 35 to 50	Age 15 to 19	Age 20 to 34	Age 35 to 50
	Wisconsin—cont'd										
55117	Sheboygan County	25,565	5.1	75.3	17.5	3.1	83.1	13.9	1.0	11.6	1.5
55127	Walworth County	24,360	3.3	66.2	5.1	11.6	77.1	11.3	2.5	6.4	0.8
55131	Washington County	30,013	5.0	72.0	7.0	3.7	77.6	18.7	1.4	11.8	1.8
55133	Waukesha County	87,126	4.1	85.9	8.8	1.7	77.6	20.7	0.5	9.3	1.6
55135	Waupaca County	10,756	6.6	76.6	16.5	5.9	86.2	7.9	2.7	15.9	1.0
55139	Winnebago County	40,824	5.3	69.9	19.1	2.0	81.3	16.7	0.7	10.0	2.1
55141	Wood County	15,573	4.7	62.3	15.6	2.9	82.6	14.5	1.0	9.9	1.4
56000	**Wyoming**	130,749	5.5	72.5	13.4	3.4	84.3	12.3	1.4	10.4	1.6
56021	Laramie County	21,734	5.1	85.7	10.7	0.0	84.9	15.1	0.0	10.1	1.8
56025	Natrona County	18,417	5.0	61.2	19.5	8.5	74.3	17.2	3.5	8.1	2.1

Table C-3: Metropolitan Areas—Marriages and Births

CBSA FIPS code	Metropolitan area	Total population 15 years and older	Marital status, percent			Male population 15 years and older	Male, marital status, percent			Female population 15 years and older	Female, marital status, percent		
			Never married	Now married (except separated)	Separated, widowed, or divorced		Never married	Now married (except separated)	Separated, widowed, or divorced		Never married	Now married (except separated)	Separated, widowed, or divorced
10180	Abilene, TX	134,199	31.7	47.4	20.9	67,749	36.4	47.3	16.3	66,450	27.0	47.5	25.5
10420	Akron, OH	581,677	33.6	46.8	19.6	278,746	36.2	49.1	14.7	302,931	31.2	44.7	24.1
10500	Albany, GA	123,607	37.0	40.1	22.9	57,536	39.1	44.0	16.9	66,071	35.1	36.8	28.1
10540	Albany, OR	95,096	25.7	53.7	20.6	46,670	28.5	55.7	15.7	48,426	23.0	51.7	25.3
10580	Albany-Schenectady-Troy, NY	727,602	35.7	46.4	17.9	352,303	38.8	48.2	13.0	375,299	32.7	44.7	22.6
10740	Albuquerque, NM	720,575	33.9	45.4	20.7	351,391	36.9	47.2	15.9	369,184	31.0	43.7	25.3
10780	Alexandria, LA	122,322	31.9	43.2	24.8	59,825	36.8	43.8	19.4	62,497	27.3	42.6	30.1
10900	Allentown-Bethlehem-Easton, PA-NJ	677,108	30.6	50.7	18.7	327,080	33.8	52.9	13.2	350,028	27.5	48.6	23.9
11020	Altoona, PA	104,948	28.0	50.0	22.0	50,375	31.3	52.3	16.4	54,573	25.0	47.9	27.1
11100	Amarillo, TX	200,163	29.3	49.5	21.3	99,276	32.6	50.7	16.7	100,887	26.0	48.2	25.7
11180	Ames, IA	78,093	47.1	42.5	10.4	40,310	51.7	41.6	6.7	37,783	42.2	43.5	14.3
11260	Anchorage, AK	307,020	33.4	49.0	17.6	156,535	37.9	47.7	14.4	150,485	28.7	50.4	20.9
11460	Ann Arbor, MI	292,935	41.8	43.8	14.4	143,391	45.0	44.9	10.1	149,544	38.7	42.8	18.5
11500	Anniston-Oxford-Jacksonville, AL	95,402	27.9	46.8	25.3	45,186	31.1	49.0	20.0	50,216	25.0	44.9	30.1
11540	Appleton, WI	181,738	27.5	56.8	15.7	90,163	31.6	56.6	11.7	91,575	23.4	56.9	19.7
11700	Asheville, NC	361,503	26.4	51.0	22.6	172,750	30.0	54.2	15.8	188,753	23.0	48.2	28.8
12020	Athens-Clarke County, GA	162,722	44.7	39.4	15.9	77,292	46.1	42.5	11.4	85,430	43.4	36.6	20.0
12060	Atlanta-Sandy Springs-Roswell, GA	4,274,920	34.4	47.4	18.3	2,049,682	37.0	50.0	12.9	2,225,238	31.9	45.0	23.1
12100	Atlantic City-Hammonton, NJ	224,182	34.9	45.4	19.7	107,248	37.9	48.3	13.8	116,934	32.2	42.7	25.1
12220	Auburn-Opelika, AL	120,747	39.7	44.3	16.1	59,314	43.5	45.5	11.0	61,433	35.9	43.1	21.0
12260	Augusta-Richmond County, GA-SC	459,692	32.9	45.8	21.3	221,356	35.6	48.4	16.0	238,336	30.5	43.3	26.2
12420	Austin-Round Rock, TX	1,448,723	35.9	47.4	16.7	721,815	39.3	48.4	12.3	726,908	32.5	46.3	21.2
12540	Bakersfield, CA	643,446	35.8	46.4	17.8	332,082	39.8	46.4	13.7	311,364	31.6	46.4	22.0
12580	Baltimore-Columbia-Towson, MD	2,239,639	35.8	45.2	19.0	1,065,465	37.9	48.1	14.1	1,174,174	33.9	42.6	23.5
12620	Bangor, ME	129,678	30.7	48.2	21.2	63,501	34.3	48.9	16.9	66,177	27.3	47.5	25.2
12700	Barnstable Town, MA	186,612	26.2	52.8	21.1	87,879	30.1	56.1	13.8	98,733	22.7	49.8	27.5
12940	Baton Rouge, LA	649,477	36.1	43.5	20.4	315,188	38.9	45.7	15.4	334,289	33.5	41.4	25.1
12980	Battle Creek, MI	108,982	29.4	46.7	23.9	52,462	33.5	47.5	19.0	56,520	25.6	45.9	28.5
13020	Bay City, MI	88,195	29.1	50.6	20.4	42,791	33.9	51.7	14.4	45,404	24.5	49.5	26.0
13140	Beaumont-Port Arthur, TX	323,742	29.7	47.2	23.1	163,191	33.3	48.4	18.4	160,551	26.1	46.1	27.8
13220	Beckley, WV	103,149	26.1	50.3	23.6	51,621	30.9	49.4	19.7	51,528	21.3	51.2	27.5
13380	Bellingham, WA	170,226	34.1	48.1	17.8	83,737	37.5	50.0	12.5	86,489	30.8	46.3	23.0
13460	Bend-Redmond, OR	132,615	24.6	54.1	21.3	64,987	27.6	55.4	17.0	67,628	21.7	53.0	25.4
13740	Billings, MT	131,383	27.5	50.1	22.4	63,680	31.0	51.9	17.1	67,703	24.3	48.4	27.3
13780	Binghamton, NY	207,634	33.3	47.3	19.4	100,963	36.9	48.8	14.3	106,671	29.9	46.0	24.2
13820	Birmingham-Hoover, AL	912,575	29.0	49.0	22.0	432,950	31.5	52.1	16.4	479,625	26.7	46.2	27.1
13900	Bismarck, ND	96,900	29.8	53.5	16.7	47,654	32.8	54.7	12.5	49,246	26.9	52.3	20.8
13980	Blacksburg-Christiansburg-Radford, VA	154,383	39.4	43.4	17.3	77,003	43.3	43.6	13.2	77,380	35.5	43.1	21.4
14010	Bloomington, IL	153,726	37.0	47.8	15.1	74,255	39.6	49.6	10.9	79,471	34.7	46.2	19.1
14020	Bloomington, IN	139,483	45.7	38.4	15.9	68,960	49.1	38.9	11.9	70,523	42.3	37.9	19.7
14100	Bloomsburg-Berwick, PA	72,310	32.6	48.7	18.8	34,163	34.7	51.5	13.8	38,147	30.7	46.1	23.3
14260	Boise City, ID	493,230	27.5	53.8	18.7	244,009	30.6	55.6	13.8	249,221	24.3	52.1	23.5
14460	Boston-Cambridge-Newton, MA-NH	3,840,464	36.4	47.3	16.3	1,841,187	38.9	49.8	11.3	1,999,277	34.1	45.0	20.9
14500	Boulder, CO	252,792	37.2	47.7	15.2	126,358	40.4	48.6	11.0	126,434	34.0	46.7	19.3
14540	Bowling Green, KY	131,485	31.4	49.1	19.5	63,830	34.4	50.9	14.7	67,655	28.6	47.4	24.0
14740	Bremerton-Silverdale, WA	209,342	27.9	52.5	19.6	106,445	33.1	52.7	14.2	102,897	22.5	52.3	25.2
14860	Bridgeport-Stamford-Norwalk, CT	749,174	32.5	50.9	16.6	360,364	35.2	53.5	11.3	388,810	30.0	48.5	21.5
15180	Brownsville-Harlingen, TX	303,059	32.5	49.0	18.5	143,095	34.9	52.6	12.5	159,964	30.3	45.8	23.9
15260	Brunswick, GA	91,299	26.4	49.9	23.6	43,451	29.3	52.6	18.1	47,848	23.8	47.5	28.7
15380	Buffalo-Cheektowaga-Niagara Falls, NY	940,747	35.4	44.9	19.7	450,134	38.8	46.9	14.2	490,613	32.3	43.1	24.7
15500	Burlington, NC	124,385	29.8	48.9	21.3	58,265	31.5	53.5	15.0	66,120	28.4	44.9	26.7
15540	Burlington-South Burlington, VT	178,561	36.2	48.1	15.7	86,535	38.8	49.0	12.2	92,026	33.7	47.3	19.0
15680	California-Lexington Park, MD	85,721	28.3	56.5	15.2	42,528	30.3	58.4	11.4	43,193	26.3	54.7	19.0
15940	Canton-Massillon, OH	330,059	28.1	50.5	21.4	158,288	30.9	52.7	16.5	171,771	25.6	48.4	26.0
15980	Cape Coral-Fort Myers, FL	543,015	26.0	50.3	23.7	264,117	29.5	52.0	18.5	278,898	22.6	48.7	28.6
16020	Cape Girardeau, MO-IL	79,029	30.8	49.4	19.8	37,930	34.6	51.4	14.0	41,099	27.2	47.6	25.2
16060	Carbondale-Marion, IL	105,722	35.8	44.6	19.6	52,533	40.3	46.1	13.6	53,189	31.5	43.1	25.4
16180	Carson City, NV	44,972	28.2	46.0	25.8	22,931	34.4	45.7	19.8	22,041	21.7	46.2	32.1
16220	Casper, WY	62,878	27.5	51.8	20.7	31,548	30.7	50.9	18.4	31,330	24.2	52.6	23.1
16300	Cedar Rapids, IA	209,233	28.8	51.7	19.5	103,045	31.5	52.5	16.0	106,188	26.2	51.0	22.8
16540	Chambersburg-Waynesboro, PA	122,040	25.5	54.8	19.7	59,150	27.7	58.2	14.1	62,890	23.4	51.6	25.0
16580	Champaign-Urbana, IL	195,715	43.3	41.9	14.8	97,310	46.5	42.8	10.7	98,405	40.1	41.0	18.9
16620	Charleston, WV	185,951	26.2	48.8	25.0	88,622	30.0	51.4	18.6	97,329	22.7	46.5	30.8
16700	Charleston-North Charleston, SC	562,785	33.7	45.9	20.3	273,047	36.9	47.7	15.4	289,738	30.7	44.3	25.0
16740	Charlotte-Concord-Gastonia, NC-SC	1,813,943	31.6	49.6	18.7	870,219	34.1	52.4	13.5	943,724	29.4	47.0	23.6
16820	Charlottesville, VA	185,028	35.4	47.9	16.7	88,735	37.8	50.1	12.1	96,293	33.3	45.8	20.9
16860	Chattanooga, TN-GA	440,057	27.9	50.4	21.7	210,154	31.3	52.8	15.9	229,903	24.8	48.2	27.0
16940	Cheyenne, WY	75,309	25.7	53.7	20.6	37,708	29.5	54.4	16.1	37,601	21.8	53.0	25.2
16980	Chicago-Naperville-Elgin, IL-IN-WI	7,598,803	36.4	46.9	16.6	3,676,577	39.3	49.2	11.5	3,922,226	33.8	44.9	21.4

Table C-3: Metropolitan Areas—Marriages and Births—*Continued*

CBSA FIPS code	Metropolitan area	Total women age 15 to 50 years	Percent of all women who had a birth in the past year	Percent of women who had a birth who were married (including separated and spouse absent):	Percent of women who had a birth who were partners in an unmarried partner household	Age of women who had a birth in the last year as a percent of all women who had a birth			Women who had a birth in the last year as a percent of all women in their age group		
						Age 15 to 19	Age 20 to 34	Age 35 to 50	Age 15 to 19	Age 20 to 34	Age 35 to 50
10180	Abilene, TX	39,400	6.0	55.9	13.2	9.3	86.7	4.0	3.7	11.1	0.6
10420	Akron, OH	170,535	4.9	55.9	11.3	5.6	77.8	16.6	1.8	9.1	1.9
10500	Albany, GA	39,488	6.0	35.3	18.9	2.2	82.2	15.6	0.9	11.4	2.2
10540	Albany, OR	26,388	4.3	76.8	2.8	0.6	77.1	22.3	0.2	7.9	2.2
10580	Albany-Schenectady-Troy, NY	213,245	4.0	68.2	11.1	3.5	72.9	23.6	1.0	7.1	2.1
10740	Albuquerque, NM	216,003	5.7	60.4	12.9	4.7	75.5	19.8	2.0	9.9	2.6
10780	Alexandria, LA	35,957	4.2	57.9	5.8	6.5	84.0	9.5	1.9	8.4	0.9
10900	Allentown-Bethlehem-Easton, PA-NJ	192,234	4.8	59.8	13.2	4.9	73.1	22.0	1.6	9.2	2.2
11020	Altoona, PA	28,059	4.3	62.3	16.7	6.4	71.5	22.1	2.1	7.7	2.1
11100	Amarillo, TX	61,527	6.4	62.0	12.2	7.7	76.3	16.0	3.5	10.8	2.5
11180	Ames, IA	26,203	2.9	87.8	9.0	0.4	86.3	13.4	0.1	4.5	1.6
11260	Anchorage, AK	99,506	5.3	65.8	12.8	2.9	74.9	22.2	1.2	9.0	2.8
11460	Ann Arbor, MI	96,980	3.8	69.6	7.6	3.1	69.8	27.1	0.8	5.5	2.8
11500	Anniston-Oxford-Jacksonville, AL	28,048	3.9	60.6	3.0	17.6	63.7	18.8	5.0	5.8	1.7
11540	Appleton, WI	54,332	5.1	80.2	13.4	0.6	82.0	17.4	0.2	10.7	1.9
11700	Asheville, NC	94,856	4.7	69.0	7.8	9.1	69.1	21.8	3.6	7.9	2.2
12020	Athens-Clarke County, GA	57,692	3.9	58.3	9.8	10.2	68.4	21.4	2.0	5.5	2.6
12060	Atlanta-Sandy Springs-Roswell, GA										
12100	Atlantic City-Hammonton, NJ	65,716	4.4	58.8	15.2	3.4	75.3	21.3	1.1	8.6	2.0
12220	Auburn-Opelika, AL	42,140	4.4	70.7	10.3	11.5	81.0	7.5	3.3	7.1	1.0
12260	Augusta-Richmond County, GA-SC	139,537	5.1	57.3	2.2	6.9	77.7	15.4	2.7	9.2	1.8
12420	Austin-Round Rock, TX										
12540	Bakersfield, CA	204,900	6.8	56.5	14.3	10.4	76.0	13.6	4.4	11.8	2.3
12580	Baltimore-Columbia-Towson, MD	693,023	5.4	62.5	8.3	5.8	69.9	24.2	2.4	9.0	2.9
12620	Bangor, ME	37,117	4.5	58.6	16.6	1.4	89.7	8.9	0.5	9.7	0.9
12700	Barnstable Town, MA	39,792	2.8	66.1	14.7	0.0	77.7	22.3	0.0	6.0	1.2
12940	Baton Rouge, LA	208,620	5.1	54.5	9.1	5.7	81.9	12.5	2.0	9.2	1.5
12980	Battle Creek, MI	31,098	4.7	58.9	17.0	4.6	75.7	19.7	1.5	8.8	2.0
13020	Bay City, MI	23,199	5.4	43.9	17.9	3.3	90.1	6.7	1.3	12.1	0.8
13140	Beaumont-Port Arthur, TX	93,052	5.4	53.2	9.1	14.6	73.9	11.5	5.4	9.5	1.4
13220	Beckley, WV	26,350	4.5	64.7	8.7	4.2	77.3	18.5	1.6	8.5	1.7
13380	Bellingham, WA	51,263	4.6	72.9	5.6	2.3	72.9	24.7	0.7	7.2	3.0
13460	Bend-Redmond, OR	36,225	4.6	69.3	4.5	3.5	64.1	32.4	1.3	7.5	3.1
13740	Billings, MT	37,512	5.0	60.9	20.6	4.3	76.1	19.6	1.7	8.8	2.2
13780	Binghamton, NY	57,380	4.4	63.6	18.7	3.8	73.4	22.8	1.0	7.7	2.4
13820	Birmingham-Hoover, AL	277,747	5.7	61.9	4.7	6.3	79.0	14.7	2.8	10.7	1.9
13900	Bismarck, ND	28,350	6.2	66.6	16.4	0.5	84.1	15.4	0.2	11.6	2.3
13980	Blacksburg-Christiansburg-Radford, VA	48,458	3.7	75.2	12.5	4.8	76.3	18.9	1.0	5.7	2.1
14010	Bloomington, IL	51,570	4.3	55.4	13.2	7.5	78.9	13.7	2.2	7.1	1.6
14020	Bloomington, IN	47,510	4.5	71.4	4.0	2.8	76.5	20.8	0.7	6.4	3.3
14100	Bloomsburg-Berwick, PA	21,105	3.7	61.4	23.8	5.4	84.2	10.3	1.1	7.4	0.9
14260	Boise City, ID	153,784	6.0	73.6	7.5	5.2	83.1	11.6	2.3	11.9	1.6
14460	Boston-Cambridge-Newton, MA-NH	1,187,430	4.6	73.7	7.1	2.5	65.2	32.4	0.9	7.2	3.4
14500	Boulder, CO	78,926	4.6	79.3	7.9	4.3	57.3	38.3	1.3	6.1	4.3
14540	Bowling Green, KY	42,079	4.0	63.0	7.7	9.5	78.0	12.5	2.2	7.4	1.3
14740	Bremerton-Silverdale, WA	56,459	6.0	82.7	7.4	0.0	82.4	17.6	0.0	11.8	2.4
14860	Bridgeport-Stamford-Norwalk, CT	224,540	4.5	76.2	6.3	3.7	59.8	36.5	1.2	7.7	3.3
15180	Brownsville-Harlingen, TX	102,159	6.5	56.1	6.9	13.6	71.8	14.6	5.1	11.5	2.2
15260	Brunswick, GA	26,308	3.8	44.2	12.2	12.0	78.0	10.1	3.5	7.3	0.8
15380	Buffalo-Cheektowaga-Niagara Falls, NY	266,527	5.0	58.8	14.1	3.8	74.6	21.6	1.3	8.9	2.5
15500	Burlington, NC	37,849	4.4	53.0	3.8	2.4	74.4	23.2	0.7	8.4	2.2
15540	Burlington-South Burlington, VT	55,507	4.2	74.7	9.1	2.6	68.0	29.3	0.7	6.8	3.0
15680	California-Lexington Park, MD	27,590	6.0	61.4	6.4	1.4	79.9	18.7	0.6	12.3	2.4
15940	Canton-Massillon, OH	90,309	5.7	56.5	12.3	2.7	86.8	10.5	1.1	12.5	1.3
15980	Cape Coral-Fort Myers, FL	127,828	4.7	57.8	12.7	7.3	70.4	22.4	2.5	8.3	2.2
16020	Cape Girardeau, MO-IL	23,555	5.7	47.2	2.5	3.1	86.4	10.6	1.1	10.9	1.6
16060	Carbondale-Marion, IL	31,479	4.2	60.8	15.1	2.7	81.3	16.0	0.7	7.3	1.8
16180	Carson City, NV	11,410	4.2	75.8	2.5	8.3	82.7	9.0	2.2	8.9	0.8
16220	Casper, WY	18,417	5.0	61.2	19.5	8.5	74.3	17.2	3.5	8.1	2.1
16300	Cedar Rapids, IA	61,205	5.7	72.2	6.6	3.9	75.7	20.4	1.6	10.5	2.6
16540	Chambersburg-Waynesboro, PA	34,015	4.9	78.2	9.7	0.0	63.7	36.3	0.0	8.1	3.8
16580	Champaign-Urbana, IL	64,587	3.2	70.9	7.9	8.1	77.4	14.5	1.6	4.9	1.5
16620	Charleston, WV	50,008	4.3	57.9	10.8	8.7	85.4	5.9	3.1	9.0	0.5
16700	Charleston-North Charleston, SC	176,075	4.9	59.7	5.9	6.7	77.5	15.7	2.7	8.4	1.8
16740	Charlotte-Concord-Gastonia, NC-SC	587,268	5.5	65.8	6.9	5.1	71.5	23.4	2.2	9.9	2.7
16820	Charlottesville, VA	56,701	4.3	70.2	8.9	3.4	75.8	20.8	1.1	7.0	2.2
16860	Chattanooga, TN-GA	127,378	5.8	56.7	11.6	6.7	74.2	19.1	2.9	10.4	2.4
16940	Cheyenne, WY	21,734	5.1	85.7	10.7	0.0	84.9	15.1	0.0	10.1	1.8
16980	Chicago-Naperville-Elgin, IL-IN-WI	2,399,120	5.0	64.5	8.2	5.1	70.9	23.9	1.9	8.5	2.7

Table C-3: Metropolitan Areas—Marriages and Births—*Continued*

CBSA FIPS code	Metropolitan area	Total population 15 years and older	Marital status, percent — Never married	Now married (except separated)	Separated, widowed, or divorced	Male population 15 years and older	Male, marital status, percent — Never married	Now married (except separated)	Separated, widowed, or divorced	Female population 15 years and older	Female, marital status, percent — Never married	Now married (except separated)	Separated, widowed, or divorced
17020	Chico, CA	183,730	35.6	42.0	22.3	90,333	40.5	43.1	16.5	93,397	30.9	41.0	28.0
17140	Cincinnati, OH-KY-IN	1,695,536	31.5	49.1	19.4	820,531	34.3	51.0	14.7	875,005	28.9	47.3	23.8
17300	Clarksville, TN-KY	206,601	26.8	54.2	19.0	103,028	31.6	54.1	14.3	103,573	22.0	54.4	23.7
17420	Cleveland, TN	95,707	24.9	51.8	23.3	46,177	28.1	52.9	18.9	49,530	22.0	50.7	27.3
17460	Cleveland-Elyria, OH	1,687,589	33.8	45.5	20.7	801,907	36.7	48.1	15.2	885,682	31.1	43.1	25.7
17660	Coeur d'Alene, ID	114,226	23.9	55.4	20.6	55,807	27.3	57.1	15.6	58,419	20.8	53.8	25.4
17780	College Station-Bryan, TX	192,239	46.7	39.1	14.2	97,007	50.5	39.1	10.4	95,232	42.8	39.1	18.1
17820	Colorado Springs, CO	527,639	28.1	53.9	18.0	263,459	32.4	54.4	13.2	264,180	23.9	53.3	22.8
17860	Columbia, MO	138,707	43.3	42.0	14.7	66,065	44.9	44.6	10.5	72,642	41.9	39.7	18.4
17900	Columbia, SC	635,250	35.3	44.8	20.0	306,076	38.8	46.7	14.5	329,174	32.0	42.9	25.1
17980	Columbus, GA-AL	244,662	35.1	42.2	22.7	119,928	40.1	43.5	16.4	124,734	30.2	41.1	28.7
18020	Columbus, IN	62,536	25.7	53.0	21.3	30,846	29.8	55.0	15.1	31,690	21.6	51.0	27.4
18140	Columbus, OH	1,549,449	33.6	47.5	18.9	753,737	36.3	49.1	14.5	795,712	30.9	46.0	23.1
18580	Corpus Christi, TX	344,326	31.5	46.9	21.6	168,117	34.9	49.1	16.0	176,209	28.3	44.9	26.9
18700	Corvallis, OR	74,251	41.8	43.5	14.7	37,374	45.1	43.8	11.1	36,877	38.5	43.1	18.4
18880	Crestview-Fort Walton Beach-Destin, FL	201,674	26.7	51.6	21.7	102,091	32.0	51.1	16.9	99,583	21.2	52.1	26.6
19060	Cumberland, MD-WV	86,343	36.2	41.8	22.0	44,335	41.7	41.7	16.6	42,008	30.3	41.9	27.8
19100	Dallas-Fort Worth-Arlington, TX	5,165,278	31.4	50.4	18.2	2,519,825	34.3	52.6	13.2	2,645,453	28.7	48.4	22.9
19140	Dalton, GA	110,194	25.3	52.2	22.5	54,388	28.3	53.9	17.8	55,806	22.4	50.6	27.0
19180	Danville, IL	64,579	28.6	47.5	24.0	31,761	32.8	47.7	19.5	32,818	24.5	47.2	28.3
19300	Daphne-Fairhope-Foley, AL	155,044	23.3	55.5	21.2	75,202	26.6	57.3	16.1	79,842	20.2	53.7	26.1
19340	Davenport-Moline-Rock Island, IA-IL	308,440	28.7	50.3	21.0	150,214	32.0	52.0	16.0	158,226	25.6	48.7	25.7
19380	Dayton, OH	654,145	31.7	46.3	22.1	312,460	34.5	49.0	16.5	341,685	29.0	43.8	27.2
19460	Decatur, AL	124,075	23.9	52.3	23.8	60,091	27.5	54.3	18.2	63,984	20.5	50.4	29.0
19500	Decatur, IL	89,332	29.5	47.9	22.6	42,218	32.6	50.6	16.9	47,114	26.7	45.6	27.8
19660	Deltona-Daytona Beach-Ormond Beach, FL	505,651	27.2	47.7	25.1	243,524	30.8	50.0	19.2	262,127	23.9	45.5	30.6
19740	Denver-Aurora-Lakewood, CO	2,104,730	31.9	49.5	18.6	1,040,027	35.2	50.7	14.1	1,064,703	28.6	48.3	23.1
19780	Des Moines-West Des Moines, IA	461,669	28.7	53.2	18.1	224,299	31.0	55.0	14.0	237,370	26.6	51.5	21.9
19820	Detroit-Warren-Dearborn, MI	3,470,303	34.2	46.3	19.5	1,661,537	37.3	48.4	14.3	1,808,766	31.4	44.3	24.3
20020	Dothan, AL	118,502	26.3	49.2	24.5	55,924	30.0	52.6	17.4	62,578	23.0	46.2	30.8
20100	Dover, DE	133,550	31.6	48.1	20.4	63,445	33.2	50.7	16.1	70,105	30.1	45.7	24.2
20220	Dubuque, IA	76,690	31.6	51.7	16.8	37,486	33.9	53.5	12.6	39,204	29.3	49.9	20.8
20260	Duluth, MN-WI	232,865	32.2	47.7	20.0	116,806	36.4	48.0	15.6	116,059	28.0	47.4	24.5
20500	Durham-Chapel Hill, NC	429,348	37.2	45.4	17.4	203,536	39.2	48.1	12.8	225,812	35.4	43.0	21.6
20700	East Stroudsburg, PA	138,895	33.1	49.8	17.1	68,081	36.4	51.6	12.0	70,814	29.8	48.1	22.1
20740	Eau Claire, WI	134,281	32.6	49.7	17.8	66,891	36.0	50.0	14.0	67,390	29.1	49.4	21.5
20940	El Centro, CA	134,231	36.6	45.2	18.1	69,144	41.1	45.1	13.8	65,087	31.9	45.4	22.7
21060	Elizabethtown-Fort Knox, KY	119,077	25.6	52.9	21.4	59,026	29.5	54.1	16.4	60,051	21.8	51.8	26.4
21140	Elkhart-Goshen, IN	152,256	28.7	52.3	19.0	74,514	30.9	54.9	14.2	77,742	26.7	49.8	23.5
21300	Elmira, NY	72,582	30.7	48.7	20.6	35,934	35.2	50.1	14.7	36,648	26.3	47.4	26.3
21340	El Paso, TX	627,143	32.5	47.4	20.2	302,774	35.6	50.0	14.4	324,369	29.6	44.9	25.5
21500	Erie, PA	229,567	34.7	46.6	18.8	111,875	37.6	48.7	13.7	117,692	31.9	44.5	23.6
21660	Eugene, OR	298,345	33.3	45.1	21.5	145,224	37.4	46.4	16.1	153,121	29.4	43.9	26.6
21780	Evansville, IN-KY	253,501	27.9	50.8	21.3	121,623	31.1	52.7	16.1	131,878	25.0	49.0	26.0
21820	Fairbanks, AK	78,574	34.9	47.9	17.2	42,045	40.1	46.0	13.9	36,529	29.0	50.0	21.0
22020	Fargo, ND-MN	176,860	37.9	47.2	14.8	88,495	41.0	47.9	11.2	88,365	34.9	46.6	18.5
22140	Farmington, NM	97,470	36.1	46.1	17.8	48,145	39.2	47.8	13.0	49,325	33.1	44.4	22.5
22180	Fayetteville, NC	289,188	31.6	47.6	20.8	139,007	35.4	49.6	15.0	150,181	28.1	45.8	26.1
22220	Fayetteville-Springdale-Rogers, AR-MO	374,866	27.6	55.0	17.4	185,042	31.0	56.1	12.9	189,824	24.3	54.0	21.7
22380	Flagstaff, AZ	110,185	43.6	42.0	14.4	54,106	45.5	42.9	11.6	56,079	41.7	41.2	17.1
22420	Flint, MI	335,571	33.2	44.3	22.5	159,164	35.9	46.7	17.4	176,407	30.8	42.2	27.0
22500	Florence, SC	164,671	33.2	45.3	21.5	75,950	35.2	49.7	15.1	88,721	31.5	41.4	27.0
22520	Florence-Muscle Shoals, AL	121,618	25.6	52.4	22.1	57,367	27.7	56.4	15.9	64,251	23.7	48.8	27.6
22540	Fond du Lac, WI	83,219	27.8	54.1	18.1	40,651	31.1	55.1	13.8	42,568	24.6	53.1	22.3
22660	Fort Collins, CO	256,728	33.6	50.9	15.6	127,026	36.8	51.9	11.4	129,702	30.4	49.9	19.7
22900	Fort Smith, AR-OK	222,539	23.7	52.4	23.9	108,676	27.7	54.0	18.3	113,863	19.9	50.8	29.3
23060	Fort Wayne, IN	329,931	29.8	50.1	20.0	159,842	32.6	52.2	15.2	170,089	27.2	48.2	24.6
23420	Fresno, CA	715,918	37.8	44.1	18.1	354,962	41.5	45.1	13.4	360,956	34.2	43.1	22.7
23460	Gadsden, AL	85,085	26.0	49.7	24.3	40,492	29.7	51.2	19.2	44,593	22.6	48.4	29.0
23540	Gainesville, FL	227,988	46.0	37.2	16.8	109,872	48.6	38.7	12.8	118,116	43.5	35.8	20.6
23580	Gainesville, GA	142,844	28.7	50.7	20.5	70,923	31.9	52.2	16.0	71,921	25.7	49.3	25.0
23900	Gettysburg, PA	83,971	27.2	55.4	17.3	41,141	29.7	57.2	13.1	42,830	24.9	53.8	21.4
24020	Glens Falls, NY	108,072	28.6	49.3	22.1	53,989	32.5	51.3	16.2	54,083	24.7	47.3	28.0
24140	Goldsboro, NC	98,843	31.7	45.0	23.3	47,872	35.9	47.5	16.6	50,971	27.8	42.6	29.6
24220	Grand Forks, ND-MN	81,766	37.4	47.0	15.6	41,996	42.2	46.5	11.3	39,770	32.4	47.5	20.1
24260	Grand Island, NE	65,238	25.8	55.0	19.2	32,401	29.2	55.9	14.9	32,837	22.5	54.2	23.3
24300	Grand Junction, CO	119,314	26.9	52.7	20.3	58,819	32.3	53.5	14.2	60,495	21.7	52.0	26.2
24340	Grand Rapids-Wyoming, MI	795,107	31.5	52.4	16.1	388,125	34.3	53.7	12.0	406,982	28.9	51.1	20.0
24420	Grants Pass, OR	69,540	23.2	51.8	25.0	33,584	27.3	53.7	19.0	35,956	19.3	50.1	30.6
24500	Great Falls, MT	66,347	26.9	52.0	21.2	32,911	30.8	53.3	15.9	33,436	23.0	50.6	26.4
24540	Greeley, CO	202,984	28.4	54.8	16.8	101,340	31.0	54.9	14.1	101,644	25.8	54.6	19.6

Table C-3: Metropolitan Areas—Marriages and Births—*Continued*

CBSA FIPS code	Metropolitan area	Total women age 15 to 50 years	Percent of all women who had a birth in the past year	Percent of women who had a birth who were married (including separated and spouse absent):	Percent of women who had a birth who were partners in an unmarried partner household	Age of women who had a birth in the last year as a percent of all women who had a birth			Women who had a birth in the last year as a percent of all women in their age group		
						Age 15 to 19	Age 20 to 34	Age 35 to 50	Age 15 to 19	Age 20 to 34	Age 35 to 50
17020	Chico, CA	52,654	5.6	66.2	11.6	7.4	70.3	22.2	2.7	8.3	3.4
17140	Cincinnati, OH-KY-IN	514,003	5.6	61.3	9.1	4.6	80.6	14.7	1.9	10.9	1.8
17300	Clarksville, TN-KY	69,826	7.3	72.8	8.4	6.7	76.1	17.3	4.1	11.3	3.2
17420	Cleveland, TN	27,958	8.0	58.2	10.6	8.3	76.0	15.7	4.7	15.2	2.7
17460	Cleveland-Elyria, OH	477,726	4.8	55.7	12.2	5.8	74.1	20.0	2.0	9.0	2.1
17660	Coeur d'Alene, ID	32,195	8.6	71.4	8.8	6.7	68.1	25.2	4.2	14.2	4.8
17780	College Station-Bryan, TX	68,436	4.8	68.4	6.4	9.0	72.8	18.2	2.7	6.2	3.1
17820	Colorado Springs, CO	163,553	5.9	79.6	5.3	4.2	79.6	16.2	1.8	10.8	2.2
17860	Columbia, MO	50,400	4.8	73.3	5.7	9.3	74.7	16.0	3.0	6.8	2.4
17900	Columbia, SC	200,544	5.0	54.6	9.3	5.4	76.8	17.8	1.9	8.8	2.1
17980	Columbus, GA-AL	75,688	7.2	58.1	6.6	8.2	78.7	13.0	4.4	12.4	2.2
18020	Columbus, IN	17,937	5.7	61.6	13.8	0.0	83.2	16.8	0.0	12.2	2.0
18140	Columbus, OH										
18580	Corpus Christi, TX	104,047	6.0	49.6	11.4	7.8	82.0	10.1	3.2	11.5	1.4
18700	Corvallis, OR	22,846	3.4	69.7	5.1	4.4	78.3	17.3	0.8	5.2	1.8
18880	Crestview-Fort Walton Beach-Destin, FL	55,293	6.0	70.3	13.8	3.2	80.3	16.4	1.6	11.0	2.2
19060	Cumberland, MD-WV	21,670	5.5	48.0	16.5	2.5	70.1	27.4	0.8	9.7	3.4
19100	Dallas-Fort Worth-Arlington, TX										
19140	Dalton, GA	34,394	4.9	67.1	12.6	9.6	76.4	14.0	3.3	9.3	1.5
19180	Danville, IL	17,390	5.5	54.0	22.4	6.9	88.8	4.3	2.5	12.3	0.5
19300	Daphne-Fairhope-Foley, AL	42,338	5.8	67.0	3.8	5.8	68.9	25.3	2.6	10.5	3.0
19340	Davenport-Moline-Rock Island, IA-IL	86,895	5.3	63.3	13.1	5.3	79.7	15.0	2.0	10.0	1.8
19380	Dayton, OH	189,133	5.0	56.8	12.9	4.8	80.0	15.2	1.7	9.4	1.8
19460	Decatur, AL	35,836	5.0	77.1	2.9	8.8	66.5	24.7	3.1	8.7	2.6
19500	Decatur, IL	25,347	5.4	42.6	15.5	11.4	80.2	8.4	4.4	10.5	1.0
19660	Deltona-Daytona Beach-Ormond Beach, FL	122,236	4.3	58.2	9.9	4.0	72.4	23.7	1.3	7.8	2.1
19740	Denver-Aurora-Lakewood, CO	666,748	5.4	72.5	8.0	3.7	72.6	23.6	1.7	9.2	2.8
19780	Des Moines-West Des Moines, IA	147,195	6.1	73.4	8.1	3.6	79.7	16.7	1.8	11.2	2.3
19820	Detroit-Warren-Dearborn, MI	1,028,199	5.3	58.0	11.6	5.9	73.6	20.6	2.2	10.1	2.3
20020	Dothan, AL	34,355	6.5	59.6	6.5	5.7	80.9	13.3	2.8	13.1	1.9
20100	Dover, DE	41,134	6.4	60.7	7.5	4.8	67.2	28.0	2.1	10.1	4.1
20220	Dubuque, IA	21,801	6.1	70.1	18.3	1.6	82.0	16.4	0.6	12.2	2.3
20260	Duluth, MN-WI	62,559	4.8	64.2	15.5	4.9	80.7	14.4	1.5	9.0	1.6
20500	Durham-Chapel Hill, NC										
20700	East Stroudsburg, PA	40,397	3.5	60.7	8.0	0.0	77.1	22.9	0.0	7.9	1.7
20740	Eau Claire, WI	39,753	4.8	69.7	14.9	4.5	81.8	13.8	1.4	8.3	1.7
20940	El Centro, CA	41,289	7.2	49.9	10.1	7.5	75.9	16.5	3.3	13.0	2.9
21060	Elizabethtown-Fort Knox, KY	35,779	6.3	67.4	10.3	2.3	83.7	14.0	1.0	12.8	1.9
21140	Elkhart-Goshen, IN	45,931	7.9	60.8	12.9	10.8	77.4	11.8	5.8	14.9	2.1
21300	Elmira, NY	19,532	5.0	62.0	18.5	10.5	73.3	16.1	3.6	9.1	1.8
21340	El Paso, TX	208,660	6.1	63.8	6.0	9.6	72.4	18.0	3.7	10.3	2.7
21500	Erie, PA	65,841	4.1	47.0	10.5	2.9	75.7	21.4	0.8	7.3	2.1
21660	Eugene, OR	84,737	4.4	62.9	11.5	0.6	82.6	16.8	0.2	7.9	1.9
21780	Evansville, IN-KY	73,850	5.1	55.4	17.5	7.1	80.8	12.1	2.7	9.6	1.4
21820	Fairbanks, AK	25,087	6.6	76.8	12.4	2.2	64.2	33.5	1.2	8.6	5.7
22020	Fargo, ND-MN	58,298	6.2	73.5	7.1	2.7	78.5	18.8	1.2	9.5	3.4
22140	Farmington, NM	29,972	5.1	56.8	12.6	5.9	79.9	14.1	2.1	9.4	1.7
22180	Fayetteville, NC	99,527	6.0	70.9	7.5	7.9	79.1	12.9	3.8	10.1	2.0
22220	Fayetteville-Springdale-Rogers, AR-MO	121,057	5.0	72.4	8.6	5.6	78.2	16.2	2.0	8.8	1.9
22380	Flagstaff, AZ	36,927	5.2	43.8	12.3	8.7	64.6	26.7	2.1	7.3	4.3
22420	Flint, MI	99,072	4.4	44.7	17.6	9.5	76.7	13.8	3.0	8.6	1.3
22500	Florence, SC	50,380	6.2	48.1	17.4	7.4	72.0	20.6	3.3	10.9	2.8
22520	Florence-Muscle Shoals, AL	34,629	4.2	70.1	3.5	2.1	91.0	6.8	0.6	9.4	0.6
22540	Fond du Lac, WI	23,293	5.1	68.2	20.5	1.3	78.9	19.9	0.5	10.0	2.2
22660	Fort Collins, CO	78,189	5.1	75.5	10.3	4.0	75.4	20.5	1.4	8.1	2.7
22900	Fort Smith, AR-OK	64,646	6.1	58.1	10.6	6.8	83.3	9.8	3.0	12.4	1.3
23060	Fort Wayne, IN	100,096	6.0	56.4	7.9	7.4	76.2	16.4	3.1	11.1	2.3
23420	Fresno, CA	234,380	6.1	63.9	10.9	4.4	78.8	16.8	1.7	10.6	2.6
23460	Gadsden, AL	24,331	4.3	60.1	10.1	10.0	78.1	11.9	3.2	8.6	1.1
23540	Gainesville, FL	76,836	3.3	71.4	8.5	2.8	84.5	12.7	0.6	5.1	1.4
23580	Gainesville, GA	43,871	6.6	65.3	13.1	5.7	75.9	18.4	2.6	12.5	2.7
23900	Gettysburg, PA	22,854	4.5	71.4	6.5	10.1	72.3	17.6	2.8	8.8	1.7
24020	Glens Falls, NY	27,934	3.8	55.3	13.7	6.4	83.2	10.4	1.8	8.6	0.8
24140	Goldsboro, NC	29,047	5.6	60.8	5.8	2.3	87.2	10.5	1.0	11.5	1.3
24220	Grand Forks, ND-MN	24,363	6.2	64.3	16.6	13.7	77.4	9.0	5.4	9.5	1.6
24260	Grand Island, NE	18,293	7.2	50.7	19.8	10.5	76.9	12.6	4.7	14.2	2.0
24300	Grand Junction, CO	33,239	7.1	63.0	17.2	8.9	89.4	1.7	4.1	14.5	0.3
24340	Grand Rapids-Wyoming, MI	247,470	6.0	68.2	11.7	5.3	78.5	16.3	2.1	11.0	2.3
24420	Grants Pass, OR	15,907	5.9	78.2	19.9	0.0	89.1	10.9	0.0	13.5	1.4
24500	Great Falls, MT	18,379	5.6	65.1	8.6	4.7	89.2	6.1	1.9	11.0	0.8
24540	Greeley, CO	64,889	7.3	60.3	9.3	1.8	82.1	16.1	0.9	13.9	2.7

Table C-3: Metropolitan Areas—Marriages and Births—*Continued*

CBSA FIPS code	Metropolitan area	Total population 15 years and older	Marital status, percent			Male population 15 years and older	Male, marital status, percent			Female population 15 years and older	Female, marital status, percent		
			Never married	Now married (except separated)	Separated, widowed, or divorced		Never married	Now married (except separated)	Separated, widowed, or divorced		Never married	Now married (except separated)	Separated, widowed, or divorced
24580	Green Bay, WI	248,524	30.2	53.4	16.4	123,186	33.2	53.9	12.9	125,338	27.4	52.8	19.9
24660	Greensboro-High Point, NC	595,740	32.1	47.4	20.5	281,483	34.5	50.8	14.7	314,257	30.1	44.3	25.7
24780	Greenville, NC	140,538	43.3	39.5	17.2	64,834	45.0	43.0	11.9	75,704	41.9	36.5	21.6
24860	Greenville-Anderson-Mauldin, SC	679,709	30.3	49.9	19.8	327,181	32.6	52.6	14.8	352,528	28.1	47.4	24.5
25060	Gulfport-Biloxi-Pascagoula, MS	301,785	29.8	47.6	22.6	148,230	33.3	49.1	17.6	153,555	26.5	46.1	27.4
25180	Hagerstown-Martinsburg, MD-WV	206,817	28.2	50.4	21.3	103,744	31.9	51.0	17.1	103,073	24.5	49.9	25.6
25220	Hammond, LA	98,050	34.3	44.2	21.6	46,630	37.7	46.6	15.8	51,420	31.2	42.0	26.8
25260	Hanford-Corcoran, CA	116,037	36.2	44.5	19.3	66,823	41.6	41.6	16.8	49,214	28.8	48.5	22.6
25420	Harrisburg-Carlisle, PA	455,941	31.0	50.8	18.2	220,832	34.1	52.6	13.3	235,109	28.2	49.1	22.8
25500	Harrisonburg, VA	106,643	39.8	44.1	16.1	50,852	41.2	46.4	12.3	55,791	38.4	42.0	19.6
25540	Hartford-West Hartford-East Hartford, CT	1,002,004	34.4	47.1	18.5	482,969	37.7	49.2	13.2	519,035	31.3	45.3	23.4
25620	Hattiesburg, MS	116,493	34.5	45.1	20.4	55,031	36.5	47.6	15.9	61,462	32.8	42.9	24.3
25860	Hickory-Lenoir-Morganton, NC	298,031	26.7	50.1	23.3	146,275	30.8	51.3	17.9	151,756	22.6	48.9	28.4
25940	Hilton Head Island-Bluffton-Beaufort, SC	159,535	27.4	52.0	20.6	78,812	31.5	53.6	15.0	80,723	23.4	50.5	26.0
25980	Hinesville, GA	60,469	28.5	54.0	17.5	30,023	31.8	54.1	14.1	30,446	25.3	53.8	20.9
26140	Homosassa Springs, FL	122,172	18.6	54.7	26.7	58,711	22.0	57.0	21.0	63,461	15.5	52.5	32.0
26300	Hot Springs, AR	80,388	22.7	49.6	27.7	38,327	26.3	52.0	21.6	42,061	19.4	47.3	33.3
26380	Houma-Thibodaux, LA	165,422	31.5	47.6	21.0	80,803	34.9	48.7	16.3	84,619	28.2	46.4	25.4
26420	Houston-The Woodlands-Sugar Land, TX	4,758,379	32.9	49.6	17.5	2,349,495	35.9	51.3	12.8	2,408,884	29.9	48.0	22.1
26580	Huntington-Ashland, WV-KY-OH	298,886	25.4	50.6	24.0	144,730	29.0	52.3	18.7	154,156	22.1	49.0	28.9
26620	Huntsville, AL	348,376	29.7	50.5	19.8	170,051	33.1	52.2	14.8	178,325	26.5	48.9	24.6
26820	Idaho Falls, ID	99,184	24.2	57.3	18.5	48,846	27.6	57.8	14.6	50,338	21.0	56.8	22.2
26900	Indianapolis-Carmel-Anderson, IN	1,518,324	31.3	48.8	19.9	733,309	34.0	50.9	15.1	785,015	28.8	46.8	24.4
26980	Iowa City, IA	130,641	41.2	46.2	12.7	64,657	44.2	46.8	9.0	65,984	38.2	45.5	16.3
27060	Ithaca, NY	89,613	48.3	38.9	12.8	43,819	52.3	39.8	7.9	45,794	44.4	38.0	17.6
27100	Jackson, MI	130,470	30.6	47.2	22.2	66,604	34.6	46.5	19.0	63,866	26.5	48.0	25.5
27140	Jackson, MS	453,738	35.8	43.4	20.8	213,985	38.1	46.7	15.2	239,753	33.8	40.4	25.8
27180	Jackson, TN	104,752	31.3	45.6	23.1	49,036	33.4	48.8	17.8	55,716	29.5	42.8	27.7
27260	Jacksonville, FL	1,112,957	31.2	46.8	22.0	535,519	34.5	49.1	16.5	577,438	28.1	44.8	27.1
27340	Jacksonville, NC	141,182	29.9	53.3	16.8	77,599	37.7	49.8	12.5	63,583	20.5	57.6	22.0
27500	Janesville-Beloit, WI	128,243	28.8	50.9	20.3	62,357	31.9	52.8	15.3	65,886	25.8	49.1	25.1
27620	Jefferson City, MO	121,556	29.6	50.9	19.5	62,116	33.9	51.1	15.1	59,440	25.1	50.8	24.1
27740	Johnson City, TN	167,501	25.9	51.9	22.2	80,725	28.9	53.6	17.5	86,776	23.1	50.4	26.6
27780	Johnstown, PA	119,041	30.3	48.3	21.5	58,677	34.5	49.9	15.5	60,364	26.1	46.6	27.2
27860	Jonesboro, AR	98,531	28.3	49.3	22.4	47,290	31.7	51.7	16.5	51,241	25.1	47.0	27.8
27900	Joplin, MO	138,239	25.0	53.2	21.8	67,125	28.4	55.0	16.6	71,114	21.8	51.6	26.6
27980	Kahului-Wailuku-Lahaina, HI	128,429	31.0	50.8	18.2	64,186	35.0	51.6	13.3	64,243	26.9	49.9	23.2
28020	Kalamazoo-Portage, MI	267,736	35.1	46.0	19.0	130,124	38.4	47.4	14.2	137,612	31.9	44.6	23.6
28100	Kankakee, IL	89,841	34.0	45.7	20.3	43,546	38.0	47.7	14.2	46,295	30.2	43.7	26.1
28140	Kansas City, MO-KS	1,608,954	29.7	50.3	20.0	779,787	32.1	52.6	15.3	829,167	27.4	48.2	24.4
28420	Kennewick-Richland, WA	201,843	29.7	51.9	18.4	102,320	33.3	52.5	14.3	99,523	26.0	51.4	22.7
28660	Killeen-Temple, TX	320,099	29.3	51.3	19.4	157,949	34.5	51.4	14.1	162,150	24.2	51.3	24.5
28700	Kingsport-Bristol-Bristol, TN-VA	257,361	21.5	54.0	24.5	123,758	24.7	56.3	19.0	133,603	18.5	51.9	29.7
28740	Kingston, NY	153,644	33.8	46.9	19.3	76,116	37.0	48.3	14.7	77,528	30.6	45.5	23.9
28940	Knoxville, TN	698,395	27.0	51.8	21.2	337,453	30.5	53.6	15.9	360,942	23.8	50.1	26.1
29020	Kokomo, IN	67,111	24.8	52.6	22.6	31,808	26.2	54.5	19.3	35,303	23.5	50.9	25.5
29100	La Crosse-Onalaska, WI-MN	111,641	35.2	48.8	16.0	54,122	37.0	50.8	12.2	57,519	33.4	47.0	19.6
29180	Lafayette, LA	373,636	33.1	46.2	20.7	180,141	35.7	48.7	15.6	193,495	30.7	43.8	25.4
29200	Lafayette-West Lafayette, IN	169,753	40.3	44.1	15.6	86,284	44.4	43.5	12.1	83,469	36.0	44.7	19.2
29340	Lake Charles, LA	159,789	30.2	47.4	22.4	76,900	33.0	49.9	17.1	82,889	27.5	45.1	27.4
29420	Lake Havasu City-Kingman, AZ	170,100	24.0	48.8	27.2	85,570	27.9	48.8	23.3	84,530	20.0	48.8	31.2
29460	Lakeland-Winter Haven, FL	498,335	29.6	48.0	22.4	241,644	33.4	50.2	16.4	256,691	26.1	45.9	28.0
29540	Lancaster, PA	419,972	29.0	55.3	15.7	202,765	31.6	57.5	11.0	217,207	26.6	53.3	20.1
29620	Lansing-East Lansing, MI	384,257	37.9	44.5	17.7	185,433	40.6	45.9	13.6	198,824	35.4	43.1	21.5
29700	Laredo, TX	183,744	36.0	47.3	16.7	88,085	38.2	50.9	10.9	95,659	34.0	44.0	22.0
29740	Las Cruces, NM	166,751	35.4	45.8	18.8	81,186	39.3	47.6	13.2	85,565	31.8	44.1	24.1
29820	Las Vegas-Henderson-Paradise, NV	1,590,689	33.6	44.7	21.7	795,724	37.0	45.5	17.5	794,965	30.1	43.9	26.0
29940	Lawrence, KS	95,061	46.7	39.8	13.5	47,071	49.3	41.2	9.5	47,990	44.2	38.4	17.4
30020	Lawton, OK	104,380	30.3	46.6	23.1	54,166	35.9	47.0	17.0	50,214	24.2	46.2	29.7
30140	Lebanon, PA	109,387	27.5	52.1	20.5	52,807	30.6	54.8	14.6	56,580	24.5	49.5	26.0
30300	Lewiston, ID-WA	50,837	23.1	53.1	23.8	24,615	26.3	54.2	19.5	26,222	20.1	52.0	27.9
30340	Lewiston-Auburn, ME	87,615	29.6	48.4	22.0	42,503	32.7	49.8	17.5	45,112	26.6	47.1	26.3
30460	Lexington-Fayette, KY	392,916	33.4	47.1	19.5	190,669	36.5	49.3	14.2	202,247	30.4	45.1	24.5
30620	Lima, OH	84,841	32.8	45.4	21.7	42,615	37.3	46.5	16.2	42,226	28.3	44.4	27.3
30700	Lincoln, NE	249,239	35.6	48.3	16.1	124,457	39.1	48.7	12.2	124,782	32.1	48.0	20.0
30780	Little Rock-North Little Rock-Conway, AR	571,494	30.5	48.0	21.5	274,018	33.6	50.4	16.1	297,476	27.7	45.8	26.5
30860	Logan, UT-ID	93,920	32.4	56.9	10.7	46,478	34.6	58.1	7.3	47,442	30.2	55.8	14.0
30980	Longview, TX	171,242	27.3	49.0	23.7	85,114	31.3	50.6	18.0	86,128	23.4	47.4	29.2
31020	Longview, WA	82,049	26.1	51.1	22.8	40,382	29.7	53.5	16.7	41,667	22.5	48.8	28.7
31080	Los Angeles-Long Beach-Anaheim, CA	10,513,650	39.8	44.0	16.2	5,144,227	43.3	45.6	11.1	5,369,423	36.5	42.4	21.1

Table C-3: Metropolitan Areas—Marriages and Births—*Continued*

CBSA FIPS code	Metropolitan area	Total women age 15 to 50 years	Percent of all women who had a birth in the past year	Percent of women who had a birth who were married (including separated and spouse absent):	Percent of women who had a birth who were partners in an unmarried partner household	Age of women who had a birth in the last year as a percent of all women who had a birth			Women who had a birth in the last year as a percent of all women in their age group		
						Age 15 to 19	Age 20 to 34	Age 35 to 50	Age 15 to 19	Age 20 to 34	Age 35 to 50
24580	Green Bay, WI	73,015	5.9	59.2	18.6	5.8	77.7	16.5	2.4	11.2	2.2
24660	Greensboro-High Point, NC	185,063	5.4	61.4	12.5	2.5	75.4	22.1	1.0	9.9	2.6
24780	Greenville, NC	50,933	4.1	45.9	10.7	1.7	85.6	12.7	0.4	7.2	1.5
24860	Greenville-Anderson-Mauldin, SC	205,151	5.1	61.2	9.0	5.9	72.6	21.5	2.1	8.9	2.4
25060	Gulfport-Biloxi-Pascagoula, MS	90,971	4.8	58.9	9.2	8.3	79.6	12.1	3.1	9.0	1.3
25180	Hagerstown-Martinsburg, MD-WV	59,377	5.4	63.6	9.8	1.2	83.8	15.0	0.5	11.6	1.7
25220	Hammond, LA	31,157	3.4	67.6	4.0	2.9	76.3	20.7	0.7	5.5	1.8
25260	Hanford-Corcoran, CA	33,011	7.9	52.5	11.9	10.9	74.9	14.2	5.4	13.1	2.9
25420	Harrisburg-Carlisle, PA	130,097	5.1	60.5	13.6	5.9	76.7	17.4	2.1	9.7	2.0
25500	Harrisonburg, VA	36,334	3.7	65.4	2.5	19.0	66.5	14.4	3.2	5.5	1.6
25540	Hartford-West Hartford-East Hartford, CT	292,572	4.7	63.2	7.7	3.8	71.7	24.5	1.2	8.7	2.5
25620	Hattiesburg, MS	39,431	4.5	55.4	5.3	4.2	83.1	12.6	1.4	7.8	1.5
25860	Hickory-Lenoir-Morganton, NC	82,208	4.2	70.7	9.0	8.6	69.3	22.1	2.7	8.1	1.9
25940	Hilton Head Island-Bluffton-Beaufort, SC	39,925	6.8	76.9	4.6	1.4	87.2	11.4	0.8	13.4	1.8
25980	Hinesville, GA	21,622	8.5	62.7	10.8	8.8	86.9	4.3	6.7	14.0	1.0
26140	Homosassa Springs, FL	22,401	3.5	55.2	20.2	10.1	74.7	15.2	2.3	8.0	1.0
26300	Hot Springs, AR	20,450	4.7	63.2	6.8	4.4	88.0	7.6	1.4	10.6	0.8
26380	Houma-Thibodaux, LA	51,107	5.2	55.9	20.4	6.1	84.1	9.7	2.4	9.8	1.2
26420	Houston-The Woodlands-Sugar Land, TX	1,584,127	6.1	66.6	7.5	7.8	72.2	20.0	3.5	10.3	2.7
26580	Huntington-Ashland, WV-KY-OH	82,912	4.9	69.4	5.9	7.2	79.3	13.4	2.7	9.7	1.4
26620	Huntsville, AL	106,463	4.9	67.6	11.7	6.4	83.8	9.8	2.3	10.2	1.0
26820	Idaho Falls, ID	31,232	8.6	77.9	7.6	3.6	77.7	18.8	2.0	15.3	3.9
26900	Indianapolis-Carmel-Anderson, IN	480,977	5.7	64.1	10.7	6.5	74.2	19.3	2.8	10.1	2.4
26980	Iowa City, IA	44,231	4.7	73.6	11.8	0.0	77.1	22.9	0.0	6.9	3.3
27060	Ithaca, NY	30,408	4.3	73.8	13.9	2.8	80.6	16.7	0.5	7.1	2.5
27100	Jackson, MI	35,164	5.0	48.5	13.4	5.2	84.4	10.4	1.7	11.1	1.1
27140	Jackson, MS	146,042	5.5	49.3	3.6	8.7	81.7	9.5	3.4	10.4	1.2
27180	Jackson, TN	32,295	5.0	60.4	11.6	6.2	82.5	11.3	2.0	9.4	1.4
27260	Jacksonville, FL	342,284	4.7	61.2	9.2	4.1	75.4	20.6	1.5	8.5	2.1
27340	Jacksonville, NC	44,815	9.6	81.4	12.3	8.0	88.2	3.8	7.4	14.7	1.1
27500	Janesville-Beloit, WI	37,978	6.4	64.6	11.1	4.5	75.3	20.1	2.1	12.2	2.8
27620	Jefferson City, MO	34,508	6.3	55.8	13.0	3.1	86.4	10.6	1.3	13.4	1.5
27740	Johnson City, TN	47,866	3.9	68.1	10.7	4.2	82.4	13.4	1.2	7.7	1.2
27780	Johnstown, PA	29,294	4.8	56.1	20.3	7.7	77.1	15.1	2.5	9.5	1.6
27860	Jonesboro, AR	31,238	6.1	65.2	8.4	1.7	93.6	4.7	0.8	12.6	0.7
27900	Joplin, MO	41,035	6.3	64.8	5.6	2.8	79.5	17.7	1.2	11.7	2.6
27980	Kahului-Wailuku-Lahaina, HI	36,195	6.5	51.5	21.1	6.0	76.2	17.8	3.1	12.5	2.4
28020	Kalamazoo-Portage, MI	82,411	4.7	62.7	16.6	3.2	81.6	15.2	1.0	8.3	1.8
28100	Kankakee, IL	26,904	4.7	52.7	12.6	9.7	76.5	13.8	3.1	8.6	1.5
28140	Kansas City, MO-KS	492,405	5.6	66.2	10.1	5.1	75.9	19.1	2.2	10.3	2.4
28420	Kennewick-Richland, WA	62,254	6.0	73.2	13.5	1.7	82.9	15.4	0.7	11.5	2.2
28660	Killeen-Temple, TX	110,414	5.1	77.3	4.5	4.2	84.0	11.8	1.8	8.8	1.5
28700	Kingsport-Bristol-Bristol, TN-VA	67,674	5.0	59.3	10.5	10.1	80.9	9.1	3.9	10.8	0.9
28740	Kingston, NY	41,755	4.5	62.2	19.1	2.5	69.3	28.1	0.8	8.1	2.7
28940	Knoxville, TN	200,724	4.8	63.6	14.2	6.7	80.6	12.7	2.4	9.4	1.3
29020	Kokomo, IN	18,298	6.8	63.2	6.7	11.1	74.6	14.3	5.3	13.0	2.1
29100	La Crosse-Onalaska, WI-MN	33,612	4.4	72.9	18.3	2.2	72.5	25.2	0.6	7.0	2.9
29180	Lafayette, LA	118,153	6.3	55.2	14.4	4.2	84.3	11.6	2.0	11.7	1.7
29200	Lafayette-West Lafayette, IN	55,331	5.2	68.7	17.1	2.1	85.7	12.2	0.7	8.6	2.0
29340	Lake Charles, LA	48,319	6.1	47.1	12.4	9.2	77.7	13.1	4.0	10.8	1.9
29420	Lake Havasu City-Kingman, AZ	36,464	4.4	67.4	15.4	3.4	74.4	22.2	1.0	8.6	2.1
29460	Lakeland-Winter Haven, FL	137,163	5.7	53.3	13.9	6.7	75.8	17.4	2.8	10.4	2.2
29540	Lancaster, PA	121,369	6.5	70.4	8.4	5.1	79.1	15.8	2.2	12.5	2.3
29620	Lansing-East Lansing, MI	122,292	4.9	63.1	10.1	6.0	73.8	20.2	1.8	7.9	2.6
29700	Laredo, TX	67,047	6.8	62.1	7.3	11.5	75.2	13.3	4.5	12.4	2.2
29740	Las Cruces, NM	53,570	6.3	46.3	9.8	9.4	74.1	16.5	3.5	10.4	2.7
29820	Las Vegas-Henderson-Paradise, NV	497,333	5.3	65.8	14.2	5.5	69.7	24.8	2.3	8.6	2.9
29940	Lawrence, KS	33,320	4.5	70.1	9.8	4.3	74.0	21.7	1.2	6.1	3.3
30020	Lawton, OK	32,041	6.6	60.1	9.8	6.1	85.4	8.4	3.1	11.9	1.4
30140	Lebanon, PA	29,825	5.9	63.7	12.7	4.4	88.5	7.1	1.8	13.2	0.9
30300	Lewiston, ID-WA	13,514	4.7	57.7	17.9	4.7	89.5	5.8	1.6	10.1	0.6
30340	Lewiston-Auburn, ME	25,401	5.7	59.1	25.2	1.3	90.7	8.0	0.6	12.4	1.0
30460	Lexington-Fayette, KY	125,363	5.1	73.0	10.0	4.1	81.4	14.5	1.6	9.1	1.8
30620	Lima, OH	23,036	6.4	44.0	14.6	12.7	76.9	10.4	5.6	12.0	1.5
30700	Lincoln, NE	77,936	6.3	68.0	14.7	4.0	78.0	18.0	1.7	10.1	3.1
30780	Little Rock-North Little Rock-Conway, AR	178,508	4.9	66.8	5.8	3.4	86.2	10.4	1.3	9.6	1.2
30860	Logan, UT-ID	33,959	7.3	88.6	7.5	3.3	79.5	17.1	1.3	11.2	4.2
30980	Longview, TX	48,643	6.1	57.8	14.0	11.9	78.2	9.8	5.1	11.5	1.4
31020	Longview, WA	21,980	6.9	39.9	27.1	20.2	69.6	10.2	9.4	12.4	1.5
31080	Los Angeles-Long Beach-Anaheim, CA	3,399,744	4.8	63.3	10.5	4.8	67.5	27.7	1.7	7.6	3.0

Table C-3: Metropolitan Areas—Marriages and Births—*Continued*

CBSA FIPS code	Metropolitan area	Total population 15 years and older	Marital status, percent			Male population 15 years and older	Male, marital status, percent			Female population 15 years and older	Female, marital status, percent		
			Never married	Now married (except separated)	Separated, widowed, or divorced		Never married	Now married (except separated)	Separated, widowed, or divorced		Never married	Now married (except separated)	Separated, widowed, or divorced
31140	Louisville/Jefferson County, KY-IN...	1,009,020	30.6	47.4	21.9	486,677	33.9	49.6	16.5	522,343	27.6	45.5	26.9
31180	Lubbock, TX.................................	237,509	37.0	44.3	18.8	116,519	40.6	45.7	13.7	120,990	33.5	42.9	23.6
31340	Lynchburg, VA..............................	211,666	30.8	49.9	19.3	100,886	33.5	53.1	13.4	110,780	28.3	47.1	24.6
31420	Macon, GA...................................	184,878	35.6	42.2	22.2	87,300	38.7	45.0	16.3	97,578	32.9	39.7	27.4
31460	Madera, CA..................................	116,469	37.1	46.3	16.6	55,814	39.8	48.7	11.5	60,655	34.6	44.1	21.4
31540	Madison, WI.................................	507,514	35.4	49.1	15.5	250,327	37.8	50.4	11.8	257,187	33.0	47.8	19.2
31700	Manchester-Nashua, NH.................	329,089	30.5	51.3	18.3	162,002	34.0	52.3	13.7	167,087	27.0	50.2	22.7
31740	Manhattan, KS..............................	79,807	45.1	43.2	11.7	41,797	49.4	41.9	8.7	38,010	40.3	44.6	15.1
31860	Mankato-North Mankato, MN.........	80,956	40.7	46.7	12.6	40,334	44.2	46.7	9.0	40,622	37.1	46.7	16.1
31900	Mansfield, OH..............................	100,442	28.7	47.1	24.2	50,607	33.8	47.3	18.9	49,835	23.6	46.8	29.6
32580	McAllen-Edinburg-Mission, TX......	573,696	31.5	52.4	16.1	275,675	33.9	55.4	10.7	298,021	29.3	49.7	21.0
32780	Medford, OR................................	170,026	26.4	50.6	23.0	82,343	29.2	53.6	17.2	87,683	23.9	47.7	28.4
32820	Memphis, TN-MS-AR	1,051,041	37.1	41.7	21.2	496,707	39.6	44.4	16.1	554,334	34.9	39.2	25.9
32900	Merced, CA..................................	195,260	37.6	45.5	17.0	98,111	41.7	46.0	12.2	97,149	33.3	44.9	21.7
33100	Miami-Fort Lauderdale-West Palm Beach, FL	4,758,671	34.3	43.0	22.7	2,284,944	38.2	45.6	16.2	2,473,727	30.8	40.5	28.7
33140	Michigan City-La Porte, IN............	90,895	30.2	48.2	21.6	47,284	35.4	46.6	17.9	43,611	24.6	49.9	25.5
33220	Midland, MI.................................	68,448	25.4	56.8	17.7	33,488	28.7	57.7	13.6	34,960	22.3	56.0	21.7
33260	Midland, TX.................................	115,377	29.6	52.8	17.6	56,528	33.4	53.4	13.3	58,849	25.9	52.3	21.8
33340	Milwaukee-Waukesha-West Allis, WI	1,252,910	36.0	46.7	17.3	602,818	38.6	48.8	12.6	650,092	33.7	44.7	21.6
33460	Minneapolis-St. Paul-Bloomington, MN-WI	2,724,672	32.9	51.2	15.8	1,335,595	35.9	52.3	11.8	1,389,077	30.1	50.2	19.7
33540	Missoula, MT...............................	92,781	36.9	44.8	18.3	46,245	39.5	44.5	15.9	46,536	34.2	45.0	20.7
33660	Mobile, AL..................................	329,814	32.4	44.8	22.9	155,738	35.3	47.7	16.9	174,076	29.7	42.1	28.2
33700	Modesto, CA................................	401,606	34.0	47.8	18.1	196,710	38.2	48.9	12.9	204,896	30.1	46.8	23.2
33740	Monroe, LA..................................	140,069	35.1	43.4	21.5	66,208	39.1	46.3	14.6	73,861	31.6	40.8	27.6
33780	Monroe, MI..................................	122,532	26.8	53.4	19.8	59,900	30.7	54.5	14.8	62,632	23.0	52.3	24.7
33860	Montgomery, AL...........................	299,493	34.2	43.5	22.2	141,370	37.0	46.5	16.6	158,123	31.8	40.9	27.3
34060	Morgantown, WV..........................	115,347	43.6	40.6	15.8	59,500	47.8	40.6	11.6	55,847	39.1	40.6	20.3
34100	Morristown, TN............................	93,498	23.7	52.5	23.8	45,186	27.4	55.7	16.9	48,312	20.3	49.4	30.3
34580	Mount Vernon-Anacortes, WA......	95,740	25.6	53.0	21.3	47,266	29.1	55.5	15.4	48,474	22.3	50.6	27.1
34620	Muncie, IN..................................	98,978	38.2	42.4	19.3	46,965	41.6	44.5	13.9	52,013	35.2	40.6	24.2
34740	Muskegon, MI	136,365	31.4	46.9	21.6	66,632	34.6	48.3	17.2	69,733	28.4	45.7	25.9
34820	Myrtle Beach-Conway-North Myrtle Beach, SC-NC	331,075	25.9	51.9	22.2	159,771	29.2	53.9	16.9	171,304	22.7	50.1	27.2
34900	Napa, CA....................................	113,529	30.3	50.2	19.5	56,258	33.5	53.1	13.4	57,271	27.1	47.4	25.5
34940	Naples-Immokalee-Marco Island, FL	281,278	24.7	52.5	22.8	137,551	28.8	55.8	15.4	143,727	20.7	49.5	29.8
34980	Nashville-Davidson–Murfreesboro–Franklin, TN	1,379,615	30.8	49.4	19.8	666,645	33.4	51.8	14.8	712,970	28.4	47.1	24.4
35100	New Bern, NC...............................	103,952	25.9	54.6	19.5	52,065	29.3	56.4	14.4	51,887	22.4	52.8	24.8
35300	New Haven-Milford, CT	711,413	36.4	44.9	18.8	338,939	39.8	47.2	13.0	372,474	33.2	42.7	24.0
35380	New Orleans-Metairie, LA	993,074	37.3	41.5	21.2	476,643	40.2	44.3	15.5	516,431	34.6	39.0	26.4
35620	New York-Newark-Jersey City, NY-NJ-PA	16,167,618	37.9	45.5	16.7	7,710,681	40.7	48.4	10.9	8,456,937	35.3	42.8	21.9
35660	Niles-Benton Harbor, MI...............	126,545	29.9	49.4	20.7	61,026	32.7	52.0	15.3	65,519	27.3	47.0	25.7
35840	North Port-Sarasota-Bradenton, FL	616,684	23.4	52.4	24.2	293,098	26.8	55.3	17.9	323,586	20.2	49.8	29.9
35980	Norwich-New London, CT.............	227,573	31.3	49.5	19.1	113,179	35.3	49.9	14.8	114,394	27.4	49.2	23.4
36100	Ocala, FL....................................	282,988	23.9	51.0	25.0	134,273	26.7	54.0	19.4	148,715	21.5	48.4	30.2
36140	Ocean City, NJ.............................	82,034	27.1	54.4	18.5	39,750	31.5	56.6	12.0	42,284	23.1	52.3	24.6
36220	Odessa, TX..................................	108,613	30.1	48.6	21.3	53,866	33.7	49.9	16.3	54,747	26.5	47.3	26.1
36260	Ogden-Clearfield, UT...................	446,074	25.7	59.0	15.3	222,277	29.1	59.2	11.7	223,797	22.4	58.8	18.8
36420	Oklahoma City, OK	1,024,107	29.9	49.3	20.8	499,801	33.2	50.7	16.1	524,306	26.6	48.1	25.3
36500	Olympia-Tumwater, WA................	211,206	27.8	52.1	20.1	101,571	30.7	53.5	15.8	109,635	25.2	50.8	24.0
36540	Omaha-Council Bluffs, NE-IA	691,619	31.4	50.9	17.7	338,066	34.5	52.5	13.0	353,553	28.3	49.4	22.3
36740	Orlando-Kissimmee-Sanford, FL	1,804,223	35.0	44.9	20.1	874,389	38.8	46.7	14.5	929,834	31.4	43.3	25.3
36780	Oshkosh-Neenah, WI	138,705	33.0	48.8	18.2	69,417	36.9	49.0	14.2	69,288	29.2	48.6	22.2
36980	Owensboro, KY............................	92,406	24.7	53.2	22.1	44,543	28.0	55.7	16.4	47,863	21.7	50.9	27.4
37100	Oxnard-Thousand Oaks-Ventura, CA.	664,319	32.2	50.4	17.4	327,635	36.0	51.6	12.4	336,684	28.5	49.3	22.2
37340	Palm Bay-Melbourne-Titusville, FL.	462,383	26.6	48.0	25.4	223,882	30.8	50.0	19.3	238,501	22.7	46.2	31.1
37460	Panama City, FL...........................	154,646	27.1	49.0	23.9	77,771	31.8	48.8	19.4	76,875	22.4	49.2	28.4
37620	Parkersburg-Vienna, WV...............	76,074	25.4	51.1	23.4	36,395	29.3	53.5	17.2	39,679	21.9	49.0	29.2
37860	Pensacola-Ferry Pass-Brent, FL	377,663	31.0	46.7	22.3	188,202	35.1	47.7	17.2	189,461	27.0	45.6	27.4
37900	Peoria, IL....................................	306,229	29.6	51.7	18.7	148,474	32.6	53.1	14.3	157,755	26.9	50.4	22.8
37980	Philadelphia-Camden-Wilmington, PA-NJ-DE-MD..............................	4,889,370	37.3	44.9	17.7	2,330,414	40.0	47.7	12.2	2,558,956	34.9	42.4	22.7
38060	Phoenix-Mesa-Scottsdale, AZ........	3,399,964	33.3	47.5	19.2	1,678,524	36.9	48.9	14.3	1,721,440	29.8	46.1	24.1
38220	Pine Bluff, AR..............................	79,334	36.0	41.1	22.9	40,274	41.5	41.0	17.5	39,060	30.3	41.2	28.5
38300	Pittsburgh, PA.............................	1,982,349	31.6	48.5	19.9	950,883	34.9	50.9	14.2	1,031,466	28.5	46.3	25.2
38340	Pittsfield, MA..............................	110,898	31.9	45.7	22.4	52,819	35.0	48.1	16.9	58,079	29.1	43.5	27.3
38540	Pocatello, ID...............................	64,315	28.8	51.4	19.8	31,753	32.1	51.5	16.4	32,562	25.5	51.4	23.1
38860	Portland-South Portland, ME........	432,347	28.7	51.2	20.1	207,840	31.5	53.3	15.2	224,507	26.2	49.2	24.6

Table C-3: Metropolitan Areas—Marriages and Births—*Continued*

CBSA FIPS code	Metropolitan area	Total women age 15 to 50 years	Percent of all women who had a birth in the past year	Percent of women who had a birth who were married (including separated and spouse absent):	Percent of women who had a birth who were partners in an unmarried partner household	Age of women who had a birth in the last year as a percent of all women who had a birth			Women who had a birth in the last year as a percent of all women in their age group		
						Age 15 to 19	Age 20 to 34	Age 35 to 50	Age 15 to 19	Age 20 to 34	Age 35 to 50
31140	Louisville/Jefferson County, KY-IN...	300,238	5.1	62.1	7.7	5.6	74.2	20.2	2.2	9.3	2.3
31180	Lubbock, TX..................................	78,401	4.9	64.6	6.3	9.1	75.5	15.4	2.9	7.4	2.1
31340	Lynchburg, VA..............................	61,526	4.9	74.3	10.5	1.2	86.9	11.8	0.4	10.3	1.4
31420	Macon, GA...................................	55,983	4.6	47.5	5.4	10.5	76.9	12.6	3.2	8.5	1.3
31460	Madera, CA..................................	38,238	6.7	52.4	12.6	12.3	67.9	19.9	5.9	10.6	3.1
31540	Madison, WI.................................	158,451	4.6	74.3	8.3	2.6	76.7	20.7	0.9	7.7	2.3
31700	Manchester-Nashua, NH	97,795	4.8	74.4	11.6	4.5	74.4	21.1	1.6	9.6	2.1
31740	Manhattan, KS..............................	27,406	5.9	87.6	1.0	2.1	92.7	5.2	0.7	9.6	1.3
31860	Mankato-North Mankato, MN	25,742	4.1	61.1	20.9	7.5	78.5	14.0	1.7	6.5	1.9
31900	Mansfield, OH...............................	25,617	5.7	55.9	14.9	10.9	80.8	8.3	4.5	11.7	1.0
32580	McAllen-Edinburg-Mission, TX	203,986	7.4	72.8	4.0	10.5	74.9	14.6	4.6	13.0	2.6
32780	Medford, OR.................................	44,231	4.2	53.0	27.9	4.6	82.9	12.5	1.4	8.2	1.2
32820	Memphis, TN-MS-AR	340,640	6.7	47.8	9.8	5.8	72.0	22.2	2.8	11.5	3.4
32900	Merced, CA..................................	64,288	6.4	65.0	13.4	10.1	71.9	18.0	3.7	10.6	2.9
33100	Miami-Fort Lauderdale-West Palm Beach, FL	1,403,796	4.7	59.2	9.8	5.0	67.8	27.2	1.9	7.9	2.7
33140	Michigan City-La Porte, IN............	23,475	4.9	55.9	17.2	5.8	76.0	18.3	2.1	9.4	1.9
33220	Midland, MI.................................	19,235	6.0	82.1	10.7	3.0	83.4	13.6	1.3	13.2	1.7
33260	Midland, TX..................................	36,970	6.2	77.4	5.3	8.1	83.6	8.3	3.5	11.2	1.3
33340	Milwaukee-Waukesha-West Allis, WI...	382,447	4.9	61.7	12.3	4.0	75.9	20.1	1.4	8.7	2.2
33460	Minneapolis-St. Paul-Bloomington, MN-WI..	851,572	5.8	72.9	9.0	4.3	74.8	20.8	1.9	10.3	2.7
33540	Missoula, MT................................	28,991	4.2	67.3	21.5	3.7	79.1	17.3	1.2	6.4	2.0
33660	Mobile, AL...................................	101,514	5.0	52.1	9.0	6.8	78.0	15.1	2.5	9.1	1.8
33700	Modesto, CA................................	128,351	6.0	62.2	15.1	7.2	79.2	13.6	2.8	11.2	1.9
33740	Monroe, LA..................................	44,063	5.1	36.1	9.0	9.1	81.2	9.7	3.3	9.4	1.2
33780	Monroe, MI..................................	34,315	6.9	74.9	11.5	4.3	78.7	17.0	2.0	14.8	2.4
33860	Montgomery, AL...........................	95,421	5.3	47.5	12.9	8.5	80.2	11.3	3.2	9.9	1.4
34060	Morgantown, WV..........................	35,674	4.0	45.4	8.5	1.9	76.9	21.3	0.5	5.8	2.7
34100	Morristown, TN............................	25,806	4.3	59.3	9.4	15.3	74.6	10.0	5.1	8.3	0.9
34580	Mount Vernon-Anacortes, WA......	25,431	5.9	55.4	32.3	3.8	79.0	17.2	1.5	11.4	2.3
34620	Muncie, IN...................................	31,498	4.4	66.7	13.8	7.7	77.1	15.2	1.8	7.1	2.0
34740	Muskegon, MI	38,887	5.3	49.9	21.5	5.9	79.8	14.4	2.0	10.5	1.7
34820	Myrtle Beach-Conway-North Myrtle Beach, SC-NC	85,232	5.4	51.2	14.1	7.9	81.9	10.2	3.7	10.9	1.2
34900	Napa, CA.....................................	31,853	5.1	72.1	7.8	2.7	65.8	31.4	1.0	8.7	3.5
34940	Naples-Immokalee-Marco Island, FL	61,910	4.8	55.2	11.1	9.3	67.0	23.7	3.4	8.5	2.3
34980	Nashville-Davidson—Murfreesboro—Franklin, TN	443,624	5.1	67.7	8.9	5.3	75.4	19.3	2.2	8.9	2.2
35100	New Bern, NC...............................	27,289	6.8	80.1	7.5	3.6	86.8	9.6	1.9	12.7	1.6
35300	New Haven-Milford, CT	213,493	4.3	57.9	8.8	4.1	73.0	22.9	1.2	7.9	2.2
35380	New Orleans-Metairie, LA	305,496	5.3	48.8	11.8	4.9	76.9	18.3	2.1	9.2	2.3
35620	New York-Newark-Jersey City, NY-NJ-PA	5,042,404	4.9	68.9	7.4	3.1	66.4	30.5	1.2	7.7	3.3
35660	Niles-Benton Harbor, MI...............	34,589	4.5	58.0	11.5	2.5	82.4	15.1	0.7	9.6	1.4
35840	North Port-Sarasota-Bradenton, FL	133,272	4.6	62.6	9.0	8.4	66.5	25.1	3.0	8.1	2.3
35980	Norwich-New London, CT.............	63,970	4.4	65.3	19.0	3.0	78.1	18.9	0.9	8.9	1.7
36100	Ocala, FL.....................................	65,720	5.8	47.4	14.4	6.3	77.2	16.5	2.8	11.4	2.0
36140	Ocean City, NJ..............................	18,730	5.4	75.8	2.2	5.9	80.5	13.6	2.4	11.3	1.5
36220	Odessa, TX...................................	35,221	11.8	59.0	15.3	4.4	87.9	7.6	3.6	21.9	2.4
36260	Ogden-Clearfield, UT	148,488	7.1	85.5	3.9	3.4	84.5	12.1	1.6	13.5	2.1
36420	Oklahoma City, OK	320,392	6.1	68.5	9.4	5.9	80.1	14.0	2.8	10.8	2.1
36500	Olympia-Tumwater, WA	63,057	5.5	73.5	13.4	4.8	69.8	25.3	1.9	9.2	3.2
36540	Omaha-Council Bluffs, NE-IA	217,163	5.8	72.4	9.2	2.5	78.9	18.6	1.1	10.5	2.5
36740	Orlando-Kissimmee-Sanford, FL	573,043	5.2	54.9	13.3	6.1	70.1	23.9	2.5	8.5	2.8
36780	Oshkosh-Neenah, WI	40,824	5.3	69.9	19.1	2.0	81.3	16.7	0.7	10.0	1.5
36980	Owensboro, KY	26,476	5.4	57.7	15.1	14.1	81.5	4.4	5.8	10.8	0.5
37100	Oxnard-Thousand Oaks-Ventura, CA..	201,691	5.1	70.3	5.7	5.2	71.1	23.7	1.8	9.1	2.7
37340	Palm Bay-Melbourne-Titusville, FL .	113,631	4.4	67.0	9.0	6.1	73.2	20.7	2.0	8.5	1.9
37460	Panama City, FL............................	42,333	6.6	60.1	8.6	5.2	82.0	12.8	3.0	12.7	1.8
37620	Parkersburg-Vienna, WV...............	20,841	5.4	45.3	20.2	17.7	68.9	13.4	8.0	9.4	1.5
37860	Pensacola-Ferry Pass-Brent, FL	107,411	5.3	69.7	8.8	5.8	72.3	21.9	2.1	9.0	2.7
37900	Peoria, IL.....................................	87,582	5.5	58.2	12.9	4.7	79.8	15.5	1.9	10.6	1.9
37980	Philadelphia-Camden-Wilmington, PA-NJ-DE-MD..............................	1,490,649	5.0	60.9	8.8	5.7	69.7	24.7	2.1	8.4	2.8
38060	Phoenix-Mesa-Scottsdale, AZ	1,049,706	5.7	62.3	11.2	5.4	71.4	23.2	2.2	9.5	3.0
38220	Pine Bluff, AR..............................	21,964	3.9	40.4	13.8	3.4	83.9	12.7	0.8	8.0	1.1
38300	Pittsburgh, PA..............................	532,728	4.6	64.8	10.9	4.6	75.0	20.4	1.5	8.3	2.0
38340	Pittsfield, MA...............................	28,608	4.7	52.9	22.3	7.3	60.9	31.9	2.1	7.6	3.3
38540	Pocatello, ID................................	20,146	5.5	77.0	7.0	2.6	86.0	11.4	1.0	9.9	1.7
38860	Portland-South Portland, ME	120,534	4.7	71.0	13.4	4.0	71.1	24.9	1.4	9.0	2.4

Table C-3: Metropolitan Areas—Marriages and Births—*Continued*

CBSA FIPS code	Metropolitan area	Total population 15 years and older	Marital status, percent			Male population 15 years and older	Male, marital status, percent			Female population 15 years and older	Female, marital status, percent		
			Never married	Now married (except separated)	Separated, widowed, or divorced		Never married	Now married (except separated)	Separated, widowed, or divorced		Never married	Now married (except separated)	Separated, widowed, or divorced
38900	Portland-Vancouver-Hillsboro, OR-WA	1,849,343	31.5	49.3	19.1	905,767	34.8	50.8	14.4	943,576	28.4	48.0	23.6
38940	Port St. Lucie, FL	361,970	25.8	50.3	23.9	176,009	29.6	51.9	18.4	185,961	22.2	48.8	29.1
39140	Prescott, AZ	181,345	21.1	54.1	24.8	87,886	25.3	55.9	18.7	93,459	17.0	52.4	30.6
39300	Providence-Warwick, RI-MA	1,327,432	35.0	45.3	19.7	635,160	38.3	48.0	13.7	692,272	31.9	42.9	25.2
39340	Provo-Orem, UT	384,905	31.9	58.2	9.9	191,528	34.1	58.8	7.1	193,377	29.7	57.5	12.8
39380	Pueblo, CO	129,266	30.4	46.4	23.1	63,040	33.7	47.6	18.8	66,226	27.3	45.4	27.3
39460	Punta Gorda, FL	144,449	18.8	55.3	25.9	69,446	21.8	58.9	19.3	75,003	16.0	52.0	32.0
39540	Racine, WI	155,723	31.8	49.4	18.8	76,472	34.8	51.0	14.2	79,251	28.9	47.8	23.3
39580	Raleigh, NC	932,545	31.7	51.7	16.6	449,882	34.8	53.8	11.4	482,663	28.7	49.8	21.5
39660	Rapid City, SD	111,012	28.1	51.4	20.5	55,466	31.9	51.8	16.4	55,546	24.3	51.0	24.7
39740	Reading, PA	334,186	31.2	49.6	19.2	162,594	33.9	51.7	14.4	171,592	28.6	47.5	23.8
39820	Redding, CA	146,570	27.0	49.6	23.3	71,333	31.3	51.0	17.7	75,237	23.0	48.3	28.6
39900	Reno, NV	351,243	31.6	46.7	21.7	176,052	35.9	46.6	17.5	175,191	27.3	46.8	25.9
40060	Richmond, VA	1,002,063	34.5	45.5	20.0	478,619	37.4	48.1	14.4	523,444	31.7	43.1	25.1
40140	Riverside-San Bernardino-Ontario, CA	3,354,331	35.1	47.0	18.0	1,657,274	38.5	48.2	13.3	1,697,057	31.8	45.7	22.5
40220	Roanoke, VA	255,872	26.5	51.7	21.8	121,598	29.3	55.1	15.6	134,274	23.9	48.7	27.4
40340	Rochester, MN	165,933	28.1	56.2	15.7	81,026	31.2	57.9	10.9	84,907	25.2	54.6	20.2
40380	Rochester, NY	889,995	35.0	46.2	18.8	428,177	37.6	48.4	14.0	461,818	32.6	44.2	23.2
40420	Rockford, IL	275,152	30.5	49.3	20.2	133,463	33.4	51.1	15.5	141,689	27.7	47.7	24.7
40580	Rocky Mount, NC	122,177	33.4	43.6	23.0	57,191	35.4	46.6	17.9	64,986	31.5	41.0	27.5
40660	Rome, GA	76,891	28.4	48.0	23.6	36,477	31.2	51.6	17.2	40,414	26.0	44.6	29.4
40900	Sacramento-Roseville-Arden-Arcade, CA	1,757,121	33.2	47.2	19.5	852,063	36.8	49.2	14.0	905,058	29.9	45.4	24.7
40980	Saginaw, MI	161,364	32.9	45.7	21.3	77,088	36.5	47.8	15.7	84,276	29.7	43.8	26.5
41060	St. Cloud, MN	153,245	35.4	50.7	13.9	76,960	39.1	50.2	10.7	76,285	31.7	51.1	17.1
41100	St. George, UT	108,947	23.6	59.1	17.4	53,257	26.2	60.7	13.0	55,690	21.0	57.5	21.5
41140	St. Joseph, MO-KS	103,882	30.1	47.8	22.1	53,449	34.7	48.0	17.4	50,433	25.2	47.7	27.2
41180	St. Louis, MO-IL	2,260,348	31.9	48.7	19.4	1,079,216	34.5	51.1	14.4	1,181,132	29.6	46.4	24.0
41420	Salem, OR	313,283	30.2	50.0	19.8	153,546	33.2	51.5	15.3	159,737	27.4	48.5	24.1
41500	Salinas, CA	330,266	37.6	47.4	15.0	169,924	42.0	46.4	11.6	160,342	33.0	48.5	18.6
41540	Salisbury, MD-DE	317,827	31.1	46.9	22.0	153,845	34.9	48.8	16.3	163,982	27.6	45.1	27.2
41620	Salt Lake City, UT	846,600	31.1	52.4	16.6	422,994	34.2	52.6	13.2	423,606	28.0	52.1	19.9
41660	San Angelo, TX	92,325	30.9	46.8	22.3	45,055	34.2	48.2	17.6	47,270	27.8	45.4	26.8
41700	San Antonio-New Braunfels, TX	1,745,976	32.6	47.7	19.7	850,883	35.8	49.8	14.4	895,093	29.5	45.7	24.7
41740	San Diego-Carlsbad, CA	2,572,530	35.9	47.0	17.1	1,287,094	40.3	47.9	11.8	1,285,436	31.4	46.1	22.5
41860	San Francisco-Oakland-Hayward, CA	3,681,779	36.0	47.3	16.7	1,804,521	39.6	48.7	11.7	1,877,258	32.6	45.9	21.5
41940	San Jose-Sunnyvale-Santa Clara, CA	1,514,636	32.6	53.1	14.2	757,480	36.4	53.9	9.7	757,156	28.8	52.4	18.8
42020	San Luis Obispo-Paso Robles-Arroyo Grande, CA	232,320	34.1	48.2	17.7	118,559	38.5	48.5	13.0	113,761	29.7	47.8	22.5
42100	Santa Cruz-Watsonville, CA	221,276	38.9	44.5	16.6	109,309	42.5	45.7	11.8	111,967	35.4	43.2	21.4
42140	Santa Fe, NM	121,789	30.4	46.8	22.7	59,042	33.3	49.9	16.8	62,747	27.7	44.0	28.3
42200	Santa Maria-Santa Barbara, CA	349,349	38.9	44.9	16.2	174,797	42.6	45.6	11.8	174,552	35.1	44.2	20.7
42220	Santa Rosa, CA	405,248	32.2	46.6	21.2	197,656	36.2	48.5	15.2	207,592	28.5	44.7	26.9
42340	Savannah, GA	289,130	34.5	44.4	21.1	138,670	37.6	47.1	15.3	150,460	31.6	41.9	26.5
42540	Scranton–Wilkes-Barre–Hazleton, PA	471,314	32.8	46.4	20.8	228,295	36.3	48.9	14.9	243,019	29.5	44.2	26.3
42660	Seattle-Tacoma-Bellevue, WA	2,888,011	32.4	49.5	18.0	1,432,081	36.1	50.4	13.4	1,455,930	28.8	48.6	22.6
42680	Sebastian-Vero Beach, FL	119,783	22.4	52.2	25.4	57,063	27.7	54.7	17.7	62,720	17.6	49.9	32.4
42700	Sebring, FL	83,327	21.6	52.2	26.2	40,408	24.9	53.0	22.1	42,919	18.4	51.4	30.1
43100	Sheboygan, WI	93,201	27.5	54.4	18.1	46,511	30.9	54.7	14.3	46,690	24.0	54.1	21.8
43300	Sherman-Denison, TX	97,708	25.4	50.9	23.7	46,818	27.8	52.9	19.2	50,890	23.1	49.1	27.8
43340	Shreveport-Bossier City, LA	354,247	33.6	42.9	23.5	168,211	36.3	46.0	17.7	186,036	31.2	40.1	28.8
43420	Sierra Vista-Douglas, AZ	106,607	28.2	49.3	22.4	54,582	34.5	47.7	17.8	52,025	21.6	51.0	27.3
43580	Sioux City, IA-NE-SD	131,359	28.1	52.2	19.7	64,215	32.0	52.8	15.2	67,144	24.3	51.7	24.1
43620	Sioux Falls, SD	186,168	30.9	52.6	16.4	92,475	33.9	53.1	13.0	93,693	28.0	52.1	19.9
43780	South Bend-Mishawaka, IN-MI	255,723	32.5	47.8	19.7	123,014	35.1	49.6	15.2	132,709	30.2	46.0	23.8
43900	Spartanburg, SC	254,502	29.9	48.3	21.8	121,717	32.9	50.8	16.3	132,785	27.2	46.0	26.8
44060	Spokane-Spokane Valley, WA	432,452	29.8	49.4	20.7	212,596	33.1	50.4	16.5	219,856	26.7	48.5	24.8
44100	Springfield, IL	170,934	30.2	48.1	21.7	80,906	32.8	50.9	16.4	90,028	27.9	45.6	26.4
44140	Springfield, MA	518,174	38.5	42.1	19.4	244,264	41.1	45.2	13.8	273,910	36.3	39.3	24.4
44180	Springfield, MO	359,280	27.7	51.8	20.5	174,069	30.4	53.5	16.1	185,211	25.0	50.3	24.7
44220	Springfield, OH	110,855	27.9	48.9	23.2	53,047	32.0	50.9	17.1	57,808	24.2	47.0	28.8
44300	State College, PA	135,180	46.6	41.1	12.4	70,397	50.2	40.5	9.3	64,783	42.6	41.8	15.6
44420	Staunton-Waynesboro, VA	98,656	26.0	52.1	21.8	47,710	29.9	53.6	16.6	50,946	22.5	50.8	26.8
44700	Stockton-Lodi, CA	535,071	34.4	47.6	18.0	263,808	37.9	48.8	13.4	271,263	31.0	46.4	22.6
44940	Sumter, SC	85,243	33.0	44.8	22.2	40,740	35.9	47.8	16.3	44,503	30.4	42.1	27.5
45060	Syracuse, NY	542,481	35.5	45.2	19.3	261,152	38.3	46.9	14.8	281,329	32.8	43.6	23.5
45220	Tallahassee, FL	311,694	43.0	39.6	17.5	150,552	45.0	41.3	13.7	161,142	41.0	38.0	21.0
45300	Tampa-St. Petersburg-Clearwater, FL	2,361,056	30.1	46.2	23.7	1,130,920	33.5	48.7	17.8	1,230,136	27.0	43.9	29.1
45460	Terre Haute, IN	141,648	30.8	46.9	22.3	71,801	34.8	47.2	18.0	69,847	26.7	46.6	26.7

Table C-3: Metropolitan Areas—Marriages and Births—*Continued*

CBSA FIPS code	Metropolitan area	Total women age 15 to 50 years	Percent of all women who had a birth in the past year	Percent of women who had a birth who were married (including separated and spouse absent):	Percent of women who had a birth who were partners in an unmarried partner household	Age of women who had a birth in the last year as a percent of all women who had a birth			Women who had a birth in the last year as a percent of all women in their age group		
						Age 15 to 19	Age 20 to 34	Age 35 to 50	Age 15 to 19	Age 20 to 34	Age 35 to 50
38900	Portland-Vancouver-Hillsboro, OR-WA....................	572,551	5.1	73.6	10.0	2.6	73.8	23.6	1.1	8.8	2.6
38940	Port St. Lucie, FL	86,787	5.1	55.6	7.3	1.4	76.9	21.7	0.5	10.3	2.3
39140	Prescott, AZ	37,210	5.2	62.2	9.1	18.6	71.8	9.6	6.8	9.9	1.0
39300	Providence-Warwick, RI-MA..........	393,761	4.6	56.1	14.2	4.7	75.4	19.9	1.5	8.6	2.0
39340	Provo-Orem, UT..........................	145,642	8.5	92.2	3.3	1.2	86.9	11.9	0.6	14.4	3.2
39380	Pueblo, CO	36,427	5.6	61.2	9.1	10.1	76.7	13.2	3.8	10.2	1.7
39460	Punta Gorda, FL	24,729	4.4	54.5	4.7	6.6	78.9	14.5	2.0	10.2	1.2
39540	Racine, WI	44,682	4.7	56.8	16.9	5.5	80.4	14.1	1.9	9.9	1.4
39580	Raleigh, NC	315,015	5.0	71.1	8.9	2.8	75.3	21.9	1.1	9.5	2.3
39660	Rapid City, SD	31,087	6.7	54.0	23.3	17.9	73.5	8.5	8.7	11.5	1.3
39740	Reading, PA	97,776	5.4	59.2	11.8	4.7	79.1	16.1	1.7	11.1	1.9
39820	Redding, CA	38,644	3.7	70.1	17.3	5.2	78.4	16.4	1.4	7.1	1.4
39900	Reno, NV	103,194	5.5	71.2	12.2	4.6	75.5	19.9	1.9	9.5	2.5
40060	Richmond, VA.............................	310,152	4.7	62.6	8.9	3.7	78.9	17.4	1.3	8.9	1.8
40140	Riverside-San Bernardino-Ontario, CA........	1,092,954	5.9	60.1	11.9	6.8	73.8	19.4	2.6	10.4	2.7
40220	Roanoke, VA...............................	70,727	5.7	68.1	7.2	9.2	68.4	22.4	3.9	9.9	2.7
40340	Rochester, MN	48,096	6.1	76.5	14.9	2.4	71.3	26.2	1.1	10.3	3.6
40380	Rochester, NY	260,884	5.0	57.6	11.2	3.8	75.5	20.6	1.3	9.2	2.4
40420	Rockford, IL	80,613	5.5	56.5	11.9	9.7	73.5	16.8	3.8	10.3	2.0
40580	Rocky Mount, NC	35,338	5.4	39.9	11.9	18.8	72.0	9.2	7.0	10.4	1.0
40660	Rome, GA..................................										
40900	Sacramento–Roseville–Arden-Arcade, CA........	543,474	5.0	64.9	12.2	3.8	74.9	21.2	1.4	8.9	2.5
40980	Saginaw, MI	45,366	4.3	49.6	9.9	11.9	74.1	14.1	3.3	7.9	1.4
41060	St. Cloud, MN	47,163	4.8	70.8	21.5	1.8	84.8	13.4	0.5	9.0	1.7
41100	St. George, UT............................	30,394	7.1	84.6	4.1	7.8	77.5	14.7	3.2	12.3	2.8
41140	St. Joseph, MO-KS	28,290	5.2	47.9	10.5	10.5	74.8	14.7	3.8	9.0	1.8
41180	St. Louis, MO-IL	676,906	5.3	62.4	11.4	5.0	73.8	21.2	2.0	9.4	2.5
41420	Salem, OR	93,284	5.7	57.9	18.4	12.4	68.2	19.4	4.5	9.2	2.7
41500	Salinas, CA	100,599	6.3	66.8	13.3	6.9	66.6	26.5	2.9	9.4	4.1
41540	Salisbury, MD-DE........................	82,187	5.2	57.3	9.7	8.7	74.9	16.4	3.1	9.5	1.9
41620	Salt Lake City, UT........................	286,562	6.9	78.3	6.7	3.8	77.7	18.5	2.0	11.5	3.2
41660	San Angelo, TX	27,878	4.6	76.5	8.7	9.8	86.7	3.5	3.0	8.3	0.4
41700	San Antonio-New Braunfels, TX	561,350	6.0	62.9	9.0	7.4	73.4	19.3	3.1	10.4	2.7
41740	San Diego-Carlsbad, CA................	805,703	5.1	77.0	6.5	4.4	72.7	22.9	1.8	8.3	2.8
41860	San Francisco-Oakland-Hayward, CA........	1,126,252	4.9	76.1	7.4	1.8	63.9	34.3	0.8	7.4	3.6
41940	San Jose-Sunnyvale-Santa Clara, CA........	478,053	5.7	77.9	6.2	3.0	66.2	30.8	1.4	9.3	3.7
42020	San Luis Obispo-Paso Robles-Arroyo Grande, CA	61,624	4.6	71.0	10.5	4.2	70.0	25.8	1.1	7.3	3.1
42100	Santa Cruz-Watsonville, CA	67,391	4.5	65.5	10.2	2.9	70.9	26.2	0.8	7.4	2.9
42140	Santa Fe, NM	31,238	4.1	62.9	7.0	15.1	73.5	11.4	4.7	7.8	0.9
42200	Santa Maria-Santa Barbara, CA.....	107,256	5.1	71.7	8.3	7.5	69.5	23.1	2.2	7.6	3.1
42220	Santa Rosa, CA...........................	112,766	5.1	63.3	13.5	2.3	69.2	28.5	0.8	8.6	3.2
42340	Savannah, GA	92,978	5.1	52.7	10.8	5.1	79.6	15.3	2.0	8.8	2.0
42540	Scranton–Wilkes-Barre–Hazleton, PA........	126,489	4.5	52.3	15.8	6.1	77.2	16.7	2.0	8.7	1.6
42660	Seattle-Tacoma-Bellevue, WA.......	899,237	5.3	74.8	10.3	2.9	71.9	25.1	1.3	8.8	2.9
42680	Sebastian-Vero Beach, FL	25,881	5.5	62.4	17.9	3.6	69.7	26.7	1.5	10.3	2.9
42700	Sebring, FL	16,081	5.1	55.9	10.5	0.0	85.7	14.3	0.0	11.4	1.6
43100	Sheboygan, WI	25,565	5.1	75.3	17.5	3.1	83.1	13.9	1.0	11.6	1.5
43300	Sherman-Denison, TX	27,825	5.2	52.5	2.4	17.0	69.3	13.6	5.8	9.0	1.6
43340	Shreveport-Bossier City, LA...........	108,022	6.0	46.7	9.3	5.8	78.8	15.4	2.7	10.6	2.2
43420	Sierra Vista-Douglas, AZ...............	27,301	4.4	63.0	17.6	17.7	74.7	7.7	4.7	8.0	0.8
43580	Sioux City, IA-NE-SD....................	38,329	6.2	66.3	11.4	5.0	79.8	15.2	2.1	12.0	2.2
43620	Sioux Falls, SD	57,391	7.2	68.5	16.2	0.0	84.8	15.2	0.0	13.7	2.6
43780	South Bend-Mishawaka, IN-MI......	76,066	5.2	57.3	11.2	8.3	77.7	14.0	2.7	9.7	1.7
43900	Spartanburg, SC	75,729	6.3	58.7	9.6	8.6	75.0	16.5	3.8	11.9	2.3
44060	Spokane-Spokane Valley, WA........	125,510	4.7	70.6	10.9	3.4	82.7	14.0	1.1	8.9	1.6
44100	Springfield, IL.............................	49,702	4.7	63.6	9.6	2.9	81.3	15.8	1.0	9.2	1.6
44140	Springfield, MA...........................	159,951	3.9	55.4	11.2	5.9	74.0	20.1	1.4	6.8	1.9
44180	Springfield, MO..........................	108,512	5.5	65.7	9.3	7.2	76.0	16.8	2.8	9.1	2.3
44220	Springfield, OH	30,619	4.5	42.9	17.1	5.3	85.4	9.3	1.6	9.7	0.9
44300	State College, PA	43,139	3.7	64.9	18.7	3.8	76.3	19.9	0.7	5.4	2.5
44420	Staunton-Waynesboro, VA............	26,723	5.7	62.0	12.5	0.0	83.8	16.2	0.0	12.3	2.0
44700	Stockton-Lodi, CA........................	171,385	6.4	61.6	10.1	6.7	76.0	17.4	2.7	11.6	2.6
44940	Sumter, SC	25,753	6.1	40.9	18.6	2.5	88.0	9.5	1.1	12.1	1.4
45060	Syracuse, NY..............................	161,968	4.8	55.2	15.2	5.3	76.2	18.6	1.5	9.0	2.0
45220	Tallahassee, FL............................	104,535	3.6	60.9	7.4	6.4	73.4	20.2	1.5	5.2	2.1
45300	Tampa-St. Petersburg-Clearwater, FL	661,564	4.7	58.2	11.1	4.2	73.7	22.2	1.6	8.6	2.2
45460	Terre Haute, IN...........................	39,479	5.7	54.3	6.5	5.5	84.3	10.2	2.1	11.1	1.4

Table C-3: Metropolitan Areas—Marriages and Births—*Continued*

CBSA FIPS code	Metropolitan area	Total population 15 years and older	Marital status, percent			Male population 15 years and older	Male, marital status, percent			Female population 15 years and older	Female, marital status, percent		
			Never married	Now married (except separated)	Separated, widowed, or divorced		Never married	Now married (except separated)	Separated, widowed, or divorced		Never married	Now married (except separated)	Separated, widowed, or divorced
45500	Texarkana, TX-AR......................	119,773	27.9	46.6	25.5	59,317	31.9	47.1	21.0	60,456	24.0	46.1	29.9
45540	The Villages, FL	95,580	14.3	63.2	22.5	48,966	19.3	63.1	17.6	46,614	9.1	63.3	27.6
45780	Toledo, OH.................................	493,240	35.7	43.6	20.7	236,960	38.8	45.4	15.8	256,280	32.8	41.9	25.2
45820	Topeka, KS.................................	186,622	26.7	52.0	21.3	90,191	30.3	53.5	16.3	96,431	23.3	50.7	26.0
45940	Trenton, NJ	301,670	36.6	47.2	16.1	146,304	40.4	48.6	10.9	155,366	33.1	45.9	21.0
46060	Tucson, AZ	808,251	33.7	44.7	21.6	394,525	37.4	46.2	16.4	413,726	30.1	43.4	26.6
46140	Tulsa, OK	752,041	27.2	51.1	21.7	364,671	30.3	53.0	16.7	387,370	24.3	49.3	26.4
46220	Tuscaloosa, AL	191,693	39.1	42.2	18.7	91,340	41.8	44.6	13.6	100,353	36.6	40.0	23.4
46340	Tyler, TX...................................	169,149	27.2	50.8	22.0	80,430	29.3	54.2	16.5	88,719	25.3	47.8	26.9
46520	Urban Honolulu, HI	795,585	33.8	50.2	16.1	399,577	38.3	50.4	11.3	396,008	29.2	49.9	20.9
46540	Utica-Rome, NY	245,940	32.8	45.3	21.9	121,635	36.7	46.6	16.6	124,305	28.9	44.0	27.1
46660	Valdosta, GA..............................	113,438	37.6	41.4	21.0	55,244	40.9	42.5	16.7	58,194	34.5	40.3	25.1
46700	Vallejo-Fairfield, CA...................	338,805	33.7	46.8	19.4	168,029	37.4	48.1	14.5	170,776	30.1	45.6	24.3
47020	Victoria, TX	75,737	27.4	49.6	22.9	36,655	31.8	50.9	17.3	39,082	23.4	48.5	28.2
47220	Vineland-Bridgeton, NJ	126,111	40.8	38.8	20.3	65,053	44.7	39.2	16.1	61,058	36.7	38.5	24.8
47260	Virginia Beach-Norfolk-Newport News, VA-NC..............................	1,373,234	33.6	46.6	19.8	669,349	37.5	48.3	14.2	703,885	29.9	45.1	25.0
47300	Visalia-Porterville, CA..................	330,027	35.2	48.3	16.6	164,388	38.8	49.7	11.5	165,639	31.6	46.9	21.5
47380	Waco, TX...................................	203,995	33.7	45.8	20.5	97,626	36.3	48.5	15.2	106,369	31.3	43.4	25.3
47460	Walla Walla, WA.........................	52,232	32.7	47.1	20.2	26,777	37.5	47.5	15.0	25,455	27.6	46.7	25.7
47580	Warner Robins, GA......................	145,950	30.7	49.8	19.5	69,717	32.4	53.3	14.3	76,233	29.0	46.6	24.3
47900	Washington-Arlington-Alexandria, DC-VA-MD-WV............................	4,710,438	36.2	48.2	15.6	2,272,736	38.4	50.5	11.1	2,437,702	34.2	46.0	19.9
47940	Waterloo-Cedar Falls, IA..............	138,155	33.9	48.9	17.2	66,927	37.0	50.7	12.3	71,228	31.0	47.2	21.8
48060	Watertown-Fort Drum, NY...........	93,603	28.8	53.2	18.0	48,702	34.7	51.2	14.1	44,901	22.4	55.4	22.2
48140	Wausau, WI	108,446	26.7	55.6	17.8	54,067	30.1	56.3	13.6	54,379	23.3	54.8	21.9
48260	Weirton-Steubenville, WV-OH	103,250	26.7	49.9	23.4	49,313	29.7	52.7	17.6	53,937	24.0	47.3	28.7
48300	Wenatchee, WA..........................	89,343	26.5	55.9	17.6	44,292	30.2	56.6	13.2	45,051	22.9	55.2	21.9
48540	Wheeling, WV-OH	123,396	27.3	50.1	22.5	60,713	31.7	51.1	17.3	62,683	23.2	49.2	27.6
48620	Wichita, KS................................	494,107	28.7	51.2	20.1	242,866	32.1	52.8	15.1	251,241	25.4	49.7	24.9
48660	Wichita Falls, TX	121,983	30.8	48.2	21.0	62,594	36.1	47.5	16.4	59,389	25.2	48.9	25.8
48700	Williamsport, PA.........................	97,034	30.3	48.3	21.4	47,348	34.3	49.5	16.1	49,686	26.4	47.1	26.5
48900	Wilmington, NC	219,462	33.4	47.0	19.6	105,915	35.8	48.7	15.5	113,547	31.2	45.3	23.5
49020	Winchester, VA-WV	105,829	29.8	50.8	19.4	52,247	34.0	50.8	15.2	53,582	25.7	50.8	23.5
49180	Winston-Salem, NC	521,878	29.5	50.0	20.6	247,599	32.0	53.0	15.0	274,279	27.2	47.2	25.5
49340	Worcester, MA-CT	755,198	33.3	47.8	18.8	369,214	36.7	49.3	14.0	385,984	30.2	46.4	23.4
49420	Yakima, WA	183,851	32.2	49.0	18.8	91,548	36.0	50.1	14.0	92,303	28.4	48.0	23.6
49620	York-Hanover, PA	355,540	28.1	52.6	19.3	173,776	30.9	54.3	14.8	181,764	25.5	51.0	23.6
49660	Youngstown-Warren-Boardman, OH-PA	463,484	29.9	47.4	22.7	223,574	33.4	49.8	16.8	239,910	26.7	45.1	28.3
49700	Yuba City, CA	129,180	29.2	51.5	19.3	64,257	32.7	52.3	15.0	64,923	25.6	50.7	23.6
49740	Yuma, AZ...................................	156,471	27.2	56.1	16.6	80,137	31.1	55.8	13.1	76,334	23.2	56.5	20.3

Table C-3: Metropolitan Areas—Marriages and Births—*Continued*

CBSA FIPS code	Metropolitan area	Total women age 15 to 50 years	Percent of all women who had a birth in the past year	Percent of women who had a birth who were married (including separated and spouse absent):	Percent of women who had a birth who were partners in an unmarried partner household	Age of women who had a birth in the last year as a percent of all women who had a birth			Women who had a birth in the last year as a percent of all women in their age group		
						Age 15 to 19	Age 20 to 34	Age 35 to 50	Age 15 to 19	Age 20 to 34	Age 35 to 50
45500	Texarkana, TX-AR	33,737	6.9	63.1	12.0	13.0	71.1	15.9	6.2	12.4	2.4
45540	The Villages, FL	8,825	3.9	73.1	2.7	7.3	80.4	12.3	2.0	8.8	0.9
45780	Toledo, OH	149,146	4.9	58.0	11.5	5.0	78.0	17.0	1.6	8.9	2.0
45820	Topeka, KS	52,084	5.8	63.4	13.0	5.6	83.4	11.0	2.3	11.7	1.4
45940	Trenton, NJ	92,157	4.4	67.7	6.0	4.3	67.6	28.0	1.3	7.6	2.7
46060	Tucson, AZ	230,793	5.2	57.8	16.0	5.1	78.1	16.8	1.8	9.2	2.1
46140	Tulsa, OK	226,697	5.7	62.9	12.0	6.8	78.7	14.5	2.9	10.5	1.9
46220	Tuscaloosa, AL	63,909	5.8	66.0	0.8	2.1	85.2	12.7	0.7	10.2	2.0
46340	Tyler, TX	51,559	6.2	61.4	5.8	9.3	77.3	13.4	4.1	10.8	2.0
46520	Urban Honolulu, HI	228,294	6.5	72.2	8.3	4.5	71.6	23.9	2.5	10.4	3.6
46540	Utica-Rome, NY	66,457	5.6	55.0	22.4	6.1	73.1	20.9	2.2	10.4	2.6
46660	Valdosta, GA	38,129	5.0	52.0	6.8	7.5	80.7	11.8	2.4	8.4	1.6
46700	Vallejo-Fairfield, CA	101,096	5.2	60.7	14.7	5.1	74.9	20.0	1.9	9.2	2.3
47020	Victoria, TX	21,750	4.4	48.0	20.6	9.5	84.9	5.6	3.0	8.9	0.6
47220	Vineland-Bridgeton, NJ	35,544	5.9	52.5	8.3	4.4	83.7	11.9	1.9	11.8	1.6
47260	Virginia Beach-Norfolk-Newport News, VA-NC	429,166	5.4	62.9	7.5	5.1	78.2	16.7	2.1	9.5	2.1
47300	Visalia-Porterville, CA	109,902	7.2	57.4	18.2	7.4	80.0	12.6	3.2	13.2	2.3
47380	Waco, TX	65,348	5.0	60.3	9.5	11.4	73.3	15.3	3.5	8.1	2.0
47460	Walla Walla, WA	13,884	4.2	53.3	24.3	1.9	79.1	19.0	0.4	8.4	2.0
47580	Warner Robins, GA	47,897	4.5	64.7	8.2	1.2	88.9	10.0	0.4	9.4	1.0
47900	Washington-Arlington-Alexandria, DC-VA-MD-WV	1,552,891	5.2	70.4	7.3	3.4	68.0	28.5	1.5	8.5	3.3
47940	Waterloo-Cedar Falls, IA	41,501	5.2	62.3	10.2	5.2	87.3	7.5	1.7	9.6	1.1
48060	Watertown-Fort Drum, NY	28,116	8.0	76.5	11.1	5.8	82.0	12.2	3.9	13.3	2.5
48140	Wausau, WI	30,343	5.5	75.7	19.6	1.5	75.1	23.4	0.6	10.8	2.7
48260	Weirton-Steubenville, WV-OH	26,435	4.8	58.5	11.5	5.8	82.0	12.3	1.9	10.4	1.3
48300	Wenatchee, WA	24,591	4.4	57.9	16.4	13.6	73.0	13.5	3.9	8.0	1.4
48540	Wheeling, WV-OH	30,377	2.9	53.1	16.9	9.9	72.7	17.4	2.0	5.4	1.1
48620	Wichita, KS	148,105	6.4	66.6	7.9	7.0	78.8	14.2	3.1	11.7	2.1
48660	Wichita Falls, TX	34,012	5.2	66.7	18.0	11.9	75.0	13.1	4.4	8.5	1.7
48700	Williamsport, PA	26,386	5.4	55.0	19.2	2.0	78.7	19.3	0.8	10.1	2.3
48900	Wilmington, NC	65,846	4.7	63.1	13.4	8.9	67.4	23.7	2.9	7.3	2.6
49020	Winchester, VA-WV	30,641	5.3	58.5	15.5	5.7	77.9	16.4	2.2	10.7	1.8
49180	Winston-Salem, NC	155,642	4.9	63.4	7.3	7.6	75.8	16.6	2.7	9.6	1.7
49340	Worcester, MA-CT	225,579	4.8	64.8	14.5	2.9	73.6	23.5	1.0	9.3	2.4
49420	Yakima, WA	56,601	6.9	57.2	12.3	13.6	70.4	16.0	5.7	11.3	2.7
49620	York-Hanover, PA	102,200	4.7	57.4	14.4	7.4	79.5	13.1	2.6	9.9	1.3
49660	Youngstown-Warren-Boardman, OH-PA	119,279	4.4	50.7	11.8	8.4	73.6	18.0	2.5	8.3	1.7
49700	Yuba City, CA	39,716	7.0	64.1	10.2	8.9	78.1	13.0	4.5	12.2	2.2
49740	Yuma, AZ	44,952	6.2	67.9	17.1	6.5	77.8	15.8	2.4	11.3	2.4

Table C-4: Cities with a Population of 50,000 or More—Marriages and Births

State/place FIPS code	State/Place	Total population 15 years and older	Marital status, percent			Male population 15 years and older	Male, marital status, percent			Female population 15 years and older	Female, marital status, percent		
			Never married	Now married (except separated)	Separated, widowed, or divorced		Never married	Now married (except separated)	Separated, widowed, or divorced		Never married	Now married (except separated)	Separated, widowed, or divorced
0000000	**United States**................	252,732,021	32.7	48.1	19.2	123,212,971	36.0	49.9	14.1	129,519,050	29.6	46.4	24.0
0100000	**Alabama**........................	3,891,144	29.5	48.2	22.3	1,862,214	32.5	50.9	16.6	2,028,930	26.7	45.8	27.5
0103076	Auburn city........................	48,352	57.3	33.6	9.1	24,287	61.0	33.9	5.2	24,065	53.6	33.3	13.1
0107000	Birmingham city.................	173,463	43.8	29.1	27.1	79,140	46.0	32.1	21.9	94,323	42.0	26.6	31.4
0120104	Decatur city........................	44,678	27.2	47.9	24.8	20,980	29.6	51.9	18.5	23,698	25.2	44.4	30.4
0121184	Dothan city.........................	54,045	29.6	46.2	24.1	25,204	33.4	50.0	16.6	28,841	26.3	42.9	30.7
0135896	Hoover city.........................	64,966	24.2	59.1	16.7	31,013	25.7	63.1	11.1	33,953	22.8	55.5	21.8
0137000	Huntsville city.....................	151,189	35.7	42.0	22.3	73,526	39.8	43.7	16.5	77,663	31.7	40.4	27.9
0150000	Mobile city.........................	157,277	39.4	36.8	23.8	74,508	43.7	39.4	16.8	82,769	35.5	34.3	30.2
0151000	Montgomery city................	161,671	40.3	37.0	22.7	74,253	42.5	41.1	16.5	87,418	38.5	33.5	28.0
0177256	Tuscaloosa city...................	80,085	53.0	31.0	16.1	37,855	56.8	33.0	10.2	42,230	49.5	29.1	21.3
0200000	**Alaska**...........................	571,984	33.9	48.4	17.8	299,425	38.2	47.1	14.7	272,559	29.2	49.8	21.1
0203000	Anchorage municipality...........	235,095	35.3	47.4	17.3	119,334	39.8	46.4	13.8	115,761	30.5	48.5	20.9
0400000	**Arizona**.........................	5,201,287	32.6	47.4	20.0	2,569,288	36.2	48.7	15.1	2,631,999	29.0	46.2	24.8
0404720	Avondale city......................	57,751	39.4	43.9	16.7	27,408	40.9	46.8	12.4	30,343	38.1	41.4	20.5
0407940	Buckeye town......................	40,980	33.8	49.5	16.6	22,334	39.7	47.6	12.7	18,646	26.9	51.8	21.3
0410670	Casas Adobes CDP................	55,859	27.7	49.1	23.1	26,230	30.7	52.5	16.7	29,629	25.1	46.1	28.8
0411230	Catalina Foothills CDP..........	45,169	22.4	58.9	18.6	21,722	25.0	62.0	13.0	23,447	20.1	56.1	23.9
0412000	Chandler city.......................	188,971	32.1	51.7	16.2	93,749	36.3	52.5	11.3	95,222	28.0	51.0	21.0
0423620	Flagstaff city.......................	56,550	52.8	34.2	13.0	27,673	55.6	34.6	9.9	28,877	50.2	33.8	16.0
0427400	Gilbert town........................	160,594	27.5	58.5	13.9	78,151	28.7	60.4	10.9	82,443	26.4	56.8	16.8
0427820	Glendale city.......................	181,462	37.4	42.6	20.0	89,045	41.4	44.2	14.4	92,417	33.5	41.0	25.4
0428380	Goodyear city......................	53,972	28.2	58.9	12.9	25,687	29.2	61.3	9.4	28,285	27.3	56.6	16.1
0439370	Lake Havasu City city...........	45,486	20.6	55.1	24.3	21,831	24.1	57.0	18.9	23,655	17.5	53.2	29.3
0446000	Mesa city............................	356,787	32.6	47.0	20.4	173,311	36.0	48.8	15.2	183,476	29.3	45.3	25.4
0454050	Peoria city..........................	126,713	27.1	52.2	20.6	60,440	31.3	54.4	14.3	66,273	23.4	50.2	26.5
0455000	Phoenix city........................	1,150,726	38.9	41.7	19.4	570,884	42.7	42.8	14.5	579,842	35.3	40.6	24.2
0464210	San Tan Valley CDP..............	60,841	28.6	56.7	14.7	30,226	29.2	61.3	9.5	30,615	28.0	52.1	19.8
0465000	Scottsdale city.....................	191,220	28.7	50.9	20.3	91,754	32.4	53.4	14.2	99,466	25.3	48.7	26.0
0471510	Surprise city........................	91,231	19.0	61.5	19.4	42,998	21.0	65.6	13.4	48,233	17.2	57.9	24.8
0473000	Tempe city..........................	143,741	54.1	30.7	15.2	74,763	58.2	29.7	12.1	68,978	49.6	31.9	18.5
0477000	Tucson city.........................	427,576	41.3	35.6	23.1	211,385	46.1	36.2	17.7	216,191	36.7	35.0	28.3
0485540	Yuma city...........................	71,234	28.1	54.1	17.8	36,759	32.9	54.3	12.8	34,475	22.9	53.9	23.2
0500000	**Arkansas**.......................	2,355,484	27.0	50.5	22.5	1,143,822	30.4	52.6	17.1	1,211,662	23.9	48.5	27.6
0515190	Conway city........................	50,642	41.6	42.1	16.3	24,821	45.1	43.0	11.9	25,821	38.2	41.3	20.5
0523290	Fayetteville city...................	65,784	47.3	36.1	16.6	32,456	50.9	36.5	12.5	33,328	43.8	35.6	20.5
0524550	Fort Smith city....................	69,133	29.1	46.6	24.3	33,830	33.7	47.9	18.3	35,303	24.6	45.4	30.0
0535710	Jonesboro city.....................	55,745	33.7	44.4	21.9	26,204	37.7	47.3	15.1	29,541	30.2	41.9	27.9
0541000	Little Rock city....................	158,949	39.0	39.1	21.9	75,061	42.8	41.5	15.7	83,888	35.5	37.0	27.5
0550450	North Little Rock city...........	49,505	35.9	39.1	25.1	23,093	39.1	41.9	19.0	26,412	33.0	36.6	30.4
0560410	Rogers city.........................	43,805	28.5	54.4	17.1	21,349	31.9	56.3	11.8	22,456	25.2	52.6	22.2
0566080	Springdale city....................	53,245	29.4	52.9	17.8	26,604	31.7	54.8	13.5	26,641	27.0	50.9	22.1
0600000	**California**......................	30,396,377	36.5	46.3	17.2	15,012,016	40.2	47.6	12.2	15,384,361	32.9	45.1	22.0
0600562	Alameda city.......................	62,913	33.6	49.0	17.4	30,519	38.2	50.4	11.4	32,394	29.2	47.7	23.1
0600884	Alhambra city......................	71,784	38.1	46.3	15.6	34,351	42.4	48.7	8.9	37,433	34.2	44.1	21.7
0602000	Anaheim city.......................	267,602	36.5	46.9	16.6	131,315	41.2	48.2	10.6	136,287	31.9	45.7	22.3
0602252	Antioch city........................	83,409	35.6	45.8	18.6	39,028	37.8	49.2	13.0	44,381	33.6	42.8	23.6
0602364	Apple Valley town................	56,189	29.2	50.7	20.1	27,447	32.1	52.8	15.1	28,742	26.5	48.7	24.9
0602462	Arcadia city........................	47,781	28.4	58.1	13.5	22,316	31.2	61.8	7.0	25,465	25.9	54.8	19.2
0602553	Arden-Arcade CDP................	74,663	34.4	41.9	23.8	35,042	38.2	45.3	16.5	39,621	31.0	38.8	30.2
0603526	Bakersfield city....................	267,526	36.2	46.3	17.5	131,068	38.6	47.8	13.5	136,458	33.9	44.8	21.3
0603666	Baldwin Park city.................	60,509	43.7	42.6	13.7	30,000	47.6	43.3	9.1	30,509	39.9	41.8	18.3
0604982	Bellflower city.....................	59,228	40.9	41.1	17.9	28,168	44.6	43.8	11.5	31,060	37.6	38.7	23.8
0606000	Berkeley city.......................	103,672	55.5	32.0	12.4	50,359	58.3	33.3	8.4	53,313	52.9	30.8	16.2
0608142	Brentwood city....................	40,812	27.2	57.3	15.5	19,939	29.5	58.7	11.8	20,873	25.0	55.9	19.0
0608786	Buena Park city...................	66,479	35.5	47.7	16.8	32,493	39.7	49.2	11.1	33,986	31.4	46.3	22.3
0608954	Burbank city.......................	87,270	34.8	47.1	18.1	41,456	37.9	49.4	12.7	45,814	32.1	45.0	22.9
0610046	Camarillo city......................	53,043	28.8	52.7	18.6	25,565	32.4	54.3	13.3	27,478	25.4	51.2	23.4
0611194	Carlsbad city.......................	88,241	25.7	56.2	18.2	44,135	31.3	57.0	11.8	44,106	20.1	55.4	24.5
0611390	Carmichael CDP...................	51,996	30.9	44.3	24.8	24,139	35.2	48.0	16.8	27,857	27.2	41.1	31.7
0611530	Carson city..........................	75,838	39.3	43.3	17.4	36,604	43.1	45.7	11.2	39,234	35.7	41.1	23.2
0611964	Castro Valley CDP................	50,072	29.7	51.8	18.5	24,333	31.3	54.3	14.4	25,739	28.2	49.5	22.3
0612048	Cathedral City city...............	40,469	36.0	43.7	20.2	21,430	42.8	41.7	15.5	19,039	28.4	46.0	25.5
0613014	Chico city...........................	73,160	45.4	35.4	19.2	34,685	49.6	37.5	12.8	38,475	41.6	33.5	24.9
0613210	Chino city...........................	65,108	35.8	47.4	16.8	34,202	37.5	47.9	14.5	30,906	34.0	46.8	19.3
0613214	Chino Hills city....................	60,874	33.6	53.2	13.1	30,766	38.4	53.7	7.9	30,108	28.8	52.7	18.5
0613392	Chula Vista city...................	197,519	32.8	50.5	16.6	94,615	36.4	53.3	10.4	102,904	29.6	48.0	22.4
0613588	Citrus Heights city...............	69,385	32.3	45.5	22.3	33,003	35.9	47.7	16.4	36,382	29.0	43.4	27.6
0614218	Clovis city...........................	76,038	31.9	49.4	18.7	36,294	34.6	51.9	13.5	39,744	29.5	47.0	23.4
0614890	Colton city..........................	38,404	43.5	41.3	15.2	18,558	46.5	43.0	10.5	19,846	40.7	39.7	19.6
0615044	Compton city.......................	70,995	47.6	37.0	15.4	34,448	50.9	39.2	9.9	36,547	44.5	34.9	20.6
0616000	Concord city........................	99,830	31.9	50.1	17.9	50,158	36.8	50.5	12.7	49,672	27.1	49.7	23.2
0616350	Corona city.........................	121,323	34.4	51.2	14.4	60,044	37.7	52.6	9.7	61,279	31.2	49.8	19.0

State/place FIPS code	State/Place	Total women age 15 to 50 years	Percent of all women who had a birth in the past year	Percent of women who had a birth who were married (including separated and spouse absent):	Percent of women who had a birth who were partners in an unmarried partner household	Age of women who had a birth in the last year as a percent of all women who had a birth			Women who had a birth in the last year as a percent of all women in their age group		
						Age 15 to 19	Age 20 to 34	Age 35 to 50	Age 15 to 19	Age 20 to 34	Age 35 to 50
0000000	**United States**	76,155,872	5.3	64.1	10.1	5.5	73.8	20.7	2.1	9.4	2.5
0100000	**Alabama**	1,165,746	5.5	58.9	6.2	7.1	78.5	14.4	2.8	10.3	1.8
0103076	Auburn city	19,344	3.2	80.8	15.3	22.1	63.6	14.3	3.4	3.6	2.0
0107000	Birmingham city	55,931	6.2	36.4	7.9	8.5	76.6	14.9	4.2	9.8	2.4
0120104	Decatur city	13,461	5.5	72.3	0.0	14.9	56.9	28.2	5.8	7.8	3.3
0121184	Dothan city	16,359	5.5	55.6	5.3	3.6	80.8	15.7	1.6	10.4	1.9
0135896	Hoover city	20,057	5.0	83.7	0.0	0.0	68.9	31.1	0.0	7.8	3.4
0137000	Huntsville city	46,281	4.9	52.1	19.0	2.0	87.3	10.7	0.8	9.4	1.3
0150000	Mobile city	47,978	4.9	43.4	12.2	8.4	76.1	15.4	3.4	8.1	1.9
0151000	Montgomery city	53,306	6.1	34.9	15.6	9.6	81.0	9.3	4.2	10.8	1.4
0177256	Tuscaloosa city	29,101	3.7	56.0	0.8	5.5	81.5	13.0	0.9	6.0	1.7
0200000	**Alaska**	176,655	6.2	62.3	14.7	3.7	73.5	22.8	1.7	10.3	3.4
0203000	Anchorage municipality	77,456	5.5	64.8	13.2	3.1	74.7	22.2	1.3	8.9	2.9
0400000	**Arizona**	1,536,237	5.6	60.7	12.1	5.9	73.1	21.0	2.3	9.6	2.7
0404720	Avondale city	22,389	6.2	52.6	5.1	20.9	71.4	7.7	9.2	9.8	1.2
0407940	Buckeye town	12,012	5.1	56.7	0.0	0.0	86.4	13.6	0.0	10.7	1.6
0410670	Casas Adobes CDP	15,756	5.8	75.3	18.9	0.2	79.7	20.1	0.1	10.8	2.6
0411230	Catalina Foothills CDP	9,176	5.2	95.8	4.2	0.0	77.9	22.1	0.0	10.8	2.5
0412000	Chandler city	63,579	5.3	67.7	8.8	4.4	78.9	16.7	1.9	10.3	1.9
0423620	Flagstaff city	21,270	5.3	51.0	15.8	4.5	67.3	28.2	0.9	7.2	6.2
0427400	Gilbert town	59,231	5.6	84.7	6.9	4.2	81.6	14.1	1.6	12.4	1.7
0427820	Glendale city	59,328	5.7	50.9	10.4	4.6	77.8	17.6	1.9	10.5	2.3
0428380	Goodyear city	17,700	5.0	69.0	19.2	4.3	57.7	37.9	2.3	6.5	4.1
0439370	Lake Havasu City city	9,209	4.0	55.3	9.5	0.0	78.9	21.1	0.0	8.5	1.7
0446000	Mesa city	107,849	5.9	66.6	13.2	4.4	83.1	12.5	1.9	10.6	1.8
0454050	Peoria city	37,481	5.3	66.1	15.0	4.1	76.2	19.7	1.5	11.0	2.1
0455000	Phoenix city	388,996	6.3	57.9	12.1	5.7	66.6	27.7	2.7	9.8	4.0
0464210	San Tan Valley CDP	21,648	5.5	78.4	16.4	0.0	66.6	33.4	0.0	8.9	4.0
0465000	Scottsdale city	50,319	4.5	71.7	3.3	0.5	62.3	37.1	0.2	6.7	3.5
0471510	Surprise city	25,704	5.2	81.3	7.2	4.5	75.9	19.5	2.0	9.5	2.2
0473000	Tempe city	49,154	4.7	43.8	11.0	10.9	67.1	22.0	2.9	5.7	3.8
0477000	Tucson city	134,235	4.8	50.3	19.6	7.5	77.1	15.4	2.4	7.6	2.0
0485540	Yuma city	21,926	6.6	67.5	17.6	8.9	77.1	14.0	3.8	11.3	2.4
0500000	**Arkansas**	692,569	5.4	62.6	9.5	6.9	81.5	11.6	2.7	10.5	1.4
0515190	Conway city	18,504	4.4	71.1	6.7	1.4	96.4	2.2	0.4	7.9	0.3
0523290	Fayetteville city	24,495	4.2	78.6	1.9	4.9	81.7	13.4	1.1	6.3	2.2
0524550	Fort Smith city	20,751	5.4	62.9	10.1	10.5	78.8	10.7	4.2	9.3	1.4
0535710	Jonesboro city	19,262	6.3	69.1	8.1	1.7	95.0	3.3	0.7	12.1	0.6
0541000	Little Rock city	49,613	4.3	60.6	3.6	2.5	80.5	17.0	0.9	7.5	1.7
0550450	North Little Rock city	16,037	3.7	59.8	2.3	0.0	95.7	4.3	0.0	7.3	0.4
0560410	Rogers city	15,582	5.5	75.7	11.0	0.0	89.7	10.3	0.0	10.7	1.4
0566080	Springdale city	18,323	6.5	64.8	16.8	5.2	73.7	21.1	2.8	10.6	3.2
0600000	**California**	9,553,926	5.2	66.1	10.3	5.0	70.4	24.6	1.9	8.7	3.0
0600562	Alameda city	18,637	4.5	84.5	3.0	0.0	49.5	50.5	0.0	5.8	4.3
0600884	Alhambra city	21,665	3.2	75.0	2.0	7.1	59.5	33.4	2.2	4.4	2.4
0602000	Anaheim city	90,062	4.5	62.2	11.5	10.0	60.0	30.0	3.2	6.3	3.2
0602252	Antioch city	27,846	6.0	44.6	11.2	7.4	71.3	21.3	2.5	11.0	3.0
0602364	Apple Valley town	16,178	6.0	68.8	4.2	1.2	91.8	6.9	0.5	12.3	1.1
0602462	Arcadia city	14,203	2.4	100.0	0.0	0.0	51.9	48.1	0.0	3.7	2.2
0602553	Arden-Arcade CDP	21,907	5.7	60.3	13.3	4.6	77.0	18.4	2.2	9.3	2.6
0603526	Bakersfield city	92,966	6.3	54.3	15.5	10.5	77.1	12.4	4.2	10.9	2.0
0603666	Baldwin Park city	20,391	4.9	66.2	4.3	2.4	67.9	29.6	0.7	8.1	3.5
0604982	Bellflower city	20,391	6.3	47.8	15.3	9.6	81.6	8.9	4.3	11.1	1.4
0606000	Berkeley city	35,911	2.4	81.9	7.4	0.0	38.0	62.0	0.0	1.7	5.2
0608142	Brentwood city	13,258	3.2	85.3	0.0	0.0	57.9	42.1	0.0	6.9	2.5
0608786	Buena Park city	20,849	5.4	67.9	11.7	3.4	73.8	22.8	1.4	9.6	2.7
0608954	Burbank city	27,839	3.1	88.3	4.5	0.0	54.7	45.3	0.0	3.9	3.0
0610046	Camarillo city	15,272	5.9	84.6	9.2	0.0	77.9	22.1	0.0	11.7	2.7
0611194	Carlsbad city	23,439	4.4	68.1	8.1	8.3	43.0	48.8	4.2	5.6	3.8
0611390	Carmichael CDP	14,679	4.8	33.4	19.5	11.1	77.4	11.5	3.9	9.2	1.2
0611530	Carson city	23,079	5.1	58.5	17.1	1.4	69.8	28.8	0.5	8.2	3.3
0611964	Castro Valley CDP	14,563	5.9	85.5	5.9	0.0	71.1	28.9	0.0	11.0	3.4
0612048	Cathedral City city	12,044	6.1	51.4	13.8	8.2	66.7	25.1	3.5	9.9	3.4
0613014	Chico city	25,744	4.6	75.1	4.5	0.8	67.3	31.8	0.2	5.7	4.8
0613210	Chino city	20,726	4.9	84.1	0.0	0.0	80.0	20.0	0.0	8.8	2.3
0613214	Chino Hills city	20,726	4.9	84.1	0.0	0.0	80.0	20.0	0.0	8.8	2.3
0613392	Chula Vista city	66,720	4.9	68.9	10.6	3.4	69.7	26.9	1.2	8.3	2.9
0613588	Citrus Heights city	21,243	4.7	67.0	11.8	1.6	80.0	18.4	0.7	8.0	2.1
0614218	Clovis city	25,605	4.4	81.1	5.1	3.8	70.9	25.3	1.0	7.8	2.5
0614890	Colton city	14,461	5.9	56.5	26.8	3.4	89.9	6.7	1.5	11.2	1.0
0615044	Compton city	25,470	7.9	42.7	9.1	8.8	83.6	7.5	4.1	14.5	1.6
0616000	Concord city	29,601	7.7	70.8	19.0	0.8	81.4	17.9	0.6	13.7	3.1
0616350	Corona city	42,211	4.5	78.4	4.6	5.5	75.1	19.3	1.7	8.5	1.9

State/ place FIPS code	State/Place	Total population 15 years and older	Marital status, percent			Male population 15 years and older	Male, marital status, percent			Female population 15 years and older	Female, marital status, percent		
			Never married	Now married (except separated)	Separated, widowed, or divorced		Never married	Now married (except separated)	Separated, widowed, or divorced		Never married	Now married (except separated)	Separated, widowed, or divorced
	California—cont'd												
0616532	Costa Mesa city	90,832	40.1	42.3	17.6	45,712	45.1	43.0	11.8	45,120	34.9	41.7	23.4
0617610	Cupertino city	46,329	22.9	65.4	11.7	22,619	28.0	66.7	5.3	23,710	18.0	64.2	17.8
0617918	Daly City city	87,051	37.9	47.5	14.5	43,414	42.3	47.5	10.1	43,637	33.6	47.6	18.9
0618100	Davis city	56,714	54.7	35.3	10.0	27,040	55.3	38.1	6.6	29,674	54.2	32.7	13.1
0618394	Delano city	40,142	43.9	41.2	14.9	24,033	50.6	37.6	11.8	16,109	33.9	46.5	19.6
0619192	Diamond Bar city	47,502	32.9	53.7	13.4	22,308	34.9	57.1	8.0	25,194	31.2	50.7	18.1
0619766	Downey city	88,793	38.6	44.6	16.8	42,669	40.3	47.7	11.9	46,124	37.1	41.6	21.3
0620802	East Los Angeles CDP	98,981	49.0	37.4	13.6	48,501	52.1	39.2	8.7	50,480	46.1	35.5	18.3
0621230	Eastvale city	39,265	29.4	60.2	10.5	18,965	31.9	61.8	6.4	20,300	27.1	58.6	14.3
0621712	El Cajon city	79,620	37.1	41.6	21.3	38,448	41.6	43.6	14.8	41,172	33.0	39.7	27.3
0622020	Elk Grove city	121,154	30.8	52.3	16.9	58,690	33.8	54.9	11.3	62,464	28.0	49.8	22.2
0622230	El Monte city	91,901	39.1	45.6	15.4	45,188	43.3	47.6	9.1	46,713	35.0	43.6	21.4
0622678	Encinitas city	50,126	30.3	54.4	15.3	24,578	34.3	55.9	9.8	25,548	26.5	52.9	20.7
0622804	Escondido city	114,636	35.3	48.3	16.4	56,027	39.1	50.8	10.1	58,609	31.7	45.9	22.4
0623182	Fairfield city	85,145	33.0	50.2	16.7	41,111	36.5	52.1	11.4	44,034	29.8	48.5	21.7
0624477	Florence-Graham CDP	45,790	49.0	38.2	12.8	22,823	51.7	39.4	8.9	22,967	46.4	37.0	16.7
0624498	Florin CDP	38,960	36.8	40.0	23.2	18,877	41.2	42.5	16.3	20,083	32.7	37.7	29.6
0624638	Folsom city	57,656	27.7	54.2	18.1	31,685	33.4	51.4	15.2	25,971	20.8	57.6	21.6
0624680	Fontana city	149,480	39.2	47.3	13.5	73,370	42.4	49.0	8.6	76,110	36.1	45.6	18.3
0625380	Fountain Valley city	47,681	30.1	51.3	18.6	23,146	33.7	53.0	13.3	24,535	26.8	49.8	23.5
0626000	Fremont city	176,037	27.0	59.6	13.3	86,445	30.3	61.1	8.5	89,592	23.8	58.2	18.0
0627000	Fresno city	379,647	40.1	40.4	19.5	184,470	43.6	42.0	14.4	195,177	36.9	38.8	24.3
0628000	Fullerton city	111,681	38.6	46.9	14.6	54,000	41.7	48.4	9.8	57,681	35.6	45.5	19.0
0628168	Gardena city	48,955	36.8	43.2	20.0	23,650	41.4	45.3	13.3	25,305	32.5	41.3	26.2
0629000	Garden Grove city	139,540	36.3	46.8	16.9	69,285	40.4	48.2	11.5	70,255	32.3	45.4	22.3
0629504	Gilroy city	37,927	34.3	50.1	15.6	18,895	38.4	51.5	10.2	19,032	30.3	48.7	20.9
0630000	Glendale city	164,129	33.0	49.9	17.1	77,721	36.8	53.0	10.2	86,408	29.6	47.0	23.4
0630014	Glendora city	42,142	33.1	50.7	16.1	20,416	36.5	52.9	10.6	21,726	30.0	48.7	21.3
0631596	Hacienda Heights CDP	44,810	33.0	51.8	15.2	21,020	34.4	55.8	9.8	23,790	31.7	48.3	20.0
0631960	Hanford city	40,174	31.0	49.6	19.4	19,435	35.1	51.1	13.7	20,739	27.1	48.2	24.7
0632548	Hawthorne city	66,210	44.9	38.1	17.0	31,153	46.0	40.1	13.8	35,057	43.9	36.3	19.8
0633000	Hayward city	120,579	37.8	46.2	16.0	58,420	40.7	48.5	10.8	62,159	35.1	44.1	20.8
0633182	Hemet city	64,395	27.6	42.6	29.8	30,927	32.5	44.6	22.9	33,468	23.1	40.7	36.2
0633434	Hesperia city	68,976	34.9	45.6	19.4	34,882	38.1	45.3	16.6	34,094	31.6	46.0	22.4
0633588	Highland city	39,565	38.2	46.8	15.0	19,073	39.0	49.1	12.0	20,492	37.5	44.7	17.8
0636000	Huntington Beach city	163,750	31.9	49.6	18.6	80,909	34.6	50.5	14.9	82,841	29.2	48.6	22.2
0636056	Huntington Park city	44,067	48.9	37.6	13.5	21,370	51.4	39.5	9.1	22,697	46.5	35.9	17.6
0636448	Indio city	61,888	31.8	50.9	17.3	30,343	34.7	53.1	12.2	31,545	29.1	48.8	22.1
0636546	Inglewood city	86,694	44.3	35.9	19.8	40,201	46.3	39.0	14.6	46,493	42.6	33.1	24.3
0636770	Irvine city	187,450	37.0	50.7	12.3	91,468	40.6	51.5	7.9	95,982	33.5	50.0	16.5
0637692	Jurupa Valley city	74,610	36.4	47.3	16.4	37,131	38.1	48.2	13.6	37,479	34.6	46.3	19.1
0639248	Laguna Niguel city	52,663	26.7	57.9	15.5	25,306	30.3	60.1	9.6	27,357	23.3	55.8	20.9
0639290	La Habra city	48,390	37.5	45.9	16.6	23,719	41.4	47.4	11.2	24,671	33.7	44.5	21.7
0639486	Lake Elsinore city	40,885	33.9	50.8	15.3	20,487	38.5	51.3	10.3	20,398	29.3	50.3	20.4
0639496	Lake Forest city	64,161	29.9	56.0	14.2	31,577	32.7	57.0	10.2	32,584	27.1	54.9	18.0
0639892	Lakewood city	65,005	33.0	48.2	18.8	31,041	36.2	50.5	13.2	33,964	30.0	46.0	23.9
0640004	La Mesa city	47,632	32.7	43.3	24.0	21,938	34.2	47.2	18.6	25,694	31.5	39.9	28.6
0640130	Lancaster city	120,826	38.6	43.9	17.5	60,443	42.1	44.9	13.0	60,383	35.1	42.9	22.0
0641992	Livermore city	66,660	27.7	54.6	17.7	33,276	31.8	54.3	14.0	33,384	23.6	54.9	21.4
0642202	Lodi city	49,073	30.6	48.3	21.1	23,775	33.3	50.3	16.4	25,298	28.0	46.4	25.6
0643000	Long Beach city	373,968	44.5	37.3	18.2	182,285	47.4	38.9	13.7	191,683	41.8	35.8	22.4
0644000	Los Angeles city	3,145,978	45.7	38.2	16.0	1,554,229	49.2	39.5	11.2	1,591,749	42.3	37.0	20.8
0644574	Lynwood city	51,245	48.5	37.8	13.6	24,608	49.2	39.9	10.9	26,637	47.9	35.9	16.2
0645022	Madera city	44,359	44.6	41.6	13.8	22,631	49.3	42.6	8.1	21,728	39.7	40.6	19.7
0645484	Manteca city	53,861	32.4	49.6	18.0	25,922	34.1	52.2	13.7	27,939	30.8	47.1	22.0
0646842	Menifee city	65,235	26.8	51.1	22.2	31,767	30.0	52.7	17.4	33,468	23.7	49.5	26.7
0646898	Merced city	59,182	39.4	41.4	19.2	28,664	43.5	43.0	13.5	30,518	35.5	39.9	24.6
0647766	Milpitas city	56,236	32.2	54.0	13.8	28,557	36.6	54.1	9.3	27,679	27.6	53.9	18.4
0648256	Mission Viejo city	79,149	25.8	58.2	16.0	38,066	28.5	60.8	10.7	41,083	23.3	55.8	20.9
0648354	Modesto city	160,037	35.7	44.7	19.6	76,593	39.5	46.5	14.0	83,444	32.3	43.0	24.7
0648816	Montebello city	51,407	41.0	39.0	20.1	24,679	44.3	42.5	13.2	26,728	37.9	35.7	26.4
0648914	Monterey Park city	52,035	36.6	48.3	15.1	25,403	40.0	50.9	9.1	26,632	33.5	45.8	20.7
0649270	Moreno Valley city	150,612	39.5	43.8	16.6	71,582	41.5	46.7	11.8	79,030	37.7	41.2	21.0
0649670	Mountain View city	62,522	34.2	51.0	14.8	31,762	38.8	51.3	9.9	30,760	29.5	50.7	19.8
0650076	Murrieta city	80,809	28.0	54.5	17.4	38,899	31.2	57.0	11.9	41,910	25.1	52.3	22.6
0650258	Napa city	62,748	31.2	48.8	20.0	30,862	33.8	52.3	13.9	31,886	28.7	45.4	25.9
0650398	National City city	48,140	39.1	42.9	17.9	24,329	42.6	46.4	11.0	23,811	35.7	39.3	25.0
0651182	Newport Beach city	73,394	29.7	50.9	19.4	36,649	35.9	51.1	13.0	36,745	23.5	50.6	25.9
0652526	Norwalk city	83,401	41.1	43.1	15.8	41,277	45.3	44.4	10.3	42,124	37.1	41.8	21.1
0652582	Novato city	43,418	25.6	53.7	20.7	20,938	29.0	56.5	14.5	22,480	22.6	51.0	26.4
0653000	Oakland city	330,150	43.9	37.1	19.0	158,164	46.1	39.4	14.5	171,986	41.9	34.9	23.2
0653322	Oceanside city	139,260	32.8	48.5	18.7	71,108	37.7	48.3	14.0	68,152	27.7	48.8	23.5
0653896	Ontario city	128,071	39.1	43.9	17.0	60,956	41.6	47.2	11.1	67,115	36.8	41.0	22.2
0653980	Orange city	114,627	38.1	46.3	15.6	57,628	41.9	47.1	10.9	56,999	34.1	45.5	20.4

Table C-4: Cities with a Population of 50,000 or More—Marriages and Births—Continued

State/place FIPS code	State/Place	Total women age 15 to 50 years	Percent of all women who had a birth in the past year	Percent of women who had a birth who were married (including separated and spouse absent):	Percent of women who had a birth who were partners in an unmarried partner household	Age of women who had a birth in the last year as a percent of all women who had a birth			Women who had a birth in the last year as a percent of all women in their age group		
						Age 15 to 19	Age 20 to 34	Age 35 to 50	Age 15 to 19	Age 20 to 34	Age 35 to 50
	California—cont'd										
0616532	Costa Mesa city	30,988	5.0	56.6	18.1	3.9	71.7	24.5	2.1	7.5	2.9
0617610	Cupertino city	14,168	3.7	98.5	0.0	0.0	44.9	55.1	0.0	7.0	3.2
0617918	Daly City city	25,666	3.6	79.2	4.7	0.0	61.2	38.8	0.0	5.0	3.2
0618100	Davis city	21,967	2.2	68.7	3.1	0.0	43.6	56.4	0.0	1.6	4.7
0618394	Delano city	11,129	9.6	43.2	17.6	12.4	73.0	14.6	6.3	16.0	3.8
0619192	Diamond Bar city	14,879	3.6	98.1	0.0	0.0	58.5	41.5	0.0	5.2	3.3
0619766	Downey city	31,326	5.7	59.9	14.9	9.7	69.6	20.7	4.5	8.6	2.8
0620802	East Los Angeles CDP	35,661	5.1	52.7	13.7	7.3	62.0	30.6	2.1	7.4	4.0
0621230	Eastvale city	14,821	6.6	89.2	4.8	0.0	78.7	21.3	0.0	13.4	3.0
0621712	El Cajon city	26,502	5.5	66.9	15.3	1.9	83.2	14.9	0.7	10.1	2.1
0622020	Elk Grove city	40,668	4.9	77.6	6.7	7.4	67.5	25.1	2.1	9.7	2.5
0622230	El Monte city	29,891	3.7	56.8	6.0	1.6	74.3	24.0	0.4	6.4	2.0
0622678	Encinitas city	14,129	5.0	95.2	2.1	0.0	51.1	48.9	0.0	6.3	4.8
0622804	Escondido city	38,753	6.0	65.6	6.2	10.9	69.9	19.2	4.2	9.5	2.8
0623182	Fairfield city	28,318	6.6	61.5	11.0	3.8	76.0	20.2	1.8	11.2	3.2
0624477	Florence-Graham CDP	17,149	7.8	37.3	14.1	6.5	66.7	26.7	2.9	11.3	5.7
0624498	Florin CDP	12,831	7.7	64.1	13.3	1.1	75.9	23.0	0.6	13.3	4.3
0624638	Folsom city	15,939	5.4	77.1	22.9	0.0	71.2	28.8	0.0	12.1	2.8
0624680	Fontana city	54,638	6.0	54.2	11.6	6.3	70.3	23.3	2.4	10.0	3.3
0625380	Fountain Valley city	13,407	5.8	69.0	7.3	0.0	67.6	32.4	0.0	10.8	3.8
0626000	Fremont city	57,457	4.7	89.0	5.1	1.0	64.1	35.0	0.5	7.5	3.3
0627000	Fresno city	131,000	6.4	60.2	10.9	6.3	79.7	14.0	2.7	10.7	2.4
0628000	Fullerton city	37,367	5.8	69.9	11.3	4.1	71.5	24.4	1.5	8.8	3.7
0628168	Gardena city	14,455	7.5	50.8	9.6	4.3	73.0	22.7	3.6	12.9	3.5
0629000	Garden Grove city	43,636	4.7	64.4	10.7	6.8	72.3	20.8	2.2	8.5	2.1
0629504	Gilroy city	12,431	5.9	70.7	7.1	11.8	76.4	11.8	4.3	12.2	1.5
0630000	Glendale city	48,556	4.8	84.3	4.4	0.0	48.6	51.4	0.0	5.8	5.0
0630014	Glendora city	12,136	3.2	85.8	2.8	0.0	83.0	17.0	0.0	6.8	1.2
0631596	Hacienda Heights CDP	12,722	3.5	79.2	2.9	2.7	76.7	20.5	0.8	6.2	1.6
0631960	Hanford city	13,240	7.1	47.2	21.6	14.9	65.9	19.2	6.3	11.0	3.3
0632548	Hawthorne city	25,392	5.8	49.7	10.3	12.3	79.9	7.9	6.1	9.6	1.2
0633000	Hayward city	39,813	5.7	73.8	2.7	0.9	82.7	16.4	0.4	10.2	2.3
0633182	Hemet city	16,124	5.1	53.9	18.0	4.1	92.3	3.5	1.4	10.1	0.5
0633434	Hesperia city	22,155	6.0	57.1	8.8	8.5	77.7	13.8	3.3	10.4	2.1
0633588	Highland city	14,531	4.4	42.2	8.2	8.5	75.4	16.1	2.3	7.8	1.7
0636000	Huntington Beach city	47,601	3.9	88.2	8.3	0.9	70.2	28.9	0.3	6.8	2.3
0636056	Huntington Park city	16,180	8.9	46.0	18.0	5.3	71.6	23.0	3.1	13.9	5.3
0636448	Indio city	19,763	6.1	63.0	20.9	4.1	75.4	20.5	2.1	10.6	2.8
0636546	Inglewood city	29,532	5.1	40.9	11.5	3.2	69.8	27.1	1.3	7.9	3.2
0636770	Irvine city	66,352	3.4	91.2	1.3	0.0	62.8	37.2	0.0	5.1	3.0
0637692	Jurupa Valley city	25,768	5.6	61.5	11.7	15.4	64.4	20.3	5.1	8.1	3.0
0639248	Laguna Niguel city	14,975	4.6	95.8	0.0	0.0	63.6	36.4	0.0	8.1	3.1
0639290	La Habra city	15,607	5.1	58.8	15.6	3.9	80.5	15.6	1.5	8.5	2.0
0639486	Lake Elsinore city	14,555	7.7	65.7	8.9	12.5	65.1	22.4	4.8	13.9	3.9
0639496	Lake Forest city	20,309	3.7	86.2	0.0	2.1	87.0	10.9	0.6	9.4	0.8
0639892	Lakewood city	20,278	3.8	64.5	19.3	1.3	78.1	20.6	0.4	8.1	1.5
0640004	La Mesa city	15,310	5.9	74.4	10.3	0.0	74.3	25.7	0.0	8.2	4.0
0640130	Lancaster city	39,260	5.8	58.0	11.3	3.5	82.2	14.3	1.2	11.6	2.0
0641992	Livermore city	19,850	6.9	79.1	5.9	3.1	81.7	15.2	1.6	15.2	2.1
0642202	Lodi city	15,060	6.5	70.4	10.1	11.5	61.8	26.8	4.1	10.8	4.0
0643000	Long Beach city	127,611	5.2	56.3	16.8	2.4	74.5	23.1	0.9	8.8	2.8
0644000	Los Angeles city	1,043,637	4.8	58.9	12.7	5.4	66.8	27.8	2.1	7.0	3.2
0644574	Lynwood city	20,217	5.4	40.8	8.8	15.1	65.6	19.2	5.1	8.2	2.5
0645022	Madera city	14,981	8.3	51.6	7.9	17.1	69.0	13.9	9.3	13.1	2.9
0645484	Manteca city	17,482	5.7	69.2	6.8	9.7	72.3	18.0	3.3	9.5	2.5
0646842	Menifee city	18,111	5.9	56.4	14.4	28.3	69.8	2.0	10.7	9.3	0.3
0646898	Merced city	20,496	7.6	63.8	12.1	9.6	67.6	22.8	4.4	11.0	4.8
0647766	Milpitas city	17,662	5.6	77.4	4.3	3.3	56.3	40.4	1.7	7.6	4.7
0648256	Mission Viejo city	21,907	3.4	92.6	3.4	2.6	53.4	44.1	0.5	5.4	3.0
0648354	Modesto city	51,225	6.1	59.2	21.6	9.7	74.0	16.3	4.0	10.3	2.4
0648816	Montebello city	15,334	6.1	54.8	12.7	4.4	66.2	29.4	1.9	9.9	3.9
0648914	Monterey Park city	14,505	3.7	70.3	8.6	1.7	64.4	34.0	0.7	5.4	2.7
0649270	Moreno Valley city	55,660	5.7	45.3	15.4	6.8	81.9	11.4	2.3	10.7	1.7
0649670	Mountain View city	19,798	5.0	98.2	0.8	0.0	46.9	53.1	0.0	5.1	5.7
0650076	Murrieta city	26,942	6.2	76.8	2.2	6.8	64.0	29.2	3.1	10.1	3.8
0650258	Napa city	18,922	5.1	74.0	13.1	3.1	65.9	31.0	1.2	7.8	3.6
0650398	National City city	15,431	5.6	59.0	4.8	17.8	59.7	22.5	6.1	8.1	3.0
0651182	Newport Beach city	18,675	3.5	95.3	0.0	0.0	58.7	41.3	0.0	5.3	2.9
0652526	Norwalk city	27,274	5.7	66.8	7.3	4.2	68.2	27.6	1.7	9.4	3.5
0652582	Novato city	11,540	6.9	74.2	9.3	3.0	63.2	33.8	1.6	16.1	3.9
0653000	Oakland city	108,500	5.3	66.0	11.4	3.6	70.4	26.0	1.9	8.1	3.2
0653322	Oceanside city	40,846	5.7	77.6	6.6	3.7	64.9	31.4	1.7	8.6	4.1
0653896	Ontario city	47,192	6.0	57.2	8.2	7.9	71.6	20.5	3.0	10.0	3.0
0653980	Orange city	36,718	5.0	74.7	8.7	3.0	62.5	34.5	1.1	7.6	3.9

State/place FIPS code	State/Place	Total population 15 years and older	Marital status, percent: Never married	Marital status, percent: Now married (except separated)	Marital status, percent: Separated, widowed, or divorced	Male population 15 years and older	Male, marital status, percent: Never married	Male, marital status, percent: Now married (except separated)	Male, marital status, percent: Separated, widowed, or divorced	Female population 15 years and older	Female, marital status, percent: Never married	Female, marital status, percent: Now married (except separated)	Female, marital status, percent: Separated, widowed, or divorced
	California—cont'd												
0654652	Oxnard city	154,404	38.3	45.5	16.2	78,936	43.0	45.3	11.7	75,468	33.3	45.7	21.0
0655156	Palmdale city	114,391	40.6	43.6	15.7	55,256	42.6	45.7	11.8	59,135	38.8	41.8	19.4
0655282	Palo Alto city	53,898	26.9	57.2	15.9	25,894	31.7	59.2	9.1	28,004	22.4	55.3	22.3
0655618	Paramount city	40,823	44.1	42.1	13.8	20,092	46.9	43.0	10.1	20,731	41.4	41.3	17.4
0656000	Pasadena city	117,629	39.9	42.2	17.9	57,114	43.9	43.7	12.4	60,515	36.2	40.8	23.0
0656700	Perris city	50,314	40.6	43.4	16.0	24,074	40.7	46.6	10.3	26,240	38.4	40.4	21.2
0656784	Petaluma city	46,469	28.9	50.0	21.1	22,007	31.1	54.4	14.6	24,462	26.9	46.1	27.0
0656924	Pico Rivera city	50,975	40.1	43.5	16.5	24,371	43.0	46.9	10.0	26,604	37.4	40.3	22.3
0657456	Pittsburg city	50,993	38.1	42.8	19.1	24,427	40.1	44.8	15.1	26,566	36.3	40.9	22.8
0657526	Placentia city	41,701	33.7	50.6	15.7	20,765	36.8	51.6	11.6	20,936	30.6	49.6	19.8
0657792	Pleasanton city	57,350	23.7	61.1	15.2	28,120	27.7	62.2	10.1	29,230	19.8	60.1	20.1
0658072	Pomona city	117,194	44.2	40.7	15.1	57,893	48.2	41.3	10.5	59,301	40.4	40.1	19.5
0658240	Porterville city	39,335	36.4	45.7	17.9	19,386	42.2	47.1	10.7	19,949	30.8	44.2	24.9
0659444	Rancho Cordova city	52,813	34.3	44.9	20.8	25,446	38.0	46.9	15.1	27,367	30.8	43.1	26.1
0659451	Rancho Cucamonga city	136,570	34.3	49.2	16.5	67,914	38.2	50.8	11.0	68,656	30.5	47.6	21.9
0659920	Redding city	73,961	30.2	46.1	23.7	36,112	35.5	47.4	17.1	37,849	25.2	44.9	30.0
0659962	Redlands city	55,629	31.9	49.8	18.3	26,588	32.9	52.7	14.4	29,041	31.0	47.1	21.9
0660018	Redondo Beach city	55,021	30.6	51.8	17.6	26,259	33.7	53.9	12.3	28,762	27.7	49.8	22.5
0660102	Redwood City city	63,311	33.6	48.5	17.9	31,592	38.1	49.2	12.7	31,719	29.2	47.8	23.0
0660466	Rialto city	74,394	39.8	43.6	16.6	36,213	42.8	45.1	12.1	38,181	37.0	42.1	20.9
0660620	Richmond city	84,467	39.2	40.8	20.0	40,278	42.2	44.0	13.8	44,189	36.4	37.9	25.6
0662000	Riverside city	246,207	40.2	42.8	17.0	121,516	44.0	44.1	11.9	124,691	36.5	41.5	21.9
0662364	Rocklin city	45,405	27.8	55.0	17.1	22,128	31.5	56.6	11.9	23,277	24.4	53.6	22.1
0662896	Rosemead city	45,293	35.3	50.9	13.7	22,177	39.6	52.3	8.1	23,116	31.2	49.7	19.1
0662938	Roseville city	98,754	28.2	53.3	18.5	45,993	31.0	57.2	11.8	52,761	25.8	49.9	24.3
0663218	Rowland Heights CDP	44,538	34.6	50.8	14.6	23,203	38.9	50.5	10.6	21,335	30.0	51.1	18.9
0664000	Sacramento city	379,219	40.3	39.2	20.5	181,855	44.0	41.1	14.9	197,364	36.8	37.5	25.7
0664224	Salinas city	113,566	42.9	44.8	12.3	58,160	46.9	43.9	9.3	55,406	38.7	45.8	15.5
0665000	San Bernardino city	159,508	45.0	35.1	19.9	77,853	48.4	36.1	15.5	81,655	41.9	34.1	24.0
0665042	San Buenaventura (Ventura) city	89,338	32.7	45.3	22.0	43,605	37.6	46.9	15.5	45,733	28.0	43.8	28.1
0665084	San Clemente city	50,428	23.8	57.7	18.5	24,600	26.7	59.4	13.8	25,828	21.0	56.1	22.9
0666000	San Diego city	1,098,596	40.7	42.8	16.5	552,410	45.3	43.3	11.4	546,186	36.1	42.2	21.7
0667000	San Francisco city	732,604	46.5	38.1	15.3	372,667	51.1	38.3	10.7	359,937	41.8	38.0	20.1
0668000	San Jose city	783,585	34.6	50.9	14.6	392,263	38.2	51.7	10.1	391,322	30.8	50.1	19.0
0668084	San Leandro city	71,682	32.9	50.2	16.8	35,585	36.6	51.9	11.5	36,097	29.3	48.6	22.1
0668196	San Marcos city	68,346	33.4	49.6	17.0	31,940	35.9	53.6	10.4	36,406	31.1	46.0	22.8
0668252	San Mateo city	82,700	31.4	49.5	19.1	40,338	36.7	51.4	12.0	42,362	26.3	47.8	25.9
0668364	San Rafael city	47,973	33.7	47.5	18.9	23,614	38.0	49.4	12.5	24,359	29.4	45.6	25.0
0668378	San Ramon city	55,671	24.4	63.6	12.0	26,861	25.8	66.4	7.8	28,810	23.0	61.0	16.0
0669000	Santa Ana city	251,083	42.0	44.4	13.5	125,940	45.3	45.9	8.7	125,143	38.7	42.9	18.3
0669070	Santa Barbara city	75,004	40.5	41.8	17.7	37,418	44.7	42.6	12.6	37,586	36.3	41.1	22.7
0669084	Santa Clara city	95,617	34.4	53.1	12.5	47,902	38.1	53.5	8.5	47,715	30.7	52.7	16.5
0669088	Santa Clarita city	141,828	32.8	51.5	15.6	69,910	36.9	52.3	10.8	71,918	28.9	50.8	20.3
0669112	Santa Cruz city	54,657	55.7	29.6	14.7	26,995	59.1	30.5	10.3	27,662	52.4	28.7	18.9
0669196	Santa Maria city	74,665	38.2	46.8	15.0	37,532	42.4	47.6	10.1	37,133	33.9	46.1	19.9
0670000	Santa Monica city	80,799	45.8	35.2	19.0	39,221	50.6	36.1	13.2	41,578	41.3	34.3	24.4
0670098	Santa Rosa city	137,959	34.3	44.0	21.6	67,863	39.3	45.3	15.4	70,096	29.5	42.8	27.7
0670224	Santee city	44,602	29.9	47.5	22.6	20,855	33.5	50.7	15.8	23,747	26.7	44.8	28.6
0672016	Simi Valley city	100,917	28.0	54.8	17.2	48,721	31.5	56.6	11.9	52,196	24.8	53.1	22.1
0673080	South Gate city	73,190	44.9	41.2	13.9	36,345	48.9	42.4	8.7	36,845	41.1	39.9	19.0
0673262	South San Francisco city	52,997	32.5	50.7	16.8	25,667	35.3	52.6	12.1	27,330	29.9	48.9	21.2
0673430	South Whittier CDP	47,806	40.3	44.6	15.0	23,086	43.1	47.3	9.6	24,720	37.8	42.1	20.1
0675000	Stockton city	221,978	38.5	43.2	18.3	106,013	42.0	45.7	12.3	115,965	35.4	40.8	23.8
0677000	Sunnyvale city	117,710	30.0	57.4	12.6	60,151	33.8	57.7	8.5	57,559	26.0	57.2	16.8
0678120	Temecula city	80,500	31.3	54.0	14.7	38,914	34.5	55.7	9.8	41,586	28.4	52.3	19.3
0678582	Thousand Oaks city	103,573	27.8	56.3	16.0	49,197	30.0	59.5	10.4	54,376	25.7	53.3	21.0
0680000	Torrance city	121,241	29.2	52.2	18.6	57,159	32.1	55.8	12.1	64,082	26.6	49.0	24.4
0680238	Tracy city	63,545	30.7	54.5	14.7	32,615	36.2	52.8	10.9	30,930	24.9	56.3	18.8
0680644	Tulare city	43,962	33.8	49.9	16.3	21,266	37.3	51.5	11.2	22,696	30.6	48.3	21.1
0680812	Turlock city	54,314	34.6	47.3	18.1	26,770	40.7	48.1	11.2	27,544	28.7	46.6	24.7
0680854	Tustin city	60,563	35.4	49.0	15.6	28,772	38.8	51.9	9.4	31,791	32.4	46.3	21.3
0681204	Union City city	57,492	31.9	55.3	12.9	28,045	35.6	57.2	7.2	29,447	28.3	53.4	18.3
0681344	Upland city	60,723	35.9	46.4	17.8	27,161	35.3	51.9	12.7	33,562	36.3	41.9	21.9
0681554	Vacaville city	76,446	32.9	45.9	21.2	40,606	36.1	45.5	18.4	35,860	29.3	46.3	24.4
0681666	Vallejo city	97,364	38.6	40.7	20.8	47,088	42.9	42.6	14.5	50,276	34.5	38.8	26.6
0682590	Victorville city	86,296	37.3	42.5	20.3	42,194	40.0	44.1	15.9	44,102	34.6	40.9	24.4
0682954	Visalia city	96,145	32.7	47.6	19.7	46,760	37.1	49.7	13.2	49,385	28.6	45.5	25.9
0682996	Vista city	77,756	37.5	46.2	16.3	39,177	41.9	47.2	10.9	38,579	33.0	45.3	21.7
0683346	Walnut Creek city	56,623	26.8	51.3	21.9	25,970	30.3	56.2	13.5	30,653	23.8	47.2	29.0
0683668	Watsonville city	38,492	42.9	44.3	12.8	18,843	44.9	46.2	8.9	19,649	40.9	42.5	16.6
0684200	West Covina city	87,219	37.6	45.8	16.6	41,643	41.3	48.8	10.0	45,576	34.3	43.1	22.6
0684550	Westminster city	74,973	33.4	49.9	16.7	36,963	37.9	51.4	10.7	38,010	29.1	48.3	22.6
0685292	Whittier city	68,930	39.0	44.3	16.7	33,218	41.8	46.6	11.6	35,712	36.4	42.1	21.4
0686328	Woodland city	44,221	31.3	48.5	20.2	21,446	36.9	51.2	11.9	22,775	26.0	46.0	28.0

Table C-4: Cities with a Population of 50,000 or More—Marriages and Births—*Continued*

State/place FIPS code	State/Place	Total women age 15 to 50 years	Percent of all women who had a birth in the past year	Percent of women who had a birth who were married (including separated and spouse absent):	Percent of women who had a birth who were partners in an unmarried partner household	Age of women who had a birth in the last year as a percent of all women who had a birth			Women who had a birth in the last year as a percent of all women in their age group		
						Age 15 to 19	Age 20 to 34	Age 35 to 50	Age 15 to 19	Age 20 to 34	Age 35 to 50
	California—cont'd										
0654652	Oxnard city	50,941	6.9	61.6	6.5	13.9	67.5	18.7	6.8	10.1	3.2
0655156	Palmdale city	40,928	7.0	48.1	10.7	10.4	69.9	19.6	3.8	12.7	3.2
0655282	Palo Alto city	15,302	4.4	100.0	0.0	0.0	58.7	41.3	0.0	6.9	3.5
0655618	Paramount city	15,534	3.1	46.0	8.9	10.9	66.4	22.7	2.0	5.7	1.5
0656000	Pasadena city	37,140	4.9	75.4	6.0	4.5	64.3	31.2	2.1	6.6	3.6
0656700	Perris city	19,570	4.9	65.0	10.9	3.2	55.6	41.2	0.8	6.8	5.1
0656784	Petaluma city	13,165	6.1	62.4	11.5	0.0	63.4	36.6	0.0	10.1	4.5
0656924	Pico Rivera city	16,583	4.0	51.9	12.7	3.9	67.4	28.7	1.1	6.6	2.6
0657456	Pittsburg city	17,641	6.6	46.8	15.9	1.3	76.8	22.0	0.7	11.2	3.4
0657526	Placentia city	12,950	5.3	81.9	9.3	0.0	43.9	56.1	0.0	5.8	6.2
0657792	Pleasanton city	17,178	2.7	100.0	0.0	0.0	45.1	54.9	0.0	4.6	2.6
0658072	Pomona city	41,177	4.9	55.2	7.4	16.8	66.4	16.8	5.0	7.2	2.1
0658240	Porterville city	13,352	8.2	63.1	30.3	0.0	79.8	20.2	0.0	14.7	4.0
0659444	Rancho Cordova city	17,437	4.6	58.1	11.6	9.9	74.2	15.9	4.0	7.3	1.8
0659451	Rancho Cucamonga city	45,021	5.0	76.6	4.0	2.1	86.0	11.9	0.7	11.5	1.2
0659920	Redding city	20,780	3.5	65.6	19.0	0.0	73.3	26.7	0.0	5.8	2.3
0659962	Redlands city	16,650	4.3	69.9	8.6	2.4	59.9	37.7	0.7	6.0	3.8
0660018	Redondo Beach city	18,313	3.3	94.6	3.4	2.0	48.3	49.8	0.9	4.3	3.0
0660102	Redwood City city	19,768	5.0	85.6	2.4	3.3	73.4	23.3	1.4	9.2	2.4
0660466	Rialto city	26,560	7.9	63.8	10.1	4.0	75.3	20.7	1.9	13.1	4.3
0660620	Richmond city	27,590	7.8	65.4	10.3	2.5	70.8	26.7	1.7	11.8	4.9
0662000	Riverside city	85,411	5.7	60.6	9.1	7.8	73.8	18.5	2.8	9.3	2.7
0662364	Rocklin city	14,976	3.0	74.9	25.1	0.0	63.3	36.7	0.0	5.6	2.2
0662896	Rosemead city	13,289	3.9	77.4	2.5	0.0	61.2	38.8	0.0	6.4	3.1
0662938	Roseville city	31,763	4.8	71.1	7.9	1.2	79.3	19.5	0.3	9.9	2.1
0663218	Rowland Heights CDP	12,016	3.7	91.4	0.0	0.0	61.9	38.1	0.0	5.5	3.1
0664000	Sacramento city	125,892	5.6	58.5	14.3	4.3	79.7	16.1	2.0	9.3	2.2
0664224	Salinas city	39,643	6.3	52.8	22.6	7.6	73.2	19.2	3.0	10.3	3.1
0665000	San Bernardino city	56,047	6.2	43.3	15.0	11.4	76.6	12.0	3.8	10.6	2.0
0665042	San Buenaventura (Ventura) city	25,685	3.3	72.9	3.2	0.0	73.7	26.3	0.0	6.1	1.8
0665084	San Clemente city	14,882	4.4	79.5	10.2	0.0	74.3	25.7	0.0	9.2	2.1
0666000	San Diego city	357,403	4.9	79.1	6.1	4.1	72.6	23.3	1.7	7.2	2.9
0667000	San Francisco city	226,683	3.7	79.6	4.3	0.1	51.3	48.5	0.1	3.7	4.3
0668000	San Jose city	251,082	6.0	72.0	7.6	2.9	68.7	28.4	1.5	9.9	3.7
0668084	San Leandro city	20,430	5.3	61.7	11.3	0.0	64.6	35.4	0.0	9.0	3.5
0668196	San Marcos city	24,274	3.8	89.9	0.7	8.1	59.6	32.3	2.4	5.8	2.5
0668252	San Mateo city	24,270	5.3	85.0	5.4	0.0	67.1	32.9	0.0	8.8	3.6
0668364	San Rafael city	13,164	6.6	75.6	3.6	3.5	61.8	34.8	2.1	10.6	4.5
0668378	San Ramon city	19,613	5.0	98.8	0.0	0.0	35.3	64.7	0.0	6.4	5.4
0669000	Santa Ana city	91,526	6.0	61.8	9.4	2.9	75.1	22.0	1.3	10.0	3.3
0669070	Santa Barbara city	22,533	5.4	78.6	6.4	6.7	66.5	26.8	3.1	7.1	3.9
0669084	Santa Clara city	32,875	5.7	88.0	2.6	3.5	71.1	25.4	1.7	9.2	3.2
0669088	Santa Clarita city	32,875	5.7	88.0	2.6	3.5	71.1	25.4	1.7	9.2	3.2
0669112	Santa Cruz city	19,552	1.7	77.5	0.0	0.0	66.4	33.6	0.0	2.3	2.1
0669196	Santa Maria city	25,465	7.2	65.0	4.7	8.2	76.2	15.6	4.1	11.6	2.9
0670000	Santa Monica city	25,376	2.3	84.9	6.6	0.0	45.9	54.1	0.0	2.3	2.7
0670098	Santa Rosa city	39,761	4.6	73.7	8.9	0.0	73.3	26.7	0.0	8.3	2.7
0670224	Santee city	15,666	6.6	86.9	1.4	0.0	79.1	20.9	0.0	13.3	2.9
0672016	Simi Valley city	30,821	5.5	86.1	1.4	0.0	52.7	47.3	0.0	8.0	5.2
0673080	South Gate city	25,014	5.3	34.0	14.2	13.8	76.2	9.9	4.6	9.4	1.3
0673262	South San Francisco city	15,570	6.9	78.6	7.9	0.0	57.0	43.0	0.0	8.8	6.5
0673430	South Whittier CDP	16,555	6.9	53.3	5.3	5.4	79.1	15.5	2.5	13.0	2.5
0675000	Stockton city	75,209	7.0	56.7	11.4	6.7	77.7	15.6	2.9	12.1	2.8
0677000	Sunnyvale city	37,711	7.2	91.4	2.5	0.9	74.2	24.9	0.7	11.2	4.2
0678120	Temecula city	28,111	4.4	53.7	27.4	2.6	76.2	21.3	0.6	10.8	1.9
0678582	Thousand Oaks city	29,966	2.5	70.2	1.9	1.6	83.4	15.0	0.3	6.1	0.7
0680000	Torrance city	35,837	3.9	73.1	5.7	0.0	62.0	38.0	0.0	6.4	2.9
0680238	Tracy city	20,887	5.5	66.3	4.8	0.0	85.5	14.5	0.0	13.5	1.6
0680644	Tulare city	15,290	9.2	43.7	18.3	11.5	85.1	3.4	7.2	17.3	0.8
0680812	Turlock city	17,015	7.0	79.6	2.9	5.1	68.4	26.5	2.6	10.3	4.6
0680854	Tustin city	21,820	5.3	77.1	6.3	0.0	73.0	27.0	0.0	9.0	3.1
0681204	Union City city	18,194	6.2	77.7	16.5	0.0	90.2	9.8	0.0	12.9	1.4
0681344	Upland city	21,161	4.5	54.0	9.9	2.2	68.1	29.8	0.7	7.3	3.1
0681554	Vacaville city	22,171	4.4	65.0	16.9	4.1	69.9	26.0	1.2	7.7	2.5
0681666	Vallejo city	28,126	4.9	59.0	14.7	9.0	70.8	20.2	3.6	7.9	2.2
0682590	Victorville city	30,685	6.7	66.7	10.3	0.0	81.9	18.1	0.0	13.4	3.1
0682954	Visalia city	32,014	7.0	62.8	14.4	7.3	79.7	13.0	3.4	12.7	2.2
0682996	Vista city	25,767	4.4	74.3	2.2	6.1	74.5	19.4	2.5	6.9	2.0
0683346	Walnut Creek city	14,107	4.8	100.0	0.0	0.0	51.6	48.4	0.0	7.0	4.6
0683668	Watsonville city	13,845	6.6	50.3	5.6	7.2	76.3	16.5	2.6	12.5	2.7
0684200	West Covina city	27,803	4.5	63.3	8.6	7.2	62.3	30.4	2.3	6.4	3.2
0684550	Westminster city	21,790	5.2	64.1	28.2	0.0	71.5	28.5	0.0	9.3	3.2
0685292	Whittier city	23,021	4.5	61.0	22.5	10.7	71.3	18.0	3.1	7.9	1.9
0686328	Woodland city	13,791	6.7	57.2	5.7	4.6	68.6	26.8	2.1	11.9	3.9

State/ place FIPS code	State/Place	Total population 15 years and older	Marital status, percent			Male population 15 years and older	Male, marital status, percent			Female population 15 years and older	Female, marital status, percent		
			Never married	Now married (except separated)	Separated, widowed, or divorced		Never married	Now married (except separated)	Separated, widowed, or divorced		Never married	Now married (except separated)	Separated, widowed, or divorced
	California—cont'd												
0686832	Yorba Linda city	54,113	25.6	61.4	13.0	26,003	27.1	64.5	8.4	28,110	24.1	58.6	17.2
0686972	Yuba City city	50,997	31.2	50.6	18.2	25,147	35.3	51.7	13.0	25,850	27.1	49.6	23.3
0687042	Yucaipa city	41,708	28.1	52.1	19.8	20,288	30.6	54.1	15.4	21,420	25.7	50.3	24.0
0800000	**Colorado**	4,156,448	31.1	50.7	18.3	2,075,336	34.8	51.3	13.9	2,081,112	27.3	50.0	22.7
0803455	Arvada city	88,859	27.8	52.3	19.9	43,013	30.9	54.0	15.1	45,846	24.8	50.7	24.4
0804000	Aurora city	262,085	34.2	45.5	20.2	126,971	37.5	47.4	15.1	135,114	31.2	43.7	25.1
0807850	Boulder city	89,679	55.7	32.8	11.5	44,804	59.1	33.5	7.5	44,875	52.4	32.1	15.5
0809280	Broomfield city	45,498	27.6	56.5	15.9	22,352	30.3	58.7	11.0	23,146	25.0	54.3	20.7
0812415	Castle Rock town	37,770	21.0	63.8	15.2	18,491	23.6	66.6	9.8	19,279	18.5	61.1	20.4
0812815	Centennial city	84,520	25.0	58.4	16.6	41,236	28.3	60.2	11.5	43,284	21.9	56.7	21.4
0816000	Colorado Springs city	344,341	29.3	51.0	19.6	169,805	33.2	52.2	14.6	174,536	25.6	49.9	24.6
0820000	Denver city	517,861	41.8	38.5	19.7	258,098	45.0	39.5	15.4	259,763	38.5	37.4	24.0
0827425	Fort Collins city	124,785	44.0	42.3	13.7	61,427	47.5	43.0	9.6	63,358	40.7	41.7	17.6
0831660	Grand Junction city	48,284	30.0	47.7	22.3	23,372	35.6	48.9	15.6	24,912	24.7	46.6	28.6
0832155	Greeley city	75,425	37.3	44.6	18.0	37,237	40.1	45.2	14.7	38,188	34.6	44.1	21.3
0836410	Highlands Ranch CDP	76,432	21.5	64.2	14.2	37,498	24.1	66.2	9.7	38,934	19.0	62.4	18.6
0843000	Lakewood city	121,213	31.9	45.4	22.6	60,472	37.7	46.0	16.3	60,741	26.2	44.9	28.9
0845970	Longmont city	69,892	28.6	52.5	18.9	35,441	33.2	53.3	13.5	34,451	23.8	51.6	24.6
0846465	Loveland city	55,950	25.7	55.3	19.0	27,348	30.2	57.6	12.2	28,602	21.4	53.1	25.5
0862000	Pueblo city	86,837	34.0	40.5	25.5	42,289	38.2	41.5	20.3	44,548	30.0	39.6	30.4
0877290	Thornton city	93,053	30.0	54.7	15.3	46,415	33.7	55.1	11.2	46,638	26.3	54.3	19.4
0883835	Westminster city	87,654	29.7	51.4	19.0	42,762	32.8	53.2	13.9	44,892	26.6	49.6	23.8
0900000	**Connecticut**	2,944,753	33.7	48.1	18.2	1,419,698	37.0	50.2	12.8	1,525,055	30.6	46.2	23.2
0908000	Bridgeport city	115,255	47.4	32.7	19.8	55,336	50.3	35.5	14.2	59,919	44.8	30.2	25.0
0908420	Bristol city	50,190	32.0	46.8	21.2	24,211	36.9	48.0	15.1	25,979	27.5	45.6	26.9
0918430	Danbury city	69,255	36.3	44.7	19.0	33,718	39.3	47.8	12.9	35,537	33.4	41.8	24.8
0922700	East Hartford CDP	42,444	41.2	37.4	21.5	20,100	45.2	39.3	15.5	22,344	37.5	35.6	26.8
0937000	Hartford city	99,196	57.8	23.0	19.2	47,432	59.9	24.8	15.4	51,764	55.9	21.4	22.7
0946450	Meriden city	50,256	37.3	44.9	17.8	24,172	40.4	47.6	12.0	26,084	34.5	42.4	23.1
0947515	Milford city	43,451	27.5	50.4	22.1	20,626	31.5	53.7	14.8	22,825	23.9	47.4	28.7
0950370	New Britain city	58,827	43.9	35.3	20.8	27,005	47.5	38.1	14.4	31,822	40.8	32.9	26.3
0952000	New Haven city	106,260	54.4	28.6	17.0	49,644	57.7	30.6	11.7	56,616	51.5	26.8	21.7
0955990	Norwalk city	73,274	33.6	47.6	18.8	35,958	37.6	49.9	12.5	37,316	29.7	45.3	24.9
0973000	Stamford city	101,791	35.4	47.2	17.4	49,570	39.3	49.4	11.3	52,221	31.7	45.2	23.1
0974260	Stratford CDP	43,909	29.3	51.3	19.4	20,430	30.5	54.8	14.6	23,479	28.2	48.2	23.6
0980000	Waterbury city	86,315	42.8	35.9	21.3	41,028	46.2	37.4	16.4	45,287	39.7	34.5	25.8
0982660	West Hartford CDP	52,070	30.2	51.4	18.4	23,895	33.7	56.5	9.8	28,175	27.3	47.0	25.7
0982800	West Haven city	44,933	40.1	39.8	20.1	21,028	42.2	43.4	14.4	23,905	38.3	36.6	25.1
1000000	**Delaware**	746,911	33.3	47.1	19.6	357,481	35.9	49.5	14.6	389,430	30.9	44.9	24.2
1077580	Wilmington city	56,685	51.2	26.1	22.6	25,808	55.3	28.8	15.9	30,877	47.9	23.9	28.2
1100000	**District of Columbia**	541,211	57.5	26.0	16.5	253,125	58.6	28.4	13.0	288,086	56.6	23.8	19.6
1150000	Washington city	541,211	57.5	26.0	16.5	253,125	58.6	28.4	13.0	288,086	56.6	23.8	19.6
1200000	**Florida**	16,009,758	31.2	46.1	22.8	7,757,981	34.9	48.2	16.9	8,251,777	27.6	44.1	28.3
1200410	Alafaya CDP	59,941	35.3	49.0	15.7	28,747	35.5	51.5	12.9	31,194	35.1	46.6	18.3
1207300	Boca Raton city	75,724	30.9	47.4	21.7	37,214	34.6	49.0	16.4	38,510	27.4	45.8	26.9
1207875	Boynton Beach city	59,023	34.0	41.6	24.4	27,352	35.6	45.7	18.7	31,671	32.7	38.0	29.3
1207950	Bradenton city	42,217	30.2	41.5	28.2	20,178	35.3	44.0	20.8	22,039	25.6	39.3	35.1
1208150	Brandon CDP	87,742	36.5	43.7	19.8	41,594	39.6	46.5	13.9	46,148	33.6	41.2	25.2
1210275	Cape Coral city	130,026	24.6	52.6	22.8	62,341	27.3	55.2	17.6	67,685	22.1	50.2	27.7
1212875	Clearwater city	90,849	30.0	41.7	28.4	42,693	35.5	44.5	20.0	48,156	25.1	39.1	35.8
1213275	Coconut Creek city	45,681	30.1	44.0	25.9	21,484	33.6	47.4	19.0	24,197	26.9	41.1	32.0
1214400	Coral Springs city	98,727	33.7	47.4	18.9	46,971	37.1	50.3	12.6	51,756	30.5	44.8	24.6
1216475	Davie town	77,880	33.2	45.8	21.0	36,981	37.7	48.5	13.8	40,899	29.2	43.4	27.4
1216525	Daytona Beach city	54,262	44.3	29.3	26.4	26,388	49.6	30.3	20.0	27,874	39.3	28.3	32.4
1216725	Deerfield Beach city	64,412	31.5	40.4	28.1	30,045	37.4	43.2	19.4	34,367	26.3	37.9	35.8
1217100	Delray Beach city	54,929	34.0	38.6	27.4	25,357	34.8	42.4	22.8	29,572	33.3	35.4	31.3
1217200	Deltona city	68,409	29.2	49.2	21.7	33,541	32.9	50.7	16.4	34,868	25.6	47.7	26.7
1224000	Fort Lauderdale city	146,026	41.4	34.6	24.1	78,618	46.6	33.2	20.2	67,408	35.3	36.2	28.5
1224125	Fort Myers city	55,355	37.5	37.0	25.5	28,445	42.6	36.6	20.8	26,910	32.1	37.4	30.4
1224562	Fountainebleau CDP	45,721	31.1	41.4	27.5	20,625	32.1	47.1	20.8	25,096	30.3	36.8	32.9
1225175	Gainesville city	113,215	62.2	24.0	13.8	53,197	63.9	25.6	10.5	60,018	60.7	22.6	16.7
1230000	Hialeah city	197,076	34.9	42.1	23.0	92,336	39.9	45.7	14.4	104,740	30.5	38.9	30.6
1232000	Hollywood city	119,692	31.5	43.4	25.1	57,835	35.0	45.4	19.6	61,857	28.2	41.5	30.3
1232275	Homestead city	47,098	38.7	42.8	18.5	23,896	42.9	44.3	12.8	23,202	34.3	41.2	24.5
1235000	Jacksonville city	671,732	34.5	42.9	22.6	321,083	37.9	45.2	16.9	350,649	31.4	40.7	27.9
1235875	Jupiter town	47,797	23.8	54.2	22.1	23,578	27.6	56.1	16.4	24,219	20.1	52.3	27.6
1236062	Kendale Lakes CDP	51,494	31.4	44.8	23.8	23,747	37.4	49.2	13.5	27,747	26.3	41.0	32.7
1236100	Kendall CDP	62,021	30.5	46.3	23.2	29,824	35.2	49.4	15.5	32,197	26.1	43.5	30.4
1236950	Kissimmee city	49,595	36.6	40.3	23.2	23,924	38.0	44.3	17.7	25,671	35.3	36.5	28.2
1238250	Lakeland city	82,209	34.6	40.0	25.3	38,029	37.3	43.5	19.2	44,180	32.3	37.1	30.6
1239425	Largo city	67,989	27.9	40.7	31.5	32,606	30.8	42.9	26.2	35,383	25.2	38.6	36.3
1239550	Lauderhill city	54,982	44.4	30.7	24.9	25,132	47.9	34.4	17.7	29,850	41.5	27.6	30.9

Table C-4: Cities with a Population of 50,000 or More—Marriages and Births—Continued

State/place FIPS code	State/Place	Total women age 15 to 50 years	Percent of all women who had a birth in the past year	Percent of women who had a birth who were married (including separated and spouse absent):	Percent of women who had a birth who were partners in an unmarried partner household	Age of women who had a birth in the last year as a percent of all women who had a birth			Women who had a birth in the last year as a percent of all women in their age group		
						Age 15 to 19	Age 20 to 34	Age 35 to 50	Age 15 to 19	Age 20 to 34	Age 35 to 50
	California—cont'd										
0686832	Yorba Linda city	15,668	5.7	75.9	6.8	12.1	76.1	11.8	4.2	12.8	1.3
0686972	Yuba City city	15,889	6.2	59.3	8.5	10.4	72.4	17.1	4.5	10.5	2.5
0687042	Yucaipa city	12,761	5.3	49.6	11.0	14.3	63.2	22.5	4.3	8.7	2.8
0800000	**Colorado**	1,267,458	5.5	72.7	8.5	4.4	74.2	21.4	1.9	9.6	2.7
0803455	Arvada city	25,396	4.9	67.2	13.3	2.1	74.4	23.5	0.8	9.2	2.4
0804000	Aurora city	87,559	6.8	67.9	13.1	2.8	81.5	15.6	1.4	12.6	2.5
0807850	Boulder city	32,152	2.7	76.7	13.0	2.4	36.4	61.3	0.3	1.9	6.1
0809280	Broomfield city	14,768	6.2	70.3	0.0	2.5	76.7	20.8	1.5	11.0	2.8
0812415	Castle Rock town	12,800	7.2	86.4	5.9	0.0	87.4	12.6	0.0	18.7	1.7
0812815	Centennial city	23,764	5.0	84.5	7.8	1.7	62.8	35.5	0.6	9.0	3.5
0816000	Colorado Springs city	107,709	6.3	75.1	5.9	5.7	76.9	17.4	2.6	10.7	2.7
0820000	Denver city	173,606	5.3	68.2	5.4	4.1	68.8	27.2	2.4	7.1	3.7
0827425	Fort Collins city	43,881	4.4	79.8	10.9	1.6	68.8	29.6	0.5	5.6	4.2
0831660	Grand Junction city	14,057	5.6	68.6	11.9	17.2	79.4	3.3	5.9	9.1	0.5
0832155	Greeley city	25,197	6.1	60.9	14.3	0.0	79.2	20.8	0.0	10.5	3.6
0836410	Highlands Ranch CDP	26,021	5.6	86.8	1.0	8.9	62.0	29.1	3.6	12.0	2.9
0843000	Lakewood city	33,700	5.3	60.3	7.0	2.2	67.0	30.8	1.0	7.9	3.7
0845970	Longmont city	20,313	6.2	70.9	4.5	5.4	68.0	26.6	2.7	10.4	3.5
0846465	Loveland city	15,977	5.2	82.7	13.3	0.0	85.6	14.4	0.0	10.2	1.7
0862000	Pueblo city	24,950	6.2	58.1	11.5	12.8	75.6	11.6	5.2	10.9	1.7
0877290	Thornton city	32,080	6.5	71.3	10.7	0.0	81.9	18.1	0.0	12.2	2.6
0883835	Westminster city	28,265	5.5	88.7	2.4	6.2	74.8	19.0	3.2	9.1	2.3
0900000	**Connecticut**	864,070	4.5	65.5	8.6	3.6	69.9	26.5	1.1	8.2	2.5
0908000	Bridgeport city	39,482	5.7	50.2	11.2	9.3	73.0	17.7	4.0	8.9	2.5
0908420	Bristol city	13,910	2.9	71.4	18.7	0.0	79.3	20.7	0.0	5.7	1.3
0918430	Danbury city	22,607	4.4	76.7	11.9	3.0	59.5	37.4	1.0	6.2	3.7
0922700	East Hartford CDP	13,312	7.5	40.1	5.4	5.3	75.5	19.2	4.1	13.3	3.0
0937000	Hartford city	35,934	6.3	18.5	15.9	11.2	77.9	10.9	3.8	10.6	2.0
0946450	Meriden city	15,042	4.2	56.3	5.8	1.6	82.8	15.6	0.5	8.3	1.5
0947515	Milford city	11,995	5.5	68.9	0.0	2.6	63.1	34.3	1.2	10.6	3.3
0950370	New Britain city	19,787	5.9	41.5	10.4	13.7	72.7	13.6	4.7	9.3	2.2
0952000	New Haven city	39,343	4.3	50.9	10.2	1.2	83.5	15.3	0.4	6.8	2.0
0955990	Norwalk city	20,989	5.3	79.7	5.7	5.8	46.5	47.6	3.4	6.0	5.1
0973000	Stamford city	31,296	4.8	74.6	10.6	3.6	56.4	39.9	1.8	6.0	4.2
0974260	Stratford CDP	12,468	3.6	85.7	0.0	3.3	79.9	16.8	0.8	9.2	1.1
0980000	Waterbury city	28,301	6.4	39.3	14.2	5.3	78.4	16.3	2.6	11.2	2.5
0982660	West Hartford CDP	14,679	3.8	89.5	7.5	0.0	75.5	24.5	0.0	8.3	1.9
0982800	West Haven city	14,528	5.6	55.3	2.6	0.0	78.6	21.4	0.0	10.0	3.0
1000000	**Delaware**	221,083	5.3	62.6	10.9	4.0	71.4	24.6	1.6	9.1	2.9
1077580	Wilmington city	19,520	6.1	38.9	21.3	8.6	70.0	21.3	4.6	9.4	3.1
1100000	**District of Columbia**	193,803	4.2	52.0	7.1	3.2	66.0	30.7	1.3	5.1	3.8
1150000	Washington city	193,803	4.2	52.0	7.1	3.2	66.0	30.7	1.3	5.1	3.8
1200000	**Florida**	4,449,952	4.8	58.7	10.7	5.3	71.5	23.2	2.0	8.4	2.4
1200410	Alafaya CDP	22,841	4.6	55.2	33.6	0.0	90.9	9.1	0.0	8.7	1.0
1207300	Boca Raton city	19,006	4.6	65.2	9.4	1.7	56.9	41.4	0.4	7.5	4.1
1207875	Boynton Beach city	16,115	3.4	57.3	28.3	0.2	64.0	35.9	0.1	4.7	2.8
1207950	Bradenton city	10,848	5.7	63.3	8.2	4.7	89.2	6.1	2.0	11.7	0.8
1208150	Brandon CDP	29,440	4.9	65.2	12.4	7.8	55.0	37.3	3.0	5.8	4.6
1210275	Cape Coral city	34,372	5.4	43.3	12.3	3.7	78.9	17.4	1.6	11.3	1.9
1212875	Clearwater city	24,370	6.0	45.3	5.2	7.5	75.2	17.3	4.4	11.0	2.1
1213275	Coconut Creek city	13,658	3.8	63.0	5.1	17.3	68.0	14.6	5.7	6.4	1.1
1214400	Coral Springs city	34,031	4.5	54.4	24.6	0.0	70.4	29.6	0.0	9.0	2.7
1216475	Davie town	25,263	3.3	72.1	12.5	3.1	64.4	32.5	0.7	5.5	2.4
1216525	Daytona Beach city	15,211	3.7	51.7	3.8	1.3	79.4	19.3	0.3	5.8	2.1
1216725	Deerfield Beach city	16,167	7.3	57.2	16.3	0.0	78.7	21.3	0.0	13.6	3.2
1217100	Delray Beach city	14,069	6.4	43.7	7.9	2.6	79.9	17.4	1.5	11.3	2.6
1217200	Deltona city	19,716	4.4	28.1	28.8	2.2	87.7	10.1	0.7	9.2	1.0
1224000	Fort Lauderdale city	38,001	4.9	59.5	11.4	6.1	64.0	29.8	2.6	7.3	3.2
1224125	Fort Myers city	14,905	4.5	49.3	16.2	5.8	77.7	16.5	1.9	8.5	1.6
1224562	Fountainebleau CDP	14,549	3.0	61.8	5.4	3.2	62.7	34.2	1.1	4.1	2.3
1225175	Gainesville city	44,694	1.8	49.4	11.1	2.7	90.1	7.2	0.3	2.6	0.8
1230000	Hialeah city	58,467	3.6	61.9	9.9	3.3	65.1	31.6	1.0	6.4	2.3
1232000	Hollywood city	34,747	4.1	47.1	14.9	17.4	63.0	19.6	6.1	6.8	1.6
1232275	Homestead city	16,170	6.5	50.7	25.3	0.0	87.3	12.7	0.0	12.3	1.8
1235000	Jacksonville city	215,501	5.4	58.9	8.6	3.2	78.2	18.6	1.5	9.4	2.3
1235875	Jupiter town	11,519	4.7	83.6	4.8	1.9	62.5	35.7	0.8	8.6	3.0
1236062	Kendale Lakes CDP	15,793	3.1	62.6	3.0	0.0	54.7	45.3	0.0	4.8	2.9
1236100	Kendall CDP	16,253	4.4	91.5	0.0	0.1	63.0	36.8	0.1	6.9	3.3
1236950	Kissimmee city	17,499	5.1	54.3	28.8	2.3	74.4	23.2	0.9	9.2	2.6
1238250	Lakeland city	23,771	6.1	53.6	10.4	6.8	74.8	18.3	2.5	10.4	2.9
1239425	Largo city	16,057	3.1	39.0	20.3	7.2	69.7	23.1	2.3	4.9	1.6
1239550	Lauderhill city	8,716	8.5	23.3	25.3	9.8	68.1	22.1	6.3	12.2	4.8

State/place FIPS code	State/Place	Total population 15 years and older	Marital status, percent — Never married	Marital status, percent — Now married (except separated)	Marital status, percent — Separated, widowed, or divorced	Male population 15 years and older	Male, marital status, percent — Never married	Male, marital status, percent — Now married (except separated)	Male, marital status, percent — Separated, widowed, or divorced	Female population 15 years and older	Female, marital status, percent — Never married	Female, marital status, percent — Now married (except separated)	Female, marital status, percent — Separated, widowed, or divorced
	Florida—cont'd												
1239925	Lehigh Acres CDP	80,352	34.0	44.3	21.7	39,050	38.1	45.2	16.7	41,302	30.2	43.4	26.4
1243125	Margate city	46,423	30.6	42.8	26.6	22,316	36.0	45.2	18.8	24,107	25.6	40.5	33.8
1243975	Melbourne city	66,393	31.4	40.2	28.5	31,829	37.8	42.6	19.7	34,564	25.4	38.0	36.6
1245000	Miami city	347,860	41.0	34.2	24.8	172,808	45.6	35.6	18.8	175,052	36.5	32.7	30.8
1245025	Miami Beach city	77,362	37.9	36.5	25.7	40,925	44.1	35.6	20.3	36,437	30.9	37.5	31.6
1245060	Miami Gardens city	88,926	47.2	31.7	21.1	40,660	48.4	35.4	16.2	48,266	46.2	28.5	25.2
1245975	Miramar city	100,820	35.0	45.4	19.7	46,310	37.7	50.9	11.3	54,510	32.6	40.6	26.7
1249450	North Miami city	49,682	46.4	34.7	18.9	24,409	50.4	36.8	12.8	25,273	42.7	32.6	24.8
1249675	North Port city	47,538	27.8	50.9	21.4	23,083	27.6	53.0	19.4	24,455	28.0	48.9	23.2
1250750	Ocala city	45,829	32.6	39.7	27.7	21,884	37.9	42.1	19.9	23,945	27.7	37.5	34.8
1253000	Orlando city	202,231	43.9	33.8	22.3	95,421	47.5	36.3	16.2	106,810	40.6	31.6	27.8
1254000	Palm Bay city	84,734	27.2	47.5	25.3	38,852	30.4	51.8	17.8	45,882	24.5	43.8	31.7
1254200	Palm Coast city	64,754	23.4	53.8	22.8	30,449	25.0	58.2	16.7	34,305	22.0	49.9	28.2
1254350	Palm Harbor CDP	52,183	24.3	51.4	24.3	24,033	26.8	55.7	17.5	28,150	22.2	47.7	30.1
1255775	Pembroke Pines city	130,991	28.6	48.7	22.8	60,870	32.3	53.2	14.6	70,121	25.3	44.8	29.9
1255925	Pensacola city	44,150	35.8	39.0	25.3	21,031	37.9	41.0	21.2	23,119	33.9	37.1	29.0
1256825	Pine Hills CDP	51,727	41.9	37.7	20.5	24,762	44.9	40.2	15.0	26,965	39.1	35.4	25.6
1257425	Plantation city	73,308	32.1	47.1	20.8	34,805	34.2	50.4	15.4	38,503	30.2	44.2	25.7
1257900	Poinciana CDP	43,122	32.5	51.8	15.7	20,191	34.0	56.7	9.3	22,931	31.1	47.6	21.3
1258050	Pompano Beach city	86,776	39.1	34.6	26.2	44,835	44.0	34.7	21.3	41,941	33.9	34.6	31.5
1258350	Port Charlotte CDP	47,242	23.6	49.2	27.2	21,937	26.4	53.7	19.8	25,305	21.1	45.2	33.6
1258575	Port Orange city	48,518	24.8	49.5	25.7	23,249	30.2	52.1	17.7	25,269	19.8	47.2	33.0
1258715	Port St. Lucie city	134,732	27.3	52.2	20.5	65,570	29.9	54.1	16.0	69,162	24.8	50.5	24.8
1260950	Riverview CDP	56,497	28.9	54.0	17.1	27,474	30.7	55.5	13.8	29,023	27.2	52.7	20.2
1263000	St. Petersburg city	209,327	36.0	38.3	25.7	99,561	40.6	40.4	18.9	109,766	31.8	36.4	31.7
1263650	Sanford city	42,681	38.8	36.5	24.7	20,226	43.3	39.3	17.4	22,455	34.7	34.0	31.3
1264175	Sarasota city	46,062	33.6	38.6	27.8	22,205	39.5	40.4	20.1	23,857	28.1	37.0	34.9
1268350	Spring Hill CDP	84,144	23.4	52.8	23.8	40,081	26.7	55.2	18.1	44,063	20.4	50.6	28.9
1269700	Sunrise city	72,700	30.4	44.6	25.0	31,560	32.8	52.0	15.2	41,140	28.6	38.8	32.6
1270600	Tallahassee city	158,839	55.8	30.0	14.3	74,517	58.5	31.8	9.7	84,322	53.3	28.4	18.3
1270675	Tamarac city	53,436	26.9	41.3	31.8	23,323	32.1	47.6	20.3	30,113	22.9	36.4	40.7
1270700	Tamiami CDP	47,066	30.9	48.3	20.8	22,568	34.1	52.5	13.4	24,498	28.0	44.4	27.6
1271000	Tampa city	286,249	41.6	36.6	21.8	139,381	44.9	38.7	16.4	146,868	38.4	34.6	27.0
1271569	The Hammocks CDP	45,671	34.1	47.6	18.3	21,330	37.3	53.3	9.4	24,341	31.2	42.6	26.2
1271625	The Villages CDP	58,167	4.0	77.8	18.2	27,175	5.6	83.6	10.9	30,992	2.6	72.7	24.7
1272145	Town 'n' Country CDP	67,281	34.6	42.3	23.1	32,789	39.8	43.7	16.5	34,492	29.7	40.9	29.4
1275812	Wellington village	46,702	27.3	58.0	14.7	21,721	29.4	62.7	7.9	24,981	25.4	53.9	20.6
1276582	Weston city	51,906	26.0	61.4	12.6	25,818	29.0	62.4	8.6	26,088	23.1	60.3	16.6
1276600	West Palm Beach city	85,525	42.3	33.8	23.9	41,266	46.9	35.6	17.5	44,259	38.0	32.1	29.9
1300000	**Georgia**	7,829,101	33.5	46.9	19.6	3,780,350	36.4	49.2	14.4	4,048,751	30.7	44.8	24.6
1301052	Albany city	60,288	45.0	30.8	24.1	26,785	46.7	35.8	17.5	33,503	43.7	26.8	29.4
1301696	Alpharetta city	46,635	25.5	60.6	13.9	22,962	30.4	62.1	7.5	23,673	20.7	59.2	20.1
1303440	Athens-Clarke County	100,885	56.8	29.6	13.6	47,455	58.3	32.7	9.0	53,430	55.6	26.8	17.6
1304000	Atlanta city	370,176	54.0	27.3	18.7	183,644	58.5	27.9	13.6	186,532	49.5	26.7	23.8
1304204	Augusta-Richmond County	156,221	41.4	34.3	24.3	75,033	44.7	36.6	18.7	81,188	38.4	32.1	29.5
1310944	Brookhaven city	41,224	42.5	42.9	14.6	21,294	47.5	42.6	9.9	19,930	37.2	43.2	19.7
1319000	Columbus city	157,052	37.5	39.0	23.5	75,785	42.9	40.2	16.9	81,267	32.4	38.0	29.6
1342425	Johns Creek city	62,585	23.9	63.7	12.4	30,171	25.5	67.1	7.4	32,414	22.4	60.5	17.1
1349000	Macon city	70,449	45.9	29.0	25.1	31,078	48.4	33.1	18.5	39,371	43.9	25.8	30.3
1349756	Marietta city	46,851	42.2	40.3	17.5	22,818	46.1	41.5	12.4	24,033	38.6	39.0	22.4
1367284	Roswell city	74,520	30.9	53.9	15.2	36,939	33.9	56.5	9.5	37,581	27.9	51.4	20.7
1368516	Sandy Springs city	79,077	37.1	45.5	17.4	37,281	39.2	49.6	11.3	41,796	35.2	41.9	22.9
1369000	Savannah city	115,397	45.2	31.7	23.1	54,116	48.6	34.7	16.7	61,281	42.2	29.1	28.7
1371492	Smyrna city	41,886	34.7	45.8	19.5	19,063	36.4	49.8	13.8	22,823	33.3	42.5	24.2
1378800	Valdosta city	46,021	49.2	29.4	21.4	22,196	52.6	31.1	16.3	23,825	46.0	27.8	26.1
1380508	Warner Robins city	54,346	33.0	45.4	21.5	25,862	35.5	49.0	15.6	28,484	30.8	42.2	27.0
1500000	**Hawaii**	1,133,822	33.1	50.0	16.8	568,002	37.5	50.4	12.1	565,820	28.8	49.7	21.6
1571550	Urban Honolulu CDP	293,174	36.7	44.5	18.8	144,305	41.3	45.3	13.3	148,869	32.2	43.7	24.0
1600000	**Idaho**	1,238,968	26.0	55.2	18.9	616,275	29.2	56.1	14.7	622,693	22.7	54.3	23.0
1608830	Boise City city	174,133	33.1	47.2	19.7	85,346	36.8	49.2	14.0	88,787	29.6	45.2	25.2
1639700	Idaho Falls city	43,722	24.8	51.3	23.9	21,368	28.0	52.5	19.6	22,354	21.7	50.3	28.0
1652120	Meridian city	57,602	21.7	63.2	15.1	27,255	22.2	68.3	9.5	30,347	21.3	58.6	20.1
1656260	Nampa city	61,303	28.1	52.2	19.7	29,973	32.7	54.2	13.1	31,330	23.7	50.3	25.9
1664090	Pocatello city	42,633	31.6	48.3	20.1	21,185	35.4	48.2	16.4	21,448	27.8	48.4	23.8
1700000	**Illinois**	10,343,979	34.7	47.8	17.6	5,027,821	37.7	49.7	12.6	5,316,158	31.7	45.9	22.3
1702154	Arlington Heights village	62,853	26.9	58.5	14.6	30,020	29.2	62.3	8.5	32,833	24.9	55.0	20.1
1703012	Aurora city	147,670	34.2	51.2	14.6	73,452	37.2	52.2	10.6	74,218	31.3	50.2	18.5
1705573	Berwyn city	43,467	38.6	43.8	17.6	21,376	42.1	45.6	12.3	22,091	35.1	42.1	22.8
1706613	Bloomington city	61,303	34.0	48.2	17.8	29,681	37.4	49.4	13.1	31,622	30.7	47.0	22.3
1707133	Bolingbrook village	56,061	32.0	54.4	13.6	28,121	36.5	55.4	8.1	27,940	27.5	53.4	19.2
1712385	Champaign city	71,011	52.7	34.0	13.4	36,104	56.9	33.9	9.2	34,907	48.3	34.1	17.6
1714000	Chicago city	2,202,660	48.9	34.5	16.6	1,060,676	51.4	36.7	11.9	1,141,984	46.6	32.5	21.0

Table C-4: Cities with a Population of 50,000 or More—Marriages and Births—*Continued*

State/place FIPS code	State/Place	Total women age 15 to 50 years	Percent of all women who had a birth in the past year	Percent of women who had a birth who were married (including separated and spouse absent):	Percent of women who had a birth who were partners in an unmarried partner household	Age of women who had a birth in the last year as a percent of all women who had a birth			Women who had a birth in the last year as a percent of all women in their age group		
						Age 15 to 19	Age 20 to 34	Age 35 to 50	Age 15 to 19	Age 20 to 34	Age 35 to 50
	Florida—cont'd										
1239925	Lehigh Acres CDP	26,774	7.0	63.4	12.6	11.0	54.8	34.2	7.1	8.6	5.4
1243125	Margate city	12,119	4.5	67.3	6.5	0.0	89.9	10.1	0.0	10.1	0.9
1243975	Melbourne city	17,015	3.4	54.7	6.8	4.6	87.0	8.4	1.7	6.5	0.6
1245000	Miami city	102,527	5.3	46.9	7.6	9.3	71.7	19.0	5.5	8.2	2.2
1245025	Miami Beach city	102,527	5.3	46.9	7.6	9.3	71.7	19.0	5.5	8.2	2.2
1245060	Miami Gardens city	102,527	5.3	46.9	7.6	9.3	71.7	19.0	5.5	8.2	2.2
1245975	Miramar city	37,406	4.2	72.0	2.7	0.0	59.1	40.9	0.0	6.8	3.4
1249450	North Miami city	12,010	9.3	61.9	4.6	4.6	71.2	24.2	2.8	14.4	5.8
1249675	North Port city	12,349	5.4	17.7	5.3	48.7	32.5	18.8	13.6	5.0	2.2
1250750	Ocala city	12,912	8.6	58.3	3.7	3.0	59.6	37.4	2.1	11.5	7.6
1253000	Orlando city	74,243	5.2	44.3	16.1	6.2	76.8	17.0	3.7	7.9	2.2
1254000	Palm Bay city............................	24,304	4.4	49.2	8.7	12.8	71.7	15.4	4.5	8.0	1.4
1254200	Palm Coast city	15,465	5.3	84.8	0.0	0.0	84.2	15.8	0.0	12.5	1.7
1254350	Palm Harbor CDP	12,751	4.3	79.5	5.7	0.0	88.8	11.2	0.0	10.7	1.0
1255775	Pembroke Pines city	39,560	3.9	78.7	5.1	4.4	74.3	21.3	1.4	7.6	1.7
1255925	Pensacola city	12,430	4.7	59.4	13.4	0.0	67.9	32.1	0.0	7.0	3.5
1256825	Pine Hills CDP	17,251	4.9	55.6	10.6	4.5	67.5	28.0	1.8	7.5	3.1
1257425	Plantation city	22,583	4.3	76.1	16.2	0.0	69.5	30.5	0.0	7.3	2.8
1257900	Poinciana CDP	13,588	4.0	43.2	0.0	21.6	62.6	15.8	5.3	7.1	1.3
1258050	Pompano Beach city	22,686	6.5	50.2	8.2	5.7	65.8	28.5	3.2	9.8	4.1
1258350	Port Charlotte CDP	9,839	4.9	46.7	0.0	5.2	88.8	6.0	1.6	12.3	0.6
1258575	Port Orange city	0	0.0	0.0	0.0	0.0	0.0	0.0	0.0	0.0	0.0
1258715	Port St. Lucie city	38,979	5.1	55.8	5.2	2.3	83.3	14.4	0.9	11.8	1.5
1260950	Riverview CDP	19,893	3.8	76.8	6.3	6.7	67.6	25.7	2.0	6.7	2.0
1263000	St. Petersburg city	60,088	5.4	52.1	10.6	4.2	79.5	16.3	1.9	10.6	1.8
1263650	Sanford city	15,196	6.7	58.4	2.7	11.5	67.8	20.7	5.8	10.6	3.2
1264175	Sarasota city	11,603	3.3	74.5	3.6	1.8	69.8	28.4	0.6	5.6	2.0
1268350	Spring Hill CDP	20,827	4.5	47.7	22.0	0.0	90.3	9.7	0.0	10.8	0.9
1269700	Sunrise city	23,138	4.9	37.4	12.4	1.1	87.4	11.6	0.4	9.8	1.3
1270600	Tallahassee city	62,145	2.9	63.6	6.4	5.1	78.6	16.3	0.9	3.9	2.0
1270675	Tamarac city	62,145	2.9	63.6	6.4	5.1	78.6	16.3	0.9	3.9	2.0
1270700	Tamiami CDP	14,316	2.8	64.7	30.5	0.0	65.7	34.3	0.0	4.8	2.0
1271000	Tampa city	94,775	5.0	54.5	5.7	6.3	70.9	22.8	2.4	7.7	2.7
1271569	The Hammocks CDP	15,832	3.3	100.0	4.8	0.0	78.6	21.4	0.0	6.4	1.6
1271625	The Villages CDP	0	0.0	0.0	0.0	0.0	0.0	0.0	0.0	0.0	0.0
1272145	Town 'n' Country CDP	21,310	2.3	62.0	24.6	0.0	80.3	19.7	0.0	4.3	1.0
1275812	Wellington village	15,252	2.8	70.4	14.9	6.4	66.2	27.4	1.0	6.4	1.4
1276582	Weston city	17,408	2.8	93.8	0.0	0.0	63.3	36.7	0.0	7.0	1.7
1276600	West Palm Beach city	25,139	5.5	61.8	9.5	7.1	80.2	12.7	3.7	9.2	1.7
1300000	**Georgia ....**	2,525,451	5.6	60.6	8.9	6.0	72.5	21.5	2.4	9.8	2.6
1301052	Albany city	21,149	7.6	25.9	20.4	1.4	81.8	16.9	0.7	13.1	3.4
1301696	Alpharetta city	15,234	6.0	93.2	6.8	0.0	59.5	40.5	0.0	10.5	4.5
1303440	Athens-Clarke County	39,611	3.7	53.0	7.9	14.3	63.1	22.6	2.4	4.3	3.6
1304000	Atlanta city	127,205	4.7	46.1	3.4	6.2	74.1	19.7	2.5	6.7	2.6
1304204	Augusta-Richmond County	49,662	5.7	37.2	1.6	8.9	82.3	8.8	4.2	9.7	1.3
1310944	Brookhaven city	14,308	4.9	97.0	0.0	0.0	62.9	37.1	0.0	5.8	4.5
1319000	Columbus city	50,371	6.8	54.5	9.8	8.8	79.9	11.3	4.5	11.8	1.9
1342425	Johns Creek city	21,458	3.2	95.7	4.3	0.0	52.1	47.9	0.0	7.2	2.6
1349000	Macon city	24,194	6.2	36.1	2.9	10.1	76.7	13.2	3.4	10.7	2.2
1349756	Marietta city	16,105	3.3	56.5	19.8	18.3	52.5	29.3	6.1	3.6	2.2
1367284	Roswell city	22,676	4.2	84.9	1.9	2.7	65.4	31.9	0.8	8.0	2.6
1368516	Sandy Springs city	26,732	4.1	89.6	5.3	0.0	75.4	24.6	0.0	6.4	2.3
1369000	Savannah city	38,487	5.6	36.2	11.9	7.0	76.3	16.8	2.4	8.1	2.9
1371492	Smyrna city	16,416	3.9	77.1	8.3	0.0	63.8	36.2	0.0	5.2	2.9
1378800	Valdosta city	16,500	5.4	46.1	7.3	4.8	82.0	13.2	1.4	7.8	3.0
1380508	Warner Robins city	19,134	5.8	66.6	2.0	2.2	92.2	5.5	1.0	11.2	0.8
1500000	**Hawaii...................................**	319,934	6.4	68.1	10.5	4.8	73.4	21.8	2.4	10.8	3.2
1571550	Urban Honolulu CDP...................	82,065	5.4	73.5	8.7	2.9	64.0	33.1	1.3	7.5	4.1
1600000	**Idaho....................................**	369,379	6.8	73.8	8.9	4.9	81.7	13.5	2.2	12.9	2.2
1608830	Boise City city	54,944	5.3	72.1	6.5	3.2	83.0	13.8	1.3	9.4	1.8
1639700	Idaho Falls city	13,643	10.0	62.1	14.1	3.7	76.2	20.1	2.4	16.7	5.2
1652120	Meridian city	19,152	6.3	74.0	15.6	0.0	90.7	9.3	0.0	14.8	1.2
1656260	Nampa city	20,738	7.1	82.5	3.1	7.0	86.7	6.3	3.0	14.4	1.1
1664090	Pocatello city	13,824	5.9	79.3	2.1	2.1	84.7	13.3	0.9	9.5	2.3
1700000	**Illinois...................................**	3,162,329	5.0	63.2	10.0	5.5	72.8	21.7	2.0	8.7	2.5
1702154	Arlington Heights village..............	17,635	4.1	93.1	4.5	0.0	59.9	40.1	0.0	6.9	3.4
1703012	Aurora city	53,308	5.6	63.9	10.1	5.3	68.7	26.0	2.2	9.8	3.1
1705573	Berwyn city	14,939	6.0	32.7	9.2	0.0	78.0	22.0	0.0	11.5	2.9
1706613	Bloomington city........................	20,200	4.9	48.6	16.9	6.2	82.5	11.4	2.9	8.7	1.3
1707133	Bolingbrook village	18,789	9.2	73.3	4.8	8.2	58.9	32.9	5.6	15.0	6.0
1712385	Champaign city..........................	25,246	2.7	70.0	3.1	9.4	76.7	14.0	1.4	3.7	1.5
1714000	Chicago city..............................	756,296	5.2	54.4	9.1	6.4	69.6	24.0	2.9	7.2	3.2

Table C-4: Cities with a Population of 50,000 or More—Marriages and Births—*Continued*

State/ place FIPS code	State/Place	Total population 15 years and older	Marital status, percent			Male population 15 years and older	Male, marital status, percent			Female population 15 years and older	Female, marital status, percent		
			Never married	Now married (except separated)	Separated, widowed, or divorced		Never married	Now married (except separated)	Separated, or divorced		Never married	Now married (except separated)	Separated, widowed, or divorced
	Illinois—cont'd												
1714351	Cicero town	60,011	41.2	43.8	15.0	30,171	43.9	44.8	11.3	29,840	38.6	42.7	18.7
1718823	Decatur city	61,275	32.9	41.4	25.7	28,345	35.9	44.6	19.5	32,930	30.3	38.7	31.0
1719642	Des Plaines city	48,894	28.8	53.9	17.4	23,691	33.7	54.9	11.4	25,203	24.2	52.9	22.9
1723074	Elgin city	83,122	33.6	49.0	17.4	41,407	37.1	49.6	13.3	41,715	30.1	48.4	21.5
1724582	Evanston city	62,215	42.8	42.0	15.2	29,537	44.6	45.4	10.0	32,678	41.2	39.0	19.8
1735411	Hoffman Estates village	42,215	27.8	58.8	13.4	20,385	31.4	61.1	7.5	21,830	24.5	56.7	18.8
1738570	Joliet city	110,921	35.9	48.3	15.8	53,705	37.9	51.0	11.2	57,216	34.1	45.8	20.1
1751089	Mount Prospect village	44,118	27.7	58.6	13.8	21,970	31.8	59.9	8.3	22,148	23.6	57.2	19.2
1751622	Naperville city	113,028	28.0	60.4	11.6	55,163	31.5	61.9	6.6	57,865	24.7	59.0	16.4
1753234	Normal town	46,587	54.2	34.5	11.3	22,138	55.1	37.2	7.7	24,449	53.4	32.0	14.5
1754820	Oak Lawn village	46,892	31.6	49.0	19.4	22,312	35.7	51.5	12.7	24,580	27.9	46.7	25.5
1754885	Oak Park village	41,699	34.8	50.5	14.7	18,873	35.1	56.5	8.3	22,826	34.6	45.5	19.9
1756640	Orland Park village	48,742	26.5	57.6	15.9	22,402	28.6	62.7	8.7	26,340	24.7	53.2	22.1
1757225	Palatine village	55,171	31.7	50.9	17.4	26,849	35.6	53.2	11.2	28,322	28.0	48.7	23.3
1759000	Peoria city	90,827	41.8	40.5	17.7	42,699	44.3	42.6	13.1	48,128	39.5	38.7	21.9
1765000	Rockford city	118,044	35.9	40.5	23.6	55,841	39.7	42.7	17.6	62,203	32.5	38.5	29.0
1768003	Schaumburg village	61,291	30.6	52.2	17.2	28,792	34.9	56.1	9.0	32,499	26.8	48.7	24.4
1770122	Skokie village	54,193	28.3	53.8	17.9	25,264	31.9	58.0	10.1	28,929	25.1	50.1	24.7
1772000	Springfield city	95,110	34.4	41.2	24.4	44,844	37.6	43.8	18.6	50,266	31.5	38.9	29.6
1775484	Tinley Park village	46,224	29.3	53.6	17.2	21,604	32.0	58.2	9.8	24,620	26.8	49.5	23.7
1779293	Waukegan city	68,069	40.3	43.0	16.7	33,978	43.4	44.1	12.5	34,091	37.2	41.9	20.8
1781048	Wheaton city	43,360	32.5	54.1	13.4	20,530	34.3	57.0	8.7	22,830	30.8	51.5	17.7
1800000	**Indiana**	5,222,309	30.2	49.7	20.2	2,546,882	33.2	51.4	15.4	2,675,427	27.3	48.0	24.7
1801468	Anderson city	45,226	33.8	37.9	28.3	21,187	39.8	39.7	20.4	24,039	28.4	36.3	35.3
1805860	Bloomington city	72,483	65.4	22.7	12.0	36,127	68.0	22.9	9.1	36,356	62.8	22.5	14.7
1810342	Carmel city	64,441	23.0	65.9	11.0	30,780	24.4	68.5	7.0	33,661	21.8	63.6	14.6
1820728	Elkhart city	39,052	36.2	38.7	25.1	18,713	37.1	42.3	20.6	20,339	35.4	35.4	29.2
1822000	Evansville city	97,505	33.8	40.8	25.4	45,661	37.4	43.6	19.0	51,844	30.7	38.2	31.0
1823278	Fishers town	59,866	25.5	61.6	12.8	28,605	25.9	63.9	10.2	31,261	25.2	59.5	15.2
1825000	Fort Wayne city	199,553	34.4	44.0	21.6	94,921	37.2	46.6	16.1	104,632	31.8	41.5	26.7
1827000	Gary city	60,957	45.9	26.9	27.2	26,454	47.4	30.8	21.8	34,503	44.8	23.9	31.3
1829898	Greenwood city	41,867	26.4	53.6	20.0	19,866	30.4	55.9	13.7	22,001	22.7	51.6	25.7
1831000	Hammond city	61,149	39.7	39.7	20.6	29,680	43.1	41.4	15.5	31,469	36.4	38.1	25.5
1836003	Indianapolis city	658,545	39.0	39.5	21.4	312,703	41.7	41.9	16.4	345,842	36.7	37.4	26.0
1840392	Kokomo city	45,140	26.7	46.8	26.5	21,193	27.9	48.8	23.2	23,947	25.6	44.9	29.5
1840788	Lafayette city	55,485	35.3	44.1	20.6	26,374	37.2	46.9	15.9	29,111	33.5	41.6	24.9
1851876	Muncie city	60,639	48.3	31.8	19.8	28,311	51.5	33.5	15.0	32,328	45.6	30.4	24.1
1854180	Noblesville city	42,930	22.7	59.6	17.6	20,781	24.5	63.3	12.2	22,149	21.1	56.2	22.7
1871000	South Bend city	77,635	40.0	37.9	22.1	36,949	43.5	40.3	16.2	40,686	36.9	35.8	27.3
1875428	Terre Haute city	50,775	44.2	33.7	22.1	26,279	48.7	34.1	17.2	24,496	39.3	33.3	27.4
1900000	**Iowa**	2,474,777	28.7	52.7	18.6	1,216,354	32.0	54.0	14.0	1,258,423	25.5	51.5	23.0
1901855	Ames city	54,235	59.6	32.9	7.5	28,518	64.1	31.6	4.3	25,717	54.6	34.4	11.0
1912000	Cedar Rapids city	103,230	34.5	45.8	19.8	50,190	37.0	47.3	15.7	53,040	32.1	44.3	23.6
1916860	Council Bluffs city	50,059	33.3	42.8	23.9	24,268	38.8	44.4	16.8	25,791	28.1	41.3	30.6
1919000	Davenport city	80,565	35.4	42.5	22.0	39,395	38.8	43.2	18.0	41,170	32.2	42.0	25.8
1921000	Des Moines city	161,467	34.7	43.1	22.2	78,567	38.3	44.7	16.9	82,900	31.2	41.6	27.2
1922395	Dubuque city	48,062	37.3	42.6	20.1	22,801	40.2	45.3	14.5	25,261	34.7	40.1	25.2
1938595	Iowa City city	61,155	56.4	33.0	10.6	30,377	60.0	33.2	6.8	30,778	52.8	32.8	14.4
1973335	Sioux City city	64,768	33.0	44.2	22.8	31,805	37.2	44.4	18.4	32,963	29.0	44.0	26.9
1982425	Waterloo city	54,910	35.3	43.1	21.6	27,009	40.8	43.5	15.6	27,901	29.9	42.7	27.4
1983910	West Des Moines city	47,517	31.4	53.7	14.9	23,621	34.3	54.6	11.1	23,896	28.5	52.8	18.7
2000000	**Kansas**	2,276,556	28.5	52.4	19.1	1,123,515	31.9	53.6	14.5	1,153,041	25.2	51.1	23.6
2036000	Kansas City city	111,459	37.0	40.1	22.9	54,639	40.3	41.2	18.5	56,820	33.8	39.1	27.2
2038900	Lawrence city	76,556	52.2	35.0	12.9	37,637	54.8	36.6	8.6	38,919	49.6	33.4	17.0
2044250	Manhattan city	48,534	56.4	33.7	9.9	24,934	59.2	33.4	7.4	23,600	53.5	34.0	12.5
2052575	Olathe city	98,021	25.5	59.2	15.3	48,318	27.8	61.2	11.0	49,703	23.2	57.3	19.5
2053775	Overland Park city	143,134	27.4	55.3	17.3	67,920	29.7	59.3	11.0	75,214	25.4	51.7	22.9
2064500	Shawnee city	48,898	27.2	56.6	16.3	23,584	28.1	60.1	11.8	25,314	26.3	53.3	20.5
2071000	Topeka city	101,968	31.3	44.3	24.4	48,106	35.8	45.8	18.4	53,862	27.2	43.0	29.7
2079000	Wichita city	298,686	31.9	46.9	21.2	146,805	35.4	48.5	16.1	151,881	28.4	45.5	26.2
2100000	**Kentucky**	3,531,594	27.8	50.0	22.2	1,719,880	31.4	51.7	16.9	1,811,714	24.5	48.4	27.1
2108902	Bowling Green city	49,667	46.0	33.0	21.0	23,969	49.1	35.1	15.8	25,698	43.1	31.1	25.8
2146027	Lexington-Fayette urban county	250,142	38.1	43.2	18.8	121,843	41.3	44.6	14.1	128,299	35.0	41.8	23.2
2148006	Louisville/Jefferson County	487,122	35.3	42.0	22.8	232,306	38.9	44.1	17.0	254,816	31.9	40.0	28.0
2158620	Owensboro city	46,213	27.9	46.2	25.9	21,497	33.0	49.8	17.2	24,716	23.5	43.0	33.5
2200000	**Louisiana**	3,668,677	34.5	43.9	21.6	1,775,133	37.6	46.2	16.2	1,893,544	31.5	41.8	26.7
2205000	Baton Rouge city	187,856	48.5	30.1	21.3	89,377	51.9	32.0	16.1	98,479	45.4	28.5	26.1
2208920	Bossier City city	50,936	31.6	44.0	24.4	23,967	35.7	47.4	16.9	26,969	27.9	41.0	31.1
2239475	Kenner city	54,551	32.7	44.8	22.5	25,899	35.4	48.8	15.8	28,652	30.2	41.2	28.6
2240735	Lafayette city	100,924	40.6	39.1	20.3	48,497	43.2	42.0	14.9	52,427	38.3	36.4	25.4
2241155	Lake Charles city	58,943	38.5	36.5	25.0	28,312	41.8	39.4	18.8	30,631	35.5	33.9	30.7
2250115	Metairie CDP	116,321	34.5	43.5	21.9	56,859	39.1	45.8	15.1	59,462	30.2	41.3	28.5
2255000	New Orleans city	304,686	48.8	30.1	21.1	144,452	51.6	32.5	15.9	160,234	46.3	27.9	25.8

State/place FIPS code	State/Place	Total women age 15 to 50 years	Percent of all women who had a birth in the past year	Percent of women who had a birth who were married (including separated and spouse absent):	Percent of women who had a birth who were partners in an unmarried partner household	Age of women who had a birth in the last year as a percent of all women who had a birth			Women who had a birth in the last year as a percent of all women in their age group		
						Age 15 to 19	Age 20 to 34	Age 35 to 50	Age 15 to 19	Age 20 to 34	Age 35 to 50
	Illinois—cont'd										
1714351	Cicero town..................................	22,572	5.2	55.4	3.3	13.2	82.9	3.8	4.3	9.6	0.5
1718823	Decatur city.................................	17,928	6.1	37.4	17.6	10.6	84.2	5.2	5.0	11.2	0.8
1719642	Des Plaines city	12,716	5.7	85.4	1.8	1.9	75.4	22.7	1.1	9.5	2.9
1723074	Elgin city.....................................	27,522	6.0	71.0	10.1	3.0	73.0	24.0	1.4	10.0	3.3
1724582	Evanston city...............................	20,879	3.9	86.3	3.0	0.0	74.8	25.2	0.0	6.9	2.4
1735411	Hoffman Estates village...............	12,761	6.3	79.3	0.0	0.0	69.3	30.8	0.0	10.4	4.2
1738570	Joliet city....................................	39,684	5.5	63.8	7.4	5.0	80.2	14.7	1.8	11.1	1.8
1751089	Mount Prospect village................	12,449	5.0	80.7	13.9	0.0	67.0	33.0	0.0	8.2	3.4
1751622	Naperville city.............................	35,862	4.1	89.1	0.0	6.4	64.2	29.4	1.7	8.4	2.2
1753234	Normal town................................	18,779	2.2	56.6	3.6	14.5	81.9	3.6	1.6	3.1	0.4
1754820	Oak Lawn village.........................	12,940	5.0	71.6	15.6	0.0	84.0	16.0	0.0	9.1	1.8
1754885	Oak Park village...........................	12,940	5.0	71.6	15.6	0.0	84.0	16.0	0.0	9.1	1.8
1756640	Orland Park village......................	12,895	3.4	68.3	14.7	0.0	68.6	31.4	0.0	7.5	2.0
1757225	Palatine village............................	17,160	5.1	90.9	5.8	0.0	68.2	31.8	0.0	8.7	3.4
1759000	Peoria city...................................	29,309	5.2	32.2	15.1	5.5	87.3	7.2	2.1	9.5	1.0
1765000	Rockford city...............................	35,659	6.8	44.8	11.9	6.0	80.2	13.8	3.2	11.9	2.3
1768003	Schaumburg village......................	18,927	5.3	89.0	2.8	0.0	65.1	34.9	0.0	6.9	4.4
1770122	Skokie village..............................	14,095	5.6	81.6	1.0	11.9	46.4	41.6	5.0	7.1	4.7
1772000	Springfield city............................	27,251	5.1	48.2	13.6	2.2	87.8	10.0	0.9	9.9	1.2
1775484	Tinley Park village.......................	13,934	6.5	91.7	6.8	0.0	72.5	27.5	0.0	12.3	3.8
1779293	Waukegan city.............................	23,528	5.5	40.9	12.2	9.5	77.8	12.8	3.3	9.6	1.7
1781048	Wheaton city...............................	13,166	3.8	100.0	0.0	0.0	71.9	28.1	0.0	6.9	2.5
1800000	**Indiana**...................................	1,558,798	5.6	60.9	11.3	6.9	78.0	15.1	2.7	10.4	1.9
1801468	Anderson city...............................	13,973	4.8	48.3	12.8	8.4	82.9	8.7	2.8	9.1	1.0
1805860	Bloomington city..........................	28,789	3.2	68.6	3.1	1.5	72.0	26.5	0.2	3.8	5.2
1810342	Carmel city..................................	20,146	6.3	95.8	0.0	1.9	43.3	54.8	0.8	8.8	6.5
1820728	Elkhart city..................................	12,812	8.6	44.4	17.5	13.7	82.2	4.1	8.9	15.4	0.9
1822000	Evansville city..............................	29,632	5.3	50.0	18.6	8.7	84.6	6.7	3.9	8.9	0.9
1823278	Fishers town................................	23,241	6.4	88.4	5.8	5.8	48.5	45.7	2.5	9.9	5.4
1825000	Fort Wayne city............................	62,483	6.3	44.8	10.0	9.3	75.9	14.8	4.1	10.8	2.3
1827000	Gary city......................................	18,893	6.0	14.9	13.5	11.6	83.6	4.8	4.6	11.8	0.7
1829898	Greenwood city...........................	13,647	4.5	78.5	6.7	2.0	77.0	21.0	0.7	7.8	2.1
1831000	Hammond city..............................	20,249	5.9	34.6	11.4	9.6	77.0	13.4	3.6	10.5	1.9
1836003	Indianapolis city..........................	219,279	6.2	53.7	12.0	6.3	78.2	15.5	3.3	10.2	2.4
1840392	Kokomo city................................	12,479	8.3	62.9	6.5	13.5	72.8	13.7	8.3	12.9	2.8
1840788	Lafayette city...............................	18,785	8.2	62.0	23.0	2.9	86.0	11.0	2.4	12.6	2.7
1851876	Muncie city..................................	21,161	4.2	61.5	12.0	10.5	75.0	14.5	2.1	5.7	2.6
1854180	Noblesville city............................	14,025	5.5	75.7	17.7	17.8	68.6	13.6	9.5	9.3	1.5
1871000	South Bend city............................	24,140	8.3	52.7	11.7	11.8	76.5	11.8	6.9	14.1	2.4
1875428	Terre Haute city...........................	15,345	6.1	45.7	6.6	10.2	83.7	6.1	3.7	10.0	1.1
1900000	**Iowa**.......................................	705,099	5.4	68.1	12.1	3.6	80.5	15.9	1.3	10.4	2.0
1901855	Ames city.....................................	19,852	2.1	94.5	2.4	0.0	87.4	12.6	0.0	3.0	1.5
1912000	Cedar Rapids city.........................	31,996	5.7	68.3	6.2	6.7	74.9	18.4	2.9	9.5	2.5
1916860	Council Bluffs city........................	14,975	5.3	44.5	12.0	0.0	85.1	14.9	0.0	10.2	1.9
1919000	Davenport city..............................	24,470	4.0	62.9	11.4	7.1	74.6	18.3	2.3	6.2	1.9
1921000	Des Moines city............................	52,315	7.3	63.4	6.8	5.4	82.1	12.5	3.4	12.4	2.2
1922395	Dubuque city...............................	14,063	5.6	62.3	23.8	0.0	78.0	22.0	0.0	9.5	3.2
1938595	Iowa City city..............................	22,679	3.0	59.1	8.6	0.0	77.5	22.5	0.0	4.1	3.0
1973335	Sioux City city..............................	19,787	6.6	53.0	16.2	5.8	86.4	7.8	2.6	12.5	1.3
1982425	Waterloo city...............................	15,698	7.2	47.9	11.4	5.0	92.0	3.0	3.4	13.3	0.5
1983910	West Des Moines city....................	15,853	4.5	85.6	8.0	3.4	63.6	33.0	1.3	5.6	4.0
2000000	**Kansas**....................................	669,908	6.5	69.2	9.6	5.6	76.3	18.1	2.4	11.5	2.8
2036000	Kansas City city...........................	35,348	5.7	49.5	11.2	5.8	76.7	17.5	2.5	9.6	2.4
2038900	Lawrence city...............................	28,351	4.1	76.6	5.5	5.6	74.2	20.2	1.4	5.2	3.3
2044250	Manhattan city.............................	18,470	5.0	86.5	0.0	3.7	92.1	4.2	0.9	7.4	1.3
2052575	Olathe city...................................	33,010	6.6	88.9	2.9	2.5	83.8	13.7	1.2	14.6	1.8
2053775	Overland Park city........................	43,633	5.6	84.3	2.1	1.8	83.2	15.0	0.9	10.6	1.9
2064500	Shawnee city...............................	16,140	5.1	80.9	0.0	1.2	85.9	12.8	0.5	11.2	1.3
2071000	Topeka city..................................	30,393	6.8	62.4	16.7	4.9	84.1	10.9	2.4	12.3	1.8
2079000	Wichita city.................................	91,975	6.5	64.0	8.3	5.4	80.7	13.9	2.7	11.4	2.2
2100000	**Kentucky**.................................	1,041,060	5.4	64.4	10.1	6.9	77.9	15.2	2.7	10.1	1.8
2108902	Bowling Green city.......................	18,148	4.0	50.2	10.6	0.0	79.5	20.5	0.0	6.5	2.8
2146027	Lexington-Fayette urban county....	82,464	5.2	72.1	12.6	4.7	80.8	14.5	2.0	8.5	2.0
2148006	Louisville/Jefferson County...........	149,127	5.5	56.8	8.3	6.5	72.6	20.9	2.9	9.2	2.6
2158620	Owensboro city............................	13,388	5.1	44.9	25.1	10.2	88.4	1.5	4.7	10.5	0.2
2200000	**Louisiana**.................................	1,126,108	5.5	50.9	10.9	6.1	80.2	13.7	2.5	9.9	1.8
2205000	Baton Rouge city..........................	62,327	4.7	49.0	5.9	8.2	77.8	14.0	2.7	6.7	2.1
2208920	Bossier City city...........................	16,364	8.5	62.5	4.8	5.6	81.0	13.4	3.8	14.0	2.9
2239475	Kenner city..................................	16,306	4.2	64.5	11.7	0.0	85.5	14.5	0.0	7.6	1.4
2240735	Lafayette city...............................	32,931	5.4	47.8	11.4	3.9	79.1	16.9	1.6	9.0	2.3
2241155	Lake Charles city..........................	17,124	6.1	24.9	17.9	13.2	79.3	7.5	4.9	10.5	1.2
2250115	Metairie CDP................................	32,350	5.8	55.9	17.2	6.8	76.6	16.6	3.4	9.8	2.3
2255000	New Orleans city..........................	99,700	5.2	39.4	11.7	2.0	74.6	23.4	0.9	7.6	3.2

Table C-4: Cities with a Population of 50,000 or More—Marriages and Births—*Continued*

State/place FIPS code	State/Place	Total population 15 years and older	Marital status, percent			Male population 15 years and older	Male, marital status, percent			Female population 15 years and older	Female, marital status, percent		
			Never married	Now married (except separated)	Separated, widowed, or divorced		Never married	Now married (except separated)	Separated, widowed, or divorced		Never married	Now married (except separated)	Separated, widowed, or divorced
	Louisiana—cont'd												
2270000	Shreveport city..........	159,457	40.6	35.3	24.0	73,294	43.2	39.4	17.4	86,163	38.4	31.9	29.7
2300000	**Maine**..........	1,112,439	27.7	50.8	21.5	539,761	30.7	52.5	16.9	572,678	24.8	49.3	25.9
2360545	Portland city..........	56,691	43.8	36.2	20.0	27,918	48.5	37.1	14.4	28,773	39.2	35.3	25.5
2400000	**Maryland**	4,770,688	35.1	46.5	18.3	2,282,623	37.5	49.3	13.3	2,488,065	33.0	44.0	23.0
2402825	Aspen Hill CDP..........	42,398	37.2	47.1	15.7	20,177	39.8	49.0	11.1	22,221	34.8	45.3	19.9
2404000	Baltimore city..........	510,014	52.1	26.0	21.9	236,383	53.6	29.1	17.3	273,631	50.8	23.4	25.9
2407125	Bethesda CDP..........	51,680	28.2	57.9	13.9	23,873	28.7	62.8	8.6	27,807	27.8	53.7	18.5
2408775	Bowie city..........	45,522	32.9	48.9	18.2	21,472	37.3	52.4	10.3	24,050	28.9	45.8	25.2
2419125	Columbia CDP..........	82,581	29.0	54.4	16.6	39,900	31.3	56.1	12.6	42,681	26.8	52.8	20.4
2423975	Dundalk CDP..........	49,871	32.8	40.4	26.8	23,906	36.7	42.0	21.3	25,965	29.2	38.9	31.9
2426000	Ellicott City CDP..........	54,671	23.1	65.2	11.7	26,392	25.2	68.2	6.7	28,279	21.1	62.4	16.5
2430325	Frederick city..........	53,073	35.2	43.8	21.0	25,274	38.7	46.6	14.6	27,799	32.0	41.2	26.8
2431175	Gaithersburg city..........	49,037	31.0	50.8	18.2	23,001	34.5	54.4	11.1	26,036	27.9	47.6	24.5
2432025	Germantown CDP..........	70,128	32.4	53.2	14.4	33,187	34.8	56.4	8.9	36,941	30.2	50.4	19.4
2432650	Glen Burnie CDP..........	55,988	34.8	40.2	25.0	26,015	36.8	43.4	19.8	29,973	33.1	37.4	29.5
2467675	Rockville city..........	52,317	29.2	54.7	16.0	25,430	33.0	56.1	10.9	26,887	25.7	53.4	20.9
2472450	Silver Spring CDP..........	61,937	41.9	44.3	13.8	29,689	42.4	48.5	9.2	32,248	41.4	40.6	18.1
2478425	Towson CDP..........	49,911	45.4	38.1	16.5	22,500	44.7	42.7	12.6	27,411	46.0	34.4	19.7
2481175	Waldorf CDP..........	56,695	38.5	43.9	17.6	25,512	39.9	48.8	11.3	31,183	37.3	39.9	22.8
2483775	Wheaton CDP..........	40,598	40.5	45.9	13.6	20,759	44.6	46.2	9.2	19,839	36.2	45.6	18.2
2500000	**Massachusetts**..........	5,500,845	36.0	46.6	17.5	2,634,936	38.7	49.0	12.3	2,865,909	33.5	44.3	22.2
2507000	Boston city..........	548,826	56.6	28.3	15.1	259,860	57.8	30.9	11.3	288,966	55.6	25.9	18.5
2509000	Brockton city..........	73,662	40.3	38.7	21.0	34,673	44.7	41.3	14.0	38,989	36.3	36.5	27.2
2509210	Brookline CDP..........	50,007	42.5	45.2	12.3	20,477	38.2	55.3	6.4	29,530	45.4	38.2	16.4
2511000	Cambridge city..........	96,139	57.1	31.0	11.9	46,100	59.1	33.1	7.9	50,039	55.2	29.2	15.6
2513660	Chicopee city..........	47,035	34.6	42.4	23.0	22,248	34.9	45.9	19.3	24,787	34.4	39.2	26.3
2523000	Fall River city..........	72,660	36.2	38.7	25.0	33,231	39.4	42.9	17.6	39,429	33.5	35.2	31.3
2524960	Framingham CDP..........	57,252	34.2	49.0	16.8	26,102	33.6	53.9	12.5	31,150	34.7	44.8	20.4
2529405	Haverhill city..........	50,170	35.8	43.0	21.2	23,958	38.8	46.0	15.1	26,212	33.1	40.3	26.7
2534550	Lawrence city..........	59,424	46.9	33.5	19.6	27,557	50.4	37.3	12.3	31,867	43.8	30.3	25.9
2537000	Lowell city..........	88,270	43.7	37.0	19.2	43,928	48.1	36.9	15.0	44,342	39.4	37.1	23.5
2537490	Lynn city..........	70,968	41.0	39.7	19.3	34,427	45.5	41.5	13.0	36,541	36.8	38.0	25.2
2537875	Malden city..........	50,790	40.4	45.3	14.3	24,368	43.9	47.2	8.9	26,422	37.1	43.5	19.3
2539835	Medford city..........	49,650	41.3	44.6	14.1	23,207	43.9	47.9	8.2	26,443	39.0	41.8	19.2
2545000	New Bedford city..........	77,410	39.9	37.3	22.8	36,705	43.6	40.4	16.0	40,705	36.6	34.5	28.9
2545560	Newton city..........	70,976	32.9	55.2	11.9	33,193	33.7	58.7	7.6	37,783	32.1	52.2	15.7
2552490	Peabody city..........	44,291	30.5	48.4	21.2	20,409	33.5	52.4	14.0	23,882	27.9	44.9	27.3
2555745	Quincy city..........	79,831	39.0	43.7	17.3	38,503	41.7	45.8	12.5	41,328	36.5	41.7	21.8
2556585	Revere city..........	44,516	37.2	39.9	22.9	22,898	43.3	40.3	16.4	21,618	30.7	39.5	29.9
2562535	Somerville city..........	68,749	56.0	31.8	12.2	33,753	58.8	32.9	8.2	34,996	53.3	30.8	15.9
2567000	Springfield city..........	119,559	46.3	32.2	21.5	56,121	49.5	35.5	15.0	63,438	43.5	29.4	27.2
2569170	Taunton city..........	46,507	34.2	43.9	21.9	22,543	40.0	46.0	14.0	23,964	28.8	42.0	29.3
2572600	Waltham city..........	54,271	46.7	38.9	14.4	25,845	49.3	40.7	10.0	28,426	44.4	37.3	18.4
2578972	Weymouth Town city..........	45,985	33.1	45.9	21.0	21,725	37.7	48.9	13.4	24,260	29.1	43.1	27.8
2582000	Worcester city..........	148,875	43.8	35.5	20.7	69,878	47.3	37.7	15.0	78,997	40.8	33.5	25.7
2600000	**Michigan**..........	8,028,676	32.5	48.1	19.4	3,901,469	35.8	49.6	14.6	4,127,207	29.5	46.7	23.8
2603000	Ann Arbor city..........	102,974	55.8	31.9	12.4	51,696	60.1	32.0	7.9	51,278	51.4	31.7	16.9
2605920	Battle Creek city..........	40,635	32.7	41.3	26.0	19,114	36.4	42.9	20.8	21,521	29.5	39.9	30.6
2621000	Dearborn city..........	72,497	31.7	52.0	16.3	35,370	34.2	54.1	11.7	37,127	29.3	50.0	20.7
2621020	Dearborn Heights city..........	45,037	31.5	47.0	21.5	21,783	36.6	47.9	15.6	23,254	26.7	46.2	27.2
2622000	Detroit city..........	551,373	54.5	22.7	22.8	256,351	57.3	24.8	18.0	295,022	52.0	21.0	27.0
2627440	Farmington Hills city..........	67,876	27.2	54.2	18.6	31,671	29.5	58.6	11.9	36,205	25.1	50.4	24.5
2629000	Flint city..........	78,747	48.3	26.4	25.4	37,446	50.0	28.7	21.3	41,301	46.7	24.2	29.1
2634000	Grand Rapids city..........	150,986	44.8	36.7	18.5	72,637	48.0	38.1	13.9	78,349	41.9	35.4	22.8
2642160	Kalamazoo city..........	62,418	56.2	25.6	18.2	31,302	62.1	25.8	12.1	31,116	50.2	25.4	24.4
2646000	Lansing city..........	90,981	43.9	34.7	21.4	42,471	46.1	36.5	17.5	48,510	42.0	33.1	24.9
2649000	Livonia city..........	80,307	27.6	54.5	18.0	39,596	32.0	55.1	12.9	40,711	23.2	53.9	22.9
2659440	Novi city..........	45,654	25.7	57.3	17.0	21,640	27.1	61.0	11.9	24,014	24.5	54.0	21.5
2665440	Pontiac city..........	46,939	48.9	27.2	23.9	22,747	52.6	28.4	19.1	24,192	45.5	26.0	28.5
2669035	Rochester Hills city..........	58,641	27.1	58.5	14.4	28,096	30.3	61.2	8.5	30,545	24.1	56.0	19.8
2670040	Royal Oak city..........	50,503	39.2	42.4	18.3	24,742	43.6	43.4	13.0	25,761	35.1	41.5	23.4
2670520	Saginaw city..........	39,134	46.1	27.5	26.4	18,441	50.9	28.6	20.5	20,693	41.7	26.5	31.7
2670760	St. Clair Shores city..........	50,626	30.5	46.7	22.8	24,127	35.7	49.0	15.3	26,499	25.8	44.5	29.7
2674900	Southfield city..........	60,097	36.8	38.0	25.2	26,221	39.1	43.4	17.5	33,876	35.0	33.8	31.2
2676460	Sterling Heights city..........	108,613	29.5	53.9	16.7	53,415	32.9	55.2	11.9	55,198	26.1	52.6	21.3
2679000	Taylor city..........	49,836	34.4	42.7	22.9	23,410	37.6	44.7	17.6	26,426	31.5	40.9	27.7
2680700	Troy city..........	67,189	25.5	61.5	12.9	32,550	28.6	63.3	8.1	34,639	22.6	59.9	17.5
2684000	Warren city..........	109,881	35.4	43.8	20.8	52,733	39.3	45.8	14.9	57,148	31.8	41.9	26.2
2686000	Westland city..........	68,725	35.7	40.4	23.9	31,277	37.9	44.7	17.4	37,448	33.9	36.8	29.3
2688940	Wyoming city..........	57,887	33.8	49.8	16.4	29,698	38.6	48.3	13.1	28,189	28.8	51.4	19.8
2700000	**Minnesota**..........	4,318,219	31.5	52.1	16.4	2,129,781	34.8	53.0	12.2	2,188,438	28.3	51.3	20.4
2706382	Blaine city..........	45,213	28.0	57.7	14.3	22,221	31.2	59.0	9.7	22,992	24.9	56.4	18.7
2706616	Bloomington city..........	71,774	31.2	49.5	19.3	34,534	35.0	50.6	14.4	37,240	27.8	48.4	23.8

State/place FIPS code	State/Place	Total women age 15 to 50 years	Percent of all women who had a birth in the past year	Percent of women who had a birth who were married (including separated and spouse absent):	Percent of women who had a birth who were partners in an unmarried partner household	Age of women who had a birth in the last year as a percent of all women who had a birth			Women who had a birth in the last year as a percent of all women in their age group		
						Age 15 to 19	Age 20 to 34	Age 35 to 50	Age 15 to 19	Age 20 to 34	Age 35 to 50
	Louisiana—cont'd										
2270000	Shreveport city........................	51,126	5.5	41.7	5.7	5.4	79.1	15.5	2.2	9.3	2.2
2300000	**Maine**	298,992	4.7	64.1	17.0	3.9	78.2	17.9	1.3	9.7	1.8
2360545	Portland city............................	17,538	4.4	49.7	23.1	5.0	86.4	8.6	2.7	7.4	1.0
2400000	**Maryland**	1,476,529	5.3	63.2	9.5	5.1	70.5	24.5	2.0	9.1	2.8
2402825	Aspen Hill CDP.........................	13,171	6.0	62.9	11.7	4.2	71.5	24.3	2.0	10.3	3.1
2404000	Baltimore city...........................	170,330	5.9	37.8	8.2	10.3	69.4	20.3	5.2	8.1	3.2
2407125	Bethesda CDP...........................	15,351	4.8	93.6	2.2	0.0	39.6	60.4	0.0	5.1	5.6
2408775	Bowie city................................	14,368	3.7	78.8	1.5	1.3	57.9	40.8	0.3	7.1	2.7
2419125	Columbia CDP...........................	25,963	6.4	76.3	0.0	4.8	73.5	21.6	3.1	11.1	2.9
2423975	Dundalk CDP.............................	13,967	4.4	49.1	21.6	4.9	69.2	25.9	2.2	6.5	2.6
2426000	Ellicott City CDP.......................	16,174	4.9	98.2	1.8	0.0	52.6	47.4	0.0	9.4	4.2
2430325	Frederick city............................	17,462	4.6	58.5	20.5	1.6	86.4	12.0	0.9	8.6	1.2
2431175	Gaithersburg city......................	16,187	6.8	86.3	2.3	1.4	74.5	24.1	0.9	11.5	3.6
2432025	Germantown CDP.......................	25,513	5.1	69.0	11.8	3.3	70.9	25.8	1.6	9.5	2.6
2432650	Glen Burnie CDP........................	18,078	6.6	69.1	1.8	14.1	74.8	11.1	8.2	10.7	1.7
2467675	Rockville city............................	15,104	8.3	94.2	5.6	0.0	66.3	33.7	0.0	13.3	5.7
2472450	Silver Spring CDP......................	22,221	5.3	72.4	12.2	5.5	59.5	35.0	3.1	7.3	4.0
2478425	Towson CDP..............................	17,362	3.4	88.2	6.1	0.0	53.1	46.9	0.0	4.1	4.6
2481175	Waldorf CDP.............................	22,236	4.7	48.5	12.5	0.0	78.5	21.5	0.0	9.9	2.1
2483775	Wheaton CDP............................	13,116	6.3	59.1	15.1	4.3	73.7	22.0	2.7	9.0	3.7
2500000	**Massachusetts**	1,666,805	4.6	69.1	9.3	2.9	67.5	29.6	1.0	7.5	3.0
2507000	Boston city...............................	202,493	3.9	56.0	7.2	3.4	70.4	26.2	1.0	4.8	3.3
2509000	Brockton city............................	23,583	4.5	28.0	10.1	0.0	78.7	21.3	0.0	9.0	2.0
2509210	Brookline CDP...........................	18,897	3.0	100.0	0.0	0.0	56.6	43.4	0.0	2.9	4.0
2511000	Cambridge city..........................	36,085	3.2	89.4	3.4	2.0	58.3	39.7	0.5	3.0	5.1
2513660	Chicopee city............................	13,696	4.3	57.4	8.1	3.9	89.9	6.3	1.1	8.7	0.7
2523000	Fall River city...........................	22,710	5.0	42.6	22.7	0.0	89.9	10.1	0.0	9.9	1.1
2524960	Framingham CDP........................	19,036	7.4	84.3	0.0	1.6	70.0	28.4	1.0	11.3	4.9
2529405	Haverhill city............................	15,431	4.8	58.3	10.6	4.8	71.3	23.9	1.9	8.7	2.4
2534550	Lawrence city............................	21,435	7.6	47.5	16.4	7.4	87.4	5.2	3.2	15.1	1.0
2537000	Lowell city...............................	28,866	6.1	53.6	14.3	5.9	69.6	24.5	2.5	8.8	4.0
2537490	Lynn city..................................	23,063	7.5	46.2	17.9	2.7	75.3	21.9	2.0	11.6	4.1
2537875	Malden city...............................	17,478	4.9	82.5	0.0	0.0	56.9	43.1	0.0	5.8	5.1
2539835	Medford city.............................	16,081	3.6	97.2	0.0	0.0	65.8	34.2	0.0	4.4	3.3
2545000	New Bedford city.......................	23,583	6.3	42.9	12.9	7.3	77.5	15.3	3.9	10.7	2.2
2545560	Newton city..............................	21,295	2.5	87.1	5.6	0.0	51.5	48.5	0.0	3.8	2.6
2552490	Peabody city.............................	12,101	3.0	52.0	0.0	0.0	96.5	3.5	0.0	7.6	0.2
2555745	Quincy city...............................	24,484	7.1	91.1	0.9	0.0	70.0	30.0	0.0	10.2	5.2
2556585	Revere city................................	12,589	6.1	75.6	4.3	4.2	66.1	29.7	3.7	9.4	3.6
2562535	Somerville city...........................	25,690	4.5	81.6	7.2	0.4	64.6	34.9	0.3	4.6	5.4
2567000	Springfield city..........................	40,278	5.1	29.6	14.4	15.4	69.9	14.7	4.9	7.9	1.9
2569170	Taunton city..............................	13,130	5.4	43.9	19.9	0.0	78.2	21.8	0.0	10.6	2.4
2572600	Waltham city.............................	18,912	3.4	92.5	2.0	0.0	81.5	18.5	0.0	5.5	1.8
2578972	Weymouth Town city	12,857	4.0	80.7	8.4	0.0	53.5	46.5	0.0	7.1	3.2
2582000	Worcester city...........................	49,277	5.7	62.6	17.6	1.8	83.6	14.7	0.7	9.9	2.3
2600000	**Michigan**	2,327,914	5.2	60.7	12.7	5.7	75.9	18.5	2.0	9.7	2.1
2603000	Ann Arbor city..........................	36,122	2.6	84.3	3.6	3.3	69.2	27.5	0.5	3.1	3.0
2605920	Battle Creek city........................	12,710	5.3	61.0	14.6	4.3	68.8	26.9	1.8	8.2	3.3
2621000	Dearborn city............................	22,804	7.4	86.6	4.9	0.0	81.1	18.9	0.0	13.2	3.7
2621020	Dearborn Heights city.................	22,804	7.4	86.6	4.9	0.0	81.1	18.9	0.0	13.2	3.7
2622000	Detroit city...............................	176,577	6.1	25.1	12.9	13.7	72.0	14.3	5.4	10.2	2.1
2627440	Farmington Hills city..................	18,913	4.7	80.5	4.1	10.6	72.0	17.4	3.6	8.8	1.7
2629000	Flint city..................................	25,412	4.6	17.3	22.3	12.2	77.0	10.8	3.6	8.1	1.2
2634000	Grand Rapids city......................	51,393	6.2	61.0	14.2	4.6	70.9	24.5	2.0	8.4	4.5
2642160	Kalamazoo city..........................	21,696	3.8	45.3	20.7	3.3	75.2	21.5	0.8	5.3	2.8
2646000	Lansing city..............................	32,030	5.9	56.0	5.7	13.6	74.3	12.1	6.9	8.5	1.9
2649000	Livonia city..............................	20,330	3.7	90.6	7.3	2.2	60.5	37.4	0.7	5.9	2.7
2659440	Novi city..................................	13,899	4.7	93.6	6.4	0.0	74.5	25.5	0.0	10.4	2.3
2665440	Pontiac city..............................	14,998	8.6	31.1	16.6	10.6	76.0	13.4	5.7	14.4	3.0
2669035	Rochester Hills city....................	16,086	4.7	83.0	7.2	0.0	74.9	25.1	0.0	9.5	2.4
2670040	Royal Oak city...........................	15,320	4.5	84.8	1.9	1.7	73.5	24.7	0.9	6.4	2.8
2670520	Saginaw city.............................	12,509	5.7	15.1	12.4	13.7	75.6	10.7	4.9	10.5	1.4
2670760	St. Clair Shores city...................	12,883	6.0	56.0	21.4	0.0	76.0	24.0	0.0	10.5	3.1
2674900	Southfield city...........................	17,397	5.6	47.8	14.0	10.9	56.8	32.3	4.7	8.7	3.6
2676460	Sterling Heights city...................	30,887	3.7	76.5	8.0	0.0	81.5	18.5	0.0	7.5	1.5
2679000	Taylor city................................	15,718	5.5	45.0	24.2	13.5	70.8	15.7	6.1	9.5	1.9
2680700	Troy city..................................	19,392	5.7	86.6	4.3	2.3	52.6	45.1	1.0	8.9	4.9
2684000	Warren city...............................	31,861	4.7	52.4	16.2	1.7	81.4	16.9	0.6	9.2	1.8
2686000	Westland city............................	21,165	5.4	55.1	11.0	8.6	72.3	19.2	3.9	8.4	2.4
2688940	Wyoming city............................	6,462	4.5	59.3	38.6	7.6	63.4	29.0	2.5	7.8	2.6
2700000	**Minnesota**.............................	1,277,310	5.7	70.8	11.8	4.6	76.2	19.2	1.9	10.4	2.5
2706382	Blaine city................................	14,425	6.4	78.5	0.0	0.0	78.4	21.6	0.0	12.9	2.8
2706616	Bloomington city........................	18,795	6.1	65.5	21.0	4.8	72.3	22.9	2.7	10.0	3.1

Table C-4: Cities with a Population of 50,000 or More—Marriages and Births—Continued

State/place FIPS code	State/Place	Total population 15 years and older	Marital status, percent			Male population 15 years and older	Male, marital status, percent			Female population 15 years and older	Female, marital status, percent		
			Never married	Now married (except separated)	Separated, widowed, or divorced		Never married	Now married (except separated)	Separated, widowed, or divorced		Never married	Now married (except separated)	Separated, widowed, or divorced
	Minnesota—cont'd												
2707966	Brooklyn Park city	60,221	37.5	46.9	15.7	29,259	40.1	48.4	11.5	30,962	35.0	45.4	19.6
2708794	Burnsville city	49,868	32.9	48.9	18.2	24,514	36.2	50.0	13.8	25,354	29.7	47.9	22.5
2713114	Coon Rapids city	49,748	32.1	49.5	18.4	24,271	35.2	51.3	13.5	25,477	29.2	47.7	23.1
2717000	Duluth city	72,797	43.3	38.9	17.9	35,712	47.5	39.5	13.0	37,085	39.1	38.3	22.6
2717288	Eagan city	51,765	29.0	56.4	14.6	25,714	32.3	56.7	11.0	26,051	25.7	56.0	18.3
2718116	Eden Prairie city	48,943	27.0	59.5	13.5	24,126	29.4	59.9	10.7	24,817	24.7	59.2	16.2
2735180	Lakeville city	42,878	26.0	63.0	11.0	20,785	26.7	65.3	8.0	22,093	25.3	60.9	13.8
2740166	Maple Grove city	50,481	23.9	64.1	12.0	24,299	25.7	65.8	8.5	26,182	22.2	62.6	15.2
2743000	Minneapolis city	324,506	51.8	33.2	15.0	162,822	54.9	33.3	11.8	161,684	48.7	33.1	18.2
2743252	Minnetonka city	42,190	25.4	56.6	17.9	19,846	26.9	60.6	12.5	22,344	24.2	53.1	22.7
2751730	Plymouth city	59,019	26.5	58.8	14.7	28,128	27.4	61.9	10.7	30,891	25.7	55.9	18.4
2754880	Rochester city	86,532	32.3	51.3	16.4	41,563	35.1	53.9	11.0	44,969	29.6	49.0	21.4
2756896	St. Cloud city	54,493	48.0	37.4	14.5	28,361	52.3	36.2	11.5	26,132	43.4	38.8	17.8
2758000	St. Paul city	228,926	44.8	37.8	17.4	111,546	48.2	38.8	13.0	117,380	41.6	36.9	21.5
2771428	Woodbury city	49,149	25.6	61.7	12.7	23,155	25.6	65.7	8.7	25,994	25.7	58.1	16.3
2800000	**Mississippi**	2,365,073	33.3	44.7	22.1	1,134,219	36.1	47.5	16.4	1,230,854	30.7	42.1	27.3
2829700	Gulfport city	55,210	33.9	41.8	24.3	26,659	38.3	44.1	17.7	28,551	29.8	39.7	30.5
2836000	Jackson city	135,144	48.4	28.5	23.1	60,797	49.4	32.5	18.0	74,347	47.6	25.3	27.2
2869280	Southaven city	38,493	27.0	52.5	20.5	17,615	28.4	58.0	13.6	20,878	25.8	47.9	26.4
2900000	**Missouri**	4,859,594	29.8	49.7	20.6	2,357,488	32.8	51.5	15.8	2,502,106	27.0	47.9	25.1
2906652	Blue Springs city	40,755	26.0	54.8	19.2	19,679	27.3	57.3	15.4	21,076	24.8	52.6	22.6
2915670	Columbia city	94,492	51.5	35.5	13.0	44,646	53.1	38.1	8.8	49,846	50.0	33.2	16.8
2924778	Florissant city	42,140	33.8	43.8	22.3	19,376	35.8	47.6	16.6	22,764	32.2	40.7	27.2
2935000	Independence city	95,616	27.9	45.3	26.9	45,169	32.9	47.9	19.3	50,447	23.4	42.9	33.7
2937592	Joplin city	41,789	29.9	46.2	23.9	20,431	34.5	47.6	17.8	21,358	25.4	44.9	29.7
2938000	Kansas City city	371,713	39.0	39.6	21.4	177,753	41.1	41.6	17.3	193,960	37.1	37.7	25.2
2941348	Lee's Summit city	71,414	25.7	57.1	17.2	33,467	27.1	62.1	10.8	37,947	24.5	52.7	22.8
2954074	O'Fallon city	61,795	25.1	58.8	16.0	30,295	28.2	59.7	12.1	31,500	22.2	58.0	19.8
2964082	St. Charles city	56,118	35.0	45.3	19.7	27,611	41.0	45.6	13.4	28,507	29.1	45.0	25.8
2964550	St. Joseph city	61,938	33.5	42.8	23.7	30,711	37.8	44.6	17.6	31,227	29.2	41.1	29.7
2965000	St. Louis city	263,545	50.0	28.5	21.5	125,635	52.7	30.4	16.9	137,910	47.5	26.9	25.7
2965126	St. Peters city	44,086	27.1	55.1	17.9	20,265	28.3	60.2	11.5	23,821	26.0	50.8	23.2
2970000	Springfield city	137,425	38.4	37.4	24.2	65,527	42.2	39.5	18.4	71,898	34.9	35.5	29.6
3000000	**Montana**	820,867	28.1	51.8	20.1	410,108	31.9	52.3	15.7	410,759	24.3	51.2	24.5
3006550	Billings city	86,480	30.5	45.8	23.7	41,303	34.7	48.0	17.4	45,177	26.7	43.7	29.5
3032800	Great Falls city	47,725	28.5	48.6	22.9	22,965	32.2	51.4	16.4	24,760	25.1	46.0	28.9
3050200	Missoula city	58,371	44.7	37.7	17.7	28,525	46.9	38.1	15.0	29,846	42.5	37.2	20.2
3100000	**Nebraska**	1,466,890	29.4	53.0	17.6	722,428	32.6	54.2	13.1	744,462	26.3	51.8	22.0
3103950	Bellevue city	40,976	29.2	52.9	17.8	19,309	29.4	56.7	13.8	21,667	29.0	49.6	21.4
3119595	Grand Island city	38,593	28.9	50.7	20.4	19,242	31.9	51.8	16.2	19,351	25.8	49.6	24.5
3128000	Lincoln city	213,903	37.5	45.8	16.7	106,496	41.2	46.4	12.4	107,407	33.9	45.1	20.9
3137000	Omaha city	338,769	36.8	43.7	19.5	165,190	40.2	45.6	14.2	173,579	33.7	41.9	24.4
3200000	**Nevada**	2,204,875	32.2	45.9	21.9	1,106,651	35.8	46.4	17.7	1,098,224	28.6	45.4	26.0
3209700	Carson City	44,972	28.2	46.0	25.8	22,931	34.4	45.7	19.8	22,041	21.7	46.2	32.1
3223770	Enterprise CDP	95,331	33.9	48.3	17.8	49,117	38.0	47.4	14.6	46,214	29.5	49.3	21.2
3231900	Henderson city	216,705	28.7	49.3	21.9	102,390	29.8	52.8	17.4	114,315	27.8	46.2	26.0
3240000	Las Vegas city	473,491	33.1	43.3	23.6	236,916	36.6	44.1	19.4	236,575	29.7	42.5	27.8
3251800	North Las Vegas city	165,109	34.2	47.0	18.8	82,100	38.5	47.7	13.8	83,009	30.0	46.2	23.8
3254600	Paradise CDP	183,197	39.4	38.2	22.4	93,994	43.1	38.9	18.1	89,203	35.6	37.6	26.9
3260600	Reno city	186,097	35.8	42.1	22.1	93,798	40.2	42.0	17.7	92,299	31.3	42.2	26.5
3268400	Sparks city	73,422	29.5	46.9	23.5	35,474	33.5	48.7	17.8	37,948	25.8	45.2	28.9
3268585	Spring Valley CDP	154,228	35.3	42.7	22.0	75,281	38.5	44.2	17.3	78,947	32.3	41.3	26.4
3271400	Sunrise Manor CDP	142,887	36.9	42.2	20.9	72,121	41.0	42.7	16.4	70,766	32.7	41.8	25.5
3300000	**New Hampshire**	1,097,738	29.0	52.4	18.6	537,698	31.8	54.1	14.1	560,040	26.2	50.8	23.0
3345140	Manchester city	92,010	38.0	40.2	21.8	45,991	43.9	40.1	16.0	46,019	32.0	40.3	27.7
3350260	Nashua city	70,130	32.3	47.8	19.9	33,559	34.9	50.6	14.5	36,571	30.0	45.2	24.8
3400000	**New Jersey**	7,192,367	34.0	49.1	16.9	3,469,363	37.1	51.6	11.2	3,723,004	31.1	46.7	22.2
3403580	Bayonne city	52,902	38.6	42.5	19.0	25,825	42.0	43.2	14.8	27,077	35.3	41.8	22.9
3410000	Camden city	56,615	60.5	21.8	17.7	26,472	61.2	25.5	13.3	30,143	59.9	18.5	21.6
3413690	Clifton city	68,951	35.0	49.1	16.0	34,160	39.7	50.7	9.6	34,791	30.3	47.5	22.2
3419390	East Orange city	52,040	51.3	25.3	23.4	21,814	52.4	29.9	17.7	30,226	50.6	21.9	27.6
3421000	Elizabeth city	96,068	43.5	36.0	20.5	46,121	45.9	39.1	14.9	49,947	41.2	33.2	25.6
3432250	Hoboken city	45,574	56.4	33.4	10.2	22,443	58.3	33.8	7.9	23,131	54.5	33.0	12.5
3436000	Jersey City city	210,566	42.8	41.3	15.9	103,828	45.8	43.1	11.1	106,738	39.9	39.6	20.4
3451000	Newark city	217,635	53.5	27.6	18.9	107,829	56.6	29.4	14.0	109,806	50.3	26.0	23.7
3451210	New Brunswick city	44,515	68.4	21.1	10.5	22,189	70.9	23.0	6.1	22,326	65.9	19.2	14.9
3456550	Passaic city	51,473	51.2	34.3	14.5	25,497	55.4	35.9	8.7	25,976	47.0	32.8	20.2
3457000	Paterson city	112,777	50.7	33.0	16.3	52,935	52.2	36.8	11.0	59,842	49.3	29.7	20.9
3458200	Perth Amboy city	40,301	44.8	38.9	16.2	19,693	47.7	41.1	11.2	20,608	42.0	36.9	21.1
3459190	Plainfield city	40,408	49.6	31.2	19.2	20,665	53.5	32.0	14.5	19,743	45.6	30.3	24.1
3473110	Toms River CDP	73,751	30.6	50.4	19.0	35,529	33.9	53.0	13.0	38,222	27.4	48.0	24.5

Table C-4: Cities with a Population of 50,000 or More—Marriages and Births—*Continued*

State/place FIPS code	State/Place	Total women age 15 to 50 years	Percent of all women who had a birth in the past year	Percent of women who had a birth who were married (including separated and spouse absent):	Percent of women who had a birth who were partners in an unmarried partner household	Age of women who had a birth in the last year as a percent of all women who had a birth			Women who had a birth in the last year as a percent of all women in their age group		
						Age 15 to 19	Age 20 to 34	Age 35 to 50	Age 15 to 19	Age 20 to 34	Age 35 to 50
	Minnesota—cont'd										
2707966	Brooklyn Park city	8,397	7.9	52.3	10.1	20.4	51.7	27.9	11.3	9.2	5.4
2708794	Burnsville city	14,668	5.9	59.8	12.6	19.3	61.3	19.3	8.7	8.4	2.6
2713114	Coon Rapids city	15,553	5.1	78.1	1.8	0.0	84.8	15.2	0.0	9.5	1.8
2717000	Duluth city	22,576	4.9	64.1	15.8	6.5	81.1	12.3	1.8	8.1	1.8
2717288	Eagan city	16,360	6.5	72.3	10.1	0.6	68.7	30.7	0.3	11.1	4.1
2718116	Eden Prairie city	15,193	6.9	90.0	7.4	0.0	73.6	26.4	0.0	12.8	3.8
2735180	Lakeville city	15,279	5.5	89.7	4.5	2.3	75.7	22.1	0.7	13.0	2.4
2740166	Maple Grove city	16,157	5.4	84.8	0.0	8.0	76.8	15.2	3.4	11.7	1.6
2743000	Minneapolis city	112,730	5.4	59.2	8.4	5.9	74.4	19.7	2.8	7.4	3.2
2743252	Minnetonka city	11,009	5.6	94.1	5.9	0.0	69.1	30.9	0.0	9.1	3.8
2751730	Plymouth city	17,656	5.4	89.7	2.1	1.9	79.8	18.3	0.9	10.5	2.1
2754880	Rochester city	26,743	6.6	80.0	17.3	0.0	67.0	33.0	0.0	9.4	5.4
2756896	St. Cloud city	17,509	4.6	62.6	20.7	0.0	87.8	12.2	0.0	7.3	2.0
2758000	St. Paul city	78,908	6.5	62.5	12.2	6.7	73.1	20.2	3.3	9.4	3.6
2771428	Woodbury city	16,934	3.6	95.4	3.9	0.0	60.7	39.3	0.0	5.9	2.8
2800000	**Mississippi**	724,800	5.3	51.8	7.2	8.1	79.2	12.7	2.9	10.1	1.6
2829700	Gulfport city	17,409	5.0	57.9	16.3	6.2	92.3	1.5	3.0	9.7	0.2
2836000	Jackson city	47,501	5.1	27.1	5.3	14.0	79.9	6.0	4.7	8.6	0.8
2869280	Southaven city	13,684	5.1	86.6	6.2	0.0	66.0	34.0	0.0	8.2	3.7
2900000	**Missouri**	1,426,918	5.5	61.8	11.1	6.7	76.5	16.8	2.7	10.0	2.1
2906652	Blue Springs city	12,879	3.9	84.0	4.4	2.2	93.6	4.2	0.6	9.4	0.4
2915670	Columbia city	36,780	4.4	78.6	2.5	11.9	72.1	16.0	3.1	5.5	2.7
2924778	Florissant city	12,242	6.0	65.0	19.3	5.2	64.7	30.1	1.9	10.1	4.0
2935000	Independence city	25,778	6.1	54.0	12.0	3.9	93.0	3.1	2.2	12.1	0.4
2937592	Joplin city	12,426	6.6	59.5	11.8	1.2	88.6	10.2	0.7	11.8	1.7
2938000	Kansas City city	121,522	6.1	51.3	13.1	7.0	72.7	20.3	3.8	9.4	3.0
2941348	Lee's Summit city	22,901	4.2	65.1	9.9	3.1	63.8	33.0	0.8	7.5	2.9
2954074	O'Fallon city	20,838	5.4	68.2	18.5	5.4	70.2	24.4	2.9	9.9	2.6
2964082	St. Charles city	16,591	4.8	66.9	15.5	0.0	81.5	18.5	0.0	8.3	2.3
2964550	St. Joseph city	18,110	5.9	46.8	12.0	13.7	72.0	14.3	5.9	9.2	2.1
2965000	St. Louis city	87,421	5.4	43.4	6.5	9.6	75.1	15.4	4.6	7.8	2.2
2965126	St. Peters city	14,048	4.2	79.1	11.5	0.0	75.9	24.1	0.0	7.7	2.2
2970000	Springfield city	44,283	4.9	52.1	16.6	9.6	79.3	11.1	3.2	7.2	1.8
3000000	**Montana**	223,088	5.4	67.8	12.6	4.4	78.4	17.2	1.7	10.0	2.2
3006550	Billings city	25,391	5.2	63.1	20.1	4.3	75.6	20.1	1.8	8.4	2.5
3032800	Great Falls city	13,722	5.5	55.8	10.5	5.5	91.1	3.5	2.2	10.6	0.5
3050200	Missoula city	19,749	4.3	57.6	28.4	5.2	74.6	20.2	1.8	5.7	2.7
3100000	**Nebraska**	432,821	6.1	71.8	11.5	3.9	79.1	17.0	1.6	11.2	2.5
3103950	Bellevue city	13,615	6.4	60.7	16.0	2.3	83.5	14.2	0.9	12.9	2.2
3119595	Grand Island city	11,483	7.7	39.7	22.8	12.2	79.0	8.9	6.4	14.2	1.6
3128000	Lincoln city	68,607	6.6	68.6	14.0	3.9	78.0	18.1	1.8	10.1	3.4
3137000	Omaha city	107,318	5.2	65.9	8.9	3.9	79.1	17.0	1.5	8.7	2.3
3200000	**Nevada**	667,295	5.4	65.4	14.6	5.3	71.9	22.8	2.2	9.1	2.7
3209700	Carson City	11,410	4.2	75.8	2.5	8.3	82.7	9.0	2.2	8.9	0.8
3223770	Enterprise CDP	31,783	6.0	75.7	11.3	3.4	75.2	21.4	2.2	10.2	2.7
3231900	Henderson city	65,275	5.0	67.6	19.0	2.0	76.2	21.8	0.8	9.6	2.3
3240000	Las Vegas city	145,660	5.5	60.8	14.7	7.1	67.2	25.7	3.0	8.8	3.1
3251800	North Las Vegas city	58,090	4.4	64.3	15.7	5.6	72.3	22.1	1.8	7.7	2.2
3254600	Paradise CDP	57,019	4.8	68.3	15.7	4.4	67.7	27.9	1.7	7.3	3.1
3260600	Reno city	58,136	5.4	67.3	14.7	5.5	74.3	20.2	2.2	8.4	2.8
3268400	Sparks city	22,530	6.3	78.5	3.6	6.1	71.1	22.8	2.9	11.4	3.0
3268585	Spring Valley CDP	49,782	4.7	69.1	11.0	4.8	63.5	31.6	2.0	6.2	3.6
3271400	Sunrise Manor CDP	46,045	5.9	50.7	19.5	8.4	72.8	18.9	3.3	10.2	2.5
3300000	**New Hampshire**	311,299	4.6	71.3	11.5	3.3	71.3	25.3	1.0	8.8	2.4
3345140	Manchester city	27,647	5.3	67.5	15.2	5.6	76.1	18.3	2.6	8.9	2.2
3350260	Nashua city	22,395	5.1	75.5	12.2	7.9	78.6	13.5	2.9	9.8	1.5
3400000	**New Jersey**	2,149,755	4.9	69.3	8.5	2.8	69.3	27.9	1.1	8.8	2.9
3403580	Bayonne city	16,426	5.6	66.6	12.1	1.8	76.8	21.4	0.9	10.7	2.4
3410000	Camden city	21,249	7.3	16.9	17.8	10.6	72.2	17.2	5.4	11.6	3.1
3413690	Clifton city	20,921	4.7	77.0	1.2	3.2	74.8	22.0	1.5	8.2	2.2
3419390	East Orange city	18,124	4.8	34.7	14.8	1.4	65.0	33.7	0.6	7.5	3.5
3421000	Elizabeth city	33,962	7.4	47.6	21.7	4.3	77.4	18.3	2.7	11.8	3.4
3432250	Hoboken city	18,541	4.1	88.2	0.0	0.0	58.0	42.0	0.0	3.6	5.6
3436000	Jersey City city	72,972	6.0	73.0	7.3	3.2	70.1	26.6	2.1	8.2	4.1
3451000	Newark city	74,179	5.8	28.7	12.7	3.1	78.8	18.1	1.4	9.9	2.5
3451210	New Brunswick city	18,341	5.6	39.3	24.7	7.2	84.4	8.3	2.1	8.2	2.0
3456550	Passaic city	18,434	4.1	70.8	9.9	2.1	76.6	21.3	0.5	7.4	2.2
3457000	Paterson city	40,076	6.7	42.0	9.6	5.4	82.0	12.6	2.5	12.2	2.1
3458200	Perth Amboy city	13,350	6.5	61.8	6.1	9.7	66.4	23.9	4.7	9.9	3.6
3459190	Plainfield city	12,974	9.7	19.3	21.4	4.1	86.8	9.2	3.0	19.7	2.0
3473110	Toms River CDP	20,326	3.6	87.5	3.7	1.7	48.1	50.3	0.4	4.8	3.6

State/ place FIPS code	State/Place	Total population 15 years and older	Marital status, percent			Male population 15 years and older	Male, marital status, percent			Female population 15 years and older	Female, marital status, percent		
			Never married	Now married (except separated)	Separated, widowed, or divorced		Never married	Now married (except separated)	Separated, widowed, or divorced		Never married	Now married (except separated)	Separated, widowed, or divorced
	New Jersey—cont'd												
3474000	Trenton city	66,682	52.8	28.3	18.9	34,490	56.4	29.0	14.6	32,192	48.9	27.5	23.6
3474630	Union City city	55,369	44.4	35.0	20.6	28,030	49.5	37.0	13.4	27,339	39.1	33.0	27.9
3476070	Vineland city	48,206	38.5	41.9	19.6	22,434	36.4	46.6	17.0	25,772	40.3	37.8	21.9
3479610	West New York town	42,185	41.8	38.8	19.3	20,822	45.1	41.1	13.9	21,363	38.7	36.7	24.7
3500000	**New Mexico**	1,655,442	33.6	45.7	20.8	813,817	36.8	47.5	15.8	841,625	30.5	43.9	25.6
3502000	Albuquerque city	444,333	35.7	43.1	21.1	213,457	39.0	45.5	15.5	230,876	32.7	41.0	26.3
3539380	Las Cruces city	79,354	38.5	40.7	20.9	38,851	43.8	41.7	14.6	40,503	33.4	39.7	26.9
3563460	Rio Rancho city	70,148	29.2	50.5	20.3	33,651	31.1	52.6	16.4	36,497	27.6	48.5	23.9
3570500	Santa Fe city	58,383	33.2	40.7	26.1	26,791	35.6	45.6	18.8	31,592	31.1	36.5	32.3
3600000	**New York**	16,065,870	38.0	44.4	17.6	7,698,201	41.0	46.9	12.1	8,367,669	35.3	42.0	22.7
3601000	Albany city	83,807	58.7	25.3	16.0	40,036	62.6	26.9	10.4	43,771	55.1	23.8	21.1
3608026	Brentwood CDP	47,306	45.1	40.2	14.7	24,079	48.5	41.2	10.3	23,227	41.6	39.1	19.3
3611000	Buffalo city	210,810	50.9	28.2	20.9	99,392	54.2	29.7	16.1	111,418	48.1	26.8	25.1
3615000	Cheektowaga CDP	64,108	35.8	43.4	20.8	29,763	38.4	46.9	14.7	34,345	33.5	40.4	26.1
3633139	Hempstead village	43,283	48.4	33.8	17.9	21,445	52.3	35.5	12.2	21,838	44.5	32.1	23.4
3637737	Irondequoit CDP	42,968	31.5	47.3	21.2	19,596	32.5	51.9	15.6	23,372	30.7	43.4	25.9
3642081	Levittown CDP	43,402	30.0	55.3	14.7	21,101	33.1	56.9	10.0	22,301	27.1	53.8	19.1
3649121	Mount Vernon city	54,827	44.0	35.4	20.6	24,097	44.5	41.4	14.0	30,730	43.6	30.6	25.8
3650617	New Rochelle city	64,238	35.3	47.4	17.2	30,774	37.9	50.6	11.5	33,464	33.0	44.5	22.5
3651000	New York city	6,850,565	44.1	38.6	17.2	3,213,783	46.8	41.9	11.3	3,636,782	41.8	35.7	22.5
3663000	Rochester city	167,113	53.8	25.0	21.2	79,931	56.7	26.7	16.6	87,182	51.2	23.4	25.4
3665508	Schenectady city	53,627	45.3	33.7	21.0	26,380	48.8	35.2	16.0	27,247	41.9	32.3	25.8
3673000	Syracuse city	116,398	53.8	25.9	20.2	54,033	55.2	28.2	16.6	62,365	52.7	24.0	23.3
3674183	Tonawanda CDP	49,159	31.0	47.7	21.4	23,033	35.3	50.9	13.8	26,126	27.2	44.9	28.0
3676540	Utica city	48,957	44.1	33.0	22.9	23,317	48.7	34.8	16.5	25,640	40.0	31.4	28.6
3681677	White Plains city	47,292	34.9	46.6	18.5	22,272	37.8	49.6	12.5	25,020	32.3	43.9	23.9
3684000	Yonkers city	161,536	39.7	42.0	18.3	75,078	42.3	46.1	11.5	86,458	37.5	38.3	24.2
3700000	**North Carolina**	7,842,120	31.0	48.9	20.1	3,776,005	34.1	51.3	14.7	4,066,115	28.1	46.7	25.2
3702140	Asheville city	71,020	38.0	37.2	24.7	32,615	41.7	40.7	17.6	38,405	34.9	34.3	30.8
3709060	Burlington city	41,823	31.7	43.1	25.2	18,808	32.5	49.2	18.3	23,015	31.1	38.1	30.7
3710740	Cary town	113,145	25.9	61.0	13.1	55,664	29.4	62.4	8.2	57,481	22.4	59.7	17.9
3711800	Chapel Hill town	50,701	54.2	37.2	8.5	23,348	53.6	41.2	5.2	27,353	54.8	33.9	11.4
3712000	Charlotte city	610,571	39.9	42.3	17.8	288,840	41.6	45.7	12.7	321,731	38.4	39.2	22.4
3714100	Concord city	63,263	29.5	51.9	18.6	30,384	33.4	54.7	12.0	32,879	25.9	49.3	24.8
3719000	Durham city	192,926	41.8	40.2	18.0	89,111	43.9	43.1	13.0	103,815	40.0	37.7	22.3
3722920	Fayetteville city	158,733	32.5	45.7	21.9	77,080	37.1	47.4	15.4	81,653	28.1	44.0	27.9
3725580	Gastonia city	56,453	33.6	44.0	22.4	26,581	37.3	46.4	16.3	29,872	30.3	41.8	27.9
3728000	Greensboro city	224,715	41.3	39.5	19.2	104,315	43.8	43.1	13.2	120,400	39.2	36.4	24.5
3728080	Greenville city	73,593	55.5	29.7	14.8	32,260	56.7	33.8	9.6	41,333	54.6	26.6	18.9
3731400	High Point city	85,729	35.0	43.2	21.8	39,003	37.2	48.3	14.5	46,726	33.3	38.9	27.9
3734200	Jacksonville city	53,403	37.1	48.7	14.2	32,127	47.3	42.2	10.5	21,276	21.6	58.5	19.9
3755000	Raleigh city	339,663	42.4	40.5	17.1	162,331	46.1	42.6	11.3	177,332	39.0	38.6	22.3
3757500	Rocky Mount city	46,123	39.2	37.1	23.8	20,750	41.3	41.0	17.6	25,373	37.4	33.8	28.8
3774440	Wilmington city	93,628	42.9	37.5	19.7	43,829	44.8	40.4	14.7	49,799	41.1	34.9	24.0
3775000	Winston-Salem city	185,250	40.0	40.1	19.9	85,488	42.3	43.5	14.2	99,762	38.1	37.2	24.7
3800000	**North Dakota**	571,203	31.6	52.0	16.4	290,486	36.0	51.8	12.2	280,717	27.1	52.2	20.7
3807200	Bismarck city	53,249	32.8	48.3	18.9	25,495	36.8	50.5	12.7	27,754	29.1	46.3	24.6
3825700	Fargo city	91,611	43.6	41.3	15.1	45,629	47.1	42.2	10.8	45,982	40.1	40.5	19.4
3832060	Grand Forks city	45,515	45.7	39.4	14.9	23,420	49.8	39.0	11.2	22,095	41.4	39.7	18.8
3900000	**Ohio**	9,357,346	31.3	48.1	20.6	4,524,839	34.4	50.0	15.6	4,832,507	28.5	46.3	25.2
3901000	Akron city	161,010	43.1	33.7	23.2	75,982	46.6	36.1	17.3	85,028	40.0	31.5	28.5
3912000	Canton city	56,820	37.2	36.3	26.5	24,815	36.6	41.3	22.1	32,005	37.6	32.5	29.9
3915000	Cincinnati city	240,140	51.4	27.3	21.3	113,621	53.7	29.6	16.6	126,519	49.3	25.2	25.5
3916000	Cleveland city	315,644	49.2	25.6	25.2	148,963	52.4	27.4	20.2	166,681	46.4	23.9	29.7
3918000	Columbus city	649,697	43.8	36.5	19.7	313,956	46.8	38.2	15.0	335,741	41.0	35.0	24.0
3921000	Dayton city	117,742	48.1	26.3	25.6	56,671	51.7	27.7	20.6	61,071	44.7	25.0	30.2
3925256	Elyria city	43,954	36.6	41.1	22.3	20,432	38.7	44.1	17.3	23,522	34.8	38.6	26.6
3933012	Hamilton city	48,990	31.5	41.3	27.2	22,847	35.8	44.2	20.0	26,143	27.8	38.9	33.4
3940040	Kettering city	46,403	30.4	46.4	23.2	21,910	33.6	49.6	16.9	24,493	27.6	43.6	28.8
3941664	Lakewood city	42,728	41.9	36.7	21.4	20,198	46.0	39.2	14.8	22,530	38.2	34.4	27.4
3944856	Lorain city	50,504	35.6	40.2	24.1	22,919	41.2	43.6	15.2	27,585	30.9	37.5	31.6
3961000	Parma city	67,725	32.3	47.3	20.4	32,259	36.0	50.3	13.7	35,466	29.0	44.6	26.4
3974118	Springfield city	47,188	34.8	37.6	27.5	21,653	38.4	40.5	21.1	25,535	31.9	35.2	32.9
3977000	Toledo city	227,839	41.9	34.1	24.0	109,635	45.8	35.4	18.8	118,204	38.2	33.0	28.8
3988000	Youngstown city	53,587	44.6	26.7	28.7	25,795	47.7	29.8	22.5	27,792	41.7	23.7	34.6
4000000	**Oklahoma**	3,027,585	27.3	50.6	22.0	1,486,092	30.8	52.0	17.1	1,541,493	24.0	49.3	26.7
4009050	Broken Arrow city	79,764	23.5	58.3	18.2	38,796	26.4	59.7	13.8	40,968	20.7	57.0	22.2
4023200	Edmond city	67,597	27.5	56.6	15.9	32,898	30.7	57.6	11.6	34,699	24.4	55.7	19.9
4041850	Lawton city	76,947	32.6	42.6	24.8	40,461	39.4	42.8	17.8	36,486	25.0	42.4	32.5
4048350	Midwest City city	44,733	30.0	44.3	25.7	20,850	34.2	47.6	18.1	23,883	26.2	41.4	32.4
4049200	Moore city	44,757	26.3	52.6	21.0	21,222	28.3	55.8	15.8	23,535	24.5	49.8	25.7
4052500	Norman city	96,325	40.8	42.3	16.9	47,608	44.8	42.7	12.5	48,717	36.8	42.0	21.2

Table C-4: Cities with a Population of 50,000 or More—Marriages and Births—*Continued*

State/place FIPS code	State/Place	Total women age 15 to 50 years	Percent of all women who had a birth in the past year	Percent of women who had a birth who were married (including separated and spouse absent):	Percent of women who had a birth who were partners in an unmarried partner household	Age of women who had a birth in the last year as a percent of all women who had a birth			Women who had a birth in the last year as a percent of all women in their age group		
						Age 15 to 19	Age 20 to 34	Age 35 to 50	Age 15 to 19	Age 20 to 34	Age 35 to 50
	New Jersey—cont'd										
3474000	Trenton city	21,919	5.0	33.0	8.9	16.2	66.9	16.9	5.9	7.7	2.0
3474630	Union City city	17,632	4.9	45.8	25.5	4.2	87.0	8.8	1.8	9.4	1.0
3476070	Vineland city	14,983	4.6	61.2	15.9	6.1	72.4	21.4	1.9	8.2	2.2
3479610	West New York town	14,281	4.9	76.1	7.3	5.6	78.4	16.0	2.8	7.9	1.9
3500000	**New Mexico**.............................	483,237	5.9	53.0	13.7	8.3	75.2	16.5	3.3	10.5	2.3
3502000	Albuquerque city	139,135	5.7	60.3	13.7	4.2	76.2	19.6	1.9	9.4	2.7
3539380	Las Cruces city	25,709	6.0	55.1	6.6	8.8	75.1	16.2	3.5	9.2	2.7
3563460	Rio Rancho city	21,934	6.9	75.1	9.1	0.0	71.3	28.7	0.0	12.5	4.4
3570500	Santa Fe city	15,264	4.1	64.7	7.5	26.8	59.3	13.9	7.7	6.0	1.3
3600000	**New York**..................................	4,921,807	4.9	65.5	9.2	3.7	68.4	27.8	1.4	7.8	3.0
3601000	Albany city	27,812	4.0	42.9	20.0	4.6	66.7	28.7	1.0	5.0	3.9
3608026	Brentwood CDP	16,403	5.8	36.7	27.8	2.1	71.8	26.1	1.0	8.9	3.6
3611000	Buffalo city	68,859	5.7	47.0	12.2	5.5	76.5	18.0	2.2	8.8	2.8
3615000	Cheektowaga CDP	18,656	4.3	32.8	22.7	0.0	82.8	17.2	0.0	8.3	1.6
3633139	Hempstead village	13,543	6.6	35.7	18.0	4.9	80.9	14.2	3.1	11.5	2.2
3637737	Irondequoit CDP	12,501	6.5	62.9	8.4	1.1	83.4	15.5	0.6	13.7	2.1
3642081	Levittown CDP	12,866	4.6	83.2	0.0	0.0	68.0	32.0	0.0	8.4	2.9
3649121	Mount Vernon city	18,725	6.8	46.6	7.7	15.7	57.8	26.5	7.9	10.0	3.9
3650617	New Rochelle city	18,443	4.2	77.5	9.5	0.0	66.1	33.9	0.0	6.6	3.3
3651000	New York city	2,278,684	4.9	64.1	6.9	3.8	67.3	28.9	1.7	7.0	3.4
3663000	Rochester city	57,953	6.1	29.1	8.7	6.2	74.6	19.1	2.9	8.8	3.4
3665508	Schenectady city	17,108	4.7	54.0	10.4	0.0	89.1	10.9	0.0	9.0	1.3
3673000	Syracuse city	41,223	6.3	36.5	12.5	8.8	77.4	13.9	2.8	9.8	2.8
3674183	Tonawanda CDP	12,698	4.3	65.7	20.6	0.0	86.0	14.0	0.0	8.3	1.4
3676540	Utica city	14,422	7.3	46.4	21.7	14.3	62.9	22.9	6.3	10.0	4.5
3681677	White Plains city	14,138	6.5	73.3	4.9	1.6	63.5	34.9	1.3	9.6	4.6
3684000	Yonkers city	49,584	7.3	61.8	8.5	6.3	66.7	27.0	3.6	11.1	4.5
3700000	**North Carolina**........................	2,387,385	5.4	63.0	9.4	5.9	74.3	19.9	2.4	9.9	2.4
3702140	Asheville city	21,806	4.8	69.1	8.3	2.5	69.0	28.5	1.4	6.5	3.4
3709060	Burlington city	12,598	4.9	73.9	4.5	2.9	87.8	9.2	1.1	9.0	1.2
3710740	Cary town	37,072	5.4	86.2	4.3	0.0	74.0	26.0	0.0	11.2	2.6
3711800	Chapel Hill town	0	0.0	0.0	0.0	0.0	0.0	0.0	0.0	0.0	0.0
3712000	Charlotte city	218,823	5.5	60.5	7.3	4.6	69.0	26.4	2.2	8.4	3.3
3714100	Concord city	21,112	5.3	66.3	5.8	17.6	63.8	18.5	8.1	9.6	1.8
3719000	Durham city	0	0.0	0.0	0.0	0.0	0.0	0.0	0.0	0.0	0.0
3722920	Fayetteville city	53,560	6.7	71.9	6.4	8.6	79.9	11.5	5.1	10.6	2.1
3725580	Gastonia city	17,702	7.0	47.3	12.6	9.6	79.4	11.0	5.0	13.8	1.6
3728000	Greensboro city	76,377	5.6	58.4	12.1	5.2	72.8	22.1	2.0	8.5	3.2
3728080	Greenville city	76,377	5.6	58.4	12.1	5.2	72.8	22.1	2.0	8.5	3.2
3731400	High Point city	29,134	6.8	63.7	15.5	0.2	79.9	19.9	0.1	13.3	3.0
3734200	Jacksonville city	15,510	12.4	80.1	10.5	7.6	87.4	5.0	7.5	17.6	2.4
3755000	Raleigh city	0	0.0	0.0	0.0	0.0	0.0	0.0	0.0	0.0	0.0
3757500	Rocky Mount city	14,119	6.2	41.0	7.8	5.3	89.2	5.5	2.2	13.3	0.8
3774440	Wilmington city	30,743	4.7	49.5	19.6	12.2	77.1	10.7	3.6	7.1	1.5
3775000	Winston-Salem city	60,709	5.0	60.3	12.5	9.3	79.4	11.2	3.3	8.7	1.4
3800000	**North Dakota**..........................	161,588	6.6	68.3	14.0	5.0	81.3	13.7	2.3	11.4	2.3
3807200	Bismarck city	15,251	5.6	55.9	20.3	0.0	82.2	17.8	0.0	9.0	2.7
3825700	Fargo city	31,011	6.0	79.2	6.6	3.7	80.3	16.0	1.6	8.6	3.2
3832060	Grand Forks city	14,741	5.2	55.9	28.7	11.6	82.1	6.2	3.7	7.7	1.2
3900000	**Ohio**	2,710,248	5.3	59.5	11.6	5.4	77.3	17.3	2.0	10.0	2.0
3901000	Akron city	50,321	6.5	36.1	12.3	6.5	85.1	8.4	3.0	12.2	1.4
3912000	Canton city	18,617	4.6	32.0	21.1	6.4	90.6	3.0	2.1	8.8	0.4
3915000	Cincinnati city	80,541	5.8	38.7	6.2	4.7	82.5	12.8	2.0	9.1	2.2
3916000	Cleveland city	99,615	5.4	21.9	14.4	12.6	74.2	13.2	5.0	8.6	1.8
3918000	Columbus city	0	0.0	0.0	0.0	0.0	0.0	0.0	0.0	0.0	0.0
3921000	Dayton city	37,648	5.6	34.0	12.0	7.3	81.3	11.4	2.4	9.3	1.8
3925256	Elyria city	13,231	6.2	33.2	20.9	0.6	88.8	10.6	0.3	11.9	1.7
3933012	Hamilton city	14,714	8.7	40.8	16.0	5.5	83.6	10.8	5.1	15.1	2.2
3940040	Kettering city	12,971	5.9	54.6	8.9	5.6	84.4	9.9	2.4	11.7	1.3
3941664	Lakewood city	14,235	4.3	73.4	20.4	0.0	79.3	20.7	0.0	6.5	2.3
3944856	Lorain city	15,275	4.9	28.6	12.2	17.0	59.9	23.1	5.4	7.9	2.4
3961000	Parma city	18,681	4.5	67.8	10.5	4.9	72.7	22.4	1.5	8.0	2.3
3974118	Springfield city	14,530	5.7	30.4	18.6	6.5	82.5	11.0	2.5	10.1	1.6
3977000	Toledo city	70,658	5.5	47.5	12.3	4.3	85.1	10.6	1.7	10.2	1.4
3988000	Youngstown city	14,799	7.6	26.7	13.9	11.8	71.8	16.4	5.2	12.4	3.2
4000000	**Oklahoma**	898,579	6.0	63.8	11.8	7.0	80.4	12.6	3.0	10.9	1.8
4009050	Broken Arrow city	24,600	5.0	82.4	6.9	4.3	75.4	20.3	1.7	9.2	2.1
4023200	Edmond city	21,071	5.2	79.4	6.2	3.6	82.6	13.7	1.2	10.6	1.6
4041850	Lawton city	23,965	7.7	61.2	8.4	5.8	88.3	5.9	3.8	13.2	1.3
4048350	Midwest City city	13,858	4.7	61.3	10.0	6.9	77.5	15.6	2.7	8.5	1.6
4049200	Moore city	16,089	5.4	71.4	0.0	8.1	81.3	10.6	4.3	8.4	1.6
4052500	Norman city	31,787	3.6	85.3	6.4	2.6	85.7	11.7	0.6	5.8	1.4

Table C-4: Cities with a Population of 50,000 or More—Marriages and Births—*Continued*

State/place FIPS code	State/Place	Total population 15 years and older	Marital status, percent			Male population 15 years and older	Male, marital status, percent			Female population 15 years and older	Female, marital status, percent		
			Never married	Now married (except separated)	Separated, widowed, or divorced		Never married	Now married (except separated)	Separated, widowed, or divorced		Never married	Now married (except separated)	Separated, widowed, or divorced
	Oklahoma—cont'd												
4055000	Oklahoma City city..............	468,392	31.9	47.3	20.8	228,537	34.9	48.7	16.4	239,855	29.1	45.9	25.0
4075000	Tulsa city..........................	312,956	33.5	42.9	23.6	149,400	36.7	45.5	17.8	163,556	30.6	40.5	28.9
4100000	**Oregon**..............................	3,186,598	30.0	49.5	20.5	1,564,755	33.4	50.9	15.7	1,621,843	26.8	48.1	25.1
4101000	Albany city........................	40,487	28.8	48.6	22.6	20,147	32.9	49.4	17.7	20,340	24.7	47.8	27.4
4101650	Aloha CDP........................	39,378	31.2	52.2	16.6	19,437	34.4	53.4	12.1	19,941	28.1	51.0	20.9
4105350	Beaverton city..................	74,092	32.9	47.2	19.9	35,772	35.7	49.2	15.1	38,320	30.4	45.3	24.3
4105800	Bend city..........................	63,807	28.0	50.1	21.9	31,051	31.0	52.1	16.8	32,756	25.1	48.2	26.7
4115800	Corvallis city.....................	48,430	51.9	34.5	13.6	24,543	56.6	34.6	8.8	23,887	47.2	34.4	18.4
4123850	Eugene city.......................	135,523	43.2	37.1	19.7	66,505	48.8	37.5	13.7	69,018	37.9	36.7	25.4
4131250	Gresham city.....................	84,723	33.6	44.3	22.1	41,333	36.8	46.4	16.8	43,390	30.5	42.2	27.2
4134100	Hillsboro city....................	74,089	31.1	51.0	18.0	35,968	34.5	53.0	12.5	38,121	27.9	49.0	23.1
4147000	Medford city.....................	61,321	28.4	48.5	23.1	29,523	31.1	51.7	17.3	31,798	25.9	45.6	28.5
4159000	Portland city.....................	507,280	40.7	40.5	18.8	250,070	43.8	41.5	14.7	257,210	37.6	39.5	22.9
4164900	Salem city.........................	124,902	32.7	44.7	22.6	61,202	35.9	46.3	17.8	63,700	29.7	43.2	27.1
4169600	Springfield city..................	48,092	33.2	43.7	23.0	23,011	35.2	46.0	18.8	25,081	31.4	41.7	26.9
4200000	**Pennsylvania**	10,514,479	33.3	48.0	18.8	5,082,914	36.4	50.1	13.5	5,431,565	30.4	46.0	23.6
4202000	Allentown city...................	92,664	45.4	34.4	20.2	43,804	47.8	37.1	15.1	48,860	43.2	32.0	24.8
4206088	Bethlehem city..................	63,350	43.0	36.5	20.5	30,524	48.6	38.9	12.5	32,826	37.8	34.3	27.9
4224000	Erie city............................	81,582	43.5	35.9	20.6	39,482	47.5	38.1	14.4	42,100	39.7	33.9	26.4
4241216	Lancaster city....................	47,079	50.9	29.7	19.4	22,386	53.2	31.7	15.1	24,693	48.8	28.0	23.2
4242928	Levittown CDP...................	41,875	33.8	46.8	19.4	19,907	38.1	49.0	12.9	21,968	29.9	44.7	25.3
4260000	Philadelphia city................	1,257,813	52.2	28.7	19.1	583,308	54.8	31.6	13.7	674,505	50.1	26.2	23.7
4261000	Pittsburgh city..................	264,914	51.2	30.9	17.9	126,860	54.9	32.7	12.4	138,054	47.9	29.3	22.8
4263624	Reading city......................	65,651	46.5	30.5	22.9	31,570	49.6	33.0	17.4	34,081	43.7	28.2	28.1
4269000	Scranton city.....................	62,746	41.6	37.0	21.4	29,653	44.1	40.5	15.4	33,093	39.3	34.0	26.7
4400000	**Rhode Island**....................	873,678	35.7	44.7	19.6	417,748	39.0	47.4	13.7	455,930	32.6	42.3	25.1
4419180	Cranston city.....................	67,374	35.1	44.8	20.0	33,598	39.6	46.0	14.3	33,776	30.6	43.7	25.7
4454640	Pawtucket city..................	57,201	39.1	38.9	22.1	27,950	42.4	40.5	17.1	29,251	35.9	37.4	26.8
4459000	Providence city..................	144,761	54.7	28.6	16.7	69,964	57.9	30.5	11.6	74,797	51.6	26.9	21.5
4474300	Warwick city.....................	69,549	28.8	48.6	22.6	32,580	32.4	52.3	15.3	36,969	25.6	45.4	29.0
4500000	**South Carolina**.................	3,824,255	31.8	47.3	21.0	1,839,923	34.7	49.6	15.7	1,984,332	29.0	45.1	25.8
4513330	Charleston city..................	106,136	42.5	38.5	19.0	49,726	45.0	40.9	14.1	56,410	40.3	36.3	23.4
4516000	Columbia city....................	113,016	54.9	28.2	17.0	59,068	59.0	28.8	12.2	53,948	50.4	27.4	22.2
4530850	Greenville city...................	50,241	41.5	36.4	22.1	24,609	43.7	38.8	17.6	25,632	39.4	34.1	26.4
4548535	Mount Pleasant town.........	57,376	26.8	54.0	19.2	26,971	26.9	56.8	16.4	30,405	26.7	51.5	21.8
4550875	North Charleston city.........	80,081	41.6	37.0	21.4	39,768	46.8	38.4	14.7	40,313	36.5	35.6	27.9
4561405	Rock Hill city....................	54,780	39.0	40.6	20.4	25,057	39.5	44.3	16.2	29,723	38.5	37.5	24.0
4600000	**South Dakota**	662,338	30.1	51.8	18.0	330,968	33.6	52.3	14.1	331,370	26.7	51.4	22.0
4652980	Rapid City city...................	55,508	31.4	44.7	23.9	27,489	36.1	45.5	18.4	28,019	26.9	43.8	29.3
4659020	Sioux Falls city..................	127,007	34.0	48.4	17.7	62,664	36.8	49.2	13.9	64,343	31.2	47.5	21.3
4700000	**Tennessee**	5,211,459	28.9	49.4	21.7	2,511,894	31.9	51.5	16.6	2,699,565	26.2	47.4	26.5
4703440	Bartlett city......................	45,611	24.5	58.0	17.5	21,502	26.3	61.1	12.6	24,109	22.9	55.3	21.9
4714000	Chattanooga city...............	140,854	37.7	38.2	24.2	67,101	41.9	40.6	17.5	73,753	33.8	36.0	30.2
4715160	Clarksville city..................	106,934	28.1	52.8	19.1	52,151	31.5	53.7	14.7	54,783	24.8	51.9	23.3
4727740	Franklin city.....................	51,825	23.1	60.2	16.7	24,193	25.8	63.7	10.4	27,632	20.7	57.2	22.1
4733280	Hendersonville city............	42,389	24.1	56.5	19.4	19,915	26.3	61.2	12.4	22,474	22.1	52.4	25.5
4737640	Jackson city......................	53,294	37.4	39.2	23.4	23,809	38.8	44.5	16.8	29,485	36.2	35.0	28.8
4738320	Johnson City city...............	54,371	33.5	43.7	22.8	25,555	37.0	45.8	17.2	28,816	30.4	41.9	27.7
4739560	Kingsport city...................	43,499	21.3	51.8	26.9	19,927	24.8	56.0	19.2	23,572	18.4	48.3	33.4
4740000	Knoxville city....................	154,719	40.6	36.6	22.7	73,843	43.4	38.4	18.2	80,876	38.1	35.0	26.9
4748000	Memphis city....................	515,512	45.5	31.0	23.5	241,148	48.3	33.5	18.1	274,364	43.0	28.7	28.3
4751560	Murfreesboro city..............	92,746	38.1	44.4	17.5	45,326	42.6	45.1	12.3	47,420	33.8	43.6	22.5
4752006	Nashville-Davidson...........	507,576	40.4	39.1	20.6	242,927	42.5	42.0	15.5	264,649	38.4	36.4	25.2
4800000	**Texas**	20,196,175	31.7	49.4	18.9	9,951,393	35.0	51.0	14.0	10,244,782	28.6	47.7	23.7
4801000	Abilene city......................	97,602	36.2	43.0	20.8	50,417	40.7	43.2	16.1	47,185	31.4	42.9	25.8
4801924	Allen city..........................	66,522	24.8	61.3	13.9	30,904	25.5	66.0	8.5	35,618	24.2	57.2	18.6
4803000	Amarillo city.....................	150,160	29.1	48.9	22.0	72,338	32.3	51.4	16.3	77,822	26.2	46.5	27.3
4804000	Arlington city....................	290,981	34.9	47.3	17.7	141,483	37.7	49.3	13.0	149,498	32.4	45.4	22.2
4804462	Atascocita CDP..................	51,069	29.6	55.8	14.7	24,778	29.2	58.5	12.3	26,291	29.9	53.2	16.9
4805000	Austin city........................	701,692	43.6	39.1	17.3	352,954	47.5	39.9	12.6	348,738	39.7	38.2	22.0
4806128	Baytown city.....................	55,304	30.5	46.5	23.0	26,659	32.9	49.1	18.1	28,645	28.3	44.1	27.6
4807000	Beaumont city...................	93,145	36.1	38.7	25.2	43,993	37.4	42.4	20.1	49,152	34.8	35.4	29.8
4810768	Brownsville city.................	131,718	33.2	47.9	18.9	60,853	35.3	52.2	12.5	70,865	31.4	44.2	24.4
4810912	Bryan city.........................	61,253	40.8	39.3	19.9	31,671	46.5	38.7	14.8	29,582	34.7	40.0	25.3
4813024	Carrollton city..................	99,715	29.8	52.9	17.4	48,851	33.3	54.8	11.9	50,864	26.4	51.0	22.6
4813552	Cedar Park city.................	43,669	27.2	58.3	14.5	20,773	31.2	62.1	6.7	22,896	23.5	54.8	21.7
4815976	College Station city............	84,926	62.5	30.1	7.4	43,448	65.0	29.9	5.1	41,478	59.9	30.3	9.8
4816432	Conroe city.......................	46,782	33.7	44.1	22.2	21,670	36.3	50.1	13.6	25,112	31.4	39.0	29.6
4817000	Corpus Christi city.............	245,880	33.1	45.2	21.7	119,674	36.6	47.6	15.8	126,206	29.8	42.9	27.3
4819000	Dallas city........................	964,074	40.9	39.6	19.5	479,934	44.2	41.2	14.6	484,140	37.5	38.1	24.4
4819972	Denton city.......................	101,425	48.9	36.3	14.7	48,313	50.6	39.3	10.1	53,112	47.4	33.6	19.0

Table C-4: Cities with a Population of 50,000 or More—Marriages and Births—*Continued*

State/place FIPS code	State/Place	Total women age 15 to 50 years	Percent of all women who had a birth in the past year	Percent of women who had a birth who were married (including separated and spouse absent):	Percent of women who had a birth who were partners in an unmarried partner household	Age of women who had a birth in the last year as a percent of all women who had a birth			Women who had a birth in the last year as a percent of all women in their age group		
						Age 15 to 19	Age 20 to 34	Age 35 to 50	Age 15 to 19	Age 20 to 34	Age 35 to 50
	Oklahoma—cont'd										
4055000	Oklahoma City city..............	149,782	6.9	67.3	10.4	5.8	79.9	14.3	3.5	11.4	2.5
4075000	Tulsa city.......................	97,739	6.1	54.9	14.6	7.7	80.2	12.1	3.7	10.3	1.9
4100000	**Oregon**........................	919,777	5.0	68.1	11.9	3.8	74.8	21.5	1.5	8.8	2.4
4101000	Albany city.....................	12,189	3.8	78.6	6.5	0.0	62.2	37.8	0.0	5.2	3.2
4101650	Aloha CDP.......................	13,555	8.7	62.4	9.8	0.0	81.1	18.9	0.0	14.5	3.9
4105350	Beaverton city..................	10,535	3.2	59.9	18.7	14.3	60.5	25.1	2.3	5.4	1.9
4105800	Bend city.......................	18,757	3.7	78.2	4.0	0.0	65.9	34.1	0.0	5.8	2.8
4115800	Corvallis city..................	16,384	3.1	69.3	7.6	6.7	70.3	23.1	1.1	4.0	2.7
4123850	Eugene city.....................	42,635	3.0	60.1	16.1	1.8	76.7	21.5	0.3	4.6	1.9
4131250	Gresham city....................	26,366	6.4	59.1	14.6	4.8	78.8	16.4	2.5	10.8	2.6
4134100	Hillsboro city..................	26,364	7.7	69.9	6.3	0.0	83.8	16.2	0.0	13.7	3.0
4147000	Medford city....................	18,065	6.0	54.7	33.7	0.6	84.1	15.3	0.2	11.0	2.2
4159000	Portland city...................	167,096	4.4	75.5	7.5	1.5	66.5	32.0	0.7	6.1	3.3
4164900	Salem city......................	37,768	6.4	65.0	15.6	3.2	71.1	25.6	1.4	10.1	4.1
4169600	Springfield city................	15,712	5.0	49.6	13.6	0.0	84.5	15.5	0.0	9.0	2.0
4200000	**Pennsylvania**.................	2,981,873	4.9	60.8	11.2	5.6	73.8	20.6	1.9	8.8	2.2
4202000	Allentown city..................	31,211	6.5	35.3	15.4	12.1	78.1	9.8	5.0	11.4	1.6
4206088	Bethlehem city..................	6,558	4.3	72.1	14.8	0.0	75.6	24.4	0.0	9.3	2.0
4224000	Erie city.......................	25,059	5.3	47.6	12.4	1.8	77.6	20.6	0.6	8.7	2.8
4241216	Lancaster city..................	16,792	8.4	33.4	8.5	11.9	81.5	6.7	5.9	13.9	1.7
4242928	Levittown CDP...................	12,179	4.9	57.8	13.8	0.0	82.0	18.0	0.0	9.5	2.0
4260000	Philadelphia city...............	423,500	5.3	38.1	9.8	12.2	68.8	18.9	5.2	7.3	2.7
4261000	Pittsburgh city.................	85,093	4.2	51.2	11.9	6.6	79.8	13.6	1.8	6.1	1.9
4263624	Reading city....................	23,274	8.6	35.8	19.2	8.0	86.7	5.2	4.0	17.4	1.1
4269000	Scranton city...................	18,527	4.4	60.4	20.5	1.1	77.3	21.6	0.3	7.0	2.6
4400000	**Rhode Island**.................	258,792	4.6	56.0	14.2	6.2	74.0	19.8	1.9	8.2	2.1
4419180	Cranston city...................	19,080	5.7	65.6	21.3	7.2	76.1	16.7	2.8	12.3	1.9
4454640	Pawtucket city..................	17,635	5.8	41.3	11.4	7.5	79.8	12.8	4.1	10.2	1.7
4459000	Providence city.................	53,562	4.9	41.4	15.5	10.6	71.1	18.3	3.0	6.8	2.8
4474300	Warwick city....................	18,209	4.4	69.5	15.5	2.8	88.3	8.9	1.0	9.6	0.8
4500000	**South Carolina**..............	1,134,527	5.5	54.6	8.6	6.5	76.6	17.0	2.6	10.0	2.1
4513330	Charleston city.................	35,360	3.4	67.1	2.3	0.0	76.6	23.4	0.0	4.7	2.4
4516000	Columbia city...................	8,294	3.0	54.8	15.2	0.0	86.8	13.2	0.0	7.5	0.8
4530850	Greenville city.................	16,250	4.5	86.0	1.0	0.0	53.2	46.8	0.0	4.6	5.6
4548535	Mount Pleasant town.............	18,152	4.0	76.7	0.0	23.3	60.3	16.4	9.1	5.8	1.3
4550875	North Charleston city...........	26,999	6.5	49.1	6.0	5.9	82.9	11.2	3.6	10.5	1.9
4561405	Rock Hill city..................	19,639	4.8	67.0	9.0	3.0	69.8	27.2	0.9	6.9	3.6
4600000	**South Dakota**.................	187,109	6.9	61.9	17.3	6.1	80.2	13.8	2.7	12.8	2.3
4652980	Rapid City city.................	15,508	7.7	44.1	23.9	22.6	73.3	4.1	12.7	12.2	0.8
4659020	Sioux Falls city................	39,668	8.0	68.4	16.8	0.0	89.3	10.7	0.0	14.1	2.2
4700000	**Tennessee**....................	1,562,075	5.4	60.2	9.9	6.7	76.2	17.1	2.8	10.0	2.1
4703440	Bartlett city...................	13,742	4.5	74.7	0.0	0.0	65.9	34.1	0.0	9.5	3.0
4714000	Chattanooga city................	41,759	5.6	45.7	9.0	6.8	75.2	18.0	2.7	9.5	2.4
4715160	Clarksville city................	25,704	5.2	81.3	7.2	4.5	75.9	19.5	2.0	9.5	2.2
4727740	Franklin city...................	16,608	3.4	84.0	5.0	0.0	64.9	35.1	0.0	6.5	2.2
4733280	Hendersonville city.............	12,994	4.7	68.9	2.8	0.0	86.9	13.1	0.0	12.3	1.2
4737640	Jackson city....................	17,770	5.2	46.0	15.7	3.6	80.9	15.5	1.2	9.1	2.1
4738320	Johnson City city...............	17,185	3.2	76.8	8.6	3.4	65.1	31.5	0.7	4.3	2.8
4739560	Kingsport city..................	11,420	4.7	50.7	4.3	5.6	79.1	15.4	2.8	9.3	1.4
4740000	Knoxville city..................	50,355	5.7	53.8	20.9	5.0	81.6	13.4	2.2	8.7	2.3
4748000	Memphis city....................	171,290	7.7	36.8	10.3	6.1	71.6	22.2	3.6	11.8	4.3
4751560	Murfreesboro city...............	32,994	4.5	72.7	8.5	2.6	88.8	8.6	1.0	7.6	1.1
4752006	Nashville-Davidson..............	172,315	5.1	60.8	11.6	3.8	74.1	22.1	1.8	7.5	2.9
4800000	**Texas**........................	6,524,003	6.0	65.0	8.2	8.0	73.0	19.0	3.4	10.3	2.6
4801000	Abilene city....................	29,463	6.6	60.1	14.9	10.2	87.7	2.1	4.3	11.3	0.4
4801924	Allen city......................	25,459	7.0	81.2	5.4	0.0	72.2	27.8	0.0	16.4	3.6
4803000	Amarillo city...................	47,960	6.8	62.3	9.4	9.3	73.9	16.8	4.7	10.9	2.8
4804000	Arlington city..................	100,454	6.3	56.4	14.3	8.4	76.4	15.3	3.9	10.8	2.3
4804462	Atascocita CDP..................	18,991	6.2	62.6	1.1	4.2	86.6	9.3	1.8	11.9	1.4
4805000	Austin city.....................	0	0.0	0.0	0.0	0.0	0.0	0.0	0.0	0.0	0.0
4806128	Baytown city....................	18,921	6.0	56.5	10.3	12.5	70.8	16.7	5.1	9.8	2.4
4807000	Beaumont city...................	29,224	6.0	45.1	14.4	20.6	69.1	10.4	7.7	9.0	1.6
4810768	Brownsville city................	46,768	5.5	72.6	4.7	8.6	70.4	21.0	2.7	9.7	2.8
4810912	Bryan city......................	20,096	7.1	61.6	10.8	2.3	66.1	31.6	1.9	8.6	6.2
4813024	Carrollton city.................	0	0.0	0.0	0.0	0.0	0.0	0.0	0.0	0.0	0.0
4813552	Cedar Park city.................	0	0.0	0.0	0.0	0.0	0.0	0.0	0.0	0.0	0.0
4815976	College Station city............	34,764	2.7	86.1	0.0	0.0	100.0	0.0	0.0	4.1	0.0
4816432	Conroe city.....................	16,631	4.6	60.0	9.3	8.7	73.7	17.6	3.0	7.4	2.0
4817000	Corpus Christi city.............	76,416	5.5	48.8	10.4	8.3	83.5	8.2	3.1	10.3	1.1
4819000	Dallas city.....................	0	0.0	0.0	0.0	0.0	0.0	0.0	0.0	0.0	0.0
4819972	Denton city.....................	4,826	4.1	57.1	0.0	0.0	88.4	11.6	0.0	7.8	1.1

Table C-4: Cities with a Population of 50,000 or More—Marriages and Births—*Continued*

State/place FIPS code	State/Place	Total population 15 years and older	Marital status, percent			Male population 15 years and older	Male, marital status, percent			Female population 15 years and older	Female, marital status, percent		
			Never married	Now married (except separated)	Separated, widowed, or divorced		Never married	Now married (except separated)	Separated, widowed, or divorced		Never married	Now married (except separated)	Separated, widowed, or divorced
	Texas—cont'd												
4820092	DeSoto city	41,864	31.3	46.0	22.6	18,942	35.9	51.1	13.0	22,922	27.6	41.8	30.6
4822660	Edinburg city	58,794	38.4	47.3	14.3	29,166	40.0	49.0	11.0	29,628	36.8	45.7	17.6
4824000	El Paso city	514,328	31.9	47.0	21.1	244,330	34.7	50.2	15.0	269,998	29.4	44.0	26.5
4824768	Euless city	41,925	33.6	43.1	23.2	20,656	37.9	44.9	17.3	21,269	29.5	41.5	29.0
4826232	Flower Mound town	50,945	23.2	64.4	12.4	24,522	24.7	67.4	7.9	26,423	21.8	61.5	16.6
4827000	Fort Worth city	584,376	33.9	46.1	20.0	278,736	35.9	49.2	14.9	305,640	32.0	43.3	24.8
4827684	Frisco city	92,131	21.8	65.0	13.2	44,751	23.9	67.9	8.2	47,380	19.7	62.3	18.0
4829000	Garland city	175,444	32.4	49.5	18.1	85,351	37.1	51.6	11.3	90,093	27.9	47.5	24.6
4829336	Georgetown city	43,021	19.3	61.9	18.8	20,579	22.3	66.1	11.6	22,442	16.5	58.0	25.5
4830464	Grand Prairie city	135,989	34.1	49.7	16.2	67,038	37.4	50.8	11.8	68,951	30.9	48.6	20.5
4832372	Harlingen city	48,023	32.6	46.9	20.5	23,025	36.3	49.6	14.0	24,998	29.2	44.3	26.5
4835000	Houston city	1,695,474	39.5	41.5	19.0	846,410	43.0	42.8	14.1	849,064	36.0	40.2	23.8
4837000	Irving city	173,136	33.0	49.2	17.8	86,093	35.1	51.0	13.9	87,043	30.9	47.4	21.7
4839148	Killeen city	98,351	29.3	51.1	19.6	47,662	34.5	51.1	14.4	50,689	24.5	51.1	24.5
4841464	Laredo city	174,024	35.8	47.6	16.6	83,206	37.9	51.3	10.7	90,818	33.8	44.1	22.1
4841980	League City city	68,734	25.9	58.2	15.9	33,751	29.8	60.2	10.0	34,983	22.2	56.2	21.7
4842508	Lewisville city	76,100	31.7	49.2	19.1	36,460	32.8	52.0	15.2	39,640	30.6	46.6	22.8
4843888	Longview city	64,143	31.0	45.4	23.6	31,540	36.7	46.4	16.9	32,603	25.5	44.5	30.0
4845000	Lubbock city	188,532	40.1	41.2	18.7	91,905	43.7	42.8	13.5	96,627	36.8	39.7	23.5
4845384	McAllen city	103,016	29.9	52.1	18.0	49,578	32.6	54.2	13.2	53,438	27.5	50.1	22.4
4845744	McKinney city	105,842	25.5	59.3	15.1	50,987	28.9	61.8	9.3	54,855	22.4	57.0	20.6
4846452	Mansfield city	43,948	23.9	61.0	15.1	21,609	26.5	62.1	11.4	22,339	21.4	59.9	18.8
4847892	Mesquite city	107,511	33.0	47.6	19.4	48,966	33.6	53.0	13.4	58,545	32.6	43.0	24.4
4848072	Midland city	91,278	30.3	51.6	18.1	43,656	33.6	53.2	13.2	47,622	27.3	50.1	22.7
4848768	Mission city	57,182	27.2	59.4	13.5	27,118	29.4	62.8	7.8	30,064	25.1	56.2	18.6
4848804	Missouri City city	55,549	31.9	53.4	14.8	26,141	34.1	57.2	8.6	29,408	29.9	49.9	20.2
4850820	New Braunfels city	46,360	26.4	53.1	20.5	21,536	26.8	58.1	15.1	24,824	26.1	48.7	25.2
4852356	North Richland Hills city	53,064	26.5	54.0	19.6	25,874	28.4	56.2	15.3	27,190	24.6	51.8	23.6
4853388	Odessa city	81,314	31.3	47.0	21.8	40,413	35.6	48.1	16.3	40,901	27.0	45.9	27.1
4856000	Pasadena city	114,354	33.8	46.0	20.2	56,391	38.3	48.0	13.7	57,963	29.5	44.0	26.5
4856348	Pearland city	73,586	22.7	61.8	15.4	35,882	26.2	65.6	8.2	37,704	19.5	58.2	22.3
4857176	Pflugerville city	39,726	25.0	57.6	17.4	18,999	29.2	61.0	9.8	20,727	21.1	54.5	24.4
4857200	Pharr city	50,750	31.7	50.8	17.5	23,437	34.8	56.8	8.4	27,313	29.0	45.6	25.4
4858016	Plano city	214,809	26.6	58.1	15.3	104,957	29.8	60.0	10.2	109,852	23.5	56.4	20.2
4858820	Port Arthur city	41,191	34.3	41.0	24.8	20,573	37.4	44.7	17.9	20,618	31.1	37.3	31.6
4861796	Richardson city	83,519	29.9	53.3	16.8	41,503	33.7	54.4	11.9	42,016	26.0	52.2	21.8
4863500	Round Rock city	78,479	29.4	55.1	15.5	37,223	29.7	59.2	11.1	41,256	29.0	51.5	19.5
4863572	Rowlett city	47,440	28.2	57.5	14.3	22,927	31.6	59.7	8.7	24,513	25.1	55.4	19.5
4864472	San Angelo city	76,885	33.3	43.6	23.1	37,334	36.9	45.1	18.0	39,551	29.8	42.3	27.9
4865000	San Antonio city	1,080,722	36.1	42.8	21.0	520,564	39.5	45.3	15.2	560,158	33.0	40.5	26.5
4865600	San Marcos city	44,709	67.7	19.8	12.5	21,571	70.8	19.9	9.3	23,138	64.9	19.6	15.5
4869596	Spring CDP	43,409	29.3	53.9	16.8	21,061	32.1	56.3	11.6	22,348	26.6	51.7	21.7
4870808	Sugar Land city	66,489	23.3	64.5	12.3	31,743	25.4	67.3	7.2	34,746	21.3	61.8	16.9
4872176	Temple city	54,030	26.9	50.8	22.3	26,319	30.0	52.4	17.6	27,711	24.0	49.3	26.7
4872656	The Woodlands CDP	80,371	23.6	63.4	13.1	38,907	25.9	65.9	8.3	41,464	21.4	61.0	17.5
4874144	Tyler city	80,168	34.0	42.3	23.7	36,155	35.8	47.6	16.6	44,013	32.5	37.9	29.5
4875428	Victoria city	50,304	30.1	45.0	24.9	24,221	34.1	46.3	19.5	26,083	26.3	43.8	29.8
4876000	Waco city	100,994	41.0	37.4	21.6	47,815	43.5	40.0	16.5	53,179	38.8	35.0	26.2
4879000	Wichita Falls city	84,643	35.5	42.8	21.7	44,439	41.8	41.5	16.7	40,204	28.6	44.2	27.2
4900000	**Utah**	2,102,136	29.4	55.8	14.8	1,048,510	32.4	56.2	11.4	1,053,626	26.3	55.5	18.2
4943660	Layton city	50,350	26.2	58.8	15.0	24,839	29.8	58.9	11.3	25,511	22.8	58.6	18.6
4944320	Lehi city	31,882	23.6	68.6	7.9	16,367	26.5	67.2	6.3	15,515	20.4	70.0	9.5
4950150	Millcreek CDP	51,262	31.7	47.0	21.3	25,126	35.2	48.3	16.5	26,136	28.3	45.7	25.9
4955980	Ogden city	63,885	33.3	44.7	22.0	32,673	37.8	44.1	18.1	31,212	28.7	45.2	26.1
4957300	Orem city	67,592	33.9	53.8	12.3	33,167	36.6	54.8	8.5	34,425	31.3	52.8	16.0
4962470	Provo city	92,336	46.9	44.6	8.5	45,522	47.9	45.7	6.4	46,814	46.0	43.5	10.6
4965330	St. George city	57,654	25.5	56.9	17.5	27,711	27.7	59.2	13.1	29,943	23.6	54.8	21.6
4967000	Salt Lake City city	153,620	41.3	41.0	17.8	78,965	45.4	40.4	14.2	74,655	36.9	41.6	21.5
4967440	Sandy city	68,726	26.8	58.6	14.6	34,245	29.5	58.6	11.8	34,481	24.2	58.5	17.3
4970850	South Jordan city	40,100	23.7	66.8	9.5	20,423	27.0	65.4	7.5	19,677	20.3	68.2	11.5
4975360	Taylorsville city	45,739	29.0	52.3	18.7	22,330	31.7	53.6	14.7	23,409	26.4	51.0	22.6
4982950	West Jordan city	77,467	29.4	56.0	14.6	38,876	32.2	55.6	12.2	38,591	26.6	56.5	16.9
4983470	West Valley City city	95,726	32.7	49.9	17.4	48,096	35.2	50.1	14.7	47,630	30.3	49.6	20.1
5000000	**Vermont**	525,206	31.2	50.0	18.8	256,552	34.4	51.0	14.6	268,654	28.1	49.1	22.8
5100000	**Virginia**	6,634,998	31.7	49.9	18.3	3,230,845	34.9	51.8	13.3	3,404,153	28.7	48.2	23.1
5101000	Alexandria city	124,035	40.2	44.0	15.8	59,747	41.9	46.3	11.7	64,288	38.5	41.8	19.7
5103000	Arlington CDP	189,378	45.9	41.7	12.4	94,634	47.9	43.2	8.9	94,744	44.0	40.2	15.9
5114440	Centreville CDP	57,324	30.9	55.0	14.1	28,096	35.2	56.3	8.6	29,228	26.7	53.8	19.5
5116000	Chesapeake city	181,560	29.2	52.4	18.5	87,594	32.2	54.2	13.6	93,966	26.4	50.7	22.9
5121088	Dale City CDP	52,871	34.5	50.9	14.6	25,535	37.2	52.9	9.9	27,336	32.0	49.1	18.9
5135000	Hampton city	111,395	36.9	40.8	22.2	52,739	40.0	43.4	16.6	58,656	34.2	38.5	27.3
5135624	Harrisonburg city	43,933	60.2	26.9	12.9	20,450	60.0	29.4	10.6	23,483	60.4	24.8	14.8

State/place FIPS code	State/Place	Total women age 15 to 50 years	Percent of all women who had a birth in the past year	Percent of women who had a birth who were married (including separated and spouse absent):	Percent of women who had a birth who were partners in an unmarried partner household	Age of women who had a birth in the last year as a percent of all women who had a birth			Women who had a birth in the last year as a percent of all women in their age group		
						Age 15 to 19	Age 20 to 34	Age 35 to 50	Age 15 to 19	Age 20 to 34	Age 35 to 50
	Texas—cont'd										
4820092	DeSoto city	0	0.0	0.0	0.0	0.0	0.0	0.0	0.0	0.0	0.0
4822660	Edinburg city	21,665	7.3	77.5	2.9	11.5	63.4	25.1	5.7	10.1	4.7
4824000	El Paso city	169,595	6.1	65.6	6.4	9.4	72.7	17.8	3.8	10.2	2.6
4824768	Euless city	14,669	5.0	77.9	7.6	9.4	58.4	32.2	3.6	6.9	3.6
4826232	Flower Mound town	18,095	3.7	85.8	8.1	2.2	56.9	40.9	0.5	9.7	2.5
4827000	Fort Worth city	210,382	6.4	54.4	11.7	8.2	77.2	14.6	4.1	11.0	2.2
4827684	Frisco city	8,559	3.4	75.9	0.0	0.0	90.5	9.5	0.0	9.4	0.6
4829000	Garland city	0	0.0	0.0	0.0	0.0	0.0	0.0	0.0	0.0	0.0
4829336	Georgetown city	0	0.0	0.0	0.0	0.0	0.0	0.0	0.0	0.0	0.0
4830464	Grand Prairie city	0	0.0	0.0	0.0	0.0	0.0	0.0	0.0	0.0	0.0
4832372	Harlingen city	15,047	7.7	62.1	3.2	4.1	83.3	12.7	2.1	15.8	2.2
4835000	Houston city	563,889	6.2	60.9	9.1	9.2	70.2	20.6	4.8	9.1	3.1
4837000	Irving city	0	0.0	0.0	0.0	0.0	0.0	0.0	0.0	0.0	0.0
4839148	Killeen city	38,449	5.3	77.1	5.5	1.2	84.7	14.0	0.7	8.5	2.0
4841464	Laredo city	8,562	9.1	75.7	12.9	3.1	93.0	4.0	1.6	22.8	0.8
4841980	League City city	23,034	4.2	93.5	4.2	0.0	91.9	8.1	0.0	9.7	0.7
4842508	Lewisville city	0	0.0	0.0	0.0	0.0	0.0	0.0	0.0	0.0	0.0
4843888	Longview city	19,184	6.3	58.0	21.7	6.7	85.1	8.3	3.1	12.2	1.3
4845000	Lubbock city	64,472	4.8	60.6	7.0	10.7	76.5	12.7	3.3	7.0	1.9
4845384	McAllen city	34,765	6.3	76.4	1.9	12.9	73.9	13.2	5.5	11.0	1.9
4845744	McKinney city	38,553	5.8	81.9	0.8	0.8	60.2	39.0	0.4	9.8	4.4
4846452	Mansfield city	15,659	5.1	83.8	14.2	0.0	79.5	20.5	0.0	13.4	1.9
4847892	Mesquite city	0	0.0	0.0	0.0	0.0	0.0	0.0	0.0	0.0	0.0
4848072	Midland city	30,287	6.6	76.8	5.3	6.3	87.1	6.6	3.1	12.2	1.1
4848768	Mission city	20,395	7.8	74.1	0.0	13.9	71.3	14.8	5.7	16.0	2.5
4848804	Missouri City city	16,869	5.0	70.3	0.0	20.7	50.8	28.4	7.0	7.7	2.7
4850820	New Braunfels city	15,328	6.1	36.2	14.9	7.4	86.9	5.8	3.2	11.8	0.9
4852356	North Richland Hills city	16,593	4.2	74.3	6.9	5.9	63.0	31.1	1.6	6.6	2.9
4853388	Odessa city	26,002	11.9	62.4	12.6	5.8	87.7	6.5	4.9	21.6	2.1
4856000	Pasadena city	37,990	6.6	59.5	8.6	7.7	79.2	13.1	3.2	12.3	2.1
4856348	Pearland city	25,161	8.2	85.9	0.0	1.6	69.7	28.7	1.1	15.6	4.6
4857176	Pflugerville city	0	0.0	0.0	0.0	0.0	0.0	0.0	0.0	0.0	0.0
4857200	Pharr city	18,362	5.7	78.8	4.5	11.1	72.6	16.3	3.9	9.2	2.4
4858016	Plano city	67,839	5.8	66.6	15.2	3.2	77.7	19.0	1.5	12.3	2.2
4858820	Port Arthur city	12,447	7.9	53.6	7.4	4.9	80.5	14.6	3.0	14.5	2.7
4861796	Richardson city	0	0.0	0.0	0.0	0.0	0.0	0.0	0.0	0.0	0.0
4863500	Round Rock city	0	0.0	0.0	0.0	0.0	0.0	0.0	0.0	0.0	0.0
4863572	Rowlett city	0	0.0	0.0	0.0	0.0	0.0	0.0	0.0	0.0	0.0
4864472	San Angelo city	23,830	5.2	78.0	6.7	10.1	86.3	3.6	3.6	9.1	0.5
4865000	San Antonio city	360,390	6.1	61.2	8.8	8.4	73.3	18.3	3.7	9.9	2.8
4865600	San Marcos city	0	0.0	0.0	0.0	0.0	0.0	0.0	0.0	0.0	0.0
4869596	Spring CDP	15,176	6.9	69.9	17.1	6.8	64.9	28.3	3.1	11.7	4.2
4870808	Sugar Land city	18,682	5.2	97.6	0.0	0.0	72.7	27.3	0.0	10.5	2.8
4872176	Temple city	16,444	6.3	87.2	1.3	8.2	81.9	9.9	4.1	10.8	1.6
4872656	The Woodlands CDP	25,093	4.3	84.4	0.0	11.2	56.5	32.4	3.2	8.8	2.5
4874144	Tyler city	26,601	4.8	39.4	8.2	8.0	85.1	6.9	2.6	8.2	0.9
4875428	Victoria city	15,192	4.6	44.1	28.4	9.5	83.6	6.9	3.1	8.6	0.8
4876000	Waco city	35,015	4.7	49.0	11.3	14.3	72.5	13.3	3.5	6.9	2.0
4879000	Wichita Falls city	24,085	5.0	59.1	22.5	16.2	68.3	15.5	5.4	7.2	2.0
4900000	**Utah**	712,683	7.4	83.8	5.3	3.2	82.1	14.7	1.6	12.9	2.9
4943660	Layton city	17,546	5.7	93.2	0.0	0.0	82.0	18.0	0.0	9.9	2.7
4944320	Lehi city	12,166	9.5	94.2	5.8	0.0	89.5	10.5	0.0	17.9	2.5
4950150	Millcreek CDP	15,509	6.5	77.9	1.9	6.2	69.2	24.6	3.6	9.3	4.0
4955980	Ogden city	21,136	9.2	70.6	10.7	3.4	86.3	10.3	2.6	15.1	2.7
4957300	Orem city	24,288	8.7	88.5	4.6	0.0	90.5	9.5	0.0	14.6	3.0
4962470	Provo city	38,600	6.1	86.2	6.6	3.3	89.5	7.1	1.0	8.7	2.8
4965330	St. George city	15,995	6.9	82.9	6.8	13.9	73.1	13.1	4.7	11.2	2.6
4967000	Salt Lake City city	51,635	6.1	80.7	5.6	4.1	76.0	19.8	2.4	8.3	3.5
4967440	Sandy city	21,323	5.8	84.6	7.0	0.0	79.7	20.3	0.0	11.0	2.7
4970850	South Jordan city	13,559	6.5	91.1	0.0	0.0	78.2	21.8	0.0	12.4	3.2
4975360	Taylorsville city	15,065	7.2	74.1	12.9	6.7	81.0	12.3	3.4	12.4	2.2
4982950	West Jordan city	28,493	8.3	75.6	3.7	3.6	82.5	13.9	2.1	15.7	2.7
4983470	West Valley City city	34,068	7.4	69.4	8.3	7.8	74.6	17.7	3.8	12.2	3.3
5000000	**Vermont**	144,883	3.9	66.9	14.3	4.7	73.3	22.0	1.2	7.3	1.9
5100000	**Virginia**	2,039,556	5.3	68.6	8.1	4.7	73.7	21.5	1.9	9.3	2.5
5101000	Alexandria city	44,183	5.5	84.1	8.1	2.8	72.9	24.3	3.0	7.8	3.0
5103000	Arlington CDP	67,617	5.1	79.4	1.2	5.8	53.9	40.2	5.4	4.8	5.5
5114440	Centreville CDP	19,684	7.1	86.2	6.1	0.0	64.7	35.3	0.0	12.1	5.2
5116000	Chesapeake city	57,339	5.0	64.7	6.8	3.1	78.6	18.3	1.1	10.1	2.0
5121088	Dale City CDP	18,602	7.4	56.1	5.7	0.0	79.7	20.3	0.0	15.2	3.4
5135000	Hampton city	35,267	4.3	38.0	7.4	17.9	66.7	15.4	5.4	6.2	1.6
5135624	Harrisonburg city	18,698	2.4	57.3	2.7	29.3	60.0	10.7	2.5	2.8	1.3

Table C-4: Cities with a Population of 50,000 or More—Marriages and Births—*Continued*

State/place FIPS code	State/Place	Total population 15 years and older	Marital status, percent			Male population 15 years and older	Male, marital status, percent			Female population 15 years and older	Female, marital status, percent		
			Never married	Now married (except separated)	Separated, widowed, or divorced		Never married	Now married (except separated)	Separated, widowed, or divorced		Never married	Now married (except separated)	Separated, widowed, or divorced
	Virginia—cont'd												
5147672	Lynchburg city	64,373	45.7	36.2	18.1	29,783	49.5	39.1	11.4	34,590	42.5	33.6	23.9
5156000	Newport News city	144,476	37.0	40.7	22.3	69,006	40.9	43.0	16.1	75,470	33.4	38.6	28.0
5157000	Norfolk city	201,984	46.0	33.8	20.2	105,558	51.3	33.7	15.0	96,426	40.3	33.9	25.8
5164000	Portsmouth city	76,896	38.1	36.4	25.5	36,580	42.9	39.1	18.0	40,316	33.7	34.0	32.3
5166672	Reston CDP	50,187	30.8	53.2	16.1	23,218	32.2	57.7	10.1	26,969	29.5	49.3	21.2
5167000	Richmond city	176,537	52.0	25.7	22.3	83,098	55.5	27.9	16.6	93,439	48.9	23.7	27.4
5168000	Roanoke city	79,227	34.7	39.5	25.8	37,193	38.5	42.7	18.8	42,034	31.3	36.7	31.9
5176432	Suffolk city	67,076	28.5	50.8	20.6	31,856	29.8	53.5	16.7	35,220	27.4	48.4	24.2
5182000	Virginia Beach city	358,884	31.6	49.5	18.8	174,285	35.9	51.3	12.7	184,599	27.5	47.9	24.6
5300000	Washington	5,573,172	30.7	50.3	19.0	2,764,295	34.4	51.3	14.4	2,808,877	27.1	49.4	23.5
5303180	Auburn city	58,065	32.0	48.2	19.8	28,099	35.4	50.3	14.3	29,966	28.9	46.1	24.9
5305210	Bellevue city	109,754	27.7	56.8	15.5	56,394	33.1	56.0	10.9	53,360	22.0	57.7	20.3
5305280	Bellingham city	71,060	46.7	34.2	19.0	34,308	51.3	35.9	12.8	36,752	42.5	32.7	24.8
5322640	Everett city	85,091	34.7	41.9	23.4	42,851	40.6	42.8	16.6	42,240	28.8	40.9	30.3
5323515	Federal Way city	73,509	34.2	45.9	19.9	35,755	39.2	47.5	13.3	37,754	29.5	44.3	26.2
5335275	Kennewick city	58,346	29.9	48.5	21.6	29,007	33.9	49.9	16.2	29,339	26.0	47.0	26.9
5335415	Kent city	96,372	34.2	48.3	17.6	47,748	36.3	50.3	13.4	48,624	32.1	46.3	21.6
5335940	Kirkland city	67,589	28.2	54.8	16.9	33,179	32.5	56.1	11.4	34,410	24.1	53.7	22.3
5338038	Lakewood city	48,472	30.0	44.9	25.1	23,500	31.8	46.8	21.4	24,972	28.3	43.1	28.6
5343955	Marysville city	48,191	29.7	51.1	19.2	24,043	34.8	51.8	13.4	24,148	24.7	50.4	24.9
5353545	Pasco city	46,043	34.1	49.3	16.7	23,472	37.0	50.9	12.0	22,571	31.0	47.5	21.5
5357535	Redmond city	46,049	29.3	56.6	14.1	23,864	35.5	55.5	9.0	22,185	22.7	57.8	19.5
5357745	Renton city	77,168	34.5	45.5	20.0	38,308	36.9	47.1	15.9	38,860	32.2	43.9	24.0
5358235	Richland city	40,750	28.5	52.8	18.7	20,475	33.2	53.1	13.7	20,275	23.7	52.6	23.7
5363000	Seattle city	549,006	44.2	39.5	16.3	271,896	47.3	40.1	12.5	277,110	41.1	38.9	20.0
5363960	Shoreline city	46,173	33.3	48.0	18.8	22,562	38.9	49.3	11.9	23,611	27.9	46.7	25.4
5365922	South Hill CDP	41,382	26.2	59.0	14.8	20,843	31.8	58.3	9.9	20,539	20.5	59.7	19.8
5367000	Spokane city	170,629	34.3	42.6	23.1	82,933	37.5	43.9	18.6	87,696	31.2	41.4	27.4
5367167	Spokane Valley city	73,854	28.0	49.2	22.7	36,551	32.4	49.9	17.7	37,303	23.8	48.6	27.6
5370000	Tacoma city	163,818	35.2	41.8	23.0	79,223	38.6	43.5	17.9	84,595	32.0	40.3	27.7
5374060	Vancouver city	133,298	30.3	45.4	24.3	64,132	33.3	47.7	19.0	69,166	27.5	43.3	29.3
5380010	Yakima city	71,553	34.1	44.4	21.5	35,884	39.4	45.3	15.3	35,669	28.7	43.5	27.8
5400000	**West Virginia**	1,538,216	27.4	50.0	22.6	752,757	31.2	51.4	17.3	785,459	23.8	48.6	27.6
5414600	Charleston city	42,345	32.7	40.3	27.0	20,259	35.9	42.6	21.4	22,086	29.8	38.1	32.1
5500000	**Wisconsin**	4,636,493	31.4	50.9	17.7	2,285,832	34.6	52.0	13.5	2,350,661	28.4	49.8	21.8
5502375	Appleton city	57,913	33.1	47.7	19.2	28,197	37.1	48.1	14.8	29,716	29.3	47.3	23.4
5522300	Eau Claire city	56,180	43.9	38.7	17.4	26,625	46.8	40.6	12.5	29,555	41.2	37.0	21.7
5531000	Green Bay city	83,582	37.4	44.0	18.6	40,802	40.1	44.8	15.0	42,780	34.9	43.1	22.0
5537825	Janesville city	50,650	29.4	49.3	21.3	24,092	32.8	52.1	15.1	26,558	26.3	46.9	26.9
5539225	Kenosha city	78,256	37.0	42.2	20.9	37,614	41.0	44.6	14.4	40,642	33.2	39.9	26.9
5540775	La Crosse city	45,021	51.6	32.6	15.8	21,342	53.1	34.6	12.3	23,679	50.3	30.8	18.9
5548000	Madison city	204,368	48.3	37.6	14.1	99,843	50.6	39.0	10.4	104,525	46.1	36.2	17.6
5553000	Milwaukee city	463,986	51.7	30.2	18.0	219,602	53.3	32.3	14.4	244,384	50.3	28.4	21.3
5560500	Oshkosh city	56,075	44.5	35.9	19.6	28,998	48.0	35.2	16.8	27,077	40.8	36.6	22.6
5566000	Racine city	60,147	39.7	39.6	20.7	28,418	41.9	42.2	15.9	31,729	37.7	37.3	25.0
5584250	Waukesha city	57,122	33.2	48.8	18.0	28,096	37.0	50.4	12.5	29,026	29.5	47.3	23.2
5585300	West Allis city	49,821	36.2	43.1	20.7	24,135	39.9	44.6	15.6	25,686	32.8	41.8	25.5
5600000	**Wyoming**	459,841	27.2	53.0	19.8	234,022	30.9	52.8	16.3	225,819	23.4	53.2	23.4
5613150	Casper city	46,234	28.9	50.4	20.6	23,269	32.4	49.8	17.8	22,965	25.4	51.1	23.5
5613900	Cheyenne city	48,939	27.9	50.0	22.1	23,811	32.7	52.0	15.2	25,128	23.4	48.1	28.5

Table C-4: Cities with a Population of 50,000 or More—Marriages and Births—*Continued*

State/place FIPS code	State/Place	Total women age 15 to 50 years	Percent of all women who had a birth in the past year	Percent of women who had a birth who were married (including separated and spouse absent):	Percent of women who had a birth who were partners in an unmarried partner household	Age of women who had a birth in the last year as a percent of all women who had a birth			Women who had a birth in the last year as a percent of all women in their age group		
						Age 15 to 19	Age 20 to 34	Age 35 to 50	Age 15 to 19	Age 20 to 34	Age 35 to 50
	Virginia—cont'd										
5147672	Lynchburg city..............................	22,190	5.7	80.2	4.7	0.0	92.4	7.6	0.0	10.4	1.5
5156000	Newport News city.......................	48,141	6.0	51.5	9.7	8.6	73.1	18.3	3.9	9.0	2.9
5157000	Norfolk city.................................	63,621	6.3	58.9	4.1	5.4	81.7	12.9	2.7	9.6	2.4
5164000	Portsmouth city............................	23,851	6.0	52.9	19.5	3.6	78.9	17.6	1.9	9.6	2.6
5166672	Reston CDP..................................	16,851	4.5	82.7	7.6	0.0	56.8	43.2	0.0	6.2	4.0
5167000	Richmond city..............................	60,164	4.6	47.8	11.9	2.8	80.5	16.8	1.0	6.7	2.3
5168000	Roanoke city................................	23,912	6.8	54.9	9.6	12.6	66.6	20.8	8.4	9.9	3.2
5176432	Suffolk city..................................	21,237	5.6	61.0	5.2	4.6	79.0	16.4	2.1	11.6	1.9
5182000	Virginia Beach city........................	115,588	5.4	72.3	7.7	2.8	80.9	16.3	1.3	9.7	2.1
5300000	Washington..................................	1,659,615	5.4	71.7	11.8	4.2	74.0	21.7	1.7	9.4	2.7
5303180	Auburn city.................................	17,780	5.1	61.2	27.7	0.0	84.2	15.8	0.0	10.1	1.8
5305210	Bellevue city................................	31,319	5.0	91.1	2.4	0.0	67.2	32.8	0.0	8.0	3.4
5305280	Bellingham city............................	31,319	5.0	91.1	2.4	0.0	67.2	32.8	0.0	8.0	3.4
5322640	Everett city..................................	27,031	6.2	65.4	13.3	3.5	88.3	8.2	2.3	11.5	1.2
5323515	Federal Way city..........................	22,968	6.3	59.1	17.9	9.1	71.7	19.2	4.3	10.7	2.7
5335275	Kennewick city.............................	18,203	6.9	76.5	7.1	1.3	85.8	12.9	0.6	14.3	2.1
5335415	Kent city.....................................	32,613	7.2	64.8	7.7	5.2	75.0	19.7	3.0	12.2	3.3
5335940	Kirkland city................................	20,573	5.5	88.7	10.0	5.1	71.6	23.3	2.9	9.1	2.7
5338038	Lakewood city..............................	13,694	5.0	42.2	22.2	10.1	70.4	19.4	4.8	7.0	2.5
5343955	Marysville city..............................	15,221	5.2	72.6	14.7	1.4	87.2	11.4	0.6	10.4	1.4
5353545	Pasco city....................................	16,315	7.7	69.6	18.8	0.0	77.5	22.5	0.0	12.7	4.5
5357535	Redmond city...............................	14,941	5.8	82.0	4.9	2.4	65.7	31.8	2.2	7.5	4.3
5357745	Renton city..................................	25,475	5.5	76.8	13.3	0.0	78.8	21.2	0.0	9.7	2.6
5358235	Richland city................................	11,792	5.1	64.4	15.1	6.7	86.5	6.8	2.6	10.2	0.8
5363000	Seattle city..................................	182,682	4.7	76.8	8.8	3.3	61.5	35.2	1.8	5.6	4.2
5363960	Shoreline city...............................	12,832	3.7	78.5	4.4	0.0	79.3	20.7	0.0	7.8	1.6
5365922	South Hill CDP.............................	14,176	7.3	76.6	18.3	3.2	84.8	12.0	1.7	15.8	1.9
5367000	Spokane city................................	51,912	6.2	68.1	13.8	3.6	86.7	9.7	1.8	10.7	1.6
5367167	Spokane Valley city.......................	21,037	4.4	74.2	11.6	4.0	64.0	32.0	1.3	7.0	3.1
5370000	Tacoma city.................................	52,020	6.3	65.9	14.5	5.0	71.3	23.6	2.5	9.8	3.6
5374060	Vancouver city..............................	41,764	6.7	67.1	9.4	4.9	82.9	12.1	2.6	12.4	1.9
5380010	Yakima city..................................	21,230	7.7	57.3	7.1	13.7	68.7	17.7	6.3	11.8	3.5
5400000	**West Virginia**............................	417,010	4.5	61.0	9.8	5.6	80.7	13.7	1.9	8.9	1.3
5414600	Charleston city.............................	11,720	5.7	53.4	14.5	10.3	82.9	6.7	4.2	10.7	0.9
5500000	**Wisconsin**.................................	1,337,285	5.1	67.5	13.2	3.8	78.1	18.1	1.4	9.6	2.1
5502375	Appleton city...............................	17,998	4.5	66.4	27.0	0.0	88.6	11.4	0.0	9.0	1.2
5522300	Eau Claire city..............................	19,408	4.0	58.4	16.5	3.6	79.4	17.0	0.8	6.0	2.4
5531000	Green Bay city..............................	26,084	6.2	58.9	19.2	6.8	83.0	10.2	3.1	10.3	1.7
5537825	Janesville city...............................	15,546	6.1	68.5	13.1	6.3	79.0	14.7	3.2	10.9	2.1
5539225	Kenosha city................................	25,660	4.0	65.5	8.2	9.1	72.8	18.1	2.4	7.2	1.7
5540775	La Crosse city...............................	15,780	3.3	57.0	35.4	4.8	68.8	26.5	0.7	4.4	3.5
5548000	Madison city................................	72,133	4.1	70.8	7.5	3.6	79.2	17.2	1.2	5.6	2.4
5553000	Milwaukee city.............................	165,128	5.4	42.6	15.1	6.7	76.0	17.3	2.5	8.4	2.5
5560500	Oshkosh city................................	17,533	5.3	65.4	22.6	1.3	85.4	13.3	0.4	9.4	2.0
5566000	Racine city...................................	20,016	5.5	31.9	24.3	8.0	82.0	9.9	3.4	10.6	1.3
5584250	Waukesha city..............................	18,152	4.7	82.2	10.7	2.7	78.7	18.6	0.9	7.8	2.3
5585300	West Allis city..............................	14,735	3.8	77.3	19.9	4.7	70.5	24.9	2.0	5.2	2.4
5600000	**Wyoming**..................................	130,749	5.5	72.5	13.4	3.4	84.3	12.3	1.4	10.4	1.6
5613150	Casper city..................................	13,398	4.5	61.0	19.1	8.1	77.6	14.3	3.2	7.2	1.6
5613900	Cheyenne city..............................	14,630	5.1	78.9	15.8	0.0	86.5	13.5	0.0	9.5	1.7

Children

PART D. CHILDREN

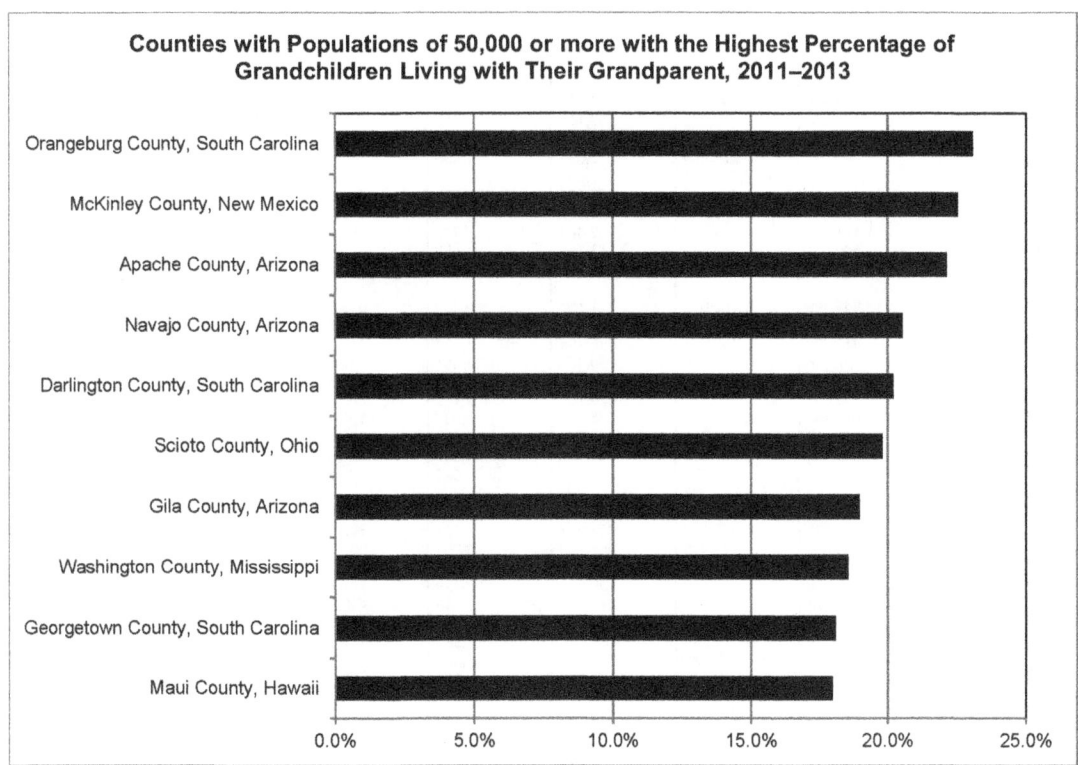

Counties with Populations of 50,000 or more with the Highest Percentage of Grandchildren Living with Their Grandparent, 2011–2013

In the United States, there are about 70 million children under the age of 18, and about two-thirds of them live with both parents. In Utah, 81 percent of children under 6 live with both parents, and 5 other states have proportions above 70 percent. In the District of Columbia, Mississippi, and Louisiana, the percentage of children under 6 living with both parents is 50 percent or lower.

In 21 cities, 90 percent or more of children under 6 live with both parents, topped by San Ramon, CA at 96.1 percent. The 20 other cities are in 11 states and include most regions of the country. In a few cities, fewer than 20 percent of children under 6 live with two parents: Camden NJ, Flint MI, Youngstown OH, and Hartford CT. South Jordan UT has the highest proportion of children ages 6 to 17 living with two parents, at 89.9 percent, followed closely by Flower Mound TX, Bethesda MD, Cupertino CA, and Sugar Land TX. Camden NJ has the lowest proportion at 18.6 percent of children age 6 to 17.

Among children under 6 years old, 36.8 percent live with both parents, and both parents are in the labor force. For children ages 6 to 17, the proportion is slightly higher—42.4 percent live in two-parent families with both parents in the labor force. About 28 percent of children of all ages live in single-parent families with the parent in the labor force. In Iowa, Minnesota, and North Dakota, about half of all children under 6 live with

two parents who are in the labor force, compared with about 30 percent of children in New Mexico, Louisiana, Mississippi, and Arizona. In 8 states, more than half of older children (age 6 to 17) live with two parents who are in the labor force. Again, the highest proportions are in North Dakota, Minnesota, and Iowa.

Nationally, 1.3 percent of children under 6 were born in foreign countries, with levels over 2 percent in New York, New Jersey, and the District of Columbia. For ages 6 to 17, the national proportion of foreign-born children is 4.4 percent, with levels over 6 percent in California, Hawaii, New Jersey, Florida, and New York. 25 percent of children under 6 have at least one parent who is foreign-born, ranging from 46.6 percent in California to 2.4 percent in West Virginia. The proportions are about the same for children ages 6 to 17, though California's proportion is slightly over half for this age group.

About 8 percent of American children live in their grandparent's household, and the grandparent is responsible for the child in about half of those households. Among the states, Hawaii has the highest proportion at 16.5 percent of all children, and Minnesota has the lowest at 4 percent. In Miami Gardens FL, 22.7 percent of children live with their grandparents, and 8 other cities in California and Florida have levels of 17 percent or higher.

Table D-1: States—Children

State FIPS code	State	Total own children under 18 in families and subfamilies	Own children under 6 years in families and subfamilies						
			Total own children under 6 years	Nativity and parentage, under 6 years					
				Child is native	Child is foreign born	Only native parent(s)	One or more foreign-born parent:	One or more foreign-born parent: - Child is native	One or more foreign-born parent: - Child is foreign born
	United States...............	70,173,842	23,215,525	22,898,556	306,019	17,404,256	5,800,319	5,533,916	266,403
1	Alabama..........................	1,050,918	344,683	342,782	1,882	314,073	30,591	29,229	1,362
2	Alaska.............................	179,648	63,336	63,117	219	56,579	6,757	6,608	149
4	Arizona...........................	1,531,962	508,962	502,603	6,248	372,547	136,304	130,851	5,453
5	Arkansas.........................	664,652	223,469	222,039	1,430	195,903	27,566	26,331	1,235
6	California........................	8,780,993	2,927,371	2,873,617	52,182	1,562,978	1,362,821	1,314,467	48,354
8	Colorado.........................	1,182,138	395,515	390,482	4,907	308,947	86,442	82,499	3,943
9	Connecticut....................	768,816	230,927	226,512	4,165	170,251	60,426	56,696	3,730
10	Delaware	191,554	64,151	63,409	742	50,955	13,196	12,519	677
11	District of Columbia........	100,091	43,530	42,160	1,159	31,536	11,783	10,750	1,033
12	Florida	3,804,656	1,249,125	1,229,149	19,393	851,260	397,282	379,522	17,760
13	Georgia...........................	2,349,999	780,912	771,154	9,439	615,631	164,962	156,687	8,275
15	Hawaii............................	288,797	103,598	101,679	1,887	75,323	28,243	26,589	1,654
16	Idaho..............................	410,390	136,541	135,195	1,304	116,193	20,306	19,249	1,057
17	Illinois............................	2,932,336	944,645	930,482	13,651	683,552	260,581	249,257	11,324
18	Indiana...........................	1,508,064	492,870	488,151	4,631	438,357	54,425	50,948	3,477
19	Iowa................................	694,083	230,397	228,200	2,120	206,290	24,030	22,193	1,837
20	Kansas............................	693,288	237,252	235,175	2,055	199,989	37,241	35,547	1,694
21	Kentucky.........................	945,623	316,066	313,368	2,503	288,266	27,605	25,634	1,971
22	Louisiana	1,045,345	359,520	358,153	1,307	334,045	25,415	24,213	1,202
23	Maine..............................	251,774	76,476	75,942	515	71,661	4,796	4,471	325
24	Maryland.........................	1,285,577	427,978	420,391	7,199	307,582	120,008	113,616	6,392
25	Massachusetts	1,349,577	430,160	421,003	8,321	302,033	127,291	119,959	7,332
26	Michigan.........................	2,165,093	673,975	665,749	8,004	586,577	87,176	80,506	6,670
27	Minnesota	1,234,372	410,101	403,865	6,046	331,783	78,128	73,552	4,576
28	Mississippi......................	690,498	231,060	230,621	439	221,300	9,760	9,395	365
29	Missouri..........................	1,328,024	440,994	438,037	2,718	400,520	40,235	38,215	2,020
30	Montana..........................	210,713	72,359	72,149	208	69,583	2,774	2,628	146
31	Nebraska.........................	442,576	151,288	149,880	1,367	127,156	24,091	22,995	1,096
32	Nevada............................	628,665	212,789	210,746	2,030	133,562	79,214	77,283	1,931
33	New Hampshire	264,738	78,243	77,291	891	67,857	10,325	9,693	632
34	New Jersey......................	1,968,419	631,427	615,460	15,698	389,867	241,291	226,818	14,473
35	New Mexico.....................	485,198	164,028	162,755	1,252	132,509	31,498	30,646	852
36	New York.........................	4,080,838	1,349,393	1,320,074	28,097	867,149	481,022	455,448	25,574
37	North Carolina................	2,169,314	719,380	711,248	7,545	576,878	141,915	135,699	6,216
38	North Dakota..................	151,243	53,991	53,607	384	51,553	2,438	2,074	364
39	Ohio................................	2,536,221	818,899	813,160	5,638	747,709	71,089	66,685	4,404
40	Oklahoma........................	884,279	303,188	300,274	2,658	261,169	41,763	39,645	2,118
41	Oregon............................	817,706	267,721	264,707	2,918	202,839	64,786	62,343	2,443
42	Pennsylvania	2,615,591	840,520	831,355	8,805	737,265	102,895	95,880	7,015
44	Rhode Island...................	206,631	65,038	63,808	1,187	49,840	15,155	14,185	970
45	South Carolina................	1,015,015	338,816	336,848	1,838	301,570	37,116	35,621	1,495
46	South Dakota..................	194,342	68,459	68,029	406	64,099	4,336	4,033	303
47	Tennessee	1,403,158	464,004	459,482	4,415	406,373	57,524	54,471	3,053
48	Texas..............................	6,646,543	2,252,764	2,219,342	32,913	1,501,869	750,386	719,903	30,483
49	Utah................................	858,051	303,468	301,386	2,037	252,860	50,563	48,919	1,644
50	Vermont..........................	118,957	36,717	36,460	212	34,069	2,603	2,436	167
51	Virginia...........................	1,779,171	598,316	589,570	8,384	456,525	141,429	134,167	7,262
53	Washington.....................	1,518,172	510,783	501,813	8,607	362,961	147,459	140,110	7,349
54	West Virginia	357,417	117,410	117,000	383	114,511	2,872	2,621	251
55	Wisconsin........................	1,261,858	407,831	404,189	3,489	359,478	48,200	45,980	2,220
56	Wyoming.........................	130,758	45,079	44,888	191	40,874	4,205	4,130	75

Table D-1: States—Children—*Continued*

State FIPS code	State	Own children under 6 years in families and subfamilies										
		Own children under 6 years living with two parents					Own children under 6 living with one parent					
		Total under 6 years living with two parents:	Both parents in labor force	Father only in labor force	Mother only in labor force	Neither parent in labor force	Total under 6 years living with one parent	Total under 6 years living with father	Living with father in labor force	Living with father not in labor force	Total under 6 years living with mother	Living with mother in labor force	Living with mother not in labor force
	United States............	14,719,177	8,538,727	5,507,611	447,302	225,537	8,496,348	1,855,007	1,653,040	201,967	6,641,341	4,833,315	1,808,026
1	Alabama......................	199,380	114,635	75,290	6,508	2,947	145,303	20,611	17,373	3,238	124,692	90,589	34,103
2	Alaska........................	41,225	21,906	16,575	1,868	876	22,111	6,916	6,297	619	15,195	11,116	4,079
4	Arizona......................	307,202	154,666	134,367	11,332	6,837	201,760	50,031	43,593	6,438	151,729	105,758	45,971
5	Arkansas....................	135,761	77,333	51,395	4,479	2,554	87,708	18,013	15,106	2,907	69,695	50,222	19,473
6	California...................	1,883,674	1,023,423	770,471	54,752	35,028	1,043,697	270,567	242,961	27,606	773,130	520,418	252,712
8	Colorado	278,887	154,857	110,894	9,426	3,710	116,628	28,867	26,386	2,481	87,761	64,648	23,113
9	Connecticut................	153,537	98,803	49,183	4,439	1,112	77,390	14,659	13,063	1,596	62,731	49,092	13,639
10	Delaware....................	37,138	22,864	12,662	922	690	27,013	6,349	5,674	675	20,664	16,437	4,227
11	District of Columbia........	21,277	15,506	4,811	744	216	22,253	3,527	2,992	535	18,726	13,402	5,324
12	Florida	720,459	424,457	259,637	25,145	11,220	528,666	114,807	101,586	13,221	413,859	310,937	102,922
13	Georgia	464,030	264,671	179,630	12,912	6,817	316,882	61,469	53,980	7,489	255,413	187,019	68,394
15	Hawaii.......................	69,451	41,253	24,832	2,180	1,186	34,147	8,392	7,668	724	25,755	17,665	8,090
16	Idaho........................	102,191	50,439	48,309	2,191	1,252	34,350	9,061	7,884	1,177	25,289	18,358	6,931
17	Illinois.......................	612,439	370,479	219,407	15,394	7,159	332,206	72,327	66,187	6,140	259,879	200,778	59,101
18	Indiana......................	311,085	184,468	112,592	9,570	4,455	181,785	39,834	35,190	4,644	141,951	108,360	33,591
19	Iowa.........................	159,063	114,449	38,895	4,028	1,691	71,334	18,098	16,777	1,321	53,236	42,196	11,040
20	Kansas.......................	159,681	96,824	57,567	4,124	1,166	77,571	18,685	17,153	1,532	58,886	44,720	14,166
21	Kentucky....................	196,885	117,638	65,899	7,417	5,931	119,181	26,331	22,236	4,095	92,850	66,110	26,740
22	Louisiana....................	180,269	108,310	64,338	4,684	2,937	179,251	32,311	27,865	4,446	146,940	105,580	41,360
23	Maine........................	50,784	33,161	14,500	2,061	1,062	25,692	7,393	6,804	589	18,299	12,819	5,480
24	Maryland....................	268,120	177,249	81,870	6,400	2,601	159,858	33,802	31,300	2,502	126,056	98,028	28,028
25	Massachusetts	294,437	197,497	84,690	8,511	3,739	135,723	25,051	22,193	2,858	110,672	79,677	30,995
26	Michigan....................	419,459	248,858	145,463	16,005	9,133	254,516	53,899	46,287	7,612	200,617	151,368	49,249
27	Minnesota..................	289,743	203,414	75,577	7,671	3,081	120,358	31,250	29,189	2,061	89,108	70,499	18,609
28	Mississippi..................	113,286	69,907	37,272	3,995	2,112	117,774	16,691	14,348	2,343	101,083	73,979	27,104
29	Missouri.....................	277,009	170,790	92,628	8,434	5,157	163,985	36,660	32,287	4,373	127,325	97,617	29,708
30	Montana....................	49,304	27,824	18,847	1,700	933	23,055	5,518	4,994	524	17,537	13,503	4,034
31	Nebraska	104,277	70,084	30,866	2,164	1,163	47,011	11,424	10,681	743	35,587	28,312	7,275
32	Nevada......................	133,747	73,710	54,494	3,762	1,781	79,042	21,875	20,185	1,690	57,167	43,186	13,981
33	New Hampshire..............	53,399	33,615	17,623	1,483	678	24,844	6,855	6,335	520	17,989	13,387	4,602
34	New Jersey..................	434,246	264,461	149,959	15,770	4,056	197,181	42,396	37,939	4,457	154,785	115,177	39,608
35	New Mexico.................	88,931	45,878	37,721	3,391	1,941	75,097	16,349	13,826	2,523	58,748	42,094	16,654
36	New York....................	859,566	496,415	315,354	34,280	13,517	489,827	97,446	85,419	12,027	392,381	275,314	117,067
37	North Carolina..............	434,956	252,473	163,358	13,393	5,732	284,424	60,924	55,022	5,902	223,500	165,184	58,316
38	North Dakota...............	38,461	26,775	10,415	933	338	15,530	4,185	3,890	295	11,345	8,436	2,909
39	Ohio.........................	497,148	312,360	162,020	15,458	7,310	321,751	63,457	56,080	7,377	258,294	193,868	64,426
40	Oklahoma...................	191,303	106,059	75,464	6,191	3,589	111,885	26,465	23,518	2,947	85,420	58,807	26,613
41	Oregon......................	184,181	103,011	70,225	7,429	3,516	83,540	21,714	19,190	2,524	61,826	41,794	20,032
42	Pennsylvania................	530,881	331,710	176,432	14,331	8,408	309,639	64,817	56,762	8,055	244,822	179,446	65,376
44	Rhode Island...............	37,235	25,193	10,062	1,366	614	27,803	5,771	5,278	493	22,032	16,357	5,675
45	South Carolina..............	185,550	110,083	66,179	5,835	3,453	153,266	27,198	24,045	3,153	126,068	95,980	30,088
46	South Dakota...............	43,955	31,714	10,657	1,101	483	24,504	6,300	5,546	754	18,204	14,328	3,876
47	Tennessee...................	281,572	159,024	109,320	8,803	4,425	182,432	36,633	31,634	4,999	145,799	106,030	39,769
48	Texas........................	1,417,401	717,821	641,989	36,551	21,040	835,363	164,458	149,157	15,301	670,905	466,880	204,025
49	Utah.........................	245,817	107,896	129,765	5,623	2,533	57,651	14,218	13,560	658	43,433	32,159	11,274
50	Vermont	24,148	16,690	6,467	705	286	12,569	3,145	2,613	532	9,424	6,929	2,495
51	Virginia......................	402,869	238,515	151,180	9,461	3,713	195,447	39,457	36,194	3,263	155,990	119,270	36,720
53	Washington.................	356,487	186,391	154,171	10,091	5,834	154,296	40,855	36,050	4,805	113,441	81,060	32,381
54	West Virginia...............	72,331	38,382	28,334	3,563	2,052	45,079	10,558	8,956	1,602	34,521	20,384	14,137
55	Wisconsin...................	272,913	186,052	75,608	8,170	3,083	134,918	33,325	30,062	3,263	101,593	80,872	20,721
56	Wyoming....................	32,027	18,734	12,347	556	390	13,052	4,063	3,725	338	8,989	7,166	1,823

Table D-1: States—Children—*Continued*

State FIPS code	State	Total own children under 6 years	Own children under 6 years in families and subfamilies					
			Nativity and parentage, under 6 years					
			Child is native	Child is foreign born	Only native parent(s)	One or more foreign-born parent:	One or more foreign-born parent: - Child is native	One or more foreign-born parent: - Child is foreign born
	United States...............	100.0	98.6	1.3	75.0	25.0	23.8	1.1
1	Alabama...........................	100.0	99.4	0.5	91.1	8.9	8.5	0.4
2	Alaska.............................	100.0	99.7	0.3	89.3	10.7	10.4	0.2
4	Arizona...........................	100.0	98.8	1.2	73.2	26.8	25.7	1.1
5	Arkansas.........................	100.0	99.4	0.6	87.7	12.3	11.8	0.6
6	California........................	100.0	98.2	1.8	53.4	46.6	44.9	1.7
8	Colorado	100.0	98.7	1.2	78.1	21.9	20.9	1.0
9	Connecticut	100.0	98.1	1.8	73.7	26.2	24.6	1.6
10	Delaware	100.0	98.8	1.2	79.4	20.6	19.5	1.1
11	District of Columbia........	100.0	96.9	2.7	72.4	27.1	24.7	2.4
12	Florida............................	100.0	98.4	1.6	68.1	31.8	30.4	1.4
13	Georgia	100.0	98.8	1.2	78.8	21.1	20.1	1.1
15	Hawaii............................	100.0	98.1	1.8	72.7	27.3	25.7	1.6
16	Idaho..............................	100.0	99.0	1.0	85.1	14.9	14.1	0.8
17	Illinois............................	100.0	98.5	1.4	72.4	27.6	26.4	1.2
18	Indiana...........................	100.0	99.0	0.9	88.9	11.0	10.3	0.7
19	Iowa...............................	100.0	99.0	0.9	89.5	10.4	9.6	0.8
20	Kansas............................	100.0	99.1	0.9	84.3	15.7	15.0	0.7
21	Kentucky.........................	100.0	99.1	0.8	91.2	8.7	8.1	0.6
22	Louisiana	100.0	99.6	0.4	92.9	7.1	6.7	0.3
23	Maine.............................	100.0	99.3	0.7	93.7	6.3	5.8	0.4
24	Maryland.........................	100.0	98.2	1.7	71.9	28.0	26.5	1.5
25	Massachusetts.................	100.0	97.9	1.9	70.2	29.6	27.9	1.7
26	Michigan.........................	100.0	98.8	1.2	87.0	12.9	11.9	1.0
27	Minnesota	100.0	98.5	1.5	80.9	19.1	17.9	1.1
28	Mississippi......................	100.0	99.8	0.2	95.8	4.2	4.1	0.2
29	Missouri..........................	100.0	99.3	0.6	90.8	9.1	8.7	0.5
30	Montana..........................	100.0	99.7	0.3	96.2	3.8	3.6	0.2
31	Nebraska	100.0	99.1	0.9	84.0	15.9	15.2	0.7
32	Nevada...........................	100.0	99.0	1.0	62.8	37.2	36.3	0.9
33	New Hampshire	100.0	98.8	1.1	86.7	13.2	12.4	0.8
34	New Jersey......................	100.0	97.5	2.5	61.7	38.2	35.9	2.3
35	New Mexico.....................	100.0	99.2	0.8	80.8	19.2	18.7	0.5
36	New York........................	100.0	97.8	2.1	64.3	35.6	33.8	1.9
37	North Carolina................	100.0	98.9	1.0	80.2	19.7	18.9	0.9
38	North Dakota..................	100.0	99.3	0.7	95.5	4.5	3.8	0.7
39	Ohio...............................	100.0	99.3	0.7	91.3	8.7	8.1	0.5
40	Oklahoma........................	100.0	99.0	0.9	86.1	13.8	13.1	0.7
41	Oregon	100.0	98.9	1.1	75.8	24.2	23.3	0.9
42	Pennsylvania...................	100.0	98.9	1.0	87.7	12.2	11.4	0.8
44	Rhode Island...................	100.0	98.1	1.8	76.6	23.3	21.8	1.5
45	South Carolina................	100.0	99.4	0.5	89.0	11.0	10.5	0.4
46	South Dakota..................	100.0	99.4	0.6	93.6	6.3	5.9	0.4
47	Tennessee	100.0	99.0	1.0	87.6	12.4	11.7	0.7
48	Texas..............................	100.0	98.5	1.5	66.7	33.3	32.0	1.4
49	Utah...............................	100.0	99.3	0.7	83.3	16.7	16.1	0.5
50	Vermont..........................	100.0	99.3	0.6	92.8	7.1	6.6	0.5
51	Virginia...........................	100.0	98.5	1.4	76.3	23.6	22.4	1.2
53	Washington.....................	100.0	98.2	1.7	71.1	28.9	27.4	1.4
54	West Virginia	100.0	99.7	0.3	97.5	2.4	2.2	0.2
55	Wisconsin........................	100.0	99.1	0.9	88.1	11.8	11.3	0.5
56	Wyoming.........................	100.0	99.6	0.4	90.7	9.3	9.2	0.2

Table D-1: States—Children—*Continued*

		Own children under 6 years in families and subfamilies										
		Own children under 6 years living with two parents					Own children under 6 years living with one parent					
State FIPS code	State	Total under 6 years living with two parents:	Both parents in labor force	Father only in labor force	Mother only in labor force	Neither parent in labor force	Total under 6 years living with one parent	Total under 6 years living with father	Living with father in labor force	Living with father not in labor force	Total under 6 years living with mother	Living with mother in labor force	Living with mother not in labor force
	United States............	63.4	36.8	23.7	1.9	1.0	36.6	8.0	7.1	0.9	28.6	20.8	7.8
1	Alabama........................	57.8	33.3	21.8	1.9	0.9	42.2	6.0	5.0	0.9	36.2	26.3	9.9
2	Alaska..........................	65.1	34.6	26.2	2.9	1.4	34.9	10.9	9.9	1.0	24.0	17.6	6.4
4	Arizona........................	60.4	30.4	26.4	2.2	1.3	39.6	9.8	8.6	1.3	29.8	20.8	9.0
5	Arkansas......................	60.8	34.6	23.0	2.0	1.1	39.2	8.1	6.8	1.3	31.2	22.5	8.7
6	California......................	64.3	35.0	26.3	1.9	1.2	35.7	9.2	8.3	0.9	26.4	17.8	8.6
8	Colorado	70.5	39.2	28.0	2.4	0.9	29.5	7.3	6.7	0.6	22.2	16.3	5.8
9	Connecticut..................	66.5	42.8	21.3	1.9	0.5	33.5	6.3	5.7	0.7	27.2	21.3	5.9
10	Delaware......................	57.9	35.6	19.7	1.4	1.1	42.1	9.9	8.8	1.1	32.2	25.6	6.6
11	District of Columbia........	48.9	35.6	11.1	1.7	0.5	51.1	8.1	6.9	1.2	43.0	30.8	12.2
12	Florida	57.7	34.0	20.8	2.0	0.9	42.3	9.2	8.1	1.1	33.1	24.9	8.2
13	Georgia	59.4	33.9	23.0	1.7	0.9	40.6	7.9	6.9	1.0	32.7	23.9	8.8
15	Hawaii	67.0	39.8	24.0	2.1	1.1	33.0	8.1	7.4	0.7	24.9	17.1	7.8
16	Idaho............................	74.8	36.9	35.4	1.6	0.9	25.2	6.6	5.8	0.9	18.5	13.4	5.1
17	Illinois..........................	64.8	39.2	23.2	1.6	0.8	35.2	7.7	7.0	0.6	27.5	21.3	6.3
18	Indiana.........................	63.1	37.4	22.8	1.9	0.9	36.9	8.1	7.1	0.9	28.8	22.0	6.8
19	Iowa.............................	69.0	49.7	16.9	1.7	0.7	31.0	7.9	7.3	0.6	23.1	18.3	4.8
20	Kansas..........................	67.3	40.8	24.3	1.7	0.5	32.7	7.9	7.2	0.6	24.8	18.8	6.0
21	Kentucky.......................	62.3	37.2	20.8	2.3	1.9	37.7	8.3	7.0	1.3	29.4	20.9	8.5
22	Louisiana......................	50.1	30.1	17.9	1.3	0.8	49.9	9.0	7.8	1.2	40.9	29.4	11.5
23	Maine...........................	66.4	43.4	19.0	2.7	1.4	33.6	9.7	8.9	0.8	23.9	16.8	7.2
24	Maryland	62.6	41.4	19.1	1.5	0.6	37.4	7.9	7.3	0.6	29.5	22.9	6.5
25	Massachusetts	68.4	45.9	19.7	2.0	0.9	31.6	5.8	5.2	0.7	25.7	18.5	7.2
26	Michigan.......................	62.2	36.9	21.6	2.4	1.4	37.8	8.0	6.9	1.1	29.8	22.5	7.3
27	Minnesota.....................	70.7	49.6	18.4	1.9	0.8	29.3	7.6	7.1	0.5	21.7	17.2	4.5
28	Mississippi....................	49.0	30.3	16.1	1.7	0.9	51.0	7.2	6.2	1.0	43.7	32.0	11.7
29	Missouri........................	62.8	38.7	21.0	1.9	1.2	37.2	8.3	7.3	1.0	28.9	22.1	6.7
30	Montana.......................	68.1	38.5	26.0	2.3	1.3	31.9	7.6	6.9	0.7	24.2	18.7	5.6
31	Nebraska	68.9	46.3	20.4	1.4	0.8	31.1	7.6	7.1	0.5	23.5	18.7	4.8
32	Nevada.........................	62.9	34.6	25.6	1.8	0.8	37.1	10.3	9.5	0.8	26.9	20.3	6.6
33	New Hampshire	68.2	43.0	22.5	1.9	0.9	31.8	8.8	8.1	0.7	23.0	17.1	5.9
34	New Jersey....................	68.8	41.9	23.7	2.5	0.6	31.2	6.7	6.0	0.7	24.5	18.2	6.3
35	New Mexico...................	54.2	28.0	23.0	2.1	1.2	45.8	10.0	8.4	1.5	35.8	25.7	10.2
36	New York......................	63.7	36.8	23.4	2.5	1.0	36.3	7.2	6.3	0.9	29.1	20.4	8.7
37	North Carolina...............	60.5	35.1	22.7	1.9	0.8	39.5	8.5	7.6	0.8	31.1	23.0	8.1
38	North Dakota.................	71.2	49.6	19.3	1.7	0.6	28.8	7.8	7.2	0.5	21.0	15.6	5.4
39	Ohio	60.7	38.1	19.8	1.9	0.9	39.3	7.7	6.8	0.9	31.5	23.7	7.9
40	Oklahoma.....................	63.1	35.0	24.9	2.0	1.2	36.9	8.7	7.8	1.0	28.2	19.4	8.8
41	Oregon.........................	68.8	38.5	26.2	2.8	1.3	31.2	8.1	7.2	0.9	23.1	15.6	7.5
42	Pennsylvania	63.2	39.5	21.0	1.7	1.0	36.8	7.7	6.8	1.0	29.1	21.3	7.8
44	Rhode Island.................	57.3	38.7	15.5	2.1	0.9	42.7	8.9	8.1	0.8	33.9	25.1	8.7
45	South Carolina...............	54.8	32.5	19.5	1.7	1.0	45.2	8.0	7.1	0.9	37.2	28.3	8.9
46	South Dakota.................	64.2	46.3	15.6	1.6	0.7	35.8	9.2	8.1	1.1	26.6	20.9	5.7
47	Tennessee	60.7	34.3	23.6	1.9	1.0	39.3	7.9	6.8	1.1	31.4	22.9	8.6
48	Texas...........................	62.9	31.9	28.5	1.6	0.9	37.1	7.3	6.6	0.7	29.8	20.7	9.1
49	Utah.............................	81.0	35.6	42.8	1.9	0.8	19.0	4.7	4.5	0.2	14.3	10.6	3.7
50	Vermont	65.8	45.5	17.6	1.9	0.8	34.2	8.6	7.1	1.4	25.7	18.9	6.8
51	Virginia.........................	67.3	39.9	25.3	1.6	0.6	32.7	6.6	6.0	0.5	26.1	19.9	6.1
53	Washington...................	69.8	36.5	30.2	2.0	1.1	30.2	8.0	7.1	0.9	22.2	15.9	6.3
54	West Virginia	61.6	32.7	24.1	3.0	1.7	38.4	9.0	7.6	1.4	29.4	17.4	12.0
55	Wisconsin......................	66.9	45.6	18.5	2.0	0.8	33.1	8.2	7.4	0.8	24.9	19.8	5.1
56	Wyoming.......................	71.0	41.6	27.4	1.2	0.9	29.0	9.0	8.3	0.7	19.9	15.9	4.0

State FIPS code	State	Total own children 6 to 17 years	Own children 6 to 17 years in families and subfamilies					
			Nativity and parentage, age 6 to 17					
			Child is native	Child is foreign born	Only native parent(s)	One or more foreign-born parent	One or more foreign-born parent: - Child is native	One or more foreign-born parent: - Child is foreign born
	United States..............	46,958,317	44,846,225	2,087,226	35,437,839	11,495,612	9,602,404	1,893,208
1	Alabama........................	706,235	693,639	12,193	658,143	47,689	37,602	10,087
2	Alaska...........................	116,312	111,872	4,434	101,261	15,045	11,361	3,684
4	Arizona.........................	1,023,000	975,017	47,672	723,136	299,553	254,623	44,930
5	Arkansas.......................	441,183	431,024	10,052	391,406	49,670	40,572	9,098
6	California......................	5,853,622	5,448,676	401,428	2,851,319	2,998,785	2,609,385	389,400
8	Colorado.......................	786,623	752,201	33,932	613,925	172,208	143,069	29,139
9	Connecticut...................	537,889	511,478	26,072	418,054	119,496	97,357	22,139
10	Delaware	127,403	124,056	3,326	106,740	20,642	17,987	2,655
11	District of Columbia........	56,561	53,471	3,002	43,617	12,856	10,158	2,698
12	Florida..........................	2,555,531	2,382,606	171,566	1,715,268	838,904	675,534	163,370
13	Georgia	1,569,087	1,511,669	56,453	1,270,789	297,333	246,621	50,712
15	Hawaii..........................	185,199	172,659	12,485	128,174	56,970	45,175	11,795
16	Idaho............................	273,849	267,308	6,520	236,322	37,506	31,821	5,685
17	Illinois..........................	1,987,691	1,902,125	84,218	1,462,047	524,296	448,975	75,321
18	Indiana.........................	1,015,194	992,328	22,645	926,274	88,699	70,446	18,253
19	Iowa.............................	463,686	452,742	10,723	420,856	42,609	34,076	8,533
20	Kansas..........................	456,036	442,150	13,711	388,108	67,753	55,641	12,112
21	Kentucky.......................	629,557	616,049	13,166	589,082	40,133	30,094	10,039
22	Louisiana	685,825	676,658	9,048	647,771	37,935	30,202	7,733
23	Maine...........................	175,298	171,896	3,230	163,135	11,991	9,772	2,219
24	Maryland	857,599	809,451	47,164	651,998	204,617	162,276	42,341
25	Massachusetts	919,417	870,018	47,947	689,426	228,539	186,252	42,287
26	Michigan.......................	1,491,118	1,448,912	41,763	1,317,140	173,535	141,109	32,426
27	Minnesota	824,271	790,057	33,525	698,736	124,846	98,903	25,943
28	Mississippi....................	459,438	454,918	4,339	443,602	15,655	12,144	3,511
29	Missouri........................	887,030	867,999	18,702	822,048	64,653	50,408	14,245
30	Montana.......................	138,354	137,128	1,177	133,167	5,138	4,754	384
31	Nebraska	291,288	281,263	9,965	249,333	41,895	33,170	8,725
32	Nevada.........................	415,876	391,908	23,865	253,525	162,248	139,095	23,153
33	New Hampshire	186,495	181,335	4,887	166,925	19,297	16,399	2,898
34	New Jersey....................	1,336,992	1,246,532	89,850	870,595	465,787	382,868	82,919
35	New Mexico...................	321,170	307,549	13,425	250,728	70,246	57,829	12,417
36	New York.......................	2,731,445	2,550,426	178,881	1,772,063	957,244	791,484	165,760
37	North Carolina...............	1,449,934	1,398,512	50,607	1,210,200	238,919	194,784	44,135
38	North Dakota.................	97,252	95,350	1,902	92,504	4,748	3,077	1,671
39	Ohio.............................	1,717,322	1,684,816	32,005	1,602,932	113,889	89,793	24,096
40	Oklahoma.....................	581,091	566,160	14,662	509,821	71,001	57,767	13,234
41	Oregon	549,985	523,948	25,749	419,912	129,785	107,716	22,069
42	Pennsylvania.................	1,775,071	1,727,662	46,490	1,583,580	190,572	153,917	36,655
44	Rhode Island.................	141,593	134,323	7,191	105,384	36,130	30,293	5,837
45	South Carolina...............	676,199	661,445	14,588	615,456	60,577	47,963	12,614
46	South Dakota.................	125,883	123,246	2,388	119,234	6,400	4,446	1,954
47	Tennessee	939,154	915,420	23,401	847,640	91,181	71,510	19,671
48	Texas............................	4,393,779	4,135,905	256,009	2,869,385	1,522,529	1,277,331	245,198
49	Utah.............................	554,583	537,068	17,376	459,508	94,936	79,428	15,508
50	Vermont	82,240	80,378	1,689	76,761	5,306	4,477	829
51	Virginia.........................	1,180,855	1,127,728	52,805	935,361	245,172	198,542	46,630
53	Washington	1,007,389	952,567	54,192	735,404	271,355	222,970	48,385
54	West Virginia	240,007	238,135	1,859	233,582	6,412	5,159	1,253
55	Wisconsin	854,027	832,819	20,959	767,907	85,871	70,811	15,060
56	Wyoming.......................	85,679	83,623	1,988	78,555	7,056	5,258	1,798

Table D-1: States—Children—*Continued*

| State FIPS code | State | Own children 6 to 17 years in families and subfamilies | | | | | | | | | | | |
| | | Own children 6 to 17 years living with two parents | | | | | Own children 6 to 17 living with one parent | | | | | | |
		Total 6 to 17 years living with two parents:	Both parents in labor force	Father only in labor force	Mother only in labor force	Neither parent in labor force	Total 6 to 17 years living with one parent	Total 6 to 17 years living with father	Living with father in labor force	Living with father not in labor force	Total 6 to 17 years living with mother	Living with mother in labor force	Living with mother not in labor force
	United States...............	30,813,108	19,926,045	9,051,973	1,243,503	591,587	16,145,209	3,405,642	2,996,611	409,031	12,739,567	10,178,703	2,560,864
1	Alabama	432,153	271,248	129,956	19,902	11,047	274,082	45,919	38,848	7,071	228,163	176,092	52,071
2	Alaska..........................	78,539	48,975	22,761	4,667	2,136	37,773	11,007	8,746	2,261	26,766	21,757	5,009
4	Arizona........................	638,268	368,337	225,991	28,283	15,657	384,732	88,818	77,808	11,010	295,914	230,656	65,258
5	Arkansas......................	277,511	176,412	76,656	15,586	8,857	163,672	34,789	29,382	5,407	128,883	99,912	28,971
6	California.....................	3,875,672	2,295,285	1,341,035	153,669	85,683	1,977,950	477,914	426,209	51,705	1,500,036	1,156,527	343,509
8	Colorado......................	549,964	357,313	166,214	18,083	8,354	236,659	55,662	50,924	4,738	180,997	149,364	31,633
9	Connecticut..................	366,074	258,226	91,992	12,104	3,752	171,815	31,833	28,645	3,188	139,982	118,627	21,355
10	Delaware	77,541	54,784	17,753	3,014	1,990	49,862	10,995	10,107	888	38,867	32,086	6,781
11	District of Columbia........	20,239	14,752	3,963	984	540	36,322	5,218	4,178	1,040	31,104	23,837	7,267
12	Florida.........................	1,573,233	1,025,923	440,517	73,837	32,956	982,298	192,536	169,068	23,468	789,762	644,907	144,855
13	Georgia........................	973,358	620,645	293,363	40,370	18,980	595,729	105,321	90,058	15,263	490,408	394,780	95,628
15	Hawaii	130,709	90,577	31,852	5,167	3,113	54,490	13,397	11,434	1,963	41,093	32,861	8,232
16	Idaho...........................	201,615	121,230	68,995	8,153	3,237	72,234	21,575	19,319	2,256	50,659	40,727	9,932
17	Illinois.........................	1,331,419	878,257	389,664	45,673	17,825	656,272	127,942	114,818	13,124	528,330	440,061	88,269
18	Indiana........................	674,510	449,368	190,003	24,622	10,517	340,684	75,888	67,327	8,561	264,796	213,352	51,444
19	Iowa............................	325,890	250,488	60,288	10,788	4,326	137,796	34,995	31,020	3,975	102,801	86,928	15,873
20	Kansas.........................	321,449	224,664	83,427	10,328	3,030	134,587	31,810	29,076	2,734	102,777	87,656	15,121
21	Kentucky......................	407,305	266,425	105,648	20,631	14,601	222,252	52,139	43,002	9,137	170,113	128,832	41,281
22	Louisiana	380,948	252,310	103,945	15,928	8,765	304,877	51,262	43,207	8,055	253,615	200,596	53,019
23	Maine..........................	117,029	82,941	25,662	6,050	2,376	58,269	15,948	13,107	2,841	42,321	33,952	8,369
24	Maryland	552,961	399,657	127,409	20,049	5,846	304,638	59,492	54,588	4,904	245,146	207,234	37,912
25	Massachusetts	626,895	453,249	142,948	22,079	8,619	292,522	51,191	45,156	6,035	241,331	187,777	53,554
26	Michigan......................	984,742	646,809	267,402	45,777	24,754	506,376	106,788	91,534	15,254	399,588	315,216	84,372
27	Minnesota	591,014	447,631	117,626	18,794	6,963	233,257	59,452	54,237	5,215	173,805	146,724	27,081
28	Mississippi	248,031	162,350	64,796	14,312	6,573	211,407	31,010	25,525	5,485	180,397	137,003	43,394
29	Missouri.......................	588,398	406,847	146,067	22,551	12,933	298,632	65,927	57,792	8,135	232,705	190,418	42,287
30	Montana.......................	96,814	66,820	24,104	3,953	1,937	41,540	12,128	10,615	1,513	29,412	24,220	5,192
31	Nebraska......................	207,111	153,352	45,225	5,866	2,668	84,177	21,470	19,712	1,758	62,707	54,549	8,158
32	Nevada........................	259,896	160,476	82,485	11,797	5,138	155,980	36,422	33,517	2,905	119,558	97,667	21,891
33	New Hampshire	134,134	96,088	31,270	4,338	2,438	52,361	13,535	11,871	1,664	38,826	32,440	6,386
34	New Jersey....................	932,311	623,150	265,067	33,658	10,436	404,681	80,662	73,708	6,954	324,019	266,567	57,452
35	New Mexico..................	187,930	112,810	60,792	9,509	4,819	133,240	31,139	26,849	4,290	102,101	78,308	23,793
36	New York......................	1,762,106	1,121,912	521,304	83,308	35,582	969,339	181,533	158,202	23,331	787,806	614,801	173,005
37	North Carolina...............	908,082	591,898	255,620	42,345	18,219	541,852	107,707	94,017	13,690	434,145	350,707	83,438
38	North Dakota.................	71,138	53,627	15,074	1,683	754	26,114	8,057	7,701	356	18,057	15,122	2,935
39	Ohio............................	1,110,239	749,920	292,898	45,263	22,158	607,083	125,162	107,825	17,337	481,921	384,984	96,937
40	Oklahoma.....................	379,485	238,860	114,884	17,425	8,316	201,606	49,836	43,428	6,408	151,770	117,086	34,684
41	Oregon........................	373,685	238,844	112,604	14,759	7,478	176,300	44,951	38,747	6,204	131,349	103,888	27,461
42	Pennsylvania.................	1,182,432	797,436	315,307	46,420	23,269	592,639	126,026	107,926	18,100	466,613	361,431	105,182
44	Rhode Island.................	87,328	64,571	18,303	3,521	933	54,265	8,920	7,827	1,093	45,345	36,574	8,771
45	South Carolina...............	400,573	260,542	112,748	17,958	9,325	275,626	48,866	42,554	6,312	226,760	182,557	44,203
46	South Dakota.................	85,644	67,476	14,589	2,310	1,269	40,239	11,327	9,945	1,382	28,912	24,882	4,030
47	Tennessee	602,039	379,227	177,844	28,520	16,448	337,115	68,412	58,819	9,593	268,703	210,258	58,445
48	Texas...........................	2,866,593	1,698,952	1,016,867	101,522	49,252	1,527,186	289,006	258,566	30,440	1,238,180	994,448	243,732
49	Utah............................	439,210	237,355	183,934	12,926	4,995	115,373	27,129	24,777	2,352	88,244	72,843	15,401
50	Vermont.......................	56,646	43,266	10,264	2,332	784	25,594	7,049	6,096	953	18,545	14,711	3,834
51	Virginia........................	817,239	542,406	232,025	29,005	13,803	363,616	75,243	67,591	7,652	288,373	238,662	49,711
53	Washington	701,973	433,986	224,819	29,574	13,594	305,416	76,457	66,914	9,543	228,959	180,841	48,118
54	West Virginia	157,371	93,351	46,920	11,087	6,013	82,636	20,849	16,667	4,182	61,787	42,948	18,839
55	Wisconsin.....................	588,156	434,075	125,157	21,069	7,855	265,871	67,803	60,949	6,854	198,068	164,702	33,366
56	Wyoming......................	59,506	40,942	15,936	1,954	674	26,173	7,125	6,673	452	19,048	15,625	3,423

Table D-1: States—Children—*Continued*

State FIPS code	State	Total own children 6 to 17 years	Own children 6 to 17 years in families and subfamilies					
			Nativity and parentage, age 6 to 17					
			Child is native	Child is foreign born	Only native parent(s)	One or more foreign-born parent	One or more foreign-born parent: - Child is native	One or more foreign-born parent: - Child is foreign born
	United States..............	100.0	95.5	4.4	75.5	24.5	20.4	4.0
1	Alabama.........................	100.0	98.2	1.7	93.2	6.8	5.3	1.4
2	Alaska...........................	100.0	96.2	3.8	87.1	12.9	9.8	3.2
4	Arizona..........................	100.0	95.3	4.7	70.7	29.3	24.9	4.4
5	Arkansas........................	100.0	97.7	2.3	88.7	11.3	9.2	2.1
6	California.......................	100.0	93.1	6.9	48.7	51.2	44.6	6.7
8	Colorado........................	100.0	95.6	4.3	78.0	21.9	18.2	3.7
9	Connecticut....................	100.0	95.1	4.8	77.7	22.2	18.1	4.1
10	Delaware	100.0	97.4	2.6	83.8	16.2	14.1	2.1
11	District of Columbia........	100.0	94.5	5.3	77.1	22.7	18.0	4.8
12	Florida	100.0	93.2	6.7	67.1	32.8	26.4	6.4
13	Georgia..........................	100.0	96.3	3.6	81.0	18.9	15.7	3.2
15	Hawaii	100.0	93.2	6.7	69.2	30.8	24.4	6.4
16	Idaho.............................	100.0	97.6	2.4	86.3	13.7	11.6	2.1
17	Illinois...........................	100.0	95.7	4.2	73.6	26.4	22.6	3.8
18	Indiana..........................	100.0	97.7	2.2	91.2	8.7	6.9	1.8
19	Iowa..............................	100.0	97.6	2.3	90.8	9.2	7.3	1.8
20	Kansas...........................	100.0	97.0	3.0	85.1	14.9	12.2	2.7
21	Kentucky	100.0	97.9	2.1	93.6	6.4	4.8	1.6
22	Louisiana	100.0	98.7	1.3	94.5	5.5	4.4	1.1
23	Maine............................	100.0	98.1	1.8	93.1	6.8	5.6	1.3
24	Maryland	100.0	94.4	5.5	76.0	23.9	18.9	4.9
25	Massachusetts	100.0	94.6	5.2	75.0	24.9	20.3	4.6
26	Michigan........................	100.0	97.2	2.8	88.3	11.6	9.5	2.2
27	Minnesota	100.0	95.8	4.1	84.8	15.1	12.0	3.1
28	Mississippi.....................	100.0	99.0	0.9	96.6	3.4	2.6	0.8
29	Missouri.........................	100.0	97.9	2.1	92.7	7.3	5.7	1.6
30	Montana.........................	100.0	99.1	0.9	96.3	3.7	3.4	0.3
31	Nebraska........................	100.0	96.6	3.4	85.6	14.4	11.4	3.0
32	Nevada	100.0	94.2	5.7	61.0	39.0	33.4	5.6
33	New Hampshire	100.0	97.2	2.6	89.5	10.3	8.8	1.6
34	New Jersey.....................	100.0	93.2	6.7	65.1	34.8	28.6	6.2
35	New Mexico....................	100.0	95.8	4.2	78.1	21.9	18.0	3.9
36	New York........................	100.0	93.4	6.5	64.9	35.0	29.0	6.1
37	North Carolina................	100.0	96.5	3.5	83.5	16.5	13.4	3.0
38	North Dakota..................	100.0	98.0	2.0	95.1	4.9	3.2	1.7
39	Ohio..............................	100.0	98.1	1.9	93.3	6.6	5.2	1.4
40	Oklahoma.......................	100.0	97.4	2.5	87.7	12.2	9.9	2.3
41	Oregon	100.0	95.3	4.7	76.3	23.6	19.6	4.0
42	Pennsylvania	100.0	97.3	2.6	89.2	10.7	8.7	2.1
44	Rhode Island..................	100.0	94.9	5.1	74.4	25.5	21.4	4.1
45	South Carolina...............	100.0	97.8	2.2	91.0	9.0	7.1	1.9
46	South Dakota..................	100.0	97.9	1.9	94.7	5.1	3.5	1.6
47	Tennessee	100.0	97.5	2.5	90.3	9.7	7.6	2.1
48	Texas.............................	100.0	94.1	5.8	65.3	34.7	29.1	5.6
49	Utah..............................	100.0	96.8	3.1	82.9	17.1	14.3	2.8
50	Vermont	100.0	97.7	2.1	93.3	6.5	5.4	1.0
51	Virginia..........................	100.0	95.5	4.5	79.2	20.8	16.8	3.9
53	Washington	100.0	94.6	5.4	73.0	26.9	22.1	4.8
54	West Virginia	100.0	99.2	0.8	97.3	2.7	2.1	0.5
55	Wisconsin.......................	100.0	97.5	2.5	89.9	10.1	8.3	1.8
56	Wyoming........................	100.0	97.6	2.3	91.7	8.2	6.1	2.1

Table D-1: States—Children—*Continued*

| State FIPS code | State | Own children 6 to 17 years in families and subfamilies | | | | | | | | | | | |
| | | Own children 6 to 17 years living with two parents | | | | | Own children 6 to 17 living with one parent | | | | | | |
		Total 6 to 17 years living with two parents:	Both parents in labor force	Father only in labor force	Mother only in labor force	Neither parent in labor force	Total 6 to 17 years living with one parent	Total 6 to 17 years living with father	Living with father in labor force	Living with father not in labor force	Total 6 to 17 years living with mother	Living with mother in labor force	Living with mother not in labor force
	United States............	65.6	42.4	19.3	2.6	1.3	34.4	7.3	6.4	0.9	27.1	21.7	5.5
1	Alabama........................	61.2	38.4	18.4	2.8	1.6	38.8	6.5	5.5	1.0	32.3	24.9	7.4
2	Alaska..........................	67.5	42.1	19.6	4.0	1.8	32.5	9.5	7.5	1.9	23.0	18.7	4.3
4	Arizona.........................	62.4	36.0	22.1	2.8	1.5	37.6	8.7	7.6	1.1	28.9	22.5	6.4
5	Arkansas.......................	62.9	40.0	17.4	3.5	2.0	37.1	7.9	6.7	1.2	29.2	22.6	6.6
6	California......................	66.2	39.2	22.9	2.6	1.5	33.8	8.2	7.3	0.9	25.6	19.8	5.9
8	Colorado	69.9	45.4	21.1	2.3	1.1	30.1	7.1	6.5	0.6	23.0	19.0	4.0
9	Connecticut...................	68.1	48.0	17.1	2.3	0.7	31.9	5.9	5.3	0.6	26.0	22.1	4.0
10	Delaware	60.9	43.0	13.9	2.4	1.6	39.1	8.6	7.9	0.7	30.5	25.2	5.3
11	District of Columbia........	35.8	26.1	7.0	1.7	1.0	64.2	9.2	7.4	1.8	55.0	42.1	12.8
12	Florida.........................	61.6	40.1	17.2	2.9	1.3	38.4	7.5	6.6	0.9	30.9	25.2	5.7
13	Georgia	62.0	39.6	18.7	2.6	1.2	38.0	6.7	5.7	1.0	31.3	25.2	6.1
15	Hawaii..........................	70.6	48.9	17.2	2.8	1.7	29.4	7.2	6.2	1.1	22.2	17.7	4.4
16	Idaho...........................	73.6	44.3	25.2	3.0	1.2	26.4	7.9	7.1	0.8	18.5	14.9	3.6
17	Illinois..........................	67.0	44.2	19.6	2.3	0.9	33.0	6.4	5.8	0.7	26.6	22.1	4.4
18	Indiana.........................	66.4	44.3	18.7	2.4	1.0	33.6	7.5	6.6	0.8	26.1	21.0	5.1
19	Iowa............................	70.3	54.0	13.0	2.3	0.9	29.7	7.5	6.7	0.9	22.2	18.7	3.4
20	Kansas..........................	70.5	49.3	18.3	2.3	0.7	29.5	7.0	6.4	0.6	22.5	19.2	3.3
21	Kentucky.......................	64.7	42.3	16.8	3.3	2.3	35.3	8.3	6.8	1.5	27.0	20.5	6.6
22	Louisiana	55.5	36.8	15.2	2.3	1.3	44.5	7.5	6.3	1.2	37.0	29.2	7.7
23	Maine...........................	66.8	47.3	14.6	3.5	1.4	33.2	9.1	7.5	1.6	24.1	19.4	4.8
24	Maryland	64.5	46.6	14.9	2.3	0.7	35.5	6.9	6.4	0.6	28.6	24.2	4.4
25	Massachusetts	68.2	49.3	15.5	2.4	0.9	31.8	5.6	4.9	0.7	26.2	20.4	5.8
26	Michigan.......................	66.0	43.4	17.9	3.1	1.7	34.0	7.2	6.1	1.0	26.8	21.1	5.7
27	Minnesota	71.7	54.3	14.3	2.3	0.8	28.3	7.2	6.6	0.6	21.1	17.8	3.3
28	Mississippi.....................	54.0	35.3	14.1	3.1	1.4	46.0	6.7	5.6	1.2	39.3	29.8	9.4
29	Missouri........................	66.3	45.9	16.5	2.5	1.5	33.7	7.4	6.5	0.9	26.2	21.5	4.8
30	Montana........................	70.0	48.3	17.4	2.9	1.4	30.0	8.8	7.7	1.1	21.3	17.5	3.8
31	Nebraska	71.1	52.6	15.5	2.0	0.9	28.9	7.4	6.8	0.6	21.5	18.7	2.8
32	Nevada	62.5	38.6	19.8	2.8	1.2	37.5	8.8	8.1	0.7	28.7	23.5	5.3
33	New Hampshire	71.9	51.5	16.8	2.3	1.3	28.1	7.3	6.4	0.9	20.8	17.4	3.4
34	New Jersey....................	69.7	46.6	19.8	2.5	0.8	30.3	6.0	5.5	0.5	24.2	19.9	4.3
35	New Mexico...................	58.5	35.1	18.9	3.0	1.5	41.5	9.7	8.4	1.3	31.8	24.4	7.4
36	New York......................	64.5	41.1	19.1	3.0	1.3	35.5	6.6	5.8	0.9	28.8	22.5	6.3
37	North Carolina...............	62.6	40.8	17.6	2.9	1.3	37.4	7.4	6.5	0.9	29.9	24.2	5.8
38	North Dakota.................	73.1	55.1	15.5	1.7	0.8	26.9	8.3	7.9	0.4	18.6	15.5	3.0
39	Ohio............................	64.6	43.7	17.1	2.6	1.3	35.4	7.3	6.3	1.0	28.1	22.4	5.6
40	Oklahoma......................	65.3	41.1	19.8	3.0	1.4	34.7	8.6	7.5	1.1	26.1	20.1	6.0
41	Oregon.........................	67.9	43.4	20.5	2.7	1.4	32.1	8.2	7.0	1.1	23.9	18.9	5.0
42	Pennsylvania	66.6	44.9	17.8	2.6	1.3	33.4	7.1	6.1	1.0	26.3	20.4	5.9
44	Rhode Island.................	61.7	45.6	12.9	2.5	0.7	38.3	6.3	5.5	0.8	32.0	25.8	6.2
45	South Carolina...............	59.2	38.5	16.7	2.7	1.4	40.8	7.2	6.3	0.9	33.5	27.0	6.5
46	South Dakota.................	68.0	53.6	11.6	1.8	1.0	32.0	9.0	7.9	1.1	23.0	19.8	3.2
47	Tennessee.....................	64.1	40.4	18.9	3.0	1.8	35.9	7.3	6.3	1.0	28.6	22.4	6.2
48	Texas...........................	65.2	38.7	23.1	2.3	1.1	34.8	6.6	5.9	0.7	28.2	22.6	5.5
49	Utah............................	79.2	42.8	33.2	2.3	0.9	20.8	4.9	4.5	0.4	15.9	13.1	2.8
50	Vermont	68.9	52.6	12.5	2.8	1.0	31.1	8.6	7.4	1.2	22.5	17.9	4.7
51	Virginia.........................	69.2	45.9	19.6	2.5	1.2	30.8	6.4	5.7	0.6	24.4	20.2	4.2
53	Washington....................	69.7	43.1	22.3	2.9	1.3	30.3	7.6	6.6	0.9	22.7	18.0	4.8
54	West Virginia	65.6	38.9	19.5	4.6	2.5	34.4	8.7	6.9	1.7	25.7	17.9	7.8
55	Wisconsin......................	68.9	50.8	14.7	2.5	0.9	31.1	7.9	7.1	0.8	23.2	19.3	3.9
56	Wyoming.......................	69.5	47.8	18.6	2.3	0.8	30.5	8.3	7.8	0.5	22.2	18.2	4.0

Table D-1: States—Children—*Continued*

State FIPS code	State	Grandchildren under 18 living with a grandparent householder	Grandparent householder responsible for own grandchildren under 18		Grandparent householder not responsible for own grandchildren under 18 years	Grandchildren under 18 living with a grandparent householder	Grandparent householder responsible for own grandchildren under 18		Grandparent householder not responsible for own grandchildren under 18 years
			Grandparent responsible	Grandparent responsible but parent present			Grandparent responsible	Grandparent responsible but parent present	
	United States...............	5,562,532	2,886,167	1,960,450	2,676,365	100.0	51.9	35.2	48.1
1	Alabama........................	114,322	71,861	43,416	42,461	100.0	62.9	38.0	37.1
2	Alaska..........................	12,875	7,248	5,521	5,627	100.0	56.3	42.9	43.7
4	Arizona........................	139,511	71,931	52,471	67,580	100.0	51.6	37.6	48.4
5	Arkansas......................	60,727	41,640	24,404	19,087	100.0	68.6	40.2	31.4
6	California......................	765,460	315,161	241,525	450,299	100.0	41.2	31.6	58.8
8	Colorado......................	70,888	35,811	23,747	35,077	100.0	50.5	33.5	49.5
9	Connecticut...................	42,141	19,648	13,314	22,493	100.0	46.6	31.6	53.4
10	Delaware	19,940	10,516	7,004	9,424	100.0	52.7	35.1	47.3
11	District of Columbia........	11,228	5,131	3,525	6,097	100.0	45.7	31.4	54.3
12	Florida.........................	336,635	179,868	122,006	156,767	100.0	53.4	36.2	46.6
13	Georgia	217,865	132,951	87,391	84,914	100.0	61.0	40.1	39.0
15	Hawaii..........................	47,670	15,613	11,998	32,057	100.0	32.8	25.2	67.2
16	Idaho...........................	20,822	10,626	7,148	10,196	100.0	51.0	34.3	49.0
17	Illinois.........................	213,052	107,367	78,921	105,685	100.0	50.4	37.0	49.6
18	Indiana.........................	111,312	63,628	41,057	47,684	100.0	57.2	36.9	42.8
19	Iowa............................	32,341	17,205	10,558	15,136	100.0	53.2	32.6	46.8
20	Kansas.........................	40,225	22,638	15,135	17,587	100.0	56.3	37.6	43.7
21	Kentucky.......................	89,226	57,729	30,970	31,497	100.0	64.7	34.7	35.3
22	Louisiana	119,313	76,612	49,659	42,701	100.0	64.2	41.6	35.8
23	Maine...........................	14,282	7,193	4,763	7,089	100.0	50.4	33.3	49.6
24	Maryland.......................	107,342	49,500	36,337	57,842	100.0	46.1	33.9	53.9
25	Massachusetts	79,754	33,431	23,379	46,323	100.0	41.9	29.3	58.1
26	Michigan.......................	144,930	72,593	48,902	72,337	100.0	50.1	33.7	49.9
27	Minnesota	48,920	23,505	15,032	25,415	100.0	48.0	30.7	52.0
28	Mississippi.....................	92,275	57,482	37,255	34,793	100.0	62.3	40.4	37.7
29	Missouri........................	97,357	51,278	32,671	46,079	100.0	52.7	33.6	47.3
30	Montana........................	13,284	8,038	4,857	5,246	100.0	60.5	36.6	39.5
31	Nebraska	20,035	10,642	6,859	9,393	100.0	53.1	34.2	46.9
32	Nevada.........................	44,276	25,321	18,652	18,955	100.0	57.2	42.1	42.8
33	New Hampshire	14,245	5,935	3,835	8,310	100.0	41.7	26.9	58.3
34	New Jersey.....................	119,888	48,589	34,463	71,299	100.0	40.5	28.7	59.5
35	New Mexico....................	50,901	30,575	22,050	20,326	100.0	60.1	43.3	39.9
36	New York.......................	305,826	130,656	97,007	175,170	100.0	42.7	31.7	57.3
37	North Carolina................	175,785	105,795	68,359	69,990	100.0	60.2	38.9	39.8
38	North Dakota..................	6,959	3,620	2,395	3,339	100.0	52.0	34.4	48.0
39	Ohio............................	183,181	106,007	65,635	77,174	100.0	57.9	35.8	42.1
40	Oklahoma......................	75,115	45,609	25,914	29,506	100.0	60.7	34.5	39.3
41	Oregon	48,787	23,457	15,047	25,330	100.0	48.1	30.8	51.9
42	Pennsylvania	190,170	91,461	61,658	98,709	100.0	48.1	32.4	51.9
44	Rhode Island..................	13,367	5,678	3,815	7,689	100.0	42.5	28.5	57.5
45	South Carolina................	110,685	64,332	39,914	46,353	100.0	58.1	36.1	41.9
46	South Dakota..................	12,458	8,033	5,601	4,425	100.0	64.5	45.0	35.5
47	Tennessee	133,235	80,190	48,871	53,045	100.0	60.2	36.7	39.8
48	Texas...........................	626,060	351,282	244,504	274,778	100.0	56.1	39.1	43.9
49	Utah............................	51,012	20,569	16,360	30,443	100.0	40.3	32.1	59.7
50	Vermont........................	6,307	3,076	1,788	3,231	100.0	48.8	28.3	51.2
51	Virginia.........................	131,873	66,804	45,363	65,069	100.0	50.7	34.4	49.3
53	Washington	82,069	40,904	27,621	41,165	100.0	49.8	33.7	50.2
54	West Virginia	33,480	20,476	12,358	13,004	100.0	61.2	36.9	38.8
55	Wisconsin......................	56,875	27,177	17,365	29,698	100.0	47.8	30.5	52.2
56	Wyoming.......................	6,246	3,775	2,050	2,471	100.0	60.4	32.8	39.6

This page is intentionally left blank

Table D-2: Counties with a Population of 50,000 or More—Children

State/county FIPS code	State/County	Total own children under 18 in families and subfamilies	Total own children under 6 years	Nativity and parentage, under 6 years		Own children under 6 years living with two parents			Own children under 6 living with one parent	
				Child is foreign born, percent	One or more foreign-born parent, percent	Total under 6 years living with two parents, percent	Both parents in labor force, percent	One parent in labor force, percent	Total under 6 years living with one parent, percent	Parent in labor force, percent
00000	**United States**	70,173,842	23,215,525	1.3	25.0	63.4	36.8	25.7	36.6	27.9
01000	**Alabama**	1,050,918	344,683	0.5	8.9	57.8	33.3	23.7	42.2	31.3
01001	Autauga County	13,022	4,068	0.0	1.8	64.7	36.6	26.1	35.3	27.6
01003	Baldwin County	41,970	13,637	0.9	8.4	66.0	37.8	28.2	34.0	23.2
01009	Blount County	12,999	4,013	1.6	16.7	63.1	34.1	27.9	36.9	23.4
01015	Calhoun County	23,927	7,931	0.0	5.3	50.3	29.5	20.4	49.7	42.9
01031	Coffee County	11,517	3,870	0.2	9.6	57.2	31.7	25.5	42.8	34.5
01033	Colbert County	11,162	3,408	0.0	4.5	62.3	33.1	28.4	37.7	17.2
01043	Cullman County	17,397	5,733	0.4	11.0	66.9	31.9	34.9	33.1	24.4
01045	Dale County	11,381	3,710	1.4	9.9	67.5	27.4	39.9	32.5	22.8
01049	DeKalb County	16,931	4,784	1.4	26.9	73.5	41.4	32.0	26.5	14.0
01051	Elmore County	17,568	5,338	0.0	7.6	64.1	30.7	32.3	35.9	28.0
01055	Etowah County	21,908	6,644	0.0	5.5	59.7	38.8	18.6	40.3	30.7
01069	Houston County	23,432	7,607	0.2	5.1	54.1	36.2	17.2	45.9	34.3
01071	Jackson County	11,030	3,094	0.0	0.6	80.5	41.6	36.1	19.5	15.3
01073	Jefferson County	144,042	50,325	0.5	11.3	56.2	32.8	22.7	43.8	33.0
01077	Lauderdale County	18,136	5,508	0.0	4.7	62.0	39.9	21.6	38.0	15.9
01081	Lee County	30,348	10,798	0.7	8.4	65.2	35.8	28.3	34.8	31.0
01083	Limestone County	19,523	6,471	2.2	12.4	64.8	32.9	31.7	35.2	27.8
01089	Madison County	75,406	24,086	0.5	8.8	62.9	38.4	23.9	37.1	31.8
01095	Marshall County	22,258	7,468	0.3	27.6	63.5	33.2	29.3	36.5	24.1
01097	Mobile County	94,063	31,561	0.8	6.4	47.2	27.4	18.5	52.8	40.0
01101	Montgomery County	53,540	18,041	0.8	10.1	47.2	27.0	19.9	52.8	38.3
01103	Morgan County	26,506	8,418	0.5	19.0	65.6	34.9	30.7	34.4	28.5
01113	Russell County	13,635	4,969	0.0	5.3	52.5	30.9	20.8	47.5	41.2
01115	St. Clair County	18,680	6,164	0.0	0.0	70.3	50.0	19.7	29.7	23.3
01117	Shelby County	48,693	15,511	1.3	15.2	83.7	46.7	36.1	16.3	13.6
01121	Talladega County	16,047	5,007	0.0	0.0	46.0	21.6	24.4	54.0	42.3
01125	Tuscaloosa County	40,286	13,869	0.4	10.5	61.6	40.0	20.0	38.4	23.4
01127	Walker County	13,797	4,604	0.0	3.6	54.5	26.0	23.8	45.5	27.0
02000	**Alaska**	179,648	63,336	0.3	10.7	65.1	34.6	29.1	34.9	27.5
02020	Anchorage Municipality	72,539	25,464	0.3	14.9	66.5	38.7	26.2	33.5	29.1
02090	Fairbanks North Star Borough	24,366	9,318	0.2	10.4	66.0	34.1	31.9	34.0	26.9
02122	Kenai Peninsula Borough	12,611	4,030	0.3	5.2	75.3	32.9	41.1	24.7	16.3
02170	Matanuska-Susitna Borough	24,830	8,164	0.1	6.5	75.1	31.2	41.7	24.9	18.5
04000	**Arizona**	1,531,962	508,962	1.2	26.8	60.4	30.4	28.6	39.6	29.3
04001	Apache County	19,997	6,702	0.6	6.5	40.1	17.4	19.9	59.9	35.5
04003	Cochise County	27,981	8,908	1.5	25.1	65.7	29.7	34.3	34.3	27.8
04005	Coconino County	29,100	9,808	0.3	11.7	50.5	28.8	20.2	49.5	34.9
04007	Gila County	10,181	3,333	0.8	5.1	40.4	23.9	14.5	59.6	45.7
04013	Maricopa County	961,136	319,826	1.4	30.6	61.6	31.4	28.9	38.4	28.7
04015	Mohave County	36,788	11,354	0.0	13.5	58.6	30.1	27.6	41.4	32.8
04017	Navajo County	28,255	9,278	0.1	4.7	43.6	21.2	20.5	56.4	36.3
04019	Pima County	208,664	69,613	1.5	22.7	58.6	30.0	27.7	41.4	31.3
04021	Pinal County	93,397	31,854	0.3	16.7	65.1	29.2	34.5	34.9	24.8
04025	Yavapai County	35,712	11,112	0.7	11.7	60.6	29.8	24.3	39.4	31.1
04027	Yuma County	52,096	17,932	1.5	41.3	62.2	32.1	29.0	37.8	25.3
05000	**Arkansas**	664,652	223,469	0.6	12.3	60.8	34.6	25.0	39.2	29.2
05007	Benton County	61,231	20,844	2.8	26.9	79.0	38.4	39.5	21.0	16.6
05031	Craighead County	23,020	8,298	0.0	4.8	58.2	35.7	22.4	41.8	32.6
05033	Crawford County	14,750	4,421	0.0	12.4	60.7	35.3	23.2	39.3	28.8
05035	Crittenden County	13,483	4,522	0.0	10.3	40.5	26.4	13.6	59.5	44.2
05045	Faulkner County	27,051	9,225	0.2	6.6	67.0	39.3	27.6	33.0	27.0
05051	Garland County	17,618	5,819	0.0	3.3	58.7	36.8	21.3	41.3	33.2
05069	Jefferson County	16,260	5,061	0.1	3.0	34.4	22.6	11.4	65.6	51.2
05085	Lonoke County	17,983	5,820	1.3	1.1	79.6	55.5	23.5	20.4	13.7
05115	Pope County	13,509	4,303	0.0	4.1	73.3	38.1	33.7	26.7	19.5
05119	Pulaski County	87,759	31,759	0.4	11.1	54.2	33.1	20.5	45.8	34.0
05125	Saline County	25,294	8,435	0.0	6.2	68.6	48.3	20.3	31.4	28.5
05131	Sebastian County	29,742	10,325	0.9	25.8	59.5	27.0	28.6	40.5	30.7
05143	Washington County	51,599	17,958	1.7	30.9	67.2	35.1	31.4	32.8	23.9
05145	White County	17,215	5,677	1.7	7.4	70.5	35.5	31.6	29.5	17.3
06000	**California**	8,780,993	2,927,371	1.8	46.6	64.3	35.0	28.2	35.7	26.1
06001	Alameda County	328,232	114,090	2.7	52.9	71.3	42.7	27.5	28.7	21.4
06007	Butte County	41,993	13,432	0.3	15.2	64.4	34.2	27.5	35.6	22.3
06013	Contra Costa County	249,888	77,271	1.9	43.6	72.9	42.4	29.2	27.1	21.5
06017	El Dorado County	38,292	11,140	0.5	21.0	84.9	52.8	28.5	15.1	11.9
06019	Fresno County	264,483	93,137	1.1	41.3	52.0	25.7	24.9	48.0	32.4
06023	Humboldt County	24,504	8,163	0.4	14.6	54.1	29.1	23.3	45.9	32.2
06025	Imperial County	48,311	17,323	1.0	48.7	52.2	28.9	23.0	47.8	33.1
06029	Kern County	242,192	84,165	1.1	39.9	55.8	27.5	26.2	44.2	30.7

Table D-2: Counties with a Population of 50,000 or More—Children—*Continued*

State/ county FIPS code	State/County	Total own children 6 to 17	Own children age 6 to 17 years in families and subfamilies							Grand-children under 18 living with a grandparent householder	Grand-children under 18 living with a grandparent householder, as a percent of all children	Children for whom grandparent householders are responsible, as a percent of all children
			Nativity and parentage, age 6 to 17 years		Own children age 6 to 17 years living with two parents			Own children age 6 to 17 years living with one parent				
			Child is foreign born, percent	One or more foreign-born parent, percent	Age 6 to 17 years living with two parents, percent	Both parents in labor force, percent	One parent in labor force, percent	Age 6 to 17 years living with one parent, percent	Parent in labor force, percent			
00000	**United States**	46,958,317	4.4	24.5	65.6	42.4	21.9	34.4	28.1	5,562,532	7.9	4.1
01000	**Alabama**	706,235	1.7	6.8	61.2	38.4	21.2	38.8	30.4	114,322	10.9	6.8
01001	Autauga County	8,954	0.5	3.5	74.3	44.3	29.3	25.7	19.1	1,527	11.7	8.0
01003	Baldwin County	28,333	0.9	5.8	72.7	44.4	27.2	27.3	21.4	3,694	8.8	5.8
01009	Blount County	8,986	0.3	9.0	73.2	44.0	25.9	26.8	18.8	1,464	11.3	7.5
01015	Calhoun County	15,996	0.3	4.9	61.4	39.2	20.7	38.6	33.0	3,493	14.6	7.8
01031	Coffee County	7,647	2.9	11.3	58.8	33.6	23.8	41.2	35.5	1,181	10.3	7.3
01033	Colbert County	7,754	3.7	3.9	69.0	40.5	25.4	31.0	24.5	1,104	9.9	7.9
01043	Cullman County	11,664	0.6	5.0	67.3	38.8	27.6	32.7	23.9	1,380	7.9	4.9
01045	Dale County	7,671	0.5	8.1	61.0	38.8	21.0	39.0	27.3	1,041	9.1	5.6
01049	DeKalb County	12,147	2.6	25.6	78.6	54.7	21.9	21.4	16.0	1,559	9.2	6.5
01051	Elmore County	12,230	0.4	4.0	68.5	50.6	16.8	31.5	23.7	1,730	9.8	6.4
01055	Etowah County	15,264	0.9	5.8	55.6	31.7	21.0	44.4	33.8	3,151	14.4	9.0
01069	Houston County	15,825	0.9	4.4	57.9	38.7	17.9	42.1	30.7	2,175	9.3	5.5
01071	Jackson County	7,936	3.0	7.6	71.2	40.8	30.2	28.8	21.5	981	8.9	5.7
01073	Jefferson County	93,717	2.6	7.9	56.7	37.4	18.6	43.3	35.6	15,487	10.8	6.6
01077	Lauderdale County	12,628	1.0	3.5	68.9	44.2	23.4	31.1	25.4	1,791	9.9	6.1
01081	Lee County	19,550	3.3	7.4	68.5	41.6	25.2	31.5	27.0	2,730	9.0	6.1
01083	Limestone County	13,052	2.9	11.0	69.2	45.3	23.1	30.8	27.6	1,655	8.5	6.4
01089	Madison County	51,320	2.1	9.3	69.0	44.2	24.1	31.0	27.8	5,525	7.3	4.9
01095	Marshall County	14,790	3.9	17.1	67.4	36.6	29.5	32.6	24.7	1,668	7.5	4.5
01097	Mobile County	62,502	1.0	5.2	53.8	34.1	17.8	46.2	35.5	12,941	13.8	8.8
01101	Montgomery County	35,499	2.7	7.5	46.0	28.2	17.0	54.0	42.4	5,203	9.7	5.6
01103	Morgan County	18,088	3.5	11.3	68.4	43.3	24.3	31.6	27.7	2,464	9.3	6.0
01113	Russell County	8,666	0.3	6.2	50.2	30.3	17.0	49.8	39.1	2,177	16.0	7.5
01115	St. Clair County	12,516	0.0	0.0	67.9	39.3	27.0	32.1	23.4	2,212	11.8	7.1
01117	Shelby County	33,182	3.4	9.7	77.7	49.3	28.2	22.3	20.0	2,337	4.8	2.9
01121	Talladega County	11,040	0.0	0.0	59.7	43.4	16.3	40.3	28.6	2,150	13.4	9.3
01125	Tuscaloosa County	26,417	1.8	5.7	59.8	41.4	16.1	40.2	29.4	3,323	8.2	4.8
01127	Walker County	9,193	0.4	0.6	61.4	32.0	25.4	38.6	29.8	1,789	13.0	8.4
02000	**Alaska**	116,312	3.8	12.9	67.5	42.1	23.6	32.5	26.2	12,875	7.2	4.0
02020	Anchorage Municipality	47,075	4.8	19.1	67.5	45.6	20.1	32.5	27.6	4,215	5.8	2.8
02090	Fairbanks North Star Borough	15,048	4.0	8.4	66.5	40.8	25.0	33.5	24.7	1,201	4.9	3.4
02122	Kenai Peninsula Borough	8,581	1.7	3.4	69.5	35.3	32.5	30.5	26.4	390	3.1	2.2
02170	Matanuska-Susitna Borough	16,666	3.5	9.0	74.4	35.7	36.6	25.6	17.6	1,437	5.8	3.3
04000	**Arizona**	1,023,000	4.7	29.3	62.4	36.0	24.9	37.6	30.2	139,511	9.1	4.7
04001	Apache County	13,295	0.3	2.4	47.2	22.1	20.4	52.8	37.5	4,428	22.1	11.8
04003	Cochise County	19,073	4.9	21.4	65.4	36.4	26.7	34.6	26.4	2,993	10.7	7.4
04005	Coconino County	19,292	1.1	10.3	59.0	40.2	17.0	41.0	31.8	5,110	17.6	9.3
04007	Gila County	6,848	3.0	7.3	56.5	34.8	17.6	43.5	34.4	1,932	19.0	10.6
04013	Maricopa County	641,310	5.3	32.3	63.2	36.3	25.5	36.8	29.7	75,531	7.9	3.7
04015	Mohave County	25,434	1.0	12.0	65.0	39.6	23.9	35.0	25.5	3,706	10.1	7.0
04017	Navajo County	18,977	1.0	4.0	51.6	26.9	22.5	48.4	35.4	5,802	20.5	14.4
04019	Pima County	139,051	4.9	29.4	59.7	36.2	22.2	40.3	33.6	19,795	9.5	5.1
04021	Pinal County	61,543	2.0	18.8	64.1	32.5	30.3	35.9	28.2	6,683	7.2	4.7
04025	Yavapai County	24,600	3.4	13.9	65.1	42.4	19.6	34.9	29.9	4,562	12.8	7.7
04027	Yuma County	34,164	6.0	54.1	63.2	36.6	24.8	36.8	28.4	5,455	10.5	3.6
05000	**Arkansas**	441,183	2.3	11.3	62.9	40.0	20.9	37.1	29.3	60,727	9.1	6.3
05007	Benton County	40,387	6.3	25.0	79.0	47.5	30.3	21.0	17.6	3,169	5.2	3.4
05031	Craighead County	14,722	2.8	9.4	58.3	37.9	18.9	41.7	33.4	1,610	7.0	5.1
05033	Crawford County	10,329	1.6	13.7	60.1	32.2	20.6	39.9	30.9	1,971	13.4	7.7
05035	Crittenden County	8,961	0.2	1.7	42.9	32.3	9.4	57.1	42.7	1,851	13.7	8.0
05045	Faulkner County	17,826	1.2	4.5	67.3	49.9	16.6	32.7	29.7	1,507	5.6	3.8
05051	Garland County	11,799	1.7	8.9	55.4	34.1	18.3	44.6	36.7	2,385	13.5	9.3
05069	Jefferson County	11,199	0.1	4.5	42.3	28.6	12.9	57.7	48.3	2,513	15.5	9.5
05085	Lonoke County	12,163	1.0	3.4	67.6	47.9	18.9	32.4	27.1	1,612	9.0	6.3
05115	Pope County	9,206	0.7	9.7	70.3	48.8	20.3	29.7	26.1	1,114	8.2	6.4
05119	Pulaski County	56,000	2.2	9.8	55.8	36.5	18.3	44.2	34.4	7,036	8.0	5.3
05125	Saline County	16,859	1.9	7.0	69.1	50.0	18.2	30.9	28.5	2,283	9.0	5.9
05131	Sebastian County	19,417	1.9	24.6	63.7	35.0	24.2	36.3	28.2	2,542	8.5	5.9
05143	Washington County	33,641	6.8	27.6	69.2	44.5	23.4	30.8	25.2	2,464	4.8	3.5
05145	White County	11,538	1.1	4.7	73.8	44.7	27.7	26.2	20.0	1,511	8.8	5.9
06000	**California**	5,853,622	6.9	51.2	66.2	39.2	25.5	33.8	27.0	765,460	8.7	3.6
06001	Alameda County	214,142	8.2	56.3	69.5	44.8	23.7	30.5	24.7	22,443	6.8	2.9
06007	Butte County	28,561	2.5	19.0	64.4	39.0	22.8	35.6	26.8	3,563	8.5	5.0
06013	Contra Costa County	172,617	7.2	44.5	73.2	44.9	27.1	26.8	23.0	15,866	6.3	2.9
06017	El Dorado County	27,152	2.2	20.1	77.6	48.7	26.1	22.4	18.7	2,405	6.3	1.9
06019	Fresno County	171,346	5.7	46.0	58.2	34.2	22.0	41.8	31.5	24,554	9.3	4.4
06023	Humboldt County	16,341	1.6	13.9	59.7	36.9	21.1	40.3	31.9	1,638	6.7	3.6
06025	Imperial County	30,988	8.0	57.2	61.0	37.6	22.5	39.0	26.8	7,076	14.6	8.3
06029	Kern County	158,027	6.1	46.2	62.3	35.4	25.2	37.7	29.9	21,097	8.7	4.3

State/ county FIPS code	State/County	Total own children under 18 in families and subfamilies	Total own children under 6 years	Nativity and parentage, under 6 years		Own children under 6 years living with two parents			Own children under 6 living with one parent	
				Child is foreign born, percent	One or more foreign-born parent, percent	Total under 6 years living with two parents, percent	Both parents in labor force, percent	One parent in labor force, percent	Total under 6 years living with one parent, percent	Parent in labor force, percent
	California—cont'd									
06031	Kings County	39,766	14,414	0.0	33.1	56.7	32.0	23.9	43.3	27.5
06033	Lake County	11,714	4,382	0.0	7.2	41.1	22.9	17.5	58.9	45.9
06037	Los Angeles County	2,241,499	740,909	1.9	54.4	59.5	31.5	27.0	40.5	29.3
06039	Madera County	40,970	13,741	1.7	47.0	56.7	26.0	25.2	43.3	20.2
06041	Marin County	51,259	15,108	1.8	41.0	77.2	52.3	24.4	22.8	19.4
06045	Mendocino County	17,441	5,782	2.0	37.8	57.7	33.5	23.7	42.3	33.0
06047	Merced County	76,769	25,114	0.8	51.0	56.4	29.2	25.2	43.6	28.5
06053	Monterey County	107,010	37,511	1.8	58.1	60.4	30.0	29.2	39.6	30.3
06055	Napa County	30,085	9,165	1.6	56.8	68.3	35.1	32.7	31.7	22.5
06057	Nevada County	17,482	4,945	0.0	20.1	73.4	50.9	20.8	26.6	17.5
06059	Orange County	701,273	224,824	2.0	54.5	71.8	38.7	32.4	28.2	21.0
06061	Placer County	83,548	24,924	0.7	24.5	78.8	43.5	34.9	21.2	17.8
06065	Riverside County	584,617	188,819	1.1	39.0	63.1	31.8	29.9	36.9	26.7
06067	Sacramento County	344,190	115,688	1.6	38.8	61.7	34.3	25.6	38.3	28.3
06069	San Benito County	15,218	4,778	0.1	39.2	71.9	41.4	30.3	28.1	23.1
06071	San Bernardino County	553,584	182,661	0.9	34.9	58.3	28.4	27.8	41.7	29.4
06073	San Diego County	693,655	241,503	2.2	41.4	71.3	37.2	32.8	28.7	21.4
06075	San Francisco County	105,161	41,438	3.5	54.6	77.0	49.6	26.2	23.0	20.4
06077	San Joaquin County	189,541	62,263	1.2	41.9	63.2	36.1	26.1	36.8	27.5
06079	San Luis Obispo County	48,828	16,522	1.9	28.5	69.5	41.9	26.7	30.5	26.4
06081	San Mateo County	155,379	54,233	2.3	58.7	77.3	52.3	24.7	22.7	19.3
06083	Santa Barbara County	92,345	32,035	1.7	48.0	63.0	36.2	26.3	37.0	29.6
06085	Santa Clara County	418,854	145,296	4.1	63.9	76.0	44.6	31.0	24.0	18.7
06087	Santa Cruz County	52,870	17,749	0.6	47.1	70.0	41.9	27.8	30.0	23.4
06089	Shasta County	36,094	11,239	0.9	11.3	63.9	28.5	29.5	36.1	29.3
06095	Solano County	93,328	30,559	0.6	34.3	59.1	33.3	25.2	40.9	32.4
06097	Sonoma County	100,267	32,434	1.6	38.3	69.3	39.4	29.3	30.7	24.0
06099	Stanislaus County	136,246	44,579	1.2	36.4	55.9	28.5	26.8	44.1	31.1
06101	Sutter County	24,094	7,516	1.8	43.0	64.3	32.6	31.1	35.7	26.5
06103	Tehama County	14,059	5,047	0.9	14.5	62.9	34.3	24.1	37.1	26.6
06107	Tulare County	135,587	46,936	0.9	45.1	54.4	26.9	26.1	45.6	33.3
06109	Tuolumne County	8,318	2,671	1.8	9.0	69.7	41.6	25.2	30.3	25.9
06111	Ventura County	197,764	63,541	1.9	43.8	67.5	39.9	26.9	32.5	23.5
06113	Yolo County	43,285	13,832	2.9	41.7	69.8	41.6	27.1	30.2	22.3
06115	Yuba County	19,815	7,322	0.3	22.8	66.9	33.2	33.5	33.1	22.1
08000	Colorado	1,182,138	395,515	1.2	21.9	70.5	39.2	30.4	29.5	23.0
08001	Adams County	122,795	44,099	1.2	31.5	67.1	38.6	27.7	32.9	26.7
08005	Arapahoe County	143,156	47,240	1.8	32.8	69.3	38.6	30.2	30.7	24.6
08013	Boulder County	61,282	19,544	1.3	25.2	77.7	42.3	35.3	22.3	18.4
08014	Broomfield County	14,528	4,401	0.3	18.2	77.3	47.4	29.6	22.7	11.3
08031	Denver County	128,418	50,582	2.8	36.2	63.7	35.9	26.7	36.3	27.3
08035	Douglas County	86,437	25,126	1.1	12.6	88.4	51.5	35.8	11.6	8.7
08041	El Paso County	158,207	54,045	0.8	14.4	70.4	34.3	35.3	29.6	22.8
08045	Garfield County	14,601	4,916	1.9	36.4	76.9	33.9	43.1	23.1	19.0
08059	Jefferson County	112,271	34,385	0.9	12.6	72.8	46.5	25.0	27.2	22.9
08067	La Plata County	9,915	3,246	0.6	7.0	70.9	37.6	29.1	29.1	25.8
08069	Larimer County	62,711	20,146	1.6	11.8	77.5	48.7	27.2	22.5	17.6
08077	Mesa County	32,303	11,229	0.0	7.7	66.1	33.0	33.0	33.9	22.6
08101	Pueblo County	35,674	11,583	0.4	10.9	53.0	28.1	23.6	47.0	36.1
08123	Weld County	68,582	22,851	0.6	19.5	68.5	32.5	35.4	31.5	23.6
09000	Connecticut	768,816	230,927	1.8	26.2	66.5	42.8	23.2	33.5	26.9
09001	Fairfield County	218,731	66,091	2.3	37.5	74.2	41.4	32.3	25.8	20.7
09003	Hartford County	191,942	58,447	1.7	26.7	61.8	43.1	18.3	38.2	30.7
09005	Litchfield County	37,192	9,921	0.3	12.6	73.1	48.7	24.3	26.9	23.4
09007	Middlesex County	32,682	9,537	0.3	12.2	81.3	61.9	19.4	18.7	16.2
09009	New Haven County	179,718	54,905	2.3	25.0	61.4	40.2	20.2	38.6	29.5
09011	New London County	55,301	16,603	1.0	14.5	62.7	43.2	19.3	37.3	31.0
09013	Tolland County	28,935	7,960	1.9	11.9	69.4	43.8	25.6	30.6	27.9
09015	Windham County	24,315	7,463	0.0	8.2	50.0	37.1	12.7	50.0	41.5
10000	Delaware	191,554	64,151	1.2	20.6	57.9	35.6	21.2	42.1	34.5
10001	Kent County	37,576	12,618	0.2	10.5	58.0	31.8	24.4	42.0	33.0
10003	New Castle County	116,879	38,895	1.8	22.9	58.9	37.4	20.5	41.1	34.9
10005	Sussex County	37,099	12,638	0.3	23.3	54.8	34.0	20.1	45.2	34.5
11000	District of Columbia	100,091	43,530	2.7	27.1	48.9	35.6	12.8	51.1	37.7
11001	District of Columbia	100,091	43,530	2.7	27.1	48.9	35.6	12.8	51.1	37.7
12000	Florida	3,804,656	1,249,125	1.6	31.8	57.7	34.0	22.8	42.3	33.0
12001	Alachua County	42,334	16,145	1.1	13.2	61.3	36.6	24.3	38.7	30.0
12005	Bay County	35,646	12,305	0.1	11.6	61.0	34.5	25.1	39.0	29.9

Table D-2: Counties with a Population of 50,000 or More—Children—*Continued*

State/county FIPS code	State/County	Total own children 6 to 17	Nativity and parentage, age 6 to 17 years		Own children age 6 to 17 years living with two parents			Own children age 6 to 17 years living with one parent		Grand-children under 18 living with a grandparent householder	Grand-children under 18 living with a grandparent householder, as a percent of all children	Children for whom grandparent householders are responsible, as a percent of all children
			Child is foreign born, percent	One or more foreign-born parent, percent	Age 6 to 17 years living with two parents, percent	Both parents in labor force, percent	One parent in labor force, percent	Age 6 to 17 years living with one parent, percent	Parent in labor force, percent			
	California—cont'd											
06031	Kings County	25,352	6.3	40.3	63.4	35.9	26.3	36.6	27.4	3,763	9.5	4.8
06033	Lake County	7,332	2.6	21.7	52.7	34.0	16.0	47.3	37.8	1,061	9.1	4.8
06037	Los Angeles County	1,500,590	7.5	62.1	62.3	35.8	25.3	37.7	30.1	228,011	10.2	3.8
06039	Madera County	27,229	7.8	48.4	65.6	29.8	28.5	34.4	22.7	3,606	8.8	3.9
06041	Marin County	36,151	5.7	31.5	73.3	46.3	25.8	26.7	24.0	1,217	2.4	1.1
06045	Mendocino County	11,659	7.0	31.6	62.4	38.8	21.2	37.6	31.0	2,217	12.7	8.9
06047	Merced County	51,655	7.8	57.3	61.2	33.1	25.7	38.8	29.4	5,895	7.7	3.7
06053	Monterey County	69,499	9.7	63.1	67.2	39.9	24.3	32.8	27.0	8,254	7.7	2.7
06055	Napa County	20,920	6.7	54.0	71.2	50.9	19.8	28.8	23.4	1,486	4.9	1.9
06057	Nevada County	12,537	0.8	13.2	76.3	47.7	27.1	23.7	20.0	863	4.9	2.2
06059	Orange County	476,449	8.3	56.1	72.0	41.2	29.6	28.0	23.5	53,999	7.7	2.8
06061	Placer County	58,624	3.5	22.6	74.2	48.1	25.7	25.8	23.5	3,459	4.1	1.2
06065	Riverside County	395,798	4.9	46.6	67.1	38.3	27.3	32.9	26.0	62,348	10.7	4.5
06067	Sacramento County	228,502	7.0	39.8	61.3	38.2	21.0	38.7	30.1	24,624	7.2	3.1
06069	San Benito County	10,440	5.5	41.3	68.5	46.9	21.1	31.5	24.2	2,103	13.8	3.7
06071	San Bernardino County	370,923	4.5	44.8	61.4	33.6	26.0	38.6	29.1	59,438	10.7	5.1
06073	San Diego County	452,152	7.5	47.8	67.9	39.2	27.1	32.1	26.0	55,139	7.9	3.4
06075	San Francisco County	63,723	10.5	59.2	69.1	47.8	19.9	30.9	25.2	7,520	7.2	2.5
06077	San Joaquin County	127,278	5.8	46.0	65.5	38.3	25.5	34.5	26.4	15,215	8.0	3.7
06079	San Luis Obispo County	32,306	3.6	25.1	72.5	50.4	21.9	27.5	22.1	3,019	6.2	3.8
06081	San Mateo County	101,146	8.0	56.8	75.0	50.3	24.1	25.0	22.2	10,099	6.5	2.3
06083	Santa Barbara County	60,310	7.8	51.2	67.8	43.9	23.0	32.2	26.5	7,021	7.6	3.3
06085	Santa Clara County	273,558	10.0	64.1	75.3	46.2	28.1	24.7	20.5	27,206	6.5	2.3
06087	Santa Cruz County	35,121	5.2	44.7	69.7	46.8	20.9	30.3	26.4	3,245	6.1	1.6
06089	Shasta County	24,855	1.8	11.5	61.4	35.1	22.9	38.6	28.0	3,158	8.7	5.6
06095	Solano County	62,769	5.2	39.2	65.3	40.2	24.1	34.7	29.3	8,312	8.9	3.7
06097	Sonoma County	67,833	7.0	40.2	70.5	44.3	24.8	29.5	26.0	5,080	5.1	2.3
06099	Stanislaus County	91,667	5.5	43.8	63.8	37.4	25.1	36.2	28.5	11,713	8.6	4.0
06101	Sutter County	16,578	7.1	42.8	70.2	44.7	24.1	29.8	22.4	2,079	8.6	3.6
06103	Tehama County	9,012	0.2	22.0	69.8	37.7	24.9	30.2	21.5	1,473	10.5	5.6
06107	Tulare County	88,651	5.4	51.5	63.5	37.2	24.7	36.5	28.2	15,198	11.2	5.2
06109	Tuolumne County	5,647	0.6	8.3	65.6	38.9	26.5	34.4	27.5	949	11.4	7.2
06111	Ventura County	134,223	5.8	44.8	71.9	46.5	24.6	28.1	23.6	17,284	8.7	2.8
06113	Yolo County	29,453	7.5	45.2	66.9	42.4	21.8	33.1	27.9	3,391	7.8	2.4
06115	Yuba County	12,493	3.6	25.5	60.9	31.2	27.6	39.1	25.7	1,850	9.3	3.2
08000	**Colorado**	786,623	4.3	21.9	69.9	45.4	23.4	30.1	25.5	70,888	6.0	3.0
08001	Adams County	78,696	6.3	37.1	69.0	42.9	23.9	31.0	25.1	11,681	9.5	4.7
08005	Arapahoe County	95,916	6.3	30.1	66.7	43.4	22.7	33.3	29.1	7,159	5.0	2.6
08013	Boulder County	41,738	6.0	25.2	73.3	46.8	26.0	26.7	24.0	1,988	3.2	1.4
08014	Broomfield County	10,127	1.6	19.7	76.4	54.4	21.4	23.6	18.6	437	3.0	2.0
08031	Denver County	77,836	9.0	40.9	59.8	36.3	22.5	40.2	34.1	10,103	7.9	3.1
08035	Douglas County	61,311	2.1	10.7	81.5	54.9	26.1	18.5	16.5	2,523	2.9	1.6
08041	El Paso County	104,162	2.9	13.8	70.9	43.6	26.2	29.1	23.3	8,453	5.3	2.5
08045	Garfield County	9,685	8.0	34.8	75.9	47.6	28.2	24.1	21.0	967	6.6	3.2
08059	Jefferson County	77,886	3.0	12.5	69.7	49.0	19.7	30.3	26.1	6,144	5.5	2.6
08067	La Plata County	6,669	4.2	8.8	74.0	40.7	30.5	26.0	24.0	329	3.3	1.8
08069	Larimer County	42,565	2.9	11.7	72.9	49.0	23.1	27.1	23.4	3,362	5.4	3.3
08077	Mesa County	21,074	1.1	7.3	63.3	44.9	17.7	36.7	30.3	2,321	7.2	3.0
08101	Pueblo County	24,091	0.8	7.9	61.2	39.8	19.5	38.8	33.6	3,339	9.4	4.8
08123	Weld County	45,731	3.2	24.4	73.3	45.6	26.9	26.7	22.0	4,840	7.1	4.1
09000	**Connecticut**	537,889	4.8	22.2	68.1	48.0	19.4	31.9	27.4	42,141	5.5	2.6
09001	Fairfield County	152,640	6.6	31.2	73.0	44.4	27.8	27.0	23.7	11,069	5.1	2.0
09003	Hartford County	133,495	5.2	23.4	62.3	46.1	15.6	37.7	32.0	11,556	6.0	3.0
09005	Litchfield County	27,271	2.7	12.6	79.0	57.2	21.6	21.0	18.9	2,285	6.1	2.3
09007	Middlesex County	23,145	3.3	11.9	76.6	59.1	16.8	23.4	20.6	1,074	3.3	1.7
09009	New Haven County	124,813	4.3	20.6	63.9	47.7	15.4	36.1	29.9	9,635	5.4	2.6
09011	New London County	38,698	3.3	13.8	66.4	48.2	17.1	33.6	29.5	3,601	6.5	3.5
09013	Tolland County	20,975	3.5	8.8	74.2	58.9	15.3	25.8	24.2	1,259	4.4	1.3
09015	Windham County	16,852	1.5	8.8	66.9	53.5	12.1	33.1	28.4	1,662	6.8	4.6
10000	**Delaware**	127,403	2.6	16.2	60.9	43.0	16.3	39.1	33.1	19,940	10.4	5.5
10001	Kent County	24,958	1.2	7.6	61.3	39.6	19.4	38.7	33.4	3,729	9.9	5.4
10003	New Castle County	77,984	3.1	19.1	60.9	44.1	15.9	39.1	33.6	11,828	10.1	5.1
10005	Sussex County	24,461	2.4	15.6	60.2	43.0	14.5	39.8	31.2	4,383	11.8	6.9
11000	**District of Columbia**	56,561	5.3	22.7	35.8	26.1	8.7	64.2	49.5	11,228	11.2	5.1
11001	District of Columbia	56,561	5.3	22.7	35.8	26.1	8.7	64.2	49.5	11,228	11.2	5.1
12000	**Florida**	2,555,531	6.7	32.8	61.6	40.1	20.1	38.4	31.9	336,635	8.8	4.7
12001	Alachua County	26,189	3.2	17.2	61.6	40.7	18.6	38.4	30.8	3,814	9.0	5.6
12005	Bay County	23,341	1.8	9.1	61.5	40.9	20.0	38.5	33.1	2,693	7.6	5.6

Table D-2: Counties with a Population of 50,000 or More—Children—*Continued*

State/county FIPS code	State/County	Total own children under 18 in families and subfamilies	Own children under 6 years in families and subfamilies							
			Total own children under 6 years	Nativity and parentage, under 6 years		Own children under 6 years living with two parents			Own children under 6 living with one parent	
				Child is foreign born, percent	One or more foreign-born parent, percent	Total under 6 years living with two parents, percent	Both parents in labor force, percent	One parent in labor force, percent	Total under 6 years living with one parent, percent	Parent in labor force, percent
	Florida—cont'd									
12009	Brevard County	98,964	31,576	0.3	15.1	57.2	32.4	24.3	42.8	34.2
12011	Broward County	380,469	124,479	2.3	50.0	58.2	37.3	20.4	41.8	35.5
12015	Charlotte County	20,542	6,101	1.6	24.2	59.3	32.7	24.4	40.7	33.9
12017	Citrus County	18,755	5,707	0.0	8.0	46.7	20.0	25.7	53.3	45.4
12019	Clay County	47,103	12,763	0.5	10.9	64.7	40.5	23.4	35.3	29.6
12021	Collier County	60,602	19,914	0.9	49.1	59.6	31.8	27.7	40.4	31.1
12023	Columbia County	13,860	4,407	0.0	2.8	40.0	22.5	17.2	60.0	52.7
12031	Duval County	191,204	69,253	0.8	16.0	53.3	31.1	21.3	46.7	35.1
12033	Escambia County	59,039	22,219	0.1	7.6	47.9	27.1	20.2	52.1	41.7
12035	Flagler County	17,877	5,374	4.1	22.4	61.9	28.8	33.1	38.1	29.0
12053	Hernando County	31,276	8,811	0.6	10.1	49.8	25.3	22.8	50.2	42.1
12055	Highlands County	17,008	5,499	2.6	29.8	58.0	29.0	24.8	42.0	27.3
12057	Hillsborough County	280,261	94,099	1.9	27.1	58.1	35.0	22.1	41.9	33.5
12061	Indian River County	23,975	7,615	1.3	27.2	63.1	33.6	27.7	36.9	32.5
12069	Lake County	58,982	18,311	1.0	15.0	63.4	39.6	22.8	36.6	30.7
12071	Lee County	117,509	38,611	1.3	28.7	54.6	31.9	21.8	45.4	33.7
12073	Leon County	51,013	17,051	0.5	13.8	63.2	39.4	22.9	36.8	28.5
12081	Manatee County	62,111	20,222	1.2	31.2	60.5	33.9	25.4	39.5	30.9
12083	Marion County	58,748	19,507	0.4	9.7	53.7	28.3	24.6	46.3	35.1
12085	Martin County	24,902	7,335	0.0	31.3	60.5	37.5	22.2	39.5	31.4
12086	Miami-Dade County	525,574	177,712	3.6	64.2	58.1	33.7	22.8	41.9	31.8
12087	Monroe County	10,608	3,646	2.9	34.5	66.9	37.6	28.6	33.1	31.7
12089	Nassau County	14,126	4,422	0.0	4.3	52.6	31.0	20.8	47.4	32.7
12091	Okaloosa County	39,717	14,254	0.5	15.6	61.9	29.1	32.8	38.1	31.0
12095	Orange County	264,229	87,902	1.9	33.3	58.2	35.7	21.7	41.8	33.9
12097	Osceola County	70,723	21,015	1.0	27.6	51.7	31.1	19.9	48.3	37.2
12099	Palm Beach County	259,460	84,006	1.7	44.5	58.1	36.7	21.0	41.9	33.6
12101	Pasco County	93,595	29,222	1.0	17.6	65.5	38.9	25.7	34.5	25.5
12103	Pinellas County	151,047	48,748	1.2	21.7	54.0	32.8	20.9	46.0	34.8
12105	Polk County	134,329	44,047	0.2	21.3	54.9	31.3	22.9	45.1	33.5
12107	Putnam County	15,082	5,144	0.0	11.7	39.4	19.7	18.7	60.6	38.0
12109	St. Johns County	43,472	12,593	0.2	9.0	74.2	44.9	28.6	25.8	19.7
12111	St. Lucie County	58,328	18,397	0.5	28.0	53.8	33.6	18.7	46.2	36.6
12113	Santa Rosa County	35,217	10,488	0.0	8.0	64.3	27.4	36.1	35.7	26.1
12115	Sarasota County	56,493	16,977	1.4	22.9	59.0	36.8	20.1	41.0	32.7
12117	Seminole County	91,282	26,995	1.4	21.1	68.1	38.7	29.2	31.9	25.7
12119	Sumter County	7,542	2,524	0.0	17.9	67.2	48.1	18.9	32.8	30.0
12127	Volusia County	85,903	27,819	0.7	13.4	58.0	32.5	24.9	42.0	30.0
12131	Walton County	11,019	3,490	1.2	8.3	62.8	44.2	15.0	37.2	21.5
13000	**Georgia**	2,349,999	780,912	1.2	21.1	59.4	33.9	24.7	40.6	30.9
13013	Barrow County	18,859	6,284	0.3	13.2	71.2	39.4	30.1	28.8	21.5
13015	Bartow County	24,212	7,482	0.0	13.6	59.9	40.1	18.2	40.1	34.6
13021	Bibb County	37,299	13,461	0.8	6.9	36.1	21.8	13.6	63.9	46.3
13031	Bulloch County	13,719	4,835	0.0	6.5	53.5	29.2	22.9	46.5	41.7
13039	Camden County	12,701	4,465	0.3	7.1	71.1	32.5	38.6	28.9	23.0
13045	Carroll County	25,538	8,588	0.0	12.9	63.1	40.0	21.1	36.9	24.3
13047	Catoosa County	15,113	4,414	0.0	2.1	68.5	38.9	29.6	31.5	24.0
13051	Chatham County	58,055	21,561	1.3	15.8	54.3	29.0	25.3	45.7	33.2
13057	Cherokee County	56,407	17,377	0.1	18.1	79.7	41.1	36.9	20.3	16.2
13059	Clarke County	19,823	8,208	2.3	25.3	56.2	30.2	25.4	43.8	34.7
13063	Clayton County	67,934	24,352	0.7	28.9	45.5	23.6	21.7	54.5	43.8
13067	Cobb County	170,554	56,085	1.7	34.7	66.8	43.8	22.4	33.2	29.4
13073	Columbia County	33,938	10,273	0.3	14.6	79.7	37.8	41.9	20.3	18.3
13077	Coweta County	33,691	10,927	1.2	12.9	61.9	31.6	28.8	38.1	22.3
13089	DeKalb County	159,665	59,479	3.8	34.4	57.2	33.1	22.9	42.8	35.7
13095	Dougherty County	20,530	7,728	0.4	4.2	33.1	24.1	7.9	66.9	51.4
13097	Douglas County	34,949	10,996	0.3	17.9	57.7	40.2	17.5	42.3	30.5
13103	Effingham County	13,820	4,049	0.5	2.5	76.3	37.4	39.0	23.7	20.1
13113	Fayette County	26,353	5,435	0.0	20.5	73.3	38.9	33.9	26.7	25.3
13115	Floyd County	20,806	7,078	1.2	21.4	62.5	42.9	19.1	37.5	27.5
13117	Forsyth County	54,570	15,817	0.8	29.9	87.7	46.1	41.4	12.3	9.4
13121	Fulton County	219,298	75,393	1.7	24.9	56.6	34.2	22.0	43.4	33.7
13127	Glynn County	17,475	5,770	1.3	16.2	46.6	29.5	15.2	53.4	41.5
13129	Gordon County	13,360	4,469	3.6	27.1	70.0	32.2	37.4	30.0	27.3
13135	Gwinnett County	232,019	73,448	2.4	44.7	71.1	38.8	31.4	28.9	23.6
13139	Hall County	48,000	16,180	1.1	39.1	65.6	37.7	27.4	34.4	25.9
13151	Henry County	55,316	16,349	0.3	12.9	59.0	34.4	20.7	41.0	28.9
13153	Houston County	36,178	11,770	0.6	9.4	53.6	33.0	19.4	46.4	31.6
13157	Jackson County	15,289	4,931	0.0	13.1	74.3	43.5	30.7	25.7	20.3
13179	Liberty County	18,088	7,907	0.4	7.0	61.4	22.3	37.8	38.6	31.0
13185	Lowndes County	26,283	9,684	0.0	6.7	49.2	24.1	24.3	50.8	40.8
13215	Muscogee County	46,883	16,909	2.1	8.5	48.4	21.8	26.6	51.6	37.4

Table D-2: Counties with a Population of 50,000 or More—Children—*Continued*

State/county FIPS code	State/County	Total own children 6 to 17	Nativity and parentage, age 6 to 17 years		Own children age 6 to 17 years living with two parents			Own children age 6 to 17 years living with one parent		Grandchildren under 18 living with a grandparent householder	Grandchildren under 18 living with a grandparent householder, as a percent of all children	Children for whom grandparent householders are responsible, as a percent of all children
			Child is foreign born, percent	One or more foreign-born parent, percent	Age 6 to 17 years living with two parents, percent	Both parents in labor force, percent	One parent in labor force, percent	Age 6 to 17 years living with one parent, percent	Parent in labor force, percent			
	Florida—cont'd											
12009	Brevard County	67,388	2.4	15.5	61.3	38.8	21.9	38.7	33.1	11,062	11.2	6.6
12011	Broward County	255,990	10.6	53.0	61.2	42.7	17.9	38.8	34.6	28,876	7.6	3.7
12015	Charlotte County	14,441	3.4	18.1	59.9	41.5	16.2	40.1	32.8	2,008	9.8	5.3
12017	Citrus County	13,048	1.0	7.6	58.3	35.4	20.3	41.7	32.6	2,317	12.4	6.0
12019	Clay County	34,340	2.4	13.1	70.7	43.7	24.9	29.3	24.0	4,331	9.2	7.0
12021	Collier County	40,688	10.2	47.5	64.9	38.3	26.0	35.1	30.5	3,851	6.4	2.7
12023	Columbia County	9,453	1.8	8.1	63.6	35.9	26.8	36.4	30.3	2,208	15.9	10.5
12031	Duval County	121,951	3.7	16.4	56.6	37.1	18.2	43.4	34.6	17,263	9.0	5.2
12033	Escambia County	36,820	1.1	10.5	61.0	41.4	18.7	39.0	32.0	7,802	13.2	7.9
12035	Flagler County	12,503	4.0	16.2	64.4	40.1	24.1	35.6	28.1	1,637	9.2	6.3
12053	Hernando County	22,465	1.2	10.0	66.1	39.8	21.8	33.9	26.4	3,062	9.8	5.7
12055	Highlands County	11,509	3.1	25.0	64.2	39.9	22.0	35.8	27.9	1,744	10.3	7.0
12057	Hillsborough County	186,162	5.4	27.6	61.3	39.4	20.7	38.7	32.1	23,635	8.4	4.1
12061	Indian River County	16,360	4.4	22.2	68.9	47.0	21.5	31.1	25.1	1,817	7.6	4.3
12069	Lake County	40,671	1.4	17.8	68.7	46.9	19.8	31.3	27.0	5,920	10.0	4.6
12071	Lee County	78,898	5.7	33.5	61.5	39.8	20.5	38.5	31.9	6,669	5.7	3.5
12073	Leon County	33,962	2.9	9.7	58.8	38.0	18.8	41.2	36.9	3,307	6.5	3.3
12081	Manatee County	41,889	4.6	28.6	64.7	41.3	22.3	35.3	27.5	5,115	8.2	6.1
12083	Marion County	39,241	2.7	12.9	58.2	35.0	22.5	41.8	34.2	5,948	10.1	4.9
12085	Martin County	17,567	5.1	29.3	69.6	40.8	27.7	30.4	28.0	1,543	6.2	4.4
12086	Miami-Dade County	347,862	17.0	68.5	58.9	38.3	18.9	41.1	33.8	55,020	10.5	4.1
12087	Monroe County	6,962	11.5	38.5	64.6	42.6	20.9	35.4	32.7	742	7.0	3.8
12089	Nassau County	9,704	0.1	3.9	71.5	42.6	26.5	28.5	23.9	1,627	11.5	9.3
12091	Okaloosa County	25,463	2.1	13.1	65.2	37.5	27.1	34.8	28.3	3,027	7.6	4.4
12095	Orange County	176,327	6.5	33.2	59.6	40.0	18.7	40.4	34.4	19,963	7.6	3.9
12097	Osceola County	49,708	4.8	35.0	61.7	39.2	19.6	38.3	31.1	6,572	9.3	4.5
12099	Palm Beach County	175,454	8.5	43.2	62.9	42.6	19.5	37.1	31.7	18,880	7.3	3.9
12101	Pasco County	64,373	3.0	15.9	68.9	43.9	22.8	31.1	26.0	7,085	7.6	4.6
12103	Pinellas County	102,299	4.1	20.5	59.2	41.2	16.8	40.8	33.5	14,303	9.5	5.5
12105	Polk County	90,282	4.0	21.4	54.9	34.4	18.7	45.1	35.0	14,343	10.7	5.6
12107	Putnam County	9,938	2.1	16.3	51.1	26.3	23.5	48.9	36.6	2,563	17.0	13.8
12109	St. Johns County	30,879	0.9	13.2	75.7	51.5	23.2	24.3	21.2	2,762	6.4	4.0
12111	St. Lucie County	39,931	4.1	32.3	63.1	42.7	19.4	36.9	29.3	4,058	7.0	3.3
12113	Santa Rosa County	24,729	1.5	10.2	75.6	40.3	33.8	24.4	18.3	2,361	6.7	4.5
12115	Sarasota County	39,516	6.3	22.4	68.5	48.2	18.3	31.5	27.2	3,949	7.0	4.2
12117	Seminole County	64,287	2.9	21.0	65.8	42.8	22.5	34.2	29.0	5,818	6.4	3.9
12119	Sumter County	5,018	1.5	15.2	59.8	40.3	17.4	40.2	34.8	853	11.3	7.8
12127	Volusia County	58,084	2.0	14.9	59.6	35.2	23.4	40.4	27.7	8,764	10.2	5.9
12131	Walton County	7,529	1.4	9.6	59.0	38.9	18.7	41.0	23.3	758	6.9	5.0
13000	**Georgia**	1,569,087	3.6	18.9	62.0	39.6	21.3	38.0	30.9	217,865	9.3	5.7
13013	Barrow County	12,575	3.8	16.1	71.4	43.3	26.8	28.6	20.4	1,675	8.9	5.7
13015	Bartow County	16,730	0.7	10.2	67.0	47.1	17.7	33.0	26.8	2,989	12.3	8.4
13021	Bibb County	23,838	1.5	7.8	46.4	32.2	13.9	53.6	38.7	4,617	12.4	6.0
13031	Bulloch County	8,884	1.4	9.6	65.0	33.3	31.1	35.0	30.9	1,038	7.6	4.8
13039	Camden County	8,236	0.6	2.5	64.4	45.6	18.5	35.6	32.2	1,010	8.0	6.6
13045	Carroll County	16,950	1.7	7.8	59.6	38.4	19.7	40.4	27.8	4,021	15.7	6.8
13047	Catoosa County	10,699	1.6	5.2	61.9	45.2	16.4	38.1	34.1	1,246	8.2	6.4
13051	Chatham County	36,494	3.3	10.2	54.6	38.3	15.8	45.4	37.7	6,174	10.6	7.0
13057	Cherokee County	39,030	3.5	17.1	73.2	44.3	26.8	26.8	23.2	3,240	5.7	3.3
13059	Clarke County	11,615	6.1	23.9	57.5	35.9	20.6	42.5	33.7	1,512	7.6	4.6
13063	Clayton County	43,582	5.6	29.4	51.1	32.8	17.9	48.9	41.2	8,789	12.9	8.0
13067	Cobb County	114,469	5.7	29.4	68.4	45.3	22.5	31.6	27.9	10,569	6.2	3.2
13073	Columbia County	23,665	3.4	13.8	77.8	48.4	28.3	22.2	19.2	1,831	5.4	3.7
13077	Coweta County	22,764	2.2	10.4	70.0	41.3	27.4	30.0	24.9	2,581	7.7	4.0
13089	DeKalb County	100,186	8.4	27.8	52.9	34.6	16.6	47.1	40.0	15,786	9.9	5.5
13095	Dougherty County	12,802	0.5	5.1	36.7	24.9	9.6	63.3	50.7	2,685	13.1	9.9
13097	Douglas County	23,953	2.4	18.5	58.8	40.1	18.0	41.2	32.2	3,688	10.6	6.9
13103	Effingham County	9,771	1.9	6.5	64.2	43.0	20.8	35.8	32.5	1,136	8.2	6.8
13113	Fayette County	20,918	4.2	19.3	76.8	49.2	27.5	23.2	17.7	2,112	8.0	4.4
13115	Floyd County	13,728	2.8	18.1	65.8	43.1	20.9	34.2	25.3	2,701	13.0	9.5
13117	Forsyth County	38,753	5.1	24.5	81.5	47.6	33.6	18.5	16.5	2,005	3.7	1.6
13121	Fulton County	143,905	5.0	23.3	58.1	35.5	22.0	41.9	35.7	14,543	6.6	3.7
13127	Glynn County	11,705	2.3	10.9	51.1	38.9	11.9	48.9	43.0	2,606	14.9	12.1
13129	Gordon County	8,891	2.2	22.2	78.5	46.1	30.1	21.5	18.0	1,073	8.0	5.9
13135	Gwinnett County	158,571	6.9	41.1	70.0	42.7	26.7	30.0	25.6	10,958	4.7	2.5
13139	Hall County	31,820	3.5	37.1	72.1	42.7	28.8	27.9	22.0	3,544	7.4	3.7
13151	Henry County	38,967	0.7	9.9	59.6	36.9	20.1	40.4	34.6	6,437	11.6	5.7
13153	Houston County	24,408	2.5	12.6	62.6	45.2	17.1	37.4	28.8	3,288	9.1	5.2
13157	Jackson County	10,358	1.2	9.0	70.8	45.0	25.4	29.2	25.7	1,105	7.2	3.6
13179	Liberty County	10,181	1.4	14.1	63.8	34.1	28.2	36.2	29.2	1,111	6.1	3.4
13185	Lowndes County	16,599	1.3	5.4	57.6	36.1	20.5	42.4	38.3	2,308	8.8	4.6
13215	Muscogee County	29,974	1.9	7.8	49.4	29.0	19.7	50.6	40.2	4,530	9.7	6.4

State/county FIPS code	State/County	Total own children under 18 in families and subfamilies	Total own children under 6 years	Own children under 6 years in families and subfamilies						
				Nativity and parentage, under 6 years		Own children under 6 years living with two parents			Own children under 6 living with one parent	
				Child is foreign born, percent	One or more foreign-born parent, percent	Total under 6 years living with two parents, percent	Both parents in labor force, percent	One parent in labor force, percent	Total under 6 years living with one parent, percent	Parent in labor force, percent
	Georgia—cont'd									
13217	Newton County	25,579	7,796	0.5	9.4	55.2	29.9	23.5	44.8	39.8
13223	Paulding County	40,403	12,189	0.4	8.6	73.1	48.9	24.2	26.9	20.0
13245	Richmond County	45,427	16,512	0.8	8.7	35.5	19.0	15.6	64.5	45.8
13247	Rockdale County	21,496	6,495	0.3	27.2	62.7	40.8	20.7	37.3	28.2
13255	Spalding County	14,113	4,386	0.0	9.3	51.5	34.9	16.6	48.5	23.0
13285	Troup County	16,555	5,887	1.5	7.2	47.7	30.6	17.1	52.3	43.9
13295	Walker County	13,909	4,652	0.0	0.0	56.9	28.6	25.3	43.1	36.8
13297	Walton County	20,968	5,890	0.0	4.4	70.4	39.6	30.8	29.6	24.2
13313	Whitfield County	26,525	8,447	1.7	44.5	65.5	38.1	27.3	34.5	24.8
15000	**Hawaii**	288,797	103,598	1.8	27.3	67.0	39.8	26.1	33.0	24.5
15001	Hawaii County	39,159	13,802	1.4	23.7	57.5	37.2	19.8	42.5	34.6
15003	Honolulu County	201,647	72,934	1.8	27.7	70.5	39.9	29.3	29.5	20.2
15007	Kauai County	14,403	5,364	2.8	25.3	64.5	42.6	20.7	35.5	30.2
15009	Maui County	33,588	11,498	1.9	29.4	57.9	41.0	15.8	42.1	36.8
16000	**Idaho**	410,390	136,541	1.0	14.9	74.8	36.9	37.0	25.2	19.2
16001	Ada County	102,149	32,086	1.4	10.0	77.7	42.9	34.1	22.3	17.0
16005	Bannock County	21,941	7,538	0.4	3.6	67.0	34.7	31.3	33.0	25.5
16019	Bonneville County	32,473	11,353	0.5	11.7	79.5	34.2	44.6	20.5	17.4
16027	Canyon County	57,055	19,121	1.0	24.3	72.3	30.8	41.0	27.7	19.6
16055	Kootenai County	32,219	10,729	2.3	7.3	71.4	35.3	35.9	28.6	20.6
16083	Twin Falls County	20,822	7,426	0.5	22.2	67.9	32.1	34.9	32.1	25.9
17000	**Illinois**	2,932,336	944,645	1.4	27.6	64.8	39.2	24.9	35.2	28.3
17001	Adams County	14,503	4,977	0.0	0.0	59.0	37.5	21.4	41.0	33.2
17007	Boone County	14,080	4,095	0.0	34.1	67.7	47.1	20.6	32.3	23.3
17019	Champaign County	37,275	13,554	2.2	20.2	67.7	39.9	27.6	32.3	26.3
17029	Coles County	9,292	3,127	0.0	4.2	57.1	34.3	22.8	42.9	40.8
17031	Cook County	1,154,865	392,489	2.1	38.8	60.8	35.2	24.7	39.2	30.8
17037	DeKalb County	22,197	7,307	1.0	9.8	63.8	43.3	20.6	36.2	31.4
17043	DuPage County	218,900	66,927	1.7	35.7	81.5	48.8	32.0	18.5	15.6
17063	Grundy County	12,998	3,944	0.0	12.5	76.1	48.8	27.4	23.9	19.3
17073	Henry County	11,148	3,518	0.5	8.6	61.9	36.7	22.8	38.1	33.3
17077	Jackson County	9,865	3,569	2.4	18.7	70.2	39.5	23.1	29.8	24.0
17089	Kane County	140,779	43,585	1.4	41.2	68.6	37.9	30.1	31.4	25.0
17091	Kankakee County	26,468	8,106	0.2	14.3	53.7	35.3	16.7	46.3	39.0
17093	Kendall County	35,241	11,150	0.4	19.0	80.7	53.8	26.9	19.3	18.6
17095	Knox County	9,972	2,824	0.5	8.7	51.1	27.5	23.5	48.9	38.6
17097	Lake County	180,472	52,742	1.6	38.5	71.5	44.7	26.2	28.5	23.5
17099	LaSalle County	24,043	6,848	0.0	8.0	64.2	44.9	17.5	35.8	28.5
17111	McHenry County	78,239	22,027	0.5	18.3	77.0	48.9	28.0	23.0	17.0
17113	McLean County	36,953	12,330	2.4	13.5	69.8	47.2	22.3	30.2	26.8
17115	Macon County	23,495	7,865	0.8	6.2	50.3	33.8	16.3	49.7	44.7
17119	Madison County	56,464	18,331	0.9	7.2	65.4	43.0	21.5	34.6	28.0
17141	Ogle County	12,022	3,345	0.9	11.3	73.2	47.5	25.7	26.8	24.0
17143	Peoria County	42,225	14,289	2.3	12.4	53.3	28.3	23.7	46.7	36.1
17161	Rock Island County	31,751	10,880	3.0	18.9	56.8	35.3	20.6	43.2	38.0
17163	St. Clair County	63,097	20,949	0.3	6.5	52.8	31.7	19.4	47.2	36.3
17167	Sangamon County	44,050	14,375	0.4	6.2	59.8	42.1	17.8	40.2	35.3
17179	Tazewell County	30,356	9,934	0.6	2.5	73.2	38.6	32.8	26.8	22.5
17183	Vermilion County	18,180	6,095	0.0	3.9	46.2	28.5	17.0	53.8	45.7
17195	Whiteside County	12,458	3,441	0.0	6.4	51.3	32.9	18.4	48.7	39.8
17197	Will County	184,602	54,309	0.6	26.8	73.9	45.6	28.2	26.1	20.5
17199	Williamson County	13,784	4,455	0.0	2.6	58.6	39.8	18.6	41.4	31.9
17201	Winnebago County	67,222	22,564	0.9	15.6	52.2	34.0	17.3	47.8	39.8
18000	**Indiana**	1,508,064	492,870	0.9	11.0	63.1	37.4	24.8	36.9	29.1
18003	Allen County	91,452	30,899	1.5	12.3	62.1	33.3	28.1	37.9	28.1
18005	Bartholomew County	17,635	5,552	2.8	17.6	65.8	37.9	27.3	34.2	28.7
18011	Boone County	15,482	4,762	1.7	6.7	86.4	58.0	28.4	13.6	12.6
18019	Clark County	24,853	8,780	1.2	9.1	65.5	41.3	23.0	34.5	26.1
18035	Delaware County	21,471	7,026	1.6	2.6	59.9	36.8	19.8	40.1	30.2
18039	Elkhart County	53,568	18,386	1.0	24.1	62.6	30.6	30.2	37.4	28.1
18043	Floyd County	16,907	5,066	0.4	4.0	67.1	47.9	18.9	32.9	24.4
18053	Grant County	13,842	4,458	0.4	6.5	53.6	35.8	17.2	46.4	32.2
18057	Hamilton County	82,577	26,564	2.3	14.8	86.1	54.2	31.2	13.9	12.5
18059	Hancock County	17,465	5,262	0.0	3.0	68.6	46.9	21.6	31.4	30.1
18063	Hendricks County	39,486	11,504	0.7	9.1	83.0	52.9	29.8	17.0	13.6
18067	Howard County	17,901	5,500	0.0	3.6	64.8	45.4	19.1	35.2	31.7
18081	Johnson County	35,903	11,479	0.3	7.4	73.5	46.9	26.6	26.5	20.5
18085	Kosciusko County	18,449	5,957	0.0	9.2	71.0	41.9	28.4	29.0	23.1
18089	Lake County	118,268	38,074	1.0	12.1	51.9	28.6	22.9	48.1	35.3
18091	LaPorte County	23,542	7,401	0.5	8.1	55.5	33.8	21.8	44.5	33.7
18095	Madison County	26,931	9,093	0.0	3.3	56.2	34.5	21.5	43.8	32.7

State/county FIPS code	State/County	Total own children 6 to 17	Child is foreign born, percent	One or more foreign-born parent, percent	Age 6 to 17 years living with two parents, percent	Both parents in labor force, percent	One parent in labor force, percent	Age 6 to 17 years living with one parent, percent	Parent in labor force, percent	Grandchildren under 18 living with a grandparent householder	Grandchildren under 18 living with a grandparent householder, as a percent of all children	Children for whom grandparent householders are responsible, as a percent of all children
	Georgia—cont'd											
13217	Newton County	17,783	1.2	11.0	51.2	35.1	15.9	48.8	43.8	3,799	14.9	9.8
13223	Paulding County	28,214	2.3	14.0	73.3	48.5	24.7	26.7	24.9	2,709	6.7	3.5
13245	Richmond County	28,915	1.2	5.1	41.0	25.6	13.9	59.0	40.0	5,849	12.9	8.4
13247	Rockdale County	15,001	3.3	20.4	55.0	37.2	16.6	45.0	37.5	2,387	11.1	7.5
13255	Spalding County	9,727	2.0	5.2	58.2	41.9	13.4	41.8	30.6	2,250	15.9	9.4
13285	Troup County	10,668	2.7	7.5	49.9	33.9	12.9	50.1	41.1	1,593	9.6	6.2
13295	Walker County	9,257	0.0	0.0	70.1	50.3	19.1	29.9	20.8	2,090	15.0	13.1
13297	Walton County	15,078	0.2	7.8	64.2	41.2	22.8	35.8	27.9	1,839	8.8	4.8
13313	Whitfield County	18,078	4.2	44.5	66.5	46.0	20.3	33.5	29.2	2,475	9.3	6.7
15000	**Hawaii**	185,199	6.7	30.8	70.6	48.9	20.0	29.4	23.9	47,670	16.5	5.4
15001	Hawaii County	25,357	6.4	21.2	63.9	42.0	20.0	36.1	28.2	5,773	14.7	6.3
15003	Honolulu County	128,713	6.6	32.3	71.9	48.9	21.4	28.1	22.6	33,294	16.5	5.4
15007	Kauai County	9,039	10.0	34.2	72.8	56.1	14.7	27.2	24.8	2,559	17.8	6.6
15009	Maui County	22,090	6.4	31.4	69.8	53.8	14.0	30.2	26.5	6,044	18.0	4.1
16000	**Idaho**	273,849	2.4	13.7	73.6	44.3	28.2	26.4	21.9	20,822	5.1	2.6
16001	Ada County	70,063	3.7	11.6	71.3	42.3	27.9	28.7	24.0	3,392	3.3	1.4
16005	Bannock County	14,403	1.9	7.7	74.3	50.0	23.7	25.7	20.2	998	4.5	2.2
16019	Bonneville County	21,120	1.4	11.4	77.5	43.8	33.2	22.5	20.4	1,396	4.3	1.5
16027	Canyon County	37,934	1.1	21.9	70.2	39.9	28.6	29.8	23.8	3,853	6.8	3.6
16055	Kootenai County	21,490	0.7	2.8	72.1	49.4	22.2	27.9	23.0	1,941	6.0	2.8
16083	Twin Falls County	13,396	4.8	15.8	70.0	35.6	33.6	30.0	27.2	1,380	6.6	3.5
17000	**Illinois**	1,987,691	4.2	26.4	67.0	44.2	21.9	33.0	27.9	213,052	7.3	3.7
17001	Adams County	9,526	0.0	0.0	75.7	54.2	19.1	24.3	18.9	830	5.7	2.9
17007	Boone County	9,985	1.7	26.9	72.0	48.0	23.5	28.0	24.2	1,951	13.9	6.8
17019	Champaign County	23,721	4.8	15.6	63.7	46.2	17.3	36.3	31.6	1,823	4.9	3.8
17029	Coles County	6,165	0.4	5.1	65.2	42.9	21.9	34.8	27.1	578	6.2	4.6
17031	Cook County	762,376	6.0	39.3	60.6	37.7	22.0	39.4	32.8	112,724	9.8	4.7
17037	DeKalb County	14,890	1.7	12.0	70.2	44.8	25.2	29.8	25.3	1,140	5.1	2.6
17043	DuPage County	151,973	6.1	32.5	79.2	52.6	25.9	20.8	18.4	8,966	4.1	1.5
17063	Grundy County	9,054	1.1	6.1	68.2	42.7	25.2	31.8	28.9	590	4.5	2.5
17073	Henry County	7,630	0.3	4.4	73.1	54.2	18.7	26.9	20.5	408	3.7	1.9
17077	Jackson County	6,296	2.9	8.3	62.1	44.9	14.8	37.9	32.6	561	5.7	3.8
17089	Kane County	97,194	5.6	39.0	74.7	47.6	26.5	25.3	22.3	7,317	5.2	2.1
17091	Kankakee County	18,362	2.7	14.0	61.0	40.6	18.6	39.0	33.2	2,002	7.6	4.1
17093	Kendall County	24,091	2.4	21.3	78.0	51.8	25.6	22.0	20.7	1,633	4.6	2.6
17095	Knox County	7,148	0.3	4.1	55.1	37.1	17.5	44.9	30.2	699	7.0	3.8
17097	Lake County	127,730	4.8	34.0	75.7	48.5	26.3	24.3	21.5	8,122	4.5	1.9
17099	LaSalle County	17,195	2.5	9.8	70.2	47.0	21.6	29.8	25.2	1,521	6.3	3.8
17111	McHenry County	56,212	3.9	17.8	79.7	53.1	26.4	20.3	17.5	3,314	4.2	1.8
17113	McLean County	24,623	5.0	9.3	72.3	57.0	15.0	27.7	25.1	2,042	5.5	2.9
17115	Macon County	15,630	1.1	5.5	54.5	36.9	16.5	45.5	41.0	2,416	10.3	8.0
17119	Madison County	38,133	1.4	6.2	67.3	47.6	17.9	32.7	28.0	4,166	7.4	3.6
17141	Ogle County	8,677	1.0	11.2	74.5	55.3	17.9	25.5	23.4	506	4.2	3.2
17143	Peoria County	27,936	3.2	11.6	60.1	38.1	20.5	39.9	34.5	2,948	7.0	4.2
17161	Rock Island County	20,871	5.2	13.8	58.3	41.2	16.6	41.7	38.0	2,194	6.9	3.6
17163	St. Clair County	42,148	1.0	4.6	53.1	35.2	15.5	46.9	34.4	5,183	8.2	4.9
17167	Sangamon County	29,675	1.7	6.2	59.6	47.0	12.4	40.4	35.1	1,926	4.4	2.6
17179	Tazewell County	20,422	1.5	3.1	71.8	46.5	24.1	28.2	23.5	1,492	4.9	3.0
17183	Vermilion County	12,085	0.7	4.6	56.9	40.3	15.7	43.1	38.3	1,542	8.5	4.6
17195	Whiteside County	9,017	1.0	7.9	68.3	50.5	16.5	31.7	27.7	699	5.6	3.5
17197	Will County	130,293	2.6	24.2	77.1	52.2	24.4	22.9	19.7	10,569	5.7	2.9
17199	Williamson County	9,329	1.1	1.9	62.8	46.3	15.7	37.2	29.0	882	6.4	3.6
17201	Winnebago County	44,658	2.9	16.5	58.8	39.1	18.8	41.2	35.4	4,703	7.0	3.6
18000	**Indiana**	1,015,194	2.2	8.7	66.4	44.3	21.1	33.6	27.6	111,312	7.4	4.2
18003	Allen County	60,553	4.1	11.4	64.0	40.9	22.0	36.0	29.0	5,212	5.7	3.0
18005	Bartholomew County	12,083	4.5	10.5	73.0	50.1	22.5	27.0	22.1	1,428	8.1	4.7
18011	Boone County	10,720	2.7	6.1	82.7	56.8	25.8	17.3	15.3	835	5.4	3.3
18019	Clark County	16,073	1.9	6.8	67.7	46.6	19.5	32.3	26.8	2,750	11.1	8.7
18035	Delaware County	14,445	0.8	2.3	61.7	41.4	19.3	38.3	30.0	1,715	8.0	4.2
18039	Elkhart County	35,182	4.2	19.1	67.5	40.9	25.8	32.5	26.1	3,348	6.3	3.1
18043	Floyd County	11,841	3.9	6.5	70.6	47.4	22.0	29.4	21.8	1,273	7.5	5.3
18053	Grant County	9,384	0.5	2.4	59.8	37.6	20.6	40.2	27.6	1,022	7.4	3.9
18057	Hamilton County	56,013	3.9	12.7	80.9	54.4	26.4	19.1	17.3	2,755	3.3	1.9
18059	Hancock County	12,203	0.0	1.7	69.1	51.1	17.8	30.9	29.9	1,034	5.9	2.2
18063	Hendricks County	27,982	2.0	8.5	78.8	61.6	17.0	21.2	19.4	1,709	4.3	1.7
18067	Howard County	12,401	0.7	3.1	64.5	45.4	17.6	35.5	29.6	1,100	6.1	4.5
18081	Johnson County	24,424	0.8	3.8	72.6	52.2	19.7	27.4	21.8	2,649	7.4	4.6
18085	Kosciusko County	12,492	1.1	10.5	73.1	44.9	27.0	26.9	23.0	1,424	7.7	4.4
18089	Lake County	80,194	1.7	12.6	57.5	36.7	19.6	42.5	33.2	10,725	9.1	4.2
18091	LaPorte County	16,141	1.3	6.6	62.0	43.0	18.5	38.0	31.7	2,530	10.7	3.9
18095	Madison County	17,838	1.8	4.2	62.5	42.8	17.7	37.5	29.5	2,240	8.3	5.3

Table D-2: Counties with a Population of 50,000 or More—Children—*Continued*

State/county FIPS code	State/County	Total own children under 18 in families and subfamilies	Own children under 6 years in families and subfamilies							
			Total own children under 6 years	Nativity and parentage, under 6 years		Own children under 6 years living with two parents			Own children under 6 living with one parent	
				Child is foreign born, percent	One or more foreign-born parent, percent	Total under 6 years living with two parents, percent	Both parents in labor force, percent	One parent in labor force, percent	Total under 6 years living with one parent, percent	Parent in labor force, percent
	Indiana—cont'd									
18097	Marion County	215,592	77,545	1.3	19.4	50.0	32.0	16.8	50.0	41.6
18105	Monroe County	22,097	7,584	2.0	15.8	76.4	38.0	36.6	23.6	19.0
18109	Morgan County	16,268	4,814	0.8	3.6	67.4	42.3	25.2	32.6	26.2
18127	Porter County	37,087	10,996	0.9	6.1	69.2	36.6	32.0	30.8	24.6
18141	St. Joseph County...................	61,002	20,411	1.3	14.9	61.2	36.2	24.0	38.8	31.4
18157	Tippecanoe County.................	34,915	12,358	2.0	19.5	65.8	38.1	25.7	34.2	29.1
18163	Vanderburgh County	37,558	13,402	0.2	5.2	58.4	38.1	18.8	41.6	34.6
18167	Vigo County...........................	21,307	7,162	0.1	6.3	55.2	28.4	25.9	44.8	35.5
18173	Warrick County......................	14,130	4,354	1.1	9.0	77.2	47.7	29.6	22.8	16.1
18177	Wayne County........................	14,256	5,124	0.8	7.1	54.1	28.7	22.5	45.9	27.1
19000	**Iowa**..................................	694,083	230,397	0.9	10.4	69.0	49.7	18.6	31.0	25.6
19013	Black Hawk County.................	27,387	9,470	1.1	12.6	67.3	47.9	17.8	32.7	26.4
19049	Dallas County	20,583	7,588	1.6	15.5	84.4	58.3	26.1	15.6	13.3
19061	Dubuque County	21,507	7,117	1.6	2.7	70.1	54.3	15.1	29.9	24.1
19103	Johnson County	26,714	10,009	1.6	18.2	73.8	53.1	20.5	26.2	22.1
19113	Linn County...........................	49,606	16,151	0.8	6.0	69.0	52.6	16.2	31.0	27.5
19153	Polk County	108,692	37,731	2.3	18.3	69.1	49.3	18.8	30.9	25.0
19155	Pottawattamie County.............	20,747	6,780	0.0	4.9	56.8	47.8	8.9	43.2	36.9
19163	Scott County..........................	39,324	13,514	0.5	5.6	62.3	45.1	16.2	37.7	29.0
19169	Story County..........................	15,414	5,367	1.7	14.2	85.4	54.0	30.6	14.6	12.9
19193	Woodbury County	24,994	9,044	1.7	20.3	55.8	37.6	17.0	44.2	37.3
20000	**Kansas**..............................	693,288	237,252	0.9	15.7	67.3	40.8	26.0	32.7	26.1
20015	Butler County	16,358	4,919	0.4	2.4	69.7	43.4	26.2	30.3	23.6
20045	Douglas County	20,386	6,744	2.9	16.0	64.0	43.0	19.3	36.0	29.1
20091	Johnson County.....................	140,567	45,693	1.4	17.1	80.2	51.8	27.7	19.8	17.9
20103	Leavenworth County...............	18,403	5,947	0.7	9.3	66.7	39.8	26.5	33.3	22.5
20155	Reno County..........................	14,356	4,889	0.0	4.2	69.4	35.2	34.2	30.6	25.4
20161	Riley County..........................	13,158	6,395	0.9	11.1	75.9	30.8	44.7	24.1	17.2
20169	Saline County	12,958	4,582	0.0	10.4	57.5	41.2	16.0	42.5	29.8
20173	Sedgwick County....................	129,538	45,904	0.7	18.6	61.8	36.4	25.0	38.2	31.8
20177	Shawnee County.....................	41,652	13,929	0.2	12.9	63.6	41.1	22.4	36.4	31.2
20209	Wyandotte County..................	42,150	15,881	2.2	31.0	46.3	30.8	14.5	53.7	39.6
21000	**Kentucky**...........................	945,623	316,066	0.8	8.7	62.3	37.2	23.2	37.7	28.0
21015	Boone County........................	33,021	10,635	3.4	9.8	72.2	46.3	25.5	27.8	22.7
21029	Bullitt County.........................	17,053	4,862	0.0	4.6	66.1	45.1	20.1	33.9	28.4
21037	Campbell County....................	19,283	6,680	0.5	5.1	61.3	42.2	18.3	38.7	30.3
21047	Christian County.....................	20,051	7,902	0.0	10.5	73.3	28.0	42.9	26.7	18.1
21059	Daviess County	21,699	7,150	0.4	3.4	61.2	41.6	19.7	38.8	32.3
21067	Fayette County	60,844	21,245	2.0	23.6	66.7	43.7	21.5	33.3	27.5
21093	Hardin County........................	26,209	9,566	0.3	5.0	54.6	29.9	23.5	45.4	36.7
21111	Jefferson County....................	161,231	55,953	1.7	17.1	57.3	37.1	19.0	42.7	36.1
21117	Kenton County.......................	37,525	13,820	0.6	8.7	55.8	32.2	22.4	44.2	34.8
21125	Laurel County.........................	13,448	4,728	0.0	3.0	62.5	30.0	31.2	37.5	23.1
21145	McCracken County..................	13,336	4,192	0.4	2.7	57.1	40.2	16.6	42.9	33.8
21151	Madison County	16,466	5,638	0.0	2.6	64.5	42.8	20.3	35.5	25.7
21185	Oldham County	16,086	3,519	0.2	12.7	85.4	62.9	21.4	14.6	13.4
21195	Pike County	12,669	4,083	0.1	1.7	66.3	24.5	35.9	33.7	15.2
21199	Pulaski County	13,247	4,529	0.0	8.1	62.4	40.1	21.8	37.6	20.7
21227	Warren County.......................	24,402	8,245	2.8	15.9	59.5	37.2	21.4	40.5	34.7
22000	**Louisiana**..............................	1,045,345	359,520	0.4	7.1	50.1	30.1	19.2	49.9	37.1
22001	Acadia Parish	14,971	5,372	0.0	0.0	52.0	30.3	21.7	48.0	35.5
22005	Ascension Parish	30,412	10,525	0.8	7.3	67.4	52.2	13.8	32.6	25.3
22015	Bossier Parish	29,051	10,286	1.1	12.3	59.7	33.7	25.9	40.3	32.5
22017	Caddo Parish	58,253	21,025	0.1	4.2	40.1	25.4	14.5	59.9	40.7
22019	Calcasieu Parish	46,494	14,684	0.1	3.1	47.2	23.6	23.2	52.8	39.6
22033	East Baton Rouge Parish.........	96,273	33,219	0.4	10.0	47.7	31.2	16.1	52.3	40.9
22045	Iberia Parish	18,648	6,473	0.8	4.9	37.7	23.7	12.9	62.3	48.5
22051	Jefferson Parish	92,040	33,709	0.7	21.2	48.9	30.5	17.7	51.1	37.9
22055	Lafayette Parish	52,011	18,288	0.1	6.6	54.5	33.6	20.5	45.5	37.4
22057	Lafourche Parish	21,682	7,062	0.3	6.0	57.1	34.6	22.2	42.9	37.1
22063	Livingston Parish....................	32,555	10,449	1.1	5.1	57.6	36.8	20.8	42.4	35.8
22071	Orleans Parish	71,953	26,528	0.4	8.4	36.7	24.8	10.4	63.3	47.4
22073	Ouachita Parish	37,297	12,803	0.4	1.8	42.8	24.7	17.4	57.2	38.3
22079	Rapides Parish	31,662	10,428	0.5	5.4	54.3	33.9	18.7	45.7	30.8
22089	St. Charles Parish	12,925	4,075	0.0	8.3	48.0	31.3	16.1	52.0	42.5
22097	St. Landry Parish	21,647	7,898	0.0	1.9	43.7	24.0	18.5	56.3	35.0
22099	St. Martin Parish	12,712	4,468	0.0	0.0	53.8	32.0	21.8	46.2	29.6
22101	St. Mary Parish.......................	12,435	4,313	1.0	12.1	45.5	19.1	25.7	54.5	37.7
22103	St. Tammany Parish	56,979	16,576	0.4	3.9	65.7	40.5	24.0	34.3	25.9
22105	Tangipahoa Parish	28,227	9,974	0.0	3.2	55.6	34.7	20.5	44.4	37.0
22109	Terrebonne Parish	27,097	9,375	0.0	9.2	49.7	23.7	23.9	50.3	37.1

Table D-2: Counties with a Population of 50,000 or More—Children—*Continued*

State/county FIPS code	State/County	Total own children 6 to 17	Nativity and parentage, age 6 to 17 years		Own children age 6 to 17 years living with two parents			Own children age 6 to 17 years living with one parent		Grand-children under 18 living with a grandparent householder	Grand-children under 18 living with a grandparent householder, as a percent of all children	Children for whom grandparent householders are responsible, as a percent of all children
			Child is foreign born, percent	One or more foreign-born parent, percent	Age 6 to 17 years living with two parents, percent	Both parents in labor force, percent	One parent in labor force, percent	Age 6 to 17 years living with one parent, percent	Parent in labor force, percent			
	Indiana—cont'd											
18097	Marion County	138,047	4.2	14.8	51.8	35.4	15.2	48.2	39.9	17,961	8.3	4.8
18105	Monroe County	14,513	2.6	7.0	67.4	46.5	20.0	32.6	26.5	661	3.0	1.0
18109	Morgan County	11,454	1.8	3.2	72.6	50.1	22.0	27.4	25.1	1,851	11.4	6.6
18127	Porter County	26,091	0.9	7.5	74.9	46.6	27.5	25.1	22.0	3,093	8.3	5.3
18141	St. Joseph County	40,591	3.0	12.8	64.1	44.0	19.2	35.9	29.4	3,827	6.3	3.9
18157	Tippecanoe County	22,557	3.9	17.7	70.0	45.4	23.4	30.0	25.4	1,887	5.4	3.3
18163	Vanderburgh County	24,156	2.3	4.3	59.3	36.3	21.9	40.7	34.3	2,443	6.5	3.3
18167	Vigo County	14,145	0.6	3.8	63.9	37.9	24.6	36.1	27.2	1,388	6.5	3.8
18173	Warrick County	9,776	1.4	5.5	77.2	49.2	27.0	22.8	20.2	1,168	8.3	5.5
18177	Wayne County	9,132	0.8	2.7	67.0	43.9	20.7	33.0	23.3	1,167	8.2	4.7
19000	**Iowa**	463,686	2.3	9.2	70.3	54.0	15.3	29.7	25.4	32,341	4.7	2.5
19013	Black Hawk County	17,917	3.0	12.0	68.3	49.3	17.4	31.7	26.7	1,511	5.5	3.6
19049	Dallas County	12,995	2.2	9.5	74.8	52.6	22.0	25.2	22.4	0	0.0	0.0
19061	Dubuque County	14,390	1.0	3.1	68.7	56.6	12.0	31.3	25.9	768	3.6	1.8
19103	Johnson County	16,705	4.9	20.1	71.9	56.6	14.8	28.1	24.9	550	2.1	0.8
19113	Linn County	33,455	0.7	5.2	70.9	55.6	14.9	29.1	26.1	2,582	5.2	2.9
19153	Polk County	70,961	4.6	16.4	68.1	52.2	14.9	31.9	27.8	5,689	5.2	2.8
19155	Pottawattamie County	13,967	1.1	6.1	60.3	45.2	14.4	39.7	34.2	1,397	6.7	2.8
19163	Scott County	25,810	1.1	5.5	64.2	49.5	13.7	35.8	27.7	1,920	4.9	2.5
19169	Story County	10,047	4.4	12.5	76.8	61.6	13.2	23.2	21.7	0	0.0	0.0
19193	Woodbury County	15,950	3.3	19.4	60.5	43.5	16.3	39.5	34.1	1,813	7.3	3.1
20000	**Kansas**	456,036	3.0	14.9	70.5	49.3	20.6	29.5	25.6	40,225	5.8	3.3
20015	Butler County	11,439	1.0	3.6	74.9	53.4	20.2	25.1	24.6	1,206	7.4	4.8
20045	Douglas County	13,642	2.4	9.3	69.4	55.2	14.0	30.6	25.4	1,117	5.5	3.7
20091	Johnson County	94,874	3.8	14.5	77.1	53.3	23.4	22.9	21.2	4,342	3.1	1.3
20103	Leavenworth County	12,456	1.2	4.0	72.0	44.9	26.4	28.0	25.6	1,052	5.7	4.1
20155	Reno County	9,467	1.9	7.6	76.2	50.1	24.5	23.8	20.4	439	3.1	2.1
20161	Riley County	6,763	2.5	13.4	77.4	46.6	29.7	22.6	20.7	0	0.0	0.0
20169	Saline County	8,376	3.1	9.5	60.2	45.4	14.5	39.8	35.5	996	7.7	6.0
20173	Sedgwick County	83,634	3.4	20.0	65.3	44.7	20.1	34.7	30.0	9,160	7.1	3.5
20177	Shawnee County	27,723	2.7	12.3	66.1	49.6	16.1	33.9	28.5	2,633	6.3	3.1
20209	Wyandotte County	26,269	6.7	33.1	52.8	36.7	15.3	47.2	38.1	3,760	8.9	5.6
21000	**Kentucky**	629,557	2.1	6.4	64.7	42.3	20.1	35.3	27.3	89,226	9.4	6.1
21015	Boone County	22,386	1.0	5.4	70.6	52.7	17.5	29.4	24.4	1,348	4.1	2.5
21029	Bullitt County	12,191	0.2	3.7	62.5	47.4	14.9	37.5	32.2	1,589	9.3	5.6
21037	Campbell County	12,603	0.8	1.7	66.2	51.4	13.7	33.8	27.4	1,649	8.6	6.0
21047	Christian County	12,149	1.4	8.2	72.5	32.6	36.3	27.5	21.8	1,419	7.1	4.9
21059	Daviess County	14,549	1.4	3.9	67.1	42.3	24.4	32.9	28.9	2,233	10.3	5.0
21067	Fayette County	39,599	5.0	18.6	61.5	42.4	18.4	38.5	33.4	3,964	6.5	4.4
21093	Hardin County	16,643	1.6	6.6	60.1	35.2	22.5	39.9	30.4	1,966	7.5	4.1
21111	Jefferson County	105,278	5.3	12.7	56.1	39.7	15.8	43.9	37.1	14,221	8.8	5.7
21117	Kenton County	23,705	1.6	4.6	62.5	44.2	17.5	37.5	31.8	2,786	7.4	4.6
21125	Laurel County	8,720	0.5	1.6	66.0	36.2	26.5	34.0	22.7	1,592	11.8	7.2
21145	McCracken County	9,144	2.8	2.3	64.2	43.4	20.3	35.8	28.3	1,543	11.6	8.4
21151	Madison County	10,828	0.6	2.7	67.2	48.9	16.5	32.8	26.3	1,683	10.2	6.3
21185	Oldham County	12,567	2.5	8.0	80.6	55.5	23.9	19.4	17.7	593	3.7	2.1
21195	Pike County	8,586	0.2	1.5	66.6	32.9	24.6	33.4	17.3	1,669	13.2	7.8
21199	Pulaski County	8,718	0.0	2.7	63.0	44.9	14.8	37.0	25.4	1,340	10.1	8.0
21227	Warren County	16,157	8.7	16.8	64.5	44.8	17.7	35.5	29.4	1,714	7.0	4.3
22000	**Louisiana**	685,825	1.3	5.5	55.5	36.8	17.5	44.5	35.5	119,313	11.4	7.3
22001	Acadia Parish	9,599	0.0	0.0	57.8	35.5	21.7	42.2	32.7	1,771	11.8	6.7
22005	Ascension Parish	19,887	0.9	5.5	66.1	47.2	17.6	33.9	29.9	2,076	6.8	4.5
22015	Bossier Parish	18,765	2.8	7.0	60.8	42.5	18.0	39.2	32.9	4,129	14.2	11.2
22017	Caddo Parish	37,228	0.5	3.0	44.1	28.8	14.1	55.9	43.4	7,835	13.4	8.8
22019	Calcasieu Parish	31,810	0.8	3.5	60.1	42.2	16.9	39.9	33.4	4,564	9.8	6.1
22033	East Baton Rouge Parish	63,054	1.5	7.2	49.0	32.7	15.6	51.0	42.9	11,904	12.4	6.6
22045	Iberia Parish	12,175	2.3	4.5	45.6	27.1	17.7	54.4	42.9	2,514	13.5	10.8
22051	Jefferson Parish	58,331	3.2	16.7	53.0	35.2	16.8	47.0	38.2	9,638	10.5	5.8
22055	Lafayette Parish	33,723	2.0	6.5	61.8	41.6	19.6	38.2	32.8	4,014	7.7	4.2
22057	Lafourche Parish	14,620	1.6	3.6	56.0	33.9	20.9	44.0	38.1	2,725	12.6	7.2
22063	Livingston Parish	22,106	0.2	4.9	66.6	48.3	17.3	33.4	27.0	2,843	8.7	6.4
22071	Orleans Parish	45,425	1.6	6.6	38.6	26.6	10.4	61.4	49.2	9,024	12.5	7.7
22073	Ouachita Parish	24,494	0.6	2.9	50.7	32.3	16.3	49.3	36.6	4,447	11.9	7.1
22079	Rapides Parish	21,234	1.8	5.9	57.8	38.2	19.0	42.2	32.8	2,988	9.4	5.9
22089	St. Charles Parish	8,850	1.9	12.5	62.4	41.3	20.9	37.6	30.9	1,162	9.0	3.7
22097	St. Landry Parish	13,749	0.0	1.7	51.6	36.0	11.8	48.4	34.1	1,439	6.6	4.1
22099	St. Martin Parish	8,244	0.0	0.0	54.7	36.4	16.5	45.3	37.1	1,667	13.1	9.6
22101	St. Mary Parish	8,122	2.2	6.2	54.9	31.5	22.4	45.1	35.1	1,517	12.2	8.2
22103	St. Tammany Parish	40,403	1.2	5.7	68.7	45.1	22.8	31.3	25.1	4,934	8.7	5.9
22105	Tangipahoa Parish	18,253	1.6	2.3	54.9	40.1	13.2	45.1	35.3	3,718	13.2	8.3
22109	Terrebonne Parish	17,722	0.6	5.4	57.7	30.6	25.3	42.3	31.9	2,915	10.8	8.3

				Own children under 6 years in families and subfamilies						
				Nativity and parentage, under 6 years		Own children under 6 years living with two parents			Own children under 6 living with one parent	
State/county FIPS code	State/County	Total own children under 18 in families and subfamilies	Total own children under 6 years	Child is foreign born, percent	One or more foreign-born parent, percent	Total under 6 years living with two parents, percent	Both parents in labor force, percent	One parent in labor force, percent	Total under 6 years living with one parent, percent	Parent in labor force, percent
	Louisiana—cont'd									
22113	Vermilion Parish	14,290	4,727	1.0	6.4	46.5	31.1	14.2	53.5	39.8
22115	Vernon Parish	13,952	5,722	0.6	12.5	73.1	25.5	44.9	26.9	19.1
23000	**Maine**	251,774	76,476	0.7	6.3	66.4	43.4	21.7	33.6	25.7
23001	Androscoggin County	22,762	7,622	0.7	2.5	55.3	38.0	15.8	44.7	34.2
23003	Aroostook County	12,674	3,955	0.2	5.7	64.0	42.3	19.4	36.0	25.8
23005	Cumberland County	55,195	16,700	1.6	15.0	70.5	49.3	20.3	29.5	22.6
23009	Hancock County	9,391	2,827	1.7	3.0	66.3	47.1	18.4	33.7	26.3
23011	Kennebec County	22,958	6,786	0.4	6.0	69.4	45.9	21.1	30.6	22.4
23017	Oxford County	11,055	3,288	0.0	0.5	66.4	33.4	31.9	33.6	22.6
23019	Penobscot County	27,263	8,516	0.6	5.5	68.2	44.4	22.1	31.8	23.1
23025	Somerset County	9,969	2,826	0.0	2.5	55.1	26.0	26.3	44.9	34.5
23031	York County	38,902	11,510	0.2	3.5	73.0	49.8	22.2	27.0	25.0
24000	**Maryland**	1,285,577	427,978	1.7	28.0	62.6	41.4	20.6	37.4	30.2
24001	Allegany County	12,246	3,858	1.2	3.2	60.0	36.1	21.2	40.0	32.0
24003	Anne Arundel County	121,273	41,991	0.6	19.2	73.4	46.3	27.1	26.6	22.0
24005	Baltimore County	169,378	57,780	2.1	22.5	63.1	43.2	19.0	36.9	29.0
24009	Calvert County	21,701	5,352	0.0	3.0	68.1	41.5	26.2	31.9	31.1
24013	Carroll County	37,734	9,966	0.1	4.3	71.9	51.6	20.2	28.1	20.3
24015	Cecil County	23,650	7,414	0.7	4.3	63.3	41.0	21.1	36.7	28.1
24017	Charles County	37,528	11,205	0.7	12.6	57.5	39.0	18.3	42.5	31.8
24021	Frederick County	56,745	17,617	0.4	23.1	70.6	44.4	25.6	29.4	27.3
24025	Harford County	56,512	16,826	0.5	11.8	70.8	43.4	27.0	29.2	22.7
24027	Howard County	74,043	21,801	2.4	33.7	80.3	51.2	28.8	19.7	16.0
24031	Montgomery County	230,298	75,711	3.6	56.4	75.9	50.9	24.0	24.1	21.0
24033	Prince George's County	191,389	68,286	1.6	40.5	49.9	36.1	13.7	50.1	42.2
24037	St. Mary's County	26,621	9,005	0.1	14.9	74.7	46.4	27.9	25.3	21.9
24043	Washington County	31,087	10,020	2.6	13.3	59.6	37.1	22.2	40.4	29.8
24045	Wicomico County	20,914	7,140	2.2	23.5	49.1	30.0	18.9	50.9	44.3
24047	Worcester County	8,832	2,606	0.0	17.3	72.1	51.1	21.0	27.9	27.1
24510	Baltimore city	121,225	47,246	1.1	14.0	35.5	23.4	10.7	64.5	47.5
25000	**Massachusetts**	1,349,577	430,160	1.9	29.6	68.4	45.9	21.7	31.6	23.7
25001	Barnstable County	34,312	9,396	0.1	15.3	69.8	48.6	21.3	30.2	25.6
25003	Berkshire County	22,710	6,886	0.9	12.2	56.8	38.4	17.9	43.2	33.2
25005	Bristol County	113,995	34,778	0.6	16.6	62.5	43.9	18.2	37.5	28.3
25009	Essex County	163,269	50,643	1.6	31.8	64.5	42.5	21.5	35.5	26.2
25011	Franklin County	12,913	3,873	1.2	10.3	65.2	39.3	25.9	34.8	25.5
25013	Hampden County	101,801	32,250	1.2	16.2	47.5	31.2	14.5	52.5	34.9
25015	Hampshire County	24,221	7,344	1.3	14.4	77.6	57.4	17.0	22.4	14.9
25017	Middlesex County	313,010	102,567	2.6	37.7	80.2	52.6	27.0	19.8	15.5
25021	Norfolk County	147,746	45,233	3.4	32.2	83.5	56.9	25.8	16.5	13.0
25023	Plymouth County	112,099	32,866	0.6	20.4	70.4	49.5	20.3	29.6	23.7
25025	Suffolk County	123,863	48,896	3.2	47.6	51.6	34.9	15.6	48.4	36.5
25027	Worcester County	174,281	53,654	1.4	24.3	67.9	45.0	21.4	32.1	24.1
26000	**Michigan**	2,165,093	673,975	1.2	12.9	62.2	36.9	24.0	37.8	29.3
26005	Allegan County	26,939	7,987	0.8	8.6	71.7	41.6	28.6	28.3	19.0
26015	Barry County	13,428	3,806	0.0	4.8	78.8	46.8	30.4	21.2	19.1
26017	Bay County	22,123	6,945	0.0	2.3	64.1	44.7	18.2	35.9	20.2
26021	Berrien County	34,256	11,394	1.8	10.6	58.3	31.9	24.0	41.7	33.1
26025	Calhoun County	29,833	9,608	0.3	5.3	50.9	33.8	16.8	49.1	40.1
26027	Cass County	11,100	3,386	0.6	7.0	63.1	31.0	32.1	36.9	25.8
26037	Clinton County	17,214	4,459	0.0	4.7	73.2	50.4	22.3	26.8	24.2
26045	Eaton County	23,230	6,957	0.0	3.2	72.0	47.2	24.0	28.0	25.0
26049	Genesee County	95,068	29,631	0.3	3.2	46.3	28.9	16.3	53.7	39.5
26055	Grand Traverse County	17,803	5,703	0.0	4.9	70.8	48.1	22.8	29.2	25.4
26065	Ingham County	54,739	18,957	1.9	12.0	60.0	37.4	21.2	40.0	32.6
26067	Ionia County	14,674	4,525	0.1	4.7	71.9	47.4	24.3	28.1	20.1
26073	Isabella County	11,574	3,966	1.2	4.2	56.9	36.2	18.0	43.1	34.3
26075	Jackson County	34,229	10,993	0.1	2.6	59.5	33.7	24.6	40.5	29.2
26077	Kalamazoo County	54,267	17,844	0.9	10.0	60.6	37.6	21.1	39.4	31.8
26081	Kent County	150,911	51,577	1.5	17.5	66.2	42.8	22.3	33.8	27.3
26087	Lapeer County	19,804	5,392	0.4	5.8	69.5	42.2	24.6	30.5	22.3
26091	Lenawee County	20,855	6,353	0.0	1.5	62.7	37.8	23.2	37.3	30.7
26093	Livingston County	43,432	11,321	0.6	5.5	80.4	51.2	28.7	19.6	16.9
26099	Macomb County	183,981	54,539	2.2	20.2	65.1	38.3	26.0	34.9	28.5
26103	Marquette County	11,632	3,951	0.0	3.0	77.9	54.3	22.9	22.1	16.2
26111	Midland County	18,206	5,036	1.6	9.1	73.4	33.6	39.6	26.6	18.8
26115	Monroe County	33,386	10,265	0.6	4.1	61.2	34.0	26.4	38.8	31.5
26117	Montcalm County	13,610	4,183	0.4	2.6	65.8	38.8	24.0	34.2	26.7
26121	Muskegon County	38,699	12,001	0.2	3.6	52.1	36.1	15.6	47.9	35.8
26125	Oakland County	269,422	80,395	2.3	22.1	74.0	45.3	27.7	26.0	22.5

Table D-2: Counties with a Population of 50,000 or More—Children—*Continued*

			Own children age 6 to 17 years in families and subfamilies								Grand-children under 18 living with a grandparent householder	Grand-children under 18 living with a grandparent householder, as a percent of all children	Children for whom grandparent householders are responsible, as a percent of all children
			Nativity and parentage, age 6 to 17 years		Own children age 6 to 17 years living with two parents			Own children age 6 to 17 years living with one parent				
State/county FIPS code	State/County	Total own children 6 to 17	Child is foreign born, percent	One or more foreign-born parent, percent	Age 6 to 17 years living with two parents, percent	Both parents in labor force, percent	One parent in labor force, percent	Age 6 to 17 years living with one parent, percent	Parent in labor force, percent	Grand-children under 18 living with a grandparent householder		
	Louisiana—cont'd											
22113	Vermilion Parish	9,563	1.2	4.4	62.9	46.3	14.3	37.1	33.1	1,521	10.6	6.7
22115	Vernon Parish	8,230	2.6	6.4	76.5	35.8	39.9	23.5	17.0	823	5.9	4.6
23000	**Maine**	175,298	1.8	6.8	66.8	47.3	18.1	33.2	26.8	14,282	5.7	2.9
23001	Androscoggin County	15,140	2.7	7.1	62.6	46.1	15.2	37.4	30.8	1,581	6.9	3.5
23003	Aroostook County	8,719	0.5	4.6	68.0	45.8	20.3	32.0	25.0	791	6.2	2.7
23005	Cumberland County	38,495	3.8	11.7	67.1	49.5	16.6	32.9	27.0	2,387	4.3	2.3
23009	Hancock County	6,564	0.5	4.6	68.7	53.3	14.0	31.3	26.8	383	4.1	1.9
23011	Kennebec County	16,172	0.5	6.5	65.5	47.4	16.4	34.5	26.3	1,130	4.9	2.5
23017	Oxford County	7,767	0.4	3.7	65.7	43.4	21.5	34.3	24.9	901	8.2	4.8
23019	Penobscot County	18,747	2.1	6.1	69.0	46.5	20.6	31.0	22.6	1,526	5.6	3.0
23025	Somerset County	7,143	0.5	3.3	58.9	40.1	16.4	41.1	31.0	538	5.4	2.5
23031	York County	27,392	1.3	6.6	71.4	51.1	19.8	28.6	25.3	2,376	6.1	2.8
24000	**Maryland**	857,599	5.5	23.9	64.5	46.6	17.2	35.5	30.5	107,342	8.3	3.9
24001	Allegany County	8,388	1.4	3.7	63.5	40.4	21.1	36.5	28.7	1,173	9.6	4.2
24003	Anne Arundel County	79,282	3.3	13.6	72.0	50.7	20.8	28.0	25.5	9,014	7.4	3.2
24005	Baltimore County	111,598	6.4	20.2	61.6	44.2	16.7	38.4	32.6	13,489	8.0	4.0
24009	Calvert County	16,349	0.7	6.2	78.3	55.5	22.3	21.7	19.0	1,814	8.4	2.7
24013	Carroll County	27,768	1.4	5.9	77.2	58.1	18.8	22.8	20.4	2,644	7.0	3.0
24015	Cecil County	16,236	1.6	6.0	70.0	45.4	20.5	30.0	22.6	1,936	8.2	3.3
24017	Charles County	26,323	2.2	10.7	64.7	49.1	15.0	35.3	31.2	2,943	7.8	3.1
24021	Frederick County	39,128	3.9	18.3	74.6	53.6	20.8	25.4	21.6	3,412	6.0	2.7
24025	Harford County	39,686	1.9	7.8	68.2	49.5	17.5	31.8	27.1	4,559	8.1	4.2
24027	Howard County	52,242	7.9	33.5	75.6	55.0	20.5	24.4	22.7	3,646	4.9	2.6
24031	Montgomery County	154,587	11.5	50.9	74.7	54.8	19.3	25.3	22.7	10,008	4.3	1.7
24033	Prince George's County	123,103	6.6	35.5	53.2	41.3	11.6	46.8	42.1	22,695	11.9	4.7
24037	St. Mary's County	17,616	0.8	7.1	76.9	51.2	25.4	23.1	19.5	1,539	5.8	2.6
24043	Washington County	21,067	2.9	8.3	65.8	47.8	17.1	34.2	28.8	2,581	8.3	5.1
24045	Wicomico County	13,774	6.5	16.0	58.4	41.3	16.9	41.6	35.0	1,335	6.4	4.4
24047	Worcester County	6,226	1.8	8.0	60.8	40.7	18.5	39.2	35.2	809	9.2	5.5
24510	Baltimore city	73,979	2.2	8.9	31.7	21.4	9.2	68.3	52.5	19,454	16.0	8.1
25000	**Massachusetts**	919,417	5.2	24.9	68.2	49.3	17.9	31.8	25.3	79,754	5.9	2.5
25001	Barnstable County	24,916	3.0	9.9	62.6	48.0	13.8	37.4	31.4	2,048	6.0	2.7
25003	Berkshire County	15,824	1.4	8.1	65.7	48.2	15.2	34.3	29.5	1,354	6.0	4.0
25005	Bristol County	79,217	2.8	19.7	66.2	49.4	16.1	33.8	26.7	8,271	7.3	2.7
25009	Essex County	112,626	6.7	29.3	65.3	47.8	16.4	34.7	28.6	10,073	6.2	2.5
25011	Franklin County	9,040	2.5	6.3	66.4	49.9	16.1	33.6	27.4	879	6.8	2.4
25013	Hampden County	69,551	3.6	15.3	51.1	37.5	12.1	48.9	33.8	7,949	7.8	4.4
25015	Hampshire County	16,877	2.7	10.9	64.7	49.2	14.7	35.3	27.7	1,021	4.2	1.7
25017	Middlesex County	210,443	6.8	30.4	78.2	55.0	22.8	21.8	18.1	14,424	4.6	1.7
25021	Norfolk County	102,513	4.3	25.1	80.0	56.8	22.3	20.0	16.6	6,182	4.2	1.2
25023	Plymouth County	79,233	2.1	14.2	73.9	53.3	19.8	26.1	21.2	8,369	7.5	3.0
25025	Suffolk County	74,967	9.3	50.5	42.9	31.4	11.0	57.1	44.5	9,689	7.8	3.4
25027	Worcester County	120,627	5.3	19.4	68.4	49.8	17.0	31.6	25.0	9,395	5.4	2.5
26000	**Michigan**	1,491,118	2.8	11.6	66.0	43.4	21.0	34.0	27.3	144,930	6.7	3.4
26005	Allegan County	18,952	2.1	6.3	77.2	51.2	25.3	22.8	17.2	1,465	5.4	2.8
26015	Barry County	9,622	0.7	3.0	79.4	52.8	25.7	20.6	19.8	643	4.8	1.8
26017	Bay County	15,178	0.9	3.5	65.1	48.8	15.4	34.9	28.6	1,284	5.8	3.2
26021	Berrien County	22,862	2.9	11.3	62.3	42.8	18.2	37.7	28.5	2,404	7.0	4.2
26025	Calhoun County	20,225	2.2	6.4	60.4	42.5	16.7	39.6	31.3	2,333	7.8	3.6
26027	Cass County	7,714	0.6	5.8	69.6	48.4	20.2	30.4	23.3	801	7.2	4.5
26037	Clinton County	12,755	0.8	2.8	75.7	58.8	15.8	24.3	22.0	909	5.3	1.8
26045	Eaton County	16,273	2.5	5.6	72.0	49.2	19.7	28.0	23.9	1,176	5.1	2.6
26049	Genesee County	65,437	0.5	2.7	55.9	37.2	17.4	44.1	34.4	8,027	8.4	4.7
26055	Grand Traverse County	12,100	1.2	4.8	67.1	44.2	21.6	32.9	28.2	1,085	6.1	3.6
26065	Ingham County	35,782	4.4	13.8	62.6	43.5	17.5	37.4	30.8	4,053	7.4	4.3
26067	Ionia County	10,149	0.1	3.7	73.2	51.1	21.1	26.8	23.2	985	6.7	2.9
26073	Isabella County	7,608	0.8	2.9	64.4	48.6	13.6	35.6	28.6	455	3.9	2.1
26075	Jackson County	23,236	0.3	1.3	65.5	45.6	17.7	34.5	25.9	2,527	7.4	4.6
26077	Kalamazoo County	36,423	2.7	8.6	66.2	45.0	20.7	33.8	29.3	2,854	5.3	2.9
26081	Kent County	99,334	3.5	15.5	70.0	46.3	22.5	30.0	24.8	7,436	4.9	2.3
26087	Lapeer County	14,412	1.5	8.1	74.4	47.8	25.4	25.6	19.5	1,478	7.5	2.9
26091	Lenawee County	14,502	0.4	3.8	70.1	48.7	19.5	29.9	26.2	1,689	8.1	3.9
26093	Livingston County	32,111	1.2	5.7	78.1	52.3	24.9	21.9	19.2	1,752	4.0	1.4
26099	Macomb County	129,442	3.8	17.8	70.6	47.9	21.1	29.4	23.5	11,472	6.2	2.7
26103	Marquette County	7,681	0.5	2.6	67.6	48.2	18.3	32.4	23.1	442	3.8	2.6
26111	Midland County	13,170	3.1	6.2	74.9	46.5	27.3	25.1	20.9	838	4.6	2.9
26115	Monroe County	23,121	1.2	3.4	70.2	50.1	18.5	29.8	26.0	2,655	8.0	4.4
26117	Montcalm County	9,427	0.5	1.4	74.7	43.9	25.4	25.3	19.5	884	6.5	3.1
26121	Muskegon County	26,698	0.4	2.8	61.0	42.6	16.8	39.0	30.7	3,231	8.3	3.5
26125	Oakland County	189,027	5.7	19.6	72.8	48.4	23.4	27.2	23.7	11,666	4.3	1.9

State/county FIPS code	State/County	Total own children under 18 in families and subfamilies	Own children under 6 years in families and subfamilies							
			Total own children under 6 years	Nativity and parentage, under 6 years		Own children under 6 years living with two parents			Own children under 6 living with one parent	
				Child is foreign born, percent	One or more foreign-born parent, percent	Total under 6 years living with two parents, percent	Both parents in labor force, percent	One parent in labor force, percent	Total under 6 years living with one parent, percent	Parent in labor force, percent
	Michigan—cont'd									
26139	Ottawa County	65,720	19,954	3.0	11.4	78.1	44.0	33.8	21.9	19.0
26145	Saginaw County	42,397	13,455	0.0	2.5	52.0	34.6	15.8	48.0	37.3
26147	St. Clair County	35,039	10,294	0.6	5.1	62.9	37.4	23.7	37.1	30.7
26149	St. Joseph County	14,526	4,900	0.0	11.7	63.2	32.9	29.0	36.8	22.5
26155	Shiawassee County	15,000	4,262	0.0	0.0	65.1	40.6	22.4	34.9	28.9
26157	Tuscola County	10,962	3,185	0.0	0.0	66.9	43.4	21.6	33.1	25.9
26159	Van Buren County	17,687	5,387	0.0	9.1	66.5	28.8	36.9	33.5	24.6
26161	Washtenaw County	68,372	21,426	2.9	23.6	71.4	39.6	30.6	28.6	23.9
26163	Wayne County	415,861	135,771	0.9	18.8	49.0	26.1	20.9	51.0	37.0
27000	**Minnesota**	1,234,372	410,101	1.5	19.1	70.7	49.6	20.3	29.3	24.3
27003	Anoka County	81,619	25,427	0.5	17.4	70.9	51.3	19.6	29.1	24.3
27013	Blue Earth County	12,354	4,479	0.2	5.1	72.3	60.0	11.0	27.7	24.2
27019	Carver County	26,903	7,805	0.6	12.8	85.7	59.1	26.2	14.3	11.9
27025	Chisago County	12,769	3,695	0.6	4.0	72.0	56.9	14.9	28.0	25.2
27027	Clay County	13,245	4,667	0.3	13.4	77.4	55.6	20.7	22.6	16.2
27035	Crow Wing County	13,761	4,541	0.0	3.3	71.1	50.4	19.7	28.9	25.3
27037	Dakota County	101,069	32,178	1.1	22.0	74.5	52.0	22.0	25.5	22.9
27053	Hennepin County	255,801	90,946	2.5	31.7	68.2	44.4	23.3	31.8	25.3
27109	Olmsted County	35,950	12,666	1.1	23.7	74.4	56.0	17.6	25.6	23.1
27111	Otter Tail County	11,810	3,803	0.9	6.9	75.3	52.0	21.4	24.7	19.9
27123	Ramsey County	116,982	42,090	3.8	38.4	65.6	43.5	20.0	34.4	27.8
27131	Rice County	14,326	4,504	0.2	17.5	65.9	46.4	19.5	34.1	27.5
27137	St. Louis County	37,125	12,467	0.4	2.6	61.5	37.6	22.4	38.5	33.0
27139	Scott County	38,534	12,473	2.1	20.5	84.4	63.3	20.5	15.6	14.0
27141	Sherburne County	24,162	7,398	1.1	6.4	78.4	63.9	14.5	21.6	19.9
27145	Stearns County	33,894	11,544	0.5	11.2	71.5	55.9	15.3	28.5	24.4
27163	Washington County	61,711	17,796	1.5	14.2	76.3	55.5	20.6	23.7	19.3
27169	Winona County	9,140	2,836	0.3	7.6	78.6	58.9	19.4	21.4	18.2
27171	Wright County	36,345	12,219	1.3	8.4	78.4	55.8	22.1	21.6	18.6
28000	**Mississippi**	690,498	231,060	0.2	4.2	49.0	30.3	17.9	51.0	38.2
28033	DeSoto County	43,428	12,613	0.1	9.0	65.3	44.9	19.9	34.7	29.4
28035	Forrest County	16,625	6,290	0.0	4.1	44.0	22.3	21.7	56.0	46.5
28047	Harrison County	42,804	15,420	0.0	6.9	51.5	25.2	22.9	48.5	37.3
28049	Hinds County	58,929	19,237	0.0	1.4	35.2	23.2	10.0	64.8	53.3
28059	Jackson County	32,154	9,882	1.0	5.4	57.3	28.3	27.8	42.7	33.1
28067	Jones County	16,180	5,221	0.0	5.8	46.5	25.9	20.6	53.5	30.7
28071	Lafayette County	8,592	3,314	0.0	2.7	52.7	31.5	21.2	47.3	32.9
28073	Lamar County	14,481	4,819	0.0	2.6	67.8	43.2	24.5	32.2	30.0
28075	Lauderdale County	18,143	6,078	0.5	4.9	44.8	28.5	16.3	55.2	42.0
28081	Lee County	20,815	7,428	0.0	9.3	58.3	42.2	15.3	41.7	36.7
28087	Lowndes County	13,207	4,940	0.5	3.8	48.2	30.9	17.3	51.8	45.8
28089	Madison County	24,423	7,514	0.8	7.7	66.2	45.3	20.3	33.8	25.2
28109	Pearl River County	12,852	4,238	0.0	5.2	50.7	30.7	20.0	49.3	35.5
28121	Rankin County	34,586	11,282	0.0	6.1	79.6	57.6	21.8	20.4	18.5
28151	Washington County	12,201	4,080	0.0	0.0	21.7	15.8	4.9	78.3	64.4
29000	**Missouri**	1,328,024	440,994	0.6	9.1	62.8	38.7	22.9	37.2	29.5
29019	Boone County	33,536	11,874	1.0	10.5	70.0	38.7	27.4	30.0	24.1
29021	Buchanan County	19,547	6,999	0.0	7.3	50.1	29.7	19.5	49.9	43.4
29031	Cape Girardeau County	16,155	5,600	0.0	3.4	59.9	47.0	12.3	40.1	28.9
29037	Cass County	24,677	7,560	0.8	8.0	69.0	46.0	23.0	31.0	26.1
29043	Christian County	20,530	6,477	0.4	3.1	62.9	45.3	17.3	37.1	30.3
29047	Clay County	55,547	18,711	0.1	11.5	68.2	41.4	25.9	31.8	25.8
29051	Cole County	16,478	5,766	0.0	4.4	60.8	40.3	19.4	39.2	28.8
29071	Franklin County	23,328	7,483	0.0	2.0	67.9	45.1	18.7	32.1	26.6
29077	Greene County	55,867	20,447	0.7	7.8	63.1	36.9	25.0	36.9	29.3
29095	Jackson County	154,906	54,645	0.7	13.9	54.2	31.8	21.2	45.8	34.0
29097	Jasper County	27,724	9,858	0.9	11.4	58.7	34.5	22.0	41.3	33.1
29099	Jefferson County	51,800	17,095	0.0	3.2	67.2	43.3	22.5	32.8	28.1
29101	Johnson County	11,291	4,397	0.2	4.9	75.3	35.8	39.5	24.7	20.8
29113	Lincoln County	13,566	4,239	0.0	3.4	69.5	41.1	27.9	30.5	22.3
29145	Newton County	13,829	4,223	0.0	11.9	73.6	39.5	33.6	26.4	21.1
29165	Platte County	21,438	6,998	1.1	13.3	70.6	46.5	23.7	29.4	27.3
29169	Pulaski County	12,123	5,077	2.7	9.4	71.9	36.7	35.0	28.1	21.5
29183	St. Charles County	89,960	28,010	1.2	8.6	78.5	52.4	25.4	21.5	18.7
29187	St. Francois County	12,760	4,392	0.0	0.0	47.0	31.2	14.0	53.0	42.1
29189	St. Louis County	219,432	67,504	1.3	14.9	65.4	41.2	23.8	34.6	28.4
29213	Taney County	10,514	3,607	0.0	0.0	55.2	30.6	23.7	44.8	35.0
29510	St. Louis city	60,063	23,701	1.0	14.5	43.2	27.0	14.7	56.8	44.4
30000	**Montana**	210,713	72,359	0.3	3.8	68.1	38.5	28.4	31.9	25.6
30013	Cascade County	17,574	6,571	0.0	2.4	60.8	29.6	26.8	39.2	32.1

State/county FIPS code	State/County	Total own children 6 to 17	Nativity and parentage, age 6 to 17 years		Own children age 6 to 17 years living with two parents			Own children age 6 to 17 years living with one parent		Grandchildren under 18 living with a grandparent householder	Grandchildren under 18 living with a grandparent householder, as a percent of all children	Children for whom grandparent householders are responsible, as a percent of all children
			Child is foreign born, percent	One or more foreign-born parent, percent	Age 6 to 17 years living with two parents, percent	Both parents in labor force, percent	One parent in labor force, percent	Age 6 to 17 years living with one parent, percent	Parent in labor force, percent			
	Michigan—cont'd											
26139	Ottawa County	45,766	4.4	9.8	78.4	52.9	25.3	21.6	18.4	3,516	5.3	2.5
26145	Saginaw County	28,942	0.7	3.5	57.1	41.1	14.0	42.9	35.7	3,312	7.8	4.0
26147	St. Clair County	24,745	1.2	4.9	68.2	47.1	20.0	31.8	27.6	1,914	5.5	2.2
26149	St. Joseph County	9,626	0.8	8.3	63.5	40.7	21.7	36.5	31.0	1,166	8.0	4.3
26155	Shiawassee County	10,738	0.0	0.0	71.7	50.1	18.9	28.3	24.8	934	6.2	2.4
26157	Tuscola County	7,777	0.0	0.0	70.2	46.0	21.9	29.8	22.8	1,069	9.8	4.6
26159	Van Buren County	12,300	2.5	12.0	64.3	35.4	25.6	35.7	26.1	1,613	9.1	6.1
26161	Washtenaw County	46,946	4.9	19.7	70.9	46.5	23.8	29.1	24.7	3,030	4.4	2.3
26163	Wayne County	280,090	3.4	17.7	52.9	30.5	19.9	47.1	35.7	39,311	9.5	4.9
27000	**Minnesota**	824,271	4.1	15.1	71.7	54.3	16.6	28.3	24.4	48,920	4.0	1.9
27003	Anoka County	56,192	4.5	14.9	73.5	57.6	15.4	26.5	23.0	4,748	5.8	2.3
27013	Blue Earth County	7,875	2.0	9.4	79.7	67.7	11.3	20.3	17.9	212	1.7	1.1
27019	Carver County	19,098	3.5	9.0	84.9	62.3	21.6	15.1	13.8	565	2.1	0.7
27025	Chisago County	9,074	2.4	2.9	81.0	65.8	14.6	19.0	16.2	339	2.7	0.8
27027	Clay County	8,578	0.6	4.9	71.8	57.7	13.8	28.2	22.4	559	4.2	2.7
27035	Crow Wing County	9,220	1.3	2.5	72.1	52.5	17.4	27.9	24.9	505	3.7	1.1
27037	Dakota County	68,891	3.8	17.1	72.9	55.9	16.6	27.1	24.3	2,870	2.8	1.7
27053	Hennepin County	164,855	6.4	26.3	67.1	46.4	20.2	32.9	27.5	9,911	3.9	1.9
27109	Olmsted County	23,284	5.4	19.2	71.7	57.3	13.2	28.3	24.6	1,115	3.1	0.8
27111	Otter Tail County	8,007	2.8	7.5	75.2	60.7	12.8	24.8	20.4	436	3.7	1.4
27123	Ramsey County	74,892	11.1	32.8	64.1	45.0	17.0	35.9	29.9	5,605	4.8	2.2
27131	Rice County	9,822	3.5	15.3	74.4	58.2	16.2	25.6	24.4	551	3.8	1.5
27137	St. Louis County	24,658	1.2	2.6	64.5	44.9	18.7	35.5	30.1	1,516	4.1	1.9
27139	Scott County	26,061	1.6	14.6	81.6	62.7	18.1	18.4	15.9	955	2.5	1.2
27141	Sherburne County	16,764	0.7	5.9	77.5	63.6	13.7	22.5	21.6	929	3.8	1.2
27145	Stearns County	22,350	3.6	8.7	78.6	68.0	10.2	21.4	18.9	927	2.7	1.6
27163	Washington County	43,915	3.4	12.1	74.0	55.0	18.6	26.0	24.8	2,217	3.6	1.4
27169	Winona County	6,304	0.5	8.0	81.8	61.9	19.4	18.2	16.8	292	3.2	1.3
27171	Wright County	24,126	2.9	5.9	77.5	62.0	15.3	22.5	20.3	874	2.4	0.9
28000	**Mississippi**	459,438	0.9	3.4	54.0	35.3	17.2	46.0	35.4	92,275	13.4	8.3
28033	DeSoto County	30,815	1.3	7.7	66.7	47.8	18.7	33.3	30.2	3,720	8.6	4.4
28035	Forrest County	10,335	1.0	2.4	54.4	30.7	22.2	45.6	35.6	2,122	12.8	10.8
28047	Harrison County	27,384	1.0	5.4	58.2	33.7	22.2	41.8	33.4	5,754	13.4	9.4
28049	Hinds County	39,692	1.1	2.8	41.7	29.3	11.2	58.3	48.5	8,882	15.1	9.8
28059	Jackson County	22,272	2.7	7.3	61.0	34.4	25.5	39.0	31.1	4,468	13.9	8.1
28067	Jones County	10,959	1.3	4.5	51.0	30.3	20.7	49.0	33.4	1,928	11.9	8.3
28071	Lafayette County	5,278	0.0	1.7	69.8	47.2	22.5	30.2	26.1	751	8.7	5.1
28073	Lamar County	9,662	1.6	3.1	61.9	41.2	20.5	38.1	34.6	1,145	7.9	5.1
28075	Lauderdale County	12,065	2.8	2.4	46.8	36.2	10.3	53.2	44.7	2,044	11.3	6.7
28081	Lee County	13,387	0.4	3.7	61.8	45.0	16.5	38.2	31.5	1,973	9.5	6.0
28087	Lowndes County	8,267	0.1	1.8	54.4	38.4	14.5	45.6	36.9	1,761	13.3	8.1
28089	Madison County	16,909	1.5	7.0	67.8	49.4	16.4	32.2	25.0	2,129	8.7	5.0
28109	Pearl River County	8,614	1.5	1.4	53.3	36.3	16.8	46.7	30.4	2,063	16.1	8.8
28121	Rankin County	23,304	0.8	2.6	68.9	47.1	20.8	31.1	27.2	2,294	6.5	2.9
28151	Washington County	8,121	0.0	0.0	31.3	24.3	5.4	68.7	52.9	2,265	18.6	13.0
29000	**Missouri**	887,030	2.1	7.3	66.3	45.9	19.0	33.7	28.0	97,357	7.3	3.9
29019	Boone County	21,662	3.7	11.4	68.3	51.4	14.5	31.7	28.4	1,645	4.9	2.8
29021	Buchanan County	12,548	1.5	7.1	65.9	48.8	15.2	34.1	23.9	2,098	10.7	6.6
29031	Cape Girardeau County	10,555	0.4	1.7	70.0	53.9	15.3	30.0	23.9	1,067	6.6	2.2
29037	Cass County	17,117	0.9	4.9	71.5	46.1	24.8	28.5	25.0	1,913	7.8	2.5
29043	Christian County	14,053	0.7	2.3	69.5	48.1	20.5	30.5	28.8	1,052	5.1	3.2
29047	Clay County	36,836	2.3	8.6	66.7	50.5	14.8	33.3	29.6	3,576	6.4	2.2
29051	Cole County	10,712	1.4	4.9	66.3	51.5	12.4	33.7	27.9	1,634	9.9	7.8
29071	Franklin County	15,845	0.7	3.0	74.7	54.3	19.7	25.3	22.8	1,693	7.3	3.4
29077	Greene County	35,420	1.8	7.6	68.7	47.0	20.0	31.3	25.9	3,148	5.6	3.0
29095	Jackson County	100,261	3.5	12.5	56.5	38.6	16.6	43.5	35.9	11,327	7.3	4.0
29097	Jasper County	17,866	1.1	10.9	69.1	43.9	24.1	30.9	26.1	1,803	6.5	3.7
29099	Jefferson County	34,705	1.1	2.7	69.7	50.6	18.5	30.3	27.0	4,227	8.2	4.1
29101	Johnson County	6,894	0.3	5.0	80.6	44.2	35.0	19.4	15.9	387	3.4	1.7
29113	Lincoln County	9,327	1.4	3.8	71.9	47.6	23.5	28.1	23.1	1,123	8.3	3.9
29145	Newton County	9,606	2.2	6.5	76.7	51.3	24.2	23.3	19.4	1,185	8.6	4.8
29165	Platte County	14,440	2.0	9.9	71.4	52.7	18.0	28.6	22.3	1,438	6.7	2.4
29169	Pulaski County	7,046	3.0	10.0	74.5	47.4	26.7	25.5	19.4	453	3.7	0.5
29183	St. Charles County	61,950	1.5	6.6	78.3	57.8	19.7	21.7	19.6	4,269	4.7	2.2
29187	St. Francois County	8,368	0.0	0.0	69.4	53.5	13.5	30.6	24.8	848	6.6	3.6
29189	St. Louis County	151,928	3.9	11.5	63.5	44.6	18.2	36.5	30.9	13,459	6.1	3.0
29213	Taney County	6,907	0.0	0.0	62.0	45.0	15.8	38.0	33.2	651	6.2	3.8
29510	St. Louis city	36,362	4.3	10.7	37.9	25.2	11.1	62.1	51.3	6,553	10.9	6.5
30000	**Montana**	138,354	0.9	3.7	70.0	48.3	20.3	30.0	25.2	13,284	6.3	3.8
30013	Cascade County	11,003	0.4	1.7	64.9	43.5	18.9	35.1	29.6	802	4.6	2.7

Table D-2: Counties with a Population of 50,000 or More—Children—*Continued*

State/ county FIPS code	State/County	Total own children under 18 in families and subfamilies	Own children under 6 years in families and subfamilies							
			Total own children under 6 years	Nativity and parentage, under 6 years		Own children under 6 years living with two parents			Own children under 6 living with one parent	
				Child is foreign born, percent	One or more foreign-born parent, percent	Total under 6 years living with two parents, percent	Both parents in labor force, percent	One parent in labor force, percent	Total under 6 years living with one parent, percent	Parent in labor force, percent
	Montana—cont'd									
30029	Flathead County.........................	20,102	6,529	0.4	4.8	80.1	41.6	36.8	19.9	16.3
30031	Gallatin County.........................	18,690	6,736	0.5	9.9	86.7	52.6	33.3	13.3	10.8
30049	Lewis and Clark County............	13,968	4,839	0.0	3.0	72.0	52.2	18.8	28.0	23.8
30063	Missoula County........................	20,733	7,356	1.3	2.8	66.3	36.0	29.0	33.7	29.4
30111	Yellowstone County...................	33,155	11,390	0.0	4.6	61.9	37.3	24.0	38.1	32.4
31000	**Nebraska**........................	442,576	151,288	0.9	15.9	68.9	46.3	21.8	31.1	25.8
31055	Douglas County.........................	131,543	47,037	1.8	22.8	64.8	42.5	21.1	35.2	28.6
31079	Hall County..............................	15,354	5,146	0.0	21.1	57.6	46.0	11.4	42.4	31.1
31109	Lancaster County......................	65,209	23,801	0.8	16.7	71.6	48.9	22.3	28.4	24.1
31153	Sarpy County............................	45,627	15,223	0.9	8.7	74.4	47.2	26.9	25.6	21.6
32000	**Nevada**...........................	628,665	212,789	1.0	37.2	62.9	34.6	27.4	37.1	29.8
32003	Clark County............................	464,016	158,753	1.1	40.6	62.2	33.9	27.3	37.8	30.7
32007	Elko County.............................	14,091	4,483	0.5	11.1	78.2	38.1	39.8	21.8	14.4
32019	Lyon County.............................	11,294	3,336	0.0	22.3	58.2	31.9	25.3	41.8	30.4
32031	Washoe County.........................	94,426	32,198	0.8	34.0	65.4	40.6	24.4	34.6	28.0
32510	Carson City..............................	11,174	3,401	0.0	27.3	65.7	30.5	35.0	34.3	22.2
33000	**New Hampshire**.....................	264,738	78,243	1.1	13.2	68.2	43.0	24.4	31.8	25.2
33001	Belknap County.........................	11,387	3,222	1.0	4.1	63.2	39.3	22.5	36.8	26.4
33005	Cheshire County........................	13,339	4,054	0.4	8.8	64.6	37.9	26.5	35.4	31.5
33009	Grafton County.........................	15,286	4,556	0.0	14.9	69.1	33.5	33.0	30.9	25.4
33011	Hillsborough County...................	87,657	27,606	2.1	17.7	67.1	41.8	24.5	32.9	25.2
33013	Merrimack County.....................	29,004	8,523	1.4	9.2	66.6	44.6	21.5	33.4	27.3
33015	Rockingham County...................	62,469	16,740	0.3	14.0	78.8	51.7	26.3	21.2	16.1
33017	Strafford County.......................	23,738	7,599	1.3	12.9	59.9	40.2	19.6	40.1	35.1
34000	**New Jersey**	1,968,419	631,427	2.5	38.2	68.8	41.9	26.2	31.2	24.2
34001	Atlantic County.........................	59,204	19,104	2.1	29.5	54.1	35.6	17.8	45.9	34.8
34003	Bergen County..........................	199,153	59,146	3.7	49.2	81.9	50.2	31.4	18.1	13.0
34005	Burlington County......................	96,730	29,299	1.1	18.4	70.5	48.2	22.2	29.5	25.9
34007	Camden County.........................	117,905	39,263	1.3	20.0	55.7	39.0	16.4	44.3	33.9
34009	Cape May County......................	16,676	5,145	2.0	13.0	76.3	52.1	23.9	23.7	15.3
34011	Cumberland County	34,860	11,840	0.8	23.0	48.3	28.2	20.0	51.7	39.2
34013	Essex County............................	184,055	61,738	1.9	40.2	50.3	33.6	16.4	49.7	41.1
34015	Gloucester County.....................	66,106	20,150	1.2	11.8	72.9	49.9	22.8	27.1	20.7
34017	Hudson County.........................	128,214	51,147	6.1	61.5	60.7	35.0	25.0	39.3	31.3
34019	Hunterdon County......................	27,185	7,071	1.3	20.8	84.1	54.8	29.2	15.9	14.9
34021	Mercer County..........................	78,850	25,525	2.0	40.1	68.0	43.7	24.0	32.0	25.1
34023	Middlesex County.......................	180,333	59,016	4.3	57.7	74.7	43.2	30.9	25.3	19.2
34025	Monmouth County.....................	141,399	40,566	1.2	29.2	76.7	46.0	30.4	23.3	17.2
34027	Morris County...........................	112,125	32,299	3.2	35.0	86.4	51.2	34.4	13.6	11.0
34029	Ocean County...........................	132,053	46,464	0.1	18.1	80.3	37.6	40.6	19.7	15.3
34031	Passaic County..........................	120,295	40,068	4.0	48.3	58.1	32.5	23.3	41.9	28.5
34033	Salem County...........................	14,029	4,606	0.7	12.6	50.2	32.0	18.2	49.8	34.3
34035	Somerset County	76,855	22,555	2.2	48.8	81.4	51.9	28.8	18.6	15.5
34037	Sussex County...........................	32,428	8,810	1.1	20.6	81.2	50.4	30.8	18.8	16.1
34039	Union County...........................	126,428	41,265	1.4	48.6	64.8	40.4	24.2	35.2	27.7
34041	Warren County.........................	23,536	6,350	0.8	18.5	77.1	52.3	24.5	22.9	17.1
35000	**New Mexico**.........................	485,198	164,028	0.8	19.2	54.2	28.0	25.1	45.8	34.1
35001	Bernalillo County	150,626	51,727	1.1	21.2	56.1	30.3	24.3	43.9	33.3
35005	Chaves County..........................	16,904	5,670	0.0	25.2	58.2	25.7	32.5	41.8	30.6
35009	Curry County............................	13,139	5,324	0.0	17.1	54.9	26.9	24.2	45.1	31.5
35013	Do±a Ana County......................	53,121	18,507	1.8	30.3	53.4	30.5	22.3	46.6	38.3
35015	Eddy County............................	13,752	4,733	0.0	16.2	54.8	28.8	26.1	45.2	31.7
35025	Lea County..............................	18,426	6,417	0.5	34.0	56.0	23.0	31.2	44.0	34.8
35031	McKinley County	20,944	7,259	0.0	2.5	39.3	18.2	18.7	60.7	28.6
35035	Otero County............................	15,681	5,579	1.9	19.2	48.8	23.5	24.6	51.2	38.9
35043	Sandoval County.......................	33,235	9,854	0.2	9.9	55.0	24.3	29.3	45.0	33.4
35045	San Juan County........................	33,624	11,497	0.6	7.8	58.0	30.1	26.9	42.0	29.5
35049	Santa Fe County	28,282	9,069	0.5	31.4	61.8	39.7	21.5	38.2	30.0
35061	Valencia County........................	18,192	5,856	0.5	15.2	60.2	28.2	30.9	39.8	28.8
36000	**New York**..........................	4,080,838	1,349,393	2.1	35.6	63.7	36.8	25.9	36.3	26.7
36001	Albany County..........................	56,642	17,645	1.8	16.8	61.9	39.8	21.7	38.1	33.1
36005	Bronx County...........................	344,986	119,854	2.3	50.8	38.1	21.3	16.0	61.9	42.9
36007	Broome County.........................	37,095	11,810	0.7	9.0	58.4	31.3	25.6	41.6	28.6
36009	Cattaraugus County....................	17,352	5,660	0.4	4.7	62.7	33.7	27.8	37.3	26.7
36011	Cayuga County..........................	15,730	4,924	0.1	2.6	58.1	38.2	17.0	41.9	32.6
36013	Chautauqua County....................	26,466	8,310	0.2	2.1	62.4	35.6	25.0	37.6	25.7
36015	Chemung County	18,464	5,982	3.1	7.3	59.9	33.6	26.1	40.1	32.3
36019	Clinton County..........................	14,132	4,463	0.0	3.1	58.2	39.8	17.6	41.8	30.7
36021	Columbia County.......................	11,069	3,401	0.0	7.6	56.2	34.6	19.8	43.8	38.5
36027	Dutchess County........................	60,388	16,460	1.6	23.6	68.9	48.5	19.7	31.1	25.5

Table D-2: Counties with a Population of 50,000 or More—Children—*Continued*

State/county FIPS code	State/County	Total own children 6 to 17	Nativity and parentage, age 6 to 17		Own children age 6 to 17 years living with two parents			Own children age 6 to 17 years living with one parent		Grandchildren under 18 living with a grandparent householder	Grandchildren under 18 living with a grandparent householder, as a percent of all children	Children for whom grandparent householders are responsible, as a percent of all children
			Child is foreign born, percent	One or more foreign-born parent, percent	Age 6 to 17 years living with two parents, percent	Both parents in labor force, percent	One parent in labor force, percent	Age 6 to 17 years living with one parent, percent	Parent in labor force, percent			
	Montana—cont'd											
30029	Flathead County	13,573	1.0	5.9	70.3	42.6	25.6	29.7	24.8	576	2.9	1.4
30031	Gallatin County	11,954	2.3	4.8	77.2	55.3	20.5	22.8	21.3	332	1.8	1.3
30049	Lewis and Clark County	9,129	0.9	2.0	66.6	52.5	12.8	33.4	30.5	530	3.8	1.3
30063	Missoula County	13,377	0.2	4.4	68.5	52.9	15.3	31.5	28.5	1,029	5.0	3.1
30111	Yellowstone County	21,765	0.8	3.7	69.6	49.9	19.3	30.4	25.9	2,495	7.5	4.3
31000	**Nebraska**	291,288	3.4	14.4	71.1	52.6	17.5	28.9	25.5	20,035	4.5	2.4
31055	Douglas County	84,506	5.2	19.8	66.2	46.8	18.7	33.8	29.9	6,288	4.8	2.2
31079	Hall County	10,208	5.8	29.2	68.6	53.3	14.9	31.4	25.2	543	3.5	1.2
31109	Lancaster County	41,408	3.9	14.2	70.5	50.1	19.4	29.5	26.7	2,383	3.7	2.1
31153	Sarpy County	30,404	3.2	11.3	73.6	51.8	21.2	26.4	22.7	1,989	4.4	2.1
32000	**Nevada**	415,876	5.7	39.0	62.5	38.6	22.7	37.5	31.5	44,276	7.0	4.0
32003	Clark County	305,263	6.2	42.1	60.8	37.1	22.5	39.2	33.1	32,051	6.9	3.8
32007	Elko County	9,608	3.0	25.6	81.3	49.1	29.6	18.7	16.3	994	7.1	3.8
32019	Lyon County	7,958	1.7	20.8	64.3	36.2	27.2	35.7	28.5	1,039	9.2	4.2
32031	Washoe County	62,228	5.3	36.4	65.7	43.1	21.7	34.3	28.6	6,096	6.5	3.9
32510	Carson City	7,773	6.7	33.5	60.0	47.4	11.4	40.0	36.2	1,175	10.5	8.0
33000	**New Hampshire**	186,495	2.6	10.3	71.9	51.5	19.1	28.1	23.8	14,245	5.4	2.2
33001	Belknap County	8,165	4.5	7.9	70.9	51.1	18.5	29.1	20.9	669	5.9	3.2
33005	Cheshire County	9,285	1.2	7.0	68.0	52.8	14.9	32.0	26.6	613	4.6	2.6
33009	Grafton County	10,730	3.9	7.8	64.2	40.7	22.7	35.8	30.5	692	4.5	1.8
33011	Hillsborough County	60,051	3.6	16.2	71.1	50.8	18.8	28.9	24.8	4,918	5.6	2.2
33013	Merrimack County	20,481	2.6	7.8	72.3	53.1	17.5	27.7	23.7	2,046	7.1	2.7
33015	Rockingham County	45,729	1.5	7.8	76.8	55.3	20.6	23.2	19.5	3,143	5.0	2.0
33017	Strafford County	16,139	2.8	10.4	70.6	51.0	17.5	29.4	25.3	1,042	4.4	2.3
34000	**New Jersey**	1,336,992	6.7	34.8	69.7	46.6	22.3	30.3	25.5	119,888	6.1	2.5
34001	Atlantic County	40,100	7.3	27.0	56.5	39.4	16.2	43.5	37.4	5,918	10.0	4.7
34003	Bergen County	140,007	8.3	45.8	78.3	49.5	28.1	21.7	17.8	8,050	4.0	1.7
34005	Burlington County	67,431	3.6	17.3	72.6	53.2	18.9	27.4	24.4	7,329	7.6	3.0
34007	Camden County	78,642	3.2	19.6	60.1	43.6	15.5	39.9	32.7	9,178	7.8	3.2
34009	Cape May County	11,531	2.4	9.5	67.9	46.5	21.0	32.1	28.2	1,766	10.6	3.8
34011	Cumberland County	23,020	4.7	19.5	52.1	36.7	14.4	47.9	40.1	4,314	12.4	4.9
34013	Essex County	122,317	7.6	39.8	56.5	39.2	16.7	43.5	35.9	13,687	7.4	3.4
34015	Gloucester County	45,956	2.0	10.7	70.5	50.3	19.8	29.5	25.1	4,100	6.2	2.5
34017	Hudson County	77,067	14.9	62.6	53.6	33.3	19.2	46.4	38.8	10,719	8.4	3.8
34019	Hunterdon County	20,114	3.2	14.0	83.2	55.7	27.5	16.8	16.1	1,130	4.2	1.0
34021	Mercer County	53,325	8.7	37.6	69.3	50.5	17.9	30.7	25.6	4,419	5.6	2.0
34023	Middlesex County	121,317	10.9	53.2	73.9	48.7	24.4	26.1	22.4	9,294	5.2	1.8
34025	Monmouth County	100,833	3.2	21.2	77.5	48.5	28.0	22.5	19.6	6,475	4.6	1.8
34027	Morris County	79,826	5.4	31.0	82.9	54.7	27.8	17.1	15.1	3,289	2.9	1.0
34029	Ocean County	85,589	2.0	15.9	76.4	47.1	28.5	23.6	19.9	7,455	5.6	2.3
34031	Passaic County	80,227	10.3	50.4	60.4	40.0	18.9	39.6	29.0	9,241	7.7	3.0
34033	Salem County	9,423	3.0	7.7	61.0	41.5	19.0	39.0	34.1	1,373	9.8	3.6
34035	Somerset County	54,300	5.8	39.2	82.1	55.9	25.7	17.9	16.3	2,495	3.2	1.3
34037	Sussex County	23,618	2.8	17.3	79.2	55.1	23.7	20.8	19.7	1,276	3.9	1.2
34039	Union County	85,163	7.7	46.7	67.5	45.3	21.4	32.5	28.4	7,533	6.0	2.1
34041	Warren County	17,186	3.5	16.2	76.1	53.8	21.7	23.9	19.2	847	3.6	2.0
35000	**New Mexico**	321,170	4.2	21.9	58.5	35.1	21.9	41.5	32.7	50,901	10.5	6.3
35001	Bernalillo County	98,899	5.4	23.8	57.2	35.0	20.5	42.8	34.9	11,227	7.5	4.4
35005	Chaves County	11,234	5.1	33.4	64.8	33.3	30.3	35.2	28.9	1,409	8.3	5.7
35009	Curry County	7,815	1.0	23.1	69.1	39.8	27.8	30.9	25.3	1,266	9.6	5.9
35013	Do±a Ana County	34,614	5.7	39.0	56.6	33.4	22.7	43.4	36.6	6,637	12.5	7.4
35015	Eddy County	9,019	0.5	11.2	66.0	48.5	17.3	34.0	25.3	1,248	9.1	6.7
35025	Lea County	12,009	6.2	39.0	65.6	32.0	33.2	34.4	27.7	2,178	11.8	8.7
35031	McKinley County	13,685	0.6	4.0	50.0	27.6	18.6	50.0	30.7	4,722	22.5	14.4
35035	Otero County	10,102	5.1	19.9	56.0	24.9	30.0	44.0	37.5	1,761	11.2	7.3
35043	Sandoval County	23,381	2.9	12.3	60.7	38.4	21.5	39.3	30.2	3,630	10.9	4.4
35045	San Juan County	22,127	1.2	9.7	59.6	32.9	25.1	40.4	29.0	5,248	15.6	8.6
35049	Santa Fe County	19,213	9.9	32.3	54.8	38.8	14.9	45.2	36.8	2,186	7.7	5.4
35061	Valencia County	12,336	1.0	16.3	64.6	38.5	23.6	35.4	23.6	1,762	9.7	6.9
36000	**New York**	2,731,445	6.5	35.0	64.5	41.1	22.1	35.5	28.3	305,826	7.5	3.2
36001	Albany County	38,997	5.2	15.1	63.3	46.7	16.1	36.7	30.4	3,248	5.7	3.2
36005	Bronx County	225,132	11.1	55.5	35.8	21.5	13.0	64.2	47.8	35,450	10.3	4.7
36007	Broome County	25,285	2.7	9.2	62.0	44.8	15.9	38.0	29.1	1,850	5.0	1.9
36009	Cattaraugus County	11,692	0.7	2.8	64.8	40.3	23.3	35.2	27.3	841	4.8	2.5
36011	Cayuga County	10,806	1.2	3.8	65.1	43.9	19.9	34.9	28.6	1,300	8.3	4.3
36013	Chautauqua County	18,156	0.3	2.7	64.2	37.9	23.8	35.8	26.4	2,047	7.7	3.9
36015	Chemung County	12,482	0.7	3.5	66.1	48.2	17.2	33.9	24.4	1,059	5.7	2.4
36019	Clinton County	9,669	1.0	5.7	65.4	47.4	16.6	34.6	27.2	915	6.5	2.6
36021	Columbia County	7,668	1.5	9.1	62.2	40.7	20.8	37.8	35.3	781	7.1	3.6
36027	Dutchess County	43,928	4.4	21.3	72.7	51.6	20.5	27.3	22.8	2,984	4.9	2.2

State/county FIPS code	State/County	Total own children under 18 in families and subfamilies	Own children under 6 years in families and subfamilies							
			Total own children under 6 years	Nativity and parentage, under 6 years		Own children under 6 years living with two parents			Own children under 6 living with one parent	
				Child is foreign born, percent	One or more foreign-born parent, percent	Total under 6 years living with two parents, percent	Both parents in labor force, percent	One parent in labor force, percent	Total under 6 years living with one parent, percent	Parent in labor force, percent
	New York—cont'd									
36029	Erie County............................	185,485	57,788	1.8	12.4	59.9	36.9	21.2	40.1	29.8
36033	Franklin County......................	9,589	3,191	0.0	3.2	55.8	26.4	26.1	44.2	28.4
36035	Fulton County.........................	10,857	3,329	0.0	0.8	58.5	34.9	23.3	41.5	30.4
36037	Genesee County......................	12,220	3,780	0.1	3.3	68.3	43.7	23.9	31.7	21.9
36043	Herkimer County.....................	13,087	3,958	0.0	7.6	55.9	35.0	20.2	44.1	33.6
36045	Jefferson County.....................	28,483	11,419	0.6	10.5	64.3	34.7	28.7	35.7	23.9
36047	Kings County..........................	575,494	216,445	2.8	49.9	62.2	31.2	29.6	37.8	26.9
36051	Livingston County...................	12,069	3,451	0.0	6.8	63.1	43.7	19.2	36.9	31.3
36053	Madison County......................	14,617	4,305	0.0	3.3	65.6	42.5	22.3	34.4	21.1
36055	Monroe County.......................	156,878	49,261	1.4	12.6	57.4	38.9	17.5	42.6	32.3
36059	Nassau County........................	296,844	85,993	1.9	39.4	77.9	50.6	26.7	22.1	17.3
36061	New York County....................	226,728	92,047	3.8	44.3	65.2	37.5	27.0	34.8	23.9
36063	Niagara County.......................	42,987	13,056	0.3	5.7	58.0	39.0	18.1	42.0	34.5
36065	Oneida County........................	48,202	15,400	2.6	14.9	56.9	36.0	19.7	43.1	33.4
36067	Onondaga County....................	99,953	31,949	1.7	14.1	62.1	39.7	21.2	37.9	27.5
36069	Ontario County.......................	22,294	6,315	0.7	9.0	65.8	40.1	25.7	34.2	30.0
36071	Orange County........................	96,734	30,218	0.7	21.1	74.4	33.7	39.8	25.6	19.2
36075	Oswego County.......................	25,881	7,650	0.0	4.9	51.0	28.2	21.9	49.0	30.4
36077	Otsego County........................	10,370	3,007	0.8	4.7	63.8	46.0	17.8	36.2	33.1
36079	Putnam County.......................	22,171	5,676	0.0	24.5	87.6	62.1	25.3	12.4	10.8
36081	Queens County.......................	446,571	160,354	3.6	67.2	65.8	32.9	32.0	34.2	26.8
36083	Rensselaer County...................	31,591	10,059	1.9	8.5	62.9	40.3	21.9	37.1	30.0
36085	Richmond County.....................	104,544	33,614	1.5	32.5	70.1	40.6	28.0	29.9	18.3
36087	Rockland County.....................	86,627	28,726	1.5	34.3	80.5	45.8	33.5	19.5	14.9
36089	St. Lawrence County................	21,742	7,152	0.2	5.2	65.4	38.9	24.2	34.6	28.8
36091	Saratoga County.....................	46,892	13,943	1.6	12.3	77.5	55.9	21.6	22.5	17.1
36093	Schenectady County................	33,284	10,391	1.1	13.4	56.4	42.6	13.0	43.6	30.7
36101	Steuben County.......................	21,134	6,432	0.3	4.7	61.2	34.5	25.7	38.8	28.6
36103	Suffolk County........................	333,180	97,123	0.8	29.8	72.9	44.4	27.9	27.1	20.0
36105	Sullivan County.......................	15,810	4,783	0.2	11.9	60.0	43.6	14.6	40.0	32.8
36107	Tioga County..........................	10,776	3,141	0.0	3.3	72.8	51.4	19.9	27.2	21.1
36109	Tompkins County.....................	14,744	4,552	2.4	21.2	72.8	47.4	23.4	27.2	13.6
36111	Ulster County.........................	33,053	9,788	0.8	15.7	60.7	38.1	21.5	39.3	30.1
36113	Warren County........................	12,196	3,489	0.0	2.9	63.1	47.1	16.0	36.9	31.2
36115	Washington County.................	11,580	3,760	0.7	5.5	59.2	32.8	25.2	40.8	33.6
36117	Wayne County........................	20,101	6,099	0.9	1.2	64.5	41.3	22.6	35.5	32.4
36119	Westchester County.................	216,457	66,173	2.5	44.3	72.2	41.5	30.2	27.8	21.8
37000	**North Carolina**......................	2,169,314	719,380	1.0	19.7	60.5	35.1	24.6	39.5	30.6
37001	Alamance County....................	33,329	11,035	0.1	23.2	55.1	33.6	21.2	44.9	35.3
37019	Brunswick County...................	18,809	6,029	1.3	11.6	59.7	32.1	27.3	40.3	25.0
37021	Buncombe County...................	47,128	15,762	1.3	15.1	64.4	39.3	23.3	35.6	28.1
37023	Burke County..........................	17,097	5,152	0.0	16.4	56.6	29.4	26.8	43.4	35.0
37025	Cabarrus County.....................	47,933	14,760	1.0	20.0	70.0	44.5	24.0	30.0	23.8
37027	Caldwell County......................	16,319	4,609	0.0	5.6	62.6	35.7	26.5	37.4	25.1
37031	Carteret County......................	11,959	3,706	0.3	4.9	59.8	42.7	16.8	40.2	33.1
37035	Catawba County.....................	34,560	10,686	0.9	18.0	64.7	41.5	23.0	35.3	24.3
37037	Chatham County.....................	12,993	3,765	0.6	27.7	68.0	43.6	24.4	32.0	23.5
37045	Cleveland County....................	20,429	6,565	0.0	5.0	44.0	31.9	12.1	56.0	44.9
37047	Columbus County....................	12,097	3,711	0.0	9.8	55.8	32.9	22.5	44.2	22.3
37049	Craven County........................	22,658	8,853	0.8	8.6	59.9	33.0	26.7	40.1	31.0
37051	Cumberland County.................	81,099	31,263	0.4	9.7	58.2	25.2	32.1	41.8	32.5
37057	Davidson County.....................	35,052	11,115	0.4	16.8	62.6	35.5	26.2	37.4	31.0
37061	Duplin County.........................	13,639	4,851	0.0	35.7	58.1	30.5	25.6	41.9	29.5
37063	Durham County......................	60,104	23,304	1.4	31.1	55.3	35.1	19.0	44.7	36.4
37065	Edgecombe County..................	12,132	4,264	2.4	6.8	20.2	14.5	5.7	79.8	68.1
37067	Forsyth County.......................	81,980	27,936	0.4	26.9	56.3	29.7	25.6	43.7	31.3
37069	Franklin County......................	13,878	4,655	0.0	10.5	61.3	35.2	26.1	38.7	29.5
37071	Gaston County........................	46,475	15,175	0.7	12.7	58.4	40.9	16.9	41.6	33.4
37077	Granville County.....................	12,147	3,688	1.4	16.9	49.3	30.2	19.2	50.7	26.9
37081	Guilford County......................	110,361	36,469	1.7	23.5	58.8	34.6	23.5	41.2	33.3
37083	Halifax County........................	10,997	3,437	0.0	1.0	31.7	22.1	9.6	68.3	51.6
37085	Harnett County.......................	32,166	11,280	0.2	16.2	71.3	38.5	32.3	28.7	20.9
37087	Haywood County.....................	10,126	3,102	0.0	4.5	49.7	26.0	23.6	50.3	26.1
37089	Henderson County...................	20,556	6,509	0.4	23.3	70.2	43.9	25.2	29.8	24.2
37093	Hoke County..........................	14,136	5,250	0.9	17.6	53.0	25.1	25.0	47.0	33.7
37097	Iredell County.........................	37,983	10,555	1.3	13.7	60.6	37.0	22.9	39.4	28.0
37101	Johnston County.....................	45,642	15,332	0.1	26.6	67.3	36.4	30.4	32.7	22.3
37105	Lee County.............................	14,503	5,034	0.3	33.1	51.4	29.0	20.9	48.6	42.3
37107	Lenoir County.........................	13,239	4,410	0.6	11.1	37.6	13.7	20.9	62.4	46.6
37109	Lincoln County........................	16,926	5,110	0.0	13.2	66.6	43.3	21.7	33.4	24.9
37119	Mecklenburg County...............	232,077	81,997	2.1	28.9	63.0	36.5	26.2	37.0	31.5

| State/county FIPS code | State/County | Own children age 6 to 17 years in families and subfamilies | | | | | | | | Grand-children under 18 living with a grandparent householder | Grand-children under 18 living with a grandparent householder, as a percent of all children | Children for whom grandparent householders are responsible, as a percent of all children |
| | | | Nativity and parentage, age 6 to 17 years | | Own children age 6 to 17 years living with two parents | | | Own children age 6 to 17 years living with one parent | | | | |
		Total own children 6 to 17	Child is foreign born, percent	One or more foreign-born parent, percent	Age 6 to 17 years living with two parents, percent	Both parents in labor force, percent	One parent in labor force, percent	Age 6 to 17 living with one parent, percent	Parent in labor force, percent			
	New York—cont'd											
36029	Erie County..........	127,697	3.8	9.5	63.6	44.1	17.5	36.4	28.9	9,119	4.9	2.5
36033	Franklin County.....	6,398	1.8	3.4	61.0	39.4	20.1	39.0	24.3	701	7.3	5.5
36035	Fulton County.........	7,528	0.9	4.4	66.2	45.1	18.0	33.8	28.3	698	6.4	3.8
36037	Genesee County......	8,440	0.2	4.8	70.6	52.0	18.5	29.4	24.2	598	4.9	2.0
36043	Herkimer County......	9,129	2.4	10.0	68.7	47.8	18.4	31.3	24.6	747	5.7	2.0
36045	Jefferson County......	17,064	1.9	10.9	66.4	40.8	24.0	33.6	24.2	1,803	6.3	3.6
36047	Kings County........	359,049	10.2	56.9	59.7	32.4	25.8	40.3	31.7	55,153	9.6	4.0
36051	Livingston County....	8,618	0.4	5.9	66.4	47.4	17.9	33.6	27.7	574	4.8	2.3
36053	Madison County	10,312	0.7	2.7	73.6	50.7	22.5	26.4	21.1	767	5.2	2.2
36055	Monroe County	107,617	3.9	12.6	59.9	44.1	14.7	40.1	31.2	9,592	6.1	3.5
36059	Nassau County.......	210,851	5.0	37.4	79.3	52.8	25.5	20.7	18.1	18,185	6.1	1.9
36061	New York County.....	134,681	10.1	50.9	52.8	30.7	21.0	47.2	36.4	20,305	9.0	4.3
36063	Niagara County	29,931	1.3	7.0	61.1	42.5	17.6	38.9	31.7	2,641	6.1	3.2
36065	Oneida County	32,802	6.9	15.1	59.5	41.2	16.6	40.5	33.2	2,483	5.2	2.4
36067	Onondaga County	68,004	4.2	12.4	64.6	45.0	18.4	35.4	29.0	5,824	5.8	3.4
36069	Ontario County	15,979	1.4	7.5	65.4	48.2	16.7	34.6	29.4	1,043	4.7	3.0
36071	Orange County	66,516	2.9	23.1	74.9	46.4	27.3	25.1	20.7	5,060	5.2	2.5
36075	Oswego County	18,231	0.1	2.9	64.8	41.2	21.8	35.2	27.6	1,674	6.5	2.3
36077	Otsego County	7,363	1.1	7.1	66.5	51.0	14.4	33.5	28.1	808	7.8	3.8
36079	Putnam County.......	16,495	2.7	23.2	81.6	56.4	25.0	18.4	15.3	1,534	6.9	1.0
36081	Queens County.......	286,217	13.9	72.0	65.0	36.6	27.1	35.0	29.0	42,379	9.5	3.7
36083	Rensselaer County	21,532	2.8	8.8	65.8	50.4	14.6	34.2	29.5	1,770	5.6	3.4
36085	Richmond County	70,930	4.2	35.7	70.1	40.7	27.8	29.9	20.8	7,977	7.6	2.2
36087	Rockland County	57,901	5.2	33.3	81.1	48.6	31.6	18.9	15.5	3,273	3.8	1.5
36089	St. Lawrence County ..	14,590	1.2	5.0	65.6	41.2	18.3	34.4	27.3	1,785	8.2	4.4
36091	Saratoga County	32,949	3.3	8.3	74.4	52.2	21.8	25.6	22.5	2,358	5.0	2.2
36093	Schenectady County ..	22,893	4.4	15.9	67.6	52.7	13.2	32.4	24.4	2,189	6.6	4.0
36101	Steuben County.......	14,702	0.8	5.1	65.0	44.5	17.7	35.0	26.6	1,260	6.0	3.1
36103	Suffolk County	236,057	3.7	25.4	75.4	50.5	24.0	24.6	20.0	26,438	7.9	2.3
36105	Sullivan County	11,027	4.2	14.0	64.3	40.8	20.9	35.7	30.3	1,314	8.3	2.5
36107	Tioga County.........	7,635	3.1	5.1	77.4	55.6	21.8	22.6	20.4	901	8.4	3.6
36109	Tompkins County.....	10,192	4.4	16.3	66.8	48.0	17.3	33.2	27.6	785	5.3	3.5
36111	Ulster County.........	23,265	2.4	12.1	68.7	49.4	18.3	31.3	25.7	1,802	5.5	2.8
36113	Warren County........	8,707	3.7	2.4	65.1	47.8	16.3	34.9	34.2	997	8.2	3.0
36115	Washington County ...	7,820	1.3	1.9	68.4	49.0	16.8	31.6	27.7	1,144	9.9	5.7
36117	Wayne County........	14,002	1.6	3.4	65.2	42.2	22.1	34.8	30.8	2,008	10.0	5.3
36119	Westchester County ...	150,284	6.4	41.4	71.8	44.5	26.3	28.2	23.8	10,259	4.7	1.9
37000	**North Carolina........**	1,449,934	3.5	16.5	62.6	40.8	20.6	37.4	30.7	175,785	8.1	4.9
37001	Alamance County.....	22,294	2.5	20.6	58.3	38.8	18.6	41.7	35.1	3,012	9.0	4.8
37019	Brunswick County	12,780	1.3	11.4	65.3	37.3	25.0	34.7	28.1	2,115	11.2	9.2
37021	Buncombe County	31,366	3.6	11.6	61.6	42.4	17.0	38.4	33.1	3,299	7.0	3.9
37023	Burke County........	11,945	2.3	15.7	54.4	37.2	15.4	45.6	33.0	1,683	9.8	6.6
37025	Cabarrus County	33,173	2.6	16.6	74.8	52.2	22.1	25.2	22.0	3,544	7.4	4.5
37027	Caldwell County	11,710	1.2	7.2	67.3	43.2	21.2	32.7	24.8	1,554	9.5	6.8
37031	Carteret County......	8,253	2.8	5.3	60.9	48.2	11.7	39.1	30.4	1,127	9.4	7.2
37035	Catawba County......	23,874	3.7	19.2	68.3	47.0	20.6	31.7	22.3	2,518	7.3	3.0
37037	Chatham County......	9,228	6.2	26.0	73.9	54.2	19.6	26.1	23.1	744	5.7	3.5
37045	Cleveland County.....	13,864	1.0	4.0	63.5	46.4	16.4	36.5	31.9	2,346	11.5	7.1
37047	Columbus County.....	8,386	0.0	6.2	58.3	31.6	25.4	41.7	26.2	1,812	15.0	10.5
37049	Craven County........	13,805	6.3	13.6	62.7	42.8	17.2	37.3	26.9	2,644	11.7	7.8
37051	Cumberland County ...	49,836	1.5	8.9	54.2	31.8	20.5	45.8	37.1	7,417	9.1	5.1
37057	Davidson County	23,937	1.8	13.4	65.1	46.4	17.9	34.9	28.0	2,975	8.5	4.7
37061	Duplin County	8,788	4.8	26.0	59.6	38.7	18.3	40.4	31.6	1,083	11.2	4.7
37063	Durham County	36,800	7.1	25.3	56.2	40.2	14.6	43.8	36.6	4,307	7.2	4.6
37065	Edgecombe County ...	7,868	1.3	5.9	42.1	30.0	11.3	57.9	47.9	1,764	14.5	10.3
37067	Forsyth County.......	54,044	4.8	22.8	61.7	41.2	19.3	38.3	31.4	6,234	7.6	5.3
37069	Franklin County......	9,223	2.3	11.7	67.2	42.1	22.8	32.8	28.3	1,522	11.0	7.7
37071	Gaston County	31,300	3.3	11.5	60.0	41.5	17.5	40.0	31.4	4,134	8.9	5.5
37077	Granville County......	8,459	1.2	12.9	61.9	37.4	23.2	38.1	31.4	1,314	10.8	6.6
37081	Guilford County......	73,892	5.1	19.4	57.1	37.4	18.8	42.9	35.0	7,591	6.9	3.8
37083	Halifax County........	7,560	0.9	3.8	39.7	26.5	11.3	60.3	43.8	1,969	17.9	9.9
37085	Harnett County.......	20,886	2.2	15.0	64.9	36.9	26.8	35.1	29.0	1,973	6.1	3.6
37087	Haywood County.....	7,024	2.7	4.4	58.2	31.8	25.9	41.8	28.0	1,334	13.2	9.7
37089	Henderson County....	14,047	3.4	16.6	71.4	47.8	22.6	28.6	24.4	1,711	8.3	5.8
37093	Hoke County	8,886	1.7	12.3	62.2	41.1	20.0	37.8	29.1	1,293	9.1	5.0
37097	Iredell County........	27,428	1.8	13.3	67.3	42.5	24.1	32.7	27.2	2,713	7.1	4.7
37101	Johnston County......	30,310	3.6	18.8	64.5	44.1	19.3	35.5	25.2	2,672	5.9	3.2
37105	Lee County...........	9,469	6.2	28.7	60.7	41.1	19.0	39.3	34.9	984	6.8	1.9
37107	Lenoir County........	8,829	1.9	7.6	48.3	27.9	18.0	51.7	42.1	1,613	12.2	9.3
37109	Lincoln County.......	11,816	1.2	9.7	74.3	52.4	20.1	25.7	22.4	1,906	11.3	5.3
37119	Mecklenburg County....	150,080	5.5	25.0	61.5	39.7	21.0	38.5	33.7	15,521	6.7	3.5

State/county FIPS code	State/County	Total own children under 18 in families and subfamilies	Own children under 6 years in families and subfamilies							
			Total own children under 6 years	Nativity and parentage, under 6 years		Own children under 6 years living with two parents			Own children under 6 living with one parent	
				Child is foreign born, percent	One or more foreign-born parent, percent	Total under 6 years living with two parents, percent	Both parents in labor force, percent	One parent in labor force, percent	Total under 6 years living with one parent, percent	Parent in labor force, percent
	North Carolina—cont'd									
37125	Moore County	18,999	6,193	1.0	19.0	65.0	33.9	30.6	35.0	26.5
37127	Nash County	20,795	6,079	1.7	15.0	51.3	30.5	20.8	48.7	41.3
37129	New Hanover County	39,929	14,441	1.5	15.2	60.7	39.0	21.7	39.3	29.9
37133	Onslow County	45,145	19,898	0.2	7.8	71.3	27.9	42.7	28.7	18.5
37135	Orange County	27,646	7,982	4.0	27.6	71.1	42.8	26.0	28.9	22.6
37141	Pender County	11,512	3,650	0.3	12.4	63.2	39.0	23.2	36.8	28.1
37147	Pitt County	36,215	13,095	0.8	10.6	53.3	37.9	14.6	46.7	42.2
37151	Randolph County	32,124	9,445	0.9	25.0	60.5	34.5	24.3	39.5	31.2
37155	Robeson County	32,916	11,397	0.5	18.6	31.2	16.5	13.3	68.8	47.4
37157	Rockingham County	18,335	5,552	0.0	16.7	49.4	36.3	13.1	50.6	37.4
37159	Rowan County	29,610	9,586	0.3	19.4	56.2	39.9	15.3	43.8	34.0
37161	Rutherford County	13,024	3,792	1.9	10.7	69.9	36.1	33.4	30.1	24.1
37163	Sampson County	14,880	4,763	0.0	26.1	56.1	34.7	20.2	43.9	33.6
37167	Stanly County	12,608	3,588	0.6	5.9	51.6	39.6	12.1	48.4	43.4
37171	Surry County	15,672	5,124	0.0	15.4	59.2	34.0	23.7	40.8	26.9
37179	Union County	59,262	16,686	0.4	27.0	72.4	40.2	30.8	27.6	21.3
37183	Wake County	235,664	75,751	2.3	28.3	72.8	43.0	29.5	27.2	22.8
37189	Watauga County	6,537	2,338	0.4	6.8	71.0	46.4	20.9	29.0	24.4
37191	Wayne County	28,073	9,520	0.0	21.0	46.7	25.9	20.8	53.3	46.3
37193	Wilkes County	13,633	3,855	0.3	16.0	53.7	31.5	22.3	46.3	37.5
37195	Wilson County	18,604	6,202	0.0	20.3	55.0	26.8	28.0	45.0	27.8
38000	**North Dakota**	151,243	53,991	0.7	4.5	71.2	49.6	21.0	28.8	22.8
38015	Burleigh County	18,683	6,818	0.0	2.7	70.8	57.6	13.2	29.2	24.7
38017	Cass County	33,800	12,956	2.2	10.3	72.0	56.1	15.1	28.0	23.3
38035	Grand Forks County	13,053	4,691	1.3	4.2	71.9	46.0	25.8	28.1	21.9
38101	Ward County	14,657	5,682	0.0	1.5	79.2	46.7	31.0	20.8	19.1
39000	**Ohio**	2,536,221	818,899	0.7	8.7	60.7	38.1	21.7	39.3	30.5
39003	Allen County	23,737	7,970	0.0	3.2	55.6	34.8	20.4	44.4	36.8
39005	Ashland County	11,378	3,442	0.0	5.5	74.7	45.0	29.1	25.3	20.0
39007	Ashtabula County	21,247	6,771	0.2	3.8	53.9	32.0	20.4	46.1	34.5
39009	Athens County	9,163	2,764	1.5	5.0	51.1	37.2	12.2	48.9	33.6
39013	Belmont County	12,524	3,697	0.0	0.0	71.8	47.8	24.1	28.2	19.8
39017	Butler County	86,969	27,774	0.5	12.7	62.7	38.4	23.5	37.3	29.5
39023	Clark County	29,907	9,456	0.0	5.0	47.9	27.1	20.2	52.1	38.7
39025	Clermont County	47,191	14,838	0.6	3.9	68.8	44.4	23.9	31.2	23.9
39029	Columbiana County	21,209	6,365	0.2	1.3	57.5	35.0	22.2	42.5	28.2
39035	Cuyahoga County	265,116	85,437	1.0	12.6	54.2	34.4	18.6	45.8	35.3
39037	Darke County	12,472	3,987	0.0	1.5	66.9	43.0	23.8	33.1	25.8
39041	Delaware County	50,197	15,254	1.0	15.1	82.7	53.1	29.6	17.3	15.1
39043	Erie County	15,686	4,760	0.0	2.0	61.1	42.1	19.0	38.9	32.0
39045	Fairfield County	35,917	10,646	0.5	8.6	69.7	50.2	18.7	30.3	22.8
39049	Franklin County	271,186	99,754	1.3	22.6	60.8	38.9	21.3	39.2	30.9
39055	Geauga County	22,969	5,993	0.8	5.1	86.3	38.2	48.1	13.7	12.4
39057	Greene County	33,135	10,208	1.4	7.7	66.8	36.9	28.1	33.2	28.9
39061	Hamilton County	177,362	62,105	1.2	10.2	52.4	33.2	18.1	47.6	35.6
39063	Hancock County	16,384	5,419	0.1	4.7	61.1	41.8	19.2	38.9	36.3
39077	Huron County	13,966	4,573	0.0	10.4	62.1	41.6	19.4	37.9	31.5
39081	Jefferson County	12,362	3,981	0.0	0.0	54.8	25.9	28.0	45.2	29.2
39083	Knox County	13,683	4,586	0.0	2.0	70.5	37.8	32.7	29.5	25.3
39085	Lake County	47,985	14,535	0.4	14.0	69.3	47.7	21.1	30.7	27.6
39087	Lawrence County	13,277	4,185	0.0	0.0	61.5	29.2	32.3	38.5	29.7
39089	Licking County	38,152	11,515	0.2	2.3	68.0	47.3	18.9	32.0	26.8
39093	Lorain County	66,491	20,670	0.0	4.8	60.1	41.7	17.3	39.9	30.7
39095	Lucas County	97,047	33,322	0.2	5.7	52.4	34.2	17.1	47.6	37.9
39099	Mahoning County	47,087	14,533	0.4	4.1	50.9	32.9	17.0	49.1	38.0
39101	Marion County	12,889	4,367	0.0	3.0	53.4	38.8	13.7	46.6	35.2
39103	Medina County	41,325	11,149	0.6	8.0	75.5	45.6	29.2	24.5	18.2
39109	Miami County	23,119	6,791	0.0	1.5	62.4	34.8	26.7	37.6	34.7
39113	Montgomery County	114,918	38,520	0.9	7.5	48.7	29.0	18.6	51.3	40.7
39119	Muskingum County	18,547	6,153	0.0	0.0	48.9	30.9	17.7	51.1	39.0
39129	Pickaway County	11,579	3,196	0.0	0.0	70.9	45.7	24.8	29.1	21.0
39133	Portage County	30,961	9,295	0.7	3.7	62.3	42.9	18.3	37.7	28.9
39139	Richland County	24,440	7,832	0.1	0.7	60.5	33.8	25.0	39.5	26.7
39141	Ross County	15,985	4,668	0.0	0.0	64.6	43.9	18.2	35.4	27.7
39143	Sandusky County	13,427	4,448	0.3	2.5	65.3	38.5	26.7	34.7	31.5
39145	Scioto County	14,886	4,756	0.0	0.6	59.1	32.0	24.2	40.9	25.4
39147	Seneca County	12,132	3,634	0.0	0.0	54.7	37.9	16.7	45.3	39.0
39151	Stark County	79,762	24,483	0.2	3.5	56.0	35.7	19.3	44.0	35.3
39153	Summit County	114,312	36,177	0.8	9.0	57.8	37.4	19.6	42.2	33.7
39155	Trumbull County	42,302	12,660	0.5	1.9	49.8	28.8	20.2	50.2	32.4

Table D-2: Counties with a Population of 50,000 or More—Children—*Continued*

State/county FIPS code	State/County	Total own children 6 to 17	Nativity and parentage, age 6 to 17 years — Child is foreign born, percent	One or more foreign-born parent, percent	Own children age 6 to 17 years living with two parents — Age 6 to 17 years living with two parents, percent	Both parents in labor force, percent	One parent in labor force, percent	Own children age 6 to 17 years living with one parent — Age 6 to 17 years living with one parent, percent	Parent in labor force, percent	Grandchildren under 18 living with a grandparent householder	Grandchildren under 18 living with a grandparent householder, as a percent of all children	Children for whom grandparent householders are responsible, as a percent of all children
	North Carolina—cont'd											
37125	Moore County	12,806	1.2	13.4	68.1	43.6	24.1	31.9	24.5	1,324	7.0	2.4
37127	Nash County	14,716	1.4	10.8	58.4	40.8	16.3	41.6	34.2	2,424	11.7	7.4
37129	New Hanover County	25,488	2.6	13.9	61.4	39.6	20.9	38.6	31.6	2,170	5.4	3.7
37133	Onslow County	25,247	1.1	8.4	67.5	30.6	35.1	32.5	26.0	1,974	4.4	2.9
37135	Orange County	19,664	8.1	25.3	75.2	49.6	23.7	24.8	21.4	951	3.4	1.7
37141	Pender County	7,862	1.1	10.1	61.1	42.0	18.1	38.9	26.5	1,079	9.4	7.0
37147	Pitt County	23,120	2.2	10.6	51.5	40.6	8.8	48.5	42.6	3,282	9.1	6.2
37151	Randolph County	22,679	3.1	18.3	62.2	41.5	18.9	37.8	31.2	2,894	9.0	5.0
37155	Robeson County	21,519	1.7	13.0	47.3	29.0	17.1	52.7	33.6	5,215	15.8	9.5
37157	Rockingham County	12,783	1.1	9.7	60.9	41.8	18.1	39.1	32.6	1,649	9.0	5.9
37159	Rowan County	20,024	2.2	16.2	60.7	36.2	24.1	39.3	32.3	2,291	7.7	5.5
37161	Rutherford County	9,232	0.6	6.0	56.7	36.6	17.1	43.3	31.9	1,881	14.4	10.3
37163	Sampson County	10,117	5.5	19.9	56.4	42.7	12.4	43.6	33.2	2,412	16.2	10.2
37167	Stanly County	9,020	2.5	12.8	62.5	46.3	15.1	37.5	32.8	1,505	11.9	6.8
37171	Surry County	10,548	1.7	16.6	71.1	44.3	25.0	28.9	20.9	1,252	8.0	5.9
37179	Union County	42,576	4.8	18.6	77.3	45.9	31.0	22.7	20.7	3,490	5.9	3.5
37183	Wake County	159,913	5.2	23.1	70.1	46.1	23.2	29.9	26.9	9,188	3.9	1.7
37189	Watauga County	4,199	2.7	8.0	71.4	45.1	22.6	28.6	27.3	569	8.7	7.7
37191	Wayne County	18,553	1.3	13.8	52.3	32.9	18.7	47.7	38.3	2,547	9.1	6.4
37193	Wilkes County	9,778	2.3	10.6	68.8	39.9	25.9	31.2	24.6	1,639	12.0	9.8
37195	Wilson County	12,402	3.2	21.2	54.5	35.4	18.3	45.5	38.3	1,572	8.4	4.6
38000	**North Dakota**	97,252	2.0	4.9	73.1	55.1	17.2	26.9	23.5	6,959	4.6	2.4
38015	Burleigh County	11,865	0.6	2.1	73.3	60.6	12.5	26.7	24.8	812	4.3	1.3
38017	Cass County	20,844	5.8	10.3	74.8	57.0	17.3	25.2	23.6	1,001	3.0	2.2
38035	Grand Forks County	8,362	1.8	5.4	72.7	58.6	14.0	27.3	24.5	837	6.4	3.2
38101	Ward County	8,975	1.3	4.0	77.5	54.4	22.3	22.5	21.7	0	0.0	0.0
39000	**Ohio**	1,717,322	1.9	6.6	64.6	43.7	19.7	35.4	28.7	183,181	7.2	4.2
39003	Allen County	15,767	0.2	3.0	59.4	43.7	14.8	40.6	32.0	1,687	7.1	4.8
39005	Ashland County	7,936	0.2	3.1	72.8	49.2	23.1	27.2	23.3	861	7.6	4.0
39007	Ashtabula County	14,476	0.6	2.5	64.1	41.1	21.2	35.9	29.0	1,883	8.9	4.6
39009	Athens County	6,399	0.2	5.8	64.6	41.1	17.8	35.4	23.2	783	8.5	5.6
39013	Belmont County	8,827	0.0	0.0	71.5	46.0	22.7	28.5	22.4	839	6.7	3.4
39017	Butler County	59,195	2.9	8.5	70.2	49.4	20.2	29.8	25.2	6,034	6.9	4.5
39023	Clark County	20,451	0.7	4.4	63.4	44.7	17.3	36.6	29.1	2,580	8.6	4.8
39025	Clermont County	32,353	1.1	3.9	71.6	46.5	24.2	28.4	21.8	3,050	6.5	3.6
39029	Columbiana County	14,844	0.3	0.6	63.7	39.0	24.2	36.3	29.7	2,015	9.5	6.2
39035	Cuyahoga County	179,679	2.4	9.5	55.5	37.9	16.5	44.5	35.2	20,059	7.6	4.2
39037	Darke County	8,485	0.5	0.9	77.1	51.2	24.5	22.9	17.2	666	5.3	3.4
39041	Delaware County	34,943	1.5	11.3	80.1	55.1	24.9	19.9	18.2	1,234	2.5	1.4
39043	Erie County	10,926	0.2	1.8	64.3	49.1	14.4	35.7	31.6	1,068	6.8	4.3
39045	Fairfield County	25,271	1.6	9.9	72.1	51.7	19.5	27.9	24.4	2,220	6.2	3.5
39049	Franklin County	171,432	5.2	17.8	59.3	39.2	18.6	40.7	33.8	17,969	6.6	4.1
39055	Geauga County	16,976	1.5	4.7	84.4	46.5	37.5	15.6	12.5	1,102	4.8	1.1
39057	Greene County	22,927	1.9	7.8	71.0	44.9	25.4	29.0	25.9	2,000	6.0	3.3
39061	Hamilton County	115,257	2.7	7.7	55.8	37.9	16.9	44.2	35.8	13,571	7.7	4.7
39063	Hancock County	10,965	0.9	4.3	69.9	50.6	19.0	30.1	25.8	444	2.7	1.3
39077	Huron County	9,393	0.9	7.0	68.6	53.4	13.0	31.4	26.6	1,086	7.8	3.5
39081	Jefferson County	8,381	0.0	0.0	68.0	37.2	30.1	32.0	25.2	1,136	9.2	6.2
39083	Knox County	9,097	1.3	1.9	68.6	44.8	23.3	31.4	21.4	738	5.4	1.9
39085	Lake County	33,450	2.1	9.3	71.7	52.1	18.8	28.3	25.7	2,032	4.2	1.6
39087	Lawrence County	9,092	0.0	0.0	65.5	35.6	25.3	34.5	27.7	1,637	12.3	6.5
39089	Licking County	26,637	0.7	1.6	71.9	52.4	18.3	28.1	23.7	2,601	6.8	4.4
39093	Lorain County	45,821	1.0	3.9	61.5	42.1	18.5	38.5	30.1	5,932	8.9	5.1
39095	Lucas County	63,725	0.9	4.9	52.4	37.0	13.9	47.6	38.7	7,715	7.9	4.6
39099	Mahoning County	32,554	0.7	5.1	54.7	37.5	15.5	45.3	37.2	3,261	6.9	4.3
39101	Marion County	8,522	0.3	4.3	67.7	44.7	19.1	32.3	25.3	1,454	11.3	7.2
39103	Medina County	30,176	1.2	4.0	78.0	54.6	22.6	22.0	19.6	2,512	6.1	2.4
39109	Miami County	16,328	1.8	4.2	65.4	46.8	17.9	34.6	28.2	1,302	5.6	2.9
39113	Montgomery County	76,398	2.0	6.6	57.2	37.9	18.2	42.8	33.7	8,777	7.6	4.5
39119	Muskingum County	12,394	0.0	0.0	57.3	40.8	15.4	42.7	34.6	1,398	7.5	3.8
39129	Pickaway County	8,383	0.0	0.0	66.7	43.5	19.0	33.3	26.5	1,795	15.5	10.8
39133	Portage County	21,666	1.6	3.1	71.1	49.7	19.6	28.9	21.9	2,202	7.1	4.3
39139	Richland County	16,608	0.4	2.3	61.5	42.6	18.8	38.5	33.1	2,474	10.1	5.9
39141	Ross County	11,317	0.0	0.0	64.1	43.3	17.5	35.9	27.6	1,884	11.8	7.3
39143	Sandusky County	8,979	0.7	1.0	63.8	48.7	14.4	36.2	34.6	1,395	10.4	5.7
39145	Scioto County	10,130	0.2	1.4	61.5	39.8	18.5	38.5	21.6	2,950	19.8	15.5
39147	Seneca County	8,498	0.0	0.0	68.5	50.2	17.5	31.5	24.5	630	5.2	2.8
39151	Stark County	55,279	1.0	3.2	64.4	43.6	19.8	35.6	29.3	5,765	7.2	3.7
39153	Summit County	78,135	3.1	7.5	62.8	42.5	18.9	37.2	29.7	8,152	7.1	4.1
39155	Trumbull County	29,642	0.4	2.1	61.0	37.5	21.7	39.0	29.9	3,821	9.0	5.9

State/county FIPS code	State/County	Total own children under 18 in families and subfamilies	Own children under 6 years in families and subfamilies							
			Total own children under 6 years	Nativity and parentage, under 6 years		Own children under 6 years living with two parents			Own children under 6 years living with one parent	
				Child is foreign born, percent	One or more foreign-born parent, percent	Total under 6 years living with two parents, percent	Both parents in labor force, percent	One parent in labor force, percent	Total under 6 years living with one parent, percent	Parent in labor force, percent
	Ohio—cont'd									
39157	Tuscarawas County	20,622	6,462	0.5	3.3	62.8	34.0	28.8	37.2	32.0
39159	Union County	13,202	3,810	1.7	9.8	81.6	55.4	26.2	18.4	12.9
39165	Warren County	56,116	16,188	2.4	12.3	80.6	50.7	29.9	19.4	16.1
39167	Washington County	11,536	3,407	0.0	2.5	72.0	39.9	32.1	28.0	19.7
39169	Wayne County	27,579	9,015	0.2	3.1	76.5	36.2	38.0	23.5	18.7
39173	Wood County	25,805	8,588	0.8	8.7	68.0	43.8	24.1	32.0	26.2
40000	**Oklahoma**	884,279	303,188	0.9	13.8	63.1	35.0	26.9	36.9	27.2
40017	Canadian County	31,472	10,609	1.3	10.9	75.4	52.0	22.3	24.6	20.2
40027	Cleveland County	56,884	19,131	0.8	10.7	67.5	40.7	26.6	32.5	24.4
40031	Comanche County	29,157	11,098	1.3	8.0	60.8	27.9	31.2	39.2	32.2
40037	Creek County	16,054	5,152	0.2	4.7	70.3	37.1	32.5	29.7	19.0
40047	Garfield County	14,427	5,134	2.7	20.6	70.1	41.3	28.2	29.9	24.4
40051	Grady County	12,434	3,921	1.9	4.2	69.4	40.9	26.4	30.6	23.4
40101	Muskogee County	15,876	5,554	0.6	9.5	54.6	32.1	22.5	45.4	34.5
40109	Oklahoma County	180,041	66,691	1.2	24.2	61.8	32.8	27.8	38.2	30.0
40119	Payne County	14,723	5,241	0.1	7.3	60.9	30.1	28.7	39.1	23.6
40125	Pottawatomie County	16,298	5,539	0.0	5.1	64.4	37.2	26.3	35.6	28.2
40131	Rogers County	21,273	6,109	1.1	5.8	72.9	40.9	31.6	27.1	23.0
40143	Tulsa County	148,407	52,460	1.2	19.2	61.0	33.7	26.5	39.0	28.4
40145	Wagoner County	18,362	5,820	0.0	10.1	67.7	42.4	24.8	32.3	21.6
40147	Washington County	11,340	3,477	1.2	6.0	57.4	31.7	24.8	42.6	26.8
41000	**Oregon**	817,706	267,721	1.1	24.2	68.8	38.5	29.0	31.2	22.8
41003	Benton County	14,164	4,631	2.1	24.1	75.6	32.3	36.8	24.4	14.6
41005	Clackamas County	84,615	24,613	1.2	20.1	76.0	44.4	29.2	24.0	17.8
41011	Coos County	10,574	3,513	0.6	11.8	63.8	33.1	28.0	36.2	22.2
41017	Deschutes County	34,674	10,860	0.8	13.7	69.2	37.3	31.2	30.8	22.9
41019	Douglas County	19,501	5,717	0.2	9.4	69.9	33.7	33.2	30.1	22.4
41029	Jackson County	41,903	13,767	0.5	15.7	63.2	35.3	27.1	36.8	24.8
41033	Josephine County	15,861	4,594	0.0	5.0	63.1	27.4	31.2	36.9	23.4
41035	Klamath County	13,557	4,496	0.1	12.0	54.2	29.4	24.0	45.8	37.1
41039	Lane County	65,127	20,644	1.5	12.7	60.5	30.4	27.6	39.5	28.3
41043	Linn County	26,248	8,856	0.1	10.4	63.0	31.3	29.1	37.0	23.5
41047	Marion County	79,527	25,974	0.4	33.6	60.9	35.3	24.5	39.1	27.5
41051	Multnomah County	143,909	52,952	1.9	30.5	70.6	41.6	28.3	29.4	21.2
41053	Polk County	17,651	5,157	0.2	16.3	76.9	39.6	35.5	23.1	18.8
41059	Umatilla County	18,639	6,375	0.3	26.4	53.5	30.8	22.2	46.5	37.5
41067	Washington County	131,717	43,418	1.8	37.7	78.4	43.5	34.6	21.6	16.5
41071	Yamhill County	22,681	6,840	0.0	25.1	71.9	47.1	24.5	28.1	22.8
42000	**Pennsylvania**	2,615,591	840,520	1.0	12.2	63.2	39.5	22.7	36.8	28.1
42001	Adams County	20,567	6,423	0.4	16.2	68.0	45.3	22.3	32.0	25.7
42003	Allegheny County	229,155	76,115	1.1	9.9	64.5	41.2	22.5	35.5	27.5
42005	Armstrong County	12,916	4,040	0.1	0.6	63.3	40.2	22.9	36.7	29.0
42007	Beaver County	32,598	10,413	0.4	3.4	66.0	44.3	20.8	34.0	23.7
42011	Berks County	91,682	28,426	0.6	15.7	59.9	37.4	20.8	40.1	30.8
42013	Blair County	24,827	8,264	0.0	1.9	57.3	37.8	19.2	42.7	35.4
42015	Bradford County	12,896	4,205	0.1	1.4	66.8	34.2	28.8	33.2	24.9
42017	Bucks County	134,619	38,437	1.1	17.5	78.0	52.4	25.2	22.0	17.4
42019	Butler County	38,204	11,349	1.5	4.9	77.6	49.0	27.2	22.4	19.3
42021	Cambria County	26,448	8,282	0.0	2.5	60.5	39.0	20.9	39.5	29.6
42025	Carbon County	12,328	3,629	0.0	1.3	59.5	30.0	28.1	40.5	35.0
42027	Centre County	23,232	7,518	2.4	13.9	78.8	49.5	28.5	21.2	16.5
42029	Chester County	118,737	36,841	1.5	19.1	81.7	52.3	29.4	18.3	15.9
42033	Clearfield County	14,825	4,397	0.0	1.3	63.3	40.3	21.7	36.7	26.1
42037	Columbia County	11,563	3,523	0.3	4.6	71.4	47.8	21.4	28.6	21.2
42039	Crawford County	18,235	5,401	0.1	2.2	68.4	33.7	33.6	31.6	19.4
42041	Cumberland County	47,291	14,875	1.8	10.4	69.3	45.4	23.8	30.7	26.4
42043	Dauphin County	58,218	19,268	1.6	13.0	56.3	41.2	14.0	43.7	37.4
42045	Delaware County	121,387	39,266	0.8	18.9	63.1	42.9	19.3	36.9	28.8
42049	Erie County	58,835	18,721	1.8	9.5	54.3	33.3	20.1	45.7	36.0
42051	Fayette County	24,607	7,787	0.0	1.5	58.2	28.0	28.0	41.8	23.8
42055	Franklin County	33,828	11,410	0.5	9.6	70.1	38.5	30.9	29.9	25.9
42063	Indiana County	15,656	4,941	0.2	1.4	70.0	36.1	32.5	30.0	21.0
42069	Lackawanna County	41,702	13,268	1.1	12.3	66.4	45.7	19.9	33.6	25.7
42071	Lancaster County	123,787	41,313	0.8	8.7	76.1	36.3	38.7	23.9	19.6
42073	Lawrence County	17,550	5,175	0.2	1.8	62.4	39.1	23.0	37.6	27.3
42075	Lebanon County	29,688	10,134	0.7	8.5	68.2	40.3	27.5	31.8	24.3
42077	Lehigh County	78,965	25,083	1.5	19.3	56.4	39.9	14.7	43.6	32.6
42079	Luzerne County	60,348	18,576	0.5	12.9	48.9	31.9	16.3	51.1	35.3
42081	Lycoming County	22,982	7,541	1.6	3.4	62.3	46.5	15.0	37.7	29.1
42085	Mercer County	22,524	6,855	0.0	2.2	62.5	36.4	25.7	37.5	28.1
42089	Monroe County	35,730	8,956	0.0	20.9	56.5	32.6	23.3	43.5	36.9

State/county FIPS code	State/County	Total own children 6 to 17	Nativity and parentage, age 6 to 17 years		Own children age 6 to 17 years living with two parents			Own children age 6 to 17 years living with one parent		Grand-children under 18 living with a grandparent householder	Grand-children under 18 living with a grandparent householder, as a percent of all children	Children for whom grandparent householders are responsible, as a percent of all children
			Child is foreign born, percent	One or more foreign-born parent, percent	Age 6 to 17 years living with two parents, percent	Both parents in labor force, percent	One parent in labor force, percent	Age 6 to 17 years living with one parent, percent	Parent in labor force, percent			
	Ohio—cont'd											
39157	Tuscarawas County	14,160	1.5	2.6	73.6	51.9	20.4	26.4	22.8	1,128	5.5	2.2
39159	Union County	9,392	1.7	7.7	78.9	54.0	24.9	21.1	18.8	518	3.9	2.8
39165	Warren County	39,928	2.5	10.9	81.7	55.6	25.9	18.3	15.8	2,069	3.7	1.9
39167	Washington County	8,129	0.9	2.3	67.6	44.5	20.9	32.4	27.4	1,187	10.3	4.1
39169	Wayne County	18,564	0.8	3.1	78.6	44.7	31.6	21.4	18.0	1,645	6.0	3.3
39173	Wood County	17,217	1.1	5.8	72.5	53.5	17.8	27.5	24.2	1,208	4.7	2.6
40000	**Oklahoma**	581,091	2.5	12.2	65.3	41.1	22.8	34.7	27.6	75,115	8.5	5.2
40017	Canadian County	20,863	1.1	10.9	73.2	53.9	18.8	26.8	22.4	1,534	4.9	2.2
40027	Cleveland County	37,753	2.6	12.4	69.8	45.6	23.2	30.2	25.1	4,281	7.5	4.1
40031	Comanche County	18,059	2.2	9.4	54.6	34.8	18.0	45.4	39.4	3,181	10.9	6.1
40037	Creek County	10,902	1.3	4.5	70.5	43.2	26.1	29.5	18.7	1,756	10.9	7.0
40047	Garfield County	9,293	3.8	16.9	69.1	45.5	22.9	30.9	27.7	1,317	9.1	6.9
40051	Grady County	8,513	1.0	7.2	71.9	50.2	20.1	28.1	23.3	880	7.1	5.0
40101	Muskogee County	10,322	0.7	6.8	61.0	41.0	17.2	39.0	29.6	1,540	9.7	5.2
40109	Oklahoma County	113,350	5.8	23.3	61.4	37.2	22.9	38.6	31.9	13,396	7.4	4.3
40119	Payne County	9,482	1.4	7.1	71.8	43.5	28.0	28.2	19.8	651	4.4	3.3
40125	Pottawatomie County	10,759	0.2	3.5	65.2	40.4	22.6	34.8	25.7	1,534	9.4	6.7
40131	Rogers County	15,164	1.0	4.9	75.4	48.9	26.2	24.6	19.4	1,666	7.8	4.6
40143	Tulsa County	95,947	3.5	16.4	62.8	40.4	21.5	37.2	30.0	9,181	6.2	3.6
40145	Wagoner County	12,542	1.7	8.3	71.0	42.0	27.8	29.0	23.3	1,814	9.9	6.4
40147	Washington County	7,863	1.9	6.3	72.0	45.6	25.6	28.0	23.9	652	5.7	3.9
41000	**Oregon**	549,985	4.7	23.6	67.9	43.4	23.2	32.1	25.9	48,787	6.0	2.9
41003	Benton County	9,533	5.9	21.4	79.2	48.2	27.9	20.8	14.5	788	5.6	2.9
41005	Clackamas County	60,002	3.6	19.6	72.6	44.7	27.0	27.4	23.3	5,143	6.1	2.6
41011	Coos County	7,061	0.7	6.0	65.1	48.0	16.0	34.9	23.1	1,144	10.8	4.2
41017	Deschutes County	23,814	2.9	9.9	75.8	49.1	25.2	24.2	19.9	1,606	4.6	2.3
41019	Douglas County	13,784	1.5	5.1	62.9	41.5	17.7	37.1	30.4	1,836	9.4	4.2
41029	Jackson County	28,136	2.7	12.0	57.2	36.7	19.4	42.8	33.7	2,486	5.9	2.7
41033	Josephine County	11,267	0.6	6.7	66.9	37.4	23.2	33.1	22.9	1,397	8.8	3.7
41035	Klamath County	9,061	1.8	11.6	68.5	45.0	22.9	31.5	24.7	891	6.6	3.0
41039	Lane County	44,483	2.5	12.1	65.3	39.7	23.1	34.7	26.8	3,954	6.1	2.8
41043	Linn County	17,392	1.6	8.7	65.3	42.9	21.9	34.7	23.5	1,900	7.2	3.7
41047	Marion County	53,553	6.0	37.4	63.8	41.4	21.5	36.2	30.0	4,247	5.3	2.5
41051	Multnomah County	90,957	9.0	33.4	63.1	40.4	21.4	36.9	30.1	9,158	6.4	3.2
41053	Polk County	12,494	2.0	20.3	75.6	47.9	27.4	24.4	19.9	612	3.5	2.0
41059	Umatilla County	12,264	3.5	28.3	61.7	48.9	11.7	38.3	32.3	1,418	7.6	3.7
41067	Washington County	88,299	6.8	36.0	73.8	46.0	27.3	26.2	23.4	4,006	3.0	1.4
41071	Yamhill County	15,841	3.0	22.4	67.7	45.1	19.7	32.3	23.9	1,862	8.2	4.0
42000	**Pennsylvania**	1,775,071	2.6	10.7	66.6	44.9	20.4	33.4	26.4	190,170	7.3	3.5
42001	Adams County	14,144	1.1	10.4	70.5	50.2	19.7	29.5	25.2	1,275	6.2	3.0
42003	Allegheny County	153,040	3.2	8.1	66.1	44.2	20.8	33.9	27.4	13,001	5.7	3.0
42005	Armstrong County	8,876	0.2	0.8	67.5	43.5	22.6	32.5	24.6	737	5.7	2.3
42007	Beaver County	22,185	0.2	3.1	64.0	46.5	17.3	36.0	28.9	2,749	8.4	4.0
42011	Berks County	63,256	3.2	16.5	66.4	46.3	19.1	33.6	27.2	6,691	7.3	3.8
42013	Blair County	16,563	0.8	2.9	69.3	47.4	20.4	30.7	25.5	1,985	8.0	4.5
42015	Bradford County	8,691	1.0	2.9	68.8	38.6	26.6	31.2	26.3	1,247	9.7	5.5
42017	Bucks County	96,182	2.6	14.6	77.0	54.2	22.4	23.0	19.5	8,586	6.4	2.5
42019	Butler County	26,855	0.8	2.6	79.1	51.9	25.8	20.9	17.8	1,644	4.3	2.3
42021	Cambria County	18,166	0.6	0.9	67.9	48.9	17.9	32.1	26.3	1,392	5.3	2.0
42025	Carbon County	8,699	0.4	6.0	62.4	35.9	21.9	37.6	27.2	813	6.6	3.3
42027	Centre County	15,714	3.4	6.2	76.0	53.7	21.7	24.0	19.6	772	3.3	1.6
42029	Chester County	81,896	3.5	15.0	79.3	51.3	27.3	20.7	18.6	5,123	4.3	1.6
42033	Clearfield County	10,428	0.0	1.2	71.7	48.8	21.1	28.3	20.8	983	6.6	4.0
42037	Columbia County	8,040	0.8	4.4	69.7	52.6	15.0	30.3	22.2	724	6.3	3.3
42039	Crawford County	12,834	0.7	1.2	71.4	44.7	24.2	28.6	20.4	905	5.0	2.5
42041	Cumberland County	32,416	4.4	9.4	72.7	51.6	19.3	27.3	24.7	2,285	4.8	2.6
42043	Dauphin County	38,950	3.7	11.3	61.6	45.6	14.2	38.4	33.3	4,803	8.3	4.1
42045	Delaware County	82,121	3.6	14.9	66.5	45.3	20.5	33.5	27.1	9,959	8.2	4.6
42049	Erie County	40,114	3.2	8.7	61.5	42.4	17.8	38.5	30.5	4,575	7.8	3.7
42051	Fayette County	16,820	0.4	2.0	64.6	36.2	25.2	35.4	22.6	2,214	9.0	4.8
42055	Franklin County	22,418	0.8	8.5	70.8	49.1	20.4	29.2	26.2	1,641	4.9	1.9
42063	Indiana County	10,715	1.0	4.7	76.4	45.2	29.4	23.6	17.0	951	6.1	3.6
42069	Lackawanna County	28,434	3.0	7.0	65.7	46.0	17.3	34.3	26.6	2,571	6.2	2.1
42071	Lancaster County	82,474	2.2	7.3	76.7	45.8	30.0	23.3	19.3	7,515	6.1	2.5
42073	Lawrence County	12,375	0.0	2.6	59.4	39.1	18.8	40.6	30.8	1,427	8.1	3.9
42075	Lebanon County	19,554	1.7	5.4	65.2	45.6	18.4	34.8	29.0	1,247	4.2	2.2
42077	Lehigh County	53,882	3.9	20.6	62.0	40.8	19.1	38.0	29.9	5,701	7.2	3.0
42079	Luzerne County	41,772	2.7	12.9	60.5	40.3	17.6	39.5	29.8	4,660	7.7	3.6
42081	Lycoming County	15,441	0.7	3.5	68.9	51.4	17.1	31.1	27.2	1,664	7.2	2.7
42085	Mercer County	15,669	0.4	1.5	71.0	47.0	22.7	29.0	21.8	1,157	5.1	2.3
42089	Monroe County	26,774	2.2	21.4	67.5	42.4	22.7	32.5	27.1	2,949	8.3	4.7

State/county FIPS code	State/County	Total own children under 18 in families and subfamilies	Total own children under 6 years	Nativity and parentage, under 6 years		Own children under 6 years living with two parents			Own children under 6 living with one parent	
				Child is foreign born, percent	One or more foreign-born parent, percent	Total under 6 years living with two parents, percent	Both parents in labor force, percent	One parent in labor force, percent	Total under 6 years living with one parent, percent	Parent in labor force, percent
	Pennsylvania—cont'd									
42091	Montgomery County	176,499	54,881	1.8	19.2	80.1	53.7	25.8	19.9	17.7
42095	Northampton County	60,671	18,052	1.1	13.6	68.4	43.3	24.3	31.6	24.0
42097	Northumberland County	17,585	6,032	1.1	4.5	60.5	34.1	26.4	39.5	31.9
42101	Philadelphia County	323,234	120,618	1.9	20.6	39.1	24.1	13.1	60.9	43.4
42103	Pike County	11,674	2,853	0.0	19.8	72.1	41.4	27.9	27.9	23.7
42107	Schuylkill County	27,695	8,693	0.1	5.1	61.6	39.4	21.0	38.4	26.0
42111	Somerset County	13,913	4,185	0.0	1.7	73.8	46.9	26.3	26.2	20.6
42121	Venango County	10,418	3,141	0.0	0.6	58.5	37.4	20.3	41.5	29.7
42125	Washington County	39,577	12,316	0.4	3.4	68.6	43.5	24.2	31.4	22.5
42127	Wayne County	9,058	2,430	0.0	4.8	67.2	42.1	24.6	32.8	29.2
42129	Westmoreland County	67,213	19,950	0.7	2.5	65.3	39.9	24.9	34.7	26.4
42133	York County	95,538	30,576	0.3	6.0	62.2	42.1	20.0	37.8	27.2
44000	**Rhode Island**	206,631	65,038	1.8	23.3	57.3	38.7	17.6	42.7	33.3
44003	Kent County	31,338	9,649	1.8	13.6	66.3	47.3	16.4	33.7	28.0
44005	Newport County	14,841	4,392	0.3	12.0	81.8	57.9	23.7	18.2	14.4
44007	Providence County	127,605	42,791	2.3	29.9	49.0	32.7	15.7	51.0	38.9
44009	Washington County	23,311	5,763	0.5	2.6	75.2	46.6	26.9	24.8	22.4
45000	**South Carolina**	1,015,015	338,816	0.5	11.0	54.8	32.5	21.3	45.2	35.4
45003	Aiken County	34,299	10,907	0.0	13.3	61.3	36.9	23.7	38.7	28.9
45007	Anderson County	41,739	13,512	1.5	5.8	57.2	36.2	19.9	42.8	35.5
45013	Beaufort County	32,955	12,304	0.0	21.9	63.3	34.4	28.2	36.7	29.8
45015	Berkeley County	44,643	15,825	0.3	13.7	64.7	37.2	26.2	35.3	27.8
45019	Charleston County	70,085	27,014	0.4	10.3	55.5	34.4	20.5	44.5	38.8
45021	Cherokee County	12,312	3,956	0.0	5.3	43.3	27.5	14.9	56.7	38.5
45031	Darlington County	14,988	4,734	0.0	1.8	42.8	28.9	13.9	57.2	46.1
45035	Dorchester County	35,655	11,673	0.1	6.7	61.5	37.5	23.8	38.5	27.2
45041	Florence County	31,575	10,697	0.1	4.2	43.8	32.9	10.3	56.2	40.2
45043	Georgetown County	11,384	3,248	0.0	8.7	26.9	19.8	7.1	73.1	53.0
45045	Greenville County	106,392	35,196	1.1	16.2	61.5	34.1	26.3	38.5	31.2
45047	Greenwood County	14,860	4,863	0.9	9.1	47.0	27.2	19.0	53.0	46.3
45051	Horry County	52,563	17,570	0.2	14.0	50.3	32.9	16.3	49.7	39.0
45055	Kershaw County	14,147	4,831	2.9	2.2	60.2	30.8	29.2	39.8	34.1
45057	Lancaster County	16,763	5,475	0.0	8.1	56.2	34.5	19.1	43.8	33.1
45059	Laurens County	13,995	5,004	0.0	3.7	36.5	23.2	12.6	63.5	46.2
45063	Lexington County	61,614	19,696	0.6	11.5	69.7	44.6	23.0	· 30.3	21.8
45073	Oconee County	14,536	5,016	1.3	10.4	51.4	24.1	26.9	48.6	44.1
45075	Orangeburg County	19,046	6,627	0.0	4.4	31.4	24.1	4.8	68.6	48.0
45077	Pickens County	22,347	6,919	0.0	4.6	60.4	33.1	24.9	39.6	33.4
45079	Richland County	83,145	27,329	1.0	10.8	52.2	30.6	20.6	47.8	39.5
45083	Spartanburg County	65,024	21,136	0.4	17.2	56.7	30.0	25.5	43.3	33.2
45085	Sumter County	24,906	9,202	0.7	9.0	50.8	29.3	19.6	49.2	37.5
45091	York County	56,267	17,750	1.0	12.9	68.3	41.2	26.3	31.7	27.6
46000	**South Dakota**	194,342	68,459	0.6	6.3	64.2	46.3	17.2	35.8	29.0
46099	Minnehaha County	42,607	16,010	1.4	12.4	63.6	47.8	15.8	36.4	30.4
46103	Pennington County	23,803	8,201	0.0	2.7	51.7	35.3	15.5	48.3	41.2
47000	**Tennessee**	1,403,158	464,004	1.0	12.4	60.7	34.3	25.5	39.3	29.7
47001	Anderson County	15,200	4,600	0.2	5.1	49.3	27.8	21.5	50.7	32.3
47009	Blount County	24,983	6,909	0.7	6.8	68.9	42.9	24.4	31.1	22.3
47011	Bradley County	21,145	6,573	0.2	11.7	68.3	38.1	27.0	31.7	21.5
47019	Carter County	10,322	3,373	0.0	0.0	61.3	35.6	25.8	38.7	31.4
47031	Coffee County	11,521	3,641	0.6	11.5	58.1	26.2	29.8	41.9	30.9
47035	Cumberland County	9,638	3,042	1.0	7.6	49.4	33.7	13.5	50.6	25.6
47037	Davidson County	132,550	52,394	2.9	27.9	57.3	32.8	23.5	42.7	33.4
47043	Dickson County	11,755	4,139	0.1	9.0	63.4	34.9	28.0	36.6	31.0
47059	Greene County	12,999	4,020	1.0	7.5	65.1	36.1	25.5	34.9	16.8
47063	Hamblen County	13,246	4,092	0.6	25.2	66.5	35.1	30.9	33.5	21.4
47065	Hamilton County	69,073	23,551	1.1	11.8	59.0	32.1	25.8	41.0	31.8
47073	Hawkins County	11,098	3,195	0.0	0.0	67.5	36.3	28.3	32.5	25.5
47089	Jefferson County	10,385	3,447	0.0	5.6	51.8	36.8	14.0	48.2	37.8
47093	Knox County	89,514	29,726	0.6	13.8	70.7	42.9	27.6	29.3	20.5
47107	McMinn County	10,602	3,532	0.0	0.0	75.9	41.4	31.3	24.1	21.6
47113	Madison County	21,553	7,659	0.2	10.8	53.3	28.1	24.8	46.7	35.2
47119	Maury County	18,653	6,669	0.0	9.4	62.1	37.8	22.9	37.9	27.3
47125	Montgomery County	48,470	18,851	0.4	10.2	63.9	28.5	35.2	36.1	25.7
47141	Putnam County	15,046	5,423	2.3	14.0	62.9	27.9	32.9	37.1	27.2
47145	Roane County	9,906	2,944	0.0	2.9	50.7	26.2	23.4	49.3	39.6
47147	Robertson County	15,970	4,924	0.0	11.4	63.4	37.8	24.1	36.6	31.3
47149	Rutherford County	67,535	22,516	1.3	14.5	71.0	44.9	26.0	29.0	22.4
47155	Sevier County	18,445	6,326	1.4	11.5	61.5	29.8	30.6	38.5	26.8
47157	Shelby County	229,566	78,777	0.9	16.4	45.3	27.5	17.5	54.7	44.5

Table D-2: Counties with a Population of 50,000 or More—Children—*Continued*

State/county FIPS code	State/County	Total own children 6 to 17	Own children age 6 to 17 years in families and subfamilies							Grandchildren under 18 living with a grandparent householder	Grandchildren under 18 living with a grandparent householder, as a percent of all children	Children for whom grandparent householders are responsible, as a percent of all children
			Nativity and parentage, age 6 to 17 years		Own children age 6 to 17 years living with two parents			Own children age 6 to 17 years living with one parent				
			Child is foreign born, percent	One or more foreign-born parent, percent	Age 6 to 17 years living with two parents, percent	Both parents in labor force, percent	One parent in labor force, percent	Age 6 to 17 years living with one parent, percent	Parent in labor force, percent			
	Pennsylvania—cont'd											
42091	Montgomery County	121,618	3.8	16.8	77.7	55.6	21.6	22.3	20.0	8,321	4.7	2.0
42095	Northampton County	42,619	2.8	13.2	71.3	47.6	23.0	28.7	22.9	4,661	7.7	2.8
42097	Northumberland County	11,553	0.7	1.7	72.0	49.5	21.1	28.0	23.1	1,108	6.3	2.4
42101	Philadelphia County	202,616	4.9	20.0	39.0	25.7	11.4	61.0	43.0	45,095	14.0	6.7
42103	Pike County	8,821	1.5	11.6	73.2	50.4	21.2	26.8	23.1	748	6.4	2.3
42107	Schuylkill County	19,002	0.9	4.6	67.6	46.5	19.1	32.4	26.7	2,326	8.4	4.6
42111	Somerset County	9,728	0.1	1.2	77.1	54.0	21.4	22.9	18.8	833	6.0	2.3
42121	Venango County	7,277	0.3	0.7	61.7	45.6	13.6	38.3	28.6	924	8.9	4.7
42125	Washington County	27,261	1.2	2.7	73.9	50.5	22.1	26.1	19.6	2,506	6.3	3.8
42127	Wayne County	6,628	0.5	3.8	64.9	41.1	22.7	35.1	27.9	423	4.7	2.8
42129	Westmoreland County	47,263	0.9	3.2	70.1	49.4	20.2	29.9	23.2	3,634	5.4	3.1
42133	York County	64,962	1.5	6.1	67.2	47.5	18.9	32.8	26.7	6,343	6.6	3.3
44000	**Rhode Island**	141,593	5.1	25.5	61.7	45.6	15.4	38.3	31.4	13,367	6.5	2.7
44003	Kent County	21,689	2.0	13.5	70.0	55.3	14.1	30.0	26.8	2,168	6.9	2.7
44005	Newport County	10,449	4.2	12.4	66.2	49.7	16.2	33.8	30.2	1,279	8.6	3.3
44007	Providence County	84,814	6.6	34.7	55.6	39.9	15.0	44.4	35.4	8,578	6.7	3.1
44009	Washington County	17,548	3.0	6.5	70.0	51.2	18.1	30.0	25.4	824	3.5	0.8
45000	**South Carolina**	676,199	2.2	9.0	59.2	38.5	19.3	40.8	33.3	110,685	10.9	6.3
45003	Aiken County	23,392	0.8	7.1	56.0	35.0	20.2	44.0	34.6	3,551	10.4	6.0
45007	Anderson County	28,227	0.9	4.7	62.1	40.2	21.0	37.9	29.0	5,217	12.5	7.5
45013	Beaufort County	20,651	9.0	22.1	64.3	38.3	21.7	35.7	32.5	2,122	6.4	3.6
45015	Berkeley County	28,818	2.0	9.7	62.3	40.5	21.1	37.7	30.9	4,524	10.1	6.0
45019	Charleston County	43,071	1.3	7.0	57.4	36.5	19.9	42.6	35.9	7,303	10.4	7.2
45021	Cherokee County	8,356	0.8	7.5	59.0	33.1	25.2	41.0	24.7	1,736	14.1	8.5
45031	Darlington County	10,254	1.0	2.4	48.5	33.1	15.5	51.5	42.0	3,029	20.2	10.9
45035	Dorchester County	23,982	1.7	5.8	62.1	43.5	17.6	37.9	31.2	3,807	10.7	7.2
45041	Florence County	20,878	1.5	5.0	53.7	39.0	12.5	46.3	38.5	4,481	14.2	5.0
45043	Georgetown County	8,136	1.4	5.8	51.3	30.2	18.1	48.7	37.0	2,061	18.1	9.3
45045	Greenville County	71,196	3.9	14.7	65.6	38.4	26.4	34.4	28.1	8,081	7.6	4.7
45047	Greenwood County	9,997	1.4	8.6	50.9	34.5	14.5	49.1	42.0	1,578	10.6	5.6
45051	Horry County	34,993	2.9	12.7	61.6	42.4	17.3	38.4	31.0	4,924	9.4	5.1
45055	Kershaw County	9,316	0.6	4.8	64.3	46.0	16.8	35.7	32.1	1,510	10.7	6.0
45057	Lancaster County	11,288	1.8	7.9	55.9	39.1	15.2	44.1	39.0	1,182	7.1	3.2
45059	Laurens County	8,991	0.7	7.7	50.5	30.1	17.8	49.5	38.0	2,175	15.5	11.5
45063	Lexington County	41,918	1.9	9.2	64.2	46.5	16.7	35.8	29.6	4,765	7.7	4.0
45073	Oconee County	9,520	2.4	7.8	61.1	28.3	31.6	38.9	29.5	793	5.5	4.0
45075	Orangeburg County	12,419	0.2	2.0	47.5	32.4	11.9	52.5	42.9	4,397	23.1	14.5
45077	Pickens County	15,428	1.7	6.1	72.4	47.0	21.8	27.6	22.0	2,370	10.6	8.4
45079	Richland County	55,816	2.2	7.8	54.6	37.8	15.9	45.4	39.0	6,392	7.7	4.1
45083	Spartanburg County	43,888	3.6	15.4	62.1	39.5	21.6	37.9	32.0	6,838	10.5	6.6
45085	Sumter County	15,704	1.4	4.8	57.1	36.9	19.1	42.9	34.7	3,305	13.3	8.0
45091	York County	38,517	2.1	10.0	69.3	46.2	22.7	30.7	26.6	4,291	7.6	4.7
46000	**South Dakota**	125,883	1.9	5.1	68.0	53.6	13.4	32.0	27.7	12,458	6.4	4.1
46099	Minnehaha County	26,597	5.0	14.8	66.9	54.4	12.3	33.1	29.2	1,822	4.3	2.3
46103	Pennington County	15,602	0.8	2.1	58.5	47.4	10.0	41.5	36.2	1,563	6.6	3.2
47000	**Tennessee**	939,154	2.5	9.7	64.1	40.4	22.0	35.9	28.7	133,235	9.5	5.7
47001	Anderson County	10,600	0.9	3.9	63.7	37.9	21.7	36.3	25.4	1,661	10.9	6.6
47009	Blount County	18,074	1.1	5.8	76.8	43.1	30.2	23.2	20.3	2,218	8.9	6.0
47011	Bradley County	14,572	1.2	7.4	66.3	44.1	19.4	33.7	28.9	1,908	9.0	5.0
47019	Carter County	6,949	0.0	0.0	70.4	46.4	20.1	29.6	21.3	1,149	11.1	7.7
47031	Coffee County	7,880	0.9	7.1	62.4	36.0	25.3	37.6	33.6	1,842	16.0	11.1
47035	Cumberland County	6,596	1.7	5.1	68.8	52.4	12.5	31.2	24.4	1,479	15.3	10.3
47037	Davidson County	80,156	7.8	27.3	54.4	32.2	20.9	45.6	38.3	10,781	8.1	4.3
47043	Dickson County	7,616	0.3	4.9	68.5	42.5	23.5	31.5	26.8	985	8.4	4.5
47059	Greene County	8,979	2.9	4.8	66.3	38.0	27.7	33.7	22.1	1,459	11.2	7.9
47063	Hamblen County	9,154	3.0	18.9	66.9	44.2	21.2	33.1	22.4	1,654	12.5	7.6
47065	Hamilton County	45,522	2.4	8.7	64.6	42.6	20.6	35.4	28.4	6,282	9.1	5.9
47073	Hawkins County	7,903	0.0	0.0	70.8	48.5	18.9	29.2	21.3	1,436	12.9	8.5
47089	Jefferson County	6,938	0.7	6.6	66.2	48.9	16.4	33.8	26.7	761	7.3	2.9
47093	Knox County	59,788	2.5	10.5	71.6	45.7	25.2	28.4	22.0	7,404	8.3	5.5
47107	McMinn County	7,070	0.0	0.0	66.5	42.1	23.0	33.5	26.1	755	7.1	4.0
47113	Madison County	13,894	1.6	6.0	59.0	39.7	19.1	41.0	29.7	2,032	9.4	6.1
47119	Maury County	11,984	2.9	9.0	63.1	43.8	17.9	36.9	29.5	1,491	8.0	3.8
47125	Montgomery County	29,619	1.9	11.1	63.8	33.6	28.2	36.2	26.8	2,292	4.7	2.9
47141	Putnam County	9,623	3.1	9.2	69.6	38.9	21.9	30.4	22.6	1,565	10.4	3.3
47145	Roane County	6,962	0.4	2.6	68.9	37.1	27.9	31.1	20.0	1,294	13.1	8.5
47147	Robertson County	11,046	1.1	7.7	68.4	46.3	17.7	31.6	27.0	2,000	12.5	8.6
47149	Rutherford County	45,019	2.7	14.2	72.0	49.2	21.5	28.0	23.9	3,579	5.3	3.3
47155	Sevier County	12,119	5.3	13.0	61.8	44.5	16.2	38.2	32.8	2,537	13.8	10.1
47157	Shelby County	150,789	2.9	11.3	48.5	32.5	15.6	51.5	43.4	23,596	10.3	5.7

State/county FIPS code	State/County	Total own children under 18 in families and subfamilies	Own children under 6 years in families and subfamilies							
			Total own children under 6 years	Nativity and parentage, under 6 years		Own children under 6 years living with two parents			Own children under 6 living with one parent	
				Child is foreign born, percent	One or more foreign-born parent, percent	Total under 6 years living with two parents, percent	Both parents in labor force, percent	One parent in labor force, percent	Total under 6 years living with one parent, percent	Parent in labor force, percent
	Tennessee—cont'd									
47163	Sullivan County........................	29,636	8,537	0.2	3.1	63.3	40.4	20.7	36.7	25.9
47165	Sumner County.........................	38,876	11,947	0.4	10.2	67.4	39.7	26.6	32.6	27.1
47167	Tipton County	15,171	4,467	0.0	0.3	53.6	31.6	21.6	46.4	35.2
47179	Washington County	23,596	7,477	0.5	6.4	68.3	47.1	19.7	31.7	25.0
47187	Williamson County	54,232	15,259	3.5	13.8	84.9	43.4	41.2	15.1	13.4
47189	Wilson County	27,319	8,352	0.3	11.4	74.1	40.3	33.3	25.9	19.0
48000	**Texas ....**	6,646,543	2,252,764	1.5	33.3	62.9	31.9	30.1	37.1	27.3
48001	Anderson County......................	10,461	3,169	0.3	21.6	60.9	33.3	27.2	39.1	29.7
48005	Angelina County	21,970	7,030	0.0	20.5	58.2	31.0	24.8	41.8	37.7
48021	Bastrop County	17,784	5,411	0.9	31.5	74.8	34.7	40.0	25.2	17.8
48027	Bell County..............................	85,583	32,938	0.8	14.6	68.6	33.1	34.6	31.4	23.5
48029	Bexar County	450,527	152,655	1.2	24.1	57.9	30.3	26.4	42.1	31.2
48037	Bowie County	20,693	6,585	0.0	8.9	48.4	31.3	17.1	51.6	37.7
48039	Brazoria County	84,658	28,844	0.9	29.3	70.8	44.3	26.2	29.2	22.1
48041	Brazos County	39,522	14,681	1.0	24.6	63.9	33.8	28.7	36.1	31.0
48061	Cameron County	126,746	41,270	1.4	43.0	53.3	22.1	27.4	46.7	29.2
48073	Cherokee County	12,245	4,268	0.0	26.1	45.0	26.6	16.8	55.0	38.2
48085	Collin County............................	227,823	70,508	2.2	34.1	79.5	43.8	35.0	20.5	16.3
48091	Comal County	25,105	7,501	0.4	10.5	71.5	29.8	40.8	28.5	22.7
48099	Coryell County	19,268	7,258	0.3	9.9	75.5	25.3	47.6	24.5	12.8
48113	Dallas County	634,694	225,371	2.1	48.1	58.0	28.9	28.5	42.0	33.2
48121	Denton County	183,406	58,756	1.4	30.2	75.7	43.5	31.3	24.3	20.1
48135	Ector County	39,941	14,308	0.3	23.7	60.6	24.9	35.2	39.4	27.7
48139	Ellis County	40,683	12,458	0.2	18.4	63.9	36.6	26.7	36.1	30.3
48141	El Paso County..........................	230,018	77,580	1.2	36.7	61.5	28.8	31.5	38.5	25.4
48157	Fort Bend County	174,733	52,487	3.8	45.7	75.4	44.8	30.2	24.6	19.2
48167	Galveston County	70,749	23,153	0.8	19.6	68.5	42.3	25.5	31.5	25.4
48181	Grayson County	27,181	9,200	1.4	14.8	57.0	34.2	21.3	43.0	33.5
48183	Gregg County	29,912	10,408	0.3	21.6	54.8	32.7	22.1	45.2	34.7
48187	Guadalupe County....................	36,175	10,586	0.2	17.4	67.6	40.4	27.0	32.4	22.4
48199	Hardin County	13,214	4,443	0.0	2.0	70.6	30.3	40.3	29.4	17.8
48201	Harris County	1,119,997	393,894	2.0	45.9	60.9	28.8	31.3	39.1	29.3
48203	Harrison County........................	15,282	4,952	0.4	18.4	57.3	37.3	20.0	42.7	35.1
48209	Hays County	39,444	12,865	0.0	24.0	69.9	38.0	31.5	30.1	24.6
48213	Henderson County	16,464	5,293	0.1	18.7	68.7	31.4	32.9	31.3	17.6
48215	Hidalgo County	264,594	91,059	2.3	53.7	64.2	25.8	36.9	35.8	22.5
48221	Hood County	10,585	3,469	3.7	20.7	77.4	28.2	49.3	22.6	12.9
48231	Hunt County.............................	19,825	6,343	1.3	12.3	66.2	31.5	34.1	33.8	29.0
48245	Jefferson County	55,661	18,751	1.0	27.0	50.5	21.7	27.3	49.5	36.0
48251	Johnson County........................	38,226	11,827	0.3	17.0	66.2	34.5	28.9	33.8	27.0
48257	Kaufman County	27,719	8,916	2.2	21.9	61.5	34.4	26.0	38.5	26.4
48291	Liberty County	18,272	6,405	0.2	14.9	52.9	23.0	28.4	47.1	33.4
48303	Lubbock County	66,125	23,042	0.8	8.9	60.1	36.7	23.0	39.9	32.5
48309	McLennan County	57,168	19,798	0.3	23.2	58.3	32.2	25.3	41.7	31.1
48323	Maverick County	17,679	5,955	1.2	49.0	55.5	17.0	38.5	44.5	30.4
48329	Midland County........................	38,112	13,830	0.4	19.3	64.6	27.2	36.4	35.4	24.9
48339	Montgomery County	127,065	40,733	1.5	28.7	71.5	31.3	39.3	28.5	19.3
48347	Nacogdoches County.................	14,904	5,574	3.4	26.6	48.9	19.7	29.2	51.1	36.4
48355	Nueces County	84,431	27,741	0.5	11.1	46.9	25.8	20.5	53.1	37.3
48361	Orange County	18,992	6,416	0.0	9.7	61.7	34.5	26.7	38.3	28.4
48367	Parker County	27,841	8,271	0.3	14.4	73.5	35.8	37.7	26.5	18.8
48375	Potter County	31,737	11,616	3.2	27.1	52.2	27.3	24.0	47.8	33.9
48381	Randall County	28,660	9,962	0.5	7.8	71.2	47.8	22.7	28.8	24.4
48397	Rockwall County	22,991	6,953	1.8	21.8	72.2	47.2	25.0	27.8	23.9
48401	Rusk County	11,539	4,099	0.0	26.0	56.7	32.7	23.0	43.3	15.5
48409	San Patricio County...................	16,586	5,320	0.7	11.4	57.4	29.6	27.2	42.6	28.9
48423	Smith County	50,301	16,780	0.4	28.5	62.4	32.0	28.8	37.6	28.9
48427	Starr County	19,625	6,952	1.7	60.9	56.5	22.9	33.6	43.5	28.9
48439	Tarrant County	495,998	164,700	1.5	33.3	64.0	33.7	29.6	36.0	27.3
48441	Taylor County...........................	29,881	10,841	0.4	9.0	57.3	30.2	27.1	42.7	30.7
48451	Tom Green County	24,990	9,376	1.0	13.0	58.2	29.1	28.0	41.8	30.3
48453	Travis County	245,347	90,157	1.8	38.4	68.0	37.1	30.2	32.0	24.6
48467	Van Zandt County.....................	11,399	3,460	0.8	13.5	64.0	31.9	31.4	36.0	23.7
48469	Victoria County	21,904	7,522	0.4	10.1	52.7	26.1	26.5	47.3	33.6
48471	Walker County..........................	10,130	3,537	0.8	21.1	56.8	24.8	31.9	43.2	31.3
48479	Webb County	84,582	29,510	1.1	44.6	55.1	23.0	30.1	44.9	24.2
48485	Wichita County	28,427	10,220	1.0	10.1	58.1	34.2	22.7	41.9	32.5
48491	Williamson County	124,124	41,044	1.6	23.9	78.7	44.7	33.1	21.3	18.0
48497	Wise County	14,106	4,296	0.0	26.4	69.6	32.8	34.7	30.4	24.9
49000	**Utah ....**	858,051	303,468	0.7	16.7	81.0	35.6	44.6	19.0	15.1
49003	Box Elder County	16,481	5,696	0.0	8.1	83.6	39.2	44.3	16.4	16.0

State/county FIPS code	State/County	Total own children 6 to 17	Nativity and parentage, age 6 to 17 years		Own children age 6 to 17 years living with two parents			Own children age 6 to 17 years living with one parent		Grand-children under 18 living with a grandparent householder	Grand-children under 18 living with a grandparent householder, as a percent of all children	Children for whom grandparent householders are responsible, as a percent of all children
			Child is foreign born, percent	One or more foreign-born parent, percent	Age 6 to 17 years living with two parents, percent	Both parents in labor force, percent	One parent in labor force, percent	Age 6 to 17 years living with one parent, percent	Parent in labor force, percent			
	Tennessee—cont'd											
47163	Sullivan County	21,099	0.9	3.0	67.3	42.1	22.2	32.7	27.0	3,708	12.5	8.2
47165	Sumner County	26,929	1.8	7.5	70.3	46.7	22.9	29.7	25.0	3,356	8.6	3.6
47167	Tipton County	10,704	2.3	4.6	65.1	47.8	17.0	34.9	31.0	2,160	14.2	7.3
47179	Washington County	16,119	2.0	8.0	66.8	40.4	23.7	33.2	28.4	1,733	7.3	4.2
47187	Williamson County	38,973	3.0	9.5	82.2	45.4	36.2	17.8	15.5	1,663	3.1	1.1
47189	Wilson County	18,967	2.4	7.9	73.4	48.4	24.2	26.6	22.7	2,433	8.9	3.3
48000	**Texas**	4,393,779	5.8	34.7	65.2	38.7	25.5	34.8	28.5	626,060	9.4	5.3
48001	Anderson County	7,292	4.0	20.7	58.7	33.3	24.5	41.3	31.9	949	9.1	7.2
48005	Angelina County	14,940	3.8	19.8	57.9	32.3	23.2	42.1	36.9	2,179	9.9	3.9
48021	Bastrop County	12,373	3.7	36.6	70.9	41.0	28.0	29.1	21.6	1,573	8.8	5.2
48027	Bell County	52,645	1.8	17.0	63.3	36.5	24.9	36.7	28.3	5,843	6.8	4.8
48029	Bexar County	297,872	5.0	27.1	61.0	37.1	22.7	39.0	31.5	50,010	11.1	5.8
48037	Bowie County	14,108	0.9	4.2	53.4	37.5	14.3	46.6	38.1	2,962	14.3	10.0
48039	Brazoria County	55,814	5.3	30.7	69.7	43.9	24.9	30.3	27.0	7,635	9.0	5.6
48041	Brazos County	24,841	5.7	28.1	63.5	36.8	26.0	36.5	30.9	2,888	7.3	4.7
48061	Cameron County	85,476	5.6	53.0	59.4	29.1	26.7	40.6	28.9	18,795	14.8	6.3
48073	Cherokee County	7,977	5.0	31.2	67.1	40.0	25.1	32.9	25.0	1,305	10.7	5.9
48085	Collin County	157,315	5.6	31.4	77.4	49.8	27.0	22.6	19.9	10,168	4.5	2.0
48091	Comal County	17,604	3.7	13.9	74.4	48.5	24.3	25.6	17.9	2,172	8.7	5.7
48099	Coryell County	12,010	0.8	15.9	69.1	38.7	27.2	30.9	20.9	878	4.6	3.3
48113	Dallas County	409,323	8.5	50.1	60.4	34.0	25.6	39.6	33.5	56,200	8.9	5.2
48121	Denton County	124,650	4.9	26.5	75.9	50.1	25.3	24.1	21.2	8,012	4.4	2.8
48135	Ector County	25,633	2.1	31.7	60.1	34.2	25.2	39.9	29.7	5,028	12.6	7.8
48139	Ellis County	28,225	3.8	22.9	69.0	46.9	21.6	31.0	26.6	4,388	10.8	4.9
48141	El Paso County	152,438	5.5	49.1	60.1	31.3	27.4	39.9	31.3	29,182	12.7	6.5
48157	Fort Bend County	122,246	9.5	46.1	75.4	48.0	26.7	24.6	20.9	12,714	7.3	3.9
48167	Galveston County	47,596	3.0	21.8	69.9	47.2	21.5	30.1	25.9	5,940	8.4	4.8
48181	Grayson County	17,981	3.1	13.2	63.1	40.2	20.3	36.9	31.2	2,424	8.9	4.9
48183	Gregg County	19,504	4.5	23.4	60.7	37.2	23.0	39.3	31.2	2,858	9.6	5.6
48187	Guadalupe County	25,589	2.9	18.5	71.7	48.5	22.2	28.3	24.5	3,838	10.6	5.6
48199	Hardin County	8,771	0.4	2.4	69.3	39.4	29.7	30.7	21.8	1,641	12.4	6.0
48201	Harris County	726,103	8.2	47.6	63.0	35.0	27.0	37.0	31.2	94,130	8.4	4.4
48203	Harrison County	10,330	2.1	15.7	63.9	38.1	23.5	36.1	32.3	2,258	14.8	12.1
48209	Hays County	26,579	1.8	19.5	74.5	51.7	22.2	25.5	21.9	2,235	5.7	2.7
48213	Henderson County	11,171	2.9	14.9	65.9	38.2	23.8	34.1	23.8	1,781	10.8	7.3
48215	Hidalgo County	173,535	9.4	59.2	64.7	32.2	30.7	35.3	26.8	37,180	14.1	5.7
48221	Hood County	7,116	4.9	14.4	75.3	43.0	30.9	24.7	16.9	567	5.4	3.1
48231	Hunt County	13,482	4.6	15.6	71.0	48.2	22.3	29.0	26.2	2,592	13.1	5.0
48245	Jefferson County	36,910	5.1	26.7	55.4	31.1	23.1	44.6	37.1	5,853	10.5	6.5
48251	Johnson County	26,399	2.3	16.3	71.5	42.2	28.3	28.5	23.4	4,551	11.9	7.2
48257	Kaufman County	18,803	2.7	17.1	69.0	47.8	20.6	31.0	25.5	3,530	12.7	8.8
48291	Liberty County	11,867	1.2	19.5	67.4	33.0	32.9	32.6	24.1	2,861	15.7	10.3
48303	Lubbock County	43,083	2.0	11.0	62.9	41.8	19.8	37.1	32.4	6,665	10.1	7.4
48309	McLennan County	37,370	4.6	22.6	61.7	40.3	20.8	38.3	31.2	5,384	9.4	6.2
48323	Maverick County	11,724	5.3	61.4	62.1	28.4	31.7	37.9	27.6	2,467	14.0	7.1
48329	Midland County	24,282	1.8	25.6	66.1	40.9	24.3	33.9	29.4	4,092	10.7	5.9
48339	Montgomery County	86,332	6.2	28.1	72.2	37.2	34.3	27.8	22.0	7,643	6.0	3.9
48347	Nacogdoches County	9,330	5.6	25.6	68.2	36.4	30.7	31.8	24.7	1,109	7.4	4.0
48355	Nueces County	56,690	2.2	12.9	56.1	36.2	19.1	43.9	35.9	10,137	12.0	7.6
48361	Orange County	12,576	1.4	4.7	67.1	42.0	23.6	32.9	28.1	2,259	11.9	8.1
48367	Parker County	19,570	0.3	13.6	74.6	43.4	30.0	25.4	20.5	2,284	8.2	4.7
48375	Potter County	20,121	6.8	29.5	60.2	37.9	21.7	39.8	33.5	3,010	9.5	6.0
48381	Randall County	18,698	1.4	9.5	69.6	46.7	22.9	30.4	23.5	1,763	6.2	4.1
48397	Rockwall County	16,038	3.9	12.5	80.3	53.1	26.5	19.7	17.6	1,173	5.1	2.6
48401	Rusk County	7,440	2.4	16.4	63.6	43.0	19.6	36.4	26.1	1,902	16.5	13.2
48409	San Patricio County	11,266	1.6	12.3	58.1	36.3	20.8	41.9	33.8	1,797	10.8	6.2
48423	Smith County	33,521	3.7	24.8	69.5	43.3	25.3	30.5	26.6	5,569	11.1	6.5
48427	Starr County	12,673	6.5	66.8	56.7	28.8	27.3	43.3	37.0	3,324	16.9	9.6
48439	Tarrant County	331,298	6.2	33.3	65.6	40.6	24.4	34.4	28.7	38,836	7.8	4.5
48441	Taylor County	19,040	1.8	12.8	62.5	38.0	22.6	37.5	30.0	3,175	10.6	7.8
48451	Tom Green County	15,614	1.5	15.5	59.2	35.2	23.3	40.8	35.1	2,084	8.3	3.7
48453	Travis County	155,190	7.7	38.9	65.7	40.0	24.8	34.3	29.0	14,887	6.1	3.3
48467	Van Zandt County	7,939	4.1	12.8	75.0	38.7	35.8	25.0	21.2	1,343	11.8	8.4
48469	Victoria County	14,382	1.5	12.8	56.1	33.3	22.8	43.9	35.1	2,804	12.8	6.6
48471	Walker County	6,593	3.5	19.6	64.2	50.8	13.0	35.8	33.2	743	7.3	6.6
48479	Webb County	55,072	7.4	50.2	59.6	27.5	30.3	40.4	26.6	12,797	15.1	7.8
48485	Wichita County	18,207	2.4	13.4	63.9	44.2	18.8	36.1	32.0	2,328	8.2	4.2
48491	Williamson County	83,080	4.8	23.1	76.3	48.5	26.9	23.7	21.8	7,298	5.9	2.9
48497	Wise County	9,810	1.7	18.9	75.5	42.0	33.5	24.5	19.5	1,691	12.0	5.8
49000	**Utah**	554,583	3.1	17.1	79.2	42.8	35.5	20.8	17.6	51,012	5.9	2.4
49003	Box Elder County	10,785	0.2	6.0	77.8	45.7	31.5	22.2	18.8	834	5.1	2.0

Table D-2: Counties with a Population of 50,000 or More—Children—*Continued*

State/county FIPS code	State/County	Total own children under 18 in families and subfamilies	Total own children under 6 years	Nativity and parentage, under 6 years — Child is foreign born, percent	One or more foreign-born parent, percent	Own children under 6 years living with two parents — Total under 6 years living with two parents, percent	Both parents in labor force, percent	One parent in labor force, percent	Own children under 6 living with one parent — Total under 6 years living with one parent, percent	Parent in labor force, percent
	Utah—cont'd									
49005	Cache County	35,635	13,196	0.5	15.1	85.7	34.4	49.1	14.3	11.9
49011	Davis County	105,123	36,985	0.4	9.2	85.2	37.0	47.6	14.8	11.1
49035	Salt Lake County	293,583	103,562	1.2	25.3	75.6	36.0	39.3	24.4	19.6
49045	Tooele County	20,237	6,236	0.0	7.7	80.8	39.7	39.7	19.2	16.1
49049	Utah County	184,187	67,338	0.5	14.0	88.7	31.5	55.8	11.3	9.0
49053	Washington County	40,325	14,431	0.0	14.7	80.5	32.9	47.0	19.5	15.8
49057	Weber County	67,028	24,192	0.7	14.3	74.5	38.5	34.8	25.5	18.8
50000	**Vermont**	118,957	36,717	0.6	7.1	65.8	45.5	19.5	34.2	26.0
50007	Chittenden County	29,491	9,530	1.5	15.0	71.8	50.5	20.7	28.2	20.1
50021	Rutland County	10,437	3,144	0.9	4.5	61.5	40.2	20.6	38.5	31.6
50023	Washington County	11,470	3,727	0.3	6.5	68.3	51.0	14.8	31.7	23.9
50027	Windsor County	10,453	3,089	0.5	5.3	60.3	43.1	17.2	39.7	30.7
51000	**Virginia**	1,779,171	598,316	1.4	23.6	67.3	39.9	26.8	32.7	26.0
51003	Albemarle County	20,931	6,823	1.1	21.5	69.8	42.2	27.0	30.2	23.0
51013	Arlington County	34,871	14,947	2.5	40.3	83.9	54.5	29.2	16.1	13.3
51015	Augusta County	14,225	4,197	0.0	6.0	69.3	38.6	30.4	30.7	25.0
51019	Bedford County	14,329	3,693	0.0	11.3	79.9	44.6	34.5	20.1	18.1
51031	Campbell County	11,029	3,096	0.0	3.0	68.2	40.2	27.0	31.8	23.2
51041	Chesterfield County	77,523	23,437	1.1	18.3	67.3	45.6	21.6	32.7	28.1
51059	Fairfax County	263,342	89,509	2.9	52.5	81.0	48.9	31.6	19.0	15.6
51061	Fauquier County	15,977	4,667	0.4	13.6	64.8	30.9	33.9	35.2	30.7
51067	Franklin County	10,801	3,182	0.0	5.3	67.8	38.6	26.1	32.2	23.5
51069	Frederick County	18,558	6,126	0.7	17.6	77.0	50.8	26.2	23.0	18.9
51085	Hanover County	22,975	5,939	0.5	7.4	77.0	51.6	24.7	23.0	15.3
51087	Henrico County	71,431	23,880	2.3	22.2	62.7	40.5	21.3	37.3	31.3
51089	Henry County	10,201	3,137	0.7	10.1	57.7	33.7	21.2	42.3	30.6
51095	James City County	14,150	4,305	2.1	15.1	68.1	42.2	25.9	31.9	30.3
51107	Loudoun County	99,394	32,930	2.0	41.7	87.6	51.1	36.4	12.4	10.9
51121	Montgomery County	14,517	5,045	4.3	14.1	76.2	42.0	28.5	23.8	20.7
51143	Pittsylvania County	11,819	3,681	0.0	7.3	58.7	38.3	20.4	41.3	26.7
51153	Prince William County	118,417	42,090	1.7	39.9	73.4	44.6	28.3	26.6	21.8
51161	Roanoke County	18,992	5,285	1.1	15.0	78.1	47.3	30.0	21.9	18.1
51165	Rockingham County	17,003	5,354	0.3	14.1	68.3	38.8	28.9	31.7	23.6
51177	Spotsylvania County	32,104	9,603	0.5	13.8	70.1	39.9	30.2	29.9	22.6
51179	Stafford County	35,586	10,338	0.5	20.2	76.0	43.5	32.4	24.0	18.9
51191	Washington County	9,792	3,163	0.0	2.2	66.0	39.6	25.1	34.0	28.6
51199	York County	15,691	4,049	0.4	12.1	79.5	33.7	44.7	20.5	18.8
51510	Alexandria city	24,870	11,731	3.0	43.7	70.8	42.5	27.8	29.2	27.3
51550	Chesapeake city	54,505	17,122	0.8	11.3	61.6	32.8	28.6	38.4	33.3
51650	Hampton city	28,107	10,180	0.1	8.3	45.9	26.8	18.1	54.1	43.8
51660	Harrisonburg city	7,710	2,941	4.5	48.7	65.0	29.6	35.4	35.0	30.3
51680	Lynchburg city	14,193	5,268	1.1	8.7	58.8	34.3	23.9	41.2	32.8
51700	Newport News city	40,895	15,729	1.4	11.4	48.2	24.9	22.8	51.8	43.8
51710	Norfolk city	47,029	19,000	0.9	11.3	49.9	27.7	21.4	50.1	36.7
51740	Portsmouth city	21,089	7,969	0.0	3.2	40.0	24.2	15.7	60.0	48.1
51760	Richmond city	36,368	15,428	0.4	16.6	37.5	20.7	16.8	62.5	47.5
51770	Roanoke city	20,073	8,004	1.5	20.3	56.8	41.1	15.7	43.2	31.3
51800	Suffolk city	20,669	6,936	0.0	9.8	55.4	31.7	23.4	44.6	35.0
51810	Virginia Beach city	100,252	33,915	1.4	15.3	65.0	36.8	27.7	35.0	24.2
53000	**Washington**	1,518,172	510,783	1.7	28.9	69.8	36.5	32.2	30.2	22.9
53005	Benton County	46,510	15,981	1.3	25.1	67.8	35.3	32.1	32.2	27.8
53007	Chelan County	16,975	5,527	2.3	45.5	70.3	24.7	45.6	29.7	21.5
53009	Clallam County	12,080	3,684	0.5	7.1	59.6	36.6	22.0	40.4	27.0
53011	Clark County	107,889	33,914	1.2	22.0	70.3	35.2	33.9	29.7	24.9
53015	Cowlitz County	22,734	7,475	0.0	12.2	50.7	22.6	27.3	49.3	36.6
53021	Franklin County	28,115	10,522	0.5	53.1	63.0	31.0	31.0	37.0	30.5
53025	Grant County	27,182	9,812	0.1	46.9	67.7	34.8	32.9	32.3	29.1
53027	Grays Harbor County	14,321	4,728	0.2	16.3	61.9	28.2	31.2	38.1	35.3
53029	Island County	15,009	5,172	0.9	9.9	77.4	41.5	34.5	22.6	16.7
53033	King County	409,951	143,525	3.7	42.6	75.9	41.2	33.7	24.1	17.6
53035	Kitsap County	51,947	16,519	1.0	11.7	74.5	35.2	38.0	25.5	14.9
53041	Lewis County	15,611	4,856	0.0	14.6	60.6	38.8	19.8	39.4	23.0
53045	Mason County	11,145	3,468	0.0	13.6	61.2	29.6	28.7	38.8	27.0
53053	Pierce County	188,696	63,371	0.9	18.8	66.3	32.4	32.3	33.7	25.5
53057	Skagit County	25,422	8,310	2.0	24.9	61.2	32.1	28.6	38.8	28.2
53061	Snohomish County	166,117	55,294	1.3	30.8	71.8	39.0	31.8	28.2	21.5
53063	Spokane County	103,259	34,732	0.7	10.5	69.7	37.3	31.1	30.3	22.8
53067	Thurston County	55,764	17,969	0.6	16.0	72.1	36.3	34.6	27.9	23.5
53071	Walla Walla County	12,318	3,976	0.0	33.1	60.2	39.2	17.5	39.8	34.2
53073	Whatcom County	40,258	13,066	0.7	19.3	68.3	34.1	33.8	31.7	22.1
53077	Yakima County	70,264	24,537	0.6	41.2	58.2	30.1	26.5	41.8	31.4

State/county FIPS code	State/County	Total own children 6 to 17	Nativity and parentage, age 6 to 17 years		Own children age 6 to 17 years living with two parents			Own children age 6 to 17 years living with one parent		Grand-children under 18 living with a grandparent householder	Grand-children under 18 living with a grandparent householder, as a percent of all children	Children for whom grandparent householders are responsible, as a percent of all children
			Child is foreign born, percent	One or more foreign-born parent, percent	Age 6 to 17 years living with two parents, percent	Both parents in labor force, percent	One parent in labor force, percent	Age 6 to 17 years living with one parent, percent	Parent in labor force, percent			
	Utah—cont'd											
49005	Cache County	22,439	2.5	13.6	85.1	48.3	35.6	14.9	13.1	1,324	3.7	2.1
49011	Davis County	68,138	1.3	10.4	80.0	42.1	37.4	20.0	18.0	5,238	5.0	2.2
49035	Salt Lake County	190,021	5.1	25.6	75.6	43.0	31.9	24.4	21.1	20,531	7.0	2.4
49045	Tooele County	14,001	0.8	7.8	84.1	43.9	38.4	15.9	13.6	1,514	7.5	3.8
49049	Utah County	116,849	2.5	15.9	86.6	38.0	47.2	13.4	11.2	9,271	5.0	2.0
49053	Washington County	25,894	2.2	13.3	71.1	38.6	31.6	28.9	22.9	2,039	5.1	2.3
49057	Weber County	42,836	3.1	16.1	73.7	45.8	27.5	26.3	22.5	4,376	6.5	3.2
50000	**Vermont**	82,240	2.1	6.5	68.9	52.6	15.3	31.1	25.3	6,307	5.3	2.6
50007	Chittenden County	19,961	5.1	11.6	72.7	56.7	15.3	27.3	23.6	1,317	4.5	1.8
50021	Rutland County	7,293	0.7	4.9	67.3	49.2	17.0	32.7	27.5	1,047	10.0	7.1
50023	Washington County	7,743	1.1	6.6	65.5	53.8	10.9	34.5	28.1	0	0.0	0.0
50027	Windsor County	7,364	0.9	5.3	65.8	46.1	19.4	34.2	28.8	543	5.2	2.0
51000	**Virginia**	1,180,855	4.5	20.8	69.2	45.9	22.1	30.8	25.9	131,873	7.4	3.8
51003	Albemarle County	14,108	2.4	18.4	80.7	54.8	24.7	19.3	14.7	1,183	5.7	1.8
51013	Arlington County	19,924	14.8	40.7	76.2	50.4	24.6	23.8	21.8	1,216	3.5	1.2
51015	Augusta County	10,028	0.6	3.5	72.1	46.9	24.1	27.9	20.5	1,423	10.0	4.2
51019	Bedford County	10,636	0.7	3.9	78.3	55.9	20.9	21.7	17.5	861	6.0	2.2
51031	Campbell County	7,933	0.4	3.3	68.8	43.1	21.0	31.2	26.3	1,036	9.4	5.8
51041	Chesterfield County	54,086	2.8	13.9	72.1	52.4	18.9	27.9	24.2	4,797	6.2	3.4
51059	Fairfax County	173,833	10.1	48.3	80.7	51.9	28.1	19.3	16.8	10,258	3.9	1.6
51061	Fauquier County	11,310	1.2	10.8	81.0	56.5	23.6	19.0	18.0	1,442	9.0	4.9
51067	Franklin County	7,619	1.7	5.2	73.9	44.7	24.9	26.1	22.8	969	9.0	4.3
51069	Frederick County	12,432	3.3	11.7	79.3	54.0	25.1	20.7	17.4	1,224	6.6	3.1
51085	Hanover County	17,036	1.6	8.2	80.8	58.6	21.3	19.2	16.1	1,441	6.3	2.0
51087	Henrico County	47,551	6.8	18.4	65.4	47.7	17.2	34.6	29.9	4,670	6.5	3.1
51089	Henry County	7,064	1.4	10.8	58.8	36.8	19.9	41.2	36.5	855	8.4	4.7
51095	James City County	9,845	2.7	9.2	72.8	51.5	20.5	27.2	23.6	1,359	9.6	4.3
51107	Loudoun County	66,464	6.8	38.0	84.6	55.7	28.4	15.4	14.7	2,950	3.0	1.6
51121	Montgomery County	9,472	3.0	12.3	73.2	51.4	17.9	26.8	22.6	0	0.0	0.0
51143	Pittsylvania County	8,138	1.9	4.7	66.2	45.7	18.3	33.8	24.8	1,450	12.3	7.2
51153	Prince William County	76,327	6.2	40.3	74.4	51.4	22.1	25.6	22.4	7,070	6.0	3.2
51161	Roanoke County	13,707	2.4	11.1	74.3	55.9	17.8	25.7	22.0	1,713	9.0	3.6
51165	Rockingham County	11,649	1.9	15.1	80.1	57.3	20.9	19.9	17.0	1,351	7.9	3.6
51177	Spotsylvania County	22,501	1.5	13.0	72.0	49.2	22.6	28.0	25.1	2,687	8.4	4.8
51179	Stafford County	25,248	3.5	16.9	74.8	47.5	26.6	25.2	21.4	2,699	7.6	4.8
51191	Washington County	6,629	1.7	4.4	71.4	43.3	28.0	28.6	20.3	750	7.7	4.6
51199	York County	11,642	2.4	15.3	81.8	48.2	33.4	18.2	15.0	580	3.7	2.3
51510	Alexandria city	13,139	17.7	45.6	63.8	37.4	24.7	36.2	30.6	1,172	4.7	2.6
51550	Chesapeake city	37,383	1.5	10.0	69.0	46.0	22.7	31.0	27.3	5,654	10.4	4.0
51650	Hampton city	17,927	2.4	9.8	47.2	31.1	15.7	52.8	42.9	2,909	10.3	5.1
51660	Harrisonburg city	4,769	21.3	53.4	60.4	32.4	26.0	39.6	38.8	0	0.0	0.0
51680	Lynchburg city	8,925	1.9	7.6	60.5	38.4	21.4	39.5	35.0	883	6.2	1.7
51700	Newport News city	25,166	2.6	12.5	49.5	32.3	16.3	50.5	43.9	4,052	9.9	5.3
51710	Norfolk city	28,029	2.6	10.3	45.7	30.3	13.9	54.3	46.4	5,719	12.2	6.7
51740	Portsmouth city	13,120	0.4	2.8	35.0	24.6	9.7	65.0	57.5	2,872	13.6	8.1
51760	Richmond city	20,940	1.3	11.9	37.2	25.5	11.0	62.8	43.8	3,104	8.5	5.0
51770	Roanoke city	12,069	6.0	12.8	45.7	35.6	9.7	54.3	45.8	1,879	9.4	6.7
51800	Suffolk city	13,733	1.0	5.5	60.6	42.1	16.8	39.4	33.0	1,924	9.3	6.5
51810	Virginia Beach city	66,337	2.9	14.9	62.9	40.9	21.2	37.1	31.3	7,379	7.4	3.8
53000	**Washington**	1,007,389	5.4	26.9	69.7	43.1	25.3	30.3	24.6	82,069	5.4	2.7
53005	Benton County	30,529	4.1	22.8	67.2	40.2	26.3	32.8	28.1	3,380	7.3	3.7
53007	Chelan County	11,448	5.1	35.7	73.1	48.3	24.4	26.9	22.7	881	5.2	2.7
53009	Clallam County	8,396	1.3	7.3	65.4	43.5	21.1	34.6	24.4	767	6.3	3.5
53011	Clark County	73,975	3.7	21.9	70.9	42.6	26.8	29.1	23.9	6,239	5.8	3.2
53015	Cowlitz County	15,259	2.9	10.9	66.5	41.5	23.2	33.5	27.3	2,165	9.5	4.9
53021	Franklin County	17,593	9.4	51.6	62.1	36.6	24.9	37.9	34.1	1,238	4.4	2.2
53025	Grant County	17,370	6.6	42.8	71.8	51.2	20.3	28.2	23.0	1,210	4.5	2.3
53027	Grays Harbor County	9,593	3.8	13.7	58.1	34.9	20.9	41.9	35.9	887	6.2	3.7
53029	Island County	9,837	3.0	10.8	76.7	49.6	25.5	23.3	16.2	428	2.9	1.6
53033	King County	266,426	8.9	38.1	72.5	44.9	26.7	27.5	22.9	17,185	4.2	1.7
53035	Kitsap County	35,428	1.7	11.6	70.4	41.2	28.0	29.6	22.9	2,556	4.9	3.0
53041	Lewis County	10,755	3.3	16.9	66.9	44.0	19.6	33.1	25.0	1,411	9.0	4.4
53045	Mason County	7,677	3.4	12.3	65.6	31.6	30.6	34.4	26.0	700	6.3	3.4
53053	Pierce County	125,325	4.2	19.8	67.4	42.2	24.1	32.6	26.3	11,886	6.3	3.0
53057	Skagit County	17,112	2.6	20.2	63.5	36.2	25.8	36.5	30.1	1,464	5.8	2.8
53061	Snohomish County	110,823	5.4	27.4	72.1	45.1	25.6	27.9	22.4	7,045	4.2	1.9
53063	Spokane County	68,527	2.6	10.3	68.4	41.9	24.5	31.6	25.7	5,131	5.0	2.7
53067	Thurston County	37,795	4.1	15.8	67.9	41.9	24.4	32.1	26.1	2,464	4.4	2.5
53071	Walla Walla County	8,342	4.7	26.2	72.1	44.4	24.3	27.9	20.3	535	4.3	3.0
53073	Whatcom County	27,192	5.2	28.0	74.0	46.0	26.7	26.0	20.2	1,888	4.7	2.8
53077	Yakima County	45,727	4.3	48.1	61.6	38.8	21.0	38.4	30.2	6,749	9.6	4.1

State/county FIPS code	State/County	Total own children under 18 in families and subfamilies	Own children under 6 years in families and subfamilies							
			Total own children under 6 years	Nativity and parentage, under 6 years		Own children under 6 years living with two parents			Own children under 6 living with one parent	
				Child is foreign born, percent	One or more foreign-born parent, percent	Total under 6 years living with two parents, percent	Both parents in labor force, percent	One parent in labor force, percent	Total under 6 years living with one parent, percent	Parent in labor force, percent
54000	**West Virginia**.........................	357,417	117,410	0.3	2.4	61.6	32.7	27.2	38.4	25.0
54003	Berkeley County.........................	24,379	8,079	0.6	6.9	64.2	38.9	24.2	35.8	28.4
54011	Cabell County...........................	17,989	6,138	0.5	2.7	59.9	33.8	25.0	40.1	26.7
54033	Harrison County.........................	13,412	4,634	0.0	1.7	62.3	39.3	22.1	37.7	23.0
54037	Jefferson County.........................	12,107	3,785	1.8	10.1	61.2	43.0	18.2	38.8	30.9
54039	Kanawha County.........................	36,563	11,662	0.0	1.5	57.6	32.9	23.9	42.4	32.9
54049	Marion County...........................	10,993	3,764	0.0	0.0	60.3	29.4	30.9	39.7	31.4
54055	Mercer County...........................	11,936	4,306	0.0	0.0	57.4	28.1	26.7	42.6	21.9
54061	Monongalia County....................	15,273	5,587	1.7	8.9	69.4	40.9	28.5	30.6	15.6
54079	Putnam County...........................	12,303	3,676	0.7	2.8	73.0	44.3	28.6	27.0	13.8
54081	Raleigh County...........................	15,515	5,443	0.0	0.0	61.5	27.9	30.0	38.5	28.8
54107	Wood County.............................	16,999	5,832	0.0	1.5	55.0	29.6	23.5	45.0	34.8
55000	**Wisconsin**..............................	1,261,858	407,831	0.9	11.8	66.9	45.6	20.5	33.1	27.2
55009	Brown County............................	59,346	19,806	0.5	18.3	67.0	48.7	18.1	33.0	27.4
55017	Chippewa County.......................	13,574	4,244	0.1	1.6	73.3	55.6	17.1	26.7	24.3
55021	Columbia County........................	12,492	4,081	0.2	2.1	69.8	52.4	16.8	30.2	26.2
55025	Dane County..............................	104,399	35,326	1.3	18.4	73.1	55.3	17.7	26.9	23.1
55027	Dodge County............................	17,953	5,591	1.8	4.3	65.8	42.6	22.5	34.2	31.3
55035	Eau Claire County......................	20,131	7,012	0.8	9.3	75.3	50.3	25.0	24.7	21.5
55039	Fond du Lac County....................	21,963	6,948	3.4	11.4	71.2	47.7	23.5	28.8	25.2
55043	Grant County.............................	9,998	3,075	0.0	1.6	74.3	55.0	17.0	25.7	21.4
55055	Jefferson County........................	18,542	5,538	0.4	14.5	72.7	50.0	22.5	27.3	25.4
55059	Kenosha County.........................	39,413	12,441	0.9	14.3	58.5	34.9	23.5	41.5	32.6
55063	La Crosse County.......................	23,350	7,631	1.3	6.2	78.4	65.2	13.1	21.6	16.5
55071	Manitowoc County.....................	16,850	5,311	1.4	6.0	73.8	47.3	26.2	26.2	19.7
55073	Marathon County.......................	30,987	9,940	0.2	13.6	73.6	49.5	23.7	26.4	21.7
55079	Milwaukee County......................	223,653	80,171	1.2	18.3	49.4	32.3	16.4	50.6	40.5
55087	Outagamie County.....................	42,704	13,896	0.7	8.2	72.0	50.7	20.8	28.0	23.9
55089	Ozaukee County........................	19,199	5,091	0.5	5.1	83.1	51.9	29.0	16.9	14.2
55097	Portage County..........................	13,572	4,277	0.1	7.4	72.6	43.0	29.5	27.4	25.4
55101	Racine County............................	45,381	14,464	0.3	13.1	58.8	36.9	21.5	41.2	32.7
55105	Rock County..............................	36,293	11,395	0.3	9.0	56.7	35.5	20.6	43.3	30.5
55109	St. Croix County.........................	22,243	6,883	1.6	1.6	74.6	56.4	17.6	25.4	22.7
55111	Sauk County.............................	14,355	4,634	0.2	8.8	70.9	52.5	16.0	29.1	23.7
55117	Sheboygan County.....................	25,757	8,493	0.9	15.9	68.4	46.8	21.5	31.6	26.1
55127	Walworth County.......................	22,485	6,653	0.9	18.0	67.1	44.3	22.7	32.9	28.2
55131	Washington County....................	30,734	8,726	0.7	6.2	79.9	58.6	20.9	20.1	18.4
55133	Waukesha County......................	88,476	25,489	1.5	13.2	85.4	57.5	27.3	14.6	12.9
55135	Waupaca County........................	10,652	3,423	0.1	5.2	71.6	44.5	27.1	28.4	26.5
55139	Winnebago County.....................	34,003	11,478	0.6	8.5	69.8	46.2	23.1	30.2	23.2
55141	Wood County.............................	15,634	4,971	0.8	7.2	66.4	49.0	17.0	33.6	30.9
56000	**Wyoming**..............................	130,758	45,079	0.4	9.3	71.0	41.6	28.6	29.0	24.2
56021	Laramie County..........................	21,237	7,360	0.4	9.6	73.0	42.0	28.5	27.0	23.7
56025	Natrona County.........................	17,445	6,231	0.0	8.8	61.8	33.3	28.5	38.2	30.1

Table D-2: Counties with a Population of 50,000 or More—Children—*Continued*

State/county FIPS code	State/County	Own children age 6 to 17 years in families and subfamilies								Grand-children under 18 living with a grandparent householder	Grand-children under 18 living with a grandparent householder, as a percent of all children	Children for whom grandparent householders are responsible, as a percent of all children
		Total own children 6 to 17	Nativity and parentage, age 6 to 17 years		Own children age 6 to 17 years living with two parents			Own children age 6 to 17 years living with one parent				
			Child is foreign born, percent	One or more foreign-born parent, percent	Age 6 to 17 years living with two parents, percent	Both parents in labor force, percent	One parent in labor force, percent	Age 6 to 17 years living with one parent, percent	Parent in labor force, percent			
54000	**West Virginia**	240,007	0.8	2.7	65.6	38.9	24.2	34.4	24.8	33,480	9.4	5.7
54003	Berkeley County	16,300	1.5	7.8	64.5	40.3	23.0	35.5	27.4	1,510	6.2	3.0
54011	Cabell County	11,851	0.9	5.2	56.9	39.1	16.7	43.1	30.1	1,051	5.8	3.7
54033	Harrison County	8,778	0.3	0.7	65.8	41.0	23.2	34.2	25.4	1,625	12.1	5.3
54037	Jefferson County	8,322	5.5	9.9	69.5	43.0	26.4	30.5	25.8	1,070	8.8	5.1
54039	Kanawha County	24,901	1.0	2.9	59.7	39.8	18.9	40.3	31.3	3,202	8.8	5.7
54049	Marion County	7,229	0.0	0.0	61.9	41.9	18.9	38.1	32.5	831	7.6	4.5
54055	Mercer County	7,630	0.0	0.0	63.8	30.4	29.8	36.2	22.5	1,372	11.5	7.9
54061	Monongalia County	9,686	2.4	9.3	71.6	43.9	26.7	28.4	21.7	673	4.4	3.0
54079	Putnam County	8,627	1.3	2.6	68.9	43.3	25.4	31.1	22.8	737	6.0	4.7
54081	Raleigh County	10,072	0.0	0.0	64.9	34.5	28.5	35.1	22.8	1,605	10.3	7.2
54107	Wood County	11,167	0.3	2.0	62.1	40.6	20.1	37.9	33.2	1,447	8.5	5.3
55000	**Wisconsin**	854,027	2.5	10.1	68.9	50.8	17.1	31.1	26.4	56,875	4.5	2.2
55009	Brown County	39,540	2.7	12.8	71.2	54.3	15.7	28.8	24.6	2,861	4.8	2.9
55017	Chippewa County	9,330	0.6	3.4	74.4	55.6	17.8	25.6	22.4	607	4.5	2.3
55021	Columbia County	8,411	0.7	3.3	71.7	57.7	14.0	28.3	24.9	321	2.6	1.2
55025	Dane County	69,073	4.7	15.6	70.0	54.5	14.5	30.0	25.6	2,752	2.6	1.0
55027	Dodge County	12,362	2.1	4.1	72.8	55.6	16.6	27.2	23.9	1,166	6.5	3.2
55035	Eau Claire County	13,119	3.1	6.9	72.1	53.9	18.0	27.9	25.6	572	2.8	1.3
55039	Fond du Lac County	15,015	2.3	6.4	71.4	57.5	13.7	28.6	26.3	605	2.8	0.7
55043	Grant County	6,923	1.5	1.6	80.4	64.5	14.6	19.6	17.8	347	3.5	1.8
55055	Jefferson County	13,004	0.9	8.0	73.9	59.5	14.2	26.1	24.0	872	4.7	2.0
55059	Kenosha County	26,972	1.3	14.8	61.1	43.3	17.6	38.9	33.6	2,699	6.8	2.8
55063	La Crosse County	15,719	2.6	8.3	69.8	57.1	12.6	30.2	26.2	835	3.6	2.2
55071	Manitowoc County	11,539	1.1	5.7	74.2	55.4	17.4	25.8	23.5	487	2.9	0.6
55073	Marathon County	21,047	1.6	10.1	75.5	56.5	18.2	24.5	21.7	862	2.8	1.3
55079	Milwaukee County	143,482	4.6	17.9	50.3	34.7	14.7	49.7	39.5	14,739	6.6	3.7
55087	Outagamie County	28,808	1.8	8.4	75.2	56.9	17.8	24.8	22.5	1,483	3.5	1.5
55089	Ozaukee County	14,108	1.9	8.1	83.7	57.0	26.1	16.3	14.6	468	2.4	0.8
55097	Portage County	9,295	0.9	9.2	79.4	54.9	24.4	20.6	19.2	441	3.2	1.3
55101	Racine County	30,917	1.5	10.8	64.2	44.1	19.1	35.8	29.1	2,816	6.2	3.5
55105	Rock County	24,898	2.7	12.2	64.9	44.9	18.6	35.1	27.5	2,392	6.6	3.1
55109	St. Croix County	15,360	1.0	3.6	77.0	59.1	16.1	23.0	22.2	940	4.2	1.1
55111	Sauk County	9,721	0.9	7.6	69.6	54.3	14.1	30.4	28.3	484	3.4	1.3
55117	Sheboygan County	17,264	4.2	12.6	72.9	56.6	16.1	27.1	23.6	725	2.8	1.3
55127	Walworth County	15,832	1.7	13.9	68.4	48.8	19.2	31.6	27.8	1,606	7.1	2.4
55131	Washington County	22,008	1.3	4.8	76.0	58.1	17.7	24.0	21.7	854	2.8	0.9
55133	Waukesha County	62,987	2.4	9.6	82.6	60.2	22.0	17.4	15.6	2,212	2.5	0.7
55135	Waupaca County	7,229	0.7	3.3	78.5	59.8	18.0	21.5	16.9	521	4.9	2.7
55139	Winnebago County	22,525	1.5	8.9	70.7	50.9	19.7	29.3	23.5	1,101	3.2	1.3
55141	Wood County	10,663	2.2	5.6	68.8	52.7	14.5	31.2	28.2	643	4.1	2.2
56000	**Wyoming**	85,679	2.3	8.2	69.5	47.8	20.9	30.5	26.0	6,246	4.8	2.9
56021	Laramie County	13,877	0.8	3.3	64.8	47.1	16.9	35.2	31.1	977	4.6	2.3
56025	Natrona County	11,214	0.4	5.6	65.3	49.3	16.0	34.7	27.2	919	5.3	3.8

Table D-3: Metropolitan Areas—Children

CBSA FIPS code	Metropolitan area	Total own children under 18 in families and subfamilies	Own children under 6 years in families and subfamilies							
			Total own children under 6 years	Nativity and parentage, under 6 years		Own children under 6 years living with two parents			Own children under 6 living with one parent	
				Child is foreign born, percent	One or more foreign-born parent, percent	Total under 6 years living with two parents, percent	Both parents in labor force, percent	One parent in labor force, percent	Total under 6 years living with one parent, percent	Parent in labor force, percent
10180	Abilene, TX	36,145	12,605	0.5	8.7	59.1	30.7	28.5	40.9	28.4
10420	Akron, OH	145,273	45,472	0.8	7.9	58.7	38.5	19.3	41.3	32.7
10500	Albany, GA	35,737	12,658	0.5	5.7	37.6	25.1	11.5	62.4	47.8
10540	Albany, OR	26,248	8,856	0.1	10.4	63.0	31.3	29.1	37.0	23.5
10580	Albany-Schenectady-Troy, NY	174,159	53,924	1.6	13.0	65.3	44.5	20.2	34.7	27.9
10740	Albuquerque, NM	205,107	68,252	0.9	18.9	56.2	29.2	25.7	43.8	33.0
10780	Alexandria, LA	36,328	12,065	0.5	4.6	54.3	33.5	19.4	45.7	30.1
10900	Allentown-Bethlehem-Easton, PA-NJ	175,500	53,114	1.2	16.0	63.2	41.8	20.0	36.8	28.0
11020	Altoona, PA	24,827	8,264	0.0	1.9	57.3	37.8	19.2	42.7	35.4
11100	Amarillo, TX	62,541	22,136	1.9	17.9	61.6	37.0	23.7	38.4	29.1
11180	Ames, IA	15,414	5,367	1.7	14.2	85.4	54.0	30.6	14.6	12.9
11260	Anchorage, AK	97,369	33,668	0.3	12.9	68.6	36.9	30.0	31.4	26.5
11460	Ann Arbor, MI	68,372	21,426	2.9	23.6	71.4	39.6	30.6	28.6	23.9
11500	Anniston-Oxford-Jacksonville, AL	23,927	7,931	0.0	5.3	50.3	29.5	20.4	49.7	42.9
11540	Appleton, WI	55,249	17,741	0.7	9.0	75.1	52.2	22.2	24.9	21.7
11700	Asheville, NC	81,663	26,536	0.9	15.5	64.5	38.9	24.3	35.5	26.5
12020	Athens-Clarke County, GA	38,328	13,532	1.5	20.4	63.4	36.2	26.6	36.6	26.5
12060	Atlanta-Sandy Springs-Roswell, GA	1,344,696	437,264	1.6	27.5	63.5	37.1	25.4	36.5	29.0
12100	Atlantic City-Hammonton, NJ	59,204	19,104	2.1	29.5	54.1	35.6	17.8	45.9	34.8
12220	Auburn-Opelika, AL	30,348	10,798	0.7	8.4	65.2	35.8	28.3	34.8	31.0
12260	Augusta-Richmond County, GA-SC	131,202	43,453	0.4	11.0	53.9	29.3	24.0	46.1	34.5
12420	Austin-Round Rock, TX	435,358	152,418	1.6	32.6	71.2	39.1	31.3	28.8	22.5
12540	Bakersfield, CA	242,192	84,165	1.1	39.9	55.8	27.5	26.2	44.2	30.7
12580	Baltimore-Columbia-Towson, MD	591,230	198,774	1.3	19.0	61.8	40.5	20.6	38.2	29.4
12620	Bangor, ME	27,263	8,516	0.6	5.5	68.2	44.4	22.1	31.8	23.1
12700	Barnstable Town, MA	34,312	9,396	0.1	15.3	69.8	48.6	21.3	30.2	25.6
12940	Baton Rouge, LA	185,429	63,143	0.5	7.7	52.6	35.9	16.2	47.4	36.8
12980	Battle Creek, MI	29,833	9,608	0.3	5.3	50.9	33.8	16.8	49.1	40.1
13020	Bay City, MI	22,123	6,945	0.0	2.3	64.1	44.7	18.2	35.9	20.2
13140	Beaumont-Port Arthur, TX	90,869	30,709	0.6	18.9	54.7	25.2	28.5	45.3	32.8
13220	Beckley, WV	24,253	8,573	0.0	0.0	62.4	27.5	32.5	37.6	27.3
13380	Bellingham, WA	40,258	13,066	0.7	19.3	68.3	34.1	33.8	31.7	22.1
13460	Bend-Redmond, OR	34,674	10,860	0.8	13.7	69.2	37.3	31.2	30.8	22.9
13740	Billings, MT	35,213	11,957	0.0	4.6	62.0	37.6	23.9	38.0	32.1
13780	Binghamton, NY	47,871	14,951	0.6	7.8	61.4	35.5	24.4	38.6	27.0
13820	Birmingham-Hoover, AL	252,619	85,549	0.7	11.2	62.9	35.5	26.5	37.1	27.3
13900	Bismarck, ND	26,617	9,840	0.0	2.0	71.3	56.5	14.7	28.7	24.1
13980	Blacksburg-Christiansburg-Radford, VA	28,741	9,269	2.4	8.8	72.5	38.1	30.8	27.5	23.6
14010	Bloomington, IL	40,547	13,482	2.2	12.4	68.7	46.0	22.5	31.3	27.5
14020	Bloomington, IN	26,698	8,923	1.7	13.9	74.8	37.8	35.5	25.2	19.3
14100	Bloomsburg-Berwick, PA	14,953	4,587	0.2	4.0	71.7	46.2	23.9	28.3	20.6
14260	Boise City, ID	167,123	53,655	1.2	15.4	75.4	37.9	36.9	24.6	18.2
14460	Boston-Cambridge-Newton, MA-NH	946,194	304,544	2.3	33.7	71.9	48.0	23.1	28.1	21.7
14500	Boulder, CO	61,282	19,544	1.3	25.2	77.7	42.3	35.3	22.3	18.4
14540	Bowling Green, KY	34,069	11,322	2.0	11.6	64.9	40.7	22.5	35.1	29.5
14740	Bremerton-Silverdale, WA	51,947	16,519	1.0	11.7	74.5	35.2	38.0	25.5	14.9
14860	Bridgeport-Stamford-Norwalk, CT	218,731	66,091	2.3	37.5	74.2	41.4	32.3	25.8	20.7
15180	Brownsville-Harlingen, TX	126,746	41,270	1.4	43.0	53.3	22.1	27.4	46.7	29.2
15260	Brunswick, GA	24,551	8,057	1.0	13.3	44.7	26.8	15.4	55.3	40.3
15380	Buffalo-Cheektowaga-Niagara Falls, NY	228,472	70,844	1.5	11.1	59.6	37.3	20.6	40.4	30.7
15500	Burlington, NC	33,329	11,035	0.1	23.2	55.1	33.6	21.2	44.9	35.3
15540	Burlington-South Burlington, VT	41,980	13,307	1.1	11.8	68.0	48.1	19.4	32.0	21.9
15680	California-Lexington Park, MD	26,621	9,005	0.1	14.9	74.7	46.4	27.9	25.3	21.9
15940	Canton-Massillon, OH	85,708	26,273	0.3	3.3	57.7	36.0	20.0	42.3	33.8
15980	Cape Coral-Fort Myers, FL	117,509	38,611	1.3	28.7	54.6	31.9	21.8	45.4	33.7
16020	Cape Girardeau, MO-IL	20,469	7,142	0.0	2.9	57.7	43.7	13.0	42.3	28.2
16060	Carbondale-Marion, IL	23,649	8,024	1.1	9.8	63.8	39.7	20.6	36.2	28.4
16180	Carson City, NV	11,174	3,401	0.0	27.3	65.7	30.5	35.0	34.3	22.2
16220	Casper, WY	17,445	6,231	0.0	8.8	61.8	33.3	28.5	38.2	30.1
16300	Cedar Rapids, IA	60,114	19,263	0.7	5.7	69.9	53.2	16.5	30.1	26.4
16540	Chambersburg-Waynesboro, PA	33,828	11,410	0.5	9.6	70.1	38.5	30.9	29.9	25.9
16580	Champaign-Urbana, IL	44,020	15,465	1.9	17.7	68.5	41.8	26.5	31.5	25.8
16620	Charleston, WV	44,083	14,492	0.0	1.2	59.9	32.5	26.1	40.1	29.6
16700	Charleston-North Charleston, SC	150,383	54,512	0.3	10.5	59.5	35.9	22.8	40.5	33.1
16740	Charlotte-Concord-Gastonia, NC-SC	550,050	179,330	1.3	22.2	63.5	38.4	24.3	36.5	29.6
16820	Charlottesville, VA	43,179	14,864	2.3	17.9	69.5	39.4	29.2	30.5	22.7
16860	Chattanooga, TN-GA	109,773	36,218	0.9	8.3	59.2	32.3	25.3	40.8	31.8
16940	Cheyenne, WY	21,237	7,360	0.4	9.6	73.0	42.0	28.5	27.0	23.7
16980	Chicago-Naperville-Elgin, IL-IN-WI	2,234,037	719,639	1.7	33.8	65.5	38.6	26.2	34.5	27.2
17020	Chico, CA	41,993	13,432	0.3	15.2	64.4	34.2	27.5	35.6	22.3

Table D-3: Metropolitan Areas—Children—*Continued*

CBSA FIPS code	Metropolitan area	Total own children 6 to 17	Child is foreign born, percent	One or more foreign-born parent, percent	Age 6 to 17 years living with two parents, percent	Both parents in labor force, percent	One parent in labor force, percent	Age 6 to 17 years living with one parent, percent	Parent in labor force, percent	Grand-children under 18 living with a grandparent householder	Grand-children under 18 living with a grandparent householder, as a percent of all children	Children for whom grandparent householders are responsible, as a percent of all children
10180	Abilene, TX	23,540	1.6	11.4	64.3	39.5	23.2	35.7	27.9	3,764	10.4	7.8
10420	Akron, OH	99,801	2.8	6.6	64.6	44.1	19.1	35.4	28.0	10,354	7.1	4.1
10500	Albany, GA	23,079	1.0	4.9	48.3	32.1	14.5	51.7	41.3	4,436	12.4	9.0
10540	Albany, OR	17,392	1.6	8.7	65.3	42.9	21.9	34.7	23.5	1,900	7.2	3.7
10580	Albany-Schenectady-Troy, NY	120,235	3.9	11.9	67.9	50.1	16.9	32.1	26.8	10,172	5.8	3.2
10740	Albuquerque, NM	136,855	4.5	20.9	58.7	36.2	20.9	41.3	32.9	17,001	8.3	4.7
10780	Alexandria, LA	24,263	1.6	5.2	58.4	38.3	19.5	41.6	32.1	3,438	9.5	5.9
10900	Allentown-Bethlehem-Easton, PA-NJ	122,386	3.2	16.4	67.2	44.7	21.0	32.8	25.8	12,022	6.9	2.8
11020	Altoona, PA	16,563	0.8	2.9	69.3	47.4	20.4	30.7	25.5	1,985	8.0	4.5
11100	Amarillo, TX	40,405	4.0	19.3	64.8	42.4	22.1	35.2	28.7	4,932	7.9	5.0
11180	Ames, IA	10,047	4.4	12.5	76.8	61.6	13.2	23.2	21.7	...	...	...
11260	Anchorage, AK	63,741	4.4	16.5	69.3	43.0	24.4	30.7	25.0	5,652	5.8	2.9
11460	Ann Arbor, MI	46,946	4.9	19.7	70.9	46.5	23.8	29.1	24.7	3,030	4.4	2.3
11500	Anniston-Oxford-Jacksonville, AL	15,996	0.3	4.9	61.4	39.2	20.7	38.6	33.0	3,493	14.6	7.8
11540	Appleton, WI	37,508	1.6	8.5	76.3	57.6	18.4	23.7	21.1	1,762	3.2	1.4
11700	Asheville, NC	55,127	3.4	11.8	64.1	42.3	20.1	35.9	29.7	6,624	8.1	5.2
12020	Athens-Clarke County, GA	24,796	3.3	15.8	67.7	42.0	24.0	32.3	25.0	2,896	7.6	4.2
12060	Atlanta-Sandy Springs-Roswell, GA	907,432	4.8	24.3	64.0	40.5	22.6	36.0	30.4	108,242	8.0	4.5
12100	Atlantic City-Hammonton, NJ	40,100	7.3	27.0	56.5	39.4	16.2	43.5	37.4	5,918	10.0	4.7
12220	Auburn-Opelika, AL	19,550	3.3	7.4	68.5	41.6	25.2	31.5	27.0	2,730	9.0	6.1
12260	Augusta-Richmond County, GA-SC	87,749	1.7	7.8	55.7	35.0	19.4	44.3	32.9	13,564	10.3	6.6
12420	Austin-Round Rock, TX	282,940	6.0	31.9	69.6	43.7	25.1	30.4	26.1	27,739	6.4	3.5
12540	Bakersfield, CA	158,027	6.1	46.2	62.3	35.4	25.2	37.7	29.9	21,097	8.7	4.3
12580	Baltimore-Columbia-Towson, MD	392,456	4.3	16.0	62.0	44.3	16.9	38.0	31.9	53,658	9.1	4.4
12620	Bangor, ME	18,747	2.1	6.1	69.0	46.5	20.6	31.0	22.6	1,526	5.6	3.0
12700	Barnstable Town, MA	24,916	3.0	9.9	62.6	48.0	13.8	37.4	31.4	2,048	6.0	2.7
12940	Baton Rouge, LA	122,286	1.0	5.7	55.9	38.5	16.6	44.1	36.9	20,834	11.2	6.7
12980	Battle Creek, MI	20,225	2.2	6.4	60.4	42.5	16.7	39.6	31.3	2,333	7.8	3.6
13020	Bay City, MI	15,178	0.9	3.5	65.1	48.8	15.4	34.9	28.6	1,284	5.8	3.2
13140	Beaumont-Port Arthur, TX	60,160	3.5	17.8	59.0	34.1	23.9	41.0	33.9	10,599	11.7	7.2
13220	Beckley, WV	15,680	0.0	0.0	63.7	31.1	29.5	36.3	23.3	2,787	11.5	8.0
13380	Bellingham, WA	27,192	5.2	28.0	74.0	46.0	26.7	26.0	20.2	1,888	4.7	2.8
13460	Bend-Redmond, OR	23,814	2.9	9.9	75.8	49.1	25.2	24.2	19.9	1,606	4.6	2.3
13740	Billings, MT	23,256	0.7	3.5	69.6	50.4	18.8	30.4	26.0	2,519	7.2	4.1
13780	Binghamton, NY	32,920	2.8	8.2	65.6	47.3	17.2	34.4	27.1	2,751	5.7	2.3
13820	Birmingham-Hoover, AL	167,070	2.5	7.6	63.4	39.8	22.5	36.6	29.2	25,226	10.0	6.2
13900	Bismarck, ND	16,777	0.4	1.7	71.4	58.1	13.1	28.6	26.0	1,403	5.3	2.3
13980	Blacksburg-Christiansburg-Radford, VA	19,472	1.7	6.9	68.6	47.4	18.0	31.4	25.6	2,429	8.5	5.4
14010	Bloomington, IL	27,065	4.6	8.4	72.2	56.2	15.7	27.8	24.8	2,151	5.3	2.9
14020	Bloomington, IN	17,775	2.1	6.1	68.5	45.9	22.0	31.5	24.6	1,103	4.1	1.5
14100	Bloomsburg-Berwick, PA	10,366	0.9	4.7	69.3	51.9	15.7	30.7	24.0	925	6.2	3.1
14260	Boise City, ID	113,468	2.7	15.4	70.6	41.1	28.1	29.4	24.4	7,697	4.6	2.3
14460	Boston-Cambridge-Newton, MA-NH	641,650	5.6	27.6	71.3	51.0	19.5	28.7	23.4	52,922	5.6	2.2
14500	Boulder, CO	41,738	6.0	25.2	73.3	46.8	26.0	26.7	24.0	1,988	3.2	1.4
14540	Bowling Green, KY	22,747	6.3	12.3	69.9	45.8	20.6	30.1	24.4	2,104	6.2	4.1
14740	Bremerton-Silverdale, WA	35,428	1.7	11.6	70.4	41.2	28.0	29.6	22.9	2,556	4.9	3.0
14860	Bridgeport-Stamford-Norwalk, CT	152,640	6.6	31.2	73.0	44.4	27.8	27.0	23.7	11,069	5.1	2.0
15180	Brownsville-Harlingen, TX	85,476	5.6	53.0	59.4	29.1	26.7	40.6	28.9	18,795	14.8	6.3
15260	Brunswick, GA	16,494	1.8	8.3	56.2	39.2	15.7	43.8	37.5	3,760	15.3	13.0
15380	Buffalo-Cheektowaga-Niagara Falls, NY	157,628	3.3	9.1	63.1	43.8	17.5	36.9	29.4	11,760	5.1	2.6
15500	Burlington, NC	22,294	2.5	20.6	58.3	38.8	18.6	41.7	35.1	3,012	9.0	4.8
15540	Burlington-South Burlington, VT	28,673	3.8	9.5	72.2	56.4	15.1	27.8	23.1	2,262	5.4	2.4
15680	California-Lexington Park, MD	17,616	0.8	7.1	76.9	51.2	25.4	23.1	19.5	1,539	5.8	2.6
15940	Canton-Massillon, OH	59,435	1.0	3.0	65.6	44.1	20.5	34.4	28.3	5,997	7.0	3.6
15980	Cape Coral-Fort Myers, FL	78,898	5.7	33.5	61.5	39.8	20.5	38.5	31.9	6,669	5.7	3.5
16020	Cape Girardeau, MO-IL	13,327	0.3	1.8	66.8	49.3	15.8	33.2	25.4	1,295	6.3	2.5
16060	Carbondale-Marion, IL	15,625	1.9	4.5	62.5	45.8	15.3	37.5	30.4	1,443	6.1	3.6
16180	Carson City, NV	7,773	6.7	33.5	60.0	47.4	11.4	40.0	36.2	1,175	10.5	8.0
16220	Casper, WY	11,214	0.4	5.6	65.3	49.3	16.0	34.7	27.2	919	5.3	3.8
16300	Cedar Rapids, IA	40,851	0.6	4.6	71.2	56.2	14.7	28.8	25.5	2,858	4.8	2.6
16540	Chambersburg-Waynesboro, PA	22,418	0.8	8.5	70.8	49.1	20.4	29.2	26.2	1,641	4.9	1.9
16580	Champaign-Urbana, IL	28,555	4.1	13.3	66.8	48.7	17.6	33.2	29.0	2,071	4.7	3.6
16620	Charleston, WV	29,591	0.9	2.8	60.2	37.8	20.6	39.8	29.5	4,082	9.3	6.1
16700	Charleston-North Charleston, SC	95,871	1.6	7.6	60.0	39.5	19.7	40.0	33.2	15,634	10.4	6.9
16740	Charlotte-Concord-Gastonia, NC-SC	370,720	3.8	18.2	65.7	42.6	22.2	34.3	29.5	40,619	7.4	4.5
16820	Charlottesville, VA	28,315	3.3	12.3	70.5	45.8	23.0	29.5	23.5	3,035	7.0	2.7
16860	Chattanooga, TN-GA	73,555	1.8	6.8	64.3	43.9	19.3	35.7	28.3	11,874	10.8	7.8
16940	Cheyenne, WY	13,877	0.8	3.3	64.8	47.1	16.9	35.2	31.1	977	4.6	2.3
16980	Chicago-Naperville-Elgin, IL-IN-WI	1,514,398	5.0	32.8	67.4	43.1	23.4	32.6	27.5	172,024	7.7	3.6
17020	Chico, CA	28,561	2.5	19.0	64.4	39.0	22.8	35.6	26.8	3,563	8.5	5.0

Table D-3: Metropolitan Areas—Children—*Continued*

			Own children under 6 years in families and subfamilies							
				Nativity and parentage, under 6 years		Own children under 6 years living with two parents			Own children under 6 living with one parent	
CBSA FIPS code	Metropolitan area	Total own children under 18 in families and subfamilies	Total own children under 6 years	Child is foreign born, percent	One or more foreign-born parent, percent	Total under 6 years living with two parents, percent	Both parents in labor force, percent	One parent in labor force, percent	Total under 6 years living with one parent, percent	Parent in labor force, percent
17140	Cincinnati, OH-KY-IN	495,259	164,082	1.1	9.4	61.1	38.6	21.7	38.9	29.9
17300	Clarksville, TN-KY	71,543	27,566	0.2	10.0	66.8	28.2	37.7	33.2	23.5
17420	Cleveland, TN	24,212	7,364	0.1	10.6	69.1	39.2	27.0	30.9	21.8
17460	Cleveland-Elyria, OH	443,886	137,784	0.8	10.8	59.8	38.0	20.8	40.2	31.4
17660	Coeur d'Alene, ID	32,219	10,729	2.3	7.3	71.4	35.3	35.9	28.6	20.6
17780	College Station-Bryan, TX	47,205	17,285	0.9	23.4	61.7	33.3	27.2	38.3	32.1
17820	Colorado Springs, CO	162,706	55,251	0.8	14.3	70.1	34.4	34.9	29.9	23.2
17860	Columbia, MO	33,536	11,874	1.0	10.5	70.0	38.7	27.4	30.0	24.1
17900	Columbia, SC	170,886	55,938	0.9	10.6	58.7	35.1	22.3	41.3	32.5
17980	Columbus, GA-AL	72,292	25,833	1.4	7.8	54.5	26.0	28.3	45.5	34.4
18020	Columbus, IN	17,635	5,552	2.8	17.6	65.8	37.9	27.3	34.2	28.7
18140	Columbus, OH	452,292	154,605	1.1	17.2	65.0	42.9	21.6	35.0	27.4
18580	Corpus Christi, TX	105,163	34,322	0.5	11.1	49.4	26.0	22.8	50.6	35.3
18700	Corvallis, OR	14,164	4,631	2.1	24.1	75.6	32.3	36.8	24.4	14.6
18880	Crestview-Fort Walton Beach-Destin, FL	50,736	17,744	0.6	14.2	62.1	32.1	29.3	37.9	29.1
19060	Cumberland, MD-WV	17,770	5,615	0.8	2.2	59.6	34.2	23.5	40.4	27.7
19100	Dallas-Fort Worth-Arlington, TX	1,746,025	582,530	1.7	37.2	65.2	34.3	30.1	34.8	27.3
19140	Dalton, GA	36,122	11,305	1.3	39.7	64.1	37.4	26.3	35.9	25.8
19180	Danville, IL	18,180	6,095	0.0	3.9	46.2	28.5	17.0	53.8	45.7
19300	Daphne-Fairhope-Foley, AL	41,970	13,637	0.9	8.4	66.0	37.8	28.2	34.0	23.2
19340	Davenport-Moline-Rock Island, IA-IL	85,539	28,757	1.5	10.9	60.5	40.6	18.9	39.5	32.6
19380	Dayton, OH	171,172	55,519	0.9	6.8	53.7	31.2	21.3	46.3	37.8
19460	Decatur, AL	33,729	10,681	0.4	15.0	64.6	34.9	29.7	35.4	28.5
19500	Decatur, IL	23,495	7,865	0.8	6.2	50.3	33.8	16.3	49.7	44.7
19660	Deltona-Daytona Beach-Ormond Beach, FL	103,780	33,193	1.2	14.9	58.6	31.9	26.2	41.4	29.8
19740	Denver-Aurora-Lakewood, CO	618,257	208,450	1.6	26.9	70.6	41.1	28.6	29.4	23.1
19780	Des Moines-West Des Moines, IA	146,927	50,702	2.0	16.2	71.9	51.2	20.0	28.1	23.0
19820	Detroit-Warren-Dearborn, MI	967,539	297,712	1.5	18.8	60.8	35.2	24.1	39.2	30.3
20020	Dothan, AL	32,544	10,350	0.1	4.8	55.0	38.6	15.7	45.0	33.0
20100	Dover, DE	37,576	12,618	0.2	10.5	58.0	31.8	24.4	42.0	33.0
20220	Dubuque, IA	21,507	7,117	1.6	2.7	70.1	54.3	15.1	29.9	24.1
20260	Duluth, MN-WI	53,663	17,926	0.4	2.4	61.0	39.1	20.7	39.0	33.6
20500	Durham-Chapel Hill, NC	109,200	37,652	1.8	29.0	59.4	37.9	20.1	40.6	31.7
20700	East Stroudsburg, PA	35,730	8,956	0.0	20.9	56.5	32.6	23.3	43.5	36.9
20740	Eau Claire, WI	33,705	11,256	0.6	6.4	74.5	52.3	22.0	25.5	22.6
20940	El Centro, CA	48,311	17,323	1.0	48.7	52.2	28.9	23.0	47.8	33.1
21060	Elizabethtown-Fort Knox, KY	36,560	12,575	0.3	4.1	53.6	27.8	23.9	46.4	36.7
21140	Elkhart-Goshen, IN	53,568	18,386	1.0	24.1	62.6	30.6	30.2	37.4	28.1
21300	Elmira, NY	18,464	5,982	3.1	7.3	59.9	33.6	26.1	40.1	32.3
21340	El Paso, TX	231,141	77,991	1.2	36.8	61.5	28.7	31.6	38.5	25.4
21500	Erie, PA	58,835	18,721	1.8	9.5	54.3	33.3	20.1	45.7	36.0
21660	Eugene, OR	65,127	20,644	1.5	12.7	60.5	30.4	27.6	39.5	28.3
21780	Evansville, IN-KY	67,210	23,089	0.3	6.1	60.8	39.2	20.3	39.2	31.6
21820	Fairbanks, AK	24,366	9,318	0.2	10.4	66.0	34.1	31.9	34.0	26.9
22020	Fargo, ND-MN	47,045	17,623	1.7	11.1	73.4	56.0	16.6	26.6	21.4
22140	Farmington, NM	33,624	11,497	0.6	7.8	58.0	30.1	26.9	42.0	29.5
22180	Fayetteville, NC	95,235	36,513	0.4	10.9	57.5	25.2	31.0	42.5	32.6
22220	Fayetteville-Springdale-Rogers, AR-MO	122,284	41,647	2.2	28.1	73.3	37.2	35.2	26.7	20.1
22380	Flagstaff, AZ	29,100	9,808	0.3	11.7	50.5	28.8	20.2	49.5	34.9
22420	Flint, MI	95,068	29,631	0.3	3.2	46.3	28.9	16.3	53.7	39.5
22500	Florence, SC	46,563	15,431	0.1	3.5	43.5	31.7	11.4	56.5	42.0
22520	Florence-Muscle Shoals, AL	29,298	8,916	0.0	4.6	62.1	37.3	24.2	37.9	16.4
22540	Fond du Lac, WI	21,963	6,948	3.4	11.4	71.2	47.7	23.5	28.8	25.2
22660	Fort Collins, CO	62,711	20,146	1.6	11.8	77.5	48.7	27.2	22.5	17.6
22900	Fort Smith, AR-OK	64,813	21,209	0.7	18.1	60.2	29.3	27.7	39.8	28.9
23060	Fort Wayne, IN	105,658	35,297	1.4	10.9	62.4	34.0	27.8	37.6	28.7
23420	Fresno, CA	264,483	93,137	1.1	41.3	52.0	25.7	24.9	48.0	32.4
23460	Gadsden, AL	21,908	6,644	0.0	5.5	59.7	38.8	18.6	40.3	30.7
23540	Gainesville, FL	45,266	17,200	1.1	12.9	62.6	36.2	24.8	37.4	28.6
23580	Gainesville, GA	48,000	16,180	1.1	39.1	65.6	37.7	27.4	34.4	25.9
23900	Gettysburg, PA	20,567	6,423	0.4	16.2	68.0	45.3	22.3	32.0	25.7
24020	Glens Falls, NY	23,776	7,249	0.4	4.3	61.1	39.7	20.7	38.9	32.4
24140	Goldsboro, NC	28,073	9,520	0.0	21.0	46.7	25.9	20.8	53.3	46.3
24220	Grand Forks, ND-MN	20,242	7,193	1.4	5.0	70.4	44.0	26.3	29.6	24.0
24260	Grand Island, NE	20,652	6,713	0.1	17.1	62.8	47.1	15.4	37.2	27.8
24300	Grand Junction, CO	32,303	11,229	0.0	7.7	66.1	33.0	33.0	33.9	22.6
24340	Grand Rapids-Wyoming, MI	243,669	79,520	1.8	14.6	69.8	43.1	25.7	30.2	24.8
24420	Grants Pass, OR	15,861	4,594	0.0	5.0	63.1	27.4	31.2	36.9	23.4
24500	Great Falls, MT	17,574	6,571	0.0	2.4	60.8	29.6	26.8	39.2	32.1

Table D-3: Metropolitan Areas—Children—*Continued*

CBSA FIPS code	Metropolitan area	Total own children 6 to 17	Nativity and parentage, age 6 to 17		Own children age 6 to 17 years living with two parents			Own children age 6 to 17 years living with one parent		Grand-children under 18 living with a grandparent householder	Grand-children under 18 living with a grandparent householder, as a percent of all children	Children for whom grandparent householders are responsible, as a percent of all children
			Child is foreign born, percent	One or more foreign-born parent, percent	Age 6 to 17 years living with two parents, percent	Both parents in labor force, percent	One parent in labor force, percent	Age 6 to 17 years living with one parent, percent	Parent in labor force, percent			
17140	Cincinnati, OH-KY-IN	331,177	2.1	6.7	65.9	45.5	19.6	34.1	27.8	34,649	7.0	4.3
17300	Clarksville, TN-KY	43,977	1.7	9.9	65.5	33.4	29.8	34.5	25.8	4,020	5.6	3.4
17420	Cleveland, TN	16,848	1.2	7.0	66.6	44.3	19.6	33.4	28.5	2,480	10.2	5.5
17460	Cleveland-Elyria, OH	306,102	2.0	7.9	62.0	42.2	18.8	38.0	30.6	31,637	7.1	3.7
17660	Coeur d'Alene, ID	21,490	0.7	2.8	72.1	49.4	22.2	27.9	23.0	1,941	6.0	2.8
17780	College Station-Bryan, TX	29,920	5.6	26.4	63.4	37.9	24.9	36.6	30.6	3,672	7.8	5.2
17820	Colorado Springs, CO	107,455	2.8	13.4	70.7	43.6	26.0	29.3	23.5	8,733	5.4	2.5
17860	Columbia, MO	21,662	3.7	11.4	68.3	51.4	14.5	31.7	28.4	1,645	4.9	2.8
17900	Columbia, SC	114,948	2.0	8.2	58.6	40.9	16.7	41.4	34.7	14,506	8.5	4.6
17980	Columbus, GA-AL	46,459	1.8	7.5	53.7	31.7	20.8	46.3	36.4	7,919	11.0	6.4
18020	Columbus, IN	12,083	4.5	10.5	73.0	50.1	22.5	27.0	22.1	1,428	8.1	4.7
18140	Columbus, OH	297,687	3.5	13.0	65.6	44.5	19.9	34.4	28.8	29,609	6.5	4.0
18580	Corpus Christi, TX	70,841	2.0	12.8	56.8	35.5	20.2	43.2	34.6	12,324	11.7	7.3
18700	Corvallis, OR	9,533	5.9	21.4	79.2	48.2	27.9	20.8	14.5	788	5.6	2.9
18880	Crestview-Fort Walton Beach-Destin, FL	32,992	1.9	12.3	63.8	37.8	25.2	36.2	27.2	3,785	7.5	4.5
19060	Cumberland, MD-WV	12,155	1.0	2.6	64.3	40.0	23.0	35.7	27.9	1,711	9.6	4.4
19100	Dallas-Fort Worth-Arlington, TX	1,163,495	6.4	36.2	67.4	41.2	25.5	32.6	27.7	134,275	7.7	4.4
19140	Dalton, GA	24,817	3.7	36.9	67.4	46.2	20.8	32.6	26.4	3,313	9.2	6.0
19180	Danville, IL	12,085	0.7	4.6	56.9	40.3	15.7	43.1	38.3	1,542	8.5	4.6
19300	Daphne-Fairhope-Foley, AL	28,333	0.9	5.8	72.7	44.4	27.2	27.3	21.4	3,694	8.8	5.8
19340	Davenport-Moline-Rock Island, IA-IL	56,782	2.4	8.2	63.3	47.1	15.5	36.7	30.8	4,765	5.6	2.9
19380	Dayton, OH	115,653	2.0	6.5	61.1	40.6	19.6	38.9	31.4	12,079	7.1	4.1
19460	Decatur, AL	23,048	2.8	9.7	65.9	39.7	25.2	34.1	29.9	3,239	9.6	6.4
19500	Decatur, IL	15,630	1.1	5.5	54.5	36.9	16.5	45.5	41.0	2,416	10.3	8.0
19660	Deltona-Daytona Beach-Ormond Beach, FL	70,587	2.4	15.1	60.4	36.1	23.5	39.6	27.8	10,401	10.0	6.0
19740	Denver-Aurora-Lakewood, CO	409,807	5.4	26.5	69.1	45.2	22.8	30.9	26.4	38,539	6.2	3.0
19780	Des Moines-West Des Moines, IA	96,225	4.0	13.6	69.3	52.6	15.9	30.7	27.0	7,179	4.9	2.5
19820	Detroit-Warren-Dearborn, MI	669,827	3.9	17.0	64.2	40.9	21.5	35.8	28.5	67,593	7.0	3.3
20020	Dothan, AL	22,194	0.8	3.9	59.1	40.1	17.8	40.9	29.6	2,991	9.2	5.3
20100	Dover, DE	24,958	1.2	7.6	61.3	39.6	19.4	38.7	33.4	3,729	9.9	5.4
20220	Dubuque, IA	14,390	1.0	3.1	68.7	56.6	12.0	31.3	25.9	768	3.6	1.8
20260	Duluth, MN-WI	35,737	1.3	2.6	64.1	46.7	16.6	35.9	30.7	2,605	4.9	2.2
20500	Durham-Chapel Hill, NC	71,548	6.8	23.7	63.5	44.6	17.6	36.5	30.7	6,748	6.2	3.9
20700	East Stroudsburg, PA	26,774	2.2	21.4	67.5	42.4	22.7	32.5	27.1	2,949	8.3	4.7
20740	Eau Claire, WI	22,449	2.0	5.4	73.0	54.6	17.9	27.0	24.2	1,179	3.5	1.7
20940	El Centro, CA	30,988	8.0	57.2	61.0	37.6	22.5	39.0	26.8	7,076	14.6	8.3
21060	Elizabethtown-Fort Knox, KY	23,985	1.2	6.1	61.2	37.1	22.0	38.8	29.0	2,859	7.8	4.2
21140	Elkhart-Goshen, IN	35,182	4.2	19.1	67.5	40.9	25.8	32.5	26.1	3,348	6.3	3.1
21300	Elmira, NY	12,482	0.7	3.5	66.1	48.2	17.2	33.9	24.4	1,059	5.7	2.4
21340	El Paso, TX	153,150	5.5	49.1	60.1	31.2	27.4	39.9	31.4	29,420	12.7	6.6
21500	Erie, PA	40,114	3.2	8.7	61.5	42.4	17.8	38.5	30.5	4,575	7.8	3.7
21660	Eugene, OR	44,483	2.5	12.1	65.3	39.7	23.1	34.7	26.8	3,954	6.1	2.8
21780	Evansville, IN-KY	44,121	1.7	4.2	65.0	41.9	21.5	35.0	29.9	5,431	8.1	4.9
21820	Fairbanks, AK	15,048	4.0	8.4	66.5	40.8	25.0	33.5	24.7	1,201	4.9	3.4
22020	Fargo, ND-MN	29,422	4.3	8.7	73.9	57.2	16.3	26.1	23.3	1,560	3.3	2.3
22140	Farmington, NM	22,127	1.2	9.7	59.6	32.9	25.1	40.4	29.0	5,248	15.6	8.6
22180	Fayetteville, NC	58,722	1.6	9.4	55.4	33.2	20.4	44.6	35.9	8,710	9.1	5.1
22220	Fayetteville-Springdale-Rogers, AR-MO	80,637	6.4	25.5	74.5	46.1	27.0	25.5	21.0	6,472	5.3	3.5
22380	Flagstaff, AZ	19,292	1.1	10.3	59.0	40.2	17.0	41.0	31.8	5,110	17.6	9.3
22420	Flint, MI	65,437	0.5	2.7	55.9	37.2	17.4	44.1	34.4	8,027	8.4	4.7
22500	Florence, SC	31,132	1.3	4.1	52.0	37.0	13.5	48.0	39.6	7,510	16.1	6.9
22520	Florence-Muscle Shoals, AL	20,382	2.0	3.7	69.0	42.8	24.1	31.0	25.1	2,895	9.9	6.8
22540	Fond du Lac, WI	15,015	2.3	6.4	71.4	57.5	13.7	28.6	26.3	605	2.8	0.7
22660	Fort Collins, CO	42,565	2.9	11.7	72.9	49.0	23.1	27.1	23.4	3,362	5.4	3.3
22900	Fort Smith, AR-OK	43,604	1.4	15.5	64.3	36.3	23.1	35.7	27.7	6,474	10.0	6.2
23060	Fort Wayne, IN	70,361	3.6	10.0	64.9	41.9	21.8	35.1	28.5	6,040	5.7	3.0
23420	Fresno, CA	171,346	5.7	46.0	58.2	34.2	22.0	41.8	31.5	24,554	9.3	4.4
23460	Gadsden, AL	15,264	0.9	5.8	55.6	31.7	21.0	44.4	33.8	3,151	14.4	9.0
23540	Gainesville, FL	28,066	3.0	16.6	62.9	41.0	19.4	37.1	29.8	3,986	8.8	5.5
23580	Gainesville, GA	31,820	3.5	37.1	72.1	42.7	28.8	27.9	22.0	3,544	7.4	3.7
23900	Gettysburg, PA	14,144	1.1	10.4	70.5	50.2	19.7	29.5	25.2	1,275	6.2	3.0
24020	Glens Falls, NY	16,527	2.5	2.2	66.6	48.3	16.5	33.4	31.1	2,141	9.0	4.3
24140	Goldsboro, NC	18,553	1.3	13.8	52.3	32.9	18.7	47.7	38.3	2,547	9.1	6.4
24220	Grand Forks, ND-MN	13,049	1.4	5.8	73.1	57.1	15.8	26.9	23.4	1,155	5.7	3.0
24260	Grand Island, NE	13,939	4.3	22.2	70.4	55.5	14.1	29.6	24.4	767	3.7	1.4
24300	Grand Junction, CO	21,074	1.1	7.3	63.3	44.9	17.7	36.7	30.3	2,321	7.2	3.0
24340	Grand Rapids-Wyoming, MI	164,149	3.4	12.4	73.2	48.4	23.6	26.8	22.4	12,479	5.1	2.3
24420	Grants Pass, OR	11,267	0.6	6.7	66.9	37.4	23.2	33.1	22.9	1,397	8.8	3.7
24500	Great Falls, MT	11,003	0.4	1.7	64.9	43.5	18.9	35.1	29.6	802	4.6	2.7

Table D-3: Metropolitan Areas—Children—*Continued*

CBSA FIPS code	Metropolitan area	Total own children under 18 in families and subfamilies	Total own children under 6 years	Own children under 6 years in families and subfamilies						
				Nativity and parentage, under 6 years		Own children under 6 years living with two parents			Own children under 6 living with one parent	
				Child is foreign born, percent	One or more foreign-born parent, percent	Total under 6 years living with two parents, percent	Both parents in labor force, percent	One parent in labor force, percent	Total under 6 years living with one parent, percent	Parent in labor force, percent
24540	Greeley, CO	68,582	22,851	0.6	19.5	68.5	32.5	35.4	31.5	23.6
24580	Green Bay, WI	71,486	23,195	0.5	16.0	68.2	50.6	17.4	31.8	26.5
24660	Greensboro-High Point, NC	160,820	51,466	1.4	23.0	58.1	34.8	22.6	41.9	33.4
24780	Greenville, NC	36,215	13,095	0.8	10.6	53.3	37.9	14.6	46.7	42.2
24860	Greenville-Anderson-Mauldin, SC	184,473	60,631	1.0	11.5	58.4	33.6	23.6	41.6	33.6
25060	Gulfport-Biloxi-Pascagoula, MS	84,851	28,360	0.4	6.0	55.6	27.2	26.1	44.4	33.8
25180	Hagerstown-Martinsburg, MD-WV	55,466	18,099	1.7	10.4	61.6	37.9	23.1	38.4	29.2
25220	Hammond, LA	28,227	9,974	0.0	3.2	55.6	34.7	20.5	44.4	37.0
25260	Hanford-Corcoran, CA	39,766	14,414	0.0	33.1	56.7	32.0	23.9	43.3	27.5
25420	Harrisburg-Carlisle, PA	115,116	37,258	1.5	11.1	62.7	42.7	19.3	37.3	31.9
25500	Harrisonburg, VA	24,713	8,295	1.8	26.4	67.1	35.6	31.2	32.9	26.0
25540	Hartford-West Hartford-East Hartford, CT	253,559	75,944	1.5	23.3	65.0	45.5	19.2	35.0	28.6
25620	Hattiesburg, MS	33,912	12,004	0.0	3.2	53.9	30.2	23.7	46.1	39.1
25860	Hickory-Lenoir-Morganton, NC	75,811	22,947	0.5	13.9	62.4	36.6	25.2	37.6	27.2
25940	Hilton Head Island-Bluffton-Beaufort, SC	38,774	14,335	0.0	22.4	61.3	32.8	27.8	38.7	31.4
25980	Hinesville, GA	22,382	9,574	0.9	7.0	58.7	22.4	35.2	41.3	31.2
26140	Homosassa Springs, FL	18,755	5,707	0.0	8.0	46.7	20.0	25.7	53.3	45.4
26300	Hot Springs, AR	17,618	5,819	0.0	3.3	58.7	36.8	21.3	41.3	33.2
26380	Houma-Thibodaux, LA	48,779	16,437	0.1	7.8	52.9	28.3	23.2	47.1	37.1
26420	Houston-The Woodlands-Sugar Land, TX	1,622,102	554,443	2.0	42.1	64.0	31.9	31.3	36.0	26.9
26580	Huntington-Ashland, WV-KY-OH	72,706	23,152	0.3	1.9	63.5	34.2	28.0	36.5	23.6
26620	Huntsville, AL	94,929	30,557	0.9	9.6	63.3	37.3	25.5	36.7	31.0
26820	Idaho Falls, ID	42,540	14,724	0.4	11.9	82.4	34.1	47.5	17.6	14.9
26900	Indianapolis-Carmel-Anderson, IN	469,628	157,302	1.2	14.1	63.4	40.7	22.0	36.6	30.3
26980	Iowa City, IA	31,839	11,586	1.4	16.2	73.9	52.5	20.7	26.1	22.1
27060	Ithaca, NY	14,744	4,552	2.4	21.2	72.8	47.4	23.4	27.2	13.6
27100	Jackson, MI	34,229	10,993	0.1	2.6	59.5	33.7	24.6	40.5	29.2
27140	Jackson, MS	137,240	44,961	0.1	3.7	52.7	36.6	15.0	47.3	38.4
27180	Jackson, TN	28,792	10,134	0.1	12.2	58.2	32.1	25.7	41.8	32.3
27260	Jacksonville, FL	301,492	101,072	0.6	13.7	57.5	34.0	22.7	42.5	32.0
27340	Jacksonville, NC	45,145	19,898	0.2	7.8	71.3	27.9	42.7	28.7	18.5
27500	Janesville-Beloit, WI	36,293	11,395	0.3	9.0	56.7	35.5	20.6	43.3	30.5
27620	Jefferson City, MO	32,543	10,570	0.0	4.3	64.4	43.6	20.1	35.6	27.6
27740	Johnson City, TN	37,557	11,837	0.3	5.2	67.3	44.8	21.5	32.7	25.9
27780	Johnstown, PA	26,448	8,282	0.0	2.5	60.5	39.0	20.9	39.5	29.6
27860	Jonesboro, AR	28,003	10,111	0.0	4.7	55.5	33.5	21.9	44.5	33.9
27900	Joplin, MO	41,553	14,081	0.6	11.6	63.2	36.0	25.5	36.8	29.5
27980	Kahului-Wailuku-Lahaina, HI	33,588	11,498	1.9	29.4	57.9	41.0	15.8	42.1	36.8
28020	Kalamazoo-Portage, MI	71,954	23,231	0.7	9.8	62.0	35.5	24.7	38.0	30.1
28100	Kankakee, IL	26,468	8,106	0.2	14.3	53.7	35.3	16.7	46.3	39.0
28140	Kansas City, MO-KS	491,059	165,655	0.9	15.0	64.4	40.4	23.3	35.6	28.0
28420	Kennewick-Richland, WA	74,625	26,503	1.0	36.2	65.9	33.6	31.7	34.1	28.9
28660	Killeen-Temple, TX	109,301	41,402	0.7	13.9	69.7	31.6	37.0	30.3	21.9
28700	Kingsport-Bristol-Bristol, TN-VA	58,280	17,303	0.1	2.3	63.0	38.1	22.9	37.0	28.0
28740	Kingston, NY	33,053	9,788	0.8	15.7	60.7	38.1	21.5	39.3	30.1
28940	Knoxville, TN	169,503	53,685	0.5	10.4	65.5	37.9	27.0	34.5	24.3
29020	Kokomo, IN	17,901	5,500	0.0	3.6	64.8	45.4	19.1	35.2	31.7
29100	La Crosse-Onalaska, WI-MN	27,320	8,823	1.2	5.8	77.6	63.4	14.0	22.4	17.6
29180	Lafayette, LA	112,632	39,328	0.3	4.8	50.3	31.0	18.8	49.7	38.4
29200	Lafayette-West Lafayette, IN	41,520	14,291	1.7	18.6	66.4	38.5	26.2	33.6	28.1
29340	Lake Charles, LA	48,039	15,300	0.1	3.0	48.7	24.4	24.0	51.3	38.5
29420	Lake Havasu City-Kingman, AZ	36,788	11,354	0.0	13.5	58.6	30.1	27.6	41.4	32.8
29460	Lakeland-Winter Haven, FL	134,329	44,047	0.2	21.3	54.9	31.3	22.9	45.1	33.5
29540	Lancaster, PA	123,787	41,313	0.8	8.7	76.1	36.3	38.7	23.9	19.6
29620	Lansing-East Lansing, MI	95,183	30,373	1.2	8.9	64.7	41.6	22.0	35.3	29.7
29700	Laredo, TX	84,582	29,510	1.1	44.6	55.1	23.0	30.1	44.9	24.2
29740	Las Cruces, NM	53,121	18,507	1.8	30.3	53.4	30.5	22.3	46.6	38.3
29820	Las Vegas-Henderson-Paradise, NV	464,016	158,753	1.1	40.6	62.2	33.9	27.3	37.8	30.7
29940	Lawrence, KS	20,386	6,744	2.9	16.0	64.0	43.0	19.3	36.0	29.1
30020	Lawton, OK	30,462	11,527	1.2	7.9	60.6	28.1	30.8	39.4	32.0
30140	Lebanon, PA	29,688	10,134	0.7	8.5	68.2	40.3	27.5	31.8	24.3
30300	Lewiston, ID-WA	12,410	4,169	1.6	1.3	67.0	52.4	14.3	33.0	29.1
30340	Lewiston-Auburn, ME	22,762	7,622	0.7	2.5	55.3	38.0	15.8	44.7	34.2
30460	Lexington-Fayette, KY	101,938	34,560	1.5	18.0	68.2	45.5	21.4	31.8	25.5
30620	Lima, OH	23,737	7,970	0.0	3.2	55.6	34.8	20.4	44.4	36.8
30700	Lincoln, NE	69,049	25,031	0.9	15.9	72.1	49.4	22.3	27.9	23.8
30780	Little Rock-North Little Rock-Conway, AR	164,353	57,156	0.4	8.4	61.5	38.9	22.2	38.5	29.6
30860	Logan, UT-ID	40,144	14,313	0.4	15.5	86.0	34.4	49.6	14.0	11.7
30980	Longview, TX	50,584	17,047	0.2	20.0	58.4	35.0	23.0	41.6	27.5

CBSA FIPS code	Metropolitan area	Total own children 6 to 17	Own children age 6 to 17 years in families and subfamilies							Grand-children under 18 living with a grandparent householder	Grand-children under 18 living with a grandparent householder, as a percent of all children	Children for whom grandparent householders are responsible, as a percent of all children
			Nativity and parentage, age 6 to 17 years		Own children age 6 to 17 years living with two parents			Own children age 6 to 17 years living with one parent				
			Child is foreign born, percent	One or more foreign-born parent, percent	Age 6 to 17 years living with two parents, percent	Both parents in labor force, percent	One parent in labor force, percent	Age 6 to 17 years living with one parent, percent	Parent in labor force, percent			
24540	Greeley, CO	45,731	3.2	24.4	73.3	45.6	26.9	26.7	22.0	4,840	7.1	4.1
24580	Green Bay, WI	48,291	2.3	10.7	73.4	57.2	15.3	26.6	22.6	3,217	4.5	2.7
24660	Greensboro-High Point, NC	109,354	4.2	18.0	58.6	38.8	18.8	41.4	33.9	12,134	7.5	4.3
24780	Greenville, NC	23,120	2.2	10.6	51.5	40.6	8.8	48.5	42.6	3,282	9.1	6.2
24860	Greenville-Anderson-Mauldin, SC	123,842	2.7	10.8	64.6	39.3	24.0	35.4	28.2	17,843	9.7	6.3
25060	Gulfport-Biloxi-Pascagoula, MS	56,491	1.7	6.1	59.6	34.8	23.0	40.4	32.2	11,581	13.6	8.8
25180	Hagerstown-Martinsburg, MD-WV	37,367	2.3	8.1	65.2	44.5	19.7	34.8	28.2	4,091	7.4	4.2
25220	Hammond, LA	18,253	1.6	2.3	54.9	40.1	13.2	45.1	35.3	3,718	13.2	8.3
25260	Hanford-Corcoran, CA	25,352	6.3	40.3	63.4	35.9	26.3	36.6	27.4	3,763	9.5	4.8
25420	Harrisburg-Carlisle, PA	77,858	3.7	9.9	67.1	48.6	16.9	32.9	28.7	7,561	6.6	3.4
25500	Harrisonburg, VA	16,418	7.6	26.3	74.4	50.1	22.4	25.6	23.4	1,515	6.1	2.7
25540	Hartford-West Hartford-East Hartford, CT	177,615	4.7	20.2	65.6	49.3	15.7	34.4	29.6	13,889	5.5	2.6
25620	Hattiesburg, MS	21,908	1.2	2.5	58.3	34.6	22.6	41.7	34.0	3,717	11.0	8.4
25860	Hickory-Lenoir-Morganton, NC	52,864	2.5	14.5	64.8	43.5	19.3	35.2	26.1	6,513	8.6	4.7
25940	Hilton Head Island-Bluffton-Beaufort, SC	24,439	8.0	21.6	62.1	38.0	20.4	37.9	34.7	2,757	7.1	4.3
25980	Hinesville, GA	12,808	1.5	13.4	62.9	34.4	27.4	37.1	29.7	1,186	5.3	3.0
26140	Homosassa Springs, FL	13,048	1.0	7.6	58.3	35.4	20.3	41.7	32.6	2,317	12.4	6.0
26300	Hot Springs, AR	11,799	1.7	8.9	55.4	34.1	18.3	44.6	36.7	2,385	13.5	9.3
26380	Houma-Thibodaux, LA	32,342	1.1	4.6	56.9	32.1	23.3	43.1	34.7	5,640	11.6	7.8
26420	Houston-The Woodlands-Sugar Land, TX	1,067,659	7.7	43.2	66.1	37.8	27.3	33.9	28.5	132,861	8.2	4.5
26580	Huntington-Ashland, WV-KY-OH	49,554	0.6	2.2	64.1	38.7	23.3	35.9	25.0	6,979	9.6	6.4
26620	Huntsville, AL	64,372	2.2	9.6	69.1	44.5	23.9	30.9	27.7	7,180	7.6	5.2
26820	Idaho Falls, ID	27,816	1.4	10.3	78.1	42.7	35.0	21.9	19.3	1,556	3.7	1.4
26900	Indianapolis-Carmel-Anderson, IN	312,326	3.1	10.6	64.5	45.2	18.6	35.5	30.1	33,277	7.1	4.0
26980	Iowa City, IA	20,253	4.2	17.8	72.2	58.2	13.3	27.8	24.7	808	2.5	1.0
27060	Ithaca, NY	10,192	4.4	16.3	66.8	48.0	17.3	33.2	27.6	785	5.3	3.5
27100	Jackson, MI	23,236	0.3	1.3	65.5	45.6	17.7	34.5	25.9	2,527	7.4	4.6
27140	Jackson, MS	92,279	1.1	3.5	53.4	37.7	14.6	46.6	37.6	16,899	12.3	7.1
27180	Jackson, TN	18,658	2.4	7.2	60.7	41.4	18.7	39.3	29.8	2,550	8.9	5.7
27260	Jacksonville, FL	200,420	2.8	14.5	62.9	40.8	20.7	37.1	30.1	27,176	9.0	5.7
27340	Jacksonville, NC	25,247	1.1	8.4	67.5	30.6	35.1	32.5	26.0	1,974	4.4	2.9
27500	Janesville-Beloit, WI	24,898	2.7	12.2	64.9	44.9	18.6	35.1	27.5	2,392	6.6	3.1
27620	Jefferson City, MO	21,973	1.2	3.4	71.3	51.8	17.9	28.7	24.1	2,652	8.1	6.3
27740	Johnson City, TN	25,720	2.3	7.7	68.9	42.2	23.5	31.1	25.0	2,914	7.8	4.8
27780	Johnstown, PA	18,166	0.6	0.9	67.9	48.9	17.9	32.1	26.3	1,392	5.3	2.0
27860	Jonesboro, AR	17,892	2.3	8.0	58.4	37.7	18.4	41.6	33.0	2,630	9.4	6.9
27900	Joplin, MO	27,472	1.5	9.4	71.8	46.5	24.1	28.2	23.7	2,988	7.2	4.0
27980	Kahului-Wailuku-Lahaina, HI	22,090	6.4	31.4	69.8	53.8	14.0	30.2	26.5	6,044	18.0	4.1
28020	Kalamazoo-Portage, MI	48,723	2.7	9.5	65.7	42.5	21.9	34.3	28.5	4,467	6.2	3.7
28100	Kankakee, IL	18,362	2.7	14.0	61.0	40.6	18.6	39.0	33.2	2,002	7.6	4.1
28140	Kansas City, MO-KS	325,404	3.2	12.6	66.4	46.2	19.4	33.6	28.8	30,262	6.2	3.1
28420	Kennewick-Richland, WA	48,122	6.0	33.3	65.3	38.9	25.8	34.7	30.3	4,618	6.2	3.2
28660	Killeen-Temple, TX	67,899	1.8	16.5	64.9	37.3	25.6	35.1	26.5	7,140	6.5	4.7
28700	Kingsport-Bristol-Bristol, TN-VA	40,977	0.8	3.1	68.0	43.4	22.0	32.0	25.0	6,623	11.4	7.2
28740	Kingston, NY	23,265	2.4	12.1	68.7	49.4	18.3	31.3	25.7	1,802	5.5	2.8
28940	Knoxville, TN	115,818	1.9	7.6	72.1	42.9	27.0	27.9	21.0	16,506	9.7	6.5
29020	Kokomo, IN	12,401	0.7	3.1	64.5	45.4	17.6	35.5	29.6	1,100	6.1	4.5
29100	La Crosse-Onalaska, WI-MN	18,497	2.2	7.4	69.2	56.6	12.3	30.8	27.1	912	3.3	2.0
29180	Lafayette, LA	73,304	1.5	4.5	57.9	38.4	18.5	42.1	35.0	11,487	10.2	6.5
29200	Lafayette-West Lafayette, IN	27,229	3.4	16.1	71.3	47.1	23.1	28.7	24.4	2,510	6.0	3.9
29340	Lake Charles, LA	32,739	0.8	3.4	61.1	43.0	17.2	38.9	32.6	4,748	9.9	6.0
29420	Lake Havasu City-Kingman, AZ	25,434	1.0	12.0	65.0	39.6	23.9	35.0	25.5	3,706	10.1	7.0
29460	Lakeland-Winter Haven, FL	90,282	4.0	21.4	54.9	34.4	18.7	45.1	35.0	14,343	10.7	5.6
29540	Lancaster, PA	82,474	2.2	7.3	76.7	45.8	30.0	23.3	19.3	7,515	6.1	2.5
29620	Lansing-East Lansing, MI	64,810	3.2	9.6	67.5	48.0	17.7	32.5	27.3	6,138	6.4	3.5
29700	Laredo, TX	55,072	7.4	50.2	59.6	27.5	30.3	40.4	26.6	12,797	15.1	7.8
29740	Las Cruces, NM	34,614	5.7	39.0	56.6	33.4	22.7	43.4	36.6	6,637	12.5	7.4
29820	Las Vegas-Henderson-Paradise, NV	305,263	6.2	42.1	60.8	37.1	22.5	39.2	33.1	32,051	6.9	3.8
29940	Lawrence, KS	13,642	2.4	9.3	69.4	55.2	14.0	30.6	25.4	1,117	5.5	3.7
30020	Lawton, OK	18,935	2.1	9.1	54.8	34.8	18.3	45.2	39.3	3,340	11.0	5.7
30140	Lebanon, PA	19,554	1.7	5.4	65.2	45.6	18.4	34.8	29.0	1,247	4.2	2.2
30300	Lewiston, ID-WA	8,241	0.0	1.8	68.2	49.7	17.8	31.8	27.5	1,074	8.7	5.7
30340	Lewiston-Auburn, ME	15,140	2.7	7.1	62.6	46.1	15.2	37.4	30.8	1,581	6.9	3.5
30460	Lexington-Fayette, KY	67,378	3.6	13.1	65.7	45.6	19.4	34.3	28.6	6,608	6.5	4.4
30620	Lima, OH	15,767	0.2	3.0	59.4	43.7	14.8	40.6	32.0	1,687	7.1	4.8
30700	Lincoln, NE	44,018	3.7	13.7	71.0	51.0	19.1	29.0	26.1	2,487	3.6	2.0
30780	Little Rock-North Little Rock-Conway, AR	107,197	1.8	7.4	61.8	42.4	18.5	38.2	31.3	12,948	7.9	5.2
30860	Logan, UT-ID	25,831	2.2	12.8	84.9	49.5	34.4	15.1	13.4	1,521	3.8	2.0
30980	Longview, TX	33,537	3.2	18.4	62.5	40.2	21.5	37.5	29.4	5,724	11.3	7.6

CBSA FIPS code	Metropolitan area	Total own children under 18 in families and subfamilies	Own children under 6 years in families and subfamilies							
			Total own children under 6 years	Nativity and parentage, under 6 years		Own children under 6 years living with two parents			Own children under 6 living with one parent	
				Child is foreign born, percent	One or more foreign-born parent, percent	Total under 6 years living with two parents, percent	Both parents in labor force, percent	One parent in labor force, percent	Total under 6 years living with one parent, percent	Parent in labor force, percent
31020	Longview, WA	22,734	7,475	0.0	12.2	50.7	22.6	27.3	49.3	36.6
31080	Los Angeles-Long Beach-Anaheim, CA	2,942,772	965,733	1.9	54.4	62.3	33.2	28.2	37.7	27.4
31140	Louisville/Jefferson County, KY-IN	275,575	89,891	1.3	13.2	61.4	40.3	20.1	38.6	32.2
31180	Lubbock, TX	69,570	24,345	0.7	8.6	59.7	36.9	22.3	40.3	32.7
31340	Lynchburg, VA	49,919	15,461	0.4	6.7	66.8	37.2	29.0	33.2	26.3
31420	Macon, GA	53,678	18,084	0.6	6.1	41.2	26.7	14.0	58.8	44.1
31460	Madera, CA	40,970	13,741	1.7	47.0	56.7	26.0	25.2	43.3	20.2
31540	Madison, WI	130,885	43,905	1.0	15.3	72.9	55.0	17.6	27.1	23.4
31700	Manchester-Nashua, NH	87,657	27,606	2.1	17.7	67.1	41.8	24.5	32.9	25.2
31740	Manhattan, KS	19,569	8,716	0.7	9.0	80.9	33.4	47.0	19.1	13.4
31860	Mankato-North Mankato, MN	19,378	6,915	0.6	7.1	71.9	58.6	12.6	28.1	25.6
31900	Mansfield, OH	24,440	7,832	0.1	0.7	60.5	33.8	25.0	39.5	26.7
32580	McAllen-Edinburg-Mission, TX	264,594	91,059	2.3	53.7	64.2	25.8	36.9	35.8	22.5
32780	Medford, OR	41,903	13,767	0.5	15.7	63.2	35.3	27.1	36.8	24.8
32820	Memphis, TN-MS-AR	328,802	108,891	0.6	13.6	47.5	29.3	17.9	52.5	42.3
32900	Merced, CA	76,769	25,114	0.8	51.0	56.4	29.2	25.2	43.6	28.5
33100	Miami-Fort Lauderdale-West Palm Beach, FL	1,165,503	386,197	2.8	55.3	58.1	35.5	21.7	41.9	33.3
33140	Michigan City-La Porte, IN	23,542	7,401	0.5	8.1	55.5	33.8	21.8	44.5	33.7
33220	Midland, MI	18,206	5,036	1.6	9.1	73.4	33.6	39.6	26.6	18.8
33260	Midland, TX	39,390	14,186	0.4	19.1	64.6	26.9	36.7	35.4	25.1
33340	Milwaukee-Waukesha-West Allis, WI	362,062	119,477	1.2	15.7	60.8	40.4	19.6	39.2	31.9
33460	Minneapolis-St. Paul-Bloomington, MN-WI	812,111	269,853	2.0	24.1	71.7	49.8	21.2	28.3	23.4
33540	Missoula, MT	20,733	7,356	1.3	2.8	66.3	36.0	29.0	33.7	29.4
33660	Mobile, AL	94,063	31,561	0.8	6.4	47.2	27.4	18.5	52.8	40.0
33700	Modesto, CA	136,246	44,579	1.2	36.4	55.9	28.5	26.8	44.1	31.1
33740	Monroe, LA	41,993	14,416	0.4	1.9	42.8	24.9	17.1	57.2	38.5
33780	Monroe, MI	33,386	10,265	0.6	4.1	61.2	34.0	26.4	38.8	31.5
33860	Montgomery, AL	86,720	28,290	0.5	8.1	52.0	28.6	22.7	48.0	35.7
34060	Morgantown, WV	21,302	7,596	1.2	6.8	70.4	40.2	30.0	29.6	16.9
34100	Morristown, TN	23,631	7,539	0.3	16.3	59.8	35.9	23.2	40.2	28.9
34580	Mount Vernon-Anacortes, WA	25,422	8,310	2.0	24.9	61.2	32.1	28.6	38.8	28.2
34620	Muncie, IN	21,471	7,026	1.6	2.6	59.9	36.8	19.8	40.1	30.2
34740	Muskegon, MI	38,699	12,001	0.2	3.6	52.1	36.1	15.6	47.9	35.8
34820	Myrtle Beach-Conway-North Myrtle Beach, SC-NC	71,372	23,599	0.5	13.4	52.7	32.7	19.1	47.3	35.4
34900	Napa, CA	30,085	9,165	1.6	56.8	68.3	35.1	32.7	31.7	22.5
34940	Naples-Immokalee-Marco Island, FL	60,602	19,914	0.9	49.1	59.6	31.8	27.7	40.4	31.1
34980	Nashville-Davidson–Murfreesboro–Franklin, TN	394,640	135,145	1.8	17.7	65.7	37.8	27.1	34.3	26.5
35100	New Bern, NC	26,672	10,056	0.7	8.6	59.9	33.3	26.4	40.1	30.9
35300	New Haven-Milford, CT	179,718	54,905	2.3	25.0	61.4	40.2	20.2	38.6	29.5
35380	New Orleans-Metairie, LA	266,327	92,055	0.5	12.3	49.5	31.2	17.5	50.5	37.8
35620	New York-Newark-Jersey City, NY-NJ-PA	4,282,921	1,425,681	2.6	45.4	66.7	37.9	28.0	33.3	24.7
35660	Niles-Benton Harbor, MI	34,256	11,394	1.8	10.6	58.3	31.9	24.0	41.7	33.1
35840	North Port-Sarasota-Bradenton, FL	118,604	37,199	1.3	27.4	59.8	35.2	23.0	40.2	31.7
35980	Norwich-New London, CT	55,301	16,603	1.0	14.5	62.7	43.2	19.3	37.3	31.0
36100	Ocala, FL	58,748	19,507	0.4	9.7	53.7	28.3	24.6	46.3	35.1
36140	Ocean City, NJ	16,676	5,145	2.0	13.0	76.3	52.1	23.9	23.7	15.3
36220	Odessa, TX	39,941	14,308	0.3	23.7	60.6	24.9	35.2	39.4	27.7
36260	Ogden-Clearfield, UT	191,984	68,094	0.4	10.8	81.4	38.0	42.7	18.6	14.2
36420	Oklahoma City, OK	307,975	108,458	1.1	18.5	65.4	37.2	27.2	34.6	26.8
36500	Olympia-Tumwater, WA	55,764	17,969	0.6	16.0	72.1	36.3	34.6	27.9	23.5
36540	Omaha-Council Bluffs, NE-IA	220,920	75,810	1.3	16.4	67.1	44.8	21.4	32.9	26.8
36740	Orlando-Kissimmee-Sanford, FL	485,216	154,223	1.6	28.2	59.7	36.0	22.9	40.3	32.5
36780	Oshkosh-Neenah, WI	34,003	11,478	0.6	8.5	69.8	46.2	23.1	30.2	23.2
36980	Owensboro, KY	25,969	8,482	0.4	3.1	62.3	41.5	20.4	37.7	31.1
37100	Oxnard-Thousand Oaks-Ventura, CA	197,764	63,541	1.9	43.8	67.5	39.9	26.9	32.5	23.5
37340	Palm Bay-Melbourne-Titusville, FL	98,964	31,576	0.3	15.1	57.2	32.4	24.3	42.8	34.2
37460	Panama City, FL	37,892	13,037	0.1	10.9	60.2	33.7	25.1	39.8	30.9
37620	Parkersburg-Vienna, WV	18,163	6,281	0.0	1.4	55.5	30.8	22.8	44.5	34.5
37860	Pensacola-Ferry Pass-Brent, FL	94,256	32,707	0.0	7.7	53.2	27.2	25.3	46.8	36.7
37900	Peoria, IL	85,858	28,264	1.4	7.4	64.2	34.2	28.6	35.8	28.4
37980	Philadelphia-Camden-Wilmington, PA-NJ-DE-MD	1,309,775	429,670	1.5	19.1	61.2	40.3	20.0	38.8	29.8
38060	Phoenix-Mesa-Scottsdale, AZ	1,054,533	351,680	1.3	29.4	61.9	31.2	29.4	38.1	28.3
38220	Pine Bluff, AR	20,448	6,408	0.1	2.5	38.5	24.3	12.4	61.5	49.0
38300	Pittsburgh, PA	444,270	141,970	0.9	6.7	65.8	41.3	23.5	34.2	25.8
38340	Pittsfield, MA	22,710	6,886	0.9	12.2	56.8	38.4	17.9	43.2	33.2

CBSA FIPS code	Metropolitan area	Total own children 6 to 17	Nativity and parentage, age 6 to 17 years		Own children age 6 to 17 years living with two parents			Own children age 6 to 17 years living with one parent		Grandchildren under 18 living with a grandparent householder	Grandchildren under 18 living with a grandparent householder, as a percent of all children	Children for whom grandparent householders are responsible, as a percent of all children
			Child is foreign born, percent	One or more foreign-born parent, percent	Age 6 to 17 years living with two parents, percent	Both parents in labor force, percent	One parent in labor force, percent	Age 6 to 17 years living with one parent, percent	Parent in labor force, percent			
31020	Longview, WA	15,259	2.9	10.9	66.5	41.5	23.2	33.5	27.3	2,165	9.5	4.9
31080	Los Angeles-Long Beach-Anaheim, CA	1,977,039	7.7	60.6	64.6	37.1	26.3	35.4	28.5	282,010	9.6	3.6
31140	Louisville/Jefferson County, KY-IN	185,684	3.9	9.8	61.7	43.6	17.3	38.3	32.1	23,760	8.6	5.8
31180	Lubbock, TX	45,225	2.1	11.0	62.8	42.0	19.6	37.2	32.4	7,207	10.4	7.6
31340	Lynchburg, VA	34,458	0.9	4.2	67.8	45.5	20.2	32.2	26.7	3,813	7.6	3.2
31420	Macon, GA	35,594	1.1	6.1	51.8	35.6	15.3	48.2	35.0	6,419	12.0	6.2
31460	Madera, CA	27,229	7.8	48.4	65.6	29.8	28.5	34.4	22.7	3,606	8.8	3.9
31540	Madison, WI	86,980	3.9	13.0	71.2	56.2	14.2	28.8	24.8	3,445	2.6	1.0
31700	Manchester-Nashua, NH	60,051	3.6	16.2	71.1	50.8	18.8	28.9	24.8	4,918	5.6	2.2
31740	Manhattan, KS	10,853	1.6	10.3	78.2	46.0	31.4	21.8	19.2	592	3.0	1.6
31860	Mankato-North Mankato, MN	12,463	1.5	7.5	78.5	67.5	10.5	21.5	20.0	547	2.8	1.2
31900	Mansfield, OH	16,608	0.4	2.3	61.5	42.6	18.8	38.5	33.1	2,474	10.1	5.9
32580	McAllen-Edinburg-Mission, TX	173,535	9.4	59.2	64.7	32.2	30.7	35.3	26.8	37,180	14.1	5.7
32780	Medford, OR	28,136	2.7	12.0	57.2	36.7	19.4	42.8	33.7	2,486	5.9	2.7
32820	Memphis, TN-MS-AR	219,911	2.4	9.5	51.9	35.4	16.0	48.1	40.6	34,937	10.6	5.9
32900	Merced, CA	51,655	7.8	57.3	61.2	33.1	25.7	38.8	29.4	5,895	7.7	3.7
33100	Miami-Fort Lauderdale-West Palm Beach, FL	779,306	13.0	57.7	60.6	40.7	18.7	39.4	33.6	102,776	8.8	3.9
33140	Michigan City-La Porte, IN	16,141	1.3	6.6	62.0	43.0	18.5	38.0	31.7	2,530	10.7	3.9
33220	Midland, MI	13,170	3.1	6.2	74.9	46.5	27.3	25.1	20.9	838	4.6	2.9
33260	Midland, TX	25,204	1.8	25.3	66.2	40.9	24.0	33.8	29.2	4,150	10.5	5.8
33340	Milwaukee-Waukesha-West Allis, WI	242,585	3.6	14.0	63.0	44.8	17.5	37.0	30.2	18,273	5.0	2.6
33460	Minneapolis-St. Paul-Bloomington, MN-WI	542,258	5.2	19.0	71.5	53.1	17.6	28.5	24.7	31,875	3.9	1.8
33540	Missoula, MT	13,377	0.2	4.4	68.5	52.9	15.3	31.5	28.5	1,029	5.0	3.1
33660	Mobile, AL	62,502	1.0	5.2	53.8	34.1	17.8	46.2	35.5	12,941	13.8	8.8
33700	Modesto, CA	91,667	5.5	43.8	63.8	37.4	25.1	36.2	28.5	11,713	8.6	4.0
33740	Monroe, LA	27,577	0.6	2.6	51.7	33.1	16.4	48.3	35.1	4,809	11.5	7.1
33780	Monroe, MI	23,121	1.2	3.4	70.2	50.1	18.5	29.8	26.0	2,655	8.0	4.4
33860	Montgomery, AL	58,430	1.8	6.0	54.9	35.2	18.9	45.1	34.9	8,896	10.3	6.2
34060	Morgantown, WV	13,706	1.8	6.9	72.4	42.3	27.3	27.6	21.6	1,212	5.7	3.6
34100	Morristown, TN	16,092	2.0	13.6	66.6	46.2	19.1	33.4	24.2	2,415	10.2	5.5
34580	Mount Vernon-Anacortes, WA	17,112	2.6	20.2	63.5	36.2	25.8	36.5	30.1	1,464	5.8	2.8
34620	Muncie, IN	14,445	0.8	2.3	61.7	41.4	19.3	38.3	30.0	1,715	8.0	4.2
34740	Muskegon, MI	26,698	0.4	2.8	61.0	42.6	16.8	39.0	30.7	3,231	8.3	3.5
34820	Myrtle Beach-Conway-North Myrtle Beach, SC-NC	47,773	2.5	12.4	62.6	41.0	19.4	37.4	30.2	7,039	9.9	6.2
34900	Napa, CA	20,920	6.7	54.0	71.2	50.9	19.8	28.8	23.4	1,486	4.9	1.9
34940	Naples-Immokalee-Marco Island, FL	40,688	10.2	47.5	64.9	38.3	26.0	35.1	30.5	3,851	6.4	2.7
34980	Nashville-Davidson–Murfreesboro–Franklin, TN	259,495	3.9	14.8	67.4	42.5	23.5	32.6	27.4	29,422	7.5	4.0
35100	New Bern, NC	16,616	5.5	12.1	61.3	41.2	18.0	38.7	28.9	3,190	12.0	7.7
35300	New Haven-Milford, CT	124,813	4.3	20.6	63.9	47.7	15.4	36.1	29.9	9,635	5.4	2.6
35380	New Orleans-Metairie, LA	174,272	2.1	9.9	53.7	36.3	16.3	46.3	37.2	28,184	10.6	6.4
35620	New York-Newark-Jersey City, NY-NJ-PA	2,857,240	8.0	44.6	66.8	41.7	24.0	33.2	26.8	310,389	7.2	2.9
35660	Niles-Benton Harbor, MI	22,862	2.9	11.3	62.3	42.8	18.2	37.7	28.5	2,404	7.0	4.2
35840	North Port-Sarasota-Bradenton, FL	81,405	5.4	25.6	66.6	44.7	20.3	33.4	27.3	9,064	7.6	5.2
35980	Norwich-New London, CT	38,698	3.3	13.8	66.4	48.2	17.1	33.6	29.5	3,601	6.5	3.5
36100	Ocala, FL	39,241	2.7	12.9	58.2	35.0	22.5	41.8	34.2	5,948	10.1	4.9
36140	Ocean City, NJ	11,531	2.4	9.5	67.9	46.5	21.0	32.1	28.2	1,766	10.6	3.8
36220	Odessa, TX	25,633	2.1	31.7	60.1	34.2	25.2	39.9	29.7	5,028	12.6	7.8
36260	Ogden-Clearfield, UT	123,890	1.8	11.8	77.7	43.8	33.4	22.3	19.6	10,647	5.5	2.5
36420	Oklahoma City, OK	199,517	4.0	17.7	65.9	42.1	22.5	34.1	28.3	22,944	7.4	4.2
36500	Olympia-Tumwater, WA	37,795	4.1	15.8	67.9	41.9	24.4	32.1	26.1	2,464	4.4	2.5
36540	Omaha-Council Bluffs, NE-IA	145,110	3.9	14.8	68.4	48.9	18.6	31.6	27.7	11,034	5.0	2.4
36740	Orlando-Kissimmee-Sanford, FL	330,993	4.9	29.2	62.2	41.3	19.7	37.8	31.9	38,273	7.9	4.1
36780	Oshkosh-Neenah, WI	22,525	1.5	8.9	70.7	50.9	19.7	29.3	23.5	1,101	3.2	1.3
36980	Owensboro, KY	17,487	1.2	3.8	65.4	41.7	23.0	34.6	30.3	2,533	9.8	4.8
37100	Oxnard-Thousand Oaks-Ventura, CA	134,223	5.8	44.8	71.9	46.5	24.6	28.1	23.6	17,284	8.7	2.8
37340	Palm Bay-Melbourne-Titusville, FL	67,388	2.4	15.5	61.3	38.8	21.9	38.7	33.1	11,062	11.2	6.6
37460	Panama City, FL	24,855	2.1	8.6	61.0	40.2	20.1	39.0	33.7	3,040	8.0	5.9
37620	Parkersburg-Vienna, WV	11,882	0.3	1.9	62.4	41.4	19.6	37.6	33.0	1,480	8.1	5.0
37860	Pensacola-Ferry Pass-Brent, FL	61,549	1.3	10.4	66.9	41.0	24.8	33.1	26.5	10,163	10.8	6.6
37900	Peoria, IL	57,594	2.3	7.1	67.4	43.4	22.9	32.6	27.5	4,928	5.7	3.5
37980	Philadelphia-Camden-Wilmington, PA-NJ-DE-MD	880,105	3.6	16.8	63.7	44.3	18.4	36.3	28.9	112,828	8.6	4.8
38060	Phoenix-Mesa-Scottsdale, AZ	702,853	5.0	31.1	63.3	36.0	25.9	36.7	29.5	82,214	7.8	3.8
38220	Pine Bluff, AR	14,040	0.1	4.1	47.2	32.3	13.2	52.8	43.9	2,862	14.0	8.6
38300	Pittsburgh, PA	302,300	2.0	5.5	68.4	46.0	21.3	31.6	24.9	26,485	6.0	3.2
38340	Pittsfield, MA	15,824	1.4	8.1	65.7	48.2	15.2	34.3	29.5	1,354	6.0	4.0

CBSA FIPS code	Metropolitan area	Total own children under 18 in families and subfamilies	Total own children under 6 years	Nativity and parentage, under 6 years		Own children under 6 years living with two parents			Own children under 6 living with one parent	
				Child is foreign born, percent	One or more foreign-born parent, percent	Total under 6 years living with two parents, percent	Both parents in labor force, percent	One parent in labor force, percent	Total under 6 years living with one parent, percent	Parent in labor force, percent
38540	Pocatello, ID................	21,941	7,538	0.4	3.6	67.0	34.7	31.3	33.0	25.5
38860	Portland–South Portland, ME...........	100,970	30,179	1.0	9.7	70.9	48.8	21.2	29.1	24.1
38900	Portland–Vancouver–Hillsboro, OR–WA................	503,734	165,362	1.5	28.5	73.5	41.3	31.2	26.5	20.1
38940	Port St. Lucie, FL................	83,230	25,732	0.4	28.9	55.7	34.7	19.7	44.3	35.1
39140	Prescott, AZ................	35,712	11,112	0.7	11.7	60.6	29.8	24.3	39.4	31.1
39300	Providence–Warwick, RI–MA............	320,626	99,816	1.4	21.0	59.1	40.5	17.8	40.9	31.5
39340	Provo–Orem, UT................	187,822	68,578	0.5	13.8	88.6	31.6	55.6	11.4	9.0
39380	Pueblo, CO................	35,674	11,583	0.4	10.9	53.0	28.1	23.6	47.0	36.1
39460	Punta Gorda, FL................	20,542	6,101	1.6	24.2	59.3	32.7	24.4	40.7	33.9
39540	Racine, WI................	45,381	14,464	0.3	13.1	58.8	36.9	21.5	41.2	32.7
39580	Raleigh, NC................	295,184	95,738	1.9	27.2	71.3	41.6	29.5	28.7	23.0
39660	Rapid City, SD................	31,212	10,764	0.0	2.5	55.9	37.7	17.6	44.1	37.2
39740	Reading, PA................	91,682	28,426	0.6	15.7	59.9	37.4	20.8	40.1	30.8
39820	Redding, CA................	36,094	11,239	0.9	11.3	63.9	28.5	29.5	36.1	29.3
39900	Reno, NV................	95,035	32,436	0.8	33.8	65.6	40.7	24.5	34.4	27.8
40060	Richmond, VA................	265,325	87,434	1.1	15.5	59.8	38.0	21.4	40.2	32.0
40140	Riverside–San Bernardino–Ontario, CA................	1,138,201	371,480	1.0	37.0	60.8	30.1	28.9	39.2	28.0
40220	Roanoke, VA................	62,444	20,068	0.9	14.3	67.2	42.6	23.9	32.8	24.8
40340	Rochester, MN................	51,309	17,398	0.9	17.8	73.2	55.6	16.8	26.8	23.8
40380	Rochester, NY................	225,278	69,409	1.2	10.5	58.8	38.8	19.2	41.2	32.4
40420	Rockford, IL................	81,302	26,659	0.8	18.5	54.6	36.0	17.8	45.4	37.3
40580	Rocky Mount, NC................	32,927	10,343	2.0	11.6	38.5	23.9	14.6	61.5	52.4
40660	Rome, GA................	20,806	7,078	1.2	21.4	62.5	42.9	19.1	37.5	27.5
40900	Sacramento–Roseville–Arden–Arcade, CA................	509,315	165,584	1.5	35.7	66.6	37.5	27.3	33.4	25.1
40980	Saginaw, MI................	42,397	13,455	0.0	2.5	52.0	34.6	15.8	48.0	37.3
41060	St. Cloud, MN................	43,373	14,737	0.4	9.7	69.5	54.0	14.8	30.5	25.4
41100	St. George, UT................	40,325	14,431	0.0	14.7	80.5	32.9	47.0	19.5	15.8
41140	St. Joseph, MO–KS................	27,070	9,015	0.0	6.1	54.0	34.4	18.9	46.0	40.4
41180	St. Louis, MO–IL................	620,816	200,290	0.9	9.9	63.8	41.2	21.5	36.2	29.5
41420	Salem, OR................	97,178	31,131	0.4	30.7	63.5	36.0	26.3	36.5	26.1
41500	Salinas, CA................	107,010	37,511	1.8	58.1	60.4	30.0	29.2	39.6	30.3
41540	Salisbury, MD–DE................	70,780	23,695	0.8	21.6	53.3	33.3	19.6	46.7	37.0
41620	Salt Lake City, UT................	313,820	109,798	1.1	24.3	75.9	36.2	39.4	24.1	19.4
41660	San Angelo, TX................	25,493	9,494	1.0	12.8	58.0	29.1	27.8	42.0	30.6
41700	San Antonio–New Braunfels, TX.......	557,274	183,292	1.1	22.3	59.9	31.3	27.5	40.1	29.7
41740	San Diego–Carlsbad, CA................	693,655	241,503	2.2	41.4	71.3	37.2	32.8	28.7	21.4
41860	San Francisco–Oakland–Hayward, CA	889,919	302,140	2.5	51.2	73.9	45.8	27.1	26.1	20.8
41940	San Jose–Sunnyvale–Santa Clara, CA	434,072	150,074	4.0	63.1	75.9	44.5	31.0	24.1	18.8
42020	San Luis Obispo–Paso Robles–Arroyo Grande, CA................	48,828	16,522	1.9	28.5	69.5	41.9	26.7	30.5	26.4
42100	Santa Cruz–Watsonville, CA...........	52,870	17,749	0.6	47.1	70.0	41.9	27.8	30.0	23.4
42140	Santa Fe, NM................	28,282	9,069	0.5	31.4	61.8	39.7	21.5	38.2	30.0
42200	Santa Maria–Santa Barbara, CA........	92,345	32,035	1.7	48.0	63.0	36.2	26.3	37.0	29.6
42220	Santa Rosa, CA................	100,267	32,434	1.6	38.3	69.3	39.4	29.3	30.7	24.0
42340	Savannah, GA................	81,087	28,656	1.1	14.0	58.2	31.0	27.1	41.8	31.6
42540	Scranton–Wilkes-Barre–Hazleton, PA	107,721	33,556	0.7	12.2	56.6	38.0	17.9	43.4	31.2
42660	Seattle–Tacoma–Bellevue, WA........	764,764	262,190	2.5	34.3	72.7	38.6	33.0	27.3	20.3
42680	Sebastian–Vero Beach, FL	23,975	7,615	1.3	27.2	63.1	33.6	27.7	36.9	32.5
42700	Sebring, FL................	17,008	5,499	2.6	29.8	58.0	29.0	24.8	42.0	27.3
43100	Sheboygan, WI................	25,757	8,493	0.9	15.9	68.4	46.8	21.5	31.6	26.1
43300	Sherman–Denison, TX................	27,181	9,200	1.4	14.8	57.0	34.2	21.3	43.0	33.5
43340	Shreveport–Bossier City, LA............	102,535	36,134	0.4	6.3	46.8	28.1	18.6	53.2	38.1
43420	Sierra Vista–Douglas, AZ................	27,981	8,908	1.5	25.1	65.7	29.7	34.3	34.3	27.8
43580	Sioux City, IA–NE-SD................	42,247	14,564	1.0	22.1	61.6	43.2	17.2	38.4	33.3
43620	Sioux Falls, SD................	59,705	21,758	1.1	10.2	68.8	51.6	17.2	31.2	25.7
43780	South Bend–Mishawaka, IN–MI........	72,102	23,797	1.2	13.8	61.5	35.5	25.2	38.5	30.6
43900	Spartanburg, SC................	70,830	23,098	0.4	15.9	55.5	29.9	24.5	44.5	34.7
44060	Spokane–Spokane Valley, WA........	115,014	37,983	0.7	9.8	69.5	36.4	31.7	30.5	22.5
44100	Springfield, IL................	46,835	15,141	0.3	5.9	60.6	43.1	17.4	39.4	34.4
44140	Springfield, MA................	126,022	39,594	1.2	15.9	53.1	36.1	14.9	46.9	31.2
44180	Springfield, MO................	96,451	33,424	0.5	5.9	64.7	37.8	25.7	35.3	28.2
44220	Springfield, OH................	29,907	9,456	0.0	5.0	47.9	27.1	20.2	52.1	38.7
44300	State College, PA................	23,232	7,518	2.4	13.9	78.8	49.5	28.5	21.2	16.5
44420	Staunton–Waynesboro, VA...............	23,126	7,392	0.0	5.4	64.3	37.5	25.0	35.7	29.0
44700	Stockton–Lodi, CA................	189,541	62,263	1.2	41.9	63.2	36.1	26.1	36.8	27.5
44940	Sumter, SC................	24,906	9,202	0.7	9.0	50.8	29.3	19.6	49.2	37.5
45060	Syracuse, NY................	140,451	43,904	1.2	11.4	60.5	38.0	21.5	39.5	27.4
45220	Tallahassee, FL................	70,021	23,221	1.0	12.5	57.1	36.4	19.6	42.9	33.1
45300	Tampa–St. Petersburg–Clearwater, FL	556,179	180,880	1.5	23.3	57.8	34.6	22.4	42.2	33.0
45460	Terre Haute, IN................	34,747	11,278	0.1	4.0	58.0	31.0	26.5	42.0	29.8

CBSA FIPS code	Metropolitan area	Total own children 6 to 17	Nativity and parentage, age 6 to 17 years		Own children age 6 to 17 years living with two parents			Own children age 6 to 17 years living with one parent		Grand-children under 18 living with a grandparent householder	Grand-children under 18 living with a grandparent householder, as a percent of all children	Children for whom grandparent householders are responsible, as a percent of all children
			Child is foreign born, percent	One or more foreign-born parent, percent	Age 6 to 17 years living with two parents, percent	Both parents in labor force, percent	One parent in labor force, percent	Age 6 to 17 living with one parent, percent	Parent in labor force, percent			
38540	Pocatello, ID	14,403	1.9	7.7	74.3	50.0	23.7	25.7	20.2	998	4.5	2.2
38860	Portland–South Portland, ME	70,791	2.6	9.2	69.4	50.6	17.9	30.6	25.9	5,156	5.1	2.4
38900	Portland-Vancouver-Hillsboro, OR-WA	338,372	5.8	28.0	69.8	43.5	25.1	30.2	25.3	27,465	5.5	2.7
38940	Port St. Lucie, FL	57,498	4.4	31.4	65.1	42.1	21.9	34.9	28.9	5,601	6.7	3.6
39140	Prescott, AZ	24,600	3.4	13.9	65.1	42.4	19.6	34.9	29.9	4,562	12.8	7.7
39300	Providence-Warwick, RI-MA	220,810	4.2	23.4	63.3	47.0	15.7	36.7	29.7	21,638	6.7	2.7
39340	Provo-Orem, UT	119,244	2.5	15.7	86.4	38.3	46.8	13.6	11.3	9,439	5.0	2.0
39380	Pueblo, CO	24,091	0.8	7.9	61.2	39.8	19.5	38.8	33.6	3,339	9.4	4.8
39460	Punta Gorda, FL	14,441	3.4	18.1	59.9	41.5	16.2	40.1	32.8	2,008	9.8	5.3
39540	Racine, WI	30,917	1.5	10.8	64.2	44.1	19.1	35.8	29.1	2,816	6.2	3.5
39580	Raleigh, NC	199,446	4.8	21.9	69.1	45.6	22.6	30.9	26.7	13,382	4.5	2.2
39660	Rapid City, SD	20,448	0.7	2.0	62.1	49.0	11.8	37.9	33.1	1,729	5.5	2.7
39740	Reading, PA	63,256	3.2	16.5	66.4	46.3	19.1	33.6	27.2	6,691	7.3	3.8
39820	Redding, CA	24,855	1.8	11.5	61.4	35.1	22.9	38.6	28.0	3,158	8.7	5.6
39900	Reno, NV	62,599	5.3	36.2	65.6	43.0	21.6	34.4	28.7	6,120	6.4	3.8
40060	Richmond, VA	177,891	3.3	12.8	64.9	46.4	17.8	35.1	28.9	19,430	7.3	3.7
40140	Riverside-San Bernardino-Ontario, CA	766,721	4.7	45.7	64.3	36.0	26.7	35.7	27.5	121,786	10.7	4.8
40220	Roanoke, VA	42,376	3.1	9.4	66.7	47.7	17.8	33.3	28.7	5,500	8.8	4.7
40340	Rochester, MN	33,911	3.9	14.2	73.1	59.4	12.6	26.9	23.8	1,653	3.2	1.0
40380	Rochester, NY	155,869	3.0	10.4	61.5	44.1	16.4	38.5	30.8	14,131	6.3	3.6
40420	Rockford, IL	54,643	2.7	18.4	61.2	40.8	19.7	38.8	33.3	6,654	8.2	4.1
40580	Rocky Mount, NC	22,584	1.3	9.1	52.7	37.0	14.6	47.3	38.9	4,188	12.7	8.5
40660	Rome, GA	13,728	2.8	18.1	65.8	43.1	20.9	34.2	25.3	2,701	13.0	9.5
40900	Sacramento–Roseville–Arden-Arcade, CA	343,731	6.0	35.7	65.3	41.1	22.3	34.7	27.9	33,879	6.7	2.7
40980	Saginaw, MI	28,942	0.7	3.5	57.1	41.1	14.0	42.9	35.7	3,312	7.8	4.0
41060	St. Cloud, MN	28,636	3.0	7.7	76.9	66.1	10.2	23.1	19.9	1,384	3.2	1.8
41100	St. George, UT	25,894	2.2	13.3	71.1	38.6	31.6	28.9	22.9	2,039	5.1	2.3
41140	St. Joseph, MO-KS	18,055	1.1	5.0	70.9	53.7	15.6	29.1	21.4	2,553	9.4	5.4
41180	St. Louis, MO-IL	420,526	2.4	7.6	64.5	46.1	17.4	35.5	29.8	43,522	7.0	3.7
41420	Salem, OR	66,047	5.3	34.2	66.0	42.6	22.6	34.0	28.1	4,859	5.0	2.4
41500	Salinas, CA	69,499	9.7	63.1	67.2	39.9	24.3	32.8	27.0	8,254	7.7	2.7
41540	Salisbury, MD-DE	47,085	3.4	14.1	59.1	41.5	15.9	40.9	33.4	7,500	10.6	6.6
41620	Salt Lake City, UT	204,022	4.8	24.4	76.2	43.1	32.4	23.8	20.5	22,045	7.0	2.5
41660	San Angelo, TX	15,999	1.5	15.2	59.4	35.7	23.0	40.6	34.8	2,094	8.2	3.6
41700	San Antonio-New Braunfels, TX	373,982	4.4	24.6	63.4	39.1	23.1	36.6	29.5	61,633	11.1	5.8
41740	San Diego-Carlsbad, CA	452,152	7.5	47.8	67.9	39.2	27.1	32.1	26.0	55,139	7.9	3.4
41860	San Francisco-Oakland-Hayward, CA	587,779	8.0	51.7	71.7	46.2	24.5	28.3	23.8	57,145	6.4	2.6
41940	San Jose-Sunnyvale-Santa Clara, CA	283,998	9.8	63.2	75.0	46.2	27.9	25.0	20.6	29,309	6.8	2.4
42020	San Luis Obispo-Paso Robles-Arroyo Grande, CA	32,306	3.6	25.1	72.5	50.4	21.9	27.5	22.1	3,019	6.2	3.8
42100	Santa Cruz-Watsonville, CA	35,121	5.2	44.7	69.7	46.8	20.9	30.3	26.4	3,245	6.1	1.6
42140	Santa Fe, NM	19,213	9.9	32.3	54.8	38.8	14.9	45.2	36.8	2,186	7.7	5.4
42200	Santa Maria-Santa Barbara, CA	60,310	7.8	51.2	67.8	43.9	23.0	32.2	26.5	7,021	7.6	3.3
42220	Santa Rosa, CA	67,833	7.0	40.2	70.5	44.3	24.8	29.5	26.0	5,080	5.1	2.3
42340	Savannah, GA	52,431	2.8	9.5	58.4	40.9	16.8	41.6	34.7	7,980	9.8	6.7
42540	Scranton–Wilkes-Barre–Hazleton, PA	74,165	2.8	10.0	62.6	42.4	17.7	37.4	28.7	7,748	7.2	3.1
42660	Seattle-Tacoma-Bellevue, WA	502,574	7.0	31.2	71.1	44.2	25.8	28.9	23.6	36,116	4.7	2.1
42680	Sebastian-Vero Beach, FL	16,360	4.4	22.2	68.9	47.0	21.5	31.1	25.1	1,817	7.6	4.3
42700	Sebring, FL	11,509	3.1	25.0	64.2	39.9	22.0	35.8	27.9	1,744	10.3	7.0
43100	Sheboygan, WI	17,264	4.2	12.6	72.9	56.6	16.1	27.1	23.6	725	2.8	1.3
43300	Sherman-Denison, TX	17,981	3.1	13.2	63.1	40.2	20.3	36.9	31.2	2,424	8.9	4.9
43340	Shreveport-Bossier City, LA	66,401	1.1	3.9	50.1	32.7	16.0	49.9	39.0	13,330	13.0	9.0
43420	Sierra Vista-Douglas, AZ	19,073	4.9	21.4	65.4	36.4	26.7	34.6	26.4	2,993	10.7	7.4
43580	Sioux City, IA-NE-SD	27,683	2.6	19.1	66.9	50.5	15.8	33.1	29.2	2,517	6.0	2.9
43620	Sioux Falls, SD	37,947	3.6	11.3	70.0	54.5	15.3	30.0	26.7	1,981	3.3	1.8
43780	South Bend-Mishawaka, IN-MI	48,305	2.6	11.7	65.0	44.7	19.3	35.0	28.4	4,628	6.4	4.0
43900	Spartanburg, SC	47,732	3.3	14.4	61.0	38.7	21.4	39.0	32.7	7,669	10.8	6.8
44060	Spokane-Spokane Valley, WA	77,031	2.5	9.9	68.7	41.6	25.0	31.3	25.3	6,157	5.4	3.1
44100	Springfield, IL	31,694	1.7	5.9	60.4	47.4	12.7	39.6	34.3	2,073	4.4	2.6
44140	Springfield, MA	86,428	3.5	14.4	53.8	39.8	12.6	46.2	32.6	8,970	7.1	3.9
44180	Springfield, MO	63,027	1.2	5.2	69.6	44.6	23.1	30.4	25.4	5,872	6.1	3.4
44220	Springfield, OH	20,451	0.7	4.4	63.4	44.7	17.3	36.6	29.1	2,580	8.6	4.8
44300	State College, PA	15,714	3.4	6.2	76.0	53.7	21.7	24.0	19.6	772	3.3	1.6
44420	Staunton-Waynesboro, VA	15,734	0.8	3.6	64.0	42.3	20.6	36.0	26.6	1,922	8.3	3.5
44700	Stockton-Lodi, CA	127,278	5.8	46.0	65.5	38.3	25.5	34.5	26.4	15,215	8.0	3.7
44940	Sumter, SC	15,704	1.4	4.8	57.1	36.9	19.1	42.9	34.7	3,305	13.3	8.0
45060	Syracuse, NY	96,547	3.1	9.6	65.6	44.9	19.5	34.4	27.9	8,265	5.9	3.1
45220	Tallahassee, FL	46,800	2.6	9.2	55.6	36.5	17.2	44.4	37.6	5,783	8.3	4.2
45300	Tampa-St. Petersburg-Clearwater, FL	375,299	4.4	22.6	62.3	40.7	20.0	37.7	31.1	48,085	8.6	4.7
45460	Terre Haute, IN	23,469	0.4	2.5	67.4	42.2	24.1	32.6	25.9	2,473	7.1	4.1

| CBSA FIPS code | Metropolitan area | Total own children under 18 in families and subfamilies | Own children under 6 years in families and subfamilies | | | | | | | |
| | | | Total own children under 6 years | Nativity and parentage, under 6 years | | Own children under 6 years living with two parents | | | Own children under 6 living with one parent | |
				Child is foreign born, percent	One or more foreign-born parent, percent	Total under 6 years living with two parents, percent	Both parents in labor force, percent	One parent in labor force, percent	Total under 6 years living with one parent, percent	Parent in labor force, percent
45500	Texarkana, TX-AR............................	33,267	10,725	0.0	6.7	50.8	31.6	19.2	49.2	35.7
45540	The Villages, FL	7,542	2,524	0.0	17.9	67.2	48.1	18.9	32.8	30.0
45780	Toledo, OH....................................	133,188	45,059	0.3	6.2	56.8	37.8	18.2	43.2	34.4
45820	Topeka, KS.....................................	54,539	17,786	0.2	10.2	66.1	44.1	21.9	33.9	28.6
45940	Trenton, NJ	78,850	25,525	2.0	40.1	68.0	43.7	24.0	32.0	25.1
46060	Tucson, AZ.....................................	208,664	69,613	1.5	22.7	58.6	30.0	27.7	41.4	31.3
46140	Tulsa, OK.......................................	227,003	76,524	0.9	15.0	62.3	34.6	26.9	37.7	27.2
46220	Tuscaloosa, AL................................	47,400	16,160	0.3	9.9	58.8	38.3	19.1	41.2	26.0
46340	Tyler, TX..	50,301	16,780	0.4	28.5	62.4	32.0	28.8	37.6	27.9
46520	Urban Honolulu, HI..........................	201,647	72,934	1.8	27.7	70.5	39.9	29.3	29.5	20.2
46540	Utica-Rome, NY	61,289	19,358	2.1	13.4	56.7	35.8	19.8	43.3	33.4
46660	Valdosta, GA...................................	32,888	12,290	0.0	7.9	48.9	25.5	22.2	51.1	38.0
46700	Vallejo-Fairfield, CA.........................	93,328	30,559	0.6	34.3	59.1	33.3	25.2	40.9	32.4
47020	Victoria, TX....................................	23,186	7,925	0.4	9.6	53.3	26.2	27.0	46.7	32.7
47220	Vineland-Bridgeton, NJ	34,860	11,840	0.8	23.0	48.3	28.2	20.0	51.7	39.2
47260	Virginia Beach-Norfolk-Newport News, VA-NC	370,116	126,752	0.9	11.4	57.1	31.8	24.8	42.9	33.6
47300	Visalia-Porterville, CA......................	135,587	46,936	0.9	45.1	54.4	26.9	26.1	45.6	33.3
47380	Waco, TX.......................................	60,607	20,932	0.3	22.4	58.1	32.2	25.0	41.9	30.7
47460	Walla Walla, WA.............................	12,911	4,111	0.0	32.0	59.6	38.5	17.6	40.4	34.8
47580	Warner Robins, GA..........................	43,833	14,580	0.5	9.5	50.4	31.0	18.5	49.6	34.8
47900	Washington-Arlington-Alexandria, DC-VA-MD-WV.............................	1,327,334	459,532	2.3	40.6	69.8	44.4	25.1	30.2	25.0
47940	Waterloo-Cedar Falls, IA...................	35,483	12,140	0.9	10.3	71.2	50.8	19.2	28.8	23.7
48060	Watertown-Fort Drum, NY..............	28,483	11,419	0.6	10.5	64.3	34.7	28.7	35.7	23.9
48140	Wausau, WI....................................	30,987	9,940	0.2	13.6	73.6	49.5	23.7	26.4	21.7
48260	Weirton-Steubenville, WV-OH	22,266	6,638	0.0	0.0	54.9	28.2	26.2	45.1	27.8
48300	Wenatchee, WA..............................	26,836	8,575	1.5	43.9	71.0	32.5	38.6	29.0	23.3
48540	Wheeling, WV-OH	26,203	8,157	0.0	1.2	63.3	42.5	20.6	36.7	30.7
48620	Wichita, KS....................................	161,716	55,915	0.7	15.9	63.6	37.0	26.2	36.4	30.2
48660	Wichita Falls, TX	32,554	11,224	0.9	9.6	59.0	35.0	22.8	41.0	31.1
48700	Williamsport, PA.............................	22,982	7,541	1.6	3.4	62.3	46.5	15.0	37.7	29.1
48900	Wilmington, NC..............................	51,441	18,091	1.2	14.6	61.2	39.0	22.0	38.8	29.5
49020	Winchester, VA-WV	28,873	9,448	0.4	22.1	70.9	44.4	26.1	29.1	22.9
49180	Winston-Salem, NC	143,241	46,736	0.5	22.0	59.1	32.5	25.8	40.9	30.5
49340	Worcester, MA-CT	198,596	61,117	1.2	22.3	65.7	44.0	20.3	34.3	26.2
49420	Yakima, WA....................................	70,264	24,537	0.6	41.2	58.2	30.1	26.5	41.8	31.4
49620	York-Hanover, PA............................	95,538	30,576	0.3	6.0	62.2	42.1	20.0	37.8	27.2
49660	Youngstown-Warren-Boardman, OH-PA..	111,913	34,048	0.4	2.9	52.8	32.1	20.0	47.2	33.9
49700	Yuba City, CA	43,909	14,838	1.1	33.1	65.6	32.9	32.3	34.4	24.4
49740	Yuma, AZ.......................................	52,096	17,932	1.5	41.3	62.2	32.1	29.0	37.8	25.3

Table D-3: Metropolitan Areas—Children—*Continued*

CBSA FIPS code	Metropolitan area	Total own children 6 to 17	Nativity and parentage, age 6 to 17 years		Own children age 6 to 17 years living with two parents			Own children age 6 to 17 years living with one parent		Grandchildren under 18 living with a grandparent householder	Grandchildren under 18 living with a grandparent householder, as a percent of all children	Children for whom grandparent householders are responsible, as a percent of all children
			Child is foreign born, percent	One or more foreign-born parent, percent	Age 6 to 17 years living with two parents, percent	Both parents in labor force, percent	One parent in labor force, percent	Age 6 to 17 years living with one parent, percent	Parent in labor force, percent			
45500	Texarkana, TX-AR	22,542	0.7	4.3	54.0	36.6	16.4	46.0	38.1	4,530	13.6	9.7
45540	The Villages, FL	5,018	1.5	15.2	59.8	40.3	17.4	40.2	34.8	853	11.3	7.8
45780	Toledo, OH	88,129	0.9	5.0	58.2	42.0	14.6	41.8	34.4	9,428	7.1	4.1
45820	Topeka, KS	36,753	2.1	9.5	69.1	51.1	17.3	30.9	26.2	3,612	6.6	3.3
45940	Trenton, NJ	53,325	8.7	37.6	69.3	50.5	17.9	30.7	25.6	4,419	5.6	2.0
46060	Tucson, AZ	139,051	4.9	29.4	59.7	36.2	22.2	40.3	33.6	19,795	9.5	5.1
46140	Tulsa, OK	150,479	2.6	12.2	65.1	40.8	23.1	34.9	27.6	17,703	7.8	4.6
46220	Tuscaloosa, AL	31,240	1.5	5.1	58.2	41.1	14.9	41.8	30.3	4,755	10.0	6.6
46340	Tyler, TX	33,521	3.7	24.8	69.5	43.3	25.3	30.5	26.6	5,569	11.1	6.5
46520	Urban Honolulu, HI	128,713	6.6	32.3	71.9	48.9	21.4	28.1	22.6	33,294	16.5	5.4
46540	Utica-Rome, NY	41,931	5.9	14.0	61.5	42.6	17.0	38.5	31.3	3,230	5.3	2.3
46660	Valdosta, GA	20,598	1.6	7.1	57.7	35.2	20.7	42.3	37.2	3,551	10.8	5.4
46700	Vallejo-Fairfield, CA	62,769	5.2	39.2	65.3	40.2	24.1	34.7	29.3	8,312	8.9	3.7
47020	Victoria, TX	15,261	1.4	12.2	56.3	33.8	22.6	43.7	35.4	2,966	12.8	6.5
47220	Vineland-Bridgeton, NJ	23,020	4.7	19.5	52.1	36.7	14.4	47.9	40.1	4,314	12.4	4.9
47260	Virginia Beach-Norfolk-Newport News, VA-NC	243,364	2.2	10.8	59.8	39.5	19.5	40.2	34.3	35,467	9.6	5.0
47300	Visalia-Porterville, CA	88,651	5.4	51.5	63.5	37.2	24.7	36.5	28.2	15,198	11.2	5.2
47380	Waco, TX	39,675	4.5	22.7	62.1	40.8	20.7	37.9	30.5	6,098	10.1	6.6
47460	Walla Walla, WA	8,800	4.6	24.8	71.8	44.1	24.1	28.2	20.7	609	4.7	3.2
47580	Warner Robins, GA	29,253	2.5	12.4	61.9	43.2	18.4	38.1	30.2	4,223	9.6	5.8
47900	Washington-Arlington-Alexandria, DC-VA-MD-WV	867,802	7.7	36.7	70.4	48.7	21.1	29.6	25.8	87,120	6.6	2.9
47940	Waterloo-Cedar Falls, IA	23,343	2.4	9.4	71.5	53.7	16.5	28.5	24.2	1,643	4.6	2.9
48060	Watertown-Fort Drum, NY	17,064	1.9	10.9	66.4	40.8	24.0	33.6	24.2	1,803	6.3	3.6
48140	Wausau, WI	21,047	1.6	10.1	75.5	56.5	18.2	24.5	21.7	862	2.8	1.3
48260	Weirton-Steubenville, WV-OH	15,628	0.0	0.0	68.7	39.6	27.5	31.3	24.1	2,032	9.1	5.8
48300	Wenatchee, WA	18,261	5.1	38.4	70.7	46.4	23.7	29.3	25.2	1,574	5.9	3.4
48540	Wheeling, WV-OH	18,046	0.4	1.1	67.9	47.1	19.4	32.1	27.2	1,927	7.4	3.6
48620	Wichita, KS	105,801	3.2	17.0	67.5	46.8	20.0	32.5	28.3	11,016	6.8	3.5
48660	Wichita Falls, TX	21,330	2.3	12.3	66.1	46.3	18.8	33.9	29.8	2,696	8.3	4.5
48700	Williamsport, PA	15,441	0.7	3.5	68.9	51.4	17.1	31.1	27.2	1,664	7.2	2.7
48900	Wilmington, NC	33,350	2.3	13.0	61.3	40.2	20.3	38.7	30.4	3,249	6.3	4.5
49020	Winchester, VA-WV	19,425	2.2	12.7	76.2	47.9	27.9	23.8	19.6	2,009	7.0	3.9
49180	Winston-Salem, NC	96,505	3.6	18.3	63.9	42.9	19.8	36.1	29.4	11,831	8.3	5.4
49340	Worcester, MA-CT	137,479	4.8	18.1	68.2	50.2	16.4	31.8	25.5	11,057	5.6	2.8
49420	Yakima, WA	45,727	4.3	48.1	61.6	38.8	21.0	38.4	30.2	6,749	9.6	4.1
49620	York-Hanover, PA	64,962	1.5	6.1	67.2	47.5	18.9	32.8	26.7	6,343	6.6	3.3
49660	Youngstown-Warren-Boardman, OH-PA	77,865	0.5	3.2	60.4	39.4	19.3	39.6	31.3	8,239	7.4	4.5
49700	Yuba City, CA	29,071	5.6	35.4	66.2	38.9	25.6	33.8	23.8	3,929	8.9	3.4
49740	Yuma, AZ	34,164	6.0	54.1	63.2	36.6	24.8	36.8	28.4	5,455	10.5	3.6

Table D-4: Cities with a Population of 50,000 or More—Children

State/Place FIPS code	State/Place	Total own children under 18 in families and subfamilies	Own children under 6 years in families and subfamilies						
			Total own children under 6 years	Nativity and parentage, under 6 years		Own children under 6 years living with two parents			Own children under 6 living with one parent	
				Child is foreign born, percent	One or more foreign-born parent, percent	Total under 6 years living with two parents, percent	Both parents in labor force, percent	One parent in labor force, percent	Total under 6 years living with one parent, percent	Parent in labor force, percent
0000000	United States.........	70,173,842	23,215,525	1.3	25.0	63.4	36.8	25.7	36.6	27.9
0100000	Alabama................	1,050,918	344,683	0.5	8.9	57.8	33.3	23.7	42.2	31.3
0103076	Auburn city...........	10,042	3,255	1.0	13.2	73.2	41.3	29.4	26.8	23.5
0107000	Birmingham city......	41,020	16,722	0.4	7.8	31.5	18.3	11.8	68.5	48.8
0120104	Decatur city...........	11,933	4,161	1.0	31.6	64.5	36.4	28.1	35.5	28.8
0121184	Dothan city...........	14,859	5,126	0.3	4.9	52.3	35.3	16.7	47.7	37.8
0135896	Hoover city...........	21,062	6,884	1.9	21.8	85.9	51.1	34.2	14.1	13.7
0137000	Huntsville city.......	37,039	13,036	0.8	12.2	52.2	32.2	19.1	47.8	41.9
0150000	Mobile city...........	41,946	14,921	1.1	7.2	39.0	22.2	16.0	61.0	45.9
0151000	Montgomery city......	48,538	16,752	0.8	10.6	45.3	25.1	19.9	54.7	39.6
0177256	Tuscaloosa city.......	16,034	5,570	0.5	16.0	54.3	36.6	15.5	45.7	26.9
0200000	Alaska...................	179,648	63,336	0.3	10.7	65.1	34.6	29.1	34.9	27.5
0203000	Anchorage municipality..........	72,539	25,464	0.3	14.9	66.5	38.7	26.2	33.5	29.1
0400000	Arizona.................	1,531,962	508,962	1.2	26.8	60.4	30.4	28.6	39.6	29.3
0404720	Avondale city.........	22,697	7,813	0.1	27.6	47.6	24.9	22.1	52.4	35.0
0407940	Buckeye town.........	15,107	4,717	2.2	21.7	69.0	28.7	38.9	31.0	18.7
0410670	Casas Adobes CDP.....	15,946	5,028	1.8	18.3	73.4	40.6	32.8	26.6	22.7
0411230	Catalina Foothills CDP...........	7,853	1,983	3.7	27.9	92.3	38.8	53.6	7.7	6.2
0412000	Chandler city.........	63,246	20,769	0.9	29.2	70.6	39.1	31.0	29.4	21.9
0423620	Flagstaff city.........	12,815	4,957	0.6	20.0	54.5	33.3	21.2	45.5	34.9
0427400	Gilbert town..........	70,877	21,964	0.6	15.1	85.8	46.0	39.3	14.2	12.5
0427820	Glendale city.........	58,679	18,851	0.9	34.5	52.3	25.6	23.7	47.7	37.1
0428380	Goodyear city........	17,591	5,155	0.8	19.0	79.6	45.5	33.0	20.4	16.6
0439370	Lake Havasu City city	8,492	2,454	0.0	16.6	56.6	40.2	16.4	43.4	38.8
0446000	Mesa city.............	107,239	37,775	1.1	26.5	60.6	32.1	26.9	39.4	30.1
0454050	Peoria city............	38,617	11,369	0.2	16.4	67.1	34.0	31.6	32.9	26.9
0455000	Phoenix city...........	382,159	132,937	2.0	39.9	54.4	27.7	25.5	45.6	32.8
0464210	San Tan Valley CDP....	31,938	11,210	0.0	13.9	72.6	29.4	41.6	27.4	21.5
0465000	Scottsdale city........	38,412	12,598	1.2	28.0	68.0	27.8	40.1	32.0	26.3
0471510	Surprise city..........	33,740	10,527	1.9	14.6	73.9	38.7	34.0	26.1	20.1
0473000	Tempe city............	25,805	9,582	1.5	26.2	53.3	29.6	23.2	46.7	41.7
0477000	Tucson city...........	107,654	37,948	1.9	27.4	50.8	26.6	23.6	49.2	38.4
0485540	Yuma city.............	24,425	8,602	0.9	32.0	69.5	37.6	31.7	30.5	22.9
0500000	Arkansas...............	664,652	223,469	0.6	12.3	60.8	34.6	25.0	39.2	29.2
0515190	Conway city...........	13,784	4,695	0.4	5.7	62.1	37.5	24.4	37.9	32.5
0523290	Fayetteville city.......	13,058	4,395	3.6	12.2	80.4	44.5	35.2	19.6	13.3
0524550	Fort Smith city........	20,461	7,571	1.2	32.3	57.4	25.1	28.3	42.6	32.0
0535710	Jonesboro city........	16,416	6,272	0.0	4.7	52.8	33.2	19.6	47.2	35.8
0541000	Little Rock city........	42,200	15,268	0.9	14.3	46.7	30.1	15.7	53.3	37.7
0550450	North Little Rock city..	16,060	6,238	0.0	8.8	45.7	18.4	27.2	54.3	40.7
0560410	Rogers city............	17,655	6,288	2.2	34.2	70.0	32.4	36.5	30.0	26.7
0566080	Springdale city........	24,991	9,312	1.4	54.2	59.2	26.8	32.4	40.8	30.2
0600000	California...............	8,780,993	2,927,371	1.8	46.6	64.3	35.0	28.2	35.7	26.1
0600562	Alameda city..........	14,923	5,423	1.1	43.4	79.6	50.5	28.8	20.4	13.9
0600884	Alhambra city.........	15,004	5,015	3.6	53.5	70.7	41.5	28.8	29.3	23.1
0602000	Anaheim city..........	86,022	29,915	1.0	63.4	62.7	33.2	28.7	37.3	26.5
0602252	Antioch city...........	26,093	6,752	1.0	34.9	65.6	40.8	20.6	34.4	24.5
0602364	Apple Valley town.....	16,954	4,778	0.0	8.4	60.0	24.5	25.3	40.0	20.9
0602462	Arcadia city...........	11,609	2,696	8.3	74.6	92.0	61.0	29.3	8.0	6.2
0602553	Arden-Arcade CDP.....	19,039	7,239	0.6	29.3	66.0	33.6	32.2	34.0	28.5
0603526	Bakersfield city........	103,543	37,369	0.9	35.3	59.9	30.2	27.6	40.1	28.8
0603666	Baldwin Park city......	19,314	5,655	2.8	62.2	52.6	22.7	29.9	47.4	29.9
0604982	Bellflower city........	21,217	6,850	1.2	49.1	48.7	18.3	28.8	51.3	39.1
0606000	Berkeley city..........	13,372	4,907	2.1	33.0	77.6	57.9	18.2	22.4	13.6
0608142	Brentwood city........	15,433	4,329	3.4	27.1	65.4	36.9	26.5	34.6	28.4
0608786	Buena Park city.......	18,744	5,861	0.4	53.3	60.3	37.9	22.2	39.7	26.2
0608954	Burbank city..........	20,268	6,377	1.8	51.6	85.7	58.2	27.3	14.3	19.4
0610046	Camarillo city.........	14,860	4,737	0.0	14.1	69.5	41.7	27.8	30.5	19.4
0611194	Carlsbad city..........	24,209	7,702	1.2	24.2	86.0	45.7	33.7	14.0	13.5
0611390	Carmichael CDP.......	12,730	4,163	3.5	23.2	48.3	23.5	18.5	51.7	39.8
0611530	Carson city...........	18,922	6,058	1.2	51.9	61.3	44.3	16.3	38.7	32.8
0611964	Castro Valley CDP.....	12,965	4,587	0.5	57.1	80.9	45.5	34.9	19.1	14.3
0612048	Cathedral City city.....	14,142	4,647	0.9	63.4	57.0	25.8	31.1	43.0	27.7
0613014	Chico city.............	16,244	5,971	0.0	12.2	66.5	40.4	24.2	33.5	22.7
0613210	Chino city.............	18,296	6,435	1.0	32.2	71.3	47.8	23.5	28.7	25.5
0613214	Chino Hills city........	19,246	4,886	1.2	43.7	79.5	50.3	25.4	20.5	17.1
0613392	Chula Vista city........	64,652	20,275	1.4	44.3	66.3	38.8	26.9	33.7	25.3
0613588	Citrus Heights city.....	17,596	5,930	3.1	27.9	67.7	36.0	30.4	32.3	27.4
0614218	Clovis city............	26,923	8,019	0.5	24.0	71.0	47.2	22.3	29.0	21.9
0614890	Colton city............	16,649	6,095	0.3	46.5	50.2	25.3	24.9	49.8	37.1

Table D-4: Cities with a Population of 50,000 or More—Children—*Continued*

State/Place FIPS code	State/Place	Total own children 6 to 17	Nativity and parentage, age 6 to 17 years		Own children age 6 to 17 years living with two parents			Own children age 6 to 17 years living with one parent		Grandchildren under 18 living with a grandparent householder	Grandchildren under 18 living with a grandparent householder, as a percent of all children	Children for whom grandparent householders are responsible, as a percent of all children
			Child is foreign born, percent	One or more foreign-born parent, percent	Age 6 to 17 years living with two parents, percent	Both parents in labor force, percent	One parent in labor force, percent	Age 6 to 17 years living with one parent, percent	Parent in labor force, percent			
0000000	**United States**	46,958,317	4.4	24.5	65.6	42.4	21.9	34.4	28.1	5,562,532	7.9	4.1
0100000	**Alabama**	706,235	1.7	6.8	61.2	38.4	21.2	38.8	30.4	114,322	10.9	6.8
0103076	Auburn city	6,787	9.0	13.8	70.0	35.2	34.8	30.0	27.5	0	0.0	0.0
0107000	Birmingham city	24,298	0.9	3.5	29.4	21.8	6.9	70.6	52.9	5,833	14.2	9.9
0120104	Decatur city	7,772	2.1	17.7	61.1	36.9	24.2	38.9	34.2	920	7.7	5.0
0121184	Dothan city	9,733	0.5	5.1	56.3	37.1	17.7	43.7	31.9	1,320	8.9	5.6
0135896	Hoover city	14,178	4.5	16.6	76.2	45.2	31.0	23.8	22.0	549	2.6	1.6
0137000	Huntsville city	24,003	2.1	9.1	58.1	36.7	20.7	41.9	38.4	3,121	8.4	5.6
0150000	Mobile city	27,025	1.3	3.3	42.5	26.4	15.0	57.5	45.4	5,236	12.5	7.8
0151000	Montgomery city	31,786	2.9	8.2	42.4	25.0	16.5	57.6	45.0	4,740	9.8	5.7
0177256	Tuscaloosa city	10,464	2.1	6.5	46.9	29.1	14.5	53.1	35.5	1,149	7.2	4.9
0200000	**Alaska**	116,312	3.8	12.9	67.5	42.1	23.6	32.5	26.2	12,875	7.2	4.0
0203000	Anchorage municipality	47,075	4.8	19.1	67.5	45.6	20.1	32.5	27.6	4,215	5.8	2.8
0400000	**Arizona**	1,023,000	4.7	29.3	62.4	36.0	24.9	37.6	30.2	139,511	9.1	4.7
0404720	Avondale city	14,884	3.2	32.2	46.0	30.0	14.8	54.0	43.5	3,595	15.8	7.2
0407940	Buckeye town	10,390	1.4	22.1	67.2	41.3	25.2	32.8	24.8	1,498	9.9	5.9
0410670	Casas Adobes CDP	10,918	4.1	13.3	62.3	42.1	19.9	37.7	31.9	939	5.9	2.2
0411230	Catalina Foothills CDP	5,870	5.9	23.5	81.0	50.4	28.1	19.0	16.1	0	0.0	0.0
0412000	Chandler city	42,477	5.2	28.4	72.9	44.6	27.7	27.1	22.3	4,976	7.9	3.4
0423620	Flagstaff city	7,858	0.6	15.4	62.1	46.0	15.8	37.9	34.1	726	5.7	2.5
0427400	Gilbert town	48,913	3.2	16.0	78.4	43.8	33.5	21.6	19.4	2,623	3.7	1.1
0427820	Glendale city	39,828	7.3	37.8	54.6	32.7	20.3	45.4	34.4	5,799	9.9	5.3
0428380	Goodyear city	12,436	3.4	19.0	70.3	43.2	25.2	29.7	24.9	523	3.0	2.3
0439370	Lake Havasu City city	6,038	1.4	8.7	63.0	44.2	18.1	37.0	28.3	1,188	14.0	9.5
0446000	Mesa city	69,464	3.2	28.7	62.6	34.0	26.8	37.4	32.0	7,689	7.2	3.8
0454050	Peoria city	27,248	1.7	16.2	69.1	48.7	19.0	30.9	27.1	2,784	7.2	3.9
0455000	Phoenix city	249,222	7.9	45.4	56.9	31.7	23.7	43.1	33.6	32,304	8.5	4.2
0464210	San Tan Valley CDP	20,728	1.5	15.8	74.0	36.6	36.2	26.0	21.5	994	3.1	2.1
0465000	Scottsdale city	25,814	3.0	21.5	72.2	39.7	30.3	27.8	23.0	1,252	3.3	1.9
0471510	Surprise city	23,213	3.8	14.4	73.6	43.5	28.5	26.4	20.9	2,715	8.0	4.1
0473000	Tempe city	16,223	5.2	24.6	52.3	31.5	20.1	47.7	42.9	1,682	6.5	2.2
0477000	Tucson city	69,706	6.3	34.0	52.8	32.0	20.0	47.2	39.0	10,888	10.1	5.9
0485540	Yuma city	15,823	4.3	40.4	64.6	39.4	24.6	35.4	32.3	1,794	7.3	4.4
0500000	**Arkansas**	441,183	2.3	11.3	62.9	40.0	20.9	37.1	29.3	60,727	9.1	6.3
0515190	Conway city	9,089	2.1	6.8	60.5	49.4	11.0	39.5	37.9	0	0.0	0.0
0523290	Fayetteville city	8,663	5.1	15.8	71.3	48.0	22.7	28.7	22.9	750	5.7	4.8
0524550	Fort Smith city	12,890	2.8	33.9	57.8	28.3	25.4	42.2	31.9	1,590	7.8	5.4
0535710	Jonesboro city	10,144	4.1	12.9	51.3	32.3	17.4	48.7	40.0	1,133	6.9	4.6
0541000	Little Rock city	26,932	2.6	11.3	54.1	35.5	17.7	45.9	35.8	3,545	8.4	6.0
0550450	North Little Rock city	9,822	2.2	7.0	41.9	25.2	14.5	58.1	45.5	1,053	6.6	4.9
0560410	Rogers city	11,367	7.8	44.7	79.8	47.1	30.9	20.2	18.2	665	3.8	2.6
0566080	Springdale city	15,679	13.0	48.5	61.8	38.3	23.0	38.2	32.3	935	3.7	3.0
0600000	**California**	5,853,622	6.9	51.2	66.2	39.2	25.5	33.8	27.0	765,460	8.7	3.6
0600562	Alameda city	9,500	7.8	44.2	70.1	50.7	17.9	29.9	25.9	455	3.0	1.9
0600884	Alhambra city	9,989	12.1	70.6	69.7	47.0	22.5	30.3	27.1	1,525	10.2	4.1
0602000	Anaheim city	56,107	8.2	72.0	67.2	38.4	28.0	32.8	26.1	8,718	10.1	4.0
0602252	Antioch city	19,341	7.0	38.1	61.7	40.4	17.8	38.3	31.4	2,140	8.2	4.7
0602364	Apple Valley town	12,176	0.2	18.5	60.1	31.6	24.4	39.9	27.1	1,323	7.8	3.3
0602462	Arcadia city	8,913	14.6	73.4	80.7	47.5	31.3	19.3	14.7	390	3.4	1.0
0602553	Arden-Arcade CDP	11,800	8.4	30.9	59.2	32.2	24.2	40.8	33.7	728	3.8	1.6
0603526	Bakersfield city	66,174	5.2	43.6	62.4	36.2	25.4	37.6	30.4	7,474	7.2	2.5
0603666	Baldwin Park city	13,659	7.3	74.3	62.6	34.8	27.2	37.4	27.9	2,645	13.7	5.8
0604982	Bellflower city	14,367	6.0	55.2	57.8	36.2	19.3	42.2	34.3	1,849	8.7	3.6
0606000	Berkeley city	8,465	3.0	30.1	67.4	44.7	22.2	32.6	25.1	698	5.2	1.9
0608142	Brentwood city	11,104	5.7	36.6	82.1	52.2	29.3	17.9	16.8	923	6.0	4.1
0608786	Buena Park city	12,883	10.4	60.9	70.1	39.9	27.9	29.9	23.1	1,599	8.5	2.1
0608954	Burbank city	13,891	8.4	54.9	71.2	49.4	21.4	28.8	26.1	1,054	5.2	1.6
0610046	Camarillo city	10,123	2.8	29.8	69.9	46.2	22.2	30.1	26.4	1,031	6.9	2.8
0611194	Carlsbad city	16,507	4.1	22.8	73.2	41.7	26.5	26.8	22.4	475	2.0	0.9
0611390	Carmichael CDP	8,567	5.4	19.3	55.4	37.7	16.9	44.6	39.4	839	7.7	6.6
0611530	Carson city	12,864	6.8	54.5	65.1	44.2	20.3	34.9	28.1	3,353	17.7	6.9
0611964	Castro Valley CDP	8,378	7.8	49.6	71.5	48.2	23.0	28.5	23.4	797	6.1	2.9
0612048	Cathedral City city	9,495	11.0	64.4	66.4	37.7	27.5	33.6	30.1	859	6.1	2.3
0613014	Chico city	10,273	1.7	13.0	66.9	47.1	17.9	33.1	27.0	702	4.3	1.5
0613210	Chino city	11,861	2.8	38.2	71.3	49.3	20.8	28.7	24.6	1,747	9.5	4.8
0613214	Chino Hills city	14,360	4.8	48.1	73.8	47.6	25.3	26.2	22.0	1,062	5.5	2.6
0613392	Chula Vista city	44,377	6.9	57.8	70.6	43.6	24.8	29.4	23.8	5,419	8.4	4.4
0613588	Citrus Heights city	11,666	7.6	31.7	61.7	33.7	26.7	38.3	31.5	1,278	7.3	3.1
0614218	Clovis city	18,904	1.9	23.2	69.5	51.4	16.5	30.5	22.4	1,049	3.9	2.1
0614890	Colton city	10,554	5.6	50.4	49.1	27.7	21.0	50.9	45.0	2,456	14.8	9.3

State/ Place FIPS code	State/Place	Total own children under 18 in families and subfamilies	Total own children under 6 years	Nativity and parentage, under 6 years		Own children under 6 years living with two parents			Own children under 6 living with one parent	
				Child is foreign born, percent	One or more foreign-born parent, percent	Total under 6 years living with two parents, percent	Both parents in labor force, percent	One parent in labor force, percent	Total under 6 years living with one parent, percent	Parent in labor force, percent
	California—cont'd									
0615044	Compton city	29,038	10,001	0.7	52.9	47.5	24.8	21.1	52.5	39.3
0616000	Concord city	28,110	10,896	1.8	49.1	76.6	42.5	31.4	23.4	17.0
0616350	Corona city	42,977	13,585	2.3	47.9	74.2	38.5	35.1	25.8	19.8
0616532	Costa Mesa city	23,505	8,491	0.4	45.6	72.8	43.0	29.8	27.2	22.5
0617610	Cupertino city	16,360	4,280	10.2	89.2	91.5	50.4	40.0	8.5	7.7
0617918	Daly City city	18,598	6,598	1.0	81.3	78.8	55.9	22.9	21.2	17.6
0618100	Davis city	10,805	3,234	6.2	32.8	80.2	43.0	35.8	19.8	15.6
0618394	Delano city	14,934	5,442	1.3	64.6	47.7	30.3	17.3	52.3	33.0
0619192	Diamond Bar city	11,634	2,620	1.4	54.4	85.2	51.3	33.9	14.8	12.0
0619766	Downey city	27,890	9,462	1.0	47.4	60.2	35.4	23.5	39.8	31.5
0620802	East Los Angeles CDP	36,675	12,206	2.2	62.0	51.5	21.2	30.0	48.5	35.1
0621230	Eastvale city	16,795	6,419	2.6	35.5	84.1	44.9	34.4	15.9	12.4
0621712	El Cajon city	25,531	9,327	10.2	48.9	60.4	26.0	33.6	39.6	30.3
0622020	Elk Grove city	44,587	11,481	0.4	40.1	72.6	47.0	23.9	27.4	20.6
0622230	El Monte city	27,184	9,135	0.8	70.6	59.5	18.1	40.8	40.5	25.7
0622678	Encinitas city	12,355	4,880	0.8	37.3	94.5	50.0	42.2	5.5	4.9
0622804	Escondido city	36,857	13,660	1.0	53.8	64.2	31.6	31.5	35.8	29.4
0623182	Fairfield city	25,252	8,945	0.9	42.9	62.4	34.0	27.5	37.6	29.9
0624477	Florence-Graham CDP	20,335	7,466	3.5	65.1	39.8	16.9	20.9	60.2	40.4
0624498	Florin CDP	13,670	4,943	1.5	52.5	46.6	21.7	22.0	53.4	38.7
0624638	Folsom city	18,075	5,634	1.5	31.7	86.7	46.1	40.7	13.3	12.6
0624680	Fontana city	59,733	18,270	0.6	50.1	61.0	24.9	35.1	39.0	28.4
0625380	Fountain Valley city	10,490	2,908	3.0	58.6	76.9	39.5	36.4	23.1	21.6
0626000	Fremont city	52,630	18,193	6.2	70.5	83.7	44.6	37.7	16.3	12.2
0627000	Fresno city	141,903	51,977	1.1	35.8	48.1	23.6	23.0	51.9	34.0
0628000	Fullerton city	30,699	10,431	4.9	57.6	70.5	34.8	32.6	29.5	24.3
0628168	Gardena city	12,006	4,036	2.4	56.7	68.0	40.2	27.0	32.0	26.6
0629000	Garden Grove city	40,715	12,185	2.9	68.9	65.3	36.0	28.5	34.7	23.1
0629504	Gilroy city	14,107	4,834	0.6	51.8	64.3	35.0	27.2	35.7	24.7
0630000	Glendale city	35,867	12,492	3.7	67.3	78.8	42.9	33.9	21.2	18.4
0630014	Glendora city	11,075	2,671	1.8	27.2	79.5	42.8	36.7	20.5	15.5
0631596	Hacienda Heights CDP	10,504	2,933	3.1	63.3	70.9	36.4	29.8	29.1	18.3
0631960	Hanford city	16,227	5,086	0.0	20.3	56.6	43.0	12.7	43.4	32.8
0632548	Hawthorne city	22,256	7,444	1.7	50.4	50.9	31.9	19.0	49.1	34.3
0633000	Hayward city	32,666	11,252	2.9	63.7	66.2	40.0	24.9	33.8	26.7
0633182	Hemet city	19,385	6,201	0.0	24.8	49.8	19.1	27.5	50.2	38.3
0633434	Hesperia city	25,546	8,090	0.6	23.0	57.4	17.0	33.4	42.6	33.6
0633588	Highland city	16,284	4,755	0.0	31.8	47.9	24.1	23.6	52.1	30.2
0636000	Huntington Beach city	37,425	11,464	1.5	37.2	78.4	44.2	32.8	21.6	17.3
0636056	Huntington Park city	16,758	6,087	0.9	67.1	41.9	18.9	21.7	58.1	43.3
0636448	Indio city	22,825	8,106	1.3	45.5	54.4	34.6	19.4	45.6	33.4
0636546	Inglewood city	27,691	9,516	0.4	44.1	48.0	26.4	20.9	52.0	40.3
0636770	Irvine city	49,273	14,941	5.9	60.7	87.9	46.4	39.6	12.1	10.4
0637692	Jurupa Valley city	25,594	8,884	1.0	51.0	62.6	27.4	35.0	37.4	25.4
0639248	Laguna Niguel city	13,399	4,236	2.5	42.2	89.6	45.1	44.5	10.4	10.1
0639290	La Habra city	15,020	5,324	1.1	48.3	64.7	38.4	25.7	35.3	26.8
0639486	Lake Elsinore city	17,322	5,327	0.3	36.0	63.5	30.7	32.6	36.5	22.0
0639496	Lake Forest city	17,824	5,113	1.7	44.4	84.1	53.6	29.6	15.9	11.7
0639892	Lakewood city	18,774	6,141	1.9	28.8	58.2	41.8	16.0	41.8	29.5
0640004	La Mesa city	11,460	4,757	0.5	26.6	68.7	39.1	29.6	31.3	20.8
0640130	Lancaster city	43,249	15,250	0.7	25.6	58.2	26.5	29.1	41.8	26.7
0641992	Livermore city	19,648	7,121	0.3	30.6	76.5	44.7	31.4	23.5	19.9
0642202	Lodi city	17,003	4,992	0.8	39.2	70.1	37.0	32.4	29.9	21.3
0643000	Long Beach city	109,420	37,219	0.8	44.3	53.3	30.2	22.0	46.7	35.7
0644000	Los Angeles city	813,744	286,239	2.1	60.8	56.3	29.7	25.8	43.7	31.8
0644574	Lynwood city	22,601	7,362	2.2	61.4	42.8	14.4	27.8	57.2	42.9
0645022	Madera city	20,265	7,133	1.4	59.0	49.5	30.5	18.9	50.5	28.0
0645484	Manteca city	19,440	6,392	2.2	28.9	74.5	39.2	35.2	25.5	23.0
0646842	Menifee city	18,674	6,175	1.1	20.0	75.5	35.8	39.1	24.5	19.2
0646898	Merced city	24,225	8,787	1.1	47.6	51.4	27.1	21.5	48.6	34.4
0647766	Milpitas city	14,058	5,246	2.4	72.1	73.1	45.2	27.9	26.9	23.5
0648256	Mission Viejo city	19,807	5,641	1.5	32.1	83.7	41.9	41.3	16.3	10.8
0648354	Modesto city	49,415	16,770	1.3	29.9	50.5	24.0	26.1	49.5	34.0
0648816	Montebello city	13,385	4,621	1.1	48.3	52.3	23.6	27.2	47.7	24.0
0648914	Monterey Park city	10,370	3,494	1.4	60.9	71.0	47.5	22.0	29.0	17.1
0649270	Moreno Valley city	56,131	18,021	0.6	34.4	45.8	17.5	24.0	54.2	40.1
0649670	Mountain View city	15,426	6,021	6.7	63.6	87.9	52.4	35.5	12.1	10.3
0650076	Murrieta city	28,473	8,256	0.6	23.7	79.8	46.4	30.8	20.2	15.1
0650258	Napa city	18,164	5,909	2.6	56.0	65.8	38.5	26.5	34.2	23.2
0650398	National City city	13,589	4,275	2.2	57.3	55.6	24.5	29.1	44.4	25.3
0651182	Newport Beach city	15,341	4,592	0.3	26.6	85.4	38.3	44.9	14.6	10.5

Table D-4: Cities with a Population of 50,000 or More—Children—*Continued*

State/Place FIPS code	State/Place	Total own children 6 to 17	Nativity and parentage, age 6 to 17 years		Own children age 6 to 17 years living with two parents			Own children age 6 to 17 years living with one parent		Grandchildren under 18 living with a grandparent householder	Grandchildren under 18 living with a grandparent householder, as a percent of all children	Children for whom grandparent householders are responsible, as a percent of all children
			Child is foreign born, percent	One or more foreign-born parent, percent	Age 6 to 17 years living with two parents, percent	Both parents in labor force, percent	One parent in labor force, percent	Age 6 to 17 years living with one parent, percent	Parent in labor force, percent			
	California—cont'd											
0615044	Compton city	19,037	7.5	63.2	54.7	29.7	23.4	45.3	36.6	5,191	17.9	9.3
0616000	Concord city	17,214	11.5	51.2	69.8	44.5	24.5	30.2	25.9	1,963	7.0	3.5
0616350	Corona city	29,392	6.0	49.0	72.8	43.1	29.5	27.2	23.8	3,015	7.0	1.9
0616532	Costa Mesa city	15,014	8.4	55.4	64.7	39.1	25.1	35.3	32.3	1,449	6.2	2.9
0617610	Cupertino city	12,080	16.8	85.2	87.5	51.3	34.6	12.5	10.9	0	0.0	0.0
0617918	Daly City city	12,000	13.8	76.5	67.6	53.5	14.1	32.4	27.1	2,234	12.0	5.6
0618100	Davis city	7,571	6.7	35.0	77.3	53.6	21.4	22.7	19.7	0	0.0	0.0
0618394	Delano city	9,492	14.7	83.7	67.1	48.0	19.1	32.9	26.5	1,556	10.4	4.5
0619192	Diamond Bar city	9,014	8.8	63.8	73.0	51.6	21.0	27.0	22.1	814	7.0	1.1
0619766	Downey city	18,428	5.7	65.1	62.5	36.8	24.8	37.5	32.6	3,240	11.6	4.0
0620802	East Los Angeles CDP	24,469	6.9	74.2	53.3	26.6	26.1	46.7	34.3	5,981	16.3	4.5
0621230	Eastvale city	10,376	6.7	50.4	78.6	48.9	29.7	21.4	18.4	1,557	9.3	2.9
0621712	El Cajon city	16,204	20.7	59.3	61.3	34.1	24.6	38.7	31.7	1,337	5.2	2.0
0622020	Elk Grove city	33,106	3.1	37.2	66.1	46.7	18.2	33.9	28.9	2,778	6.2	3.3
0622230	El Monte city	18,049	10.7	76.3	64.3	25.3	37.4	35.7	27.1	3,056	11.2	4.9
0622678	Encinitas city	7,475	1.5	28.5	77.5	47.3	28.5	22.5	20.3	0	0.0	0.0
0622804	Escondido city	23,197	9.4	62.8	67.3	31.6	33.9	32.7	25.4	3,403	9.2	3.1
0623182	Fairfield city	16,307	5.2	47.5	72.5	41.0	29.3	27.5	21.5	2,018	8.0	3.8
0624477	Florence-Graham CDP	12,869	9.3	82.3	49.9	22.3	25.0	50.1	33.9	2,432	12.0	4.2
0624498	Florin CDP	8,727	11.5	61.9	51.0	23.1	23.2	49.0	36.3	1,349	9.9	5.4
0624638	Folsom city	12,441	5.4	28.9	77.0	49.1	27.5	23.0	21.1	0	0.0	0.0
0624680	Fontana city	41,463	6.2	59.3	67.8	36.5	30.3	32.2	25.0	7,330	12.3	4.6
0625380	Fountain Valley city	7,582	3.2	53.3	78.8	52.0	25.3	21.2	16.1	754	7.2	1.8
0626000	Fremont city	34,437	10.9	73.3	83.0	53.7	28.6	17.0	14.6	2,616	5.0	2.0
0627000	Fresno city	89,926	5.3	43.4	52.6	29.9	20.6	47.4	35.2	12,498	8.8	4.2
0628000	Fullerton city	20,268	11.6	58.0	68.3	39.5	24.8	31.7	29.0	2,298	7.5	2.8
0628168	Gardena city	7,970	7.8	55.1	57.7	37.2	19.2	42.3	39.3	1,160	9.7	4.9
0629000	Garden Grove city	28,530	10.2	74.9	67.1	38.7	27.4	32.9	25.3	4,821	11.8	3.5
0629504	Gilroy city	9,273	5.4	52.9	65.4	43.4	21.4	34.6	31.4	1,316	9.3	5.3
0630000	Glendale city	23,375	19.1	77.9	79.1	50.0	27.2	20.9	16.9	1,918	5.3	1.6
0630014	Glendora city	8,404	3.1	32.9	69.8	43.7	25.6	30.2	26.2	594	5.4	1.9
0631596	Hacienda Heights CDP	7,571	7.4	63.4	72.5	50.0	19.7	27.5	19.8	1,832	17.4	2.5
0631960	Hanford city	11,141	6.0	37.4	61.3	41.7	18.1	38.7	29.0	1,320	8.1	3.7
0632548	Hawthorne city	14,812	9.4	67.2	56.1	35.2	20.3	43.9	36.0	2,050	9.2	5.7
0633000	Hayward city	21,414	9.6	73.6	64.9	41.6	22.1	35.1	29.6	2,762	8.5	3.1
0633182	Hemet city	13,184	1.4	33.0	56.2	33.3	20.3	43.8	32.5	2,035	10.5	5.7
0633434	Hesperia city	17,456	3.2	34.2	64.2	27.4	32.4	35.8	26.7	3,589	14.0	9.1
0633588	Highland city	11,529	4.7	47.7	56.2	36.0	19.2	43.8	30.0	2,022	12.4	7.7
0636000	Huntington Beach city	25,961	2.9	33.9	73.9	44.9	26.9	26.1	21.4	2,386	6.4	2.7
0636056	Huntington Park city	10,671	11.6	84.7	51.7	27.5	23.1	48.3	39.9	2,473	14.8	3.8
0636448	Indio city	14,719	8.0	52.3	61.7	44.1	16.6	38.3	30.2	2,465	10.8	3.9
0636546	Inglewood city	18,175	3.8	55.8	55.0	33.6	20.8	45.0	38.4	2,993	10.8	4.2
0636770	Irvine city	34,332	17.3	64.3	79.6	44.9	33.9	20.4	16.8	0	0.0	0.0
0637692	Jurupa Valley city	16,710	6.9	65.1	72.1	36.6	34.4	27.9	20.3	4,570	17.9	6.0
0639248	Laguna Niguel city	9,163	3.6	30.4	82.3	43.5	38.7	17.7	15.4	0	0.0	0.0
0639290	La Habra city	9,696	5.3	54.6	67.7	40.4	26.2	32.3	27.2	1,312	8.7	2.8
0639486	Lake Elsinore city	11,995	3.0	45.3	65.5	41.6	22.7	34.5	24.6	2,144	12.4	8.6
0639496	Lake Forest city	12,711	3.4	39.3	75.9	49.3	26.1	24.1	23.1	0	0.0	0.0
0639892	Lakewood city	12,633	4.1	41.4	67.9	45.7	21.8	32.1	28.0	1,961	10.4	4.4
0640004	La Mesa city	6,703	4.2	23.0	69.0	40.3	28.5	31.0	26.6	676	9.5	4.0
0640130	Lancaster city	27,999	3.3	34.2	61.8	32.6	26.0	38.2	25.7	5,488	12.7	4.6
0641992	Livermore city	12,527	4.2	32.6	71.7	44.3	27.4	28.3	24.0	1,163	5.9	2.5
0642202	Lodi city	12,011	7.6	44.4	71.4	40.7	27.8	28.6	23.8	855	5.0	2.8
0643000	Long Beach city	72,201	5.8	54.3	54.8	30.8	22.9	45.2	34.8	10,204	9.3	4.1
0644000	Los Angeles city	527,505	8.7	69.3	58.1	32.9	23.9	41.9	33.5	76,384	9.4	3.3
0644574	Lynwood city	15,239	6.7	75.0	48.7	22.0	26.3	51.3	40.6	3,528	15.6	5.7
0645022	Madera city	13,132	10.7	60.6	55.2	26.5	26.1	44.8	27.8	1,592	7.9	4.2
0645484	Manteca city	13,048	3.0	33.2	63.5	36.9	26.5	36.5	30.1	2,037	10.5	3.6
0646842	Menifee city	12,499	2.2	26.3	76.0	45.1	30.5	24.0	20.5	1,573	8.4	2.8
0646898	Merced city	15,438	8.9	53.3	53.6	32.1	17.8	46.4	35.3	1,733	7.2	2.9
0647766	Milpitas city	8,812	9.9	75.1	72.5	52.2	19.8	27.5	23.0	1,437	10.2	5.2
0648256	Mission Viejo city	14,166	3.8	33.2	83.1	50.8	32.2	16.9	15.0	1,641	8.3	3.5
0648354	Modesto city	32,645	5.6	41.0	58.5	32.3	25.2	41.5	30.9	4,443	9.0	4.2
0648816	Montebello city	8,764	2.4	51.1	49.4	25.3	23.1	50.6	37.6	2,273	17.0	4.2
0648914	Monterey Park city	6,876	10.0	67.5	65.7	44.0	20.1	34.3	31.5	1,490	14.4	5.1
0649270	Moreno Valley city	38,110	4.0	50.0	55.8	29.4	21.9	44.2	32.7	9,252	16.5	6.9
0649670	Mountain View city	9,405	8.6	65.1	74.2	45.3	28.1	25.8	21.7	0	0.0	0.0
0650076	Murrieta city	20,217	2.6	25.6	79.5	47.6	31.0	20.5	16.4	1,907	6.7	3.2
0650258	Napa city	12,259	7.0	53.0	68.5	52.8	15.5	31.5	24.9	734	4.3	1.5
0650398	National City city	9,314	11.7	67.1	55.9	27.9	26.8	44.1	34.4	2,492	18.3	7.0
0651182	Newport Beach city	10,749	7.3	26.7	74.6	31.5	40.8	25.4	20.8	710	4.6	1.4

State/Place FIPS code	State/Place	Total own children under 18 in families and subfamilies	Own children under 6 years in families and subfamilies							
			Total own children under 6 years	Nativity and parentage, under 6 years		Own children under 6 years living with two parents			Own children under 6 living with one parent	
				Child is foreign born, percent	One or more foreign-born parent, percent	Total under 6 years living with two parents, percent	Both parents in labor force, percent	One parent in labor force, percent	Total under 6 years living with one parent, percent	Parent in labor force, percent
	California—cont'd									
0652526	Norwalk city...................	26,304	8,147	0.7	55.2	63.4	35.9	26.4	36.6	26.9
0652582	Novato city....................	11,547	3,350	5.3	45.3	79.5	47.9	30.8	20.5	16.8
0653000	Oakland city..................	79,231	29,648	1.3	43.3	57.7	36.0	20.9	42.3	31.9
0653322	Oceanside city...............	36,976	12,394	2.5	40.5	69.4	32.9	35.7	30.6	24.3
0653896	Ontario city..................	43,839	14,916	1.1	40.6	53.9	28.7	24.6	46.1	35.1
0653980	Orange city...................	28,268	9,940	2.7	55.9	63.7	35.9	26.7	36.3	27.2
0654652	Oxnard city...................	52,733	19,525	2.3	62.8	58.0	38.8	18.6	42.0	28.1
0655156	Palmdale city.................	47,969	15,928	0.6	39.8	50.7	21.2	29.1	49.3	30.1
0655282	Palo Alto city................	14,916	3,802	6.3	56.9	93.7	57.5	34.4	6.3	5.4
0655618	Paramount city...............	16,351	4,782	0.8	64.0	53.1	22.1	31.0	46.9	32.0
0656000	Pasadena city................	24,514	8,579	4.0	50.3	73.3	44.6	27.4	26.7	22.5
0656700	Perris city....................	23,626	7,541	0.2	39.8	55.0	22.6	30.5	45.0	32.8
0656784	Petaluma city................	14,121	4,721	1.1	43.6	76.8	42.0	34.4	23.2	21.4
0656924	Pico Rivera city..............	14,669	4,958	0.3	50.0	56.4	28.5	26.4	43.6	32.9
0657456	Pittsburg city................	16,485	5,770	1.1	53.8	58.2	34.4	23.1	41.8	35.1
0657526	Placentia city................	12,205	3,854	0.4	59.2	72.6	40.3	32.3	27.4	22.2
0657792	Pleasanton city..............	18,560	4,399	3.1	47.6	83.7	47.6	35.4	16.3	15.4
0658072	Pomona city..................	39,405	13,262	1.1	59.3	55.4	23.5	31.8	44.6	29.1
0658240	Porterville city...............	17,244	6,431	1.8	34.1	52.2	27.7	21.9	47.8	37.1
0659444	Rancho Cordova city........	15,667	6,310	2.3	40.1	66.4	42.6	20.9	33.6	21.3
0659451	Rancho Cucamonga city..........	40,591	12,807	2.6	36.8	73.3	49.1	23.3	26.7	24.4
0659920	Redding city..................	18,896	5,705	1.6	14.0	61.7	28.3	30.9	38.3	32.1
0659962	Redlands city.................	15,913	5,391	0.0	19.6	75.5	39.4	31.3	24.5	17.5
0660018	Redondo Beach city.........	13,937	5,730	0.8	38.4	90.3	59.7	30.6	9.7	8.6
0660102	Redwood City city...........	18,258	6,820	2.0	53.0	73.2	49.2	23.4	26.8	26.0
0660466	Rialto city....................	30,032	10,175	0.9	47.8	54.1	28.1	25.8	45.9	38.1
0660620	Richmond city................	24,377	9,041	1.9	62.8	54.7	30.6	22.2	45.3	35.3
0662000	Riverside city................	77,523	25,865	1.2	41.7	59.8	30.1	28.3	40.2	26.8
0662364	Rocklin city..................	15,739	4,303	0.7	24.6	79.6	48.0	30.7	20.4	14.4
0662896	Rosemead city................	11,047	3,139	3.0	68.4	69.9	35.9	33.8	30.1	17.2
0662938	Roseville city.................	30,984	9,415	1.3	27.5	78.7	38.8	39.6	21.3	19.0
0663218	Rowland Heights CDP...........	8,481	2,678	5.5	67.7	69.5	41.2	26.5	30.5	15.9
0664000	Sacramento city..............	108,193	39,486	1.8	43.7	55.0	31.2	22.4	45.0	32.4
0664224	Salinas city..................	45,679	16,529	1.0	61.5	51.1	26.6	22.7	48.9	37.6
0665000	San Bernardino city.........	61,344	20,459	0.7	39.8	42.7	16.8	22.4	57.3	34.1
0665042	San Buenaventura (Ventura) city..	21,550	7,023	0.5	27.4	67.7	47.9	19.1	32.3	26.4
0665084	San Clemente city............	16,092	5,159	0.6	21.1	84.9	45.2	39.7	15.1	10.5
0666000	San Diego city................	273,303	98,410	2.7	45.9	71.1	38.6	31.4	28.9	21.7
0667000	San Francisco city...........	105,161	41,438	3.5	54.6	77.0	49.6	26.2	23.0	20.4
0668000	San Jose city.................	227,401	79,950	2.7	62.8	70.7	42.7	27.7	29.3	22.2
0668084	San Leandro city	17,454	5,387	1.9	54.7	73.1	46.6	24.9	26.9	19.9
0668196	San Marcos city...............	21,391	6,858	1.3	47.2	78.6	36.7	38.3	21.4	13.4
0668252	San Mateo city...............	19,695	8,139	3.4	57.0	75.3	48.3	27.0	24.7	21.2
0668364	San Rafael city...............	11,947	4,379	0.5	63.4	65.5	49.7	15.5	34.5	32.1
0668378	San Ramon city...............	21,982	5,686	4.1	65.3	96.1	53.9	42.2	3.9	2.9
0669000	Santa Ana city...............	89,601	30,475	2.1	77.3	56.1	23.9	31.7	43.9	31.0
0669070	Santa Barbara city...........	16,561	6,812	2.2	49.0	66.9	44.3	22.4	33.1	28.6
0669084	Santa Clara city..............	25,326	10,846	5.6	72.5	79.6	42.2	37.2	20.4	18.1
0669088	Santa Clarita city............	44,349	12,902	1.9	46.2	71.5	38.8	31.0	28.5	21.2
0669112	Santa Cruz city...............	8,488	3,022	0.0	28.9	71.0	45.4	25.6	29.0	25.7
0669196	Santa Maria city..............	28,723	9,122	1.0	70.0	59.3	33.8	24.6	40.7	29.3
0670000	Santa Monica city	12,663	4,776	3.2	46.7	84.6	55.4	28.9	15.4	15.1
0670098	Santa Rosa city...............	38,190	12,381	2.7	43.0	67.7	37.2	29.9	32.3	25.7
0670224	Santee city...................	13,235	4,264	1.2	12.4	74.6	43.2	30.1	25.4	16.3
0672016	Simi Valley city..............	29,131	9,100	2.4	34.5	80.5	49.8	29.7	19.5	15.7
0673080	South Gate city..............	26,455	8,425	1.6	53.5	45.2	23.1	21.1	54.8	43.5
0673262	South San Francisco city............	14,351	4,973	2.1	56.5	69.0	49.4	19.5	31.0	27.7
0673430	South Whittier CDP...........	15,667	4,824	1.3	47.9	62.2	35.2	26.4	37.8	28.9
0675000	Stockton city.................	84,279	28,584	1.2	44.1	53.7	31.7	20.0	46.3	33.9
0677000	Sunnyvale city...............	31,652	13,825	10.8	76.6	84.0	46.2	37.8	16.0	13.9
0678120	Temecula city................	30,441	7,911	0.7	20.9	71.6	36.6	34.7	28.4	17.0
0678582	Thousand Oaks city...........	29,473	7,195	2.8	39.3	78.4	39.7	38.1	21.6	19.3
0680000	Torrance city.................	30,062	9,303	7.3	49.8	87.8	49.2	37.1	12.2	11.8
0680238	Tracy city....................	24,513	7,722	1.0	41.7	73.6	47.2	26.1	26.4	19.4
0680644	Tulare city	17,712	6,442	0.5	40.4	55.7	26.4	28.2	44.3	36.8
0680812	Turlock city..................	17,727	5,952	0.9	41.4	60.9	35.2	24.6	39.1	29.8
0680854	Tustin city...................	19,355	7,153	1.7	57.9	68.1	35.6	32.5	31.9	24.5
0681204	Union City city...............	16,212	5,838	2.2	67.4	75.3	45.7	27.9	24.7	18.4
0681344	Upland city..................	17,619	5,508	2.5	30.3	56.9	30.6	23.6	43.1	22.8

Table D-4: Cities with a Population of 50,000 or More—Children—*Continued*

State/ Place FIPS code	State/Place	Total own children 6 to 17	Child is foreign born, percent	One or more foreign-born parent, percent	Age 6 to 17 years living with two parents, percent	Both parents in labor force, percent	One parent in labor force, percent	Age 6 to 17 years living with one parent, percent	Parent in labor force, percent	Grand-children under 18 living with a grandparent householder	Grand-children under 18 living with a grandparent householder, as a percent of all children	Children for whom grandparent householders are responsible, as a percent of all children
	California—cont'd											
0652526	Norwalk city	18,157	3.5	65.6	65.9	38.8	25.4	34.1	29.9	3,738	14.2	4.6
0652582	Novato city	8,197	6.9	37.9	75.7	43.1	31.8	24.3	22.4	381	3.3	2.2
0653000	Oakland city	49,583	8.2	49.5	55.1	33.3	20.6	44.9	34.7	7,297	9.2	3.9
0653322	Oceanside city	24,582	4.4	44.6	70.9	40.5	27.6	29.1	21.2	4,140	11.2	5.2
0653896	Ontario city	28,923	7.9	59.3	59.6	35.4	22.9	40.4	30.7	5,779	13.2	6.2
0653980	Orange city	18,328	7.4	53.2	70.8	40.9	28.4	29.2	24.4	2,299	8.1	3.2
0654652	Oxnard city	33,208	9.4	69.5	65.6	45.0	20.0	34.4	28.1	7,343	13.9	4.5
0655156	Palmdale city	32,041	5.0	53.8	59.6	24.9	32.4	40.4	32.6	5,058	10.5	5.0
0655282	Palo Alto city	11,114	9.0	56.0	82.7	46.3	35.3	17.3	13.2	0	0.0	0.0
0655618	Paramount city	11,569	7.2	75.9	62.5	32.1	30.4	37.5	25.4	2,085	12.8	4.4
0656000	Pasadena city	15,935	5.2	53.2	66.1	44.5	20.6	33.9	28.8	1,719	7.0	2.4
0656700	Perris city	16,085	3.7	56.7	59.5	26.8	31.8	40.5	29.9	3,828	16.2	8.5
0656784	Petaluma city	9,400	5.6	35.8	75.2	46.6	28.1	24.8	21.5	757	5.4	3.5
0656924	Pico Rivera city	9,711	2.8	59.5	62.2	38.4	22.8	37.8	31.6	2,455	16.7	6.0
0657456	Pittsburg city	10,715	8.6	60.5	62.3	34.1	26.1	37.7	33.7	1,549	9.4	2.9
0657526	Placentia city	8,351	7.2	44.9	72.9	42.4	29.5	27.1	24.8	794	6.5	1.4
0657792	Pleasanton city	14,161	8.0	45.3	82.4	48.2	33.3	17.6	14.8	447	2.4	1.4
0658072	Pomona city	26,143	7.0	67.7	61.6	33.9	27.0	38.4	27.0	4,278	10.9	3.5
0658240	Porterville city	10,813	2.9	47.7	64.5	37.5	23.4	35.5	30.0	1,424	8.3	5.3
0659444	Rancho Cordova city	9,357	11.5	40.9	59.6	35.7	21.2	40.4	35.8	941	6.0	2.8
0659451	Rancho Cucamonga city	27,784	3.3	39.4	70.4	47.7	22.5	29.6	27.6	2,486	6.1	3.3
0659920	Redding city	13,191	0.5	10.0	55.4	34.4	18.4	44.6	33.0	1,387	7.3	4.1
0659962	Redlands city	10,522	4.8	33.0	63.2	32.6	29.0	36.8	34.4	1,617	10.2	4.7
0660018	Redondo Beach city	8,207	4.3	32.9	74.2	44.0	29.5	25.8	24.2	0	0.0	0.0
0660102	Redwood City city	11,438	7.1	59.7	74.7	52.8	21.8	25.3	21.2	1,089	6.0	1.8
0660466	Rialto city	19,857	5.3	61.2	64.5	38.6	24.7	35.5	30.1	5,017	16.7	7.9
0660620	Richmond city	15,336	12.6	66.8	60.9	35.6	22.9	39.1	31.2	1,980	8.1	4.0
0662000	Riverside city	51,658	5.5	47.7	65.3	37.2	26.9	34.7	28.3	8,649	11.2	4.2
0662364	Rocklin city	11,436	3.5	21.5	69.7	44.6	25.1	30.3	27.4	520	3.3	0.7
0662896	Rosemead city	7,908	8.8	77.2	71.2	40.4	27.8	28.8	23.4	1,157	10.5	6.0
0662938	Roseville city	21,569	3.8	25.9	74.4	48.7	25.3	25.6	24.4	912	2.9	0.8
0663218	Rowland Heights CDP	5,803	13.1	80.5	74.0	48.8	24.0	26.0	21.6	1,120	13.2	3.5
0664000	Sacramento city	68,707	7.1	46.6	55.4	35.5	17.3	44.6	34.0	9,365	8.7	3.9
0664224	Salinas city	29,150	10.4	69.4	65.1	38.1	22.6	34.9	27.5	3,087	6.8	2.0
0665000	San Bernardino city	40,885	5.3	48.5	49.4	22.9	24.3	50.6	35.4	6,520	10.6	3.5
0665042	San Buenaventura (Ventura) city	14,527	5.9	29.6	65.6	45.2	19.9	34.4	28.6	1,733	8.0	2.2
0665084	San Clemente city	10,933	2.3	22.4	72.3	39.5	31.2	27.7	22.2	0	0.0	0.0
0666000	San Diego city	174,893	9.5	53.9	65.8	39.3	25.7	34.2	27.7	22,781	8.3	3.1
0667000	San Francisco city	63,723	10.5	59.2	69.1	47.8	19.9	30.9	25.2	7,520	7.2	2.5
0668000	San Jose city	147,451	10.1	66.7	72.1	45.0	26.0	27.9	22.6	17,842	7.8	2.4
0668084	San Leandro city	12,067	8.4	60.4	72.2	52.4	18.7	27.8	24.9	1,324	7.6	3.5
0668196	San Marcos city	14,533	2.7	48.3	71.3	41.1	26.3	28.7	21.3	1,144	5.3	1.7
0668252	San Mateo city	11,556	8.2	59.0	76.0	52.0	23.8	24.0	21.9	899	4.6	2.0
0668364	San Rafael city	7,568	11.9	50.8	67.8	48.0	19.1	32.2	28.9	0	0.0	0.0
0668378	San Ramon city	16,296	9.8	57.7	87.2	53.7	32.7	12.8	11.6	306	1.4	0.5
0669000	Santa Ana city	59,126	12.8	87.8	64.4	32.7	30.6	35.6	28.5	12,065	13.5	4.9
0669070	Santa Barbara city	9,749	8.8	53.5	64.5	46.5	17.9	35.5	31.3	1,278	7.7	3.2
0669084	Santa Clara city	14,480	13.8	68.5	74.6	42.5	31.7	25.4	21.6	1,572	6.2	2.8
0669088	Santa Clarita city	31,447	4.0	40.7	72.7	43.8	27.3	27.3	24.5	2,096	4.7	1.2
0669112	Santa Cruz city	5,466	4.0	35.6	73.2	52.4	20.5	26.8	26.1	0	0.0	0.0
0669196	Santa Maria city	19,601	10.6	70.6	62.8	42.3	19.2	37.2	28.2	2,410	8.4	3.8
0670000	Santa Monica city	7,887	6.8	37.3	70.3	46.8	21.5	29.7	25.7	0	0.0	0.0
0670098	Santa Rosa city	25,809	9.6	48.2	67.8	42.1	23.5	32.2	29.0	2,364	6.2	2.3
0670224	Santee city	8,971	1.3	17.1	64.9	44.2	19.5	35.1	29.1	661	5.0	3.4
0672016	Simi Valley city	20,031	2.7	32.7	76.3	52.6	23.2	23.7	19.2	1,419	4.9	1.9
0673080	South Gate city	18,030	5.7	73.6	58.1	28.5	28.8	41.9	34.6	3,704	14.0	4.8
0673262	South San Francisco city	9,378	8.3	61.6	69.5	51.6	17.3	30.5	28.5	1,266	8.8	2.8
0673430	South Whittier CDP	10,843	4.6	53.5	65.2	34.9	30.3	34.8	25.9	1,784	11.4	4.9
0675000	Stockton city	55,695	6.0	49.4	56.1	33.5	20.3	43.9	33.1	7,803	9.3	4.4
0677000	Sunnyvale city	17,827	13.6	67.0	79.5	47.8	31.5	20.5	17.8	1,416	4.5	1.8
0678120	Temecula city	22,530	3.7	33.1	77.4	45.6	30.9	22.6	18.4	1,612	5.3	3.2
0678582	Thousand Oaks city	22,278	4.8	37.4	80.5	52.6	27.5	19.5	17.9	1,389	4.7	0.9
0680000	Torrance city	20,759	12.5	52.7	79.6	52.3	26.3	20.4	17.6	825	2.7	1.0
0680238	Tracy city	16,791	4.9	45.5	76.3	48.2	27.7	23.7	18.6	1,518	6.2	2.5
0680644	Tulare city	11,270	4.4	45.8	64.0	37.9	23.9	36.0	25.9	1,847	10.4	4.2
0680812	Turlock city	11,775	7.6	45.0	64.7	39.6	23.4	35.3	27.4	1,789	10.1	5.3
0680854	Tustin city	12,202	9.4	56.7	63.8	37.1	25.7	36.2	33.6	1,285	6.6	4.5
0681204	Union City city	10,374	12.5	74.5	77.3	54.0	22.5	22.7	14.8	1,556	9.6	3.3
0681344	Upland city	12,111	5.2	38.0	58.5	30.8	25.4	41.5	31.7	1,262	7.2	4.3

State/Place FIPS code	State/Place	Total own children under 18 in families and subfamilies	Total own children under 6 years	Nativity and parentage, under 6 years		Own children under 6 years living with two parents			Own children under 6 living with one parent	
				Child is foreign born, percent	One or more foreign-born parent, percent	Total under 6 years living with two parents, percent	Both parents in labor force, percent	One parent in labor force, percent	Total under 6 years living with one parent, percent	Parent in labor force, percent
	California—cont'd									
0681554	Vacaville city	20,103	6,417	0.0	21.1	69.8	37.6	32.2	30.2	25.5
0681666	Vallejo city	23,324	7,974	0.9	39.1	47.9	27.6	18.9	52.1	39.5
0682590	Victorville city	37,459	12,438	0.0	24.2	54.3	31.6	22.1	45.7	30.2
0682954	Visalia city	34,902	12,388	0.5	31.3	58.7	31.7	25.3	41.3	29.2
0682996	Vista city	20,240	7,058	0.9	54.2	70.1	26.6	39.8	29.9	22.7
0683346	Walnut Creek city	11,086	3,336	0.0	36.2	90.1	62.7	27.3	9.9	9.5
0683668	Watsonville city	15,623	5,809	0.7	75.2	66.4	35.2	31.0	33.6	22.6
0684200	West Covina city	23,905	6,962	0.8	47.7	54.9	36.2	18.7	45.1	36.3
0684550	Westminster city	19,567	5,684	2.2	71.3	63.5	36.3	27.2	36.5	26.1
0685292	Whittier city	20,887	6,835	1.4	32.5	66.1	34.2	30.2	33.9	28.8
0686328	Woodland city	14,190	4,749	1.7	43.4	65.0	40.2	24.8	35.0	25.9
0686832	Yorba Linda city	15,232	4,163	2.2	37.3	86.4	55.9	30.5	13.6	12.7
0686972	Yuba City city	16,045	4,998	2.7	48.7	61.3	31.4	29.0	38.7	28.8
0687042	Yucaipa city	12,980	4,082	0.0	11.3	61.7	40.2	20.7	38.3	30.5
0800000	**Colorado**	1,182,138	395,515	1.2	21.9	70.5	39.2	30.4	29.5	23.0
0803455	Arvada city	23,473	7,467	0.2	7.4	69.4	43.9	24.3	30.6	25.3
0804000	Aurora city	86,400	31,529	1.4	39.5	62.5	32.1	30.2	37.5	31.0
0807850	Boulder city	13,981	4,958	1.1	24.9	76.7	46.5	30.3	23.3	20.8
0809280	Broomfield city	14,528	4,401	0.3	18.2	77.3	47.4	29.6	22.7	11.3
0812415	Castle Rock town	15,569	5,219	0.0	11.4	85.2	52.8	31.0	14.8	12.1
0812815	Centennial city	24,061	6,795	1.3	17.6	83.5	53.7	29.8	16.5	11.1
0816000	Colorado Springs city	101,731	36,531	0.8	16.9	67.6	34.2	32.4	32.4	24.9
0820000	Denver city	128,418	50,582	2.8	36.2	63.7	35.9	26.7	36.3	27.3
0827425	Fort Collins city	28,114	9,595	2.2	10.0	79.6	43.6	33.5	20.4	15.3
0831660	Grand Junction city	12,284	4,567	0.0	11.3	66.8	38.1	28.7	33.2	23.3
0832155	Greeley city	22,083	7,210	0.7	32.2	60.1	25.5	33.4	39.9	25.7
0836410	Highlands Ranch CDP	32,488	9,991	1.1	13.6	89.6	50.6	39.0	10.4	5.9
0843000	Lakewood city	26,710	9,912	0.9	16.6	63.4	40.9	21.8	36.6	30.6
0845970	Longmont city	21,699	7,424	1.3	30.5	67.8	30.4	37.2	32.2	24.9
0846465	Loveland city	16,291	5,181	1.1	9.6	73.9	50.4	23.6	26.1	22.3
0862000	Pueblo city	23,674	8,305	0.4	12.4	49.5	26.9	21.5	50.5	37.3
0877290	Thornton city	35,128	12,264	0.7	31.5	71.3	45.7	25.7	28.7	24.2
0883835	Westminster city	24,530	8,685	1.2	22.6	76.1	47.0	27.9	23.9	20.9
0900000	**Connecticut**	768,816	230,927	1.8	26.2	66.5	42.8	23.2	33.5	26.9
0908000	Bridgeport city	35,207	12,491	1.0	43.9	45.8	27.7	17.2	54.2	43.3
0908420	Bristol city	12,057	3,558	0.0	17.1	54.7	42.1	11.2	45.3	40.4
0918430	Danbury city	15,774	5,563	3.1	51.2	60.7	45.7	13.8	39.3	32.2
0922700	East Hartford CDP	9,891	3,250	1.4	32.1	44.7	35.6	8.6	55.3	43.3
0937000	Hartford city	29,990	10,424	2.2	29.0	19.6	10.3	8.8	80.4	60.0
0946450	Meriden city	12,077	4,694	1.1	23.8	49.5	28.2	20.9	50.5	40.2
0947515	Milford city	9,789	2,989	1.0	26.3	81.9	56.8	24.1	18.1	14.5
0950370	New Britain city	15,941	5,154	0.6	25.7	39.0	22.5	15.9	61.0	48.4
0952000	New Haven city	27,568	9,564	4.4	30.4	44.3	28.5	15.0	55.7	42.9
0955990	Norwalk city	15,736	6,062	3.0	41.7	75.3	43.1	32.2	24.7	21.2
0973000	Stamford city	26,580	9,997	4.1	53.2	72.9	43.7	29.2	27.1	20.5
0974260	Stratford CDP	9,678	2,461	0.0	27.7	79.2	51.7	27.5	20.8	15.4
0980000	Waterbury city	26,138	9,543	1.0	21.7	42.1	23.4	17.6	57.9	34.8
0982660	West Hartford CDP	13,613	3,894	2.5	24.6	85.2	60.3	24.8	14.8	11.2
0982800	West Haven city	11,811	4,024	0.0	31.7	61.2	49.0	12.2	38.8	37.9
1000000	**Delaware**	191,554	64,151	1.2	20.6	57.9	35.6	21.2	42.1	34.5
1077580	Wilmington city	15,727	5,732	2.3	10.9	25.3	14.3	10.0	74.7	62.5
1100000	**District of Columbia**	100,091	43,530	2.7	27.1	48.9	35.6	12.8	51.1	37.7
1150000	Washington city	100,091	43,530	2.7	27.1	48.9	35.6	12.8	51.1	37.7
1200000	**Florida**	3,804,656	1,249,125	1.6	31.8	57.7	34.0	22.8	42.3	33.0
1200410	Alafaya CDP	20,258	6,292	2.6	24.2	66.6	49.8	14.3	33.4	27.1
1207300	Boca Raton city	15,143	4,046	3.1	31.9	87.3	55.3	31.7	12.7	11.8
1207875	Boynton Beach city	12,518	4,640	1.3	48.3	58.0	39.5	18.5	42.0	39.5
1207950	Bradenton city	9,674	3,532	1.9	28.2	59.1	38.3	17.2	40.9	30.7
1208150	Brandon CDP	24,077	8,234	1.2	19.5	54.9	35.4	16.9	45.1	35.8
1210275	Cape Coral city	36,426	11,356	1.5	19.3	53.0	30.8	20.7	47.0	35.0
1212875	Clearwater city	19,496	7,484	2.5	26.8	47.1	28.6	18.0	52.9	34.8
1213275	Coconut Creek city	11,428	3,852	2.5	58.1	74.7	58.2	16.5	25.3	22.8
1214400	Coral Springs city	32,285	9,993	1.7	48.7	58.3	39.0	18.7	41.7	35.7
1216475	Davie town	20,986	6,187	2.9	38.0	72.1	47.0	24.6	27.9	25.7
1216525	Daytona Beach city	8,675	3,539	0.0	14.5	39.4	14.1	25.3	60.6	40.7
1216725	Deerfield Beach city	14,114	4,547	1.0	48.8	54.1	32.7	21.2	45.9	30.2
1217100	Delray Beach city	8,464	3,117	4.0	43.5	49.9	31.9	17.9	50.1	38.0
1217200	Deltona city	18,988	6,388	0.8	10.5	60.9	30.7	30.2	39.1	27.5

State/Place FIPS code	State/Place	Total own children 6 to 17	Nativity and parentage, age 6 to 17 years		Own children age 6 to 17 years living with two parents			Own children age 6 to 17 years living with one parent		Grand-children under 18 living with a grandparent householder	Grand-children under 18 living with a grandparent householder, as a percent of all children	Children for whom grandparent householders are responsible, as a percent of all children
			Child is foreign born, percent	One or more foreign-born parent, percent	Age 6 to 17 years living with two parents, percent	Both parents in labor force, percent	One parent in labor force, percent	Age 6 to 17 years living with one parent, percent	Parent in labor force, percent			
	California—cont'd											
0681554	Vacaville city	13,686	4.9	29.6	67.9	43.4	24.2	32.1	29.1	1,937	9.6	1.9
0681666	Vallejo city	15,350	8.2	48.0	56.3	34.3	20.9	43.7	34.1	2,376	10.2	5.2
0682590	Victorville city	25,021	1.7	37.7	49.9	24.1	24.9	50.1	31.6	4,570	12.2	4.8
0682954	Visalia city	22,514	2.1	32.7	60.9	38.9	20.6	39.1	30.6	3,329	9.5	5.6
0682996	Vista city	13,182	4.5	55.7	66.6	28.9	34.6	33.4	24.6	1,625	8.0	4.7
0683346	Walnut Creek city	7,750	7.9	36.6	80.4	56.6	22.8	19.6	18.7	400	3.6	1.7
0683668	Watsonville city	9,814	10.9	72.4	68.8	45.7	18.7	31.2	26.2	0	0.0	0.0
0684200	West Covina city	16,943	9.1	55.2	68.5	46.6	21.5	31.5	27.4	2,647	11.1	5.3
0684550	Westminster city	13,883	7.3	74.4	69.0	38.4	28.8	31.0	27.3	1,379	7.0	1.5
0685292	Whittier city	14,052	2.9	41.6	65.9	42.4	23.4	34.1	29.8	1,692	8.1	2.9
0686328	Woodland city	9,441	5.3	49.4	62.7	43.9	18.2	37.3	32.3	1,137	8.0	3.6
0686832	Yorba Linda city	11,069	3.5	31.3	83.5	50.6	32.2	16.5	15.1	554	3.6	0.9
0686972	Yuba City city	11,047	6.2	46.4	69.4	43.3	24.7	30.6	21.3	1,540	9.6	4.0
0687042	Yucaipa city	8,898	2.3	26.9	72.1	48.6	19.9	27.9	22.7	1,168	9.0	3.8
0800000	**Colorado**	786,623	4.3	21.9	69.9	45.4	23.4	30.1	25.5	70,888	6.0	3.0
0803455	Arvada city	16,006	3.2	8.3	63.5	45.1	18.2	36.5	32.9	1,443	6.1	3.2
0804000	Aurora city	54,871	9.7	42.8	59.2	35.8	22.4	40.8	34.8	5,970	6.9	3.6
0807850	Boulder city	9,023	8.0	29.4	74.4	47.9	24.7	25.6	22.9	328	2.3	1.7
0809280	Broomfield city	10,127	1.6	19.7	76.4	54.4	21.4	23.6	18.6	437	3.0	2.0
0812415	Castle Rock town	10,350	2.0	10.0	80.5	52.5	28.0	19.5	18.9	0	0.0	0.0
0812815	Centennial city	17,266	4.0	17.4	75.3	51.1	23.7	24.7	21.8	931	3.9	2.4
0816000	Colorado Springs city	65,200	3.2	16.5	68.0	43.7	23.1	32.0	25.6	5,857	5.8	2.8
0820000	Denver city	77,836	9.0	40.9	59.8	36.3	22.5	40.2	34.1	10,103	7.9	3.1
0827425	Fort Collins city	18,519	3.4	11.9	74.1	48.7	24.6	25.9	20.9	1,110	3.9	3.1
0831660	Grand Junction city	7,717	1.0	8.1	63.2	47.9	14.2	36.8	28.6	850	6.9	4.0
0832155	Greeley city	14,873	4.2	34.4	63.5	36.2	26.0	36.5	27.6	1,811	8.2	4.3
0836410	Highlands Ranch CDP	22,497	2.0	12.0	81.6	55.8	25.6	18.4	15.0	699	2.2	0.7
0843000	Lakewood city	16,798	4.9	19.8	61.1	46.7	13.6	38.9	31.8	1,851	6.9	4.1
0845970	Longmont city	14,275	8.6	31.3	69.3	41.1	28.3	30.7	27.0	1,192	5.5	2.5
0846465	Loveland city	11,110	2.1	9.9	68.2	48.7	18.6	31.8	29.3	826	5.1	2.1
0862000	Pueblo city	15,369	0.9	9.3	54.5	34.9	16.9	45.5	39.7	2,053	8.7	5.0
0877290	Thornton city	22,864	3.5	27.7	76.1	50.8	24.6	23.9	21.0	2,573	7.3	3.2
0883835	Westminster city	15,845	3.0	21.9	72.6	49.1	22.6	27.4	22.8	1,752	7.1	3.2
0900000	**Connecticut**	537,889	4.8	22.2	68.1	48.0	19.4	31.9	27.4	42,141	5.5	2.6
0908000	Bridgeport city	22,716	7.2	41.2	40.9	29.9	10.6	59.1	51.1	3,664	10.4	3.6
0908420	Bristol city	8,499	1.8	15.5	65.9	50.0	13.6	34.1	28.9	692	5.7	2.7
0918430	Danbury city	10,211	9.5	53.5	66.8	53.4	12.5	33.2	30.6	1,228	7.8	3.5
0922700	East Hartford CDP	6,641	6.2	31.1	46.3	38.6	7.7	53.7	45.3	988	10.0	8.1
0937000	Hartford city	19,566	8.6	27.7	24.6	16.8	7.2	75.4	58.1	3,262	10.9	5.5
0946450	Meriden city	7,383	4.1	17.0	53.2	34.4	15.4	46.8	37.6	893	7.4	3.2
0947515	Milford city	6,800	4.0	23.5	75.2	54.0	20.7	24.8	22.6	599	6.1	2.8
0950370	New Britain city	10,787	7.5	25.8	45.8	33.0	12.8	54.2	41.2	1,507	9.5	5.2
0952000	New Haven city	18,004	7.6	21.0	34.9	22.8	11.6	65.1	53.2	2,009	7.3	4.3
0955990	Norwalk city	9,674	12.5	43.4	68.1	47.1	21.0	31.9	29.6	1,103	7.0	2.5
0973000	Stamford city	16,583	11.8	51.8	63.2	39.8	23.1	36.8	32.7	1,050	4.0	1.6
0974260	Stratford CDP	7,217	2.9	21.1	68.6	47.0	21.2	31.4	28.7	895	9.2	6.2
0980000	Waterbury city	16,595	6.0	24.1	42.5	27.0	14.6	57.5	38.1	1,614	6.2	4.0
0982660	West Hartford CDP	9,719	9.0	32.2	75.2	51.4	23.4	24.8	23.2	410	3.0	0.6
0982800	West Haven city	7,787	3.8	28.2	65.1	49.6	13.6	34.9	34.0	571	4.8	3.4
1000000	**Delaware**	127,403	2.6	16.2	60.9	43.0	16.3	39.1	33.1	19,940	10.4	5.5
1077580	Wilmington city	9,995	2.3	10.8	23.3	12.6	9.4	76.7	59.3	2,192	13.9	7.6
1100000	**District of Columbia**	56,561	5.3	22.7	35.8	26.1	8.7	64.2	49.5	11,228	11.2	5.1
1150000	Washington city	56,561	5.3	22.7	35.8	26.1	8.7	64.2	49.5	11,228	11.2	5.1
1200000	**Florida**	2,555,531	6.7	32.8	61.6	40.1	20.1	38.4	31.9	336,635	8.8	4.7
1200410	Alafaya CDP	13,966	5.8	30.0	66.4	54.2	9.8	33.6	27.9	669	3.3	2.3
1207300	Boca Raton city	11,097	8.1	34.0	71.3	42.8	26.6	28.7	25.2	0	0.0	0.0
1207875	Boynton Beach city	7,878	10.2	46.7	57.6	46.9	10.8	42.4	36.9	978	7.8	3.5
1207950	Bradenton city	6,142	5.4	32.4	54.2	37.0	16.0	45.8	35.9	629	6.5	4.7
1208150	Brandon CDP	15,843	3.6	18.8	63.2	41.6	20.2	36.8	28.4	1,808	7.5	4.5
1210275	Cape Coral city	25,070	4.1	27.4	63.2	42.2	20.2	36.8	31.0	1,873	5.1	2.9
1212875	Clearwater city	12,012	2.7	23.3	51.8	32.2	16.4	48.2	38.7	1,848	9.5	7.0
1213275	Coconut Creek city	7,576	7.5	41.8	62.1	47.6	14.2	37.9	34.1	0	0.0	0.0
1214400	Coral Springs city	22,292	7.9	45.2	64.0	46.0	17.4	36.0	32.9	1,850	5.7	2.2
1216475	Davie town	14,799	8.8	42.7	66.7	48.2	16.9	33.3	30.4	905	4.3	2.0
1216525	Daytona Beach city	5,136	2.4	12.2	27.7	17.0	10.5	72.3	43.6	498	5.7	4.3
1216725	Deerfield Beach city	9,567	10.0	53.9	58.7	36.7	21.7	41.3	34.1	1,277	9.0	6.0
1217100	Delray Beach city	5,347	14.8	37.6	52.9	38.9	13.9	47.1	35.7	1,447	17.1	6.7
1217200	Deltona city	12,600	2.5	18.8	67.2	31.4	35.2	32.8	22.8	3,291	17.3	8.5

Table D-4: Cities with a Population of 50,000 or More—Children—*Continued*

State/Place FIPS code	State/Place	Total own children under 18 in families and subfamilies	Own children under 6 years in families and subfamilies							
			Total own children under 6 years	Nativity and parentage, under 6 years		Own children under 6 years living with two parents			Own children under 6 living with one parent	
				Child is foreign born, percent	One or more foreign-born parent, percent	Total under 6 years living with two parents, percent	Both parents in labor force, percent	One parent in labor force, percent	Total under 6 years living with one parent, percent	Parent in labor force, percent
	Florida—cont'd									
1224000	Fort Lauderdale city..............	28,090	10,337	1.1	39.5	46.8	30.2	16.2	53.2	43.9
1224125	Fort Myers city....................	12,034	4,383	4.2	26.9	44.6	28.4	14.0	55.4	40.6
1224562	Fountainebleau CDP..............	8,562	3,398	3.6	86.3	64.5	34.5	30.1	35.5	25.8
1225175	Gainesville city...................	15,070	6,457	1.7	11.4	52.4	29.8	21.8	47.6	35.0
1230000	Hialeah city.......................	41,312	13,758	6.2	79.7	55.2	34.4	18.6	44.8	34.1
1232000	Hollywood city....................	29,042	9,636	2.9	47.2	55.3	37.2	18.1	44.7	38.7
1232275	Homestead city...................	18,058	6,215	1.1	56.2	69.3	40.9	27.3	30.7	23.0
1235000	Jacksonville city..................	183,967	67,006	0.8	15.9	52.7	30.8	21.0	47.3	35.6
1235875	Jupiter town......................	10,931	3,363	0.6	31.3	81.2	42.8	38.0	18.8	16.5
1236062	Kendale Lakes CDP...............	10,268	2,665	3.6	83.7	74.4	43.3	31.1	25.6	22.7
1236100	Kendall CDP.......................	13,766	4,798	0.0	56.4	74.4	49.0	25.4	25.6	18.5
1236950	Kissimmee city....................	15,393	5,090	1.7	41.9	38.3	22.0	16.4	61.7	45.3
1238250	Lakeland city......................	19,939	7,082	0.7	17.5	50.1	28.4	21.5	49.9	36.7
1239425	Largo city.........................	11,263	3,212	0.0	17.9	47.5	36.8	10.7	52.5	50.5
1239550	Lauderhill city....................	16,072	5,791	0.9	46.6	27.2	22.6	4.6	72.8	64.7
1239925	Lehigh Acres CDP................	29,508	10,803	0.9	33.5	47.3	27.5	19.6	52.7	39.8
1243125	Margate city......................	10,192	2,990	0.5	44.0	54.1	25.6	27.7	45.9	39.8
1243975	Melbourne city...................	11,915	4,284	0.4	11.4	59.5	38.6	19.0	40.5	31.7
1245000	Miami city.........................	73,749	29,199	4.4	62.5	45.5	24.6	19.6	54.5	41.5
1245025	Miami Beach city.................	14,657	6,457	4.3	65.6	65.8	37.0	23.1	34.2	31.8
1245060	Miami Gardens city..............	24,393	8,060	1.2	39.5	32.4	19.0	11.1	67.6	52.6
1245975	Miramar city......................	31,893	9,720	1.6	62.0	62.8	42.9	19.9	37.2	35.1
1249450	North Miami city.................	12,933	4,046	2.1	63.7	49.9	27.3	19.6	50.1	39.0
1249675	North Port city...................	13,030	3,810	2.4	13.1	55.4	33.5	21.8	44.6	23.6
1250750	Ocala city.........................	12,424	4,583	0.0	7.5	49.1	21.9	26.6	50.9	38.0
1253000	Orlando city......................	52,027	19,788	1.0	25.9	45.9	31.6	14.2	54.1	44.4
1254000	Palm Bay city.....................	22,136	7,169	0.0	10.8	54.0	20.6	33.4	46.0	34.9
1254200	Palm Coast city..................	14,848	4,525	4.8	25.7	68.0	30.9	37.1	32.0	27.9
1254350	Palm Harbor CDP................	8,983	2,553	3.9	21.2	56.6	34.9	21.7	43.4	42.3
1255775	Pembroke Pines city.............	33,546	9,764	1.7	58.1	76.2	56.1	19.7	23.8	18.6
1255925	Pensacola city....................	9,536	3,273	0.0	4.0	56.8	37.7	19.1	43.2	32.9
1256825	Pine Hills CDP....................	17,986	5,722	1.6	51.2	43.1	27.0	15.9	56.9	49.1
1257425	Plantation city...................	17,714	5,825	1.9	41.2	72.1	35.5	36.3	27.9	23.3
1257900	Poinciana CDP....................	14,671	3,399	0.0	18.7	41.4	20.9	20.5	58.6	51.8
1258050	Pompano Beach city.............	17,979	7,509	1.0	44.1	44.2	30.1	13.6	55.8	41.9
1258350	Port Charlotte CDP..............	7,693	1,999	0.0	15.4	54.0	29.6	20.5	46.0	37.8
1258575	Port Orange city.................	9,816	2,912	0.0	17.5	63.6	40.0	22.8	36.4	30.7
1258715	Port St. Lucie city...............	40,445	11,770	0.3	29.7	60.6	41.3	17.6	39.4	36.2
1260950	Riverview CDP....................	18,523	6,674	0.9	27.0	68.7	38.5	29.8	31.3	25.7
1263000	St. Petersburg city...............	44,654	14,358	0.5	14.6	47.4	27.9	19.6	52.6	40.5
1263650	Sanford city......................	13,376	4,599	0.0	23.7	54.0	36.7	17.3	46.0	30.4
1264175	Sarasota city.....................	7,861	3,094	0.2	36.7	48.8	34.9	13.9	51.2	42.2
1268350	Spring Hill CDP..................	21,500	5,864	0.5	13.6	51.0	24.9	23.5	49.0	43.0
1269700	Sunrise city.......................	17,934	6,600	0.7	54.9	61.4	41.7	17.8	38.6	30.3
1270600	Tallahassee city..................	29,919	10,824	0.5	15.6	62.5	38.4	22.7	37.5	27.2
1270675	Tamarac city......................	10,854	2,939	1.6	56.7	45.6	38.6	7.0	54.4	53.9
1270700	Tamiami CDP......................	8,700	3,040	2.5	75.4	50.3	36.0	13.8	49.7	37.3
1271000	Tampa city.........................	69,631	24,029	1.1	21.7	52.4	31.7	20.6	47.6	37.1
1271569	The Hammocks CDP..............	10,419	3,399	11.4	75.1	72.9	42.2	29.0	27.1	18.7
1272145	Town 'n' Country CDP...........	14,897	4,169	4.1	22.5	54.5	31.8	21.3	45.5	39.1
1275812	Wellington village...............	15,261	3,777	3.0	36.9	80.6	40.9	39.5	19.4	16.8
1276582	Weston city.......................	20,125	4,243	9.4	58.6	93.3	39.3	54.1	6.7	4.2
1276600	West Palm Beach city............	17,626	6,641	2.5	40.6	38.2	25.3	12.6	61.8	52.5
1300000	**Georgia**.................................	2,349,999	780,912	1.2	21.1	59.4	33.9	24.7	40.6	30.9
1301052	Albany city........................	17,105	6,625	0.4	4.9	30.7	23.7	5.6	69.3	53.9
1301696	Alpharetta city...................	17,633	5,910	5.5	48.7	88.8	46.7	42.1	11.2	6.3
1303440	Athens-Clarke County...........	19,503	8,078	2.3	25.6	55.7	29.9	25.2	44.3	35.2
1304000	Atlanta city.......................	76,195	30,910	0.8	12.9	44.6	28.5	15.4	55.4	40.5
1304204	Augusta-Richmond County........	44,085	15,861	0.8	7.8	34.5	18.1	15.4	65.5	46.7
1310944	Brookhaven city..................	9,616	4,478	1.6	52.8	86.2	53.9	32.3	13.8	10.8
1319000	Columbus CDP....................	46,883	16,909	2.1	8.5	48.4	21.8	26.6	51.6	37.4
1342425	Johns Creek city.................	23,711	6,102	3.1	51.1	89.7	58.7	30.9	10.3	9.1
1349000	Macon city........................	22,857	9,156	1.2	5.0	27.2	16.5	10.7	72.8	52.5
1349756	Marietta city......................	11,944	4,735	0.0	46.3	62.3	40.0	21.1	37.7	34.5
1367284	Roswell city.......................	22,290	7,069	2.9	30.0	79.7	42.8	36.9	20.3	17.8
1368516	Sandy Springs city...............	21,993	7,982	2.5	41.5	68.4	39.5	28.7	31.6	24.3
1369000	Savannah city.....................	29,323	10,937	1.0	15.4	43.9	20.6	23.2	56.1	40.1
1371492	Smyrna city.......................	11,487	5,069	4.1	38.2	72.1	45.9	26.2	27.9	27.3
1378800	Valdosta city......................	11,662	5,068	0.0	7.0	37.9	20.9	17.1	62.1	50.5
1380508	Warner Robins city..............	19,214	7,059	0.9	11.0	50.4	29.9	18.6	49.6	34.2

Table D-4: Cities with a Population of 50,000 or More—Children—*Continued*

State/ Place FIPS code	State/Place	Total own children 6 to 17	Nativity and parentage, age 6 to 17 years		Own children age 6 to 17 years living with two parents			Own children age 6 to 17 years living with one parent		Grand-children under 18 living with a grandparent householder	Grand-children under 18 living with a grandparent householder, as a percent of all children	Children for whom grandparent householders are responsible, as a percent of all children
			Child is foreign born, percent	One or more foreign-born parent, percent	Age 6 to 17 years living with two parents, percent	Both parents in labor force, percent	One parent in labor force, percent	Age 6 to 17 years living with one parent, percent	Parent in labor force, percent			
	Florida—cont'd											
1224000	Fort Lauderdale city	17,753	9.7	39.7	49.9	35.6	13.2	50.1	42.5	3,992	14.2	8.1
1224125	Fort Myers city	7,651	5.5	33.0	45.7	30.1	15.2	54.3	42.0	1,413	11.7	8.5
1224562	Fountainebleau CDP	5,164	24.7	92.6	64.2	38.5	25.6	35.8	34.2	407	4.8	2.5
1225175	Gainesville city	8,613	3.7	15.0	44.3	27.2	15.3	55.7	49.1	933	6.2	4.9
1230000	Hialeah city	27,554	32.3	87.2	54.4	36.7	17.2	45.6	35.8	5,619	13.6	5.9
1232000	Hollywood city	19,406	10.3	49.0	61.8	41.6	19.9	38.2	34.6	2,097	7.2	2.5
1232275	Homestead city	11,843	11.1	57.7	59.0	36.7	20.5	41.0	31.9	850	4.7	1.9
1235000	Jacksonville city	116,961	3.8	16.8	56.1	36.8	18.0	43.9	34.9	16,731	9.1	5.3
1235875	Jupiter town	7,568	1.3	16.6	75.5	41.9	33.1	24.5	17.1	284	2.6	1.6
1236062	Kendale Lakes CDP	7,603	20.9	82.7	60.8	47.6	12.8	39.2	36.4	635	6.2	1.1
1236100	Kendall CDP	8,968	16.2	55.7	77.6	52.5	24.6	22.4	19.4	859	6.2	2.1
1236950	Kissimmee city	10,303	6.5	40.5	49.6	32.0	16.7	50.4	33.0	1,532	10.0	5.9
1238250	Lakeland city	12,857	3.7	15.1	47.0	31.8	13.9	53.0	40.3	2,727	13.7	7.1
1239425	Largo city	8,051	5.9	23.5	53.0	40.2	12.2	47.0	40.4	0	0.0	0.0
1239550	Lauderhill city	10,281	13.2	58.4	37.0	32.5	4.6	63.0	54.1	1,663	10.3	5.0
1239925	Lehigh Acres CDP	18,705	8.8	40.8	51.8	33.9	16.5	48.2	37.7	1,472	5.0	3.4
1243125	Margate city	7,202	10.7	62.1	55.0	40.8	14.1	45.0	42.8	621	6.1	0.8
1243975	Melbourne city	7,631	3.2	17.4	55.6	36.1	18.0	44.4	39.2	1,285	10.8	8.1
1245000	Miami city	44,550	21.9	69.6	45.3	27.5	15.9	54.7	44.3	8,804	11.9	4.0
1245025	Miami Beach city	8,200	16.3	66.9	60.8	38.2	22.4	39.2	34.4	0	0.0	0.0
1245060	Miami Gardens city	16,333	4.6	44.1	34.3	23.1	9.4	65.7	54.9	5,529	22.7	10.1
1245975	Miramar city	22,173	9.8	69.5	64.3	45.0	18.2	35.7	34.3	2,572	8.1	4.4
1249450	North Miami city	8,887	16.1	69.4	51.2	33.6	15.8	48.8	37.9	1,796	13.9	4.7
1249675	North Port city	9,220	3.0	12.5	63.2	44.8	17.8	36.8	28.7	1,200	9.2	5.0
1250750	Ocala city	7,841	2.2	10.9	45.8	30.7	15.0	54.2	45.3	1,082	8.7	6.3
1253000	Orlando city	32,239	8.5	31.7	42.4	30.6	11.2	57.6	48.1	4,105	7.9	5.2
1254000	Palm Bay city	14,967	2.6	14.5	60.1	32.7	26.9	39.9	32.6	3,228	14.6	7.3
1254200	Palm Coast city	10,323	4.3	17.6	64.2	40.2	23.7	35.8	29.0	813	5.5	2.5
1254350	Palm Harbor CDP	6,430	7.4	22.2	73.9	53.7	19.1	26.1	23.3	671	7.5	2.4
1255775	Pembroke Pines city	23,782	8.5	58.7	69.3	50.3	18.5	30.7	27.9	1,266	3.8	2.0
1255925	Pensacola city	6,263	1.8	8.4	62.1	50.2	11.7	37.9	31.9	885	9.3	6.6
1256825	Pine Hills CDP	12,264	7.3	52.0	47.5	33.2	14.2	52.5	46.1	2,052	11.4	6.0
1257425	Plantation city	11,889	8.0	41.8	69.5	47.2	21.9	30.5	26.8	1,176	6.6	3.5
1257900	Poinciana CDP	11,272	3.1	30.9	54.6	31.4	14.9	45.4	34.3	1,309	8.9	6.0
1258050	Pompano Beach city	10,470	8.5	47.1	51.8	30.3	20.7	48.2	36.5	1,428	7.9	4.3
1258350	Port Charlotte CDP	5,694	4.5	24.2	64.4	51.0	10.5	35.6	26.7	1,103	14.3	10.1
1258575	Port Orange city	6,904	2.2	13.4	64.8	41.6	22.8	35.2	28.5	359	3.7	2.5
1258715	Port St. Lucie city	28,675	4.1	33.9	68.6	46.9	20.9	31.4	27.4	2,842	7.0	3.0
1260950	Riverview CDP	11,849	5.4	32.1	77.5	51.3	24.1	22.5	18.0	1,781	9.6	4.2
1263000	St. Petersburg city	30,296	4.3	17.5	53.0	39.5	13.1	47.0	37.3	4,434	9.9	6.6
1263650	Sanford city	8,777	3.1	24.2	43.3	29.4	12.6	56.7	41.7	1,880	14.1	11.8
1264175	Sarasota city	4,767	18.6	43.5	60.6	41.1	19.3	39.4	35.4	446	5.7	3.2
1268350	Spring Hill CDP	15,636	0.8	12.7	69.6	41.5	21.8	30.4	24.0	2,041	9.5	5.7
1269700	Sunrise city	11,334	13.2	60.8	59.2	42.3	16.5	40.8	36.4	1,457	8.1	4.1
1270600	Tallahassee city	19,095	3.7	12.0	53.4	34.3	15.9	46.6	41.5	1,360	4.5	2.5
1270675	Tamarac city	7,915	10.5	65.6	49.5	40.2	9.0	50.5	46.3	1,025	9.4	1.6
1270700	Tamiami CDP	5,660	20.3	87.6	71.6	47.5	23.0	28.4	24.4	0	0.0	0.0
1271000	Tampa city	45,602	5.7	24.0	53.6	31.4	21.0	46.4	37.5	5,514	7.9	3.9
1271569	The Hammocks CDP	7,020	16.6	77.1	75.6	49.7	23.8	24.4	21.8	0	0.0	0.0
1272145	Town 'n' Country CDP	10,728	11.1	30.6	53.6	34.5	16.6	46.4	41.6	1,427	9.6	4.0
1275812	Wellington village	11,484	5.8	40.9	79.1	50.6	26.9	20.9	19.7	686	4.5	3.0
1276582	Weston city	15,882	24.1	63.8	85.8	51.0	34.3	14.2	12.2	0	0.0	0.0
1276600	West Palm Beach city	10,985	8.1	43.8	43.8	27.1	15.6	56.2	46.3	2,211	12.5	8.1
1300000	**Georgia**	1,569,087	3.6	18.9	62.0	39.6	21.3	38.0	30.9	217,865	9.3	5.7
1301052	Albany city	10,480	0.6	5.0	30.7	20.5	7.5	69.3	55.6	2,024	11.8	9.0
1301696	Alpharetta city	11,723	8.2	34.8	82.6	50.6	32.0	17.4	14.4	0	0.0	0.0
1303440	Athens-Clarke County	11,425	6.1	23.8	57.0	35.3	20.6	43.0	34.1	1,512	7.8	4.7
1304000	Atlanta city	45,285	2.0	10.0	43.9	25.7	17.3	56.1	46.4	8,473	11.1	6.0
1304204	Augusta-Richmond County	28,224	1.2	5.2	40.5	25.6	13.6	59.5	40.3	5,509	12.5	8.1
1310944	Brookhaven city	5,138	13.8	48.0	79.2	56.6	20.3	20.8	18.5	0	0.0	0.0
1319000	Columbus city	29,974	1.9	7.8	49.4	29.0	19.7	50.6	40.2	4,530	9.7	6.4
1342425	Johns Creek city	17,609	9.8	40.2	80.3	52.5	27.3	19.7	17.3	571	2.4	2.0
1349000	Macon city	13,701	0.6	5.3	33.1	18.6	13.9	66.9	47.2	2,984	13.1	6.8
1349756	Marietta city	7,209	13.7	38.6	57.4	37.4	18.9	42.6	37.4	0	0.0	0.0
1367284	Roswell city	15,221	8.7	29.1	82.3	49.4	32.5	17.7	16.0	342	1.5	0.7
1368516	Sandy Springs city	14,011	7.9	31.1	64.4	41.6	21.5	35.6	30.4	0	0.0	0.0
1369000	Savannah city	18,386	2.7	7.9	45.5	32.2	13.1	54.5	44.8	3,401	11.6	8.3
1371492	Smyrna city	6,418	7.2	31.6	64.9	35.1	29.8	35.1	28.9	0	0.0	0.0
1378800	Valdosta city	6,594	1.1	8.1	37.7	25.0	12.6	62.3	54.6	802	6.9	3.3
1380508	Warner Robins city	12,155	3.9	12.0	50.8	35.0	15.5	49.2	38.4	1,770	9.2	6.2

State/Place FIPS code	State/Place	Total own children under 18 in families and subfamilies	Own children under 6 years in families and subfamilies							
			Total own children under 6 years	Nativity and parentage, under 6 years		Own children under 6 years living with two parents			Own children under 6 living with one parent	
				Child is foreign born, percent	One or more foreign-born parent, percent	Total under 6 years living with two parents, percent	Both parents in labor force, percent	One parent in labor force, percent	Total under 6 years living with one parent, percent	Parent in labor force, percent
1500000	**Hawaii**..............................	288,797	103,598	1.8	27.3	67.0	39.8	26.1	33.0	24.5
1571550	Urban Honolulu CDP...............	57,929	21,320	3.9	44.5	70.7	42.4	27.2	29.3	20.6
1600000	**Idaho**..............................	410,390	136,541	1.0	14.9	74.8	36.9	37.0	25.2	19.2
1608830	Boise City city.......................	45,111	14,546	2.9	14.3	70.7	41.7	27.8	29.3	20.3
1639700	Idaho Falls city......................	16,089	6,153	0.9	15.2	72.2	35.7	36.5	27.8	24.2
1652120	Meridian city.........................	24,958	7,986	0.0	6.0	83.6	46.9	36.7	16.4	13.6
1656260	Nampa city...........................	26,438	8,232	0.8	22.5	68.2	24.5	43.4	31.8	23.3
1664090	Pocatello city.........................	13,569	4,780	0.6	5.8	69.6	32.5	35.7	30.4	22.3
1700000	**Illinois**.............................	2,932,336	944,645	1.4	27.6	64.8	39.2	24.9	35.2	28.3
1702154	Arlington Heights village...........	15,786	4,920	1.8	40.3	92.9	49.3	43.6	7.1	6.4
1703012	Aurora city............................	57,721	17,734	1.9	47.2	67.7	36.7	29.9	32.3	25.1
1705573	Berwyn city...........................	15,217	4,832	0.3	44.0	52.9	29.1	23.5	47.1	35.0
1706613	Bloomington city.....................	18,172	6,010	3.6	20.0	65.3	39.9	25.3	34.7	32.3
1707133	Bolingbrook village..................	20,501	7,545	0.6	44.5	71.5	47.1	24.4	28.5	22.2
1712385	Champaign city.......................	13,133	4,748	2.6	27.7	68.2	46.0	21.8	31.8	23.5
1714000	Chicago city..........................	573,777	209,658	1.7	34.9	51.5	29.9	20.6	48.5	37.4
1714351	Cicero town...........................	27,302	8,794	1.6	74.3	61.6	23.3	37.6	38.4	32.8
1718823	Decatur city..........................	15,592	5,335	0.9	7.4	40.0	24.7	15.0	60.0	54.0
1719642	Des Plaines city......................	11,260	3,950	1.6	55.1	86.8	49.7	34.6	13.2	9.0
1723074	Elgin city..............................	31,346	11,922	1.8	59.5	64.1	37.8	25.5	35.9	25.9
1724582	Evanston city.........................	14,925	5,630	4.1	37.1	77.1	46.6	27.9	22.9	16.4
1735411	Hoffman Estates village............	12,461	3,420	5.6	39.9	70.7	50.9	19.9	29.3	27.5
1738570	Joliet city.............................	41,933	14,402	0.1	23.5	68.1	41.4	26.3	31.9	27.4
1751089	Mount Prospect village.............	12,401	3,728	4.8	49.1	88.9	58.0	29.7	11.1	10.6
1751622	Naperville city........................	38,884	9,664	2.1	37.8	93.5	50.2	43.1	6.5	6.2
1753234	Normal town..........................	9,196	3,427	1.0	11.5	68.2	51.6	15.8	31.8	26.2
1754820	Oak Lawn village....................	11,862	3,820	0.0	42.5	81.8	34.2	43.0	18.2	15.0
1754885	Oak Park village.....................	12,249	3,856	1.8	22.3	86.0	58.5	26.5	14.0	13.6
1756640	Orland Park village..................	10,852	2,942	0.0	35.7	83.0	48.7	34.3	17.0	6.8
1757225	Palatine village.......................	16,720	5,935	5.3	50.8	66.9	46.7	19.9	33.1	25.4
1759000	Peoria city............................	27,582	9,395	2.4	17.3	43.8	21.6	20.1	56.2	41.7
1765000	Rockford city.........................	37,528	13,545	1.5	21.7	45.4	28.1	15.7	54.6	43.6
1768003	Schaumburg village..................	15,044	6,466	6.4	49.5	83.7	53.5	30.3	16.3	10.9
1770122	Skokie village........................	13,346	4,142	3.0	71.8	77.5	47.9	29.3	22.5	21.5
1772000	Springfield city.......................	24,366	8,435	0.4	7.2	54.0	40.1	13.9	46.0	40.8
1775484	Tinley Park village...................	12,965	4,084	1.8	20.2	78.9	53.9	25.1	21.1	18.5
1779293	Waukegan city.......................	24,522	8,059	1.7	55.3	50.4	32.7	17.2	49.6	40.3
1781048	Wheaton city.........................	12,606	3,798	3.3	25.5	92.4	57.4	34.6	7.6	7.6
1800000	**Indiana**.............................	1,508,064	492,870	0.9	11.0	63.1	37.4	24.8	36.9	29.1
1801468	Anderson city.........................	11,449	3,997	0.0	6.1	46.8	31.0	15.3	53.2	36.1
1805860	Bloomington city.....................	8,755	4,015	2.6	23.6	73.9	33.0	37.8	26.1	21.4
1810342	Carmel city...........................	23,483	6,340	5.1	24.8	84.2	45.4	38.8	15.8	15.0
1820728	Elkhart city...........................	13,407	5,075	1.5	27.8	37.5	18.4	14.0	62.5	46.2
1822000	Evansville city........................	25,052	9,598	0.0	2.4	46.5	27.2	18.8	53.5	44.0
1823278	Fishers town..........................	25,693	8,722	1.2	9.1	89.5	62.5	27.0	10.5	9.5
1825000	Fort Wayne city......................	62,630	22,032	1.3	14.0	54.2	28.7	25.1	45.8	33.9
1827000	Gary city..............................	20,000	6,755	0.6	3.8	20.5	11.0	8.7	79.5	57.9
1829898	Greenwood city......................	12,510	5,176	0.0	13.9	75.1	50.7	24.4	24.9	21.1
1831000	Hammond city........................	20,795	7,603	3.0	23.7	47.8	19.4	28.4	52.2	38.7
1836003	Indianapolis city.....................	193,913	69,558	1.3	20.0	49.6	31.8	16.6	50.4	41.3
1840392	Kokomo city..........................	12,008	4,380	0.0	4.5	60.9	43.2	17.4	39.1	35.9
1840788	Lafayette city.........................	16,041	6,318	1.6	16.9	56.7	41.3	15.4	43.3	35.3
1851876	Muncie city...........................	10,647	3,903	1.6	2.9	50.7	28.0	16.7	49.3	35.0
1854180	Noblesville city.......................	15,912	5,770	1.2	10.0	83.0	57.0	23.2	17.0	16.8
1871000	South Bend city......................	24,938	9,259	0.6	18.1	51.5	33.8	17.0	48.5	39.7
1875428	Terre Haute city......................	10,833	4,273	0.1	4.5	49.1	22.8	24.8	50.9	36.9
1900000	**Iowa**...............................	694,083	230,397	0.9	10.4	69.0	49.7	18.6	31.0	25.6
1901855	Ames city.............................	7,682	2,680	3.3	23.1	88.2	53.0	34.9	11.8	9.5
1912000	Cedar Rapids city....................	28,321	9,917	1.0	6.0	64.4	50.9	13.1	35.6	30.2
1916860	Council Bluffs city....................	13,575	4,438	0.0	4.7	49.1	40.1	9.0	50.9	44.3
1919000	Davenport city........................	23,593	8,959	0.4	5.3	52.0	35.4	15.3	48.0	36.4
1921000	Des Moines city......................	49,170	18,587	3.1	24.0	56.3	37.5	17.3	43.7	34.1
1922395	Dubuque city.........................	11,326	3,946	0.3	3.4	55.4	37.1	17.3	44.6	35.2
1938595	Iowa City city........................	10,792	4,136	2.2	23.3	67.6	45.8	21.2	32.4	26.6
1973335	Sioux City city........................	19,624	7,485	1.7	23.9	53.2	35.1	16.6	46.8	39.0
1982425	Waterloo city.........................	15,134	5,346	1.5	16.4	54.7	38.3	16.2	45.3	37.4
1983910	West Des Moines city................	14,357	5,570	5.8	20.0	79.5	51.7	27.8	20.5	17.7
2000000	**Kansas**.............................	693,288	237,252	0.9	15.7	67.3	40.8	26.0	32.7	26.1
2036000	Kansas City city......................	39,128	14,737	2.3	32.7	44.1	29.2	13.8	55.9	41.0

| State/Place FIPS code | State/Place | Total own children 6 to 17 | Own children age 6 to 17 years in families and subfamilies | | | | | | | | Grandchildren under 18 living with a grandparent householder | Grandchildren under 18 living with a grandparent householder, as a percent of all children | Children for whom grandparent householders are responsible, as a percent of all children |
| | | | Nativity and parentage, age 6 to 17 years | | Own children age 6 to 17 years living with two parents | | | Own children age 6 to 17 years living with one parent | | | | |
			Child is foreign born, percent	One or more foreign-born parent, percent	Age 6 to 17 years living with two parents, percent	Both parents in labor force, percent	One parent in labor force, percent	Age 6 to 17 years living with one parent, percent	Parent in labor force, percent			
1500000	**Hawaii**................................	185,199	6.7	30.8	70.6	48.9	20.0	29.4	23.9	47,670	16.5	5.4
1571550	Urban Honolulu CDP................	36,609	13.4	49.7	69.5	47.8	20.2	30.5	24.4	9,746	16.8	5.4
1600000	**Idaho**..................................	273,849	2.4	13.7	73.6	44.3	28.2	26.4	21.9	20,822	5.1	2.6
1608830	Boise City city.......................	30,565	6.9	13.0	66.7	43.1	22.0	33.3	26.0	1,568	3.5	1.2
1639700	Idaho Falls city......................	9,936	1.0	12.6	66.4	39.2	27.2	33.6	30.8	647	4.0	1.4
1652120	Meridian city.........................	16,972	1.5	10.9	80.6	50.9	29.1	19.4	17.4	1,007	4.0	1.9
1656260	Nampa city............................	18,206	1.3	23.0	68.7	38.4	29.6	31.3	25.5	1,340	5.1	3.3
1664090	Pocatello city.........................	8,789	2.7	9.3	69.9	44.0	25.6	30.1	22.4	595	4.4	1.9
1700000	**Illinois**..............................	1,987,691	4.2	26.4	67.0	44.2	21.9	33.0	27.9	213,052	7.3	3.7
1702154	Arlington Heights village............	10,866	6.7	28.1	83.9	55.8	28.0	16.1	15.9	218	1.4	0.7
1703012	Aurora city............................	39,987	7.8	50.5	69.4	42.4	26.5	30.6	27.6	3,951	6.8	2.6
1705573	Berwyn city............................	10,385	2.5	58.6	59.2	35.8	22.8	40.8	38.0	2,154	14.2	3.4
1706613	Bloomington city.....................	12,162	5.9	11.7	67.2	53.7	13.5	32.8	29.0	943	5.2	3.2
1707133	Bolingbrook village..................	12,956	5.2	44.7	76.5	50.8	25.3	23.5	19.7	1,394	6.8	2.4
1712385	Champaign city.......................	8,385	8.4	24.0	60.5	44.2	15.6	39.5	34.2	907	6.9	5.9
1714000	Chicago city...........................	364,119	6.2	39.7	50.2	29.1	20.0	49.8	40.4	69,674	12.1	5.9
1714351	Cicero town...........................	18,508	8.0	81.7	67.7	37.9	29.0	32.3	27.7	2,087	7.6	1.8
1718823	Decatur city...........................	10,257	0.8	3.6	41.2	25.7	14.3	58.8	52.9	1,995	12.8	9.9
1719642	Des Plaines city......................	7,310	6.2	54.0	83.2	55.8	26.8	16.8	16.6	470	4.2	1.2
1723074	Elgin city...............................	19,424	9.0	60.1	70.8	47.2	22.8	29.2	24.6	1,310	4.2	2.2
1724582	Evanston city..........................	9,295	6.1	29.0	65.7	48.7	16.5	34.3	27.2	0	0.0	0.0
1735411	Hoffman Estates village.............	9,041	9.5	45.5	74.7	52.0	22.2	25.3	24.8	0	0.0	0.0
1738570	Joliet city..............................	27,531	2.7	29.8	69.2	41.6	26.6	30.8	27.0	2,971	7.1	3.6
1751089	Mount Prospect village.............	8,673	11.7	53.9	84.9	59.9	24.9	15.1	14.2	0	0.0	0.0
1751622	Naperville city........................	29,220	6.7	32.4	85.0	51.0	33.5	15.0	13.2	427	1.1	0.9
1753234	Normal town...........................	5,769	6.1	11.8	78.3	65.7	12.6	21.7	20.0	0	0.0	0.0
1754820	Oak Lawn village.....................	8,042	0.9	35.7	79.2	46.0	31.9	20.8	17.8	903	7.6	4.4
1754885	Oak Park village......................	8,393	4.0	18.8	74.7	57.4	16.9	25.3	23.0	0	0.0	0.0
1756640	Orland Park village..................	7,910	3.0	23.8	81.9	57.1	23.9	18.1	16.2	450	4.1	1.2
1757225	Palatine village.......................	10,785	8.4	41.5	71.9	50.4	21.3	28.1	22.2	1,150	6.9	3.7
1759000	Peoria city.............................	18,187	4.6	15.9	52.4	30.1	20.7	47.6	41.3	1,980	7.2	4.5
1765000	Rockford city..........................	23,983	4.3	22.8	48.9	30.9	16.9	51.1	43.5	2,769	7.4	3.8
1768003	Schaumburg village..................	8,578	8.6	40.3	76.6	57.5	18.8	23.4	22.2	469	3.1	1.7
1770122	Skokie village.........................	9,204	12.1	59.3	79.0	62.3	16.6	21.0	17.6	665	5.0	2.5
1772000	Springfield city.......................	15,931	2.9	7.6	54.0	42.7	11.1	46.0	38.7	1,227	5.0	2.9
1775484	Tinley Park village...................	8,881	5.7	22.6	75.6	55.8	19.8	24.4	21.4	859	6.6	3.9
1779293	Waukegan city........................	16,463	5.7	59.7	53.7	33.7	17.7	46.3	42.2	1,864	7.6	3.3
1781048	Wheaton city..........................	8,808	6.0	18.1	83.6	52.5	28.9	16.4	14.7	327	2.6	1.0
1800000	**Indiana**...............................	1,015,194	2.2	8.7	66.4	44.3	21.1	33.6	27.6	111,312	7.4	4.2
1801468	Anderson city.........................	7,452	3.5	7.0	48.3	24.5	20.8	51.7	40.4	1,137	9.9	7.7
1805860	Bloomington city.....................	4,740	3.9	12.7	59.0	35.9	22.4	41.0	27.8	147	1.7	0.8
1810342	Carmel city............................	17,143	7.2	20.7	83.1	51.7	31.5	16.9	14.6	478	2.0	0.5
1820728	Elkhart city............................	8,332	7.5	36.0	49.6	32.7	15.1	50.4	41.7	870	6.5	3.1
1822000	Evansville city.........................	15,454	1.2	4.2	46.4	25.9	19.6	53.6	44.0	1,966	7.8	4.3
1823278	Fishers town...........................	16,971	3.9	13.2	85.3	58.5	26.8	14.7	13.7	0	0.0	0.0
1825000	Fort Wayne city.......................	40,598	5.5	14.3	56.7	34.9	20.6	43.3	34.7	4,068	6.5	3.5
1827000	Gary city...............................	13,305	0.3	2.2	21.9	12.4	7.7	78.1	58.9	2,511	12.5	6.6
1829898	Greenwood city.......................	7,334	2.1	7.0	75.8	51.0	23.3	24.2	21.3	785	6.3	3.4
1831000	Hammond city.........................	13,192	5.1	25.9	57.2	30.8	24.6	42.8	33.1	2,780	13.4	5.4
1836003	Indianapolis city......................	124,355	4.3	15.2	51.6	35.4	15.0	48.4	39.6	16,155	8.3	4.8
1840392	Kokomo city...........................	7,628	0.8	4.1	58.3	39.7	17.0	41.7	35.9	673	5.6	4.0
1840788	Lafayette city.........................	9,723	1.0	19.7	57.0	38.0	17.9	43.0	37.3	1,003	6.3	4.6
1851876	Muncie city............................	6,744	1.7	4.2	49.8	29.1	18.7	50.2	36.2	848	8.0	3.4
1854180	Noblesville city.......................	10,142	1.4	7.3	77.2	52.9	23.8	22.8	20.1	0	0.0	0.0
1871000	South Bend city.......................	15,679	3.2	17.6	50.7	35.1	13.5	49.3	39.0	1,856	7.4	4.6
1875428	Terre Haute city.......................	6,560	0.9	4.0	55.7	27.7	25.2	44.3	34.3	927	8.6	4.7
1900000	**Iowa**...................................	463,686	2.3	9.2	70.3	54.0	15.3	29.7	25.4	32,341	4.7	2.5
1901855	Ames city..............................	5,002	6.8	16.4	79.8	65.1	12.6	20.2	18.6	0	0.0	0.0
1912000	Cedar Rapids city....................	18,404	0.6	7.4	64.2	50.7	13.0	35.8	31.0	1,643	5.8	3.1
1916860	Council Bluffs city....................	9,137	1.6	7.7	50.1	35.3	14.0	49.9	44.9	977	7.2	2.5
1919000	Davenport city........................	14,634	0.4	6.4	55.9	42.6	12.0	44.1	33.7	1,312	5.6	2.8
1921000	Des Moines city.......................	30,583	6.8	26.5	56.6	39.2	16.3	43.4	37.6	4,179	8.5	4.7
1922395	Dubuque city..........................	7,380	1.7	3.7	58.6	47.3	11.3	41.4	32.1	668	5.9	2.6
1938595	Iowa City city.........................	6,656	9.5	28.9	64.5	45.7	18.8	35.5	29.2	0	0.0	0.0
1973335	Sioux City city........................	12,139	3.5	24.1	57.5	41.0	15.9	42.5	36.8	1,685	8.6	3.8
1982425	Waterloo city..........................	9,788	2.0	17.1	57.4	40.0	14.5	42.6	35.4	915	6.0	4.1
1983910	West Des Moines city................	8,787	7.0	12.3	74.6	52.4	20.7	25.4	21.2	0	0.0	0.0
2000000	**Kansas**................................	456,036	3.0	14.9	70.5	49.3	20.6	29.5	25.6	40,225	5.8	3.3
2036000	Kansas City city.......................	24,391	7.2	34.7	52.0	35.8	15.4	48.0	38.3	3,570	9.1	5.7

State/ Place FIPS code	State/Place	Total own children under 18 in families and subfamilies	Own children under 6 years in families and subfamilies							
			Total own children under 6 years	Nativity and parentage, under 6 years		Own children under 6 years living with two parents			Own children under 6 living with one parent	
				Child is foreign born, percent	One or more foreign-born parent, percent	Total under 6 years living with two parents, percent	Both parents in labor force, percent	One parent in labor force, percent	Total under 6 years living with one parent, percent	Parent in labor force, percent
	Kansas—cont'd									
2038900	Lawrence city	14,779	5,318	3.7	20.3	63.4	40.5	20.7	36.6	30.3
2044250	Manhattan city	7,832	3,719	1.6	16.6	70.7	36.2	33.8	29.3	22.4
2052575	Olathe city	36,721	12,385	1.0	16.5	85.6	55.7	29.4	14.4	13.4
2053775	Overland Park city	41,879	13,840	2.7	27.7	76.4	44.9	30.1	23.6	22.6
2064500	Shawnee city	16,725	5,071	0.6	10.7	80.0	47.4	32.1	20.0	16.2
2071000	Topeka city	28,901	10,961	0.3	15.0	59.2	37.6	21.4	40.8	35.2
2079000	Wichita city	97,031	35,848	0.7	22.1	58.8	34.0	24.3	41.2	34.4
2100000	**Kentucky**	945,623	316,066	0.8	8.7	62.3	37.2	23.2	37.7	28.0
2108902	Bowling Green city	11,662	4,697	4.2	22.1	50.1	28.0	20.6	49.9	42.3
2146027	Lexington-Fayette urban county	60,844	21,245	2.0	23.6	66.7	43.7	21.5	33.3	27.5
2148006	Louisville/Jefferson County	132,299	45,892	1.7	17.7	54.1	35.8	17.2	45.9	38.6
2158620	Owensboro city	12,986	4,644	0.3	4.6	54.0	36.2	17.8	46.0	38.4
2200000	**Louisiana**	1,045,345	359,520	0.4	7.1	50.1	30.1	19.2	49.9	37.1
2205000	Baton Rouge city	45,419	16,980	0.8	8.4	37.5	25.8	11.7	62.5	50.5
2208920	Bossier City city	15,055	5,907	1.9	10.9	59.7	33.9	25.6	40.3	30.9
2239475	Kenner city	13,253	4,754	1.4	35.0	58.8	31.2	27.6	41.2	30.9
2240735	Lafayette city	24,786	7,775	0.3	6.8	47.7	30.7	16.7	52.3	43.7
2241155	Lake Charles city	16,182	5,495	0.0	5.4	28.6	17.6	11.0	71.4	57.7
2250115	Metairie CDP	27,263	10,473	1.4	24.1	64.3	41.0	22.0	35.7	30.8
2255000	New Orleans city	71,953	26,528	0.4	8.4	36.7	24.8	10.4	63.3	47.4
2270000	Shreveport city	47,101	17,093	0.0	4.9	36.3	24.4	11.7	63.7	43.8
2300000	**Maine**	251,774	76,476	0.7	6.3	66.4	43.4	21.7	33.6	25.7
2360545	Portland city	10,365	3,695	3.1	30.2	66.1	43.8	19.4	33.9	22.6
2400000	**Maryland**	1,285,577	427,978	1.7	28.0	62.6	41.4	20.6	37.4	30.2
2402825	Aspen Hill CDP	12,082	4,252	2.1	68.5	53.0	31.7	20.7	47.0	44.4
2404000	Baltimore city	121,225	47,246	1.1	14.0	35.5	23.4	10.7	64.5	47.5
2407125	Bethesda CDP	14,175	4,477	7.5	43.8	93.7	52.5	38.5	6.3	2.9
2408775	Bowie city	12,576	3,937	1.9	36.3	78.3	62.9	15.4	21.7	16.1
2419125	Columbia CDP	24,283	8,917	3.3	31.9	71.9	47.9	24.0	28.1	21.1
2423975	Dundalk CDP	12,629	4,097	0.0	11.2	53.8	32.3	21.6	46.2	35.4
2426000	Ellicott City CDP	18,745	4,319	0.5	37.6	89.3	58.6	29.7	10.7	8.3
2430325	Frederick city	14,834	5,667	0.7	36.2	51.9	34.9	17.0	48.1	46.3
2431175	Gaithersburg city	16,058	6,134	4.5	64.5	78.9	41.9	35.7	21.1	14.6
2432025	Germantown CDP	23,880	7,475	1.2	67.8	73.3	52.4	18.5	26.7	24.7
2432650	Glen Burnie CDP	14,043	5,492	0.0	18.4	52.8	30.5	22.3	47.2	35.9
2467675	Rockville city	12,597	4,690	5.1	49.9	82.5	52.1	29.8	17.5	17.1
2472450	Silver Spring CDP	16,202	6,576	4.5	57.7	68.5	50.9	16.1	31.5	26.6
2478425	Towson CDP	9,967	3,082	4.3	26.7	89.0	54.5	29.6	11.0	5.3
2481175	Waldorf CDP	20,175	6,317	1.2	17.9	51.8	35.3	16.4	48.2	36.0
2483775	Wheaton CDP	11,431	4,646	2.5	71.7	56.9	36.6	18.4	43.1	37.8
2500000	**Massachusetts**	1,349,577	430,160	1.9	29.6	68.4	45.9	21.7	31.6	23.7
2507000	Boston city	101,901	39,773	2.8	43.4	50.4	34.2	15.4	49.6	37.4
2509000	Brockton city	23,085	8,595	2.0	53.5	45.6	35.6	10.0	54.4	43.0
2509210	Brookline CDP	10,603	3,760	16.4	56.9	92.3	57.4	33.1	7.7	2.0
2511000	Cambridge city	11,226	4,791	7.3	53.3	83.9	53.0	26.8	16.1	10.6
2513660	Chicopee city	10,313	3,306	0.0	6.8	50.3	36.3	8.7	49.7	34.9
2523000	Fall River city	18,198	6,493	0.6	23.2	44.9	28.8	15.0	55.1	39.2
2524960	Framingham CDP	14,085	5,379	2.4	53.2	77.0	50.5	26.5	23.0	15.6
2529405	Haverhill city	12,912	4,814	0.2	18.3	59.3	37.9	20.9	40.7	31.2
2534550	Lawrence city	20,509	7,565	2.4	59.6	32.5	20.8	11.8	67.5	48.0
2537000	Lowell city	23,437	8,934	2.3	38.0	43.1	30.9	12.2	56.9	43.3
2537490	Lynn city	22,541	8,459	5.4	54.4	46.0	24.7	20.0	54.0	43.6
2537875	Malden city	11,159	4,032	8.2	70.0	73.4	44.5	25.1	26.6	19.4
2539835	Medford city	8,400	3,521	2.6	41.0	86.6	54.7	31.3	13.4	12.5
2545000	New Bedford city	19,381	6,753	1.5	26.8	44.0	28.6	15.3	56.0	42.6
2545560	Newton city	18,791	6,240	3.2	44.2	87.9	60.6	26.3	12.1	10.0
2552490	Peabody city	9,192	2,659	0.7	34.4	71.3	53.3	18.0	28.7	26.7
2555745	Quincy city	14,973	6,813	3.0	49.4	75.7	47.5	27.2	24.3	20.5
2556585	Revere city	9,762	3,872	4.1	66.1	60.1	42.3	13.8	39.9	31.7
2562535	Somerville city	10,172	4,569	2.2	56.8	65.6	42.8	22.7	34.4	30.4
2567000	Springfield city	38,080	12,945	1.0	18.5	30.8	16.5	12.0	69.2	43.9
2569170	Taunton city	11,161	3,834	0.0	15.3	56.4	39.2	17.2	43.6	31.2
2572600	Waltham city	8,039	3,622	3.4	56.6	85.0	57.5	26.9	15.0	13.7
2578972	Weymouth Town city	10,699	3,136	1.5	28.8	68.7	48.0	19.4	31.3	22.4
2582000	Worcester city	37,923	14,418	2.3	41.5	52.3	28.9	19.9	47.7	34.8
2600000	**Michigan**	2,165,093	673,975	1.2	12.9	62.2	36.9	24.0	37.8	29.3
2603000	Ann Arbor city	15,768	5,483	5.9	35.4	82.1	42.6	38.4	17.9	13.8
2605920	Battle Creek city	12,707	4,570	0.6	6.9	42.2	27.1	15.1	57.8	52.8
2621000	Dearborn city	28,102	9,607	2.8	62.5	81.5	24.9	53.5	18.5	10.2

State/ Place FIPS code	State/Place	Own children age 6 to 17 years in families and subfamilies								Grand-children under 18 living with a grandparent householder	Grand-children under 18 living with a grandparent householder, as a percent of all children	Children for whom grandparent householders are responsible, as a percent of all children
		Total own children 6 to 17	Nativity and parentage, age 6 to 17 years		Own children age 6 to 17 years living with two parents			Own children age 6 to 17 years living with one parent				
			Child is foreign born, percent	One or more foreign-born parent, percent	Age 6 to 17 years living with two parents, percent	Both parents in labor force, percent	One parent in labor force, percent	Age 6 to 17 years living with one parent, percent	Parent in labor force, percent			
	Kansas—cont'd											
2038900	Lawrence city....................	9,461	3.5	13.1	66.1	54.1	12.0	33.9	29.4	825	5.6	4.4
2044250	Manhattan city..................	4,113	4.1	20.0	75.5	45.1	28.7	24.5	23.0	0	0.0	0.0
2052575	Olathe city.........................	24,336	4.9	18.6	78.9	59.1	19.8	21.1	20.1	1,298	3.5	1.8
2053775	Overland Park city.............	28,039	5.2	18.6	73.6	48.4	25.0	26.4	25.0	1,154	2.8	1.0
2064500	Shawnee city.....................	11,654	0.9	6.5	80.3	54.9	24.2	19.7	17.7	0	0.0	0.0
2071000	Topeka city........................	17,940	3.9	15.3	61.4	44.1	16.6	38.6	32.0	1,831	6.3	3.4
2079000	Wichita city.......................	61,183	4.5	25.1	62.5	41.5	20.4	37.5	31.9	7,222	7.4	3.8
2100000	**Kentucky.......................**	629,557	2.1	6.4	64.7	42.3	20.1	35.3	27.3	89,226	9.4	6.1
2108902	Bowling Green city............	6,965	17.3	28.1	53.2	37.3	12.8	46.8	38.5	499	4.3	3.5
2146027	Lexington-Fayette urban county.	39,599	5.0	18.6	61.5	42.4	18.4	38.5	33.4	3,964	6.5	4.4
2148006	Louisville/Jefferson County........	86,407	5.5	12.8	53.6	37.9	15.0	46.4	38.9	12,602	9.5	6.1
2158620	Owensboro city..................	8,342	1.6	4.6	60.3	33.9	25.9	39.7	33.6	1,259	9.7	3.2
2200000	**Louisiana.......................**	685,825	1.3	5.5	55.5	36.8	17.5	44.5	35.5	119,313	11.4	7.3
2205000	Baton Rouge city...............	28,439	2.1	6.0	38.4	26.3	11.4	61.6	51.4	6,643	14.6	6.7
2208920	Bossier City city.................	9,148	2.4	7.7	58.9	44.5	14.0	41.1	35.4	2,309	15.3	12.4
2239475	Kenner city........................	8,499	5.8	25.5	58.2	35.8	22.3	41.8	35.5	1,906	14.4	8.8
2240735	Lafayette city.....................	17,011	2.8	6.3	52.7	36.1	16.4	47.3	40.8	1,888	7.6	4.1
2241155	Lake Charles city...............	10,687	0.4	5.0	37.4	26.9	9.5	62.6	55.6	1,863	11.5	7.1
2250115	Metairie CDP......................	16,790	3.3	16.8	63.1	42.2	20.1	36.9	33.7	1,772	6.5	3.9
2255000	New Orleans city................	45,425	1.6	6.6	38.6	26.6	10.4	61.4	49.2	9,024	12.5	7.7
2270000	Shreveport city..................	30,008	0.6	3.0	39.0	27.2	10.6	61.0	47.4	6,016	12.8	8.7
2300000	**Maine.............................**	175,298	1.8	6.8	66.8	47.3	18.1	33.2	26.8	14,282	5.7	2.9
2360545	Portland city......................	6,670	14.6	31.2	62.1	42.4	17.3	37.9	29.3	753	7.3	4.5
2400000	**Maryland ....**	857,599	5.5	23.9	64.5	46.6	17.2	35.5	30.5	107,342	8.3	3.9
2402825	Aspen Hill CDP...................	7,830	13.1	56.7	59.9	49.8	9.6	40.1	35.5	1,002	8.3	3.0
2404000	Baltimore city....................	73,979	2.2	8.9	31.7	21.4	9.2	68.3	52.5	19,454	16.0	8.1
2407125	Bethesda CDP.....................	9,698	8.7	34.8	87.5	61.5	25.7	12.5	11.1	0	0.0	0.0
2408775	Bowie city..........................	8,639	5.6	23.6	75.9	61.0	14.5	24.1	20.3	661	5.3	1.9
2419125	Columbia CDP.....................	15,366	9.5	34.9	67.8	53.0	14.8	32.2	29.8	1,475	6.1	3.2
2423975	Dundalk CDP.......................	8,532	3.7	8.3	46.6	28.5	17.7	53.4	39.9	1,306	10.3	5.8
2426000	Ellicott City CDP.................	14,426	10.4	42.7	79.2	53.6	25.6	20.8	18.1	414	2.2	1.6
2430325	Frederick city.....................	9,167	8.2	36.6	57.5	40.7	16.7	42.5	35.0	0	0.0	0.0
2431175	Gaithersburg city...............	9,924	9.5	52.8	59.7	39.4	17.9	40.3	33.3	0	0.0	0.0
2432025	Germantown CDP................	16,405	14.1	64.6	71.5	54.3	16.5	28.5	26.1	574	2.4	1.6
2432650	Glen Burnie CDP.................	8,551	2.0	12.5	54.6	37.6	16.4	45.4	38.3	2,072	14.8	5.7
2467675	Rockville city......................	7,907	13.2	57.4	74.7	63.2	11.5	25.3	22.0	467	3.7	2.4
2472450	Silver Spring CDP................	9,626	19.0	56.7	65.2	51.0	14.0	34.8	29.9	901	5.6	1.6
2478425	Towson CDP........................	6,885	8.5	19.6	73.9	45.7	26.8	26.1	23.3	0	0.0	0.0
2481175	Waldorf CDP.......................	13,858	3.6	14.5	57.2	44.6	12.5	42.8	36.8	1,440	7.1	2.0
2483775	Wheaton CDP......................	6,785	16.0	76.2	68.5	55.8	12.1	31.5	29.1	1,331	11.6	2.2
2500000	**Massachusetts................**	919,417	5.2	24.9	68.2	49.3	17.9	31.8	25.3	79,754	5.9	2.5
2507000	Boston city.........................	62,128	9.2	49.2	39.3	28.1	10.6	60.7	47.0	7,511	7.4	3.7
2509000	Brockton city......................	14,490	8.0	43.0	46.2	34.5	11.4	53.8	41.7	2,228	9.7	4.6
2509210	Brookline CDP.....................	6,843	14.9	46.4	79.1	43.7	35.0	20.9	10.4	0	0.0	0.0
2511000	Cambridge city...................	6,435	14.0	41.4	68.7	51.2	15.7	31.3	27.7	378	3.4	2.4
2513660	Chicopee city.....................	7,007	2.0	14.2	40.5	31.6	7.6	59.5	46.3	1,323	12.8	7.1
2523000	Fall River city.....................	11,705	3.7	31.8	46.5	25.3	18.9	53.5	39.4	1,228	6.7	3.4
2524960	Framingham CDP.................	8,706	8.5	39.9	72.2	53.3	18.5	27.8	23.3	0	0.0	0.0
2529405	Haverhill city......................	8,098	2.0	17.4	58.2	45.0	11.2	41.8	35.7	1,215	9.4	1.6
2534550	Lawrence city.....................	12,944	17.8	62.2	33.4	24.5	8.8	66.6	51.4	1,676	8.2	4.1
2537000	Lowell city.........................	14,503	7.5	43.8	50.9	37.2	12.6	49.1	37.4	1,582	6.8	2.9
2537490	Lynn city............................	14,082	14.1	56.8	47.6	31.6	13.6	52.4	42.7	1,676	7.4	2.9
2537875	Malden city........................	7,127	20.6	66.0	67.3	47.8	19.5	32.7	24.3	867	7.8	4.4
2539835	Medford city.......................	4,879	4.7	44.4	83.8	63.1	20.7	16.2	12.0	622	7.4	0.8
2545000	New Bedford city................	12,628	7.0	33.9	47.7	31.2	15.1	52.3	37.6	1,372	7.1	3.2
2545560	Newton city........................	12,551	10.3	36.4	82.8	55.2	27.3	17.2	14.4	195	1.0	0.5
2552490	Peabody city......................	6,533	4.8	33.5	71.5	61.4	9.7	28.5	26.4	613	6.7	1.4
2555745	Quincy city.........................	8,160	8.2	47.1	69.9	50.4	17.1	30.1	24.7	1,178	7.9	2.9
2556585	Revere city.........................	5,890	8.5	56.5	68.5	57.2	10.9	31.5	25.7	991	10.2	1.7
2562535	Somerville city....................	5,603	8.2	57.6	54.0	33.5	20.3	46.0	30.6	949	9.3	4.8
2567000	Springfield city...................	25,135	3.9	18.2	36.1	22.7	11.1	63.9	40.7	3,888	10.2	6.6
2569170	Taunton city.......................	7,327	1.5	16.1	57.2	44.2	13.0	42.8	27.8	1,206	10.8	4.1
2572600	Waltham city......................	4,417	9.9	34.8	76.5	60.5	15.4	23.5	22.8	524	6.5	2.6
2578972	Weymouth Town city..........	7,563	2.1	12.4	73.6	61.5	10.5	26.4	16.3	544	5.1	2.3
2582000	Worcester city....................	23,505	11.1	41.5	49.1	33.7	13.7	50.9	38.8	2,261	6.0	3.1
2600000	**Michigan ....**	1,491,118	2.8	11.6	66.0	43.4	21.0	34.0	27.3	144,930	6.7	3.4
2603000	Ann Arbor city...................	10,285	10.1	33.5	65.3	41.7	23.2	34.7	29.1	381	2.4	1.2
2605920	Battle Creek city................	8,137	3.3	10.7	55.2	39.4	15.4	44.8	37.2	782	6.2	2.8
2621000	Dearborn city.....................	18,495	9.9	64.9	79.2	22.4	50.6	20.8	14.4	1,319	4.7	2.2

Table D-4: Cities with a Population of 50,000 or More—Children—*Continued*

State/Place FIPS code	State/Place	Total own children under 18 in families and subfamilies	Own children under 6 years in families and subfamilies							
			Total own children under 6 years	Nativity and parentage, under 6 years		Own children under 6 years living with two parents			Own children under 6 living with one parent	
				Child is foreign born, percent	One or more foreign-born parent, percent	Total under 6 years living with two parents, percent	Both parents in labor force, percent	One parent in labor force, percent	Total under 6 years living with one parent, percent	Parent in labor force, percent
	Michigan—cont'd									
2621020	Dearborn Heights city	13,529	4,907	1.0	43.6	74.8	28.6	40.0	25.2	17.6
2622000	Detroit city	163,765	55,395	0.6	14.3	24.4	11.1	10.6	75.6	52.6
2627440	Farmington Hills city	15,479	4,656	4.2	43.5	84.6	49.7	34.9	15.4	12.7
2629000	Flint city	23,486	8,580	0.0	2.2	18.0	11.7	5.2	82.0	58.1
2634000	Grand Rapids city	44,301	17,834	2.3	23.1	50.7	30.1	19.0	49.3	38.7
2642160	Kalamazoo city	14,156	4,973	0.9	8.1	41.6	29.7	10.9	58.4	41.0
2646000	Lansing city	24,969	10,010	1.7	10.2	45.0	29.5	13.6	55.0	43.5
2649000	Livonia city	18,731	5,465	1.9	10.0	81.8	49.6	31.1	18.2	13.8
2659440	Novi city	13,555	3,546	4.0	40.1	92.5	62.6	29.4	7.5	6.9
2665440	Pontiac city	14,862	5,110	0.0	11.4	29.6	18.8	10.2	70.4	62.7
2669035	Rochester Hills city	16,038	5,096	3.7	26.8	81.4	45.3	36.1	18.6	17.3
2670040	Royal Oak city	9,236	3,310	0.4	14.5	83.1	58.2	23.5	16.9	10.7
2670520	Saginaw city	12,845	4,090	0.0	1.1	23.9	14.6	6.0	76.1	50.9
2670760	St. Clair Shores city	10,791	3,374	0.0	6.2	73.4	50.9	22.5	26.6	25.2
2674900	Southfield city	14,453	4,664	3.9	19.3	48.0	26.8	16.8	52.0	45.3
2676460	Sterling Heights city	26,863	7,915	6.1	45.9	76.2	37.3	37.5	23.8	16.7
2679000	Taylor city	14,204	4,989	0.3	3.8	38.0	24.1	13.8	62.0	52.6
2680700	Troy city	18,212	4,986	7.4	54.0	90.3	50.6	39.0	9.7	8.3
2684000	Warren city	28,898	9,621	4.3	23.6	57.3	29.1	26.4	42.7	33.6
2686000	Westland city	16,671	6,227	0.2	10.6	50.7	35.6	15.1	49.3	40.6
2688940	Wyoming city	17,356	6,598	0.3	25.8	71.6	53.9	15.7	28.4	25.5
2700000	**Minnesota**	1,234,372	410,101	1.5	19.1	70.7	49.6	20.3	29.3	24.3
2706382	Blaine city	16,061	5,958	0.0	22.6	77.2	57.6	19.6	22.8	19.4
2706616	Bloomington city	15,917	5,350	1.2	32.3	74.4	46.5	24.5	25.6	21.8
2707966	Brooklyn Park city	19,996	6,962	2.7	36.9	54.0	38.3	14.9	46.0	38.9
2708794	Burnsville city	13,173	4,392	2.1	37.8	61.9	39.0	22.9	38.1	32.7
2713114	Coon Rapids city	13,826	4,829	1.3	20.5	69.5	49.7	19.8	30.5	26.8
2717000	Duluth city	15,413	5,588	0.5	4.9	61.6	41.8	18.2	38.4	31.9
2717288	Eagan city	16,050	5,381	1.3	28.7	80.6	56.2	23.9	19.4	17.3
2718116	Eden Prairie city	15,665	5,058	5.0	38.4	88.6	58.6	30.1	11.4	9.6
2735180	Lakeville city	17,355	4,870	2.0	21.9	86.5	57.0	29.1	13.5	12.0
2740166	Maple Grove city	16,638	5,524	1.4	25.0	90.7	57.9	31.8	9.3	7.6
2743000	Minneapolis city	74,781	31,090	2.4	36.1	56.1	37.1	18.8	43.9	33.8
2743252	Minnetonka city	10,253	3,138	1.8	17.2	80.7	55.6	25.1	19.3	16.8
2751730	Plymouth city	16,404	5,253	7.6	29.4	79.3	47.9	31.1	20.7	19.9
2754880	Rochester city	26,085	9,577	1.0	29.4	73.1	52.9	19.0	26.9	24.1
2756896	St. Cloud city	12,999	5,106	0.4	15.5	60.3	44.5	14.4	39.7	28.7
2758000	St. Paul city	70,681	26,194	4.7	44.3	62.9	41.2	19.0	37.1	30.5
2771428	Woodbury city	18,113	5,579	3.5	26.3	87.2	62.7	24.3	12.8	8.9
2800000	**Mississippi**	690,498	231,060	0.2	4.2	49.0	30.3	17.9	51.0	38.2
2829700	Gulfport city	15,580	6,107	0.0	5.6	44.8	19.1	21.1	55.2	45.1
2836000	Jackson city	42,987	14,393	0.0	1.8	28.7	20.0	6.8	71.3	57.8
2869280	Southaven city	13,529	3,755	0.0	9.5	64.0	38.8	25.2	36.0	30.9
2900000	**Missouri**	1,328,024	440,994	0.6	9.1	62.8	38.7	22.9	37.2	29.5
2906652	Blue Springs city	13,778	4,517	0.0	8.5	74.7	38.9	32.0	25.3	18.9
2915670	Columbia city	20,792	8,054	1.4	13.1	73.9	36.6	31.6	26.1	20.4
2924778	Florissant city	12,353	4,041	0.0	7.1	62.1	40.2	21.4	37.9	30.3
2935000	Independence city	23,988	8,969	0.8	13.7	48.6	29.9	17.5	51.4	39.8
2937592	Joplin city	10,579	3,821	0.0	3.6	50.5	33.0	17.4	49.5	43.3
2938000	Kansas City city	103,003	37,977	0.8	17.7	52.5	29.2	22.6	47.5	35.3
2941348	Lee's Summit city	25,281	7,831	0.6	9.6	73.6	54.3	19.0	26.4	22.2
2954074	O'Fallon city	23,386	7,225	1.4	10.4	82.3	54.1	28.2	17.7	15.6
2964082	St. Charles city	12,485	4,389	3.8	20.3	64.8	43.8	20.9	35.2	29.3
2964550	St. Joseph city	16,976	6,479	0.0	7.8	49.2	29.7	18.6	50.8	44.8
2965000	St. Louis city	60,063	23,701	1.0	14.5	43.2	27.0	14.7	56.8	44.4
2965126	St. Peters city	11,679	4,120	0.7	3.5	76.1	56.4	18.8	23.9	20.2
2970000	Springfield city	27,509	11,476	0.5	7.8	54.5	28.3	24.6	45.5	36.7
3000000	**Montana**	210,713	72,359	0.3	3.8	68.1	38.5	28.4	31.9	25.6
3006550	Billings city	22,687	8,005	0.0	5.0	59.9	32.1	27.3	40.1	33.2
3032800	Great Falls city	12,673	4,963	0.0	1.6	51.3	25.4	20.5	48.7	40.7
3050200	Missoula city	11,384	4,290	0.0	0.0	61.6	31.0	28.3	38.4	32.8
3100000	**Nebraska**	442,576	151,288	0.9	15.9	68.9	46.3	21.8	31.1	25.8
3103950	Bellevue city	13,420	4,338	0.9	15.5	56.3	29.8	26.1	43.7	34.6
3119595	Grand Island city	12,752	4,525	0.0	23.4	55.2	44.8	10.2	44.8	32.0
3128000	Lincoln city	57,753	21,845	0.8	18.1	70.3	47.5	22.4	29.7	25.2
3137000	Omaha city	101,977	36,353	2.2	27.0	58.8	37.0	21.1	41.2	32.9
3200000	**Nevada**	628,665	212,789	1.0	37.2	62.9	34.6	27.4	37.1	29.8
3209700	Carson City	11,174	3,401	0.0	27.3	65.7	30.5	35.0	34.3	22.2

Table D-4: Cities with a Population of 50,000 or More—Children—*Continued*

State/Place FIPS code	State/Place	Total own children 6 to 17	Nativity and parentage, age 6 to 17 years		Own children age 6 to 17 years living with two parents			Own children age 6 to 17 years living with one parent		Grandchildren under 18 living with a grandparent householder	Grandchildren under 18 living with a grandparent householder, as a percent of all children	Children for whom grandparent householders are responsible, as a percent of all children
			Child is foreign born, percent	One or more foreign-born parent, percent	Age 6 to 17 years living with two parents, percent	Both parents in labor force, percent	One parent in labor force, percent	Age 6 to 17 years living with one parent, percent	Parent in labor force, percent			
	Michigan—cont'd											
2621020	Dearborn Heights city	8,622	8.1	51.7	73.2	29.9	38.9	26.8	23.5	507	3.7	2.1
2622000	Detroit city	108,370	2.1	12.7	29.3	15.4	10.9	70.7	50.5	24,221	14.8	7.8
2627440	Farmington Hills city	10,823	7.8	30.9	74.7	49.4	24.7	25.3	23.1	780	5.0	2.4
2629000	Flint city	14,906	0.0	1.0	27.5	15.3	10.4	72.5	52.4	2,764	11.8	8.0
2634000	Grand Rapids city	26,467	5.0	20.6	52.5	34.2	17.1	47.5	37.2	2,580	5.8	2.6
2642160	Kalamazoo city	9,183	3.8	10.0	45.2	32.0	12.1	54.8	42.9	1,016	7.2	4.1
2646000	Lansing city	14,959	6.6	17.5	45.8	30.4	13.1	54.2	42.2	2,635	10.6	7.3
2649000	Livonia city	13,266	2.0	8.3	78.4	54.9	22.6	21.6	20.5	777	4.1	1.5
2659440	Novi city	10,009	10.8	36.5	82.2	58.3	22.9	17.8	15.5	0	0.0	0.0
2665440	Pontiac city	9,752	1.9	15.3	38.3	19.7	15.0	61.7	48.3	1,350	9.1	6.2
2669035	Rochester Hills city	10,942	4.8	26.4	84.2	59.6	24.4	15.8	13.5	503	3.1	1.5
2670040	Royal Oak city	5,926	3.6	13.3	67.5	49.2	17.6	32.5	28.2	0	0.0	0.0
2670520	Saginaw city	8,755	0.0	2.6	31.0	19.2	8.2	69.0	50.3	1,738	13.5	8.3
2670760	St. Clair Shores city	7,417	1.8	4.8	70.4	51.1	15.7	29.6	26.3	417	3.9	2.9
2674900	Southfield city	9,789	3.4	11.5	49.2	36.6	11.0	50.8	43.5	912	6.3	3.3
2676460	Sterling Heights city	18,948	10.8	45.5	78.5	50.6	25.3	21.5	17.5	1,551	5.8	1.0
2679000	Taylor city	9,215	1.8	5.8	50.3	35.8	14.1	49.7	42.0	1,281	9.0	5.1
2680700	Troy city	13,226	16.1	48.1	83.3	57.4	24.6	16.7	14.6	441	2.4	0.6
2684000	Warren city	19,277	5.8	20.4	61.3	39.1	19.4	38.7	28.9	1,857	6.4	2.8
2686000	Westland city	10,444	3.2	9.9	54.2	42.7	9.9	45.8	38.5	1,073	6.4	2.5
2688940	Wyoming city	10,758	3.7	30.4	73.6	49.7	19.5	26.4	23.8	1,176	6.8	2.1
2700000	**Minnesota**	824,271	4.1	15.1	71.7	54.3	16.6	28.3	24.4	48,920	4.0	1.9
2706382	Blaine city	10,103	8.9	22.3	77.3	59.9	17.1	22.7	20.4	740	4.6	1.8
2706616	Bloomington city	10,567	6.3	24.2	69.1	56.4	12.2	30.9	28.0	574	3.6	1.1
2707966	Brooklyn Park city	13,034	8.4	38.6	65.8	52.9	12.5	34.2	31.1	1,123	5.6	2.2
2708794	Burnsville city	8,781	3.5	31.8	66.2	45.4	19.6	33.8	30.4	522	4.0	2.0
2713114	Coon Rapids city	8,997	6.7	15.9	62.9	52.8	9.8	37.1	31.4	933	6.7	2.7
2717000	Duluth city	9,825	1.3	3.3	58.2	38.0	19.5	41.8	33.9	486	3.2	1.9
2717288	Eagan city	10,669	4.6	17.1	71.4	54.6	16.7	28.6	26.3	0	0.0	0.0
2718116	Eden Prairie city	10,607	6.7	22.9	73.1	43.1	29.8	26.9	23.3	0	0.0	0.0
2735180	Lakeville city	12,485	4.1	15.8	78.5	59.7	18.4	21.5	18.7	544	3.1	1.9
2740166	Maple Grove city	11,114	3.1	18.0	80.3	53.7	25.7	19.7	17.7	0	0.0	0.0
2743000	Minneapolis city	43,691	8.5	33.5	52.6	35.2	16.2	47.4	36.5	4,513	6.0	3.4
2743252	Minnetonka city	7,115	3.5	12.5	75.1	50.6	24.5	24.9	23.0	0	0.0	0.0
2751730	Plymouth city	11,151	6.4	24.7	75.4	49.2	25.6	24.6	21.5	0	0.0	0.0
2754880	Rochester city	16,508	7.2	25.3	68.9	54.2	13.3	31.1	26.7	857	3.3	0.6
2756896	St. Cloud city	7,893	7.1	16.3	64.9	48.0	15.5	35.1	27.1	563	4.3	2.4
2758000	St. Paul city	44,487	14.2	41.3	58.0	39.1	16.2	42.0	34.3	4,034	5.7	2.7
2771428	Woodbury city	12,534	4.5	16.0	77.4	56.9	20.0	22.6	21.3	0	0.0	0.0
2800000	**Mississippi**	459,438	0.9	3.4	54.0	35.3	17.2	46.0	35.4	92,275	13.4	8.3
2829700	Gulfport city	9,473	0.0	2.8	51.6	26.5	22.0	48.4	35.1	2,521	16.2	10.0
2836000	Jackson city	28,594	1.2	2.3	35.4	25.6	8.1	64.6	53.0	6,564	15.3	10.9
2869280	Southaven city	9,774	1.4	8.3	63.8	47.6	16.0	36.2	32.7	904	6.7	3.3
2900000	**Missouri**	887,030	2.1	7.3	66.3	45.9	19.0	33.7	28.0	97,357	7.3	3.9
2906652	Blue Springs city	9,261	0.7	2.5	65.7	46.3	18.3	34.3	26.7	485	3.5	2.1
2915670	Columbia city	12,738	5.8	17.6	70.6	48.4	18.1	29.4	27.1	810	3.9	2.4
2924778	Florissant city	8,312	0.0	6.6	55.5	42.4	12.5	44.5	36.3	935	7.6	2.3
2935000	Independence city	15,019	2.5	12.2	59.9	40.9	16.7	40.1	31.4	1,584	6.6	3.5
2937592	Joplin city	6,758	0.3	3.8	66.8	44.4	21.8	33.2	29.0	787	7.4	3.6
2938000	Kansas City city	65,026	4.8	17.1	51.4	33.7	16.5	48.6	40.5	8,593	8.3	3.8
2941348	Lee's Summit city	17,450	1.6	6.5	72.4	57.2	14.4	27.6	24.8	1,074	4.2	1.4
2954074	O'Fallon city	16,161	1.7	8.0	77.6	58.4	19.1	22.4	20.8	986	4.2	2.8
2964082	St. Charles city	8,096	4.1	8.4	66.4	48.3	18.1	33.6	28.6	783	6.3	3.7
2964550	St. Joseph city	10,497	1.7	8.4	62.0	45.4	14.7	38.0	26.6	2,018	11.9	7.3
2965000	St. Louis city	36,362	4.3	10.7	37.9	25.2	11.1	62.1	51.3	6,553	10.9	6.5
2965126	St. Peters city	7,559	1.1	5.1	78.0	62.6	14.1	22.0	19.6	848	7.3	1.4
2970000	Springfield city	16,033	2.8	10.2	58.7	35.9	20.1	41.3	34.5	1,505	5.5	2.3
3000000	**Montana**	138,354	0.9	3.7	70.0	48.3	20.3	30.0	25.2	13,284	6.3	3.8
3006550	Billings city	14,682	0.8	3.9	64.4	46.0	18.1	35.6	29.3	1,650	7.3	4.1
3032800	Great Falls city	7,710	0.0	0.8	56.1	40.2	12.6	43.9	37.0	670	5.3	3.3
3050200	Missoula city	7,094	0.0	0.0	63.5	48.8	14.0	36.5	33.9	0	0.0	0.0
3100000	**Nebraska**	291,288	3.4	14.4	71.1	52.6	17.5	28.9	25.5	20,035	4.5	2.4
3103950	Bellevue city	9,082	3.1	19.6	59.0	39.4	18.4	41.0	33.0	805	6.0	3.2
3119595	Grand Island city	8,227	6.4	35.2	66.9	50.7	15.6	33.1	27.1	448	3.5	1.3
3128000	Lincoln city	35,908	4.2	15.6	68.4	48.1	19.5	31.6	28.4	2,069	3.6	2.1
3137000	Omaha city	65,624	5.7	22.1	62.2	42.8	18.8	37.8	33.0	5,549	5.4	2.5
3200000	**Nevada**	415,876	5.7	39.0	62.5	38.6	22.7	37.5	31.5	44,276	7.0	4.0
3209700	Carson City	7,773	6.7	33.5	60.0	47.4	11.4	40.0	36.2	1,175	10.5	8.0

State/Place FIPS code	State/Place	Total own children under 18 in families and subfamilies	Own children under 6 years in families and subfamilies								
			Total own children under 6 years	Nativity and parentage, under 6 years		Own children under 6 years living with two parents			Own children under 6 living with one parent	
				Child is foreign born, percent	One or more foreign-born parent, percent	Total under 6 years living with two parents, percent	Both parents in labor force, percent	One parent in labor force, percent	Total under 6 years living with one parent, percent	Parent in labor force, percent
	Nevada—cont'd									
3223770	Enterprise CDP....................	28,518	10,663	2.2	39.5	74.6	52.0	21.5	25.4	20.6
3231900	Henderson city....................	56,090	16,203	1.0	20.6	66.5	35.0	31.5	33.5	27.4
3240000	Las Vegas city....................	139,875	46,804	0.6	41.1	59.1	31.6	26.6	40.9	31.8
3251800	North Las Vegas city....................	65,205	21,780	0.4	41.8	64.5	33.3	29.2	35.5	30.0
3254600	Paradise CDP....................	46,928	16,699	0.7	48.8	58.2	31.2	26.6	41.8	32.5
3260600	Reno city....................	51,350	18,187	1.1	35.0	63.2	41.8	21.3	36.8	29.9
3268400	Sparks city....................	21,142	7,866	0.6	41.2	69.2	39.6	29.0	30.8	27.0
3268585	Spring Valley CDP....................	35,757	14,200	3.9	48.4	66.0	34.9	30.9	34.0	31.9
3271400	Sunrise Manor CDP....................	48,238	16,552	0.3	50.0	47.1	22.3	23.1	52.9	44.1
3300000	**New Hampshire.................**	264,738	78,243	1.1	13.2	68.2	43.0	24.4	31.8	25.2
3345140	Manchester city....................	21,302	7,389	3.6	23.8	51.0	30.6	19.7	49.0	35.8
3350260	Nashua city....................	18,579	7,070	3.2	24.7	63.9	40.2	23.4	36.1	27.3
3400000	**New Jersey.................**	1,968,419	631,427	2.5	38.2	68.8	41.9	26.2	31.2	24.2
3403580	Bayonne city....................	13,488	4,854	3.4	49.2	61.3	34.0	26.7	38.7	27.6
3410000	Camden city....................	23,233	8,294	1.4	18.2	14.6	10.1	4.5	85.4	57.2
3413690	Clifton city....................	18,270	6,309	3.4	60.3	77.7	47.3	29.0	22.3	16.8
3419390	East Orange city....................	13,657	5,025	0.0	25.5	21.4	12.9	7.4	78.6	66.6
3421000	Elizabeth city....................	33,536	13,290	1.8	71.2	45.1	31.8	13.2	54.9	43.4
3432250	Hoboken city....................	6,834	4,180	1.8	34.3	78.1	48.9	29.2	21.9	16.1
3436000	Jersey City city....................	49,958	19,943	8.8	58.7	61.8	32.6	27.9	38.2	30.7
3451000	Newark city....................	66,273	24,522	1.9	41.7	28.7	18.1	10.4	71.3	57.2
3451210	New Brunswick city....................	11,564	4,555	1.8	74.4	30.9	14.4	16.5	69.1	45.9
3456550	Passaic city....................	22,345	7,597	3.6	61.0	37.9	17.2	18.9	62.1	40.7
3457000	Paterson city....................	37,791	13,629	6.2	49.1	39.1	17.1	17.2	60.9	42.8
3458200	Perth Amboy city....................	13,111	4,708	7.2	56.0	40.7	20.3	17.7	59.3	38.2
3459190	Plainfield city....................	10,827	3,810	1.0	62.6	31.2	20.1	10.6	68.8	52.6
3473110	Toms River CDP....................	18,855	5,197	0.4	15.5	74.7	45.3	28.8	25.3	18.5
3474000	Trenton city....................	20,226	7,437	1.5	35.1	29.9	15.3	14.6	70.1	54.4
3474630	Union City city....................	14,685	5,259	2.8	74.3	35.4	20.8	14.6	64.6	49.8
3476070	Vineland city....................	14,855	4,435	0.0	29.3	58.7	30.6	28.1	41.3	34.2
3479610	West New York town....................	10,540	4,609	9.4	79.7	63.0	39.4	22.2	37.0	28.4
3500000	**New Mexico.................**	485,198	164,028	0.8	19.2	54.2	28.0	25.1	45.8	34.1
3502000	Albuquerque city....................	125,047	43,960	1.3	20.0	55.5	31.3	22.6	44.5	34.2
3539380	Las Cruces city....................	24,661	9,146	0.4	19.9	60.1	36.1	23.2	39.9	32.9
3563460	Rio Rancho city....................	24,118	7,068	0.0	8.8	60.7	25.9	33.1	39.3	29.3
3570500	Santa Fe city....................	12,454	3,972	1.2	28.1	56.9	37.9	19.0	43.1	33.4
3600000	**New York.................**	4,080,838	1,349,393	2.1	35.6	63.7	36.8	25.9	36.3	26.7
3601000	Albany city....................	16,272	6,058	1.5	21.0	46.8	29.8	17.0	53.2	46.5
3608026	Brentwood CDP....................	14,535	5,412	4.9	76.6	40.2	22.8	17.1	59.8	50.4
3611000	Buffalo city....................	55,518	19,416	3.0	17.5	38.7	18.4	18.3	61.3	42.3
3615000	Cheektowaga CDP....................	13,578	4,281	1.9	11.1	52.4	34.1	17.5	47.6	33.7
3633139	Hempstead village....................	12,244	4,920	1.7	56.0	36.0	25.6	9.9	64.0	44.9
3637737	Irondequoit CDP....................	10,154	3,463	0.3	9.6	68.9	52.3	15.6	31.1	28.2
3642081	Levittown CDP....................	10,912	2,765	0.5	34.5	94.4	69.5	25.0	5.6	5.0
3649121	Mount Vernon city....................	15,082	5,626	0.4	42.3	48.6	32.6	15.6	51.4	40.1
3650617	New Rochelle city....................	16,809	5,853	2.1	53.1	67.5	34.0	32.7	32.5	25.0
3651000	New York city....................	1,698,323	622,314	3.0	52.8	59.3	31.2	27.1	40.7	29.0
3663000	Rochester city....................	47,431	16,829	1.3	10.9	26.5	15.2	9.8	73.5	53.1
3665508	Schenectady city....................	14,248	5,032	0.2	11.7	37.4	24.6	11.0	62.6	40.8
3673000	Syracuse city....................	30,445	11,673	3.2	19.4	36.3	21.5	13.3	63.7	42.7
3674183	Tonawanda CDP....................	10,886	2,769	1.0	7.8	75.2	45.2	30.0	24.8	17.6
3676540	Utica city....................	14,886	5,095	5.8	37.3	46.3	21.3	23.2	53.7	39.3
3681677	White Plains city....................	11,179	3,952	1.1	58.1	69.3	35.9	33.1	30.7	26.8
3684000	Yonkers city....................	42,801	15,191	2.3	48.5	54.3	31.2	21.8	45.7	32.8
3700000	**North Carolina.................**	2,169,314	719,380	1.0	19.7	60.5	35.1	24.6	39.5	30.6
3702140	Asheville city....................	16,272	6,781	2.4	19.0	61.8	41.7	19.6	38.2	31.6
3709060	Burlington city....................	11,008	3,985	0.0	22.0	42.1	26.3	15.8	57.9	52.0
3710740	Cary town....................	38,862	12,300	3.3	39.6	80.8	45.7	35.0	19.2	16.1
3711800	Chapel Hill town....................	9,255	2,443	12.9	37.0	81.8	51.2	22.8	18.2	18.2
3712000	Charlotte city....................	185,259	66,923	2.3	31.5	59.8	34.2	25.3	40.2	34.6
3714100	Concord city....................	21,844	6,768	0.9	20.2	69.4	46.8	22.3	30.6	22.6
3719000	Durham city....................	51,543	20,602	1.4	29.5	53.0	34.2	17.4	47.0	39.2
3722920	Fayetteville city....................	48,508	19,462	0.3	9.3	56.3	24.3	31.6	43.7	33.9
3725580	Gastonia city....................	18,717	6,642	1.6	14.8	45.9	30.4	14.4	54.1	42.1
3728000	Greensboro city....................	58,358	21,045	1.5	24.0	53.5	29.7	22.9	46.5	36.9
3728080	Greenville city....................	15,530	6,005	1.7	8.8	41.7	29.1	12.6	58.3	53.2
3731400	High Point city....................	25,020	8,075	3.1	27.1	56.7	35.2	20.8	43.3	34.9
3734200	Jacksonville city....................	17,129	7,908	0.0	9.0	71.0	23.7	46.8	29.0	18.5
3755000	Raleigh city....................	92,990	33,308	2.2	31.1	61.8	35.6	26.0	38.2	31.5
3757500	Rocky Mount city....................	12,806	3,938	0.8	8.6	28.1	14.4	13.6	71.9	64.3

Table D-4: Cities with a Population of 50,000 or More—Children—*Continued*

State/ Place FIPS code	State/Place	Total own children 6 to 17	Nativity and parentage, age 6 to 17 years		Own children age 6 to 17 years living with two parents			Own children age 6 to 17 years living with one parent		Grand-children under 18 living with a grandparent householder	Grand-children under 18 living with a grandparent householder, as a percent of all children	Children for whom grandparent householders are responsible, as a percent of all children
			Child is foreign born, percent	One or more foreign-born parent, percent	Age 6 to 17 years living with two parents, percent	Both parents in labor force, percent	One parent in labor force, percent	Age 6 to 17 years living with one parent, percent	Parent in labor force, percent			
	Nevada—cont'd											
3223770	Enterprise CDP	17,855	7.4	38.8	62.0	38.8	21.6	38.0	34.3	924	3.2	2.1
3231900	Henderson city	39,887	2.2	23.1	65.3	41.0	24.0	34.7	31.3	3,203	5.7	3.6
3240000	Las Vegas city	93,071	6.7	42.4	59.2	35.6	22.7	40.8	33.7	10,165	7.3	3.9
3251800	North Las Vegas city	43,425	4.4	44.9	61.0	36.0	22.7	39.0	32.1	4,322	6.6	4.0
3254600	Paradise CDP	30,229	9.8	47.4	56.7	36.4	19.6	43.3	38.1	3,410	7.3	5.0
3260600	Reno city	33,163	6.3	37.2	62.0	41.7	19.0	38.0	31.1	2,253	4.4	2.7
3268400	Sparks city	13,276	5.5	42.1	64.0	39.2	24.6	36.0	31.2	2,121	10.0	6.1
3268585	Spring Valley CDP	21,557	9.2	53.1	59.6	36.5	22.6	40.4	35.8	3,045	8.5	3.4
3271400	Sunrise Manor CDP	31,686	6.8	58.6	57.7	35.2	19.5	42.3	34.2	4,410	9.1	5.3
3300000	**New Hampshire**	186,495	2.6	10.3	71.9	51.5	19.1	28.1	23.8	14,245	5.4	2.2
3345140	Manchester city	13,913	6.7	25.0	57.2	39.1	16.9	42.8	34.9	1,033	4.8	2.4
3350260	Nashua city	11,509	3.8	28.7	61.6	41.5	17.8	38.4	32.9	1,491	8.0	3.8
3400000	**New Jersey**	1,336,992	6.7	34.8	69.7	46.6	22.3	30.3	25.5	119,888	6.1	2.5
3403580	Bayonne city	8,634	15.4	46.4	57.2	36.4	18.2	42.8	32.6	732	5.4	2.1
3410000	Camden city	14,939	1.5	18.7	18.6	13.7	4.2	81.4	61.6	2,275	9.8	4.6
3413690	Clifton city	11,961	9.7	65.6	69.4	43.4	25.2	30.6	26.7	1,000	5.5	2.2
3419390	East Orange city	8,632	8.2	34.7	32.6	24.6	7.3	67.4	55.8	2,149	15.7	4.0
3421000	Elizabeth city	20,246	14.0	68.5	49.6	34.1	14.4	50.4	42.1	2,638	7.9	2.9
3432250	Hoboken city	2,654	4.6	20.3	59.2	31.2	27.5	40.8	29.1	0	0.0	0.0
3436000	Jersey City city	30,015	13.2	51.2	50.1	29.2	19.6	49.9	41.3	4,273	8.6	4.5
3451000	Newark city	41,751	9.3	41.3	35.9	23.5	11.4	64.1	51.6	6,461	9.7	5.5
3451210	New Brunswick city	7,009	16.2	79.9	34.9	22.2	12.5	65.1	52.3	748	6.5	2.4
3456550	Passaic city	14,748	14.6	69.4	46.2	25.3	19.3	53.8	38.2	1,596	7.1	3.5
3457000	Paterson city	24,162	15.7	52.1	42.8	23.4	16.2	57.2	38.8	3,926	10.4	3.5
3458200	Perth Amboy city	8,403	18.4	60.4	43.7	22.6	20.0	56.3	43.1	1,231	9.4	4.8
3459190	Plainfield city	7,017	12.7	65.4	40.7	34.2	5.4	59.3	52.9	1,567	14.5	2.7
3473110	Toms River CDP	13,658	2.0	17.7	72.8	53.0	18.8	27.2	21.7	1,151	6.1	2.9
3474000	Trenton city	12,789	12.2	35.2	36.2	23.1	11.9	63.8	52.4	1,888	9.3	3.9
3474630	Union City city	9,426	22.4	83.5	42.9	23.5	19.5	57.1	49.2	1,815	12.4	4.1
3476070	Vineland city	10,420	6.6	22.9	53.5	35.9	16.2	46.5	38.6	1,662	11.2	4.4
3479610	West New York town	5,931	16.8	80.1	48.3	26.7	20.8	51.7	44.6	933	8.9	4.7
3500000	**New Mexico**	321,170	4.2	21.9	58.5	35.1	21.9	41.5	32.7	50,901	10.5	6.3
3502000	Albuquerque city	81,087	5.3	23.2	56.8	35.2	19.9	43.2	35.5	7,859	6.3	3.6
3539380	Las Cruces city	15,515	6.1	24.4	53.3	31.7	21.4	46.7	39.4	1,678	6.8	4.0
3563460	Rio Rancho city	17,050	3.2	13.1	63.8	40.8	22.5	36.2	28.2	1,229	5.1	2.5
3570500	Santa Fe city	8,482	11.0	32.0	49.5	39.5	9.1	50.5	40.7	839	6.7	4.7
3600000	**New York**	2,731,445	6.5	35.0	64.5	41.1	22.1	35.5	28.3	305,826	7.5	3.2
3601000	Albany city	10,214	8.7	21.8	41.8	24.1	16.8	58.2	46.0	1,489	9.2	4.3
3608026	Brentwood CDP	9,123	7.1	72.3	58.4	43.5	14.3	41.6	37.4	2,096	14.4	3.1
3611000	Buffalo city	36,102	8.7	15.3	38.2	18.6	15.9	61.8	45.6	3,992	7.2	4.4
3615000	Cheektowaga CDP	9,297	1.9	8.1	59.6	43.4	14.8	40.4	33.8	453	3.3	1.2
3633139	Hempstead village	7,324	5.7	64.5	46.0	32.6	11.6	54.0	45.8	1,982	16.2	8.1
3637737	Irondequoit CDP	6,691	1.5	7.5	56.2	46.5	8.6	43.8	39.8	819	8.1	4.6
3642081	Levittown CDP	8,147	3.1	28.2	77.6	50.4	26.2	22.4	21.2	828	7.6	1.3
3649121	Mount Vernon city	9,456	6.5	55.3	40.9	27.3	12.7	59.1	47.6	1,567	10.4	4.1
3650617	New Rochelle city	10,956	7.8	45.5	70.4	45.7	24.5	29.6	23.8	737	4.4	2.0
3651000	New York city	1,076,009	11.0	58.5	55.9	31.6	23.0	44.1	34.2	161,264	9.5	4.0
3663000	Rochester city	30,602	5.3	15.4	27.5	17.2	7.6	72.5	50.0	4,700	9.9	5.2
3665508	Schenectady city	9,216	6.1	26.0	50.9	37.8	9.8	49.1	33.7	1,059	7.4	5.3
3673000	Syracuse city	18,772	10.1	19.6	39.2	23.8	13.1	60.8	42.9	2,827	9.3	6.4
3674183	Tonawanda CDP	8,117	1.4	4.3	63.8	48.3	13.5	36.2	29.9	292	2.7	1.7
3676540	Utica city	9,791	16.4	35.1	44.9	24.9	18.7	55.1	40.1	903	6.1	4.2
3681677	White Plains city	7,227	8.6	65.0	73.8	40.9	32.7	26.2	23.0	840	7.5	5.7
3684000	Yonkers city	27,610	8.9	53.7	54.6	31.2	21.4	45.4	36.0	2,947	6.9	3.2
3700000	**North Carolina**	1,449,934	3.5	16.5	62.6	40.8	20.6	37.4	30.7	175,785	8.1	4.9
3702140	Asheville city	9,491	3.8	13.6	53.5	39.5	13.0	46.5	38.6	621	3.8	2.2
3709060	Burlington city	7,023	1.3	28.2	48.3	31.8	16.2	51.7	45.5	1,227	11.1	5.1
3710740	Cary town	26,562	9.3	35.2	82.4	53.1	28.0	17.6	15.0	815	2.1	0.6
3711800	Chapel Hill town	6,812	11.2	33.1	77.0	54.7	21.1	23.0	22.0	0	0.0	0.0
3712000	Charlotte city	118,336	6.2	27.1	57.3	36.8	19.4	42.7	37.3	13,755	7.4	3.8
3714100	Concord city	15,076	4.2	20.9	71.8	51.5	20.2	28.2	22.3	1,263	5.8	4.2
3719000	Durham city	30,941	7.2	26.4	54.4	37.9	14.8	45.6	38.2	3,499	6.8	4.2
3722920	Fayetteville city	29,046	2.1	9.2	50.6	27.8	21.4	49.4	38.7	4,163	8.6	5.5
3725580	Gastonia city	12,075	5.8	16.0	48.9	36.8	10.6	51.1	43.1	1,250	6.7	4.8
3728000	Greensboro city	37,313	6.6	20.5	50.9	33.3	17.0	49.1	39.4	3,703	6.3	3.8
3728080	Greenville city	9,525	2.6	10.0	46.2	32.5	11.4	53.8	47.4	992	6.4	3.4
3731400	High Point city	16,945	6.6	23.7	52.0	35.0	15.9	48.0	39.4	1,656	6.6	3.3
3734200	Jacksonville city	9,221	1.8	12.0	64.0	22.4	40.6	36.0	26.6	449	2.6	2.1
3755000	Raleigh city	59,682	5.6	25.7	55.5	36.7	18.2	44.5	40.8	3,526	3.8	2.0
3757500	Rocky Mount city	8,868	1.5	7.0	46.3	29.9	15.1	53.7	46.8	1,418	11.1	8.2

Table D-4: Cities with a Population of 50,000 or More—Children—Continued

State/Place FIPS code	State/Place	Total own children under 18 in families and subfamilies	Own children under 6 years in families and subfamilies							
			Total own children under 6 years	Nativity and parentage, under 6 years		Own children under 6 years living with two parents			Own children under 6 living with one parent	
				Child is foreign born, percent	One or more foreign-born parent, percent	Total under 6 years living with two parents, percent	Both parents in labor force, percent	One parent in labor force, percent	Total under 6 years living with one parent, percent	Parent in labor force, percent
	North Carolina—cont'd									
3774440	Wilmington city	19,256	7,083	3.0	17.3	48.4	31.9	16.4	51.6	40.2
3775000	Winston-Salem city	54,411	20,245	0.4	30.5	49.8	27.4	21.6	50.2	36.2
3800000	**North Dakota**	151,243	53,991	0.7	4.5	71.2	49.6	21.0	28.8	22.8
3807200	Bismarck city	13,193	4,868	0.0	3.2	63.8	51.7	12.0	36.2	30.2
3825700	Fargo city	21,346	8,656	2.0	12.5	71.5	55.0	15.2	28.5	21.6
3832060	Grand Forks city	9,385	3,334	1.8	5.0	68.3	44.4	23.8	31.7	23.4
3900000	**Ohio**	2,536,221	818,899	0.7	8.7	60.7	38.1	21.7	39.3	30.5
3901000	Akron city	41,262	15,472	0.7	7.7	33.6	19.4	13.3	66.4	53.3
3912000	Canton city	17,268	6,376	0.4	5.0	31.4	19.2	11.5	68.6	52.3
3915000	Cincinnati city	60,955	24,550	1.2	9.6	32.8	19.9	12.0	67.2	48.5
3916000	Cleveland city	84,062	29,693	0.7	7.0	23.2	14.2	7.5	76.8	55.3
3918000	Columbus city	178,008	71,913	1.2	25.1	55.3	34.1	20.3	44.7	34.9
3921000	Dayton city	28,240	10,769	0.9	5.8	30.1	18.5	9.3	69.9	49.2
3925256	Elyria city	11,167	4,222	0.0	0.0	41.0	32.3	8.5	59.0	43.3
3933012	Hamilton city	13,746	5,342	0.4	6.4	46.0	35.1	10.6	54.0	42.9
3940040	Kettering city	11,680	3,536	1.0	4.6	57.3	34.0	23.3	42.7	27.7
3941664	Lakewood city	9,650	3,502	2.0	17.8	75.4	44.6	29.9	24.6	19.5
3944856	Lorain city	15,218	4,833	0.0	3.7	36.9	25.8	6.8	63.1	49.1
3961000	Parma city	15,449	5,121	1.2	18.5	70.7	48.7	20.0	29.3	23.4
3974118	Springfield city	13,834	4,875	0.0	5.7	33.3	18.4	13.8	66.7	48.9
3977000	Toledo city	62,077	22,950	0.1	5.3	42.8	27.4	14.8	57.2	45.1
3988000	Youngstown city	13,838	5,037	0.0	3.0	18.6	9.7	7.4	81.4	63.2
4000000	**Oklahoma**	884,279	303,188	0.9	13.8	63.1	35.0	26.9	36.9	27.2
4009050	Broken Arrow city	26,033	8,164	0.9	12.7	73.8	45.0	28.1	26.2	18.9
4023200	Edmond city	20,449	6,598	0.0	10.9	86.5	51.5	32.5	13.5	12.0
4041850	Lawton city	22,748	9,290	1.5	9.0	58.2	25.4	30.7	41.8	35.3
4048350	Midwest City city	12,707	4,200	0.0	6.2	53.7	31.7	22.0	46.3	38.9
4049200	Moore city	14,541	5,160	0.0	6.7	61.7	42.5	19.2	38.3	32.6
4052500	Norman city	21,423	7,550	1.0	8.3	70.4	38.8	31.3	29.6	21.3
4055000	Oklahoma City city	147,120	55,032	1.5	28.6	62.5	35.2	26.3	37.5	28.5
4075000	Tulsa city	90,835	34,116	1.4	24.1	53.0	26.2	25.8	47.0	33.8
4100000	**Oregon**	817,706	267,721	1.1	24.2	68.8	38.5	29.0	31.2	22.8
4101000	Albany city	12,377	4,258	0.0	14.2	54.2	33.2	20.6	45.8	31.5
4101650	Aloha CDP	13,744	5,199	1.4	42.6	72.2	49.9	21.9	27.8	14.9
4105350	Beaverton city	20,474	6,677	2.5	43.9	75.9	35.5	40.0	24.1	21.6
4105800	Bend city	17,949	6,089	1.4	16.1	67.5	41.7	25.5	32.5	28.3
4115800	Corvallis city	7,770	2,832	3.5	28.0	73.4	30.9	39.3	26.6	14.4
4123850	Eugene city	26,443	8,781	2.1	15.5	60.0	28.0	28.9	40.0	27.0
4131250	Gresham city	26,581	9,466	2.3	37.0	56.9	31.7	25.0	43.1	32.0
4134100	Hillsboro city	24,294	8,826	0.5	48.2	76.6	37.4	39.2	23.4	20.0
4147000	Medford city	17,056	5,924	1.0	19.7	60.9	35.1	24.2	39.1	32.0
4159000	Portland city	106,788	40,261	1.9	29.2	73.9	44.8	28.1	26.1	18.7
4164900	Salem city	38,922	13,390	0.3	29.5	62.3	37.1	23.2	37.7	27.4
4169600	Springfield city	13,584	4,743	2.1	17.0	53.9	29.5	22.9	46.1	35.5
4200000	**Pennsylvania**	2,615,591	840,520	1.0	12.2	63.2	39.5	22.7	36.8	28.1
4202000	Allentown city	29,747	10,413	2.4	22.2	31.3	18.2	10.6	68.7	46.9
4206088	Bethlehem city	13,958	4,272	1.7	10.8	43.2	26.5	15.4	56.8	42.9
4224000	Erie city	21,389	7,643	2.9	14.0	42.6	25.3	15.4	57.4	42.8
4241216	Lancaster city	14,294	4,988	0.9	15.7	36.8	26.3	10.5	63.2	50.1
4242928	Levittown CDP	10,260	3,140	0.5	6.6	58.1	38.7	14.7	41.9	31.5
4260000	Philadelphia city	323,234	120,618	1.9	20.6	39.1	24.1	13.1	60.9	43.4
4261000	Pittsburgh city	46,610	17,864	2.2	11.6	47.5	32.8	13.0	52.5	39.7
4263624	Reading city	25,272	8,837	0.8	30.4	32.2	14.4	14.8	67.8	46.4
4269000	Scranton city	14,893	5,326	1.8	19.2	55.0	37.8	15.5	45.0	36.1
4400000	**Rhode Island**	206,631	65,038	1.8	23.3	57.3	38.7	17.6	42.7	33.3
4419180	Cranston city	15,433	5,373	1.6	28.7	65.0	49.0	14.5	35.0	32.7
4454640	Pawtucket city	15,094	5,808	0.4	33.0	38.0	26.0	11.4	62.0	45.7
4459000	Providence city	38,876	12,531	4.9	39.3	36.4	21.2	15.1	63.6	46.6
4474300	Warwick city	14,798	4,763	2.2	14.3	68.1	50.1	16.7	31.9	30.0
4500000	**South Carolina**	1,015,015	338,816	0.5	11.0	54.8	32.5	21.3	45.2	35.4
4513330	Charleston city	21,290	8,835	0.3	7.9	61.5	43.1	17.7	38.5	35.6
4516000	Columbia city	21,181	8,657	1.6	14.8	48.9	28.8	19.5	51.1	40.4
4530850	Greenville city	11,590	4,319	3.2	15.4	55.2	32.1	19.0	44.8	31.9
4548535	Mount Pleasant town	16,749	4,913	1.1	8.1	78.5	44.1	33.9	21.5	21.3
4550875	North Charleston city	23,301	10,290	0.3	14.4	45.9	29.4	16.2	54.1	42.8
4561405	Rock Hill city	15,009	5,253	0.2	7.2	54.4	31.0	23.3	45.6	41.6
4600000	**South Dakota**	194,342	68,459	0.6	6.3	64.2	46.3	17.2	35.8	29.0
4652980	Rapid City city	15,459	5,841	0.0	2.2	49.9	35.4	14.5	50.1	42.2

State/ Place FIPS code	State/Place	Total own children 6 to 17	Nativity and parentage, age 6 to 17 years		Own children age 6 to 17 years living with two parents			Own children age 6 to 17 years living with one parent		Grand-children under 18 living with a grandparent householder	Grand-children under 18 living with a grandparent householder, as a percent of all children	Children for whom grandparent householders are responsible, as a percent of all children
			Child is foreign born, percent	One or more foreign-born parent, percent	Age 6 to 17 years living with two parents, percent	Both parents in labor force, percent	One parent in labor force, percent	Age 6 to 17 years living with one parent, percent	Parent in labor force, percent			
	North Carolina—cont'd											
3774440	Wilmington city	12,173	3.7	13.8	50.5	28.6	20.3	49.5	42.5	974	5.1	2.5
3775000	Winston-Salem city	34,166	5.7	28.2	55.6	36.9	17.3	44.4	36.1	4,238	7.8	5.8
3800000	**North Dakota**	97,252	2.0	4.9	73.1	55.1	17.2	26.9	23.5	6,959	4.6	2.4
3807200	Bismarck city	8,325	0.8	2.2	67.9	56.4	11.5	32.1	29.7	687	5.2	1.6
3825700	Fargo city	12,690	5.5	12.1	69.7	50.3	18.8	30.3	27.9	795	3.7	3.1
3832060	Grand Forks city	6,051	2.4	6.4	68.8	58.1	10.7	31.2	28.5	627	6.7	3.5
3900000	**Ohio**	1,717,322	1.9	6.6	64.6	43.7	19.7	35.4	28.7	183,181	7.2	4.2
3901000	Akron city	25,790	3.6	7.6	39.2	25.1	11.8	60.8	46.1	4,018	9.7	6.1
3912000	Canton city	10,892	1.0	2.4	37.9	20.9	14.6	62.1	48.2	1,686	9.8	5.7
3915000	Cincinnati city	36,405	2.9	7.9	31.8	20.8	9.8	68.2	52.3	5,029	8.3	5.4
3916000	Cleveland city	54,369	1.7	6.2	29.5	18.0	9.8	70.5	52.4	9,298	11.1	6.5
3918000	Columbus city	106,095	6.9	22.3	49.9	31.1	16.9	50.1	40.6	13,087	7.4	4.6
3921000	Dayton city	17,471	2.1	6.3	38.9	23.5	13.0	61.1	42.5	3,262	11.6	7.0
3925256	Elyria city	6,945	0.0	0.0	46.3	32.5	13.8	53.7	37.4	1,295	11.6	6.9
3933012	Hamilton city	8,404	1.2	6.0	47.9	35.2	12.0	52.1	39.3	1,212	8.8	6.0
3940040	Kettering city	8,144	3.5	5.3	59.8	39.7	19.6	40.2	32.4	563	4.8	2.8
3941664	Lakewood city	6,148	5.8	13.1	64.3	44.7	19.0	35.7	30.5	0	0.0	0.0
3944856	Lorain city	10,385	0.5	3.3	43.2	29.0	10.7	56.8	42.1	1,672	11.0	6.4
3961000	Parma city	10,328	4.7	12.7	60.0	42.1	17.2	40.0	31.2	842	5.5	2.7
3974118	Springfield city	8,959	0.3	5.4	48.6	30.0	16.7	51.4	40.3	1,205	8.7	5.9
3977000	Toledo city	39,127	0.6	4.9	42.2	29.6	11.3	57.8	45.8	5,956	9.6	5.7
3988000	Youngstown city	8,801	0.0	2.4	22.4	12.9	8.3	77.6	58.5	1,608	11.6	7.6
4000000	**Oklahoma**	581,091	2.5	12.2	65.3	41.1	22.8	34.7	27.6	75,115	8.5	5.2
4009050	Broken Arrow city	17,869	2.2	12.5	70.9	48.7	21.5	29.1	24.5	1,118	4.3	2.7
4023200	Edmond city	13,851	2.6	10.6	80.1	53.0	25.3	19.9	17.9	505	2.5	1.5
4041850	Lawton city	13,458	2.8	10.8	50.5	30.9	17.8	49.5	44.3	2,422	10.6	5.4
4048350	Midwest City city	8,507	1.6	5.2	48.6	32.5	13.8	51.4	46.3	1,169	9.2	3.7
4049200	Moore city	9,381	1.4	10.4	62.9	41.2	20.7	37.1	31.8	1,177	8.1	4.6
4052500	Norman city	13,873	3.6	9.9	68.0	44.7	21.8	32.0	25.2	1,390	6.5	4.5
4055000	Oklahoma City city	92,088	6.7	28.4	62.4	38.4	23.2	37.6	30.5	10,822	7.4	4.1
4075000	Tulsa city	56,719	4.8	21.1	55.7	34.6	20.3	44.3	34.8	6,430	7.1	3.9
4100000	**Oregon**	549,985	4.7	23.6	67.9	43.4	23.2	32.1	25.9	48,787	6.0	2.9
4101000	Albany city	8,119	2.0	11.3	55.0	38.6	15.4	45.0	28.0	596	4.8	2.9
4101650	Aloha CDP	8,545	3.4	37.2	71.4	49.6	21.3	28.6	20.5	622	4.5	1.5
4105350	Beaverton city	13,797	13.0	43.9	63.3	36.7	26.1	36.7	33.9	395	1.9	1.0
4105800	Bend city	11,860	4.8	11.2	79.2	54.2	24.8	20.8	19.3	0	0.0	0.0
4115800	Corvallis city	4,938	8.7	30.0	79.5	49.3	25.5	20.5	13.2	0	0.0	0.0
4123850	Eugene city	17,662	4.4	16.9	65.6	38.5	24.5	34.4	27.6	559	2.1	1.3
4131250	Gresham city	17,115	7.0	36.1	61.1	36.4	23.1	38.9	32.4	2,512	9.5	4.9
4134100	Hillsboro city	15,468	7.5	37.1	71.7	41.8	29.6	28.3	25.4	1,253	5.2	2.1
4147000	Medford city	11,132	5.2	15.1	56.7	33.3	22.1	43.3	30.0	954	5.6	2.0
4159000	Portland city	66,527	9.9	34.4	63.1	41.2	20.8	36.9	29.7	5,846	5.5	2.7
4164900	Salem city	25,532	6.6	32.5	63.2	40.5	21.6	36.8	31.4	1,368	3.5	1.5
4169600	Springfield city	8,841	0.5	13.4	60.8	35.5	22.3	39.2	28.7	1,296	9.5	3.8
4200000	**Pennsylvania**	1,775,071	2.6	10.7	66.6	44.9	20.4	33.4	26.4	190,170	7.3	3.5
4202000	Allentown city	19,334	5.3	25.8	37.9	18.8	15.4	62.1	43.8	3,426	11.5	5.3
4206088	Bethlehem city	9,686	4.1	15.8	52.6	33.7	17.1	47.4	37.5	865	6.2	3.1
4224000	Erie city	13,746	7.5	14.1	44.4	25.4	16.6	55.6	38.1	1,980	9.3	4.5
4241216	Lancaster city	9,306	3.1	13.3	39.1	28.3	9.1	60.9	46.1	1,441	10.1	4.2
4242928	Levittown CDP	7,120	2.2	7.3	67.1	49.6	15.9	32.9	25.7	1,436	14.0	6.2
4260000	Philadelphia city	202,616	4.9	20.0	39.0	25.7	11.4	61.0	43.0	45,095	14.0	6.7
4261000	Pittsburgh city	28,746	3.1	8.5	46.2	31.5	12.8	53.8	41.1	4,095	8.8	5.1
4263624	Reading city	16,435	9.0	38.4	36.9	20.0	14.3	63.1	45.5	2,872	11.4	6.5
4269000	Scranton city	9,567	6.4	13.1	57.1	40.7	13.1	42.9	32.6	1,059	7.1	2.8
4400000	**Rhode Island**	141,593	5.1	25.5	61.7	45.6	15.4	38.3	31.4	13,367	6.5	2.7
4419180	Cranston city	10,060	4.2	30.5	69.3	47.5	20.5	30.7	27.5	1,036	6.7	2.2
4454640	Pawtucket city	9,286	9.4	48.6	45.1	31.1	12.6	54.9	44.0	1,490	9.9	6.0
4459000	Providence city	26,345	11.8	54.0	42.8	27.2	14.4	57.2	45.9	2,381	6.1	2.4
4474300	Warwick city	10,035	1.9	15.0	65.5	52.2	12.1	34.5	31.6	955	6.5	1.9
4500000	**South Carolina**	676,199	2.2	9.0	59.2	38.5	19.3	40.8	33.3	110,685	10.9	6.3
4513330	Charleston city	12,455	0.8	4.3	56.6	37.3	19.0	43.4	38.1	1,793	8.4	6.6
4516000	Columbia city	12,524	1.9	7.1	49.3	31.0	18.0	50.7	41.0	1,105	5.2	2.9
4530850	Greenville city	7,271	3.3	12.4	58.3	30.9	26.1	41.7	31.9	758	6.5	5.2
4548535	Mount Pleasant town	11,836	1.9	4.3	77.0	48.0	28.1	23.0	19.4	0	0.0	0.0
4550875	North Charleston city	13,011	2.3	12.3	46.5	32.9	13.1	53.5	43.3	2,922	12.5	8.7
4561405	Rock Hill city	9,756	0.6	7.7	50.8	37.3	13.0	49.2	46.5	1,051	7.0	5.1
4600000	**South Dakota**	125,883	1.9	5.1	68.0	53.6	13.4	32.0	27.7	12,458	6.4	4.1
4652980	Rapid City city	9,618	1.2	1.6	53.2	42.1	10.4	46.8	39.9	748	4.8	2.1

State/ Place FIPS code	State/Place	Total own children under 18 in families and subfamilies	Own children under 6 years in families and subfamilies							
			Total own children under 6 years	Nativity and parentage, under 6 years		Own children under 6 years living with two parents			Own children under 6 living with one parent	
				Child is foreign born, percent	One or more foreign-born parent, percent	Total under 6 years living with two parents, percent	Both parents in labor force, percent	One parent in labor force, percent	Total under 6 years living with one parent, percent	Parent in labor force, percent
	South Dakota—cont'd									
4659020	Sioux Falls city	37,825	15,346	1.4	12.8	64.6	47.6	17.1	35.4	29.0
4700000	**Tennessee**	1,403,158	464,004	1.0	12.4	60.7	34.3	25.5	39.3	29.7
4703440	Bartlett city	14,401	4,457	2.9	12.7	72.3	43.8	27.4	27.7	25.5
4714000	Chattanooga city	33,680	12,466	0.6	12.6	49.2	28.2	18.9	50.8	38.2
4715160	Clarksville city	37,790	15,384	0.4	9.9	59.9	24.4	35.4	40.1	27.6
4727740	Franklin city	17,162	5,121	2.1	23.5	85.3	40.0	45.3	14.7	11.9
4733280	Hendersonville city	12,869	3,552	0.0	10.1	80.7	57.0	23.7	19.3	15.8
4737640	Jackson city	15,510	5,656	0.0	13.5	49.2	24.0	24.7	50.8	38.3
4738320	Johnson City city	11,312	3,462	1.1	8.5	63.7	44.3	16.3	36.3	29.0
4739560	Kingsport city	10,622	3,147	0.6	3.9	54.5	36.0	18.5	45.5	31.2
4740000	Knoxville city	29,657	12,065	0.2	13.9	57.6	34.0	23.3	42.4	28.0
4748000	Memphis city	153,621	56,837	0.6	16.8	35.6	21.7	13.7	64.4	51.6
4751560	Murfreesboro city	24,751	9,112	1.0	11.7	78.4	54.9	23.5	21.6	18.1
4752006	Nashville-Davidson	127,733	51,010	2.9	28.5	56.5	32.7	22.7	43.5	34.0
4800000	**Texas**	6,646,543	2,252,764	1.5	33.3	62.9	31.9	30.1	37.1	27.3
4801000	Abilene city	25,484	10,080	0.5	8.7	55.5	28.6	26.9	44.5	32.0
4801924	Allen city	27,412	8,144	1.5	34.3	89.3	52.8	36.5	10.7	10.7
4803000	Amarillo city	50,245	18,267	2.1	20.8	58.2	34.2	23.1	41.8	31.7
4804000	Arlington city	96,124	34,773	0.5	38.4	60.2	30.7	29.0	39.8	31.7
4804462	Atascocita CDP	19,847	5,714	2.2	21.8	70.9	44.0	25.7	29.1	24.1
4805000	Austin city	179,568	67,985	1.8	39.0	64.9	34.8	29.6	35.1	27.4
4806128	Baytown city	21,068	7,565	1.1	37.5	60.8	25.7	35.0	39.2	29.9
4807000	Beaumont city	26,642	9,152	0.8	19.7	44.5	20.0	23.1	55.5	38.9
4810768	Brownsville city	55,806	17,740	1.6	47.0	54.0	23.2	29.0	46.0	28.2
4810912	Bryan city	18,068	6,742	0.6	29.3	51.6	26.7	25.0	48.4	40.7
4813024	Carrollton city	29,935	9,291	1.8	53.0	73.0	46.4	24.5	27.0	24.4
4813552	Cedar Park city	16,436	4,665	1.2	26.0	80.1	45.7	34.4	19.9	17.3
4815976	College Station city	14,681	5,201	2.2	21.2	73.2	34.6	35.8	26.8	23.6
4816432	Conroe city	16,335	6,575	1.0	42.2	51.9	24.8	26.6	48.1	36.3
4817000	Corpus Christi city	76,231	24,618	0.6	11.5	46.9	26.2	20.1	53.1	38.0
4819000	Dallas city	303,605	115,790	1.8	50.5	53.4	24.3	28.3	46.6	36.4
4819972	Denton city	22,244	7,744	3.0	26.6	64.5	38.5	23.7	35.5	29.4
4820092	DeSoto city	11,441	2,789	0.0	18.6	52.4	42.5	9.9	47.6	41.6
4822660	Edinburg city	23,180	8,868	1.2	29.2	69.7	45.9	23.8	30.3	25.5
4824000	El Paso city	179,532	60,745	1.3	34.5	63.2	31.0	31.1	36.8	24.5
4824768	Euless city	12,421	3,816	3.3	32.8	64.0	29.6	33.8	36.0	33.4
4826232	Flower Mound town	20,347	4,766	0.0	19.6	85.4	51.4	33.9	14.6	10.5
4827000	Fort Worth city	216,376	76,823	2.1	36.3	60.8	30.9	29.0	39.2	29.4
4827684	Frisco city	42,658	13,543	0.3	26.9	87.1	49.6	37.4	12.9	10.4
4829000	Garland city	65,623	21,607	1.5	52.0	53.9	26.8	27.0	46.1	38.9
4829336	Georgetown city	9,922	3,446	4.3	21.0	76.9	51.0	25.9	23.1	18.5
4830464	Grand Prairie city	50,821	16,578	1.4	46.0	64.2	39.8	24.0	35.8	29.5
4832372	Harlingen city	19,640	6,768	2.0	30.1	61.5	20.6	33.4	38.5	21.0
4835000	Houston city	521,019	193,763	2.5	51.0	55.8	25.8	29.4	44.2	32.4
4837000	Irving city	57,074	22,696	4.8	63.6	66.8	33.6	32.6	33.2	28.2
4839148	Killeen city	39,256	16,000	0.6	13.1	67.2	34.0	32.3	32.8	26.3
4841464	Laredo city	79,154	27,421	1.1	43.7	56.7	23.9	31.1	43.3	24.9
4841980	League City city	22,767	7,579	0.6	8.5	85.5	60.2	25.3	14.5	11.0
4842508	Lewisville city	26,186	9,585	3.9	47.6	69.0	36.3	32.6	31.0	22.3
4843888	Longview city	19,897	6,849	0.5	27.1	52.5	32.5	20.0	47.5	38.8
4845000	Lubbock city	53,846	19,425	0.9	8.8	56.7	34.2	21.9	43.3	35.1
4845384	McAllen city	36,627	12,440	4.1	42.8	65.2	30.4	32.4	34.8	24.4
4845744	McKinney city	43,295	13,776	0.2	24.2	80.5	47.2	32.9	19.5	14.6
4846452	Mansfield city	18,024	5,414	0.3	25.8	80.8	47.6	33.2	19.2	18.6
4847892	Mesquite city	40,715	13,492	1.2	36.7	54.4	31.1	23.2	45.6	37.2
4848072	Midland city	30,956	11,576	0.5	16.7	61.7	25.0	36.1	38.3	28.8
4848768	Mission city	26,891	8,523	2.1	52.4	75.5	29.7	44.8	24.5	13.2
4848804	Missouri City city	15,773	3,770	2.7	42.3	64.0	42.1	21.8	36.0	33.7
4850820	New Braunfels city	16,205	5,203	0.6	13.4	71.7	36.5	34.9	28.3	22.9
4852356	North Richland Hills city	14,886	5,330	2.0	22.8	73.6	44.0	29.7	26.4	23.0
4853388	Odessa city	29,035	10,649	0.1	21.9	59.2	26.2	32.3	40.8	28.9
4856000	Pasadena city	43,220	14,229	1.4	45.2	56.0	19.2	35.2	44.0	33.9
4856348	Pearland city	27,839	9,826	2.7	32.9	84.5	61.0	23.5	15.5	13.3
4857176	Pflugerville city	14,481	5,084	0.0	23.3	81.6	49.6	28.1	18.4	14.8
4857200	Pharr city	24,600	8,165	1.6	55.8	56.3	19.8	36.4	43.7	22.8
4858016	Plano city	67,207	20,463	5.2	47.2	74.9	38.4	36.4	25.1	20.3
4858820	Port Arthur city	14,428	5,155	2.3	51.7	52.0	15.2	34.9	48.0	32.9
4861796	Richardson city	23,186	7,968	6.5	45.3	78.3	42.5	34.9	21.7	20.8
4863500	Round Rock city	32,807	12,542	0.8	28.6	74.6	42.9	31.6	25.4	20.2
4863572	Rowlett city	14,618	3,765	1.2	14.1	78.7	57.8	20.9	21.3	15.9

Table D-4: Cities with a Population of 50,000 or More—Children—*Continued*

State/Place FIPS code	State/Place	Total own children 6 to 17	Nativity and parentage, age 6 to 17 years		Own children age 6 to 17 years living with two parents			Own children age 6 to 17 years living with one parent		Grand-children under 18 living with a grandparent householder	Grand-children under 18 living with a grandparent householder, as a percent of all children	Children for whom grandparent householders are responsible, as a percent of all children
			Child is foreign born, percent	One or more foreign-born parent, percent	Age 6 to 17 years living with two parents, percent	Both parents in labor force, percent	One parent in labor force, percent	Age 6 to 17 years living with one parent, percent	Parent in labor force, percent			
	South Dakota—cont'd											
4659020	Sioux Falls city	22,479	5.7	17.1	61.6	48.5	12.8	38.4	33.9	1,319	3.5	2.4
4700000	**Tennessee**	939,154	2.5	9.7	64.1	40.4	22.0	35.9	28.7	133,235	9.5	5.7
4703440	Bartlett city	9,944	1.7	8.7	71.7	50.5	20.3	28.3	27.4	890	6.2	3.7
4714000	Chattanooga city	21,214	2.2	8.6	51.5	35.3	13.6	48.5	36.3	3,475	10.3	6.9
4715160	Clarksville city	22,406	2.5	11.8	59.0	29.7	26.7	41.0	29.4	1,531	4.1	2.6
4727740	Franklin city	12,041	6.1	14.6	82.4	45.2	37.2	17.6	15.8	0	0.0	0.0
4733280	Hendersonville city	9,317	1.7	10.6	71.8	48.1	23.5	28.2	23.0	771	6.0	1.7
4737640	Jackson city	9,854	1.9	7.8	55.9	38.0	17.7	44.1	30.4	1,287	8.3	5.5
4738320	Johnson City city	7,850	3.8	10.9	63.4	39.2	20.3	36.6	32.2	742	6.6	3.5
4739560	Kingsport city	7,475	1.4	5.3	61.2	43.1	16.4	38.8	31.6	1,282	12.1	10.1
4740000	Knoxville city	17,592	2.9	9.0	54.7	34.6	19.1	45.3	33.7	2,839	9.6	7.0
4748000	Memphis city	96,784	2.9	11.5	36.1	23.4	12.3	63.9	52.7	17,973	11.7	6.5
4751560	Murfreesboro city	15,639	2.8	13.6	73.3	48.6	22.5	26.7	23.8	557	2.3	1.3
4752006	Nashville-Davidson	76,723	8.1	28.3	53.5	32.5	19.6	46.5	39.3	10,288	8.1	4.3
4800000	**Texas**	4,393,779	5.8	34.7	65.2	38.7	25.5	34.8	28.5	626,060	9.4	5.3
4801000	Abilene city	15,404	1.9	13.4	59.5	36.1	22.2	40.5	32.0	2,949	11.6	8.6
4801924	Allen city	19,268	4.9	29.3	82.6	52.6	29.2	17.4	16.7	859	3.1	2.1
4803000	Amarillo city	31,978	4.8	23.4	62.9	40.1	22.4	37.1	30.6	3,937	7.8	5.5
4804000	Arlington city	61,351	6.4	42.2	63.3	40.4	22.6	36.7	31.3	7,315	7.6	4.6
4804462	Atascocita CDP	14,133	1.8	18.1	70.5	49.7	20.7	29.5	26.9	1,423	7.2	4.2
4805000	Austin city	111,583	8.3	41.5	61.6	36.9	23.8	38.4	32.5	10,966	6.1	3.3
4806128	Baytown city	13,503	4.1	39.2	53.7	29.7	23.9	46.3	38.8	2,403	11.4	7.9
4807000	Beaumont city	17,490	4.7	21.6	49.0	29.4	18.8	51.0	41.0	2,706	10.2	6.8
4810768	Brownsville city	38,066	6.5	61.3	59.7	29.4	27.6	40.3	29.9	6,529	11.7	4.7
4810912	Bryan city	11,326	3.6	34.2	52.5	27.7	24.8	47.5	37.0	1,624	9.0	5.4
4813024	Carrollton city	20,644	10.6	52.2	70.1	48.5	21.0	29.9	26.4	1,765	5.9	3.4
4813552	Cedar Park city	11,771	5.1	16.6	82.2	53.7	28.1	17.8	16.2	1,475	9.0	3.5
4815976	College Station city	9,480	8.9	23.4	73.5	42.7	29.3	26.5	24.9	551	3.8	3.1
4816432	Conroe city	9,760	6.0	44.7	59.0	31.0	28.0	41.0	36.0	1,179	7.2	4.0
4817000	Corpus Christi city	51,613	2.3	13.3	56.0	36.5	18.8	44.0	36.6	8,488	11.1	7.1
4819000	Dallas city	187,815	9.5	54.1	55.1	27.3	26.8	44.9	36.8	26,507	8.7	5.0
4819972	Denton city	14,500	4.7	28.0	63.2	40.4	21.9	36.8	30.6	1,546	7.0	5.0
4820092	DeSoto city	8,652	0.0	14.0	65.0	56.7	8.4	35.0	30.3	1,170	10.2	5.0
4822660	Edinburg city	14,312	7.5	43.1	66.1	46.1	19.4	33.9	27.4	1,930	8.3	2.3
4824000	El Paso city	118,787	5.3	47.3	59.5	32.3	25.8	40.5	32.4	20,515	11.4	6.0
4824768	Euless city	8,605	12.7	34.9	54.8	35.4	18.6	45.2	41.7	527	4.2	2.8
4826232	Flower Mound town	15,581	5.2	23.5	88.6	58.5	30.0	11.4	10.5	421	2.1	1.5
4827000	Fort Worth city	139,553	7.0	36.7	62.8	37.7	24.3	37.2	30.1	19,929	9.2	5.3
4827684	Frisco city	29,115	2.6	25.7	80.5	54.7	25.2	19.5	17.4	719	1.7	0.9
4829000	Garland city	44,016	8.5	57.7	63.7	39.8	23.0	36.3	31.9	5,698	8.7	5.1
4829336	Georgetown city	6,476	4.5	24.2	68.1	42.9	24.2	31.9	28.1	905	9.4	4.6
4830464	Grand Prairie city	34,243	7.2	44.8	62.5	36.7	25.5	37.5	33.6	5,415	10.7	5.5
4832372	Harlingen city	12,872	5.0	36.0	57.4	26.5	22.8	42.6	29.9	2,150	10.9	4.6
4835000	Houston city	327,256	10.0	54.1	57.9	31.0	25.8	42.1	34.7	50,031	9.6	5.2
4837000	Irving city	34,378	14.2	64.7	67.9	41.7	25.0	32.1	28.5	3,872	6.8	4.0
4839148	Killeen city	23,256	1.8	16.6	57.4	32.9	22.2	42.6	34.2	2,605	6.6	5.1
4841464	Laredo city	51,733	7.5	48.7	59.5	27.3	30.4	40.5	27.0	11,592	14.6	7.2
4841980	League City city	15,188	1.5	16.8	82.4	60.8	19.7	17.6	15.6	632	2.8	2.1
4842508	Lewisville city	16,601	6.5	38.8	64.4	45.3	18.6	35.6	30.7	919	3.5	1.8
4843888	Longview city	13,048	5.1	25.1	57.7	33.8	23.2	42.3	33.6	1,746	8.8	4.5
4845000	Lubbock city	34,421	2.6	11.4	58.9	39.1	18.3	41.1	36.4	5,621	10.4	7.7
4845384	McAllen city	24,187	8.7	53.2	68.3	35.9	28.9	31.7	25.7	4,900	13.4	5.6
4845744	McKinney city	29,519	3.0	22.0	75.9	48.6	27.1	24.1	20.3	2,044	4.7	1.7
4846452	Mansfield city	12,610	5.7	25.0	75.9	52.0	23.8	24.1	22.5	662	3.7	1.9
4847892	Mesquite city	27,223	4.7	38.0	58.5	37.5	20.4	41.5	36.1	4,320	10.6	6.9
4848072	Midland city	19,380	2.2	24.3	64.5	37.6	26.1	35.5	30.0	3,420	11.0	5.7
4848768	Mission city	18,368	10.5	55.8	77.2	47.1	28.6	22.8	17.5	3,823	14.2	5.3
4848804	Missouri City city	12,003	7.4	38.4	67.3	53.5	13.3	32.7	30.3	1,877	11.9	3.3
4850820	New Braunfels city	11,002	4.4	20.9	71.2	47.7	21.8	28.8	22.2	1,398	8.6	5.7
4852356	North Richland Hills city	9,556	5.8	24.9	75.9	53.9	20.5	24.1	21.2	735	4.9	3.1
4853388	Odessa city	18,386	1.4	30.2	60.7	35.9	24.1	39.3	31.8	3,176	10.9	7.1
4856000	Pasadena city	28,991	9.1	52.8	59.5	27.9	30.6	40.5	34.1	4,322	10.0	3.9
4856348	Pearland city	18,013	4.7	35.9	73.1	50.0	22.8	26.9	26.4	1,404	5.0	2.6
4857176	Pflugerville city	9,397	9.2	33.0	77.6	58.0	19.4	22.4	20.7	1,423	9.8	6.7
4857200	Pharr city	16,435	10.5	66.8	58.0	24.2	33.2	42.0	32.4	3,739	15.2	5.5
4858016	Plano city	46,744	10.2	44.0	74.4	47.9	26.2	25.6	23.1	2,813	4.2	1.4
4858820	Port Arthur city	9,273	10.7	50.3	57.5	25.7	29.6	42.5	34.6	1,829	12.7	6.3
4861796	Richardson city	15,218	9.0	45.1	73.2	43.3	28.3	26.8	25.2	1,131	4.9	3.4
4863500	Round Rock city	20,265	7.1	32.5	74.9	49.5	25.2	25.1	22.9	1,474	4.5	2.2
4863572	Rowlett city	10,853	2.8	27.0	72.1	48.6	23.1	27.9	26.2	1,207	8.3	3.7

State/ Place FIPS code	State/Place	Total own children under 18 in families and subfamilies	Own children under 6 years in families and subfamilies								
			Total own children under 6 years	Nativity and parentage, under 6 years		Own children under 6 years living with two parents			Own children under 6 years living with one parent	
				Child is foreign born, percent	One or more foreign-born parent, percent	Total under 6 years living with two parents, percent	Both parents in labor force, percent	One parent in labor force, percent	Total under 6 years living with one parent, percent	Parent in labor force, percent
	Texas—cont'd									
4864472	San Angelo city	21,038	8,326	1.1	12.7	57.7	27.5	29.7	42.3	30.5
4865000	San Antonio city	343,718	118,031	1.4	26.1	54.5	28.1	25.1	45.5	33.1
4865600	San Marcos city	6,981	2,614	0.0	5.5	40.2	26.2	12.4	59.8	54.9
4869596	Spring CDP	17,239	5,402	0.0	24.9	65.6	43.1	21.7	34.4	25.7
4870808	Sugar Land city	18,316	5,195	7.9	65.7	89.7	52.1	35.1	10.3	8.7
4872176	Temple city	16,134	5,819	2.1	18.7	77.6	43.4	33.2	22.4	15.4
4872656	The Woodlands CDP	30,456	8,961	1.4	28.9	86.8	33.9	52.6	13.2	7.1
4874144	Tyler city	21,188	7,005	0.9	34.2	51.4	23.3	27.8	48.6	38.5
4875428	Victoria city	15,921	5,571	0.6	8.0	48.3	23.6	24.7	51.7	39.2
4876000	Waco city	29,859	12,008	0.6	28.0	52.8	29.0	23.0	47.2	33.2
4879000	Wichita Falls city	22,196	7,990	1.3	12.8	53.8	33.7	18.6	46.2	35.6
4900000	**Utah**	858,051	303,468	0.7	16.7	81.0	35.6	44.6	19.0	15.1
4943660	Layton city	21,350	8,625	1.6	12.2	81.8	37.8	44.0	18.2	11.2
4944320	Lehi city	22,190	8,719	0.0	6.2	93.4	34.4	56.9	6.6	5.8
4950150	Millcreek CDP	12,742	4,815	3.0	14.8	77.5	30.6	44.8	22.5	15.3
4955980	Ogden city	21,757	9,275	0.3	21.4	62.3	30.8	29.6	37.7	30.5
4957300	Orem city	26,359	10,880	1.3	19.2	82.2	29.4	51.6	17.8	13.4
4962470	Provo city	25,519	11,526	0.6	25.4	85.7	25.5	57.0	14.3	11.6
4965330	St. George city	20,395	7,249	0.0	20.2	82.9	34.3	48.4	17.1	14.7
4967000	Salt Lake City city	40,160	16,041	2.4	30.9	71.8	37.6	33.7	28.2	21.3
4967440	Sandy city	24,462	7,399	1.1	9.5	78.8	35.2	43.6	21.2	19.6
4970850	South Jordan city	18,402	5,491	0.5	9.9	90.0	35.8	54.3	10.0	8.9
4975360	Taylorsville city	16,016	6,098	0.5	35.9	67.8	38.0	29.8	32.2	29.7
4982950	West Jordan city	35,414	12,404	0.4	19.1	77.3	42.8	34.4	22.7	18.7
4983470	West Valley City city	40,053	14,951	0.3	50.8	64.6	29.1	35.4	35.4	26.3
5000000	**Vermont**	118,957	36,717	0.6	7.1	65.8	45.5	19.5	34.2	26.0
5100000	**Virginia**	1,779,171	598,316	1.4	23.6	67.3	39.9	26.8	32.7	26.0
5101000	Alexandria city	24,870	11,731	3.0	43.7	70.8	42.5	27.8	29.2	27.3
5103000	Arlington CDP	34,871	14,947	2.5	40.3	83.9	54.5	29.2	16.1	13.3
5114440	Centreville CDP	18,813	5,822	3.6	49.9	86.7	52.9	33.1	13.3	10.2
5116000	Chesapeake city	54,505	17,122	0.8	11.3	61.6	32.8	28.6	38.4	33.3
5121088	Dale City CDP	18,773	5,872	2.0	45.3	62.9	41.3	21.4	37.1	32.2
5135000	Hampton city	28,107	10,180	0.1	8.3	45.9	26.8	18.1	54.1	43.8
5135624	Harrisonburg city	7,710	2,941	4.5	48.7	65.0	29.6	35.4	35.0	30.3
5147672	Lynchburg city	14,193	5,268	1.1	8.7	58.8	34.3	23.9	41.2	32.8
5156000	Newport News city	40,895	15,729	1.4	11.4	48.2	24.9	22.8	51.8	43.8
5157000	Norfolk city	47,029	19,000	0.9	11.3	49.9	27.7	21.4	50.1	36.7
5164000	Portsmouth city	21,089	7,969	0.0	3.2	40.0	24.2	15.7	60.0	48.1
5166672	Reston CDP	12,986	5,333	4.5	53.7	85.0	47.2	37.9	15.0	14.3
5167000	Richmond city	36,368	15,428	0.4	16.6	37.5	20.7	16.8	62.5	47.5
5168000	Roanoke city	20,073	8,004	1.5	20.3	56.8	41.1	15.7	43.2	31.3
5176432	Suffolk city	20,669	6,936	0.0	9.8	55.4	31.7	23.4	44.6	35.0
5182000	Virginia Beach city	100,252	33,915	1.4	15.3	65.0	36.8	27.7	35.0	24.2
5300000	**Washington**	1,518,172	510,783	1.7	28.9	69.8	36.5	32.2	30.2	22.9
5303180	Auburn city	16,644	6,038	1.1	45.1	61.9	25.4	35.7	38.1	26.0
5305210	Bellevue city	26,242	9,038	11.2	65.9	87.1	41.5	43.3	12.9	8.6
5305280	Bellingham city	13,008	5,025	1.2	22.6	66.3	33.1	32.5	33.7	21.3
5322640	Everett city	21,385	8,928	2.5	38.4	58.0	23.4	33.0	42.0	34.2
5323515	Federal Way city	21,398	7,033	1.9	44.6	52.7	26.6	25.3	47.3	36.0
5335275	Kennewick city	19,976	7,520	1.5	32.4	64.8	37.1	27.7	35.2	29.5
5335415	Kent city	30,814	10,761	8.2	54.9	69.4	30.8	35.3	30.6	22.2
5335940	Kirkland city	17,593	6,331	3.7	38.1	82.5	39.9	41.5	17.5	16.3
5338038	Lakewood city	11,926	4,660	1.5	27.1	52.3	22.4	29.3	47.7	35.0
5343955	Marysville city	16,116	6,322	1.8	24.4	68.3	35.8	32.1	31.7	24.6
5353545	Pasco city	22,412	8,571	0.6	52.5	63.2	32.9	30.3	36.8	32.1
5357535	Redmond city	12,041	4,741	11.9	77.6	90.2	41.5	48.6	9.8	5.6
5357745	Renton city	21,068	8,283	2.1	51.8	69.9	40.9	27.9	30.1	19.9
5358235	Richland city	12,462	4,465	1.9	14.7	67.6	32.2	33.7	32.4	27.7
5363000	Seattle city	96,852	38,575	2.3	34.5	77.2	49.1	27.3	22.8	15.9
5363960	Shoreline city	10,082	2,866	4.1	34.9	80.7	43.3	35.2	19.3	15.0
5365922	South Hill CDP	16,754	4,984	0.0	16.8	67.4	30.8	36.6	32.6	22.3
5367000	Spokane city	43,640	16,899	1.0	12.7	65.8	36.1	27.7	34.2	26.4
5367167	Spokane Valley city	19,978	6,154	0.4	9.6	62.0	43.2	17.5	38.0	27.4
5370000	Tacoma city	42,480	15,040	0.6	27.4	58.5	33.1	22.4	41.5	31.2
5374060	Vancouver city	36,694	12,824	1.1	27.4	61.9	32.1	28.4	38.1	30.6
5380010	Yakima city	23,597	9,277	0.6	42.3	58.2	31.9	24.9	41.8	32.5
5400000	**West Virginia**	357,417	117,410	0.3	2.4	61.6	32.7	27.2	38.4	25.0
5414600	Charleston city	9,873	3,019	0.0	2.3	47.7	26.8	19.4	52.3	41.1

Table D-4: Cities with a Population of 50,000 or More—Children—*Continued*

State/ Place FIPS code	State/Place	Total own children 6 to 17	Nativity and parentage, age 6 to 17 years		Own children age 6 to 17 years living with two parents			Own children age 6 to 17 years living with one parent		Grand-children under 18 living with a grandparent householder	Grand-children under 18 living with a grandparent householder, as a percent of all children	Children for whom grandparent householders are responsible, as a percent of all children
			Child is foreign born, percent	One or more foreign-born parent, percent	Age 6 to 17 years living with two parents, percent	Both parents in labor force, percent	One parent in labor force, percent	Age 6 to 17 years living with one parent, percent	Parent in labor force, percent			
	Texas—cont'd											
4864472	San Angelo city	12,712	1.5	16.8	56.0	31.7	24.0	44.0	38.0	1,644	7.8	3.7
4865000	San Antonio city	225,687	5.4	28.2	57.8	35.6	20.9	42.2	33.9	40,542	11.8	6.0
4865600	San Marcos city	4,367	0.0	7.6	50.5	40.1	8.8	49.5	41.4	0	0.0	0.0
4869596	Spring CDP	11,837	3.6	22.6	63.1	43.5	17.3	36.9	36.2	1,056	6.1	3.6
4870808	Sugar Land city	13,121	11.6	61.7	87.5	53.8	31.9	12.5	11.6	1,289	7.0	2.7
4872176	Temple city	10,315	2.4	21.5	63.5	40.3	22.0	36.5	25.9	1,447	9.0	6.8
4872656	The Woodlands CDP	21,495	11.7	28.4	83.9	42.7	40.2	16.1	13.2	472	1.5	1.0
4874144	Tyler city	14,183	4.3	31.3	61.6	38.2	22.6	38.4	31.8	2,618	12.4	6.6
4875428	Victoria city	10,350	0.5	9.8	52.0	31.7	20.3	48.0	39.9	2,005	12.6	6.8
4876000	Waco city	17,851	6.5	32.2	56.2	34.2	21.4	43.8	33.7	2,473	8.3	5.5
4879000	Wichita Falls city	14,206	3.1	16.1	60.1	41.8	17.2	39.9	35.3	1,858	8.4	4.5
4900000	**Utah**	554,583	3.1	17.1	79.2	42.8	35.5	20.8	17.6	51,012	5.9	2.4
4943660	Layton city	12,725	2.2	13.8	73.2	43.2	29.6	26.8	23.7	1,370	6.4	3.6
4944320	Lehi city	13,471	0.7	8.7	87.1	31.8	53.9	12.9	12.3	728	3.3	0.7
4950150	Millcreek CDP	7,927	11.6	22.5	79.0	39.9	36.3	21.0	18.9	642	5.0	2.5
4955980	Ogden city	12,482	5.6	32.9	65.9	37.6	27.4	34.1	30.0	1,710	7.9	4.0
4957300	Orem city	15,479	4.5	24.3	80.5	30.1	49.0	19.5	14.0	2,369	9.0	4.6
4962470	Provo city	13,993	9.5	35.5	82.4	36.5	43.9	17.6	14.7	1,831	7.2	2.0
4965330	St. George city	13,146	3.4	17.0	73.3	41.7	30.9	26.7	24.0	1,053	5.2	2.9
4967000	Salt Lake City city	24,119	8.7	39.1	64.9	38.2	26.1	35.1	28.0	2,657	6.6	2.0
4967440	Sandy city	17,063	2.9	15.4	80.6	42.1	38.3	19.4	17.4	1,362	5.6	1.2
4970850	South Jordan city	12,911	0.9	12.1	89.9	44.8	44.9	10.1	9.5	1,016	5.5	1.3
4975360	Taylorsville city	9,918	8.2	32.2	69.6	45.7	23.7	30.4	26.0	1,556	9.7	3.1
4982950	West Jordan city	23,010	3.0	21.2	78.2	50.0	27.3	21.8	19.7	2,577	7.3	2.3
4983470	West Valley City city	25,102	8.0	47.6	66.5	37.3	28.4	33.5	28.7	4,725	11.8	5.2
5000000	**Vermont**	82,240	2.1	6.5	68.9	52.6	15.3	31.1	25.3	6,307	5.3	2.6
5100000	**Virginia**	1,180,855	4.5	20.8	69.2	45.9	22.1	30.8	25.9	131,873	7.4	3.8
5101000	Alexandria city	13,139	17.7	45.6	63.8	37.4	24.7	36.2	30.6	1,172	4.7	2.6
5103000	Arlington CDP	19,924	14.8	40.7	76.2	50.4	24.6	23.8	21.8	1,216	3.5	1.2
5114440	Centreville CDP	12,991	13.3	53.3	78.2	49.2	28.7	21.8	19.4	0	0.0	0.0
5116000	Chesapeake city	37,383	1.5	10.0	69.0	46.0	22.7	31.0	27.3	5,654	10.4	4.0
5121088	Dale City CDP	12,901	8.5	51.8	68.6	51.0	17.1	31.4	26.9	1,686	9.0	4.5
5135000	Hampton city	17,927	2.4	9.8	47.2	31.1	15.7	52.8	42.9	2,909	10.3	5.1
5135624	Harrisonburg city	4,769	21.3	53.4	60.4	32.4	26.0	39.6	38.8	0	0.0	0.0
5147672	Lynchburg city	8,925	1.9	7.6	60.5	38.4	21.4	39.5	35.0	883	6.2	1.7
5156000	Newport News city	25,166	2.6	12.5	49.5	32.3	16.3	50.5	43.9	4,052	9.9	5.3
5157000	Norfolk city	28,029	2.6	10.3	45.7	30.3	13.9	54.3	46.4	5,719	12.2	6.7
5164000	Portsmouth city	13,120	0.4	2.8	35.0	24.6	9.7	65.0	57.5	2,872	13.6	8.1
5166672	Reston CDP	7,653	5.6	42.9	72.3	47.0	25.3	27.7	27.7	398	3.1	1.1
5167000	Richmond city	20,940	1.3	11.9	37.2	25.5	11.0	62.8	43.8	3,104	8.5	5.0
5168000	Roanoke city	12,069	6.0	12.8	45.7	35.6	9.7	54.3	45.8	1,879	9.4	6.7
5176432	Suffolk city	13,733	1.0	5.5	60.6	42.1	16.8	39.4	33.0	1,924	9.3	6.5
5182000	Virginia Beach city	66,337	2.9	14.9	62.9	40.9	21.2	37.1	31.3	7,379	7.4	3.8
5300000	**Washington**	1,007,389	5.4	26.9	69.7	43.1	25.3	30.3	24.6	82,069	5.4	2.7
5303180	Auburn city	10,606	7.9	37.9	65.5	38.9	26.1	34.5	24.6	905	5.4	2.4
5305210	Bellevue city	17,204	12.8	53.3	82.0	49.6	30.3	18.0	14.8	435	1.7	0.3
5305280	Bellingham city	7,983	7.7	29.2	50.4	28.1	21.7	49.6	38.2	345	2.7	0.9
5322640	Everett city	12,457	10.1	46.0	66.5	36.5	27.0	33.5	25.3	854	4.0	1.2
5323515	Federal Way city	14,365	7.0	43.0	61.3	38.9	21.1	38.7	30.4	1,290	6.0	3.5
5335275	Kennewick city	12,456	4.8	27.0	67.4	42.3	24.8	32.6	27.7	1,345	6.7	3.8
5335415	Kent city	20,053	12.4	53.6	63.6	38.2	23.4	36.4	29.2	1,916	6.2	2.3
5335940	Kirkland city	11,262	7.2	33.6	72.5	40.4	31.8	27.5	26.1	434	2.5	0.8
5338038	Lakewood city	7,266	6.1	28.0	59.0	34.9	23.2	41.0	32.5	926	7.8	2.2
5343955	Marysville city	9,794	1.5	23.4	63.9	39.4	23.3	36.1	27.7	787	4.9	1.6
5353545	Pasco city	13,841	9.5	54.9	59.0	37.2	21.7	41.0	38.1	1,015	4.5	2.0
5357535	Redmond city	7,300	15.3	58.1	81.5	40.5	40.7	18.5	14.7	0	0.0	0.0
5357745	Renton city	12,785	11.7	42.9	65.0	40.9	22.3	35.0	26.3	1,267	6.0	1.5
5358235	Richland city	7,997	2.4	16.5	62.6	37.2	23.4	37.4	32.4	0	0.0	0.0
5363000	Seattle city	58,277	8.1	34.1	68.7	46.6	21.4	31.3	26.5	3,623	3.7	1.6
5363960	Shoreline city	7,216	11.0	35.8	66.0	44.2	21.3	34.0	28.3	692	6.9	1.6
5365922	South Hill CDP	11,770	0.8	17.7	68.6	49.9	17.7	31.4	26.2	470	2.8	1.5
5367000	Spokane city	26,741	4.6	12.2	58.8	37.0	19.8	41.2	33.9	1,956	4.5	2.6
5367167	Spokane Valley city	13,824	1.5	13.5	66.0	43.7	20.0	34.0	26.5	1,030	5.2	3.0
5370000	Tacoma city	27,440	7.3	29.9	60.3	41.5	17.5	39.7	30.4	3,386	8.0	3.6
5374060	Vancouver city	23,870	4.6	25.6	62.4	38.3	22.2	37.6	30.1	2,747	7.5	4.3
5380010	Yakima city	14,320	2.9	48.3	55.3	35.6	18.9	44.7	33.9	2,585	11.0	4.4
5400000	**West Virginia**	240,007	0.8	2.7	65.6	38.9	24.2	34.4	24.8	33,480	9.4	5.7
5414600	Charleston city	6,854	1.3	4.8	54.7	40.1	13.5	45.3	36.9	653	6.6	4.2

Table D-4: Cities with a Population of 50,000 or More—Children—*Continued*

State/ Place FIPS code	State/Place	Total own children under 18 in families and subfamilies	Own children under 6 years in families and subfamilies							
			Total own children under 6 years	Nativity and parentage, under 6 years		Own children under 6 years living with two parents			Own children under 6 living with one parent	
				Child is foreign born, percent	One or more foreign-born parent, percent	Total under 6 years living with two parents, percent	Both parents in labor force, percent	One parent in labor force, percent	Total under 6 years living with one parent, percent	Parent in labor force, percent
5500000	**Wisconsin**.................................	1,261,858	407,831	0.9	11.8	66.9	45.6	20.5	33.1	27.2
5502375	Appleton city.............................	17,407	5,600	0.8	10.6	62.4	43.1	18.5	37.6	33.4
5522300	Eau Claire city............................	12,527	4,057	1.5	11.2	69.7	53.3	16.4	30.3	26.3
5531000	Green Bay city............................	23,305	8,855	0.3	27.5	64.5	41.4	23.1	35.5	26.2
5537825	Janesville city.............................	14,291	5,081	0.0	5.8	54.4	34.9	18.2	45.6	31.6
5539225	Kenosha city..............................	25,103	8,357	1.0	19.9	55.2	33.9	21.3	44.8	37.3
5540775	La Crosse city.............................	7,715	2,715	0.4	6.8	65.7	49.4	16.3	34.3	25.4
5548000	Madison city..............................	40,171	15,427	2.1	28.0	68.1	51.3	16.7	31.9	27.1
5553000	Milwaukee city...........................	150,344	54,052	1.4	19.4	35.8	23.5	11.5	64.2	50.9
5560500	Oshkosh city..............................	11,770	3,997	1.3	7.3	57.6	43.1	14.5	42.4	32.7
5566000	Racine city.................................	20,511	6,690	0.2	21.9	44.9	24.1	20.5	55.1	40.1
5584250	Waukesha city............................	15,452	5,785	2.8	23.4	73.7	47.5	25.0	26.3	22.0
5585300	West Allis city............................	11,936	4,844	0.2	8.2	67.0	44.9	21.2	33.0	29.4
5600000	**Wyoming**.................................	130,758	45,079	0.4	9.3	71.0	41.6	28.6	29.0	24.2
5613150	Casper city................................	12,869	4,677	0.0	9.1	63.2	33.8	29.4	36.8	28.4
5613900	Cheyenne city............................	13,991	4,846	0.2	10.0	67.3	38.7	24.7	32.7	29.6

State/ Place FIPS code	State/Place	Own children age 6 to 17 years in families and subfamilies								Grand-children under 18 living with a grandparent householder	Grand-children under 18 living with a grandparent householder, as a percent of all children	Children for whom grandparent householders are responsible, as a percent of all children
		Total own children 6 to 17	Nativity and parentage, age 6 to 17 years		Own children age 6 to 17 years living with two parents			Own children age 6 to 17 years living with one parent				
			Child is foreign born, percent	One or more foreign-born parent, percent	Age 6 to 17 years living with two parents, percent	Both parents in labor force, percent	One parent in labor force, percent	Age 6 to 17 years living with one parent, percent	Parent in labor force, percent			
5500000	Wisconsin	854,027	2.5	10.1	68.9	50.8	17.1	31.1	26.4	56,875	4.5	2.2
5502375	Appleton city	11,807	2.2	15.3	70.2	48.4	21.3	29.8	25.1	682	3.9	1.6
5522300	Eau Claire city	8,470	3.6	7.5	62.9	48.9	14.0	37.1	33.7	373	3.0	1.5
5531000	Green Bay city	14,450	4.5	23.4	60.0	40.7	18.1	40.0	31.6	1,499	6.4	3.6
5537825	Janesville city	9,210	1.8	7.4	64.6	44.4	20.1	35.4	27.4	1,105	7.7	4.8
5539225	Kenosha city	16,746	1.2	19.9	49.7	34.9	14.5	50.3	43.8	1,595	6.4	2.7
5540775	La Crosse city	5,000	0.9	8.2	58.1	43.9	14.1	41.9	34.8	242	3.1	1.3
5548000	Madison city	24,744	7.0	22.7	63.0	48.5	13.1	37.0	28.8	687	1.7	0.7
5553000	Milwaukee city	96,292	5.4	19.9	38.2	24.8	12.2	61.8	48.2	11,958	8.0	4.7
5560500	Oshkosh city	7,773	0.0	5.6	58.9	43.2	15.7	41.1	31.8	565	4.8	2.6
5566000	Racine city	13,821	1.8	17.9	53.3	30.8	21.3	46.7	36.5	1,517	7.4	4.6
5584250	Waukesha city	9,667	3.5	21.1	71.3	49.4	20.4	28.7	24.0	315	2.0	0.9
5585300	West Allis city	7,092	2.0	8.3	64.1	44.3	19.8	35.9	28.0	768	6.4	3.3
5600000	Wyoming	85,679	2.3	8.2	69.5	47.8	20.9	30.5	26.0	6,246	4.8	2.9
5613150	Casper city	8,192	0.6	6.6	65.2	48.8	16.1	34.8	25.7	626	4.9	3.6
5613900	Cheyenne city	9,145	0.6	3.6	62.5	44.0	17.4	37.5	33.0	596	4.3	2.3

Income, Poverty, and Health Insurance

PART E. INCOME, POVERTY, AND HEALTH INSURANCE

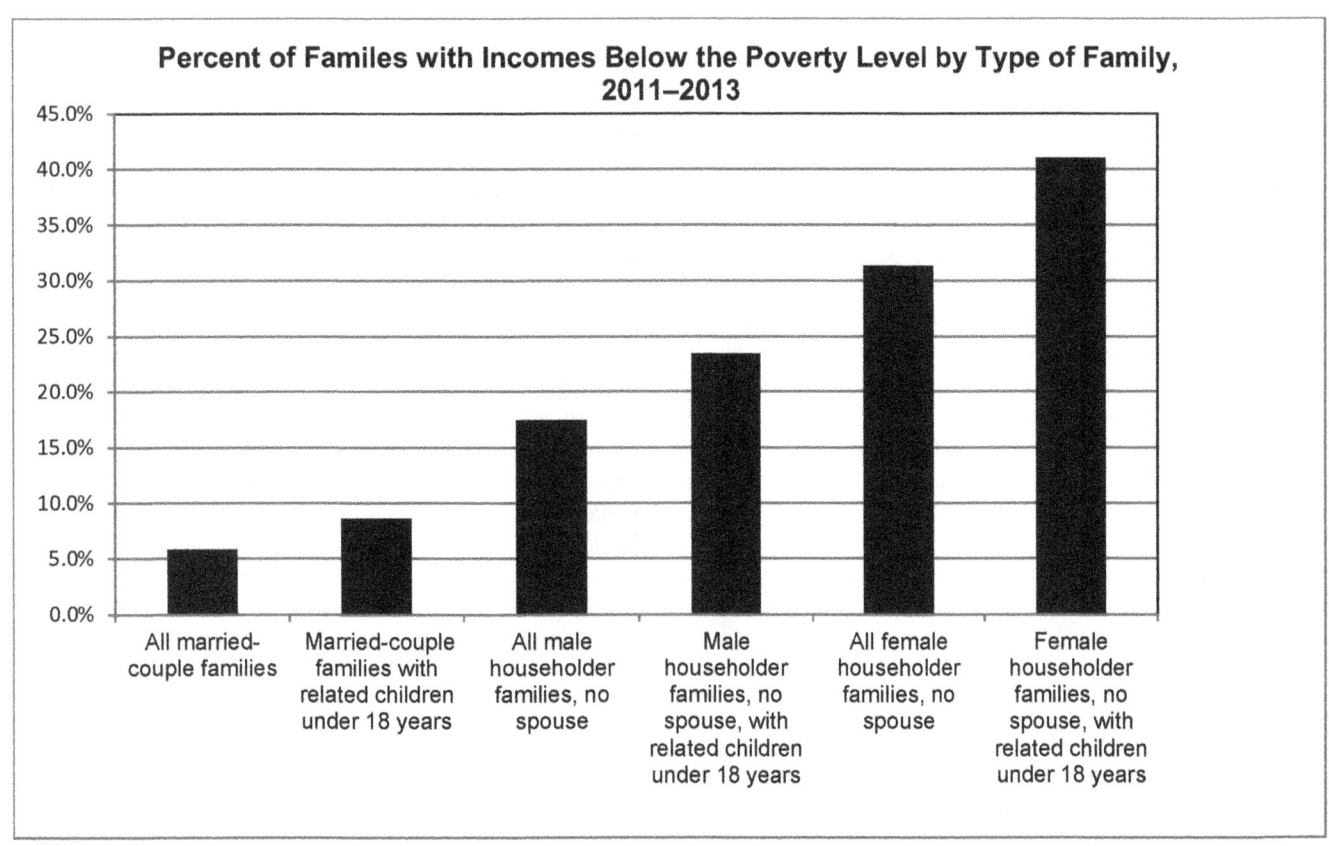

Percent of Familes with Incomes Below the Poverty Level by Type of Family, 2011–2013

In the 2011–2013 time period, the median family income in the United States was $63,784. Half of all families had incomes below this level, and half had higher incomes. All income levels in this book have been adjusted for inflation and represent the 2013 value. Among the states, Maryland had the highest median income at $87,060, while Connecticut, New Jersey, Massachusetts and Alaska also had median incomes above $80,000. The state with the lowest median income was Mississippi, the only state with a median below $50,000.

Families with no earners had a median income of $31,313 while the median for families with 3 or more earners was $102,461. At the state level, both the lowest and the highest median incomes were estimated for families in the District of Columbia—$15,606 for families with no earners, and $137,418 for families with two earners. When compared with other cities of 50,000 or more residents, 61 cities had lower median incomes than the District of Columbia for families with no earners, with

Passaic and Camden, NJ and Florence-Graham, CA below $10,000. In Palo Alto, CA and Bethesda, MD, families with 2 earners had median incomes above $225,000.

Married couple families with children had a median income of $82,511, the highest of all the family types. Women householders with children under 18 and no spouse had the lowest median income, at $23,787. In five states and the District of Columbia, the median income for married-couple families with children was over $100,000, and 16 other states had medians above the national level. The lowest median income for married-couple families with children was $63,851 in Idaho, and the median was below $70,000 in 5 other states. For female householder families with children, the highest median income was $36,393 in Maryland. Only 3 other states had medians above $30,000 for this group. Six states had medians below $20,000, with the lowest level at $17,591 in West Virginia.

In 5 cities, married-couple families with children had median incomes over $200,000, with Palo Alto, CA at $219,038. In 6 cities, the median income for married-couple families with children was below $40,000, with the lowest in Scranton, PA at $34,195. In 5 cities, female householder families with children had median incomes above $70,000, topped by Bowie, MD at $80,234. In 6 cities, these mothers with children had median incomes below $15,000, with Allentown, PA at $6,987.

Almost 9 million families had incomes below the poverty level, 11.7 percent of all families, ranging from 5.8 percent among all married-couple families to 41.1 percent among female householder families with no spouse and with children under 18 years old. The lowest poverty levels for states were married-couple families in New Hampshire, Vermont, Alaska, and Maryland, all under 3 percent. The highest poverty levels for married-couple families were in New Mexico (9.2 percent) and Texas (8 percent.) In Mississippi and West Virginia, more than half of female householders with children had incomes below the poverty level. This proportion was below 30 percent in Alaska, Maryland and New Hampshire.

The Supplemental Nutrition Assistance Program (SNAP) provides eligible households with coupons or cards that can be used to purchase food. Formerly known as the Federal Food Stamp program, this benefit was received by 14.4 percent of households in the 2011–2013 time period, ranging from above 20 percent in the District of Columbia, Oregon, and Mississippi to less than 10 percent in Wyoming, New Hampshire, and North Dakota. Among married-couple families, 7.4 percent received food stamps, while one-third of householders with no spouse received them. Nearly half of the married-couple families that received food stamps had two or more workers in the family, and 72.5 percent of the householders with no spouse had at least one worker. More than one in four married-couple families in Hialeah and Homestead, FL and Pharr, TX had workers in their families and also received food stamps, and more than half of the single householder families in Springfield OR had SNAP benefits and included workers.

85.2 percent of the household population had health insurance—65.2 percent with private health insurance and 31 percent with public insurance. Some people have both, like retirees who have private insurance to supplement Medicare. In married-couple families, 88.6 percent of people were insured, while only 78.1 percent of people in male or female householder families were insured. Fully 96 percent of Massachusetts residents had health insurance, while only 77.5 percent of people in Texas were insured.

Table E-1: States—Income, Poverty, and Health Insurance

State FIPS code	State	Median family income in the past 12 months (in 2013 inflation-adjusted dollars)					Married couple families		
		All families	Families with no earners	Families with one earner	Families with two earners	Families with three or more earners	All married-couple families	With own children under 18 years	With no own children under 18 years
	United States..............	$63,784	$31,313	$45,505	$84,323	$102,461	$77,279	$82,511	$73,737
1	Alabama.........................	$53,991	$26,970	$40,869	$76,759	$94,234	$67,358	$73,523	$64,082
2	Alaska...........................	$81,721	$38,919	$55,788	$98,171	$121,285	$94,671	$92,503	$95,802
4	Arizona.........................	$57,317	$36,056	$42,897	$79,086	$92,730	$69,482	$72,137	$67,759
5	Arkansas.......................	$50,600	$27,052	$37,644	$69,917	$88,984	$60,620	$64,920	$58,222
6	California......................	$67,746	$29,455	$48,976	$91,345	$100,397	$83,378	$82,294	$84,225
8	Colorado	$71,939	$38,176	$50,890	$88,748	$105,466	$83,615	$87,137	$81,327
9	Connecticut...................	$86,354	$35,655	$59,935	$108,103	$126,870	$103,903	$112,382	$98,072
10	Delaware	$70,668	$42,381	$51,357	$89,317	$112,572	$84,833	$93,443	$80,279
11	District of Columbia.......	$78,892	$15,606	$49,300	$137,418	$130,757	$140,915	$157,541	$133,927
12	Florida..........................	$55,758	$34,825	$42,072	$75,621	$90,957	$66,910	$71,937	$64,468
13	Georgia	$57,432	$26,281	$41,334	$79,557	$93,926	$71,892	$76,385	$69,054
15	Hawaii	$78,501	$40,960	$54,697	$90,367	$123,507	$88,092	$87,567	$88,376
16	Idaho	$55,296	$34,365	$41,860	$67,736	$84,642	$62,206	$63,851	$60,955
17	Illinois..........................	$69,142	$32,285	$48,001	$89,454	$106,113	$83,143	$88,403	$79,806
18	Indiana.........................	$59,490	$31,602	$42,256	$77,001	$95,990	$70,485	$76,786	$66,246
19	Iowa.............................	$65,550	$35,528	$43,336	$80,074	$96,280	$74,991	$81,489	$70,530
20	Kansas..........................	$64,346	$34,928	$43,825	$79,709	$98,311	$74,603	$79,250	$71,207
21	Kentucky.......................	$53,994	$25,353	$40,940	$75,776	$94,284	$65,281	$73,748	$60,957
22	Louisiana.......................	$55,414	$23,278	$39,756	$82,102	$102,388	$73,992	$83,839	$67,493
23	Maine...........................	$60,235	$30,232	$41,626	$77,758	$97,789	$69,372	$76,056	$66,093
24	Maryland	$87,060	$38,003	$59,175	$109,732	$129,316	$106,183	$113,714	$100,930
25	Massachusetts	$83,867	$30,356	$56,245	$106,084	$125,258	$101,792	$112,824	$93,475
26	Michigan.......................	$60,398	$34,550	$44,945	$81,067	$99,413	$72,617	$81,062	$67,897
27	Minnesota.....................	$74,434	$38,024	$49,205	$89,615	$106,873	$85,397	$94,432	$79,330
28	Mississippi.....................	$47,531	$21,966	$35,899	$69,064	$90,332	$61,944	$67,574	$59,167
29	Missouri........................	$58,626	$31,395	$41,478	$76,531	$97,006	$69,777	$76,510	$65,651
30	Montana........................	$59,345	$36,454	$42,491	$71,651	$89,239	$67,022	$72,172	$64,183
31	Nebraska	$64,862	$34,645	$42,221	$77,553	$94,332	$75,143	$79,890	$72,124
32	Nevada	$58,779	$33,957	$43,382	$76,260	$95,605	$70,102	$69,580	$70,353
33	New Hampshire	$79,485	$36,525	$54,131	$94,971	$115,664	$89,862	$100,154	$83,788
34	New Jersey....................	$85,615	$35,626	$61,012	$110,220	$128,876	$103,598	$111,781	$97,168
35	New Mexico...................	$53,555	$28,370	$39,494	$76,365	$92,119	$67,142	$68,669	$66,194
36	New York.......................	$69,813	$27,817	$48,566	$94,722	$114,449	$87,355	$93,157	$83,480
37	North Carolina...............	$56,001	$29,254	$40,907	$76,504	$92,148	$69,592	$75,259	$66,109
38	North Dakota.................	$71,797	$34,628	$45,305	$86,061	$107,129	$81,493	$88,252	$76,190
39	Ohio	$60,999	$31,221	$43,529	$80,839	$100,646	$73,701	$81,778	$68,971
40	Oklahoma......................	$56,036	$28,741	$40,886	$74,125	$91,712	$66,782	$69,435	$65,104
41	Oregon.........................	$60,863	$35,850	$45,406	$78,059	$91,603	$71,066	$74,506	$69,161
42	Pennsylvania	$66,098	$31,283	$48,059	$85,612	$105,643	$78,610	$88,326	$72,734
44	Rhode Island.................	$72,152	$29,672	$48,154	$94,309	$113,937	$89,007	$96,919	$83,968
45	South Carolina...............	$53,972	$28,960	$39,851	$75,602	$91,824	$67,664	$73,641	$64,631
46	South Dakota.................	$62,594	$32,153	$39,614	$74,608	$91,688	$72,954	$77,266	$69,113
47	Tennessee	$54,458	$27,901	$40,492	$73,639	$91,857	$65,725	$71,531	$62,530
48	Texas............................	$60,656	$27,707	$41,916	$81,593	$93,924	$74,925	$75,463	$74,508
49	Utah.............................	$66,321	$38,285	$51,414	$73,777	$99,597	$73,696	$73,995	$73,334
50	Vermont	$67,953	$32,368	$45,522	$83,452	$103,174	$78,116	$83,160	$75,099
51	Virginia.........................	$75,778	$35,774	$52,904	$96,379	$113,489	$90,806	$98,043	$85,755
53	Washington	$71,100	$39,274	$53,164	$91,187	$106,694	$82,523	$85,824	$80,485
54	West Virginia	$51,949	$27,721	$42,971	$76,260	$93,908	$61,252	$71,003	$56,764
55	Wisconsin......................	$65,877	$35,499	$44,059	$81,992	$99,328	$76,326	$84,375	$71,363
56	Wyoming.......................	$70,531	$36,362	$49,622	$86,697	$105,900	$80,538	$84,210	$77,086

Table E-1: States—Income, Poverty, and Health Insurance—*Continued*

State FIPS code	State	Median family income in the past 12 months (in 2013 inflation-adjusted dollars)							Total family households
		Other families							
		All other families	Male householder, no spouse present			Female householder, no spouse present			
			All male householder families, no spouse present	With own children under 18 years	With no own children under 18 years	All female householder families, no spouse present	With own children under 18 years	With no own children under 18 years	
	United States...............	$34,152	$43,567	$36,858	$50,825	$30,993	$23,767	$41,947	76,444,922
1	Alabama........................	$27,094	$38,065	$32,653	$41,500	$24,654	$18,502	$33,328	1,236,566
2	Alaska...........................	$46,246	$59,488	$51,540	$69,797	$40,780	$31,776	$59,414	167,553
4	Arizona.........................	$33,513	$40,102	$35,918	$44,142	$31,309	$25,228	$40,762	1,560,655
5	Arkansas.......................	$26,432	$34,327	$29,332	$40,243	$23,831	$18,687	$33,869	755,344
6	California......................	$38,786	$46,418	$37,371	$54,751	$35,633	$26,341	$47,308	8,602,735
8	Colorado	$38,442	$46,529	$41,877	$54,296	$34,807	$28,222	$47,322	1,271,180
9	Connecticut...................	$43,142	$60,460	$51,622	$66,366	$38,546	$30,019	$52,035	894,728
10	Delaware	$41,753	$50,889	$42,821	$59,689	$37,376	$29,037	$48,838	226,510
11	District of Columbia.......	$38,431	$50,447	$36,852	$58,530	$36,513	$25,582	$50,336	114,484
12	Florida..........................	$32,848	$39,529	$32,892	$45,038	$31,035	$24,860	$39,879	4,594,006
13	Georgia	$30,208	$38,345	$33,883	$44,292	$27,631	$22,191	$35,749	2,386,724
15	Hawaii..........................	$51,697	$61,398	$48,840	$71,100	$46,359	$27,683	$63,463	311,096
16	Idaho...........................	$30,821	$37,887	$36,592	$42,030	$27,430	$20,543	$39,393	404,512
17	Illinois..........................	$35,617	$46,011	$37,113	$53,609	$32,074	$24,017	$43,966	3,114,415
18	Indiana.........................	$30,891	$40,649	$35,568	$47,567	$27,589	$21,383	$38,280	1,647,579
19	Iowa............................	$33,175	$42,068	$38,392	$49,465	$29,434	$24,069	$42,424	792,745
20	Kansas..........................	$33,067	$42,133	$35,997	$52,099	$30,193	$23,860	$42,057	727,902
21	Kentucky.......................	$27,273	$36,010	$32,067	$39,465	$24,451	$18,590	$33,577	1,131,310
22	Louisiana......................	$27,791	$42,144	$38,120	$45,772	$24,551	$19,279	$33,069	1,127,030
23	Maine...........................	$31,141	$38,560	$32,702	$50,467	$28,238	$22,301	$41,256	345,776
24	Maryland.......................	$49,942	$58,467	$50,869	$67,579	$46,709	$36,393	$60,575	1,432,364
25	Massachusetts	$41,156	$55,625	$45,121	$63,518	$36,959	$27,158	$51,113	1,606,383
26	Michigan.......................	$30,741	$39,646	$33,763	$45,610	$27,697	$20,352	$38,428	2,489,254
27	Minnesota.....................	$37,554	$46,541	$40,684	$56,250	$33,336	$26,795	$49,145	1,367,091
28	Mississippi.....................	$24,985	$36,200	$32,295	$39,341	$22,650	$18,312	$29,149	743,178
29	Missouri........................	$30,992	$40,610	$34,515	$46,813	$27,948	$21,892	$38,913	1,527,728
30	Montana........................	$31,164	$40,063	$34,563	$50,693	$26,973	$20,044	$39,519	255,929
31	Nebraska	$33,383	$41,489	$37,024	$49,823	$29,610	$24,258	$43,783	472,470
32	Nevada.........................	$37,416	$45,025	$37,086	$53,200	$34,181	$28,248	$44,905	641,060
33	New Hampshire	$41,489	$49,953	$44,404	$57,717	$37,552	$28,473	$50,747	346,775
34	New Jersey.....................	$45,477	$56,026	$45,334	$65,471	$41,432	$30,016	$56,159	2,203,456
35	New Mexico...................	$29,036	$37,543	$32,605	$46,555	$26,394	$20,758	$35,414	494,555
36	New York.......................	$38,795	$49,764	$38,808	$57,643	$35,439	$25,937	$48,451	4,594,587
37	North Carolina...............	$29,041	$35,589	$31,549	$40,521	$26,871	$21,820	$34,675	2,467,843
38	North Dakota.................	$37,819	$52,278	$48,533	$58,333	$30,257	$24,136	$45,356	176,378
39	Ohio.............................	$30,586	$40,561	$35,072	$46,997	$27,374	$20,852	$39,188	2,920,189
40	Oklahoma......................	$30,446	$40,452	$36,376	$44,964	$26,676	$20,619	$37,151	959,015
41	Oregon.........................	$31,976	$40,316	$33,666	$47,270	$29,268	$22,326	$39,450	959,743
42	Pennsylvania..................	$35,492	$45,716	$38,974	$51,616	$31,979	$23,858	$43,594	3,186,145
44	Rhode Island..................	$37,574	$48,835	$37,600	$57,198	$34,500	$26,155	$48,692	257,316
45	South Carolina...............	$27,626	$37,326	$31,724	$42,999	$25,403	$20,273	$31,945	1,199,885
46	South Dakota.................	$31,015	$40,076	$37,542	$47,474	$27,343	$23,473	$37,902	210,494
47	Tennessee	$28,837	$36,547	$31,427	$42,539	$26,388	$20,006	$35,311	1,646,360
48	Texas............................	$32,452	$42,760	$36,672	$49,092	$29,569	$23,538	$39,197	6,235,820
49	Utah............................	$37,931	$46,456	$40,880	$53,593	$34,577	$26,784	$47,988	667,046
50	Vermont	$35,042	$41,160	$36,990	$48,168	$31,404	$24,590	$43,639	159,883
51	Virginia.........................	$39,403	$50,170	$42,199	$57,583	$36,045	$27,583	$46,955	2,033,567
53	Washington....................	$37,389	$49,004	$41,732	$56,234	$33,467	$25,856	$46,140	1,694,518
54	West Virginia	$27,700	$39,081	$35,189	$41,900	$24,142	$17,591	$32,583	479,062
55	Wisconsin......................	$33,219	$42,131	$36,513	$51,293	$29,468	$23,702	$42,084	1,458,497
56	Wyoming.......................	$35,461	$50,488	$45,175	$57,143	$29,535	$23,418	$44,353	145,481

State FIPS code	State	Married-couple family households		All other family households	Other family households			
					Male householder families, no spouse present		Female householder families, no spouse present	
		All married-couple family households	Married-couple family with related children under 18 years		All male householder families	Male householder families with related children under 18 years	All female householder families	Female householder families with related children under 18 years
	United States...............	55,747,944	24,010,463	20,696,978	5,552,073	3,115,261	15,144,905	9,938,754
1	Alabama.........................	877,131	351,331	359,435	78,039	41,036	281,396	185,653
2	Alaska...........................	124,654	58,045	42,899	14,623	9,555	28,276	20,814
4	Arizona.........................	1,124,577	465,843	436,078	128,659	78,753	307,419	209,486
5	Arkansas.......................	553,817	222,613	201,527	50,444	29,809	151,083	102,404
6	California.......................	6,122,335	3,001,312	2,480,400	756,455	417,471	1,723,945	1,082,923
8	Colorado	977,214	436,958	293,966	88,625	54,783	205,341	140,581
9	Connecticut...................	659,668	283,282	235,060	57,806	29,189	177,254	114,481
10	Delaware.......................	162,724	63,560	63,786	16,704	10,336	47,082	30,281
11	District of Columbia........	60,812	23,692	53,672	10,422	5,208	43,250	26,206
12	Florida..........................	3,316,161	1,206,230	1,277,845	328,016	176,142	949,829	597,644
13	Georgia	1,677,631	765,528	709,093	168,761	95,149	540,332	366,617
15	Hawaii...........................	231,601	103,736	79,495	24,052	12,291	55,443	31,299
16	Idaho............................	321,679	142,828	82,833	25,891	17,429	56,942	39,581
17	Illinois..........................	2,289,104	1,016,971	825,311	217,971	118,978	607,340	391,452
18	Indiana..........................	1,226,311	512,561	421,268	113,561	68,657	307,707	212,091
19	Iowa.............................	626,297	251,090	166,448	50,332	32,041	116,116	83,618
20	Kansas..........................	563,171	245,976	164,731	48,528	30,439	116,203	82,088
21	Kentucky.......................	830,215	337,161	301,095	81,609	46,581	219,486	147,022
22	Louisiana	746,288	313,104	380,742	88,115	48,419	292,627	200,190
23	Maine...........................	269,688	93,467	76,088	23,613	15,629	52,475	36,027
24	Maryland.......................	1,012,523	449,957	419,841	103,457	56,702	316,384	200,220
25	Massachusetts	1,181,198	514,068	425,185	103,656	50,073	321,529	200,986
26	Michigan	1,824,333	728,339	664,921	173,808	98,020	491,113	316,347
27	Minnesota	1,073,564	451,774	293,527	89,810	54,785	203,717	144,336
28	Mississippi	486,734	202,464	256,444	53,538	28,707	202,906	138,812
29	Missouri........................	1,137,352	458,227	390,376	100,528	59,878	289,848	197,259
30	Montana........................	200,808	74,031	55,121	17,875	11,133	37,246	25,903
31	Nebraska.......................	369,775	156,354	102,695	30,903	19,492	71,792	51,952
32	Nevada..........................	449,385	199,016	191,675	60,512	35,305	131,163	88,695
33	New Hampshire	273,749	107,219	73,026	21,673	13,015	51,353	33,850
34	New Jersey.....................	1,615,471	745,557	587,985	156,004	75,930	431,981	260,326
35	New Mexico...................	343,336	139,746	151,219	42,386	26,101	108,833	75,549
36	New York.......................	3,162,525	1,395,512	1,432,062	361,667	177,657	1,070,395	651,420
37	North Carolina...............	1,789,108	734,012	678,735	166,110	97,059	512,625	347,448
38	North Dakota.................	141,699	56,732	34,679	11,927	7,516	22,752	16,716
39	Ohio.............................	2,132,541	848,376	787,648	202,091	116,230	585,557	394,867
40	Oklahoma......................	707,880	299,068	251,135	71,460	43,578	179,675	125,582
41	Oregon..........................	732,053	292,106	227,690	67,964	42,041	159,726	105,221
42	Pennsylvania	2,377,594	922,732	808,551	214,497	116,095	594,054	370,426
44	Rhode Island..................	180,743	72,004	76,573	19,692	10,503	56,881	36,651
45	South Carolina...............	843,305	330,273	356,580	83,197	45,601	273,383	181,863
46	South Dakota.................	163,039	64,247	47,455	15,319	9,842	32,136	24,808
47	Tennessee	1,203,173	488,380	443,187	110,893	61,893	332,294	217,449
48	Texas............................	4,486,257	2,206,474	1,749,563	459,059	260,075	1,290,504	904,009
49	Utah	541,105	290,823	125,941	38,112	22,883	87,829	59,962
50	Vermont	126,295	45,353	33,588	10,325	6,610	23,263	16,266
51	Virginia.........................	1,527,465	669,238	506,102	130,373	71,603	375,729	241,650
53	Washington	1,300,793	555,740	393,725	119,005	72,378	274,720	181,841
54	West Virginia	359,823	127,367	119,239	34,505	19,047	84,734	52,232
55	Wisconsin......................	1,127,742	443,948	330,755	99,617	60,826	231,138	161,158
56	Wyoming.......................	115,498	46,038	29,983	9,884	6,788	20,099	14,492

			Families with income in the past 12 months below the poverty level						
			Married-couple families with income below the poverty level		Other families with income below the poverty level				
						Male householder families		Female householder families	
State FIPS code	State	All families with income below the poverty level	All married-couple families	Married-couple families with related children under 18 years	All other families	All male householder families, no spouse	Male householder families, no spouse, with related childred under 18 years	All female householder families, no spouse	Female householder families, no spouse, with related children under 18 years
	United States..............	8,954,624	3,241,638	2,077,333	5,712,986	968,808	730,430	4,744,178	4,080,388
1	Alabama.........................	180,204	55,956	33,435	124,248	16,177	10,972	108,071	92,000
2	Alaska...........................	11,318	3,530	2,454	7,788	1,981	1,717	5,807	5,474
4	Arizona.........................	214,360	87,957	59,252	126,403	27,229	20,927	99,174	84,515
5	Arkansas.......................	110,419	40,486	25,432	69,933	11,602	8,415	58,331	50,191
6	California.......................	1,088,817	463,551	332,173	625,266	133,337	102,548	491,929	417,662
8	Colorado	115,206	46,610	32,291	68,596	13,080	10,025	55,516	48,747
9	Connecticut...................	69,874	19,609	11,482	50,265	6,494	4,605	43,771	37,290
10	Delaware.......................	18,349	5,274	3,280	13,075	2,087	1,681	10,988	9,189
11	District of Columbia.......	17,479	2,650	1,358	14,829	1,798	1,291	13,031	10,169
12	Florida..........................	570,894	227,789	125,659	343,105	64,108	47,238	278,997	231,680
13	Georgia	349,633	121,813	79,087	227,820	35,596	25,590	192,224	163,212
15	Hawaii..........................	24,976	10,635	6,069	14,341	2,865	2,245	11,476	9,800
16	Idaho...........................	45,579	21,032	13,595	24,547	5,037	3,966	19,510	17,774
17	Illinois..........................	338,244	114,647	77,185	223,597	36,270	26,794	187,327	160,707
18	Indiana.........................	191,347	62,651	39,968	128,696	21,998	17,453	106,698	94,253
19	Iowa............................	66,731	22,973	13,402	43,758	7,489	6,173	36,269	33,230
20	Kansas.........................	68,677	25,299	17,449	43,378	7,323	5,812	36,055	32,933
21	Kentucky.......................	164,772	61,161	35,002	103,611	18,544	14,007	85,067	73,275
22	Louisiana.......................	175,184	43,188	21,994	131,996	16,954	12,079	115,042	98,631
23	Maine...........................	33,007	12,570	6,775	20,437	4,070	3,468	16,367	14,379
24	Maryland	102,524	29,138	16,832	73,386	10,200	7,716	63,186	53,812
25	Massachusetts	135,352	38,632	21,639	96,720	12,528	9,600	84,192	72,481
26	Michigan	310,007	101,397	64,885	208,610	35,907	26,613	172,703	147,023
27	Minnesota.....................	103,194	33,568	20,736	69,626	12,305	9,488	57,321	51,850
28	Mississippi.....................	135,373	36,978	22,528	98,395	12,062	8,195	86,333	72,952
29	Missouri........................	176,851	62,008	36,257	114,843	18,999	14,627	95,844	83,961
30	Montana........................	26,927	10,881	6,023	16,046	3,145	2,623	12,901	11,412
31	Nebraska	42,413	15,589	10,487	26,824	4,693	3,760	22,131	20,333
32	Nevada.........................	76,772	32,220	22,312	44,552	9,582	7,629	34,970	30,294
33	New Hampshire	19,935	6,962	3,757	12,973	1,993	1,513	10,980	10,127
34	New Jersey.....................	181,511	59,597	36,246	121,914	19,891	14,789	102,023	87,365
35	New Mexico....................	81,858	31,640	19,323	50,218	9,648	7,002	40,570	35,325
36	New York.......................	560,670	198,260	126,584	362,410	56,785	40,623	305,625	252,001
37	North Carolina...............	325,882	110,543	68,611	215,339	35,408	27,195	179,931	154,314
38	North Dakota.................	13,066	4,330	2,431	8,736	1,658	1,248	7,078	6,448
39	Ohio............................	345,206	102,247	63,602	242,959	38,806	29,765	204,153	180,637
40	Oklahoma......................	123,157	45,749	28,755	77,408	12,905	9,714	64,503	56,677
41	Oregon.........................	112,989	46,633	29,054	66,356	13,862	10,648	52,494	44,888
42	Pennsylvania..................	301,001	92,856	51,410	208,145	33,198	25,854	174,947	150,504
44	Rhode Island..................	26,247	8,023	4,673	18,224	2,481	1,964	15,743	13,890
45	South Carolina...............	170,221	51,371	30,296	118,850	17,192	12,095	101,658	85,563
46	South Dakota.................	19,659	6,263	3,606	13,396	2,835	2,289	10,561	9,640
47	Tennessee.....................	223,217	81,184	49,865	142,033	23,361	17,282	118,672	101,837
48	Texas............................	873,675	359,742	258,803	513,933	78,787	59,851	435,146	383,784
49	Utah............................	64,855	32,931	24,063	31,924	6,385	4,456	25,539	22,228
50	Vermont	11,503	3,543	1,882	7,960	1,482	1,282	6,478	5,979
51	Virginia.........................	171,053	57,129	34,349	113,924	16,771	12,376	97,153	83,772
53	Washington....................	159,013	62,348	39,845	96,665	17,591	14,033	79,074	68,946
54	West Virginia	62,673	24,901	13,746	37,772	6,644	5,007	31,128	26,349
55	Wisconsin......................	130,506	41,237	24,829	89,269	16,450	13,166	72,819	64,967
56	Wyoming.......................	12,244	4,357	2,562	7,887	1,215	1,021	6,672	5,918

Table E-1: States—Income, Poverty, and Health Insurance—*Continued*

State FIPS code	State	Percent of families with income in the past 12 months below the poverty level								Total families	Household received Food Stamps/SNAP in the past 12 months:	Percent of families whose household received Food Stamps/SNAP in the past 12 months:
		All families with income below the poverty level	Married-couple families with income below the poverty level		Other families with income below the poverty level							
			All married-couple families	Married-couple families with related children under 18 years	All other families	Male householder families		Female householder families				
						All male householder families, no spouse	Male householder families, no spouse, with related childred under 18 years	All female householder families, no spouse	Female householder families, no spouse, with related children under 18 years			
	United States...............	11.7	5.8	8.7	27.6	17.4	23.4	31.3	41.1	76,444,922	11,012,355	14.4
1	Alabama......................	14.6	6.4	9.5	34.6	20.7	26.7	38.4	49.6	1,236,566	218,017	17.6
2	Alaska........................	6.8	2.8	4.2	18.2	13.5	18.0	20.5	26.3	167,553	18,359	11.0
4	Arizona.......................	13.7	7.8	12.7	29.0	21.2	26.6	32.3	40.3	1,560,655	251,977	16.1
5	Arkansas.....................	14.6	7.3	11.4	34.7	23.0	28.2	38.6	49.0	755,344	122,064	16.2
6	California....................	12.7	7.6	11.1	25.2	17.6	24.6	28.5	38.6	8,602,735	969,120	11.3
8	Colorado.....................	9.1	4.8	7.4	23.3	14.8	18.3	27.0	34.7	1,271,180	122,362	9.6
9	Connecticut..................	7.8	3.0	4.1	21.4	11.2	15.8	24.7	32.6	894,728	103,363	11.6
10	Delaware.....................	8.1	3.2	5.2	20.5	12.5	16.3	23.3	30.3	226,510	32,817	14.5
11	District of Columbia.......	15.3	4.4	5.7	27.6	17.3	24.8	30.1	38.8	114,484	26,090	22.8
12	Florida.......................	12.4	6.9	10.4	26.9	19.5	26.8	29.4	38.8	4,594,006	758,207	16.5
13	Georgia	14.6	7.3	10.3	32.1	21.1	26.9	35.6	44.5	2,386,724	420,924	17.6
15	Hawaii........................	8.0	4.6	5.9	18.0	11.9	18.3	20.7	31.3	311,096	36,642	11.8
16	Idaho.........................	11.3	6.5	9.5	29.6	19.5	22.8	34.3	44.9	404,512	56,442	14.0
17	Illinois.......................	10.9	5.0	7.6	27.1	16.6	22.5	30.8	41.1	3,114,415	436,602	14.0
18	Indiana.......................	11.6	5.1	7.8	30.5	19.4	25.4	34.7	44.4	1,647,579	224,938	13.7
19	Iowa..........................	8.4	3.7	5.3	26.3	14.9	19.3	31.2	39.7	792,745	95,453	12.0
20	Kansas........................	9.4	4.5	7.1	26.3	15.1	19.1	31.0	40.1	727,902	73,421	10.1
21	Kentucky	14.6	7.4	10.4	34.4	22.7	30.1	38.8	49.8	1,131,310	200,706	17.7
22	Louisiana.....................	15.5	5.8	7.0	34.7	19.2	24.9	39.3	49.3	1,127,030	206,722	18.3
23	Maine.........................	9.5	4.7	7.2	26.9	17.2	22.2	31.2	39.9	345,776	57,323	16.6
24	Maryland......................	7.2	2.9	3.7	17.5	9.9	13.6	20.0	26.9	1,432,364	166,924	11.7
25	Massachusetts	8.4	3.3	4.2	22.7	12.1	19.2	26.2	36.1	1,606,383	200,880	12.5
26	Michigan	12.5	5.6	8.9	31.4	20.7	27.2	35.2	46.5	2,489,254	447,586	18.0
27	Minnesota	7.5	3.1	4.6	23.7	13.7	17.3	28.1	35.9	1,367,091	124,019	9.1
28	Mississippi	18.2	7.6	11.1	38.4	22.5	28.5	42.5	52.6	743,178	149,440	20.1
29	Missouri......................	11.6	5.5	7.9	29.4	18.9	24.4	33.1	42.6	1,527,728	229,350	15.0
30	Montana......................	10.5	5.4	8.1	29.1	17.6	23.6	34.6	44.1	255,929	29,503	11.5
31	Nebraska.....................	9.0	4.2	6.7	26.1	15.2	19.3	30.8	39.1	472,470	45,260	9.6
32	Nevada.......................	12.0	7.2	11.2	23.2	15.8	21.6	26.7	34.2	641,060	84,331	13.2
33	New Hampshire	5.7	2.5	3.5	17.8	9.2	11.6	21.4	29.9	346,775	27,949	8.1
34	New Jersey...................	8.2	3.7	4.9	20.7	12.8	19.5	23.6	33.6	2,203,456	201,173	9.1
35	New Mexico..................	16.6	9.2	13.8	33.2	22.8	26.8	37.3	46.8	494,555	89,040	18.0
36	New York.....................	12.2	6.3	9.1	25.3	15.7	22.9	28.6	38.7	4,594,587	737,665	16.1
37	North Carolina...............	13.2	6.2	9.3	31.7	21.3	28.0	35.1	44.4	2,467,843	397,605	16.1
38	North Dakota.................	7.4	3.1	4.3	25.2	13.9	16.6	31.1	38.6	176,378	14,767	8.4
39	Ohio..........................	11.8	4.8	7.5	30.8	19.2	25.6	34.9	45.7	2,920,189	462,392	15.8
40	Oklahoma.....................	12.8	6.5	9.6	30.8	18.1	22.3	35.9	45.1	959,015	145,503	15.2
41	Oregon........................	11.8	6.4	9.9	29.1	20.4	25.3	32.9	42.7	959,743	193,915	20.2
42	Pennsylvania..................	9.4	3.9	5.6	25.7	15.5	22.3	29.4	40.6	3,186,145	408,477	12.8
44	Rhode Island.................	10.2	4.4	6.5	23.8	12.6	18.7	27.7	37.9	257,316	39,397	15.3
45	South Carolina...............	14.2	6.1	9.2	33.3	20.7	26.5	37.2	47.0	1,199,885	206,700	17.2
46	South Dakota.................	9.3	3.8	5.6	28.2	18.5	23.3	32.9	38.9	210,494	24,649	11.7
47	Tennessee	13.6	6.7	10.2	32.0	21.1	27.9	35.7	46.8	1,646,360	305,140	18.5
48	Texas.........................	14.0	8.0	11.7	29.4	17.2	23.0	33.7	42.5	6,235,820	1,004,806	16.1
49	Utah..........................	9.7	6.1	8.3	25.3	16.8	19.5	29.1	37.1	667,046	66,724	10.0
50	Vermont	7.2	2.8	4.1	23.7	14.4	19.4	27.8	36.8	159,883	21,163	13.2
51	Virginia.......................	8.4	3.7	5.1	22.5	12.9	17.3	25.9	34.7	2,033,567	215,807	10.6
53	Washington	9.4	4.8	7.2	24.6	14.8	19.4	28.8	37.9	1,694,518	260,559	15.4
54	West Virginia	13.1	6.9	10.8	31.7	19.3	26.3	36.7	50.4	479,062	77,337	16.1
55	Wisconsin.....................	8.9	3.7	5.6	27.0	16.5	21.6	31.5	40.3	1,458,497	193,366	13.3
56	Wyoming......................	8.4	3.8	5.6	26.3	12.3	15.0	33.2	40.8	145,481	9,379	6.4

Table E-1: States—Income, Poverty, and Health Insurance—*Continued*

State FIPS code	State	Total married couple families	Household received Food Stamps/ SNAP in the past 12 months	Percent of married-couple families whose household received Food Stamps/ SNAP in the past 12 months	Number of workers in married-couple families who received Food Stamps/SNAP in the past 12 months				Number of workers in family as a percent of married-couple families who received Food Stamps/SNAP in the past 12 months			
					No workers	1 worker	2 workers:	3 or more workers:	No workers	1 worker	2 workers:	3 or more workers:
	United States...............	55,747,944	4,110,058	7.4	655,612	1,530,168	1,393,925	530,353	16.0	37.2	33.9	12.9
1	Alabama........................	877,131	73,924	8.4	13,795	29,099	24,733	6,297	18.7	39.4	33.5	8.5
2	Alaska..........................	124,654	7,664	6.1	775	2,681	2,775	1,433	10.1	35.0	36.2	18.7
4	Arizona........................	1,124,577	104,755	9.3	13,544	42,777	34,371	14,063	12.9	40.8	32.8	13.4
5	Arkansas......................	553,817	45,676	8.2	9,039	18,430	15,056	3,151	19.8	40.3	33.0	6.9
6	California.....................	6,122,335	401,157	6.6	46,445	160,443	127,074	67,195	11.6	40.0	31.7	16.8
8	Colorado	977,214	49,718	5.1	5,228	18,875	18,649	6,966	10.5	38.0	37.5	14.0
9	Connecticut..................	659,668	29,850	4.5	5,498	9,264	9,869	5,219	18.4	31.0	33.1	17.5
10	Delaware......................	162,724	10,933	6.7	1,184	3,739	3,895	2,115	10.8	34.2	35.6	19.3
11	District of Columbia........	60,812	4,003	6.6	733	1,437	1,375	458	18.3	35.9	34.3	11.4
12	Florida	3,316,161	312,035	9.4	52,896	114,459	105,810	38,870	17.0	36.7	33.9	12.5
13	Georgia	1,677,631	151,576	9.0	24,017	59,514	50,799	17,246	15.8	39.3	33.5	11.4
15	Hawaii	231,601	16,308	7.0	2,445	4,409	5,448	4,006	15.0	27.0	33.4	24.6
16	Idaho...........................	321,679	27,738	8.6	2,316	9,765	11,538	4,119	8.3	35.2	41.6	14.8
17	Illinois	2,289,104	154,383	6.7	22,250	55,970	53,222	22,941	14.4	36.3	34.5	14.9
18	Indiana	1,226,311	79,150	6.5	11,877	30,968	27,755	8,550	15.0	39.1	35.1	10.8
19	Iowa	626,297	35,218	5.6	4,876	11,063	14,340	4,939	13.8	31.4	40.7	14.0
20	Kansas	563,171	28,139	5.0	3,179	9,545	11,337	4,078	11.3	33.9	40.3	14.5
21	Kentucky	830,215	80,081	9.6	21,090	29,474	22,749	6,768	26.3	36.8	28.4	8.5
22	Louisiana	746,288	59,090	7.9	11,664	19,587	21,004	6,835	19.7	33.1	35.5	11.6
23	Maine	269,688	24,512	9.1	5,056	8,811	8,369	2,276	20.6	35.9	34.1	9.3
24	Maryland	1,012,523	51,913	5.1	7,156	16,293	19,511	8,953	13.8	31.4	37.6	17.2
25	Massachusetts	1,181,198	64,102	5.4	14,491	19,590	20,284	9,737	22.6	30.6	31.6	15.2
26	Michigan	1,824,333	160,847	8.8	28,985	61,371	51,640	18,851	18.0	38.2	32.1	11.7
27	Minnesota	1,073,564	42,271	3.9	5,916	14,228	16,346	5,781	14.0	33.7	38.7	13.7
28	Mississippi	486,734	44,223	9.1	7,511	16,867	15,516	4,329	17.0	38.1	35.1	9.8
29	Missouri........................	1,137,352	82,602	7.3	14,501	29,895	29,920	8,286	17.6	36.2	36.2	10.0
30	Montana.......................	200,808	11,502	5.7	1,409	4,071	4,435	1,587	12.3	35.4	38.6	13.8
31	Nebraska	369,775	15,516	4.2	1,827	5,494	6,106	2,089	11.8	35.4	39.4	13.5
32	Nevada	449,385	34,683	7.7	4,714	14,995	11,244	3,730	13.6	43.2	32.4	10.8
33	New Hampshire	273,749	10,494	3.8	1,840	3,346	3,668	1,640	17.5	31.9	35.0	15.6
34	New Jersey....................	1,615,471	66,792	4.1	11,708	23,572	21,126	10,386	17.5	35.3	31.6	15.5
35	New Mexico...................	343,336	33,225	9.7	5,321	13,667	9,905	4,332	16.0	41.1	29.8	13.0
36	New York......................	3,162,525	260,250	8.2	53,282	92,823	80,672	33,473	20.5	35.7	31.0	12.9
37	North Carolina...............	1,789,108	139,753	7.8	23,687	52,990	48,789	14,287	16.9	37.9	34.9	10.2
38	North Dakota.................	141,699	5,515	3.9	564	2,165	2,177	609	10.2	39.3	39.5	11.0
39	Ohio.............................	2,132,541	152,245	7.1	30,517	54,262	51,993	15,473	20.0	35.6	34.2	10.2
40	Oklahoma......................	707,880	55,797	7.9	8,627	21,239	19,841	6,090	15.5	38.1	35.6	10.9
41	Oregon.........................	732,053	89,351	12.2	12,275	30,805	33,780	12,491	13.7	34.5	37.8	14.0
42	Pennsylvania	2,377,594	133,200	5.6	27,502	46,489	43,395	15,814	20.6	34.9	32.6	11.9
44	Rhode Island.................	180,743	12,686	7.0	1,892	5,376	3,350	2,068	14.9	42.4	26.4	16.3
45	South Carolina...............	843,305	66,728	7.9	12,300	27,219	20,994	6,215	18.4	40.8	31.5	9.3
46	South Dakota.................	163,039	7,799	4.8	812	2,163	3,634	1,190	10.4	27.7	46.6	15.3
47	Tennessee	1,203,173	120,172	10.0	22,998	45,231	38,991	12,952	19.1	37.6	32.4	10.8
48	Texas...........................	4,486,257	419,766	9.4	49,813	166,531	145,467	57,955	11.9	39.7	34.7	13.8
49	Utah	541,105	32,793	6.1	2,163	12,224	12,647	5,759	6.6	37.3	38.6	17.6
50	Vermont	126,295	8,687	6.9	1,551	2,855	3,148	1,133	17.9	32.9	36.2	13.0
51	Virginia	1,527,465	74,741	4.9	11,523	25,741	26,598	10,879	15.4	34.4	35.6	14.6
53	Washington	1,300,793	112,931	8.7	15,109	39,311	42,271	16,240	13.4	34.8	37.4	14.4
54	West Virginia	359,823	32,318	9.0	9,052	13,274	8,122	1,870	28.0	41.1	25.1	5.8
55	Wisconsin	1,127,742	68,224	6.0	8,436	24,790	26,683	8,315	12.4	36.3	39.1	12.2
56	Wyoming.......................	115,498	3,022	2.6	223	981	1,504	314	7.4	32.5	49.8	10.4

Table E-1: States—Income, Poverty, and Health Insurance—*Continued*

State FIPS code	State	Total other families	Household received Food Stamps/ SNAP in the past 12 months	Percent of other families whose household received Food Stamps/ SNAP in the past 12 months	Number of workers in other families who received Food Stamps/SNAP in the past 12 months				Number of workers in family as a percent of other families who received Food Stamps/SNAP in the past 12 months			
					No workers	1 worker	2 workers:	3 or more workers:	No workers	1 worker	2 workers:	3 or more workers:
	United States..............	20,696,978	6,902,297	33.3	1,898,726	3,756,111	973,994	273,466	27.5	54.4	14.1	4.0
1	Alabama........................	359,435	144,093	40.1	46,096	76,450	17,534	4,013	32.0	53.1	12.2	2.8
2	Alaska...........................	42,899	10,695	24.9	1,858	6,382	1,651	804	17.4	59.7	15.4	7.5
4	Arizona..........................	436,078	147,222	33.8	38,819	80,962	21,172	6,269	26.4	55.0	14.4	4.3
5	Arkansas........................	201,527	76,388	37.9	23,126	42,236	8,901	2,125	30.3	55.3	11.7	2.8
6	California.......................	2,480,400	567,963	22.9	165,992	282,043	87,027	32,901	29.2	49.7	15.3	5.8
8	Colorado........................	293,966	72,644	24.7	16,267	41,223	12,064	3,090	22.4	56.7	16.6	4.3
9	Connecticut....................	235,060	73,513	31.3	20,472	39,537	10,713	2,791	27.8	53.8	14.6	3.8
10	Delaware	63,786	21,884	34.3	4,704	12,560	3,798	822	21.5	57.4	17.4	3.8
11	District of Columbia.......	53,672	22,087	41.2	7,432	10,358	3,513	784	33.6	46.9	15.9	3.5
12	Florida..........................	1,277,845	446,172	34.9	118,587	238,093	70,150	19,342	26.6	53.4	15.7	4.3
13	Georgia..........................	709,093	269,348	38.0	77,626	146,572	35,961	9,189	28.8	54.4	13.4	3.4
15	Hawaii	79,495	20,334	25.6	4,870	10,207	3,130	2,127	24.0	50.2	15.4	10.5
16	Idaho............................	82,833	28,704	34.7	6,152	17,557	3,827	1,168	21.4	61.2	13.3	4.1
17	Illinois...........................	825,311	282,219	34.2	71,671	155,182	42,411	12,955	25.4	55.0	15.0	4.6
18	Indiana	421,268	145,788	34.6	40,942	83,712	17,770	3,364	28.1	57.4	12.2	2.3
19	Iowa..............................	166,448	60,235	36.2	11,903	37,310	8,865	2,157	19.8	61.9	14.7	3.6
20	Kansas...........................	164,731	45,282	27.5	10,004	27,081	6,733	1,464	22.1	59.8	14.9	3.2
21	Kentucky........................	301,095	120,625	40.1	43,780	61,585	12,614	2,646	36.3	51.1	10.5	2.2
22	Louisiana.......................	380,742	147,632	38.8	41,901	82,576	19,043	4,112	28.4	55.9	12.9	2.8
23	Maine............................	76,088	32,811	43.1	9,254	18,376	4,299	882	28.2	56.0	13.1	2.7
24	Maryland........................	419,841	115,011	27.4	26,519	62,051	20,029	6,412	23.1	54.0	17.4	5.6
25	Massachusetts	425,185	136,778	32.2	42,821	68,368	19,306	6,283	31.3	50.0	14.1	4.6
26	Michigan	664,921	286,739	43.1	84,346	155,791	37,503	9,099	29.4	54.3	13.1	3.2
27	Minnesota......................	293,527	81,748	27.9	18,871	49,002	10,774	3,101	23.1	59.9	13.2	3.8
28	Mississippi.....................	256,444	105,217	41.0	33,420	56,107	12,633	3,057	31.8	53.3	12.0	2.9
29	Missouri.........................	390,376	146,748	37.6	39,830	83,639	19,138	4,141	27.1	57.0	13.0	2.8
30	Montana........................	55,121	18,001	32.7	3,241	11,550	2,138	1,072	18.0	64.2	11.9	6.0
31	Nebraska........................	102,695	29,744	29.0	5,457	18,901	4,577	809	18.3	63.5	15.4	2.7
32	Nevada..........................	191,675	49,648	25.9	13,888	26,323	7,775	1,662	28.0	53.0	15.7	3.3
33	New Hampshire	73,026	17,455	23.9	4,555	10,045	2,130	725	26.1	57.5	12.2	4.2
34	New Jersey.....................	587,985	134,381	22.9	40,606	68,445	19,255	6,075	30.2	50.9	14.3	4.5
35	New Mexico....................	151,219	55,815	36.9	13,854	31,227	8,512	2,222	24.8	55.9	15.3	4.0
36	New York........................	1,432,062	477,415	33.3	143,371	240,014	68,968	25,062	30.0	50.3	14.4	5.2
37	North Carolina...............	678,735	257,852	38.0	71,685	143,617	34,847	7,703	27.8	55.7	13.5	3.0
38	North Dakota.................	34,679	9,252	26.7	1,648	6,446	957	201	17.8	69.7	10.3	2.2
39	Ohio..............................	787,648	310,147	39.4	92,251	172,799	37,049	8,048	29.7	55.7	11.9	2.6
40	Oklahoma.......................	251,135	89,706	35.7	24,732	50,970	11,627	2,377	27.6	56.8	13.0	2.6
41	Oregon..........................	227,690	104,564	45.9	25,882	57,613	17,123	3,946	24.8	55.1	16.4	3.8
42	Pennsylvania..................	808,551	275,277	34.0	85,941	146,950	34,338	8,048	31.2	53.4	12.5	2.9
44	Rhode Island..................	76,573	26,711	34.9	8,025	13,919	3,512	1,255	30.0	52.1	13.1	4.7
45	South Carolina...............	356,580	139,972	39.3	41,923	76,119	17,351	4,579	30.0	54.4	12.4	3.3
46	South Dakota.................	47,455	16,850	35.5	3,450	10,250	2,358	792	20.5	60.8	14.0	4.7
47	Tennessee......................	443,187	184,968	41.7	53,850	99,676	25,046	6,396	29.1	53.9	13.5	3.5
48	Texas.............................	1,749,563	585,040	33.4	129,781	335,170	92,497	27,592	22.2	57.3	15.8	4.7
49	Utah..............................	125,941	33,931	26.9	6,503	19,569	5,855	2,004	19.2	57.7	17.3	5.9
50	Vermont.........................	33,588	12,476	37.1	3,609	7,164	1,419	284	28.9	57.4	11.4	2.3
51	Virginia..........................	506,102	141,066	27.9	34,888	77,143	22,734	6,301	24.7	54.7	16.1	4.5
53	Washington	393,725	147,628	37.5	36,398	84,253	21,105	5,872	24.7	57.1	14.3	4.0
54	West Virginia.................	119,239	45,019	37.8	16,960	22,653	4,545	861	37.7	50.3	10.1	1.9
55	Wisconsin......................	330,755	125,142	37.8	27,910	76,222	16,774	4,236	22.3	60.9	13.4	3.4
56	Wyoming.......................	29,983	6,357	21.2	1,055	4,113	943	246	16.6	64.7	14.8	3.9

Table E-1: States—Income, Poverty, and Health Insurance—*Continued*

State FIPS code	State	Total civilian noninstitutionalized population	Health insurance coverage of population in family households								
			Population in married-couple family households								
			Total in married couple families	All relatives in married-couple families				Non-relatives in married-couple families			
				Total relatives in married couple families	With private health insurance coverage	With public health insurance coverage	No health insurance coverage	Total non-relatives in married couple families	With private health insurance coverage	With public health insurance coverage	No health insurance coverage
	United States...............	308,858,098	182,438,098	180,979,252	134,442,635	46,632,202	20,322,631	1,458,846	529,609	493,968	501,016
1	Alabama........................	4,737,268	2,744,504	2,729,488	2,085,369	751,220	263,209	15,016	4,943	6,480	4,453
2	Alaska..........................	706,544	421,961	416,668	305,785	93,031	59,457	5,293	2,017	1,483	2,015
4	Arizona.........................	6,441,287	3,693,704	3,662,856	2,487,228	1,122,155	508,689	30,848	9,211	12,493	10,539
5	Arkansas.......................	2,896,439	1,718,822	1,707,554	1,160,512	545,311	221,739	11,268	3,384	4,476	3,988
6	California......................	37,487,065	22,260,411	21,957,761	14,775,852	5,811,300	3,196,316	302,650	110,982	88,453	114,043
8	Colorado.......................	5,098,744	3,114,661	3,087,820	2,358,779	705,340	336,436	26,841	10,510	9,016	8,520
9	Connecticut....................	3,536,463	2,130,204	2,115,433	1,735,623	483,053	128,585	14,771	6,629	4,614	4,175
10	Delaware	902,314	520,138	515,514	408,229	149,367	35,991	4,624	1,625	1,728	1,441
11	District of Columbia........	622,605	187,890	183,260	150,055	50,698	8,018	4,630	3,528	938	619
12	Florida.........................	19,010,848	10,613,267	10,518,833	6,953,282	3,289,264	1,659,482	94,434	28,704	28,867	41,169
13	Georgia	9,710,901	5,587,037	5,546,316	3,996,637	1,317,042	781,141	40,721	10,917	12,733	18,712
15	Hawaii..........................	1,337,598	827,901	810,128	665,519	212,706	41,155	17,773	10,997	6,131	1,823
16	Idaho...........................	1,577,379	1,052,288	1,042,381	763,656	265,961	138,988	9,907	2,980	4,850	2,792
17	Illinois..........................	12,690,730	7,603,403	7,560,653	5,793,562	1,858,452	689,270	42,750	16,143	13,702	14,533
18	Indiana.........................	6,441,965	3,897,434	3,871,288	3,002,604	917,670	398,618	26,146	8,815	8,870	9,562
19	Iowa............................	3,031,378	1,895,869	1,887,073	1,572,272	472,725	105,683	8,796	3,499	3,353	2,486
20	Kansas..........................	2,824,697	1,773,412	1,762,815	1,416,339	396,968	156,187	10,597	3,867	4,574	2,802
21	Kentucky	4,295,357	2,580,707	2,563,943	1,907,926	705,133	264,044	16,764	4,311	8,448	5,021
22	Louisiana	4,498,089	2,386,292	2,373,569	1,722,588	633,675	280,943	12,723	3,699	4,954	4,711
23	Maine...........................	1,314,314	786,948	780,689	590,285	253,200	57,344	6,259	2,326	3,265	1,300
24	Maryland.......................	5,790,545	3,348,591	3,315,541	2,747,514	715,650	237,982	33,050	15,917	8,644	9,984
25	Massachusetts................	6,568,640	3,813,028	3,785,020	3,183,893	963,200	91,835	28,008	14,228	12,150	3,323
26	Michigan.......................	9,773,359	5,765,923	5,733,734	4,579,953	1,552,490	430,834	32,189	10,850	15,108	8,471
27	Minnesota	5,323,891	3,341,406	3,321,950	2,812,875	726,122	180,073	19,456	8,619	7,544	4,165
28	Mississippi.....................	2,918,229	1,552,916	1,543,599	1,062,543	462,912	201,875	9,317	2,246	4,195	3,297
29	Missouri........................	5,913,412	3,530,501	3,508,887	2,726,982	875,064	337,443	21,614	6,438	9,016	6,775
30	Montana........................	990,602	602,860	598,054	432,569	164,935	82,043	4,806	1,728	2,097	1,305
31	Nebraska.......................	1,826,997	1,148,648	1,140,953	931,265	251,174	91,442	7,695	3,236	3,285	1,930
32	Nevada	2,719,575	1,524,973	1,506,612	1,062,386	345,575	255,880	18,361	6,259	5,306	7,316
33	New Hampshire	1,306,205	828,567	822,455	691,400	177,535	55,581	6,112	2,589	2,227	1,750
34	New Jersey.....................	8,759,905	5,457,721	5,419,446	4,337,879	1,133,518	484,263	38,275	15,262	10,050	14,543
35	New Mexico....................	2,047,997	1,128,148	1,119,456	702,994	378,155	174,907	8,692	2,638	3,669	2,711
36	New York.......................	19,323,884	10,695,356	10,589,109	7,896,596	3,014,597	833,253	106,247	37,839	35,225	37,902
37	North Carolina................	9,550,684	5,540,976	5,509,831	4,046,005	1,468,721	666,161	31,145	8,983	11,350	11,962
38	North Dakota..................	688,158	421,434	419,196	364,513	85,213	25,533	2,238	836	944	496
39	Ohio............................	11,384,722	6,654,339	6,620,087	5,285,975	1,632,304	510,877	34,252	11,393	14,660	9,781
40	Oklahoma......................	3,736,108	2,237,352	2,221,964	1,563,478	619,523	315,727	15,388	4,050	6,531	5,470
41	Oregon.........................	3,861,618	2,288,141	2,259,844	1,669,679	633,814	252,213	28,297	10,686	9,928	9,032
42	Pennsylvania..................	12,555,282	7,441,494	7,402,318	6,041,668	1,852,307	535,758	39,176	15,623	16,075	9,972
44	Rhode Island..................	1,035,491	564,233	560,449	452,023	141,393	40,771	3,784	1,566	1,236	1,246
45	South Carolina................	4,624,813	2,605,126	2,590,934	1,900,191	734,570	312,266	14,192	4,411	4,549	5,785
46	South Dakota..................	816,471	494,870	492,021	404,458	118,490	34,749	2,849	905	1,125	968
47	Tennessee......................	6,348,051	3,759,440	3,738,552	2,770,765	1,047,734	385,975	20,888	6,675	8,101	6,984
48	Texas...........................	25,573,996	15,568,572	15,470,900	10,048,167	3,723,006	3,000,950	97,672	30,853	32,032	38,643
49	Utah............................	2,829,593	2,030,260	2,013,270	1,595,648	356,345	232,252	16,990	8,704	3,622	5,080
50	Vermont........................	620,244	369,957	366,972	282,922	121,266	16,698	2,985	1,024	1,458	652
51	Virginia.........................	7,974,644	4,890,301	4,847,543	3,981,756	991,340	430,961	42,758	20,270	9,158	15,591
53	Washington....................	6,789,761	4,142,087	4,099,363	3,150,858	1,021,182	420,331	42,724	17,724	13,876	13,387
54	West Virginia	1,826,219	1,089,590	1,082,167	785,536	346,108	117,982	7,423	1,962	3,219	2,630
55	Wisconsin	5,650,835	3,450,967	3,434,146	2,798,301	865,884	198,272	16,821	5,990	7,418	4,234
56	Wyoming.......................	566,182	353,468	350,837	279,741	77,804	36,449	2,631	1,018	742	927

State FIPS code	State	Total in other families: Male householder, no spouse present:	Health insurance coverage of population in family households — Population in other family households — In other families: male householder, no spouse present — All relatives in other families: male householder, no spouse present — Total relatives in other families: Male householder, no spouse present	With private health insurance coverage	With public health insurance coverage	No health insurance coverage	All non-relatives in other families: male householder, no spouse present — Total non-relatives in other families: - Male householder, no spouse present	With private health insurance coverage	With public health insurance coverage	No health insurance coverage
	United States...............	19,433,713	17,124,414	8,290,762	5,695,946	4,211,655	2,309,299	860,000	644,120	861,911
1	Alabama........................	261,328	239,051	117,002	83,903	55,858	22,277	9,036	5,316	8,487
2	Alaska...........................	56,262	48,032	21,217	14,947	14,393	8,230	2,993	1,940	3,475
4	Arizona..........................	470,354	410,869	185,640	137,962	107,305	59,485	20,228	19,902	20,534
5	Arkansas........................	172,952	155,068	66,057	62,562	37,130	17,884	5,800	4,723	7,968
6	California......................	2,893,784	2,535,004	1,122,156	849,024	676,596	358,780	124,316	95,918	144,983
8	Colorado	289,926	254,929	134,755	69,503	64,054	34,997	15,465	8,914	11,619
9	Connecticut....................	191,606	169,629	96,487	54,739	31,571	21,977	10,069	6,432	5,952
10	Delaware	60,024	51,796	29,342	19,641	6,996	8,228	3,740	3,480	1,448
11	District of Columbia........	35,933	32,858	17,350	15,468	4,270	3,075	1,583	1,490	307
12	Florida	1,258,818	1,111,116	456,053	365,521	352,439	147,702	49,241	35,969	65,855
13	Georgia	617,295	549,411	245,274	166,282	168,010	67,884	22,131	13,580	33,645
15	Hawaii	93,048	83,516	54,835	30,289	8,362	9,532	5,952	2,983	1,177
16	Idaho............................	86,146	75,575	36,475	24,088	19,950	10,571	2,908	2,428	5,410
17	Illinois..........................	764,766	674,940	327,978	225,709	159,701	89,826	32,117	30,848	28,972
18	Indiana..........................	381,980	331,454	170,957	106,033	75,091	50,526	18,983	13,973	18,779
19	Iowa.............................	158,690	138,048	81,906	44,832	22,104	20,642	9,771	5,614	5,961
20	Kansas...........................	156,011	137,981	79,725	37,713	28,871	18,030	8,462	3,125	6,732
21	Kentucky........................	264,857	234,080	112,307	86,032	51,478	30,777	10,570	9,224	11,805
22	Louisiana	303,075	267,683	117,345	100,787	66,844	35,392	11,437	11,114	14,428
23	Maine............................	74,804	62,590	29,668	26,668	11,074	12,214	5,105	5,425	2,125
24	Maryland	364,013	316,486	179,552	92,624	65,336	47,527	19,182	11,632	17,649
25	Massachusetts	337,201	298,041	176,561	125,041	24,264	39,160	18,560	17,919	4,145
26	Michigan	574,713	503,374	253,315	193,871	98,350	71,339	26,369	28,164	19,352
27	Minnesota	293,105	252,497	149,549	73,861	45,198	40,608	18,118	12,799	10,499
28	Mississippi.....................	182,188	164,400	73,078	64,484	39,377	17,788	5,906	4,863	7,885
29	Missouri.........................	330,128	286,682	155,410	87,695	62,040	43,446	18,944	11,292	14,327
30	Montana........................	57,242	51,081	24,403	15,720	14,464	6,161	2,271	869	3,197
31	Nebraska	98,708	85,668	49,947	23,732	16,951	13,040	6,161	2,480	4,736
32	Nevada	225,083	198,521	99,941	46,853	61,525	26,562	10,019	4,206	12,846
33	New Hampshire...............	68,344	58,574	32,304	19,060	11,108	9,770	4,242	2,369	3,493
34	New Jersey.....................	538,305	474,414	242,766	133,809	126,205	63,891	22,943	13,680	28,563
35	New Mexico....................	157,234	140,289	60,528	55,020	34,299	16,945	5,747	4,989	6,485
36	New York.......................	1,256,947	1,117,709	542,022	417,905	235,876	139,238	54,314	45,124	44,298
37	North Carolina...............	575,817	505,261	220,322	183,553	134,016	70,556	19,815	18,764	33,159
38	North Dakota.................	36,846	32,410	20,235	7,637	6,831	4,436	2,493	883	1,103
39	Ohio.............................	652,031	570,715	298,463	203,427	113,887	81,316	31,554	29,157	23,203
40	Oklahoma......................	245,146	217,971	98,853	70,987	61,475	27,175	8,212	6,291	12,962
41	Oregon..........................	230,696	197,523	96,538	67,694	47,307	33,173	13,675	8,920	11,590
42	Pennsylvania	701,725	621,661	352,288	219,925	108,894	80,064	35,748	27,130	19,916
44	Rhode Island..................	64,157	56,848	30,108	19,637	11,835	7,309	3,109	2,383	2,033
45	South Carolina...............	280,608	252,406	116,967	86,610	67,600	28,202	8,700	8,987	10,953
46	South Dakota..................	50,488	43,865	22,545	15,198	9,226	6,623	2,817	1,705	2,285
47	Tennessee......................	369,420	325,820	155,702	115,664	76,192	43,600	14,133	14,661	15,707
48	Texas............................	1,662,339	1,490,537	622,170	434,304	502,291	171,802	56,530	30,059	88,054
49	Utah.............................	140,659	122,069	70,381	27,157	31,322	18,590	8,056	3,068	7,743
50	Vermont	31,651	27,140	12,100	13,639	3,578	4,511	1,808	2,143	688
51	Virginia.........................	437,454	387,607	225,721	102,604	87,048	49,847	21,728	9,804	19,489
53	Washington....................	407,641	349,138	182,485	108,328	82,205	58,503	23,620	15,868	20,913
54	West Virginia	115,729	102,310	50,631	40,321	19,901	13,419	4,751	4,479	4,470
55	Wisconsin	321,351	280,102	155,351	100,489	45,078	41,249	18,165	15,765	8,702
56	Wyoming........................	35,085	29,665	17,997	7,394	5,879	5,420	2,403	1,269	1,804

State FIPS code	State	Total civilian noninstitutionalized population	Total in other families: Female householder, no spouse present:	All relatives in other families: female householder, no spouse present				All non-relatives in other families: female householder, no spouse present			
				Total relatives in other families: Female householder, no spouse present	With private health insurance coverage	With public health insurance coverage	No health insurance coverage	Total non-relatives in other families: female householder, no spouse present	With private health insurance coverage	With public health insurance coverage	No health insurance coverage
	United States...............	308,858,098	52,981,252	49,737,443	21,046,562	22,643,938	9,407,870	3,243,809	1,227,608	753,402	1,356,134
1	Alabama.........................	4,737,268	967,248	929,258	365,374	453,219	178,559	37,990	13,465	8,404	17,318
2	Alaska............................	706,544	105,078	95,978	40,815	36,366	24,617	9,100	3,041	2,137	4,251
4	Arizona..........................	6,441,287	1,155,433	1,074,848	426,840	493,361	216,754	80,585	26,390	22,818	33,211
5	Arkansas........................	2,896,439	513,667	489,796	170,090	246,983	102,232	23,871	8,119	4,511	11,769
6	California.......................	37,487,065	6,500,533	6,011,706	2,535,875	2,571,214	1,240,385	488,827	174,816	120,519	207,563
8	Colorado........................	5,098,744	693,077	645,968	302,166	256,722	126,079	47,109	20,199	8,695	19,437
9	Connecticut....................	3,536,463	584,036	552,087	254,368	272,984	64,490	31,949	13,583	9,885	9,668
10	Delaware........................	902,314	164,884	153,247	73,970	75,415	17,367	11,637	5,135	4,386	2,811
11	District of Columbia........	622,605	155,190	149,368	62,611	92,178	10,402	5,822	2,979	2,212	834
12	Florida...........................	19,010,848	3,617,650	3,394,458	1,320,858	1,402,776	855,684	223,192	71,201	49,822	108,223
13	Georgia..........................	9,710,901	1,960,173	1,866,611	743,873	773,048	453,087	93,562	30,975	16,963	48,936
15	Hawaii	1,337,598	219,321	202,490	125,094	83,579	15,842	16,831	9,798	5,555	2,731
16	Idaho.............................	1,577,379	191,183	177,359	81,154	74,631	36,490	13,824	6,006	2,339	5,864
17	Illinois...........................	12,690,730	2,142,113	2,023,735	811,711	995,584	345,319	118,378	44,125	26,205	50,200
18	Indiana	6,441,965	1,024,117	955,984	400,674	434,663	184,440	68,133	26,178	13,328	30,123
19	Iowa..............................	3,031,378	371,423	344,602	164,572	169,948	43,994	26,821	13,384	5,476	8,773
20	Kansas...........................	2,824,697	384,446	359,258	174,867	142,452	67,582	25,188	11,941	4,160	9,773
21	Kentucky	4,295,357	710,254	667,203	264,935	322,059	129,179	43,051	15,263	9,707	19,183
22	Louisiana........................	4,498,089	1,041,267	996,327	339,744	505,050	213,543	44,940	16,796	8,681	20,844
23	Maine............................	1,314,314	162,637	147,239	59,732	85,582	15,859	15,398	5,345	6,196	4,553
24	Maryland........................	5,790,545	1,095,591	1,029,053	551,921	425,296	127,440	66,538	30,720	15,562	22,840
25	Massachusetts	6,568,640	1,037,430	975,271	476,651	535,666	50,725	62,159	30,857	23,636	10,494
26	Michigan	9,773,359	1,657,016	1,555,489	646,509	812,128	237,446	101,527	35,429	31,398	38,235
27	Minnesota	5,323,891	657,590	605,323	298,825	276,277	76,510	52,267	23,020	15,399	15,044
28	Mississippi.....................	2,918,229	734,843	704,688	237,378	353,676	151,831	30,155	10,321	5,833	14,510
29	Missouri.........................	5,913,412	955,256	893,930	388,452	394,514	170,316	61,326	25,159	11,520	25,998
30	Montana.........................	990,602	124,200	114,875	47,292	47,073	28,493	9,325	3,597	1,582	4,376
31	Nebraska........................	1,826,997	233,250	216,522	102,776	92,088	36,334	16,728	7,102	3,194	6,767
32	Nevada	2,719,575	484,357	447,508	215,566	140,621	117,891	36,849	15,454	5,145	17,667
33	New Hampshire	1,306,205	160,680	146,685	75,818	58,506	23,612	13,995	6,928	2,409	4,981
34	New Jersey......................	8,759,905	1,472,611	1,391,515	680,783	549,582	251,734	81,096	32,815	14,752	35,523
35	New Mexico.....................	2,047,997	416,032	391,094	126,988	197,972	90,136	24,938	8,029	5,625	11,746
36	New York........................	19,323,884	3,678,564	3,478,030	1,584,653	1,738,919	430,850	200,534	79,977	59,891	67,872
37	North Carolina................	9,550,684	1,741,534	1,651,100	648,825	771,303	333,048	90,434	30,449	17,380	44,972
38	North Dakota..................	688,158	69,732	64,023	33,179	25,378	10,406	5,709	3,122	564	2,145
39	Ohio..............................	11,384,722	1,914,815	1,794,145	755,240	919,742	263,057	120,670	44,200	34,303	45,369
40	Oklahoma.......................	3,736,108	609,793	570,798	216,050	261,789	132,897	38,995	14,147	7,798	18,000
41	Oregon...........................	3,861,618	534,287	485,065	218,045	218,113	88,250	49,222	19,261	10,877	20,708
42	Pennsylvania...................	12,555,282	1,994,121	1,874,978	868,781	937,320	245,713	119,143	50,978	30,655	41,459
44	Rhode Island..................	1,035,491	183,741	172,547	82,727	79,813	24,337	11,194	5,562	2,541	3,387
45	South Carolina................	4,624,813	956,139	910,914	347,630	429,750	190,625	45,225	15,014	9,266	22,197
46	South Dakota.................	816,471	108,954	100,752	41,334	47,211	19,760	8,202	3,623	1,248	3,606
47	Tennessee	6,348,051	1,127,569	1,066,887	426,849	536,775	179,758	60,682	20,249	14,086	27,732
48	Texas.............................	25,573,996	4,693,379	4,444,284	1,646,138	1,833,542	1,190,685	249,095	86,821	37,722	129,876
49	Utah	2,829,593	319,111	298,622	152,290	100,516	66,672	20,489	8,277	3,682	8,977
50	Vermont.........................	620,244	70,256	63,834	26,662	38,798	4,484	6,422	2,468	2,728	1,392
51	Virginia..........................	7,974,644	1,258,336	1,182,772	609,453	443,178	212,815	75,564	33,303	12,099	32,324
53	Washington	6,789,761	924,933	844,538	394,985	356,909	161,464	80,395	31,703	17,113	34,220
54	West Virginia	1,826,219	280,573	261,411	99,544	134,107	51,142	19,162	6,041	5,729	8,113
55	Wisconsin.......................	5,650,835	753,006	698,629	296,666	373,853	82,887	54,377	22,181	17,057	16,952
56	Wyoming........................	566,182	69,823	64,639	29,229	25,709	14,648	5,184	2,062	609	2,587

Table E-1: States—Income, Poverty, and Health Insurance—*Continued*

State FIPS code	State	Total population in non-family households and other living arrangements:	Householder living alone				Householder not living alone			
			Total non-family householders living alone	With private health insurance coverage	With public health insurance coverage	No health insurance coverage	Total non-family householders not living alone	With private health insurance coverage	With public health insurance coverage	No health insurance coverage
	United States......	54,005,035	31,993,176	20,820,885	14,793,753	4,078,763	7,169,956	4,850,681	1,293,037	1,533,905
1	Alabama..........	764,188	524,604	334,494	262,521	62,942	74,195	46,952	14,821	17,576
2	Alaska..........	123,243	63,653	37,694	22,117	13,955	17,885	11,975	2,523	4,469
4	Arizona..........	1,121,796	651,916	402,669	297,827	97,603	166,910	107,611	38,475	35,953
5	Arkansas..........	490,998	317,778	180,510	163,806	47,303	56,386	32,848	11,810	15,428
6	California..........	5,832,337	3,053,521	1,977,808	1,338,818	387,498	910,705	621,141	160,967	193,054
8	Colorado..........	1,001,080	558,661	375,930	214,674	80,502	156,274	110,603	21,244	32,963
9	Connecticut..........	630,617	376,177	253,055	188,412	35,007	76,527	55,350	14,581	12,617
10	Delaware..........	157,268	88,873	63,998	44,581	7,004	21,469	15,030	5,225	3,218
11	District of Columbia.......	243,592	119,527	91,933	40,160	7,169	33,537	29,246	3,870	1,868
12	Florida..........	3,521,113	2,097,966	1,240,651	1,033,642	333,598	468,709	276,085	108,610	128,306
13	Georgia	1,546,396	942,070	597,053	378,629	152,903	188,790	116,459	28,562	53,989
15	Hawaii	197,328	104,962	76,703	47,595	8,064	28,774	21,149	6,719	3,899
16	Idaho	247,762	141,408	87,992	68,201	22,604	37,235	24,252	6,192	9,730
17	Illinois	2,180,448	1,376,502	939,420	592,034	174,111	271,329	194,034	39,250	54,356
18	Indiana	1,138,434	692,654	452,079	320,599	96,641	141,626	93,657	23,815	33,259
19	Iowa	605,396	355,356	251,327	176,011	32,768	78,802	59,184	12,755	11,801
20	Kansas	510,828	314,849	217,338	143,554	38,135	64,920	46,397	8,538	13,706
21	Kentucky	739,539	474,110	285,603	244,053	61,915	87,162	54,410	16,524	22,232
22	Louisiana	767,455	496,149	288,883	225,191	83,451	90,737	54,069	16,972	25,062
23	Maine	289,925	161,353	92,412	89,657	21,127	45,314	27,699	11,167	10,116
24	Maryland	982,350	587,134	439,039	247,547	49,810	127,164	97,327	21,620	18,940
25	Massachusetts	1,380,981	728,666	504,785	386,182	28,089	192,458	151,612	39,526	13,851
26	Michigan	1,775,707	1,104,293	749,866	548,883	134,946	221,266	147,663	46,215	46,272
27	Minnesota	1,031,790	597,596	425,912	282,051	52,117	144,979	108,542	24,798	20,470
28	Mississippi	448,282	298,143	167,078	152,691	44,081	44,199	24,493	10,380	12,699
29	Missouri..........	1,097,527	680,800	438,131	321,889	86,870	142,951	98,603	24,711	28,824
30	Montana..........	206,300	121,799	74,341	59,655	19,642	27,110	18,170	4,370	6,444
31	Nebraska	346,391	211,435	147,433	93,317	26,426	44,756	33,298	6,059	8,018
32	Nevada	485,162	276,569	170,071	110,522	47,626	76,513	46,815	15,306	20,314
33	New Hampshire	248,614	132,023	87,796	62,268	16,236	39,202	28,629	6,600	6,859
34	New Jersey..........	1,291,268	821,203	557,293	395,956	87,632	155,510	107,957	26,936	33,049
35	New Mexico..........	346,583	218,961	124,930	107,166	34,501	45,653	27,612	10,530	11,385
36	New York..........	3,693,017	2,147,453	1,393,318	1,044,152	203,473	468,987	332,799	89,008	80,610
37	North Carolina	1,692,357	1,031,393	660,700	469,940	147,827	211,009	136,803	34,019	53,546
38	North Dakota	160,146	90,757	66,745	37,670	10,856	23,579	19,038	2,112	3,401
39	Ohio..........	2,163,537	1,365,076	883,780	651,098	173,687	264,890	177,513	49,892	56,713
40	Oklahoma..........	643,817	406,199	247,646	194,751	63,668	77,482	46,051	13,625	22,484
41	Oregon..........	808,494	425,425	275,733	207,312	56,733	130,707	87,169	24,329	29,827
42	Pennsylvania	2,417,942	1,469,335	1,017,543	749,146	136,324	288,829	210,900	57,366	44,585
44	Rhode Island..........	223,360	123,731	80,702	61,167	12,914	29,025	20,042	4,936	5,873
45	South Carolina..........	782,940	488,770	299,821	231,800	76,735	89,956	56,007	15,562	24,436
46	South Dakota..........	162,159	94,998	64,782	43,354	11,344	20,171	14,386	3,380	3,979
47	Tennessee	1,091,622	703,266	436,374	325,923	101,808	128,317	80,365	26,515	30,830
48	Texas..........	3,649,706	2,237,639	1,400,201	878,175	381,240	480,773	304,390	70,392	131,934
49	Utah	339,563	175,166	116,343	76,327	23,062	48,483	33,239	5,343	11,872
50	Vermont	148,380	72,691	44,200	41,765	5,371	23,907	15,442	6,549	3,542
51	Virginia	1,388,553	794,958	583,578	334,405	81,842	186,718	140,242	26,298	33,193
53	Washington	1,315,100	726,811	491,388	318,344	89,391	206,813	142,221	36,568	43,941
54	West Virginia	340,327	223,688	132,114	124,147	29,782	36,894	21,110	9,634	9,180
55	Wisconsin	1,125,511	664,296	451,949	317,789	71,041	158,487	113,519	25,617	29,206
56	Wyoming..........	107,806	60,813	39,741	26,279	9,389	15,882	10,573	2,221	4,026

State FIPS code	State	Other living arrangements in non-family households — Total population with other living arrangements	With private health insurance coverage	With public health insurance coverage	No health insurance coverage	Total population in households	Percent with health insurance	Type of health insurance (some have both) — Percent with private health insurance	Percent with public health insurance	Married-couple families, percent	Male householder or female householder families, no spouse present	Nonfamily households
	United States..............	14,841,903	9,185,336	2,852,712	3,413,591	308,858,098	85.2	65.2	31.0	88.6	78.1	83.3
1	Alabama..........................	165,389	99,736	29,593	42,636	4,737,268	86.3	64.9	34.1	90.2	78.8	83.9
2	Alaska............................	41,705	23,843	7,060	12,978	706,544	80.2	63.6	25.7	85.4	71.0	74.5
4	Arizona..........................	302,970	168,188	73,411	77,784	6,441,287	82.8	59.5	34.4	85.9	76.8	81.2
5	Arkansas........................	116,834	64,605	24,753	32,019	2,896,439	83.4	58.4	36.9	86.9	76.8	80.7
6	California.......................	1,868,111	1,094,993	381,280	467,683	37,487,065	82.3	60.1	30.5	85.1	75.8	82.0
8	Colorado........................	286,145	190,975	37,688	66,770	5,098,744	85.4	69.0	26.1	88.9	77.5	82.0
9	Connecticut....................	177,913	119,456	36,633	28,467	3,536,463	90.9	72.0	30.3	93.8	85.6	87.9
10	Delaware	46,926	31,327	10,476	7,442	902,314	90.7	70.1	34.8	92.8	87.3	88.8
11	District of Columbia........	90,528	73,739	11,801	7,430	622,605	93.4	69.6	35.1	95.4	91.7	93.2
12	Florida..........................	954,438	474,968	206,426	322,772	19,010,848	79.7	57.2	34.3	84.0	71.7	77.7
13	Georgia	415,536	245,443	57,680	124,307	9,710,901	81.1	61.9	28.5	85.7	72.7	78.6
15	Hawaii...........................	63,592	40,296	18,154	9,227	1,337,598	93.1	75.5	30.9	94.8	91.0	89.3
16	Idaho............................	69,119	43,180	12,601	16,305	1,577,379	83.6	66.5	29.2	86.5	75.6	80.4
17	Illinois..........................	532,617	342,577	92,627	114,430	12,690,730	87.1	67.0	30.5	90.7	79.9	84.3
18	Indiana..........................	304,154	193,574	52,834	67,605	6,441,965	85.8	67.8	29.4	89.5	78.1	82.7
19	Iowa.............................	171,238	123,451	30,989	24,427	3,031,378	91.5	75.2	30.4	94.3	84.8	88.6
20	Kansas...........................	131,059	89,146	18,436	27,896	2,824,697	87.5	72.5	26.9	91.0	79.1	84.4
21	Kentucky	178,267	104,235	35,246	46,264	4,295,357	85.8	64.2	33.4	89.6	78.3	82.4
22	Louisiana	180,569	94,804	36,848	56,108	4,498,089	83.0	58.9	34.3	88.0	76.5	78.5
23	Maine............................	83,258	48,831	23,451	15,831	1,314,314	89.4	65.5	38.4	92.5	85.8	83.8
24	Maryland	268,052	183,256	50,358	46,881	5,790,545	89.7	73.6	27.4	92.6	84.0	88.2
25	Massachusetts	459,857	352,939	91,294	32,866	6,568,640	96.0	74.8	33.4	97.5	93.5	94.6
26	Michigan	450,148	271,984	107,485	94,100	9,773,359	88.7	68.8	34.1	92.4	82.4	84.5
27	Minnesota	289,215	198,133	63,140	38,814	5,323,891	91.7	76.0	27.8	94.5	84.5	89.2
28	Mississippi.....................	105,940	58,851	20,668	30,243	2,918,229	82.7	56.3	37.0	86.8	76.7	80.6
29	Missouri.........................	273,776	173,646	50,931	59,574	5,913,412	86.6	68.2	30.2	90.3	78.8	84.0
30	Montana.........................	57,391	35,028	9,857	14,949	990,602	82.3	64.5	30.9	86.2	72.2	80.1
31	Nebraska	90,200	63,916	13,048	16,399	1,826,997	88.6	73.6	26.7	91.9	80.5	85.3
32	Nevada..........................	132,080	69,449	26,119	43,138	2,719,575	78.5	62.4	25.7	82.7	70.4	77.1
33	New Hampshire	77,389	55,867	10,533	13,967	1,306,205	89.5	75.5	26.1	93.1	81.1	85.1
34	New Jersey.....................	314,555	192,737	59,646	75,004	8,759,905	87.0	70.7	26.7	90.9	78.0	84.8
35	New Mexico....................	81,969	42,267	18,992	24,657	2,047,997	80.9	53.8	38.2	84.3	75.1	79.6
36	New York.......................	1,076,577	680,302	253,872	187,918	19,323,884	89.0	65.2	34.7	91.9	84.2	87.2
37	North Carolina	449,955	268,931	76,357	120,258	9,550,684	83.8	63.3	31.9	87.8	76.5	81.0
38	North Dakota..................	45,810	33,864	5,270	8,050	688,158	90.0	79.1	24.1	93.8	80.8	86.1
39	Ohio.............................	533,571	343,285	101,412	108,606	11,384,722	88.5	68.8	31.9	92.2	82.6	84.3
40	Oklahoma.......................	160,136	88,058	30,842	46,597	3,736,108	81.8	61.2	32.4	85.6	73.6	79.4
41	Oregon..........................	252,362	145,395	52,639	68,011	3,861,618	84.9	65.7	31.9	88.6	78.1	80.9
42	Pennsylvania	659,778	466,987	131,975	93,292	12,555,282	90.2	72.2	32.0	92.7	84.6	88.7
44	Rhode Island..................	70,604	50,132	9,982	12,982	1,035,491	88.9	70.1	31.2	92.6	83.2	85.8
45	South Carolina................	204,214	126,149	31,466	53,731	4,624,813	83.5	62.2	33.6	87.8	76.4	80.2
46	South Dakota..................	46,990	31,734	9,226	8,618	816,471	88.4	71.8	29.5	92.8	78.1	85.2
47	Tennessee	260,039	151,519	48,549	69,173	6,348,051	85.9	64.0	33.7	89.5	80.0	81.5
48	Texas............................	931,294	527,733	140,564	294,345	25,573,996	77.5	57.6	28.1	80.5	69.9	77.9
49	Utah.............................	115,914	80,561	13,439	25,164	2,829,593	85.4	73.3	20.8	88.3	75.0	82.3
50	Vermont........................	51,782	36,896	11,480	5,559	620,244	93.2	68.3	38.7	95.3	90.0	90.2
51	Virginia.........................	406,877	288,768	51,116	82,546	7,974,644	87.5	74.0	24.8	90.9	79.3	85.8
53	Washington	381,476	233,506	81,788	87,516	6,789,761	86.0	68.8	29.0	89.5	77.6	83.2
54	West Virginia	79,745	44,167	19,324	20,043	1,826,219	85.6	62.7	37.6	88.9	78.9	82.7
55	Wisconsin......................	302,728	203,423	57,987	53,808	5,650,835	91.0	71.9	31.5	94.1	85.7	86.3
56	Wyoming........................	31,111	18,486	5,366	8,401	566,182	85.1	70.9	26.0	89.4	76.2	79.8

This page is intentionally left blank

Table E-2: Counties with a Population of 50,000 or More—Income, Poverty, and Health Insurance

State/ County FIPS code	State/Place	Median family income in the past 12 months (in 2,013 inflation-adjusted dollars)					Families with own children under 18 years			Total population in households	Persons who had health insurance, as a percent of all persons in that household type		
		All families	Families with no earners	Families with one earner	Families with two earners	Families with three or more earners	Married-couple families with children	Male householder, no spouse present, with children	Female householder, no spouse present, with children		Married-couple families, percent	Male householder or female householder families, no spouse present	Nonfamily households
00000	United States...........	$63,784	$31,313	$45,505	$84,323	$102,461	$82,511	$36,858	$23,767	308,858,098	88.6	78.1	83.3
01000	Alabama.................	$53,991	$26,970	$40,869	$76,759	$94,234	$73,523	$32,653	$18,502	4,737,268	90.2	78.8	83.9
01001	Autauga County	$62,635	$31,058	$38,401	$82,867	$88,839	$77,930	$120,030	$19,680	54,572	91.1	79.8	79.3
01003	Baldwin County	$62,280	$41,272	$44,748	$78,822	$101,068	$74,994	$36,537	$21,276	188,766	91.2	75.3	79.2
01009	Blount County	$51,710	$24,093	$42,574	$71,634	$87,778	$61,856	$51,862	$18,233	57,277	90.7	83.4	85.6
01015	Calhoun County	$50,156	$26,336	$37,318	$68,789	$79,909	$61,927	$30,139	$14,058	115,813	90.9	78.4	82.2
01031	Coffee County	$58,925	$26,393	$46,757	$78,394	$103,110	$74,705	$28,641	$18,949	48,740	91.9	78.4	84.4
01033	Colbert County	$50,623	$30,747	$39,624	$77,389	$85,952	$62,822	$37,938	$17,839	54,042	90.5	82.7	82.6
01043	Cullman County	$49,425	$26,216	$39,629	$69,164	$88,971	$59,886	$49,697	$14,256	79,845	88.5	74.6	84.3
01045	Dale County............	$53,883	$32,512	$39,209	$72,713	$73,917	$68,750	$28,825	$16,613	47,578	89.9	82.1	74.8
01049	DeKalb County.........	$45,970	$27,575	$37,957	$58,584	$73,775	$54,141	$28,750	$17,804	70,478	85.7	72.3	81.6
01051	Elmore County.........	$63,884	$36,220	$45,795	$82,945	$104,191	$74,808	$48,657	$18,051	75,047	92.8	79.5	89.7
01055	Etowah County	$48,635	$24,717	$37,337	$66,623	$83,583	$62,313	$43,014	$18,134	103,042	89.7	76.5	82.3
01069	Houston County	$52,274	$27,070	$38,158	$73,818	$92,602	$74,088	$30,170	$17,425	102,172	91.1	77.9	81.0
01071	Jackson County	$48,542	$26,002	$39,831	$68,714	$86,667	$61,281	$22,931	$21,657	52,604	86.1	71.7	85.4
01073	Jefferson County.......	$59,484	$26,677	$41,858	$85,711	$102,790	$90,368	$31,604	$20,932	651,148	91.7	81.3	84.4
01077	Lauderdale County.....	$56,556	$36,002	$48,563	$68,697	$78,171	$65,329	$43,588	$14,460	91,957	90.6	80.4	85.8
01081	Lee County	$62,709	$19,336	$48,317	$80,268	$89,498	$77,247	$28,968	$21,723	145,149	92.6	78.0	87.4
01083	Limestone County......	$58,388	$31,149	$47,495	$79,930	$98,295	$77,110	$36,303	$23,235	82,673	89.8	78.3	88.1
01089	Madison County	$73,498	$45,988	$55,202	$92,579	$112,593	$94,097	$37,614	$25,000	339,354	92.3	76.6	83.4
01095	Marshall County	$48,006	$26,867	$34,410	$67,344	$91,348	$59,785	$30,719	$18,966	93,464	86.2	70.2	83.5
01097	Mobile County.........	$51,779	$24,256	$37,251	$73,772	$100,285	$72,212	$33,053	$17,823	405,816	88.3	78.1	82.3
01101	Montgomery County ...	$56,051	$24,935	$38,390	$80,101	$95,221	$80,180	$33,576	$20,779	223,537	91.8	80.4	83.6
01103	Morgan County	$55,014	$32,921	$36,619	$73,642	$97,935	$74,010	$40,089	$21,818	118,290	88.6	74.2	81.8
01113	Russell County	$43,108	$22,585	$34,046	$70,960	$79,428	$61,205	$46,250	$17,061	55,689	89.4	75.0	75.2
01115	St. Clair County	$58,995	$26,439	$48,422	$80,440	$104,021	$73,339	$30,068	$19,750	83,390	91.2	77.7	87.1
01117	Shelby County	$80,817	$38,615	$62,823	$93,612	$104,417	$93,060	$54,068	$32,207	199,461	92.4	85.0	87.4
01121	Talladega County	$43,181	$23,732	$34,290	$65,184	$109,265	$57,976	$17,169	$15,707	78,813	87.8	81.3	85.7
01125	Tuscaloosa County.....	$57,547	$27,776	$41,613	$81,168	$97,038	$81,056	$31,757	$18,947	197,323	92.7	78.6	88.5
01127	Walker County.........	$45,721	$29,808	$38,958	$66,158	$98,611	$57,550	$24,321	$18,880	65,572	89.2	75.7	82.0
02000	Alaska	$81,721	$38,919	$55,788	$98,171	$121,285	$92,503	$51,540	$31,776	706,544	85.4	71.0	74.5
02020	Anchorage Municipality	$89,235	$58,084	$54,366	$104,588	$133,354	$100,284	$60,353	$35,906	287,519	87.5	74.7	79.5
02090	Fairbanks North Star Borough	$78,726	$33,903	$57,109	$91,716	$131,742	$90,161	$54,038	$30,283	93,367	91.2	73.0	77.2
02122	Kenai Peninsula Borough	$74,753	$39,282	$60,118	$92,298	$126,411	$86,573	$67,763	$28,033	55,596	82.6	69.4	71.9
02170	Matanuska-Susitna Borough	$80,582	$42,908	$65,883	$96,738	$118,143	$88,620	$45,214	$25,880	92,202	84.3	69.3	71.8
04000	Arizona	$57,317	$36,056	$42,897	$79,086	$92,730	$72,137	$35,918	$25,228	6,441,287	85.9	76.8	81.2
04001	Apache County	$36,541	$16,295	$34,463	$59,116	$80,417	$46,850	$13,319	$24,456	71,628	77.3	71.9	73.6
04003	Cochise County	$53,203	$36,082	$41,223	$73,488	$88,944	$67,625	$34,844	$22,104	118,042	88.9	77.8	87.1
04005	Coconino County.......	$58,234	$30,474	$42,142	$74,245	$95,112	$80,721	$33,611	$22,074	134,902	82.4	74.3	77.0
04007	Gila County	$48,432	$37,806	$42,192	$63,236	$77,366	$54,298	$41,750	$25,000	52,494	86.3	75.3	84.1
04013	Maricopa County.......	$62,533	$35,845	$45,043	$84,810	$99,424	$78,454	$37,630	$27,594	3,911,355	86.0	76.0	80.2
04015	Mohave County........	$45,306	$35,751	$39,917	$65,128	$76,747	$54,525	$22,217	$21,032	194,408	84.5	77.4	81.1
04017	Navajo County.........	$40,902	$21,615	$35,183	$65,859	$71,991	$52,101	$24,770	$15,419	105,067	83.5	78.7	78.7
04019	Pima County...........	$55,965	$39,408	$40,951	$73,809	$84,456	$69,620	$34,697	$22,284	974,635	88.3	79.5	83.6
04021	Pinal County	$53,455	$37,505	$46,065	$73,075	$95,033	$64,628	$37,419	$24,447	365,504	86.6	78.2	83.7
04025	Yavapai County........	$53,354	$44,828	$43,121	$70,215	$72,323	$60,254	$35,648	$23,491	211,426	87.1	76.1	82.7
04027	Yuma County..........	$43,067	$31,614	$31,743	$58,582	$64,566	$50,972	$30,212	$16,540	192,544	78.0	77.3	83.5
05000	Arkansas...............	$50,600	$27,052	$37,644	$69,917	$88,984	$64,920	$29,332	$18,687	2,896,439	86.9	76.8	80.7
05007	Benton County	$62,903	$39,497	$49,025	$77,309	$89,311	$75,402	$33,816	$27,622	230,888	88.0	76.1	80.8
05031	Craighead County......	$52,346	$29,715	$37,879	$72,420	$85,257	$70,340	$36,406	$16,208	98,945	86.3	77.5	78.0
05033	Crawford County.......	$43,155	$25,173	$35,923	$56,693	$76,067	$53,700	$27,292	$16,089	61,245	86.5	72.8	84.0
05035	Crittenden County......	$48,459	$17,588	$31,606	$76,412	$85,219	$70,759	$27,636	$21,105	49,542	89.2	78.9	80.7
05045	Faulkner County	$63,194	$36,538	$43,373	$79,167	$102,049	$74,167	$45,836	$22,109	117,041	90.2	82.5	82.3
05051	Garland County........	$48,605	$30,864	$33,917	$67,431	$100,833	$59,762	$16,045	$18,642	95,523	86.3	72.4	75.8
05069	Jefferson County.......	$48,770	$23,077	$35,770	$74,228	$90,700	$66,308	$37,200	$19,097	70,103	89.7	83.2	84.7
05085	Lonoke County	$61,183	$31,018	$43,728	$76,922	$102,177	$68,904	$51,513	$27,570	68,407	89.5	79.7	81.2
05115	Pope County...........	$49,097	$30,334	$37,755	$63,949	$75,092	$53,925	$49,769	$20,542	61,970	88.4	71.6	81.0
05119	Pulaski County.........	$57,621	$26,660	$42,946	$80,932	$100,483	$83,023	$22,665	$23,334	383,654	89.9	79.3	79.4
05125	Saline County	$66,011	$43,250	$46,994	$82,096	$95,598	$82,781	$41,109	$32,737	110,748	91.1	78.9	82.4
05131	Sebastian County.......	$50,555	$27,097	$37,051	$70,029	$88,544	$61,690	$33,656	$16,971	126,052	84.9	75.9	77.4
05143	Washington County.....	$55,381	$28,132	$40,924	$68,954	$85,217	$64,941	$29,738	$20,083	210,162	84.5	73.7	84.5
05145	White County	$54,703	$28,098	$43,098	$79,053	$94,286	$73,443	$33,462	$19,116	77,821	86.4	76.5	78.1
06000	California...............	$67,746	$29,455	$48,976	$91,345	$100,397	$82,294	$37,371	$26,341	37,487,065	85.1	75.8	82.0
06001	Alameda County	$88,271	$32,687	$61,521	$115,826	$116,386	$112,840	$48,080	$30,575	1,542,472	90.4	81.0	85.6
06007	Butte County	$53,530	$33,923	$42,718	$71,852	$86,679	$66,112	$27,820	$20,788	218,749	87.2	80.8	80.7
06013	Contra Costa County ...	$92,359	$40,737	$69,699	$117,510	$122,899	$115,115	$53,850	$35,603	1,073,714	91.1	80.5	86.4
06017	El Dorado County	$83,230	$44,516	$68,670	$106,072	$112,639	$102,484	$48,897	$36,647	180,028	92.1	79.6	84.3
06019	Fresno County	$47,786	$19,585	$35,011	$70,053	$80,484	$58,966	$26,343	$18,162	936,524	82.8	77.6	76.4
06023	Humboldt County......	$51,462	$32,323	$39,342	$74,553	$92,042	$68,156	$33,819	$17,368	133,660	85.7	74.3	73.1

State/ County FIPS code	State/Place	Total number of families	Families with incomes below the poverty level, as a percent of all families of that family type				Families that received Food Stamps (SNAP), as a percent of all families of that family type			Families that received food stamps (SNAP) and had at least one worker	
			All families	Married-couple families with related children under 18	Male householder families, no spouse present, with related children	Female householder families, no spouse present	All families	Married-couple families	Male householder or female householder families, no spouse present	Married-couple families, percent	Male householder or female householder families, no spouse present
00000	**United States**............................	76,444,922	11.7	8.7	23.4	41.1	14.4	7.4	6.2	33.3	24.2
01000	**Alabama**................................	1,236,566	14.6	9.5	26.7	49.6	17.6	8.4	6.9	40.1	27.3
01001	Autauga County	13,943	10.6	6.7	14.0	47.2	14.6	8.5	7.8	38.0	21.5
01003	Baldwin County	51,611	9.6	7.4	34.0	41.5	10.2	4.4	3.6	32.0	23.2
01009	Blount County	15,618	12.2	8.7	18.3	56.1	17.1	11.3	9.1	39.9	25.1
01015	Calhoun County	29,760	16.9	13.0	21.9	57.8	22.1	11.7	9.7	45.8	35.6
01031	Coffee County	12,918	14.2	7.6	29.8	52.7	14.8	6.5	5.1	35.0	24.3
01033	Colbert County	14,875	13.9	15.7	5.1	43.7	16.6	10.3	8.4	33.4	18.4
01043	Cullman County	22,529	13.3	11.1	12.8	51.8	15.3	10.1	8.2	31.9	18.6
01045	Dale County................................	12,771	15.2	10.9	34.6	51.9	16.1	8.4	7.2	35.0	27.3
01049	DeKalb County	17,580	11.8	11.2	10.9	57.8	13.6	8.1	7.2	37.5	24.2
01051	Elmore County	20,491	10.5	8.4	14.7	46.6	12.6	5.8	5.5	35.5	28.1
01055	Etowah County	27,861	16.0	12.7	14.9	50.6	18.0	9.4	6.6	38.6	25.9
01069	Houston County	26,390	14.1	6.1	34.8	52.4	16.0	5.8	4.7	40.5	27.0
01071	Jackson County	13,878	12.5	10.7	34.3	46.6	15.4	9.9	7.3	36.3	17.4
01073	Jefferson County	164,418	14.4	7.4	31.6	45.1	17.7	8.0	7.0	36.8	25.5
01077	Lauderdale County.......................	25,328	12.9	9.3	23.1	58.4	13.7	7.7	6.3	35.0	22.5
01081	Lee County	34,949	13.0	7.3	23.4	42.2	13.2	6.8	5.2	30.4	23.6
01083	Limestone County	23,701	10.9	8.3	29.0	38.0	14.9	8.5	7.7	37.6	28.9
01089	Madison County	87,921	10.1	6.5	22.0	39.4	12.4	5.2	4.5	31.9	25.8
01095	Marshall County	24,345	15.2	16.1	30.1	49.7	17.3	9.9	8.2	39.1	27.4
01097	Mobile County	104,433	16.7	8.8	22.9	50.7	22.0	10.3	8.2	44.2	30.9
01101	Montgomery County	55,883	18.2	8.6	42.7	47.6	24.4	8.8	7.5	47.2	35.4
01103	Morgan County	31,552	12.8	9.6	20.7	47.3	13.7	6.5	5.7	35.3	27.0
01113	Russell County	14,049	18.6	11.6	16.5	51.6	26.9	11.4	9.0	52.7	34.3
01115	St. Clair County	23,427	14.0	12.0	37.2	46.0	15.7	9.4	8.4	39.5	24.0
01117	Shelby County	53,181	5.6	4.8	15.4	25.5	7.5	4.1	3.5	22.2	17.0
01121	Talladega County	22,179	19.6	13.4	46.9	59.2	22.7	10.8	9.2	45.3	30.7
01125	Tuscaloosa County	45,145	13.4	7.2	17.9	46.9	13.6	4.3	3.5	36.0	23.0
01127	Walker County............................	18,203	16.5	15.2	36.7	51.7	21.0	13.5	9.7	40.3	28.6
02000	**Alaska**	167,553	6.8	4.2	18.0	26.3	11.0	6.1	5.5	24.9	20.6
02020	Anchorage Municipality	69,047	5.0	3.0	11.6	20.9	9.1	4.9	4.5	20.7	18.3
02090	Fairbanks North Star Borough	22,302	5.8	1.2	18.3	29.2	7.1	2.5	1.7	23.4	18.0
02122	Kenai Peninsula Borough	14,320	5.6	3.9	18.9	22.7	7.6	4.6	4.1	19.3	17.1
02170	Matanuska-Susitna Borough	22,639	7.2	4.5	21.3	36.0	10.4	6.9	6.2	24.0	16.3
04000	**Arizona**	1,560,655	13.7	12.7	26.6	40.3	16.1	9.3	8.1	33.8	24.9
04001	Apache County...........................	13,094	29.2	28.0	59.8	42.6	30.3	19.3	12.3	45.6	23.4
04003	Cochise County	31,971	14.2	16.7	23.9	41.0	17.3	10.3	9.1	38.3	30.5
04005	Coconino County........................	29,944	17.2	14.2	37.8	47.9	17.5	8.4	6.9	38.7	31.5
04007	Gila County	13,419	14.9	20.3	35.9	42.5	20.9	11.3	7.8	47.3	34.4
04013	Maricopa County	928,330	12.9	11.8	24.8	38.1	14.5	8.3	7.4	30.2	22.2
04015	Mohave County	50,304	14.8	19.1	42.0	44.7	20.1	12.2	10.0	46.6	31.8
04017	Navajo County	24,333	26.5	26.3	37.6	53.5	30.7	19.3	15.4	52.1	34.9
04019	Pima County...............................	237,220	13.9	11.9	25.1	43.2	18.0	9.5	8.3	38.1	29.2
04021	Pinal County	91,355	11.6	11.5	18.5	36.8	13.6	8.3	7.4	30.1	20.8
04025	Yavapai County	57,757	12.1	14.8	33.2	40.5	14.1	9.6	8.4	31.8	24.7
04027	Yuma County..............................	54,707	17.4	14.3	37.5	53.7	22.5	14.5	12.8	45.3	32.7
05000	**Arkansas**	755,344	14.6	11.4	28.2	49.0	16.2	8.2	6.6	37.9	26.4
05007	Benton County	61,337	8.6	8.8	17.8	36.7	8.3	4.5	4.1	26.5	21.3
05031	Craighead County.......................	25,780	14.7	9.4	20.2	51.7	16.8	7.5	6.3	37.7	27.7
05033	Crawford County.........................	17,654	16.3	16.8	33.7	49.0	17.8	11.0	8.6	37.3	30.4
05035	Crittenden County.......................	12,713	17.7	5.7	12.2	49.3	24.0	8.4	7.3	44.2	28.1
05045	Faulkner County	29,284	9.8	6.9	10.1	36.3	10.6	6.0	4.7	25.9	22.0
05051	Garland County...........................	25,331	16.2	15.1	58.5	46.6	15.4	6.6	5.3	38.3	26.5
05069	Jefferson County........................	17,724	19.3	10.9	32.8	48.2	20.7	9.5	7.5	38.8	29.2
05085	Lonoke County	18,563	10.0	9.7	13.5	31.6	11.9	9.0	8.2	21.9	14.4
05115	Pope County	15,342	15.0	13.9	26.2	51.4	15.8	8.9	7.4	37.9	29.5
05119	Pulaski County............................	91,168	12.1	7.6	32.0	36.5	15.8	6.6	5.0	34.5	24.3
05125	Saline County	29,657	5.6	3.9	11.0	26.5	10.6	5.0	4.1	30.9	27.9
05131	Sebastian County........................	32,369	17.0	14.2	35.2	58.9	17.8	9.3	6.7	40.9	29.3
05143	Washington County......................	50,574	14.1	11.2	26.0	49.8	13.7	8.6	8.0	28.8	21.7
05145	White County	20,753	13.6	7.6	20.2	45.8	11.2	6.4	4.6	28.7	16.1
06000	**California**...............................	8,602,735	12.7	11.1	24.6	38.6	11.3	6.6	5.8	22.9	16.2
06001	Alameda County.........................	358,510	9.1	6.5	17.9	33.0	9.7	5.4	4.8	21.0	14.4
06007	Butte County	50,510	13.8	12.0	24.5	43.0	14.0	7.7	6.5	29.2	18.1
06013	Contra Costa County..................	268,549	8.2	6.6	18.8	30.9	7.5	3.7	3.1	19.3	13.9
06017	El Dorado County	47,308	6.8	8.3	16.1	23.6	5.6	3.4	2.5	17.5	11.9
06019	Fresno County	212,657	22.4	20.4	37.3	53.4	24.0	14.8	13.3	40.2	27.6
06023	Humboldt County........................	29,695	14.5	10.9	18.5	50.5	12.4	5.3	4.6	29.9	23.1

| State/County FIPS code | State/Place | Median family income in the past 12 months (in 2,013 inflation-adjusted dollars) | | | | | | | | Total population in households | Persons who had health insurance, as a percent of all persons in that household type | | |
		All families	Families with no earners	Families with one earner	Families with two earners	Families with three or more earners	Married-couple families with children	Male householder, no spouse present, with children	Female householder, no spouse present, with children		Married-couple families, percent	Male householder or female householder families, no spouse present	Nonfamily households
							Families with own children under 18 years						
	California—cont'd												
06025	Imperial County	$44,215	$18,951	$34,396	$62,701	$80,104	$60,867	$43,214	$17,307	165,486	80.3	77.1	79.8
06029	Kern County	$51,340	$20,812	$38,481	$71,390	$86,520	$63,442	$29,040	$18,620	827,422	83.1	76.3	78.6
06031	Kings County	$48,585	$18,545	$37,428	$72,654	$81,175	$57,011	$30,811	$20,128	130,140	84.4	77.7	74.2
06033	Lake County	$46,469	$30,244	$40,531	$65,685	$92,554	$56,250	$25,335	$21,904	63,357	83.8	75.1	81.1
06037	Los Angeles County	$60,572	$21,718	$41,629	$82,089	$92,854	$73,219	$35,069	$25,314	9,881,122	80.9	72.4	78.8
06039	Madera County	$47,178	$26,815	$38,330	$67,337	$79,931	$49,217	$21,118	$18,944	143,593	81.1	76.3	71.4
06041	Marin County	$114,481	$68,796	$92,431	$148,134	$123,143	$150,190	$72,685	$44,066	250,860	93.8	84.5	89.4
06045	Mendocino County	$54,076	$31,477	$43,197	$68,954	$76,194	$57,467	$42,127	$17,690	86,368	84.8	77.9	78.3
06047	Merced County	$45,484	$19,790	$33,679	$63,938	$81,952	$52,402	$32,268	$18,274	258,521	82.1	79.1	76.3
06053	Monterey County	$61,107	$39,622	$44,340	$75,582	$83,934	$62,968	$36,268	$25,312	406,115	81.2	70.0	78.3
06055	Napa County	$76,894	$46,681	$55,660	$97,080	$96,511	$82,938	$40,740	$34,206	137,107	88.7	77.8	82.1
06057	Nevada County	$69,358	$46,050	$58,515	$91,135	$92,032	$91,480	$32,458	$27,563	97,373	89.5	76.5	79.8
06059	Orange County	$83,210	$36,802	$61,061	$105,821	$113,309	$99,882	$44,908	$32,348	3,067,305	85.5	74.0	84.4
06061	Placer County	$84,678	$50,079	$68,236	$111,275	$124,502	$107,279	$45,992	$32,885	359,067	92.5	81.1	83.7
06065	Riverside County	$61,166	$32,616	$45,017	$79,876	$96,670	$70,548	$37,534	$26,305	2,240,719	82.0	74.3	81.1
06067	Sacramento County	$62,244	$28,889	$47,862	$84,550	$97,269	$76,531	$36,493	$26,784	1,432,810	87.7	80.8	82.6
06069	San Benito County	$71,379	$35,108	$50,577	$86,285	$108,839	$81,335	$41,029	$34,167	56,724	87.1	80.7	79.6
06071	San Bernardino County	$57,251	$22,182	$42,331	$79,453	$96,502	$67,572	$36,507	$23,961	2,036,626	82.1	75.9	78.9
06073	San Diego County	$71,422	$31,153	$52,198	$93,288	$105,973	$83,473	$40,548	$28,443	3,074,879	86.4	75.5	82.3
06075	San Francisco County	$89,497	$24,112	$57,044	$128,898	$111,848	$126,167	$54,121	$33,272	821,781	92.5	84.0	88.9
06077	San Joaquin County	$57,448	$26,183	$44,536	$77,719	$89,553	$65,706	$35,717	$23,187	691,495	84.2	80.0	80.3
06079	San Luis Obispo County	$74,912	$54,146	$57,788	$90,333	$104,399	$86,150	$33,385	$27,517	266,873	90.1	76.7	84.3
06081	San Mateo County	$103,221	$51,337	$75,523	$129,856	$123,409	$130,434	$52,011	$49,288	734,124	92.4	80.6	87.7
06083	Santa Barbara County	$73,078	$43,447	$51,745	$92,290	$99,483	$79,802	$43,299	$31,925	423,692	83.4	70.5	86.4
06085	Santa Clara County	$103,443	$38,685	$81,706	$136,815	$122,153	$132,730	$53,106	$36,390	1,827,575	91.6	79.8	86.8
06087	Santa Cruz County	$81,675	$50,254	$59,963	$103,961	$92,991	$87,770	$34,271	$33,162	265,649	88.4	79.0	83.3
06089	Shasta County	$51,646	$32,096	$44,093	$79,971	$105,042	$64,902	$37,829	$20,864	177,069	85.9	81.3	79.8
06095	Solano County	$74,793	$39,208	$54,405	$98,891	$111,533	$87,901	$46,652	$27,845	406,740	90.3	81.6	82.2
06097	Sonoma County	$73,901	$43,830	$53,662	$91,814	$107,722	$85,505	$50,100	$33,263	486,885	88.5	78.6	84.4
06099	Stanislaus County	$53,082	$26,310	$40,616	$72,966	$92,384	$62,993	$32,768	$19,784	518,291	84.4	78.6	75.6
06101	Sutter County	$56,264	$33,792	$42,088	$72,694	$90,808	$63,849	$26,234	$24,300	93,601	84.8	76.1	82.4
06103	Tehama County	$48,102	$29,941	$41,830	$71,638	$76,528	$56,526	$40,187	$18,350	62,644	87.7	72.2	83.7
06107	Tulare County	$42,590	$20,353	$31,526	$62,946	$70,365	$49,935	$23,920	$20,313	446,527	80.3	76.1	74.3
06109	Tuolumne County	$55,329	$38,211	$49,209	$77,912	$106,912	$63,610	$23,827	$19,875	50,904	91.2	79.1	83.2
06111	Ventura County	$85,243	$42,250	$64,643	$103,716	$108,593	$99,587	$50,412	$32,203	827,808	86.3	76.3	83.6
06113	Yolo County	$71,366	$33,590	$41,896	$99,456	$93,446	$86,811	$44,942	$34,706	201,907	87.8	79.2	89.5
06115	Yuba County	$49,346	$27,119	$44,468	$62,258	$78,446	$56,619	$36,691	$18,918	70,272	86.9	81.5	75.1
08000	**Colorado**	$71,939	$38,176	$50,890	$88,748	$105,466	$87,137	$41,877	$28,222	5,098,744	88.9	77.5	82.0
08001	Adams County	$63,412	$29,838	$43,673	$79,588	$92,272	$73,972	$40,805	$29,392	456,643	82.4	71.9	79.4
08005	Arapahoe County	$72,833	$44,498	$51,939	$88,039	$108,978	$90,538	$44,581	$33,040	591,407	87.9	76.4	80.7
08013	Boulder County	$93,165	$54,216	$72,799	$110,554	$118,571	$117,097	$53,788	$30,736	303,089	92.3	81.2	88.0
08014	Broomfield County	$94,751	$44,091	$68,546	$110,151	$145,591	$119,948	$43,864	$40,645	57,972	94.1	80.7	86.6
08031	Denver County	$65,203	$24,696	$41,494	$91,851	$87,672	$82,889	$41,643	$23,560	627,940	86.2	77.8	83.2
08035	Douglas County	$111,324	$46,982	$93,805	$124,444	$139,394	$125,473	$83,023	$49,308	297,913	95.7	85.2	85.2
08037	Eagle County	$84,925	$41,555	$46,174	$95,354	$130,452	$92,016	$42,463	$24,446	51,929	84.4	76.4	78.2
08041	El Paso County	$70,007	$42,114	$52,171	$83,699	$109,844	$80,105	$43,602	$27,438	615,058	91.5	79.2	79.3
08045	Garfield County	$59,977	$41,036	$42,483	$68,934	$114,665	$64,629	$28,333	$38,221	55,938	71.3	63.3	70.0
08059	Jefferson County	$83,896	$46,551	$60,189	$102,293	$121,250	$105,816	$50,290	$35,115	538,940	92.8	79.7	84.1
08067	La Plata County	$70,012	$41,323	$62,880	$77,059	$101,290	$77,850	$43,984	$31,750	52,005	88.9	68.9	72.8
08069	Larimer County	$74,831	$46,083	$59,181	$88,084	$101,538	$91,089	$44,160	$29,217	308,159	91.6	80.6	84.2
08077	Mesa County	$56,869	$29,556	$40,476	$77,845	$103,966	$72,259	$32,457	$19,147	146,338	87.0	79.0	82.1
08101	Pueblo County	$52,038	$31,253	$38,569	$69,123	$87,325	$64,028	$32,171	$23,755	156,900	91.5	81.0	82.8
08123	Weld County	$65,676	$31,029	$44,141	$84,186	$101,632	$76,647	$40,161	$23,809	260,749	87.3	77.5	82.0
09000	**Connecticut**	$86,354	$35,655	$59,935	$108,103	$126,870	$112,382	$51,622	$30,019	3,536,463	93.8	85.6	87.9
09001	Fairfield County	$103,676	$38,122	$80,162	$128,620	$129,470	$146,042	$51,917	$31,942	924,802	91.9	80.2	84.1
09003	Hartford County	$81,407	$32,622	$54,445	$105,168	$122,773	$108,183	$51,173	$29,409	881,569	94.6	87.3	88.4
09005	Litchfield County	$86,877	$43,200	$61,616	$100,015	$126,943	$103,228	$72,992	$35,728	186,243	94.1	87.3	89.0
09007	Middlesex County	$99,610	$49,148	$67,232	$119,858	$135,493	$121,421	$70,417	$37,442	163,878	95.3	87.5	89.7
09009	New Haven County	$77,436	$29,651	$52,403	$102,362	$127,582	$100,514	$51,508	$25,924	852,445	93.7	87.0	88.7
09011	New London County	$81,042	$44,583	$56,279	$101,493	$120,833	$98,251	$40,122	$34,910	262,653	95.7	88.4	88.9
09013	Tolland County	$93,589	$48,821	$66,353	$109,779	$134,522	$116,255	$59,049	$44,861	148,650	96.4	91.0	93.5
09015	Windham County	$70,062	$32,972	$45,140	$86,955	$112,862	$85,873	$41,453	$21,349	116,223	93.6	85.2	88.2
10000	**Delaware**	$70,668	$42,381	$51,357	$89,317	$112,572	$93,443	$42,821	$29,037	902,314	92.8	87.3	88.8
10001	Kent County	$61,970	$40,476	$44,488	$82,567	$103,686	$80,861	$42,034	$24,414	163,872	93.0	90.1	88.7
10003	New Castle County	$78,110	$39,173	$54,805	$99,719	$120,165	$104,869	$44,934	$32,020	537,786	93.2	87.5	89.2
10005	Sussex County	$61,776	$47,328	$47,564	$74,330	$101,914	$77,400	$37,050	$25,475	200,656	91.6	84.2	87.6
11000	**District of Columbia**	$78,892	$15,606	$49,300	$137,418	$130,757	$157,541	$36,852	$25,582	622,605	95.4	91.7	93.2
11001	District of Columbia	$78,892	$15,606	$49,300	$137,418	$130,757	$157,541	$36,852	$25,582	622,605	95.4	91.7	93.2

State/ County FIPS code	State/Place	Total number of families	Families with incomes below the poverty level, as a percent of all families of that family type				Families that received Food Stamps (SNAP), as a percent of all families of that family type			Families that received food stamps (SNAP) and had at least one worker	
			All families	Married-couple families with related children under 18	Male householder families, no spouse present, with related children	Female householder families, no spouse present	All families	Married-couple families	Male householder or female householder families, no spouse present	Married-couple families, percent	Male householder or female householder families, no spouse present
	California—cont'd										
06025	Imperial County	36,695	21.6	17.6	25.7	52.5	22.0	14.2	13.0	37.4	27.4
06029	Kern County	193,078	19.8	15.4	32.3	55.2	18.8	10.9	9.6	35.0	23.5
06031	Kings County	32,007	17.6	14.5	26.4	46.1	19.0	10.8	9.8	34.5	22.6
06033	Lake County	16,459	16.5	25.9	23.9	44.3	17.4	9.2	5.9	33.7	23.4
06037	Los Angeles County	2,158,798	14.9	13.8	26.0	39.9	11.1	6.7	6.0	19.8	14.2
06039	Madera County	32,142	18.8	20.3	40.7	48.9	20.1	13.8	10.7	36.5	26.0
06041	Marin County	64,059	5.1	3.3	18.3	20.0	4.3	2.2	1.9	12.9	9.9
06045	Mendocino County	20,189	14.5	14.5	19.5	55.1	13.4	6.1	5.8	33.2	25.5
06047	Merced County	58,279	21.8	18.8	33.7	55.1	23.5	14.2	12.6	42.1	24.8
06053	Monterey County	90,577	13.4	12.8	23.6	41.9	9.0	5.9	5.6	16.9	13.7
06055	Napa County	33,750	7.6	6.0	17.6	27.0	7.0	4.1	3.8	16.1	12.0
06057	Nevada County	25,752	9.2	9.8	29.6	31.8	6.5	2.6	1.5	22.8	16.0
06059	Orange County	717,556	9.4	8.9	20.9	31.5	7.3	4.7	4.3	15.5	12.4
06061	Placer County	94,780	6.5	4.5	19.7	25.2	4.9	2.1	1.9	16.0	10.1
06065	Riverside County	506,544	13.5	12.2	26.7	38.2	12.8	8.0	7.0	25.7	18.3
06067	Sacramento County	335,289	14.3	11.9	25.3	40.4	15.9	9.0	7.7	30.5	19.9
06069	San Benito County	13,442	7.8	7.7	22.2	21.3	13.7	10.2	10.0	25.1	19.6
06071	San Bernardino County	457,183	16.0	13.1	27.5	43.1	16.9	10.0	8.8	31.5	21.2
06073	San Diego County	716,575	11.2	9.3	20.9	34.1	7.9	4.6	4.0	17.4	12.3
06075	San Francisco County	157,580	8.6	5.6	20.2	31.2	7.1	4.1	3.5	15.2	10.9
06077	San Joaquin County	160,636	14.9	12.7	23.8	42.5	15.6	8.6	7.8	31.1	21.4
06079	San Luis Obispo County	65,095	7.9	7.2	15.5	36.0	7.1	3.3	3.0	21.5	15.8
06081	San Mateo County	174,659	5.0	4.4	16.6	19.2	3.6	2.4	2.1	7.9	6.4
06083	Santa Barbara County	92,577	9.8	8.9	21.4	33.6	8.6	5.4	4.8	18.0	14.2
06085	Santa Clara County	438,863	7.2	5.2	17.6	27.5	6.3	3.8	3.4	15.0	11.6
06087	Santa Cruz County	58,785	8.8	8.2	11.5	34.0	8.4	4.6	4.4	20.4	15.4
06089	Shasta County	45,440	12.2	13.7	20.7	41.6	13.5	6.9	5.5	32.0	20.8
06095	Solano County	100,829	10.3	7.7	12.7	36.3	11.2	5.5	4.8	24.6	16.6
06097	Sonoma County	116,190	7.9	8.0	19.5	25.3	8.0	4.8	4.4	17.6	13.1
06099	Stanislaus County	123,974	17.2	15.6	29.8	47.2	18.4	11.7	10.0	33.0	22.2
06101	Sutter County	23,492	14.6	11.8	36.0	39.0	12.6	7.6	7.1	24.9	15.1
06103	Tehama County	16,250	13.8	15.1	24.4	52.2	14.7	10.3	6.4	28.1	17.1
06107	Tulare County	103,648	23.6	23.7	41.3	50.3	27.5	19.2	17.6	44.5	32.4
06109	Tuolumne County	14,749	11.0	14.5	12.9	44.8	11.8	4.8	3.3	35.3	26.9
06111	Ventura County	195,715	8.4	7.5	15.9	32.0	8.1	4.6	4.1	19.0	14.8
06113	Yolo County	43,792	10.2	10.4	19.7	29.2	12.3	7.8	6.7	25.4	20.1
06115	Yuba County	17,958	16.0	9.5	24.8	55.1	21.1	11.3	8.7	44.1	27.8
08000	**Colorado**	1,271,180	9.1	7.4	18.3	34.7	9.6	5.1	4.6	24.7	19.2
08001	Adams County	108,797	11.1	10.0	16.7	35.5	12.7	7.6	7.2	25.8	19.3
08005	Arapahoe County	147,789	8.9	8.0	14.9	28.1	9.5	5.0	4.6	21.5	18.7
08013	Boulder County	71,394	6.4	5.2	14.5	27.8	6.0	2.6	2.4	19.0	16.5
08014	Broomfield County	15,028	6.5	2.6	16.2	37.5	4.8	1.5	1.5	19.5	11.4
08031	Denver County	127,738	14.0	12.1	25.1	41.5	14.6	7.8	6.9	30.1	22.7
08035	Douglas County	81,418	3.2	1.0	6.0	18.6	2.3	1.1	1.0	9.9	8.1
08037	Eagle County	11,373	9.2	7.1	0.0	43.3	...	...	...	...	...
08041	El Paso County	163,447	8.5	6.3	15.1	34.7	10.0	5.2	4.7	26.9	21.0
08045	Garfield County	14,237	10.0	13.8	26.8	19.2	10.8	7.1	7.1	27.1	25.4
08059	Jefferson County	142,737	5.9	4.8	10.6	27.7	6.3	2.7	2.2	19.0	13.9
08067	La Plata County	12,896	6.0	5.0	17.1	24.6	7.2	3.2	2.5	24.0	22.0
08069	Larimer County	76,880	6.7	5.2	14.8	33.7	7.4	4.5	4.3	19.4	15.3
08077	Mesa County	39,484	11.5	6.3	29.7	45.8	11.4	5.2	4.4	30.3	20.6
08101	Pueblo County	39,553	14.1	12.4	29.6	42.7	19.1	11.0	9.1	38.0	28.6
08123	Weld County	66,341	10.0	7.3	23.4	43.1	10.4	6.2	5.7	25.6	17.9
09000	**Connecticut**	894,728	7.8	4.1	15.8	32.6	11.6	4.5	3.7	31.3	22.6
09001	Fairfield County	228,970	6.6	3.0	16.3	28.7	8.5	3.2	2.8	25.9	19.5
09003	Hartford County	225,390	9.3	4.6	17.5	33.5	14.4	5.2	4.2	36.0	25.4
09005	Litchfield County	50,182	4.1	2.7	9.9	22.2	5.8	3.4	2.9	16.2	12.2
09007	Middlesex County	43,325	4.1	2.2	12.1	23.4	5.5	2.5	1.9	18.2	12.9
09009	New Haven County	210,654	10.1	6.0	16.1	38.9	14.6	5.7	4.5	35.7	25.1
09011	New London County	70,160	6.7	4.4	20.8	24.4	11.0	5.1	4.2	27.9	20.9
09013	Tolland County	36,473	3.9	1.9	1.7	24.0	6.6	2.3	2.0	22.3	16.9
09015	Windham County	29,574	8.8	3.6	13.5	43.2	17.4	8.9	7.5	39.8	29.8
10000	**Delaware**	226,510	8.1	5.2	16.3	30.3	14.5	6.7	6.0	34.3	26.9
10001	Kent County	41,345	9.3	7.1	6.0	31.9	18.4	9.1	8.2	41.3	34.2
10003	New Castle County	133,033	7.3	3.6	19.4	27.7	12.9	5.7	5.2	30.5	23.8
10005	Sussex County	52,132	9.1	8.9	15.2	36.7	15.4	7.3	6.2	39.1	29.7
11000	**District of Columbia**	114,484	15.3	5.7	24.8	38.8	22.8	6.6	5.4	41.2	27.3
11001	District of Columbia	114,484	15.3	5.7	24.8	38.8	22.8	6.6	5.4	41.2	27.3

Table E-2: Counties with a Population of 50,000 or More—Income, Poverty, and Health Insurance—*Continued*

State/ County FIPS code	State/Place	Median family income in the past 12 months (in 2,013 inflation-adjusted dollars): All families	Families with no earners	Families with one earner	Families with two earners	Families with three or more earners	Families with own children under 18 years: Married-couple families with children	Male householder, no spouse present, with children	Female householder, no spouse present, with children	Total population in households	Persons who had health insurance, as a percent of all persons in that household type: Married-couple families, percent	Male householder or female householder families, no spouse present	Nonfamily households
12000	**Florida**	$55,758	$34,825	$42,072	$75,621	$90,957	$71,937	$32,892	$24,860	19,010,848	84.0	71.7	77.7
12001	Alachua County	$61,658	$28,279	$46,352	$86,411	$99,597	$85,952	$42,758	$19,102	248,965	89.5	79.7	80.9
12005	Bay County	$55,424	$34,086	$41,002	$73,162	$85,683	$71,156	$28,059	$22,751	168,104	86.0	77.4	74.6
12009	Brevard County	$58,760	$39,775	$46,874	$80,755	$98,105	$77,710	$35,876	$23,355	541,779	87.7	74.6	80.1
12011	Broward County	$60,374	$26,734	$42,690	$79,282	$98,909	$80,237	$39,063	$30,710	1,802,056	81.3	70.6	76.3
12015	Charlotte County	$54,056	$45,451	$48,272	$70,171	$84,056	$64,642	$40,679	$29,289	159,190	88.1	70.3	82.2
12017	Citrus County	$48,882	$39,242	$46,756	$66,100	$87,438	$65,991	$26,908	$19,722	137,567	89.5	77.3	80.2
12019	Clay County	$64,732	$39,503	$49,382	$81,355	$105,227	$81,204	$49,776	$32,408	191,481	89.1	79.8	80.3
12021	Collier County	$63,442	$60,610	$50,654	$75,723	$74,623	$63,004	$35,737	$27,103	331,446	82.6	66.4	76.1
12023	Columbia County	$46,582	$35,435	$35,192	$66,489	$99,464	$64,959	$32,995	$28,502	63,106	85.8	73.6	80.2
12031	Duval County	$57,685	$24,873	$41,861	$79,711	$103,296	$73,749	$33,578	$22,014	862,385	87.6	77.4	78.0
12033	Escambia County	$55,257	$38,102	$40,607	$73,525	$86,495	$73,672	$32,972	$22,337	286,682	87.2	81.0	77.3
12035	Flagler County	$51,941	$43,149	$42,014	$71,896	$93,125	$60,998	$28,566	$29,420	98,210	86.3	71.3	83.6
12053	Hernando County	$46,860	$36,041	$41,708	$67,508	$90,663	$60,274	$26,483	$21,500	171,888	85.5	76.3	84.8
12055	Highlands County	$43,079	$35,069	$34,930	$65,995	$76,098	$52,254	$24,619	$21,783	96,876	86.9	73.5	80.1
12057	Hillsborough County	$59,190	$28,245	$42,117	$81,853	$93,944	$79,411	$34,326	$26,328	1,268,996	85.8	75.2	78.1
12061	Indian River County	$54,274	$44,645	$41,864	$72,500	$76,798	$64,261	$30,753	$21,280	139,087	86.0	69.9	77.8
12069	Lake County	$53,420	$37,727	$41,539	$75,844	$85,753	$72,522	$33,409	$20,968	300,210	88.1	76.0	83.0
12071	Lee County	$55,878	$45,006	$43,847	$74,842	$87,969	$62,435	$31,402	$25,060	640,429	84.4	66.6	79.8
12073	Leon County	$68,817	$34,922	$46,964	$84,039	$107,235	$91,948	$48,837	$28,033	277,873	91.8	79.5	84.3
12081	Manatee County	$57,554	$42,639	$46,678	$76,778	$89,464	$73,403	$42,878	$24,135	331,722	85.2	72.0	79.1
12083	Marion County	$45,783	$37,543	$38,111	$64,002	$85,417	$57,705	$38,261	$22,522	327,600	86.1	72.5	75.5
12085	Martin County	$65,029	$49,151	$52,418	$85,339	$118,650	$85,216	$30,815	$30,338	146,214	89.2	71.1	81.1
12086	Miami-Dade County	$47,469	$17,044	$34,920	$67,379	$86,127	$65,132	$31,563	$22,878	2,565,217	74.0	64.5	70.5
12087	Monroe County	$65,288	$51,709	$46,155	$78,060	$110,064	$64,083	$40,119	$21,477	73,560	81.6	62.1	68.2
12089	Nassau County	$62,607	$42,500	$53,391	$80,372	$96,672	$70,614	$35,462	$35,653	74,201	86.3	76.1	76.2
12091	Okaloosa County	$63,281	$43,901	$48,050	$75,665	$95,919	$72,267	$31,932	$20,954	178,327	89.6	75.1	77.0
12095	Orange County	$55,704	$25,663	$37,808	$72,676	$85,984	$70,788	$29,485	$24,443	1,186,966	82.0	70.5	75.2
12097	Osceola County	$46,635	$25,197	$33,472	$62,249	$76,694	$55,461	$25,488	$21,998	285,884	78.5	69.8	73.7
12099	Palm Beach County	$63,231	$44,290	$48,998	$82,604	$89,423	$78,901	$36,346	$26,848	1,342,097	84.9	69.3	79.9
12101	Pasco County	$54,574	$34,725	$45,083	$78,968	$92,769	$78,345	$38,716	$28,386	464,843	88.4	76.4	79.9
12103	Pinellas County	$59,439	$35,866	$45,658	$80,209	$100,198	$80,684	$31,404	$26,898	911,337	88.0	74.3	78.6
12105	Polk County	$49,890	$33,797	$38,696	$70,402	$82,067	$61,762	$30,255	$22,987	605,950	84.7	73.5	81.4
12107	Putnam County	$40,952	$29,967	$33,550	$63,420	$85,577	$60,656	$30,441	$18,048	72,100	80.9	76.2	74.7
12109	St. Johns County	$78,021	$48,519	$64,136	$93,642	$124,129	$99,702	$51,679	$29,081	200,731	92.0	80.0	83.2
12111	St. Lucie County	$49,985	$34,858	$41,755	$69,901	$75,734	$56,032	$17,111	$20,495	281,914	82.7	69.6	77.9
12113	Santa Rosa County	$65,309	$42,517	$55,413	$74,749	$101,109	$69,435	$41,076	$27,173	149,573	90.1	77.2	75.6
12115	Sarasota County	$60,421	$51,129	$49,588	$73,801	$88,069	$71,977	$31,363	$27,255	382,246	87.4	75.9	82.5
12117	Seminole County	$66,246	$32,993	$50,915	$86,784	$97,170	$87,639	$40,625	$31,581	428,488	86.0	73.9	81.7
12119	Sumter County	$57,658	$54,132	$59,035	$72,517	$70,491	$62,825	$30,893	$20,412	93,575	93.9	71.8	87.6
12127	Volusia County	$50,180	$36,173	$42,378	$70,700	$90,396	$63,958	$26,974	$21,790	491,275	85.2	75.9	78.1
12131	Walton County	$57,985	$36,461	$40,452	$69,854	$72,188	$65,267	$31,676	$17,697	55,709	86.1	67.3	75.8
13000	**Georgia**	$57,432	$26,281	$41,334	$79,557	$93,926	$76,385	$33,883	$22,191	9,710,901	85.7	72.7	78.6
13013	Barrow County	$58,301	$29,449	$42,330	$69,496	$91,887	$66,007	$53,216	$32,769	70,211	83.0	74.7	78.6
13015	Bartow County	$55,012	$27,156	$41,508	$72,202	$83,468	$66,718	$36,765	$21,441	99,711	83.7	70.1	74.4
13021	Bibb County	$48,397	$21,266	$32,302	$70,836	$78,997	$71,297	$19,071	$15,611	151,893	87.1	74.3	77.8
13031	Bulloch County	$51,686	$21,950	$35,694	$71,095	$86,667	$71,136	$26,886	$20,316	71,430	86.3	72.9	80.6
13039	Camden County	$60,190	$32,425	$42,013	$70,349	$100,832	$65,366	$4,682	$17,751	47,690	91.9	72.4	74.1
13045	Carroll County	$54,243	$27,459	$42,850	$74,833	$102,006	$69,706	$52,319	$21,433	110,313	88.3	62.1	80.4
13047	Catoosa County	$57,970	$29,729	$47,601	$77,868	$91,781	$76,414	$36,513	$31,506	64,567	88.7	75.5	81.0
13051	Chatham County	$55,367	$37,111	$41,447	$72,093	$98,533	$76,240	$23,863	$19,212	268,165	86.8	69.9	79.4
13057	Cherokee County	$77,656	$41,014	$58,723	$92,894	$109,253	$96,004	$47,340	$35,554	220,487	88.8	73.2	80.4
13059	Clarke County	$48,986	$17,977	$31,869	$70,522	$85,078	$59,992	$16,373	$15,119	119,059	86.7	72.8	83.6
13063	Clayton County	$43,656	$17,856	$31,966	$60,365	$81,988	$50,600	$33,961	$21,600	261,038	76.6	68.1	71.3
13067	Cobb County	$75,001	$38,683	$56,048	$96,281	$107,108	$96,858	$37,849	$31,312	701,789	86.5	70.0	78.9
13073	Columbia County	$76,528	$43,121	$60,502	$96,619	$109,748	$84,624	$55,893	$24,247	129,129	92.9	79.4	81.0
13077	Coweta County	$70,055	$30,544	$54,967	$86,509	$103,792	$80,803	$55,625	$19,649	130,515	89.9	79.6	81.7
13089	DeKalb County	$57,919	$25,019	$39,780	$84,957	$90,317	$80,896	$32,265	$26,193	697,995	83.8	71.6	79.0
13095	Dougherty County	$35,263	$18,864	$28,104	$70,450	$73,517	$67,664	$27,618	$12,697	92,132	82.6	74.4	76.6
13097	Douglas County	$56,341	$28,269	$39,963	$81,063	$91,689	$79,923	$27,151	$29,139	133,253	84.9	76.4	74.8
13103	Effingham County	$71,102	$48,367	$46,123	$92,048	$103,375	$83,371	$51,125	$21,833	52,933	87.5	66.5	79.0
13113	Fayette County	$91,047	$50,481	$80,167	$108,041	$125,668	$107,710	$46,994	$32,459	106,848	92.2	82.9	93.2
13115	Floyd County	$49,533	$24,695	$37,407	$64,067	$100,417	$61,250	$42,208	$13,653	93,854	82.2	75.3	77.1
13117	Forsyth County	$99,047	$45,142	$82,500	$117,821	$108,817	$116,329	$59,197	$41,750	187,993	88.7	72.1	77.3
13121	Fulton County	$74,557	$24,020	$53,757	$108,725	$116,081	$120,354	$35,193	$23,945	962,193	89.5	72.8	80.0
13127	Glynn County	$54,776	$42,627	$38,480	$70,703	$73,563	$67,144	$18,399	$23,984	79,924	85.6	68.1	75.0
13129	Gordon County	$46,962	$25,346	$33,816	$68,159	$89,464	$57,575	$20,876	$13,346	55,065	82.9	66.5	73.7
13135	Gwinnett County	$64,500	$26,054	$42,964	$85,395	$93,637	$78,260	$35,910	$30,389	836,588	81.7	72.3	75.1
13139	Hall County	$55,868	$35,222	$37,492	$72,693	$82,500	$62,922	$27,455	$16,356	183,792	83.1	68.5	77.6
13151	Henry County	$62,298	$31,282	$48,552	$80,954	$100,258	$72,892	$41,404	$33,116	207,567	86.3	77.0	83.4
13153	Houston County	$63,716	$32,851	$47,213	$84,029	$99,592	$80,073	$24,792	$20,741	143,054	87.7	78.4	84.0

346 Families in America

Table E-2: Counties with a Population of 50,000 or More—Income, Poverty, and Health Insurance—*Continued*

State/ County FIPS code	State/Place	Total number of families	Families with incomes below the poverty level, as a percent of all families of that family type				Families that received Food Stamps (SNAP), as a percent of all families of that family type			Families that received food stamps (SNAP) and had at least one worker	
			All families	Married-couple families with related children under 18	Male householder families, no spouse present, with related children	Female householder families, no spouse present	All families	Married-couple families	Male householder or female householder families, no spouse present	Married-couple families, percent	Male householder or female householder families, no spouse present
12000	**Florida**................	4,594,006	12.4	10.4	26.8	38.8	16.5	9.4	7.8	34.9	25.6
12001	Alachua County............	50,154	13.4	7.2	19.0	47.5	13.5	5.4	4.2	33.1	19.5
12005	Bay County..................	43,551	11.0	9.0	18.3	38.8	15.6	8.2	6.6	36.4	27.4
12009	Brevard County..............	138,311	10.2	8.8	19.8	38.5	14.1	6.4	5.2	36.2	26.8
12011	Broward County.............	415,615	11.5	8.2	19.2	30.1	15.4	8.8	7.5	29.2	23.7
12015	Charlotte County............	45,601	8.8	10.3	22.1	34.3	12.0	6.5	5.1	36.8	24.8
12017	Citrus County................	38,478	10.8	9.0	43.9	45.4	14.5	7.0	5.6	45.4	28.5
12019	Clay County..................	50,407	6.9	5.1	20.3	21.4	11.5	6.3	5.8	28.1	21.0
12021	Collier County...............	82,392	9.2	13.2	25.7	30.5	11.7	6.9	6.3	30.4	25.4
12023	Columbia County............	14,744	14.9	16.8	24.0	36.8	20.0	10.7	7.7	40.8	33.1
12031	Duval County................	205,389	13.8	7.4	25.1	44.4	17.7	8.4	6.7	37.1	25.1
12033	Escambia County............	67,495	12.7	8.9	27.0	43.9	18.0	8.6	7.1	40.5	30.3
12035	Flagler County...............	24,716	10.4	16.7	23.3	40.9	10.6	6.2	4.9	32.2	23.3
12053	Hernando County...........	47,703	12.9	14.7	29.0	42.8	18.1	10.5	7.6	42.0	28.2
12055	Highlands County...........	24,921	11.8	13.8	25.0	39.5	15.6	9.2	6.2	42.5	27.9
12057	Hillsborough County........	301,959	13.4	10.0	26.9	38.2	18.0	10.9	9.0	34.5	25.5
12061	Indian River County.........	36,580	9.7	11.5	21.3	42.0	14.6	8.4	7.5	36.8	31.4
12069	Lake County.................	80,861	10.2	9.1	28.2	43.9	14.5	9.2	7.9	37.1	28.8
12071	Lee County..................	158,675	11.0	12.2	26.8	38.7	13.8	7.6	6.3	35.6	25.2
12073	Leon County.................	61,549	10.9	6.3	22.8	35.1	14.8	6.3	5.5	33.6	24.7
12081	Manatee County............	85,261	10.6	12.1	24.8	38.3	11.5	5.9	4.9	32.3	24.1
12083	Marion County..............	87,747	13.2	14.4	34.6	45.1	17.6	10.4	8.7	40.4	25.9
12085	Martin County...............	37,923	8.4	9.1	35.5	39.6	9.7	5.0	4.3	29.4	24.0
12086	Miami-Dade County.........	565,614	17.4	14.4	28.9	41.9	27.5	20.0	16.0	41.0	30.9
12087	Monroe County..............	16,195	9.1	12.5	20.1	37.5	8.5	5.2	4.6	21.7	18.8
12089	Nassau County..............	20,325	10.2	12.2	36.2	28.5	12.4	6.6	5.8	33.1	23.4
12091	Okaloosa County............	49,401	11.9	7.6	28.9	46.3	13.0	6.7	6.2	31.5	21.5
12095	Orange County..............	266,253	13.8	10.5	30.5	39.8	17.3	9.4	8.2	34.4	26.9
12097	Osceola County.............	66,440	16.2	14.3	32.8	42.8	23.7	15.7	14.1	40.6	29.7
12099	Palm Beach County.........	324,496	11.0	9.7	24.8	36.1	12.0	6.3	5.5	27.3	21.3
12101	Pasco County................	119,289	9.7	8.8	20.8	31.9	13.5	8.0	6.8	32.7	23.6
12103	Pinellas County..............	220,241	9.9	7.7	27.2	34.6	13.0	6.2	5.0	31.0	22.2
12105	Polk County..................	150,257	14.0	12.4	28.4	42.4	17.9	10.2	8.7	38.1	26.5
12107	Putnam County..............	17,541	19.3	19.6	42.5	49.9	21.6	10.1	8.4	51.2	35.1
12109	St. Johns County............	52,647	6.4	3.2	17.4	36.0	7.9	3.8	3.4	25.4	17.8
12111	St. Lucie County.............	71,740	14.5	14.1	47.2	43.7	15.6	9.1	8.0	34.5	22.9
12113	Santa Rosa County..........	42,758	8.1	8.0	13.8	32.5	11.5	7.2	6.4	28.9	21.7
12115	Sarasota County............	103,374	7.7	5.7	26.4	31.7	9.7	5.0	4.2	29.6	23.2
12117	Seminole County...........	97,825	8.8	5.5	16.0	26.9	9.2	5.1	4.2	20.9	14.6
12119	Sumter County..............	31,441	6.8	17.5	27.6	45.3	6.4	3.7	2.9	29.9	18.5
12127	Volusia County..............	119,637	12.2	11.0	32.8	43.4	16.8	10.0	8.3	37.4	24.8
12131	Walton County..............	15,019	11.4	9.2	39.4	43.7	13.5	5.5	4.8	39.3	29.2
13000	**Georgia**................	2,386,724	14.6	10.3	26.9	44.5	17.6	9.0	7.6	38.0	27.0
13013	Barrow County..............	18,147	10.8	8.9	12.5	40.3	15.8	9.6	8.9	33.0	22.2
13015	Bartow County..............	25,424	14.4	9.7	20.0	54.8	17.0	10.3	6.9	37.9	29.6
13021	Bibb County.................	35,123	22.7	12.0	39.0	56.7	27.3	9.2	7.7	54.0	37.8
13031	Bulloch County..............	14,770	17.6	13.9	24.7	42.4	18.4	7.4	6.5	43.0	34.7
13039	Camden County.............	13,829	14.1	8.2	51.6	62.1	12.8	7.1	6.1	31.5	24.9
13045	Carroll County...............	27,265	13.5	9.6	14.7	44.5	22.0	12.8	11.1	43.7	30.3
13047	Catoosa County.............	17,427	10.3	10.1	25.5	21.2	13.2	7.2	5.8	31.5	23.3
13051	Chatham County............	63,154	15.0	8.9	36.4	48.8	14.2	6.0	5.2	30.9	21.5
13057	Cherokee County...........	56,810	8.1	6.1	12.6	30.0	8.3	4.7	4.0	20.2	17.8
13059	Clarke County...............	20,661	23.4	13.5	52.6	62.1	23.0	10.5	9.1	46.0	29.0
13063	Clayton County.............	57,269	22.3	19.5	26.4	47.9	31.0	19.3	17.5	44.7	32.8
13067	Cobb County................	177,359	9.9	8.2	25.6	29.8	11.9	6.0	5.7	28.6	24.0
13073	Columbia County............	35,129	7.1	4.4	4.1	31.0	6.8	3.4	2.8	20.2	17.3
13077	Coweta County..............	35,526	11.3	6.1	37.5	45.1	13.2	5.8	4.3	38.7	26.3
13089	DeKalb County..............	153,398	15.8	14.1	31.3	38.5	20.6	10.9	9.6	36.9	27.8
13095	Dougherty County..........	22,351	25.8	12.7	28.7	56.8	31.3	12.5	8.6	53.1	35.0
13097	Douglas County.............	34,560	15.5	8.9	34.9	42.1	21.4	11.1	10.2	40.9	27.3
13103	Effingham County...........	14,029	8.1	3.8	11.6	34.1	8.2	5.5	5.1	16.6	14.0
13113	Fayette County..............	30,070	7.0	4.9	14.1	38.3	7.2	3.5	3.1	25.2	17.8
13115	Floyd County................	22,697	17.2	16.8	9.0	50.9	21.2	13.4	10.1	42.0	24.4
13117	Forsyth County..............	45,523	6.0	3.9	19.0	22.6	5.8	3.2	3.1	21.2	17.5
13121	Fulton County...............	205,394	13.5	6.0	20.5	42.5	16.9	5.5	4.8	39.1	28.1
13127	Glynn County................	21,437	15.5	8.0	35.1	43.0	20.2	8.6	7.9	44.6	36.7
13129	Gordon County..............	13,829	18.2	19.6	47.1	57.1	19.5	10.6	9.3	46.8	26.4
13135	Gwinnett County............	204,965	11.5	11.1	18.9	31.3	14.2	9.9	9.3	26.5	21.1
13139	Hall County..................	44,172	15.8	14.8	38.0	51.7	16.3	9.8	8.5	35.5	24.1
13151	Henry County................	54,005	11.8	12.6	12.0	35.4	15.3	9.4	7.8	29.4	19.6
13153	Houston County.............	36,197	13.4	7.7	23.6	42.3	16.7	9.2	8.1	38.6	26.4

| State/County FIPS code | State/Place | Median family income in the past 12 months (in 2,013 inflation-adjusted dollars) | | | | | | | | Total population in households | Persons who had health insurance, as a percent of all persons in that household type | | |
		All families	Families with no earners	Families with one earner	Families with two earners	Families with three or more earners	Married-couple families with children	Male householder, no spouse present, with children	Female householder, no spouse present, with children		Married-couple families, percent	Male householder or female householder families, no spouse present	Nonfamily households
	Georgia—cont'd												
13157	Jackson County	$58,958	$27,727	$43,186	$79,239	$97,713	$75,839	$41,338	$26,293	60,189	88.6	66.0	75.0
13179	Liberty County	$47,331	$17,385	$36,721	$64,496	$95,766	$52,651	$40,378	$17,316	58,726	91.9	78.1	75.8
13185	Lowndes County	$48,242	$24,903	$33,062	$69,895	$87,924	$62,386	$29,531	$19,218	108,427	86.6	74.4	71.7
13215	Muscogee County	$52,041	$25,766	$37,022	$70,954	$83,068	$67,903	$36,185	$21,842	184,655	90.9	77.2	78.7
13217	Newton County	$54,916	$29,764	$42,522	$69,508	$104,022	$74,210	$41,180	$26,899	100,598	86.9	73.1	82.0
13223	Paulding County	$64,107	$28,278	$48,397	$80,877	$93,750	$78,877	$38,024	$29,636	144,528	88.4	71.6	84.8
13245	Richmond County	$45,355	$20,819	$35,890	$66,186	$90,945	$72,610	$35,667	$15,217	192,600	87.9	76.7	79.9
13247	Rockdale County	$54,551	$28,927	$41,357	$77,925	$107,365	$71,408	$31,563	$31,841	85,385	82.9	71.1	74.2
13255	Spalding County	$48,372	$24,214	$41,805	$61,936	$84,625	$58,411	$40,272	$18,352	62,877	83.4	79.9	83.4
13285	Troup County	$50,604	$23,324	$32,854	$72,159	$85,755	$78,629	$29,262	$15,549	67,028	89.2	74.7	81.3
13295	Walker County	$51,886	$29,871	$38,661	$66,345	$89,497	$63,518	$24,292	$17,800	67,013	86.7	72.6	77.7
13297	Walton County	$59,184	$33,256	$40,193	$81,464	$81,469	$72,942	$31,897	$19,986	84,176	88.4	73.8	80.6
13313	Whitfield County	$43,874	$23,615	$30,823	$56,967	$78,438	$49,975	$30,926	$20,579	102,174	76.1	70.2	77.0
15000	**Hawaii**	$78,501	$40,960	$54,697	$90,367	$123,507	$87,567	$48,840	$27,683	1,337,598	94.8	91.0	89.3
15001	Hawaii County	$57,151	$29,163	$41,292	$76,199	$95,065	$73,137	$24,750	$20,143	187,678	93.1	87.3	85.5
15003	Honolulu County	$83,981	$45,510	$60,569	$96,422	$130,518	$92,731	$62,082	$30,800	925,216	95.6	92.3	91.5
15007	Kauai County	$72,619	$38,594	$51,418	$82,939	$107,111	$80,739	$34,583	$31,769	67,837	91.9	89.6	82.6
15009	Maui County	$75,856	$40,776	$49,032	$83,583	$114,393	$83,543	$40,972	$29,590	156,787	92.9	89.5	84.5
16000	**Idaho**	$55,296	$34,365	$41,860	$67,736	$84,642	$63,851	$36,592	$20,543	1,577,379	86.5	75.6	80.4
16001	Ada County	$65,604	$37,312	$50,891	$78,140	$102,266	$79,442	$36,814	$24,126	403,114	91.3	77.6	83.3
16005	Bannock County	$57,454	$38,385	$38,765	$70,705	$81,183	$65,800	$27,278	$20,038	82,020	88.5	81.0	80.5
16019	Bonneville County	$57,206	$40,271	$49,168	$65,479	$94,722	$69,501	$44,702	$22,076	105,686	89.1	73.2	78.0
16027	Canyon County	$46,676	$32,405	$34,638	$59,339	$66,849	$52,315	$29,659	$15,716	193,270	83.4	73.7	78.3
16055	Kootenai County	$57,243	$35,763	$47,880	$68,943	$82,464	$64,242	$36,004	$28,309	141,463	86.9	75.3	75.3
16083	Twin Falls County	$50,543	$28,516	$36,382	$61,501	$83,472	$59,206	$46,604	$16,098	77,947	84.3	73.7	75.8
17000	**Illinois**	$69,142	$32,285	$48,001	$89,454	$106,113	$88,403	$37,113	$24,017	12,690,730	90.7	79.9	84.3
17001	Adams County	$59,187	$33,331	$38,891	$73,607	$88,108	$73,135	$29,293	$16,957	65,926	93.8	85.6	80.3
17007	Boone County	$66,256	$28,860	$47,252	$76,171	$119,338	$71,841	$56,335	$25,208	53,705	90.7	78.2	84.5
17019	Champaign County	$68,167	$40,110	$45,000	$81,201	$105,255	$87,809	$35,020	$23,397	201,731	94.6	87.0	87.8
17029	Coles County	$54,768	$34,087	$37,298	$70,602	$85,833	$66,157	$19,119	$19,668	53,038	88.6	81.7	86.5
17031	Cook County	$64,754	$25,329	$43,690	$90,453	$102,207	$83,689	$33,640	$24,874	5,184,657	87.0	76.7	83.3
17037	DeKalb County	$67,720	$36,473	$50,369	$80,493	$105,924	$81,689	$52,676	$15,078	103,756	91.9	83.6	88.9
17043	DuPage County	$93,834	$44,104	$71,074	$108,859	$121,498	$111,840	$60,163	$36,871	921,771	92.9	81.8	87.7
17063	Grundy County	$78,084	$41,200	$50,035	$97,081	$106,377	$91,685	$37,003	$29,501	49,939	93.1	86.7	89.5
17073	Henry County	$62,493	$32,982	$51,645	$82,571	$100,804	$86,488	$38,958	$21,497	49,398	95.7	83.3	85.1
17077	Jackson County	$52,468	$30,946	$34,594	$75,439	$89,344	$68,324	$13,810	$15,678	59,377	91.3	86.7	89.8
17089	Kane County	$78,996	$42,378	$53,135	$92,825	$107,740	$92,129	$37,546	$25,613	518,467	89.3	77.9	82.1
17091	Kankakee County	$59,623	$29,733	$44,007	$82,138	$99,711	$80,101	$43,039	$19,571	110,590	92.6	82.8	84.7
17093	Kendall County	$90,952	$40,250	$62,059	$105,077	$127,171	$102,115	$43,651	$36,557	117,828	94.9	88.2	91.2
17095	Knox County	$51,107	$31,767	$34,391	$77,821	$89,919	$68,091	$30,969	$16,130	49,621	93.2	83.3	86.2
17097	Lake County	$90,331	$39,452	$65,689	$109,351	$116,547	$108,401	$39,595	$27,321	686,657	91.4	80.6	85.2
17099	LaSalle County	$61,134	$34,394	$44,243	$79,270	$99,934	$80,404	$36,857	$20,264	110,214	93.4	82.8	81.7
17111	McHenry County	$87,211	$42,571	$62,229	$98,491	$113,540	$101,660	$50,349	$33,878	306,385	94.2	82.3	83.4
17113	McLean County	$82,705	$52,591	$54,495	$99,495	$116,111	$102,751	$44,253	$27,446	171,402	95.9	87.3	89.9
17115	Macon County	$57,722	$37,869	$38,893	$84,387	$104,800	$80,780	$31,553	$16,043	107,679	94.1	83.7	84.9
17119	Madison County	$65,892	$34,422	$50,596	$83,420	$111,662	$85,909	$32,820	$25,228	264,762	94.0	84.7	83.5
17141	Ogle County	$68,436	$37,637	$45,894	$85,858	$104,375	$84,145	$30,387	$28,458	52,296	95.2	79.7	84.3
17143	Peoria County	$64,524	$37,429	$45,115	$87,287	$105,909	$89,182	$31,458	$20,221	185,193	94.4	84.8	82.9
17161	Rock Island County	$60,395	$41,290	$41,000	$76,208	$93,761	$72,544	$35,785	$24,293	145,203	93.5	84.0	86.4
17163	St. Clair County	$61,655	$25,518	$43,038	$83,762	$117,057	$84,626	$42,672	$18,065	262,810	92.8	83.4	82.3
17167	Sangamon County	$69,958	$41,609	$47,492	$91,987	$109,913	$94,188	$37,641	$21,482	196,908	95.1	86.0	84.3
17179	Tazewell County	$69,168	$40,504	$50,900	$83,678	$110,172	$82,751	$41,615	$24,250	133,900	94.6	83.2	84.6
17183	Vermilion County	$54,199	$34,140	$40,089	$75,603	$98,684	$72,953	$40,625	$20,408	78,707	92.8	83.2	83.1
17195	Whiteside County	$58,753	$36,922	$41,108	$74,506	$86,437	$73,516	$39,973	$21,071	56,988	93.7	84.7	85.3
17197	Will County	$85,134	$38,379	$63,301	$99,650	$115,543	$98,787	$53,401	$31,926	675,414	93.7	83.5	84.7
17199	Williamson County	$53,869	$33,036	$39,837	$73,903	$99,375	$84,568	$38,625	$20,288	65,045	94.1	81.3	78.1
17201	Winnebago County	$56,758	$29,254	$41,481	$80,187	$95,364	$76,397	$32,080	$22,173	288,897	91.7	82.7	81.1
18000	**Indiana**	$59,490	$31,602	$42,256	$77,001	$95,990	$76,786	$35,568	$21,383	6,441,965	89.5	78.1	82.7
18003	Allen County	$58,691	$30,743	$42,217	$78,209	$97,425	$75,158	$35,432	$22,429	357,190	88.4	77.2	80.8
18005	Bartholomew County	$65,958	$37,783	$45,816	$81,342	$107,061	$83,960	$31,605	$25,554	77,767	92.7	73.5	87.7
18011	Boone County	$79,930	$37,491	$57,042	$91,609	$114,435	$105,574	$41,222	$38,345	58,501	95.3	82.2	82.3
18019	Clark County	$63,769	$35,238	$44,305	$75,152	$100,721	$74,825	$33,382	$30,341	110,622	90.4	76.5	85.8
18035	Delaware County	$49,735	$30,273	$39,682	$70,042	$83,481	$71,082	$42,667	$18,924	116,041	91.4	77.3	84.5
18039	Elkhart County	$52,609	$26,568	$39,370	$67,009	$90,059	$62,678	$38,964	$18,589	196,980	80.5	76.4	78.2
18043	Floyd County	$69,138	$32,157	$56,930	$82,437	$108,138	$85,387	$56,030	$17,356	74,573	91.2	80.0	82.8
18053	Grant County	$48,369	$28,577	$39,836	$65,245	$75,929	$61,744	$27,339	$19,043	68,374	90.2	75.7	84.2
18057	Hamilton County	$100,976	$44,383	$74,247	$115,219	$135,337	$118,828	$50,829	$42,010	288,153	94.8	83.0	86.4
18059	Hancock County	$73,541	$40,704	$50,950	$91,285	$100,956	$92,685	$41,341	$36,219	70,342	93.7	84.0	82.4
18063	Hendricks County	$79,047	$44,512	$56,127	$93,168	$120,500	$95,377	$50,635	$37,327	148,011	95.3	79.4	86.8

Table E-2: Counties with a Population of 50,000 or More—Income, Poverty, and Health Insurance—*Continued*

State/ County FIPS code	State/Place	Total number of families	Families with incomes below the poverty level, as a percent of all families of that family type				Families that received Food Stamps (SNAP), as a percent of all families of that family type			Families that received food stamps (SNAP) and had at least one worker	
			All families	Married-couple families with related children under 18	Male householder families, no spouse present, with related children	Female householder families, no spouse present	All families	Married-couple families	Male householder or female householder families, no spouse present	Married-couple families, percent	Male householder or female householder families, no spouse present
	Georgia—cont'd										
13157	Jackson County	16,600	13.6	8.1	27.7	42.4	13.9	9.3	7.2	30.0	21.2
13179	Liberty County	17,113	14.8	9.1	14.3	50.6	15.8	6.9	6.3	38.5	30.5
13185	Lowndes County	24,648	17.2	12.4	19.0	50.7	21.0	10.8	8.5	41.8	32.2
13215	Muscogee County	45,804	15.5	7.6	20.3	42.2	21.6	8.9	8.0	41.5	30.5
13217	Newton County	24,351	12.9	6.2	39.4	33.7	22.2	10.5	10.2	43.3	35.3
13223	Paulding County	39,219	12.3	8.3	27.7	39.6	11.6	6.7	5.7	28.6	23.5
13245	Richmond County	43,024	21.3	10.8	20.5	58.9	25.2	9.3	8.2	45.7	31.1
13247	Rockdale County	21,228	13.5	12.0	34.7	31.3	16.8	10.7	7.7	29.9	22.2
13255	Spalding County	16,507	18.4	12.8	35.9	45.5	22.8	11.4	9.7	42.6	21.1
13285	Troup County	16,951	19.7	9.5	22.2	62.0	21.5	6.3	5.3	46.2	31.9
13295	Walker County	17,832	12.8	6.1	32.8	48.3	16.7	10.0	8.0	37.5	25.1
13297	Walton County	23,214	11.6	7.9	14.4	49.2	13.8	6.7	6.0	35.1	26.8
13313	Whitfield County	25,212	15.6	14.6	33.7	42.4	16.4	10.5	9.0	32.7	24.2
15000	**Hawaii**	311,096	8.0	5.9	18.3	31.3	11.8	7.0	6.0	25.6	19.5
15001	Hawaii County	43,533	14.6	12.0	38.3	43.5	18.3	10.5	8.8	37.1	25.0
15003	Honolulu County	215,872	6.8	4.8	10.1	30.3	9.9	6.2	5.3	20.9	16.0
15007	Kauai County	15,759	8.0	8.1	28.2	24.0	12.1	7.7	6.8	27.6	20.4
15009	Maui County	35,918	7.4	5.3	17.4	24.5	15.0	7.6	6.8	36.4	31.3
16000	**Idaho**	404,512	11.3	9.5	22.8	44.9	14.0	8.6	7.9	34.7	27.2
16001	Ada County	104,414	9.1	6.1	24.9	38.0	11.5	6.0	5.6	31.1	22.7
16005	Bannock County	19,869	11.8	12.0	22.1	40.2	16.9	9.9	9.0	40.6	34.7
16019	Bonneville County	26,566	9.4	7.2	5.9	39.5	15.3	8.8	8.5	39.1	33.6
16027	Canyon County	47,244	16.4	14.0	31.8	58.8	23.4	15.9	14.8	48.8	39.5
16055	Kootenai County	38,204	9.3	4.6	33.8	35.9	12.8	7.1	6.6	33.3	24.4
16083	Twin Falls County	20,203	13.0	9.4	15.9	57.7	17.2	9.4	8.8	42.3	36.0
17000	**Illinois**	3,114,415	10.9	7.6	22.5	41.1	14.0	6.7	5.8	34.2	25.5
17001	Adams County	17,548	11.0	7.7	30.1	50.1	13.8	6.5	5.2	42.3	34.6
17007	Boone County	13,647	9.7	6.4	26.6	38.1	12.7	6.2	4.9	40.4	30.6
17019	Champaign County	42,372	10.5	6.3	25.8	41.9	11.2	4.8	4.1	30.2	24.9
17029	Coles County	11,758	13.5	12.2	34.9	38.9	17.5	7.1	6.2	46.2	33.9
17031	Cook County	1,176,075	13.8	10.3	25.8	42.0	18.4	9.2	7.8	37.1	27.0
17037	DeKalb County	22,683	12.9	7.6	25.9	56.1	14.5	8.5	7.8	31.8	23.0
17043	DuPage County	239,278	5.1	4.4	14.9	25.4	6.4	4.3	3.9	15.7	12.9
17063	Grundy County	13,128	7.2	3.2	17.3	29.8	11.1	5.1	4.6	30.8	22.4
17073	Henry County	13,882	7.3	3.2	6.1	46.0	8.6	3.8	3.4	28.3	21.5
17077	Jackson County	11,551	18.9	17.9	50.0	56.6	20.4	10.6	8.3	48.3	38.1
17089	Kane County	126,599	8.8	7.7	15.8	39.6	12.4	7.5	7.0	30.4	25.8
17091	Kankakee County	27,997	13.2	9.4	14.0	48.4	19.2	9.3	8.5	41.6	30.3
17093	Kendall County	29,550	4.2	3.6	13.3	18.8	5.4	2.7	2.3	19.2	19.2
17095	Knox County	12,456	14.0	8.7	25.0	63.8	18.0	8.2	6.8	45.4	26.6
17097	Lake County	179,169	7.6	5.2	23.5	35.5	9.0	4.6	4.1	26.5	20.0
17099	LaSalle County	28,805	10.1	6.7	18.4	48.9	12.6	6.3	5.2	32.8	24.0
17111	McHenry County	81,791	6.0	4.6	16.4	28.8	5.7	2.8	2.5	18.6	16.4
17113	McLean County	40,034	7.2	2.6	23.3	33.9	9.9	3.9	3.4	32.1	27.0
17115	Macon County	27,857	14.0	8.2	14.2	57.3	16.0	6.6	5.7	40.5	29.9
17119	Madison County	70,984	9.7	6.5	27.2	38.7	14.6	7.4	6.1	35.1	25.9
17141	Ogle County	13,537	6.9	5.2	30.4	35.0	9.3	5.9	5.6	25.9	21.7
17143	Peoria County	46,480	13.6	8.3	32.0	49.3	13.6	3.2	2.4	39.1	29.0
17161	Rock Island County	37,635	11.0	8.9	12.5	42.7	13.8	6.2	5.6	33.9	27.1
17163	St. Clair County	68,389	15.9	8.5	22.5	51.8	17.9	6.1	4.5	41.1	28.5
17167	Sangamon County	51,239	11.3	7.2	24.6	43.1	13.7	5.2	4.7	34.8	27.6
17179	Tazewell County	36,923	6.4	3.5	12.8	30.8	9.0	3.7	2.8	31.1	27.4
17183	Vermilion County	20,457	14.2	7.6	24.3	51.1	17.2	8.0	6.5	39.8	27.9
17195	Whiteside County	15,621	8.4	5.9	12.7	41.4	11.7	4.0	3.0	38.2	31.4
17197	Will County	170,292	6.4	4.0	13.8	30.3	8.5	4.5	4.1	23.8	17.4
17199	Williamson County	17,964	11.0	5.6	15.1	43.8	13.8	6.6	5.6	36.3	24.3
17201	Winnebago County	75,010	13.4	9.0	21.5	43.7	17.9	7.8	6.2	42.7	31.6
18000	**Indiana**	1,647,579	11.6	7.8	25.4	44.4	13.7	6.5	5.5	34.6	24.9
18003	Allen County	89,711	13.1	9.1	26.7	42.6	14.1	5.7	4.9	35.7	24.3
18005	Bartholomew County	20,179	9.1	7.0	29.4	34.4	8.0	3.1	2.2	23.7	16.9
18011	Boone County	16,221	3.8	1.5	24.2	21.7	5.0	3.6	3.3	11.7	10.3
18019	Clark County	28,045	8.4	7.0	26.9	29.7	10.6	6.6	5.8	23.0	18.1
18035	Delaware County	27,561	13.1	8.7	33.1	46.9	18.9	9.0	6.8	44.3	31.6
18039	Elkhart County	51,212	13.9	10.4	22.6	48.6	16.4	8.0	7.1	38.9	27.3
18043	Floyd County	19,486	11.5	5.3	14.0	52.3	11.9	4.5	3.4	34.2	20.5
18053	Grant County	17,727	15.9	10.5	40.8	47.8	18.5	7.6	5.9	45.7	29.7
18057	Hamilton County	77,314	3.6	2.1	13.7	18.6	3.8	2.1	1.8	12.6	10.7
18059	Hancock County	19,018	4.8	2.2	6.2	26.1	7.6	2.5	2.2	25.3	21.1
18063	Hendricks County	40,524	2.7	1.7	11.8	14.6	5.0	3.3	3.2	12.9	9.3

Table E-2: Counties with a Population of 50,000 or More—Income, Poverty, and Health Insurance—*Continued*

State/County FIPS code	State/Place	Median family income in the past 12 months (in 2,013 inflation-adjusted dollars)								Total population in households	Persons who had health insurance, as a percent of all persons in that household type		
		All families	Families with no earners	Families with one earner	Families with two earners	Families with three or more earners	Families with own children under 18 years						
							Married-couple families with children	Male householder, no spouse present, with children	Female householder, no spouse present, with children		Married-couple families, percent	Male householder or female householder families, no spouse present	Nonfamily households
	Indiana—cont'd												
18067	Howard County	$57,053	$38,750	$39,579	$79,814	$98,627	$77,584	$31,400	$20,923	81,935	92.3	80.0	78.7
18081	Johnson County	$72,315	$34,068	$49,182	$88,891	$101,111	$86,684	$42,713	$23,378	141,223	92.9	80.0	84.3
18085	Kosciusko County	$61,512	$35,932	$46,121	$68,198	$97,237	$69,447	$40,240	$32,752	76,908	86.6	80.8	84.5
18089	Lake County	$59,807	$26,822	$44,695	$81,569	$102,789	$81,101	$40,532	$18,062	489,490	89.0	78.4	81.6
18091	LaPorte County	$58,280	$31,620	$40,269	$78,443	$87,763	$73,833	$30,909	$15,719	102,289	90.8	81.4	79.5
18095	Madison County	$53,362	$37,911	$37,047	$72,110	$88,194	$63,756	$24,983	$22,521	125,387	88.9	78.5	79.9
18097	Marion County	$51,338	$24,834	$35,073	$72,444	$94,281	$71,028	$27,206	$21,300	909,706	87.7	77.4	79.5
18105	Monroe County	$61,943	$31,946	$50,809	$75,911	$82,764	$85,015	$52,361	$23,590	140,244	92.3	77.7	88.0
18109	Morgan County	$63,432	$38,143	$45,838	$74,290	$100,962	$78,781	$30,394	$22,485	68,845	91.5	81.2	79.5
18127	Porter County	$77,160	$36,173	$56,954	$93,547	$111,883	$93,422	$48,468	$22,862	164,566	92.4	79.1	85.2
18141	St. Joseph County	$54,917	$30,965	$38,927	$71,778	$92,205	$72,052	$25,201	$18,961	264,085	90.3	75.9	82.9
18157	Tippecanoe County	$62,283	$38,304	$43,298	$76,646	$92,409	$75,760	$36,367	$19,919	176,068	91.1	79.5	86.5
18163	Vanderburgh County	$56,864	$31,285	$37,557	$74,478	$101,695	$77,032	$27,756	$20,073	178,210	92.1	79.6	81.1
18167	Vigo County	$54,722	$30,246	$38,197	$69,853	$83,807	$65,781	$29,531	$20,158	104,025	88.2	78.6	79.2
18173	Warrick County	$70,614	$46,242	$47,447	$87,956	$104,000	$87,574	$21,622	$26,240	59,836	95.4	78.7	84.0
18177	Wayne County	$46,104	$24,932	$32,163	$67,931	$90,922	$62,077	$31,438	$11,724	67,173	83.0	78.3	81.3
19000	**Iowa**	$65,550	$35,528	$43,336	$80,074	$96,280	$81,489	$38,392	$24,069	3,031,378	94.3	84.8	88.6
19013	Black Hawk County	$61,309	$36,606	$41,840	$75,677	$95,736	$78,072	$35,948	$21,344	130,548	95.5	84.4	90.7
19049	Dallas County	$85,440	$39,219	$69,188	$99,022	$112,038	$99,701	$74,500	$33,759	71,602	96.6	90.7	87.3
19061	Dubuque County	$66,923	$37,255	$43,711	$80,607	$89,520	$84,801	$43,552	$19,862	93,823	95.4	90.5	91.7
19103	Johnson County	$81,742	$45,282	$53,156	$93,984	$115,319	$98,328	$51,471	$25,196	134,609	94.3	87.5	92.0
19113	Linn County	$76,006	$43,277	$50,052	$90,739	$108,708	$93,531	$37,845	$27,231	213,033	96.3	84.8	88.7
19153	Polk County	$72,230	$34,680	$43,366	$88,260	$105,382	$90,461	$36,388	$26,428	439,491	94.3	85.3	90.6
19155	Pottawattamie County	$63,054	$29,615	$45,643	$77,056	$96,773	$84,327	$49,741	$27,753	91,802	92.2	83.9	83.3
19163	Scott County	$72,049	$38,173	$44,549	$92,797	$109,797	$97,134	$45,448	$25,129	166,847	93.8	84.8	85.5
19169	Story County	$75,721	$52,732	$53,151	$85,854	$108,369	$85,594	$40,990	$17,571	90,900	97.7	88.8	92.7
19193	Woodbury County	$55,637	$29,586	$35,202	$70,202	$92,431	$69,764	$39,139	$20,780	101,369	92.4	83.4	83.6
20000	**Kansas**	$64,346	$34,928	$43,825	$79,709	$98,311	$79,250	$35,997	$23,860	2,824,697	91.0	79.1	84.4
20015	Butler County	$70,148	$43,984	$51,645	$87,026	$101,406	$80,180	$52,443	$21,847	64,070	94.0	83.0	88.6
20045	Douglas County	$70,291	$42,786	$49,984	$82,393	$111,568	$92,152	$36,743	$33,171	112,525	92.2	79.2	86.5
20091	Johnson County	$91,411	$48,593	$67,059	$104,607	$124,816	$111,055	$49,858	$37,319	555,360	94.6	81.8	87.2
20103	Leavenworth County	$75,977	$37,529	$61,013	$90,970	$108,681	$89,858	$51,514	$25,468	70,506	94.1	81.7	87.5
20155	Reno County	$55,824	$31,365	$41,160	$70,316	$85,962	$67,743	$30,921	$20,500	61,779	87.4	78.0	83.4
20161	Riley County	$61,357	$39,205	$43,131	$80,396	$96,170	$64,093	$34,250	$29,609	68,214	95.6	91.3	89.1
20169	Saline County	$56,739	$32,193	$37,500	$70,111	$93,279	$72,354	$28,736	$21,921	54,971	88.8	80.8	80.4
20173	Sedgwick County	$62,016	$35,612	$42,698	$79,404	$97,998	$75,509	$35,755	$22,440	496,464	89.4	79.1	80.8
20177	Shawnee County	$62,219	$38,103	$42,082	$81,900	$97,847	$81,559	$35,559	$21,090	175,737	92.0	79.2	81.5
20209	Wyandotte County	$45,419	$22,222	$29,670	$64,220	$78,472	$56,288	$25,649	$17,496	158,015	79.3	71.0	75.6
21000	**Kentucky**	$53,994	$25,353	$40,940	$75,776	$94,284	$73,748	$32,067	$18,590	4,295,357	89.6	78.3	82.4
21015	Boone County	$75,791	$40,551	$53,161	$93,908	$104,415	$94,701	$50,807	$23,635	122,286	95.3	81.8	83.4
21029	Bullitt County	$64,619	$33,955	$43,985	$79,549	$99,670	$85,948	$34,100	$29,298	75,671	94.2	85.0	86.7
21037	Campbell County	$68,400	$31,449	$46,743	$90,229	$111,131	$96,677	$27,617	$18,813	89,639	91.8	78.1	85.3
21047	Christian County	$46,640	$22,094	$33,247	$58,902	$87,449	$50,479	$25,597	$15,296	65,848	88.0	73.0	77.6
21059	Daviess County	$58,313	$29,843	$42,229	$74,505	$101,733	$71,233	$30,953	$21,081	96,069	91.8	79.3	83.6
21067	Fayette County	$67,463	$36,016	$43,399	$86,466	$107,509	$90,341	$37,254	$21,005	299,612	90.6	79.7	83.6
21093	Hardin County	$58,052	$29,816	$44,788	$77,682	$95,245	$76,913	$40,662	$20,614	101,130	90.7	82.6	82.4
21111	Jefferson County	$61,185	$32,237	$42,523	$82,769	$102,465	$87,756	$41,821	$22,698	742,833	92.0	79.2	81.9
21117	Kenton County	$64,684	$30,093	$45,831	$82,601	$106,193	$85,982	$44,833	$21,394	160,243	91.1	78.4	84.3
21125	Laurel County	$41,855	$23,297	$35,648	$67,267	$79,583	$53,950	$30,485	$15,732	58,735	84.7	68.3	78.9
21145	McCracken County	$54,613	$30,899	$45,299	$73,852	$84,043	$81,924	$45,664	$14,794	64,490	91.2	75.6	82.3
21151	Madison County	$54,392	$26,917	$42,676	$75,469	$91,424	$76,206	$20,387	$19,398	84,023	90.2	78.0	81.4
21185	Oldham County	$91,518	$50,214	$70,010	$107,592	$118,033	$114,454	$63,529	$37,115	57,269	96.1	84.3	81.3
21195	Pike County	$42,998	$23,739	$40,906	$71,538	$104,868	$55,276	$33,918	$13,441	63,302	87.5	78.7	87.6
21199	Pulaski County	$43,373	$18,654	$34,991	$57,947	$84,397	$57,951	$27,600	$12,483	62,847	88.6	76.1	83.4
21227	Warren County	$58,593	$30,110	$39,421	$70,248	$90,373	$81,812	$38,354	$17,207	115,653	89.5	77.8	83.1
22000	**Louisiana**	$55,414	$23,278	$39,756	$82,102	$102,388	$83,839	$38,120	$19,279	4,498,089	88.0	76.5	78.5
22001	Acadia Parish	$44,577	$19,559	$37,040	$70,000	$100,019	$76,823	$45,100	$19,442	61,075	87.2	76.5	75.3
22005	Ascension Parish	$76,724	$30,239	$49,979	$102,068	$106,618	$105,477	$41,420	$25,190	111,432	92.6	76.5	79.2
22015	Bossier Parish	$66,685	$29,262	$46,759	$81,024	$113,701	$86,681	$40,363	$20,520	117,420	90.1	76.2	80.3
22017	Caddo Parish	$52,251	$25,166	$36,494	$80,786	$96,037	$86,486	$48,458	$19,891	251,187	88.2	75.5	80.3
22019	Calcasieu Parish	$55,119	$28,275	$39,113	$82,352	$111,193	$80,784	$37,156	$22,877	192,169	87.7	75.7	75.8
22033	East Baton Rouge Parish	$62,210	$29,966	$41,108	$87,215	$109,610	$90,620	$36,992	$22,093	440,648	90.8	80.2	84.9
22045	Iberia Parish	$49,889	$21,741	$39,526	$77,825	$105,467	$80,721	$37,425	$20,234	72,858	86.5	79.4	77.0
22051	Jefferson Parish	$59,940	$27,630	$40,295	$82,919	$105,517	$83,606	$38,168	$20,335	431,017	87.0	76.6	75.1
22055	Lafayette Parish	$68,684	$22,921	$46,440	$88,898	$109,858	$91,315	$58,047	$17,953	224,952	89.9	75.9	80.0
22057	Lafourche Parish	$59,556	$25,964	$43,554	$90,934	$97,206	$90,846	$34,696	$23,588	96,145	88.3	76.6	78.5
22063	Livingston Parish	$65,507	$28,081	$46,196	$84,608	$123,115	$85,745	$61,556	$18,876	131,064	88.1	74.2	76.7
22071	Orleans Parish	$46,979	$15,712	$32,089	$84,406	$95,643	$88,220	$33,633	$17,189	364,405	87.9	78.3	78.6
22073	Ouachita Parish	$49,557	$20,267	$32,252	$74,254	$97,293	$77,396	$41,409	$14,126	148,962	85.4	68.0	72.0
22079	Rapides Parish	$49,114	$24,742	$35,652	$75,134	$100,966	$74,972	$28,023	$18,989	129,683	87.1	75.9	80.9

State/County FIPS code	State/Place	Total number of families	Families with incomes below the poverty level, as a percent of all families of that family type				Families that received Food Stamps (SNAP), as a percent of all families of that family type			Families that received food stamps (SNAP) and had at least one worker	
			All families	Married-couple families with related children under 18	Male householder families, no spouse present, with related children	Female householder families, no spouse present	All families	Married-couple families	Male householder or female householder families, no spouse present	Married-couple families, percent	Male householder or female householder families, no spouse present
	Indiana—cont'd										
18067	Howard County	22,421	12.3	11.0	38.0	44.6	15.5	6.6	6.1	42.3	29.4
18081	Johnson County	37,780	9.0	5.8	28.7	44.1	9.1	4.3	4.2	28.9	20.0
18085	Kosciusko County	20,485	7.6	6.9	25.5	29.5	8.7	4.8	4.2	24.7	18.9
18089	Lake County	122,415	14.7	9.5	19.3	50.3	17.5	7.6	6.3	37.7	25.4
18091	LaPorte County	27,858	14.1	10.4	25.4	56.4	15.0	5.8	4.9	41.3	30.9
18095	Madison County	32,267	13.3	10.3	37.7	42.9	16.3	8.0	7.0	38.6	26.3
18097	Marion County	212,908	16.9	10.0	35.8	44.9	20.6	9.3	8.2	39.9	29.8
18105	Monroe County	27,550	11.9	7.4	17.9	44.8	11.1	4.6	4.1	29.9	18.3
18109	Morgan County	18,978	8.6	5.3	34.9	48.3	12.6	6.4	5.2	40.6	30.9
18127	Porter County	44,218	8.6	5.8	9.7	39.5	8.8	4.4	3.9	24.0	19.6
18141	St. Joseph County	65,425	14.0	10.9	34.4	50.1	16.3	7.1	6.2	40.1	30.5
18157	Tippecanoe County	38,710	11.5	8.3	15.9	50.8	12.9	5.5	5.1	36.4	28.0
18163	Vanderburgh County	44,599	11.9	5.3	27.2	44.1	13.2	5.8	4.2	31.8	23.2
18167	Vigo County	24,211	13.8	10.6	38.1	51.5	16.8	8.6	7.1	40.0	28.7
18173	Warrick County	16,906	7.2	5.1	64.9	44.7	7.7	4.9	4.5	22.8	15.5
18177	Wayne County	18,288	18.7	16.8	32.1	66.4	18.5	10.0	7.9	40.9	22.5
19000	**Iowa**	792,745	8.4	5.3	19.3	39.7	12.0	5.6	4.8	36.2	29.0
19013	Black Hawk County	30,508	9.9	7.4	22.0	44.3	13.1	5.4	4.3	40.1	29.3
19049	Dallas County	19,602	3.8	1.6	0.3	18.8	6.4	4.0	3.1	17.6	15.3
19061	Dubuque County	23,929	8.0	3.2	8.5	49.4	9.6	3.4	3.2	34.1	27.8
19103	Johnson County	30,216	6.7	3.7	8.9	35.6	10.6	5.4	5.1	30.3	25.4
19113	Linn County	53,145	6.0	1.7	18.5	30.3	11.1	4.2	3.7	35.3	30.7
19153	Polk County	112,798	9.6	6.7	24.6	35.4	15.6	7.0	6.0	41.3	33.2
19155	Pottawattamie County	24,295	9.0	6.6	8.3	35.4	15.7	7.7	6.4	36.2	26.0
19163	Scott County	41,848	8.9	4.1	16.9	39.5	12.0	5.0	4.3	33.7	25.0
19169	Story County	18,866	7.5	5.1	13.3	50.3	8.2	4.6	4.0	29.5	27.1
19193	Woodbury County	25,115	12.3	7.7	16.4	44.6	18.2	9.9	8.8	38.0	31.4
20000	**Kansas**	727,902	9.4	7.1	19.1	40.1	10.1	5.0	4.4	27.5	21.4
20015	Butler County	17,290	6.5	3.4	9.7	41.5	8.1	3.8	3.7	25.7	21.7
20045	Douglas County	23,749	8.4	6.4	21.2	35.1	8.4	4.5	4.0	20.7	16.9
20091	Johnson County	147,978	4.0	2.4	13.2	18.8	4.5	2.0	1.9	15.3	12.6
20103	Leavenworth County	19,111	8.2	5.9	6.0	42.4	7.7	4.1	4.0	21.0	14.3
20155	Reno County	16,656	8.3	4.8	27.5	44.0	11.8	6.4	5.6	32.7	22.7
20161	Riley County	14,156	6.6	3.5	12.4	28.8	6.9	3.6	3.0	19.1	16.4
20169	Saline County	14,364	12.4	6.4	25.6	50.2	9.6	3.0	2.3	27.0	18.9
20173	Sedgwick County	124,097	11.6	9.9	19.0	40.5	13.8	7.1	6.3	31.9	25.6
20177	Shawnee County	44,480	11.5	8.2	22.6	44.7	12.6	6.1	5.0	32.4	24.0
20209	Wyandotte County	36,841	19.6	14.7	20.7	55.4	21.3	10.7	9.8	37.3	26.4
21000	**Kentucky**	1,131,310	14.6	10.4	30.1	49.8	17.7	9.6	7.1	40.1	25.5
21015	Boone County	32,931	6.8	2.6	13.9	36.0	8.7	3.8	3.7	24.6	17.9
21029	Bullitt County	20,648	7.5	2.4	26.1	29.6	9.7	3.8	2.8	27.8	19.6
21037	Campbell County	22,604	11.2	4.1	40.1	47.2	10.5	2.9	2.1	30.7	20.1
21047	Christian County	18,170	17.3	9.4	32.1	63.3	18.3	9.1	7.6	43.0	30.4
21059	Daviess County	25,342	13.1	10.0	39.3	47.4	14.0	6.0	5.1	39.9	27.1
21067	Fayette County	71,027	11.3	6.7	18.8	42.6	13.5	5.8	5.0	32.4	25.7
21093	Hardin County	28,220	12.1	6.6	9.8	48.9	15.3	7.6	7.1	35.9	27.5
21111	Jefferson County	185,940	12.5	8.3	22.6	40.9	16.2	7.1	6.3	34.7	24.6
21117	Kenton County	39,748	11.7	5.7	24.1	45.5	14.8	6.0	5.1	35.6	24.2
21125	Laurel County	16,616	17.2	10.5	35.8	58.8	22.0	15.4	11.2	41.1	27.5
21145	McCracken County	16,770	14.4	5.2	46.6	59.8	14.3	4.2	2.8	41.9	27.7
21151	Madison County	20,188	13.8	9.1	39.5	47.5	18.3	10.0	8.1	43.8	29.3
21185	Oldham County	15,754	4.3	2.9	5.6	34.5	4.2	1.7	1.7	17.3	13.8
21195	Pike County	17,643	17.5	15.6	25.5	59.3	26.7	17.7	10.8	54.8	28.4
21199	Pulaski County	17,837	20.6	17.8	36.0	55.5	22.3	11.7	7.8	56.5	28.5
21227	Warren County	28,553	13.7	5.7	27.9	52.0	17.0	8.0	6.6	40.0	29.6
22000	**Louisiana**	1,127,030	15.5	7.0	24.9	49.3	18.3	7.9	6.4	38.8	27.8
22001	Acadia Parish	15,698	15.2	4.7	14.0	45.7	21.9	12.9	9.4	41.7	28.0
22005	Ascension Parish	29,660	9.9	5.7	3.7	37.9	11.6	4.9	3.4	31.2	23.0
22015	Bossier Parish	30,693	12.0	2.9	21.7	44.4	13.4	3.6	3.0	37.2	27.7
22017	Caddo Parish	61,621	16.1	5.3	17.1	47.1	19.4	6.8	5.6	37.3	25.9
22019	Calcasieu Parish	50,437	13.0	5.9	17.8	44.6	16.1	7.4	6.8	34.3	27.1
22033	East Baton Rouge Parish	103,329	14.2	6.8	23.1	44.3	17.9	6.9	5.7	37.0	28.8
22045	Iberia Parish	19,129	16.6	3.6	31.8	49.9	21.3	8.6	7.0	44.9	34.2
22051	Jefferson Parish	104,771	13.8	7.7	22.1	46.6	16.9	8.4	7.0	32.6	25.4
22055	Lafayette Parish	54,658	13.0	3.1	19.7	48.5	13.4	4.7	4.3	32.4	27.1
22057	Lafourche Parish	24,737	11.2	6.2	29.4	38.7	17.8	9.6	7.7	39.7	30.7
22063	Livingston Parish	34,105	11.8	5.7	14.9	45.2	16.2	8.5	7.8	36.9	27.7
22071	Orleans Parish	77,344	23.2	9.6	27.0	56.6	25.6	9.6	7.3	43.2	29.2
22073	Ouachita Parish	37,451	20.4	8.7	29.0	60.0	19.1	6.3	5.4	41.8	27.8
22079	Rapides Parish	30,992	16.1	7.8	36.1	50.4	19.9	9.7	8.0	40.7	27.1

Table E-2: Counties with a Population of 50,000 or More—Income, Poverty, and Health Insurance—*Continued*

State/ County FIPS code	State/Place	Median family income in the past 12 months (in 2,013 inflation-adjusted dollars)								Total population in households	Persons who had health insurance, as a percent of all persons in that household type		
							Families with own children under 18 years						
		All families	Families with no earners	Families with one earner	Families with two earners	Families with three or more earners	Married-couple families with children	Male householder, no spouse present, with children	Female householder, no spouse present, with children		Married-couple families, percent	Male householder or female householder families, no spouse present	Nonfamily households
	Louisiana—cont'd												
22089	St. Charles Parish	$63,875	$24,477	$45,642	$96,623	$93,494	$95,509	$43,068	$25,842	51,911	89.2	79.2	77.1
22097	St. Landry Parish	$46,199	$17,710	$37,315	$73,605	$90,871	$74,463	$44,355	$14,988	82,368	91.0	77.1	80.6
22099	St. Martin Parish	$51,310	$20,102	$33,760	$79,261	$104,673	$80,570	$37,157	$30,088	52,586	86.1	80.0	77.4
22101	St. Mary Parish	$46,671	$17,245	$42,840	$69,221	$84,013	$68,438	$29,271	$18,216	52,942	84.9	73.1	69.3
22103	St. Tammany Parish	$71,958	$33,792	$52,771	$92,720	$110,893	$96,233	$42,400	$26,141	237,099	91.3	76.7	80.9
22105	Tangipahoa Parish	$50,443	$17,105	$36,996	$73,489	$102,163	$72,699	$30,556	$15,051	123,162	85.7	77.8	75.5
22109	Terrebonne Parish	$57,339	$25,028	$47,537	$80,220	$101,343	$85,108	$50,203	$22,341	110,798	86.2	74.4	80.2
22113	Vermilion Parish	$55,822	$24,546	$34,870	$86,805	$100,367	$86,962	$21,930	$22,026	58,259	86.4	79.4	74.3
22115	Vernon Parish	$49,877	$26,487	$44,336	$70,470	$103,047	$55,087	$29,375	$21,493	47,217	90.9	78.3	76.7
23000	**Maine**	$60,235	$30,232	$41,626	$77,758	$97,789	$76,056	$32,702	$22,301	1,314,314	92.5	85.8	83.8
23001	Androscoggin County	$57,432	$25,199	$38,772	$75,733	$95,817	$77,375	$26,643	$19,013	106,613	93.8	88.2	84.1
23003	Aroostook County	$49,823	$25,814	$38,469	$65,233	$82,903	$60,873	$39,167	$15,893	69,703	90.2	89.9	84.2
23005	Cumberland County	$75,103	$36,209	$48,202	$90,450	$115,378	$93,719	$39,537	$28,092	280,636	94.6	86.7	85.5
23009	Hancock County	$58,401	$37,672	$40,974	$70,984	$106,625	$66,989	$30,455	$18,198	54,242	88.8	78.8	78.4
23011	Kennebec County	$59,604	$30,328	$40,444	$76,954	$98,268	$74,516	$27,895	$21,550	120,207	92.5	88.4	84.1
23017	Oxford County	$49,065	$23,512	$37,450	$69,329	$95,385	$57,019	$22,480	$16,010	57,120	91.4	86.0	79.8
23019	Penobscot County	$54,517	$26,076	$39,578	$72,676	$100,199	$68,943	$36,281	$20,451	151,814	92.8	83.5	84.2
23025	Somerset County	$49,380	$23,608	$37,352	$67,852	$83,155	$57,115	$25,357	$22,586	51,251	89.4	85.0	84.4
23031	York County	$70,640	$34,338	$46,819	$84,619	$99,591	$85,405	$38,528	$27,055	197,389	93.7	85.6	85.2
24000	**Maryland**	$87,060	$38,003	$59,175	$109,732	$129,316	$113,714	$50,869	$36,393	5,790,545	92.6	84.0	88.2
24001	Allegany County	$53,706	$34,566	$42,146	$71,768	$94,453	$67,170	$32,225	$24,593	68,501	93.2	88.6	89.1
24003	Anne Arundel County	$99,226	$51,787	$72,776	$118,109	$138,802	$117,819	$56,422	$46,561	530,498	95.3	86.3	90.9
24005	Baltimore County	$78,583	$36,535	$55,756	$100,571	$125,059	$105,983	$52,743	$36,009	809,274	93.0	85.9	89.8
24009	Calvert County	$105,904	$51,048	$73,032	$122,056	$153,329	$124,140	$53,313	$43,826	88,455	95.4	87.8	86.9
24013	Carroll County	$97,038	$39,585	$72,870	$110,289	$136,195	$117,964	$50,741	$40,286	165,359	96.1	89.4	88.0
24015	Cecil County	$79,772	$35,913	$53,967	$99,623	$114,174	$96,866	$34,076	$31,729	100,632	92.8	83.4	86.9
24017	Charles County	$101,429	$41,016	$66,859	$123,561	$160,842	$124,274	$59,266	$51,146	148,684	95.4	89.4	90.1
24021	Frederick County	$95,470	$44,900	$68,909	$110,227	$136,458	$116,117	$53,965	$34,910	237,160	94.6	85.1	89.0
24025	Harford County	$91,284	$38,609	$66,253	$106,763	$137,490	$110,359	$65,425	$35,006	245,658	95.2	91.8	90.5
24027	Howard County	$125,843	$59,494	$87,453	$146,360	$169,923	$145,486	$61,750	$61,306	296,989	94.7	87.6	89.3
24031	Montgomery County	$115,685	$66,298	$82,530	$138,009	$137,004	$137,362	$51,802	$44,046	995,448	91.4	78.0	89.4
24033	Prince George's County	$82,530	$41,286	$55,904	$104,310	$123,216	$103,852	$46,664	$43,803	874,844	87.9	80.0	84.6
24037	St. Mary's County	$95,187	$49,368	$62,625	$114,702	$145,214	$111,511	$60,920	$30,810	105,997	93.3	87.0	92.8
24043	Washington County	$66,219	$31,131	$50,068	$80,834	$105,069	$82,904	$37,474	$29,176	140,738	93.0	88.2	85.3
24045	Wicomico County	$58,961	$35,405	$37,274	$79,292	$98,309	$75,760	$30,699	$25,081	99,239	90.5	82.7	89.9
24047	Worcester County	$67,216	$47,681	$47,230	$93,045	$106,169	$91,522	$40,168	$35,093	50,977	91.1	84.8	85.2
24510	Baltimore city	$49,245	$16,323	$37,579	$79,623	$95,487	$82,933	$38,889	$22,037	611,839	90.9	85.7	87.4
25000	**Massachusetts**	$83,867	$30,356	$56,245	$106,084	$125,258	$112,824	$45,121	$27,158	6,568,640	97.5	93.5	94.6
25001	Barnstable County	$75,626	$47,155	$60,949	$91,234	$116,825	$97,544	$50,877	$31,519	212,563	96.6	91.1	94.4
25003	Berkshire County	$64,922	$34,831	$44,430	$80,994	$104,375	$81,909	$32,039	$22,145	127,781	98.0	95.1	97.6
25005	Bristol County	$70,710	$26,316	$47,695	$93,239	$120,445	$100,294	$36,447	$23,355	543,539	97.5	92.8	93.9
25009	Essex County	$83,718	$30,780	$56,523	$102,943	$129,974	$108,882	$46,547	$26,849	748,662	97.4	92.9	93.5
25011	Franklin County	$68,098	$26,534	$50,960	$84,015	$99,324	$83,142	$41,776	$29,442	70,737	96.9	95.0	94.4
25013	Hampden County	$60,586	$21,991	$41,159	$87,932	$110,787	$91,960	$34,454	$19,978	460,579	97.0	94.0	94.3
25015	Hampshire County	$80,774	$33,707	$57,047	$96,684	$118,965	$100,310	$52,361	$31,258	158,401	98.3	93.3	96.0
25017	Middlesex County	$103,581	$34,607	$73,324	$124,082	$136,725	$131,254	$55,848	$33,443	1,521,666	97.6	93.2	94.9
25021	Norfolk County	$107,189	$37,018	$76,136	$126,404	$142,422	$133,594	$64,338	$41,770	673,461	98.3	95.4	97.1
25023	Plymouth County	$89,467	$38,349	$63,659	$106,964	$127,657	$112,493	$43,542	$31,866	491,390	97.6	93.6	93.3
25025	Suffolk County	$59,562	$16,144	$38,236	$93,633	$97,399	$93,490	$38,038	$21,690	738,472	96.4	92.7	94.5
25027	Worcester County	$80,005	$29,794	$52,817	$101,875	$122,817	$106,292	$47,043	$27,870	794,363	97.6	94.6	93.5
26000	**Michigan**	$60,398	$34,550	$44,945	$81,067	$99,413	$81,062	$33,763	$20,352	9,773,359	92.4	82.4	84.5
26005	Allegan County	$59,808	$37,999	$44,041	$73,678	$97,002	$72,183	$30,948	$20,048	111,277	92.2	82.0	82.1
26015	Barry County	$62,188	$36,813	$46,348	$75,555	$100,459	$69,407	$36,786	$19,229	58,458	92.9	86.5	82.4
26017	Bay County	$55,910	$34,574	$42,234	$76,860	$91,739	$79,403	$33,413	$17,309	106,018	93.1	81.9	83.6
26021	Berrien County	$56,056	$32,336	$41,085	$76,208	$92,766	$73,782	$38,967	$19,957	154,578	91.2	81.0	82.0
26025	Calhoun County	$52,930	$32,229	$36,079	$75,108	$98,099	$77,213	$26,652	$18,868	133,519	91.9	82.6	84.3
26027	Cass County	$52,655	$29,932	$42,795	$75,645	$96,673	$67,429	$38,319	$21,062	52,029	89.1	84.3	81.6
26037	Clinton County	$72,876	$45,081	$54,634	$91,757	$108,676	$92,481	$43,804	$27,500	75,649	93.2	88.5	86.9
26045	Eaton County	$63,878	$40,442	$50,686	$82,670	$93,880	$83,300	$33,382	$24,911	107,434	93.2	85.7	86.5
26049	Genesee County	$51,824	$34,668	$39,713	$77,684	$91,500	$74,414	$28,307	$16,738	415,547	93.2	85.8	85.8
26055	Grand Traverse County	$63,712	$47,227	$46,085	$71,904	$90,918	$71,888	$41,250	$20,095	86,733	91.8	83.0	76.8
26065	Ingham County	$60,856	$44,134	$41,516	$82,386	$95,160	$80,155	$32,206	$19,308	280,283	94.5	84.4	89.3
26067	Ionia County	$54,784	$35,210	$42,006	$69,972	$94,314	$66,211	$21,841	$25,000	60,202	92.8	81.8	86.5
26073	Isabella County	$51,840	$34,478	$36,635	$72,678	$88,589	$73,380	$23,182	$17,462	69,924	91.9	79.2	85.3
26075	Jackson County	$55,658	$32,489	$42,402	$76,167	$89,651	$72,395	$35,574	$14,797	152,544	92.2	81.3	84.7
26077	Kalamazoo County	$61,586	$37,173	$46,934	$81,375	$95,714	$87,770	$33,718	$19,181	252,844	93.6	83.5	85.2
26081	Kent County	$64,083	$31,449	$44,507	$78,928	$93,482	$80,841	$31,629	$22,236	610,625	93.5	82.4	85.0
26087	Lapeer County	$60,379	$41,744	$50,464	$79,684	$96,885	$70,313	$39,537	$17,323	86,714	92.0	82.9	82.2
26091	Lenawee County	$58,719	$41,648	$42,222	$73,602	$92,896	$71,710	$35,735	$20,864	96,005	92.0	84.0	87.6
26093	Livingston County	$83,157	$49,026	$65,564	$98,972	$115,136	$100,293	$56,563	$32,394	182,502	95.0	84.1	85.0
26099	Macomb County	$66,115	$36,989	$49,692	$84,827	$109,171	$84,907	$36,661	$23,999	842,107	92.3	82.6	84.3

Table E-2: Counties with a Population of 50,000 or More—Income, Poverty, and Health Insurance—*Continued*

| State/County FIPS code | State/Place | Total number of families | Families with incomes below the poverty level, as a percent of all families of that family type | | | | Families that received Food Stamps (SNAP), as a percent of all families of that family type | | | Families that received food stamps (SNAP) and had at least one worker | |
			All families	Married-couple families with related children under 18	Male householder families, no spouse present, with related children	Female householder families, no spouse present	All families	Married-couple families	Male householder or female householder families, no spouse present	Married-couple families, percent	Male householder or female householder families, no spouse present
	Louisiana—cont'd										
22089	St. Charles Parish	13,456	10.3	2.7	4.8	32.5	11.3	6.8	6.1	20.6	12.5
22097	St. Landry Parish	21,683	21.7	10.7	23.1	69.7	21.4	5.9	4.4	49.0	32.4
22099	St. Martin Parish	13,198	13.8	9.4	5.5	34.8	14.5	6.6	4.6	32.3	22.9
22101	St. Mary Parish	13,643	20.7	7.9	43.9	53.4	26.0	10.7	8.5	50.4	31.9
22103	St. Tammany Parish	64,603	8.8	4.6	21.3	37.3	11.7	5.5	4.3	30.7	24.9
22105	Tangipahoa Parish	30,402	19.5	6.6	38.9	57.2	23.6	9.9	8.5	50.7	30.4
22109	Terrebonne Parish	28,059	12.7	8.4	27.2	41.1	16.2	7.3	5.6	35.7	28.5
22113	Vermilion Parish	15,352	13.2	3.2	27.3	46.7	16.6	7.4	5.6	38.7	31.2
22115	Vernon Parish	13,205	12.3	8.2	25.6	43.1	11.9	6.3	4.6	30.5	20.0
23000	**Maine**	345,776	9.5	7.2	22.2	39.9	16.6	9.1	7.2	43.1	31.0
23001	Androscoggin County	27,533	12.7	8.4	22.4	50.5	21.0	10.3	8.1	51.1	37.6
23003	Aroostook County	19,539	11.4	9.2	15.9	56.4	19.9	11.2	7.7	53.6	36.5
23005	Cumberland County	71,226	8.2	4.9	22.0	34.9	12.4	6.0	5.0	34.5	25.6
23009	Hancock County	14,617	9.5	7.1	34.3	47.5	14.2	8.2	6.9	42.3	31.9
23011	Kennebec County	32,055	8.8	6.7	17.5	38.4	18.8	10.5	8.2	46.7	34.1
23017	Oxford County	14,524	10.9	9.5	21.5	49.1	20.7	13.0	10.4	47.3	28.8
23019	Penobscot County	38,437	10.8	10.2	18.8	40.6	19.0	11.2	8.9	46.6	27.9
23025	Somerset County	13,822	13.5	13.3	31.5	40.6	23.0	12.6	9.0	54.2	34.6
23031	York County	52,677	6.4	4.0	17.0	28.2	12.8	6.9	5.9	36.1	30.4
24000	**Maryland**	1,432,364	7.2	3.7	13.6	26.9	11.7	5.1	4.4	27.4	21.1
24001	Allegany County	16,766	11.1	8.3	31.7	41.9	19.8	10.9	8.8	44.3	34.2
24003	Anne Arundel County	139,306	4.1	1.9	7.7	19.1	7.4	3.5	3.2	19.8	15.7
24005	Baltimore County	201,831	6.6	5.0	10.7	22.5	11.7	5.4	4.7	26.4	19.9
24009	Calvert County	23,037	3.5	2.1	0.0	21.3	9.8	5.9	5.8	23.1	16.8
24013	Carroll County	44,201	3.7	2.1	10.1	21.4	6.0	3.1	2.6	19.6	13.8
24015	Cecil County	26,287	6.5	4.2	20.8	28.3	11.1	5.4	4.0	28.9	21.4
24017	Charles County	37,520	6.2	3.5	17.4	22.5	8.8	3.7	3.1	21.3	16.1
24021	Frederick County	62,984	4.6	1.2	5.6	28.0	6.9	3.3	3.0	19.9	16.1
24025	Harford County	66,682	6.8	4.0	18.2	28.4	9.0	3.9	3.7	25.4	18.1
24027	Howard County	79,977	3.5	2.4	4.5	18.1	5.8	3.0	2.6	16.8	13.9
24031	Montgomery County	249,564	4.5	2.7	10.7	19.3	6.4	3.2	2.7	17.2	14.6
24033	Prince George's County	199,293	7.1	4.2	8.9	19.6	12.7	5.6	5.3	22.6	18.3
24037	St. Mary's County	27,958	6.0	1.5	13.0	38.5	11.3	6.1	5.4	34.6	29.1
24043	Washington County	37,596	9.4	5.9	26.0	34.4	13.7	6.8	5.4	32.5	25.1
24045	Wicomico County	24,694	12.3	8.3	24.9	42.9	16.9	8.5	7.9	35.2	29.5
24047	Worcester County	12,905	7.5	9.5	5.3	23.7	12.8	7.6	6.8	32.7	29.1
24510	Baltimore city	122,258	19.8	8.8	30.6	43.2	32.1	14.1	11.0	47.6	34.2
25000	**Massachusetts**	1,606,383	8.4	4.2	19.2	36.1	12.5	5.4	4.2	32.2	22.1
25001	Barnstable County	58,096	6.0	4.3	16.9	31.8	7.3	3.3	2.8	22.7	17.4
25003	Berkshire County	32,959	9.9	5.5	22.3	43.3	14.0	6.2	5.0	35.4	24.4
25005	Bristol County	137,494	9.8	4.8	22.7	36.8	15.5	6.7	4.9	37.6	24.4
25009	Essex County	190,634	8.9	4.6	18.7	36.1	13.8	5.5	4.1	34.8	26.0
25011	Franklin County	17,869	7.8	1.9	29.9	33.8	13.0	6.2	5.4	32.7	20.5
25013	Hampden County	115,408	14.3	7.9	24.4	45.6	23.4	11.0	7.8	45.5	28.8
25015	Hampshire County	34,765	5.4	3.2	12.9	27.1	7.9	4.2	2.8	20.5	13.5
25017	Middlesex County	372,144	5.7	3.4	14.9	28.1	7.4	3.5	2.9	22.7	16.2
25021	Norfolk County	170,157	4.6	2.7	9.7	25.3	6.9	4.1	3.2	18.0	12.9
25023	Plymouth County	128,311	5.4	2.4	16.1	28.3	9.4	3.8	3.3	27.3	20.3
25025	Suffolk County	142,320	16.9	7.6	24.8	43.7	25.2	11.3	8.7	43.0	30.2
25027	Worcester County	200,065	8.8	4.8	19.6	39.0	12.4	5.6	4.4	31.7	19.5
26000	**Michigan**	2,489,254	12.5	8.9	27.2	46.5	18.0	8.8	7.2	43.1	30.4
26005	Allegan County	30,966	10.7	7.5	31.3	47.0	13.7	7.9	6.4	39.1	28.6
26015	Barry County	15,869	7.7	7.2	28.8	42.8	14.5	8.7	7.6	45.4	36.3
26017	Bay County	28,591	10.4	6.1	26.9	47.5	15.7	6.6	5.2	43.6	29.4
26021	Berrien County	39,526	12.6	9.4	17.5	49.8	17.1	6.7	5.0	46.5	32.9
26025	Calhoun County	34,142	14.6	8.2	27.0	49.8	19.8	9.2	7.3	43.6	30.6
26027	Cass County	13,528	10.2	9.6	22.4	42.7	13.6	7.7	6.2	34.8	19.6
26037	Clinton County	19,796	6.3	6.5	11.6	27.0	9.8	5.5	4.9	28.8	20.7
26045	Eaton County	28,229	8.4	6.2	14.6	32.8	15.2	9.2	7.8	35.5	26.4
26049	Genesee County	106,369	16.8	9.5	38.1	52.7	24.2	10.4	8.1	51.4	33.0
26055	Grand Traverse County	22,204	8.2	5.8	13.7	44.3	12.7	5.8	5.2	38.5	30.4
26065	Ingham County	61,032	14.7	10.8	33.0	47.6	20.4	9.8	8.7	44.9	36.8
26067	Ionia County	15,669	11.2	9.1	33.3	38.8	17.2	11.9	10.8	36.5	25.2
26073	Isabella County	13,648	15.1	10.9	36.9	50.7	20.4	9.9	8.4	49.0	38.2
26075	Jackson County	40,054	13.9	11.1	28.3	53.9	20.3	11.1	8.9	44.8	29.8
26077	Kalamazoo County	59,997	11.7	7.0	18.3	46.6	16.7	6.9	5.8	43.7	34.2
26081	Kent County	153,140	10.6	6.6	29.7	42.2	16.3	7.2	6.2	44.1	33.0
26087	Lapeer County	24,379	8.3	8.2	15.9	47.9	13.3	8.0	7.0	35.1	22.8
26091	Lenawee County	25,478	9.8	6.6	16.8	42.4	15.6	8.4	7.2	40.9	34.6
26093	Livingston County	50,312	4.2	2.9	9.5	26.0	7.0	3.7	3.3	22.5	19.2
26099	Macomb County	221,611	10.7	8.2	23.7	40.8	15.9	8.3	6.8	37.1	27.2

Table E-2: Counties with a Population of 50,000 or More—Income, Poverty, and Health Insurance—*Continued*

State/ County FIPS code	State/Place	Median family income in the past 12 months (in 2,013 inflation-adjusted dollars)					Families with own children under 18 years			Total population in households	Persons who had health insurance, as a percent of all persons in that household type		
		All families	Families with no earners	Families with one earner	Families with two earners	Families with three or more earners	Married-couple families with children	Male householder, no spouse present, with children	Female householder, no spouse present, with children		Married-couple families, percent	Male householder or female householder families, no spouse present	Nonfamily households
	Michigan—cont'd												
26103	Marquette County	$59,612	$39,040	$50,058	$78,983	$92,339	$83,981	$30,735	$19,278	65,611	91.7	80.6	79.8
26111	Midland County	$66,599	$40,315	$52,728	$87,236	$92,604	$82,698	$40,145	$23,528	83,342	94.0	84.6	82.5
26115	Monroe County	$65,167	$35,463	$50,674	$82,513	$107,434	$78,565	$43,073	$21,185	150,069	95.3	83.4	85.5
26117	Montcalm County	$49,243	$32,924	$40,610	$61,901	$82,117	$58,439	$33,533	$16,193	60,673	90.6	80.0	84.1
26121	Muskegon County	$49,800	$28,351	$37,265	$71,741	$90,208	$66,471	$28,092	$15,695	165,417	92.5	87.6	83.8
26125	Oakland County	$83,455	$42,753	$63,860	$105,839	$120,191	$108,480	$40,266	$30,932	1,215,231	93.9	82.6	85.8
26139	Ottawa County	$67,594	$38,155	$48,928	$77,704	$99,942	$80,583	$32,221	$24,013	268,076	95.4	82.7	86.1
26145	Saginaw County	$52,315	$33,015	$40,599	$73,861	$92,031	$75,678	$30,039	$17,060	194,549	93.0	84.7	86.6
26147	St. Clair County	$58,611	$36,400	$45,128	$76,559	$93,426	$78,395	$35,393	$20,780	159,706	92.8	83.4	81.3
26149	St. Joseph County	$50,091	$30,521	$36,939	$66,005	$80,089	$61,075	$43,634	$12,203	60,421	89.9	79.9	85.5
26155	Shiawassee County	$53,791	$31,469	$43,243	$75,399	$89,405	$65,409	$25,156	$20,799	68,958	91.3	82.3	82.4
26157	Tuscola County	$51,292	$34,098	$41,593	$69,700	$83,427	$65,432	$33,333	$17,934	53,830	89.4	83.1	84.3
26159	Van Buren County	$53,216	$27,796	$40,366	$71,873	$85,580	$60,556	$29,783	$20,308	75,108	88.5	79.0	81.4
26161	Washtenaw County	$85,332	$43,660	$60,397	$106,701	$122,579	$108,198	$40,714	$26,496	347,745	95.9	86.4	90.4
26163	Wayne County	$51,566	$24,580	$38,077	$80,519	$103,960	$77,711	$30,243	$17,758	1,777,608	90.3	80.6	81.7
27000	**Minnesota**	$74,434	$38,024	$49,205	$89,615	$106,873	$94,432	$40,684	$26,795	5,323,891	94.5	84.5	89.2
27003	Anoka County	$81,286	$38,648	$55,064	$95,244	$114,738	$100,258	$39,972	$32,115	333,869	94.5	86.2	89.9
27013	Blue Earth County	$70,383	$37,532	$43,497	$77,673	$103,750	$81,642	$29,200	$20,733	64,447	95.9	86.8	89.4
27019	Carver County	$98,207	$43,281	$69,787	$109,957	$124,119	$115,989	$57,000	$35,617	93,832	97.3	85.2	89.9
27025	Chisago County	$78,305	$40,959	$54,724	$92,120	$106,359	$96,837	$45,205	$28,764	52,338	95.2	86.2	86.8
27027	Clay County	$68,867	$32,789	$41,688	$81,212	$94,605	$84,428	$51,558	$25,726	59,762	95.8	79.7	92.0
27035	Crow Wing County	$58,960	$43,168	$40,426	$72,529	$88,537	$75,753	$29,643	$22,485	62,224	93.8	84.9	87.4
27037	Dakota County	$88,352	$45,668	$60,208	$100,952	$122,938	$108,970	$42,748	$34,083	403,366	95.4	85.4	88.5
27053	Hennepin County	$84,423	$36,027	$56,246	$105,121	$115,439	$111,216	$43,416	$26,530	1,174,442	94.3	83.5	89.6
27109	Olmsted County	$82,935	$44,655	$52,191	$97,197	$112,588	$97,395	$38,750	$37,614	145,354	96.1	84.1	88.9
27111	Otter Tail County	$62,882	$37,215	$43,962	$72,897	$93,942	$75,697	$39,832	$23,304	56,677	95.4	88.9	87.9
27123	Ramsey County	$71,638	$36,382	$43,234	$90,427	$104,431	$90,000	$36,313	$26,866	516,714	92.9	82.9	88.2
27131	Rice County	$70,422	$34,490	$44,866	$84,078	$91,628	$85,863	$38,750	$22,460	61,795	91.3	86.1	93.7
27137	St. Louis County	$62,433	$39,142	$45,864	$80,238	$92,649	$83,776	$33,022	$20,947	196,905	95.5	85.8	90.2
27139	Scott County	$95,730	$47,687	$60,020	$106,313	$127,293	$116,199	$51,100	$40,909	133,644	95.7	86.4	90.3
27141	Sherburne County	$79,125	$42,713	$47,119	$86,106	$112,713	$87,844	$48,243	$34,328	87,797	95.7	90.1	90.3
27145	Stearns County	$70,436	$35,927	$44,348	$83,757	$103,071	$90,181	$46,439	$26,707	150,478	95.7	85.2	90.0
27163	Washington County	$93,586	$50,785	$64,278	$107,851	$124,730	$113,099	$55,921	$35,827	241,102	96.2	87.6	91.7
27169	Winona County	$67,975	$42,620	$44,818	$78,558	$89,891	$75,210	$48,000	$23,056	50,797	92.5	87.4	87.4
27171	Wright County	$80,986	$37,093	$54,305	$93,368	$110,993	$96,776	$58,885	$37,958	126,601	95.3	87.0	90.1
28000	**Mississippi**	$47,531	$21,966	$35,899	$69,064	$90,332	$67,574	$32,295	$18,312	2,918,229	86.8	76.7	80.6
28033	DeSoto County	$63,658	$33,990	$46,117	$80,180	$101,243	$78,817	$43,267	$31,362	165,285	89.0	78.1	79.1
28035	Forrest County	$45,582	$23,050	$31,227	$61,896	$92,799	$65,216	$25,996	$19,046	75,862	85.8	76.6	82.1
28047	Harrison County	$50,044	$27,120	$35,839	$66,609	$94,082	$59,571	$35,871	$16,984	186,190	84.4	72.0	74.5
28049	Hinds County	$45,121	$17,371	$32,004	$67,161	$82,782	$73,786	$31,485	$20,279	244,592	87.9	76.3	76.1
28059	Jackson County	$58,382	$32,834	$49,167	$71,130	$99,135	$70,590	$70,101	$27,056	138,827	86.1	71.1	77.3
28067	Jones County	$44,073	$23,233	$35,076	$67,965	$96,213	$59,322	$29,327	$13,477	67,699	83.6	77.7	80.3
28071	Lafayette County	$63,235	$30,977	$41,914	$80,268	$93,319	$86,287	$46,354	$16,383	49,416	89.7	76.7	88.8
28073	Lamar County	$59,184	$28,556	$47,257	$72,584	$97,622	$76,331	$39,362	$24,185	56,940	86.4	83.4	72.1
28075	Lauderdale County	$45,594	$19,009	$30,722	$73,760	$91,686	$71,477	$27,475	$16,545	76,735	92.7	79.0	82.4
28081	Lee County	$55,706	$21,906	$36,405	$69,271	$87,167	$72,193	$41,194	$14,336	83,690	90.3	79.6	83.7
28087	Lowndes County	$45,835	$24,152	$35,098	$61,055	$79,868	$66,017	$44,103	$14,083	57,972	86.7	75.4	78.9
28089	Madison County	$77,066	$21,823	$53,072	$94,663	$111,948	$101,411	$68,452	$28,061	97,497	93.6	85.0	88.8
28109	Pearl River County	$46,872	$20,934	$38,328	$65,170	$95,297	$57,813	$29,228	$17,434	54,531	80.3	73.0	76.0
28121	Rankin County	$65,497	$31,314	$44,439	$87,033	$100,801	$82,915	$35,082	$30,871	139,427	91.6	81.2	84.4
28151	Washington County	$34,626	$14,942	$26,697	$65,653	$91,285	$59,891	$10,625	$17,468	49,606	85.2	73.9	80.2
29000	**Missouri**	$58,626	$31,395	$41,478	$76,531	$97,006	$76,510	$34,515	$21,892	5,913,412	90.3	78.8	84.0
29019	Boone County	$69,964	$42,075	$47,651	$85,122	$95,583	$86,645	$30,179	$23,918	167,047	93.4	81.9	90.6
29021	Buchanan County	$56,912	$29,147	$38,888	$70,770	$91,516	$75,866	$16,717	$20,086	86,869	89.6	72.1	81.0
29031	Cape Girardeau County	$56,442	$32,779	$37,968	$70,098	$90,118	$73,561	$40,978	$14,876	75,898	93.0	80.4	86.5
29037	Cass County	$68,197	$42,144	$51,672	$85,103	$108,389	$82,672	$41,667	$26,849	99,282	91.4	80.6	86.4
29043	Christian County	$59,000	$37,257	$39,582	$73,220	$88,067	$71,673	$31,092	$28,716	79,288	89.1	79.8	81.2
29047	Clay County	$71,546	$40,696	$48,067	$88,863	$108,325	$90,907	$42,235	$30,051	226,209	93.3	78.2	83.5
29051	Cole County	$63,724	$45,044	$43,750	$79,359	$104,534	$74,924	$45,893	$27,807	72,605	93.3	81.9	87.0
29071	Franklin County	$60,425	$35,368	$41,440	$75,170	$94,455	$76,160	$39,102	$27,096	100,847	92.2	80.9	82.6
29077	Greene County	$53,425	$32,332	$37,467	$69,029	$84,066	$67,271	$21,868	$17,526	276,784	89.1	74.4	80.8
29095	Jackson County	$59,025	$28,217	$39,976	$81,394	$101,487	$81,457	$31,918	$21,237	670,971	89.3	76.0	79.9
29097	Jasper County	$49,114	$28,900	$35,221	$66,359	$86,055	$61,176	$25,709	$21,447	115,424	86.0	77.3	82.3
29099	Jefferson County	$61,972	$36,143	$49,062	$78,704	$95,837	$80,858	$42,556	$23,575	218,805	92.6	81.6	84.1
29101	Johnson County	$59,246	$32,308	$46,588	$72,045	$94,873	$64,331	$45,543	$18,764	50,807	91.2	84.2	85.7
29113	Lincoln County	$57,935	$31,582	$42,621	$73,012	$93,941	$69,375	$35,688	$20,162	52,969	92.9	79.6	85.0
29145	Newton County	$49,793	$30,007	$37,265	$65,942	$81,440	$55,047	$37,806	$21,078	58,220	83.2	78.8	78.9
29165	Platte County	$82,273	$37,430	$54,881	$100,464	$116,351	$101,411	$56,526	$28,933	91,032	94.1	84.8	88.2
29169	Pulaski County	$57,617	$27,202	$38,817	$70,645	$88,281	$61,398	$28,264	$14,583	40,245	89.2	78.9	79.7
29183	St. Charles County	$83,020	$42,948	$60,954	$97,096	$118,755	$101,513	$51,342	$30,421	367,170	95.1	83.0	89.1

State/County FIPS code	State/Place	Total number of families	Families with incomes below the poverty level, as a percent of all families of that family type				Families that received Food Stamps (SNAP), as a percent of all families of that family type			Families that received food stamps (SNAP) and had at least one worker	
			All families	Married-couple families with related children under 18	Male householder families, no spouse present, with related children	Female householder families, no spouse present	All families	Married-couple families	Male householder or female householder families, no spouse present	Married-couple families, percent	Male householder or female householder families, no spouse present
	Michigan—cont'd										
26103	Marquette County	15,820	10.3	5.9	30.8	47.3	10.8	5.7	4.8	33.1	22.7
26111	Midland County	22,703	10.2	8.6	31.5	42.2	12.4	7.1	6.0	36.8	21.9
26115	Monroe County	41,071	9.1	5.8	14.8	44.9	12.6	5.9	5.2	34.4	23.7
26117	Montcalm County	16,487	11.4	10.4	22.1	50.0	17.4	10.0	7.5	44.2	31.7
26121	Muskegon County	43,270	16.1	10.8	28.5	57.1	23.2	12.1	9.6	49.8	33.3
26125	Oakland County	319,859	7.8	5.6	19.5	32.6	11.3	5.7	4.8	29.8	23.6
26139	Ottawa County	70,038	7.0	5.1	24.8	39.8	10.2	5.2	4.6	34.7	29.0
26145	Saginaw County	49,742	13.9	7.5	33.0	52.7	21.4	9.2	7.3	50.5	32.2
26147	St. Clair County	43,289	11.6	8.6	19.0	45.3	17.4	9.0	7.4	45.2	33.4
26149	St. Joseph County	15,863	14.1	12.1	19.7	53.7	16.4	8.9	7.7	40.9	27.2
26155	Shiawassee County	19,520	12.1	10.7	29.9	45.2	15.9	8.8	7.2	39.2	25.3
26157	Tuscola County	14,667	11.3	11.4	25.9	47.4	19.7	13.2	11.2	46.5	35.6
26159	Van Buren County	19,607	15.4	15.5	38.1	51.7	21.6	13.7	10.7	45.5	29.9
26161	Washtenaw County	78,477	9.0	5.6	17.6	38.7	13.0	5.6	4.7	37.5	29.4
26163	Wayne County	415,933	20.3	14.0	36.2	52.8	28.9	13.6	11.0	51.5	33.9
27000	**Minnesota**	1,367,091	7.5	4.6	17.3	35.9	9.1	3.9	3.4	27.9	21.4
27003	Anoka County	87,662	6.3	3.2	18.5	30.4	8.5	3.8	3.4	25.5	19.2
27013	Blue Earth County	14,021	8.4	3.6	26.0	46.7	9.0	3.8	3.1	33.0	26.7
27019	Carver County	25,712	3.3	1.5	3.4	23.8	3.3	1.6	1.2	12.9	11.4
27025	Chisago County	14,247	3.6	0.9	7.7	18.3	6.1	2.7	2.2	24.4	22.1
27027	Clay County	14,712	8.3	6.2	3.7	39.2	9.4	5.6	4.8	22.2	16.7
27035	Crow Wing County	18,072	9.5	6.4	36.6	40.3	9.9	5.2	4.1	27.7	20.9
27037	Dakota County	107,936	5.3	4.0	10.1	26.2	6.1	2.8	2.5	18.4	14.4
27053	Hennepin County	280,241	8.5	4.5	18.6	38.7	10.5	3.8	3.1	30.5	22.0
27109	Olmsted County	37,499	4.7	2.8	12.1	21.3	6.4	3.4	2.8	18.9	16.0
27111	Otter Tail County	16,222	6.4	3.0	19.4	44.4	7.1	3.7	3.1	24.7	15.7
27123	Ramsey County	119,188	11.5	9.9	18.4	38.8	14.4	7.0	6.0	32.8	24.4
27131	Rice County	15,520	8.2	7.2	13.5	35.9	8.9	4.2	3.9	25.1	15.9
27137	St. Louis County	48,996	9.6	4.5	22.9	46.1	10.9	4.2	3.8	33.0	25.1
27139	Scott County	35,218	4.3	2.5	11.5	18.6	3.7	1.8	1.6	13.5	11.3
27141	Sherburne County	23,121	5.3	1.6	11.5	25.0	7.1	2.6	2.5	26.6	22.1
27145	Stearns County	36,752	6.3	3.6	10.7	31.9	7.6	3.6	3.1	25.0	20.6
27163	Washington County	65,911	4.0	1.5	4.8	21.4	5.2	1.7	1.4	20.1	16.6
27169	Winona County	11,163	6.2	5.5	15.7	35.8	7.0	2.2	2.0	33.7	28.3
27171	Wright County	34,777	4.9	4.3	5.4	24.7	7.0	4.4	4.0	18.3	14.6
28000	**Mississippi**	743,178	18.2	11.1	28.5	52.6	20.1	9.1	7.5	41.0	28.0
28033	DeSoto County	43,757	7.9	5.9	9.4	25.9	10.0	6.8	6.0	18.6	15.0
28035	Forrest County	17,005	22.6	14.4	49.9	52.0	22.5	10.2	9.2	43.7	35.2
28047	Harrison County	48,182	17.5	12.0	17.8	52.8	20.8	10.9	9.2	39.8	31.0
28049	Hinds County	57,184	21.7	10.3	26.3	50.8	25.3	9.7	8.3	42.7	30.5
28059	Jackson County	34,641	11.2	9.4	3.9	33.7	16.3	9.5	8.5	31.6	21.7
28067	Jones County	17,413	16.7	9.5	22.3	65.4	18.4	9.5	7.5	38.7	25.0
28071	Lafayette County	9,196	12.9	4.7	11.2	59.8	...	...	...	...	...
28073	Lamar County	15,868	11.3	6.1	36.2	37.6	17.2	7.4	7.0	43.2	33.1
28075	Lauderdale County	20,051	21.4	9.8	21.6	62.6	23.7	9.8	8.1	46.4	33.9
28081	Lee County	22,678	16.5	6.6	21.3	58.6	18.3	5.0	4.8	47.8	36.8
28087	Lowndes County	15,184	21.2	10.8	4.2	67.1	26.0	10.5	8.8	56.7	44.5
28089	Madison County	25,834	9.9	4.5	20.6	37.2	11.6	4.3	3.8	30.3	20.0
28109	Pearl River County	14,433	19.6	13.0	32.3	66.6	24.4	14.5	12.7	49.3	27.7
28121	Rankin County	38,911	7.5	8.0	15.2	23.4	10.3	6.3	5.4	21.5	15.5
28151	Washington County	12,345	30.4	18.1	61.1	59.6	37.8	14.5	12.2	59.1	36.5
29000	**Missouri**	1,527,728	11.6	7.9	24.4	42.6	15.0	7.3	6.0	37.6	27.4
29019	Boone County	36,732	8.8	5.1	27.7	37.3	13.4	5.4	4.7	39.4	32.8
29021	Buchanan County	21,025	14.3	6.2	48.4	49.5	18.4	7.1	6.1	46.7	32.7
29031	Cape Girardeau County	19,138	11.5	6.0	23.9	59.3	13.2	5.1	4.4	42.5	33.5
29037	Cass County	27,728	6.6	3.2	15.3	34.3	11.6	4.6	4.6	38.2	31.3
29043	Christian County	22,639	7.7	7.7	15.7	32.8	12.2	8.1	7.1	29.4	23.3
29047	Clay County	58,824	7.1	6.2	12.4	23.3	10.0	5.3	4.8	23.7	19.7
29051	Cole County	19,090	9.5	4.8	20.2	33.5	11.8	5.3	4.4	31.1	26.5
29071	Franklin County	27,308	8.5	6.1	22.7	28.3	12.0	6.6	6.1	31.5	24.6
29077	Greene County	69,487	13.5	7.9	36.4	52.5	15.1	7.4	5.7	38.3	29.1
29095	Jackson County	161,409	13.9	8.5	25.1	44.8	16.9	6.3	5.1	37.9	26.0
29097	Jasper County	29,801	12.7	10.4	23.0	38.9	18.3	10.4	8.7	39.4	28.9
29099	Jefferson County	59,707	9.0	4.7	11.8	44.7	12.6	6.7	5.9	32.7	24.6
29101	Johnson County	13,092	10.3	9.5	27.8	44.8	15.5	10.3	9.3	39.7	30.2
29113	Lincoln County	13,767	11.7	8.2	46.0	42.2	13.8	9.7	8.6	27.7	18.6
29145	Newton County	15,612	11.2	11.0	25.9	44.6	12.0	9.0	8.2	25.1	16.5
29165	Platte County	24,854	5.7	1.8	8.3	34.3	7.7	2.6	2.4	25.8	19.8
29169	Pulaski County	10,173	11.1	5.4	15.9	54.5	14.7	6.8	6.4	43.9	34.3
29183	St. Charles County	100,088	4.9	2.3	17.3	27.3	6.1	2.8	2.5	20.5	16.4

| State/ County FIPS code | State/Place | Median family income in the past 12 months (in 2,013 inflation-adjusted dollars) | | | | | | | | Total population in households | Persons who had health insurance, as a percent of all persons in that household type | | |
| | | | | | | | Families with own children under 18 years | | | | | | |
		All families	Families with no earners	Families with one earner	Families with two earners	Families with three or more earners	Married-couple families with children	Male householder, no spouse present, with children	Female householder, no spouse present, with children		Married-couple families, percent	Male householder or female householder families, no spouse present	Nonfamily households
	Missouri—cont'd												
29187	St. Francois County	$44,652	$23,685	$36,100	$59,891	$77,891	$57,470	$29,176	$17,369	57,697	88.2	81.0	84.0
29189	St. Louis County	$74,165	$36,988	$53,249	$94,336	$113,417	$101,623	$46,322	$27,398	988,465	93.9	82.1	87.4
29213	Taney County	$44,807	$33,102	$37,257	$52,478	$86,406	$59,868	$41,067	$20,385	52,645	81.0	72.2	74.8
29510	St. Louis city	$43,246	$14,638	$30,693	$72,706	$85,380	$71,364	$25,045	$17,857	314,065	86.8	75.2	81.8
30000	**Montana**	$59,345	$36,454	$42,491	$71,651	$89,239	$72,172	$34,563	$20,044	990,602	86.2	72.2	80.1
30013	Cascade County	$56,846	$39,663	$41,880	$67,978	$82,931	$66,308	$37,969	$18,750	78,033	88.8	75.5	80.6
30029	Flathead County	$56,886	$48,053	$45,244	$64,688	$72,355	$65,232	$26,607	$19,832	91,334	84.4	70.7	71.7
30031	Gallatin County	$70,067	$50,567	$49,776	$75,164	$90,475	$79,820	$37,439	$19,781	92,551	89.1	78.8	84.5
30049	Lewis and Clark County	$67,880	$43,424	$45,963	$79,831	$97,642	$77,300	$35,283	$22,500	64,169	92.3	83.4	86.6
30063	Missoula County	$62,649	$41,009	$42,401	$72,832	$93,444	$75,431	$31,307	$23,019	110,415	87.6	73.5	78.4
30111	Yellowstone County	$65,097	$40,591	$47,401	$77,471	$104,954	$80,546	$38,434	$21,164	149,684	88.5	72.6	81.5
31000	**Nebraska**	$64,862	$34,645	$42,221	$77,553	$94,332	$79,890	$37,024	$24,258	1,826,997	91.9	80.5	85.3
31055	Douglas County	$68,438	$33,237	$41,831	$85,431	$101,705	$91,471	$41,738	$26,470	525,100	90.8	80.6	85.4
31079	Hall County	$54,360	$31,969	$34,220	$67,919	$84,899	$62,708	$33,134	$20,385	59,379	89.0	71.5	74.8
31109	Lancaster County	$67,552	$40,933	$41,555	$80,186	$109,569	$85,890	$34,059	$24,214	288,904	92.4	82.4	85.4
31153	Sarpy County	$78,365	$45,922	$55,844	$89,155	$113,408	$91,502	$47,670	$28,769	162,028	95.0	86.1	88.2
32000	**Nevada**	$58,779	$33,957	$43,382	$76,260	$95,605	$69,580	$37,086	$28,248	2,719,575	82.7	70.4	77.1
32003	Clark County	$57,824	$32,234	$42,344	$74,812	$95,570	$67,918	$36,283	$29,266	1,974,661	82.2	70.3	76.0
32007	Elko County	$75,376	$39,529	$60,545	$93,506	$118,095	$86,629	$36,406	$17,156	50,263	86.7	68.2	77.5
32019	Lyon County	$45,680	$29,182	$42,172	$70,232	$90,196	$57,146	$60,294	$19,040	51,134	86.4	66.7	75.0
32031	Washoe County	$62,993	$36,724	$45,970	$79,654	$98,509	$72,480	$41,449	$25,517	426,006	82.4	72.0	80.3
32510	Carson City	$60,720	$44,750	$43,843	$71,173	$87,625	$60,372	$19,825	$28,955	52,473	85.8	66.4	81.2
33000	**New Hampshire**	$79,485	$36,525	$54,131	$94,971	$115,664	$100,152	$44,404	$28,473	1,306,205	93.1	81.1	85.1
33001	Belknap County	$67,046	$28,380	$48,518	$81,486	$122,968	$82,867	$43,881	$21,231	59,545	91.7	80.1	78.7
33005	Cheshire County	$69,182	$34,756	$50,890	$81,930	$116,177	$87,575	$46,034	$26,865	75,918	92.7	83.7	85.6
33009	Grafton County	$68,504	$39,856	$49,447	$85,558	$105,417	$82,125	$42,553	$35,380	88,426	90.1	78.5	86.9
33011	Hillsborough County	$84,577	$34,500	$58,924	$100,378	$119,261	$108,186	$43,978	$28,133	399,048	93.8	82.5	84.5
33013	Merrimack County	$80,760	$38,228	$50,359	$93,289	$114,127	$94,653	$39,771	$30,176	143,651	93.9	80.5	85.6
33015	Rockingham County	$91,982	$42,009	$64,856	$109,057	$120,298	$111,853	$57,821	$32,319	295,803	94.5	82.0	87.1
33017	Strafford County	$71,048	$35,065	$50,213	$86,265	$118,403	$89,659	$40,590	$24,579	122,837	92.4	80.4	85.3
34000	**New Jersey**	$85,615	$35,626	$61,012	$110,220	$128,876	$111,781	$45,334	$30,016	8,759,905	90.9	78.0	84.8
34001	Atlantic County	$64,539	$31,982	$45,887	$83,571	$105,962	$83,373	$32,361	$25,394	272,144	89.6	79.0	82.1
34003	Bergen County	$100,425	$36,485	$72,834	$124,006	$145,141	$128,053	$56,694	$36,474	913,322	90.6	79.2	85.0
34005	Burlington County	$92,594	$44,053	$68,468	$109,427	$141,875	$116,124	$52,334	$46,671	436,812	94.9	86.1	87.5
34007	Camden County	$75,500	$29,959	$51,950	$98,191	$115,230	$101,143	$40,374	$25,761	507,901	91.2	82.9	84.4
34009	Cape May County	$74,090	$18,244	$58,233	$87,870	$116,147	$87,338	$50,718	$27,128	94,140	92.3	85.7	87.9
34011	Cumberland County	$56,632	$27,873	$41,717	$83,536	$106,556	$77,591	$46,718	$26,039	146,132	87.7	81.1	83.6
34013	Essex County	$65,832	$20,806	$42,957	$102,829	$123,623	$111,210	$33,273	$24,674	776,212	87.5	77.0	78.4
34015	Gloucester County	$87,257	$38,248	$62,658	$108,969	$130,673	$113,907	$55,311	$32,157	288,324	94.0	85.2	89.7
34017	Hudson County	$61,048	$18,678	$41,311	$88,941	$103,914	$78,774	$39,177	$22,777	649,396	81.3	69.9	82.3
34019	Hunterdon County	$123,363	$52,886	$94,368	$141,776	$158,594	$142,042	$84,659	$59,821	122,138	96.5	89.2	89.2
34021	Mercer County	$94,000	$38,533	$64,332	$117,403	$122,061	$121,855	$46,228	$28,358	362,260	92.0	80.4	88.7
34023	Middlesex County	$91,195	$38,070	$69,986	$113,168	$130,428	$112,728	$45,257	$35,532	813,272	90.0	76.2	86.3
34025	Monmouth County	$103,428	$48,717	$78,379	$125,212	$148,245	$127,809	$45,269	$35,831	625,467	93.5	79.4	85.7
34027	Morris County	$115,178	$57,131	$90,607	$134,630	$147,673	$138,008	$59,124	$48,267	493,477	94.6	79.1	89.2
34029	Ocean County	$75,320	$44,153	$60,630	$98,648	$124,589	$93,710	$48,772	$32,056	575,595	94.3	78.4	91.2
34031	Passaic County	$66,309	$18,244	$42,097	$95,223	$117,467	$91,554	$32,869	$22,441	500,894	85.1	73.0	81.1
34033	Salem County	$73,104	$33,776	$54,814	$99,351	$108,214	$100,446	$38,722	$18,029	64,464	92.4	82.9	81.6
34035	Somerset County	$114,759	$54,930	$88,449	$138,124	$150,798	$139,424	$64,861	$45,410	325,749	93.5	82.1	88.9
34037	Sussex County	$99,875	$45,736	$78,484	$110,112	$130,682	$117,218	$76,250	$39,647	145,637	93.4	79.2	88.1
34039	Union County	$80,615	$31,520	$54,424	$108,654	$120,552	$109,778	$43,344	$27,433	539,815	88.6	75.1	78.9
34041	Warren County	$81,884	$39,048	$58,018	$99,597	$130,844	$101,265	$36,694	$31,140	106,754	93.9	82.5	83.0
35000	**New Mexico**	$53,555	$28,370	$39,494	$76,365	$92,119	$68,669	$32,605	$20,758	2,047,997	84.3	75.1	79.6
35001	Bernalillo County	$58,536	$29,720	$40,526	$80,542	$97,202	$75,431	$33,843	$22,749	664,256	86.4	80.0	80.6
35005	Chaves County	$50,215	$29,063	$36,705	$75,443	$86,827	$58,750	$34,592	$23,171	64,804	84.4	71.7	79.5
35009	Curry County	$47,590	$25,394	$33,962	$75,353	$83,188	$63,090	$19,167	$15,183	48,036	90.2	73.2	79.3
35013	Do±a Ana County	$43,350	$25,691	$31,040	$57,081	$71,231	$49,310	$27,788	$16,716	209,951	81.4	73.0	79.1
35015	Eddy County	$63,581	$23,609	$51,004	$90,092	$97,059	$82,135	$36,777	$22,236	54,173	90.1	74.4	77.8
35025	Lea County	$61,422	$25,322	$42,908	$86,137	$106,591	$69,524	$47,058	$20,926	65,020	80.7	71.4	75.8
35031	McKinley County	$34,544	$10,484	$31,170	$61,439	$68,963	$57,274	$15,179	$16,453	72,816	67.0	60.1	72.3
35035	Otero County	$45,987	$34,537	$38,021	$63,624	$89,266	$65,283	$18,516	$19,343	60,894	83.3	79.4	85.2
35043	Sandoval County	$65,506	$35,736	$54,599	$87,734	$100,916	$83,102	$43,056	$27,868	134,581	89.6	77.6	84.5
35045	San Juan County	$57,854	$19,941	$42,957	$78,618	$105,848	$74,942	$40,917	$22,228	126,427	78.2	65.3	74.1
35049	Santa Fe County	$62,280	$40,453	$44,914	$86,214	$82,330	$71,889	$40,531	$25,208	144,517	82.8	71.4	79.1
35061	Valencia County	$50,606	$24,628	$37,886	$72,246	$82,113	$64,622	$19,161	$15,367	74,918	85.9	79.9	77.9
36000	**New York**	$69,813	$27,817	$48,566	$94,722	$114,449	$93,157	$38,808	$25,937	19,323,884	91.9	84.2	87.2
36001	Albany County	$79,987	$41,272	$54,394	$104,331	$121,455	$106,998	$41,532	$27,925	302,222	96.0	89.5	90.4
36005	Bronx County	$37,285	$11,747	$30,401	$62,875	$83,680	$55,991	$27,628	$19,694	1,384,115	86.0	84.2	85.2

State/County FIPS code	State/Place	Total number of families	Families with incomes below the poverty level, as a percent of all families of that family type				Families that received Food Stamps (SNAP), as a percent of all families of that family type			Families that received food stamps (SNAP) and had at least one worker	
			All families	Married-couple families with related children under 18	Male householder families, no spouse present, with related children	Female householder families, no spouse present	All families	Married-couple families	Male householder or female householder families, no spouse present	Married-couple families, percent	Male householder or female householder families, no spouse present
	Missouri—cont'd										
29187	St. Francois County........	15,713	15.6	13.3	33.1	49.4	24.8	12.5	9.1	58.8	38.6
29189	St. Louis County.............	261,614	8.7	5.1	17.1	33.2	12.5	4.7	4.1	31.9	23.8
29213	Taney County...............	13,574	14.2	8.6	43.1	42.9	18.3	12.1	11.2	36.8	27.3
29510	St. Louis city..............	64,535	22.6	15.3	40.1	52.0	32.6	14.3	11.1	52.9	38.0
30000	**Montana**	255,929	10.5	8.1	23.6	44.1	11.5	5.7	5.0	32.7	26.8
30013	Cascade County.............	21,114	12.7	12.0	25.2	49.9	12.6	5.9	5.2	33.7	27.2
30029	Flathead County............	24,015	10.0	6.5	31.2	48.0	9.2	4.8	4.7	30.4	25.1
30031	Gallatin County.............	22,556	6.4	6.2	16.0	30.3	6.7	3.7	3.5	21.3	18.1
30049	Lewis and Clark County	16,761	8.5	3.1	28.0	34.8	10.1	4.7	4.3	30.2	26.6
30063	Missoula County............	26,566	9.5	5.4	11.0	41.7	15.0	8.0	6.7	35.2	31.7
30111	Yellowstone County.........	38,527	9.2	5.2	18.4	38.6	12.0	4.8	4.5	32.1	27.6
31000	**Nebraska**	472,470	9.0	6.7	19.3	39.1	9.6	4.2	3.7	29.0	23.6
31055	Douglas County.............	126,717	10.7	7.6	21.0	36.3	12.6	5.3	4.7	31.1	24.6
31079	Hall County................	14,681	13.3	11.0	22.9	46.5	14.4	6.7	5.7	38.4	32.7
31109	Lancaster County...........	70,178	9.5	6.9	23.0	39.3	9.7	4.0	3.5	29.1	24.3
31153	Sarpy County..............	44,248	5.6	2.6	18.7	32.0	6.5	2.9	2.6	20.4	17.4
32000	**Nevada**....................	641,060	12.0	11.2	21.6	34.2	13.2	7.7	6.7	25.9	18.7
32003	Clark County...............	456,983	12.5	11.6	21.9	32.9	14.0	8.6	7.6	25.5	18.5
32007	Elko County...............	12,583	8.3	7.7	4.1	48.9	6.4	2.2	1.4	24.6	18.0
32019	Lyon County...............	13,652	15.6	13.6	12.4	49.2	14.5	8.5	6.5	32.9	25.4
32031	Washoe County.............	100,520	11.0	9.4	22.2	36.6	10.3	5.3	4.2	23.6	16.1
32510	Carson City...............	12,572	10.2	14.8	43.9	23.3	12.6	7.6	7.0	27.3	19.8
33000	**New Hampshire**..........	346,775	5.7	3.5	11.6	29.9	8.1	3.8	3.2	23.9	17.7
33001	Belknap County............	16,843	8.0	6.2	7.6	39.4	9.5	4.8	4.4	26.4	16.1
33005	Cheshire County............	19,199	5.7	2.6	3.7	34.5	10.4	5.0	4.7	28.2	22.1
33009	Grafton County.............	21,927	6.0	6.2	13.8	30.7	7.5	4.0	3.4	20.5	15.6
33011	Hillsborough County.........	103,411	5.9	3.3	11.3	29.4	8.2	3.6	2.9	23.8	18.1
33013	Merrimack County..........	37,970	6.2	4.0	12.2	28.2	9.2	5.2	4.0	24.9	18.4
33015	Rockingham County.........	81,603	3.9	2.1	9.9	25.9	4.8	2.2	1.9	16.7	12.3
33017	Strafford County............	31,040	7.2	4.2	19.6	35.3	11.6	5.2	3.8	32.3	24.0
34000	**New Jersey**	2,203,456	8.2	4.9	19.5	33.6	9.1	4.1	3.4	22.9	15.9
34001	Atlantic County.............	68,182	12.7	8.3	24.3	40.3	14.3	6.5	5.7	30.1	21.0
34003	Bergen County.............	240,064	5.8	3.7	14.1	27.3	4.8	2.4	1.9	13.1	8.5
34005	Burlington County..........	114,299	4.1	1.7	8.5	20.8	5.5	2.5	2.2	15.1	10.6
34007	Camden County............	124,590	10.7	4.5	21.6	39.1	13.2	5.3	4.0	30.1	20.3
34009	Cape May County..........	25,924	6.8	5.3	16.7	33.1	6.8	4.0	3.4	19.1	13.3
34011	Cumberland County.........	34,534	14.9	8.7	23.4	38.8	18.4	9.5	7.1	33.6	24.6
34013	Essex County	181,322	14.4	6.2	27.2	41.9	17.0	6.2	5.0	33.1	21.7
34015	Gloucester County..........	75,931	5.9	2.3	15.7	30.6	7.5	3.3	2.9	19.9	11.9
34017	Hudson County............	151,007	15.2	11.0	22.2	42.8	17.1	8.7	7.6	30.8	23.5
34019	Hunterdon County..........	34,208	2.3	1.5	0.0	16.1	2.3	1.2	1.1	8.4	8.2
34021	Mercer County.............	88,312	7.6	4.1	16.5	37.3	9.0	3.8	3.3	23.5	17.5
34023	Middlesex County..........	203,389	6.6	4.2	24.3	25.3	5.6	3.0	2.5	14.0	10.3
34025	Monmouth County..........	163,657	5.1	2.7	18.1	26.8	4.8	2.2	1.8	14.3	11.2
34027	Morris County.............	129,380	3.2	2.5	12.0	15.0	3.2	2.2	1.8	8.2	6.6
34029	Ocean County..............	148,276	7.3	9.6	10.3	27.5	8.8	5.6	4.7	20.6	15.1
34031	Passaic County.............	119,004	13.7	8.6	23.2	42.0	18.2	9.2	7.4	34.9	21.6
34033	Salem County..............	16,660	10.8	2.7	25.2	47.4	11.8	3.2	2.5	32.5	22.2
34035	Somerset County	84,424	3.7	1.9	13.3	18.7	3.3	1.4	1.2	12.0	8.4
34037	Sussex County	40,139	4.5	3.4	17.9	24.3	4.0	1.9	1.6	13.4	9.1
34039	Union County..............	131,065	8.8	5.1	18.6	30.9	8.9	4.2	3.3	19.8	14.9
34041	Warren County.............	29,089	6.1	3.4	33.6	30.8	7.0	3.9	3.3	18.3	11.7
35000	**New Mexico**...............	494,555	16.6	13.8	26.8	46.8	18.0	9.7	8.1	36.9	27.7
35001	Bernalillo County	163,032	15.1	13.0	20.7	42.9	17.8	9.0	7.7	35.9	27.4
35005	Chaves County.............	16,309	16.2	12.3	28.3	49.2	18.9	9.0	7.7	40.0	30.9
35009	Curry County..............	12,813	16.6	6.3	47.2	57.8	16.1	7.4	6.3	39.0	28.6
35013	Do±a Ana County...........	51,559	23.2	22.2	31.5	56.1	21.7	12.5	10.5	41.6	33.1
35015	Eddy County...............	13,882	10.2	3.2	11.7	45.6	15.4	6.7	6.1	36.0	24.2
35025	Lea County................	15,924	12.0	8.2	11.3	48.6	12.4	7.8	6.9	24.8	21.6
35031	McKinley County	12,305	33.5	24.1	51.6	55.4	26.1	17.3	12.8	38.2	23.4
35035	Otero County..............	16,021	17.3	11.9	48.9	51.3	21.5	11.2	9.5	49.4	38.6
35043	Sandoval County...........	33,579	11.6	7.5	22.4	35.9	14.3	7.8	6.9	32.3	24.4
35045	San Juan County...........	28,966	15.7	11.2	25.6	43.8	14.7	8.1	7.0	28.8	18.0
35049	Santa Fe County	35,394	13.7	13.7	18.9	39.9	12.4	6.8	6.3	27.5	17.9
35061	Valencia County............	18,719	19.7	14.7	37.7	63.6	20.2	12.8	9.9	41.2	30.8
36000	**New York**	4,594,587	12.2	9.1	22.9	38.7	16.1	8.2	6.5	33.3	23.3
36001	Albany County.............	68,366	8.7	4.4	17.9	36.9	11.3	3.9	3.3	30.9	21.2
36005	Bronx County..............	311,197	28.1	18.8	32.6	50.0	40.8	23.9	19.0	52.6	36.0

Table E-2: Counties with a Population of 50,000 or More—Income, Poverty, and Health Insurance—*Continued*

| State/County FIPS code | State/Place | Median family income in the past 12 months (in 2,013 inflation-adjusted dollars) | | | | | Families with own children under 18 years | | | Total population in households | Persons who had health insurance, as a percent of all persons in that household type | | |
		All families	Families with no earners	Families with one earner	Families with two earners	Families with three or more earners	Married-couple families with children	Male householder, no spouse present, with children	Female householder, no spouse present, with children		Married-couple families, percent	Male householder or female householder families, no spouse present	Nonfamily households
	New York—cont'd												
36007	Broome County	$61,294	$30,891	$46,263	$77,944	$105,908	$76,235	$37,040	$20,966	195,302	94.6	86.5	89.7
36009	Cattaraugus County	$51,359	$28,367	$39,015	$71,368	$88,864	$66,545	$30,352	$19,887	78,605	90.1	85.0	86.6
36011	Cayuga County	$62,709	$34,920	$47,629	$81,078	$100,224	$82,430	$48,504	$24,179	76,651	92.9	85.6	88.4
36013	Chautauqua County	$51,508	$29,588	$42,205	$70,850	$89,867	$59,461	$23,922	$18,136	130,915	93.1	88.9	89.0
36015	Chemung County	$61,633	$31,924	$41,800	$85,838	$110,369	$87,271	$32,115	$21,232	83,954	95.7	89.5	84.0
36019	Clinton County	$63,285	$36,048	$46,485	$83,056	$102,220	$80,877	$48,041	$17,045	77,028	95.4	90.8	90.7
36021	Columbia County	$72,270	$33,559	$55,864	$87,391	$109,762	$88,913	$37,347	$34,569	60,677	95.3	89.4	85.4
36027	Dutchess County	$87,630	$44,726	$63,052	$106,368	$120,456	$107,701	$43,785	$30,444	289,632	94.3	84.3	87.8
36029	Erie County	$65,685	$33,821	$45,078	$87,739	$111,530	$90,827	$39,020	$22,739	907,651	96.3	89.3	90.8
36033	Franklin County	$54,193	$29,945	$41,871	$76,520	$93,611	$66,676	$31,987	$23,028	46,730	93.3	81.1	87.6
36035	Fulton County	$56,086	$33,226	$37,979	$77,040	$108,588	$67,897	$24,929	$25,521	54,045	95.3	81.9	85.9
36037	Genesee County	$60,232	$32,307	$42,813	$72,621	$93,875	$70,806	$44,269	$24,738	59,191	94.0	86.6	83.4
36043	Herkimer County	$55,419	$29,820	$39,767	$71,431	$87,681	$71,998	$35,107	$19,904	63,760	93.9	87.8	85.9
36045	Jefferson County	$54,676	$32,009	$37,460	$70,096	$89,927	$63,129	$33,183	$19,144	107,086	93.6	87.7	86.1
36047	Kings County	$51,565	$14,692	$37,604	$78,868	$100,827	$62,680	$31,961	$25,700	2,557,446	89.8	83.7	82.5
36051	Livingston County	$65,345	$35,510	$41,051	$85,400	$109,200	$84,106	$27,083	$24,743	62,390	96.1	85.2	91.2
36053	Madison County	$66,258	$34,692	$47,628	$85,248	$97,600	$82,493	$46,042	$24,622	71,888	96.5	86.6	92.3
36055	Monroe County	$67,748	$32,890	$46,304	$89,470	$109,732	$94,958	$38,301	$21,755	740,741	95.4	89.2	90.5
36059	Nassau County	$110,959	$47,713	$84,579	$131,282	$146,491	$132,649	$49,043	$43,563	1,338,058	93.5	82.9	90.4
36061	New York County	$83,370	$16,724	$54,703	$146,735	$87,533	$159,357	$45,124	$26,391	1,606,918	92.6	84.3	90.5
36063	Niagara County	$63,096	$33,125	$47,096	$84,122	$104,194	$88,144	$43,942	$23,182	212,789	95.3	88.0	89.0
36065	Oneida County	$61,583	$32,826	$42,318	$80,078	$100,434	$80,116	$34,774	$24,747	225,676	94.1	90.3	89.4
36067	Onondaga County	$69,917	$31,226	$50,310	$91,587	$109,373	$94,225	$36,516	$23,398	462,032	95.0	86.9	88.9
36069	Ontario County	$68,371	$42,657	$47,624	$84,725	$105,781	$96,092	$41,429	$27,118	107,656	95.0	86.1	90.2
36071	Orange County	$81,487	$37,578	$56,910	$101,070	$127,788	$98,235	$40,793	$32,208	364,406	93.4	84.7	85.4
36075	Oswego County	$58,358	$28,703	$44,190	$76,336	$101,538	$73,480	$36,838	$19,326	120,739	92.8	89.6	89.2
36077	Otsego County	$60,644	$37,512	$42,854	$74,529	$95,132	$78,063	$36,133	$25,159	61,209	94.4	89.6	90.9
36079	Putnam County	$110,538	$46,476	$76,317	$128,333	$149,375	$131,636	$55,104	$51,260	99,037	93.7	84.4	79.9
36081	Queens County	$62,443	$23,095	$45,077	$81,527	$107,031	$70,697	$40,693	$31,781	2,261,451	85.0	78.9	78.3
36083	Rensselaer County	$75,035	$36,914	$54,355	$94,760	$109,599	$94,480	$38,485	$23,451	157,933	96.2	90.2	90.6
36085	Richmond County	$85,006	$30,186	$62,009	$110,985	$141,719	$102,709	$49,327	$30,235	467,614	93.6	87.5	90.2
36087	Rockland County	$95,298	$47,688	$64,970	$118,208	$139,838	$108,414	$56,658	$35,047	315,251	93.2	79.7	88.2
36089	St. Lawrence County	$53,412	$33,519	$40,415	$74,846	$92,157	$66,827	$37,028	$20,593	108,557	88.7	86.7	89.1
36091	Saratoga County	$86,811	$50,254	$62,185	$105,077	$116,048	$110,464	$53,813	$32,334	218,980	95.9	90.5	92.7
36093	Schenectady County	$73,787	$35,915	$53,000	$89,041	$103,708	$93,023	$27,426	$25,107	153,332	94.6	89.7	87.4
36101	Steuben County	$56,170	$34,671	$42,832	$75,363	$89,370	$71,447	$34,485	$23,228	97,785	91.5	82.5	86.8
36103	Suffolk County	$100,012	$43,564	$72,925	$117,960	$137,019	$118,851	$63,451	$42,259	1,483,782	92.9	82.6	89.2
36105	Sullivan County	$60,745	$32,978	$47,226	$79,352	$95,455	$78,044	$36,436	$21,728	74,570	92.3	79.5	84.6
36107	Tioga County	$67,045	$40,972	$51,842	$81,087	$101,266	$87,544	$28,750	$24,092	50,165	94.6	87.2	82.9
36109	Tompkins County	$72,719	$40,487	$48,363	$90,669	$115,000	$88,857	$41,208	$24,375	101,836	93.4	87.5	94.0
36111	Ulster County	$72,369	$34,840	$53,028	$93,414	$108,490	$95,742	$37,569	$28,182	177,420	93.8	85.7	79.1
36113	Warren County	$64,222	$39,811	$44,635	$80,834	$100,769	$83,325	$26,528	$26,538	64,878	93.6	83.2	89.0
36115	Washington County	$61,340	$36,674	$42,279	$75,208	$89,865	$76,307	$30,350	$25,447	60,224	93.2	82.8	86.3
36117	Wayne County	$63,463	$36,731	$47,333	$80,051	$99,875	$81,517	$46,198	$24,697	91,792	93.5	85.3	85.0
36119	Westchester County	$103,739	$41,555	$73,964	$134,314	$140,862	$146,335	$48,062	$36,035	948,567	92.0	82.1	88.8
37000	**North Carolina**	$56,001	$29,254	$40,907	$76,504	$92,148	$75,259	$31,549	$21,820	9,550,684	87.8	76.5	81.0
37001	Alamance County	$52,590	$28,703	$36,207	$73,868	$92,852	$67,303	$30,559	$21,782	152,588	87.7	74.4	80.3
37019	Brunswick County	$55,315	$44,177	$46,272	$73,051	$73,542	$65,650	$24,550	$18,008	111,524	87.7	75.1	80.4
37021	Buncombe County	$57,118	$36,674	$40,920	$72,576	$89,170	$71,326	$36,804	$23,477	240,865	87.8	77.5	76.7
37023	Burke County	$48,508	$24,921	$38,500	$64,581	$82,661	$61,004	$30,297	$16,914	87,980	86.7	79.4	80.1
37025	Cabarrus County	$65,151	$31,669	$46,603	$81,212	$97,913	$82,126	$38,360	$25,816	182,848	87.4	74.9	78.9
37027	Caldwell County	$46,099	$23,129	$36,218	$62,281	$74,042	$60,474	$19,167	$21,178	81,202	86.8	74.6	78.8
37031	Carteret County	$56,600	$39,808	$40,203	$77,986	$95,650	$79,674	$29,202	$16,263	65,956	87.5	72.6	76.0
37035	Catawba County	$54,036	$28,086	$39,906	$70,879	$82,005	$66,500	$33,013	$18,188	152,992	88.6	76.2	79.9
37037	Chatham County	$64,629	$48,371	$55,019	$83,306	$79,962	$84,261	$26,382	$25,804	65,227	88.8	75.7	83.1
37045	Cleveland County	$48,357	$24,381	$37,614	$65,790	$104,832	$67,064	$27,298	$13,115	97,023	87.9	78.1	80.9
37047	Columbus County	$44,029	$22,618	$35,300	$65,800	$104,273	$59,578	$26,640	$14,441	54,873	81.8	75.6	80.6
37049	Craven County	$58,201	$44,771	$42,440	$69,674	$110,565	$61,565	$33,857	$13,778	96,725	88.7	71.6	83.4
37051	Cumberland County	$51,711	$24,574	$40,162	$72,216	$92,961	$66,422	$35,403	$22,188	295,292	90.7	80.4	80.2
37057	Davidson County	$51,341	$26,785	$38,291	$71,246	$89,112	$61,847	$34,315	$21,429	161,494	89.6	78.9	78.2
37061	Duplin County	$41,640	$28,058	$30,158	$60,942	$66,682	$49,391	$20,749	$14,446	59,146	81.4	69.3	72.9
37063	Durham County	$64,848	$26,912	$41,174	$90,293	$89,554	$87,707	$30,613	$26,521	276,929	88.3	75.2	81.6
37065	Edgecombe County	$41,372	$18,763	$31,247	$65,492	$93,972	$68,802	$30,494	$11,846	54,588	84.8	76.8	76.0
37067	Forsyth County	$57,934	$31,398	$38,781	$80,492	$103,706	$76,596	$28,412	$19,936	354,836	88.6	74.9	83.0
37069	Franklin County	$50,024	$29,109	$34,415	$72,323	$108,618	$68,438	$26,818	$22,031	60,567	84.2	74.9	80.5
37071	Gaston County	$51,152	$24,205	$39,174	$71,304	$86,569	$67,160	$34,223	$16,323	206,045	86.4	74.8	81.3
37077	Granville County	$51,873	$26,213	$42,776	$81,408	$95,969	$79,294	$33,003	$26,322	54,739	90.4	81.6	84.8
37081	Guilford County	$56,883	$28,270	$40,791	$78,155	$93,131	$79,352	$30,941	$23,381	497,159	88.9	76.8	79.2
37083	Halifax County	$40,627	$17,763	$33,640	$65,564	$67,163	$63,604	$9,934	$16,701	52,422	88.9	78.7	85.7
37085	Harnett County	$52,295	$26,296	$40,613	$75,763	$85,154	$64,493	$33,088	$25,140	116,169	87.2	75.5	80.9

Table E-2: Counties with a Population of 50,000 or More—Income, Poverty, and Health Insurance—*Continued*

State/County FIPS code	State/Place	Total number of families	Families with incomes below the poverty level, as a percent of all families of that family type				Families that received Food Stamps (SNAP), as a percent of all families of that family type			Families that received food stamps (SNAP) and had at least one worker	
			All families	Married-couple families with related children under 18	Male householder families, no spouse present, with related children	Female householder families, no spouse present	All families	Married-couple families	Male householder or female householder families, no spouse present	Married-couple families, percent	Male householder or female householder families, no spouse present
	New York—cont'd										
36007	Broome County....................	47,693	11.7	9.9	23.3	46.0	15.9	7.6	5.9	39.5	25.2
36009	Cattaraugus County.................	20,069	13.6	16.1	26.5	45.6	14.5	9.1	7.2	29.4	16.7
36011	Cayuga County...................	19,649	8.5	6.7	18.6	35.0	11.4	5.4	4.3	27.4	19.6
36013	Chautauqua County..............	34,101	14.6	14.9	36.0	49.1	18.5	10.5	8.9	40.6	24.1
36015	Chemung County..................	22,180	12.3	7.7	19.3	49.6	14.2	6.6	4.5	35.5	21.0
36019	Clinton County....................	20,528	10.7	8.3	11.9	49.2	15.9	6.1	4.8	44.3	32.3
36021	Columbia County.................	16,251	6.7	6.8	14.8	26.0	8.7	4.3	3.4	21.6	15.8
36027	Dutchess County.................	71,106	5.8	3.9	15.6	27.3	9.3	3.8	3.3	27.8	21.6
36029	Erie County....................	230,091	11.1	6.7	19.7	42.1	15.1	5.9	4.5	36.3	24.7
36033	Franklin County.................	11,641	15.0	14.8	35.4	46.9	15.8	7.9	6.3	37.2	22.8
36035	Fulton County....................	14,710	11.1	9.6	34.6	36.2	13.4	7.7	5.1	28.5	16.9
36037	Genesee County..................	16,091	9.2	9.9	15.3	39.5	10.0	5.0	4.4	27.0	18.1
36043	Herkimer County.................	17,647	12.0	9.7	26.6	43.5	16.5	9.6	6.3	35.7	23.3
36045	Jefferson County................	30,477	12.3	8.2	20.0	47.5	15.3	8.9	6.8	35.4	25.6
36047	Kings County....................	576,129	20.3	19.8	30.0	39.8	27.5	19.6	15.4	38.9	26.7
36051	Livingston County...............	15,598	9.9	5.3	33.0	36.6	11.8	4.4	3.9	38.2	27.4
36053	Madison County..................	17,490	7.7	8.1	14.2	35.2	10.2	4.2	3.7	30.2	23.7
36055	Monroe County..................	181,404	11.4	5.5	22.9	44.6	15.1	4.8	3.8	38.9	25.4
36059	Nassau County..................	336,922	4.5	3.3	15.6	23.9	5.1	2.6	2.2	14.6	11.1
36061	New York County................	297,758	14.9	7.7	25.9	42.1	19.5	9.3	6.6	37.5	26.5
36063	Niagara County..................	55,334	9.9	3.5	17.3	43.2	12.7	4.8	3.8	32.9	22.9
36065	Oneida County..................	55,433	11.7	9.3	21.8	40.7	16.2	6.8	5.3	39.0	28.0
36067	Onondaga County................	112,156	10.7	5.7	26.0	41.4	13.6	5.3	4.1	33.9	22.0
36069	Ontario County..................	29,384	6.3	2.9	18.8	32.7	9.1	3.7	3.1	24.8	18.9
36071	Orange County..................	89,926	9.6	10.2	29.1	28.5	11.5	7.1	6.3	25.2	18.5
36075	Oswego County..................	30,360	13.2	8.5	26.3	49.3	15.5	6.7	5.0	38.4	23.8
36077	Otsego County..................	14,670	8.4	7.5	11.7	35.4	10.3	5.6	4.2	26.1	20.7
36079	Putnam County...................	26,197	3.3	2.6	14.7	19.8	3.8	2.1	1.7	12.0	8.8
36081	Queens County...................	519,989	12.8	12.5	19.5	31.6	16.1	10.9	8.8	26.4	20.9
36083	Rensselaer County...............	39,634	9.1	4.3	22.1	43.6	11.7	4.9	3.9	30.5	20.1
36085	Richmond County.................	120,248	9.5	5.6	18.8	36.9	12.3	6.5	5.7	28.0	16.8
36087	Rockland County.................	74,387	10.2	14.5	15.1	28.9	11.7	9.8	9.0	19.1	15.4
36089	St. Lawrence County.............	26,264	13.9	12.6	32.0	44.0	15.0	8.2	5.3	34.0	22.6
36091	Saratoga County.................	58,110	4.2	2.8	11.6	24.1	6.2	2.9	2.3	19.8	15.7
36093	Schenectady County.............	34,963	9.7	4.3	37.6	43.8	12.0	4.5	3.3	35.1	23.3
36101	Steuben County.................	26,590	11.6	10.6	27.5	43.0	12.6	6.9	4.8	28.5	18.5
36103	Suffolk County..................	372,318	4.9	3.2	9.4	22.2	6.0	3.2	2.8	15.5	10.3
36105	Sullivan County.................	17,588	12.2	7.7	22.5	45.3	14.0	6.3	5.0	34.2	27.8
36107	Tioga County....................	14,093	5.3	4.1	2.4	29.9	8.7	4.8	3.7	24.6	18.6
36109	Tompkins County.................	20,394	8.9	6.0	28.8	42.0	10.2	4.5	3.9	33.2	23.1
36111	Ulster County...................	43,813	7.3	5.0	26.5	27.4	11.0	5.2	3.8	27.0	20.1
36113	Warren County...................	17,779	9.2	6.5	19.3	35.6	11.2	5.1	4.1	28.9	23.2
36115	Washington County...............	16,344	9.9	7.1	28.0	41.7	13.8	5.8	4.3	37.6	31.4
36117	Wayne County...................	24,985	7.5	3.9	16.6	39.7	10.5	4.7	4.1	30.1	23.2
36119	Westchester County..............	236,675	7.4	4.3	18.5	29.6	8.4	3.7	3.1	21.8	16.2
37000	**North Carolina........................**	2,467,843	13.2	9.3	28.0	44.4	16.1	7.8	6.5	38.0	27.4
37001	Alamance County.................	40,693	13.9	12.4	27.0	43.2	14.7	6.7	5.1	33.7	27.3
37019	Brunswick County................	34,006	12.6	10.8	44.8	45.8	15.4	8.9	6.6	39.0	25.6
37021	Buncombe County................	59,011	12.1	10.3	18.0	43.2	14.4	7.5	6.7	35.0	25.9
37023	Burke County....................	22,335	14.1	10.1	19.6	53.8	16.9	8.5	6.8	37.8	22.9
37025	Cabarrus County.................	46,583	9.5	7.3	20.9	36.5	14.1	8.2	7.9	36.4	27.9
37027	Caldwell County.................	20,233	16.2	13.1	54.9	48.5	19.2	11.9	8.3	40.9	26.4
37031	Carteret County.................	19,239	13.4	7.7	28.5	54.7	15.7	6.1	4.8	44.8	33.8
37035	Catawba County.................	40,148	11.5	9.2	30.2	47.3	17.4	9.9	8.8	41.2	27.1
37037	Chatham County.................	18,365	9.3	9.6	42.0	37.2	9.5	4.3	3.9	32.8	25.1
37045	Cleveland County................	24,586	16.0	11.3	30.8	56.8	18.6	9.0	7.8	44.0	30.2
37047	Columbus County................	13,918	19.2	13.8	51.7	54.9	22.1	12.2	9.6	42.4	26.1
37049	Craven County..................	28,014	11.2	5.4	24.5	53.4	15.2	7.0	6.5	43.1	35.5
37051	Cumberland County..............	81,165	14.4	6.7	28.0	41.8	18.3	7.8	6.8	38.6	28.3
37057	Davidson County.................	43,695	12.6	6.9	28.3	46.4	17.9	9.5	7.6	43.5	35.1
37061	Duplin County...................	15,014	16.9	12.9	48.0	58.1	20.3	11.4	9.5	40.9	30.5
37063	Durham County.................	65,863	13.0	9.4	30.4	35.8	14.5	5.1	4.9	33.4	24.8
37065	Edgecombe County..............	14,057	20.6	12.8	34.9	58.9	31.1	12.6	11.5	56.4	40.9
37067	Forsyth County..................	89,321	14.3	11.7	28.6	47.7	13.5	5.7	5.0	32.2	22.3
37069	Franklin County.................	15,932	12.7	8.6	27.1	41.8	21.9	13.7	11.8	46.9	37.9
37071	Gaston County..................	53,980	13.9	9.1	26.1	53.7	19.2	9.5	8.0	41.6	29.8
37077	Granville County.................	14,226	12.7	8.3	29.7	36.4	16.2	8.7	6.8	33.9	23.6
37081	Guilford County.................	125,957	13.9	8.5	28.7	42.8	15.9	6.2	5.2	36.4	25.6
37083	Halifax County..................	14,229	23.5	7.3	59.2	58.8	33.8	14.4	8.9	60.3	38.1
37085	Harnett County..................	29,187	13.4	10.4	23.5	38.0	16.5	9.1	8.0	37.9	28.8

Table E-2: Counties with a Population of 50,000 or More—Income, Poverty, and Health Insurance—*Continued*

| State/County FIPS code | State/Place | Median family income in the past 12 months (in 2,013 inflation-adjusted dollars) | | | | | Families with own children under 18 years | | | Total population in households | Persons who had health insurance, as a percent of all persons in that household type | | |
		All families	Families with no earners	Families with one earner	Families with two earners	Families with three or more earners	Married-couple families with children	Male householder, no spouse present, with children	Female householder, no spouse present, with children		Married-couple families, percent	Male householder or female householder families, no spouse present	Nonfamily households
	North Carolina—cont'd												
37087	Haywood County	$50,161	$33,566	$40,821	$74,006	$99,076	$71,500	$29,643	$20,155	58,341	86.0	75.4	81.8
37089	Henderson County	$54,975	$41,439	$42,862	$68,677	$94,801	$64,167	$23,140	$22,859	107,318	86.2	72.3	80.4
37093	Hoke County	$54,578	$14,815	$35,874	$71,979	$80,352	$63,125	$28,559	$17,831	46,377	87.6	80.8	79.5
37097	Iredell County	$60,520	$27,777	$48,553	$81,148	$83,897	$88,168	$35,359	$22,135	161,654	89.1	75.1	81.0
37101	Johnston County	$58,515	$28,577	$41,052	$79,418	$87,437	$71,729	$36,201	$19,404	173,488	87.7	72.2	77.4
37105	Lee County	$54,872	$35,106	$34,528	$72,576	$90,859	$69,425	$21,692	$16,659	57,988	84.6	74.4	74.6
37107	Lenoir County	$44,492	$28,042	$33,193	$62,585	$69,282	$58,120	$33,271	$20,665	58,300	87.1	75.4	73.0
37109	Lincoln County	$61,664	$25,285	$44,628	$78,536	$100,165	$73,303	$26,726	$21,628	78,720	87.4	78.2	79.4
37119	Mecklenburg County	$66,994	$31,405	$46,067	$88,040	$96,548	$94,281	$35,009	$26,265	962,168	87.9	75.6	79.3
37125	Moore County	$61,020	$44,614	$51,468	$79,477	$91,729	$77,282	$37,170	$14,812	87,875	90.6	83.8	82.9
37127	Nash County	$52,098	$29,877	$35,024	$69,424	$78,125	$68,487	$36,302	$20,869	93,952	86.4	76.7	85.8
37129	New Hanover County	$66,206	$42,933	$47,698	$85,007	$96,219	$89,346	$33,539	$22,724	207,061	89.3	72.9	81.7
37133	Onslow County	$49,698	$30,745	$41,710	$59,243	$106,025	$52,364	$41,417	$26,860	151,756	89.3	79.2	78.0
37135	Orange County	$85,299	$35,368	$50,317	$115,458	$118,750	$114,505	$34,688	$28,509	137,171	91.2	76.6	91.5
37141	Pender County	$52,606	$33,616	$34,739	$71,263	$75,718	$70,182	$28,582	$18,993	52,600	84.2	75.9	80.9
37147	Pitt County	$55,873	$27,036	$33,617	$81,220	$100,207	$88,111	$32,181	$20,635	171,250	89.4	77.1	85.4
37151	Randolph County	$50,808	$23,879	$37,269	$69,785	$91,476	$61,994	$31,947	$21,909	141,247	84.6	71.8	82.4
37155	Robeson County	$36,310	$15,776	$29,263	$61,554	$77,003	$54,032	$15,970	$15,843	132,551	80.5	75.6	75.0
37157	Rockingham County	$46,162	$27,385	$36,013	$64,912	$86,629	$62,059	$27,164	$18,583	91,614	88.7	78.2	82.5
37159	Rowan County	$48,981	$27,743	$37,544	$73,411	$87,679	$65,843	$32,114	$18,596	135,629	87.2	77.6	78.2
37161	Rutherford County	$40,480	$23,723	$35,092	$61,141	$72,402	$51,925	$31,789	$22,500	66,288	84.9	78.8	80.6
37163	Sampson County	$42,414	$25,252	$31,895	$59,078	$82,791	$55,913	$12,245	$19,560	63,274	82.1	77.4	74.1
37167	Stanly County	$50,714	$27,272	$34,383	$71,235	$83,656	$71,914	$30,331	$16,868	59,116	87.1	81.3	78.9
37171	Surry County	$43,389	$22,715	$34,930	$62,541	$83,207	$56,406	$22,317	$22,307	72,695	85.4	74.0	78.8
37179	Union County	$72,989	$30,216	$56,244	$86,172	$96,272	$91,863	$32,165	$29,656	207,814	89.4	75.7	80.4
37183	Wake County	$82,439	$42,177	$56,983	$100,396	$113,455	$104,074	$37,620	$30,248	942,898	89.7	78.4	85.1
37189	Watauga County	$62,196	$45,528	$43,094	$75,655	$79,455	$75,466	$25,761	$19,013	51,780	88.4	76.0	90.3
37191	Wayne County	$50,721	$23,351	$37,156	$67,140	$90,551	$67,334	$22,056	$17,022	119,476	88.1	80.3	79.0
37193	Wilkes County	$38,764	$23,018	$32,589	$60,852	$70,981	$49,830	$23,295	$14,446	68,205	85.8	79.4	76.6
37195	Wilson County	$47,370	$28,398	$36,640	$63,638	$97,692	$55,543	$48,046	$14,904	80,443	85.9	75.9	81.8
38000	**North Dakota**	$71,797	$34,628	$45,305	$86,061	$107,129	$88,252	$48,533	$24,136	688,158	93.8	80.8	86.1
38015	Burleigh County	$84,650	$51,164	$46,244	$95,280	$122,079	$101,844	$43,370	$29,425	84,113	96.5	83.7	86.6
38017	Cass County	$73,536	$45,861	$45,651	$89,097	$101,138	$91,725	$51,516	$24,724	156,213	95.2	82.7	87.3
38035	Grand Forks County	$70,989	$32,821	$38,986	$83,829	$109,688	$85,298	$31,477	$25,102	66,050	96.4	85.4	89.1
38101	Ward County	$69,066	$36,285	$44,292	$80,913	$113,955	$81,189	$51,690	$25,234	62,055	95.0	83.6	85.0
39000	**Ohio**	$60,999	$31,221	$43,529	$80,839	$100,646	$81,778	$35,072	$20,852	11,384,722	92.2	82.6	84.3
39003	Allen County	$54,519	$32,072	$37,528	$69,592	$84,456	$70,356	$36,328	$19,409	102,849	92.8	83.6	81.6
39005	Ashland County	$56,314	$36,612	$41,445	$68,235	$76,583	$64,773	$25,565	$21,120	52,686	88.3	83.2	86.8
39007	Ashtabula County	$48,315	$27,467	$37,409	$66,510	$85,443	$60,130	$37,538	$14,193	97,221	89.0	81.1	80.8
39009	Athens County	$50,281	$25,035	$38,644	$70,500	$89,840	$61,615	$18,333	$12,210	64,049	91.2	82.6	92.3
39013	Belmont County	$53,217	$30,184	$45,297	$70,470	$94,038	$68,198	$32,418	$17,596	65,960	93.5	82.9	76.4
39017	Butler County	$68,909	$33,791	$48,912	$85,503	$112,784	$89,771	$42,544	$26,121	367,668	93.0	81.6	88.0
39023	Clark County	$53,576	$33,716	$38,220	$71,915	$96,467	$71,929	$28,279	$19,321	135,263	92.2	84.7	83.8
39025	Clermont County	$70,529	$33,765	$50,712	$87,370	$108,524	$91,189	$34,460	$25,605	198,097	93.5	79.5	84.7
39029	Columbiana County	$54,886	$26,629	$41,799	$67,144	$91,261	$67,668	$24,783	$17,897	103,096	89.3	83.7	80.0
39035	Cuyahoga County	$59,286	$25,968	$41,446	$84,630	$101,870	$87,219	$32,549	$21,359	1,250,692	93.5	83.7	84.5
39037	Darke County	$53,346	$28,483	$40,853	$71,772	$88,851	$67,524	$35,156	$17,937	51,960	90.7	84.7	82.7
39041	Delaware County	$101,827	$44,721	$74,904	$121,529	$124,099	$122,091	$60,214	$40,545	180,646	96.6	87.5	92.4
39043	Erie County	$61,066	$39,519	$42,472	$78,145	$92,397	$81,856	$37,905	$20,375	75,452	93.2	82.7	80.7
39045	Fairfield County	$72,614	$36,483	$48,554	$88,115	$109,207	$90,615	$42,584	$26,842	145,368	93.6	87.2	83.0
39049	Franklin County	$64,270	$27,685	$42,090	$85,631	$106,017	$87,838	$36,742	$24,699	1,187,908	91.8	78.7	83.8
39055	Geauga County	$83,945	$42,122	$65,149	$105,444	$110,281	$100,847	$47,992	$26,754	93,154	86.8	86.9	83.9
39057	Greene County	$74,465	$42,815	$59,203	$94,726	$118,077	$94,007	$31,736	$23,810	159,387	95.5	85.9	88.4
39061	Hamilton County	$64,280	$27,841	$41,788	$90,095	$111,090	$94,575	$32,936	$19,312	794,678	93.5	82.7	84.4
39063	Hancock County	$64,912	$39,583	$41,387	$80,503	$99,020	$80,759	$33,165	$22,768	74,740	94.4	79.7	83.4
39077	Huron County	$56,377	$34,720	$40,275	$73,315	$85,000	$72,679	$25,244	$18,923	58,682	92.6	83.3	82.8
39081	Jefferson County	$51,754	$30,717	$41,556	$68,266	$94,529	$70,746	$37,813	$17,725	67,667	90.2	83.0	87.8
39083	Knox County	$57,081	$36,476	$43,121	$69,600	$101,302	$67,318	$33,281	$16,138	60,372	86.4	77.7	88.1
39085	Lake County	$69,818	$35,499	$48,076	$87,690	$102,323	$89,449	$46,627	$26,065	227,785	93.9	83.5	85.7
39087	Lawrence County	$55,157	$28,266	$49,492	$75,386	$95,536	$69,299	$40,568	$37,608	61,561	92.7	80.7	78.3
39089	Licking County	$67,556	$34,854	$47,851	$83,539	$106,420	$84,859	$42,588	$17,996	166,476	92.8	82.6	82.9
39093	Lorain County	$62,862	$35,349	$46,881	$82,174	$104,067	$88,139	$40,372	$19,776	295,182	93.7	84.7	84.8
39095	Lucas County	$53,946	$28,390	$37,889	$76,141	$101,250	$78,115	$32,089	$17,170	432,530	92.8	82.0	82.5
39099	Mahoning County	$52,078	$30,065	$39,994	$70,516	$93,699	$75,682	$30,600	$18,521	229,463	93.1	85.3	83.5
39101	Marion County	$52,297	$28,492	$40,684	$73,156	$97,129	$70,044	$27,120	$16,771	59,621	88.9	84.3	84.3
39103	Medina County	$75,968	$38,950	$57,490	$90,935	$106,485	$92,767	$47,065	$29,689	172,915	94.3	86.5	85.4
39109	Miami County	$61,051	$34,744	$41,145	$79,453	$96,869	$81,079	$31,443	$17,729	102,371	93.6	80.7	83.5
39113	Montgomery County	$54,921	$30,706	$39,547	$77,753	$97,004	$75,610	$30,838	$19,202	527,939	92.1	82.7	84.1
39119	Muskingum County	$50,214	$25,885	$33,324	$74,535	$78,814	$71,215	$19,398	$20,918	84,932	90.3	87.0	81.5

State/County FIPS code	State/Place	Total number of families	Families with incomes below the poverty level, as a percent of all families of that family type				Families that received Food Stamps (SNAP), as a percent of all families of that family type			Families that received food stamps (SNAP) and had at least one worker	
			All families	Married-couple families with related children under 18	Male householder families, no spouse present, with related children	Female householder families, no spouse present	All families	Married-couple families	Male householder or female householder families, no spouse present	Married-couple families, percent	Male householder or female householder families, no spouse present
	North Carolina—cont'd										
37087	Haywood County	17,585	15.4	11.9	44.3	50.6	15.6	7.4	5.4	38.4	23.5
37089	Henderson County	30,511	10.4	10.0	11.2	38.2	10.5	6.6	5.9	28.9	23.0
37093	Hoke County	12,402	17.6	10.2	38.1	50.3	23.0	13.1	12.1	45.3	30.7
37097	Iredell County	43,311	10.1	4.8	22.7	46.8	11.9	5.8	4.9	32.1	21.6
37101	Johnston County	45,494	12.5	8.7	33.4	42.7	14.3	7.5	6.3	34.3	24.0
37105	Lee County	14,911	15.8	12.3	27.0	54.8	17.6	9.6	8.8	37.8	29.2
37107	Lenoir County	15,257	18.1	19.2	19.5	49.1	29.6	15.2	11.7	52.1	39.2
37109	Lincoln County	21,555	9.9	6.5	53.6	44.3	12.3	7.2	5.4	33.1	23.8
37119	Mecklenburg County	229,183	12.3	7.7	23.8	36.9	15.8	7.3	6.5	34.6	27.7
37125	Moore County	24,745	11.4	9.9	22.7	53.4	8.6	3.3	2.6	33.1	15.8
37127	Nash County	24,503	14.0	8.0	8.9	46.9	21.8	10.1	8.7	48.1	39.1
37129	New Hanover County	50,464	11.5	6.5	18.1	43.7	15.5	6.9	5.6	38.3	30.0
37133	Onslow County	43,700	12.1	8.7	17.0	41.6	10.0	5.8	5.1	23.7	19.9
37135	Orange County	31,341	9.7	6.4	19.7	37.9	10.2	5.1	4.5	28.5	20.8
37141	Pender County	13,946	14.0	11.8	35.8	46.2	16.7	8.7	7.7	41.1	31.6
37147	Pitt County	39,835	15.5	7.6	27.5	48.6	21.5	8.1	6.9	47.1	34.0
37151	Randolph County	38,357	14.8	15.1	29.4	42.8	14.6	8.9	7.4	31.8	20.9
37155	Robeson County	32,247	25.7	19.8	49.8	54.6	34.4	19.3	14.7	54.6	36.4
37157	Rockingham County	25,477	15.3	10.1	32.2	49.0	18.4	10.3	7.7	38.5	27.6
37159	Rowan County	35,226	13.4	10.4	20.2	50.7	17.1	7.7	5.5	41.0	29.6
37161	Rutherford County	18,986	14.7	18.0	18.3	45.1	25.8	18.0	14.7	47.4	32.3
37163	Sampson County	15,622	18.6	13.3	64.7	49.3	20.8	7.7	5.8	49.0	39.9
37167	Stanly County	16,430	13.1	11.3	24.0	47.7	17.2	7.9	6.6	43.3	30.8
37171	Surry County	20,181	15.5	17.9	38.3	41.7	17.8	10.5	7.7	39.6	22.4
37179	Union County	54,446	8.0	5.0	27.3	32.2	11.2	5.8	4.9	34.3	27.3
37183	Wake County	235,958	7.9	4.9	27.2	31.3	8.8	3.9	3.6	24.7	18.8
37189	Watauga County	10,427	10.4	10.3	28.7	52.1	9.7	4.7	4.3	33.5	25.6
37191	Wayne County	31,903	17.7	12.9	45.1	51.2	21.8	9.8	7.4	44.9	31.4
37193	Wilkes County	19,195	19.6	20.1	46.1	59.1	23.2	14.9	11.0	50.6	27.2
37195	Wilson County	20,941	16.6	16.7	15.5	55.2	19.3	8.5	7.3	40.2	28.5
38000	**North Dakota**	176,378	7.4	4.3	16.6	38.6	8.4	3.9	3.5	26.7	21.9
38015	Burleigh County	21,978	4.5	1.8	8.1	24.8	5.7	2.4	2.4	18.8	17.5
38017	Cass County	36,585	7.3	3.8	19.4	37.1	10.5	5.3	5.0	29.1	25.7
38035	Grand Forks County	15,025	7.2	5.0	25.8	29.1	9.0	4.9	3.9	25.5	19.2
38101	Ward County	15,358	4.9	2.8	6.2	29.0	7.1	3.8	3.3	20.7	20.4
39000	**Ohio**	2,920,189	11.8	7.5	25.6	45.7	15.8	7.1	5.7	39.4	27.7
39003	Allen County	26,240	13.1	6.5	22.5	49.0	18.2	6.4	5.6	45.5	36.2
39005	Ashland County	14,013	10.5	8.5	29.6	45.7	13.1	6.9	5.9	37.6	31.1
39007	Ashtabula County	25,286	15.1	11.5	31.5	52.7	19.1	11.7	8.7	38.7	24.1
39009	Athens County	12,385	18.8	10.9	55.6	70.1	23.5	11.1	6.3	56.9	32.5
39013	Belmont County	17,894	9.9	7.0	14.5	63.5	13.9	9.0	7.2	32.3	23.7
39017	Butler County	93,190	9.8	6.3	17.8	37.6	12.7	6.0	5.0	33.9	24.4
39023	Clark County	35,303	13.7	10.8	38.9	48.7	21.2	10.1	8.5	49.6	34.7
39025	Clermont County	52,785	7.8	5.6	17.7	30.7	8.9	4.2	3.3	24.7	15.7
39029	Columbiana County	28,395	12.4	7.4	29.6	58.8	17.4	8.9	6.8	42.7	26.6
39035	Cuyahoga County	305,190	14.4	7.7	30.7	45.7	19.6	7.6	5.9	41.9	28.0
39037	Darke County	13,863	11.2	12.8	12.7	48.8	11.0	4.6	3.9	38.7	26.2
39041	Delaware County	49,245	3.4	1.2	6.5	23.0	5.2	2.1	2.0	23.0	17.8
39043	Erie County	20,691	8.4	3.0	11.9	44.8	15.2	5.2	4.2	42.9	37.4
39045	Fairfield County	39,400	7.4	4.9	9.1	34.3	14.2	7.2	6.2	39.4	28.9
39049	Franklin County	272,165	13.1	8.4	24.5	40.6	17.9	8.4	6.9	38.2	27.5
39055	Geauga County	25,400	5.0	3.2	5.6	34.9	4.8	1.9	1.7	21.7	15.6
39057	Greene County	41,299	9.0	8.1	22.7	41.0	11.7	6.1	4.9	33.1	23.9
39061	Hamilton County	192,858	14.5	5.3	31.7	49.9	17.4	5.0	4.1	42.6	29.5
39063	Hancock County	19,449	10.2	6.6	27.7	47.4	10.5	3.9	3.9	34.5	31.8
39077	Huron County	15,846	10.7	6.4	39.5	43.0	18.1	9.8	8.7	44.8	32.1
39081	Jefferson County	18,079	11.1	6.5	34.1	50.6	17.3	9.1	7.2	42.7	23.8
39083	Knox County	15,617	11.3	6.6	30.5	62.1	15.6	7.1	5.8	49.8	41.4
39085	Lake County	60,850	6.6	4.4	14.2	32.7	8.3	3.8	3.2	23.3	16.4
39087	Lawrence County	16,073	11.7	9.7	8.7	34.2	18.3	9.8	6.2	40.6	24.8
39089	Licking County	44,614	9.3	6.3	19.8	47.1	14.1	7.0	6.0	39.5	28.9
39093	Lorain County	79,496	11.4	6.1	24.2	48.0	15.3	6.4	5.3	37.9	27.3
39095	Lucas County	105,252	17.6	10.9	33.9	52.5	23.0	9.7	7.6	47.1	33.3
39099	Mahoning County	60,949	13.5	8.7	21.7	53.4	20.4	8.7	6.7	45.2	34.2
39101	Marion County	16,830	12.0	8.6	30.2	52.5	19.6	11.7	9.1	44.5	31.1
39103	Medina County	47,795	5.3	4.2	18.8	22.5	8.2	4.4	3.9	25.8	21.8
39109	Miami County	28,194	10.7	6.0	26.2	50.7	9.5	2.7	2.2	30.9	22.8
39113	Montgomery County	133,273	14.4	8.3	28.7	48.4	18.2	7.1	5.5	40.7	28.8
39119	Muskingum County	23,037	15.2	10.1	46.8	47.9	23.2	11.9	9.9	49.3	34.3

Table E-2: Counties with a Population of 50,000 or More—Income, Poverty, and Health Insurance—*Continued*

State/County FIPS code	State/Place	Median family income in the past 12 months (in 2,013 inflation-adjusted dollars)					Families with own children under 18 years			Total population in households	Persons who had health insurance, as a percent of all persons in that household type		
		All families	Families with no earners	Families with one earner	Families with two earners	Families with three or more earners	Married-couple families with children	Male householder, no spouse present, with children	Female householder, no spouse present, with children		Married-couple families, percent	Male householder or female householder families, no spouse present	Nonfamily households
	Ohio—cont'd												
39129	Pickaway County	$65,625	$33,661	$49,167	$79,934	$101,078	$78,470	$47,989	$23,110	52,236	93.0	81.3	89.3
39133	Portage County	$66,696	$37,652	$47,413	$80,720	$103,501	$83,392	$40,667	$19,544	162,971	93.4	84.5	85.4
39139	Richland County	$51,725	$27,173	$41,424	$72,113	$88,071	$61,023	$40,464	$17,749	116,031	89.6	83.0	84.7
39141	Ross County	$53,714	$27,863	$42,429	$71,728	$99,138	$67,632	$32,227	$16,404	71,875	91.3	83.3	81.4
39143	Sandusky County	$55,774	$32,540	$41,416	$72,608	$91,525	$73,018	$41,638	$13,760	59,502	93.8	84.3	84.2
39145	Scioto County	$49,398	$21,885	$40,578	$78,318	$85,188	$65,610	$31,340	$14,553	75,789	87.5	82.5	81.5
39147	Seneca County	$56,822	$31,750	$39,488	$72,200	$89,500	$72,943	$36,875	$15,281	55,105	93.3	83.6	88.3
39151	Stark County	$58,187	$32,577	$42,772	$76,103	$98,835	$79,344	$36,496	$20,180	370,235	92.3	83.4	83.6
39153	Summit County	$62,988	$31,857	$45,846	$85,552	$100,764	$88,326	$30,588	$20,630	536,267	93.3	82.0	84.2
39155	Trumbull County	$52,605	$34,653	$41,986	$75,542	$91,605	$73,082	$26,694	$14,889	203,909	89.3	81.9	82.8
39157	Tuscarawas County	$52,703	$34,451	$38,673	$66,366	$90,438	$69,154	$34,410	$19,876	91,447	90.4	82.1	82.0
39159	Union County	$77,878	$41,145	$53,393	$97,215	$118,594	$97,969	$37,262	$35,415	49,775	93.0	88.5	89.8
39165	Warren County	$85,575	$39,146	$67,623	$102,632	$122,165	$105,748	$58,783	$25,176	211,919	95.7	83.8	87.2
39167	Washington County	$54,443	$32,470	$43,174	$75,566	$89,805	$71,140	$20,750	$19,837	60,799	92.3	78.8	81.1
39169	Wayne County	$59,748	$35,750	$41,420	$70,992	$93,083	$68,634	$29,938	$22,046	113,818	85.6	82.6	85.0
39173	Wood County	$69,364	$35,923	$50,190	$83,918	$105,290	$86,483	$38,837	$22,005	127,297	95.2	83.0	89.7
40000	**Oklahoma**	$56,036	$28,741	$40,886	$74,125	$91,712	$69,435	$36,376	$20,619	3,736,108	85.6	73.6	79.4
40017	Canadian County	$71,148	$42,663	$50,409	$86,895	$100,959	$82,747	$48,295	$31,878	120,826	91.1	78.9	84.7
40027	Cleveland County	$67,057	$34,422	$49,046	$80,360	$103,040	$78,253	$43,812	$23,771	260,311	90.1	76.6	86.0
40031	Comanche County	$55,604	$30,895	$38,406	$72,304	$107,943	$66,414	$32,473	$21,560	112,141	89.8	75.5	76.3
40037	Creek County	$52,350	$26,783	$41,766	$74,152	$96,293	$66,009	$32,201	$23,433	69,755	84.9	73.0	80.9
40047	Garfield County	$56,085	$34,297	$36,801	$68,410	$77,865	$67,738	$45,019	$19,567	59,158	88.6	77.1	82.0
40051	Grady County	$59,311	$28,110	$40,889	$80,505	$83,333	$75,179	$47,602	$23,068	52,580	87.3	69.3	79.8
40101	Muskogee County	$47,497	$21,357	$38,169	$63,669	$77,123	$54,761	$29,792	$17,708	67,709	80.6	73.2	77.0
40109	Oklahoma County	$58,163	$31,135	$40,033	$75,173	$90,406	$70,359	$35,824	$20,353	731,241	84.4	73.2	77.7
40119	Payne County	$54,855	$31,534	$36,735	$70,250	$70,421	$66,377	$17,254	$12,298	77,278	88.5	77.6	86.8
40125	Pottawatomie County	$53,314	$30,359	$40,006	$70,142	$96,445	$66,243	$35,801	$18,787	68,149	85.7	72.8	81.5
40131	Rogers County	$65,839	$38,930	$46,363	$84,392	$105,545	$80,639	$43,643	$29,965	87,381	90.2	73.9	85.1
40143	Tulsa County	$59,638	$28,872	$42,143	$78,319	$94,743	$75,521	$37,238	$21,204	609,774	86.1	75.3	77.4
40145	Wagoner County	$60,979	$35,000	$46,725	$80,227	$102,074	$71,134	$38,523	$30,585	74,633	87.6	76.3	79.9
40147	Washington County	$58,293	$34,887	$42,742	$75,133	$89,393	$69,107	$21,583	$19,612	51,207	87.8	71.7	79.9
41000	**Oregon**	$60,863	$35,850	$45,406	$78,059	$91,603	$74,506	$33,666	$22,326	3,861,618	88.6	78.1	80.9
41003	Benton County	$74,325	$53,091	$52,917	$89,041	$101,137	$90,649	$26,707	$23,479	86,091	93.4	82.0	88.9
41005	Clackamas County	$75,420	$43,167	$60,133	$92,687	$113,865	$90,650	$51,033	$29,872	382,420	90.9	82.4	84.1
41011	Coos County	$47,027	$36,087	$37,292	$60,861	$69,399	$60,578	$27,202	$21,177	61,558	86.7	79.7	79.1
41017	Deschutes County	$59,767	$42,139	$42,259	$71,859	$79,453	$74,175	$26,600	$24,035	161,762	86.5	74.5	73.6
41019	Douglas County	$48,916	$32,954	$43,087	$67,235	$91,121	$59,383	$25,899	$17,271	106,469	88.4	78.9	81.6
41029	Jackson County	$52,047	$36,624	$40,577	$67,579	$83,016	$65,030	$24,371	$23,054	205,620	85.8	72.6	78.4
41033	Josephine County	$45,051	$36,707	$34,850	$69,275	$85,196	$58,657	$18,221	$18,280	82,238	86.9	79.1	81.6
41035	Klamath County	$47,213	$31,937	$35,843	$69,721	$82,623	$64,248	$28,094	$19,335	65,629	88.0	73.6	76.6
41039	Lane County	$54,993	$36,831	$42,358	$72,218	$83,695	$66,679	$28,378	$19,465	353,308	89.5	78.8	80.8
41043	Linn County	$52,519	$32,993	$40,241	$70,372	$82,531	$64,669	$33,323	$16,180	117,689	87.7	81.9	81.5
41047	Marion County	$53,405	$34,252	$39,658	$69,455	$80,644	$59,586	$35,256	$19,599	314,925	85.0	76.0	82.8
41051	Multnomah County	$65,503	$31,197	$46,777	$86,480	$95,000	$82,454	$41,610	$24,855	752,403	89.4	79.2	79.5
41053	Polk County	$62,482	$36,240	$52,940	$73,886	$103,872	$66,606	$45,508	$24,444	76,083	89.5	83.4	85.9
41059	Umatilla County	$58,438	$32,224	$36,533	$76,913	$84,480	$67,387	$36,947	$20,373	72,755	86.2	77.3	77.1
41067	Washington County	$76,071	$36,786	$59,245	$90,396	$101,016	$90,039	$45,885	$25,002	544,039	90.0	76.9	84.1
41071	Yamhill County	$59,972	$32,472	$40,341	$74,119	$100,974	$72,372	$27,033	$19,887	98,359	88.6	76.9	87.6
42000	**Pennsylvania**	$66,098	$31,283	$48,059	$85,612	$105,643	$88,326	$38,974	$23,858	12,555,282	92.7	84.6	88.7
42001	Adams County	$67,661	$38,104	$51,035	$78,843	$99,964	$79,041	$37,138	$26,383	100,262	92.5	83.5	89.0
42003	Allegheny County	$70,468	$31,770	$50,858	$91,526	$106,884	$96,965	$37,585	$21,664	1,215,609	95.2	86.9	89.3
42005	Armstrong County	$53,697	$31,013	$42,346	$69,563	$94,484	$67,188	$44,744	$21,803	67,833	91.9	87.3	91.3
42007	Beaver County	$64,293	$33,992	$48,556	$81,204	$99,846	$83,676	$36,279	$23,938	169,115	94.9	85.4	90.2
42011	Berks County	$66,936	$32,061	$46,812	$84,490	$103,404	$85,558	$44,406	$20,509	408,120	92.7	84.2	86.5
42013	Blair County	$54,803	$33,625	$40,677	$72,507	$91,521	$71,951	$30,028	$20,454	125,144	92.3	85.8	90.4
42015	Bradford County	$57,855	$32,007	$47,447	$76,760	$95,000	$70,744	$37,946	$26,207	62,095	89.9	80.6	87.7
42017	Bucks County	$91,122	$39,626	$63,426	$107,681	$131,074	$114,898	$51,898	$40,333	620,339	95.1	88.0	90.5
42019	Butler County	$74,422	$39,411	$56,321	$89,610	$110,658	$98,361	$31,380	$27,782	183,056	95.2	83.7	88.8
42021	Cambria County	$53,875	$31,306	$42,246	$72,314	$93,358	$71,019	$31,988	$20,916	136,672	94.3	88.4	90.0
42025	Carbon County	$55,081	$34,810	$41,727	$74,178	$82,951	$71,481	$25,481	$26,264	64,147	91.3	83.2	88.5
42027	Centre County	$71,961	$39,508	$50,622	$83,823	$99,767	$88,238	$44,630	$25,891	152,007	94.2	86.7	93.9
42029	Chester County	$101,926	$46,353	$77,959	$117,949	$133,680	$125,724	$55,737	$41,224	501,220	94.2	85.4	88.8
42033	Clearfield County	$52,146	$30,135	$41,789	$68,147	$90,247	$65,000	$28,526	$19,121	76,254	92.1	81.5	89.3
42037	Columbia County	$57,391	$26,775	$42,760	$75,019	$90,822	$77,290	$29,423	$23,940	66,077	95.2	82.3	94.5
42039	Crawford County	$55,118	$31,155	$40,965	$71,258	$86,837	$70,201	$34,819	$16,786	86,031	86.7	84.8	86.7
42041	Cumberland County	$74,251	$46,060	$52,474	$87,524	$118,596	$90,623	$48,083	$27,115	232,833	94.4	87.8	90.9
42043	Dauphin County	$68,670	$37,178	$45,842	$83,302	$108,516	$83,822	$40,767	$25,688	266,477	93.3	83.0	87.0
42045	Delaware County	$81,176	$33,835	$54,199	$105,215	$127,020	$107,619	$45,052	$30,333	553,305	94.3	84.8	90.2
42049	Erie County	$56,859	$30,452	$42,356	$74,342	$92,176	$73,936	$45,045	$19,267	275,506	93.8	87.9	88.0
42051	Fayette County	$50,333	$26,189	$42,695	$69,150	$93,003	$67,306	$31,528	$13,344	132,294	92.6	85.1	84.4

Table E-2: Counties with a Population of 50,000 or More—Income, Poverty, and Health Insurance—*Continued*

State/ County FIPS code	State/Place	Total number of families	Families with incomes below the poverty level, as a percent of all families of that family type				Families that received Food Stamps (SNAP), as a percent of all families of that family type			Families that received food stamps (SNAP) and had at least one worker	
			All families	Married-couple families with related children under 18	Male householder families, no spouse present, with related children	Female householder families, no spouse present	All families	Married-couple families	Male householder or female householder families, no spouse present	Married-couple families, percent	Male householder or female householder families, no spouse present
	Ohio—cont'd										
39129	Pickaway County	14,227	9.8	10.9	13.5	35.2	15.7	10.6	8.4	36.0	27.9
39133	Portage County	39,649	11.0	6.8	23.9	48.9	13.1	6.3	4.8	35.8	26.7
39139	Richland County	30,250	13.6	11.7	24.1	52.1	18.8	10.6	8.6	42.7	29.0
39141	Ross County	19,311	14.3	11.8	28.4	54.5	21.1	15.8	12.1	38.1	23.3
39143	Sandusky County	16,078	11.1	6.7	21.3	50.7	13.0	6.6	5.3	32.1	25.7
39145	Scioto County	18,425	18.2	17.7	34.3	57.0	24.7	17.1	10.6	48.6	23.7
39147	Seneca County	14,516	12.4	5.3	29.1	59.8	15.6	7.2	6.4	43.6	34.8
39151	Stark County	98,902	11.2	8.2	23.7	44.2	16.2	7.6	6.4	40.5	30.2
39153	Summit County	136,733	11.3	5.1	29.8	45.3	15.9	6.2	4.9	41.0	28.1
39155	Trumbull County	55,586	13.7	8.3	29.4	55.1	17.0	6.7	5.6	42.3	28.2
39157	Tuscarawas County	25,438	10.6	8.8	16.3	49.2	13.6	6.5	5.5	39.0	33.7
39159	Union County	13,418	4.7	4.4	9.0	17.6	7.3	3.7	2.9	22.8	19.1
39165	Warren County	58,231	4.7	3.0	14.7	36.3	5.0	2.5	1.8	18.8	13.8
39167	Washington County	16,354	10.6	10.3	44.5	41.1	15.1	8.4	5.8	39.1	23.5
39169	Wayne County	30,090	9.0	10.4	17.1	39.6	11.4	5.7	4.9	37.1	29.5
39173	Wood County	30,985	8.7	5.6	22.5	40.0	9.7	4.6	4.0	29.0	22.2
40000	**Oklahoma**	959,015	12.8	9.6	22.3	45.1	15.2	7.9	6.7	35.7	25.9
40017	Canadian County	31,534	4.9	2.4	10.6	27.8	8.9	5.0	4.3	25.1	21.1
40027	Cleveland County	64,930	8.2	4.9	8.2	35.1	11.4	5.7	5.2	29.1	21.5
40031	Comanche County	28,513	14.5	9.4	21.4	42.6	17.1	8.0	7.5	38.8	33.1
40037	Creek County	18,593	11.6	10.1	19.6	41.9	12.7	7.7	6.6	30.4	15.4
40047	Garfield County	16,759	9.3	7.1	21.7	40.4	15.4	9.0	7.9	35.6	29.4
40051	Grady County	14,271	8.3	7.8	10.5	42.3	14.1	7.7	6.4	37.0	30.4
40101	Muskogee County	18,033	17.9	14.5	22.5	54.1	22.9	13.6	10.5	44.8	28.5
40109	Oklahoma County	176,531	14.4	11.6	22.1	46.3	16.8	7.8	6.8	37.3	28.7
40119	Payne County	16,529	15.9	9.3	53.7	61.1	15.7	7.9	6.4	43.7	36.2
40125	Pottawatomie County	17,876	14.3	12.1	30.0	51.2	17.7	10.1	8.2	42.0	28.0
40131	Rogers County	25,101	6.8	4.3	12.3	34.0	10.2	5.3	4.6	29.1	23.4
40143	Tulsa County	154,681	12.3	7.9	22.0	43.6	14.6	6.8	6.2	33.1	22.9
40145	Wagoner County	20,305	8.5	7.3	16.6	33.4	10.9	5.6	4.6	30.2	19.5
40147	Washington County	14,079	11.6	7.9	44.0	45.6	11.8	6.0	5.5	31.6	24.8
41000	**Oregon**	959,743	11.8	9.9	25.3	42.7	20.2	12.2	10.5	45.9	34.6
41003	Benton County	18,757	9.8	7.8	10.1	44.4	14.7	7.8	7.2	45.1	29.0
41005	Clackamas County	101,323	6.7	5.5	12.2	27.9	13.6	8.1	6.7	34.3	25.1
41011	Coos County	15,553	10.7	11.2	24.8	30.4	24.1	14.5	11.9	56.5	42.3
41017	Deschutes County	42,559	11.3	10.0	45.2	25.3	19.3	12.2	10.3	46.8	37.4
41019	Douglas County	28,971	13.8	13.6	32.7	55.7	23.1	13.0	10.0	56.2	40.2
41029	Jackson County	53,332	13.3	11.8	31.3	41.2	23.1	13.7	12.0	52.7	41.0
41033	Josephine County	22,048	14.7	15.0	53.4	39.2	22.4	14.5	11.9	49.0	36.0
41035	Klamath County	18,280	14.6	15.0	14.1	48.8	27.7	17.3	13.9	55.7	41.8
41039	Lane County	85,586	13.1	9.6	35.1	49.0	23.8	13.1	11.4	54.2	41.5
41043	Linn County	30,690	13.4	11.4	25.6	56.6	21.7	11.9	10.5	53.3	36.2
41047	Marion County	78,384	16.0	14.8	26.5	49.2	26.8	17.1	15.6	52.0	40.3
41051	Multnomah County	166,003	13.0	11.1	25.0	41.4	21.2	13.0	11.3	42.7	31.6
41053	Polk County	19,061	11.3	12.4	36.6	45.9	19.3	13.5	12.4	42.5	27.2
41059	Umatilla County	18,213	12.4	7.2	8.2	48.7	21.1	12.6	11.5	44.2	35.3
41067	Washington County	136,024	9.2	6.5	15.0	38.7	14.4	8.7	7.8	35.9	28.9
41071	Yamhill County	24,298	10.8	8.5	27.2	42.9	23.1	16.6	14.9	44.4	31.7
42000	**Pennsylvania**	3,186,145	9.4	5.6	22.3	40.6	12.8	5.6	4.4	34.0	23.4
42001	Adams County	27,315	6.1	5.5	19.5	30.7	8.0	4.2	3.6	23.5	18.5
42003	Allegheny County	303,638	9.4	4.1	27.7	42.8	13.0	4.5	3.7	35.9	25.6
42005	Armstrong County	19,344	9.8	8.2	14.2	43.5	13.5	7.3	6.3	33.6	22.4
42007	Beaver County	46,159	8.0	4.8	19.0	38.2	12.1	5.5	4.5	33.1	24.0
42011	Berks County	104,401	10.3	6.3	18.1	48.1	14.1	6.6	5.4	36.7	25.7
42013	Blair County	33,008	9.5	7.3	24.3	43.0	15.3	7.6	6.0	39.0	32.6
42015	Bradford County	16,581	10.5	12.8	17.8	36.2	10.7	6.8	5.7	25.3	17.4
42017	Bucks County	166,307	4.3	2.5	17.0	21.4	5.0	2.5	1.8	15.5	11.1
42019	Butler County	49,910	5.7	2.5	25.5	35.6	7.6	3.0	2.6	28.7	19.4
42021	Cambria County	36,723	10.0	7.8	31.0	44.8	14.6	6.4	4.8	39.0	26.1
42025	Carbon County	17,399	8.3	7.1	46.6	27.7	9.4	3.8	2.6	28.3	18.8
42027	Centre County	32,582	7.5	6.5	13.2	38.9	7.5	4.0	3.7	23.1	18.7
42029	Chester County	129,774	4.5	2.2	21.6	25.8	4.5	2.0	1.7	17.0	12.7
42033	Clearfield County	21,335	10.1	8.4	21.2	50.1	12.9	7.4	6.2	33.4	24.1
42037	Columbia County	16,753	9.6	8.7	15.5	42.8	10.3	4.9	3.6	29.4	18.3
42039	Crawford County	23,020	10.4	7.8	25.3	49.8	15.7	8.3	6.5	42.8	28.3
42041	Cumberland County	61,887	6.5	4.5	27.0	32.4	7.1	2.6	2.3	26.0	20.8
42043	Dauphin County	68,992	9.2	5.7	15.9	37.2	12.6	5.4	4.6	30.5	24.4
42045	Delaware County	135,031	7.6	3.7	19.3	31.6	11.8	5.0	4.1	29.3	20.6
42049	Erie County	69,824	12.4	8.2	20.6	50.6	18.3	8.6	7.1	43.8	31.4
42051	Fayette County	34,884	13.7	9.6	29.5	59.3	19.8	11.1	7.7	43.5	25.5

Table E-2: Counties with a Population of 50,000 or More—Income, Poverty, and Health Insurance—*Continued*

State/County FIPS code	State/Place	Median family income in the past 12 months (in 2,013 inflation-adjusted dollars)					Families with own children under 18 years			Total population in households	Persons who had health insurance, as a percent of all persons in that household type		
		All families	Families with no earners	Families with one earner	Families with two earners	Families with three or more earners	Married-couple families with children	Male householder, no spouse present, with children	Female householder, no spouse present, with children		Married-couple families, percent	Male householder or female householder families, no spouse present	Nonfamily households
	Pennsylvania—cont'd												
42055	Franklin County	$62,717	$39,678	$45,134	$79,704	$100,230	$78,011	$36,136	$27,284	150,203	88.0	81.8	88.8
42063	Indiana County	$56,318	$31,845	$45,806	$72,108	$92,007	$68,368	$41,154	$15,599	86,513	89.1	84.3	89.9
42069	Lackawanna County	$58,173	$30,211	$43,744	$78,613	$96,756	$79,401	$42,264	$23,941	210,580	93.5	87.0	89.0
42071	Lancaster County	$67,504	$35,748	$50,020	$80,148	$103,810	$80,147	$40,380	$24,725	519,113	85.9	84.4	89.5
42073	Lawrence County	$56,189	$29,407	$44,463	$75,981	$95,632	$81,263	$33,000	$17,308	88,790	93.2	85.5	87.9
42075	Lebanon County	$64,581	$35,554	$47,548	$76,978	$98,323	$77,257	$50,496	$24,043	133,525	89.9	83.6	87.7
42077	Lehigh County	$65,774	$30,890	$49,490	$85,348	$95,043	$89,361	$34,052	$24,774	349,640	92.1	80.8	87.1
42079	Luzerne County	$57,461	$26,535	$41,773	$77,228	$98,728	$79,717	$34,023	$18,410	313,264	93.3	85.8	88.5
42081	Lycoming County	$57,781	$29,105	$40,983	$72,765	$89,905	$76,277	$36,929	$21,682	113,859	93.4	82.4	86.9
42085	Mercer County	$54,728	$32,462	$42,316	$70,536	$92,633	$72,982	$23,977	$20,503	111,772	92.5	86.2	90.1
42089	Monroe County	$62,460	$33,471	$49,167	$82,835	$98,985	$82,542	$41,006	$26,752	167,422	88.8	83.3	82.8
42091	Montgomery County	$98,454	$44,015	$71,439	$116,842	$132,429	$122,437	$57,069	$38,988	795,691	95.6	84.7	91.9
42095	Northampton County	$71,867	$33,700	$53,207	$89,090	$110,362	$93,579	$41,173	$27,645	296,177	94.4	83.3	87.8
42097	Northumberland County	$53,070	$27,906	$38,885	$74,490	$90,217	$71,897	$24,836	$18,274	89,576	91.2	85.2	85.4
42101	Philadelphia County	$44,747	$16,404	$35,796	$75,859	$95,152	$68,311	$30,352	$21,721	1,532,142	87.6	83.0	86.5
42103	Pike County	$69,745	$45,566	$54,447	$86,181	$92,941	$86,853	$36,875	$28,333	56,557	91.0	88.2	83.3
42107	Schuylkill County	$58,047	$28,522	$43,509	$76,509	$95,122	$76,295	$42,436	$22,724	140,725	92.8	85.8	86.0
42111	Somerset County	$54,897	$30,792	$43,005	$71,288	$89,268	$67,656	$31,974	$17,037	72,374	91.6	81.6	90.2
42121	Venango County	$50,691	$29,599	$38,838	$67,677	$83,625	$69,311	$26,418	$20,057	53,550	91.5	87.0	89.2
42125	Washington County	$68,858	$34,885	$53,776	$86,040	$107,382	$92,254	$40,263	$19,843	206,587	95.4	84.3	88.6
42127	Wayne County	$58,328	$36,303	$47,277	$66,826	$85,938	$71,271	$30,643	$24,946	48,323	92.2	85.3	86.9
42129	Westmoreland County	$64,664	$33,169	$49,296	$84,962	$105,591	$85,758	$39,131	$23,321	358,687	94.9	88.9	90.1
42133	York County	$68,203	$33,991	$48,610	$84,363	$102,982	$85,563	$38,391	$24,025	432,798	94.1	81.7	87.1
44000	**Rhode Island**	$72,152	$29,672	$48,154	$94,309	$113,937	$96,919	$37,600	$26,155	1,035,491	92.6	83.2	85.8
44003	Kent County	$80,515	$38,129	$56,606	$98,976	$120,076	$105,727	$45,881	$37,028	163,672	95.4	88.4	86.6
44005	Newport County	$88,186	$42,412	$62,444	$109,918	$131,071	$108,060	$47,620	$32,700	80,077	93.9	84.5	85.3
44007	Providence County	$61,619	$22,982	$40,462	$86,579	$107,826	$86,171	$35,380	$23,673	618,274	90.4	81.4	84.9
44009	Washington County	$89,339	$53,009	$64,665	$107,161	$130,867	$113,650	$47,089	$36,263	125,065	96.0	89.7	88.4
45000	**South Carolina**	$53,972	$28,960	$39,851	$75,602	$91,824	$73,641	$31,724	$20,273	4,624,813	87.8	76.4	80.2
45003	Aiken County	$55,739	$31,974	$41,642	$82,590	$91,681	$67,466	$33,214	$21,762	161,489	89.5	76.4	83.2
45007	Anderson County	$51,130	$27,714	$39,725	$76,126	$90,860	$73,214	$40,861	$18,440	188,270	89.0	74.2	82.2
45013	Beaufort County	$65,287	$63,520	$50,198	$76,739	$79,342	$58,904	$42,534	$27,493	160,609	86.7	71.2	80.0
45015	Berkeley County	$58,019	$29,480	$43,064	$77,159	$96,038	$70,382	$36,429	$26,058	183,759	84.4	76.1	80.9
45019	Charleston County	$65,220	$35,994	$46,843	$84,513	$99,827	$92,197	$32,076	$21,746	358,047	89.0	75.1	80.9
45021	Cherokee County	$43,820	$19,571	$33,803	$67,715	$76,371	$58,986	$22,966	$11,310	55,364	87.5	74.8	81.6
45031	Darlington County	$43,372	$21,610	$35,627	$63,214	$82,634	$74,167	$14,678	$17,400	67,363	88.3	74.9	77.8
45035	Dorchester County	$61,976	$30,779	$46,152	$80,831	$101,411	$81,079	$35,279	$23,693	139,824	89.4	77.6	79.2
45041	Florence County	$51,266	$23,859	$37,139	$72,282	$92,874	$75,938	$29,221	$20,744	136,305	90.5	79.8	80.9
45043	Georgetown County	$52,425	$43,046	$37,019	$69,771	$92,292	$69,353	$35,491	$14,345	59,647	84.2	63.8	79.8
45045	Greenville County	$61,087	$27,169	$44,371	$81,408	$96,253	$80,089	$35,962	$18,721	462,285	88.2	76.1	78.3
45047	Greenwood County	$46,277	$26,347	$29,882	$77,441	$86,570	$82,040	$27,350	$15,246	68,379	87.9	74.1	82.5
45051	Horry County	$49,411	$36,774	$36,133	$64,971	$83,900	$57,913	$25,982	$17,421	281,163	82.3	68.3	74.0
45055	Kershaw County	$52,603	$32,422	$36,560	$69,583	$99,915	$70,299	$55,896	$24,457	61,678	89.2	75.5	74.0
45057	Lancaster County	$51,464	$28,509	$40,994	$74,331	$80,679	$77,671	$36,182	$19,195	77,229	87.5	75.2	76.1
45059	Laurens County	$43,121	$24,619	$32,292	$67,151	$85,098	$59,050	$24,542	$18,422	65,062	86.4	76.0	83.4
45063	Lexington County	$64,926	$30,071	$46,032	$83,918	$102,788	$81,599	$37,647	$23,701	267,029	90.3	79.2	79.1
45073	Oconee County	$49,162	$31,274	$40,334	$68,693	$90,433	$60,660	$30,219	$17,235	74,043	86.8	74.7	82.7
45075	Orangeburg County	$41,735	$21,961	$33,580	$61,767	$70,367	$57,466	$28,388	$14,075	90,616	85.4	74.6	78.8
45077	Pickens County	$52,437	$29,592	$39,266	$71,080	$86,601	$66,272	$31,739	$23,552	118,890	87.8	78.5	87.5
45079	Richland County	$61,268	$30,708	$40,683	$83,942	$98,586	$86,065	$33,013	$25,598	369,390	90.5	81.4	84.3
45083	Spartanburg County	$51,297	$26,454	$36,654	$74,029	$91,917	$70,318	$28,222	$21,101	284,440	86.1	78.6	79.4
45085	Sumter County	$49,178	$28,906	$37,978	$68,981	$95,827	$61,976	$35,613	$17,237	103,980	90.4	77.7	77.6
45091	York County	$63,315	$31,808	$45,185	$84,866	$95,493	$85,669	$26,765	$26,793	233,238	90.0	79.4	79.7
46000	**South Dakota**	$62,594	$32,153	$39,614	$74,608	$91,688	$77,266	$37,542	$23,473	816,471	92.8	78.1	85.2
46099	Minnehaha County	$66,368	$31,311	$38,358	$78,467	$97,088	$80,874	$37,888	$24,697	172,919	93.5	82.6	84.6
46103	Pennington County	$63,284	$37,293	$40,744	$74,397	$95,724	$73,921	$38,777	$25,792	101,179	91.5	78.8	82.6
47000	**Tennessee**	$54,458	$27,901	$40,492	$73,639	$91,857	$71,531	$31,427	$20,006	6,348,051	89.5	80.0	81.5
47001	Anderson County	$50,939	$26,555	$38,962	$73,929	$98,009	$69,298	$27,349	$20,907	74,572	91.9	79.5	84.9
47009	Blount County	$55,623	$31,650	$43,550	$75,843	$87,864	$65,248	$32,016	$25,747	123,038	89.7	80.4	82.6
47011	Bradley County	$50,858	$28,342	$36,115	$71,705	$79,153	$62,220	$32,275	$16,759	100,080	89.5	78.4	80.6
47019	Carter County	$41,295	$25,234	$33,719	$58,614	$75,764	$51,215	$17,656	$10,408	56,322	88.4	74.1	84.4
47031	Coffee County	$47,145	$23,482	$37,192	$69,291	$92,825	$63,425	$32,100	$14,612	52,558	87.4	78.8	77.2
47035	Cumberland County	$42,211	$37,377	$38,297	$60,127	$84,836	$51,052	$35,531	$20,745	56,403	88.6	72.5	83.4
47037	Davidson County	$58,472	$27,419	$40,557	$76,785	$91,289	$74,178	$31,343	$22,201	639,040	87.4	78.3	81.1
47043	Dickson County	$49,948	$30,304	$39,510	$70,941	$81,250	$68,146	$42,500	$16,692	49,714	91.8	80.3	79.9
47059	Greene County	$42,910	$27,935	$33,842	$62,872	$90,297	$49,438	$21,875	$14,233	67,432	87.6	80.9	81.7
47063	Hamblen County	$46,034	$25,444	$37,387	$66,186	$72,623	$57,988	$35,377	$13,533	62,206	83.3	75.5	85.3
47065	Hamilton County	$60,252	$32,868	$43,056	$78,342	$96,981	$80,599	$23,653	$21,596	341,499	90.6	82.1	83.1

Table E-2: Counties with a Population of 50,000 or More—Income, Poverty, and Health Insurance—*Continued*

State/County FIPS code	State/Place	Total number of families	Families with incomes below the poverty level, as a percent of all families of that family type				Families that received Food Stamps (SNAP), as a percent of all families of that family type			Families that received food stamps (SNAP) and had at least one worker	
			All families	Married-couple families with related children under 18	Male householder families, no spouse present, with related children	Female householder families, no spouse present	All families	Married-couple families	Male householder or female householder families, no spouse present	Married-couple families, percent	Male householder or female householder families, no spouse present
	Pennsylvania—cont'd										
42055	Franklin County	39,858	8.5	7.5	17.8	38.2	10.5	5.7	4.9	31.1	23.5
42063	Indiana County	21,209	9.7	5.4	22.6	52.3	10.6	5.4	4.0	31.6	21.6
42069	Lackawanna County	53,058	9.9	6.9	18.3	40.0	13.1	6.3	4.6	31.8	20.8
42071	Lancaster County	136,311	7.8	5.7	16.5	39.8	9.3	4.6	4.0	29.9	21.1
42073	Lawrence County	24,126	10.9	7.1	26.4	46.7	16.1	5.9	4.5	48.2	31.3
42075	Lebanon County	35,976	8.2	5.0	12.6	43.1	11.3	4.8	4.4	33.2	26.7
42077	Lehigh County	88,864	9.9	5.6	30.6	42.2	12.8	5.8	4.4	31.9	21.6
42079	Luzerne County	82,405	12.2	6.8	23.1	49.5	17.0	8.5	6.7	37.3	26.5
42081	Lycoming County	28,905	9.8	4.1	27.0	48.6	13.4	6.5	5.5	35.4	24.6
42085	Mercer County	30,476	9.3	6.3	34.5	44.4	16.2	7.4	6.2	43.8	29.1
42089	Monroe County	43,153	9.3	5.9	15.6	34.7	13.6	8.7	7.6	27.6	22.1
42091	Montgomery County	208,052	4.4	2.5	13.0	22.4	5.5	2.6	2.2	17.9	14.1
42095	Northampton County	77,879	7.1	4.5	8.6	36.2	9.9	4.6	3.9	28.1	19.8
42097	Northumberland County	25,179	9.6	7.2	25.4	46.3	10.4	5.0	3.3	28.0	19.8
42101	Philadelphia County	303,420	21.6	14.3	31.9	46.5	30.6	15.0	10.9	46.8	29.1
42103	Pike County	15,041	7.0	6.6	26.7	22.9	10.1	5.6	4.9	29.7	15.4
42107	Schuylkill County	38,567	9.2	6.6	23.8	40.2	12.5	5.2	3.8	33.8	23.5
42111	Somerset County	20,728	8.3	6.2	25.2	45.9	11.4	6.9	5.4	32.2	19.2
42121	Venango County	15,058	11.7	8.7	33.0	47.9	15.1	6.3	5.0	43.0	28.8
42125	Washington County	55,002	7.3	3.6	15.8	41.9	10.1	3.9	2.7	33.0	22.1
42127	Wayne County	13,560	8.8	10.1	24.7	27.4	11.1	5.0	3.3	36.0	25.6
42129	Westmoreland County	100,507	7.0	4.1	18.5	38.4	11.1	4.7	3.8	33.8	22.2
42133	York County	115,856	7.7	3.2	16.1	41.1	10.3	4.1	3.4	30.9	22.3
44000	**Rhode Island**	257,316	10.2	6.5	18.7	37.9	15.3	7.0	6.0	34.9	24.4
44003	Kent County	43,078	5.6	4.7	10.3	27.7	9.7	5.3	4.5	23.6	16.6
44005	Newport County	21,003	6.6	2.1	1.6	34.2	7.2	2.0	1.7	26.1	20.9
44007	Providence County	147,142	13.7	9.0	23.0	41.8	20.6	9.9	8.5	40.0	27.5
44009	Washington County	33,366	4.6	3.9	10.0	25.0	7.5	3.1	2.4	23.6	17.9
45000	**South Carolina**	1,199,885	14.2	9.2	26.5	47.0	17.2	7.9	6.5	39.3	27.5
45003	Aiken County	42,140	14.3	12.6	36.9	47.6	18.3	10.0	8.7	39.4	26.2
45007	Anderson County	51,499	13.1	7.0	18.8	47.9	16.8	7.7	6.2	41.4	27.3
45013	Beaufort County	43,814	8.8	11.3	21.0	31.7	10.1	4.1	3.5	31.8	27.7
45015	Berkeley County	48,303	11.7	8.8	24.0	38.4	15.2	7.8	6.5	36.3	24.9
45019	Charleston County	84,300	13.0	7.6	19.5	47.8	13.0	4.6	3.8	31.4	22.8
45021	Cherokee County	14,357	20.0	15.4	34.7	59.7	23.9	11.2	8.3	52.4	30.0
45031	Darlington County	18,510	22.8	12.2	41.7	54.6	27.8	13.9	11.4	50.4	34.0
45035	Dorchester County	36,947	9.7	3.1	15.4	38.0	14.9	6.8	5.2	37.5	25.7
45041	Florence County	35,112	15.2	8.5	26.9	43.5	21.8	8.9	7.5	45.2	32.6
45043	Georgetown County	16,200	15.3	4.6	26.0	63.0	17.0	5.4	4.3	46.3	34.2
45045	Greenville County	119,078	12.7	8.5	23.4	50.0	13.3	5.5	4.5	36.2	25.5
45047	Greenwood County	18,139	20.6	11.9	24.6	62.8	22.3	8.3	6.2	48.6	36.3
45051	Horry County	73,438	14.1	11.1	36.5	54.0	16.4	8.5	7.5	39.4	29.0
45055	Kershaw County	16,879	12.6	8.6	22.9	38.9	16.6	9.2	7.7	34.2	26.0
45057	Lancaster County	20,442	17.0	10.3	31.9	45.3	17.4	8.0	6.9	38.8	23.0
45059	Laurens County	17,875	18.3	15.1	21.3	52.1	22.0	10.6	7.6	41.6	29.0
45063	Lexington County	71,979	10.4	7.2	17.4	40.1	14.6	7.8	6.3	34.1	23.7
45073	Oconee County	20,900	14.0	13.3	31.8	51.4	17.3	9.4	5.8	40.2	30.2
45075	Orangeburg County	21,594	18.7	10.7	22.6	53.0	25.9	13.9	10.2	45.0	31.4
45077	Pickens County	28,555	10.2	8.2	15.1	43.7	13.4	8.4	6.8	31.1	24.2
45079	Richland County	87,629	13.2	5.2	17.7	41.4	17.2	6.8	5.8	36.5	27.0
45083	Spartanburg County	75,566	15.1	11.4	31.3	45.0	15.0	6.5	5.3	34.1	24.8
45085	Sumter County	27,505	13.2	7.2	19.1	44.6	20.8	10.2	9.2	40.8	29.1
45091	York County	62,908	11.2	6.9	37.6	39.2	14.2	7.2	5.6	35.4	26.3
46000	**South Dakota**	210,494	9.3	5.6	23.3	38.9	11.7	4.8	4.3	35.5	28.2
46099	Minnehaha County	43,741	8.6	3.2	18.3	36.2	11.3	4.8	4.3	29.8	21.6
46103	Pennington County	25,847	9.4	5.3	22.1	37.2	14.5	5.1	4.6	40.3	34.7
47000	**Tennessee**	1,646,360	13.6	10.2	27.9	46.8	18.5	10.0	8.1	41.7	29.6
47001	Anderson County	19,457	14.4	13.7	36.0	48.0	18.9	9.4	6.0	44.2	28.7
47009	Blount County	33,951	12.0	12.6	9.4	39.3	17.0	11.4	8.4	40.4	30.2
47011	Bradley County	26,065	15.6	15.3	11.2	57.2	19.4	10.2	8.7	44.9	33.2
47019	Carter County	16,002	18.5	16.9	49.0	63.3	20.5	12.3	9.1	48.4	33.3
47031	Coffee County	14,357	16.8	13.5	17.7	54.6	20.8	11.8	8.5	42.9	27.9
47035	Cumberland County	16,194	11.9	15.0	25.0	47.7	17.2	9.9	7.5	48.8	32.7
47037	Davidson County	141,462	13.6	11.6	29.6	41.3	19.5	10.2	9.0	38.4	29.2
47043	Dickson County	13,859	14.4	13.1	25.6	54.8	20.2	12.6	10.3	40.8	28.3
47059	Greene County	19,315	17.8	25.5	34.0	56.1	21.3	14.3	10.9	44.7	31.5
47063	Hamblen County	16,811	18.3	12.6	46.6	61.1	23.6	16.0	13.2	42.6	26.9
47065	Hamilton County	88,084	12.1	9.0	33.2	42.6	17.6	8.3	7.1	42.2	31.9

Table E-2: Counties with a Population of 50,000 or More—Income, Poverty, and Health Insurance—*Continued*

State/ County FIPS code	State/Place	Median family income in the past 12 months (in 2,013 inflation-adjusted dollars)					Families with own children under 18 years			Total population in households	Persons who had health insurance, as a percent of all persons in that household type		
		All families	Families with no earners	Families with one earner	Families with two earners	Families with three or more earners	Married-couple families with children	Male householder, no spouse present, with children	Female householder, no spouse present, with children		Married-couple families, percent	Male householder or female householder families, no spouse present	Nonfamily households
	Tennessee—cont'd												
47073	Hawkins County	$48,775	$26,413	$40,541	$63,644	$86,903	$63,632	$26,069	$17,204	56,159	92.4	82.4	78.7
47089	Jefferson County..............	$49,881	$28,970	$36,224	$62,138	$91,534	$63,022	$19,067	$17,519	51,338	90.8	73.4	85.0
47093	Knox County....................	$63,454	$29,956	$46,249	$80,833	$96,148	$84,638	$35,791	$20,037	437,292	91.5	81.7	86.2
47107	McMinn County................	$47,363	$29,776	$40,743	$58,376	$83,328	$55,594	$22,292	$16,755	51,479	89.2	72.6	76.9
47113	Madison County...............	$57,445	$28,933	$39,694	$77,420	$94,400	$74,950	$31,713	$16,556	97,274	88.7	83.4	82.3
47119	Maury County..................	$55,808	$25,571	$43,713	$70,396	$101,081	$69,320	$41,416	$16,826	81,175	90.9	83.2	79.9
47125	Montgomery County	$56,175	$22,160	$43,301	$69,215	$95,345	$63,989	$39,159	$18,845	168,691	90.8	82.1	77.9
47141	Putnam County................	$46,262	$21,963	$35,347	$66,930	$78,478	$67,052	$23,237	$13,669	72,364	88.2	76.7	77.2
47145	Roane County	$51,798	$31,095	$43,670	$79,717	$71,312	$59,702	$30,600	$11,185	52,982	89.8	81.6	84.3
47147	Robertson County.............	$58,871	$31,174	$47,101	$69,694	$106,541	$70,826	$34,673	$29,024	66,274	90.7	80.1	78.9
47149	Rutherford County............	$66,542	$36,632	$46,284	$80,230	$99,293	$78,887	$48,113	$31,015	272,286	88.7	82.2	80.6
47155	Sevier County	$49,996	$34,239	$35,895	$61,719	$72,443	$57,448	$20,596	$18,750	91,578	85.6	65.0	75.6
47157	Shelby County	$56,482	$20,055	$37,143	$81,074	$97,746	$87,039	$30,331	$20,755	925,844	88.7	80.0	79.2
47163	Sullivan County...............	$51,678	$30,346	$39,110	$73,438	$90,625	$69,058	$28,864	$14,742	154,947	92.0	77.7	82.3
47165	Sumner County	$64,655	$37,186	$51,008	$79,725	$95,640	$82,245	$51,544	$25,110	164,683	91.9	84.9	79.5
47167	Tipton County	$60,047	$30,510	$44,521	$73,857	$96,211	$79,453	$36,328	$19,861	60,571	91.5	83.3	82.7
47179	Washington County............	$52,289	$31,729	$42,104	$71,949	$90,098	$72,936	$30,982	$18,750	123,032	91.9	74.2	82.9
47187	Williamson County	$105,688	$51,870	$86,771	$121,635	$126,771	$126,396	$92,750	$29,821	192,778	95.6	82.2	90.7
47189	Wilson County..................	$66,444	$38,662	$51,019	$88,272	$95,640	$87,483	$48,775	$21,706	118,310	92.3	81.6	79.9
48000	**Texas ....**	$60,656	$27,707	$41,916	$81,593	$93,924	$75,463	$36,672	$23,538	25,573,996	80.5	69.9	77.9
48001	Anderson County...............	$51,522	$27,165	$34,586	$73,391	$84,905	$60,785	$30,849	$14,617	45,317	81.3	74.2	88.7
48005	Angelina County...............	$46,570	$32,416	$36,916	$58,096	$82,967	$54,564	$33,594	$22,252	85,307	79.9	79.2	81.4
48021	Bastrop County................	$60,713	$41,956	$39,765	$78,370	$102,300	$62,761	$32,258	$22,918	73,120	78.8	71.4	77.0
48027	Bell County....................	$57,710	$33,661	$41,296	$77,547	$102,545	$62,189	$27,321	$27,669	300,469	88.1	77.3	79.0
48029	Bexar County..................	$57,036	$26,016	$40,867	$74,551	$90,981	$71,862	$36,907	$25,662	1,753,560	83.1	73.7	80.2
48037	Bowie County..................	$51,462	$26,751	$40,177	$76,987	$91,930	$74,265	$25,756	$20,219	87,836	87.7	73.3	79.6
48039	Brazoria County...............	$78,284	$32,790	$51,682	$104,812	$114,242	$101,570	$40,668	$31,696	314,557	84.2	70.3	77.1
48041	Brazos County.................	$58,320	$30,484	$35,132	$77,275	$91,939	$71,396	$26,389	$22,670	196,520	85.0	75.6	86.2
48061	Cameron County...............	$35,811	$14,841	$26,491	$58,661	$68,275	$43,710	$26,897	$16,048	412,429	66.5	64.3	74.4
48073	Cherokee County...............	$46,389	$23,810	$33,741	$63,215	$87,102	$57,056	$20,656	$14,910	48,816	79.7	68.6	80.2
48085	Collin County..................	$97,763	$38,476	$74,063	$115,197	$123,005	$114,033	$57,386	$44,973	830,970	88.7	73.3	81.4
48091	Comal County	$74,935	$47,464	$58,717	$94,387	$105,893	$90,213	$39,740	$20,078	113,854	86.9	69.9	80.2
48099	Coryell County	$57,659	$38,933	$47,844	$81,831	$99,370	$62,081	$53,490	$33,059	59,381	91.7	78.0	83.5
48113	Dallas County..................	$53,999	$22,288	$35,688	$75,996	$86,208	$62,231	$31,481	$24,026	2,426,944	74.8	67.0	75.9
48121	Denton County................	$88,647	$41,230	$62,301	$105,303	$114,670	$106,696	$56,040	$33,892	703,035	87.6	74.8	80.8
48135	Ector County..................	$60,519	$23,071	$44,116	$77,682	$89,399	$71,336	$46,778	$24,093	143,137	75.5	69.4	78.1
48139	Ellis County...................	$69,055	$33,180	$46,186	$84,897	$109,283	$82,827	$37,054	$22,836	152,869	83.5	72.0	79.5
48141	El Paso County................	$45,090	$18,402	$33,437	$62,456	$74,651	$54,219	$31,932	$20,081	799,275	74.2	67.0	75.4
48157	Fort Bend County.............	$96,123	$30,454	$73,599	$112,352	$116,086	$110,757	$53,275	$35,499	623,553	84.8	74.5	82.3
48167	Galveston County.............	$75,281	$35,067	$55,364	$96,088	$115,405	$97,060	$34,545	$21,451	296,850	86.9	75.2	77.9
48181	Grayson County................	$57,389	$34,223	$39,680	$78,364	$95,111	$68,459	$27,207	$29,350	120,535	84.9	74.9	80.9
48183	Gregg County	$54,527	$31,333	$39,451	$77,331	$89,049	$77,058	$31,652	$20,104	120,894	82.6	72.4	78.8
48187	Guadalupe County.............	$69,991	$39,157	$50,659	$87,879	$103,978	$87,577	$32,365	$27,362	137,327	86.5	69.9	82.5
48199	Hardin County.................	$63,537	$28,988	$50,385	$85,986	$91,979	$71,500	$62,202	$18,641	54,795	84.7	74.8	77.5
48201	Harris County..................	$59,883	$22,438	$40,794	$80,984	$92,623	$71,314	$38,774	$23,679	4,235,082	77.4	67.7	74.5
48203	Harrison County...............	$52,677	$29,508	$40,432	$84,278	$77,256	$73,372	$31,411	$20,481	66,510	82.0	71.7	82.1
48209	Hays County...................	$73,958	$50,759	$45,272	$90,344	$105,372	$91,209	$43,317	$17,474	168,039	86.4	72.4	80.5
48213	Henderson County.............	$47,972	$30,111	$39,693	$66,703	$86,775	$58,739	$23,191	$16,817	77,896	81.4	68.8	75.3
48215	Hidalgo County................	$36,510	$16,184	$24,151	$54,418	$67,514	$43,507	$24,750	$16,057	798,386	63.8	60.8	70.4
48221	Hood County...................	$63,675	$43,438	$53,779	$86,673	$76,641	$73,726	$87,586	$26,117	51,449	84.4	72.7	80.0
48231	Hunt County...................	$55,668	$34,063	$44,681	$71,555	$100,136	$62,990	$55,668	$22,792	86,079	78.7	70.7	81.5
48245	Jefferson County...............	$52,485	$25,974	$40,208	$75,878	$105,199	$67,656	$41,831	$19,863	238,414	81.0	72.8	78.2
48251	Johnson County................	$64,474	$36,133	$48,715	$85,174	$102,834	$75,321	$53,133	$20,658	150,821	80.8	64.4	73.6
48257	Kaufman County	$66,446	$28,427	$46,734	$85,198	$107,456	$80,818	$35,714	$31,113	105,848	82.5	69.1	76.3
48291	Liberty County	$57,079	$26,309	$46,005	$82,014	$95,789	$73,586	$35,253	$20,000	70,327	78.8	65.3	68.6
48303	Lubbock County...............	$57,040	$31,521	$36,559	$72,576	$96,563	$76,169	$31,106	$22,649	281,956	84.9	72.8	80.6
48309	McLennan County	$52,241	$29,586	$35,004	$71,980	$91,736	$69,768	$26,941	$20,135	235,098	82.8	74.4	85.5
48323	Maverick County	$36,428	$14,902	$24,187	$54,134	$58,813	$44,750	$50,804	$17,576	54,654	61.0	72.0	80.2
48329	Midland County................	$76,111	$31,205	$54,903	$86,687	$98,096	$89,273	$47,847	$28,056	145,123	79.9	69.2	81.5
48339	Montgomery County	$78,777	$36,698	$60,269	$98,227	$116,688	$100,492	$41,540	$29,846	482,547	85.9	68.7	74.7
48347	Nacogdoches County...........	$51,847	$20,852	$36,075	$77,347	$81,995	$61,405	$31,250	$16,982	64,715	76.4	72.6	78.2
48355	Nueces County	$54,820	$24,241	$40,553	$77,500	$85,847	$76,376	$42,441	$21,759	342,407	83.3	73.9	75.7
48361	Orange County	$59,189	$32,304	$51,059	$78,593	$93,272	$77,905	$42,182	$30,615	82,098	85.6	74.0	73.8
48367	Parker County.................	$79,748	$38,561	$63,410	$97,749	$112,928	$91,680	$71,429	$21,365	116,662	86.6	71.7	76.6
48375	Potter County.................	$45,414	$24,838	$31,463	$62,400	$83,295	$56,853	$25,197	$19,165	115,758	78.1	69.0	71.1
48381	Randall County................	$72,663	$37,230	$53,451	$88,153	$116,537	$89,730	$37,475	$28,072	124,122	90.7	78.7	77.8
48397	Rockwall County...............	$95,196	$53,920	$74,143	$104,434	$128,632	$107,101	$73,523	$36,831	82,403	88.5	71.3	85.6
48401	Rusk County...................	$54,115	$32,779	$36,524	$74,558	$83,805	$70,324	$32,245	$18,948	49,304	77.7	72.6	78.9
48409	San Patricio County...........	$54,500	$23,074	$37,383	$73,949	$94,156	$73,793	$31,517	$23,333	64,421	83.1	68.1	80.7
48423	Smith County..................	$57,576	$34,205	$43,192	$75,820	$95,901	$72,991	$28,571	$23,509	212,208	81.9	71.9	77.3
48427	Starr County...................	$27,008	$14,128	$21,355	$45,876	$53,083	$36,352	$32,404	$13,651	61,175	59.1	61.6	80.7

Table E-2: Counties with a Population of 50,000 or More—Income, Poverty, and Health Insurance—*Continued*

State/County FIPS code	State/Place	Total number of families	Families with incomes below the poverty level, as a percent of all families of that family type				Families that received Food Stamps (SNAP), as a percent of all families of that family type			Families that received food stamps (SNAP) and had at least one worker	
			All families	Married-couple families with related children under 18	Male householder families, no spouse present, with related children	Female householder families, no spouse present	All families	Married-couple families	Male householder or female householder families, no spouse present	Married-couple families, percent	Male householder or female householder families, no spouse present
	Tennessee—cont'd										
47073	Hawkins County	16,172	12.8	6.1	44.1	50.3	17.4	8.9	5.6	46.1	29.4
47089	Jefferson County	14,009	12.2	7.5	44.4	49.7	16.9	9.1	7.5	44.7	31.9
47093	Knox County	109,330	10.5	7.8	18.0	48.5	13.7	6.4	5.0	37.9	25.5
47107	McMinn County	13,890	14.6	13.7	40.4	55.9	17.8	12.6	9.3	38.8	32.6
47113	Madison County	23,593	14.9	3.9	28.1	57.8	19.6	8.0	6.9	46.9	30.1
47119	Maury County	21,715	12.2	7.5	20.1	49.3	19.9	10.5	8.5	42.6	28.3
47125	Montgomery County	47,921	13.0	7.2	20.6	50.6	16.2	8.0	7.5	39.7	30.5
47141	Putnam County	18,919	20.6	19.4	48.7	63.1	15.9	10.6	8.2	30.9	20.5
47145	Roane County	14,876	12.8	11.6	30.0	59.1	16.9	11.3	8.6	40.0	24.4
47147	Robertson County	18,023	10.2	7.4	35.4	36.6	15.3	7.0	5.3	41.7	34.7
47149	Rutherford County	67,233	8.4	7.6	15.6	33.0	12.5	7.3	6.4	30.1	24.8
47155	Sevier County	26,634	11.4	5.4	30.0	54.7	18.2	11.8	10.5	38.4	33.0
47157	Shelby County	218,960	17.1	8.3	32.8	46.4	24.5	10.0	8.7	45.7	33.5
47163	Sullivan County	43,642	13.9	11.4	35.1	55.1	17.2	9.8	7.3	41.0	27.6
47165	Sumner County	45,967	7.1	4.3	10.2	32.5	13.6	6.9	6.1	35.9	30.0
47167	Tipton County	16,251	10.6	3.1	37.9	39.0	17.4	7.0	5.9	43.3	34.2
47179	Washington County	33,130	13.2	10.6	31.5	48.1	15.3	8.8	7.2	35.1	25.0
47187	Williamson County	52,674	4.9	2.9	8.5	35.0	4.2	2.3	2.1	17.9	15.1
47189	Wilson County	31,202	8.6	4.2	28.4	35.9	11.8	6.0	5.0	33.5	23.3
48000	**Texas**	6,235,820	14.0	11.7	23.0	42.5	16.1	9.4	8.2	33.4	26.0
48001	Anderson County	11,972	16.7	12.5	14.0	61.4	17.0	9.5	8.2	37.8	28.0
48005	Angelina County	22,345	14.2	17.1	12.0	43.2	21.3	12.3	10.8	41.9	32.7
48021	Bastrop County	17,906	12.1	16.0	40.5	34.7	11.8	7.8	6.5	26.7	23.0
48027	Bell County	74,496	11.7	7.6	35.9	37.2	13.0	7.1	6.6	29.0	21.8
48029	Bexar County	413,223	14.5	11.0	22.1	40.2	18.6	10.6	9.4	35.0	26.7
48037	Bowie County	23,002	17.5	9.1	34.9	51.0	18.9	7.6	6.0	41.7	33.1
48039	Brazoria County	81,089	8.3	5.6	15.2	30.3	11.0	6.5	5.6	25.5	19.9
48041	Brazos County	38,990	15.3	12.0	29.7	43.7	15.2	7.6	7.4	34.2	28.1
48061	Cameron County	94,551	29.8	28.2	38.9	60.2	31.4	24.6	20.8	44.9	30.3
48073	Cherokee County	12,988	19.8	16.7	46.8	61.4	20.0	11.2	9.0	43.1	34.9
48085	Collin County	219,198	6.0	4.0	15.6	22.7	4.9	2.6	2.3	14.9	12.9
48091	Comal County	31,601	7.6	4.6	5.7	39.4	7.6	3.8	3.6	24.4	20.9
48099	Coryell County	16,041	9.9	9.4	19.3	31.2	9.7	6.3	4.7	20.5	17.4
48113	Dallas County	565,857	16.2	14.5	24.7	41.6	18.0	10.1	9.3	33.6	26.3
48121	Denton County	176,243	5.9	4.2	11.6	23.9	7.4	3.8	3.4	20.4	17.3
48135	Ector County	35,845	11.8	8.0	4.3	38.2	16.5	9.8	8.8	30.3	26.0
48139	Ellis County	41,082	9.9	7.5	17.5	37.6	13.2	7.6	7.0	33.7	28.8
48141	El Paso County	194,581	20.3	18.1	25.8	48.7	26.4	18.3	16.0	42.2	32.2
48157	Fort Bend County	162,570	7.1	5.2	12.6	29.0	8.2	4.4	4.3	23.2	19.2
48167	Galveston County	75,654	10.6	6.2	19.9	44.8	13.4	6.8	6.2	33.7	27.6
48181	Grayson County	31,692	12.1	9.7	33.3	36.5	15.4	8.0	7.3	34.7	26.7
48183	Gregg County	30,573	14.4	8.8	28.8	47.8	15.4	6.1	5.7	36.7	28.1
48187	Guadalupe County	35,214	7.0	4.0	10.5	33.9	9.7	5.1	4.4	26.4	21.0
48199	Hardin County	15,271	8.1	6.6	13.5	43.8	13.0	9.1	7.9	27.4	17.6
48201	Harris County	990,859	15.6	13.8	23.4	42.9	16.6	9.5	8.6	31.7	25.1
48203	Harrison County	17,355	13.3	8.3	31.1	41.6	15.3	8.5	7.7	34.4	26.2
48209	Hays County	37,645	9.6	8.9	13.9	43.2	10.9	6.2	6.0	26.6	23.5
48213	Henderson County	19,971	15.2	14.9	38.1	57.8	18.8	12.3	10.8	41.5	31.3
48215	Hidalgo County	180,050	31.3	32.1	42.1	60.6	36.0	29.9	25.3	50.7	39.6
48221	Hood County	14,443	7.8	8.3	4.2	42.1	9.8	5.8	4.9	33.5	22.0
48231	Hunt County	20,781	14.6	14.9	19.7	41.5	15.5	9.5	8.0	37.8	29.3
48245	Jefferson County	58,453	17.3	11.8	23.2	47.1	21.8	10.8	9.3	41.3	32.0
48251	Johnson County	39,555	9.6	6.5	16.1	44.2	13.0	7.4	6.5	33.7	26.7
48257	Kaufman County	27,405	10.1	4.2	27.2	34.3	12.5	6.7	5.2	30.1	19.3
48291	Liberty County	18,245	14.6	10.2	26.1	47.5	20.7	12.8	11.0	43.6	31.1
48303	Lubbock County	66,312	13.1	9.1	32.1	44.4	17.7	10.2	9.4	35.7	30.5
48309	McLennan County	57,103	15.3	11.4	27.7	46.3	17.3	8.6	7.9	38.3	29.5
48323	Maverick County	13,027	24.7	19.6	31.3	51.3	32.3	25.9	21.3	46.9	36.4
48329	Midland County	36,196	6.9	5.3	4.3	27.2	9.0	5.0	4.5	20.9	18.7
48339	Montgomery County	123,733	10.4	8.8	17.3	41.3	9.0	5.0	4.6	22.9	17.5
48347	Nacogdoches County	14,739	20.6	19.7	35.6	50.3	16.4	8.5	7.3	33.3	23.9
48355	Nueces County	85,531	13.9	9.7	19.3	43.3	20.1	11.1	9.7	36.8	28.3
48361	Orange County	22,086	11.9	11.2	26.9	34.4	17.1	9.1	7.8	40.5	31.9
48367	Parker County	31,906	7.7	8.3	3.6	43.3	8.2	4.7	4.0	23.3	16.5
48375	Potter County	27,619	18.7	14.3	27.1	49.9	21.7	12.7	11.2	38.9	29.2
48381	Randall County	33,046	7.1	5.0	14.9	31.0	8.9	4.6	4.5	24.2	17.9
48397	Rockwall County	22,496	4.1	1.9	8.3	16.5	6.1	3.5	3.3	17.9	14.7
48401	Rusk County	11,870	14.6	11.9	20.4	51.1	12.6	6.5	6.0	29.2	17.8
48409	San Patricio County	17,132	13.9	6.0	19.3	44.5	12.2	5.4	4.4	27.2	21.0
48423	Smith County	53,752	12.1	11.9	28.0	36.2	12.3	5.6	5.2	30.6	23.7
48427	Starr County	13,333	40.1	37.8	28.2	65.5	47.8	41.8	33.2	58.4	49.1

Table E-2: Counties with a Population of 50,000 or More—Income, Poverty, and Health Insurance—*Continued*

| State/ County FIPS code | State/Place | Median family income in the past 12 months (in 2,013 inflation-adjusted dollars) | | | | | Families with own children under 18 years | | | Total population in households | Persons who had health insurance, as a percent of all persons in that household type | | |
		All families	Families with no earners	Families with one earner	Families with two earners	Families with three or more earners	Married-couple families with children	Male householder, no spouse present, with children	Female householder, no spouse present, with children		Married-couple families, percent	Male householder or female householder families, no spouse present	Nonfamily households
	Texas—cont'd												
48439	Tarrant County	$67,059	$31,148	$44,828	$85,748	$104,092	$80,344	$35,639	$26,678	1,865,216	82.0	70.3	78.8
48441	Taylor County	$54,516	$28,100	$37,562	$71,220	$81,888	$66,237	$31,239	$20,894	129,594	84.9	75.1	79.0
48451	Tom Green County	$56,930	$33,888	$42,912	$71,339	$80,146	$71,806	$48,642	$19,513	108,139	84.9	68.5	79.8
48453	Travis County	$73,719	$39,237	$48,874	$94,235	$96,177	$95,403	$39,658	$24,680	1,085,641	85.5	73.8	77.6
48467	Van Zandt County	$51,343	$27,953	$37,917	$73,152	$96,434	$68,710	$28,438	$15,702	51,850	81.7	67.8	72.0
48469	Victoria County	$55,268	$30,641	$36,694	$77,737	$90,434	$79,571	$25,592	$22,641	87,847	81.7	69.1	82.5
48471	Walker County	$55,670	$34,046	$36,030	$74,417	$71,947	$67,771	$53,120	$13,312	49,960	85.0	67.4	89.0
48479	Webb County	$40,321	$10,214	$31,072	$58,061	$68,036	$49,791	$23,818	$16,662	256,577	65.3	64.6	66.1
48485	Wichita County	$55,800	$34,779	$37,987	$74,196	$92,793	$69,888	$23,622	$21,441	117,034	85.8	71.2	78.6
48491	Williamson County	$82,460	$52,120	$62,381	$97,064	$109,585	$99,026	$42,125	$41,365	452,800	87.9	76.7	83.0
48497	Wise County	$63,804	$35,771	$50,283	$82,428	$110,542	$71,568	$35,952	$22,857	59,448	82.5	73.2	78.7
49000	**Utah**	$66,321	$38,285	$51,414	$73,777	$99,597	$73,995	$40,880	$26,784	2,829,593	88.3	75.0	82.3
49003	Box Elder County	$61,952	$37,429	$50,095	$66,558	$99,924	$69,313	$60,472	$28,048	50,046	93.0	79.2	85.0
49005	Cache County	$56,538	$38,359	$47,915	$57,677	$88,380	$59,554	$36,596	$23,345	115,030	89.0	78.0	87.7
49011	Davis County	$76,972	$47,796	$61,337	$82,325	$115,045	$82,374	$62,083	$31,557	313,219	93.1	82.0	81.8
49035	Salt Lake County	$69,544	$34,830	$50,458	$77,553	$100,493	$76,844	$35,349	$26,975	1,055,889	87.0	74.3	82.4
49045	Tooele County	$65,326	$32,241	$52,215	$75,949	$102,537	$68,682	$50,625	$27,472	59,390	91.8	78.0	84.2
49049	Utah County	$65,330	$42,872	$54,390	$66,496	$100,447	$72,849	$36,498	$29,366	536,964	88.8	75.4	84.3
49053	Washington County	$56,078	$43,371	$45,215	$65,927	$84,174	$63,049	$37,310	$30,353	143,173	85.5	74.6	78.0
49057	Weber County	$61,354	$39,702	$46,391	$71,257	$98,184	$69,068	$48,508	$24,151	233,522	87.7	75.3	82.2
50000	**Vermont**	$67,953	$32,368	$45,522	$83,452	$103,174	$83,160	$36,990	$24,590	620,244	95.3	90.0	90.2
50007	Chittenden County	$84,978	$41,182	$52,954	$95,816	$120,208	$101,360	$43,066	$28,073	157,557	96.3	91.1	92.8
50021	Rutland County	$61,648	$33,915	$47,126	$77,714	$103,007	$70,926	$28,952	$23,173	60,229	94.7	89.1	90.9
50023	Washington County	$71,500	$37,720	$48,109	$86,647	$96,884	$85,275	$41,971	$33,994	58,924	96.5	89.2	89.9
50027	Windsor County	$70,662	$34,514	$49,077	$87,199	$105,239	$84,132	$31,691	$23,580	55,317	95.2	89.0	86.6
51000	**Virginia**	$75,778	$35,774	$52,904	$96,379	$113,489	$98,043	$42,199	$27,583	7,974,644	90.9	79.3	85.8
51003	Albemarle County	$93,377	$49,381	$75,858	$109,722	$117,266	$112,462	$32,331	$37,976	100,606	95.0	79.8	91.0
51013	Arlington County	$139,542	$44,052	$94,433	$170,669	$150,265	$170,414	$52,679	$34,990	217,172	92.1	67.5	93.2
51015	Augusta County	$57,780	$36,309	$45,614	$71,168	$95,566	$74,363	$28,179	$20,918	69,873	92.3	80.8	82.6
51019	Bedford County	$70,626	$42,585	$52,107	$83,923	$89,520	$83,876	$28,975	$27,370	69,323	92.6	81.9	87.9
51031	Campbell County	$53,754	$31,979	$41,547	$77,934	$83,466	$71,269	$36,458	$31,354	54,665	89.6	81.0	85.9
51041	Chesterfield County	$82,177	$47,223	$59,645	$98,532	$119,000	$98,980	$54,716	$37,357	321,186	92.9	80.7	84.4
51059	Fairfax County	$125,756	$70,866	$101,060	$150,018	$149,070	$138,778	$84,309	$49,165	1,104,465	90.5	76.1	87.7
51061	Fauquier County	$104,091	$64,632	$68,765	$114,897	$145,304	$113,972	$46,016	$27,465	66,128	93.7	75.9	84.3
51067	Franklin County	$56,494	$40,915	$45,927	$66,718	$90,361	$64,092	$34,950	$19,219	56,024	89.1	77.1	83.6
51069	Frederick County	$78,085	$39,702	$52,594	$94,545	$109,874	$96,988	$32,175	$32,350	79,433	92.0	79.2	85.0
51085	Hanover County	$87,225	$39,688	$61,458	$101,943	$119,712	$111,241	$59,068	$41,028	99,776	95.2	87.7	89.8
51087	Henrico County	$73,917	$38,329	$53,278	$94,274	$113,088	$102,196	$51,184	$32,020	312,779	91.9	79.5	86.2
51089	Henry County	$42,183	$24,664	$36,721	$59,954	$73,973	$52,396	$20,825	$20,694	52,288	86.9	80.9	80.0
51095	James City County	$90,074	$78,426	$75,430	$97,033	$125,638	$102,343	$18,698	$42,010	67,629	95.5	85.2	89.0
51107	Loudoun County	$131,775	$67,318	$100,487	$152,587	$156,108	$146,793	$76,828	$54,010	336,135	92.7	80.9	88.8
51121	Montgomery County	$65,637	$35,915	$42,330	$85,562	$98,950	$77,607	$29,229	$19,309	94,771	93.1	83.2	92.1
51143	Pittsylvania County	$50,424	$27,286	$41,989	$68,333	$86,797	$68,300	$29,135	$23,241	62,027	90.2	79.2	82.6
51153	Prince William County	$104,934	$56,260	$69,891	$123,706	$140,442	$113,314	$49,375	$49,952	421,462	88.6	78.8	87.0
51161	Roanoke County	$74,656	$43,908	$59,746	$88,657	$105,096	$94,322	$61,606	$32,088	91,561	95.1	84.4	90.7
51165	Rockingham County	$60,822	$33,553	$47,573	$70,272	$90,655	$68,051	$47,771	$27,247	77,007	88.1	82.7	86.3
51177	Spotsylvania County	$85,421	$49,517	$59,370	$94,583	$127,379	$96,476	$51,511	$35,827	124,920	89.4	82.6	83.0
51179	Stafford County	$105,674	$50,053	$78,905	$127,066	$146,978	$114,700	$51,451	$44,763	127,862	93.5	83.6	87.8
51191	Washington County	$55,097	$29,583	$43,804	$68,732	$86,758	$71,263	$38,583	$31,720	54,241	89.1	80.2	86.6
51199	York County	$92,127	$48,725	$67,034	$109,634	$121,399	$103,189	$66,165	$24,281	62,998	95.8	87.7	94.0
51510	Alexandria city	$106,308	$41,506	$65,933	$144,464	$95,581	$128,570	$38,613	$35,213	143,819	87.1	72.3	88.5
51550	Chesapeake city	$78,370	$41,833	$54,954	$97,159	$116,607	$94,804	$47,889	$29,109	216,749	93.9	81.8	87.6
51650	Hampton city	$60,311	$30,015	$39,901	$81,829	$107,288	$75,716	$31,698	$24,938	131,633	91.3	83.8	83.4
51660	Harrisonburg city	$47,660	$32,022	$36,017	$60,092	$74,171	$57,630	$33,986	$22,205	50,085	83.5	69.7	91.3
51680	Lynchburg city	$48,148	$26,560	$31,600	$63,619	$99,438	$64,806	$35,625	$15,619	75,542	89.2	82.4	85.7
51700	Newport News city	$56,726	$34,339	$38,192	$75,230	$97,280	$72,716	$32,308	$23,947	172,561	90.4	79.3	82.6
51710	Norfolk city	$50,382	$23,457	$35,985	$69,947	$85,944	$66,405	$36,910	$19,278	219,463	88.2	77.0	81.4
51740	Portsmouth city	$51,115	$26,965	$36,489	$75,361	$87,368	$78,367	$33,204	$21,731	92,566	89.9	79.7	82.6
51760	Richmond city	$47,985	$16,494	$34,246	$76,326	$84,847	$91,416	$27,036	$15,947	207,996	90.0	77.6	80.9
51770	Roanoke city	$49,513	$26,276	$34,555	$65,376	$66,940	$66,993	$29,744	$18,515	96,354	89.2	77.2	80.6
51800	Suffolk city	$74,879	$32,984	$54,227	$92,347	$113,134	$99,624	$48,194	$29,901	82,889	91.5	84.2	87.5
51810	Virginia Beach city	$75,552	$41,972	$54,405	$90,500	$114,506	$91,479	$52,535	$31,248	422,238	93.2	82.4	84.8
53000	**Washington**	$71,100	$39,274	$53,164	$91,187	$106,694	$85,824	$41,732	$25,856	6,789,761	89.5	77.6	83.2
53005	Benton County	$71,535	$40,727	$52,641	$94,632	$106,892	$83,847	$44,042	$21,897	180,843	88.8	73.0	81.5
53007	Chelan County	$60,863	$40,233	$43,608	$76,866	$77,773	$65,608	$36,157	$27,788	73,097	82.3	69.8	74.7
53009	Clallam County	$58,859	$48,049	$52,965	$76,695	$81,875	$70,268	$38,185	$22,955	70,976	89.4	80.1	80.6
53011	Clark County	$67,344	$37,116	$51,798	$83,540	$102,066	$82,060	$41,542	$27,337	435,793	89.2	79.4	82.5
53015	Cowlitz County	$56,716	$36,910	$44,292	$78,367	$96,869	$68,643	$42,650	$20,571	101,080	89.4	79.7	85.3
53021	Franklin County	$56,255	$30,144	$36,747	$71,368	$90,652	$64,198	$44,602	$17,225	83,025	82.9	73.0	73.9
53025	Grant County	$52,638	$33,632	$33,931	$67,688	$72,641	$61,853	$27,381	$20,154	90,873	82.3	70.9	80.2

Table E-2: Counties with a Population of 50,000 or More—Income, Poverty, and Health Insurance—*Continued*

State/County FIPS code	State/Place	Total number of families	Families with incomes below the poverty level, as a percent of all families of that family type				Families that received Food Stamps (SNAP), as a percent of all families of that family type			Families that received food stamps (SNAP) and had at least one worker	
			All families	Married-couple families with related children under 18	Male householder families, no spouse present, with related children	Female householder families, no spouse present	All families	Married-couple families	Male householder or female householder families, no spouse present	Married-couple families, percent	Male householder or female householder families, no spouse present
	Texas—cont'd										
48439	Tarrant County	457,728	12.4	10.7	21.3	37.4	13.9	7.7	7.0	29.5	23.3
48441	Taylor County	31,266	12.2	9.2	27.8	40.7	15.5	9.1	7.3	33.8	27.0
48451	Tom Green County	27,392	11.5	5.8	13.2	44.4	16.2	7.0	6.2	39.3	33.9
48453	Travis County	238,489	12.2	9.7	24.0	41.3	14.0	7.4	7.1	30.7	24.3
48467	Van Zandt County	13,177	13.5	13.4	30.8	51.1	13.8	8.8	6.6	33.5	26.6
48469	Victoria County	22,844	13.5	11.8	19.4	37.9	16.0	6.9	6.5	37.0	29.9
48471	Walker County	12,229	18.8	13.1	19.0	69.6	12.3	5.0	5.0	30.2	14.8
48479	Webb County	56,095	28.3	24.6	48.2	57.2	34.6	26.3	22.3	50.3	36.1
48485	Wichita County	31,604	12.5	8.0	27.4	42.0	14.8	6.4	5.6	35.7	27.4
48491	Williamson County	114,479	5.4	3.7	14.0	18.9	7.3	4.3	4.2	19.7	17.2
48497	Wise County	15,968	8.4	7.3	24.6	34.0	12.9	9.2	8.3	31.6	24.0
49000	**Utah**	667,046	9.7	8.3	19.5	37.1	10.0	6.1	5.7	26.9	21.8
49003	Box Elder County	12,996	7.2	4.1	19.9	30.2	11.7	6.5	5.8	38.8	30.5
49005	Cache County	26,222	11.1	10.2	16.6	40.7	10.1	7.5	7.0	26.3	20.4
49011	Davis County	77,828	6.3	4.9	9.8	31.0	7.6	4.7	4.5	22.9	20.4
49035	Salt Lake County	243,850	10.0	9.0	23.3	36.6	10.2	6.0	5.6	24.7	19.7
49045	Tooele County	14,566	7.5	7.0	6.7	22.9	10.1	5.9	5.2	27.6	23.4
49049	Utah County	118,635	10.8	8.8	17.2	35.7	9.7	6.6	6.4	28.4	24.5
49053	Washington County	35,791	11.0	13.6	14.9	43.1	11.1	8.2	7.8	25.6	20.5
49057	Weber County	58,459	9.7	7.7	16.3	40.6	11.9	6.0	5.5	32.0	25.0
50000	**Vermont**	159,883	7.2	4.1	19.4	36.8	13.2	6.9	5.7	37.1	26.4
50007	Chittenden County	37,214	5.5	2.0	16.6	33.4	10.4	4.9	4.3	32.3	22.7
50021	Rutland County	15,913	7.5	4.3	22.6	34.6	13.5	7.2	6.3	35.9	28.1
50023	Washington County	15,040	6.0	3.9	12.8	25.5	8.7	4.6	3.5	23.0	16.7
50027	Windsor County	15,439	6.4	2.4	11.7	39.0	13.3	5.9	4.7	43.5	33.4
51000	**Virginia**	2,033,567	8.4	5.1	17.3	34.7	10.6	4.9	4.1	27.9	21.0
51003	Albemarle County	24,460	6.0	3.6	35.4	35.2	5.2	1.6	1.2	24.0	17.6
51013	Arlington County	44,308	6.0	3.5	19.8	26.6	5.5	3.0	2.1	15.3	11.1
51015	Augusta County	20,706	7.7	4.9	30.9	47.3	8.7	3.6	3.1	28.9	23.2
51019	Bedford County	19,942	6.1	4.7	20.5	29.7	7.9	4.3	3.5	26.5	21.5
51031	Campbell County	15,360	11.0	7.8	41.9	37.5	12.9	6.4	5.1	33.5	24.8
51041	Chesterfield County	80,854	5.1	3.2	8.7	24.1	8.3	4.1	3.8	23.1	18.0
51059	Fairfax County	277,600	4.2	3.6	7.8	21.5	4.9	2.9	2.6	13.3	11.7
51061	Fauquier County	16,887	3.6	2.1	1.9	22.9	5.5	2.7	2.7	21.4	19.6
51067	Franklin County	16,597	9.4	9.3	9.1	39.8	13.2	7.8	6.3	37.7	31.6
51069	Frederick County	21,345	3.6	2.5	12.7	23.1	5.5	1.9	1.8	23.4	17.2
51085	Hanover County	27,501	3.6	2.7	7.3	18.9	3.9	1.9	1.9	12.3	9.0
51087	Henrico County	78,233	8.6	4.6	16.3	31.0	11.0	4.3	3.6	26.9	21.5
51089	Henry County	15,451	13.9	16.9	47.0	44.8	19.0	10.6	8.6	40.4	31.2
51095	James City County	19,395	4.3	2.0	31.9	18.5	4.0	1.0	1.0	16.2	14.3
51107	Loudoun County	84,670	2.8	1.5	10.2	14.1	2.7	1.7	1.6	8.4	7.7
51121	Montgomery County	19,162	9.6	7.6	31.6	48.2	9.3	4.8	4.5	27.0	19.7
51143	Pittsylvania County	17,790	9.5	6.7	18.4	39.9	13.0	7.2	6.0	30.7	23.8
51153	Prince William County	104,908	5.0	4.7	10.5	17.1	7.3	4.5	4.4	16.7	14.7
51161	Roanoke County	25,577	5.4	4.8	8.3	19.3	7.4	2.7	2.2	25.5	19.8
51165	Rockingham County	20,745	6.9	7.1	18.8	30.9	6.3	3.8	3.5	17.1	11.6
51177	Spotsylvania County	33,925	5.6	4.7	6.0	20.6	8.9	4.2	4.0	26.2	19.0
51179	Stafford County	34,970	4.0	1.6	7.2	21.5	5.3	3.2	3.0	14.6	11.3
51191	Washington County	15,043	6.5	6.5	10.1	21.5	12.4	7.3	6.6	30.5	24.1
51199	York County	18,671	6.6	1.6	31.1	42.5	4.3	1.5	1.5	17.6	15.0
51510	Alexandria city	31,206	5.8	4.3	3.9	27.1	6.9	3.3	2.8	18.5	11.6
51550	Chesapeake city	59,294	8.0	4.3	12.7	31.4	10.0	4.9	4.6	24.2	19.5
51650	Hampton city	32,502	12.7	6.0	27.2	40.7	15.7	5.2	4.7	34.7	27.9
51660	Harrisonburg city	8,142	14.1	15.5	10.1	43.0	20.1	13.5	10.5	33.1	31.5
51680	Lynchburg city	16,060	18.5	11.1	26.7	54.5	19.3	7.3	6.1	43.8	30.0
51700	Newport News city	42,910	12.9	7.8	20.3	40.3	17.9	7.2	6.5	34.5	28.3
51710	Norfolk city	50,082	16.5	6.7	14.3	48.3	22.0	8.4	7.4	41.6	32.1
51740	Portsmouth city	23,410	15.9	4.4	22.7	42.7	19.6	6.1	4.6	36.0	29.0
51760	Richmond city	40,552	20.8	8.2	25.3	52.3	25.7	8.3	7.1	42.9	27.6
51770	Roanoke city	23,556	16.6	11.8	36.2	48.5	22.2	9.3	7.4	42.0	33.9
51800	Suffolk city	22,314	7.4	2.2	11.2	32.0	14.5	5.7	4.5	36.8	27.5
51810	Virginia Beach city	112,851	6.9	3.4	13.8	27.6	7.8	3.3	2.9	19.7	14.8
53000	**Washington**	1,694,518	9.4	7.2	19.4	37.9	15.4	8.7	7.5	37.5	28.3
53005	Benton County	45,747	9.8	7.1	18.1	42.6	17.3	10.0	9.0	42.1	35.1
53007	Chelan County	18,660	10.5	13.3	3.5	37.7	13.2	7.4	7.2	34.9	30.4
53009	Clallam County	18,671	8.2	5.9	26.0	39.0	13.9	8.4	6.0	38.1	23.4
53011	Clark County	110,144	9.3	6.5	13.4	35.2	17.5	10.3	9.2	40.2	30.1
53015	Cowlitz County	26,087	12.2	9.4	25.3	44.4	23.2	14.4	12.7	50.5	34.5
53021	Franklin County	18,483	18.2	14.3	24.0	56.1	26.1	17.7	16.4	45.1	39.0
53025	Grant County	22,180	14.5	13.8	20.0	49.4	21.5	13.6	12.2	44.4	38.7

State/County FIPS code	State/Place	Median family income in the past 12 months (in 2,013 inflation-adjusted dollars)					Families with own children under 18 years			Total population in households	Persons who had health insurance, as a percent of all persons in that household type		
		All families	Families with no earners	Families with one earner	Families with two earners	Families with three or more earners	Married-couple families with children	Male householder, no spouse present, with children	Female householder, no spouse present, with children		Married-couple families, percent	Male householder or female householder families, no spouse present	Nonfamily households
	Washington—cont'd												
53027	Grays Harbor County	$53,028	$34,775	$41,299	$69,331	$81,625	$61,899	$52,728	$23,457	68,647	86.1	69.5	79.5
53029	Island County	$68,921	$47,371	$53,161	$85,320	$100,638	$75,983	$39,063	$21,207	73,986	92.4	83.4	86.2
53033	King County	$91,917	$43,439	$68,431	$113,112	$122,622	$114,306	$50,588	$30,500	1,994,122	91.6	78.5	85.1
53035	Kitsap County	$73,118	$43,351	$61,629	$95,074	$118,110	$84,623	$44,418	$25,520	240,660	92.7	81.2	85.1
53041	Lewis County	$52,304	$37,747	$42,321	$71,435	$105,590	$57,988	$36,750	$25,429	74,559	88.1	77.7	81.1
53045	Mason County	$56,564	$44,957	$40,929	$80,837	$98,547	$67,440	$26,700	$21,042	59,259	87.4	65.7	76.4
53053	Pierce County	$68,729	$37,371	$51,699	$89,843	$115,724	$79,522	$45,294	$29,997	789,401	89.6	79.5	82.5
53057	Skagit County	$62,465	$37,667	$46,481	$84,100	$96,096	$74,236	$37,276	$26,827	116,981	87.9	75.5	79.0
53061	Snohomish County	$79,627	$38,508	$60,726	$96,801	$115,221	$93,448	$55,300	$29,935	724,054	90.0	79.3	83.6
53063	Spokane County	$62,241	$37,970	$46,389	$79,008	$97,579	$76,287	$35,821	$22,064	467,826	90.7	78.6	81.5
53067	Thurston County	$72,126	$45,217	$56,420	$90,574	$107,464	$80,708	$41,735	$24,401	252,879	90.6	82.1	83.6
53071	Walla Walla County	$59,932	$38,455	$40,502	$82,611	$80,938	$73,347	$24,848	$16,835	56,078	89.1	79.6	83.4
53073	Whatcom County	$66,420	$35,885	$52,500	$81,323	$89,978	$77,266	$37,094	$17,558	203,191	89.3	76.7	82.4
53077	Yakima County	$48,659	$26,879	$34,718	$61,483	$78,815	$53,052	$29,424	$21,886	243,664	78.5	68.2	76.7
54000	**West Virginia**	$51,949	$27,721	$42,971	$76,260	$93,908	$71,003	$35,189	$17,591	1,826,219	88.9	78.9	82.7
54003	Berkeley County	$59,935	$34,481	$46,129	$80,813	$88,942	$73,739	$50,539	$20,070	106,403	91.5	77.6	80.1
54011	Cabell County	$52,567	$29,375	$41,439	$76,366	$98,971	$81,046	$26,094	$14,030	95,391	88.9	78.6	81.9
54033	Harrison County	$55,114	$29,337	$43,435	$77,843	$103,327	$82,419	$51,188	$13,061	68,574	89.3	74.1	81.3
54037	Jefferson County	$74,915	$31,715	$52,714	$98,685	$100,313	$93,285	$42,361	$28,204	54,472	90.0	78.5	87.2
54039	Kanawha County	$57,624	$32,101	$43,245	$81,485	$100,682	$77,956	$27,869	$20,043	190,014	90.8	82.3	84.1
54049	Marion County	$53,703	$29,406	$42,381	$79,561	$101,528	$77,908	$31,759	$26,476	56,407	89.0	79.1	83.0
54055	Mercer County	$43,453	$25,235	$37,363	$69,533	$75,625	$58,583	$22,466	$12,931	61,813	88.8	80.1	83.1
54061	Monongalia County	$67,730	$32,151	$52,746	$84,887	$105,701	$89,375	$51,422	$23,125	99,005	91.0	83.8	85.5
54079	Putnam County	$65,480	$29,302	$56,392	$89,586	$100,025	$86,856	$82,234	$19,422	56,143	91.6	85.1	83.7
54081	Raleigh County	$48,405	$27,192	$45,008	$74,398	$85,625	$70,473	$20,017	$15,868	75,776	89.4	81.7	84.0
54107	Wood County	$50,411	$30,486	$39,501	$76,857	$88,372	$65,987	$35,753	$20,676	86,226	88.7	81.9	81.8
55000	**Wisconsin**	$65,877	$35,499	$44,059	$81,992	$99,328	$84,375	$36,513	$23,702	5,650,835	94.1	85.7	86.3
55009	Brown County	$66,668	$37,856	$41,399	$83,496	$97,608	$86,727	$38,380	$25,207	249,418	94.4	84.9	85.6
55017	Chippewa County	$62,839	$37,147	$43,578	$74,908	$90,905	$73,885	$42,098	$24,261	60,674	94.6	85.5	85.9
55021	Columbia County	$70,605	$40,631	$49,916	$85,872	$93,662	$86,194	$48,125	$28,670	55,226	94.3	88.3	84.8
55025	Dane County	$82,314	$47,652	$53,541	$94,623	$114,872	$102,487	$39,029	$26,931	499,312	96.3	88.4	89.3
55027	Dodge County	$64,686	$34,656	$48,535	$77,277	$93,750	$79,038	$45,255	$30,000	83,896	95.2	87.2	88.6
55035	Eau Claire County	$66,499	$45,608	$42,148	$77,188	$99,054	$83,984	$31,661	$28,278	99,890	93.3	82.1	88.6
55039	Fond du Lac County	$64,411	$36,792	$45,961	$77,546	$95,515	$79,792	$37,113	$20,629	100,140	95.3	84.0	89.2
55043	Grant County	$60,249	$36,563	$39,788	$70,933	$90,425	$71,916	$29,375	$24,280	49,991	91.6	87.0	87.0
55055	Jefferson County	$67,782	$40,343	$45,086	$79,543	$98,887	$80,340	$40,109	$26,497	83,755	95.9	84.2	90.6
55059	Kenosha County	$66,490	$30,049	$45,117	$88,834	$100,103	$87,097	$38,750	$24,823	165,621	92.8	84.7	83.5
55063	La Crosse County	$67,723	$31,240	$46,342	$80,773	$97,286	$85,540	$38,209	$27,868	114,876	96.3	87.8	87.7
55071	Manitowoc County	$62,617	$34,184	$44,066	$74,768	$91,543	$74,995	$47,747	$28,058	80,221	95.8	87.0	88.8
55073	Marathon County	$63,249	$32,271	$43,388	$77,329	$99,435	$83,394	$34,663	$26,208	133,610	93.3	87.6	84.8
55079	Milwaukee County	$54,365	$22,402	$33,024	$80,422	$97,981	$78,926	$27,443	$20,771	944,722	91.7	83.8	84.5
55087	Outagamie County	$71,330	$38,355	$47,746	$83,477	$97,106	$88,217	$41,471	$27,385	177,486	95.3	89.7	86.1
55089	Ozaukee County	$90,808	$45,201	$72,284	$103,859	$113,930	$113,106	$80,060	$29,356	86,367	97.4	92.2	89.5
55097	Portage County	$62,899	$41,791	$45,442	$76,997	$91,250	$79,384	$41,333	$16,989	69,939	96.5	84.3	87.2
55101	Racine County	$66,240	$36,489	$46,162	$85,065	$104,036	$83,582	$36,977	$27,122	190,709	92.0	84.0	83.5
55105	Rock County	$58,244	$35,482	$40,852	$75,840	$93,803	$73,724	$34,773	$19,617	158,962	93.5	83.6	84.2
55109	St. Croix County	$79,675	$48,159	$50,310	$95,725	$114,717	$98,250	$37,165	$34,148	84,659	95.8	83.8	85.9
55111	Sauk County	$63,100	$34,347	$42,893	$75,328	$91,711	$74,342	$43,686	$21,734	62,011	92.6	88.7	83.2
55117	Sheboygan County	$63,416	$36,837	$43,048	$76,717	$94,474	$81,000	$32,185	$21,496	112,674	95.7	87.5	83.2
55127	Walworth County	$68,789	$39,381	$46,872	$81,701	$95,179	$82,350	$36,775	$25,625	102,106	93.7	86.8	86.5
55131	Washington County	$80,636	$41,049	$53,860	$95,522	$106,267	$98,528	$36,266	$28,986	131,515	97.3	89.2	91.0
55133	Waukesha County	$91,885	$44,324	$71,922	$103,770	$116,113	$108,736	$53,634	$32,793	389,701	96.7	90.0	90.1
55135	Waupaca County	$60,690	$37,038	$46,341	$73,760	$97,670	$71,714	$30,069	$15,551	50,829	93.9	87.2	87.5
55139	Winnebago County	$67,139	$38,194	$44,833	$82,408	$100,231	$84,183	$40,799	$22,677	163,331	96.0	88.0	85.5
55141	Wood County	$60,655	$36,094	$41,570	$73,360	$90,750	$73,319	$40,463	$22,049	73,639	95.6	91.8	86.8
56000	**Wyoming**	$70,531	$36,362	$49,622	$86,697	$105,900	$84,210	$45,175	$23,418	566,182	89.4	76.2	79.8
56021	Laramie County	$74,871	$52,951	$49,833	$86,609	$110,854	$82,762	$59,764	$28,490	91,333	92.5	78.7	80.9
56025	Natrona County	$70,593	$33,627	$50,377	$87,467	$120,304	$92,611	$52,365	$19,803	77,635	88.8	79.7	76.6

State/ County FIPS code	State/Place	Total number of families	Families with incomes below the poverty level, as a percent of all families of that family type				Families that received Food Stamps (SNAP), as a percent of all families of that family type			Families that received food stamps (SNAP) and had at least one worker	
			All families	Married-couple families with related children under 18	Male householder families, no spouse present, with related children	Female householder families, no spouse present	All families	Married-couple families	Male householder or female householder families, no spouse present	Married-couple families, percent	Male householder or female householder families, no spouse present
	Washington—cont'd										
53027	Grays Harbor County	17,369	12.5	12.7	23.9	42.2	19.5	12.3	9.9	37.5	29.4
53029	Island County	22,703	6.7	5.1	14.3	43.0	10.7	6.8	5.7	30.9	19.7
53033	King County	476,064	7.8	5.2	23.2	32.9	12.0	6.3	5.4	31.8	24.0
53035	Kitsap County	65,374	7.6	4.1	17.9	40.3	12.5	6.2	5.5	35.2	25.5
53041	Lewis County	19,760	10.3	8.1	19.4	38.9	23.3	13.6	10.7	54.0	41.7
53045	Mason County	15,183	11.5	14.7	25.7	53.6	17.9	12.1	10.2	40.6	33.2
53053	Pierce County	200,874	9.2	7.3	17.1	32.2	16.1	8.9	7.8	36.7	27.7
53057	Skagit County	31,008	10.5	8.7	17.9	37.6	17.3	9.5	8.3	41.2	32.3
53061	Snohomish County	182,208	7.4	6.3	12.4	32.6	13.7	7.8	6.8	33.1	24.3
53063	Spokane County	117,342	10.2	7.5	16.5	43.0	17.8	9.6	8.1	43.5	33.1
53067	Thurston County	67,297	8.8	5.9	21.3	39.0	12.9	7.3	6.7	31.1	25.4
53071	Walla Walla County	13,503	13.3	10.9	34.6	55.9	16.7	8.6	7.7	46.3	36.7
53073	Whatcom County	48,716	11.4	7.1	20.8	53.3	15.9	9.0	7.9	41.7	28.2
53077	Yakima County	56,753	16.9	16.0	23.0	46.7	26.6	16.8	15.0	51.6	39.7
54000	**West Virginia**	479,062	13.1	10.8	26.3	50.4	16.1	9.0	6.5	37.8	23.5
54003	Berkeley County	28,898	10.0	8.9	10.2	42.4	12.8	6.3	5.8	30.2	22.0
54011	Cabell County	23,418	16.1	9.3	27.3	62.5	18.4	6.9	5.6	44.2	29.6
54033	Harrison County	18,028	14.3	12.3	29.7	61.4	13.7	7.7	6.3	32.3	18.4
54037	Jefferson County	14,378	7.4	6.7	25.3	29.4	12.9	6.0	5.8	35.9	27.5
54039	Kanawha County	50,596	10.8	7.2	30.8	42.9	16.5	6.9	5.2	39.7	30.7
54049	Marion County	14,334	10.8	7.5	30.9	40.6	12.4	7.1	3.5	27.9	19.8
54055	Mercer County	17,137	17.1	16.9	28.9	55.2	20.0	12.2	8.2	43.5	21.0
54061	Monongalia County	19,174	9.9	7.2	14.5	40.2	7.5	3.8	2.8	20.6	12.1
54079	Putnam County	15,979	8.2	3.7	6.0	44.0	8.8	3.8	2.5	27.6	14.3
54081	Raleigh County	20,722	14.0	8.5	29.0	53.2	18.4	7.9	5.1	50.0	34.2
54107	Wood County	22,834	13.7	13.3	18.0	47.7	18.2	11.1	9.0	39.8	25.3
55000	**Wisconsin**	1,458,497	8.9	5.6	21.6	40.3	13.3	6.0	5.3	37.8	29.4
55009	Brown County	64,686	8.7	5.0	19.3	39.3	12.0	5.8	5.4	33.3	26.3
55017	Chippewa County	16,506	7.3	6.2	19.4	26.1	10.6	6.3	4.7	29.7	25.7
55021	Columbia County	15,328	5.3	3.4	4.3	30.6	7.4	3.5	3.0	22.2	19.0
55025	Dane County	120,118	7.0	4.1	24.0	35.2	10.0	4.2	3.9	30.4	24.8
55027	Dodge County	21,818	6.0	4.5	7.0	31.7	9.5	5.0	4.4	29.5	25.8
55035	Eau Claire County	23,583	7.2	5.0	18.3	32.0	11.3	6.2	5.5	32.0	28.1
55039	Fond du Lac County	27,535	6.6	2.3	12.7	44.9	9.4	4.3	4.1	28.0	24.2
55043	Grant County	12,046	8.0	6.8	31.7	36.3	9.1	4.9	4.4	30.1	24.2
55055	Jefferson County	21,777	6.9	5.9	14.3	32.2	11.0	6.2	5.9	31.6	25.8
55059	Kenosha County	41,784	10.6	3.9	27.4	38.1	17.0	6.9	6.1	42.8	31.8
55063	La Crosse County	27,786	7.5	4.0	23.5	38.8	10.5	4.1	3.6	34.1	25.4
55071	Manitowoc County	21,942	5.3	5.5	5.4	29.1	9.2	5.9	5.1	24.4	17.9
55073	Marathon County	35,997	7.9	5.3	25.0	40.5	9.8	4.3	3.4	32.2	25.4
55079	Milwaukee County	216,430	17.6	9.8	31.8	48.3	27.4	11.4	9.9	52.9	39.3
55087	Outagamie County	47,164	5.8	3.3	12.2	30.6	8.1	3.7	3.5	25.8	21.4
55089	Ozaukee County	24,206	3.3	2.0	2.3	26.3	5.6	2.4	2.1	23.6	22.1
55097	Portage County	17,403	7.6	3.3	31.6	47.1	12.8	7.4	7.3	35.6	30.8
55101	Racine County	48,757	9.7	6.8	22.8	38.2	14.8	6.6	6.0	39.4	27.5
55105	Rock County	42,332	11.5	6.9	23.4	45.5	20.0	10.4	9.1	45.6	32.7
55109	St. Croix County	23,288	5.2	3.4	14.6	23.4	6.7	2.6	2.4	23.6	19.6
55111	Sauk County	16,526	8.7	6.9	7.7	43.6	12.7	7.1	5.9	37.1	28.9
55117	Sheboygan County	30,433	8.0	5.0	24.5	38.3	13.7	6.6	6.2	41.4	35.9
55127	Walworth County	25,780	7.7	4.6	19.5	34.8	11.7	5.2	4.6	34.5	27.9
55131	Washington County	37,350	4.4	3.4	13.5	29.5	6.7	2.6	2.3	25.5	22.3
55133	Waukesha County	107,461	3.7	2.1	13.2	27.5	4.9	2.3	1.9	21.0	16.6
55135	Waupaca County	14,376	8.1	6.3	21.1	58.0	11.2	5.7	5.0	36.8	31.4
55139	Winnebago County	40,792	7.5	4.5	18.4	41.5	11.0	4.5	4.1	36.2	29.2
55141	Wood County	20,380	8.1	4.9	10.3	43.3	13.2	6.3	5.2	40.8	34.8
56000	**Wyoming**	145,481	8.4	5.6	15.0	40.8	6.4	2.6	2.4	21.2	17.7
56021	Laramie County	24,077	6.5	2.8	3.3	40.4	6.8	2.7	2.5	22.5	20.8
56025	Natrona County	20,464	8.4	4.9	9.8	42.1	7.5	2.1	1.8	22.9	19.9

Table E-3: Metropolitan Areas—Income, Poverty, and Health Insurance

CBSA FIPS code	Metropolitan area	Median family income in the past 12 months (in 2,013 inflation-adjusted dollars)								Total population in households	Persons who had health insurance, as a percent of all persons in that household type		
		All families	Families with no earners	Families with one earner	Families with two earners	Families with three or more earners	Families with own children under 18 years						
							Married-couple families with children	Male householder, no spouse present, with children	Female householder, no spouse present, with children		Married-couple families, percent	Male householder or female householder families, no spouse present	Nonfamily households
10180	Abilene, TX	$54,594	$29,116	$38,351	$72,131	$83,157	$68,199	$31,208	$19,588	155,396	83.7	75.2	79.2
10420	Akron, OH	$63,683	$33,024	$46,157	$84,113	$101,748	$87,079	$31,676	$20,442	699,238	93.3	82.5	84.5
10500	Albany, GA	$42,048	$19,569	$31,801	$72,397	$75,347	$70,966	$27,263	$17,297	153,161	84.3	73.6	76.8
10540	Albany, OR	$52,519	$32,993	$40,241	$70,372	$82,531	$64,669	$33,323	$16,180	117,689	87.7	81.9	81.5
10580	Albany-Schenectady-Troy, NY	$78,833	$41,882	$55,902	$99,271	$112,978	$101,368	$42,107	$27,292	864,527	95.7	89.9	90.4
10740	Albuquerque, NM	$58,697	$29,737	$42,144	$80,737	$97,025	$74,802	$34,748	$22,295	888,979	86.8	79.6	80.8
10780	Alexandria, LA	$48,703	$26,995	$35,971	$75,288	$100,059	$73,392	$28,605	$18,909	148,465	86.8	76.4	81.0
10900	Allentown-Bethlehem-Easton, PA-NJ	$69,096	$33,394	$51,147	$87,377	$105,595	$90,972	$35,106	$26,011	816,718	93.2	82.0	87.0
11020	Altoona, PA	$54,803	$33,625	$40,677	$72,507	$91,521	$71,951	$30,028	$20,454	125,144	92.3	85.8	90.4
11100	Amarillo, TX	$59,843	$31,184	$41,500	$80,261	$98,950	$79,706	$35,904	$21,721	249,192	85.3	72.8	75.0
11180	Ames, IA	$75,721	$52,732	$53,151	$85,854	$108,369	$85,594	$40,990	$17,571	90,900	97.7	88.8	92.7
11260	Anchorage, AK	$86,627	$46,467	$58,114	$103,527	$131,267	$96,520	$54,375	$33,269	379,721	86.7	73.6	78.0
11460	Ann Arbor, MI	$85,332	$43,660	$60,397	$106,701	$122,579	$108,198	$40,714	$26,496	347,745	95.9	86.4	90.4
11500	Anniston-Oxford-Jacksonville, AL	$50,156	$26,336	$37,318	$68,789	$79,909	$61,927	$30,139	$14,058	115,813	90.9	78.4	82.2
11540	Appleton, WI	$72,644	$37,410	$49,701	$84,367	$98,845	$90,091	$42,663	$27,697	226,939	95.8	90.1	86.2
11700	Asheville, NC	$54,786	$36,991	$41,397	$71,980	$93,136	$69,368	$31,860	$21,991	427,197	87.1	76.1	78.5
12020	Athens-Clarke County, GA	$54,693	$24,184	$40,028	$77,157	$98,068	$65,028	$26,091	$16,978	194,811	88.6	74.0	82.6
12060	Atlanta-Sandy Springs-Roswell, GA	$65,126	$30,028	$46,301	$87,210	$98,367	$86,130	$36,965	$27,515	5,403,983	85.7	72.3	78.8
12100	Atlantic City-Hammonton, NJ	$64,539	$31,982	$45,887	$83,571	$105,962	$83,373	$32,361	$25,394	272,144	89.6	79.0	82.1
12220	Auburn-Opelika, AL	$62,709	$19,336	$48,317	$80,268	$89,498	$77,247	$28,968	$21,723	145,149	92.6	78.0	87.4
12260	Augusta-Richmond County, GA-SC	$56,247	$27,619	$41,962	$79,803	$96,932	$75,962	$36,104	$17,751	558,870	89.8	76.7	81.1
12420	Austin-Round Rock, TX	$75,180	$44,990	$51,059	$93,288	$101,739	$94,301	$40,521	$27,304	1,816,408	86.0	74.2	78.4
12540	Bakersfield, CA	$51,340	$20,812	$38,481	$71,390	$86,520	$63,442	$29,040	$18,620	827,422	83.1	76.3	78.6
12580	Baltimore-Columbia-Towson, MD	$84,510	$33,365	$57,997	$108,063	$130,981	$113,905	$52,055	$33,315	2,707,468	94.0	86.6	89.1
12620	Bangor, ME	$54,517	$26,076	$39,578	$72,676	$100,199	$68,943	$36,281	$20,451	151,814	92.8	83.5	84.2
12700	Barnstable Town, MA	$75,626	$47,155	$60,949	$91,234	$116,825	$97,544	$50,877	$31,519	212,563	96.6	91.1	94.4
12940	Baton Rouge, LA	$64,025	$27,628	$42,782	$88,489	$111,234	$90,983	$41,860	$21,791	799,370	90.6	78.6	82.7
12980	Battle Creek, MI	$52,930	$32,229	$36,079	$75,108	$98,099	$77,213	$26,652	$18,868	133,519	91.9	82.6	84.3
13020	Bay City, MI	$55,910	$34,574	$42,234	$76,860	$91,739	$79,403	$33,413	$17,309	106,018	93.1	81.9	83.6
13140	Beaumont-Port Arthur, TX	$55,901	$29,616	$43,052	$77,468	$100,468	$70,409	$42,453	$20,794	389,149	82.7	73.4	76.9
13220	Beckley, WV	$46,501	$26,574	$41,828	$72,984	$86,406	$67,826	$21,362	$16,298	120,160	88.3	78.6	83.1
13380	Bellingham, WA	$66,420	$35,885	$52,500	$81,323	$89,978	$77,266	$37,094	$17,558	203,191	89.3	76.7	82.4
13460	Bend-Redmond, OR	$59,767	$42,139	$42,259	$71,859	$79,453	$74,175	$26,600	$24,035	161,762	86.5	74.5	73.6
13740	Billings, MT	$64,613	$38,879	$47,042	$77,386	$103,630	$80,696	$38,687	$21,376	160,705	88.7	72.1	81.2
13780	Binghamton, NY	$62,819	$32,010	$46,899	$78,654	$104,865	$78,201	$36,176	$21,784	245,467	94.6	86.6	88.9
13820	Birmingham-Hoover, AL	$60,792	$27,239	$45,068	$84,340	$101,382	$83,221	$35,328	$21,095	1,121,313	91.2	81.3	85.0
13900	Bismarck, ND	$80,250	$41,357	$47,750	$90,358	$119,635	$96,795	$47,336	$29,814	117,939	95.5	83.5	86.6
13980	Blacksburg-Christiansburg-Radford, VA	$56,582	$29,352	$43,576	$77,191	$90,482	$76,772	$33,493	$21,730	177,437	91.9	79.8	88.6
14010	Bloomington, IL	$80,898	$50,847	$52,970	$97,739	$114,875	$101,341	$43,865	$26,043	187,649	95.6	87.4	89.3
14020	Bloomington, IN	$59,272	$30,269	$47,480	$71,085	$84,517	$75,401	$51,753	$20,565	161,465	90.7	77.9	87.4
14100	Bloomsburg-Berwick, PA	$58,990	$28,718	$45,974	$76,181	$98,431	$79,055	$29,327	$24,633	83,944	94.7	84.2	93.6
14260	Boise City, ID	$58,095	$35,086	$44,080	$72,117	$89,174	$68,267	$36,164	$20,025	631,107	88.2	75.5	81.4
14460	Boston-Cambridge-Newton, MA-NH	$91,308	$32,182	$62,126	$112,719	$128,562	$120,047	$49,981	$29,163	4,592,291	97.2	92.4	94.1
14500	Boulder, CO	$93,165	$54,216	$72,799	$110,554	$118,571	$117,097	$53,788	$30,736	303,089	92.3	81.2	88.0
14540	Bowling Green, KY	$53,984	$26,411	$38,523	$68,572	$86,610	$74,063	$39,056	$14,587	160,333	88.6	77.2	82.5
14740	Bremerton-Silverdale, WA	$73,118	$43,351	$61,629	$95,074	$118,110	$84,623	$44,418	$25,520	240,660	92.7	81.2	85.1
14860	Bridgeport-Stamford-Norwalk, CT	$103,676	$38,122	$80,162	$128,620	$129,470	$146,042	$51,917	$31,942	924,802	91.9	80.2	84.1
15180	Brownsville-Harlingen, TX	$35,811	$14,841	$26,491	$58,661	$68,275	$43,710	$26,897	$16,048	412,429	66.5	64.3	74.4
15260	Brunswick, GA	$52,647	$35,420	$40,543	$69,232	$77,923	$64,211	$25,444	$21,778	112,323	82.9	69.2	75.4
15380	Buffalo-Cheektowaga-Niagara Falls, NY	$65,168	$33,635	$45,560	$86,908	$110,382	$90,406	$39,377	$22,822	1,120,440	96.1	89.1	90.5
15500	Burlington, NC	$52,590	$28,703	$36,207	$73,868	$92,852	$67,303	$30,559	$21,782	152,588	87.7	74.4	80.3
15540	Burlington-South Burlington, VT	$80,110	$33,685	$48,132	$92,970	$116,848	$96,982	$41,348	$24,711	212,170	96.0	91.1	92.2
15680	California-Lexington Park, MD	$95,187	$49,368	$62,625	$114,702	$145,214	$111,511	$60,920	$30,810	105,997	93.3	87.0	92.8
15940	Canton-Massillon, OH	$57,632	$32,506	$42,624	$75,897	$98,623	$76,933	$36,982	$19,689	398,521	91.8	83.5	83.4
15980	Cape Coral-Fort Myers, FL	$55,878	$45,006	$43,847	$74,842	$87,969	$62,435	$31,402	$25,060	640,429	84.4	66.6	79.8
16020	Cape Girardeau, MO-IL	$53,299	$29,742	$38,538	$68,986	$88,440	$72,031	$40,854	$15,150	95,490	92.1	80.1	86.4
16060	Carbondale-Marion, IL	$53,223	$32,568	$38,229	$74,629	$96,071	$77,253	$28,837	$17,115	124,422	93.0	83.6	85.9
16180	Carson City, NV	$60,720	$44,750	$43,843	$71,173	$87,625	$60,372	$19,825	$28,955	52,473	85.8	66.4	81.2
16220	Casper, WY	$70,593	$33,627	$50,377	$87,467	$120,304	$92,611	$52,365	$19,803	77,635	88.8	79.7	76.6
16300	Cedar Rapids, IA	$74,454	$41,870	$49,894	$89,085	$105,766	$92,657	$37,629	$26,844	257,945	96.3	85.2	88.9
16540	Chambersburg-Waynesboro, PA	$62,717	$39,678	$45,134	$79,704	$100,230	$78,011	$36,136	$27,284	150,203	88.0	81.8	88.8
16580	Champaign-Urbana, IL	$67,959	$39,974	$46,070	$80,515	$108,103	$86,302	$37,266	$23,205	231,752	94.6	87.0	87.7
16620	Charleston, WV	$56,507	$30,874	$44,090	$79,708	$101,484	$75,847	$25,948	$18,866	223,537	90.4	82.3	83.9
16700	Charleston-North Charleston, SC	$62,270	$32,620	$45,521	$81,878	$99,308	$81,530	$35,450	$22,729	681,630	87.7	75.9	80.7
16740	Charlotte-Concord-Gastonia, NC-SC	$62,299	$28,746	$45,112	$82,584	$93,828	$85,858	$34,118	$24,020	2,277,816	88.1	76.1	79.5
16820	Charlottesville, VA	$76,502	$41,990	$58,864	$92,343	$106,974	$98,961	$30,910	$31,225	217,189	93.4	79.9	88.7

| CBSA FIPS code | Metropolitan area | Total number of families | Families with incomes below the poverty level, as a percent of all families of that family type | | | | Families that received Food Stamps (SNAP), as a percent of all families of that family type | | | Families that received food stamps (SNAP) and had at least one worker | |
			All families	Married-couple families	Male householder families, no spouse present	Female householder families, no spouse present	All families	Married-couple families	Male householder or female householder families, no spouse present	Married-couple families, percent	Male householder or female householder families, no spouse present, percent
10180	Abilene, TX	38,480	12.8	9.04	28.0	45.2	14.9	8.7	33.4	6.8	26.8
10420	Akron, OH	176,382	11.3	5.52	28.9	46.0	15.2	6.2	40.0	4.9	27.8
10500	Albany, GA	38,689	21.6	12.17	30.0	51.3	27.1	12.1	49.7	8.8	32.5
10540	Albany, OR	30,690	13.4	11.43	25.6	56.6	21.7	11.9	53.3	10.5	36.2
10580	Albany-Schenectady-Troy, NY	209,298	7.7	3.94	21.5	36.9	10.1	4.0	29.0	3.2	20.1
10740	Albuquerque, NM	218,830	15.0	12.43	22.6	43.5	17.5	9.2	36.0	7.8	27.3
10780	Alexandria, LA	35,968	15.8	7.90	32.7	50.5	20.4	10.3	41.9	8.4	28.0
10900	Allentown-Bethlehem-Easton, PA-NJ	213,231	8.3	4.96	24.5	37.6	10.6	4.9	28.7	3.9	19.6
11020	Altoona, PA	33,008	9.5	7.33	24.3	43.0	15.3	7.6	39.0	6.0	32.6
11100	Amarillo, TX	63,241	12.1	9.24	20.4	41.8	14.3	7.7	32.0	7.0	24.0
11180	Ames, IA	18,866	7.5	5.09	13.3	50.3	8.2	4.6	29.5	4.0	27.1
11260	Anchorage, AK	91,686	5.5	3.39	13.9	23.6	9.4	5.4	21.3	4.9	17.9
11460	Ann Arbor, MI	78,477	9.0	5.56	17.6	38.7	13.0	5.6	37.5	4.7	29.4
11500	Anniston-Oxford-Jacksonville, AL	29,760	16.9	12.96	21.9	57.8	22.1	11.7	45.8	9.7	35.6
11540	Appleton, WI	61,005	5.5	3.20	12.5	30.6	7.6	3.8	24.0	3.6	19.8
11700	Asheville, NC	112,745	12.1	10.58	21.2	43.9	13.5	7.4	34.4	6.3	25.1
12020	Athens-Clarke County, GA	40,531	16.6	9.73	38.4	55.8	17.1	8.1	40.4	6.9	24.9
12060	Atlanta-Sandy Springs-Roswell, GA	1,304,670	12.6	9.43	23.7	38.3	16.0	8.3	34.4	7.4	25.7
12100	Atlantic City-Hammonton, NJ	68,182	12.7	8.27	24.3	40.3	14.3	6.5	30.1	5.7	21.0
12220	Auburn-Opelika, AL	34,949	13.0	7.32	23.4	42.2	13.2	6.8	30.4	5.2	23.6
12260	Augusta-Richmond County, GA-SC	140,653	15.6	8.99	26.5	52.1	18.5	8.0	40.8	6.8	28.4
12420	Austin-Round Rock, TX	416,957	10.1	8.10	21.1	36.0	12.0	6.6	28.1	6.2	22.9
12540	Bakersfield, CA	193,078	19.8	15.39	32.3	55.2	18.8	10.9	35.0	9.6	23.5
12580	Baltimore-Columbia-Towson, MD	667,216	7.9	3.85	15.2	29.4	13.1	5.3	31.1	4.5	23.1
12620	Bangor, ME	38,437	10.8	10.24	18.8	40.6	19.0	11.2	46.6	8.9	27.9
12700	Barnstable Town, MA	58,096	6.0	4.27	16.9	31.8	7.3	3.3	22.7	2.8	17.4
12940	Baton Rouge, LA	197,766	13.4	6.78	19.0	44.3	17.1	7.4	36.6	6.1	27.6
12980	Battle Creek, MI	34,142	14.6	8.24	27.0	49.8	19.8	9.2	43.6	7.3	30.6
13020	Bay City, MI	28,591	10.4	6.13	26.9	47.5	15.7	6.6	43.6	5.2	29.4
13140	Beaumont-Port Arthur, TX	98,963	14.4	10.59	22.4	44.9	19.2	10.0	39.6	8.6	30.3
13220	Beckley, WV	32,295	14.9	9.68	27.3	52.2	19.8	9.6	48.4	6.8	31.4
13380	Bellingham, WA	48,716	11.4	7.15	20.8	53.3	15.9	9.0	41.7	7.9	28.2
13460	Bend-Redmond, OR	42,559	11.3	10.02	45.2	25.3	19.3	12.2	46.8	10.3	37.4
13740	Billings, MT	41,613	9.1	5.12	18.4	38.8	11.4	4.7	31.2	4.4	26.7
13780	Binghamton, NY	61,786	10.3	8.50	20.2	43.0	14.3	6.9	36.7	5.4	24.0
13820	Birmingham-Hoover, AL	292,018	12.8	8.30	27.7	44.2	16.0	8.1	36.0	6.8	24.5
13900	Bismarck, ND	31,249	5.5	2.72	8.3	29.5	6.5	2.4	22.4	2.3	18.5
13980	Blacksburg-Christiansburg-Radford, VA	40,878	9.4	6.56	21.7	40.2	11.1	5.3	30.7	4.2	19.6
14010	Bloomington, IL	44,486	7.7	3.49	22.5	36.7	10.3	4.3	32.3	3.8	26.7
14020	Bloomington, IN	33,692	11.8	7.56	22.6	46.4	12.3	5.9	31.6	5.0	20.3
14100	Bloomsburg-Berwick, PA	21,306	9.0	7.31	21.1	39.4	9.4	4.4	27.7	3.3	16.7
14260	Boise City, ID	160,413	11.6	8.70	26.8	46.5	15.2	9.1	36.7	8.5	28.1
14460	Boston-Cambridge-Newton, MA-NH	1,116,209	7.4	3.63	16.9	33.5	10.8	4.6	29.4	3.7	21.3
14500	Boulder, CO	71,394	6.4	5.15	14.5	27.8	6.0	2.6	19.0	2.4	16.5
14540	Bowling Green, KY	41,052	14.3	8.22	26.1	54.9	16.9	9.2	39.7	7.1	29.2
14740	Bremerton-Silverdale, WA	65,374	7.6	4.05	17.9	40.3	12.5	6.2	35.2	5.5	25.5
14860	Bridgeport-Stamford-Norwalk, CT	228,970	6.6	3.02	16.3	28.7	8.5	3.2	25.9	2.8	19.5
15180	Brownsville-Harlingen, TX	94,551	29.8	28.17	38.9	60.2	31.4	24.6	44.9	20.8	30.3
15260	Brunswick, GA	29,881	14.7	6.24	37.8	46.4	20.4	10.0	44.0	8.4	33.9
15380	Buffalo-Cheektowaga-Niagara Falls, NY	285,425	10.8	6.15	19.2	42.3	14.7	5.7	35.7	4.4	24.4
15500	Burlington, NC	40,693	13.9	12.36	27.0	43.2	14.7	6.7	33.7	5.1	27.3
15540	Burlington-South Burlington, VT	52,165	6.3	2.27	20.0	36.9	11.8	5.5	35.9	4.6	24.8
15680	California-Lexington Park, MD	27,958	6.0	1.51	13.0	38.5	11.3	6.1	34.6	5.4	29.1
15940	Canton-Massillon, OH	106,785	11.2	8.92	23.1	45.4	16.0	7.7	40.7	6.5	30.1
15980	Cape Coral-Fort Myers, FL	158,675	11.0	12.24	26.8	38.7	13.8	7.6	35.6	6.3	25.2
16020	Cape Girardeau, MO-IL	23,951	12.8	6.97	25.1	58.5	15.1	6.2	45.7	5.1	33.3
16060	Carbondale-Marion, IL	29,515	14.1	10.62	28.7	48.7	16.4	8.2	41.2	6.6	29.9
16180	Carson City, NV	12,572	10.2	14.83	43.9	23.3	12.6	7.6	27.3	7.0	19.8
16220	Casper, WY	20,464	8.4	4.94	9.8	42.1	7.5	2.1	22.9	1.8	19.9
16300	Cedar Rapids, IA	65,882	6.1	1.98	19.6	31.0	10.7	4.4	34.4	3.8	29.8
16540	Chambersburg-Waynesboro, PA	39,858	8.5	7.47	17.8	38.2	10.5	5.7	31.1	4.9	23.5
16580	Champaign-Urbana, IL	50,697	9.8	6.18	23.7	41.3	11.1	4.9	31.3	4.2	25.8
16620	Charleston, WV	59,739	11.9	9.24	34.4	45.5	17.0	8.0	40.2	5.7	29.6
16700	Charleston-North Charleston, SC	169,550	11.9	6.83	20.0	43.2	14.0	6.0	33.9	4.9	23.9
16740	Charlotte-Concord-Gastonia, NC-SC	576,100	11.9	7.35	26.5	40.8	15.3	7.4	36.3	6.3	27.3
16820	Charlottesville, VA	51,857	7.5	5.92	26.9	32.3	9.2	3.7	30.1	2.9	19.9

| CBSA FIPS code | Metropolitan area | Median family income in the past 12 months (in 2,013 inflation-adjusted dollars) | | | | | | | | Total population in households | Persons who had health insurance, as a percent of all persons in that household type | | |
| | | All families | Families with no earners | Families with one earner | Families with two earners | Families with three or more earners | Families with own children under 18 years | | | | | | |
							Married-couple families with children	Male householder, no spouse present, with children	Female householder, no spouse present, with children		Married-couple families, percent	Male householder or female householder families, no spouse present	Nonfamily households
16860	Chattanooga, TN-GA	$57,693	$31,557	$42,161	$75,602	$95,484	$75,304	$27,356	$22,058	531,645	89.7	80.0	81.9
16940	Cheyenne, WY	$74,871	$52,951	$49,833	$86,609	$110,854	$82,762	$59,764	$28,490	91,333	92.5	78.7	80.9
16980	Chicago-Naperville-Elgin, IL-IN-WI ...	$73,096	$30,238	$50,660	$94,588	$108,244	$92,574	$39,146	$25,701	9,431,501	89.6	78.3	83.9
17020	Chico, CA	$53,530	$33,923	$42,718	$71,852	$86,679	$66,112	$27,820	$20,788	218,749	87.2	80.8	80.7
17140	Cincinnati, OH-KY-IN	$68,152	$31,550	$47,957	$88,316	$110,812	$92,298	$37,242	$21,695	2,106,703	93.4	81.5	85.2
17300	Clarksville, TN-KY	$52,939	$23,184	$41,699	$67,470	$94,360	$61,663	$35,018	$18,278	248,744	89.6	79.8	77.9
17420	Cleveland, TN	$49,699	$28,710	$36,573	$70,665	$80,308	$60,654	$35,093	$17,137	116,519	89.4	79.0	81.2
17460	Cleveland-Elyria, OH	$63,923	$30,386	$45,069	$86,171	$103,405	$89,749	$35,898	$22,185	2,039,728	93.3	84.0	84.7
17660	Coeur d'Alene, ID	$57,243	$35,763	$40,887	$68,943	$82,464	$64,242	$36,004	$28,309	141,463	86.9	75.3	75.3
17780	College Station-Bryan, TX	$57,070	$30,311	$35,270	$76,332	$95,461	$71,595	$29,338	$22,442	229,952	84.2	75.8	86.4
17820	Colorado Springs, CO	$70,297	$42,083	$53,059	$83,413	$110,472	$80,393	$43,105	$27,773	638,087	91.4	79.2	79.4
17860	Columbia, MO	$69,964	$42,075	$47,651	$85,122	$95,583	$86,645	$30,179	$23,918	167,047	93.4	81.9	90.6
17900	Columbia, SC	$60,787	$30,361	$41,604	$81,449	$99,733	$81,663	$35,850	$24,810	755,827	89.9	80.1	81.3
17980	Columbus, GA-AL	$52,961	$25,584	$38,646	$72,865	$90,637	$67,816	$37,984	$22,001	288,308	90.6	76.5	77.9
18020	Columbus, IN	$65,958	$37,783	$45,816	$81,342	$107,061	$83,960	$31,605	$25,554	77,767	92.7	73.5	87.7
18140	Columbus, OH	$68,010	$31,445	$45,955	$88,682	$107,610	$91,938	$40,923	$24,997	1,919,571	92.6	80.4	84.3
18580	Corpus Christi, TX	$54,699	$24,996	$40,163	$76,414	$86,263	$75,413	$40,018	$21,540	430,254	83.4	72.8	76.2
18700	Corvallis, OR	$74,325	$53,091	$52,917	$89,041	$101,137	$90,649	$26,707	$23,479	86,091	93.4	82.0	88.9
18880	Crestview-Fort Walton Beach-Destin, FL	$61,931	$40,959	$46,552	$74,590	$92,210	$69,856	$31,804	$20,390	234,036	88.8	73.1	76.7
19060	Cumberland, MD-WV	$52,154	$31,571	$40,255	$72,546	$95,675	$68,205	$32,100	$23,349	96,222	91.2	82.8	85.1
19100	Dallas-Fort Worth-Arlington, TX	$68,229	$29,610	$45,796	$89,534	$101,375	$83,927	$37,178	$27,136	6,640,146	81.4	69.4	78.1
19140	Dalton, GA	$43,600	$21,307	$30,103	$59,467	$76,971	$51,237	$27,152	$21,626	141,305	78.2	70.0	77.9
19180	Danville, IL	$54,199	$34,140	$40,089	$75,603	$98,684	$72,953	$40,625	$20,408	78,707	92.8	83.2	83.1
19300	Daphne-Fairhope-Foley, AL	$62,280	$41,272	$44,748	$78,822	$101,068	$74,994	$36,537	$21,276	188,766	91.2	75.3	79.2
19340	Davenport-Moline-Rock Island, IA-IL	$65,196	$38,925	$44,043	$85,116	$103,342	$87,433	$39,500	$24,570	377,447	94.1	84.4	85.9
19380	Dayton, OH	$59,675	$33,299	$42,860	$81,297	$101,716	$80,554	$30,960	$19,365	789,697	93.1	82.9	84.9
19460	Decatur, AL	$53,397	$30,675	$37,167	$73,552	$93,502	$71,414	$53,208	$21,633	151,852	88.7	75.6	82.6
19500	Decatur, IL	$57,722	$37,869	$38,893	$84,387	$104,800	$80,780	$31,553	$16,043	107,679	94.1	83.7	84.9
19660	Deltona-Daytona Beach-Ormond Beach, FL	$50,449	$37,391	$42,286	$70,970	$90,800	$63,665	$27,451	$22,647	589,485	85.4	75.2	78.7
19740	Denver-Aurora-Lakewood, CO	$77,320	$38,938	$52,859	$96,280	$108,828	$96,183	$44,921	$30,961	2,624,457	89.0	77.2	82.4
19780	Des Moines-West Des Moines, IA	$73,564	$36,407	$46,184	$89,571	$106,166	$91,173	$40,773	$28,169	583,558	94.8	86.0	90.2
19820	Detroit-Warren-Dearborn, MI	$65,178	$33,586	$48,311	$89,477	$109,715	$90,081	$35,589	$21,356	4,263,868	92.3	81.6	83.5
20020	Dothan, AL	$51,434	$27,633	$37,921	$73,565	$81,643	$73,871	$26,630	$15,925	145,831	91.4	77.5	81.7
20100	Dover, DE	$61,970	$40,476	$44,488	$82,567	$103,686	$80,861	$42,034	$24,414	163,872	93.0	90.1	88.7
20220	Dubuque, IA	$66,923	$37,255	$43,711	$80,607	$89,520	$84,801	$43,552	$19,862	93,823	95.4	90.5	91.7
20260	Duluth, MN-WI	$61,880	$38,898	$45,131	$79,608	$91,511	$81,905	$39,828	$21,462	274,937	95.0	86.2	88.9
20500	Durham-Chapel Hill, NC	$67,065	$34,669	$45,129	$92,686	$95,748	$94,005	$30,365	$26,595	518,288	89.2	76.2	85.0
20700	East Stroudsburg, PA	$62,460	$33,471	$49,167	$82,835	$98,985	$82,542	$41,006	$26,752	167,422	88.8	83.3	82.8
20740	Eau Claire, WI	$64,660	$40,005	$42,926	$76,207	$94,396	$78,698	$34,081	$25,757	160,564	93.8	83.4	87.8
20940	El Centro, CA	$44,215	$18,951	$34,396	$62,701	$80,104	$60,867	$43,214	$17,307	165,486	80.3	77.1	79.8
21060	Elizabethtown-Fort Knox, KY	$56,266	$30,007	$43,758	$75,571	$95,132	$74,559	$40,222	$18,364	143,482	90.5	80.8	81.8
21140	Elkhart-Goshen, IN	$52,609	$26,568	$39,370	$67,009	$90,059	$62,678	$38,964	$18,589	196,980	80.5	76.4	78.2
21300	Elmira, NY	$61,633	$31,924	$41,800	$85,838	$110,369	$87,271	$32,115	$21,232	83,954	95.7	89.5	84.0
21340	El Paso, TX	$45,018	$18,369	$33,325	$62,422	$74,683	$54,150	$31,887	$20,056	802,564	74.2	67.0	75.5
21500	Erie, PA	$56,859	$30,452	$42,356	$74,342	$92,176	$73,936	$45,045	$19,267	275,506	93.8	87.9	88.0
21660	Eugene, OR	$54,993	$36,831	$42,358	$72,218	$83,695	$66,679	$28,378	$19,465	353,308	89.5	78.8	80.8
21780	Evansville, IN-KY	$60,393	$35,914	$43,993	$78,497	$100,245	$80,352	$31,005	$19,002	308,829	92.6	80.0	82.2
21820	Fairbanks, AK	$78,726	$33,903	$57,109	$91,716	$131,742	$90,161	$54,038	$30,283	93,367	91.2	73.0	77.2
22020	Fargo, ND-MN	$72,328	$39,521	$44,295	$86,132	$99,825	$89,940	$51,525	$25,068	215,975	95.4	81.8	88.4
22140	Farmington, NM	$57,854	$19,941	$42,957	$78,618	$105,848	$74,942	$40,917	$22,228	126,427	78.2	65.3	74.1
22180	Fayetteville, NC	$52,115	$23,942	$39,692	$72,165	$90,444	$65,736	$32,471	$21,884	341,669	90.3	80.5	80.1
22220	Fayetteville-Springdale-Rogers, AR-MO	$57,851	$32,791	$42,669	$72,609	$87,005	$67,973	$30,762	$21,957	479,251	86.2	73.8	82.9
22380	Flagstaff, AZ	$58,234	$30,474	$42,142	$74,245	$95,112	$80,721	$33,611	$22,074	134,902	82.4	74.3	77.0
22420	Flint, MI	$51,824	$34,668	$39,713	$77,684	$91,500	$74,414	$28,307	$16,738	415,547	93.2	85.8	85.8
22500	Florence, SC	$48,678	$22,977	$36,505	$69,426	$89,533	$75,369	$25,644	$20,104	203,668	89.8	78.2	80.0
22520	Florence-Muscle Shoals, AL	$54,340	$33,499	$44,890	$70,587	$81,293	$63,518	$39,248	$16,000	145,999	90.6	81.4	84.8
22540	Fond du Lac, WI	$64,411	$36,792	$45,961	$77,546	$95,515	$79,792	$37,113	$20,629	100,140	95.3	84.0	89.2
22660	Fort Collins, CO	$74,831	$46,083	$59,181	$88,084	$101,538	$91,089	$44,160	$29,217	308,159	91.6	80.6	84.2
22900	Fort Smith, AR-OK	$46,544	$25,745	$36,421	$63,417	$83,906	$57,857	$30,000	$16,632	277,262	83.1	72.6	77.7
23060	Fort Wayne, IN	$58,653	$32,674	$42,739	$76,994	$96,659	$74,785	$38,052	$22,862	417,291	88.9	78.1	81.3
23420	Fresno, CA	$47,786	$19,585	$35,011	$70,053	$80,484	$58,966	$26,343	$18,162	936,524	82.8	77.6	76.4
23460	Gadsden, AL	$48,635	$24,710	$37,337	$66,623	$83,583	$62,313	$43,014	$18,134	103,042	89.7	76.5	82.3
23540	Gainesville, FL	$61,169	$29,092	$46,434	$85,589	$98,319	$84,015	$43,313	$18,672	264,781	89.0	79.1	80.8
23580	Gainesville, GA	$55,868	$35,222	$37,492	$72,693	$82,500	$62,922	$27,455	$16,356	183,792	83.1	68.5	77.6
23900	Gettysburg, PA	$67,661	$38,104	$51,035	$78,843	$99,964	$79,041	$37,138	$26,383	100,262	92.5	83.5	89.0
24020	Glens Falls, NY	$62,412	$37,239	$43,458	$78,032	$93,110	$80,558	$27,192	$25,671	125,102	93.4	83.0	87.8
24140	Goldsboro, NC	$50,721	$23,351	$37,156	$67,140	$90,551	$67,334	$22,056	$17,022	119,476	88.1	80.3	79.0
24220	Grand Forks, ND-MN	$69,300	$34,264	$41,312	$81,187	$107,163	$82,689	$36,060	$26,273	97,019	95.5	85.1	89.5

Table E-3: Metropolitan Areas—Income, Poverty, and Health Insurance—*Continued*

CBSA FIPS code	Metropolitan area	Total number of families	Families with incomes below the poverty level, as a percent of all families of that family type				Families that received Food Stamps (SNAP), as a percent of all families of that family type			Families that received food stamps (SNAP) and had at least one worker	
			All families	Married-couple families	Male householder families, no spouse present	Female householder families, no spouse present	All families	Married-couple families	Male householder or female householder families, no spouse present	Married-couple families, percent	Male householder or female householder families, no spouse present, percent
16860	Chattanooga, TN-GA	140,310	11.8	8.41	29.8	41.2	16.7	8.5	39.9	7.0	29.5
16940	Cheyenne, WY	24,077	6.5	2.84	3.3	40.4	6.8	2.7	22.5	2.5	20.8
16980	Chicago-Naperville-Elgin, IL-IN-WI ...	2,259,905	11.0	7.69	22.5	39.7	14.3	7.0	33.2	6.1	24.5
17020	Chico, CA	50,510	13.8	12.04	24.5	43.0	14.0	7.7	29.2	6.5	18.1
17140	Cincinnati, OH-KY-IN	535,343	10.8	5.23	22.8	44.3	13.1	4.9	35.9	4.0	25.0
17300	Clarksville, TN-KY	70,234	14.1	7.94	23.9	53.2	16.5	8.0	40.3	7.3	30.4
17420	Cleveland, TN	30,962	14.9	15.07	11.3	54.0	19.5	11.1	43.5	9.1	32.2
17460	Cleveland-Elyria, OH	518,731	11.7	6.39	26.3	43.7	15.8	6.2	38.3	5.0	26.3
17660	Coeur d'Alene, ID	38,204	9.3	4.59	33.8	35.9	12.8	7.1	33.3	6.6	24.4
17780	College Station-Bryan, TX	47,726	15.3	12.38	27.9	43.8	16.3	8.0	37.3	7.7	30.2
17820	Colorado Springs, CO	169,677	8.4	6.23	15.2	34.2	9.9	5.1	26.6	4.7	20.9
17860	Columbia, MO	36,732	8.8	5.07	27.7	37.3	13.4	5.4	39.4	4.7	32.8
17900	Columbia, SC	191,450	12.5	6.90	21.7	40.5	16.6	7.6	36.6	6.3	26.5
17980	Columbus, GA-AL	72,446	14.7	7.82	20.4	43.1	20.6	8.5	42.4	7.4	29.9
18020	Columbus, IN	20,179	9.1	6.96	29.4	34.4	8.0	3.1	23.7	2.2	16.9
18140	Columbus, OH	471,158	10.7	6.82	20.6	39.5	15.3	7.4	37.1	6.1	26.7
18580	Corpus Christi, TX	109,315	14.0	9.64	20.4	44.1	18.8	10.4	35.5	8.7	27.2
18700	Corvallis, OR	18,757	9.8	7.80	10.1	44.4	14.7	7.8	45.1	7.2	29.0
18880	Crestview-Fort Walton Beach-Destin, FL	64,420	11.8	7.93	31.3	45.7	13.1	6.4	33.2	5.9	23.2
19060	Cumberland, MD-WV	22,457	10.7	9.12	31.6	38.7	17.1	9.7	38.3	7.8	29.6
19100	Dallas-Fort Worth-Arlington, TX	1,634,940	11.7	9.57	20.7	36.6	13.1	7.1	29.2	6.4	23.1
19140	Dalton, GA	35,886	16.6	13.59	34.5	43.5	17.4	11.2	34.7	9.0	23.4
19180	Danville, IL	20,457	14.2	7.56	24.3	51.1	17.2	8.0	39.8	6.5	27.9
19300	Daphne-Fairhope-Foley, AL	51,611	9.6	7.36	34.0	41.5	10.2	4.4	32.0	3.6	23.2
19340	Davenport-Moline-Rock Island, IA-IL	98,026	9.4	5.72	13.6	41.2	11.9	5.2	33.0	4.6	25.5
19380	Dayton, OH	202,766	12.8	7.94	27.5	47.7	15.7	6.2	38.5	4.9	27.4
19460	Decatur, AL	41,092	13.2	10.92	14.9	48.7	14.9	8.2	34.3	7.1	25.3
19500	Decatur, IL	27,857	14.0	8.22	14.2	57.3	16.0	6.6	40.5	5.7	29.9
19660	Deltona-Daytona Beach-Ormond Beach, FL	144,353	11.9	11.98	31.6	43.1	15.7	9.3	36.7	7.7	24.6
19740	Denver-Aurora-Lakewood, CO	637,875	8.8	7.19	16.0	32.2	9.2	4.7	23.1	4.2	17.9
19780	Des Moines-West Des Moines, IA	152,801	8.3	5.49	20.9	33.0	13.5	6.3	37.4	5.3	30.2
19820	Detroit-Warren-Dearborn, MI	1,075,383	13.2	9.01	27.4	45.4	19.1	9.0	42.7	7.3	29.8
20020	Dothan, AL	38,600	14.9	8.01	36.8	56.2	16.7	6.7	41.7	5.4	28.4
20100	Dover, DE	41,345	9.3	7.06	6.0	31.9	18.4	9.1	41.3	8.2	34.2
20220	Dubuque, IA	23,929	8.0	3.18	8.5	49.4	9.6	3.4	34.1	3.2	27.8
20260	Duluth, MN-WI	69,325	9.9	5.02	22.9	44.1	11.1	4.6	31.6	4.2	24.2
20500	Durham-Chapel Hill, NC	125,830	11.6	8.08	30.0	37.1	13.2	4.9	34.1	4.5	25.0
20700	East Stroudsburg, PA	43,153	9.3	5.87	15.6	34.7	13.6	8.7	27.6	7.6	22.1
20740	Eau Claire, WI	40,089	7.2	5.48	18.7	29.4	11.0	6.2	31.1	5.2	27.2
20940	El Centro, CA	36,695	21.6	17.62	25.7	52.5	22.0	14.2	37.4	13.0	27.4
21060	Elizabethtown-Fort Knox, KY	39,930	12.9	7.45	17.5	52.0	16.3	8.2	38.2	7.6	26.7
21140	Elkhart-Goshen, IN	51,212	13.9	10.39	22.6	48.6	16.4	8.0	38.9	7.1	27.3
21300	Elmira, NY	22,180	12.3	7.69	19.3	49.6	14.2	6.6	35.5	4.5	21.0
21340	El Paso, TX	195,316	20.4	18.25	26.1	48.8	26.4	18.4	42.3	16.0	32.3
21500	Erie, PA	69,824	12.4	8.15	20.6	50.6	18.3	8.6	43.8	7.1	31.4
21660	Eugene, OR	85,586	13.1	9.59	35.1	49.0	23.8	13.1	54.2	11.4	41.5
21780	Evansville, IN-KY	81,330	11.2	5.79	29.8	47.4	12.7	5.9	33.2	4.6	24.3
21820	Fairbanks, AK	22,302	5.8	1.19	18.3	29.2	7.1	2.5	23.4	1.7	18.0
22020	Fargo, ND-MN	51,297	7.6	4.51	16.5	37.8	10.2	5.3	27.1	5.0	23.0
22140	Farmington, NM	28,966	15.7	11.16	25.6	43.8	14.7	8.1	28.8	7.0	18.0
22180	Fayetteville, NC	93,567	14.8	7.22	29.4	42.8	18.9	8.5	39.4	7.5	28.6
22220	Fayetteville-Springdale-Rogers, AR-MO	122,320	11.8	10.57	23.1	45.3	11.5	6.9	28.8	6.2	22.0
22380	Flagstaff, AZ	29,944	17.2	14.22	37.8	47.9	17.5	8.4	38.7	6.9	31.5
22420	Flint, MI	106,369	16.8	9.53	38.1	52.7	24.2	10.4	51.4	8.1	33.0
22500	Florence, SC	53,622	17.8	9.66	31.5	47.4	23.9	10.6	47.1	8.8	33.1
22520	Florence-Muscle Shoals, AL	40,203	13.3	11.51	14.7	52.0	14.8	8.6	34.3	7.0	20.8
22540	Fond du Lac, WI	27,535	6.6	2.32	12.7	44.9	9.4	4.3	28.0	4.1	24.2
22660	Fort Collins, CO	76,880	6.7	5.22	14.8	33.7	7.4	4.5	19.4	4.3	15.3
22900	Fort Smith, AR-OK	73,566	17.0	15.61	32.2	53.9	18.6	10.8	40.8	8.0	28.7
23060	Fort Wayne, IN	106,870	12.1	8.61	24.3	42.1	13.4	5.6	34.7	4.9	23.8
23420	Fresno, CA	212,657	22.4	20.38	37.3	53.4	24.0	14.8	40.2	13.3	27.6
23460	Gadsden, AL	27,861	16.0	12.69	14.9	50.6	18.0	9.4	38.6	6.6	25.9
23540	Gainesville, FL	54,250	13.6	8.15	19.3	48.4	13.8	6.1	33.2	4.8	19.6
23580	Gainesville, GA	44,172	15.8	14.83	38.0	51.7	16.3	9.8	35.5	8.5	24.1
23900	Gettysburg, PA	27,315	6.1	5.48	19.5	30.7	8.0	4.2	23.5	3.6	18.5
24020	Glens Falls, NY	34,123	9.5	6.81	23.5	38.6	12.4	5.4	33.1	4.2	27.1
24140	Goldsboro, NC	31,903	17.7	12.93	45.1	51.2	21.8	9.8	44.9	7.4	31.4
24220	Grand Forks, ND-MN	23,226	8.0	5.22	22.9	33.5	10.3	6.1	27.1	5.1	21.8

| CBSA FIPS code | Metropolitan area | Median family income in the past 12 months (in 2,013 inflation-adjusted dollars) | | | | | | | | Total population in households | Persons who had health insurance, as a percent of all persons in that household type | | |
		All families	Families with no earners	Families with one earner	Families with two earners	Families with three or more earners	Married-couple families with children	Male householder, no spouse present, with children	Female householder, no spouse present, with children		Married-couple families, percent	Male householder or female householder families, no spouse present	Nonfamily households
							Families with own children under 18 years						
24260	Grand Island, NE	$56,459	$34,315	$35,314	$68,927	$87,791	$67,860	$32,614	$19,591	82,383	91.1	74.5	78.6
24300	Grand Junction, CO	$56,869	$29,556	$40,476	$77,845	$103,966	$72,259	$32,457	$19,147	146,338	87.0	79.0	82.1
24340	Grand Rapids-Wyoming, MI	$63,715	$33,592	$45,021	$77,191	$95,393	$78,787	$32,324	$21,981	997,832	93.8	82.5	85.1
24420	Grants Pass, OR	$45,051	$36,707	$34,850	$69,275	$85,196	$58,657	$18,221	$18,280	82,238	86.9	79.1	81.6
24500	Great Falls, MT	$56,846	$39,663	$41,880	$67,978	$82,931	$66,308	$37,969	$18,750	78,033	88.8	75.5	80.6
24540	Greeley, CO	$65,676	$31,029	$44,141	$84,186	$101,632	$76,647	$40,161	$23,809	260,749	87.3	77.5	82.0
24580	Green Bay, WI	$66,460	$36,641	$41,938	$81,954	$96,776	$84,860	$38,500	$24,957	307,049	94.7	85.3	85.5
24660	Greensboro-High Point, NC	$53,944	$26,828	$39,538	$74,218	$91,889	$72,036	$30,630	$22,121	730,020	87.9	76.1	80.0
24780	Greenville, NC	$55,873	$27,036	$33,617	$81,220	$100,207	$88,111	$32,181	$20,635	171,250	89.4	77.1	85.4
24860	Greenville-Anderson-Mauldin, SC	$55,908	$27,677	$41,220	$77,111	$91,773	$74,915	$33,349	$19,057	834,507	88.2	75.9	81.2
25060	Gulfport-Biloxi-Pascagoula, MS	$52,393	$29,709	$40,162	$68,900	$100,129	$63,147	$37,144	$20,338	370,056	85.3	71.0	75.2
25180	Hagerstown-Martinsburg, MD-WV	$63,597	$32,418	$47,772	$80,823	$99,733	$79,697	$45,336	$24,836	247,141	92.3	83.3	83.2
25220	Hammond, LA	$50,443	$17,105	$36,996	$73,489	$102,163	$72,699	$30,556	$15,051	123,162	85.7	77.8	75.5
25260	Hanford-Corcoran, CA	$48,585	$18,545	$37,428	$72,654	$81,175	$57,011	$30,811	$20,128	130,140	84.4	77.7	74.2
25420	Harrisburg-Carlisle, PA	$70,790	$40,727	$49,154	$84,837	$112,018	$86,764	$41,947	$25,927	544,526	93.5	84.8	88.7
25500	Harrisonburg, VA	$57,932	$33,085	$44,467	$66,660	$86,591	$64,950	$36,481	$25,605	127,092	86.9	77.4	89.7
25540	Hartford-West Hartford-East Hartford, CT	$85,357	$36,346	$57,948	$107,793	$127,063	$111,464	$52,479	$30,968	1,194,097	94.9	87.6	89.4
25620	Hattiesburg, MS	$50,995	$26,574	$38,155	$68,674	$90,565	$70,063	$29,107	$22,026	144,835	85.5	78.3	79.5
25860	Hickory-Lenoir-Morganton, NC	$49,881	$25,900	$38,210	$66,406	$81,671	$62,731	$28,940	$19,040	358,107	88.1	77.2	80.1
25940	Hilton Head Island-Bluffton-Beaufort, SC	$60,489	$55,797	$45,240	$73,000	$79,101	$56,810	$42,193	$26,538	185,734	85.7	71.2	80.6
25980	Hinesville, GA	$47,093	$20,673	$36,998	$61,964	$91,164	$53,052	$36,841	$18,516	73,795	90.7	75.6	75.4
26140	Homosassa Springs, FL	$48,882	$39,242	$46,756	$66,100	$87,438	$65,991	$26,908	$19,722	137,567	89.5	77.3	80.2
26300	Hot Springs, AR	$48,605	$30,864	$33,917	$67,431	$100,833	$59,762	$16,045	$18,642	95,523	86.3	72.4	75.8
26380	Houma-Thibodaux, LA	$58,639	$25,531	$45,711	$84,151	$100,420	$86,848	$46,110	$22,976	206,943	87.2	75.3	79.4
26420	Houston-The Woodlands-Sugar Land, TX	$66,432	$26,314	$45,773	$88,596	$98,525	$82,250	$39,778	$24,859	6,131,606	80.0	68.7	75.2
26580	Huntington-Ashland, WV-KY-OH	$54,267	$28,625	$46,593	$77,749	$98,306	$77,345	$34,825	$15,974	359,562	90.2	79.0	81.4
26620	Huntsville, AL	$70,620	$43,095	$52,224	$90,030	$107,182	$90,420	$36,808	$24,532	422,027	91.8	76.9	84.1
26820	Idaho Falls, ID	$56,501	$36,517	$48,436	$65,444	$92,123	$67,865	$45,114	$20,644	135,152	88.4	73.9	77.5
26900	Indianapolis-Carmel-Anderson, IN	$64,393	$32,863	$42,718	$84,181	$104,099	$86,511	$35,251	$24,326	1,903,266	91.1	78.5	81.3
26980	Iowa City, IA	$79,544	$40,455	$51,053	$90,657	$107,217	$93,863	$51,961	$26,033	156,211	93.9	86.3	92.0
27060	Ithaca, NY	$72,719	$40,487	$48,363	$90,669	$115,000	$88,857	$41,208	$24,375	101,836	93.4	87.5	94.0
27100	Jackson, MI	$55,658	$32,489	$42,402	$76,167	$89,651	$72,395	$35,574	$14,797	152,544	92.2	81.3	84.7
27140	Jackson, MS	$55,106	$21,398	$38,125	$78,737	$95,081	$80,788	$34,809	$21,650	561,772	89.9	77.8	80.1
27180	Jackson, TN	$53,529	$27,866	$37,982	$74,127	$94,638	$71,448	$31,590	$17,339	128,790	88.7	82.8	81.5
27260	Jacksonville, FL	$62,156	$32,076	$46,648	$81,825	$104,802	$78,556	$37,862	$25,138	1,353,370	88.6	77.9	79.0
27340	Jacksonville, NC	$49,698	$30,745	$41,710	$59,243	$106,025	$52,364	$41,417	$26,860	151,756	89.3	79.2	78.0
27500	Janesville-Beloit, WI	$58,244	$35,482	$40,852	$75,840	$93,803	$73,724	$34,773	$19,617	158,962	93.5	83.6	84.2
27620	Jefferson City, MO	$60,773	$39,098	$42,998	$73,298	$99,917	$70,973	$41,883	$26,517	142,710	91.8	82.3	87.2
27740	Johnson City, TN	$48,689	$29,214	$38,640	$66,947	$84,325	$63,179	$26,312	$15,589	197,227	90.7	74.4	83.7
27780	Johnstown, PA	$53,875	$31,306	$42,246	$72,314	$93,358	$71,019	$31,988	$20,916	136,672	94.3	88.4	90.0
27860	Jonesboro, AR	$49,143	$27,255	$36,949	$69,707	$84,971	$66,240	$32,304	$15,670	122,904	85.6	77.7	78.3
27900	Joplin, MO	$49,379	$29,256	$38,999	$66,267	$85,206	$59,091	$30,666	$21,293	173,644	85.0	77.7	81.3
27980	Kahului-Wailuku-Lahaina, HI	$75,856	$40,776	$49,032	$83,574	$114,393	$83,543	$40,972	$29,590	156,867	92.9	89.5	84.6
28020	Kalamazoo-Portage, MI	$59,136	$33,240	$44,565	$79,396	$92,114	$81,674	$31,904	$19,343	327,952	92.3	82.4	84.7
28100	Kankakee, IL	$59,623	$29,733	$44,007	$82,138	$99,711	$80,101	$43,039	$19,571	110,590	92.6	82.8	84.7
28140	Kansas City, MO-KS	$70,394	$35,538	$47,260	$88,438	$108,835	$90,965	$39,966	$25,604	2,013,950	91.5	77.6	82.8
28420	Kennewick-Richland, WA	$66,439	$37,390	$47,514	$87,516	$99,633	$75,269	$44,138	$20,534	263,868	87.0	73.0	79.8
28660	Killeen-Temple, TX	$57,523	$35,630	$42,711	$78,322	$100,229	$62,175	$37,575	$27,975	379,393	88.4	76.9	79.7
28700	Kingsport-Bristol-Bristol, TN-VA	$50,198	$28,283	$39,874	$68,966	$86,537	$67,521	$30,103	$16,503	305,309	90.8	79.6	83.3
28740	Kingston, NY	$72,369	$34,840	$53,028	$93,414	$108,490	$95,742	$37,569	$28,182	177,420	93.8	85.7	79.1
28940	Knoxville, TN	$57,399	$29,546	$42,574	$76,321	$89,659	$72,955	$32,381	$19,679	837,289	90.8	81.1	85.3
29020	Kokomo, IN	$57,053	$38,750	$39,579	$79,814	$98,627	$77,584	$31,400	$20,923	81,935	92.3	80.0	78.7
29100	La Crosse-Onalaska, WI-MN	$66,730	$33,680	$45,305	$79,242	$97,086	$82,526	$37,022	$26,583	133,513	96.3	88.0	87.6
29180	Lafayette, LA	$58,353	$21,579	$39,672	$83,750	$105,010	$86,223	$46,491	$20,445	469,730	88.1	77.6	78.3
29200	Lafayette-West Lafayette, IN	$61,437	$36,674	$43,016	$76,772	$90,920	$76,192	$34,957	$20,767	204,795	90.8	78.5	86.1
29340	Lake Charles, LA	$55,837	$28,575	$39,589	$82,390	$111,204	$81,190	$37,156	$22,894	199,327	87.9	75.5	76.1
29420	Lake Havasu City-Kingman, AZ	$45,306	$35,751	$39,917	$65,128	$76,747	$54,525	$22,217	$21,032	194,408	84.5	77.4	81.1
29460	Lakeland-Winter Haven, FL	$49,890	$33,797	$38,696	$70,402	$82,067	$61,762	$30,255	$22,987	605,950	84.7	73.5	81.4
29540	Lancaster, PA	$67,504	$35,748	$50,020	$80,148	$103,810	$80,147	$40,380	$24,725	519,113	85.9	84.4	89.5
29620	Lansing-East Lansing, MI	$63,700	$43,183	$46,007	$84,415	$98,403	$83,583	$33,611	$21,811	463,366	93.9	85.2	88.6
29700	Laredo, TX	$40,321	$10,214	$31,072	$58,061	$68,036	$49,791	$23,818	$16,662	256,570	65.3	64.6	66.1
29740	Las Cruces, NM	$43,350	$25,691	$31,040	$57,081	$71,231	$49,310	$27,788	$16,716	209,951	81.4	73.0	79.1
29820	Las Vegas-Henderson-Paradise, NV	$57,824	$32,234	$42,344	$74,812	$95,570	$67,918	$36,283	$29,266	1,974,661	82.2	70.3	76.0
29940	Lawrence, KS	$70,291	$42,786	$49,984	$82,393	$111,568	$92,152	$36,743	$33,171	112,525	92.2	79.2	86.5
30020	Lawton, OK	$55,616	$30,551	$38,445	$72,348	$108,972	$66,246	$32,787	$21,489	118,192	89.5	75.2	75.9
30140	Lebanon, PA	$64,581	$35,554	$47,548	$76,978	$98,323	$77,257	$50,496	$24,043	133,525	89.9	83.6	87.7
30300	Lewiston, ID-WA	$57,656	$36,836	$40,201	$69,566	$91,023	$66,628	$36,573	$22,373	60,700	88.7	81.1	80.9
30340	Lewiston-Auburn, ME	$57,432	$25,199	$38,772	$75,733	$95,817	$77,375	$26,643	$19,013	106,613	93.8	88.2	84.1

Table E-3: Metropolitan Areas—Income, Poverty, and Health Insurance—*Continued*

CBSA FIPS code	Metropolitan area	Total number of families	Families with incomes below the poverty level, as a percent of all families of that family type				Families that received Food Stamps (SNAP), as a percent of all families of that family type			Families that received food stamps (SNAP) and had at least one worker	
			All families	Married-couple families	Male householder families, no spouse present	Female householder families, no spouse present	All families	Married-couple families	Male householder or female householder families, no spouse present	Married-couple families, percent	Male householder or female householder families, no spouse present, percent
24260	Grand Island, NE	21,309	11.2	8.76	21.0	47.4	12.5	5.4	38.2	4.4	32.6
24300	Grand Junction, CO	39,484	11.5	6.29	29.7	45.8	11.4	5.2	30.3	4.4	20.6
24340	Grand Rapids-Wyoming, MI	255,534	9.4	6.41	27.7	42.2	14.6	6.9	42.1	5.9	32.2
24420	Grants Pass, OR	22,048	14.7	15.04	53.4	39.2	22.4	14.5	49.0	11.9	36.0
24500	Great Falls, MT	21,114	12.7	11.98	25.2	49.9	12.6	5.9	33.7	5.2	27.2
24540	Greeley, CO	66,341	10.0	7.31	23.4	43.1	10.4	6.2	25.6	5.7	17.9
24580	Green Bay, WI	80,715	8.1	4.80	19.0	39.4	11.1	5.4	32.7	5.0	25.7
24660	Greensboro-High Point, NC	189,791	14.3	10.04	29.3	43.5	16.0	7.4	35.9	6.0	25.1
24780	Greenville, NC	39,835	15.5	7.55	27.5	48.6	21.5	8.1	47.1	6.9	34.0
24860	Greenville-Anderson-Mauldin, SC	217,007	12.9	8.48	21.0	49.1	14.8	6.8	37.5	5.4	26.2
25060	Gulfport-Biloxi-Pascagoula, MS	95,697	15.4	11.74	16.8	46.2	19.5	10.9	37.4	9.5	27.7
25180	Hagerstown-Martinsburg, MD-WV	66,494	9.7	7.19	17.8	37.7	13.3	6.6	31.5	5.6	23.7
25220	Hammond, LA	30,402	19.5	6.55	38.9	57.2	23.6	9.9	50.7	8.5	30.4
25260	Hanford-Corcoran, CA	32,007	17.6	14.51	26.4	46.1	19.0	10.8	34.5	9.8	22.6
25420	Harrisburg-Carlisle, PA	143,814	7.8	5.11	20.5	35.4	9.9	4.0	28.6	3.4	22.5
25500	Harrisonburg, VA	28,887	8.9	9.42	13.8	36.1	10.2	6.1	23.7	5.2	19.8
25540	Hartford-West Hartford-East Hartford, CT	305,188	7.9	3.86	14.9	31.8	12.2	4.4	33.0	3.5	23.4
25620	Hattiesburg, MS	35,831	17.2	9.44	46.7	45.5	20.1	8.7	44.2	8.0	33.8
25860	Hickory-Lenoir-Morganton, NC	92,496	13.3	11.03	32.5	49.3	17.6	10.2	39.6	8.3	26.2
25940	Hilton Head Island-Bluffton-Beaufort, SC	49,974	10.0	13.02	19.0	33.2	11.9	5.1	34.9	4.3	29.5
25980	Hinesville, GA	21,051	15.5	9.96	15.9	48.7	16.4	7.8	37.2	6.7	30.0
26140	Homosassa Springs, FL	38,478	10.8	8.98	43.9	45.4	14.5	7.0	45.4	5.6	28.5
26300	Hot Springs, AR	25,331	16.2	15.09	58.5	46.6	15.4	6.6	38.3	5.3	26.5
26380	Houma-Thibodaux, LA	52,796	12.0	7.36	28.1	40.0	16.9	8.4	37.5	6.6	29.4
26420	Houston-The Woodlands-Sugar Land, TX	1,480,292	13.5	11.22	21.5	41.2	14.5	8.2	30.4	7.4	24.0
26580	Huntington-Ashland, WV-KY-OH	95,599	13.7	10.14	23.7	52.5	16.3	8.8	38.1	6.1	23.3
26620	Huntsville, AL	111,622	10.2	6.92	23.3	39.1	12.9	5.9	32.9	5.3	26.4
26820	Idaho Falls, ID	33,903	10.0	8.53	6.4	43.8	15.4	9.6	37.7	9.3	32.2
26900	Indianapolis-Carmel-Anderson, IN	479,793	11.0	5.89	28.5	39.8	13.6	6.0	34.0	5.3	25.5
26980	Iowa City, IA	36,280	6.5	4.04	8.8	33.2	10.6	5.6	29.9	5.2	25.0
27060	Ithaca, NY	20,394	8.9	6.00	28.8	42.0	10.2	4.5	33.2	3.9	23.1
27100	Jackson, MI	40,054	13.9	11.10	28.3	53.9	20.3	11.1	44.8	8.9	29.8
27140	Jackson, MS	140,993	15.8	8.67	25.1	45.5	18.3	7.6	36.9	6.6	25.7
27180	Jackson, TN	31,604	14.9	5.99	27.2	55.0	20.1	9.4	45.9	8.2	30.4
27260	Jacksonville, FL	334,591	11.4	6.54	24.5	40.0	15.0	7.2	34.7	5.9	23.9
27340	Jacksonville, NC	43,700	12.1	8.75	17.0	41.6	10.0	5.8	23.7	5.1	19.9
27500	Janesville-Beloit, WI	42,332	11.5	6.92	23.4	45.5	20.0	10.4	45.6	9.1	32.7
27620	Jefferson City, MO	37,288	9.2	5.04	20.1	35.3	11.6	5.3	33.5	4.4	26.0
27740	Johnson City, TN	53,823	14.8	12.91	35.1	53.6	17.3	10.3	39.6	8.0	27.4
27780	Johnstown, PA	36,723	10.0	7.83	31.0	44.8	14.6	6.4	39.0	4.8	26.1
27860	Jonesboro, AR	32,148	15.9	11.66	25.1	54.1	18.4	8.4	40.9	6.6	29.3
27900	Joplin, MO	45,413	12.2	10.63	23.7	40.3	16.1	9.9	35.7	8.5	25.7
27980	Kahului-Wailuku-Lahaina, HI	35,932	7.4	5.29	17.4	24.5	15.0	7.6	36.4	6.8	31.3
28020	Kalamazoo-Portage, MI	79,604	12.6	9.11	23.2	47.8	17.9	8.6	44.1	7.0	33.2
28100	Kankakee, IL	27,997	13.2	9.37	14.0	48.4	19.2	9.3	41.6	8.5	30.3
28140	Kansas City, MO-KS	516,669	9.3	5.54	17.7	37.4	11.4	4.6	30.5	4.1	22.3
28420	Kennewick-Richland, WA	64,230	12.2	9.46	19.9	47.4	19.9	12.1	43.2	10.9	36.5
28660	Killeen-Temple, TX	95,967	11.4	8.40	33.4	36.9	12.3	7.0	27.3	6.3	21.0
28700	Kingsport-Bristol-Bristol, TN-VA	86,586	12.9	9.85	30.8	50.4	16.9	9.3	41.1	6.9	27.9
28740	Kingston, NY	43,813	7.3	4.96	26.5	27.4	11.0	5.2	27.0	3.8	20.1
28940	Knoxville, TN	219,693	12.1	11.07	21.5	48.8	16.2	9.4	39.8	6.9	26.4
29020	Kokomo, IN	22,421	12.3	11.00	38.0	44.6	15.5	6.6	42.3	6.1	29.4
29100	La Crosse-Onalaska, WI-MN	33,344	7.8	4.86	29.7	37.3	10.4	4.3	33.1	3.7	24.7
29180	Lafayette, LA	118,035	14.0	4.03	21.4	46.5	16.3	7.0	36.6	5.6	28.5
29200	Lafayette-West Lafayette, IN	46,424	11.1	7.95	22.0	48.7	12.9	6.0	35.3	5.6	27.2
29340	Lake Charles, LA	52,424	12.7	5.72	17.6	44.0	16.0	7.3	34.8	6.7	27.7
29420	Lake Havasu City-Kingman, AZ	50,304	14.8	19.12	42.0	44.7	20.1	12.2	46.6	10.0	31.8
29460	Lakeland-Winter Haven, FL	150,257	14.0	12.39	28.4	42.4	17.9	10.2	38.1	8.7	26.5
29540	Lancaster, PA	136,311	7.8	5.73	16.5	39.8	9.3	4.6	29.9	4.0	21.1
29620	Lansing-East Lansing, MI	109,057	11.6	8.74	26.2	41.7	17.1	8.8	40.7	7.7	32.4
29700	Laredo, TX	56,095	28.3	24.63	48.2	57.2	34.6	26.3	50.3	22.3	36.1
29740	Las Cruces, NM	51,559	23.2	22.19	31.5	56.1	21.7	12.5	41.6	10.5	33.1
29820	Las Vegas-Henderson-Paradise, NV	456,983	12.5	11.64	21.9	32.9	14.0	8.6	25.5	7.6	18.5
29940	Lawrence, KS	23,749	8.4	6.39	21.2	35.1	8.4	4.5	20.7	4.0	16.9
30020	Lawton, OK	30,109	14.3	9.23	21.7	42.5	17.1	8.1	38.9	7.5	33.0
30140	Lebanon, PA	35,976	8.2	4.96	12.6	43.1	11.3	4.8	33.2	4.4	26.7
30300	Lewiston, ID-WA	16,402	8.4	7.86	16.7	32.0	13.6	8.0	33.5	7.2	25.2
30340	Lewiston-Auburn, ME	27,533	12.7	8.43	22.4	50.5	21.0	10.3	51.1	8.1	37.6

| CBSA FIPS code | Metropolitan area | Median family income in the past 12 months (in 2,013 inflation-adjusted dollars) | | | | | | | | Total population in households | Persons who had health insurance, as a percent of all persons in that household type | | |
		All families	Families with no earners	Families with one earner	Families with two earners	Families with three or more earners	Married-couple families with children	Male householder, no spouse present, with children	Female householder, no spouse present, with children		Married-couple families, percent	Male householder or female householder families, no spouse present	Nonfamily households
30460	Lexington-Fayette, KY	$65,762	$30,563	$45,008	$83,748	$103,191	$87,434	$31,494	$20,407	477,332	91.4	79.2	83.4
30620	Lima, OH	$54,519	$32,072	$37,528	$69,592	$84,456	$70,356	$36,328	$19,409	102,849	92.8	83.6	81.6
30700	Lincoln, NE	$68,007	$40,470	$42,009	$80,504	$109,232	$85,792	$34,599	$23,917	305,579	92.7	82.3	85.6
30780	Little Rock-North Little Rock-Conway, AR	$60,471	$31,409	$43,971	$79,753	$100,401	$77,851	$38,380	$24,085	707,907	90.0	79.7	80.6
30860	Logan, UT-ID	$56,551	$39,030	$46,565	$58,019	$84,258	$59,408	$35,931	$23,556	127,807	88.4	78.6	87.2
30980	Longview, TX	$55,243	$30,237	$40,858	$76,454	$89,322	$74,678	$31,686	$19,126	209,699	81.6	72.1	78.0
31020	Longview, WA	$56,716	$36,910	$44,292	$78,367	$96,869	$68,643	$42,650	$20,571	101,080	89.4	79.7	85.3
31080	Los Angeles-Long Beach-Anaheim, CA	$65,415	$24,326	$45,643	$87,673	$97,600	$79,855	$36,473	$26,625	12,948,427	82.1	72.7	80.0
31140	Louisville/Jefferson County, KY-IN	$63,357	$32,763	$44,808	$81,998	$101,664	$85,199	$41,531	$23,182	1,234,951	92.1	79.5	82.3
31180	Lubbock, TX	$56,511	$30,990	$36,203	$72,091	$95,567	$75,382	$30,320	$22,421	295,047	84.5	72.6	80.5
31340	Lynchburg, VA	$58,906	$33,510	$42,713	$76,912	$93,614	$74,069	$37,483	$20,787	252,288	90.6	82.0	86.1
31420	Macon, GA	$50,550	$23,529	$36,425	$75,172	$87,083	$72,318	$20,000	$17,534	226,598	88.6	73.5	79.0
31460	Madera, CA	$47,178	$26,815	$38,330	$67,337	$79,931	$49,217	$21,118	$18,944	143,593	81.1	76.3	71.4
31540	Madison, WI	$78,952	$44,604	$51,754	$91,886	$109,760	$97,574	$40,847	$26,849	614,766	96.1	88.0	88.9
31700	Manchester-Nashua, NH	$84,577	$34,500	$58,924	$100,378	$119,261	$108,186	$43,978	$28,133	399,048	93.8	82.5	84.5
31740	Manhattan, KS	$63,379	$38,782	$44,666	$80,072	$96,486	$70,417	$35,359	$30,382	90,228	94.6	90.4	88.7
31860	Mankato-North Mankato, MN	$70,061	$36,644	$43,637	$78,585	$105,202	$80,616	$40,438	$21,195	97,269	95.7	88.0	91.1
31900	Mansfield, OH	$51,725	$27,173	$41,424	$72,113	$88,071	$61,023	$40,464	$17,749	116,031	89.6	83.0	84.7
32580	McAllen-Edinburg-Mission, TX	$36,510	$16,184	$24,151	$54,418	$67,514	$43,507	$24,750	$16,057	798,386	63.8	60.8	70.4
32780	Medford, OR	$52,047	$36,624	$40,577	$67,579	$83,016	$65,030	$24,371	$23,054	205,620	85.8	72.6	78.4
32820	Memphis, TN-MS-AR	$56,881	$22,641	$38,646	$79,676	$97,900	$83,484	$32,056	$21,831	1,321,778	89.0	79.9	79.4
32900	Merced, CA	$45,484	$19,790	$33,679	$63,938	$81,952	$52,402	$32,268	$18,274	258,521	82.1	79.1	76.3
33100	Miami-Fort Lauderdale-West Palm Beach, FL	$55,493	$26,388	$40,252	$75,394	$90,679	$73,130	$35,204	$26,134	5,709,370	78.9	67.3	75.1
33140	Michigan City-La Porte, IN	$58,280	$31,620	$40,269	$78,443	$87,763	$73,833	$30,909	$15,719	102,289	90.8	81.4	79.5
33220	Midland, MI	$66,599	$40,315	$52,728	$87,236	$92,604	$82,698	$40,145	$23,528	83,342	94.0	84.6	82.5
33260	Midland, MI	$75,546	$31,044	$54,799	$86,102	$98,231	$88,679	$47,917	$28,346	149,467	79.7	68.7	81.4
33340	Milwaukee-Waukesha-West Allis, WI	$69,812	$31,537	$43,253	$91,421	$106,062	$94,732	$32,890	$22,061	1,552,305	94.3	85.1	86.2
33460	Minneapolis-St. Paul-Bloomington, MN-WI	$82,664	$39,707	$54,169	$98,908	$114,586	$104,371	$43,396	$30,287	3,394,832	94.7	84.7	89.3
33540	Missoula, MT	$62,649	$41,009	$42,401	$72,832	$93,444	$75,431	$31,307	$23,019	110,415	87.6	73.5	78.4
33660	Mobile, AL	$51,779	$24,256	$37,251	$73,772	$100,285	$72,212	$33,053	$17,823	405,816	88.3	78.1	82.3
33700	Modesto, CA	$53,082	$26,310	$40,616	$72,966	$92,384	$62,993	$32,768	$19,784	518,291	84.4	78.6	75.6
33740	Monroe, LA	$49,026	$19,200	$32,227	$74,204	$96,447	$76,461	$40,424	$13,381	171,047	85.8	69.1	71.8
33780	Monroe, MI	$65,167	$35,463	$50,674	$82,513	$107,434	$78,565	$43,073	$21,185	150,069	95.3	83.4	85.5
33860	Montgomery, AL	$58,433	$27,819	$39,447	$80,649	$96,757	$78,896	$36,831	$20,052	363,872	91.8	80.1	84.1
34060	Morgantown, WV	$62,485	$32,554	$50,318	$79,655	$103,989	$78,638	$50,553	$21,142	130,704	89.8	81.8	84.9
34100	Morristown, TN	$48,587	$26,563	$36,856	$63,400	$80,884	$60,101	$23,209	$15,300	113,544	86.8	74.6	85.2
34580	Mount Vernon-Anacortes, WA	$62,465	$37,667	$46,481	$84,100	$96,096	$74,236	$37,276	$26,827	116,981	87.9	75.5	79.0
34620	Muncie, IN	$49,735	$30,273	$39,682	$70,042	$83,481	$71,082	$42,667	$18,924	116,041	91.4	77.3	84.5
34740	Muskegon, MI	$49,800	$28,351	$37,265	$71,741	$90,208	$66,471	$28,092	$15,695	165,417	92.5	87.6	83.8
34820	Myrtle Beach-Conway-North Myrtle Beach, SC-NC	$51,012	$39,136	$40,059	$66,747	$80,726	$60,669	$25,669	$17,528	392,687	84.0	70.0	75.5
34900	Napa, CA	$76,894	$46,681	$55,660	$97,080	$96,511	$82,938	$40,740	$34,206	137,107	88.7	77.8	82.1
34940	Naples-Immokalee-Marco Island, FL	$63,442	$60,610	$50,654	$75,723	$74,623	$63,004	$35,737	$27,103	331,446	82.6	66.4	76.1
34980	Nashville-Davidson–Murfreesboro–Franklin, TN	$64,117	$31,791	$46,115	$80,962	$98,041	$81,451	$40,267	$23,332	1,708,436	90.3	80.5	81.0
35100	New Bern, NC	$56,395	$42,708	$42,062	$70,280	$107,770	$61,855	$33,994	$14,364	119,355	88.5	72.4	83.5
35300	New Haven-Milford, CT	$77,436	$29,651	$52,403	$102,362	$127,582	$100,514	$51,508	$25,924	852,445	93.7	87.0	88.7
35380	New Orleans-Metairie, LA	$58,571	$23,982	$40,061	$85,541	$102,418	$87,323	$37,423	$20,351	1,213,858	88.8	78.0	77.8
35620	New York-Newark-Jersey City, NY-NJ-PA	$78,531	$27,336	$53,714	$106,553	$124,228	$104,700	$41,474	$28,483	19,653,808	90.5	81.0	85.6
35660	Niles-Benton Harbor, MI	$56,056	$32,336	$41,085	$76,208	$92,766	$73,782	$38,967	$19,957	154,578	91.2	81.0	82.0
35840	North Port-Sarasota-Bradenton, FL	$59,234	$47,627	$48,213	$75,281	$88,325	$72,336	$35,357	$25,642	713,968	86.3	73.9	81.1
35980	Norwich-New London, CT	$81,042	$44,583	$56,279	$101,493	$120,833	$98,251	$40,122	$34,910	262,653	95.7	88.4	88.9
36100	Ocala, FL	$45,783	$37,543	$38,111	$64,002	$88,261	$57,705	$38,261	$22,522	327,600	86.1	72.5	75.5
36140	Ocean City, NJ	$74,090	$43,906	$58,233	$87,870	$116,147	$87,338	$50,718	$27,128	94,140	92.3	85.7	87.9
36220	Odessa, TX	$60,519	$23,071	$44,116	$77,682	$89,399	$71,336	$46,778	$24,093	143,137	75.5	69.4	78.1
36260	Ogden-Clearfield, UT	$70,030	$42,173	$53,095	$76,566	$108,905	$76,916	$51,907	$27,060	606,572	91.1	78.7	82.2
36420	Oklahoma City, OK	$61,686	$32,774	$42,916	$78,265	$94,450	$74,535	$40,088	$21,820	1,277,721	86.7	74.3	80.2
36500	Olympia-Tumwater, WA	$72,126	$45,217	$56,420	$90,574	$107,464	$80,708	$41,735	$24,401	252,879	90.6	82.1	83.6
36540	Omaha-Council Bluffs, NE-IA	$70,926	$34,835	$46,175	$85,044	$104,242	$90,252	$44,493	$27,074	873,323	92.3	82.3	85.7
36740	Orlando-Kissimmee-Sanford, FL	$55,913	$30,391	$40,334	$74,266	$86,156	$71,607	$30,665	$24,575	2,201,548	83.3	71.6	77.2
36780	Oshkosh-Neenah, WI	$67,139	$38,194	$44,833	$82,408	$100,231	$84,183	$40,799	$22,677	163,331	96.0	88.0	85.5
36980	Owensboro, KY	$57,581	$28,377	$43,279	$74,806	$100,467	$71,313	$30,769	$21,783	114,079	91.9	79.7	83.7
37100	Oxnard-Thousand Oaks-Ventura, CA	$85,243	$42,250	$64,643	$103,716	$108,593	$99,587	$50,412	$32,203	827,808	86.3	76.3	83.6
37340	Palm Bay-Melbourne-Titusville, FL	$58,760	$39,775	$46,874	$80,755	$98,105	$77,710	$35,876	$23,355	541,779	87.7	74.6	80.1
37460	Panama City, FL	$54,450	$33,032	$40,389	$72,142	$84,981	$70,516	$28,569	$22,724	181,598	85.7	77.8	75.0

CBSA FIPS code	Metropolitan area	Total number of families	Families with incomes below the poverty level, as a percent of all families of that family type				Families that received Food Stamps (SNAP), as a percent of all families of that family type			Families that received food stamps (SNAP) and had at least one worker	
			All families	Married-couple families	Male householder families, no spouse present	Female householder families, no spouse present	All families	Married-couple families	Male householder or female householder families, no spouse present	Married-couple families, percent	Male householder or female householder families, no spouse present, percent
30460	Lexington-Fayette, KY	118,959	11.2	6.42	22.3	44.2	14.2	6.5	35.2	5.5	26.2
30620	Lima, OH	26,240	13.1	6.53	22.5	49.0	18.2	6.4	45.5	5.6	36.2
30700	Lincoln, NE	74,517	9.2	6.79	21.8	39.4	9.5	3.9	29.1	3.5	24.0
30780	Little Rock-North Little Rock-Conway, AR	176,489	10.2	6.97	19.6	34.7	13.4	6.5	31.4	5.2	23.3
30860	Logan, UT-ID	29,545	11.0	10.93	11.8	39.0	9.4	7.0	24.0	6.5	18.4
30980	Longview, TX	52,601	13.8	9.22	25.1	49.9	14.8	6.5	36.5	5.9	26.4
31020	Longview, WA	26,087	12.2	9.43	25.3	44.4	23.2	14.4	50.5	12.7	34.5
31080	Los Angeles-Long Beach-Anaheim, CA	2,876,354	13.5	12.50	25.0	38.3	10.2	6.1	18.9	5.5	13.9
31140	Louisville/Jefferson County, KY-IN	317,075	11.2	6.90	22.1	40.5	14.0	6.3	33.0	5.3	23.1
31180	Lubbock, TX	69,627	13.3	9.40	32.0	44.6	18.0	10.4	36.1	9.6	31.0
31340	Lynchburg, VA	65,702	11.4	7.68	24.3	43.9	13.2	6.0	35.6	4.9	25.9
31420	Macon, GA	55,618	19.5	10.48	38.0	54.1	24.1	9.0	51.9	6.9	36.6
31460	Madera, CA	32,142	18.8	20.31	40.7	48.9	20.1	13.8	36.5	10.7	26.0
31540	Madison, WI	152,094	6.9	4.19	20.5	35.0	9.7	4.4	29.1	4.0	23.9
31700	Manchester-Nashua, NH	103,411	5.9	3.31	11.3	29.4	8.2	3.6	23.8	2.9	18.1
31740	Manhattan, KS	19,794	6.2	4.41	13.2	26.6	6.7	3.8	19.4	3.2	16.5
31860	Mankato-North Mankato, MN	22,418	8.3	4.52	22.5	40.8	10.0	4.6	34.7	4.1	29.3
31900	Mansfield, OH	30,250	13.6	11.74	24.1	52.1	18.8	10.6	42.7	8.6	29.0
32580	McAllen-Edinburg-Mission, TX	180,050	31.3	32.13	42.1	60.6	36.0	29.9	50.7	25.3	39.6
32780	Medford, OR	53,332	13.3	11.75	31.3	41.2	23.1	13.7	52.7	12.0	41.0
32820	Memphis, TN-MS-AR	323,279	15.4	7.60	27.8	44.1	21.6	9.1	42.2	7.9	30.9
32900	Merced, CA	58,279	21.8	18.84	33.7	55.1	23.5	14.2	42.1	12.6	24.8
33100	Miami-Fort Lauderdale-West Palm Beach, FL	1,305,725	13.9	11.29	24.8	36.7	19.8	12.7	34.5	10.5	26.6
33140	Michigan City-La Porte, IN	27,858	14.1	10.42	25.4	56.4	15.0	5.8	41.3	4.9	30.9
33220	Midland, MI	22,703	10.2	8.55	31.5	42.2	12.4	7.1	36.8	6.0	21.9
33260	Midland, TX	37,226	7.2	5.65	5.1	26.8	9.0	4.9	21.0	4.4	18.7
33340	Milwaukee-Waukesha-West Allis, WI	385,447	11.6	6.09	26.1	44.6	17.7	6.7	45.9	5.8	34.5
33460	Minneapolis-St. Paul-Bloomington, MN-WI	855,908	7.1	4.23	15.2	33.0	8.9	3.7	26.8	3.2	20.3
33540	Missoula, MT	26,566	9.5	5.45	11.0	41.7	15.0	8.0	35.2	6.7	31.7
33660	Mobile, AL	104,433	16.7	8.81	22.9	50.7	22.0	10.3	44.2	8.2	30.9
33700	Modesto, CA	123,974	17.2	15.60	29.8	47.2	18.4	11.7	33.0	10.0	22.2
33740	Monroe, LA	43,313	21.1	9.87	35.0	62.9	18.9	6.3	43.1	5.1	27.9
33780	Monroe, MI	41,071	9.1	5.83	14.8	44.9	12.6	5.9	34.4	5.2	23.7
33860	Montgomery, AL	92,854	15.4	8.14	34.9	47.5	20.4	8.0	44.6	7.1	32.8
34060	Morgantown, WV	27,731	10.1	8.17	13.7	43.1	9.8	6.2	23.6	4.3	15.4
34100	Morristown, TN	30,820	15.5	10.62	45.8	56.5	20.6	12.7	43.4	10.5	28.9
34580	Mount Vernon-Anacortes, WA	31,008	10.5	8.68	17.9	37.6	17.3	9.5	41.2	8.3	32.3
34620	Muncie, IN	27,561	13.1	8.66	33.1	46.9	18.9	9.0	44.3	6.8	31.6
34740	Muskegon, MI	43,270	16.1	10.83	28.5	57.1	23.2	12.1	49.8	9.6	33.3
34820	Myrtle Beach-Conway-North Myrtle Beach, SC-NC	107,444	13.6	11.02	39.2	51.9	16.1	8.6	39.3	7.2	28.0
34900	Napa, CA	33,750	7.6	6.00	17.6	27.0	7.0	4.1	16.1	3.8	12.0
34940	Naples-Immokalee-Marco Island, FL	82,392	9.2	13.20	25.7	30.5	11.7	6.9	30.4	6.3	25.4
34980	Nashville-Davidson–Murfreesboro–Franklin, TN	425,554	10.5	7.76	22.9	39.7	15.2	8.0	36.6	6.9	27.9
35100	New Bern, NC	34,302	11.5	5.84	25.7	53.3	16.3	7.9	44.6	7.0	35.6
35300	New Haven-Milford, CT	210,654	10.1	6.02	16.1	38.9	14.6	5.7	35.7	4.5	25.1
35380	New Orleans-Metairie, LA	293,753	15.1	6.89	23.7	47.7	17.7	7.9	35.1	6.3	25.4
35620	New York-Newark-Jersey City, NY-NJ-PA	4,673,828	11.4	8.23	21.9	36.1	14.4	7.5	29.8	6.1	21.0
35660	Niles-Benton Harbor, MI	39,526	12.6	9.35	17.5	49.8	17.1	6.7	46.5	5.0	32.9
35840	North Port-Sarasota-Bradenton, FL	188,635	9.0	8.78	25.7	35.1	10.5	5.4	30.9	4.5	23.7
35980	Norwich-New London, CT	70,160	6.7	4.40	20.8	24.4	11.0	5.1	27.9	4.2	20.9
36100	Ocala, FL	87,747	13.2	14.44	34.6	45.1	17.6	10.4	40.4	8.7	25.9
36140	Ocean City, NJ	25,924	6.8	5.32	16.7	33.1	6.8	4.0	19.1	3.4	13.3
36220	Odessa, TX	35,845	11.8	8.03	4.3	38.2	16.5	9.8	30.3	8.8	26.0
36260	Ogden-Clearfield, UT	151,820	7.6	5.80	12.8	35.5	9.6	5.3	28.3	5.0	23.2
36420	Oklahoma City, OK	317,189	11.5	8.83	17.0	42.6	14.5	7.1	34.7	6.2	26.7
36500	Olympia-Tumwater, WA	67,297	8.8	5.87	21.3	39.0	12.9	7.3	31.1	6.7	25.4
36540	Omaha-Council Bluffs, NE-IA	221,502	8.9	5.95	18.8	35.4	10.9	4.8	29.5	4.2	23.2
36740	Orlando-Kissimmee-Sanford, FL	511,379	12.6	9.83	28.4	38.5	16.1	9.3	33.2	8.1	25.4
36780	Oshkosh-Neenah, WI	40,792	7.5	4.54	18.4	41.5	11.0	4.5	36.2	4.1	29.2
36980	Owensboro, KY	30,553	13.3	10.50	39.4	47.6	14.8	6.9	40.3	5.7	27.8
37100	Oxnard-Thousand Oaks-Ventura, CA	195,715	8.4	7.55	15.9	32.0	8.1	4.6	19.0	4.1	14.8
37340	Palm Bay-Melbourne-Titusville, FL	138,311	10.2	8.78	19.8	38.5	14.1	6.4	36.2	5.2	26.8
37460	Panama City, FL	47,729	11.3	9.37	17.7	38.7	15.7	8.5	35.4	6.9	26.0

Table E-3: Metropolitan Areas—Income, Poverty, and Health Insurance—*Continued*

| CBSA FIPS code | Metropolitan area | Median family income in the past 12 months (in 2,013 inflation-adjusted dollars) | | | | | | | | Total population in households | Persons who had health insurance, as a percent of all persons in that household type | | |
| | | All families | Families with no earners | Families with one earner | Families with two earners | Families with three or more earners | Families with own children under 18 years | | | | Married-couple families, percent | Male householder or female householder families, no spouse present | Nonfamily households |
							Married-couple families with children	Male householder, no spouse present, with children	Female householder, no spouse present, with children				
37620	Parkersburg-Vienna, WV	$50,075	$30,252	$39,167	$74,920	$88,451	$64,583	$35,753	$21,344	92,000	88.8	82.3	81.6
37860	Pensacola-Ferry Pass-Brent, FL	$59,293	$39,455	$45,335	$74,071	$92,231	$71,412	$35,496	$23,888	436,255	88.4	80.1	76.9
37900	Peoria, IL	$67,347	$39,475	$49,469	$85,190	$105,697	$86,958	$35,035	$21,924	375,705	94.6	84.1	84.1
37980	Philadelphia-Camden-Wilmington, PA-NJ-DE-MD	$78,511	$30,460	$54,001	$102,375	$122,860	$107,692	$43,911	$28,649	5,938,616	93.1	84.4	88.2
38060	Phoenix-Mesa-Scottsdale, AZ	$61,558	$36,061	$45,196	$83,943	$98,975	$76,914	$37,567	$27,459	4,276,859	86.1	76.2	80.5
38220	Pine Bluff, AR	$47,791	$22,408	$34,953	$73,482	$90,300	$66,774	$36,480	$19,734	88,702	88.2	83.1	83.8
38300	Pittsburgh, PA	$67,042	$32,297	$50,340	$87,200	$104,822	$91,772	$37,852	$21,819	2,333,181	94.9	86.6	89.2
38340	Pittsfield, MA	$64,922	$34,831	$44,430	$80,994	$104,375	$81,909	$32,039	$22,145	127,781	98.0	95.1	97.6
38540	Pocatello, ID	$57,454	$38,385	$38,765	$70,705	$81,183	$65,800	$27,278	$20,038	82,020	88.5	81.0	80.5
38860	Portland-South Portland, ME	$72,387	$35,347	$46,974	$87,057	$107,388	$88,977	$38,310	$27,025	512,873	94.2	86.3	85.3
38900	Portland-Vancouver-Hillsboro, OR-WA	$70,493	$36,537	$52,320	$87,474	$101,177	$85,565	$43,333	$26,033	2,273,115	89.8	79.1	81.8
38940	Port St. Lucie, FL	$54,260	$39,800	$44,378	$73,821	$84,070	$65,800	$21,378	$22,816	428,128	85.0	70.0	79.1
39140	Prescott, AZ	$53,354	$44,828	$43,121	$70,215	$72,323	$60,254	$35,648	$23,491	211,426	87.1	76.1	82.7
39300	Providence-Warwick, RI-MA	$71,693	$28,373	$48,003	$93,836	$115,744	$98,211	$37,263	$25,267	1,579,030	94.3	86.4	88.3
39340	Provo-Orem, UT	$65,082	$42,504	$54,171	$66,449	$99,961	$72,669	$36,159	$29,099	547,160	88.7	75.4	84.4
39380	Pueblo, CO	$52,038	$31,253	$38,569	$69,123	$87,325	$64,028	$32,171	$23,755	156,900	91.5	81.0	82.8
39460	Punta Gorda, FL	$54,056	$45,451	$48,272	$70,171	$84,056	$64,642	$40,679	$29,289	159,190	88.1	70.3	82.2
39540	Racine, WI	$66,240	$36,489	$46,162	$85,065	$104,036	$83,582	$36,977	$27,122	190,709	92.0	84.0	83.5
39580	Raleigh, NC	$75,478	$37,133	$52,736	$95,193	$107,808	$97,921	$36,237	$27,700	1,176,953	89.1	77.1	84.1
39660	Rapid City, SD	$61,744	$37,035	$41,688	$74,662	$97,822	$74,664	$38,587	$26,387	134,259	92.0	78.6	83.5
39740	Reading, PA	$66,936	$32,061	$46,812	$84,490	$103,404	$85,558	$44,406	$20,509	408,120	92.7	84.2	86.5
39820	Redding, CA	$51,646	$32,096	$44,093	$79,971	$105,042	$64,902	$37,829	$20,864	177,069	85.9	81.3	79.8
39900	Reno, NV	$63,042	$36,840	$46,127	$79,724	$98,303	$72,611	$41,630	$25,674	430,364	82.5	72.0	80.3
40060	Richmond, VA	$72,101	$36,023	$50,446	$92,775	$111,010	$96,951	$42,744	$28,328	1,205,841	92.4	79.9	83.6
40140	Riverside-San Bernardino-Ontario, CA	$59,438	$28,400	$43,645	$79,684	$96,601	$69,195	$37,018	$25,174	4,277,345	82.0	75.1	80.1
40220	Roanoke, VA	$60,441	$37,704	$45,815	$76,275	$92,417	$78,347	$41,629	$21,528	306,065	92.2	80.8	85.0
40340	Rochester, MN	$78,994	$42,046	$49,965	$92,815	$106,809	$94,372	$40,000	$33,280	207,255	95.5	85.3	88.9
40380	Rochester, NY	$66,149	$34,390	$45,578	$86,630	$106,761	$90,021	$38,378	$22,680	1,066,940	94.7	88.4	90.0
40420	Rockford, IL	$58,243	$29,218	$42,210	$79,590	$98,184	$75,651	$32,520	$22,198	342,602	91.5	82.1	81.5
40580	Rocky Mount, NC	$48,396	$26,534	$33,152	$67,979	$82,278	$68,545	$32,067	$18,720	148,540	85.9	76.7	82.6
40660	Rome, GA	$49,533	$24,695	$37,407	$64,067	$100,417	$61,250	$42,208	$13,653	93,854	82.2	75.3	77.1
40900	Sacramento–Roseville–Arden-Arcade, CA	$68,280	$35,180	$51,620	$92,577	$103,166	$85,448	$39,304	$28,409	2,173,812	89.1	80.6	83.8
40980	Saginaw, MI	$52,315	$33,015	$40,599	$73,861	$92,031	$75,678	$30,039	$17,060	194,549	93.0	84.7	86.6
41060	St. Cloud, MN	$69,546	$34,778	$42,997	$83,709	$101,743	$89,618	$44,082	$25,279	188,971	95.4	83.5	89.2
41100	St. George, UT	$56,078	$43,371	$45,215	$65,927	$84,174	$63,049	$37,310	$30,353	143,173	85.5	74.6	78.0
41140	St. Joseph, MO-KS	$58,514	$30,182	$40,330	$71,883	$91,188	$75,943	$25,127	$20,562	121,351	90.5	73.5	82.7
41180	St. Louis, MO-IL	$67,855	$33,845	$48,464	$86,575	$108,624	$91,148	$41,442	$23,775	2,763,290	93.3	81.6	85.2
41420	Salem, OR	$55,104	$34,708	$41,648	$70,307	$84,037	$61,156	$35,914	$20,103	391,008	86.0	77.1	83.5
41500	Salinas, CA	$61,107	$39,622	$44,340	$75,582	$83,934	$62,968	$36,268	$25,312	406,115	81.2	70.0	78.3
41540	Salisbury, MD-DE	$61,264	$43,958	$43,476	$77,195	$102,512	$76,969	$36,138	$24,615	371,937	91.1	84.2	87.7
41620	Salt Lake City, UT	$69,169	$34,643	$50,837	$77,332	$100,497	$76,305	$36,690	$27,024	1,115,279	87.3	74.5	82.4
41660	San Angelo, TX	$57,211	$33,811	$42,915	$71,744	$80,276	$71,806	$49,030	$19,399	109,940	84.7	68.3	79.7
41700	San Antonio-New Braunfels, TX	$60,257	$29,743	$42,559	$77,876	$93,300	$75,380	$36,965	$25,264	2,194,528	83.9	73.2	80.4
41740	San Diego-Carlsbad, CA	$71,422	$31,153	$52,198	$93,288	$105,973	$83,473	$40,548	$28,443	3,074,879	86.4	75.5	82.3
41860	San Francisco-Oakland-Hayward, CA	$93,575	$37,526	$67,083	$121,876	$119,244	$120,056	$52,048	$35,356	4,422,951	91.4	81.5	87.3
41940	San Jose-Sunnyvale-Santa Clara, CA	$102,369	$38,253	$80,568	$134,773	$121,436	$130,916	$52,517	$36,164	1,884,299	91.5	79.8	86.7
42020	San Luis Obispo-Paso Robles-Arroyo Grande, CA	$74,912	$54,146	$57,788	$90,333	$104,399	$86,150	$33,385	$27,517	266,873	90.1	76.7	84.3
42100	Santa Cruz-Watsonville, CA	$81,675	$50,254	$59,963	$103,961	$92,991	$87,770	$34,271	$33,162	265,649	88.4	79.0	83.3
42140	Santa Fe, NM	$62,280	$40,453	$44,914	$86,214	$82,330	$71,889	$40,531	$25,208	144,517	82.8	71.4	79.1
42200	Santa Maria-Santa Barbara, CA	$73,078	$43,447	$51,745	$92,290	$99,483	$79,802	$43,299	$31,925	423,692	83.4	70.5	86.4
42220	Santa Rosa, CA	$73,901	$43,830	$53,662	$91,814	$107,722	$85,505	$50,100	$33,263	486,885	88.5	78.6	84.4
42340	Savannah, GA	$60,461	$37,941	$42,260	$79,619	$98,061	$78,356	$36,250	$19,536	351,947	87.9	69.4	79.2
42540	Scranton–Wilkes-Barre–Hazleton, PA	$57,839	$28,345	$42,574	$77,780	$97,911	$79,465	$39,980	$20,321	551,730	93.3	86.0	88.6
42660	Seattle-Tacoma-Bellevue, WA	$82,241	$40,631	$61,458	$103,311	$119,201	$101,028	$49,210	$30,214	3,507,577	90.8	78.9	84.4
42680	Sebastian-Vero Beach, FL	$54,274	$44,645	$41,864	$72,500	$76,798	$64,261	$30,753	$21,280	139,087	86.0	69.9	77.8
42700	Sebring, FL	$43,079	$35,069	$34,930	$65,995	$76,098	$52,254	$24,619	$21,783	96,876	86.9	73.5	80.1
43100	Sheboygan, WI	$63,416	$36,837	$43,048	$76,717	$94,474	$81,000	$32,185	$21,496	112,674	95.7	87.5	83.2
43300	Sherman-Denison, TX	$57,389	$34,223	$39,680	$78,364	$95,111	$68,459	$27,207	$29,350	120,535	84.9	74.9	80.9
43340	Shreveport-Bossier City, LA	$55,695	$25,545	$39,423	$80,718	$99,425	$85,135	$40,000	$20,016	435,490	88.6	75.5	79.9
43420	Sierra Vista-Douglas, AZ	$53,203	$36,082	$41,223	$73,488	$88,944	$67,625	$34,844	$22,104	118,042	88.9	77.8	87.1
43580	Sioux City, IA-NE-SD	$59,442	$31,391	$38,359	$73,421	$81,789	$70,464	$38,594	$20,994	167,144	92.3	82.6	83.9
43620	Sioux Falls, SD	$70,722	$35,043	$40,694	$80,401	$97,242	$83,720	$38,784	$25,720	234,616	94.6	82.4	85.7
43780	South Bend-Mishawaka, IN-MI	$54,469	$30,673	$40,099	$72,166	$93,786	$71,606	$27,245	$19,184	316,114	90.1	77.2	82.7
43900	Spartanburg, SC	$50,302	$25,898	$36,116	$73,267	$92,001	$70,155	$28,200	$20,950	312,258	86.1	78.6	80.2
44060	Spokane-Spokane Valley, WA	$60,700	$36,514	$46,514	$77,769	$97,745	$74,697	$35,867	$22,076	523,878	90.4	78.5	81.4

CBSA FIPS code	Metropolitan area	Total number of families	Families with incomes below the poverty level, as a percent of all families of that family type				Families that received Food Stamps (SNAP), as a percent of all families of that family type			Families that received food stamps (SNAP) and had at least one worker	
			All families	Married-couple families	Male householder families, no spouse present	Female householder families, no spouse present	All families	Married-couple families	Male householder or female householder families, no spouse present	Married-couple families, percent	Male householder or female householder families, no spouse present, percent
37620	Parkersburg-Vienna, WV	24,438	13.6	12.75	18.0	46.1	18.5	11.1	40.8	8.9	25.6
37860	Pensacola-Ferry Pass-Brent, FL	110,253	10.9	8.49	21.9	40.7	15.5	8.0	37.0	6.8	27.7
37900	Peoria, IL	99,195	9.7	5.58	24.7	42.2	10.8	3.4	35.0	2.6	27.1
37980	Philadelphia-Camden-Wilmington, PA-NJ-DE-MD	1,433,384	9.3	4.51	21.7	35.4	12.9	5.2	31.7	4.1	21.1
38060	Phoenix-Mesa-Scottsdale, AZ	1,019,685	12.8	11.74	24.2	38.0	14.4	8.3	30.2	7.4	22.1
38220	Pine Bluff, AR	23,087	19.5	10.77	37.9	49.0	20.9	10.0	40.8	7.6	29.0
38300	Pittsburgh, PA	609,444	8.7	4.33	23.8	42.4	12.3	4.9	35.1	3.9	24.3
38340	Pittsfield, MA	32,959	9.9	5.49	22.3	43.3	14.0	6.2	35.4	5.0	24.4
38540	Pocatello, ID	19,869	11.8	12.01	22.1	40.2	16.9	9.9	40.6	9.0	34.7
38860	Portland-South Portland, ME	133,377	7.7	4.81	19.6	34.3	12.8	6.6	35.5	5.5	27.9
38900	Portland-Vancouver-Hillsboro, OR-WA	554,326	9.9	7.74	18.5	37.3	17.3	10.5	39.3	9.2	29.5
38940	Port St. Lucie, FL	109,663	12.4	12.44	43.6	42.7	13.6	7.6	33.1	6.7	23.2
39140	Prescott, AZ	57,757	12.1	14.78	33.2	40.5	14.1	9.6	31.8	8.4	24.7
39300	Providence-Warwick, RI-MA	394,810	10.1	5.89	20.0	37.5	15.4	6.9	35.8	5.6	24.4
39340	Provo-Orem, UT	121,185	10.9	8.89	16.8	36.3	9.8	6.7	28.7	6.4	24.9
39380	Pueblo, CO	39,553	14.1	12.40	29.6	42.7	19.1	11.0	38.0	9.1	28.6
39460	Punta Gorda, FL	45,601	8.8	10.32	22.1	34.3	12.0	6.5	36.8	5.1	24.8
39540	Racine, WI	48,757	9.7	6.75	22.8	38.2	14.8	6.6	39.4	6.0	27.5
39580	Raleigh, NC	297,384	8.9	5.63	28.3	33.7	10.3	5.0	27.6	4.4	20.7
39660	Rapid City, SD	35,775	9.1	5.33	28.1	37.0	13.0	4.7	38.8	4.3	32.5
39740	Reading, PA	104,401	10.3	6.26	18.1	48.1	14.1	6.6	36.7	5.4	25.7
39820	Redding, CA	45,440	12.2	13.70	20.7	41.6	13.5	6.9	32.0	5.5	20.8
39900	Reno, NV	101,695	10.9	9.44	21.8	36.4	10.2	5.3	23.7	4.2	16.2
40060	Richmond, VA	299,356	9.2	4.29	17.0	36.1	12.7	5.0	31.2	4.2	22.4
40140	Riverside-San Bernardino-Ontario, CA	963,727	14.7	12.63	27.1	40.7	14.7	8.9	28.7	7.8	19.8
40220	Roanoke, VA	83,413	9.9	8.09	19.4	39.1	12.9	5.9	33.9	4.8	27.2
40340	Rochester, MN	54,912	5.2	3.29	15.6	25.2	6.6	3.4	20.9	2.9	17.9
40380	Rochester, NY	268,937	10.5	5.32	22.9	42.7	14.0	5.0	37.0	4.0	24.9
40420	Rockford, IL	88,657	12.9	8.47	22.1	43.2	17.1	7.5	42.4	6.0	31.5
40580	Rocky Mount, NC	38,560	16.4	9.35	17.5	52.0	25.2	10.9	51.7	9.6	39.9
40660	Rome, GA	22,697	17.2	16.83	9.0	50.9	21.2	13.4	42.0	10.1	24.4
40900	Sacramento-Roseville-Arden-Arcade, CA	521,169	11.9	10.08	23.8	36.7	12.7	6.9	27.5	5.9	18.2
40980	Saginaw, MI	49,742	13.9	7.52	33.0	52.7	21.4	9.2	50.5	7.3	32.2
41060	St. Cloud, MN	46,730	6.8	3.18	9.1	37.3	7.9	3.5	25.7	2.9	21.0
41100	St. George, UT	35,791	11.0	13.57	14.9	43.1	11.1	8.2	25.6	7.8	20.5
41140	St. Joseph, MO-KS	30,281	12.3	5.31	43.2	47.2	14.9	6.1	41.7	5.1	29.9
41180	St. Louis, MO-IL	720,356	10.2	5.75	21.5	39.6	14.0	5.8	35.5	4.9	26.2
41420	Salem, OR	97,445	15.1	14.32	27.7	48.8	25.4	16.3	50.5	14.9	38.3
41500	Salinas, CA	90,577	13.4	12.79	23.6	41.9	9.0	5.9	16.9	5.6	13.7
41540	Salisbury, MD-DE	94,562	10.3	8.99	17.9	39.9	16.0	7.8	38.4	6.7	30.1
41620	Salt Lake City, UT	258,416	9.9	8.86	22.3	35.9	10.2	6.0	24.8	5.5	19.9
41660	San Angelo, TX	27,863	11.5	5.82	13.0	44.9	16.1	7.0	39.2	6.2	33.7
41700	San Antonio-New Braunfels, TX	531,588	13.1	9.89	20.4	40.2	16.8	9.5	34.0	8.4	26.0
41740	San Diego-Carlsbad, CA	716,575	11.2	9.32	20.9	34.1	7.9	4.6	17.4	4.0	12.3
41860	San Francisco-Oakland-Hayward, CA	1,023,357	7.8	5.83	18.2	29.5	7.3	4.0	17.2	3.5	12.3
41940	San Jose-Sunnyvale-Santa Clara, CA	452,305	7.2	5.27	17.8	27.2	6.5	3.9	15.4	3.6	11.9
42020	San Luis Obispo-Paso Robles-Arroyo Grande, CA	65,095	7.9	7.17	15.5	36.0	7.1	3.3	21.5	3.0	15.8
42100	Santa Cruz-Watsonville, CA	58,785	8.8	8.23	11.5	34.0	8.4	4.6	20.4	4.4	15.4
42140	Santa Fe, NM	35,394	13.7	13.69	18.9	39.9	12.4	6.8	27.5	6.3	17.9
42200	Santa Maria-Santa Barbara, CA	92,577	9.8	8.92	21.4	33.6	8.6	5.4	18.0	4.8	14.2
42220	Santa Rosa, CA	116,190	7.9	8.01	19.5	25.3	8.0	4.8	17.6	4.4	13.1
42340	Savannah, GA	86,418	13.0	6.77	26.0	46.9	12.9	5.7	29.1	5.0	21.1
42540	Scranton–Wilkes-Barre–Hazleton, PA	142,780	11.1	6.76	21.2	45.6	15.2	7.5	35.0	5.8	24.4
42660	Seattle-Tacoma-Bellevue, WA	859,146	8.0	5.88	18.9	32.6	13.3	7.2	33.4	6.2	25.0
42680	Sebastian-Vero Beach, FL	36,580	9.7	11.51	21.3	42.0	14.6	8.4	36.8	7.5	31.4
42700	Sebring, FL	24,921	11.8	13.84	25.0	39.5	15.6	9.2	42.5	6.2	27.9
43100	Sheboygan, WI	30,433	8.0	5.02	24.5	38.3	13.7	6.6	41.4	6.2	35.9
43300	Sherman-Denison, TX	31,692	12.1	9.69	33.3	36.5	15.4	8.0	34.7	7.3	26.7
43340	Shreveport-Bossier City, LA	109,449	15.0	4.80	22.8	46.6	17.8	5.9	38.5	4.8	26.6
43420	Sierra Vista-Douglas, AZ	31,971	14.2	16.74	23.9	41.0	17.3	10.3	38.3	9.1	30.5
43580	Sioux City, IA-NE-SD	42,807	10.3	6.26	20.2	43.9	13.9	7.3	34.3	6.6	28.1
43620	Sioux Falls, SD	60,535	7.0	2.44	17.1	33.0	9.2	3.7	27.7	3.4	20.3
43780	South Bend-Mishawaka, IN-MI	78,953	13.4	10.66	32.2	49.2	15.8	7.2	39.4	6.2	29.0
43900	Spartanburg, SC	83,080	15.2	11.20	31.9	45.2	15.5	6.6	34.9	5.4	24.7
44060	Spokane-Spokane Valley, WA	132,880	10.5	7.80	17.4	43.6	18.0	10.0	43.9	8.3	32.9

CBSA FIPS code	Metropolitan area	Median family income in the past 12 months (in 2,013 inflation-adjusted dollars)					Families with own children under 18 years			Total population in households	Persons who had health insurance, as a percent of all persons in that household type		
		All families	Families with no earners	Families with one earner	Families with two earners	Families with three or more earners	Married-couple families with children	Male householder, no spouse present, with children	Female householder, no spouse present, with children		Married-couple families, percent	Male householder or female householder families, no spouse present	Nonfamily households
44100	Springfield, IL	$70,640	$41,714	$47,760	$91,494	$108,241	$92,446	$36,406	$21,656	209,420	95.1	86.1	84.3
44140	Springfield, MA	$65,637	$23,805	$43,408	$90,206	$112,926	$95,230	$36,709	$22,252	618,980	97.4	93.9	95.0
44180	Springfield, MO	$53,308	$32,332	$38,040	$68,437	$83,289	$65,507	$26,493	$19,578	438,722	87.3	75.5	81.3
44220	Springfield, OH	$53,576	$33,716	$38,220	$71,915	$96,467	$71,929	$28,279	$19,321	135,263	92.2	84.7	83.8
44300	State College, PA	$71,961	$39,508	$50,622	$83,823	$99,767	$88,238	$44,630	$25,891	152,007	94.2	86.7	93.9
44420	Staunton-Waynesboro, VA	$57,949	$32,945	$44,743	$71,520	$92,588	$73,570	$32,202	$23,678	114,455	90.9	78.7	81.6
44700	Stockton-Lodi, CA	$57,448	$26,183	$44,536	$77,719	$89,553	$65,706	$35,717	$23,187	691,495	84.2	80.0	80.3
44940	Sumter, SC	$49,178	$28,906	$37,978	$68,981	$95,827	$61,976	$35,613	$17,237	103,980	90.4	77.7	77.6
45060	Syracuse, NY	$66,798	$30,802	$48,546	$87,649	$107,632	$88,441	$36,728	$22,955	654,659	94.8	87.4	89.3
45220	Tallahassee, FL	$62,674	$30,843	$43,910	$80,160	$105,154	$84,325	$39,099	$23,943	361,757	90.2	80.1	83.1
45300	Tampa-St. Petersburg-Clearwater, FL	$57,337	$33,293	$43,516	$79,872	$95,094	$78,224	$32,846	$26,476	2,817,064	86.9	75.1	78.8
45460	Terre Haute, IN	$54,270	$29,855	$39,862	$69,871	$84,013	$67,787	$28,839	$18,688	165,394	88.4	78.6	78.2
45500	Texarkana, TX-AR	$50,520	$26,165	$38,846	$74,098	$93,750	$69,730	$39,053	$18,745	142,947	86.6	74.3	79.6
45540	The Villages, FL	$57,658	$54,132	$59,035	$72,517	$70,491	$62,825	$30,893	$20,412	93,575	93.9	71.8	87.6
45780	Toledo, OH	$58,377	$30,356	$40,577	$77,820	$102,037	$79,685	$33,500	$18,313	601,985	93.6	82.4	84.4
45820	Topeka, KS	$63,036	$38,087	$43,164	$79,657	$95,841	$80,430	$36,895	$22,163	230,662	92.4	79.0	82.6
45940	Trenton, NJ	$94,000	$38,533	$64,332	$117,403	$122,061	$121,855	$46,228	$28,358	362,260	92.0	80.4	88.7
46060	Tucson, AZ	$55,965	$39,408	$40,951	$79,326	$84,456	$69,620	$34,697	$22,284	974,435	88.3	79.5	83.6
46140	Tulsa, OK	$59,319	$30,248	$42,981	$78,285	$95,705	$74,008	$37,828	$21,770	943,583	86.6	75.2	78.2
46220	Tuscaloosa, AL	$53,914	$24,458	$40,368	$79,008	$91,690	$78,744	$30,730	$18,200	231,514	92.4	78.7	88.5
46340	Tyler, TX	$57,576	$34,205	$43,192	$75,820	$95,901	$72,991	$28,571	$23,509	212,208	81.9	71.9	77.3
46520	Urban Honolulu, HI	$83,981	$45,510	$60,569	$96,422	$130,518	$92,731	$62,082	$30,800	925,216	95.6	92.3	91.5
46540	Utica-Rome, NY	$60,377	$31,615	$41,673	$77,498	$94,116	$78,609	$34,860	$23,713	289,436	94.0	89.8	88.7
46660	Valdosta, GA	$47,824	$22,736	$33,946	$68,186	$87,935	$60,924	$30,757	$19,022	138,023	84.7	73.8	72.3
46700	Vallejo-Fairfield, CA	$74,793	$39,208	$54,405	$98,891	$111,533	$87,901	$46,652	$27,845	406,740	90.3	81.6	82.2
47020	Victoria, TX	$55,839	$31,736	$37,548	$79,327	$90,645	$79,668	$25,658	$23,292	95,092	82.5	69.8	82.1
47220	Vineland-Bridgeton, NJ	$56,632	$27,873	$41,717	$83,536	$106,556	$77,591	$46,718	$26,039	146,132	87.7	81.1	83.6
47260	Virginia Beach-Norfolk-Newport News, VA-NC	$68,653	$39,026	$47,786	$86,930	$109,468	$87,316	$43,526	$25,823	1,610,911	92.2	81.1	84.4
47300	Visalia-Porterville, CA	$42,590	$20,353	$31,526	$62,946	$70,365	$49,935	$23,920	$20,313	446,527	80.3	76.1	74.3
47380	Waco, TX	$51,885	$28,997	$34,791	$71,449	$91,211	$68,688	$26,809	$20,199	250,781	82.9	73.7	85.7
47460	Walla Walla, WA	$58,808	$37,554	$39,591	$81,752	$82,662	$73,471	$24,757	$15,807	60,047	89.3	79.4	83.4
47580	Warner Robins, GA	$61,489	$32,258	$43,536	$81,689	$98,814	$80,193	$30,701	$19,993	180,288	87.3	76.2	83.1
47900	Washington-Arlington-Alexandria, DC-VA-MD-WV	$105,101	$48,173	$71,849	$129,058	$136,446	$127,266	$52,050	$41,275	5,788,076	91.0	80.9	89.1
47940	Waterloo-Cedar Falls, IA	$63,714	$38,144	$44,705	$78,502	$95,915	$81,890	$36,288	$21,911	166,905	96.0	85.2	90.8
48060	Watertown-Fort Drum, NY	$54,676	$32,009	$37,460	$70,096	$89,927	$63,129	$33,183	$19,144	107,086	93.6	87.7	86.1
48140	Wausau, WI	$63,249	$32,271	$43,388	$77,329	$99,435	$83,394	$34,663	$26,208	133,610	93.3	87.6	84.8
48260	Weirton-Steubenville, WV-OH	$51,334	$30,177	$41,169	$70,133	$94,314	$65,353	$40,597	$18,034	121,494	90.3	81.7	87.3
48300	Wenatchee, WA	$58,148	$42,213	$43,010	$74,052	$74,705	$62,156	$36,837	$26,784	112,148	81.8	71.0	77.0
48540	Wheeling, WV-OH	$54,542	$32,668	$43,852	$70,926	$95,334	$69,747	$41,186	$20,411	141,642	91.9	83.1	80.1
48620	Wichita, KS	$62,999	$36,720	$43,665	$79,394	$97,443	$76,054	$38,469	$21,958	625,558	90.3	79.5	81.7
48660	Wichita Falls, TX	$56,794	$34,102	$38,666	$76,240	$93,097	$71,731	$28,333	$21,163	136,185	86.1	71.7	79.8
48700	Williamsport, PA	$57,781	$29,105	$40,983	$72,765	$89,905	$76,277	$36,929	$21,682	113,859	93.4	82.4	86.9
48900	Wilmington, NC	$62,141	$40,912	$43,031	$82,523	$89,863	$85,112	$32,524	$22,028	259,661	88.1	73.6	81.6
49020	Winchester, VA-WV	$70,748	$33,531	$45,924	$90,151	$107,572	$90,981	$32,466	$26,450	129,108	89.6	77.7	78.1
49180	Winston-Salem, NC	$54,580	$29,039	$39,248	$75,787	$92,398	$70,410	$30,470	$20,760	641,642	88.7	76.3	82.0
49340	Worcester, MA-CT	$78,234	$30,175	$51,914	$99,689	$121,633	$104,009	$46,497	$25,926	910,586	97.1	93.4	92.8
49420	Yakima, WA	$48,659	$26,879	$34,718	$61,483	$78,815	$53,052	$29,424	$21,886	243,664	78.5	68.2	76.7
49620	York-Hanover, PA	$68,203	$33,991	$48,610	$84,363	$102,982	$85,563	$38,391	$24,025	432,798	94.1	81.7	87.1
49660	Youngstown-Warren-Boardman, OH-PA	$52,800	$32,396	$41,374	$72,310	$92,482	$73,949	$27,963	$17,443	545,144	91.5	84.2	84.7
49700	Yuba City, CA	$52,622	$29,689	$43,443	$67,907	$84,301	$60,012	$27,059	$21,719	163,873	85.7	78.5	79.2
49740	Yuma, AZ	$43,067	$31,614	$31,743	$58,582	$64,566	$50,972	$30,212	$16,540	192,544	78.0	77.3	83.5

| CBSA FIPS code | Metropolitan area | Total number of families | Families with incomes below the poverty level, as a percent of all families of that family type | | | | Families that received Food Stamps (SNAP), as a percent of all families of that family type | | | Families that received food stamps (SNAP) and had at least one worker | |
			All families	Married-couple families	Male householder families, no spouse present	Female householder families, no spouse present	All families	Married-couple families	Male householder or female householder families, no spouse present	Married-couple families, percent	Male householder or female householder families, no spouse present, percent
44100	Springfield, IL	54,709	11.0	7.17	24.4	42.8	13.4	5.1	34.5	4.7	27.4
44140	Springfield, MA	150,173	12.2	6.63	22.4	43.2	19.8	9.2	41.6	6.4	26.4
44180	Springfield, MO	114,947	12.5	9.27	28.3	49.2	15.4	8.7	38.2	6.9	28.2
44220	Springfield, OH	35,303	13.7	10.80	38.9	48.7	21.2	10.1	49.6	8.5	34.7
44300	State College, PA	32,582	7.5	6.54	13.2	38.9	7.5	4.0	23.1	3.7	18.7
44420	Staunton-Waynesboro, VA	32,182	9.5	6.36	25.3	42.1	11.2	4.8	31.1	4.1	23.8
44700	Stockton-Lodi, CA	160,636	14.9	12.66	23.8	42.5	15.6	8.6	31.1	7.8	21.4
44940	Sumter, SC	27,505	13.2	7.22	19.1	44.6	20.8	10.2	40.8	9.2	29.1
45060	Syracuse, NY	160,006	10.9	6.48	24.7	42.4	13.6	5.5	34.4	4.2	22.5
45220	Tallahassee, FL	83,690	12.5	7.58	28.7	39.4	16.1	6.8	36.0	5.8	25.0
45300	Tampa-St. Petersburg-Clearwater, FL	689,192	11.6	9.46	26.2	36.5	15.6	8.8	33.6	7.2	24.3
45460	Terre Haute, IN	41,246	13.6	10.23	32.9	52.4	16.5	8.3	42.0	6.5	30.2
45500	Texarkana, TX-AR	37,443	16.4	8.21	24.7	52.2	17.5	6.7	40.4	5.4	31.4
45540	The Villages, FL	31,441	6.8	17.50	27.6	45.3	6.4	3.7	29.9	2.9	18.5
45780	Toledo, OH	147,887	14.9	9.43	30.4	49.8	19.2	8.3	43.5	6.7	31.2
45820	Topeka, KS	59,764	10.1	7.01	19.3	43.2	11.4	5.6	30.7	4.7	23.2
45940	Trenton, NJ	88,312	7.6	4.09	16.5	37.3	9.0	3.8	23.5	3.3	17.5
46060	Tucson, AZ	237,220	13.9	11.89	25.1	43.2	18.0	9.5	38.1	8.3	29.2
46140	Tulsa, OK	245,909	11.4	7.62	20.8	42.5	13.7	6.6	33.1	5.8	22.9
46220	Tuscaloosa, AL	54,052	14.8	7.55	23.0	48.6	15.4	4.9	39.1	3.9	24.4
46340	Tyler, TX	53,752	12.1	11.90	28.0	36.2	12.3	5.6	30.6	5.2	23.7
46520	Urban Honolulu, HI	215,872	6.8	4.83	10.1	30.3	9.9	6.2	20.9	5.3	16.0
46540	Utica-Rome, NY	73,080	11.7	9.43	22.9	41.3	16.3	7.5	38.3	5.5	27.0
46660	Valdosta, GA	31,850	18.4	13.40	16.9	52.6	21.5	11.4	42.6	8.8	32.0
46700	Vallejo-Fairfield, CA	100,829	10.3	7.70	12.7	36.3	11.2	5.5	24.6	4.8	16.6
47020	Victoria, TX	24,940	13.0	11.67	19.4	37.4	15.2	6.5	36.5	6.0	29.5
47220	Vineland-Bridgeton, NJ	34,534	14.9	8.73	23.4	38.8	18.4	9.5	33.6	7.1	24.6
47260	Virginia Beach-Norfolk-Newport News, VA-NC	420,389	9.7	4.42	17.8	36.8	12.3	4.7	29.7	4.2	23.5
47300	Visalia-Porterville, CA	103,648	23.6	23.66	41.3	50.3	27.5	19.2	44.5	17.6	32.4
47380	Waco, TX	60,448	15.3	11.25	27.3	46.5	17.3	8.5	38.9	7.7	29.5
47460	Walla Walla, WA	14,633	13.7	10.34	34.1	57.8	17.5	9.1	48.0	7.8	37.6
47580	Warner Robins, GA	45,938	14.0	8.29	24.2	43.8	18.6	10.1	42.1	8.9	29.5
47900	Washington-Arlington-Alexandria, DC-VA-MD-WV	1,384,775	5.9	3.38	11.0	23.6	8.6	3.8	21.9	3.4	17.0
47940	Waterloo-Cedar Falls, IA	40,693	8.5	6.11	18.2	42.9	11.5	4.7	38.1	3.8	28.1
48060	Watertown-Fort Drum, NY	30,477	12.3	8.21	20.0	47.5	15.3	8.9	35.4	6.8	25.6
48140	Wausau, WI	35,997	7.9	5.29	25.0	40.5	9.8	4.3	32.2	3.4	25.4
48260	Weirton-Steubenville, WV-OH	32,674	11.8	6.82	31.1	53.7	16.6	8.9	39.2	7.4	22.0
48300	Wenatchee, WA	29,610	10.2	13.44	6.9	35.7	14.6	8.2	38.3	7.9	33.0
48540	Wheeling, WV-OH	37,891	9.7	8.07	16.9	48.5	13.0	8.0	30.8	6.6	22.7
48620	Wichita, KS	158,991	10.8	9.03	17.7	41.5	12.8	6.5	31.2	5.8	24.8
48660	Wichita Falls, TX	37,000	11.5	7.41	24.1	42.7	13.6	5.7	35.4	4.9	26.9
48700	Williamsport, PA	28,905	9.8	4.12	27.0	48.6	13.4	6.5	35.4	5.5	24.6
48900	Wilmington, NC	64,410	12.0	7.59	21.7	44.1	15.8	7.3	38.9	6.1	30.3
49020	Winchester, VA-WV	31,339	6.0	4.01	15.1	29.8	8.3	3.2	28.7	2.7	21.7
49180	Winston-Salem, NC	167,848	13.7	10.81	29.6	46.0	14.4	7.1	34.7	5.9	25.1
49340	Worcester, MA-CT	229,639	8.8	4.63	18.5	39.6	13.1	6.0	32.8	4.8	20.9
49420	Yakima, WA	56,753	16.9	15.98	23.0	46.7	26.6	16.8	51.6	15.0	39.7
49620	York-Hanover, PA	115,856	7.7	3.23	16.1	41.1	10.3	4.1	30.9	3.4	22.3
49660	Youngstown-Warren-Boardman, OH-PA	147,011	12.7	8.01	27.1	52.7	18.2	7.6	43.8	6.2	31.1
49700	Yuba City, CA	41,450	15.2	10.72	30.8	46.3	16.3	9.2	33.4	7.8	20.7
49740	Yuma, AZ	54,707	17.4	14.26	37.5	53.7	22.5	14.5	45.3	12.8	32.7

Table E-4: Cities with a Population of 50,000 or More—Income, Poverty, and Health Insurance

State/Place FIPS code	State/place	Median family income in the past 12 months (in 2,013 inflation-adjusted dollars)					Families with own children under 18 years			Total population in households	Persons who had health insurance, as a percent of all persons in that household type		
		All families	Families with no earners	Families with one earner	Families with two earners	Families with three or more earners	Married-couple families with children	Male householder, no spouse present, with children	Female householder, no spouse present, with children		Married-couple families, percent	Male householder or female householder families, no spouse present	Nonfamily households
0000000	United States...............	$63,784	$31,313	$45,505	$84,323	$102,461	$82,511	$36,858	$23,767	308,858,098	88.6	78.1	83.3
0100000	Alabama.........	$53,991	$26,970	$40,869	$76,759	$94,234	$73,523	$32,653	$18,502	4,737,268	90.2	78.8	83.9
0103076	Auburn city..................	$73,585	$26,417	$60,315	$89,931	$122,174	$89,589	$43,005	$23,723	56,654	96.7	85.7	88.7
0107000	Birmingham city.........	$36,648	$16,367	$29,116	$65,499	$66,780	$57,558	$21,098	$16,276	208,366	87.0	79.5	82.2
0120104	Decatur city................	$54,877	$36,211	$29,297	$71,044	$77,386	$71,456	$29,025	$13,133	54,876	87.3	76.5	82.9
0121184	Dothan city.................	$54,197	$28,796	$38,673	$76,636	$95,066	$79,021	$32,083	$16,486	66,462	91.3	79.1	81.6
0135896	Hoover city.................	$99,435	$54,697	$84,560	$110,935	$127,255	$116,704	$74,276	$37,247	82,620	94.9	81.5	94.2
0137000	Huntsville city.............	$63,800	$46,277	$43,529	$82,177	$112,962	$90,948	$28,515	$21,868	181,428	90.2	74.6	82.4
0150000	Mobile city.................	$47,782	$21,818	$32,309	$72,472	$94,094	$71,817	$27,910	$15,714	188,469	88.9	77.7	80.6
0151000	Montgomery city..........	$52,689	$23,021	$37,538	$75,527	$90,652	$77,210	$32,762	$20,204	200,240	90.9	80.1	83.8
0177256	Tuscaloosa city............	$51,160	$20,227	$40,399	$76,299	$90,386	$80,813	$30,051	$18,443	92,980	90.4	78.6	89.2
0200000	Alaska	$81,721	$38,919	$55,788	$98,171	$121,285	$92,503	$51,540	$31,776	706,544	85.4	71.0	74.5
0203000	Anchorage municipality	$89,235	$50,084	$54,366	$104,588	$133,354	$100,284	$60,353	$35,906	287,519	87.5	74.7	79.5
0400000	Arizona.........	$57,317	$36,056	$42,897	$79,086	$92,730	$72,137	$35,918	$25,228	6,441,287	85.9	76.8	81.2
0404720	Avondale city...............	$56,976	$16,055	$40,048	$74,004	$87,553	$61,911	$55,353	$33,938	77,756	83.1	75.5	77.2
0407940	Buckeye town..............	$65,355	$41,444	$48,860	$77,999	$69,643	$79,174	$16,938	$26,346	48,821	84.7	84.5	81.5
0410670	Casas Adobes CDP.........	$61,869	$41,880	$45,643	$77,792	$97,500	$75,641	$37,089	$32,203	68,739	91.3	86.2	88.3
0411230	Catalina Foothills CDP...	$101,680	$69,205	$99,055	$126,221	$145,244	$133,342	$99,537	$57,629	51,136	97.1	88.7	92.3
0412000	Chandler city..............	$81,967	$38,079	$60,679	$101,276	$115,820	$99,992	$49,858	$38,288	244,673	90.9	82.2	84.9
0423620	Flagstaff city...............	$65,958	$51,875	$43,851	$77,090	$94,663	$81,233	$34,346	$22,860	66,869	83.0	73.1	77.6
0427400	Gilbert town................	$87,457	$41,952	$66,436	$102,500	$110,470	$98,495	$61,651	$45,066	221,339	91.8	85.2	84.7
0427820	Glendale city...............	$52,478	$24,811	$35,886	$74,069	$91,421	$59,400	$32,350	$25,376	229,541	82.4	75.8	75.6
0428380	Goodyear city..............	$72,379	$44,531	$49,067	$92,222	$123,229	$89,204	$49,265	$34,235	65,877	90.5	85.9	85.2
0439370	Lake Havasu City city	$49,626	$39,253	$47,950	$63,430	$82,644	$53,478	$44,595	$20,906	52,677	89.7	76.9	76.1
0446000	Mesa city...................	$57,132	$40,609	$40,849	$75,600	$98,873	$69,142	$36,833	$26,708	449,871	85.8	75.1	78.5
0454050	Peoria city..................	$74,922	$41,449	$52,715	$94,989	$110,718	$96,487	$41,572	$35,000	158,582	90.7	78.0	86.6
0455000	Phoenix city................	$52,251	$18,782	$36,778	$76,804	$89,236	$63,678	$33,359	$23,648	1,478,646	80.0	72.5	76.5
0464210	San Tan Valley CDP........	$59,184	$34,977	$47,129	$71,588	$91,453	$64,613	$44,224	$31,597	89,103	85.2	83.3	85.7
0465000	Scottsdale city.............	$91,108	$46,534	$75,263	$122,483	$134,748	$121,360	$66,538	$32,819	222,623	95.1	84.2	84.6
0471510	Surprise city...............	$62,265	$50,195	$53,152	$83,909	$98,783	$75,923	$39,375	$31,268	120,913	93.4	86.9	88.0
0473000	Tempe city..................	$62,350	$37,656	$46,915	$82,568	$105,846	$86,669	$34,750	$21,929	165,803	87.3	79.5	81.3
0477000	Tucson city.................	$44,920	$25,959	$32,017	$62,464	$73,811	$56,021	$27,049	$20,751	510,805	84.2	77.6	81.2
0485540	Yuma city...................	$47,040	$31,678	$33,629	$64,118	$72,757	$55,161	$33,611	$23,519	86,933	82.2	78.1	84.9
0500000	Arkansas	$50,600	$27,052	$37,644	$69,917	$88,984	$64,920	$29,332	$18,687	2,896,439	86.9	76.8	80.7
0515190	Conway city................	$65,510	$44,946	$48,781	$81,848	$117,717	$78,036	$46,075	$21,881	61,821	91.1	86.5	83.4
0523290	Fayetteville city............	$68,780	$37,534	$56,508	$75,917	$113,235	$85,433	$29,352	$20,286	76,125	87.4	78.3	87.3
0524550	Fort Smith city.............	$45,595	$25,373	$32,632	$65,431	$87,622	$54,501	$25,000	$16,510	86,517	82.0	73.3	77.4
0535710	Jonesboro city..............	$51,961	$30,507	$36,122	$75,031	$96,098	$75,815	$44,430	$15,122	69,592	87.6	77.6	80.7
0541000	Little Rock city.............	$59,593	$23,441	$46,034	$83,440	$97,733	$100,993	$21,963	$22,984	194,544	90.6	77.8	80.4
0550450	North Little Rock city.....	$50,853	$28,953	$35,704	$68,161	$88,681	$57,781	$31,932	$19,679	63,755	87.1	82.2	72.8
0560410	Rogers city.................	$60,569	$43,051	$40,546	$78,473	$88,111	$71,753	$32,200	$21,929	58,557	84.6	70.9	79.8
0566080	Springdale city.............	$43,412	$18,296	$30,612	$60,078	$77,340	$55,110	$29,499	$18,733	75,092	80.3	72.6	77.8
0600000	California.........	$67,746	$29,455	$48,976	$91,345	$100,397	$82,294	$37,371	$26,341	37,487,065	85.1	75.8	82.0
0600562	Alameda city...............	$86,780	$50,865	$58,347	$115,549	$150,588	$121,814	$48,182	$38,979	74,207	90.1	83.1	85.7
0600884	Alhambra city..............	$57,098	$20,207	$40,767	$81,090	$107,944	$71,686	$39,383	$39,874	83,639	82.9	77.0	82.0
0602000	Anaheim city...............	$61,844	$22,979	$40,977	$77,690	$99,863	$66,006	$34,972	$26,291	340,927	79.8	70.4	78.1
0602252	Antioch city................	$69,169	$28,322	$47,567	$90,212	$112,905	$82,944	$39,484	$33,135	105,088	88.4	85.3	82.1
0602364	Apple Valley town.........	$51,814	$22,363	$47,188	$84,270	$120,580	$73,212	$36,552	$16,042	70,066	89.0	75.9	80.7
0602462	Arcadia city................	$92,373	$31,641	$71,649	$123,219	$116,351	$117,746	$106,250	$34,083	56,889	90.6	81.1	85.8
0602553	Arden-Arcade CDP.........	$57,050	$31,641	$48,396	$84,748	$90,201	$73,333	$31,875	$18,944	90,713	89.4	77.9	79.9
0603526	Bakersfield city............	$59,626	$22,167	$41,041	$77,383	$99,119	$72,031	$35,228	$20,603	356,567	85.3	77.7	79.3
0603666	Baldwin Park city..........	$51,632	$16,233	$38,425	$54,462	$80,977	$54,451	$54,180	$26,698	75,872	72.0	73.6	66.8
0604982	Bellflower city..............	$50,446	$22,891	$37,013	$68,872	$92,912	$60,593	$29,303	$30,586	76,948	82.8	74.3	76.3
0606000	Berkeley city...............	$108,358	$59,209	$74,279	$141,250	$144,850	$157,006	$47,171	$35,837	114,898	94.9	83.1	91.1
0608142	Brentwood city.............	$103,660	$47,552	$81,882	$113,774	$130,321	$116,750	$91,753	$43,456	53,742	94.2	84.1	94.8
0608786	Buena Park city............	$73,596	$22,861	$50,297	$89,476	$118,117	$85,882	$42,279	$30,029	81,990	83.3	76.6	73.6
0608954	Burbank city...............	$80,339	$25,213	$55,069	$97,705	$116,357	$98,172	$45,341	$43,644	103,954	86.7	80.5	79.1
0610046	Camarillo city..............	$100,637	$59,926	$76,847	$113,958	$148,420	$117,643	$62,530	$25,253	65,137	90.1	81.7	86.9
0611194	Carlsbad city...............	$101,026	$33,991	$82,982	$131,996	$132,768	$127,605	$65,290	$29,245	108,022	93.1	76.8	85.1
0611390	Carmichael CDP............	$71,296	$39,247	$51,058	$89,639	$90,738	$85,061	$27,165	$30,173	62,393	91.7	80.6	83.4
0611530	Carson city.................	$77,195	$33,750	$60,199	$88,875	$102,593	$83,877	$53,235	$53,193	92,153	83.6	81.3	78.8
0611964	Castro Valley CDP.........	$95,611	$54,681	$72,765	$114,957	$138,458	$114,971	$37,097	$53,578	60,099	93.3	78.4	87.1
0612048	Cathedral City city........	$42,636	$27,193	$31,005	$61,411	$63,351	$46,602	$26,269	$25,260	52,467	70.4	64.9	79.0
0613014	Chico city..................	$57,206	$25,016	$34,101	$77,472	$89,301	$70,698	$25,417	$18,329	86,737	88.3	79.6	81.2
0613210	Chino city..................	$73,249	$28,077	$55,911	$89,244	$100,964	$87,063	$40,481	$35,686	71,911	85.4	77.0	85.7
0613214	Chino Hills city............	$97,993	$33,107	$73,725	$115,021	$138,668	$107,386	$52,482	$48,395	76,037	88.7	78.6	82.6
0613392	Chula Vista city............	$70,930	$23,314	$50,067	$91,634	$116,654	$86,579	$49,070	$24,714	248,496	85.4	75.5	81.2
0613588	Citrus Heights city........	$57,784	$39,624	$45,832	$69,855	$99,093	$62,879	$31,810	$27,375	84,302	85.7	78.4	80.6
0614218	Clovis city..................	$71,174	$26,781	$52,305	$94,063	$117,761	$94,608	$28,288	$30,813	98,147	90.0	82.8	79.2

State/ Place FIPS code	State/place	Total number of families	Families with incomes below the poverty level, as a percent of all families of that family type				Families that received Food Stamps (SNAP), as a percent of all families of that family type			Families that received food stamps (SNAP) and had at least one worker	
			All families	Married-couple families	Male householder families, no spouse present	Female householder families, no spouse present	All families	Married-couple families	Male householder or female householder families, no spouse present	Married-couple families, percent	Male householder or female householder families, no spouse present
0000000	United States............................	76,444,922	11.7	8.7	23.4	41.1	14.4	7.4	33.3	6.2	24.2
0100000	**Alabama**............................	1,236,566	14.6	9.5	26.7	49.6	17.6	8.4	40.1	6.9	27.3
0103076	Auburn city............................	10,656	12.0	6.9	16.4	43.2	...	...	...	...	...
0107000	Birmingham city............................	46,966	26.2	15.8	49.5	56.9	32.1	15.7	47.3	13.2	31.2
0120104	Decatur city............................	13,879	17.5	14.6	24.2	61.5	17.9	8.8	41.5	8.2	32.4
0121184	Dothan city............................	17,108	14.9	5.0	33.6	57.0	17.1	4.8	43.6	4.1	30.5
0135896	Hoover city............................	22,371	4.0	4.0	0.0	15.0	5.3	3.1	14.2	3.1	13.7
0137000	Huntsville city............................	44,240	13.1	8.2	26.1	42.9	15.9	6.0	35.6	4.9	30.0
0150000	Mobile city............................	45,823	21.0	9.8	28.8	55.4	24.5	8.7	45.9	7.1	31.8
0151000	Montgomery city............................	49,199	19.9	9.6	44.6	48.2	26.4	9.5	48.6	8.1	36.8
0177256	Tuscaloosa city............................	18,322	16.7	8.7	19.3	49.3	16.9	4.4	36.8	3.9	23.1
0200000	**Alaska**............................	167,553	6.8	4.2	18.0	26.3	11.0	6.1	24.9	5.5	20.6
0203000	Anchorage municipality.................	69,047	5.0	3.0	11.6	20.9	9.1	4.9	20.7	4.5	18.3
0400000	**Arizona**............................	1,560,655	13.7	12.7	26.6	40.3	16.1	9.3	33.8	8.1	24.9
0404720	Avondale city............................	17,638	15.4	12.6	17.6	35.4	20.3	11.9	33.3	11.1	26.2
0407940	Buckeye town........................	11,682	14.0	9.8	50.4	42.0	13.2	9.8	23.7	9.2	14.2
0410670	Casas Adobes CDP.....................	17,460	8.7	8.3	9.9	23.7	11.9	7.0	25.9	6.4	20.7
0411230	Catalina Foothills CDP.................	14,683	3.5	2.0	23.1	24.7	...	...	...	...	...
0412000	Chandler city............................	60,280	7.1	6.5	15.1	23.4	9.6	6.0	21.0	5.7	16.5
0423620	Flagstaff city............................	13,620	15.6	10.7	34.3	42.6	16.7	6.7	35.8	6.0	31.1
0427400	Gilbert town............................	55,207	5.2	3.8	12.4	21.5	5.9	3.6	15.4	3.2	12.2
0427820	Glendale city............................	53,243	17.8	16.9	31.7	41.8	22.3	13.6	38.1	12.0	28.8
0428380	Goodyear city............................	18,235	6.8	5.0	19.3	31.9	5.9	5.5	7.7	5.0	5.9
0439370	Lake Havasu City city..................	14,863	10.6	13.4	23.1	38.2	9.4	3.8	31.2	3.6	23.1
0446000	Mesa city............................	108,002	13.0	12.4	22.3	36.7	14.1	8.1	28.5	7.3	22.7
0454050	Peoria city............................	40,775	7.8	6.4	16.8	24.1	8.3	4.3	20.7	3.7	15.9
0455000	Phoenix city............................	328,055	18.7	17.0	30.3	44.7	21.1	12.6	36.6	11.1	26.0
0464210	San Tan Valley CDP..................	20,741	10.4	10.5	9.4	27.8	15.7	12.2	28.3	12.2	24.5
0465000	Scottsdale city............................	58,014	6.5	5.7	9.3	29.5	5.0	2.2	15.7	2.0	12.5
0471510	Surprise city............................	32,484	8.1	8.5	11.8	25.9	8.2	5.1	20.3	4.7	17.8
0473000	Tempe city............................	30,548	12.3	8.0	24.0	44.2	13.7	6.4	27.0	6.1	21.7
0477000	Tucson city............................	112,012	19.3	16.3	28.2	47.6	24.7	13.3	42.4	11.9	32.4
0485540	Yuma city............................	24,209	14.0	10.3	17.2	44.8	21.6	14.1	42.2	12.7	33.0
0500000	**Arkansas**............................	755,344	14.6	11.4	28.2	49.0	16.2	8.2	37.9	6.6	26.4
0515190	Conway city............................	13,735	9.9	7.7	11.3	35.4	10.2	4.6	25.8	3.9	22.1
0523290	Fayetteville city............................	14,805	11.6	4.3	31.8	46.7	10.0	3.4	29.9	3.3	22.0
0524550	Fort Smith city............................	21,387	20.3	18.3	42.8	60.1	21.5	12.0	43.0	9.3	31.7
0535710	Jonesboro city............................	17,209	18.2	11.5	23.9	60.1	19.8	7.5	42.0	6.4	31.1
0541000	Little Rock city............................	44,547	12.8	5.8	32.1	34.7	17.2	7.3	34.4	4.7	24.6
0550450	North Little Rock city..................	14,102	16.8	15.1	23.4	48.9	19.8	9.5	38.4	8.9	24.6
0560410	Rogers city............................	14,103	13.6	11.0	22.5	45.2	9.7	3.9	29.9	3.8	25.4
0566080	Springdale city............................	18,427	20.1	16.9	24.4	56.7	19.2	13.1	31.7	12.4	24.0
0600000	**California**............................	8,602,735	12.7	11.1	24.6	38.6	11.3	6.6	22.9	5.8	16.2
0600562	Alameda city............................	18,673	7.0	5.1	13.7	22.9	7.9	5.1	15.9	4.8	11.2
0600884	Alhambra city............................	20,027	12.2	12.4	22.0	24.9	6.9	5.5	10.0	4.6	8.2
0602000	Anaheim city............................	74,753	14.5	13.3	27.8	41.1	13.0	8.7	23.2	7.7	17.5
0602252	Antioch city............................	24,887	12.1	11.6	19.5	35.6	13.6	6.8	27.8	5.0	20.2
0602364	Apple Valley town.....................	18,179	19.7	16.9	33.8	55.3	19.1	11.4	37.6	8.4	19.2
0602462	Arcadia city............................	14,927	9.2	7.3	0.0	27.3	1.1	1.2	0.7	1.1	0.3
0602553	Arden-Arcade CDP....................	21,580	15.8	15.0	25.7	45.0	19.4	11.7	34.8	8.9	23.1
0603526	Bakersfield city............................	82,170	17.5	11.1	25.4	52.5	15.8	8.2	31.0	7.7	21.7
0603666	Baldwin Park city.....................	15,157	15.7	18.3	3.5	36.7	16.3	13.1	22.0	12.0	16.2
0604982	Bellflower city............................	17,337	15.5	16.9	22.8	36.6	13.9	9.0	21.4	7.6	16.6
0606000	Berkeley city............................	19,733	7.7	1.8	26.4	28.3	5.6	2.1	16.4	2.0	10.5
0608142	Brentwood city............................	13,679	4.0	2.6	3.0	20.2	...	...	...	...	...
0608786	Buena Park city............................	19,267	9.6	8.0	25.7	35.6	9.7	5.1	20.6	4.4	14.3
0608954	Burbank city............................	25,043	6.8	4.7	18.2	21.2	4.5	2.2	10.5	2.0	6.5
0610046	Camarillo city............................	16,363	3.7	1.7	2.3	26.9	4.2	3.0	9.1	3.0	7.7
0611194	Carlsbad city............................	28,823	11.0	9.9	31.3	24.7	2.9	1.5	9.0	1.5	6.8
0611390	Carmichael CDP........................	16,180	10.9	10.5	24.3	31.2	13.2	5.4	28.1	4.5	19.0
0611530	Carson city............................	20,111	7.3	8.0	17.3	23.6	6.9	4.8	11.1	4.3	9.5
0611964	Castro Valley CDP.....................	15,729	4.6	6.4	8.7	11.3	5.9	3.5	13.3	3.2	11.7
0612048	Cathedral City city....................	11,279	19.0	19.9	31.6	33.6	15.2	10.8	25.3	9.4	21.0
0613014	Chico city............................	17,451	14.2	7.4	24.1	47.3	12.4	4.9	27.7	4.7	17.1
0613210	Chino city............................	16,571	9.4	6.8	12.8	36.7	6.1	2.2	18.2	2.0	15.5
0613214	Chino Hills city............................	18,852	6.0	3.5	16.6	20.8	...	...	...	...	...
0613392	Chula Vista city............................	59,672	11.0	7.4	24.8	37.7	9.3	4.8	21.1	4.3	12.1
0613588	Citrus Heights city.....................	20,295	11.7	13.9	19.1	35.3	12.8	8.2	23.5	6.9	20.7
0614218	Clovis city............................	24,357	11.5	6.9	34.3	35.4	12.0	8.3	21.5	6.0	13.1

| State/Place FIPS code | State/place | Median family income in the past 12 months (in 2,013 inflation-adjusted dollars) | | | | | | | | Total population in households | Persons who had health insurance, as a percent of all persons in that household type | | |
		All families	Families with no earners	Families with one earner	Families with two earners	Families with three or more earners	Married-couple families with children	Male householder, no spouse present, with children	Female householder, no spouse present, with children		Married-couple families, percent	Male householder or female householder families, no spouse present	Nonfamily households
	California—cont'd												
0614890	Colton city	$42,436	$15,182	$28,672	$55,495	$74,222	$52,544	$50,089	$17,453	52,765	70.2	73.9	76.1
0615044	Compton city	$42,895	$12,167	$35,525	$52,435	$81,289	$50,207	$32,981	$21,743	97,377	73.1	73.9	77.1
0616000	Concord city	$73,160	$37,539	$55,552	$101,054	$110,958	$88,622	$42,234	$23,732	123,912	89.4	75.5	81.3
0616350	Corona city	$81,795	$29,252	$53,290	$98,542	$119,304	$92,380	$36,234	$34,141	156,984	84.9	74.7	82.8
0616532	Costa Mesa city	$74,390	$35,897	$46,748	$94,229	$97,862	$80,352	$37,833	$31,382	111,146	80.6	70.4	78.6
0617610	Cupertino city	$159,255	$46,298	$129,311	$208,415	$194,196	$188,285	$160,991	$77,851	59,401	97.6	89.5	93.5
0617918	Daly City city	$76,743	$42,939	$52,841	$87,267	$112,704	$83,809	$34,038	$42,736	103,225	89.9	74.3	84.6
0618100	Davis city	$104,483	$66,531	$78,348	$132,589	$132,750	$128,621	$51,131	$36,362	65,560	95.0	81.7	90.9
0618394	Delano city	$35,837	$15,327	$27,134	$42,251	$60,766	$42,761	$20,677	$15,504	44,508	73.3	75.2	80.6
0619192	Diamond Bar city	$96,482	$38,841	$62,592	$121,165	$131,569	$110,707	$51,518	$35,357	56,105	88.7	79.5	83.1
0619766	Downey city	$64,591	$30,789	$43,821	$78,035	$102,055	$77,337	$36,276	$38,621	112,216	80.5	76.4	78.5
0620802	East Los Angeles CDP	$39,307	$15,350	$25,720	$49,261	$71,748	$44,178	$22,970	$17,049	130,389	65.8	62.4	57.0
0621230	Eastvale city	$111,572	$41,473	$71,303	$121,573	$147,102	$120,756	$96,348	$62,096	54,849	88.3	83.5	76.6
0621712	El Cajon city	$47,950	$19,096	$33,995	$67,671	$93,480	$51,391	$27,027	$21,962	99,708	81.9	71.5	79.4
0622020	Elk Grove city	$80,022	$36,036	$61,490	$105,519	$118,557	$102,114	$62,628	$39,986	158,050	92.7	86.1	90.1
0622230	El Monte city	$38,208	$17,891	$30,557	$51,323	$86,508	$37,220	$31,483	$22,506	114,168	72.9	70.2	65.9
0622678	Encinitas city	$110,126	$56,125	$91,885	$129,585	$153,764	$128,037	$56,779	$32,750	60,509	91.0	79.4	85.1
0622804	Escondido city	$50,942	$12,764	$34,171	$71,820	$88,022	$52,709	$25,879	$26,493	146,179	77.2	68.5	80.7
0623182	Fairfield city	$71,721	$41,667	$54,793	$93,235	$102,577	$75,156	$47,745	$22,940	103,911	89.6	82.4	85.7
0624477	Florence-Graham CDP	$32,545	$9,194	$23,383	$47,308	$75,630	$37,372	$26,339	$16,435	63,750	66.9	64.5	61.2
0624498	Florin CDP	$42,274	$22,052	$35,835	$61,446	$79,476	$52,845	$27,236	$20,691	50,694	79.3	80.7	78.0
0624638	Folsom city	$111,970	$48,750	$98,987	$136,017	$125,000	$132,996	$74,729	$63,061	66,675	95.5	91.2	89.1
0624680	Fontana city	$66,331	$18,322	$41,809	$81,695	$95,708	$74,480	$34,960	$27,481	200,874	78.0	69.9	78.0
0625380	Fountain Valley city	$92,759	$41,747	$75,208	$114,675	$138,125	$113,042	$32,399	$38,220	56,162	91.8	82.3	83.3
0626000	Fremont city	$109,759	$32,866	$89,675	$143,817	$134,092	$132,280	$53,622	$38,923	220,575	93.7	85.4	86.9
0627000	Fresno city	$43,192	$16,570	$33,298	$67,333	$74,716	$56,428	$24,562	$17,034	501,107	83.1	78.3	76.3
0628000	Fullerton city	$75,724	$40,514	$53,822	$98,188	$102,994	$88,933	$26,154	$28,464	137,172	82.9	71.5	81.8
0628168	Gardena city	$53,300	$27,803	$35,911	$81,880	$91,211	$63,066	$34,048	$32,163	58,950	80.8	71.4	79.6
0629000	Garden Grove city	$60,490	$20,273	$41,329	$72,366	$102,637	$63,401	$39,200	$31,514	173,288	81.8	74.6	80.0
0629504	Gilroy city	$84,934	$24,013	$60,319	$102,232	$100,634	$89,552	$50,921	$26,599	50,446	88.2	76.3	83.6
0630000	Glendale city	$60,536	$19,406	$43,875	$88,092	$93,600	$76,814	$42,610	$32,872	193,310	83.1	73.5	81.8
0630014	Glendora city	$78,320	$43,614	$61,083	$100,234	$126,405	$91,300	$53,871	$31,941	50,057	91.1	85.1	88.9
0631596	Hacienda Heights CDP	$79,527	$37,875	$61,002	$93,603	$131,640	$87,188	$45,804	$31,429	53,932	86.5	75.7	80.8
0631960	Hanford city	$55,826	$21,500	$40,212	$88,478	$77,986	$75,220	$22,376	$23,060	53,261	86.5	82.2	83.9
0632548	Hawthorne city	$46,940	$14,471	$31,355	$63,756	$80,943	$52,864	$30,729	$25,700	85,263	76.4	71.5	71.7
0633000	Hayward city	$67,330	$23,841	$45,244	$80,551	$109,888	$73,745	$33,125	$20,990	148,274	83.5	78.2	81.4
0633182	Hemet city	$40,438	$28,196	$36,942	$58,813	$70,523	$46,793	$39,583	$19,224	80,530	81.6	77.3	83.0
0633434	Hesperia city	$45,952	$21,804	$37,988	$75,005	$85,922	$52,314	$28,417	$23,000	91,771	84.2	68.0	68.9
0633588	Highland city	$56,809	$25,021	$41,616	$84,982	$77,554	$69,375	$36,528	$19,036	53,916	84.4	76.7	78.9
0636000	Huntington Beach city	$94,831	$51,201	$72,805	$122,953	$127,863	$121,603	$80,464	$34,239	194,624	91.3	80.9	84.5
0636056	Huntington Park city	$35,130	$13,411	$24,190	$41,612	$67,726	$36,430	$21,600	$18,533	58,584	69.2	62.8	61.7
0636448	Indio city	$52,354	$31,863	$38,522	$64,092	$84,742	$61,383	$24,088	$20,363	81,797	79.3	69.8	76.7
0636546	Inglewood city	$46,324	$22,055	$31,398	$70,085	$85,525	$53,421	$23,650	$24,940	110,627	75.9	73.3	77.9
0636770	Irvine city	$105,796	$30,134	$90,170	$133,668	$151,275	$124,941	$90,538	$41,629	228,320	92.3	81.9	91.8
0637692	Jurupa Valley city	$57,474	$22,002	$39,919	$68,657	$81,667	$55,651	$45,332	$26,149	96,520	72.9	70.2	78.2
0639248	Laguna Niguel city	$124,533	$60,593	$96,424	$146,228	$160,500	$143,111	$76,194	$46,607	64,149	93.9	80.6	87.9
0639290	La Habra city	$66,819	$36,050	$40,133	$80,031	$105,493	$70,000	$24,891	$28,878	61,102	78.7	71.8	82.4
0639486	Lake Elsinore city	$61,091	$15,655	$42,846	$83,236	$112,143	$68,133	$44,521	$21,967	55,868	82.9	72.3	73.4
0639496	Lake Forest city	$105,534	$50,685	$70,359	$117,044	$132,522	$116,944	$49,950	$45,719	78,590	88.3	79.3	93.6
0639892	Lakewood city	$84,142	$35,291	$61,649	$104,953	$108,412	$103,382	$59,620	$43,768	80,757	91.1	77.7	88.0
0640004	La Mesa city	$68,981	$37,325	$54,518	$82,246	$140,050	$82,192	$20,351	$36,194	57,130	88.2	79.1	84.0
0640130	Lancaster city	$51,962	$14,205	$43,157	$75,272	$109,277	$62,925	$35,225	$20,945	151,967	83.5	80.2	85.2
0641992	Livermore city	$106,676	$60,366	$86,520	$134,262	$129,405	$134,556	$85,895	$41,349	83,517	92.9	84.1	90.1
0642202	Lodi city	$54,400	$40,729	$43,235	$71,513	$81,250	$58,498	$40,478	$21,586	62,614	84.7	73.7	80.3
0643000	Long Beach city	$56,629	$19,297	$37,079	$79,063	$96,257	$71,795	$31,995	$23,858	464,227	82.2	76.3	81.6
0644000	Los Angeles city	$52,185	$18,721	$35,362	$74,222	$81,855	$62,822	$27,972	$21,484	3,826,966	77.7	69.5	76.0
0644574	Lynwood city	$40,799	$16,364	$27,418	$51,994	$72,320	$47,608	$30,140	$21,157	68,444	70.5	64.0	65.9
0645022	Madera city	$41,625	$19,119	$33,008	$55,029	$73,098	$47,272	$21,583	$18,507	62,342	80.2	75.6	63.3
0645484	Manteca city	$66,483	$36,679	$46,628	$79,341	$99,301	$74,970	$52,407	$29,923	70,361	86.8	82.8	79.8
0646842	Menifee city	$63,652	$37,833	$54,826	$77,500	$97,574	$76,861	$45,179	$61,142	80,952	87.0	78.8	85.4
0646898	Merced city	$42,136	$16,408	$31,431	$66,811	$85,897	$50,735	$36,955	$17,693	79,641	87.3	84.5	73.3
0647766	Milpitas city	$97,935	$23,898	$67,927	$122,961	$124,719	$114,433	$58,883	$53,666	66,462	91.7	80.1	88.1
0648256	Mission Viejo city	$106,899	$52,887	$92,074	$131,238	$142,279	$118,117	$80,982	$56,948	94,766	93.7	82.6	89.1
0648354	Modesto city	$52,041	$24,512	$40,262	$74,703	$96,651	$65,783	$32,439	$17,245	201,807	84.9	78.7	77.8
0648816	Montebello city	$52,515	$21,853	$40,608	$69,531	$105,259	$66,147	$30,069	$32,070	62,769	78.7	72.7	66.9
0648914	Monterey Park city	$62,528	$25,743	$43,788	$80,245	$92,124	$68,831	$51,875	$31,688	60,578	82.8	74.9	65.9
0649270	Moreno Valley city	$53,648	$19,112	$39,760	$67,276	$90,517	$56,946	$40,860	$25,237	198,650	76.7	74.6	76.6
0649670	Mountain View city	$118,075	$22,019	$82,841	$169,650	$117,250	$160,882	$34,615	$40,806	76,330	92.5	77.2	91.6
0650076	Murrieta city	$75,219	$40,972	$61,529	$95,168	$103,112	$90,460	$46,118	$36,156	105,127	86.1	82.8	84.8
0650258	Napa city	$72,348	$48,526	$50,122	$85,995	$88,575	$79,963	$41,827	$30,990	77,564	86.6	78.4	82.9
0650398	National City city	$40,148	$15,194	$26,501	$57,015	$75,363	$44,706	$23,831	$18,449	54,892	70.4	64.5	72.6

Table E-4: Cities with a Population of 50,000 or More—Income, Poverty, and Health Insurance—*Continued*

State/ Place FIPS code	State/place	Total number of families	Families with incomes below the poverty level, as a percent of all families of that family type				Families that received Food Stamps (SNAP), as a percent of all families of that family type			Families that received food stamps (SNAP) and had at least one worker	
			All families	Married-couple families	Male householder families, no spouse present	Female householder families, no spouse present	All families	Married-couple families	Male householder or female householder families, no spouse present	Married-couple families, percent	Male householder or female householder families, no spouse present
	California—cont'd										
0614890	Colton city	11,135	22.8	16.8	26.5	52.8	25.4	18.4	34.6	17.8	25.8
0615044	Compton city	18,831	26.1	24.5	29.0	46.6	25.1	20.3	30.5	18.3	20.6
0616000	Concord city	31,388	10.3	9.8	30.9	35.0	8.9	6.3	15.6	5.6	12.2
0616350	Corona city	35,961	9.6	8.1	21.8	31.4	10.0	6.3	21.7	6.0	17.5
0616532	Costa Mesa city	23,745	10.3	9.6	27.8	30.4	6.6	3.4	14.7	3.1	12.5
0617610	Cupertino city	16,015	2.7	0.8	34.3	16.4	...	...	...	...	...
0617918	Daly City city	22,069	5.2	3.4	29.7	18.1	3.7	2.5	6.8	2.3	5.3
0618100	Davis city	11,743	7.2	5.7	13.3	18.7	...	...	...	...	...
0618394	Delano city	9,309	28.5	21.7	44.0	69.5	25.1	14.8	44.4	14.8	34.4
0619192	Diamond Bar city	14,602	5.0	3.0	21.5	23.6	2.0	1.0	5.5	0.8	4.9
0619766	Downey city	25,745	10.0	8.4	15.5	27.8	8.7	3.8	17.5	3.4	15.7
0620802	East Los Angeles CDP	25,480	27.4	22.8	41.6	54.2	17.8	15.2	21.2	14.2	14.3
0621230	Eastvale city	11,400	4.7	2.7	31.9	15.4	...	...	...	...	...
0621712	El Cajon city	23,220	22.4	27.4	25.3	40.7	25.1	19.7	34.1	15.1	25.4
0622020	Elk Grove city	38,226	7.7	5.9	14.2	25.1	6.9	5.0	12.0	4.3	8.1
0622230	El Monte city	25,024	24.0	29.1	35.1	43.6	16.8	11.7	25.4	11.1	18.1
0622678	Encinitas city	14,895	5.7	4.2	14.6	24.9	...	...	...	...	...
0622804	Escondido city	32,530	16.5	14.5	31.6	32.2	8.3	4.9	17.2	4.8	13.6
0623182	Fairfield city	25,778	10.7	10.4	13.9	40.0	11.9	7.6	25.1	6.7	17.1
0624477	Florence-Graham CDP	12,475	34.3	30.1	33.8	60.2	31.6	23.1	40.3	20.7	28.8
0624498	Florin CDP	11,253	22.1	23.0	41.3	43.4	29.0	18.0	42.9	14.3	28.6
0624638	Folsom city	17,263	1.7	1.0	10.9	4.9	...	...	...	...	...
0624680	Fontana city	41,070	13.0	9.1	23.2	39.7	15.2	9.9	27.1	9.2	21.1
0625380	Fountain Valley city	14,204	5.8	6.6	9.6	27.4	4.4	2.8	10.1	2.8	8.4
0626000	Fremont city	56,233	4.2	2.2	10.4	25.4	4.6	2.8	12.4	2.5	9.3
0627000	Fresno city	112,016	25.6	22.6	39.8	55.7	27.8	16.6	43.6	14.8	28.8
0628000	Fullerton city	31,486	12.3	12.6	31.6	36.0	7.6	4.0	18.2	3.8	15.9
0628168	Gardena city	14,023	11.3	10.3	25.1	30.6	5.5	3.6	9.1	3.0	8.6
0629000	Garden Grove city	36,757	14.2	15.5	23.2	33.8	13.5	11.0	19.1	9.9	15.0
0629504	Gilroy city	11,797	11.8	13.3	7.2	35.4	13.8	8.0	27.2	7.9	19.2
0630000	Glendale city	48,359	11.3	13.9	23.5	27.3	9.7	9.1	11.1	7.6	8.8
0630014	Glendora city	12,721	7.2	5.7	15.6	24.8	4.0	2.4	9.1	1.9	8.0
0631596	Hacienda Heights CDP	12,610	6.0	3.6	5.5	25.1	4.6	3.9	6.5	3.5	6.1
0631960	Hanford city	13,272	17.6	9.3	42.7	45.1	18.2	6.9	40.7	5.8	27.3
0632548	Hawthorne city	19,068	18.3	17.4	23.9	39.3	16.6	11.4	22.8	11.0	14.8
0633000	Hayward city	33,541	12.0	10.3	19.4	39.4	15.5	9.4	28.1	8.7	19.8
0633182	Hemet city	18,898	21.9	18.9	39.1	49.3	21.1	10.9	40.5	9.3	29.3
0633434	Hesperia city	20,752	21.5	20.2	30.2	46.9	22.4	15.7	36.4	13.2	25.3
0633588	Highland city	11,989	18.0	9.9	23.2	58.1	20.5	12.7	36.8	11.7	21.5
0636000	Huntington Beach city	49,435	6.8	5.0	24.5	26.4	5.4	2.9	13.2	2.5	11.7
0636056	Huntington Park city	12,295	28.1	28.4	39.5	49.8	24.4	18.7	31.1	16.7	25.6
0636448	Indio city	19,427	16.2	12.7	34.9	46.4	15.9	7.6	34.5	6.5	25.8
0636546	Inglewood city	24,860	18.5	21.3	30.6	30.9	15.7	8.8	23.5	7.8	17.8
0636770	Irvine city	54,868	6.2	4.0	8.1	25.6	2.5	1.4	6.7	0.9	5.2
0637692	Jurupa Valley city	19,611	15.0	16.2	25.9	31.2	19.2	15.0	29.8	14.0	20.0
0639248	Laguna Niguel city	17,030	4.0	2.6	0.0	22.5	...	...	...	...	...
0639290	La Habra city	13,898	13.3	12.5	40.4	38.5	12.2	8.7	21.0	8.6	18.4
0639486	Lake Elsinore city	12,266	12.9	7.0	33.3	47.1	12.1	6.9	26.1	6.6	18.5
0639496	Lake Forest city	19,955	4.9	2.8	18.2	16.3	...	...	...	...	...
0639892	Lakewood city	19,934	5.3	4.2	4.1	16.0	5.2	2.4	11.5	2.3	9.1
0640004	La Mesa city	13,643	8.4	3.1	42.9	28.6	8.5	3.9	18.9	3.7	12.9
0640130	Lancaster city	34,930	19.1	14.7	31.5	48.2	12.7	6.3	25.3	4.9	13.0
0641992	Livermore city	21,901	4.5	3.5	4.5	17.5	4.9	4.0	7.9	4.0	5.8
0642202	Lodi city	15,024	13.6	17.2	11.4	44.4	14.3	10.2	25.1	9.7	19.5
0643000	Long Beach city	99,083	17.5	14.5	30.5	42.1	16.6	8.6	28.9	7.6	20.4
0644000	Los Angeles city	794,502	18.6	18.0	31.7	46.1	12.7	7.7	21.0	7.1	15.0
0644574	Lynwood city	12,848	24.3	18.2	27.9	53.0	22.5	15.7	31.8	15.2	22.6
0645022	Madera city	12,950	23.3	20.0	35.4	51.3	25.2	17.7	36.4	15.7	25.0
0645484	Manteca city	16,670	10.0	8.3	9.4	32.8	10.4	5.6	22.9	5.1	19.4
0646842	Menifee city	18,769	6.8	5.0	17.6	25.5	6.1	4.8	11.0	3.4	9.0
0646898	Merced city	17,526	25.5	23.7	34.7	56.6	30.4	18.8	48.0	15.7	29.3
0647766	Milpitas city	15,703	7.1	4.1	9.9	29.5	5.3	2.6	14.5	2.4	12.4
0648256	Mission Viejo city	25,564	3.7	3.9	2.2	17.8	1.5	0.7	5.4	0.7	4.3
0648354	Modesto city	48,241	17.9	14.5	30.4	50.5	21.2	12.1	38.6	9.6	26.8
0648816	Montebello city	14,311	10.9	8.3	14.6	25.7	12.5	4.6	23.3	4.0	16.4
0648914	Monterey Park city	14,404	12.1	16.3	10.7	32.5	5.8	3.5	10.1	2.5	7.6
0649270	Moreno Valley city	42,657	17.2	16.0	22.2	38.9	18.5	12.3	29.0	11.0	19.6
0649670	Mountain View city	18,431	7.9	5.6	16.8	30.5	5.2	3.9	10.9	3.1	8.4
0650076	Murrieta city	24,933	6.4	5.7	33.1	24.9	6.1	4.6	12.9	4.0	9.8
0650258	Napa city	18,913	7.2	4.5	12.4	30.1	7.9	4.4	17.8	3.9	11.9
0650398	National City city	11,519	24.8	24.4	28.7	52.6	16.4	13.5	20.9	11.1	14.0

Table E-4: Cities with a Population of 50,000 or More—Income, Poverty, and Health Insurance—*Continued*

| State/ Place FIPS code | State/place | Median family income in the past 12 months (in 2,013 inflation-adjusted dollars) | | | | | | | | Total population in households | Persons who had health insurance, as a percent of all persons in that household type | | |
		All families	Families with no earners	Families with one earner	Families with two earners	Families with three or more earners	Married-couple families with children	Male householder, no spouse present, with children	Female householder, no spouse present, with children		Married-couple families, percent	Male householder or female householder families, no spouse present	Nonfamily households
	California—cont'd												
0651182	Newport Beach city	$137,246	$69,479	$130,476	$168,947	$149,430	$190,307	$75,221	$50,755	86,467	94.3	81.3	88.1
0652526	Norwalk city	$61,455	$22,451	$46,081	$72,920	$89,250	$74,144	$50,799	$36,569	105,234	78.5	71.4	81.8
0652582	Novato city	$96,425	$65,739	$73,035	$117,970	$133,077	$110,746	$49,853	$34,980	52,990	92.8	84.2	91.6
0653000	Oakland city	$58,320	$19,721	$40,250	$96,590	$81,946	$77,180	$32,230	$23,339	399,039	85.9	79.1	81.9
0653322	Oceanside city	$64,111	$33,523	$47,963	$78,615	$97,173	$73,737	$30,809	$32,139	167,418	85.6	75.4	83.6
0653896	Ontario city	$54,715	$21,989	$39,887	$65,827	$86,525	$61,821	$27,221	$27,534	166,425	75.5	71.7	82.0
0653980	Orange city	$83,419	$34,199	$61,722	$103,803	$110,362	$98,829	$59,643	$30,370	135,221	85.5	75.0	82.5
0654652	Oxnard city	$59,177	$26,993	$39,025	$66,458	$83,819	$60,909	$50,143	$28,892	199,889	76.4	72.8	80.0
0655156	Palmdale city	$52,289	$19,213	$38,999	$76,430	$93,877	$58,908	$35,599	$20,060	155,480	83.2	77.6	84.7
0655282	Palo Alto city	$168,932	$64,474	$137,356	$226,939	$181,719	$219,038	$210,156	$60,156	65,540	96.4	94.5	93.8
0655618	Paramount city	$46,045	$15,842	$30,226	$59,859	$81,603	$49,023	$41,950	$25,388	54,425	73.5	71.8	71.2
0656000	Pasadena city	$88,046	$33,967	$60,308	$105,711	$108,451	$113,242	$30,466	$30,211	137,690	88.7	71.4	87.1
0656700	Perris city	$45,936	$11,893	$32,046	$59,468	$82,935	$51,576	$29,933	$23,698	71,125	74.3	71.4	74.9
0656784	Petaluma city	$86,402	$40,762	$66,028	$103,253	$122,031	$106,048	$52,188	$44,317	58,389	89.5	80.5	88.4
0656924	Pico Rivera city	$62,047	$29,601	$42,779	$75,747	$94,471	$71,421	$45,121	$32,721	63,111	79.1	68.9	70.7
0657456	Pittsburg city	$61,746	$21,173	$45,940	$83,656	$115,357	$64,561	$50,230	$32,594	65,427	83.5	80.4	82.9
0657526	Placentia city	$83,993	$41,659	$65,757	$95,916	$131,217	$97,293	$51,361	$53,725	51,689	84.1	82.6	85.5
0657792	Pleasanton city	$136,330	$64,504	$116,222	$167,202	$162,616	$162,226	$104,745	$50,204	72,325	95.9	80.1	90.2
0658072	Pomona city	$51,170	$17,432	$32,912	$63,401	$78,958	$54,511	$40,481	$22,341	148,737	73.7	73.7	78.6
0658240	Porterville city	$41,830	$25,921	$30,799	$69,764	$54,653	$49,645	$30,471	$21,903	54,083	82.2	76.3	73.2
0659444	Rancho Cordova city	$52,939	$19,123	$42,461	$73,701	$87,077	$61,479	$50,319	$26,105	66,629	88.0	79.6	82.3
0659451	Rancho Cucamonga city	$88,590	$36,210	$60,857	$107,709	$111,583	$107,691	$60,260	$37,360	166,875	90.5	81.2	83.6
0659920	Redding city	$51,136	$31,180	$41,426	$82,753	$99,750	$65,201	$37,741	$25,696	89,625	85.5	82.8	79.7
0659962	Redlands city	$85,344	$42,209	$70,971	$106,537	$128,269	$92,401	$65,603	$43,167	69,155	89.4	85.8	87.2
0660018	Redondo Beach city	$121,187	$42,308	$82,793	$144,738	$146,149	$146,917	$81,109	$36,998	67,241	96.6	85.8	88.8
0660102	Redwood City city	$93,621	$46,150	$57,313	$127,648	$106,023	$118,043	$41,900	$43,036	78,264	89.1	76.7	85.3
0660466	Rialto city	$50,201	$21,031	$35,925	$59,735	$89,789	$52,254	$25,438	$23,313	101,159	75.5	74.0	74.6
0660620	Richmond city	$58,756	$22,255	$40,518	$77,003	$93,856	$64,327	$55,052	$21,039	105,415	83.4	74.4	80.0
0662000	Riverside city	$60,691	$25,087	$42,097	$77,209	$100,988	$64,844	$35,821	$28,133	310,548	81.7	75.3	81.7
0662364	Rocklin city	$82,865	$37,406	$61,497	$113,276	$120,199	$108,980	$62,821	$28,025	58,580	94.5	84.3	85.0
0662896	Rosemead city	$41,479	$19,108	$31,521	$61,266	$79,483	$38,750	$32,132	$24,682	54,057	74.9	74.7	72.6
0662938	Roseville city	$89,588	$45,012	$74,066	$109,743	$146,000	$111,162	$109,107	$39,526	123,905	95.4	82.2	83.1
0663218	Rowland Heights CDP	$62,391	$28,705	$51,423	$81,957	$102,241	$77,662	$56,531	$33,341	51,533	79.9	67.7	61.1
0664000	Sacramento city	$55,717	$21,020	$40,550	$78,423	$92,792	$70,417	$30,814	$22,938	471,369	85.6	81.3	82.9
0664224	Salinas city	$48,557	$21,909	$35,663	$62,210	$73,906	$52,909	$34,277	$21,858	152,218	78.1	70.8	69.5
0665000	San Bernardino city	$38,472	$12,867	$30,690	$60,574	$84,782	$48,067	$28,116	$16,236	209,179	75.1	76.0	72.8
0665042	San Buenaventura (Ventura) city	$79,528	$39,270	$58,872	$98,617	$116,567	$99,241	$40,859	$37,320	107,180	89.2	80.1	83.4
0665081	San Clemente city	$112,340	$49,792	$103,750	$133,930	$111,609	$132,116	$116,147	$39,844	64,216	90.2	80.6	84.1
0666000	San Diego city	$75,887	$31,904	$53,062	$97,643	$104,692	$89,312	$44,242	$26,580	1,299,051	86.5	76.4	82.6
0667000	San Francisco city	$89,497	$24,112	$57,044	$128,898	$111,848	$126,167	$54,121	$33,272	821,781	92.5	84.0	88.9
0668000	San Jose city	$88,755	$29,664	$62,065	$119,358	$113,057	$111,033	$47,672	$34,021	980,579	89.3	79.4	83.7
0668084	San Leandro city	$77,207	$43,440	$51,052	$94,455	$109,641	$86,225	$48,371	$39,007	86,615	90.1	76.0	88.1
0668196	San Marcos city	$61,030	$10,465	$53,119	$86,036	$87,942	$83,006	$29,754	$45,336	86,611	85.0	73.1	84.1
0668252	San Mateo city	$97,678	$58,302	$83,482	$117,597	$101,338	$127,549	$47,361	$52,474	99,353	91.0	80.9	88.0
0668364	San Rafael city	$94,546	$66,593	$73,824	$132,889	$75,856	$130,724	$41,875	$36,250	57,807	91.6	82.4	85.0
0668378	San Ramon city	$150,286	$50,107	$115,042	$171,885	$171,801	$161,923	$150,197	$62,000	73,726	97.8	84.9	90.9
0669000	Santa Ana city	$49,234	$20,020	$29,154	$53,420	$80,040	$51,199	$36,008	$21,539	328,037	69.4	63.2	74.5
0669070	Santa Barbara city	$81,047	$42,490	$56,651	$94,153	$86,935	$93,709	$46,019	$36,905	89,089	80.8	62.1	82.3
0669084	Santa Clara city	$107,633	$40,929	$100,679	$130,820	$109,348	$126,665	$62,788	$44,702	118,722	93.2	79.1	90.5
0669088	Santa Clarita city	$90,996	$36,064	$66,819	$105,721	$136,599	$101,317	$62,362	$45,103	178,327	89.7	81.7	84.0
0669112	Santa Cruz city	$88,441	$53,003	$59,722	$111,750	$88,468	$114,219	$48,963	$38,438	61,706	92.5	82.4	84.8
0669196	Santa Maria city	$51,993	$25,354	$32,127	$62,934	$77,215	$57,798	$31,607	$21,250	100,617	74.7	66.9	73.1
0670000	Santa Monica city	$114,346	$40,302	$86,845	$131,498	$153,516	$150,898	$131,422	$50,625	90,715	91.8	82.8	87.9
0670098	Santa Rosa city	$67,314	$44,939	$50,634	$80,741	$94,651	$73,709	$50,252	$30,907	168,721	87.0	77.5	84.1
0670224	Santee city	$83,966	$38,661	$61,765	$98,031	$138,168	$96,295	$66,750	$34,554	54,000	91.2	85.4	85.5
0672016	Simi Valley city	$97,083	$39,875	$74,013	$120,060	$122,342	$112,500	$67,500	$40,486	125,251	91.9	78.1	86.4
0673080	South Gate city	$43,756	$17,450	$32,783	$51,669	$84,011	$51,343	$31,540	$25,273	95,253	70.3	66.0	75.2
0673262	South San Francisco city	$82,377	$40,833	$49,559	$105,583	$115,039	$91,848	$33,828	$38,690	65,264	93.1	84.5	89.0
0673430	South Whittier CDP	$64,404	$23,125	$41,478	$86,368	$94,228	$73,793	$38,918	$30,417	61,107	80.6	71.6	81.6
0675000	Stockton city	$49,370	$19,818	$35,125	$69,938	$83,279	$59,149	$25,274	$19,201	294,867	81.8	81.1	81.3
0677000	Sunnyvale city	$117,327	$43,750	$97,149	$160,134	$125,833	$144,969	$50,447	$40,438	145,284	94.1	73.9	88.0
0678120	Temecula city	$84,717	$35,547	$64,286	$100,982	$103,989	$95,387	$45,547	$31,751	103,461	89.0	82.8	76.4
0678582	Thousand Oaks city	$115,758	$56,890	$103,330	$132,225	$137,007	$139,406	$75,120	$50,349	127,659	91.8	75.5	89.8
0680000	Torrance city	$90,260	$42,083	$76,124	$104,634	$132,185	$108,011	$70,038	$46,930	146,125	91.2	82.4	87.7
0680238	Tracy city	$78,290	$20,806	$58,933	$94,500	$102,677	$80,422	$55,005	$42,031	84,069	89.7	84.4	81.1
0680644	Tulare city	$47,275	$18,745	$34,242	$70,340	$85,900	$52,006	$31,377	$18,333	60,369	81.4	74.5	73.3
0680812	Turlock city	$57,537	$28,868	$45,746	$75,694	$85,761	$74,286	$27,222	$28,477	69,283	87.0	75.8	75.9
0680854	Tustin city	$74,171	$28,750	$45,705	$101,351	$95,793	$90,088	$31,557	$32,094	77,263	85.3	75.2	84.2
0681204	Union City city	$90,265	$33,988	$53,203	$115,009	$119,346	$108,219	$39,551	$35,515	71,461	90.3	86.4	84.7
0681344	Upland city	$64,686	$28,299	$52,428	$93,972	$123,173	$73,302	$52,525	$26,008	74,514	85.0	83.6	84.6
0681554	Vacaville city	$83,788	$45,132	$59,518	$103,765	$125,625	$95,648	$41,000	$34,041	84,886	93.9	82.9	84.3

State/Place FIPS code	State/place	Total number of families	Families with incomes below the poverty level, as a percent of all families of that family type				Families that received Food Stamps (SNAP), as a percent of all families of that family type			Families that received food stamps (SNAP) and had at least one worker	
			All families	Married-couple families	Male householder families, no spouse present	Female householder families, no spouse present	All families	Married-couple families	Male householder or female householder families, no spouse present	Married-couple families, percent	Male householder or female householder families, no spouse present
	California—cont'd										
0651182	Newport Beach city	21,759	5.7	2.8	5.0	18.9	...	...	...	...	...
0652526	Norwalk city	22,235	10.9	9.1	18.1	29.3	11.2	8.1	16.7	7.3	11.8
0652582	Novato city	13,816	3.5	3.0	0.0	6.5	...	...	...	...	...
0653000	Oakland city	85,012	16.8	14.7	23.7	42.7	17.5	9.6	29.7	8.6	19.6
0653322	Oceanside city	39,407	10.4	8.1	12.4	29.3	7.1	3.7	17.2	3.3	13.8
0653896	Ontario city	34,649	15.6	14.5	36.5	36.5	14.6	8.9	25.3	8.1	17.9
0653980	Orange city	30,919	9.4	8.2	15.3	36.4	6.3	3.4	14.5	3.0	10.4
0654652	Oxnard city	40,794	14.0	15.9	10.0	36.8	15.4	10.4	26.0	9.6	21.5
0655156	Palmdale city	34,050	19.8	15.6	18.9	52.6	17.7	8.7	33.5	8.1	22.1
0655282	Palo Alto city	17,012	4.4	1.5	0.0	24.5	...	...	...	...	...
0655618	Paramount city	11,099	22.7	25.4	23.2	44.7	18.6	14.0	26.0	13.3	18.1
0656000	Pasadena city	30,287	8.2	8.2	24.3	24.0	6.4	3.6	14.1	3.1	11.2
0656700	Perris city	14,198	22.9	20.7	32.2	42.9	20.2	16.5	26.0	15.0	18.2
0656784	Petaluma city	13,997	6.3	10.7	7.2	8.6	5.2	4.3	8.1	3.7	6.4
0656924	Pico Rivera city	13,527	11.3	8.6	22.7	26.3	10.7	8.0	15.4	6.9	11.8
0657456	Pittsburg city	15,000	15.3	18.8	18.0	30.4	16.7	10.5	27.4	7.3	19.3
0657526	Placentia city	12,133	8.5	9.6	21.5	19.9	7.8	5.7	14.2	5.2	10.4
0657792	Pleasanton city	20,011	3.9	1.5	30.3	25.1	...	...	...	...	...
0658072	Pomona city	29,656	17.9	16.6	18.0	40.0	16.5	11.8	25.2	11.3	17.8
0658240	Porterville city	12,379	23.2	20.5	29.2	53.8	25.3	16.6	40.9	15.1	29.1
0659444	Rancho Cordova city	16,050	13.0	10.6	26.8	33.8	15.8	8.8	29.9	8.4	21.3
0659451	Rancho Cucamonga city	40,546	6.5	4.7	9.0	21.4	6.8	3.2	17.2	3.1	15.9
0659920	Redding city	21,984	13.0	10.7	20.5	40.0	15.9	8.2	34.8	6.3	22.2
0659962	Redlands city	16,610	9.1	9.0	18.1	32.8	10.0	5.2	25.5	4.6	22.3
0660018	Redondo Beach city	17,241	3.1	1.9	9.1	10.8	2.0	0.7	6.1	0.4	5.5
0660102	Redwood City city	18,524	5.9	5.6	15.1	19.5	4.5	3.5	7.6	3.5	5.9
0660466	Rialto city	20,615	17.7	15.1	27.6	41.6	23.2	16.5	36.1	15.8	26.5
0660620	Richmond city	24,159	14.8	10.9	21.5	43.6	13.7	7.0	24.0	6.7	16.0
0662000	Riverside city	64,518	15.0	13.7	26.5	37.3	14.0	9.5	24.0	8.7	17.4
0662364	Rocklin city	15,776	8.0	3.2	3.4	30.3	...	...	...	...	...
0662896	Rosemead city	12,199	19.0	25.9	18.8	43.7	9.7	10.3	8.7	7.8	8.1
0662938	Roseville city	31,384	5.6	4.6	13.9	17.4	5.0	2.6	13.5	2.3	9.0
0663218	Rowland Heights CDP	12,171	7.7	8.0	9.4	9.6	6.2	4.0	11.8	3.4	11.1
0664000	Sacramento city	101,979	19.0	16.0	32.6	47.3	20.5	11.1	36.4	10.0	22.2
0664224	Salinas city	31,777	17.6	15.5	24.8	47.5	12.9	8.4	21.2	7.9	17.4
0665000	San Bernardino city	42,570	28.6	23.7	31.6	56.4	31.3	19.6	45.1	17.0	29.9
0665042	San Buenaventura (Ventura) city	25,677	7.3	4.1	16.2	25.1	8.8	4.6	19.0	3.3	13.9
0665084	San Clemente city	16,888	5.8	6.0	13.8	20.7	...	...	...	...	...
0666000	San Diego city	282,541	10.9	9.1	21.1	37.2	8.5	4.7	18.5	4.0	12.9
0667000	San Francisco city	157,580	8.6	5.6	20.2	31.2	7.1	4.1	15.2	3.5	10.9
0668000	San Jose city	227,581	8.9	6.8	20.4	29.2	8.4	5.5	16.8	5.0	12.8
0668084	San Leandro city	20,712	7.3	9.5	12.0	22.2	7.2	4.9	13.5	4.4	11.0
0668196	San Marcos city	19,510	14.1	8.9	24.0	29.3	3.1	1.7	7.2	1.3	5.4
0668252	San Mateo city	23,538	4.3	3.4	15.9	17.2	4.8	3.7	8.2	3.4	7.7
0668364	San Rafael city	13,743	9.1	7.6	27.9	33.5	...	...	...	...	...
0668378	San Ramon city	19,324	3.1	1.4	0.0	19.3	...	...	...	...	...
0669000	Santa Ana city	59,661	19.6	19.6	24.4	45.5	18.6	15.4	25.0	14.8	20.3
0669070	Santa Barbara city	18,842	8.1	6.5	24.3	22.4	5.7	3.5	11.4	3.1	10.6
0669084	Santa Clara city	28,304	5.7	3.0	14.8	29.4	3.9	1.8	11.8	1.5	7.8
0669088	Santa Clarita city	44,625	7.1	6.1	19.5	20.5	5.1	2.6	12.7	2.3	9.8
0669112	Santa Cruz city	9,811	7.7	7.7	7.3	24.0	8.0	4.6	17.8	4.4	15.5
0669196	Santa Maria city	20,749	17.4	15.2	24.9	48.8	17.1	12.9	25.7	11.5	18.2
0670000	Santa Monica city	17,328	5.8	2.9	9.0	22.9	...	...	...	...	...
0670098	Santa Rosa city	38,941	9.3	8.7	18.2	27.1	10.7	6.7	20.6	6.0	15.0
0670224	Santee city	13,962	6.8	5.4	5.5	25.5	6.5	3.7	13.5	2.7	10.2
0672016	Simi Valley city	32,138	4.3	2.5	14.9	16.9	4.1	2.0	11.7	1.5	10.2
0673080	South Gate city	19,602	19.2	15.7	28.4	43.6	18.4	14.1	25.2	12.6	20.3
0673262	South San Francisco city	15,220	5.5	5.7	21.1	16.1	4.0	1.6	11.8	1.6	11.2
0673430	South Whittier CDP	13,233	12.7	13.2	18.9	31.5	12.0	7.6	20.8	6.9	16.0
0675000	Stockton city	66,092	21.8	18.0	35.9	46.8	22.4	12.1	38.6	10.8	25.3
0677000	Sunnyvale city	36,494	5.0	3.3	22.3	21.0	3.7	1.6	13.3	1.4	12.2
0678120	Temecula city	25,367	6.9	4.5	15.9	22.9	5.5	2.7	16.3	2.7	13.5
0678582	Thousand Oaks city	32,758	5.2	2.8	23.1	27.6	3.7	1.3	15.6	1.2	11.6
0680000	Torrance city	38,617	5.1	3.6	6.1	21.9	2.7	1.7	5.7	1.1	4.5
0680238	Tracy city	19,720	5.6	3.1	10.6	19.5	8.7	5.7	19.3	5.5	16.7
0680644	Tulare city	14,162	19.4	17.6	24.6	49.3	25.9	16.4	45.5	15.0	30.7
0680812	Turlock city	17,100	13.2	11.9	40.7	37.0	12.4	9.5	19.1	8.7	11.3
0680854	Tustin city	18,317	8.8	7.3	22.1	22.0	7.9	3.7	17.4	3.7	16.4
0681204	Union City city	16,354	5.8	2.4	13.0	25.9	8.4	6.1	15.7	5.3	9.8
0681344	Upland city	18,211	12.3	11.4	13.2	34.9	12.0	5.9	26.1	5.2	18.0
0681554	Vacaville city	21,778	9.1	5.7	5.0	31.1	8.7	3.6	22.0	3.6	14.6

State/ Place FIPS code	State/place	Median family income in the past 12 months (in 2,013 inflation-adjusted dollars)								Total population in households	Persons who had health insurance, as a percent of all persons in that household type		
		All families	Families with no earners	Families with one earner	Families with two earners	Families with three or more earners	Families with own children under 18 years				Married-couple families, percent	Male householder or female householder families, no spouse present	Nonfamily households
							Married-couple families with children	Male householder, no spouse present, with children	Female householder, no spouse present, with children				
	California—cont'd												
0681666	Vallejo city	$63,116	$30,079	$46,096	$90,371	$106,875	$77,076	$46,297	$22,813	117,283	86.6	78.0	80.2
0682590	Victorville city	$49,941	$17,746	$37,734	$70,453	$109,048	$64,179	$39,237	$19,060	114,926	80.9	82.3	70.0
0682954	Visalia city	$53,802	$21,603	$41,719	$77,997	$79,755	$67,803	$21,398	$25,125	125,742	85.7	80.7	79.7
0682996	Vista city	$49,797	$17,683	$34,322	$70,256	$86,875	$47,826	$31,440	$25,885	93,508	78.4	72.0	76.9
0683346	Walnut Creek city	$112,614	$56,146	$98,125	$152,456	$193,284	$159,937	$100,534	$54,860	64,895	95.6	89.1	90.3
0683668	Watsonville city	$47,080	$28,500	$35,004	$55,505	$77,716	$55,164	$29,422	$20,582	51,759	79.2	75.6	82.0
0684200	West Covina city	$71,546	$27,967	$50,198	$85,936	$102,248	$86,110	$40,489	$35,605	106,901	84.1	76.8	81.2
0684550	Westminster city	$55,384	$23,357	$47,495	$72,037	$103,935	$65,880	$31,417	$31,917	91,084	82.6	77.0	83.8
0685292	Whittier city	$73,907	$32,353	$50,923	$93,595	$113,097	$94,667	$61,161	$27,783	85,668	88.5	77.5	86.4
0686328	Woodland city	$65,402	$32,057	$37,925	$94,011	$85,846	$74,728	$43,875	$33,924	55,230	87.1	75.4	85.0
0686832	Yorba Linda city	$128,026	$52,359	$97,019	$141,467	$172,212	$139,928	$123,125	$48,889	66,206	94.4	86.9	93.6
0686972	Yuba City city	$53,415	$29,841	$39,708	$69,880	$81,047	$63,220	$25,889	$23,225	64,015	85.5	75.9	84.1
0687042	Yucaipa city	$65,201	$39,967	$47,754	$82,292	$101,397	$76,072	$13,438	$35,938	51,869	83.8	86.3	84.1
0800000	**Colorado**	$71,939	$38,176	$50,890	$88,748	$105,466	$87,137	$41,877	$28,222	5,098,744	88.9	77.5	82.0
0803455	Arvada city	$81,043	$44,634	$54,600	$98,098	$116,027	$101,651	$37,456	$34,889	109,238	94.1	83.9	83.8
0804000	Aurora city	$57,654	$37,966	$40,263	$70,701	$88,722	$62,634	$35,474	$30,382	336,058	81.3	71.7	77.6
0807850	Boulder city	$106,371	$75,583	$85,129	$127,731	$130,500	$143,538	$58,639	$31,639	101,011	94.9	82.2	91.6
0809280	Broomfield city	$94,751	$44,091	$68,546	$110,151	$145,591	$119,948	$43,864	$40,645	57,972	94.1	80.7	86.6
0812415	Castle Rock town	$97,288	$48,929	$74,797	$107,051	$129,010	$108,940	$76,809	$35,803	50,834	94.2	75.1	84.6
0812815	Centennial city	$100,672	$57,117	$75,678	$115,097	$136,563	$116,318	$70,346	$52,557	103,377	94.3	83.6	86.7
0816000	Colorado Springs city	$67,758	$40,226	$52,341	$80,464	$108,731	$80,815	$41,092	$26,980	420,605	91.4	77.2	78.8
0820000	Denver city	$65,203	$24,696	$41,494	$91,851	$87,672	$82,889	$41,643	$23,560	627,940	86.2	77.8	83.2
0827425	Fort Collins city	$76,840	$41,375	$60,806	$89,050	$107,874	$92,717	$41,098	$29,341	147,179	92.5	86.2	87.1
0831660	Grand Junction city	$55,833	$29,875	$40,760	$77,988	$89,743	$71,915	$33,944	$17,858	58,768	86.7	80.5	83.3
0832155	Greeley city	$55,435	$25,026	$35,190	$77,982	$105,487	$59,732	$30,693	$19,068	93,483	85.8	74.8	84.7
0836410	Highlands Ranch CDP	$114,746	$45,000	$97,904	$124,270	$158,319	$126,485	$79,441	$48,849	104,237	95.9	83.6	90.4
0843000	Lakewood city	$67,744	$41,467	$48,924	$89,462	$108,468	$88,504	$50,233	$28,386	142,431	89.0	72.6	84.0
0845970	Longmont city	$72,648	$39,206	$54,353	$83,773	$98,967	$76,657	$46,423	$26,278	88,174	85.6	78.4	80.4
0846465	Loveland city	$67,288	$43,368	$50,875	$79,081	$87,926	$78,904	$50,800	$27,967	69,809	88.8	76.2	80.5
0862000	Pueblo city	$43,603	$25,838	$34,578	$59,753	$82,917	$55,225	$27,255	$22,578	104,158	90.3	79.4	82.3
0877290	Thornton city	$72,314	$29,009	$45,583	$91,050	$98,443	$83,251	$41,045	$33,303	123,932	86.3	76.5	84.1
0883835	Westminster city	$74,775	$43,362	$52,208	$88,342	$116,512	$86,192	$41,647	$35,345	108,822	89.7	79.3	83.2
0900000	**Connecticut**	$86,354	$35,655	$59,935	$108,103	$126,870	$112,382	$51,622	$30,019	3,536,463	93.8	85.6	87.9
0908000	Bridgeport city	$44,453	$14,866	$30,893	$63,491	$86,981	$60,915	$27,275	$20,825	144,681	77.9	78.5	74.7
0908420	Bristol city	$68,222	$37,231	$49,903	$95,402	$122,054	$90,458	$50,462	$29,587	59,933	94.5	87.7	89.9
0918430	Danbury city	$77,678	$33,438	$50,929	$91,014	$105,786	$91,180	$53,043	$26,957	80,946	86.7	70.9	74.3
0922700	East Hartford CDP	$55,098	$26,563	$38,018	$78,020	$91,644	$76,065	$31,291	$28,223	50,769	89.0	86.4	82.3
0937000	Hartford city	$31,347	$10,475	$27,182	$55,642	$74,781	$55,766	$20,119	$19,174	123,081	83.2	84.0	81.4
0946450	Meriden city	$58,847	$26,701	$41,574	$86,070	$120,739	$60,975	$34,602	$27,454	59,816	92.8	85.6	86.6
0947515	Milford city	$97,479	$37,609	$72,170	$116,186	$133,654	$125,491	$26,746	$26,845	51,252	96.5	89.8	90.9
0950370	New Britain city	$48,418	$17,292	$34,313	$69,732	$97,885	$65,027	$38,500	$20,693	72,363	88.5	87.5	86.4
0952000	New Haven city	$43,629	$16,173	$32,389	$71,975	$98,698	$59,828	$34,737	$20,635	128,966	87.4	84.3	87.4
0955990	Norwalk city	$91,385	$31,333	$70,614	$116,815	$106,830	$106,519	$64,792	$38,056	86,650	84.6	74.5	87.0
0973000	Stamford city	$92,391	$36,565	$66,827	$124,024	$117,448	$123,563	$40,257	$27,995	124,480	87.6	72.9	81.3
0974260	Stratford CDP	$83,241	$35,137	$56,587	$100,496	$131,814	$92,537	$36,528	$34,947	51,709	92.9	86.5	90.0
0980000	Waterbury city	$46,979	$13,545	$36,455	$69,445	$106,203	$67,212	$28,092	$19,082	108,594	87.5	87.7	85.6
0982660	West Hartford CDP	$107,434	$44,528	$76,826	$130,952	$148,136	$131,156	$110,679	$42,056	62,333	96.7	89.0	92.2
0982800	West Haven city	$64,943	$28,724	$40,601	$83,526	$115,341	$85,913	$69,922	$20,809	54,873	92.7	82.9	84.6
1000000	**Delaware**	$70,668	$42,381	$51,357	$89,317	$112,572	$93,443	$42,821	$29,037	902,314	92.8	87.3	88.8
1077580	Wilmington city	$46,895	$11,598	$35,607	$73,677	$87,965	$71,747	$42,311	$24,552	69,403	88.2	88.4	88.0
1100000	**District of Columbia**	$78,892	$15,606	$49,300	$137,418	$130,757	$157,541	$36,852	$25,582	622,605	95.4	91.7	93.2
1150000	Washinton city	$78,892	$15,606	$49,300	$137,418	$130,757	$157,541	$36,852	$25,582	622,605	95.4	91.7	93.2
1200000	**Florida**	$55,758	$34,825	$42,072	$75,621	$90,957	$71,937	$32,892	$24,860	19,010,848	84.0	71.7	77.7
1200410	Alafaya CDP	$67,296	$28,117	$43,987	$93,813	$97,049	$88,472	$42,792	$30,761	76,999	85.6	68.9	87.0
1207300	Boca Raton city	$90,740	$71,466	$71,031	$109,480	$119,322	$107,782	$41,524	$47,800	87,364	90.9	76.3	86.3
1207875	Boynton Beach city	$50,958	$34,210	$41,135	$73,295	$75,045	$66,260	$51,750	$32,705	69,351	81.0	67.1	82.5
1207950	Bradenton city	$49,273	$42,741	$38,660	$68,041	$76,583	$58,983	$32,344	$20,810	49,730	81.0	66.6	73.8
1208150	Brandon CDP	$61,764	$32,868	$44,322	$81,151	$93,611	$78,444	$38,800	$29,250	104,729	86.7	78.6	82.9
1210275	Cape Coral city	$53,129	$34,098	$42,464	$72,720	$82,088	$60,979	$31,796	$26,891	161,222	85.1	67.6	76.0
1212875	Clearwater city	$56,637	$41,207	$40,686	$78,692	$105,086	$77,198	$28,929	$28,580	107,811	87.0	72.2	71.8
1213275	Coconut Creek city	$62,493	$30,426	$44,688	$83,825	$106,327	$83,239	$51,964	$35,680	54,990	84.0	75.0	81.9
1214400	Coral Springs city	$67,781	$19,476	$42,852	$83,764	$106,401	$84,450	$42,077	$31,879	124,973	82.4	72.2	81.9
1216475	Davie town	$75,891	$28,081	$47,856	$91,366	$125,039	$91,801	$65,997	$37,132	95,143	86.3	78.0	77.7
1216525	Daytona Beach city	$36,833	$21,390	$30,819	$59,574	$89,957	$46,369	$18,809	$15,268	60,458	86.1	73.1	74.7
1216725	Deerfield Beach city	$48,516	$27,582	$35,006	$70,548	$69,184	$64,496	$32,713	$22,524	76,426	78.6	67.4	74.6
1217100	Delray Beach city	$59,976	$34,453	$52,255	$74,375	$75,901	$84,479	$26,806	$30,655	62,243	84.2	66.0	78.4
1217200	Deltona city	$47,003	$28,697	$39,865	$62,780	$87,419	$58,451	$31,308	$29,955	85,509	81.9	71.3	71.2
1224000	Fort Lauderdale city	$59,795	$27,495	$45,645	$77,268	$105,328	$70,245	$29,896	$20,265	169,242	80.4	69.9	77.1

State/Place FIPS code	State/place	Total number of families	Families with incomes below the poverty level, as a percent of all families of that family type				Families that received Food Stamps (SNAP), as a percent of all families of that family type			Families that received food stamps (SNAP) and had at least one worker	
			All families	Married-couple families	Male householder families, no spouse present	Female householder families, no spouse present	All families	Married-couple families	Male householder or female householder families, no spouse present	Married-couple families, percent	Male householder or female householder families, no spouse present
	California—cont'd										
0681666	Vallejo city	27,112	14.2	11.8	19.3	40.5	14.4	5.9	27.9	4.7	19.2
0682590	Victorville city	24,501	22.6	19.8	26.7	47.5	24.6	13.9	41.9	12.1	25.1
0682954	Visalia city	30,711	17.7	14.6	39.7	41.2	22.2	13.2	40.1	12.0	29.0
0682996	Vista city	21,435	14.6	11.4	12.2	32.0	4.3	3.2	7.5	2.7	5.6
0683346	Walnut Creek city	16,611	3.2	3.4	0.0	10.3	...	...	...	...	...
0683668	Watsonville city	11,004	19.5	17.2	8.4	54.2	21.7	13.9	38.2	13.6	27.8
0684200	West Covina city	24,357	7.8	5.2	19.7	29.6	5.8	3.8	10.1	3.0	7.8
0684550	Westminster city	21,238	14.5	17.0	28.6	28.8	12.8	9.3	21.1	8.3	18.4
0685292	Whittier city	20,029	10.9	9.0	17.1	32.0	8.1	4.3	16.5	3.7	13.7
0686328	Woodland city	13,700	9.7	8.9	19.7	29.5	13.3	7.2	29.3	6.4	24.2
0686832	Yorba Linda city	18,102	2.3	3.3	0.0	12.3	...	...	...	...	...
0686972	Yuba City city	15,738	16.5	13.0	34.2	43.2	14.1	8.1	27.1	7.5	15.4
0687042	Yucaipa city	13,055	13.2	15.0	49.9	26.9	13.8	8.3	31.5	7.8	23.8
0800000	**Colorado**	1,271,180	9.1	7.4	18.3	34.7	9.6	5.1	24.7	4.6	19.2
0803455	Arvada city	29,439	6.8	5.1	12.2	29.0	6.1	2.9	16.1	2.3	11.9
0804000	Aurora city	79,783	12.5	13.0	18.0	30.5	14.9	8.7	27.0	7.9	22.6
0807850	Boulder city	17,408	5.6	2.6	6.4	32.0	6.3	2.3	22.7	1.7	21.0
0809280	Broomfield city	15,028	6.5	2.6	16.2	37.5	4.8	1.5	19.5	1.5	11.4
0812415	Castle Rock town	13,835	5.3	1.0	0.0	27.2	...	...	...	...	...
0812815	Centennial city	28,466	4.2	2.3	4.8	19.0	2.5	1.5	7.2	1.4	6.6
0816000	Colorado Springs city	108,123	9.7	7.4	18.2	36.9	11.8	6.0	29.5	5.6	22.4
0820000	Denver city	127,738	14.0	12.1	25.1	41.5	14.6	7.8	30.1	6.9	22.7
0827425	Fort Collins city	31,648	7.5	5.2	21.1	30.7	7.6	4.5	19.7	4.0	13.6
0831660	Grand Junction city	14,700	14.1	8.1	19.9	48.7	12.1	5.2	30.5	3.6	20.2
0832155	Greeley city	21,739	15.4	13.8	33.0	52.7	15.5	8.0	34.2	7.5	22.7
0836410	Highlands Ranch CDP	27,986	2.6	1.0	7.6	14.7	1.3	0.5	6.0	0.5	4.5
0843000	Lakewood city	35,475	9.9	11.2	18.6	36.0	10.2	4.3	24.3	3.8	18.2
0845970	Longmont city	22,649	11.1	11.7	27.4	33.3	9.6	5.4	21.5	5.2	18.3
0846465	Loveland city	18,997	6.7	7.0	10.6	31.4	9.1	6.1	18.8	6.1	14.8
0862000	Pueblo city	24,923	18.2	17.6	34.8	47.2	23.2	13.5	40.3	10.7	30.5
0877290	Thornton city	30,638	7.2	5.3	21.8	27.5	10.0	4.9	26.6	4.6	20.5
0883835	Westminster city	27,540	6.7	5.2	13.6	24.0	7.1	4.0	15.5	3.9	11.0
0900000	**Connecticut**	894,728	7.8	4.1	15.8	32.6	11.6	4.5	31.3	3.7	22.6
0908000	Bridgeport city	31,588	20.6	11.7	30.7	44.5	30.5	16.3	44.5	14.3	31.1
0908420	Bristol city	15,368	8.5	7.4	10.8	30.0	14.5	7.6	32.4	5.9	22.5
0918430	Danbury city	18,505	8.3	5.5	13.8	25.0	11.0	5.4	25.4	4.2	22.9
0922700	East Hartford CDP	13,048	14.3	7.5	26.0	32.6	25.6	7.7	48.3	5.8	36.2
0937000	Hartford city	26,188	33.5	15.3	43.6	51.0	48.4	26.2	59.8	20.7	39.9
0946450	Meriden city	15,734	12.9	13.9	19.6	33.8	22.0	11.3	43.3	7.5	31.2
0947515	Milford city	13,056	4.4	2.2	17.4	27.4	5.9	1.8	22.1	1.4	19.4
0950370	New Britain city	16,579	19.0	10.7	26.7	43.9	30.8	14.6	49.1	11.9	31.1
0952000	New Haven city	27,109	22.7	13.9	31.2	45.7	31.4	11.5	49.6	9.0	35.1
0955990	Norwalk city	20,987	6.5	2.8	3.0	19.5	6.3	2.3	18.1	2.0	15.1
0973000	Stamford city	29,603	7.3	2.2	29.3	32.7	7.9	2.7	22.7	2.4	18.9
0974260	Stratford CDP	13,516	5.1	3.9	12.6	17.9	9.1	4.1	25.0	3.6	21.8
0980000	Waterbury city	25,686	21.1	12.5	32.2	51.2	31.4	15.2	49.8	12.6	29.7
0982660	West Hartford CDP	16,322	5.2	3.9	4.1	23.9	6.5	3.6	17.0	2.5	15.8
0982800	West Haven city	12,750	12.3	7.9	3.0	44.9	18.9	7.9	41.3	6.4	33.3
1000000	**Delaware**	226,510	8.1	5.2	16.3	30.3	14.5	6.7	34.3	6.0	26.9
1077580	Wilmington city	15,694	22.1	6.8	23.1	42.9	34.6	13.6	48.7	11.8	34.5
1100000	**District of Columbia**	114,484	15.3	5.7	24.8	38.8	22.8	6.6	41.2	5.4	27.3
1150000	Washinton city	114,484	15.3	5.7	24.8	38.8	22.8	6.6	41.2	5.4	27.3
1200000	**Florida**	4,594,006	12.4	10.4	26.8	38.8	16.5	9.4	34.9	7.8	25.6
1200410	Alafaya CDP	18,745	8.8	6.2	17.8	35.2	...	...	...	...	...
1207300	Boca Raton city	21,214	6.1	5.4	21.4	23.2	5.4	2.7	16.0	2.4	15.5
1207875	Boynton Beach city	15,585	13.7	15.2	11.1	27.7	16.1	9.7	29.9	8.8	26.2
1207950	Bradenton city	11,114	14.2	14.3	47.3	46.3	16.8	6.9	40.4	6.2	29.7
1208150	Brandon CDP	25,629	9.2	4.5	10.6	32.6	12.2	6.7	24.6	5.6	19.4
1210275	Cape Coral city	40,759	11.2	10.2	32.9	26.9	14.3	9.0	31.9	7.5	21.5
1212875	Clearwater city	25,313	12.3	13.8	31.7	28.9	16.9	8.7	33.7	6.8	24.2
1213275	Coconut Creek city	12,730	7.0	4.9	4.3	17.4	8.5	5.8	16.4	4.6	13.0
1214400	Coral Springs city	31,300	8.9	6.3	13.4	27.0	11.9	5.6	24.7	4.2	19.5
1216475	Davie town	22,507	7.6	5.0	3.1	22.1	10.1	5.9	21.3	5.3	18.0
1216525	Daytona Beach city	11,789	22.9	19.2	50.6	56.3	26.1	13.6	45.0	9.6	23.0
1216725	Deerfield Beach city	16,930	15.3	10.3	28.1	41.2	16.8	10.2	29.3	9.5	20.8
1217100	Delray Beach city	13,238	12.1	10.9	40.4	34.5	14.2	6.7	31.9	5.4	26.5
1217200	Deltona city	20,653	12.1	13.4	28.2	38.0	21.7	16.5	38.6	14.2	28.5
1224000	Fort Lauderdale city	33,194	15.5	12.3	30.1	46.5	23.1	14.3	40.1	13.4	27.4

Table E-4: Cities with a Population of 50,000 or More—Income, Poverty, and Health Insurance—*Continued*

State/ Place FIPS code	State/place	All families	Families with no earners	Families with one earner	Families with two earners	Families with three or more earners	Married-couple families with children	Male householder, no spouse present, with children	Female householder, no spouse present, with children	Total population in households	Married-couple families, percent	Male householder or female householder families, no spouse present	Nonfamily households
	Florida—cont'd												
1224125	Fort Myers city	$44,789	$34,894	$30,711	$69,575	$84,009	$41,110	$23,750	$20,205	62,208	82.2	64.8	75.9
1224562	Fountainebleau CDP	$44,986	$21,969	$38,657	$59,661	$78,274	$47,308	$33,425	$24,880	53,306	64.5	63.0	63.1
1225175	Gainesville city	$52,960	$14,085	$40,774	$72,928	$99,036	$76,757	$44,484	$18,343	124,912	87.9	79.1	81.6
1230000	Hialeah city	$32,323	$14,881	$26,369	$45,121	$70,545	$40,197	$26,096	$17,121	231,193	65.9	60.2	64.4
1232000	Hollywood city	$54,138	$27,438	$40,350	$72,132	$78,256	$68,725	$32,958	$25,266	144,436	79.1	68.5	72.8
1232275	Homestead city	$40,810	$10,925	$35,088	$58,750	$76,164	$47,381	$17,442	$19,392	62,385	68.7	62.9	61.8
1235000	Jacksonville city	$56,805	$23,836	$41,367	$78,667	$102,979	$72,998	$32,735	$22,127	819,692	87.4	77.3	77.6
1235875	Jupiter town	$86,127	$67,585	$65,150	$105,171	$124,333	$81,528	$62,105	$41,923	57,045	90.8	80.0	81.1
1236062	Kendale Lakes CDP	$50,821	$19,601	$37,782	$65,537	$85,124	$61,094	$26,663	$21,996	59,401	76.6	59.6	63.6
1236100	Kendall CDP	$74,510	$24,098	$51,495	$97,459	$96,250	$91,712	$58,804	$30,753	73,599	87.2	73.3	83.3
1236950	Kissimmee city	$38,025	$14,243	$28,434	$57,845	$69,449	$47,244	$30,599	$17,277	63,010	74.4	68.3	68.9
1238250	Lakeland city	$45,584	$31,548	$37,571	$67,045	$69,917	$57,923	$29,219	$23,093	98,767	87.1	77.5	84.3
1239425	Largo city	$49,836	$40,189	$36,484	$66,990	$79,625	$74,840	$26,875	$23,669	76,740	85.7	74.3	74.7
1239550	Lauderhill city	$43,046	$16,598	$30,398	$61,642	$87,510	$67,867	$25,417	$25,293	68,841	76.7	69.4	70.9
1239925	Lehigh Acres CDP	$41,037	$19,978	$31,738	$60,361	$71,309	$51,133	$30,859	$23,796	106,989	74.4	66.0	71.2
1243125	Margate city	$50,424	$30,136	$39,846	$68,381	$67,813	$57,446	$31,028	$30,543	54,868	80.1	67.3	79.0
1243975	Melbourne city	$51,149	$30,513	$40,818	$69,816	$98,125	$79,180	$34,977	$22,731	76,291	87.7	71.4	82.4
1245000	Miami city	$33,475	$14,775	$26,408	$53,028	$66,812	$45,146	$22,985	$16,559	407,493	68.7	62.8	67.4
1245025	Miami Beach city	$56,542	$20,858	$43,216	$79,617	$79,320	$100,833	$37,797	$26,504	89,940	81.8	58.4	68.6
1245060	Miami Gardens city	$44,158	$18,287	$31,680	$56,513	$84,112	$54,128	$37,216	$27,648	110,650	72.5	70.3	75.4
1245975	Miramar city	$65,220	$23,520	$50,145	$73,976	$107,830	$72,603	$50,807	$48,956	127,939	80.3	73.6	69.7
1249450	North Miami city	$37,885	$13,591	$26,302	$56,589	$66,833	$39,114	$36,343	$20,847	60,122	59.3	57.6	70.4
1249675	North Port city	$56,530	$40,888	$44,452	$72,074	$79,186	$71,209	$42,975	$21,178	58,236	87.9	79.2	85.3
1250750	Ocala city	$43,645	$25,267	$34,257	$73,790	$88,393	$66,250	$41,809	$17,212	54,235	87.8	72.2	72.6
1253000	Orlando city	$47,568	$21,670	$31,246	$66,675	$74,254	$62,091	$27,237	$23,305	246,090	80.8	73.6	73.7
1254000	Palm Bay city	$50,154	$32,398	$38,174	$69,867	$74,474	$61,614	$46,065	$21,500	103,658	85.8	78.5	79.9
1254200	Palm Coast city	$50,968	$43,441	$39,981	$71,711	$83,548	$57,120	$28,995	$31,902	77,529	87.4	71.6	83.8
1254350	Palm Harbor CDP	$71,412	$41,261	$59,090	$89,140	$122,404	$94,559	$52,174	$28,571	58,757	89.3	82.6	88.5
1255775	Pembroke Pines city	$75,186	$26,272	$50,219	$89,461	$110,556	$94,579	$34,735	$46,191	158,975	85.9	76.1	81.7
1255925	Pensacola city	$61,860	$46,083	$42,999	$76,617	$87,750	$95,510	$30,761	$26,180	51,666	86.6	78.1	78.7
1256825	Pine Hills CDP	$38,480	$18,413	$26,983	$51,831	$63,977	$45,560	$17,921	$21,633	67,470	75.4	72.7	66.6
1257425	Plantation city	$78,159	$34,368	$53,993	$93,305	$113,160	$93,636	$56,235	$39,554	87,988	87.1	76.1	80.1
1257900	Poinciana CDP	$43,727	$36,584	$35,889	$63,843	$66,813	$43,481	$28,750	$20,179	55,444	83.3	65.3	81.9
1258050	Pompano Beach city	$44,494	$24,761	$33,836	$56,690	$76,319	$54,630	$30,325	$22,629	99,862	72.2	63.1	68.6
1258350	Port Charlotte CDP	$51,423	$38,581	$45,407	$67,188	$76,726	$51,963	$40,286	$28,305	53,733	82.6	70.9	78.9
1258575	Port Orange city	$52,327	$36,343	$47,795	$75,863	$104,386	$75,114	$50,972	$28,140	56,629	88.6	78.0	81.4
1258715	Port St. Lucie city	$53,580	$31,951	$42,181	$74,713	$74,926	$58,162	$16,810	$30,906	168,695	83.2	68.6	76.4
1260950	Riverview CDP	$72,889	$32,970	$51,469	$90,534	$87,510	$83,597	$41,667	$38,010	72,392	89.1	79.1	78.2
1263000	St. Petersburg city	$57,798	$28,586	$39,843	$78,740	$92,076	$76,479	$28,519	$22,963	244,330	87.3	75.1	77.8
1263650	Sanford city	$42,993	$16,087	$32,607	$57,386	$67,794	$50,731	$23,971	$21,912	53,841	76.9	69.4	79.1
1264175	Sarasota city	$49,091	$43,750	$35,073	$58,977	$72,337	$53,108	$16,348	$21,708	51,211	80.3	70.4	74.6
1268350	Spring Hill CDP	$46,469	$34,356	$41,000	$66,843	$79,524	$55,389	$29,255	$22,544	101,542	86.3	76.9	85.9
1269700	Sunrise city	$55,378	$21,348	$42,315	$70,265	$96,117	$69,412	$40,979	$35,186	87,879	81.2	69.9	81.1
1270600	Tallahassee city	$62,732	$26,816	$44,296	$80,643	$98,906	$94,307	$39,715	$24,541	182,593	91.7	79.8	83.8
1270675	Tamarac city	$53,335	$30,615	$43,108	$70,592	$101,958	$66,112	$39,722	$36,848	62,245	80.1	74.9	82.7
1270700	Tamiami CDP	$50,269	$18,452	$37,954	$66,405	$90,333	$61,096	$40,285	$29,330	54,175	75.5	63.2	64.7
1271000	Tampa city	$52,674	$18,650	$37,733	$83,492	$86,866	$81,541	$31,673	$21,245	346,070	86.7	76.2	80.2
1271569	The Hammocks CDP	$60,929	$20,763	$36,113	$75,779	$92,029	$70,435	$28,906	$28,385	54,230	76.4	60.2	78.5
1271625	The Villages CDP	$65,380	$60,450	$78,571	$82,156	$...	$...	$...	$...	...	...	...	...
1272145	Town 'n' Country CDP	$55,464	$25,289	$42,388	$66,122	$95,729	$69,127	$63,773	$31,434	79,855	79.1	75.7	72.5
1275812	Wellington village	$85,780	$46,317	$67,828	$108,145	$105,026	$88,084	$50,858	$41,152	58,808	89.7	85.4	76.5
1276582	Weston city	$101,831	$55,461	$84,456	$120,287	$124,344	$115,706	$94,125	$30,076	67,565	86.2	86.0	85.8
1276600	West Palm Beach city	$51,270	$31,782	$39,476	$69,869	$72,635	$65,943	$32,633	$24,294	100,490	79.2	71.7	71.5
1300000	**Georgia**	$57,432	$26,281	$41,334	$79,557	$93,926	$76,385	$33,883	$22,191	9,710,901	85.7	72.7	78.6
1301052	Albany city	$32,982	$14,947	$26,833	$65,190	$73,598	$66,772	$27,124	$12,771	75,313	82.1	74.1	76.3
1301696	Alpharetta city	$105,314	$51,289	$84,500	$123,503	$148,182	$124,401	$68,476	$34,146	61,156	94.3	82.7	83.6
1303440	Athens-Clarke County	$48,719	$17,848	$31,665	$69,948	$84,904	$59,675	$16,373	$15,179	117,716	86.7	72.7	83.6
1304000	Atlanta city	$58,940	$16,121	$34,128	$106,791	$85,579	$125,383	$29,980	$16,220	434,244	89.5	73.6	81.8
1304204	Augusta-Richmond County	$45,105	$20,556	$35,658	$66,197	$90,466	$73,105	$35,667	$15,181	187,021	88.4	76.7	79.9
1310944	Brookhaven city	$95,179	$45,378	$76,006	$117,437	$87,823	$114,701	$17,241	$18,373	49,864	84.0	48.9	85.0
1319000	Columbus city	$52,041	$25,766	$37,022	$70,954	$83,068	$67,903	$36,185	$21,842	184,655	90.9	77.2	78.7
1342425	Johns Creek city	$114,255	$50,242	$80,049	$138,795	$148,889	$130,845	$77,773	$43,309	81,494	90.6	77.4	87.2
1349000	Macon city	$30,686	$13,814	$24,827	$59,490	$59,492	$58,327	$15,000	$12,917	88,694	82.3	73.9	75.0
1349756	Marietta city	$47,626	$29,329	$31,328	$67,071	$54,337	$77,892	$27,815	$17,598	56,946	79.7	62.6	75.1
1367284	Roswell city	$101,175	$66,321	$66,450	$121,569	$153,476	$126,181	$60,000	$33,718	92,632	90.5	59.8	77.4
1368516	Sandy Springs city	$96,298	$45,509	$84,732	$119,648	$175,285	$113,557	$41,563	$31,012	98,308	92.4	62.2	75.9
1369000	Savannah city	$46,049	$21,716	$33,528	$63,333	$75,786	$61,777	$23,214	$17,332	137,271	84.1	72.1	78.5
1371492	Smyrna city	$78,125	$37,770	$45,804	$110,089	$90,104	$106,607	$16,809	$34,507	52,412	86.7	72.1	78.4
1378800	Valdosta city	$36,105	$17,230	$26,770	$60,816	$71,127	$56,135	$27,458	$18,329	54,814	85.8	73.2	72.0

392 Families in America

State/ Place FIPS code	State/place	Total number of families	Families with incomes below the poverty level, as a percent of all families of that family type				Families that received Food Stamps (SNAP), as a percent of all families of that family type			Families that received food stamps (SNAP) and had at least one worker	
			All families	Married-couple families	Male householder families, no spouse present	Female householder families, no spouse present	All families	Married-couple families	Male householder or female householder families, no spouse present	Married-couple families, percent	Male householder or female householder families, no spouse present
	Florida—cont'd										
1224125	Fort Myers city	13,258	20.0	22.7	23.2	46.3	26.3	11.6	50.9	8.6	33.9
1224562	Fountainebleau CDP	12,495	10.7	12.0	28.5	30.9	25.8	18.9	36.2	17.0	33.4
1225175	Gainesville city	19,306	17.2	9.7	17.8	45.7	16.3	5.6	34.1	4.3	20.4
1230000	Hialeah city	51,729	24.0	19.7	34.0	50.5	43.6	37.3	53.8	28.0	40.8
1232000	Hollywood city	32,408	12.7	11.2	18.4	30.5	19.2	11.2	35.9	9.5	30.9
1232275	Homestead city	13,187	28.6	25.7	54.5	51.5	37.5	33.0	45.4	26.3	36.6
1235000	Jacksonville city	195,316	14.1	7.6	25.5	44.5	18.2	8.7	37.5	6.9	25.4
1235875	Jupiter town	14,777	5.8	5.4	6.2	31.3	4.2	2.2	13.1	2.2	9.1
1236062	Kendale Lakes CDP	14,334	12.7	12.2	27.8	38.0	23.6	20.8	28.5	17.1	23.1
1236100	Kendall CDP	17,566	6.7	4.1	0.0	31.9	11.6	7.5	23.0	6.2	16.4
1236950	Kissimmee city	14,227	24.2	17.5	44.7	52.0	33.2	16.7	57.4	13.2	39.7
1238250	Lakeland city	22,958	16.1	13.5	33.5	40.3	18.3	7.0	40.7	5.8	27.6
1239425	Largo city	17,743	10.8	6.4	31.4	35.8	16.9	8.2	37.6	6.4	31.5
1239550	Lauderhill city	14,855	17.1	9.5	23.7	34.8	27.1	16.2	37.1	12.7	29.4
1239925	Lehigh Acres CDP	23,523	17.1	11.7	26.0	42.3	28.8	18.2	47.8	15.3	36.2
1243125	Margate city	12,777	12.5	10.7	24.8	31.5	13.0	10.0	19.7	7.7	18.0
1243975	Melbourne city	17,684	12.4	6.2	5.4	40.7	17.4	8.3	37.7	5.6	23.5
1245000	Miami city	85,065	26.0	23.6	37.3	54.9	37.3	26.9	50.2	20.3	35.3
1245025	Miami Beach city	18,409	12.7	7.8	24.7	37.0	20.2	13.3	34.9	9.3	28.4
1245060	Miami Gardens city	23,267	19.2	22.0	13.9	29.7	33.8	23.3	43.9	18.3	33.7
1245975	Miramar city	29,892	8.1	5.6	4.2	17.9	12.8	8.5	20.8	7.9	16.5
1249450	North Miami city	11,331	25.2	23.7	14.2	50.4	30.0	20.2	43.4	18.1	34.7
1249675	North Port city	14,885	9.8	1.5	21.1	44.6	18.5	10.6	45.6	10.1	33.1
1250750	Ocala city	13,037	21.7	17.9	23.8	51.4	25.7	15.8	41.0	13.2	25.0
1253000	Orlando city	52,288	16.9	12.8	31.8	39.7	22.1	9.2	39.5	8.2	32.2
1254000	Palm Bay city	25,637	13.9	16.2	23.2	38.2	20.6	10.6	44.0	9.3	31.9
1254200	Palm Coast city	19,337	11.1	19.5	26.9	39.0	11.7	7.2	32.7	6.1	25.7
1254350	Palm Harbor CDP	15,885	5.0	2.7	0.0	26.0	5.3	3.1	14.6	2.6	9.6
1255775	Pembroke Pines city	39,086	7.2	4.0	12.2	19.0	9.9	5.9	20.7	5.3	18.6
1255925	Pensacola city	11,871	10.6	6.2	31.6	36.5	17.6	8.9	34.1	8.1	25.1
1256825	Pine Hills CDP	14,630	20.1	16.8	50.4	40.1	29.9	17.2	44.2	16.1	36.4
1257425	Plantation city	21,502	7.4	8.5	3.4	20.9	9.1	6.0	17.0	5.6	13.7
1257900	Poinciana CDP	13,643	16.3	17.2	31.2	42.4	22.8	16.9	37.9	13.2	25.4
1258050	Pompano Beach city	21,318	20.3	20.1	26.9	49.1	23.4	14.2	38.2	11.9	27.5
1258350	Port Charlotte CDP	13,854	11.6	13.6	41.7	28.3	17.7	10.0	43.4	8.2	31.8
1258575	Port Orange city	14,698	6.2	6.4	12.4	24.0	11.4	7.2	26.7	6.5	21.3
1258715	Port St. Lucie city	42,836	13.2	14.0	51.4	31.1	15.0	10.0	29.7	9.0	22.6
1260950	Riverview CDP	18,186	7.3	3.9	8.2	21.3	9.2	6.9	17.4	5.4	10.9
1263000	St. Petersburg city	55,396	12.1	7.1	26.9	41.6	16.3	7.6	33.3	6.3	23.1
1263650	Sanford city	11,029	20.0	5.8	60.6	42.7	23.7	12.9	40.0	9.8	27.5
1264175	Sarasota city	11,491	15.4	13.4	41.9	47.7	16.9	8.8	36.0	7.0	31.7
1268350	Spring Hill CDP	27,395	13.4	17.6	21.8	40.1	19.4	13.3	37.5	9.1	26.2
1269700	Sunrise city	21,125	11.3	8.1	9.1	25.6	15.0	9.4	26.3	7.8	21.4
1270600	Tallahassee city	35,016	14.6	7.5	29.3	40.7	16.8	6.3	34.8	5.5	24.6
1270675	Tamarac city	15,305	10.9	14.5	22.0	17.5	15.8	9.2	27.6	8.2	22.9
1270700	Tamiami CDP	12,711	13.4	11.9	31.0	27.7	22.2	16.8	35.9	13.6	33.1
1271000	Tampa city	75,671	17.4	11.2	30.5	44.5	22.4	11.4	40.9	8.7	27.4
1271569	The Hammocks CDP	12,590	10.2	10.3	21.3	27.8	17.5	13.9	27.8	13.1	21.9
1271625	The Villages CDP	23,083	3.6	...	...	...	...	...	...	...	...
1272145	Town 'n' Country CDP	19,229	10.9	15.0	11.8	26.0	18.7	13.6	29.0	11.1	21.8
1275812	Wellington village	15,484	7.2	4.0	17.4	29.5	6.9	4.5	18.4	3.9	14.7
1276582	Weston city	17,477	5.5	3.3	0.0	44.3	...	...	...	...	...
1276600	West Palm Beach city	21,112	14.8	13.5	26.6	34.8	16.6	8.8	28.4	7.2	20.0
1300000	**Georgia**	2,386,724	14.6	10.3	26.9	44.5	17.6	9.0	38.0	7.6	27.0
1301052	Albany city	17,604	28.7	13.3	27.6	57.8	36.2	16.2	55.0	11.4	36.0
1301696	Alpharetta city	15,703	5.7	2.4	0.0	35.3	...	...	...	...	...
1303440	Athens-Clarke County	20,320	23.6	13.4	52.6	62.0	23.3	10.7	46.3	9.2	29.3
1304000	Atlanta city	77,537	19.7	7.3	35.9	53.6	25.0	7.2	49.2	5.6	33.7
1304204	Augusta-Richmond County	41,815	21.4	10.4	21.1	58.8	25.5	9.5	45.6	8.3	30.8
1310944	Brookhaven city	10,306	12.2	13.6	59.9	47.4	8.4	7.5	12.0	6.6	10.6
1319000	Columbus city	45,804	15.5	7.6	20.3	42.2	21.6	8.9	41.5	8.0	30.5
1342425	Johns Creek city	21,480	4.6	1.4	0.0	32.4	...	...	...	...	...
1349000	Macon city	19,420	33.9	16.9	47.4	64.9	40.0	14.7	62.2	11.8	41.0
1349756	Marietta city	12,943	18.2	11.9	17.4	56.0	18.3	7.0	39.4	6.3	32.0
1367284	Roswell city	23,112	6.5	7.8	6.3	22.5	6.1	3.2	17.4	3.0	12.0
1368516	Sandy Springs city	22,209	8.7	9.3	9.1	27.9	8.5	5.4	17.3	5.3	14.0
1369000	Savannah city	29,242	20.8	11.6	39.8	54.8	20.2	7.6	36.4	6.3	24.0
1371492	Smyrna city	12,596	9.9	9.3	47.0	25.2	...	...	...	...	...
1378800	Valdosta city	11,361	25.0	18.7	10.6	54.9	28.7	12.4	48.7	9.8	36.0

Table E-4: Cities with a Population of 50,000 or More—Income, Poverty, and Health Insurance—*Continued*

State/ Place FIPS code	State/place	Median family income in the past 12 months (in 2,013 inflation-adjusted dollars)								Total population in households	Persons who had health insurance, as a percent of all persons in that household type		
							Families with own children under 18 years						
		All families	Families with no earners	Families with one earner	Families with two earners	Families with three or more earners	Married-couple families with children	Male householder, no spouse present, with children	Female householder, no spouse present, with children		Married-couple families, percent	Male householder or female householder families, no spouse present	Nonfamily households
	Georgia—cont'd												
1380508	Warner Robins city	$52,649	$16,887	$38,042	$68,081	$95,690	$62,177	$31,369	$17,976	70,662	83.8	78.9	82.7
1500000	**Hawaii**	$78,501	$40,960	$54,697	$90,367	$123,507	$87,567	$48,840	$27,683	1,337,598	94.8	91.0	89.3
1571550	Urban Honolulu CDP	$73,585	$39,761	$56,299	$84,884	$126,831	$82,299	$60,009	$31,202	333,703	94.8	92.0	90.7
1600000	**Idaho**	$55,296	$34,365	$41,860	$67,736	$84,642	$63,851	$36,592	$20,543	1,577,379	86.5	75.6	80.4
1608830	Boise City city	$64,423	$32,875	$47,692	$77,926	$97,602	$82,103	$30,338	$21,597	210,581	90.0	81.3	82.3
1639700	Idaho Falls city	$51,466	$40,956	$40,310	$60,413	$92,757	$65,469	$45,076	$21,980	57,028	89.3	70.2	77.5
1652120	Meridian city	$66,591	$45,458	$55,841	$79,529	$101,439	$79,951	$45,991	$19,775	80,453	92.3	67.1	90.1
1656260	Nampa city	$42,088	$33,300	$30,655	$57,973	$59,603	$49,246	$27,018	$17,310	83,729	84.1	74.2	77.4
1664090	Pocatello city	$54,775	$40,157	$38,267	$61,725	$84,595	$60,021	$24,425	$20,371	53,976	87.8	82.7	81.3
1700000	**Illinois**	$69,142	$32,285	$48,001	$89,454	$106,113	$88,403	$37,113	$24,017	12,690,730	90.7	79.9	84.3
1702154	Arlington Heights village	$95,956	$56,007	$73,060	$115,600	$142,500	$109,254	$65,718	$47,198	74,857	94.0	84.1	91.2
1703012	Aurora city	$69,587	$35,337	$44,355	$86,803	$99,209	$75,598	$34,909	$24,945	197,639	85.2	76.7	74.6
1705573	Berwyn city	$60,034	$20,375	$39,076	$72,664	$94,806	$67,453	$31,438	$26,205	56,704	84.8	81.0	84.9
1706613	Bloomington city	$81,323	$49,322	$53,356	$102,576	$120,650	$106,441	$43,322	$25,531	77,382	95.0	89.2	88.8
1707133	Bolingbrook village	$82,177	$26,161	$57,008	$93,178	$106,167	$92,050	$41,401	$28,359	73,518	90.7	81.0	79.4
1712385	Champaign city	$70,125	$28,380	$45,344	$81,074	$105,568	$87,059	$16,417	$23,942	82,122	93.4	86.9	87.1
1714000	Chicago city	$52,299	$17,090	$35,825	$84,486	$88,825	$72,918	$30,026	$21,331	2,689,006	83.2	75.1	81.9
1714351	Cicero town	$41,739	$12,172	$31,958	$51,913	$87,566	$47,880	$35,485	$24,978	83,676	76.6	71.8	70.7
1718823	Decatur city	$49,261	$33,065	$33,765	$76,315	$92,479	$68,110	$33,333	$15,434	73,168	92.1	84.2	83.8
1719642	Des Plaines city	$75,127	$39,027	$60,592	$84,857	$115,530	$78,879	$0	$49,250	58,219	89.0	81.6	85.6
1723074	Elgin city	$65,041	$25,705	$40,892	$75,111	$91,594	$65,959	$28,953	$22,528	109,497	84.1	76.0	80.1
1724582	Evanston city	$102,945	$32,461	$70,935	$126,134	$139,135	$133,828	$85,734	$40,221	73,945	94.4	83.9	93.4
1735411	Hoffman Estates village	$90,671	$48,092	$65,335	$110,496	$105,938	$105,176	$62,115	$31,250	52,148	90.6	78.4	88.9
1738570	Joliet city	$70,860	$25,432	$51,720	$84,829	$97,854	$83,628	$52,306	$29,833	145,739	90.3	80.5	83.5
1751089	Mount Prospect village	$82,302	$40,138	$60,858	$93,761	$121,766	$93,324	$45,276	$42,756	54,596	88.3	79.8	82.1
1751622	Naperville city	$124,945	$49,020	$108,806	$142,076	$151,410	$148,690	$44,625	$53,083	142,718	95.5	79.6	91.2
1753234	Normal town	$90,739	$57,455	$57,500	$101,844	$117,583	$109,904	$47,625	$32,805	54,022	97.7	84.1	91.3
1754820	Oak Lawn village	$70,686	$35,793	$44,872	$95,294	$119,321	$76,969	$69,914	$40,016	56,463	89.9	84.6	88.2
1754885	Oak Park village	$108,637	$36,391	$75,678	$136,613	$136,146	$161,109	$90,917	$47,500	51,671	96.2	87.8	86.7
1756640	Orland Park village	$95,843	$48,413	$71,602	$115,737	$123,691	$104,838	$70,417	$57,685	57,068	95.3	86.1	92.1
1757225	Palatine village	$89,898	$30,895	$64,331	$105,141	$121,912	$106,250	$58,722	$29,259	68,873	91.4	75.6	81.8
1759000	Peoria city	$58,503	$27,123	$40,339	$88,074	$100,212	$89,686	$26,995	$18,299	114,551	93.1	85.7	83.6
1765000	Rockford city	$45,637	$22,561	$33,111	$72,363	$87,340	$61,138	$28,125	$18,944	148,492	89.5	82.5	79.9
1768003	Schaumburg village	$86,538	$45,135	$74,980	$95,594	$124,743	$93,042	$58,950	$40,986	74,131	92.7	82.2	90.1
1770122	Skokie village	$74,422	$34,152	$58,213	$93,396	$98,933	$81,870	$40,051	$34,111	64,492	86.5	74.7	86.0
1772000	Springfield city	$63,188	$37,934	$39,731	$88,503	$108,750	$89,318	$33,786	$19,751	115,263	94.1	82.8	83.0
1775484	Tinley Park village	$85,928	$45,637	$65,335	$102,621	$130,694	$100,972	$19,132	$42,308	56,867	95.5	91.1	90.4
1779293	Waukegan city	$49,921	$17,472	$30,684	$62,190	$77,838	$56,502	$32,971	$20,419	87,324	79.3	74.9	75.5
1781048	Wheaton city	$108,420	$46,919	$91,615	$121,048	$134,211	$128,962	$74,901	$36,667	52,576	95.7	80.8	90.3
1800000	**Indiana**	$59,490	$31,602	$42,256	$77,001	$95,990	$76,786	$35,568	$21,383	6,441,965	89.5	78.1	82.7
1801468	Anderson city	$41,753	$30,688	$31,184	$63,975	$75,417	$52,852	$25,833	$18,520	54,547	84.3	77.0	77.9
1805860	Bloomington city	$56,995	$22,415	$47,198	$67,606	$79,634	$75,039	$65,560	$11,556	79,772	93.7	77.8	88.4
1810342	Carmel city	$127,356	$46,438	$102,340	$138,093	$171,333	$147,439	$115,254	$51,458	83,361	97.2	89.2	92.8
1820728	Elkhart city	$36,434	$17,073	$29,435	$55,584	$73,831	$50,582	$27,607	$16,835	51,169	77.2	72.1	77.4
1822000	Evansville city	$44,475	$27,491	$30,907	$66,389	$88,519	$64,411	$27,383	$18,591	117,932	89.7	78.9	77.2
1823278	Fishers town	$105,945	$60,584	$71,971	$116,356	$137,012	$120,155	$41,779	$54,877	82,039	94.8	80.6	88.9
1825000	Fort Wayne city	$53,037	$25,359	$37,303	$73,232	$96,313	$68,893	$28,114	$21,474	251,860	87.0	76.1	80.8
1827000	Gary city	$30,255	$13,673	$26,658	$57,099	$83,882	$52,398	$28,087	$12,090	78,643	85.4	78.2	77.4
1829898	Greenwood city	$63,262	$33,274	$46,190	$80,405	$88,348	$73,377	$43,404	$17,773	52,060	90.9	75.1	87.6
1831000	Hammond city	$42,633	$17,636	$34,265	$64,468	$83,716	$50,631	$31,385	$16,354	79,427	80.0	74.9	77.8
1836003	Indianapolis city	$50,896	$24,371	$35,037	$72,294	$93,770	$71,004	$26,415	$21,001	824,801	87.4	77.4	79.4
1840392	Kokomo city	$49,511	$35,095	$34,972	$74,566	$97,602	$65,509	$32,813	$19,884	55,365	90.6	81.7	77.9
1840788	Lafayette city	$52,016	$29,482	$35,048	$61,926	$74,320	$61,733	$35,127	$16,935	69,165	87.7	75.7	77.4
1851876	Muncie city	$40,047	$24,653	$32,394	$58,464	$72,690	$47,459	$17,917	$17,808	68,632	89.1	76.1	85.1
1854180	Noblesville city	$84,040	$37,483	$56,058	$95,768	$122,639	$93,507	$48,629	$33,750	56,485	94.4	81.3	86.7
1871000	South Bend city	$40,512	$18,881	$28,781	$58,889	$79,028	$52,406	$21,472	$15,939	98,503	88.4	75.5	77.0
1875428	Terre Haute city	$42,215	$27,714	$29,797	$61,131	$72,750	$49,625	$26,262	$15,655	56,721	84.2	76.1	78.2
1900000	**Iowa**	$65,550	$35,528	$43,336	$80,074	$96,280	$81,489	$38,392	$24,069	3,031,378	94.3	84.8	88.6
1901855	Ames city	$79,573	$58,000	$50,857	$87,654	$110,000	$87,099	$41,687	$16,476	60,697	97.6	87.9	92.9
1912000	Cedar Rapids city	$69,906	$38,609	$44,985	$83,958	$105,383	$89,546	$41,529	$25,159	126,625	95.5	85.3	87.8
1916860	Council Bluffs city	$56,724	$28,349	$38,904	$73,927	$92,226	$75,712	$51,778	$27,145	61,153	89.3	82.6	83.0
1919000	Davenport city	$60,086	$32,222	$36,941	$82,408	$105,000	$82,238	$42,479	$23,261	99,851	91.0	87.1	84.2
1921000	Des Moines city	$54,066	$24,874	$33,899	$70,654	$87,924	$67,781	$35,227	$22,345	204,633	91.7	84.1	88.8
1922395	Dubuque city	$58,860	$38,406	$39,913	$77,825	$80,848	$80,225	$34,215	$18,739	56,855	93.1	90.0	91.1
1938595	Iowa City city	$69,967	$40,737	$51,785	$82,493	$116,914	$92,402	$50,625	$22,199	69,974	94.7	82.0	92.5
1973335	Sioux City city	$52,146	$29,092	$33,213	$66,364	$77,530	$61,239	$39,321	$20,979	81,850	91.2	82.6	83.7
1982425	Waterloo city	$51,200	$30,867	$35,501	$65,341	$83,542	$64,726	$28,059	$17,539	67,563	93.4	83.7	87.8
1983910	West Des Moines city	$86,730	$40,521	$65,471	$109,753	$116,074	$105,581	$39,965	$32,596	59,226	96.5	91.2	92.2
2000000	**Kansas**	$64,346	$34,928	$43,825	$79,709	$98,311	$79,250	$35,997	$23,860	2,824,697	91.0	79.1	84.4
2036000	Kansas City city	$43,612	$21,431	$29,431	$63,108	$77,542	$52,569	$25,808	$16,710	146,421	77.9	70.7	75.1

State/Place FIPS code	State/place	Total number of families	Families with incomes below the poverty level, as a percent of all families of that family type				Families that received Food Stamps (SNAP), as a percent of all families of that family type			Families that received food stamps (SNAP) and had at least one worker	
			All families	Married-couple families	Male householder families, no spouse present	Female householder families, no spouse present	All families	Married-couple families	Male householder or female householder families, no spouse present	Married-couple families, percent	Male householder or female householder families, no spouse present
	Georgia—cont'd										
1380508	Warner Robins city...............	16,775	20.3	14.5	32.9	46.5	21.3	12.7	38.0	11.3	27.1
1500000	**Hawaii**...........................	311,096	8.0	5.9	18.3	31.3	11.8	7.0	25.6	6.0	19.5
1571550	Urban Honolulu CDP............	73,342	8.4	7.7	11.7	32.2	11.2	8.0	19.2	6.1	14.6
1600000	**Idaho**.............................	404,512	11.3	9.5	22.8	44.9	14.0	8.6	34.7	7.9	27.2
1608830	Boise City city....................	51,924	10.0	7.5	24.7	38.5	12.6	6.5	30.4	6.0	19.8
1639700	Idaho Falls city...................	14,531	12.4	9.3	7.4	42.5	18.5	10.5	40.1	10.1	36.5
1652120	Meridian city......................	21,359	7.2	4.7	9.6	44.4	11.8	6.3	36.3	6.2	28.3
1656260	Nampa city........................	20,066	19.9	20.0	38.3	56.8	24.9	16.7	47.8	15.3	38.8
1664090	Pocatello city.....................	12,746	13.8	14.7	24.4	47.0	18.0	10.8	39.0	10.5	32.8
1700000	**Illinois**...........................	3,114,415	10.9	7.6	22.5	41.1	14.0	6.7	34.2	5.8	25.5
1702154	Arlington Heights village.......	20,163	2.4	2.2	3.2	15.5	2.8	1.7	10.1	1.1	10.1
1703012	Aurora city........................	45,440	11.2	10.1	21.8	34.6	17.3	12.1	32.0	11.3	28.0
1705573	Berwyn city........................	12,845	11.7	10.2	21.2	28.4	21.2	14.3	34.6	12.2	24.8
1706613	Bloomington city.................	18,378	7.8	2.4	20.1	37.3	11.8	4.2	36.0	3.6	30.2
1707133	Bolingbrook village..............	17,624	8.4	7.4	22.0	33.9	11.4	7.8	24.1	7.1	19.2
1712385	Champaign city...................	15,149	13.4	6.5	51.1	45.2	12.6	4.0	37.1	3.3	30.7
1714000	Chicago city.......................	558,839	19.5	14.4	30.2	48.1	25.6	12.6	44.2	10.4	31.4
1714351	Cicero town........................	17,321	20.2	17.5	21.5	44.3	28.3	22.8	38.3	21.8	28.0
1718823	Decatur city.......................	17,969	19.0	14.2	17.5	60.4	22.6	9.9	46.3	8.6	34.0
1719642	Des Plaines city..................	14,562	4.4	6.9	6.0	18.7	6.4	4.9	13.8	4.7	11.2
1723074	Elgin city..........................	23,855	12.2	11.1	10.5	45.5	16.7	10.9	32.2	10.1	29.7
1724582	Evanston city......................	15,600	5.8	3.6	14.3	21.9	9.5	4.2	25.1	3.7	18.2
1735411	Hoffman Estates village.........	14,173	3.1	2.4	9.7	16.7	8.2	5.1	22.3	4.8	21.7
1738570	Joliet city.........................	33,848	9.4	5.7	18.1	29.8	14.4	7.7	30.9	6.8	23.2
1751089	Mount Prospect village..........	14,280	4.0	5.5	5.4	15.9	7.5	6.8	11.2	6.5	10.4
1751622	Naperville city....................	37,768	3.3	1.8	9.0	18.7	3.8	2.0	14.5	1.8	12.2
1753234	Normal town.......................	9,914	7.9	1.9	43.0	24.9	...	...	...	...	...
1754820	Oak Lawn village.................	14,242	7.5	13.2	22.4	27.2	9.5	5.6	21.4	5.5	17.3
1754885	Oak Park village..................	12,845	5.9	1.9	7.3	33.4	6.8	3.7	17.8	3.4	11.8
1756640	Orland Park village..............	15,633	4.6	3.0	21.2	34.5	4.7	2.2	18.1	2.1	10.9
1757225	Palatine village..................	17,104	8.0	7.5	20.5	27.7	6.9	5.2	12.3	4.1	7.8
1759000	Peoria city........................	26,890	18.9	11.4	33.9	54.4	18.8	4.3	45.0	2.9	32.6
1765000	Rockford city......................	35,962	21.2	15.4	30.5	52.2	27.9	13.3	52.1	10.5	36.6
1768003	Schaumburg village..............	18,424	4.3	2.1	0.0	28.8	8.0	5.1	20.1	4.7	12.6
1770122	Skokie village.....................	16,549	9.3	8.7	19.3	28.0	12.2	8.4	24.4	7.2	20.7
1772000	Springfield city...................	28,234	14.2	9.0	32.4	46.3	17.5	6.1	39.0	5.5	30.8
1775484	Tinley Park village...............	14,833	6.5	4.7	33.0	21.7	4.4	2.6	11.8	2.6	9.7
1779293	Waukegan city....................	20,351	19.9	14.8	36.0	47.4	22.1	11.5	40.1	10.7	29.5
1781048	Wheaton city......................	13,093	5.4	4.5	9.4	19.5	7.5	5.7	17.1	4.7	13.5
1800000	**Indiana**...........................	1,647,579	11.6	7.8	25.4	44.4	13.7	6.5	34.6	5.5	24.9
1801468	Anderson city.....................	12,965	21.7	19.1	45.0	51.9	25.8	13.2	45.8	11.9	29.7
1805860	Bloomington city.................	10,842	19.9	10.7	26.3	65.1	16.6	6.0	40.5	5.0	24.1
1810342	Carmel city........................	23,270	2.7	0.5	0.0	24.9	...	...	...	...	...
1820728	Elkhart city........................	12,041	26.4	22.6	31.1	55.4	28.9	15.1	46.6	12.4	32.0
1822000	Evansville city....................	28,767	16.4	8.7	24.6	46.2	18.5	8.8	35.5	6.1	26.0
1823278	Fishers town......................	21,286	1.9	1.4	10.5	5.3	...	...	...	...	...
1825000	Fort Wayne city..................	61,441	16.4	11.5	30.9	44.1	17.9	7.6	38.4	6.4	26.2
1827000	Gary city...........................	18,436	36.3	26.6	41.1	68.2	40.7	18.2	55.1	13.5	34.4
1829898	Greenwood city...................	13,237	13.4	13.2	7.1	53.3	10.8	6.0	26.9	5.9	20.8
1831000	Hammond city.....................	18,174	20.9	20.5	18.6	50.7	23.7	14.1	37.9	13.3	27.9
1836003	Indianapolis city..................	191,440	17.3	10.1	37.6	45.5	20.9	9.3	40.4	8.2	29.8
1840392	Kokomo city.......................	14,492	16.1	14.3	35.5	48.8	19.6	8.6	43.0	8.2	27.8
1840788	Lafayette city.....................	16,966	15.9	7.1	18.3	61.0	20.9	8.8	45.6	8.2	33.4
1851876	Muncie city........................	13,854	20.1	18.0	49.8	53.6	26.3	13.1	49.5	9.8	32.6
1854180	Noblesville city...................	14,791	6.1	3.7	22.1	29.8	...	...	...	...	...
1871000	South Bend city..................	22,728	23.7	19.4	40.3	61.0	27.6	12.8	50.5	11.3	35.3
1875428	Terre Haute city..................	11,813	19.7	15.2	38.1	62.2	25.3	15.3	45.2	12.3	32.5
1900000	**Iowa**...............................	792,745	8.4	5.3	19.3	39.7	12.0	5.6	36.2	4.8	29.0
1901855	Ames city..........................	10,115	9.0	8.0	6.6	47.5	7.9	4.5	27.7	3.6	26.0
1912000	Cedar Rapids city................	30,278	7.8	1.9	20.5	34.6	14.1	5.3	39.1	4.6	34.3
1916860	Council Bluffs city...............	15,252	11.6	10.1	8.6	36.6	20.9	10.6	40.2	8.8	29.9
1919000	Davenport city....................	23,313	12.8	7.2	18.7	43.1	17.9	8.2	39.8	7.1	30.6
1921000	Des Moines city..................	48,674	15.6	12.4	25.2	45.1	27.0	14.0	51.8	12.0	41.7
1922395	Dubuque city......................	13,192	10.8	4.5	12.4	50.1	14.9	5.5	40.6	5.5	33.1
1938595	Iowa City city.....................	12,752	11.1	5.7	0.0	43.8	12.9	6.6	30.4	6.1	26.7
1973335	Sioux City city....................	19,696	13.4	10.1	15.0	43.6	20.9	11.6	39.7	10.2	32.9
1982425	Waterloo city.....................	16,133	14.3	11.2	25.7	49.1	19.4	8.4	45.0	6.5	32.3
1983910	West Des Moines city............	15,072	6.3	5.1	0.0	24.6	...	...	...	...	...
2000000	**Kansas**............................	727,902	9.4	7.1	19.1	40.1	10.1	5.0	27.5	4.4	21.4
2036000	Kansas City city..................	33,766	20.8	16.3	21.1	57.0	22.5	11.4	38.3	10.6	26.8

State/Place FIPS code	State/place	Median family income in the past 12 months (in 2,013 inflation-adjusted dollars)								Total population in households	Persons who had health insurance, as a percent of all persons in that household type		
		All families	Families with no earners	Families with one earner	Families with two earners	Families with three or more earners	Families with own children under 18 years				Married-couple families, percent	Male householder or female householder families, no spouse present	Nonfamily households
							Married-couple families with children	Male householder, no spouse present, with children	Female householder, no spouse present, with children				
	Kansas—cont'd												
2038900	Lawrence city	$66,492	$43,536	$45,172	$79,084	$102,643	$89,239	$36,216	$28,933	89,286	91.7	79.1	86.4
2044250	Manhattan city	$66,224	$41,892	$43,279	$85,694	$96,907	$79,419	$36,813	$30,294	53,367	94.4	91.5	88.7
2052575	Olathe city	$90,615	$46,300	$63,484	$99,082	$121,365	$104,071	$50,972	$40,224	129,022	92.5	79.0	82.1
2053775	Overland Park city	$89,367	$49,641	$66,993	$106,044	$129,778	$114,925	$54,314	$34,025	177,436	95.5	82.0	91.1
2064500	Shawnee city	$88,153	$40,459	$65,601	$97,966	$128,357	$102,232	$51,372	$34,800	63,199	95.6	83.1	79.2
2071000	Topeka city	$54,181	$30,085	$36,745	$69,804	$90,000	$71,427	$29,474	$18,448	124,988	89.4	77.6	80.5
2079000	Wichita city	$57,599	$33,489	$38,374	$75,568	$96,167	$70,225	$31,875	$20,741	380,103	87.9	77.9	79.7
2100000	**Kentucky**	$53,994	$25,353	$40,940	$75,776	$94,284	$73,748	$32,067	$18,590	4,295,357	89.6	78.3	82.4
2108902	Bowling Green city	$42,573	$24,496	$27,951	$59,693	$90,625	$68,060	$20,574	$13,278	59,335	88.5	74.3	82.0
2146027	Lexington-Fayette urban county	$67,463	$36,016	$43,399	$86,466	$107,509	$90,341	$37,254	$21,005	299,612	90.6	79.7	83.6
2148006	Louisville/Jefferson County	$57,427	$29,346	$40,511	$80,300	$98,982	$84,223	$40,133	$22,055	598,478	91.5	78.9	80.8
2158620	Owensboro city	$53,632	$27,703	$36,125	$69,504	$97,235	$65,341	$25,587	$18,623	56,843	90.0	80.3	83.9
2200000	**Louisiana**	$55,414	$23,278	$39,756	$82,102	$102,388	$83,839	$38,120	$19,279	4,498,089	88.0	76.5	78.5
2205000	Baton Rouge city	$48,910	$22,652	$36,185	$75,531	$84,747	$83,608	$31,939	$20,524	227,830	88.7	77.6	83.9
2208920	Bossier City city	$61,686	$19,015	$44,025	$76,113	$104,788	$86,085	$29,293	$20,429	61,382	89.9	76.7	77.9
2239475	Kenner city	$59,278	$30,490	$41,971	$81,330	$87,193	$70,591	$76,903	$16,989	66,507	82.0	74.1	70.1
2240735	Lafayette city	$63,045	$25,972	$44,407	$84,875	$104,601	$92,973	$49,935	$20,311	121,341	89.6	75.0	78.6
2241155	Lake Charles city	$45,565	$26,301	$30,369	$72,801	$107,900	$79,018	$17,384	$22,732	71,541	88.8	77.7	75.1
2250115	Metairie CDP	$72,083	$37,625	$48,916	$91,907	$120,145	$92,381	$50,650	$18,393	138,963	88.6	77.4	73.3
2255000	New Orleans city	$46,979	$15,712	$32,089	$84,406	$95,643	$88,220	$33,633	$17,189	364,405	87.9	78.3	78.6
2270000	Shreveport city	$47,040	$21,713	$32,523	$79,397	$93,609	$88,320	$45,405	$19,491	196,934	87.4	75.5	79.9
2300000	**Maine**	$60,235	$30,232	$41,626	$77,758	$97,789	$76,056	$32,702	$22,301	1,314,314	92.5	85.8	83.8
2360545	Portland city	$62,248	$19,840	$39,941	$84,973	$103,000	$85,040	$39,615	$22,100	65,248	95.0	84.2	81.5
2400000	**Maryland**	$87,060	$38,003	$59,175	$109,732	$129,316	$113,714	$50,869	$36,393	5,790,545	92.6	84.0	88.2
2402825	Aspen Hill CDP	$87,546	$63,600	$47,321	$120,193	$94,955	$97,050	$29,226	$17,439	52,883	88.2	75.2	79.0
2404000	Baltimore city	$49,245	$16,323	$37,579	$79,623	$95,487	$82,933	$38,889	$22,037	611,839	90.9	85.7	87.4
2407125	Bethesda CDP	$191,250	$104,085	$167,909	$225,237	$225,625	$212,984	$176,719	$71,500	62,342	96.7	93.9	95.6
2408775	Bowie city	$117,939	$64,668	$85,842	$130,200	$157,880	$132,426	$97,623	$80,234	55,727	93.4	91.0	86.5
2419125	Columbia CDP	$117,604	$57,738	$80,161	$137,872	$169,375	$141,241	$59,913	$38,156	103,294	94.6	88.8	92.3
2423975	Dundalk CDP	$54,438	$30,537	$46,630	$71,817	$96,061	$71,474	$50,348	$28,814	61,085	92.0	86.7	87.7
2426000	Ellicott City CDP	$132,336	$60,417	$91,627	$161,380	$184,583	$153,286	$113,768	$64,163	69,250	94.4	83.3	93.4
2430325	Frederick city	$72,564	$38,504	$58,569	$86,375	$110,875	$82,071	$36,128	$30,219	65,267	91.4	80.1	86.5
2431175	Gaithersburg city	$86,063	$43,477	$59,097	$122,873	$121,944	$104,855	$34,125	$32,335	62,846	90.4	78.9	84.2
2432025	Germantown CDP	$91,635	$15,607	$58,295	$113,967	$114,497	$115,956	$45,088	$40,991	90,516	86.9	78.1	89.3
2432650	Glen Burnie CDP	$71,433	$42,015	$55,488	$85,963	$118,602	$85,291	$55,050	$33,051	67,794	90.7	86.9	91.1
2467675	Rockville city	$118,818	$70,278	$93,072	$139,002	$131,926	$128,816	$71,008	$45,940	62,345	93.1	82.8	92.0
2472450	Silver Spring CDP	$84,348	$29,107	$56,974	$108,300	$111,994	$119,950	$42,388	$50,325	76,323	86.1	69.3	84.3
2478425	Towson CDP	$100,453	$41,406	$77,172	$119,775	$135,167	$130,909	$70,625	$58,375	55,749	95.9	83.5	93.6
2481175	Waldorf CDP	$91,611	$24,654	$65,565	$119,783	$150,240	$116,531	$56,658	$51,416	72,262	95.0	89.1	92.6
2483775	Wheaton CDP	$75,600	$68,967	$45,361	$84,854	$97,763	$85,542	$33,576	$32,202	50,222	75.8	63.0	79.9
2500000	**Massachusetts**	$83,867	$30,356	$56,245	$106,084	$125,258	$112,824	$45,121	$27,158	6,568,640	97.5	93.5	94.6
2507000	Boston city	$59,635	$15,582	$37,633	$97,632	$99,308	$100,370	$37,067	$21,393	631,129	96.7	93.3	94.7
2509000	Brockton city	$60,504	$22,880	$40,214	$76,701	$104,149	$79,030	$36,942	$24,180	92,918	95.6	93.3	87.4
2509210	Brookline CDP	$131,822	$27,622	$113,750	$168,125	$154,529	$172,301	$52,026	$51,170	58,402	98.8	97.5	98.8
2511000	Cambridge city	$93,406	$17,303	$60,292	$120,173	$122,344	$130,990	$59,125	$35,066	106,001	97.8	92.4	96.7
2513660	Chicopee city	$57,285	$26,084	$42,992	$77,750	$96,304	$77,869	$33,875	$31,366	54,957	97.4	95.6	95.3
2523000	Fall River city	$41,814	$18,039	$34,924	$64,975	$107,553	$58,938	$22,344	$20,336	87,595	96.2	91.8	92.9
2524960	Framingham CDP	$85,108	$33,588	$59,776	$96,985	$113,119	$99,515	$37,589	$30,056	68,679	94.4	89.3	92.9
2529405	Haverhill city	$70,405	$25,096	$40,797	$93,083	$119,500	$95,920	$29,292	$26,013	60,994	97.8	92.4	94.4
2534550	Lawrence city	$34,416	$15,261	$25,880	$53,501	$76,787	$55,081	$36,957	$20,301	76,625	90.8	89.0	88.9
2537000	Lowell city	$55,875	$16,989	$35,267	$76,012	$101,947	$77,545	$38,611	$25,824	106,977	93.6	91.5	92.3
2537490	Lynn city	$54,009	$15,096	$35,535	$80,851	$110,739	$74,640	$33,214	$21,925	90,854	95.0	92.5	91.2
2537875	Malden city	$61,193	$15,205	$37,953	$80,442	$103,776	$66,103	$63,571	$27,359	60,113	95.0	91.7	87.2
2539835	Medford city	$87,108	$31,848	$61,307	$109,909	$125,532	$97,788	$27,023	$23,036	56,479	98.0	94.4	95.6
2545000	New Bedford city	$44,644	$18,984	$34,237	$67,841	$88,750	$60,000	$30,353	$19,531	93,436	95.4	91.8	91.2
2545560	Newton city	$155,931	$45,278	$118,864	$186,439	$188,194	$201,372	$96,250	$44,141	86,469	99.2	97.2	97.4
2552490	Peabody city	$84,011	$39,766	$62,054	$93,530	$126,630	$97,401	$52,083	$49,949	51,295	96.0	95.3	97.0
2555745	Quincy city	$71,636	$23,075	$53,548	$85,994	$129,155	$86,659	$60,818	$38,680	92,496	97.8	93.0	95.5
2556585	Revere city	$57,251	$25,956	$42,115	$72,960	$99,900	$73,878	$47,938	$28,452	53,006	96.0	91.4	91.7
2562535	Somerville city	$68,076	$24,917	$43,538	$96,917	$114,028	$103,841	$49,344	$19,713	77,648	96.9	90.7	95.3
2567000	Springfield city	$37,291	$15,286	$31,128	$68,472	$100,680	$59,321	$30,228	$16,433	152,634	94.9	92.9	93.6
2569170	Taunton city	$65,150	$26,271	$45,640	$85,294	$110,392	$88,562	$40,692	$23,527	55,417	97.2	91.7	93.5
2572600	Waltham city	$87,128	$31,750	$67,896	$109,119	$123,047	$107,063	$63,450	$42,352	61,543	97.7	90.6	95.9
2578972	Weymouth Town city	$89,363	$32,621	$62,037	$106,550	$132,135	$114,531	$71,193	$30,900	54,448	97.4	96.1	97.8
2582000	Worcester city	$54,035	$15,728	$37,725	$80,839	$118,800	$77,367	$28,645	$21,357	180,195	97.1	94.0	93.2
2600000	**Michigan**	$60,398	$34,550	$44,945	$81,067	$99,413	$81,062	$33,763	$20,352	9,773,359	92.4	82.4	84.5
2603000	Ann Arbor city	$95,115	$58,296	$62,954	$111,358	$128,150	$107,367	$46,417	$35,050	115,973	96.3	90.0	92.6
2605920	Battle Creek city	$48,280	$27,555	$31,747	$72,347	$93,036	$72,578	$23,727	$17,388	51,164	89.9	86.6	84.4

State/Place FIPS code	State/place	Total number of families	Families with incomes below the poverty level, as a percent of all families of that family type				Families that received Food Stamps (SNAP), as a percent of all families of that family type			Families that received food stamps (SNAP) and had at least one worker	
			All families	Married-couple families	Male householder families, no spouse present	Female householder families, no spouse present	All families	Married-couple families	Male householder or female householder families, no spouse present	Married-couple families, percent	Male householder or female householder families, no spouse present
	Kansas—cont'd										
2038900	Lawrence city................	17,363	9.0	5.6	21.5	40.0	9.6	4.8	22.9	4.3	18.5
2044250	Manhattan city................	9,744	6.5	3.2	1.9	26.5	...	...	...	...	...
2052575	Olathe city................	33,826	4.6	3.3	9.3	19.4	4.6	2.5	14.4	2.5	12.0
2053775	Overland Park city................	47,738	3.8	1.9	16.5	15.4	4.5	2.2	13.1	2.1	10.7
2064500	Shawnee city................	16,344	4.4	1.9	8.7	30.8	6.1	2.0	25.0	1.8	18.6
2071000	Topeka city................	29,906	15.4	10.9	27.0	49.4	16.5	8.0	36.1	6.5	26.3
2079000	Wichita city................	92,211	13.8	12.0	22.7	43.9	16.1	8.7	33.8	7.7	27.1
2100000	**Kentucky**................	1,131,310	14.6	10.4	30.1	49.8	17.7	9.6	40.1	7.1	25.5
2108902	Bowling Green city................	12,407	23.1	11.1	48.4	60.7	25.0	10.5	46.1	8.9	35.3
2146027	Lexington-Fayette urban county......	71,027	11.3	6.7	18.8	42.6	13.5	5.8	32.4	5.0	25.7
2148006	Louisville/Jefferson County........	147,404	14.1	9.4	25.7	41.9	18.3	8.3	36.6	7.3	25.7
2158620	Owensboro city................	14,138	16.5	11.1	44.2	51.8	18.3	6.2	47.4	5.3	32.3
2200000	**Louisiana**................	1,127,030	15.5	7.0	24.9	49.3	18.3	7.9	38.8	6.4	27.8
2205000	Baton Rouge city................	48,297	18.3	5.7	27.6	47.2	25.2	9.1	43.8	7.2	33.5
2208920	Bossier City city................	15,219	15.8	4.8	35.5	44.4	17.2	4.2	43.8	4.1	34.4
2239475	Kenner city................	16,279	11.8	8.1	3.0	48.8	19.4	12.3	35.0	10.8	30.2
2240735	Lafayette city................	27,982	13.6	4.7	13.7	47.5	15.4	5.4	34.8	5.2	30.1
2241155	Lake Charles city................	17,769	18.8	5.7	40.4	47.5	23.7	9.3	43.0	8.4	35.9
2250115	Metairie CDP................	33,218	10.1	7.4	17.5	46.5	12.1	6.4	25.9	5.3	20.7
2255000	New Orleans city................	77,344	23.2	9.6	27.0	56.6	25.6	9.6	43.2	7.3	29.2
2270000	Shreveport city................	47,086	18.9	5.9	22.2	48.3	22.2	7.3	39.4	6.0	27.9
2300000	**Maine**................	345,776	9.5	7.2	22.2	39.9	16.6	9.1	43.1	7.2	31.0
2360545	Portland city................	13,449	15.1	13.1	28.4	42.6	22.1	11.1	47.6	8.4	32.3
2400000	**Maryland**................	1,432,364	7.2	3.7	13.6	26.9	11.7	5.1	27.4	4.4	21.1
2402825	Aspen Hill CDP................	12,660	7.7	3.1	15.2	35.5	8.4	3.3	19.3	2.6	16.4
2404000	Baltimore city................	122,258	19.8	8.8	30.6	43.2	32.1	14.1	47.6	11.0	34.2
2407125	Bethesda CDP................	16,486	1.6	0.5	0.0	16.7	...	...	...	...	...
2408775	Bowie city................	14,181	1.3	1.0	0.0	7.2	3.8	2.5	7.5	2.0	5.2
2419125	Columbia CDP................	27,567	4.3	2.8	0.0	18.2	7.6	3.4	20.5	2.4	18.6
2423975	Dundalk CDP................	15,006	10.9	9.5	11.4	36.5	22.9	12.7	37.7	11.2	24.2
2426000	Ellicott City CDP................	19,600	3.7	2.5	0.0	26.3	3.7	2.2	13.0	2.2	9.8
2430325	Frederick city................	16,056	7.7	1.9	7.9	35.4	12.3	5.6	25.7	4.9	21.2
2431175	Gaithersburg city................	15,723	9.0	5.6	22.7	31.0	12.5	5.6	29.1	4.8	24.1
2432025	Germantown CDP................	22,868	5.8	3.9	6.5	20.4	9.3	5.6	18.6	5.4	13.1
2432650	Glen Burnie CDP................	16,659	7.8	3.7	0.0	20.7	17.8	7.3	33.5	6.8	29.0
2467675	Rockville city................	16,215	3.9	2.7	12.8	10.5	4.5	1.9	16.1	1.1	14.3
2472450	Silver Spring CDP................	16,750	7.2	4.5	14.8	14.2	11.0	7.9	18.1	6.5	17.1
2478425	Towson CDP................	11,555	5.5	3.8	13.8	15.6	4.2	1.6	12.1	1.3	6.1
2481175	Waldorf CDP................	17,469	8.0	3.3	28.0	22.5	12.2	5.0	25.2	4.2	18.3
2483775	Wheaton CDP................	10,809	8.3	7.9	24.4	19.3	9.4	5.8	16.9	5.4	14.3
2500000	**Massachusetts**................	1,606,383	8.4	4.2	19.2	36.1	12.5	5.4	32.2	4.2	22.1
2507000	Boston city................	118,622	17.6	8.0	23.4	44.0	26.1	11.4	44.0	8.6	30.7
2509000	Brockton city................	22,582	15.3	8.9	29.3	39.7	23.8	9.7	42.0	8.7	32.7
2509210	Brookline CDP................	13,206	4.5	2.1	35.4	32.5	...	...	...	...	...
2511000	Cambridge city................	17,737	8.8	6.6	9.8	31.7	7.7	3.2	20.3	2.3	14.9
2513660	Chicopee city................	13,519	10.4	4.9	28.3	33.1	20.0	8.6	41.6	6.4	29.7
2523000	Fall River city................	21,937	19.8	15.1	39.4	44.8	29.5	15.4	48.9	9.5	29.5
2524960	Framingham CDP................	17,241	9.0	7.0	26.4	39.3	10.9	6.0	25.0	4.5	14.4
2529405	Haverhill city................	14,900	10.3	2.6	31.7	32.8	17.5	5.5	40.7	4.0	32.9
2534550	Lawrence city................	18,280	27.6	16.4	27.4	50.4	45.3	29.5	56.4	22.3	43.9
2537000	Lowell city................	23,808	16.6	10.4	26.5	39.6	24.3	12.2	42.0	10.3	27.4
2537490	Lynn city................	21,523	18.0	12.7	26.6	42.3	27.8	15.9	42.1	9.8	29.4
2537875	Malden city................	13,623	15.2	17.8	31.6	32.6	16.3	10.1	31.7	9.5	22.9
2539835	Medford city................	12,888	5.5	2.3	23.6	27.7	8.2	3.8	24.6	2.4	16.1
2545000	New Bedford city................	22,829	19.7	12.5	22.7	48.8	28.0	11.9	49.4	8.9	34.2
2545560	Newton city................	21,729	3.8	2.3	7.4	25.8	4.4	2.8	15.2	1.8	10.5
2552490	Peabody city................	13,117	4.7	1.4	10.9	23.9	9.9	5.9	22.5	4.6	20.6
2555745	Quincy city................	21,469	8.9	5.9	24.5	25.2	14.0	10.1	23.5	7.7	15.2
2556585	Revere city................	11,907	12.4	8.2	30.4	33.3	17.1	9.3	31.2	6.0	23.4
2562535	Somerville city................	14,599	12.1	10.1	13.7	41.6	14.2	8.1	25.0	7.3	17.8
2567000	Springfield city................	35,589	26.7	19.7	37.1	54.0	41.0	25.2	54.6	18.2	33.0
2569170	Taunton city................	14,012	10.4	1.6	18.9	39.7	17.9	9.0	37.1	7.8	20.7
2572600	Waltham city................	12,816	5.2	4.7	12.4	23.7	8.0	2.2	25.1	1.8	20.3
2578972	Weymouth Town city................	13,445	5.2	2.5	11.1	25.2	10.2	4.5	26.0	4.4	18.2
2582000	Worcester city................	39,656	18.6	11.9	35.8	50.0	24.5	10.9	43.0	8.3	25.2
2600000	**Michigan**................	2,489,254	12.5	8.9	27.2	46.5	18.0	8.8	43.1	7.2	30.4
2603000	Ann Arbor city................	19,988	6.9	4.7	25.8	26.2	7.6	2.6	24.6	2.1	19.5
2605920	Battle Creek city................	12,351	20.1	8.2	33.8	55.4	26.5	11.1	51.5	9.5	37.3

State/ Place FIPS code	State/place	Median family income in the past 12 months (in 2,013 inflation-adjusted dollars)					Families with own children under 18 years			Total population in households	Persons who had health insurance, as a percent of all persons in that household type		
		All families	Families with no earners	Families with one earner	Families with two earners	Families with three or more earners	Married-couple families with children	Male householder, no spouse present, with children	Female householder, no spouse present, with children		Married-couple families, percent	Male householder or female householder families, no spouse present	Nonfamily households
	Michigan—cont'd												
2621000	Dearborn city	$53,952	$30,056	$35,236	$83,877	$94,211	$54,084	$38,547	$21,765	96,371	87.1	78.0	85.0
2621020	Dearborn Heights city	$46,116	$30,337	$35,261	$71,109	$89,103	$51,853	$22,330	$18,389	56,448	86.5	73.3	83.0
2622000	Detroit city	$30,376	$14,746	$26,901	$57,042	$80,147	$42,874	$15,188	$15,182	690,969	84.3	79.4	77.6
2627440	Farmington Hills city	$91,402	$50,659	$69,554	$118,750	$127,417	$100,607	$61,750	$44,589	80,546	94.0	87.8	90.6
2629000	Flint city	$28,540	$16,676	$24,853	$51,225	$77,219	$42,194	$17,305	$11,623	99,445	90.2	86.3	81.8
2634000	Grand Rapids city	$47,530	$22,818	$32,496	$64,711	$82,050	$63,330	$23,116	$18,208	188,111	91.4	82.9	83.4
2642160	Kalamazoo city	$44,692	$24,075	$28,912	$64,327	$72,786	$68,642	$36,389	$16,445	74,054	89.7	85.3	84.5
2646000	Lansing city	$39,934	$24,856	$26,967	$59,684	$72,750	$54,092	$18,629	$13,847	113,237	92.7	82.8	84.7
2649000	Livonia city	$81,285	$47,485	$63,200	$100,008	$122,603	$101,078	$55,671	$45,246	94,979	95.3	85.9	92.0
2659440	Novi city	$103,927	$45,496	$85,849	$129,762	$154,614	$137,400	$82,266	$47,724	56,630	95.3	88.3	86.6
2665440	Pontiac city	$31,384	$16,454	$25,570	$54,045	$70,784	$53,895	$21,709	$14,111	58,336	87.9	78.7	74.8
2669035	Rochester Hills city	$99,403	$52,941	$78,694	$122,525	$135,595	$118,659	$40,326	$37,557	71,892	95.1	82.7	89.8
2670040	Royal Oak city	$86,957	$42,671	$64,819	$103,772	$106,842	$103,067	$59,756	$36,789	58,281	94.0	83.4	86.1
2670520	Saginaw city	$32,405	$14,246	$27,600	$49,522	$61,875	$44,457	$14,722	$11,968	49,891	88.4	87.3	77.8
2670760	St. Clair Shores city	$67,603	$36,786	$53,874	$86,021	$92,794	$82,466	$44,519	$29,025	59,577	92.5	81.9	86.1
2674900	Southfield city	$58,191	$34,281	$48,674	$82,079	$102,843	$75,536	$41,069	$31,288	71,966	91.2	83.4	86.2
2676460	Sterling Heights city	$67,142	$36,522	$53,969	$86,754	$109,111	$73,522	$37,079	$28,416	129,934	90.1	79.6	89.2
2679000	Taylor city	$47,265	$32,223	$35,621	$64,837	$91,114	$68,297	$24,038	$12,970	61,664	90.5	83.6	78.3
2680700	Troy city	$96,170	$46,131	$76,828	$124,688	$131,979	$113,608	$78,269	$41,151	81,954	90.7	78.9	92.5
2684000	Warren city	$51,094	$30,376	$39,626	$73,386	$94,349	$66,800	$30,921	$23,890	133,388	90.4	81.7	79.3
2686000	Westland city	$55,445	$29,829	$43,758	$73,613	$93,888	$78,586	$43,214	$27,714	82,426	92.2	82.6	80.7
2688940	Wyoming city	$55,920	$31,742	$37,782	$67,539	$80,775	$65,560	$31,774	$22,614	73,236	88.4	75.8	82.9
2700000	**Minnesota**	$74,434	$38,024	$49,205	$89,615	$106,873	$94,432	$40,684	$26,795	5,323,891	94.5	84.5	89.2
2706382	Blaine city	$83,245	$35,926	$60,847	$98,728	$107,316	$99,669	$45,638	$42,743	59,222	96.5	88.7	93.6
2706616	Bloomington city	$78,036	$48,885	$58,082	$95,113	$106,875	$101,399	$66,082	$31,469	84,773	94.1	85.5	91.0
2707966	Brooklyn Park city	$69,885	$33,898	$43,290	$85,584	$112,917	$87,269	$42,267	$28,068	77,595	91.6	82.3	83.3
2708794	Burnsville city	$72,471	$41,941	$50,472	$87,601	$116,961	$90,240	$31,083	$20,464	60,768	93.1	86.5	83.1
2713114	Coon Rapids city	$72,919	$37,386	$51,923	$84,646	$104,196	$91,467	$32,313	$29,327	61,575	91.5	87.5	91.9
2717000	Duluth city	$62,097	$40,763	$38,252	$77,661	$84,174	$83,203	$27,013	$19,102	84,595	95.8	88.6	90.7
2717288	Eagan city	$105,233	$52,076	$71,427	$116,860	$134,094	$123,439	$59,880	$44,868	64,847	96.6	87.8	92.3
2718116	Eden Prairie city	$116,177	$56,094	$100,148	$126,961	$147,500	$140,411	$66,467	$36,339	61,986	98.0	77.9	91.8
2735180	Lakeville city	$101,864	$46,788	$66,274	$107,200	$132,500	$113,489	$65,645	$31,056	57,464	95.6	87.0	86.7
2740166	Maple Grove city	$107,210	$37,292	$80,386	$119,452	$132,396	$137,008	$68,333	$12,317	64,329	97.1	90.4	97.3
2743000	Minneapolis city	$66,809	$19,028	$37,491	$94,890	$95,353	$94,937	$33,333	$20,202	389,075	91.2	81.8	88.1
2743252	Minnetonka city	$102,384	$36,663	$74,489	$125,821	$156,328	$128,205	$53,250	$55,300	50,629	94.9	88.7	89.5
2751730	Plymouth city	$103,863	$47,750	$81,783	$127,685	$135,375	$140,413	$61,196	$34,389	72,237	96.5	87.3	95.1
2754880	Rochester city	$80,547	$44,857	$50,732	$97,127	$107,530	$95,058	$36,790	$35,694	107,355	96.4	83.0	90.2
2756896	St. Cloud city	$59,993	$31,202	$38,090	$76,808	$95,857	$86,815	$53,182	$18,082	63,994	95.2	82.4	87.5
2758000	St. Paul city	$60,965	$22,821	$35,315	$82,498	$92,861	$77,736	$34,025	$24,467	289,359	90.4	82.7	86.7
2771428	Woodbury city	$108,508	$50,697	$86,837	$115,362	$151,236	$126,750	$68,409	$50,837	64,352	97.2	87.2	94.6
2800000	**Mississippi**	$47,531	$21,966	$35,899	$69,064	$90,332	$67,574	$32,295	$18,312	2,918,229	86.8	76.7	80.6
2829700	Gulfport city	$44,597	$21,005	$29,846	$62,451	$69,947	$51,250	$35,095	$15,783	67,575	84.1	69.9	76.0
2836000	Jackson city	$35,926	$12,376	$28,544	$56,206	$76,453	$61,853	$32,295	$17,275	172,799	87.4	76.0	74.3
2869280	Southaven city	$64,515	$33,948	$41,082	$83,479	$101,566	$80,440	$43,125	$32,759	50,064	89.8	82.7	80.1
2900000	**Missouri**	$58,626	$31,395	$41,478	$76,531	$97,006	$76,510	$34,515	$21,892	5,913,412	90.3	78.8	84.0
2906652	Blue Springs city	$72,069	$30,200	$46,571	$85,125	$114,897	$84,978	$42,101	$26,325	52,843	93.4	82.4	78.8
2915670	Columbia city	$73,913	$38,153	$48,846	$95,097	$100,744	$95,558	$23,861	$21,520	112,156	93.6	80.8	92.2
2924778	Florissant city	$59,818	$32,614	$40,590	$77,446	$89,274	$72,008	$43,259	$28,012	51,649	93.0	84.9	82.5
2935000	Independence city	$54,701	$32,992	$40,836	$71,852	$102,917	$70,427	$32,238	$20,462	115,966	87.5	78.3	82.3
2937592	Joplin city	$48,024	$28,714	$35,514	$60,936	$80,332	$60,166	$20,407	$19,727	50,534	85.4	75.1	83.9
2938000	Kansas City city	$56,623	$24,682	$36,722	$82,651	$94,115	$82,784	$31,069	$21,974	460,045	88.3	75.0	80.7
2941348	Lee's Summit city	$91,601	$47,145	$57,624	$107,389	$116,905	$112,098	$42,371	$26,011	92,299	95.8	88.4	86.5
2954074	O'Fallon city	$86,886	$39,912	$62,849	$96,670	$118,735	$105,472	$48,333	$31,147	81,616	94.7	85.7	89.4
2964082	St. Charles city	$70,484	$37,500	$48,221	$88,491	$128,894	$101,108	$34,375	$25,644	65,736	92.0	79.5	87.1
2964550	St. Joseph city	$53,722	$28,227	$35,483	$67,201	$90,771	$72,537	$15,175	$18,974	74,406	89.2	72.6	81.1
2965000	St. Louis city	$43,246	$14,638	$30,693	$72,706	$85,380	$71,364	$25,045	$17,857	314,065	86.8	75.2	81.8
2965126	St. Peters city	$82,406	$39,118	$62,286	$93,135	$110,203	$100,242	$47,115	$37,731	53,900	94.2	85.1	92.2
2970000	Springfield city	$42,180	$26,803	$31,660	$57,913	$76,063	$54,692	$20,831	$14,767	159,047	87.2	71.5	79.8
3000000	**Montana**	$59,345	$36,454	$42,491	$71,651	$89,239	$72,172	$34,563	$20,044	990,602	86.2	72.2	80.1
3006550	Billings city	$63,950	$40,833	$42,634	$76,858	$105,142	$81,071	$35,556	$19,518	105,233	88.9	72.0	81.5
3032800	Great Falls city	$56,049	$40,359	$39,650	$68,708	$85,455	$70,525	$36,792	$18,684	57,030	88.1	75.7	81.0
3050200	Missoula city	$62,686	$42,042	$37,148	$72,713	$94,472	$76,529	$30,289	$20,466	67,843	89.6	76.4	78.0
3100000	**Nebraska**	$64,862	$34,645	$42,221	$77,553	$94,332	$79,890	$37,024	$24,258	1,826,997	91.9	80.5	85.3
3103950	Bellevue city	$64,097	$45,654	$46,086	$76,583	$104,179	$69,925	$36,814	$25,187	52,067	90.5	85.8	83.8
3119595	Grand Island city	$50,504	$30,469	$33,179	$63,775	$84,819	$59,409	$32,340	$18,961	49,295	88.4	69.3	74.6
3128000	Lincoln city	$64,244	$39,251	$40,165	$77,311	$107,350	$83,298	$33,542	$23,914	261,103	91.8	82.1	85.4
3137000	Omaha city	$61,150	$30,927	$37,008	$78,328	$94,803	$80,577	$39,956	$24,720	423,816	89.0	79.9	84.8
3200000	**Nevada**	$58,779	$33,957	$43,382	$76,260	$95,605	$69,580	$37,086	$28,248	2,719,575	82.7	70.4	77.1
3209700	Carson City	$60,720	$44,750	$43,843	$71,173	$87,625	$60,372	$19,825	$28,955	52,473	85.8	66.4	81.2

State/ Place FIPS code	State/place	Total number of families	Families with incomes below the poverty level, as a percent of all families of that family type				Families that received Food Stamps (SNAP), as a percent of all families of that family type			Families that received food stamps (SNAP) and had at least one worker	
			All families	Married-couple families	Male householder families, no spouse present	Female householder families, no spouse present	All families	Married-couple families	Male householder or female householder families, no spouse present	Married-couple families, percent	Male householder or female householder families, no spouse present
	Michigan—cont'd										
2621000	Dearborn city	21,247	24.7	32.1	35.9	49.5	28.3	25.2	38.6	22.6	28.9
2621020	Dearborn Heights city	13,870	18.5	20.4	56.2	52.5	23.2	16.5	39.7	14.1	28.3
2622000	Detroit city	144,477	36.2	29.5	53.1	60.6	49.9	27.7	62.8	20.7	39.7
2627440	Farmington Hills city	21,467	5.5	3.7	19.6	21.3	6.1	4.1	14.8	3.4	13.1
2629000	Flint city	22,422	36.0	26.8	65.0	64.7	48.3	21.1	67.8	14.9	40.7
2634000	Grand Rapids city	40,748	19.6	13.2	44.4	53.4	29.5	12.0	59.5	10.0	43.2
2642160	Kalamazoo city	13,156	22.2	11.1	15.5	57.6	30.6	13.4	52.0	12.1	36.4
2646000	Lansing city	25,385	25.9	19.4	49.3	59.6	36.7	19.1	58.9	16.8	46.7
2649000	Livonia city	25,701	3.1	3.4	3.6	10.5	5.6	3.2	16.5	2.8	12.3
2659440	Novi city	14,802	3.2	3.7	0.0	19.1	7.7	4.1	27.4	3.6	25.5
2665440	Pontiac city	13,736	33.3	28.4	46.3	58.9	41.2	20.9	55.4	17.6	37.9
2669035	Rochester Hills city	19,095	3.4	1.6	10.5	23.2	6.1	3.9	18.1	3.5	16.4
2670040	Royal Oak city	13,025	3.4	1.2	0.0	14.7	7.1	3.9	18.4	3.6	12.4
2670520	Saginaw city	11,151	32.8	19.3	57.3	62.5	48.6	24.1	67.0	17.5	37.6
2670760	St. Clair Shores city	15,362	8.7	6.9	13.3	36.0	12.3	6.4	28.3	4.9	21.1
2674900	Southfield city	18,358	14.4	13.9	16.4	34.0	20.6	13.6	29.9	10.2	22.1
2676460	Sterling Heights city	34,796	11.2	16.6	18.0	32.0	16.2	11.6	31.9	9.6	24.6
2679000	Taylor city	15,601	19.7	10.9	28.4	60.8	28.4	13.4	53.0	11.5	40.2
2680700	Troy city	22,481	7.2	7.5	20.5	28.1	8.5	5.6	25.4	4.6	18.6
2684000	Warren city	33,924	16.0	13.0	36.8	47.3	22.2	12.7	41.1	9.5	27.0
2686000	Westland city	20,023	11.2	8.0	10.6	33.0	20.3	11.4	35.2	9.3	25.4
2688940	Wyoming city	17,977	10.3	10.1	17.8	34.6	15.1	10.2	30.5	8.7	27.1
2700000	**Minnesota**	1,367,091	7.5	4.6	17.3	35.9	9.1	3.9	27.9	3.4	21.4
2706382	Blaine city	15,907	4.3	1.9	0.0	32.2	6.8	3.6	18.8	3.3	13.8
2706616	Bloomington city	21,604	6.2	5.5	7.9	33.5	8.0	4.6	19.5	4.1	16.1
2707966	Brooklyn Park city	19,198	9.3	6.5	19.2	31.6	16.2	7.1	34.5	6.7	27.1
2708794	Burnsville city	15,222	9.2	4.7	27.1	45.3	10.0	3.4	30.1	3.1	21.6
2713114	Coon Rapids city	15,645	7.8	2.9	31.4	33.2	9.9	4.4	26.3	4.0	18.4
2717000	Duluth city	18,503	12.7	4.8	32.0	51.2	15.6	4.8	43.9	4.7	35.4
2717288	Eagan city	17,638	4.4	4.1	8.0	17.0	4.0	2.5	10.2	2.1	7.8
2718116	Eden Prairie city	17,029	3.4	0.6	5.5	27.7	3.8	1.7	13.3	1.3	7.8
2735180	Lakeville city	15,634	5.0	4.1	7.9	29.7	4.0	3.0	9.6	2.8	8.5
2740166	Maple Grove city	18,012	5.3	1.5	14.0	56.4	4.4	1.9	19.9	1.6	7.7
2743000	Minneapolis city	74,049	15.8	8.3	24.5	49.9	19.7	7.0	43.8	5.4	31.3
2743252	Minnetonka city	14,052	3.7	1.6	19.9	12.9	5.6	2.4	20.1	1.9	15.7
2751730	Plymouth city	20,053	4.9	3.8	18.4	26.6	3.3	1.6	11.7	0.9	9.8
2754880	Rochester city	26,764	5.5	3.8	11.3	23.7	7.4	4.2	18.9	3.4	16.2
2756896	St. Cloud city	13,236	14.0	6.1	7.8	52.9	15.6	6.5	37.5	4.9	28.0
2758000	St. Paul city	61,096	17.1	14.7	21.8	44.5	21.7	11.7	39.6	10.2	29.5
2771428	Woodbury city	17,587	1.5	0.9	0.0	9.8	3.0	1.6	10.5	1.1	10.5
2800000	**Mississippi**	743,178	18.2	11.1	28.5	52.6	20.1	9.1	41.0	7.5	28.0
2829700	Gulfport city	17,375	21.1	16.3	22.7	54.2	27.4	15.0	45.6	13.0	34.5
2836000	Jackson city	38,632	27.5	12.7	28.7	55.8	31.9	13.3	46.6	11.1	32.7
2869280	Southaven city	13,026	9.0	8.4	5.1	26.1	11.1	7.3	21.6	6.8	17.6
2900000	**Missouri**	1,527,728	11.6	7.9	24.4	42.6	15.0	7.3	37.6	6.0	27.4
2906652	Blue Springs city	14,191	7.0	4.7	4.3	32.3	11.0	6.1	26.0	4.2	20.5
2915670	Columbia city	21,659	11.0	5.9	30.6	43.2	14.7	6.3	39.1	5.1	31.6
2924778	Florissant city	13,550	8.1	11.4	12.5	20.4	17.1	8.2	32.7	7.5	21.7
2935000	Independence city	29,138	13.3	13.4	13.1	45.5	15.3	5.8	36.2	4.7	24.8
2937592	Joplin city	12,563	12.4	6.3	35.1	36.7	18.8	8.2	44.5	7.0	33.5
2938000	Kansas City city	106,699	15.6	9.5	25.4	45.2	18.9	7.2	38.8	6.0	26.6
2941348	Lee's Summit city	24,755	5.5	1.4	14.0	32.9	7.8	2.2	29.7	2.2	22.5
2954074	O'Fallon city	22,089	4.1	0.0	22.3	18.7	5.5	2.2	18.8	2.2	15.4
2964082	St. Charles city	16,286	8.6	6.0	36.9	35.3	10.7	4.4	29.2	4.2	24.6
2964550	St. Joseph city	17,488	16.2	7.0	55.6	51.2	20.6	7.8	48.8	6.9	34.2
2965000	St. Louis city	64,535	22.6	15.3	40.1	52.0	32.6	14.3	52.9	11.1	38.0
2965126	St. Peters city	14,240	3.1	0.0	14.2	19.3	4.9	1.9	18.2	1.6	14.9
2970000	Springfield city	35,904	18.7	12.1	40.6	56.8	21.7	11.6	42.0	8.8	31.4
3000000	**Montana**	255,929	10.5	8.1	23.6	44.1	11.5	5.7	32.7	5.0	26.8
3006550	Billings city	26,108	11.5	6.7	20.6	42.8	13.8	4.8	35.8	4.6	30.4
3032800	Great Falls city	14,892	14.4	13.9	24.6	50.0	15.2	7.0	35.2	6.0	28.8
3050200	Missoula city	14,587	10.7	4.5	4.4	46.8	...	...	...	...	...
3100000	**Nebraska**	472,470	9.0	6.7	19.3	39.1	9.6	4.2	29.0	3.7	23.6
3103950	Bellevue city	14,101	9.6	6.5	29.0	37.3	12.3	6.2	27.7	6.0	21.4
3119595	Grand Island city	11,983	15.5	12.6	26.4	49.4	16.7	8.1	41.1	6.9	35.0
3128000	Lincoln city	62,112	10.4	7.8	24.9	40.4	10.7	4.5	29.8	4.0	24.7
3137000	Omaha city	99,886	12.7	9.8	22.9	38.9	14.9	6.4	33.4	5.8	26.4
3200000	**Nevada**	641,060	12.0	11.2	21.6	34.2	13.2	7.7	25.9	6.7	18.7
3209700	Carson City	12,572	10.2	14.8	43.9	23.3	12.6	7.6	27.3	7.0	19.8

Table E-4: Cities with a Population of 50,000 or More—Income, Poverty, and Health Insurance—*Continued*

State/ Place FIPS code	State/place	Median family income in the past 12 months (in 2,013 inflation-adjusted dollars) All families	Families with no earners	Families with one earner	Families with two earners	Families with three or more earners	Families with own children under 18 years Married-couple families with children	Male householder, no spouse present, with children	Female householder, no spouse present, with children	Total population in households	Persons who had health insurance, as a percent of all persons in that household type Married-couple families, percent	Male householder or female householder families, no spouse present	Nonfamily households
	Nevada—cont'd												
3223770	Enterprise CDP	$74,893	$26,399	$50,301	$90,447	$115,848	$90,036	$40,694	$35,965	120,558	84.8	75.8	77.3
3231900	Henderson city	$71,951	$44,263	$58,012	$90,597	$112,620	$89,707	$45,848	$34,028	263,913	89.8	81.8	82.9
3240000	Las Vegas city	$56,053	$32,263	$40,723	$74,848	$92,702	$64,129	$36,070	$29,563	587,875	81.6	68.2	75.9
3251800	North Las Vegas city	$53,861	$22,223	$40,701	$67,773	$95,382	$67,400	$39,419	$29,004	218,452	80.3	69.3	75.4
3254600	Paradise CDP	$52,529	$26,540	$37,861	$68,544	$93,931	$62,968	$28,434	$28,609	224,207	81.6	66.2	70.3
3260600	Reno city	$58,461	$29,785	$45,283	$75,133	$93,492	$70,484	$42,391	$25,450	228,019	80.0	69.2	77.6
3268400	Sparks city	$60,337	$41,914	$37,599	$78,730	$95,434	$71,862	$33,085	$25,326	91,784	83.9	74.6	85.7
3268585	Spring Valley CDP	$55,862	$30,413	$42,945	$68,352	$87,634	$61,483	$43,671	$31,372	184,912	80.7	68.8	75.8
3271400	Sunrise Manor CDP	$42,508	$19,490	$31,936	$57,751	$81,192	$49,091	$28,218	$19,440	184,124	72.3	65.3	72.6
3300000	**New Hampshire**	$79,485	$36,525	$54,131	$94,971	$115,664	$100,152	$44,404	$28,473	1,306,205	93.1	81.1	85.1
3345140	Manchester city	$64,476	$23,677	$42,870	$79,475	$110,417	$80,935	$44,813	$24,084	108,543	90.4	78.8	83.1
3350260	Nashua city	$81,195	$37,774	$51,633	$103,154	$107,671	$102,079	$32,175	$24,399	86,261	93.5	83.8	82.2
3400000	**New Jersey**	$85,615	$35,626	$61,012	$110,220	$128,876	$111,781	$45,334	$30,016	8,759,905	90.9	78.0	84.8
3403580	Bayonne city	$61,145	$23,553	$45,547	$97,863	$133,155	$81,866	$18,599	$27,452	64,465	87.0	79.9	82.8
3410000	Camden city	$28,363	$9,661	$26,542	$51,497	$92,708	$57,701	$25,469	$16,004	75,438	81.0	81.3	76.7
3413690	Clifton city	$78,841	$30,838	$51,487	$97,686	$134,155	$89,888	$31,905	$35,666	84,776	85.8	71.2	85.1
3419390	East Orange city	$44,439	$16,056	$32,052	$71,526	$94,925	$71,613	$36,723	$23,528	63,580	87.9	78.4	79.3
3421000	Elizabeth city	$42,983	$15,438	$31,454	$59,466	$87,184	$55,472	$35,690	$21,462	125,023	76.8	69.6	68.9
3432250	Hoboken city	$135,250	$13,514	$89,423	$184,449	$166,354	$201,250	$73,684	$15,867	51,901	97.6	90.5	95.2
3436000	Jersey City city	$63,370	$16,021	$42,208	$91,756	$108,894	$82,557	$45,430	$21,711	253,686	83.0	74.7	82.3
3451000	Newark city	$36,655	$12,271	$30,135	$60,199	$89,199	$50,847	$25,360	$18,975	270,077	75.3	74.2	68.8
3451210	New Brunswick city	$33,631	$13,973	$26,105	$46,285	$70,586	$50,921	$23,750	$22,844	55,454	62.9	57.4	87.5
3456550	Passaic city	$34,546	$8,811	$28,789	$52,201	$81,831	$53,030	$32,994	$18,359	70,298	71.8	63.8	66.9
3457000	Paterson city	$35,243	$10,441	$29,187	$60,179	$92,557	$49,014	$27,591	$19,238	144,438	75.3	72.7	72.0
3458200	Perth Amboy city	$46,957	$10,227	$32,426	$69,038	$97,018	$56,899	$47,250	$22,061	51,273	71.3	62.2	73.0
3459190	Plainfield city	$54,773	$15,303	$25,316	$69,347	$98,148	$67,571	$24,879	$19,685	49,953	79.6	63.9	64.9
3473110	Toms River CDP	$83,720	$41,236	$64,776	$107,461	$145,938	$111,399	$56,818	$32,115	87,997	93.8	84.1	88.8
3474000	Trenton city	$40,679	$11,215	$31,950	$57,452	$85,153	$48,209	$29,207	$19,908	79,560	79.0	77.9	74.4
3474630	Union City city	$39,592	$13,147	$27,684	$50,833	$74,444	$54,763	$31,045	$18,676	67,508	68.9	55.4	70.5
3476070	Vineland city	$56,045	$27,971	$40,976	$86,084	$115,982	$84,518	$46,458	$24,526	60,075	88.3	84.3	86.4
3479610	West New York town	$46,066	$18,117	$33,787	$56,736	$70,234	$51,318	$34,955	$27,484	51,398	73.1	56.3	67.0
3500000	**New Mexico**	$53,555	$28,370	$39,494	$76,365	$92,119	$68,669	$32,605	$20,758	2,047,997	84.3	75.1	79.6
3502000	Albuquerque city	$58,551	$30,343	$40,581	$81,146	$97,303	$77,687	$34,324	$22,776	550,817	87.4	80.7	81.0
3539380	Las Cruces city	$49,142	$40,272	$33,318	$67,100	$87,292	$59,809	$30,081	$19,588	98,702	87.2	79.3	78.4
3563460	Rio Rancho city	$68,013	$32,669	$56,926	$88,094	$100,841	$90,287	$45,250	$26,491	90,306	91.4	83.8	85.7
3570500	Santa Fe city	$64,880	$43,724	$42,688	$89,773	$90,134	$72,372	$41,070	$17,340	69,083	83.4	75.1	79.7
3600000	**New York**	$69,813	$27,817	$48,566	$94,722	$114,449	$93,157	$38,808	$25,937	19,323,884	91.9	84.2	87.2
3601000	Albany city	$58,867	$20,374	$38,554	$83,349	$96,030	$78,451	$22,114	$21,632	96,707	93.8	88.1	89.3
3608026	Brentwood CDP	$66,457	$31,901	$38,625	$71,594	$99,697	$70,659	$39,032	$46,140	59,583	79.3	68.5	66.0
3611000	Buffalo city	$37,304	$16,619	$29,794	$66,985	$95,064	$55,143	$34,131	$16,794	257,359	93.5	88.9	87.1
3615000	Cheektowaga CDP	$61,628	$37,174	$45,231	$76,002	$98,539	$80,876	$32,656	$25,336	75,232	96.5	89.8	89.5
3633139	Hempstead village	$57,555	$18,523	$32,202	$64,298	$103,099	$60,199	$26,862	$22,435	53,929	73.3	75.7	73.2
3637737	Irondequoit CDP	$67,364	$33,512	$45,864	$82,983	$107,305	$93,060	$40,830	$25,352	51,129	95.3	92.1	93.5
3642081	Levittown CDP	$105,840	$48,518	$77,602	$115,077	$156,275	$119,679	$86,346	$75,591	52,135	95.6	92.2	97.5
3649121	Mount Vernon city	$60,746	$20,514	$40,017	$84,450	$109,464	$82,367	$24,353	$31,317	67,386	86.7	87.0	83.9
3650617	New Rochelle city	$82,210	$34,058	$48,553	$114,718	$142,661	$104,491	$30,694	$29,747	77,274	89.9	83.7	91.4
3651000	New York city	$56,760	$16,675	$41,014	$86,731	$103,314	$74,836	$35,715	$24,759	8,277,544	88.5	82.9	85.2
3663000	Rochester city	$33,805	$13,037	$26,087	$62,528	$85,371	$56,045	$27,836	$15,747	207,168	90.6	88.0	86.8
3665508	Schenectady city	$50,919	$18,655	$30,823	$67,289	$90,055	$68,022	$16,477	$15,197	65,233	89.2	88.4	84.3
3673000	Syracuse city	$37,684	$12,144	$29,676	$69,364	$85,577	$58,871	$25,495	$15,711	141,537	90.6	86.9	87.7
3674183	Tonawanda CDP	$66,724	$41,133	$51,215	$80,485	$107,070	$90,018	$40,216	$33,333	57,907	98.5	91.2	91.5
3676540	Utica city	$39,894	$15,276	$27,602	$63,356	$65,250	$53,903	$20,208	$16,169	60,730	90.1	91.8	89.3
3681677	White Plains city	$102,404	$42,250	$70,640	$138,145	$120,995	$128,241	$23,706	$21,915	56,678	85.6	73.1	91.1
3684000	Yonkers city	$68,812	$23,988	$47,021	$102,904	$123,542	$93,688	$34,750	$31,844	197,560	89.8	81.8	86.8
3700000	**North Carolina**	$56,001	$29,254	$40,907	$76,504	$92,148	$75,259	$31,549	$21,820	9,550,684	87.8	76.5	81.0
3702140	Asheville city	$57,478	$34,122	$40,515	$75,507	$82,500	$67,335	$38,763	$20,975	84,103	87.6	81.5	77.7
3709060	Burlington city	$46,787	$27,990	$31,087	$65,589	$92,981	$66,620	$23,028	$16,990	51,358	88.7	76.2	75.8
3710740	Cary town	$111,714	$59,747	$90,804	$133,745	$129,776	$134,579	$32,222	$45,620	145,790	90.8	79.1	81.3
3711800	Chapel Hill town	$112,583	$68,839	$71,625	$137,942	$130,511	$132,708	$50,579	$41,923	57,992	93.9	77.9	94.6
3712000	Charlotte city	$61,993	$26,659	$41,511	$82,901	$90,276	$89,038	$32,046	$25,615	769,743	86.6	75.2	78.7
3714100	Concord city	$66,283	$33,681	$48,880	$87,255	$97,314	$88,354	$46,250	$26,341	81,208	88.0	72.3	77.6
3719000	Durham city	$62,217	$22,973	$38,446	$89,810	$89,727	$88,512	$29,992	$26,371	237,729	87.9	74.9	80.8
3722920	Fayetteville city	$50,465	$23,750	$41,039	$68,978	$87,141	$62,171	$36,207	$21,770	179,674	90.6	81.1	81.7
3725580	Gastonia city	$47,814	$22,250	$34,257	$68,511	$84,948	$73,586	$28,962	$15,880	71,462	85.5	75.4	80.6
3728000	Greensboro city	$51,854	$22,106	$37,021	$72,545	$89,109	$72,356	$29,233	$22,451	273,964	88.3	78.3	79.3
3728080	Greenville city	$53,098	$22,361	$33,162	$83,313	$100,885	$88,867	$29,542	$20,247	87,030	90.1	78.7	87.8
3731400	High Point city	$50,534	$24,858	$35,481	$75,480	$70,815	$71,605	$32,727	$20,318	106,787	84.7	73.9	78.1
3734200	Jacksonville city	$44,356	$30,777	$40,630	$57,451	$93,667	$49,343	$41,116	$26,385	49,230	94.6	83.6	83.4
3755000	Raleigh city	$66,980	$34,069	$45,520	$89,380	$96,515	$88,067	$33,012	$27,557	415,792	86.9	78.3	85.6
3757500	Rocky Mount city	$40,806	$25,303	$31,582	$55,625	$90,259	$60,142	$37,978	$19,000	56,283	85.3	79.1	85.1

State/Place FIPS code	State/place	Total number of families	Families with incomes below the poverty level, as a percent of all families of that family type				Families that received Food Stamps (SNAP), as a percent of all families of that family type			Families that received food stamps (SNAP) and had at least one worker	
			All families	Married-couple families	Male householder families, no spouse present	Female householder families, no spouse present	All families	Married-couple families	Male householder or female householder families, no spouse present	Married-couple families, percent	Male householder or female householder families, no spouse present
	Nevada—cont'd										
3223770	Enterprise CDP	28,236	6.5	4.6	2.7	21.2	7.1	4.3	14.2	4.3	10.3
3231900	Henderson city	66,873	7.6	5.2	17.0	24.4	7.5	4.7	15.2	4.2	11.2
3240000	Las Vegas city	135,847	13.8	14.3	23.6	35.0	15.3	9.3	27.0	8.2	20.0
3251800	North Las Vegas city	49,320	14.3	13.4	24.0	31.2	16.6	10.6	29.3	9.4	21.0
3254600	Paradise CDP	48,108	13.4	10.6	23.3	33.6	15.3	10.8	22.6	9.4	17.7
3260600	Reno city	50,473	13.5	9.7	24.8	38.5	12.0	6.1	25.3	4.5	17.0
3268400	Sparks city	22,003	10.6	12.1	18.8	29.4	10.0	5.6	19.8	4.4	14.9
3268585	Spring Valley CDP	41,371	10.4	9.0	26.0	27.7	10.9	6.7	19.4	6.3	15.9
3271400	Sunrise Manor CDP	40,655	20.8	19.5	26.8	48.5	25.1	15.1	41.4	12.3	25.9
3300000	**New Hampshire**	346,775	5.7	3.5	11.6	29.9	8.1	3.8	23.9	3.2	17.7
3345140	Manchester city	25,835	11.0	7.3	14.0	39.5	16.3	7.2	33.9	5.8	23.9
3350260	Nashua city	21,310	7.7	5.4	14.9	31.1	11.0	4.4	29.1	3.5	24.7
3400000	**New Jersey**	2,203,456	8.2	4.9	19.5	33.6	9.1	4.1	22.9	3.4	15.9
3403580	Bayonne city	16,283	13.8	8.8	46.7	31.8	14.8	8.8	24.6	7.4	16.2
3410000	Camden city	16,234	37.2	16.6	35.4	60.2	49.2	29.7	58.1	22.7	36.5
3413690	Clifton city	20,600	6.7	7.0	11.0	20.3	9.2	6.5	16.5	5.8	12.1
3419390	East Orange city	14,252	20.0	6.4	12.3	40.8	26.4	14.0	34.1	10.6	24.2
3421000	Elizabeth city	26,937	16.4	11.1	17.5	37.7	19.5	10.8	29.2	8.6	22.2
3432250	Hoboken city	9,546	11.2	0.0	11.6	58.3	...	...	...	...	...
3436000	Jersey City city	58,824	16.2	11.9	22.8	43.8	16.2	7.1	30.7	6.1	22.4
3451000	Newark city	57,766	27.1	15.0	36.2	52.8	33.8	15.5	46.3	13.0	30.0
3451210	New Brunswick city	8,301	27.3	20.1	45.1	43.9	28.0	15.5	37.1	13.3	27.0
3456550	Passaic city	14,819	28.8	18.9	24.5	53.1	36.9	23.3	48.4	19.5	31.1
3457000	Paterson city	31,886	27.3	19.2	37.4	49.6	36.3	23.8	46.6	17.5	27.3
3458200	Perth Amboy city	12,200	22.5	14.9	29.7	41.7	16.0	11.1	21.3	7.5	16.1
3459190	Plainfield city	10,134	21.6	11.2	34.0	45.6	22.9	10.7	34.2	9.7	26.6
3473110	Toms River CDP	23,077	4.0	1.4	6.4	22.8	7.9	3.6	20.8	3.1	12.0
3474000	Trenton city	17,448	22.5	16.4	28.7	45.9	28.1	14.4	38.6	12.4	27.2
3474630	Union City city	15,633	24.4	20.2	21.5	52.1	31.9	21.7	41.0	20.3	33.8
3476070	Vineland city	14,604	14.9	7.6	11.8	38.5	19.1	9.9	35.6	6.9	26.3
3479610	West New York town	11,625	18.5	21.4	24.5	36.1	22.4	16.0	31.0	13.5	28.3
3500000	**New Mexico**	494,555	16.6	13.8	26.8	46.8	18.0	9.7	36.9	8.1	27.7
3502000	Albuquerque city	134,324	14.8	11.6	19.8	42.5	18.0	8.5	36.6	7.2	27.9
3539380	Las Cruces city	23,142	19.1	15.4	31.0	51.0	21.3	11.3	39.8	10.0	31.2
3563460	Rio Rancho city	22,416	10.3	4.9	15.8	34.6	14.4	7.8	33.0	7.1	24.5
3570500	Santa Fe city	15,461	14.1	8.3	19.7	48.3	13.0	5.4	29.2	5.3	17.8
3600000	**New York**	4,594,587	12.2	9.1	22.9	38.7	16.1	8.2	33.3	6.5	23.3
3601000	Albany city	16,884	17.7	10.4	36.6	44.2	25.3	9.6	45.3	7.3	30.2
3608026	Brentwood CDP	11,838	9.2	8.2	12.6	19.6	14.3	9.2	22.3	7.7	18.4
3611000	Buffalo city	57,862	26.6	24.8	27.4	53.5	38.3	20.3	53.7	15.5	35.7
3615000	Cheektowaga CDP	19,703	8.4	4.8	22.9	35.5	12.6	4.5	29.8	4.0	22.0
3633139	Hempstead village	11,144	16.1	8.1	28.5	36.5	20.0	6.4	33.5	3.6	20.8
3637737	Irondequoit CDP	13,379	7.5	3.9	20.7	39.8	10.3	2.6	30.4	2.2	19.9
3642081	Levittown CDP	13,618	1.8	1.5	0.0	11.8	2.9	1.6	7.5	1.2	5.2
3649121	Mount Vernon city	15,877	13.7	7.6	17.9	30.5	22.0	9.0	36.8	6.4	28.1
3650617	New Rochelle city	19,441	8.1	5.9	12.2	33.5	9.8	4.9	21.6	3.8	16.3
3651000	New York city	1,825,321	17.9	14.5	26.5	41.4	24.2	14.5	38.6	11.4	27.2
3663000	Rochester city	42,928	31.5	21.3	41.8	58.5	42.6	19.9	58.7	15.5	37.4
3665508	Schenectady city	12,607	20.8	14.7	51.6	58.0	27.4	11.9	51.5	8.2	33.6
3673000	Syracuse city	26,880	29.3	22.1	48.5	58.4	37.1	19.1	53.4	15.6	33.0
3674183	Tonawanda CDP	15,092	7.1	5.2	24.0	33.7	9.1	3.7	23.8	3.4	12.5
3676540	Utica city	12,909	26.0	23.3	33.8	57.2	35.5	17.7	58.0	13.3	40.7
3681677	White Plains city	12,949	9.3	5.2	11.0	40.5	5.4	3.1	11.2	2.9	7.8
3684000	Yonkers city	47,867	14.1	10.8	23.7	35.9	19.7	9.8	34.9	8.0	24.7
3700000	**North Carolina**	2,467,843	13.2	9.3	28.0	44.4	16.1	7.8	38.0	6.5	27.4
3702140	Asheville city	17,745	13.5	7.6	2.6	48.9	17.7	8.9	38.0	8.1	29.4
3709060	Burlington city	13,462	17.7	7.5	27.4	54.0	20.6	7.4	43.4	5.9	33.6
3710740	Cary town	38,033	4.9	3.1	37.5	21.4	3.3	1.4	14.2	1.4	13.3
3711800	Chapel Hill town	10,640	7.6	1.9	9.6	31.5	...	...	...	...	...
3712000	Charlotte city	179,807	14.0	8.6	27.2	37.8	17.8	8.2	36.4	7.2	28.9
3714100	Concord city	19,942	9.6	4.5	26.2	35.0	15.2	8.7	37.4	8.6	26.8
3719000	Durham city	54,771	14.2	9.9	30.6	35.8	16.1	5.5	34.5	5.4	25.6
3722920	Fayetteville city	50,503	15.5	6.6	29.9	43.5	18.8	7.5	39.1	6.7	28.8
3725580	Gastonia city	18,442	18.2	9.4	37.4	55.7	24.7	11.1	48.1	9.3	34.7
3728000	Greensboro city	65,527	15.7	8.6	31.6	42.3	17.6	5.9	36.8	4.8	25.4
3728080	Greenville city	17,223	17.5	5.7	20.8	47.1	25.1	4.8	54.7	4.1	40.4
3731400	High Point city	26,875	18.4	13.9	23.3	49.1	21.2	9.0	42.3	8.0	31.3
3734200	Jacksonville city	15,212	13.3	8.2	12.4	44.3	9.3	4.1	24.4	3.6	19.0
3755000	Raleigh city	94,411	11.5	7.2	29.1	35.2	12.7	5.4	27.9	4.6	20.8
3757500	Rocky Mount city	14,204	20.6	15.3	17.2	52.0	32.8	14.7	55.5	13.0	43.0

Table E-4: Cities with a Population of 50,000 or More—Income, Poverty, and Health Insurance—*Continued*

| State/ Place FIPS code | State/place | Median family income in the past 12 months (in 2,013 inflation-adjusted dollars) | | | | | | | | Total population in households | Persons who had health insurance, as a percent of all persons in that household type | | |
| | | | | | | | Families with own children under 18 years | | | | | | |
		All families	Families with no earners	Families with one earner	Families with two earners	Families with three or more earners	Married-couple families with children	Male householder, no spouse present, with children	Female householder, no spouse present, with children		Married-couple families, percent	Male householder or female householder families, no spouse present	Nonfamily households
	North Carolina—cont'd												
3774440	Wilmington city	$55,633	$39,301	$37,417	$77,209	$94,728	$91,973	$30,330	$19,452	109,509	88.5	75.5	82.5
3775000	Winston-Salem city	$50,180	$27,793	$32,168	$73,488	$89,352	$66,322	$23,927	$18,479	231,623	86.3	73.7	82.4
3800000	**North Dakota**	$71,797	$34,628	$45,305	$86,061	$107,129	$88,252	$48,533	$24,136	688,158	93.8	80.8	86.1
3807200	Bismarck city	$80,264	$49,318	$44,056	$91,818	$116,364	$97,486	$39,803	$28,745	63,279	96.1	85.9	86.7
3825700	Fargo city	$67,133	$43,750	$41,176	$85,808	$97,292	$87,641	$44,332	$24,063	109,420	94.0	80.3	87.7
3832060	Grand Forks city	$70,900	$30,357	$38,723	$82,957	$106,162	$87,961	$24,915	$22,153	53,105	96.5	85.2	89.7
3900000	**Ohio**	$60,999	$31,221	$43,529	$80,839	$100,646	$81,778	$35,072	$20,852	11,384,722	92.2	82.6	84.3
3901000	Akron city	$42,008	$18,189	$32,261	$63,714	$88,453	$58,734	$20,243	$17,700	196,502	89.4	80.6	81.3
3912000	Canton city	$37,946	$20,439	$28,586	$55,441	$84,487	$82,928	$23,500	$45,690	71,503	87.8	82.9	76.9
3915000	Cincinnati city	$41,987	$12,250	$29,165	$75,679	$90,646	$64,213	$70,873	$22,796	293,062	91.7	81.2	82.7
3916000	Cleveland city	$32,235	$13,719	$27,087	$60,022	$76,981	$89,203	$23,774	$14,726	384,837	87.7	83.0	78.6
3918000	Columbus city	$53,202	$17,555	$35,817	$74,891	$93,440	$96,157	$20,179	$29,474	804,800	89.6	78.0	83.4
3921000	Dayton city	$33,618	$16,075	$27,989	$60,306	$87,305	$78,512	$40,598	$19,358	140,415	86.1	80.7	83.1
3925256	Elyria city	$48,582	$28,462	$36,446	$68,637	$97,063	$144,258	$101,633	$56,136	53,459	93.4	82.8	80.3
3933012	Hamilton city	$47,324	$24,031	$31,958	$72,271	$90,865	$96,850	$47,188	$29,466	61,010	90.7	79.6	80.4
3940040	Kettering city	$60,151	$39,796	$43,967	$81,139	$89,821	$67,961	$0	$16,594	55,738	94.0	82.9	85.6
3941664	Lakewood city	$60,919	$24,017	$36,775	$79,368	$101,204	$76,605	$35,469	$23,479	51,117	89.3	82.5	82.0
3944856	Lorain city	$42,205	$25,038	$32,700	$66,736	$107,672	$49,157	$24,353	$14,875	63,394	87.3	84.2	81.8
3961000	Parma city	$60,373	$32,382	$45,369	$72,151	$102,823	$90,991	$17,688	$32,639	79,702	92.0	82.7	88.3
3974118	Springfield city	$41,000	$20,382	$28,537	$62,224	$80,884	$79,246	$22,989	$58,500	58,578	90.0	85.9	82.4
3977000	Toledo city	$42,709	$22,990	$29,758	$65,458	$86,554	$110,173	$33,750	$65,518	280,597	90.8	81.1	81.1
3988000	Youngstown city	$30,538	$20,358	$23,494	$53,454	$78,359	$56,514	$26,484	$12,630	61,721	88.7	86.4	78.6
4000000	**Oklahoma**	$56,036	$28,741	$40,886	$74,125	$91,712	$69,435	$36,376	$20,619	3,736,108	85.6	73.6	79.4
4009050	Broken Arrow city	$73,008	$38,573	$52,073	$86,964	$104,319	$110,789	$51,786	$35,425	101,404	89.7	81.8	86.0
4023200	Edmond city	$89,355	$49,138	$68,333	$101,933	$125,673	$61,957	$36,079	$15,975	84,570	93.2	78.9	86.1
4041850	Lawton city	$47,865	$29,655	$36,633	$67,061	$94,866	$65,856	$45,379	$19,591	85,155	89.6	75.3	75.2
4048350	Midwest City city	$53,125	$35,428	$42,161	$63,566	$90,977	$60,366	$33,506	$22,244	55,071	87.6	81.8	78.6
4049200	Moore city	$61,933	$33,523	$40,746	$77,037	$90,445	$62,453	$47,368	$24,127	57,085	89.7	74.6	85.7
4052500	Norman city	$68,021	$34,671	$50,632	$85,383	$98,417	$55,337	$25,369	$14,339	114,710	91.3	76.9	87.9
4055000	Oklahoma City city	$57,094	$30,381	$38,862	$74,503	$89,512	$84,105	$39,750	$21,240	590,405	83.6	72.7	76.3
4075000	Tulsa city	$51,858	$25,693	$36,928	$70,616	$89,053	$63,705	$11,987	$12,486	391,517	82.6	73.1	75.8
4100000	**Oregon**	$60,863	$35,850	$45,406	$78,059	$91,603	$74,506	$33,666	$22,326	3,861,618	88.6	78.1	80.9
4101000	Albany city	$52,970	$29,142	$36,265	$72,582	$90,915	$84,150	$39,659	$23,940	50,788	89.8	79.5	81.7
4101650	Aloha CDP	$66,932	$21,944	$47,515	$77,328	$93,719	$69,526	$33,234	$16,063	51,652	87.5	82.4	84.9
4105350	Beaverton city	$72,331	$29,484	$53,879	$87,151	$114,554	$69,479	$32,833	$21,379	92,257	88.4	76.6	81.2
4105800	Bend city	$65,479	$58,733	$43,473	$72,970	$86,358	$85,765	$78,690	$21,048	79,024	86.1	70.5	71.4
4115800	Corvallis city	$74,596	$44,436	$52,898	$85,562	$98,000	$138,695	$0	$79,734	54,801	92.3	83.8	90.0
4123850	Eugene city	$59,255	$39,190	$44,008	$77,676	$86,966	$90,455	$26,667	$20,610	157,221	91.8	79.7	81.1
4131250	Gresham city	$53,183	$31,942	$38,904	$71,421	$93,346	$54,053	$20,078	$18,396	107,891	86.3	76.6	80.9
4134100	Hillsboro city	$71,260	$34,105	$49,396	$80,504	$103,636	$64,178	$39,665	$19,950	94,640	87.9	72.0	87.0
4147000	Medford city	$48,284	$35,903	$33,397	$62,772	$65,097	$57,193	$21,988	$17,392	75,899	83.4	71.5	81.2
4159000	Portland city	$69,204	$29,253	$48,912	$89,838	$93,551	$72,601	$67,666	$23,971	598,470	89.9	79.7	79.5
4164900	Salem city	$53,968	$31,779	$39,659	$71,390	$86,339	$66,848	$11,042	$19,053	153,449	86.5	75.8	84.0
4169600	Springfield city	$48,333	$29,773	$34,167	$65,637	$71,369	$65,166	$29,016	$23,195	59,783	85.4	81.2	74.4
4200000	**Pennsylvania**	$66,098	$31,283	$48,059	$85,612	$105,643	$88,326	$38,974	$23,858	12,555,282	92.7	84.6	88.7
4202000	Allentown city	$40,771	$17,249	$31,266	$59,635	$73,886	$40,377	$37,935	$6,987	116,634	83.7	77.6	82.7
4206088	Bethlehem city	$56,574	$24,510	$41,575	$73,750	$97,787	$94,573	$40,833	$41,020	74,079	91.4	83.2	88.2
4224000	Erie city	$41,980	$19,526	$34,631	$59,665	$75,439	$62,606	$31,090	$19,980	99,556	92.9	86.1	87.0
4241216	Lancaster city	$36,716	$13,241	$28,329	$59,018	$77,958	$51,979	$16,419	$10,442	56,962	87.3	84.8	82.1
4242928	Levittown CDP	$76,713	$29,826	$53,167	$87,958	$112,876	$62,978	$36,569	$13,638	50,380	94.0	89.8	93.4
4260000	Philadelphia city	$44,747	$16,404	$35,796	$75,859	$95,152	$60,742	$40,033	$29,459	1,532,142	87.6	83.0	86.5
4261000	Pittsburgh city	$54,555	$21,692	$38,554	$82,577	$91,566	$68,311	$30,352	$21,721	298,695	92.7	86.9	89.6
4263624	Reading city	$28,285	$11,613	$23,894	$44,979	$76,382	$75,625	$19,821	$23,487	87,447	80.0	80.3	78.3
4269000	Scranton city	$46,891	$25,026	$36,455	$69,802	$83,582	$34,195	$31,389	$13,512	73,571	90.5	85.2	85.3
4400000	**Rhode Island**	$72,152	$29,672	$48,154	$94,309	$113,937	$96,919	$37,600	$26,155	1,035,491	92.6	83.2	85.8
4419180	Cranston city	$76,989	$31,592	$50,382	$94,061	$109,265	$94,906	$37,306	$36,060	76,331	92.8	84.8	84.2
4454640	Pawtucket city	$49,962	$18,820	$38,186	$74,188	$74,761	$65,980	$40,994	$23,913	70,774	86.6	79.4	84.3
4459000	Providence city	$44,096	$10,248	$27,985	$66,617	$83,370	$64,627	$35,897	$17,826	176,865	82.8	78.1	80.5
4474300	Warwick city	$79,333	$37,787	$59,300	$96,352	$121,609	$101,295	$46,352	$40,393	81,333	95.9	89.2	88.2
4500000	**South Carolina**	$53,972	$28,960	$39,851	$75,602	$91,824	$73,641	$31,724	$20,273	4,624,813	87.8	76.4	80.2
4513330	Charleston city	$74,488	$32,328	$47,913	$98,408	$122,742	$104,076	$30,227	$18,872	124,764	92.5	77.9	85.8
4516000	Columbia city	$54,297	$22,030	$35,941	$83,895	$95,160	$90,000	$22,330	$20,028	111,629	90.0	83.4	85.5
4530850	Greenville city	$57,188	$20,163	$34,936	$96,720	$64,531	$90,256	$34,531	$17,643	59,350	88.6	78.0	76.3
4548535	Mount Pleasant town	$99,098	$62,197	$85,706	$109,375	$105,833	$117,029	$31,779	$55,000	71,250	94.6	87.5	86.1
4550875	North Charleston city	$46,025	$21,444	$29,605	$65,305	$89,603	$67,668	$24,674	$18,196	96,080	83.5	70.4	73.0
4561405	Rock Hill city	$52,642	$25,061	$37,135	$72,673	$89,286	$76,069	$16,064	$30,131	67,669	89.6	76.8	78.8
4600000	**South Dakota**	$62,594	$32,153	$39,614	$74,608	$91,688	$77,266	$37,542	$23,473	816,471	92.8	78.1	85.2
4652980	Rapid City city	$58,529	$36,737	$37,517	$72,324	$92,717	$72,868	$35,653	$26,828	67,417	92.7	79.0	85.3

Table E-4: Cities with a Population of 50,000 or More—Income, Poverty, and Health Insurance—*Continued*

State/ Place FIPS code	State/place	Total number of families	Families with incomes below the poverty level, as a percent of all families of that family type				Families that received Food Stamps (SNAP), as a percent of all families of that family type			Families that received food stamps (SNAP) and had at least one worker	
			All families	Married-couple families	Male householder families, no spouse present	Female householder families, no spouse present	All families	Married-couple families	Male householder or female householder families, no spouse present	Married-couple families, percent	Male householder or female householder families, no spouse present
	North Carolina—cont'd										
3774440	Wilmington city	24,043	15.7	10.4	23.2	48.1	22.0	9.9	46.2	7.4	36.3
3775000	Winston-Salem city	54,787	19.1	15.9	33.4	53.3	18.3	7.7	36.7	6.9	24.5
3800000	**North Dakota**	176,378	7.4	4.3	16.6	38.6	8.4	3.9	26.7	3.5	21.9
3807200	Bismarck city	16,010	5.2	0.8	9.4	26.3	6.8	2.4	20.9	2.4	19.3
3825700	Fargo city	23,728	9.5	4.8	29.3	39.2	13.6	6.5	35.0	6.3	30.4
3832060	Grand Forks city	11,109	8.6	5.8	34.4	30.8	10.7	6.2	26.4	4.8	19.3
3900000	**Ohio**	2,920,189	11.8	7.5	25.6	45.7	15.8	7.1	39.4	5.7	27.7
3901000	Akron city	45,102	21.5	11.5	40.8	52.7	31.3	13.6	53.0	10.6	34.5
3912000	Canton city	17,441	26.8	21.8	45.0	59.2	34.3	16.3	56.4	12.1	40.3
3915000	Cincinnati city	60,851	26.0	7.6	46.6	59.7	31.7	9.0	53.6	7.1	36.4
3916000	Cleveland city	84,228	30.7	21.7	47.5	58.2	40.5	18.9	56.7	14.0	36.4
3918000	Columbus city	172,594	17.1	12.2	26.7	44.1	23.6	11.8	42.4	9.6	30.4
3921000	Dayton city	28,859	29.5	24.1	42.6	62.5	34.4	16.6	51.1	11.6	34.4
3925256	Elyria city	14,125	17.1	9.7	33.9	52.7	24.5	11.0	45.2	10.0	30.1
3933012	Hamilton city	15,354	17.7	10.4	16.0	52.0	23.8	10.8	44.5	9.1	31.3
3940040	Kettering city	14,507	9.0	5.4	13.6	40.6	9.3	2.6	25.7	2.5	15.6
3941664	Lakewood city	10,843	14.5	12.8	11.9	50.0	17.1	9.2	34.1	8.2	23.9
3944856	Lorain city	16,466	24.2	20.0	28.4	61.0	29.5	16.0	47.6	11.6	33.0
3961000	Parma city	21,201	9.8	5.8	14.8	44.1	14.0	5.9	34.4	4.5	25.3
3974118	Springfield city	13,756	24.4	21.9	47.5	56.4	33.1	15.5	57.1	12.4	39.7
3977000	Toledo city	64,803	24.0	16.1	44.4	57.0	31.5	15.0	52.4	11.6	36.4
3988000	Youngstown city	14,380	30.8	30.9	37.9	63.0	44.3	25.8	58.1	19.5	42.9
4000000	**Oklahoma**	959,015	12.8	9.6	22.3	45.1	15.2	7.9	35.7	6.7	25.9
4009050	Broken Arrow city	28,158	6.1	4.2	12.6	28.3	7.1	3.5	20.7	3.2	12.4
4023200	Edmond city	22,052	5.7	3.2	22.3	34.7	4.6	2.2	15.7	1.9	13.9
4041850	Lawton city	21,192	16.1	11.2	17.0	42.1	19.5	9.4	39.6	9.0	33.7
4048350	Midwest City city	14,407	12.4	6.8	17.1	33.9	16.2	6.1	33.0	4.8	26.4
4049200	Moore city	15,382	8.0	5.1	9.5	29.1	14.7	8.4	30.2	7.8	25.0
4052500	Norman city	25,480	10.3	6.2	6.7	43.3	11.0	4.1	31.3	3.8	21.1
4055000	Oklahoma City city	142,157	14.6	12.5	23.7	46.9	17.0	8.2	38.0	7.2	28.5
4075000	Tulsa city	94,831	16.2	11.5	24.5	47.5	19.4	8.8	38.9	7.8	27.2
4100000	**Oregon**	959,743	11.8	9.9	25.3	42.7	20.2	12.2	45.9	10.5	34.6
4101000	Albany city	13,283	16.3	13.0	18.8	57.3	24.5	8.9	59.9	7.9	42.6
4101650	Aloha CDP	12,375	9.4	7.5	24.8	42.2	21.8	15.8	41.4	14.9	25.5
4105350	Beaverton city	21,482	13.0	9.3	24.7	44.6	17.2	8.8	42.7	7.7	35.8
4105800	Bend city	19,108	7.9	6.2	37.9	19.4	14.6	9.2	33.7	8.2	32.7
4115800	Corvallis city	10,141	11.9	6.1	17.1	50.4	16.4	9.0	41.5	8.3	26.0
4123850	Eugene city	33,260	13.5	7.5	30.4	46.8	22.6	10.8	51.7	9.5	39.6
4131250	Gresham city	25,949	17.0	15.8	17.7	44.3	29.9	17.9	52.7	16.7	42.7
4134100	Hillsboro city	22,868	11.1	6.7	1.7	45.1	18.6	10.8	43.5	10.0	40.2
4147000	Medford city	19,225	16.9	15.2	53.9	40.0	27.0	16.0	56.8	14.6	45.9
4159000	Portland city	127,334	12.2	9.9	26.4	40.4	19.8	12.4	40.3	10.5	28.7
4164900	Salem city	37,247	16.2	13.2	30.3	44.7	28.6	17.7	53.2	15.9	40.3
4169600	Springfield city	14,334	18.2	9.8	50.8	55.5	33.4	18.1	67.1	15.9	53.0
4200000	**Pennsylvania**	3,186,145	9.4	5.6	22.3	40.6	12.8	5.6	34.0	4.4	23.4
4202000	Allentown city	26,285	22.1	12.9	40.3	53.5	29.8	13.7	47.8	10.3	32.4
4206088	Bethlehem city	16,729	15.9	10.4	36.1	46.1	21.9	10.6	41.2	7.3	26.0
4224000	Erie city	22,898	22.3	18.9	19.0	57.7	30.5	15.6	52.5	12.0	35.2
4241216	Lancaster city	11,791	26.4	17.3	31.3	58.4	38.2	23.1	55.2	18.9	39.1
4242928	Levittown CDP	13,320	6.0	5.2	5.6	18.9	7.4	5.0	13.0	3.3	8.7
4260000	Philadelphia city	303,074	21.6	14.3	31.9	46.5	30.6	15.0	46.8	10.9	29.1
4261000	Pittsburgh city	61,768	16.1	7.8	29.1	49.9	22.2	7.0	46.1	5.4	30.5
4263624	Reading city	18,945	37.6	29.3	37.6	68.3	51.4	32.6	66.9	24.7	44.3
4269000	Scranton city	16,433	16.0	12.0	32.5	52.6	22.1	11.2	43.0	7.9	28.1
4400000	**Rhode Island**	257,316	10.2	6.5	18.7	37.9	15.3	7.0	34.9	6.0	24.4
4419180	Cranston city	19,352	6.8	5.3	17.9	31.3	10.5	6.1	21.7	5.2	14.2
4454640	Pawtucket city	17,043	15.7	10.3	20.7	40.8	27.0	16.6	41.0	13.9	28.3
4459000	Providence city	34,531	25.7	17.8	23.6	54.5	36.7	17.4	56.5	15.3	39.8
4474300	Warwick city	21,415	4.4	3.6	6.3	20.8	9.3	4.8	22.7	3.9	17.2
4500000	**South Carolina**	1,199,885	14.2	9.2	26.5	47.0	17.2	7.9	39.3	6.5	27.5
4513330	Charleston city	26,484	12.0	5.6	16.9	52.0	10.0	2.5	29.6	1.6	22.5
4516000	Columbia city	22,234	17.5	5.7	35.8	49.3	22.0	6.2	46.6	4.8	32.3
4530850	Greenville city	12,978	17.6	8.5	9.0	54.7	17.2	5.1	39.3	3.7	25.8
4548535	Mount Pleasant town	18,395	5.6	0.9	31.8	29.3	...	...	...	...	...
4550875	North Charleston city	22,566	19.7	10.2	21.3	51.2	23.2	9.0	42.9	7.7	34.1
4561405	Rock Hill city	16,651	13.6	5.2	46.2	36.3	22.2	11.5	39.3	10.0	30.6
4600000	**South Dakota**	210,494	9.3	5.6	23.3	38.9	11.7	4.8	35.5	4.3	28.2
4652980	Rapid City city	16,626	11.2	6.2	27.1	35.4	16.9	4.6	46.1	4.1	38.6

State/ Place FIPS code	State/place	Median family income in the past 12 months (in 2,013 inflation-adjusted dollars)					Families with own children under 18 years			Total population in households	Persons who had health insurance, as a percent of all persons in that household type		
		All families	Families with no earners	Families with one earner	Families with two earners	Families with three or more earners	Married-couple families with children	Male householder, no spouse present, with children	Female householder, no spouse present, with children		Married-couple families, percent	Male householder or female householder families, no spouse present	Nonfamily households
	South Dakota—cont'd												
4659020	Sioux Falls city	$66,542	$33,618	$37,208	$79,208	$93,085	$80,447	$36,619	$23,063	157,959	93.6	80.9	85.1
4700000	**Tennessee**	$54,458	$27,901	$40,492	$73,639	$91,857	$71,531	$31,427	$20,006	6,348,051	89.5	80.0	81.5
4703440	Bartlett city	$85,499	$46,925	$63,284	$101,905	$121,074	$102,118	$61,442	$42,384	57,003	94.4	88.2	93.3
4714000	Chattanooga city	$49,691	$26,017	$35,614	$72,376	$84,970	$74,580	$24,393	$17,825	169,507	88.3	81.9	80.9
4715160	Clarksville city	$51,750	$17,342	$41,845	$65,431	$95,283	$61,320	$35,651	$17,921	128,565	90.4	82.7	76.9
4727740	Franklin city	$108,660	$50,406	$86,429	$120,288	$124,263	$132,705	$51,481	$21,648	66,040	94.0	74.7	92.2
4733280	Hendersonville city	$71,501	$46,123	$52,687	$82,143	$107,782	$90,617	$55,234	$28,107	53,014	93.6	81.8	78.8
4737640	Jackson city	$52,507	$25,833	$36,061	$79,677	$93,698	$82,234	$30,845	$15,467	66,223	88.4	83.1	83.5
4738320	Johnson City city	$54,663	$41,322	$45,985	$71,638	$101,071	$81,382	$25,865	$19,286	63,610	92.2	74.8	81.5
4739560	Kingsport city	$53,771	$33,051	$41,171	$80,322	$100,357	$77,898	$30,817	$11,713	52,166	91.6	75.4	84.3
4740000	Knoxville city	$48,739	$24,835	$32,449	$64,932	$78,281	$63,201	$28,527	$12,913	180,392	88.8	82.2	85.5
4748000	Memphis city	$42,065	$15,466	$29,991	$66,755	$80,986	$67,012	$24,079	$18,482	643,330	85.0	78.5	77.5
4751560	Murfreesboro city	$65,998	$36,533	$46,279	$78,516	$111,086	$81,536	$30,846	$28,483	112,509	89.6	86.1	80.8
4752006	Nashville-Davidson	$57,220	$26,588	$39,867	$75,892	$89,669	$72,286	$31,197	$22,449	615,410	87.1	78.4	80.9
4800000	**Texas**	$60,656	$27,707	$41,916	$81,593	$93,924	$75,463	$36,672	$23,538	25,573,996	80.5	69.9	77.9
4801000	Abilene city	$51,841	$27,033	$35,397	$68,862	$80,018	$65,125	$30,598	$20,595	110,511	84.7	75.3	79.3
4801924	Allen city	$112,744	$42,297	$86,089	$126,864	$123,011	$123,691	$39,543	$56,259	89,481	90.7	72.7	84.1
4803000	Amarillo city	$55,462	$32,121	$37,251	$76,568	$89,752	$75,163	$35,777	$20,446	193,440	84.1	72.1	73.7
4804000	Arlington city	$60,920	$36,286	$37,028	$78,575	$104,560	$70,629	$28,839	$27,600	374,257	78.8	68.3	75.5
4804462	Atascocita CDP	$82,627	$41,620	$65,947	$96,764	$117,861	$94,351	$41,724	$54,462	65,818	91.4	82.0	86.7
4805000	Austin city	$70,089	$31,726	$44,213	$92,195	$89,174	$92,850	$38,363	$25,007	858,097	84.9	73.7	78.0
4806128	Baytown city	$50,893	$23,063	$35,015	$73,052	$87,261	$65,237	$36,363	$26,072	73,173	71.5	68.3	76.1
4807000	Beaumont city	$47,508	$22,583	$35,301	$72,494	$105,579	$65,659	$33,333	$20,401	115,223	81.2	71.5	78.6
4810768	Brownsville city	$35,578	$12,911	$25,832	$55,110	$69,309	$43,460	$26,944	$15,933	179,177	62.5	62.2	70.9
4810912	Bryan city	$48,977	$29,206	$29,380	$66,190	$77,203	$58,333	$24,107	$19,281	74,464	78.2	75.4	76.9
4813024	Carrollton city	$76,556	$28,727	$51,057	$88,990	$99,254	$78,036	$51,588	$38,775	124,446	75.9	70.1	81.1
4813552	Cedar Park city	$92,559	$47,420	$69,140	$104,650	$116,931	$102,164	$41,974	$49,294	57,373	89.2	73.0	87.0
4815976	College Station city	$64,809	$23,519	$38,223	$87,183	$122,609	$78,364	$26,465	$29,498	97,562	90.0	74.1	89.7
4816432	Conroe city	$50,871	$25,187	$39,740	$73,850	$84,295	$62,226	$31,319	$30,783	59,878	76.5	64.9	67.1
4817000	Corpus Christi city	$55,660	$24,726	$40,642	$78,115	$85,892	$77,099	$45,010	$21,877	307,054	83.8	73.3	76.1
4819000	Dallas city	$44,881	$16,557	$30,965	$68,125	$77,375	$51,752	$27,282	$19,591	1,227,164	70.6	64.8	74.2
4819972	Denton city	$65,262	$52,756	$41,153	$77,430	$97,403	$78,845	$61,350	$26,766	117,844	83.5	69.4	82.2
4820092	DeSoto city	$75,996	$28,811	$45,605	$93,516	$116,250	$93,945	$40,665	$36,199	50,491	86.1	73.4	89.7
4822660	Edinburg city	$47,395	$15,259	$26,970	$64,066	$80,196	$54,590	$17,195	$20,141	78,542	72.0	68.7	72.2
4824000	El Paso city	$46,760	$19,564	$35,135	$64,751	$77,055	$56,783	$32,201	$20,807	652,753	76.3	67.7	76.1
4824768	Euless city	$59,818	$38,618	$40,013	$79,269	$96,667	$75,125	$42,941	$29,982	52,585	83.3	70.7	79.0
4826232	Flower Mound town	$130,482	$53,654	$107,330	$150,752	$137,500	$150,746	$150,079	$65,781	67,388	94.4	88.3	89.6
4827000	Fort Worth city	$59,953	$21,040	$40,100	$78,983	$89,274	$69,527	$34,613	$23,734	769,046	78.4	69.5	78.0
4827684	Frisco city	$119,715	$50,018	$91,336	$134,373	$131,535	$133,943	$60,359	$54,940	129,196	93.4	81.1	84.2
4829000	Garland city	$53,152	$29,569	$34,746	$68,673	$79,413	$57,934	$30,783	$26,548	232,238	73.8	67.6	72.7
4829336	Georgetown city	$77,418	$67,241	$57,788	$98,268	$117,661	$93,011	$27,328	$31,250	51,589	88.4	79.7	85.2
4830464	Grand Prairie city	$60,603	$20,840	$36,648	$77,681	$96,698	$71,159	$27,620	$28,553	180,862	75.8	70.8	79.1
4832372	Harlingen city	$39,011	$17,302	$31,339	$72,152	$79,228	$45,477	$48,860	$18,838	65,070	74.6	69.2	75.1
4835000	Houston city	$49,322	$18,484	$32,807	$70,410	$80,545	$56,420	$31,737	$19,666	2,147,847	74.0	65.8	73.2
4837000	Irving city	$57,248	$23,672	$41,682	$73,963	$75,484	$61,953	$29,179	$26,300	224,027	73.6	66.8	76.6
4839148	Killeen city	$50,782	$26,069	$37,011	$66,324	$89,580	$57,824	$36,932	$27,269	124,174	87.5	79.3	75.5
4841464	Laredo city	$41,094	$10,621	$31,352	$59,335	$68,778	$50,474	$23,729	$17,072	242,190	65.9	64.7	65.6
4841980	League City city	$96,962	$70,635	$75,949	$116,242	$128,958	$112,641	$76,303	$40,160	88,172	93.2	83.4	87.9
4842508	Lewisville city	$65,306	$31,312	$45,768	$77,635	$112,551	$77,083	$41,172	$28,137	98,951	82.7	69.8	78.4
4843888	Longview city	$52,153	$27,009	$36,286	$75,022	$82,838	$75,457	$30,616	$19,978	80,135	81.0	71.1	77.8
4845000	Lubbock city	$56,364	$31,302	$36,406	$71,535	$91,995	$75,823	$27,348	$23,164	233,128	85.6	73.6	81.5
4845384	McAllen city	$45,294	$17,569	$30,602	$70,614	$76,795	$60,338	$28,232	$18,673	134,128	68.7	56.1	67.6
4845744	McKinney city	$95,407	$33,064	$69,722	$112,079	$125,369	$106,216	$78,722	$52,550	141,776	88.1	71.2	81.9
4846452	Mansfield city	$104,640	$53,820	$65,608	$119,367	$131,935	$111,559	$49,490	$30,273	58,731	89.8	73.2	78.8
4847892	Mesquite city	$53,501	$19,252	$36,526	$73,254	$86,372	$61,600	$39,835	$24,567	142,044	77.9	69.6	74.4
4848072	Midland city	$74,171	$31,385	$55,108	$84,240	$103,090	$88,517	$53,295	$27,195	118,298	82.6	71.0	80.4
4848768	Mission city	$45,970	$21,670	$34,523	$64,869	$69,811	$66,153	$50,045	$17,484	80,093	72.7	64.1	78.8
4848804	Missouri City city	$96,788	$39,450	$65,077	$106,606	$118,843	$110,325	$30,391	$45,938	68,141	89.9	75.9	81.6
4850820	New Braunfels city	$64,096	$42,353	$41,527	$86,129	$91,990	$77,038	$33,047	$21,250	60,346	83.2	69.6	79.5
4852356	North Richland Hills city	$72,035	$45,107	$56,113	$85,755	$106,304	$83,630	$44,081	$26,340	65,396	83.9	70.0	84.3
4853388	Odessa city	$61,997	$24,050	$43,900	$82,064	$92,746	$77,773	$46,806	$25,114	105,857	80.1	69.9	77.6
4856000	Pasadena city	$52,015	$25,907	$35,217	$66,812	$82,655	$56,054	$42,685	$22,178	151,395	68.9	67.5	70.6
4856348	Pearland city	$103,122	$44,248	$64,834	$119,832	$130,552	$116,597	$75,568	$47,138	97,729	91.2	78.3	87.8
4857176	Pflugerville city	$81,962	$44,141	$61,518	$90,976	$111,922	$86,828	$60,734	$60,904	52,562	90.7	70.7	89.5
4857200	Pharr city	$36,539	$14,107	$24,033	$51,148	$63,500	$42,890	$17,083	$17,418	72,918	61.5	60.7	71.8
4858016	Plano city	$98,757	$43,513	$75,082	$122,840	$123,888	$118,725	$67,066	$37,937	270,195	88.8	73.3	81.2
4858820	Port Arthur city	$36,901	$16,814	$32,262	$54,442	$89,000	$44,504	$22,103	$14,563	53,610	67.8	68.5	71.0
4861796	Richardson city	$86,360	$43,431	$61,250	$109,278	$107,398	$108,176	$51,500	$35,496	102,672	86.7	70.3	81.0
4863500	Round Rock city	$81,540	$22,933	$60,426	$94,888	$96,237	$92,738	$35,618	$36,551	106,520	85.0	78.8	80.7

State/ Place FIPS code	State/place	Total number of families	Families with incomes below the poverty level, as a percent of all families of that family type				Families that received Food Stamps (SNAP), as a percent of all families of that family type			Families that received food stamps (SNAP) and had at least one worker	
			All families	Married-couple families	Male householder families, no spouse present	Female householder families, no spouse present	All families	Married-couple families	Male householder or female householder families, no spouse present	Married-couple families, percent	Male householder or female householder families, no spouse present
	South Dakota—cont'd										
4659020	Sioux Falls city	39,892	8.8	2.6	19.1	35.8	11.7	4.7	30.6	4.1	21.9
4700000	**Tennessee**	1,646,360	13.6	10.2	27.9	46.8	18.5	10.0	41.7	8.1	29.6
4703440	Bartlett city	15,653	2.2	1.7	20.4	7.8	6.5	4.2	16.3	4.2	14.3
4714000	Chattanooga city	39,658	18.9	14.7	33.5	50.8	25.3	10.6	49.8	8.7	36.5
4715160	Clarksville city	36,544	14.8	7.1	21.7	53.4	17.8	8.1	41.8	7.5	31.4
4727740	Franklin city	17,375	6.4	3.0	12.3	44.1	4.9	2.2	20.3	2.2	16.2
4733280	Hendersonville city	14,845	5.3	3.4	8.5	19.1	7.1	3.7	19.4	3.7	16.6
4737640	Jackson city	14,929	18.2	4.2	41.1	60.8	23.8	9.7	50.2	8.1	31.3
4738320	Johnson City city	15,224	15.6	13.5	44.8	48.8	17.2	9.4	37.3	7.7	29.5
4739560	Kingsport city	14,355	15.0	8.5	6.4	62.8	19.9	11.2	43.9	8.0	30.9
4740000	Knoxville city	39,037	16.7	12.1	23.2	60.0	23.1	9.0	51.4	6.7	34.6
4748000	Memphis city	144,108	23.2	13.6	37.7	51.3	33.2	15.5	50.6	13.4	36.6
4751560	Murfreesboro city	25,762	9.8	8.4	33.5	36.1	14.0	6.7	37.5	5.6	29.6
4752006	Nashville-Davidson	135,106	14.0	12.0	29.8	41.5	20.1	10.5	39.0	9.3	29.7
4800000	**Texas**	6,235,820	14.0	11.7	23.0	42.5	16.1	9.4	33.4	8.2	26.0
4801000	Abilene city	26,036	13.7	11.0	29.5	42.1	17.6	10.6	35.7	8.4	28.2
4801924	Allen city	23,447	5.0	5.0	3.5	17.9	4.9	2.6	15.7	2.3	14.1
4803000	Amarillo city	48,854	13.7	10.9	18.9	44.6	16.2	8.7	33.8	8.1	26.1
4804000	Arlington city	90,783	14.1	14.9	29.1	32.5	16.1	9.8	29.8	9.1	25.3
4804462	Atascocita CDP	16,917	5.0	4.9	22.9	10.3	7.0	4.5	15.5	3.2	12.2
4805000	Austin city	179,061	13.3	10.7	24.7	41.5	15.4	8.1	31.0	7.7	24.3
4806128	Baytown city	17,620	18.4	14.0	21.7	38.7	21.7	12.8	37.9	12.2	29.7
4807000	Beaumont city	27,390	18.1	10.8	22.6	46.5	25.2	10.6	45.5	8.6	35.0
4810768	Brownsville city	40,984	30.7	27.0	35.4	60.4	30.4	22.9	43.7	20.2	28.9
4810912	Bryan city	16,209	19.0	13.2	37.3	52.2	23.1	10.9	44.5	10.5	35.8
4813024	Carrollton city	32,181	6.5	8.1	19.4	18.9	7.1	4.0	16.6	3.9	14.5
4813552	Cedar Park city	14,275	4.6	3.3	0.0	16.1	...	...	...	...	...
4815976	College Station city	16,012	14.6	13.8	19.3	35.2	9.8	5.9	21.8	5.9	17.8
4816432	Conroe city	14,335	18.1	15.2	24.9	41.2	15.0	5.4	32.1	5.1	22.1
4817000	Corpus Christi city	5,634	22.4	13.3	38.7	64.9	19.7	10.4	36.6	9.1	28.3
4819000	Dallas city	267,664	21.1	19.8	30.6	49.0	22.4	12.7	37.8	11.6	29.0
4819972	Denton city	23,843	9.9	5.6	14.7	35.8	13.1	5.3	31.0	3.8	26.0
4820092	DeSoto city	13,363	7.5	7.5	4.0	21.4	10.7	4.1	25.5	3.8	17.8
4822660	Edinburg city	17,680	23.0	20.8	43.9	50.3	28.3	21.8	43.7	18.5	33.1
4824000	El Paso city	160,918	18.6	16.1	28.8	45.8	24.9	16.9	40.4	14.6	30.8
4824768	Euless city	12,364	12.1	16.1	12.9	32.7	13.5	10.3	19.4	8.9	19.1
4826232	Flower Mound town	18,422	1.6	1.5	4.8	5.5	...	...	...	...	...
4827000	Fort Worth city	179,408	16.0	13.4	23.1	42.7	18.5	10.6	35.3	9.4	27.2
4827684	Frisco city	34,982	3.5	1.2	27.8	15.7	3.3	1.3	12.9	1.1	12.0
4829000	Garland city	56,274	14.6	12.9	26.6	39.3	16.4	9.7	31.2	9.1	25.5
4829336	Georgetown city	13,978	6.5	3.2	42.2	30.8	...	...	...	...	...
4830464	Grand Prairie city	42,982	13.8	10.4	29.7	31.8	16.1	9.2	31.9	8.6	25.1
4832372	Harlingen city	15,205	25.0	27.1	28.6	54.4	27.5	21.2	40.2	15.8	24.8
4835000	Houston city	478,982	19.9	18.9	28.5	49.4	20.4	11.9	35.1	10.7	27.3
4837000	Irving city	52,531	12.4	12.1	20.5	35.4	16.2	10.5	29.5	10.1	26.0
4839148	Killeen city	30,587	13.2	7.6	27.6	38.4	14.7	7.6	30.1	7.2	24.0
4841464	Laredo city	53,182	27.8	24.0	48.6	55.9	33.7	25.4	49.6	21.4	35.7
4841980	League City city	22,739	3.2	0.9	0.0	22.7	...	...	...	...	...
4842508	Lewisville city	24,373	9.7	8.2	14.3	31.1	13.5	8.2	26.6	8.2	21.5
4843888	Longview city	20,001	14.0	6.4	37.4	47.3	17.5	7.0	37.7	6.5	28.6
4845000	Lubbock city	53,374	13.4	6.0	36.2	43.0	18.6	10.4	35.9	9.6	30.5
4845384	McAllen city	31,175	23.8	22.8	40.0	57.9	25.5	18.7	42.0	14.4	33.0
4845744	McKinney city	36,773	7.3	5.0	8.5	21.2	3.6	2.4	8.2	2.4	6.7
4846452	Mansfield city	15,662	5.7	1.6	18.5	31.6	4.5	3.2	10.5	3.1	10.0
4847892	Mesquite city	35,892	14.1	10.8	17.2	38.9	16.3	8.5	30.3	8.2	24.7
4848072	Midland city	29,269	8.1	5.8	5.8	29.1	10.2	5.6	22.0	5.0	19.8
4848768	Mission city	19,343	22.2	20.4	6.6	58.8	24.5	19.8	41.6	16.0	28.8
4848804	Missouri City city	18,056	3.9	2.6	41.2	7.9	7.7	3.9	19.7	3.8	16.1
4850820	New Braunfels city	15,311	7.4	3.7	0.0	31.2	9.9	3.9	26.9	3.8	23.7
4852356	North Richland Hills city	17,612	6.1	3.5	3.9	34.5	6.8	3.4	18.6	3.1	17.8
4853388	Odessa city	26,451	11.1	7.4	3.8	36.1	15.5	9.2	28.0	7.9	24.8
4856000	Pasadena city	34,501	18.0	17.7	18.1	48.0	20.3	12.2	37.0	10.6	31.1
4856348	Pearland city	26,994	3.6	2.6	14.1	13.0	6.7	4.8	14.3	4.4	14.3
4857176	Pflugerville city	13,765	7.2	9.3	0.0	21.0	...	...	...	...	...
4857200	Pharr city	16,304	33.5	33.7	34.1	58.1	40.4	32.5	55.9	27.5	45.7
4858016	Plano city	73,012	5.5	3.0	12.1	25.5	4.6	1.9	15.8	1.7	14.2
4858820	Port Arthur city	11,652	28.3	22.0	35.7	61.2	31.4	19.5	47.8	16.8	35.8
4861796	Richardson city	26,598	6.2	7.7	5.5	17.9	6.4	4.4	13.6	3.8	12.0
4863500	Round Rock city	25,515	6.8	5.0	18.8	22.3	9.9	6.4	22.6	6.3	17.3

State/ Place FIPS code	State/place	Median family income in the past 12 months (in 2,013 inflation-adjusted dollars) All families	Families with no earners	Families with one earner	Families with two earners	Families with three or more earners	Families with own children under 18 years Married-couple families with children	Male householder, no spouse present, with children	Female householder, no spouse present, with children	Total population in households	Persons who had health insurance, as a percent of all persons in that household type Married-couple families, percent	Male householder or female householder families, no spouse present	Nonfamily households
	Texas—cont'd												
4863572	Rowlett city	$92,463	$31,094	$61,250	$98,531	$122,438	$99,142	$73,158	$56,449	58,486	85.9	78.0	83.3
4864472	San Angelo city	$54,354	$34,800	$42,087	$69,261	$80,581	$68,625	$51,348	$17,448	91,068	85.1	68.6	80.0
4865000	San Antonio city	$52,538	$23,208	$36,987	$70,166	$88,693	$66,696	$35,110	$23,988	1,365,820	81.6	73.2	79.6
4865600	San Marcos city	$45,970	$53,664	$28,155	$55,552	$93,906	$58,551	$29,630	$16,610	49,829	84.0	65.7	78.0
4869596	Spring CDP	$70,906	$31,250	$52,148	$89,641	$84,354	$83,394	$63,340	$44,003	58,307	81.9	75.1	81.3
4870808	Sugar Land city	$117,152	$31,998	$94,214	$132,510	$143,078	$128,732	$135,789	$53,315	81,205	87.9	72.2	88.5
4872176	Temple city	$61,753	$35,754	$41,977	$81,559	$120,146	$75,124	$38,579	$22,554	67,460	85.8	76.0	82.8
4872656	The Woodlands CDP	$134,145	$43,018	$130,841	$153,344	$155,169	$153,270	$73,655	$27,141	104,721	94.7	80.8	90.0
4874144	Tyler city	$55,300	$37,826	$45,099	$68,736	$88,250	$70,890	$23,194	$23,536	97,457	81.9	72.4	77.8
4875428	Victoria city	$53,630	$30,578	$32,723	$76,549	$84,625	$79,914	$26,060	$22,418	63,296	82.4	68.3	82.9
4876000	Waco city	$42,245	$20,474	$30,969	$58,839	$81,190	$56,399	$23,750	$15,822	124,319	78.9	73.9	86.8
4879000	Wichita Falls city	$54,777	$36,227	$37,931	$73,538	$95,000	$70,478	$24,135	$20,379	90,494	85.4	71.7	78.7
4900000	**Utah**	$66,321	$38,285	$51,414	$73,777	$99,597	$73,995	$40,880	$26,784	2,829,593	88.3	75.0	82.3
4943660	Layton city	$75,368	$43,851	$60,440	$82,873	$109,934	$78,419	$48,886	$33,039	68,699	94.0	83.1	81.8
4944320	Lehi city	$79,389	$53,417	$69,003	$78,617	$110,924	$84,523	$42,786	$36,958	51,753	93.0	83.3	83.9
4950150	Millcreek CDP	$72,517	$40,327	$60,452	$86,034	$94,474	$93,333	$51,875	$20,323	61,656	88.4	81.1	77.1
4955980	Ogden city	$44,237	$32,768	$33,320	$53,826	$80,920	$50,486	$31,708	$21,202	81,794	80.5	71.3	77.2
4957300	Orem city	$57,001	$32,361	$50,059	$56,575	$95,402	$60,282	$33,689	$27,024	90,313	85.1	72.3	76.5
4962470	Provo city	$41,990	$38,942	$35,755	$37,162	$80,741	$50,946	$34,132	$14,818	114,435	85.3	71.3	86.5
4965330	St. George city	$56,952	$46,201	$44,906	$65,927	$80,745	$63,287	$28,750	$35,134	74,739	84.3	70.4	75.9
4967000	Salt Lake City city	$62,919	$24,650	$42,337	$75,912	$82,820	$71,250	$32,929	$21,221	188,613	82.9	70.9	84.1
4967440	Sandy city	$83,789	$46,200	$63,526	$91,813	$123,194	$90,955	$52,893	$36,350	89,144	91.5	85.4	91.9
4970850	South Jordan city	$93,200	$47,679	$77,878	$102,620	$133,971	$95,461	$40,983	$45,476	56,184	92.8	84.6	81.1
4975360	Taylorsville city	$64,458	$40,257	$43,496	$70,720	$93,900	$69,333	$36,071	$33,609	60,032	82.7	75.7	83.7
4982950	West Jordan city	$72,631	$35,373	$51,077	$76,365	$97,162	$76,412	$40,396	$32,576	107,728	89.6	78.6	81.8
4983470	West Valley City city	$51,579	$24,579	$31,983	$60,046	$92,211	$55,517	$28,263	$20,777	132,014	77.9	63.4	82.9
5000000	**Vermont**	$67,953	$32,368	$45,522	$83,452	$103,174	$83,160	$36,990	$24,590	620,244	95.3	90.0	90.2
5100000	**Virginia**	$75,778	$35,774	$52,904	$96,379	$113,489	$98,043	$42,199	$27,583	7,974,644	90.9	79.3	85.8
5101000	Alexandria city	$106,308	$41,506	$65,933	$144,464	$95,581	$128,570	$38,613	$35,213	143,819	87.1	72.3	88.5
5103000	Arlington CDP	$139,542	$44,052	$94,433	$170,669	$150,265	$170,414	$52,679	$34,990	217,172	92.1	67.5	93.2
5114440	Centreville CDP	$114,560	$49,292	$84,977	$130,529	$133,080	$122,610	$123,144	$56,507	72,368	88.9	76.2	87.4
5116000	Chesapeake city	$78,370	$41,833	$54,954	$97,159	$116,607	$94,804	$47,889	$29,109	216,749	93.9	81.8	87.6
5121088	Dale City CDP	$87,221	$42,518	$54,188	$103,088	$134,403	$100,805	$41,512	$44,213	68,545	85.9	84.0	81.1
5135000	Hampton city	$60,311	$30,015	$39,901	$81,829	$107,288	$75,716	$31,698	$24,938	131,633	91.3	83.8	83.4
5135624	Harrisonburg city	$47,660	$32,022	$36,017	$60,092	$74,171	$57,630	$33,986	$22,205	50,085	83.5	69.7	91.3
5147672	Lynchburg city	$48,148	$26,560	$31,600	$63,619	$99,438	$64,806	$35,625	$15,619	75,542	89.2	82.4	85.7
5156000	Newport News city	$56,726	$34,339	$38,192	$75,230	$97,280	$72,716	$32,308	$23,947	172,561	90.4	79.3	82.6
5157000	Norfolk city	$50,382	$23,457	$35,985	$69,947	$85,944	$66,405	$36,910	$19,278	219,463	88.2	77.0	81.4
5164000	Portsmouth city	$51,115	$26,965	$36,489	$75,361	$87,368	$78,367	$33,204	$21,731	92,566	89.9	79.7	82.6
5166672	Reston CDP	$126,875	$58,750	$91,879	$151,531	$160,039	$133,963	$72,411	$46,534	61,701	92.2	83.3	93.9
5167000	Richmond city	$47,985	$16,494	$34,246	$76,326	$84,847	$91,416	$27,036	$15,947	207,996	90.0	77.6	80.9
5168000	Roanoke city	$49,513	$26,276	$34,555	$65,376	$66,940	$66,993	$29,744	$18,515	96,354	89.2	77.2	80.6
5176432	Suffolk city	$74,879	$32,984	$54,227	$92,347	$113,134	$99,624	$48,194	$29,901	82,889	91.5	84.2	87.5
5182000	Virginia Beach city	$75,552	$41,972	$54,405	$90,500	$114,506	$91,479	$52,535	$31,248	422,238	93.2	82.4	84.8
5300000	**Washington**	$71,100	$39,274	$53,164	$91,187	$106,694	$85,824	$41,732	$25,856	6,789,761	89.5	77.6	83.2
5303180	Auburn city	$62,139	$35,764	$41,010	$85,645	$110,779	$77,947	$46,211	$24,460	72,323	87.8	77.4	85.8
5305210	Bellevue city	$103,242	$55,461	$92,206	$126,800	$144,583	$130,963	$42,973	$36,613	131,764	92.7	79.8	86.9
5305280	Bellingham city	$61,651	$36,725	$49,826	$76,916	$72,566	$82,674	$38,365	$16,147	80,827	90.6	79.0	83.4
5322640	Everett city	$55,970	$20,675	$37,852	$83,523	$90,625	$59,709	$35,176	$23,874	101,117	84.0	78.8	79.7
5323515	Federal Way city	$60,741	$25,353	$41,355	$84,150	$112,731	$66,205	$45,268	$22,492	91,107	85.7	76.9	78.2
5335275	Kennewick city	$59,452	$32,311	$41,000	$83,895	$96,741	$63,962	$42,804	$19,211	74,687	85.4	72.6	81.0
5335415	Kent city	$65,317	$22,857	$42,038	$84,004	$107,683	$71,849	$30,500	$27,095	121,350	81.3	77.5	84.5
5335940	Kirkland city	$104,011	$49,083	$78,575	$123,769	$128,606	$128,564	$91,639	$41,408	82,942	93.7	81.8	84.6
5338038	Lakewood city	$56,416	$28,094	$48,597	$74,387	$94,214	$52,190	$20,568	$20,642	55,827	87.5	78.5	85.5
5343955	Marysville city	$69,313	$32,854	$52,271	$84,131	$120,859	$75,427	$48,614	$28,399	61,647	88.2	80.3	85.2
5353545	Pasco city	$54,962	$33,266	$32,996	$69,748	$86,803	$63,413	$29,353	$20,847	65,874	83.4	73.8	71.4
5357535	Redmond city	$118,449	$40,083	$101,576	$152,311	$134,462	$140,922	$128,833	$38,882	56,411	95.2	82.9	89.0
5357745	Renton city	$74,794	$27,422	$56,116	$89,153	$100,870	$84,001	$39,589	$31,360	95,204	88.0	77.9	81.3
5358235	Richland city	$85,981	$50,240	$66,750	$112,529	$141,304	$104,819	$42,955	$32,500	51,250	95.0	79.1	82.7
5363000	Seattle city	$96,251	$42,021	$67,491	$118,669	$113,077	$126,343	$51,579	$32,495	630,183	93.4	79.9	86.0
5363960	Shoreline city	$76,744	$45,024	$52,484	$98,917	$127,708	$100,822	$46,167	$31,483	53,696	92.5	77.3	81.5
5365922	South Hill CDP	$81,201	$39,154	$59,137	$100,105	$123,362	$90,680	$56,324	$32,255	54,613	89.5	88.5	82.4
5367000	Spokane city	$54,789	$33,294	$39,319	$74,915	$90,043	$71,301	$32,407	$20,618	206,999	90.7	78.7	81.1
5367167	Spokane Valley city	$58,324	$37,471	$42,319	$73,458	$94,705	$73,803	$32,044	$19,604	90,390	88.0	75.3	79.5
5370000	Tacoma city	$60,973	$29,746	$44,362	$83,755	$111,875	$71,864	$38,523	$21,685	197,247	86.0	76.5	80.0
5374060	Vancouver city	$55,336	$32,005	$42,288	$75,701	$88,337	$70,315	$38,157	$25,394	164,163	85.5	77.2	80.5
5380010	Yakima city	$46,246	$29,511	$30,709	$61,262	$65,926	$51,537	$27,955	$20,133	91,014	77.0	70.7	78.1
5400000	**West Virginia**	$51,949	$27,721	$42,971	$76,260	$93,908	$71,003	$35,189	$17,591	1,826,219	88.9	78.9	82.7
5414600	Charleston city	$66,128	$30,313	$38,726	$91,900	$109,327	$108,080	$15,865	$14,440	49,984	92.4	82.2	82.2

Table E-4: Cities with a Population of 50,000 or More—Income, Poverty, and Health Insurance—Continued

State/ Place FIPS code	State/place	Total number of families	Families with incomes below the poverty level, as a percent of all families of that family type				Families that received Food Stamps (SNAP), as a percent of all families of that family type			Families that received food stamps (SNAP) and had at least one worker	
			All families	Married-couple families	Male householder families, no spouse present	Female householder families, no spouse present	All families	Married-couple families	Male householder or female householder families, no spouse present	Married-couple families, percent	Male householder or female householder families, no spouse present
	Texas—cont'd										
4863572	Rowlett city..................	15,673	4.9	3.3	3.1	12.8	6.9	5.1	13.6	4.9	10.3
4864472	San Angelo city..............	22,344	12.9	6.8	12.7	47.3	17.6	6.7	42.0	6.0	36.3
4865000	San Antonio city.............	315,470	16.6	12.9	24.6	42.6	20.7	12.1	36.2	10.7	27.4
4865600	San Marcos city..............	6,970	15.7	12.8	19.0	40.8	21.4	10.4	34.8	9.3	32.7
4869596	Spring CDP...................	13,995	8.4	7.9	3.3	25.4	10.1	5.1	25.2	4.7	23.3
4870808	Sugar Land city..............	22,247	3.7	4.1	0.0	7.8	2.8	1.2	12.8	1.1	10.2
4872176	Temple city..................	16,324	10.9	6.6	35.2	48.4	14.4	8.9	30.5	8.2	19.5
4872656	The Woodlands CDP............	28,332	4.8	3.2	0.0	40.7	...	...	...	...	...
4874144	Tyler city...................	23,022	14.0	12.6	37.4	37.9	13.7	5.9	29.4	5.4	23.4
4875428	Victoria city................	16,172	14.8	12.0	23.8	39.4	17.8	7.3	38.4	6.7	32.7
4876000	Waco city....................	27,059	21.3	12.6	33.6	56.1	25.0	12.0	47.4	11.0	35.3
4879000	Wichita Falls city...........	23,889	14.4	10.4	25.7	45.7	16.6	6.4	38.9	6.0	30.4
4900000	**Utah**	667,046	9.7	8.3	19.5	37.1	10.0	6.1	26.9	5.7	21.8
4943660	Layton city..................	17,396	7.3	5.6	12.1	24.7	9.8	4.9	29.1	4.6	26.7
4944320	Lehi city....................	11,462	4.4	3.8	20.0	18.7	...	...	...	...	...
4950150	Millcreek CDP................	14,375	7.8	7.3	0.0	36.3	9.0	5.4	21.6	4.4	18.6
4955980	Ogden city...................	19,060	16.6	15.5	23.5	46.4	21.1	11.5	41.5	11.1	32.9
4957300	Orem city....................	20,276	13.8	12.3	19.8	43.8	12.8	8.8	29.7	8.6	23.2
4962470	Provo city...................	22,988	23.5	21.2	25.7	55.6	13.8	9.7	33.7	9.3	31.2
4965330	St. George city..............	17,936	10.4	13.6	19.2	36.8	11.4	9.7	20.7	9.3	17.9
4967000	Salt Lake City city..........	39,013	14.3	14.6	22.5	43.2	13.6	8.2	27.6	7.5	19.6
4967440	Sandy city...................	22,503	5.6	5.1	14.7	25.4	5.9	3.3	18.1	2.9	15.2
4970850	South Jordan city............	13,276	3.5	1.5	17.5	23.3	5.1	4.2	14.7	4.2	14.7
4975360	Taylorsville city............	13,797	9.3	8.7	27.8	27.2	13.3	7.3	33.6	7.2	30.6
4982950	West Jordan city.............	24,530	8.2	6.0	19.1	33.8	8.2	5.8	17.5	5.6	14.9
4983470	West Valley City city........	29,392	18.3	16.4	33.0	52.9	15.8	8.7	31.5	7.8	25.3
5000000	**Vermont**..................	159,883	7.2	4.1	19.4	36.8	13.2	6.9	37.1	5.7	26.4
5100000	**Virginia**	2,033,567	8.4	5.1	17.3	34.7	10.6	4.9	27.9	4.1	21.0
5101000	Alexandria city..............	31,206	5.8	4.3	3.9	27.1	6.9	3.3	18.5	2.8	11.6
5103000	Arlington CDP................	44,308	6.0	3.5	19.8	26.6	5.5	3.0	15.3	2.1	11.1
5114440	Centreville CDP..............	18,102	3.6	2.7	0.0	15.9	...	...	...	...	...
5116000	Chesapeake city..............	59,294	8.0	4.3	12.7	31.4	10.0	4.9	24.2	4.6	19.5
5121088	Dale City CDP................	16,702	4.0	1.0	8.4	24.6	11.4	8.0	20.5	7.9	18.9
5135000	Hampton city.................	32,502	12.7	6.0	27.2	40.7	15.7	5.2	34.7	4.7	27.9
5135624	Harrisonburg city............	8,142	14.1	15.5	10.1	43.0	20.1	13.5	33.1	10.5	31.5
5147672	Lynchburg city...............	16,060	18.5	11.1	26.7	54.5	19.3	7.3	43.8	6.1	30.0
5156000	Newport News city............	42,910	12.9	7.8	20.3	40.3	17.9	7.2	34.5	6.5	28.3
5157000	Norfolk city.................	50,082	16.5	6.7	14.3	48.3	22.0	8.4	41.6	7.4	32.1
5164000	Portsmouth city..............	23,410	15.9	4.4	22.7	42.7	19.6	6.1	36.0	4.6	29.0
5166672	Reston CDP...................	15,222	5.1	6.9	5.2	16.8	...	...	...	...	...
5167000	Richmond city................	40,552	20.8	8.2	25.3	52.3	25.7	8.3	42.9	7.1	27.6
5168000	Roanoke city.................	23,556	16.6	11.8	36.2	48.5	22.2	9.3	42.0	7.4	33.9
5176432	Suffolk city.................	22,314	7.4	2.2	11.2	32.0	14.5	5.7	36.8	4.5	27.5
5182000	Virginia Beach city..........	112,851	6.9	3.4	13.8	27.6	7.8	3.3	19.7	2.9	14.8
5300000	**Washington**	1,694,518	9.4	7.2	19.4	37.9	15.4	8.7	37.5	7.5	28.3
5303180	Auburn city..................	18,183	11.0	10.1	13.0	39.5	21.3	12.6	42.1	10.8	29.1
5305210	Bellevue city................	34,631	5.7	4.0	20.6	33.9	5.9	3.1	20.1	2.6	16.5
5305280	Bellingham city..............	16,381	15.5	7.1	11.7	57.3	17.1	8.2	37.4	7.9	24.0
5322640	Everett city.................	22,485	14.2	12.9	19.3	44.1	27.3	18.0	48.2	15.2	36.8
5323515	Federal Way city.............	22,617	13.7	11.9	38.2	39.3	23.6	13.1	44.4	11.6	33.4
5335275	Kennewick city...............	17,765	12.4	9.4	11.2	48.3	23.8	13.7	51.8	12.8	42.8
5335415	Kent city....................	28,059	14.6	13.2	31.2	35.4	24.5	17.7	41.3	15.1	32.1
5335940	Kirkland city................	21,800	4.9	3.9	3.1	18.5	6.0	3.5	15.8	3.0	12.7
5338038	Lakewood city................	13,781	16.4	18.4	41.2	39.6	24.1	12.8	50.8	10.5	33.5
5343955	Marysville city..............	15,801	7.4	5.5	10.1	37.3	15.9	7.9	38.9	7.1	27.1
5353545	Pasco city...................	14,473	19.0	15.1	26.5	50.7	28.2	19.1	46.1	17.9	40.8
5357535	Redmond city.................	14,181	5.2	2.5	21.6	34.4	3.1	2.2	8.7	1.1	4.2
5357745	Renton city..................	21,987	9.3	5.2	29.8	28.9	15.7	7.0	36.2	6.2	24.0
5358235	Richland city................	13,466	8.2	4.2	27.4	33.3	12.7	6.0	35.5	4.8	28.2
5363000	Seattle city.................	127,803	8.0	5.0	22.6	32.8	10.9	5.2	30.6	4.0	23.2
5363960	Shoreline city...............	13,013	6.8	3.6	29.5	30.7	12.3	8.5	24.3	8.0	18.9
5365922	South Hill CDP...............	14,825	6.0	4.0	7.2	20.0	9.5	6.6	18.9	6.4	11.0
5367000	Spokane city.................	48,409	13.6	8.9	19.3	49.6	23.0	11.9	49.6	9.8	39.9
5367167	Spokane Valley city..........	23,301	10.3	9.1	18.3	37.9	19.4	10.6	43.4	9.1	31.6
5370000	Tacoma city..................	45,245	13.7	10.2	25.8	43.5	22.9	13.1	44.3	11.2	31.8
5374060	Vancouver city...............	39,617	13.7	10.4	16.8	39.4	24.1	15.3	44.3	12.9	32.5
5380010	Yakima city..................	20,677	18.6	13.5	32.7	50.9	28.8	17.5	54.3	15.5	42.0
5400000	**West Virginia**.............	479,062	13.1	10.8	26.3	50.4	16.1	9.0	37.8	6.5	23.5
5414600	Charleston city..............	12,192	15.7	8.3	60.8	54.5	20.4	6.0	48.0	4.7	36.3

State/ Place FIPS code	State/place	Median family income in the past 12 months (in 2,013 inflation-adjusted dollars)								Total population in households	Persons who had health insurance, as a percent of all persons in that household type		
		All families	Families with no earners	Families with one earner	Families with two earners	Families with three or more earners	Families with own children under 18 years				Married- couple families, percent	Male householder or female householder families, no spouse present	Nonfamily households
							Married- couple families with children	Male householder, no spouse present, with children	Female householder, no spouse present, with children				
5500000	**Wisconsin**............	$65,877	$35,499	$44,059	$81,992	$99,328	$84,375	$36,513	$23,702	5,650,835	94.1	85.7	86.3
5502375	Appleton city	$68,012	$31,405	$49,777	$79,373	$96,313	$87,128	$50,058	$23,359	71,707	94.8	89.0	83.5
5522300	Eau Claire city	$64,226	$46,736	$41,225	$73,003	$97,355	$84,139	$29,601	$27,439	66,205	96.1	83.8	89.1
5531000	Green Bay city..................	$52,120	$32,549	$34,096	$67,626	$79,171	$66,305	$28,657	$17,651	103,330	91.2	83.3	83.4
5537825	Janesville city	$57,416	$33,720	$38,558	$76,367	$85,865	$72,988	$40,033	$17,525	63,251	95.7	85.0	83.8
5539225	Kenosha city....................	$57,164	$23,372	$41,629	$82,248	$90,126	$82,488	$37,378	$22,288	98,260	91.5	85.4	83.4
5540775	La Crosse city	$55,342	$28,254	$40,256	$69,597	$89,375	$69,324	$36,447	$24,566	50,559	94.1	85.2	87.7
5548000	Madison city	$76,339	$41,648	$47,034	$91,959	$114,425	$93,672	$25,951	$21,770	238,612	96.5	88.1	89.7
5553000	Milwaukee city.................	$39,852	$16,888	$27,461	$68,085	$82,029	$60,875	$25,050	$19,437	593,727	88.4	83.1	82.5
5560500	Oshkosh city....................	$57,430	$31,257	$36,755	$76,948	$86,202	$76,842	$27,072	$16,664	62,059	95.0	90.9	85.4
5566000	Racine city	$49,900	$20,316	$33,556	$68,159	$100,354	$62,558	$30,083	$21,241	77,118	85.2	82.0	79.6
5584250	Waukesha city..................	$71,447	$34,871	$52,604	$85,435	$103,576	$83,661	$41,078	$26,915	70,095	94.7	84.6	85.0
5585300	West Allis city	$60,730	$25,117	$38,028	$77,865	$89,028	$74,329	$31,212	$19,599	60,110	93.9	86.2	84.4
5600000	**Wyoming**	$70,531	$36,362	$49,622	$86,697	$105,900	$84,210	$45,175	$23,418	566,182	89.4	76.2	79.8
5613150	Casper city......................	$70,793	$32,705	$50,495	$89,450	$109,009	$90,890	$45,375	$19,358	57,353	89.3	80.1	76.8
5613900	Cheyenne city	$76,094	$55,922	$48,462	$88,105	$102,394	$85,945	$57,973	$32,942	59,696	92.3	81.1	82.0

State/ Place FIPS code	State/place	Total number of families	Families with incomes below the poverty level, as a percent of all families of that family type				Families that received Food Stamps (SNAP), as a percent of all families of that family type			Families that received food stamps (SNAP) and had at least one worker	
			All families	Married-couple families	Male householder families, no spouse present	Female householder families, no spouse present	All families	Married-couple families	Male householder or female householder families, no spouse present	Married-couple families, percent	Male householder or female householder families, no spouse present
5500000	**Wisconsin**......................................	1,458,497	8.9	5.6	21.6	40.3	13.3	6.0	37.8	5.3	29.4
5502375	Appleton city	17,773	9.1	5.5	18.3	35.9	12.8	6.2	30.8	5.6	24.7
5522300	Eau Claire city	14,125	8.4	5.0	18.4	30.6	14.2	7.7	34.0	6.8	30.3
5531000	Green Bay city..................................	25,005	14.5	10.4	27.9	48.5	19.8	10.2	41.5	9.7	30.7
5537825	Janesville city	16,593	13.1	7.1	14.3	50.4	22.4	12.7	46.3	10.5	33.3
5539225	Kenosha city	24,117	14.2	5.4	27.5	39.3	22.3	8.5	45.6	7.1	34.4
5540775	La Crosse city	9,732	10.6	5.7	26.9	37.6	15.8	5.4	39.8	4.5	29.9
5548000	Madison city	49,331	10.1	5.1	36.0	43.1	13.3	4.9	36.5	4.4	28.9
5553000	Milwaukee city.................................	128,423	25.4	15.6	35.6	52.3	38.3	17.8	58.0	15.6	42.9
5560500	Oshkosh city	13,368	11.1	3.9	28.4	53.7	17.9	6.8	44.7	6.1	34.6
5566000	Racine city	17,763	20.1	14.4	29.1	50.2	28.8	15.0	51.8	13.2	34.3
5584250	Waukesha city..................................	17,092	8.2	5.5	16.8	39.4	11.1	6.1	28.3	5.3	18.6
5585300	West Allis city	14,021	11.0	2.1	34.2	42.1	20.1	8.1	49.0	7.0	34.1
5600000	**Wyoming**	145,481	8.4	5.6	15.0	40.8	6.4	2.6	21.2	2.4	17.7
5613150	Casper city.......................................	14,827	8.4	4.3	12.4	44.4	7.0	1.6	22.1	1.5	18.4
5613900	Cheyenne city	14,968	6.5	3.8	6.5	35.3	8.6	3.2	26.9	3.0	25.5

APPENDIX A. SOURCE NOTES AND EXPLANATIONS

All data in this book are from the American Community Survey (ACS). 3-year estimates for the years 2011 through 2013. This section of source notes is generally excerpted from: http://www2.census.gov/programs-surveys/acs/tech_docs/subject_definitions/2013_ACSSubjectDefinitions.pdf.

The data were assembled from the ACS detailed tables and the following notes reference the numbers of those detailed tables. Also included with each table number and title is the table's universe, which is the total number of units (e.g., individuals, households, businesses, in the population of interest). Many of the data items can also be found in ACS profiles, subject tables, geographic comparison tables, and other formats available on the ACS website.

Symbols

A ". . ." in a cell indicates that either there were no sample cases or the number of sample cases was too small.

Part A — LIVING ARRANGEMENTS

Table A-1. States

HOUSEHOLD TYPE, Items 1 through 15

Source: Table B11001. Household Type (including Living Alone) and B11005. Households By Presence Of People Under 18 Years By Household Type

Universe: Households

Household – A household includes all the people who occupy a housing unit. (People not living in households are classified as living in group quarters.) A housing unit is a house, an apartment, a mobile home, a group of rooms, or a single room that is occupied (or if vacant, is intended for occupancy) as separate living quarters. Separate living quarters are those in which the occupants live separately from any other people in the building and which have direct access from the outside of the building or through a common hall. The occupants may be a single family, one person living alone, two or more families living together, or any other group of related or unrelated people who share living arrangements.

Householder – One person in each household is designated as the householder. In most cases, this is the person or one of the people in whose name the home is owned, being bought, or rented and who is listed on line one of the survey questionnaire.

If there is no such person in the household, any adult household member 15 years old and over could be designated as the householder.

Households are classified by type according to the sex of the householder and the presence of relatives. Two types of householders are distinguished: a family householder and a nonfamily householder. A family householder is a householder living with one or more individuals related to him or her by birth, marriage, or adoption. The householder and all people in the household related to him or her are family members. A nonfamily householder is a householder living alone or with nonrelatives only.

Family Households – A family consists of a householder and one or more other people living in the same household who are related to the householder by birth, marriage, or adoption. All people in a household who are related to the householder are regarded as members of his or her family. A family household may contain people not related to the householder, but those people are not included as part of the householder's family in tabulations. Thus, the number of family households is equal to the number of families, but family households may include more members than do families. A household can contain only one family for purposes of tabulations. Not all households contain families since a household may comprise a group of unrelated people or of one person living alone – these are called nonfamily households. Families are classified by type as either a "married-couple family" or "other family" according to the sex of the householder and the presence of relatives. The data on family type are based on answers to questions on sex and relationship that were asked of all people.

- Married-Couple Family – A family in which the householder and his or her spouse are listed as members of the same household.
- Other Family:
  - Male Householder, No Spouse Present – A family with a male householder and no spouse of householder present.
  - Female Householder, No Spouse Present – A family with a female householder and no spouse of householder present.

Family households and married-couple families include same-sex married couples, beginning with the 2013 data products used in these tables.

Nonfamily Household – A householder living alone or with nonrelatives only. Unmarried couples households, whether opposite-sex or same-sex, with no relatives of the householder present are tabulated in nonfamily households.

Related Child – Any child under 18 years old who is related to the householder by birth, marriage, or adoption. Related children of the householder include ever-married as well as never-married children. Children, by definition, exclude persons under 18 years who maintain households or are spouses or unmarried partners of householders. Households with children under 18 can include own children of the householder, related children of the householder, or children who are not related, such as a foster child.

MULTIGENERATIONAL HOUSEHOLDS, Items 16 and 17

Source: Table B11017. Multigenerational households
Universe: Households

Multigenerational Household – Multigenerational households are family households consisting of three or more generations. These households include (1) a householder, a parent or parent-in-law of the householder, and an own child of the householder, (2) a householder, an own child of the householder, and a grandchild of the householder, or (3) a householder, a parent or parent-in-law of the householder, an own child of the householder, and a grandchild of the householder.

UNMARRIED PARTNER HOUSEHOLDS, Items 18 through 20

Source: Table B11009. Unmarried-Partner Households and Household Type by Sex of Partner.

Universe: Households

Unmarried-Partner Household – An unmarried-partner household is a household other than a "married-couple household" that includes a householder and an "unmarried partner." An "unmarried partner" can be of the same sex or of the opposite sex as the householder. An "unmarried partner" in an "unmarried-partner household" is an adult who is unrelated to the householder, but shares living quarters and has a close personal relationship with the householder. An unmarried-partner household also may be a family household or a nonfamily household, depending on the presence or absence of another person in the household who is related to the householder by birth or adoption. There may be only one unmarried partner per household, and an unmarried partner may not be included in a married-couple household, as the householder cannot have both a spouse and an unmarried partner.

SUBFAMILIES, Items 21 through 23

Source: Table C11013. Subfamily Type.

Universe: Subfamilies

Subfamily – A subfamily is a married couple (husband and wife interviewed as members of the same household) with or without never-married children under 18 years old, or one parent with one or more never-married children under 18 years old. A subfamily does not maintain its own household, but lives in a household where the householder or householder's spouse is a relative. The number of subfamilies is not included in the count of families, since subfamily members are counted as part of the householder's family. Subfamilies are defined during processing of data. Same-sex married couples are only shown as the householder and spouse, and are not included in subfamilies. In selected tabulations, subfamilies are further classified by type: married-couple subfamilies, with or without own children; mother-child subfamilies; and father-child subfamilies.

FAMILIES WITH CHILDREN UNDER 18, Items 24 through 28.

Source: Table C23007. Presence of Own Children Under 18 Years by Family Type by Employment Status.

Universe: Families

Own Child – A never-married child under 18 years who is a son or daughter by birth, a stepchild, or an adopted child of the householder. In certain tabulations, own children are further classified as living with two parents or with one parent only. Own children of the householder living with two parents are by definition found only in married-couple families (Note: When used in "EMPLOYMENT STATUS" tabulations, own child refers to a never married child under the age of 18 in a family or a subfamily who is a son or daughter, by birth, marriage, or adoption, of a member of the householder's family, but not necessarily of the householder).

Civilian Labor Force – Consists of people classified as employed or unemployed in accordance with the criteria described below.

Employed – This category includes all civilians 16 years old and over who either (1) were "at work," that is, those who did any work at all during the reference week as paid employees, worked in their own business or profession, worked on their own farm, or worked 15 hours or more as unpaid workers on a family farm or in a family business; or (2) were "with a job but not at work," that is, those who did not work during the reference week but had jobs or businesses from which they were temporarily absent due to illness, bad weather, industrial dispute, vacation, or other personal reasons. Excluded from the employed are people whose only activity consisted of work around the house or unpaid volunteer work for religious, charitable, and similar organizations; also excluded are all institutionalized people and people on active duty in the United States Armed Forces.

Civilian Employed – This term is defined exactly the same as the term "employed" above.

Unemployed – All civilians 16 years old and over are classified as unemployed if they (1) were neither "at work" nor "with a job but not at work" during the reference week, and (2) were actively looking for work during the last 4 weeks, and (3) were available to start a job. Also included as unemployed are civilians who did not work at all during the reference week, were waiting to be called back to a job from which they had been laid off, and were available for work except for temporary illness. Examples of job seeking activities are:

- Registering at a public or private employment office
- Meeting with prospective employers
- Investigating possibilities for starting a professional practice or opening a business
- Placing or answering advertisements
- Writing letters of application
- Being on a union or professional register

RACE AND HISPANIC ORIGIN OF HOUSEHOLDER, Items 29 through 37

Source: Table B11001, B11001B, B11001C, B11001D, B11001E, B11001F, B11001G, B11001H, B11001I. Household Type (Including Living Alone) for individual race and Hispanic origin groups.

Universe: Households

Households are classified by the race or Hispanic origin of the householder rather than the race or Hispanic origin of each individual.

White. A person having origins in any of the original peoples of Europe, the Middle East, or North Africa. It includes people who indicate their race as "White" or report entries such as Irish, German, Italian, Lebanese, Arab, Moroccan, or Caucasian.

Black or African American. A person having origins in any of the Black racial groups of Africa. It includes people who indicate their race as "Black, African Am., or Negro" or report entries such as African American, Kenyan, Nigerian, or Haitian.

American Indian or Alaska Native. A person having origins in any of the original peoples of North and South America (including Central America) and who maintains tribal affiliation or community attachment. This category includes people who indicate their race as "American Indian or Alaska Native" or report entries such as Navajo, Blackfeet, Inupiat, Yup'ik,

or Central American Indian groups, or South American Indian groups. Respondents who identified themselves as "American Indian or Alaska Native" were asked to report their enrolled or principal tribe.

Asian. A person having origins in any of the original peoples of the Far East, Southeast Asia, or the Indian subcontinent including, for example, Cambodia, China, India, Japan, Korea, Malaysia, Pakistan, the Philippine Islands, Thailand, and Vietnam. It includes people who indicate their race as "Asian Indian," "Chinese," "Filipino," "Korean," "Japanese," "Vietnamese," and "Other Asian" or provide other detailed Asian responses.

Native Hawaiian or Other Pacific Islander. A person having origins in any of the original peoples of Hawaii, Guam, Samoa, or other Pacific Islands. It includes people who indicate their race as "Native Hawaiian," "Guamanian or Chamorro," "Samoan," and "Other Pacific Islander" or provide other detailed Pacific Islander responses.

Some Other Race. Includes all other responses not included in the "White," "Black or African American," "American Indian or Alaska Native," "Asian," and "Native Hawaiian or Other Pacific Islander" race categories described above. Respondents reporting entries such as multiracial, mixed, interracial, or a Hispanic, Latino, or Spanish group (for example, Mexican, Puerto Rican, Cuban, or Spanish) in response to the race question are included in this category.

Two or More Races. People may choose to provide two or more races either by checking two or more race response check boxes, by providing multiple responses, or by some combination of check boxes and other responses. The race response categories shown on the questionnaire are collapsed into the five minimum race groups identified by OMB, and the Census Bureau's "Some Other Race" category. For data product purposes, "Two or More Races" refers to combinations of two or more of the following race categories:

1. White
2. Black or African American
3. American Indian or Alaska Native
4. Asian
5. Native Hawaiian or Other Pacific Islander
6. Some Other Race

There are 57 possible combinations involving the race categories shown above. Thus, according to this approach, a response of "White" and "Asian" was tallied as Two or More Races, while a response of "Japanese" and "Chinese" was not because "Japanese" and "Chinese" are both Asian responses.

Race Concepts. Given the many possible ways of displaying data on race, data products will provide varying levels of detail.

There are several concepts used to display and tabulate race information for the six major race categories (White; Black or African American; American Indian or Alaska Native; Asian; Native Hawaiian or Other Pacific Islander; and Some Other Race) and the various details within these groups.

The concept "race alone" includes people who reported a single entry (i.e., Korean) and no other race, as well as people who reported two or more entries within the same major race group (i.e., Asian). For example, respondents who reported Korean and Vietnamese are part of the larger "Asian alone" race group.

The concept "race alone or in combination" includes people who reported a single race alone (i.e., Asian) and people who reported that race in combination with one or more of the other major race groups (i.e., White, Black or African American, American Indian and Alaska Native, Native Hawaiian and Other Pacific Islander, and Some Other Race). The "race alone or in combination" concept, therefore, represents the maximum number of people who reported as that race group, either alone, or in combination with another race(s). The sum of the six individual race "alone or in combination" categories may add to more than the total population because people who reported more than one race were tallied in each race category.

This table uses the concept "race alone."

Hispanic or Latino origin. The terms "Hispanic," "Latino," and "Spanish" are used interchangeably. Some respondents identify with all three terms while others may identify with only one of these three specific terms. Hispanics or Latinos who identify with the terms "Hispanic," "Latino," or "Spanish" are those who classify themselves in one of the specific Hispanic, Latino, or Spanish categories listed on the questionnaire ("Mexican," "Puerto Rican," or "Cuban") as well as those who indicate that they are "another Hispanic, Latino, or Spanish origin." People who do not identify with one of the specific origins listed on the questionnaire but indicate that they are "another Hispanic, Latino, or Spanish origin" are those whose origins are from Spain, the Spanish-speaking countries of Central or South America, or the Dominican Republic. Up to two write-in responses to the "another Hispanic, Latino, or Spanish origin" category are coded.

Origin can be viewed as the heritage, nationality group, lineage, or country of birth of the person or the person's parents or ancestors before their arrival in the United States. People who identify their origin as Hispanic, Latino, or Spanish may be of any race.

HOUSEHOLD TYPE BY RACE AND HISPANIC ORIGIN OF HOUSEHOLDER, Items 38 through 77

Source: Table B11001, B11001B, B11001C, B11001D, B11001E, B11001F, B11001G, B11001H, B11001I.

Household Type (Including Living Alone) for individual race and Hispanic origin groups.

Universe: Households

See above definitions of Household Type, Race, and Hispanic Origin.

HOUSEHOLD TYPE BY AGE OF HOUSEHOLDER, Items 78 through 95

Source: B25011. Tenure by Household Type (Including Living Alone) and Age of Householder

Universe: Occupied housing units

The age classification is based on the age of the person in complete years at the time of interview. Both age and date of birth are used in combination to calculate the most accurate age at the time of the interview. Respondents are asked to give an age in whole, completed years as of interview date as well as the month, day and year of birth. People are not to round an age up if the person is close to having a birthday, and to estimate an age if the exact age is not known. An additional instruction on babies also asks respondents to print "0" for babies less than one year old.

HOMEOWNERSHIP RATES, Items 96 through 99

Source: B25011. Tenure by Household Type (Including Living Alone) and Age of Householder

Universe: Occupied housing units

Owner-Occupied – A housing unit is owner-occupied if the owner or co-owner lives in the unit, even if it is mortgaged or not fully paid for. The owner or co-owner must live in the unit and usually is Person 1 on the questionnaire. The unit is "Owned by you or someone in this household with a mortgage or loan" if it is being purchased with a mortgage or some other debt arrangement such as a deed of trust, trust deed, contract to purchase, land contract, or purchase agreement. The unit also is considered owned with a mortgage if it is built on leased land and there is a mortgage on the unit. Mobile homes occupied by owners with installment loan balances also are included in this category.

A housing unit is "Owned by you or someone in this household free and clear (without a mortgage or loan)" if there is no mortgage or other similar debt on the house, apartment, or mobile home including units built on leased land if the unit is owned outright without a mortgage.

HOUSEHOLDS WITH PERSONS UNDER 18 YEARS OLD, Item 100

Source: B11005. Households by Presence of People under 18 Years by Household Type

Universe: Households

HOUSEHOLDS WITH PERSONS AGE 65 OR OLDER, Item 101

Source: B11007. Households by Presence of People 65 Years and Over, Household Size and Household Type

Universe: Households

AVERAGE HOUSEHOLD SIZE, Item 102

Source: B25010. Average Household Size of Occupied Housing Units by Tenure

Universe: Occupied housing units

Average Household Size – A measure obtained by dividing the number of people in households by the number of households. Average household size is rounded to the nearest hundredth.

Table A-2, A-3, and A-4. Counties with populations of 50,000 or more, Metropolitan Areas, Cities with Populations of 50,000 or more

HOUSEHOLD TYPE, Items 1 through 7

Source: Table B11001. Household Type (including Living Alone)

Universe: Households

Household – A household includes all the people who occupy a housing unit. (People not living in households are classified as living in group quarters.) A housing unit is a house, an apartment, a mobile home, a group of rooms, or a single room that is occupied (or if vacant, is intended for occupancy) as separate living quarters. Separate living quarters are those in which the occupants live separately from any other people in the building and which have direct access from the outside of the building or through a common hall. The occupants may be a single family, one person living alone, two or more families living together, or any other group of related or unrelated people who share living arrangements.

Householder – One person in each household is designated as the householder. In most cases, this is the person or one of the people in whose name the home is owned, being bought, or rented and who is listed on line one of the survey questionnaire. If there is no such person in the household, any adult household member 15 years old and over could be designated as the householder.

Households are classified by type according to the sex of the householder and the presence of relatives. Two types of householders are distinguished: a family householder and a nonfamily householder. A family householder is a householder living with one or more individuals related to him or her by birth, marriage, or adoption. The householder and all people in the household related to him or her are family members. A nonfamily householder is a householder living alone or with nonrelatives only.

Family Households – A family consists of a householder and one or more other people living in the same household who are related to the householder by birth, marriage, or adoption. All people in a household who are related to the householder are regarded as members of his or her family. A family household may contain people not related to the householder, but those people are not included as part of the householder's family in tabulations. Thus, the number of family households is equal to the number of families, but family households may include more members than do families. A household can contain only one family for purposes of tabulations. Not all households contain families since a household may comprise a group of unrelated people or of one person living alone – these are called nonfamily households. Families are classified by type as either a "married-couple family" or "other family" according to the sex of the householder and the presence of relatives. The data on family type are based on answers to questions on sex and relationship that were asked of all people.

- Married-Couple Family – A family in which the householder and his or her spouse are listed as members of the same household.
- Other Family:
  - Male Householder, No Spouse Present – A family with a male householder and no spouse of householder present.
  - Female Householder, No Spouse Present – A family with a female householder and no spouse of householder present.

Family households and married-couple families include same-sex married couples, beginning with the 2013 data.

Nonfamily Household – A householder living alone or with nonrelatives only. Unmarried couples households, whether opposite-sex or same-sex, with no relatives of the householder present are tabulated in nonfamily households.

UNMARRIED PARTNER HOUSEHOLDS, Items 8 and 9

Source: Table B11009. Unmarried-Partner Households and Household Type by Sex of Partner.

Universe: Households

Unmarried-Partner Household – An unmarried-partner household is a household other than a "married-couple household" that includes a householder and an "unmarried partner." An "unmarried partner" can be of the same sex or of the opposite sex as the householder. An "unmarried partner" in an "unmarried-partner household" is an adult who is unrelated to the householder, but shares living quarters and has a close personal relationship with the householder. An unmarried-partner household also may be a family household or a nonfamily household, depending on the presence or absence of another person in the household who is related to the householder by birth or adoption. There may be only one unmarried partner per household, and an unmarried partner may not be included in a married-couple household, as the householder cannot have both a spouse and an unmarried partner.

AVERAGE HOUSEHOLD SIZE, Item 10

Source: B25010. Average Household Size of Occupied Housing Units by Tenure

Universe: Occupied housing units

Average Household Size – A measure obtained by dividing the number of people in households by the number of households. Average household size is rounded to the nearest hundredth.

RACE AND HISPANIC ORIGIN OF HOUSEHOLDER, Items 11 through 14

Source: Table B11001B, B11001D, B11001H, B11001I. Household Type (Including Living Alone) for individual race and Hispanic origin groups.

Universe: Households

Households are classified by the race or Hispanic origin of the householder rather than the race or Hispanic origin of each individual.

White. A person having origins in any of the original peoples of Europe, the Middle East, or North Africa. It includes people who indicate their race as "White" or report entries such as Irish, German, Italian, Lebanese, Arab, Moroccan, or Caucasian.

Black or African American. A person having origins in any of the Black racial groups of Africa. It includes people who indicate their race as "Black, African Am., or Negro" or report entries such as African American, Kenyan, Nigerian, or Haitian.

Asian. A person having origins in any of the original peoples of the Far East, Southeast Asia, or the Indian subcontinent including, for example, Cambodia, China, India, Japan, Korea,

Malaysia, Pakistan, the Philippine Islands, Thailand, and Vietnam. It includes people who indicate their race as "Asian Indian," "Chinese," "Filipino," "Korean," "Japanese," "Vietnamese," and "Other Asian" or provide other detailed Asian responses.

The concept "race alone" includes people who reported a single entry (i.e., Korean) and no other race, as well as people who reported two or more entries within the same major race group (i.e., Asian). For example, respondents who reported Korean and Vietnamese are part of the larger "Asian alone" race group.

This table uses the concept "race alone."

Hispanic or Latino origin. The terms "Hispanic," "Latino," and "Spanish" are used interchangeably. Some respondents identify with all three terms while others may identify with only one of these three specific terms. Hispanics or Latinos who identify with the terms "Hispanic," "Latino," or "Spanish" are those who classify themselves in one of the specific Hispanic, Latino, or Spanish categories listed on the questionnaire ("Mexican," "Puerto Rican," or "Cuban") as well as those who indicate that they are "another Hispanic, Latino, or Spanish origin." People who do not identify with one of the specific origins listed on the questionnaire but indicate that they are "another Hispanic, Latino, or Spanish origin" are those whose origins are from Spain, the Spanish-speaking countries of Central or South America, or the Dominican Republic. Up to two write-in responses to the "another Hispanic, Latino, or Spanish origin" category are coded.

Origin can be viewed as the heritage, nationality group, lineage, or country of birth of the person or the person's parents or ancestors before their arrival in the United States. People who identify their origin as Hispanic, Latino, or Spanish may be of any race.

AGE OF HOUSEHOLDER, Items 15 through 17

Source: B25011. Tenure by Household Type (Including Living Alone) and Age of Householder

Universe: Occupied housing units

The age classification is based on the age of the person in complete years at the time of interview. Both age and date of birth are used in combination to calculate the most accurate age at the time of the interview. Respondents are asked to give an age in whole, completed years as of interview date as well as the month, day and year of birth. People are not to round an age up if the person is close to having a birthday, and to estimate an age if the exact age is not known. An additional instruction on babies also asks respondents to print "0" for babies less than one year old.

HOUSEHOLDS WITH PERSONS UNDER 18 YEARS OLD, Item 18

Source: B11005. Households by Presence of People under 18 Years by Household Type

Universe: Households

HOUSEHOLDS WITH PERSONS AGE 65 OR OLDER, Item 19

Source: B11007. Households by Presence of People 65 Years and Over, Household Size and Household Type

Universe: Households

HOMEOWNERSHIP RATES, Item 20

Source: B25011. Tenure by Household Type (Including Living Alone) and Age of Householder

Universe: Occupied housing units

Owner-Occupied – A housing unit is owner-occupied if the owner or co-owner lives in the unit, even if it is mortgaged or not fully paid for. The owner or co-owner must live in the unit and usually is Person 1 on the questionnaire. The unit is "Owned by you or someone in this household with a mortgage or loan" if it is being purchased with a mortgage or some other debt arrangement such as a deed of trust, trust deed, contract to purchase, land contract, or purchase agreement. The unit also is considered owned with a mortgage if it is built on leased land and there is a mortgage on the unit. Mobile homes occupied by owners with installment loan balances also are included in this category.

A housing unit is "Owned by you or someone in this household free and clear (without a mortgage or loan)" if there is no mortgage or other similar debt on the house, apartment, or mobile home including units built on leased land if the unit is owned outright without a mortgage.

Part B — RELATIONSHIPS

Table B-1. States

POPULATION, Items 1 through 3, 37 through 39

Source: Table B09019. Household Type (Including Living Alone) by Relationship

Universe: Total Population

In the ACS, the total population is based on the Census Bureau's official annual population estimates, adjusted to reflect the appropriate time period.

Population in households. The data shown for population in households is the total population minus any people living in group quarters. All people occupying housing units are counted, including the householder, occupants related to the householder, and lodgers, roomers, boarders, and so forth.

Population in Group Quarters. All people not living in households. Two general categories of people in group quarters are recognized: (1) the institutionalized population which includes people under formally authorized supervised care or custody in institutions at the time of enumeration (such as correctional institutions, nursing homes, and juvenile institutions) and (2) the noninstitutionalized population which includes all people who live in group quarters other than institutions (such as college dormitories, military quarters, and group homes). The noninstitutionalized population includes all people who live in group quarters other than institutions.

RELATIONSHIP BY HOUSEHOLD TYPE, Items 4 through 36, 40 through 73

Source: Table B09019. Household Type (Including Living Alone) by Relationship

Universe: Total Population

Relationship is the relationship to the Householder

Householder – One person in each household is designated as the householder. In most cases, this is the person or one of the people in whose name the home is owned, being bought, or rented and who is listed on line one of the survey questionnaire. If there is no such person in the household, any adult household member 15 years old and over could be designated as the householder.

Households are classified by type according to the sex of the householder and the presence of relatives. Two types of householders are distinguished: a family householder and a nonfamily householder. A family householder is a householder living with one or more individuals related to him or her by birth, marriage, or adoption. The householder and all people in the household related to him or her are family members. A nonfamily householder is a householder living alone or with nonrelatives only.

Spouse – Includes a person married to and living with the householder. The category "married couple" includes people in formal marriages, as well as people in common-law marriages. In these tabulations, "Spouse" and "married couple" includes same-sex married couples.

Child – Includes a son or daughter by birth, a stepchild, or adopted child of the householder, regardless of the child's age or marital status. The category excludes sons-in-law, daughters-in-law, and foster children.

- Biological son or daughter – The son or daughter of the householder by birth.
- Adopted son or daughter – The son or daughter of the householder by legal adoption. If a stepson or stepdaughter has been legally adopted by the householder, the child is then classified as an adopted child.
- Stepson or stepdaughter – The son or daughter of the householder through marriage but not by birth, excluding sons-in-law and daughters-in-law. If a stepson or stepdaughter of the householder has been legally adopted by the householder, the child is then classified as an adopted child.

Own Child – A never-married child under 18 years who is a son or daughter by birth, a stepchild, or an adopted child of the householder. In certain tabulations, own children are further classified as living with two parents or with one parent only. Own children of the householder living with two parents are by definition found only in married-couple families.

Related Child – Any child under 18 years old who is related to the householder by birth, marriage, or adoption. Related children of the householder include ever-married as well as never-married children. Children, by definition, exclude persons under 18 years who maintain households or are spouses or unmarried partners of householders.

Other Relatives – In tabulations, the category "other relatives" includes any household member related to the householder by birth, marriage, or adoption, but not included specifically in another relationship category. In this table, the following categories are shown:

- Grandchild – The grandson or granddaughter of the householder.
- Brother/Sister – The brother or sister of the householder, including stepbrothers, stepsisters, and brothers and sisters by adoption. Brothers-in-law and sisters-in-law are included in the "Other Relative" category on the questionnaire.
- Parent – The father or mother of the householder, including a stepparent or adoptive parent. Fathers-in-law and mothers-in-law are included in the "Parent-in-law" category on the questionnaire.
- Parent-in-law – The mother-in-law or father-in-law of the householder.
- Son-in-law or daughter-in-law – The spouse of the child of the householder.
- Other Relatives – Anyone not listed in a reported category above who is related to the householder by birth, marriage, or adoption (brother-in-law, grandparent, nephew, aunt, cousin, and so forth).

Nonrelatives – This category includes any household member, including foster children, not related to the householder

by birth, marriage, or adoption. The following categories are included in this table:

- Roomer or Boarder – A roomer or boarder is a person who lives in a room in the household of the householder. Some sort of cash or noncash payment (e.g., chores) is usually made for their living accommodations.
- Housemate or Roommate – A housemate or roommate is a person age 15 years old and over, who is not related to the householder, and who shares living quarters primarily in order to share expenses.
- Unmarried Partner – An unmarried partner is a person age 15 years old and over, who is not related to the householder, who shares living quarters, and who has a close personal relationship with the householder.
- Foster Child – A foster child is a person under 21 years old, who is placed by the local government in a household to receive parental care. Foster children may be living in the household for just a brief period or for several years. Foster children are nonrelatives of the householder. If the foster child is also related to the householder, the child is classified as that specific relative.
- Other Nonrelatives – Anyone who is not related by birth, marriage, or adoption to the householder and who is not described by the categories given above. When relationship is not reported for an individual, it is imputed according to the responses for age, sex, and marital status for that person while maintaining consistency with responses for other individuals in the household.

Unrelated Individual – An unrelated individual is: (1) a householder living alone or with nonrelatives only, (2) a household member who is not related to the householder, or (3) a person living in group quarters who is not an inmate of an institution.

Family Households – A family consists of a householder and one or more other people living in the same household who are related to the householder by birth, marriage, or adoption. All people in a household who are related to the householder are regarded as members of his or her family. A family household may contain people not related to the householder, but those people are not included as part of the householder's family in tabulations. Thus, the number of family households is equal to the number of families, but family households may include more members than do families. A household can contain only one family for purposes of tabulations. Not all households contain families since a household may be comprised of a group of unrelated people or of one person living alone – these are called nonfamily households. Families are classified by type as either a "married-couple family" or "other family" according to the sex of the householder and the presence of relatives.

- Married-Couple Family – A family in which the householder and his or her spouse are listed as members of the same household.

- Other Family:
  - Male Householder, No Wife Present – A family with a male householder and no spouse of householder present.
  - Female Householder, No Husband Present – A family with a female householder and no spouse of householder present.

Family households and married-couple families include same-sex married couples, beginning with the 2013 data.

Nonfamily Household – A householder living alone or with nonrelatives only. Unmarried couples households, whether opposite-sex or same-sex, with no relatives of the householder present are tabulated in nonfamily households.

RELATIONSHIP IN SUBFAMILIES, Items 74 through 95

Source: Table B11014. Population in Subfamilies by Subfamily Type by Relationship

Universe: Population in subfamilies

Subfamily – A subfamily is a married couple (husband and wife interviewed as members of the same household) with or without never-married children under 18 years old, or one parent with one or more never-married children under 18 years old. A subfamily does not maintain its own household, but lives in a household where the householder or householder's spouse is a relative. The number of subfamilies is not included in the count of families, since subfamily members are counted as part of the householder's family.

Subfamilies are defined during processing of data. Same-sex married couples are only shown as the householder and spouse, and are not included in subfamilies.

In this table, subfamilies are further classified by type: married-couple subfamilies, with or without own children; mother-child subfamilies; and father-child subfamilies.

Table B-2, B-3, and B-4. Counties with populations of 50,000 or more, Metropolitan Areas, Cities with Populations of 50,000 or more

POPULATION, Items 1 and 2

Source: Table B09019. Household Type (Including Living Alone) by Relationship

Universe: Total Population

In the ACS, the total population is based on the Census Bureau's official annual population estimates, adjusted to reflect the appropriate time period.

Population in households. The data shown for population in households is the total population minus any people living in group quarters. All people occupying housing units are counted, including the householder, occupants related to the householder, and lodgers, roomers, boarders, and so forth.

RELATIONSHIP BY HOUSEHOLD TYPE, Items 3 through 14

Source: Table B09019. Household Type (Including Living Alone) by Relationship

Universe: Total Population

Relationship is the relationship to the Householder.

Householder – One person in each household is designated as the householder. In most cases, this is the person or one of the people in whose name the home is owned, being bought, or rented and who is listed on line one of the survey questionnaire. If there is no such person in the household, any adult household member 15 years old and over could be designated as the householder.

Households are classified by type according to the sex of the householder and the presence of relatives. Two types of householders are distinguished: a family householder and a nonfamily householder. A family householder is a householder living with one or more individuals related to him or her by birth, marriage, or adoption. The householder and all people in the household related to him or her are family members. A nonfamily householder is a householder living alone or with nonrelatives only.

Spouse – Includes a person married to and living with the householder. The category "married couple" includes people in formal marriages, as well as people in common-law marriages. In tabulations, beginning in 2013, unless otherwise specified, "Spouse" and "married couple" includes same-sex married couples.

Child – Includes a son or daughter by birth, a stepchild, or adopted child of the householder, regardless of the child's age or marital status. The category excludes sons-in-law, daughters-in-law, and foster children.

- Biological son or daughter – The son or daughter of the householder by birth.
- Adopted son or daughter – The son or daughter of the householder by legal adoption. If a stepson or stepdaughter has been legally adopted by the householder, the child is then classified as an adopted child.
- Stepson or stepdaughter – The son or daughter of the householder through marriage but not by birth, excluding sons-in-law and daughters-in-law. If a stepson or stepdaughter of the householder has been legally adopted by

the householder, the child is then classified as an adopted child.

Own Child – A never-married child under 18 years who is a son or daughter by birth, a stepchild, or an adopted child of the householder. In certain tabulations, own children are further classified as living with two parents or with one parent only. Own children of the householder living with two parents are by definition found only in married-couple families.

Related Child – Any child under 18 years old who is related to the householder by birth, marriage, or adoption. Related children of the householder include ever-married as well as never-married children. Children, by definition, exclude persons under 18 years who maintain households or are spouses or unmarried partners of householders.

Other Relatives – This category includes any household member related to the householder by birth, marriage, or adoption, but not the spouse or child of the householder. The following are included:

- Grandchild – The grandson or granddaughter of the householder.
- Brother/Sister – The brother or sister of the householder, including stepbrothers, stepsisters, and brothers and sisters by adoption. Brothers-in-law and sisters-in-law are included in the "Other Relative" category on the questionnaire.
- Parent – The father or mother of the householder, including a stepparent or adoptive parent. Fathers-in-law and mothers-in-law are included in the "Parent-in-law" category on the questionnaire.
- Parent-in-law – The mother-in-law or father-in-law of the householder.
- Son-in-law or daughter-in-law – The spouse of the child of the householder.
- Other Relatives – Anyone not listed in a reported category above who is related to the householder by birth, marriage, or adoption (brother-in-law, grandparent, nephew, aunt, cousin, and so forth).

Nonrelatives – This category includes any household member, including foster children, not related to the householder by birth, marriage, or adoption. The following categories are included:

- Roomer or Boarder – A roomer or boarder is a person who lives in a room in the household of the householder. Some sort of cash or noncash payment (e.g., chores) is usually made for their living accommodations.
- Housemate or Roommate – A housemate or roommate is a person age 15 years old and over, who is not related to the householder, and who shares living quarters primarily in order to share expenses.
- Unmarried Partner – An unmarried partner is a person age 15 years old and over, who is not related to the householder, who shares living quarters, and who has a close personal relationship with the householder.
- Foster Child – A foster child is a person under 21 years old, who is placed by the local government in a household to receive parental care. Foster children may be living in the household for just a brief period or for several years. Foster children are nonrelatives of the householder. If the foster child is also related to the householder, the child is classified as that specific relative.
- Other Nonrelatives – Anyone who is not related by birth, marriage, or adoption to the householder and who is not described by the categories given above.

When relationship is not reported for an individual, it is imputed according to the responses for age, sex, and marital status for that person while maintaining consistency with responses for other individuals in the household.

Unrelated Individual – An unrelated individual is: (1) a householder living alone or with nonrelatives only, (2) a household member who is not related to the householder, or (3) a person living in group quarters who is not an inmate of an institution.

Family Households – A family consists of a householder and one or more other people living in the same household who are related to the householder by birth, marriage, or adoption. All people in a household who are related to the householder are regarded as members of his or her family. A family household may contain people not related to the householder, but those people are not included as part of the householder's family in tabulations. Thus, the number of family households is equal to the number of families, but family households may include more members than do families. A household can contain only one family for purposes of tabulations. Not all households contain families since a household may be comprised of a group of unrelated people or of one person living alone – these are called nonfamily households. Families are classified by type as either a "married-couple family" or "other family" according to the sex of the householder and the presence of relatives.

- Married-Couple Family – A family in which the householder and his or her spouse are listed as members of the same household.
- Other Family:
  - Male Householder, No Wife Present – A family with a male householder and no spouse of householder present.
  - Female Householder, No Husband Present – A family with a female householder and no spouse of householder present.

Family households and married-couple families include same-sex married couples beginning with the 2013 data.

Nonfamily Household – A householder living alone or with nonrelatives only. Unmarried couples households, whether opposite-sex or same-sex, with no relatives of the householder present are tabulated in nonfamily households.

RELATIONSHIP IN SUBFAMILIES, Items 15 through 20

Source: Table B11014. Population in Subfamilies by Subfamily Type by Relationship

Universe: Population in subfamilies

Subfamily – A subfamily is a married couple (husband and wife interviewed as members of the same household) with or without never-married children under 18 years old, or one parent with one or more never-married children under 18 years old. A subfamily does not maintain its own household, but lives in a household where the householder or householder's spouse is a relative. The number of subfamilies is not included in the count of families, since subfamily members are counted as part of the householder's family.

Subfamilies are defined during processing of data. Same-sex married couples are only shown as the householder and spouse, and are not included in subfamilies.

In this table, subfamilies are further classified by type: married-couple subfamilies, with or without own children, and parent-child subfamilies.

Part C — MARRIAGES AND BIRTHS

Table C-1. States.

MARITAL STATUS, Items 1 through 33

Source: Table B12001. Sex by Marital Status for the Population 15 Years and Over

Universe: Population 15 years and over

People 15 and over are asked whether they are "now married," "widowed," "divorced," "separated," or "never married." People in common-law marriages are allowed to report the marital status they considered the most appropriate. When marital status is not reported, it is imputed according to the person's relationship to the householder, sex, and age. Differences in the number of married males and females occur because there is no step in the weighting process to equalize the weighted estimates of husbands and wives.

Never Married – Includes all people who have never been married, including people whose only marriage(s) was annulled.

Ever Married – Includes people ever married at the time of interview (including those now married, separated, widowed, or divorced).

Now Married, Except Separated – Includes people whose current marriage has not ended through widowhood or divorce (regardless of previous marital history), and who are not currently separated. The category may also include couples who live together or people in common-law marriages if they consider this category the most appropriate. In certain tabulations, currently married people are further classified as "spouse present" or "spouse absent."

Separated – Includes people legally separated or otherwise absent from their spouse because of marital discord. Those without a final divorce decree are classified as "separated." This category also includes people who have been deserted or who have parted because they no longer want to live together, but who have not obtained a divorce.

Widowed – Includes widows and widowers who have not remarried.

Divorced – Includes people who are legally divorced and who have not remarried. Those without a final divorce decree are classified as "separated."

Now Married – All people whose current marriage has not ended by widowhood or divorce.

This category includes people defined above as "separated."

- Spouse Present – Married people whose wife or husband was reported as a member of the same household, including those whose spouses may have been temporarily absent for such reasons as travel or hospitalization.
- Spouse Absent – Married people whose wife or husband was not reported as a member of the same household or people reporting they were married and living in a group quarters facility.
  - Separated – Defined above.
  - Spouse Absent, Other – Married people whose wife or husband was not reported as a member of the same household, excluding separated. Included is any person whose spouse was employed and living away from home or in an institution or serving away from home in the Armed Forces.

Note that beginning in 2013, same-sex married couples are included in the married spouse present category.

Differences between the number of married males and the number of married females occur because: some husbands and wives have their usual residence in different areas; and husbands and wives do not have the same weights. By definition, the numbers would be the same.

MEDIAN AGE AT FIRST MARRIAGE, Items 34 and 35

Source: Table B12007. Median Age at First Marriage

Universe: Population 15 to 54 years

Median Age at First Marriage – The median age at first marriage is calculated indirectly by estimating the proportion of young people who will marry during their lifetime, calculating one-half of this proportion, and determining the age (at the time of the survey) of people at this half-way mark by osculatory interpolation. It does not represent the actual median age of the population who married during the calendar year. It is shown to the nearest tenth of a year. Henry S. Shryock and Jacob S. Siegel outline the osculatory procedure in Methods and Materials of Demography, First Edition (May 1973), Volume 1, pages 291–296.

MARITAL HISTORY, Items 36 THROUGH 64

Source: Table B12505. Number of Times Married by Sex by Marital Status; Table B12501. Marriages in the Last Year by Sex by Marital Status; Table B12502. Marriages Ending in Widowhood in the Last Year by Sex by Marital Status; Table B12503. Divorces in the Last Year by Sex by Marital Status;

Universe: Population 15 years and over

Table B12504. Median Duration of Current Marriage in Years by Sex by Marital Status

Universe: Population 15 years and over who are now married or separated

Marital History – Beginning in 2008, people 15 years and over who were ever married (married, widowed, separated, or divorced) were asked if they had been married, widowed, or divorced in the past 12 months. They are asked how many times (once, two times, or three or more times) they have been married, and the year of their last marriage.

BIRTHS, Items 65 through 92

Source: Table B13002. Women 15 to 50 Years who Had a Birth in the Past 12 Months by Marital Status and Age; Table B13004. Women 15 to 50 Years who Had a Birth in the Past 12 Months by Marital Status and Presence of Unmarried Partner

Universe: Women 15 to 50 years in households

Women 15 to 50 years old were asked if they had given birth in the past 12 months. The question was asked of all women 15 to 50 years old regardless of marital status.

Table C-2, C-3, and C-4. Counties with populations of 50,000 or more, Metropolitan Areas, Cities with Populations of 50,000 or more

MARITAL STATUS, Items 1 through 12

Source: Table B12001. Sex by Marital Status for the Population 15 Years and Over

Universe: Population 15 years and over

People 15 and over are asked whether they are "now married," "widowed," "divorced," "separated," or "never married." People in common-law marriages are allowed to report the marital status they considered the most appropriate. When marital status is not reported, it is imputed according to the person's relationship to the householder, sex, and age. Differences in the number of married males and females occur because there is no step in the weighting process to equalize the weighted estimates of husbands and wives. Never Married – Includes all people who have never been married, including people whose only marriage(s) was annulled.

Ever Married – Includes people ever married at the time of interview (including those now married, separated, widowed, or divorced).

Now Married, Except Separated – Includes people whose current marriage has not ended through widowhood or divorce (regardless of previous marital history), and who are not currently separated. The category may also include couples who live together or people in common-law marriages if they consider this category the most appropriate. In certain tabulations, currently married people are further classified as "spouse present" or "spouse absent."

Separated – Includes people legally separated or otherwise absent from their spouse because of marital discord. Those without a final divorce decree are classified as "separated." This category also includes people who have been deserted or who have parted because they no longer want to live together, but who have not obtained a divorce.

Widowed – Includes widows and widowers who have not remarried.

Divorced – Includes people who are legally divorced and who have not remarried. Those without a final divorce decree are classified as "separated."

Now Married – All people whose current marriage has not ended by widowhood or divorce.

This category includes people defined above as "separated."

- Spouse Present – Married people whose wife or husband was reported as a member of the same household, including those whose spouses may have been temporarily absent for such reasons as travel or hospitalization.
- Spouse Absent – Married people whose wife or husband was not reported as a member of the same household or

people reporting they were married and living in a group quarters facility.

- Separated – Defined above.
- Spouse Absent, Other – Married people whose wife or husband was not reported as a member of the same household, excluding separated. Included is any person whose spouse was employed and living away from home or in an institution or serving away from home in the Armed Forces.

Note that beginning in 2013, same-sex married couples are included in the married spouse present category.

Differences between the number of married males and the number of married females occur because: some husbands and wives have their usual residence in different areas; and husbands and wives do not have the same weights. By definition, the numbers would be the same.

BIRTHS, Items 13 through 22

Source: Table B13002. Women 15 to 50 Years who Had a Birth in the Past 12 Months by Marital Status and Age; Table B13004. Women 15 to 50 Years who Had a Birth in the Past 12 Months by Marital Status and Presence of Unmarried Partner

Universe: Women 15 to 50 years in households

Women 15 to 50 years old were asked if they had given birth in the past 12 months. The question was asked of all women 15 to 50 years old regardless of marital status.

Part D — CHILDREN

Table D-1. States

NATIVITY AND PARENTAGE, Items 1 through 8, 21 through 27, 40 through 46, 59 through 65

Source: Table C05009. Age and Nativity of Own Children under 18 Years in Families and Subfamilies by Nativity of Parents

Universe: Own children under 18 years in families and subfamilies

Nativity – Information on place of birth and citizenship status was used to classify the population into two major categories: native and foreign born.

Native – The native population includes anyone who was a U.S. citizen at birth. The native population includes those born in the United States, Puerto Rico, American Samoa, Guam, the Northern Marianas, or the U.S. Virgin Islands, as well as those born abroad of at least one U.S. citizen parent.

Foreign Born – The foreign-born population includes anyone who was not a U.S. citizen at birth. This includes respondents who indicated they were a U.S. citizen by naturalization or not a U.S. citizen.

Nativity of parent indicates the nativity (native or foreign born) of the parent(s) of children living in a family or subfamily with one or more parents present in the household. It applies to "own children," that is, never married children under 18 years of age living with one or more of their parents. The nativity of the child's parent(s) is determined by the citizenship status of the parent(s). A person is considered native if he/she is a native United States citizen at birth, and foreign born if he/she is not a United States citizen at birth.

LABOR FORCE STATUS OF PARENTS, Items 9 through 20, 28 through 39, 47 through 58, 66 through 77

Source: Table B23008. Age of Own Children under 18 Years in Families and Subfamilies by Living Arrangements by Employment Status of Parents

Universe: Own children under 18 years in families and subfamilies

The series of questions on employment status was designed to identify, in this sequence: (1) people who worked at any time during the reference week (week before their interview); (2) people on temporary layoff who were available for work; (3) people who did not work during the reference week but who had jobs or businesses from which they were temporarily absent (excluding layoff); (4) people who did not work during the reference week, but who were looking for work during the last four weeks and were available for work during the reference week; and (5) people not in the labor force. The employment status data shown in ACS tabulations relate to people 16 years old and over.

Civilian Labor Force – Consists of people classified as employed or unemployed in accordance with the criteria described above.

Employed – This category includes all civilians 16 years old and over who either (1) were "at work," that is, those who did any work at all during the reference week as paid employees, worked in their own business or profession, worked on their own farm, or worked 15 hours or more as unpaid workers on a family farm or in a family business; or (2) were "with a job but not at work," that is, those who did not work during the reference week but had jobs or businesses from which they were temporarily absent due to illness, bad weather, industrial dispute, vacation, or other personal reasons. Excluded from the employed are people whose only activity consisted of work around the house or unpaid volunteer work for religious, charitable, and similar organizations; also excluded are all institutionalized people and people on active duty in the United States Armed Forces.

Unemployed – All civilians 16 years old and over are classified as unemployed if they (1) were neither "at work" nor "with a job but not at work" during the reference week, and (2) were actively looking for work during the last 4 weeks, and (3) were available to start a job. Also included as unemployed are civilians who did not work at all during the reference week, were waiting to be called back to a job from which they had been laid off, and were available for work except for temporary illness. Examples of job seeking activities are:

- Registering at a public or private employment office
- Meeting with prospective employers
- Investigating possibilities for starting a professional practice or opening a business
- Placing or answering advertisements
- Writing letters of application
- Being on a union or professional register

GRANDPARENTS AS CAREGIVERS, Items 78 through 85

Source: Table B10002. Grandchildren under 18 Years Living with a Grandparent Householder by Grandparent Responsibility and Presence of Parent

Universe: Grandchildren under 18 living with grandparent householder

Data are collected on whether a grandchild lives with a grandparent in the household, whether the grandparent has responsibility for the basic needs of the grandchild, and the duration of that responsibility.

Existence of a Grandparent Living with a Grandchild in the Household – This was determined by a "Yes" answer to the question, "Does this person have any of his/her own grandchildren under the age of 18 living in this house or apartment?" This question was asked of people 15 years of age and over. Because of the low numbers of persons under 30 years old living with their grandchildren, data were only tabulated for people 30 and over.

Responsibility for Basic Needs – This question determines if the grandparent is financially responsible for food, shelter, clothing, day care, etc., for any or all grandchildren living in the household. Grandparent responsibility is further classified by presence of parent (of the grandchild).

Table D-2, D-3, and D-4. Counties with populations of 50,000 or more, Metropolitan Areas, Cities with Populations of 50,000 or more

NATIVITY AND PARENTAGE, Items 1 through 4, 10 through 12

Source: Table C05009. Age and Nativity of Own Children under 18 Years in Families and Subfamilies by Nativity of Parents

Universe: Own children under 18 years in families and subfamilies

Nativity – Information on place of birth and citizenship status was used to classify the population into two major categories: native and foreign born.

Native – The native population includes anyone who was a U.S. citizen at birth. The native population includes those born in the United States, Puerto Rico, American Samoa, Guam, the Northern Marianas, or the U.S. Virgin Islands, as well as those born abroad of at least one U.S. citizen parent.

Foreign Born – The foreign-born population includes anyone who was not a U.S. citizen at birth. This includes respondents who indicated they were a U.S. citizen by naturalization or not a U.S. citizen.

Nativity of parent indicates the nativity (native or foreign born) of the parent(s) of children living in a family or subfamily with one or more parents present in the household. It applies to "own children," that is, never married children under 18 years of age living with one or more of their parents. The nativity of the child's parent(s) is determined by the citizenship status of the parent(s). A person is considered native if he/she is a native United States citizen at birth, and foreign born if he/she is not a United States citizen at birth.

LABOR FORCE STATUS OF PARENTS, Items 5 through 9, 13 through 17

Source: Table B23008. Age of Own Children under 18 Years in Families and Subfamilies by Living Arrangements by Employment Status of Parents

Universe: Own children under 18 years in families and subfamilies

The series of questions on employment status was designed to identify, in this sequence: (1) people who worked at any time during the reference week (week before their interview); (2) people on temporary layoff who were available for work; (3) people who did not work during the reference week but who had jobs or businesses from which they were temporarily absent (excluding layoff); (4) people who did not work during the reference week, but who were looking for work during the last four weeks and were available for work during the reference week; and (5) people not in the labor force. The employment status data shown in ACS tabulations relate to people 16 years old and over.

Civilian Labor Force – Consists of people classified as employed or unemployed in accordance with the criteria described above.

Employed – This category includes all civilians 16 years old and over who either (1) were "at work," that is, those who did any work at all during the reference week as paid employees, worked in their own business or profession, worked on their own farm, or worked 15 hours or more as unpaid workers on a family farm or in a family business; or (2) were "with a job but not at work," that is, those who did not work during the reference week but had jobs or businesses from which they were temporarily absent due to illness, bad weather, industrial dispute, vacation, or other personal reasons. Excluded from the employed are people whose only activity consisted of work around the house or unpaid volunteer work for religious, charitable, and similar organizations; also excluded are all institutionalized people and people on active duty in the United States Armed Forces.

Unemployed – All civilians 16 years old and over are classified as unemployed if they (1) were neither "at work" nor "with a job but not at work" during the reference week, and (2) were actively looking for work during the last 4 weeks, and (3) were available to start a job. Also included as unemployed are civilians who did not work at all during the reference week, were waiting to be called back to a job from which they had been laid off, and were available for work except for temporary illness. Examples of job seeking activities are:

- Registering at a public or private employment office
- Meeting with prospective employers
- Investigating possibilities for starting a professional practice or opening a business
- Placing or answering advertisements
- Writing letters of application
- Being on a union or professional register

GRANDPARENTS AS CAREGIVERS, Items 18 through 20

Source: Table B10002. Grandchildren under 18 Years Living with a Grandparent Householder by Grandparent Responsibility and Presence of Parent

Universe: Grandchildren under 18 living with grandparent householder

Data are collected on whether a grandchild lives with a grandparent in the household, whether the grandparent has responsibility for the basic needs of the grandchild, and the duration of that responsibility.

Existence of a Grandparent Living with a Grandchild in the Household – This was determined by a "Yes" answer to the question, "Does this person have any of his/her own grandchildren under the age of 18 living in this house or apartment?" This question was asked of people 15 years of age and over. Because of the low numbers of persons under 30 years old living with their grandchildren, data were only tabulated for people 30 and over.

Responsibility for Basic Needs – This question determines if the grandparent is financially responsible for food, shelter, clothing, day care, etc., for any or all grandchildren living in the household. Grandparent responsibility is further classified by presence of parent (of the grandchild).

Part E — INCOME, POVERTY, AND HEALTH INSURANCE

Table E-1. States

MEDIAN INCOME, Items 1 through 15

Source: Table B19126. Median Family Income in the Past 12 Months (In 2013 Inflation-Adjusted Dollars) by Family Type by Presence of Own Children under 18 Years; Table B1912. Median Family Income in the Past 12 Months (In 2013 Inflation-Adjusted Dollars) by Number of Earners in Family.

Universe: Families

"Total income" is the sum of the amounts reported separately for wage or salary income; net self-employment income; interest, dividends, or net rental or royalty income or income from estates and trusts; Social Security or Railroad Retirement income; Supplemental Security Income (SSI); public assistance or welfare payments; retirement, survivor, or disability pensions; and all other income.

Receipts from the following sources are not included as income: capital gains, money received from the sale of property (unless the recipient was engaged in the business of selling such property); the value of income "in kind" from food stamps, public housing subsidies, medical care, employer contributions for individuals, etc.; withdrawal of bank deposits; money borrowed; tax refunds; exchange of money between relatives living in the same household; gifts and lump-sum inheritances, insurance payments, and other types of lump-sum receipts.

Income Type in the Past 12 Months

The eight types of income reported in the ACS are defined as follows:

1. Wage or salary income: Wage or salary income includes total money earnings received for work performed as an

employee during the past 12 months. It includes wages, salary, Armed Forces pay, commissions, tips, piece-rate payments, and cash bonuses earned before deductions were made for taxes, bonds, pensions, union dues, etc.

2. Self-employment income: Self-employment income includes both farm and non-farm self-employment income. Farm self-employment income includes net money income (gross receipts minus operating expenses) from the operation of a farm by a person on his or her own account, as an owner, renter, or sharecropper. Gross receipts include the value of all products sold, government farm programs, money received from the rental of farm equipment to others, and incidental receipts from the sale of wood, sand, gravel, etc. Operating expenses include cost of feed, fertilizer, seed, and other farming supplies, cash wages paid to farmhands, depreciation charges, rent, interest on farm mortgages, farm building repairs, farm taxes (not state and federal personal income taxes), etc. The value of fuel, food, or other farm products used for family living is not included as part of net income.

   Non-farm self-employment income includes net money income (gross receipts minus expenses) from one's own business, professional enterprise, or partnership. Gross receipts include the value of all goods sold and services rendered. Expenses include costs of goods purchased, rent, heat, light, power, depreciation charges, wages and salaries paid, business taxes (not personal income taxes), etc.

3. Interest, dividends, net rental income, royalty income, or income from estates and trusts: Interest, dividends, or net rental income includes interest on savings or bonds, dividends from stockholdings or membership in associations, net income from rental of property to others and receipts from boarders or lodgers, net royalties, and periodic payments from an estate or trust fund.

4. Social Security income: Social Security income includes Social Security pensions and survivor benefits, permanent disability insurance payments made by the Social Security Administration prior to deductions for medical insurance, and railroad retirement insurance checks from the U.S. government. Medicare reimbursements are not included.

5. Supplemental Security Income (SSI): Supplemental Security Income (SSI) is a nationwide U.S. assistance program administered by the Social Security Administration that guarantees a minimum level of income for needy aged, blind, or disabled individuals.

6. Public assistance income: Public assistance income includes general assistance and Temporary Assistance to Needy Families (TANF). Separate payments received for hospital or other medical care (vendor payments) are excluded. This does not include Supplemental Security Income (SSI) or noncash benefits such as Food Stamps. The terms "public assistance income" and "cash public assistance" are used interchangeably in the 2013 ACS data products.

7. Retirement, survivor, or disability income: Retirement income includes: (1) retirement pensions and survivor benefits from a former employer; labor union; or federal, state, or local government; and the U.S. military; (2) disability income from companies or unions; federal, state, or local government; and the U.S. military; (3) periodic receipts from annuities and insurance; and (4) regular income from IRA and Keogh plans. This does not include Social Security income.

8. All other income: All other income includes unemployment compensation, worker's compensation, Department of Veterans Affairs (VA) payments, alimony and child support, contributions received periodically from people not living in the household, military family allotments, and other kinds of periodic income other than earnings.

Income of Families – In compiling statistics on family income, the incomes of all members 15 years old and over related to the householder are summed and treated as a single amount. Although the family income statistics cover the past 12 months, the characteristics of individuals and the composition of families refer to the time of interview. Thus, the income of the family does not include amounts received by individuals who were members of the family during all or part of the past 12 months if these individuals no longer resided with the family at the time of interview. Similarly, income amounts reported by individuals who did not reside with the family during the past 12 months but who were members of the family at the time of interview are included. However, the composition of most families was the same during the past 12 months as at the time of interview.

Median Income – The median divides the income distribution into two equal parts: one-half of the cases falling below the median income and one-half above the median. For families, the median income is based on the distribution of the total number of families including those with no income. Median income for families is computed on the basis of a standard distribution of 100 groupings of $2500 ranging from zero to a maximum category of $250,000 or more. Median income is rounded to the nearest whole dollar. Median income figures are calculated using linear interpolation.

POVERTY STATUS, Items 16 through 39

Source: Table C17010. Poverty Status in the Past 12 Months of Families by Family Type by Presence of Related Children under 18 Years

Universe: Families

The Census Bureau uses a set of dollar value thresholds that vary by family size and composition to determine who is in poverty. Further, poverty thresholds for people living alone or with nonrelatives (unrelated individuals) vary by age (under 65 years or 65 years and older). The poverty thresholds for two-person families also vary by the age of the householder. If a family's total income is less than the dollar value of the appropriate threshold, then that family and every individual in it are considered to be in poverty. Similarly, if an unrelated individual's total income is less than the appropriate threshold, then that individual is considered to be in poverty. In 2013, the average poverty threshold for a family of four was $23,834.

In determining the poverty status of families and unrelated individuals, the Census Bureau uses thresholds (income cutoffs) arranged in a two-dimensional matrix. The matrix consists of family size (from one person to nine or more people) cross-classified by presence and number of family members under 18 years old (from no children present to eight or more children present). Unrelated individuals and two-person families are further differentiated by age of reference person (householder) (under 65 years old and 65 years old and over). To determine a person's poverty status, one compares the person's total family income in the last 12 months with the poverty threshold appropriate for that person's family size and composition. If the total income of that person's family is less than the threshold appropriate for that family, then the person is considered "below the poverty level," together with every member of his or her family. If a person is not living with anyone related by birth, marriage, or adoption, then the person's own income is compared with his or her poverty threshold. The total number of people below the poverty level is the sum of people in families and the number of unrelated individuals with incomes in the last 12 months below the poverty threshold.

Since ACS is a continuous survey, people respond throughout the year. Because the income questions specify a period covering the last 12 months, the appropriate poverty thresholds are determined by multiplying the base-year poverty thresholds (1982) by the average of the monthly inflation factors for the 12 months preceding the data collection.

Individuals for Whom Poverty Status is Determined – Poverty status was determined for all people except institutionalized people, people in military group quarters, people in college dormitories, and unrelated individuals under 15 years old. These groups were excluded from the numerator and denominator when calculating poverty rates.

FOOD STAMPS/SNAP, Items 40 through 64

Source: Table B22007. Receipt of Food Stamps/Snap in the Past 12 Months by Family Type by Number of Workers in Family in the Past 12 Months

Universe: Families

The Food Stamp Act of 1977 defines this federally-funded program as one intended to "permit low-income households to obtain a more nutritious diet" (from Title XIII of Public Law 95-113, The Food Stamp Act of 1977, declaration of policy). Food purchasing power is increased by providing eligible households with coupons or cards that can be used to purchase food. The Food and Nutrition Service (FNS) of the U.S. Department of Agriculture (USDA) administers the Food Stamp Program through state and local welfare offices. The Food Stamp Program is the major national income support program to which all low-income and low-resource households, regardless of household characteristics, are eligible.

The questions on participation in the Food Stamp Program were designed to identify households in which one or more of the current members received food stamps during the past 12 months.

In 2008, the Food Stamp Program was renamed the Supplemental Nutrition Assistance Program (SNAP).

HEALTH INSURANCE, Items 65 through 112

Source: Table B27021. Health Insurance Coverage Status and Type by Living Arrangement

Universe: Civilian noninstitutionalized population

ACS Respondents were instructed to report their current health insurance coverage and to mark "yes" or "no" for each of the eight types listed:

a. Insurance through a current or former employer or union (of this person or another family member)
b. Insurance purchased directly from an insurance company (by this person or another family member)
c. Medicare, for people 65 and older, or people with certain disabilities
d. Medicaid, Medical Assistance, or any kind of government-assistance plan for those with low incomes or a disability
e. TRICARE or other military health care
f. VA (including those who have ever used or enrolled for VA health care)
g. Indian Health Service
h. Any other type of health insurance or health coverage plan (respondents were asked to provide their other type of coverage type in a write-in field.)

Health insurance coverage in the ACS and other Census Bureau surveys define coverage to include plans and programs that provide comprehensive health coverage. Plans that provide insurance for specific conditions or situations such as cancer and long-term care policies are not considered coverage. Likewise, other types of insurance like dental, vision, life, and disability insurance are not considered health insurance coverage.

In defining types of coverage, write-in responses were reclassified into one of the first seven types of coverage or determined not to be a coverage type. Write-in responses that referenced the coverage of a family member were edited to assign coverage based on responses from other family members.

An eligibility edit was applied to give Medicaid, Medicare, and TRICARE coverage to individuals based on program eligibility rules. TRICARE or other military health care was given to active-duty military personnel and their spouses and children. Medicaid or other means-tested public coverage was given to foster children, certain individuals receiving Supplementary Security Income or Public Assistance, and the spouses and children of certain Medicaid beneficiaries. Medicare coverage was given to people 65 and older who received Social Security or Medicaid benefits.

People were considered insured if they reported at least one "yes." People who had no reported health coverage, or those whose only health coverage was Indian Health Service, were considered uninsured. For reporting purposes, the Census Bureau broadly classifies health insurance coverage as private health insurance or public coverage. Private health insurance is a plan provided through an employer or union, a plan purchased by an individual from a private company, or TRICARE or other military health care. Respondents reporting a "yes" to the types listed in parts a, b, or e were considered to have private health insurance. Public health coverage includes the federal programs Medicare, Medicaid, and VA Health Care (provided through the Department of Veterans Affairs); the Children's Health Insurance Program (CHIP); and individual state health plans. Respondents reporting a "yes" to the types listed in c, d, or f were considered to have public coverage. The types of health insurance are not mutually exclusive; people may be covered by more than one at the same time.

Table E-2, E-3, and E-4. Counties with populations of 50,000 or more, Metropolitan Areas, Cities with Populations of 50,000 or more

MEDIAN INCOME, Items 1 through 8

Source: Table B19126. Median Family Income in the Past 12 Months (In 2013 Inflation-Adjusted Dollars) by Family Type by Presence of Own Children under 18 Years; Table B1912. Median Family Income in the Past 12 Months (In 2013 Inflation-Adjusted Dollars) by Number of Earners in Family

Universe: Families

"Total income" is the sum of the amounts reported separately for wage or salary income; net self-employment income; interest, dividends, or net rental or royalty income or income from estates and trusts; Social Security or Railroad Retirement income; Supplemental Security Income (SSI); public

assistance or welfare payments; retirement, survivor, or disability pensions; and all other income.

Receipts from the following sources are not included as income: capital gains, money received from the sale of property (unless the recipient was engaged in the business of selling such property); the value of income "in kind" from food stamps, public housing subsidies, medical care, employer contributions for individuals, etc.; withdrawal of bank deposits; money borrowed; tax refunds; exchange of money between relatives living in the same household; gifts and lump-sum inheritances, insurance payments, and other types of lump-sum receipts.

Income Type in the Past 12 Months

The eight types of income reported in the ACS are defined as follows:

1. Wage or salary income: Wage or salary income includes total money earnings received for work performed as an employee during the past 12 months. It includes wages, salary, Armed Forces pay, commissions, tips, piece-rate payments, and cash bonuses earned before deductions were made for taxes, bonds, pensions, union dues, etc.

2. Self-employment income: Self-employment income includes both farm and non-farm self-employment income. Farm self-employment income includes net money income (gross receipts minus operating expenses) from the operation of a farm by a person on his or her own account, as an owner, renter, or sharecropper. Gross receipts include the value of all products sold, government farm programs, money received from the rental of farm equipment to others, and incidental receipts from the sale of wood, sand, gravel, etc. Operating expenses include cost of feed, fertilizer, seed, and other farming supplies, cash wages paid to farmhands, depreciation charges, rent, interest on farm mortgages, farm building repairs, farm taxes (not state and federal personal income taxes), etc. The value of fuel, food, or other farm products used for family living is not included as part of net income.

   Non-farm self-employment income includes net money income (gross receipts minus expenses) from one's own business, professional enterprise, or partnership. Gross receipts include the value of all goods sold and services rendered. Expenses include costs of goods purchased, rent, heat, light, power, depreciation charges, wages and salaries paid, business taxes (not personal income taxes), etc.

3. Interest, dividends, net rental income, royalty income, or income from estates and trusts: Interest, dividends, or net rental income includes interest on savings or bonds, dividends from stockholdings or membership in associations, net income from rental of property to others and receipts from boarders or lodgers, net royalties, and periodic payments from an estate or trust fund.

4. Social Security income: Social Security income includes Social Security pensions and survivor benefits, permanent

disability insurance payments made by the Social Security Administration prior to deductions for medical insurance, and railroad retirement insurance checks from the U.S. government. Medicare reimbursements are not included.

5. Supplemental Security Income (SSI): Supplemental Security Income (SSI) is a nationwide U.S. assistance program administered by the Social Security Administration that guarantees a minimum level of income for needy aged, blind, or disabled individuals.

6. Public assistance income: Public assistance income includes general assistance and Temporary Assistance to Needy Families (TANF). Separate payments received for hospital or other medical care (vendor payments) are excluded. This does not include Supplemental Security Income (SSI) or noncash benefits such as Food Stamps. The terms "public assistance income" and "cash public assistance" are used interchangeably in the 2013 ACS data products.

7. Retirement, survivor, or disability income: Retirement income includes: (1) retirement pensions and survivor benefits from a former employer; labor union; or federal, state, or local government; and the U.S. military; (2) disability income from companies or unions; federal, state, or local government; and the U.S. military; (3) periodic receipts from annuities and insurance; and (4) regular income from IRA and Keogh plans. This does not include Social Security income.

8. All other income: All other income includes unemployment compensation, worker's compensation, Department of Veterans Affairs (VA) payments, alimony and child support, contributions received periodically from people not living in the household, military family allotments, and other kinds of periodic income other than earnings.

Income of Families – In compiling statistics on family income, the incomes of all members 15 years old and over related to the householder are summed and treated as a single amount. Although the family income statistics cover the past 12 months, the characteristics of individuals and the composition of families refer to the time of interview. Thus, the income of the family does not include amounts received by individuals who were members of the family during all or part of the past 12 months if these individuals no longer resided with the family at the time of interview. Similarly, income amounts reported by individuals who did not reside with the family during the past 12 months but who were members of the family at the time of interview are included. However, the composition of most families was the same during the past 12 months as at the time of interview.

Median Income – The median divides the income distribution into two equal parts: one-half of the cases falling below the median income and one-half above the median. For families, the median income is based on the distribution of the total number of families including those with no income. Median income for families is computed on the basis of a standard distribution of 100 groupings of $2500 ranging from zero to a maximum category of $250,000 or more. Median income is rounded to the nearest whole dollar. Median income figures are calculated using linear interpolation.

HEALTH INSURANCE, Items 9 through 12

Source: Table B27021. Health Insurance Coverage Status and Type by Living Arrangement

Universe: Civilian noninstitutionalized population

ACS Respondents were instructed to report their current health insurance coverage and to mark "yes" or "no" for each of the eight types listed:

a. Insurance through a current or former employer or union (of this person or another family member)
b. Insurance purchased directly from an insurance company (by this person or another family member)
c. Medicare, for people 65 and older, or people with certain disabilities
d. Medicaid, Medical Assistance, or any kind of government-assistance plan for those with low incomes or a disability
e. TRICARE or other military health care
f. VA (including those who have ever used or enrolled for VA health care)
g. Indian Health Service
h. Any other type of health insurance or health coverage plan (respondents were asked to provide their other type of coverage type in a write-in field.)

Health insurance coverage in the ACS and other Census Bureau surveys define coverage to include plans and programs that provide comprehensive health coverage. Plans that provide insurance for specific conditions or situations such as cancer and long-term care policies are not considered coverage. Likewise, other types of insurance like dental, vision, life, and disability insurance are not considered health insurance coverage.

In defining types of coverage, write-in responses were reclassified into one of the first seven types of coverage or determined not to be a coverage type. Write-in responses that referenced the coverage of a family member were edited to assign coverage based on responses from other family members.

An eligibility edit was applied to give Medicaid, Medicare, and TRICARE coverage to individuals based on program eligibility rules. TRICARE or other military health care was given to active-duty military personnel and their spouses and children. Medicaid or other means-tested public coverage was given to foster children, certain individuals receiving Supplementary Security Income or Public Assistance, and the spouses and children of certain Medicaid beneficiaries. Medicare coverage was given to people 65 and older who received Social Security or Medicaid benefits.

People were considered insured if they reported at least one "yes". People who had no reported health coverage, or those whose only health coverage was Indian Health Service, were considered uninsured. For reporting purposes, the Census Bureau broadly classifies health insurance coverage as private health insurance or public coverage. Private health insurance is a plan provided through an employer or union, a plan purchased by an individual from a private company, or TRICARE or other military health care. Respondents reporting a "yes" to the types listed in parts a, b, or e were considered to have private health insurance. Public health coverage includes the federal programs Medicare, Medicaid, and VA Health Care (provided through the Department of Veterans Affairs); the Children's Health Insurance Program (CHIP); and individual state health plans. Respondents reporting a "yes" to the types listed in c, d, or f were considered to have public coverage. The types of health insurance are not mutually exclusive; people may be covered by more than one at the same time.

POVERTY STATUS, Items 13 through 17

Source: Table C17010. Poverty Status in the Past 12 Months of Families by Family Type by Presence of Related Children under 18 Years

Universe: Families

The Census Bureau uses a set of dollar value thresholds that vary by family size and composition to determine who is in poverty. Further, poverty thresholds for people living alone or with nonrelatives (unrelated individuals) vary by age (under 65 years or 65 years and older). The poverty thresholds for two-person families also vary by the age of the householder. If a family's total income is less than the dollar value of the appropriate threshold, then that family and every individual in it are considered to be in poverty. Similarly, if an unrelated individual's total income is less than the appropriate threshold, then that individual is considered to be in poverty.

In determining the poverty status of families and unrelated individuals, the Census Bureau uses thresholds (income cutoffs) arranged in a two-dimensional matrix. The matrix consists of family size (from one person to nine or more people) cross-classified by presence and number of family members under 18 years old (from no children present to eight or more children present). Unrelated individuals and two-person families are further differentiated by age of reference person (householder) (under 65 years old and 65 years old and over). To determine a person's poverty status, one compares the person's total family income in the last 12 months with the poverty threshold appropriate for that person's family size and composition. If the total income of that person's family is less than the threshold appropriate for that family, then the person is considered "below the poverty level," together with every member of his or her family. If a person is not living with anyone related by birth, marriage, or adoption, then the person's own income is compared with his or her poverty threshold. The total number of people below the poverty level is the sum of people in families and the number of unrelated individuals with incomes in the last 12 months below the poverty threshold.

Since ACS is a continuous survey, people respond throughout the year. Because the income questions specify a period covering the last 12 months, the appropriate poverty thresholds are determined by multiplying the base-year poverty thresholds (1982) by the average of the monthly inflation factors for the 12 months preceding the data collection.

Individuals for Whom Poverty Status is Determined – Poverty status was determined for all people except institutionalized people, people in military group quarters, people in college dormitories, and unrelated individuals under 15 years old. These groups were excluded from the numerator and denominator when calculating poverty rates.

FOOD STAMPS/SNAP, Items 18 through 22

Source: Table B22007. Receipt of Food Stamps/Snap in the Past 12 Months by Family Type by Number of Workers in Family in the Past 12 Months

Universe: Families

The Food Stamp Act of 1977 defines this federally-funded program as one intended to "permit low-income households to obtain a more nutritious diet" (from Title XIII of Public Law 95–113, The Food Stamp Act of 1977, declaration of policy). Food purchasing power is increased by providing eligible households with coupons or cards that can be used to purchase food. The Food and Nutrition Service (FNS) of the U.S. Department of Agriculture (USDA) administers the Food Stamp Program through state and local welfare offices. The Food Stamp Program is the major national income support program to which all low-income and low-resource households, regardless of household characteristics, are eligible.

The questions on participation in the Food Stamp Program were designed to identify households in which one or more of the current members received food stamps during the past 12 months.

In 2008, the Food Stamp Program was renamed the Supplemental Nutrition Assistance Program (SNAP).

Core Based Statistical Areas and Components (as defined February 2013)

Core based statistical area	State/County FIPS code	Title and Geographic Components
10180		Abilene, TX Metro area
	48059	Callahan County, TX
	48253	Jones County, TX
	48441	Taylor County, TX
10420		Akron, OH Metro area
	39133	Portage County, OH
	39153	Summit County, OH
10500		Albany, GA Metro area
	13007	Baker County, GA
	13095	Dougherty County, GA
	13177	Lee County, GA
	13273	Terrell County, GA
	13321	Worth County, GA
10580		Albany-Schenectady-Troy, NY Metro area
	36001	Albany County, NY
	36083	Rensselaer County, NY
	36091	Saratoga County, NY
	36093	Schenectady County, NY
	36095	Schoharie County, NY
10740		Albuquerque, NM Metro area
	35001	Bernalillo County, NM
	35043	Sandoval County, NM
	35057	Torrance County, NM
	35061	Valencia County, NM
10780		Alexandria, LA Metro area
	22043	Grant Parish, LA
	22079	Rapides Parish, LA
10900		Allentown-Bethlehem-Easton, PA-NJ Metro area
	34041	Warren County, NJ
	42025	Carbon County, PA
	42077	Lehigh County, PA
	42095	Northampton County, PA
11020		Altoona, PA Metro area
	42013	Blair County, PA
11100		Amarillo, TX Metro area
	48011	Armstrong County, TX
	48065	Carson County, TX
	48359	Oldham County, TX
	48375	Potter County, TX
	48381	Randall County, TX
11180		Ames, IA Metro area
	19169	Story County, IA
11260		Anchorage, AK Metro area
	02020	Anchorage Municipality, AK
	02170	Matanuska-Susitna Borough, AK
11460		Ann Arbor, MI Metro area
	26161	Washtenaw County, MI
11500		Anniston-Oxford-Jacksonville, AL Metro area
	01015	Calhoun County, AL
11540		Appleton, WI Metro area
	55015	Calumet County, WI
	55087	Outagamie County, WI
11700		Asheville, NC Metro area
	37021	Buncombe County, NC
	37087	Haywood County, NC
	37089	Henderson County, NC
	37115	Madison County, NC
12020		Athens-Clarke County, GA Metro area
	13059	Clarke County, GA
	13195	Madison County, GA
	13219	Oconee County, GA
	13221	Oglethorpe County, GA
12060		Atlanta-Sandy Springs-Roswell, GA Metro area
	13013	Barrow County, GA
	13015	Bartow County, GA
	13035	Butts County, GA
	13045	Carroll County, GA
	13057	Cherokee County, GA
	13063	Clayton County, GA
	13067	Cobb County, GA
	13077	Coweta County, GA
	13085	Dawson County, GA
	13089	DeKalb County, GA
	13097	Douglas County, GA
	13113	Fayette County, GA
	13117	Forsyth County, GA
	13121	Fulton County, GA

Core Based Statistical Areas and Components (as defined February 2013)

Core based statistical area	State/County FIPS code	Title and Geographic Components
	13135	Gwinnett County, GA
	13143	Haralson County, GA
	13149	Heard County, GA
	13151	Henry County, GA
	13159	Jasper County, GA
	13171	Lamar County, GA
	13199	Meriwether County, GA
	13211	Morgan County, GA
	13217	Newton County, GA
	13223	Paulding County, GA
	13227	Pickens County, GA
	13231	Pike County, GA
	13247	Rockdale County, GA
	13255	Spalding County, GA
	13297	Walton County, GA
12100		Atlantic City-Hammonton, NJ Metro area
	34001	Atlantic County, NJ
12220		Auburn-Opelika, AL Metro area
	01081	Lee County, AL
12260		Augusta-Richmond County, GA-SC Metro area
	13033	Burke County, GA
	13073	Columbia County, GA
	13181	Lincoln County, GA
	13189	McDuffie County, GA
	13245	Richmond County, GA
	45003	Aiken County, SC
	45037	Edgefield County, SC
12420		Austin-Round Rock, TX Metro area
	48021	Bastrop County, TX
	48055	Caldwell County, TX
	48209	Hays County, TX
	48453	Travis County, TX
	48491	Williamson County, TX
12540		Bakersfield, CA Metro area
	06029	Kern County, CA
12580		Baltimore-Columbia-Towson, MD Metro area
	24003	Anne Arundel County, MD
	24005	Baltimore County, MD
	24013	Carroll County, MD
	24025	Harford County, MD
	24027	Howard County, MD
	24035	Queen Anne's County, MD
	24510	Baltimore city, MD
12620		Bangor, ME Metro area
	23019	Penobscot County, ME
12700		Barnstable Town, MA Metro area
	25001	Barnstable County, MA
12940		Baton Rouge, LA Metro area
	22005	Ascension Parish, LA
	22033	East Baton Rouge Parish, LA
	22037	East Feliciana Parish, LA
	22047	Iberville Parish, LA
	22063	Livingston Parish, LA
	22077	Pointe Coupee Parish, LA
	22091	St. Helena Parish, LA
	22121	West Baton Rouge Parish, LA
	22125	West Feliciana Parish, LA
12980		Battle Creek, MI Metro area
	26025	Calhoun County, MI
13020		Bay City, MI Metro area
	26017	Bay County, MI
13140		Beaumont-Port Arthur, TX Metro area
	48199	Hardin County, TX
	48245	Jefferson County, TX
	48351	Newton County, TX
	48361	Orange County, TX
13380		Bellingham, WA Metro area
	53073	Whatcom County, WA
13460		Bend-Redmond, OR Metro area
	41017	Deschutes County, OR
13740		Billings, MT Metro area
	30009	Carbon County, MT
	30037	Golden Valley County, MT
	30111	Yellowstone County, MT
13780		Binghamton, NY Metro area
	36007	Broome County, NY
	36107	Tioga County, NY
13820		Birmingham-Hoover, AL Metro area

Core based statistical area	State/County FIPS code	Title and Geographic Components
	01007	Bibb County, AL
	01009	Blount County, AL
	01021	Chilton County, AL
	01073	Jefferson County, AL
	01115	St. Clair County, AL
	01117	Shelby County, AL
	01127	Walker County, AL
13900		Bismarck, ND Metro area
	38015	Burleigh County, ND
	38059	Morton County, ND
	38065	Oliver County, ND
	38085	Sioux County, ND
13980		Blacksburg-Christiansburg-Radford, VA Metro area
	51063	Floyd County, VA
	51071	Giles County, VA
	51121	Montgomery County, VA
	51155	Pulaski County, VA
	51750	Radford city, VA
14010		Bloomington, IL Metro area
	17039	De Witt County, IL
	17113	McLean County, IL
14020		Bloomington, IN Metro area
	18105	Monroe County, IN
	18119	Owen County, IN
14260		Boise City, ID Metro area
	16001	Ada County, ID
	16015	Boise County, ID
	16027	Canyon County, ID
	16045	Gem County, ID
	16073	Owyhee County, ID
14460		Boston-Cambridge Newton, MA-NH Metro area
14460		Boston, MA Metro Div 14454
	25021	Norfolk County, MA
	25023	Plymouth County, MA
	25025	Suffolk County, MA
14460		Cambridge-Newton-Framingham, MA Metro Div 15764
	25009	Essex County, MA
	25017	Middlesex County, MA
14460		Rockingham County-Strafford County-NH Metro Div 40484
	33015	Rockingham County, NH
	33017	Strafford County, NH
14500		Boulder, CO Metro area
	08013	Boulder County, CO
14540		Bowling Green, KY Metro area
	21003	Allen County, KY
	21031	Butler County, KY
	21061	Edmonson County, KY
	21227	Warren County, KY
14740		Bremerton-Silverdale, WA Metro area
	53035	Kitsap County, WA
14860		Bridgeport-Stamford-Norwalk, CT Metro area
	09001	Fairfield County, CT
15180		Brownsville-Harlingen, TX Metro area
	48061	Cameron County, TX
15260		Brunswick, GA Metro area
	13025	Brantley County, GA
	13127	Glynn County, GA
	13191	McIntosh County, GA
15380		Buffalo-Cheektowaga-Niagara Falls, NY Metro area
	36029	Erie County, NY
	36063	Niagara County, NY
15500		Burlington, NC Metro area
	37001	Alamance County, NC
15540		Burlington-South Burlington, VT Metro area
	50007	Chittenden County, VT
	50011	Franklin County, VT
	50013	Grand Isle County, VT
15940		Canton-Massillon, OH Metro area
	39019	Carroll County, OH
	39151	Stark County, OH
15980		Cape Coral-Fort Myers, FL Metro area
	12071	Lee County, FL
16020		Cape Girardeau, MO-IL Metro area
	17003	Alexander County, IL
	29017	Bollinger County, MO
	29031	Cape Girardeau County, MO
16220		Casper, WY Metro area
	56025	Natrona County, WY
16300		Cedar Rapids, IA Metro area
	19011	Benton County, IA
	19105	Jones County, IA
	19113	Linn County, IA
16580		Champaign-Urbana, IL Metro area
	17019	Champaign County, IL
	17053	Ford County, IL
	17147	Piatt County, IL
16620		Charleston, WV Metro area

Core based statistical area	State/County FIPS code	Title and Geographic Components
	54005	Boone County, WV
	54015	Clay County, WV
	54039	Kanawha County, WV
16700		Charleston-North Charleston, SC Metro area
	45015	Berkeley County, SC
	45019	Charleston County, SC
	45035	Dorchester County, SC
16740		Charlotte-Concord-Gastonia, NC-SC Metro area
	37025	Cabarrus County, NC
	37071	Gaston County, NC
	37097	Iredell County, NC
	37109	Lincoln County, NC
	37119	Mecklenburg County, NC
	37159	Rowan County, NC
	37179	Union County, NC
	45023	Chester County, SC
	45057	Lancaster County, SC
	45091	York County, SC
16820		Charlottesville, VA Metro area
	51003	Albemarle County, VA
	51029	Buckingham County, VA
	51065	Fluvanna County, VA
	51079	Greene County, VA
	51125	Nelson County, VA
	51540	Charlottesville city, VA
16860		Chattanooga, TN-GA Metro area
	13047	Catoosa County, GA
	13083	Dade County, GA
	13295	Walker County, GA
	47065	Hamilton County, TN
	47115	Marion County, TN
	47153	Sequatchie County, TN
16940		Cheyenne, WY Metro area
	56021	Laramie County, WY
16980		Chicago-Naperville-Elgin, IL-IN-WI Metro area
16980		Chicago-Naperville-Arlington Heights, IL Metro Div 16974
	17031	Cook County, IL
	17043	DuPage County, IL
	17063	Grundy County, IL
	17093	Kendall County, IL
	17111	McHenry County, IL
	17197	Will County, IL
16980		Gary, IN Metro Div 23844
	18073	Jasper County, IN
	18089	Lake County, IN
	18111	Newton County, IN
	18127	Porter County, IN
16980		Lake County-Kenosha County, IL-WI Metro Div 29404
	17097	Lake County, IL
	55059	Kenosha County, WI
17020		Chico, CA Metro area
	06007	Butte County, CA
17140		Cincinnati, OH-KY-IN Metro area
	18029	Dearborn County, IN
	18115	Ohio County, IN
	18161	Union County, IN
	21015	Boone County, KY
	21023	Bracken County, KY
	21037	Campbell County, KY
	21077	Gallatin County, KY
	21081	Grant County, KY
	21117	Kenton County, KY
	21191	Pendleton County, KY
	39015	Brown County, OH
	39017	Butler County, OH
	39025	Clermont County, OH
	39061	Hamilton County, OH
	39165	Warren County, OH
17300		Clarksville, TN-KY Metro area
	21047	Christian County, KY
	21221	Trigg County, KY
	47125	Montgomery County, TN
17420		Cleveland, TN Metro area
	47011	Bradley County, TN
	47139	Polk County, TN
17460		Cleveland-Elyria, OH Metro area
	39035	Cuyahoga County, OH
	39055	Geauga County, OH
	39085	Lake County, OH
	39093	Lorain County, OH
	39103	Medina County, OH
17660		Coeur d'Alene, ID Metro area
	16055	Kootenai County, ID
17780		College Station-Bryan, TX Metro area
	48041	Brazos County, TX
	48051	Burleson County, TX
	48395	Robertson County, TX
17820		Colorado Springs, CO Metro area

Core based statistical area	State/County FIPS code	Title and Geographic Components
	08041	El Paso County, CO
	08119	Teller County, CO
17860		Columbia, MO Metro area
	29019	Boone County, MO
17900		Columbia, SC Metro area
	45017	Calhoun County, SC
	45039	Fairfield County, SC
	45055	Kershaw County, SC
	45063	Lexington County, SC
	45079	Richland County, SC
	45081	Saluda County, SC
17980		Columbus, GA-AL Metro area
	01113	Russell County, AL
	13053	Chattahoochee County, GA
	13145	Harris County, GA
	13197	Marion County, GA
	13215	Muscogee County, GA
18020		Columbus, IN Metro area
	18005	Bartholomew County, IN
18140		Columbus, OH Metro area
	39041	Delaware County, OH
	39045	Fairfield County, OH
	39049	Franklin County, OH
	39073	Hocking County, OH
	39089	Licking County, OH
	39097	Madison County, OH
	39117	Morrow County, OH
	39127	Perry County, OH
	39129	Pickaway County, OH
	39159	Union County, OH
18580		Corpus Christi, TX Metro area
	48007	Aransas County, TX
	48355	Nueces County, TX
	48409	San Patricio County, TX
18700		Corvallis, OR Metro area
	41003	Benton County, OR
18880		Crestview-Fort Walton Beach-Destin, FL Metro area
	12091	Okaloosa County, FL
	12131	Walton County, FL
19060		Cumberland, MD-WV Metro area
	24001	Allegany County, MD
	54057	Mineral County, WV
19100		Dallas-Fort Worth-Arlington, TX Metro area
19100		Dallas-Plano-Irving, TX Metro Div 19124
	48085	Collin County, TX
	48113	Dallas County, TX
	48121	Denton County, TX
	48139	Ellis County, TX
	48231	Hunt County, TX
	48257	Kaufman County, TX
	48397	Rockwall County, TX
19100		Fort Worth-Arlington, TX Metro Div 23104
	48221	Hood County, TX
	48251	Johnson County, TX
	48367	Parker County, TX
	48425	Somervell County, TX
	48439	Tarrant County, TX
	48497	Wise County, TX
19140		Dalton, GA Metro area
	13213	Murray County, GA
	13313	Whitfield County, GA
19180		Danville, IL Metro area
	17183	Vermilion County, IL
19260		Danville, VA Micro area
	51143	Pittsylvania County, VA
	51590	Danville city, VA
19340		Davenport-Moline-Rock Island, IA-IL Metro area
	17073	Henry County, IL
	17131	Mercer County, IL
	17161	Rock Island County, IL
	19163	Scott County, IA
19380		Dayton, OH Metro area
	39057	Greene County, OH
	39109	Miami County, OH
	39113	Montgomery County, OH
19460		Decatur, AL Metro area
	01079	Lawrence County, AL
	01103	Morgan County, AL
19500		Decatur, IL Metro area
	17115	Macon County, IL
19660		Deltona-Daytona Beach-Ormond Beach, FL Metro area
	12035	Flagler County, FL
	12127	Volusia County, FL
19740		Denver-Aurora-Lakewood, CO Metro area
	08001	Adams County, CO
	08005	Arapahoe County, CO
	08014	Broomfield County, CO
	08019	Clear Creek County, CO

Core based statistical area	State/County FIPS code	Title and Geographic Components
	08031	Denver County, CO
	08035	Douglas County, CO
	08039	Elbert County, CO
	08047	Gilpin County, CO
	08059	Jefferson County, CO
	08093	Park County, CO
19780		Des Moines-West Des Moines, IA Metro area
	19049	Dallas County, IA
	19077	Guthrie County, IA
	19121	Madison County, IA
	19153	Polk County, IA
	19181	Warren County, IA
19820		Detroit-Warren-Dearborn, MI Metro area
19820		Detroit-Dearborn-Livonia, MI Metro Div 19804
	26163	Wayne County, MI
19820		Warren-Troy-Farmington Hills, MI Metro Div 47664
	26087	Lapeer County, MI
	26093	Livingston County, MI
	26099	Macomb County, MI
	26125	Oakland County, MI
	26147	St. Clair County, MI
20020		Dothan, AL Metro area
	01061	Geneva County, AL
	01067	Henry County, AL
	01069	Houston County, AL
20100		Dover, DE Metro area
	10001	Kent County, Delaware
20220		Dubuque, IA Metro area
	19061	Dubuque County, IA
20260		Duluth, MN-WI Metro area
	27017	Carlton County, MN
	27137	St. Louis County, MN
	55031	Douglas County, WI
20500		Durham-Chapel Hill, NC Metro area
	37037	Chatham County, NC
	37063	Durham County, NC
	37135	Orange County, NC
	37145	Person County, NC
20740		Eau Claire, WI Metro area
	55017	Chippewa County, WI
	55035	Eau Claire County, WI
20940		El Centro, CA Metro area
	06025	Imperial County, CA
21060		Elizabethtown-Fort Knox, KY Metro area
	21093	Hardin County, KY
	21123	Larue County, KY
	21163	Meade County, KY
21140		Elkhart-Goshen, IN Metro area
	18039	Elkhart County, IN
21300		Elmira, NY Metro area
	36015	Chemung County, NY
21340		El Paso, TX Metro area
	48141	El Paso County, TX
	48229	Hudspeth County, TX
21500		Erie, PA Metro area
	42049	Erie County, PA
21660		Eugene, OR Metro area
	41039	Lane County, OR
21780		Evansville, IN-KY Metro area
	18129	Posey County, IN
	18163	Vanderburgh County, IN
	18173	Warrick County, IN
	21101	Henderson County, KY
21820		Fairbanks, AK Metro area
	02090	Fairbanks North Star Borough, AK
22020		Fargo, ND-MN Metro area
	27027	Clay County, MN
	38017	Cass County, ND
22140		Farmington, NM Metro area
	35045	San Juan County, NM
22180		Fayetteville, NC Metro area
	37051	Cumberland County, NC
	37093	Hoke County, NC
22220		Fayetteville-Springdale-Rogers, AR-MO Metro area
	05007	Benton County, AR
	05087	Madison County, AR
	05143	Washington County, AR
	29119	McDonald County, MO
22380		Flagstaff, AZ Metro area
	04005	Coconino County, AZ
22420		Flint, MI Metro area
	26049	Genesee County, MI
22500		Florence, SC Metro area
	45031	Darlington County, SC
	45041	Florence County, SC
22520		Florence-Muscle Shoals, AL Metro area
	01033	Colbert County, AL
	01077	Lauderdale County, AL

Core based statistical area	State/County FIPS code	Title and Geographic Components
22540		Fond du Lac, WI Metro area
	55039	Fond du Lac County, WI
22660		Fort Collins, CO Metro area
	08069	Larimer County, CO
22900		Fort Smith, AR-OK Metro area
	05033	Crawford County, AR
	05131	Sebastian County, AR
	40079	Le Flore County, OK
	40135	Sequoyah County, OK
23060		Fort Wayne, IN Metro area
	18003	Allen County, IN
	18179	Wells County, IN
	18183	Whitley County, IN
23420		Fresno, CA Metro area
	06019	Fresno County, CA
23460		Gadsden, AL Metro area
	01055	Etowah County, AL
23540		Gainesville, FL Metro area
	12001	Alachua County, FL
	12041	Gilchrist County, FL
23580		Gainesville, GA Metro area
	13139	Hall County, GA
24020		Glens Falls, NY Metro area
	36113	Warren County, NY
	36115	Washington County, NY
24140		Goldsboro, NC Metro area
	37191	Wayne County, NC
24220		Grand Forks, ND-MN Metro area
	27119	Polk County, MN
	38035	Grand Forks County, ND
24300		Grand Junction, CO Metro area
	08077	Mesa County, CO
24340		Grand Rapids-Wyoming, MI Metro area
	26015	Barry County, MI
	26081	Kent County, MI
	26117	Montcalm County, MI
	26139	Ottawa County, MI
24500		Great Falls, MT Metro area
	30013	Cascade County, MT
24540		Greeley, CO Metro area
	08123	Weld County, CO
24580		Green Bay, WI Metro area
	55009	Brown County, WI
	55061	Kewaunee County, WI
	55083	Oconto County, WI
24660		Greensboro-High Point, NC Metro area
	37081	Guilford County, NC
	37151	Randolph County, NC
	37157	Rockingham County, NC
24780		Greenville, NC Metro area
	37147	Pitt County, NC
24860		Greenville-Anderson-Mauldin, SC Metro area
	45007	Anderson County, SC
	45045	Greenville County, SC
	45059	Laurens County, SC
	45077	Pickens County, SC
25060		Gulfport-Biloxi-Pascagoula, MS Metro area
	28045	Hancock County, MS
	28047	Harrison County, MS
	28059	Jackson County, MS
25180		Hagerstown-Martinsburg, MD-WV Metro area
	24043	Washington County, MD
	54003	Berkeley County, WV
25260		Hanford-Corcoran, CA Metro area
	06031	Kings County, CA
25420		Harrisburg-Carlisle, PA Metro area
	42041	Cumberland County, PA
	42043	Dauphin County, PA
	42099	Perry County, PA
25500		Harrisonburg, VA Metro area
	51165	Rockingham County, VA
	51660	Harrisonburg city, VA
25540		Hartford-West Hartford-East Hartford, CT Metro area
	09003	Hartford County, CT
	09007	Middlesex County, CT
	09013	Tolland County, CT
25620		Hattiesburg, MS Metro area
	28035	Forrest County, MS
	28073	Lamar County, MS
	28111	Perry County, MS
25860		Hickory-Lenoir-Morganton, NC Metro area
	37003	Alexander County, NC
	37023	Burke County, NC
	37027	Caldwell County, NC
	37035	Catawba County, NC
25980		Hinesville, GA Metro area
	13179	Liberty County, GA
	13183	Long County, GA

Core based statistical area	State/County FIPS code	Title and Geographic Components
26090		Holland, MI Micro area
	26005	Allegan County, MI
26300		Hot Springs, AR Metro area
	05051	Garland County, AR
26380		Houma-Thibodaux, LA Metro area
	22057	Lafourche Parish, LA
	22109	Terrebonne Parish, LA
26420		Houston-The Woodlands-Sugar Land, TX Metro area
	48015	Austin County, TX
	48039	Brazoria County, TX
	48071	Chambers County, TX
	48157	Fort Bend County, TX
	48167	Galveston County, TX
	48201	Harris County, TX
	48291	Liberty County, TX
	48339	Montgomery County, TX
	48473	Waller County, TX
26580		Huntington-Ashland, WV-KY-OH Metro area
	21019	Boyd County, KY
	21089	Greenup County, KY
	39087	Lawrence County, OH
	54011	Cabell County, WV
	54043	Lincoln County, WV
	54079	Putnam County, WV
	54099	Wayne County, WV
26620		Huntsville, AL Metro area
	01083	Limestone County, AL
	01089	Madison County, AL
26820		Idaho Falls, ID Metro area
	16019	Bonneville County, ID
	16023	Butte County, ID
	16051	Jefferson County, ID
26900		Indianapolis-Carmel-Anderson, IN Metro area
	18011	Boone County, IN
	18013	Brown County, IN
	18057	Hamilton County, IN
	18059	Hancock County, IN
	18063	Hendricks County, IN
	18081	Johnson County, IN
	18095	Madison County, IN
	18097	Marion County, IN
	18109	Morgan County, IN
	18133	Putnam County, IN
	18145	Shelby County, IN
26980		Iowa City, IA Metro area
	19103	Johnson County, IA
	19183	Washington County, IA
27060		Ithaca, NY Metro area
	36109	Tompkins County, NY
27100		Jackson, MI Metro area
	26075	Jackson County, MI
27140		Jackson, MS Metro area
	28029	Copiah County, MS
	28049	Hinds County, MS
	28089	Madison County, MS
	28121	Rankin County, MS
	28127	Simpson County, MS
	28163	Yazoo County, MS
27180		Jackson, TN Metro area
	47023	Chester County, TN
	47033	Crockett County, TN
	47113	Madison County, TN
27260		Jacksonville, FL Metro area
	12003	Baker County, FL
	12019	Clay County, FL
	12031	Duval County, FL
	12089	Nassau County, FL
	12109	St. Johns County, FL
27340		Jacksonville, NC Metro area
	37133	Onslow County, NC
27500		Janesville-Beloit, WI Metro area
	55105	Rock County, WI
27620		Jefferson City, MO Metro area
	29027	Callaway County, MO
	29051	Cole County, MO
	29135	Moniteau County, MO
	29151	Osage County, MO
27740		Johnson City, TN Metro area
	47019	Carter County, TN
	47171	Unicoi County, TN
	47179	Washington County, TN
27780		Johnstown, PA Metro area
	42021	Cambria County, PA
27860		Jonesboro, AR Metro area
	05031	Craighead County, AR
	05111	Poinsett County, AR
27900		Joplin, MO Metro area
	29097	Jasper County, MO

Core based statistical area	State/County FIPS code	Title and Geographic Components
	29145	Newton County, MO
27920		Junction City, KS Micro area
	20061	Geary County, KS
27940		Juneau, AK Micro area
	02110	Juneau City and Borough, AK
27980		Kahului-Wailuku-Lahaina, HI Metro area
	15005	Kalawao County, HI
	15009	Maui County, HI
28020		Kalamazoo-Portage, MI Metro area
	26077	Kalamazoo County, MI
	26159	Van Buren County, MI
28100		Kankakee, IL Metro area
	17091	Kankakee County, IL
28140		Kansas City, MO-KS Metro area
	20091	Johnson County, KS
	20103	Leavenworth County, KS
	20107	Linn County, KS
	20121	Miami County, KS
	20209	Wyandotte County, KS
	29013	Bates County, MO
	29025	Caldwell County, MO
	29037	Cass County, MO
	29047	Clay County, MO
	29049	Clinton County, MO
	29095	Jackson County, MO
	29107	Lafayette County, MO
	29165	Platte County, MO
	29177	Ray County, MO
28420		Kennewick-Richland, WA Metro area
	53005	Benton County, WA
	53021	Franklin County, WA
28660		Killeen-Temple, TX Metro area
	48027	Bell County, TX
	48099	Coryell County, TX
	48281	Lampasas County, TX
28700		Kingsport-Bristol-Bristol, TN-VA Metro area
	47073	Hawkins County, TN
	47163	Sullivan County, TN
	51169	Scott County, VA
	51191	Washington County, VA
	51520	Bristol city, VA
28740		Kingston, NY Metro area
	36111	Ulster County, NY
28940		Knoxville, TN Metro area
	47001	Anderson County, TN
	47009	Blount County, TN
	47013	Campbell County, TN
	47057	Grainger County, TN
	47093	Knox County, TN
	47105	Loudon County, TN
	47129	Morgan County, TN
	47145	Roane County, TN
	47173	Union County, TN
29020		Kokomo, IN Metro area
	18067	Howard County, IN
29100		La Crosse-Onalaska, WI-MN Metro area
	27055	Houston County, MN
	55063	La Crosse County, WI
29180		Lafayette, LA Metro area
	22001	Acadia Parish, LA
	22045	Iberia Parish, LA
	22055	Lafayette Parish, LA
	22099	St. Martin Parish, LA
	22113	Vermilion Parish, LA
29200		Lafayette-West Lafayette, IN Metro area
	18007	Benton County, IN
	18015	Carroll County, IN
	18157	Tippecanoe County, IN
29340		Lake Charles, LA Metro area
	22019	Calcasieu Parish, LA
	22023	Cameron Parish, LA
29420		Lake Havasu City-Kingman, AZ Metro area
	04015	Mohave County, AZ
29460		Lakeland-Winter Haven, FL Metro area
	12105	Polk County, FL
29540		Lancaster, PA Metro area
	42071	Lancaster County, PA
29620		Lansing-East Lansing, MI Metro area
	26037	Clinton County, MI
	26045	Eaton County, MI
	26065	Ingham County, MI
29700		Laredo, TX Metro area
	48479	Webb County, TX
29740		Las Cruces, NM Metro area
	35013	Doña Ana County, NM
29820		Las Vegas-Henderson-Paradise, NV Metro area
	32003	Clark County, NV
29940		Lawrence, KS Metro area

Core based statistical area	State/County FIPS code	Title and Geographic Components
	20045	Douglas County, KS
30020		Lawton, OK Metro area
	40031	Comanche County, OK
	40033	Cotton County, OK
30060		Lebanon, MO Micro area
	29105	Laclede County, MO
30340		Lewiston-Auburn, ME Metro area
	23001	Androscoggin County, ME
30460		Lexington-Fayette, KY Metro area
	21017	Bourbon County, KY
	21049	Clark County, KY
	21067	Fayette County, KY
	21113	Jessamine County, KY
	21209	Scott County, KY
	21239	Woodford County, KY
30620		Lima, OH Metro area
	39003	Allen County, OH
30660		Lincoln, IL Micro area
	17107	Logan County, IL
30780		Little Rock-North Little Rock-Conway, AR Metro area
	05045	Faulkner County, AR
	05053	Grant County, AR
	05085	Lonoke County, AR
	05105	Perry County, AR
	05119	Pulaski County, AR
	05125	Saline County, AR
30860		Logan, UT-ID Metro area
30980		Longview, TX Metro area
	48183	Gregg County, TX
	48401	Rusk County, TX
	48459	Upshur County, TX
31020		Longview, WA Metro area
	53015	Cowlitz County, WA
31080		Los Angeles-Long Beach-Anaheim, CA Metro area
31080		Anaheim-Santa Ana-Irvine, CA Metro Div 11244
	06059	Orange County, CA
31080		Los Angeles-Long Beach-Glendale, CA Metro Div 31084
	06037	Los Angeles County, CA
31140		Louisville/Jefferson County, KY-IN Metro area
	18019	Clark County, IN
	18043	Floyd County, IN
	18061	Harrison County, IN
	18143	Scott County, IN
	18175	Washington County, IN
	21029	Bullitt County, KY
	21103	Henry County, KY
	21111	Jefferson County, KY
	21185	Oldham County, KY
	21211	Shelby County, KY
	21215	Spencer County, KY
	21223	Trimble County, KY
31180		Lubbock, TX Metro area
	48107	Crosby County, TX
	48303	Lubbock County, TX
	48305	Lynn County, TX
31340		Lynchburg, VA Metro area
	51009	Amherst County, VA
	51011	Appomattox County, VA
	51019	Bedford County, VA
	51031	Campbell County, VA
	51515	Bedford city, VA
	51680	Lynchburg city, VA
31420		Macon, GA Metro area
	13021	Bibb County, GA
	13079	Crawford County, GA
	13169	Jones County, GA
	13207	Monroe County, GA
	13289	Twiggs County, GA
31460		Madera, CA Metro area
	06039	Madera County, CA
31540		Madison, WI Metro area
	55021	Columbia County, WI
	55025	Dane County, WI
	55045	Green County, WI
	55049	Iowa County, WI
31700		Manchester-Nashua, NH Metro area
	33011	Hillsborough County, NH
31740		Manhattan, KS Metro area
	20149	Pottawatomie County, KS
	20161	Riley County, KS
31860		Mankato-North Mankato, MN Metro area
	27013	Blue Earth County, MN
	27103	Nicollet County, MN
31900		Mansfield, OH Metro area
	39139	Richland County, OH
32580		McAllen-Edinburg-Mission, TX Metro area
	48215	Hidalgo County, TX
32780		Medford, OR Metro area

Core based statistical area	State/County FIPS code	Title and Geographic Components
	41029	Jackson County, OR
32820		Memphis, TN-MS-AR Metro area
	05035	Crittenden County, AR
	28009	Benton County, MS
	28033	DeSoto County, MS
	28093	Marshall County, MS
	28137	Tate County, MS
	28143	Tunica County, MS
	47047	Fayette County, TN
	47157	Shelby County, TN
	47167	Tipton County, TN
32900		Merced, CA Metro area
	06047	Merced County, CA
33100		Miami-Fort Lauderdale-West Palm Beach, FL Metro area
		Fort Lauderdale-Pompano Beach-Deerfield Beach, FL
33100		Metro Div 22744
	12011	Broward County, FL
33100		Miami-Miami Beach-Kendall, FL Metro Div 33124
	12086	Miami-Dade County, FL
		West Palm Beach-Boca Raton-Delray Beach, FL Metro Div
33100		48424
	12099	Palm Beach County, FL
33140		Michigan City-La Porte, IN Metro area
	18091	LaPorte County, IN
33260		Midland, TX Metro area
	48317	Martin County, TX
	48329	Midland County, TX
33340		Milwaukee-Waukesha-West Allis, WI Metro area
	55079	Milwaukee County, WI
	55089	Ozaukee County, WI
	55131	Washington County, WI
	55133	Waukesha County, WI
33460		Minneapolis-St. Paul-Bloomington, MN Metro area
	27003	Anoka County, MN
	27019	Carver County, MN
	27025	Chisago County, MN
	27037	Dakota County, MN
	27053	Hennepin County, MN
	27059	Isanti County, MN
	27079	Le Sueur County, MN
	27095	Mille Lacs County, MN
	27123	Ramsey County, MN
	27139	Scott County, MN
	27141	Sherburne County, MN
	27143	Sibley County, MN
	27163	Washington County, MN
	27171	Wright County, MN
	55093	Pierce County, WI
	55109	St. Croix County, WI
33540		Missoula, MT Metro area
	30063	Missoula County, MT
33660		Mobile, AL Metro area
	01097	Mobile County, AL
33700		Modesto, CA Metro area
	06099	Stanislaus County, CA
33740		Monroe, LA Metro area
	22073	Ouachita Parish, LA
	22111	Union Parish, LA
33780		Monroe, MI Metro area
	26115	Monroe County, MI
33860		Montgomery, AL Metro area
	01001	Autauga County, AL
	01051	Elmore County, AL
	01085	Lowndes County, AL
	01101	Montgomery County, AL
34060		Morgantown, WV Metro area
	54061	Monongalia County, WV
	54077	Preston County, WV
34100		Morristown, TN Metro area
	47063	Hamblen County, TN
	47089	Jefferson County, TN
34540		Mount Vernon, OH Micro area
	39083	Knox County, OH
34620		Muncie, IN Metro area
	18035	Delaware County, IN
34740		Muskegon, MI Metro area
	26121	Muskegon County, MI
		Myrtle Beach-Conway-North Myrtle Beach, NC-SC Metro
34820		area
	37019	Brunswick County, NC
	45051	Horry County, SC
34900		Napa, CA Metro area
	06055	Napa County, CA
34940		Naples-Immokalee-Marco Island, FL Metro area
	12021	Collier County, FL
34980		Nashville-Davidson–Murfreesboro–Franklin, TN Metro area
	47015	Cannon County, TN
	47021	Cheatham County, TN

Core based statistical area	State/County FIPS code	Title and Geographic Components
	47037	Davidson County, TN
	47043	Dickson County, TN
	47081	Hickman County, TN
	47111	Macon County, TN
	47119	Maury County, TN
	47147	Robertson County, TN
	47149	Rutherford County, TN
	47159	Smith County, TN
	47165	Sumner County, TN
	47169	Trousdale County, TN
	47187	Williamson County, TN
	47189	Wilson County, TN
35300		New Haven-Milford, CT Metro area
	09009	New Haven County, CT
35380		New Orleans-Metairie, LA Metro area
	22051	Jefferson Parish, LA
	22071	Orleans Parish, LA
	22075	Plaquemines Parish, LA
	22087	St. Bernard Parish, LA
	22089	St. Charles Parish, LA
	22093	St. James Parish, LA
	22095	St. John the Baptist Parish, LA
	22103	St. Tammany Parish, LA
35620		New York-Newark-Jersey City, NY-NJ-PA Metro area
35620		Dutchess County-Putnam County, NY Metro Div 20524
	36027	Dutchess County, NY
	36079	Putnam County, NY
35620		Nassau County-Suffolk County, NY Metro Div 35004
	36059	Nassau County, NY
	36103	Suffolk County, NY
35620		Newark, NJ-PA Metro Div 35084
	34013	Essex County, NJ
	34019	Hunterdon County, NJ
	34027	Morris County, NJ
	34035	Somerset County, NJ
	34037	Sussex County, NJ
	34039	Union County, NJ
	42103	Pike County, PA
35620		New York-Jersey City-White Plains, NY-NJ Metro Div 35614
	34003	Bergen County, NJ
	34017	Hudson County, NJ
	34023	Middlesex County, NJ
	34025	Monmouth County, NJ
	34029	Ocean County, NJ
	34031	Passaic County, NJ
	36005	Bronx County, NY
	36047	Kings County, NY
	36061	New York County, NY
	36071	Orange County, NY
	36081	Queens County, NY
	36085	Richmond County, NY
	36087	Rockland County, NY
	36119	Westchester County, NY
35660		Niles-Benton Harbor, MI Metro area
	26021	Berrien County, MI
35840		North Port-Sarasota-Bradenton, FL Metro area
	12081	Manatee County, FL
	12115	Sarasota County, FL
35980		Norwich-New London, CT Metro area
	09011	New London County, CT
36100		Ocala, FL Metro area
	12083	Marion County, FL
36140		Ocean City, NJ Metro area
	34009	Cape May County, NJ
36220		Odessa, TX Metro area
	48135	Ector County, TX
36260		Ogden-Clearfield, UT Metro area
	49003	Box Elder County, UT
	49011	Davis County, UT
	49029	Morgan County, UT
	49057	Weber County, UT
36420		Oklahoma City, OK Metro area
	40017	Canadian County, OK
	40027	Cleveland County, OK
	40051	Grady County, OK
	40081	Lincoln County, OK
	40083	Logan County, OK
	40087	McClain County, OK
	40109	Oklahoma County, OK
36500		Olympia-Tumwater, WA Metro area
	53067	Thurston County, WA
36540		Omaha-Council Bluffs, NE-IA Metro area
	19085	Harrison County, IA
	19129	Mills County, IA
	19155	Pottawattamie County, IA
	31025	Cass County, NE
	31055	Douglas County, NE
	31153	Sarpy County, NE

Core based statistical area	State/County FIPS code	Title and Geographic Components
	31155	Saunders County, NE
	31177	Washington County, NE
36740		Orlando-Kissimmee-Sanford, FL Metro
	12069	Lake County, FL
	12095	Orange County, FL
	12097	Osceola County, FL
	12117	Seminole County, FL
36780		Oshkosh-Neenah, WI Metro area
	55139	Winnebago County, WI
36980		Owensboro, KY Metro area
	21059	Daviess County, KY
	21091	Hancock County, KY
	21149	McLean County, KY
37100		Oxnard-Thousand Oaks-Ventura, CA Metro area
	06111	Ventura County, CA
37340		Palm Bay-Melbourne-Titusville, FL Metro area
	12009	Brevard County, FL
37460		Panama City, FL Metro area
37620		Parkersburg-Vienna, WV Metro area
37860		Pensacola-Ferry Pass-Brent, FL Metro area
	12033	Escambia County, FL
	12113	Santa Rosa County, FL
37900		Peoria, IL Metro area
	17123	Marshall County, IL
	17143	Peoria County, IL
	17175	Stark County, IL
	17179	Tazewell County, IL
	17203	Woodford County, IL
		Philadelphia-Camden-Wilmington, PA-NJ-DE-MD Metro
37980		area
37980		Camden, NJ Metro Div 15804
	34005	Burlington County, NJ
	34007	Camden County, NJ
	34015	Gloucester County, NJ
		Montgomery County-Bucks County-Chester County, PA
37980		Metro Div 33874
	42017	Bucks County, PA
	42029	Chester County, PA
	42091	Montgomery County, PA
37980		Philadelphia, PA Metro Div 37964
	42045	Delaware County, PA
	42101	Philadelphia County, PA
37980		Wilmington, DE-MD-NJ Metro Div 48864
	10003	New Castle County, Delaware
	24015	Cecil County, MD
	34033	Salem County, NJ
38060		Phoenix-Mesa-Scottsdale, AZ Metro area
	04013	Maricopa County, AZ
	04021	Pinal County, AZ
38220		Pine Bluff, AR Metro area
	05025	Cleveland County, AR
	05069	Jefferson County, AR
	05079	Lincoln County, AR
38300		Pittsburgh, PA Metro area
	42003	Allegheny County, PA
	42005	Armstrong County, PA
	42007	Beaver County, PA
	42019	Butler County, PA
	42051	Fayette County, PA
	42125	Washington County, PA
	42129	Westmoreland County, PA
38340		Pittsfield, MA Metro area
	25003	Berkshire County, MA
38540		Pocatello, ID Metro area
	16005	Bannock County, ID
38860		Portland-South Portland, ME Metro area
	23005	Cumberland County, ME
	23023	Sagadahoc County, ME
	23031	York County, ME
38900		Portland-Vancouver-Hillsboro, OR-WA Metro area
	41005	Clackamas County, OR
	41009	Columbia County, OR
	41051	Multnomah County, OR
	41067	Washington County, OR
	41071	Yamhill County, OR
	53011	Clark County, WA
	53059	Skamania County, WA
38940		Port St. Lucie, FL Metro area
	12085	Martin County, FL
	12111	St. Lucie County, FL
39140		Prescott, AZ Metro area
	04025	Yavapai County, AZ
39300		Providence-Warwick, RI-MA Metro area
	25005	Bristol County, MA
	44001	Bristol County, RI
	44003	Kent County, RI
	44005	Newport County, RI
	44007	Providence County, RI

Core based statistical area	State/County FIPS code	Title and Geographic Components
	44009	Washington County, RI
39340		Provo-Orem, UT Metro area
	49023	Juab County, UT
	49049	Utah County, UT
39380		Pueblo, CO Metro area
	08101	Pueblo County, CO
39460		Punta Gorda, FL Metro area
	12015	Charlotte County, FL
39540		Racine, WI Metro area
	55101	Racine County, WI
39580		Raleigh, NC Metro area
	37069	Franklin County, NC
	37101	Johnston County, NC
	37183	Wake County, NC
39660		Rapid City, SD Metro area
	46033	Custer County, SD
	46093	Meade County, SD
	46103	Pennington County, SD
39740		Reading, PA Metro area
	42011	Berks County, PA
39820		Redding, CA Metro area
	06089	Shasta County, CA
39900		Reno, NV Metro area
	32029	Storey County, NV
	32031	Washoe County, NV
40060		Richmond, VA Metro area
	51007	Amelia County, VA
	51033	Caroline County, VA
	51036	Charles City County, VA
	51041	Chesterfield County, VA
	51053	Dinwiddie County, VA
	51075	Goochland County, VA
	51085	Hanover County, VA
	51087	Henrico County, VA
	51101	King William County, VA
	51127	New Kent County, VA
	51145	Powhatan County, VA
	51149	Prince George County, VA
	51183	Sussex County, VA
	51570	Colonial Heights city, VA
	51670	Hopewell city, VA
	51730	Petersburg city, VA
	51760	Richmond city, VA
40140		Riverside-San Bernardino-Ontario, CA
	06065	Riverside County, CA
	06071	San Bernardino County, CA
40220		Roanoke, VA Metro area
	51023	Botetourt County, VA
	51045	Craig County, VA
	51067	Franklin County, VA
	51161	Roanoke County, VA
	51770	Roanoke city, VA
	51775	Salem city, VA
40340		Rochester, MN Metro area
	27039	Dodge County, MN
	27045	Fillmore County, MN
	27109	Olmsted County, MN
	27157	Wabasha County, MN
40380		Rochester, NY Metro area
	36051	Livingston County, NY
	36055	Monroe County, NY
	36069	Ontario County, NY
	36073	Orleans County, NY
	36117	Wayne County, NY
	36123	Yates County, NY
40420		Rockford, IL Metro area
	17007	Boone County, IL
	17201	Winnebago County, IL
40580		Rocky Mount, NC Metro area
	37065	Edgecombe County, NC
	37127	Nash County, NC
40660		Rome, GA Metro area
	13115	Floyd County, GA
40900		Sacramento–Roseville–Arden-Arcade, CA Metro area
	06017	El Dorado County, CA
	06061	Placer County, CA
	06067	Sacramento County, CA
	06113	Yolo County, CA
40980		Saginaw, MI Metro area
	26145	Saginaw County, MI
41060		St. Cloud, MN Metro area
	27009	Benton County, MN
	27145	Stearns County, MN
41100		St. George, UT Metro area
	49053	Washington County, UT
41140		St. Joseph, MO-KS Metro area
	20043	Doniphan County, KS
	29003	Andrew County, MO

Core based statistical area	State/County FIPS code	Title and Geographic Components
	29021	Buchanan County, MO
	29063	DeKalb County, MO
41180		St. Louis, MO-IL Metro area
	17005	Bond County, IL
	17013	Calhoun County, IL
	17027	Clinton County, IL
	17083	Jersey County, IL
	17117	Macoupin County, IL
	17119	Madison County, IL
	17133	Monroe County, IL
	17163	St. Clair County, IL
	29071	Franklin County, MO
	29099	Jefferson County, MO
	29113	Lincoln County, MO
	29183	St. Charles County, MO
	29189	St. Louis County, MO
	29219	Warren County, MO
	29510	St. Louis city, MO
41420		Salem, OR Metro area
	41047	Marion County, OR
	41053	Polk County, OR
41500		Salinas, CA Metro area
	06053	Monterey County, CA
41540		Salisbury, MD-DE Metro area
	10005	Sussex County, DE
	24039	Somerset County, MD
	24045	Wicomico County, MD
	24047	Worcester County, MD
41620		Salt Lake City, UT Metro area
	49035	Salt Lake County, UT
	49045	Tooele County, UT
41660		San Angelo, TX Metro area
	48235	Irion County, TX
	48451	Tom Green County, TX
41700		San Antonio-New Braunfels, TX Metro
	48013	Atascosa County, TX
	48019	Bandera County, TX
	48029	Bexar County, TX
	48091	Comal County, TX
	48187	Guadalupe County, TX
	48259	Kendall County, TX
	48325	Medina County, TX
	48493	Wilson County, TX
41740		San Diego-Carlsbad, CA Metro area
	06073	San Diego County, CA
41780		Sandusky, OH Micro area
	39043	Erie County, OH
41860		San Francisco-Oakland-Hayward, CA Metro area
41860		Oakland-Hayward-Berkeley, CA Metro Div 36084
	06001	Alameda County, CA
	06013	Contra Costa County, CA
41860		San Francisco-Redwood City-South San Francisco, CA Metro Div 41884
	06075	San Francisco County, CA
	06081	San Mateo County, CA
41860		San Rafael, CA Metropolitan Div 42034
	06041	Marin County, CA
41940		San Jose-Sunnyvale-Santa Clara, CA Metro area
	06069	San Benito County, CA
	06085	Santa Clara County, CA
42020		San Luis Obispo-Paso Robles-Arroyo Grande, CA Metro area
	06079	San Luis Obispo County, CA
42100		Santa Cruz-Watsonville, CA Metro area
	06087	Santa Cruz County, CA
42140		Santa Fe, NM Metro area
	35049	Santa Fe County, NM
42200		Santa Maria-Santa Barbara, CA Metro
	06083	Santa Barbara County, CA
42220		Santa Rosa, CA Metro area
	06097	Sonoma County, CA
42340		Savannah, GA Metro area
	13029	Bryan County, GA
	13051	Chatham County, GA
	13103	Effingham County, GA
42540		Scranton–Wilkes-Barre–Hazleton, PA Metro area
	42069	Lackawanna County, PA
	42079	Luzerne County, PA
	42131	Wyoming County, PA
42660		Seattle-Tacoma-Bellevue, WA Metro area
42660		Seattle-Bellevue-Everett, WA Metro Div 42644
	53033	King County, WA
	53061	Snohomish County, WA
42660		Tacoma-Lakewood, WA Metro Div 45104
	53053	Pierce County, WA
42680		Sebastian-Vero Beach, FL Metro area
	12061	Indian River County, FL
43100		Sheboygan, WI Metro area

Core based statistical area	State/County FIPS code	Title and Geographic Components
	55117	Sheboygan County, WI
43300		Sherman-Denison, TX Metro area
	48181	Grayson County, TX
43340		Shreveport-Bossier City, LA Metro area
	22015	Bossier Parish, LA
	22017	Caddo Parish, LA
	22031	De Soto Parish, LA
	22119	Webster Parish, LA
43580		Sioux City, IA-NE-SD Metro area
	19149	Plymouth County, IA
	19193	Woodbury County, IA
	31043	Dakota County, NE
	31051	Dixon County, NE
	46127	Union County, SD
43620		Sioux Falls, SD Metro area
	46083	Lincoln County, SD
	46087	McCook County, SD
	46099	Minnehaha County, SD
	46125	Turner County, SD
43780		South Bend-Mishawaka, IN-MI Metro area
	18141	St. Joseph County, IN
	26027	Cass County, MI
43900		Spartanburg, SC Metro area
	45083	Spartanburg County, SC
	45087	Union County, SC
44060		Spokane-Spokane Valley, WA Metro area
	53051	Pend Oreille County, WA
	53063	Spokane County, WA
	53065	Stevens County, WA
44100		Springfield, IL Metro area
	17129	Menard County, IL
	17167	Sangamon County, IL
44140		Springfield, MA Metro area
	25013	Hampden County, MA
	25015	Hampshire County, MA
44180		Springfield, MO Metro area
	29043	Christian County, MO
	29059	Dallas County, MO
	29077	Greene County, MO
	29167	Polk County, MO
	29225	Webster County, MO
44220		Springfield, OH Metro area
	39023	Clark County, OH
44300		State College, PA Metro area
	42027	Centre County, PA
44700		Stockton-Lodi, CA Metro area
	06077	San Joaquin County, CA
44940		Sumter, SC Metro area
	45085	Sumter County, SC
45060		Syracuse, NY Metro area
	36053	Madison County, NY
	36067	Onondaga County, NY
	36075	Oswego County, NY
45220		Tallahassee, FL Metro area
	12039	Gadsden County, FL
	12065	Jefferson County, FL
	12073	Leon County, FL
	12129	Wakulla County, FL
45300		Tampa-St. Petersburg-Clearwater, FL Metro area
	12053	Hernando County, FL
	12057	Hillsborough County, FL
	12101	Pasco County, FL
	12103	Pinellas County, FL
45460		Terre Haute, IN Metro area
	18021	Clay County, IN
	18153	Sullivan County, IN
	18165	Vermillion County, IN
	18167	Vigo County, IN
45500		Texarkana, TX-AR Metro area
	05081	Little River County, AR
	05091	Miller County, AR
	48037	Bowie County, TX
45780		Toledo, OH Metro area
	39051	Fulton County, OH
	39095	Lucas County, OH
	39173	Wood County, OH
45820		Topeka, KS Metro area
	20085	Jackson County, KS
	20087	Jefferson County, KS
	20139	Osage County, KS
	20177	Shawnee County, KS
	20197	Wabaunsee County, KS
45940		Trenton, NJ Metro area
	34021	Mercer County, NJ
46060		Tucson, AZ Metro area
	04019	Pima County, AZ
46140		Tulsa, OK Metro area
	40037	Creek County, OK

Core based statistical area	State/County FIPS code	Title and Geographic Components
	40111	Okmulgee County, OK
	40113	Osage County, OK
	40117	Pawnee County, OK
	40131	Rogers County, OK
	40143	Tulsa County, OK
	40145	Wagoner County, OK
46220		Tuscaloosa, AL Metro area
	01065	Hale County, AL
	01107	Pickens County, AL
	01125	Tuscaloosa County, AL
46340		Tyler, TX Metro area
	48423	Smith County, TX
46520		Urban Honolulu, HI Metro area
	15003	Honolulu County, HI
46540		Utica-Rome, NY Metro area
	36043	Herkimer County, NY
	36065	Oneida County, NY
46660		Valdosta, GA Metro area
	13027	Brooks County, GA
	13101	Echols County, GA
	13173	Lanier County, GA
	13185	Lowndes County, GA
46700		Vallejo-Fairfield, CA Metro area
	06095	Solano County, CA
47020		Victoria, TX Metro area
	48175	Goliad County, TX
	48469	Victoria County, TX
47220		Vineland-Bridgeton, NJ Metro area
	34011	Cumberland County, NJ
47260		Virginia Beach-Norfolk-Newport News, VA-NC Metro area
	37053	Currituck County, NC
	37073	Gates County, NC
	51073	Gloucester County, VA
	51093	Isle of Wight County, VA
	51095	James City County, VA
	51115	Mathews County, VA
	51199	York County, VA
	51550	Chesapeake city, VA
	51650	Hampton city, VA
	51700	Newport News city, VA
	51710	Norfolk city, VA
	51735	Poquoson city, VA
	51740	Portsmouth city, VA
	51800	Suffolk city, VA
	51810	Virginia Beach city, VA
	51830	Williamsburg city, VA
47300		Visalia-Porterville, CA Metro area
	06107	Tulare County, CA
47380		Waco, TX Metro area
	48145	Falls County, TX
	48309	McLennan County, TX
47580		Warner Robins, GA Metro area
	13153	Houston County, GA
	13225	Peach County, GA
	13235	Pulaski County, GA
47900		Washington-Arlington-Alexandria, DC-VA-MD-WV Metro area
47900		Silver Spring-Frederick-Rockville, MD Metro Div 43524
	24021	Frederick County, MD
	24031	Montgomery County, MD
47900		Washington-Arlington-Alexandria, DC-VA-MD-WV Metro Div 47894
	11001	District of Columbia, DC
	24009	Calvert County, MD
	24017	Charles County, MD
	24033	Prince George's County, MD
	51013	Arlington County, VA
	51043	Clarke County, VA
	51047	Culpeper County, VA
	51059	Fairfax County, VA
	51061	Fauquier County, VA
	51107	Loudoun County, VA
	51153	Prince William County, VA

Core based statistical area	State/County FIPS code	Title and Geographic Components
	51157	Rappahannock County, VA
	51177	Spotsylvania County, VA
	51179	Stafford County, VA
	51187	Warren County, VA
	51510	Alexandria city, VA
	51600	Fairfax city, VA
	51610	Falls Church city, VA
	51630	Fredericksburg city, VA
	51683	Manassas city, VA
	51685	Manassas Park city, VA
	54037	Jefferson County, WV
47920		Washington Court House, OH Micro area
	39047	Fayette County, OH
47940		Waterloo-Cedar Falls, IA Metro area
	19013	Black Hawk County, IA
	19017	Bremer County, IA
	19075	Grundy County, IA
48140		Wausau, WI Metro area
	55073	Marathon County, WI
48300		Wenatchee, WA Metro area
	53007	Chelan County, WA
	53017	Douglas County, WA
48260		Weirton-Steubenville, WV-OH Metro area
	39081	Jefferson County, OH
	54009	Brooke County, WV
	54029	Hancock County, WV
48540		Wheeling, WV-OH Metro area
	39013	Belmont County, OH
	54051	Marshall County, WV
	54069	Ohio County, WV
48620		Wichita, KS Metro area
	20015	Butler County, KS
	20079	Harvey County, KS
	20095	Kingman County, KS
	20173	Sedgwick County, KS
	20191	Sumner County, KS
48660		Wichita Falls, TX Metro area
	48009	Archer County, TX
	48077	Clay County, TX
	48485	Wichita County, TX
48700		Williamsport, PA Metro area
	42081	Lycoming County, PA
48900		Wilmington, NC Metro area
	37129	New Hanover County, NC
	37141	Pender County, NC
49020		Winchester, VA-WV Metro area
	51069	Frederick County, VA
	51840	Winchester city, VA
	54027	Hampshire County, WV
49180		Winston-Salem, NC Metro area
	37057	Davidson County, NC
	37059	Davie County, NC
	37067	Forsyth County, NC
	37169	Stokes County, NC
	37197	Yadkin County, NC
49340		Worcester, MA-CT Metro area
	09015	Windham County, CT
	25027	Worcester County, MA
49420		Yakima, WA Metro area
	53077	Yakima County, WA
49460		Yankton, SD Micro area
	46135	Yankton County, SD
49620		York-Hanover, PA Metro area
	42133	York County, PA
49660		Youngstown-Warren-Boardman, OH-PA Metro area
	39099	Mahoning County, OH
	39155	Trumbull County, OH
	42085	Mercer County, PA
49700		Yuba City, CA Metro area
	06101	Sutter County, CA
	06115	Yuba County, CA
49740		Yuma, AZ Metro area
	04027	Yuma County, AZ

APPENDIX C. CITIES BY COUNTY

State code	County Code	Place Code	Geographic area name	2010 Census population
01			**ALABAMA**	4779736
01		03076	Auburn city	53380
01	081	03076	Lee County	53380
01		07000	Birmingham city	212237
01	073	07000	Jefferson County	210609
01	117	07000	Shelby County	1628
01		20104	Decatur city	55683
01	083	20104	Limestone County	84
01	103	20104	Morgan County	55599
01		21184	Dothan city	65496
01	045	21184	Dale County	887
01	067	21184	Henry County	5
01	069	21184	Houston County	64604
01		35896	Hoover city	81619
01	073	35896	Jefferson County	58582
01	117	35896	Shelby County	23037
01		37000	Huntsville city	180105
01	083	37000	Limestone County	1521
01	089	37000	Madison County	178584
01		50000	Mobile city	195111
01	097	50000	Mobile County	195111
01		51000	Montgomery city	205764
01	101	51000	Montgomery County	205764
01		77256	Tuscaloosa city	90468
01	125	77256	Tuscaloosa County	90468
02			**ALASKA**	710231
02		03000	Anchorage municipality	291826
02	020	03000	Anchorage Municipality	291826
04			**ARIZONA**	6392017
04		04720	Avondale city	76238
04	013	04720	Maricopa County	76238
04		07940	Buckeye town	50876
04	013	07940	Maricopa County	50876
04		12000	Chandler city	236123
04	013	12000	Maricopa County	236123
04		23620	Flagstaff city	65870
04	005	23620	Coconino County	65870
04		27400	Gilbert town	208453
04	013	27400	Maricopa County	208453
04		27820	Glendale city	226721
04	013	27820	Maricopa County	226721
04		28380	Goodyear city	65275
04	013	28380	Maricopa County	65275
04		39370	Lake Havasu City city	52527
04	015	39370	Mohave County	52527
04		46000	Mesa city	439041
04	013	46000	Maricopa County	439041
04		54050	Peoria city	154065
04	013	54050	Maricopa County	154058
04	025	54050	Yavapai County	7
04		55000	Phoenix city	1445632
04	013	55000	Maricopa County	1445632
04		65000	Scottsdale city	217385
04	013	65000	Maricopa County	217385

State code	County Code	Place Code	Geographic area name	2010 Census population
04		71510	Surprise city	117517
04	013	71510	Maricopa County	117517
04		73000	Tempe city	161719
04	013	73000	Maricopa County	161719
04		77000	Tucson city	520116
04	019	77000	Pima County	520116
04		85540	Yuma city	93064
04	027	85540	Yuma County	93064
05			**ARKANSAS**	2915918
05		15190	Conway city	58908
05	045	15190	Faulkner County	58908
05		23290	Fayetteville city	73580
05	143	23290	Washington County	73580
05		24550	Fort Smith city	86209
05	131	24550	Sebastian County	86209
05		35710	Jonesboro city	67263
05	031	35710	Craighead County	67263
05		41000	Little Rock city	193524
05	119	41000	Pulaski County	193524
05		50450	North Little Rock city	62304
05	119	50450	Pulaski County	62304
05		60410	Rogers city	55964
05	007	60410	Benton County	55964
05		66080	Springdale city	69797
05	007	66080	Benton County	6054
05	143	66080	Washington County	63743
06			**CALIFORNIA**	37253956
06		00562	Alameda city	73812
06	001	00562	Alameda County	73812
06		00884	Alhambra city	83089
06	037	00884	Los Angeles County	83089
06		02000	Anaheim city	336265
06	059	02000	Orange County	336265
06		02252	Antioch city	102372
06	013	02252	Contra Costa County	102372
06		02364	Apple Valley town	69135
06	071	02364	San Bernardino County	69135
06		02462	Arcadia city	56364
06	037	02462	Los Angeles County	56364
06		03526	Bakersfield city	347483
06	029	03526	Kern County	347483
06		03666	Baldwin Park city	75390
06	037	03666	Los Angeles County	75390
06		04982	Bellflower city	76616
06	037	04982	Los Angeles County	76616
06		06000	Berkeley city	112580
06	001	06000	Alameda County	112580
06		08142	Brentwood city	51481
06	013	08142	Contra Costa County	51481
06		08786	Buena Park city	80530
06	059	08786	Orange County	80530
06		08954	Burbank city	103340
06	037	08954	Los Angeles County	103340

State code	County Code	Place Code	Geographic area name	2010 Census population	State code	County Code	Place Code	Geographic area name	2010 Census population
06		10046	Camarillo city	65201	06		26000	Fremont city	214089
06	111	10046	Ventura County	65201	06	001	26000	Alameda County	214089
06		11194	Carlsbad city	105328	06		27000	Fresno city	494665
06	073	11194	San Diego County	105328	06	019	27000	Fresno County	494665
06		11530	Carson city	91714	06		28000	Fullerton city	135161
06	037	11530	Los Angeles County	91714	06	059	28000	Orange County	135161
06		12048	Cathedral City city	51200	06		28168	Gardena city	58829
06	065	12048	Riverside County	51200	06	037	28168	Los Angeles County	58829
06		13014	Chico city	86187	06		29000	Garden Grove city	170883
06	007	13014	Butte County	86187	06	059	29000	Orange County	170883
06		13210	Chino city	77983	06		30000	Glendale city	191719
06	071	13210	San Bernardino County	77983	06	037	30000	Los Angeles County	191719
06		13214	Chino Hills city	74799	06		30014	Glendora city	50073
06	071	13214	San Bernardino County	74799	06	037	30014	Los Angeles County	50073
06		13392	Chula Vista city	243916	06		31960	Hanford city	53967
06	073	13392	San Diego County	243916	06	031	31960	Kings County	53967
06		13588	Citrus Heights city	83301	06		32548	Hawthorne city	84293
06	067	13588	Sacramento County	83301	06	037	32548	Los Angeles County	84293
06		14218	Clovis city	95631	06		33000	Hayward city	144186
06	019	14218	Fresno County	95631	06	001	33000	Alameda County	144186
06		14890	Colton city	52154	06		33182	Hemet city	78657
06	071	14890	San Bernardino County	52154	06	065	33182	Riverside County	78657
06		15044	Compton city	96455	06		33434	Hesperia city	90173
06	037	15044	Los Angeles County	96455	06	071	33434	San Bernardino County	90173
06		16000	Concord city	122067	06		33588	Highland city	53104
06	013	16000	Contra Costa County	122067	06	071	33588	San Bernardino County	53104
06		16350	Corona city	152374	06		36000	Huntington Beach city	189992
06	065	16350	Riverside County	152374	06	059	36000	Orange County	189992
06		16532	Costa Mesa city	109960	06		36056	Huntington Park city	58114
06	059	16532	Orange County	109960	06	037	36056	Los Angeles County	58114
06		17610	Cupertino city	58302	06		36546	Inglewood city	109673
06	085	17610	Santa Clara County	58302	06	037	36546	Los Angeles County	109673
06		17918	Daly City city	101123	06		36770	Irvine city	212375
06	081	17918	San Mateo County	101123	06	059	36770	Orange County	212375
06		18100	Davis city	65622	06		39248	Laguna Niguel city	62979
06	113	18100	Yolo County	65622	06	059	39248	Orange County	62979
06		18394	Delano city	53041	06		39290	La Habra city	60239
06	029	18394	Kern County	53041	06	059	39290	Orange County	60239
06		19192	Diamond Bar city	55544	06		39486	Lake Elsinore city	51821
06	037	19192	Los Angeles County	55544	06	065	39486	Riverside County	51821
06		19766	Downey city	111772	06		39496	Lake Forest city	77264
06	037	19766	Los Angeles County	111772	06	059	39496	Orange County	77264
06		21712	El Cajon city	99478	06		39892	Lakewood city	80048
06	073	21712	San Diego County	99478	06	037	39892	Los Angeles County	80048
06		22020	Elk Grove city	153015	06		40004	La Mesa city	57065
06	067	22020	Sacramento County	153015	06	073	40004	San Diego County	57065
06		22230	El Monte city	113475	06		40130	Lancaster city	156633
06	037	22230	Los Angeles County	113475	06	037	40130	Los Angeles County	156633
06		22678	Encinitas city	59518	06		41992	Livermore city	80968
06	073	22678	San Diego County	59518	06	001	41992	Alameda County	80968
06		22804	Escondido city	143911	06		42202	Lodi city	62134
06	073	22804	San Diego County	143911	06	077	42202	San Joaquin County	62134
06		23182	Fairfield city	105321	06		43000	Long Beach city	462257
06	095	23182	Solano County	105321	06	037	43000	Los Angeles County	462257
06		24638	Folsom city	72203	06		44000	Los Angeles city	3792621
06	067	24638	Sacramento County	72203	06	037	44000	Los Angeles County	3792621
06		24680	Fontana city	196069	06		44574	Lynwood city	69772
06	071	24680	San Bernardino County	196069	06	037	44574	Los Angeles County	69772
06		25380	Fountain Valley city	55313	06		45022	Madera city	61416
06	059	25380	Orange County	55313	06	039	45022	Madera County	61416

State code	County Code	Place Code	Geographic area name	2010 Census population
06 06	 077	45484 45484	Manteca city San Joaquin County	67096 67096
06 06	 065	46842 46842	Menifee city Riverside County	77519 77519
06 06	 047	46898 46898	Merced city Merced County	78958 78958
06 06	 085	47766 47766	Milpitas city Santa Clara County	66790 66790
06 06	 059	48256 48256	Mission Viejo city Orange County	93305 93305
06 06	 099	48354 48354	Modesto city Stanislaus County	201165 201165
06 06	 037	48816 48816	Montebello city Los Angeles County	62500 62500
06 06	 037	48914 48914	Monterey Park city Los Angeles County	60269 60269
06 06	 065	49270 49270	Moreno Valley city Riverside County	193365 193365
06 06	 085	49670 49670	Mountain View city Santa Clara County	74066 74066
06 06	 065	50076 50076	Murrieta city Riverside County	103466 103466
06 06	 055	50258 50258	Napa city Napa County	76915 76915
06 06	 073	50398 50398	National City city San Diego County	58582 58582
06 06	 059	51182 51182	Newport Beach city Orange County	85186 85186
06 06	 037	52526 52526	Norwalk city Los Angeles County	105549 105549
06 06	 041	52582 52582	Novato city Marin County	51904 51904
06 06	 001	53000 53000	Oakland city Alameda County	390724 390724
06 06	 073	53322 53322	Oceanside city San Diego County	167086 167086
06 06	 071	53896 53896	Ontario city San Bernardino County	163924 163924
06 06	 059	53980 53980	Orange city Orange County	136416 136416
06 06	 111	54652 54652	Oxnard city Ventura County	197899 197899
06 06	 037	55156 55156	Palmdale city Los Angeles County	152750 152750
06 06	 085	55282 55282	Palo Alto city Santa Clara County	64403 64403
06 06	 037	55618 55618	Paramount city Los Angeles County	54098 54098
06 06	 037	56000 56000	Pasadena city Los Angeles County	137122 137122
06 06	 065	56700 56700	Perris city Riverside County	68386 68386
06 06	 097	56784 56784	Petaluma city Sonoma County	57941 57941
06 06	 037	56924 56924	Pico Rivera city Los Angeles County	62942 62942
06 06	 013	57456 57456	Pittsburg city Contra Costa County	63264 63264
06 06	 059	57526 57526	Placentia city Orange County	50533 50533

State code	County Code	Place Code	Geographic area name	2010 Census population
06 06	 001	57792 57792	Pleasanton city Alameda County	70285 70285
06 06	 037	58072 58072	Pomona city Los Angeles County	149058 149058
06 06	 107	58240 58240	Porterville city Tulare County	54165 54165
06 06	 067	59444 59444	Rancho Cordova city Sacramento County	64776 64776
06 06	 071	59451 59451	Rancho Cucamonga city San Bernardino County	165269 165269
06 06	 089	59920 59920	Redding city Shasta County	89861 89861
06 06	 071	59962 59962	Redlands city San Bernardino County	68747 68747
06 06	 037	60018 60018	Redondo Beach city Los Angeles County	66748 66748
06 06	 081	60102 60102	Redwood City city San Mateo County	76815 76815
06 06	 071	60466 60466	Rialto city San Bernardino County	99171 99171
06 06	 013	60620 60620	Richmond city Contra Costa County	103701 103701
06 06	 065	62000 62000	Riverside city Riverside County	303871 303871
06 06	 061	62364 62364	Rocklin city Placer County	56974 56974
06 06	 037	62896 62896	Rosemead city Los Angeles County	53764 53764
06 06	 061	62938 62938	Roseville city Placer County	118788 118788
06 06	 067	64000 64000	Sacramento city Sacramento County	466488 466488
06 06	 053	64224 64224	Salinas city Monterey County	150441 150441
06 06	 071	65000 65000	San Bernardino city San Bernardino County	209924 209924
06 06	 111	65042 65042	San Buenaventura (Ventura) Ventura County	106433 106433
06 06	 059	65084 65084	San Clemente city Orange County	63522 63522
06 06	 073	66000 66000	San Diego city San Diego County	1307402 1307402
06 06	 075	67000 67000	San Francisco city San Francisco County	805235 805235
06 06	 085	68000 68000	San Jose city Santa Clara County	945942 945942
06 06	 001	68084 68084	San Leandro city Alameda County	84950 84950
06 06	 073	68196 68196	San Marcos city San Diego County	83781 83781
06 06	 081	68252 68252	San Mateo city San Mateo County	97207 97207
06 06	 041	68364 68364	San Rafael city Marin County	57713 57713
06 06	 013	68378 68378	San Ramon city Contra Costa County	72148 72148
06 06	 059	69000 69000	Santa Ana city Orange County	324528 324528
06 06	 083	69070 69070	Santa Barbara city Santa Barbara County	88410 88410

State code	County Code	Place Code	Geographic area name	2010 Census population
06		69084	Santa Clara city	116468
06	085	69084	Santa Clara County	116468
06		69088	Santa Clarita city	176320
06	037	69088	Los Angeles County	176320
06		69112	Santa Cruz city	59946
06	087	69112	Santa Cruz County	59946
06		69196	Santa Maria city	99553
06	083	69196	Santa Barbara County	99553
06		70000	Santa Monica city	89736
06	037	70000	Los Angeles County	89736
06		70098	Santa Rosa city	167815
06	097	70098	Sonoma County	167815
06		70224	Santee city	53413
06	073	70224	San Diego County	53413
06		72016	Simi Valley city	124237
06	111	72016	Ventura County	124237
06		73080	South Gate city	94396
06	037	73080	Los Angeles County	94396
06		73262	South San Francisco city	63632
06	081	73262	San Mateo County	63632
06		75000	Stockton city	291707
06	077	75000	San Joaquin County	291707
06		77000	Sunnyvale city	140081
06	085	77000	Santa Clara County	140081
06		78120	Temecula city	100097
06	065	78120	Riverside County	100097
06		78582	Thousand Oaks city	126683
06	111	78582	Ventura County	126683
06		80000	Torrance city	145438
06	037	80000	Los Angeles County	145438
06		80238	Tracy city	82922
06	077	80238	San Joaquin County	82922
06		80644	Tulare city	59278
06	107	80644	Tulare County	59278
06		80812	Turlock city	68549
06	099	80812	Stanislaus County	68549
06		80854	Tustin city	75540
06	059	80854	Orange County	75540
06		81204	Union City city	69516
06	001	81204	Alameda County	69516
06		81344	Upland city	73732
06	071	81344	San Bernardino County	73732
06		81554	Vacaville city	92428
06	095	81554	Solano County	92428
06		81666	Vallejo city	115942
06	095	81666	Solano County	115942
06		82590	Victorville city	115903
06	071	82590	San Bernardino County	115903
06		82954	Visalia city	124442
06	107	82954	Tulare County	124442
06		82996	Vista city	93834
06	073	82996	San Diego County	93834
06		83346	Walnut Creek city	64173
06	013	83346	Contra Costa County	64173
06		83668	Watsonville city	51199
06	087	83668	Santa Cruz County	51199
06		84200	West Covina city	106098
06	037	84200	Los Angeles County	106098
06		84550	Westminster city	89701
06	059	84550	Orange County	89701

State code	County Code	Place Code	Geographic area name	2010 Census population
06		85292	Whittier city	85331
06	037	85292	Los Angeles County	85331
06		86328	Woodland city	55468
06	113	86328	Yolo County	55468
06		86832	Yorba Linda city	64234
06	059	86832	Orange County	64234
06		86972	Yuba City city	64925
06	101	86972	Sutter County	64925
06		87042	Yucaipa city	51367
06	071	87042	San Bernardino County	51367
08			**COLORADO**	5029196
08		03455	Arvada city	106433
08	001	03455	Adams County	2849
08	059	03455	Jefferson County	103584
08		04000	Aurora city	325078
08	001	04000	Adams County	39871
08	005	04000	Arapahoe County	285090
08	035	04000	Douglas County	117
08		07850	Boulder city	97385
08	013	07850	Boulder County	97385
08		09280	Broomfield city	55889
08	014	09280	Broomfield County	55889
08		12815	Centennial city	100377
08	005	12815	Arapahoe County	100377
08		16000	Colorado Springs city	416427
08	041	16000	El Paso County	416427
08		20000	Denver city	600158
08	031	20000	Denver County	600158
08		27425	Fort Collins city	143986
08	069	27425	Larimer County	143986
08		31660	Grand Junction city	58566
08	077	31660	Mesa County	58566
08		32155	Greeley city	92889
08	123	32155	Weld County	92889
08		43000	Lakewood city	142980
08	059	43000	Jefferson County	142980
08		45970	Longmont city	86270
08	013	45970	Boulder County	86240
08	123	45970	Weld County	30
08		46465	Loveland city	66859
08	069	46465	Larimer County	66859
08		62000	Pueblo city	106595
08	101	62000	Pueblo County	106595
08		77290	Thornton city	118772
08	001	77290	Adams County	118772
08	123	77290	Weld County	
08		83835	Westminster city	106114
08	001	83835	Adams County	63696
08	059	83835	Jefferson County	42418
09			**CONNECTICUT**	3574097
09		08000	Bridgeport city	144229
09	001	08000	Fairfield County	144229
09		08420	Bristol city	60477
09	003	08420	Hartford County	60477
09		18430	Danbury city	80893
09	001	18430	Fairfield County	80893
09		37000	Hartford city	124775
09	003	37000	Hartford County	124775
09		46450	Meriden city	60868
09	009	46450	New Haven County	60868
09		50370	New Britain city	73206

State code	County Code	Place Code	Geographic area name	2010 Census population
09	003	50370	Hartford County	73206
09		52000	New Haven city	129779
09	009	52000	New Haven County	129779
09		55990	Norwalk city	85603
09	001	55990	Fairfield County	85603
09		73000	Stamford city	122643
09	001	73000	Fairfield County	122643
09		80000	Waterbury city	110366
09	009	80000	New Haven County	110366
09		82800	West Haven city	55564
09	009	82800	New Haven County	55564
10			**DELAWARE**	897934
10		77580	Wilmington city	70851
10	003	77580	New Castle County	70851
11			**DISTRICT OF COLUMBIA**	601723
11		50000	Washington city	601723
11	001	50000	District of Columbia	601723
12			**FLORIDA**	18801310
12		07300	Boca Raton city	84392
12	099	07300	Palm Beach County	84392
12		07875	Boynton Beach city	68217
12	099	07875	Palm Beach County	68217
12		10275	Cape Coral city	154305
12	071	10275	Lee County	154305
12		12875	Clearwater city	107685
12	103	12875	Pinellas County	107685
12		13275	Coconut Creek city	52909
12	011	13275	Broward County	52909
12		14400	Coral Springs city	121096
12	011	14400	Broward County	121096
12		16475	Davie town	91992
12	011	16475	Broward County	91992
12		16525	Daytona Beach city	61005
12	127	16525	Volusia County	61005
12		16725	Deerfield Beach city	75018
12	011	16725	Broward County	75018
12		17100	Delray Beach city	60522
12	099	17100	Palm Beach County	60522
12		17200	Deltona city	85182
12	127	17200	Volusia County	85182
12		24000	Fort Lauderdale city	165521
12	011	24000	Broward County	165521
12		24125	Fort Myers city	62298
12	071	24125	Lee County	62298
12		25175	Gainesville city	124354
12	001	25175	Alachua County	124354
12		30000	Hialeah city	224669
12	086	30000	Miami-Dade County	224669
12		32000	Hollywood city	140768
12	011	32000	Broward County	140768
12		32275	Homestead city	60512
12	086	32275	Miami-Dade County	60512
12		35000	Jacksonville city	821784
12	031	35000	Duval County	821784
12		35875	Jupiter town	55156
12	099	35875	Palm Beach County	55156
12		36950	Kissimmee city	59682
12	097	36950	Osceola County	59682
12		38250	Lakeland city	97422
12	105	38250	Polk County	97422
12		39425	Largo city	77648
12	103	39425	Pinellas County	77648
12		39550	Lauderhill city	66887
12	011	39550	Broward County	66887
12		43125	Margate city	53284
12	011	43125	Broward County	53284
12		43975	Melbourne city	76068
12	009	43975	Brevard County	76068
12		45000	Miami city	399457
12	086	45000	Miami-Dade County	399457
12		45025	Miami Beach city	87779
12	086	45025	Miami-Dade County	87779
12		45060	Miami Gardens city	107167
12	086	45060	Miami-Dade County	107167
12		45975	Miramar city	122041
12	011	45975	Broward County	122041
12		49450	North Miami city	58786
12	086	49450	Miami-Dade County	58786
12		49675	North Port city	57357
12	115	49675	Sarasota County	57357
12		50750	Ocala city	56315
12	083	50750	Marion County	56315
12		53000	Orlando city	238300
12	095	53000	Orange County	238300
12		54000	Palm Bay city	103190
12	009	54000	Brevard County	103190
12		54200	Palm Coast city	75180
12	035	54200	Flagler County	75180
12		55775	Pembroke Pines city	154750
12	011	55775	Broward County	154750
12		55925	Pensacola city	51923
12	033	55925	Escambia County	51923
12		57425	Plantation city	84955
12	011	57425	Broward County	84955
12		58050	Pompano Beach city	99845
12	011	58050	Broward County	99845
12		58575	Port Orange city	56048
12	127	58575	Volusia County	56048
12		58715	Port St. Lucie city	164603
12	111	58715	St. Lucie County	164603
12		63000	St. Petersburg city	244769
12	103	63000	Pinellas County	244769
12		63650	Sanford city	53570
12	117	63650	Seminole County	53570
12		64175	Sarasota city	51917
12	115	64175	Sarasota County	51917
12		69700	Sunrise city	84439
12	011	69700	Broward County	84439
12		70600	Tallahassee city	181376
12	073	70600	Leon County	181376
12		70675	Tamarac city	60427
12	011	70675	Broward County	60427
12		71000	Tampa city	335709
12	057	71000	Hillsborough County	335709
12		75812	Wellington village	56508
12	099	75812	Palm Beach County	56508
12		76582	Weston city	65333
12	011	76582	Broward County	65333
12		76600	West Palm Beach city	99919

State code	County Code	Place Code	Geographic area name	2010 Census population
12	099	76600	Palm Beach County	99919
13			**GEORGIA**	9687653
13		01052	Albany city	77434
13	095	01052	Dougherty County	77434
13		01696	Alpharetta city	57551
13	121	01696	Fulton County	57551
13		04000	Atlanta city	420003
13	089	04000	DeKalb County	28292
13	121	04000	Fulton County	391711
13		19000	Columbus city	189885
13	215	19000	Muscogee County	189885
13		42425	Johns Creek city	76728
13	121	42425	Fulton County	76728
13		49000	Macon city	91351
13	021	49000	Bibb County	90885
13	169	49000	Jones County	466
13		49756	Marietta city	56579
13	067	49756	Cobb County	56579
13		67284	Roswell city	88346
13	121	67284	Fulton County	88346
13		68516	Sandy Springs city	93853
13	121	68516	Fulton County	93853
13		69000	Savannah city	136286
13	051	69000	Chatham County	136286
13		71492	Smyrna city	51271
13	067	71492	Cobb County	51271
13		78800	Valdosta city	54518
13	185	78800	Lowndes County	54518
13		80508	Warner Robins city	66588
13	153	80508	Houston County	66224
13	225	80508	Peach County	364
15			**HAWAII**	1360301
15		71550	Urban Honolulu CDP	337256
15	003	71550	Honolulu County	337256
16			**IDAHO**	1567582
16		08830	Boise City city	205671
16	001	08830	Ada County	205671
16		39700	Idaho Falls city	56813
16	019	39700	Bonneville County	56813
16		52120	Meridian city	75092
16	001	52120	Ada County	75092
16		56260	Nampa city	81557
16	027	56260	Canyon County	81557
16		64090	Pocatello city	54255
16	005	64090	Bannock County	54239
16	077	64090	Power County	16
17			**ILLINOIS**	12830632
17		02154	Arlington Heights village	75101
17	031	02154	Cook County	75101
17	097	02154	Lake County	
17		03012	Aurora city	197899
17	043	03012	DuPage County	49433
17	089	03012	Kane County	130976
17	093	03012	Kendall County	6019
17	197	03012	Will County	11471
17		05573	Berwyn city	56657
17	031	05573	Cook County	56657
17		06613	Bloomington city	76610
17	113	06613	McLean County	76610
17		07133	Bolingbrook village	73366
17	043	07133	DuPage County	1571
17	197	07133	Will County	71795
17		12385	Champaign city	81055
17	019	12385	Champaign County	81055
17		14000	Chicago city	2695598
17	031	14000	Cook County	2695598
17	043	14000	DuPage County	
17		14351	Cicero town	83891
17	031	14351	Cook County	83891
17		18823	Decatur city	76122
17	115	18823	Macon County	76122
17		19642	Des Plaines city	58364
17	031	19642	Cook County	58364
17		23074	Elgin city	108188
17	031	23074	Cook County	24032
17	089	23074	Kane County	84156
17		24582	Evanston city	74486
17	031	24582	Cook County	74486
17		35411	Hoffman Estates village	51895
17	031	35411	Cook County	51895
17	089	35411	Kane County	
17		38570	Joliet city	147433
17	093	38570	Kendall County	9749
17	197	38570	Will County	137684
17		51089	Mount Prospect village	54167
17	031	51089	Cook County	54167
17		51622	Naperville city	141853
17	043	51622	DuPage County	94533
17	197	51622	Will County	47320
17		53234	Normal town	52497
17	113	53234	McLean County	52497
17		54820	Oak Lawn village	56690
17	031	54820	Cook County	56690
17		54885	Oak Park village	51878
17	031	54885	Cook County	51878
17		56640	Orland Park village	56767
17	031	56640	Cook County	56583
17	197	56640	Will County	184
17		57225	Palatine village	68557
17	031	57225	Cook County	68557
17	097	57225	Lake County	
17		59000	Peoria city	115007
17	143	59000	Peoria County	115007
17		65000	Rockford city	152871
17	201	65000	Winnebago County	152871
17		68003	Schaumburg village	74227
17	031	68003	Cook County	74227
17	043	68003	DuPage County	
17		70122	Skokie village	64784
17	031	70122	Cook County	64784
17		72000	Springfield city	116250
17	167	72000	Sangamon County	116250
17		75484	Tinley Park village	56703
17	031	75484	Cook County	49236
17	197	75484	Will County	7467
17		79293	Waukegan city	89078
17	097	79293	Lake County	89078
17		81048	Wheaton city	52894
17	043	81048	DuPage County	52894
18			**INDIANA**	6483802
18		01468	Anderson city	56129
18	095	01468	Madison County	56129
18		05860	Bloomington city	80405
18	105	05860	Monroe County	80405

State code	County Code	Place Code	Geographic area name	2010 Census population
18		10342	Carmel city	79191
18	057	10342	Hamilton County	79191
18		20728	Elkhart city	50949
18	039	20728	Elkhart County	50949
18		22000	Evansville city	117429
18	163	22000	Vanderburgh County	117429
18		23278	Fishers town	76794
18	057	23278	Hamilton County	76794
18		25000	Fort Wayne city	253691
18	003	25000	Allen County	253691
18		27000	Gary city	80294
18	089	27000	Lake County	80294
18		31000	Hammond city	80830
18	089	31000	Lake County	80830
18		40788	Lafayette city	67140
18	157	40788	Tippecanoe County	67140
18		51876	Muncie city	70085
18	035	51876	Delaware County	70085
18		54180	Noblesville city	51969
18	057	54180	Hamilton County	51969
18		71000	South Bend city	101168
18	141	71000	St. Joseph County	101168
18		75428	Terre Haute city	60785
18	167	75428	Vigo County	60785
19			**IOWA**	3046355
19		01855	Ames city	58965
19	169	01855	Story County	58965
19		12000	Cedar Rapids city	126326
19	113	12000	Linn County	126326
19		16860	Council Bluffs city	62230
19	155	16860	Pottawattamie County	62230
19		19000	Davenport city	99685
19	163	19000	Scott County	99685
19		21000	Des Moines city	203433
19	153	21000	Polk County	203419
19	181	21000	Warren County	14
19		22395	Dubuque city	57637
19	061	22395	Dubuque County	57637
19		38595	Iowa City city	67862
19	103	38595	Johnson County	67862
19		73335	Sioux City city	82684
19	149	73335	Plymouth County	6
19	193	73335	Woodbury County	82678
19		82425	Waterloo city	68406
19	013	82425	Black Hawk County	68406
19		83910	West Des Moines city	56609
19	049	83910	Dallas County	11569
19	153	83910	Polk County	44999
19	181	83910	Warren County	41
20			**KANSAS**	2853118
20		36000	Kansas City city	145786
20	209	36000	Wyandotte County	145786
20		38900	Lawrence city	87643
20	045	38900	Douglas County	87643
20		44250	Manhattan city	52281
20	149	44250	Pottawatomie County	146
20	161	44250	Riley County	52135
20		52575	Olathe city	125872
20	091	52575	Johnson County	125872
20		53775	Overland Park city	173372
20	091	53775	Johnson County	173372
20		64500	Shawnee city	62209
20	091	64500	Johnson County	62209
20		71000	Topeka city	127473
20	177	71000	Shawnee County	127473
20		79000	Wichita city	382368
20	173	79000	Sedgwick County	382368
21			**KENTUCKY**	4339367
21		08902	Bowling Green city	58067
21	227	08902	Warren County	58067
21		46027	Lexington-Fayette urban county	295803
21	067	46027	Fayette County	295803
21		58620	Owensboro city	57265
21	059	58620	Daviess County	57265
22			**LOUISIANA**	4533372
22		05000	Baton Rouge city	229493
22	033	05000	East Baton Rouge Parish	229493
22		08920	Bossier City city	61315
22	015	08920	Bossier Parish	61315
22		39475	Kenner city	66702
22	051	39475	Jefferson Parish	66702
22		40735	Lafayette city	120623
22	055	40735	Lafayette Parish	120623
22		41155	Lake Charles city	71993
22	019	41155	Calcasieu Parish	71993
22		55000	New Orleans city	343829
22	071	55000	Orleans Parish	343829
22		70000	Shreveport city	199311
22	015	70000	Bossier Parish	2702
22	017	70000	Caddo Parish	196609
23			**MAINE**	1328361
23		60545	Portland city	66194
23	005	60545	Cumberland County	66194
24			**MARYLAND**	5773552
24		04000	Baltimore city	620961
24	510	04000	Baltimore city	620961
24		08775	Bowie city	54727
24	033	08775	Prince George's County	54727
24		30325	Frederick city	65239
24	021	30325	Frederick County	65239
24		31175	Gaithersburg city	59933
24	031	31175	Montgomery County	59933
24		67675	Rockville city	61209
24	031	67675	Montgomery County	61209
25			**MASSACHUSETTS**	6547629
25		07000	Boston city	617594
25	025	07000	Suffolk County	617594
25		09000	Brockton city	93810
25	023	09000	Plymouth County	93810
25		11000	Cambridge city	105162
25	017	11000	Middlesex County	105162
25		13660	Chicopee city	55298
25	013	13660	Hampden County	55298
25		23000	Fall River city	88857
25	005	23000	Bristol County	88857
25		29405	Haverhill city	60879
25	009	29405	Essex County	60879
25		34550	Lawrence city	76377
25	009	34550	Essex County	76377

State code	County Code	Place Code	Geographic area name	2010 Census population
25		37000	Lowell city	106519
25	017	37000	Middlesex County	106519
25		37490	Lynn city	90329
25	009	37490	Essex County	90329
25		37875	Malden city	59450
25	017	37875	Middlesex County	59450
25		39835	Medford city	56173
25	017	39835	Middlesex County	56173
25		45000	New Bedford city	95072
25	005	45000	Bristol County	95072
25		45560	Newton city	85146
25	017	45560	Middlesex County	85146
25		52490	Peabody city	51251
25	009	52490	Essex County	51251
25		55745	Quincy city	92271
25	021	55745	Norfolk County	92271
25		56585	Revere city	51755
25	025	56585	Suffolk County	51755
25		62535	Somerville city	75754
25	017	62535	Middlesex County	75754
25		67000	Springfield city	153060
25	013	67000	Hampden County	153060
25		69170	Taunton city	55874
25	005	69170	Bristol County	55874
25		72600	Waltham city	60632
25	017	72600	Middlesex County	60632
25		78972	Weymouth Town city	53743
25	021	78972	Norfolk County	53743
25		82000	Worcester city	181045
25	027	82000	Worcester County	181045
26			**MICHIGAN**	9883640
26		03000	Ann Arbor city	113934
26	161	03000	Washtenaw County	113934
26		05920	Battle Creek city	52347
26	025	05920	Calhoun County	52347
26		21000	Dearborn city	98153
26	163	21000	Wayne County	98153
26		21020	Dearborn Heights city	57774
26	163	21020	Wayne County	57774
26		22000	Detroit city	713777
26	163	22000	Wayne County	713777
26		27440	Farmington Hills city	79740
26	125	27440	Oakland County	79740
26		29000	Flint city	102434
26	049	29000	Genesee County	102434
26		42160	Kalamazoo city	74262
26	077	42160	Kalamazoo County	74262
26		46000	Lansing city	114297
26	045	46000	Eaton County	4734
26	065	46000	Ingham County	109563
26		49000	Livonia city	96942
26	163	49000	Wayne County	96942
26		59440	Novi city	55224
26	125	59440	Oakland County	55224
26		65440	Pontiac city	59515
26	125	65440	Oakland County	59515
26		69035	Rochester Hills city	70995
26	125	69035	Oakland County	70995
26		70040	Royal Oak city	57236
26	125	70040	Oakland County	57236
26		70520	Saginaw city	51508
26	145	70520	Saginaw County	51508
26		70760	St. Clair Shores city	59715
26	099	70760	Macomb County	59715
26		74900	Southfield city	71739
26	125	74900	Oakland County	71739
26		76460	Sterling Heights city	129699
26	099	76460	Macomb County	129699
26		79000	Taylor city	63131
26	163	79000	Wayne County	63131
26		80700	Troy city	80980
26	125	80700	Oakland County	80980
26		84000	Warren city	134056
26	099	84000	Macomb County	134056
26		86000	Westland city	84094
26	163	86000	Wayne County	84094
26		88940	Wyoming city	72125
26	081	88940	Kent County	72125
27			**MINNESOTA**	5303925
27		06382	Blaine city	57186
27	003	06382	Anoka County	57186
27	123	06382	Ramsey County	
27		06616	Bloomington city	82893
27	053	06616	Hennepin County	82893
27		07966	Brooklyn Park city	75781
27	053	07966	Hennepin County	75781
27		08794	Burnsville city	60306
27	037	08794	Dakota County	60306
27		13114	Coon Rapids city	61476
27	003	13114	Anoka County	61476
27		17288	Eagan city	64206
27	037	17288	Dakota County	64206
27		18116	Eden Prairie city	60797
27	053	18116	Hennepin County	60797
27		35180	Lakeville city	55954
27	037	35180	Dakota County	55954
27		40166	Maple Grove city	61567
27	053	40166	Hennepin County	61567
27		43000	Minneapolis city	382578
27	053	43000	Hennepin County	382578
27		51730	Plymouth city	70576
27	053	51730	Hennepin County	70576
27		54880	Rochester city	106769
27	109	54880	Olmsted County	106769
27		56896	St. Cloud city	65842
27	009	56896	Benton County	6396
27	141	56896	Sherburne County	6785
27	145	56896	Stearns County	52661
27		58000	St. Paul city	285068
27	123	58000	Ramsey County	285068
27		71428	Woodbury city	61961
27	163	71428	Washington County	61961
28			**MISSISSIPPI**	2967297
28		29700	Gulfport city	67793
28	047	29700	Harrison County	67793
28		36000	Jackson city	173514
28	049	36000	Hinds County	172891
28	089	36000	Madison County	622
28	121	36000	Rankin County	1
29			**MISSOURI**	5988927
29		06652	Blue Springs city	52575

State code	County Code	Place Code	Geographic area name	2010 Census population
29	095	06652	Jackson County	52575
29		15670	Columbia city	108500
29	019	15670	Boone County	108500
29		24778	Florissant city	52158
29	189	24778	St. Louis County	52158
29		35000	Independence city	116830
29	047	35000	Clay County	
29	095	35000	Jackson County	116830
29		37592	Joplin city	50150
29	097	37592	Jasper County	43955
29	145	37592	Newton County	6195
29		38000	Kansas City city	459787
29	037	38000	Cass County	197
29	047	38000	Clay County	113415
29	095	38000	Jackson County	302499
29	165	38000	Platte County	43676
29		41348	Lee's Summit city	91364
29	037	41348	Cass County	1917
29	095	41348	Jackson County	89447
29		54074	O'Fallon city	79329
29	183	54074	St. Charles County	79329
29		64082	St. Charles city	65794
29	183	64082	St. Charles County	65794
29		64550	St. Joseph city	76780
29	021	64550	Buchanan County	76780
29		65000	St. Louis city	319294
29	510	65000	St. Louis city	319294
29		65126	St. Peters city	52575
29	183	65126	St. Charles County	52575
29		70000	Springfield city	159498
29	043	70000	Christian County	2
29	077	70000	Greene County	159496
30			**MONTANA**	989415
30		06550	Billings city	104170
30	111	06550	Yellowstone County	104170
30		32800	Great Falls city	58505
30	013	32800	Cascade County	58505
30		50200	Missoula city	66788
30	063	50200	Missoula County	66788
31			**NEBRASKA**	1826341
31		03950	Bellevue city	50137
31	153	03950	Sarpy County	50137
31		28000	Lincoln city	258379
31	109	28000	Lancaster County	258379
31		37000	Omaha city	408958
31	055	37000	Douglas County	408958
32			**NEVADA**	2700551
32		09700	Carson City	55274
32	510	09700	Carson City	55274
32		31900	Henderson city	257729
32	003	31900	Clark County	257729
32		40000	Las Vegas city	583756
32	003	40000	Clark County	583756
32		51800	North Las Vegas city	216961
32	003	51800	Clark County	216961
32		60600	Reno city	225221
32	031	60600	Washoe County	225221
32		68400	Sparks city	90264
32	031	68400	Washoe County	90264
33			**NEW HAMPSHIRE**	1316470
33		45140	Manchester city	109565

State code	County Code	Place Code	Geographic area name	2010 Census population
33	011	45140	Hillsborough County	109565
33		50260	Nashua city	86494
33	011	50260	Hillsborough County	86494
34			**NEW JERSEY**	8791894
34		03580	Bayonne city	63024
34	017	03580	Hudson County	63024
34		10000	Camden city	77344
34	007	10000	Camden County	77344
34		13690	Clifton city	84136
34	031	13690	Passaic County	84136
34		19390	East Orange city	64270
34	013	19390	Essex County	64270
34		21000	Elizabeth city	124969
34	039	21000	Union County	124969
34		32250	Hoboken city	50005
34	017	32250	Hudson County	50005
34		36000	Jersey City city	247597
34	017	36000	Hudson County	247597
34		51000	Newark city	277140
34	013	51000	Essex County	277140
34		51210	New Brunswick city	55181
34	023	51210	Middlesex County	55181
34		56550	Passaic city	69781
34	031	56550	Passaic County	69781
34		57000	Paterson city	146199
34	031	57000	Passaic County	146199
34		58200	Perth Amboy city	50814
34	023	58200	Middlesex County	50814
34		74000	Trenton city	84913
34	021	74000	Mercer County	84913
34		74630	Union City city	66455
34	017	74630	Hudson County	66455
34		76070	Vineland city	60724
34	011	76070	Cumberland County	60724
35			**NEW MEXICO**	2059179
35		02000	Albuquerque city	545852
35	001	02000	Bernalillo County	545852
35		39380	Las Cruces city	97618
35	013	39380	Do±a Ana County	97618
35		63460	Rio Rancho city	87521
35	001	63460	Bernalillo County	130
35	043	63460	Sandoval County	87391
35		70500	Santa Fe city	67947
35	049	70500	Santa Fe County	67947
36			**NEW YORK**	19378102
36		01000	Albany city	97856
36	001	01000	Albany County	97856
36		11000	Buffalo city	261310
36	029	11000	Erie County	261310
36		33139	Hempstead village	53891
36	059	33139	Nassau County	53891
36		49121	Mount Vernon city	67292
36	119	49121	Westchester County	67292
36		50617	New Rochelle city	77062
36	119	50617	Westchester County	77062
36		51000	New York city	8175133
36	005	51000	Bronx County	1385108
36	047	51000	Kings County	2504700
36	061	51000	New York County	1585873
36	081	51000	Queens County	2230722
36	085	51000	Richmond County	468730

State code	County Code	Place Code	Geographic area name	2010 Census population
36		51055	Niagara Falls city	50193
36	063	51055	Niagara County	50193
36		63000	Rochester city	210565
36	055	63000	Monroe County	210565
36		65508	Schenectady city	66135
36	093	65508	Schenectady County	66135
36		73000	Syracuse city	145170
36	067	73000	Onondaga County	145170
36		75484	Troy city	50129
36	083	75484	Rensselaer County	50129
36		76540	Utica city	62235
36	065	76540	Oneida County	62235
36		81677	White Plains city	56853
36	119	81677	Westchester County	56853
37			**NORTH CAROLINA**	9535483
37		02140	Asheville city	83393
37	021	02140	Buncombe County	83393
37		10740	Cary town	135234
37	037	10740	Chatham County	1422
37	183	10740	Wake County	133812
37		11800	Chapel Hill town	57233
37	063	11800	Durham County	2836
37	135	11800	Orange County	54397
37		12000	Charlotte city	731424
37	119	12000	Mecklenburg County	731424
37		14100	Concord city	79066
37	025	14100	Cabarrus County	79066
37		19000	Durham city	228330
37	063	19000	Durham County	228300
37	135	19000	Orange County	30
37	183	19000	Wake County	
37		22920	Fayetteville city	200564
37	051	22920	Cumberland County	200564
37		25580	Gastonia city	71741
37	071	25580	Gaston County	71741
37		28000	Greensboro city	269666
37	081	28000	Guilford County	269666
37		28080	Greenville city	84554
37	147	28080	Pitt County	84554
37		31400	High Point city	104371
37	057	31400	Davidson County	5310
37	067	31400	Forsyth County	8
37	081	31400	Guilford County	99042
37	151	31400	Randolph County	11
37		34200	Jacksonville city	70145
37	133	34200	Onslow County	70145
37		55000	Raleigh city	403892
37	063	55000	Durham County	1067
37	183	55000	Wake County	402825
37		57500	Rocky Mount city	57477
37	065	57500	Edgecombe County	17524
37	127	57500	Nash County	39953
37		74440	Wilmington city	106476
37	129	74440	New Hanover County	106476
37		75000	Winston-Salem city	229617
37	067	75000	Forsyth County	229617
38			**NORTH DAKOTA**	672591
38		07200	Bismarck city	61272
38	015	07200	Burleigh County	61272
38		25700	Fargo city	105549
38	017	25700	Cass County	105549
38		32060	Grand Forks city	52838
38	035	32060	Grand Forks County	52838
39			**OHIO**	11536504
39		01000	Akron city	199110
39	153	01000	Summit County	199110
39		12000	Canton city	73007
39	151	12000	Stark County	73007
39		15000	Cincinnati city	296943
39	061	15000	Hamilton County	296943
39		16000	Cleveland city	396815
39	035	16000	Cuyahoga County	396815
39		18000	Columbus city	787033
39	041	18000	Delaware County	7245
39	045	18000	Fairfield County	9666
39	049	18000	Franklin County	770122
39		21000	Dayton city	141527
39	113	21000	Montgomery County	141527
39		25256	Elyria city	54533
39	093	25256	Lorain County	54533
39		33012	Hamilton city	62477
39	017	33012	Butler County	62477
39		40040	Kettering city	56163
39	057	40040	Greene County	467
39	113	40040	Montgomery County	55696
39		41664	Lakewood city	52131
39	035	41664	Cuyahoga County	52131
39		44856	Lorain city	64097
39	093	44856	Lorain County	64097
39		61000	Parma city	81601
39	035	61000	Cuyahoga County	81601
39		74118	Springfield city	60608
39	023	74118	Clark County	60608
39		77000	Toledo city	287208
39	095	77000	Lucas County	287208
39		88000	Youngstown city	66982
39	099	88000	Mahoning County	66971
39	155	88000	Trumbull County	11
40			**OKLAHOMA**	3751351
40		09050	Broken Arrow city	98850
40	143	09050	Tulsa County	80634
40	145	09050	Wagoner County	18216
40		23200	Edmond city	81405
40	109	23200	Oklahoma County	81405
40		41850	Lawton city	96867
40	031	41850	Comanche County	96867
40		48350	Midwest City city	54371
40	109	48350	Oklahoma County	54371
40		49200	Moore city	55081
40	027	49200	Cleveland County	55081
40		52500	Norman city	110925
40	027	52500	Cleveland County	110925
40		55000	Oklahoma City city	579999
40	017	55000	Canadian County	44541
40	027	55000	Cleveland County	63723
40	109	55000	Oklahoma County	471671
40	125	55000	Pottawatomie County	64
40		75000	Tulsa city	391906
40	113	75000	Osage County	6136
40	131	75000	Rogers County	
40	143	75000	Tulsa County	385613
40	145	75000	Wagoner County	157
41			**OREGON**	3831074
41		01000	Albany city	50158
41	003	01000	Benton County	6463

State code	County Code	Place Code	Geographic area name	2010 Census population
41	043	01000	Linn County	43695
41		05350	Beaverton city	89803
41	067	05350	Washington County	89803
41		05800	Bend city	76639
41	017	05800	Deschutes County	76639
41		15800	Corvallis city	54462
41	003	15800	Benton County	54462
41		23850	Eugene city	156185
41	039	23850	Lane County	156185
41		31250	Gresham city	105594
41	051	31250	Multnomah County	105594
41		34100	Hillsboro city	91611
41	067	34100	Washington County	91611
41		47000	Medford city	74907
41	029	47000	Jackson County	74907
41		59000	Portland city	583776
41	005	59000	Clackamas County	744
41	051	59000	Multnomah County	581485
41	067	59000	Washington County	1547
41		64900	Salem city	154637
41	047	64900	Marion County	130398
41	053	64900	Polk County	24239
41		69600	Springfield city	59403
41	039	69600	Lane County	59403
42			**PENNSYLVANIA**	12702379
42		02000	Allentown city	118032
42	077	02000	Lehigh County	118032
42		06088	Bethlehem city	74982
42	077	06088	Lehigh County	19343
42	095	06088	Northampton County	55639
42		24000	Erie city	101786
42	049	24000	Erie County	101786
42		41216	Lancaster city	59322
42	071	41216	Lancaster County	59322
42		60000	Philadelphia city	1526006
42	101	60000	Philadelphia County	1526006
42		61000	Pittsburgh city	305704
42	003	61000	Allegheny County	305704
42		63624	Reading city	88082
42	011	63624	Berks County	88082
42		69000	Scranton city	76089
42	069	69000	Lackawanna County	76089
44			**RHODE ISLAND**	1052567
44		19180	Cranston city	80387
44	007	19180	Providence County	80387
44		54640	Pawtucket city	71148
44	007	54640	Providence County	71148
44		59000	Providence city	178042
44	007	59000	Providence County	178042
44		74300	Warwick city	82672
44	003	74300	Kent County	82672
45			**SOUTH CAROLINA**	4625364
45		13330	Charleston city	120083
45	015	13330	Berkeley County	8095
45	019	13330	Charleston County	111988
45		16000	Columbia city	129272
45	063	16000	Lexington County	559
45	079	16000	Richland County	128713
45		30850	Greenville city	58409
45	045	30850	Greenville County	58409
45		48535	Mount Pleasant town	67843
45	019	48535	Charleston County	67843
45		50875	North Charleston city	97471
45	015	50875	Berkeley County	0
45	019	50875	Charleston County	78393
45	035	50875	Dorchester County	19078
45		61405	Rock Hill city	66154
45	091	61405	York County	66154
46			**SOUTH DAKOTA**	814180
46		52980	Rapid City city	67956
46	103	52980	Pennington County	67956
46		59020	Sioux Falls city	153888
46	083	59020	Lincoln County	21095
46	099	59020	Minnehaha County	132793
47			**TENNESSEE**	6346105
47		03440	Bartlett city	54613
47	157	03440	Shelby County	54613
47		14000	Chattanooga city	167674
47	065	14000	Hamilton County	167674
47		15160	Clarksville city	132929
47	125	15160	Montgomery County	132929
47		27740	Franklin city	62487
47	187	27740	Williamson County	62487
47		33280	Hendersonville city	51372
47	165	33280	Sumner County	51372
47		37640	Jackson city	65211
47	113	37640	Madison County	65211
47		38320	Johnson City city	63152
47	019	38320	Carter County	1252
47	163	38320	Sullivan County	367
47	179	38320	Washington County	61533
47		40000	Knoxville city	178874
47	093	40000	Knox County	178874
47		48000	Memphis city	646889
47	157	48000	Shelby County	646889
47		51560	Murfreesboro city	108755
47	149	51560	Rutherford County	108755
48			**TEXAS**	25145561
48		01000	Abilene city	117063
48	253	01000	Jones County	5145
48	441	01000	Taylor County	111918
48		01924	Allen city	84246
48	085	01924	Collin County	84246
48		03000	Amarillo city	190695
48	375	03000	Potter County	105486
48	381	03000	Randall County	85209
48		04000	Arlington city	365438
48	439	04000	Tarrant County	365438
48		05000	Austin city	790390
48	209	05000	Hays County	2
48	453	05000	Travis County	754691
48	491	05000	Williamson County	35697
48		06128	Baytown city	71802
48	071	06128	Chambers County	4116
48	201	06128	Harris County	67686
48		07000	Beaumont city	118296
48	245	07000	Jefferson County	118296
48		10768	Brownsville city	175023
48	061	10768	Cameron County	175023
48		10912	Bryan city	76201
48	041	10912	Brazos County	76201
48		13024	Carrollton city	119097
48	085	13024	Collin County	2
48	113	13024	Dallas County	49352

State code	County Code	Place Code	Geographic area name	2010 Census population
48	121	13024	Denton County	69743
48		15976	College Station city	93857
48	041	15976	Brazos County	93857
48		16432	Conroe city	56207
48	339	16432	Montgomery County	56207
48		17000	Corpus Christi city	305215
48	007	17000	Aransas County	0
48	273	17000	Kleberg County	0
48	355	17000	Nueces County	305215
48	409	17000	San Patricio County	0
48		19000	Dallas city	1197816
48	085	19000	Collin County	46885
48	113	19000	Dallas County	1124296
48	121	19000	Denton County	26579
48	257	19000	Kaufman County	0
48	397	19000	Rockwall County	56
48		19972	Denton city	113383
48	121	19972	Denton County	113383
48		22660	Edinburg city	77100
48	215	22660	Hidalgo County	77100
48		24000	El Paso city	649121
48	141	24000	El Paso County	649121
48		24768	Euless city	51277
48	439	24768	Tarrant County	51277
48		26232	Flower Mound town	64669
48	121	26232	Denton County	64457
48	439	26232	Tarrant County	212
48		27000	Fort Worth city	741206
48	121	27000	Denton County	7813
48	367	27000	Parker County	7
48	439	27000	Tarrant County	733386
48	497	27000	Wise County	0
48		27684	Frisco city	116989
48	085	27684	Collin County	72489
48	121	27684	Denton County	44500
48		29000	Garland city	226876
48	085	29000	Collin County	266
48	113	29000	Dallas County	226608
48	397	29000	Rockwall County	2
48		30464	Grand Prairie city	175396
48	113	30464	Dallas County	123487
48	139	30464	Ellis County	45
48	439	30464	Tarrant County	51864
48		32372	Harlingen city	64849
48	061	32372	Cameron County	64849
48		35000	Houston city	2099451
48	157	35000	Fort Bend County	38124
48	201	35000	Harris County	2057280
48	339	35000	Montgomery County	4047
48		37000	Irving city	216290
48	113	37000	Dallas County	216290
48		39148	Killeen city	127921
48	027	39148	Bell County	127921
48		41464	Laredo city	236091
48	479	41464	Webb County	236091
48		41980	League City city	83560
48	167	41980	Galveston County	81998
48	201	41980	Harris County	1562
48		42508	Lewisville city	95290
48	113	42508	Dallas County	841
48	121	42508	Denton County	94449
48		43888	Longview city	80455
48	183	43888	Gregg County	78585
48	203	43888	Harrison County	1870
48		45000	Lubbock city	229573
48	303	45000	Lubbock County	229573
48		45384	McAllen city	129877
48	215	45384	Hidalgo County	129877
48		45744	McKinney city	131117
48	085	45744	Collin County	131117
48		46452	Mansfield city	56368
48	139	46452	Ellis County	95
48	251	46452	Johnson County	1652
48	439	46452	Tarrant County	54621
48		47892	Mesquite city	139824
48	113	47892	Dallas County	139731
48	257	47892	Kaufman County	93
48		48072	Midland city	111147
48	317	48072	Martin County	
48	329	48072	Midland County	111147
48		48768	Mission city	77058
48	215	48768	Hidalgo County	77058
48		48804	Missouri City city	67358
48	157	48804	Fort Bend County	61755
48	201	48804	Harris County	5603
48		50820	New Braunfels city	57740
48	091	50820	Comal County	47586
48	187	50820	Guadalupe County	10154
48		52356	North Richland Hills city	63343
48	439	52356	Tarrant County	63343
48		53388	Odessa city	99940
48	135	53388	Ector County	98270
48	329	53388	Midland County	1670
48		56000	Pasadena city	149043
48	201	56000	Harris County	149043
48		56348	Pearland city	91252
48	039	56348	Brazoria County	86706
48	157	56348	Fort Bend County	721
48	201	56348	Harris County	3825
48		57200	Pharr city	70400
48	215	57200	Hidalgo County	70400
48		58016	Plano city	259841
48	085	58016	Collin County	254525
48	121	58016	Denton County	5316
48		58820	Port Arthur city	53818
48	245	58820	Jefferson County	53814
48	361	58820	Orange County	4
48		61796	Richardson city	99223
48	085	61796	Collin County	28569
48	113	61796	Dallas County	70654
48		63500	Round Rock city	99887
48	453	63500	Travis County	1362
48	491	63500	Williamson County	98525
48		63572	Rowlett city	56199
48	113	63572	Dallas County	49188
48	397	63572	Rockwall County	7011
48		64472	San Angelo city	93200
48	451	64472	Tom Green County	93200
48		65000	San Antonio city	1327407
48	029	65000	Bexar County	1327381
48	091	65000	Comal County	
48	325	65000	Medina County	26
48		70808	Sugar Land city	78817
48	157	70808	Fort Bend County	78817
48		72176	Temple city	66102
48	027	72176	Bell County	66102
48		74144	Tyler city	96900
48	423	74144	Smith County	96900
48		75428	Victoria city	62592
48	469	75428	Victoria County	62592
48		76000	Waco city	124805
48	309	76000	McLennan County	124805

State code	County Code	Place Code	Geographic area name	2010 Census population
48		79000	Wichita Falls city	104553
48	485	79000	Wichita County	104553
49			**UTAH**	2763885
49		43660	Layton city	67311
49	011	43660	Davis County	67311
49		55980	Ogden city	82825
49	057	55980	Weber County	82825
49		57300	Orem city	88328
49	049	57300	Utah County	88328
49		62470	Provo city	112488
49	049	62470	Utah County	112488
49		65330	St. George city	72897
49	053	65330	Washington County	72897
49		67000	Salt Lake City city	186440
49	035	67000	Salt Lake County	186440
49		67440	Sandy city	87461
49	035	67440	Salt Lake County	87461
49		70850	South Jordan city	50418
49	035	70850	Salt Lake County	50418
49		75360	Taylorsville city	58652
49	035	75360	Salt Lake County	58652
49		82950	West Jordan city	103712
49	035	82950	Salt Lake County	103712
49		83470	West Valley City city	129480
49	035	83470	Salt Lake County	129480
50			**VERMONT**	625741
51			**VIRGINIA**	8001024
51		01000	Alexandria city	139966
51	510	01000	Alexandria city	139966
51		16000	Chesapeake city	222209
51	550	16000	Chesapeake city	222209
51		35000	Hampton city	137436
51	650	35000	Hampton city	137436
51		47672	Lynchburg city	75568
51	680	47672	Lynchburg city	75568
51		56000	Newport News city	180719
51	700	56000	Newport News city	180719
51		57000	Norfolk city	242803
51	710	57000	Norfolk city	242803
51		64000	Portsmouth city	95535
51	740	64000	Portsmouth city	95535
51		67000	Richmond city	204214
51	760	67000	Richmond city	204214
51		68000	Roanoke city	97032
51	770	68000	Roanoke city	97032
51		76432	Suffolk city	84585
51	800	76432	Suffolk city	84585
51		82000	Virginia Beach city	437994
51	810	82000	Virginia Beach city	437994
53			**WASHINGTON**	6724540
53		03180	Auburn city	70180
53	033	03180	King County	62761
53	053	03180	Pierce County	7419
53		05210	Bellevue city	122363
53	033	05210	King County	122363
53		05280	Bellingham city	80885
53	073	05280	Whatcom County	80885
53		22640	Everett city	103019
53	061	22640	Snohomish County	103019

State code	County Code	Place Code	Geographic area name	2010 Census population
53		23515	Federal Way city	89306
53	033	23515	King County	89306
53		35275	Kennewick city	73917
53	005	35275	Benton County	73917
53		35415	Kent city	92411
53	033	35415	King County	92411
53		38038	Lakewood city	58163
53	053	38038	Pierce County	58163
53		43955	Marysville city	60020
53	061	43955	Snohomish County	60020
53		53545	Pasco city	59781
53	021	53545	Franklin County	59781
53		57535	Redmond city	54144
53	033	57535	King County	54144
53		57745	Renton city	90927
53	033	57745	King County	90927
53		63000	Seattle city	608660
53	033	63000	King County	608660
53		63960	Shoreline city	53007
53	033	63960	King County	53007
53		67000	Spokane city	208916
53	063	67000	Spokane County	208916
53		67167	Spokane Valley city	89755
53	063	67167	Spokane County	89755
53		70000	Tacoma city	198397
53	053	70000	Pierce County	198397
53		74060	Vancouver city	161791
53	011	74060	Clark County	161791
53		80010	Yakima city	91067
53	077	80010	Yakima County	91067
54			**WEST VIRGINIA**	1852994
54		14600	Charleston city	51400
54	039	14600	Kanawha County	51400
55			**WISCONSIN**	5686986
55		02375	Appleton city	72623
55	015	02375	Calumet County	11088
55	087	02375	Outagamie County	60045
55	139	02375	Winnebago County	1490
55		22300	Eau Claire city	65883
55	017	22300	Chippewa County	1981
55	035	22300	Eau Claire County	63902
55		31000	Green Bay city	104057
55	009	31000	Brown County	104057
55		37825	Janesville city	63575
55	105	37825	Rock County	63575
55		39225	Kenosha city	99218
55	059	39225	Kenosha County	99218
55		40775	La Crosse city	51320
55	063	40775	La Crosse County	51320
55		48000	Madison city	233209
55	025	48000	Dane County	233209
55		53000	Milwaukee city	594833
55	079	53000	Milwaukee County	594833
55	131	53000	Washington County	0
55	133	53000	Waukesha County	0
55		60500	Oshkosh city	66083
55	139	60500	Winnebago County	66083
55		66000	Racine city	78860
55	101	66000	Racine County	78860
55		84250	Waukesha city	70718
55	133	84250	Waukesha County	70718

State code	County Code	Place Code	Geographic area name	2010 Census population
55		85300	West Allis city	60411
55	079	85300	Milwaukee County	60411
56			**WYOMING**	563626
56		13150	Casper city	55316

State code	County Code	Place Code	Geographic area name	2010 Census population
56	025	13150	Natrona County	55316
56		13900	Cheyenne city	59466
56	021	13900	Laramie County	59466

APPENDIX D. GEOGRAPHIC CONCEPTS AND CODES

GEOGRAPHIC AREAS COVERED

Families in America presents data for all states, counties with populations of 50,000 or more, all metropolitan areas, and cities with populations of 50,000 or more.

STATES AND COUNTIES

Data are presented for each of the 50 states, the District of Columbia, and the United States as a whole. The states are arranged alphabetically and counties are arranged alphabetically within each state. Data are presented for 980 counties and county equivalents with populations of 50,000 or more.

County Equivalents

In Louisiana, the primary divisions of the state are known as parishes rather than counties. In Alaska, the county equivalents are the organized boroughs, together with the census areas that were developed for general statistical purposes by the state of Alaska and the U.S. Census Bureau. Four states—Maryland, Missouri, Nevada, and Virginia—have one or more incorporated places that are legally independent of any county and thus constitute primary divisions of their states. Within each state, independent cities are listed alphabetically following the list of counties. The District of Columbia is not divided into counties or county equivalents—data for the entire district are presented as a county equivalent. New York City contains five counties: Bronx, Kings, New York, Queens, and Richmond.

Independent Cities

The following independent cities are not included in any county; their data are presented separately in this volume.

Maryland
Baltimore (separate from Baltimore County)

Missouri
St. Louis (separate from St. Louis County)

Nevada
Carson City

Virginia
Alexandria
Chesapeake

Hampton
Harrisonburg
Lynchburg
Newport News
Norfolk
Portsmouth
Richmond
Roanoke
Suffolk
Virginia Beach

METROPOLITAN AREAS

Data are included for all 381 metropolitan statistical areas. The metropolitan statistical areas are listed alphabetically.

The U.S. Office of Management and Budget (OMB) defines metropolitan and micropolitan statistical areas according to published standards. The major purpose of defining these areas is to enable all U.S. government agencies to use the same geographic definitions in tabulating and publishing data. The general concept of a metropolitan or micropolitan statistical area is that of a core area containing a substantial population nucleus, together with adjacent communities that have a high degree of economic and social integration with the core. New delineations of these Core Based Statistical Areas (CBSAs) based on the 2010 census were released in February 2013. Appendix B lists the metropolitan areas and metropolitan divisions with their component counties.

Standard definitions of metropolitan areas were first issued in 1949 by the Bureau of the Budget (the predecessor of OMB), under the designation "standard metropolitan area" (SMA). The term was changed to "standard metropolitan statistical area" (SMSA) in 1959, and to "metropolitan statistical area" (MSA) in 1983. The term "metropolitan area" (MA) was adopted in 1990 and referred collectively to metropolitan statistical areas (MSAs), consolidated metropolitan statistical areas (CMSAs), and primary metropolitan statistical areas (PMSAs). The term "core based statistical area" (CBSA) became effective in 2000 and refers collectively to metropolitan and micropolitan statistical areas.

The 2010 standards provide that each CBSA must contain at least one urban area of 10,000 or more population. Each metropolitan statistical area must have at least one urbanized area of 50,000 or more inhabitants. Each micropolitan statistical area must have at least one urban cluster of at least 10,000 but less than 50,000 people.

Under the standards, A metro area contains a core urban area of 50,000 or more population, and a micro area contains an urban core of at least 10,000 (but less than 50,000) population. Each metro or micro area consists of one or more counties and includes the counties containing the core urban area, as well as any adjacent counties that have a high degree of social and economic integration (as measured by commuting to work) with the urban core.

If specified criteria are met, a metropolitan statistical area containing a single core with a population of 2.5 million or more may be subdivided to form smaller groupings of counties referred to as "metropolitan divisions."

As of February 28, 2013, there were 381 metropolitan statistical areas and 541 micropolitan statistical areas in the United States. This book includes the 381 metropolitan statistical areas. The metropolitan areas are listed in Appendix B with their component counties (and component metropolitan divisions for the largest metropolitan areas.)

The largest city in each metropolitan statistical area is designated a "principal city." Additional cities qualify if specified requirements are met concerning population size and employment. The title of each metropolitan statistical area consists of the names of up to three of its principal cities and the name of each state into which the metropolitan statistical area extends. The principal city need not be an incorporated place if it meets the requirements of population size and employment. Usually such a principal city is a census designated place in decennial census data and American Community Survey data.

In view of the importance of cities and town in New England, the 2010 standards also provide for a set of geographic areas that are defined using cities and towns in the six New England states. These New England city and town areas (NECTAs) are not included in this volume.

Appendix B lists the 381 metropolitan statistical areas, together with their component metropolitan divisions, where appropriate, and the component counties of each area

CITIES

Data are included for 795 cities with populations of 50,000 or more. Corresponding data for states are also provided. The states are arranged alphabetically and the cities are ordered alphabetically within each state.

As used in this volume, the term *city* refers to places that have been incorporated as cities, boroughs, towns, or villages under the laws of their respective states. Towns in the New England states and New York are treated as minor civil divisions (MCDs) and are not included in the cities database. Data for census designated places (CDPs) with populations of 50,000 or more are included. CDPs are delineated by the Census Bureau, in cooperation with states and localities, as statistical counterparts of incorporated places for purposes of the decennial census. CDPs comprise densely settled concentrations of population that are identifiable by name but are not legally incorporated as places.

Appendix C lists the 795 cities followed by the county where each city is located. If a city includes portions of more than one county, the population in each part is specified.

A consolidated city is an incorporated place that has combined its government functions with a county or subcounty entity but contains one or more other semi-independent incorporated places that continue to function as local governments within the consolidated government. Each consolidated city contains a core city, the area of a consolidated city not included in another separately incorporated place. The census geographic term for this core is the "balance" of the consolidated city. Thus the "balance" is essentially the core city of the consolidated government. Because the ACS includes only the "balance," all data in this book are for the "balance."

Consolidated cities included in this volume are Milford, CT; Athens-Clarke County, GA; Augusta-Richmond County, GA; Indianapolis, IN; Louisville-Jefferson County, KY; and Nashville-Davidson, TN.

GEOGRAPHIC CODES

All tables provide, at the beginning of the table, a geographic code or codes for each area.

For states, a two-digit code is included. The state code is a sequential numbering, with some gaps, of the states and the District of Columbia in alphabetical order from Alabama (01) to Wyoming (56). For states and counties, a five-digit code is given for each state and county. The first two digits indicate the state; the remaining three represent the county. Within each state, the counties are listed in order, beginning with 001, with even numbers usually omitted. Independent cities follow the counties and begin with the number 510.

These codes have been established by the U.S. government as Federal Information Processing Standards and are often referred to as *FIPS codes*. They are used by U.S. government agencies and many other organizations for data presentation. The codes are provided in this volume for use in matching the data given here with other data sources in which geographic areas are identified by FIPS code.

For cities, a seven-digit state and place code is included. The first two digits identify the state and are the same as the FIPS codes described above. The remaining five digits are the place FIPS codes established by the U.S. government.

INDEX